TWO THOUSAND NOTABLE AMERICANS

TWO THOUSAND

NOTABLE AMERICANS

Second Edition

published by:

the **American Biographical Institute**

main offices

5126 Bur Oak Circle, Post Office Box 31226
Raleigh, North Carolina 27622 USA

ISBN Prefix: 934544

6/85
gift R.M.

Library of Congress Catalog Card Number 81-71697

International Standard Book Number 0-934544-35-2

Printed and bound in the United States of America by
Book Crafters, Inc.
Chelsea, Michigan

PRINTED
IN
U.S.A.

Table of Contents

Preface   vii

Biographies   1

Addendum   439

Appendix I   ix
   Editorial Advisory Board
   The American Biographical Institute

Appendix II   xiii
   Honorary Educational Advisory Board
   The American Biographical Institute

Appendix III   xvii
   Research Board of Advisors
   The American Biographical Institute

Appendix IV   xxiii
   Roster of Life and Annual Members
   The American Biographical Institute
   Research Association

Appendix V   xxix
   Roster of Fellow Members
   The American Biographical Institute

Preface

The Second Edition of *TWO THOUSAND NOTABLE AMERICANS* represents a distinctive look at America's strength . . . its citizens. The individuals whose names and endeavors are recorded in this volume were chosen for inclusion because of their contributions to a better society reflected by their own personal achievement on local, state and/or national levels. Each is truly a notable citizen of our day.

As with all other biographical reference works published by the Institute, entry is decided by the Governing Board of Editors and based entirely on individual merit through a non-discriminating process. There is *never* a fee for listing in any of the Institute's titles. True efforts are made by the editors to give an accurate presentation of the life histories behind the wealth of American spirit and leadership.

Copies of *TWO THOUSAND NOTABLE AMERICANS* will be placed in major library reference centers throughout the United States, and in many instances, sent complimentarily to a library of the biographee's choice. Interest in this publication has been overwhelming. As an exclusive collection of national profiles on distinguished men and women of our time, *TWO THOUSAND NOTABLE AMERICANS* will hold great historical value for future generations in addition to serving, justifiably, as a personal symbol of accomplishment for each person mentioned herein.

The Governing Board of Editors takes pride in presenting this Second Edition to the biographical reference field, and especially to those whose lives and deeds made this volume possible.

J. M. Evans
Editorial Director
Governing Board of Editors
The American Biographical Institute, Inc.

IFTIKHARUL HAQUE ABBASY

Surgeon. Personal: Born October 28, 1935; Son of Mumtaz Begum; Married Karen Hampton, Daughter of Ethel Johnson; Father of Shameem Ara. Education: M.B.B.S.; F.R.C.S.(C); Diplomate, The American Board of Surgeons; Diplomate, The American Board of Abdominal Surgeons; F.A.C.S.; F.I.C.S. Career: Surgeon/Medical Doctor; Active Staff, Memorial Hospital, Elmhurst, Illinois; Consulting Staff, Harvard Community Hospital, Harvard, Illinois. Organizational Memberships: American Medical Associaiton; Illinois Medical Society; DuPage County Medical Society; American College of Surgeons; International College of Surgeons; Pan Pacific Association; Royal College of Surgeons of Canada. Religion: Member of Muslim Community of Western Suburb. Honors and Awards: Listed in *Men and Women of Distinction, Who's Who in the Midwest, Dictionary of International Biography, International Who's Who of Community Service.* Address: 905 Burr Oak Court, Oak Brook, Illinois 60521.■

THEODORA MEAD ABEL

Clinical Psychologist. Personal: Born September 9, 1899; Daughter of Mr. and Mrs. Robert G. Mead (both deceased); Married Theodore Abel; Mother of Peter, Caroline, Zita. Education: B.A., Vassar College, 1921; M.A. 1924, Ph.D. 1925, Columbia University; Diploma in Psychology, University of Paris, 1923. Career: Clinical Psychologist, Individual, Marital and Family Psychotherapy; Former Psychology Instructor, Sarah Lawrence College, University of Illinois, Long Island Univeristy; Several Research Projects funded by the National Research Council, Laura Spellman Fund, Office of Naval Research, Keith Fund. Organizational Memberships: Fellow, American Psychological Association; Former Vice President, American Orthopsychiatric Association; Past Vice President, American Psychopathological Association; Past President, New York Society of Clinical Psychology; Diplomate in Clinical Psychology, American Board of Professional Psychology; Others. Community Activities: Former President, Trustee, School Board, Palisades, New York; Workshops at Home at Abroad; Donations to United Way, Various Funds for Animals, Environmental Preservation. Religion: Unitarian. Published Works: Author of One Book; Co-Author of Three Books; Contributor of 85 Articles to Scientific Journals or Chapters to Books. Honors and Awards: Psychologist of the Year, New York Society of Clinical Psychologists, 1972; Phi Beta Kappa; Sigma Xi; Sigma Delta Epsilon. Address: 4200 Sunningdale N.E., Albuquerque, New Mexico 87110.■

MAC J. ABELS

Retail Florist. Personal: Born March 17, 1930; Son of Mrs. Joe Abels; Married Patricia A.; Father of Lallene J. Rector, Melody Hubnik (Mrs. Ray). Education: B.S., Texas Christian University. Career: Retail Florist, Fort Worth, Texas; Former Employee, Conoco Oil Company. Organizational Memberships: American Institute of Floral Designers; Society of American Florists; Professional Floral Commentators International; Fort Worth Florists Association; Texas State Florists Association; West Texas-New Mexico Florists Association; Teleflora North Texas Unit. Community Activities: Kiwanis Club of Greater Fort Worth. Religion: Active Member of Boulevard United Methodist Church. Address: 1732 Sheffield Place, Fort Worth, Texas 76112.■

ROSALIE S. ABRAMS

Legislator. Personal: Born in Baltimore, Maryland; Daughter of Isaac and Dora Rodbell Silber; Mother of Elizabeth Joan. Education: R.N., Sinai Hospital School of Nursing; B.S. summa cum laude 1963, M.A. 1969, The Johns Hopkins University. Military: Served in the United States Navy Nurse Corps, World War II. Career: Director, Office on Aging, State of Maryland, 1983 to present; Senator 1970-83; Senate Majority Leader 1979-82, Chairman Finance Committee 1983; State of Maryland; Served on Budget and Taxation Committee, Legislative Policy Committee, Spending Affordability Committee, Environment and Health Subcommittee, Special Joint Committee on Mental Health Laws, Others; Elected to House of Delegates, 1966-70; Nursing Supervisor, Sinai Hospital; Public Health Nursing, Baltimore City; Business Manager, Silber's Bakery, Inc.; Realtor, Baltimore, Maryland, 1980 to present. Organizational Memberships: Democratic Party of Maryland, Chairman, 1979-83; Democratic National Strategy Council, 1981 to present; Humane Practices of Maryland, Chairman, 1979 to present; National Conference of State Legislatures, State Federal Committee on Human Resources. Honors and Awards: Most Distinguished Woman in Government, Maryland Chapter of the National Organization for Women; Award for Legislative Excellence, Maryland Council of Jewish National Fund; Award for Distinguished Service, Baltimore Area Council on Alcoholism; Award for Legislative Excellence, Maryland Nurses Association; Award of Distinction, *Baltimore News-American*; Achievement Award, American Academy of Comprehensive Health Planning; Hilda Katz Blaustein Distinguished Women-in-Community Service Award, American Jewish Committee; Margaret Sanger Award, Planned Parenthood of Maryland; Leader in Lifesaving Award, Safety First Club of Maryland; Honored by the Maryland Public Health Association; Honorary Membership, Pi Chapter, Sigma Theta Tau National Honor Society of Nursing; Listed in *Who's Who, Who's Who in the East, Who's Who in America Jewry, Who's Who in Politics, Biography of Women in Politics, Who's Who Internationally, Who's Who of American Women, Anglo-American Who's Who, International Yearbook and Statesmen's Who's Who.* Address: 111 Hamlet Hill Road, Baltimore, Maryland 21210.■

KAREL B. ABSOLON

Cardiopulmonary Consultant. Personal: Born March 21, 1926; Married; Father of Mary, John, Peter, Martha. Education: M.D., Yale University Medical School, 1952; M.S. Physiology and Pathology 1956, Ph.D. Surgery and Psychology 1963, University of Minnesota. Career: Consultant, National Institutes of Health, Heart, Lung and Blood Institutes Devices and Technology Branch, 1980 to present; Consultant, United States Air Force, 1983; Former Positions include Academic Chairman of Surgery at University of Illinois-Urbana 1977-80, Associate Professor of Surgery at George Washington University, Assistant Professor of Surgery at University of Minnesota. Organizational Memberships: Vice President, Society of Arts and Sciences, Washington, D.C. 1980-82; Vice President, Washington Thoracic Society, 1977; Numerous Other Professional Memberships. Military: Served in the United States Naval Reserve, 1954-56, attaining the rank of Lieutenant MC and Lieutenant Colonal. Published Works: Author of *Text on Development of Modern Surgery, The Conquest, Field Enterprises - Research Projects* 1984; Author of over 150 Publications. Honors and Awards: Awards, American Board of Surgeons, Board of Thoracic and Cardiovascular Surgery; Fellow, National Institutes of Health, American Cancer Society, American Heart Association, Academy of Surgeons Society, Others. Address: 11225 Huntover Drive, Rockville, Maryland 20852.■

BRENDA T. ACKEN

Accounting and Corporate Executive. Personal: Born March 16, 1947; Daughter of Murl and Pauline Thomas. Education: Graduate, Princeton High School; B.S.B.A., Concord College, Athens; Certified Public Accountant in West Virginia, 1973. Career: Corporate Officer and Member of Board of Directors, South Atlantic Coal Company Inc., Race Fork Coal Corporation, Permac Inc., REP Aviation Inc., Bakertown Coal Company Inc., REP Sales Inc.; Comptroller, Tri-States Sales Company; Trustee, Three Pension Plans; Senior Accountant, Higgins and Gorman, Attorneys and CPAs, 1968-74. Organizational Memberships: Bluefield Community Hospital, Chairman of Executive Committee and Long-Range Planning Committee, Vice Chairman Board of Directors (second term), Treasurer 2 Years, Chairman of Hospital Finance Committee 2 Years; West Virginia Society of C.P.A.s, Southern Chapter President, 1976-77, State Board of Directors 1978 to present, President-elect 1982-83; American Institue of CPAs, Industry Committee 1981-84, Special Task Force on CPE for CPAs in Industry 1979-82, Course Development Subcommittee 1982-83; American Woman's Society of CPAs; American Society of Professional and Executive Women; National Society of Women Accountants; National Association of Accountants. Community Activities: Advisory Board, Bluefield Salvation Army, 1979-83; President, Quota Club of Bluefield, 1978-79; Quota International Inc., Lieutenant Governor of First District 1979-80, Governor of First District 1980-81, By-Laws Committee 1981-82, Service Committee 1982-83; Museum Subcommittee, Pocahontas Coalfield Centennial Celebration; Participant, Various Greater Bluefield Chamber of Commerce Activities on Behalf of Companies; Selective Service Board. Honors and Awards: Outstanding Committee Chairman for Chairman of Public Relations Committee of CPAs, 1978-79; First Woman Officer as Vice President, West Virginia Society of CPAs, 1981-82; Listed in *Personalities of the South, World Who's Who of Women, Who's Who in the South and Southwest*. Address: 628 Parkway, Bluefield, WV 24701.■

NANCY JANE ACKER

Educator and Department Chairman. Personal: Born October 22, 1934; Daughter of Mildred Acker. Education: B.S. Health Education, Slippery Rock State College, 1956; M.S. Physical Education, Indiana University. Career: Department Chairman and Teacher, Edinboro University of Pennsylvania (formerly Edinboro State College); Former High School Teacher and Summer Girl Scout Camp Director. Organizational Memberships: Vice President for Physical Education in Pennsylvania, 1979; President-elect State Health and Physical Education Association, 1981; President, State Health and Physical Education Association, 1982. Community Activities: Director, Penncrest School, Venango Boro School; President, Community Bowling and Golf Leagues; Worthy Grand Matron, Pennsylvania Order of the Eastern Star; Education Committee, General Grand Chapter, Order of the Eastern Star; President, Edinboro State College Senate. Religion: Church Treasurer 6 Years, Choir Member 30 Years. Honors and Awards: Edinboro Distinguished Faculty Award, 1978; Commendation, House of Representatives, Commonwealth of Pennsylvania, 1976; Professional Honor Award, Pennsylvania Association for Health, Physical Education, Recreation and Dance, 1979; Listed in *International Who's Who of Education, Who's Who of American Women, World Who's Who of Women*. Address: 114 Doughty Road, Meadville, Pennsylvania 16335.■

HELEN RUTH PENNER ACKERMAN

Independent Practitioner, Psychological Consultant. Personal: Born March 5, 1939, in New York City, New York; Married Ross S. Ackerman; Mother of Eric, Ruth. Education: B.A., Hofstra University, 1960; M.A., George Washington University, 1962; Ed.D., University of Maryland, 1967. Career: High School Instructor, Army Education Center, Bad Kissingen, Germany, 1961-63; Lecturer in Psychology, University of Maryland European Campus, Schweinfurt and Bad Kissingen, Germany, 1962-63; Psychologist, Crownsville State Hospital, Maryland, 1963-65; Research Psychologist, Johns Hopkins University, 1965; Assistant Professor of Psychology, Anne Arundel Community College, 1968; School Psychologist, Baltimore County Board of Education, 1966-68, and The Mills School, Fort Lauderdale, Florida, 1968-69; Consultant, Hospital Management and Planning Associates, Miami, Florida, 1968-75; Independent Practitioner, Fort Lauderdale, 1975 to present; Maryland Psychological Consultant, 1979-80; Psychological Consultant, Broward County School System, 1980-81. Organizational Memberships: American Psychological Association; Florida Association of School Psychologists; Southeastern Psychological Association; Canadian Psychological Association; Maryland Psychological Association; New Hampshire Psychological Association. Community Activities: Community Activities: Anne Arundel County Police Community Relations Council, Planning Director, 1967-68; Plantation American Association of University Women, First Vice President, 1974-75; Florida Mental Health Association, Legislative Representative, 1981; Red Cross Volunteer, Bad Kissingen, Germany and Annapolis, Maryland, 1961-66; Plantation Golf Estates Civic Association, Chairperson, 1968-69); Psi Chi, George Washington University; Plantation Chamber of Commerce; Plantation Education Committee, 1978-79, 1980-81; Voices of Interested Parents; Peters Elementary School Parent-Teacher Association, Corresponding Secretary, Volunteer Chairperson, President 1983; West Broward Symphony Guild, By-Laws Chairperson, 1978-79; Mental Health Associaton of Broward County, Board of Directors, 1978-80; Broward County Psychological Association, Ethics Committee, Second Vice President, 1978-79; Gables Academy, Advisory Board Member, 1979-81. Religion: Plantation Jewish Congregation; Founder's Group First Vice President, Editor of Bulletin *Life* 1974-1976-1977, Non-Salaried Pre-School Director 1975-77. Published Works: Number of Articles including "Taking the Guesswork out of Studying for Undergraduate Psychology Courses," *Directory of Teaching Innovations in Psychology*; "Children of All Ages Need TV Supervision," *Today's Child*; "Kids and TV Sometimes Don't Mix," *Miami Herald*; Author *American-Jewish Holiday Fun for the Public School*. Honors and Awards: University of Maryland Felowship, 1964-65; Second Place Winner, Florida Osteopathic Medical Associaton Logo Contest, 1976; Listed in *Who's Who of American Women, World Who's Who of Women, Personalities of the South, Who's Who Among Students in American Universities and Colleges*. Address: 5921 Almond Terrace, Plantation, Florida 33317.■

RICHARD M. ACUNA

Attorney. Personal: Born August 7, 1948; Son of Miguel Acuna. Education: B.S., St. Mary's College, 1971; J.D., Hastings College of Law, 1974; M.B.A., Golden Gate University, 1982. Career: Law Partner, Vogt, Sanchez and Meadville, 1982 to present; Attorney, Security Pacific National Bank, 1979-82; Attorney, National Broadcasting Company, 1976-79. Community Activities: Board of Directors, Bilingual Foundation of Arts; Board of Directors, Mexican-American Opportunity Foundation. Religion: Catholic. Address: Vogt, Sanchez and Meadville, 16255 Ventura Boulevard, Suite 1100, Encino, California 91436.■

GERALD R. ADAMS

Professor. Personal: Born June 2, 1946; Son of Arthur and Florence Adams; Married Jane Elizabeth; Father of Shawnelle, Sheryl, Shelli, Elizabeth. Education: B.S. Education/Sociology, Midland College, 1969; M.A. Psychology, University of Nebraska at Omaha, 1971; Ph.D. Human Development, Pennsylvania State University, 1975. Career: Assistant through Full Professor 1975 to present, Department Head 1980-82, Utah State University at Logan, Department of Family and Human Development; Consulting Editor, *American Education Research Journal*, 1981 to present; Associate Editor, *Family Relations*, 1981 to present; Associate Editor, *Journal of Early Adolescence*, 1981 to present; Elementary School Teacher, Ralston, Nebraska, 1967-69; Former School Psychologist. Organizational Memberships: American Sociological Association; Amerian Psychological Association; National Council on Family Relations; Society for Research in Child Development, Program Committee for 1981 Conference, Boston, Massachusetts; Sigma Xi; Rocky Mountain Psychology Association; Southwestern Society for Research in Human Development, Program Chairman for 1984 Convention; American Educational Research Association. Community Activities: Utah Council on Family Relations, Board Member 1978-82; Utah State University Graduate Council, 1980-85. Honors and Awards: Researcher of the Year, College of Family Life, Utah State University, 1976, 1979, 1983; Pennsylvania State University Graduate Fellowship, 1974-75; Listed in *American Men and Women of Sciences, Personalities of America, Who's Who in the West*. Address: 1685 East 1500 North, Logan, Utah 84321.■

MARIANNE KATHRYN ADAMS

Consultant in Administrative Management. Personal: Born January 10, 1924; Daughter of Harold J. and Marion S. Adams. Education: B.A. 1945, M.A. 1946, New York State College for Teachers (now State University of New York-Albany). Military: Volunteer, Air Defense Command. Career: Consultant in Administrative Management; Former Public Administrator, Management Analyst, Program Coordinator, Personnel Administrator. Organizational Memberships: International Personnel Management Association, Director, Capital District Chapter; American Society for Public Administration, Director, Capital District Chapter 1972-74; New York State Academy of Health Administration, Vice President, 1975-77; American Academy of Health Administration; American Public Health Association; New York State Public Health Association, Secretary of Health Administration Section; New York State Academy of Public Administration, Task Force Member, 1974-80; Business and Professional Women of Albany, 1965-81; National Association of Female Executives; Cornell Club of New York, Associate Member, 1977-80; American Association of University Women, Member 1980 to present, Treasurer 1981-83, Vice President-Program 1983-84, President 1984-85, Rancho Bernardo Branch. Community Activities: Bundles for Britain, Volunteer, 1944; Volunteer, Air Defense Command Filter Center, 1943-45, 1953-54; United Way Budget Panel, 1960-62; Mohawk-Hudson Council of Girl Scouts, Secretary, Employed Personnel Committee, 1961-62; Employees Federated Fund, New York State Department of Civil Service, Treasurer 1961, Chairman 1962; State University of New York-Albany Alumni Association, Board of Directors, 1974-77; Alumni House Fund Raiser, 1973; Albany Symphony Orchestra Vanguard, Member/Campaign Worker, 1968-80; Saratoga Performing Arts Center, Member/Campaign Worker, 1970-80; United Way, New York State Department of Social Services, Vice Chairman, 1964; New York State Department of Health, Vice Chairman 1975, Chairman 1976; San Diego Symphony Orchestra Association, Member/Campaign Worker, 1981 to present; Recreation Council of Rancho Bernardo, 1981; Rancho Bernardo Center for

Continuing Education, 1981 to present; Salk Institute, Contributor, 1975 to present; San Diego Zoological Society, 1980 to present. Religion: Trinity United Methodist Church, Albany, Member, Secretary of Administrative Board, 1973-75; Rancho Bernardo Community Church, 1981-83; Hope United Methodist Church, 1983 to present; Chair of Council on Ministries, 1984. Honors and Awards: Air Defense Command 1500-Hour Award; New York State Merit Suggestion Award, 1962; 25-Year and 30-Year New York State Service Awards, Letter of Commendation, Secretary of the Department of Health, Education and Welfare, 1976; Certificate of Outstanding Contribution, State University of New York-Albany Alumni Association Board of Directors, 1978; Citation from the Governor of New York, 1980. Address: 12417 Lomica Drive, San Diego, California 92128.■

WILLIAM RICHARD ADAMS

Research and Instruction in Zooarcheology. Personal: Born February 21, 1923; Son of William B. and Mildred Adams; Married Connie Christie; Father of W. H., James E., Margaret E., Richard B., Scott C., Teresa M. Education: A.B. 1944, M.A. 1949, Indiana University. Career: Research and Teaching in Zooarcheology; Former Bank President, Zooarcheologist. Organizational Memberships: American Bankers Association; Indiana Bankers Association; Society of American Archeology; S.O.P.A.; Indiana Academy of Science; Indiana Historical Society. Community Activities: Monroe County Auxiliary Police; Monroe County Merit Board. Religion: First Methodist Church of Bloomington, Board of Trustees. Honors and Awards: Indiana Gearworks, Arctic Expedition, 1957; Monroe County Auxiliary Police Award, 1979. Address: 215 W. Chester Drive, Ellettsville, Indiana 47429.■

ARTHUR L. ADEN

Engineering Manager. Personal: Born February 1, 1924; Married Leona (Betty); Father of Donald, Charles, Sherry, Gary. Education: Master of Arts 1948, Master of Engineering Sciences 1949, Ph.D. 1950, Harvard University. Career: Senior Staff and Line Positions 1973 to present, Vice President of Xerox Electro Optical Systems 1963-72, Xerox Corporation; Vice President, Motorola Instrumentation and Control Inc., Motorola Inc., 1958-63; Manager of Operations for Solid State Systems Division and Associate Director of Research and Development, Military Electronics Division, Sylvania Electric Products Inc., 1953-58; Assistant Laboratory Manager and Engineering Manager, Sylvania Microwave Physics Laboratory, 1950-53; Section Head and Senior Staff Member, Cambridge Research Center. Organizational Memberships: Institute of Electrical and Electronice Engineers, Fellow, Former Chairman, P.G.M.T.T. National Symposium, Former Chairman of San Gabriel Section, Former Secretary of Phoenix Section; Sigma Zeta; Sigma Xi; American Physical Society; American Management Association. Military: Served in the United States Army Air Corps, 1943-46, with assignments as Assistant Chief of Flying Training Division of Weather Reconnaissance School, as Electronics Officer and as Meteorology Officer. Honors and Awards: Fellow 1966, Annual Award for Outstanding Contributions to Electronics from Phoenix (Arizona) Section 1963, Institute of Electrical and Electronic Engineers; National Research Council Fellowship in Electronics at Harvard University, 1948-50; Gordon McKay Scholarship, Harvard University, 1947-48; Scholarship, Northern Illinois State College, 1941-43. Address: 1421 Lincoln Drive, Carrollton, Texas 75006.■

V. HARRY ADROUNIE

Environmental Administrator. Personal: Born April 29, 1915; Son of Dr. H. A. (deceased) and Dorothy Adrounie; Married Agne M. Slone; Father of Harry Michael, Vee Patrick. Education: B.S. 1940, B.A. 1959, St. Ambrose College; Command and Staff College Air University, United States Air Force 27 Years; Achieved the Rank of Lieutenant Colonel. Career: Environmental Specialist, School of Public Health, University of Hawaii, 1978-80; Director, Division of Environmental Protection, Chester County, Pennsylvania, Department of Health, 1970; Director, Environmental Health, Berrien County, Michigan, 1975; Past Deputy Commander, First Aeromedical Evacuation Group T.A.C.; Technical Director, Large Organizational Selling Services to Hospitals and Other Medical Care Facilities throughout the United States, 1968-70; Deputy Commander, World-wide United States Air Force Medical Unit, 1966-68; Acting Chairman and Visiting Associate Professor, Department of Environmental Health, American University, Beirut, Lebanon, 1963-66; Commander, Detachments 10 and 11, First Aeromedical Transport Group, 1961-63; Environmental Health Specialist, U.S. Air Force Surgeon General and U.S. Air Force Environmental Health Representative to National Academy of Sciences and U.S. Interdepartment Committee on Nutrition for National Defense, Consultant U.S. Public Health Service Mobilization, 1957-61; Environmental Health Specialists Medical Division and Biological and Chemical Warfare Specialist in Special Weapons Division, Office of the Inspector General Headquarters, U.S. Air Force, 1953-56; Chief of Planning and Reporting Branch, Field Test and Meteorology Division, Fort Detrick, Maryland, 1951-52; Preventive Medicine Officer, U.S. Army I Corps, Japan, 1947-50; Commander, 20th Medical Laboratory, Fort Lewis, Washington, 1946-47; Calhoun County Health Department Bacteriologist TB Research, 1946; Base Medical Inspector, Lincoln Air Force Base, Nebraska, 1943-46; Only Air Force Medical Service Corps Officer Qualified as Medical Administrative Staff Officer, Staff Biomedical Science and Biological Environmental Engineer; Consultant, Ministry of Health, Indonesia, 1978-80. Organizational Memberships: American Public Health Association, Fellow; Royal Society of Health, Fellow; American Association for the Advancement of Science, Fellow; National Environmental Health Association, Life Member, Board of Directors, President; International Health Society, Charter Member, Board of Governors; New York Academy of Science; American Association of University Professors; American Management Association; Association of Military Surgeons of the United States; North Carolina Public Health Association; Institute of Sanitation Management; Chester County Water Resources Authority, Chairman, Board of Directors; Pennsylvania Environmental Health Association, Board of Directors; Legal and Public Relations Committee, Pennsylvania Health Council and Environmental Health Review and Study Committee of the Regional Comprehensive Health Planning Council, Board of Directors; Sanitarians Regional Board of Pennsylvania, Chairman; National Association of Sanitarians, President, 1961-62; American Academy of Sanitarians, Founder, Diplomate; Chester County Board of Health, Member; Michigan Association of Local Environmental Health Administrators, Founder, First President; American Board of Industrial Hygiene, Diplomate; Pennsylvania Public Health Association, Section on Environment, Chairman; Certified by the American Academy of Sanitarians, American Board of Industrial Hygiene in Comprehensive Practice of Industrial Hygiene; American Academy of Sanitarians, American Board of Industrial Hygiene in Comprehensive Practice of Industrial Hygiene; Registered Sanitarian in the States of California, Pennsylvania, Michigan, Nevada, North Carolina, Others; Number of Other Professional Activities and Offices. Community Activities: Chester County Solid Waste Management Plan, Coordinator, 1973-75; Barry County, Michigan, Solid Waste Planning Committee, Chairman, 1980 to present; Western Michigan University Citizen Center for Science, Policy Council, 1981 to present; National Rifle Association of America, Life Member, Certified Rifle Marksmanship Instructor; American Museum of Natural History, Associate Member; National Geographic Society; Board of Directors, Hastings Kiwanis, 1983 to present; Trustee, B.P.O. Elks, 1983 to present; American Legion; United States Air Force Association; Number of Other Civic Activities. Honors and Awards: Walter S. Mangold Award, 1963; Alumnus of the Year, Hastings High School, Michigan, 1961; Received Oak Leaf Cluster to Air Force Commendation Medal; Legion of Merit, Only Serviceman Appointed as University Department Chairman, American University, Beirut; United States Air Force Commendation Medal (last 2 positions responsible for world-wide operations of United States Air Force); Commendation for Responsibility for Southern Half of Japan, 1947-50; Listed in *American Men of Science, Who's Who in the South and Southwest, Personalities of the West and Midwest, Notable Americans, Community Leaders and Noteworthy Americans, Personalities of America, Who's Who in Health Care, Who's Who in Technology Today, Who's Who in the East, Dictionary of International Biography.* Address: 1905 N. Broadway Hastings, Michigan 49058.■

SALEEM AHMED

Research Associate. Personal: Born December 28, 1939, in Nagpur, India; Son of Syed Izzuddin (deceased) and Hameeda I. Ahmed; Married Carol (Yasmin), Daughter of Izumi (deceased) and Shizuka Matsumoto; Father of Aisha Akiko, Seema Sueko. Education: Graduate of St. Patrick's High School, Karachi, 1955; B.Sc. Geology and Chemistry with honors, 1960, M.Sc. Geology with honors 1961, University of Karachi; Ph.D. Soils Science, University of Hawaii, 1965. Career: Research Associate in Planing and Coordinating Production and Management, 1973 to present; Regional Agronomist to Technical Services Advisor (responsible for planning and implementing agronomic research and extension, advertising and sales promotion, marketing planning, and training), Exxon Chemicals Pakistan Ltd, 1966-73; Lecturer, University of Karachi Department of Geology, 1965-66. Organizational Memberships: American Association for the Advancement of Science; American Association of Agronomy; International Soil Science Society; Council for Agriculture, Science, and Tehnology; Charter Member, Planetary Society. Community Activities: Vice President, Honolulu Children's Opera Chorus, 1982-83; Board of Directors, Kamiloiki Community Associatoin, Honolulu, 1981 to present; President, East-West Center Students Association, Honolulu, 1962-63; General Secretary, Karachi University Students Association, 1960-61; Joint Secretary, Karachi University Students Association, 1959-60; Founder-President, Garden Road Community Youth Center, Karachi, 1958-61; Senior Crew Leader, Karachi Sea Scouts, 1952-58. Religion: Muslim. Honors and Awards: Most Outstanding Team Project at East-West Center, Honolulu, 1980; Scholarship for Graduate Studies at Univerity of Hawaii, East-West Center, 1961-64; Most Outstanding Student at East-West Center, 1963; Honorable Mention, Most Outstanding pakistani

Student in U.S.A. and Canada Award, Pakistani Students Association of North America, 1963; Most Outstanding Student at Karachi University, 1960; Pakistan Representative, 8th World Boy Scouts Jamboree, Canada, 1955. Address: 781 Eleele Place, Honolulu, Hawaii 96825.■

DAVID H. AHNER

Osteopathic Physician. Personal: Born April 29, 1943; Son of Hurley Thomas Ahner (deceased) and Elizabeth Show Gade; Married Conchita Uy de Leon. Education: B.A., Univerity of Delaware-Newark, 1965; D.O., Philadelphia College of Osteopathic Medicine, 1965-70; Intern, Tri-County Hospital (Springfield, Pennsylvania) 1970-71, Albert Einstein Medical Center (Philadelphia, Pennsylvania) 1971-72; Resident in Psychiatry, The Institute of the Pennsylvania Hospital, Philadelphia, Pennsylvania, 1972-74. Career: Osteopathic Physician specializing in Psychiatry, Community Services for Human Growth Inc., (Paoli, Pennsylvania) 1981 to present, Fair Acres Farm (Glen Riddle-Lima, Pennsylania) 1976 to present, The Fairmount Institute (Philadelphia, Pennsylvania) 1980 to present, Metropolitan Hospital (Springfield, Pennsylvania), 1976 to present, Riddle Memorial Hospital (Media, Pennsylvania) 1977 to present, Sacred Heart General Hospital (Chester, Pennsylvania) 1977 to present, Taylor Hospital (Ridley Park, Pennsylvania) 1976 to present; By-Laws Commitee 1981 to present, Chairman of Utilization and Admissions Committee 1979-81, Department of Psychiatry 1975 to present, Medical Director of Comprehensive Alcoholism Program for Community Mental Health Center 1975-81, Crozer-Chester Medical Center, Upland, Chester, Pennsylvania. Organizational Memberships: American Psychiatric Association; Pennsylvania Psychiatric Society; Philadelphia Psychiatric Society; American Osteopathic Association; American College of Neuropsychiatrists; Pennsylvania Osteopathic Medical Associaton; Philadelphia County Osteopathic Medical Society; American College of Utilization Review Physicians; American Medical Society on Alcoholism; National Council on Alcoholism. Honors and Awards: Legion of Honor, The Chapel of Four Chaplains, 1979; Listed in *Biographical Roll of Honor, Book of Honor, Community Leaders of America, International Register of Profiles, Outstanding Young Men of America, Personalities of America, Who's Who in the East.* Address: 1139 Dorset Drive, West Chester, Pennsylvania 19380.■

SAMUEL SIMEON AIDLIN

Executive. Personal: Born August 29, 1913; Married Ruth Baker; Father of Stephen Howard. Education: B.M.E., City College of New York, 1937; M.M.E., Stevens Institute/Polytechnic/N.S. of New York, 1945; D.M.E., World University, 1982. Career: President and Director, A—I—D Labs (America); Chairman and Chief Executive Officer, Aidlin Automation Corporation; Consultant to Industry Engaged in Design, Development and Testing of Consumer Products for Various National and International Companies. Organizational Memberships: President, Manufacturing Engineers Council, 1963 to present; President, Kings County Professional Engineers, 1973-74; A.S.E.E.; A.S.T.M.; S.A.E. Community Activities: Member 1940 to present, Chancellor Commander 1945-46, Knights of Pythias; B'nai B'rith, 1960 to present. Honors and Awards: Engineer of Year, N.S.P.E. 1973, Lambda Rho 1963. Address: 5079 Village Gardens Drive, Sarasota, Florida 33580.■

ELIAS C. AIFANTIS

Professor of Engineering Mechanics. Personal: Born October 10, 1950; Son of Charalambos and Aikaterini Aifantis; Married. Education: Diploma in Mining Engineering and Metallurgy, N.T.U., Athens, 1973; Ph.D. Mathematical Science and Mechanics, University of Minnesota, 1975. Career: Professor of Engineering Mechanics, Michigan Tech and Corrosion Center and Mathematical Institute University of Minnesota; Academic Appointments at University of Minnesota 1975-76 and 1980-82, University of Illinois 1976-80, Michigan Tech 1982 to present. Published Works: Author of Over 70 Scientific Publications in Technical Journals. Honors and Awards: Invited Speaker, Symposia in U.S.A. and Abroad; Advisor, Over 15 Graduate Students (six Ph.D. candidates); Research Leader in Mechanics of Materials. Address: University of Minnesota, Minneapolis, Minnesota 55455; Michigan Tech, Houghton, Michigan 49931.■

MOLLY BENNETT-MARKS AITKEN

Corporation Executive. Personal: Born July 25, 1944; Married Gerard James Aitken III; Mother of Bridget Marks, Sean Marks, Frederick Marks, Jacqueline Marks, Gerard James Aitken IV, Mary Hannah Aitken. Education: Attended Nevada Southern University, New York University. Career: Board of Directors, Marks Polarized Corporation; Board of Directors, Phototherm Inc.; Vice President, Thora Energy Corporation; President, The World Energy Foundation; Past Contributing Editor, *North Shore Club Life* and Numerous Horseman Publications, including *Horsemen's Yankee Pedlar* and *Chronicle of the Horse*; Interviewer/Moderator, KLAS Television Channel 8, Las Vegas. Community Activities: North Shore Auxiliary United Cerebral Palsy, President, 1973; First Annual Association for the Help of Retarded Children Horse Show, Manager, 1973; American Horseshows Association, Life Member; Screen Actors Guild; Century Horse Show to Benefit the United States Equestrian Team, Manager, 1974-77. Religion: Catholic. Honors and Awards: Papal Blessing from the Vatican, 1964; Certificate of Merit, United Cerebral Palsy, 1973; Numerous Awards for Horsemanship. Address: Green Gables Farm, Athol, Massachusetts 01331.■

LOIS ELDORA WILSON ALBERT

Archeologist. Personal: Born June 2, 1938, in Alva, Oklahoma; Daughter of Clinton L. and Daisy M. Wilson; Married Abbott H. Albert. Education: B.S., Northwestern State College, 1960; M.S., Oklahoma State University, 1963; Further Study, Oklahoma City University, Central State University; M.A., University of Oklahoma, 1974. Career: Principal Investigator, James Fork Creek Watershed Project, 1982 to present; Co-Principal Investigator, Red River Survey Project, 1980-83; Oklahoma Archeological Survey of University of Oklahoma, Archeologist II 1981 to present, Research Assistant 1979-81, Acting Driector 1978-79, Research Assistant I 1976-78, Secretary I 1975-76; Co-Principal Investigator, Spiro Mounds Project, Phase I, 1979; Project Director, Prehistoric People of Oklahoma Film Series Planning Project, 1979; Editor, *Studies in Oklahoma's Past,* 1978-79; Clerk-Typist, Oklahoma Highway Department, 1975; Archeological Assistant, Oklahoma River Basin Survey, University of Oklahoma, 1973; Archaeological Assistant to Dr. Robert Bell, Department of Anthropology, University of Oklahoma, 1971; Research Assistant, Department of Microbiology, University of Oklahoma Health Sciences Center, 1966-70, 1974; Research Assistant, Cancer Section, Oklahoma Medical Research Foundation, 1964-66. Organizational Memberships: American Chemical Society; Sigma Xi; American Association of Stratigraphic Palynologists; Society of American Archeology; Oklahoma Anthropological Society; Oklahoma Academy of Science; Arizona Archaeolgoical and Historical Society; Society for Archeological Sciences; American Association for the Advancement of Science. Honors and Awards: Phi Sigma; Listed in *Who's Who Among Students in American Universities and Colleges, Outstanding Young Women in America, Who's Who in the South and Southwest.* Address: 1808 Newton Drive Room 116, Norman, Oklahoma 73019.■

DONALD ALLAN ALBERTS, SR.

Oil Spill Consultant. Personal: Born March 29, 1932, in Cleveland, Ohio; Son of Milton Charles and Ruth Louise Graves Alberts; Married Shirley Ethel Tripp, March 25, 1952; Father of Donald, Beverly Ann, Keith, Dawn. Education: B.S.B.A., Bowling Green University, 1968; LL.D., LaSalle University, 1971; Ph.D., World University, 1982. Military: Served in the United States Coast Guard, 1949-73. Career: Executive President, All Point Associates Inc., Worldwide Environmental Consultants, Oil Spill Consultants, 1979 to present; Texaco Inc., Senior Environmental Specialists 1978-79, with the company 1973-79. Organizational Memberships: International Association of Pollution Control; American Standards and Testing Association; American Petroleum Institute. Religion: Roman Catholic. Address: Route 1 Box 3309, Monroeville, Ohio 44847.■

JAMES E. ALDERMAN

State Supreme Court Chief Justice. Personal: Born November 1, 1936; Son of B. E. and Frances Alderman; Married Jean; Father of James Allen. Education: B.A., University of Florida, 1958; LL.B., University of Florida College of Law, 1961. Career: Supreme Court of Florida, Tallahassee, Florida, Chief Justice 1982-84, Justice 1978-82; Judge, Fourth District Court of Appeal, Florida, 1976-78; Circuit Judge, Nineteenth Judicial Circuit of Florida, 1973-76; County Judge, St. Lucie County, Florida, 1971-72; U.S. Commissioner and U.S. Magistrate (part-time), Southern District of Florida, 1961-71. Organizational Memberships: President, St. Lucie

County Bar Association; Community Activities: President, Ft. Pierce-St. Lucie County Chamber of Commerce; President, St. Lucie County Fair Association; President, Ft. Pierce Mutual Concert Association; Ft. Pierce Rotary Club. Religion: Episcopal. Address: 3058 Carlow Circle, Tallahassee, Florida 32308.■

LOUIS CLEVELAND ALDERMAN, JR.

College President. Personal: Born August 12, 1924; Married Anne Whipple; Father of Amelia Anne, Louis C. III, Fielding D., Jonathan A. Education: A.A., South Georgia College, 1942; A.B., Emory University, 1946; M.S., University of Georgia, 1949; Ed.D., Auburn University, 1959. Career: President, Middle Georgia College, Cochran, Georgia; Former Positions include Instructor in Biology at University of Georgia-Rome Center, Director and Instructor in Biology at University of Georgia-Savannah Center, Director of Univerity of Georgia-Columbus Center, Director of University of Kentucky Henderson College. Organizational Memberships: Past President, G.A.J.C.; G.A.E.; N.A.E.; Association of Higher Education; Georgia Association of Colleges, Vice President 1981-82, President 1982-83; American Association for the Advancement of Science. Community Activities: Conference Chairman of College of Governors 1981 and Past District Governor of District 692, Scholarship Committee, Rotary International; Past President, Cochran Rotary Club; Board of Trustees, Rotary Student Loan Fund; Georgia Historical Society; Sons of the American Revolution, Middle Georgia Chapter, Organizing President; Order of Kentucky Colonels; Board of Directors, Cochran-Bleckley Chamber of Commerce; Board of Managers and Vice President, Georgia State Society, National Society of Sons of the American Revolution; Presidents Academy, A.A.C.J.C. Military: Served in the United States Army, 1942-46, during World War II in Asiatic-Pacific Theater. Religion: First Baptist Church (Cochran, Georgia), Chairman of Board of Deacons, Building and Finance Committee, Teacher of Men's Bible Class. Honors and Awards: Graduate Research Assistantship, U.S. Public Health Service, 1948-49; Good Citizenship Award, Civitan Club, 1955; Special Award, Rotary Club, 1969; Fellowship Fund for the Advancement of Education, Ford Foundation, Auburn University, 1958-59; Kendall Award, National Society Son sof the American Revolution, 1980; Paul Harris Fellow, Rotary International, 1981; Listed in *Community Leaders of America, Creative and Successful Personalities of the World.* Address: Old Chester Road, Cochran, Georgia 31014.■

MARY HENNEN ALDRIDGE

Educator. Personal: Born January 11, 1919; Mother of Cecily Joan Ward. Education: B.S., University of Georgia, 1939; M.A., Duke University, 1941; Ph.D., Georgetown University, 1954. Career: Professor 1962 to present, Chairman of Chemistry Department 1979 to present, American University, Washington, D.C.; Associate Professor 1955-62, Assistant Professor of Chemistry 1947-55, University of Maryland-College Park; Chemist, E.I. du Pont de Nemours and Company, Buffalo, New York, 1941-47. Organizational Memberships: American University Senate, Member 1963-72 and 1980-83, Chairman of Research Committee 1983, Executive Secretary 1970-72; American University Faculty Relations Committee, Member 1966-69, Chairman 1969; American University Graduate Studies Committee, 1979-80; American University Interdisciplinary Committee, Chairman, 1980-81; American University Committee on Facilities and Service, Chairman, 1981-82; Chemical Society of Washington, Chairman of Organic Topical Group 1962-63, Board of Managers 1962-77, Secretary 1967-68, Councilor 1967-77, President 1970; American Chemical Society, Chairman of National Committee for Women's Activities 1962, Member Joint Board Council Committee on Chemistry and Public Affairs 1971-74, Board of Trustees for Insurance Affairs 1977-82, Chairman of Public Affairs Symposia at National Meeting 1974; Washington Academy of Sciences, General Chairman of Science Achievement Award 1972-74, Chairman of Physical Science Achievement Awards 1980-83; Washington Chromatography Discussion Group, Organization Chairman of 4-Day Course in Theory and Practice of Gas, Liquid and Thin-Layer Chromatography sponsored by American University Department of Chemistry 1966-74, President 1974-75, Board of Governors 1966 to present. Honors and Awards: Charles Gordon Memorial Award for Service, Chemical Society of Washington, 1982; Honor Scroll Award, District of Columbia Institute of Chemists, 1982; Professional Service Award, Alpha Chi Sigma, 1977. Address: 2930 45th Street Northwest, Washington, D.C. 20016.■

ANDREW LAMAR ALEXANDER

Governor of Tennessee. Personal: Born July 3, 1940, in Knox County, Tennessee; Son of Andy and Flo Alexander; Married Leslee Kathryn (Honey) Buhler, January 4, 1969; Father of Drew, Leslee, Kathryn, Will. Education: B.A., Vanderbilt University; J.D., New York University, 1965. Career: Admitted to Tennessee State Bar, 1965; Associate, Firm of Fowler, Rountree, Fowler and Robertson, Knoxville, Tennessee, 1965; Former Law Clerk, United States Court of Appeals for the 5th Circuit, New Orleans; Campaign Coordinator, Howard Baker's United States Senate Race, 1966; Legislative Assistant to United States Senator Howard Baker, 1967-69; Executive Assistant to Counselor in Charge of Congressional Relations at the White House, 1969-70; Manager, Gubernatorial Campaign of Winfield Dunn, Tennessee, 1970; Partner, Firm of Dearborn and Ewing, Nashville, 1971-78; Political Commentator, Television Station, Nashville, 1975-77; Special Counsel to Senate Majority Leader Howard Baker, 1977; Governor, State of Tennessee, 1979 to present. Organizational Memberships: Tennessee Citizens for Revenue Sharing, Founder, Co-Chairman, 1971; Tennessee Council on Crime and Delinquency, Founder, First Chairman, 1973; American Bar Association; Phi Beta Kappa; Appalachian Regional Commission, Co-Chairman, 1980-81; President's Advisory Committe on Intergovernmental Relations, Vice-Chairman; President's Task Force on Federalism; National Governor's Association Committee on Executive Management and Fiscal Affairs, Chairman. Religion: Presbyterian. Address: Office of the Governor, State Capitol Building, Nashville, Tennessee 37219.■

SAMUEL PRESTON ALEXANDER

Architect, Planner and Interior Designer. Personal: Born November 4, 1953, in Johnson City, Tennessee; Son of Clyde Ernest and Betty Irene White Alexander; Father of Joshua Lloyd. Education: B.Arch., University of Tennessee-Knoxville, 1977; Naval School, Civil Engineer Corps Officers, 1978. Military: Served in the United States Navy, 1978-81, attaining the rank of Lieutenant C.E.C.; United States Naval Reserve, 1981 to present, Lieutenant C.E.C. with Naval Reserve Construction Battalion 23. Career: Architect, Planner, and Interior Designer; Engineer-in-Charge, Navy Public Works Center, Norfolk, Virginia, 1982 to present; Naval Officer, 1978-81. Organizational Memberships: Construction Specification Institute; Society of American Military Engineers. Community Activities: International Platform Associaton; Big Brothers/Big Sisters of America. Honors and Awards: Listed in Published Works: *Who's Who in the South and Southwest, Distinguished American Personalities, International Book of Honor.* Address: 7000 Auburn Avenue Apartment 101, Norfolk, Virginia 23513.■

RALPH JOSEPH ALFIDI

Professor and Department Chairman. Personal: Born April 20, 1932; Son of Luca Alfidi; Married Rose; Father of Suzanne, Christine, Lisa, Katherine, Mary, John. Education: A.B., Ripon College, Wisconsin, 1955; M.D., Marquette University, Wisconsin, 1959. Military: Served in the United States Army, 1963-65, attaining the rank of Captain. Career: Professor and Chairman of Department of Radiology, Case Western Reserve University School of Medicine, 1978 to present; Director of Department of Radiology, University Hospitals of Cleveland, Cleveland, Ohio, 1978 to present; Director, Hospital Department of Radiology, Cleveland Clinic Foundation, Cleveland, Ohio, 1968-78. Organizational Memberships: American College of Radiology; Radiological Society of North America; American Roentgen Ray Society; Society of Cardiovascular Radiology; Society of Computer Body Tomography, First President. Honors and Awards: Fellow, American College of Radiology, 1974; Society of San Andiu, 1978; Pasteur Club, 1978. Address: 742 Coy Lane, Chagrin Falls, Ohio 44022.■

BELLE ALLEN

Executive. Personal: Born August 1; Daughter of Isaac and Clara Allen (both deceased). Education: Attended the University of Chicago. Career: Chairman of the Board and President, William Karp Consulting Company, Inc.; President, Belle Allen Communications; Vice President and Treasurer, Cultural Arts Surveys, Inc., Chicago; Governor's Grievance Panel for State of Illinois Employees, 1979 to present; Federal Reserve System Nominee to the Consumer Advisory Council of the Board of Governors, 1979; Illinois Coalition on the Employment of Women, Member of the Advisory Governing Board, 1980 to present; Illinois Commission on Technological Progress, Special Assistant 1965-67; Special Program Consultant, The City Club of Chicago Civic Assembly, 1962-65. Organizational Memberships: Affirmative Action Association, Member 1980 to present, Board of Directors 1981 to present, Chairperson of Membership Committee 1981-84, Chairperson Program Committee 1981-84, Elected President 1983; Society of Personnel Administrators, 1979 to present; Women's Equity Action League, 1975 to present; Chicago Press Club, Member 1967 to present, Chairperson Women's Activities 1969-71; Publicity Club of Chicago, Member 1958 to present, Chairperson Inter-city Relations Committee 1960-61, Employment Committee, Program Committee, Admissions Committee, Education Committee, Membership Committee, Entertainment Committee; The Fashion Group, Member 1969 to present, Chairperson "A Retrospective View of a Historical Decade, 1960-70" 1970, Board of Directors 1981-83, Editor Bulletin 1981 to present; Industrial Relations Research Associates, Member 1958-62 and 1981 to present, Director Personnel Placement 1960-61; National Association of Inter-Group Relations Officials, Member 1958-62, National Conference Program Committee 1959; Welfare Public Relations Forum, 1958-62. Community Activities: Illinois State Chamber of Commerce, Member 1961-74, Community Relations Committee, Alternate for the Labor Relations Committee; Chicago Association of Commerce and Industry 1961-63, Merit Employment Committee, Public Relations Committee; Field Museum of Natural History, 1966-74; Chicago Historical Society, 1962-64; Regional Ballet Ensemble of Chicago, Board of Directors, Executive Committee, Chairperson Public Affairs Committee, 1961-62; Society for the Chicago Strings, Chicago Symphony Orchestra Members, Board of Directors 1963-64; United Cerebral Palsy Association of Chicago, Women's Division, Founding Member, Board of Directors 1954-58; Adlai E. Stevenson Campaign Staff, 1952, 1956; John F. Kennedy Campaign Staff, 1960; Press Conference Staff for Eleanor Roosevelt, 1960; Democratic Federation of Illinois, President 1958-61; Independent Democratic Coalition, 1968-69; Citizens for Political Change, Founding Member and Board of Directors, 1969; City Council Aldermanic Election, 42nd Ward, Campaign Manager, 1969. Published Works: Editor and Contributor of More than 65 Articles and Papers in Professional and Business Publications and Journals, Speeches, Hearing Materials, Commission Reports, Manuals, and a Book (*Operations Research on the Management of Mental Health Systems*). Honors and Awards: Reference Source, American Bicentennial Research Institute Library of Human Resources, 1973; Special Communications Program, The White House, 1961; Distinguished Service Award, Publicity Club of Chicago, 1968; Citation for Outstanding Service, United Cerebral Palsy Association of Chicago, 1954; Listed in *Who's Who in America, Who's Who of American Women, World Who's Who of Women, Who's Who in the Midwest, Who's Who in Finance and Industry, Foremost Women in Communications, Two Thousand Women of Achievement, International Who's Who in Community Service, Who's Who in Public Relations, Dictionary of International Biography, Women's Organizations and Leaders, Directory of Public Affairs, Notable Americans, Personalities of America, Personalities of the West and Midwest, Community Leaders and Noteworthy Americans, Men and Women of Distinction, Contemporary Personages*, the *Directory of Distinguished Americans*, the *Registry of American Achievement, Five Thousand Personalities of the World, Community Leaders of the World*. Address: 111 East Chestnut Street #56-B, Chicago, Illinois 60611.■

DENIS MCGEE ALLEN

Electronic Trainer. Personal: Born June 2, 1944; Son of Donald Allen; Married Geraldine Jones. Education: Attended University of Minnesota, Chapman College, Palomar College, Orange Coast College, Daley College; B.A., University of Illinois, 1969; M.S.Ed., Chicago State University, 1978. Military: Served in the United States Marine Corps, 1962-66, attaining rank of Corporal. Career: Electronics Trainer, ARCO Alaska Inc.; Former Radiological Engineer, Providence Cancer Therapy Center (Anchorage, Alaska); Chief Engineer, Anchorage Public Radio, KSKA-FM; Faculty Member, University of Alaska, 1980-83; Director, Electronics Industries Association, Color Television Training Center; Faculty, Industrial Skill Center, Chicago Board of Education; Consultant, Alaska Pacific University, Bureau of Land Management; Commercial Pilot, U.S. Geological Survey. Organizational Memberships: Institute of Electrical and Electronic Engineers; Society of Broadcast Engineers; American Association for the Advancement of Science; American Federation of Teachers; Chicago Teachers Union. Community Activities: Experimental Aircraft Association; Airplane Owners and Pilots Association; American Radio Relay League, Life Member; Sierra Club, 1968; Anchorage Manpower Development Commission, 1982; Amateur Radio Satellite Corporation, 1973; Midwest Sled Dog Club, 1978; Anchorage Radio Club, 1978-82; American Cancer Society Bikeathon, 1978; DeMolay, 1962. Published Works: Poems Published in *Patterns*, 1968. Honors and Awards: DX Century Club (100 countries in radio contacts since 1945); Poetry Reading, Chicago Museum Contemporary Art, 1969; Listed in *Who's Who in the Midwest, International Who's Who of Intellectuals, Community Leaders of America, International Who's Who of Engineering, Men of Achievement, Who's Who in the West, Directory of Distinguished Americans*. Address: SR 1762, Eagle River, Alaska 99577.■

FRANK CARROLL ALLEN

Banker. Personal: Born November 10, 1913, in Hazlehurst, Mississippi; Son of Walter Scott and May Ellis Allen; Married Clara Marnee Alford, June 23, 1937; Father of Marnee Louise, Susan Carroll, Elizabeth Jane. Education: A.A. with high honors, Copiah-Lincoln Junior College, 1933; Attended American Institute of Banking, 1935, 1936, 1937, 1947, 1949. Military: Served in the United States Army, 1942-46, attaining the rank of First Lieutenant. Career: Georgetown Bank, Mississippi, Bookkeeper, Teller 1933-34, Cashier, Director 1936-41; Bookkeeper, Deposit Guaranty Bank and Trust Company, Jackson, Mississippi, 1934-37; Bank Examiner, Mississippi, 1942-46; Cashier, Director, Brookhaven Bank and Trust Company, Mississippi, 1947-49; President, Director, Lawrence County Bank, Monticello, Mississippi, 1949-65; President, Monticello Bank, Branch Deposit Guaranty National Bank, Monticello/Newhebron Branches, 1966 to present; Chairman, Advisory Board, Monticello/Newhebron Bank, 1966 to present; Advisory Board, Deposit Guaranty National Bank, Jackson, 1966 to present; Commissioner of Banking and Consumer Finance, State of Mississippi, February-July 1980. Organizational Memberships: American Bankers Association, Chairman, Mississippi District 7 on United States Savings Bonds, 1952 to present; Mississippi Bankers Association, Chairman of Bank Management Committee 1948-49, Group Vice President 1948-49; Insurance and Realty Underwriters, Chairman of the Board 1971-75, Director 1961-76; Mississippi Economic Council, Board of Directors, 1950-53; Monticello Planning Board, Commissioner, 1964-74; Southwest Mississippi Development Assocaiton, Board of Directors, 1960-72. Community Activities: Monticello Manufacturing Company, Chairman, Scholarship Board, 1960-72; Andrew Jackson Council, Boy Scouts of America, Executive Board, 1975 to present; Monticello Chamber of Commerce, President 1951-53 and 1960-61, Director 1951-81; Newcomen Society of North America; Lion's Club, President 1954-55. Address: P.O. Box 297, Monticello, Mississippi 29654.■

GARY IRVING ALLEN

President. Personal: Born April 7, 1942; Son of Ralph W. Allen; Married Elaine Irene; Father of Michelle Irene, Elisa Joy, Scott Jeremy. Education: B.S. Electrical Engineering, Cornell University, 1965; Ph.D. Physiology, State University of New York-Buffalo, 1969. Career: Neurophysiologist; Assistant Professor, 1971-76, Director 1976-76, Laboratory of Neurobiology, Department of Physiology, School of Medicine, State University of New York-Buffalo; Lecturer/Visiting Scholar, Department of Physiology and Anatomy, University of California-Berkeley, 1976-79; Director, Christian Embassy, United Nations, 1979-83; Adjunct Assistant Professor, Department of Physiology, New York Medical College; President, Christian Mission for the United Nations Community. Organizational Memberships: American Physiological Society; Society for Neuroscience; International Brain Research Organization. Community Activities: Asia Society; America-Nepal Society; American Scientific Affiliation, Metropolitan New York Executive Council; Ridgeway Alliance Church, Chairman, Missions Committee; Asia Christian Medical Congress, Philippines, Speaker, 1978, 1979, 1981; Medical Lecturer, United States, Canada, Germany, Singapore; Christian Conference Speaker, United States, India, Korea, Singapore; Christian Lecturer, Indonesia, Japan, Thailand. Address: 965 Knollwood Road, White Plains, New York 10603.■

JOHNNY MAC ALLEN

Coordinator of Public Information/Relations. Personal: Born September 25, 1937; Married Hughanne; Father of Anthony Marc, Nichole Juliana, Andrea Danielle. Education: B.S. Liberal Studies (Journalism emphasis), Central State University in Edmond, Oklahoma; M.S. Journalism, University of Oklahoma; Doctorate in Higher Education Administration, Oklahoma State University in Stillwater. Military: Served in the United States Army, 101st Airborne Division, 1959-61, Sp-4. Career: Coordinator of Public Information/Relations, Instructor of Mass Communication and News Reporting and Writing, Oscar Rose Junior College, Midwest

City, Oklahoma, 1980 to present; 20-Year Veteran of Radio and Television including such Markets as Denver, Omaha, Detroit, San Antonio, Kansas City, Wichita, and Numerous Medium to Smaller Markets including Oklahoma City; Extensive Broadcast Experience Encompassing Management and News Directing to Progamming, Music and Sales; Host and Guest on Numerous Television Programs Dealing with Public Relations, Education and the Mass Media. Organizational Memberships: Member of Numerous Professional Organizations. Community Activities: Board Member, Del City Chamber of Commerce, Chairman Public Image Committee; Co-Chairman, Midwest City, Oklahoma Public Image Committee of City Council Tree Board; Voting Member, Higher Education Alumni Council of Oklahoma. Published Works: Author of Several Articles in the Fields of Education and Mass Communication; Research in the Fields of Educational Technology and Higher Educational Delivery Systems. Honors and Awards: Kappa Tau Alpha Journalism Society; Phi Delta Kappa National Educational Society; Recipient of Bronze Derrick Award Distinguished Achievement for the Best Public Relations Promotional Campaign in Oklahoma for 1981, Bronze Derrick Award of Merit for Best Promotional Campaign in Oklahoma for 1982, Public Relations Society of America, Oklahoma Chapter; Special Recognition Award, University of Oklahoma Chapter, Alpha Epsilon Rho Broadcasting Society; Award of Merit for Service to Del City, Oklahoma Chamber of Commerce, 1982; Listed in *Who's Who in the South and Southwest*. Address: 3348 Del Aire Place, Del City, Oklahoma 73115.■

WILLIAM EUGENE ALLEN

Chief Operating Officer. Personal: Born February 8, 1933; Married Carolyn Ann; Father of Catherine Anne (Allen) Smith, Cheryl Diane (Allen) Hackenberg, William Eugene II. Education: J.D. 1978, B.S. in Laws, Western State University College of Law; Certificate in Business Administration, San Diego State University, 1973; Diploma in Electronic Technology, DeVry Technical Institute, 1960. Military: Served with the United States Army, E-4, 1953-55. Career: Self-Employed Attorney and Business Consultant; Chief Operating Officer, Helle Engineering; Operations Manager, Cohu, Inc. Electronic Division; Controller/Director of Administration, Digital Scientific Corporation (DSC); Director of Engineering, DSC; Project Coordinator, ITT, Aerospace/Optical Division. Organizational Memberships: California State Bar; San Diego County Bar Association; Board of Directors Western State University Alumni Association; Steering Committee, San Diego State University Alumni Association. Community Activities: Active in Political Campaigning at Local, State and National Levels; Sustaining Member of Republican National Committee. Religion: Lutheran, Chairman of the Board of Terrasanta Lutheran Church 1971-74, San Diego Lay Delegate to Lutheran Church National Convention 1974. Honors and Awards: Outstanding Alumni Award, Lincoln High School, Vincennes, Indiana 1973 (honoring 10 most outstanding alumni in 100 years); Certificate of Appreciation, Jet Propulsion Lab, Space Sciences Division 1965 (for participation in the successful mission of Mariner IV's photographing of Mars). Address: 12917 Evalyn Court, Poway, California 92064.■

ROBERT ALLENDER

Organization National Conference Planner and Educational Director. Personal: Born April 12, 1946; Son of Ede Allender; Married Lisa Pack, Daughter of Lucille Pack; Father of Sara Pack, Rebecca Pack. Education: B.A. English Literature, Elmhurst College, Elmhurst, Illinois, 1969; M.A. Educational Media 1972, Ed.D. Psychology of Open Education, Group Dynamics and Organizational Development 1976, Temple University, Philadelphia, Pennsylvania; Training at National Training Laboratories, Bethel, Maine 1973-75, Hayim Greenberg Institute, Jerusalem, Israel 1970-71. Career: National Conference Planner and Educational Director, Big Brothers/Big Sisters of America, 1978 to present; Director of Education, Reform Congregation, Beth Or, Spring House, Pennsylvania Kindergarten, High School, 1977-78; Eastern Pennsylvania Regional Director of Hadassah Zionist Youth Commission, Young Judaea and Hamagshimim, 1975-76; Co-Founder and Co-Director, Growth Unlimited, 1974 to present; Co-Founder and Co-Director, Jewish Educational Workshop, 1972 to present; Assistant Professor, LaSalle College, Department of English, 1980 to present; Teaching Associate, Temple University, Department of Psychoeductional Processes, 1976-77; Adjunct Faculty, Antioch Graduate School, Department of Counseling, 1974-75; Graduate Assistant, Temple University, Department of Psychoeducational Processes, 1973-75; Graduate Assistant, Temple University, Department of Educational Media, 1971-72; Teacher, Project Learn, Alternative Elementary School, Philadlephia 1971-73, Or Ami Religious School, Lafayette Hill, Pennsylvania 1971-72, Oak Park Reform Religious School, Oak Park, Illinois 1967-68, Beth Tikvah Congregation Religious School, Hoffman Estates, Illinois 1965-68. Organizational Memberships: Association of Humanistic Education, 1980 to present; American Society for Training and Development, 1980; Wilderness Society, 1975-77, Association of Humastic Psychology, 1974-77; Graduate Student Association, 1972-76; PEP Center, Steering Committee, 1974-76; Department of Psychoeducational Processes, Program Committee, 1973-75; Treasurer, Jewish Educational Workshop, 1972-74. Religion: Hayim Greenberg Institute, Jerusalem, Israel 1970-71, Director of Education Congregation Beth Or, Spring House, Pennsylvania 1977-78. Published Works: Numerous Publications in His Field; Video Tape Productions. Honors and Awards: Summer Stipend for Research, College of Education, Temple University, 1975; Teaching Associate, Department of Psychoeducational Processes, Temple University, 1974-75; Graduate Assistant, Department of Psychoeducational Processes, Temple University, 1973-74; Graduate Assistant, Department of Educational Media, Temple University, 1972; Scholarship to the Hayim Greenberg Institute, Jerusalem, Israel, 1970. Address: 415 Houston Road, Ambler, Pennsylvania 19002.■

FRANKLIN LLOYD ALLNUTT

Writer, Television and Film Producer. Personal: Born April 16, 1940; Son of Mrs. G. G. Allnutt; Married Ruth Cutler, Daughter of Mr. and Mrs. Charles Cutler; Father of Garrett Franklin, Theodore William, Lara Ruth. Education: B.A. Radio-Television-Film, University of Denver, 1965; Public Relations Courses, Universit of California at Los Angeles, 1966. Military: Served with the United States Naval Reserve, Parachute Rigger 3rd Class, Active Duty 1958-61. Career: Owner, Frank Allnutt Company (Evergreen, Colorado), Publisher/Editor of Books for *Better Living Magazine*, Publishes Books and Provides Public Relations/Advertising Consulting Services, 1981 to present; Executive Director and Producer of Weekly Television Program "The Calvary Temple Hour," Charles Blair Foundation (Denver), 1980-81; Owner/Manager, Allnutt Advertising, 1979-80; General Manager/Editor-in-Chief, Here's Life Publishers, Inc., 1976-79; President, Christian Resource Communications, Inc., 1975-76; Owner/Manager, Franklin L. Allnutt Public Relations and Advertising, 1969-75; Position with Walt Disney Productions, 1963-69. Organizational Memberships: The American Film Institute; Christian Booksellers Association; Christian Ministries Management Association; Evangelical Christian Publishers Association; Public Relations Society of America, Past Member; National Writers Club. Published Works: Author, *Kissinger: Man of Destiny* 1975, *After The Omen* 1976, *The Force of Star Wars* 1977, *The Peacemaker* 1977, *Infinite Encounters* 1978, *In Search of a Superman* 1980, *In My Enemy's Camp* (with Josef Korbel) 1976, *A Movement of Miracles* (with Bill Bright) 1978, *The Holy Spirit* 1980. Honors and Awards: Athletic Award, University of Denver (diver on swimming team); Included in Several Bestseller Lists for *The Force of Star Wars, After the Omen* and *The Peacemaker*; Listed in *Who's Who in the West, Who's Who in America, Personalities of America, International Book of Honor, The Biographical Roll of Honor, Men of Achievement, Community Leaders of America, Community Leaders of the World, Personalities of the West and Midwest, Five Thousand Personalities of the World, International Who's Who of Contemporary Achievement*. Address: Box 247, Indian Hills, Colorado 80454.■

EARL ARTHUR ALLUISI

Chief Scientist. Personal: Born June 11, 1927; Son of Humber P. (deceased) and Elizabeth M. (Dini); Married Mary Jane Boyle; Father of John C., Jean E., Paul D. J., Janet A. Education: B.S. Psychology, The College of William and Mary, 1949; M.A. Psychology 1950, Ph.D. Psychology 1954, The Ohio State University. Military: United States Army Medical Research Laboratory, Fort Knox, Kentucky, Psychology Division, Captain MSC, Head Environmental Factors 1957-58, Psychology Division, First Lieutenant MSC, Research Psychologist 1950-53; United States Army, Sergeant, Infantry, 1944-47. Career: Chief Scientist, Air Force Human Resources Laboratory, Brooks Air Force Base, Texas; Senior Psychologist, Stanford Research Institute, Menlo Park, California, 1958-59; Assistant to Associate Professor of Psychology, Emory University, Atlanta, Georgia, 1959-61; Associate Scientist, Lockheed-Georgia Company, Marietta, Georgia, 1961-63; Professor of Psychology (to VP Planning), University of Louisville, Louisville, Kentucky, 1963-74; University Professor of Psychology, Old Dominion University, Norfolk, Virginia, 1974-83. Organizational Memberships: American Association for the Advancement of Science, Fellow; American Association for Higher Education, Charter Life Member; American Association of University Professors; American Psychological Association, Fellow Numerous Divisions and Committees; COSMOS

Club, 1978 to present; Georgia Psychological Association, Director 1962-63; Human Factors Society, Active in Tidewater Chapter and Alamo Chapter; International Association of Applied Psychology; International Society for Chronobiologia; Inter-University Seminar on Armed Forces and Society, Fellow; Kentucky Academy of Science, Life Member, Section Chair 1964-65; Kentucky Psychological Association, President 1966-67; National Council of University Research Administrators; Psychometric Society; Psychonomic Society, Charter Member; Society for Applied Learning Technology, Senior Member; Southern Society for Philosophy and Psychology, Secretary 1962-65, Council Member 1965-66, President 1967-68; Virginia Psychological Association, Former Member. Community Activities: Louisville HELP Organization, Steering Committee 1965; Woodrow Wilson National Fellowship Foundation, Region VII Committee 1965-67; Kentucky Civil Liberties Union, Inc., Board of Directors 1967-74, Vice Chairperson 1971-72, Chairperson 1972-74; Kentucky Science and Technology Advisory Council 1967-72; Kentucky Humanities Council, Inc., Founding Director 1972-74, President and Chairperson of Board of Directors 1972-73; Department of Defense, Defense Science Board, Chairperson Task Force on Training Technology 1974-76, Chairperson Panel on Environmental and Life Sciences, Task Force on Technology Base Strategy, 1975; National Science Foundation, Advisory Subcommittee of the Applied Social and Behavioral Sciences, 1978-79; Department of the Air Force, Scientific Advisory Board, Committee on the Human Resources Laboratory, 1978-79; United States Army Reserve, Retired List, Medical Service Corps. Published Works: Numerous Editorships and Extensive Research in His Field. Honors and Awards: Phi Beta Kappa, 1949; Psi Chi, Psychology Scholastic Honorary, 1953; Ohio State University Fellow, 1953-54; Alpha Psi Delta, Psychology Research Honorary, 1954; Society of the Sigma Xi, 1955, Life Member; Jerome H. Ely Award of the Human Factors Society, 1970; Franklin V. Taylor Award of the Society of Engineering Psychologists, 1971; Phi Kappa Phi, 1972. Address: 15211 Sandia, San Antonio, Texas 78232.■

RALPH A. ALPHER

Physicist. Personal: Born February 3, 1921; Married Louise Ellen Simons; Father of Harriet Rose Lebetkin, Victor Seth Alpher. Education: M.S. 1945, B.S. 1943, Ph.D. 1948, George Washington University; Career: Physicist. Organizational Memberships: American Physical Society, Fellow, Elected to Council 1979-83, Various Committees; American Association for the Advancement of Science, Fellow, Elected to Section B Committee (Physics) 1981-84; Sigma Xi; Federation American Scientists; New York Academy of Sciences; Past Memberships in American Astronomical Society, American Geochemical Society, Sigma Pi Sigma. Community Activities: Mohawk Hudson Council for Educational Television (WMHT) Board 1972 to present; Chairperson, Board 1979-80; Boy Scouts of America; Local Civic Associations. Honors and Awards: Eagle Scout, 1934; Magellanic Premium, American Philosophical Society 1975, Prix Georges Vanderlinden, Belgian Royal Academy of Scieces, Letters and Fine Arts 1975, John Price Wetherill Medal, The Franklin Institute 1980, New York Academy of Sciences Award in Physical and Mathematical Sciences 1981 (all shared with Robert Herman). Address: 2159 Orchard Park Drive, Schenectedy, New York 12301.■

THOMAS ATKINS ALSPAUGH

Environmental Manager. Personal: Born September 18, 1925; Son of Mr. and Mrs. Everett C. Alspaugh; Married Peggy Adams Johnston, Daughter of Mrs. Henry Johnston; Father of Thomas Jr., Martha West, John Curtis. Education: B.S. Chemistry, University of North Carolina at Chapel Hill, 1949; M.S. Public Health, University of North Carolina School of Public Health, 1951. Military: United States, Seaman 1C (AOM), 1943-46. Career: Environmental Manager, present; Chemist, Ohio Department of Health, Stream Pollution Unit, 1951-53; Research Chemist, Cone Mills Laboratory, 1953-58; Operational Supervisor and Manager Water Supply and Waste Treatment Plants, 1959-72. Organizational Memberships: American Chemical Society; American Water Works Association; Water Pollution Control Association; American Association of Textile Chemists and Colorists; North Carolina Piedmont, Waste Operators Association; North Carolina Piedmont, Water Plant Operators Association; Air Pollution Control Association; A.A.A.S.; New York Academy of Science; North Carolina Textile Manufacturers Association, Water and Air Resources Committee 1970 to present; Member Symposium Committee RA-58 1971 to present, American Textile Manufactureres Institute, Inc., Member Environmental Preservation Committee 1970 to present, Chairman Water Subcommittee 1974 to present, Co-Chairman Operations Subcommittee for Research Grant on 1983 Treatment Guidelines; Reviewer, EPA Grant Program, Textile Wastes, 1973 to present; Reviewer, A.A.T.C.C., Textile Chemists and Colorists, 1975 to present; Member, Sanitary Engineering Technology Curriculum Committee, North Carolina Technical Schools; Member, G.T.I., Curriculum Committee, Operator Training; Guilford County Environmental Affairs Committee, 1980 to present; Yadkin-Pee Dee River Citizens Advisory Committee, 1982 to present. Community Activities: League of Women Voters Hazardous Waste Committee, 1981 to present; Committee Chairman, Cub Scout Pack 157 and 160, 1966-67 and 1976-77; Sunday School Teacher, 1947-50, 1976, 1977, 1980; Boy Scouts, Explorer Chairman, Eastern District, 1968-69; Sea Scouts, Committee, 1962-64; Cub Scouts, Pack Secretary, Pack 157 1963-64, Assistant Cub Master, Pack 157 1964-65, Cub Master, Pack 157 1965-67; High Rock Yacht Club; Young Men's Christian Association, Indian Guide Program, 1974-75; Church, Commission on Missions, Board of Stewards, Trustee 1955-56, 1963-64, 1978-81. Honors and Awards: Co-Winner Industrial Waste Medal, 1959, 1963; Best Industrial Waste Paper, Water Pollution Control Federation. Address: 2003 Mimosa Drive, Greensboro, North Carolina 27403.■

AMY L. ALTENHAUS

Clinical Psychologist and Consultant. Personal: Born July 7, 1950; Daughter of Julian and Corrinne Altenhaus; Married Stephen J. Potter on October 17, 1982. Education: B.A. with honors, University of Wisconsin-Madison, 1972; M.A. 1977, Ph.D. 1978, Rutgers University. Career: Chief Psychologist, Director of Pregnant Adolescent Program; Private Practice of Clinical Psychology; Staff of Outpatient Department, Freehold Area Hospital; Consultant, The Mt. Sinai Medical School, New York City; Consultant to Medical Centers and Industry; Former Staff Psychologist and Director of Rutgers Hotline. Organizational Memberships: American Psychological Association, Chairperson Task Force on Clinical Psychology and Competent Female Behavior; New Jersey Psychological Association; Monmouth-Ocean Psychological Association; Pi Lambda Theta. Community Activities: Academic Review, New York City, Advisory Board; Monmouth Adolescent Programs and Service Network. Honors and Awards: Diplomate, American Academy of Behavioral Medicine. Address: 89 East Main Street, Freehold, New Jersey 07728.■

GORDON MAC KAY AMBACH

University President and Commissioner of Education. Personal: Born October 11, 1934; Son of Russell Ambach; Married Lucy DeWitt Emory, Daughter of Mrs. Katherine Emory; Father of Kenneth Emory, Alison Repass, Douglas Mac Kay. Education: B.A., Yale University, 1952-56; M.A. 1956-57, C.A.S. 1964-66, Harvard University Graduate School of Education. Military: Served with the United States Army Reserve, 1957-63 (including 6 months active duty and 5½ years as Education Specialist). Career: President, University of the State of New York and Commissioner of Education, New York State, 1977 to present, Former Executive Deputy Commissioner; with the United States Office of Education, Washington D.C. 1961-64, Assistant Program Planning Officer, Assistant Legislative Specialist, Executive Secretary for the Higher Education Facilities Act Task Force (appointment by Commissioner Francis Keppel); Administrative Assistant to a Member of The Boston School Committee; Staff Member, Harvard University Graduate School of Education (managed staff seminar of the USEO report "Equality of Educational Opportunity"), 1966-67; Special Assistant to Commissioner James E. Allen Jr.; Assistant Commissioner for Long Range Planning; Executive Deputy Commissioner, New York State Education Department. Community Activities: Co-Chairman, Albany United Way; Former Director, Albany Symphony Orchestra; Serves on Local and University Committees for Yale and Harvard Universities; Member Board of Directors, Lincoln Center Institute, National Commission on Libraries and Information Science and the Saratoga Performing Arts Center; Member, Education Commission of the States; President-elect, Council of Chief State School Officers; Member of the Governor's Cabinet, and on 18 State Boards and Commissions including the New York State Science and Technology Foundation, New York State Health Planning Commission, New York State Commission on Highway Safety, New York State Board for Historic Preservation. Honors and Awards: Recipient of First Distinguished Public Service Award, Independent Student Coalition, 1982. Address: Box 528, 33 Fiddlers Lane, Newtonville, New York 12128.■

JOSEPH MARK AMBROSE

Major General (retired). Personal: Born May 10, 1921. Education: Arlington (Massachusetts) High School, 1938; A.B. cum laude Government, Harvard College, 1942; J.D., Harvard Law School, 1948; United States Army Field Artillery School, 1942, 1945, 1958; Armor School, 1945; Command and General Staff College, 1962. Military: Served with the United States Army and Army National Guard, 1942-81, Second Lieutenant to Major General. Career: Major General (retired); Attorney, Private Practice, 1948-53; Executive Department Commonwealth of Massachusetts, 1953-73. Organizational Memberships: National Guard Association; Association of the United States Army; Navy League; Numerous Veteran Associations; College Class Committee. Religion: Roman Catholic, Annunciation Parish Council 1950-52, Boston Archdiocesan Choir School Club 1978 to present. Community Activities: Town of Danvers (Massachusetts), Town Meeting Member,

Finance Committee, Author of Town Manager Government, 1947-56; North Shore (Massachusetts) Regional Vocational School Planning Committee, 1973; Commonwealth of Massachusetts, Attorney and Special Services Supervisor, Divison of Youth Service 1953-64, The Adjutant General 1964-69, Executive Secretary, Council on Juvenile Behavior 1970-73; Massachusetts Halfway House Association 1960 to present, Founder, President, Director; Big Brother, 1946 to present. Honors and Awards: United States Army, Distinguished Service Medal 1981, Legion of Merit 1970; Massachusetts National Guard, Massachusetts Military Medal, 1981; International Half-Way House Association, Meritorious Service Award, 1976. Address: 114 Howe Street, Framingham, Massachusetts 01701.■

MARC LESTER AMES

Trial Attorney. Personal: Born March 14, 1943; Married Eileen. Education: B.B.A., Baruch College, 1965; LL.B. 1967, J.D., Brooklyn Law School; LL.M. New York University Law School, 1968. Career: Trial Attorney; Former Faculty Member, Long Island University and New York City Community College. Organizational Memberships: Member New York Bar; Admitted to Federal District Courts, Southern and Eastern Districts of New York, United States Court of Appeals, 20 Circuit United States Supreme Court; American Arbitration Association, Arbitrator; New York County Lawyer's Association; New York State Bar Association; New York Social Security Bar Association, Board Directors. Honors and Awards: Citation from New York State Trial Lawyers for Participation in Professional Education Program; Listed in *Who's Who in American Law, Men of Achievement*. Address: 225 Broadway, New York, New York 10007.■

ALI REZA AMIR-MOEZ

Professor. Personal: Born April 7, 1919, in Teheran, Iran; Son of Mohammad and Fatemeh Amir-Moez. Education: B.A., University of Teheran, 1941; M.A. 1951, Ph.D. 1955, both from the University of California, Los Angeles. Military: Served as a Second Lieutenant in the Persian Army. Career: Instructor, Assistant Professor, Associate Professor, and Professor at the University of California-Santa Barbara, University of Idaho, Queens College, University of City of New York, Purdue University, University of Florida, Clarkson College of Technology, Texas Tech University. Organizational Memberships: American Mathematical Society; Mathematical Association of America; Sigma Xi; Pi Mu Epsilon; Kappa Mu Epsilon; Texas Academy of Science; New York Academy of Science. Religion: Universal Theist. Published Works: Author Books, *Elements of Linear Spaces* 1962, *Extreme Properties of Linear Transformations and Geometry in Unitary Space* 1971, *Classes Residues et Figure anec Ficelli* 1968; Plays, "Kaleelah and Demneh," "Three Persian Tales"; Over 150 Papers, Articles and Books. Honors and Awards: The Medal of Pro Mundi Beneficio, Academia Brasileira de Ciencos Humanas, 1975. Address: Math Department, Texas Tech University, Lubbock, Texas 79409.■

MARK AMITIN

Co-Author and Interviewer. Education: Diploma Profound Studies 1976, Doctorate in Theatre 1978, University of Paris. Career: Co-Author and Interviewer, "Signaling Through the Flames"; Archive Housed at University of California-Davis; General Manager, Radical Theatre Repertory and Tour Manager for Living Theatre, 1968-69; Founding Director, Universal Movement Theatre, New York, 1970-76; Coordinator, Rhode Island Festival-Theatre, 1971; Producer of Tours for Living Theatre, Open Theatre, Performance Group, Manhattan Project, Ridiculous Theatre Company, El Teatro Campesino, San Francisco Mime Troupe, Le Plan K, Theatre Laboratorire Vicinal, Studio 2, People Show; Guest Lecturer, Univeristy of Paris VII, France, 1975-77; North American Rep. Festival Mondial du Theatre, France, 1975-76; Festival of Fools, Holland, 1977; Producer, Albee Directs Albee Tour of North America and Asia, 1978-79; Lecturer, Over 140 Universities. Published Works: Contributor to Professional Journals. Honors and Awards: Recipient of New England Theatre Conference Award for Rhode Island Festival, 1972. Address: Box 774, Time Square Station, New York, New York 10036.■

MARVIN C. AMOS

Airline Executive. Personal: Born July 29, 1924, in Seymour, Indiana; Son of Mary Eva Amos; Married Anne Addison; Father of Patrick M., Joanne L., Judy M., Mark A., Steven L. Education: B.A., Hanover College. Military: Served in the United States Army, 1943-46. Career: Senior Vice President, Personnel and Corporate Administration, Eastern Air Lines, Inc.; Former Director, Industrial Relations, Curtiss-Wright Corporation; Has also been associated with General Electric Company, R.C.A., Goodyear Engineering Company. Organizational Memberships: Gamma Sigma Pi. Community Activities: Hanover College, Board of Trustees, Executive Committee, Chairman of Buildings and Grounds Committee; Governor Graham's Advisory Council on Productivity in the State of Florida, Chairman of Subcommittee #2, 1980; Working Group for Business Roundtable Task Force on National Planning and Employment Policy, Eastern Air Lines Representative. Religion: Roman Catholic. Honors and Awards: Awarded Battlefield Commission, 1945. Address: 7745 S.W. 138 Terrace, Miami, Florida 33158.■

L. D. ANAGNOSTOPOULOS

Physician (Cardiologist). Personal: Born March 29, 1930; Son of Kaltezai; Father of Nikki. Education: B.S. Microbiology 1957, M.D. 1961, University of Chicago. Military: Served with the United States Army, 1952-54, Sergeant (Military Intelligence). Career: Physician (Cardiologist). Organizational Memberships: American Medical Association; American Heart Association; American College of Physicians; American College of Chest Physicians; American College of Cardiology; American Academy of Political and Social Sciences; New York Academy of Sciences. Honors and Awards: Hellenic Cultural Circle, Outstanding Services to Humanity 1970; Brotherhod of May 26, 1921, for Achievement and Service to Humanity, 1971; Argolis Society for Services to Humanity, 1979, 1982; Hellenic Voters of America, Outstanding Physician of Greek Descent, 1980; Men of Achievement Award, Cambridge England, 1980; Kalynnian Society, Services to Humanity, 1982; Listed in *Who's Who Among Intellectuals*. Address: 4035 Evergreen Lane, Northbrook, Illinois 60062.■

RAJEN S. ANAND

Professor of Physiology. Personal: Born June 8, 1937; Son of Dial Singh Anand; Married Asha, Daughter of Mrs H. Kaur; Father of Sunjay, Shabeen. Education: B.Sc. Biology, India, 1956; D.V.M., 1960; Ph.D. Physiology, University of California at Davis, 1969. Career: Professor of Physiology, Department of Biology, California State University at Long Beach; Research Physiologist, University of California at Davis, 1968-70; Fellow in Endocrinology, University of California at Los Angeles-Harbor Medical Center, 1977-78; Demonstrator in Biochemistry, M. P. Vet College, Mhow, India, 1960-63. Organizational Memberships: American Physiological Society; American Association for the Advancement of Science; Sigma Xi; Phi Kappa Phi; President, Association of Scientists of Indian Origin in America, President 1982-83. Community Activities: Federation of Indian Associations, Secretary 1980-; Sikh Temple of Orange County, Secretary 1980-; International Club of the University of California at Davis, President 1967-68; Chairman, Committee for Salute to Governor Brown (California), 1980; Member Several Democratic Clubs in Southern California. Honors and Awards: Outstanding Professor, California State University at Long Beach, 1980; Hertzendorf Memorial Award in Physiology, 1969; John W. Gilmore Foreign Student Award, 1967, 1968; Listed in Various Biographical Reference Publications.■

SURESH C. ANAND

Physician, Executive. Personal: Born September 13, 1931; Son of Dr. and Mrs. Sat-Chit-Anand (both deceased); Married Wiltrud Behr; Father of Miriam, Michael. Education: M.B., B.S., University of Lucknow, India, 1954; M.Sc., University of Colorado, 1962; Diplomate, American Board of Allergy and Immunology 1975, Recertified 1980 and 1983. Career: Medical Officer, U.P. India, 1954-57; National Jewish Hospital, Denver, Colorado; Fellow in Pulmonary Disease, 1957-58; Resident in Chest Medicine, 1958-60; Chief Resident, Allergy and Asthma, 1960-62; Mt. Sinai Hospital, Toronto, Ontario, Canada, Internship 1962-63, Resident in Medicine 1963-64, Chief Resident in Medicine 1964-65; Research Associate, Department of Allergy and Asthma, National Jewish Hospital 1966-69; Demonstrator in Clinical Technique 1963-64, and Fellow in Medicine 1964-65, University of Toronto; Clinical Instructor in Medicine, University of Colorado Medical Center, 1967-69; President, Allergy Associates and Laboratory, Ltd.; Staff Member, Phoenix Baptist Hospital, John C. Lincoln Hospital, Good Samaritan Hospital, Doctor's Hospital, Memorial Hospital, St. Lukes Hospital, St. Joseph's Hospital, Scottsdale Memorial Hospital, Mesa Lutheran Hospital, Desert Samaritan Hospital, Maryvale Hospital, Tempe St. Lukes Hospital. Organizational Memberships: Vice President, Phoenix Allergy Society; Association for the Care of Asthma; Interasma

Association; World Medical Association; American Medical Association; Arizona Medical Association, Chairman Scientific Assembly Committee 1980-81; Maricopa County Medical Society; Arizona Allergy Society; Arizona Thoracic Society; Western Society of Allergy and Immunology; New York Academy of Sciences; National Geographical Society; Smithsonian Institute. Community Activities: Camelback Hospital Citizens' Advisory Board, 1972-80; Scottsdale Sertoma Club, 1972-76; Sertoma International, Life Member. Honors and Awards: Physicians Recognition Award, American Medical Association, 1972, 1975, 1978, 1980; Fellow, American College of Physicians, American College of Chest Physicians, American College of Allergists, American Academy of Allergy, American Association of Allergy and Clinical Immunology; Listed in *Who's Who in the West.* Address: 2200 West Bethany Home Road, Phoenix, Arizona 85015 and Lakes Professional Plaza, 1006, East Guadalupe Road, Tempe, Arizona 85283.■

STEPHEN ANDERL

Roman Catholic Priest. Personal: Born July 13, 1910; Son of Henry A. Anderl (deceased). Education: B.A., St. John's University, 1932; M.Div., St. John's University, 1974; Ph.D., World University, 1982. Career: Curate, Saints Peter and Paul Parish, 1936-37; Holy Trinity Parish, 1937-40; Instructor, Vice-Principal, Guidance Counselor, Aquinas High School, 1937-49. Pastor, Sacred Heart Parish 1949-52, St. Michael's Parish 1952-53, St. Mary's Parish 1953 to present; Dean, Durand Deanery, 1953 to present. Organizational Memberships: Diocesan Board of Education; Executive, Catholic Social Agency; Diocesan Personnel Board; Vicar General for Religious; Censor Librorum; Committee for Continued Education of the Clergy; Committee for the Elderly; Executive Board, Founder, West Central Wisconsin Action Agency; Executive Secretary, Diocesan Sodality and C.Y.O.; Governor's Commission on Children and Youth; State Committee on Mental Health and Retardation; Faithful Friar of the Pope John XXIII General Assembly Fourth Degree Knights of Columbus; American Academy of Religion; Wisconsin Genological Society; Wisconsin Academy of Arts, Science and Letters; American Numismatic Society; Collectors of Religion on Stamps; Fellow, International Institute of Community Serivce; Honorary Fellow, Anglo-American Academy. Community Activities: Diocesan Chaplain, Boy Scouts and Girl Scouts; Vice-Chairman, Diocesan Catholic Committee on Scouting; Chaplain, Council Catholic Committee on Scouting; National Catholic Committee on Scouting; Board of Directors, Silver Waters Girl Scout Council; Board of Directors, Indian Waters Girl Scout Council; Chaplain, XII World Jamboree of Boy Scouts, 1967; Chaplain, Seventh and Eighth National Jamborees of Boy Scouts of America, 1969-73. Honors and Awards: Domestic Prelate by Pope John XXIII; St. George Award, 1970; Silver Beaver, 1968; Citation for Outstanding Service to the Poor, 1972; American Honorarium, 1968; St. Ann Award, 1982; Listed in *Who's Who in the Midwest, American Catholic Who's Who, Who's Who in Religion, Two Thousand Men of Achievement, Personalities of the West and Midwest, Blue Book, National Social Directory, Notable Americans of the Bicentennial Era, National Register of Notable Americans, Dictionary of International Biography, Hereditary Register of the U.S.A., Wisconsin Men of Achievement, Men and Women of Achievement, Book of Honor, International Who's Who of Intellectuals, International Register of Profiles, Creative and Successful Personalities, International Who's Who in Community Service, Verlag for Industrie und Kultur, Who's Who in the Catholic World, Academia Italia, Annuario Pontifice.* Address: 2214 Peter Drive, Apartment 309, Eau Claire, Wisconsin 54703-2450.■

APPA LEONE ANDERSON

Chiropractic Roentgenologist. Personal: Born July 10, 1924; Daughter of Grace Baird and Floyd Benjamin Stober (both deceased); Married Harry S. Anderson (divorced), Son of Lydia French and Henry Carl Anderson (deceased); Mother of Linda Lee McCaffrey, John George Anderson, Bonnie Gail Williams, Janet Grace Anderson. Education: Attended Warner Pacific College, Portland, Oregon; Portland State University, Portland, Oregon; Doctor of Chiropractic Degree, Western States Chiropractic College, 1953; Postgraduate Diplomate American Chiropractic Board of Roentgenologists, 1960. Military: Served as Technical Sergeant, Radiologic Technologist in W.A.C. Medical Corps during World War II, 1944-46. Career: Chiropractic Physician; Faculty Member, Western States Chriopractic College, Portland, Oregon, 1951 to present; Professor Clinical Science Division (X-ray); Faculty Continuing Education Division, Western States Chiropractic College and Los Angeles College of Chiropractic, Glendale, California, D.A.C.B.R. X-ray Consultant 1960 to present, Medicare Consultant, Aetna Insurance, Oregon and Alaska 1973 to present; Licensed in Oregon, California; Lecturer on Topic of Diagnostic X-ray, Numerous Seminars, Workshops and Conventions. Organizational Memberships: Worldwide Christian Chiropractic Association, Oregon Representative; American Chiropractic Association; Oregon Association of Chiropractic Physicians; A.C.A. Council on Roentgentology; O.A.C.P. X-ray Council, President 1964; American Chiropractic College of Roentgenologists, Secretary Committee on Education 1964-81; Western States Chiropractic Alumni Association, President 1963-64; W.S.C.C. Ceremony Committee Chairperson (participation in 57 commencements to date). Community Activities: Medicare Seminars, Houston, Texas for Development of Radiological Manifestations of Subluxations 1972, Los Angeles, California Medicare Instructors Workshop 1973, Portland, Oregon 1973, Seattle, Washington 1973; Northwest Regional Medicare Consultants Workship, Boise, Idaho, 1976; Medicare Consultant Aetna Insurance Oregon and A.K. 1973 to present. Religion: Southern Baptist, Sunday School Nursery Worker 1959-79. Honors and Awards: Oregon Chiropractor of the Year, 1976 and 1983; Fellow, International Chiropractic College, 1976; A.C.A. Clyde Martin Distinguished Service Award, 1979-80; Western States Chiropractic College Alumnus of the Year, 1982; Chriopractic Woman of the Year, Oregon CA Association, 1981; Listed in *World Who's Who of Women, Who's Who in Chiropractic.* Address: 14028 Southeast Bush, Portland, Oregon 97236.■

FRANCES SWEM ANDERSON

Retired Nuclear Medical Technologist. Personal: Born November 27, 1913; Daughter of Frank and Carrie S. Swem, (both deceased); Married Clarence A. F. Anderson; Mother of Robert Curtis, Clarelyn Christine Schmelling, Stanley Herbert. Education: Attended Muskegon School of Business; Certificate Course, Muskegon Community College, 1964. Career: Hackley Hospital, Muskegon, Michigan, X-Ray File Clerk and Film Librarian 1957-59, Radioisotope Technolgist and Secretary 1959-65; Nuclear Medical Technologist, Butler Memorial Hospital, Muskegon Heights, 1966-70; Senior Nuclear Medical Technologist, Mercy Hospital, Muskegon, 1970-79; Retired 1979. Organizational Memberships: American Registry of Radiologic Technologists; Certified Nuclear Medical Technologists; American Society Radiologic Technologists, 1964-80; Society of Nuclear Medicine, 1971-80; Society of Nuclear Medical Technologists, Charter Member. Community Activities: Parent-Teacher Association, Mother-Teacher Singer 1941-48, Treasurer 1944-48; Civic A Cappella Choir, Muskegon, 1932-39; Civic Opera Association, Muskegon, 1950-51; Jackson Hill Reunion, Co-Chairman 1982 and 1983; International Platform Association, 1971 to present. Religion: Muskegon Forest Park Covenant Church, Member 1953 to present, Choir 1953-79, 1983 to present, Secretary 1963-79, Sunday School Teacher 1954-75, Sunday School Superintendent 1975-78, Sunday School Treasurer 1981 to present, Church Secretary 1982, 1983 and 1984. Honors and Awards: Frances Anderson Day, Proclaimed by Peers and Department Co-Workers, Mercy Hospital, 1979. Listed in *Who's Who of American Women, Who's Who in the Midwest, The World Who's Who of Women.* Address: 5757 East Sternberg Road, Fruitport, Michigan 49415.■

GORDON WOOD ANDERSON

Research Physicist, Electronic Engineer. Personal: Born March 8, 1936; Son of Gordon Hilmer (deceased) and Avis Elizabeth Hillman Anderson; Married Gillian Anne Bunshaft. Education: B.E.E., Cornell University, 1959; M.S. 1961, Ph.D. 1969, University of Illinois at Urbana-Champaign. Career: Research Physicist, Naval Research Laboratory, Washington, D.C., 1971 to present; Consultant, Planning and Human Systems, Inc., 1978-79; National Research Council Research Associate, Naval Research Laboratory, 1969-70; Ford Foundation Fellow, Research Assistant, Teaching Assistant, University of Illinois at Urbana-Champaign, 1959-69; Physics Teacher, Tougaloo College, 1965. Organizational Memberships: American Physical Society; Institute of Electrical and Electronics Engineers; American Association for the Advancement of Science; Foundation for Science and the Handicapped; Federation of American Scientists; Union of Concerned Scientists. Community Activities: Epilepsy Foundation of America, Board of Directors 1979 to present; Epilepsy Foundation for the National Capital Area, President 1976-78, Executive Committee 1974 to present, Founding Member of the Board of Directors 1972-73, 1974 to present; Colonial Singers and Players, Inc., Secretary-Treasurer, Founding Member of the Board of Directors 1974 to present; District of Columbia Services for Independent Living, Inc., Founding Member of the Board of Directors 1981 to present, Vice President 1982-83; Cornell Club of Washington; University of Illiois Alumni Association; Capitol Hill Restoration Society; American Civil Liberties Union; Amnesty International; National Organization for Women; Alpine Club of Canada; Oesterreichischer Alpenverein; Sierra Club; Wilderness Society; Friends of the Earth; Environmental Defense Fund; Alpha Delta Phi. Religion: St. Mark's Episcopal Church of Washington D.C., Convener 1980, Member 1979-81, Seminarian Lay Training Committee. Honors and Awards: Navy Achievement Award, 1983; Life Fellow, American Biographical Institute Research Association; Sigma Xi; Tau Beta Pi; Eta Kappa Nu; Ford Foundation Fellowship; National Science Foundation Grantee; National Research Council Postdoctoral Research Associate, 1969-70; Sloan Foundation National Scholarship; Cornell National Scholarship; William College Book Award; Red Key, Sphinx Head Undergraduate

TWO THOUSAND NOTABLE AMERICANS

Honor Societies; Author, Papers in Field; Patent; Listed in *Who's Who in the East, Men and Women of Science, Who's Who in Technology Today, Resource Directory of Handicapped Scientists, Directory of Distinguished Americans, Personalities of America, Community Leaders of America.* Address: 1320 North Carolina Avenue, N.E., Washington, D.C. 20002.■

JAMES WILLIAM ANDERSON

Ordained Minister. Personal: Born July 16, 1930; Son of William John Wylly Anderson (deceased); Married Carroll Wombacher; Father of James Carroll, Mark Christian. Education: B.S., Tulane University, 1952; B.D., Austin Presbyterian Theological Seminary, 1955; Attended Duke University Graduate School of Religion, 1958-61; Th.D., New Orleans Baptist Theological Seminary, 1976. Career: Pastor, Benton and Rocky Mount Presbyterian Churches, Louisiana, 1955-58; Pastor, Pittsboro Presbyterian Church, North Carolina, 1958-61; Pastor, Lockhart and Mount Tabor Presbyterian Churches, South Carolina, 1961-67; Teacher, Presbyterian College, Clinton, South Carolina, 1963-64; Pastor, Albany Presbyterian Church, Louisiana, 1968-74; Pastor, First Presbyterian Church, Ponchatoula, Louisiana, 1967 to present. Organizational Memberships: Presbyterian Historical Society; American Church Historical Society; Medieval Historical Society; Presbyterian Historical Society of the Southwest. Community Activities: Big Brother/Big Sister Program, Board Member 1978-81, Youth Service Bureau of Tangipahoa Parish, Board Member 1980 to present; Boy Scouts of America, Executive Board of Istrouma Area Council 1978-80, Chairman Chappepeela District 1978-80; District 684 of Rotary International, Health, Humanity and Hunger Program 1978 to present; Ponchatoula Rotary Club, Present 1977-78, Treasurer 1978 to present. Religion: Chairman, Executive Committee and Council, Presbytery of South Louisiana, 1981; Chairman, Division of Care for Churches, 1979-80. Honors and Awards: Silver Beaver Award, Boy Scouts of America, 1981; Presidential and Lily Scholarships, Duke University, 1958-60; Tulane Presidential Scholarships, 1950-52; Aaron Hartmann Medal in Psychology, Tulane University, 1952. Address: P.O. Box 326, Ponchatoula, Louisiana 70454.■

LORIN W. ANDERSON

Professor. Personal: Born May 21, 1945; Son of Willard R. Anderson; Married Jo Anne Craig, Daughter of E. B. Craig IV; Father of Christopher Craig, Nicholas Craig. Education: B.A., Macalester College, St. Paul, Minnesota, 1967; M.A., University of Minnesota, 1971; Ph.D., University of Chicago, 1973. Career: Assistant Dean, College of Education, University of South Carolina, 1982 to present; Professor of Educational Research, College of Education, University of South Carolina; Former High School Mathematics Teacher. Organizational Memberships: American Educational Research Association; National Council on Measurement in Education, Association for Supervision and Curriculum Development. Community Activities: Pre-School Advisory Board, Bethel Methodist Church, 1980-82; Member, Christian Education Committee, St. Michael and All Angels Episcopal Church, 1980-82. Religion: Member, St. Michael and All Angels Episcopal Church, 1979-83. Honors and Awards: Recipient of President's Award for Emerging Young Researcher, University of South Carolina, 1980; Recipient of Outstanding Teacher Award, University of South Carolina, 1978; Listed in *Who's Who in the South and Southwest.* Address: 4437 Willingham Drive, Columbia, South Carolina 29206.■

MEL ANDERSON

College President. Personal: Born September 28, 1928. Education: B.S., Saint Mary's College, 1952; D.Litt. honoris causa, St. Albert's College, Berkeley, California, 1976; L.H.D. honoris causa, Lewis University, Lockport, Illinois, 1979. Career: President, St. Mary's College of California, 1969 to present; Teacher, Sacred Heart High School, San Francisco, California, 1952-56; Vice Principal, La Salle High School, Pasadena, California, 1956-62; Principal, San Joaquin Memorial High School, Fresno, California, 1962-64; Principal and Superior, St. Mary's High School, Residence School and Grammar School, Berkeley, California, 1964-69. Organizational Memberships: Chairman, Regional Association of East Bay Colleges and Universities, 1979-81; Vice President, Executive Committee, Association of Independent California Colleges and Universities, 1982-84; Member, Independent Colleges of Northern California. Community Activities: Member, Commonwealth Club of California; President, Board of Trustees, St. Mary's College, 1969 to present. Religion: Member of the Brothers of the Christian Schools (F.S.C., Fratres Scholarum Christianarum, a non-clerical world-wide order of the Catholic Church devoted entirely to teaching), 1947 to present. Honors and Awards: D.Litt. and L.H.D. degrees honoris causa. Address: Saint Mary's College, Moraga, California 94575.■

THOMAS JEFFERSON ANDERSON

Governmental Affairs Consultant, Commissioner. Personal: Born November 21, 1919; Married Margaret Anderson; Father of Laurel B. Moore, Eugene Thomas, Craig Jeffrey. Education: Ford Motor Company Engineering School, 1946-48; United States Marine Corps Institute, 1946-51; United States Marine Corps Electronic Schools, 1950-51; United States Army Electronic Schools, 1943-45. Military: Served with the United States Army, achieving the rank of Master Sergeant 1946-51, active 1950-51. Career: Quality Analysis Engineer; Engineering Coordinator; Technical Writer, Ford Motor Company; Commissioner, Michigan Natural Resources Commission, 1983 to present; Legislator, State of Michigan, 1965-82; Governmental Affairs Consultant. Organizational Memberships: Mayor, City of Southgate, Michigan, 1958-61; City Council, President 1963-64; Ecorse Township, Supervisor 1953-58; Intergovernmental Science, Engineering and Technology Advisory Panel 1975-81; National Conference of State Legislators, Chairmanships 1970-82. Religion: Protestant. Honors and Awards: United States Environmental Protection Agency Awards in Environmental Act, State, Federal and Organizational Awards; Audubon Society Awards; Michigan United Conservation Clubs and Soil Conservation Service Awards. Address: 13726 Sycamore, Southgate, Michigan 48195.■

WENDELL BERNHARD ANDERSON

Poet, Writer. Personal: Born January 10, 1920; Son of Gustav B. and Ebba Reed Anderson (both deceased); Married Emily Mansfield Ferry. Education: Attended the University of Oregon, Reed College; B.A., Franklin Pierce College, 1969. Career: Writer, Poet; Former Teacher, Creative Writing, Hampshire Country School, Rindge, New Hampshire; Family Services Caseworker, New Mexico Department of Public Welfare, 1969-73; Social Worker, New Mexico Department of Social Service, Child Welfare, 1973-75; Operator, Harwood Foundation Library Bookmobile Program, University of New Mexico, 1949-51; Served with 5 National Forests as Fire Control Aide; Clerk-Patrolman, United States Fish and Wildlife Service; United States Park Service Fire Control Aide, Bandelier National Monument, 1955. Organizational Memberships: Otero County Board for Alcoholism and Alcohol Abuse, Board Member 1973-74; New Mexico Social Service Agency; Rio Grande Writers Association. Published Works: Collections of Poetry, *The Heart Must Be Half Eagle, Hawk's Hunger, Yes or No, Endangered Island, Season of the Crow, Rocky Mountain Vigil.* Honors and Awards: Ye Taborde Inn Writers Honorary, University of Oregon, 1940-42; Peter B. Allen Student Award for Excellence in English, Franklin Pierce College, 1969; Honors for Thesis for B.A. in English, 1969; Poems have been Anthologized. Address: 102 La Quinta Street, Las Cruces, New Mexico 88005.■

IKE ANDREWS

Attorney. Personal: Born September 2, 1925, in Bonlee, Chatham County, North Carolina; Married Patricia Goodwin; Father of Alice, Nina Patricia. Education: Attended Bonlee High School, Fork Union Military Academy and Mars Hill College; B.S. Commerce, University of North Carolina, 1950; J.D., University of North Carolina School of Law, 1952. Military: Served with the United States Army, Field Artillery Forward Observer, European Theatre in World War II. Career: Admitted to North Carolina Bar, 1952; Partner, Law Firm of Andrews and Stone in Siler City, North Carolina, 1952-72. Community Activities:

United States House of Representatives 1973 to present, Member Committee on Education and Labor 1973 to present, Chairman Subcommittee on Human Resources 1977 to present, Member Subcommittee on Elementary, Secondary and Vocational Education 1973 to present, Member Subcommittee on Post-Secondary Education 1973 to present, Member Select Committee on Aging 1974 to present; General Assembly, State of North Carolina, State Senate 1959-61, State House of Representatives 1961-63, 1967-72, House Majority Leader 1971-72, House Speaker Pro Tem 1971-72, Chairman Committee on Constitutional Amendments 1969-72, Chairman Committee on Rules and Operations 1969-72; Solicitor, 22nd State District (Orange, Chatham, Alamance, Person Counties), 1963-67; Board of Trustees, Consolidated University of North Carolina 1959-72, Executive Committee 1971-72; Member, Governor's Commission on the Restructuring of Higher Education 1969-72; Chairman, Chancellor Selection Committee, University of North Carolina at Chapel Hill; Member, American Legion; Rotary Club; Chamber of Commerce; Masonic Lodge. Religion: Member, First Baptist Church, Siler City, North Carolina, Former Chairman of Board of Deacons, Former Sunday School Teacher. Honors and Awards: Named Siler City Young Man of the Year; Recieved Distinguished Service Award from Asheboro/Randolph County Jaycees; Awarded Bronze Star and Purple Heart, 1944.■

IRVING HENRY ANELLIS

Research Associate. Personal: Born October 31, 1946. Education: B.A., Northeastern University, 1969; M.A., Duquesne University, 1971; Ph.D., Brandeis University, 1977. Career: Research Associate, History of Mathematics; Visiting Research Consultant, Rivista Internazionale de Logica (Italy), Spring 1982; Assistant Professor, Mathematics, University of Minnesota-Duluth, 1981-82; Visiting Lecturer, Mathematics, University of Iowa, Spring 1981; Assistant Professor and Chairperson, Mathematics, Mount St. Clare College, 1980-81; Assistant Professor, Mathematics, Mississippi Valley State University, 1979-80; Adjunct Research Scholar, Philosophy, University of Florida, 1978-79. Organizational Memberships: American Mathematical Society; Canadian Mathematical Society; Association for Symbolic Logic; Unione Matematic Italiana; Organizer, American Mathematics Society Special Session on Proof Theory, Denver, 1983. Honors and Awards: Brandeis University, Graduate Fellowship, 1976-77; Brandeis University Scholarships, 1975-76, 1976-77; Certificate of Merit, *Men of Achievement*, International Biographical Centre (British), 1980; "Outstanding Scientific Achievement," *Personalities of America*, 1982; Member, International Board of Collaborators, Advisor *Riv. Int. de Logica* (Italian), 1980-82; Referee, Mathematics Notes, *American Mathematics Monthly*, 1981.■

THOMAS MICHAEL ANGEL

Business Executive. Personal: Born April 16, 1939; Son of Joseph Vincent and Mary Lucille (Stucid) Angel (both deceased); Married Bette Jean Miller, Daughter of Leo and Alberta (deceased) Miller; Father of Nicole Lee, Tommie Jean, Martine Renee. Education: Graduate, Mount Pleasant High School, 1957; Lifetime Faculty Member, Florida Institute of Technology, 1977. Military: Served with the United States Navy Seabees, Construction Mechanic, 1956-62. Career: Vice President, Santa Fe Underwater Services, 1979 to present; Manager World-wide, Sanford Brothers Divers, 1963-66; Vice President, Sanford Marine Services, 1966-70; Manager World-wide, Fluor Ocean Services, 1970-73; Manager World-wide, Santa Fe Engineering and Construction Company, 1973-79. Organizational Memberships: Association of Diving Contractors 1973-74, President and Board Member; Florida Institute of Technology 1977 to present, Chairman Board of Advisors; American Bureau of Shipping 1980 to present, Technical Committee Member; Santa Barbara City College 1974 to present, Board of Advisors; Marine Technology Society, 1964 to present; Underseas Medical Society, 1975 to present. Community Activities: Chamber of Commerce, 1970 to present; American Petroleum Institute, 1975 to present. Religion: Vice President, Holy Names Society, 1961; Member, Knights of Columbus, 1965. Address: 25 Mary Hughes Court, Houma, Louisiana 70360.■

MORTON ANTELL

Physician. Personal: Born May 17, 1937; Son of Abraham and Ray Morton; Married Marilyn; Father of Debra, Diane, Craig. Education: B.A. Economics, New York University; B.S. Columbia University; D.O., Chicago College of Osteopathy. Career: Physician, Kings and Queens County. Community Activities: Health Care Review; United States Senate Business Advisory Board. Religion: Hebrew. Honors and Awards: New York State Regents Scholar, 1981-82; Listed in *Who's Who in the East*. Address: 3384 Jason Court, Bellmore, New York 11710.■

M. LAWREACE ANTOUN

Woman Religious, College President. Personal: Born December 30, 1927; Daughter of George K. and Freda Habib Antoun. Education: B.S., Villa Marie College, 1954; M.S. 1959, Ph.D. (A.B.D.) 1965, University of Notre Dame. Career: Entered the Sisters of Saint Joseph, 1947; Villa Maria College, Instructor of Chemistry 1955-61, Assistant Professor of Chemistry 1965-66, President 1966 to present. Organizational Memberships: National Fuel Gas, Board of Directors Audit Committee; Pennsylvania Post-Secondary Education Planning Commission/1203 Commission, Chairperson; Pennsylvania State Board of Education, Chairperson of Council of Higher Education and of Advisory Committee; Governor's Commission on the Financing of Higher Education. Community Activities: Commission for Independent Colleges and Universities, Executive Board; Commonwealth Judicial Council; Cornell University, Advisory Board, Human Ecology; Erie Conference on Community Development, Board of Directors; Hamot Medical Center, Board of Corporators; King's Collge, Board of Trustees, Student Affairs; McMannis Education Trust Fund, Chairperson Advisory Council; Middle States Association, Commission of Higher Education, Planning Consultant; Saint Vincent Health Center, Board of Corporators. Religion: Catholic. Honors and Awards: Atomic Energy Commission Grant for Research in Chemistry; Honorary Doctorate, Gannon University; Award for Distinguished Service, Pennsylvania Association of Adult Education; Listed in *International Who's Who of Women*, *The World Who's Who of Women*, *Outstanding Educators of America*, *Who's Who in Religion*, *Who's Who of American Women*, *Community Leaders and Noteworthy Americans*, *Contemporary Personalities*. Address: Villa Maria Collge, 2551 West Lake Road, Erie, Pennsylvania 16505.■

CLARA TAUBMAN APPELL

Family Therapist, Executive, Consultant. Personal: Born July 31, 1921; Daughter of Max and Yetta Schuber Taubman (both deceased); Married Morey L. Appell (deceased); Mother of Laurie, Randy Johnson, Glenn, Jodie, Jonathan. Education: B.S. 1942, M.A. 1946, Ohio State University; Ed.D., Columbia University, 1959; Undertook Post-Doctoral Studies, Academic-Clinical Program, Ackerman Institute for Family Therapy, 1971-73. Career: Consultant on Human Development; Private Practice in Family Therapy; President, Morey L. Appell Human Relations Foundation; Lecturer, University of Connecticut, 1982-83; Adjunct Professor, Queens College, City University of New York, 1975-79; Title XX Project Associate, University of Connecticut-Stamford, 1978-79; Consultant, Butterick Publications, Risp Series of Filmstrips, 1979-80; Co-Director of Family Life Center, New York Society of Ethical Culture, 1972-73; Coordinator of Child Development and Family Life Education, Greenwich Health Association, 1969-71; Consultant to the Greenwich (Connecticut) Association for Retarded Citizens, 1982-83; Consultant, Connecticut State Department of Education, 1968-69; Director, Home Care Training and Child Development Family Specialist, Bank State College, 1967-68; Professor of Child Development and Family Relations and Head Start Coordinator, University of Wisconsin-Stout, 1966-67; Associate Professor of Child Development and Family Life and Co-Director of Family Life Institute, Indiana State University, 1964-66; Child Guidance League Parent Educator, Brooklyn, New York, 1954-61; Brooklyn College, City University of New York, 1954-61; Home Economics Teacher, Long Island City High School, 1947-48; Educational Director, Day Care Center, Colony House, Brooklyn, 1946-47; High School Teacher, 1943-46. Organizational Memberships: American Association for Marriage and Family Therapy, Programs Chairperson, Conecticut Division 1978; American Association of Sex Educators, Counselors and Therapists; American Orthopsychiatric Association, Fellow; American Home Economics Association; American Psychological Association; Forum for Death Education and Counseling; International Council of Psychologists; Groves Conference on Marriage and Family; National Council on Family Relations; Tri-State Council on Family Relations, Treasurer 1958-59; Society for Research in Child Development. Community Activities: Morey L. Appell Human Relations Foundation, Founder and President 1978 to present; Hospice of Stamford, Inc., Volunteeer Consultant 1981-82; Connecticut Media and Communications Task Force for White House Conference on Families, 1979-80; Mothering Center, Inc., Cos Cob, Connecticut, Board Member 1979 to present; Stamford Family Life Workshops Inc., Board Member 1979-80; Public Service Radio Program Hostess/Moderator, "Family Talk," WGCH-AM, Greenwich, Connecticut, 1974-80; Connecticut Association of Marriage and Family Counselors, Court Judicial Department, Family Conciliation Court, Chairperson, State Conference, Divorce Collaboration; Groves Conference, Program Committee 1978; National

Family Life Education Workshop, Planning Committee 1971; Indiana State University Auspices Radio and Television Series, Co-Host, "Family Talk," 1964-66; Talks, Seminars, Workshops to Professionals and Community Groups, 1953 to present; Child Study Association of America, Book Committee 1950-61; Community Newspaper Column Co-Author, "Living with Our Children," 1951-53. Religion: Speaker at Numerous Religiously Sponsored Meetings of Church Groups, Jewish Groups, Young Women's Christian Association; Member of Mental Health Professionals, Sponsored by Jewish Family Service of Stamford, Conecticut. Honors and Awards: Fellow International Council of Sex Education and Parenthood, 1981; Certificate of Appreciation, Gateway Dental Hygienists, 1980; Greenwich Kiwanis Certificate of Appreciation, 1975; Ohio State University Diamond Anniversary Award Recipient in Home Economics, 1971; Omicron Nu; Delta Kappa Pi; Pi Lambda Theta; Graduate Fellowships, Ohio State University, 1945-46; Listed in *Who's Who of American Women*. Address: 145 Old Church Road, Greenwich, Connecticut 06830.■

WAYNE DOUGLAS APPLEMAN

Government Official. Personal: Born July 8, 1937; Son of W. Ross Appleman; Father of Todd Douglas, Scott Douglas. Education: B.A., Ohio Wesleyan University; Graduate Study in Business and Law, Ohio State University. Military: Served with the United States Army, National Guard, 1960-63. Career: Chief of Management and Staff Development 1983 to present, Manager of Quality of Work Life Center 1981-82, California Department of Personnel Administration; Assistant Division Chief and Manager Training Policy 1978-81, Manager Instructional Design 1975-78, Manager Management Development Services 1972-75, Coordinator Regional Training Centers 1971-72, California State Personnel Board, Sacramento, California; Assistant Director, Training and Development, Wetterau Foods, St. Louis, Missouri, 1969-70; Corporate Director of Training, American Investment Company, St. Louis, Missouri, 1966-68; Personnel Staff Work, Nationwide Insurance Company, Columbis, Ohio, 1961-66. Organizational Memberships: American Society for Training and Development, Chapter Co-Founder 1972, Vice President 1974, President 1975, Regional Assistant Vice President 1977-78 and Assistant Vice President Administration 1981-82, National Member of Ethics Committee 1979, Member of Communications Task Force 1978, Chairperson of National Heritage Task Force 1982, Sacramento Quality Circle Facilitator Network Founder and Facilitator 1982; Member Board of Directors, Center for Management Development, Fairfield, California, 1976-81; Intergovernmental Training and Development Center, San Diego, 1971-81; Management Development Institute, Oakland, 1971-81; Valley Regional Training Center, Fresno, 1971-81; Channel Coast Regional Training Center, Santa Barbara, 1979-81; Southwest Regional Training Center, Carson, 1977-81; Consultant in Quality Circles. Community Activities: Chairman, Advisory Group, Department of Management and Supervision, Sierra College, 1977-80; Campaign Manager, Sacramento State Employees United Way, 1975; President, Parent-Teacher Association, 1976. Religion: Ordained Elder, United Presbyterian Church, 1979; Church Session Board Member, 1979-82. Honors and Awards: Torch Award, American Society for Training and Development, 1979, for Distinguished Contribution to the Profession and the Society. Address: 6819 Coachlite Way, Sacramento, California 95831.■

GUYLAINE RAYMONDE ARAGONA

Assistant Researcher, Assistant to Chief of Staff, Assistant to Executive Director, Assistant Director, Curator. Personal: Born August 31, 1954; Son of Armand and Magella Rouleau; Married Ronald J., Son of Paul Sr. and Marie Antoinette Aragona; Mother of Ronald J. Jr., Jason Bryant Palmer, Bradford Ashley Hamilton, Danielle Vita Valente, Shani Jamie Valente, Conan Michael Christopher Valente. Education: Assistant Researcher, Vertebral Subluxation Complex, The R. J. Aragona Cooperative Chiropractic Health Center; Chemistry for Health Sciences, New Hampshire Technical Institute of Health Sciences. Career: Executive Controller, Eastern Gypsum "76," Inc., 1976-81; Assistant Researcher, R. J. Aragona Chiropractic Spinal Biomechanics Research Laboratories for Congenital Anomalies, Developmental Defects and Vertebral Subluxation Degeneration; Assistant to Chief of Staff as Examiner for Spinal Biomechanical Misalignment and Gradation; Assistant to Executive Director, the Department of Education, R. J. Aragona Cooperative Chiropractic Health Center; Assistant Director of Department of Spinal Roentgenology (X-ray), R. J. Aragona Chiropractic Health Center; Curator, R & G Aragona Gallery of Infinite Unparalleled Expressions of Perceptive Art; Vice President and Treasurer, R. J. Aragona Publishers, Inc. Organizational Memberships: Active Member, Patient Education Planning Subcommittee, B. J. Palmer Chiropractic Philosophy Research Committee, Inc., 1976 to present; Executive Board Member, Chapter 1, Patient Education Planning Subcommittee of the B. J. Palmer Chiropractic Philosophy Research Committee, Inc.; Volunteer Worker, Cooperative Patient Group, R.J.A.C.C.H.C., 1972 to present. Community Activities: Political Supporter, Senior Representative Member for State Governor of New Hampshire; Supporter, Young Men's Christian Association, Manchester, New Hampshire, Building Expansion Program, 1982; Sustaining Member, New Hampshire Association of Chiefs of Police, 1979 to present. Honors and Awards: Listed in *Community Leaders of America, Biographical Roll of Honor*. Address: 4 Brimstone Hill Road, Amherst, New Hampshire 03031.■

RONALD J. ARAGONA

Educator, Author-Editor-Publisher, Chiropractic Instructor, Administrator, Chiropractic Consultant, Inventor, Chiropractic Historian. Personal: Born May 12, 1944; Son of Paul C. Sr. and Marie Antoinette Aragona; Married Guylaine R. Aragona on March 21, 1981, Daughter of Armand and Magella Rouleau; Father of Ronald J. Jr., Jason Bryant Palmer, Bradford Ashley Hamilton, Danielle V. Valente, Shani J. Valente, Conan M. C. Valente. Education: Doctorate Degree in Chiropractic 1965, Postgraduate Degrees, Ph.C. and X-ray and Spinography 1965, A.S.C.C., Columbia College of Chiropractic, New York City, New York; Diplomat Degree in Chiropractic National Board of Chiropractic Examiners, 1966; License, State of Vermont, 1966; License, State of New Hampshire, 1967; Extensive Postgraduate Continuing Education. Career: Educator; Author-Editor-Publisher; Chiropractic Instructor; Administrator; Chiropractic Consultant; Inventor; Chiropractic Historian; Assistant, Department of X-Ray, Columbia College of Chiropractic, 1964-65; Private Practice, New York, New York, 1965-69; Sherman College of Straight Chiropractic, Spartanburg, South Carolina Extension Faculty Member, 1978 to present; Lecturer on the Principles of Chiropractic, Degenerative and Developmental Defects of the Spine, the Vertebral Subluxation Complex, Genetic and Developmental Subluxation Complex; Executive Director, Founder, Developer, Chief of Staff, R. J. Aragona Cooperative Chiropractic Health Center for Health, Chiropractic Education and Research, Manchester, New Hampshire, 1969 to present; Appointment to Position of Chairman, Chiropractic Advisor to the Scientific Advisory Board of Renaissance International, Inc., 1980 to present; Head of Research, R. J. Aragona Chiropractic Spinal Biomechanics Research Laboratories for Congenital Anomalies, Developmental Defects and Vertebral Subluxation Degeneration, 1976 to present. Organizational Memberships: International Chiropractors Association, 1962 to present; Columbia Chiropractic College Alumni Association, 1965 to present; C.I.C., Atlantic States Institute of Chiropractic, 1966 to present; Chiropractic Association of New York, 1966-69; New York Chiropractic Society, 1967-69; Granite State Chiropractic Society, 1969; American Chiropractic Association, 1967; Sustaining Member, New Hampshire Association of Chiefs of Police, Inc., 1969 to present; Member, New Hampshire Chiropractic Association, Inc., 1970-75; Palmer College of Chiropractic Ambassador, 1971 to present; Founder and First Chairman, B. J. Palmer Chiropractic Philosophy Research Committee, Inc. 1971, Chairman of Board of Directors 1971 to present, Chairman of Chiropractic Legislative Subcommittee 1971 to present, Member Recruitment and Scholarship Subcommittee 1971-79; Founder and Member, Board of Directors, The Granite State Chapter of National Health Federation, 1972; International Chiropractors Association, State Representative Assemblyman for the State of New Hampshire, Executive Office Held for 3 Consecutive Terms, 1972-74, 1974-76, 1976-78; Liaison to I.C.A. Legislative Committee, New Hampshire Legislative Affairs, 1973-78; B. J. Palmer Chiropractic Philosophy Research Committee, Inc., Member Continuing Education Subcommittee, 1973-79, Chairman Thesis Review Committee 1973 to present; New Hampshire Regional Advisor, Sherman College of Straight Chiropractic, 1973 to present; Invited to Attend and Critique Gonstead Chiropractic Education Seminars, 1972; International Chiropractors Association, Chairman of Handbook Committee 1974-76, Liaison to Research Committee and University of Colorado's Biomechanics Conference on the Spine 1974-78, Invitation to Attend Mid-Winter Reserach Workshop as Chairman of B. J. Palmer Chiropractic Philosophy Research Committee, Inc. 1974-78; HMO Input Provider 1974, Member State of New Hampshire Health Planning Organization; Honorary Member, Sherman College of Straight Chriopractic Alumni Asssociation, 1974; Founder and Developer, N.H.S.C.S., Inc., 1975-79; Liaison to Committee on Unity, New Hampshire Chiropractic Association, 1975; Chiropractic Liaison to New Hampshire Commissioner of Labor to Establish Equal Representation for First Chiropractic Peer Review Committee, 1975; New Hampshire Straight Chiropractic Society, Inc., Member Board of Directors 1976-78, Chairman of Ethics Committee 1975-78, Postgraduate Education Convention Chairman 1976, Continuing Education Committee 1976-78; Advisor to Patient Education Planning Subcommittee, B. J. Palmer Chiropractic Philosophy Research Committee, Inc., 1976 to present; Advisor of the Federation of Straight Chiropractor's Organization, Liaison to International Chiropractors Association Counsel on Chiropractic Education Study Committee 1976, Chairman of I.C.A. Constitution and By-Laws Committee, 1976; Student Referral Counselor, A.D.I.O. Institute of Straight Chiropractic, 1978 to present; Advisor to Board of Directors, Patients for Cooperative Chiropractic Education, Inc., 1978 to present; Member, Sacro-Occipital Technique Associaton, 1982; Addressed Members of Hamilton Chiropractic Society Seminar and Exposition at Hamilton Convention Center, Hamilton, Ontario, 1981; Health Instructor, Community Education Program, United States Government, 1972; Lectured at D. E. Life Foundation, 1973-74; Class President, Columbia College of Chiropractic, 1962-64. Community Activities: Manchester, New Hampshire Jaycees; Others. Published Works: Author and Publisher of Numerous Articles, Pamphlets and Journals on Technical, Scientific, Philosophical and Educational Aspects of Chiropractic, Internationally Distributed; Numerous Other Publications. Honors and Awards: Clarence N. Flick Memorial

Award, Foundation for Health Research, 1965; Columbia College Meritorious Certificate, 1966; Bronze "Chiropractic Oath," 1968; Physical Fitness Leadership Award, United States Jaycees Metropolitan Life Award, 1969; Original Founders and First Chairman Award, B. J. Palmer Chiropractic Philosophy Research Committee, Inc., 1971; Guest Speaker Award of Appreciation, Jaycees, 1974; Certified Thesis Review Board Member Award, B.J.P.C., Inc., 1975; Acknowledgement of Election Certification for Three Consecutive Terms as Executive Officer of Represenetative Assembly for State of New Hampshire in International Chiropractors Association, 1976; Certificate of Commendation for Health Center Expansion, Manchester, New Hampshire, Junior Women's Club, The Generation of Women's Clubs and Cities Service Company, 1976; P.E.P.S. Meritorious Award, 1976; Nominated by Governor of State of New Hampshire, Meldrim Thomson Jr., to Health and Welfare Advisory Commission; Certificate of Gratitude and Appreciation from Sherman College of Straight Chiropractic Rugby Supporters Club, 1980; Numerous Others; Listed in *Who's Who in Chiropractic International, Communty Leaders of America, Biographical Roll of Honor, Personalities of America, Directory of Distinguished Americans*. Address: 132 Webster Street, Manchester, New Hampshire 03104.■

ABELARDO DE JESUS ARANGO

General and Vascular Surgeon. Personal: Born July 6, 1944; Son of Dr. Abelardo Arango and Julia Arango (deceased); Married Janet, Daughter of Louis and Lois Rossi; Father of Julia, Jannette, Abelardo, David Anthony. Education: M.D. cum laude, University of Antioquia, Medellin, Colombia; Manuel Uribe Award, University of Antioquia, 1967; N.I.H. Research Fellow in Liver Diseases, University of Miami, 1968; Fellow in Surgery, University of Texas Southwestern, Medical School at Dallas, 1974; American Board of Surgery, 1974; Fellow American College of Surgeons, 1977; Fellow, American College of Gastroenterology, 1980; Fellow, American Society of Abdominal Surgeons, 1981. Career: Chief Surgical Resident, Jackson Memorial Hospital University of Miami Schol of Medicine, 1972-73; Clinical Instructor, Department of Surgery, University of Miami School of Medicine, 1973-74; Visiting Assistant Professor, University of Texas Southwestern Medical School, 1975-80; Assistant Professor of Surgery, Department of Surgery, University of Miami School of Medicine, 1975-80; Clinical Assistant Professor, Department of Surgery, University of Miami School of Medicine, 1981 to present. Organizational Memberships: Dade County Medical Society; Florida Medical Association; American Medical Association; Southern Medical Association; American Gastroenterology Association; New York Academy of Science; American Trauma Society; Florida Association of General Surgery; Dade-Monroe Professional Standards Review Organization; University of Miami School of Medicine Visiting Committee for the School of Medicine. Religion: Active Member of the Catholic Church. Honors and Awards: University of Antioquia, Medellin, Colombia, M.D. cum laude; Manuel Uribe Award, University of Antioquia. Address: Mercy Professional Building, 3661 South Miami Avenue, Miami, Florida 33133.■

CARLOS J. ARBOLEYA

Banker. Personal: Born February 1, 1929; Son of Fermin (deceased) and Ana Quiros; Married Marta Quintana, on August 29, 1954; Father of Carlos. Education: Attended Public High School 89 (Brooklyn, New York), Stuyvesant High School (New York), Havana University (Cuba). Career: Instructor in Principles of Banking and American Business; Held Positions from Office Boy to Manager, First National City Bank of New York (Havana, Cuba), 1946-57; Assistant Manager, The Trust Company of Cuba (Havana), 1957-59; Chief Auditor, Comptroller's Division, Banco Continental Cubano (Havana), 1959-60; Held Positions from Clerk to Office Manager and Comptroller, Allure Shoe Corporation (Miami, Florida), 1960-62; Operations Officer, Personnel Director, Cashier, Vice President and Cashier, Secretary to the Board of Directors, Boulevard National Bank (Miami, Florida), 1962-66; Executive Vice President and Cashier, President and Director, President and Vice Chairman of Board, Fidelity National Bank of South Miami (Florida), 1966-73; Co-Owner, Organizer, President and Director, Chairman of the Board and President, The Flagler Bank (Miami), 1973-75; President and Director, Barnett Bank at Westchester (Miami) and Barnett Bank at Midway, 1975-76; Chairman of the Board, Barnett Bank/Bank Americard Center (Miami), 1975-76; President and Chief Operating Officer and Director, Consolidated Barnett Banks of Miami; Chairman of the Board and Chief Executive Officer, Barnett Bank/Bank Americard Center; President, Barnett Leasing Company, 1977-81; Vice Chairman and Chief Operating Officer and Director, Consolidated Barnett Bank of South Florida, 1981 to present; President, Barnett Leasing Company; Director, L. Luria and Son. Organizational Memberships: National Amateur Athletic Association, Director; National Softball Association, Director; Havana University Honor Athletes Association, Director; American Institute of Banking, Board of Governors and Vice President; National Association for Bank Audit Control, Director; Bank Administration Institute, Past President and Director; Inter American Association of Businessmen, Director; Dade County Bankers Association, Director; Florida Bankers Association, Economic Development Committee, Board Member; Delta Sigma Pi; American Bankers Association, Banking Advisor; Numerous Other Professional Organizations. Community Activities: Children's Rehabilitation Center Committee; Baseball Little League; Bankers Club, Sports Commissioner; Cuban Olympic Committee, Director; Kiwanis Club; March of Dimes, Director; Dade County Association of Retarded Children, Director; United Fund, Co-Chairman; Heart Association of Greater Miami, Director; Boy Scouts of America, Assistant Council Commissioner, Council Advancement, Chairman Council Executive Board; Miami Heart Institute, Board of Directors; Numerous Other Civic Organizations. Honors and Awards: Certificate of Merit, American Heart Association, 1965; Distinguished Service to Youth Award, Y.M.C.A., 1968; Bank Administration Institute, Distinguished Service Award, 1968; May 7, 1971, Carlos J. Arboleya Day in Dade Count for Civic and Youth Work, Awarded by Mayor Steve Clark; Keys to the Cities of Miami, Coral Gables, Miami Beach, South Miami and to Dade County; WQBA and WQAM Outstanding Citizen Honor Awards; Saint George Emblem, The Catholic Church's Highest Honor for Scouting; Numerous Awards from the Boy Scouts of America; Presidential Four Leaf Clover, White House, Washington D.C., 1973; George Washington Honor Medals for Americanism Activities, Public Address, Advertising Campaign on Americanism; Horatio Alger Award, American Schools and Colleges Association, 1976; Greater Miami Business Hall of Fame Award, 1982; State of Israel's Peace Award, 1982; Florida Congressional Delegation "Distinguished Service Award," 1983; Numerous Other Civic and Professional Awards; Listed in *Florida Lives, Who's Who in Florida, National Social Directory, Personalities of the South, Who's Who in the South and Southwest, Who's Who in Banking, Who's Who in Industry and Finance, Community Leaders of America, Two Thousand Men of Achievement, Prominent Cuban Familties, Who's Who in Commerce and Industry, International Who's Who in Community Service*. Address: 1941 Southwest 23 Street, Miami, Florida 33145.■

CARL MARION ARCHER

Oil Company Executive, Farming Executive. Personal: Born December 16, 1920, in Spearman, Texas; Son of Robert Barton and Gertrude Lucille Sheets Archer; Married Mary Frances Garrett, August 22, 1939; Father of Mary Frances, Carla Lee. Education: Attended Texas University at Austin, 1937-39. Career: President, Anchor Oil Company, 1959 to present; President, Carl M. Archer Farms, 1960 to present; General Manager, Speartex Grain Company, 1967 to present; General Manager, Speartex Oil and Gas Company, 1974 to present. Organizational Memberships: Texas Grain Dealers Association; National Grain Dealers Association; Texas Independent Producers and Royalty Owners Association; Panhandle Producers and Royalty Owners Association; American Petroleum Landmen Association; National Bankers Association; Texas Bankers Association. Community Activities: Director, Panhandle Bank and Trust Comapny, Borger, Texas; Democratic County Chairman, 1969 to present. Religion: Member Church of Christ. Honors and Awards: Listed in *Who's Who in Finance and Industry, Who's Who in the World, Dun and Bradstreet*. Address: 304 South Endicott Street, Spearman, Texas 79081.■

LLOYD DANIEL ARCHER

Media Consultant, Photographer, Professor. Personal: Born May 15, 1942, in Cromwell, Indiana; Son of Dallas Lloyd Archer and Wilma Christine (Halsey) Archer; Married Carol Sue Bonney Archer; Father of Elisa Carol. Education: B.S. Music/Radio and Television, Indiana University, 1971; M.S., Instructional Systems Technology, Indiana University, 1973. Career: Director of the Instructional Media Services Center, Indiana University, Bloomington Campus, 1970-73; Director of Media and Assistant Professor, Fort Valley State College, 1973 to present; Consultant/Educational Media Specialist, Southeast Consortium for International Development, Republic of Mali, Africa, 1982. Organizational Memberships: Association for Educational Communications and Technology; Georgia Association for Instructional Technology; Georgia Association for Counselor Education, Executive Committee; American Association of University Professors, Fort Valley State Chapter, Vice President; End Zoners Club, Fort Valley State, Charter Member; Community Activities: The National Association for the Advancement of Colored People; Phi Mu Alpha Sinfonia Fraternity. Honors and Awards: Listed in *Community Leaders of America, Directory of Distinguished Americans, International Men of Achievement, Two Thousand Notable Americans, International Book of Honor*. Address: 224 Kingsbury Circle, Warner Robins, Georgia 31903.■

TWO THOUSAND NOTABLE AMERICANS

TROY EUGENE ARGENBRIGHT

Educator. Personal: Born January 25, 1921; Son of George O. and Altha L. Argenbright (both deceased); Married Betty M. Education: B.S.; M.A. Military: Served in the United States Army Air Force. Career: Biology Teacher, Garland High School (Garland, Texas). Community Activities: Scottish Rite; Shriner. Religion: Methodist. Honors and Awards: President, Garland Scottish Rite Club. Address: 3505 Classic Drive, Garland, Texas 75042.■

L. JULES ARKIN

Attorney. Personal: Born March 19, 1929; Father of Gary, Richard. Education: LL.B., University of Miami; Attended Emory University. Military: Lieutenant Commander, United States Naval Reserve (retired). Career: President (1980-84) and Director (1969-84), Financial Federal Savings and Loan Association of Dade County; Attorney at Law, Partner, Firm of Meyer, Weiss, Rose, Arkin & Shockett, P.A. Organizational Memberships: American Bar Association; Florida Bar; Dade County and Miami Beach Bar Associations. Community Activities: Past President Greater Miami Jewish Federation, Past Chairman Budget Committee, Past General Campaign Chairman, Past Chairman of Foundation of Jewish Philanthropies; Trustee, Past President, Former Member Board of Governors, Miami Beach Chamber of Commerce; Mount Sinai Hospital of Greater Miami, Life Trustee, Past Vice President Board of Trustees, Past President Sustaining Board of Fellows; Director, H.I.A.S. and Council of Jewish Federations; Member Board of Governors, Greater Miami Chamber of Commerce; Member and Past President, Miami Beach Kiwanis Club; Former Chairman and Former Member of the Board, City of Miami Beach Social Services Advisory Board; Member, Temple Beth Sholom; Member, Hibiscus Lodge No. 275 Free and Accepted Masons. Honors and Awards: President's Leadership Award, Greater Miami Jewish Federation, 1967; Civic League of Miami Beach, Outstanding Civic Leader of Miami Beach, 1971; Silver Medallion Award, National Conference of Christians and Jews. Address: 407 Lincoln Road, Miami Beach, Florida 33139.■

ALMETTA ARMSTRONG

Educator. Personal: Daughter of Mr. and Mrs. R. B. Armstrong. Education: A.B., Shaw University; Master's Degree, North Carolina A&T State University; Additional Study, North Carolina State University. Career: Teacher. Organizational Memberships: Election Chairperson/Resolution Chairperson, District 8 N.C.A.E., 1974-81; Faculty Representative, State N.C.A.E Human Relations Council; President, State Treasurer, Montgomery County North Carolina Association of Educators; President, State Treasurer, Montgomery County Association of Classroom Teachers. Community Activities: North Carolina Human Relations Council; North Carolina Inmate Labor Commission; Sandhills Mental Health Area Board; Alcohol and Drug Abuse Advisory Board, 1977-82; North Carolina Black Leadership Caucus, Chairperson Eighth Congressional District; State Democratic Platform; Delegate to National Democratic Mini and National Convention, 1980; Carter Key/Hunt Key, 1980 Election. Religion: Baptist (Life). Honors and Awards: Miss Shaw University National Alumni Queen, 1969; Outstanding Leadership Plaque, State Black Leadership Caucus, State Level, National Association for the Advancement of Colored People/State Council on Status of Women, 1979-80; District 8 Caucus; Montgomery County Black Caucus; Montgomery County N.C.A.E. Address: Route 2 Box 128, Candor, North Carolina 27229.■

ANNE L. ARMSTRONG

Executive. Personal: Born December 27, 1927; Daughter of Armant and Olive (Martindale) Legendre; Married Tobin Armstrong; Mother of John Barclay, Katharine A., Sarita S., Tobin Jr. and James L. (twins). Education: Graduate, Foxcroft School, Middleburg, Virginia, 1945; B.A., Vassar College, 1949. Career: Counsellor to the President, Cabinet Rank to Presidents Nixon and Ford, 1973-74; United States Ambassador to Great Britain, 1976-77; President's Foreign Intelligence Advisory Board, Chairman 1981 to present; Board of Directors, Boise Cascade, First City Bancorporation of Texas, General Foods, General Motors, Halliburton, American Express. Organizational Memberships: Center for Strategic and International Studies, Georgetown University, Chairman of Advisory Board, Vice Chairman of Executive Board 1977 to present; Smithsonian Institution, Citizen Regent, Board of Regents 1978 to present; Southern Methodist University, Board of Trustees 1977 to present; John F. Kennedy School of Government, Harvard University, Visiting Committee 1978-82; Bob Hope U.S.O. Center Campaign, Co-Chairman 1979-82; Guggenheim Foundation, Board of Trustees 1980 to present. Religion: Episcopalian. Honors and Awards: Honorary Doctor of Laws Degrees, Bristol University (England) 1976, Washington and Lee University 1976, Williams College 1977, St. Mary's University 1978, Tulane University 1978; Republican Women of the Year Award, 1979; Texan of the Year, 1981; Gold Medal, National Institute of Social Sciences for Distinguished Service to Humanity, 1977. Address: Armstrong Ranch, Armstrong, Texas 78338.■

SHEILA ARNOLD

Legislator. Personal: Born January 15, 1929; Married George Longan Arnold; Mother of Michael, Peter, (Stepsons) Drew, George, Joe. Education: Undertook Several College Courses. Career: Wyoming State Legislature, 1978 to present; Former Secretary, Researcher. Organizational Memberships: State Land Use Advisory Committee, Member, Secretary 1975-79; Legislative Mines, Minerals and Industrial Development Committee; Agriculture, Public Lands and Water Committee; Select Water Development Committee. Community Activities: Member of the Board, First Interstate Bank of Laramie; Laramie Area Chamber of Commerce, President 1982, Former Member of Executive Board, Former Chairman, Legislative Action Committee; League of Women Voters, State Land Use Chairman 1974; University of Wyoming Faculty Women's Club, Past President; Zonta; Jane Jefferson Democratic Women's Club, Past President; Laramie Women's Club; Albany County Democratic Central Committee, Past Vice Chairman; Democratic State Committeewoman, 1977-79. Honors and Awards: Top Hand Award, Laramie Area Chamber of Commerce, 1977. Address: 1058 Alta Vista Drive, Laramie, Wyoming 87020.■

GUY THEODORE ASHTON

Associate Professor. Personal: Born February 25, 1941; Son of Dr. Jon R. Ashton; Married Ruth Maria Urrego de Ashton, Daughter of Dr. Alfonso Urrego-Chavarriaga; Father of Juan Enrique, Mayra Alicia. Education: B.A. Sociology/Anthropology, Grinnell College, Grinnell, Iowa, 1963; M.A. Anthropology 1968, Ph.D. Anthropology 1972, University of Illinois-Urbana. Career: Associate Professor, Sociology/Anthropology, InterAmerican University. Organizational Memberships: American Anthropology Association, Fellow 1972 to present; Society for Applied Anthropology, Fellow 1974 to present; Latin American Studies Association, 1972 to present; Carribbean Studies Association, 1974 to present. Community Activities: Baldrich Tennis Club, Tennis Clinics. Honors and Awards: Fulbright Lecturer, Colombia, University of Los Angeles, 1969-71; Member Editorial Advisory Board, *Revista/Review Interamericana*, 1978 to present; Sectional Tennis Singles Champion (35 years and older), Puerto Rico 1978, Sectional Tennis Doubles Champion (35 years and older), Puerto Rico 1979 and 1980. Address: 1001 Fordham, University Gardens, Rio Piedras, Puerto Rico 00927.■

TWO THOUSAND NOTABLE AMERICANS

THOMAS LEE ATKINS

Roman Catholic Priest, Training Specialist. Personal: Born December 4, 1921; Son of Samuel Merritt III and Alphonsine Atkins (both deceased); Married Marylin E. Bowman; Father of Elizabeth, Catherine. Education: B.A., University of Notre Dame, 1943; Graduate Studies, Catholic University; Ordained Priest, 1951. Military: Served in the United States Naval Reserve, 1943-46, Lieutenant (j.g.). Career: Training Specialist, Personnel, 1974-81; Employment Counselor, 1967-74; Catholic Parish Priest/Pastor, 1951-66; Catholic Chaplain, Veterans Hospital, Saginaw, Michigan, 1954-58; Catholic Chaplain, United States Naval Reserve Training Center, Bay City, Michigan, 1958-64. Organizational Memberships: Amvets Post #60, Provost Marshall; International Association of Personnel in Employment Security, Michigan Chapter. Community Activities: Lansing Masters Swimming Club; Saginaw Valley Indian Association, President 1981-84; Social Workers Roundtable of Bay City, President 1969-74; Michigan Retired Officers Association; Sebewaing Hospital Corporation, President 1960-61; Bishop's Representative for Civil Defense, 1956-66; President, Kingswood Subdivision Homeowners Association, 1984 to present. Honors and Awards: Honor Man, Recruit Training Command, 1943; WXYZ Radio-TV Good Citizen, 1981. Address: 4695 Kingswood Drive, Okemos, Michigan 48864.■

EVELYN ROREX ATKINSON

Architect. Personal: Born December 29, 1931; Married Atmar L. Atkinson; Mother of Penny A. Redmon, Charles Michael. Education: B.Arch., Texas Technological College, 1955. Career: Texas Technological College Department of Landscaping and City of Lubbock Parks Department, 1953-55; Archeson, Atkinson & Cartwright, Architects & Engineers, 1955-69; Atcheson, Atkinson, Cartwright & Rorek, Architects and Engineers, 1969-74; Atkinson & Atkinson, Architects, 1974 to present. Organizational Memberships: American Institute of Architects, Member Lubbock Chapter 1958 to present, Treasurer 1966; Texas Society of Architets. Community Activities: West Texas Watercolor Association; Lubbock Cultural Affairs Council, Board of Directors 1971-76; Texas Fine arts Association. Honors and Awards: American Institute of Architects Award to Outstanding Graduate in Architecture, 1955; Award of Merit, Southwestern Bell Telephone Company, 1969; Listed in *Who's Who in the South and Southwest, Two Thousand Women of Achievement*. Address: 3201 29th Street, Lubbock, Texas 79410.■

NORMAN RALPH AUGUSTINE

Aerospace Executive. Personal: Born July 27, 1935; Son of Ralph and Freda Augustine; Married Margareta E. Engman; Father of Gregory E., Rene I. Education: B.S.E. 1957, M.S.E. 1959, Princeton University; Undertook Postgraduate Courses, Columbia University, University of California-Los Angeles, University of Southern California. Career: Engineer; Government Official. Organizational Memberships: American Institute of Aeronautics and Astronautics, President, Board Member, 1977 to present; American Helicopter Society, Board of Directors 1974-79. Community Activities: Under Secretary of the Army, 1975-77; Assistant Secretary of the Army, 1973-75; Assistant Director of Defense and Engineering, Office of Secretary of Defense, 1965-70; Association of the United States Army, President 1981 to present; Boy Scouts of America, National Committee Chairman; Defense Science Board, Chairman 1980 to present; Young Men's Christian Association, Fund Raiser; Advisory Boards to American University, Princeton University, Colorado University, Duke University, Georgia Tech University, Florida State University. Religion: Presbyterian. Honors and Awards: Phi Beta Kappa; Sigma Xi; Tau Beta Pi; Department of Defense Meritorious Service Medal; Department of Defense Distinguished Service Medal; Department of Army Distinguished Service Medal; Fellow, American Institute of Aeronautics and Astronautics; Fellow, American Astronautical Society. Address: 2102 Green Oaks Lane, Littleton, Colorado 80121.■

GEORGE EDWARD AUMAN

Community Leader. Personal: Born February 2, 1920; Son of George Emmett and Millie Senada Reitz Auman (deceased); Married Martyle Vera Simon; Father of Sheri Doreen, Sandra Ellen. Education: B.S., Bucknell University, 1941; Postgraduate Certificate, University of Chicago, 1945; Postgraduate Certificate, Industrial College of Armed Forces, 1956, Community Activities: Federal and Association Administrator; Chairman, Committee on Suspected Child Abuse and Neglect, Executive Club of Capitol Hill, 1980, 1981; National President, Federal Professional Association, 1978-79; Board of Directors, Fund for Assuring an Independent Retirement, 1980 to present; I.P.A., 1976-80; Director of Field Operations, National Association of Retired Federal Employees, 1980 to present; Area Vice President, Montgomery County Parent-Teacher Association, 1958-60; Study Committee, 1958; Chairman, Garrett Park Estates-White Flint, Michigan. Honors and Awards: Silver Medal Award, United States Department of Commerce, 1966; Certificate of Commendation, National Bureau of Standards, 1969; Mu Tiao Medal, Republic of China, 1974; Decorated Bronze Star Medal, Lieutenant United States Naval Reserve, 1946. Address: 843 Diamond Drive, Gaithersburg, Maryland 20878.■

WILLIAM GERALD AUSTEN

Surgeon. Personal: Born January 20, 1930; Son of Mrs. Bertyl Arnstein; Married Patricia Ramsdell; Father of Karl R., W. Gerald, Jr., Christopher M., Elizabeth P. Education: B.S., Massachusetts Institute of Technology, 1951; M.D., Harvard Medical School, 1955. Military: Served with the United States Public Health Service Commissioned Corps, 1961-62, as a Surgeon. Career: Edward D. Churchill Professor of Surgery 1974 to present, Professor of Surgery 1966-74, Associate Professor of Surgery 1965-66, Associate in Surgery 1963-65, Teaching Fellow in Surgery 1960-61, Harvard Medical School; Chief of Surgical Services 1969 to present, Visiting Surgeon 1966-69, Chief, Surgical Cardiovascular Research Unit 1963-70, Massachusetts General Hospital, Surgeon, Clinic of Surgery, National Heart Institute, Bethesda, Maryland, 1961-62; Visiting Professorships, University of Leyden (Holland), University of North Carolina, University of Miami, University of Texas at San Antonio, University of Vermont, Ohio State University, Brown University, University of Illinois, University of Chicago, University of Pittsburgh, University of Texas at Galveston, University of California at San Diego, Loyola University, Mount Sinai University, University of Wisconsin at Milwaukee, Ohio State University, University of Texas Health Science Center, Yale University, Case Western Reserve, University of Pennsylvania, University of Athens; Sample Lecturer, Yale University; Sir James Wattie Visiting Professor, New Zealand; Editorial Board Member, Circulation, 1972-76, *The New England Journal of Medicine* 1972-75, *The Annals of Thoracic Surgery* 1970-80, *Review of Surgery* 1970-72, *Annals of Surgery* 1972 to present, *Current Surgery* 1972 to present, *American Heart Journal* 1980 to present. Organizational Memberships: American Heart Association, President 1977-78; New England Cardiovascular Society, President 1972-73; Massachusetts Heart Association, President 1972-74; Association for Academic Surgery, President 1970; The Society of University Surgeons, President 1972-73; American Medical Association; New England Surgical Society; The American Surgical Association; American College of Cardiology; Boston Surgical Society; Society of Thoracic Surgeons; American College of Surgeons; New York Academy of Sciences; Societe Internationale de Chirurgie; Massachusetts Medical Society; Society for Vascular Surgery; Pan American Medical Association; American Academy of Arts and Sciences; Society of Clinical Surgery; Allen O. Whipple Surgical Society; American Trauma Society; Italian Research Society; Canadian Cardiovascular Society; Institute of Medicine of the National Academy of Sciences; American Association for Thoracic Surgery; American Heart Association; American Society for Clinical Investigation; Association for Academic Surgery; Halsted Society; International Cardiovascular Society; James IV Association of Surgeons, Inc.; Pan-Pacific Surgical Association; Society for Surgery of the Alimentary Tract; Society of Surgical Chairmen; The Society of University Surgeons; Surgical Biology Club II. Honors and Awards: Honorary Member, Panhellenic Surgical Society, Canadian Cardiovascular Society, Dutch Cardiology Society; Fellow, American Academy of Arts and Sciences; Markle Scholar in Academic Medicine, The Outstanding Young Men Award, Boston, 1965; Affiliate, of the Royal Society of Medicine; Secretary, The American Surgical Association; Honorary Doctor of Humanities, University of Akron; Gold Heart Award, American Heart Association; Paul Dudley White Cardiac Award, Massachusetts Heart Association; Louis Mark Memorial Lecture Award, American College of Chest Physicians; Honorary Doctor of Science, University of Athens, Greece; Massachusetts Institute of Technology, Life Member of the Corporation, Board of Trustees.

TWO THOUSAND NOTABLE AMERICANS

Address: 163 Wellesley Street, Weston, Massachusetts 02193.■

LORA EVELYN AUSTIN

Regional Chief Immunoserologist. Personal: Born September 6, 1926; Daughter of Carlton and Florence (Tyson) Austin (deceased). Education: B.A., Olivet College, Olivet, Michigan, 1948; M.S., California State University, Dominquez Hills, Carson, California, 1981. Military: Served with the United States Marine Corps Reserve, Private First Class, 1957-60. Career: Regional Chief Immunoserologist for Southern California Permanente Medical Group, Los Angeles, 1970 to present; Adjunct Faculty Member, California State University, Dominquez Hills, School of Technology, 1970 to present; Staff Medical Technologist, Southern California Permanente Medical Group, 1952-70; Internship, Butterworth Hospital, Grand Rapids, Michigan, 1948-50; Staff Medical Technologist, Butterworth Hospital, 1950-52. Organizational Memberships: California Association for Medical Technologist, State Delegate 1980 and 1982; American Society for Medical Technologists; Associate Member, American Society of Clinical Pathologists. Community Activities: Leader, Campfire Girls, Grand Rapids, Michigan, 1949-52; Assistant Leader, Girl Scouts of America, Los Angeles, California, 1970-81; Member National Rifle Association; California Rifle and Pistol Association; National Wildlife Federation; National Audubon Society; Associate Member, Smithsonian Institute; Member, Olivet College Alumni Association; Former Member, Theta Chi Epsilon, Former Secretary, Treasurer, Vice President and President of Zeta Chapter, Hollywood, California (all offices held during the 1960's); Los Angeles Area Council, Secretary 1964, Vice President 1965, President 1966-67; National Scrapbook Chairman, 1965. Religion: Active in Second Congregational Young People's Program and Choirs until 1944; Active in Choir Park Congregational Church, Grand Rapids, Michigan, 1948-52. Honors and Awards: Recipient, Distinguished Alumni Award, Olivet College, 1978; National Achievement Award, 1966 and 1967; Listed in *Who's Who of American Women, World Who's Who of Women, Biographical Roll of Honor, Who's Who in the West.* Address: 10707 Moorpark Street, Toluca Lake, California 91602.■

ARTHUR WILLIAM AVERY

Laboratory Director. Personal: Born June 11, 1949; Son of Arthur Wolcot and Merylyn Meeks Avery. Education: B.A. cum laude 1971, M.S. 1973, Ph.D. 1975, Pennsylvania State University. Career: Graduate and Groves Fellow, Pennsylvania State University, 1975; Assistant Professor of Family Studies, Texas Tech University, 1975-77; Director, Graduate Program in Human Development and Family Studies, Texas Tech University, 1977-79; Director, Human Development Laboratory, University of Arizona, 1979 to present. Organizational Memberships: American Psychological Association, Division 27, Program Committee, Continuing Education Committee; American Association for Marriage and Family Therapy, Directors of Clinical Training Committee; National Council on Family Relations, Chairperson National Meeting Site Selection Committee; Groves Conference on Marriage and Family, National Planning Committee; Approved Site Training Reviewer, Commission on Accreditation in Marriage and Family Therapy Education, Accrediting Agency, United States Department of Health and Human Services. Honors and Awards: Phi Beta Kappa; Psi Chi; Alpha Kappa Delta; Associate Editor, *Family Relations: Journal of Applied Family and Child Studies;* National Institute of Health Grant; Certified/Licensed Psychologist, Arizona, Texas; Listed in *Who's Who in the West, Community Leaders of America.* Address: 444 West Orange Grove #915, Tucson, Arizona 85704.■

BOULOS AYAD AYAD

Professor. Personal: Born May 3, 1928; Son of Ayad Ayad; Married Suzanne E., Daughter of Eduard Naguib; Father of Mary, Thereza, Boulos. Education: M.A., University of Cairo, 1957; M.A., University of Ain Shams, 1953; M.A., Higher Institute of Coptic Studies, Cairo, 1960; Ph.D. with honors, University of Cairo, 1963. Career: Professor of Archaeology and Ancient Languages, University of Colorado, 1977 to present; Assistant Professor, University of Utah, Salt Lake City, 1967-68; Assistant Professor, University of Colorado, Boulder 1968-72, Associate Professor 1972-77. Organizational Memberships: African Studies Association; La Societe d'Archaeologie Copte; American Association of University Professors; American Association of Teachers of Arabic; Smithsonian Institution. Religion: Active in the Coptic Orthodox Church of Egypt; Served in The Society of the Friends of the Holy Bible, Sunday Schools, The Social Service Society and the Coptic Memorial Hall of St. Mark; St. Mark Coptic Church, Denver, Colorado, Sunday School Teacher, Attended Conferences, Chairman of Coptic Inheritance and Language Committee and Cultural Affairs Committee (lecturer on international and local culture and civilization); Social and Spiritual Life; Participated in Meeting for the Interpretation of the Bible (Old and New Testaments). Published Works: Author of Numerous Articles and Books on Topics in his Field. Honors and Awards: University Fellow, 1974-75; Listed in *The Fifth International Directory of Anthropologists, The International Directory of Scholars and Specialists in African Studies, Marquis Who's Who in the West, Marquis Who's Who in America, Men of Achievement, Personalities of America, Community Leaders of America, International Book of Honor, The Biographical Roll of Honor.* Address: 1332 Scrub Oak Circle, Boulder, Colorado 80303.■

MARIE ANN BADALAMENTE

Assistant Professor, Director of Neuromuscular Research. Personal: Born July 17, 1949; Daughter of Elizabeth Badalamente. Education: B.A. 1971, M.S. 1973, Long Island University; Ph.D., Fordham University, 1977. Career: Assistant Professor, Department of Orthopaedics and Director of Neuromuscular Research, State University of New York-Stony Brook; Assistant Professor, Director of Electron Microscopy, Department of Cell Biology, State University of New York Downstate Medical Center, 1978-79; Assistant Professor, Department of Biology, C. W. Post Center, Long Island University, 1975-78. Organizational Memberships: New York Academy of Sciences; Electron Microscopy Society of America; New York Society of Electron Microscopy; Sigma Xi; Scientific Research Society; American Association for the Advancement of Science; Orthopaedic Research Society. Honors and Awards: Easter Seals Research Foundation Grantee, 1981-84; Muscular Dystrophy Association Grantee, 1979-81; National Institute of Health Research Association, Fordham University (while Ph.D. Candidate), 1976-78. Address: 109 St. Marks Place, Roslyn Heights, New York 11577.■

JOSEPH RIGSBY BAGBY

Investor, Author. Personal: Born August 23, 1935; Son of Mrs. P. R. Bagby; Married Martha Lane Green, Daughter of Mrs. Hampton Green; Father of Meredith Elaine. Education: B.A. Economics, University of Miami, 1959. Military: Served in the 82nd Airborn Division, 1959-61, with the rank of Private First Class; Certificate of Achievement, 1961. Career: Investments; Director of Real Estate 1966-70, Manager of Real Estate 1966, Real Estate Representative 1964, Burger King Corporation; Vice President, Jack Thomas Realty, 1963-65; General Real Estate, Oscar Dooly Associates, 1961-63. Organizational Memberships: National Association of Corporate Real Estate Executives, Founder, President 1977 to present, Chairman of Board of Trustees. Published Works: Author *Real Estate Financing Desk Book* 1975, *The Real Estate Dictionary* 1981, *The Complete Book of Real Estate* 1982. Honors and Awards: Recipient of Iron Arrow, Highest Honor Attained by Men, University of Miami; Sigma Chi Chapter Balfour Award, 1959.■

PETER M. BAINUM

University Professor. Personal: Born February 4, 1938; Son of Charles J. Bainum and Mildred T. Salyer (deceased); Married Carmen Cecilia Perez R.; Father of David P. Education; B.S. Aerospace Engineering, Texas A&M University, 1959; S.M. Aeronautics and Astronautics, Massachusetts Institute of Technology, 1960; Ph.D. Aerospace Engineering, Catholic University, 1967. Career: Graduate Professor of Aerospace Engineering, Howard University; Vice President and Consultant, WHF and Associates, 1977 to present; John Hopkins University Applied Physics Laboratory, Senior Staff Engineer 1965-69, Consultant 1969-72; Staff Engineer, IBM, Federal Systems Division, 1962-65; Senior Engineer, Martin-Marietta, Orlando Division, 1960-62. Organizational Memberships: American Astronautical Society, Fellow and Executive Vice President 1982 to present, First Vice President 1980-82, Vice President Technical 1978-80, Vice President Publications 1976-78; Associate Fellow and Member Astrodynamics Technical Committee, American Institute of Aeronautics and Astronautics; Vice Chairman, International Astronautical Federation Astrodynamics Technical Committee; Fellow, British Interplanetary Society. Community Activities: American Institute of Aeronautics and Astronautics, National Capital Section, Community Action Committee, 1975-76; Judge, D.C. Science Fair, 1973. Honors and Awards: Award for Outstanding Research, Howard University, 1980-81; Outstanding Faculty Award, Howard University Graduate School, 1979-80; Sigma Xi, Scientific Research Society, 1978 to present; Teetor Award for Engineering Educators, Society Automotive Engineers, 1971; NASA/ASEE Summer Faculty Fellowship, 1970-71. Address: 9804 Raleigh Tavern Court, Bethesda, Maryland 20814.■

MARY HELEN BAIR

Program Director. Personal: Born November 1, 1929; Daughter of Mr. and Mrs. O. D. Griffin; Married Charles E. Bair; Mother of Michael Wayne. Education: Graduate, Idabel High School, Oklahoma, 1946; Graduate, B.M.I. Business College, 1948; Attended Numerous Seminars and Workshops on Radio; Graduate, Dale Carnegie Course, 1949. Career: Radio Station KFRO, Secretary to Manager 1948-62, Program Director 1962 to present; Holds 3rd Class Radio License; 30-minute "Christmas Shopping with Mary Helen" Show, Thanksgiving until Christmas Eve, 1952 to present. Organizational Memberships: Texas Press Women, District 9, President 1972-73, Membership Chairman 1974-75, Nominating Committee Chairman 1974-75, Treasurer 1976-78 and 1982-83, Vice President 1978-80, State Sites Chairman 1974-75, State Resolutions Chairman 1977-79; National Federation of Press Women, 1968 to present; Texas Press Women, Inc., Member 1968 to present, Life Member 1982 to present; Epsilon Sigma Alpha, Theta Lambda Chapter, Chapter President (6 times), Vice President (5 times), Secretary (1 time), Treasurer 1979-81, District Vice President 1956-57, District President 1957-58, District P.P.A.C. Chairman 1970-71, District Co-ordinator 1974-75, District Chaplain 1977-78; Professional Journalists, Inc. Community Activities: Muscular Dystrophy Association of America, Northeast Texas Chapter, Charter Member, First Treasurer; American Cancer Society, Director Gregg-North Chapter 1976-82, Public Information Committee; Gregg County Association for Retarded Citizens, Team Captain on Membership Drive 1977-78, Membership Advisory Committee 1978-79; Longview Woman's Forum, 1977 to present; Young Men's Christian Association, Team Member on Membership Drive 1979-82; Longview Public Schools, Public Information Advisory Council 1979-80; Pine Tree Independent School District, Communications Advisory Board 1980-81; Longview Chamber of Commerce, Information and Public Relations Committee 1980-81 and 1981-82. Religion: St. Andrew Presbyterian Church, Deacon 1968-71, Elder and Member of the Session 1972. Honors and Awards: Texas Press Women, Inc., Woman of Achievement Award 1977, Annual Communications Award, First Place in Radio Feature and Radio News 1981; Life Fellow, American Biographical Institute Research Association; Listed in *Who's Who of American Women, The World Who's Who of Women, Community Leaders of America, Personalities of America.* Address: 1105 West Garfield, Longview, Texas 75603.■

WILMA WILLIAM BAITSELL

Retired Art Teacher/Supervisor. Personal: Daughter of Glen H. and Luetta Newell Williamson (deceased); Married Victor H. Baitsell (deceased); Mother of Corin Victor, Coby Allan, Corrine B. Robideau. Education: B.S., M.S. Career: Retired Art Teacher/Supervisor. Organizational Memberships: New York State Art Association; National Art Association; New York State Retired Teachers Association; National Retired Teachers Association. Community Activities: Order of the

Eastern Star; Grand Old Party; County Historical Society; Local Historical Society; Art Guild; Alumni Association. Honors and Awards: World Anglo-American Academy; Listed in *Dictionary of International Biography, Who's Who in America, Who's Who in Art, Directory of Distinguished Amricans.* Address: 3027 Whittemore Road, R.F.D. 4 Box 330, Oswego, New York 13126.■

BERNARD ROBERT BAKER

District Court Judge. Personal: Born April 5, 1937; Son of Mr. and Mrs. B. F. Baker; Married Caroline Roberta Spanier, Daughter of Mr. and Mrs. R. W. Spanier; Father of Susan Caroline, Deborah Ann, Pamela Ruth. Education: Graduate, Calumet High School, Chicago, Illinois, 1954; B.S., Northwestern University, 1958; J.D., Indiana University School of Law, 1964. Military: Served in the United States Army, 1965-67, attaining the rank of Captain in the Judge Advocate General's Corps. Career: District Court Judge, 4th District, State of Colorado, 1976 to present; Deputy and Chief Deputy, Office of the District Attorney, 1969-75; Associate, Law Firm of Agee & Fann, Colorado Springs, Colorado, 1968; Claims Investigator and Supervisor, Allstate Insurance Company, Indianapolis, Indiana, 1961-64; Accountant, Chevrolet Division, General Motors Corporation, Indianapolis, 1960-61; Insurance Counselor, Equitable Life Insurance, New York, 1968-60. Organizational Memberships: Colorado Bar Association, Environmental Problems Committee; Indiana Bar Association; Member of Bar of Supreme Court of the United States, United States Court of Military Appeals, United States District Court of Colorado and Indiana; American Bar Association; El Paso County Bar Association; American Judicature Society. Community Activities: President, Citizen's Lobby for Sensible Growth; Board of Directors, Salvation Army; Board of Directors, Mental Retardation Foundation; Chairman, Sierra Club, Pikes Peak Chapter; Pikes Peak Children's Advocates; Guest Lecturer/Teacher, Colorado College, United States Air Force Academy; Advisory Board, Pikes Peak Community College. Honors and Awards: Army Commendation Medal, 1967; Faculty Member, National Judicial College, 1982. Address: 1423 North Tejon, Colorado Springs, Colorado 80907.■

FRANK HAMON BAKER

Animal Scientist, International Stockmen's School Director. Personal: Born May 2, 1923; Son of Dewitt and Maude Baker (both deceased); Married Melonee Gray; Father of Rilda, Necia, Twila, Dayna. Education: B.S. 1947, M.S. 1951, Ph.D. 1954, all from Oklahoma State University. Military: Served with the United States Army, 1943-45. Career: Oklahoma Extension Agent, 1947-48; Veterans Agriculture Teacher, 1948-50; Graduate Student, 1950-53; Animal Scientist, Kansas State University 1953-55, University of Kentucky 1955-58; Extension Animal Scientist, Oklahoma State University, 1958-62; Coordinator Extension Animal Science, United States Department of Agriculture, Washington, D.C., 1962-66; Chairman, Animal Science Department, University of Nebraska, 1966-74; Dean of Agriculture, Oklahoma State University, 1974-79; Director, International Stockmen's School, Winrock Morrilton, Arkansas, 1981 to present. Organizational Memberships: American Society of Animal Science, Vice President 1973, President 1974; Council for Agricultural Science and Technology, President-Elect 1978, President 1979; National Beef Improvement Federation, Executive Secretary 1968-74; American Meat Science Association; American Association for the Advancement of Science. Community Activities: 4-H Club; Block and Bridle Club; Agriculture Student Association, President 1946; Alpha Zeta; Blue Key; Phi Kappa Phi; Farm House Fraternity; Sigma Xi; Gamma Sigma Delta; Epsilon Sigma Phi; Omicron Delta Kappa; American Legion; Kiwanis; Advisory Committee to U.S. Secretary of Agriculture, 1972-76; National Beef Records Committee, Chairman 1963-65; American Polled Hereford Association, Advisory Committees; American Hereford Association; American Angus Association; National Cattlemen's Association; Great Plains Range & Livestock Committee, Chairman 1971-73; North Central Research Advisory Committee, Chairman 1972-73; Consultant to U.S.A.I.D. and Agriculture Agencies of Turkey, Colombia, Ecuador, Botswana. Religion: Methodist. Honors and Awards: American Society of Animal Science, Fellow 1977, Animal Industry Service Award 1981; Oklahoma Farmers Union Service Award, 1980; Hall of Merit, American Polled Hereford Association, 1974; Agriculture Achievement Award, Knights of AKSARBEN, 1974; Oklahoma State University Animal Science Alumni Hall of Fame, 1968; American Association for the Advancement of Science Fellow; United States Department of Agriculture, Special Merit 1966, Outstanding Service Award 1965; Distillers Feed Research Council Distinguished Nutritionist, 1964; Beef Improvement Federation Service Award, 1974; Future Farmers of America Honorary Farmer Award, 1976; National 4-H Award, 1941; Purple Heart, 1945. Address: Winrock International, Route 3, Morrilton, Arkansas 72110.■

H. KENT BAKER

Professor of Finance. Personal: Born November 13, 1944; Son of Ruby L. Baker; Married Linda A. Weitzel, Daughter of Jack and Betty Weitzel. Education: B.S.B.A., Georgetown University, 1967; M.B.A. 1969, D.B.A. 1972, M.Ed. 1974, University of Maryland; M.S. The American University, 1979; C.F.A., Institute of Chartered Financial Analysts, 1978; C.M.A., Institute for Management Accounting, 1979. Career: Professor of Finance, The American University, Kogod College of Business Administration; Former Positions include Assistant Dean and Assistant Professor of the School of Business Administration at Georgetown University and Assistant to the Dean of the College of Business and Public Administration of the University of Maryland. Organizational Memberships: American Finance Association; American Management Association; Financial Analysts Federation; Financial Management Association; Washington Society of Investment Analysts; Eastern Finance Association; Southern Finance Association. Community Activities: Chairman Board of Directors, Childrens Television International, 1979 to present; Board of Directors, The American University Employee's Federal Credit Union, 1979-82; Research and Publications Committee, The Institute of Chartered Financial Analysts, 1979 to present; Advisory Board Member and Advisory Director, District of Columbia National Bank, 1966-70. Honors and Awards: Alpha Iota Delta; Alpha Sigma Nu; American University Award for Outstanding Research, Scholarship and Other Contributions, 1978-79, 1979-80; Beta Gamma Sigma; Danforth Associates; Financial Management Association Honor Society; Phi Alpha Alpha; Phi Delta Kappa; Phi Kappa Phi. Address: 5816 Edson Lane, Rockville, Maryland 20852.■

JOHN STEVENSON BAKER

Author, Poet. Personal: Born June 18, 1931; Son of Everette B. (deceased) and Ione M. Baker. Education: B.A. cum laude, Pomona College, 1953; M.D., University of California School of Medicine, Berkeley and San Francisco, 1957. Career: 57 Poems (most published under the name Michael Dyregrov), including "A Lake for Those Who Died of Syphilis," "Os," "Stahr," "The Sun's a Bug" (published in *Tenth Assembling*, 1980), "Solomon's Seal," "Recall," "The Sprocket of a Metaphor," "Nuthatch," "Rose-breasted Grosbeak," "Ermine," "Owl Pillow;" Author of a Fictional Diary "The Diary of Sesso-Vesucci," *Trace,* Autumn 1963; Short Story, "Mister Carcoleotes," *The Human Voice Quarterly,* May 1965; Number of Articles in Professional Journals, including "Electroencephalograms during hypoxia in healthy men" in *Archives of Neurology,* December 1961 and "Patterns of the electroencephalogram during tilt, hypoxia and hypercapnia: response characteristics for normal aging subjects" in *Neurology,* April 1963. Honors and Awards: First Prize, Jennings English Prize, Pomona College, 1950; Distinguished Service Award, Minnesota State Horticultural Society, 1976; Certificate of Appreciation, United States National Arboretum, Washington, D.C., 1978. Address: P.O. Box 16007, Minneapolis, Minnesota 55416.■

MARY NELL BAKER

Music Educator. Personal: Born April 4, 1926; Daughter of Truman Benjamin Tarpley; Married Joseph Edwin Baker, Jr.; Mother of Mary Baker Swain, Ann Baker Street. Education: Attended Bob Jones Academy, 1944; Piano Certificate of Performance, 1944; Attended Bob Jones College, Cadek Conservatory; Extensive Study with Outstanding Concert Artists and Professors; Certification by Tennessee Music Teachers Association and Music Teachers National Association by Examination, 1973. Career: Independent Music Teacher; Former Executive Director of Girls Club, Director of Youth Ministry, Organist and Director of Church Music Ministry, Certified Laboratory Instructor for Workers with Youth. Organizational Memberships: Chattanooga Music Teachers, Workshop Chairperson, Auditions Chairperson; Knoxville Music Teachers, Certification Chairperson; East Tennessee Representative, Board Member 1980-82, Tennessee Music Teachers Association; Knoxville Choral Society, 1976-79; Delta Omicron Professional Music Fraternity. Community Activities: Ministers Wives, Vice President of Conference, Local President; Church Women United, President; Concert Board; Opera Association; Women's Club; Home Demonstration Club; National Honor Society; National Thespian Society; Board Member 1981-83, Asbury Centers Inc. (retirement and health care homes); Business and Professional Women's Club; Programs for Community Affairs. Religion: United Methodist Church, Lifetime Member, Minister's Wife. Honors and Awards: Woman of the Year, McFarland United Methodist Church, 1966. Address: 2017 Avalon Avenue, Chattanooga, Tennessee 37415.■

ROBERT HART BAKER

Music Director. Personal: Born March 19, 1954, in Bronxville, New York; Son of Jeanne Baker. Education: A.B. cum laude, Harvard College, 1974; M.Mus. 1976,

M.M.A. 1978, Yale School of Music. Career: Music Director, Asheville Symphony Orchestra; Formerly with the Youth Symphony Orchestra of New York at Carnegie Hall; Connecticut Philharmonic Orchestra; Bach Society Orchestra, Cambridge, Massachusetts; Putnam (New York) Symphony Orchestra. Organizational Memberships: American Symphony Orchestra League Conductor's Guild; American Society of Composers, Authors and Publishers; American Verdi Institute; International Double Reed Society. Community Activities: Guest Conductor, Rhode Island Philharmonic, St. Louis Philharmonic, Spoleto (Italy) Festival Orchestra, York (Pennsylvania) Philharmonic, Connecticut Music Educators Association Orchestra; Guest Speaker, Kiwanis International, Civitan International, National Association of American Pen Women. Honors and Awards: American Society of Composers, Authors and Publishers Award for Modern Music Programming, 1981; Yale School of Music Alumni Association Award, 1978; National Federation of Music Clubs Composition Award, 1976; McCord Book Prize at Harvard, 1974; Jellinek Gold Medal for Composition, New York City, 1971. Address: 129 Evelyn Place, Asheville, North Carolina 28801.■

WILLIAM OLIVER BAKER

Retired Chairman of the Board. Personal: Born July 15, 1915, in Chestertown, Maryland; Son of Harold M. and Helen Stokes Baker (both deceased); Married Frances Burrill in 1941; Father of Joseph, Wendy (deceased). Education: B.S., Washington College, 1935; Ph.D., Princeton University, 1948; Recipient of 23 Honorary Degrees. Career: Bell Laboratories (1939-80), in charge of Polymer Research and Development 1948-51, Assistant Director of Chemical and Metallurgical Research 1951-54, Director of Research in Physical Sciences 1954-55, Vice President of Research 1955-73, President 1973-79, Chairman of the Board 1979-80. Organizational Memberships: Director, Summit and Elizabeth Trust Company 1958 to present, Babcock and Wilcox Company 1962-78, Mead Johnson & Company 1966-68, Annual Reviews Inc. 1969 to present, Council on Library Resources 1970 to present, Bell Telephone Laboratories Inc. 1973-80, Clinical Scholars Program of the Robert Wood Johnson Foundation 1973-76, Sandia Corporation 1973-80, The Third Century 1974-76, American Bell International Inc. 1975-79, Western Electric Company Inc. 1975-80, Harry Frank Guggenheim Foundation 1976 to present, Western Electric International Inc. 1978-80, Johnson and Johnson 1980 to present, General American Investors 1980 to present; Trustee, Rockefeller University 1960 to present (Vice Chairman 1970-80, Chairman 1980 to present), Urban Studies Inc. 1960-78, Aerospace Corporation 1961-76, Princeton University 1964 to present, The Andrew W. Mellon Foundation 1965 to present (Chairman 1975 to present), Old Dominion Foundation 1965, Avalon Foundation 1967, Carnegie-Mellon University 1967 to present, The Fund for New Jersey 1974 to present, General Motors Cancer Research Foundation 1978 to present, The Charles Babbage Institute 1978 to present, The Newark Museum 1979 to present; Board of Overseers, Engineering and Applied Science University, Pennsylvania; President's Foreign Intelligence Advisory Board, 1957-77, 1981 to present; Advisory Board, Federal Emergency Management Agency, 1980 to present; National Commission on Excellence in Education, 1982 to present; National Science Board, 1960-66; National Cancer Advisory Board, 1973-79; American Chemical Society, Member 1938 to present, Carbon Committee of Third Carbon Conference 1958, Councilor of North Jersey Section, Committee Advisory to the Chemical Corps 1961-63, Committee on National Defense 1963-69, Committee on Chemistry and Public Affairs 1965-77, Consultant 1978-79, Education Steering Committee 1969-80; Industrial Research Institute, Member 1955-80, Director 1960-63, Membership Committee 1961-62, Advisory Editorial Board of *Research Management* 1962-63; Directors of Industrial Research, 1956 to present; Cosmos Club, 1959 to present; American Society for Testing and Materials, Administrative Committee on Research 1959-60; National Academy of Sciences, Member 1961 to present, Council Member 1969-72; Scientific Research Society of America, Board of Governors 1961-67, R.E.S.A. Proctor Award Committee 1962, 1963, 1964, R.E.S.A. Nominating Committee 1965; American Physical Society, Fellow 1962 to present; American Philosophical Society, 1963 to present; American Academy of Arts and Sciences, 1965 to present; American Institute of Chemists, Fellow 1968 to present; Institute of Medicine, Member 1972 to present, Council 1973-75, Finance Committee 1976-79; The Chemists' Club, Honorary Member 1974 to present; National Academy of Engineering, 1975 to present; The Franklin Institute, Fellow 1977 to present. Published Works: *Listen to Leaders in Engineering, Science and Society: A Symposium, Perspectives in Polymer Science*, Numerous Other Books in the Professional Realm; Approximately 100 Research Papers. Honors and Awards: One of Top Ten Scientists in United States Industry, 1954; A.I.C. Honor Scroll, 1962; Perkin Medal, 1963; Priestley Medal, 1966; Edgar Marburg Award, 1967; A.S.T.M. Award to Executives, 1967; Industrial Research Institute Medal, 1970; Frederik Philips Award, 1972; Industrial Research Man of the Year Award, 1973; Proctor Prize, 1973; James Madison Medal, Princeton University, 1975; Gold Medal, American Institute of Chemists, 1975; Mellon Institute Award, 1975; Award for Distinguished Contributions to Research Administration, Society of Research Administrators, 1976; American Chemical Society Parsons Award, 1976; Franklin Institute Delmer S. Fahrney Medal, 1977; J. Willard Gibbs Medal, American Chemical Society, 1978; von Hippel Award, Materials Research Society, 1978; New Jersey Science/Technology Medal, 1980; Madison Marshall Award, 1980; Vannevar Bush Award, 1981; Jefferson Medal, 1981; Sarnoff Award, A.F.C.E.A., 1981; President's National Security Medal, 1982; Holder of 13 Patents. Address: Spring Valley Road, Morristown, New Jersey 07060.■

GEORGE C. BALDWIN

Physicist. Personal: Born May 5, 1917; Married Winifred; Father of George T., John E., Celia M. Education: B.A., Kalamazoo College, 1939; Ph.D., University of Illinois, 1943. Career: Physicist, Los Alamos National Laboratory; Professor, Nuclear Engineering, Rensselaer Polytechnic Institute, 1964-77; Research Associate, Nuclear Engineer, Applied Physicist, General Electric Company, 1944-67. Organizational Memberships: American Physical Society, Fellow; American Nuclear Society; American Association for the Advancement of Science. Community Activities: Councilman, Town of Niskayuna, New York, 1965-69; Zoning Board, Niskayuna, New York, 1968-77. Published Works: Author 75 Articles in Technical Journals; Book *An Introduction to Nonlinear Optics*. Honors and Awards: Phi Beta Kappa, Illinois University, 1942. Address: 1016 Calle Bajo, Santa Fe, New Mexico 87501.■

JACK LYELL BALDWIN

Extension Entomologist. Personal: Born February 14, 1949; Son of Mr. and Mrs. James E. Frierson; Married Anne Frierson; Father of Belinda Marie, Priscilla Michelle, Kimberly Leigh. Education: B.S. 1971, M.S. 1972, Texas A&M University; Ph.D., Oklahoma State University, 1980. Career: Extension Entomologist, Louisiana State University; Field Biologist, Agricultural Chemicals Division, I.C.I. America, Inc., 1974-76. Organizational Memberships: American Registry of Professional Entomologists; Entomological Society of America; Louisiana Entomology Society; Southwestern Entomological Society. Honors and Awards: Distinguished Graduate, Texas A&M University, 1971; Silver Caduceus Society of Korea; Listed in *Who's Who in the South and Southwest*. Address: 17212 Gaines Mill Avenue, Baton Rouge, Louisiana 70816.■

ALICE L. BALL

Educator. Personal: Born 1942. Education: Graduate Hays High School, Hays, Kansas, 1959; General Diploma, Cottey College, Nevada, Missouri, 1961; B.S. Art 1964, M.A. Special Education 1975, Candidate for Specialist Degree, Fort Hays State University. Career: Full-time Substitute Teacher for Art Classes, Cheney, Kansas, 2 Years; Art Classes for Adults, Cheney and Satanta (Kansas); Graduate Assistant, Education Department, Hays, Kansas; Teaching Director, Harrison Junior High School, Great Bend, Kansas; Teacher of Educable Mentally Handicapped, Santata, Hugoton High School, Hugoton Middle School, Hutchinson High School 1980-81; Adult Art Classes for the Handicapped, Hutchinson, Kansas, 1981-82; Sponsor for Traveling Groups with the International Order of Job's Daughters, 1982-83; Sponsor for Briny Birds, Hutchinson High School, 1981-83; Director of Hutchinson Recreation Summer Playgrounds, 1982-83; Assistant Director of Hutchinson Recreation Summer Playgrounds, 1981-82; Landscape Director, Hugoton, Kansas, 1974-80; Number Other Former Positions. Organizational Memberships: Beta Sigma Phi; Delta Psi Omega; Alpha Psi Omega; Delphian Society; Candidate for Phi Kappa Phi; Council for Exceptional Children; Kansas National Educators Association, Represenative and Negotiator; Kansas National Educators Association of Middle Level Educators. Community Activities: Little Theatre; Drama Club; Radio Club; Choral Reading; Rainbow Girls; Daughters of the American Revolution; New England Women; Recreational Board, Association for Retarded Citizens; Day Camp; International Order of Eastern Star; Brownie Scouts; Coordinator of Teachers of Educable Mentally Handicapped in Garden City (Kansas) Cooperative; Guest Speaker, Fort Hays University for the English Workshop; Library Club; Federated Women of America; Pep Club, Coordinator; Cheerleader, Coordinator; Sponsor, Kansas Special Olympics (10 years); International Special Olympics, Sponsor (2 years); Producer, 5-State Special Rodeo (only one of its kind in the world). Honors and Awards: Nominated as Outstanding Educator in Hutchinson, Kansas, 1982-83; Listed in *Outstanding Young Women of America, Directory of Distinguished Americans, Biographical Roll of Honor, Community Leaders of America*. Address: 612 West 21st Avenue, Hutchinson, Kansas 67501.■

THERESA GALLAGHER BALOG

Assistant Dean of Nursing. Personal: Born December 18, 1937; Daughter of Bernard and Dorothy Gallagher; Married David Balog, Son of Andrew and Josephine Balog; Mother of Megan, Paul. Education: R.N Diploma, Allegheny Valley Hospital School of Nursing, 1960; B.S.N., Duquesne University School of Nursing, 1963; M.N., University of Pittsburgh School of Nursing, 1968; Pediatric Care Specialist; Ph.D. in Higher Education Administration, University of Pittsburgh School of Education, 1984. Career: Assistant Dean of Nursing, Community College of Allegheny County-Center-North; Associate Professor/ Coordinator of Maternal-Child Nursing, Duquesne University; Assistant Professor/Director of Pediatric Affiliate Program, Instructor of Maternal-Newborn Nursing, Instructor of Pediatric Nursing, University of Pittsburgh; Instructor of Pediatric Nursing, Inservice Education Coordinator, Staff Nurse, Children's

TWO THOUSAND NOTABLE AMERICANS

Hospital, Pittsburgh. Organizational Memberships: Pennsylvania Association of Associate Degree Nursing Educators (State-wide and West Sections); Western Pennsylvania Nursing Administrators; Pennsylvania Association of Directors of Practical Nursing Programs; National League for Nursing; Alumni Associations — Allegheny Valley Hospital, Duquesne University, University of Pittsburgh. Community Activities: Sigma Theta Tau Nominating Committee, 1980; Advisory Boards, Carlow College Weekend Program for Registered Nurses, Beatty Vo-Tech School, Parkway West Vo-Tech School, Lenape School of Practical Nursing; Pediatric Nursing Master's Thesis Committee, 1978, 1979, 1980, 1981; Research Committee, Profile of R.N. Students in a Baccalaureate Program, University of Pittsburgh School of Nursing, 1979; Research Study, Relationship of Measures of Self-Actualization to Nursing Competency of Students Completing an Associate Degree Career Mobility Nursing Program. Honors and Awards: Sigma Theta Tau, Eta Chapter, National Honorary Nursing Society; Research Award, Sigma Theta Tau, Eta Chapter, 1983; Listed in *Who's Who of Women in Education, International Who's Who in Education, International Who's Who in Education*. Address: 6356 Caton Street, Pittsburgh, Pennsylvania 15217.■

BRUCE LORD BANDURSKI

Advisor. Personal: Born June 28, 1940; Son of Stanley Alexander Bandurski and Virginia VanRensselaer Hinckley. Education: B.S. with honors, Honors College, Michigan State University, 1962. Career: Presently on Secondment as Advisor (Transboundary Monitoring Network) to U.S. Section, International Joint Commission, U.S. and Canada; Former Positions include Federal Civil Service as Mail Carrier, Smokechaser, Lookout, Park Ranger, Scientific Reference Analyst, Intelligence Operations Specialist, Survey Data Analyst, Intelligence Operations Specialist, Outdoor Recreation Planner, Watch Director, and Deputy/Acting Mission Director of the U.S. Man-in-the-Sea Program, Environmental Review Officer, Coordinator of the Federal Recreation Fee Program, Natural Resource Specialist, Environmental Specialist, Headquarters Office Branch Chief for Environmental Planning and Coordination, National Environmental Policy Act Officer. Organizational Memberships: Faculty Member, U.S.D.A. Graduate School Evening Program, 1968 to present; Charter Member, Metropolitan Washington Chapter, Ecological Society of America. Community Activities: President, Outdoor Ethic Guild (advocating systems approach to problems of ecomanagement). Honors and Awards: Listed in *Outstanding Young Men of America, Men of Achievement, International Who's Who of Intellectuals, Dictionary of International Biography, Personalities of America, Community Leaders of America, Community Leaders of the World*. Address: 800 South Saint Asaph Street, #203, Alexandria, Virginia 22314.■

SARA LYNN BANKS

Adjunct Professor of Psychology, Psychologist in Private Practice. Personal: Born April 19, 1939; Daughter of Lee and Irving Groves; Married Douglas Trent Banks; Mother of Douglas Trent III, Elizabeth, Erin. Education: B.A. Psychology 1971, M.A. Counseling 1973, Psy.D. 1982. Career: Adjunct Professor of Psychology, Rollins College; Former Positions include Psychology Doctoral Intern, Teacher of Socially Maladjusted, Adjustment Counselor for Disabled, Educational Counselor for Residential Psychiatric and Substance Abuse Patients. Organizational Memberships: American Personnel and Guidance Association; International Transactional Analysis Association; Institute for Rational Living; American Psychological Association. Community Activities: Red Cross Social Worker, 1971-72; Friends for Youth, 1973-74. Honors and Awards: B.A. magna cum laude. Address: 325 Miami Avenue, Indialantic, Florida 32903.■

GORDON DEWEY BANKSTON

Artist, Cartoonist. Personal: Born January 10, 1932; Son of L. D. and Gurtha (Threadgill) Bankston; Father of Debra Dolores, Gary Gordon. Education: Graduate of Monahans High School, 1950; Studies at Hardin-Simmons University, North Texas University. Military: Service in the Texas National Guard, 1979-87. Career: Artist and Cartoonist; Former Positions as Pumper for the Chevron Oil Company and Owner of City Sign Service; Owner, Gordon Bankston Enterprises, Designs Unlimited; Co-Owner, Sandbank Productions. Organizational Memberships: Kappa Alpha; International Platform Association. Community Activities: West Texas Rehabilitation for Crippled Children; West Texas Chamber of Commerce; Odessa Chamber of Commerce. Religion: Member Sherwood Baptist Church. Published Works: Author *Red, in the Oil Patch* 1970, *The Oil Patch* 1974, *Yep, It's the Oil Patch* 1984, *The Art of Marketing Your Art* 1984. Honors and Awards: Gordon Bankston Collection at the University of Wyoming Petroleum History and Research Center; Given Title "Artist of the Southwest," 1974; Listed in *Who's Who in the South and Southwest, Personalities of the South, Personalities of America, Personalities of the World, Men of Achievement, Directory of Distinguished Americans, International Register of Profiles, International Book of Honor, International Who's Who of Contemporary Achievements, Community Leaders of the World*. Address: 3813 Springdale, Odessa, Texas 79762.■

ANDREY I. BARANOV

Botanist. Personal: Born October 17, 1917; Son of I. and V. Baranov (both deceased); Married Nina M.; Father of Elena. Education: First Class Diploma (equivalent LL.B.), Harbin Law School, 1938; Attended University of Washington, Seattle, Washington, 1960-61; M.S. Biology, Northeastern University, Boston, Massachusetts, 1973. Career: Research Fellow, Harbin Regional Museum, 1946-50; Research Fellow, Academia Sinica (Institute of Forestry and Soil Science), 1950-58; Herbarium Assistant, Arnold Arboretum, Harvard University, 1963-67; Bibliography Researcher, World Life Research Institute, 1967-68. Organizational Memberships: Council Member, New England Botanical Club, 1974; Member, Botanical Society of America; Member, International Association for Plant Taxonomy; Member, Friends of the Arnold Arboretum Society; Member, American Fern Society. Published Works: Author of Over 100 Articles and Monographs on Plant Taxonomy and Ethnobotany Published in Various Professional Journals, 1942-84; Books, *Basic Latin for Plant Taxonomists* 1971, *Studies in the Begoniaceae* 1981. Honors and Awards: Listed in *The Directory of Distinguished Americans, International Who's Who of Intellectuals*. Address: 18 Locke Street, #2, Cambridge, Massachusetts 02140.■

PANOS DEMETRIOS BARDIS

Professor, Editor, Author, Poet. Personal: Born September 24, 1924 in Lefcohorion, Arcadia, Greece; Married Donna Jean; Father of Byron Galen, Jason Dante. Education: Panteios Supreme School, Athens, 1945-47, B.A., magna cum laude, Bethany College, 1950; M.A., Notre Dame University, 1953; Ph.D., Purdue University, 1955. Career: Professor, Editor, Author, Poet; Instructor to Associate Professor of Sociology, Albion College, 1955-59; Associate Professor of Sociology, 1959-62; Professor of Sociology Toledo University, 1963 to present; Editor and Book Review Editor, *International Social Science Review*, 1982 to present; Editorial Advisor, American Biographical Institute, 1980 to present; *Journal of Sociological Studies* 1979 to present, *Renaissance Universal Journal* 1982 to present, *Sociological Inquiry* 1981 to present, *South African Journal of Sociology* 1971 to present, *Synthesis; the Interdisciplinary Journal of Sociology* 1973 to present; Editorial Consultant, *College Journal of Education* 1973 to present, *Society and Culture* 1972 to present; Book Review Editor 1974 to present and Editorial Board 1965 to present, *Darshana International*; Assistant American Editor and Book Review Editor, *Indian Journal of Social Research* 1965 to present; Associate Editor, *Indian Psychological Bulletin* 1965 to present, *International Journal of Contemporary Sociology* 1971 to present, *International Journal of Sociology of the Family* 1970 to present, *Journal of Political and Military Sociology* 1972 to present, *Literary Endeavour* 1981 to present, *Poetry International* 1982 to present, *Revista del Instituto de Ciencias Sociales* 1965 to present; Associate Editor 1968 to present and Book Review Editor 1966 to present, *International Review of History and Political Science*; Coeditor, *International Review of Modern Sociology* 1972 to present; Editorial Board, *Journal of Education* 1965 to present, *Poetry Americas* 1981 to present, *Review of Social Sciences* 1978 to present, *Sociologia Religiosa* 1966 to present; Associate Editor and Book Review Editor, *Sociological Perspectives* 1981 to present; American Editor, *Sociology International* 1967 to present; Editor in Chief and Book Review Editor, *International Journal on World Peace*, 1983 to present. Organizational Memberships: Academy of American Poets, 1982 to present; Accademia Tiberina, 1982 to present; Alpha Kappa Delta, 1954 to present; Fellow, American Association for the Advancement of Science, 1960 to present; American Association of University Professors, 1955 to present; American Biographical Institute, Member 1979 to present, Publications Committee, 1983 to present; Awards Committee, 1983 to present; Board of Advisors, American Society for Neo-Hellenic Studies, 1969 to present; American Sociological Association, Fellow, 1953 to present, Membership Committee, 1966-1971; Conference Internationale de Sociologie de la Religion, 1969 to present; Council of Social Science Journal Editors, 1979 to present; Democritos, 1973 to present; Editorial Advisor, Free Press International, 1980 to present; Academic Advisory Board, Georgetown University Institute, 1981 to present; Global Congress of the World's Religions, Member, 1980 to present, Associate Trustee, 1982 to present, Chairman of Task Force on the Family, 1982 to present; Group for the Study of Sociolinguistics, 1967 to present; Ernest Groves Fund Committee, 1977 to present, Groves Conference; Hellenic Professional Association of America International, Member 1981 to present, Advisory Board on Professional, Educational and Governmental Matters, 1982 to present, Chairman, Biographical, Credential Upgrading and Academy Referral Subcommittee, 1982 to present, Trustee, 1982 to present; Institut International de Sociologie, Fellow, 1969 to present, Chairman of Membership Committee, 1970 to present, Coordinator for the U.S.A., 1974 to present, Executive Committee, 1982 to present; Advisory Council, Institute for Mediterranean Affairs, 1968 to present; Honorary Associate, Institute for the Study of Plural Societies, University of Pretoria, South Africa, 1974 to present; Fellow, Intercontinental Biographical

TWO THOUSAND NOTABLE AMERICANS

Association, 1976 to present; International Association of Family Sociology, 1976 to present; Founding Life Fellow, International College of Proctors and Preceptors, 1982 to present; Life Fellow, International Institute of Arts and Letters, 1966 to present; Honorary Advisor, International Personnel Research, 1971 to present; International Scientific Commission on the Family, 1969 to present; International Sociological Association, Member 1970 to present, Research Committee on Social Change, 1972 to present, Research Committee on Sociology of Education, 1972 to present, Research Committee on Family Sociology, 1974 to present; Kappa Delta Pi, 1975 to present; KRIKOS, 1975 to present; Advisory Council for Academic Affairs, 1977 to present; Advisory Member, Marquis Biographical Library Society, 1973 to present; Board of Trustees, Marriage Museum, 1969 to present; Advisory Board, Minority Alliance International, 1981 to present; Modern Greek Society, 1973 to present; Board of Directors, National Academy of Economics and Political Science, 1959 to present; Consultant, National Association on Standard Medical Vocabulary, 1963 to present; National Council on Family Relations, 1953 to present; National Society of Literature and the Arts, 1975 to present; National Society of Published Poets, 1976 to present; Professional Member, National Writer's Club, 1963 to present; Active Member, New York Academy of Sciences, elected 1963; Advisory Board, News World Communications, 1980 to present; North Central Sociological Association, 1972 to present; Ohio Council on Family Relations, 1959 to present; Ohio Society of Poets, 1976 to present; Life Member, Phi Kappa Phi, 1972 to present; Pi Gamma Mu, 1959 to present; Professors' World Peace Academy, Founding Member 1979 to present, Great Lakes Coordinator 1983 to present, Executive Committee 1983 to present; Royal Asiatic Society, 1982 to present; Sigma Xi, 1979 to present; Associate, Smithsonian Institution, 1977 to present; Fellow, World Academy of Scholars, 1976 to present; World Alliance for Civil Rights, 1981 to present; World Poetry Society Intercontinental, 1980 to present; Chief of International Board and Member of Governing Body (representing North America) World University, 1981 to present. Published Works: Author of *Atlas of Human Reproductive Anatomy* 1983, *Evolution of the Family in the West* 1983, *Global Marriage and Family Customs* 1983, *Studies in Marriage and the Family* 1975, 2nd edition 1978, *The Family in Changing Civilizations* 1969, *Encyclopedia of Campus Unrest, Ivan and Artemis, History of the Family* 1975, *The Future of the Greek Language in the United States* 1976, *Nine Oriental Muses* 1983, *History of Thanatology; Philosophical, Religious, Psychological and Sociological Ideas Concerning Death from Primitive Times to the Present* 1981; Co-editor of *Poetry Americas* 1982, *The Family in Asia* 1978. Honors and Awards: Couphos Prize; Winner of Seminario de Investigacion Historica y Arqueologica Award, Museo de Historia, Barcelona, Spain, 1967; Award for Outstanding Achievement in Education, Bethany College, 1975; Outstanding Teaching Award, Toledo University, 1975; Outstanding Journalism Award, American Biographical Institute, 1982; Poetry Award, Hoosier Challenger Magazine, 1983; Listed in *American Biographical Institute Research Association, American Hellenic Who's Who in Business and the Professions, American Men of Science, American Men and Women of Science, American Registry Series, Author's and Writer's Who's Who, Biographical Encyclopedia of the United States, Book of Honor, Community Leaders of America, Community Leaders and Noteworthy Americans, Community Leaders of the World, Contemporary Authors, Contemporary Notables, Creative and Successful Personalities of the World, Dictionary of International Biography, Directory of Distinguished Americans, Ellenicon Who's Who, International Author's and Writer's Who's Who, International Biographical Association Yearbook and Biographical Directory, International Book of Honor, International Directory of Sex Research and Related Fields, International Directory of Sociology, International Portrait Gallery, International Scholars Directory, International Who's Who in Community Service, International Who's Who in Education, International Who's Who in Poetry, International Who's Who in Sociology, International Who's Who of Contemporary Achievement, Leaders of American Science, Men and Women of Distinction, Men of Achievement, National Register of Eductional Researchers, National Register of Prominent Americans and International Notables, Notable Americans, Notable Americans of the Bicentennial Era, Notable Americans of 1976-1977, Ohio Lives, Personalities of America, Personalities of the West and Midwest, Registry of American Achievement, Two Thousand Notable Americans, Who is Who of Greek Origin in Institutions of Higher Learning in the United States and Canada, Who's Who in America, Who's Who in the Midwest, Who's Who in the World, World Directory of Linguists, World Who's Who in Science, World Who's Who of Authors, Writer's Directory.* Address: 2533 Orkney, Ottawa Hills, Toledo, Ohio, 43606.■

KENNY DALE BARFIELD

Instructor, Minister, Administrator. Personal: Born November 17, 1947; Son of H. P. and Bernice Barfield; Married Nancy Ann Cordray, Daughter of Mildred Cordray; Father of Amber Elizabeth, Lora Allyn. Education: B.A., David Lipscomb College, 1969; M.A., University of Alabama, 1972. Career: Director, T. B. Larimore Forensic Society, Mars Hill Bible School; Assistant Minister, Sherrod Avenue Church of Christ; Instructor in Speech, University of North Alabama; Former Positions as Minister of Highland Park Church of Christ (Muscle Shoals, Alabama) and Jackson Heights Church of Christ (Florence, Alabama). Organizational Memberships: Alabama Forensic Educators Association, President 1976-77 and 1982-85; National Forensic League, Chairman Deep South District 1977-79 and 1981-85; Amerian Forensic Association; Speech Communication Association; Southern Speech Association; Columbia Scholastic Press Advisor's Association; Alabama Journalism Educators Association. Published Works: Author *50 Golden Years: The NFL Nationals*, 1980; Articles, "Go to the B-1 Subpoint" (1979) and "Agreeable Surprise" (1970). Honors and Awards: Outstanding Young Religious Leader, Alabama Jaycees, 1976; Alabama Speech Teacher of the Year, 1977; Key Coach, The Barkley Forum for High Schools, Emory University, 1981; Double Diamond Coach and Distinguished Service Award, National Forensic League, 1981; Listed in *International Men of Achievement, Personalities of the South, Personalities of America, Who's Who Among Students in American Universities and Colleges.* Address: 2030 Saxton Drive, Florence, Alabama 35630.■

JAMIE S. BARKIN

Educator, Administrator, Physician. Personal: Born June 1, 1943. Education: Graduated magna cum laude, University of Miami, 1965; M.D., University of Miami School of Medicine, 1970; Intern 1970-71, Junior Residency in Medicine 1971-72, Senior Residency in Medicine 1972-73, Junior Fellow in Gastroenterology 1973-74, Senior Fellow in Gastroenterology 1974-75, Jackson Memorial Hospital, Veterans Administration Hospital (associated with University of Miami). Military: Served in the United States Army Reserve, 324th General Hospital, attaining the rank of Major. Career: Assistant Professor (Department of Medicine) 1975-80, Assistant Professor (Department of Oncology) 1978-81, Associate Professor (Department of Medicine) 1980 to present, Associate Professor (Department of Oncology) 1981 to present, Biomedical Engineering Faculty, University of Miami School of Medicine; Coordinator of Endoscopy, Miami Veterans Hospital, 1975 to present; Active Attending Staff, Jackson Memorial Hospital, Miami, 1975 to present; Active Attending Staff, Veterans Administration Hospital, Miami, 1975 to present; Active Attending Staff, National Children's Cardiac Hospital, Miami; Reviewer for *Diabetes Care* 1978 to present, *Digestive Diseases and Sciences* 1980; Editorial Board, *American Journal of Gastroenterology* 1980. Organizational Memberships: Gastrointestinal Tract Study Group (G.I. Cancer), National Cancer Institute, Member 1975 to present, Chairman 1981; American College of Gastroenterology, Board of Trustees 1980-83, Post-graduate Course Director 1982, Chairman Constitution and Bylaws Committee 1982-83, Awards and Protocol Committee 1978-79, Program Committee 1978-82; Council of Regional Endoscopic Societies, Secretary 1982-84; American Society for Gastrointestinal Endoscopy, Constitution and By-laws Committee 1980-81 and 1981-82, Scientific Program Committee 1981-82, Postgraduate Education Committee 1982-84, Nominating Committee 1983; Alpha Omega Alpha; American Society of Internal Medicine; American College of Physicians; American Medical Association; Fellow, American College of Gastroenterology; American Gastroenterological Association; Southern Medical Association; American Pancreatic Society; Florida Society of Gastrointestinal Endoscopy, Vice President 1978, President 1979-81, Councillor 1981-82; American Federation of Clinical Research; Bockus International Society of Gastroenterology; American Association for the History of Medicine; Florida Medical Association, Program Chairman of Section of GI 108th Meeting; International Biliary Society. Published Works: Author/Co-Author Numerous Professional Publications. Honors and Awards: Best Fellow, University of Miami, 1974; Veterans Administration Performance Award, Special Advancement for Performance, 1977; Fellow, American College of Physicians, 1973; "Percutaneous Transhepatic Insertion of a Permanent Internal Prosthesis in the Biliary Tree: A non-surgical method for the relief of Obstructive Jaundice," Honorable Mention, Radiological Society of North America Meeting, 1978; "Non-surgical Transhepatic Crushing and Removal of Common Duct Stones: A New Technique," Honorable Mention, Radiological Society of America Inc., 1980. Address: 171 Southeast 21st Road, Miami, Florida 33129.■

CHARLES M. BARNES

College President. Personal: Born October 15, 1917, in Baltimore, Maryland; Son of Charles M. and Florence M. Boyle Barnes; Married Nellie E. Dorsey, July 6, 1940, in Oak Park, Illinois; Father of Roger Clifford. Education: Attended Roosevelt College, Chicago, 1938-40; B.S.Ed. 1950, M.S. 1950, Kansas State College, Pittsburgh; Attended the University of Kansas (Summers 1951 and 1952), University of Colorado (Summers 1953 and 1954); Fellowship, Community College Leadership Program, Michigan State University, 1961. Military: Served with the United States Army in the European Theatre of Operations (Scotland, Belgium, England, France, Germany), 1943-46, attaining the rank of Sergent. Career: Instructor, Ottawa Senior High School 1950-51, Fort Scott Junior College (Kansas) 1951-53;

TWO THOUSAND NOTABLE AMERICANS

Assistant Dean, Fort Scott Junior College, 1953-56; Executive Dean, Pratt Junior College (Kansas) 1956-59, Dodge City College (Kansas) 1959-65; President, Dodge City Community College, 1965 to present. Organizational Memberships: Kappa Delta Pi, National Education Fraternity, 1950; Phi Alpha Theta, National History Fraternity, 1950; National Education Association, 1950; Kansas State Teachers Association, 1950; Kansas History Teachers Association, Executive Council 1951; Kansas Public Junior College Association, Secretary 1956-58, Vice President 1958-61, President 1961-63; Council of North Central Junior Colleges, President 1965-66; Kansas Association of Colleges and Universities, President 1966-67; Kansas-Nebraska Educational Consortium, Vice President 1967-69, President 1969-7, Treasurer 1970 to present; Commission on Institutions of Higher Education, North Central Association of Colleges and Schools, Consultant/ Examiner 1966 to present, Council on Research and Service 1972-78; A.A.C.J.C. Program with Developing Institutions, Coordinator 1968-70; Plains Consortium, Title III Program with Developing Institutions, Coordinator 1970-73; Board of Directors, North Central Association of Colleges and Schools, 1975-77; Board of Directors, Kansas Association of Community Colleges, 1974-76. Community Activities: Rotary Club, President 1963-64. Religion: Methodist. Published Works: Articles in *Kansas Teacher and Junior College Journal*. Honors and Awards: Danforth Foundation Leave Grant, 1971; Recipient of the First Annual Clyde U. Phillips Award for Outstanding Alumnus in Education, Pittsburg State University, Pittsburg, Kansas, 1975; Recipient of an Award of Merit for Outstanding Contributions to Community Colleges, Kansas Association of Community Colleges, 1978. Address: 2514 Thompson, Dodge City, Kansas 67801.■

MELVER RAYMOND BARNES

Private Scientific Researcher. Personal: Born November 15, 1917; Son of Oscar Lester and Sarah Albertine Rowe Barnes (both deceased). Education: Graduate, Tyro High School, Davidson County, North Carolina, 1935; B.A. Chemistry 1947, Special Student in Chemistry (6 Months) 1947, University of North Carolina at Chapel Hill; Courses in Mathematics, Chemistry, Physics, McCoy College (Baltimore, Maryland) 1952 and 1953, University of California at Los Angeles, University of Utah, Brigham Young University, Massachusetts Institute of Technology, George Washington University, Georgia Technical Institute; Diplomas in Basic Electronics and Computers, Microprocesors and Minicomputers, Data Processing and Computer Programming; Diplomas in Radio and Television Servicing, Industrial Electronics, Electronic Communications, Radio Electronic Television Schools, 1957-61. Military: Served in the United States Army, 1942-45. Career: Chemist, Pittsburgh Testing Laboratories, Greensboro, North Carolina 1948-49; Chemist, North Carolina State Highway and Public Works Commission, Raleigh, 1949-51; Chemist, Edgewood Arsenal,· Edgewood, Maryland, 1951-61; Chemist, Dugway Proving Ground, Dugway, Utah, 1961-70; Private Scientific Research. Organizational Memberships: American Chemical Society; American Physical Society; American Association for the Advancement of Science; New York Academy of Sciences. Community Activities: Donation of $1000 to National Space Institute, 1979. Honors and Awards: Doctoral Membership in Theoretical Physics, World University, 1982. Address: Route 1 Box 424, Linwood, North Carolina 27299.■

MICHAEL C. BARNEY

Senior Research Microbiologist. Personal: Born September 27, 1946; Son of Frederick C. (deceased) and Dorothy E. Barney; Married Jill A. Guenther. Education: Attended University of Illinois and Parsons College; B.S. 1970, M.S. 1972, University of Wisconsin; Undertook Five Years of Postgraduate Work at the Medical College of Wisconsin. Career: Biology and Bacteriology Instructor, University of Wisconsin; Research Chemist, Kimberly Clark Corporation; Senior Research Microbiologist, Miller Brewing Company. Organizational Memberships: American Society for Microbiology; Society for Industrial Microbiology; American Society of Brewing Chemists, Chairman of the Committee for Microbiological Controls 1976-79; Miller Management Club, President 1980-81. Religion: Presbyterian. Published Works: Articles Published in Scientific Journals. Honors and Awards: National Honor Society, 1963-64; Scholarship to the University of Wisconsin, 1971; Registered Microbiologist, National Registry of the American Academy of Microbiology; Invited to Participate in Seminars at Universities. Address: 2325 North 83rd Street, Wauwatosa, Wisconsin 53213.■

BERNARD M. BARRETT, JR.

Plastic and Reconstructive Surgeon, Author, Bank and Insurance Director. Personal: Born May 3, 1944, in Pensacola, Florida; Son of Bernard M. Barrett, Sr., M.D., and Blanche Lischkoff Barrett; Married Julie Prokop, November 25, 1972; Father of Beverly Frances, Julie Blaine, Audrey Blake, Bernard Joseph. Education: B.S., Tulane University, 1965; M.D., University of Miami School of Medicine, 1969; Diplomate, American Board of Plastic Surgery; Fellow, American College of Surgeons. Military: Served in the United States Navy Reserve, 1969-74, attaining the rank of Lieutenant Commander. Career: President and Chairman of the Board, Plastic and Reconstructive Surgeons, P.A., Houston, Texas, 1976 to present; Director, American Physicians, Inc., Dallas, Texas, 1977 to present; Director, API Life Insurance Company, Dallas, Texas, 1979 to present; Director, Southwestern Bank, Houston, Texas, 1980 to present; Director, Southwestern Bank-North Belt, Houston, Texas, 1983 to present. Organizational Memberships: American Society of Plastic and Reconstructive Surgeons; American Society for Aesthetic Plastic Surgery; Royal Society of Medicine; Denton A. Cooley Cardiovascular Surgical Society; Michael E. DeBakey International Cardiovascular Society; Director, Plastic Surgery Education Foundation, Chicago, Illinois. Community Activities: Steering Committee, Finance Committee, Reagan/Bush Presidential Campaign, 1980; Director Channel 14 Educational TV, Houston, Texas, 1982 to present; Republican; Houstonian (Houston, Texas); Royal Biscayne Racquet Club (Key Biscayne, Florida). Religion: Methodist. Published Works: Author, *Patient Care in Plastic Surgery* (a leading medical textbook in plastic and reconstructive surgery), 1982; Author Numerous Medical Publications. Honors and Awards: Outstanding Surgical Intern, Methodist Hospital, Houston, Texas, 1969-70; Foreign Exchange Scholarship, Royal College of Surgeons (London, England) and Oxford University (Oxford, England), 1968. Address: 6655 Travis Street, Suite 950, Houston, Texas 77030.■

MELANIE TAYLOR BARRETT

Association Management. Personal: Born September 22, 1943; Daughter of Gail R. and Lois E. Taylor; Mother of Michael Gail, Eric Edward. Education: Studies in Business Administration and Journalism, Walla-Walla Community College; Public Administration Studies, City College, Seattle. Career: Management, Social Services National Association; Chief Administrator, Social Services Agency. Organizational Memberships: Washington Association C.A.A., Quad Chair 1978-80, Chairman of Personnel Committee, Executive Board 1979-80; National Association C.A.A.; Washington Association of Social Welfare; American Society of Association Executives. Community Activities: Washington State Governors Commission of Prison Reform; Fair Housing, Mason County; Mason County Planning Task Force; Washington State Pioneers Association; Veterans of Foreign Wars Auxiliary; Mason County Independent Mothers Association; National Council of Aging. Religion: Member, Garden Grove Community Church, Garden Grove, California. Address: 5945 Mullen Road, Lacey, Washington 98503.■

LOWELL SUNDE BARRICK

Fisheries Engineer. Personal: Born March 3, 1936; Son of L. R. Barrick; Married Kay Parkinson, Daughter of Van Parkinson; Father of Burke, Kevin, Kathy. Education: Attended Ricks College 1954-55, University of Hawaii 1955-56, University of Idaho 1956-59; B.S.C.E., Utah State University, 1962; M.S. Engineering Management, University of Alaska, 1977. Military: Served in the United States National Guard, Idaho, Hawaii, Alaska, 1952-73, Captain in the 38th Special

Forces. Career: Fisheries Engineer, 1974 to present; Airport Engineer, 1964-74; Highway Engineer, 1962-64. Organizational Memberships: Association of Conservation Engineers, President 1980-81; American Society of Engineering Management, Charter Member; American Fisheries Society; Anglo-American Academy. Community Activities: Gastineau Channel Little League, President 1976-78; Civil Air Patrol Search and Rescue Pilot. Religion: Protestant. Honors and Awards: Registered Civil Engineer, 1968; Registered Land Surveyer, 1972. Address: 9505 Mendenhall Loop Road, Juneau, Alaska.■

Nelda Ann Lambert Barton

Nursing Home Administrator, Medical Technologist. Personal: Born May 12, 1929, in Providence, Kentucky; Daughter of Eulis Grant Lambert and Rubie Lois West; Married Harold Bryan Barton, May 11, 1951; Mother of William Grant (deceased), Barbara Lynn, Harold Bryan Jr., Stephen Lamberg, Suzanne. Education: Graduate, Providence High School, 1947; Attended Western Kentucky University, 1947-49; Graduate, Norton Memorial Infirmary School of Medical Technology, 1950; Attended Cumberland College 1978; Continuing Education in Long-term Care. Career: President and Chairman of the Board, Health Systems Inc., Corbin, Kentucky; Consultant in Long-term Care Nursing; Licensed Nursing Home Administrator, Kentucky Board; Registered Medical Technologist, A.S.C.P.; President, Barton and Associates Inc. (Hillcrest Nursing Home), Corbin; President, Hazard Nursing Home Inc., Hazard, Kentucky; President, Harold B. Barton M.D. Memorial Nursing Home, Williamsburg, Kentucky; President, Corbin Nursing Home Inc. (Mountain Laurel Manor), Corbin; President, Barbourville Nursing Home Inc., Barbourville, Kentucky, 1981 to present; President, The Whitley Whiz Inc., Williamsburg, Kentucky, 1983 to present. Community Activities: Director, Kentucky Chamber of Commerce, 1983 to present; Republican National Committeewomen for Kentucky, 1968 to present; Republican National Committee, Executive Committee 1976-80; 1981 Presidential Inaugural Coordinator for Kentucky; Corbin Republican Women's Club, President 1968; Whitley County Republican Party, Chairwoman 1968-72, Campaign Chairwoman 1968-72; 5th District Kentucky Federation of Republican Women, Governor 1968-70, 2nd Vice President 1968-70, Executive Committee 1963 to present, Chairman of State Convention 1970; Republican Party of Kentucky, Advisory Committee 1974 to present; 5th District Lincoln Club Advisory Committee, 1970 to present; Kentucky Candidate Search Committee, Co-Chairman 1974-75; American Medical Political Action Committee; Kentucky Educational Medical Political Action Committee; Kentucky Association Nursing Home Political Action Committee; Kentucky Federation College Republican Advisory Committee, 1981; Kentucky Federal Advisory Committee, 1981; Western Kentucky University Beta Omega Chi, President 1948-49; Fair Housing Task Force, City of Corbin, 1980 to present; Corbin Deposit Bank Board, Director 1980-84; Kentucky Peer Review Organization, Long Term Care Advisory Committee 1978-81; Cumberland College Associate Degree Nursing Advisory Committee 1973-78; Numerous Offices Previously Held in Other Political and Civic Organizations; Member, Federal Council on Aging, 1981 to present. Religion: First Christian Church; Christian Women's Fellowship #2; Stewardship, Property, Education, Chairman Youth Fellowship, Circle Chairman, Others. Honors and Awards: Honorary Kentucky Mother of the Year, Kentucky Mothers Association, 1983; Kentucky Woman of Achievement, Kentucky Business and Professional Women; Valedictorian, Providence High School, 1947; Academic Scholarship to Western Kentucky University, 1947-49; Parent-Teacher Association Life Membership, 1964; Kentucky Republican Woman of the Year, Kentucky Federation of Republican Women, 1968-69; Bluegrass Council Boy Scout Thank You Award, 1974; Kentucky Colonel, 1968; Indiana Sagamore of the Wabash, 1973; The Dwight David Eisenhower Award, 1970; Mayor of Corbin Proclaimed "Nelda Barton Day," October 22, 1973; Recognition Award, Joint Republican Leadership of the United States Congress, 1979; Listed in *Who's Who in the Southeast, Who's Who in America, World Who's Who of Women, Directory of Distinguished Americans, Book of Honor*. Address: 1311 Seventh Street Road, Corbin, Kentucky 40701.■

Sydney Claire Johnson Bass

Educational Administrator. Personal: Born October 21, 1935, in Dalhart, Texas; Mother of James Stewart, Brenda Katherine, Sherman Cecil Kenneth. Education: Graduate, Dalhart High School, 1953; A.B. (high honors) 1959, Graduate Work toward M.A., Life Teaching Certificate, University of Texas-Austin. Career: Administrator, Opportunity School, Inc., Amarillo, Texas, 1973 to present; Assistant, Max Sherman for Texas Senate Campaign, 1973; Part-time Worker, State Senator Max Sherman, Amarillo, 1971; Panhellenic Advisor, West Texas State University, Canyon, Texas, 1964-66; Instructor, United States History, Texas Tech University, 1961-62; Teacher 7th and 8th Grades, History, English, Biology, Lamar Junior High School, Austin, Texas, 1959-60; Secretary, Honorable J. W. Buchanan, Texas House of Representatives, 1959; Private Secretary to Plant Manager, General Electric Company, 1956-57. Organizational Memberships: Delta Delta Delta, Theta Zeta Chapter; Texas Association of Child Care Administrators. Community Activities: American Association of University Women, Membership Chairman 1963-65, Third Vice President 1963-65, Judging for Forensic Speaking Tournament 1964 and 1965, Recording Secretary 1965-67, Delegate to National Convention, Denver, Fund Raising Projects for Mary E. Bivins Library, Study Groups; Delta Delta Delta Amarillo Alumnae Alliance, President 1963-65, Chaplain, Chairman Financial Project, Chairman Story Hour Service Project 1973-75, P.E.O. Education Committee Chairman 1966-67, Chaplain 1970-71 and 1971-72, Skit-song Chairman for State Convention, Dallas, 1974; Junior League of Amarillo, Active Member 1966-76, Sustaining Member 1976 to present, Assistant Yearbook Chairman 1970-71, Goddess of the Month of September 1971, Circulation Manager for Newssheet 1971-72, Education Committee Secretary 1972-73, Mail Chairman and Assistant Newssheet Chairman 1972-73, Editor Newssheet *The Limit* 1973-74, Board of Directors 1973-74, Nominating Committee 1973-75, Delegate to Funding Seminar 1975, Advisor to Committee Concerned with Professional Members Status 1974-75, Articles Published in Newssheet 1968, 1969, 1970, 1973, 1974, 1980; S. F. Austin Band and Orchestra Parents, Member 1973-77 and 1980-83, Treasurer 1975-76; Amarillo City Panhellenic, 1963 to present; Amarillo Alliance of Community Service Executive, Member 1978 to present, Program Chairman, Former Work with Newcomers Club, CLASP, March of Dimes Teen Dances, Wolflin School P.T.A. and Room Mother, Block Worker for Mental Health and Cancer, American Heart Association, Stephen F. Austin Junior High P.T.A. and Room Mother, Advisory Board for Hilltop Board of Community Action, Y.M.C.A., Advisory Board for North Heights, Y.W.C.A. (May Day Luncheons), Starlighters Dance Club, Brownie Scouts and Girl Scouts (Amarillo Girl Scout Council), Opportunity School, Amarillo Symphony Guild, Amarillo Law Wives, Potter-Randall Child Welfare Board (Vice President, President, Skit Chairman); Board of Trustees, The Don Harrington Discovery Center, 1983-84. Religion: Westminster Presbyterian Church, Member 1962-77, Women's Association 1962-77, Circle Member 1962-77, Circle Officer 1962 and 1970, Leader Prayer Retreat 1970 and 1972, Family Life and Missionary Education Committee, Adult Church School Teacher 1964-67, Christian Education Committee 4 Years, Children's Council 1970-71 and 1971-72, Chairman Program Committee for All Sunday School Classes 1972, 2nd Grade Lead Sunday School Teacher 1969-75, Observer National Presbyterian General Assembly 1970, Preaching at Church and in Surrounding Community Churches 1971 and 1972, Ordained Deacon 1975; Adult Teacher, State Presbyterian Synod School, Trinity University, San Antonio, Texas, 1971; Studied at Presbyterian State Synod School in San Antonio; First Presbyterian Church, Member 1977 to present, RISK Evangelism Committee 1978-83; Ordained Deacon, 1975; Honors and Awards: Delta Delta Delta Scholarship Awards, University of Texas 1957, 1958; 2nd Place, Battle of the Flowers State Oratorical Competition, University of Texas, 1958; KIXZ Housewife Hall of Fame, 1964; KGNC Housewife Hall of Fame, 1965; Alpha Lambda Delta, Secretary 1954-55; Pi Lambda Theta; Phi Alpha Theta; Phi Beta Kappa; Delta Kappa Gamma, Honorary Life Member; Scottish Rite Dormitory Advisory; 10-Year Service Award, Girl Scouts of America; Nominated by Amarillo Y.W.C.A. and Amarillo Branch American Association of University Women to *Outstanding Young Women of America*; Listed in *Personalities of America, Outstanding Young Women of America*. Address: 2208 South Hayden, Amarillo, Texas 79109.■

Carl Edward Baum

Senior Scientist. Personal: Born February 6, 1940. Education: B.S. with honors 1962, M.S. 1963, Ph.D. 1969, California Institute of Technology. Military: Served in the United States Air Force, 1962-71, achieving the rank of Captain. Career: Senior Scientist for Electromagnetics, Kirkland Air Force Base, Albuquerque, New Mexico. Organizational Memberships: New Mexico Academy of Science; Institute of Electrical and Electronic Engineers, Senior Member; Organizer of Special Session at the E.M.C. Symposium in Rotterdam (Holland) 1979, Zurich Symposium 1981 and 1983; U.S.R.I. Commission B&E; Electromagnetic Society, President; U.R.S.I. U.S. Delegate to General Assembly, Lima 1975, Helsinki 1978, Washington 1981, Florence (Italy) 1984. Religion: Composer of Sacred Music; Director of Choir, Our Lady of Assumption Catholic Church, 4 Years. Honors and Awards: National Honor Society, Valedictorian, Academic Medals, Christian Brothers Academy, Syracuse, New York; Wheaton Football Trophy 1960-61, Sloan Scholarship 1959-62, Scholarship 1958-59, Tau Beta Pi, Honeywell Award as Best Undergraduate in Engineering 1962, Society of Military Engineers Award 1962, Distinguished A.F.R.O.T.C. Graduate (commissioned 2nd Lieutenant) 1962, Sigma Xi, California Institute of Technology; Air Force Commendation Medal, 1969; Air Force Research and Development Award, 1970; Air Force Nomination to Ten Outstanding Young Men of America, 1971. Address: 51116 Eastern S.E. Unit D, Albuquerque, New Mexico 87105.■

Eleanor E. Bauwens

Associate Dean. Personal: Born December 13, 1931; Daughter of Mr. and Mrs. R.W. King; Married Maurice J. Bauwens; Mother of Paul Joseph. Education: Diploma, St. Mary's Hospital School of Nursing, 1952; B.S.N. with high distinction 1966, M.A. 1970, The University of Arizona; Undertook Graduate Study in Nursing, The University of Arizona, 1972-73; Ph.D., The University of Arizona, 1974. Career: Associate Dean and Professor, College of Nursing, University of Arizona; Former Associate Professor, Research Assistant, University of Arizona; Office Nurse; Industrial Nurse. Organizational Memberships: American Academy of Nursing, Fellow 1979 to present; American Anthropological Association, Fellow 1975 to present; Society for Applied Anthropology, Fellow 1978 to present; Sigma Theta Tau, Past President Beta Mu Chapter; Phi Kappa Phi; National Research Awards Review Committee; Arizona Nurses Association, Council on Practice 1978-80; Editorial Board Reviewer, *Image*, 1978 to present; Council on Nursing and Anthropology, President-Elect 1981-83, President 1983-85; Sigma Xi; University of Arizona Undergraduate Council, Chairman 1981-84. Community Activities: Pima County Home Health Advisory Committee, Chairman 1979 to present; Speaker, Seminars and Conferences; WISE Center, Panel Member; Conducted Community Swine Flu Immunization Clinics, Wellness Subcommittee, Heath Systems Agency Southeastern Arizona. Published Works: 28 Publications including 2 Books. Honors and Awards: Certificate of Honors, University of Arizona, 1966; Nurse Scientist Pre-Doctoral Fellowship, United States Public Health Service, 1967-72; Publishing Grant, C.V. Mosby Company, 1980; 6 Funded Research Projects; Western Writers Regional Conference Committee, Sigma Theta Tau; Listed in *Who's Who in Health Care, Who's Who of American Women, World Who's Who of Women, Who's Who in America, International Gold Award Book*. Address: University of Arizona College of Nursing, Tucson, Arizona 85721.■

TWO THOUSAND NOTABLE AMERICANS

ABDO FARES BAYAZEED

Petroleum Engineer. Personal: Born August 20, 1924, in Damascus, Syria; Father of Fares, David, Raina, Jason (deceased), Nadia. Education: Graduate of Wentworth Military Academy Junior College; B.S. Petroleum Engineering, University of Oklahoma, 1955. Career: Petroleum Engineer, Sinclair Oil and Gas Company, Tulsa, Oklahoma, 1955-60; Petroleum Engineer, Layton Oil Company, Independence, Kansas, 1960-62; Petroleum Engineer, Department of Energy, Bartlesville Energy Research Center, Bartlesville, Oklahoma, 1962 to present. Organizational Memberships: Society of Petroleum Engineers of A.I.M.E.; Oklahoma Chapter of Society of Petroleum Engineers, Advisory Committee 1967, Board of Directors 1968-71, Chairman of Education Committee. Community Activities: Science Fair (Bartlesville), Chairman of Arrangements and Registration 1967, Judge 1968; Bartlesville Young Men's Christian Association; Junior Hi-Y Club, Youth Committee 1969-70, Advisor 1969-70. Published Works: Author/Co-Author Number of Technical Papers. Honors and Awards: Award of Honor, Wentworth Military Acdemy, 1950; Listed in *Who's Who in the South and Southwest, Personalities of the South, Book of Honor, Community Leaders and Noteworthy Americans, Notable Americans, Personalities of America, American Register of Profiles, Who's Who in Technology Today, Who's Who in America, Dictionary of International Biography, Men of Achievement, Men and Women of Distinction, International Who's Who of Intellectuals, International Register of Profiles, International Who's Who in Community Service.* Address: 1026 South Johnstone, Apartment 8, Bartlesville, Oklahoma 74003.■

ANNA MARY BAYGENTS

Educator. Personal: Born July 13, 1926; Daughter of George Francis AuBuchon and Bertha Louise Franck (both deceased); Married Roy Emerson Baygents, Son of Thomas Fullwood Baygents and Iva Mae Partney (both deceased); Mother of Ralph George (deceased); Stepmother of Steven Warren, Edris Marie Beck, Roy E. Jr., William Michael, Jeffrey Thomas, Timothy Gregory, Patricia Joy Scheer. Education: Graduate, Poplar Bluff High School, 1944; Extension Classes, University of North Carolina, University of Missouri, SEMO State University, Three Rivers Community College; A.A., Three Rivers Community College, 1984. Career: Instructor, Dental Assisting, Three Rivers Community College, 1972 to present; Baygents Service, Owner and Bookkeeper 1978-83, Bookkeeper 1968-1978; Certified Dental Assistant, 1944-68. Organizational Memberships: American Dental Assistants Association, Treasurer 1963-68; Missouri Dental Assistants Association, President 1957; Missouri Dental Assisting Educators; Missouri Vocational Association, Health Occupation Division; Missouri Association of Community and Junior Colleges. Community Activities: Butler County United Fund, Board Member 1958-1961, Secretary 1960 and 1961; Butler County Council for Retarded Children, President 1981 and 1982; Wilhaven, Residence for Mentally Handicapped Adults, Organizing Board Member and Secretary, 1980-83; Daughters of the American Revolution, Poplar Bluff Chapter, Organizing Member and Chapter Treasurer, 1980-83; Troop Committee Chairman for Handicapped Boy and Girl Scout Troop, 1979-83; Butler County Genealogical Society, First Vice President 1980-83. Religion: Catholic; Legion of Mary, 1950-65; Secretary and President, Treasurer 1960-61, Legion of Mary Curia (District Level); Sacred Heart School Board, Secretary, 1971-72. Honors and Awards: Daughters of the American Revolution History Award, 1940; High School Salutatorian, 1944; Achievement Award, American Dental Assistants Association, 1967; Cooperation Award 1974, Achievement Award 1976, Missouri Dental Assistants Association; Listed in *Who's Who in the Midwest.* Address: P.O. Box 506, Poplar Bluff, Missouri 63901.■

PARKER REYNOLDS BEAMER

Pathologist, Educator, Director of Resident Training. Personal: Born Jul 27, 1914; Son of Powhatan Reynolds and Bessie Louise Poole Beamer (dec); Married Mary Jo Scovill; Father of Jo Beamer Zurbrugg, Mary Susan, Grant Scovill. Education: A.B. with high honors 1935, M.S. 1937, Ph.D. 1940, University of Illinois; M.D. cum laude, Washington University, St. Louis, 1943. Military: Served in the Medical Corps, Reserve Commanding Officer and Chief of Microbiology, Serology and Parasitology , Antilles Gen Medical Laboratory, San Juan, Puerto Rico, 1945-57, First Lieutenant to Lieutenant Colonel. Career: Assistant In Bacteriology and Immunology, University of Illinois, 1935-39; Assistant in Pathology 1941-43, Assistant Professor Pathology 1943-49, Washington University School of Medicine; Director and Professor Microbiology and Immunology and Associate Professor of Pathology 1949-53, Associate Dean 1951-53, Bowman Gray School of Medicine; Microbiologist and Associate Pathologist, North Carolina Baptist Hospital, 1949-53; Consultant in Pathology, Veterans Administration Regional Office, Winston-Salem, North Carolina, and Veterans Administration Hospital, Mountain Home, Tennessee, 1950-53; Professor of Pathology 1953-65, Department Chairman 1960-65, Indiana University School of Medicine; Pathologist, Indiana University Medical Center Hospitals, 1953-65; Chief Pathologist, Director of Pathology and Laborties, Los Angeles County University Southern California Medical Center, 1965-69; Professor of Pathology 1979-80, Professor Emeritus 1980 to present, University Health Sciences/Chicago Medical School; Associate Pathologist and Director Resident Training, West Suburban Hospital Medical Center, Oak Park, Illinois, 1980 to present; Clinical Professor of Pathology, Loyola University Stritch School of Medicine, 1981 to present. Organizational Memberships: Alpha Omega Alpha; Sigma Xi; Fellow, College of American Pathologists; American Society of Clinical Pathologists; Founding Fellow, Association of Clinical Scientists; American Association of Pathologists; American Medical Association; Society Experimental Biology and Medicine; Gamma Alpha; Phi Chi; Kiwanis International; World Medical Association; Chicago Institute of Medicine; Chicago Pathological Society; New York Academy of Science; Association of American Medical Colleges; American Association of University Professors; Executive Council, Washington University Medical Center, 1972-76, 1978-79; North Carolina Society Bacteriologists, Member 1949-53, President 1951-53. Religion: Baptist. Published Works: Author of Over 250 Articles in Various American and Foreign Journals; Co-Author, *Principles of Human Pathology* 1959, *Microscopic Pathology* 1965; Contributor 5 Medical Books, 1952, 1955, 1977, 1979, 1981; Consulting and Contributing Editor, *Stedman's Medical Dictionary*, 1961, 1966, 1972, 1976, 1982; Editor-in-Chief 1956-65, Board of Editors 1953-55 and 1966-76, *American Journal of Clinical Pathology*; Founding Editor-in-Chief, *Survey of Pathology in Medicine and Surgery* 1964; Editor Pathology, *Current Medical Digest*, 1959-68; Co-Editor, *The Microbiology-Immunology Series*, 1973 to present. Honors and Awards: Bronze Tablet for Military and Scholastic Excellence, University of Illinois, 1935; Alpha Omega Alpha Honorary Medical Society, 1943; Three World War II Medals, 1945, 1946; Gold Medal for Meritorious Research, North Carolina Medical Society, 1950; Outstanding Facult Member Plaque, Indiana University Medical Center, 1961; Honorary Medallion, Air Force Institute Pathology, 1962; Teaching Award from Residents, Indiana University Medical Center, 1964; Commemoration and Appreciation Plaque, Los Angeles, Co-University Southern California Medical Center, 1969; Three International Symposium Awards for Meritorious Research on Leukemia and Lymphona, 1973, 1975, 1979; Charter Member with Medal of Merit, Presidential Task Force, 1981; Diploma with Special Competence Certification in Microbiology and Immunology, 1950; Trustee 1962-69, Life Trustee Award for Distinguished Service 1970, American Board of Pathology; Chancellor's Committee of Five Hundred, Washington University, St. Louis, 1968; Jackson Johnson Scholar and Fellow, Washington University School of Medicine, 1939-41; Listed in *Who's Who in America, Who's Who in the World, Who's Who in the Midwest, National Cyclopaedia of American Biography, American Men and Women of Science, Directory of Medical Services.* Address: 539 Franklin Avenue, River Forest, Illinois 60305.■

ADELINE CHARLOTTE BECHT

Counselor-Rehabilitation Therapist, Researcher, Community Educator, Consultant. Personal: Born March 11, 1937; Deaf and Blind. Education: B.A. Psychology, Cascade College, 1964; M.Ed. Counseling and Guidance, Lewis and Clark College, 1976; M.A. Clincial Psychology, University of Oregon, 1982; Ph.D. Clincial Psychology and Ph.D. Counseling and Guidance, University of Oregon, 1982. Career: Counselor-Rehabilitation Therapist, Researcher, Community Educator, Consultant in Private Practice, 1981 to present; Executive Director/Director of Programs and Program Development, The Living Rehabilitation Center, 1971-81; Visiting Lecturer to Department of Special Education for the Hearing Impaired, Lewis and Clark College, 1971 to present; Consultant on Deafness, Blindness, Deaf-Blindness and Mental Health to the Handicapped, Riverside Psychiatric Hospital, 1974 to present; Visiting Lecturer, Western Oregon State College, 1974-80; Library Assistant/Researcher, Tektronix, Inc., 1965-72. Organizational Memberships: American Personnel and Guidance Association; American Psychological Association; American Tinnitus Association; International Platform Association; Order of Ameranth Fraternity. Community Activities: Psychology Intern, Riverside Psychiatric Hospital, 1980-81; Practicum Counselor, Washington State School for the Blind, 1976; Sponsor/Counselor, Alcoholics Anonymous, 1962-70; Counselor, Hillcrest State School for Girls, 1962-65; College Team Leader/Assistant to Social Worker, White Shield for Unwed Mothers, 1959-64; Entertainer to Institutions of Socially and Physically Handicapped, 1959-64. Published Works: Author of *An Exploratory Study: The Effects of Subjective Tinnitus on Health in Deaf and Hearing Adults* 1982, *Fifteen Ways to Communicate with a Deaf-Blind Person* 1982, *How the Deaf Perceive Their World and Why They Act the Way They Do* 1982, *The Effectiveness of Deep Muscle Relaxation with Positive Imagery and Cognitive Meditative Therapy in Treatment of Stress Resulting from Subjective Continuous Tinnitus in Hearing Adults* 1982. Honors and Awards: First Deaf and Blind Person in the World to Earn Ph.D.; Service to Mankind Award, Sertoma International, 1977; How Great is One Award, National Organization of Christians and Jews, 1976; Special Citation Award, Oregon's Governor's Committee on Employment of the Handicapped, 1970; Honor Girl of the Term, Cascade College, 1962; Listed in *Who's Who in the West, Who's Who of American Women, Book of Honor, Personalities of the World, Who's Who in Frontier Science and Technology, Notable Americans.* Address: 9028 Southeast Market Street, Portland, Oregon 97216.■

TWO THOUSAND NOTABLE AMERICANS

MARION POLLY BEHRMANN

Special Education Consultant, Author. Personal: Born November 24, 1925; Daughter of Marjory R. Piper; Married John W. Behrmann; Father of James Piper, Charles Robert, Judith B. Richardson, Roland A. Education: B.S.Ed., B.S. Recreational Leadership, University of Massachusetts; Undertook Education Courses, Boston University, 1946; Studies in Learning Disabilities, Reading Research Institute, 1965-66; Psychology Courses, Clark University, 1973-74; Special Education Courses, Boston College, 1974-75; Special Education Courses, Lesley College, 1977. Career: Kindergarten Director, Teacher, Reading Tutor for Emotionally Disturbed, Mentally Retarded, Physically Handicapped, Tutor and Home Teacher, Substitute Teacher, Camp Director, 1948-65; Supervisor, Learning Disabilities for Reading Research Institute, 1966; Master Teacher, American International College, Summer Institute for Learning Disabilities, 1968-69; Remedial Reading and Learning Disabilities, Framingham, 1966-71; Teacher/Diagnostician, Liberty Council of Schools, 1970-71; Master Teacher, Framingham State College, Summer Institute for Learning Disabilities, 1971; Coordinator, Learning Disabilities, Framingham Middle Schools, 1971-73; Teacher, Clark University, 1973; Special Educator, Resource Center, Wellesley, Massachusetts, 1973 to present; Instructor, League of Women Voters Paraprofessionals, 1974; Lecturer/Consultant, Harvard University, Boston College, Boston University, Clark University, University of Massachusetts, Lesley College, Assumption College, Boston State College, Tufts University, American International College, Mount Holyoke College, Framingham State College, and for over 200 School Systems in Massachusetts Communities, Association for Children with Learning Disabilities Conferences throughout the United States and Canada, Massachusetts Teachers Association Conferences, Others, 1967 to present; Conductor of Workshops, Demonstrations and College Courses, 196 to present; Television Demonstrations and Radio Programs, 1968 to present. Organizational Memberships: Massachusetts Association for Children with Learning Disabilities, Co-Founder Framingham Chapter, Advisory Board Member 1973-79, Board of Directors 1968-72; Massachusetts Council for Exceptional Children, Treasurer 1974-75; Selected Participant in H.E.W. Conference on Technology for Children, 1972. Community Activities: Cub Scout Leader; Girl Scout Leader; Framingham Square Dance, Co-Founder; Local Republican Leader. Religion: Sunday School Teacher, Choir Member. Published Works; Author *Why Is It Always Me?, Number and Letter Dice, Activities for Developing Auditory Perception, Activities for Developing Visual Perception, How-to-Make-it Cards*; Co-Author *Parents As Playmates, How Many Spoons Make a Family?, EXCEL I—Experience for Children in Learing, EXCEL II*; Co-Department Editor, *Day Care Magazine, Highlights, Parents*. Honors and Awards: Massachusetts Mother of the Year, 1979; Massachusetts Association for Children with Learning Disabilities Award for Outstanding Contribution to the Field of Learning Disabilities, 1970; Phi Kappa Phi; Listed in *Who's Who in Learning Disabilities, Who's Who in American Colleges, Who's Who in Outdoor Education, Who's Who of American Women, Who's Who of International Women, Who's Who in Education*. Address: 115 Lake Road, Framingham, Massachusetts 01701.■

TIMOTHY A. BELL

State Representative. Personal: Born August 2, 1942; Son of Barbara Johnson Bell. Education: B.A. Social Studies 1970, M.S. Guidance and Counseling 1973, Western New Mexico University. Career: Member, Illinois House of Representatives; Member, Moline School Board; Member, Rock Island County Board of Realtors; Salesman, National Biscuit Company (Nabisco); Administrative Assistant to Dean of Student Affairs, Western New Mexico University; Member, Moline Board of Education, 8 Years. Organizational Memberships: Legislative Memberships include Vice Chairman of Revenue Committee, Member Executive Committee and Higher Education Committee; American Legislative Council; Member and Building Representative, Moline Education Association; Illinois Teachers Federation; Illinois Guidance-Personnel Association. Honors and Awards: Listed in *Outstanding Young Men of America, Who's Who in American Politics, Who's Who in the Midwest, Personalities of America, Personalities of the West and Midwest, Men of Achievement, Biographical Roll of Honor, Dictionary of International Biography*. Address: 2545 - 18th Avenue A, Moline, Illinois 61265.■

JEANETTE LOBACH BELY

Professor. Personal: Born January 15, 1916; Daughter of John M. and Antonina M. Lobach; Mother of Jeanette Zinaida, Leona Bely. Education: B.B.A., St. John's University, 1938; M.A., Teacher's College, Columbia University, 1939; Ph.D., St. John's University, 1961; Licensed Teacher of Accounting, Law and Allied Subjects, School Administrator and Supervisor, District School Administrator. Career: Professor of Education, Bernard M. Baruch College of the City of New York, 1954 to present; Temporary Lecturer, Hunter College, 1954; Teacher in Charge, Miller Schools, Inc., 1941-48; Instructor, Lamb's Business Training School, 1940; Instructor, Pace College, 1951-54; Technical Editor, Simon and Schuster, Inc., Houghton, Mifflin and Company. Organizational Memberships: International Society for Business Education; Administrative Management Society; Business Education Association of Metropolitan New York; National Business Education Association, Eastern Business Education Association; Business Teachers Association of New York State; Eastern Business Teachers Association; Delta Pi Epsilon. Community Activities: Block Association; Presidential Task Force; Sustaining Member, Republican National Committee, 1983; U.S. Senatorial Club, 1983. Published Works: Author of *Pitman Secretarial Shorthand for Colleges 1978; Instructor's Handbook and Supplementary Dictation 1978*; Co-editor of *Review for CPA Exams 1977*; Contributing Author of *The World Secretaries Handbook*; Co-editor of *Business Education Association Yearbook* 26th edition, 1965-66; Authored Articles "Population Change and Justifiable Expectations", *The Journal of Business Education* February 1973; "Let's Not Always Blame the Business Schools", *Administrative Management* February 1973; "Word Processing and Its Implications on Stenography", *The Balance Sheet* April 1973, Others; Authored Professional Papers "The Effect of Typing Techniques and Comprehensions on Transcription"; "How This Job Can be a Stepping Stone Upward"; "How to Get Along with People", and others. Honors and Awards: National Honorary Graduate Business Education Fraternity; Merit Award of Administrative Management Society, 1969; Meritorious Service Award for Outstanding Professionalism and Significant Achievement, National Business Education Association, 1978; Listed in *Leaders in Education, World Who's Who of American Women, Dictionary of International Biography, Contemporary Authors, The World's Who's Who of Women, World Who's Who of Women in Education, Community Leaders and Noteworthy Americans, International Who's Who of Women, Anglo-American Who's Who, Men and Women of Distinction, Book of Honor, Five Thousand Men and Women of Distinction, The International Who's Who of Intellectuals, The Directory of Distinguished Americans, Personalities of America, Community Leaders of America, International Book of Honor, Five Thousand Personalities of the World*. Address: 1024 East 93rd Street, Brooklyn, New York 11236.■

JOHN JOSEPH BENDIK

Associate Pastor. Personal: Born October 15, 1941; Son of Mrs. John Bendik. Education: B.A. Philosophy, St. Meinrad College, Indiana, 1963; M.Div., St. Meinrad School of Theology, Indiana, 1972. Career: Chaplain, College Misericordia, Dallas, Pennsylvania; Associate Pastor, St. Matthew's Parish, East Stroudsburg, Pennsylvania; Campus Minister, East Stroudsburg State College. Organizational Memberships: President, Senate of Priests, Diocese of Scranton; Chairperson, Pennsylvania Catholic Campus Ministry Association, 1979 to present; Chairperson, National Advisory Board of Directors, Campus Ministry of the United States Catholic Conference, 1981 to present; Catholic Campus Ministry Association, 1969 to present; Director, Campus Ministry, Diocese of Scranton; National Institute of Campus Ministries. Community Activities: Member Board of Directors, Monroe County Headstart Program; Monroe County Volunteers for Youth; Monroe County Juvenile Task Force; Practical Nursing Program of Monroe County Area Vocational/Technical School; Member Commission of Ecumenism and Human Affairs, Diocese of Scranton; Member Board of Trustees, Mount Saint Mary's College and Seminary, Emmitsburg, Maryland; Other Activities. Religion: Catholic Priest and Chaplain to College Students. Honors and Awards: East Stroudsburg State College Alumni President's Award, 1981; Cullen Shamrock Award, Pocono Irish American Club, 1980; Charles Forsyth Award from Catholic Campus Ministry Association, 1979; Distinguished Service Award, Pocono Mountains Junior Chamber of Commerce, 1972; Liberty Bell Award, Monroe County Bar Association, 1973; Outstanding Young Man of the Year Award, United States Chamber of Commerce, 1973; Listed in *Men of Achievement, Dictionary of International Biography, International Who's Who in Community Service, Men and Women of Distinction, Book of Honor, Personalities of America, Notable Americans*. Address: College Misericordia, Dallas, Pennsylvania 18612.■

MARK J. BENEDICT

Attorney-at-Law. Personal: Born October 1, 1951; Son of Dr. and Mrs. I. J. Benedict. Education: A.A. with honors, San Antonio College, 1971; B.A. summa cum laude, Trinity University, 1973; J.D., University of Texas School of Law. Career: Attorney-at-Law; Administrative Aide, State Representative, Nowlin; Systems Analyst, Trinity University; Computer Programmer/Systems Analyst, City of San Antonio. Organizational Memberships: San Antonio Bar Association, 1978; State Bar of Texas, 1978; Federal Bar, 1979; American Bar Association, 1978; San Antonio Young Lawyers, 1978; Texas City Attorney's Association, 1982. Community Activities: Director, Prevent Blindness Association, 1978-80; Director, Alamo Area Big Brothers and Sisters, 1979-81; St. Benedict's Hospice Advisory Board, 1979-81; Director, University of Texas Ex-Students Association, 1978-80; Vice President Finance, Alamo Area Big Brothers and Sisters, 1981; City Attorney, City of Hill County Village, Texas, 1981-82; San Antonio Chamber of Commerce, President's Club, 1978-82. Honors and Awards: Phi Beta Kappa, 1973; Phi Theta Kappa, 1971;

Alpha Chi, 1972; Benedict Fellowship, 1973; Top Producer, United States Chamber of Commerce, 1979; Listed in *Who's Who in American Law, Outstanding Young Men of America, Men of Achievement, Biographical Roll of Honor*. Address: 16403 Hidden View, San Antonio, Texas 78232.■

HARRY BELL BENFORD

Professor of Naval Architecture and Marine Engineering. Personal: Born August 7, 1917; Married Elizabeth Smallman; Father of Howard Lee, Frank Alfred, Robert James. Education: B.S.E. Naval Architecture and Marine Engineering, University of Michigan, 1940. Career: Professor of Naval Architecture and Marine Engineering, Ann Arbor, Michigan; Former Positions as Shipyard Expeditor and Cost Estimator, Executive Director for National Research Council Committee. Organizational Memberships: Society of Naval Architects and Marine Engineers, Fellow, Honorary Member, Honorary Vice President; Fellow, Royal Institution of Naval Architects. Community Activities: Member of National Research Council Committees, 1961-68, 1981 to present, Member-at-Large 1963-70. Honors and Awards: Society of Naval Architects and Marine Engineers, Presidents Award 1957, Linnard Prize 1962, Taylor Medal, 1976. Address: 1710 Shadford, Ann Arbor, Michigan 48104.■

JACK E. BENHAM

Executive. Personal: Son of Edward H. and Mary A. Stanton Benham; Married June Gridley, February 14, 1950 (deceased); Father of Cynthia Ann. Education: Attended the University of Cincinnati College of Liberal Arts, University of Cincinnati College of Engineering, United States Armed Forces Institute, Dale Carnegie Institute, Alexander Hamilton Institute, Famous Writer's School. Military: Served in the United States Naval Reserve, achieving the rank of Yeoman 3rd Class, Discharged in 1945; Served in the Ohio State Guard, Medical Corps, achieving the rank of Sergeant. Career: Draftsman, Kettering Laboratories of Applied Physiology, 1943; Pilot Plant, Proctor and Gamble Corporation, 1943; Laboratory Technician, Hilton-Davis Corporation, 1944; Laboratory Technician, Engineering Co-Op, Ault and Wiborg, 1944; Paint Technician, Interchemical Corporation, 1945-46; Laboratory Director, Paint Chemist, Southern Manufacturing Company, 1947; Technical Director, Sun and Sea Paint and Varnish Company, 1950-54; Technical Director, Bruning Paint Company, 1954-56; Vice President, Stockholder, Southseas Chemical Corporation, 1956; Vice President, Stockholder, Graphic Arts Screen Process, Inc., 1956; Technical Director, Bruning Paint Company, 1956-64; Stockholder, Boca Raton Office Supply, 1959-61; Vice President, Sales Manager, Stockholder, Palmer Supplies Company of Florida, 1964-71; President, Sales Manager, Chairman of the Board, Majority Stockholder, J.B. International Marketing Corporation, 1971; Vice President, Stockholder, Billie Rose Dinner Theatre, 1969-71; President, Vice President of Southeast Sales Division, J.B. International Marketing Corporation, 1971-82; Board Member, E-Bond Epoxies, Inc., 1971-82; Board Member, Hercules Polymers, Inc., 1978-82; Board Member, Sunburst Paints, Ltd., Nassau, Bahamas, 1978-82; J.B. Sales & Consulting, 1982-83; Technical Director 1983-84, Vice President 1984 to present, Commercial Coatings Corporation. Organizational Memberships: National Association of Chemical Distributors, Founder, Past National President; Southern Society for Paint Technology, Founder, Former Chairman, Miami Section; United Nations Day, U.N.A.-U.S.A., Former Vice Chairman; American Security Council, National Advisory Board; American Institute of Chemists, Fellow; New York Academy of Sciences; American Chemical Society; International Platform Association. Community Activities: Boca Raton Elks Lodge 2166, Founder, Member-at-large; Masonic Lodge 576; Florida Atlantic University, Founder '64 Committee; Boca Raton Jaycees, Life Member; Jaycee's International, Senator; United States Senatorial Club. Published Works: Author of *Beings, Boundaries and Beauty; Macaronical, Metaphorical, Montage*; Author of Article "Young Men at Work" *All Florida Magazine*, 1957; Game of Three-Dimensional Chess, Cookbook. Honors and Awards: Salesman of the Year, Southern Society of Paint Technology, 1966; Listed in *American Men of Science, Who's Who in Commerce and Industry, Who's Who in the South and Southwest, International Register of Profiles, Dictionary of International Biography*. Address: 701 N.W. 214th Street, Apt. 1-101, Miami, Florida 33169-2012.■

INGRID I. BENN

International Market Director. Personal: Born May 1, 1953; Son of Roberto and Virginia Benn. Education: B.A., Wilmington College, Wilmington, Ohio, 1975; M.B.A., The Ohio State University, Columbus, Ohio, 1977. Career: International Market Director, School Division; Senior Product Manager School Division, Senior Product Manager, Science Product Manager, Trade Marketing Manager, Charles E. Merrill Company. Organizational Memberships: National Association of Female Executives; Association of American Publishers; T.E.S.O.L. Community Activities: Volunteer Publishing and Marketing Consultant to DANA Rhinehart, Franklin County Treasurer, Columbus, Ohio, 1981; Addressed Students from Ohio State University on Careers and Educational Publishing. Honors and Awards: American Association of University Women's Award, 1974; Green Key Honor Society, Wilmington College, Wilmington, Ohio, 1973; Beta Gamma Sigma, Ohio State University, 1977. Address: 545 Woodingham Place, Columbus, Ohio 43213.■

IVAN STANLEY BENNETT

Senior Counselor. Personal: Born January 27, 1949; Son of Ivan F. and Audrey P. Bennett; Married Susan E. Bennett; Father of Jonathan Lee, Jason Charles, Joseph Wesley. Education: A.B., Thomas More College, 1972; M.Ed., Xavier University, 1974. Career: Senior Counselor, Holmes High School, Covington, Kentucky; Former Manager, Job Preparation School (for school dropouts); Director of Admissions-Release, Northern Kentucky State Vocational Technical School; Junior Counselor, Holmes High School. Organizational Memberships: Northern Kentucky Personnel and Guidance Association, President 1975-76; Kentucky Personnel and Guidance Association, President 1980-81; American Personnel and Guidance Association, Government Relations Committee 1977-79; American Personnel and Guidance Association, Board of Directors 1981-84. Community Activities: Covington Teacher Advisory Committee, 1973-75; Covington Child Welfare Citizens Committee, Secretary, Chairperson 1973-75; Law Enforcement Assistance Administration, Sponsored Alternative School Program Advisory Committee, Chairperson 1975-76; American College Testing, Advisory Council for Kentucky 1980 to present, Subcommittee on Career Exploration Programs in Kentucky Schools 1981 to present; Kentucky Council on Higher Education, Pre-College Curriculum Committee; Northern Kentucky Advisory and Reource Council for Teenage Parents, 1975-78; Juvenile Delinquency Task Force; Kentucky Advisory Commission on Criminal Justice Standards and Goals, 1975-77; Regional Council on Substance Abuse, 1976-77. Religion: Lutheran. Honors and Awards: Certificates of Appreciation, Northern Kentucky Personnel and Guidance Association, Kentucky Personnel and Guidance Association, American Personnel and Guidance Association; Awards, Southern Region Branch Assembly, American Personnel and Guidance Association, National Vocational Guidance Association. Address: 2502 Belleview Road, Burlington, Kentucky 41005.■

MARILYN F. BENNETT

Registered Nurse. Personal: Born January 27, 1944. Education: A.S., Southwestern Union College Academy, 1962; B.S. 1967, M.P.H. 1975, Loma Linda University School of Health; Attended Loma Linda School of Graduate Studies, 1982. Career: Registered Nurse. Organizational Memberships: Association of Seventh-day Adventist Nurses, 1980-82; American Nurses Association; National League for Nursing. Community Activities: Director, School of Nursing, Saigou Adventist Hospital, 1968-70; Jungle Nurse, Borneo, 1971; Nurse-Advisor, Maternal Child Health Project, United States Agency for International Development, 1976-79; Nursing Instructor, Maluti Adventist Hospital, Lesotho, Southern Africa, 1982. Religion: Sabbath School Superintendent; Pianist for Church; Prayer Group Leader; Leader, Campus Community Fellowship, Loma Linda University Church; Sabbath School Teacher. Honors and Awards: Listed in *Outstanding Young Women of America, Who's Who in American Women, World Who's Who of Women, Men and Women of International Distinction, Men and Women of Achievement*. Address: 2589 Ithica Road, Avon Park, Florida 33825.■

RONALD THOMAS BENNETT

Photojournalist. Personal: Born November 6, 1944; Son of E. Al and Donna Mae Bennett; Father of Ronald T. Jr., Gardina W. Education: Attended Multnomah

College 1963-64, and Portland State University 1964-67. Military: Served in the United States Air Force Reserve, 1966-72. Career: Senior United Press International White House Photographer; Senior United States Senate Photographer; Staff Photojournalist, Photo Editor, 1971 to present; Coverage of Presidents Kennedy, Johnson, Nixon, Ford, Carter, Reagan, 1963 to present; Photo Editor, Staff Photojournalist, United Press International News Pictures, Los Angeles, 1968-71; Staff Photojournalist, *Oregon Journal*, 1965-68. Organizational Memberships: Los Angeles Press Photographers, Board of Directors; California Press Photographers Association; National Press Photographers Association; White House News Photographers Association, Board of Directors; United States Senate Press Photographers, Standing Committee 1980 to present. Honors and Awards: Pulitzer Prize Nomination for Photographs of Senator Robert F. Kennedy Assassination, 1968; Gold Medal, Spot News, World Press Photo, The Hague, 1969; First Place, Spot News, Outstanding Achievement in News Photography, National Headliner, 1969; First Place, Spot News and Sports, California Press Photographers Association Gold Seal Competition, 1969; Eight Ball, Spot News, Greater Los Angeles Press Club, 1969; Picture of the Year for Feature, National Press Photographers, 1970-75; Award for Feature, Forest Lawn Photographers Competition and Exhibition; United Press International Certificates of Merit for Spot News, Sports and Features; First Place in Features Category, National Press Photographers, Outboard Marine Contest; Pulitzer Prize Nominations for Photojournalism, 1968, 1976, 1977, 1978; Photo Exhibition, Library of Congress, 1972-82; First in Presidential, Award for Presidential and Sports Features, Award for Personality Photography, White House News Photographers Association, 1976-82; Award for Outstanding Syndicate Photography, National Headliners, 1978; Listed in *Who's Who in the World, Who's Who in America*. Address: 7203 Early Street, Annandale, Virginia 22003.∎

PAUL S. BENOIT

Computer Specialist. Personal: Born December 20, 1938; Son of Saul (deceased) and Lena Ancelet Benoit; Married Jane Alice Morrison. Education: B.S., Southwestern University, 1960; Postgraduate Study, University of Houston, 1961. Military: Served in the United States Navy, 1962-65, attaining the rank of Lieutenant. Career: Accountant, Pan American Petroleum Corporation, Houston, 1960-62; Senior Data Processing Technician, Tulsa, 1965-67; Lead Programmer, Supervisor of Systems and Planning, Manager of Systems Procedures and Data Processing, Singer Corporation, Silver Springs, Maryland, 1967-74; Senior Finance Systems Analyst, Timesharing Administrator, Computer Specialist, G.A.O., Washington, D.C., 1974 to present. Organizational Memberships: Association for Systems Management, Charter President of Patuxent Chapter 1972-73, Chairman of By-Laws Committee 1972-73, Chairman of Awards Committee 1972-73, Chesapeake Division Council, President Patuxent Chapter 1973-74, Council Vice Chairman, Chairman of Awards Committee, Chesapeake Division Council 1973-74, Chairman of Nominating Committee of Patuxent Chapter 1975-76, Arrangement Coordinator of Annual Conference 1977, Chairman Awards Committee of Chesapeake Division Council 1979, President 1980-81, Secretary 1982-83, 1983-84, Patuxent Chapter. Honors and Awards: Systems Man of the Year, Association for Systems Management, Patuxent Chapter, 1972-73; Certificate of Recognition, American Production and Inventory Control Society, 1973 Metro D.C. Chapter; Service Award, Association for Systems Management, Patuxent Chapter, 1973-74; Merit Award, Association for Systems Management's International Distinguished Service Award Program, 1976; Systems Man of the Year, Association for Systems Managment, Patuxent Chapter, 1976-77; Certificate of Appreciation, Association for Systems Management International Organization; Certificate of Appreciation, Association for Systems Management, Patuxent Chapter, 1979; G.A.O. Certificate of Merit with Cash Award for Best Professional Article or Publication, *Journal of Systems Management*, 1979; Achievement Award, Association for Systems Management's International Distinguished Service Award Program, 1981; Certificate of Appreciation, Association for Systems Management, Patuxent Chapter, 1981. Address: 12007 Aspenwood Lane, Laurel, Maryland 20708.∎

GEORGE STUART BENSON

Executive. Personal: Born September 26, 1898, Dewey County, Oklahoma; Son of Mr. and Mrs. S. F. Benson (both deceased); Married First Wife Sally E. Benson (deceased); Married Second Wife Marguerite E. O'Banion, February 22, 1983; Father of Lois McEuen, Ruth Crowder. Education: B.S., Oklahoma A&M University, 1924; B.A., Harding University, 1925; M.A., University of Chicago, 1931; LL.D., Harding University, 1932; LL.D., Knox College, 1948; LL.D., Waynesburg College, 1960; LL.D., Oklahoma Christian College, 1968; LL.D., Freed-Hardeman College, 1981; Career: President, Executive Director, The National Education Program, 1936 to present; Chairman, Board of Zambia Christian College (Africa), 1966 to present; Chancellor, Alabama Christian College, 1975 to present; Chancellor, Oklahoma Christian College, 1956-67; Owner and Director, Camp Tahkodah (boy's summer camp), 1942-64; President, Harding University, 1936-65; President, Canton Bible School, 1930-36; Professor of English, National Sun Yat Sen University, 1929-30; Missionary, Canton, China, 1925-36; Principal, Harding Academy, 1924-25; Teacher, Oklahoma Public School, 1918-21; Founder, Canton Bible School (1930) and Canton English College (1932), both in Canton, China; Conducted Radio Progam "Land of the Free" on 300 Stations, 1945-53; Radio Program "Behind the News" on 120 Sations, 1955 to present; Weekly Column "Looking Ahead" in 2000 Newspapers; Monthly Newsletter to 50,000 Readers. Organizational Memberships: Pi Kappa Delta. Community Activities: Kiwanis Club, Honorary; Civitan Club, Honorary; Searcy Chamber of Commerce; American Security Council. Religion: College Church of Christ, Searcy, Arkansas, Elder. Honors and Awards: Freedom Foundation Award; National Recognition Award, Freedom Foundation at Valley Forge, 1974; Arkansan of the Year, 1953-54; Oklahoma Hall of Fame, 1972; Outstanding Alumnus, Oklahoma State University, 1976; Distinguished Alumnus, Harding University, 1963; Christian Leadership Award, 1968; Oklahoma State University Hall of Fame, 1976; Wisdom Award of Honor, Wisdom Society; Horatio Alger Award, 1981; Man of the Year in Education, *Christian Voice*, 1981; Listed in *Personalities of the South, Who's Who in America, National Register of Prominent Americans and International Notables*. Address: Harding University, Box 760, Searcy, Arkansas 72143.∎

MARGUERITE E. O'BANION BENSON

Executive Assistant. Personal: Born August 18, 1918; Daughter of J. W. O'Banion, Mrs. J. W. O'Banion (deceased); Married George Benson. Education: Graduate of Swifton High School (Arkansas), 1935; B.A., Harding University, 1942; Graduate of Dale Carnegie Program, 1954; LL.D., Alabama Christian College, 1979. Career: Executive Secretary to Dr. George S. Benson, 38 Years. Organizational Memberships: Business and Professional Women's Club, Past President; American Association of University Women, Past Secretary of Searcy Branch; Harding Business Women's Club, Founding President, Reporter; Associated Women for Harding, Charter Member, First Life Member, Secretary Searcy Chapter (One Year); Arkansas Chapter, Freedoms Foundation at Valley Forge. Religion: Church of Christ. Honors and Awards: Distinguished Citizenship Award, National Education Program; LL.D., Alabama Christian College, 1979; First Woman Among Churches of Christ to Receive LL.D. Degree. Address: Harding University, Box 751, Searcy, Arkansas 72143.∎

KENTON E. BENTLEY

Administrator. Personal: Born June 1, 1927; Son of Marion Isabell Norris; Married Elizabeth Jule Montrose. Education: B.S., University of Michigan, 1950; Ph.D., University of New Mexico, 1959. Military: Served in the United States Navy, 1945-46. Career: Director of Science and Applications, Program Manager of E.P.A. Environmental Programs, Lockheed-E.M.S.C.O.; Former Director, Iran Earth Resources, Lockheed; Head, Electrochemistry Group, Hughes Aircraft; Task Leader/Scientist, Jet Propulsion Laboratory, California Institute of Technology; Research Scientist, Lockheed California Company; Assistant Professor of Chemistry, American University, Beirut, Lebanon; Visiting Professor of Chemistry, Highlands University, New Mexico; Los Alamos Research Fellow, University of New Mexico. Organizational Memberships: American Chemical Society, Analytical Division; American Association for the Advancement of Science, Life Member; American Association of University Professors (inactive); American Institute of Aeronautics and Astronautics; N.M.A.; Sigma Xi, Life Member; Alpha Chi Sigma. Published Works: Co-Author "Pyrolysis Studies: Controlled Thermal Degradation of Mesoporphyrin," "A Gas Chromatography-Mass Spectrometer System for Space Exploration," "Oxygen Detection" (U.S. Patent), "Spectrophotemetric Investigation of Vanadium (II), Vanadium (III) and Vanadium (IV) in Various Media," "Apparatus for Oxygen-Sensitive Volumetric Solutions." Honors and Awards: Los Alamos Research Fellow, University of New Mexico, 1954-56; Rockefeller Foundation Grant, American University of Beirut, 1960. Address: 15811 Dunmoor Drive, Houston, Texas 77059.∎

LUIS A. BERDECIA

Assistant Professor. Personal: Born March 17, 1939; Son of Enrique Berdecia; Married Irma Falcon; Father of Irma Maricelli, Luis Antonia, Rafael Enrique. Education: University of Puerto Rico, Normal Diploma 1960, Secondary Education/English 1966; M.A. Higher Education/English, New York University, 1969; University of Puerto Rico, Attended Linguistics Institute Summers 1965, 1969, IV International American Institute of Linguistics Summer 1971, Seminar on Theory and Practice of Cooperativism Summer 1971, Seminar-Workshop on Teaching of Skills in Reading, Department of Education 1973-74, Seminar-Workshop on Role of Zone Supervisor of English-Caguas Educational Region 1973-74, Seminar-Workshop on Individualized Instruction, Department of Education 1975, and Others; Several Certificates in Education. Career: Rural Elementary School Teacher, 1960-61; English Elementary School Teacher, 1962-65; Junior High School English Teacher, 1965-66; Senior High School English Teacher, 1966-68; Evening School Teacher, Basic Education 1965-67, Conversational English 1968-70; Zone Supervisor of English, 1968-75; General Supervisor of English Job Corps, 1975-76; Part-time English Instructor, 1971-76; Full time English Instructor, 1976 to present.

TWO THOUSAND NOTABLE AMERICANS

Organizational Memberships: Teachers Association of Puerto Rico; National Education Association; T.E.S.O.L.; Bilingual Education Association. Community Activities: Alumni Association of New York University; National Wild Life Association. Honors and Awards: Study Grant, University of Puerto Rico, 1958-60; Study Grant, University of New York, 1969; Candidate Manuel A. Pérez Award-Education, Naranjito School District, 1972. Address: San Cristóbal, Calle A #5, Box 696, Barranquitas, Puerto Rico 00618.■

M. MAJELLA BERG

College President. Personal: Born July 7, 1916; Daughter of Gustov Peter and Mary Josephine Berg (both deceased). Education: B.A., Marymount College, 1938; M.A., Fordham University, 1948; D.H.L. (honorary), Georgetown University, 1970. Career: President, Marymount College of Virginia, 1960 to present; Registrar, Marymount College, Tarrytown, New York, 1958-60; Registrar, Marymount College of Virginia, 1957-58; Professor of Classics and Registrar, Marymount College, Manhattan, New York, 1948-57; Registrar, Marymount School, New York City, 1943-48. Organizational Memberships: Virginia College Fund, Secretary/Treasurer, Executive Committee, 1966-67 and 1973; Council of Independent Colleges in Virginia, Vice-president 1972-73, Secretary of the Executive Committee 1974. Community Activities: Committee of the Private College Advisory Committee, State Council of Higher Education in Virginia; Executive Committee, Arlington Citizen Participation Council; Executive Committee, Arlington Chorus; Arlington Committee of 100; League of Women Voters; American Association of University Women; Arlington Health and Welfare Council's Day Care Committee, 1967-69; Board of Directors, Arlington Chamber of Commerce; Virginia State Chamber of Commerce, Membership Committee 1967-68, Education Committee 1969 and 1971; Appointed to the Advisory Committee on Staff Development for Two-Year Colleges, Catholic University of America, 1972; Appointed to Board of Directors, Northern Virginia Educational Television Association, 1972; Chairman of Arbitration Panel, Arlington School Board and Arlington Education Association, 1967; Board of Directors, HOPE, 1983 to present; Board of Directors, Virginia Foundation for Independent Colleges, 1982 to present; Arlington Committee for the Organization of Northern Virginia Technical Institute (now Northern Virginia Community College); Arlington Hall for Arlington Committee. Religion: Diocese of Arlington's Evangelization Commission, 1979 to present; Bishop's Pastoral Council, 1979-83; Executive Committee Sister Council, 1978 to present. Honors and Awards: Listed in *Who's Who in American Education, Who's Who of American Women, Leaders in Education, Presidents and Deans of American Colleges, Who's Who International, Personalities of the South, Contemporary Authors, Dictionary of International Biography, Men of Achievement, Who's Who in the South and Southwest, World Who's Who of Women, American Catholic Who's Who Among Authors and Journalists.* Address: Marymount College of Virginia, 2807 North Glebe Road, Arlington, Virginia 22207.■

GRAENUM BERGER

Consultant, Writer. Personal: Born April 21, 1908; Son of Harry Isaac and Bascia Berger (both deceased); Married Emma; Father of Ramon F, Baruch Michael. Education: B.A., University of Missouri, 1930; Certificate towards MSS, Graduate School of Jewish Social Work, 1932. Career: Consultant on Social Welfare; Writer; Consultant on Social Welfare, Federation Jewish Philanthropies, New York, 1949-73; Director Wiener Institute for Executives, New York, 1969-73; Executive Director Bronx House and Camp Bronx House, New York, 1938-49; Executive Director, Jewish Community Center, Staten Island, New York, 1932-38; Instructor, New York School of Social Work 1938-49; City College of New York and Yeshivah University, New York 1944-46, Wurzweiler School of Social Work 1968. Organizational Memberships: President, National Association of Jewish Center Workers, 1946-48; President, Research Institute Social Group Work. Community Activities: President, Jewish Student Organization, University of Missouri, 1928-30; President, Pelham (New York) Jewish Center, 1953-54; President and Founder, American Association of Ethiopian Jews, 1969-78. Honors and Awards: Author of *The Jewish Center as a Fourth Force* 1966, *Innovation by Tradition* 1973, *Black Jews in America* 1978; Editor of *The Turbulent Decades: Jewish Communal Services in the United States and Canada, 1958-78* 1981; Frank L. Weil Award, Jewish Welfare Board, 1962; Lehman Medal and $1000 Award, New York, 1966; Honorary Doctorate in Humane Letters, Yeshiva University, New York, 1973. Address: 340 Corlies Avenue, Pelham, New York 10803.■

JAMES HENRY BERGER

Entertainment Promoter. Personal: Born July 27, 1951; Son of Joan Marie Berger; Married Rochelle Ann; Father of Justin Henry. Education: Graduate of Cooper School of Art, Cleveland, Ohio, 1973. Military: Served in the United States Navy, 1968-71, attaining the rank of Seaman. Career: Entertainment Promoter; Night Club Operator of Eight Clubs; Promoter of Outdoor Rock Concerts; Art and Advertising Graphics. Organizational Memberships: The American Film Institute. Honors and Awards: Yearly Guest Lecturer, Independent Promotion at University of California-Los Angeles Film School; Listed in *Who's Who in America, Personalities in America, Directory of Distinguished Americans.* Address: 7928 Sangamon Drive, Sun Valley, California 91352.■

STEVEN BARRY BERGER

Research Physicist. Personal: Born December 29, 1946; Son of Bernard and Sylvia Berger. Education: B.S. 1967, Ph.D. 1973, Massachusetts Institute of Technology. Career: Research Physicist, Naval Research Laboratory; Former Instructor, Department of Electrical Engineering, George Washington University; N.D.E.A. Russian Language Fellow, Indiana University and Soviet Union, 1965; Technical Staff, MITRE Corporation; Technical Staff, TRW; Systems Engineer, TRW Space and Technology Group; Assistant Editor, *American Journal of Physics*; Technical Staff, ITEK Corporation. Organizational Memberships: American Physical Society; Treasurer, Northern Virginia Chapter, Control Systems Society, Institute of Electrical and Electronics Engineering; Sigma Xi. Community Activities: American Film Institute; Common Cause; Cousteau Society; Mensa; Sierra Club; Smithsonian Associates; Toastmasters International. Religion: Jewish. Honors and Awards: National Science Foundation Graduate Fellowship, 1972; Sloan Foundation Graduate Fellowship, 1973; Fight-for-Sight, Inc. Post Doctoral Fellowship, 1974-76; Listed in *American Men and Women of Science, Who's Who in the South and Southwest.* Address: 19009 Laurel Park Road, Space 174, Dominguez Hills, California 90220.■

KAY V. BERGIN

Writer, Lecturer, Consultant. Personal: Born November 29, 1921; Married Francis X. Bergin; Mother of Sandy. Education: B.S., Central Connecticut State College, 1943; M.A.L.S., Wesleyan University, 1957. Career: Former District Manager, Neighborhood Reinvestment Corporation; Former Deputy Banking Commissioner, State of Connecticut; Executive Director, Permanent Commission on the Status of Women, Connecticut; Associate Professor, Mattatuck Community College. Organizational Memberships: Board Member, Women in Housing and Finance; Board Member, Connecticut Housing Investment Fund, 1976-78; Board Member, Hartford Neighborhood Housing Service, 1976-78; Community Activities: Connecticut Preservation Action Board; Board Member, Waterbury Action to Conserve Our Heritage; Appointed to Board by Governor, Connecticut Marketing Authority; Delegate Representing Connecticut, National Women's Conference, Houston, 1977; Board Member, Connecticut Women's Legal Education Fund, 1975-78. Religion: St. John's Church, Vestry and Finance Committee. Honors and Awards: Distinguished Women, State of Connecticut, 1976; Business and Professional Women's Award, Outstanding Woman in Connecticut, 1976. Address: 25 Steuben Street, Waterbury, Connecticut 06708.■

JANE COHEN BERGNER

Attorney. Personal: Born April 6, 1943; Married Alfred P. Bergner; Mother of Justin Laurence, Lauren Jill. Education: A.B., Vassar College, 1964; L.L.B., Columbia Law School, 1967. Career: Trial Attorney, Tax Division, U.S. Department of Justice, Review Section 1967-69, Court of Claims Section 1969-74; Arnold and Porter, 1974-76; Rogovin, Hughe and Lezner, 1976 to present. Organizational Memberships: Admitted to District of Columbia Bar, U.S. Claims Court, U.S. Court of Appeals for the Federal Circuit, U.S. Tax Court, U.S. Court of Appeals for District of Columbia Circuit Court, U.S. District Court for the District of Columbia; Chairman Subcommittee on Continuing Legal Education of Committee on Court Procedure of Section of Taxation, American Bar Association. Community Activities: Jewish Social Service Agency, Legal Counsel, Board of Directors, Executive Committee, Budget and Priorities Committee; United Jewish Appeal

Federation, Member, Former Trainee, Young Leadership Division; Service Guild of Washington; Life Member, Hadassah; Lawyers Division, American Friends of Hebrew University; National Women's Committee of Brandeis University, Life Member, Former Officer, Board Member of D.C. Chapter. Religion: Temple Sinai, Former Deputy Comptroller. Published Works: Author "Not for Men Only; Why Women Need A Will", *Women's Work* 1977. Honors and Awards: Harlan Fiske Stone Honor Moot Court Competition Semi-Finalist; Winner, New York State Regents College Scholarship; New York State Scholar Incentive Award for College and Law School; Semi-Finalist, National Merit Scholarship. Address: 1730 Rhode Island Avenue, Northwest, Washington, D.C. 20036.■

RILEY NORMAN BERGRUN

Executive. Personal: Born August 4, 1921; Son of Theodore and Naomi Ruth Stemm Bergrun (both deceased); Married Claire Michaelson; Father of Clark, Jay, Joan. Education: B.S.M.E., Cornell University, 1943; L.L.B., LaSalle University (Extension), 1955; Postgraduate Study, Stanford University, 1947; Continuing Education, Foothill College, 1982. Military: Served in the United States Navy, 1944-46, attaining the rank of Chief Specialist. Career: Executive, Bergrun Companies (Research, Engineering, Contruction, Properties); Thermodynamicist, Douglas Aircraft Company, El Segundo, 1943-44; Aero Research Scientist, NACA Ames Laboratory, 1944-56; Lockheed Missile and Space Company, Van Nuys (CA), Supervisor Flight Test 1956-68, Manager Flight Test Analysis 1958-62, Manager Test Plans and Direction 1962-63, Manager Re-Entry Test Operations 1963-67, Staff Scientist Satellite Systems Applications 1967-69; Director, Management Information Systems, Nielsen Engineering and Research, Mt. View, California. Organizational Memberships: American Institute of Aeronautics and Astronautics, Chairman San Francisco Section 1962, Regional Director 1963, Associate Fellow; California Society of Professional Engineers, State Director 1973-74 and 1979-83; National Society of Professional Engineers, National Director, 1975-76; California Space and Defense Council, 1982; Charter Member Aviation Hall of Fame. Community Activities: Foreign-Student Host, International Center for the Advancement of Management Education, Stanford University, 1964-67; National Hearing on Noise Abatement and Control, Washington, D.C., 1971; Steering Committee Member for Representative Charles S. Gubser, 10th District California, 83rd-93rd Congress, 1960-74; California Space and Defense Council, 1982; Presidential Task Force, 1982; Television Public Service Announcement, Holiday Project, 1981. Religion: Stanford Memorial Chapel, Teaching Assistant, Youth Program; Member Chapel Summer Choir, 1982; Foothill Evening Chorale, 1980-82. Honors and Awards: Engineer of the Year, California Society of Professional Engineers, Penisula Chapter, 1978; Appreciation for Sustained Contributions, Institute of Aeronautics and Astronautics, 1972; Extraordinary Service Award, National Management Association, 1968; Recognition of Distinctive Service, Institute of Aerospace Sciences, 1962; Appreciation for Contributions to First Polaris Launching, Navy Department, 1960. Address: 26865 St. Francis Road, Los Altos Hills, California 94022.■

C. FRED BERGSTEN

Economist. Personal: Born April 23, 1941; Son of Carl A. Bergsten; Married Virginia Wood; Father of Mark David. Education: B.A., Central Methodist College, 1961; M.A. 1962, M.A. L.D. 1963, Ph.D. 1969, Fletcher School of Law and Diplomacy. Career: Director, Institute for International Economics, 1981 to present; Senior Associate, Carnegie Endowment for International Peace, 1981; Assistant Secretary of Treasury for International Affairs, 1977-81; Senior Fellow, Brookings Institution, 1972-76; Assistant for International Economic Affairs, National Security Council, 1969-71; Visiting Fellow, Council on Foreign Relations, 1967-68. Organizational Memberships: American Economic Association; National Economists Club; Council on Foreign Relations; Washington Institute of Foreign Affairs, Board of Directors. Community Activities: Atlantic Council, Board of Directors 1982 to present; Consumers for World Trade, Board of Directors 1981 to present; Consumers Union of the United States, Board of Directors 1976; Overseas Development Council, Board of Directors 1974-76; Atlantic Institute, Board of Governors 1973-76; Central Methodist College, Board of Curators 1980 to present; Brasilinveit, International Advisory Board 1981 to present; Overseas Private Investment Corporation, Board of Directors 1977-81; United States-Israel Binational Research and Development Foundation, Board of Directors 1977-81; United States-Saudi Arabia Joint Economic Commission, United States Coordinator 1977-81; Worldwatch Institute, Board of Directors 1975-76. Honors and Awards: Exceptional Service Award, Department of Treasury, 1980; Meritorious Honor Award, Department of State, 1965; Distinguished Alumnus Award, Central Methodist College, 1975; *Time's* 200 Young American Leaders, 1974. Address: 4106 Sleepy Hollow Road, Annandale, Virginia 22003.■

WILLIAM ROBERT BERLINER

College Dean and Professor. Personal: Born March 10, 1915; Married Leah Silver; Father of Robert Jr, Alice (Berliner) Hadler, Henry J, Nancy. Education: B.S., Yale University, 1936; M.D., Columbia University, 1939. Military: Served in the United States Public Health Service, 1952-54. Career: Dean and Professor of Physiology and Medicine, Yale University School of Medicine, 1973 to present; National Institutes of Health, Bethesda, Maryland, Deputy Director for Science 1969-73, Director of Laboratories and Clinics 1968-69; National Heart Institute at National Institutes of Health, Director of Intramural Research 1954-68, Chief Laboratory of Kidney and Electrolyte Metabolism 1950-62; Professorial Lecturer, Georgetown University Schools of Medicine and Dentistry, Washington, D.C., 1964-73; Special Lecturer, George Washington University School of Medicine, Washington, D.C., 1951-73; Assistant Professor of Medicine, Columbia University, New York, New York, 1947-50; Research Associate, Department of Hospitals, City of New York, 1947-50; Goldwater Memorial Hospital, New York, New York, Research Assistant, Third Division Research Service 1944-47, Research Fellow 1943-44, Resident Physician 1942-43; New York University College of Medicine, New York, New York, Instructor in Medicine 1944-47, Assistant in Medicine 1943-44; Intern, Presbyterian Hospital, New York, New York, 1939-41. Organizational Memberships: American Academy of Arts and Sciences; Vice-President, American Association for the Advancement of Science, 1972; American Physiological Society, Publications Committee 1961-66, Chairman 1963-66, Council Member 1965-66, President 1967; American Society for Clinical Investigation, President 1959, Representative National Research Council 1957-60; President, American Society for Nephrology, 1968; Association of American Physicians; Institute of Medicine; National Academy of Sciences, Committee on Science and Public Policy 1973-77, National Research Council Assembly of Life Sciences Executive Committee 1973-78, Chairman Division of Medical Sciences 1976-78, Council of the Academy 1978 to present; Society for Experimental Biology and Medicine, Council 1969-73, President 1979-81; Society of General Physiologists; Royal Society of Medicine; Washington Academy of Medicine; Washington Academy of Sciences; Alpha Omega Alpha; Sigma Xi. Community Activities: The Harvey Society; The Philosophical Society of Washington; Editorial Boards of *Journal of Clinical Investigation, American Journal of Physiology*. Honors and Awards: Distinguished Service Award, Department of Health, Education and Welfare, 1962; Homer W. Smith Award in Renal Physiology, New York Heart Association, 1965; College of Physicians and Surgeons, Columbia University, Alumni Award for Distinguished Achievement 1966, Bicentennial Medal for Achievement in Internal Medicine 1967, Joseph Mather Smith Prize 1978; Distinguished Achievement Award, Modern Medicine, 1969; Research Achievement Award, American Heart Association, 1970; A. Ross McIntyre Award for Outstanding Contributions in the Field of Health, University of Nebraska Medical Center, 1974; A.C.D.P. Service Award, Association of Chairmen, Department of Physiology, 1981; Ray G. Daggs Award, American Physiological Society, 1981. Address: 36 Edgehill Terrace, New Haven, Connecticut 96511.■

MURIEL MALLIN BERMAN

Executive. Personal: Married Philip I. Berman; Mother of Nancy, Nina, Steven. Education: Honorary Doctor of Fine Arts, Cedar Crest College, 1972; Honorary Degree, Wilson College, 1969; Doctor's Degree, Pennsylvania College of Optometry; Honorary Fellow, Hebrew University, 1975; Licensed to Practice Optometry in Pennsylvania and New Jersey; Attended University of Pittsburgh, Carnegie Tech Universtiy; Studies in Music Appreciation and Art History, University of Pittsburgh Graduate School; Studies in Comparative Religion and History, Cedar Crest College; Studies in Philosophy, Muhlenberg College. Career: Underwriting Member, Lloyd's of London, 1974 to present; Hess's Inc, Vice Chairman, Vice President, Assistant Secretary, Board Member; Fleetways, Inc, Secretary, Board Member; Philip and Muriel Berman Foundation, Secretary-Treasurer, Board Member; Secretary, F.F. Bast Inc. and Fleet-Power, Inc; Producer and Moderator, Television Program "Guest Spot". Community Activities: United Nations We Believe; League of Women Voters; Young Women's Christian Association; Wellesley Club, New York; Lehigh County Historical Society; Keneseth Israel Sisterhood, Past Vice President, State Budget Chairman; Art Collector's Club of America; American Federation of Art; Friends of Whitney Museum; Archives of American Art, Detroit and New York; Museum of Primitive Art, New York; Allentown Art Museum; Reading Art Museum; Jewish Museum, New York; Skirball Museum, Los Angeles; Patron for Life, Pennsylvania Academy of Fine Arts, Philadelphia; Metropolitan Opera Guild; Associate, Philadelphia Museum of Art; University Museum, Philadelphia; Kemmerer Museum, Bethlehem; Historic Bethlehem; Lehigh Art Alliance; Philadelphia Art Alliance; Metropolitan Museum, New York; Neuberger Museum; New York; Board of Trustees, Pennsylvania Ballet; Jewish Publication Society, Board of Trustees, Treasurer, Chairman; Board of Trustees, Endowment Fund of Legigh Valley; Smithsonian Art Council, Board of Trustees, National Council Member; Women's Club, Board of Trustees, Fine Arts Chairman; Board of Trustees, Foreign Policy Association of Lehigh County; Lehigh Valley Educational Television, Channel 39, Chairman Program Committee, Board of Trustees; Board of Trustees, Lehigh County Community College Foundation; Board of Trustees, Hadassah National Board; Board of Trustees, Pennsylvania Council on Women, 1968-79; Allentown Art Museum Auxiliary, Art Appreciation Director,

Board of Trustees; Allentown Symphony, Vice Chairman, Former Treasurer of Symphony Ball, Board of Trustees; Heart Association of Pennsylvania, Board of Directors; Board of Trustees, Dieruff High School Art Advisory Committee; Board of Trustees, Baum Art School; Board of Trustees, Bonds for Israel; Board of Trustees, Young Audiences; United Nations International Women's Year Conference, Mexico City, United States Department Delegate by Presidential Appointment, 1975; National Commission on the Observance of Women's Year, Arts and Humanities Committee, 1975; United States Center for International Womens Year, Advisory Committee; United Nations Activities, Elected 1977, National Board U.N.A.-U.S.A.; N.G.O. Delegate to U.N.I.C.E.F. and Executive Board, N.G.O. Representative to the U.S. Mission of United Nations for Hadassah, E.C.O.S.O.C. Mission in Geneva with Husband, N.G.O. Delegate to the Executive Board Meeting of U.N.I.C.E.F. in Santiago, Chile 1970, N.G.O. U.N.I.C.E.F. Board on Latin American and Africa, Other Meetings; Pennsylvania Council on the Arts, 1972-78; Art in the U.S. Embassies Program; Muhlenberg College, Art Selection Committee with the National Endowment for the Arts; Carnegie-Berman College "Art Slide Library Exchange," Founder, Donor; Berman Circulation Traveling Art Exhibitions; Chairman, Hadassah-Israel Art Show; Official Delegate, Democratic National Convention, 1972, 1976, Platform Committee; Honorary Chairman, Bucks County Collectors Art Show; Chairman, Girl Scouts Great Valley Council "Brownies Create Art" Exhibit; Lehigh County Community College, Chairman of the Board, Trustee, Founding Board Member; Kutztown State College, Trustee, Vice Chairman of the Board, 1960-66; Cedar Crest College, Advisory Council; Conference for Women Trustees; College and University Governing Boards; Aspen Institute of Humanisitic Studies. Honors and Awards: Woman of Valor, Bonds for Israel; Henrietta Szold Award, Allentown Chapter, Hadassah; Outstanding Woman Award, Allentown Young Women's Christian Association, 1973; Myrtle Wreath Award, Pennsylvania Region of Hassadah; Listed in *Who's Who in American Art, Who's Who of American Women, Who's Who in the East, Royal Blue Book, National Social Directory, The Israel Honorarium.* Address: 20 Hundred, Nottingham Road, Allentown, Pennsylvania 18103.■

DOROTHY C. BERNARD (MRS. VERNON)

Court Clerk. Personal: Born September 27, 1917; Daughter of Arthur Butler Carter and Rosa Belle Cantwell (both deceased); Married Vernon Bernard, Son of Jim and Eliza George Bernard (both deceased); Father of Steve Butler. Education: Training undertaken at Baptist Memorial Hospital (Memphis, Tennessee); Attended Arkansas State University, Southern State University and the University of Arkansas. Career: County and Probate Court Clerk, St. Francis County, Arkansas; Former Positions include Market Research for Department of Commerce, Bureau of Census and News Reporter. Organizational Memberships: Arkansas County Clerk's Association, Past Vice President, President 1983-85. Community Activities: 4-H and Home Demonstration Clubs of St. Francis County; Past President, Parent-Teacher Associations; President, Spadet Dream Garden Club, 1957-58, 1968-69; President, Forrest City Business and Professional Women's Club, 1973-74; County Fair Bord, 1960 to present; Executive Board, St. Francis County Unit, American Cancer Society, 1960 to present; Charter President, Quota Club of Forrest City, 1975; Memorial Chairman, County Unit, American Cancer Society, 1961 to present. Religion: Methodist. Honors and Awards: Outstanding 4-H Leader in State, 1949; Woman of the Year, Business and Professional Women's Club, 1975; Quotarian of the Year, Quota Club, 1982; Elected Lt. Governor of Quota International Inc. for 23rd District, 1983. Address: Route 1, Box 120, Blackfish Lake, Heth, Arkansas 72346.■

ELLEN M. SCHIMMEL BERNS

Designer/Artist. Personal: Born October 3, 1948; Daughter of Milton O. and Ruth M. Schimmel. Education: Attended the University of Oklahoma at Norman, 1966-68; B.A. Art History and Art, University of Texas at Austin, 1968-70; Three-Year Advanced Certificate in Interior Design, Two-Year Applied Arts and Sciences Certification in Interior Design, Work toward Applied Arts Degree, El Centro College, 1975-78; Further Studies undertaken at the Parsons/School of Design (New York City) Summer 1977, Parsons/School of Design and Bank Street College (New York City) Summer 1978, Parsons/School of Design 1978-79, National Academy of Design and Art Students League (New York City) 1980-82. Career: Senior and Intermediate Designer/Artist, Swanke Hayden Connell Architects, 1981 to present; Senior Designer/Artist, The Permanent Mission of the State of Kuwait to the United Nations; Intermediate Designer, Manufacturers Hanover Trust (New York City), Wachtell Lipton Rosen & Katz (New York City), Standard/Nabisco Brands (New York City), Dewey Ballantine Bushby Palmer & Wood (New York City); Artist, Irving Trust Bank (New York City) and Northwestern Mutual Life Insurance Stained Glass Windows (Milwaukee, Wisconsin); Senior Designer, Haight Gardner Poor & Havens (New York City); Artist and Designer, Sidewalk Pedestal Clock (520 Madison Avenue, New York City); Instructor of Drawing for Home Furnishings, Parsons/School of Design-Midtown Campus, 1982-83; Volunteer Children's Art Instructor, 92nd Street Y.H.C.A., New York City, Summer 1983. Ellen S. Berns Interiors, 1974-78; Freelance Artist/Designer of Custom Rugs, Sylvan Garret Showroom, 1978; Expanded/Theatrical/Fantasy Costume Design, Ellen S. Berns Interiors, 1977; Freelance Artist/Designer, Peter Wolf and Associates, 1975; Fashion Illustration Instructor, El Centro College, Spring 1978; Religious School Art Instructor, Dallas, Texas, 1973-74; Exhibitions include Women in Design at Keystone (Keystone College) 1983, Judith Selkowitz Fine Art Gallery (New York City) 1982, Women in Design at Parsons (New York City) 1982, Suzanne's Gallery (New York City) 1980, Parsons/School of Design Student Exhibition 1979, Dallas Museum of Fine Arts 1977 & 1978. Organizational Memberships: American Society of Interior Designers, Educational Committee of New York City Metropolitan Chapter 1981-83; Associate Member, Women in Design: New York City 1982-83. Community Activities: Designer, Certificate Award for Parsons Exhibition, 1982; Designer, Luncheon Program/Room Decorations, Marble Collegiate Church, 1982; Tour Guide, Holy Land Museum, Marble Collegiate Church, 1981-83. Artist/Designer, Nursery Wall Mural, Marble Collegiate Church, 1980. Honors and Awards: American Watercolor Society Scholarship, National Academy of the School of Fine Arts, 1982; Listed in *Who's Who of American Women, Who's Who in the East;* Nominated to *Personalities of America, World Who's Who of Women, Directory of Distinguished Americans.* Address: 1305 York Avenue, Apt. 35H, New York, New York 10021.■

BRADY SCOTT BERRESFORD

Custom Leather Carving. Personal: Born July 28, 1940; Son of M. H. Berresford; Married Patricia A. Powers; Father of Terri L. Kelly M., Kimberly A. Education: Attending San Jacinto College, Pasadena, Texas. Military: Served in the United States Air Force, 1958-78, as Industrial Safety Manager. Career: Custom Leather Carving. Organizational Memberships: American Society of Safety Engineers; Leather Artisans International. Community Activities: Defensive Driving Instructor, National Safety Council; Instructor, American Heart Association. Honors and Awards: Listed in *Who's Who in the South and Southwest, Biographical Roll of Honor, Personalities of America, Personalities of the South.* Address: 517 South Richey, #102, Pasadena, Texas 77506.■

MICHAEL ALDEN BERRY

Physician. Personal: Born June 2, 1946; Son of Charles A. Berry; Married Frankie; Father of Jennifer Alice, Michael David. Education: B.S., Texas Christian University, 1968; M.D., University of Texas Southwestern Medical School, 1971; M.S., O.S.U., 1977. Military: Served in the United States Air Force, 1970-76, attaining the rank of Major. Career: Physician, N.A.S.A. Flight Surgeon; Vice President, Preventive and Aerospace Medicine Consultants. Organizational Memberships: Vice President, National Foundation for Prevention of Disease; Aerospace Medical Association, Educational Committee 1979 to present, Scientific Program Committee 1979 to present, Award Committee 1980 to present, President's Reception Committee 1979-81; International Academy of Aviation and Space Medicine; American College of Preventive Medicine, Fellow, Scientific Program Chairman 1981; American College of Emergency Physicians; Texas Medical Association; Harris County Medical Society; Society of N.A.S.A. Flight Surgeons; Society of Air Force Flight Surgeons. Community Activities: Clear Lake Unit, American Heart Association, Board of Directors 1978, Vice President for campaign 1979, President 1981. Honors and Awards: Special N.A.S.A. Award for Approach and Landing Text Program, 1978; Physician's Recognition Award, American Medical Association, 1979 and 1982; Lyndon B. Johnson Space Center Group Achievement Award, 1981; N.A.S.A. Group Achievement Award, 1981; N.A.S.A. Group Achievement Award, 1981; First Shuttle Flight Achievement Award, 1981; Outstanding Young Men of America Award, 1981; United States Air Force, Outstanding Unit Award, National Defense Service Medal; Julian Ward Award of the Aerospace Medical Association, 1978; N.A.S.A. Exceptional Service Award, 1980; Fellow, Aerospace Medical Association, 1981. Address: 8810 Hydethorpe Drive, Houston, Texas 77083.■

TWO THOUSAND NOTABLE AMERICANS

GERHARD KLAUS BIENEK

Consultant, University Instructor. Personal: Born October 20, 1943; Son of Fritz (deceased) and Hildegard Bienek; Married Rosemarie Edeltraud; Father of Klaus Gerhard, Peter Ralph, Diane Rose. Education; B.A. magna cum laude 1971, Ph.D. 1974, University of Utah. Career: Instructor, Utah State University; Former Positions include Endangered Species Coordinator, Scientific Advisor to U.S. Interior Officials (Washington, D.C.), Wildlife Biologist, Environmental Coordinator, Research Biologist, Director of Environmental Sciences. Organizational Memberships: New York Academy of Science; Sigma Xi; American Society of Parasitologists; Rocky Mountain Society of Parasitologists; Ecological Society of America. Community Activities: Cub Scout Master; Boy Scouts of America, District Committee Member; Expert Witness for Endangered Species for Community of Barrow, Alaska; Endangered Species Advisor for Delta, Utah, Residents. Religion: Church of Jesus Christ of Latter-Day Saints. Honors and Awards: Full Member, Sigma Xi; Affiliate Associate Professor of Ecology, University of Alaska; Listed in *Who's Who in America, Who's Who in the West, Personalities of America*. Address: 485 K Street, Salt Lake City, Utah 84103.∎

ARTHUR B. BILLET

Principal Engineer. Born May 20, 1920; Son of Mr. and Mrs. Arthur J. Billet (deceased); Married E. Christine Carter; Father of Thomas A. and Carol C. Education: Aeronautical Engineering, University of Michigan, 1941. Military; Served in United States Air Force, 1942-44, attaining the rank of First Lieutenant. Career: Principal Engineer, Hydro Products, Honeywell Marine Systems, at present; Supervisor Engineer, Rohr Industries/Rohr Marine, 1973-81; Systems Engineer, Teldyne Ryan Aeronautical, 1970-73; Supervisor, 747 Hydraulics, The Boeing Company, 1967-70; Executive Engineer, Laboratory Manager, Group Supervisor, Sperry Vickers, 1944-67. Organizational Memberships: Society of Automotive Engineers, Fellow Member 1983 to present, National Board of Directors 1975-78; Institute of Environmental Science, First Fellow Member, National President 1961-62; Fellow, American Institute of Aeronautics and Astronautics; President San Diego Section, American Defense Preparedness Association, 1977-78. Religion: Member of United Methodist Church Board, 1962-64. Published Works: Author of 72 Technical Papers given in U.S., Canada, England, Germany, Sweden and Japan; Author of 14 Technical Magazine Articles. Honors and Awards: Listed in *Who's Who in Engineering, Who's Who in the West, Jane's Who's Who in Aviation and Aerospace, Who's Who in Technology Today, Men and Women of Distinction, Men of Achievement, Who's Who in California, Personalities of the West and Midwest, International Who's Who in Engineering*. Address: 2322 Via Siena, La Jolla, California 92037.∎

DONALD LEO BIRKIMER

Technical Director. Personal: Born September 6, 1941; Son of Edgar Earl and Virginia Eileen Birkimer; Married Edith Marie Lowe; Father of Mark Austin, Thomas Edgar, Julie Lee. Education; B.S.C.E., Ohio University, 1963; M.S. 1965, Ph.D. 1968, University of Cincinnati; P.M.D., Harvard Graduate School of Business Administration, 1973; Federal Executive Institute Program in Senior Managers in Government, Harvard Graduate School of Business Administration/ Kennedy School of Government, 1976. Career: Technical Director, Naval Civil Engineering Laboratory; Technical Director, United States Coast Guard Research & Development Center; Assistant Director, Naval Surface Weapons Center; Acting Chief, Construction Materials Branch, United States Army Constuction Engineering Research Laboratory; Research Structural Engineer, Battelle Memorial Institute; Research Civil Engineer, United States Army Corps of Engineers; Civil Engineer, Wright-Patterson Air Force Base. Organizational Memberships: American Association for the Advancement of Science; American Management Association; The Institute of Management Sciences; American Society for Testing Materials; National Society of Professional Engineers. Community Activities: Rotary; Benevolent Protective Order of the Elks. Honors and Awards: WASON Medal, American Concrete Institute, 1973; Registered Professional Engineer, Chi Epsilon Honorary Fraternity, 1967; Coast Guard Meritorious Unit Commendation Award, 1976. Address: 1291 Seybolt Avenue, Camarillo, California 93010.∎

JAY LYMAN BISHOP

Chemical Engineer. Personal: Born July 7, 1932; Son of Marvin James and Klar Lyman Bishop; Married Geneil True Walton; Father of Peggy Lou, Lynn Walton, Janet Gay, Nancy, Deanna True, Linda Elaine, Lyman Michael, Jay Stanley, Michelle. Education: B.S. Chemistry and Mathematics 1953, Ph.D. Chemistry and Physics 1962, University of Utah at Salt Lake City; Various Courses Fordham University, Rutgers University, American Chemical Society. Military: Served in the United States Army, 1956-57. Career: Chemical Engineer, United States Army Civil Service; Former Positions in Synthetic Fuel Development (6 Years), Synthesis of Potential Anticancer Agents and Chief Chemist and Metallurgist (6 Years), Senior Chemist in Pharmaceutical Industry (5 Years), Research Associate and Instructor at Arizona State University (5 Years), Lecturer at the University of Utah and Arizona Academy of Science (6 Years), Translator of Documents in 22 Languages. Organizational Memberships: American Association for the Advancement of Science; American Chemical Society; Utah Genealogical Association of Professional Genealogists; Sigma Xi Honorary Research Society of America. Community Activities: Youth Counselor, 30 Years; Scoutmaster, 1964-1966; Over 100 Public Vocal or Instrumental Performances; Volunteer Paleographer, 2 Years; State Delegate Twice and Legislative Candidate, American Party; Volunteer Welfare Worker, 20 Years. Religion: Church of Jesus Christ of Latter-Day Saints, Missionary (East German Mission), Elder, Teacher 1944 to present. Published Works: Author of 20 Publications and 3 Patents. Honors and Awards: B.S. Honors, 1953; Eagle Scout; Eisenhower Medal; 7 Aaronic Priesthood Individual Awards; Several Academic Scholarships and Fellowships; Two-Year Letterman Varsity Wrestling, University of Utah; 2nd Place, Varsity Wrestling, Utah A.A.U., 1951; Various Ceramic and Music Arts Awards and Scholarship Awards; Private Airplane Pilot; Radio Operator. Address: South 75 East, Bountiful, Utah 84010.∎

ROBERT CHARLES BISHOP

Museum Administrator, Educator. Personal: Born August 25, 1938. Education: Ph.D. American Culture, University of Michigan, 1975. Career: Director, Museum of American Folk Art (New York City), 1976 to present; Adjunct Professor, Department of Art and Art Education, New York University, 1980 to present; Museum Editor, Greenfield Village and Henry Ford Museum, 1974-76; Adjunct Professor, History of Art Department, University of Michigan, 1975-77; Adjunct Professor, History of Art Department, University of Michigan, Dearborn Campus, 1977; Curator of American Decorative Arts, Greenfield Village and Henry Ford Museum, 1966-74. Organizational Memberships: International Society of Appraisers; International Society for the Preservation of Living Traditions, Chairman of the Board 1981 to present; Trustee, Opportunity Resources (New York City), 1979 to present; Chairman, Museums Council of New York City, 1978-81. Community Activities: Board of Directors, Pioneer Educational Foundation (Estero, Florida), 1978 to present; Board of Directors, Koreshan Unity (Estero, Florida), 1978 to present; Trustee, Grove House (Coconut Grove, Florida), 1977 to present; Board of Directors, Friends of the Shakers, 1977 to present; Inkster Fine Arts Council (Inkster, Michigan), 1975-76; Board of Trustees, D.P.C.A. (New York City), 1977 to present. Published Works: Member of the Editorial Board of *Antique Collecting, Art and Antiques, Horizon, Portfolio*, 1977 to present; Associate Editor, *Antique Monthly, The Gray Letter*, 1969 to present; Co-Author (with Patricia Coblentz) *A Gallery of American Weathervanes and Whirligigs* 1980, *Folk Painters of America* 1979, *The World of Antiques,*

TWO THOUSAND NOTABLE AMERICANS

Art, and Architecture in Victorian America 1979, World Furniture 1979; Author *Treasures of American Folk Art 1979, The Borden Limner and His Contemporaries 1976;* Designer and Co-Author (with Elizabeth Safanda), *A Gallery of Amish Quilts,* 1976; Designer and Co-Author (with William Distin), *The American Clock,* 1976; Author and Designer, *New Discoveries in American Quilts 1974, American Folk Sculpture 1974, Guide to American Antique Furniture 1973, How to Know American Antique Furniture 1973;* Designer, *Twentieth Century American Folk Art and Artists 1974, Centuries and Styles of the American Chair 1640-1970, 1972;* Designer and Co-Author (with Dean Fales, *American Painted and Decorated Furniture,* 1972; Designer and Co-Author (with Carleton Safford), *American's Quilts and Coverlets,* 1972; Editor and Designer, *Greenfield Village and Henry Ford Museum, Preserving America's Heritage,* 1972; Picture Editor, *American Heritage History of American Antiques from the Revolution to the Civil War 1968, American Heritage History of Colonial Antiques 1967, American Heritage History of Antiques from the Civil War to World War I 1960;* Various Works in Progress. Honors and Awards: Silver Medal, International Film and Television Festival for Project "What is American Folk Art?" 1978; International Cultural Society Impressario Award for Creative Writing, 1975. Address: 213 West 22nd Street, New York, New York 10011.■

JOSE BISQUERRA

Physician. Personal: Born May 12, 1927, in Palma de Mallorca, Spain; Son of Jose and Dolores Bisquerra (both deceased); Married Amalia Riaza; Father of Maria Jose, Jose Miguel. Education: B.A., B.S., LaSalle University of Barcelona, Spain, 1948; M.S., M.D., University of Seville School of Medicine, 1955; Ph.D., Univesity of Seville, 1956. Career: Professor of Obstetrics/Gynecology, Exploratory Maneuvers and Differential Diagnosis of Abdominal Pathology and Surgery, 1955; Professor, Pharmacology Department, University of Seville School of Medicine, 1955; Professor, Internal Medicine, University of Seville School of Medicine, 1955; Approved American Medical Association Rotating Internship, Memorial Hospital, Charleston, West Virginia, 1957; Approved American Medical Association General Practice Residency, Memorial Hospital, Charleston, 1958; Medical Director and Surgeon, Reynolds Metals Company General Hospital, Guyana, South America, 1960; Staff Physician, Obstetrics and Gynecology, Wilmington Medical Center, Wilmington General Hospital (Wilmington, Delaware), 1963; Staff Physician 1964, Clinical Director 1965, Hospital for the Mentally Retarded, (Georgetown, Delaware); Resident in Psychiatry, Five-Year Program, University of Missouri School of Medicine at Kansas City General Hospital and Medical Center, 1966; Fellowship in Child Psychiatry, University of Missouri School of Medicine at Kansas City General Hospital and Medical Center, 1970; Fellow in Child Psychiatry, Institute of Living (Hartford, Connecticut), 1971; Chief, Child and Adolescent Psychiatry, Scott and White Clinic and Hospital, 1972; Private Practice, Adult and Child Psychiatry, Bisquerra Clinic (Temple Professional Plaza, Texas), 1978-81; Private Practice, Veterans Administration Medical Center (Shreveport, Louisiana), 1981 to present. Organizational Memberships: American Medical Association; Texas Medical Association; American Psychiatric Association, Texas District Branch; American Academy of Child Psychiatry; Texas Society of Child Psychiatry; Houston Chapter, American Society for Adolescent Psychiatry; Helen Scott Saulsbury Day Care Center, Board of Directors; Missouri Psychiatric Association, President-Elect 1967-68; St. Joseph State Hospital, Secretary of Medical Staff by Election 1969-70; American Association of Psychiatric Services for Children; Bell County Medical Society; American Association of Foreign Graduates, Charter Member. Honors and Awards: American Medical Association Recognition Award, 1969-81; St. Joseph State Hospital Outstanding Physician of the Year Award, 1971; Recognition Award, State of Missouri Division of Mental Health, 1971; Recognition Award, Western Missouri Mental Health Center, 1971; University of Missouri School of Medicine, Department of Psychiatry Recognition Award, 1971; Medal of Honor, Outstanding Humanitarian Service, Georgetown, Guyana, South America, 1962; Medal of Honor, Kwakwani, Guyana, South America, 1962; Gold Medal, Guyana Miners Union, 1962; Gold Medal, "We The People," Guyana, 1962; Member of and Advisor to the United Nations, Public Health, Guyana, 1960-63; Miguel de Cervantes International Award, Madrid, 1947. Address: 220 Norcross, Bossier City, Louisiana 71111.■

BRUNO V. BITKER

Lawyer. Personal: Born February 5, 1898, in Milwaukee, Wisconsin; Married Marjorie. Education: L.L.B., Cornell University, 1921. Military: Served in the United States Army during World War I, attaining the rank of Lieutenant. Career: Member Sewerage Commission of Milwaukee, 1931-53; Federal Court Trustee, Milwaukee Rapid Transit Line, 1950-52; Special Counsel to Governor of Wisconsin, 1937; Counsel, State Banking Commission, 1938; Consultant, OPM, Washington, 1941; Wisconsin State Counsel and District Director OPA, 1942-44; Special Prosecuting Attorney, Milwaukee, 1949; Chairman, State Public Utility Arbitration Board, 1947; Member, Officer, Governor's Commission on Human Rights, 1947-56; Chairman, Milwaukee Committee on Living Cost and Food Conservation, Milwaukee, 1947; Chairman, Commission on Economic Study, Milwaukee, 1948; Member Mayor's Commission on Human Relations, 1948-52; U.S. Delegate to the International Conference of Local Governments, Geneva, 1949; U.S. Representative to the First World Conference of Lawyers, Athens (Greece) 1963, Geneva (Switzerland) 1967, Belgrade (Yugoslavia) 1971, Abidjan (Ivory Coast) 1973; Chairman, Municipal Commission of Mass Transportation, 1954; Lecturer, Division of Continuing Education, Marquette University, 1961; Chairman Governor's Commission United Nations, 1959-75; Honorary Chairman, Governor's Commission United Nations, 1976 to present; Wisconsin Advisory Committee, U.S. Commission on Civil Rights, Chairman 1960-71; National Citizen's Commission of International Cooperation, 1965; U.S. National Commission for UNESCO, 1965-71; President's Commission for Observance of Human Rights Year, 1968-69; U.S. Civil Leadership Delegate to Germany, 1964; U.S. Representative to the International Conference on Human Rights, Teheran, Iran, 1968; Consultant, Department of State, 1968-69; Delegate, Human Rights Confernece, Uppsala University, 1972; U.S. Representative to United Nations Seminar on Human Rights, Geneva, 1978; Trustee, Advisory Council of the Milwaukee Arts Institute, 1957-78. Organizational Memberships: American Bar Association, Chairman Genocide Subcommittee; Wisconsin Bar Association; Milwaukee Bar Association; Federal Bar Association of Milwaukee, President 1945; American Society of International Law, Human Rights Panel; World Peace Through Law Center, Charter Geneva. Community Activities: Cornell Alumni Association of Wisconsin. Published Works: Articles in Legal Journals and Treatises on U.N. Affairs. Honors and Awards: City of Milwaukee Citation for Distinguished Public Service, 1944; Amity Award, 1950; Jr. Achievement Award, 1959; Citation, Wisconsin Supreme Court, for Lifetime Services to the Court and the States, 1978. Address: 2330 East Back Bay, Milwaukee, Wisconsin 53202.■

DAVID L. BLACK

International Public Servant. Personal: Born April 3, 1934; Son of Wilma Black; Father of Roger David. Education: B.A., Baylor University, 1954; Undertook Post-graduate Studies at the University of Texas at Austin and Trinity University. Career: Deputy Director, Science/Technology, Organization of American States; Former Director of Special Programs and Assistant to the President, Southwest Research Institute, San Antonio. Organizational Memberships: American Society for Metals, Chairman Latin American Relations Committee; American Association for the Advancement of Science. Community Activities: Planned Parenthood Association, Board Member; Community Guidance Center, San Antonio, Board Member; Friends of McNay, Board Member; San Antonio Chamber Music Society, President. Religion: Christ Episcopal Church, Washington D.C. Honors and Awards: Centennial Award, American Society of Mechanical Engineers, 1980. Address: 1021 Arlington Blvd., E-341, Rosslyn, Virginia 22209.■

LOUIS ECKERT BLACK

Travel Agency Executive. Personal: Born September 6, 1942; Son of Louis Eckert and Leonie Louise Black, Jacksonville, Florida; Married Susan Sims Harrell, Daughter of William H. and Elizabeth Sims Harrell. Education: B.A. with honors, College of Wooster, 1965; M.A.T., University of Florida, 1966. Career: President, Avondale Travel Bureau; Account Executive, Hayden, Stone, Inc., Jacksonville, Florida, 1970-74; Field Claim Representative, State Farm Insurance Company, Jacksonville, Florida, 1969-70; Chairman, Department of Foreign Languages, Ribault Junior High School, Jacksonville, Florida, 1967-69; Administrative Assistant, United States Information Agency, Barranquilla, Colorado, 1963-64. Organizational Memberships: Eastern-Pan Am World Airways Travel Advisory Board; Norwegian Carribbean Cruise Lines Advisory Board; American Society of Travel Agents Education Committee; Instructor, American Society of Travel Agents Seminars at Sea; National A.S.T.A.P.A.C. Committee, 1982. Community Activities: Charter Member, Jacksonville Sports and Entertainment Committee, 1981-82; Rotary Club of Jacksonville. Religion: Episcopalian. Honors and Awards: "CREST" Award (Creative Excellence in Selling Travel), American Society of Travel Agents; Order of the Dolphin, Jacksonville University, 1983. Address: 3530 St. Johns Avenue, Jacksonville, Florida 32205.■

F. OTIS BLACKWELL

Professor of Environmental Health. Personal: Born February 27, 1925; Son of Floyd W. and Mary Noel Blackwell (both deceased); Married Eleanor L. Edwards; Father of Susan, Betsy, Mary Ruth, Stephen. Education: B.S., Washington State University, 1950; M.S., University of Massachusetts, 1954; M.P.H. 1965, D.P.H. 1969, University of California at Berkeley School of Public Health. Military: Served in the United States Navy, 1943-46, 1950-52. Career: Professor and Chairman, Department of Environmental Health Science, Eastern Kentucky University; Former Positions include Professor of Environmental Health at East Carolina

University, Associate Professor of Community Medicine at the University of Vermont, Associate Professor of Environmental Science at Rutgers University, Assistant Professor and Acting Chairman in the Department of Environmental Health of the American University at Beirut, Environmental Health Advisor to the Government of Pakistan, Sanitarian for the Benton-Franklin District Health Department (Pasco, Washington). Organizational Memberships: National Environmental Health Association, President 1975-76; American Academy of Sanitarians, Founder, Diplomate, Board of Directors 1974-78; American Public Health Association, Sanitation Section Council 1980; International Health Society Inc. Community Activities: Human Relations Council (East Brunswick, New Jersey), President 1970; N.I.H. Public Health Review Committee, 1971-73; Red Oak Church Boy Scout Troop 228 (Greenville, North Carolina), Scoutmaster 1975-76; Mayor's Committee on Environment, Greenville, 1981. Religion: Religious Society of Friends (Quaker). Honors and Awards: Harry R. H. Nicholas Award for Excellence, New Jersey Association of Sanitarians, 1970; Certificate of Merit, National Environmental Health Association, 1970; Certificate of Appreciation, Virginia Environmental Health Association, 1979. Address: 905 Vickers Village, Richmond, Kentucky 40475.■

DUDLEY BENEDICTUS BLAKE

Corporation Executive. Personal: Born January 28, 1920; Married Marilyn Luntz; Father of Charles Roger, Russell Phillipp, Geoffrey Robert, Christopher Luntz, Matthew Field. Education: Attended Columbia University. Military: Served in the Adjutant General's Department, General Headquarters, 1942-46, attaining the rank of Captain. Career: President, United Solvents of America, Inc., Sanford, Florida. Organizational Memberships: Florida Paint and Coatings Association, Charter Member 1960, Past President 1963; National Paint and Coatings Association, 1966 to present. Community Activities: American Diabetes Association, President Central Florida Chapter 1982-83, Florida Affiliate State Board of Directors 1981-82, Charter Member Triangle Club of Florida Affiliate 1981-82; Founder and Charter Member, Edyth Bush Civic Theatre, Orlando, Florida, 1970 to present; Board of Directors, Central Florida Civic Theatre, 1962 to present; Masonic Lodge; Scottish Rite; Shriner. Honors and Awards: Masonic 25-Year Award, Orlando Lodge 69, F&AM, 1983; Past President's Award for Outstanding Achievement, Central Florida Chapter, American Diabetes Association, 1983; Award for Superior Achievement as War Bond Officer, 4th Service Command, 1943. Address: 1619 Morningside Drive, Orlando, Florida 32806.■

JAMES FREDERICK BLAKE, JR.

Naval Logistician/Management Analyst. Personal: Born November 21, 1933; Son of James Frederick (deceased) and Alpha Snipes Blake; Married Barbara Lee Darkis, Daughter of Frederick R. (deceased) and Mildred Darkis; Father of Susan Lynn Blake Crabb, Mrs. William Gordon II), James Frederick III. Education: B.S., University of North Carolina, 1955; M.S., Rensselaer Polytechnic Institute, 1967; P.M.D., Harvard Business School, 1972; Distinguished Graduate, Naval War College, 1974. Military: Served in the United States Navy, Commissioned Ensign 1955, promoted through the ranks to Captain 1976, retired 1978. Career: Manager, Logistics Sciences Department Group, CACI, Inc.; Deputy Staff Supply Officer and Assistant Chief of Staff for Suppy and Financial Managment, Surface Force, U.S. Atlantic Fleet, 1976-78; Planning Officer/Comptroller and Executive Officer, Naval Supply Depot, Yokosuka, Japan, 1974-76; Head, Supply Operations Branch, Navy Material Command, 1971-73. Organizational Memberships: Harvard Business School Club of Washington, D.C. Religion: Member Aldersgate Methodist Church, Alexandria, Virginia 22308. Address: 7903 Bayberry Drive, Alexandria, Virginia 22306.■

TERRI BLAKE (THERESA LANDS BLALACK)

Author, Actress. Personal: Born September 10, 1903, in New York City, New York; Daughter of Fran and Anna Lands; Married Russell E. Blalack, July 1, 1920 (deceased 1976); Mother of Russell E., David E., Ronald E. Education: Attended Orange Coast College 1963-64, Los Angeles City College 1965. Career: Real Estate Owner/Developer, Hollywood, California, 1953-62; Actress Appearing in Various Motion Pictures, 1955-62; Hostess, Radio Program, KOCM-FM, Newport Beach, California, "Take A Break with Terri Blake"; Hostess, Television Program, "Take a Break with Terri Blake," Dayton, Ohio, 1966; Speaker to Various Groups and Organizations, 1966-78; Producer Shows for U.S.O. 1955-56, Veterans Administration 1955-59; Started Campaign for Grandmothers Day 1955, Bill Changed to Grandparents Day 1968 (signed into law September 5, 1979), Campaign to Prohibit Mandatory Retirement, Campaign to Allow Elderly/Handicapped to Have Pets in Federally Funded Housing (Bill Passed by Congress); Gained Worldwide Publicity for Grandparents Day. Organizational Memberships: National League of American Pen Women, President Los Angeles Branch 1974-76; International Poetry Society. Community Activities: Republican National Committee; Hollywood Wilshire Symphony Association, Board of Directors, In Charge of Publicity; Order of Eastern Star; Thursday Morning Club, Newport Beach, California. Published Works: Author *You Can Do It Too*, First Edition 1970, Second Edition 1979. Religion: Lector, St. Thomas Episcopal Church of Hollywood. Honors and Awards: Honored by N.A.S.A. for Poem to Apollo 11, "A Dream, A Flag and You," 1969; V.I.P. Treatment to Witness Landing of *Columbia*, President Reagan and Jean Dixon also Praised Poem; Received High School Diploma at Age 80; Award for Contribution to Humanitarian Progress, Human Relations Commission of City of Los Angeles, 1980; Special Invitation to National Nutrition Week, Assist Mayor Bradley's Wife in Cutting the Cake, 1984; Mayor's Community Service Award, Los Angeles, 1972; Community Service Award, New Neighbor Club, Dayton, OHio, 1971; World's Most Glamorous Grandmother, Hollywood Chamber of Commerce, 1957; Ever Youthful Senior Inspiration of the Year, Greater New York Citizens Society, 1972; Woman of the Year, International Authors Guild, Oceanside, California, 1973; Pin-Up Grandmother of.the Year, American Legion of Oceanside, 1979; White House Honoree as Founder National Grandparents Day, 1979; Plaque for Entertaining Veterans, California Legislature, 1981; Congressional Record Award, 1978, 1979; Guest Appearance on Tom Snyder Show, 1979; National League of American Pen Women, President's Citation, Woman of Achievement Award 1981; First Prize, International Poetry Society, 1969, 1977; Featured in *Playboy* Magazine in Bunny Outfit, 1979, 1982; Holder of Title at Age 80 of "Eternal Youth"; Attended President Nixon's Inaugural Ball and Governor's Reception, 1969; Only White Woman to Have Television Show on Black Radio Station KIIX, Los Angeles, California, 1963, "Never Give Up"; Only Great Grandmother to be in *National Enquirer* as Cheese Cake Glamour Girl, 1981; Famous as "Grandmother Bunny." Address: 570 North Rossmore Avenue, Hollywood, California 90004.■

DANNY BLANCHARD

College Professor. Personal: Born April 11, 1949; Son of Louise Blanchard; Married Deborah Hamilton; Father of Lashanice. Education: B.A., Oakwood College, 1971; M.A., Loma Linda University, 1973; Ed.S. 1976, Ph.D. 1980, Vanderbilt University. Military: Served in the United States Army. Career: College Professor; Former Psychologist, Program Department, Riverside, California. Organizational Memberships: American Personnel and Guidance Association; A.P.A. Community Activities: Huntsville Human Relations Counsel; Huntsville Rural Senior Services, President, Board Member; Oakwood College Alumni Association, Vice President. Religion: Seventh-day Adventist, Church School Teacher. Honors and Awards: United States Army Letter of Commendation, 1978. Address: 11007 Rockcliff Drive, Huntsville, Alabama 45801.■

LAUREL LEMIEUX BLAND-SCHRICKER

Executive, Author. Personal: Born Febr"ary 23, 1926, in Spokane, Washington; Daughter of Alfred T. and Bernice K. Lawrence LeMieux; Married Frank H. Schricker in Alaska in 1976; Mother of Laurel K. Bland Eisinger, Daniel M. Bland. Education: A.A., Anchorage Community College, 1966; B.Ed. cum laude 1968, M.A. 1969, University of Alaska; Undertook Postgraduate Studies at the University of Alaska and the Hebrew University in Israel; Ph.D., University of New Mexico, 1974. Career: Pioneer in the Initiation and Development of Supportive Strategies for Cultural Heritage Documentation and Preservation by and for the Northern Eskimos of Alaska; Known for Landmark Studies Related to the Special Learning Skills of the American Indian and Eskimo Children; Alaska Legal Services Liaison, 2nd Judicial District, 1967-68; Consultant to State and Federal Government Agencies, Local Cities and Communities, American Indian Organizations, Alaska Native Villages and Organizations, 1964 to present; Director, Special Historical and Cultural Inventory of Seward Peninsula, Alaska, 1968 to present; Associate Professor, University of Alaska, 1974; Faculty, Alaska Methodist University, 1969-73; Professor, Sheldon Jackson College, Sitka, Alaska, 1975; President and Director, Human Environmental Resources Services, 1969 to present. Organizational Memberships: Society of Intercultural Education; Alaska Historical Society; National Indian Education Association; Society for Indian and Northern Education. Community Activities: Board of Directors, Altrusa Club; Officer, Sheldon Jackson College Adjunct Faculty, Lifetime Professor of Crosscultural Education 1975; Inducted into the Yakutat Tlinget Indian Tribe, 1975; University of Alaska, Fellowship 1968-69; Brookings Institute Alaska Seminar, Legislative Appointee 1969; Named into Kaweramuit Eskimo Community, 1972; Officer, Tri-City Minority Purchasing

Council, 1981 to present. Published Works: *People of Kauwerak* (with William Oquilluk), *Northern Eskimo of Alaska, Alaska Native Population & Manpower* (volumes 1, 2 & 3), *Manpower Needs to Construct the Transalaska Pipeline*; Contributor of Articles of General Interest to Various Journals; Scholarly Articles on File with the United States Office of Education E.R.I.C./C.R.E.S.S. National Repository. Honors and Awards: Listed in *Who's Who of American Women, Who's Who in the West, Men and Women of Distinction, Personalities of the West and Midwest, Directory of Distinguished Americans, Community Leaders of America, World Who's Who of Women*. Address: 1921 West 17th, Kennewick, Washington 99336.■

FRANKLIN BLANK

Free-Lance Writer. Personal: Born October 19, 1921; Married Annette C.; Father of Emily C. Gonichelis. Education: B.B.A., Southeastern University, 1956; A.A. Liberal Arts, University of Baltimore, 1966; Postgraduate Studies in Communications, College of Notre Dame. Military: Served in the United States Air Force, 1942-46; Served in the Air Force Reserves, 1946-49. Career: Free-lance Writer. Organizational Memberships: National Writers Club; Author's Guild; European Academy of Arts, Sciences and Humanities; Life Fellow, International Biographical Association. Community Activities: Congressional Advisory Board; Maryland Coalition Committee; American Security Council, 1980-84; A Director, Fund for Assurance of Independent Retirement; International Platform Association, Speaking Ladder; Chairman, Branch Savings Bond Campaign, Social Security Administration, 1979; Co-Chairman, Fund-raising, Volunteer of Social Security, 1979; Petition Leader, American Federation of Government Employees, 1982; Political Action Committee, A.F.G.E.; Sponsor, Adopt-a-Family, Office of the Mayor, Baltimore, 1981-83; Supported the President's Economic Recovery Policies; University of Baltimore Alumni Association, 1967 to present; Grand and Petit Juror, Baltimore Criminal Court, 1976; Former Member, Maryland Big Brothers, 1978; Blood Donor (8 Gallons); American Red Cross; Nominated for President of Postal Union Local, 1962; Petition Leader to Oppose Ratification of SALT II, American Security Council, 1980. Religion: Reformed Jewish Religion. Honors and Awards: Nominated for American Legion Safety Award, 1963; Elected Life Fellow, International Biographical Association, 1983; Distinguished Leadership Award, American Security Congressional Advisory Board, 1984; Honorable Mention, *Writers Digest* Writing Competition, U.S. and Canada, 1980; Superior Achievement Award for Performance, Social Security Administration (Group and Individual), 1974, 1982; Superior Accomplishment Award, Baltimore Post Office, 1963; Bronze Plaque and Award for Blood Donation from Commissioner, Social Security Administration, 1977; Commendation from Commissioner, Social Security Administration, for Volunteer Work, 1977, 1978; Letter of Appreciation from the President of the United States for Congressional Advisory Board Activities for Maryland State Group, 1983; Letter of Appreciation (individual appreciation) from the Mayor of Baltimore for Newspaper Support, 1983; Chief Judge, Supreme Bench, Baltimore City, 1976; Listed in *International Who's Who of Intellectuals, Community Leaders of the World, Dictionary of International Biography, International Book of Honor*. Address: 5477 Cedonia Avenue, Baltimore, Maryland 21206.■

LYTLE HOUSTON BLANKENSHIP

Professor, Wildlife Research Scientist. Personal: Born March 1, 1927; Son of Sydney and Amanda Elizabeth Blankenship (deceased); Married Margaret, Daughter of Bill and Mary Luecke; Father of Terry Lynn, Kerry Jon, Jerry Alan, Sheri Ann. Education: B.S., Texas A&M University, 1950; M.S., University of Minnesota, 1952; Ph.D., Michigan State University, 1957. Military: Served in the United States Navy, 1945-46. Career: Game Biologist, Minnesota Division Game and Fish, St. Paul, 1956-61; Research Biologist, United States Fish and Wildlife Service, Tucson, Arizona, 1961-69; Research Scientist, Caesar Kleberg Wildlife Program, Texas A&M University, Nairobi, Kenya, 1969-72; Consultant for World Bank in Kenya and for Organization of American States in Dominican Republic; Visiting Lecturer, University Dar es Salaam, Tanzania, 1978; Consultant for U.S. Fish and Wildlife Service to India on Wildlife Management Techniques Workshop, 1981-82; Professor and Wildlife Research Scientist, Texas A&M University. Organizational Memberships: The Wildlife Society, International Affairs Committee 1971 to present, Southwest Section Representative to Society Council 1979-85; Texas Chapter, Wildlife Society; Wildlife Disease Association; East African Wildlife Society; Wildlife Society of South Africa; Council for Agricultural Science and Technology; Sigma Xi. Community Activities: Uvalde Lions Club; Lions Club International, District Governor 2-A2, 1981-82; Director, Texas Lions Camp for Crippled Children, 1981-83; Director Lions Eye Bank, 1981-83; Director Lions Ear Board, 1981-83; President, Lions Sight and Tissue, 1983-84; Trustee and Vice President, Uvalde Community Christian School; President, Uvalde Band and Choir Boosters, 1974-75; Uvalde County Aggie Club, Scholarship Committee. Religion: Baptist, Deacon, Sunday School Teacher, Superintendent, Director, Choir Member, Various Committees and Chairmanships; Gideons International, Uvalde Camp. Honors and Awards: Who's Who, and Outstanding Senior School of Agriculture, Texas A&M University, 1949; University Fellowship, Michigan State University; People-to-People Program, 1968; Various Lions Club Awards, including Lion of the Year 1975-76; Lions International President's Award, 1983; Melvin Jones Fellow Award, 1982; Certified Wildlife Biologist. Address: Batesville Star Route, Box 979, Uvalde, Texas 78801.■

ALFRED JOSEPH BLASCO

Business and Finance Consultant, Bank Executive. Personal: Born October 9, 1904, in Kansas City, Missouri; Son of Joseph and Mary Bevacqua Blasco; Married Kathryn Oleno, June 28, 1926; Father of Barbara Mehrer (Mrs. Charles F. III), Phyllis O'Connor (Mrs. Michael). Education: Attended the Kansas City School of Accountancy 1921-25, American Institute of Banking 1926-30; Honorary Ph.D., Avila College, 1969. Career: Office Boy to Assistant Controller, Commerce Trust Company (Kansas City), 1921-35; Interstates Securities Company (Kansas City), Controller 1935-45, Vice President 1945-53, President 1953 to present, Chairman of the Board 1961-68; ISC Finance Corporation, Senior Vice President 1968-69, Honorary Chairman of the Board 1970-77, President 1979 to present; Chairman of the Board, Red Bridge Bank, 1966-72; Chairman of the Board, Mark Plaza State Bank (Overland Park, Kansas), 1973-77; Vice Chairman of the Board, Anchor Savings Association; Special Lecturer in Consumer Credit, Columbia University (New York City) 1956, University of Kansas at Lawrence 1963-64. Organizational Memberships: Society of St. Vincent de Paul, President 1959-67; American Industrial Bankers Association, National President 1956-57; American Institute of Banking, President Kansas City Chapter 1932-33; Bank Auditors and Controllers Association; Financial Executives Institute of America, President Kansas City Chapter 1928-29; National Association of Accountants; Kansas City Chamber of Commerce. Community Activities: Fair Public Accomodations Committee (Kansas City), 1964-68; President, Catholic Community Library, 1955-56; Ward Committeeman (Kansas City), 1972-76; President, Honorary Board of Directors, Baptist Memorial Hospital, 1970-74; Chairman of the Board of Directors, St. Anthony's Home, 1965-69; Chairman of the Board of Trustees, Avila College, 1969 to present. Honors and Awards: Decorated Papal Knight 1957, Knight Commander 1964, Knight Grand Cross 1966, Lieutenant in the Northern Lieutenancy of the United States 1970-77, Vice Governor General 1977 to present, Knight of the Collar 1982, Equestrian Order Holy Sepulchre of Jerusalem; Businessman of the Year, State of Missouri, 1957; Man of the Year, City of Hope, 1973; Community Service Aard, Rockne Club of Notre Dame, 1959; Brotherhood Award, National Council of Christians and Jews, 1979; Wisdom Award of Honor, 1979. Address: 11705 Central Street, Kansas City, Missouri 64114.■

(ELLEN) ALENE BLEDSOE

Family Physician. Personal: Born May 5, 1914; Daughter of Joseph S. and Clyde Bledsoe (both deceased). Education: B.A., Columbia University, 1941; M.D., Loma Linda University, 1950; Graduate Work in Obstetrics, Chicago Maternity Center, 1950; Certified by the American Board of Anatomical and Clinical Pathology, 1963. Career: Family Physician, 1978 to present; Medical Director, Clinica de Salad para Familias, Hollister, California, 1975-76; Director, Anatomical, Clinical, Forensic Pathology, Cumberland Region NS, 1970-72; Director, Anatomical, Clinical, Forensic Pathology (with own lab), Fort Bragg, California, 1961-69; General Practice, Skagway (Alaska) 1951, Jacksonville (Illinois) State Hospital 1951-52. Organizational Memberships: Diplomate, National Board of Medical Examiners, 1951; Pan American Medical Association; Associate, World Medical Association; American Medical Association; Various State and County Medical Associations; American Heart Association; American Lung Association; American Cancer Society; Canadian Medical Association, 1970-72. Community Activities: Volunteer Teacher, California Society Meetings 1961-69, Ambulance Corps & Women's Clubs Meetings 1970-72, Heart Association Nutrition Meetings 1975-76; Donations to Various

Service Organizations (including American Field Service, United Way), 1978-83. Religion: Seventh-day Adventist, Master Guide for Pathfinder Youth 1943; Help to Bristol Bay (Alaska) Mission School, 1958-72. Honors and Awards: Fellow, College of American Pathologists, 1972; Fellow (now Emeritus Fellow), American Society of Clinical Pathologists, 1973; Listed in *Who's Who of American Women, Who's Who in California.* Address: 33201 Jefferson Way, Fort Bragg, California 95437. ∎

DALLAS R. BLEVINS

Associate Professor of Finance. Personal: Born December 22, 1938; Son of Mr. and Mrs. Virgil J. Blevins; Married Eunice, Daughter of Mr. and Mrs. Dewey J. Stalvey; Father of Deborah Lynn, Teresa Lee, Jennifer Kay. Education: Bachelor of General Education, University of Omaha, 1965; M.B.A, University of South Florida, 1967; D.B.A., Florida State University, 1976; Ayers Fellow, Stonier Graduate School of Banking, Rutgers University, 1981. Military: Served in the United States Air Force, 1958-66, rising through the ranks from Aviation Cadet to Captain. Career: Associate Professor of Finance, University of Northern Florida. Organizational Memberships: Institute of Cost Analysis, Journal Editor; American Society of Military Comptrollers, Advisor to Education Committee. Community Activities: Birmingham Regional Hospital Council, Cost Containment Committee, Uniform Accounting Standards Committee; Board of Directors, Finance Committee, Regional Health Systems Agency. Religion: Member of Church of Christ, Preacher and Teacher of the Gospel of Christ, 1960 to present. Honors and Awards: Academic Scholarship Award, 1956; Citation for High Grade Point, 1960, 1967; Officially Classified Among the Top Five Percent of All Air Force Fighter Pilots, 1965; One of Five Outstanding Young Men of Valdosta, Georgia, 1971; Outstanding Contribution Award, Squadron Officers School, 1965; Outstanding Contributions Award, American Society of Military Comptrollers, 1981. Address: 6663 Diane Road, Jacksonville, Florida 32211. ∎

EDITH HELEN BLICKSILVER

Associate Professor of English. Personal: Born January 6, 1926, in New York City, New York; Daughter of Simon and Fanny Settner (both deceased); Married Jack Blicksilver, June 27, 1948; Mother of Paul, Diane, Robert. Education: B.A., Queens College, 1947; M.A., Smith College, 1948. Career: Lecturer in History and English, Smith College, Northampton, Massachusetts, 1947-48; Professor of English, Southern State Teachers College, Springfield, South Dakota, 1953-54; Instructor in English, Northeastern University, Boston, 1962-63; Associate Professor of English, Georgia Institute of Technology, 1961-62 and 1963 to present. Organizational Memberships: Multi-Ethnic Literary Society of the United States, Secretary; College English Association, Board of Directors, President Georgia-South Carolina Regional Branch; American Association of University Women, Corporate Representative from Georgia Institute of Technology; Modern Language Association of America. Published Works: Author *The Ethnic American Women: Problems, Protests, Lifestyle.* Honors and Awards: Grantee, Georgia Institute of Technology and the American Association of University Women; Winner, Best Non-Fiction Book Award of the Year, Dixie Council of Authors and Journalists. Address: 1800 Timothy Drive, N.E., Atlanta, Georgia 30329. ∎

VIRGIL CLARENCE BLUM

Religious Administrator. Personal: Born March 27, 1913. Education: B.A. 1938, M.A. 1944, Theological Studies 1944-48, Ph.D. in Political Science 1954, St. Louis University; Student-at-Large, University of Chicago, 1950-51. Career: Founder, President, Catholic League for Religious and Civil Rights; Associate Professor and Professor of Political Science 1956-78, Professor Emeritus 1978 to present, Marquette University; Assistant Professor of Political Science, Creighton University, 1953-56; Teacher, Campion High School, Prairie du Chien, Wisconsin, 1941-44. Community Activities: Chairman, Citizens for Educational Freedom, 1969-73; National Council on Religion and Public Education, 1973 to present; Citizens for Higher Education, 1958-62; Chairman and Founder, Children's Equal Opportunities Committee, 1965 to present; Founder and President, Catholic League for Religious and Civil Rights, 1973 to present; Associates for Research on Private Education, 1977 to present. Religion: Entered the Society of Jesus (Jesuits), 1934; Ordained Roman Catholic Priest, 1947; Priestly Functions, 1947 to present. Honors and Awards: Teaching Excellence Award, Marquette University, 1966; West German Government Grant for Study of German Education, 1961; St. Elizabeth Seton Award, Brooklyn Diocese Federation of Home School Associations, 1978; Doctor of Public Service, Walsh College, 1979; Doctor of Laws, Loyola University of Chicago, 1980; Alumni Merit Award, St. Louis University, 1980. Address: 1404 West Wisconsin Avenue, Milwaukee, Wisconsin 53233. ∎

JAMES HAROLD BLY

Product Manager. Personal: Born May 12, 1917; Married Jeanette C.; Father of J. Philip, Jonathan C., C. Graham, James C. Education: Studies in Physics and Chemistry, University of Chicago, 1940. Career: Product Manager, Marketing Department, Radiation Dynamics Inc. (manufacturer of Industrial Electron Beam Accelerators); Former Positions include Consultant in Radiation, Accelerators and Nondestructive Testing, Radiographic and Research Accelerator Sales Manager for Applied Radiation Corporation, Acting General Manager and Sales Manager of ARCO Division of the High Voltage Engineering Corporation, Director of Science Applications of High Voltage Engineering Corporation and Supervisor of Radiography and Electronics with Pratt and Whitney Aircraft. Organizational Memberships: Chairman of Committee E-7 on Nondestructive Testing, A.S.T.M., 1948-62 and 1965-70; A.S.N.T., Director 1948-50; A.P.S.; Religion: Chairman, Board of Trustees, Christ Church Memorial Foundation; Vestryman, Christ Church, Oyster Bay, New York. Honors and Awards: Coolidge Award, A.S.N.T., 1964; Fellow, A.S.N.T., 1974; Fellow and Award of Merit, A.S.T.M., 1975; Honorary Member, A.S.T.M, 1978. Address: 56 Fieldstone Drive, Syosset, New York 11791. ∎

PAULA JOHANNA BOGHOSIAN

Principle Historic Environment Consultant, Architectural Historian and Preservation Planner. Personal: Born February 14, 1934; Daughter of Cecil G. Sorgatz; Mother of Gregory, Michael. Education: B.A., University of Calfiornia at Berkeley, 1959; Graduate Studies in Education, Junior High School Teaching Credential, Secondary Teaching Credential, California State University, Sacramento, 1961-62; Attended the Attingham School, Royal Oaks Foundation, Great Britain, 1981. Career: Architectural Design and Drafting, Franklin Design Service, Safeway Stores, 1955; Junior High School Instructor, Art and English, Sacramento City Unified School District, 1962; Graphics and Free-lance Commercial Art, 1971-77; Lectures, Historic Architecture and Preservation, University of California Extension, California State University-Sacramento Extension, National Trust for Historic Preservation, California Historical Society, 1974-83; Administrator, National Register of Historic Places, California State Historical Landmarks Programs, State of California Office of Historical Preservation, 1976. Organizational Memberships: American Association of University Women, National Board of Directors, Cultural Interests Representative 1973-76, Education Foundation 1973-76; National Trust for Historic Preservation; Society of Architectural Historians; California Historical Society. Community Activities: Sacramento County Grand Jury, Chairman Education Committee 1968; Sacramento City Preservation Board, Chairman 1975-78; Sacramento Heritage Inc., Chairman 1975-78; Cityscape Inc., Grants Officer 1980-82; Kingsley Art Club, Board of Directors 1976-79; KVIE, Art Auction Chairperson 1972. Published Works: Author *Vanishing Victorians, Carson City's Architectural Heritage, Winter's Archiectural Heritage, Vallejo's Architectural Heritage* (co-author). Honors and Awards; Historic Preservation Citation Award, Sacramento County Historical Society, 1971; Rosalie Stern Award, $500, University of California Alumni Association, 1972; Woman of the Year, California Council, Women's Architectural League, 1973; Resolution of Commendation, Sacramento City Planning Commission, 1974; Certificate of Award for Literary Achievement, Sacramento Regional Arts Council, 1974; Certificate of Appreciation for Community Service, Sacramento Old City Association, 1974; Award of Merit, American Association for State and Local History, 1974; Award of Merit, Sacramento Valley Section, American Institute of Planners, 1975; Award of Merit, Sacramento County Historical Society, 1977; Certificate of Appreciation, American Association of University Women, Sacramento Branch, 1978 (for outstanding service to A.A.U.W. and the community); Certificate of Appreciation, Sacramento City Council, 1980, 1982; Resolution of Commendation, California State Historic Resources Commission and the State of California, 1982; Listed in *Women's Organizations and Leaders Directory, Who's Who of American Women, Outstanding Young Women of America.* Address: 8579 La Riviera Drive, Sacramento, California 95826. ∎

TWO THOUSAND NOTABLE AMERICANS

DOUGLAS JOHN BOLTON

Educational Administrator. Personal: Born October 20, 1953; Son of Mr. and Mrs. Robert K. Bolton. Education: Attended the College of Europe (Brugge, Belgium) 1974, State University of Cortland 1975; B.S., State University of New York at Buffalo, 1981; M.Ed., 1981; Ed.D., College of Mt. St. Joseph, 1983. Career: Social Studies Teacher, Cross Country and Track Coach, West Genesee Junior High School (Camillus, New York), 1975-76; Social Studies Teacher, Track and Basketball Coach, Geneva Junior High School (Geneva, New York), 1976-77; Social Studies Teacher, Track and Basketball Coach, East Aurora High School (East Aurora, New York), 1977-79; Assistant Athletic Trainer, State University of New York at Buffalo Department of Physical Education and Athletics, 1979; Instructor and Supervisor of Student Teachers, State University of New York at Buffalo, 1979-81; Curriculum Specialist, Rush-Henrietta C.S.D., 1980-81; Administrative Assistant, Hamburg C.S.D., 1981; Elementary Principal, Addison C.S.D., 1983; K-12 Curriculum Supervisor in Art, Music and Social Studies Education, East Irondequoit C.S.D., 1983 to present. Organizational Memberships: Association for Supervision and Curriculum Development; New York State Association for Supervision and Curriculum Development; Western New York Association for Supervision and Curriculum Development; Genesee Valley Association for Supervision and Curriculum Development; National Council for Social Studies; New York State Council for Social Studies; New York State Council for Social Studies Supervisor's Association; Rochester Area Council for Social Studies; National Humanistic Education Center; Sagamore Institute; Association for Humanistic Education; Advisory Council for the Regional Early Childhood Direction Center; School Administrators Association of New York State. Community Activities: Track and Field Coach, Syracuse Chargers, 1975-76; Track and Field Coach, East Aurora Amateur Athletic Club, 1977-79; Rush-Henrietta C.S.D. Instructional Council, 1980-81; Instructor and Rehabilitation Counselor, Tonawanda Young Women's Christian Association, 1981; Corning-Addison Staff Development Council, 1982-83; Corning-East Steuben Business Education Committee, 1982-83; Chairman, Corning-East Steuben Futures Committee, 1982-83; Physical Education Instructor and Women's Basketball Coach, Corning Community College, 1982-83; Co-Chairman, The Chemical People, Community Task Force of East Irondequoit, 1983 to present; East Irondequoit C.S.D. Long-Range Budget Planning Comittee, 1983 to present; Middle States Steering Committee for the East Irondequoit Central School District, 1983 to present; Educational Planning and Improvement Committee of the East Irondequoit Central School District, 1983 to present; Parents, Teachers, Students Association for East Irondequoit Central School District, 1983 to present; East Irondequoit Central School District Liaison Person for Teacher's Institute at Empire State College (Rochester, New York) and for the History Teacher's Institute at Rochester Institute of Technology; Kiwanis, 1982 to present. Honors and Awards: Phi Delta Kappa; Kappa Delta Pi; Phi Alpha Theta; Pi Sigma Alpha; Certificate for Study (for successful completion of Common Market Program), College of Europe, 1976; Outstanding Teacher of the Year, 1976; Coach of the Season and Coach of the Year, 1977; Listed in *Who's Who in America, Who's Who in the East, Community Leaders of America, Personalities of America, Directory of Distinguished Americans, Biographical Roll of Honor, International Who's Who of Intellectuals.* Address: North Village Apartments #123, 2515 Culver Road, Rochester, New York 14609.■

AUDREY SHELLEY BOMBERGER

Educational Administrator. Personal: Born June 12, 1942, Lebanon, Pennsylvania; Daughter of Mr. and Mrs. Allen Shelley (deceased); Married Edward K. Bomberger, Son of Mrs. Margaret Bomberger; Mother of Beth-Ann, Gary Allen. Education: Diploma in Nursing, Reading Medical Center, Reading, Pennsylvania, 1963; B.S. Education, Millersville State College, Millersville, Pennsylvania, 1975; M.S. Education, Temple University, Philadelphia, 1979; Doctor of Health Service Administration, Columbia-Pacific University, 1983. Military: Service in the United States Army Nurse Corps, 1977 to present, attaining the rank of Major; First Female Training Officer in a Combat Unit, Training Officer 1980, Associate Chief Nurse 1982. Career: Staff Nurse, Hershey Hospital, Hershey, Pennsylvania, 1963-65; Charge Nurse and Building Supervisor of Male Psychiatric Wards 1965-69, Staff to Charge Nurse of Critical Care Unit 1970-75, Director of Education (planning, coordination and implementation of hospital educational activities) 1975-79, Lebanon Valley General Hospital, Lebanon, Pennsylvania; Department Head of Education 1979-82, Director of Education 1982-84, Saint Mary's Hospital, Reno, Nevada; Director of Nursing Education and Research, McKay-Dee Hospital Center (Ogden, Utah); Number of Professional Presentations. Organizational Memberships: National Nominating Committee, American Society of Health Education and Training, American Hospital Association, 1978-79. Published Works: Author Articles "MIC: Self-Directed Learning" 1982, "Experience at Three Mile Island" 1979, "Roving Inservice" 1982, "Inservice on Wheels" 1982; Contributing Author, *Medical-Surgical Nursing Assessment,* 1982; Author, *Radiation and Health;* Reviewer of *Being a Nursing Assistant.* Honors and Awards: Student Nurses Scholarship for Academic Achievement, 1961; Student Nurses Scholarship for Clinical Excellence, 1962; Unit Citation Award, 99th Combat Hospital, 5th Army, 79th ARCOM, for Development of Unit Training School 91-B, 1978; Honorary Fellow, Anglo-American Academy, 1980; National Education Award, American Society of Health Education and Training; Certification from American Nurses Association as Nursing Administrator, 1981; Listed in *Who's Who of American Women, Who's Who of Women of the World, Contemporary Personalities, Personalities of the West and Midwest, Personalities of America.* Address: 3415 Harrison Blvd., Ogden, Utah 84409.■

THOMAS JEFFERSON BOND, JR.

Trust Services Officer. Personal: Born August 27, 1936; Son of Thomas J. (deceased) and Clara Chisam Bond; Married Wilma McCrary, Daughter of Keller Brit (deceased) and Lee Reid McCrary; Father of T. Jefferson III, Julia Bond Franklin. Education: B.S., Tennessee Polytechnic University, 1958; M.A., Peabody College of Education, Vanderbilt University, 1959; Postgraduate Study undertaken at the University of Louisville, American University, Antioch School of Law. Military: Served in the United States Army, 1954-64. Career: Trust Services Officer, Eastern Area, Bureau of Indian Affairs, United States Department of Interior; Served 17 Years with the Fish and Wildlife Service of the United States Department of Interior; College Instructor, University of Tennessee at Chattanooga, University of Louisville, 5 Years. Organizational Memberships: Sons of the American Revolution D.C. Society, Registrar 1982, Third Vice President 1983-84, Senior Vice President 1984-85; Endowment Member, National Rifle Association; National Wildlife Federation; Wildlife Society; Federal Executive and Professional Association; World Wildlife Fund; American Forestry Association; Ducks Unlimited; National Wildlife Refuge Association; The Ruffed Grouse Society; Virginia State Rifle and Revolver Association; National Skeet Shooting Association. Community Activities: Clans of Scotland U.S.A., Treasurer 1979-80; Potomac Corral, The Westerners, Property Manager 1982, Publications Editing Committee 1983; National Museum of American History, Smithsonian Institution, Docent 1972-77, Co-Chairman (with wife) Weekend Education Program 1974-76; Smithsonian Institution Educational Advisory Board, 1974-76; Consultant, Biological Sciences Curriculum Study; Fairfax County Arbitration Commission, 1974 to present; Book Reviewer, *Chattanooga Times,* 1961-76; Citizens Study Team on Commercial Development, Appointed by Town Council, Vienna, Virginia. Religion: Wesley United Methodist Church, Member Various Church Committees and Offices. Honors and Awards: MENSA; Incentive Award, United States Fish and Wildlife Service, Department of Interior, Southwestern Regional Office, Albuquerque, New Mexico, 1971; Listed in *Who's Who in Training.* Address: P.O. Box 1301, Vienna, Virginia 22180.■

BYRON LEE BONDURANT

Professor of Agricultural Engineering, Assistant Department Chairman. Personal: Born November 11, 1925; Son of Joyce K. Gesler Bondurant; Married Lovetta M. Alexander; Father of Connie J. Jaycox, Richard T., Cindy L. Gardino. Military: Served in the United States Navy Reserve, Officer Candidate, 1943-45. Education: Bachelor of Agricultural Engineering, The Ohio State University, 1949; M.S.C.E., University of Connecticut; Further Studies at Case Institute of Technology, Rensselaer Polytechnic Institute, University of Maryland, University of Delaware, Purdue University. Career: Professor of Agricultural Engineering, Assistant Chairman of the Department of Agricultural Engineering, The Ohio State University, 1964 to present; Fulbright Professor in Agricultural Engineering, University of Nairobi, Kenya, 1979-80; Manager of UNDP/FAO Project, Leader of MUCIA/OSU Team on Strengthening Agricultural Research, Somalia, 1976-78; Visiting Professor of Agricultural Engineering, University of Nairobi, Kenya, 1974; Consultant, Institute of International Education, Punjab Agricultural University, India, 1965-72; Dean, College of Agricultural Engineering, Punjab Agricultural University, 1966; Professor and Head of the Department of Agricultural Engineering, University of Maine, 1954-64; Consultant, Harvard University, Nigeria, 1964; Consultant, United States State Department, Sierra Leone, 1962; Associate Professor of Agricultural Engineering, University of Delaware, 1953-54; Instructor of Agricultural Engineering, University of Connecticut, 1950-53; District Extension Agricultural Engineer, Cornell University, 1949-50; Laboratory Assistant, Department of Agriculturl Engineering, Ohio State University, 1948-49; Inspector of Concrete, Placement and Survey Party Chief, United States Bureau of Reclamation, Colorado, 1948. Organizational Memberships: Society of Agricultural Engineers, Chairman Ohio Section 1984-85, International Director 1980-82, Secretary-Treasurer of Tri-State Region and Ohio Section 1973-74, Chairman Acadia Section 1961, Vice Chairman of North Atlantic Section 1953, Secretary Connecticut Valley Section 1951-52; American Society of Engineering Education, Chairman of Agricultural Engineering Division 1963, Associate Editor *TECHNOS* (Journal of International Division); Maine Society of Professional Engineers, President 1963, Vice President 1962; Maine Association of Engineers, Director 1964; American Society of Civil Engineers; American Association of University Professors; Ohio Academy of Science; American Society of Agricultural Consultants; Soil Conservation Society of America. Community Activities: Civil Defense, Deputy Director, Orono, Maine, 1962-64; Faculty Council, University of Maine, 1962-64; Maine-African Institute, University of Maine, 1960-64; Parent-Teachers Association

TWO THOUSAND NOTABLE AMERICANS

(Orono, Maine), Chairman 1963, Vice Chairman 1962, Program Chairman 1961. Religion: Member of Nazarene Church, Chairman of the Board of Trustees 1962-64, Sunday School Teacher 1958-64. Honors and Awards: Future Farmers of America, State Farmer of Ohio, 1942; Life Member, Society for International Development, New York Academy of Sciences, Indian Society of Agricultural Engineers, Kenyan Society of Agricultural Engineers; Honorary Member, Tau Beta Pi, Sigma Pi, Sigma Pi Sigma, Sigma Xi, Gamma Sigma Delta, Epsilon Sigma Phi, Alpha Epsilon; 1983 Kishida International Awards; Alpha Mu; Listed in *Who's Who in America*, *Who's Who in Consulting*, *Who's Who in the East*, *Who's Who in the Midwest*, *Who's Who in the World*, *Who's Who in the United States*, *Who's Who in Engineering*. Address: 265 Franklin Street, Dublin, Ohio 43017.■

REGINALD A. BOOKER

Research Chemist. Personal: Born January 5, 1953; Son of Dorothy B. Smith. Education: B.S. Chemistry, Tuskegee Institute, 1974; M.S. Chemistry 1976, Ph.D. Chemistry 1979, University of Illinois at Champaign-Urbana. Career: Research Chemist; Chemist; Research Assistant; Teaching Assistant; Graduate Student. Organizational Memberships: American Chemical Society; National Organization for Professional Advancement of Black Chemists and Chemical Engineers; Brandywine Professional Organization; Phi Beta Sigma Fraternity; National Association for the Advancement of Colored People; National Association for the Advancement of Science. Honors and Awards: Sigma Xi Scientific Honor Society; Beta Kappa Chi Honor Society; Clarence T. Mason Memorial Science Award; I.A. Derbigny Award, 1974; Phi Beta Sigma Scholastic Award, 1973; Sophomore Chemistry Award, 1972; Analytical Chemistry Award, 1974; Listed in *Who's Who in Colleges and Universities*, *Outstanding Young Men of America*, *Personalities of America*, *Who's Who in the East*, *Biographical Roll of Honor*, *The International Book of Honor*, *Community Leaders of the World*, *International Who's Who of Contemporary Achievement*. Address: P.O. Box 183, Rockland, Delaware 19732.■

EMILY CLARK BOONE

Consultant in Private Practice. Personal: Born July 20, 1943; Daughter of Edgar Clark and Emily Florence Kidwell (both deceased); Married Edward W. Boone, Son of William and Virginia Boone; Mother of Susan Rebecca Linder. Education: B.A., University of Cincinnati, 1964; M.S.W., Washington University, George Warren Brown School of Social Work, 1970; Field Work undertaken at Barnes Hospital (St. Louis, Missouri), West St. Louis Community Center, West End Urban Renewal Project. Career: Private Consulting Practice, Training Workshops and Seminars with Businesses, Industries, Government, Unions and Civic Organizations, Therapy with Individuals, Couples, Adolescents and Children in Group, Family and Individual Settings, Retirement Planning, Discharge Planning and Consultants with Nursing Homes and Residential Care Facilities, Full-time 1979 to present, Part-time, 1972-79; Clinical Social Work, Our Lady of Peace Hospital, Louisville, Kentucky, 1977-79; Social Service Coordinator, River Region, Central State Hospital, 1976-77; Treatment Team Leader, 1976-77; Senior Social Worker, 1976; Caseworker II, Lutheran Family and Children's Services, St. Louis, 1973-75; Social Service Director, Mt. St. Rose Hospital, St. Louis, 1971-73; Social Work Supervisor, St. Louis Comprehensive Neighborhood Health Center, 1970-71. Organizational Memberships: National Association of Social Workers, Member 1970 to present, Region VII, Nominations and Leadership Identification Committee (elected 1983-85), N.A.S.W. Committee on Peace and Nuclear Disarmament 1983, Treasurer Southeast Coalition 1979 to present, Vice President Kentucky Chapter 1979-82, Kentucky Chapter ELAN Chair 1979-82, Kentucky Chapter PACE Chair 1982, Kentucky Chapter Representative to Kentucky Pro-ERA Alliance 1978-81, Kentucky Chapter Representative to Kentucky Women's Agenda Coalition 1978-81, Kentucky Chapter Representative to Denver Symposium of Clinical Social Work 19tennial Convention, Kentucky Division Delegate to Two SEC Regional Conventions 1980-82, Louisville Branch EFP Chair 1975-79, Louisville Branch Women's Chair 1979-81, Louisville Branch Delegate to Four Fall Conventions, Louisville Branch Delegate to Three Spring Workshops; American Society of Training and Development; Kentucky Association for Specialists in Group Work, Treasurer 1979-81; Lutheran Child and Family Services of Indiana/Kentucky, Louisville Office, Advisory Board Member 1981 to present; St. Matthews Business and Professional Women, 1980-81. Community Activities: Soroptimist; Block Partnership Program, Organized Resource Group 1969-70; Acid Rescue, Therapist 1972-74; City of Rolling Hills Board of Commissioners, Finance Commissioner 1981 to present; League of Women Voters, Nominating Committee 1977 to present, Cities/Urban Crisis Study Group Member, Nuclear Freeze Study Group; Kentuckian Regional Planning and Development Agency, Bicycle Transportation Committee 1979, Chairman 1980, Vice Chairman 1981-82; Louisville Wheelman, Racing Team Member 1982 to present; National Organization of Women; National Women's Political Caucus, Communications Coordinator 1978, Representative to Kentucky Caucus State Policy Council 1978-79, State Resolutions Committee Chairman 1979; Democratic Party, 48th Legislative District Secretary 1976, 48th Legislative District Group Captain 1976; Mose Green Democratic Club; Democratic National Convention, Alternate Kennedy Delegate from Kentucky Fourth Congressional District 1980; Kentucky Pro-ERA Alliance, Steering Committee Member 1978; International Women's Year, Program Chairman for the Economic Aspects of Being Female; National Women's Conference, Alternate Delegate from Kentucky to National Women's Conference, Houston, 1977; Louisville and Jefferson County Human Relations Commission, Women's Rights Task Force 1975-81; Louisville Civil Liberties Union, Board Member 1978-81; American Civil Liberties Union 1973 to present; Common Cause; Louisville Sailing Club; American Red Cross, Louisville Chapter Board Member, Chairman of Volunteers 1979-81; Parkview Heights Housing Corporation, St. Louis, Board of Directors 1969-75, Board Secretary 1969-75. Religion: Ohio Methodist Student Movement, State Officer 1962-64, Wesley Foundation Officer 1961-64. Honors and Awards: Outstanding Woman in Social Services, Louisville Young Women's Christian Association, 1978; $500 Contribution Named in Honor of Emily Clark Boone, Louisville Branch, American Association of University Women, 1978; Kentucky Chapter Delegate to National Invitational Forum on Clincial Social Work, Sponsored by National Association of Social Workers, Denver, Colorado, 1979; 10th in Time Trial of Veteran Women, 8th in Road Race of Veteran Women, United States Cycling Federation Veteran Championship, Tallahassee, Florida, 1982; Listed in *Who's Who in the South and Southwest*, *World Who's Who of Women*, *Book of Honor*, *Community Leaders and Noteworthy Americans*, *Personalities of the South*. Address: 9206 Walhampton Court, Louisville, Kentucky 40222.■

KENNETH ANDREW BORCHARDT

Clinical Microbiology Consultant, University Professor. Personal: Born September 20, 1928; Son of Leo A. and Edith R. Borchardt (deceased); Married Joyce Truitt, Daughter of Mr. and Mrs. Cecil Truitt; Father of Gregory David, Kimberly Borchardt-Hyland, Jeffrey A. Education: B.S., Loyola University, 1950; M.S., Miami University of Ohio, 1951; Ph.D., Tulane University, 1961; M.D., Loyola Universtiy; Postgraduate Fellowship in Tropical Medicine to Louisiana State University 1970; Study in Computers in Medical Microbiology, St. Thomas Hospital, London, England, 1982. Military: Served in the United States Army, 1953-65, attaining the rank of Lieutenant Colonel; Served in the United State Public Health Service, 1965-82, with the rank of Navy Captain. Career: Chief of Clinical Microbiology, United States Public Health Service Hospital, San Francisco, 1965-82; Chief of Clinical Microbiology, Letterman Army Hospital, San Francisco, 1961-65; Chief of Microbiology, Fitzsimmons Army Hospital, Denver, Colorado, 1957-58; Laboratory Officer, U.S.A.R.E.U.R. Medical Laboratory, Landstuhl, Germany, 1954-56. Organizational Memberships: Phi Sigma; American Public Health Association; Tulane Medical Alumni Association; Fellow, American Academy of Microbiology; Fellow, Tropical Medicine, Louisiana State University; Fellow, Royal Society of Tropical Medicine, 1984; New York Academy of Sciences; Sigma Xi. Community Activities: Executive Board, Boy Scouts of America, Troop 82, Novato, California. Religion: Mount Calvary Lutheran Church (New Orleans), Organist 1958-61; Shepherd of Hills Lutheran Church (Tiburon, California), Organist 1962-82. Honors and Awards: Distinguished Service Medal, United States Public Health Service, 1977; Citation for Serving as Scientific Program Chairman, United States Public Health Service, 12th Annual Meeting, 1978. Address: 15 Capilano Drive, Novato, California 94947.■

HARISIOS BOUDOULAS

Professor of Medicine, Researcher. Personal: Born November 3, 1935, in Velvendo-Kozani, Greece; Son of Konstantinos and Sophia Boudoulas; Married Olga Paspatis; Father of Sophia, Konstantinos. Education: M.D., University of Salonica, 1959; Doctorate Diploma, Faculty of Medicine, University of Salonica, Greece, 1967; Board of Internal Medicine, Greece, 1967; Board of Cardiology, Greece, 1967; Diploma of Educational Council Foreign Medical Graduates, U.S.A., 1970; Permanent License to Practice Medicine in Ohio, 1975; Michigan Permanent License, 1980. Career: Resident in Internal Medicine, Red Cross Hospital, Athens, Greece, 1960-61; Resident in Cardiology, Cardiac Clinic of 424 Military Hospital, Salonica, Greece, 1961; Resident in Internal Medicine, First Medical Clinic, University of Salonica, 1962-64; Resident in Cardiology, First Medical Clinic, University of Salonica, Greece, 1964-66; Attending Physician, Renal Unit, First Medical Clinic, University of Salonica, 1966-67; Attending Physician, Coronary Care Unit, First Medical Clinic, University of Salonica, 1967-69; Lecturer in Medicine, First Medical Clinic, University of Salonica, 1969-70; Postdoctoral Fellow and Instructor, Ohio State University College of Medicine, Division of Cardiology, 1970-73; Senior Lecturer in Medicine, Head of Coronary Care Unit, First Medical Clinic, University of Salonica, 1973-75; Postdoctoral Fellow, Division of Cardiology, Department of Medicine, Ohio State University College of Medicine, 1975; Assistant Professor of Medicine, Division of Cardiology, Department of Medicine, Ohio State University College of Medicine, 1975-78; Director, Cardiovascular Non-Invasive Research Laboratories, Division of Cardiology, Ohio State University Hospitals, 1978-80; Associate Professor of Medicine, Division of Cardiology, Ohio State University Hospitals, 1978-80; Professor of Medicine, Division of Cardiology, Wayne State University, 1980-82; Director, Clinical Cardiovascular Research, Division of Cardiology, Wayne State University, 1980-82; Chief, Cardiovascular Center, Veterans Administration Medical Center, 1980-82; Acting Director, Division of Cardiology, Wayne State University, 1982; Acting Chief, Section of Cardiology, Harper-Grace Hospitals, Detroit, Michigan, 1982; Professor of Medicine, Division of Cardiology, Ohio State University, 1983 to present; Director, Cardiovascular Research Division of Cardiology, Ohio State University, 1983 to present; Co-Director, Overstreet Teaching and Research Laboratories, 1983 to present. Organizational Memberships: American Association for the Advancement of Science; Medical Association of Salonica, Greece; Greek Society of Biochemistry; Royal Society of Medicine, Affiliate Member; Greek Renal Association; European Dialysis and Transplant Association; American Heart Association; America College of Cardiology, Fellow; Greek Heart Association; Greek Committee Against Hypertension; American Federation of Clinical Research; Council on Clinical Cardiology, Fellow; American College of Angiology, Fellow; American College of Physicians, Fellow; Central Society for Clinical Research; American College of Clinical Pharmacology, Fellow. Published Works: Author/Co-Author, Numerous Professional Articles and Abstracts. Honors and Awards: Distinguished Research Investigator, Central Ohio Heart Chapter of the American Heart Association; Listed in *Who's Who in the Midwest, International Who's Who of Intellectuals, Personalities of the West and Midwest, Men of Achievement, Dictionary of International Biography, Book of Honor, Who's Who in America.* Address: 4185 Mumford Court, Columbus, Ohio 43220.■

GEOFFREY HOWARD BOURNE

Vice Chancellor. Personal: Born November 17, 1909; Son of Walter Howard and Mary Ann Bourne (deceased); Married Maria Nelly Golarz; Father of Peter Geoffrey, Merfyn Russell Howard. Education: B.Sc. honors 1931, M.Sc. 1932, D.Sc. 1935, University of Western Australia; D.Phil., Oxford University, 1943. Military: Served in the Special Forces in Southeast Asia, 1943-45, attaining the rank of Major; Nutritional Advisor to the British Military Administration of Malaya, holding the rank of Lieutenant Colonel. Career: Vice Chancellor, St. Georges University School of Medicine, Grenada, West Indies, 1978 to present; Director, Yerkes Primate Research Center, Emory University, 1962-78; Chairman and Professor of Anatomy, Emory University, 1957-62; Reader in Histology, University of London, 1947-57; Demonstrator, Department of Physiology, Oxford, 1939-47; Biochemist, Commonwealth of Australia Advisory Council on Nutrition, 1936-38. Organizational Memberships: British Nutrition Society, Secretary 1947-57; British Society of Research in Aging, Secretary 1949-57; Royal Society of Medicine, Fellow; Zoological Society of London, Fellow; Royal Institute of Biology, Fellow; American Society of Research in Aging, Fellow; International Primatological Society, Secretary General, 1974-77; Others. Community Activities: Zoological Society of Atlanta, Founder, First President; Veterans Administration Research Advisory Group; Consultant, School of Aerospace Medicine, San Antonio, Texas. Honors and Awards: Beit Memorial Fellow in Medical Research, 1938-41; Mackenzie-Mckinnon Research Fellow, Royal College of Surgeons (England) and Royal College of Physicians (London), 1941-43; Distinguished Lecturer, Medical College of Georgia, 1961; Distinguished Lecturer, Bowman Gray College of Medicine, 1953. Address: 849 Lullwater Parkway, Atlanta, Georgia 30307.■

MAURICE BOUTIN

Professor of Philosophical Theology. Personal: Born June 10, 1938; Son of Camille Boutin and Lilianne Manseau. Education: B.A. Philosophy 1959, B.A. Theology 1963, University of Montreal; Ph.D. Theology, University of Munich, 1973. Career: Professor of Philsosophical Theology 1984 to present, Assistant Professor 1973-78, Associate Professor 1978-84, University of Montreal. Organizational Memberships: International Council of Internationale Paulus-Gesellschaft, 1974-81; International Conference of Hermeneutics, Rome, Italy, 1975 to present; Executive, Canadian Corporation for Studies in Religion, 1978 to present; Canadian Society for the Study of Religion, Board of Directors 1978 to present, Vice President 1979-81, President 1981 to present. Community Activities: Theological Committee of the Olympic Organization, 1976 Olympic Games, Montreal, 1974-76; General Committee of Christians Associated for Relationships with Eastern Europe, 1979 to present; Life Fellow, International Biographical Center, 1979; Board of Directors, Journal *Medium*, 1980 to present; Academic Advisory Board, Institute on Comparative Political and Economic Systems, Georgetown University, 1981 to present; Publications Committee, 14th International Congress of the International Association for the History of Religions, Winnipeg, Canada, August 1980, 1979-82. Honors and Awards: Ph.D. Scholarship, Ministry of Education, Government of Bavaria, West Germany, 1963-64, 1964-65. Address: 2835 Goyer, Montreal, Quebec, H3S 1H2, Canada.■

STEPHEN T. BOW

Insurance Company Executive. Personal: Born October 20, 1931, in Bow, Kentucky; Son of Mr. and Mrs. Stephen T. Bow Sr.; Married Kathy O'Connor, Daughter of Mr. and Mrs. Grover O'Connor; Father of Sandra, Carol, Deborah, Clara. Education: B.A. Sociology, Lindsey Wilson College, Berea College, 1953. Career: Agent, Lexington (Kentucky), 1953; AM Steel City (Alabama), 1955; F.T.I. South Central, 1958; T.F.S. South Central, 1959; DSM Frankfort (Kentucky), 1960; DSM, Lexington, 1964; Executive Assistant, Field Training, 1966; RSM Northern New Jersey, 1967; Agency Vice President, Canadian Home Office, 1972; Vice President 1976, Senior Vice President 1978, Midwestern Home Office, Metropolitan Life. Organizational Memberships: National Association of Life Underwriters; Dayton Life Underwriters Association; Dayton Certified Life Underwriters; Past Activities in G.A.M.A., Ottowa Life Underwriters Association, Lexington Certified Life Underwriters. Community Activities: Board Member, Dayton Power & Light Company (Chairman of Audit Committee), Duriron Company Inc., Wright State University Foundation; Board of Trustees, Berea College; Advisory Board, Ohio University's Center for Economic Education; Board Member, Dayton Philharmonic Association; National Corporation Committee, United Negro College Fund; Area Progress Council; Civic Advisory Council for Kettering Medical Center (Chairman of the Government Relations Committee). Address: Metropolitan Life, 425 Market Street, San Francisco, California 94105.■

CHARLES MALCOLM BOWDEN

Research Physicist. Personal: Born December 31, 1933; Son of Charles Edward and Emma Hoover Bowden (both deceased); Married Lou Marguerite Tolbert; Father of Melissa Gail, Steven Mark, David Malcolm. Education: B.S., University of Richmond, 1956; M.S., University of Virginia, 1959; Ph.D., Clemson University, 1967. Career: Research Physicist. Organizational Memberships: American Physical Society; Sigma Xi; Sigma Pi Sigma; New York Academy of Sciences; American Association for the Advancement of Science. Religion: University Baptist Church, Deacon 1979 to present, Vice Chairman of Deacon Council 1980, Chairman of Pastor Search Committee 1981 to present, Adult Bible Study Teacher 1972 to present, Young Adult Bible Study Teacher and Leader 1978 to present. Honors and Awards: N.A.S.A. Fellow, 1965-67; Oak Ridge National Laboratory Graduate Fellowship, Summer 1965; Paul A. Siple Scientific Achievement Award, West Point, 1978; United States Army Missile Research and Development Command Science and Engineering Award, 1980; Scientific Achievement Award, United States Army Conference, West Point, 1980; Outstanding Performance Award, 1980. Address: 716 Versailles Drive, Huntsville, Alabama 35803.■

EDITH HILLMAN BOXILL

Assistant Professor, Certified Music Therapist, Consultant, Lecturer. Personal: Daughter of Maurice and Lillian Hillman (both deceased); Married Roger Evan Boxill; Mother of Paul R. Epstein, Emily H. Duby. Education: B.A., Boston University; M.A., New York University; Certification, Dalcroze School of Music. Career: Assistant Professor of Music Therapy, New York University; Head of Music Therapy, Manhattan Developmental Center, New York; Clinical Supervisor, Music Therapy, Interns, 1977 to present; Music Instructor, Composer, Performer, 1954-71; Lecturer, Music Therapy Department, New York University, 1976-78; Music Teacher, Little Red School House and Elisabeth Irwin High School, New York City, 1957-60; Faculty, Mills College of Education, New York City, 1954-57. Organizational Memberships: American Association for Music Therapy, Board of Directors, Chairperson of State Affairs Task Force; American Association for Mental Deficiency, Chairperson of Creative Arts Therapies; American Society of Composers, Authors and Publishers; National Society for Autistic Children; Association of Musicians of Greater New York. Community Activities: New York State Coalition of Creative Arts Therapies, Chairperson for Music Therapy; Arts for the Handicapped, Official Observer, Very Special Arts Festival National Committee; United Nations Conference of the International Year of Disabled Persons, Presenter. Published Works: Author, "Developing Communications with the Autistic Child through Music Therapy," "A Continuum of Awareness: Music Therapy with the Developmentally Handicapped," "Music Therapy: A Primary Treatment Modality for the Developmentally Disabled"; Co-Author, "Essential Competencies for the Practice of Music Therapy"; Work in Progress on Music Therapy with the Mentally Retarded (*Handbook of Music Therapy with the Mentally Retarded and Developmentally Disabled*); Producer of Videotape "Music Therapy with the Multiply Handicapped." Honors and Awards: Invited to Author *Handbook on Music Therapy with the Mentally Retarded and Developmentally Disabled*; Certified Music Therapist; Composer, Arranger, Producer, Record Album, (Folkways) "Music Therapy with the Developmentally Handicapped"; Producer, Arranger and Performer, Record Album (Folkways), "Music, Adapted, Composed and Improvised for Music Therapy with the Developmentally Handicapped"; Listed in *Who's Who in the East, Directory of Outstanding Americans, World Who's Who of Women.* Address: 375 Riverside Drive, New York, New York 10025.■

TWO THOUSAND NOTABLE AMERICANS

HUNTER REED BOYLAN

College Administrator and Professor. Personal: Born April 3, 1945; Son of Mrs. B. E. Davis; Father of Heather Marie. Education: B.A., Miami University; M.Ed., Temple University; Ph.D., Bowling Green State University. Military: Served in the United States Air Force, 1967, attaining the rank of Lieutenant. Career: Professor, Director, Kellogg Institute. Organizational Memberships: A.C.P.A., Member 1969-81, Vice Chairman Commission XVI 1976-78, Chairman Commission XVI Task Force, Newsletter Editor Commission XVI; American Personnel and Guidance Association, 1969-81; American Association for Higher Education, 1975-77; National Association for Remedial/Developmental Studies, Research Chairman; National Association for Remedial/Developmental Education, President 1981-83. Published Works: Editorial Board, *Journal of Developmental and Remedial Education* and *Journal of Personalized Instruction*; Works in Developmental Education, including *Forging New Partnerships in Learning Assistance* and *Is Developmental Education Working?*. Religion: Presbyterian. Honors and Awards: Office of Education Grantee, 1975-76; Fund for the Improvement of Post-Secondary Education Grantee, 1980-81; National Association for Remedial/Developmental Education, Student Service Award 1980, Outstanding Leadership Award 1983; Outstanding Advisor Award, Temple University, 1968. Address: Route 1 Box 421, Blowing Rock, North Carolina 28605.■

JEANIE BOK DONG BRADSHAW

Beauty Consultant. Personal: Born April 9, 1944; Daughter of In Jong Chung; Married James R. Bradshaw, Son of LaVel Bradshaw; Mother of Scott James, Lisa Suk, Jonathan, Mibi. Education: Attended Seoul Central Middle and High School; Graduate, Central Beauty School, 1963; Beautician Certificate, Seoul, Korea; Attending Windward Community College and Brigham Young University-Hawaii Campus. Career: Beauty Consultant; Former Volunteer Worker for Various Organizations and Korean Language Instructor for New Missionaries. Organizational Memberships: Hawaii Business Education Association; Western Business Education Association; National Business Education Association. Community Activities: Mistress of Ceremonies, State-wide Women's Conference held at Brigham Young University-Hawaii Campus, 1980; Performance of Traditional Korean Dances, Playing of Ancient Kayaguem, Singing of Traditional Korean Folk Songs; Hostess to Visiting Officials (Government and Military). Religion: Church of Jesus Christ of Latter-day Saints, Primary Children's Organization Counselor and Teacher 1969-70, Women's Relief Society 1964 to present, Stake R.S. President 1981-83, Hawaii Temple Worker 1970 to present. Honors and Awards: Honorary Ph.D., College of Southern Utah, 1968; Joint Award (with husband for service to Korean community), Seoul Stake Latter-day Saint Church, 1975; Appreciation Plaque for Years of Service, Brigham Young University Korean Alumni, 1978; Listed in *Outstanding Young Women of America*. Address: Box 108, Brigham Young University-Hawaii, Laie, Hawaii 96762.■

JOHN ARTHUR BRADY

Personal: Born May 25, 1944; Son of Frank and Leota Brady; Married Sharon Ardean Tallman; Father of Lara Heather, Heidi Lynn, Holly Allison, Sean Kelly. Military: Served in the United States Marine Corps, 1964-66, achieving the rank of Sergeant; Served with the United States Marine Corps Reserve, 1966-71. Career: American Telephone and Telegraph, Accountant Executive/Industry Consultant 1966 to present, Executive Communications Seminar Director, Complex Equipment Installation and Repair Supervisor, Installation Force Management Supervisor, Engineer-Customer Facilities, Business Industry Consultant, Communications Consultant; Associate Professor, California Polytechnic State University Extension, 1977 to present. Organizational Memberships: American Management Association; American Public Works Association; Associated Public Safety Communications Officer; California Public Safety Radio Association. Community Activities: Public Member, San Luis Obispo County Local Area Formation Commission, 1982 to present; Oral Review Board, San Luis Obispo Police Department, 1979 to present; Prison Social Service Volunteer, State of California Department of Corrections, 1979 to present; Jail Social Service Volunteer, San Luis Obispo County Sheriff, 1979 to present; Public Speaker and Speaker Trainer, Pacific Telephone Management Speaker Bureau, 1976 to present; Vice President, Parent-Teacher Association, 1977-79; Boy Scouts of America, Eagle Scout Coordinator, Institutional Representative, Scouting Coordinator, Post Adivosr, Council Finance Committeeman, Major Membership Committeeman. Religion: Church of Jesus Christ of Latter-day Saints, Bishop, Elders Quorum President, Stake Executive Secretary, Home Teacher. Published Works: Contributing Author, *Western City Magazine* 1981 to present, *Telephone Engineer and Management* Magazine 1979 to present; Author *Telecommunications Management* (syllubus for telecommunications curriculum) 1977, *An Intercity Communications Analysis of H. S. Crocker Company Inc.* 1972, *The Economics of Your Telephone System* 1972, Others. Honors and Awards: Citizen Marine of the Year, 1968; National Defense Ribbon; Marine Corps Reserve Medal; Presidential Unit Citation; Outstanding Military Instructor Award; Officer, National Council of Leaders, American Telephone, 1982; Chairman's Outstanding Achievment Award, Pacific Telephone, 1981; President's Outstanding Achievement Award, Pacific Telephone, 1979, 1980, 1981; Outstanding Public Speakers Award, Pacific Telephone, 1978, 1979, 1980, 1981, 1982; Vice President's Outstanding Achievement Award, Pacific Telephone, 1978; P.T.A. Top Unit Achievement Award, State Parent-Teacher Association, 1979; Outstanding Achievement Award, Pacific Telephone, 1977; Excellence Public Speaking Award, Pacific Telephone, 1977; Public Speaking Awards, Pacific Telephone, 1975, 1976; Headliner of the Year, Bakersfield Chamber of Commerce, 1966; First Place Mixed Choir in Llangollen International Musical Eisteddfod at Llangollen, Wales, Bakersfield College European Concert Choir, 1965; Listed in *Outstanding Young Men of America*. Address: 1377 Woodside Drive, San Luis Obispo, California 93401.■

WINIFRED B. BRADY

Administrator. Personal: Born November 28, 1933; Married Richard Brady (deceased). Education: B.S. Industrial Relations and Journalism, Rider College; M.B.A. Industrial Relations, Temple University. Career: Director New Jersey Job Service; Former Director, Personnel and Training, Department of Labor and Industry. Organizational Memberships: American Society for Personnel Administration, National Secretary and Parliamentarian, Past Regional Vice President; National Federation of Business and Professional Women, New Jersey State President 1976-77, Board of Directors, Has Held All Principal State, District and Local Chapter Offices; International Personnel Management Association; International Association of Personnel in Employment Security. Community Activities: Young Women's Christian Association of Burlington County (New Jersey), Board of Directors 1980-83, Personnel Committee Chairman 1981-82; Soroptimists International of Trenton (New Jersey), Finance Chairman and Audit Committee Chairman; Burlington County Committee on the Status of Women, Member 1975-77, Chairman 1977. Honors and Awards: Woman of the Year, Somerset County (New Jersey) Business and Professional Women, 1977; Career Education Award Fellow, United States Civil Service Commission, 1970; Various Biographical Listings. Address: 19 Spruce Avenue, Bordentown, New Jersey 08505.■

RAYMOND LEE BRANCH

Administrator. Personal: Born August 3, 1928; Married Idaline, Daughter of Aline Harrison; Father of Joan L. Roberts, Pamela L. Gilyard, Pamela J. Whitaker, Bonnie F. Marshall. Education: B.S. Health Care Administration, Wichita State University, 1980. Military: Served in the United States Air Force as a Personnel Superintendent, 1947-74, retiring with the rank of Master Sergeant. Career: Administrator, Adult Care Home for the Mentally Retarded and Developmentally Disabled; Former Intern in the Health Systems Agency of Se Kan. Organizational Memberships: American Association of Mental Deficiencies; American College of Nursing Home Administrators; American Management Association; International Platform Association; Wichita State University Alumni Association. Honors and Awards: Bronze Star Medal, 1969; Meritorious Service Medal, 1974; First Oak Leaf Cluster to the Air Force Commendation Medal, 1972; Air Force Commendation Medal, 1968. Address: 615 East Maywood, Wichita, Kansas 67216.■

TWO THOUSAND NOTABLE AMERICANS

JAY JEROME BRANDINGER

Division Executive. Personal: Born January 2, 1927; Son of Abraham and Lillian Brandinger; Married Alice Levite; Father of Paul, Donna, Norman. Education: B.E.E., The Cooper Union, 1951; M.S. 1962, Ph.D. 1968, Rutgers University. Military: Served in the United States Signal Corps, 1943-46. Career: Group Head of Display and Systems Research 1966-70, Group Head of TV Systems Research 1970-74, RCA Laboratories, Princeton, New Jersey; Division Vice President (TV Engineering, Consumer Electronics Division) 1974-79, Division Vice President ("SelectaVision" VideoDisc Operations) 1979-81, Division Vice President and General Manager ("SelectaVision" VideoDisc Operations), RCA, Indianapolis, Indiana. Organizational Memberships: New York Academy of Sciences; Institute of Electrical and Electronics Engineers, Senior Member; Society for Information Display, Editor of Proceedings 1973-76, Editorial Board Chairman 1973-76; Institute of Mathematical Statistics; Computer and Automated Systems Association of S.M.E., Senior Member. Community Activities: Boy Scouts of America, Assistant Scoutmaster 1959-74; New Jersey Pilots Association, Program Chairman 1972. Honors and Awards: RCA Achievement Awards, 1952, 1970, 1973; Sigma Xi, 1962; Fellow, Society for Information Display, 1982. Address: 1214 Woodbridge Lane, Indianapolis, Indiana 46260.■

LEO BRANOVAN

Professor Emeritus of Mathematics. Personal: Born April 17, 1895; Son of Mr. and Mrs. Itzik Branovan (both deceased); Married Pearl L. Lhevine, Daughter of Mr. and Mrs. Justin Lhevine (both deceased); Father of Rosalind Branovan Turner. Education: B.S. Electrical Engineering, University of Wisconsin, 1924; M.S. Mathematics, University of Chicago, 1927; Postgraduate Study in Applied Mathematics, Columbia University, 1935-38. Career: Engineer, General Electric Company, Fort Wayne, Indiana, 1924-26; Instructor and Consultant in Mathematics, University of Minnesota, 1927-31; Consultant in Mathematics, J. P. Goode Company, Chicago, Illinois, 1932-34; Consulting Mathematician, New York City, 1935-38; Instructor and Consultant in Mathematics, Brooklyn Polytechnic Institute, 1939-44; Instructor to Professor in Mathematics 1944-70, Professor Emeritus of Mathematics 1970 to present, Marquette University, Milwaukee, Wisconsin. Organizational Memberships: American Mathematical Society, Life Member; American Society for Engineering Education, Life Member; American Association for the Advancement of Science; American Association of University Professors, Life Member; Wisconsin Academy of Arts, Letters and Science; Numerous Foreign Mathematical Associations. Published Works: Author Extensive Research Paper "Umbilics on Hyperellipsoids in Four Dimensions"; Present Research in Global Differential Geometry (Properties of Closed Manifolds in Hyperspace). Honors and Awards: Life Member, Pi Mu Epsilon, National Honor Society of Mathematics, 1946; President's Council, Marquette University, 1979; Fellow, International Biographical Association, 1977; Quarter Century Club, Marquette University, 1969; Half Century Club, University of Wisconsin, 1974; Life Member, Milwaukee Central Y.M.C.A., 1974. Address: 3201 North 48th Street, Milwaukee, Wisconsin 53216.■

EDWARD MARTIN BRASHIER

Chemical and Hazardous Waste Consultant. Personal: Born September 30, 1954; Son of Mr. and Mrs. M. L. Brashier; Married Deborah Warren, Daughter of Mr. and Mrs. W. E. Warren; Father of Shannon Elise, Edward Martin II, Joseph Lee II. Education: B.A. Chemistry/Biology, University of Mississippi; Chemistry Special Training in Laboratory Instrumentation, Safety and Health, Process Engineering in Treatment and Disposal of Hazardous Waste. Career: Technical Director, Consultant, American Environmental Protection Corporation and American Electric Corporation, 1982 to present; Technical Manager 1980-82, Chief Chemist 1979-80, Chemical Waste Management Inc.; Chemist, Nilok Chemicals Inc., A Division of Hilton Davis Chemical, 1978-79; Laboratory Technician, Union Carbide Corporation, Agricultural Products Division, 1977-78; Safety Coordinator, Florida Machine and Foundry, Inc., 1976-77. Organizational Memberships: American Chemical Society; American Society of Safety Engineers; Instrument Society of America; American Water Works Association; Industrial Hygiene Association; Association of Analytical Chemists; National Association of Environmental Professionals; The American Institute of Chemists; Association of Consulting Chemists and Chemical Engineers. Community Activities: Reference Material Given to Waynesboro City Library, 1982; Reference Material and Laboratory Equipment Given to Wayne Academy, 1982. Religion: Methodist. Honors and Awards: Chemical Week Research Committee, 1982; Listed in *Who's Who, Personalities of America*. Address: P.O. Box 841, Livingston, Alabama 35470.■

CHARLENA H. BRAY

Executive Director. Personal: Born April 11, 1945; Married Paul Bray (deceased). Education: B.A., Miles College, 1965; M.A., University of Alabama, 1971; Advanced Certificate in Guidance and Counseling, University of Alabama-Birmingham, 1977; Ph.D. Candidate, University of Alabama. Career: Executive Director, Alabama Center for Higher Education; Interim Director, Program Chairman, Alabama Center for Higher Education, 1972-80; Secondary Mathematics Teacher, Jefferson County Public School System, 1965-72. Organizational Memberships: American Association for Higher Education; American Personnel and Guidance Association; Council for Interinstitutional Leadership. Community Activities: Cooper Green Hospital, 10 Year Appointment to the Board of Trustees by the Jefferson Commission, Chairman of Personnel Committee, Executive Committee; Alabama Committee on the Humanities, Board Member; Birmingham Area Manpower Consortium, Secretary, Planning and Advisory Council; Council for Interinstitutional Leadership, Board of Directors; Volunteer and Information Center of Birmingham, Board Member. Religion: Union Baptist Church, Secretary, Associate Director of Church School. Honors and Awards: Xi Chapter, Kappa Delta Pi; Region IV Special Programs Award, 1976; Boquechitto Community Day Care Award, 1978; Award, Miles College Student Government Association, 1976; Rho Nu Tau Soror of the Year, 1976; Loundes County Health Services Association Award, 1978; Award, Birmingham Veterans Administration Hospital, 1977; Award, Volunteer and Information Center, 1978; Listed in *Who's Who in the South and Southwest, Outstanding Young Women of America*. Address: 3101 Lorna Road, Unit 424, Birmingham, Alabama 35216.■

HAROLD VINCENT BRAY, JR.

Clinical Psychologist. Personal: Born August 28, 1946; Son of Mr. and Mrs. Harold V. Bray, Sr.; Married Suzanne Joy, Daughter of Col. and Mrs. J. H. Couch. Education: A.B., Westminster College, 1971; M.Ed. Counseling, University of Missouri at Columbia, 1973; Further Studies undertaken at the University of Kansas at Lawrence 1974-75, University of California at Berkeley 1977; Ph.D., United States International University, 1981; Studies at the McGeorge School of Law, 1981; Continuing Education, Harvard Medical School and University of Maryland, European Division. Organizational Memberships: American Psychological Association; American Bar Association; Phi Alpha Delta Legal Fraternity; Psi Chi. Community Activities: Legislative Assistant, Missouri House of Representatives, 1970-73; Charter Member, Republican Presidential Task Force, 1982. Religion: Berkeley First Presbyterian Church, 1982. Honors and Awards: Research Award, Missouri Society for Sociology and Anthropology, 1970; Listed in *Personalities of the West and Midwest*. Address: Hagebuttenweg 45, Karlsruhe, Federal Republic of Germany; (Business Address) KMC Mental Health Clinic, A.P.O. New York 09360■

THOMAS CLARKSON BRENKER

Marketing and Communications Executive. Personal: Born April 1, 1944; Song of Frederick Joseph Murrilla and Beatrice Clarkson Brenker. Education: B.A., The American University, 1968; Postgraduate Studies, Georgetown University. Military: Served in the United States National Guard, attaining rank of First Lieutenant. Career: Communications Staff, Republican Senator James L. Buckley, 1969-75; Public Relations Director, Goodwill Industries, 1975-76; Director of Marketing and Communications, Atwood Richards, Inc., 1976-78; President, Expogroup, Inc., 1978 to present; Board of Directors, Intergroup, Bradshaw, Caffrey, Dillon and Smith; Founder, Executive Director, Mexican Food and Beverage Board. Organizational Memberships: Public Relations Society of America;

Publicity Club of New York; Advertising Club of New York. Community Activities: Empire State Society; Board of Managers, Sons of the American Revolution; Sons of the Revolution; Legion of Valor; Young Presidents Organization; Union League; St. Bartholomew Club; American Red Cross; St. Bartholomew Community House; Fraunces Tavern Museum; Medal of Honor Historical Society. Religion: Member of Episcopalian Church. Published Works: Author of *The Brenker's Since the German Reformation, 1539-*. Honors and Awards: Listed in *Who's Who in the East, The Hereditary Register of the United States of America*. Address: 314 East 41st Street, New York, New York 10017; also Massapequa, New York 11758.■

ETHEL CRAIG BREWSTER

Retired City Treasurer. Personal: Born July 30, 1889; Daughter of Benjamin Kellar and Anna Bell Young Heisler (both deceased); Widow. Career: City Treasurer, 32 Years; Former Deputy County Clerk, Deputy City Treasurer, Deputy Circuit Clerk, Circuit Clerk (appointed by governor), Others. Organizational Memberships: Quota Club, President 1955-57, 1957-59, 1969-71, 1973-75, Historian 1979-81; Stephenson County Humane Society, President 1952-83. Community Activities: American Business Women's Association, Chairman Education Committee 1981; Republic Women's Club, Parliamentarian and Historian 1979-81; Stephenson County Nursing Center, Volunteer 1956-81; Donations to All Worthy Organizations on the Local, National and International Levels. Religion: First Lutheran Church; Dorcas Circle Recorder, 1979-81. Honors and Awards: Plaque from Dalton Adding Machine Company Touch Operator 1922, March of Dimes 1960-63, American Business Women's Association (for being Woman of the Year), Quota Club (for being Honorary member 1969), Stephenson County Nursing Home Service 1973, International Quota Club (for Outstanding Achievement) 1974; Listed in *Notable Americans of the Bicentennial Era, Community Leaders and Noteworthy Americans, International Who's Who of Community Leaders, Book of Honor, World Who's Who of Women*. Address: 725 West Galena Avenue, Freeport, Illinois 61032.■

HILTON MARSHALL BRIGGS

University President Emeritus. Personal: Born January 9, 1913; Married Lillian D. Briggs; Father of Dinus M., Janice S. Education: B.S., Iowa State University, 1933; M.S., North Dakota State University, 1935; Ph.D., Cornell University, 1938. Career: Oklahoma State University, Assistant Professor 1936-41, Associate Professor 1941-45, Associate Director of Experimental Station and Associate Dean of Agriculture 1949-50; Dean of Agriculture and Director of Agriculture Experiment Station, University of Wyoming, 1950-58; South Dakota State University, President 1958-75, Distinguished Professor of Agriculture 1975 to present, Director of Foreign Program 1977-78, President Emeritus 1975 to present. Organizational Memberships: American Society of Animal Science, Secretary 1947-50, Vice President 1951, President 1952; National Research Council Committee on Animal Nutrition, 1951-57; Commission of Colleges and Universities North Central Association, 1969-73. Community Activities: Continental Dorset Club, Executive Committee 1943-48, President 1948; American Southdown Breeders Association, Director 1970-76, Director for Life 1976 to present; United States Chamber of Commerce; Rotary Club, Local President 1979. Religion: Methodist. Honors and Awards: Fellow, American Society of Animal Science, 1974; Fellow, American Association for the Advancement of Science, 1962; Alpha Zeta; Gamma Sigma Delta; Phi Kappa Phi; Sigma Xi; Builder of Man Award, Farm House Fraternity, 1960; National 4-H Club Alumni Award, 1959; Exceptional Service Award, United States Air Force, 1975; Decoration for Distingushed Civilian Service, Department of Army, 1974; Outstanding Citizen of South Dakota, 1975; Portrait to Saddle and Sirloin Gallery, 1978. Address: 1734 Garden Square, Brookings, South Dakota 57006.■

DIANE-FROST ASBURY BRISCOE

Corporation Executive. Personal: Born January 8, 1945; Daughter of Philip and Mary Louise Asbury Briscoe; Mother of Cristopher Allan Crofton Briscoe. Education: B.S. cum laude, University of Georgia, 1971; Studies at La Colline, Ecole des Langues, La Tour-de-Peilz, Vaud, Switzerland, 1963; Private Pilot's License, 1975. Career: Administrative Assistant to President, Airclaims Inc., Washington D.C., 1966-68 and 1971-72; Administrative Assistant to Claims Manager 1972-75, Claims Representative and Office Manager 1975-79, Assistant Vice President 1979-81, Vice President 1981 to present, Rowedder Aviation Adjustment Service, Inc., Atlanta, Georgia. Organizational Memberships: Atlanta Claims Association, Inc.; International Information/Word Processing Association; United States Parachute Association; Atlanta Association of Insurance Women, Inc., Speech Course Instructor 1982, Chairman Insurance Committee 1980-81, 1982-83, Corresponding Secretary 1978-79, Co-Chairman Public Relations Committee 1977-78, Region III Editor *Today's Insurance Woman* 1979-80. Community Activities: The National Society of Colonial Dames of America in the State of Maryland; Dana Marie Condominium Association, Comptroller 1981 and 1982, President 1979 and 1980, Secretary 1978, Chairman Grounds Committee 1979-81, Chairman Pool Committee 1979; Junior League of Atlanta, First Saturday Chairman Nearly New 1977-81; Volunteer, Atlanta Humane Society 1972-73 and 1973-74, Atlanta Zoological Society 1979, 1980, Georgia Mental Health Institute 1974-75. Religion: Episcopal. Honors and Awards: Region III VR Education Award, National Association of Insurance Women International, 1978; CPIW/AIM Designation 1980; Associate in Management Designation, Insurance Institute of America, 1979; Listed in *Who's Who in the South and Southwest, Who's Who of American Women, World Who's Who of Women*. Address: 408 Sycamore Drive, Decatur, Georgia 30030.■

ELI BROAD

Executive. Personal: Born June 6, 1933, in New York; Married Edythe L. Lawson; Father of Jeffrey Alan, Gary Steven. Education: Graduate, Central High School, Detroit, Michigan, 1951; B.A. Accounting, cum laude, Michigan State University, 1954. Career: Public Accounting Practice, 1954-56; Assistant Professor, Detroit Institute of Technology, 1956; Co-Founder 1957, President 1957-72, Chairman (part-time) 1973-75, Chairman and Chief Executive Officer 1976 to present, Kaufman and Broad, Inc. (a NYSE-listed company specializing in housing, financial services and life insurance); Chairman 1976-79, Director 1979 to present, Sun Life Insurance Company of America, Baltimore; Chairman, Sun Life Group of America, Inc. (Kaufman and Broad's Atlanta-based Life Insurance Group), 1978 to present. Organizational Memberships: Real Estate Advisory Board, Citibank; Director, National Energy Foundation. Community Activities: The Museum of Contemporary Art (scheduled to open in downtown Los Angeles 1984), Chairman of the Board, Founding Trustee; Boy Scouts of America, Advisory Board; Los Angeles Chamber of Commerce, Director; Young Men's Christian Association of Los Angeles, Director; United Way, Director; City of HOPE, Director; National Conference of Christians and Jews, Director; Vice Chairman Board of Trustees, California State University System; Board of Trustees, Pitzer College (Claremont, California); Visiting Committee, University of California at Los Angeles Graduate School of Management; Friends of Fine Art, University of Southern California. Honors and Awards: Housing Man of the Year, National Housing Conference; Man of the Year, City of HOPE; Humanitarian Award, National Conference of Christians and Jews; Distinguished Alumni Award, Michigan State University; Listed in *Who's Who in the World, Who's Who in the United States, Who's Who in Business and Finance*. Address: 10801 National Boulevard, Los Angeles, California 90064.■

CHARLES CLAUDE BRODEUR

Educator, Therapist, Lecturer. Personal: Born May 29, 1931, in Holyoke, Massachusetts. Education: A.A., St. Thomas Seminary, 1951; Monastic Studies, Congregation of the Sacred Hearts (Benedictine Rule), 1951-53; B.A. 1954, M.A. 1956, Fordham University; M.A. 1957, Ph.D. 1967, University of Toronto; Postgraduate Studies, Stanford University, 1960-61; Graduate, Gestalt Institute of Toronto, 1976-79; Diploma, Concept Therapy Institute, 1969-74; Certificate of Instruction in Management Sciences in Computer-Assisted Instruction, Control Data Institute for Advanced Technology, 1971; Certificate, First Hypno-Operant Therapy Workshop, New York City, 1972; Certificate, Ontario Society for Clinical Hypnosis, Basic Level 1975, Intermediate Level 1976; Certificate, Hypnosis in Psychotherapy, National Academy of Professional Psychologists, 1977. Career: Graduate Fellow in Philosophy, Fordham University, 1954-55; Graduate Assistant, in Psychology 1956-57, in Philosophy 1957-59, University of Toronto; Undergradaute Secretary, Hart House, University of Toronto, 1959-60; Instructor in Ethics, Victoria College, University of Toronto, 1959-60, 1966; Resident Assistant to the Dean of Men, Stanford University, 1960-61; Lecturer in Philosophy, University of Toronto 1961-62, University of Waterloo 1962-65; Founding Administrator for Department of Student Affairs, University of Waterloo, 1962-65; Instructor in Psychology, Ryerson Polytechnical Institute, Toronto, 1966-68; Associate Professor, Psychology, Faculty of Education, University of Toronto, 1968 to present; Elected Member of the Executive of Canadian Education Researchers Association, 1973-74; Program Chairman, Annual Conference of the Canadian Educational Researchers Association, University of Toronto, 1974; Appointed by Ontario Ministry of Education to Faculty of Toronto Principals Course, 1974-75, 1976-77; Associate, Victoria College, University of Toronto, 1977-78; Board of Directors, Humber Area Residential Placement House, 1977-78; Guest Faculty Member, The Peterborough Human Resources Institute, A Centre for Awareness and Communication Training, 1977-79; Associate for Holistic Counseling and Mind

Development, Cross Continental Corporation (Canada) Inc., 1979 to present. Organizational Memberships: American Psychological Association; Canadian Psychological Association; Ontario Council for Academic Psychologists; American Association for the Advancement of Higher Education; Phi Delta Kappa; Canadian Society for the Study of Education; Canadian Educational Researchers Association; The Society for Suggestive-Accelerative Learning and Teaching; Biofeedback Society of America; American Association of Biofeedback Clinicians, Charter Member; American Association for the Advancement of Tension Control; Ontario Biofeedback Society; American Society of Clinical Hypnosis; Ontario Society for Clinical Hypnosis; International Society for Clinical and Experimental Hypnosis; International Society for Hypnosis; International Transactional Analysis Association; Association for Transpersonal Psychology; International Association for Psychotronic Research. Published Works: Editorial Board, Founding Member and Contributor, *Student Affairs Journal*, 1963-65; Associate Editor, Founding Member and Contributor, *Canadian Association of University Student Personnel Services Journal*, 1965-67; Editor, Founding Member, Contributor, *Subject to Change*, 1978-79. Address: 131 Bloor Street West, Suite 502, Toronto, Ontario, Canada M5S 1S3.∎

RACHEL BEREZOW FRANK BROMBERG (DECEASED)

Artist, Poet, Essayist, Poetry Critic, Art Critic. Personal: Born July 24, 1917; Married Benjamin Bromberg. Education: B.A., New York University, 1940; M.A., University of Wisconsin, 1942; Requirements for Ph.D. completed at Bryn Mawr College; Postdoctoral Work undertaken at Johns Hopkins University, Middlebury Language School (Vermont). Career: Former Educator, Business Administrator at Hecht Company (Washington, D.C.), Translator for the American Red Cross, Professor of Advanced Spanish and French Literature at the University of Maryland (1944-49); Author Leading Articles in Professional and Literary Journals. Organizational Memberships: American Association of University Professors; Bryn Mawr Graduate Alumnae Society; Modern Language Association of America; Artists Equity. Community Activities: Rachel Frank Publishing Company, President; The Vestibule Gallery, Director; Bryn Mawr Graduate Discussion Society, President; Donation of Books to Colleges and New York City Libraries; Girl Scouts of America. Honors and Awards: Theodore Roosevelt Medal; Fellow, Royal Society of Arts, London; Rachel Bromberg Collection, University of Wyoming (Archive of Contemporary History); Gold Medal and Honorary Certificate, Academia Italie delle Arti e del Lavoro; Solo and Group Exhibits of Paintings (mainly in New York); Listed in *Encyclopedia of Contemporary European Artists, M.L.A. Directory of Women Scholars*.∎

SHIRLEY GERENE BRONSON

Financial Manager, Feminist Consultant. Personal: Born October 15, 1936; Daughter of Velma Geneva Smith Green; Married Bobby Ed Bronson, September 29, 1953, Son of Dorothy Brownlowe Bronson-Westmoreland; Mother of Richard Ed, David Dee, Daniel Lee, Robert Edward. Education: B.A. cum laude 1975, M.B.A. with dictinction 1977, Golden Gate University. Career: Federal Women's Program Manager 1973-74, Assistant to Comptroller 1974-76, Record's Management Officer 1976-77, Air Force Flight Test Center, Edwards Air Force Base, California; Program/Budget Analyst 1977-81, Financial Manager 1981 to present, Federal Women's Program Manager 1979 to present, Air Force Space Division; Contract Teacher, Pacific Christian College, 1977 to present; Former Data Processing Manager, Navy COMSUBPAC (Hawaii), Page Aircraft Data Processing Division (Hawaii), Western Electric (Tennessee). Organizational Memberships: National Association of Female Executives; American Society of Military Comptrollers, Los Angeles Chapter; Federal Women's Program Committee, Los Angeles Federal Executive Board; Air Force Association, Los Angeles Chapter; Federally Employed Women, President Antelope Valley Chapter 1976, 1977. Community Activities: Gamma Alpha Tau Chapter, Beta Sigma Phi, Historian, Librarian, 1970, 1971, 1972; Beta Sigma Phi, Lancaster City Council, Vice President 1972-73, Parliamentarian and Recording Secretary 1972-74, President Sigma Omicron Chapter 1973-74; Icelandic/American Club, Vice President Southern California Chapter 1976, 1977; Task Force, United Nations Decade for Women, 1977; National Women's Conference, California Delegate, 1977; Citizens for Incorporation of Lancaster (California), 1977. Published Works: Author (Article) "Space Division is Number One Federal Women's Program" 1980, (Video Tape) "Number One Federal Women's Program in the Air Force" 1981, (Film) "The Federal Women's Program" 1981. Honors and Awards: Certificate of Merit, Air Force Systems Command, 1972; Outstanding Performance Award, 1971, 1972, 1975, 1976, 1982; Sustained Superior Performance Award, Department of the Air Force, 1971, 1976, 1982; Department of the Air Force Certificate of Appreciation (Equal Employment Opportunities), 1976; Air Force Flight Test Center Federal Women's Program Space Recognition Award, 1976; Special Achievement Award, 1971, 1976, 1982; Air Force System Command Federal Women's Program Manager of the Year, 1979; Department of the Air Force Federal Women's Program Manager of the Year, Distinguished Equal Employment Opportunity Award, 1980; Los Angeles Federal Executive Board Distinguished Public Service Award, 1981; Headquarters Equal Employment Opportunities Award, 1979, 1890, 1981, 1982; Listed in *Who's Who of American Women, Who's Who in the West, Personalities of America, Directory of Distinguished Americans, The World Who's Who of Women, Personalities of the West and Midwest*. Address: 763 Brightstar Street, Thousand Oaks, California 91360.∎

BENJAMIN N. BROOK

Consultant. Personal: Born January 31, 1913; Married; Father of Robert Henry, Mark Daniel. Education: A.B. 1934, M.A. 1936, New York University; Ed.D., University of Arizona, 1972. Military: Served as an American Red Cross Director, Morocco and Italy, during World War II, holding the rank of Lieutenant Colonel. Career: Consultant; Former Positions include Executive Vice President of the Tucson Jewish Community Council, Assistant Professor of Sociology at California State University at Los Angeles, Lecturer in Public Administration at the University of Arizona, Social Welfare Administrator. Organizational Memberships: President, Arizona Conference on Social Welfare; President, United Way Professional Association; Academy of Certified Social Workers; National Association of Social Workers; Academy of Political Science. Community Activities: Referee, Puma County Juvenile Court; Treasurer, Community Food Bank; Vice President, Parents United; Delegate to the White House Conference on Aging, State of Arizona, 1981; Delegate to the White House Conference on Children, State of Arizona, 1971; Board Member, Title XX Fund Distribution; Allocations Committee, United Way. Religion: Congregation Ansher-Israel. Honors and Awards: Man of Year, Jewish Community Council; Outstanding Citizen Award, State of Arizona, City of Tucson; Commendation Award, Italian Government.∎

ARLENE SANDRA BROTMAN

Social Worker, Psychotherapist. Personal: Born June 7, 1948; Daughter of Sam and Sylvia Brotman. Education: B.A. magna cum laude, State University of New York at Albany, 1970; N.D.E.A. Fellowship for Critical Languages, Indiana University, Summer 1969; M.A., University of Pennsylvania, 1971; M.S.W., Adelphi University, 1977. Career: New York State Certified French Teacher; New York State Certified Russian Teacher; New York State Certified Attendance Teacher; New York State Certified Social Worker, Psychotherapist and Scriptwriter; Social Worker, Oceanside Public Schools, New York; Psychotherapist, Rockville Consultation Center, New York; Scriptwriter, Creative Eye, Inc. (New York). Organizational Memberships: Academy of Certified Social Workers, National Association of Social Workers; New York State School Social Workers Association; Adelphi University Alumni Association, Director at Large 1979-81; Adelphi University School of Social Work Alumni Association, Executive Board 1979-81. Honors and Awards: Dean's List, 1966-70; Mu Lambda Alpha, State University of New York at Albany, 1969 to present; National Slavic Honor Society, 1971 to present; American Biographical Institute Research Association; Listed in *Who's Who of American Women, Personalities of America, World Who's Who of Women*. Address: 53 Windsor Avenue, Rockville Centre, New York 11570.∎

ALEXANDER BROTT

Professor of Music, Musical Director and Conductor. Personal: Born March 14, 1915; Son of Samuel and Annie Brott; Married Lotte, Daughter of Walter and Else Goetzel; Father of Boris, Denis. Education: License in Music, McGill University, 1932; Laureat Degree, Quebec Academy of Music, 1933; Graduate Study 1937, Postgraduate Study 1938, Juilliard School of Music; Doctorate of Music, Chicago University, 1960; Doctor of Laws, Queen's University, 1973. Career: Concertmaster, Montreal Symphony Orchestra; Assistant Conductor, Montreal Symphony Orchestra; Conductor, Montreal Pops Concerts; Conductor, Musical Director, Kingston Symphony Orchestra; Professor of Music, Conductor-in-Residence, McGill University; Founder, Conductor, McGill Chamber Orchestra 1939 to present, Kingston "Pops" Concerts, Celebrity Connoisseur Concerts in Kingston. Organizational Memberships: McGill University Faculty Club; Musicians Guild; Societe de Musique Contemporaine; C.A.P.A.C.; Fellow, Royal Society of Arts. Published Works: Compositions include (Symphonic) "Oracle" 1938, "War and Peace" 1944, "Laurentian Idyl" 1945, "From Sea to Sea" 1946, "Delightful Delusions" 1951, "Royal Tribute" 1953, "Fancy and Folly" 1953, "Spheres in Orbit" 1961, "Martlett's Muse" 1962, "Paraphrase in Poliphony" 1967, "La Corriveau" 1967, "The Young Prometheus" 1971; (Solo and Chamber Music) "Invocation and Dance" 1939, "Mutual Salvation Orgy" 1962, "World Sophisticate" 1962, "Profundum Praedictum" 1966, "Pristine Prism" 1967, "Mini-Minus" 1968, "L'Accent" 1971, "Spasms for 6" 1971, "How Thunder and Lightning Came to Be" 1973; (Vocal) "Songs of Contemplation" 1940, "Canadiana" 1955, "Israel" 1956, "Vision of the Dry Bones" 1960, "The Prophet" 1960, "Elie, Elie" 1967, "Esperanto" 1967, "Badinage" 1968; (Group of Songs) Three Eskimo Songs ("Passangoddy Dance Song," "Malissat Love Song," and "Penobscat Medicine Song"), Four Songs of the Central Eskimos ("Ititansang's Song," "The Raven's Song," "The Fox and the Woman," "Playing the Ball"), Two Songs (Haida), "Song of the Totem Pole" and "Cradle Song." Honors and Awards: Loeb Memorial Award for Performance, 1938-39;

Elizabeth Sprague Cooledge Award for Composition, 1937, 1938; Lord Strathcona Award for Studies in England, 1939; C.A.P.A.C. Composition Award, 1941, 1942, 1943; Two Olympic Medals for Composition in Helsinki and London, 1948, 1952; Pan American Conductors Competition (First Prize), 1957; Sir Arnold Bax Society Prize for "The Composer of the Commonwealth" (Gold Medal), 1961; Canadian Jewish Congress B'nai B'rith Recognition, 1961; Prix du Disque for Serious Music, 1969; Honorary Member, Zoltan Kodaly Academy and Institute, 1970; Honorary Doctorate of Laws, Queen's University, 1973; Gold Medal of International Who's Who, 1973; Jewish People's Schools and Peretz Schools (Annual Prize), 1974; Academia brasileira de ciencias humanas (Medal & Diploma), 1975; Fellow, International Biographical Association, 1975; Canadian Music Council Medal for Contribution to Music in Canada, 1976; Queen's Anniversary Silver Jubilee Medal, 1977; Medal of the Order of Canada, 1979; Honorary Doctorate of Music, McGill University, 1980; Listed in *Notable Americans of the Bicentennial Era.* Address: 5459 Earnscliffe Avenue, Montreal, Quebec H3X 2P8, Canada.■

ALBERTA MAE BROWN

Respiratory Clinician, In-Service Instructor. Personal: Born November 11, 1932; Daughter of Sylvester C. and Malinda Mason Angel (mother deceased); Married Norman, Son of Sebron and Leslie Brown (both deceased); Mother of Stevan Arthur, Charon Lorene, Carole Yvonne. Education: Licensed Vocational Nurse, Antelope Valley College, 1961; Respiratory Therapy, San Bernardino Valley College; Registered Nurse, Los Angeles Valley College, 1975; B.S., California State University at Dominguez Hills. Career: Respiratory Clinician and In-service Instructor. Organizational Memberships: American Association for Respiratory Therapists; American Heart Association, Cardiopulmonary Resuscitation Instructor. Community Activities: President, Socialities Inc. of San Bernardino; Treasurer, Gamma Omega Chapter, Eta Phi Beta; Eastern Star; Arrowhead Allied Arts Council; National Association for the Advancement of Colored People; American Association for Respiratory Therapists; National Honor Society; National Council of Negro Women. Religion: New Hope Missionary Baptist Church, Choir Member. Honors and Awards: Outstanding Performance Award, Veterans Administration, 1974. Address: 1545 North Hancock Street, Orangewood Estates, San Bernardino, California 92411.■

JUNE GIBBS BROWN

Inspector General. Personal: Born October 5, 1933; Daughter of Tom and Lorna Gibbs; Married Ray L. Brown; Mother of Ellen Rosenthal, Linda Gibbs, Sheryl Brown, Gregory Brown, Victor Janezic, Carol Janezic. Education: B.A. summa cum laude, 1971; M.B.A., Cleveland State University, 1972; J.D., University of Denver College of Law, 1978; 92nd Advanced Management Program, Harvard University, 1983. Career: Inspector General, National Aeronautics and Space Administration, Presidential Appointment with Senate Confirmation, 1981 to present; Former Positions include Inspector General, Department of the Interior, Presidential Appointment with Senate Confirmation, 1979-81; Manager of Financial Systems Design, Department of the Interior; Director of Internal Audit, Navy Finance Center; Staff Accountant, Frank T. Cicirelli C.P.A., Ohio; Real Estate Broker/Office Manager, Northeast Realty, Ohio; Real Estate Salesman, Lester's Real Estate and Richmond Realty, Ohio. Organizational Memberships: Association of Government Accountants, National Executive Committee 1977-80 and 1981 to present, National President 1984-85, Financial Management Standards Board 1981-82, Equal Opportunity for Minorities and Women in Government Committee 2 Years, Vice Chairman National Ethics Board 2 Years; American Institute of Certified Public Accountants; American Accountants Association; Association of Federal Investigators; Beta Alpha Psi, Honorary Member. Honors and Awards: Financial Management Improvement Award, Joint Financial Management Improvement Program, 1980; Outstanding Service Award, National Association of Minority Certified Public Accounting Firms, 1980; Outstanding Achievement Award, Association of Government Accountants, Denver, 1979; Outstanding Contribution to Financial Management Award, Federal Executive Board, Denver Region, 1977; Career Service Award for Managerial Excellence, Federal Executive Board, Chicago Region, 1974; Outstanding Achievement Award, United States Navy, 1973; Service Awards, Association of Government Accountants, 1973, 1976; Woman of the Year, Bureau of Land Management, Department of the Interior, 1975. Address: N.A.S.A./Code W, 400 Maryland Avenue, S.W., Washington, D.C. 20546.■

LINDA LEE BROWN

Drafting/Graphics Supervisor. Personal: Born October 29, 1955; Married A. V. Paralez (deceased); Mother of Isaac. Education: Attended New Mexico State University 1972, Amarillo College 1973-75, West Texas State University 1975-76. Career: Drafting/Graphics 1982 to present, Drafting Supervisor 1977-85, Permits Coordinator 1980, Atlantic Richfield Company, Thunder Basin Coal Company, Black Thunder Mine; Drafter, Amarillo Oil Company, 1976-77; Drafter, Pioneer Natural Gas Company, 1975-76; Freelance Drafter, Panhandle Steel Buildings, 1974-75; Freelance Drafter, Harris and Patterson Engineers, 1974-75. Organizational Memberships: American Institute for Design and Drafting, Board of Directors 1982 and 1983-85; International Platform Association; National Association of Female Executives. Community Activities: Wright Writer's Club, Past President; Arco (Wyoming) Speaker's Bureau; Advisor to Wyoming Council of American Institute for Design and Drafting; Big Sister Volunteer; Wright Women's Consciousness Raising Group; Wyoming Powder River Arts Council; Co-Chairman of Design/Drafting Newsletter, American Institute for Design and Drafting. Published Works: Author of Two Books, *God Was Here, But He Left Early* (1976) and *A Gift of Wings* (1980); Poetry Published in Various Anthologies. Honors and Awards: Women in Industry, International Reprographics Association, 1980; Woman of the Year, Beta Sigma Phi, 180, 1981; Listed in *International Who's Who of American Women.* Address: P.O. Box 114, Wright, Wyoming 82732.■

(ROBERT) WENDELL BROWN

Lawyer. Personal: Born February 26, 1902, in Minneapolis, Minnesota; Son of Robert and Jane Amanda Anderson Brown (both deceased); Married Barbara Ann Fisher, October 20, 1934; Father of Barbara Ann Travis (Mrs. Neil), Mary Alice Fletcher (Mrs. Al). Education: A.B., University of Hawaii, 1924; J.D., University of Michigan Law School, 1926. Career: Admitted to Michigan Bar, 1926; Supreme Court of Michigan, United States Supreme Court, 6th United Circuit Court of Appeals, United States District Court, Eastern and Western Districts of Michigan, United States Board of Immigration Appeals, United States Tax Court; Lawyer, Firm of Routier, Nichols and Fildew (Detroit) 1926, Nichols and Fildew 1927-28, Frank C. Sibley 1929, Ferguson and Ferguson 1929-31; Assistant Attorney General, Michigan, 1931-32; Legal Department Union Guardian Trust Company, Detroit, 1933-34; Individual Law Practice, Detroit 1934-81, Farmington Hills (Michigan) 1981 to present. Organizational Memberships: American Bar Association; Detroit Bar Association, Former Member, Director 1939-49, Treasurer 1942-44, Secretary 1944-46, Second Vice President 1946-47, First Vice President 1947-48, President 1948-49, Chairman and/or Member of Various Committees 1935-52 and 1977-82; Oakland County Bar Association; State Bar of Michigan, Chairman or Member of Various Committees 1935-72. Community Activities: Wayne County Graft Grand Jury, Legal Advisory 1939-40; Wayne County Assistant Prosecuting Attorney of Civil Matters, 1940; Special Assistant City Attorney to Investigate Police Department, Highland Park, Michigan, 1951-52; Chairman, Citizens Committee to Form Oakland County Community College, 1962-63; Farmington School Board, President 1952-56; Oakland County Republican County Convention, Chairman 1952; Farmington Township, Oakland County, Trustee 1957-61; Oakland County Lincoln Republican Club, President 1958; Friends of Detroit Library, Treasurer, Board of Directors 1943-44; Farmington Friends of the Library, Inc., Board of Directors 1952-58, President 1956-57; Helped Organize Two Other Friends of the Library Societies; Farmington Historical Society, Honorary Member 1966; St. Anthony's Guild, Franciscan Friars, 1975. Religion: Presbyterian, Elder 30 Years of Board Activities; One of Original Incorporators, Franklin Community Church (Methodist), Franklin, Michigan. Honors and Awards: Listed in *Who's Who in the Midwest, Who's Important in Law, Who's Who in America, Who's Who in American Law, Who's Who in the World, International Who's Who of Intellectuals, Dictionary of International Biography, International Register of Profiles, International Book of Honor, Men and Women of Distinction, Men of Achievement, Personalities of America,* Others. Address: 29921 Ardmore Street, Farmington Hills, Michigan 48018.■

SANDRA M. BROWN

Investor. Personal: Born October 7, 1938; Daughter of Edgar P. Senne; Married Kenneth A. Martin; Mother of Kenneth S., Christopher S. Education: B.A. with distinction, Mount Holyoke, 1960; M.Ed., Springfield College, 1961; Ph.D., University of Connecticut, 1964. Career: President, East Thirty-Eighth Street Capital Corporation; President, Sandra Brown Advertising; Publisher, *The Executive Woman,* First National Newsletter for Women in Business; Radio Personality, NBC News and Information Service, 1976; Producer and Host, Weekly Show on "Women in Business," WPIX Television, 1975. Community Activities: Department of Health, Education and Welfare, Appointed to the Committee on the Rights and Responsibilities of Women 1975; Women's Forum, New York Chapter; Past Member Education Press Association, International Reading Association, Women Business Owners; First Woman in the United States to form a Small Business Investment Corporation licensed by the Small Business Administration. Published Works: American Express Credit Handbook for Women, 1975; Monthly Column "Money Matters" in *Viva* Magazine; Author *Read On, Skillbuilders, The Yearling Series, Metric Math, The Howey Program;* Various Other Publications in Reading and Language Arts Instruction. Honors and Awards: Award of Excellence, Education Press Association, 1967; Award for Service to the American Arbitration Association, 1978; Award for Inspiration to Youth, Junior Achievement, 1976. Address: Suite 300, 1527 Franklin Avenue, Mineola, New York 11501.■

TWO THOUSAND NOTABLE AMERICANS

VITO JOHN BRUNALE

Engineering Technical Manager. Personal: Born July 2, 1925; Son of Donato and Antoinette Wool Brunale (both deceased); Married Joan Florence, Daughter of Grace Bartlett; Father of Stephen John. Education: A.A.S. cum laude, Stewart Aeronautical Institute, 1948; B.S.A.E. cum laude, Tri-State University, 1958; M.S.M.E., University of Bridgeport, 1966; D.Sc., Nevada Institute of Technology, 1973; Graduate of Air Force Technical Schools; Attended New York University and Polytechnic of Brooklyn. Military: Served in the United States Air Force, 1943-45, attaining the rank of Technical Sergeant; Former Prisoner of War. Career: Engineer, Norden Laboratories, 1948-55; Instructor, Tri-State University, 1955-58; Engineering Consultant, United Aircraft, 1958-67; Division Consultant, Singer Aerospace, 1967-73; Engineering Manager, Magnetic Analysis Corporation, 1975-77; Consultant, Stress and Vibration Expert, Materials Expert, Former Vice President, Lithoway Corporation, 1968-77; Engineering Technical Manager, Fairchild Republic Company. Organizational Memberships: Air Force Association; United States Naval Institute; National Space Institute; American Institute of Aeronautics and Astronautics, Membership Committee 1948 to present; Institute of Environmental Sciences, Technical Committee 1959-67; National Management Association; American Ordnance Association. Community Activities: Assistant Scoutmaster, Troop 16, Mount Vernon, New York, 1959-63; Instructor of Aerodynamics and Aircraft Design, North Side Boys Club of Mount Vernon; Lecturer on Various Scientific Subjects and Topics at Local High Schools, Boy Scouts Activities and School Science Fairs, 1973 to present; Donation of Time and Money to Conservative Party Causes, 1963 to present. Religion: Member of Holy Name Society, 1948-73; Vice President Usher Society, Our Lady of Victory, Mount Vernon, 1950-58; Knights of Columbus, Council 410, 1950 to present; Assistance in Fund Raising for Catholic and Protestant Affairs. Honors and Awards: Aircraft Design Award, 1948; Institute of Aeronautical Science Lecture Award, 1948; Membership Award, American Institute of Aeronautics and Astronautics, 1975; Fairchild Achievement Awards, 1978, 1979, 1980, 1981, 1982, 1984; Norden Achievement Award, 1965, 1967; Singer Achievement Awards, 1970, 1972; Participant in National Science Foundation Grant, 1982; Listed in *Who's Who in Aviation, Who's Who in Aviation and Aerospace, Who's Who in America, Men of Achievement, Personalities of America, Biographical Roll of Honor*. Address: 459 Bronxville Road, Bronxville, New York 10708.■

SYLVIA LEIGH BRYANT

Editor, Publisher, Poet, Free-lance Writer. Personal: Born May 8, 1947, in Lynchburg, Virginia; Daughter of Mr. and Mrs. Hundley Bryant. Education: D.Lit., World University, 1981. Career: Editor/Publisher, The Anthology Society. Organizational Memberships: International Academy of Poets, Fellow; International Biographical Association, Fellow; Anglo-American Academy, Honorary Fellow; American Biographical Institute, Associate Member; United Poets Laureate International; Dr. Stella Woodall Poetry Society International; World Poetry Society; Centro Studi e Scambi Internazionali-Accademia Leonardo da Vinci; National Trust for Historic Preservation; International Platform Association; Smithsonian Institution, National Associate Member. Religion: Baptist. Published Works: Poetry can be found in *Adventures in Poetry Anthology, The Poet, Adventures in Poetry Magazine, Modern Images, Hoosier Challenger, Animal World*, Many Others. Honors and Awards: International Poet Laureate, United Poets Laureate International, 1979; Certificate of Merit, International Biographical Center, 1980; Certificate of Appreciation, American Biographical Institute, 1980; Certificate of Merit, Accademia Leonardo da Vinci, 1980; Certificate of Proclamation, American Biographical Institute, 1980; Distinguished Service Citation, World Poetry Society, 1981; Honorary Certificate of Recognition, American Biographical Institute (for work on Editorial Advisory Board), 1981; Gold Medal, Accademia Leonardo da Vinci, 1980; Poet Laureate Program, State of Virginia, 1981; Listed in *Who's Who in Poetry, International Register of Profiles, American Cultural Arts Registry, Personalities of the South, Community Leaders and Noteworthy Americans, Men and Women of Distinction, Community Leaders of America, Album of International Poets of Achievement, Personalities of America, World Who's Who of Women, Book of Honor, Directory of Distinguished Americans, International Who's Who of Poetry, International Authors and Writers Who's Who, Dictionary of International Biography, Anglo-American Who's Who, International Who's Who of Intellectuals*. Address: Route 5 Box 498A, Madison Heights, Virginia 24572.■

GARY LYNN BRYCE

Educator, Coach. Personal: Born March 28, 1941; Son of David and Ingrid Bryce (both deceased); Married Tracy K., Daughter of Mr. and Mrs. Terry Farlow; Father of Amy and David Bryce. Education: Industrial Relations Certificate, University of Michigan, 1975; M.A., University of Michigan, 1975; Teaching Fellowship, University of Pittsburgh, 1963-64; B.Sc., University of Michigan, 1963. Career: Teacher and Coach, Royal Oak Public Schools and Wayne State University; Former Positions include Recreational Director for National Music Camp, Director of Midwest All-Star Softball, Clinical Speaker at Softball Clinics. Organizational Memberships: American Alliance for Health, Physical Education and Recreation; National Education Association; Michigan Education Association; Michigan High School Coaches Association; National Coaches Association. Community Activities: Past Vice President, Lions International; American Defense Preparedness Association; National Security Advisory Committee; State Delegate to Michigan Education Association, 1973-75; Committee to Raise Money for Scholarships, Royal Oak Schools; Committee to Raise Funds for Athletics in Royal Oak; Committee to Pass Several Millage Proposals; Precinct Delegate. Religion: Unitarian, 1973 to present. Honors and Awards: All-State Football, 1958; All-American Football, 1958; Scholarship to the University of Michigan, 1959-63; Teaching Fellowship, University of Pittsburgh, 1963-64; Michigan High School Softball Coach of the Year, 1979; Softball Coach of the Year, Great Lakes Intercollegiate Athletic Conference, 1983; Listed in *Who's Who in the Midwest, Five Thousand Personalities of the World, Who's Who of Intellectuals in the World*. Address: 708 North Washington, Royal Oak, Michigan 48067.■

CONSTANCE VIRGINIA BUCEY

Teacher. Personal: Born August 22, 1936; Daughter of Mose and Lillian Russell; Married Henry Lee, Son of Lydia Bucey. Education: M.S., Pepperdine University, 1976; B.S., Virginia State College, 1959. Career: Teacher, J.R.E. Lee Elementary School, 1959-67; Teacher/Reading Resource Specialist, M. Duff Rosemead, 1967-82. Organizational Memberships: National Education Association, 1959 to present; Reading Specialists of California, 1978 to present; California Teachers Association; Garvey Teachers Association, 1967 to present; California Teacher's Federal Credit Union, President, Vice-President or Director, 1973-82; President of Board, First Financial Federal Credit Union, 1983. Religion: Member of Holy Trinity Parish, Alhambra, California, 1968 to present. Honors and Awards: Honorary Service Award, 1970; Outstanding Teacher Award, 1973; Listed in *Who's Who in the West*. Address: 871 Ashiya Road, Montebello, California 90640.■

FORREST LAWRENCE BUCHTEL

Composer, Arranger, Private Teacher. Personal: Born December 9, 1899; Son of Charles Stenton and Frances Stephens Buchtel (both deceased); Married Jessie Macdonald, Daughter of Thomas H. G. and Helene Reddeman Macdonald (both deceased); Father of Bonnie Buchtel Cataldo, Helene Buchtel Adams, Beverly Buchtel Platt, Forrest L. Jr. Education: A.B., Simpson College, 1921; M.S. Education, Northwestern University, 1931; B.Mus.Ed., VanderCook College of Music, 1932; M.Mus.Ed., 1933; Graduate Studies undertaken at Chicago University and Columbia University. Military: Served in the S.A.T.C., 1918. Career: Teacher, South High School (Grand Rapids, Michigan) 1921-25, Emporia (Kansas) State University 1925-30, Lane Technical High School (Chicago) 1930-34, Amundsen High School (Chicago) 1934-54; Teacher 1931-81, Dean of Students 1960-81, VanderCook College of Music. Organizational Memberships: American Bandmasters Association; American Society of Composers, Authors and Publishers; S.E.S.A.C.; Phi Beta Mu; Phi Mu Alpha Sinfonia; Kappa Kappa Psi; Delta Upsilon. Religion: Methodist. Published Works: 30 Sets of Band Books; 1000 Solos and Ensembles for School Bands, 30 Marches, 30 Overtures. Honors and Awards: Alumni Award, Simpson College 1966, VanderCook College 1965; Honorary Degree, Doctor of Fine Arts, Simpson College, 1983; Simpson College Candidate for Rhodes Scholarship, 1921; Listed in *International Who's Who in Music, Personalities of the West and Midwest, Who's Who in the Midwest*. Address: 1116 Cleveland Street, Evanston, Illinois 60202.■

EVELYN CLAUDENE BUFORD

General Sales Manager. Personal: Born September 21, 1940; Daughter of Claude and Evelyn Hodges; Married William Joseph Buford, Son of Thelma Buford; Mother of Vincent Shilling III, Kathryn Lynn Shilling Buford. Education: Graduate, G. B. Technical High School, 1958; Attended Hill Junior College 1975-76, Fort Worth

School of Business 1977-78. Career: Administrative Assistant to Assistant Administrator 1975-77, General Sales Manager (Commercial Division), Tarrant County Hospital District. Organizational Memberships: National Association of Female Executives; American Management Association; Executive Women International, Sergeant at Arms 1980-81, Publication Director 1981-82, Ways and Means Director 1982-83, Vice President Elect 1984. Community Activities: National Geographic Society; President's Club of Texas, Sustaining Member. Religion: United Methodist Church of Joshua. Honors and Awards: Listed in *Who's Who of American Women, Personalities of America, Personalities of the South, World Who's Who, Biographical Roll of Honor*. Address: 100 Kenneth Lane, Burleson, Texas 76028.■

WILLIAM TRUMAN BURGESS

Bank Executive. Personal: Born September 30, 1932, in Talladega, Alabama; Son of Buren Winford and Alice Folsom Burgess; Married Arlene, Daughter of Mr. and Mrs. Mike Mayernick; Father of Maria Alice, Michelle Arlene, William T., II. Education: B.S., University of Southern Mississippi, 1959; Graduate Work undertaken at Peabody College, 1963-64; J.D., Y.M.C.A. Law School, 1968. Career: Vice Chairman and President, The Citizens Bank of Hendersonville (Tennessee); Credit Union Manager, Baptist Board Employees Credit Union, 1963-68; Loan Officer, Cashier, Pensacola (Florida) Savings and Loan Bank, 1959-63. Organizational Memberships: Sumner County Bar Association. Community Activities: Veterans of Foreign Wars; American Legion; Bluegrass Country and Yacht Club; Past President, Hendersonville Civic Club; Rotary Club; Executive, Sumner County United Way; Board of Directors, Friends of Rock Castle; Board of Directors, Davidson County United Way; Appointed to Sumner County Board of Commissioners to Serve a Six-Year Term on the Sumner County Resource Authority Board, 1981-87 (Presently serving as Vice Chairman). Religion: Baptist. Honors and Awards: Outstanding Citizenship Award, Sertoma Club, 1975; Listed in *Who's Who in the South and Southwest*. Address: 160 Clifftop Drive, Hendersonville, Tennessee 37075.■

LEAH LUCILLE BURNHAM

Medical Technologist. Personal: Born July 31, 1947; Daughter of P. G. Taylor; Married Frederick Russell Burnham II, Son of Helen Gayle Burnham; Mother of Russell Adam, Laurel Helene. Education: M.T. (A.S.C.P.), Lutheran Hospital School of Medical Technology, 1968-69; B.S., Millikin University, 1969; M.S., University of Vermont, 1972; S.C. (A.S.C.P.), 1981. Career: Medical Technologist (Senior Technician, Clinical Toxicology), Arizona Health Science Center, 1974 to present; Educational Coordinator, School of Medical Technology, Tucson Medical Center, 1972-74; Teaching Fellow, University of Vermont, 1970-72; General Technologist, Lake Forest Hospital, 1970; Blood Bank Technologist, Lutheran Hospital (Cleveland, Ohio), 1969-70. Organizational Memberships: A.S.C.P.; Faculty of Workshops given by A.S.C.P., A.S.M.T.; Lecturer Preparing Medical Technologists for S.C.(A.S.C.P.) Exam, 1982. Community Activities: Boy Scouts of America. Honors and Awards: Listed in *Who's Who of American Women*. Address: 1601 West Windsor, Tucson, Arizona 85705.■

SANDRA KAYE BURNS

Attorney. Personal: Born August 9, 1949, in Bryan, Texas; Daughter of C. W. and Bert Burns; Mother of Scott. Education: B.S., University of Houston, 1970; M.A. 1972, Ph.D. 1975, University of Texas at Austin; J.D., St. Mary's University School of Law, 1978; Certified Provisional Secondary Vocational Homemaking 1970, Provisional Kindergarten Endorsement 1973, Professional School Administrator 1974, Professional Supervisor of Instruction 1979; Licensed Lawyer, State Bar of Texas, 1978. Career: Oil and Gas Attorney, Contracted to Humble Exploration, Dallas, Texas; House Counsel, First International Oil and Gas Inc., 1983; Independent Attorney, Practicing in the Areas of International Contracts, Oil and Gas, Business, Real Estate and School Laws, College Station, Texas, 1981-82; Attorney, Contracted to Republic Energy Inc., 1981-82; Visiting Lecturer, Department of Management, College of Business Administration, Texas A&M University, Fall 1981; Visiting Lecturer, Department of Educational Administration, College of Education, Texas A&M University, Summer 1981; Legal Consultant, International Law Firm of Colombotti & Associates, Aberdeen, Scotland, 1980; Committee Clerk-Counsel, Senate State Affairs Committee, Texas Senate, 66th Session, Spring 1979; Legislative Aide, The Honorable William T. Moore, Texas Senate, Fall 1978; Instructional Development Office of Educational Resources, Division of Instructional Development, University of Texas Health Science Center, San Antonio, 1976-77; Lecturer, Home Economics Department, Our Lady of the Lake College, San Antonio, Fall 1975; Professor, Departments of Child Development/Family Life and Home Economics Teacher Education, College of Nutrition, Textiles and Human Development, Texas Woman's University, 1974-75; Field Coordinator, Title III Accountability Project with Comal I.S.D. and Eanes I.S.D., Research and Evaluation, Region XIII Education Service Center, Austin, 1973-74; Doctoral Intern and Book Review Editor, American Association of Elementary-Kindergarten-Nursery Educators, National Education Association, Washington, D.C., Spring 1973; Teaching Assistant, Department of Curriculum and Instruction, College of Education, University of Texas, Austin, Fall 1972; Classroom Teacher, 8th Grade Science and 7th Grade Homemaking, Austin Independent School District, 1970-71. Organizational Memberships: Kappa Delta Pi; Phi Delta Kappa; Phi Kappa Phi; Pi Lambda Theta; American Association of Elementary-Kindergarten-Nursery Educators; American Bar Association; American Home Economics Association; American Educational Research Association; Association for Supervision and Curriculum Development; Delta Theta Phi; National Association for the Education of Young Children; Southern Association of Children under Six; State Bar of Texas; Texas State Teachers Association. Published Works: Author of Dissertation "The Relationship of Pupil Selconcept to Teacher-Pupil Dyadic Interaction in Kindergarten". Honors and Awards: Listed in *Who's Who in American Law, International Book of Honor, Directory of Distinguished Americans, World Who's Who of Women, International Register of Profiles, International Who's Who of Intellectuals, Biographical Roll of Honor, Community Leaders of America, Dictionary of International Biography*. Address: 12126 Forestwood Circle, Dallas, Texas 75234.■

STEPHEN D. BURSTEIN

Neurosurgeon. Personal: Born April 10, 1934; Son of Moe and Anna Burstein; Married Ronnie Sue Burstein; Father of Alisa Aimee. Education: B.A., University of Michigan, 1954; M.D., State University of New York, Downstate Medical Center, 1958; M.S., University of Minnesota, 1965. Military: Served in the United States Medical Corps, 1959-61, achieving the rank of Lieutenant; Battalion Surgeon 3rd Marine Division, Okinawa. Career: Neurosurgeon. Organizational Memberships: Nassau County Medical Society, Peer Review Committee; Medical Society of the State of New York, Interspecialty Committee (Neurosurgery); New York State Neurological Society, Peer Review Subcommittee President; South Nassau Community Hospital, President of Medical Staff. Community Activities: Long Island Hearing and Speech Society, First Vice President, Board of Directors. Honors and Awards: Team Physician, United States Deaf Olympic Team, 1970; Neurological Travel Award, Mayo Foundation, 1966; Alpha Omega Alpha; Sigma Xi. Address: 19 Bridle Path, Roslyn, New York 11576.■

STEVEN C. BURTNETT

Judiciary. Personal: Born July 29, 1942; Son of Joseph and Mildred Burtnett; Married Judith J., Daughter of Mrs. D. M. Lambert; Father of Steven Christian Jr. Education: B.S., Iowa State University of Science and Technology, 1964; J.D., University of California Hastings College of Law, 1967. Military: Served in the United States Marine Corps, receiving an Honorable Discharge in 1968. Career: Judiciary; Deputy District Attorney, Los Angeles County, 1968-74. Organizational Memberships: American Judges Association; California Court Commissioners Association; American Judicature Society; Los Angeles County Bar Association; Southeast District Bar Association. Community Activities: Chairman of the Board of Managers, Los Cerritos Young Men's Christian Association, 1981; Vice

President, Hastings College of Law Alumni Association, 1982; Sons of the American Revolution; Sons of Union Veterans of the Civil War. Religion: Methodist. Address: 16911 Coral Cay, Huntington Beach, California 92649. ■

WILLIAM JOSEPH BURTON

Program Manager, Professional Engineer. Personal: Born March 22, 1931; Son of Emory Goss and Olivia Copeland Burton. Education: B.S.M.E. 1957, M.S.M.E. 1964, University of South Carolina; Ph.D., Texas A&M University, 1970. Military: Served in the United States Army Military Police Corps, 1951-53, attaining the rank of Corporal. Career: Program Manager, Ocean Engineering, Department of the Navy, 1979 to present; Projects Manager, Tennessee Valley Authority, 1974-79; Assistant Professor, Mechanical and Aerospace Engineering, University of Tennessee, 1970-74; Assistant Professor, Ocean Engineering, Texas A&M University, 1970; Senior Project Engineer, General Motors Corporation, 1964-67; Dynamics Engineer Senior, Lockheed-Georgia Company, 1957-62. Organizational Memberships: American Society of Mechnical Engineers, Program Chairman and Secretary of the Ocean Engineering Division 1982 and 1983; Society of Naval Architects and Marine Engineers; National Society of Professional Engineers; International Platform Association. Community Activities: Exchange Club, Board Member, Chairman of Hospitality Committee 1975-76, Host at Quarter Horse Show 1976; University of South Carolina Society, Life Member; Combined Federal Campaign, Division Coordinator 1981; South Carolina Historical Society; National Board of Advisors, American Biographical Institute, 1982. Religion: Baptist, Choir Member 1949-51, Program Leader of Training Union 1958-62. Honors and Awards: Tau Beta Pi; Pi Tau Sigma; Sigma Xi; Fellow, International Biographical Association; Order of the Engineer; Fellow, American Biographical Institute; Citation for Outstanding Service to Combined Federal Campaign; Listed in *Notable Americans, Men of Achievement, Book of Honor.* Address: Route 1 Box 753, Iva, South Carolina 29655. ■

WENDELL E. BUSH

Attorney. Personal: Born December 10, 1943; Son of Mr. and Mrs. David Bush. Education: A.B., Philander Smith College, 1965; Further Study undertaken at Atlanta University, 1966; J.D., Emory University, 1969. Career: Attorney, Equal Employment Opportunity Commission; Former Attorney, Emory University School of Law Legal Clinic. Organizational Memberships: American Bar Association. Religion: Methodist. Honors and Awards: Listed in *Who's Who in Government, Directory of Distinguished Americans, Personalities of the South, Community Leaders of America, Who's Who in Community Service, Book of Honor, Biographical Roll of Honor.* Address: 3685 Winchester Park Circle #8, Memphis, Tennessee 38118. ■

EDWARD FRANKLYN BUTLER

Attorney at Law. Personal: Born July 1, 1937; Son of Arlene L. Butler; Father of Edward Franklyn II (Rhett), Jeffry Darrell. Education: B.A., University of Mississippi, 1958; J.D., Vanderbilt University School of Law, 1961; M.A. Criminal Justice, Memphis State University, 1984. Military: Served in the United States Air Force, receiving an Honorable Discharge in 1962; Presently Serving as Commander in the United States Naval Reserve. Career: Licensed to Practice Law in Tennessee and All Federal Courts, 1961; Admitted to Practice, United States Court of Appeals for the District of Columbia, 1978; Licensed to Practice Law in Texas, 1973; Certified as a Civil Trial Advocate by the National Board of Trial Advocacy; Private Practice as General Practitioner, Memphis, Tennessee, 1961 to present; Senior Vice President, Secretary, General Counsel, Safety First Fire Control Company, 1963 to present; Adjunct Professor, Law and Criminal Justice, Memphis State University, 1983; Secretary, General Counsel, Board of Directors, Hibbard, O'Connor & Weeks, Inc. (a nation-wide securities broker/dealer/underwriter), Houston, Texas, 1967-74; Partner, Butler and McDowell, Attorneys, 1967-71; Partner, Cobb and Butler, Attorneys, 1963-67; Associate Attorney, Erie S. Henrich, Attorney, 1963; Associate Attorney, Nelson, Norvell, Wilson and Thomason, Attorneys, 1961-63; Associate Director, Vanderbilt University Development Foundation, 1961. Organizational Memberships: American Bar Association, Member 1961 to present, Corporation, Banking and Business Law Section, Probate and Real Estate Law Section, Litigation Section, Committee on Litigation involving Securities and Subcommittee on Litigation with S.E.C. and N.A.S.D.; Tennessee Bar Association, Member 1961 to present, Legal Aid and Lawyer Referral Committee, Corporation and Banking Section, Securities Law Section, General Practice Section, Chairman State Bar College Committee 1982 to present; Memphis and Shelby County Bar Association, Member 1961 to present, Board of Directors 1979-81, Sponsor of Committee on Judicial Selections, Former Sponsor, Committee on Moral Fitness for Admission to Bar, Former Member Discipline and Ethics Committee, Former Secretary and Director Junior Bar Confernece, Lawyer Referral Service Panel; American Association of Trial Lawyers; Tennessee Association of Trial Lawyers; Memphis Trial Lawyers Association, Member 1963 to present, President 1982-83, Vice President 1970-71, Secretary 1969-70, Board of Directors 1966-71 and 1976-77, President 1982-83; Tennessee Criminal Defense Attorney's Association; Texas Bar Association, Former Member, Executive Council, Military Law Section; Memphis Area Legal Services Association, Board of Directors 1978-81, Chairman Bench and Bar Relations Committee, Co-Chairman By-laws Committee. Community Activities: Opera Memphis, Board of Directors 1978-81; West Tennessee Sportsman Association, Board of Directors 1979-81; American Heart Association, Memphis Chapter, Board of Directors 1979-82, Executive Committee 1978-79, General Counsel 1977-82, Cardiovascular Pulmonary Resuscitation Committee 1977 to prsent, Lawyers Chairman of Fund Raising Drive 1963 and 1976, Delegate to Tennessee Heart Association Annual Meeting 1978; Mid-America Ski Association, President 1978-81; Memphis Opera Guild; Chickasaw Council, Boy Scouts of America, Former Assstant Scoutmaster, Advancement Chairman, Troop Committee, Troop 34, Member Troop Committee of Troop 240, Former District Committee Member, Served as Chairman of Special Gifts Section, Sustaining Membership in Enrollment Drive, Advancement Chairman of Northeast District Committee, Eastern District Merit Badge Counselor; United States Navy League, Former Member Board of Directors of Memphis Chapter; Memphis Area Chamber of Commerce, Military Affairs Committee, Former Deputy Chairman for Navy Affairs, Houston Chamber of Commerce Military Affairs Committee; President, Memphis Chapter, Reserve Officers Association, 1983-84. Religion: Holy Communion Episcopal Church. Published Works: Author "Legal Implications of Patient Education" (1982), "Uninformed Consent" (1983), "Liability of Municipalities for Police Brutality" (in press), "The Need for Continuing Judicial Education" (1982), "Attitudes of Tennessee Criminal Court Jurists Concerning Competency of the Bar", "Insanity as a Defense: After Hinckley" (in press), "Police Abuse: Its Causes, Attempts at Correction and Two Suggestions for Reform". Honors and Awards: Invited to Speak at the American Bar Association Meeting on Litigation involving Securities Transactions, 1977; Speaker, Greater Aspen Medical-Legal Seminar, 1977; Co-Chairman, Moderator and Speaker, Memphis and Shelby County Continuing Legal Education Seminar, 1978; Invited to Testify as Expert at Arkansas Securities Division on Hearing on Revising Arkansas Securities Law, 1971; Special Attorney, Memphis Municipal Bond Dealers Association, 1971; Special Judge, General Sessions Court of Shelby County (Tennessee), Memphis and Shelby County Juvenile Court, City of Memphis Municipal Court, City of Memphis Traffic Court, Probate Court of Shelby County; Key to City of Memphis, 1973; Congressional Community Service Award, Congress of United States, 1978; Listed in *Who's Who in American Law, Who's Who in the South and Southwest, Who's Who in the United States, Men of Achievement, Dictionary of International Biography, Notable Americans, Personalities of the South, Book of Honor, Community Leaders and Noteworthy Americans.* Address: 59 North White Station Road, Memphis, Tennessee 38117. ■

REBECCA BATTS BUTLER

Educational Consultant, Adjunct Professor. Personal: Born November 29, 1910; Daughter of William Batts and Gussie Batts Overton (both deceased); Widow. Education: Teacher's Certificate, Virginia State College, 1933; B.S., Glassboro State College, 1944; M.Ed. 1950, Ed.D. 1965, Temple University. Career: Educational Consultant; Adjunct Professor, Glassboro State College; Former Positions include Director of Adult, Vocational, Continuing and Community Education, Supervisor of Guidance, Teacher of Secondary English, Teacher of Journalism, Elementary School Teacher (all in Camden, New Jersey). Organizational Memberships: National Education Association; New Jersey Education Association; New Jersey Association for Community Education; Association of Adult Education of New Jersey; American Association of University Women; New Jersey Organization of Teachers, Vice President 1980-82. Community Activities: National Council for the Advancement of Citizenship, Board Member 1981-84; National Red Cross of Camden County, Board Member 1970-84; Visiting Nurse and Health Association, Board President 1973-82; Camden County United Way, Allocation Panel Member 1970-84; American Association of Retired Persons, National Board President 1973-86; Planned Parenthood of Greater Camden, Vice President 1970-84; National Defense Advisory Committee on Women in the Services, 1972-74; Trustee Board, Thomas Edison College, 1972-76; Founded and Administered First School for Unwed Mothers in Camden, New Jersey, 1966; Founded First Spanish High School

Equivalency Program in South Jersey, 1969; International Platform Association, 1981-82. Religion: Organized the Committee on Education and Hostess Committee for Chestnut Street United African Methodist Episcopal Church (Camden, New Jersey); Presently Serving as a Stewardess of Church. Published Works: "Profiles of Outstanding Blacks in South Jersey during the 1960s, 1970s, 1980s," "Problems of Beginning Teachers" (1966); Published and Presented Scripts on Black History over Radio Stations. Honors and Awards: Certificate of Merit, Council for Advancement of Citizenship, 1982; Honorary Membership, Association of Community Education, 1982; Achievement Award, National Association of Negro Business and Professional Women, 1977; Educator of the Year, Southern New Jersey O.I.C., 1971; Service Award, Association Study of Afro-American Life and History, 1982; Outstanding Achievement in Education, Association of Adult Education of New Jersey, 1971; Appreciation Award, Spanish G.E.D. Program, 1974 and 1971; Merit Award, National Sorority Thi Delta Kappa, 1979; Distinguished Alumni, Glassboro State College, 1979; Over 30 Other Awards and Citations. Address: 15 Eddy Lane, Cherry Hill, New Jersey 08002.■

EDWARD T. BUYAMA, JR.

General, Electrical, Mechanical Contractor. Personal: Born February 1, 1933; Son of Edward T. and Gloria Buyama; Married Sandra Kay Mandeville; Father of Jeannie Sue, Carol Lynn, Helen Kay, Patricia Ann, Susan Edwina. Education: 2-year Equivalency, Furman University, 1952. Military: Served in the United States Air Force, 1950-53; Career: General, Electrical, Mechanical Engineer; Former Mechanical Inspector, Dade County, Florida. Organizational Memberships: American Society of Heating, Refrigerating, Air Conditioning Engineers; Refrigeration Service Engineers Society, Past President; State Electrical Masters Association, Immediate Past President; Associated Builders and Contractors, Political Action Committee; Florida Roofing, Sheetmetal and Air Conditioning Contractors Association, Governmental Affairs Committee. Community Activities: Building Official of Hialeah Gardens, Florida, 1980-81; Boys Club of America, Northwest Boys Club Gym, New Building, 1981; Ronald McDonald House of Miami, Board of Directors 1980. Religion: Miami Shores Baptist Church. Honors and Awards: Building Official of the Month, Bay Village, Florida. Address: 11611 West Biscayne Canal Road, Miami, Florida 33161.■

STRATTON FRANKLIN CALDWELL

Professor. Personal: Born August 25, 1926; Son of Dr. and Mrs. K. S. Caldwell (deceased); Married Sharee Deanna Ockerman, Daughter of Mrs. Emmabelle Ockerman; Father of Scott Raymond, Karole Elizabeth, Shannon Sharee Calder. Education: B.S. Education (Physical Education) 1951, Ph.D. Physical Education 1966, University of Southern California; M.S. Physical Education, University of Oregon, 1953. Military: Served in the United States Navy, 1944-46, attaining the rank of Pharmacists Mate Third Class. Career: Professor of Physical Education, Department of Physical Education, California State University, Northridge, California, 1971 to present; Visiting Associate Professor of Physical Education, Department of Ergonomics and Physical Education, University of California, Santa Barbara, California, 1969 (spring quarter); Associate Professor of Physical Education, Department of Physical Education, San Fernando Valley State College, Northridge, California, 1968-71; Visiting Associate Professor of Physical Education, Department of Physical Education (Women's), University of Washington, Seattle, Washington, Summer 1968; Assistant Professor of Physical Education, Department of Physical Education, San Fernando Valley State College, Northridge, California, 1965-68; Associate in Physical Education, Department of Physical Education, University of California, Los Angeles, California, 1957-65; Teacher (physical education, biology, social studies, health education) and Athletic Director, Queen Elizabeth Junior-Senior High School, Calgary, Alberta, Canada, 1956-57; Director of Physical Education, Regina Young Men's Christian Association, Regina, Saskatchewan, Canada, 1954-56; Teaching Assistant, Department of Physical Education, University of California, Los Angeles, California, 1953-54. Organizational Memberships: American Association for Health, Physical Education and Recreation, Fellow; American Association for the Achievement of Tension Control, Charter Member; American College of Sports Medicine, Fellow; California Association for Health, Physical Education and Recreation, International Committee on Comparative Physical Education, Charter Member; National Association for Physical Education in Higher Education, Charter Member; Vice President, Physical Education, Southern Saskatchewan Branch of Canadian Association for Health, Physical Education and Recreation, 1954-55; President, Southern Saskatchewan (Canada) Amateur Volleyball Association, 1954-55; Gymnastics Chairman, Saskatchewan Branch, Amateur Athletic Union of Canada, 1954-55; Prairie Provinces, Regina Representative Canadian Volleyball Association, 1955-56; Chairman, History and Policies Committee, California Association for Health, Physical Education and Recreation, 1962-64; Member, Physical Education Council, Southwest District, American Association for Health, Physical Education and Recreation, 1969-71; President, Los Angeles College and University Unit, California Association for Health, Physical Education and Recreation, 1969-70; Vice President, Physical Education, California Association for Health, Physical Education and Recreation, 1970-71; Member, Editorial Board, *CAHPER* (California) *Journal*, 1970-71; Member, Forum of the American Association for Health, Physical Education and Recreation, 1970-71; Member, Editorial Board, *The Physical Educator* (U.S.A.), 1972-74; Member, Editorial Board, *Canadian Journal of Health, Physical Education and Recreation*, 1973-75; Member, Centennial Commission, American Alliance for Health, Physical Education, Recreation and Dance, 1978 to present; Member, National Board of Advisors, American Biographical Institute, 1982 to present. Published Works: Author of Professional and Creative Publications including Several Books, Numerous Articles, and an Extensive Amount of Poetry. Honors and Awards: Fellow of the American Association for Health, Physical Education and Recreation 1962, American College of Sports Medicine 1965, Canadian Association for Health, Physical Education and Recreation 1971, Institute for the Advancement of Teaching and Learning California State University at Northridge (California) 1977, International Biographical Association 1978, American Biographical Institute 1979, International Academy of Poets 1980; Omega Xi Fraternity; Alpha Tau Omega Fraternity, Charter Member; Sigma Delta Psi Fraternity; Phi Epsilon Kappa Fraternity; Phi Delta Kappa Fraternity; Phi Kappa Phi Honor Society; Distinguished Service Award, Associated Students, University of California at Los Angeles, 1963; Distinguished Service Award, California Association for Health, Physical Education and Recreation, 1974; Silver Circle Award, Alpha Tau Omega Fraternity, 1976; Service Award, Phi Epsilon Kappa Fraternity, 1980; Listed in *Community Leaders and Noteworthy Americans, Dictionary of International Biography, Leaders in Education, International Who's Who in Community Service, International Who's Who of Intellectuals, Men and Women of Distinction, Men of Achievement, Personalities of America, Personalities of the West and Midwest.* Address: 80 North Kanan Road, Agoura, California 91301.■

RONALD STEVE CALINGER

Undergraduate College Dean. Personal: Born April 6, 1942; Son of Thomas and Mary Calinger; Married Betty Mikulecky; Father of John Michael. Education: A.B., Ohio University, 1963; M.A., University of Pittsburgh, 1964; Ph.D. History Science, University of Chicago, 1971. Career: Dean, Undergraduate College 1982 to present, Chairman History and Political Science Department 1977-82, Associate Professor History 1975 to present, Assistant Professor of History 1971-75, Instructor 1969-71, Rensselaer Polytechnic Institute. Organizational Memberships: American Historical Association; American Association for the Advancement of Science; History of Science Society, Co-Editor of *Isis Guide* 1983 to present; New York Academy of Sciences; American Society for 18th Century Studies (Northeast), Nominating Committee 1982; National Cabinet, University of Chicago Alumni Association. Honors and Awards: Author of *Gottfried Wilhelm Leibniz*; 1976; Editor of *Classics of Mathematics*, 1982; Prize in History of Sciences, Henry Schumann Prize 1968; Fellow, Ford Foundation 1968; Participant, National Endowment for the Humanities Pilot Grant (Division of Education), A Program in the Study of Human Dimensions of Science and Technology at Rensselaer.■

JAMES R. CALLAN

Researcher. Personal: Son of Mr. and Mrs. Ruskin Callan; Married Earlene Shewmaker; Father of James P., Kelley, Kristi, Diane. Education: Graduate, Jesuit High School, Dallas, Texas; B.A., St. Mary's University; M.A., University of Oklahoma, 1967; Undertook Studies toward Ph.D. Career: Consultant, Aerospace Research Laboratory; Researcher, Schlumberger Research Center, 1970 to present, Began Work on V.L.S.I. Design Techniques 1981; Co-founder, C. Systems, Ltd. (advertising research firm); Current Research in the Area of Artificial Intelligence; Publisher of *Advantages* (advertising research newsletter). Organizational Memberships: Institute of Electrical and Electronic Engineers; Mathematical Association of America; Association for Computing Machinery; Institute of Electrical and Electronic Engineers Computer Group. Community Activities: Volunteer Work with Teenagers; Oak Cliff Civic Theatre, Dallas, Texas, President 2 Years; Town Tennis Tournaments, Director 4 Years. Honors and Awards; Received 3 Grants from the National Science Foundation; Fellowship, National Aeronautics and Space Administration; Grant, Data Processing Management Association. Address: 332 North Salem Road, Ridgefield, Connecticut 06877.■

DOROTHY S. CAMERON

Educator. Personal: Born January 12, 1927; Daughter of William O. Simmons (deceased) and Ola N. Simmons; Married Archie N. Cameron; Mother of Toni Cameron-Vincent, Andre Cameron. Education: B.S., North Carolina Agricultural and Technical State University, 1948; M.Ed. 1964, Ed.D. 1980, University of North Carolina at Greensboro. Career: Assistant Professor of Business Education and Administrative Services; Secretary, North Carolina Agricultural Extension Service. Organizational Memberships: Alpha Kappa Mu National Honor Society; National Business Education Association; North Carolina Business Education Association; Southern Business Education Association; American Association of University Professors, Past Member; Delta Pi Epsilon, Member Zeta Chapter; Pi Omega Pi; National Collegiate Association of Secretaries. Community Activities: Washington School Parent-Teacher Association, (Planning Committee 1967-68, Chaperone on Tour to Morehead Planetarium); Dudley High School Parent-Teacher Association, Planning Committee, 1967-68; North Carolina Agricultural and Technical State University Alumni Association; University of North Carolina-Greensboro Alumni Association; Greensboro Civic Ballet Auxiliary, Committee on Communication and Social Activities, 1967-68; Brown Summit High School, Consultant, Career Day; Booker T. Washington High School, Reidsville, North Carolina, Consultant Career Day; Pearson Street Young Women's Christian Association, Membership, Collection 1968-69; Bluford School, Membership and Collection 1968-69, Consultant to Self-Study Committee on School's Philosophy 1969-70; Guilford Technical Institute, Special Study Tour on Vocational

TWO THOUSAND NOTABLE AMERICANS

Educational Opportunities 1969-70; Lincoln Parent-Teacher Association, Chairman of Hospitality Committee and Orientation Activities 1970-71, Executive Committee 1971-72, 1972-73; Family Service Traveler's Aid Association of Greensboro, Inc., Collegiate and Community Affairs Conference; Lincoln Junior High School Parent-Teacher Association, Hospitality Committee and Orientation Activities 1970-71; Chamber of Commerce Citizen's Tour of City to Study Water and Sewer Facilities Prior to Voting for Bond Issues, 1970-71; Eastern Music Festival Auxiliary, Committee on Communication 1972-73, Membership Committee 1974-75, Board Member 1974-75; Lincoln Junior High School Open House, Executive and Hospitality Committees 1973-74; National Honor Society Induction Service, 1974-75. Religion: Providence Baptist Church, Member 1972 to present, Committee Member, General Green Council, Boy Scouts of America 1972-73, Committee on Banquet Preparation 1973-74, Introduced Speaker, Missionary Circle No. 1 Anniversary Program 1972-73, Committee Member, Investitude Service, Girl Scouts of America 1974-75; St. James Presbyterian Church, Greensboro, North Carolina, Guest Speaker, Installation of Garden Council Officers, 1970-71; St. Stephen United Church of Christ, Member 1939-72, Sunday School Teacher, Usher, Choir Member, Secretary, Girl Scout Council Member. Published Works: Author of Professional Articles, Proceedings, Proposals, including "Word Processing: An Innovative Concept at North Carolina Agricultural and Technical State University," "A New School Emerges," and *A Study of Program Relevance and Student Preparation in Business Education and Administration and Administrative Services Curricular Programs with Respect to Business Employment Experiences of the Graduates of the North Carolina Agricultural and Technical State University* (Ed.D. Dissertation 1980, The University of North Carolina at Greensboro). Honors and Awards: North Carolina Agricultural and Technical State University, Alpha Kappa Mu National Honor Society 1946, Editor-in-Chief, The Register, Student Publication 1947, Pacesetters Award, University Foundation, Inc. 1967, Piedmont University Center Faculty Study Grant 1968, Summer Study Grant 1968, Summer Study Grant 1970, Pi Omega Pi 1974; Delta Pi Epsilon National Honor Society for Business Educators, University of North Carolina at Greensboro, 1966; Grant to Participate in Tri-Faculty Workshop, Texas Southern, Houston, 1970; Award to Study, Certificate, Data Processing Systems Designs for Users Department Managers, International Business Machines Center, New York City, 1971; Grant to Participate in Instructional Media Laboratory Workshop, University of Wisconsin-Milwaukee, 1971; A.I.D.P. Faculty Study Grant, Summer Session, 1975, 1977; W. K. Kellogg, Fellow 1976-77, Fellowship Certificate 1979; Board of Governors' Faculty Doctoral Study Assignment Award for Academic Year, 1979-80; Listed in *Dictionary of International Biography, Two Thousand Women of Achievement, Who's Who of American Women, World Who's Who of Education, International Who's Who in Education, Community Leaders and Noteworthy Americans.* Address: 1002 Julian Street, Greensboro, North Carolina 27406.■

ROY WILLIAM CAMBLIN, III

Director and Designer of Management Information Systems. Personal: Born January 5, 1947, in San Antonio, Texas; Married Jane Anne Day on April 20, 1981; Father of Samuel B. Education: B.S. Business Administration/Marketing, Florida State University, 1969; M.S. Systems Management, University of Southern California, 1977; Credits towards M.B.A. and Ph.D. Political Science, 1970-79; Management and Technical Service Schools, 1969-81; Air Command and Staff College, Certificate, 1978; Airline Transport Pilot, Numerous Type Ratings. Career: Supply Operations Officer, 1969-71; Instructor Pilot and Flight Examiner, 1972-81; Operations Analyst and Planner, 1976-78; Major Fiscal Program Administrator, 1979-81; Operations Analyst and Planner, 1976-78; Major Fiscal Program Administrator, 1978-81; Management Information Systems, Director/Designer, 1981 to present; Seven Years Experience in High Visibility Public Speaking. Organizational Memberships: Hereditary Member, Order of Daedalians; Hawaii Chamber of Commerce; Hawaii World Trade Association; Small Business Association. Published Works: Numerous Documents Ranging from Research Studies in Systems Management and Behavior Modification to Sensitive U.S. Defense Plans. Honors and Awards: Distguished Graduate, 1977; National Honors Society; Four National Awards for Meritorious Service. Address: P.O. Box 2048, San Francisco, California 94126.■

RONDO CAMERON

Educator. Personal: Born February 20, 1925; Son of Burr S. and Annie Mae Cameron (both deceased); Married Claydean Zumbrunnen; Father of Alan, Cindia. Education: A.B. magna cum laude, Ecomomics/Mathematics 1948, A.M. Economics/History 1949, Yale University; Ph.D., Economics/Sociology, University of Chicago, 1952. Military: Served in the United States Navy, Naval Aviation, 1942-46, attaining the rank of Lieutenant (j.g.). Career: Instructor in Ecomomics, Yale University, 1951-62; University of Wisconsin, Assistant Professor of Economics and History 1952-56, Associate Professor of Economics and History 1957-61, Professor of Economics and History 1961-69, Founder, Director, Graduate Program in Economic History, 1960-69; Visiting Professor of Economics, University of Chicago, 1956-57; Special Field Staff, Rockefeller Foundation, Santiago, Chile, 1965-67. Organizational Memberships: Economic History Association, President 1974-75; International Association of Economic History, Member and Executive Committee Member 1973 to present; *Journal of Economic History,* Editor 1975-81; Cliometric Society, Charter Member; American Historical Association; American Economic Association; Society for French National Studies. Community Activities: Albert Schweitzer Fellowship, New York Member, Board of Directors 1973 to present; Fulbright American Graduate Student Program, Member, National Screening Committee, 1980 and 1981; National Endowment for the Humanitites, Consultant-Panelist; National Science Foundation, Consultant-Panelist; Atlanta Committee on Foreign Relations, Member, Speakers Council 1977 to present; Phi Beta Kappa Associates, Lecturer 1977-81; National Convocation of Kenan Professors, Member, Program Planning Committee, 1982. Honors and Awards: Phi Beta Kappa, Yale University, 1948; Fulbright Scholarship, France, 1950-51; Social Science Research Council Awards, 1953, 1956, 1960, 1962; Guggenheim Fellowships, 1954-56, 1970-71; Fellow, Center for Advanced Studies in the Behavioral Sciences, 1958-59; Fellow, Woodrow Wilson International Center for Scholars, 1974-75; Fulbright Visiting Research Professor, University of Glasgow, Scotland, 1962-63; Rockefeller Foundation Grants for Research, 1961-65, 1980-81. Address: 1088 Clifton Road, Northeast, Atlanta, Georgia 30307.■

RENE D. CAMONIER

Field Service Engineer, Petroleum Chemical Field. Personal: Born May 26, 1929; Son of William (deceased) and Johanna P. Camonier; Father of Peter, Leslie, Juanita. Education: Manufacturing Management, Production Industry Process and Control, Industrial Engineering, Marquette University, Wisconsin; Systems Analysis, E.D.P., A.D.P., M.R.P., M.I.S., Milwaukee Institute of Technology; Higher Math, University of Amsterdam; B.S.M.E., University Delft, M.S. Maritime Engineering, Maritime Naval Academy Holland; Certified Maritime Naval Instrumentation. Career: Field Service Engineer, Petroleum Chemical Field, Heat Exchangers, Cooling Towers and Condensors; European Experience in Dry-Dock Construction, Project Management, All Phases of Steel, Foundry, Sheet Metal, Assy Manufacturing Operations, Purchasing, Refinery Site Operations, Harbour Operations; Plant Engineer, Acting Plant Manager, Houston, Texas, 1981; Chief Industrial Engineer, Rockford Dropforce Company, Rockford, Illinois, 1978-81; Staff Production Engineer, Acting Division Consulting Engineer, Colt Industries, Crucible Division Inc., Midland, Pennsylvania, 1974-78; Consulting Engineer, Project Manager, Self-Employed, Kamaz-River Complex Project, U.S.S.R., 1971-73; Associate Engineering Consultant, Westover Corporation Consultants, Milwaukee, Wisconsin, 1966-71; Assistant General Manager, Paper and Corrugated Manufacturing, Wisconsin, 1965-66 and 1962-65; Private Pilot, Ex-Captin Passenger Cargo Liner. Honors and Awards: First Class Citations, State of Wisconsin, City of Milwaukee, 1966. Address: 2220 Avenida La Quinta, #317, Houston, Texas.■

BETTY CARLSON CAMPAZZI

Commission Field Representative. Personal: Born December 16, 1926; Daughter of Simon A. (deceased) and Evelina Carlson; Married Earl James Campazzi; Mother of Earl James II. Education: Diploma, The Johns Hopkins University, Baltimore, Maryland; B.S., M.A., Ed.D., Teachers College, Columbia University, New York, New York; Additional Studies. Career: Field Representative, Joint Commission on Accreditation of Hospitals, Chicago, Illinois, Currently; Lecturer (in conjunction with doctoral study) Behrend College, Pennsylvania State University, Erie, Pennsylvania, 1979; Consultant and Project Director, Mercyhurst College, Erie, Pennsylvania, 1975; Director of Nursing, Doctors Hospital, Erie, Pennsylvania, 1972-75; Medical-Surgical Coordinator, Hamot Medical Center School of Nursing, Erie, Pennsylvania, 1971-72; Consultant and Administrator (short-term contract), Edinboro Medical Center, Edinboro, Pennsylvania, 1970-71; Teacher, Nursing, Day High School, New York City Board of Education, New York, New York, 1968-70; Assisted in Development of 2 Separate Group Physician Practices (in sequence), Claude E. Forkner, M.D., Private Clinic, New York, New York, 5 Years; Staff Nurse and Assistant Head Nurse, Medical-Surgical, The New York Hospital-Cornell Medical Center, New York, New York, 2 Years; Head, Private Medical-Surgical, The Johns Hopkins Hospital, Baltimore, Maryland, 2 Years. Organizational Memberships: Alumni Association of the Johns Hopkins University, Executive Committee, Metropolitan New York, Vice

TWO THOUSAND NOTABLE AMERICANS

President, Past Secretary; Alumni Federation of Columbia University; Nursing Education Alumni Association, Teachers College, Columbia University; American Association for the Advancement of Science, New York Academy of Science; American Association of University Women; American Nurses' Association, Member Council on Continuing Education; American Association of Allied Health; National League for Nursing; Southern Region League for Nursing; Southern Region League for Nursing; Pennsylvania Nurses Association; New York State Nurses Association; New York State Public Health Association; The Hospital Association of Pennsylvania; Pennsylvania Society for Nurse Administrators; Pennsylvania Society for Health Planning. Community Activities: Nurses, Coalition for Action in Politics (N-CAP); Politically Responsible Nurses of Pennsylvania (PRN), Past Secretary, Past Treasurer and Board of Directors; Erie County Emergency Medical Services, Erie, Pennsylvania, Board of Directors, Past Secretary and Past Treasurer; Erie Philharmonic, Membership Committee; Erie Philharmonic Women's Association, Board of Directors, Past Secretary; Mercyhurst College, Death and the Future Lecture Series, Advisory Committee; Erie County District 10, PNA, Past President and Past Chairman Legislative Committee; Lake Area Health Education Life Consortium (LAHEC), Erie, Pennsylvania, Board of Directors; United Way of Pennsylvania; Reapportionment Commission, Erie County, Pennsylvania; Vial-for-Life Project, Erie, Pennsylvania, Director; Senior Citizens Health Care Council, Erie, Pennsylvania, Chairman, Board of Trustees. Published Works: "Nurses, Nursing and Malpractice Litigation," *Nursing Administration Quarterly*, Fall 1980. Honors and Awards: Kappa Delta Pi; Pi Lambda Theta; Phi Delta Kappa; Sigma Theta Tau; Listed in *Leaders in American Science, Who's Who in the East, Community Leaders of America, Personalities of America, International Register of Profiles*. Address: R.D. #1, 3970 Crane Road, Edinboro, Pennsylvania 16412.■

CLIFTON P. CAMPBELL, JR.

Professor of Vocational-Technical Education. Personal: Born July 5, 1938; Son of Clifton P. (deceased) and Kathleen M. Campbell; Married Linda Lee Reavis, Daughter of Edward L. (deceased) and Rhuama A. Reavis; Father of Scott Alan, Douglas Eric. Education: B.S., California University of Pennsylvania, 1964; M.Ed. 1968, Ed.D. 1971, University of Maryland; Postdoctoral Studies undertaken at the University of Maryland and the University of Delaware. Military: Service in the United States Naval Reserve, 1955 to present, with the rank of Commander. Career: Professor of Vocational-Technical Education, The University of Tennessee at Knoxville; Former Positions include Training Advisor to the Royal Saudi Naval Forces (Dammam, Saudi Arabia), Education Specialist to the Ministry of Labor and Social Affairs (Riyadh, Saudi Arabia), Dean of Instruction at Delaware Technical and Community College, Coordinator of Undergraduate Occupational Teacher Education at the University of Delaware. Organizational Memberships: Technical Assistance Corps, United States Department of Labor, 1976 to present; Iota Lambda Sigma; Epsilon Pi Tau; Omicron Tau Theta; American Industrial Arts Association; American Vocational Association. Community Activities: Advisory Board, West Lake Industrial Vocational School, Taipei, Taiwan, 1971-72; Naval Reserve Association; Reserve Officers Association; Fleet Reserve Association; Navy League of the U.S.; The Naval Club, London; Columbia Lodge #285 Ancient Free & Accepted Masons; Scottish Rite; York Rite; Shriner. Religion: Presbyterian. Honors and Awards: Letter of Appreciation, Assistant Secretary of the Department of the Army, 1971; Outstanding Research Award 1975, Certificate of Appreciation 1981, American Industrial Arts Association. Address: 1420 Moorgate Drive, Knoxville, Tennessee 37922.■

DAVID G. CAMPBELL

Executive. Personal: Born May 2, 1930, in Oklahoma City, Oklahoma; Son of La Vada (Ray) Henager Campbell and Lois Raymond Henager; Married Janet Newland, March 1, 1958; Father of Carl David. Education: B.S. Geology, University of Tulsa, Oklahoma, 1953; M.S. Geology, University of Oklahoma, Norman, Oklahoma, 1957. Military; Served in the United States Naval Reserve from 1949-53 and in the United States Army from 1953-55. Career: Petroleum Geologist, Lone Star Producing Company, 1957-65; Tenneco Oil Company, Exploration Project Geologist, Denver, Colorado and Oklahoma City 1965-71, District Exploration Geologist, Oklahoma City 1971-73, Division Geological Consultant, Mid-Continent Division, Oklahoma City, 1973-77; Exploration Manager, Mid-Continent Division, Leede Exploration, Oklahoma City 1977-80; President, Earth Hawk Exploration, Oklahoma City, 1980 to present; Vice President/Division Manager, PetroCorp, 1983 to present. Organizational Memberships: American Association of Petroleum Geologists, Member 1956 to present, Information Committee 1968 National AAPG-SEPM Convention, Field Trips Chairman 1978 National AAPG-SEPM Convention, House of Delegates Member 1980-83 and 1983-86, National Chairman House of Delegates 1981-82, Member Executive Committee 1981-82, AAPG Foundation Trustee Associate, 1983 to present; Oklahoma City Geological Society Member 1957 to present, Public Relations Chairman of Speakers Bureau 1963-64, Chairman Stratigraphic Code Committee 1967-68; Presidential Appointee to Executive Board 1968-69, School Volunteer Program Oklahoma City Public Schools 1969-70, Advertising Manager of *Shale Shaker*, 1969-70 and 1970-71; Representative in AAPG House of Delegates 1980-83 and 1983-86; American Petroleum Institute; Oklahoma Independent Petroleum Association; Oklahoma Ctiy Geological Discussion Group, President 1975-76; Tulsa Geological Society; Independent Petroleum Association of America; Sigma Xi; New York Academy of Sciences; American Association for the Advancement of Science. Community Activities: Boy Scouts of America, Last Frontiers Council 1960-73, Education Chairman of Eagle District 1963-67; Assistant Scoutmaster of Wiley Post District 1971-73; Oklahoma County Representative, Cherokee Nation, 1976-78; Cherokee National Historical Society, Board of Directors, Chairman Heritage Council Solicitation Committee 1983-84; Oklahoma Historical Society; Thomas Gilcrease Museum Association; Museum of the Cherokee Indian Association; United States Chamber of Commerce; Oklahoma City Chamber of Commerce. Published Works: Three Articles (with Janet Campbell), "The MacIntosh Family Among the Cherokees," "Cherokee Participation in the Political Impact of the North American Indian," "the Wolf Clan," Each Published in *Journal of Cherokee Studies*. Honors and Awards: Petroleum Heritage Certificate of Recognition, Oklahoma-Kansas Oil and Gas Association, 1982; Listed in *Who's Who in the South and Southwest, Who's Who in Finance and Industry, Who's Who in the World, The Oklahoma Petroluem Industry* by Kenny A. Franks. Address: 6109 Woodbridge Road, Oklahoma City, Oklahoma 73132.■

MAXINE ELIZABETH CAMPBELL

Workshop Conductor, Educator. Personal: Born February 26, 1933; Daughter of William Holt and Elizabeth Jane (Napier) Shackelford (deceased); Married Oscar Hobert Campbell, Son of G. P. and Sally Ann (Combs) Campbell; Mother of Venita Kaye, Marc Eugene. Education: Associate Education, Lees Junior College, 1953; Associate Elementary Education, Miami University, 1957; Reading 1969, M.A. Curriculum and Supervision 1980, Wright State University. Career: Chairperson of Staff Development for Northwest City Schools, 1983-84; Writing Consultant (Creative and Functional Writing), Conducts Workshops in the Midwest; Wright State University Workshop Conductor, Northmont City Schools, Currently; Educator, Talawanda School District 1954-62, Oxford, Ohio 1964-, Northmont City Schools. Organizational Memberships: Northmond District Education Association; Ohio Education Association; National Education Association; Montgomery County I.R.A.; Ohio I.R.A.; International I.R.A.; Phi Delta Kappa; Kappa Delta Pi; National Council of Teachers of English; Curriculum and Supervision Association; International Platform Association. Religion: Methodist, Choir Member 1966-70, Chairperson Education Commission 1974. Honors and Awards: Prom Queen, 1951; May Queen, 1953; 25-Year Service Pin, 1980; Kentucky Colonel Award, 1960; Listed in *Who's Who, Personalities of America, Dictionary of International Biography*. Address: 6425 Noranda Drive, Dayton, Ohio 45415.■

JOSE L. CANGIANO

Medical Doctor, Medical Director. Personal: Born April 29, 1936, in Ponce, Puerto Rico; Son of Leonor and Jose L.; Married Genoveva, Daughter of Fructuoso and Carmen; Father of Lizette M., Jose L., Thomas G., Michelle D. Education: B.S. Chemistry, Catholic University of Puerto Rico, Ponce, Puerto Rico, 1956; Attended School of Medicine, University of Puerto Rico, San Juan, 1956-60; Internship: Mercy Hospital, Buffalo, New York, 1960-61; Residency, Medical, Bergen County Hospital, Paramus, New Jersey, 1963-65; Clinical Fellow, Division of Vascular Diseases and Nephrology, Hahneman Medical College and Hospital, Philadelphia, Pennsylvania, 1965-66; Research Fellow, National Institute of Health Division of Vascular Diseases and Nephrology, Hahnemann Medical College and Hospital, Philadelphia, Pennsylvania, 1966-67; Additional Medical Courses. Military: Served in the United States Medical Corps, Active Duty 1961-63. Career: Assistant in Medicine, Division of Nephrology and Hypertension, Mount Sinai Hospital of Cleveland, Ohio, 1967-69; Chief, Hypertension Unit, Mount Sinai Hospital of Cleveland, Ohio, 1968-69; Staff Nephrologist, Veterans Administration Hospital, San Juan, Puerto Rico, 1969-76; Assistant Clinical Professor, School of Medicine, University of Puerto Rico, 1971-76; Consultant in Nephrology, Medicine and Pediatric Departments, San Juan City Hospital, 1971 to present; Associate Member, American Physiological Society, 1973 to present; Chief, Hypertension Section Medical Service, VA Hospital, San Juan, Puerto Rico, 1975 to present; Member, Puerto Rico and Virgin Island End-Stage Renal Disease, Coordinating Council, 1975 to present; Associate Professor, School of Medicine, University of Puerto Rico, 1976 to present; Acting Chief, Renal Section, VA Hospital, San Juan, Puerto Rico, 1978-79; Professor of Medicine, School of Medicine, University of Puerto Rico, 1982 to present; Visiting Professor to Several Hospitals, Sessions, Courses and Universities. Organizational Memberships: American Society of Nephrology, 1967 to present; American Medical Association, 1968 to present; Society for Artificial Internal Organs, 1968 to present; Puerto Rico Medical Association, 1970 to present; American Federation for Clinical Research, 1971 to present; International Society of Nephrology, 1971 to present; International Society of Nephrology, 1971 to present; Editorial Board-Boletin Asociacion Medica de Puerto Rico, 1970 to present; Latin American Society of Nephrology, 1974 to present; International Society of Hypertension, 1976 (by invitation); Hemodialysis Technician Society of Puerto Rico, 1976, Honorary Member; Society for Experimental Biology and Medicine, 1977 to present; American Physiological Society, 1977 to present; Interamerican Society of Hypertension, 1978 to present (by invitation); Council on the Kidney, American Heart Association, 1973 to present; Council for High Blood Pressure Research, American Heart Association, 1973 to present; Southern Society for Clinical Investigation, 1979 (by invitation); American Association for the Advancement of Science, 1980; New York Academy of Sciences, 1981. Published Works: Author of Numerous Papers Presented at Medical Meetings, Numerous Abstracts and Articles, and Several Chapters in Books. Honors and Awards: Fellow of the National Foundation for Infantile Paralysis, 1958; Fellow of the National Institute of Health, 1966-67; Sociedad de Medicina Nuclear de Puerto Rico, Miembro Fundador, 1971 to present; President, Scientific Committee Puerto Rico Medical Association, 1971; Member, New Curriculum Committee Human Biology II, School of Medicine, University of Puerto Rico, 1972 to present; Member, Research and Education Committee, Veterans Administration Hospital, 1972 to present; Member, Advisory Committee in Health Problems to the President of the University of Puerto Rico, 1973-74; Consultant in Research, Upper Atlantic Region of the American Heart Association, 1973 to present; President, Scientific Committee, Puerto Rico Medical Association, 1973; President, Nephrology Section, Puerto Rico Medical Association, 1973, 1974, 1979; President, Grievance Committee, Puerto Rico Medical Association, 1973; Chairman, Research and Education Committee, VA Hospital, 1974 to present; Editor, *Buletin Asociacion Medica de Puerto Rico*, 1974-78; Chairman, Organizing Committee, Third International Cardiac Output Workshop, 1975-76; Treasurer, Organizing Committee, Fourth International Workshop on Cardiac Output, 1976-77; Scientific Council, Inter-American Society of Hypertension, 1978 to present; Assembly Delegate, Council of the Kidney in Cardiovasculary Diseases, American Heart Association, 1980; Chairman Session on Clinical Hypertension "Curso de Hipertension Arterial" Universidad Catolica de Chile, 1981; Chairman Session on Hemodynamics and Vascular Smooth Muscle in the Interamerican Society of Hypertension Meeting in Vina del Mar, 1981; Member, Nominating Committee of the Interamerican Society of Hypertension, 1981 to present. Address: R.F.D. #3-39H, Rio Piedras, Puerto Rico 00928.■

BARBARA E. M. CANNON

Higher Education Administrator. Education: B.A. Music 1957, M.A. Music 1965, San Francisco State University; French Pedagogy, University of Paris (Sorbonne), 1966-67; M.A. 1975, Ed.D. l977, Stanford University; Administrative Credential, University of California-Berkeley, l973; M.A. l975, Ed.D. l977, Stanford University. Career: Assistant Dean, College of Alameda; Research Associate/Project Coordinator, Instructional Strategies, Stanford University, 1977-78; Research Assistant, Center for Educational Research 1974-75; Administrative Assistant to National Director, Teacher Corps, United States Office of Education, 1975-76; Teacher, Staff Development Associate and Administrator, Berkeley Public Schools, 1958-74. Organizational Memberships: Blace Aces, Cultural and Educational Society, President and Founding Member 1971; Pi Lambda Theta; Phi Delta Kappa; Association of California Community College Administrators. Community Activities: Berkeley Public Schools, Coordinator of Educational Workshops for Staff Development, 1972, 1973, and 1974, Coordinator of Cadre in Organization Development 1973-74; Team Leader of Intergroup Education Project and Human Relations Project, 1968, 1969, 1970, 1971; Portland, Oregon Public Schools, Educational Consultant 1973; Far West Educational Laboratory, Educational Consultant, 1978; United States Office of Education, Educational Consultant, Teacher Corps 1978; Phillips Temple Methodist Church, Berkeley, California, Choir Director and Organist 1957-62. Honors and Awards: Presser Foundation Scholarship, 1956; Outstanding Senior Award, Mu Phi Epsilon Chapter, San Francisco State University, 1957; Senior Recital, San Francisco State University, Piano and Flute, 1957; Governmental Fellowship, University of Ghana, Summer 1969; Sabbatical Year, University of Paris (Sorbonne), 1966-67; Sabbatical Year, Stanford University, 1974-75. Address: 2101 Shoreline Drive #458, Alameda, California 94501.■

MARIA-LUISE CAPUTO-MAYR

Educator. Personal: Daughter of Leopoldine and Emil Mayr of Austria; Married Lucio Caputo; Mother of Giorgio. Education: Interpreters and Translators Degrees, 1963; Teaching Licenses in German, Italian, English; Ph.D., University of Vienna, 1966. Career: Professor of German, Temple University, Philadelphia, Pennsylvania, 1968 to present; Assistant Lecturer, German-Italian, Barking Regional College, London, 1966-67; Assistant in German, Burlington Girls School, London, 1965-66. Organizational Memberships: Founder, Executive Director, Past President, Kafka Society of America; Modern Language Association; A.A.T.G.; Interpreters Association; Executive Secretary, American Council for the Study of Austrian Literature. Community Activities: Organizer and Fund-raiser for Various Scholarly Projects. Published Works: Two Collections of Kafka Essays, 1977, 1978; Bibliography of Kafkas Works, 1982; Editor, *Newsletter of the Kafka Society of America*, 1977 to present; Articles in Numerous Scholarly Journals. Address: 160 East 65th Street, Apt. 2C, New York, New York 10021.■

MARILYN E. CARENS

Investment Broker. Personal: Born September 30, 1944; Daughter of Edward B. Daily; Married Edward M. Carens; Mother of Kelley Mary, Mark Joseph, Heidi Elizabeth. Education: Attended the Academy of Assumption, 1961; B.A. cum laude, Classics, Regis College, 1965; M.B.A., Babson College, 1977. Career: Investment Broker; Former Salesperson (top in the country), Xerox Corporation.■

JAMES GORDON CARLSON

Educator. Personal: Born January 24, 1908; Son of James August and Mabel Johns Carlson (both deceased); Married Elizabeth Shirley; Father of Shirley Johns Bowen, Bette Walker Schrader, James Marvin. Education: Bachelor of Liberal Arts 1930, Ph.D. 1935, University of Pennsylvania. Career: Assistant in Zoology, University of Pennsylvania, Philadelphia, 1929-30; Bryn Mawr College, Bryn Mawr, Pennsylvania, Demonstrator in Biology 1930-31, Instructor in Biology 1931-35; University of Alabama-Tuscaloosa, Instructor in Zoology 1935-39, Assistant Professor of Zoology 1939-45, Associate Professor of Zoology 1945-46; Instructor in Cytology, Mountain Lake Biological Station, University of Virginia, Summer 1936; Guest Investigator, Carnegie Institute of Washington, Cold Spring Harbor, Summers 1937, 1938, 1940; Rockefeller Fellow in the Natural Sciences, Genetics Laboratory, University of Missouri, 1940-41; United States Public Health Service, Associate Biologist Summer 1943, Biologist Summers 1945, 1946, Special Consultant in Biology 1943-46, 1947-48, Special Fellow University of Heidelberg, Germany 1964-65; Senior Biologist, National Institute of Health, Bethesda, Maryland, 1946-47; Consultant in Biology, Biology Division, Oak Ridge National Laboratory, Oak Ridge, Tennessee, 1947-78; University of Tennessee-Knoxville, Head, Department of Zoology and Entomology 1947-67, Professor of Zoology 1947-78, Director Institute of Radiation Biology 1955-75, Alumni Distinguished Service Professor 1962-78, Professor Emeritus of Zoology 1978 to present. Organizational Memberships: American Association for the Advancement of Science, Fellow, Vice President 1955; American Society for Cell Biology; Association of Southeastern Biologists; Radiation Research Society, Member Board of Editors *Radiation Research* 1972-74; Tennessee Academy of Science, President 1961; National Research Council, Committee on Fellowships in Biology and Agriculture 1950-52, Evaluation Panel for National Science Foundation, Predoctoral Fellowships and Postdoctoral Associateships 1962, Cooperative Graduate Fellowships and Summer Fellowships for Graduate Teaching Assistants 1963-65, Summer Fellowships for Graduate Teaching Assistants 1966. Published Works: Many Contributions to Scientific Books and Journals in the Fields of Descriptive and Experimental Cytology, and Particularly the Effects of Ultraviolet and Ionizing Radiations on Chromosomes and Cell Division. Honors and Awards: Pennsylvania State Scholarship, 1925-29;

Pennsylvania Senatorial Scholarship, 1926-29; Alpha Epsilon Delta; Phi Beta Kappa; Phi Sigma; Sigma Xi; Phi Kappa Phi. Address: 2134 Island Home Boulevard, Knoxville, Tennessee 37920.■

RICHARD LAWRENCE CARLSON

Aerospace Company Executive. Personal: Born April 12, 1937, in Providence; Son of Hans Lawrence and Bertha May (Strom) Carlson; Married Johanna Mary Cornell on August 27, 1960; Father of Richard Lawrence, Suellen Marie. Education: B.S. Management Engineering, Rensselaer Polytechnic Institute, 1964; M.B.A., University of Connecticut, 1973. Career: Industrial Engineer, Johnson and Johnson, Watervliet, New York, 1961-64; Quality Control Engineer, Corning Glass Works, New York, 1964; Industrial Engineer, United Technologies, East Hartford, Connecticut 1965-66; Supervisor Industrial Engineering 1966-68, General Supervisor Material Movement Planning 1968-76, Materials Engine Program Manager 1977 to present. Organizational Memberships: Board of Directors, Woodland Summit Water Association, 1965-67; American Management Association; Society for the Advancement of Management; American Institute of Industrial Engineers, Director 1965, Treasurer 1966-67, Seminar Chairman 1967-68; National and Connecticut Societies Professional Engineers; International Material Management Society; Phi Kappa Phi; Beta Gamma Sigam; Alpha Phi Omega. Community Activities: Democrat; Mensa; Member Executive Board, Long River Council Boy Scouts of America, Hartford, 1975 to present; First Company Governor's Horse Guards Connecticut; Rockville Fish and Game Club; British Balloon and Airship Club; National Rifle Association; Lighter Than Air Society; Balloon Federation, American; Buckskin Shirts. Religion: Lutheran. Honors and Awards: Recipient Wheel Award, *Modern Manufacturing Magazine*, 1968; Registered Professional Engineer, Massachusetts, California; Certified Manufacturing Engineer, Material Management, Material Handling; Irving Subway Corporation Grantee, 1962-63. Address: 28 Willie Circle, Tolland, Connecticut 06084.■

FRAN STEWART CARLTON

State Representative. Personal: Born January 19, 1936; Daughter of D. J. and Delma Stewart; Married Ernest E. Carlton; Mother of Lynne, Julie. Education: A.A., University of Florida, 1956; B.A., Stetson University, 1958. Career: Member, Florida House of Representatives, Chairman of the Committee on Tourism and Economic Development, Host of "The Fran Carlton Show," a Nationally Syndicated Television Show. Organizational Memberships: University of Florida Alumni Association, President; National Conference of State Legislatures; National Recreation and Park Association, Florida Representative, Southern District. Community Activities: Citizens Against Pornography, Board of Directors; University of Central Florida Dick Pope Sr. Institute of Tourism Studies, Advisory Board; Preventive Health Strategy to the President's Council on Physical Fitness and Sports, Advisory Council; Senior Citizens Advisory Board of Sea World; Community Mental Health, Board of Directors; Epilepsy Association of Central Florida, Board of Directors; Occupational Placement Specialists and Career Education Advisory Board. Religion: Guest on 700 Club and PTL Club; Featured in *Guideposts* and *Christian Living* Magazines. Honors and Awards: Outstanding Legislator of the Year, Orlando Area Tourist Trade Association 1979, Orange County Classroom Teachers Association 1977, Florida Parent Teachers Association 1980; Distinguished Alumni Award, 1974; Honor Award, President's Council on Physical Fitness and Sports, 1979; Distinguished Service Award, Florida Association of Health, Physical Education and Recreation, 1977. Address: 1250 Henry Balch Drive, Orlando, Florida 32810.■

BARBARA JOYCE CARNEY

Executive Search Consultant. Personal: Born November 6, 1942; Daughter of Mrs. Celia Sachnoff; Mother of Michael, Michelle. Education: B.A. cum laude History, University of California at Los Angeles, 1964; M.Ed., National College of Education, 1968. Career: Executive Search Consultant, Womack and Associates, Inc., 1982 to present; National Special Markets Sales Manager, Ronco, Inc., 1980-81; Midwestern Regional Sales Manager, Superscope, Inc., 1978-80; Manufacturer's Representative, Shardon Marketing, Inc., 1976-78; Teacher, North Suburban Chicago School System, 1965-68. Organizational Memberships: Women in Management, 1982 to present; American Association of University Women, 1982 to present; American Society of Professional and Executive Women, 1981 to present; National Association of Female Executives, 1981 to present. Community Activities: Board of Directors, North Shore Mental Health; Mental Health Association, 1976; Vice President and Committee Chairperson, Local Chapter of League of Women Voters, 1970-76; President, Junior Women's Honorary (CHIMES); Sorority President and Hall of Fame. Honors and Awards: Miss White Stag, 1959; Honors in History 1964 and Student Judicial Board, University of California at Los Angeles; Prytanean-Women's Service Honorary; Listed in *Who's Who of American Women, Personalities of America, Five Thousand Personalities of the World, Personalities of the West and Midwest*. Address: 2020 Lincoln Park West, Chicago, IL 60614.■

PATRICK EDWARD CARPENTER

Head of Music Composition and Theory Instructor, Malaspina College. Personal: Born May 11, 1951; Son of Terence E. Carpenter. Education: B.Mus. with distinction, University of Victoria, 1970-75; M.A., State University of New York at Stony Brook, 1978; Attended Summer Workshop in "Digital Sound Synthesis and Processing," Digital Music Systems Inc., Boston, Massachusetts. Career: Adjudicator at 10th Anniversary Okanagan Music Festival for Composers, 1982; Interviewed by CBS Producer Norman Newton about 10th Anniversary Okanagan Music Festival for Composers and about the Situation of Young Composers in Today's World, 1982; Produced and Conducted in Yearly Promotional Tours for Malaspina College Music Department, 1981-82; Attended the Canadian League of Composers 30th Anniversary Conference in Windsor, Ontario, 1981; Head Instructor of Music Theory and Composition at Malaspina College, Nanaimo, British Columbia, Canada, 1979 to present; Musical Director and Conductor of the Summerland Singers and Players Society Production of Gilbert and Sullivan's *The Sorcerer*, 1978 to present; Professional Music Copyist for the Canadian Music Centre, 1978 to present; President of Penticton Conservatory of Music, 1978 to present; Teaching Assistant for the Electronic Studios at the State University of New York at Stony Brook, Teaching Assistant for Related Courses in Electronics, 1976-77; Interviewed by Karen Keiser of the CBC on His Life as a Musician and *Touch-Stone I*, 1976; Producer for and Performer in Concert Series Mostly from the Last Decade at State University of New York at Stony Brook, 1975-76; Secretary, Performer, R. B. Composers Group, 1975 to present, Private Teacher of Music Composition, Theory and Guitar; Numerous Performances including Those of *Residual Blue* 1982, *Pegasus* 1982, *Les Pierres des Grise* 1980, *Ladyfinger Triptych* 1978, *Touch-Stone I* 1977, *So* 1974; Numerous Radio Broadcasts including *Pegasus* 1982, *Ballon et Croix: pas de Ciel* 1981, Others; Extensive Performing, Producing and Conducting Experience; Several Guest Lectures. Organizational Memberships: Canadian League of Composers and Canadian Music Centre; Composers, Authors and Publishers Association of Canada Ltd.; Victoria Musicians Association, Local 247 of A.F. of M.; Corresponding Secretary, Nanaimo Branch of the British Columbia Registered Music Teachers Association, 1980-82; Malaspina College Faculty Association; State University of New York at Stony Brook Alumni Association; University of Victoria Alumni Association; Member, Secretary, Performer in R. B. Composers Group; President, Penticton Conservatory of Music. Published Works: Numerous Musical Compositions including *Residual Blue* 1982, *Pegasus* 1980-82, *Angel of Mercy* 1977, *Close Arcturus* 1975-76, *In Just* 1972, Others. Honors and Awards: Commission from Canadian Broadcasting Corporation to Write *Ballon et Croix: pas de Ciel* for the CBC Vancouver Orchestra 1979; Member of the Canadian League of Composers and the Canadian Music Centre, 1979; Canada Council Travel Grant to Hear Premier Performance of *Ladyfinger Triptych* by the Canadian Electronic Ensemble in Toronto 1978; *Touch-Stone I* Represented Canada at the International Rostrum of Composers in Paris, France, 1977; Won Prize in CBC/Canadian Music Centre sponsored Young Composers Contest ($4500) for Electro-Acoustic Tape Piece *Touch-Stone I*, 1976; British Columbia Cultural Fund Money for Best Work by a British Columbia Composer included, 1976; Won Prize in a Bi-Annual State of New York University System Music Competition Contest for *So*, 1976; Obtained Grants from British Columbia Cultural Fund and Private Patrons to Assist with R. B. Composers Group European Study Tour, Additional Funds Received from the MacLean Foundation, University of Victoria, and Other Patrons, 1975; B.M.I. Scholarship, University of Victoria Music Department, 1975; British Columbia Government Grant, 1971; Listed in *Personalities of America, Dictionary of International Biography*. Address: 198 Cilaire Drive, Nanaimo, British Columbia, Canada V9S 3E4.■

ROBERT HUNT CARPENTER

Laboratory Administrator. Personal: Born March 22, 1948, in Kenedy, Texas; Son of William H. Carpenter, Sr.; Married Betsy Doylene Owens; Father of Robert Owens, Erin Elizabeth. Education: B.S. Veterinary Sciences 1970, D.V.M. 1971, M.S. Laboratory Animal Medicine/Experimental Surgery, 1972, Texas A&M University; Military Training, 1972-76, Veterinary Officers Basic Course (Sheppard Air Force Base, Texas), Squadron Officers School, Command and Staff College (Gunter Air Force Base, Alabama), Medical Aspects of Advanced Warfare, Global Medicine Course, U.S.A.F.S.A.M. (Brooks Air Force Base, Texas), Faculty Development Course, Academy Health Care Sciences (Fort Sam Houston, Texas). Military: Served in the United States Air Force Veterinary Corps, 1972-76; Chief of Surgery, Military Working Dog Center, Lackland Air Force Base, Texas, 1972-73; Base Veterinarian, Brooks Air Force Base, Texas, 1973-74; Chief Disaster Medicine Section, Disaster Medicine/Survival Training Brand, United States Air Force School of Aerospace Medicine 1974-76; Special Consultant to United States Air Force Surgeon General, Medical Aspects of Special Weapons Employment and Biohazardous Accidents, 1974-76. Career: President, Research Biogenics Inc, Bastrop, Texas, 1976-84; University of Texas System Cancer Center Veterinary Resources Division of the Science Park, Bastrop, Texas. Community Activities: Lions Club; Masonic Lodge, Scottish Rite; Ben Hur Shrine Temple. Published Works: Numerous Articles in Professional Journals, including "Estrus and Pregnancy

Rates Following Synchronization with Cronolone Intravaginal Sponge or Norgestomat Ear Implant in Cycling Ewes" (with J. C. Spitzer), "What is Your Diagnosis?: Chronic Oesophagostomiasis" (with R. H. Hansen, J.F. and M. J. Murphy). Honors and Awards: Listed in *Who's Who in the Southwest U.S.A., Personalities of the South, Dictionary of International Biography, Distinguished Leaders in Health Care, Personalities of America, Men of Achievement, Notable Americans.* Address: 1303 Pecan Street, Bastrop, Texas 78602.■

HOWARD WILLIAM CARROLL

Attorney, State Legislator. Personal: Born July 28, 1942; Son of Barney M. (deceased) and Lyla Price Carroll; Married Eda; Father of Jacqueline. Education: B.S.B.A., Roosevelt University; J.D., DePaul University. Community Activities: State Senator, 15th District, Illinois, 1973 to present; State Representative, 13th District, Illinois, 1971-72; Board of Governors, Co-Chairman Trades Industries and Professions Division, Co-Chairman Public Service Division 1979, Chairman Banking Division 1979, Co-Chairman Man of the Year 1979, Chairman Real Estate Division 1977, State of Israel Bonds; Chairman, Little Flower Board of Lay Advisors, 1978-79; Convener, Citywide Jewish National Fund Tribute, 1977; Jewish National Fund Executive Committee; Jewish United Fund Planning Committee for the Metropolitan Area; Budget Committee, Jewish Welfare Fund of Metropolitan Chicago; Chairman of Special Gifts, Government Agencies Division, Jewish United Fund; Board of Directors, Chicago Association for Retarded Children; Zionist Organization of Chicago; Board of Directors, Budlong Woods B'nai B'rith; Board of Directors, West Rogers Park B'nai B'rith; Board of Directors, New Tamid Congregation of North Town; Executive Committee, B'nai B'rith Council of Greater Chicago; Composit Lodge AP & AM, Scottish Rites and Medina Temple; Rogers Park-Northtown Mental Health Council; Servite Seminary, Board of Law Advisors; Convener, Young Adults Division, State of Israel Bonds. Religion: Jewish. Honors and Awards: 1971 Honoree, State of Israel Bonds, Budlong Woods Lodge, B'nai B'rith; Golden Legislator Award for Inprovement of the Environment, 1974; Suburban Publishers Right to Know Award, 1975-77; Skokie Youth Baseball Award, 1977; Illinois Bar Association Award, 1977; American Legion Citation of Recognition; Society of Fellows Award, DePaul University; Man of Year, Jewish National Fund, B'nai B'rith Council of Greater Chicago, 1974; Honoree, B'nai B'rith Anti-Defamation League Dinner, 1975; Yeshivas Brisk Special Award, 1978; Hollywood North Park Improvement Association Certificate of Appreciation, 1978; Distinguished Service Award, State of Israel Bonds, 1974, 1978; Little Flower Board of Lay Advisors, 1975-78; Susan B. Anthony Award, 1979; North River Commission Award, 1979; Outstanding Legislator Award, Illinois Credit Union League, 1977-79; Chanukah Festival Honoree, Zionist Organization of Chicago, 1979.■

WILLIAM EDWARDS CARSON

Nuclear and Electrical Engineer. Personal: Born July 31, 1930, in Danville, Virginia; Son of J. E. and Elinor Carson; Father of Kathryn C. Reed, William E. Jr., John E. Education: B.S.E.E. 1952, M.S. Nuclear Engineer 1959, Virginia Polytechnic Institute. Career: Test Engineer (aircraft simulators), E.R.C.O. Division, A.C.F. Industries Inc., Riverdale, Maryland, 1952-53; Field Engineer, E.R.C.O. Division, A.C.F. Industries Inc., Texas, Florida, North Carolina, 1953-56; Nuclear, Electrical, Instrumentation, Propositions Engineer, Babcock & Wilcox Company, Lynchburg, Virginia, 1957-71; Senior Electrical Engineer, Burns and Roe Inc., Oradell, New Jersey, 1971; Staff Engineer, Southern Nuclear Engineering Inc., Dunedin, Florida, 1971-73; Principal Engineer and Project Manager, N.U.S. Corporation, Clearwater, Florida, 1973-81; Senior Professional Staff, Southern Science Applications Inc., Dunedin, Florida, 1981-83; Nuclear Engineer, Southern Science Office, Block and Veatch, 1983 to present. Organizational Memberships: Sigma Xi; Institute of Electrical and Electronics Engineers, Senior Member. Community Activities: Young Republican Federation of Virginia, Chairman 1965-67; Lynchburg Young Republicans Club, President 1962-64; Young Republicans, 6th Congressional District of Virginia, Chairman 1964-65; Lynchburg City Republican Committee, Member 1962-68, Vice Chairman 1967-68, Publicity Chairman 1962-67; Sertoma; National Advisory Board, American Biographical Institute. Religion: United Methodist. Published Works: Contributor of Technical Articles to Several Publications. Honors and Awards: Life Fellow, American Biographical Institute Research Association; Listed in *Dictionary of International Biography, Men of Achievement, Book of Honor, Personalities of the South, Community Leaders and Noteworthy Americans, Men and Women of Distinction, International Who's Who of Intellectuals, Who's Who in the South and Southwest, Contemporary Personalities.* Address: 2625 Morningside Drive, Clearwater, Florida 33519.■

JOSEPH L. CARTER, JR.

Executive. Personal: Born December 3, 1939; Son of Judge and Mrs. Joseph L. Carter. Education: B.S. Business Administration, Bucknell University. Career: Department of Energy, Chief HQ ADP and Communication Services, Former Assistant to Director; Chief, HQ Telecommunications, United States Energy Research and Development Administration; Chief, HQ Computer Center, United States Atomic Energy Commission; Manager, Comptroller's Computer Center, State of Maryland; Systems Analyst, International Business Machines Corporation. Address: #C-1401, 12000 Old Georgetown Road, Rockville, Maryland 20852.■

MARION ELIZABETH CARTER

Language Specialist. Personal: Born in Washington, D.C. Education: Valedictorian, Dunbar High School (Washington); B.A. French, Wellesley College; M.A. Romance Languages, Howard University; M.A. Spanish, Middlebury College; M.S. Linguistics, Ph.D. Applied Linguistics, Georgetown University; Ph.D. Romance Languages, Catholic University of America; Theological Studies, Institute of Theology. Career: First Teacher to Broadcast Lessons in Spanish via Television in the Washington D.C. Public School District; Instructed Teachers at National Defense Education Act Institute, Petersburg, Virginia; Represented District of Columbia Teachers College at Sessions of National Association for Foreign Student Affairs (Minnesota, Israel, France, U.S. State Department); Professor of Foreign Languages and Linguistics, Gordon College, 1970 to present. Published Works: Books *The Role of the Symbol in French Romantic Poetry* and *A General Linguistics Textbook for College Students;* Poetry Published in *The National Anthology of Poetry.* Honors and Awards: Eugene and Agnes Meyer Fellowship for Continued Research in Spain and Puerto Rico; Fulbright Lecturer of English as a Second Language, University of La Laguna (Canary Islands); Fellow, American Biographical Institute; Ph.D., World University of Tucson, Arizona; Listed in *Directory of American Scholars, Who's Who in American Education, International Register of Profiles, International Who's Who of Intellectuals.* Address: 402 You Street Northwest, Washington, D.C. 20001.■

GEORGE BRYAN CARVER

Law Enforcement Officer. Personal: Born September 30, 1935; Son of Mr. and Mrs. Bryan Carver; Married Marjorie Crabill, Daughter of Mr. and Mrs. William Lee Crabill (deceased). Education: Graduate of Greenbrier Military School, 1955; Attended Virginia Military Institute, 1956-59; Graduate of the F.B.I. National Academy, 1974; B.A., George Washington University, 1975. Military: Served in the United States Army, 1959-60 and 1961-62. Career: Law Enforcement Officer, U.S. Capitol Police. Organizational Memberships: F.B.I. National Academy Associates, Washington Chapter, Vice President 1975-76, President 1976-77; International Association of Chiefs of Police; Fraternal Order of Police, Federal Lodge #1; Heroes Inc. Community Activities: Greenbrier Military School Alumni Association Vice President National Association 1965-66, President National Association 1966-67; Charter Member, Franklin Mint Collectors Society, 1964 to present; Wolf Trap Association; George Washington University Alumni Association; Heroes Inc.; Charter Member, American Bicentennial Commemorative Society. Honors and Awards: Meritorious Certification, Fraternal Order of Police, Federal Lodge 1, 1976; Elected Fellow, Academy of Police Science, National Law Enforcement Academy; Listed in *Community Leaders of Virginia, Men of Achievement, Dictionary of International Biography, Anglo-American Who's Who, International Who's Who of Intellectuals, International Register of Profiles, Biographical Roll of Honor.* Address: Apartment 802, 6129 Leesburg Pike, Falls Church, Virginia 22041.■

NORMAN MONDELL CASE

Associate Profesor of Anatomy. Personal: Born October 12, 1917; Son of Otto and Nola Case (deceased). Education: B.S., College of Medical Evangelists, 1950; M.S., University of Southern California, 1954; Ph.D., Loma Linda University, 1958. Military: Served in the United States Army Medical Corps, 1942-46, attaining the rank of Staff Sergeant. Career: Associate Professor of Anatomy, Loma Linda University; Former Clinical Laboratory Technologist. Organizational Memberships: Electron Microscopy Society of Southern California; Electron Microscopy Society of America; American Association of Anatomists; Royal Microscopical Society (London); Sigma Xi, Treasurer 1955. Community Activities: American Red Cross, First Aid Instructor 1940-63. Religion: Seventh Day Adventist, Deacon 1954-56, Local Elder 1956-64. Honors and Awards: Honorary Research Associate, University College (London), 1968-69; Invited Participant to Symposium on Neural Principles in Vision, University of Munich, Germany, 1975. Address: 11635 Vista Lane, Yucaipa, California 92399.■

TWO THOUSAND NOTABLE AMERICANS

JOHN KROB CASTLE

Investment Banker. Personal: Born December 22, 1940; Son of Clyo F. Castle, Emma K. Castle; Married Marianne Sherman; Father of William Sherman, John Sherman, James Sherman, David Alexander. Education: S.B., Massachusetts Institute of Technology, 1963; M.B.A. with high distinction (George F. Baker Scholar), Harvard University, 1965. Career: President and Chief Operating Officer, Donaldson, Lufkin and Jenrette, Investment Banking. Organizational Memberships: Director, Sealed Air Corporation, Baldt Inc., DLJ Inc.; Chairman of the Board, New York Medical College; Trustee, New York Eye and Ear Infirmary; American Business Conference; Young President's Organizationa; Economic Club of New York. Address: 775 Park Avenue, New York, New York 10021.■

ALFRED CATALFO, JR.

Attorney at Law. Personal: Born January 31, 1920; Son of Alfred Catalfo Sr. (deceased) and Vincenzia Amato Catalfo; Married Caroline Joanne Mosca (deceased April 30, 1968); Father of Alfred T., Carol Joanne, Gina Marie. Education: Graduate of Ecole St. Joseph, Rollinsford (New Hampshire) 1936, Berwick Academy 1940; B.A. History, University of New Hampshire, 1945; LL.B., Boston University School of Law, 1947; M.A. History, University of New Hampshire, 1952; Attended the School for Prosecuting Attorneys of Northwestern University School of Law, Harvard University, University of Alabama, Graduate School of Suffolk University School of Law, American Law Institute. Military: Served in the United States Navy Air Corps during World War II (1942-44); Served in the United States Naval Reserves, attaining the rank of Lieutenant Colonel, New Hampshire Governor's Military Staff under Governors John King and Hugh Gallen. Career: Admitted to Practice before the New Hampshire Bar 1947, United States Supreme Court 1970, United States District Court, United States Board of Appeals; Individual Law Practice, Dover, New Hampshire, 1948 to present; County Attorney, Strafford County, New Hampshire, 1949-50 and 1955-56; Past Employee, Labor Organizer, Pacific Mills, Marx Toy Company (Dover, New Hampshire). Organizational Memberships: United States Department of Justice Board of Immigration Appeals, 1953 to present; Strafford County Bar Association, Member 1947 to present, Vice President 1966-69, President 1968-69; New Hampshire Bar Association, 1947 to present; American Bar Association, 1948 to present; Interstate Commerce Commission; Phi Delta Phi International Legal Fraternity; American Trial Lawyers Association; Massachusetts Trial Lawyers Association; National Association of Criminal Defense Lawyers; American Judicature Society. Community Activities: Bellamy State Park, Past Supervisor; Disabled American Veterans, New Hampshire Department Judge Advocate 1950-56, 1957-68 and 1972 to present, Commander 1956-57, Chapter Commander 1953-54, Chairman State Department Conventions 1957, 1960, 1963, 1970; Young Democrats, President Dover Chapter 1953-55, First Vice Chairman of New Hampshire Chapter 1954-56; Dover City Democratic Committee, Chairman Ward III 1958-68; Stafford County Democratic Committee, 1948-75; New Hampshire Democratic State Committee, Vice Chairman 1954-56, Chairman 1956-58, Chairman Special Activities 1958-60, Executive Committee 1960-70; Candidate as Delegate for Adlai Stevenson, 1956; Democratic National Convention, Attended 1956 & 1976, Delegate 1960; Elected Pledge Delegate to Senator John F. Kennedy for President, 1960; Democratic Nominee, State Senate, 21st District, 1960; Democratic State Convention, Chairman 1958, Convention Director 1960; Boutin for Governor Executive Committee, 1960; Democratic Nominee for United States Senator, 1962; Committtee to Elect Jimmy Carter for President, 1976; 1972 Committee to Re-Elect Thomas McIntyre for United States Senator; Legal Advisor, Recount for United States Senator John Durkin, 1974; Football Coach, Berwick Academy 1944, Mission Catholic High School (Roxbury, Massachusetts) 1945-46; American Legion, Member Post #8 (Dover), Member 40/8, Chairman State Department Convention 1967 & 1977; Dover Lions Club; Fraternal Order of Eagles; Benevolent and Protective Order of Elks; Knights of Columbus, Council 307 (Dover), Grand Knight 1975-77, 4th Degree; Sons of Italy; Berwick Academy Alumni Association, President 1974-76; Loyal Order of the Moose; Lebanese Club; Navy League of America; Improved Order of Red Men; New Hampshire Historical Society; Dover Historical Society, Northam Colonist; Rollinsford Historical Society; University of Alabama, Class President 1940-41; Dover Catholic School Committee, Vice Chairman 1969-71; Dover Board of Adjustment, Five Years. Published Works: Author, *Laws of Divorce, Marriages and Separations in New Hampshire*; First Complete *History of the Town of Rollinsford, 1923-73*. Honors and Awards: Recipient of Keys to Four Cities, Dover, Somersworth, Concord, Manchester; Four National Plaques, Disabled American Veterans; Two Distinguished Service Plaques, American Legion; Listed in *Who's Who Among Students in American Universities and Colleges, Who's Who in American Law, Who's Who in the East*. Address: 20 Arch Street, Dover, New Hampshire 03820.■

SAFFET CATANI CATOVIC

Scientist, Educator. Personal: Born April 21, 1924, in Bilece, Yugoslavia; Son of Abid and Dervisa Cerimagic Catovic; Married Sarah Cameron Kerr, December 22, 1961; Father of Saffet Abid, Saffiya Dervisa, Suada Semra, Saliha Sarah, Surayya Hava, Sami Ismet. Education: B.S., Zagreb University, 1950; M.S., University of New Hampshire, 1961; Ph.D., Rutgers University, 1964. Career: Fellow in Entomology and Phytopathology, Zagreb University, 1951-52; Research and Extension Pathologist/Entomologist, Plant Quarantine Inspector, Sarajevo and Siaak, Yugoslavia, 1952-57; Research Entomologist, Institute for Plant Protection, Ankara, Turkey, 1957-58; Research Fellow, Botany Department, University of New Hampshire, 1958-61; Research Fellow, Plant Biology Department, Rutgers University, 1961-64; Assistant Professor 1964-69, Associate Professor 1969-74, Professor 1974 to present, Fairleigh Dickinson University Department of Biological Sciences. Organizational Memberships: American Association for the Advancement of Science; New York Academy of Sciences; New Jersey Academy of Sciences; Mycological Society of America; International Mycological Society; Medical Mycological Society of New York; Sigma Xi Scientific Research Society; Metropolitan Association of College and University Biologists; American Association of University Professors; New Jersey Society of Parasitologists; Smithsonian Associates; New York Botanical Gardens; American Museum of Natural History; National Audubon Society; Yugoslavian Association for Plant Protection; Phytopathological Association of America, Past Member Northeast Division. Address: 114 Copley Avenue, Teaneck, New Jersey 07666.■

WILLIAM QUIRINO CELLINI, JR.

Electrical Engineer, Operations Research Analyst. Personal: Born March 12, 1951, in Ardmore, Pennsylvania; Son of Mr. and Mrs. Quirino Cellini. Education: B.S.E.E., Drexel University, 1974; M.B.A., University of Pittsburgh, 1975; M.S.E.E. Candidate, George Washington University, 1977-81. Military: Attended Army Engineer Officers Basic School, Fort Belvoir, Virginia; Honorable Discharge from the United States Army Reserves, 1976, with the rank of Second Lieutenant. Career: Electrical Engineer/Operations Research Analyst, Systems Engineering Division, Systems and Applied Sciences Corporation (Riverdale, Maryland), 1982 to present; Electrical Engineer/Operations Research Analyst, J. J. Henry Company Inc. (Arlington, Virginia), 1982; Systems Analyst, Harry Diamond Laboratories (Adelphi, Maryland), 1981-82; Electrical Engineer, Gauthier, Alvarado and Associates (Falls Church, Virginia) 1981; Research Analyst, Energy Systems Presearch Inc. (Arlington, Virginia), 1980-81; Associate, Solar Electric Power Systems, P.R.C. Energy Analysis Company (McLean, Virginia), 1979-80; Systems Analyst/ Electrical Engineer, Advanced Marine Enterprises (Arlington), 1977-79. Organizational Memberships: Institute of Electrical and Electronics Engineers; National Society of Professional Engineers; American Management Association; Pennsylvania Society of Professional Engineers; American Society for Engineering Education; Society of American Military Engineers; Association of M.B.A. Executives; Association of the United States Army. Community Activities: Friends of the Kennedy Center; Smithsonian Institution; Friends of the National Zoo; National Italian American Foundation; Pennsylvania Newman Alumni Association; Crystal Plaza Social Club, Co-President 1978-79; Alpha Phi Omega, National Service Fraternity, Life Member Kansas City Chapter; Contributor, United States Olympic Society, Disabled Americans Veterans. Religion: Catholic, Arlington Diocese; Parish Representative, Coorinator of Catholic Young Adults Club 1980, Prime Time Single Catholics; Catholic Alumni Clubs International, Washington D.C. Pubished Works: Four Professional Publications including The NAVSEA HEEM Program and the Use of High Efficiency Electric Motors in the U.S. Navy; Private Consultants for the Federal Government. Honors and Awards: Associate, American Biographical Institute Research Association; Listed in *Who's Who in the South and West, Science and Technology, International Who's Who of Intellectuals, Men of Achievement, International Register of Profiles*. Address: 2111 Jefferson Davis Highway, 1012-S, Arlington, Virginia 22202.■

DAVID BAY CHALMERS

Corporation Executive. Personal: Born November 17, 1924; Son of David Twiggs (deceased) and Dorritt Bay Chalmers; Father of David Bay Jr. Education: Attended

Dartmouth College (Tuck School of Business), 1947; Studies in Advanced Management, Harvard Business School, 1966. Military: Served in the United States Armed Services, 1943-45 and 1949-50, attaining the rank of First Lieutenant. Career: Chairman of the Board and Chief Executive Officer, Coral Petroleum Inc.; President, Canadian Occidental Petroleum Ltd. and President and Chief Executive Officer of Petrogas Processing Ltd., 1968-73; Vice President, Occidental Petroleum Corporation, 1967-68; Vice President, Tenneco Oil Company, 1955-67; Positions with Bay Petroleum, 1951-55. Organizational Memberships: Director, Leeward Petroleum Company 1973 to present, Coral Petroleum Canada Inc. 1975 to present, Coral Petroleum International 1981 to present; Independent Petroleum Association of America; National Petroleum Refiners Association. Community Activities: United States Chamber of Commerce; Houston Chamber of Commerce. Honors and Awards: Elected to 25-Year Club of Petroleum Industry, 1976. Address: 5600 San Felipe, No. 4, Houston, Texas 77056.■

RUTH LOUIS CHAMBERLIN

Professor and Department Chairman. Personal: Born November 10, 1922; Daughter of Knox Dale Chamberlin (deceased) and Flossie Reed Chamberlin; Mother of David. Education: B.A., B.S., Ashland College; M.A., University of Michigan; Ph.D. Candidate, Kent State University. Career: Professor of English and Education, Chairman English Department, Liberty Baptist College. Organizational Memberships: Phi Delta Kappa; Virginia Association of Teachers of English; National Association Teacher of English; S.A. Modern Language Association. Community Activities: Public Service Speaker to Various Schools in the Community; Solicitor, Heart Association; Historical Society. Religion: Conservative Protestant. Honors and Awards: Fellow, John Hay Fellows Program in Humanities; Fellow, Asian Studies; Pi Lambda Theta; Kappa Delta Pi. Address: 5721 White Oak Drive, Lynchburg, Virginia 24502.■

HARRY SAMUEL CHAPMAN

Engineering Administrator. Personal: Born May 11, 1936; Son of Karl and Gertrude Chapman; Married Grace Ann; Father of Matthew Harry, Pamela Grace. Education: Bachelor's Degree in Chemistry, University of Vermont, 1959; Continuing Education undertaken at the Patent Institute of Fairleigh Dickinson University 1976, Kent State University 1977, New York University 1978, Temple University 1979; Further Courses with A.M.A. and T.A.P.P.I. Military: Served in the United States Army 1960, United States Army Reserve 1961-66, attaining the rank of Captain. Career: President, Ideal Design Company, 1960-67; Plant Manager, Fluorodynamics Inc., 1964-67; Vice President, Co-Founder, Chapman Industries, 1967-74; Technical Manager, Carborundum, 1974-79; Engineering Manager, Kennecott, 1979-82; Manager of Application Engineering, Standard Oil of Ohio, 1982 to present. Organizational Memberships: Director of Chapman Industries, 1967-74; Technical Association of the Pulp and Paper Industry, Extrusion Coating Committee 1981 to present; Society of the Plastics Industry, 1966-80; Society of Mechanical Engineers, 1975-79. Community Activities: Public Elected to School Board, Oxford, Pennsylvania; Member Joint Committee for the Vocational-Technical School, Southern Chester County, Pennsylvania, 1973-76; Boy Scouts of America, Cubmaster, Assistant Scoutmaster 1974-83; President, Founder, South Wallingford Youth Community Center, 1959-60; Director, Vermont Maple Sugar Makers Association, 1959-60; Pennsylvania Farmers Association, 1981-82; Aircraft Owners and Pilots Association, 1968-78; National Rifle Association. Religion: Oxford United Methodist Church, Vice Chairperson of the Administrative Board 1975-83, Finance Committee 1975-81. Honors and Awards: Gold Key Honorary Society; Thirteen Active Patents in Fluoropolymer Field, 1966-82; Fluoropolymer Article Published in International T.A.P.P.I. Journal, 1983; Scouter's Key, Boy Scouts of America, 1981; Commercial and Instrument Pilot Certificate, 1960-present.■

IVAN CHARNER

Director of Research, Educational Sociologist, Author. Personal: Born May 11, 1949, in New York City, New York; Son of Hilliard Daniel and Geraldine Resnick Charner; Married Kathleen Hammond, May 7, 1971; Father of Megin Hammond. Education: B.A., Harpur College, 1970; M.A. (Fellow), Ontario Institute for Studies in Education, 1972. Career: Research Assistant, Ontario Institute for Studies in Education, 1970-73; Research Associate, National Institute of Education, 1973-78; National Institute for Work and Learning, Senior Research Associate 1978-79, Director of Research 1978-79, Director of Research 1979 to present; Consultant, Office of Education, Boystown Center for the Study of Youth Development, Appalachian Educational Laboratory, Anne Arundel County (Missouri) Schools, 1978 to present. Organizational Memberships: American Educational Research Association; American Sociological Association; American Society for Training and Development. Published Works: Author, *Greater Resources and Opportunities for Working Women, Union Subsidies to Workers for Higher Education, Patterns of Adult Participation in Learning Activities, Documenting Youth Experiences: The Concept of a Career Passport, Another Piece of the Financial Aid Puzzle: Tuition Aid Offered by Companies and Union, Supporting Educational Oportunities for Workers*; Editor, *Education and Work in Rural America: The Social Contest of Early Career Decisions and Achievement*; Research in Employment in Fast Food Industry, Worker Education and Training, Career Development. Honors and Awards: Grant, Department of Health, Education and Welfare, 1978-80; Grant, Department of Labor, 1979-82; Grant, Women's Educational Equity Act, 1979-82; Grant, Dutchess County (New York) Private Industry Council, 1982 to present; Grant, Howard County (Missouri) Schools, 1983 to present; Listed in *Personalities of America, Who's Who in the East*. Address: 8406 Cedar Street, Silver Spring, Maryland 20910.■

HYMAN CHARTOCK

Psychiatrist, Neurologist. Personal: Born August 26, 1912; Married Laurette Y.; Father of Robert Bruce, David Seth. Education: Graduate of Washington Square College, New York University, 1933; M.D., Royal College of Physicians and Surgeons, Edinburgh, Scotland, 1939; Triple Qualifications, Licentiate, Royal College of Physicians/Royal College of Surgeons (Edinburgh), Royal Faculty of Physicians and Surgeons (Glasgow), 1939; Licensed to Practice Medicine, State of New York, 1939; Internship, Israel Zion Hospital, 1939-40; Staff Member, Brooklyn State Hospital, 1940-41; Residency in Neurology, Psychiatry and Neurosurgery, City Hospital, Welfare Island, 1941; Postgraduate Work in Neurology and Psychiatry, Columbia University, 1946-48. Military: Served in the United States Army during World War II, attaining the rank of Major; Served as Chief Neurologist (Fort Monmouth) and as Acting Regimental Surgeon (Engineers Amphibian Brigade); Medical Director, "This is the Army"; Chief Psychiatrist, Camp Ritchie (Maryland); Chief of Rehabilitation and Occupational and Recreational Therapy, Valley Forge General Hospital Psychiatric Service; Chief Psychiatrist, New Cumberland Disciplinary Barracks. Career: Assistant Chief, Neuropsychiatric Service, City Hospital, Welfare Island, 1946-57; Staff Neurologist, Psychiatrist, Presbyterian Medical Center, 1949-64; Neurologist, Long Island Jewish Hospital, 1954-55; Faculty, College of Physicans and Surgeons, Columbia University, 1949-64; Adjunct Professor, Union Graduate School, Yellow Springs, Ohio, 1972; Fellow, Academy of Orthomolecular Psychiatry; President, Bio-Phoresis Research Foundation, Inc., 1979-81; Consultant, B'nai B'rith Vocational Guidance Division, New York, 1961; Consultant, Psychiatrist, Neurologist, Commission of the Blind, New York State Department of Social Welfare, 1958; Vocational Rehabilitation Division, New York State Board of Education 1957, City of New York Compensation and Negligence 1958 to present; Author, Lecturer; Television and Radio Appearances; Specialist Rating, Workmen's Compensation Board (S.I.); Qualified Psychiatrist, Department of Mental Hygiene, State of New York, 1958. Published Works: Author *Road to Normalcy*. Honors and Awards: Listed in *American Men of Medicine, Who's Who in the East*. Address: 18-65 211th Street, Bayside, New York 11360.■

LEONA CHAZEN

Education Support Specialist. Personal: Born September 2, 1920; Daughter of Ida and Meyer L. Chazen (deceased). Education: Attended Stone Business College (New Haven, Connecticut), 1938-39. Career: Education Support Specialist, United States Department of Education; Former Positions include Assistant Executive Secretary to the Presidential Clemency Board (The White House), Administrative and Program Assistant for the U.S.-U.S.S.R. Seminar on Activating the Teaching Process and Educational Technology, Program Specialist at the National Center for Educational Technology (U.S. Office of Education), Research Instrument Review Specialist, Bureau of Research (U.S. Office of Education). Organizational Memberships: National Association for Secondary School Principals. Community Activities: Volunteer, 1961 Inaugural Committee, Executive Director's Office; Fourth General Assembly, World Future Society; Loaned Executive, Combined Federal Campaign, 1978-79; Honorary Life Member, Jewish Consumptives Relief Society; Hadassah; United Jewish Appeal. Honors and Awards: Special Award for Improvement of Agency Operations, U.S. Office of Education, 1979; Cash Award, Recommended by White House to U.S. Office of Education, 1973. Address: 4000 Tunlaw Road N.W., Apt. 1029, Washington, D.C. 20007.■

TWO THOUSAND NOTABLE AMERICANS

BRIAN HAMILTON CHERMOL

Clinical Psychologist. Personal: Born June 24, 1944; Son of Mr. and Mrs. J. Chermol; Married Annie Laurie, Daughter of Mrs. L. Dubose; Father of Laurie Ann Hammonds, Sherry Louise. Education: B.A. magna cum laude, Park College, 1970; M.A. Psychology, University of Missouri, 1972; Ph.D. Clinical Psychology, University of South Carolina, 1978. Military: Serving in the United States Army as Lieutenant Colonel, 1962 to present. Career: Clinical Psychologist, United States Army; Pathology Instructor, University of South Carolina; Infantry Officer, United States Army. Organizational Memberships: American Psychological Association; American Society of Clinical Hypnosis; Association for the Advancement of Psychology; National Register of Health Care Providers. Community Activities: United States Coast Guard Auxiliary; Civil Air Patrol; President, Scottshill Townhouse Association. Religion: Protestant. Honors and Awards: Man of the Year, Columbus, Georgia, 1963; Decorated Silver Star, Bronze Star (3) for Valor, Meritorious Service Medal, Army Commendation Medal, Air Medal (3), 1966-81; Psi Chi; Phi Kappa Phi. Address: 8120 Scottshill, San Antonio, Texas 78209.■

SUE S. (SUCHIN) CHIN

International Conceptual Designer, Painter and Photographer. Personal: Born in San Francisco, California; Daughter of William W. and Soo-Up (Swebe) Chin. Education: Graduate, California College of Arts in Los Angeles, the Minneapolis Art Institute, and the Shaeffer Design Center; Additional Studies as Student of Master Artists Yasuo Ku-niyo-shi and Rico LeBurn; Studies in Palmistry and Divination under Cheiro (Count Louis Hamon). Career: International Recognized Painter engaged in Painting and Designing of Textiles, Wallcoverings and Wall Hangings; Works Exhibited at Los Angeles County Museum of Art 1975-78, California Museum of Science and Industry (Los Angeles) 1975-78, Capricorn-Asunder (San Francisco) 1972, Peace Plaza, Japan Center and Kaiser Center, also in Hong Kong and Australia; One-Woman Show at Lucien Labaudt Gallery, San Francisco, 1975; Permanent Collections at Los Angeles County Federation of Labor, California Museum of Science and Industry, Number of Private and Corporate Collections; International Conceptual Designer, Painter, Photographer; Photojournalist, Area Television Stations, serving the *All Together Now* Art Show (KPIX-TV), *East West News* (Third World Newscasting), KNBC *Sunday Show* (Los Angeles). Organizational Memberships: Founding Vice President, Asian Women Artists, 1978-81; Secretary-Treasurer, California Chinese Artists, 1978-81; Director and Co-Chairman, Japanese American Art Council, 1978-82; San Francisco Women Artists; Artists in Print; San Francisco Graphics Guild; Chinatown Council on Performing and Visual Arts, Chinese Cultural Center Galleries; Member of Psychic Counsel; Hearthfire; Women Psychics and Healers of San Francisco; Life Fellow, International Biographical Association. Community Activities: Active in Projects affecting the Asian Community of California; Pacific Asian-American Women Bar Area Coalition; State Delegate to First PanAsian Women's Conference in Washington, D.C., 1980; Participant in National Women's Political Caucus, Delegate to State and National Conventions, Affirmative Action Chairman for San Francisco Chapter. Honors and Awards: Honorarium, AFL—CIO Labor Studies Center, Washington, D.C., 1976; Bicentennial Award, Los Angeles County Museum of Art, 1975-78; First Award for Conceptual Painting and Photography of the Far East, Asian Women Artists, 1978-81; Featured Live on Channel 4 Television Station in San Francisco, 1981; Divined at 1982 State Fair at Moscone Center; Featured as Occultist and Psychic in *California Living Magazine*, November 1981; Included in 1983 Traveling Exhibit concerning Women in History and Chinese Women in America; Included in *Chinese Women in History*; Featured on Channels 4 and 7 of Bay Area Scene Television at Holistic Center; Featured on Channel 7 Documentary, 1982; Listed in *Who's Who in the West, Who's Who Among American Women, Personalities of the West and Midwest, World Who's Who of Women, Dictionary of International Biography, Who's Who in California.* Address: Dr. Suchin Associates, Fox Plaza, San Francisco, California 94102.■

WILLIAM DEWAYNE CHISHOLM

Contracts Manager. Personal: Born March 1, 1924; Son of James A. and Evelyn May Iles Chisholm (both deceased); Married Esther Troehler; Father of James Scott, Larry Alan, Brian Duane. Education: B.S. Industrial Engineering 1949, B.S. Chemical Engineering 1949, University of Washington; M.B.A., Harvard University Graduate School of Business Administration, 1955. Military: Served in the United States Navy as Electronic Technician, 1944-46. Career: Chemist, Unit Leader, Technical Representative, The Coca-Cola Company, Atlanta and Los Angeles, 1949-59; Project Administrator 1959-61, Marketing Administrator 1961-64, Contracts Work Director 1964-66, Honeywell, Inc., Los Angeles; Clearwater (Florida) Contracts Manager 1966-73, Contracts Supervisor 1973-75, Senior Contract Management Representative 1975-80, Principal Contract Management Representative 1980-82, Contracts Manager Professional Development and Management Practices 1982-. Organizational Memberships: National Contract Management Association, Suncoast Chapter, Member 1966 to present, National Director 1976-77, 1967-69, President 1975-76, Vice President 1970-75; American Society for Training and Development, 1981 to present; Technical Marketing Society of America, 1982 to present. Community Activities: Breakfast Optimist Club of Clearwater, 1980 to present, Vice President 1980-81, Director 1982-83; Imperial Park Owners Association, Board of Directors, Vice President 1973-75, Pinellas County United Way, Honeywell Campaign Chairman 1969, Vice Chairman 1968. Religion: Village Presbyterian Church, Arcadia, California, Member 1960-65, Ordained as Elder 1964, Served on Session 1964-65; Christ Presbyterian Church, Largo, Florida, Member 1966 to present, Served in Session 1973-75, 1977-79, 1981-83, Church School Teacher 1971-74, Representative to Presbyterian Evangelism Southeast Conference 1974, Chairman Christian Faith and Life Committee 1974-79, Chairman Associate Minister/Director Christian Education Search Committee 1978-79, Chairman Stewardship Campaigns 1980 and 1981, Chairman Pastor Nominating Committee 1980-81, Member Stewardship Committee 1980-83, Member Evangelism and Outreach Committee 1983 to present; John Calvin Foundation Board of Trustees, 1974-82, Vice President 1974-80. Published Works: Article on "Return on Assets Considerations for Contract Administrators," in *National Contract Management Journal* 1975 and *Yearbook of Procurement Articles* 1975. Honors and Awards: Certified Professional Contracts Manager, 1974; Fellow Member, National Contract Management Association, 1975, National Council on Fellows 1982. Address: 11350 U.S. Highway 19 South, Clearwater, Florida 33546.■

ROBERT JOSEPH CHOUN

Minister of Education, Professor, Seminar Leader. Personal: Born August 17, 1948; Son of Mr. and Mrs. Robert J. Choun; Married Jane Willson. Education: A.A. with distinction, Luther College of the Bible and Liberal Arts, Teaneck, New Jersey, 1969; B.A. Religion, Gustavus Adolphus College, St. Peter, Minnesota, 1971; M.R.E. cum laude, Trinity Evangelical Divinity School, Deerfield, Illinois, 1974; M.A. magna cum laude, Wheaton College Graduate School, Wheaton, Illinois, 1975; D.Min. summa cum laude, Faith Evangelical Lutheran Seminary, Seattle, Washington, 1980; Ph.D. Candidate, North Texas State University, Denton, Texas. Career: Minister of Education, Pantego Bible Church, Arlington, Texas; Professor of Christian Education, Dallas Theological Seminary, Dallas, Texas; Seminar Leader, International Center for Learning, Ventura, California; Assistant to the Pastor, Holy Trinity Lutheran Church, Bridgeport, Connecticut, Summers 1966-74; Youth Director, Grace Lutheran Church, River Edge, New Jersey, 1968-69; Youth Director, First Lutheran Church, St. Peter, Minnesota, 1969-70; Youth Director (part-time), Bethany Christian and Missionary Alliance Church, St. Peter, Minnesota, 1970-71; Instructor of Extension Courses, Dallas Bible College, 1977-78; Instructor, Southern Bible Institute, Dallas, Texas, 1976-77; Instructor in International Center for Learning, Glendale, California, 1978 to present; Workshop Leader for Gospel Light Publications and Curriculum Consultant, Ventura, CA, 1977 to present; Adjunct Teacher of Christian Education, Dallas Theological Seminary, Dallas, Texas, 1978 to present. Organizational Memberships: Association for Curriculum Development and Supervision; American Management Association; Christian School Curriculum Committee, Fleming H. Revell, Publishers; Board of Evaluation, Pioneer Ministries; Consulting Editor, Gospel Light Publications; Consulting Editor for Primary, Middler and Junior Curriculum, Gospel Light Publications. Religion: Member Pantego Bible Church, Arlington, Texas; National Association of Directors of Church Education; Texas Sunday School Association. Published Works: Author, "The Primary Column," *Evangelizing Today's Child Magazine*, 1978 to present; Feature Articles in *Perspective Magazine*, 1978 to present; Articles in *Ideabank*, 1981 to present; Author, "Current Trends in Education for the 1980's," in *Bib. Sac. Journal*; "Parent Involvement," in *Texas Child Quarterly Magazine*; Book Reviews for *Bib. Sac. Journal*; Leadership Articles for Child Evangelism Fellowship. Honors and Awards: Kappa Delta Phi; Pi Delta Kappa; Listed in *Who's Who in American Junior Colleges, Who's Who in the South and Southwest, Personalities of America, Personalities of the South, Men of Achievement.* Address: 818 Clover Park Drive, Arlington, Texas 76013.■

TWO THOUSAND NOTABLE AMERICANS

LA VERNE ARDRA CHRETIEN

Senior Medical Social Worker. Personal: Born December 24, 1916; Daughter of Robert L. and Annie Williams (both deceased). Education: B.S. cum laude, Samuel Huston College (now Huston-Tillotson College), 1938; M.S.W., Atlanta University School of Social Work, Atlanta, Georgia, 1949; Postgraduate Study, Smith College School for Social Work, North Hampton, Massachusetts, 1958. Career: Senior Medical Social Worker, Los Angeles County/University of Southern California Medical Center, 1982; District Director, Public Health Social Work, County of Los Angeles, Department of Health Services, Los Angeles, California, 1973-81; Senior Medical Social Worker, Program Specialist, Sickle Cell Anemia Program, County of Los Angeles, Department of Health Services, Los Angeles, California, 1971-73; Medical Social Worker, Schwab Rehabilitation Hospital, Chicago, Illinois, 1969-71; School Social Worker, Cook County School District 143½, Posen, Illinois, 1959-69; Social Work Unit Supervisor, Chicago Committee on Urban Opportunities, Project Headstart, Chicago, Illinois, Summer 1965; Parent Involvement Coordinator, Cook County Progress Centers, Chicago, Illinois, Summer 1967; Medical Social Work Consultant, Health, Education and Welfare, Project Headstart, Region II, Chicago, Illinois, Summers 1968-70; Child Welfare Worker, Child and Family Services, Chicago, 1955-59; Social Worker, Juvenile Protective Association, Chicago, Illinois, 1953-55; Parole Agent, Illinois Department of Child Welfare, Region II, Chicago, Illinois, 1951-53; Caseworker, Chicago Welfare Department, Chicago, Illinois, 1949-51; School Teacher, L. L. Campbell Elementary School, Austin Board of Education, Austin, Texas, 1938-47. Organizational Memberships: National Association of Social Workers, Inc., 1956-78; Chairman School Social Work Council, Chicago Area, National Association Social Workers, 1968-69; Co-Chairman, Legislative Committee, National Association of Social Workers, Chicago Chapter, 1967-68; Academy of Certified Social Workers, National Association of Social Work, 1970-76; State of Illinois Certified Social Worker, 1969-70; Registered Social Worker, State of California, 1971-73. Community Activities: East Valley Community Coordinating Council, North Hollywood, California, President 1981-82; Delta Sigma Theta Sorority, Inc., Life Member; National Council Negro Women, Los Angeles, 1981-82; Life Development Project Committee, Delta Sigma Theta Sorority, Los Angeles Alumnae Chapter, Member 1981-82, Housing Committee Los Angeles Alumnae 1974-76, President Alpha Kappa Chapter 1937-38; South Carthay Neighborhood Association, Los Angeles, California, Beautification Chairperson 1979-82; Established Sickle Cell Advisory Counseling Committee, Los Angeles Health Department, 1972 to present Sickle Cell Advisory Board, Martin Luther King (County) Hospital, Los Angeles, California, 1972-73; Health Fair Planning Committee, Los Angeles, California, 1972-73; Volunteer and Contributor (public donation) to Mayor Tom Bradley's Governortorial Campaign, 1982; Volunteer, Voter Registration Drive, National Association for the Advancement of Colored People, Los Angeles, 1981-82; National Association of College Women, Chicago Branch, Chicago, Illinois, President 1966-68; United Negro College Fund, Chicago, Illinois, Volunteer Fund Raiser 1965 and 1966. Religion: Volunteer Dispatcher, Mid-Wilshire Fish, Wilshire United Methodist Church, Los Angeles, California, 1976-78. Honors and Awards: Award for Outstanding Community Service, Board of Supervisors, Los Angeles County, California, 1981; Award for Outstanding Service and Civic Responsibility, Hollywood Chamber of Commerce, North Hollywood, California, 1981; California Senatorial Citation, 20th Senate District, Senator Alan Robbins, North Hollywood, 1981; Award for Outstanding Community and Dedicated Civic Service, Federation of Community Coordinating Councils, County of Los Angeles, 1982; Award for Volunteer Service to Mid-Wilshire Fish, United Wilshire Methodist Church, Los Angeles, 1978; Award for Valuable Services to the Community and for Promoting Health Awareness to the Citizens of Los Angeles, California, Hollywood Health Fair Planning Commission and Los Angeles City College, 1973; Award for Valuable Services as School Social Worker, Robbins, Illinois, 1965; Awards for Meritorious Service to the College as Member of Human Services Aide Advisory Committee, Palos Hills, Illinois, 1969, 1970, 1971; Awards from Delta Sigma Theta Sorority, Inc., Los Angeles Alumnae Chapter for Chapter Leadership Roles, 1973-82. Address: 1034 Orlando Avenue, Los Angeles, California 90035.■

PATRICIA ANNE CHUMBLEY

Research Analyst. Personal: Born December 17, 1936; Daughter of Mrs. Cleo Chumbley Outlaw. Education: B.A., Marycrest College, Davenport, Iowa, 1966; M.A., Fordham University, New York City, 1969. Career: Research Analyst, Arizona State Legislature; Former Positions as Educator, Counselor, Social Worker and Program Administrator for City and State Governments. Community Activities: Founder of Five Emergency Pregnancy Services Centers in Various Locations in Arizona; Past Chairperson, Alternatives to Abortion, International; Community Consultant for Numerous City, County and State Civic and Government Groups in Advising regarding Social Programs, Educational Programs. Religion: Catholic. Address: 4831 West Bryce Avenue, Glendale, Arizona 85301.■

IRENE ZABOLY CHURCH

Personnel Executive. Personal: Born February 18, 1947; Daughter of Bela and Irene Zaboly; Mother of Elizabeth Anne, Irene Elizabeth. Education: Graduate of Public Schools, 1965. Career: Chairman of the Board and President, Oxford Personnel, Pepper Pike, Ohio; Chairman of the Board and President, Oxford Temporaries, Inc., Pepper Pike, Ohio; Personnel Consultant, 1965; Secretary, 1966-68; Personnel Consultant, 1968-70. Organizational Memberships: The Greater Cleveland Association of Personnel Consultants, Inc., Member 1973 to present, State Trustee 1975-80, Second Vice President and Chairperson of Business Practices and Ethics 1974-75, First Vice President and Chairperson of Business Practices and Ethics 1975-76, President 1976-77, Board Advisor and Chairperson of Vi Pender Award 1977-78, Chairperson of Vi Pender Award 1980, Chairperson of Arbitration and Fund Raising 1980 to present, Committee Member of Vi Pender Award 1981; The Ohio Association of Personnel Consultants, Inc., Member 1973 to present, Trustee and Board Member 1975-80, Secretary and Chairperson of Business Practices and Ethics 1976-77, First Vice President and Chairperson of Business Practices and Ethics 1977-78, Chairperson of Resolutions Committee 1981 to present; The National Association of Personnel Consultants, Inc., Member 1973 to present, Ethics Committee 1976-77, Co-Chairperson Ethics 1977-78, Member C.P.C. Society and Committee on Business Practices and Ethics 1981-82; National Association of Temporary Services, 1980-81; American Business Women's Association, 1980 to present. Community Activities: Guest Lecturer and Program Guest for Consumerism, Market, Ethics, Government Relations, Business Practices, and Work as it affects Family Life, 1975 to present; Generated and Assisted in the Implementaion of a Consumer/Industry Self-Improvement Ethics Program for Local, State and National Use; Member of Better Business Bureau, 1973 to present; Member Euclid Chamber of Commerce, 1973-83; Girl Scout Leader, Lake Erie Girl Scout Council, 1980 to present; Small Business Committee, Euclid Chamber of Commerce, 1981 to present Chairperson on Task Force Committee on Federal Funds in Social Security and Veterans Benefits, Euclid Chamber of Commerce, 1981; International Platform Association, 1982 to present; Created and Presented Two-Part Program, "How Work Affects Family Life," and "Re-entering the Job Market," for Public and Community, for Christian Action Committee, 1981; Created and Presented a Discussion Format regarding the Effects on Marriage and Family Life When One Party Ceases Working, 1981; Created and Produced to the Community a Two-Part Program, "Television and Violence: Its Effects on Children and Family Life," for Christian Action Committee, 1982. Religion: Member of Federated Church, Christian Action Committee 1981 to present, Fund Raiser for New Initiatives in Church Development 1981, Mary Martha Circle of Women's Fellowship 1981 (Program Director 1982-83). Published Works: Author Section on "Employment Practices" in Book, *How to Start A Business*, 1981. Honors and Awards: Awarded Designation of "Certified Personnel Consultant," 1975; Recipient Vi Pender Award for Outstanding Contributions to Personnel Industry. Address: 8 Ridgecrest Drive, Chagrin Falls, Ohio 44022.■

EMMA V. CINTRON

Counselor and Educator. Personal: Born August 8, 1926; Daughter of Jose Vargas-Bocheciamppi and Maria Teresa Rivera (deceased); Married Dr. Jorge Cintron; Mother of Lisi C., Leany C. Education: A.B. summa cum laude, M.A., Inter-American University; Candidate for Doctorate in Clinical Psychology, Caribbean Center for Graduate Studies. Career: Columnist for Newspaper *El Mundo*, Part-time Professor of Education, University Counselor, Inter-American University; Assistant to Dean of Admissions, Boston University; Advisor to Dormitories and Manager of *Law Review*, University of Puerto Rico. Organizational Memberships: Phi Delta Kappa, Newspaper Editor; Puerto Rican Psychological Association; Puerto Rico Personnel and Guidance Association, President Committee on Public Relations; American Personnel and Guidance Association; Hispanic Psychological Association. Community Activities: Grandmothers Club of San German; Lions Wives Club; Hogar Del Nino, Cupey, Rio Piedras, Board of Directors. Religion: United Methodist. Honors and Awards: Honorary Grandmother's Club, 1983; Dean's List, 1981-82; Distinguished Kappan of the Year, Phi Delta Kappa, 1980; Award for Her Work with Elderly People, Signed by the Mayor of San Juan, Puerto Rico, 1981; Listed in *Who's Who in the South and Southwest, Personalities of the South, The Directory of Distinguished Americans, Book of Honor, Personalities of America, The World Who's Who of Women, International Who's Who of Intellectuals, Community Leaders of the World, Biographical Roll of Honor, 5,000 Personalities of the World, Men and Women of Distinction, The International Book of Honor*. Address: Campus of Inter-American University, San German, Puerto Rico 00753.■

JOHN HENRY CISSIK

Aerospace Physiologist. Personal: Born August 18, 1943; Son of Mr. and Mrs. John Cissik; Married Dorothy Paulette Allen; Father of John Mark. Education: B.A., M.A., University of Texas-Austin, 1961-67; Ph.D., University of Illinois-Urbana, 1972; Studies in Management at the Industrial College of the Armed Forces.

Military: Served in the United States Air Force, 1967 to present, with the current rank of Lieutenant Colonel. Career: Aerospace Physiologist, United States Air Force Medical Center, Wright-Patterson Air Force Base, Ohio, 1967-69; Aerospace Physiologist, United States Air Force Medical Center, Andrews Air Force Base, Maryland, 1969-70; Chief, Cardiopulmonary Laboratory, United States Air Force Medical Center, Scott Air Force Base, Illinois, 1972-80; Aerospace Physiologist/ Chief, Cardiopulmonary Laboratory, United States Air Force Medical Center, Keesler Air Force Base, Mississippi. Organizational Memberships: *Journal of Cardiovascular and Pulmonary Technology*, Editorial Committee 1974-82; National Society of Cardiopulmonary Technology, Chairman Editorial Committee 1976-78; American Association for Respiratory Therapy, 1974 to present; Air Force Association, 1967 to present. Community Activities: Evans Elementary School Parent-Teacher Association, 1976-79; Cardiopulmonary Instructor, Community and School Organizations, 1977 to present; Belleville Area College/St Elizabeth Medical Center, Granite City Illinois, R. T. Coordinating Committee. Territory 14, 1979-80: Belleville's Belle Valley North Elementary School Parent-Teacher Association, 1979-80; St. Martin East Elementary School Parent-Teacher Association, 1980 to present. Honors and Awards: United States Air Force Chief Biomedical Scientist Rating, 1980; United States Air Force Meritorious Service Medal,1980; Listed in *Who's Who in the Midwest, Dictionary of International Biography, American Registry Series, Book of Honor.* Address: 12316 Marlowe Place, Ocean Springs, Mississippi 39564.■

GEORGE CLARE

Naval Aviator. Personal: Born April 8, 1930; Son of G. W. and H. M. Clare (both deceased); Married Catherine Saidee Hamel; Father of George C. Education: Attended the University of Southern California, 1960; University of Arlington, 1963-71; University of Washington, 1980. Military: Served in the United States Navy, Active Duty 1948-63; United States Naval Reserve, 1963-71; Retired with the rank of Commander, 1971; Served in Korea, 1952. Career: Senior System Safety Engineering Specialist; Former Naval Aviator. Organizational Memberships: Retired Officers Association; Naval Aviation Association; American Defense Preparedness Association; American Institute of Aeronautics and Astronautics; Certified Product Safety Managers; Military Order of World Wars. Community Activities: National Republican Committee; Republican Senatorial Committee; Republican Congressional Committee; Republican Party of Texas; Tarrent County Republican Party; Citizens for the Republic; American Security Council; National Rifle Association; Texas Rifle Association. Honors and Awards: L.T.V. President's Award, 1968; Air Medal with One Gold Star; Navy Unit Commendation; China Service Medal; European Occupation Medal; National Defense Medal; United Nations Medal; Korean Service Medal with Two Bronze Stars; South Korean Presidential Unit Commendation; Certified Product Safety Manager; Listed in *Who's Who in the South and Southwest.* Address: 817 North Bowen Road, Arlington, Texas 76012.■

FRED CLARK

Senior Legal Editor. Personal: Born December 12, 1930; Son of Thomas and Irene Clark (both deceased); Father of Paul, Rodion. Education: Central American Academy, 1944-49; University of Costa Rica, 1950-51; Stafford College, 1956-57; Inner Temple, 1957-60; University of London, 1961; Litt.B., Barrister-at-Law. Military: Served in the Royal Air Force attaining the rank of Airman. Career: Consultant in Commonwealth Law and International Operations; Private Law Practice; Trust Officer; Master of Languages; Senior Legal Editor. Organizational Memberships: International Commission of Jurists, Life Member; American Management Association. Community Activities: Special Advisor, United States Congressional Advisory Board, 1982 to present; Inter-American Society, 1974 to present; American Museum of Natural History, 1971 to present; Smithsonian Associates, 1979 to present; National Geographic Society, 1979 to present; Amateur Astronomers Association, 1980 to present; International Platform Association; National Trust for Historic Preservation, American Ballet Theatre, 1979; Metropolitan Opera Guild, 1979. Religion: United Church of Christ, Trustee 1970-78. Honors and Awards: Listed in *Who's Who in Finance and Industry, Who's Who in the East, Personalities of America, Directory of Distinguished Americans, International Who's Who of Intellectuals, Men of Achievement, International Book of Honor, Who's Who in the World.* Address: 39 West Fourth Street, Freeport, New York 11520.■

JAMES MARTIN CLARK

Corporate Executive. Personal: Born April 6, 1953; Son of Martin Clark; Married Pamela W.; Father of Michele A., James M. Jr., Madeleine E. Education: Attended the United States Naval Nuclear Power School and Prototype, 1973; B.S., University of the State of New York, 1978; M.B.A. 1979, Ph.D. 1980, Columbia Pacific University. Military: Served in the United States Navy, E-6, 1970-76. Career: President, Bajan Resorts, Inc; President, Kilburn Vacation Homeshare, Inc. Community Activities: Salt Lake City Chamber of Commerce, 1982; Sons of the American Revolution, Salt Lake Chapter Vice President 1975; Ensign Neighborhood Council, Secretary 1979; Rotary Club; Several Church Service Positions; Professional Genealogists Society, Treasurer 1976-77. Honors and Awards: Phi Kappa Phi; Tau Beta Pi; Naval Academic Award; Accredited Genealogist, Southern United States. Address: 550 Cambridge Circle, Salt Lake City, Utah 84103.■

JULIA V. CLARK

Professor. Personal: Born December 16, 1939; Daughter of Mr. and Mrs. Frank Clark. Education: B.S. Natural Science, Fort Valley State College, 1960; M.Ed. Science Education, University of Georgia, 1968; Ed.D. Science Education, Rutgers University, 1980. Career: Acting Coordinator Graduate Curriculum Programs, Howard University, 1983-84; Director of Clinical Laboratory Experiences, Clark College, 1973-81; Board of Directors, Consortium of Southern Colleges for Teacher Education, 1973-79; Professor of Science Education, Howard University, 1982 to present; Associate Professor of Education, Clark College 1975-82, Atlanta College 1976-82; Instructor of Biology and Science Education, Morris Brown College, 1970-72; Instructor of Biology and Botany, Albany State College, 1969-70; Teacher of General Science and Biology, Atlanta Public Schools, 1964-69; Chairperson, Science Department, Teacher of General Science, Biology, Chemistry and Physics, Marietta Public Schools, 1961-63; Teacher of General Science, Biology, Chemistry, Physics, Barrow County Public Schools, 1960-61; Science Teacher, Atlanta, 1978-79. Organizational Memberships: Phi Delta Kappa; Sigma Xi Scientific Research Society; National Association of Research in Science Teaching; Society for College Science Teaching, District Membership Coordinator; American Educational Research Association; National Science Teachers Association; American Association for the Advancement of Science; National Council of Negro Women; Transportation Research Board; Women's Equity Action League, Metropolitan D.C. Chapter; Minorities and Women in Science, Metropolitan D.C. Chapter. Published Works: Author of "Development of Seriation and Its Relation to the Achievement of Inferential Transitivity", *Journal of Research in Science Teaching*, 1983; "Training Teachers Through Field-Based Clinical Experiences in Science", *Teacher Corps*, 1979; Author of monographs "Trends in Mortality in Cardiovascular Diseases in Georgia", 1980; "Effects of Salt Consumption in the Epidemiology of High Blood Pressure", 1979 and others. Honors and Awards: Lily Foundation Award to Study at Rutgers University, 1979-80; United Negro College Fund Faculty Award to Study at Rutgers University, 1978-79; Certificate of Achievement in Grantsmanship, Department of Federal Affairs, Howard University, 1983; Listed in *Outstanding Young Women of America, Who's Who Among Blacks in Metropolitan Washington, The World's Who's Who of Women, Community Leaders of the World, Directory of Distinguished Americans.* Address: 5101 River Road, #208, Bethesda, Maryland 20816.■

RICHARD LeFORS CLARK

Consultant, Systems Engineer, Lecturer. Personal: Born October 29, 1936; Son of Robert M. Clark, Sr. (deceased); Married Barbara Battersby; Father of Robert James. Education: B.S. Engineering and Applied Science 1968, M.A. 1972, Jackson State College; B.S. Business Administration 1974, M.S. Psychology 1975, Ph.D. Mathematical Engineering 1978, Pacific Western University. Military: Served in the United States Army as Sargeant, 1954-57. Career: Consultant; Systems Engineer; Lecturer; Former Positions as Consultant, Systems Engineer, Author, Editor, Weapons Systems Analyst, Reconnaissance and Intelligence Engineer, Passive Reconnaissance Systems Engineer, Computer Systems Engineer, Computer Programmer. Organizational Memberships: American Nuclear Society; American Chemical Society; American Association for the Advancement of Science; New York Academy of Science; United States Psychotronic Society; American Mathematical Society; Mathematical Association of America; S.I.A.M.; Psychical Research Foundation. Community Activities: Research Consultant to M.U.F.O.N., 1982; Researcher and Reporter to Psychical Research Foundation, 1980 to present. Religion: Episcopal. Published Works: Published Author and Lecturer in New Age Science Subjects of Tesla Systems, Reich Systems, Psychotronic Systems, Alternate Energy Systems, E.V.P. Systems, E.L.F. Systems. Honors and Awards: Fellow, American Psychical Research Foundation; Fellow, United States Psychotronic Society; Listed in *Who's Who in the West, Personalities of America, Community Leaders of America, Directory of Distinguished Americans.* Address: 4015 Crown Point Drive P3, San Diego, California 92019.■

TWO THOUSAND NOTABLE AMERICANS

ROBERT FRANCIS CLARKE

Consultant and Corporation Director. Personal: Born March 20, 1915; Son of Charles Patrick and Maurine Elizabeth Clark (both deceased); Married Charlotte Adele R.; Father of Robert William, Carol Agnes (Bodeker), David Charles. Education: B.S. with honors, University of Florida, 1948; M.S., University of Arizona, 1971; Air Tactical School, 1951; Air Command and Staff College, 1973; Air War College, 1965; United States Air Force Air University; United States Army Command and General Staff College, 1968; Industrial College of the Armed Forces, 1972. Military: Served in the United States Army as Master Sergeant, 1942-46; Served in the United States Air Force, 58th Strategic Reconnaissance Squadron, 1950-52, attaining the rank of Colonel 1952-75, Retired. Career: Consultant and Director, North Star International Metals Corporation, 1978 to present; Meteorologist, United States Weather Bureau, 1940-42, 1948-50, 1952-55; Supervisory Electronics Engineer and Chief, Navigation Branch, 1956-58; Nuclear Physicist and Chief Scientist, Nuclear Surveillance Division, United States Army Electronics Proving Ground, 1958-62; Aerospace Engineer (Nuclear Propulsion and Power), NASA Lewis Research Center, 1962-66; Physicist (Optics), Hughes Aircraft Company, 1966-68; Instructor Mathematics, Pima Community College, 1970-74; Head, Electro-Mechanical Department, San Juan Campus, New Mexico State University, 1974-75; Instructor Mathematics, American International School of Kabul, Afghanistan, 1976-78. Organizational Memberships: Senior Member, Institute of Electrical and Electronics Engineers, Plasma Physics and Computer Sections; American Institute of Aeronautics and Astronautics; Society of Photo-Optical Instrumentation Engineers; Association of Unmanned Vehicle Systems; American Association of University Professors; American Meteorological Society, Southern Arizona Chapter President 1982; American Nuclear Society, Fusion Power and Reactor Physics Sections; Arizona, Nevada and New York Academies of Science; Scientists and Engineers for Secure Energy; American Physicists' Association; Federation of American Scientists; Arctic Institute of North America. Community Activities: Director, Kiwanis Club of Tucson, 1981-82; Benevolent and Protective Order of Elks; Military Order of the World Wars, Department of Arizona Adjutant 1981-82; Reserve Officers' Association of the United States, President Pima County Chapter 1981-82; Association of the United States Army, President Tucson Chapter 1981-82; Veterans of Foreign Wars; American Legion; Radiological Defense Officer (Volunteer) Pima County, Federal Emergency Management Agency, Division of Emergency Services; Director, Plans and Programs, Group I Arizona Wing Civil Air Patrol. Honors and Awards: Scholarship, Physics, University of Chicago, 1932-33; Scholarsip, University of Minnesota, 1934-35; National Science Foundation Scholarship, University of Arizona Graduate College, 1969-71; Military Order of the World Wars National Citation Award, 1982; Outstanding United States Air Force Reserve Officer with Arizona Wing Civil Air Patrol Award, 1974. Address: 5846 East South Wilshire Drive, Tucson, Arizona 85711.■

ENRICO ANTHONY CLAUSI

Army Officer. Personal: Born December 26, 1947; Son of Enrico F. and Antoinette Clausi; Married Mary E.; Father of Catherine Marie. Education: B.A. Political Science, Loyola University. Military: Graduate of Command and General Staff College, Served in United States Army, attaining rank of Captain 1974, promoted to Major 1982; Division Transportation Officer. Organizational Memberships: Association of the United States Army; American Defense Preparedness Association. Religion: Roman Catholic. Honors and Awards: United States Army Meritorious Service Medal; United States Army Commendation Medal; Awarded Honorary Rank of Colonel in the Tennessee State Militia; Listed in *Who's Who in the South and Southwest*. Address: HHC 2AD FWD, APO New York 09335.■

INA SMILEY CLAYTON

Educator. Personal: Born March 2, 1924; Daughter of O. R. and Leverett Jones Smiley; Married O. L. Clayton; Mother of Felicia Tulikka. Education: B.S. Elementary Education, Jackson State University, Jackson, Mississippi, 1946; M.A. Supervision, Syracuse University, Syracuse, New York, 1955; Ph.D. Educational Leadership and Human Behavior, United States International University, San Diego, California, 1977. Career: Classroom Teacher, Los Angeles Unified School District, 1968-77; Elementary Substitute Teacher, Compton-Willowbrook and Los Angeles, 1967-68; Elementary Principal, Laurel City Schools, Mississippi, 1963-67; Elementary Head Teacher, Laurel City Schools, Mississippi, 1955-63; Jeans Supervisor, Covington County Schools (K-12), Mississippi, 1947-54; Head Teacher, Smith County Training School, Taylorsville, Mississippi, 1946-47; Teacher and College Instructor (Inservice), Junior College Institute Social Science. Organizational Memberships: California Teachers Association, Local Representative 1969-74; Future Teachers of America, Chairman 1964-66; Hostess, District Science Association, 1966; Accreditation School Member (Southern) Mississippi, 1965-66; U.T.L.A.; National Education Association; Institute of Children's Literature. Community Activities: Sigma Gamma Rho; Smithsonian Institute Guild; Literary Guild; Collectors Guild; Doctoral Society of U.S.I.U.; Council for Basic Education; National Association for the Advancement of Colored People; Urban League. Religion: Sunday School Teacher, Grades 4-6, 1967-76; Vice President 1979 and 1980, President 1981 and 1982, United Methodist Women; Order of the Eastern Star, 1954 to present; Oral Roberts Covenant Family Membership, 1982. Honors and Awards: Member Town Hall of California Board of Governors; Listed in *Who's Who in the West, World Who's Who of Women, Who's Who in America, Community Leaders of America*. Address: 1717 West 57th Street, Los Angeles, California 90002.■

REBECCA KILGO CLAYTON

Educator. Personal: Born September 25, 1916; Daughter of Mr. and Mrs. Middleton Samuel Clayton (both deceased). Education: B.S., College of Charleston, 1944; Master of Special Education, University of Michigan, 1959; Graduate Studies, University of North Carolina, University of South Carolina, Pennsylvania State University, LaVerne College, The Citadel, Mundelyn College, University of Miami. Career: Elementary Teacher, Special Teacher and Princiapl, Orthopedic School Charleston; Special Teacher, United States Army Schools in France and Germany; Teacher and Remedial Reading Instructor, Panama Canal County Schools; Principal, Summer School Session for Migrant Workers in Charleston; Principal and Teacher, Summer Program, Orthopedic School Charleston; Resource Teacher, St. George Elementary School, 1981-84. Organizational Memberships: National Education Association; C.E.C.; President, Isthmian College Club; President and State President, National League of American Pen Women, Panama Canal Branch; National Association of Retarded Children; International Reading Association; Phi Delta Kappa; National Trust for American Women's Club; Delta Kappa Gamma. Community Activities: Girl Scout Leader, Girl Scout Counselor; Donated Painting to Help Raise Money for International Year of the Child in Panama; Pianist, Blind Center, Salvation Army Center in Panama City, Republic of Panama. Religion: Sunday School Teacher; President, Wesleyan Service Guild; President, Methodist Missionary Society; Devotion Church Fellowship of Concerned Balboa Union Church; Pianist, Junior Department, Balboa Union Church; Pianist and Choir Director, Givhans Southern Methodist Church; Pianist, Pedregal Methodist Mission Church, Republic of Panama. Honors and Awards: Valedictorian of High School Class; History Medal, Ridgeville School; Ribbons for Best Slides; Ribbons for Best Painting in Art Shows; Honor Scholarship, Coker College; Medal for Community Service, Panama Canal Commission, 1981. Address: Route Box 391, Givhans-Ridgeville, South Carolina 29472.■

WILLIAM T. CLEVELAND

Social Studies Educator. Personal: Born April 6, 1946; Son of Mrs. Francis Cleveland. Education: B.A. 1968, M.A. 1971, State University of New York at Albany; Postgraduate Studies undertaken at the University of Virginia and Claremont Graduate School. Career: Social Studies Teacher, Bethlehem High School (Delmar, New York); Former Teacher Associate, Social Science Education Consortium, Boulder, Colorado. Organizational Memberships: National Council for the Social Studies, Member 1968 to present, Board of Directors 1979-81, House of Delegates 1972-81, Chairman Carter Woodson Committee 1979-82; New York State Council for the Social Studies, President 1978-79, First Vice President 1977-78, Second Vice President 1976-77, Executive Secretary 1973-76, Newsletter Editor 1974-76, Board of Directors 1972-83; Association for Supervision and Curriculum Development; National Indian Education Association; Bethlehem Central Teachers Association, President 1973-84; National Education Association of New York, Board of Directors 1976-79 and 1981-85; National Education Association, Board of Directors 1976-78 and 1981-85, Representative Assembly 1973-85, Chairman Northeast Regional Leadership Conference 1981-82, Structure and Services Review Committee 1983-84. Community Activities: Democratic Committeeman for Albany County, 1974-78; Guilderland Democratic Chairman, 1976-78; B.C.T.A. United Way Campaign, 1982, 1983; Third Judicial District Nominating Convention, 1975-78. Religion: Member Watkins Glen First Presbyterian Church, 1960 to present. Honors and Awards: MYSKANIA, 1967; Phi Delta Kappa; National Endowment for the Humanities Fellowships, 1976, 1977, 1978; Listed in *Who's Who in the East, Community Leaders of the World, Personalities of America, International Men of Achievement*. Address: 290 State Street, Albany, New York 12210.■

RAYMOND WINFRED CLEWETT

Mechanical Design Engineer. Personal: Born November 7, 1917; Son of Howard J. (deceased) and Pansy M. Clewett; Married Hazel Royer; Father of Alan E., Charles R., Beverly C. Coutts, Patricia C. Vaughn, Richard H. Education: Attended Chaffey Junior College, 1937. Career: Research Mechanic, Master Machinist, Test Laboratory Foreman, Douglas Aircraft Company, Santa Monica, California, 1937-45; Machine Shop Foreman, Mechanical Design Engineer, Lear Inc., Los Angeles, California, 1945-51; Shop Manager, Mechanical Design Engineer, The RAND Corporation, Santa Monica, California, 1951 to present; Design Consultant, Pacific-Sierra Research Corporation; Organizer/Operator, HY-TECH Engineering and Development Laboratory, Malibu, California. Organizational Memberships: Society of Manufacturing Engineers; American Association for the Advancement of Science. Religion: Financial Secretary, First Methodist Church of West Los Angeles, 1966-69. Honors and Awards: United States Patent No. 3,766,596. Address: 7069 Fernhill Drive, Malibu, California 90265.■

CHARLES WILLIAM CLINE

Professor of English, Poet, Author. Personal: Born March 1, 1937; Son of Paul Ardell and Montarie Pittman Cline (both deceased); Married Sandra Williamson; Father of Jeffrey. Education: A.A., Reinhardt College, 1957; Student in Music at the College-Conservatory of Music, University of Cincinnati, 1957-58; B.A., George Peabody College of Vanderbilt University, 1960; M.A., Vanderbilt University, 1963. Career: Assistant Professor of English, Shorter College, 1963-64; Instructor in English, West Georgia College, 1964-68; Manuscript Procurement Editor, Fideler Company, 1968; Associate Professor of English 1969-75, Professor of English and Resident Poet 1975 to present, Kellogg Community College. Organizational Memberships: World Poetry Society Intercontinental; International Biographical Association; Centro Studi e Scambi Internazionali/Accademia Leonardo da Vinci; International Society of Literature; Tagore Institute of Creative Writing International; Poetry Society of America; Michigan Education Association; National Education Association; Midwest Conference on English. Religion: Presbyterian. Published Works: Forty Salutes to Michigan Poets (Editor 1975); Crossing the Ohio 1976, Questions for the Snow 1979, Ultima Thule 1984. Honors and Awards: Poetry Awards from Weave Anthology (1974), Modus Operandi (1975), International Belles-Lettres Society (Gold Medal 1975), Poetry Society of Michigan (two First Place Awards 1975), North American Mentor (1977, 1978); Founder Fellow, International Academy of Poets, 1976; Fellow, International Biographical Association, 1978; Poet Laureate Award and Diploma di Benemerenza, Centro Studi e Scambi Internazionali/Accademia Leonardo da Vinci, 1980; Resolutions of Recognition for Poetic Contributions to Cultural Life in Kalamazoo from the Michigan Senate, Michigan House of Representatives, Kalamazoo City Commission, 1981; Certificate of Recognition, U.S. House of Representatives (3rd Congressional District of Michigan), 1981; Litt.D., World University Roundtable, 1981; Diploma D'onore, International Great Prize "The Glory" from the Accademia Leonardo da Vinci, 1982; Life Fellow, International Society of Literature, 1982; Command Performance (Special Feature in Poetry), Voices International, 1982; Diploma di Merito, Universita delle Arti, 1982. Address: 9866 South Westnedge Avenue, Kalamazoo, Michigan 49002.■

JOHN HART CLINTON

Lawyer, Publisher. Personal: Born April 3, 1905, in Quincy, Massachusetts; Son of John Francis and Catherine Veronica Hart Clinton (both deceased); Married First Wife Helen Alice Amphlett, February 18, 1933 (deceased), Second Wife Mathilda A. Schoorel van Dillen; Father of Mary Jane, Mary Ann, John Hart Jr. Education: A.B., Boston College, 1926; J.D., Harvard University, 1929. Career: California Bar, 1930; Massachusetts Bar, 1930; Law Practice, San Francisco; Associate, Morrison, Hohfield, Foerster, Shuman and Clark, 1929-41; Partner, Morrison, Foerster, Holloway, Clinton and Clark, 1941-72; Of Counsel, Morrison and Foerster, 1972 to present; Executive Vice President, General Counsel, Industrial Employers and Distributors Association, Emeryville, 1944-72; President, Leamington Hotel, Oakland, California, 1933-37; President, Amphlett Printing Company, San Mateo, California, 1943 to present; San Mateo Times, Publisher 1943 to present, Editor 1960 to present. Organizational Memberships: Federal Communications Commission; American Bar Association; San Francisco Bar Association; San Mateo County Bar Association; State Bar California, Chairman State Bar Committee, Fair Trial/Fair Press, Co-Chairman California Bench/Bar Media Committee; American Judicature Society; National Lawyers Club; American Law Institute; California Press Association; American Newspaper Publishers Association, Government Affairs Committee, Press/Bar Relations Committee; American Bar Association-American Newspaper Publishers Association Task Force; California Newspaper Publishers Association, President 1969; American Society of Newspaper Editors; Association of Catholic Newsmen; National Press Photographers Association. Community Activities: Boy Scouts of American, Honorary Member, Executive Committee, San Mateo Council; California Jockey Club Foundation; Notre Dame College, Belmont, California, Regent Emeritus; Equestrian Order of Holy Sepulchre of Jerusalem, Decorated Knight; San Mateo County Development Association, President 1963-65; San Mateo County Historical Association, President 1960-64; International Platform Association; Newcomen Society; Commonwealth of California, Past President, San Francisco Commonwealth, Bohemian; San Mateo Rotary Club, Past President; Elks. Address: 131 Sycamore Avenue, San Mateo, California 94402.■

PATRICIA ANN CLUNN

Associate Professor and Curriculum Coordinator. Personal: Born April 17, 1930; Mother of Steven, Jeffrey. Education: B.S.N., University of Pennsylvania, Philadelphia; M.A., M.Ed., D.Ed. 1975, Teachers' College, Columbia University, New York City. Career: Program Director, Division of Psychiatric Mental Health Nursing, American Nurses Association; Assistant Professor, University of Florida; Assistant Professor, Indian River Community College; Director Nursing Services, Childrens' Residential Treatment Section, New Jersey Neuropsychiatric Institute, Princeton, New Jersey. Organizational Memberships: American Nurses Association, Council of Nurse Researchers, Council of Clinical Specialists in Psychiatric-Mental Health Nursing, Task Force for Certification Test Development for Generalist and Clinical Specialist Examinations of Division of Psychiatric Mental Health Nursing; Sigma Theta Tau; Advocates for Child Psychiatry; Advocates for Child Psychiatric Nursing, Regional Coordinator, 1977 to present; H.R.S. Task Force for Study of Needs of Disturbed Children in Florida, 1977-79; Certified Clinical Specialist in Psychiatric-Mental Health Nursing, American Nurses Association. Published Works: Co-Author (with D. Payne) Psychiatric Mental Health Nursing, Third Edition 1982, Second Edition 1979, Polish Translation 1980. Honors and Awards: American Nurses Association, Council for Advanced Practice in Psychiatric Mental Health Nursing, Contribution to Direct Practice, 1979; Recognition for Outstanding Contribution as Citizen, Alatchua County Crisis Center, 1979. Address: 8520 Southwest 149th Avenue, #1003, Miami, Florida 33193.■

CAROLYN ANN KNOPP COBB

Data Base Administrator. Personal: Born February 21, 1950; Daughter of Vincent and Margaret Knopp; Married Richard Joseph Cobb on September 29, 1978; Mother of Richard Joseph Jr. Education: B.A., Harris Teachers College, 1973; M.A., Webster College, 1975. Career: Teacher of Mathematics, St. Louis Public Schools, 1973-74; Programmer, General American Life Insurance Company, 1974-75; Programmer, Mercantile Trust Company, North America, 1975-78; Programmer/Analyst, Missouri Pacific Railroad, 1979-81; Data Base Administrator, Assistant Staff Manager, Southwestern Bell Telephone Company, 1981 to present. Organizational Memberships: Association for Systems Management; Data Processing Management Association; Charter Member, Association for Women in Computing. Community Activities: St. Paul's United Church of Christ, Oakville; St. Paul's Athletic Committee, Financial Chairman; St. Paul's Arts and Crafts Fair, Chairman; St. Paul's Co-Ed Softball Coach; St. Paul's Co-Ed Volleyball Coach; St. Paul's Choir; St. Paul's Adult Fellowship; Grace United Church of Christ, Youth Group Leader and Drop-in Advisor; Data Processing Explorer Post Advisor, Boy Scouts of America; Young Republicans. Honors and Awards: Kappa Delta Pi; Ronald Winters Memorial Scholarship; Advisory Board Scholarship; Leadership Conferences; Listed in Who's Who Among Students in American Colleges and Universities, Who's Who of American Women, World Who's Who of Women, Personalities of West and Midwest, Personalities of America. Address: 6520 Galewood Court, St. Louis, Missouri 63129.■

STEPHEN MARCUS COBAUGH

State Senate Art Director. Personal: Born November 6, 1955; Son of Charles M. and Shirley A. Cobaugh. Education: B.A. Art, Millersville State College, Millersville, Pennsylvania, 1977; M.A. Art, Indiana University of Pennsylvania, Indiana, Pennsylvania, 1979. Career: Art Director, Senate Republican Communications Office,

Senate of Pennsylvania; Chairman, Elizabethtown Area Republican Committee; Republican Committeeman, West Donegal Township, Second District, Lancaster County, Pennsylvania; Assistant Research Analyst, Senator Richard A. Snyder, Education, Welfare and Health Research, 1980; Member, Indiana University of Pennsylvania College Republican Club, 1978; Indiana University of Pennsylvania Delegate, Pennsylvania College Republican Convention, Harrisburg, Pennsylvania, 1978; Pennsylvania Delegate, Mid-Atlantic College Republican Convention, St. Davids, Pennsylvania, 1977; Millersville State College Delegate, Pennsylvania College Republican Convention, Harrisburg, Pennsylvania, 1977; President, College Republican Club, Millersville State College, Millersville, Pennsylvania, 1977; President Ford Committee, Convention Staff, Republican National Convention, Kansas City, Missouri, 1976; District 5 Coordinator (South-Central Pennsylvania), College Republican Council of Pennsylvania, 1976; County Youth Director, President Ford Committee, Lancaster County, Pennsylvania, 1976; President, College Republican Club, Millersville State College, Millersville, Pennsylvania, 1976; Millersville State College Delegate, Pennsylvania College Republican Convention, Grantville, Pennsylvania, 1976; Coordinator, Young Citizens for Specter Arlen Specter for United States Senate, Lancaster County, Pennsylvania, 1975; South-Central Pennsylvania Regional Director, College Republican Council of Pennsylvania, 1975; Millersville State College Delegate, Pennsylvania College Republican Convention, Hershey, Pennsylvania, 1975; Lancaster County Delegate, Pennsylvania Teen Age Republican Convention, Pennsylvania State University, University Park, Pennsylvania, 1975; Others. Community Activities: International President, United States Space Education Association; International Biographical Association; American Topical Association, Space Unit; International Association of Space Philatelists; American Society for Aerospace Education; Friendship Fire and Hose Company No. 1, Elizabethtown, Pennsylvania; L-5 Society; Millersville State College Alumni Association; Aviation/Space Writers Association; Smithsonian Associates. Honors and Awards: Membership's Choice Award, United States Space Education Association, 1976, 1977, 1978; Highest Communications Award at Millersville State College, 1977; Member of the Year Award, United States Space Education Association, 1977; WIXQ Service Award, Highest Communications Award at Millersville State College, 1977; WIXQ Executive Council Award, Millersville State College, 1977; WMSR Station Manager's Award, WMSR Executive Council Award, 1976; Person Contributing Most to WMSR Award, 1975; Pennsylvania Teen Age Republican of the Month, 1974; J. Warren Bishop Memorial Award for Scholarship, Leadership and Americanism, Elizabethtown Jaycees, 1973; Rotary Student of the Month, March, Elizabethtown Rotary Club; Teen of the Week Award, Lancaster New Era Newspaper. Address: 746 Turnpike Road, Elizabethtown, Pennsylvania 17022.■

DOUGLAS THANE ROMNEY CODY

Consultant, Medical Administrator. Personal: Born June 23, 1923; Married Joanne; Father of Douglas, Romney. Education: M.D., C.M., Dalhousie University, 1957; Intern, St. John General Hospital, 1956-57; Resident in Pathology, Provincial Laboratory, St. John, 1957-58; Mayo Foundation Fellowship in Otolaryngology 1958-63, Ph.D. 1966, M.D. Otorhinolaryngology. Career: Consultant in Otolaryngology, Mayo Clinic, 1963 to present; Chairman, Department of Otolaryngology, Mayo Clinic, 1968-82; Professor of Otolaryngology, Mayo Medical School; Board of Governors, Mayo Clinic, 1977 to present; Board of Trustees, Mayo Foundation, 1977 to present (Vice Chairman, 1982 to present). Organizational Memberships: American Board of Otolaryngology, Board of Directors 1981 to present; American College of Surgeons, Board of Governors 1980 to present; American Academy of Otolaryngology, Head and Neck Surgery; American Otological Society, Secretary-Treasurer 1982, Board of Trustees; American Otolaryngology Society Research Fund, 1980 to present; Alumni Association of the Mayo Foundation for Medical Education and Research; American Laryngological, Rhinological and Otological Society; Association for Research in Otolaryngology; The Barany Society; The Centurion Club of the Deafness Research Foundation; The Otosclerosis Study Group; Sigma Xi; The Society of University Otolaryngologists; Board of Directors, Dalhousie Medical Alumni Association, 1978 to present. Published Works: Author of 150 Articles including "Your Child's Ears, Nose and Throat: A Parent's Medical Guide" 1974 and "Diseases of the Ears, Nose and Throat — A Guide to Diagnosis and Management" 1981. Address: 1001 Skyline Drive Southwest, Rochester, Minnesota 55901.■

ALAN SEYMOUR COHEN

Physician (Rheumatologist). Personal: Born April 9, 1926; Son of George I. and Jennie Laskin Cohen (mother deceased); Married Joan Elizabeth Prince, Daughter of William and Anne Prince (mother deceased); Father of Evan Bruce, Andrew Hollis, Robert Adam. Education: A.B. magna cum laude, Harvard University, 1947; M.D. magna cum laude, Boston University School of Medicine, 1952. Military: Commissioned Assistant Surgeon in United States Public Health Service, 1953-55; Advanced to Senior Assistant Surgeon in Chronic Disease Division, Diabetes Field Research and Training Unit. Career: Head, Arthritis and Connective Tissue Disease Section, Evans Department of Clinical Research, Massachusetts Memorial Hospital, 1960-72; Conrad Wesselhoeft Professor of Medicine, Boston University School of Medicine, 1972 to present; Director, Division of Medicine and Thorndike Memorial Laboratory, Boston City Hospital, 1973 to present; Professor of Pharmacology, Boston University School of Medicine, 1974 to present; Director, Arthritis Center, Boston University, 1977 to present. Organizational Memberships: President, American Rheumatism Association, 1978-79; Chairman, Special Projects Review Group A, N.I.A.D.D.K., National Institutes of Health; Association of American Physicians; Past President, New England Rheumatism Society, 1966-67; American Society of Clinical Investigation; American Federation of Clinical Research; Inter-urban Clinical Club; American Society of Experimental Pathology; Phi Beta Kappa; Alpha Omega Alpha. Religion: Temple Israel of Boston. Honors and Awards: Maimonides Award, Greater Boston Medical Society, 1952; Junior Chamber of Commerce of Massachusetts Award as "Four Outstanding Young Men in Massachusetts," 1961; Outstanding Alumnus Award, Boston University School of Medicine, 1975 (21st Award in 100 Years); Honorary Member, Italian Rheumatism Society 1977, Spanish Rheumatism Society 1978, Brazilian Rheumatism Association 1978, Finnish Rheumatism Society 1980; The Purdue Frederick 1979 Arthritis Award; James H. Fairclough Jr. Memorial Award for Distinguished Service to the Massachusetts Chapter of the Arthritis Foundation, 1981 (Second Recipient); Honorary Lifetime Member, Irish Society of Rheumatology and Rehabilitation, 1981 (First Elected Honorary Member); Boston University 1981 General Alumni Award for Special Distinction (Silver Medal); Listed in *American Men of Science, Who's Who in the East, Dictionary of International Biography, Contemporary Authors, International Who's Who in Community Service, Men of Achievement, Who's Who in America, Who's Who in World Medicine, Who's Who in American Jewry, Men and Women of Distinction, Community Leaders of America, Who's Who in Technology, The Best Doctors in the U.S.*. Address: 54 Winston Road, Newton Centre, Massachusetts 02159.■

LOUIS ALEXANDER COHEN

Foreign Service Administrator. Personal: Born April 1, 1923; Son of Sultan G. and Bernice A. Cohen (deceased); Married Babara Zucrow, Daughter of Maurice J. (deceased) and Lilian Feinstein; Father of Marc Jacob. Education: B.S.C.E., Purdue University, 1948; Work Toward M.A. Degree, American University, 1966-70; Studies in Mechanical Engineering, Mississippi State University, 1944; Certificate in Environmental Engineering, University of North Carolina, 1974. Military: Served in the United States Army, 1943-46, as Technial Sergeant in the Corps of Engineers. Career: Director, U.S.A.I.D./Somalia, Foreign Service; Former Civil Engineer in Foreign Service. Organizational Memberships: National Society of Professional Engineers; American Society of Civil Engineers; American Foreign Service Association; Society of American Military Engineers; United States Committee on Large Dams; African Studies Association; American Water Resources Association; International Water Resources Association; American Association of Asian Studies; Society of International Development. Community Activities: Rotary Internatinal; B'nai B'rith; Siam Society; Botswana Society. Religion: Jewish. Published Works: Author of Chapter in *Focus on Southeast Aisa* 1972, Water Resource Portions of *Long-Term Planning for Sahel Development* 1976, *Status of Functions of AID Engineers* 1983, Articles in *Sawaddi* (Bangkok) 1971-76. Honors and Awards: Meritorious Service Award, Ministry of Public Works, Republic of Vietnam, 1972; Licensed Professional Engineer, Indiana 1949, New York 1957; Licensed Professional Land Surveyor, Indiana 1955. Address: 1099 22nd Street Northwest, Apt. 405, Washington D.C. 20037.■

ROSALIE AGGER COHEN

Educator. Personal: Born February 2, 1923; Daughter of Benjamin and Pauline Agger (both deceased); Mother of David, Anita, Michael, Joel, Brian. Education: B.A., Indiana Central College, 1951; M.Ed., Duquesne University, 1958; Ph.D., University of Pittsburgh, 1967. Career: Associate Professor of Sociology and Foundations of Education 1970 to present, Chairman of Foundations of Education Department 1974-77, Temple University (Philadelphia); Guest Professor, Institute for Advanced Studies and Scientific Research, Vienna, Austria, Summer 1970; Assistant/Associate Research Professor, G.S.S.W. 1967-69, Chairman of Masters Research and Ph.D. Program 1969, University of Pittsburgh; Research Assistant, Learning Research and Development Center, 1965-67. Organizational Memberships: American Sociological Association; Society for the Study of Social Problems, Co-Chairman Poverty and Human Relations Section 1968-71, Session Organizer 1972, Chairman Committee on Standards and Freedom of Research, Publication and Teaching 1973-76, Organization of Sessions, Open Sessions and Plenary Sessions 1974-76; American Judicature Society; Society for Applied Anthropology, Fellow; Eastern Sociological Society, Committee on the Professions 1970; Associate Editor, *Journal of Health and Social Behavior*. Community Activities: N.I.E. Field Consultant, 1974; Third International Congress on Social Psychiatry, Advisory Council 1970; Colleague Consultancies, 1967 to present; Mon-Valley Coordinated Health and Welfare Center (Monessen, Pennsylvania), Research Consultant 1969-73; Organizer, Research Conference on Urban Sub-Cultural Differences with Interdisciplinary, University, Community, International Participation (Pittsburgh, Pennsylvania), 1969; Testified for School Governance and Management, Representative College Task Force on Basic Education, Legislative Sub-Committee on Basic Education (Harrisburg), 1974. Published Works: Author of More Than 60 Articles in Professional Journals and Editor Several Professional

TWO THOUSAND NOTABLE AMERICANS

Books; Book Reviews for Publications and for Publishers of Research Centers; Writer, Working Papers, Position Papers for Presentation by University Deans and Committees. Honors and Awards: Outstanding Graduate Woman of the Year, Kappa Chapter, Phi Delta Gamma, 1967 Outstanding Faculty Woman of the Year, Temple University Women, 1978; International Dimensions Grants, Ford Foundation, 1968, 1970; Study Leave Award, Federal Impact of Education, Temple University, 1974; Listed in *American Men and Women of Science, Who's Who in the East, International Directory of Behavior and Design Research.* Address: 4024 Woodruff Avenue, Lafayette Hill, Pennsylvania 19444.■

SEYMOUR COHEN

Educational Administrator. Personal: Born December 22, 1928, in Montreal, Quebec, Canada; Married Reva; Father of Beverly, Cheryl, David. Education: B.Sc., McGill University, 1949; B.A., Loyola College (University of Montreal), 1951; M.D., University of Montreal, 1956; Intern, (Internal Medicine, General Surgery & ENT) Hopital Notre Dame 1955-56, (Obstetrics) Hopital Misericorde 1955, (Pediatrics) Hopital Pasteur 1956, (Gynecology) Hopital Dieu 1956; Resident, (Clinical Pediatrics) Montreal Children's Hospital 1956-57, (Clinical Internal Medicine) Queen Mary Veterans Hospital 1957, (Clinical Pedicatrics) Mt. Sinai Hospital 1959, (Clinical Pediatrics) Montreal Children's Hospital 1960-61; Postgraduate Fellowship, Pediatric Pathology 1958, Pediatrics 1958, Pediatrics & Pathology 1959-60, Mt. Sinai Hospital. Career: Assistant Professor of Pediatrics, The Mount Sinai School of Medicine, 1967-69; Assistant Professor of Pediatrics, The Albert Einstein College of Medicine, 1970 to present; Visiting Professor of Pediatrics, St. Justine Hospital (Montreal), 1980-81; Clinical Assistant in the Department of Pediatrics, Jewish General Hospital, 1961-67; Clinical Assistant in Pediatric Medicine, Montreal Children's Hospital, 1961-67; Research Assistant in Pathology and Pediatrics, The Mt. Sinai Hospital, New York, 1964-65; Assistant Attending Pediatrician and Assistant Attending Pathologist, City Hospital at Elmhurst (Mt. Sinai Services), 1964-69; Research Associate in Division of Renal Research, Jewish General Hospital (Montreal), 1965-67; Associate Attending Pediatrician and Associate Attending Pathologist, City Hospital of Elmhurst, 1967-69; Consultant for Pediatric Renal Disease, City Hospital at Elmhurst, 1970-72; Associate Pediatrician and Coordinator of Pediatric Ambulatory Care, The Bronx-Lebanon Hospital Center, 1972-80; Consultant in Pediatric Renal Disease, The Bronx-Lebanon Hospital Center, 1970-80; Consultant in Pediatric Renal Disease, Good Samaritan Hospital, 1972-82; Assistant Vice President 1972-78, Acting Director of Ambulatory Care and Community Medicine 1975-77, Director of Medical Education 1972-80, Vice President Professional and Medical School Affairs 1978-80, The Bronx-Lebanon Hospital Center; Associate to the Director of Professional Services and Coordinator of Ambulatory Services, Ste. Justine Hospital (Montreal) 1980-81; Vice President for Education and Research, Dean of Clinical Campus, Long Island Jewish-Hillside Medical Center, 1981 to present. Organizational Memberships: Quebec College of Physicians and Surgeons; Canadian Medical Society Licentiate of the Medical Council of Canada; New York Academy of Medicine; New York Pediatric Society; Association des Medecins de Langue Francaise du Canada; American Medical Association; Bronx County Medical Society; Medical Society of the State of New York; American Society for Pediatric Nephrology; Fellow, American Academy of Pediatrics; Certified in Pediatrics, Royal College of Physicians and Surgeons; Fellow, Royal College of Physicians and Surgeons; Fellow, New York Academy of Medicine, 1976-78. Religion: President, Orangetown (New York) Jewish Center, 1974-75 and 1978-79. Honors and Awards: Research Grant for Study of Lead Poisoning in Rats, National Institutes of Health, 1965; Fellow in Pediatrics, Royal College of Physicans and Surgeons, Canada; Principal Investigator, United States Public Health Service Grant, 1980. Address: 2 Helaine Court, Orangeburg, New York 10962.■

CHAUNCEY EUGENE COKE

Company Executive, Scientist, Author, Educator. Personal: Born in Toronto, Canada; Son of Dr. Chauncey Eugene and Edith May Redman Coke; Married Sally B. Tolmie. Education: B.S. Honors Chemistry, University of Manitoba; M.S. Organic Chemistry, Yale University; M.A. Physical Chemistry, University of Toronto; Ph.D. Polymer Chemistry, The University, Leeds, England. Military: Served in the Royal Canadian Air Force, 1942-46, attaining the rank of Major. Career: Lecturer in Physical Chemistry, McMaster University; Research Fellow, Ontario Research Foundation; Research Director, Courtaulds (Canada), 1938-42; Director of Research and Development, Guaranty Dyeing and Finishing Company, 1946-48; Guest Lecturer, Sir George Williams University, 1949-59; Director of Research and Development and Member of Executive Committee, Hartford Fibres Company, 1959-62; Technical Director Textiles, Drew Chemical Corporation, 1962-63; American Cyanamid Company, Director New Products 1963-67, Dirctor Application Development 1967-70; Coke and Associate Consultants, President 1970-78, Chairman 1979 to present; Visiting Research Professor, Stetson University, 1979 to present. Organizational Memberships: Fellow, The Royal Society of Chemistry (Great Britain); Canadian Association of Textile Colorists and Chemists, Honorary Life Member, Chairman Several Committees, Vice-Chairman Panorama of Canadian Fabrics and Fashions, Director, Second Vice-President, First Vice-President, President; Fellow, American Institute of Chemists; Fellow, The Textile Institute (Great Britain); Fellow, Society of Dyers and Colourists (Great Britain); Fellow, New Jersey Academy of Science; Life Member, New York Academy of Sciences; American Association for Textile Technology, Life Member, Chairman Council on Technology, Advisory Council, Admissions Committee, Director, Secretary, President, First Vice President; The Chemists' Club, New York City; Florida Academy of Sciences; United States Metric Association; Institute of Textile Science, Fellow, Co-Founder and Third President; Chemical Institute of Canada, Member of Council; Textile Technical Federation of Canada, Delegate 1951-57, Director 1957-59. Community Activities: Treasurer, North Peninsula Citizens Committee for Incorporation, 1972-75; Committee Member, Halifax Area Study Commission, 1973-75; Director, North Peninsula Council of Associations, 1972-74, 1976-78; Vice-Chairman, North Peninsula Advisory Board to the County Council, 1976-78; Candidate, North Peninsula Zoning Commission, 1974; Greater Daytona Beach Republican Club, President 1972-75, Director 1976-79; Republican Presidents Forum, President 1975-77, Vice-President 1978-83; Vice-Chairman, The Group of Ten, 1978 to present. Published Works: Author of 150 Published or Confidential Papers. Honors and Awards: Bronze Medal, Canadian Association of Textile Colorists and Chemists, 1963; Bronze Medal, American Association for Textile Technology, 1971; Honorary Life Member, Canadian Association of Textile Colorists and Chemists, 1977; American Biographical Institute, Editorial Advisory Board (Honorary Member) 1976, National Board of Advisory (Honorary Member) 1982; Listed in *Who's Who in America, American Men and Women of Science, Leaders in American Science, Men of Achievement, Chemical Who's Who, Dictionary of International Biography, International Register of Profiles, National Social Directory, Royal Blue Book, Leading Men in the U.S.A., Who Knows and What, Who's Who in the East, Who's Who in the South and Southwest, Who's Who in Finance and Industry, Who's Who in the World, Who's Who in Technology, Who's Who in Florida, Personalities of the South, Community Leaders and Noteworhty Americans, Notable Americans of 1976-77, Book of Honor, National Register of Prominent Americans and International Notables.* Address: HHC 2AD Forward, APO, New York 09355.■

JEANNE-MARIE COL

Educator. Personal: Born April 18, 1946; Daughter of Raymond T. and Elizabeth P. Col. Education: B.A. 1966, M.A. 1969, University of California-Davis; Ph.D., University of South Carolina, 1977. Career: Associate Professor of Public Administration, Sangamon State University, Springfield, Illinois; Former Positions Include Assistant Professor of Public Administration, State University of New York-Albany; Lecturer in Political Science and Public Administration, Makerere University, Kampala, Uganda. Organizational Memberships: Commission on United States-African Relations; American Political Science Association, President, Women's Caucus for Political Science 1982-83, Editor *Quarterly* 1981-82; American Society for Public Administration; African Studies Association; Program Chairperson, Women and Development, Association for the Advancemet of Policy, Research and Development in the Third World; International Political Science Association, Reseach Committee, Sex Roles and Political Editor *Newsletter* 1979 to present; Coalition for Labor Union Women; American Federation of Teachers; National Organization for Women; Chair-Elect, ASPA Section for Women in Public Administration, 1983; Institute for Managerial and Professional Women; Workshop Leader, National Conference on Women's Networks, 1980; Facilitator, Regional Dialogue, National Commission on Working Women, 1979. Community Activities: Consultant, Women in Public Administration, United Nations Industrial Development Organization, 1981; Roundtable Co-Chairperson, Conference on United States Affairs, Africa, United States Military Academy, 1981; Consultant, Administrative Reforms, Association of Metis and Non-Status Indians of Saskatchewan, 1981; Consultant, Program for Upwardly Mobile Clerical Women, New York State School of Industrial and Labor Relations, Cornell University, 1977-81; Consultant on Women's Cooperatives, United States Agency for International Development; Board of Directors, Center for Environmental Options, Inc, 1978-81; University Commission for Affirmative Action, State University of New York-Albany, 1979-81; Women in Public Administration Meetings, Founder, Member Springfield, Illinois 1981 to present, Member Albany, New York 1978-81; Lecturer, Public Administration Trainee Program, New York State Civil Service Commission, 1980-81; International Women's Year, United States Conference, Houston, Texas, Oral History Project, 1977; Various University and Public Lectures on Women's Issues and African Government and Public Policy, United States and Uganda; Radio Interviews Legislative Politics, Administration Development, United States-Uganda. Honors and Awards: Listed in *Who's Who in the East, Community Leaders of America.* Address: 3217 Clarendon Drive, Springfield, Illinois 62704.■

JOHNNIE COLEMON

Minister. Personal: Born February 18; Daughter of John (deceased) and Lula Parker Haley; Married Rev. Don Nedd. Education: Graduate of Rust College High School, Holly Springs, Mississippi; B.A. 1943, D.Div. 1977, Wiley College, Texas; Teaching Certificate, Ordained Minister, Unity School of Christianity, Lee's Summit, Missouri. Career: Teacher, Chicago Public School System; Price Analyst, Chicago Quartermasters, Chicago Market Center; Founder, Minister, Teacher, Christ Universal Temple for Better Living, Chicago; Speaker; Consultant; Television and Radio Appearances. Organizational Memberships: Universal Foundation for Better Living (Composed of Eighteen Churches in Chicago, Detroit, Brooklyn, Benton Harbor, Michigan, Trinidad and Guyana, South America, Miami, Toronto, Las Vegas, Evanston and Hempstead; Study Groups in New Haven, Connecticut, Atlanta and Beverly Hills); International New Thought Alliance, District President, Chairperson, 60th Anniversary Congress, Chicago. Community Activities: Community Speaker; Weekly Radio Broadcasts, "Tower of Power", WVON Radio Station, Chicago; Guest Speaker, Festival of Mind and Body, London, England; Past Director, Chicago Port Authority; Television Appearances, NBC-TV "Eyewitness News", "On Q" with Carol Cartwright, Channel 5, Chicago; Planning Christ Universal City, South Side, Chicago (Complex to Include 10,300 Seat Auditorium, Residential Housing Units, The Johnnie Colemon Institute, a Private School, Retreat House, Senior Citizen Housing and a Business Section). Honors and Awards: Class Valedictorian, Rust College High School; Most Versatile Student on Campus, Wiley College; First Black Elected President, Association of Unity Churches, Unity School of Christianity. Address: 5008 South Greenwood Avenue, Chicago, Illinois 60615.■

LOUIS M. COLLIER

University Teacher and Department Chairman. Personal: Born May 19, 1919; Son of Albert and Ludia Lewis Collier (deceased); Married Pearlie Beatrice May; Father of James Bernard, Irving Orlando, Albert Jerome, Phillip Louis, Eric Wayne. Education: B.S., Grambling State University, 1954; M.S., Oklahoma State University, 1960. Military: Served in the United States Army in World War II, attaining the rank of Sergeant. Career: State Commission by Louisiana Government, Louisiana Science Foundation Board; Chairman Science and Mathematics Department, Central High School, Calhoun, Louisiana, 1955-62; Instructor of Physics and Math, Southern University, 1962-64; Assistant Professor Physics and Masthematics and Chemical Physics Department, Southern University, 1967-72. Organizational Memberships: Louisiana Education Association, President Science and Mathematics Department; American Association for the Advancement of Science; American Association of University Professors; American Institute of Professor; National Society of Teachers of Science; National Council of Teachers of Math. Community Activities: Secretary, Cooper Road Civic Club; Shreveport Chamber of Commerce; Shreveport Negro Chamber of Commerce; Executive Board Financial Officer, Chaplain Post #525, American Legion; George Washington Carver Branch Young Men's Christian Association; Blue Ride Assembly Board, Executive Board Secretary, Co-operative Member; State Director of Education, Phi Beta Sigma; President, Shreveport Bossier Chapter, National Pan Hellenic Council; Northern Shreveport Kiwanis Club; Volunteer Counselor, Caddo-Bossier Juvenile Court; Chairman Advisory Board, Caddo Parish School Board, Emergency School Aid Action Program; Vice-President Newton Smith Parent-Teacher Association; Program Director Weekly Radio Broadcast "Youth Want to Know"; Chairman, Board of Directors, Shreveport Negro Joy Fund; Past President Board of Directors, Cooper Road Health Club; Vice-President Seventh District Bicentennial Committee; Caddo-Bossier Community Council; Shreveport-Bossier Mayors Commission on Youth Services; Caddo Community Action Agency, Vice President, Financial Committee Chairman; Caddo Parish Police Jury; MAA; CCCA Board Representive. Religion: Member of the Dubach, Louisiana Liberty Hill Baptist Church. Honors and Awards: Science Educators Leadership Award, Science and Mathematics Department of Louisiana Education Association; Classroom Teacher Award, Freedom Foundation of Valley Forge; Shell Merit Scholarship to attend Stanford University; Listed in *Two Thousand Men of Achievement, Personalities of the South*. Address: 3031 Oak Forest, Shreveport, Louisiana 71107.■

MICHAEL ROBERT COLLINGS

Associate Professor of English. Personal: Born October 2, 1947; Son of R.W. Collings; Married Judith Lynn Reeve; Father of Michael-Brent, Erika Marie, Ethan Hunt, Kendra Elayne. Education: A.A., Bakersfield College, 1967; B.A., Whittier College, 1969; M.A. 1973, Ph.D. 1977, University of California-Riverside. Career: Associate Professor of English, Pepperdine University; Poet; Author of Articles in Professional Journals; Writing Consultant, Pleasant Hawaiian Holidays 1982, Jafra Cosmetics 1981, Neil Adams Realty 1981. Organizational Memberships: Science Fiction Poetry Association; Secretary, International Conference on the Fantastic in the Arts, Member 1981, Editor *Newsletter*; Southern California C.S. Lewis Society, Member, Editor *Lamp Post*; Rocky Mountain Modern Language Association; Poets and Writers, Inc; California State Poetry Society; Science Fiction Research Association. Religion: Missionary, Church of Jesus Christ of Latter-Day Saints, Hamburg, Germany, 1969-71. Honors and Awards: Poetry Awards and Nominations, Bay Area Poets Coalition 1981, Science Fiction Poetry Association 1982, Small Press Writers and Artists Organization 1981; Listed in Who's Who in the West, 1982-83. Address: 269 Sarah, Moorpark, California 93021.■

WILLIAM EDWARD COLLINS

Laboratory Administrator. Personal: Born May 16, 1932, in Brooklyn, New York; Son of Mrs. L. Collins; Married Corliss Jean; Father of Corliss Adora. Education: B.A., St. Peter's College, 1954; M.A., Psychology 1956, Ph.D. Experimental Psychology 1959, Fordham University; Number of Post-Graduate Courses, 1960-80. Career: Psychological Research Assistant 1954-56, Teaching Fellow 1958, Research Assistant 1958-59, Graduate Instructor in Experimental Psychology 1958-59, Fordham University; Research Psychology, United States Army Medical Research Laboratory, 1959-61; Research Psychologist, 1961-63, Chief Sensory Integration Section 1963-65, Chief of Aviation Psychology Laboratory 1965 to present, Lecturer for Medical Examiners Seminars in Aeronautical Center 1969 to present; Aviation Psychology Laboratory, Federal Aviation Administration, Civil Aeromedical Institute; University of Oklahoma Health Sciences Center, Department of Psychiatry and Behavioral Sciences, Adjunct Associate Professor 1963-70, Adjunct Professor 1979 to present; Licensed by Oklahoma State Board of Psychologists, 1966 to present; Rating Panel Member, Interagency Board, United States Civil Service Examiners, State of Oklahoma, 1967 to present; Evaluator of Proposals, National Science Foundation 1968 to present, Department of Health, Education and Welfare 1971 to present; Lecturer, Railroad Accident Investigation Course, 1972 to present; Chairman, Discussant, Participant, Numerous Scientific Meetings, 1965 to present; Educational and Research Films, 1964, 1969. Organizational Memberships: American Psychological Association, Fellow Division of Experimental Psychology, Division of Comparative and Physiological Psychology; Fellow, American Association for the Advancement of Science; Sigma Xi; Fellow, Aerospace Medical Association; N.A.S.-N.R.C.; Fellow, New York Academy of Sciences; Past President, Association of Aviation Psychologists; Fellow, Barany Society; Associate Editor, *Aviation, Space and Environmental Medicine*; Chairman, Oklahoma State Board of Examiners of Psychologist, 1982-83. Community Activities: Judge, Oklahoma Science Fair, 1964; Judge, Graduate and Undergraduate Competition, Oklahoma Psychological Association, 1973, 1975, 1979; Judge, Oklahoma State Science and Engineering Fair, 1980, 1981, 1982. Published Works: Numerous Articles, Professional Journals, Presentations, Profesional Meetings (These Include "Spatial Disorientation in General Aviation Accidents", "Performance Effects of Alcohol Intoxication and Hangover at Ground Level and at Simulated Altitude", "The Selection of Air Traffic Control Specialists: History and Review of Contributions by the Civil Aeromedical Institute"). Honors and Awards: Federal Aviation Administration, Quality Performance Award 1964, 1969, 1970, 1974, Outstanding Performance Rating 1966, 1967, 1968, 1969, 1970, 1971, 1974, 1981, Sustained Superior Performance Award 1966, 1967, Expert Witness Disorientation and Visual Illusions Public Civil Aeronautics Board Hearings 1966, Award for Employee Invention 1966; Special Achievement Award 1971; Appointed Abstractor, *Psychological Abstracts* 1962 to present; Raymond F. Longacre Award, Aerospace Medical Association, 1971; Abstractor Citation, American Psychological Association, 1973; United States Patent for Caloric Irrigation Receptacle, 1968; Listed in *Who's Who in America, World Who's Who in Science, American Men of Science, Leaders in American Science, International Directory of Research and Development Scientists, Who's Who in the South and Southwest, Two Thousand Men of Achievement, Creative and Succesful Personalities of the World, Dictionary of International Biography, United States Department of Health, Education and Welfare's Office of Education Final Report of Project #9-D-046, Community Leaders of America, Personalities of the South, American Men and Women of Science, International Who's Who in Community Service, Community Leaders and Noteworthy Americans, Notable Americans of the Bicentennial Era, Notable Americans of 1976-77*. Address: 8900 Sheringham Drive, Oklahoma City, Oklahoma 73132.■

CHARLES G. COLVER

United States Forest Service Executive. Personal: Born December 12, 1920; Son of William and Myrtle Colver (deceased); Married Mary Curtiss; Father of John (deceased), Edward, Marylou. Education: A.A., Chaffey College, 1941. Military: Served in the United States Army, 1944-46, ETO. Career: Douglas Aircraft Corporation, Long Beach, California, 1941-44; United States Forest Service, 1946 to present; Manager, San Dimas Experimental Forest Station, Glendora, 1962 to present; California South Zone Fire Dispatcher, 1972 to present; Vive-President, Covin Irrigating Company, 1974 to present; Organizational Memberships: California State Forestry Association; Amerian Numismatic Association; Secretary, California State Numismatic Association, 1964 to present; Assay Commission,

1974; Community Activities: Councilman, City of Covina, California, 1974 to present; Mayor Pro Teem, 1976-78, 1982 to present; Mayor 1980-82; President's Advisory Committee, Mt. San Antonio College, Walnut; Covina Board Library Trustees, 1970-74; 45th Infantry Division Association; National Rifle Association; Covina Halley Historical Society, Founding President, Director, Committee for Preservation and Restoration of Old San Francisco Mint; Director, Society of Paper Money Collectors; Past President, Covina Coin Club; Republican. Religion: Presbyterian. Honors and Awards: United States Army, Bronze Star, Purple Heart, Combat Infantry Badge; Numismatic Ambassador Award, Krause Publications, 1974; Medal of Merit, 1970; Silver Literature Medal, 1965 and 1970; Communication Achievement Award, Toastmasters International, 1982. Address: 611 North Banna Avenue, Covina, California 91724.■

JOE CHESTER COLVIN, JR

Educator. Personal: Born January 12, 1942; Son of Joe Chester Senior (deceased) and Lillian Ann Colvin. Education: Attended Southwest Texas State University, 1959-60 and 1961-62, University of Texas-Austin 1964-65 and Summers 1966, 1967; B.A. University of Texas-Austin, 1967; M.Ed., Sam Houston State University, 1972; Ed.D. Candidate, University of Houston, 1974-76. Military: Texas National Guard, 1960-66; Career: Special Education, Houston Independent School District, Houston, Texas, 1982 to present; Special Education, North Forest Independent School District, Houston, Texas, 1980-82; Bookkeeper, Ernest Elam and Associates, Austin, Texas 1961-65; Accounting Clerk, International Harvester Company, Houston, Texas, 1965; Accounting Clerk, Tidewater Oil Company, Houston, 1966; Teacher, Aldine Independent School District, 1967-74, 1976-78; University of Houston, Teaching Assistant, Instructor, Supervisor of Student Teachers, 1974-76; Chairperson Individualized Curriculum for Social Studies, Aldine Contemporary Education Center, 1978; Consultant, Houston Local Close-up Foundation *Perspectives*, 1980. Organizational Memberships: COPE Director; American Federation of Teachers; Houston Federation of Teachers; Texas Federation of Teachers; National Council for the Social Studies, TCSS and Houston CSS. Community Activities: Harris County Central Labor Council AFL-CIO Member, 1983; Kappa Delta Pi, Member 1974 to present, President Zeta Omega Chapter 1978-80 and 1982-83; Alternate Delegate, Democratic State Convention, 1976; Houston Delegate, Democratic State Convention, 1976, 1980 and 1982; Delegate to County Democratic Conventions, 1980. Religion: Episcopal. Honors and Awards: Spoke Award, Houston Junior Chamber of Commerce, 1968; Citation for Service as COPE Director, Building Political Power for Teachers, American Federation of Teachers, 1983; Teaching Fellowship, University of Houston, 1974-76. Address: P.O. Box 66862, Houston, Texas 77266.■

DORIS-MARIE CONSTABLE-MARTIN

Artist, Educator. Personal: Born July 5, 1941; Daughter of Clifford Matthew and Doris-Marie Gray Constable (both deceased); Mother of Robert Matthew, Lisa-Marie. Education: A.A., Miami-Dade Community College, South Campus, 1971; B.A., University of Miami, University of North Carolina-Asheville, 1976; M.A. Art, Penland School, Arrowmont School of Crafts, Goddard College, 1980. Career: Art Educator, Asheville Buncombe Technical College; Former Positions include Art Educator, Asheville Country Day School; Educator in Off-Loom Fibers Techniques and Textile Printing, Asheville Art Museum; Educator in Tapestry, Opportunity House; Educator in Weaving and Crafts for Children, Unitarian Universalist Church of Asheville; Western North Carolina Fibers/Handweavers Association Inc., Founder, First President, Board Member; Commissions from and Collected by Unitarian Universalist Church of Asheville, Sterling Advertising Company, Miami-Herald Publishing Company, R. J. Reynolds, Wachovia Bank, Charter Properties, Price-McNabb Advertising, I.B.M., J. P. Stevens, Wometco; Exhibitions for Florida Craftsmen Juried Competition 1971-74, 1976, Annual Painting and Sculpture Exhibition Mint Museum, 1973, 1976, Annual Member Exhibition Artist/Craftsmen Metropolitan Museum of Miami 1972-74, 1980-81, Florida Craftsmen Exhibition Center for the Visual Arts 1975, Lowe Art Museum University of Miami 1972, Juried Painting and Sculpture Competition Southeastern Center of Contemporary Art 1973, 1975; Annual Marietta International Competitive Exhibition for Painting and Sculpture at Grover M. Hermann Fine Arts Center 1976, 1978, Springs Mills North Carolina/South Carolina Art Show 1974-76, 1980-81, Appalachian Corridors Biennial Art Exhibition 1975; Art-in-the-Bank First Union National of Asheville (North Carolina) 1972-73, Southern Highlands Invitational Arrowmont School (Gatlinburg, Tennessee) and Folk Art Center (Asheville, North Carolina) 1981, North/South Carolina Fibers Competition at Queens College Gallery 1981, International Annual Handweaving Show at The Mannings Studio 1981, Annual October Show at Asheville Art Museum 1978/University of North Carolina-Asheville Chapter 1981, Artistic Sass Juried Exhibition Hilton Head Island 1981, Asheville Art Museum 1972-74, 1978, 1980-81, National Fiberarts Competition University of Missouri 1981, University of North Carolina-Asheville Alumni Show 1980. Organizational Memberships: American Crafts Council; Southern Highland Handicraft Guild, Folk Art Center; Western North Carolina Fibers/Handweavers Association; N.S.D.A.R., Ruth Davidson Chapter; Friends of University of North Carolina-Asheville Art; Alumni Association, University of North Carolina-Asheville. Honors and Awards: Merit Award, Florida Craftsmen Juried Competition, 1971; Merit Award, Annual Members Exhibition Artists/Craftsmen Metropolitan Museum of Miami, 1976; Annual Juried Art Show Durham (North Carolina) Art Guild, Best Sculpture 1974, Merit Award 1975, Honorable Mention 1980, 1981; Merit Award, Florida Craftsmen Exhibition Center for Visual Arts, 1975; Purchase Award, Juried Painting and Sculpture Competition at Southeastern Center of Contemporary Art, 1973; Best Sculpture, Springs Mills North Carolina/South Carolina Art Show, 1974; One-Person Show Award, Art-in-the-Bank First Union National of Asheville, 1972-73; Merit Award, Fayetteville Museum of Art Annual Juried Show, 1974; Merit Award, University of North Carolina-Asheville Alumni Show, 1980; Listed in *Who's Who in American Art*, *World Who's Who of Women*, *Book of Honor*, *Dictionary of International Biography*, *American Artists of Renown*, *Personalities of the South*, *Who's Who of American Women*. Address: 65 Woodland Road, Asheville, North Carolina 28804.■

EVERLY CONWAY DE MACARIO

Research Scientist. Personal: Born April 20, 1939; Daughter of Delfin E. Conway and Maria G. Benatuil; Married Alberto J.L. Macario; Mother of Alex, Everly. Education: Ph.D. Pharmacy, 1969; Ph.D. Biochemistry, 1962. Career: Research Scientist, Laboratory Medicine Institute, New York State Department of Health, Albany, New York, 1976 to present; Visiting Scientist, Brown University, Providence, Rhode Island, 1974-76; Visiting Scientist, International Agency for Research on Cancer, World Health Organization, Lyon, France, 1973-74; Senior Research Scientist, Laboratory of Cell Biology, National Research Council of Italy (Rome, Italy), 1971-73; Research Fellow, Department of Tumor-biology, Karolinska Institute, Stockholm, Sweden, 1969-71; Chief of Immunology, School of Medicine, Buenos Aires, Argentina, 1967-68; Head of Laboratory of Oncology and Immunology, Argentinian Association Against Cancer, Buenos Aires, Argentina, 1966-77; Research Fellow, National Academy of Medicine of Argentina, Buenos Aires, Argentina, 1962-63. Organizational Memberships: Argentinian Society for Biochemistry, 1963 to present; Scandinavian Society for Immunology, 1970 to present; Italian Association of Immunologists, 1973 to present; French Society for Immunology, 1964 to present; American Association of Immunolgists, Member 1977 to present, Chairman Committee on Status of Women 1980 to present; Eastern New York Branch, American Society for Microbiology, 1980 to present; American Association of University Women, 1977 to present. Community Activities: Supervisor, Pregnancy Test Proficiency Testing Program, State of New York, 1978-80; Scientific Referee for Grants; National and International Organizations, 1980 to present; American Association of University Women Committee, 1979-81; Contributions and Donations to Several Organizations Including Cohoes Music Hall 1978, Diocesan Development Program 1981-82, and to the Needy. Honors and Awards: Professor J.M. Mezzadra Award, National University of Buenos Aires, 1969; Travel Award, French Society for Immunology, 1974; Travel Award to England, Second International Immunology Congress, 1974; Travel Award to Australia, American Association of Immunologists, 1977; Gold Medal Grant, Sweden, 1969; Sir Samuel Scott of Yews Trust Grant, Sweden, 1970; Winifred Cullis Grant, International Federation of University Women, 1972; Research Grants, National Atlantic Treaty Organization 1975 and 1981, United States Department of Energy 1981. Address: 18 Carriage Road, Delmar, New York 12054.■

DAVID HALL COOK

Training Manager. Personal: Born October 4, 1930; Son of Jennie Hall Cook; Married Joyce Fralic; Father of David II, John. Education: B.B.A. Personnel Management 1974, M.Ed. Human Resource Development 1977, George Washington University. Military: Served in the United States Navy, 1947-67, RMC. Career: Computer Sciences Training Manager Control Systems Activity 1979 to present, Engineer 1967-70, Senior Engineer 1971-74, Section Manager 1977-79; Naval Science Instructor, High School ROTC Program, 1974-77. Organizational Memberships: American Association for the Advancement of Science; Society for Interdisciplinary Studies, London; United States Naval Institute; American Society for Training and Development; Phi Delta Kappa, George Washington University Chapter, Quarterly Newsletter Editor 1977-81, Editor of Annual Publication *Educational Perspective* 1977-81, President-elect 1981, President 1982; New York Academy of Science. Community Activities: Kiwanis Club, 1970-73; Boy Scouts of America, Institutional Representative to Troop 1970-73, Scoutmaster 1966, Troop Committeeman 1964-66, Neighborhood Commissioner 1966-73; Naval Sea Cadet Corps, Member 1976-77, Training Officer 1976, Administrative Officer 1977; Anchor Lodge #182, AF&AM, 1952 to present; Key West Consistory, 1953 to present; Kena Temple Shrine, 1969 to present; George Washington University Club, 1975 to present; Smithsonian Associates, 1972 to present; National Rifle Association, 1980 to present. Honors and Awards: Boy Scouts of America, Wood Badge 1967, American Defense Commendation and Good Conduct Medals 1947-67, Numerous Certificates and Training Awards 1964-73; Meritorious Service Award, Defense Communication Agency, 1967; Kiwanis Club Outstanding Service Award, 1973; United States Air Force Letter of Appreciation, 1981; American Biographical Institute Certificate, 1979, 1980, 1981 and 1982; Harvard School of Dental Medicine, Letter of Appreciation, 1981; Listed in *Who's Who in the South and Southwest*. Address: 6217 Dana Avenue, Springfield, Virginia 22150.■

CAROLYN A. COOLEY

Executive Assistant. Personal: Born June 28, 1956, in Farmerville, Louisiana; Daughter of Eddie and Ruby Butler; Married Dr. J.F. Cooley; Mother of Stephen Lamar. Education: Studies at Louisiana Technical University and Arkansas Baptist College. Career: Clerk-Typist, Louisiana Technical University, Ruston Louisiana, 1975-76; Typist, Arkansas Baptist College, 1976 to present; Currently, Executive Secretary, County Contact Committee, Inc; Ex-Inmate Mission and Talent Center, Prison Rehabilitation Center, 1980 to present; Community Activities: Order of Easter Star; Deputy Sheriff, Pulaski County; Deputy Constable, Pulaski County, District 3-A; National Sheriff's Association, 1978-79; Associate Member, Arkansas Constable's Association; Assitant Legislative Prison Aide to Chief Legislative Aide Dr. J. F. Cooley, 1980 to present; Secretary and Editor for Women, Children and Society Columns, *Arkansas Weelky Sentinel*, 1978 to present; Secretary, Mother's Prayer and Answers Auxiliary, 1980. Honors and Awards: Certificate of Merit, Governor Dale Bumpers, 1974; Certificate of Merit, Governor David Pryor, 1976; National Historical Society, 1975-76; Honorary Probation Officer, North Little Rock Municipal Court, 1973 and 1979; Cooley's Athletic and Teenage Club, Inc, Ceritficate of Merit 1973, Certificate of Honor 1973; Nominated for International Platform Association, 1974; Certificate of Participation, Literary High School Rally, Farmerville High School, 1974; I Dare You Award, Farmerville High School, 1974; Society of Outstanding American High School Students, 1974; Outstanding Teenager of America, 1974; Arkansas Travelers Certificate, 1977; Certificate of Recognition, Governor D. Pryor, 1977; Certificate of Membership, County Contact Committee; Certificate of Recognition, Constable's Office, District 3-A; Arkansas Volunteer Award, Governor's Office of Volunteer Services, 1980; Governor Frank White, Arkansas Certificate of Merit 1981, Arkansas Certificate of Award for Outstanding Volunteer Services 1981; Special Deputy Sheriff of Pulaski County, Sheriff Tommy Robinson, 1981; Listed in *Community Leaders and Noteworthy Americans, Dictionary of International Biography, Men and Women of Distinction, Personalities of America, Outstanding Young Women of America, Personalities of the South, International Youth in Achievement, Notable Americans of the Bicentennial Era, World Who's Who of Women.* Address: P.O. Box 5150, North Little Rock, Arkansas 72119.■

J. F. COOLEY

Minister, Educator, Civil Rights Activist. Personal: Born January 11, 1926, in Rowland, North Carolina; Son of James F. and Martha Buie Cooley (both deceased); Married Carolyn Ann Butler; Father of Virginia M., James Francis, Gladys M., Franklin Donell, Stephen Lamar. Education: Graduate of Southside High School; A.B. Social Sciences 1953, B.D. Theology 1956, M.Div. 1973, Johnson Smith University; M.A. Sociology, Eastern Nebraska Christian College; D.D., Life Sciences College, Rolling Meadows, Illinois; Cultural Doctorate in Social Science, Tuscon, Arizona. Military: Served as Chaplain in the United States Army, 1944-46, attaining the rank of Lieutenant. Career: Minister, Grant Chapel Presbyterian Church (Georgia) 1956-57, St. Andrews Presbyterian Church (Arkansas), 1957-69; St. Francis County, Juvenile Probation Officer 1953-64, Associate Juvenile Judge 1963-64; Shorter College, Political Science Director, Minister of Service, Dean of Men, Academic Dean, 1969-73; Press Agent; Private Investigator, North Little Rock; Public Relations Officer, Consumer Protection Division, State Attorney General's Office, Arkansas Baptist College, 1975-82. Organizational Memberships: Arkansas Teachers Association; International Platform Association; S.A.N.E.; American Security Council; National Committee of Black Churchmen; Omega Psi Phi; National Association for the Advancement of Colored People; Arkansas Council on Human Relations; Committee for Peaceful Co-Existence; Welfare Right Organization; A.C.O.R.N.; National Sheriff's Association; Arkansas Law Enforcement Association; Ministerial Alliance of Greater Little Rock; Juvenile Correctional Association; National Conference of Christians and Jews. Community Activities: Established More Than Fifteen Community Organizations; Co-Sponsor, Community Reading and Development Center, 1976; Founder and Executive Director, County Contact Committee, Inc, 1977; Founder and Editor, *Arkansas Weekly Sentinel* 1978; Founder and Executive Director, Ex-Inmate Mission Talent Center, 1980; Editor, *State Weekly News*; Bi-Monthly Column Writer and Associate Editor, *Baptist Vanguard Magazine and Newspaper*; Pulaski County, Deputy Sheriff 1977-80 and 1969-73, Special Deputy Sheriff 1981; Pulaski County Correctional Facilities, Justice of the Peace 1973-74 and 1975-76, District #3 Constable 1978-80, Chaplain Corps and Instructor for Night Classes 1977; St. Francis County Deputy Sheriff, 1961-62; Visiting Teacher and Juvenile Officer, Juvenile Court, St. Francis County, 1963-65; Chairman, Recruitment Committee on Minorities; AF&AM Masons; National Historical Society; State Democratic Party; Veterans Organization; Urban League; Early American Society; Inspirational Trio, Singing Group; Postal Commemorative Society; National Black Veterans Organization, Inc. Honors and Awards: First Black Lieutenant, North Little Rock Police Department, 1975; Honorary D.D., Shorter College 1971, Life Science College 1972; Honorary Doctor of Civil Law, Eastern Nebraska Christian College, 1971; Honorable Lieutenant Colonel, Retired Lieutenant Colonel, 1978; Two Certificates from Federal Bureau of Prisons, Jail Operator and Jail Administrator, 1971 and 1972; Arkansas Commission on Law Enforcement Standards and Training, Five Certificates, Basic, General, Intermediate, Senior and Advanced, Certified Law Enforcement Officer, 1980, Course Certificate, National Rifle Association of America, 1971; Guest of President Lyndon B. Johnson, 1963; United Supreme Council's Thomas J. Stone Award, 1974; 33rd Degree Mason; Numerous Citations for Crime Prevention; Number of Honors, Recognitions, Certificates, Plaques from Federal, State and Local Government Officials, Private Individuals, Law Enforcement Agencies; Certificate of Membership, Prison Jaycees; January 11, 1977, Proclaimed as Dr. J.F. Cooley Day in Arkansas; 60 Trophies and Plaques Given Over 10-Year Period for Promoting Recreational Activities for Young People in Arkansas; Honorary Alumnus, Louisiana Tech University; Certificate of Eligibility, Veterans Administration; Certificate of Appreciation, Prison Inmates, 1970; Jury Commissioner, 1977; Community Service Award, Community Welfare Club of North Little Rock, 1978; Month of September 10 Through October 10, 1978, Proclaimed Dr. J. F. Cooley Month, North Little Rock; Letter of Recognition, Prison Reform and Rehabilitation, 1978; March 28 Through April 3, 1977, Proclaimed as Dr. J. F. Cooley Week; Honorary Citizen, Little Rock, 1977; Work Placed in Congressional Records, 1977; Arkansas Volunteer Award, 1980; "A Salute to a Champion", Cummins Prison Inmates, 1978; Arkansas Certificate of Merit for Outstanding Volunteer Services, 1981; Arkansas Certificate of Merit, 1981; Featured in Numerous National, State and Local Publications; First Black Certified Law Enforcement Instructor, State of Arkansas, 1981; Dr. J. F. Cooley Day, City of Little Rock, December 29, 1982. Address: P.O. Box 5150, North Little Rock, Arkansas 72119.■

C. JAMES COOPER, JR.

Attorney at Law. Personal: Born March 5, 1931; Son of Clyde and Mary Cooper; Married Rose Marie, Daughter of Raymond (deceased) and Mary Perry; Father of Julie L., Jill A., James P. Education: Attended Colorado College, 1948-50; B.A., University of Denver, 1952; LL.B., University of Denver College of Law, 1955; Admitted to the Colorado Bar, 1955. Career: Attorney at Law. Organizational Memberships: American Immigration Lawyers Association, Chairman Colorado Chapter 1980-81; International Bar Association; International Common Law Society; Colorado Bar Association; Denver Bar Association; Phi Delta Phi; Phi Gamma Delta. Community Activities: 32nd Degree Mason; Shriner. Published Works: Published Author and Lecturer on Numerous Subjects in the Field of Immigration; Board of Editors, *Immigration Law Reporter, Common Law Lawyer.* Honors and Awards: Editor, *Denver Law Journal*, 1954-55; Outstanding Scholastic Award, National Law Week, 1955; Listed in *Who's Who in American Law, Who's Who in the American West, Martindale-Hubbell Law Directory.* Address: 461 Gilpin Street, Denver, Colorado 80218.■

PAUL F. COOPER

School District Administrator. Personal: Born April 12, 1948; Son of Lewis R. and Janice W. Cooper; Married Florence M., Daughter of John and Florence Burghardt; Father of Justin Paul, Christopher Robert. Education: A.A., Nassau Community College, 1969; B.A., Marshall University, 1971; M.S., Adelphi University, 1977; P.D., C. W. Post Center-Long Island University, 1980. Career: School District Administrator, Pupil Personnel; Former Teacher of the Learning Disabled and the Emotionally Disturbed; Former Narcotics Rehabilitation Counselor. Organizational Memberships: Phi Delta Kappa; Long Island Association of Special Education Administrators, Secretary 1982-83, Vice President 1983-84, President 1984-85; A.N.Y.S.E.E.D.; Long Island Association of Pupil Personnel Service Administrators; Council of Administrators and Supervisors. Community Activities: Jericho Volunteer Fire Department, 1969-77; Boy Scouts of America; Huntington (West Virginia) Area Drug Council, 1970-71; Special Education Parent-Teacher Association, Vice President Executive Board 1979-85; Oyster Bay-East Norwich Soccer Club; East Norwich Beautification Association. Religion: Pre-Cana Trainer 1977-83, County Fair Committee. Honors and Awards: Eagle Scout Award, Boy Scouts of America, 1964; Honorary Life Member, New York State Parent-Teacher Association, 1983; S.E.P.T.A. Educator Award, 1981, 1982; Listed in *Who's Who in American Junior Colleges, Personalities of America.* Address: 10 James Avenue, East Norwich, New York 11732.■

ARNOLD GERALD CORAN

Pediatric Surgeon. Personal: Born April 16, 1938; Son of Charles Coran; Married Susan W.; Father of Michael Kenneth, David Lawrence, Randi Beth. Education: A.B. 1959, M.D. 1963, Harvard University. Military: Served in the United States Navy from 1970-72, attaining the rank of Lieutenant Commander. Career: Instructor in Surgery, Harvard Medical School, 1967-69; Associate Professor of Surgery, University of Southern California Medical School, 1972-74; University of Michigan Medical School, Professor of Surgery 1974 to present, Pediatric Surgeon, Chief of Pediatric Surgery. Organizational Memberships: American College of Surgeons; American Academy of Pediatrics; American Pediatric Surgical Association; Society of University Surgeons; American Surgical Association. Community Activities: Washtenaw County United Jewish Appeal, Board of Directors. Honors and Awards: Bronze Medal for Scientific Exhibit, American Medical Association, 1972; American Medical Writers Award, 1978. Address: 3450 Vintage Road, Ann Arbor, Michigan 48015.■

ALLEN POWELL CORBETT

Assistant Professor and Administrator. Personal: Born April 17, 1939. Education: B.S., American University, Washington, D.C., 1961; M.B.A., University of South Carolina-Columbia, 1969; C.D.P., Institution for Certification of Computer Professionals, 1979. Career: Assistant Professor of Management Science; Director, James C. Self Management Science Center, University of South Carolina; Research Supervisor, South Carolina Employment Security Commission, Columbia, South Carolina, 1971-73; Biomedical Statistician, Medical Program Assistant, Federal Aviation Administration, Washington, D.C., 1961-65. Organizational Memberships: Professional Member, Rehabilitation Engineering Society of North America; President, Association for Systems Management, 1980 to present; International Platform Association; Chairman, Legislative Committee, South Carolina Rehabilitation Association; Professional Member, Association for Computing Machinery. Community Activities: Council of Advocates, 1977-79; Finance Chairman and Chairman of the Board, South Carolina Protection and Advocacy System for the Handicapped, 1979 to present; Research Consultant, South Carolina Joint Legislative Committee to Study Problems of the Handicapped; Special Research Consultant, South Carolina Vocational Rehabilitation Department, 1979 to present; Chairman, Independent Living Advisory Committee, South Carolina Rehabilitation Department, 1979 to present; Research Consultant, South Carolina Education Department, 1982 to present; Consultant, Information Systems, United States Department of Justice, 1982; Notary Public, South Carolina; Computer Training Committee, South Carolina Vocational Rehabilitation Department; Co-Chairman, ASM/DPMA Data Processing Curriculum Committee; Chairman, Handicapped Advisory Committee, University of South Carolina, 1978-79; Co-Chairman, Intermediate Users Group of South Carolina. Religion: Director, Youth Services, Kathwood Baptist Church, Columbia, South Carolina, 1983. Honors and Awards: South Carolina Rehabilitation Association, Meritorious Service Award, 1979, Volunteer of the Year 1983; Listed in *Who's Who in the South and Southwest, Personalities of the South, Personalities of America, Men of Achievement.* Address: 2809 Magnolia Street, Columbia, South Carolina 29204.■

J. B. CORDARO

Administrator. Personal: Born October 7, 1941; Son of Mrs. Joseph B. Cordaro; Married Elizabeth Ann Dewton; Father of Susan Marie, Gregory Edward, Michael Patrick. Education: B.S.S., Loyola of New Orleans, 1963; Undertook Studies in International Economics, Georgetown School of Foreign Service, 1963-65; M.S., Cornell University, 1972. Career: Food-Nutrition Economist, United States Department of State; Food Program Manager, United States Congress/O.T.A.; Staff, Senator Hubert Humphrey; Executive Director of Food Safety Council; President, Council for Responsible Nutrition. Organizational Memberships: American Association for Advancement of Science; Institute of Food Technology; Trustee, Food Safety Council; National Meat and Poultry Advisory Board, Washington Nutrition Group. Honors and Awards: Louisiana Knights of Columbus Fellowship for Graduate Study at Georgetown University, 1963; A.I.D. Outstanding Performance Awards: Congressional Staff Observer, 1974 World Food Conference; Leader, U.S. Delegation Expert F.P.C. Conference, Morocco, 1969; Listed in *Men of Achievement, Personalities of the South, Community Leaders and Noteworthy Americans, Personalities of America, Notable Americans, Dictionary of International Biography, Community Leaders of America, Who's Who in Washington.* Address: 1336 Buttermilk Lane, Reston, Virginia 22090.■

ROSA CORONADO

Food Manufacturing Executive. Personal: Born July 27, 1938; Daughter of Arturo and Elvira Coronado. Education: Graduate of Humboldt Senior High School, 1956; Public Relations Studies at the University of Mexico, Mexico City, 1960. Career: La Cara Coronado Restaurant, Officer 1960-74, President 1975-79; Mama Coronado Food Products, Officer 1960-74, Executive Manager 1975 to present; Lecturer, Instructor, Mexican Ethnic Foods. Organizational Memberships: Minneapolis Restaurant Association, 1965-78; National Restaurant Association, 1977-79; International Geneva Executive Chefs, Minnesota Chapter, Member 1975 to present, Chairperson Membership Commitee 1976-79; Midwest Chefs Association, Member 1975 to present, Recording Secretary 1976-78; American Culinary Federation, New York Chapter; Board of Directors, Metropolitan Economic Development Association of Minneapolis, 1975 to present. Community Activities: Democratic Party; Advisory Board on Redevelopment, Minneapolis City Center, 1973-78; Small Business Task Force, State of Minnesota; Minnesota Hispanic Chamber of Commerce; Volunteer Resources, Department of Education, Twin Cities; Co-Chairperson, Geneva Ball, 1977. Religion: Our Lady of Guadalupe Catholic Church; Parish Church Council 1980-81; President of Ladies Society, 1976-78. Published Works: Author of Children's Cookbook; Board of Directors, *West Side/West St. Paul Voice* Newspaper, 1981-82. Honors and Awards: First Woman to be Elected into International Geneva for State, First to be Elected into Geneva Executive Chefs; Certificate, Research and Seminar, Mexican Foods, General Mills, Culinary Awards for Exhibits, 1970-80; Special Recognition Plaque, Minnesota International Geneva, 1979; Certificate of Recognition, Amoco, Research, New Food Ingredient, 1970; Subject of Special Feature on Women in Business, *Chamber of Commerce Magazine*, 1977; Listed in *Who's Who of American Women, Who's Who in the Midwest.* Address: 949 16th Avenue North, South St. Paul, Minnesota 55075.■

VERNA C. CORRIVEAU

Business Planner. Personal: Born December 24, 1952; Daughter of Vernon (deceased) and Doris Cutter. Education: B.A. 1974, M.A. English 1977, Clark University (graduated summa cum laude); C.L.U. American College, 1980; Ch.F.C., American College, 1982. Career: Business Planner associated with Boland Hymel and Associates; Former Position in Communications. Organizational Memberships: Society of Chartered Life Underwriters; National Association of Life Underwriters; Million Dollar Round Table. Community Activities: Chamber of Commerce (served on miscellaneous committees). Honors and Awards: Fellow of International Biographical Association; First Women Ever to Qualify as Member of Inner Circle of State Mutual of America Life Assurance Company, 1980. Address: 6720 General Haig, New Orleans, Louisiana 70124 .■

SISTER MAGDALEN COUGHLIN

College President. Personal: Born April 16, 1930; Daughter of William J. and Cecilia Coughlin. Education: B.A., The College of St. Catherine, St. Paul, Minnesota, 1952; Postgraduate Fulbright Scholar, University of Nijmegen, The Netherlands, 1952-53; M.A., Mount St. Mary's College, Los Angeles, California, 1962; Ph.D., University of Southern California, 1970. Career: Mount St. Mary's College, Los Angeles, President 1976 to present, Dean for Academic Development 1970-74, Assistant Professor of History 1963-70; Provincial Councilor/Regional Superior, Sisters of St. Joseph of Carondolet, Los Angeles Province, 1974-76; Teacher of History, St. Mary's Academy, San Fernando, 1960-61. Organizational Memberships: California Historical Society; American Historical Society; Fulbright Alumni Association. Community Activities: Council of Presidents of C.S.J. Colleges, Chairman 1980; *Educational Record* Advisory Board; Association of Catholic Colleges and Universities, Board of Directors, 1979 to present, Task Force on Minorities; Association of Independent California Colleges and Universitites, Executive Board 1979 to present; Carondolet High School, Board of Directors 1976-78; Marianne Frostig Center for Educational Therapy, Board of Trustees 1976 to present; Independent Colleges of Southern California, Board of Directors 1976 to present. Honors and Awards: Haynes Dissertation Fellowship, 1969-70; Teaching Assistant, University of Minnesota, 1953-54; Fulbright Scholarship, University of Nijmegen, The Netherlands, 1952-53; Phi Alpha Theta; Delta Epsilon Sigma; Kappa Gamma Pi; Lambda Iota Tau. Address: 12001 Chalon Road, Los Angeles, California 90049.■

NAOMI MILLER COVAL

Orthodontist. Personal: Born in Bayonne, New Jersey; Daughter of Jacob Paul Miller and Bertha Blumstein; Married Robert Simon Apel; Mother of Payson

TWO THOUSAND NOTABLE AMERICANS

Rodney, Mark Lawrence, Ilya Sandra. Education: B.A., New York University, 1939; D.D.S., Columbia University, 1943. Career: Past Instructor, New York University Dental School; Attending Dentist, Peninsula Hospital Center, 1959-81. Organizational Memberships: International Academy of Orthodontics, Vice President, Secretary; New York Association of Women Dentists, Vice President; Long Island Committee for Flouridation of Water, Chairperson; American Dental Association; Nassau-Suffolk Academy of Dentistry; American Academy of Oral Medicine; New York Association of Women Dentists; Federation of American Orthodontics; British Society for the Study of Orthodontics; American Society of Preventive Dentistry. Community Activities: American Jewish Congress, President; President Auxiliary of Peninsula Hospital Center, President; Lawrence High School Parent-Teacher Association, President; B'nai B'rith, Vice President; Charter Member, Former Member Board of Directors, National Women's Political Caucus; Charter Member, International Platform Association; Board Member, American Cancer Society; United Nations Association of the U.S.A.; American Red Cross; Natural History Society; National Council of Jewish Women; Board Member, Hadassah; National Organization of Women; Metropolitan Opera Guild; Rapa Nui Society for Easter Islanders; Wildlife Society of Kenya; National Geographic Society; Jacques Cousteau Society; Executive Board Member, Columbia University Dental Alumni. Published Works: Only Woman Editor, *The International Journal of Orthodontics*, 1962-65; Editor, *Dentistae*, 1948; Articles Published in Professional Journals and Newspapers. Honors and Awards: First Woman Selected to Represent Official Dentistry on Television, 1964; Elected Delegate to Oral Hygiene Committee (1948-51) and First Woman Dentist Invited to Give University Seminars in Soviet Socialist Bloc Countries; Honored by William Jarvie Society for Dental Research, 1942; Fellow, Society of Oral Physiology and Occlusion; Fellow, Royal Society of Health; Listed in *Who's Who of American Women, International Who's Who in Community Service, World Who's Who of Women, Who's Who in World Jewry, Dictionary of International Biography, Encyclopedia of Contemporary Personalities, Who's Who in America, Book of Honor, Who's Who in the East, Two Thousand Women of Achievement, International Who's Who of Intellectuals, Men and Women of Distinction, Personalities of America, Community Leaders and Noteworthy Americans, Directory of Distinguished Americans, Notable Americans of the Bicentennial Era*, Others. Address: 30 Westover Place, Lawrence, New York 11559.■

THERON MICHAEL COX

Psychologist. Personal: Born February 27, 1947; Son of Doris S. Knight; Married Charlotte; Father of Caroline. Career: University Professor; Social Worker; School Psychologist; Mental Health Counselor; Mental Health Project Director; Author; Editor; Researcher; Psychologist. Organizational Memberships: Kappa Delta Pi; American Association of University Professors; American Personnel and Guidance Association; N.A.S.P. Address: Route 3, Box 217, Abbeville, Alabama 36310.■

ERIC FREDERICK COX

National Field Director, Legislative Director. Personal: Born July 20, 1932, in Baltimore, Maryland; Son of C. R. and Elvira Cox. Education: Graduate of Eastern High School, 1950; B.A., Dickinson College, Carlisle, Pennsylvania, 1954; Graduate Work in Economics and Sociology. Military: Served in the United States Army, 1954-56. Career: Real Estate Salesman, Broker in Family Real Estate Business, Washington, D.C.; Community Organizer, Washington, D.C.; Radio Broadcaster for American Veterans Committee on District of Columbia Station WOOK and Weekly Radio Programs on Educational Radio WAMU-FM, Washington, D.C. ("Issues and Ideas" and "Eric Cox Interviews"); Free-lance Lecturer at Colleges; Teacher, Graduate School, United States Department of Agriculture, Free University of Georgetown University and the New School for Social Research in New York; College Administrator, Bronx Community College; Political Activist; Consultant in Politics and Community Development; Currently National Field Director for the World Federalists Association and Legislative Director for Campaign for United Nations Reform. Organizational Memberships: International Platform Association, Publicity Chairman 1 Year; Sierra Club; National Peace Academy, Former National Board Member; Metropolitan Athletic Association, Co-Founder and Past President; D.C. Citizens for Clear Air, Co-Founder. Community Activities: Founder of Local Committee for Self-Government for Washington, D.C.; D.C. Commissioners Crime Council; Washington D.C. Jaycees, Committee Chairman; Dickinson College Alumni Club, Past President; Organizer of Many Recreational, Athletic and Educational Programs for Inner-City Youth in Washington, D.C., made possible by Volunteers and Foundation Grants; Officer of D.C. Young Democrats, 3 Years; International Affairs Committee of Young Democrats, National Chairman; Democratic Precinct Chairman for Washington D.C.; Atlantic Association of Young Political Leaders, Advisory Committee; Volunteer Worker in Five Presidential Campaigns; Occasional Speech Writer for Presidential Candidates; Presidential Inaugural Committees, 1961, 1965; New York City Voluntary Action Council under Mayor Lindsay, 1972; Testified Three Times before Committees of United States Senate on Poverty 1965, Foreign Relations 1965 and 1966; Speaker at State Caucuses at G.O.P. National Conventions in Kansas City and Detroit and before State Caucuses of Democratic Conventions in New York City. Religion: Unitarian; Past President, Young Adult Organizations of All Souls Unitarian Church, Washington D.C.; Participant in National General Assemblies of Unitarian-Universalist Church. Published Works: Author, *D.C. Jaycee Report on Juvenile Delinquency in the Nation's Capital*; Over 30 Other Publications including Op-Ed Pieces in Major Newspapers and Articles in *The Educational Record, The Colorado Quarterly, The Churchmen*, Journal of the American Red Cross and Numerous Letters to the Editor in Major Papers and Magazines. Honors and Awards: National Honor Society; Five Hundred Dollar Award, National Jaycees, for Study on Delinquency which he authored for D.C. Jaycees; Special Citation, D.C. Chapter, Recreation Society, 1964; Certificate of Achievement from Commanding General, Fort Jackson, South Carolina, 1954; Various Civic Awards in Washington, D.C.; Listings in Various Reference Directories, including the *Encyclopedia of Meeting and Convention Speakers*. Address: 3133 Connecticut Avenue, N.W., Washington, D.C. 20008.■

GERALDINE V. COX

Association Executive. Personal: Born January 10, 1944; Daughter of Karl and Geraldine Vang (deceased); Married Walter G. Cox, Son of Mary H. Cox. Education: Ph.D., Drexel University, 1970; M.S., Drexel University; B.S., Drexel Institute of Technology, 1966. Career: Vice President, Technical Director, Chemical Manufacturers Association, 1979 to present; Environmental Scientist, Medicine and Biological Science Department, American Petroleum Institute, 1977-79; White House Fellow, Special Assistant to the Secretary of Labor, 1976-77; Technical Coordinator, Environmental Programs, Raytheon Oceanographic and Environmental Services, 1970-76. Organizational Memberships: Ameican Association of Engineering Societies, Coordinating Committee in Transportation 1983 to present; American Chemical Society 1968-72 and 1979 to present, Chairman Water Resources Subcommittee 1982 to present, Member Committee on Environmental Improvement 1980 to present, Member Environmental Division 1983 to present; American Society for Testing and Materials 1977 to present, Member D-19, E-34, E-35, E-47; Association for Women in Science, 1983 to present; Association of Environmental Laboratories 1974-76, Vice President 1974-76, Member of Board 1974-76; Federation of Organizations for Professional Women 1980 to present, President 1983 to present, Member Board of Directors Representing Society of Women Engineers 1980-82; Hazardous Materials Advisory Council, Member Board of Directors 1983-84; International Society of Petroleum Industry Biologists 1977-80, Convention Chairman 1979, Membership Committee 1977-80; Marine Technology Society 1970-74, Water Quality Committee 1970-74, Chairman Marine Bioassay Workshop 1972; Society for Occupational and Environmental Health 1979-83; Society of Women Engineers 1976 to present, Senior Member 1982 to present, Representative to Federation of Organizations for Professional Women 1980-82, Achievement Award Committee 1982, Executive Director Search Committee 1982-83, Long-Range Planning Committee 1982-83; Water Pollution Control Federation 1967 to present, Chairman and Founder Marine Water Quality Committee 1975-80, Chairman Oil Spill Studies Strategies and Techniques Workshop 1975, Chairman Ocean Outfalls Seminar 1978, Member Toxic Substances Committee 1978-82, Program Committee Session Chairman 1974-79, Federal Association Program Committee 1980; Women and Health Roundtble, Executive Committee 1983-84; Women's Council on Energy and the Environment 1982 to present; Served on Numerous Advisory Panels. Community Activities: Alpha Sigma Alpha 1963 to present, Chairman Development Committee 1980, Chairman of Advisors 1978-80, National Executive Vice President 1972-76, Province Director 1970-72, Advisor 1966-70, Chapter President 1965-66; American Association of University Women, 1983 to present; Boy Scouts of America, Merit Badge Counselor 1975 to present; Drexel University, Washington Area Fund Raising Chairman 1977, Area Alumni Advisor 1976 to present, Alumnae Award Committee 1978 to present; National Association Executives Club 1979 to present, Membership Recruiting Committee 1982; Republican Women's Club 1983 to present; White House Fellows Alumni Association, 1977 to present. Published Works: Numerous Publications in Field. Honors and Awards: White House Fellow, 1976-77; 1 of 10 Outstanding Young Women of America, 1975; Harriet E. Worrell Award (Outstanding Alumnae), Drexel University, 1977; Governor's Citation, State of Rhode Island, 1975, in Special Recognition of Professional Excellence in the International Year of the Woman; Phi Kappa Phi, 1969 to present; Key and Triangle Drexel Women's Leadership Honorary, 1965; Panhellenic Woman of the Year, 1966; Author of the Year, Raytheon Company, Submarine Signal Division, 1974. Address: Chemical Manufacturer's Association, 2501 M Street Northwest, Washington, D.C. 20037.■

TWO THOUSAND NOTABLE AMERICANS

ADRIENNE LEONA ANN CRAFTON-MASTERSON

Executive, Real Estate Broker. Personal: Born March 6, 1926, in Providence, Rhode Island; Daughter of John Harold and Adrienne Fitzgerald Crafton; Mother of Mary Victoria, Kathleen Joan, John Andrew, Barbara Lynn. Education: Graduate of Saint Xavier's Academy; Courses Leading to Real Estate Licensing, 1962; College Courses, Philosophy, Anthropology, English, 1971 to present; Studies, Dramatic Soprano Singing. Career: Assistant Secretary, United States Senator Theodore Francis Green of Rhode Island, 1944; Staff Member, United States Senate Committee on Campaign Expenditures, 1944-45; Assistant Clerk, House Government Operations Committee, 1944-45; Clerk, House Campaign Expenditures Committee under Chairmanship of Congressman Mike Mansfield of Montana, 1950; Assistant Appointment Secretary under Harry S. Truman and Dwight D. Eisenhower, 1951-53; Staff Member under Senator Theodore Francis Green of Rhode Island (then Chairman, Senate Foreign Relations Committee), 1954-60; Licensed Real Estate Broker, 1968; Establisher, Adrienne C. Masterson Real Estate, Alexandria, Virginia, 1968; Owner/Manager, Adrienne Investment Real Estate, Alexandria, Virginia, present. Organizational Memberships: International Investment and Business Exchange, London; National Association of Realtors; Virginia Association of Realtors, Northern Virginia Board of Realtors, Immediate Past Chairman Commercial and Industrial Committee; National Association of Industrial and Office Parks; American Society of Professional and Executive Women; National Association of Female Executives; Alexandria Chamber of Commerce. Community Activities: Kennedy Center, Founding Member; National Historical Society; National Trust for Historic Preservation; Dramatic Soprano Singer. Address: P.O. Box 1271, Alexandria, Virginia 22313. ■

ROBERT JOHN CRAIG

Associate Professor. Personal: Born July 6, 1943; Son of Robert H. and Mary L. Craig. Education: B.S.C.E. 1966, M.S.C.E. 1969, Ph.D. 1973, Purdue University. Career: Associate Professor, Department of Civil and Environmental Engineering, Director, Concrete and Structural Laboratory, New Jersey Institute of Technology, present; Stream Pollution Sampler, United States Public Health Service, Louisville, Kentucky, Summer 1965; Research and Development, Portland Cement Association, Chicago, Illinois, Summer 1967; Worked with Creep and Shrinkage Study, Deep Beam Study, and Flat Plates, Portland Cement Association, Chicago, Illinois, Summer 1968; Assistant Professor, Pennsylvania State University, Capitol Campus, 1972-75; Associate Professor, Department of Civil and Environmental Engineering, New Jersey Institute of Technology, 1975 to present; Draftsman (worked at drafting and putting together matierial for material classes), 1965-66; Teaching Assistant (put together classroom bulletin boards for materials area), 1970-72; Carried Out Reinforced Concrete Beam Tests of Shear and Flexure for Advanced Behavior of Concrete Course, 1969-72; Trunnion Test for Construction Products, Lafayette, Indiana, 1971; Assistant Professor in Building Construction Products, Pennsylvania State University Capitol Campus, 1972-75; Associate Professor of Civil and Environmental Engineering, New Jersey Institute of Technology, Newark, New Jersey, 1975 to present. Organizational Memberships: American Society of Civil Engineers; American Concrete Institute; Society for Experimental Stress Analysis; American Society for Engineering Education; American Society for Testing of Materials. Community Activities: Boy Scouts of America, Assistant Scoutmaster 1961-72, Scoutmaster 1972-75, Committee Member, Assistant Scoutmaster 1975-78, Eagle Scout, Ad Altare Dei, St. George Award, Scouter's Key, Merit Badge Advisor 1978 to present; Catholic Campus Ministry; Canoe Racing (amateur), U.S.C.A. Religion: Catholic. Published Works: Numerous Papers and Presentations in His Field. Honors and Awards: Chi Epsilon; National Civil Engineering Society; Sigma Xi; Scientific Research Society of North America; Omicron Delta Kappa; Tau Beta Pi; Outstanding Young Faculty, Mid-Atlantic Region 1978 A.S.E.E. Dow Awards; James M. Robbins Award, Civil Engineering Department, New Jersey Institute of Technology; Listed in *Who's Who in the East*. Address: 128 Newark Avenue, Apartment 3, Belleville, New Jersey 07019. ■

JEFFREY L. CRAIN

Operations Manager. Personal: Born August 2, 1943; Son of Alfred and Irene (deceased) Crain; Married Ruth Ann. Education: B.S., Youngstown State University, 1970; M.B.A., Seattle City College, 1980. Military: Served in the United States Navy, 1962-66, FTM3. Career: Operations Manager, Digital Equipment Corporation; Management Consultant, Arthur Anderson and Company; Assistant to Corporate Controller/Senior Financial Analyst, Rohr Industries, Inc.; Operations Manager, Evans Products Company; Instructor, Seattle City College, 1980-82. Organizational Memberships: Data Processing Management Association; American Production and Inventory Control Society; American Institute of Industrial Engineers; Society for Advancement of Management, 1967-70; Omicron Delta Epsilon, 1967-70. Community Activities: United Campaign, 1975. Honors and Awards: Letters of Commendation, United State Navy, 1962, 1964; Scholarship, Youngstown Area Board of Realtors, 1968; National Honor Society-Economics, Omicron Delta Epsilon, 1967-70; Scholastic Honors - Top Ten Percent of Class, Youngstown State University, 1967-70; President's Award, Seattle City College, 1980; Listed in *Who's Who in American Colleges and Universities, Who's Who in the West*. Address: 9810 Southwest Ventura Court, Tigard, Oregon 97223. ■

IRA CARLTON CRANDALL

Professional Engineer, Entrepreneur. Personal: Born October 30, 1931, in South Amboy, New Jersey; Son of Carlton Francis Crandall and Claire Elizabeth Harned; Married Jane Leigh Ford, January 1, 1954; Father of Elizabeth Anne, Amy Leigh, Matthew Garrett. Education: Graduate of South River High School, New Jersy, 1949; B.S. Radio Engineering 1954, B.S. Electrical Engineering 1958, Indiana Institute of Technology; B.S. Engineering Electronics, United States Naval; Postgraduate School, 1962; Ph.D., University of Sussex, 1964; M.A., Piedmont University, 1967; Bachelor of Law, Blackstone School of Law, 1970; Associate of Business Administration, La Salle University, 1975. Military: Served in the United States Naval Reserve, 1949-53; Re-Enlisted, Commissioned Ensign 1955, Released from Active Duty 1972, Retired 1978 with the rank of Lieutenant Commander. Career: Elementary School Teacher, 1954-55; Naval Officer, Technical and Engineering Duties, 1955-72; President, 7C-s Enterprises, 1972 to present; Vice President, Dickinson Enterprises, 1973-76; Executive Vice President and Chief of Engineering, Williamson Engineering Inc., 1972-82; Chief Electrical Engineer, Gayner Engineers Inc., 1982 to present; Engineering Consultant, President and Board Chairman, I. C. Crandall and Associates, Inc., 1976-82; Professional Engineer, N.C.E.E., North Carolina, Florida; Energy Manager, A.E.E., Professional Electrical Engineer, Professional Control Systems Engineer, Certified Energy Auditor, California; Professional Electrical Engineer, Oregon, Washington. Organizational Memberships: American College of Engineers, Fellow; American Institute of Technical Management, Senior Member; Association of Energy Engineers, Charter Member; Institute of Elecrical and Electronics Engineers; Society of American Military Engineers; United States Naval Institute; Associaton of Naval Aviation; American Biographical Research Association. Community Activities: Optimist Club, Past Charter President; Century Club; Boy Scouts of America; Neptune Society; Concord Parade and Field Association; Concord Parade and Field Association; Concord Blue Devils, Past Vice President; Concord Chamber Singers; Young Men's Christian Association, Youth Group Organizer; Parent-Teacher Association, Past President; Diablo Valley Band Review Association; Mount Diablo Unified Schools Interested Citizens, Past President; Concord Homeowners' Association; Clayton Valley Music Boosters, Past President, Board Member; Pine Hollow Band Aides, Board Member; Optimist International; International Platform Association; Sons of the American Revolution; Reserve Officers' Association; Republican Party, Member Business Advisory Council, National Republic Congressional Committee. Religion: United Methodist Church, Board Member, Past President Choir. Published Works: Articles on Engineering Management, *Journal of the American Institute of Technical Management*; Articles on Control Systems and Electronics, *Journal of the American College of Engineers*. Honors and Awards: Pioneered Use of Solid-State Electronics in Industrial Process Control Systems; Assisted in Development of Radar Systems for Ground Control of Aircraft Traffic; Responsible for Research, Development and Design for First Fully Engineered Two-Way Cable Television System in the United States; Military Decorations, Navy Unit Citation, Navy Expeditionary Medal, National Defense Service Medal, Armed Forces Expeditionary Medal, Vietnam Service Medal, Vietnam Campaign Medal, Vietnam Cross of Valor, Armed Forces Reserve Medal, Expert Rifle Shot Medal, Expert Pistol Shot Medal; Fellowships, International Biographical Association 1979, American Biographical Institute 1978, American College of Engineers 1975, University of Sussex 1964; Honorary Degrees, D.S.Sc. Piedmont University 1968, D.Litt. Saint Matthew University 1970, Ed.D. Mount Sinai University 1970; Pi Upsilon Eta, 1967 to present; Gamma Chi Epsilon, 1970 to present; Sons of the American Revolution, War Service Medal 1972, Silver Good Citizenship Medal 1975; Presidential Citation, Optimist International, 1976; Zero Defects Award, Navy Department, 1970; Listed in *Men of Achievement, International Who's Who of Intellectuals, Book of Honor, International Biographical Association Yearbook, Men and Women of Distinction, Dictionary of International Biography, Personalities of America, International Who's Who in Community Service, Community Leaders and Noteworthy Americans, Personalities of the West and Midwest, Notable Americans, Who's Who in the West, Who's Who in the United States, Who's Who in North America, Hereditary Register of the United States of America, National Social Directory, Who's Who in California, American Scientific Registry, Who's Who in California Business and Finance, American Patriots of the 1980's, Directory of Distinguished Americans, Who's Who in Technology Today, Industry's Directory of Technical Consultants, International Register of Profiles, People Who Matter, Ernest Kay's Personal Hall of Fame*. Address: 5754 Pepperridge Place, Concord, California 94521. ■

LARRY WALTER CRANDALL

Educational and Business Consultant. Personal: Born July 26, 1938; Son of Perry and Alice Crandall; Married Katherine J. Wendt, Daughter of Otto and Kathleen

Wendt; Father of Darolyn Marie, Debora Ann, Craig Steven, Danielle Lucille. Education: B.S. Health and Physical Education, University of Montana, 1960; M.Ed., Instructional Media, Eastern Washington University, 1968; Ed.D., Educational Administration, Washington State University, 1972. Military: Served with the United States Army Infantry, Active Duty 1961-63, Honorable Discharge, Captain. Career: Educational and Business Consultant; Director, Interstate Vocational Education Cooperative, Pullman, Washington, 1980-81; Director, Learning Resources, Western Nevada Community College, Carson City, Nevada, 1972-79; Instructor, Washington State University, Pullman, Washington, 1969-72; Librarian, Cheney High School, Cheney, Washington, 1965-69; Librarian, Moses Lake High School, Moses Lake, Washington, 1963-65. Organizational Memberships: Phi Delta Kappa Area Coordinator, 1981 to present; President, Phi Delta Kappa Chapter, Washington State University, 1980-81; President, Nevada Library Association, 1976; President, Nevada Audio Visual Association, 1976. Community Activities: Memberships Chairman, Pullman, Washington Rotary Club, 1982; Vice President 1980, President 1981, Pullman, Washington High School Parent-Teacher Association; President, Pullman, Washington Comets Track Club, 1980; Captain, Western Nevada Community College United Way Campaign, 1978; Member, Carson City, Nevada Park and Recreation Commission, 1978-79; Vice-Chairperson, Pullman, Washington Parks and Recreation Commission, 1980 to present; Board of University of Nevada Press, 1974-79; Member, Board of Channel 5 TV, Carson City, Nevada, 1973-76. Honors and Awards: Selected for 1978 Okobii (Wisconsin) Educational Media Leadership Conference; Selected for Institute to Train Media Specialists, Washington State University, 1969-70; Awarded Allstate Driver Education Scholarship, 1965; Listed in *Men of Achievement, Who's Who in the West.* Address: Northeast 1255 Cove Way, Pullman, Washington 99163.■

BETTY DORSEY CROOKSHANKS

State Legislator, Educator. Personal: Born October 27, 1944; Daughter of Gilda S. Buckley; Married Donald E. Crookshanks. Education: B.A., West Virginia Tech, 1968; M.A., West Virginia University, 1973. Career: West Virginia House of Delegates, State Legislator, 1976 to present; Educator, present; Life Insurance Underwriter; Secretary, National Institutes of Health; Girls' Coach. Organizational Memberships: Delta Kappa Gamma, Secretary 1980-81, First Vice President 1981-82; Greenbrier County Farm Bureau; West Virginia Education Associaton; Greenbrier Valley Life Underwriters; Business and Professional Women's Club; Greenbrier Valley Quota Club, Board of Directors 1981; Fayette County Education Association, Treasurer 1973-74; Order of Women Legislators; Member, Standing Committees, Judiciary, Health and Welfare, Roads and Transportation; Co-chairman, House Democratic Caucus; Member, Interim Committees, Health and Welfare Visitation, Coal Mining and Safety, Judiciary. Community Activities: Rupert Woman's Club, President 1978-80; Cancer Society, Greenbrier President 1981, Board of Directors West Virginia Division 1981-83; Order of the Eastern Star, Electa 1980-81; Rebekaks; West Virginia Health Systems Agency, Board of Directors 1980-82; Rupert Community Library, Board of Directors, Treasurer 1977 to present; Seneca Mental Health Council, Treasurer 1979, President Board of Directors 1980-81; West Virginia Women's Commission, Advisory Council 1977 to present; Greenbrier County Committee on Aging, Transportation Committee 1980-81; Greenbrier Valley Domestic Violence Council, 1978-80; Governor's Golden Mountaineer Card Program, 1980 to present; Rainelle Medical Center Black Lung Clinic, 1980 to present; Delegate, State Democratic Convention, 1976, 1980; Delegate, Southern Legislators Convention, 1980, 1981, 1982; Delegate, National State Legislators Convention, 1981; West Virginia Tech Alumni Association; West Virginia University Alumni Association; Marshall University Alumni Association. Religion: Big Clear Creek Baptist Church, Treasurer 1981 to present; Bays Chapel Methodist Church, Sunday School Teacher. Honors and Awards: Outstanding Young Woman of the Year, West Virginia, 1980; Meritorious Award for Conservation of Natural Resources, West Virginia Division, Issac Walton League of America, 1978; Outstanding Personality of Western Greenbrier, *Meadow River Post Newspaper,* 1977; Fayette County Young Teacher to Leadership Camp, 1969; Claude Bemedum Scholarship, 1963, 1964; Outstanding Citizen, Rupert Rotary Club, 1983. Address: Box 370, Rupert, West Virginia 25984.■

ROSE HARRIS CROSS

School Social Worker. Personal: Born March 17, 1945; Daughter of Rev. Dr. and Mrs. R. B. Harris; Mother of Una-Kariim Alencia, Kha-Lihah DaVida. Education: B.A., Jackson State University, 1967; M.S.W., Michigan State University, 1973. Career: School Social Worker, Lansing, Michigan; Former Assistant Head Advisor of Student Housing, Michigan State University; Former Medical Social Worker, St. Lawrence Hospital, Lansing; Former Field Coordinator Mississippi Action for Progress, Jackson, Mississippi. Organizational Memberships: National Association of Social Workers, Social Action Chairperson, 1974-76, Programs Chairperson 1976-78, President 1978-79; National Association of Black Social Workers; Lansing School Education Association, Representative Assembly 1974-75, Negotiating Committee 1976-79; Minority Educators Association. Community Activities: Brownie Troop Leader, Girl Scouts of America, 1979-80; Delta Sigma Theta Sorority, Inc., Charter Member Battle Creek Alumnae Chapter, Lansing Alumnae, Past Secretary, Chaplain 1981-82; Y.W.C.A. Committee to Evaluate Minority Participants in the Organization, 1981; Council for Stronger Government vs. Mayor Control, 1975-76; Public-Camp Scholarships, Parenting Classes, Transportation, 1975 to present. Religion: Summer Missionary, Southern Baptist Seminary, 1966, Vacation Bible School 1967, 1970 and 1981, Woman Day Speaker 1968, Presenter First National School Social Workers Conference 1978. Honors and Awards: Listed in *Who's Who of American Women, The World Who's Who of Women.* Address: 6435 Norburn Way, Lansing, Michigan 48910.■

MARY C. CROWLEY

Corporate Executive. Personal: Born April 1, 1915; Daughter of Rev. and Mrs. L. G. Weaver (deceased); Married First Husband Joseph Carter on May 4, 1932 (deceased), Second Husband David M. Crowley on April 10, 1948; Mother of Donald J. Carter, Ruth Carter Shanahan (Mrs. Ralph L.). Education: Attended University of Arkansas, 1931-32; Southern Methodist University, 1940-41. Career: President and Sales Manager, Home Interiors and Gifts Inc., 1957 to present; with Republic Insurance Company, 1941-46; Purse Furniture Company, 1946-50; Stanley Home Products, 1950-54; World Gift Company, Sales Manager, 1954-55; World Gift Company, Vice President, 1955-57. Community Activities: Billy Graham Evangelistic Association, Board of Directors 1974 to present; Dallas Chamber of Commerce, Board of Directors 1976; Mercantile National Bank, Board of Directors 1977; Small Business Administration, 1980; Republican. Religion: Baptist. Published Works: Author, "Moments with Mary" 1973, "Be Somebody" 1974, "Think Mink" 1977, "Women Who Win" 1979, "You Can Too" 1979, "Pocketful of Hope" 1981. Honors and Awards: Oscar of Salesmanship, American Salesmaster Organization, 1966; Altrusa Club's "Mature Woman of the Year" 1969; Direct Selling Association's "Knight of the Royal Way" 1973; Baylor University's "Woman of the Year" 1973; Direct Selling Association's Hall of Fame (first woman to be elected, 1975); Building Named in Her Honor at First Baptist Church, Dallas, Texas (Mary C. Building), 1975; Horatio Alger Awardee, 1978; Doctor of Humane Letters, Grand Canyon College, 1976; Doctor of Humanities, Dallas Baptist College, 1979; Sales and Marketing Award, 1980. Address: 10265 Inwood Road, Dallas, Texas 75229.■

IRMA RUSSELL CRUSE

Telephone Company Supervisor (Retired), Free-lance Writer, Public Speaker. Personal: Married J. Clyde Cruse; Mother of Allan Baird, Howard Russell. Education: M.A., English, Samford University, 1981; Bell System Speaker's Training Class; Photography, Editing and Writing Workshops, University of Georgia; Famous Photographers Course; Writing Courses, Christian Writers School, Newspaper Institute of America, Famous Writers School, University of Chicago, University of Wisconsin, University of Minnesota, University of Alabama's New College. Career: Southern Bell and South Central Bell Telephone 36 Years, Public Relations 4 Years, Editor *Bell Tel News,* Advertising Editor *Bama Bulletin,* Alabama Area Rate and Tariff Organization, Coordinator, Share Owner-Management Visit Program 1 Year, Traffic and Commercial Department, Toll Operator, Toll Supervisor, Toll Training Supervisor, Sales Clerk, TWX Instructor, Service Representative, Training Coach 14 Years, Rate Supervisor, Marketing Department until 1976; Stenographer for Director of Public Welfare, St. Clair County; Secretary to Public Works Officer; Naval Air Station, Birmingham; Chief of Planning, Anniston Ordnance Depot; Free-lance Writer, Articles, Playettes, Skits, Public Relations, 1956 to present. Organizational Memberships: Alabama Writers Conclave, Corresponding Secretary 1971-72, Recording Secretary 1972-73, 1979-80, President 1973-74; Alabama State Poetry Society, Program Chairman 1972-73, 1973-74, Editor *The Muse Messenger* 1976-77, 1977-778; Women in Communications, Corresponding Secretary 1968-70, President 1970-71, First Vice President and Program Chairman 1975-76, Recording Secretary 1978-79, Historian 1979-80, 1981-82); Birmingham Business Communicators (now IABC/ Birmingham), Corresponding Secretary, 1967-68, President 1970-71, National Representative of ICIE 2 Years; American Association of University Women; International Platform Association, 1971-72, 1974-75; Telephone Pioneers of America, Numerous Positions. Community Activities: Public Speaker, Service and Civic Groups, School and Church Groups; Alabama Baptist Historical Commission; Alabama Baptist Historical Society, Treasurer 1980-81, Assistant Editor *The Alabama Baptist Historian* 1979, 1980, 1981 to present; Alabama Historical Society; Birmingham Historical Society; Birmingham-Jefferson Historical Society; St. Clair County Historical Society; Birmingham-Southern College Alumni Committee; Freedoms Foundation of Valley Forge, Birmingham Chapter; Women's Chamber of Commerce, Second Vice President 1978-79, By-Laws Chairman 1978-79, 1979-80, 1980-81; Birmingham Festival of Arts, Board of Directors 1970-75; Birmingham Council of Clubs (formerly Inter-Club Council), First Vice President 1971-72, Board of Directors 1972-73, 1975-81, Recording Secretary 1973-75; Metropolitan Business and Professional Women's Club of Birmingham, Numerous Positions; Quota Club of Birmingham, President, 1976-77; Jefferson County Radio and TV Council, President 1971-72, Corresponding Secretary 1975-76; Project Volunteer Power; United Way Speakers Bureau; Salvation Army Women's Auxiliary, Chaplain 1978-79; Alabama Women's Political Caucus; Birmingham-Jefferson Women's Center; Alabama Citizens for E.R.A.; Town and Gown Players. Published Works: Writer, Producer, Director, Plays, Playlets; Numerous Articles, including (most recently) "Proclaiming the Possiblities of Life" and "Don't Be Afraid." Honors and Awards: Phi Kappa Phi Scholastic Honor Society, 1982; Birmingham Branch, National League of American Pen Women, 1982; B.P.W. Member of the Week, Metro B.P.W. Club of Birminghamm, 1965; Woman of Achievement, Twice; Liberty Bell Award, Birmingham Bar Association, 1973; David Daniel Eleemosynary Award for Community Service Activities, American Red Cross, 1973; One of "Beautiful Activists" for Alabama, 1972; Best All-Around Teletalker, Birmingham Teletalker Club; Annual Scholarship to be Named for Irma Cruse, Metropolitan Business and Professional Women's Club, 1982; Appointed by Governor Fob James to Governor's Commission on Employment of the Handicapped; Nine Awards, Birmingham Ad Club; Best Photograph, Award of Achievement for Writing, Southern Council of Industrial Editors; Honorable Mention, International Association of Industrial Editors; First Place, Association of Writers for Technical Publications; First Place for Best Feature, Jefferson County United Appeal; Outstanding Chapter President, Birmingham Business Communicators, 1968; Sigma Tau Delta; Listed in *Foremost Women in Communications, Who's Who of American Women, Who's Who in Alabama-Notable Women, Personalities of the South, Two Thousand Women of Achievement, World Who's Who of Women, Dictionary of International Biography, Community Leaders and Noteworthy Americans, International Who's Who in Community Service, Alabama's Distinguished, Notable Americans of the Bicentennial Era, Who's Who in the South and Southwest, Contemporary Americans.* Address: 136 Memory Court, Birmingham, Alabama 35213.■

FRANCES HILL CRUTCHER

Professor. Personal: Born November 2, 1905; Daughter of William H. and Daisy O'Malley Hall (deceased); Mother of John E. Hill Jr., William A. Hill, Charles J. Hill. Education: Diploma in Piano and Theory, Cadek Conservatory, Chattanooga, Tennessee, 1925; Postgraduate Diploma, Cadek Conservatory, 1927; B.M. Degree, University of Chattanooga, 1939; Graduate Study in Piano, Music History, Analysis, Counterpoint at Chautauqua, New York School of Music under James Friskin, Wendell Keene, Barbara Steinback, 1948-52. Career: Professor of Music, David Lipscomb College; Associate Professor of Piano, University of Chattanooga; Teacher of Theory, Music Appreciation, Piano, Cadek Conservatory, Chattanooga, Tennessee. Organizational Memberships: Chattanooga Music Teachers' Association, Vice President 1958-61; Middle Tennessee M.T.A., Vice President 1962-63, President 1963-65; Auditions Chairman, Tennessee Music Teachers Association, 1966-69; President, Tennessee Music Teachers Association; Secretary-Treasurer, Southern Division Music Teachers National Association, 1973-75; Board Member, Music Teachers National Association, 1973-75; President, Nashville Area Music Teachers Association 1982, Theory and Composition Chairman 1979-82. Community Activities: International Pilot Club; Chattanooga, Tennessee Chairman Committee Anchor Clubs; Professional Accompanist for Nashville Symphony Chorus, 1962-75; Accompanist for Visiting Artists in Tennessee, Alabama, Georgia, 1925 to present; Solo Concert Artist, 1923 to present; Chairman of Scholarships, Tennessee Music Teachers Association, 1976-82; Adjudicator, Auditions of Memphis State University 1980, Tennessee State Auditions 1982, Middle Tennessee State University 1981, Nashville Area Music Teachers Association, 1982. Religion: Member, Church of Christ, 1917 to present. Honors and Awards: Winner of State and Southern Division Competitions in Young Artist Piano Series, 1929; Competed in National Young Artists Series, 1930; Tennessee Music Teacher of the Year, Awarded Citation by Governor Dunn, 1971; People-to-People, Selected to Visit Schools of Music, Colleges, and Other Institutions of Musical Education in Belgium, Germany, Poland, Russia, Italy, Switzerland, and France in 1974, and in Japan and China in 1981. Address: 3401 Granny White Pike, Apartment L-229, Nashville, Tennessee 37204.■

LARRY RANDALL CRUTHERS

Associate Director Animal Health Research. Personal: Born March 15, 1945; Son of Harold and Irene Cruthers; Married Susan Margaret; Father of Carrie Lyn, Polly Jane. Education: B.S. Zoology, University of Wisconsin-Stevens Point, 1967; M.A. 1971, Ph.D. 1973, Parasitology, Kansas State University, Manhattan. Military: Served as Captain, Medical Services Corps, Honorable Discharge, 1978. Career: Associate Director, Animal Health Research, S.D.S. Biotech Corporation, Painesville, Ohio; Research Associate, Former Senior Research Parasitologist, Diamond Shamrock Corporation, Painesville, Ohio, present; Senior Research Parasitologist, Squibb Institute for Medical Research, Princeton, New Jersey; Senior Research Parasitologist, Squibb Agricultural Research Center, Three Bridges, New Jersey; Instructor of Biology, Kansas State University, Manhattan, Kansas. Organizational Memberships: American Society of Parasitology; New Jersey Society for Parasitology, Secretary/Treasurer 1976-79, President 1979-80; Helminthological Society of Washington; American Association of Veterinary Parasitologists; American Heartworm Society; Conference of Research Workers in Animal Diseases; Sigma Xi. Community Activities: Kiwanis Club, President-elect 1979-80; Society for the Prevention of Cruelty to Animals, Member, Board of Directors, Hunterdon County, New Jersey; Church School Superintendent, 1977-80. Honors and Awards: Nominee, Outstanding Undergraduate Teacher Award in Biology, Kansas State University, 1969-70. Address: 10268 Cherry Hill Drive, Painesville, Ohio 44077.■

JEANETTE GLENN CUMMINGS

Gerontologist. Personal: Born August 11, 1949; Daughter of Mr. and Mrs. Asbery Glenn; Married. Education: B.S., Tuskegee Institute, 1972; M.S.W., Atlanta University, 1973; Certificate in Community Gerontology Leadership, Georgia State University, 1983. Career: Gerontologist, Director Central Savannah River Area Agency on Aging; Former Director of Resident Services for Wesley Homes, Inc.; Former Life Insurance Agent and Nursing Home Administrator. Organizational Memberships: Academy of Certified Social Workers; Georgia Conference of Social Welfare; Past Chairperson, Augusta Unit, National Association of Social Workers, 1980-83; Chairperson, The Augusta Area Mental Health/Mental Retardation; Secretary, Senior Enrichment Association, 1982-83; Board Member, Southeastern Association of Area Agencies on Aging, 1980-83; Board Member, Vice President, Georgia Gerontology Society; Board Member, Chairperson for Nominations and Leadership, Georgia Chapter, National Association of Social Workers; Board Member of Executive Committee, Chamber of Commerce Leadership Program, 1982-83; Board Member, Leadership Augusta Alumni Association; National Association of Area Agencies on Aging; National Association of Social Workers; Gerontological Society; Professional Women Association. Community Activities: Volunteer for United Way, Red Cross, Hospice; Delta Sigma Theta; Board of Education Community School Committee, 1982; St. John Towers Advisory Board; Medical College of Georgia Human Genetic Institute Advisory Board; Augusta Tuskegee Alumni Club. Religion: Member of Christ Church Unity. Honors and Awards: Honored for Five Years of Services to Wesley Home, Inc., 1978; Employee of the Year, 1980; Selected to Participate in Chamber of Commerce Leadership Program, 1982; Citizen of the Year, Senior Enrichment Association, 1983; Outstanding Professional Social Workers of Quarter, Georgia Chapter, National Association of Social Workers, 1983; Listed in *Who's Who of American Women*. Address: 2715 Vernon Drive West, Augusta, Georgia 30906.■

GERALD LUVERN DAHL

Clinical Social Worker, Associate Professor. Personal: Born November 10, 1938; Son of Lloyd (deceased) and Leola Dahl; Married Judith Lee, Daughter of Carl and Beryl Brown; Father of Peter, Stephen, Leah. Education: B.A., Wheaton College, 1960; M.S.W., University of Nebraska, 1962; Academy of Certified Social Workers, 1964. Career: Clinical Social Worker and Associate Professor; Former Director of Patient Care at Mount Sinai Hospital and Staff Consultant to the Citizens Council on Delinquency and Crime. Organizational Memberships: Pi Gamma Mu; American Association of University Professors; National Association of Social Workers. Community Activities: Founder, Family Counseling Service, 1965. Religion: Chairman of the Board of Deacons, Edgewater Baptist Church, 1975. Published Works: *Why Christian Marriage Are Breaking Up* (1979) and *Everybody Needs Somebody Sometime* (1980). Address: 4720 Killarney Drive, Golden Valley, Minnesota 55422.∎

EDWARD LAFAYETTE DARDEN

Retired Architect and Educator. Personal: Born April 13, 1901; Son of Addison and Malissa Calaway Darden (both deceased); Widower; Father of Betty Darden Thompson, Paul Albert. Education: Graduate of Coast Artillery School (Fort Monroe, Virginia), 1918; Attended Alabama University and Auburn University, 1928-41; Special Course, University of Georgia, 1955. Military: Served in the United States Army, attaining the rank of Staff Sergeant. Career: Retired Architect and Educator; Founder, Darden Rehabilitation Center, 1953; Former Positions include President of the Alabama Vocational Association, President of the Alabama Writers Conclave, Director of the Alabama School of Trades (Gadsden, Alabama); Guest Feature Writer, *The Gadsden Times*. Organizational Memberships: United States Army Association. Community Activities: Gadsden Area Development Committee, President 1951. Religion: Methodist. Published works: *Fiction, Three Trips Up the Mountain*, *The Rose of Bagdad* and *What Do You Think?*, 1983. Honors and Awards: Gadsden State Technical School Man of the Year, Second Founders Day Award, 1967; Honorary Lieutenant Colonel, Alabama State Militia, 1962. Address: 527 Dumas Drive, Auburn, Alabama 36830.∎

RENE-YVON MARIE MARC LEFEBVRE D'ARGENCE

Museum Director and Chief Curator. Personal: Born August 21, 1928; Son of Marc Lefebvre d'Argencé (deceased) and Andrée Thierry (deceased); Married Ritva Anneli Pelanne, Daughter of Mr. and Mrs. Pentti Pelanne; Father of Chantal, Yann, Luc. Education: Attended Collège St. Aspais (Fontainebleau), Lycée Albert Sarraut (Hanoi), Pembroke College (Cambridge, England), Ecole Libre des Sciences Politiques; Licencié-es-Lettres, Sorbonne, 1952; Breveté de l'Ecole Nationale des Langues Orientales Vivantes, Chinese 1950, Japanese 1951, Finnish 1952. Military: Served with the Free French Forces in World War II. Career: Director and Chief Curator, Asian Art Museum of San Francisco, 1969 to present; Director, Avery Brundage Collection, 1965-68; Curator of Asiatic Collections, M. H. de Young Memorial Museum, San Francisco, 1964; Professor of Art History, University of California at Berkeley, 1962-65; Quai d'Orsay Grant, Taiwan, 1959; Curator, Blanchard de la Brosse Museum, Saigon, and Louis Finot Museum, Hanoi, 1954-58; Member, Ecole Français d'Extrême-Orient, 1954; Curator, Musée Cernuschi, Paris, 1953. Organizational Memberships: Trustee, Asian Art Foundation, 1979 to present; Advisory Committee, Society for Asian Art, 1964 to present; Corresponding Member, Sociedad Asiatica de la Argentina. Community Activities: Vice President, Chinese-American Bilingual School of San Francisco, 1981 to present; Board Member, Institute of Sino-American Studies, 1981-83; San Francisco-Osaka Sister City Committee, 1980 to present; San Francisco-Seoul Sister City Committee, 1980 to present; San Francisco-Shanghai Sister City Committee, 1980 to present; Trustee, Beaudry Foundation, 1977 to present; President 1976-79, Executive Vice President 1979 to present, French-American Bilingual School, San Francisco; Founder, Ecole Français of San Francisco, 1967. Honors and Awards: Médaille de la Reconnaissance Français, 1957; Chevalier de l'Etoile du Nord (Sweden), 1968; Order of Merit, Avery Brundage Foundation, 1968; Honrary Doctor's Degree, Chinese Academy, Taiwan, 1969; Chevalier de l'Ordre du Merite (France), 1970; Officer of Culture Merit Order, Korea, 1982. Address: 16 Midhill Drive, Mill Valley, California 94941.∎

AARON DAS GUPTA

Mechanical and Aerospace Engineer. Personal: Born November 20, 1943; Son of Krishna Prosad Das Gupta; Married Rumi; Father of Elora, Debraj. Education: B.Tech. (honors), Mechanical Engineering, I.I.T. (Kharaspur, India); M.Eng., Technical University of Nova Scotia, 1968; Ph.D., Engineering Mechanics, Virginia Polytechnic Institute, 1975. Career: Mechanical and Aerospace Research Engineer, Aberdeen Proving Ground; Former Positions include Mechanical Design Engineer, Stress Analyst, Project Engineer, Electronics Quality Control Engineer, Chemical Protection Engineer, Tool and Die Designer, Machine Technician. Organizational Memberships: American Academy of Mechanics; Sigma Xi; New York Academy of Science; Professional Registered Engineer, Illinois, New Mexico, Texas, Virginia, 1977 to present. Community Activities: Division Chairman, Combined Federal Campaign Committee, Aberdeen Proving Ground, 1981; State Advisor, American Security Council, Washington D.C., 1982 to present; Co-Chairman, Society for Engineering Science, 19th Annual Meeting, University of Missouri-Rolla, 1982. Published Works: Author Fifty Published Papers, Government and Industrial Reports. Honors and Awards: DRB Research Fellow, N.S.T.C., 1966-67; Quality Step Increase and Sustained High Quality Performance Award, Department of the Army, 1982; National Science Foundation Travel Grant Award to Sixth World Congress, I.F.T.O.M.M., New Delhi, India, 1983; Invited Speaker to OlinCorp, 1984; 4th National Congress, A.S.M.E.; Listed in Several Biographical Publications. Address: 104 John Street, Perryville, Maryland 21903.∎

KENNETH R. DAUT

Facilities Engineer. Personal: Born August 3, 1952, in Santa Monica, California; Married Pamela Jaye Braxton; Father of Matthew Christopher. Education: A.A., West Los Angeles Junior College, 1973; B.A., University of California at Los Angeles, 1975. Career: Facilities Engineer 1983 to present, Industrial Engineer 1980-83, Budget Analyst 1978-80, Northrop Corporation; Business Development Officer, Community Bank, 1977; Account Executive, Metropolitan Life Insurance Company, 1976. Organizational Memberships: Torrance Junior Chamber of Commerce; American Institute of Industrial Engineers. Community Activities: Youth Motivation Task Force; Pacific States Open Throw Dart Tournament; Neighborhood Watch Committee. Honors and Awards: Youth Motivation Task Force Award, Los Angeles County, 1980; Northrop Performance Award, 1978; Northrop Suggestion Award, 1979; Awarded (Three Times), Northrop 747 Stretched Upper Deck Efficiency Suggestion Awards, 1982; Listed in *Who's Who in Finance and Industry*, *Who's Who in the World*, *Who's Who in the West*, *Personalities of America*. Address: 603 Pine Drive, Torrance, California 90501.∎

MABEL E. DAVIDSON

Author, Lecturer. Personal: Born May 20, 1901; Daughter of Richard Matthew Farlow and Lida Jane Steele (deceased); Mother of Evelyn Mae. Education: Attended Purdue University and Indiana University; Graduate, Famous Writer's School. Career: Historical Researcher, Author of Books and Book Reviews, Lecturer at Purdue University and Others. Organizational Memberships: International Platform Association. Community Activities: International Toastmistress Club; International Travel Study Club; Captain, Harmon Chapter, Daughters of the American Revolution; Chorister of Issac Walton Auxiliary; Donates All Profits from Books to

Cancer Research and to Organizations Concerning Handicapped Children. Religion: United Methodist Church, Sunday School Teacher, Woman's Society. Published Works: Author of *Legend and Lore from America's Crossroads, Recollections of a Country Girl, Out of the Past Into the Future;* Author of Free-lance Material for *Indianapolis Sunday Star, The Indianapolis News, Frankfort Times,* Other Local Papers. Honors and Awards: Famous Writer's School, Charter Member with Certificate and Honorary Letter, Listed as Outstanding Graduate; Annual Associate, American Biographical Institute Research Assction; Listed in *Notable Americans of the Bicentennial Era, Community Leaders and Noteworthy Americans, Dictionary of International Biography, World Who's Who of Women.* Address: 1739 Southeast 46th Lane, Cape Coral, Florida 33904.■

BOB J. DAVIS

Professor. Personal: Born June 27, 1927; Son of Franklin H. (deceased) and Minnie C. Davis; Married Alice Joyce Reagan, Daughter of Joseph E. (deceased) and Gertrude R. Reagan; Father of Paula Lynn Kessler. Education: B.B.A. magna cum laude 1957, M.B.A. 1961, J.D. 1966, University of Houston. Military: Served in the United States Navy, 1945-47. Career: Professor, Western Illinois University, 1967 to present; Former Positions with the University of Houston (1957-62), Repubic Steel (1962-67), Texaco (1952-62), Burlington Railroad (1950-52), Oilfields (1948-50); Licensed Attorney, State of Texas. Organizational Memberships: Phi Kappa Phi; Beta Gamma Sigma; Blue Key; Sigma Iota Epsilon; Delta Theta Phi; Delta Nu Alpha; American Society of Traffic and Transportation; International Materials Management Society; Society of Logistics Engineers; Transportation Research Forum; Alumni Federation; ICC Practitioners Association; Traffic Club of Houston; Tri-State Transportation Club; Traffic Club of Galesburg. Community Activities: Boy Scout Fund Drive (Macomb), Group Leader 1971-74; Young Women's Christian Association (Houston), Fund Solicitor 1962; United Fund; Chamber of Commerce; Macomb City Planning Commission, Commissioner 1968-73; Illinois Public Airports Association, 1980-83; Macomb Airport Authority, Board Member 1980-83. Published Works: Author *An Annotated Bibliography of the Motor Carrier Industry, Information Sources in Transportation, Material Management and Physical Distribution. An Annotated Bibliography and Guide, Illinois Insurance Law Outline, Macomb Airport Study, An Annotated Pipe Line Bibliography;* Various Articles. Honors and Awards: Traffic Club of Houston Scholarship, 1955-56 and 1956-57; Houston Purchasing Agents Sam Harper Award, 1957; I.C.C. Practitioners Clyde Aitchison Award, 1966; Traffic Club of Houston Traffic Man of the Year, 1966; Regional Education Man of the Year, Delta Nu Alpha, 1979-80 and 1980-81; Teacher of the Year, Western Illinois University College of Business, 1980-81; Faculty Appreciation Award, Delta Nu Alpha, 1980, 1981, 1982; DNA Region 1, Mayleben Award, 1982. Address: 1111 East Grant Street, Macomb, Illinois 61455.■

BRUCE ALLEN DAVIS

Clinical and Industrial Psychologist. Personal: Born August 13, 1948; Son of William L. and Mable C. Davis. Education: A.B., Drury College, 1970; M.S., Southwest Missouri State University, 1974; M.B.A., Drury College, 1980. Career: Staff Psychologist and Marriage and Family Therapist, Greene County Guidance Clinic (Springfield, Missouri), 1975-80; Associate Psychologist, United States Bureau of Prisons Medical Center, 1976; Owner, Davis Psychological Testing Service, 1975 to present; Consultant to Industry, School Systems, Governmental Organizations, Medical and Legal Institutions. Organizational Memberships: American Psychological Association; Missouri Psychological Association; American Association of Marriage and Family Therapists; American Management Association; American Personnel and Guidance Association. Community Activities: Elks Club; Public Speaker to Business and Professional Groups. Published Works: Author of Numerous Articles on Business and Psychology. Honors and Awards: Listed in *Who's Who in the Midwest, Men of Achievement, Community Leaders and Noteworthy Americans, Personalities of the West and Midwest, Personalities of America, Dictionary of International Biography, Directory of Distinguished Americans, Community Leaders of America.* Address: 1240 South Saratoga, Springfield, Missouri 65804.■

EMMA LOU DAVIS

Research Associate, Foundation Administrator, Archeologist. Personal: Born November 26, 1904. Education: B.A., Vassar College; M.A., University of California at Los Angeles, 1962; Ph.D., University of California at Los Angeles, 1964. Career: Sculptor, Product Designer, Teacher in Fine Arts, until 1957; Archeologist, 1957 to present; Crew Chief for Dr. Florence Ellis, University of New Mexico, Trace Proto-Historic Navajo Intrusions on Acoma and Laguna Lands, New Mexico, 1959; Special Research for Wetherill Mesa Project, 1961-63; Independent Research, "Reconstruction of the Ethnography and Land Use Patterns of the Kuzedika Paiute of Mono Lake, California," 1962; Co-Principal Investigator, Paleo-Indian Dispersion in Southern and Baja California, 1964-65; Faculty Research Grant, University of California at Los Angeles, 1966; Curator of Archeology, San Diego Museum of Man, 1966-70; Wenner-Gren Foundation for Anthropological Research, Grant for Museum Research, 1967; Society of Sigma Xi Grant, 1967; American Philosophical Society Grant, 1968; Began China Lake Program, 1970; National Geographic Society Grant, 1971-72; National Science Foundation Grant, 1974-75; Instructor, Department of Anthropology, University of California at San Diego, 1973-75; Founder and Director, The Great Basin Foundation, 1976 to present; Guide, Friends of the Pleistocéne, Pacific Cell, Annual Field Trip, 1976; Completion of Phase I, China Lake Program, 1977; Collaboration with The Whittlesey Foundation (Wilton, Connecticut), 1977; Advisor and Preparator of Review of Literature in Five Sciences for Recon Inc. in Connection with Phase I Environmental Resources (Desert Planning Unit) for BLM, 1978; Principal Investigator on Evaluation of Early Human Activities and Remains in the California Desert for BLM California Desert Conservation Area, 1978; Archeological Consultant for Westec Services Inc., 1978, 1979; Preparation of Two Sensitivity Maps for BLM Showing Sites of 5000 Years of Age in California Desert Conservation Area, 1979; Research into Development of Bibliography of Previous Publications on California Desert Conservation Area, 1979-80; Preparation and Publication of *Evaluation of Early Human Activities and Remains in the California Desert,* 1980; Research Associate, Natural History Museum, Los Angeles County. Organizational Memberships: S.O.P.A.; Current Anthropology; American Association for the Advancement of Science; Southern California Academy of Sciences; Research Associate, Los Angeles County Museum; Research Associate, Nevada State Museum; Research Association, Archeological Research Inc.; Society of Sigma Xi; International Congress of Americanists; S.C.A. Address: 1236 Concord Street, San Diego, California 92106.■

EVELYN MARGUERITE BAILEY DAVIS

Musician and Artist. Personal: Born in Springfield, Missouri; Daughter of Philip Edward Bailey and Della Jane Morris Bailey Freeman (both deceased); Married James Harvey. Education: Secretarial Training; Private Student of Organ and Piano for Twelve Years, Webster Grove, Missouri; Special Classes at Drury College. Career: Secretary, Shea and Morris Monument Company; Soloist Member, Sextet, Radio Station KGBX; Bible Teacher, Pianist, East Avenue Baptist Church; Teacher, Bible Class, Third Baptist Church, St. Louis, Missouri; Engaged to Paint 12 by 6 Foot Mural of Jordan River, Bible Baptist Church, Maplewood, Missouri, 1954; Church Organist, Bible Teacher, Bible Baptist Church, 1956; Teacher of Organ and Piano, Voice and CromaHarp; Assistant Organist, Pianist and Soloist, Bible Church, Arnold, Missouri, 1969; Temple Baptist Church, Kirkwood, Missouri; Organist, Pianist, Soloist, Bible Teacher, Youth Orchestra Director, Music Arranger; Faculty Member, Bible Baptist Christian School, 1976-77; Organist, Vocal Soloist, Floral Arranger, Bible Teacher, Faith Missionary Baptist Church, St. Charles, Missouri, 1978 to present. Organizational Memberships: National Guild of Piano Teacher Auditions; St. Louis Chapter, National Guild of Organists. Compositions: "I Will Sing Hallelujah," "I Am Alpha and Omega," "Prelude to Prayer," "My Shephard," "O Sing Unto the Lord a New Song," "O Come Let Us Sing Unto the Lord," "The Lord in My Light and My Salvation"; Number of Hymn Arrangements for Organ and Piano. Honors and Awards: Descendant of the Sixteenth Century Christian Leader John Knox and Dr. John Witherspoon (only minister to sign the Declaration of Independence); Life Fellow, International Biographical Association; International Platform Association; Life Fellow, American Biographical Institute; Listed in *International Who's Who in Music and Musicians Directory, International Register of Profiles, Dictionary of International Biography, Who's Who of American Women, Personalities of the West and Midwest, World Who's Who of Women, International Who's Who of Intellectuals, Community Leaders and Noteworthy Americans, Men and Women of Distinction, American Patriots of the 1980s, Personalities of America, Book of Honor, The Directory of Distinguished Americans, Who's Who in the Midwest, Notable Americans, Contemporary Americans, Contemporary Personalities.* Address: #4 Ranchero Drive, Edgewood Acres, St. Charles, Missouri 63301.■

KENNETH PENN DAVIS

Management Analyst. Personal: Born August 5, 1942, in Charleston, South Carolina; Son of William Alexander and Alice Cummings Mears Davis; Married Diane Cecilia Leonard; Father of Carol Lee. Education: B.A., Oglethorpe University, 1964; M.A., Georgia State University, 1968; Ph.D., University of Virginia, 1975. Military: United States Army Officer Candidate School, Fort Benning, Commissioned 1969, Ranked 1st Lieutenant 1970; United States Army Southeastern Signal

TWO THOUSAND NOTABLE AMERICANS

Corps School, Office of the Commandant, 1969-70; 12th Signal Group, Assistant S-4 and Headquarter Detachment Commander, Danang, Vietnam; Signal Officer Basic Course, Signal Officer Advanced Course; Command and General Staff College; Ranked Captain, 1974; Ranked Major, 1981; Assigned to Alexandria, Virginia Office of Emergency Preparedness (present). Career: District Counselor, Circulation Department, *Atlanta Journal* Newspaper, 1964-65; Management Trainee, All-State Insurance Company, Atlanta, 1965-66; Program Analyst, National Archives, Washington D.C., 1974-78; Part-time Instructor, American History, Northern Virginia Community College (Alexandria), 1978; Management Analyst, General Services Administraiotn, Washington D.C., 1978 to present. Organizational Memberships: Girl Scouts of America Region Three Credit Union, Board of Directors 1979 to present; American Humanics Foundation for Youth Leadership, Kansas City, Missouri; Combined Federal Campaign, National Archives, Chairman 1978; Boy Scouts of America, Active Member 1955 to present, District Commissioner 1979-80, National Order of the Arrow Committee 1974 to present, Member-at-Large of National Council 1974 to present, Member of National Events Committee 1974 to present, Chairman Southeastern Region Order of the Arrow Committee 1974-82, National Camp School Director 1974-78, Director of Wood Badge Leadership Course 1973 to present, Camp Inspector, Associate Advisor, Assistant Scoutmaster, Training Chairman, Advisor for Training, National Order of the Arrow Conferences 1975, 1977, 1979, Staff Member of Philmont Scout Ranch (6 Years), Staff Member 1967 World Jamboree and 1973 National Jamboree; American Historical Association; Organization of American Historians; Society of Historians of American Foreign Relations; American Society of Public Administration; Phi Alpha Theta; Blue Key; Omicron Delta Kappa. Religion: Methodist. Published Works: Articles on the Cherokee Indians; Contributed Chapter to *The Cherokee Indian Nation*. Honors and Awards: National Defense Service Medal; Vietnam Service and Campaign Medals; Bronze Star with Oak Leaf Cluster; Army Reserve Components Achievement Medal; Presidential Sports Award for Jogging 200 Miles, 1981; Boy Scouts of America, Eagle Scout Award, God and Country Award, Silver Beaver, Silver Antelope, Order of the Arrow, National Distinguished Service Award, Award of Merit, Vigil of Honor of the Order of the Arrow; Lowry Scholar, 1960-64; Colonial Dames Georgia Graduate Scholar, 1967; Governor's Fellow, Virginia, 1973-74. Address: 6320 Phyllis Lane, Alexandria, Virginia 22312.■

MARYLEE DAVIS

University Administrator. Personal: Born September 17; Daughter of Mr. and Mrs. Harold Davis. Education: Attended Furman University 1961-62, Tennessee State University 1962-64; B.S. magna cum laude 1965, M.S. 1970, University of Tennessee; Ph.D. Administration and Higher Education, Michigan State University, 1974. Career: Teacher, Kingsport (Tennessee) City Schools, 1965-69; Assistant Head Resident, University of Tennessee, 1969-70; Staff Assistant, United States Congress, Summer 1971; Graduate Assistant, Judicial Programs Office, Michigan State University, 1970-71; Head Advisor, Rather Hall, Michigan State University, 1971-72; Associate Director, Owen Graduate Center, Michigan State University, 1972-74; Special Assistant to Executive Vice President 1974-78, Assistant Vice President 1978 to present, Assistant Professor of Administration and Higher Education 1974, Associate Professor 1979, Michigan State University. Organizational Memberships: Greater Lansing Chamber of Commerce, Board of Directors 1983; University Representative to East Lansing/Meridian Chamber of Commerce; Chairperson, Task Force to Explore Feasibility of External Degree Program for Michigan State Department of Education, 1975-77; American Association for Higher Education; National Association of Women Deans, Administrators and Counselors, Committee on Research and Current Issues 1974, Program Committee 1977; American Association for Higher Education; Phi Delta Kappa. Community Activities: President, Michigan Capitol Girl Scouts Council, 1982 to present; Charter Member, Michigan Statewide Extension Council; United Way, Agency Relations Committee 1982 to present; Zonta Club of East Lansing Area, Past President; Advisory Board, Salvation Army, 1982 to present; Young Women's Christian Association Diana Awards, Co-Chairman Awards Committee 1982; Vice-Chairman, Capital Area United Way, 1982. Honors and Awards: Service Award, Michigan State University Cooperative Extension Service, 1977; Certificate of Merit, Young Women's Christian Association Diana Dinner, 1977; Michigan State Universty Faculty Women's Association Award for Excellence, 1980; Business Woman of the Year, Lansing Regional Chamber of Commerce, 1982; Recipient of the First "Athena Award". Address: 6223 Cobblers Drive, East Lansing, Michigan 48823.■

SAMUEL ADAMS DAVIS

Retired. Personal: Born June 7, 1917; Son of Samuel P. and Eleanor Davis (both deceased); Married Mary Lona Forgy; Father of Lona Davis Spencer, Mary Dee Davis (deceased). Education: B.S., University of Florida, 1950. Military: Served in the United States Navy, Seaplane Pilot 1942-47, Korean Conflict 1952-55, Lieutenant Commander Retired. Career: Hillsborough County Forester, Florida State Division of Forestry, Department of Agriculture, 1969-79; Area Forester, St. Regis Paper Company, 1955-58; Air Controller, Federal Aviation Agency, 1958-59; Pole Inspector, Koppers Company, 1950-52. Organizational Memberships: International Society of Arboriculture, President Southern Chapter 1977; Florida Section of Society of American Foresters, Chairman Caribbean Chapter; Florida Farm Bureau; Florida Forestry Association; American Forestry Association; American Wildlife Federation; Audubon Society; State Cattlemen's Association. Community Activities: Rotary International; Tampa City Tree and Landscape Board, 1980-83; Florida Board of Registration for Foresters, 1978-79; Hillsborough County Children's Services Volunteer League, Board of Directors 1981-83; Military Order of World Wars, Staff of Florida Department; Naval Reserve Association; Reserve Officers Association; United States Congressional Advisory Board; National Geographic Society; United States Naval Institute; Smithsonian Institution; National Association of Retarded Citizens. Religion: Southern Baptist, Deacon, Sunday School Teacher. Honors and Awards: Navy Cross and Air Medal; Pacific Area with Two Battle Stars, 1945; Special Commendation, Hillsborough County Commissioners. Address: 2138 West Minnehaha Avenue, Tampa, Florida 38604.■

PHILIP SHERIDAN DAVY

Engineering Company Executive. Personal: Born July 12, 1915; Son of Frank J. and Mathilda Femrite Davy; Married Caecilia M. Thiemann; Father of Katherine A. Bathurst, Patricia M. Sciborski, Michael F., Barbara J. Salassa, Thomas H., Margaret T. Claeys. Education: Attended University of Wisconsin-La Crosse, University of Wisconsin-Madison; B.S. Civil Engineering with high honors, 1937; M.S. Environmental Engineering, 1938; Research Fellowship, 1937-38. Military: Served in the United States Army, 1941-46, rising through the ranks from First Lieutenant to Lieutenant Colonel; Served in the United States Army Reserves, 1946-75, retiring with the rank of Lieutenant Colonel. Career: Engineer, Frank J. Davy and Son Consulting Engineers, 1938-41; Sales Engineer, Permutit Company, 1946-47; Vice President, Davy Engineering Company, 1947-55; President, Davy Engineering Company, Consulting Engineers, 1956 to present. Organizational Memberships: Governors Commission on Wisconsin Water Resources, 1965-66; Regional Advisory Board to Wisconsin Department of Resource Development, 1966-68 (Chairman 1968); Registered Professional Engineer, Wisconsin, Minnesota, Iowa, Michigan, Indiana, Illinois; American Waterworks Association, Trustee and Chairman Wisconsin Section 1957-60; Wisconsin Society of Professional Engineers, Director/Vice President 1962-67, President 1974-75; National Society of Professional Engineers, Board of Directors 1967-70; American Society of Civil Engineers, Fellow 1971; Water Pollution Control Federation; Diplomate, American Academy of Environmental Engineers; American Public Works Association; American Association for the Advancement of Science. Community Activities: United Way of La Crosse, Director 1962-65, President 1965, Campaign Chairman 1961; Boys Scouts of America Gateway Area Council, Executive Board 1953, Vice President 1967-70, President 1971-73; Vice President of Area One, Boy Scouts of America, 1978-81; Board of Directors, Boy Scouts of America, East Central Region, 1978-81; Greater La Crosse Chamber of Commerce, Director 1959-62, Executive Board 1964-67, President 1968; La Crosse County Historical Society, Board of Directors 1980-81, President 1982-83; President, River Center, U.S.A. (La Crosse), 1981-83; Chairman, Joint Hospital Fund Drive, St. Francis and Lutheran Hospitals, La Crosse, 1977. Religion: Finance and Administration Commission 1970 to present, Chairman 1974-77, Diocese of La Crosse; Advisory Board 1962-72, President 1966-72, Lector 1976 to present, St. Joseph Cathedral. Honors and Awards: Army Commendation Award with Clusters; Eagle Scout 1931, St. George Award, Distinguished Eagle Scout, Silver Beaver, Silver Antelope, Boy Scouts of America; Papel Night of Holy Sepulcher, 1976; Knight Commander, 1980; Engineer of the Year in Private Practice 1965, Engineer of the Year 1975, Wisconsin Society of Professional Engineers; Distinguished Service Award, Wisconsin Section, American Society of Civil Engineers; Man of the Year, Greater La Crosse Chamber of Commerce, 1973; Distinguished Service Award, La Crosse Jaycees, 1982; Tau Beta Pi; Phi Kappa Phi; Chi Epsilon; Scabbard and Blade. Address: 1230 King Street, La Crosse, Wisconsin 54601.■

ROBERT EDWARD DAWSON

Ophthalmologist, Clinical Professor. Personal: Born February 23, 1918, in Rocky Mount, North Carolina; Married Julia Davis; Father of Diane Elizabeth, Janice Elaine, Robert Edward, Melanie Lorraine. Military: Served in the United States Air Force, 1955-57, attaining the rank of Major. Career: Attending Staff, Ophthalmology, Durham County General Hospital, 1976 to present, Vice President of Staff, Vice President of Medical Council 1976-78, Board of Trustees 1978 to present; Assistant Clinical Professor of Ophthalmology, Duke University Medical Center, Durham, North Carolina, 1977 to present; Clinical Associate in

TWO THOUSAND NOTABLE AMERICANS

Ophthalmology 1971-77, Duke University Hospital, Clinical Instructor in Ophthalmology 1968-70; Medical Director, Lincoln Hospital, Durham, North Carolina, 1968-70; Consultant, Division of Disability Determiniation, North Carolina Department of Human Resources, 1971 to present; Attending Staff, Ophthalmology, Watts Hospital, 1966-76; Chief, Ophthalmology and Otolaryngology, Lincoln Hospital, 1958-76; Postgraduate Training, New York Eye and Ear Infirmary, 1963; New York University Institute of Ophthalmology, 1962; Chief, Ophthalmology and Otolaryngology, 3310th Hospital, Scott Air Force Base, Illinois, 1955-57; Pathology (Ophthalmic) Armed Forces Institute of Pathology, 1956; North Carolina Central University Health Service Consultant, Ophthalmology, 1950-64; Attending Staff, Ophthalmology, Lincoln Hospital, 1946-55. Organizational Memberships: American College of Surgeons, Fellow; American Board of Ophthalmology, Diplomate 1963, Examiner 1979-82; Academy of Ophthalmology and Otolaryngology, Fellow; American Association of Ophthalmology; Pan American Medical Association, Diplomate; National Medical Association; Chi Delta Mu Scientific Fraternity; Society of Eye Surgeons; International Glaucoma Congress; American Medical Association, Board of Associates, Greensboro College 1983-; Meharry Medical College, Board of Trustees 1971 to present, Executive Committee, Chairman Hospital and Health Affairs Committee, Chairman Presidential Search Committee; National Medical Association, Board of Trustees 1970 to present, Chairman Consitituion Committee, Chairman Council on Financial Aid to Students, Chairman Insurance Committee, Council of Scientific Assembly, Budget Committee, Council on Awards, Publication Committee, Management Committee, Executive Committee, Chairman Student National Medical Association Liaison Committee, President 1979-80; North Carolina Central University, Durham, North Carolina, Board of Trustees, Executive Committee, Chairman Faculty-Trustee Relations Committee, Chairman Buildings and Grounds Committee, Nominating Committee; National Society to Prevent Blindness, North Carolina Chapter, Board of Directors 1967 to present; Foundation for Better Health, Durham County General Hospital, Board of Directors 1975-79; National Society to Prevent Blindness, Board of Directors 1976 to present, Vice President 1981 to present; Clark College, Atlanta, Georgia, Board of Visitors 1973 to present; Mutual Savings and Loan Association, Board of Trustees 1975 to present. Community Activities: Durham United Fund, Board of Directors 1975 to present; Lincoln Community Health Center, Board of Directors; Durham Academy, Board of Trustees 1969-72; American Cancer Society, Board of Directors; North Carolina State Commission for the Blind, Advisory Board; Eye Bank Association of America, Inc., Regional Surgical Director; Governor's Advisory Committee on Medical Assistance, 1978 to present; Toastmasters International, Past President Durham Chapter; Meharry National Alumni Association, President 1968-69, 1969-70, Board of Management; Durham County Tuberculosis Association, Board of Directors 1950-54; Chamber of Commerce, Operation Committee 1975; Old North State Medical Society, Past President; Alpha Phi Alpha, Past President,; Sigma Pi Phi, Treasurer, Past President; 32nd Degree Mason and Shriner; Durham Community House, Board of Directors 1966-68; Durham Council on Human Relations; National Association for the Advancement of Colored People, Life Member; Durham Business and Professional Chain; President's Committee on Employment of the Handicapped in America; Durham County Mental Health, Board of Directors 1969-80; Association of Governing Boards Commission on Boards of Trustees of Single Campus State Supported Institutions, Their Scopee and Future. Religion: St. Joseph's A.M.E. Church, Board of Stewards 1966 to present. Published Works: "Federal Impact on Medical Care" June 1980,"Bedside Manner of a Computer" March 1980, "Crisis in the Medical Arena: A Challenge for the Black Physician" December 1979, *Journal of the National Medical Association.* Honors and Awards: Distinguished Service Award, National Medical Association; Alpha Omega Alpha Honor Medical Society; Physician of the Year Award, Old North State Medical Society, 1969; Toastmaster of the Year, Durham-1206; Alpha Delta Alpha Honor Scientific Society; High School Valedictorian, Class of 1935; Listed in *Who's Who in Black America, Dictionary of Medical Specialists, International Who's Who in Community Service, International Who's Who of Intellectuals, Who's Who in the South and Southwest, Personalities of the South, North Carolina Lives.* Address: 817 Lawson Street, Durham, North Carolina 27701.∎

STEVEN PATRICK DAWSON

Educational Administrator. Personal: Born November 30, 1953; Son of Wilbert Elwood and Dorothea Mae Stevens Dawson (both deceased); Married Sandra Marie Petty, Daughter of Lewis L. and Jane Holden Petty; Father of Aaron Matthew Stevens. Education: B.A., Randolph-Macon College, 1975; Attended George Mason University 1977-78, New Life Bible Institute 1978-83, Washington College Graduate School 1984 to present. Career: Principal, New Covenant Christian Academy; Ordained to Ministry, 1979; Former Restaurant General Manager. Organizational Memberships: Maryland Association of Christian Schools; Maryland Federation of Church Schools. Community Activities: Sigma Phi Epsilon; Alumni Admissions Committee, Randolph-Macon College; Activities in Local Political Campaigns and Issues; Freshman Orientation Committee, Randolph-Macon College, 1974-75; Conduct Council, Randolph-Macon College, 1974-75. Religion: Ordained Elder, New Covenant Church, 1979 to present; Mid-Eastern Leadership Conference, 1984. Honors and Awards: Omicron Delta Kappa; U.G. Dubach Award for Scholastic Improvement, Sigma Phi Epsilon, 1974; Listed in *Personalities of the South.* Address: Route 1 Box 478, Chester, Maryland 21619.∎

BENNETT WAYNE DEAN, SR.

Employment Counselor. Personal: Born December 11, 1942; Son of Bennett and Dorothy Lucile Dean; Married Doris Jean Allinson on April 13, 1968; Father of Lillian Doris, Timpy Anna, Bennett Wayne Jr. Education: Diploma, Murphy High School, Mobile, 1961; B.S. Biology 1965, B.S. Psychology 1966, University of Alabama; Graduate Studies at the University of Arkansas and Mississippi State University. Military: Served in the United States Army, 1967-69, Specialist 4, Biologist Scientist Assistant at United States Army Natick Laboratories, Natick, Massachusetts. Career: Employment Counselor; Author, "A Mobile Mardi Gras Handbook" 1967, "Mardi Gras: Mobile's Illogical whoop-de-doo" 1971; Actor, Extra, *Close Encounters of the Third Kind* (Columbia Pictures) 1977, *Back Roads* (CBS/Warner Brothers) 1981; Director, *Mardi Gras: Mobile's Big Blast,* United States Navy, 1981; Appeared on "Today" Show, NBC, Mobile's Mardis Gras, 1982. Organizational Memberships: International Association of Personnel in Employment Security, President Alabama Chapter 1974-75, District VIII (Alabama-Mississippi-Tennessee) Representative 1978-79; President, Past Presidents Club, 1981-82; Associate Editor, *Guardian,* Alabama Chapter Association of Personnel in Employment Security, 1979-81; Advertising Federation of Greater Mobile, 1972-80; Mobile Press Club, 1975 to present. Community Activities: President, Gulf Coast Childbirth Education Association, 1973-74; Treasurer, Mobile Area Community Action Committee, 1972-73; President, Mobile Public Relations Practitioners, 1973-74; Vice President, Mobile Jaycees, 1973-74, Board of Directors 1974-76; President, Alabama-Gulf Railroad Club, 1975; President, Mobile Mardi Gras Doubloon Collector's Club, Inc., 1977-78; Vice Chairman, City of Mobile's Mardi Gras Special Events Committee, 1978 to present; Vice President, Society for the Restoration and Beautification of the Church Street Graveyard, Inc. (The Joe Cain Society), 1977 to present; Officer, Abba Temple Shrine Bowl Football Classic, 1978-80; Board of Directors, Toy Bowl Classic, 1976-78; Member of Two of Mobile's Mardi Gras Mystic Parading Societies, 1966 to present and 1969 to present; Mobile Scottish Rite Bodies 1970 to present, Mobile Lodge of Perfection, Mobile Chapter of Rose Croix, Mobile Council of Kadosh, Mobile Consistory; Abba Temple Shrine, 1972 to present; Mobile Sister Cities Federation, Charter Member 1974 to present; Historic Mobile Preservation Society, 1974 to present; Historic Mobile Preservation Society, 1974 to present; National Trust for Historic Preservation, 1976 to present; Victorian Society in America, 1976 to present; Alabama Trust for Historic Preservation, 1979 to present; Live-in-a-Landmark Council, Alabama Historical Commission, 1980 to present; State Director, Mobile Jaycees, 1974-75; Publicity and Brochure Chairman, Scottish Rite Temple Golden Anniversary Reunion, 1972; Chairman, Parade Planning Committee, Mystic Society B, 1972-73; Permanent Chairman of Publicity, Mobile Scottish Rite Bodies, Appointed 1972, Re-Appointed 1976; Public Relations Advisor, Mobile Area Youth Planning Committee, 1972-75; General Publicity Chairman, Greater Gulf State Fair, Mobile Jaycees, 1974; Christmas Parade Committee, Downtown Mobile Unlimited, 1979 to present; Fourth of July Celebration Committee, City of Mobile, 1980 to present; Parade Marshall, Order of Polka Dots, 1982 to present. Religion: Member Government Street United Methodist Church in Mobile, Administrative Board Member 1982, Member of Council on Ministries 1981-82, Chairman Ecumenical and Interreligious Concerns and Religion and Race Committee 1982, Parish Development Committee 1979; Former Member, Broad Street Methodist Church and Fulton Road Methodist Church. Honors and Awards: Distinguished Service Citation, Mobile Jaycees for Outstanding Service as General Publicity Chairman for 1974 Greater Gulf State Fair; Governor's Staff, Appointed Honorary Lieutenant Colonel Aide-de-Camp in Alabama Militia by Alabama Governor George C. Wallace, 1976; Certificate of Distinguished Service, Abba Temple Shrine Bowl, 1976; "Doubloonability Award," Mobile Mardi Gras Doubloon Collector's Club; Certificate of Appreciation, Alabama Chapter I.A.P.E.S., Past Presidents Club, 1977; Certificate of Distinguished Service, Abba Temple Shrine Bowl, 1977; Award of Merit, International Association of Personnel in Employment Security, Portland, Oregon, 1973; Outstanding Jaycee Officer, 1973-74; "M. O. Beale Scroll of Merit," Mobile Press Register, 1975; Elected to Knight Commander Court of Honour, Supreme Council of Scottish Rite, 1975; International Group Award of Merit, I.A.P.E.S., "Cinema Talent Recruiting Service," Toronto, Canada, 1981; "Patriot Award," City of Mobile, 1981; Listed in *Personalities of the South, Two Thousand Notable Americans.* Address: 1064 Palmetto Street, Oakleigh Garden District, Mobile, Alabama 36604.∎

DIANA RAMIREZ DE ARELLANO

Poet, Educator. Personal: Born June 3, 1919, in New York, New York; Daughter of Enrique and Marie Teresa (Rechani) Ramirez de Arellano. Education: B.A., University of Puerto Rico, 1941; M.A., Columbia University, 1946; Ph.D., Universidad Central de Madrid, 1952. Career: Faculty Member, University of North Carolina 1946-48, Douglass College, Rutgers University (New Jersey) 1948-58; Faculty Member 1958 to present, Professor Spanish Poetry Graduate Program 1967 to present, City College, City University of New York; Consultant, Ford Foundation, Canadian Council; Conductor of Poetry Recitals; Lecturer at Rutgers University, Boston University, University of Connecticut, New York City School System, University of Madrid, Others. Organizational Memberships: Modern

Language Association; American Association of Teachers of Spanish and Portuguese; American Association of University Professors; Royal Academy Doctors of Madrid, United States Representative; Ateneo Puertorriqueño de Nueva York, Founder, Honorary President; Journalist Association of Puerto Rico; Writers Association of Puerto Rico; P.E.N.; Hispanic Society of America, Correspondent. Community Activities: Yacht Club, Benidorm; Alicante, Spain; Golf Club, Crab Meadows, Northport, Long Island. Published Works: Author (poetry) *Albatros Sobre el Alma* 1955, *Angeles de Ceniza* 1958, *Un Vuelo Casi Humano* 1960, *Privilegio* 1965, *Del Señalado Oficio de la Muerte* 1974, *Arbol en Vispera* 1976; (criticism) *Poesia Contemporanea en Lengua Española* 1961, *Caminos de la Creción* Poètica en Pedro Salinas 1961, *Lope de Vega: Ed. Critica de Los Ramirez de Arellano* 1954, *Memorias del Teneo* 1963, 1964, 1965, 1966. Honors and Awards: Gold Medal, Diploma Ecuador, 197; Medal of Honor, Ateneo of New York, 1973; Diploma of Honor, Institute of Puerto Rico in New York City, 1970; First Prize in Literature, Institute of Literature Puerto Rico, 1958; Prize in Literary Criticism, University of Puerto Rico, 1961. Address: P.O. Box 376, Centerport, New York 11721.■

LOIS DEBAKEY

Writer, Lecturer, Editor, Educator, Literacy Scholar. Personal: Born in Louisiana. Education: B.A. Mathematics, Newcomb College, Tulane University, 1949; M.A. 1959, Ph.D. 1963, Literature and Linguistics, Tulane University. Career: Professor, Scientific Communication, Baylor College of Medicine; Tulane University School of Medicine, Scientific Communication, Assistant Professor 1963-65, Associate Professor 1965, Professor 1968, Adjunct Professor 1981 to present, Lecturer 1968 to present; Faculty, English Department, Tulane University; Director, Numerous Workshops and Courses. Organizational Memberships: Director, Plain Talk, Inc., 1979-80; Member, Special Committee on Writing, Council for Basic Education; Council of Biology Editors, Director 1973-77, Committee on Graduate Training in Scientific Writing, Chairman Committee on Editorial Policy 1971-75; National Council of Teachers of English, Member Committee on Technical and Scientific Writing, Conference on College Composition and Communication; American Medical Writers Association, Member Awards, Publications, Style and Standards Committee, Chairman Education Committee; Consultant, National Association of Standard Medical Vocabulary; Association of Teachers of Technical Writing; Committee of a Thousand for Better Health Regulations; Dictionary Society of North America; Institute of Society, Ethics and Life Sciences; International Society for General Semantics; National Association of Science Writers; National Institutes of Health Alumni Association; Society for the Advancement of Good English; Society for Health and Human Values; Society for Technical Communication, Member Board of Directors, Houston Chapter; National Advisory Council of the University of Southern California Development and Demonstration Center in Continuing Education for Health Professionals. Community Activities: Usage Panel, *The American Heritage Dictionary*, 1980 to present; National Library of Medicine, Member Biomedical Library Review Committee 1973-77, Member Board of Regents 1983 to present; Consultant, Legal Writing Committee, American Bar Association; Southern Association of Colleges and Schools, Member 1975-80, Executive Council, Commission on Colleges, Chairman Special Committee to Review Accreditation of Ph.D. Level Non-traditional and Extended Educational Programs; Panel of Judges Writing Awards, American Academy of Family Physicians; Editorial Boards, *International Journal of Cardiology* 1981 to present, *Health Communications and Biopsychosocial Health* 1981-82, *Grants Magazine* 1978-81, *Cardiovascular Research Center Bulletin* 1981-83, *Forum on Medicine* 1977-80, *Health Communications and Informatics* 1976-80, *Tulane University Studies in English* 1966-68, *Excerpta Medica's Core Journals in Cardiology* 1981 to present. Published Works: Author of *The Scientific Journal: Editioral Policies and Practices;* Editor of Thousands of Medical and Scientific Articles, Chapters and Books; Author of Articles on Biomedical Communication, Scientific Writing; Critical Reasoning, Public Speaking, Audiovisual Communication, Editing, Publishing; Ethical, Philosophic, Social and Political Aspects of Science; Medical Journalism, Fictional Treatment of Physicians and Scientists, Literacy and Its Relation to the State of Society. Honors and Awards: John P. McGovern Award, Medical Library Association, 1983; Distinguished Service Award, American Medical Writers Association, 1970; Bausch and Lomb Science Award for Outstanding Academic Performance; Phi Beta Kappa; Golden Key National Honor Society, 1982; Has Been Subject of Articles in *U.S. News and World Report*, *Time* Magazine, *The Journal of the American Medical Assn, Bulletin of the American College of Surgeons, Medical World News, Medical Tribune, Saturday Review, People, Los Angeles Times*, Publications of the United States Information Agency, and Numerous Other Lay and Medical Newspapers, Magazines and Periodicals; Listed in *Who's Who in America, Dictionary of International Biography, American Men and Women of Science, American Registry Series, Book of Honor, Creative and Successful Personalities of the World, International Who's Who in Community Service, International Who's Who in Education, Directory of Distinguished Americans, Foremost Women of the Twentieth Century, Notable Women of Texas, Men and Women of Distinction, Men of Achievement, Notable Americans, Notable Americans of the Bicentennial Era, Personalities of America, Personalities of the South, Personalities of the West and Midwest, Who Houston, Who's Who in American Education, Who's Who in Health Care, Who's Who in Library and Information Service, Who's Who in the South and Southwest, Who's Who in the World, Who's Who of American Women, World Who's Who of Women, World Who's Who of Women in Education, Community Leaders and Noteworthy Americans, International Book of Honor, Who's Who in Education*. Address: Baylor College of Medicine, One Baylor Plaza, 1200 Moursund Avenue, Houston, Texas 77030.■

MICHAEL E. DEBAKEY

Surgeon, Professor. Personal: Born September 7, 1908; Married Katrin Fehlhaber; Father of Four Sons, One Daughter. Education: B.S. 1930, M.D. 1932, M.S. 1935, Tulane University, New Orleans, Louisiana. Military: Colonel, United States Army Reserve; Chief of General Surgery, Branch of Surgical Consultants Division; Officer of Surgeon General. Career: Surgeon, Chancellor, Professor, Baylor College of Medicine. Oraganizational Memberships: (Advisory Appointments) American College of Surgeons, National Institutes of Health, American Institute of Stress, China-American Relations Society, Committee of A Thousand for Better Health Regulations, The Draper World Population Fund, Thomas Alva Edison Foundation, Father of the Year, Foundation for Biomedical Research, The Hospital for Sick Children, Institute for Advanced Research in Asian Science and Medicine, International Medical Complex of Iran, the Living Bank International, Muscular Dystrophy Association of American, Inc., National Council of Drug Abuse, National Academy of Sciences, Office of Technology Assessment, Pennsylvania Regional Tissue and Transplant Bank, Inc., Recontres Culturelles Internationales, Religious Heritage of America, Inc., St. Jude Children's Research Hospital, Task for Mechanical Circulatory Assistance, Texas Education Agency, Transylvania University, Tulane University Delta Regional Primate Research Center, United States Government Promotion of Conquest of Cancer, Stroke and Heart Disease, University of Aviation Foundation, Inc., White House Conference on Aging, Academy of Medical Sciences, U.S.S.R., Academy of Medicine of Sao Paulo, Brazil, American Association for the Advancement of Science, American Association for Thoracic Surgery, American Heart Association, American Medical Association, American Trauma Society, Asociacion Mexicana de Cirugia Cardiovascular A.C., Association for the Advancement of Medical Instrumentation, Bio-Medical Engineering Society, British Medical Association, Cuban Medical Association in Exile, Michael E. DeBakey International Cardiovascular Society, International Cardio-Pulmonary Academy, International Committee Against Mental Illness, International Platform Association, Israel Surgical Society, Peripheral Vascular Society of Great Britain and Ireland, Philosophical Society of Texas, Royal Society of Medicine, Sociedad Cirujana de Chile, Society for Biomaterials, Society for Cryobiology, Society for Experimental Biology and Medicine, Society of Medical Consultants to the Armed Forces, Southern Association for Vascular Surgery, Southern Society for Clinical Investigation, Surgical Society of Langobard, Milan, Italy, Udruzenje Kirurga Jugoslavije, Western Surgical Association, Wold Medical Association, Inc. Honors and Awards: (Honorary Degrees) Doctor of Science, Albany Medical College, Florida State University, Fort Lauderdale University, Hahnemann Medical College and Hospital of Philadelphia, MacMurray College, Medical College of Ohio at Toledo, Roger Williams College, St. John's University, University of Michigan; Doctor of Science, Honoris Causa, Assumption College, D'Youville College, Long Island University, Loyola University of the South; Doctor of Medicine, Aristotelian University of Thessaloniki; Doctor of Medicine, Honoris Causa, University of Ottawa; Faculty of Medicine, University of Chile; Doctor of Humanities, Centenary College; Doctor of Laws, Lafayette College, McNeese State University, Southwestern University, Tulane University, University of Belgrade Medal, University of Cincinnati; Doctor Honoris Causa, Ljublijana University, Yugoslavia, Universite Catholique de Louvain, University of Athens, University of Brussels, University of Ghent, University of Lyon, University of Turin; Fellowship, Institute of Medicine of Chicago; Numerous Awards, including Marian Health Care Award, St. Mary's University 1981, Gran Collare d'Oro, Accademia Internazionale di Pontzen di Lettere, Scienze ed Arti 1969, First Annual American Bicentennial Award in Medicine 1972, Certificate of Appreciation for Scientific Exhibit, American College of Surgeons 1970, Hektoen Gold Medal Award, American Medical Association 1954, 1970, Distinguished Service Award, American Surgical Association 1981, Baylor College of Medicine, Alumni Distinguished Faculty Award 1973, Faculty/Staff Recognition Award 1977, Olga Keith Wiess Chair of Surgery 1981, Michael E. DeBakey Day 1976, Michael E. DeBakey Professorship in Pharmacology 1977, DeBakey Scholar Program 1972, Britannica Achievement in Life Award for 1980, "Al Merito della Repubblica Italiana," Commendatore nell'Ordene 1972, Presidential Citation for Humanitarian Services, Government of Ecuador 1970, Harris County Hospital District 30-Year Service Award 1978, Hellenic Red Cross, Gold Cross with Laurel 1972, Supreme Red Cross 1977, Independence of Jordan Medal, First Class 1980, International Prize "LaMadonnina" 1974, Lions International Special Award 1973, Merit Order of the Republic, Egypt 1980, Panhellenic Medical Association Gold Cross Award 1972, Rotary Club Distinguished Citizens Award 1972, Secretary of Defense Meritorious Civilian Service Medal 1970, Texas Scientist of the Year, Texas Academy of Science 1979, Tulane Distinguished Alumnus of the Year 1974, U.S.S.R. Academy of Science 50th Anniversary Jubilee Medal 1973, Veterans of Foreign Wars Commander-in-Chief's Medal and Citation, 1980. Address: 5323 Cherokee, Houston, Texas 77005.■

SELMA DeBAKEY

Professor. Education: B.A., Newcomb College, Tulane University, New Orleans; Graduate Studies, Tulane University, New Orleans. Career: Professor, Former Director Department of Medical Communication, Alton Ochsner Medical Foundation, New Orleans, Louisiana. Organizational Memberships: Society of Technical Communication; Member Committee of Judges, Modern Medicine Monographs Award; Co-Editor, *Bulletin of the American Medical Writers Association*; Editor, *Ochsner Clinic Reports*; Editor, *Cardiovascular Research Center Bulletin*. Published Works: Author of Numerous Articles on Scientific Writing; Co-Author of *Current Conceptsin Breast Cancer*. Address: 1200 Moursund Avenue, Houston, Texas 77030.■

ROY JOHN DeBOER

School Principal. Personal: Born July 23, 1936; Son of Harvey Charles and Martha Hoskin DeBoer (both deceased); Father of Nicole M., Eric J., David M. Education: A.A., Olympic College; B.A., Western Washington State University; M.A., University of Puget Sound. Military: Served in the United States Air Force, 1954-58. Career: School Principal; Vice-Principal; Central Office Program Director; High School English Teacher; Longshoreman. Organizational Memberships: Elementary Principal's Organization; Phi Delta Kappa; International Reading Association; Association of Supervision and Curriculum Development. Community Activities: Washington State Native American Advisory Committee on Indian Education, Charter Member 1976, Vice Chairman 1979-83; Religion: Member of First Lutheran Church, Port Orchard, Washington, President; Board Member, American Lutheran Church, Division for Service and Mission in America; Member Scholarship Committee, American Lutheran Church, Division for College and University Services; Chairman, Development Assistance Committee, American Lutheran Church, 1976-79. Honors and Awards: Adult Leadership Award, Quill and Scroll, 1967; Outstanding Secondary Educators of American Award, 1973; Certificate of Recognition for Service to Washington State Indian Youth, State System of Schools, 1983; Listed in *Directory of Distinguished Americans, Who's Who in the West*. Address: 3528 Southeast Pine Tree Drive, Port Orchard, Washington 98366.■

JEAN CAMPBELL DECKER

Treasurer and Consultant. Personal: Born March 10, 1915; Daughter of Dm and Bertha (Campbell) Decker (deceased). Education: B.A. Business Administration, University of Chicago, 1937. Career: Calco Manufacturing Company, Employee 1950, Assistant Treasurer 1967-69, Treasurer 1969-82, Plan Administrator and Director of Pension Plan; Treasurer, Environ, Inc., Haines City, Florida, 1971-72; Gustafson Enterprises, Inc., Treasurer 1971 to present, Director 1971-78, Re-elected 1982 and 1983. Community Activities: Volunteer, Young Men's Christian Association. Religion: Protestant. Honors and Awards: Business Asssociate of the Year 1983, American Business Women's Association; Listed in *Who's Who of American Women, The World Who's Who of Women*. Address: 885 Smith Street, Glen Ellyn, Illinois 60137.■

FRANCIS J. DeGRADO

Adjunct Professor of Psychology. Personal: Born May 26, 1939; Son of Mae DeGrado. Education: B.S. 1965, M.A. 1966, Ed.D. 1969, Arizona State University. Military: Served in the United States Army Air Defense, 1959-62, Honorable Discharge. Career: Professor of Psychology, National College of Education, 1971 to present. Organizational Memberships: American Association of Sex Educators and Therapists, 1975 to present; Illinois Psychological Association, 1975 to present; Adult Education Association of the United States of America 1966, Chairman Adult Psychological Section 1971-74, Vice Chairman 1974-76. Community Activities: Facilitator, Grey Panther Film Series on Aging; Illinois Humanities Council, Rational Psychology for Aging; Human Relations Consultant, Cook County Sheriff's Department; Moderator and Panel Member, Illinois Humanities Council, "Images of Aging." Honors and Awards: Listed in *Who's Who in International Education, Men of Achievement, Who's Who in the Midwest*. Address: 1101 South 4th Avenue, Maywood, Illinois 60153.■

RUTH A. DeJOIA

Court of Common Pleas Section Director. Personal: Born August 16, 1927; Married Joseph F. A.; Mother of John F., Joanne Marie DeJoia Winans. Education: High School Graduate, 1945; Continuing Education, Pennsylvania State University, 1976 to present; One Year of Basic Correctional Training. Career: Position with Various Lawyers, Meadville, Pennsylvania, 1945-56; Clerk Typist, Crawford Company Assessment Office, 1956-59; Secretary to the Chief Adult/Juvenile Probation Officer, 1959-65; Secretary, Holiday Inn of Meadville, 1965-66; Assistant Innkeeper 1966-68; Executive Secretary, Crawford Company Tourist Association, 1970-71; Crawford County Domestic Relations Section, Court of Common Pleas 1971 to present, Administrative Assistant 1976, Assistant Director 1977, Director 1978 to Present. Organizational Memberships: Domestic Relations Association of Pennsylvania, Director 1978-81, Secretary 1980-81. Community Activities: National Recip. and Family Sup. Enf. Association, Eastern Region; Past Officer, Parent Teacher Association, Crawford County Mental Health Association, 1970 to present; Crawford County Community Council, 1978; Child Advisory Council of Pennsylvania, 1979-80; Women's Resource Group, Crawford County Drug and Alcohol Commission, 1980; Council on Welfare Fraud. Honors and Awards: Listed in *Who's Who of American Women, The Directory of Distinguished Americans, Five Thousand Personalities of the World, Personalities of America, World Who's Who of Women*. Address: P.O. Box 248, Meadville, Pennsylvania 16335.■

CAROLYN BARNES MILANES DeJOIE

Professor. Personal: Born April 17; Daughter of Alice Milanes Barnes; Mother of Deirdre Jeanelle, Prudhomme III, Duan Kendall. Education: B.A., Xavier University; M.A., Universidad Nacional Autonoma de Mexico, 1962; M.S.W., University of Wisconsin, 1970; Ph.D., Union Graduate School, 1976. Career: Professor, University of wisconsin Extension; Assistant to the President, University of Wisconsin System; Assistant Professor, Virginia State College, Norfolk; Assistant Professor, Southern University, Baton Rouge, Louisiana. Organizational Memberships: United Faculty; American Association of University Professors; American Association of University Women; National Fraternity of Graduate Women. Community Activities: Board Member, Health Writers, Dane County Mental Health, Madison Area Public Access Television, Madison Equal Opportunity Committee, American Civil Liberties Union (Madison), Human Relations Advisory Council, Madison Schools, Garel House for Girls; Chairperson, Regional Task Force, Wisconsin Division of Vocational Rehabilitation; Consultant to Latin American Association. Honors and Awards: Recognition Award, Virginia State College, 1965; Fulbright Scholarship, United States Government, 1966; Outstanding Woman Award, Zeta Phi Beta Sorority, 1980; Black Woman: Achievement Against the Odds, Wisconsin Humanities Committee, 1983. Address: 5322 Fairway Drive, Madison, Wisconsin 53711.■

RONALD J. De LAIN

Elected Official. Personal: Born October 18, 1930; Son of Harold J. and Verna F. Dulik De Lain; Married Beverly Jean Luedtke; Father of Cheryl, Micki, Vicki, Ron; Military: Served with the United States Army, 1948-52. Career: Machine Operator, Inspection of Production, Northwest Engineering Corporation, Green Bay, Wisconsin, 1952-59; Brown County, Wisconsin, Deputy Sheriff and Traffic Officer (Sheriff-Traffic Department) 1959-70, Sergeant-Chief Jailer 1967-70, Elected as County Clerk 1971, 1973, 1975, 1977, 1979, 1981, 1983. Organizational Memberships: Charter Member, Brown County Deputy Sheriffs Association, 1967 to present; Wisconsin County Clerks Association, Member 1971 to present, Secretary 1983; International Association of Clerks, Recorders, Election Officials and Treasurers, 1975-76; Wisconsin County Boards Association, 1971 to present; National Association County Recorders and Clerks, 1971 to present; National Association of Counties, 1971-81; Wisconsin Local Welfare Association, 1982 to present. Community Activities: American Heart Association of Wisconsin, Chairman Community Service Committee 1976-80, Board of Directors 1974-83, Member Executive Committee 1981-83; Brown County Division of American Heart Association of Wisconsin, County Chairman 1967, County Treasurer 1968-78, County Campaign Chairman 1965-67 and 1976-77, Chairman of Northeast Area, 1975-80. Religion: St. John the Evangelist Catholic Church, Lector 1977 to present, Canter 1979 to present, Choir Director 1978 to present, Trustee 1975-76, Parish

Council 1983-85. Honors and Awards: Cited for Meritorious Service, 1967; Awards, Community Service 1968, Distinguished Service 1979, Certificate of Voluntary Appreciation 1968, 1969, 1972, 1975, 1976; Outstanding Volunteer Award, 1983; Listed in *Who's Who in the Midwest*, *National Book of Honor*, *Community Leaders in America*, *Men of Achievement*, *Dictionary of International Biography*, *American Registry*, *Directory of Distinguished Americans*, *Who's Who in Government*, *Personalities of the West and Midwest*, *International Book of Honor*, *5,000 Personalities of the World*, *Community Leaders of the World*. Address: 817 South Jackson Street, Green Bay, Wisconsin 54301.■

JACQUES MERCIER DELPHIN

Staff Psychiatrist. Personal: Born April 16, 1929; Son of Mr. and Mrs. Alexander Delphin (deceased); Married Marlene M.; Father of Barthold, Patrick, Beverly, Miriam, Matthew, Janice. Education: B.S., Cap Haitien, Haiti, 1949; Doctorate in Medicine, University of Haiti, 1957. Career: Staff Psychiatrist; Commissioner of Mental Hygiene ad Interim, 1973-74; Medical Director, St. Cabrini Home, West Park, New York, 1974-80. Organizational Memberships: President, Dutchess County Branch of American Psychiatric Association, 1973-74. Community Activities: Board Directors, Kiwanis Club, 1970; Medical Assisting Advisory Committee Member, Dutchess Community College, 1975. Religion: Many Catholic Youth Counseling Clubs. Honors and Awards: Fellow, American Psychiatric Association, 1972; Dutchess County Mental Hygiene Award of the Year, 1983; Newsmaker of the Year, Article Appearing in *Poughkeepsie Journal*, 1973. Address: Eight Garfield Place, Poughkeepsie, New York 12601.■

JAMES KLEON DEMETRIUS

College Professor, Author, Book Review Editor. Personal: Born August 23, 1924. Education: Diploma of Higher Studies, University of Iowa, 1943; B.A., Brooklyn College, 1948; M.A., Columbia University, 1949; Ph.D., WU, Arizona, 1982. Military: Served in the United States Air Force, 1942-45. Career: College Professor of Ancient and Modern Languages; Author; Book Review Editor; Former Positions Include College Professor; Specialist in Nutrition; Author and Journalist. Organizational Memberships: Classical Association of England, 1958; Hellenic Society of England, 1958; Medieval Academy of America, 1958; American Classical League, 1958; Modern Humanities Research, 1963; Alpha Sigma Phi, 1962; Classical Association of Spain, 1961; C.E.S.C.M. De L'University of Poitins, 1963. Community Activities: Public Speaking on Grecian Scholarship to Various Campuses in Iowa and Kentucky, Pennsylvania and Others; Visitation to Numerous Schools to Lecture on Aspects of Grecian Culture. Religion: Presbyterian. Honor and Awards: Gold Watch, Students of Bloomfield College, 1968; Gold Plaque, Students of St. Francis College, 1972; Speaker at University of Kentucky on Greek Influence in Spanish Culture, 1958; Barry Chase, Honored Speaker on Plato and His Influence Upon Today, 1967; Honorary Ph.D. WU, Arizona, 1982. Address: 516 Fifth Avenue, New York, New York 10036.■

ELMER L. DENLINGER

Chiropractic Physician. Personal: Born December 16, 1927; Married Myrle Neill; Father of Jacob, Rebecca, Jonathan, Benjamin, David. Education: B.A., Beloit College, 1950; Doctor of Chiropractic, National College of Chiropractic, Chicago, Illinois, 1955-59; Military: Served in the United States Army, Working with CIA and Special Services. Career: Chiropractic Physician. Organizational Memberships: Northwest District Indiana State Chiropractic Association, Secretary/Treasurer 1966-69, District Director 1972-80; Program Chairman, Chiropractic Seminar of Edgar Cayce Foundation, Virginia Beach, Virginia, 1975-76; Secretary, Elkhart County Chiropractic Society, 1979-80; National College of Chiropractic Alumni Association, 1959 to present; Century Club of National College of Chiropractic, 1972 to present; Parker Chiropractic Research, 1961 to present; Laubach's Congress on Research for Chiropractors, 1973 to present; Referral Member, Gonstead Chiropractic Seminars, 1966 to present. Community Activities: Life Member, National Health Federation, 1950 to present; Liberty Lobby, 1970 to present; Boy Scouts of America, 1944 to present; Association for Research and Enlightenment, Virginia Beach, Virginia, 1971 to present; Fraternal Order of Police, 1975 to present; Young Men's Christian Association; Beloit College Alumni Association, 1950 to present; Elkhart Badminton Club, 1946 to present; Elkhart Tennis Club, 1943 to present; Life Member, Culver Academy Summer School Division, Black Horse Troop, 1945 to present. Published Works: Author of Articles "Are We Eating a Diseased Diet", "Blood Chemistry and Nutrition", "Color Therapy", "Do We Need Enzymes Today", all in *ISCA Journal*; Honors and Awards: Eagle Scout Award, 1945; God and Country Scouting Award, 1945; President of Alpha Chapter, National College of Chiropractic, 1958-59; Merit Award, American College of Chiropractic, 1971; Chiropractor of the Year Award, American College of Chiropractic 1971, State of Indiana (ISCA) 1979; Listed in *Who's Who in America*, *Who's Who in the Midwest*, *Who's Who in Chiropractic International*, *International Who's Who in Community Service*, *Men of Achievement*, *Dictionary of International Biography*, *International Register of Profiles*. Address: 25909 Lake Drive, Elkhart, Indiana 46514.■

HAZEL MAY DENNING

Researcher. Personal: Born March 1, 1907; Daughter of William O'Connor (deceased) and Cora May Dale (deceased); Married Burl Warren; Mother of Dora Mae Stormon. Education: A.A., Riverside City College, 1954; B.A. Social Sciences, University of California-Riverside, 1956; M.A. Educational Psychology, Claremont Graduate School, 1962; M.A. Humanistic and Transpersonal Psychology, Redlands University, 1981. Career: Researcher in Life-regression Therapy; Researcher in Parapsychology, 1940 to present; Administrator, Parks Research and Education Project, 1977 to present; Administrative Coordinator, Parapsychology Association of Riverside, 1974-81. Organizational Memberships: Parapsychology Association of Riverside, Founder 1971, President 1971-73, Board Directors 1981-82; Co-Founder and President, Association for Past-life Research and Therapy, 1980-82; A.A.U.W., Member 1962-82, President 1968-70; National League American Pen Women, Member 1972-82, President Riverside Branch 1977-79. Community Activities: Riverside Mental Health Association, Charter Member, Vice-President, First Board of Directors 1952-53; Historian and Business Manager, Riverside Community Players, 1940-50; Radio and TV Interviews on Parapsychology and Regression Therapy, 1965 to present; Lecturer, 1925 to present; Appearances in High School Psychology Classes, 1969 to present; Other Lectures in Colleges, Churches, Clubs; Taught Classes and Directed Workshops in Parapsychology, 1950 to present. Religion: First United Methodist Church; Drama Director, 1933-72; Director, Sacred Dance Choir, 1966-69; Trustee, 1961-64; Church School Superintendent 1964-66; Volunteer Service 1924-71; Youth Director, 1957-61. Honors and Awards: Best Actress, Riverside Community Players, 1942-43 and 1943-44; Honorary Life Member, Women's Society of Christian Service, 1959; Honorary Life Member, Parapsychology Association of Riverside, 1973; Pen Woman of the Year, Riverside Branch, 1976; PAR Outstanding Volunteer of the Year, 1977. Address: 7070 Espana Drive, Riverside, California 92504.■

JUDIANNE DENSEN-GERBER

Psychiatrist, Lawyer. Personal: Born November 13, 1934; Married Michael B. Badon; Mother of Judson Michael, Lindsay Robert, Trissa Austin, Sarah Densen. Education: B.A. cum laude, Bryn Mawr College, 1956; LL.B., Columbia University Law School, 1959; M.D., New York University Medical School, 1963; J.D., Columbia University Law School, 1969; Rotating Internship, French Hospital, 1963-64; Psychiatric Residency, Bellevue and Metropolitan Hospitals, 1964-67. Career: Admitted to New York State Bar, 1961 to present; Admitted to Practice Medicine and Surgery, New York 1967 to present, New Jersey 1971 to present, Utah 1971 to present, Michigan 1973 to present, Connecticut 1973 to present, Louisiana 1974 to present, New Mexico 1975 to present, New South Wales (Australia) 1977 to present, Texas 1978 to present, Pennsylvania 1978 to present; Founder and Executive Director, Odyssey House, Inc, 1967-74; Odyssey Institute of America, Inc., Founder, President, Chief Executive Officer, Chief of Psychiatry, 1974-82; Founder and President, Odyssey Resources Inc 1983 to present; Founder and President, PACT (Protect America's Children Today), 1983 to present; Odysseey Institute International, Founder, President, Chief Executive Officer, Chief of Psychiatry, 1978 to present; Visiting Associate Professor of Law, University of Utah Law School, 1974-75; Adjunct Associate Professor of Law, New York Law School, 1973 to present; Founder and President, Institute of Women's Wrongs, 1973 to present. Organizational Memberships: Delegate, White House Conference on Youth, 1971; National Advisory Commission on Criminal Justice Standards and Goals, Law Enforcement Assistance Administration, 1971-74; Consultant, National Center for Health Research and Development, Department of Health, Education and Welfare, Public Health Services, 1972 to present; Consultant, United States Army, Fort Meade, 1972-73; Drug Experience Advisory Committee, Department of Health, Education and Welfare, 1973-76; New York State Crime Control Planning Board, 1975-79; Governor's Task Force on Crime Control, 1977-79; Society of Medical Jurisprudence, 1967 to present; American Medical Association, 1968 to present; New York State Medical Society, Member 1968 to present, Sub-Committee on Drug Abuse, Subcommittee on Delivery of Health Care, Sub-Committee on Presciption Practices, Sub-Committee on Child Welfare; New York Women's Bar Association, 1969 to present; American Academy of Forensic Sciences, Member 1969-72, Fellow 1972 to present; American Psychiatric Association, 1970 to present; American Academy of Psychiatry and the Law, 1970 to present; American College of Legal Medicine, Fellow 1971 to present, Annual Convocation Committee 1973-74; American Bar Association, 1972 to present; Board of Directors, The National Coalition for Children's Justice, 1975 to present; Board of Directors, Daitch Shopwell, Inc., 1976-82; Board of Directors, American Society for the Prevention of Cruelty to Children, 1979 to present; Board of Directors, Mary E. Walker Foundatin, 1978 to present; New York Council on Alcoholism, President, A.C.C.E.P.T. Board of Directors 1978 to present; Paga House, President, Board of Directors 1978 to present; Harmony School, President, Board of Directors 1979 to present; Board of Advisor, *Contemporary Drug Problems*, 1971 to present; Board of Advisors, Hospital Audiences Inc, 1971 to present; Institute for Child Mental Health, Board of Advisors,

Professional Advisory Committee for the Study of Drug Use Among Children and Adolescents, 1972 to present; Board of Advisors, First Women's Bank of New York, 1974 to present; Board of Advisors, President's Council of School of Social Work, New York University, 1977 to present; Board of Advisors, Beard's Fun for the Arts, 1978 to present; Advisor for Law and Medicine, National Forensic Center, 1980 to present; *Focus on Women*, Editor, Board of Advisors, 1980 to present. Community Activities: Women's City Club of New York, 1956 to present; Women's Forum, 1976 to present. Religion: All Souls Unitarian Church, 1958 to present. Published Works: *Drugs, Sex, Parents and You, We Mainline Dreams, The Odyssey House Story, Walk in My Shoes, An Odyssey into Womanlife, Child Abuse and Neglect as Related to Parental Drug Abuse and Other Anti-Social Behavior*. Honors and Awards: Honorary Doctor of Science Degree, Lebanon Valley College; A.A.U.W., 1970; Myrtle Wreath Award, Hadassah, 1970; Women of Achievement Award, B'nai B'rith Women, 1971; B'nai B'rith Women of Greatness Award, 1971; Honorable Order of Kentucky Colonels, 1973; Honorary New York State Fire Chief Award, 1974; Dame of Malta, Knights of Malta, America, 1974; Outstanding Teacher of the Year, Service to New York City, Our Town Newspaper, 1977; Nobless, Order of the White Cross, Australia, 1977; Dame Commander, Knights of Malta, America, 1980; Listed in *National Social Directory, Outstanding Young Women in America, Who's Who of American Women, Dictionary of International Biography, Community Leaders of America, Who's Who in the East, Who's Who in America*. Address: 817 Fairfield Avenue, Bridgeport, Conneticut 06604.■

THOMAS STEWART DENTON

Petroleum Producer, Numismatist, Writer. Personal: Born October 12, 1945; Son of Stewart B. Denton; Jane Alma Wiggers Denton; Married Janet Lee Scott. Education: Student at University of Mississippi, 1964-68; B.S. History, Murray State University, 1968-69; Post Graduate Studies at Murray State University, 1974-77. Military: Served in the United States Air Force, 1969-73, attaining the rank of Staff Sergeant; Served in the United States Air Force Reserve, 1973-74, attaining the rank of Staff Sergeant. Career: Petroleum Producer; Numismatist; Writer. Organizational Memberships: International Platform Association; Life Patron, American Biographical Institute; Life Member, A.N.A.; American Association for the Advancement of Science. Community Activities: Life Member, Murray State Alumni Association; Public Service Research Council; Murray State University Century Club. Religion: Presbyterian; Senior High School Level Sunday School Teacher. Honors and Awards: American Biographical Institute Research Association; Listed in *Community Leaders of America, Who's Who in South and Southwest, Personalities of the South, International Who's Who of Intellectuals, Men of Achievement, Who's Who in Finance and Industry, Book of Honor, Directory of Distinguished Americans, Personalities of America, International Register of Profiles*. Address: 812 North 20th Street, Murray, Kentucky 42071.■

GARBIS H. DER YEGHIAYAN

College Administrator. Personal: Born March 29, 1949; Son of Hagop and Lydia Der Yeghiayan; Married Angela; Father of Jimmy, Johnny Samuel. Education: B.A. Political Science, M.A. Educational Administration, American University of Beirut; Ph.D. School of Management, University of La Verne. Career: Chief Executive and Dean, American Armenian International College; Former Positions Include High School Principal and Teacher. Organizational Memberships: A.A.U.P.; Armenian Professional Society. Community Activities: La Verne Rotary Club, President 1984-85, Vice-President 1983-84, Director of International Service 1982-83; Armenian General Benevolent Union; Board Member, La Verne Chamber of Commerce; Board Member, St. Gregory Armenian School, Pasadena. Religion: Executive Secretary, Bible Land Mission, 1980-83. Honors and Awards: Principal of the Year, 1972 and 1974; Teacher of the Year, 1968, 1970 and 1973; Listed in *Outstanding Young Men of America, World Community Leaders*. Address: 2018 Craig Way, La Verne, California 91750.■

VEENA BALVANTRAI DESAI

Obstetrician, Gynecologist. Personal: Born October 5, 1931; Daughter of Dr. Balvantrai P. Desai (deceased) and Maniben Ond Gujarat; Married Dr. Vinay D. Gandevia; Mother of Vijay Gandevia. Education: M.B.B.S., 1957; M.D. Obstetrics/Gynecology, 1961; M.R.C.O.G., London, 1966; F.A.C.O.G., U.S.A., 1974; D.A.B.O.G., U.S.A., 1976; F.A.C.S., 1979; F.I.C.S., 1980; Honorary Ph.D., World University, 1981. Career: Obstetrician and Gynecologist; Delegate, American Medical Delegation to China, 1981; Reporter, *Journal of the American Medical Delegation to China*, 1981-82; Dystocia Due to Fetal Suero-coccygeal Teratoma, *Journal of British Commonwealth Obstetrics and Gynecology*, 1968. Organizational Memberships: American Society of Colposcopy and Cervical Pathology, Fellow; New Hampshire Medical Society; American Medical Women's Association; Portsmouth Hospital, Cancer Care Committee 1978 to present, Quality Assurance Committee 1981 to present, Chairperson of Dietary Committee 1978-81; American Biographical Institute, Editorial Advisory Board. Community Activities: Portsmouth Hospital Guild, Patron, 1981; Portsmouth Community Health Services, Patron, 1981; Greater Chamber of Commerce, 1982; Free Health Fairs for Senior Citizens, Volunteer; Prepared Childbirth Classes, Volunteer Lecturer, 1975-79; International Platform Association, 1979-82; World University, Round Table; Donor, Portsmouth Hospital Development Fund, Portsmouth Community Services, Young Women's Christian Organization, Portsmouth Junior High School, Disabled Veterans, Various Police Organizations, Phillips-Exeter Academy, National Republican Committee. Honors and Awards: Honorary Ph.D., World University, 1981; Open Merit Scholar, 1952-57; Medal of Merit, President Ronald Reagan, 1982; Chairman, United States Congressional Advisory Board, 1983; Listed in *Who's Who of American Women, World Who's Who of Women, Directory of Distinguished Americans, International Book of Honor, Personalities of America, International Register of Profiles, International Who's Who of Intellectuals*. Address: 12 Harborview Drive, Rye, New Hampshire 03870.■

AILEEN ADA DESOMOGYI

Retired Librarian. Personal: Born November 26, 1911; Daughter of Harry Alfred and Ada Amelia Taylor (deceased); Widow. Education: B.A., London, 1936; M.A., London, 1938; A.L.A., British Library Association, 1946; M.L.S., U.W.O., 1971; Certificate of Proficiency in Archive Management, 1969; Diploma in Computer Programming, Career Learning Centre, Toronto, 1980. Military: Served with the W.R.A.C., 1955-56, achieving the rank of Corporal. Career: Librarian. Organizational Memberships: American Library Association, 1967 to present; Ontario Genealogical Society, Secretary London Branch 1967-71; East York Historical Society, 1975 to present; English-Speaking Union; International Platform Association; Royal Canadian Geographical Society. Community Activities: N.A.L.G.O., Committee Member Enfield Branch, 1949-52; C.U.P.E., Committee Member East York Branch, 1971-74. Honors and Awards: Listed in *Who's Who in Library and Information Services, Who's Who of American Women, American Catholic Who's Who, Contemporary Personalities, Dictionary of International Biography, World Who's Who of Women, Who's Who in the Commonwealth, International Who's Who in Community Service, International Who's Who of Intellectuals, Community Leaders of America, Directory of Distinguished Americans*. Address: 9 Bonnie Brae Boulevard, Toronto, Ontario, Canada M4J 4N3.■

DAVID H. DETERS

Bilingual Adult Basic Education Instructor and Counselor. Personal: Born July 22, 1947; Son of Mr. and Mrs. Harold Deters; Married Charlene Marie Clay, Daughter of Charlotte Clay. Education: B.A. with honors 1969, M.A. 1975, M.A. Community College Counseling 1977, University of Iowa; M.Div. magna cum laude, Dubuque Theological Seminary, 1973; E.S.L. Certification, University of North Iowa, 1977. Career: Bilingual Adult Basic Education Instructor/Counselor, Muscatine Community College; Former Positions include Indochinese Program Coordinator, Bilingual Career Counselor for Muscatine Community College, Spanish Teacher Assistant for University of Iowa, Bilingual Diagnostic Learning Center Instructor (Chimayo, New Mexico), Community Youth Worker (Truchas, New Mexico), and Teaching Assistant in Greek at Dubuque Theological Seminary. Organizational Memberships: Iowa Association of Lifelong Learning. Community Activities: Labor Council on Latin American Affairs, 1977-79; Vice-Chairman Advisory Committee, Iowa East Central TRAIN Agency, 1979-80; Elks Lodge #304 and Elks Chanters, 1977 to present; Volunteer, Voluntary Action Program in Muscatine. Religion: Faith United Christian Church, Muscatine, Active Member in Christian Education Activities, Choir, Liturgy, Community Involvement; St. Andrews United Presbyterian Church, Iowa City, Adult Education and Small Groups. Honors and Awards: Advisor, National Editorial Board of Advisors, American Biographical Institute, 1982; Presenter at National and Local Conferences; Fellow, International Biographical Association; Listed in Numerous Biographical Reference Works. Address: 1306 Orange, Muscatine, Iowa 52761.■

TWO THOUSAND NOTABLE AMERICANS

JULIA ANNE DeVERE

Educator. Personal: Born November 2, 1925; Daughter of Goodlet C. (deceased) and Anna R. Bonjour; Married Robert E. DeVere; Mother of David E. Education: Attended Emporia State Teachers College, University of Kansas at Lawrence, Kansas State University at Manhattan; B.A., University of Denver, 1957; M.A., University of Denver, 1961; Undertook Postgraduate Studies at University of Maryland, University of the Pacific, San Jose University, University of San Cruz, Sacramento State University, Others. Career: Teacher, One-Room School, Jackson County, Kansas, 1943-45; Teacher, Upper Elementary, Bancroft, Kansas, 1946-47; Teacher, Primary Grades, 1947-52; Teacher, Second Grade, Westmoreland, Kansas, 1953-55; Teacher, Elementary Class of Mentally Retarded Students, Stockton, California, 1957-64; Teacher, Handicapped Children, Cupertino School District, 1964 to present. Organizational Memberships: National Education Association; California Teachers Association; Cupertino Education Association; Council for Exceptional Children; Foundation for Exceptional Children, Behavioral Disorders, Mentally Retarded, Visually Handicapped and Learning Disabled; Educational Diagnostic Service. Community Activities: Walked Block for Cancer, Leukemia, Muscular Dystrophy, Heart Fund. Religion: United Brethren Church. Honors and Awards: Delta Kappa Gamma Scholarship, 1955; International Biographical Center and American Biographical Institute Awards and Honors; Listed in *Who's Who of American Women, Who's Who in the West and Midwest, International Who's Who in Community Service, Notable Americans,* Others. Address: 950 Chehalis Drive, Sunnyvale, California 94087. ■

WINSTON DeVILLE

Full-time Genealogist and Executive. Personal: Born August 8, 1937; Son of Olevia DeVille. Education: B.A., Louisiana College, 1959; M.A., Louisiana State University, 1965; Advanced Study in Canada, Mexico, France and Spain. Career: Full-time Genealogist; Chairman of the Board, Polyanthos, Inc.; Former Director, Genealogical Publishing Company; Director of Department of Special Collections, Mobile (Alabama) Public Library, 1963-64; Author of 16 Books Relating to Colonial America; Lecturer; Consultant on Special Problems in Historical Research; Expert Witness in Court Cases involving Genealogical Evidence. Organizational Memberships: National Genealogical Society, 1963 to present; Member of Numerous State and Local Historical and Genealogical Societies. Community Activities: Trustee, Board for Certification of Genealogists, 1971-80; Trustee, Association for Promotion of Scholarship in Genealogy, 1980 to present; National Chairmman of Public Relations, National Genealogical Society Conference, 1982-83; Fellow, American Society of Genealogists, 1970 to present; Lecturer, National Archives, 1971 to present; Founding President, Friends of the National Archives, 1982 to present; Co-Director, Reunion of the Old Families of Natchitoches, Louisiana, 1980 to present. Honors and Awards: American Philosophical Society Grant, 1965; Prichard Award for Outstanding Contributions to Historiography, 1975; Associate, Academia Mexicana de Genealogia y Heraldica, 1975; Recognition for Contributions to United States-Canadian Friendship, Canadian Government, 1976; Fellow, Texas State Genealogical Society, 1970. Address: P.O. Drawer 51359, New Orleans, Louisiana 70151. ■

PATRICIA PARKER DEWEY

Radio Station Executive. Personal: Born January 27, 1923; Married Ralph B. Dewey; Mother of Phillip Lee Williams. Education: B.Mus., University of Mississippi; Further Studies undertaken at Sullins Junior College, Millsaps College. Career: Owner/President, Radio Station WNNT AM/FM and WKWI-FM; Former Positions include Women's Director of Radio Station WNNT, Commentator of Daily Radio Show "Chat with Pat," Society Editor for *Jackson Daily News.* Organizational Memberships: American Women in Radio and Television; National Society Arts and Letters; National Society Composers and Conductors; National Association of Broadcasters; Virginia Association of Broadcasters. Community Activities: American Red Cross, Aquatic Director (Lancaster County, Virginia), 1950-60; Florence Crittenton Home Benefit Chairman, 1981; Home Hospitality for Servicemen, Junior Chairman 1943-46; Radio/TV Publicity Chairman, Thrift Shop Charities, 1983; Radio/TV Publicity Chairman, St. Francis House Tour Benefit, 1974, 1976; Radio/TV Publication Chairman, Landon School Garden Festival Scholarship Benefit, 1975, 1979, 1981. Religion: Christian Broadcasting Network Seminars; Grace Church Women's Committee (Lancaster County, Virginia); Life Member, Christ Church National Foundation. Honors and Awards: Guest Pianist with National Air Force Symphony Performing "Rhapsody of Youth" and "Revolution Rhapsody," 1947, 1964, 1976; Composition "Maid of Cotton" Selected as Theme Song of National Cotton Council; Featured in Musicals "Miss. Cotton Pickin' Blues" 1944-47; "Lucky X" Official Song of Chi Omega Sorority, 1943-. Address: 6211 Garnett Drive, Chevy Chase, Maryland 20815. ■

SUSAN PIERSON DE WITT

Attorney. Personal: Born May 15, 1947; Daughter of Mr. and Mrs. George W. Pierson; Married James A. De Witt (deceased). Education: A.A., Joliet Junior College, 1967; B.S., University of Illinois, 1969; J.D., John Marshall Law School, 1973. Career: Partner in Law Firm of O'Brien, Garrison, Berard, Kusta & De Witt, Joliet, Illinois, 1975-77; Assistant Attorney General, Litigation Section, Chicago Office of the Attorney General, 1977-78; Assistant Attorney General and Chief, Consumer Protection Division, Springfield Office of the Illinois Attorney General, 1978-83; United States Trustee for the Northern District of Illinois, 1983 to present. Organizational Memberships: Consumer Advisory Council to the Federal Reserve Board, Past Chairman; National Association of Attorneys General Consumer Protection Committee, Secret Warranties Subcommittee; American, Illinois, Chicago, Sangamon County and Federal Bar Associations; American Association of University Women; Board of Directors, John Marshall Law School Alumni Association. Community Activities: Zonta Club of Springfield, Past President; Land of Lincoln Girl Scout Council, Board of Directors; International Organization of Women Executives, Board of Advisors, Executive Committee; Family Service Center; Aid to Retarded Citizens; Capital Campaign; Goodman Theatre, Individual Guarantors Committee. Religion: Protestant. Published Works: Author, *Illinois Continuing Legal Education,* Bankruptcy Practice Chapter on the United States Trustee Program. Honors and Awards: Leadership Award, International Organization of Women Executives, 1980; Young Career Woman, Business and Professional Women's Organization, 1973; Featured in *Illinois Issues,* January 1981; Young Republican of the Year, 1973. Address: 505 North Lake Shore Drive, Apt. 4912, Chicago, Illinois 60611. ■

DAVID R. DeYOE

Tree Physiologist/Extension Reforestation Specialist. Personal: Born September 28, 1946; Son of Darwin and Doris DeYoe; Married Susan K. Education: Pierce Junior College, Letters and Sciences, 1964-66; B.S. Forest Management, Oregon State University, 1971; M.S. Forest Physiology, Forest Science Department, Oregon State University, 1973; Ph.D. Forest Physiology, Department of Forestry, Fisheries and Wildlife, University of Missouri, 1977. Career: Assistant Professor 1979 to present, Research Associate 1977-79, Oregon State University; Assistant Professor 1977-78, Research Assistant 1973-77, University of Missouri School of Forestry; Instructor, Oregon State University, Forest Management Department, 1971-73; Forest Physiology Technician Summer 1970 & Fall 1969, Forest Physiology/Ecology Technician Summer 1969, Oregon State University, Forest Science Department; Forest Genetics Technician, United States Forest Science Lab, Summer 1968; Timber Management Technician, United States Forest Service Region 6, Quinault R.D., Summer 1967. Organizational Memberships: American Society of Plant Physiologists, 1971 to present; Society of American Foresters, 1978 to present; Sigma Xi, 1978 to present. Community Activities: Columbia Evening Club, 1976-78; Corvallis Lions Club, Member 1978 to present, District Sight Chairman 1978-80, Club Sight Chairman 1978-79; Trustee, Sight and Hearing Foundation of Oregon, 1980-82; Faculty Representative, Delta Gamma Sorority Sight Functions, 1979 to present. Published Works: Author of Various Articles including "Glycerolipid and Fatty Acid Changes in Eastern White Pine Chloropoast Lamellae During Onset of Winter" *Plant Physiology,* "Comparison of Eight Physical Barriers Used for Protecting Douglas Fir Seedlings From Deer Browse" *Proceedings of the First Eastern Wildlife Damage Control Symposium,* "Reforestation Planning Guide; Helping Insure Reforestation Success for Woodland Owners", Oregon State University Extension Service, and others. Honors and Awards: Listed in *Outstanding Young Men of America, Who's Who in the West, Who's Who in Science and Technology, Biographical Roll of Honor, International Who's Who in Contemporary Achievement.* Address: 7233 Northwest Valley View, Corvallis, Oregon 97330. ■

JERRY RAY DIAS

Chemistry Professor. Personal: Born October 26, 1940; Son of Mr. and Mrs. F. F. Dias; Married Barbara Jean, Daughter of Mr. and Mrs. Harvey W. Turner; Father of Rene Barbara, Harvey William, Jennifer Jean. Education: B.S. honors, San Jose State University, 1965; Ph.D. Organic/Physical Chemistry, Arizona State University, 1970; N.I.H. Predoctoral Fellow 1968-70, Postdoctoral Fellow 1970-72, Stanford University. Career: Professor, Department of Chemistry, University of Missouri-Kansas City. Organizational Memberships: American Chemical Society, Advertising and Business Manager of Kansas City Section's *Kansas City Chemist* 1973 to present, Secretary 1974-76, Chairman-Elect 1977, Chairman 1978; American Electroplaters Society, National Technical Education Board 1978-81; American Institute of Chemical Engineers; American Society of Testing and Materials; National Society of Professional Engineers; Phi Lambda Upsilon; Phi Kappa Phi.

Published Works: Author Over 40 Research Papers. Honors and Awards: Fulbright Scholar to University of Ljubljana, Yugoslavia, 1981; Passed Engineer-in-Training Exam in State of Missouri; Recipient of Over $140,000 in Research Grant Money; Listed in *American Men and Women of Science; Who's Who in the Midwest, Who's Who in Technology Today, International Who's Who in Education.* Address: 10001 West 93rd, Overland Park, Kansas 66212.■

LUDMILA CHALAS DI BONA

Graduate Student. Personal: Born November 21, 1952; Daughter of Josef and Olga Chalas; Married Aidano M. Di Bona, Son of Anna and Victor Di Bona; Mother of Paul. Education: B.A. Linguistics, Lehman College, City University of New York, 1975; M.A. Slavic Linguistcs 1976, Ph.D. Slavic Linguistics 1981, Brown University; M.S. Computer Science, Pace University, expected 1984. Career: Fellow 1975-77, Teaching Assistant 1977-78, Teaching Proctor 1978-79, Brown University. Organizational Memberships: Phi Beta Kappa, Chi Chapter; Modern Language Association; Linguistic Society of America; Canadian Association of Slavists; Smithsonian Institution; American Association for Teachers of Slavic and East European Languages. Honors and Awards: Dean's List, 1973-75; German Honorary Society, 1974; Phi Beta Kappa; B.A. magna cum laude; Brown University Endowment Fellowship, 1975-76; N.D.F.L. Fellowship, N.D.E.A. Title VI, 1976-77; Assistantship, Brown University, 1977-78; Proctorship, Brown University, 1978-79; Listed in *World Who's Who of Women, World's Who's Who of Intellectuals, Biographical Roll of Honor.* Address: 94 The Crossway, Yonkers, New York 10701.■

CHARLES CAMERON DICKINSON, III

Professor. Personal: Born May 13, 1936. Education: B.A.; B.D.; Ph.D.; F.R.S.A. Career: Professor of Linguistics and Literature, Hebei Teachers University, Shijiazhuang, Hebei Province, People's Republic of China, 1983-84; Curatorial Associate for Manuscript Collections, Andover-Harvard Theological Library, Harvard University; Research Professor of Theology and Philosophy, University of Charleston, West Virginia, 1980 to present; Assistant Professor of Religion and Philosophy and Director of Honors Program, Morris Harvey College, 1975-79; Visiting Professor of Theology and Philosophy, Union Theological Seminary, Richmond, Virginia, 1974-75. Organizational Memberships: Fellow, Royal Society of Arts; American Academy of Religion; Society of Biblical Literature; Executive Committee, Karl Barth Society of North America; American Theological Society (Midwest); American Philosophical Association; American Association for the Advancement of the Humanities; American Association for the Advancement of Science; International Platform Association; International Bonhoeffer Society for Archives and Research; Past Secretary-Treasurer, West Virginia Philosophical Society; Past Danforth Liaison Officer, Morris Harvey College; Past Chairman of Student Exchange Committee, Charleston Rotary Club; Past Member Executive Committee, West Virginia Association for Higher Education; West Virginia Association for the Humanities; Past Secretary, Morris Harvey College/University of Charleston Chapter, American Association of University Professors; Speaker on "The 'Failure of Nerve' in Hellenistic Society," at West Virginia Philosophical Society and at Great Lakes and Eastern Metropolitan Meetings of American Academy of Religion, 1976-77; Attended Institute on Scholarly Publishing, Scholars Press, University of Montana at Missoula, 1977; Chairman of Session of Karl Barth Society at North America Annual Meeting of American Academy of Religion, New Orleans, Louisiana, 1978. Published Works: Contributor of Book Reviews to *Journal of Ecumenical Studies* Mid-1960's and *The New Review of Books and Religion* 1978-80; Author of Copyrighted Dissertation, *Pre-Existence, Resurrection and Recapitulation: The Pre-Existence of Christ in Karl Barth, Wolfhart Pannenberg, and the New Testament,* 1973; Contributor of "The 'Failure of Nerve' in Hellenistic Society" 1977 and "The Four-Fold Non-Root of Bio-Medical Ethics" 1979 to *Journal of the West Virginia Philosophical Society,* "What Is Myth?" and "A Passus in Christology" 1982 to *Encounter.* Address: 1111 City National Building, Wichita Falls, Texas 76301.■

JOSEPH L. DIESKA

Professor Emeritus. Personal: Born April 5, 1913; Son of John Dieska and Christina Dieskova; Married Anna, Daughter of Stephen Graca and Anna Gracova; Father of Anna, Joseph. Education: Ph.D., University of J. A. Commenius, Bratislava, 1940; Hab.Doc. 1944; Abs.Theology 1935; Certificate of Maturity 1931. Career: Professor Emeritus, University of Dayton, 1978; Former Positions include, Doctor of Philosophy at University of J. A. Commenius, Associate Professor at University of Georgetown (Washington, D.C.), Professor of Philosophy at University of Dayton, Editor of *Slovak Philosophical Review,* President of Slovak Liberty Party 1946-48, President of Philosophical Institute Maticaslovenska 1945-48, Secretary of General Slovak Philosophical Society. Organizational Memberships: Slovak Institute Rome (Italy); International Society of St. Thomas (Rome); American Catholic Philosophical Association, Washington, D.C.; CSR Christian Academy (Rome, Italy). Community Activities: Presidium Member, Free Czechoslovakia, Washington, D.C., 1950-55. Address: University of Dayton, Dayton, Ohio 45469.■

JANE A. DIETL

Consultant. Education: B.S. Education and Business, Peru State and University of Nebraska, 1962; M.A. Administration, Chapman College, 1967; Ph.D. Coursework, United States International University, 1981. Career: Consultant, Jane Dietl Enterprises, 1981 to present; Vice President, The Green Machine (Division of VM Products), 1981 to present; Consultant, Air Tamer International, Caroline, Puerto Rico, 1975 to present; Assistant Principal/Principal, Fullerton School District, Fullerton, California, 1972-77; Director of Resource Instruction, San Joaquin Unified School District, San Joaquin, California, 1971-72; Vice President, Extraction Systems Corporation, Santa Ana, California, 1970-71; Director, United States Dependents Schools, Soesterberg, Holland, 1969-70; Assistant Principal/Principal, Santa Ana Unified School District, 1967-69; Teacher, Santa Ana, 1960-67. Organizational Memberships: American Association of University Women; World Future Society; American Society for Training and Development; National Council for International Visitors; National Association of Business Owners; Academy of Management. Published Works: *Attitudinal Changes and Its Effects on Potential Dropouts, Management and Operation — Summer Guidance Opportunity School, A Study Reflecting the Dominant Personality Style Most Successful in Exemplifying Effective Situational Leadership Within a Corporate Organization.* Honors and Awards: Highest Amount of Merit Pay while Teacher in Santa Ana, 1960-67; Lifetime Teaching Credential; Lifetime University Credential; Delta Kappa Gamma Award. Address: 10322 Pacific, Suite 203, Omaha, Nebraska 68154.■

DAVID ROGERS DILLEHAY

Pyrotechnist. Personal: Born September 21, 1936; Son of Thomas Jefferson Jr. and Rachel Todd Dillehay (deceased); Married Marilyn Heath, Daughter of William Floyd (deceased) and Dolores Sieve Heath; Father of Janet Lee Dillehay Arledge, David Rogers, Jr. Education: B.A. Chemistry, Rice University, 1958; Ph.D. Chemistry, Clayton University, 1983. Career: Pyrotechnist and Special Projects Supervisor, Former Process Engineering Supervisor, Former Senior Engineer, Former Chemist, Longhorn Division of Thiokol Corporation, 1958 to present. Organizational Memberships: Secretary, International Pyrotechnic Society, 1980 to present; President 1982-83, National Representative 1983, Ark-La-Tex Chapter A.D.P.A.; Steering Committee, International Pyrotechnic Seminars; President, Thiokol Management Club, an Affiliate of the American Management Association, 1973. Community Activities: Scoutmaster, Troop 209, Boy Scouts of America, 1972-73; St. Joseph's Parish Council, 1968; President 1976-77, Treasurer 1975-76, Maverick Music Boosters. Religion: St. Joseph's Catholic Church, President C.C.D. 1963. Honors and Awards: United States Material Command Value Management Award, 1969; Marshall Chamber of Commerce, Image Maker Citation, 1983. Address: 107 Ashwood Terrace, Marshall, Texas 75670.■

PAUL ANDREW DILLON

Administrator. Personal: Born March 21, 1945; Son of Samuel D. and Helen M. Dillon; Married Barbara Ann Kleinhenz, Daughter of Frank A. and Norma Kleinhenz; Father of Jean Marie, Timothy David, Patrick Anthony. Education: A.B., John Carroll University, 1967; M.S., Northern Illinois University, 1969; Postgraduate Study in Business Management undertaken at the University of Southern California, 1969. Military: Served in the United States Army Reserve, 1969-71, achieving the rank of First Lieutenant. Career: Vice President and Director, Economic Research Division, Mid-America Appraisal and Research Corporation; Senior Consultant, Lester B. Knight & Associates, Inc., Chicago, 1974-76; Administrative Assistant, Illinois Department of Transportation, Chicago, 1971-73; Appointed to the United States Diplomatic Corps, Vietnam, 1970-71; Teaching Graduate Assistant, Northern Illinois University, 1967-68. Organizational Memberships: Metropolitan Housing and Planning Council of Chicago, 1977-82; Illinois 2000 Foundation, Chairman Transportation Implementation Team 1978-80; Transportation Research Forum, Board of Directors of Chicago Chapter 1977-78. Community Activities: Appointed by Governor of Illinois to Illinois Comittee to Strengthen Community Economies 1978, Illinois Study Commission on Public Pension Policies 1981, Illinois Tax Reform Commission 1982; Appointed by Speaker of the Illinois House of Representatives to the Illinois Legislative Commission on the Revitalization of Midway Airport; Appointed by Mayor of Chicago to O'Hare Airport Advisory Committee, 1982; Chairman, Aviation Committee, Chicago Association of Commerce and Industry. Religion: Roman Catholic. Honors and Awards: Decorated with 2 Bronze Star Medals, 1969; Eagle Scout Award, Boy Scouts of America, 1959; Named as One of Chicago's Ten Outstanding Young Citizens by Chicago Jaycees. Address: 16813 South Beverly Avenue, Tinley Park, Illinois 60477.■

ROBERT WILLIAM DILLON, SR.

Professor. Personal: Born May 31, 1942; Son of Catherine M. Dillon; Married Susan M., Daughter of Frances R. Ritonia; Father of Christopher Mark, Christian Randall, Robert William Jr. Education: A.B., Fairfield University, 1964; M.A. 1965, Ph.D., The Ohio University. Career: Full Profesor of English Language and Literature 1971 to present, Associate Professor of English 1970-71, California University of Pennsylvania Department of English (California, Pennsylvania); Assistant Professor of English 1969-70, Department of English Chairman 1968-70, Acting Dean College of Arts and Sciences 1968-70, Ohio University at Lancaster; Teaching Fellow 1965-67, Graduate Assistant 1964-65, Ohio University at Athens; Feature Writer *Lancaster (Ohio) Eagle-Gazette*, 1968-70. Organizational Memberships: Modern Language Association of America; Pennsylvania State Education Association; National Education Association; Association of American University Professors; Pennsylvania Higher Education Association; American Federation of Teachers; Association of State College and University Professors (Pennsylvania). Community Activities: President, California University of Pennsylvania Shotokan Karate Club, 1979-80; Advisor and Honorary Member, Psi Chapter, Phi Kappa Theta Fraternity, California, Pennsylvania; Former Scoutmaster, United Christian Church, Coal Center, Pennsylvania; Donor of Private Library to California Public Library, 1977; Active Member involved in Little League and Pony League, California Youth Association; Radio Forum on "The Teaching of English in the Community College," WHOK, Lancaster, Ohio, 1968; Chairman Composition Workshop and Presenter of Paper "The Essential Paragraph: A Normative Approach," Western Pennsylvania Conference on Writing, "A Look at Writing: A Time to Re-Group," 1979; English Department Curriculum Committee, Freshman Writing Committee, Faculty Promotion Committee, Sabbatical Leave Committee, Faculty Evaluation and Tenure Committees, California University of Pennsylvania. Published Works: Contributor, "A Centenary Bibliography of Carlylean Studies: 1928-74," *Bulletin of Bibliography and Magazine Notes*, 1975. Honors and Awards: Poetry Award, Fairfield University, 1962; Cum Laude Graduate, 1964; Editor-in-Chief, *New Frontiers*, Literary Quarterly, Fairfield University, 1963-64; N.D.E.A. Fellowship, The Ohio University, 1964; Graduate Assistantship and Teaching Fellowship, The Ohio University, 1964-67; Research Grant for 19th-Century British Aesthetics, The Ohio University Off-Campus Academic Programs, 1968; California University of Pennsylvania Teaching Merit Award, 1974; Listed in *International Who's Who in Education, Directory of Distinguished Americans*. Address: P.O. Box 524, 970 Wood Street, California, Pennsylvania 15419.■

ANGELO JOHN DiMASCIO

Administrator. Personal: Born June 14, 1938; Married Constance A., Daughter of Mr. and Mrs. W. Hall; Father of Laura Marie, Christopher, Steven. Education: B.S.M.E., Drexel Institute of Technology, 1963; M.S.E.M., Drexel University, 1970; D.B.A., George Washington University, 1979. Military: Served in the United States Army Corps of Engineers, 1964-66, achieving the rank of First Lieutenant. Career: Executive Director of Acquisition Management 1979 to present, Technical Director of Test and Evaluation 1977-79, Technical Director of Aviation Support Equipment Division 1973-77, Branch Head of Planning, Appraisal and Analysis in Research and Technology 1972-73, Technical Coordinator of Aviation Support Equipment 1971-72, Naval Air Systems Command; Program Manager, Naval Air Engineering Center, Philadelphia, Pennsylvania. Organizational Memberships: Pi Tau Sigma National Honor Mechanical Engineering Fraternity; Beta Gamma Sigma National Honor Business Fraternity. Community Activities: Boy Scouts of America, Troop Committee 1977; Cub Scouts, Webelos Den Leader 1980-81; Coach, Little League Baseball, 1973-74; Coach, Pee Wee League Football, 1973; Knights of Columbus, 1982 to present. Religion: Holy Family Church (Woodbridge, Virginia), Parish Building Committee 1982. Honors and Awards: Presidential Rank of Meritorious Executive, 1980; Several Outstanding Performance Awards; Various Citations and Commendations; Listed in a Number of Biographical Reference Works. Address: 4466 Dale Blvd., Woodbridge, Virginia 22193.■

ROBERT MORTON DIXON

Soil Scientist. Personal: Born May 30, 1929, in Leon, Kansas; Son of Will G. and Vivian M. Dixon (both deceased); Married Sharon Ann Youngblood; Father of James Robert, Curtis Gregory, Donna Elaine, Gregory Eric. Education: B.S. Technical Agronomy 1959, M.S. Soil Chemistry 1960, Kansas State University; Ph.D. Soil Physics and Plant Physiology, University of Wisconsin, Madison, 1966. Career: Soil Scientist for Agricultural Research Service, U.S.D.A. Arid Land Ecosystems Improvement Research Unit (Tucson, Arizona); Formerly Soil Scientist at Reno (Nevada), Sidney (Montana) and Madison (Wisconsin), United States Department of Agriculture; People-to-People Delegate to People's Republic of China, 1982; Agriculture Consultant, United States State Department, Agency for Internatinal Development, Port-au-Prince, Haiti, 1977; Irrigation Specialist, Ford Foundation, Cairo, Egypt, 1967; Instructor, Kansas State University, Manhattan, 1959-60; Developed Air-Earth Interface Concept for Controlling Rainwater Infiltration; Developed Land Imprinting Method for Conservation Tillage and Seeding in Arid and Semi-Arid Regions; Invented Land Imprinting Machine for Controlling Rainwater Infiltration to Promote Revegetation and Crop Production; Developed Method and Machine for Arresting Man-Induced Land Degradation or Desertification. Organizational Memberships: International Society of Soil Science; Soil Science Society of America; American Society of Agronomy; Soil Conservation Society of America; American Geophysical Union; American Society of Agricultural Engineers; Society for Range Management; Arizona-Nevada Academy of Science. Cmmunity Activities: Donor, Planned Parenthood World Population, Natural Resource Defense Council, American Civil Liberties Union, Audubon Society, Unitarian-Universalist Society, Public Lands Institute, Whooping Crane Conservation Association, Arizona-Sonora Desert Museum. Religion: Unitarian/Universalist Association, 1960 to present; Leon Christian Church, Sunday School Superintendent, 1947-50. Published Works: Author of Over Seventy Technical Publications in the Field of Soil Science, Hydrology, Agricultural Engineering, and Range Science; Holder of One Patent in the Field of Conservation Tillage and Planting. Honors and Awards: Gamma Sigma Delta; Sigma Xi; Phi Kappa Phi; Invitation Lecturer, National Academy of Science Seminar; Land Imprinting Selected for Special Study by National Academy of Sciences Panel; Membership, National Academy of Sciences Panel on Land Imprinting; Listed in *Who's Who in the West, American Men and Women of Science, Dictionary of International Biography, Men of Achievement, Who's Who in Technology Today, Community Leaders of America, Directory of Distinguished Americans, Personalities of America*. Address: 1231 East Big Rock Road, Tucson, Arizona 85718.■

MINNETTE FRERICHS DODERER

Legislator. Personal: Born May 16, 1923; Daughter of John and Sophie Frerichs (both deceased); Married Fred H. Doderer, Son of Herman and Augusta Doderer; Mother of Kay, Dennis. Education: B.A., University of Iowa, 1958. Career: Member Iowa House and Senate, 17 Years (10 years in Senate, 7 years in House); Lecturer and Editor for John Deere Tractor Company Publications. Organizational Memberships: Delta Kappa Gamma; Women's Political Caucus; Business and Professional Women; National Organization of Women; League of Women Voters. Community Activities: Visiting Professor, Stephens College and Iowa State University, 1979; Iowa Health Facilities Commission, 1979-80. Religion: Methodist. Honors and Awards: Sons of American Revolution Award, 1973; Iowa State Education Service Award, 1969; Iowa Women's Hall of Fame, 1979. Address: 2008 Dunlap Court, Iowa City, Iowa 52240.■

PAT EUGENE DOMENICK

Piping Superintendent. Personal: Born January 15, 1928; Son of Patsy J. and Florence Domenick; Married Mary Lou; Father of Robert P., J. Jeffrey. Education: Attended Wake Forest College, Point Park College; Various Construction Management and Construction Marketing Seminars; United Association of Plumbers

and Pipe Fitters Apprentice School. Military: Served in the United States Navy Submarine Service, 1945-47. Career: Piping Superintendent, Mac Steel Project, Eichleay Corporation, 1982 to present; Production Manager, Kansas City Officer, Schneider Inc., 1981-82; Area Manager, Blast Furnace Project, Wisconsin Steel Company, 1979-81; Piping Superintendent, Bethlehem Steel's Black Furnace (Largest Blast Furnace in Western Hemisphere), Koppers Company Inc., 1978-79; Project Manager, Beker Industries, 1974-77; Piping Superintendent, United Engineers and Constructors, 1972-74. Organizational Memberships: Master Plumber, Arkansas State Board of Health. Honors and Awards: Listed in *Who's Who in America*. Address: 22 Lincoln Avenue, Jeannette, Pennsylvania 15644. ∎

CHARLES EDWARD DONEGAN

Professor of Law. Personal: Born April 10, 1933; Son of Arthur C. and Odessa Donegan (both deceased); Married Patty L. Harris, Daughter of Cloys and Marilyn Harris (both deceased); Father of Carter Edward. Education: B.S.C., Roosevelt University, 1954; M.S.I.R., Loyola University, 1959; J.D., Howard University, 1967; LL.M., Columbia University, 1970. Career: Assistant Professor of Law, State University of New York at Buffalo Law School, 1970-73; Associate Professor of Law, Howard University Law School, 1973-77; Visiting Professor of Business Law, Ohio State University, 1977-78; Assistant Counsel, United States Environmental Agency, 1978-80; Assistant Counsel, National Association for the Advancement of Colored People Legal Defense Fund, 1967-69. Organizational Memberships: American, National, Chicago, Federal, District of Columbia, Cook County Bar Associations; Phi Alpha Delta; Phi Alpha Kappa. Community Activities: Alpha Phi Alpha; Arbitrator, Steel Industry, 1971 to present; Labor Arbitrator, American Arbitration Association. Religion: Protestant. Published Works: Author Numerous Articles in Professional Journals. Honors and Awards: Best Teacher, Southern University Law School, 1981; Most Outstanding Professor, Southern University Law School, 1982; Ford Fellow, Columbia University Law School, 1972-73; National Endowment for the Humanities Postdoctoral Fellowship in Afro-American Studies, Yale University, 1972-73; High Academic Achievement Award at 1954 Class Reunion, Roosevelt University, 1981. Address: 10837 Flintwood Avenue, Baton Rouge, Louisiana 70811. ∎

MARY AGNES DOOLEY, S.S.J.

Executive, Educator. Personal: Born March 5, 1923; Daughter of Richard and Mary O'Neill Dooley (both deceased). Education: B.A., Our Lady of the Elms College, Chicopee, Massachusetts, 1944; M.A., Assumption College, Worcester, Massachusetts, 1960; Doctorat d'Universite, University of Paris (Sorbonne), 1968. Career: Teacher, St. Joseph High School, North Adams, Massachusetts, 1946-65; Chairperson, Language Department, Elms College, 1968-70; President, Congregation of the Sisters of St. Joseph of Springfield, 1971-79; President, Elms College. Organizational Memberships: Leadership Conference of Women Religious of the United States, Member 1978-80, President, Vice President; Association of Catholic Colleges and Universities, Board Member 1980 to present; Delegate, Second, Third, Fourth Inter-American Conference, 1974, 1977, 1980. Community Activities: Official Delegate, Installation of Popes John Paul I and II, 1978; Delegate, White House Reception for Pope John Paul II, 1979; Delegate, U.J.A. Ecumenical Leadership Mission to Israel, 1975; Interfaith Council of Springfield, Massachusetts, Chairperson 1975-77; Frequent Speaker to Religious and Educational Organizations. Religion: Delegate, International Union of Superiors General, Rome 1975, 1977, 1979, Montreal 1977, 1978, Rio de Janeiro 1980. Honors and Awards: Honorary Degree, Assumption College, Worcester, Massachusetts, 1982; Chevalier dans l'Ordre des Palmes, French Government, 1981; Honorary Degree, Doctor of Letters, American International College, Springfield, Massachusetts, 1981; Distinguished Alumna Award, Elms College, 1979. Address: 291 Springfield Street, Chicopee, Massachusetts 01013. ∎

SHARON A. DORNER

Business Educator. Personal: Born November 3, 1943; Daughter of Bill and Eleanor Haddon; Mother of Wendy, Meridith. Education: Attended Trenton State College, 1961-63; B.A. Business Education magna cum laude 1965, M.A. Business Education 1970, M.A. Guidance and Counseling 1978, Montclair State College; Ed.D., Rutgers University, 1982. Career: Business Educator, Guidance Intern, Administrative Intern to the Superintendent, Woodcliff School (Woodcliff Lake, New Jersey), 1976 to present; Business Educator, Montville (New Jersey) 1976, Leonia (New Jersey) High School 1974-75, County College of Morris (Randolph, New Jersey) 1973, Katherine Gibbs Secretarial School and Kimberley School (Montclair, New Jersey) 1972-73; Adult Education Teacher, Sussex Vocational School (Sparta, New Jersey), 1969-70; Business Educator, Morris Knolls High School (Denville, New Jersey), 1965-70. Organizational Memberships: Phi Delta Kappa, Montclair State Chapter, President 1980-81 & 1981-82, Vice President for Program 1979-80, Treasurer 1975-79 and 1982 to present, National Council Delegate 1977-80, National Council Alternate 1980 to present, National District VI Newsletter Editor 1977-79; Delta Pi Epsilon, Montclair State Chapter, President 1979-80, Vice President 1978-79, Corresponding Secretary 1976-78, Newsletter Editor 1974-76, National Council Representative 1980 to present, National Standing Committee Member 1980-84 (Chairperson 1982-84); Omicron Tau Theta, Rutgers University Chapter; Kappa Delta Pi, Montclair State Chapter; Pi Omega Pi, Montclair State Chapter; Northeast Coalition of Educational Leaders; New Jersey Coalition of Educational Leaders, Northeast Regional Representative 1982-83, Treasurer 1983 to present; National Education Association; New Jersey Education Association; Bergen County Education Association; Woodcliff Lake Education Association, Secretary 1976 to present. Community Activities: Byram Township Board of Education, 1968-70; Lenape Valley Regional Board of Education, 1969-72; Essex County Board of Education, 1975 to present; Consumers League of New Jersey, Board of Directors 1976 to present; Sigma Kappa, National Alumnae District Director II 1980 to present, National Alumnae Province Officers 1977-80; Order of the Eastern Star; Daughters of the Nile. Published Works: Articles "Middle School Typewriting is No Kid Stuff" 1979 and "Keep Your Bulletin Board Ideas Alive" 1970. Honors and Awards: Phi Delta Kappa Gerald Read Scholarship Travel Award, 1982; Phi Delta Kappa Service Award, 1981; Listed in *Who's Who of American Women, World Who's Who of Women, Who's Who in the East, Directory of Distinguished Americans, Personalities of America, International Book of Honor*. Address: 28 College Avenue, Upper Montclair, New Jersey 07043. ∎

MILLICENT ELIZABETH DORSETT

Bank Officer. Personal: Born July 27, 1948, in Yadkinville, North Carolina; Daughter of Robert and Alice (Banks) Williams (both deceased); Married Steven R. Dorset, August 14, 1970; Mother of Alexander and Alexandra (twins), Steven R. Jr. Education: Graduate of Broughton High School (Raleigh, North Carolina), 1966; B.S. Psychology, Appalachian State University (Boone, North Carolina), 1970; Paralegal Certification, Meredith College, 1972; Attended Trust School, Summers 1980, 1981; Various Courses through the American Institute of Banking. Career: Trust Officer, Central Carolina Bank (Durham, North Carolina), 1982 to present; Administrative Assistant to Trust Officer, First Citizens Bank (Raleigh, North Carolina), 1976-82; Former Positions with Chevrolet Dealership, Oil Company. Organizational Memberships: North Carolina Association of Paralegals; National Association of Paralegals; American Institute of Banking. Community Activities: Hospice Volunteer; Hotline Volunteer. Religion: United Methodist Church. Address: Route 4 Box 39, Wake Forest, North Carolina 27587. ∎

BETTY JO DOSSETT

Social Insurance Representative (Retired). Personal: Born September 14, 1931; Daughter of James Daniel (deceased) and Mary Allen Ishee Mooney; Mother of Linda Gail Dossett Davis, Mark Richard Dossett. Education: B.S. 1953, M.Ed. 1972, University of Southern Mississippi. Career: Social Insurance Representative, Social Security Administration, Hattiesburg (Mississippi) 1960-66, Holiday (Florida) 1976-78, Dallas (Texas) 1978-83; Business Consultant for Paul Stephen Lee, Concert Organist, 1976-81. Organizational Memberships: National Business Education Association, 1950-52; University of Southern Mississippi Alumni Association; National Association of Female Executives, 1980-81. Bel Canto Music Club (Hattiesburg, Mississippi), Treasurer 1973-75; March of Dimes, Neighborhood Workers 1962-64. Religion: Main Street Baptist Church (Hattiesburg), Sunday School Teacher and Junior Training Union Leader 1962-66; Southern Baptist Women's Missionary Union Girls Auxiliary Director 1967-68; Director, Whitehaven Baptist Church, Memphis, Tennessee, 1966-67. Honors and Awards: 15 Year Service

Award, Social Security Administration, 1979; Federal Employee Recognition Award, Tampa Bay Federal Executive Association, Tampa, Florida, 1977; Presidential Achievement Award, 1982. Address: 409 North Street, Hattiesburg, Mississippi 39401.■

LEE S. DREYFUS

Corporation Executive, Former Governor of Wisconsin. Personal: Born June 20, 1926; Son of Mr. and Mrs. Woods Orlow Dreyfus (deceased); Married Joyce Mae Unke; Father of Susan Lynn Fosdick, Lee Sherman Jr. Education: Graduate, Washington High School, Milwaukee, Wisconsin, 1944; B.A., M.A., Ph.D., University of Wisconsin at Madison, 1946-57; Numerous Honorary Degrees. Military: Served in the United States Navy, 1944-46. Career: President and Chief Operating Officer, Sentry Worldwide Corporation, 1983 to present; Governor of Wisconsin, 1979-83; Chancellor, University of Wisconsin, 1972-79; President, Wisconsin State University at Stevens Point, 1967-72; Chairman, Division of Radio-TV-Film, University of Wisconsin at Madison, 1965-67; Professor of Speech and Radio-TV Education and Film, University of Wisconsin at Madison, 1962-67; Chairman, State Educational TV Committee, 1962-65; General Manager, WHA-TV, University of Wisconsin at Madison, 1962-65; Instructor, Assistant Professor, Associate Professor and Associate Director of Mass Communications, Wayne State University, 1952-62; General Manager, Radio Station WDET, Wayne State University, 1952-56; Instructor, University of Wisconsin at Madison, 1949-52. Organizational Memberships: Phi Beta Kappa; Phi Eta Sigma; Phi Kappa Phi; Phi Tau Phi; (while Governor) National Governor's Association, Republican Governor's Association, Vice Chairman of Midwestern Governor's Association, Member Board of Directors and Co-Chairman of National Committee of American Energy Week Inc. Community Activities: American Association of State Colleges and Universities, Board of Directors, Member Exchange Mission to Poland 1973, The People's Republic of China 1975, Taiwan 1976; Army Command Sergeants Major Academy, Board of Advisors; Association of the United States Army, Advisory Board of Directors; National Advisory Panel on Army R.O.T.C. Affairs, Chairman 1969-73; Former Member, National Association of Educational Broadcasters; Speech Association of America's Radio/TV/Film Division, Chairman 1964-65; Council of Chancellors, University of Wisconsin System, Chairman 1965; Council of Presidents of Wisconsin State University, Past President; Governor's Blue Ribbon Committee on Cable Communication, 1971; Former Board Member, Winnebago Children's Home, Stevens Point Young Men's Christian Association, Stevens Point St. Michael's Hospital, Wisconsin Health Care Review Board, Wisconsin Ballet Company, Wisconsin Fine Arts Foundation; Former Chief of Mission under Vietnam Contract for Higher Education; Wisconsin State University at Stevens Point Foundation, Inc.; Educational Advisor to Secretary of the Army, 1970-73; Honorary Co-Chairperson, Wisconsin Special Olympics, 1983; Board of Trustees, Association for Public Broadcasting; American Legion; Veterans of Foreign Wars; Masons, 33rd Degree. Religion: Episcopalian. Published Works: Articles "Education of Eagles and Dragons — Education in the People's Republic of China" 1975, "The Ruropolitan Network" (chapter in *It's a Big Responsibility*), "The Development and Promise of Technology in Education" 1968, "The University Station" (chapter in *The Farther Vision: Educational Television Today*) 1967, "Televised Instruction" 1962. Honors and Awards: Distinguished Public Service Medal, Secretary of Defense; President's Medallion, Association of the United States Army; Cross of St. Luke (for outstanding contributions to Christian education); International Supreme Council of DeMolay's Legion of Honor. Address: P.O. Box 1776, Stevens Point, Wisconsin 54481.■

JOHN NELSON DROWATZKY

Professor, Author. Personal: Born April 11, 1936; Son of Minnie Drowatzky; Married Linnea Louise Swanson, Daughter of Mr. and Mrs. Kenneth J. Swanson; Father of Kara Louise, Katrina Leigh. Education: B.S., University of Kansas, 1957; M.S. 1962, University of Oregon; J.D., University of Toledo, 1979. Military: Served in the United States Army, 1958-60, attaining the rank of Lieutenant. Career: Administrative Officer, Missile Systems Instructor, Member VIP Briefing Team, United States Army Air Defense School, 1958-60; Teacher and Coach, Enterprise School South (Wichita, Kansas), 1961-62; Director of Physical Education for Brain-Injured Children, Institute of Logopedics (Wichita), 1962-63; Teaching Assistant, University of Oregon, 1963-65; Assistant Professor 1965-68, Associate Professor 1968-71, Professor 1971 to present, Department Chairman 1972-76, University of Toledo. Organizational Memberships: American Alliance for Health, Physical Education, Recreation and Dance, Program Chairman, Research Council, Resource Fellow; American Academy of Physical Education, Editor of Newsletter; Ohio Alliance of Health, Physical Education and Recreation, Section Chairman; Toledo Bar Association; Ohio Bar Association; American Bar Association; Phi Epsilon Kappa; Phi Delta Kappa. Community Activities: Citizen's Advisory Board, Northwest Ohio Development Center, 1980 to present; Consultant for Various School Districts; Consultant, United Cerebral Palsy Foundation of Northwest Ohio, 1973-74; Advocate for Children with Learning Disabilities, 1979 to present; Camping Committee, Lucas County Association for Retarded Persons, 1977-81; Consultant, Aging Programs for Rotary Club of Fremont (Ohio), Toledo (Ohio) and the Toledo Young Men's Christian Association, 1975-81; Education Committee, American Trauma Association of Northwest Ohio, 1975-79; Education Committee, American Heart Association of Northwest Ohio, 1983 to present; Partners of the Americas Volunteer to Parana, Brazil (regarding education and rehabilitation for the handicapped), 1981; Consultant, Lucas County Association for Mentally Retarded Persons, 1966 to present. Religion: Hope Lutheran Church, Council Member 1970-76, President 1971-73, Christian Education Committee 1966-72, 1976-78, Social Ministry Committee 1973-76, Stewardship Committee 1982-84. Honors and Awards: Faculty Research Fellowship, University of Toledo, 1968; Certificate of Recognition, Lucas County Association for Mentally Retarded Persons, 1970; Hope Anchor Plaque for Service at Hope Lutheran Church, 1974; Adjunct Professor, University of Oregon, 1976; Corpus Juris Secundum Award for Significant Legal Scholarship, 1978; American Academy of Physical Education, 1983; Listed in *Who's Who in the Midwest, Men of Achievement, International Who's Who of Contemporary Achievement, Personalities of America, Community Leaders of the World*. Address: 3332 Brantford Road, Toledo, Ohio 43606.■

MARION DROZDZIEL

Personal: Born December 21, 1924, in Dunkirk, New York; Son of Stephen (deceased) and Veronica Drozdziel; Married Rita L. Korwek, August 30, 1952; Father of Eric. Education: Graduate of Dunkirk High School, 1942; Studies in Aeronautical Engineering, Tri-State University; B.S. Aeronautical Engineering, B.S. Mechanical Engineering; Advanced Courses in Structures, Ohio State University; Liberal Arts Studies, Niagara University; Work Towards M.S. in Mechanical Engineering, University of Buffalo. Military: Served in the United States Army; Attended Artillery Surveying School, Communications School, Naval Gunfire and Liaison School, Criminal Investigation School; Special Agent, Military C.I.D. and Philippine Government, 1945-46. Career: Structural Engineer, Curtiss Wright Corporation, 1948; Structural Engineer 1949, Assistant Supervisor 1960, Chief of Stress Analysis Propulsion Section 1964, Chief Engineer for Stress and Weights 1979 to present, Bell Aircraft Corporation. Organizational Memberships: American Institute of Aeronautics and Astronautics, Governing Council of Niagara Frontier Section, Past Vice Chairman of Education; Air Force Association; American Management Association; Society of Reliability Engineers; American Space Foundation; American Association for the Advancement of Science; The Planetary Society; International Society of Allied Weight Engineers; U.S. Naval Institute. Community Activities: Bell Management Club; Quarter Century Club; The Nature Conservancy; National Audubon Society; The Cousteau Society; American Academy of Political and Social Science; The Academy of Political Science; Union of Concerned Scientists; The Smithsonian Associates; Biblical Archeology Society; Archeological Institute of America. Honors and Awards: Commendation from N.A.S.A. for Work on Apollo Program, 1972; U.K. Commendation of Achievement on N.A.T.O. Program, 1982. Address: 152 Linwood Avenue, Tonawanda, New York 14150.■

CARL EDWIN DUNCAN

Attorney at Law. Personal: Born February 28, 1899; Son of Henry H. and Marian E. Duncan (both deceased); Married Ann Lee, Daughter of Oliver J. and Margaret Farmer (both deceased); Father of Margaret Ann Robertson, James Robert, Carl Michael. Education: LL.B., University of Florida, 1923. Military: Served in the United States Army, 1918. Career: Attorney at Law; Service as County Prosecuting Attorney, County Attorney, City Attorney, Member of Florida Legislature. Organizational Memberships: Board of Governors, Florida Bar Association; American Bar Association. Community Activities: President, Kiwanis Club, 1925. Religion: Methodist Church, Choir Director 1930-60. Address: 317 East Main, Tavares, Florida 32778.■

TWO THOUSAND NOTABLE AMERICANS

ESTELLE CECILIA DIGGS DUNLAP

Educator and Administrator. Personal: Born September 26, 1912; Daughter of John F. and Mary F. Diggs (deceased); Married Lee Alfred Dunlap; Mother of Gladys C. D. Kimbrough, Dolly A. D. Sparkman. Education: B.S.; M.S. Career: Visiting Lecturer of Mathematics, D.C. Teachers College; Mathematics-Science Instructor, Macfarland Junior High School, 1956-72; Instructor and Head of Mathematics Department, Garnet-Patterson Junior High School, 1941-56. Organizational Memberships: National Council of Teachers of Mathematics; American Mathematical Society; Vice President, Benjamin Banneker Mathematics Club; American Association for the Advancement of Science; National Defense Preparedness Association; National Education Association; American Association of University Women; Howard University Alumni Association; National Retired Teachers Association. Community Activities: Smithsonian Resident Association; Recording Secretary, Northwest Boundary Civic Association, 1964-69; American Museum of Natural History; International Platform Association; Founding Member, The National Historical Society; Washington Educational Television Association; National Urban League; Treasurer, Petworth Block Club; American Society of Distinguished Citizens; Marquis Biographical Library Society; Advisory Board, American Security Council; Charter Member, Republican Congressional Club; National Trust for Historical Preservation; United Nations Association U.S.A.; Foreign Policy Research Institute; National Archives Association; Academy of Political Science; Institute for American Strategy; International Institute for Community Service; Charter Citizen Member, National Police and Firefighters Association; Church Women United; American Film Institute; Boys and Girls Clubs of Metropolitan Police, D.C.; The Salvation Army Association; Charter Member, Washington Performing Arts Society; Fellow, International Biographical Association; Founding Member, United States Senatorial Club; Arena Stage Association; National Symphony Orchestra Association; Metropolitan Opera-Guild Washington Opera; United States Olympic Society; American Council for the Arts; Friends of the Kennedy Center; American Police Academy; Campaigner Member, Republican National Committee, 1980; Life Member, American Biographical Institute Research Association; New York City Opera Guild; American Association of University Women; National Association of Negro Musicians; Brunswick Bowling Clubhouse; National Council of Senior Citizens; Honorary Fellow, Anglo-American Academy; Colonial Williamsburg Foundation; Wolf Trap Association; The Winterthur Guild. Religion: Roman Catholic; St. Gabriel's Church. Honors and Awards: National Science Foundation Fellowship, 1959-62; Certificates of Award, United States School of Music, Library of Human Resources of the American Bicentennial Research Institute; Certificates of Appreciation, Superior Court of the District of Columbia, United States District Court, Institute for American Strategy, Young America's Foundation; Certificate of Merit, Editorial and Advisory Board of *Dictionary of International Biography*; Diploma of Honor, Advisory Board of *International Who's Who in Community Service*. Address: 719 Shepherd Street Northwest, Washington, D.C. 20011.■

CHARLETA J. DUNN

Professor. Personal: Born January 18, 1927; Daughter of Ruby Rice; Married Roy E. Dunn; Mother of Thomas Arthur, Roy E., III, Sharleta Elaine. Education: B.S. 1951, M.Ed. 1954, West Texas University; Ed.D., University of Houston, 1966; Postdoctorate Work (Clinical), University of Texas Medical Branch, 1970. Career: Professor, Texas Woman's University Department of Psychology, 1974 to present; Director of Appraisal, Baytown Independent School District, 1971-74; Assistant Professor of Counseling, University of Houston, 1966-69; Teacher, Amarillo Public Schools, 1953-62. Organizational Memberships: Southwestern Psychology Association, 1966 to present; American Psychology Association, 1966 to present; Texas Psychology Association, 1966 to present; American School Psychologists, 1979 to present. Community Activities: Guest Speaker, Parent-Teacher Association, Language Learning Disabilities Association; Television Talk Show Presenter on Subject of Brainwashing and Other Topics. Religion: Protestant; Workshops in Family Therapy. Honors and Awards: Research Grants, Gusreda Fellowship 1964-65, Hogg Foundation for Mental Health 1966-70; Workshop Grants, Department of Health 1970-74, Education and Welfare, Regional Education Service Center #3 1970-74 and #4 1978-79. Address: 300 Oak Drive, Friendswood, Texas 77546.■

KATHRYN JOYCE DUPREE

Retired Captain, United States Army. Personal: Born April 22, 1940; Daughter of Gordon P. Dupree, Sr. and Sara W. Booth. Education: Graduate with honors, Alameda High School, 1958; A.A., Merritt College, 1967; Certificate, American Institute of Banking, 1962; B.A., University of California at Berkeley, 1969; Diploma, Women's Army Corps Basic Officer Course, Ft. McClellan, Alabama, 1969; Diploma with honors, Chemical, Biological, Radiological Instructor Course, Ft. Gordon, Georgia, 1970; Diploma and Honor Graduate, Military Police Officer Advanced Course, Correctional Administration Course, Civil Disturbance Orientations Course, Security Management Course, all from the United States Army Military Police School; Certificate, Safe and Burglary Investigator's Seminar, 1977; Certificate/Diploma, St. Louis University School of Medicine; B.S. Physician Assistant Program, George Washington University School of Medicine, 1984; Further Courses, University of Colorado and Denver University. Military: Served with the United States Army, achieving the Rank of Captain in the Military Police Corps; Retired 1978. Career: Newspaper Route Captain, 1955-58; Cashier, Clerk, American Embassy Commissary, Tehran, Iran, 1958-59; Accounting Clerk, Navy Exchange Accounting Office, Alameda, California, 1959-60; Laboratory Assistant, Borden Laboratories, 1961; Head Resident, Westminster House, Presbyterian Student Center, University of California, Summer 1961; Loan Clerk, Computer Reconcilor, Bank of America, 1962-66; Intensive Care Unit Technician, Kaiser Foundation Hospital, Oakland, 1966-69; Corporal Cadet, W.A.C. College Junior Program, United States Army, Summer 1968; Student Officer, First Lieutenant, Officer Training Detachment, United States Women's Army Corps School and Center, Ft. McClellan, 1969; Executive Officer, Headquarters Company, W.A.C., United States Army School Training Center, Ft. Gordon, 1969-71; Battery Commander, W.A.C. Battery, Ft. Sill, Oklahoma, 1972-73; Recruiting and Induction Officer/Coordinator of Project A.H.E.A.D., United States Army District Recruiting Command, Minneapolis, 1973-76; Student, Military Police Officer Advanced Course, United States Army Military Police School, Ft. McClellan, 1976; Provost Marshal/Chief, Security Office, Tripler Army Medical Center, Health Services Command, Hawaii, 1976-77; Patient-Fitzsimons Army Medical Center, Denver, 1977-78; Temporary Disability Retired List, United States Army, 1978-82; Retired Captain, United States Army; Retired Provost Marshal, United States Army. Organizational Memberships: International Association of Chiefs of Police; Hawaiian Joint Police Officers Association; International Academy of Criminology; American Law Enforcement Officers Association; National Council on Crime and Delinquency; Child Protection and Case Management Team (law enforcement representative); Association of the United States Army; Life Member, Disabled American Veterans; American Institute of Banking; Retired Officers Association; American Association for the Advancement of Science. Community Activities: American Association of University Women; California Alumni Association, University of California at Berkeley; Veterans of Foreign Wars Auxiliary #939; Tower and Flame Honor Society, University of California at Berkeley; Alpha Gamma Sigma; Merritt College Judicial Council, Judge, 1966-67; Pre-Medical Society, University of California at Berkeley, Editor, Treasurer, 1960-63, 1967-69; Acorn Yearbook, Administrative Editor, 1957-58; Big Sister Program, Lawton, Oklahoma, Co-Founder and Council Member 1971-73; Lawton Tutorial Program, Co-Founder and Council Member, 1971-73; Chemistry Club, President, Editor, Treasurer; California Scholarship Federation, Life Member; Star and Key Honor Society, Life Member; Volunteer Reader for the Blind, University of California at Berkeley, 1960-62, 1967-69; California State Junior College Area 7, Representative for Merritt College, 1965-67; Merritt College Bond Raising Committee; Merritt College Glee Club; Merritt College Marching Band; Merritt College Orchestra; California School for the Deaf; Kaiser Hospital, Volunteer Worker; Armed Forces Day Parade Committee, Lawton, Oklahoma; Human Relations Council, Ft. Sill, Oklahoma; Girls Association, Alameda, California; Girls Athletic Association, Alameda; National Education Association; American Association for the Advancement of Science; Delegate to American Academy of Physician Assistants, Army Society of Physician Assistants. Religion: Fitzsimons Army Medical Center Chapel, Choir Director, 1977-78; Bay Farm Island Baptist Mission, Sunday School Teacher 1960-68, Superintendent, Choir Director. Honors and Awards: Gold Pin, 1954; First Chair Viola, California State Competition, 1955; Life Member, California Scholarship Federation and Star and Key Honor Society, 1958; Certificate of Excellence, Navy Exchange Accounting Office, 1960; Delta Zeta Award, 1961; Award for Efficiency Study, Bank of America, 1965; Faculty Scholarship Award, Merritt College, 1966; Irene Purington Scholarship Award, University of California at Berkeley, 1967; Distinguished Graduate of the Women Officers Basic Course and Letter of Commendation, 1969; Graduate Parade Commander, 1969; National Service Defense Medal 1969, Army Commendation Medal 1971, Army Commendation Medal with First Oak Leaf Cluster 1973, Army Commendation Medal with Second Oak Leaf Cluster 1976, United States Army; Marksman Badge, Military Police School, 1976; Listed in *World Who's Who of Women, Who's Who in American Law Enforcement, Book of Honor, Community Leaders and Noteworthy Americans, Personalities of America, International Register of Profiles, International Who's Who of Intellectuals.* Address: 2138 Alameda Avenue, Alameda, California 94501.■

JOAN MICHELE DURKIS

Professor. Personal: Born March 29, 1945; Daughter of Charles and Eleanor Chaffin; Mother of James Charles, Jerry Michael. Education: A.A.S. with highest honors, Onondaga College, 1974; B.S. with highest honors, State University of New York, 1976; M.Ed. with highest honors 1978, Ed.S. with highest honors 1980, Ed.D. with

highest honors 1982, Florida Atlantic University; Licensed Registered Professional Nurse; Certified as Coronary Care Nurse; Certified by the American Association of Critical Care Nurses in Critical Care Nursing; Teacher's Certificate in Postgraduate Nursing Education. Career: University Professor, King Abdulaziz Univerity, Jeddah, Saudi Arabia; Former Positions include Education Consultant for National Medical Enterprises, Coordinator/Instructor of Advance Medical/Surgical Nursing at Broward Community College, Assistant Professor at Palm Beach Junior College, Charge Nurse at North Broward Hospital Conorary Care Unit, Assistant to the Director at Metropolitan Miami-Dade County's Addiction Treatment Agency and Division of Addiction Sciences in the University of Miami School of Medicine, Administrator of License Divisions of Personnel Department at GAC Properties, Inc. Organizational Memberships: Association for Supervision and Curriculum Development, 1979; American Association of University Professors, 1979; American Association of Critical Care Nurses, 1980; National League for Nurses, 1982; American Society of Allied Health Professions, 1982; American College of Hospital Administrators, 1983. Honors and Awards: Honor Society of Phi Kappa Phi; Listed in *International Who's Who in Education, Who's Who in the South and Southwest, Directory of Distinguished Americans*. Address: 7800 Cardinal Road, Coral Springs, Florida 33065.■

SHELDON M. DYBSAND

Businessman. Personal: Born January 25, 1922, in Two Harbor, Minnesota; Son of Henry and Olga Magnuson Gimpel (mother deceased); Married Donna L.; Father of Eric, Sheryl, Dotta Dee. Education: Graduate, Sacred Heart Public High School, Sacred Heart, Minnesota, 1940; Completed Two Year College G.E.D., 1952; Completed Third Year of College, Parkland College, 1977. Military: Served in the United States Army Air Corps and Air Force, 1942-63, attaining the rank of Master Sergeant. Career: Farm Hand until 1940; Set-up and Supervisor, Cabinet Hardware Manufacture, Rockford, Illinois, 1940-42; Quality Control Inspector, C-141 Wing Assembly Department, Avco Aerospace, Nashville, Tennessee, 1963-65; Electrical and Mechanical Instructor 1965-66, GS-7 Training Instructor 1966, Missile Ordance Center, Redstone Arsenal, Huntsville, Alabama; Enginering Technical Services Representative of Propulsion Systems for the Tactical Air Command on C-130 Aircraft; Technical Instructor in Training School, Chanute Air Force Base, Illinois; Block Supervisor of Block III of B-52 Training Source until 1977; Certified Master Instructor; Retired 1977; Owner/Operator, Small Engine Service (part-time). Community Activities: Legislative Committee, Clay County Chapter #1890, National Association of Retired Federal Employees, 1982 to present; Boy Scouts of America, Assistant Leader 1968-69, Explorer Scout Chairman 1969-70; Tennessee Association of Rescue Squad Services; Clay County Civitan Club, 1977-78; Clay County-Dale Hollow Chamber of Commerce 1978-80; Clay County Rescue Squad, Squad Training Sergeant 1978-82, Attended and Certifed as Vehicle Extrication Instructor 1979. Honors and Awards: Meritorious Service Award, United States Army Air Force, 1945; State of Illinois Service Recognition Certificate; Citation for Meritorious Service from Governor Dwight H. Green, 1947; Lockheed Aircraft Certificate, 1000 Hour Club, 1959; Lockheed C-130 2000 Hour Club Certificate, 1962; Good Conduct Ribbon with One Silver Knot, Awarded 6 Times 1942-63; Air Force Commendation Medal for Meritorious Achievement, 1958; Air Force Commendation Medal for Meritorious Service, 1962-63; Presidential Unit Citation, Department of United States Air Force, Air Force Outstanding Unit Award, 1955; Special Act or Service Award for Special Services Accomplished, 1969-70; 10 Year Certificate of Service, 1970; 20 Year Certificate of Service, 1976; Master Instructor Certificate Award, 1976; Non-Commissioned Officer's Association Life Member Certificate 1973, Lifetime Membership Certificate 1973, Permanent Trustee Life Certificate 1974; Special Olympics Program, Cardinal Chapter (State of Illinois) Certificate of Achievement 1975, N.C.O.A. and Joseph R. Kennedy Jr. Foundation Special Olympics Certificate of Appreciation 1975; Tennessee Association of Rescue Squads and Emergency Medical Services Vehicle Extraction Instructor Certificate, 1979; Recreation Resources Management Branch of the Nashville District Corps of Engineers Certificate of Appreciation for Assistance in the 1979 Orientating Course at Dale Hollow Lake, 1979; Jackson County Rescue Squad Citation for Training Performed in Vehicle Rescue Class Recertification, 1982; Federal Emergency Management Agency Emergency Management Institute Ceriticate in Radiological Monitoring Course, 1982. Address: Rural Route 3, Box 217, Celina, Tennessee 38551.■

DE WITT S. DYKES, JR.

Educator, Administrator. Personal: Born January 2, 1938; Son of Rev. and Mrs. De Witt S. Dykes, Sr.; Married Marie Draper, Daughter of Hattie Draper Hall; Father of Laura Marie Christine. Education: B.A., Fisk University, 1960; M.A., University of Michigan, 1961; Ph.D. Candidate, University of Michigan. Career: Associate Professor of History 1973 to present, Coordinator of Afro-American Studies 1975-83, Dean's Assistant for Affirmative Action 1975-78, Assistant Professor 1969-73, Oakland University; Instructor, American Thought and Language, Michigan State University, 1965-69. Organizational Memberships: National Advisory Council, Institute of the Black World, 1977 to present; Consultant (Adjunct Faculty) to School of Public Health, University of South Carolina; Board of Editors, *Detroit in Perspective: A Journal of Regional History*, 1978 to present; Book Review Editor, *Journal of the Afro-American Historical and Genealogical Society*, 1981 to present; Vice-Chairman 1980-82, Chairman 1982 to present, Historic Designation Advisory Board, City of Detroit; President, Fred Hart William Genealogical Society, 1980 to present. Community Activities: Board of Trustees 1974-77, Chairman Research and Exhibit Committee 1974, Afro-American Museum of Detroit; Advisory Committee, Pontiac Ethnic Studies Center; Board of Trustees, Historical Society of Michigan, 1983 to present. Honors and Awards: Phi Beta Kappa; Woodrow Wilson Graduate Fellow, 1960-61; Danforth Graduate Fellow, 1960-65; Alpha Phi Alpha Graduate Fellow, 1963-64; Received One of Six Awards for Excellence in Teaching and Outstanding Contributions to Black Students, Oakland University, 1980. Address: History Department, Oakland University, Rochester, Michigan 48063.■

THOMAS CAPPER EAKIN

Sports Promotion Executive. Personal: Born December 16, 1933, in New Castle, Pennsylvania; Son of Frederick William and Beatrice Capper Eakin (both deceased); Married Brenda Lee Andrews, October 21, 1961; Father of Thomas Andrews, Scott Frederick. Education: B.A. History, Denison University, 1956. Military: Served in the United States Army, 1956-58, attaining the rank of Specialist 4th Class. Career: Life Insurance Consultant, Northwestern Mutual Life Insurance Company (Cleveland, Ohio), 1959-67; Regional Director of Sales, Empire Life Insurance Company of Ohio, 1967-68; District Manager, Putman Publishing Company (Cleveland), 1968-69; Regional Business Manager, Chilton Publishing Company, 1969-70; District Manager, Hitchcock Publishing Company (Cleveland), 1970-72; President, TCE Enterprises (Shaker Heights, Ohio), 1973 to present; Founder, President, Golf International 100 Club, 1970 to present; Founder, Director, Cy Young Museum, 1975-80; Founder, Director, "TRY," Target/Reach Youth, 1971 to present; Founder, Director, Interact Club of Shaker Heights, 1971 to present; Founder, President, Ohio Baseball Hall of Fame, 1976 to present; Founder, President, Ohio Baseball Hall of Fame "Celebration," 1977-79. Community Activities: Shaker Heights Rotary, International Student Exchange Program, United States and Canada, Founder and Chairman 1965-70; Shaker Heights Rotary Club, President 1970-71, Vice President 1969-70, Secretary 1964-65, Board of Directors 1963, 1965, 1968 and 1972; Phi Delta Theta Alumni Club of Cleveland, President 1970, Vice President 1969, Board of Directors 1971-75; Phi Delta Theta National Fraternity; Cleveland Council on Corrections, 1971-73; Cuyahoga Hills Boys School, Advisory Board 1971 to present; Camp Hope, Advisory Board 1973 to present; Cleveland Indians Old Timers Committee, 1966-67; Cy Young Centennial, Organizer and National Chairman 1967; Cy Young Golf Invitational, Founder, National Chairman 1967-79; Tuscarawas County American Revolution Bicentennial Commission, Executive Committee 1974-76; Intercontinental Biographical Association, Fellow 1973; Tuscarawas County Old Timers Baseball Association, Honorary Director 1972 to present; National Lou Gehrig Award Committee, Phi Delta Theta, Executive Committee 1975 to present; Newcomerstown Sports Corporation, Trustee 1975-80; Wahoo Club, Board of Directors 1975; Tuscarawas County Historical Society, Trustee 1978-81; Shaker Heights Youth Center Inc., Board Member 1975; Fitness Evaluation Services Inc., Advisory Board 1977-79; International Platform Association, Member 1978 to present; World Golf Hall of Fame (Pinehurst, North Carolina), Ohio Executive Sponsor Chairman 1979 to present; Tuscarawas Valley Tourist Association, Director 1979-81; Ohio Iota, Phi Delta Theta, Denison University Chapter, Trustee 1979-82; Buckeye Tourist Association, Director 1979-80; The Shaker Historical Society, Trustee 1980-82; Portage County Sports Hall of Fame, Advisory Board 1983 to present; New Hope Records, Board of Directors 1984 to present. Religion: First Baptist Church of Greater Cleveland, Board Member 1966-69. Honors and Awards: Presidential Commendation, President Richard M. Nixon, 1973; State of Ohio Commendation, Governor James A. Rhodes 1968 and 1975, Governor John J. Gilligan 1972; Baseball Commissioner Commendation, William D. Eckert, 1967; Baseball Commendation, *The Sporting News*, 1968; Citation of Merit, Louisiana Stadium and Exposition District, Louisiana Superdome, 1972; Civic Service Award, Cuyahoga Hills Boys School, 1970; Commendation Award, Cy Young Centennial Committee, 1967; Tuscarawas County (Ohio) Chamber of Commerce Commendation, 1967; Newcomerstown (Ohio) Chamber of Commerce Commendation, 1967; Sport Service Award, *Sport Magazine*, 1969; Outstanding Young Rotarian Award, Shaker Heights Rotary Club, 1962; Appreciation Award, Phi Delta Theta Alumni Club of Cleveland, 1975; Ohio Senate Commendation Award, Ohio Senate, 1976, 1979; Ohio American Revolution Bicentennial Advisory Commission Commendation, 1976; Tuscarawas County American Revolution Bicentennial Commission, Certificate of Merit 1976; American Revolution Bicentennial Administration Appreciation Award, 1977; State of Louisiana Certificate of Merit, 1978; Founder's Award, "TRY," 1979; Elected to the Chautauqua Sports Hall of Fame, Chautauqua County, New York, 1983; Honorary Director, Chautauqua Sports Hall of Fame, 1982; Listed in *Who's Who in America, Men of Achievement, Dictionary of International Biography, Community Leaders of America, International Who's Who in Community Service, Who's Who in Ohio, Two Thousand Men of Achievement, Outstanding Young Men of America, Who's Who in the United States, Who's Who in the Midwest, Personalities of America.* Address: 2729 Shelley Road, Shaker Heights, Ohio 44122. ∎

SAID MOHAMED EASA

Associate Professor of Civil Engineering. Personal: Born January 28, 1949; Son of Mohamed and Monirah Easa, Cairo, Egypt. Education: B.S.C.E., Cairo University, 1972; M.Eng. Transportation, McMaster University, 1976; Ph.D. Civil Engineering, University of California at Berkeley, 1981. Career: Instructor, Cairo University, 1972-74; Research and Teaching Assistant, McMaster University, 1974-76; Research Engineer, McMaster University, 1976-78; Research Assistant, Institute of Transportation Studies, University of California at Berkeley, 1978-81; Project Engineer, Ministry of Transportation and Communications, Ontario, Canada, 1982; Associate Professor of Civil Engineering, Lakehead University (Ontario). Organizational Memberships: Association of Professional Engineers; Institute of Transportation Engineers, President Berkeley Student Chapter 1980-81; Association of Egyptian Civil Engineers, 1972-74. Community Activities: Committee on Traffic-Flow Theory and Characteristics of the Transportation Research Board 1978-84, Chairman of Subcommittee on Goals and Objectives 1980-84; Student Representative, Institute of Transportation Studies at Berkeley, 1980-81. Published Works: Author of Numerous Papers and Research Reports, including a Book Review. Honors and Awards: Winner, Student Paper Competition, Institute of Transportation Engineers, Western United States and Canada, 1979 and 1981; McMaster Graduate Fellowship, 1974, 1975; Distinction with Honor, B.S., 1972; Author Numerous Papers and Research Reports; Listed in *Who's Who in the West, Personalities of America, International Book of Honor, Five Thousand Personalities of the World.* Address: 625 Fulton Blvd., Apt. 310, Thunder Bay, Ontario P7B 6A8, Canada. ∎

MARY L. EASTLAND

Theater Manager, Publisher. Personal: Born July 3, 1939; Daughter of James DeWitt Sr. and Mary Belle White; Mother of Charles Lamar Jr., James Denson, Laura Lynette. Education: B.S.E., Delta State University, 1961; Graduate Study undertaken at the University of Southern Mississippi, 1978. Career: Manager, Norwood Village Cinema, 1983-; Owner, Top-Flite Publishers, 1983-; Teacher, Harrison County School System (Gulfport, Mississippi), 1978-82; Business Owner, Bresler's 33 Flavors (Gulfport), 1974-76; Civil Service, I.R.S., 1963-65; Teacher, El Paso, Texas, 1961-62. Organizational Memberships: Beta Sigma Phi, Nu Delta Chapter, Member 1967-68, President 1968; Mississippi Association of Educators, 1978-82. Community Activities: Community and Youth Services, 1970-82; Gulf Pines Girl Scout Council; Orange Grove Youth Association; Northwood Hills Garden Club; Optimist Club of Gulfport; Orange Grove Optimist Club; Orange Grove Junior Chamber of Commerce; Orange Grove Girls Softball League; March of Dimes; Heart Fund. Religion: Baptist. Honors and Awards: Life Fellow, American Biographical Institute Research Association; Beta Sigma Phi Girl of the Year, 1968; President, Women's Honor Council, Delta State University, 1960-61; Listed in *Who's Who Among American Women, Personalities of America, Personalities of the South.* Address: 10 Edington Place, Gulfport, Mississippi 39503. ∎

A. REGINALD EAVES

County Commissioner, Lawyer. Personal: Born in Jacksonville, Florida; Son of Cecil and Gladys Eaves. Education: B.A., Morehouse College, 1956; Law Degree, New England Law School; Further Studies undertaken at Boston University and Atlanta University. Career: Former Administrator in Mayor's Office of Human Rights in Boston, Commissioner of Penal Institutions for Boston and Suffolk County, Teacher and Counselor in Boston's Pubic School System and Lecturer at the School of Medicine of Boston University, Executive Director of Roxbury Youth Training and Employment Center, Executive Director of Boston's South End Neighborhood Action Program; Executive Assistant to Mayor of Atlanta (Georgia), 1974; Appointed Atlanta's First Commissioner of Public Safety, 1974 (established Domestic Crisis Intervention Program, Police Chaplaincy Program, Criminal Justice Information Gathering and Retrieval Mechanism, T.H.O.R.); Elected to Fulton County Board of Commissioners, 1976 (chairman two years). Honors and Awards: Spirit of Atlanta Award; Young Man of Year Award; Distinguished Service Award; National Exchange Club Award for Crime Prevention. Address: 1158 Cardinal Way, Atlanta, Georgia 30311. ∎

MARY BEATY EDELEN

State Representative. Personal: Born December 9, 1944; Daughter of Mr. and Mrs. D. W. Beaty; Married Joseph R. Edelen, Jr.; Mother of Audra, Angelica, Anthony, Callaghan, Jarrod Arthur. Education: Attended Coffey College, 1963-64; B.A., University of South Dakota, 1967; Attended Trinity University, 1967-68; M.A., 1971. Career: South Dakota House of Representatives, 1972-81, 1983-85; Lecturer, Department of History, University of South Dakota; Lecturer, Department of Social Sciences, Yankton College. Organizational Memberships: National Order of Women Legislators, Vice President; South Dakota/National Women's Political Caucus, Past State Chairperson. Community Activities: Southeastern Council of Governments, Executive Board 1976 to present; Foster Care Task Force, Department of Social Services for the State of South Dakota; Clay County Republican Party, Vice Chairman 1981-85; South Dakotans for Modern Courts, Secretary 1973 to present; University of South Dakota Alumni Association, Recorder; Zeta Phi Eta. Religion: United Church of Christ. Honors and Awards: Grace Burgess Book Award, 1965. Address: 311 Canby Street, Vermillion, South Dakota 57069.■

ANGELA L. EDWARDS

Personal: Born October 23, in Biddeford, Maine; Married H. T. Edwards (deceased); Mother of Betti Lou Gilliam, James Robert Gilliam (deceased), John Harold Gilliam, Glenn Richard Gilliam. Education: Studies in Italy, at the Metropolitan College of Los Angeles, at San Mateo Junior College, Shasta College Extension, U.C.L.A. Extension; Current Studies in Higher Divine Philosophy; Rose-Croix University, Esoteric Hierarchy, Rosicrucian Fraternal Order, Circle of Unknown Philosophers, Martinist Fraternal Order. Career: Ward Clerk, California Lutheran Hospital; Practical Nurse, Santa Fe Hospital; Practical Nurse, St. John Hospital, Longview, Washington; Executor of Husband's Estate and Clinic. Community Activities: Hospital "Pink Lady"; P.T.A., Chairman of Child Psychology Class and Health Chairman; Active in Medical Fund Raising Drives; Brownie Scout Leader; President, Home Arts Club; Westside Grange Club; Former Member, Federated Women's Club; National Geographic Society; Lecturer, Parents Without Partners; Lecturer and Talk Show Hostess (Radio) on Astrology; Christian Singles Activities. Religion: Episcopal Church Activities and Bible Studies. Honors and Awards: Honorary Member, American Biographical Institute Board of Advisors; Life Fellow, American Biographical Institute Research Association; Fellow, International Biographical Association; Associate Degree/Mystic Degree, Martinist Fraternal Order; Superior Degree/Esoteric Hierarchy, Rosicrucian Fraternal Order; Listed in *Community Leaders of America, Personalities of the West and Midwest, Biographical Roll of Honor, International Book of Honor, The Book of Honor, Personalities of America, International Who's Who of Intellectuals.* Address: 180 South Main Street #44, Red Bluff, California 96080.■

EILEEN M. EGAN

College President. Personal: Born January 11, 1925, in Boston, Massachusetts; Daughter of Eugene O. and Mary B. Condon Egan (both deceased). Education: B.A., Spalding University, 1956; M.A., The Catholic University of America, 1963; Institute of International Education Fellow, Oxford University, 1963 Ph.D., The Catholic University of America, 1966; Academic Administration Internship Program, Smith College, 1967-68; J.D., University of Louisville School of Law, 1981. Career: Secondary School Teacher and Administrator, 1956-63; Teacher, English Department, The Catholic University of America, 1963-66; Chairman, English Department, Spalding University, 1966-67; Administrative Intern, Smith College, 1967-68; Vice President 1968-69, President 1969 to present, Spalding University; Professor, University of Louisville Law School, 1982-83. Organizational Memberships: American Council on Education; Association of American Colleges; Council for the Advancement of Small Colleges; Council of Independent Colleges and Universities; Kentuckiana Metroversity; Kentucky Independent College Fund; Kentucky State Commission on Higher Education; National Catholic Education Association; Southern Association of Colleges and Schools; National Association of Independent Colleges and Universities; American Association for Higher Education; American Association of University Women; The English-Speaking Union, Kentucky Branch; Kentucky Bar Association; American Bar Association. Community Activities: Archdiocese of Louisville; Better Business Bureau of Greater Louisville; Federal Reserve Bank of St. Louis, Louisville Branch, Chairman 1982, 1984; Louisville Area Chamber of Commerce; Louisville Center City Commission; Louisville Central Area, Inc.; Louisville Committee on Foreign Relations; Louisville and Jefferson County Human Relations Commission; Louisville and Southern Indiana Chapter, National Conference of Christians and Jews; Louisville Unit of the Recording for the Blind; Louisville's Open Spaces and Advisory Committee; Metro United Way; Old Kentucky Home Council of the Boy Scouts of America; International Center, University of Louisville; St. Joseph Infirmary; Cultural Action Plan for Louisville and Jefferson County; Jefferson County Board of Education; Jewish Hospital, Board of Trustees; Mayor's Ethics Committee. Religion: Member of the Sisters of Charity of Nazareth. Honors and Awards: Board of Trustees Scholar, The Catholic University of America, 1963-66; Equality Award, Louisville Urban League, 1978; Blance B. Ottenheimer Award, Louisville Jewish Community Center, 1978; Brotherhood Award, National Conference of Christians and Jews, 1979; Phi Delta Kappa Award, 1979; Listed in *Biographical Directory of American Education, Personalities of America, Personalities of the South, The American Catholic Who's Who, The World Who's Who of Women, Who's Who in America, Who's Who in the U.S.A..* Address: 2511 River Bend Drive #15, Louisville, Kentucky 40206.■

ROBERT JOHN EGGERT

Economist. Personal: Born December 11, 1913, in Little Rock, Arkansas; Son of John and Eleanora Fritz Lapp; Married Elizabeth Bauer, November 28, 1935; Father of Robert John, Richard F., James E. Education: B.S., University of Illinois, 1935; M.S. 1936, Candidate in Philosophy 1938, University of Minnesota. Career: Research Analyst, Bureau of Agricultural Economics, United States Department of Agriculture, Urbana, Illinois, 1935; Principal Marketing Specialist, War Meat Board, U.S. Department of Agriculture, Chicago, Illinois, 1943; Research Analyst, University of Illinois 1935-36, University of Minnesota 1936-38; Assistant Professor of Economics, Kansas State College, 1938-41; Assistant Director of Marketing, American Meat Institute, Chicago, 1941-43; Economist, Association Director, American Meat Institute, 1943-50; Ford Division, Ford Motor Company, Dearborn, Michigan, Manager Department of Marketing Research 1951-53, Manager Program Planning 1953-54, Manager Business Research 1954-57, Manager Marketing Research Marketing Staff 1957-61, Manager Marketing Research Ford Division 1961-64, Manager International Marketing Research Marketing Staff 1964-65, Manager Overseas Marketing Research Planning 1965-66, Manager Marketing Research Lincoln-Mercury Division 1966-67; Director, Agri-business Program, Michigan State University, 1967-68; Staff Vice President of Economics and Marketing Research 1968-73, Staff Vice President and Chief Economist 1974-76, R.C.A. Corp, New York City; President, Chief Economist, Eggert Economics Enterprises, Inc., Sedona, Arizona, 1976 to present; Lecturer, Marketing, University of Chicago, 1947-49; Adjunct Professor, Business Forecasting, Northern Arizona University, 1976 to present; Economic Advisor Board, United States Department of Commerce, 1969-71; Census Advisor Committee, United States Department of Commerce, 1975-78; Panel Economic Advisors, Congressional Budget Office, 1975-76; Arizona Economic Estimates Commission, 1978 to present. Organizational Memberships: Council of International Marketing Research and Planning Directors, Chairman 1965-66; American Marketing Association, Director, Vice President 1949-50, President Chicago Chapter 1947-48, Vice President Marketing Management Division 1972-73, National President 1974-75; American Statistical Association, Chairman Business and Economic Statistics Section 1957 to present, President Chicago Chapter 1948-49; Federal Statistics Users Conference, Chairman Trustees 1960-61; Conference Business Economists, Chairman 1973-74; National Association of Business Economists, Council Member 1969-72; Arizona Economic Roundtable; American Farm Economics Association; American Economics Association; American Quarter Horse Association, Director 1966-73; Alpha Zeta. Community Activities: Republican; Poco Diablo Country Club. Religion: Congregationalist. Published Works: Contributor of Articles to Professional Publications; Editor of Monthly *Blue Chip Economic Indicators* and *Blue Chip Financial Forecasts.* Honors and Awards: Economic Forecast Award, Chicago Chapter, American Statistical Association, 1950, 1960, 1968; Seer of the Year Award, Harvard Business School of Industrial Economics, 1973; Listed in *Who's Who in the World.* Address: Schnebly Hill Road, P.O. Box 1569, Sedona, Arizona 86336.■

JON JOSEPH EICHE

Personnel Manager. Personal: Born January 23, 1938; Son of Mr. and Mrs. George O. Eiche; Married Evelyn Quintrell; Father of Jon Guinn, Keith David. Education: B.S. Business and Economics, East Tennessee State University, 1959; M.A. Government, Indiana University, 1966; Attended the U.S. Institute for Advanced Russian and East European Studies 1968 (Certified), Armed Forces Staff College 1975, Department of State Foreign Service Institute 1970. Career: Personnel Manager, Porelon Inc., 1979 to present; Professor of Military Science, Tennessee Technological University, 1976-79; Various Military Positions (United States Army). Organizational Memberships: American Society for Personnel Administration, President 1983; American Society for Training and Development. Community Activities: American Legion, Member 1976 to present, Commander Post 46 1980-81; Dean of Counselors 1979, Vice Chairman 1980-81, Chairman 1981-82,

Tennessee American Legion Boys State; Eagle Kountry Runners; National Rifle Association, Life Member; United States Olympic Committee, National Sports Festival 1981, Assistant Team Manager (Rifle); Omicron Delta Epsilon; Omicron Delta Kappa; Putnam County Family Young Men's Christian Association, Member 1978 to present, President 1980-81, Board of Directors 1979-85; Putnam County United Way, Board of Directors 1980-83; Rotary International; Sigma Phi Epsilon; Tennessee Tomorrow, Advisor to Governor Lamar Alexander's Program for Youth in the State of Tennessee 1979; Hospice of Cookeville, Staff Counselor 1981-82; International Foundation of Employee Benefit Plans; Tennessee Technological University School of Nursing Foundation Trustee; Tennessee Episcopal Churchmen, Middle Tennessee Vice President. Published Works: Co-Author, *American National Security: Policy and Process*. Honors and Awards: Bronze Star Medal, 1969; Meritorious Service Medal with Oak Leaf Cluster, 1969, 1979; Air Medal, 1968; Joint Service Commendation Medal, 1971; Army Commendation Medal, 1974; Vietnam Service Medal, 1968; National Defense Service Medal, 1959; Vietnam Cross of Gallantry with Gold Palm, 1969; Republic of Vietnam Campaign Medal with Five Stars, 1968, 1969; Korea Service Medal, 1976; Listed in *Who's Who Among Students in American Universities and Colleges, Who's Who in the South and Southwest, Personalities of the South*. Address: 1081 North Wall Avenue, Cookeville, Tennessee 38501.■

JEROME ALLAN EISNER

Executive Director. Personal: Born July 6, 1945; Son of Harold and Frieda Eisner; Married Eileen Dixon, Daughter of Joseph and Connie Dixon; Father of Elizabeth Ann, Kimberly Jinmee. Education: B.S., University of Wisconsin-Oshkosh, 1968; Education Certificate, Alverno College, 1970. Career: Teacher/Coach, St. Mary's School (Milwaukee) 1968-69, Pius XI High School (Milwaukee) 1969-71; Saleman, R. L. Polk Company (Kansas City), 1971-72; Audio-Visual Editor 1972-73, Technical Writer/Trainer 1973-76, Salesman/Sales and Marketing Administrator 1976-78, 3M Company (St. Paul); Program Developer, Golle and Holmes Corporation (Minneapolis), 1978-82; Executive Director, The United States Jaycees (Tulsa), 1982 to present. Organizational Memberships: American Family Society, National Advisory Board 1982; National Foundation for Volunteerism, Secretary 1982; American Society for Training and Development, Member 1978-82; Dynamics Association, 1978-82. Community Activities: Project Concern Minnesota, Board of Directors 1980-82; Minnesota Jaycees Charitable Foundation, Board of Directors 1980-82; School District 822 Long-Range Planning and Budget Study Committee, 1979-80; Cottage Grove Hazardous Waste Citizen's Committee, 1978; Washington County Adoptive Parents Association, President 1977-78; Southeast Minnesota Adoptive Parents Group, Director 1977-78; Hennepin County Audiovisual Technicians Advisory Committee, 1973-74; Cottage Grove Jaycees, Member 1975 to present, Vice President 1976-77; Minnesota Jaycees, State Program Manager 1976-77, District Director 1977-78, State President for Administration 1979-80, State President 1980-81, State Chairman of the Board 1981-82; United States Jaycees, Midwest Regional Individual Development Coordinator 1977-78, Trainer 1978-81; Jaycees International, Certified Trainer 1981-82. Religion: Youth Counselor 1973-75, Usher 1979-81. Honors and Awards: Ten Outstanding Young Men, 1968; Greek Man of the Year, 1968; Certificate of Merit, 3M Company's Chairman of the Board, 1975; Jaycees International Senator, 1980; U.S. Jaycess Ambassador, 1982; Minnesota Jaycees Statesman, 1981; U.S. Jaycees Clayton Frost Memorial Award Winner (One of Top Five State Presidents in the Nation), 1981. Address: 2200 West Quincy, Broken Arrow, Oklahoma 74012.■

KENNETH CLARENCE ELCHERT

Aerospace Engineer. Personal: Born August 3, 1949; Son of Mr. and Mrs. Frank Elchert; Married Celia Berumen, Daughter of Mrs. Maria Berumen; Father of John. Education: B.S.A.A.E., The Ohio State University, 1973; B.A. Math/Physics, St. Joseph College (Indiana), 1970. Career: Aerospace Engineer. Organizational Memberships: American Institute of Aeronautics and Astronautics; National Space Institute. Honors and Awards: N.A.S.A. Special Award, Approach and Landing Test Program, 1978; N.A.S.A Group Achievement Award, STS-1 Performance and Analysts Integration Team, 1981; Rockwell International Engineer for the Month, 1981; Listed in *Who's Who in the West*. Address: 353 East Carter Drive, Glendora, California 91740.■

HANS GEORG ELIAS

Consultant. Personal: Born March 29, 1928; Son of George Elias; Married Maria Hanke; Father of Peter C., Rainer M. Education: Dipl.Chem., Technical University of Hanover (Germany), 1954; Dr.rer.nat., Technical University of Munich (Germany), 1957; Habilitation, Swiss Federal Institute of Technology (Zurich), 1961. Military: Served in the German Armed Forces, 1944-45. Career: Science Advisor, The Dow Chemical Company; President, Michigan Molecular Institute. 1971-83; Faculty Member, Swiss Federal Institute of Technology, 1960-71; Staff Member, Technical University of Munich, 1956-59. Organizational Memberships: American Chemical Society, Chairman Polymer Nomenclature Committee; American Physical Society; German Chemical Society; Swiss Chemists Association; Bunsen Society for Physical Chemistry; Sigma Xi. Community Activities: Honorary Advisory Board, Midland Symphony Orchestra, 1978 to present; City of Midland Beautification Advisory Commission, 1979 to present. Address: 4009 Linden Drive, Midland, Michigan 48640.■

ELLA ELIZABETH PEARCE ELIZONDO

Associate Professor of Education. Personal: Born January 23, 1927; Daughter of Dr. and Mrs. Nicholas John Pearce (both deceased); Married Leonel Elizondo, Son of Mr. and Mrs. Federico Elizondo Jr. Education: B.S., University of Mary Hardin-Baylor, 1948; M.Ed., University of Houston, 1952; Ed.D., University of Houston, 1971. Career: Associate Professor of Education, Laredo State University; Former Public School Teacher in Arkansas, Missouri, Tennessee, Texas. Organizational Memberships: Association of Supervision and Curriculum Development; Texas Association for Gifted and Talented; Texas Society of College Teachers; Laredo Association for Education of Gifted and Talented Students, Vice President 1980-81. Community Activities: President, Board of Directors, Faith Academy (Laredo), 1980-81. Religion: Teacher of Sunday School, Baptist Churches, 1944-50. Honors and Awards: National Science Academic Year in Geology, 1968; Listed in *Who's Who in the South and Southwest, World Who's Who of Women*. Address: Box 3409, Zapata, Texas 78076.■

YVONNE KISSINGER ELLIE

Elementary School Principal. Personal: Born March 21, 1936; Daughter of Alfred and Louise Kissinger; Married Gene C. Ellie; Mother of Gregory, Jean Marie, Katherine, Daniel, David, Brian. Education: B.S., College of St. Teresa, 1958; M.S., University of Wisconsin-Stevens Point, 1978; Postgraduate Studies (work toward Ph.D.), University of Wisconsin at Madison, 1979 to present. Career: Elementary School Principal, Grove and Pitsch Elementary School; Administrative Intern, Grove & Pitsch Elementary School, 1979-80; Teacher, Mead, Howe, Woodside and West Jr. High School (Wisconsin Rapids) 1978-79, Vesper Elementary School 1967-78, Moses Lake (Washington) Public Schools 1958-59, Minneapolis Public Schools 1958. Organizational Memberships: Unified Bargaining Committee, Chairman Central Wisconsin Uniserve Council 1976-79; Wisconsin Rapids Teachers Association, Member 1967-69, President 1978-79, Bargaining Committee 1977-79; National Education Association, Member 1967-79; Wisconsin Education Association, 1967-79; International Reading Association and Wisconsin Reading Association, 1975-80; Central Wisconsin Reading Association; National Association of Elementary Principal; Wisconsin School Administrators Association; Association for Supervision and Curriculum Development; Phi Delta Kappa; Network for Outcome Based Schools; National Council of Teachers of English;

TWO THOUSAND NOTABLE AMERICANS

Wisconsin Math Council. Community Activities: League of Women Voters; Central Wisconsin Arts Council; Wood County Environmental Education Committee. Religion: Confraternity of Christian Doctrine, Teacher and Coordinator. Honors and Awards: Listed in *Who's Who in the Midwest*, *World Who's Who of Women*. Address: 5885A Elm Lake Lane, Wisconsin Rapids, Wisconsin 54494.■

RICHARD PATRICK ELLIS

Air Force Officer, Educator, Coach. Personal: Born November 20, 1944; Son of Mr. and Mrs. Patrick M. Ellis; Married Cecilia R., Daughter of Mr. and Mrs. Gilbert Gulley; Father of Scott R., Kent R. Education: B.S. Basic Sciences, United States Air Force Academy, 1968; M.S. Physical Education, Texas A&M University, 1973; Ph.D. Education, University of Denver, 1981. Military: Served in the United States Air Force, 1968 to present, currently holding rank of Major. Career: Educator/ Coach, Department of Athletics, United States Air Force Academy; Former Positions include Air Force Pilot, Exercise Physiologist, Academy Physical Education Instructor, Education Administrator and Intercollegiate Coach. Organizational Memberships: United States Air Force Academy Association of Graduates, Board of Directors 1975-79; American College of Sports Medicine; American Alliance for Health, Physical Education and Recreation; American Association of College Professors. Community Activities: Phi Epsilon Kappa; Phi Delta Kappa; Special Olympics for the Handicapped, Special Assistant; Officer Representative, Air Force Academy Fellowship of Christian Athletes; American Football Coaches Association; Air Force Association. Religion: Officer Representative, United States Air Force Academy Fellowship of Christian Athletes, 1973 to present. Honors and Awards: Dean's List, Commandant's List, Superintendent's List, United States Air Force Academy, 1968; Intercollegiate All-American (Pistol), 1968; Three United States Air Force Air Medals, 1971; United States Air Force Service Medal, 1979; Air Force Commendation Medal. Address: 2536 Legend Terrace, Colorado Springs, Colorado 80914.■

FREDERICK A. ELLISTON

Senior Research Associate. Personal: Born August 22, 1944; Son of Edna Elliston; Father of David Edmund, Deborah Ann. Education: B.A., Trinity College, 1967; Ph.D., University of Toronto, 1974. Career: Senior Research Associate, Illinois Institute of Technology; Criminal Justice Research Center/Police Foundation, 1980; School of Criminal Justice, State University of New York at Albany, 1978-80; Assistant Professor of Philosophy, Union College, 1972-78; Adjunct Instructor in the Humanities and Social Science, York University, 1970-72. Organizational Memberships: American Society of Criminologists; American Philosophical Association; American Legal Studies Association; Society for Phenomenology and Existential Philosophy; Husserl Circle; Heidegger Circle. Published Works: Philosophy Editor, *Criminal Justice Ethics*; Associate Editor, *Applied Philosophy*; Author Books *Sartre, Husserl: Shorter Works, Husserl: Expositions and Appraisals, Philosophy and Sex, Feminism and Philosophy, Ethics, Public Policy and Criminal Justice*. Honors and Awards: National Institute of Mental Health Fellowship in Criminal Justice, State University of New York at Albany, 1978; National Endowment for the Humanities Summer Award, 1976; Union College Faculty Development Grant, 1975; Union College Research Grant, 1974; Ford Foundation Research Grant, 1973.■

PAUL D. ELLSWORTH

Occupational Therapist, Health Planning Consultant. Personal: Born September 5, 1941; Son of Bert W. Ellsworth; Married Judith, Daughter of Amber Ballard; Father of Todd, Tiffany. Education: B.S. Occupational Therapy, University of Florida, 1965; M.P.H. Community Mental Health Planning and Administration, University of Hawaii, 1973. Military: Service with the United States Army Medical Specialist Corps, 1965 to present, attaining the rank of LTC. Career: Occupational Therapist, Walter Reed Army Medical Center. Organizational Memberships: American Occupational Therapy Association, Chairman Commission on Practice 1976-77, Executive Board 1977, Task Force Chairman 1978-82; American Occupational Therapy Foundation, Board of Directors 1982-84, Chairman of Human Occupation Study Committee; Occupational Therapy Association of Hawaii, President 1970-72; American Public Health Association; Association of Military Surgeons. Community Activities: Allied Health Advisory Committee, Regional Medical Program of Hawaii 1971-72; Governor's State Comprehensive Health Planning Committee, Hawaii, 1971-73; Executive Board, Continuing Health Education Council of Hawaii, 1972-73; Member, State Occupational Therapy Advisory Committee, Maryland, 1979-80; Participatory Planning Commission, Division of Adult Education, Washington D.C., 1979-81; Chairman, Strategic Long Range Planning Committee, Army Occupational Therapy, 1980-81; Consultant on Administration to Occupational Therapy Section, Office of the Surgeon General, Army Medical Department, 1979-82; Task Force on Handicapped Dependent Children, United States Office of Education, 1980. Religion: Member, St. Martin's Catholic Church. Honors and Awards: Fellow, American Occupational Therapy Association, 1973; Alumnus of the Year, College of Health Related Professions, University of Florida, 1982; Army Commendation Medal, 1973; Meritorious Service Medal, 1977. Address: 224 Gold Kettle Drive, Gaithersburg, Maryland 20878.■

LINDA DIANE HENRY ELROD

Law Professor. Personal: Born March 6, 1947; Daughter of Lyndus Henry and Jane Allen; Married Mark Douglas Elrod; Mother of Carson Douglas, Bree Elizabeth. Education: B.A., Departmental Honors English, Washburn University, 1969; J.D. cum laude, Washburn University of Topeka School of Law. Career: Professor of Law, Washburn University School of Law; Research Assistant, Kansas Judicial Council; Secondary School Teacher. Organizational Memberships: American Bar Association, Member 1972 to present; Kansas Bar Association, Coordinator of and Speaker at Several Continuing Legal Education Programs; Topeka Bar Association, Chairman Title Standards Committee 1977-78, Chairman Program Committee 1978-79, Secretary 1979 to present; Washburn Law School Association, Executive Secretary 1978 to present. Community Activities: Kansas Public Disclosure Commission, Elected Vice Chairman 1981; Kansas Governmental Ethic Commission 1978-81; Young Women's Christian Association, Board of Directors 1978 to present, President 1982-83, Chairman Adult Committee 1978-79, Chairman Health, Physical Education and Recreation Committee 1979-81, Executive Board 1981 to present; Kappa Alpha Theta, Advisory Board 1981-84; University Child Development, Board of Directors 1976-78; Colonial Park Townhouse, Board of Directors 1972-74; Topeka Friends of the Zoo, 1974 to present; Shawnee County Historical Society, 1974 to present; Cub Scout Den Leader, 1982 to present. Religion: Westminster Presbyterian Church; Speaker on "Law and the Family," April 1981. Published Works: Author of *Kansas Family Law Handbook*. Honors and Awards: William O. Douglas Outstanding Professor Award, 1978-79; Nonoso, 1983; Phi Kappa Phi; Phi Alpha Delta. Address: 231 Edgewood, Topeka, Kansas 66606.■

ALBERT EVERETT ELWELL

Small Fruit and Vegetable Farmer. Personal: Born October 19, 1899; Son of Mr. and Mrs. Albert Elwell; Married Marjorie Hooper (deceased); Second Wife, Margaret Coit, Daughter of Mr. and Mrs. Archa W. Coit; Father of Nancy Bird Lewis, Richard A. Education: Attended Ipswich Schools (Ipswich, Massachusetts). Career: Small Fruit and Vegetable Farmer; Retired Public Official; West Newbury Selectman, 1928-40, 1950-80; Representative in Massachusetts Legislature, 1971-75 (2 Terms); Assessor (32 Years); Board of Health (42 Years); Board of Public Welfare (32 Years); Policeman (25 Years); Call Fireman (22 Years); Member Conservation Commission (22 Years). Community Activities: Last Surviving Charter Member, Essex County Selectman's Association, Massachusetts Legislators Association, Essex County Greenbelt Association, West Newbury Historical Society, Sons and Daughters of Old Newbury and the West Newbury Republican Town Committee; Past Master, West Newbury Grange, 1925-28. Honors and Awards: Presented Gold Medal in Public Ceremony Honoring Him as West Newbury's First Citizen on the Occasion of the Town's Celebration of its Bicentennial, 1969; Testimonial Dinner at "Albert E. Elwell Appreciation Night" in Newburyport, 1975; Undated Certificate of Appreciation from Essex County Selectman's Association on the Occasion of Their 50th Anniversary Meeting; Award for Public Service, Essex County Pomona Grange, 1981; Post Office Square in West Newbury Renamed in His Honor as Albert E. Elwell Square in Public Ceremony Attended by Officials from across Massachusetts, November 21, 1981 (also awarded Resolution of Tribute). Address: Massachusetts Hill Farm, 109 Moulton Street, West Newbury, Massachusetts 01985.■

JOE YOOK ENG

Transportation/Urban Planner. Personal: Born June 10, 1941; Son of Bob Eng; Father of Tony G., Helen W. Education: B.Arch. 1970, Master of Transportation Engineering 1971, University of California; City Planning, International City Management Association; Environmental Planning, San Francisco State University. Military: Served in the United States Army Corps of Engineers, 1964-66. Career: Transportation/Urban Planner; Architectural Designer, B. Forgensi Associates; Transport Planner, Wilbur Smith Associates; Environmental Planner, Wilsey and Ham; Traffic Engineer, Tudor Engineering; Transport Engineer, J. Warren Associates. Organizational Memberships: International Biographical Association; American Biographical Institute Research Association; American Planning

Association; American Academy of Social and Political Science; Institute of Transportation Engineers; American Society of Civil Engineers; Transportation Research Board; National Society of Professional Engineers; Metropolitan Association of Urban Designers and Environmental Planners; Association of Environmental Professionals. Community Activities: California Tomorrow, 1975; San Francisco Planning and Research Association; Richmond Planning Association; Westlake Improvement Association; Chinese for Affirmative Action; Citizens for Rail California. Honors and Awards: National Winner, Intercollegiate Architectural Design Competition, 1970; Listed in *Who's Who in the West, Men of Achievement, Dictionary of International Biography, International Who's Who of Intellectuals.* Address: 412 12th Avenue, San Francisco, California 94118.∎

RANDALL JAY ERB

Pharmaceutical Executive. Personal: Born September 19, 1946, in Elkhart, Indiana; Son of Edwin F. and Jean M. Erb; Married Connie M., Daughter of Don and Gretna Karnes. Education: B.S. with distinction 1969, M.S. 1971, Ph.D. 1977, Purdue University. Career: Registered Pharmacist, State of Indiana; Chairman, Secretary-Treasurer, Co-Founder, Computer Age Corporation of Indiana, 1982 to present; President and Director of Scientific Affairs, Pharmadynamics Research, Inc., 1978 to present; General Partner, Erb Associates (Drug Research Investment Partnership), 1979 to present; President and Director, Pharmadynamics Research Inc. of Indiana and President of Pharmadynamics Inc. (general partner of Pharmadynamics Equities Ltd.), 1976-78; Research Assistant, Purdue University Interdisciplinary Drug Assessment Laboratory, 1975-76; Research Assistant, Department of Industrial and Physical Pharmacy, Purdue University, 1975-76. Organizational Memberships: The New York Academy of Sciences; Academy of Pharmaceutical Sciences; American Pharmaceutical Association; Indiana Pharmaceutical Association; Rho Chi; Phi Lambda Upsilon; Phi Eta Sigma; Sigma Xi; Kappa Psi; American Society of Professional Consultants; American Association for the Advancement of Science. Community Activities: Indiana State Chamber of Commerce; American Entrepreneurs Association; Action Council, National Federation of Independent Business, 1981-83. Honors and Awards: Certificate of Meritorious Service, United States Army, 1974; Outstanding Scholar, United States Army Basic Training, 1971; Merck Award for Outstanding Scholarship in Medicinal Chemistry, 1969; Vice Regent/President, Kappa Psi, 1969; Dean's List Student, 9 of 10 Semesters, Purdue University, 1964-69; State and Alumni Scholarships, Purdue University, 1964-69; Outstanding Pledge, Kappa Psi, 1967; Listed in *Men of Achievement, Who's Who in the Midwest, Personalities of America, American Business Registry, American Scientific Registry, Dictionary of International Biography, International Who's Who of Intellectuals.* Address: 109 Tamiami Court, West Lafayette, Indiana 47906.∎

OSKAR M. ESSENWANGER

Supervisory Research Physicist, Adjunct Professor of Environmental Science. Personal: Born August 25, 1920; Married Katharina D. Education: Dr.rer.nat. (Ph.D. equivalent), University of Wuerzburg (West Germany), 1950. Military: Served in the German Air Force, 1939-45. Career: Supervisory Research Physicist and Adjunct Professor of Environmental Science; Research Meteorologist 1946-57, Principal Investigator 1957-60. Organizational Memberships: Sigma Xi, President University of Alabama at Huntsville Chapter 1977-82; Associate Fellow, American Institute of Aeronautics and Astronautics; Senior Member, American Society of Quality Control; Fellow, International Biographical Association. Community Activities: German Weather Service, 1946-57; Service to the United States Government, 1957 to present; Service to the University of Alabama at Huntsville, 1961 to present (part-time). Religion: Roman Catholic. Honors and Awards: Missile Command Scientific Achievement Award, 1965; Certified Quality Engineer, 1966; Certified Consulting Meteorologist, 1967; Fellow, Intercontinental Biographical Association, 1970; Outstanding Researcher, 1977; Hermann Oberth Award, Alabama Section, American Institute of Aeronautics and Astronautics, 1981; Life Fellow, American Biographical Institute, 1979. Address: 610 Mountain Gap Drive, Huntsville, Alabama 35803.∎

MARGARET TURNER ESTES

Educational Administrator. Personal: Born July 1, 1924; Daughter of William J. B. and Margaret Turner; Widow; Mother of John, Greg, David, Jennifer. Education: B.A. 1965, M.A. 1967, Ph.D. 1972, University of Kansas. Career: Associate Vice President for Academic Affairs, Mississippi State University; Professor and Chairman, Department of Sociology, Northern Arizona University, 1972-78; Assistant Professor of Anthropology, Millersville State University, 1971; Assistant Professor of Sociology, Haskell Indian College, 1970-71; Assistant Professor of Sociology, Millersville State University, 1968-70; Instructor in Sociology, University of Kansas. Organizational Memberships: American Association of Higher Education; Southern Conference of Deans and Academic Vice Presidents; Phi Kappa Phi; American Association for the Advancement of Science, Board of Directors; Phi Delta Kappa. Honors and Awards: Selected Participant in American Council on Education's Advancement of Women in Higher Education Administration, 1980; Elected to Phi Delta Kappa, 1979; Two Scholarships Awarded in Her Name to Sociology Students, 1978; Selected by Governor of Arizona as Northern Arizona's Representative on the Task Force for Marriage and Family, 1976; Northern Arizona University Representative to ACESS, 1976; Soroptimist Honoree as Successful Business Woman of the Year, 1975; Elected by Students as Faculty Woman of the Year, Northern Arizona University, 1973; Listed in *Who's Who of American Women, World Who's Who of Women, Who's Who in the South and Southwest, Personalities of the South, Directory of Distinguished Americans, Who's Who of International Women Educators.* Address: 503 Briarwick, Starkville, Mississippi 39759.∎

EDITH FRANCES ETTER

Educator. Personal: Born August 7, 1932; Daughter of Fred and Katherine Mykleby; Married Wallace Herman Etter, Son of Clare Etter; Mother of David Fred. Education: B.S. 1963, Graduate Studies, Bemidji State University. Career: First Grade Teacher, Aurora (Minnesota) Public Schools, 1952-54; First Grade Teacher, Mounds View (Minnesota) Public Schools, 1954-55; Kindergarten Teacher, St. Peter (Minnesota) Public Schools, 1956-57; First Grade Teacher, Pipestone (Minnesota) Public Schools, 1957-61; Second Grade Teacher, Thief River Falls (Minnesota) Public Schools, 1961 to present. Organizational Memberships: Thief River Falls Education Association, Teacher Rights Chairman 1980-85, Negotiating Team Co-Chairman 1983-85; Kramer-Brown UniServ; Minnesota Education Association, Resolutions Committee Secretary 1973 to present, Board of Directors 1981 to present; National Education Association, Board of Directors 1981 to present; Educators of Exceptional Children, International Peace Caucus, Higher Education Caucus; North Star Reading Council; Minnesota Reading Association; Northwestern Educational Cooperative Service Unit, Advisory Board on In-Service 1977 to present; Association for Supervision and Curriculum Development; International Reading Association. Community Activities: City Planning Commission, 1980 to present; Delta Kappa Gamma; Plummer Lioness; Northwestern Hospital Auxiliary. Religion: Member Trinity Lutheran Church. Honors and Awards: Scholastic Graduate, Bemidji State University, 1963; Leader of American Elementary Education, 1971; Citation Award, Association of Classroom Teachers, 1972; One of 11 Honor Roll Teachers of the Year in Minnesota, 1973; One of 9 Outstanding Women Educators, Women's Caucus, Minnesota Education Association, 1978. Address: 416 South Maple, Thief River Falls, Minnesota 56701.∎

DONNELL DENCIL ETZWILER

Pediatrician. Personal: Born March 29, 1927; Son of Mrs. Berniece Etzwiler; Married Marion Grassby; Father of Nancy, Diane, Lisa, David. Education: B.A. Chemistry cum laude, Indiana University, 1950; M.D., Yale University School of Medicine, 1953. Military: Served in the United States Navy, 1945-46. Career: Pediatrician, St. Louis Park Medical Center; Director, Diabetes Education Center; Medical Director, Camp Needlepoint (Minnesota's Camp for Diabetic Children), 1959 to present; Medical Staff, Project HOPE, Trujillo Medical School, Peru, 1962; Clinical Instructor in Pediatrics 1958-64, Clinical Assistant in Pediatrics 1957-58, University of Minnesota; Instructor in Pediatrics, Cornell University Medical College, 1956-57. Organizational Memberships: American Diabetes Association, Past President 1976-77, Board of Directors 1968-78, President 1976-77; Twin Cities Diabetes Association, Board Member 1959-75; International Diabetes Federation, Executive Committee, Vice President 1978 to present; American Dietetic Association, Honorary Member 1980, Advisory Committee 1981-84; American Group Practice Association; American Medical Association. Community Activities: Minneapolis Society for the Blind, Board of Directors 1976-81; Advisory Panel, Nationwide Attitude Study for General Mills on the American Family, 1978-79; Advisory Council, Television Series of Health Sciences, University of Minnesota, 1974-76; Institute of Medicine, National Academy of Sciences, 1981-86; Commissioner, National Commission on Diabetes, 1974-76; Advisory Committee for Diabetes Research and Training Centers, University of Michigan, University of Chicago, University of Indiana, Joslin Clinic, 1978 to present. Religion: Westminster Presbyterian Church, Deacon 1959-65, Elder 1967 to present. Honors and Awards: Outstanding Service Award, American Diabetes Association, 1976; Outstanding Service to Diabetic Youth, American Diabetes Association, 1979; Honorary Member, American Dietetic Association, 1979; Fellow, All India Institute of Diabetes, Bombay, 1979; Banting Medal for Outstanding Service, American Diabetes Association, 1977; WCCO's "Good Neighbor" Award, 1977; Listed in *Who's Who in the Midwest, Who's Who in America, Men of Achievement, Community Leaders of America, American Men and Women of Science, Who's Who in the World.* Address: 4820 Valley View Road, Edina, Minnesota 55424.∎

TWO THOUSAND NOTABLE AMERICANS

MARCH K. FONG EU

Secretary of State of California. Personal: Born March 29; Daughter of Yuen and Shiu Kong; Married Henry Eu; Mother of Matthew Kipling Fong, Marchesa Suyin You. Education: B.S., University of California-Berkeley; M.Ed., Mills College, 1951; Ed.D, Stanford University, 1956; Postgraduate Study, Columbia University, California State University-Hayward. Military: Served during World War II as a Dental Hygienist, Presidio, San Francisco. Career: Secretary of State of California; Former Dental Hygienist; Chairman of Dental Hygiene Division, University of California Medical Center; Dental Hygienist, Oakland Public Schools; Supervisor of Dental Health Education, Alameda County Schools; Lecturer in Health Education, Mills College; Member of California Assembly, 1966-74. Organizational Memberships: American Dental Hygienist Association, Life Member; Business and Professional Women's Club; American Association of University Women; California Teacher's Association; Delta Kappa Gamma; Northern California Dental Hygienist Association, Life Member. Community Activities; Parent-Teachers Association, Life Member; Oakland League of Women Voters; Alameda County School Board Association; Alameda County Board of Education, Member 1956-66, President 1961-62, Legislative Advocate 1963; Assembly Committees, Chairman Committee on Employement in Public Employees 1973-74, Chairman Select Committee on Agriculture, Foods and Nutrition 1973-74; Chinese Young Ladies Society; National Commission on Observance of International Women's Year, 1977; University of Southern California School of Dentistry, Board of Councillors 1976; Number of Positions in Democratic State and County Central Committees. Religion: Unitarian. Honors and Awards: Outstanding Woman Award, Number of Awards for Public Service and Professional Achievement, National Women's Political Caucus, 1980. Address: 1230 J Street, Sacramento, California 95814.■

JOHN A. EURE

Director of Environmental Health. Personal: Born October 1, 1934; Son of John and Helen Eure; Married Norma; Father of John, Joan, Ann, Paul. Education: B.S. Sanitary Engineering, University of Illinois, 1957; M.S. Sanitary Engineering, University of Texas. Military: Served with the United States Public Health Service, attaining the rank of Captain (Navy Equivalent 0-6), 1957-79. Career: Director, Environmental Health; Draftsman, Water Safety Engineer, City of Chicago; Sanitary Engineer, United States Public Health Service (Water Pollution Control and Radiological Health), 1957-79; Director, Radiological Health, Iowa State Department of Health, 1979-81. Organizational Memberships: Health Physics Society, 1963 to present; A.P.H.A., Fellow 1963-82, Section Secretary 1970, Chairman 1975; Diplomate, American Academy of Environmental Engineers, 1965 to present; Member Conference of Radiation Control Program Directors. Community Activities: Third Degree Knights of Columbus, 1953 to present; Vice President, Phi Kappa Fraternity, 1956; Cubmaster, 1970; Kenmont Club Board of Directors, 1971-78; Religious Chairman and Counselor, Boy Scouts of America, 1977. Religion: Choir Member 1975-79, Roman Catholic Eucharistic Minister 1976-78, Member Parish Council 1977-79. Honors and Awards: Ranger in Explorer Scouts, 1950; National Honor Society, 1952; Skull and Crescent Fraternity, University of Illinois, 1953; Professional Engineer, State of Texas, 1962 to present; Diplomate, American Academy of Engineers, 1965 to present. Address: 201 Glenview Drive, Des Moines, Iowa 50312.■

JANE EVANS

Corporate Executive. Personal: Born July 26, 1944; Daughter of Mrs. C. M. Pierce; Mother of One Son. Education: B.A., Vanderbilt University, 1965; Attended L'Universite d'Aix-Marseille, Aix-en-France, 1962; Postgraduate Courses in Fashion Merchandising, Fashion Institute of Technology, New York City, 1965, 1966. Career: Executive Vice President, General Mills; Group Vice President, Apparel, General Mills, 1980-81; Vice President, Administration and Corporation Development, Fingerhut Corporation, Minnesota, 1977-79; President, Butterick Fashion Marketing Company, New York City, 1974-77; President, I. Miller, New York City, 1970-73. Organizational Memberships: Young President's Organization, Executive Committee New York Chapter; The Fashion Group of New York. Community Activities: Vanderbilt University, Alumni Board of Directors, Visiting Committee; Laboratory Institute of Merchandising, Advisory Board; National Association of Women Business Owners, Advisory Board; Guthrie Theatre, Minneapolis, Board of Directors. Address: 507 Trinity Pass Road, New Canaan, Connecticut 06840.■

LOUISE EVANS

Psychologist. Personal: Daughter of Henry D. and Adela Evans; Married Tom R. Gambrell. Education: B.S. Psychology, Northwestern University, 1949; M.S. Psychology, Purdue University, 1952; Internship in Clinical Psychology, Menninger Foundation, 1953; Ph.D. Clinical Psychology, Purdue University, 1955; Postdoctoral in Clinical Child Psychology, Department of Child Psychiatry Fellowship, Menninger Clinic, 1956; Diplomate in Clinical Psychology, American Board of Examiners in Professional Psychology, 1966. Career: Private Practice Clinical and Consulting Psychology, Fullerton, California, 1960 to present; Director of Psychology Clinic (Barnes Hospital), Instructor in Medical Psychology, Department of Psychiatry and Neurology, Washington University School of Medicine, St. Louis, Missouri, 1959; Clinical Research Consultant to Episcopal City Mission, St. Louis, 1959; Head Child Guidance Clinic and Staff Psychologist, Kings County Hospital, Brooklyn, New York, 1957-58; Staff Psychologist, Kankakee State Hospital, Kankakee, Illinois, 1954; Teaching Assistant in Educational Psychology and Remedial Reading Clinic, Psychology Department, Purdue University, Lafayette, Indiana, 1950-51; Psychology Consultant to Fullerton Community Hospital (Courtesy Staff), Fullerton, California, 1961 to present; Staff Consultant in Clinical Psychology (Courtesy Staff), Martin Luther Hospital, Anaheim, California, 1963 to present. Organizational Memberships: International Council of Psychologist, Inc.; Intercontinental Biographical Association, England; Royal Society of Health, England; American Association for the Advancement of Science; American Orthopsychiatric Association; American Psychological Association, Division of Consulting Psychology, Division of Clinical Psychology, Division of Psychology of Women, Division of Humanistic Psychology, Division of Psychological Aspects of Disability; American Biographical Institute; World Wide Academy of Scholars, New Zealand; International Platform Association; American Association of University Professors; American Public Health Association; Society of Sigma Xi; California State Psychological Association; Orange County Psychological Association; Los Angeles County Psychological Association; Los Angeles Society of Clinical Psychologists; American Academy of Political and Social Science; American Judicature Society; Alumni Association, Menninger School of Psychiatry; Rehabilitation International; Center for the Study of the Presidency; New York Academy of Sciences; Pi Sigma Pi Fraternity; President's Council, Purdue University, 1981; Life Member, Purdue University Alumni Association. Published Works: Author Numerous Professional Publications. Honors and Awards: Recipient First Purdue Alumni Association Citizenship Award, 1975; Gold Medal Award, Publishers of *International Who's Who in Community Service*, 1972, 1975; Head Start Service Award Certificate of Appreciation, Yuma, Arizona, 1972; Advisory Member, Marquis Library Society, Chicago, Illinois; Chosen "Miss Heritage," Heritage Publications, 1965; Elected to Hall of Fame of Central High School, Evansville, Indiana, 1966; First Recipient of Parent-Teacher's Association Scholarship Ever Awarded by Central High School, 1945; Scholarships, Northwestern University, Evanston, Illinois, 1945; Recipient Other Scholarships (not used); Honorary Membership, Zion "Golden Age" Foundation, 1970; Recipient Numerous Certificates of Merit, Distinguished Achievement and Commendations from the Publishers of Various *Who's Who* Biographical References Nationally and Internationally; Recipient of Numerous Certificates and Letters of Appreciation from Groups Addressed; Listed in *Who's Who in American Education, Leaders in American Science, Who's Who in the West, Dictionary of International Biography, The National Gold Book — Distinguished Women of the United States, Who's Who in California, The National Register of Prominent Americans, The National Register of Prominent Americans and International Notables, The National Register of Who's Who, Royal Blue Book, Personalities of the West and Midwest, Who's Who International, Creative and Successful Personalities of the World, The Official Who's Who in Orange County, Intercontinental Biographical Association Yearbook and Directory, Community Leaders of America, Two Thousand Women of Achievement, International Who's Who in Community Service, The World Who's Who of Women, Outstanding Professionals in Human Services, Community Leaders and Noteworthy Americans, Notable Americans of the Bicentennial Era, The Hereditary Register of the United States of America, Notable Americans, Who's Who in Health Care, International Who's Who of Intellectuals, Book of Honor, Personalities of America, Who's Who in America, Council for National Register of Health Service Providers, Distinguished Leaders on Health Care, Men and Women of Distinction, Forensic Services Directory, Registry of Women in Science and Engineering, The American Registry, Contemporary Personalities, Orange County Who's Who, Two Thousand Notable Americans, International Book of Honor, The Registry of American Achievement, Biographical Roll of Honor, Community Leaders of the World, Five Thousand Personalities of the World, International Register of Biographies, International Who's Who of Contemporary Achievement, Who's Who of California Executive Women.* Address: 127 West Commonwealth, Fullerton, California 92632.■

LORNE GORDON EVERETT

Natural Resource Program Manager. Personal: Born January 1, 1943; Son of Mr. and Mrs. Leonard Reese Everett; Married Jennifer; Father of Stephen, Lauren. Education: B.Sc. Chemistry 1966, B.Sc. with honors in Water Sciences 1968, Lakehead University; M.S. Limnology 1969, Ph.D. Hydrology 1972, University of Arizona. Career: Manager, Natural Resources Program; Hydrologist, Consultant, Assistant Professor, Department of Hydrology and Water Resources. Organizational Memberships: American Medical Laboratory Association; American Society of Civil Engineers; American Society of Clinical Pathology; American

Water Resources Association; Arizona Medical Laboratory; Beta Beta Beta; National Water Well Association; International Water Resources Association. Honors and Awards: Invited Member, International Committee for UNESCO 1983 World Meeting on Technical Advance in Control and Detection of Groundwater Pollution; Advisor, United States National Center for Groundwater Research, 1982; Invited Chairman, Workshop on Monitering in Vadose Zone, First National Groudwater Monitoring Symposium, Columbus, Ohio, 1981; Invited by Directors of Peer-Reviewed Journal, *Groundwater Monitoring Review*, to Develop Charter Series of Papers on Groundwater Monitoring, 1981; Invited Moderator, "Workshop on Unsaturated Zone Monitoring", First National Groundwater Monitoring Symposium, N.W.W.A., Columbus, Ohio, 1981; Invited Lecturer, University of California, Santa Barbara, Department of Mechanical and Environmental Engineering, 1980; Charter President, California Section, American Water Resources Association, 1979. Address: 1312 Portesuello Avenue, Santa Barbara, California 93105.■

THELMA FAYE EVERETT

Educator. Personal: Born October 6, 1927; Daughter of Era M. Huntley; Mother of Denoris H. Education: B.S., Wiley College, 1951; Postgraduate, Wayne State University 1958-60, University of Michigan 1964, Oakland University 1974; M.A., University of Detroit, 1976. Career: Educator. Organizational Memberships: Highland Park Federation of Teachers, Membership Committee 1967-68, Treasurer 1968-72, Member Negotiating Team 1967-72, 1975-77, Building Representative 1981-83. Community Activities: Precinct Representative, Democratic Committee, 1973-75; Member Board of Hyde Park Co-op, 1982-85. Honors and Awards: Recipient Distinguished Service Award, Highland Park Federation of Teachers. Address: 1957 Hyde Park Road, Detroit, Michigan 48207.■

PHILLIP A. EVOLA

Theatrical and Commercial Designer/Consultant. Personal: Born September 15, 1949; Son of Paul and Pauline Evola. Education: M.F.A., Goodman School of Drama/S.A.I.C., Chicago, Illinois, 1974; B.A., St. Mary of the Plains College, Dodge City, Kansas, 1971. Career: Principal Designer, Fredericksburg Theatre Company, Fredericksburg, Virginia, Summer 1982; Principal Designer, Cockpit-in-Court Summer Theatre, Baltimore, Maryland, Summers 1978, 1979, 1980, 1981, 1982; Designer/Technical Director, Assistant Professor, Essex Community College, Department of Speech Communication and Theatre, Baltimore, Maryland, 1974-82; Resident/Designer/Technical Director, The Chesapeake Opera Company, Towson, Maryland, 1974-78; Resident Designer/Technical Director, Harford Opera Theatre, Bel Air, Maryland, Summer 1976; Resident Designer/Technical Director, Theatre-by-the-Sea, Matunuck, Rhode Island, Summer 1975; Lighting Designer/Technical Director, Alabama Shakespeare Festival, Anniston, Alabama, Summer 1974; Master Electrician/Associate Lighting Designer, Cape Cod Melody Tent, Hyannis, MA, Summer 1973; Technician, Ithaca Summer Repertory, Ithaca, New York, Summer 1971, 1972. Organizational Memberships: United Scenic Artists, Local 350; United States Institute for Theatre Technology; American Theatre Association. Honors and Awards: American College Theatre Festival, Award for Excellence in Lighting Design for *Celebration* 1981, Award for Excellence in Technical Producation of *The Madwoman of Chaillot* 1980, Awrd for Excellence in Scenic Design for *Born Yesterday*, Amoco Gold Medal of Excellence 1977, Award for Excellence in Lighting Design Citation for Outstanding Scenic Design for *What the Butler Sa w* 1976, Award for Excellence in Technical Production of *U.S.A.* 1975; Awarded Special Scholarship to Attend Helmut Grosser Master Class, Goodman School of Drama/S.A.I.C., 1973; Listed in *Who's Who in the East, Men of Achievement*. Address: 95 Third Place, Brooklyn, New York 11231.■

HAZEM A. EZZAT

Automotive Executive. Personal: Born July 12, 1942; Son of Ahmed Ezzat and Haneya Safwat; Married Shaza; Father of Jeneen H., Waleed H. Education: B.Sc. Mechanical Engineering, Cairo University, Cairo, Egypt; M.S. Mechanical Engineering, Ph.D. Mechanical Engineering, University of Wisconsin, Madison, Wisconsin. Career: Society of Automotive Engineers; American Society of Mechanical Engineers; Engineering Society of Detroit; Economic Club of Detroit; Sigma Xi; Institute Noise Control Engineering. Honors and Awards: American Society of Mechanical Engineers, Henry Hess Award, 1973; Listed in *Who's Who in Engineering, American Men and Women of Science, Who's Who in Technology Today, Men of Achievement*, Nominated for *The Directory of Distinguished Americans*. Address: 2454 Valleyview Drive, Troy, Michigan 48098.■

JEANNE RYAN FAATZ

State Legislator. Personal: Born July 30, 1941; Daughter of Charles Keith and Elizabeth M. Ryan, Evansville, Indiana; Mother of Kristin B., Susan E. Education: Graduate of Evansville Bosse High School, 1958; Bachelor's Degree, University of Illinois, 1962; Graduate Studies, University of Colorado at Denver, 1982 to present. Career: State Legislative Representative, Three Terms; Teacher of English and Speech. Organizational Memberships: Council of State Government, Transportation Committee, Western Conference; Colorado House Transportation and Energy Committee, Chairman; Member Judiciary Committee. Community Activities: Harvey Park Improvement Association, Past President; Southwest Young Women's Christian Association Adult Education Club, Past President; United Nation's Children's Fund, Past Southwest Metro Area Coordinator; Ft. Logan Mental Health Center Citizen's Advisory Board, Board Member; Southwest Young Men's Christian Association, Board of Managers. Honors and Awards: Women's Scholastic Award, Indiana University; Magna Cum Laude, Graduated with College Honors, Top 3% of Class, University of Illinois; Gallery of Fame for Community Work, *Denver Post*, 1978; Listed in *Who's Who in American Universities and Colleges*. Address: 2903 South Quitman Street, Denver, Colorado 80236.■

TUULA IRJA JOKINEN FABRIZIO

Physician and Medical Writer. Personal: Born May 13, 1931; Daughter of Arne Valfrid and Jenny Lydia Jokinen (both deceased); Married John Arthur Fabrizio; Mother of John Arne, Robert Arthur. Education: M.D. 1957, Sc.D. 1958, University of Helsinki Medical School, Finland. Career: Physician, Medical Writer, Editor of *Medical News, The Finnish Medical Journal*, 1971 to present; Emergency Room Physician, St. Vincent's Medical Center, Bridgeport 1977-79, Milford Hospital 1973-77, Norwalk Hospital 1966-69; School and Well Baby Clinic Physician, City of Norwalk, 1969-73. Organizational Memberships: Connecticut Academy of Family Physicians, Education Committee 1979 to present; American Medical Association; Fairfield County Medical Association; Connecticut State Medical Society; American Board of Family Practice, Diplomate; American Academy of Family Physicians, Fellow; American College of Preventive Medicine, Fellow; American Public Health Association; American Medical Writers Association; American Association for Automotive Medicine; New York Academy of Sciences; American Association for the Advancement of Science; Finnish Medical Association. Religion: St. Peter's Lutheran Church, Norwalk, Member 1963 to present. Honors and Awards: Bronze Plaque, Finnish Medical Association, 1980; Elected to World Academy of New Zealand, 1976; Medal Award; Listed in *International Who's Who in Community Service*, 1971. Address: 42 Stevens Street, Norwalk, Connecticut 06850.■

ALBERT SHUCRY FACUSSÉ

Attorney at Law. Personal: Born February 10, 1921; Son of Nicholas and Maria Barjum Facussé; Married May Bandak, Daughter of Issa Bandak; Father of Vivian Neuwirth, Denise Lentz. Education: Degree with honors in Pre-Law, Loyola University, 1941; Graduate in Law with Highest Grades in Class; Loyola University, 1943. Career: Self-Employed in Business, 1943-1960; Attorney-at-Law, General Practice in Law, 1960 to present. Organizational Memberships: Louisiana State Bar Association; American Bar Association; Internaitonal Bar Association; Alpha Sigma Nu; Saint Thomas Moore Law Club. Religion: Roman Catholic. Published Works: Comment Editor, *Loyola Law Review*, 1943. Honors and Awards: Listed in *Who's Who in America, Who's Who in the South and Southwest, The Best Lawyers in America, Who's Who in American Law, Martindale-Hubbell Law Directory, International Who's Who of Intellectuals, Men of Achievement, Dictionary of International Biography, International Register of Profiles, Biographical Roll of Honor, International Who's Who of Contemporary Achievement*, Others. Address: 6731 Manchester Street, New Orleans, Louisiana 70126.■

DENNIS FALCONER

Medical Food Service Division Chief. Personal: Born March 22, 1939; Son of Mr. and Mrs. Robert G. Falconer; Married Dorothy June Bland, Daughter of Mr. and Mrs. Lloyd L. Bland; Father of Dana Joe. Education: B.S. Foods and Nutrition, University of Missouri, 1961; Dietetic Internship, Ancher Hospital, St. Paul, Minnesota, 1962; Nutrition Review for Therapeutic and Research Dietitians, Walter Reed Army Medical Center, 1964; Squadron Officers School, Maxwell Air Force Base, Alabama, 1967; Air Command and Staff College, Resident Seminar, Norton Air Force Base, California, 1977; Air War College, Correspondence, 1979; M.A. Management, Columbia Pacific University, 1981; Ph.D. Candidate. Career: Staff Dietitian, Wilford Hall United States Air Force Medical Center, Lackland, Air Force Base, Texas, 1962-63; Chief, Medical Food Service, United States Air Force Regional Hospital Carswell, Carswell Air Force Base, Texas, 1963-65; Chief, Medical Food Service, United States Air Force Academy Hospital, United States Air Force Academy, Colorado, 1965-69; Chief, Medical Food Service, United States Air Force Hospital Tachikawa, Tachikawa, Japan, 1969-73; Operation Homecoming, United States Air Force Hospital Clark, Clark Air Force Base, PI, 1973; Assistant Chief, Medical Food Service, Wilford Hall United States Air Force Medical Center, Lackland Air Force Base, Texas, 1973-75; Medical Inspector, Biomedical Science Branch, HQ USAF/AFISC, Norton Air Force Base, California, 1975-78; Command Dietitian Consultant, HQ SAC/SGAF, Offutt Air Force Base, Nebraska, 1978-82; Associate Command BSC Staff Advisor, HA SAC/SGAF, Offutt Air Force Base, 1978-82; Director, Medical Food Service Division, Wilford Hall United States Air Force Medical Center, Lackland Air Force Base, Texas, 1982 to present; Associate Chief, Air Force Dietetics and Nutrition Consultant to the United States Air Force Surgeon General, 1982 to present; Consultant, Medical Food Service, Surgeon, 5th Air Force, 1969-72; Nutritional Consultant/Advisor, Operation Homecoming (repatriation of prisoners of Vietnam Conflict), 1973; Medical Food Service Facilities Consultant, Wilford Hall United States Air Force Medical Center, 1973-75; Medical Inspector, Biomedical Sciences Branch, HQ AFISC, 1975-78; Management Consultant, Omaha-Council Bluffs Stake, 1978-82; Chairman, Specialized Host Committee, The American Dietetic Association, 1982 to present. Organizational Memberships: The American Dietetic Association; Texas Dietetic Association; Association of Military Surgeons of the United States; Society of Hospital Food Service Administrators; Nutrition Today Society; San Antonio District Dietetic Association. Published Works: Author of Published Articles, Speeches, Lectures in his field. Honors and Awards: Decorated Air Force Commendation Medal, United States Air Force Academy Hospital, 1965-69; Air Force Commendation Medal with One Oak Leaf Cluster, Wilford Hall United States Air Force Medical Center, 1973-75; Meritorious Service Medal, United States Air Force Hospital Tachikawa, Japan, 1969-73; Meritorious Service Medal, with One Oak Leaf Cluster, HQ AFISC/SG, 1975-78; Meritorious Service Medal with 2nd Oak Leaf Cluster, HQ SAC/SG 1978-82; Outstanding Unit Awards, United States Air Force Academy Hospital, United States Air Force Hospital Carswell, Operation Homecoming, HQ AFISC; Listed in *Who's Who in the Midwest, Men of Achievement, The Biographical Roll of Honor, Personalities of the West and Midwest, Who's Who of Intellectuals, Personalities of America, The American Scientific Registry, The American Military Registry, Dictionary of International Biography, The American Registry*. Address: 5307 Timber Glade, San Antonio, Texas 78250.■

SALLY BASIGA FAMARIN

Real Estate and Insurance Executive. Personal: Born November 11, 1923, in Mandaue City, Philippines; Daughter of Severo and Serapia Basiga (deceased); Married

TWO THOUSAND NOTABLE AMERICANS

Carsiolo Tagle Famarin; Mother of Sally Anne, Catherine, Rodolfo Carlite, Rose Marie. Education: Graduate of University of Visayas, Cebu, Philippines, 1941; Postgraduate Study, Chamberlain Real Estate School 1961, Harlowe Real Estate School 1962, Income Tax Service 1975, San Francisco, California. Career: Director-Owner, Famarin Realty, United Homes Realty, United Homes Insurance Service, Far East America Travel, Income Tax Service; Business Opportunity, Mortgage, and Real Properties Securitites Dealer; Owner-Operator, Sally's Sunset Villa Ambulatory Home for the Aged, 1972-74; Real Estate Saleswoman, 1962 to present; Accountant, Bookkeeper, and Manager of Ladies Home, Philippines. Organizational Memberships: National Real Estate Association; National Association of Real Estate Board; The National Salesman's Association; The California Real Estate Association; The San Francisco Board of Realtors; The Multiple Listing Service of San Francisco; The American Society of Notaries; National Historic Preservations of America. Community Activities: City and County of San Francisco, Advisory Board, Child Health and Disability Prevention Program, Mayor George Moscone's Screening Committee on Boards and Commissions, Commissioner on Landmarks Preservation Advisory Board; Philippine Gardens, Golden Gate Park, San Francisco, Initiator 1976; International Hotel Landmark, First Filipino Landmark in the United States National Register of Cultural and Historical Places, Author, Endorser, 1977; Regular Veterans Association Auxiliary, President 1953-60; Cebu Association of California, Inc., Founder, President Emeritus, World Emissary; Mandaue Association de Santo Nino, Philippines, Founder; American Legion Bataan Post 600; Filipino-American Senior Citizens of San Francisco and Bay Area of St. Joseph's, Advisor; National Housing Conference Committee, Washington, D.C., 1981; Author and Endorsed, Santo Nino de Cebu Shrine, National Shrine of Filipinos in America on National Register of Cultural and Historical Places by the United States Department of the Interior, Responsible for Building of Shrine at San Franciscos St. Joseph's Church; Founder, President Emeritus and World Emissary of Santo Nino de Cebu Association International, Formed Different Chapters in the United States and Different Parts of the World including the Philippines, Australia, and Germany; Created the Biggest Annual Festival and Religious Processional Parade in the United States of the Santo Nino de Cebu (the Filipinos patron saint); Candidate, Democratic Central Committee, 19th Assembly District, San Francisco. Religion: St. Joseph's Church, Member, Parish Council President. Honors and Awards: The First Filipino te Serve as Member of the Mayors Citizens Committee to Celebrate the Birthday of San Francisco, California, 1976 to present; The First Filipino Woman Supervisorial Candidate in the City and County of San Francisco, California; Religious Achievements are Recognized by the Vatican; Received Papal Blessing from Pope John Paul II, "the Pope cordially invokes upon her God's gifts of Peace and Joy"; Procured Papal Blessing from Pope John Paul II for the Filipino People in the United States Who are the Devotees of the Santo Nino de Cebu; Robert C. Howe Memorial Plate Award for Patriot of the United States of America, 1977; Famarin Bicentennial Commemorative Flag, American Biographical Institute; Most Successful Woman Award; Mandaue's Pride Abroad; Resolution from Mandaue City Council; Certificate of Honor, San Francisco Board of Supervisors for Exemplary Leadership in the Community, 3 Times; California State Senate and State Assembly for Exemplary Leadership in Philippine-American Community of San Francisco and Distinguished Professional Achievements, Twice; Only United States Awardee, Fourth Centenary Celebration of Cebu's Republic of the Philippines, 1975; Gold Pin Award, Cebu Association, 1971; Gold Medal Award, 1980; Best of the Best and Honoring the Honored, Cambridge, England; City Planning Resolution 8621 of San Francisco for Dedication in Preserving San Francisco's Architectural and Historical Heritage, 1980; World Culture Prize Award, the Statue of Liberty for Distinguished Personality of 1984, Accademia de Italia; The First Filipino Woman Realtor in California; "Friends of Sally Famarin" Now Preparing Commemoration of Her Realtor's Silver Anniversary in Conjunction with 33 Years of Community Service in the United States; Nominated to *Community Leaders of the World*. Address: 2207 - 28th Avenue, San Francisco, California 94116.■

SATIRIS GALAHAD FASSOULIS

Company Chairman. Personal: Born August 19, 1922; Son of Peter George and Anastasia Fassoulis (both deceased). Education: B.A., Syracuse University, 1945. Military: Served in the United States Air Force, 1941-45, attaining the rank of First Lieutenant. Career: Chairman, Global Communications Company; Former President of Commerce International Corporation. Organizational Memberships: United States Congressional Advisory Board; American Defense Preparedness Committee; United States Naval Institute; Navy League of the United States. Community Activities: International Platform Association; Smithsonian Institute, 1982 to present; American Museum of Natural History, 1982 to present. Religion: Active in St. Bartholomew's Church, New York City (Episcopal). Honors and Awards: Purple Heart; Air Medal with Three Oak Leaf Clusters; Presidential Citation, 1945; Honorary Award from the Republic of China for Services Rendered, 1949. Address: 20 Waterside Plaza, New York, New York 10010.■

MRS. ROSCOE KENT FAWCETT (MARIE ANN FORMANEK)

Civic Leader. Personal: Born March 6, 1914; Daughter of Peter Paul and Mary Ann Stepanek Formanek; Married Roscoe Kent; Mother of Roscoe Kent Jr., Peter Formanek, Roger Knowlton II, Stephen Hart. Education: Graduate, Washburn High School, Minneapolis, Minnesota; Certificates from Harvard University, 1976, 1977, 1978, 1979, 1980, 1981, 1982. Community Activities: Civic Volunteer Leader. Religion: Catholic-Episcopalian. Honors and Awards: For Loyal and Devoted Service to Senior Citizens in Greenwich, Connecticut Award, Soroptimist Club; For Outstanding Volunteer Service at Nathaniel Witherell Hospital as Member of the Auxiliary from the Connecticut State Department of Health; For Distinguished Service to the Community from the United Cerebral Palsy Association of Fairfield County, Inc.; Participating Member of Huxley Institute; Work with Multiple Sclerosis and with Retarded Children; Member Board of Directors, Merry-Go-Round and Mews, Nathaniel Witherell Auxiliary, Greenwich Philharmonia, Putnam, Indian Field School; Listed in *Marquis The World Who's Who of Women, Marquis Who's Who in America, Marquis Who's Who in the East, Dictionary of International Biography, International Who's Who of Intellectuals, Internatioanl Register of Profiles, The National Register of Prominent Americans and International Notables, Royal Blue Book, Community Leaders of America, Library of Human Resources, National Social Directory, Book of Honor, Accademia Italia, Personalities of America, Directory of Distinguished Americans, Personalities of the East, National Social Directory*. Address: 12 Hawkwood Lane, Greenwich, Connecticut 06830.■

CHERIE CHRISTINA FEHRMAN

Writer, Interior Designer. Personal: Born April 13, 1945; Daughter of Mr. and Mrs. A. J. Allen; Married Kenneth R., Son of Mrs. Ruth McVey. Education: B.A. English/Creative Writing, San Francisco State University; Postgraduate Study at University of California at Berkeley. Career: Writer, Non-fiction Novels; Vice President, Design Firm; Former Manager of Savings and Loan; Actress and Singer. Organizational Memberships: Author's Guild of America; International Society of Interior Designers, Professional Member and Board Member. Community Activities: Board Member, International Society of Interior Designers; Consultant (voluntary) to Johnston House Preservation Project (a living museum restoration); Member, National Trust for Historic Preservation; Society for the Prevention of Cruelty to Animals. Honors and Awards: Listed in *Who's Who in the West, Directory of Distinguished Americans, Personalities of America, International Who's Who of Women*. Address: 4112 California Street, San Francisco, California 94118.■

MARIAN JEAN FEIST

Director of Nutrition. Personal: Born March 23, 1921; Daughter of Harlan Oscar and Bridget Matilda Hagan Mock (both deceased); Married Arthur W. Feist. Education: Graduate of Ferndale High School, Johnstown, Pennsylvania, 1938; B.S. Foods and Nutrition, Seton Hill College, Greensburgh, Pennsylvania, 1942; Dietetic Internship, Good Samaritan Hospital, Cincinnati, Ohio, 1942-43; Postgraduate Courses, University of Cincinnati School of Education, Foods and Nutrition; Registered, A.D.A., 1943, 1969 and Current, Life Membership 1949. Career: Director of Nutrition 1969-82, Acting Director, Assistant Director, Purchasing Dietitian 1948 and 1969, Good Samaritan Hospital, Cincinnati, Ohio; Assistant Administrative Dietitian, Conemaugh Valley Memorial Hospital, Johnstown, Pennsylvania, 1948; Dietitian in Administration, Therapeutics and Teaching, Allegheny General Hospital, Pittsburgh, Pennsylvania, 1943-48; Presided Over Session at Ohio Hospital Association-Hospital Institutional and Education Food Service Society, Cincinnati, Ohio, 1971; Teacher for Daycare Cooks, Foods and Nutrition Purchasing and Menu Planning, Cincinnati, Ohio, 3 Years; Presentation of Paper, "Purveyors — How They Can Help," Development of a Computerized Food Service System and the Dietitian Seminar, Cincinnati Dietetic Association, Good Samaritan Hospital, 1967; Lecturer, "Menu Planning and Purchasing," Xavier University, Cincinnati, Ohio 1963, University of Cincinnati Evening College 1967. Organizational Memberships: Greater Cincinnati Dietetic Association, President 1971-72, President's Advisory Committee 3 terms, Treasurer, Administrative Section Chairman, Legislation and Consultation, Recruitment and Career Guidance, Representative for the Sisters of Charity, Chairman of Computer Action Committee 2 Terms, Food Parade President-elect, Co-Chairman of National Nutrition

Week 1 Term, Participating Member in Speakers Bureau and Consultant Service; Pittsburgh Dietetic Association, Recording Secretary, Chairman of Therapeutic Section 1 Term; Ohio Dietetic Association, Administrative Section Committee, Co-Chairman of Exhibits Annual Convention 1976, "Foods Purchasing" Panel Participant at Ohio Dietetic Workshop 1951, Lecturer on "Two Plus Three and Convenience Food," for Institute for Dietitians in Nursing Homes, University of Dayton 1967; American Dietetic Association, Life Member; American Diabetic Association; Cincinnati Restaurant Association; Ohio Restaurant Association; National Restaurant Association; Nutrition Today Society; American Society for Food Service Administration; Society for Advancement of Management. Religion: Roman Catholic. Published Works: Co-Author, "Food Freezers," *Hospital Progress*, 1956. Honors and Awards: Daughters of the American Revolution, 1938; Sigma Kappa Pi, 1942; G.S.H. Employee Awards, 1953, 1958, 1963, 1968, 1973, 1978, 1983; International Platform Association, 1980-82; Listed in *Who's Who Among Students in American Universities and Colleges*, *Who's Who in the Midwest*, *World Who's Who of Women*, *International Who's Who of Intellectuals*, *Personalities of the West and Midwest*, *International Book of Honor*. Address: 231 Deblin Drive, Cincinnati, Ohio 34239.■

LILLIAN WAN-MING LEI FENG

Assistant Administrator. Personal: Born May 5, 1923; Daughter of Chin Chang Lei and Siu Ching (Chen) Lei (both deceased); Married Ping Tien Feng; Mother of Paul, Lucy Feng Ho, May Feng Lee, Howard. Education: R.N. Diploma, Turner School of Nursing, Hackket Medical Center, 1946; Nursing Administration Certificate, University of Hawaii, International Corporation Administration Grantee, 1959; B.A. 1978, M.A. 1979, Central Michigan University. Career: Assistant Administrator, Palolo Chinese Care Home, 1968 to present; Assistant Head Nurse and Instructor, Turner Nursing School, China, 1946-47; Head Nurse and Instructor, Hoihow American Presbyterian Hospital and Nursing School; Nurse Instructor and Head Nurse, Taiwan TB Control Center and Taipei Provincial Nursing College, R.O.C., 1950-56; Nursing Supervisor and Instructor, Taiwan TB Control Center and Taipei Provincial Nursing College, R.O.C., 1956-66; Clinical Head Nurse, United States Naval Medical Research Unit No. 2 Taiwan, R.O.C., 1966-67. Organizational Memberships: American Nurses Association, Kansas, 1983; Hawaii Nurses Association, 1983; American College of Nursing Home Administrator Association, 1983; National League for Nursing; Hawaii Pacific Gerontology Association, 1983; National Activity Coordinator Association, 1983; American Health Care Association, 1983. Community Activities: American Presbyterian Church, Hainan Island, China 1946-50; Hoihow Leper Colony, Hainan Island, China, 1946-50; Tuberculosis Control Center, Taipei, Taiwan, R.O.C., 1950-67; Public Donations to The American Cancer Society 1981-83, Christmas Seals 1968-83, Lung Society 1981-83, Aloha United Way 1969-83, Easter Seals 1983, Epilepsy Foundation of America 1983, National Federation of the Blind 1983. Religion: Choir Leader, Sunday School Teacher, Youth Counselor, 1950-68. Honors and Awards: Outstanding Nursing Service to Communities by Taiwan Governor Huang Chieh, Taiwan, R.O.C., 1965; Outstanding Service of Cholera Control Program, Taiwan, R.O.C., 1954; Listed in *Who's Who of American Women*, *Personalities of America*. Address: 2459 10th Avenue, Honolulu, Hawaii 96816.■

VIRGINIA E. FENSKE

Retired Public Welfare Administrator. Personal: Born December 14, 1909, in Chicago, Illinois; Married Hugo Fenske (deceased). Education: A.B., University of Illinois, 1931; M.A., University of Chicago, 1941; Postgraduate, University of Washington, 1955-67; Tulane University, New Orleans, 1964; St. Martin's College, Olympia, Washington, 1957-58. Career: Supervisor, Regional Office, Illinois Division of Child Welfare, 1942-44; Instructor, Social Work, St. Louis University, 1944-45; Supervisor, Social Service Department, Midwestern Medical Centre, St. Louis, 1944-45; Washington State Department of Social and Health Services; Statewide Supervisor Licensing, Voluntary Child Care Agencies, Olympia, 1945-67; State Coordinator, Adult Programs Section, Washington State Department of Social and Health Services, 1967-73; Since Retirement, Developed VIGO Subdivision, Olympia. Organizational Memberships: National Association of Social Workers; American Academy of Certified Social Workers; Charter Board Member, Washington State Employees Credit Union; Board Member, Association of Retired Persons. Community Activities: Gloria Dei Lutheran Church; Daughters of the Nile; Eastern Star Chapter 36; Board Member, Olympia, Vasa International (Swedish) Lodge; Friendship Force International. Published Works: Author, "State Protects Children Living Away from Their Own Home," "Supervision and Licensing of Children's Agencies and Institutions," "What the State and Federal Government Does in Terms of Meeting the Problems of the Unmarried Parent," "A Case Study Concerning a Rural Unwed Mother," "Social Redirection of Venereally Infected Women," "Finding Foster Homes for Adults." Honors and Awards: Listed in *Dictionary of International Biography*, *Two Thousand Women of Achievement*, *The World Who's Who of Women*, *Who's Who of American Women*, *Personalities of the West and Midwest*, *Community Leaders and Noteworthy Americans*, *International Who's Who in Community Service*, *International Who's Who of Intellectuals*, *Who's Who*, American Biographical Institute Directories. Address: 920 Fenske Drive, Olympia, Washington 98506.■

PATRICIA MARGUERITA FERGUS

Writer, Consultant, Professor. Personal: Born October 26, 1918; Daughter of Mary A. Fergus (deceased). Education: B.S. 1939, M.A. 1941, Ph.D. 1960, University of Minnesota. Career: Writer, Consultant, Professor Emeritus, Mount Saint Mary's College, Associate Dean of College, Professor of English and Writing, Director Writing Center 1979-81; Mack Truck Company, Director Written Communication Seminars, 1979-81; University of Minnesota, Director Writing Center, University College 1975-77, Assistant Professor of Advanced Writing in English Department 1972-79, Instructor 1964-72, Lecturer in English, Extension Division 1961-64, Teaching Assistant in College of Education and Instructor in Reading Center 1960-61; United States Government Department of Defense, Teaching, Writing, Editing, Administrative and Managerial Positions, 1943-59; Numerous Presentations at State, National and International Conferences on Education, Writing and Communication; Reviewer for Publishers, 1977-79; Board of Directors, 510 Groveland Associates; Private Tutoring of College Bound Students. Organizational Memberships: National Council of Teachers of English, Regional Judge 1974, 1976-77, State Coordinator and Awards in Writing Program 1977-79; Minnesota Council of Teachers of English, Secretary Legislative Committee 1973-79, Secretary Resolutions Committee 1979-81, Chairperson Careers and Job Opportunities Committee and Member Task Force on Teacher Licensure 1977-79; Minnesota Council Advisory Board; State Department of Education Liasion Committee, 1979-81; Pi Lambda Theta, National Honor and Professional Association in Education, Epsilon Chapter, Keeper of the Records 1981-82, President 1982-83, Recording Secretary 1983-84; National Writers Club; Association of Women Writers; Minneapolis Poetry Society, 1983-84; League of Minnesota Poets, 1983-84; American Association of University Women; American Association of University Professors. Community Activities: Management Team, Eitel Hospital Gift Shop, 1981; MacPhail Center for Performing Arts Adult Ensemble Club, 1982-83. Religion: Saint Olaf Catholic Church, Minneapolis, Minnesota, Member, Parish Advisory Board 1983-84, Choir 1978 to present. Honors and Awards: Twin Cities Student Assembly Award for Outstanding Contributions, University of Minnesota, 1975; Educational Development Grant, University College, 1975; Award for Outstanding Contributions to Undergraduate Education, Morse-Amoco Foundation, 1976; William Randolph Hearst Grant, Mount Saint Mary's College, 1980; Elected to League of Minnesota Poets, 1983. Address: 1235 Yale Place, #201, Minneapolis, Minnesota 55403.■

ROGER NEPHI FERGUSON

Company President. Born September 6, 1932; Son of Robert Bryon and Fawn Bernice Christensen; Married Sybil Rae Clarke; Father of Debra Kay, Michael David, Wade Clarke, Lois Christine, Julie Xarissa (Rissa). Education: Attended Brigham Young University. Career: President of Diet Center, Inc.; Partner and Co-Owner (with Mrs. Ferguson), Ferguson Laboratories, The Print Shop, Ferguson and Associates, Sybil's Inc., International Livestock Inc., Soboba Springs Country Club Championship Golf Course, Diamond Ice Plant; Owner and Chairman of the Board, Dietology School, Diet Center Inn, Ferguson Farms; Regional Manager, Bio-Chemical Farm Products Company. Organizational Memberships: President, Local Insulators in Industrial Trade. Community Activities: Sponsoring Member of "Children's Miracle Network" Telethon (Children's Hospital Benefit); Ricks College Booster Club, 1960-62; United States Chamber of Commerce, 1977-81; Rexburg Chamber of Commerce; Board of Directors, Rexburg Golf Association, 1981. Honors and Awards: Friends of Education Award, Rexburg School District; Ricks College Booster Club Award; Outstanding Business Leader Award, Chamber of Commerce, 1983; Listed in *Who's Who in the West*, *Who's Who in America*, *Who's Who in Finance and Industry*, *The Directory of Distinguished Americans*, *Community Leaders of America*, *Men of Achievement*. Address: 401 Maple Street, Rexburg, Idaho 83440.■

SYBIL RAE FERGUSON

Company Executive. Personal: Born February 7, 1934, in Canada; Came to the United States in 1938, Naturalized 1976; Daughter of Alva John and Xarissa Merkley Clarke; Married Roger Ferguson; Mother of Debra Kay, Michael David, Wade Clarke, Lois Christine, Julie Xarissa (Rissa). Education: Attended Provo (Utah) Public Schools. Career: Founder and Co-Owner, Diet Center, Inc.; Partner and Co-Owner, Ferguson Laboratories, The Print Shop, Ferguson and Associates, Sybil's Inc.,

International Livestock Inc., Soboba Springs Country Club Championship Golf Course, Diamond Ice Plant; Director, Diet Center International Conventions, Nutritional Seminars, Advertising and Public Relations, Diet Center Dietology School and Counselors; Head of New Products Formulation, Ferguson Laboratories; Teacher, Dietology School; Editor, *Ad-Vantage Magazine*. Organizatinal Memberships: Advisory Board, Ricks College, Department of Business; Board of Directors, Boise State University, Community Health Services Division; Advisory Board, Brigham Young University, Department of Business; Founding Member, Committee of Two Hundred; Rexburg Chamber of Commerce, Member, Program Director 1976. Community Activities: Soroptimists Club; Rexburg Civic Club. Religion: Member of the Mormon Church. Published Works: Author of *The Diet Center Program: Lose Weight and Keep It Off Forever* 1983; Edits and Writes "Diet Center Nutritional Newsletter", and Other Books and National Articles on Diet and Nutrition, Operating Diet Center Franchises, Instructional Behavior Modification. Honors and Awards: Business Leader Award, Ricks College; Appointed Member of United States Congressional Advisory Board on Defense, Foreign Policy and Internal Security; Friend of Education Award, Rexburg School District; Outstanding Business Leader Award, Chamber of Commerce, 1983; Listed in *Who's Who in the World, Who's Who in America, Who's Who in the West, Who's Who in Finance and Industry, Contemporary Authors, The Directory of Distinguished Americans, Community Leaders of America.* Address: 401 Maple Street, Rexburg, Idaho 83440.■

DEBORAH ANN BOONE FERRER

Recording Artist. Personal: Born September 22, 1956; Daughter of Mr. and Mrs. Charles Eugene (Pat) Boone; Married Gabriel Vicente Ferrer; Mother of Jordan Alexander. Education: Graduate, Marymount High School, 1974; Attended the Vineyard School for Discipleship, 1975-76. Career: Recording Artist. Organizational Memberships: A.F.T.R.A.; S.A.G.; Academy of Country Music; N.A.R.A.S. Community Activities: Volunteer, Hathaway House School for Autistic Children, 1974-76; Youth With a Mission, Summer Missionary Training School, 1976. Religion: Church on the Way, First Foursquare Church of Van Nuys, 1970-81. Honors and Awards: Grammy Award as Best New Artist, 1977; Gold and Platinum Single and Album, "You Light Up My Life," 1977; American Music Award, Son of the Year, 1977; National Theatre Owners Award, Best New Personality, 1977; Grammy Award, Best Inspirational Performance, "With My Song . . ." Album, 1980. Address: 205 South Beverly Drive, Suite 205, Beverly Hills, California 90210.■

DAVID MARK FETTERMAN

Anthropologist/Educational Evaluator. Personal: Born January 24, 1954; Son of Irving and Dr. Elsie Fetterman, Willimantic, Connecticut. Education: B.A. Anthropology/B.S. History, University of Connecticut, 1976; A.M. Anthropology 1977, A.M. Education 1979, Ph.D. Medical and Educational Anthropology 1981, Stanford University. Career: Anthropologist, Educational Evaluator and Project Director; Lecturer, Senior Administrator, Stanford University; Assistant Director, Palo Alto Senior Citizen Day Care Center; Director of Office of Economic Opportunity Anti-Poverty Program; High School Teacher. Organizational Memberships: American Anthropological Association, Chairman of Committee on Ethnographic Approaches to Evaluation, Contributing Newsletter Editor; Council on Athropology and Education, Board Member, Liaison to American Educational Research Association; American Educational Research Association; Society for Applied Anthropology. Community Activities: California Arts Council Evaluation Study, Director 1982; Stanford Geneological Society, President; Contemporary Chinese Studies Association, Chairman; Charitable Organizations, Coordinator of Fund-Raising Activities. Religion: Religious Educator, Ethics and Judeo-Christian Historical and Cultural History. Published Works: Author *Ethnography in Educational Evaluation*, Numerous Articles in Professional Journals. Honors and Awards: Praxis Publication Award, American Anthropological Association; Evaluation Research Society, 1981; Distinguished Scholarship Service to the Nation Award, 1981; Richard M. Weaver Fellow, 1980; Josephine de Kamin Fellow, 1979; Irish Institute of Studies Award, 1975; International Studies Award, 1973; University Scholar, 1976; Phi Beta Kappa, 1976; Phi Kappa Phi, 1976; Phi Alpha Theta International Honor Scoiety in History, 1976. Address: 3208 Alameda de las Pulgas, Menlo Park, California 94025.■

JULIA ALLEN FIELD

Environmental Planner, Futurist. Personal: Daughter of Howard Locke Allen and Julia Wright (deceased). Education: B.A. cum laude, Harvard University, 1960; Attended Rosary College Graduate School, Florence, Italy, 1961; Harvard Graduate School of Design, 1964-65. Career: Environmental Planner, Futurist; President, Foundation Amazonia 2000, Republic of Colombia; President, Academy of Arts and Sciences of the Americas, Vice President, Black Grove, Inc.; Participant Vision '67, Second World Congress on Survival and Growth, New York, 1967; Participant, Symposium of Tropical Biology, Leticia, Colombia, 1969; Participant, National Seminar on Ecology and Urbanization, Bogota, Colombia, 1973; Participant, Ibero-Latin American Congress on Environment, Bogota, Colombia, 1978; Delegate from National University of Republic of Colombia to the Second Latin American Botanical Congress in Brasilia, Brazil, 1978; Participant, Western Hemisphere Energy Symposium, Rio de Janeiro, Brazil, 1980; Participant, "Symposium of Energy for the Development of Amazonia," Leticia, Colombia, 1981; Participant, "The Amazon Universe and Latin American Integration," Caracas, Venezuela, 1981; Participant, "National Congress Ecological Society of Colombia," Bogota, Colombia, 1982. Organizational Memberships: Sociedad Colombiana de Ecologia; United Nations Association of the United States; International Association for Hydrogen Energy; American Farmland Trust. Community Activities; Blueprint for Miami 2000 Committee, 1982; Board of Visitors, Duke University Primate Center, 1979-82; Coordinator Community of Man Task Force, HORIZONS '76, City of Miami, 1975-76; Citizens Planning Study Committee for Coconut Grove, 1974; Task Force on Colonization Report to President, Colombia, 1973. Honors and Awards: President's Group of the Year 2000, Republic of Colombia, 1971-74; Fellow, Royal Geograpical Society, London; Rachel Carson Award Fund, 1967. Address: 3551 Main Highway, Miami, Florida 33133.■

WILLIAM EARLE FINDLEY

Mayor. Personal: Born August 20, 1911, in Pickens, South Carolina; Son of William Elbert and Essie (Earle) Findley; Married Mary Louise Penland; Father of William Earle Jr., Mary Ann. Education: Graduate, Pickens High School. Career: Salesman, Bookkeeper, and Operator with Trucking Business; Owner, Pickens Supply Company; Mayor, Pickens, South Carolina, 20 years. Community Activities: Member, Pickens County Planning and Development Board 25 Years, Secretary-Treasurer; Member, Pickens County Municipal Association, President; Pickens City Council Member, Elected 1953; Mayor of Pickens, Elected 1955, Re-elected 1957, Re-elected 1961, Retired 1976; Democratic Party; Member Board of Directors, Cannon Memorial Hospital; Member Board of Directors, Pickens Bank; Director, Pickens Industrial Development Corporation; Member Board of Directors, Pickens Savings and Loan; Keowee Lodge #79, Ancient Free Masons, Pickens Chapter #47, Pickens Council #34, High Priest of Pickens Chapter 3 Years; Greenville Commandery #4; Hejaz Temple of the Shrine at Greenville, South Carolina; Grand Convention of Anointed High Priests of South Carolina; Illustrious Master, Pickens Council #34; Committeeman, Boy Scouts of America. Religion: Member of Grace Methodist Church of Pickens, Chairman of Board of Stewards, Member Board of Trustees, Chairman Finance Committee, President of Methodist Men's Club. Honors and Awards: Elected Citizen of the Year for Pickens and Community, 1960 (3 years). Address: 206 Hampton Avenue, Pickens, South Carolina 29671.■

CHARLES WILLIAM FINKL II

College Professor, Writer, Editor. Personal: Born September 19, 1941; Son of Charles W. Finkl, Sr.; Father of Amanda Marie, Jonathon William Frederick. Education: B.Sc. 1964, M.Sc. 1966, Oregon State University, Corvallis; Ph.D., University of Western Australia, Perth, 1971. Career: Chief Geochemist, International Nickel Australia Limited, Perth, Western Australia; Consulting Geologist, Hall Relph and Associates, Perth; Instructor in Natural Resources, Oregon State University, Corvallis, 1966-67; Demonstrator in Physical Geography, University of Western Australia, Perth, 1967-68; Courtesy Professor in Physical Sciences, Florida International University, Miami, 1976-77, 1980; Associate Professor of Oceanography; Director and Program Professor of Coastal Studies, Institute of Coastal Studies, Nova University at Port Everglades, Florida, 1977-83; Professor, Department of Geology, Florida Atlantic University, 1983 to present; Associate Consultant, Multinational Agribusiness Systems Incorporated, Washington, D.C., 1975 to present; Chief Editor, Encyclopedia of Earth Sciences Series, Stroudsburg, Pennsylvania, 1974 to present; Series Editor, Benchmarks in Soil Science Series, Stroudsburg, Pennsylvania, 1981 to present; Executive Director and Vice President, Coastal Education and Research Foundation, Fort Lauderdale, 1983 to present; Corresponding Member, International Geographical Union, Commission on Geomorphological Survey and Mapping, and Sub-Commission on Morphotectonics; Full Commission Member, International Geographical Union, Commission on River and Coastal Plains; Corresponding Member, INQUA Neotectonics Commission; Member, Ad Hoc Committee for the Broward County Museum of Natural History and Science. Organizational Memberships: American Association for the Advancement of Science; American Association of Petroleum Geologists; American Geophysical Union; American Geographical Society; American Quaternary Association; American Littoral Society; American Shore and Beach Preservation Association; American Society of Photogrammetry; Association of Southern Agricultural Scientists; Australian Society of Soil Science; Australian

Institute of Mining and Metallurgy; British Geomorphological Research Group; British Society of Soil Science; Canadian Geophysical Union; The Coastal Society; Deutsche Bodenkundlichen Gesellschaft; Deutsche Geologische Vereinigung; European Association of Earth Science Editors; Estuarine and Brackish-Water Sciences Association; Federation of American Scientists; Florida Academy of Science; Florida Shore and Beach Preservation Association; Gamma Theta Upsilon; Geological Association of Canada; Geological Society of America; Geological Society of Australia; Geological Society of London; Geological Society of Miami; Geological Society of South Africa; Geologists Association; Geoscience Information Society; Institute of Australian Geographers; International Soil Sciece Society; International Union of Geological Sciences; Mineralogical Association of Canada; The Nature Conservancy; National Parks and Conservation Association; New York Academy of Sciences; Soil Science Society of America; Societe de Belge de Pedologie; Society of Economic Paleontologists and Mineralogists; Society of Mining Engineers of A.I.M.E. Community Activities: Co-Chair, Week of the Ocean, Fort Lauderdale, Florida, 1981; Charter Member, "Friends of Ocean Sciences," Fort Lauderdale, 1977-78; Patron, Fort Lauderdale Museum of Art, 1981 to present; Member, Fort Lauderdale Academy of Science, 1980; Member, Ad Hoc Committee to Broward Museum of Archaeology, 1979; Sigma Nu Fraternity 1960-64, Vice President, Chaplain, Historian. Religion: Presbyterian. Published Works: Editor-in-Chief, *Litoralia: An International Journal for the Coastal Sciences*, 1983 to present. Honors and Awards: Sigma Nu Man of the Year, 1964; Order of the Orange Oar, Oregon State University Varsity Rowing Team, 1964; Gamma Theta Upsilon, 1965; The Council for Agricultural Science and Technology, 1978; American Registry of Certified Professional in Agronomy, Crops, and Soils, Certified Professional Soil Scientist 1979 to present; Certified Professional Geological Scientist, American Institute of Professional Geologists, 1983 to present; United States Naval Institute, 1980. Address: 1808 Bay View Drive, Fort Lauderdale, Florida 33305.■

JOANNE ELIZABETH FINLEY

Assistant Secretary Health. Personal: Born December 28, 1922; Daughter of Frank Robert and Margaret Matthews Otte; Married Joseph Finley; Mother of Scott, Ethan, Lucinda, William. Education: B.A. Public Administration/Economics, Antioch College, Yellow Springs, Ohio, 1944; M.S. Public Health, Yale University School of Medicine, 1951; M.D., Case-Western Reserve University School of Medicine, 1962. Career: Assistant Secretary Health, Maryland Department Health and Mental Hygiene, present; New Jersey State Commissioner of Health, 1974-82; Administrative Assistant to Congressman George Outland of California; Research Director, Cleveland, Ohio, Health Goals Project; Acting Commissioner of Health, Cleveland, Ohio; Director of Health Planning, Philadelphia Department of Public Health; Vice President of Medical Affairs, Blue Cross of Greater Philadelphia; Director of Public Health, New Haven, Connecticut. Organizational Memberships: Association of State and Territorial Health Officers; American Public Health Association; American Society for Public Administration; Kellogg Commission on Education for Health Administration. Community Activities: University of Medicine and Dentistry of New Jersey, Board of Trustees; Chairman, New Jersey Health Care Facilities Financing Authority; New Jersey Health Care Administrators Board; New Jersey State Health Coordinating Council; New Jersey Board of Institutional Trustees; New Jersey Council on Postgraduate Medical Education; The Medical College of Pennsylvania, Assistant Clinical Professor; Philadelphia Mayor's Committee on Hospital Services, Staff Director 1972-73; Philadelphia Experimental Health Services Delivery System Project, Director 1972; Parent and Child Inc., Washington, D.C., Executive Director 1957; Yale University School of Medicine, Department of Epidemiolgy and Public Health, Lecturer 1982-83. Honors and Awards: Diplomate, American Board of Preventive Medicine, 1972. Address: 57 Brookstone Drive, Princeton, New Jersey 08540.■

WILLIAM F. FINN

Physician. Personal: Born Juiy 23, 1915, in Union City, New Jersey; Son of Neil C. and Catherine Marie Finn; Married Doris Henderson, Daughter of Charles H. and Ruth Henderson; Father of Neil Charles, Sharon Ruth, David Stepehn. Education: B.A. summa cum laude, Holy Cross College, 1936; M.D., Cornell University Medical School, 1940. Military: Served in the United States Medical Corps, 1944-46, attaining the rank of Captain. Career: Intern, Albany Hospital, 1940-41; Intern, Obstetrics and Gynecology, New York Hospital, 1941-42; 3rd Assistant Resident in Obstetrics and Gynecology 1942, 1st Assistant Resident in Obstetrics and Gynecology 1943, Resident in Obstetrics and Gynecology 1944, New York Hospital; J. Whitridge Williams Fellowship, Obstetrics and Gynecology, New York Hospital, 1946-47; American Cancer Society Fellowship, Gynecology, New York Hospital, 1950-51; Assistant Attending Obstetrician/Gynecologist 1948-66, Associate Attending Obstetrician/Gynecologist 1948-66, New York Hospital; Director, Obstetrics and Gynecology, North Shore University Hospital, 1952-59; Attending, Obstetrics and Gynecology, North Shore University Hospital, 1959-81; Associate Attending, St. Francis Hospital, 1973-79; Courtesy Staff, Manhasset Medical Center, 1959-70; Honorary Obstetrician/Gynecologist, North Shore University Hospital, 1981 to present; Consultant, Obstetrics and Gynecology, Mercy Hospital, 1959 to present; Attending Obstetrician/Gynecologist, St. Francis Hospital, 1979 to present; Assistant Obstetrics and Gynecology 1942-43, Instructor Obstetrics and Gynecology 1944, Assistant Professor Obstetrics and Gynecology 1948-50, Associate Professor Obstetrics and Gynecology 1950-66, Associate Professor of Clinical Obstetrics and Gynecology 1971, Cornell University; Adjunct, Health Sciences, C. W. Post Center. Organizational Memberships: Lying-In Alumni Association; New York Hospital Alumni; American Medical Association; New York State Medical Society; New York County Medical Societies; Queens Gynecology Society, Past President; New York Obstetrical Society; Nassau County Medical Society; Nassau Obstetrical and Gynecological Society, Past President; New York Academy of Science; American Fertility Society; New York Gynecological Society; American Association of Gynecological Laparoscopists; American Association of Colposcopists; American Geriatrics Society; Nassau Academy of Medicine. Community Activities: Trustee, Village of Plandome Manor; Board of Managers, Church Charity Foundation; Executive Committee, Foundation of Thanatology; Chairman, Maternal Welfare Committee; New York State Maternal and Child Welfare committee; Nassau County Medical Society; Chairman, Abortion Review Committee, Nassau Obstetrical and Gynecological Society. Religion: Episcopalian. Honors and Awards: Okinawa Battle Star; World War II Victory Medal; Occupation Medal; 25 Years of Service, New York Hospital; 25 Years of Service, North University Hospital; Physician's Recognition Award, American Medical Association; Bishop's Cross of Diocese of Long Island; Fellow, International Biographical Association; Listed in *Directory of Medical Specialists, American College Surgeons Directory, American Fertility Society Directory, American Men of Science, American Men of Medicine, Community Leaders of America, Wisdom, Who's Who in the East, National Cyclopedia of American Biography, Dictionary of International Biography, Men of Achievement, International Who's Who in Community Service, Who's Who in New York State, Who's Who in the United States, International Who's Who of Intellectuals*, Many Others. Address: 3 Aspen Gate, Manhasset, New York 11030.■

CARMINE FIORENTINO

Attorney. Personal: Born September 11, 1932, in Brooklyn, New York; Son of Pasquale and Lucy Coppola. Education: Studied Court Reporting, Hunter College, New York City, 1951; Radio Announcing, Columbia Broadcasting School, New York City, 1952; LL.B., Blackstone School of Law, Chicago, Illinois, 1954; LL.B., John Marshall Law School, Atlanta, Georgia, 1957; Studied Fiction and Non-fiction Writing, Famous Writers School, Westport, Connecticut, 1962. Career: New York State Workmen's Compensation Board; New York State Department of Labor, 1950-53; Court Reporter-Hearing Stenographer, Governor Thomas E. Dewey's Committee of State Counsel and Attorneys, 1953; Served as Public Relations Secretary, the Industrial Home for the Blind, Brooklyn, New York, 1953-55; Served as Legal Stenographer, Researcher, Law Clerk for Various Law Firms, Atlanta, Georgia, 1955, 1957-59; Served as Secretary for Import-Export Firm, Atlanta, Georgia, 1956; Private Law Practice, Atlanta, Georgia, 1959-63; Attorney-Advisor, Trial Attorney for United States Department of Housing and Urban Development, Atlanta, Georgia and Office of HUD General Counsel, Washington D.C., and Legal Counsel for The Peachtree Federal Credit Union, 1963-74; Acting Director, Elmira New York Disaster Field Office, United States Department of Housing and Urban Development, 1973; Presently Engaged in Private Law Practice. Organizational Membership: Member Bars State of Georgia, District of Columbia, United States Supreme Court, United States District Court D.C., United States Second Circuit Court of Appeals, United States District Court Northern District of Georgia, United States Fifth Circuit Court of Appeals, Georgia Supreme Court, Georgia Court of Appeals; Practiced, United States Court of Claims; Member, American Bar Association; Federal Bar Association; Atlanta Bar Association; Decatur-DeKalb Bar Association; American Judicature Society; Old War Horse Lawyers Club; Association of Trial Lawyers. Community Activities: Junior Chamber of Commerce; Toastmasters International; International Platform Association; Honorary Advisor, National Board of Advisors, American Biographical Institute; The Smithsonian Institution; Founding Member, Century Club, Republican National Committee; Sustaining Member, Republican National Committee; Columbian Repubican League; Member, Republican Presidential Task Force; Life Dynamics Fellowship; The National Historical Society; Atlanta Historical Society; Atlanta Botanical Gardens; American Museum of Natural History; Gaslight Club; National Audubon Society; Sierra Club; The Musical Heritage Society; American Association for the Advancementof Science. Published Works: Author, Non-fiction, Poetry; Composer, Words and Music to Popular Songs and Hymns; Published in *The Evening Star*, Washington D.C., and *The National Observer*. Honors and Awards: Most Progressive Student Award, New York City Public School System, 1950; Pitman Shorthand Achievement Awards, 1948, 1949, 1950; Commendation, United States House Un-American Activities Committee, 1951; Served Simultaneously as Secretary, County Committeeman, Captain, in Brooklyn Republican Assembly District Political Organization, 1954-55; Recommended for Policy-making Position in Administration of President Dwight D. Eisenhower, 1953; Recommended for White House Position in Administration of President Richard M. Nixon, 1971; Assisted in Preparation of Banquets and Meetings for President Dwight D. Eisenhower, President Richard M. Nixon, Senator Irving Ives of New York, Senator Jacob Javits of New York, Governor Thomas E. Dewey, Governor Nelson A. Rockefeller, New York; Served as Tutor and Monitor Regarding Georgia State Bar Examinations, 1959-61; Appearances on Network Television, Local Television and Radio Broadcasts; Appearances in Motion Pictures Narrated by Eva Le Gallienne and John C. Daly, Aired Nationally and Produced for the Blind and the Deaf-Blind; Acted as Public Relations Director for Robert J. Smithdas, First Deaf-Blind Person in the World Ever to Earn a Masters Degree; Served on Atlanta Lawyer Reference Panel, 1959-63; Commendation from Director of United States Department of

TWO THOUSAND NOTABLE AMERICANS

Housing and Urban Development Elmira, New York Disaster Field Office for Excellence in Disaster Relief Work During 1972 Tropical Storm Agnes Flood Disaster; Instructed Students in District of Columbia Public School System on United States Constitution, Bill of Rights, in Conjunction with Annual Program Sponsored by Federal Bar Association and Assisted by United States Supreme Court Justice Tom Clark; Served on Committee Honoring Special Assistant to the Secretary of State of the United States; Numerous Biographical Listings including *Georgia Legal Directory, Martindale Hubbell Law Directory, Outstanding Atlantans, Personalities of the South, Community Leaders and Noteworthy Americans, Men of Achievement, Book of Honor, International Who's Who in Community Service, Who's Who in the South and Southwest, Who's Who in American Law,* Others. Address: 2164 Medfield Trail, N.E. Atlanta, Georgia 30345.■

ROGER RAYMOND FISCHER

State Representative. Personal: Born June 1, 1941, in Washington, Pennsylvania; Son of Raymond and Louise Fischer; Married Catherine Louise Trettel on August 13, 1972; Father of Roger Raymond II, Steven Gregory. Education: Graduate, Washington High School, 1959; B.A., Washington and Jefferson College, 1963; Undertook Graduate Work, Carnegie Institute of Technology. Military: Served with the United States Air Force Reserve, achieving the rank of Major; presently serving with the Pennsylvania Air National Guard, 171st ARFW, Greater Pittsburgh International Airport. Career: Research Engineer, Jones and Laughlin Steel Research; Legislator, Pennsylvania House of Representatives, Elected 1966, 1968, 1970, 1972, 1974, 1976, 1978, 1980, 1982. Organizational Memberships: Pennsylvania State Board of Education; Education Committee, Chairman; Veterans Affairs Committee, Former Minority Chairman, Former Vice Chairman; Basic Education Sub-committee, Former Chairman; House Committees on Appropriations, Military, and Veterans Affairs, Industrial Development, Professional Licensure Public Utilities, Law and Order and Conservation, Game and Fisheries Commission, Former Member; Joint State Government Commissions Task Forces on Veterans Benefits to Investigate Prisons, Aid Black Lung Victims annd Study Cost of Education, Former Member; Police Sub-committee on the Pennsylvania Crime Commission's Regional Planning Council, Former Chairman. Community Activities: Washington School Board, Advisory Member, 1965-71; City Mission, Board of Directors; Boy Scout Merit Badge Counselor; Local 1141 U.S. Steel Workers; American Legion Post #175, 171st ARFW; Department of Pennsylvania American Legion 40 et 8 Vice Chairman for Legislation, Voiture #676; Reserve Officers Association, Vice President Chapter #27, 1970-71, Life Member; Washington Lodge #164 F&AM; Washington Royal Arch Chapter #150; Jacques Demolay Commander #3; Washington Council #1; Washington-Greene Shrine Caravan; Syria Temple A.A.O.N.M.S.; Appalachian Trail Conference, Life Member; Potomac Appalachian Trail Club; Keystones Trails Association; Warriors Trails Association, Life Member; Pennsylvania Appalachian Trail Committee; Triathlon Federation-U.S.A.; Sons of the American Revolution, Life Member; National Guard Association of the U.S. Religion: Lay Assistant, Lutheran Church in America. Honors and Awards: Delta Epsilon; Physics Achievement Award, Chemical Rubber Company, 1961-62. Address: Overlook Drive, Washington, Pennsylvania 15301.■

ROBERT JAY FISH

Doctor of Dental Surgery. Personal: Born June 4, 1947; Son of Sidney and Sara Fish; Married Lana Joy Halperin on May 24, 1981. Education: B.S., The Ohio State University, 1969; D.D.S., The Ohio State University College of Dentistry, 1973. Career: Externship, Department of Oral Surgery, Jackson Memorial Hospital; Licensed to Practice Dentistry in Florida, Ohio, Massachusetts, Washington D.C., New York, Michigan; Former Owner Innerspace Concepts, Inc.; Staff Member, Broward Community College of Allied Medicine, 1974; Lecturer, Dental Practice Management and Administration, Dental Health Services of Florida, 1975; Began a Charter and Air Taxi Service, Flying Fish, 1976; RJF Enterprises, 1978; Owner Fish Realty; United States Representative to Paletta Cosmetics, Paris; Member of Staff of Pennsylvania Hospital Institute and Florida Medical Center Hospital; Guest Speaker and Radio Guest Appearances on Topics of his Special Interests; Weekly Program, "Ask the Dentist"; Sole Importer for United States and Canada of Fine French Wine from Domaine de Saint Jean; Owner, Robert Jay Fish and Company; United States Representative for Sandri, S.R.L. of Genoa, Italy, Manufacturers of Sophisiticated Dental Equipment. Organizational Memberships: Alpha Omega Dental Fraternity; American Analgesia Society; Board of Certified Hypnotists; Dental Health Services of Florida, Board of Directors. Published Works: *Cosmetic and Reconstructive Dentistry.* Honors and Awards: Listed in *Who's Who in the South and Southwest, Men of Achievement, Personalities of America.* Address: 10237 N.W. 2nd Street, Coral Springs, Florida 33065.■

CHARLES FREDERICK FISHER

Education Administrator, Consultant. Personal: Born March 20, 1936; Son of F. Theodore and Helen D. Fisher. Education: B.A., Lawrence College, 1958; M.A. 1966, Ed.D. 1973, Columbia University. Military: Served as Lieutenant and United States Navy Mine Countermeasures Officer, Seventh Fleet, Western Pacific, 1958-62; Served as Naval Reserve Officer Recruiting Officer. Career: Currently Consultant, Human and Organizational Resource Development; Assistant to President, Lawrence University, Wisconsin; American Council on Education, Assistant Director of Academic Administration Fellows Program, American Council on Education, Director of Institute for College and University Administrators, Director of Higher Education Management Improvement Program, Director of Higher Education Leadership Development Programs; Director of Council Affairs, American Council on Education, Washington, D.C. Organizational Memberships: Phi Delta Kappa; American Association for Higher Education; Association for the Study of Higher Education; American Society for Training and Development; American Association of University Administrators, Board of Directors 1979-84. Community Activities: Beta Theta Pi, Chapter and Alumni President; Reserve Officers Association of the United States; Lawrence University Alumni Association, Vice President 1971-73; National Executive Service Corps; Washington International Visitors' Center, Lecturer; United States-Japan Culture Center, Board of Directors 1980 to present; Episcopal Church Vestry; Palladium Association, 1976 to present; Adjunct Professor, University of Pennsylvania and Union of Experimenting Colleges and Universities; Lawrence University Board of Trustees, 1982-86; United Charities, Chairman; Council on Religion and International Affairs, Chairman; White House Conference on Youth, Delegate; National Academy for Human Resource Development; National Identification Program for Women in Higher Education; World Affairs Council. Religion: Episcopal Church, Acolyte, Lay Reader, Committee Member, Vestryman. Published Works: "Behind the Iron Curtain," 1963; *The Remaining Steps,* 1964; *Mini Cases in College and University Administration,* 1975; *The Evaluation and Development of College and University Administrators,* 1977; "Being There Vicariously by the Case Study Method," *On College Teaching,* 1978; *A Guide to Leadership Development Opportunities for College and University Administrators,* 1976-80. Honors and Awards: Bausch and Lomb Science Award, 1952; Phi Beta Kappa Award, 1954; Pullman Foundation Award, 1954-58; Mace Honorary Society, 1957; Senior Class President, 1958; Outstanding Graduate Award, 1958; Navy People-to-People Award, 1961; New York Regents Fellowship, 1966; Heft and Delta Alpha Pi Scholarships, 1966-67; Alumni Fellowship, 1967; American Council on Education Institute Faculty Appreciation Award, 1979; Listed in *Outstanding Young Men of America, Leaders in Education, Who's Who in America, Notable Americans of the Bicentennial Era, International Men of Achievement, International Who's Who of Intellectuals, Who's Who in the World.* Address: 1325 - 18th Street Northwest, Suite 906, Washington, D.C. 20036.■

CHARLES HAROLD FISHER

Research Professor and Technical Consultant. Personal: Born November 20, 1906, in Hiawatha, West Virginia; Married Lois C. Fisher, 1968. Education: B.S., Roanoke College, Salem, Virginia, 1928; M.S. 1929, Ph.D. 1932, University of Illinois-Urbana; Certificate American Management Association, 1961. Career: Adjunct Research Professor, Roanoke College, Salem, Virginia, 1972 to present; Consultant, Paper Technology for the Library of Congress 1973-76, Food Technology for Pan-American Union 1968, Textile Research to the Republic of South Africa 1967; Director, United States Department of Agriculture Southern Utilization Research Division, New Orleans, Louisiana, 1950-72; Research Group Leader, United States Department of Agriculture Eastern Regional Laboratory, Philadelphia, Pennsylvania, 1940-50; Research Group Leader, United States Bureau of Mines, Pittsburgh, Pennsylvania, 1935-40; Instructor, Chemistry, Harvard University, 1932-35. Organizational Memberships: American Chemical Society, Board Member 1969-71; American Institute of Chemists, President 1962-63, Chairman of the Board 1963, 1973-75; American Institute of Chemical Engineers; The Chemical Society, London; American Association for the Advancement of Science; Chemists Club, New York. Community Activities: Established Lawrence D. and Mary A. Fisher Scholarship Fund, Roanoke College, Salem, Virginia; Cosmos Club, Washington, D.C.; Chamber of Commerce, New Orleans; International House, New Orleans; Round Table Club, New Orleans; Roanoke College Alumni Association, President 1978-79. Published Works: Author or Co-Author of More than 150 Publications; Inventor of Co-Inventor with 72 Patents. Honors and Awards: Honorary D.Sc. Degrees, Tulane University, 1953, Roanoke College 1963; Southern Chemists Award, 1956; Herty Medal, 1959; Chemical Pioneer Award, 1966; Honorary Member, American Institute of Chemists, 1973; Named Polymer Science Pioneer by *Polymer News* Periodical, 1981; Listed in *Who's Who in the World, Who's Who in America, Who's Who in the South and Southwest, Who's Who in Government, Dictionary of International Biography, Two Thousand Men of Achievement, American Men and Women of Science, The Blue Book of Leaders of the English-Speaking World, Engineers of Distinction Including Scientists in Related Fields, Leaders in American Science, Personalities of the South.* Address: Chemistry Department, Roanoke College, Salem, Virginia 24153.■

TWO THOUSAND NOTABLE AMERICANS

HARVEY F. FISHER

Professor, Laboratory Director. Personal: June 22, 1923; Married Camille; Father of Steven L. Education: B.S., Western Reserve University, 1947; Ph.D., University of Chicago, 1952. Military: Served with the United States Army, Combined Engineers, Corporal, 1943-46, ETO, Pac. Career: Professor Biochemistry, University of Kansas School of Medicine, Kansas City, Kansas, 1965 to present; Director, Laboratory Molecular Biochemistry, VA Medical Center, Kansas City, Missouri, 1963 to present; Postdoctoral Fellow, Physicians and Surgeons, Columbia University, New York, New York, 1952-54; Project Associate, Department of Chemistry, University of Wisconsin-Madison, 1954-56; Instructor of Chemistry, University of Massachusetts-Amherst, 1956-57; Senior Associate, Edsel B. Ford Institute for Medical Research, Detroit, Michigan, 1957-63; Associate Professor, University of Kansas School of Medicine, Kansas City, Kansas, 1963-65. Organizational Memberships: American Society of Biological Chemistry; American Chemical Society; American Association for the Advancement of Science; Biophysical Society. Community Activities: VA Liaison Representative NIH Biochemistry Study Section, 1965-68; Member VA National Basic Science Advisory Panel, 1966-68; Committee Isoenzymes and Enzyme Subunits Established by Commission of Editors of Biochemistry Journals of the International Union of Biochemistry, 1966-68; VA Biochemistry-Biophysics Research Evaluation Committee, 1969-71; National Correspondent, Public Policy Committee, American Society Biological Chemistry, Division Biological Chemistry, American Chemical Society, 1969-71; Chairman, Subcommittee on Extramural Grants for VA Council of the VA, 1969-71; Member Editorial Board, *The Journal of Biological Chemistry*, 1973-80; National Science Foundation, Molecular Biology Advisory Panel, 1974-77; Member Editorial Board, Archives of Biochemistry and Biophysics, 1981; Member, Merit Review Board for the Basic Sciences on Behalf of VA's Central Office, 1981 to present. Religion: Temple Bethel, Board of CRS. Honors and Awards: Atomic Energy Commission Predoctoral Fellow, 1951-52; VA Career Scientist Award, 1978. Address: 10031 Foster Road, Overland Park, Kansas 66212.■

WILL STRATTON FISHER

Illuminating Engineer. Personal: Born June 27, 1922; Married Patricia A., Daughter of Mr. and Mrs. E. J. Fesco; Father of Patricia Jo, Will S. Jr., Robert J. Education: Attended Vanderbilt University, 1941-43, 1946-47; B.S. Electrical Engineering (Advanced ASTP), City College of New York, 1943-44. Military: Served with the United States Army Engineers, Manhattan Project (atomic bomb), First Lieutenant, 1943-46. Career: Illuminating Engineer. Organizational Memberships: Illuminating Engineering Society of North America, President 1978-79; International Commission on Illumination, United States Expert on Technology Committee 3.3, Fundamentals of Physical Environment, 1971 to present; Institute of Electrical and Electronic Engineers, Editor of Lighting Chapter of *Graybook*, 1964, 1974, 1981; American Society of Heating, Refrigerating and Air Conditioning Engineers, Panel 9 of ASHRAE 90-75, and Lighting Expert ASHRAE 100.4. Community Activities: Orange School Boosters 1964-80, Membership Chairman 1968-70, Recreation Chairman 1970-72. Religion: Member, Garfield Memorial Methodist Church, Sunday School Superintendent 1970-74. Honors and Awards: Patent, Parabolic Wedge Louver (ultra-low brightness lighting shielding device), 1961; Fellow, Illuminating Engineering Society of North America, 1963; Distinguished Service Award, IES of North America, 1980; Tau Beta Pi; Registered Professional Engineer in Ohio. Address: 120 Meadowhill Lane, Moreland Hills, Ohio 44022.■

LEONARD DONALD FITTS

Education Administrator. Personal: Born August 19, 1940, in Montgomery, Alabama; Son of William Leonard Fitts and Mary Alice Brown; Married Sherrell Adrienne Thomas, June 4, 1966. Education: B.S. 1961, M.Ed. 1964, Tuskegee Institute; N.D.E.A. Fellow, Boston University, 1965-66; Postgraduate Study, University of Wisconsin, 1966-67; Ed.D., University of Pennsylvania, 1972; M.B.A., Drexel University, 1981. Military: Served in the United States Air Force as Communications Officer, 1961-63. Career: Assistant Superintendent of Education, Lower Camden County Regional School District Number One, Atco, New Jersey, 1981 to present; Director of Special Services, Camden City Board of Education, Camden, New Jersey, 1975-81; Psychologist of the Florida Parent Education Follow Through, Philadelphia Board of Education, 1971-75; Teaching Fellow and School Psychologist, University of Pennsylvania-Philadelphia, 1969-71; Chief of Guidance Counselors and Administrator-Staff-Equal Employment Opportunity Programs, Radio Corporation of America, 1968-69; Guidance Counselor, University of Wisconsin, 1967; School Psychometrist, Boston University, 1965-66; Graduate Assistant, Mathematics Coordination and Associate Education Director, Tuskegee Institute, 1963-65. Organizational Memberships: National Association of School Psychologists; American Psychological Association; American Personnel and Guidance Association; Association of Special Education Administrators; Camden County Guidance and Personnel Association; Council of Exceptional Children; New Jersey Association of Pupil Personnel Administrators. Community Activities: Phi Delta Kappa; Lions Club; Advisory Council of Learning Resources Center; All-Assist Recovery and Counseling Program, Southeast Neighborhood Health Center, Advisory Chairman; Lincoln Day Nursery, Board Member; The National Foundation March of Dimes, Southwest New Jersey Chapter, Board of Directors. Published Works: Author of Papers including "The School Psychologist and Drug Problems in the Schools," Published in *International Encyclopedia of Neurology, Psychiatry, Psychoanalysis, and Psychology*, 1977. Honors and Awards: Appreciation Award, the White House Conference on Handicapped Individuals, 1977; Region III Outstanding Citizens Award, United States Department of Health, Education and Welfare; The Chapel of Four Chaplains Legion of Honor Certificate Citation, 1977; Project Follow Through Certificate of Appreciation, 1975; National Association of School Psychologists Certificates of Recognition, 1973; Delta Airline Service Award, 1970; Vice President's (Hubert Humphrey) Task Force on Youth Motivation Certificate of Appreciation, 1969; Watson Kinter Scholarship, Psychological Services Assistanceship, University of Pennsylvania, 1969-72; Various Scholarships; Listed in *Who's Who in the East, Men and Women of Distinction*. Address: 1105 Hudson Avenue, Voorhees, New Jersey 08043.■

DONALD J. FLASTER

Medicolegal Consultant. Personal: Born August 29, 1932; Son of Murray and Theresa Flaster (both deceased); Father of Elisabeth Ann, Andrew Paul. Education: A.B., The Johns Hopkins University, 1953; M.D., University of Naples, 1959; LL.B., Blackstone School of Law, 1970. Career: President, Scientific and Regulatory Services Consulting, Inc.; Medicolegal Consultant; Family Physician. Orgnizational Memberships: New York Academy of Family Physicians; American Academy of Family Physicians, Fellow; Medical Society of New Jersey. Community Activities: Valley Cottage, New York Fire Department, Assistant Chief and Fire Surgeon, 1961-66; Nyack Community Ambulance Corps, Medical Advisory; "Y" Indian Guides; Morris School District Boy Scouts/Cub Scouts, Pack Committee, Instructor of Health-Related Courses. Published Works: Author, *MALPRACTICE: A Guide to the Legal Rights of Patients and Doctors*, 1983. Honors and Awards: New York State Regents Scholarship, 1949; Mead Johnson Fellowship for General Practice Residency Training, 1960; Featured as "Businessman of the Week," *Morristown Daily Record*, January 1981. Listed in *Who's Who in the East*. Address: 22B Foxwood Drive, Morris Plains, New Jersey 07950.■

MILO JOSEPH FLEMING

Attorney at Law, Municipal Attorney. Personal: Born January 4, 1911; Son of Mr. and Mrs. John E. Fleming (both deceased); Married Lucy Anna Pallissard; Father of Michael Bartlett Russell (stepson), JoAnn Clemens (stepdaughter), Elizabeth Charlene Fleming Weber. Education: A.B. 1933, LL.B. 1936, both from the University of Illinois-Urbana; Undertook Postgraduate Courses at John Marshall Law School. Military: Participated in the Reserve Officers Training Corp, University of Illinois, 1929-31, Graduating with the Rank of Sergeant. Career: Clerical, University of Illinois Health Service, 1930-36; Attorney at Law and Municipal Attorney. Organizational Memberships: American Bar Association, Chairman Committee on Ordinances and Administrative Regulations, Local Government Section 1969-72 and 1975-78, Member of the Council of Local Government Section 1976-80; Iroquois County Bar Association, State of Illinois, President 1966-67; University of Illinois Health Service, Chief Clerk 1934-36. Community Activities: Iroquois County Universities Bond Issues Campaign, Chairman 1960; Assistant Attorney General of Iroquois County, 1964-69; State of Illinois Employees Group Insurance Advisory Comission, 1975-78; Independent Order of Odd Fellows, State of Illinois, Grand Master 1964-65; Odd Fellows Old Folks Home, Mattoon, Illinois, Board of Trustees 1966-71; President, Northern Association in Illinois of Odd Fellows and Rebekahs, 1983-84; Mason (Shriner); Prepared Eight Municipal Code Books for the following Illinois Municipalities, Watseka, Milford, Martinton, Crescent City, Woodland, Cissna Park, Papineau; New Sewage Disposal Plant, New Industrial Plant of Life Time Doors, New Water Tower for Watseka, New Municipal Gas Plant for Milford, New Water Systems for Martinton and Wellington, New Water Tower for Village of Onarga; Assisted in Rebuilding Business Area of Crescent City; New Sewage Disposal Plant at Cissna Park; Developer of Belmont Acres; Belmont Water Company, President 1976-81; Iroquois County Development Corporation, President 1961-68. Religion: Methodist. Honors and Awards: First Place in State of Illinois, Examination on League of Nations, 1928; Third Place, United States in Competition for the Baldwin Prize in the Field of Municipal Government, 1932, 1933; Phi Eta Sigma, 1930; Gregory Scholarship Award, 1932; Meritorious Service Jewel, Grand Encampment of the Independent Order of Odd Fellows, 1980; 1 of 10 Finalists for Dad of the Year, University of Illinois, 1970; International Platform Association, 1980; Life Member, University of Illinois President's Council, University of Illinois Alumni Association, International Biographical Association, Iroquois

TWO THOUSAND NOTABLE AMERICANS

County Historical Association, Danville Consistory; Listed in *Personalities of America, Personalities of the West and Midwest, Dictionary of International Biography, Who's Who in the World, Who's Who in American Law, Who's Who in Finance and Industry, Who's Who in the Midwest.* Address: 120 West Jefferson Avenue, Watseka, Illinois 60970. ■

BONNIE GORDON FLICKINGER

Writer, Lecturer. Personal: Born July 27, 1932; Daughter of C. George and Violet Gordon; Mother of Burt Prentice Flickinger III, Catherine Flickinger Schweitzer, Marjorie Flickinger Ford. Education: Graduate, Buffalo Seminary; Attended Vassar College; B.A. 1964, M.Ed. 1968, State University of New York at Buffalo; Summer Study, General Theological Seminary; Certified in Teaching of German; Study at Jung Institute, Zurich. Career: Graduate Assistant, State University of New York, Department of Instruction 1969-71, Department of Educational Psychology 1976-77; Interpreter in Germany, 1972; *Redbook Magazine*, Editor, Writer, Computer Programmer, Statistician, Psychological Analysis 1975-76; Founder, Rainbow Lectures, 1977 to present; Interpreter, United States Olympic Committee, 1980; Fashion Model; Freelance Photographer; Writer; Lecturer, Television, Clubs, Church Groups. Organizational Memberships: American Association of Teachers of German; American Council of Teachers of Foreign Languages; American Educational Research Association; American Lessing Society; American Psychology Association; Association of Women Educators; Buffalo Chamber of Commerce; Delta Phi Alpha; International Platform Association; National Association of Women Business Owners; National League of American Pen Women; National Speakers Association; New York State Foreign Language Teachers Association; Pi Lambda Theta; Washington Independent Writers; Western New York Analytic Psychology Society; American Association of University Women; English-Speaking Union; Graduates Association Buffalo Seminary, Former Positions include Director, Nominating Committee Chairman, Patrons Benefit Chairman. Community Activities: Fellow, Urban College, State University of New York at Buffalo; Vassar Club of Western New York, Scholarship Chairman, Director, Prospective Student Committee, Admissions Interviewer, Former Positions include President, Fund Project Chairman, Nominating Committee Chairman; Eastern Tennis Association, Director, Regional Vice President, Management Committee, Former Positions include Captain, Delegate District 14; Buffalo World Hospitality Association, Interpreter, Hostess, Former Director; Children's Foundation, Trustee, Member Appropriations Nominations and Finance Committee; Empire Investment Club, Program Chairman, Former President; Director, Buffalo Council on World Affairs; UB Alumni Associaton, Director, Life Member, Vice President Young Alumni, Former Treasurer; Erie County Mental Health Association; Junior League of Buffalo, Former Positions include Director, Education Chairman, Chairman New Members Provisional Course; Frontier Club of Republican Women, Former Positions Include Director, Secretary; Women's Committe Museum of Science Co-Founder, Former Director; Seven College Conference Co-Founder, Former Director; Buffalo Country Club, Former Positions Include Tennis Chairman, Children's Tennis Chairman; Founder, Children's Interclub Tennis; Founder, Women's Summer Interclub Tennis; Niagara Frontier Tennis Association, Founder, Former Positions Include Director, Secretary; Life Member, Albright-Knox Art Gallery; Women's Committee, Buffalo Philharmonic Orchestra; Children's Hospital Aid Association; Landmark Society; Life Member, Buffalo Museum of Science; Metropolitan Art Museum; Museum of Modern Art; Art Gallery of Ontario; Life Member, International Institute; League of Women Voters; Life Member, New England Society. Religion: Member of Westminster Church; Sunday School Teacher; Leader Adult Bible Study; Adult Education Committee; Jersusalem Post, 1982. Published Works: Author of Articles on the Olympics in Mexico and Germany, Davis Cup Matches, "Teaching Spanish in College", *Modern Language Journal*; Other Articles include "Understanding Islam," "Bethlehem Its Message for Today," "Chronic Strife in Galilee, the Personal Province of the Prince of Peace," "IRA's for Alimony Recipients," Catalogia, the Newest Merchandising Center," "Partying in New York," "Old Friends Meet to Cheer on Reagan, Regan, Kemp, and Nowak at D.C. Balls". Honors and Awards: Scholarship, New York State Regents; Award for Best Informed Young Person, Episcopal Diocese of Western New York, 1946; Honorable Mention, New York State National League of American Pen Women, 1983; Listed in *Dictionary of International Biography, World Biographical Hall of Fame, International Who's Who in Community Service, Community Leaders of the World, International Who's Who of Intellectuals, International Book of Honor, Notable Americans, Men and Women of Distinction, Who's Who of American Women, Personalities of America, The World Who's Who of Women, Who's Who in Tennis.* Address: 31 Nottingham Terrace, Buffalo, New York 14216. ■

CHARLES E. FLOYD

Electrical Maintenance Engineer. Personal: Born September 10, 1953; Son of Mr. and Mrs. Willard Floyd. Education: B.A., Berry College, Mt. Berry, Georgia, 1975; Graduate Work, North Georgia College, Dahlonega, Georgia, 1976-77. Career: Electrical Maintenance Engineer. Community Activities: Masonic Lodge; Aircraft Owners and Pilots Association; National Rifle Association; American Association of Safety Engineers, Permanent Member T.B.L.A., Berry College; Berry Alumni Association (Y.A.B.B.I.T.); Tri-County Community College Faculty. Religion: Member, Revival Baptist Church, Blairsville, Georgia. Honors and Awards: Listed in *Who's Who in American Colleges and Universities, Who's Who in the South and Southwest, Personalities of America, Men of Distinction, Personalities of the South, Biographical Roll of Honor.* Address: Route 3, Blairsville, Georgia 30512. ■

ANDERSON B. FLY

Executive. Personal: Born November 27, 1923, in Caddo, Oklahoma; Married Celia Patterson, 1947; Father of Two Sons. Education: Graduate of Cotton Center High School, Cotton Center, Texas, 1940; United States Navy Aviation Radio School, Aviation Radar School, Aerial Gunnery School, and Operational Training In Dive Bombers, 1943; B.S. Agriculture with major in Animal Husbandry and minor in Organic Chemistry, Texas Technological College, Lubbock, Texas, 1951; United States Air Force, Technical Instructor Course Number IT 57100 completed 1955, Guidance Missile Familiarization Course completed 1956, Curricula Course in Technical Writing completed 1957; Northrop Aircraft, Inc., SM-62 Snark Guided Missile Weapons System, Guidance System Repair Technician, Electronic 31170B completed December 1957. Military: Served in the United States Navy from 1943-45 as a Combat Aircrewoman in Dive Bombers and Patrol Bomers; Awarded Two Distinguished Flying Crosses and Two Air Medals as Aviation Radioman 1/c While Serving in the South Pacific. Career: President and General Manager, Hydro-Jet Services Inc., Amarillo, Texas 1959 to present, President of Aero-Span Inc., Amarillo, Texas 1977 to present, Tuff-N-Lite Inc., Amarillo 1981 to present, Marine Metals Inc., Amarillo 1977 to present; Vice President, Tuff-N-Lite Inc., Amarillo, 1981 to present; Chief Civilian Instructor of Guidance System Electronics Repairman Course on the SM-62 Snark Guided Missile, United States Air Force, 1955-59; Automotive Mechanics Instructor in the Night School Adult Vocational Program, Amarillo Junior College, Amarillo, Texas, 1956-57; Instructor in the Veterans On-Farm Training Program, Dora, New Mexico, State Department of Vocational Education, Las Cruces, New Mexico, 1951-55; Heavy Equipment Operator, Sanders Construction Company, Portales, New Mexico, 1954-55; Derrickman, Motorman, and Roughneck on Deep Oilwell Drilling Rigs, Makin Drilling Company, Hobbs, New Mexico, 1952-54; Instructor in Veterans On-Farm Training Program, Encino, New Mexico, State Department of Vocational Education, State College, New Mexico, 1948-50; Instructor of Farm Mechanics and Welding, Hale County Vocational School, Plainview, Texas, 1948. Organizational Memberships: Society of Mining Engineers of A.I.M.E., Presented Paper "Subsurface Hydraulic Mining through Small Diameter Boreholes," 98th Annual Meeting, Washington, D.C., February 1969. Published Works: "Subsurface Hydraulic Mining through Small Diameter Boreholes," Published in *British Hydromechanics Research Association* 1970, *Mining and Minerals Engineering* 1969, *Mining Journal* 1970, Presented at First Conference on the Hydraulic Transport of Solids in Pipes, University of Warwick, Cranfield, Bedford, England, September 1970; Presented Paper, "The Hydro-Jet Mining System," Idea Conference of the 1970 Uranium Symposium sponsored by the New Mexico Institute of Mining and Techno, Socorro, New Mexico, May 1970; "Mining by Water Jet," *The Australian Miner*, 1969; "Hydro-Blast Mining Shoots Ahead," *Mining Engineering*, 1969; *Solids Pipelining Seen Around Corner*, Mid-America Oil and Gas Reporter, 1966; Two United States Patents and One Canadian Patent on Hydro-Jet Borehole Mining System; Three United States Patents and One Canadian Patent on Hydro-Torq Pumping Systems; One United States Patent on Subsurface Fluid Control Systems; Other Patents Pending. Honors and Awards: Listed in *Who's Who in the South and Southwest, Personalities of the South, Dictionary of International Biography, Who's Who in Finance and Industry, Notable Americans of 1978-79, Men of Achievement, International Who's Who of Intellectuals.* Address: Post Office Box 30400, Amarillo, Texas 79120. ■

CLAUDE L. FLY

Executive. Personal: Born June 23, 1905; Son of A. B. and Josephine Lowery Fly (both deceased); Married Miriam R.; Father of Maurita Ellen Kane, John M. Education: B.A. Agronomy/Soils/Chemistry 1927, M.S. Chemistry and Soils 1928, Oklahoma State University; Ph.D. Chemistry and Soils, Iowa State University, 1931; Postgraduate Studies in Personnel Management and Communications. Military: Served in the Oklahoma National Guard, 1923-25. Career: President, Claude L. Fly and Associates Consultants in Soil and Water Resource Development, 1963 to present; Assistant Administrator and Research Leader, U.S.D.A.-A.R.S.-S.W.C., 1958-63; Chief Agronomist and Head of Land Development, Morrison-Knudson Company, 1953-58; Soil Scientist, U.S.D.A. Soil Conservation Service, 1935-53; Head of Chemistry and Sciences Department, Panhandle A&M College, 1931-35. Organizational Memberships: American Chemical Society, Chapter Chairman; Soil Conservation Society, Chapter President; American Society of Agricultural Consultants, President; American Society of Agricultural Engineers; American Society of Agronomy and Soil Sciences; American Institute of Chemists. Community Activities: Ft. Collins Lions Club, Active Member, Drives for the Blind; Republican

TWO THOUSAND NOTABLE AMERICANS

Party, Precinct Chairman 1979, State Caucus Representative; Salvation Army, Donations and Christmas Bells Ringer; Condominium Association, Executive Board, Rules Committee Chairman. Religion: Methodist Church, Member and Supporter. Honors and Awards: Honorary Life Member, American Society of Agronomy; Fellow of the Soil Conservation Society; Fellow of the American Institute of Chemists; Distinguished Service Award, Gamma Sigma Delta; Golden Medal of Honor, Sons of the American Revolution; National 4-H Alumni Award; Listed in *Who's Who in the West, World Who's Who in Business and Commerce, Dictionary of International Biography, Men of Science, Community Leaders and Noteworthy Americans, Book of Honor.* Address: 415 South Howes Street, Fort Collins, Colorado 80521.■

JAMES L. FOBES

Research Psychologist. Personal: Born January 26, 1946; Married Jacqueline T. Mitchell. Education: Ph.D. Psychology, University of Arizona, 1975. Career: Research Psychologist, United States Army Research Institute for the Behavioral and Social Sciences; Principal Associate, Fobes Associates, Psychologists; Former Associate and Assistant Professor of Psychology, Department of Psychology, California State University at Los Angeles; Former Postdoctoral Research Fellow, Behavioral Biology Division, California Institute of Technology. Honors and Awards: Author and Co-Author of Numerou Publications in the Field of Psychology. Address: 3067 Larkin Road, Pebble Beach, California 93953.■

LeGRAND BENEDICT FONDA

Engineering Consultant (Materials). Personal: Born October 20, 1912; Son of Job Pierson and Florence Benedict Fonda (both deceased); Married Amelia Ellen Bainbridge; Father of James Benedict, Mrs. Elizabeth Jane McWethy. Education: Graduate, Lansingburgh High School, Troy, New York, 1929; B.S. Industrial Chemistry, University of Wisconsin, Madison, Wisconsin, 1934; Additional Studies through Correspondence Courses, Evening Sessions, and General Electric Company Courses; Studies at Alexander Hamilton Institute, Dale Carnegie Institute, Rensselaer Polytechnic Institute, Massachusetts Institute of Technology, Tufts University, Others. Military: Served with the New York State National Guard, Company D, 105th Infantry, PFC, 1928-30; University of Wisconsin R.O.T.C., 1930. Career: Engineering Consultant-Materials, present; Laboratory Technician, 1936-42; Metallurgical Engineer, 1942-50; Laboratory Manager, 1950-60; Provided Technical Assistance on Foreign License Agreements (Japan, Germany, Italy, Belgium), 1958 and 1960-62; Quality Control Manager, 1962-64; Advanced Jet Engines Materials and Processes Engineer, 1964-65; Deisel Engine M&P Engineer, 1965-77. Organizational Memberships: National Aeronautis Association, 1937-42; Army Ordnance Association (now National Defense Preparedness Association), 1937 to present; National Society of Professional Engineers 1947-63, Executive Committee of North Shores (Massachusetts) Chapter 1952-60; American Society for Testing and Materials 1952-64, Secretary Committee H-10 1956-60, Secretary Subcommittee XII 1952-56, Secretary Subcommittee IX 1960-64; Aerospace Materials Specifications Division of Society of Automotive Engineers 1947-64, 1979 to present, Head of Several Task Forces; Life Member, American Society for Metals 1937 to present, Member Executive Committee Northwest LA Chapter 1975 to present. Community Activities: Member Radiation Detection Team, North Shore (Massachusetts) Division of Massachusetts Civil Defense, 1954-60; Tibbits Cadets, Troy, New York, 1936-42. Religion: Clifton Lutheran Church, Marblehead, Massachusetts, Church Council 1945-60, Financial Secretary, Deacon, Trustee, Helped Raise Funds, Plan and Build New Church. Honors and Awards: Elected Fellow of the American Society for Metals (national), 1978; Named Man of the Year by Erie, Pennsylvania Engineering Societies Council; Attended 40th Anniversary of the First British Jet Airlane Flight in 1981 at Rugby, England, with Jet Pioneers. Address: 704 West Gore Boulevard, Erie, Pennsylvania 16509.■

LEE ELLEN FORD

Attorney-at-Law. Personal: Born June 16, 1917; Daughter of Arthur and Geneva Ford. Education: Ph.D., Iowa State College, 1952; J.D., University of Notre Dame Law School, 1972. Career: Attorney in Individual Practice, Auburn, Indiana; Former Writer, Professor, Auditor, Manpower Economist, Researcher and Editor. Organizational Memberships: American Bar Association; National Association of Women Lawyers; Indiana Bar Association; DeKalb County Bar Association; Association of Trial Lawyers of America, 1972-75. Community Activities: Aide to Governor of Indiana, 1973-75; Member, Board Association of Migrant Opportunity Services, 1975-80; Board Member of Indiana Federal Humane Societies, 1975 to present; Board Member of DeKalb County Humane Society, 1974-80; Butler City Planning Commission, Board Member 1973-75; Butler City Park Board, 1973-75; Coalition of Volunteers for Handicapped, Handicapped Indiana, 1975 to present; I.C.A.L.L. Indiana Caucus on Animal Legislation and Leadership. Religion: Member Lutheran Social Services, Ft. Wayne, Indiana, Personnel Board, 1982-83; Network and Social Services Committee, Indiana-Kentucky Synod Board, Lutheran Church of America; Member of Lutheran Church of America, Board of Indiana-Kentucky Synod 1976 to present, Indiana Council of Churches 1975-80, Indiana Inter-Religious Council on Human Equality 1975-80. Published Works: Has Published Over 1000 Volumes of Research Papers, Articles, etc., in the Fields of Cytogenetics Research, Dog Genetics and Breeding, Guide Dogs for the Blind, Women's Legal Rights, Animal Legal Rights, Family Law, etc. Address: 824 East Seventh Street, Auburn, Indiana 46706.■

CLAUDE ELLIS FORKNER

Foundation President. Personal: Born August 14, 1900; Son of Allen F. Forkner and Lucy Adeline Irvine (both deceased); Married Marion Sturges DuBois, Daughter of Arthur and Helen Sturges DuBois (both deceased); Father of Claude Ellis Jr., Helen Sturges Haskell (Mrs. Jack Haskell), Lucy Irvine Greene (Mrs. Thomas H. Greene). Education: B.A. cum laude 1922, M.A. 1923, University of California at Berkeley; M.D., Harvard University Medical School, 1926. Military: Served with the United States Army (S.A.T.C.), Private, 1918; United States Army Reserve, 1st Lieutenant, 1922-27; New York National Guard, Squadron A Association, Private, 1927-29; Civilian Consultant to the Surgeon General of the United States Army, Assimilated Rank of Colonel, Assigned to CBI Theater and China Theater, 1943-45; Consultant to the Surgeon General of the Chinese Army, 1943-45. Career: Assistant in Anatomy (Histology), University of California, Berkeley, 1922-23; Teaching Fellow Histology, Harvard Medical School, 1924-26; Tutorial Student under Dr. George R. Minot, Huntington Memorial Hospital, Boston, 1925-26; Resident Student Intern in General Surgery, The New England Deaconess Hospital, Boston, 1925-26; Intern, Johns Hopkins Hospital (Internal Medicine), 1926-27; Assistant in Pathology and Bacteriology, Rockefeller Institute for Medical Research, New York City, 1927-29; National Research Council Fellow in Pathology and Clinical Investigation, Freiburg, Germany, National Hospital, London, 1929-30; First Francis Weld Peabody Fellow in Medicine, Thorndike Laboratory of the Harvard Medical School, 1930-32; Associate Professor of Medicine, Peking Union Medical College (Rockefeller Foundation), Peking, China, 1932-36; Honorary Lecturer in Medicine, Peking Union Medical College (Rockefeller Foundation), Peking, China, 1936-37; Assistant Professor of Medicine, Cornell University Medical College, 1937-43; Director and Professor of Medicine, China Medical Board (Rockefeller Foundation), 1943-45; Honorary Professor of Medicine, Cheeloo University Medical College, Chengtu, China, 1943-45; Honorary Professor of Medicine, National Shanghai Medical College, Chengtu, China, 1943-45; Associate Professor of Clinical Medicine, Cornell University Medical College, 1943-53; Chief of Mission Appointed by President Harry Truman to Care for Ailing Shah of Iran, 1951; Clinical Professor of Medicine, Cornell University Medical College, 1953-66; Clinical Professor of Medicine (Emeritus), Cornell University Medical College, 1966 to present; Medical Director, The Fish Memorial Hospital (DeLand, Florida), 1969-70; Assistant Attending Physician 1937-45, Associate Attending Physician 1945-50, Attending Physician 1950-66, Consultant in Medicine 1966-74, Honorary Member of the Staff 1974 to present, The New York Hospital; Attending Physician 1946-51, Consultant in Internal Medicine 1951-69, Roosevelt Hospital; Consultant in Internal Medicine, United States Naval Hospital, St. Albans, New York, 1952-53; Consultant, The New York Infirmary, 1950-69; Consultant in Medicine Representing The New York Hospital-Cornell Medical Center, Bronx Veterans Administration Hospital, 1956-69. Organizational Memberships: American Medical Association, 1927 to present, Life Member; New York County Medical Association, 1937 to present, Life Member; New York State Medical Association, 1937 to present, Life Member; American Association for the Advancement of Science, 1927-; American Society for Clinical Investigation, 1931 to present, Emeritus 1965 to present; Association of American Physicians, 1943 to present, Emeritus 1966 to present; New York Academy of Medicine, Vice President 1953-54, Life Member; New York Society for the Study of Blood, 1948 to present, President 1951-52; International Society for Hematology, 1948 to present; New York Medical and Surgical Society, 1952 to present, Vice President 1965, President 1966, Emeritus 1974 to present; Member Board of Directors of American Board of Internal Medicine 1950-56, Chairman Examinations Committee 1954-56; Harvard Medical Society of New York, President 1958-60; The Blood Club, (National Hematological Society), 1948 to present, President 1954; New York Cancer Society, 1955-74, Vice President 1957-58, President Elect 1958-59, President 1960-61; Pan American Medical Association, 1957-74, President Section on Internal Medicine 1962-65; A Program for Harvard Medicine, National Alumni Chairman 1962-65; New York Academy of Sciences, 1954 to present, Elected Fellow 1965; The Royal Society of Health of London, 1970-74; Aesculpian Club of Harvard Medical School, 1950 to present; American Clinical and Climatological Association, 1954 to present, Emeritus 1966; Resources Committee of the Harvard Medical School, 1971-74; Association for Health Records, 1971-75; Society for Computer Medicine, 1971-74; American College of Physicians, Life Member; Association for the Advancement of Medical Instrumentation, 1971-74; Member Board of Directors, Society for Advanced Medical Systems, 1970-80; The Chinese Medical Association; Far-Eastern Association of Tropical Medicine; The Harvey Society; The Society for

TWO THOUSAND NOTABLE AMERICANS

Experimental Biology and Medicine; The Massachusetts Medical Society; The American College of Chest Physicians; The Tuberculosis and Respiratory Disease Association; American Thoracic Society; China Aid Council, Member Board of Directors 1937-43, President 1939-41; American Committee for Chinese War Orphans, Member 1938-41, President 1939-41; American Bureau for Medical Aid to China, Member Board of Directors 1938-43; United China Relief, Member Board of Directors 1941-43; Chinese Industrial Cooperatives, Member Board of Directors 1938-41; Originator, Member Board of Trustees, The Medical Passport Foundation. Community Activities: Harvard Club of New York; Century Association of New York; Harvard Club of Central Florida; Country Club of DeLand (Florida); Active in Community Affairs. Religion: Presbyterian. Published Works: Author of Approximately 125 Papers Chiefly in the Fields of Hematology, Tropical and Infectious Diseases, Pathology, Internal Medicine, Medical Education, Congenital Defects; Author of "Leukemia and Allied Disorders," 1938; Other Publications in his Field. Honors and Awards: Decorated Medal of Honored Merit, Republic of China, 1942; Companionship in the Royal Order of Homayun (Knights), Conferred by His Imperial Majesty, Shahinshah of Iran, 1957; Gold Medal, Harvard Medical Alumni Association, 1965; Sigma Xi Honorary Scientific Society, 1922; Fellow, New York Academy of Sciences, 1965 to present; Elected Honorary Member Rotary International of DeLand, Florida, 1975. Address: P.O. Box 820, Deland, Florida 32720.■

RUTH LOVE FORMAN

Educator. Personal: Born August 20, 1938; Daughter of Willie James and Gertie Lou Pippen; Married Wilbert James. Education: Diploma, Dunbar High School, Bessemer, Alabama; B.S., Alabama A&M University, Huntsville, Alabama, 1962; 15 Bible Certificates. Career: Elementary School Teacher (4th grade). Organizational Memberships: A.E.A.; J.C.E.A.; National Education Association; A.F.T.; Reading Council; Math Council. Religion: Member, Ebenezer Baptist Church, Birmingham, Alabama, Narrator for Rev. Thorne's Ministry over Radio Station WSMQ (Sunday mornings), 4 Years. Honors and Awards: Certificate of Appreciation for Outstanding and Dedicated Service, 1981; Trophy for Most Outstanding 4-H Female, 1972; American Biographical Research Association; Listed in *Personalities of the South, Book of Honor.* Address: 3012 Wenonah Circle, Birmingham, Alabama 35211.■

JOANNE C. FORTUNE

Accountant and Appraiser. Personal: Born January 24, 1947; Daughter of Mrs. J. Fortune; Married Carl J. Postighone; Mother of Renee, Carl Jr., Joseph. Education: B.S. summa cum laude, Syracuse University, 1961; Postgraduate Studies, London School of Economics. Career: Accountant and Appraiser Specializing in Tax Certiorari; Former Accountant for Cherry Burrell Corporation, Sperduto C.P.A. Firm, City Club of Yonkers Inc. Organizational Memberships: American Management Association. Community Activities: American Security Council; New York State Advisory Congress; Westchester Association of Women; American Wildlife Association; McLean Heights Youth Association; National Organization of Business; Associate, American Conference Board; Yonkers Executive Club; Youth in Trouble Board; National Caretta Association; Lincoln Park Tax Association. Honors and Awards: McLean Heights Meritorious and Sponsors Award, 1978-83; Citation, American Wildlife Association, 1983; Kenyan Wildlife Preservation Committee Citation, 1982; Listed in *Who's Who in the East, Who's Who of American Women, International Register of Profiles, International Register of Intellectuals.* Address: 105 Bajart Place, Yonkers, New York 10705.■

MAXIE ELLIOTT FOSTER

University Faculty Member. Personal: Born May 1, 1950; Son of Mrs. Rosa Rittenberry. Education: M.Ed. 1974, B.S.Ed. 1972, University of Georgia. Career: Faculty, Department of Health and Physical Education, Louisiana State University, Shreveport, Louisiana, 1982 to present; Faculty, Macon Junior College, Macon, Georgia, 1975-82; Faculty, University of Georgia, 1973-74; Teacher/Coach, Clarke County Board of Education, Athens, Georgia, 1972-73; Community Center Director, City of Athens, Athens, Georgia, 1974-75. Organizational Memberships: Phi Epsilon Kappa; American Alliance Health, Physical Education, Recreation and Dance; Council of Black American A.F.F., Atlanta, Georgia; State Committee, Life and History of Black Georgia, Atlanta, Georgia; American Association of Health, Physical Education, and Recreation; Georgia Association of Health, Physical Education and Recreation; Georgia High School Coaches Association; National Athletic Coaches Association; Georgia Association of Educators; National Educators Association; Georgia Association of Educators; Phi Epsilon Kappa. Community Activities: Board of Directors, Georgia Lung Association, Macon, Georgia, 1975-82; Board of Directors, Big Brothers Association, Macon, Georgia; Advisory Council, Jack and Jill Club of America, Macon, Georgia; Board of Managers, Health Systems Agency, Department of Health, Education and Welfare, Region IV, Macon; Board of Directors, Senior Citizens Inc., Bibb County, Macon, Georgia; Track Official, Southeastern Conference, University of Georgia; Men's Civic Club, Athens, Georgia; Christian Children's Fund Inc.; Volunteer, Georgia Sheriff Association. Religion: Vice President Baptist Training Union, Sunday School Teacher, Youth Department Organizer, Singles Ministry, Biblical Teacher/Writer, Consultant State Baptist Convention and Sunday School and B.T.V. Congress. Published Works: Author, "Running: How to Get Started" *GAHPER Journal,* Fall 1981. Honors and Awards: Scholarship to University of Georgia in Track and Field, 1968; Scholarship Awarded by Key Club of Athens High School, 1968; First Black Scholarshipped Athlete, University of Georgia, 1968; Captain of University of Georgia Track Team, 1972; First Black Physical Education Major to Attain a B.S.Ed. Degree in Physical Education from the University of Georgia, 1972; Selected as One of Three Finalists in the Martin Luther King Memorial Scholarship Award, 1968; Served on Clarke County Commission on Troubled Children, Grand Jury Appointee, Athens, Georgia, 1971; Distinguished Service Award, Samuel F. Harris Branch Young Men's Christian Association, Athens, Georgia, 1974; Served as Judge for Varsity Cheerleader Tryouts, University of Georgia, 1975; City of Athens Recreation and Parks Department, Athens Youth League, Certificate of Award in Basketball (1st place), City Wide One-on-One Championships 1975, Certificate of Award in Physical Fitness, Served as Supervisor and Coordinator of Summer Day Camp Physical Fitness Program 1975; Certificate of Award, Track and Field, Served as Supervisor and Meet Director of Summer Day Camp Track Meet 1975; Recipient Numerous Track Related Citations, Awards, Records and Services; Candidate, National Big Brother of the Year Award, 1981; Finalist, Volunteer of the Year Awards, Macon, Georgia, 1981; Kappa Delta Pi, National Professional Honor Society in Education; First State President, Black Alumni Association of Georgia, 1978; Cited as "Citizen of the Week" by *Macon Courier* Newspaper, Macon, Georgia, March 1981; Selected as First Vice President for Physical Education for the University of Georgia Health, Physical Education, Recreation and Dance Alumni Association, Fall 1981; Others; Listed in *Personalities of the South, Outstanding Young Men of America.* Address: 10200 Youree Drive #405, Shreveport, Louisiana 71115.■

FRANK EISON FOWLER

Executor, Appraiser. Personal: Born June 2, 1946; Son of Mamie Howell Fowler; Married Mary Elizabeth, Daughter of Walter H. Zimmerman; Father of Christopher Andrew, Thomas Weston. Education: Attended Baylor Prep School, Chattanooga, Tennessee, 1964; B.B.A., University of Georgia, 1969. Career: Represents Andrew Wyeth, Jamie Wyeth, Carolyn Wyeth and Estate of N. C. Wyath. Organizational Memberships: Appraisers Association of America; International Society of Appraisers. Community Activities: Member, John F. Kennedy Center for the Performing Arts; Advisory Board, Appointed by President Carter; Member Board of Directors, The Children's Home, Chattanooga, Tennessee, and Commerce Union Bank, Chattanooga, Tennessee; Chairman, The Baylor School Sustaining Fund, Chattanooga, Tennessee, 1982-83; Member, National Finance Committee for the Election of Jimmy Carter, 1976; United Way Volunteer, University of Georgia and Baylor School Alumni Societies; Produced Inaugural Portfolio for President Jimmy Carter 1976 and Presidential Portfolio 1980. Religion: Member, Church of Good Shepherd, Lookout Mountain, Tennessee. Honors and Awards: Greek Horseman Honorary Society, University of Georgia, 1968; Listed in *Men of Achievement, Personalities of America, Who's Who in South and Southwest.* Address: P.O. Box 247, Lookout Mountain, Tennessee 37350.■

RODNEY WATSON FOWLER

Associate Professor, Counselor, Crisis Intervener. Personal: Born January 30, 1938, in Lock Haven, Pennsylvania; Son of Watson Francis and Margaret Elizabeth Fowler; Married Doris Jane Reed, October 3, 1981. Education: B.S., Lock Haven State College, 1965; M.A., San Diego State University, 1968; Rank 1 Certificate, Western Kentucky University, 1971; Ed.D., Ball State University, 1974. Career: Policeman, Arizona, Pennsylvania, Kentucky, Indiana; Special Education Teacher, New York, Nevada, California; Child Care Supervisor, San Diego Children's Home; Resident Director, Home of Guiding Hands, 1960-69; Police Psychologist,

Delaware County Police (Muncie, Indiana), 1973-76; Assistant Professor of Psychology, Ball State University (Germany, England, Greece, Spain), 1974-76; Associate Professor of Counseling, University of Tennessee at Chattanooga, 1976 to present. Organizational Memberships: Diplomate, American Board of Examiners in Crisis Intervention, 1981 to present; Fellow, American Academy of Crisis Interveners, 1977 to present; Fellow, National Academy of Crisis Interveners, 1981 to present; Southeastern Academy of Crisis Interveners, President 1979 to present; National Academy of Crisis Interveners, Vice President 1982 to present; Loss Therapy Center, Director of Training 1978 to present; National Eagle Scout Association; Associate Editor, *Psychology: A Quarterly Journal of Human Behavior*; Editorial Board *Journal of Crisis Intervention*. Community Activities: Governor's Child Abuse Review Team, 1982 to present; Executive Director, Green River Crime Council; Scoutmaster, Boy Scout Council; Consultant to Eight Police Departments, Indiana Women's Prison, Elmira Reformatory, Juvenile Court, Two Hospitals and Various Other Community Agencies; Conducted Training in Crisis Intervention and Hostage Negotiations with Chattanooga City, Red Bank, Cleveland, Hamilton County and Lafayette (Georgia) Police Departments, Tennessee Highway Patrol and Numerous Others; Chief Advisor to S.W.A.T., Chattanooga Police Department, 1977 to present; S.W.A.T. Advisor, Red Bank Police Department 1978 to present, Lafayette (Georgia) Police Department 1979 to present, Cleveland Police Department 1979 to present, Tullahoma Police Department 1981 to present; Fraternal Order of Police. Published Works: Author "Police Hostage Negotiations" (1984), "Efficacious Factors for Facilitating the Emotional Adjustment of Children" (1981), "Crisis in Chattanooga: The Men from M.A.R.S." (1978), "Counselor Follow-Up On Spouse Abuse Interventions" and "Crisis Intervention on the Beat" (1979); Honors and Awards: Listed in *Who's Who in the South and Southwest, Personalities of the South, Personalities of America, Dictionary of International Biography, Notable Americans, Men of Achievement, Book of Honor, Men and Women of Distinction, International Who's Who in Community Service, The Anglo-American Who's Who, Directory of Distinguished Americans*. Address: 168 Masters Road, Hixson, Tennessee 37343.■

ABRAHAM HARVEY FOX

Motel and Real Estate Executive. Personal: Born October 6, 1918, in Wausau, Wisconsin; Son of Samuel Fox (deceased); Married First Wife, Edith Wolinsky, on October 18, 1942 (deceased 1973); Second Wife, Donna K., Daughter of Elsie Beakman; Father of Stuart Lee, Ivan Dennis, Ellen Randy (1st marriage), Danelle M. (2nd marriage). Education: Student, Public Schools, Wausau, Wisconsin. Military: Served with the United States Army, 1942-45. Career: Accountant, United Air Lines, 1946; Owner, Manager, Firebird Motel and Restaurant 1946 to present, Fox Realty Company 1958 to present, Fox Enterprises 1961-66; President, FFICO, Inc., 1966 to present; Partner, Fox Properties, Wausau, 1967-71; Owner 1971 to present; Regional Coordinator, Friendship Inns International; Loan Broker, Woodmen of the World, 1958 to present. Organizational Memberships: National Institute of Real Estate Brokers; National Association of Real Estate Boards. Community Activities: American Legion, 40 and 8, Grande Chef de Gare 1967-68; Disabled American Veterans; Chamber of Commerce, Committee Chairman 1966; Moose; Masons, 32nd Degree; Shriners, Commander 1958; Elks; Order Eastern Star; B'nai B'rith, President 1963; Active in Community Chest Drives and Other Fund Raising Activities. Honors and Awards: Decorated Bronze Star. Address: 1714 19th Street, Cheyenne, Wyoming (June through August); 4670 Freshwater Drive, Las Vegas, Nevada 89103 (remaining months).■

FRANCES JO FOX

Student. Personal: Born July 14, 1966; Son of Dr. Joseph C. (deceased) and Charlotte Fox. Education: Jellico High School (graduate in 1984). Community Activities: Beta Club (4 years), Treasurer; 4-H; School Newspaper Co-Editor; Cheerleader (5 years); Youth Community Work. Religion: Church Worker. Honors and Awards: Class President; Class Favorite; Home Economics President; Football Homecoming Queen; High School Honor Roll; School Perfect Attendance Award (9 years); Listed in *Who's Who Among American High School Students, Young Personalities of America, Biographical Roll of Honor, International Biographical Roll of Honor, Personalities of the South*. Address: P.O. Box 450, Jellico, Tennessee 37762.■

MARY ELIZABETH FOX

Jounalist and Retired Professor. Personal: Born in Williamson County, Texas; Daughter of Mr. and Mrs. J. S. Fox (both deceased). Education: Attended Southwestern University and University of Texas at Austin. Career: Journalist and Lecturer; Associate Professor of Government, History, English, Drama, Speech and Journalism, Served as Head of Journalism Department, Served as Director of Publicity, Southwestern University, 1944-77; Head of Public Relations Bureau in Washington, D.C., 1952-54; Dean's Assistant, School of Fine Arts, Southwestern University, Summer 1968; Retired from Education, 1977; Served as Accredited Correspondent to the United Nations since its Founding in 1945, Attended Numerous Sessions; Frequent Speaker on International Affairs; Popular Book Reviewer. Organizational Memberships: Women in Communications, Inc.; Writers and Press Club of England; American Judicature Society; American Association of University Women; American Newspaper Women's Club; Pi Delta Epsilon; Sigma Tau Delta; Sigma Phi Alpha; Delta Omicron; Pi Epsilon Delta; National Collegiate Players; Delta Delta Delta; Mask and Wig Players; Bell County New Media Club; P.E.O. Community Activities: International Platform Association; British Horse Society; Texas Historical Society; Mill Creek Country Club; Stagecoach Country Club; Democratic Delegate to County, State and National Conventions. Published Works: Several Projects in Progress. Honors and Awards: Named to Advisory Board of Marquis Biographical Library Society; Listed in *International Who's Who in Public Relations, Who's Who in the United States, National Register of Prominent Americans and International Notables, Dictionary of International Biography, World Who's Who of Women, Who's Who in Texas, Who's Who in Politics*, Others. Address: Plantation Square #C-3, 2411 South 61st Street, Temple, Texas 76502.■

MARION DAVID FRANCIS

Senior Scientist. Personal: Born May 9, 1923; Son of George Henry Francis (deceased) and Marian Flanagan Francis; Married Emily Liane Williams; Father of William Randall, Patricia Ann. Education: B.A. 1946, M.A. 1949, University of British Columbia; Ph.D., University of Iowa, 1952. Military: Served with the Canadian Army Reserve, 1942-46. Career: Senior Scientist, Proctor and Gamble Company, present; Former Chemical Instructor, University of British Columbia. Organizational Memberships: New York Academy of Science; Society of Nuclear Medicine; American Heart Association; American Pharmaceutical Association (Academy of Pharmaceutical Sciences); Ohio Academy of Science; International and American Association for Dental Research; American Chemical Society, Program Chairman, 1983 Central Regional Meeting; Fellow, American Institute of Chemists, Certified Professional Chemist, 1982-85; Fellow, American Association for the Advancement of Science. Community Activities: Worker, Captain, District Vice Chairman of United Appeal, 1953-66; Chairman of Various Small Organizations including the Local Chapter of I.A.D.R. 1968-70, Local Recreation Committee S.N.M. 1981, Others; Reviewer of Scientific Papers, 6 Journals, 1964 to present; Recreation Chairman, Woodson Bend Resort, Branston, Kentucky. Religion: High School Religious Instructor, 1972-74. Honors and Awards: Allied Chemical and Dye Corporation Fellowship, 1950; Chemistry Department Fellowship, University of Iowa, 1950; United States Public Health Fellowship, 1951-52; Phi Lambda Upsilon, Gamma Alpha, Sigma Xi, 1951; Chemist of the Year, Cincinnati Section of American Chemical Society, 1977; Professional Accomplishments Award in Industry, Technical and Scientific Societies of Cincinnati, 1979; Honorary Fellow, Anglo-American Academy; Co-Chairman Gordon Conference on Calcium Phosphates, 1966; Chairman, Gordon Conference on Calcium Phosphates, 1979; Gordon Conference, Session Chairman, 1981. Address: 10018 Winlake Drive, Cincinnati, Ohio 45231.■

BARBARA JEAN FRANCISCO

Quality Control Manager. Personal: August 1, 1943; Daughter of Charles and Mildred Whiteaker. Education: Graduate, Benham High School, 1961; Attended Berea College, 1961-62. Career: Quality Control Manager. Organizational Memberships: National Metal Decorators Association; American Society of Professional and Executive Women. Community Activities: Democrat Club; Order of Eastern Star. Honors and Awards: Listed in *Who's Who in Finance and Industry, Who's Who in the Midwest, World Who's Who of Women, Personalities of America, Biographical Roll of Honor, Men and Women of Distinction*. Address: 2783-D Wayfaring Lane, Lisle, Illinois 60532.■

PATRICIA ANNE COLLIER (PAT) FRANK

Legislator. Personal: Born November 12, 1929, in Cleveland, Ohio; Daughter of Paul Conrad and Mildred Patricia Roane Collier; Married Richard H. Frank; Mother of Stacy, Hillary, Courtney. Education: Graduate of Rosarian Academy, West Palm Beach, Florida, 1947; B.S.B.A. Finance and Taxation, University of Florida-Gainesville, 1951; Attended Georgetown University School of Law, Washington, D.C., 1951-52. Career: Member of Florida Senate, Three Terms, 1978 to present; Member of Florida House of Representatives, 1976-78; Member, Staff of Congressman John R. Foley, United States Capitol, 1959-60; Business Economist,

Department of Justice, Anti-Trust Division, Washington, D.C., 1951-53. Organizational Memberships: Florida Senate, Agriculture Committee. Community Activities: Chairman, Hillsborough County Legislative Delegation, 1982 to present; Agriculture Committee, Executive Business Committee, Finance, Taxation and Claims Committee, Joint Select Committee on Electronic Data Processing Systems; Chairman, Education Committee, 1980-82; National Science Foundation Task Group on Governments of the National Science Board Commission on Precollege Education in Mathematics, Science and Technology, 1982 to present; Assessment Policy Committee of the National Assessment of Educational Progress, 1983-86; Joint Executive and Legislative Task Force for Teacher Quality Improvement, 1982 to present; Florida Juvenile Justice and Delinquency Prevention Task Force, Appointed by Governor Bob Graham, 1982 to present; Appointee, Member of the Governor's Commission on Secondary Schools, 1981; School Board of Hillsborough County, Member 1972-76, Chairman 1975-76; Florida Phosphate Land Reclamation Study Commission, Appointed by Governor Askew 1978-82, Reappointed 1982-86; Southern Regional Education Board; Special Ambassador for the United States to the Independence of St. Vincent's Island, 1979; City of Tampa Election Board; Health and Rehabilitative Services, District VI Advisory Council, Appointed by Governor Askew; Tampa Young Men's Christian Association, Board of Directors; Federal Relations Network of National School Board Association, Congressional District #7, Representative; Region VIII Drug Advisory Council; Florida School Boards Association, Legislative Committee; Georgetown University Alumni Association for Central Florida, Secretary-Treasurer; Hillsborough County Advisory Council on Aging; Florida Association for Gifted Education, Board of Directors, State Legislative Chairman; League of Women Voters, Board Member; Hillsborough County Council of Parent Teacher Associations, First Vice President; Hillsborough County Bar Auxiliary, Director; St. Andrew's Episcopal Churchwomen, Vice President; Gorrie Elementary Parent Teacher Association, President. Honors and Awards: First Women Admitted to Georgetown University School of Law, 1951; Hall of Fame, Mortar Board, University of Florida-Gainesville; Valedictorian 1947, Student Body President 1945, Rosarian Academy; Appointment to National Conference of State Legislatures Committee on Education, 1981; Membership in National Advisory Panel for the Advanced Leadership Program Services of the National Conference of State Legislatures, 1981; Participation in United States-Caribbean Legislative Symposium of National Conference of State Legislatures, St. Lucia, 1981; Selection as Member of Advanced Leadership Program Services National Planning Committee, 1981; Selection as Speaker at Joint Meeting of State Higher Education Executive Officers and Council of Chief State School Officers, Colorado Springs, Colorado, 1981; Selection to Participate in First National Invitational Advanced Leadership Program Services Seminar, Co-Sponsored by the Education Commission of the States and the National Conference of State Legislatures, Houston, Texas, 1980; Tiger Award, F.E.A./United-A.F.T., 1977, 1978, 1979, 1981; Athena Award, Women in Communication, 1980; Outstanding Service Award, Florida Council of Handicapped Organizations, 1980; Educator of the Year Award, Kappa Delta Pi, Tampa Chapter, 1979; Florida N.O.W. Award, 1979; Award from Board of County Commissioners of Pasco County for Outstanding Service during 1979 Session of the Florida Legislature; Award from the School Board of Pinellas County for Contributing to Public Education during the 1979 Legislative Session; Community Leadership Award, Mental Health Association of Hillsborough County, 1979; Tampa Jaycee's Good Government Award, 1979; Allen Morris Award, Most Effective First Term Member of the House, 1978; Selection by Colleagues as Most Promising Freshman Legislator of the 1977 Legislative Session; Friends of Education Award, N.E.A.-F.T.P., 1977; Honorary Life Membership in Florida Congress of Parents and Teachers, Awarded by Hillsborough County Council of Parent-Teacher Associations, 1976; Outstanding Service Award, Adult Education, Hillsborough County, 1974; Educational Leadership Award, Hillsborough County C.T.A., 1973; Gorrie School Bell Award; Honorary Member, Delta Kappa Gamma Women Educator's Honor Society. Address: 4141 Bayshore Boulevard, Tampa, Florida 33611.■

LOYD DERWOOD FRAZIER

Administrator. Personal: Born August 12, 1912; Married Marjorie L.; Father of Larry, Robert L., Carla Stewart, Melinda Smith, Connie Doss. Education: Graduate of Corsicana High School, 1930; Fingerprint Identification, American Institute of Applied Science, Chicago, Illinois, 1930; B.S., Oklahoma University, 1934. Career: Administrative Director, Harris County District Attorney's Office, 1972 to present; Chief Deputy, Harris County Sheriff's Office, 1949-72; Instructor of Criminology, University of Houston, 1947; Assistant Superintendent, Bureau of Identification, Houston Police Department, 1940; Druggist, Memorial Hospital 1936, P.R.B. Drug Company 1935. Organizational Memberships: American Law Enforcement Officers Association, Member #P82, 00966; National District Attorneys Association; Texas District and County Attorneys Association; Texas Police Association International Association for Identification; Texas Division for Association of Identification; Texas Crime Prevention Association; Texas Police Association; Texas State Bar, Committee on Revision of the Penal Code; Harris County Mental, Board of Directors; Houston-Galveston Area Criminal Justice Advisory Committee; Texas Narcotic Association; Pharmaceutical Society. Community Activities: Masonic Lodge; Scottish Rite; York Rite; Order of Demolay; The Royal Order of Scotland; China Grotto; Arabia Temple Shrine, Assistant Marshal; Houston Parent Teacher Association; Harris County Federal Credit Union, Board of Directors; Houston Livestock Association, Life Member; Houston Farm and Ranch Club; Law Enforcement Advisory Committee, College of Mainland, Texas City, Texas, 1974-76; National Republican Congressional Committee; President Ronald Reagan's Task Force; Governor Clements of Texas Committee; Harris County Traffic Safety Advisory Committee. Address: 24600 Clay Road, Katy, Texas 77449.■

ANNIE BELLE HAMILTON FREAS

Personal: Born August 9, 1904, in Delrose, Tennessee; Daughter of James N. and Emma B. McLaughlin Hamilton. Education: Attended Martin College (Received the Underwood Typewriter Company Medal). Career: Secretary, Law Firm of Bass, Berry & Sims, 1923-24; Commercial Teacher and Bookkeeper, Martin College, 1924; Bookkepper, Head of Accounting Department and Assistant Controller, T. L. Herbert & Sons, W. G. Bush and Company, Sangravl Company; Co-Owner and Bookkeeper of Husband's General Contracting Firm, 1958 to present; Secretary and General Bookkeeper, Freas and Houghland General Contractors, Inc., 1963 to present; Secretary/Treasurer, Freas Construction Company, 1967 to present. Organizational Memberships: Women in Construction, Charter Member Nashville Chapter, Director 1961-63, Vice President 1963-64, President, Region 2 Director 1966, Chairman of Chapter Activities, Board of Directors 1966 to present. Community Activities: Charter Member, Zonta International, President Nashville Club 1970-71, Chairman of Public Affairs of Distict XI 1967-69; National Trust for Historic Preservation, Ladies Hermitage Association; Tennessee Botanical Gardens and Fine Arts Centre; Association for Preservation of Tennessee Antiquities; International Platform Association; Cheekwood Young Women's Christian Association. Religion: Presbyterian; Charter Member, Downtown Presbyterian Church of Nashville; President, Women of the Church, 1961-63. Honors and Awards: 1965 Woman in Construction of the Year; Certificate of Appreciation for Work as Chairman of Career Day, Vanderbilt University; "First Lady of the Day," Radio Station WLAC; Listed in *Who's Who of American Women*, *Dictionary of International Biography*, *The Royal Blue Book*, *Two Thousand Women of Achievement*. Address: 3003 Natchez Trace, Nashville, Tennessee 27215.■

LANNY ROSS FREEMAN

Geological Engineer. Personal: Born August 5, 1946; Son of Mr. and Mrs. R. E. Freeman. Education: B.S. Petroleum Engineering, Northwestern University, 1976; M.S. Geological Engineering, Pacific Cascade Univeristy, 1979; Doctor of Geology (Ph.D.), Northwestern University, 1981. Military: Served with the United States Air Force, Air Commando 1964-70, Vietnam 1965-68, T/Sgt E-6 Special Forces 1967-70 (Cross-Service Transfer), South Rhodesia, Air American Advisor 1969-70. Career: Geological Engineer. Organizational Memberships: Society AIME Engineers; Indiana Oil Producers Association; United States Geological Society. Honors and Awards: Decorated Medal of Honor, 1969; Air Force Cross, 1968; Distinguished Service Cross (2), 1968; Silver Star (4), 1968; Bronze Star (9), 1967-68; Distinguished Flying Cross (7), 1966-69; Legion of Merit (3), 1966-69; Purple Heart (3), 1966-69; Air Medal (9), 1965-69; Commendation Medal (11), 1965-69; Good Conduct (2), 1968-70; Viet Campaign (3), 1965, 1966 and 1967; Viet Nam Medal of Honor, 1968; Listed in *Who's Who in World Oil*. Address: 1502 Skyline, Portland, Texas 78374.■

EMMA FRANCES FREUND

Laboratory Supervisor. Personal: Born October 8, 1922; Daughter of Walter Russell and Mable Loveland Ervin (both deceased); Married Frederic Reinert; Mother of Frances, Daphne, Fern, Frederic. Education: B.S., Wilson Teachers College, Washington D.C., 1944; M.S. Biology, Catholic University, Washington D.C., 1953; Certificate in Management Development, Virginia Commonwealth University, Richmond, Virginia, 1975; Certificate in Electron Microscopy, State University of New York, New Paltz, 1977; Graduate Studies in Biology and Education, George Washington University, Washington D.C., 1944-48; Student, J. Sargent Reynolds Community College, Richmond, Virginia, 1978; Certificate in Management, Development, Virginia Commonwealth University and American Management Association, 1982; Registered Histologic Technician, American Society of Clinical Pathologists, 1969; Registered Clinical Laboratory Specialist (Histology), National

Certification Agency for Medical Laboratory Personnel, 1979, 1982. Career: Supervisor, Histology Laboratory, Medical College of Virginia Hospital, present; Technician, Parasitology Laboratory, Zoology Division, United States Department of Agriculture, Beltsville, Maryland; Histotechnologist, Pathology Department, Georgetown University Medical School, Washington D.C.; Clinical Laboratory Technician, Kent and Queen Anne's County Hospital, Chestertown, Maryland. Organizational Memberships: American Society for Medical Histology Section, 1981-83; Virginia Society for Medical Technology Representative to Scientific Assembly, Histology Section 1977-78, Histology and Cytology Sections 1980-82; Richmond Society of Medical Technologists, Corresponding Secretary 1977, Chairman Publicity 1981-82; National Society for Histotechnology, Charter Member, By-laws Committee 1981-83, Delegate 1979-81, CEUS Committee 1981-83, Co-Chairperson Third Annual Region II Seminar; Virginia Society of Histology Technicians, Charter Member, Vice President 1981-83, By-laws Committee 1975 and 1979-81, Board of Directors 1979-82, Chairman Fall Seminar 1981; American Association for the Advancement of Science; Association for Women in Science; American Society of Clinical Pathologists, Associate Member. Community Activities: Assistant Cub Scout Den Leader, Robert E. Lee Council Boy Scouts of America 1967-68, Den Leader 1968-70. Honors and Awards: Elected to Phi Beta Rho, 1940; Kappa Delta Pi, 1944; Phi Lambda Theta, 1946; Helminthological Society of Washington D.C., 1948; Sigma Xi, 1953; New York Academy of Sciences, 1979; American Biographical Institute Research Association, Life Member, 1981; American Management Association, 1982; Honored by Robert E. Lee Council of Boy Scouts of America, Banquet, May, 1970; Medical College of Virginia Hospital Service Award (30 years service), March, 1982; Listed in *Who's Who in the South and Southwest, Personalities of the South, World Who's Who of Women, International Who's Who of Intellectuals, International Register of Profiles, Personalities of America, Book of Honor, International Book of Honor, Biographical Roll of Honor*. Address: 1315 Asbury Road, Richmond, Virginia 23229.■

RONALD MARVIN FRIEDMAN

Research Scientist. Personal: Born April 26, 1930; Son of Joseph and Helen Plotkin Friedman, Brooklyn, New York; Father of Philip Max, Joelle Norma. Education: B.S. Zoology, Columbia University, 1960; M.S. Physiology 1967, Ph.D. Cell Biology 1976, New York University. Career: Postdoctoral Fellow in Biochemistry, Columbia University, 1975-76; Postdoctoral Fellow, Department M.B.B., Yale University School of Medicine, 1977-78; Visiting Fellow, Department of Biochemical Sciences, Princeton University, 1978-79; Visiting Scientist, Institute for Basic Research in Enzymology, 1979-82; Scientific Advisor to Royal Arch Masons Medical Foundation, 1982 to present; Visiting Investigator in Cell Biochemistry, Sloan-Kettering Memorial Foundation, 1983; Scientific Advisor to Royal Area Medical Research Foundation, Inc., 1982 to present; Research Scientist. Organizational Memberships: Sigma Xi; American Society of Cell Biologists; Harvey Society; New York Academy of Sciences. Community Activities: Mason; Nippon Club; New York and Japan Society, New York; Emergency Home Medical Call Survey, Bronx County, New York, 1971-72; Volunteer on Human Nutrition and its Relation to Pathology, Secretary of Agriculture's Office, Washington, D.C., 1970-71. Published Works: "Life Objectives of Dr. Ronald Friedman," a Thesis on the Global Implications of Raising Human Dignity, Submitted to and Accepted by United Nations, Translated and Sent Around the World 1981, Submitted to United States Senate 1981; Encouraged and Publicized Nationally the Fact that the Human Pediatric Neoplasm Neuroblastoma Sometimes Matures to a Benign State called Ganglioneuroma before the Age of Four, 1973-80; Pioneering Experiments Showing that Neoplastic Disease under Certain Conditions may exist or be induced in all Cellular Forms of Life, 1973-75; Pioneering Efforts Showing that Human Nutrition may have an Important Effect in the Induction of Pathology, 1970-71; Pioneering Efforts Showing the Effect of Internal Trauma to Elastic Arteries with respect to the Induction of Cerebral Vascualr Accidents and Coronary Heart Disease, 1963-66. Honors and Awards: Knights Templar Fellow, 1973-81; National Institute of Health Fellow, 1981; Listed in *Who's Who in the East.* Address: 3210 Arlington Avenue, Riverdale, New York 10463.■

ARNOLD FROMME

Jersey 07922.■

Professor of Music. Personal: Born December 2, 1925; Son of Samuel and Jeannette Fromme (both deceased); Married Catherine M. Thomasian; Father of Gregory A., Vanessa C. Education: Juilliard School of Music, 1942-48; American School of Fontainebleu, 1949; Accecit, Paris Conservatory, 1949-50; B.M., M.M., Manhattan School of Music, 1966-69; Ph.D., New York University, 1980. Military: Served in the United States Army as a Private, 1943-45. Career: Assistant Professor of Music, Jersey City State College; Trombonist and Founder, American Brass Quintet; New York Pro Musica-Sackbut; Principal Trombone, R.C.A. Victor Symphony, Columbia Records Symphony, New York City Ballet Orchestra, Little Orchestra, Esterhazt Orchestra; Trombone Extra, New York Philharmonic. Organizational Memberships: American Musical Institute Society, Founder, Vice President 1971-74; International Trombone Association Research Committee; American Musicological Society; Galoin Society A.F. of M.; American Association of University Professors; M.E.N.C.; College Music Society; National Association of College Wind and Percussion Instructors. Religion: The Unitarian Church in Summit, Music Director, 1979-81. Published Works: Original Musical Work, "3 Studies for Brass Quintet"; Editings of Renaissance Music by Gabrieli, Scheidt, Reiche, East and Others; Articles for Scholarly Journals, Music Education Journals and Popular Music Magazines, such as M.E.N.C. *Research Journal, I.T.A. Journal, Music Journal Magazine*, Conn Chord Magazine; Record Album Program Notes, Desto Records; Performance on Numerous Record Albums with New York Pro Musica, American Brass Quintet, Igor Stravinsky and Others. Honors and Awards: Diploma, *International Who's Who in Music*, 1976; Martha Baird-Rockefeller Foundation Award as Member of the American Brass Quintet, 1968. Address: 4 Janet Lane, Berkeley Heights, New

LINDA DARLENE FRUSH

Insurance Agent. Personal: Born February 25, 1947; Daughter of Mr. and Mrs. James R. Castle. Education: A.A., St. Petersburg Junior College; Currently Studying toward B.A. Degree in Elementary Education. Career: Property and Casualty Insurance Agent, Life Insurance Agent, Real Estate Agent, 1965 to present. Organizational Memberships: American Business Women of America, Dunedin Chapter, Chairperson of Nominating Committee, Chairperson of Education Committee (Scholarship Award). Community Activities: Deputy Voting Registrar of Pinellas County. Religion: Seminole First Baptist Church, General Secretary, Member Adult Choir. Honors and Awards: Phi Theta Kappa, Tau Zeta Chapter; Listed in *Personalities of the South, Community Leaders of the World, Who's Who Among Students in American Junior Colleges*. Address: 11300 124th Avenue, North Largo, Florida 33540.■

KING-SUN FU

Goss Distinguished Professor of Engineering. Personal: Born October 2, 1930; Married Viola; Father of Francis, Thomas, June. Education: B.S., National Taiwan University, 1953; M.A.Sc., University of Toronto, 1955; Ph.D., University of Illinois, 1959. Career: Goss Distinguished Professor of Engineering, Purdue University; Research Engineer, Boeing Airplane Company, 1959-60; Assistant Professor 1960-63, Associate Professor 1963-66, Professor of Electrical Engineering 1966 to present, Purdue University. Organizational Memberships: Fellow, Institute of Electrical and Electronic Engineers; National Academy of Engineering; Academia Sinica. Honors and Awards: American Society of Electrical Engineering. Senior Research Award, 1981; Institute of Electrical and Electronic Engineers Education Medal, 1982; A.F.I.P.S. Harry Goode Memorial Award, 1982. Address: 132 Rockland Drive, West Lafayette, Indiana 47906.■

MARTHA AYERS FUENTES

Writer. Personal: Born December 21, 1923; Daughter of Mr. and Mrs. William Henry Ayers (deceased); Married Manuel Solomon Fuentes, Son of Mr. and Mrs. Manuel B. Fuentes (deceased). Education: B.A. English, University of South Florida, 1969. Career: Writer, 1953 to present; Jewelry Sales Clerk in Department Store, Tampa, Florida, 1940-43; Clerk Typist, Bookkeeper, Western Union, Tampa, Florida, 1943-48. Organizational Memberships: Authors Guild; Authors League of America, Active Member; Dramatists Guild, Associate Member; Society of Children's Book Writers, Active Member; Southeastern Writers Association; The International Women's Writing Guild. Religion: Member Blue Army, Roman Catholic, Infant Jesus of Prague, Society of the Little Flower, Association of the

TWO THOUSAND NOTABLE AMERICANS

Miraculous Medal, Others (all current). Honors and Awards: George Sergel Drama Award, Full Length Play,"Go Stare at the Moon," University of Chicago, Chicago, Illinois, 1969. Address: 102 3rd Street, Belleair Beach, Florida 33535.■

LARRY FUHRER

Investment Executive. Personal: Born September 23, 1939; Married Linda Larsen; Father of Lance. Education: A.B. Psychology and Religion, Taylor University, 1961; M.B.A. (Course Work and Thesis Completed), Northern Illinois University. Career: Chairman and President, The Centre Capital Group Inc., A Private Investment Banking Group, 1973 to present; Chairman, Presidential Services, Inc., 1966 to present; Chairman, The Equity Realty Group, Ltd., 1971 to present; Chairman, Rockford Equities, Ltd.; Chairman, Family Programming, Inc., 1982 to present; Chairman, The Financial Services Group, Ltd., 1973 to present; Managing Director, The Craftsmen's Clearing House, 1979-81; President, Killian Associates, Inc., 1971-75; Executive Assistant to the President, The Robert Johnston Corporation, Los Angeles, Chicago and New York, 1968-69; Number of Other Former Positions. Organizational Memberships: National Association of Realtors. Community Activities: United States Swimming Official, Class J; Former Chairman, West Suburban Swim Conference. Religion: Member, First Presbyterian Church of Glen Ellyn. Honors and Awards: Civil Air Patrol Certificate of Proficiency; Listed in *Outstanding Young Men of America*, *Who's Who in the Midwest*, *Who's Who in Finance and Industry*, *Directory of Distinguished Americans*, *Men of Achievement*. Address: 521 Iroquois, Naperville, Illinois 60504.■

BARBARA NAOMI FUKUSHIMA

Certified Public Accountant and Entrepreneur. Personal: Born April 5, 1948, in Honolulu, Hawaii; Daughter of Harry Kazuo and Misayo (Kawasaki) Murakoshi; Married Dennis Hiroshi Fukushima on March 23, 1974; Mother of Dennis Hiroshi. Career: Realtor-Associate, Carol Ball and Associates, Kahului, 1981-83; Hotel Auditor, Hyatt Regency Maui, Kaanapali, 1980-81; Representative, Equitable Life Assurance Society for the United States, Wailuku, 1980; Realtor-Associate, Stapleton Associates, Kahului, 1980; Franchisee, Audit-Guard (Maui), Wailuku, 1980-81; President, Barbara N. Fukushima CPA, Inc., Wailuku, 1979 to present; Secretary/Treasurer, Target Pest Control, Inc., Wailuku, 1979 to present; President, Book Doors, Inc., Pukalani, 1977 to present; Partner, D & B International, Pukalani and Wailuku, 1976 to present; Internal Auditor, Accountant, Maui Land and Pineapple Company, Inc., Kahului, 1977-80; Auditor, Haskins and Sells, Kahului, Hawaii, 1974-77; Intern, Coopers and Lybrand, Honolulu, 1974. Organizational Memberships: American Institute of CPA's; Hawaii Society of CPA's; National Association of Accountants; American Women's Society of CPA's; Hawaii Association of Public Accountants; Business and Professional Women's Club. Community Activities: Donation to University of Hawaii Foundation, Harry K. Murakoshi Memorial Scholarship for Cardiology Student of the John A. Burns School of Medicine, 1980. Religion: Aloha Church (Tenrikyo), Waipahu, Hawaii. Honors and Awards: Phi Beta Kappa Book Award, 1969; Phi Kappa Phi Prize, 1970. Address: 200 Aliiolani Street, Pukalani, Hawaii 96788.■

JAMES WALKER FULLER

Surgeon. Personal: Born January 5, 1945; Son of Mrs. David W. Fuller; Married Suzanne H., Daughter of Mr. and Mrs. Danol Hotsling; Father of Kevin W., Dana M. Education: B.S., University of Tennessee, 1966; M.D., University of Tennessee Medical Units, 1970; Residency, Surgery, University of South Florida Hospitals, 1972-75. Military: Served with the United States Air Force, Robins Air Force Base, Georgia, Chief of Surgery, 1976-78. Career: Surgeon, General, Vascular, Thoracic; Surgical President; Inventor; Publisher. Organizational Memberships: Fellow, American Society of Abdominal Surgeons, 1978; Associate Fellow, American Society Colon and Rectal Surgeons, 1980; Fellow, American College of Surgeons, 1981; Fellow, International College of Surgeons, 1979; Fellow, Southeastern Surgical Congress, 1979. Community Activities: Member, Committee of One Hundred, Citrus County, Florida; Chief of Staff, Citrus Memorial Hospital; Past Chief of Surgery, Robins Air Force Base, Robins, Georgia. Honors and Awards: Associate Fellow, American Society of Colon and Rectal Surgeons, 1980; Fellow, American College of Surgeons, 1981; Fellow, International College of Surgeons, 1979; Fellow, Southeastern Surgical Congress, 1979. Address: 411 West Highland, Inverness, Florida 32650.■

HAROLD M. FULLMER

Professor. Personal: Born July 9, 1918; Son of Mrs. Rachel Fullmer; Married Rosalyn Truett, Daughter of R. E. Truett; Father of Vaneta Lynne Windham, Jaimee Truett Windham, Angela Sue Fullmer O'Connell, Pamela Rose Fullmer McLain. Education: B.S. 1942, D.D.S. 1944, Indiana University; Doctorate honoris causa, University of Athens, Greece, 1981. Career: University of Alabama at Birmingham, Professor of Pathology, Professor of Dentistry, Director of the Institute of Dental Research, Senior Scientist at Cancer Center, Member Scientific Advisory Committee of the Diabetes Research and Training Center, Associate Dean of the School of Dentistry. Organizational Memberships: Diplomate, American Board of Oral Pathology; Fellow, American College of Dentists; American Academy of Oral Pathology; American Association for the Advancement of Science, Chairman Section 1976-78, Secretary Section 1979 to present; Member American Dental Association, Consultant Council Dental Research 1973-74; International Association for Dental Research, Vice President 1974-75, President 1976-77; American Association for Dental Research, President 1976-77; International Association of Pathologists; International Association of Oral Pathologists, Co-Founder, First Vice President, Editor; Histochemistry Society; National Society for Medical Research, Director 1977-79; Biology Stain Commission, Trustee 1977 to present; Commanding Officers Association; Editor (with R. D. Lillie) Histopathologic Technic and Practical Histochemistry, 1976; Consulting Editor Oral Surgery, Oral Medicine, Oral Pathology, 1970; Editor, Founder, *Journal Oral Pathology*, 1972 to present; Associate Editor, *Journal Cutaneous Pathology*, 1973 to present; Editorial Board, Tissue Reactions, 1976 to present; Consultant Editor, Gerontology, 1981 to present. Community Activities: President, Exchange Club of New Orleans, 1952-53. Religion: Member, Mountain Brook Baptist Church, Mountain Brook, Alabama. Honors and Awards: Recipient Isaac Schour Award for Outstanding Research and Teaching in Anatomical Sciences, International Association Dental Research, 1973; Fulbright Grantee, 1972; Distinguished Alumnus of the Year, Indiana University School of Dentistry, 1978; Distinguished Alumnus Service Award, Indiana University, 1981. Address: 3514 Bethune Drive, Birmingham, Alabama 35223.■

CHARLES JOHN GABLEHOUSE

Airport Services Analyst. Personal: Born April 16, 1928, in New York City, New York; Married Marge Holman, June 21, 1964; Father of Stephanie. Education: Attended College of William and Mary 1957, Fordham University 1960. Military: Served in the United States Army, 1950-52. Career: Company Representative, DeLackner Helicopters Inc., Mt. Vernon, New York, 1956-58; Technical Editor, Project Leader, Grumman Aircraft Engineering Corporation, Bethpage, New York, 1958-61; Associate Editor, Business/Commercial Aviation Magazine, New York, 1961-62; With Aviation Department 1962 to present, Airport Services Analyst 1968 to present, Port of New York Authority, New York City. Organizational Memberships: American Institute of Aeronautics and Astronautics; American Helicopter Society; Experimental Aircraft Association; Aviation/Space Writers Association; A.S.C.E.; Society of Technical Communications; American Federation of Technical Engineers. Community Activities: Director of Public Relations, Ethical Culture Society of Bergen County, 1975 to present; Active Amnesty International; Member of Planning Board, City of Passaic (New Jersey), 1978 to present. Published Works: Author, *Helicopters and Autogiros*, 1967. Honors and Awards: National Public Relations Award, Aviation/Space Writers Association, 1974; National Award for *Helicopters and Autogiros*, Society of Technical Writers and Publications, 1970. Address: 82 Paulison Avenue, Passaic, New Jersey 07055.■

JOHN JOSEPH GALLAGHER

Systems Ecologist and Consultant. Personal: Born March 30, 1914; Son of Patrick and Cathrine Dowling Gallagher (deceased); Married Anna Helen Giordano, Daughter of Filippo and Maria Antonia D'Amico Giordano (deceased). Education: B.A. 1949, Ph.D. 1955, University of Pennsylvania; Postdoctoral Studies in Systems Ecology, University of Tennessee-Knoxville, 1967-68. Military: Served in the United States Army Air Corps, 1942-45, attaining the rank of Technical Sergeant. Career: Systems Ecologist and Consultant; Co-Director of Planning Grant for College of Nursing 1971-72, Associate Professor of Biological Sciences 1971-74, Associate Dean for College of Nursing 1972-74, Coordinator of Task Forces for Institutional Self-Evaluation, Coordinator of Environmental Development, Advisor to President for Institutional Research, Lewis University; Research Associate, State University of New York-Brockport 1968-71, Idaho State University 1957-60, University of Pennsylvania 1955-56; Consultant, Philadelphia Academy of Natural Sciences, 1950-55. Organizational Memberships: Idaho Academy of Sciences, Founding Committee 1958-59, Constitution 1958-60, Chairman of Membership Committee 1958-60; Sigma Xi; American Association for the Advancement of Science; International Limnological Association; American Society of Limnology and Oceanography; American Microscopical Society; Ecological Society of America. Community Activities: Will-Grundy-Kankakee County (Illinois) Comprehensive Health Planning Council, 1971-74. Honors and Awards: Sigma Xi, 1970 to present; Psi Chi Superior Service Award, 1936; Decorated Meritorious Achievement Bronze Star, 1945; Listed in *World Who's Who in Science, Leaders in American Science, American Men and Women of Science, Who's Who in the West, Dictionary of International Biography*. Address: 952 Agate Street, San Diego, California 92109.■

KARL WILSON GAMBLE

Professor Emeritus. Personal: Born February 22, 1911, in Pennsylvania; Married Anne Shepko. Education: B.S., California State College, 1933; M.Ed. 1937, Ed.D. 1950, University of Pittsburgh; Permanent Certification in State of Pennsylvania as Elementary Teacher, Elementary Principal, Secondary Teacher, Secondary Principal and Supervising Principal. Military: Served in the United States Army, 1942-45, in European Theater of Operations. Career: Teacher, Nottingham Township Schools, Washington County, Pennsylvania, 1933-36; Principal, South Franklin Township School, Washington County, 1938-42; Counseling Psychologist, Veterans Administration, Pittsburgh; Director, Duquesne Guidance Centre, Brownsville Guidance Centre, Washington Guidance Centre; Chief of Medical Psychology, Aspinwall Medical Hospital, 1950; Director, Veterans Guidance Centre of University of Pittsburgh, 1951-60; Industrial Psychological Consultant, Maynard Research Council; Professor of Psychology 1961-76, Professor Emeritus 1976 to present, California State College; Livestock Operation and Farm Owner and Raiser of Charolaise Cattle. Organizational Memberships: American Personnel and Guidance Association; National Society of Education; National Education Association, American College Personnel and Guidance Association; Association for Higher Education; American, Pennsylvania and Pittsburgh Psychological Associations; American Charolaise Association. Address: Rural Drawer 1, Eighty Four, Pennsylvania 15330.■

MILDRED KATHERINE GAMBRELL

Educator. Personal: Born March 10, 1939, in Austin, Texas. Education: B.Mus., University of Texas, 1962; M.Ed., Southwest Texas State University, 1966. Career: Elementary School Teacher, Victoria Public Schools (Texas) 1962-64, Dickinson Public Schools (Texas) 1964-75; Secretary, Lockheed Electronics Company, Houston, Texas, 1974-75; Piano Teacher. Organizational Memberships: Alpha Delta Kappa; Texas Education Association; Beta Sigma Phi. Community Activities: Daughters of the American Revolution; Magna Carta Dames Society; Plantagenet Society; Descendants of Most Noble Order of Knights of the Garter Society; Colonial Order of Crown Society; Genealogical Society of Mayflower Descendants; Sigma Alpha Iota; Pi Kappa Lambda. Honors and Awards: Honorary Life Member, Texas Congress of Parents and Teachers; Trophy, Barcliff, Parent-Teacher Association, 1969. Address: 620 Cibilo Street, Lockhart, Texas 78644.■

NORA KATHERINE GAMBRELL

Educator. Personal: Born April 8, 1906, in Lockhart, Texas; Married Sidney Spivey Gambrell, 1932; Mother of One Son and One Daughter. Education: B.S., Southwest Texas State University, 1950. Career: Elementary Teacher, Public School District, Lockhart, Texas, 1937-71. Organizational Memberships: Lockhart Classroom Teachers Association; Delta Kappa Gamma; Texas Education Association. Community Activities: President, Past President, Lockhart Music Club; Area Director, 1976-78; Past Secretary, Tuberculosis Association. Religion: Past President, Life Member, Methodist Women's Guild; Church Council, 1977-79. Honors and Awards: Education Scholarship in Her Honor, 1971; Citation of Appreciation, Tuberculosis Association, 1950. Address: 620 Cibilo Street, Lockhart, Texas 78664.■

RICHARD G. GANNON

Farmer, Businessman, State Senator. Personal: Born July 29, 1950; Son of Bill and Geraldine Gannon; Married Martha Wall; Father of Jessica. Education: A.A., Colby Community College, 1970; B.S., Science of Education, University of Kansas, 1973; Graduate Hours in Business/Economics, University of Kansas. Career: Farmer, Businessman, Senator from State of Kansas. Organizational Memberships: American Council on Germany; National Conference of State Legislatures; Midwestern Conference of Council of State Governments. Community Activities: Benevolent and Protective Order of Elks; Knights of Columbus; Board Member, Alumni Advisory Council; KU Chapter ACACIA; Life Member, KU Alumni Association; Citizenship Co-Leader, 4-H, Sherman County. Religion: Member of Catholic Church. Honors and Awards: Outstanding Young Men of America, 1978, 1980; Award for Meritorious Service, Veterans of World War I of Kansas, 1978; Letter of Meritorious Service, National Veterans of World War I, 1978. Address: Box 68, Route 3, Goodland, Kansas 67735.■

TWO THOUSAND NOTABLE AMERICANS

CARMEN SYLVIA GARCIA OLIVERO

Consultant, Institute President and Director. Personal: Born November 8; Daughter of Fernando Garcia Arana (deceased); Married; Mother of Martha Olivero Diaz. Education: B.S. Home Economics, University of Puerto Rico, Rio Piedras, 1948; Supervision Certificate, Personnel Office of Puerto Rico, San Juan, 1950; Master in Social Work 1956, Supervision Certificate 1960, School of Social Work, University of Puerto Rico; Advanced Curriculum in Psychiatric Case Work, School of Social Work, University of Pennsylvania, 1962-63; Marital Counseling Certificate, Residence, Department of Psychiatry, Family Division "Marriage Counsel" of Philadelphia, University of Pennsylvania, 1962-63; Research in Human Behavior, National Institute of Human Behavior, Washington 1964, Department of Psychology, Ann Arbor 1964, Department of Psychology, Duke University 1964; Studies toward Master in Public Administration, School of Public Administration, University of Puerto Rico, 1961-62; Research in Sociology (Tutor Dr. Lloyd Rogler), University of Yale, New Haven, 1964-65; Doctorate in Psychiatric Social Work (Ph.D.), 1968. Career: President and Director, The Institute of Social Research Inc., Rio Peidras, Puerto Rico; Consultant of Mental Health Program, Department of Health, Puerto Rico, 1981-82; Consultant of Assistant Secretariat of Prevention, Department of Addiction Services of Puerto Rico, 1980-82; Child Welfare Social Worker, Public Welfare, Health Department, Puerto Rico, 1948; Parole Officer, Direct of Parole Office at State Penitentiary, Puerto Rico, 1949-51; Classification Officer at State Penitentiary 1950-52, Acting Socio Penal Director 1949-50; Correctional Social Work, Young Delinquent Institution, Department of Justice, Puerto Rico, Organization and Director of Social Work Unit, 1952-56; Psychiatric Social Worker, Psychiatric Hospital, Puerto Rico, 1956-57; Psychiatric Social Work Instructor, Department of Psychiatry, School of Medicine, Puerto Rico, 1957; Director of Social Work Unit, Department of Psychiatry, School of Medicine, Puerto Rico, Department of Health, 1959-62; Director Social Research Unit (Social Psychiatry), Department of Psychiatry, School of Medicine of Puertro Rico, 1960-62; Assistant Professor in Social Research and Human Behavior, Department of Psychiatry, School of Medicine of Puerto Rico, 1968; Associate Professor in Research and Human Behavior, Department of Psychiatry, School of Medicine of Puerto Rico, 1968; Associate Professor in Research and Human Behavior, Department of Psychiatry, School of Medicine of Puerto Rico; Professor Social Research, School of Social Work, University of Puerto Rico, 1959-61; Professor and Supervision in Psychiatric Social Work, School of Special Work, University of Puerto Rico; Professor and Supervision in Social Work Research, School of Social Work, University of Puerto Rico, 1968-70; Professor Social Research and Human Behavior, Department of Psychiatry, School of Medicine, University of Puerto Rico, 1974; Consultant of Puerto Rican Problems in United States Nationalities Service in Philadelphia, 1968; Consultant Model City Program (Evaluation and Planification), Municipio de San Juan, 1970-74; Consultant Human Resources Department (Evaluation and Planification), Municipio de San Juan, 1974-76; Consultant Studies of Puerto Rican Problems, Rutger University, 1959; Consultant of Planification and Budget Office, Municipio de San Juan, 1974-78; Planification of Program, Management, Need Assessment, Evaluation and Tutoring; President and Director, Institute of Psycho-Social Research, 1977; Director of Alcoholism Program, Municipal Department of Health, San Juan Municipality, 1977; Director of Office of Technical Services and Consultant of Director of Human Resources Department, Municipality of San Juan, 1978-79; Consultant, Planning and Design of Mental Health Program, 1979; Consultant of "Departamento de Servicios Contra la Adiccion," (DSCA), Prevention and Evaluation, 1979-80; Professor of Evaluation of Program, Administrator of Mental Health Program, Survey Design, Social Research, Caribbean Institute of Psychology, 1976-78; Consultant, Design of a Mental Health Program, San Juan Department of Health, 1978; Consultant, Pyramid, California, E. U. Prevention and Evaluation on Drug Addiction and Alcoholism, 1980; Consultant, NPERN, E. U. Prevention Drug Addiction, 1980; Consultant, Advocacy Plan, Auxiliary Secretariat of Mental Health, Department of Health, Puerto Rico, 1981. Organizational Memberships: National Association of Social Work; Council Social Work Education; The Otto Rank Association; Puerto Rico Association of Social Work; The Smithsonian Institution; American Association for the Advancement of Science. Published Works: Numerous Publications in her Field. Honors and Awards: Mental Health Fellowship, Psychiatric Social Case Work, University of Pennsylvania, 1962-63; Mental Health Fellowship on Research, University of Pennsylvania, 1967-68; Special Mention in Encyclopedia Great Women of Puerto Rico, 1976; Chancellor of the Medical Science Campus Acknowledgement for Outstanding Contribution in Research and Education, 1976; Plaque Given by School of Social Work of Puerto Rico for Education Achievements, 1977; Dedication of Library Week, School of Social Work of Puerto Rico, for Contribution to Knowledge, 1978; Plaque for Outstanding Work in Alcoholism Program, Puerto Rico, 1981. Address: San Julian 421, Urbanizacion Sagrado Corazon, Rio Peidras, Puerto Rico 00926.■

NORD ARLING GARDNER

Management Consultant. Personal: Born August 10, 1923, in Afton, Wyoming; Son of Arling A. and Ruth Lee Gardner; Married Thora Marie Stephen on March 24, 1945; Father of Randall Nord, Scott Stephen, Craig Robert, Laurie Lee. Education: B.A., University of Wyoming 1945; M.S. 1972, M.P.A. 1975, California State University at Hayward; Postgraduate Work at University of Chicago, University of Michigan, University of California at Berkeley. Military: Served in the United States Army, 1942-64, advancing through the grades from Second Lieutenant to Lieutenant Colonel, Retired 1966. Career: Personnel Analyst, University Hospital, University of California at San Diego, 1964-48; Coordinator of Manpower Development, University of California at Berkeley, 1968-75; University Training Officer 1975-80, Personnel Manager 1976-80, San Francisco State University; General Manager, C.R.D.C. Maintenance Training Corporation, San Francisco; President, Director, Sandor Associates Management Consultants, Pleasant Hill, California; Instructor of Japanese, Psychology and Supervisory Courses, 1977-78. Organizational Memberships: Retired Officers Association; American Society of Training and Development; Northern California Industrial Relations Council; American Association of University Administrators; International Personnel Managers Association; College and University Personnel Association, West Coast Representative; Republican; Commonwealth of California Club; University Club, San Francisco. Community Activities: Advisory Council, San Francisco Community College. Published Works: Author, *To Gather Stones*, 1978. Honors and Awards: Distinguished Decorated Army Commendation Medal. Home: 2995 Bonnie Lane, Pleasant Hill, California 94523.■

VIRGINIA DICKENS GARDNER

Extension Agent. Personal: Born in Marianna, Florida. Education: B.S. Home Economics, Florida Agricultural and Mechanical University, Tallahassee, Florida; Graduate Study at Howard University, Prairie Uiew Agricultural Mechanical College, Tuskegee Institute, Cornell University, University of Florida-Gainesville, University of North Carolina-Greensboro; M.Ed., North Carolina State University, Raleigh; Certificate, Psychology and the Management of Human Resources Course, The Atlanta Region, United States Civil Service, Commission; Participation in More than 450 In-Service Training Programs. Career: Treasurer, The Florida Parent-Child Center, Inc.; United States Department of Agriculture Federal Extension Service, Science and Education Administration-Extension Agent, Extension Service Agent III in Home Economics, Supervising Agent for Expanded Nutrition Program, Home Economics Extension Agent II, Home Economics Extension Agent I, Assistant County Extension Home Economics Agent, 4-H Club Agent, Assistant Home Demonstration Agent, Negro Home Demonstration Agent, Pinellas, Columbia and Jackson Counties, Largo, Clearwater, Lake City and Marianna, Florida; United States Department of Agriculture Extension Service, Associate Professor of Home Economics, University of Florida at Gainesville. Organizational Memberships: National Negro Home Demonstration Agents Association; Florida State Association of Negro County and Negro Home Demonstration Agents; Florida State Association of Negro Home Demonstration Agents; Florida Home Economics Agents Association; Social, Educational and Recreational Club; The Black Caucus of University Professors; National Association of Extension Home Economists; Florida Home Economics Association; West Coast Home Economics Association; Florida Association of Extension Home Economics Agents; Alpha Delta Chapter of Epsilon Sigma Phi National Honorary Extension Fraternity, Inc.; American Home Economics Association. Community Activities: Beta Sigma Zeta Chapter of Zeta Phi Beta Sorority, Inc., Committee Member; Pinellas County Adult Vocational Home Economics, Advisory Committee; Home Economics Consumer Education Advisory Committee of Pinellas County Public Schools, Clearwater, Florida; Health Committee of Jackson County, Marianna, Florida, Chairman; Jackson County Training School Parent-Teacher Association, Former Secretary; Educational Exhibit Division for Individual, Club and Community Exhibits for Negro Girls, Women and Community Groups, The Jackson County Fair, Jackson County, Marianna, Florida, Former Chairman, 7 Years; March of Dimes Drive, Pinellas County, Clearwater, Florida, Former Chairman, 1 Year; Neighborhood Organization, Pinellas County, Former President, 3 Years; County Health Education Council; South Clearwater Organization, Guest Speaker, Citizenship Address; Summer Project Program Sponsored by Upper Pinellas Churches and Florida Council on Human Relations, Elected Representative; American Education Week, Pinellas County, Clearwater, Florida, Guest Speaker at William Elementary School; Upper Pinellas County Council on Human Relations, Board of Directors 4 Years, Advisory Committee 4 Years, Nominating Committee 1 Year; The Leadership Institute, Former Discussion Leader; Conducted Home Improvement Workshop; Dairy Days Contest, Alachua County, Gainesville, Florida, Judge, 1 Year; State of Florida 4-H Record Review Team, Judge, 1 Year; Mobile Home All-Electrical Home Award, Tampa, Florida, Judge, 1 Year; Stress and Time Management in the Home for Health Care Professionals, St. Petersburg Junior College Program, Guest Instructor; Recreational Project for Youth, Dunedin, Florida, Organizer, Director. Religion: Mt. Carmel Progressive Missionary Baptist Church, Clearwater, Florida; Women's Day, Co-Chairman 2 Years, Guest Speaker 6 Years, Chairman 3 Years; Former Church Clerk, 1 Year; Vacation Bible School, Instructor, 2 Years. Honors and Awards: Letters of Congratulations from Numerous Extension Service Administrators; Distinguished Service Award Plaque for Distinguished Service State and National, Agent of the Year Certificate; Citation for Distinguished Service and Leadership to Florida Agricultural Extension Service, National Negro Home Demonstration Agents Association; Agent of the Year, Citation for Distinguished Service in the Community as Home Demonstration Agent and Leadership in the Florida Cooperative Extension Service, Florida State Association of Negro Home Demonstration Agents; Plaque and Gift for Dedicated Service as President, National Negro Home Demonstration Agents Association; Listed in *Who's Who of American Women*, *Dictionary of International Biography*. Address: P.O. Box 15353, St. Petersburg, Florida 22733.■

TWO THOUSAND NOTABLE AMERICANS

JAMES FREDRICK GARRARD

Senior Safety and Environmental Protection Manager. Personal: Born February 26, 1938; Married Marolyn Ella McDonald; Father of James Fredrick, Janella Fae. Education: B.S. Petroleum and Geology, Lamar University, Beaumont, Texas; Graduate, Factory Mutual Loss Prevention Institute (Boston, Massachusetts), Corporate Safety at Western Electric Corporation College (Princeton, New Jersey), E. I. DuPont School of Industrial Safety (Wilmington, Delaware); Noise Measurements, Texaco Industrial Hygiene, Houston, Texas; Rig Safety Inspection, Safety Oilfield Services, Lafayette, Louisiana; Hydrogen Sulfide Methods Analysis, T.A.C., Houston, Texas; N.A.S.A. Environmental Regional Manager's Conference, N.A.S.A. Wallops Flight Center, Wallops Island, Virginia. Military: Served in the United States Army, Honorably Discharge, Non-Commissioned Officer. Career: Senior Manager of Safety and Environmental Protection, Manager of Industrial Safety, Industrial Hygiene, Environmental Control and Quality Assurance Division, Pan American World Services, 1981 to present; Assistant Divisional Safety Manager, Texaco, Inc., U.S.A., 1980-81; Senior Loss Control and Safety Consultant, A.I.G. Consultants, Inc., 1980; Director of Fire, Safety and Loss Control, Western Electric Company, Inc., 1979-80; Loss Control Consultant, Factory Mutual Engineering Systems, 1979; Technical Safety Supervisor, Pullman Kellogg (World Headquarters), 1977-79; Senior Safety Specialist, E. I. Dupont Denemours and Company, Inc., 1962-77. Organizational Memberships: Professional Member, American Society of Safety Engineers; American Chemical Society; American Institute of Chemical Engineers; American Association of Petroleum Geologists; National Fire Protection Association; Gulf Coast Society of Safety Engineers; Texas Academy of Science; Society of Fire Protection Engineers; Deep South Section, American Industrial Hygiene Association; Gulf Coast Safety and Training Group; South Central Louisiana Safety Council; National L-P Gas Association; Texas Safety Association; Safety Council of Greater Baton Rouge; National Safety Management Society; New Orleans Chapter, Houston Chapter, A.S.S.E.; Gulf Coast Federal Safety Council; N.S.T.L. Safety Manager Council; Pan Am Management Club; System Safety Society; National Safety Council; Mississippi Safety Council; State of Mississippi, State Fire Academy. Community Activities: Past President, Groves Jaycees (Texas); Past President, Port Neches Lions Club; Board of Directors, National Foundation for March of Dimes, 9 Years; Executive Board, Nederland Jaycees; Executive Board, Texas State Jaycees; Southeast Director, Texas Academy of Sciences. Religion: Southern Baptist Convention. Published Works: Author, Technical Paper and Presentation "Liquid Inclusions Within Quartz Crystals," Texas Academy of Science. Honors and Awards: Listed in *Outstanding Young Men of America, Personalities of the South, Dictionary of International Biography, Who's Who in America, Who's Who in the Southwest, Men of Achievement.* Address: 5424 Diamondhead Drive East, St. Louis, Mississippi 39520.■

CAROL ANN GARRETT

Speech-Language Pathologist. Personal: Born June 24, 1940; Daughter of Mr. and Mrs. James C. Garrett. Education: A.A. (third honor graduate), Averett College, 1960; B.S. magna cum laude, Mississippi University for Women, 1962; M.Ed., University of Virginia, 1966. Career: Speech-Language Pathologist, Lynchburg Public School, 1962 to present; Consultant, Rockbridge County Schools, 1972; Private Practice Speech Pathologist (part-time), 1963 to present. Organizational Memberships: American Speech-Language-Hearing Association, 1962 to present; Speech and Hearing Association of Virginia, 1962 to present; American Association of University Women, 1963 to present; Central Virginia Speech-Language-Hearing Association, 1979 to present; Virginia Education Association, 1962-70; Lynchburg Education Association, Member 1962-70, Handbook Committee Chairman 1967-68; Council for Exceptional Children, Lynchburg Chapter, Member 1963-68, Secretary 1966-67, Publicity Chairman 1967-68; Advisory Committee to Board of Central Virginia Speech and Hearing Center, Inc., 1970-74; Special Education Advisory Committee for Lynchburg Public Schools, 1975-79; Eastern Communication Association, 1963-75. Community Activities: Welfare Staff Agencies Club, Member 1963-67, Treasurer and Social Committee Chairman 1965-66; Beta Sigma Phi International Sorority, 1959 to present; Xi Alpha Kappa Chapter Beta Sigma Phi, Member 1963-77, President 1965-66, 1968-71, 1973-75, Vice President 1971-72, 1976-77, Recording Secretary 1973-74, Treasurer 1975-76, Extension Officer 1967-68, Social Committee Chairman 1971-72, Publicity Chairman 1975-77, Service Committee Chairman 1972-73; Lynchburg Beta Sigma Phi City Council, Member 1963-77, President 1964-65, Vice President 1974-75; Founder's Day Committee Chairman 1971-72, 1974-75, Mother's Day Tea Committee Chairman 1970-71, Service Committee Chairman 1965-66. Religion: Court Street United Methodist Church, Lynchburg, Virginia, 1963 to present; Moseley Memorial Methodist, Danville, Virginia, Member 1949-63. Honors and Awards: Third Honor Graduate, Averett College, 1960; Magna Cum Laude Graduate, Mississippi University for Women, 1962; Lynchburg Beta Sigma Phi Valentine Queen, 1965; Girl of the Year Award, Xi Alpha Kappa, 1969-70, 1971-72, 1973-74, 1974-75; Beta Sigma Phi Order of the Rose Degree, 1975; Listed in *Outstanding Young Women of America, Community Leaders of America, Personalities of the South, Dictionary of International Biography, Who's Who in Virginia, Community Leaders of Virginia, World Who's Who of Women, Dictionary of International Biography, Anglo-American Who's Who, International Who's Who of Intellectuals, Personalities of America, Two Thousand Notable Americans.* Address: 723 Custer Drive, Lynchburg, Virginia 24502.■

BARNEY WILLARD GARVIN

Oil Company Jobber. Personal: Born August 15, 1904; Son of Luther Ernest and Annabel Courtney Garvin (deceased); Widower. Education: Attended Clemson University, 1924-25; B.S., North Carolina State University, 1927. Military: Served in the United States Army Reserves, attaining the rank of First Lieutenant, Infantry. Career: District Manager, South Carolina Electricity and Gas, 1935-42; Head Engineer, South Carolina Public Service Authority, 1943; Cotton Broker, 1944-45; Farmer, 1932 to present; Owner and Operator (Exxon Jobber), Garvin Oil Company, 1958 to present; Owner, Cedar Lake Farms (4000 acres). Organizational Memberships: South Carolina Oil Jobbers Association; National Cotton Association. Community Activities: Board of Directors, Florence Chamber of Commerce, 1941-42; Board of Directors, Shriners Children's Hospital, 1945; Sigma Chi; Order of the Eastern Star, 1930 to present; Potentate, Omar Temple Shrine, 1945; Shrine Clubs, Columbia President 1937-39, Aiken First President 1946; Jesters; Rotary Club, President 1939-40; Chairman Utilities Committee, Rotary International, 1939. Religion: Baptist. Address: Route 1 Box 352, Wagener, South Carolina 29164.■

GAYLE HARRIET MARGARET GARY

Communication Executive. Personal: Born December 23, 1920, in New York City, New York; Daughter of Michael H. and Lillian E. Robbins Summers; Married Arthur John Gary, on October 28, 1943; Mother of Sandra G. M. Education: Attended University of Miami 1939, New York University 1940-43, Columbia University 1944-45. Career: President and Owner, Gayle Gary Associates Radio and Television Consultants, 1954 to present; Interviewer and Producer, Syndicated Radio Program "Views and People in the News"; Accredited Public Relations Counselor, Academy of Public Relations Society of America, 1954 to present. Organizational Memberships: Public Relations Society of America; International Radio and Television Executives Society; National Institute of Social Sciences; Religious Public Relations Society of America; American Women in Radio and Television. Community Activities: Prize Committee, Debutante Ball; Patron of Activities Committee, Women's Auxiliary of New York Infirmary, 1950 to present; Friends of Philharmonic Committee, 1950 to present; Fund Raising Committee for Women, United Hospital Fund, 1950 to present; National Advisory Committee for Narconon, 1950 to present; Special Events Committee, Eleanor Roosevelt Memorial Foundation, 1958 to present; Thrift Shop Board, Goddard Riverside, 1958-64; Special Events, Parents League, 1958-64; Board Member of Special Social Service Committee for New York University-Bellevue Medical Center; Executive Committee, Hope Cotillion, 1958 to present; National Director, National Radio-Television Committee for American Observance of Human Rights Week, 1955 to present; Chairman, Daisy Day Week; Publicity, Finance Committees, Girl Scouts of America, 1960-62; Committee Chairman, Girls Friendly Society Ball, 1958-60; Co-Leader, 70 East Assembly District, New York City, 1960-70, 1973; Chairman Public Relations, National Council Women's National Republican Club, Member 1952 to present; Republican State Committeewoman, 1970-72, 1974-76; Candidate, New York State Senate, 1974; Federation of Republican Women, Republican Committee of 100; National Advisory Board, Narcanon, 1971 to present; Board of Directors, Volunteers in Action, 1974 to present; Leadership Foundation, 1975 to present; Honorary Board of Directors, F.L.A.R.E.; National Committee to Save Abu Simbul; Horticultural Society of New York; Sea Organization; Churchwomen's Patriotic League; Navy League; Hubbard Association of Scientologists International; English-Speaking Union; National Society Literature and Arts; A.I.M.; International Platform Association; Chess Club of New York, Vice President 1968 to present. Religion: St. Bartholomew P. E. Church, Guild President 1954-56, Convocation and Diocesan Officer 1954 to present. Address: 1212 Fifth Avenue, New York City, New York 10029.■

DOROTHY MAIRE GAUDIOSE

Retired Teacher. Personal: Born November 27, 1917; Daughter of Mr. and Mrs. Michael Gaudiose. Education: B.S. Secondary Education and English, Lock Haven State Teacher's College, 1940; M.Ed., Penn State University, 1961. Career: Former High School English Teacher, Instructor for Penn State Continuation Classes in

Language Arts. Organizational Memberships: National Education Association; Pennsylvania State Educational Association, President Local Branch 1957. Community Activities: Secretary, Young People's Club, 1936; Chairman, Business and Professional Women's Club Fund-Raising Concert, 1948; American Red Cross Hospital Volunteer, 1981. Published Works: Author of Religious Book, *A Prophet of the People (A Biography of Padre Pio)*, 1974. Honors and Awards: Best Essays, 1932; Appeared on Pittsburgh Television Station KDKA and Youngstown (Ohio) Television Program. Address: 3444 West Water Street, P.O. Box 685, Lock Haven, Pennsylvania 17745.■

HAROLD WESLEY GAUSMAN

Research Leader and Plant Physiologist. Personal: Born December 23, 1921; Married Laura Ellen; Father of Donald Harris. Education: B.S. Agronomy, University of Maine-Orono, 1949; M.S. Agronomy 1950, Ph.D. Plant Physiology 1952, University of Illinois-Urbana; Postdoctoral Work in Nuclear Physics and Rediochemistry, Plant Physiology and Statistics. Military: Served in the United States Army Air Force, 1942-45, rising through the ranks from Private and Cadet to Lieutenant. Career: Research Leader and Plant Physiologist (Texas Tech University, Lubbock, Texas) 1982 to present, Research Leader and Supervisory Plant Physiologist (Weslaco, Texas) 1977-82, Plant Physiologist (Weslaco, Texas) 1967-77, United States Department of Agriculture; Professor of Soil Chemistry 1957-67, Associate Professor 1955-57, Department of Plants and Soils, University of Maine; Assistant Research Specialist on Farm Crops, Rutgers University, 1954-55; Assistant Horticulturist and Associate Agronomist, Texas A. & M. University, 1952-54; Research Assistant in Agronomy, University of Illinois, 1949-52. Organizational Memberships: American Society of Physiology; American Association for the Advancement of Science; American Society of Agronomy; American Institute of Biological Sciences; Societas Physiologiae Plantarum; American Society of Photogrammetric Engineering; Former Editor, *Journal Rio Grande Valley Horticultural Society*; Former Member, New York Academy of Sciences, Texas Vegetable Association, Phi Kappa Phi, Alpha Zeta, Gamma Sigma Delta, Phi Sigma, Sigma Xi. Published Works: Author of 210 Scientific and Technical Publications in Journals, Books and Bulletins. Honors and Awards: B.S. with high distinction, 1949; Full Member, Sigma Xi, 1952; National Science Foundation Postdoctoral Research Fellowship, Texas A. & M. University, 1964; Visiting Scientist 1964-67, Fellow 1981, American Society of Agronomy; Fellow, I.B.A. Address: 8616 Knoxville Avenue, Lubbock, Texas 79423.■

ALADINO A. GAVAZZI

Medical Center Director. Personal: Born July 24, 1922; Son of Mrs. Gavazzi; Married Nancylee, Daughter of Ann K. Ray; Father of William A., Ann Marie, Lisa Kathryn, Alan Lee, Michael J. Education: B.S. 1952, M.S.H.A. 1955, Columbia University; Ph.D. Federal Executive Development, University of Chicago, 1958; Diploma in Hospital Administration, Baylor University, 1968. Military: Served in the United State Army, 1940-81, advancing through the ranks from Private to Colonel U.R.A.R. (Retired). Career: Medical Center Director, Washington, D.C.; Former Positions include Supervisory Administration Officer, Assistant Hospital Administrator, Associate Director for Hospital Construction, Executive Assistant to Chief Medical Director, Executive Director for Administration, Veterans Administration. Organizational Memberships: Regent, American College of Hospital Administrators, 1977-80; Council on Human Resources, American Hospital Association, 1980-81 and 1982-84. Community Activities: Preceptor and Guest Lecturer on Hospital Administration, Medical College of Virginia, 1956-75; Assistant Professor/Lecturer in Health Care Administration, George Washington University, 1963-80; Preceptor and Instructor in Health Care Administration, Washington University, 1972-77; Guest Lecturer, Columbia University, University of Florida, Cornell University, Duke University, University of Brazil, University of Bologna, 1956-82; 3rd Degree, Knights of Columbus, 1960 to present; Citizens Board, Providence Hospital, Washington, D.C. Religion: Catholic. Honors and Awards: Silver Helmet Award 1974, National Commanders Award 1973, AMVETS; Ray E. Brown Award, AMSUS, 1973; Exceptional Service Award, 1981. Address: 1541 Dahlia Court, McLean, Virginia 22101.■

STEFFEN GAY

Professor. Personal: Born March 22, 1948; Son of Peter (deceased) and Ilse Weller Gay; Married Renate Erika Dörner, Daughter of Erich and Irmgard Dorner; Father of Ann-Britt, Annietta. Education: M.D., University Medical School, Leipzig, German Democratic Republic, 1972; Pre-and Postdoctoral Fellow in Pathology, University of Leipzig; Resident in Internal Medicine, Poliklinik Leipzig; Research Fellow, Section of Connective Tissue Research, Max-Planck-Institute Biochemistry, Munich, Federal Republic of Germany; Research Specialist in Biochemistry, C.M.D.N.J. Rutgers Medical School, Piscataway, New Jersey. Career: Visiting Assistant Professor of Pathology, University of Alabama at Birmingham University Medical Center Division of Clinical Immunology and Rheumatology; Associate Professor of Medicine, 1978; Associate Professor of Dermatology, 1978; Scientist, Comprehensive Cancer Center, Multipurpose Arthritis Center, Cystic Fibrosis Center, Institute of Dental Research; General Practitioner, Bartenstein, Federal Republic of Germany. Organizational Memberships: New York Academy of Science; American Association of Pathology; American Rheumatism Association; Deutsche Gesellschaft für Pathologie; Deutsche Gesellschaft für Rheumatologie. Community Activities: Editor-in-Chief and Founder of the *Journal of Collagen and Related Research*; Associate Editor of *Journal of Cutaneous Pathology*. Religion: Presbyterian. Honors and Awards: Summa Cum Laude Graduate, Medical Examinations, 1972; Alexander-Schmidt-Prize for Thrombosis Research, 1975; Carol-Nachman Prize for Rheumatology, 1978. Address: 1100 Beacon Parkway East V-102, Birmingham, Alabama 35209.■

ROBERT DUANE GEBO

Numbered Air Force Disaster Preparedness Officer. Personal: Born June 10, 1938; Son of Melvin S. and Iris C. Gebo; Father of David, Duane, Kevin. Education: B.S. Social Science, Portland State College, 1963; M.S. Industrial Management, University of North Dakota at Grand Forks, 1972. Career: Numbered Air Force Disaster Preparedness Officer, March Air Force Base, California, 1981 to present; Chief, Disaster Preparedness Division, Whiteman Air Force Base, 1979-81; Chief Missile Procedures Trainer Branch 1972-79, Wing Standardization Missile Combat Crew Commander 1971-72, Wing Instructor Missile Combat Crew Commander 1967-71; Personnel Officer, Japan 1963-64, Okinawa 1964-66, Roanoke Rapids Air Force Station (North Carolina) 1966-67; Plywood Worker, Dwyer Lumber and Plywood Company, Portland, Oregon, 1959-63; Logger, Clackamas Logging Company, Portland, Oregon, 1958-59. Organizational Memberships: Air Force Association, 1967 to present; Sedalia-Pettis County Civil Defense Agency, 1979-81; Southern California Emergency Services Association, 1981 to present; Seminar Leader, Air Command and Staff Program, 1978. Community Activities: Order of the Arrow 1955 to present, National Eagle Scout Association 1974 to present, Boy Scouts of America; Assistant Scoutmaster Troop 30, Portland Area Council Boy Scouts of America, 1956-57; Scoutmaster 1964-65, Troop 78 Far East Council (Japan) Boy Scouts of America; Unit Commissioner 1973-79, Merit Badge Counselor 1973-79, Merit Badge Counselor 1973-79, Cub Scout Pow Wow Staff Chairman WEBELOS Section 1974-75, Chairman Pack Administration Section 1976-78, Cubmaster Pack 435 1974-78, Troop Committee Member Advancement Chairman Troops 436 and 431 1974-79, Tomahawk District Scout Roundtable Staff 1975-79, Assistant Scoutmaster for Troop Leadership Development Program 1976, WEBELOS Den Leader Pack 435 1973-75, Board of Directors National Eagle Scout Association Chapter 1976-79, Silver Beaver Selection Committee 1977, Scout Woodbadge Staff North Central Region 1977-79, Northern Lights Council Boy Scouts of America; Unit Commissioner 1979-81, Cubmaster Troop 405 1979-81, Guest Chairman Eagle Scout Board of Reviews 1979-81, Lone Bear District Leadership Training Chairman 1979-81, Training Committee 1979-81, Heart of America Council Boy Scouts of America; Unit WOW Staff Chairman Skits and Costumes Section 1980, Order of the Arrow Chapter Advisor 1980-81, Heart of America Council Boy Scouts of America; Unit Commissioner 1981 to present, Cubmaster Troop 100 1981 to present, Assistant Cubmaster Pack 700 1981 to present, Cub Scout POW WOW Staff Chairman of Pack Administration Section 1982, California Inland Empire Council; Volunteer High School Varsity Football Coach, Okinawa, 1966; Minot Fin and Gill Society, 1970-74; First Aid Instructor, American Red Cross, 1971-81; Family Activities Committee, Parents Without Partners, 1976-79; Minot Air Force Base Youth Advisory Council, 1977-79; Sedalia-Pettis County Civil Defense Agency, 1979-81; Retired Officers Association, 1982. Religion: Assembly of God. Honors and Awards: United States Treasury Department Award, 1965; Tomahawk District Award of Merit, Northern Lights Council Boy Scouts of America, 1975; Silver Beaver Award, Boy Scouts of America, 1976; Air Force Commendation Medal, 1974; Meritorious Service Medal, 1979. Address: 24323 Sykes Drive, Sunnymead, California 92388.■

TWO THOUSAND NOTABLE AMERICANS

HAROLD GEIST

Clinical Psychologist. Personal: Born July 22, 1916; Son of Alexander and Edna Geist. Education: A.B., Cornell University, 1936; A.M., Columbia University, 1937; Ph.D., Stanford University, 1951. Military: Served in the Army Medical Service Corps, Psychologist. Career: Administrative Psychologist for Federal Government, Washington, D.C.; Clinical Psychologist; Consultant for various City and county School Systems in California; Lecturer, University of California at Berkeley Extension, Diablo Valley College, San Francisco State University, University of San Francisco; Visiting Professor, University of Puerto Rico; Oral Examiner for Psychology License, State of California. Organizational Memberships: Member of 14 Organizations including American Psychological Association and American Association for the Advancement of Science. Published Works: Author, *The Etiology of Idiopathic Epilepsy, The Psychological Aspects of Migraine, The Psychological Aspects of the Aging Process, The Emotional Aspects of Heart Disease, Psychological Aspects of Diabetes, Psychological Aspects of Rheumatoid Arthritis.* Honors and Awards: State Tuition Scholarship, Cornell University, 1932 Special Grant, Department of Health and Human Services, to Construct Special Test for the Deaf, 1959; Research Grant for Research on the Psychological Aspects of Rheumatoid Arthritis, Results Embodied in Monograph, "The Psychological Aspects of Rheumatoid Arthritis." Address: 2255 Heart Avenue, Berkeley, California 94709.■

CHARLES GOTTLIEB GELTZ

Professor Emeritus. Personal: Born February 21, 1896; Son of William and Mary Ditter Geltz (deceased); Married Mildred Harry, Daughter of Thomas and Hannah Harry (deceased); Father of Jane L. Keenan, Helen M. Reiley, Charles G., Betty Anne Swanson (Mrs. Joel D.). Education: B.S.F., Penn State Forest School, 1924; M.S.F., University of California at Berkeley, 1927; Silviculture Specialist (Forestry), Duke University, 1941; Education and Counseling Specialist, University of Florida College of Education, 1957. Military: Served in the United States Army, 1916-20 and 1941-46, attaining the rank of Retired Major (1956); Served in the United States Cavalry, 1920, from 2nd Lieutenant to Captain; Served in the Adjunct General's Corps, 1942-46, as Major. Career: Owner-Operator, Charles G. Geltz Associates (associated with National School of Forestry and Conservation, correspondence study, Milwaukee, Wisconsin), 1967-76; Professor of Silviculture Emeritus, University of Florida, Retired 1966; Associate Professor of Silviculture 1933-41, Assistant Professor 1930-33, Purdue University; Instructor, New York State Forest Ranger School, United States Forestry Service, 1927-29; Professor Forester, Pennsylvania 1924, Alabama 1925. Organizational Memberships: Life Member, Society of American Foresters, 1926; American Forestry Association, 1914 to present; Audubon Society, 1947; Wilderness Society, 1951; Florida Forestry Association, Member 1947 to present, First Honorary Life Member 1966, Secretary 1949-61; Executive Secretary, Florida Forestry Council, 1950-61; Phi Sigma, 1927; Xi Sigma Pi, 1927; Phi Kappa Delta, 1952; Kappa Delta Pi, 1953; American Association Professors Emeriti, 1967 to present; Registered Forester No.10, Florida Board of Registration of Foresters. Community Activities: Secretary Local Chapter 1950-51, Life Member, Reserve Officers Association; Life Member, Military Order of Veterans of World Wars; American Security Council; Advisory Committee, Congressional Committee for Security; Advisory Committee to President Reagan. Religion: Episcopalian, Lay Reader, 1942-61, Brotherhood St Andrew 1942-48, Vestryman Holy Trinity of Gainesville 1947-50. Honors and Awards: Wisdom Award of Honor, 1970; Silver Beaver Award, Boy Scouts of America; Listed in *Names of Distinction, Who's Who in America, National Register of Prominent Americans.* Address: 1521 Northwest 7th Avenue, Gainesville, Florida 32603.■

DONALD WILLIAM GENTRY

Dean of Undergraduate Studies and Professor of Mining Engineering. Personal: Born January 18, 1943; Son of William H. Gentry; Married Sheila Carol, Daughter of J. G. Schuepbach; Father of Tara Cassandre, Chad Ryan. Education: B.S. Mining Engineering, University of Illinois, 1965; M.S. Mining Engineering, University of Nevada, 1967; Ph.D. Mining Engineering, University of Arizona, 1972. Career: Dean of Undergraduate Studies 1983 to present, Professor of Mining Engineering 1978 to present, Assistant to the Dean of Faculty 1977-78, Associate Professor of Mining Engineering 1974-78, Assistant Professor of Mining Engineering 1972-74, Colorado School of Mines Mining Department; Instructor of Mining Engineering, University of Arizona, 1969-72; Special Projects Engineer and Mining Research Engineer, The Anaconda Company, 1967-69; Lecturer of Mining Engineering, University of Nevada, 1965-67; President, Mining and Subsidence Engineering Company, Inc., 1978 to present. Organizational Memberships: Member Executive Committee, Engineering Accreditation Commission of A.B.E.T. representing S.M.E./A.I.M.E., 1980 to present; Member Executive Committee, E.A.C./A.B.E.T., 1982 to present; Chairman 1981-82, Vice-Chairman 1980-81, Secretary/ Treasurer 1979-80, Program Chairman 1978-79, Colorado Section A.I.M.E.; A.S.E.E.; Sigma Xi; Sigma Gamma Epsilon. Honors and Awards: Consultant to Executive Office of White House (O.S.T.P.) 1978-81, United States Geological Survey, United States General Accounting Office 1979-81. Address: 6590 South Ridgeview Drive, Morrison, Colorado 80465.■

DONALD ROGERS GERTH

University Professor and Administrator. Personal: Born December 4, 1928; Married Beverly J. Hollman; Father of Annette Gerth Childs, Deborah Gerth Hougham. Education: A.B. Liberal Arts 1947, A.M. Political Science 1951, Ph.D. Political Science 1963, University of Chicago. Military: Served in the United States Air Force, 1952-56, attaining the rank of Captain and serving on Intelligence and Comptroller Assignments. Career: President and Professor of Political Science and Public Administration, California State University-Sacramento. 1984 to present; President and Professor of Political Science and Public Administration, California State University-Dominguez Hills, 1976-84, Vice-President for Academic Affairs 1970-76, Professor of Political Science 1964-76, Associate Vice-President for Academic Affairs and Director of International Programs (Director of Center at University of Skopje, Yugoslavia), Coordinator of Institute for Local Government and Public Service and of Public Administration, Co-Director of Danforth Foundation Research Project and Improvement of Undergraduate Teaching, Dean of Students, California State University-Chico; Associate Dean of Institutional Relations and Student Affairs, The California State University, 1963-64; Associate Dean of Students, Admissions and Records and Member of Department of Political Science, San Francisco State University, 1958-63; Admissions Counselor, University of Chicago, 1956-58; Lecturer in History, University of the Philippines, 1953-54; Assistant to the President, Shimer College, 1951; Admissions Counselor, University of Chicago, 1951; Field Representative Southeast Asia, World University Service, 1950; Part-time Assistant to the Director of Test Administration, University of Chicago, 1947-49. Organizational Memberships: Commission on Higher Education and the Adult Learner, American Council on Education, 1981 to present; Board of Directors 1979 to present, President 1981, Industry Education Council; Commission on Policies and Purposes, American Association of State Colleges and Universities, 1979 to present; President, Los Angeles Urban Consortium for Higher Education, 1978-81; Chairman of Commission on Extended Education, The California State University, 1977-82; Editorial Board, Society for College and University Planning, 1975 to present; Chairman, California Association for Public Administration, 1973-74; Chairman 1976-77 and Member 1972-77 of Commission on External Degree Programs, The California State University; American Political Science Association; American Society for Public Administration; Pi Alpha Alpha National Honor Society for Public Affairs and Administration. Community Activities: Advisory Director, Sterling Bank, Los Angeles, 1981-84; Delegate, Commission of the Californias, 1979 to present; Los Angeles World Affairs Council, 1979 to present; Board of Directors, South Bay Hospital Foundation, 1979 to present; Town Hall of Los Angeles, 1976 to present; Chairman, Chico Unified School District Personnel Commission, 1971-74; Commonwealth Club of California, 1965 to present; Los Angeles Area Council Boy Scouts of America Varsity Scouting Team, 1981-84; Chairman, Region III Public Service Agencies, United Way Campaign, 1982-83; Board of Trustees, California Family Studies Center, 1982-84. Published Works: Contributor of Papers to Professional Conferences; Author, "Institutional Approach to Faculty Development" in *New Directions for Higher Education* 1973; Co-Author and Co-Editor, *An Invisible Giant: The California State Colleges* 1971; Co-Author, *The Learning Society* for Danforth Foundation Study, 1969; Contributor and Editor, *Education for the Public Service* 1970, *Papers on the Ombudsman in Higher Education.* Address: 404 Palos Verdes Boulevard, Redondo Beach, California 90277.■

GEORGIE ANNE GEYER

Syndicated Columnist, Author, Speaker, Teacher. Personal: Born April 2, 1935; Daughter of Robert and Georgie Hazel Geyer (both deceased). Education: B.S. Journalism/History, Northwestern University, 1956; Fulbright Scholarship, University of Vienna, Austria, 1956-57. Career: Syndicated Columnist, Universal Press Syndicate and *The Washington Star*; Author; Speaker; Teacher; Television Appearances, Semi-Regular on P.B.S. *Washington Week in Review*, B.B.C. Overseas Broadcasts, *Meet the Press, Kup's Show, Panorama* Television Show in Washington, D.C., Regular on Voice of America Press Review, Many Appearances on *William Buckley's Firing Line*; Syndicated Columnist, *Los Angeles Times* Syndicate, 1975-80; *Chicago Daily News*, Foreign Correspondent 1964-75, General Assignment Reporter, 1960-64. Organizational Memberships: International Institute for Strategic Studies, London; Women in Communications; Sigma Delta Chi; The Women's Institute for Freedom of the Press. Community Activities: Lyle Spencer Professor of Journalism, Newhouse School of Communications, Syracuse University, 1977; Courses by Newspaper Project, University of California, Sponsored by National Endowment for the Humanities (national board member); John J. Fitzpatrick Lecturer,

University of Utah, 1977; Board Member, Chicago Council on Foreign Relations, 1972-75; Conferences at Army, Navy and Air War Colleges; American Enterprise Institute Latin America Group; Steering Committee, Aspen Institute's Latin American Governance Project; Lecturer on Press Ethics, Foreign Service Institute Executive Seminar; International Communications Agency Speaking Tour of Africa on Press Problems and Ethics, 1979; Commencement Speaker at Rosary College, River Forest, Illinois, 1978; Speaker to Groups such as Chicago Committee of Chicago Council on Foreign Relations, Finnish-American Chamber of Commerce (Helsinki, Finland), National Journalism Education Association, American Supply Corporation, Bank Administrators Convention, International Seminar at Lewis and Clark College, Institute for International Education in Denver, Colorado. Published Works: Author, *The New Latins* 1970, *The New 100 Years' War* 1972, *The Young Russians* 1976, *Buying the Night Flight* (autobiography) 1983; Contributor, *The Saturday Review*, *The Atlantic*, *The New Republic*, *The Progressive*, *Look*, *The Nation*, *Playgirl*, *Ladies Home Journal*, *Encyclopedia Britannica*, *People*, *Signature*. Honors and Awards: Chicago Newspaper Guild Prize for Best Human Interest Story for Masquerading as a Waitress at a Mafia Wedding, 1962; Overseas Press Club Latin America Award for Series on Living in the Mountains in Guatemala with Guerrillas and for Exclusive Interviews with Fidel Castro, 1967; National Council of Jewish Women's Hannah Solomon Award for Public Service, 1971; Maria Moors Cabot Award for Improving Relations within the Hemisphere, 1971; *Who's Who of America Women* Award for Outstanding Woman Journalist in the Country, 1971; One of Four Outstanding Women Journalists in the Country, *Newsweek* Magazine, 1967; Illinois State Merit Award, 1975; Northwestern University Merit Award, 1968; Honorary Doctor of Letters Degree, Lake Forest College, Illinois, 1980; Mortar Board. Address: 800 — 25th Street Northwest, Washington, D.C. 20037.■

MARY VIRGIL GHERING

Member of Religious Order, Librarian. Personal: Born July 18, 1910; Daughter of Henry Christian (deceased) and Frances Emily (Sharp) Ghering. Education: A.B., Central Michigan University, 1935; M.S., Marquette University, 1948; Candidate for Ph.D., Fordham University, 1959; Ph.D., St. Thomas Institute, 1968. Career: St. Thomas Institute, Faculty Member, Librarian; Aquinas College, Assistant Professor of Chemistry 1949-57, Associate Professor 1957-61, Professor 1961-68, Chairman Department Physical Sciences 1959-63; Teacher of Science and Mathematics in Various Michigan High Schools, 1931-49. Organizational Memberships: American Chemical Society; American Institute of Chemists; Pax Romana, Albertus Magnus Guild. Community Activities: Telephone Coordinator, Common Cause, Congressional District 2, Ohio, 1973-83; Daughters of the American Revolution, Sophie de Marsac Camapu Chapter, 1977 to present. Religion: Entered the Order of the Sisters of Saint Dominic, Grand Rapids, Michigan, September 8, 1929. Honors and Awards: Scholarship to Attend Central Michigan University, 1935-36; Science Faculty Fellowship to Attend Fordham University, National Science Foundation, 1957-58; Fellowship to Attend Saint Thomas Institute, 1963-68; Fellow, American Institute of Chemists, 1969; International Biographical Association. Address: 2335 Grandview Avenue, Cincinnati, Ohio 45206.■

AHMAD GHORBANI

Educator. Personal: Born April 4, 1957; Son of Esmail and Shahzadgh Ghorbani. Education: B.S.E.E., University of Texas-Austin, 1979; M.S. Industrial Education/Technology, Texas Southern University, 1981. Career: Instructor, Electronics Department, Texas Southern University. Organizational Memberships: National Association of Industrial Technology; Instrument Society of America; Teaching Industrial Arts Association; Institute of Electrical and Electronics Engineers; National Electrical Manufacturers Association. Community Activities: Attended the Texas Industrial Arts Association Conference at Texas A&M University, 1984; Mincroprocessor and Microcomputer Networks, Tarrent County Junior College, 1983; Seminar in Microcomputer and Microprocessing Networks, Hewlett-Packard Company, 1983; Certificate in Electrical Gas Turbine, Cooper Bessmer Company, 1982. Honors and Awards: National Dean's List; Distinguished Student Scholarship Award, 1979-81; Honor Graduate for Excellence in Achievement, Texas Southern University, 1981; Listed in *International Youth in Achievement, Who's Who Among Students in American Universities and Colleges*. Address: 2306 Canebreak Crossing, Sugarland, Texas 77478.■

CURTIS A. GIBSON

Aircraft Systems Engineer. Personal: Born in 1929, in Springfield, Ohio. Education: Ch.E., University of Cincinnati, Ohio, 1952. Career: Aircraft Systems Engineer, 1979 to present; Expert in Systems Acquisition and Systems Engineering Management; Authority in Design of Aircraft Oxygen Systems and in the Standardization of Aircraft Oxygen Equipment; Life Support Systems Engineer 1970-79, Mechanical Engineer 1956-70, Chemical Engineer 1956-59, United States Air Force, Wright-Patterson Air Force Base, Ohio; Chemical Engineer, Sylvania Electric Products Company, Emporium, Pennsylvania, 1952-54. Organizational Memberships: American Defense Preparedness Association; International Academy of Professional Business Executives; Air Force Association. Community Activities: Active Volunteer, Boy Scouts of America. Honors and Awards: Silver Beaver Award, Boy Scouts of America; Honorary Ph.D. and D.D. Degrees for Religious Studies, Universal Life Church, Modesto, California, 1979. Address: 2806 Oxford Drive, Springfield, Ohio 45506.■

DONALD BAKER GIBSON

Physician and Writer. Personal: Born January 24, 1930; Son of Basil and Emma Gibson; Married Jayne, Daughter of Harlan and Beth Tucker; Father of Donald, Jr., Dean, Lisa. Career: Physician and Writer; Instructor, Lee College and University of Tennessee; Instructor in Science, South Carolina and Georgia High Schools; Office Engineer, E. I. DuPont Company. Organizational Memberships: Charter Member, National Association of Disability Evaluating Physicians, 1983; Fellow, American Academy of Family Physicians, 1984; Bradley County (Tennessee) Medical Society; Tennessee Medical Association; American Medical Association; American Society of Composers, Authors and Publishers. Community Activities: Former Consultant, Teen Challenge, Cleveland, Tennessee; Business Advisory Board (Senatorial), Washington, D.C.; Former Member Board of Trustees, Lee College, Cleveland, Tennessee. Published Works: Author and Producer, Bicentennial Recording, *I Am America*, 1976; Author and Producer of Bicentennial Recording of Battle of Cowpens, *The Ballad of Daniel Morgan*, 1980; Author, *The Roosevelt Miller Story*, biography of Lee College's well-known music professor and tenor, 1982. Honors and Awards: Listed in *Personalities of the South, Two Thousand Men of Achievement, Notable Americans of the Bicentennial Era, International Who's Who of Intellectuals, Dictionary of International Biography*. Address: P.O. Box 1077, Cleveland, Tennessee 37311.■

FLOYD ROBERT GIBSON

United States Judge. Personal: Born March 3, 1910; Married Gertrude W.; Father of Charles R., John M., Catherine Gibson-Jobst. Education: A.B. 1931, J.D. 1933, University of Missouri-Columbia. Military: Served in the Missouri State Guard, 1942-46, attaining the rank of Major. Career: United States Judge, United States Courthouse, Kansas City, Missouri; Former Missouri State Senator and Lawyer. Organizational Memberships: Appellate Judges Conference, Chairman 1973-74; Commissioner, National Conference of Comissioners on Uniform State Laws, 1957 to present; Kansas City Bar Association; Missouri Bar Association; Federal Bar Association; Chairman Judicial Administration Division 1979-80, Chairman of Conference of Section Chairmen 1980-81, American Bar Association; Lawyers Association of Kansas City, Vice-President; Institute of Judicial Administration; Chairman of Chief Judges Conference, 1977-78; Judicial Conference of the United States, 1974-80. Community Activities: Trustee, University of Kansas City; Director, Board of Jacob L. and Ella C. Loose Foundation; Phi Delta Phi; Phi Kappa Psi; Council of State Governments, Board of Managers; National Legislative Conference, President, 1960; Majority Floor Leader, Missouri State Senate, 1952-56; President pro tem, Missouri Senate, 1956-60; County Counselor, Jackson County, Missouri, 1942-44. Honors and Awards: Most Valuable Member 1960, 2nd Most Valuable Member 1958, Missouri Legislature, Globe-Democrat Award; Faculty-Alumni Award, University of Missouri, 1968; Missouri Academy of Squires, 1974; Man of the Year, Phi Kappa Psi, 1974; Citation of Merit, Missouri Law School Alumni, 1975; Fellow, American Bar Association; Spurgeon Smithson Award, Missouri Bar Foundation, 1978; Honorary Member, Order of the Coif, 1979; Annual Achievement Award, Kansas City Bar Association, 1980. Address: 11521 Winner Road, Independence, Missouri 64052.■

JACQUELYN JORDAN GIBSON

Electrologist. Personal: Born August 2, 1924; Daughter of Ira Andrew (deceased) and Ercyal Brickley Jordan; Married Morgan Stone Gibson, Son of Morgan Stone and Edna Maud Gibson (both deceased); Father of Bruce Morgan, Ronald Wayne, Jeffrey Jordan. Education: Bard Avon (Baltimore, Maryland), 1943; Kree Electrolysis Institute, 1946. Career: Electrologist. Organizational Memberships: Maryland Electrolysis Association, Charter Member; Maryland Association of Professional Electrologists. Community Activities: United Grievience Committee of Maryland; Soroptimist International, Treasurer 1970-71, President 1971-72; Business and Professional Women of Jupiter-Tequesta (Florida); Junior Board, Peninsula General Medical Center; Election Worker, Baltimore and Salisbury, Maryland, 1953-81; Involved in Various Drives, including Heart Fund, Muscular Dystrophy Association, March of Dimes, Cystic Fibrosis, 1952-75; Chamber of Commerce; Helped Organizer TAR (Teen-Age Republicans), Salisbury (Maryland), 1970; Newcomers Club of Salisbury, Membership Vice President 1963. Religion: Temple Baptist Church of Baltimore, Workers Council Secretary 1942, Sunday School Teacher 1941-61. Address: 102 East Beverly Road, Jupiter-Tequesta, Florida 33458.■

WELDON BAILEY GIBSON

Administrator. Personal: Born April 23, 1917; Married Helen Mears; Father of David Mears. Education: A.B., Washington State University, 1938; M.B.A. 1940, Ph.D. 1950, Stanford University. Military: Served in the United States Air Force, 1942-46, Director of Materiel Requirements, attaining the rank of Colonel. Career: Senior Director 1982 to present, Executive Vice-President 1960-82, Vice-President 1959-60, Associate Director 1955-59, with Company as Director and Organizer of International Conferences for Senior Business Executives 1947-59, SRI International (formerly Stanford Research Institute); Lecturer on Transportation and Business Economics, Stanford University, 1947-52; Assistant Director, United States Air Force Institute of Technology, Dayton, Ohio, 1946-47; With Burroughs Corporation, San Francisco; Consultant, White House Conference on Industrial World Ahead 1972, National Security Resources Board 1949-53, Bureau of the Budget 1949-53. Organizational Memberships: American Association for the Advancement of Science; American Economic Association; American Geographical Society; Western Economic Association; Society for International Development; Explorers Club; Director, Plantronics Inc., Valley National Bank (Arizona), Vendo Company, Technical Equities Corporation Inc., Group 800 N.V. (Netherlands), Callog Limited (England); Numerous Others. Community Activities: Member of Governing Board of Many Civic and Business Associations in U.S. and Elsewhere, including, Japan-California Association, Pacific Basin Economic Council, San Francisco Bay Area Council; Chemists Club, New York; Pacific-Union Club, San Francisco; Los Altos Golf and Country Club; Palo Alto Club; Stanford Faculty Club; Villa Taverna, San Francisco; Wine and Food Society of San Francisco; Okura Club International; Six Continents Club (Inter-Continental Hotels); Nautilus Club; Numerous Others. Published Works: Author or Co-Author of Several Books and Other Publications in Fields of Economic Geography and International Economic Affairs; Author, *SRI — The Founding Years*, 1980. Honors and Awards: Medal of the Legion of Merit, United States, 1946; Order of Commander of British Empire, United Kingdom, 1947; Distinguished Alumnus Award, Alumni Achievement Award, Washington State Alumni Association; Outstanding Achievement Award, Gamma Theta Chapter of Beta Theta Pi; Presidential Award, Government of Indonesia, 1978. Address: 593 Gerona Road, Stanford, California. ■

BLAND GIDDINGS

Nuclear Physician. Personal: Son of Luther E. (deceased) and Berneice Chipman Giddings; Married Lucile Layton, Daughter of Mr. and Mrs. Lionel Layton, in 1973; Father of Luther V, Thomas C. Education: Degree in Chemistry and Pre-Medicine/Cello Studies, Brigham Young University, 1938; Ph.D. Biochemistry, University of Cincinnati, 1940s; Intern, Seattle; Studies in Nuclear Medicine, Oak Ridge, Tennessee, 1950; Board Certification, American Board of Nuclear Medicine, 1973; Board Certification Pathology, 1955. Military: Served in the United States Air Force, 1953-55, San Antonio, Texas. Career: Nuclear Medicine Physician in Private Practice, Mesa, Arizona, 1973 to present; Family Genealogist; Cellist; Former Faculty Member of Louisiana State University Medical School, New Orleans. Organizational Memberships: Charter Member, Society of Nuclear Medicine; Fellow, American College of Nuclear Medicine; President, Arizona Nuclear Medicine Physicians; Fellow, American College of Pathologists; Fellow, American College of Medical Imaging; Distinguished Fellow, American College of Nuclear Medicine. Community Activities: Founding Member, President 1967-68, Mesa Fine Arts Association; Co-Founder 1969, Vice-President, Arizona Cello Society; President, Mesa Symphony Orchestra (formerly Sun Valley Sumphony Orchestra), 1965 to present. Honors and Awards: Artist of the Year Award, 1972; Award of Appreciation for 25 Years of Dedicated Service, Mesa Symphony Orchestra, 1982; Listed in *Who's Who in the West, Community Leaders and Noteworthy Americans*. Address: 1820 East Jensen Street, Mesa, Arizona 85203. ■

WALTER EDWARD GIESTING

Executive Consultant. Personal: Born July 16, 1918; Son of Walter E. and Mae Giesting (deceased); Married Jeanne E., Daughter of Charles and Rae Fox (deceased); Father of Walter E. Jr., Judith R. Graham. Education: B.S.C., Xavier University, Cincinnati, Ohio, 1940; Attended University of Texas-Austin Graduate School of Business, 1971. Military: Served in the United States Army (Ordnance), 1942-46, in the European Theatre of Operations, attaining the rank of Captain. Career: President, Unitech International, 1978 to present; President NCR Mexico (Baja, California) 1966-76, Vice-President Pacific Division 1966-76, Division Manager of Southern Division (Dallas, Texas) 1963-66, Various Management Positions 1941-63, National Cash Register Corporation. Organizational Memberships: Past President and Director, Sales and Marketing Executives; National Association of Accountants. Community Activities: Past Vice-President and Director, Rotary Club; Past President and Director, Los Altos Golf and Country Club. Religion: Roman Catholic. Honors and Awards: Publication Award for Career Management for Today's Executive, 1976; Listed in *Who's Who in Finance and Industry, Who's Who in the World* and International Biographical Centre Publications. Address: 10115 Parkwood Drive #2, Cupertino, California 95014. ■

ROBERT FRANK GILBERT

United States Army Surgeon. Personal: Born July 19, 1935; Son of Frank and Eleanor H. Marshall Gilbert; Married Ihn Jae Byun; Father of Evelyn, Aimee, Andrew, Terence, Diane, Catherine, Elizabeth. Education: B.A., Miami University, 1957; M.D., Ohio State University of Medicine, 1962. Military: Served in the United States Army Medical Corps, 1969 to present, with rank of Colonel; Served as Army Surgeon in Korea, 1969-71 and 1972-74; Served as Surgical Advisor, A.R.V.N. Airborne Division in Viet Nam 1971-72 and Senior Medical Advisory, M.R. IV Republic of Viet Nam 1972. Career: Medical Doctor, General Surgeon, United States Army. Organizational Memberships: Diplomate, American Board of Surgery; Fellow, American College of Surgeons. Community Activities: Volunteer Physicians for Viet Nam, 1967. Honors and Awards: Military Decorations including Legion of Merit, Bronze Star. Address: 982 Sycamore Avenue, Tinton Falls, New Jersey 07724. ■

LOUIS CHARLES GILDE, JR.

Executive. Personal: Born March 23, 1924; Son of Louis Charles and Therese May Gilde (deceased); Married Patricia Ann Gilde; Father of Lisa, Mark, Patty, Susan, Troy, Sam. Education: B.S., Rutgers University, 1950. Military: Served in the United States Army, 1943-45. Career: Director of Environmental Programs, Campbell Soup Company, 1970 to present; Vice President and Member of the Board of Directors, Technological Resources Inc., subsidiary of Campbell Soup Company, 1978 to present. Organizational Memberships: National Environmental Development Association, Director 1974 to present; National Food Processors Association, Chairman Environmental Research Committee 1968-74; American Frozen Food Institute; N.A.M., Chairman Water Task Committee 1975-79; Water Pollution Control Federation; American Water Works Association; Academy of Natural Sciences, Philadelphia; Water Resources Association of the Delaware River Basin, Director 1983 to present. Community Activities: National Technical Task Committee on Industrial Waste, 1960-64; National Industrial Pollution Control Council, United States Department of Commerce, 1970-72; Camden City Environmental Commission, Commissioner and Vice-Chairman 1977 to present. Religion: Lutheran; Martin Luther Chapel, Pennsauken, New Jersey, Past Vice-President. Published Works: Author of Chapters in Four Environmental Engineering Handbooks and Over 35 Publications; Patentee in Field. Honors and Awards: Designer, Waste Treatment System that received National Gold Medal Award of Sports Foundation, 1970; Industrial Development Research Council Award for Distinguished Service in Environmental Planning, 1979; E.P.A. Certificate of Appreciation for Efforts to Improve the Environment, 1979. Address: P.O. Box 436, Haddonfield, New Jersey 08033. ■

MARIA TERESA GIL-DEL-REAL

Public Health-Epidemiology Health Researcher. Personal: Born January 5, 1941; Daughter of Antonio (deceased) and Rose Gil-del-Real; Married John R. Romano, Son of Joseph (deceased) and Connie Romano; Mother of Christina, John-Alexander. Education: Associate Degree, Bogota Business College, Colombia, 1960; B.A. summa cum laude, Rutgers University, 1979. Career: Public Health-Epidemiology Health Researcher, on Sabbatical from Masters Program in Public Health at Columbia University, New York, to do Research in Spain; Program Associate in Research, The Robert Wood Johnson Foundation, Princeton, New Jersey, 1980 to present; Bilingual Editor, Princeton International Translations, Princeton Junction, New Jersey, 1979-80; Free-lance Translator and Simultaneous Interpreter. Community Activities: Consumer Panel, Johnson and Johnson, New Brunswick, New Jersey, 1980; Regular Contributor, Greenpeace. Honors and Awards: Alpha Sigma Lambda Honor Society, 1977 to present; B.A. with highest honors. Address: 76 Princeton Avenue, Rocky Hill, New Jersey 08553. ■

TWO THOUSAND NOTABLE AMERICANS

NORMA N. GILL

Enterostomal Therapy Consultant. Personal: Born June 26, 1920; Daughter of Richard Nottingham; Widow; Married Herbert G. Thompson; Mother of Marilyn, David, Sally. Education: Studies with R. B. Turnbull, Jr., M.D., School of Enterostomal Therapy, The Cleveland Clinic Educational Foundation, Cleveland, Ohio, 1958; Birmingham General Hospital, Birmingham, England, 1970; Dale Carnegie Course, 1974; Spanish Courses, Berlitz School of Language 1979, Lakeland College (Mentor, Ohio) 1980, Akron University 1981; Principles of Management, Engineering Agreement, Leadership Course, Cleveland Clinic Foundation, 1980; Certification, International Association for Enterostomal Therapy, 1981. Career: President and Private Consultant, Worldwide Ostomy Center, Inc., Akron, Ohio, 1981 to present; Coordinator of Enterostomal Therapy, Cleveland Clinic Foundation, 1978-81; Faculty 1978-81, Assistant 1974-78, With School 1961-74, School of Enterostomal Therapy; Lecturer in Field. Organizational Memberships: Akron Ostomy Association; Allied Original Member, American Urological Association, 1972; Professional Advisory Board, International Ostomy Association, 1980-83; Chairman of First Conference, United Ostomy Association, 1962; Co-Founder, International Association for Enterostomal Therapy, 1968; Founder 1977, First President 1979-80, World Council for Enterostomal Therapists; Member Ileitis and Colitis Foundation; Honorary President, L'Association francaise de stoma therapeutes; National Association of Women Business Owners; Women's Network, Akron, Ohio. Honors and Awards: Honorary Member, World Council of Enterostomal Therapists, Munich, Germany, 1982; Honorary Member, United Ostomy Association; Honorary Member, International Association for Enterostomal Therapy; Norma N. Gill Foundation, Cleveland Conference World Council for Enterostomal Therapists, Founded 1980; Listed in *World Who's Who of Women, Who's Who of Intellectuals, Personalities of America, Personalities of the West and Midwest*. Address: 4006 Townhouse Lane, Uniontown, Ohio 44685.■

DAVID ALAN GILMAN

Professor and Educational Consultant. Personal: Born September 26, 1933; Son of Maynard and Ruth Gilman (deceased); Married Elizabeth Ann Barlow, Daughter of Marjorie Winstanley; Father of Ruth, Tom, Bill. Education: B.S., Indiana State University, 1955; M.A., Michigan State University, 1962; Ph.D., Pennsylvania State University, 1967. Military: Served as a Special Agent in the United States Army Counter Intelligence, 1956-58. Career: Professor, Indiana State University; Educational Consultant; Former Positions of Teacher, Special Agent in Counter Intelligence, Engineer, Research Director. Organizational Memberships: International Audiovisual Society, National Board Member 1979; Phi Delta Kappa Educational Honorary Fraternity, Research Director; Indiana Educational Research Association, Membership Chairman 1975-77. Community Activities: Governor's Committee on Libraries, 1979; Advisor to Indiana Legislature, 1978; Volunteer Worker, Terre Haute Boys Club, 1970-83. Honors and Awards: Caleb Mills Outstanding Teaching Award; Indiana Educational Research Association Service Award; Honorary Life Member, Indiana State University Union Board. Address: 500 Gardendale Road, Terre Haute, Indiana 47803.■

JONAS GINTAUTAS

Physician, Research Administrator. Personal: Born October 3, 1939; Son of Jonas and Elena Sinsinas; Married Kristina, Daughter of Jonas and Juze Zebrauskas; Father of Pasaka, Vadas. Education: M.D., Piragov Medical Institute (U.S.S.R.), 1967; Ph.D., Northwestern University, 1976. Career: Physician, Cook County Hospital, Chicago, 1968-69; Clinical Director, Westchester County Clinic, 1969-76; Associate Professor, Texas Tech University, 1975-79; Associate Professor and Director of Research, Texas Tech University, 1979-82. Organizational Memberships: American Association for the Advancement of Science; Society of Neurosciences; New York Academy of Science; Western Pharmacology Society. Community Activities: Board of Directors, American Heart Association; Board of Directors, Myosthenia Gravis Association, Texas Affiliate 1979-81. Religion: Member, St. John's United Methodist Church, Lubbock, Texas. Honors and Awards: Best Professor Award, Texas Tech University, 1977; First Director of Research, Department of Anesthesiology, Texas Tech University Health Science Center, 1982. Address: P.O. Box 9011, El Paso, Texas 79382.■

ANTONIO GIRAUDIER

Poet, Writer, Artist, Musician. Personal: Born September 28, 1926; Son of Antonio and Dulce M. de Giraudier. Education: Studied at Deutsche Schule, Havana, Cuba; B.L., Institute 2, Vedado, Havana, Cuba, 1944; B.L., Belen Jesuits, Havana, 1944; LL.B., Havana University Law School, 1949; Culver S. Naval School, Indiana; Admiral Bellard Academy, New London Connecticut; Private Art Studies. Career: *Modern Images* Publication of the American Fellowship Society, Editor 1978-81, Poetry Critic 1978-80; Poetry Critic of *Arbol de Fuego*, Caracas, Venezuela, 1971-76; Over 900 Poetry Readings and Music Recitals, including Readings at the New York Poetry Forum; Over 700 Performances in the United States and Europe, Piano Solo, Piano Accompaniment for Singing, Singing and Accompanying Himself on Guitar, and Singing with Piano Accompaniment; Has had 174 Exhibits; One-Man Exhibitions, Smolin Gallery (New York) 1965, New Masters Gallery (New York) 1967, Avanti Galleries (New York) 1968, 1969, 1971, 1973, 1975, Palm Beach Towers (Florida) 1969, University of Palm Beach 1970, Eastern Illinois University 1975, Senior Advisory Exhibition (Charleston, Illinois) 1977; Two-Man Exhibitions, Welfreet Gallery (Cape Cod, Massachusetts) 1967, Avanti Galleries 1972; Group Exhibitions in the United States and Europe since 1964, most recent one at Accademia Italia, Parma Italy, 1983; Creator of Around 7000 Art Works, Owner of Over 5000 of Own Works and Some of Other Artists; Over 1700 Art Works Among Private and Public Collections throughout the United States and Europe, Fordham University, Lincoln Center in New York City and the Bronx, University of Palm Beach, Greenville Museum of Art (South Carolina), Maryhill Museum of Fine Arts (Washington State), Marshall Public Library (Illinois), Eastern Illinois University, Charleston Minors Public Library, Museum of Literature and the Royal Library (Brussels, Belgium), and Others; Author of 55 Published and 71 Unpublished Titles. Organizational Memberships: Life Member, American Poets Fellowship Society; Life Patron, International Biographical Association; Eastern United States Representative, Amsterdam International Congress, 1980; Big Apple Festical, New York Poetry Forum, 1982. Published Works: Art Work Reproduced in Over 50 Publications in the United States, Switzerland, Spain, Germany, Italy, and France; Author of Numerous Books of Poetry Published in the United States, Venezuela, Cuba, France, and Spain since 1956, including 41 Definitive Works in English, 12 Definitive Works in Spanish, and 2 Definitive Works in French; Published in 6 Languages; Author of Over 6,000 Poems and Prose Works and 124 Books; Contributor to Over 100 Books including Over 80 Anthologies; Publications Appear in More than 60 Libraries; Completed Over 30 Musical Compositions and Arrangements that include "Musical Salutes and Remembrances to Composers". Honors and Awards: Over 1,000 Reviews on Authors or Works, Many Positive Reviews Internationally for Poetry and Art Works; Premier Prix de Printemps, Paris, 1959; Laureat Margerite d'Or, Paris, 1960; Honorary Member, L'Orientation litteraire, Paris; Danae Literary Designate, 1973; Golden Laurel Cup and Silver Star Laurel Cup for Poet of the Year 1979, American Poets Fellowship Society; Golden Laurel Crown for Arts and Letters, United Poets International; Academician of Italy with Gold Medal, 1980; American Biographical Institute Research Association, Gold Plaque of Outstanding Membership 1981, Gold Plaque of Distinction for Multiple Accomplishments 1982; Decree of Appointment, Accademico d'Europa, Parma, Italy, 1983; International Biographical Centre, Certificates and Dictionaries, England; Master of Painting Honoris Causa, Italy 1982; Grand Prize of the Nations 1983, Academician of the Nations 1983, Center of Study and Research, Parma, Italy; 1984 World Culture Prize, The Statue of Victory for Letters, the Arts and Sciences, Center of Studies and Research, Accad. Halen, Parma, Italy; Listed in Over 35 Biographical Reference Books including *Book of Honor, Dictionary of International Biography, International Who's Who of Intellectuals, Who's Who in American Art, International Who's Who in Poetry, Personalities of America*. Address: 215 East 68th Street, New York City, New York 10021.■

PERRY AARON GLICK (DECEASED)

Retired Entomologist-Ecologist. Personal: Born December 21, 1895; Son of M. M. and Eva Alice Morgan Glick (deceased); Married Jessie Odom (deceased); Stepfather of Dorothy Provine. Education: Attended Park College, Kansas City, Missouri 1919, University of Kansas at Lawrence (1919-20), University of Colorado Summer 1920, University of Michigan Summer 1922; B.A., M.S., University of Illinois, 1922. Military: Served in the Texas State Guard, 1944-45. Career: Retired Entomologist-Ecologist specializing in Insect Reaction to Ultra-violet Light; Conservation Research on the Influence of Cultural Practices in Anthropod Population in Cotton and on Insect Allergy to Man. Organizational Memberships: Fellow, American Association for the Advancement of Science; Fellow, Royal Entomological Society; Fellow, Entomological Society of America; Fellow, Explorers Club of New York. Community Activities: Republican Presidential

Task Force; Advisory Board, American Security Council; Advisor on Evaluating Insect Migration, National Science Foundation; Consultant on Insect Migration and Insect Density, Chance Vaught Aircraft, Military Aircraft Systems, Division of Boeing Airplane Companyu; Special Guest for Safari to Collect Butterflies in South Africa, Royal Dutch Airlines, 1978; Invited Presenter of Paper on Insect Migration, University of Chicago Science Medical Division and American Association for the Advancement of Science, 1940. Religion: Presbyterian Church, Ruling Elder, 1927-84. Honors and Awards: Certificate of Appreciation Award 1965, Length of Service Award 1964, Nominee for Superior Service Award 1964, United States Department of Agriculture; Distinguished Alumni Award, Park College, Kansas City, Missouri, 1971; Fellow, American Association for the Advancement of Science 1946, Royal Entomological Society of London 1921, Explorers Club of New York 1979, others.■

KATHLEEN CHRISTIN GOGICK

Editorial Director. Personal: Born August 3, 1945; Daughter of Emeline Wadowski; Married Robert Joseph Gogick; Mother of Jonathan Robert. Education: Attended Emmanuel College, Boston, Massachusetts; B.S., Fairleigh Dickinson University, Rutherford, New Jersey, 1967. Career: Editorial Director, Scholastic, Inc.; Beauty Editor, *Town and Country*; Creative Manager, Estee Lauder Inc.; Assistant Editor, *Cosmopolitan*. Organizational Memberships: American Society of Magazine Editors; Women in Communications; Fashion Group; Womens Economic Roundtable. Community Activities: Board of Trustees, Fairleigh Dickinson University. Honors and Awards: Numerous Editorial Awards, 1977-81; Trustees Alumni Medal, Fairleigh Dickinson University, 1984. Address: 41 East Hartshorn Drive, Short Hills, New Jersey 07078.■

LEO MONROE GOLDBERG

Attorney-at-Law. Personal: Born February 28, 1907; Son of Harris and Sarah Gere Goldberg (both deceased); Married Ruth S. Shartenberg. Education: A.B. magna cum laude, Brown University, 1928; LL.B., Yale University, 1931. Military: Served in the United States Air Force, 1941-45, as a member of the Headquarters Company, Eastern Base Section, Division of A.F.H.Q. APO763 Engineering Section and Office of Town Majors. Career: Public Defender, Rhode Island Superior Court, 1936-37; Attorney-at-Law, Goldberg and Goldberg, Providence, 1935 to present; Associate, Voigt, O'Neil and Monroe and their predecessor firm, Providence, 1931-34. Organizational Memberships: American, Rhode Island and Massachusetts Bar Associations; American Judicature Society; Association of Trial Lawyers of America. Community Activities: Admitted to Rhode Island Bar 1931, Massachusetts Bar 1936, United States District Court of Rhode Island 1932, United States District Court of Massachusetts 1949, United States First Circuit Court of Appeals 1952; F. Ronci Company Inc., General Counsel; Turks Head Club; University Club. Religion: Sons of Jacob Synagogue, Providence, Rhode Island, Chairman of the Board, 1935-40; Temple Beth El. Honors and Awards: American Economic History; Phi Beta Kappa; Francis Wyland Scholar; Jame Manning Scholar; Listed in *Who's Who in American Law*, *Men of Achievement*, *Dictionary of International Biography*, *International Who's Who of Intellectuals*. Address: 52 Lorraine Avenue, Providence, Rhode Island 02906.■

CONSTANCE J. GOLDEN

Manager of Aerospace Mission Operations. Personal: Born June 8, 1939; Daughter of Herman and Chrystle Leuer; Married Charles J. Golden; Mother of Kerri Lynn. Education: B.S. Mathematics/Physics, Beloit College, 1961; A.M. Mathematics, Harvard University, 1962; Ph.D. Course Work in Mathematics and Aerospace Engineering 1966, M.S. Operations Research 1970, Stanford University. Career: Manager, Aerospace Mission Operations; Manager, Corporate Strategic Planning; Program Manager, Various Aerospace Projects; Engineer, Development of Computer Models of Aerospace Projects. Organizational Memberships: San Francisco Bay Area Section President 1974-75, National Scholarship Chairman 1976, Society of Women Engineers; Santa Clara Valley Chapter Board of Directors, A.F.C.E.A., 1979-80; Public Policy Committee, A.I.A.A.; O.R.S.A. Community Activities: Science Advisory Council, Mills College; Past President of Local Club and A.T.M., Toastmasters International. Honors and Awards: Phi Beta Kappa Award, 1960-61; National Science Foundation Fellowship, 1961-62; Lockheed's Most Distinguished Woman, 1976; Featured in *Business Week* Article on Corporate Women, 1981; Featured on *60 Minutes* Television Program, 1981; Listed in *World Who's Who of Women*, *Who's Who in the West*. Address: 1260 Crossman Avenue, Sunnyvale, California 94086.■

ISAAC GOLDKORN

Writer and Critic. Personal: Born October 1, 1911; Son of David and Chaya Goldkorn (both deceased); Married Irene; Father of David. Education: Attended Hebrew Religious School (mainly self-educated). Career: Staff Writer, *Unzer Express*, Warsaw, Poland, 1939; Editor, *Unzer Haint*, Munich, Germany, 1951; Editor, *Widerstand*, Montreal, Quebec, Canada, 1957-59; Editor, Israelite Press, Winnipeg, Canada, 1960-64; News Editor, *Canadian Jewish Eagle*, Montreal, 1965; Staff Writer, *Jewish Daily Forward*, New York, New York, 1967-77; Writer and Literary Critic. Organizational Memberships: Yiddish P.E.N (affiliated with International P.E.N. Clubs); Canadian Ethnic Journalists and Writers Club; International Academy of Poets. Religion: Jewish. Personal: Contributor of Articles, Essays, Book Reviews and Poems to Yiddish Newspapers and Magazines in Poland (1930-39) and in Western Europe, Canada, United States and other Countries; Author, *Nocturns* (Lodz, 1938), *Lit. Silhouetten* (Munich, 1949), *Lieder* (1950), *Epigramatish* (Montreal, 1954), *Fun Welt-Kval* (Tel Aviv, 1963), *Lodzher Portreten* (Tel Aviv, 1963), *Zingers un Zogers* (Tel Aviv, 1971), *Hemishe un Fremde* (Buenos Aires, 1973), *Yellow Letters, Green Memories* (Cornwall, 1979), *Kurts un Sharf* (Toronto, 1981), *Last Harvest* (Toronto, 1984). Honors and Awards: Jacob Gladstone Prize, World Congress for Jewish Culture in New York, 1976; Listed in *Encyclopedia Britannica Year Book*, *Who's Who in World Jewry*, *Directory of Distinguished Americans*, *Who's Who in International Poetry*. Address: 3300 Don Mills Road, #1401, Willowdale, Ontario M2J 4X7, Canada.■

MARK GOLDSTEIN

Executive. Personal: Born August 22, 1941; Son of Harold M. Levin and Roberta Butterfield Goldstein. Education: B.S., University of Vermont, 1964; Ph.D., University of Miami, 1971. Military: Served in the United States Marine Corps Reserves, 1961-67. Career: President, Quantum Group; Former Positions include Senior Technical Advisory for JGC Corporation (Tokyo, Japan), Senior Researcher for East West Center (Honolulu, Hawaii), Group Leader for Brookhaven National Laboratory (Upton, New York), President of IBR Inc. (Coral Gables, Florida). Organizational Memberships: American Nuclear Society, 1975 to present; American Chemical Society, 1970 to present; American Chamber of Commerce in Japan, 1980 to present. Community Activities: Head of Nuclear Policy Study under President Ford's Science and Technology Policy Apparatus. Honors and Awards: Two National Science Foundation Fellowships; Two O.B.R. Fellowships; Sigma Xi. Address: 8110 El Paseo Grande, La Jolla, California 92037.■

NORMAN GOLDSTEIN

Dermatologist. Personal: Born July 14, 1934; Son of Mr.and Mrs. Joseph H. Goldstein; Married Ramsay; Father of Richard David, Heidi Lee. Education: B.A., Columbia University, 1955; M.D., State University of New York Downstate Medical Center, 1959; Internship, Maimonides Hospital, 1960; Dermatology Residency, New York University Skin and Cancer Unit 1961, Bellevue Hospital 1962, New York University Postgraduate Medical Center 1963; Prek, 1963. Military: Served in the United States Army Reserve, New York City, 1960-61, Chief of Dermatology Services, United States Army Hospital, Ft. Gordon, Georgia, 1963-64; United States Army Tripler General Hospital, Honolulu, Hawaii, Dermatology Service, Assistant Chief 1964-66, Chief 1966-67, Dermatology Consultant 1967 to present. Career: Private Practice Dermatologist, 1972 to present; Director, Pacific Laser; Partner, The Honolulu Medical Group, Honolulu, Hawaii, 1967-72. Organizational Memberships: American Medical Association; Society for Investigative Dermatology; International Society for Tropical Dermatology; Association of Military Dermatologists; Hawaii Dermatological Society; Honolulu County Medical Society; Hawaii Medical Association; Honorary Member, Micronesian Medical Association; Hawaii Public Health Association; American Association for the Advancement of Science; Charter Member, American Society for Photobiology; Environmental Health and Light Research Institute; American Association of Clinical Oncology; Pacific Dermatological Association;

Hawaii Association for Physicians for Indemification; Pacific Health Research Institute; Biologic Photographic Association; Health Sciences Communications Association; Hawaii Association for Protective Indemnities; International Pigment Cell Society; American Society of Preventive Oncology; American Medical Writers Association, 1979 to present; Pan-Pacific Surgical Association, 1979 to present; American College of Cryosurgery, 1979 to present; International Society for Dermatologic Surgery, 1979 to present; American College of Physicians; International Society of Cyrosurgery, 1980; Society for Computer Medicine, 1981 to present; American Association for Medical Assistants and Informatics, 1982; American College of Sports Medicine, 1982. Community Activities: International Solar Energy Society; Photographic Society of America; Honorary Member, Tokai Tattoo Club of Japan, 1979; North American Tattoo Club, 1980; Life Member, Tatoo Club of Japan, 1980; Tattoo Club of Deutschland, 1981 to present; New York Academy of Science, 1980; National Space Institute, 1980; The Friends of Photography, 1981; La Societe Internationale de la Photographie, 1981; International Platform Association, 1981 to present; Outrigger Canoe Club; Oahu Country Club; Honolulu Rotary Club; Honolulu Symphony Society; Metro Opera Guild; Smithsonian Institution; Honolulu Art Academy; Hawaii Council for Culture and Arts; Founding Board Member, Hawaii Theatre; Hawaii Jewish Welfare Board, Trustee, 1976-79; Historic Hawaii Foundation; American Institute of Architects, Liaison to National Meeting, 1982; National Trust for Historic Preservation; Hawaii Visitors Bureau; Chamber of Commerce, 1979 to present; Hawaii Historical Society; University of Hawaii Art Department, Partner; Plaza Club of Honolulu; The Honolulu Club; Chancellor's Club of the University of Hawaii, 1980 to present; Downtown Improvement Association; Friends of Alexander Young Building. Religion: Jewish; Jewish Welfare Board of Trustees, 1976-79. Published Works: Contributor to *Cosmopolitan, Mademoiselle, Self*. Honors and Awards: Illuminating Engineer Society of North America Office Lighting Design Award, Hawaii, 1982; Special Award, World of Tatoos Exhibit, Western Section of American Urologic Association, 1980; Historical and Cultural Award, World of Tattoos Exhibit, International Society of Tropical Dermatology 4th Congress, New Orleans, 1979; Third Place Photography Award, Art in Dermatology, American Academy of Dermatology, 1979; Leadership Award, Outstanding Service, United Jewish Appeal, 1976; Silver Award, Original Research in Prevention of Skin Cancers Exhibit, American Academy of Dermatology, 1972; CUTIS Manuscript Contest, Third Prize 1971, First Prize 1968; Special Award, *Dermatologia Hawaiiana*, Academy of Dermatology, 1971; Department of Army Commendation Medal, 1967; The Husik Award, Dermatology Research, 1963; Henry Silver Award for Research, The Dermatologic Society of Greater New York, 1963; Listed in *Who's Who in Frontier Science and Technology, Directory of Distinguished Americans, Personalities of America, Leaders of Hawaii, International Authors and Writers Who's Who, International Who's Who of Intellectuals, The Best Doctors in America, International Men of Achievement, Dictionary of International Biography, Community Leaders of America, Who's Who in the West, Directory of Medical Specialists*. Address: 119 Merchant Street, Suite 504, Honolulu, Hawaii 96813.■

JOHN S. GONAS

Retired Judge. Personal: Born May 14, 1907; Son of Samuel and Hazel Gonas (deceased); Married Theodosia B. Gonas; Father of John S., Jr., Roy B. Education: B.S.C.E., Tri-State University, 1930; LL.B., Blackstone College of Law, 1930; Master of Law, Chicago Law School, 1933; Graduate Work in Social Psychiatry, Patent Law and Foreign Languages. Career: Retired Presiding Judge and Chief Justice, Indiana Appellate Court; Judge of County Probate-Juvenile Court; Public Defender; State Senator; State Representative; Justice of the Peace; Assistant Prosecuting Attorney; Assessor of Voters. Organizational Memberships: American and Indiana Bar Associations; Appellate Judges Conference; Juvenile Court Foundation. Community Activities: State Budget Committee, 1940; Senate Leader, 1943; Democratic Conventions, Delegate; International Congress of Juvenile Court Judges, Brussels, Belgium, Delegate, 1954; First United Nations Conference on Crime and Delinquency, Geneva, Switzerland, Delegate upon Invitation of Dag Hammarskjold (Secretary General of United Nations); Candidate in Foraigns for Local, State and National Office, including President of the United States. Religion: Catholic Church. Honors and Awards: Kentucky Colonel, 1955; Oklahoma Colonel, 1962; Alabama Colonel, 1964; Chieftain on the Staff of Sagamores of the Wabash, Governor of Indiana, 1961; Admiral of Great Navy of Nebraska, Governor of Nebraska, 1959; Certificate of Award, Juvenile Court Institute; Man of the Year, South Bend Optimist Club; Alumni Distinguished Award, Tri-State University; Certificate of Appreciation, United States Navy; Certificate of Appreciation, Lions Club of South Bend; Certificate of Achievement for Demonstrating Vision, Resourcefulness, Hard Work, Integrity, Patience, Understanding and Common Sense as Hallmarks of American Way of Life, American University of Experience; Distinguished Political Achievement, Service to Mankind Award, American Biographical Institute; Listed in *International Who's Who of Intellectuals, Men of Achievement, Who's Who in American Law*. Address: 3120 Rue Renoir #203, South Bend, Indiana 46615-2878.■

CRISTINA GONZALEZ

Assistant Professor of Spanish. Personal: Born April 9, 1951; Daughter of César González and Cristina Sánchez; Married Richard A Cohen. Education: M.A., University of Oviedo (Spain), 1973; M.A. 1977, Ph.D. 1981, Indiana University. Career: Instructor in Spanish 1981, Assistant Professor of Spanish 1982 to preent, Purdue University; Lecturer in Spanish, Tufts University, 1980; Associate Professor of Spanish, Indiana University, 1976-79; Instructor of Spanish, Academia "Clarin" (Oviedo, Spain), 1976; Teacher of Spanish, Instituto Calderón de la Barca (Gijón, Spain) 1975, Instituto de Pola de Siero (Pola de Siero, Spain), 1974; Teacher of French, Instituto Politécnico Asturiano (Gijón, Spain), 1971; Teacher of Latin and Greek, Colegio San Vicente de Paul, Summer 1970; Tutor of Latin and Greek, High School and University Levels, 1970-76. Organizational Memberships: Société Internationale Arthurienne; The Medieval Academy of America; The Semiotic Society of America; The American Association of Teachers of Spanish and Portuguese; The Modern Language Association of America; The Midwest Modern Language Association of America; The Hispanic Enlightenment Association; Centro Español de Documentación y Estudios; Colegio Oficial de Doctores y Licenciados de Oviedo. Published Works: Author Books *Aproximación al Libro del Cavallero Zifar* and *El Libro del Cavallero Zifar* (1983), Numerous Professional Articles, Book Reviews, Book Chapters; Fifteen Original Poems Published in Several Literary Journals in Spain and the United States. Honors and Awards: Listed in *Who's Who of American Women, El Libro de Gijón*. Address: 3332 Peppermill Drive, West Lafayette, Indiana 47906.■

MARY LOWE GOOD

Research Chemist. Personal: Born June 20, 1931; Daughter of Mr. and Mrs. John W. Lowe; Married Bill J. Good; Mother of Billy John, James Patrick. Education: Ph.D. Inorganic Chemistry, University of Arkansas-Fayetteville. Career: Vice-President and Director of Research, U.O.P. Inc., Des Plaines, Illinois, 1981 to present; Boyd Professor of Materials Science, Louisiana State University, 1979-81; Associate Professor, Professor and Boyd Professor of Chemistry, University of New Orleans, 1958-78; Instructor and Assistant Professor of Chemistry, Louisiana State University, 1954-58. Organizational Memberships: Oak Ridge National Laboratory, Chemistry Division Review Committee; Harvard Board of Overseers, Committee for Chemistry Department Review; National Resource for Computation in Chemistry of Lawrence Berkeley Laboratory, Policy Board; International Union of Pure and Applied Chemistry, Chairman of Inorganic Section; President's Committee on National Medal of Science, Chairman; American Chemical Society, Chemical Abstracts Committee; *Inorganic Chemistry*, Editorial Board; National Research Council, Advisory Committee for Office of Chemistry and Chemical Technology; National Science Board. Community Activities: Zonta International, Chairman Amelia Earhart Fellowship Committee; Oak Ridge Associated Universities, Board of Directors, 1976; American Chemical Society, Chairman Board of Directors 1978, 1980; National Advisory Panels, Chemistry Section National Science Foundation 1972-76; National Institutes of Health Committee on Medicinal Chemistry, 1972-76; Office of Air Force Research, 1974-78; Brookhaven National Laboratory, Chemistry Committee, 1973-77; Science Information Task Force National Science Foundation, 1977. Published Works: Author of Approximately 100 Articles in Referred Technical Journals and One Book. Honors and Awards: Agnes Faye Morgan Research Award, Iota Sigma Pi, 1969; Distinguished Alumni Member, Phi Beta Kappa, 1972; Garvan Medal 1973, Georgia Section Herty Medal 1975, Florida Section Award for Outstanding Research, Teaching and Public Service 1979, American Chemical Society; Distinguished Alumni Citation, University of Arkansas, 1973; Teacher of the Year Award, Delta Kappa Gamma, 1974; Honorary Doctor of Laws Degree, University of Arkansas, 1979; Scientist of the Year, *Industrial Research and Development* Magazine, 1982; Gold Medal 1983, Louisiana Chapter Honor Scroll 1974, American Institute of Chemists; Listed in *Outstanding Educators*. Address: 295 Park Drive, Palatine, Illinois 60067.■

TONI KRISSEL GOODALE

Development Consultant. Personal: Born May 26, 1941 in New York City, New York; Daughter of Walter DuPont and Ricka Krissel; Married James Campbell Goodale, May 3, 1964; Mother of Timothy Fuller, Ashley Krissel, Clayton A. Education: A.B. cum laude, Smith College, 1963; Attended University of Geneva, 1962-

63; Postgraduate Work, Hunter College, 1964-65. Career: President, TKG Associates, New York City, 1979 to present; Assistant Director of Development 1978-79, New York Representative 1975-78, Smith College, New York City; Consultant to Public Education Department 1968-69, Administrative Assistant to Director of Grant Research Department 1964-67, Ford Foundation, New York City; Broadcast Analyst, Federal Communicaions Commission, Washington, D.C., 1963-64; Intern, Senator Keating, United States Senate, Washington, D.C., 1963; Lecturer, CASE, Brearley School, The New School. Community Activities: Board of Advisors, First Women's Bank; Alumnae Fund Committee, Vice President of Class, Smith College; Trustee, Alumnae Fund Chairman, Alumnae Council, Brearley School; Executive Committee, Parents Association of St. Bernard's School; Trustee, Board of Governors, Churchill School; Trustee, New York Institute of Child Development; Women's Division, Legal Aid Society; New York Committee, Joffrey Ballet; Benefit Committee, Grosvenor House; National Society of Fund Raising Executives; Board Member, American Association of Fund-raising Counsel; Brearley School Alumnae Association; Smith College Alumnae; Cosmopolitan Club; Doubles International; Smith College Club; Washington Tennis Club. Address: 1050 Park Avenue, New York, New York 10028.■

JAMES LESLIE GOODMAN

Sales Management Executive. Personal: Born November 2, 1926; Son of Leslie Hartford and Emma Rebecca Stoops Goodman (deceased); Married Maryellen Harrison, Daughter of Elmer and Bessie Harrison (deceased); Father of James Leslie, Jr. Education: Attended Chicago Technical Institute, 1948-52. Military: Served in the United States Army, 1944-48, attaining the rank of Technical Sergeant with Infantry Division. Career: Manager-President, Farrell Argast Electric Company, 1972 to present; Teacher of Economics at 9th Grade Level, Southport High School, 1979; Associated with Electric Sales Company, Green River, Wyoming, 1970-72; Operating Manager, Walker Radio Company, Denver, Colorado, 1964-70; Manager, Midland Specialty Company, Albuquerque, New Mexico, 1960-64; Associated with Radio Specialty Company, Phoenix, Arizona, 1952-60. Organizational Memberships: Electric League of Indiana; Purchasing Management Association of Indiana; National Business Management Achievement Association. Religion: Penecostal Church, Traveling Lay Evangelist and Bible Teacher. Honors and Awards: National Recognition for Volunteer Work in Junior Achievement, Front Cover Purchasing Management Magazine Magazine; Honorable Mention for Christian Activities Throughout Indiana; Teacher of Christian Ethics on Business; Listed in *Who's Who in the Midwest, Men of Distinction*. Address: 921 Fry Road, Greenwood, Indiana 46142.■

JESS THOMPSON GOODMAN

Manufacturing Executive. Personal: Born January 18, 1936; Son of Walter Raymond and Opal Mae Goodman (deceased); Married Yvonne Goodman; Father of Walter Raymond Goodman, II. Education: Graduate, Joplin High School, 1954; Attended Joplin Junior College, 1955; A.B. Political Science, University of Missouri, 1959; Graduate Work in Personnel Management, 1968; M.A. National Security Affairs, Naval Postgraduate School, 1975; Graduate Work in International Relations (Ph.D. Candidate), University of Hawaii, 1978. Military: Served in the Missouri National Guard, 1953-56, attaining the rank of Corporal; Served in the Naval Reserve, 1956-59, attaining the rank of Seaman; Served in the United States Navy, 1959-79, rising through the ranks from Ensign to Lieutenant Commander. Career: Quality Control Engineer, Labarge, Inc., 1982 to present; Quality Assurance Manager 1981-82, Production Supervisor 1980, Eagle Picher Industries (Electronics Division); Naval Science Instructor, Carl Junction (Missouri) School District, 1979-80. Organizational Memberships: Ozark Chapter, Society of Manufacturing Engineers, Secretary 1980, Treasurer 1981, Second Vice-Chairman 1982; Joplin Chapter American Society for Quality Control Education Committee, 1982; Air Force Association, 1976-80; American Association for the Advancement of Science, 1977-82; Veterans of Foreign Wars, 1968-82; Pi Kappa Alpha, 1957-82. Community Activities: Program Chairman, Joplin Kiwanis, 1981-82; Masons, 1979-82; Toastmasters, 1964-65; World Affairs Forum of Hawaii, 1976-79; World Affairs Council of Pittsburg, 1978-82; American Mensa Ltd., 1977-82; Founder, Mensa Special Interest Group in International Affairs, 1978-79; American Legion, 1968-82; Center for the Study of the Presidency, 1976-82; United States Naval Institute, 1959-82; United States Strategic Institute, 1974-82. Religion: Methodist, Choir Member, 1952 to present. Honors and Awards: Sabre, American Legion, 1953; Medal for Leadership, *Chicago Tribune*, 1954; Cadet Colonel, Joplin High School R.O.T.C., 1954; Vice-President Freshman Class, Joplin Junior College, 1955; Laverne Noyes Scholarship, University of Missouri, 1956; Commendation Medal 1969, Two Achievement Medals 1970 and 1973, Expert Rifleman and Pistolshot Medals 1970, United States Navy; Organizational Excellence Award, United States Air Force, 1978. Address: 2725 Schifferdecker, Joplin, Missouri 64801.■

JAMES TAIT GOODRICH

Neuroscientist and Physician. Personal: Born April 16, 1946, in Portland, Oregon; Son of Gail J. Goodrich; Married Judy Loudin. Education: Attended Fort Buckner Army Language Center (Japan), 1968; A.A., Orange Coast College, 1972; Attended Golden West College, Huntington Beach, California, 1971-72; B.S. cum laude, University of California at Irvine, 1974; M.Phil. 1979, Ph.D. 1980, Columbia University Graduate School of Arts and Sciences; M.S., Columbia University College of Physicians and Surgeons, 1980. Military: Served with the United States Marine Corps Reserves, 1964; Served with the United States Marine Corps, 1967-68, with active duty in Viet Nam. Career: Researcher and Physician (Neurosurgery), New York Neurological Institute, 1981 to present; Associate Research Consultant, University of California at Irvine Education Plan, 1974; S.C.U.B.A. Salvage Diver, 1969; Computer Operator, I.B.M. 360 Systems, 1966; Store Detective, 1965-66; Participant in Numberous Professional Conferences. Organizational Memberships: American Association for the History of Medicine; American Medical Association; British Research Association; European Brain and Behavior Society; New York Academy of Medicine; New Jersey Medical History Society; Columbia University Presbyterian Medical Society; Society for Ancient Medicine. Community Activities: Friends of the Columbia University Libraries; Friends of the Osler Library, McGill University; Society for Bibliography of Natural History; University of California Alumni Association; Les amis du Vin; South Coast Wine Explorers Club, Past Chairman; Friends of Bacchus Wine Club, Past Chairman; Dionysius Council of Presbyterian Hospital in the City of New York. Published Works: Contributor of Articles to Numerous Professional Journals, including *Connecticut Medicine, Gastroenterology, Anatomical Record, Journal of Pediatric Surgery, Journal of Comparative Neurology, Bulletin of New York Academy of Medicine, American Journal of Pathology*. Honors and Awards: Kiwanis Club Scholarship; Willamette Industries Scholarship; University of California President's Undergraduate Research Fellow, 1973-74; National Institute of Health Medical Scientist Trainee; Organe Coast College Class Valedictorian, 1972; Sir William Osler Medal, American Association for History of Medicine, 1977-78; Participated in National Student Research Forum, Roche Laboratories; Mead-Johnson Award for Overall Excellence of Research, National Student Research Forum, 1978; Sandoz Award for Outstanding Research, 1980; Melicow Award, New York Academy of Medicine; Listed in *Who's Who in the East, Who's Who Among Students in American Universities and Colleges*, and Others. Address: 214 Everett Place, Englewood, New Jersey 07631.■

NELSON GOODYEAR

President, California Christian University (retired). Personal: Born January 12, 1912; Son of Nelson Sr. (oxy-acetylene equipment inventor) and Katharine G. Goodyear (deceased, radio broadcaster); Married Virginia B., Daughter of Herbert O. and Florence Coxson Black (deceased); Father of Charles, Lydia, Katharine, Lawrence. Education: B.A. 1933, M.A. 1950, Columbia University; Ph.D. Political Science and Public Administration, California Christian University, Los Angeles, California, 1973. Military: Served in the United States Navy in Administrative Office of the Secretary of the Navy as Writer of Microfilming Manuals and Conductor of Industrial Engineering Surveys, attaining the rank of Seaman 1st Class. Career: President, California Christian University, Retired (to pursue real estate investments); Technical Writing Instructor, University of California at Los Angeles, Pasadena City College and Various Los Angeles City Adult Schools, 1960-72; Assistant Professor of Industrial Management, Syracuse University 1947-50, University of Southern California 1950-52; Technical Writing Instructor and Consultant on Military and Commercial Assignments. Organizational Memberships: Sigma Iota Epsilon Management Honor Society, 1947; American Association for Public Administration, 1950; Co-Founder, Association for the Advancement of Character, 1940; Board Member, Society of Applied Industrial Engineering; Junior Member, American Society of Mechanical Engineers, 1946; American Association of University Professors, 1950; Senior Member and Panel Speaker, Institute of Human Engineering Sciences, 1967. Community Activities: Kings Crown and Varsity C Club, Columbia University, 1933; Psi Upsilon Fraternity, 1931 to present. Religion: Attend Glass Cathedral, Garden Grove, California; Formerly Attended Bartholemew Community Church, New York, New York. Published Works: Holder of United States Patents for Improvements in Tool and Storage Racks 1947, United States Navy Patents for Electro-Mechanical Resuscitator, Douglas Air Conditioning, and Patent for Crash-Proof Radio Rescue Transmitter. Honors and Awards: Eighty-Seven Suggestion Awards from Aircraft Manufacturing Suggestion Committees and the United States Chief of Naval Research; Commendation for Efforts to Improve Motor Vehicle Department Driving Pamphlets, Directors of Motor Vehicles for California, New Mexico, Maryland, Maine, Alabama, Arizona; Four-Year Scholarships, Trainity School, Columbia College; Certificate, American Biographical Institute 1980, Hellenic Professional Association of America International 1981; Listed in *International Who's Who of Intellectuals, Dictionary of International Biography, Community Leaders and Noteworthy Americans, International Book of Honor.* Address: Space 23, 15111 Bushard, Westminster, California 92683. ∎

GREGORY JAMES GORUP

Executive. Personal: Born March 27, 1948; Son of Mr. and Mrs. Gorup. Education: B.A., St. Benedict College, 1970; M.B.A., University of Pennsylvania, 1972. Career: Vice-President of Marketing in Credit Suisse United States Area 1981 to present, Manager of Product Management Department 1980-81, Vice-President 1977-80, Assistant Vice-President and Director of New Product Development 1975, Irving Trust Company, New York City, New York; Product Management for Dividend Reinvestment and Corporate Stock Transfer Services 1974-75, Division Staff Corporate Product Management Division 1973-74, Product Planning and Development 1973, Marketing Officer 1973, Market Planning and Development 1972-73, Citibank, New York City. Organizational Memberships: American Management Association; Bank Administration Institute, Marshall D. Sokol and Associates, Adjunct Facility. Community Activities: Knights of Columbus, Council #4708, Grand Knight, 1968-70; New York East Side Lions Club, Treasurer 1975-76, President 1977-80; Big Brothers of New York, Fund Raising Committee, 1974-76. Religion: Archdiocese of New York; Adult Education Program, Volunteer Teacher, 1972-75. Honors and Awards: Listed in *Who's Who in Finance and Industy, Who's Who in the World, Who's Who in the East.* Address: 245 East 63rd Street Apartment 806, New York New York 10021. ∎

JANICE SANDRA CALDWELL GOULD

Stock and Investment Broker. Personal: Born December 20, 1942, in St. Louis, Missouri; Daughter of Gilbert R. and Frances E. Ellingsworth Caldwell; Mother of Troy Bryan, Jonna Ryon. Education: Graduate, Newton High School, 1961; Attended Simpson College (Indianola, Iowa) 1961-62, Drake Univerity (Des Moines, Iowa) 1964; B.A., University of Iowa (Iowa City, Iowa), 1962-67. Career: Stock and Investment Broker Edward D. Jones and Company, Ankeny, Iowa, 1982 to present; Stock and Investment Broker, Dain Bosworth Inc., Des Moines, Iowa, 1974-82; Real Estate Salesperson, Las Vegas, Nevada, 1973-74; Substitute Secondary Teacher, Las Vegas, Nevada, 1973; Legal Secretary, Las Vegas, Nevada, 1967-68; Medical Secretary, Iowa City, Iowa, 1965-67; Conductor of Investment/Market Seminars. Published Works: Author, "Law School for University of Nevada: Summary of Feasibility Study," 1972. Honors and Awards: Maytag Scholarship, 1961; Century Club, Dain Bosworth Inc., 1981; Listed in *Who's Who of American Women, World Who's Who of Women, Personalities of the West and Midwest, Biographical Roll of Honor, Five Thousand Personalities of the World, Two Thousand Notable Americans.* Address: 1307 East Detroit, Indianola, Iowa 50125. ∎

WESLEY L. GOULD

Professor Emeritus. Personal: Born May 15, 1917, in Cleveland, Ohio; Married Jean Sarah Barnard; Father of Francis Barnard, Sarra Marie, Margaret Elizabeth Guldan, Leona Larson. Education: A.B., Baldwin-Wallace College, 1939; M.A., Ohio State University, 1941; Ph.D., Harvard University, 1949. Military: Served in the United States Army, 1942-45. Career: Visiting Assistant Professor, Boston University, Summer 1953; Visiting Professor, Northwestern University, 1963-64; Ph.D. Examiner, Patna University (India), 1963-64; Consultant, International Law Study Period, Naval War College, Summer 1960; Consultant on Detroit Charter Revision, New Detroit, Inc., 1972-73; Participant/Observer, Governor's Task Force on the Option Process, Subcommittee III on Metropolitan Structure in Southeast Michigan, 1972; Participant/Observer, Committee VIII (Type of System), Regional Government Studies, Essex County, Ontario, 1973; Editorial Consultant, *Canadian Review of Studies in Nationalism*, 1973-74; Fellow, University of Liverpool, 1974-75; Visiting Scholar, University of Winnipeg, Summer 1979; Instructor, Alumni College, Baldwin-Wallace College, 1984; Instructor, Northwestern University, 1946-49; Assistant Professor 1949-58, Associate Professor 1958-61, Professor, 1961-67, Purdue University; Professor 1967-83, Professor Emeritus 1984 to present, Wayne State University. Organizational Memberships: American Society of International Law, Executive Council 1959-62; American Political Science Association; Midwest and Western Political Science Associations; International Political Science Association; London Institute of World Affairs; International Studies Association; American Society of Public Administration; Society for General Systems research, Task Force for General Systems Education 1970-72; Academy of Political Science; Law and Society Association; American Society of Legal and Political Philosophy; International Association for Philosophy of Law and Social Philosophy, American Section; Michigan Conference of Political Scientists; Indiana Academy of the Social Sciences, Member 1949-67, Board of Directors 1958-60; American Association for Higher Education; American Association of University Professors; Pi Sigma Alpha. Community Activities: Delegate, Michigan State Democratic Convention, 1971, 1972; Alternate, Oakland County Democratic Committee, 1971-73; State of Michigan Department of Education Advisory Council on Community Service and Continuing Education Programs, 1971-72; Executive Committee, The People for the New Charter Committee, 1972; Subcommittee on Education and Finance, Michigan Democratic Party, 1973-74; Subcommittee on Foreign Policy, Michigan Democratic Party, 1973-74; Regional Structure, Transportation and Communications Committees of the Regional Citizens Project of Metropolitan Fund, Inc, 1973-74; Consultant, Election Campaign of Mayor Jesse P. Miller, Highland Park, Michigan, 1975; Board of Directors, Citizen's Council for Land Use Research and Education, 1974-79; Alternate, State of Michigan, Citizen's Advisory Committee, Northwestern Highway Study, 1976-77. Published Works: Author *An Introduction to International Law* (1957), (with Judge L. Erades) *The Relation Between International Law and Municipal Law in the Netherlands and in the United States: A Comparative Study* (1961), (with Kurth Schwerin) *Law Books Recommended for Libraries* (1968), (with Michael Barkun) *International Law and the Social Sciences* (1972), (with Michael Barkun) *Social Science Literature: A Bibliography for International Law* (1973); Other Reports, Articles, Book Reviews, Contributions. Honors and Awards: Alumni Merit Award, Baldwin-Wallace College, 1984; Listed in *American Men and Women of Science: The Social and Behavioral Sciences, Dictionary of International Biography, International Scholars Directory, Men of Achievement, The Directory of Distinguished Americans, Personalities of America, Who's Who in America, Who's Who in the World, Who's Who in American Law, Who's Who in the Midwest, International Who's Who of Intellectuals, Contemporary Authors.* Address: 21611 Whitmore, Oak Park, Michigan 48237. ∎

CHARLES EDWIN GOULDING

Consulting Engineer. Personal: Born November 23, 1916; Son of Mr. and Mrs. C. E. Goulding (both deceased); Married Meta Isabelle, Daughter of Mr. and Mrs. John Hyslop (both deceased). Education: B.S. 1939, Postgraduate Certificates in C.E. and Ch.E. 1941, University of Tampa, Florida; M.S. 1944, Ph.D. 1946, University of Florida at Gainesville; Postdoctoral Work, University of Pennsylvania, 1966. Career: Consulting Engineer, Registered in 12 States and 2 Foreign Countries; Chemist, Biochemist, Bioengineer; Electronic Engineer, Chemical Engineer, Environmental Engineer, Lab Instructor, University of Tampa, University of Florida; Chemistry Instructor, Temple University (Philadelphia, Pennsylvania); Consulting Engineer to Venezuelian Government, Caracas; Construction Engineer, Fontoura Industries, Sao Paula Brazil; Chief Engineer and Project Director, Grossman Laboratories, Mexico City, Mexico; Project Director, SH&G, Seoul, Korea; International Engineering Consultant in 29 Countries. Community Activities: Civil Defense Communications Officer, Chambersburg, Pennsylvania, 1973-77; Deputy Sheriff, Sullivan County, Tennessee, 1977 to present; United States Congressional Advisory Board, 1981 to present; American Security Council, 1977 to present. Honors and Awards: Graduate Student Honor Scholar, University of Florida, 1944-46; President, Phi Sigma Honorary Biological Society, 1946; Sigma Xi Honorary Research Society, 1946 to present; Postdoctoral Scholar, University of Pennsylvania at Philadelphia, 1966-68; Honorary Mayor, Boys Town, Nebraska, 1973; Listed in *Who's Who in the East, Who's Who in the South and Southwest, International Who's Who in Biological Sciences, Bibliography of Scientists and Engineers.* Address: 2569 Volunteer Parkway, Bristol, Tennessee 37620. ∎

JOHN WILLIAM GRACE

Engineering Manager. Personal: Born May 29, 1921; Married Ruth Delores Schroeder; Father of Martha Ann G. Winters, Joan Ruth G. Chatfield, Nancy E., John W. Jr. Education: American Television Institute of Technology, 1950; B.S.E.E., Drexel University, 1960. Military: Served in the United States Navy as Fire Controlman, 1941-45. Career: Engineering Manager Las Vegas (Nevada) 1982 to present and Idaho Falls (Idaho) 1977-82, Manager of Business Development Operational Test and Evaluation in Albuquerque (New Mexico) 1973-77, Scientific Executive and Manager of Engineering at Special Projects Division in Las Vegas, Nevada 1966-73, E.G. & G. Inc.; Project Engineer 1960-66, Design Engineer 1956-60, Technician 1956-60, Instrumentation Programs, R.C.A. Missile and Surface Radar Division, Moorsetown, New Jersey. Organizational Memberships: Institute of Electrical and Electronics Engineers, Member 1950-73, Professional Goups including

Microwave Technology, Antennas and Propagation; Association of Old Crows, 1969-77; Instrument Society of America, Senior Member 1980 to present, Director of Scientific and Instrumentation Research Division. Community Activities: American Legion, Member 1945 to present, Adjutant and Vice-Commander 1950; Boy Scouts of America, 1969-71; Episcopal Couples Retreat, President Couple, 1969-70; Little League Baseball, 1968-73; Young American Football Association, 1973-75; New Mexico Energy Research Resource Registry, 1974-77. Religion: Episcopal. Honors and Awards: Patentee, Contradirectional Wave Guide Coupler; Listed in *Who's Who in the West, Who's Who Honorary Society of America, Men of Achievement, Who's Who in Finance and Industry.* Address: 2900 South Valley View — 154, Las Vegas, Nevada 89102.■

FRANCIS GLENN GRAHAM

Astronomer. Personal: Born June 1, 1951; Son of Francis E. Graham (deceased) and Marlene Miller; Married Charmaine Graham; Father of Kathryn K. Education: B.A. 1975, M.S. 1981, University of Pittsburgh; Honorary D.D., 1981. Career: Astronomer, Halo Star Research 1980, Sounding Rocket Testing 1968-71, Lunar Mapping Program; Solar Energy Consultant; Science and Mathematics Instructor; Hydrologist; Physics Instructor. Community Activities: Tripoli Science Association, Secretary 1964 to present; A.I.A.A. Publications Committee, 1979-81; *Tripolitan Journal,* Editor 1978-80. Religion: Committee on Science and Religion. Honors and Awards: Bausch and Lomb Science Award, 1969; Young Men's Christian Association Service Award, 1975. Address: 417 Franklin Street, East Pittsburgh, Pennsylvania 15112.■

WILLIAM B. GRAHAM

Executive. Personal: Born July 14, 1911; Widower; Father of William J., Robert B., Elizabeth Muckermann (Mrs. Dennis), Margaret Caswell (Mrs. Benson). Education: Graduate, Mt. Carmel High School, 1928; S.B., University of Chicago, 1932; J.D., University of Chicago, 1936. Career: Chairman of the Board, Former Chairman and Chief Executive Officer, Former President and Chief Executive Officer, Former Vice-President and General Manager, Baxter Travenol Laboratories, 1945 to present. Organizational Memberships: Pharmaceuticals Manufacturers Association, Past Chairman of Board; Illinois Manufacturing Association, Past Chairman of Board. Community Activities: Past President, Community Fund; Trustee, Crusade of Mercy, University of Chicago, Orchestral Association, Evanston Hospital; Director, Lyric Opera of Chicago. Honors and Awards: Illinois Saint Andrew Society Distinguished Citizen Award; Decision Maker of the Year Award, 1974; Marketer of the Year Award, 1976; Weizmann Institute Professorial Chair, 1978; Honorary Doctor of Law Degree, Carthage College, 1974; Pharmaceuticals Manufacturers Association Award for Special Distinction and Leadership, 1981; Recognition for Pioneering Work in Bringing New, Life-Saving Products to Health Care Industry, Health Industrial Manufacturers Association, 1981; National Kidney Foundation First Award, 1981; Chicagoan of the Year, 1981. Address: 40 Devonshire Lane, Kenilworth, Illinois 60043.■

MARGARET KAY GRATER

School Administrator. Personal: Born July 12, 1942; Daughter of Russell K. Grater. Education: B.A. English and Biology, California State University at Long Beach, 1966; M.A. School Administration, California State University at Fresno, 1972; Ph.D. Curriculum and Instruction, University of South Carolina, 1975. Career: Coordinator of Staff Development, Office of the Los Angeles County Superintendant of Schools; Former Positions include School Principal, Staff Development Coordinator for Fresno Unified School District and South Carolina Model Schools Project, University Instructor, and Junior High and High School Teacher. Organizational Memberships: Association of California School Administrators, Director 1982 to present, Region Vice-President 1980-82, Region Secretary Committee Chairperson, Charter President; Los Angeles Chamber of Commerce; Association of Supervision and Curriculum Development. Community Activities: School Administration Advisory Board Secretary, California State University at Fullerton, 1981 to present; Parliamentarian, La Mirada City Coordinating Council, 1975-80; La Mirada District and School Parent-Teachers Association, 1975-80; American Red Cross, United States and Europe, 1958-69; California Cystic Fibrosis Association, 1979-80; Teacher Trainer for Placentia Presbyterian Church, 190-81; Academic Tutor, 1961-68; Junior/Senior High School Drama Productions and Assistant Tennis Coach, 1967-70. Religion: Presbyterian Church Activities. Honors and Awards: Awards of Merit 1977-82, Outstanding Charter Award for Region 14 1979, Speaker at National Convention 1974, Association of California School Administrators; Award of Appreciation, Norwalk La Mirada Administrators Association, 1980; American Red Cross Ten-Year Service Award and Meritorious Award for European Area, 1967; Listed in *Who's Who in the West, Who's Who in America, World Who's Who of Women, Personalities of America, Community Leaders of America.* Address: 1023 Lawanda, Placentia, California 92670.■

RUSSELL ORTON GRAY, SR.

Consultant. Personal: Born April 26, 1920; Son of Karl and Christine Gray; Married Mildred Rena Magoon; Father of Russell Orton, Jr., Karl Irving. Education: Graduated from Plymouth High School, 1938; Graduated from Pittsburgh Institute of Aeronautics, 1941. Career: Consultant, Gray's Sheet Metal; Sheet Metal Worker, Scott and Williams, 1941-43; Assistant Supervisor, Portsmouth Naval Shipyard, 1943-45; Supervisor of Sheet Metal Department, Sweeney's Inc., 1946-56; Owner/Operator Gray's Sheet Metal, 1956-83. Community Activities: Claremont Chamber of Commerce, 1964-73; Small Business Service Bureau; Former Assistant Leader, 4-H Club; Former Treasurer, Parent-Teacher Association. Religion: Member of Trinity Episcopal Church, Claremont, New Hampshire; Vestry; Junior and Senior Warden; First President of Saint Andrews Society. Honors and Awards: Listed in *Who's Who in the East.* Address: 242 Elm Street, Claremont, New Hampshire 03743.■

ALBERT W. GREEN

Pastor and Educator. Personal: Born August 12, 1929; Son of Levallia C. Green; Married Elease Wesbrooks; Father of Vicki, James, Lisa. Education: A.B. Sociology, Virginia Union University (Richmond, Virginia); M.A. History Education, Eastern Illinois University (Charleston, Illinois). Military: Served in the United States Armed Forces, 1951-53. Career: Dean of Black Ministerial Alliance, Danville, Illinois; Pastor, Second Baptist Church of Danville, 5 Years; Educator, Danville, Illinois, School District 118, 13 Years. Career: O.I.C., Board of Directors; Vermillion County Emergency Service; Vermillion County Region Diabetic Association, Board Member; Danville Senior High School Human Relations Club, Sponsor. Community Activities: Governor's Master Teacher Committee, State of Illinois. Religion: Woodriver Baptist District Association, Secretary; Congress of Christian Education, Founder, Assistant Dean; Committee on Church Extension of General Baptist State Convention. Honors and Awards: Saudsow Staff Teacher of the Year Award, 1978; Danville Black Ministerial Alliance Certificate, 1978; National Appreciation Award to Reverend Albert W. Green, 1979, 1980, 1982; State Certificate of Recognition for Services Rendered in the Community and State, State of Illinois Human Relations Commission, 1982; Honors for Silver Wedding Anniversary, Second Baptist Church, July 25, 1982; Listed in *Personalities of the West and Midwest, Who's Who Among Black Baptist Ministers in America, Society of Distinguished American High School Students.* Address: 1001 North Grant Street, Danville, Illinois 61832.■

TWO THOUSAND NOTABLE AMERICANS

EDITH GREEN

United States Congresswoman (retired). Personal: Mother of James S., Richard A. Education: Gradute of Salem, Oregon, Public Schools; Attended Willamette University, 1927-29; B.S., University of Oregon, 1939. Career: United States Congresswoman, 1955-75; Educator. Organizational Memberships: United States Congress, Appropriations Committee, Subcommittee on Labor, Health, Education and Welfare, Legislative Subcommittee, Education and Labor Committee, Chairman of Subcommittee on Secondary Education; Legislation Authored in Congress, Higher Education Acts of 1965 and 1967, Higher Education Facilities Act, Higher Education Act of 1972, Amendments to End Sex Discrimination in Education and Health Manpower Training, Social Security Improvements, Equal Pay for Equal Work, Vocational Rehabilitation, National Quality Education Act of 1972, Juvenile Delinquency Prevention and Control Act, Bill to Compensate Victims of Crime, Library Service Act, Bill Requiring Improved Financial Management of Federal Programs, War Powers Act Limiting Powers of a President, Narcotic Addict Rehabilitation Act, Hospital and Nursing Home Care for the Aged, Constitutional Amendment to Provide for Special Presidential Election in Case of "No Confidence" Vote; Henry M. Jackson Oregon Presidential Primary Campaign, Chairman, 1972; Robert F. Kennedy Oregon Presidential Primary Campaign, Chairman, 1968; John F. Kennedy Oregon Presidential Campaign, Chairman, 1960; Democratic National Convention, Asked by John F. Kennedy to Second his Nomination, First Woman Chairman of State Delegation 1960, Asked by Adlai E. Stevenson to Second his Nomination 1956, Delegate 1956, 1960, 1964, 1968, 1972; World Population Conference, Bucharest, Congressional Delegate, 1974; World Health Organization, Switzerland, Congressional Delegate, 1973; United Nations Educational, Scientific and Cultural Organization General Conference, Paris, Congressional Delegate, 1964, 1966; North Atlantic Treaty Organization Conference, London, Congressional Delegate, 1958; Parliamentary Conference, Switzerland, Congressional Delegate, 1958; Non-Government-Sponsored International Conference on Higher Education, Japan, One of Two Delegates Invited 1974. Community Activities: Benjamin Franklin Savings and Loan, Portland, Oregon, Board of Directors; Linfield College, Oregon, Board of Trustees; University of Oregon Health Sciences Center, Portland, Advisory Board; Oregon Community Foundation, Board Member. Honors and Awards: Honorary Doctor of Laws Degrees, Beloit College, Wisconsin 1971, Oberlin College, Ohio 1966, Reed College, Oregon 1966, Georgetown University, Washington, D.C. 1966, Yale University, Connecticut 1965, Gonzago University, Washington 1964, Linfield College, Oregon 1964; Honorary Doctor of Public Administration Degree, Willamette University, Oregon, 1970; First Citizen Award, Portland, 1978; Annual Achievement Award, American Association of University Women, 1974; Simon LeMoyne Medal, LeMoyne College, Syracuse, New York, 1973; Annual Award, Oregon Public Health Associaton, 1973; Abram L. Sachar Award, National Women's Committee, Brandeis University, 1972; Distinguished Service Award, Oregon State University, 1972; Outstanding Service Award, National Association of Student Personnel Administrators, 1972; Portland Women of Accomplishment, One of Ten Named by *Oregon Journal*, 1972; Citation of Appreciation, American Legion, 1972; Award of Distinction, National Council of Administrative Women in Education, 1971; Distinguished Service Award, National Association of Trade and Technical Schools, 1971; Citation, World Convention of Churches of Christ, Sydney, Australia, 1970; Conde Nast Award, Georgetown University Student Body, 1969; Distinguished Service Award, National Education Association, 1967; Distinguished Service Award, Council of Chief State School Officers, 1967; Outstanding Woman in the Field of Government, *Who's Who of American Women*, 1967; President's Award, National Rehabilitation Association, 1967; Award for Distinguished Services, University of Oregon, 1967; E. B. McNaughton Award, Oregon Chapter of American Civil Liberties Union, 1966; Top Hat Award, Business and Professional Women's Clubs of America, 1965; Distinguished Achievement Award, The American College Public Relations Association, 1964; Eleanor Roosevelt — Mary McLeod-Bethune World Citizenship Award, National Council of Negro Women, 1964. Address: 8031 Sacajawea Way, Wilsonville, Oregon 97070.■

MICHAEL GEORGE GREEN

Assistant Professor of Human Development and Learning. Personal: Born February 2, 1947; Son of George W. and Margaret M. Green; Married Emily Ann Stephenson-Green, Daughter of Robert and Fleta Stephenson (both deceased). Education: B.A., University of California at Berkeley, 1969; Ed.M. 1973, Ed.D. 1977, Laboratory of Human Development of Harvard Graduate School of Education. Career: Assistant Professor of Human Development and Learning 1978 to present, Chairman of Education Foundations 1980-81, University of North Carolina at Charlotte, College of Human Development and Learning; Research Associate, Research Institute for Educational Problems, Cambridge, Massachusetts, 1977-78; Instructor in Education, Department of Education, Clark University, Worcester, Massachusetts, 1976-77; Teaching Fellow 1975-76, Research Assistant 1972-76, Laboratory of Human Development, Harvard Graduate School of Education, Cambridge, Massachusetts; Lecturer in Education, Lesley College Graduate School of Education, Cambridge, Massachusetts, 1974-75. Organizational Memberships: American Educational Research Association; American Educational Studies Association; Jean Piaget Society; Society for Philosophy and Psychology; Society for Research in Child Development. Community Activities: Chancelor's Task Force on Goals of University of North Carolina at Charlotte Education, 1980-83; Moderator of Faculty Colloquium "Discussion with Lawrence Kohlberg" 1978, Moderabor of "Focus on Metrolina Area Children's Services" for U.N.E.S.C.O.'s International Year of the Child 1979, Coordinator of Week of the Young Child 1979, University of North Carolina at Charlotte; Consultant, The Teacher Center, Monroe and Concord (North Carolina), 1979. Honors and Awards: Harvard Fellowship, 1973-76; Listed in *Men of Achievement*, *Who's Who in the South and Southwest*, *Directory of Distinguished Americans*, *The International Who's Who of Intellectuals*. Address: 1814 Sprague Avenue, Charlotte, North Carolina 28205.■

FRANK JOSEPH GREENBERG, SR.

Educational Researcher, Lecturer, Writer, Administrator, Biblical Archaeologist. Born June 15, 1933; Son of Benjamin and Mary E. Cohen Greenberg (deceased); Married Elizabeth Irene Bowser, Father of Robin Elizabeth (Greenberg) Young, Linda Ann (deceased), Diana Rose (Greenberg) DiCicco, Frank Joseph, Jr., Anita Louise (Greenberg) McSorley, Daniel Jacob Harold. Education: Diploma in Public Accountancy, Walton School of Commerce, 1956; D.CO., Caldwell Co-Ordipathic Institute, 1956; Diploma in Advanced Mechanical Engineering, Canadian Institute of Science and Technology, 1957; B.A. Sociology, Brentwood College, 1958; B.B.A. Accounting, Canton Actual Business College, 1960; Diploma in Office Management, The School of Careers, London, England, 1963; B.D. Comparative Religion, Felix Adler Memorial University, 1964; LL.B., Blackstone School of Law, 1967; Diplomas of Advanced Graduate Study in Psychoanalysis and Behavioral Science, Florida Psychoanalytic Institute, 1970; Ed.M. l970, Ed.D. 1971, College and Adult Counseling, Thomas A. Edison College; Ph.D. Industrial Psychology, Thomas A. Edison College, 1971; Diploma in Advanced Graduate Psychotherapy, Palm Beach Psychotherapy Training Center, 1972; Ph.D. Biblical Archaeology, Athenaeum Ecumenical Divinity Institute, 1979. Military: Served in the United States Coast Guard, 1950-54, attaining the rank of Seaman. Career: Independent Nontraditional Experimental Educational Research and Development, 1954 to present; Liaison Officer, Collegament Accademia Teatina Per le Scienze, Pescara, Italy, 1979 to present; Tax and Security Accountant, Self-Employed, 1963-74; Counseling Psychologist, Educational Counselor, Group Psychotherapist, Self-Employed, 1963-74; Vice President, Palm Beach Psychotherapy Training Center, 1974-77; Consultant Biblical Archaeology, Athenaeum Ecumenical Divinity Institute, 1979-80; Hellenic Professional Association of America International, Chairman Advisory Board on Professional, Educational and Governmental Matters 1980-83, Executive Director/Secretary 1982-83; Founding President/Chairman Board of Directors, International College of Proctors and Preceptors, 1982 to present; Adjunct Professor, Bernadean University, 1982 to present; Adjunct Faculty Member, North American Regional College of World University, 1983 to present. Organizational Memberships: Life Member/Academician, Accademia Tiberina, Institute for University Cultural Activities and Further Studies, Rome, Italy; Lifetime Fellow, Alpha Psi Sigma Society; Annual Member, American Association for Higher Education; Life Member, American Association for the Advancement of Criminology; Lifetime Fellow, American Association of Criminology; Annual Member, American Association of University Administrators; Lifetime Fellow/Diplomate, American Board of Examiners in Psychotherapy; Lifetime Fellow, American Biographical Institute; Lifetime Fellow, American College of Clinic Administrators; Voting Member, American Educational Research Association; American Society of Distinguished Citizens, Life Member, Chairman Credentials Evaluation Committee, 1976 to present; Annual Member, American Society of Law and Medicine; Annual Member, American Studies Association; Life Member/Research Associate, American Studies Research Centre, Hyderabad, India; Annual Member, Association for Supervision and Curriculum Development; Lifetime Fellow, Association for Social Psychology; Honorary Lifetime Fellow, Anglo-American Academy, Cambridge, England; Life Member, Athenaeum Ecumenical Divinity Institute; Annual Member, Biblical Archaeology Society; Life Member, Change Associates; Associate Member, Council for the Advancement of Experiential Learning; Lifetime Fellow; Delta Epsilon Omega Honor Society; Contributing Member, Educational Leadership Council of America; Lifetime Fellow/Diplomate, Florida Psychoanalytic Institute; Lifetime Fellow, Fraternal Order of Lambda Epsilon Chi; Professional Member, Hellenic Professional Association of America International; Professional Member, International Association for Hydrogen Energy; Lifetime Fellow, International Biographical Association; Annual Member, International Platform Association; Annual Member, Measurements and Control Society International; Annual Member, Medical Electronics and Data Society of America; Annual Member, National Council on Measurement in Education; Life Member, National Psychological Association; Annual Member, National Retired Teachers Association; College Member, National Science Teachers Association; Comprehensive Member, National Society for the Study of Education; Annual Member, National Space Institute; Navy League of the United States, Life Member, Former Committee Chairman of United States Naval Sea Cadet Units Boston and Constitution Divisions for Eastern Massachusetts Council/Navy League 1973-78, Commodore Club 1983; Annual Member, Society for Applied Learning Technology; Annual Member, Society for Intercultural Education Training and Research; Annual Member, Society for the Advancement of Education; Sustaining Member, Society of Professors of Education; Life Member/Academician, Teatine Academy of Science, Pescara, Italy; Life Member, Criminological Executives Club; Life Member, Disabled American Veterans; Annual Member, United States Naval Institute; Comprehensive Member, World Future Society; Annual Member, Inter-American Society. Community Activities: Third Degree Master Mason, Most Worshipful Grand Lodge of Ancient Free and Accepted Masons of the Commonwealth of Massachusetts, Mount Olivet Lodge; Thirty-Second Degree S.P.R.S., Scottish Bodies in the Valley of Boston; Shriner; United States Navy Sea Cadet Program, Voluntary Lieutenant Junior Grade,

TWO THOUSAND NOTABLE AMERICANS

Administrative Training Officer and Vocational Guidance Counselor, 1964-66; Universal Human Rights Foundation, Voluntary Board Member, Group Psychotherapist and Counseling Psychologist, 1965-74; Voluntary Consultant in Counseling Psychology, Dorchester Area Planning Council, 1972-73; Voluntary Consultant in Counseling Psychology and Clinical Psychotherapy, Department of the Army, United States Reynolds Army Hospital, Otolaryngology Service, 1974-77; Editorial Advisory Board, American Biographical Institute, 1977-79; Editorial Advisory Board, International Biographical Centre, Cambridge, England, 1978 to present; International Advisory Board, World University, 1983 to present. Honors and Awards: Certificate of Merit, Bureau of Business Practice, 1966; Minister Plenipotentiary, Imperial Order of Constantine, Lisbon, Portugal, 1973; Order of Saint John of Jerusalem, Knight Commander of Justice Purple Rosette Maltese Cross, 1974; Founder-Fellow Medal Community Service Diploma of Honor, International Institute of Community Service, 1975; Commander, International Order of Sursum Corda, Brussels, Belgium, 1975; Listed in *Book of Honor, Anglo-American Who's Who, Biographical Roll of Honor, Community Leaders of America, Community Leaders of the World, Community Leaders and Noteworthy Americans, Dictionary of International Biography, Directory of Organizations and Personnel in Educational Management, Distinguished Citizens of America, Five Thousand Personalities of the World, International Authors and Writers Who's Who, International Book of Honor, International Register of Personalities, International Register of Profiles, International Who's Who in Community Service, International Who's Who in Education, International Who's Who of Contemporary Achievement, International Who's Who of Intellectuals, Library of Human Resources of the American Heritage Research Association, Who's Who in the East, Men of Achievement, Men and Women of Distinction, National Social Directory, Notable Americans, Notable Americans of the Bicentennial Era, Personalities of America, Standard Who's Who in American Jewry, Two Thousand Notable Americans, Who's Who in World Jewry, Yearbook and Biographical Directory.* Address: 14 Lindsey Street, Dorchester, Massachusetts 02124-1399.■

ELLEN GREENBERGER

Professor of Social Ecology. Personal: Born November 19, 1935; Daughter of Dr. and Mrs. Edward M. Silver; Married Michael Burton; Mother of Kari, David. Education: A.B., Vassar College, 1956; M.A. 1959, Ph.D. 1961, Harvard University. Career: Professor of Social Ecology, Interdisciplinary Psychologist, University of California-Irvine; Assistant Professor of Psychology, Wellesley College, Massachusetts; Principal Research Scientist, The Johns Hopkins University, Baltimore, Maryland. Honors and Awards: Phi Beta Kappa; Margaret Floy Washburn Fellowship, 1956-58; United States Public Health Service, Pre-Doctoral Fellowship 1961-62. Address: Program in Social Ecology, University of California, Irvine, California 92717.■

KATHLEEN KING GREENE

Manager of Equal Employment Opportunity Programs. Personal: Born June 15, 1932; Daughter of Vera H. King; Mother of Christopher Tracy. Education: Management-Related Courses, Palm Beach Junior College 1950, Bryant and Stratton 1963, Massachusetts Institute of Technology Lowell Institute 1967-68, Babson College 1974-76, Barry University 1981-82. Career: Manager of Equal Employment Opportunity Programs, Former Division Management Consultant and Project Cost Engineer, Pratt and Whitney; Former Positions include Manager of Employee Relations, Division Administrator, and Assistant for Planning and Analysis for Mitre Corporation, Executive Secretary for Neelon Management Associates, Assistant Manager of Dial Employment Bureau, and Station Manager of Mackey International Airlines; Charter Member, American Business Women's Association. Organizational Memberships: Air Force Association; Florida Management Association; American Management Association; National Association of Female Executives. Community Activities: League of Women Voters; Board of Directors, Chairman of Equal Opportunity Day 1983, Urban League of Palm Beach County; Board of Directors, Steering Committee 1981-83, District X Special Olympics; Executive Committee, Community Action Council; Executive Committee, Chairman of Materials and Equipment Committee 1981-83, Florida A. & M. University Cluster; Community Relations Board, Palm Beach Halfway House. Honors and Awards: Performance Award, United Technologies Corporation, 1982; Triple Service Award, Florida A. & M. University, 1982; Service Award, Palm Beach Halfway House, 1982; Service Award, Muscular Dystrophy, 1981; Service Award, United States Savings Bond Program, 1975-78; Awards, United Fund/Way, 1970-77. Address: 2367 Laurel Lane, Lake Park, Florida 33410.■

MAURICE LUTHER GREINER

Director of Training and Safety. Personal: Born January 4, 1931; Son of William M. (deceased) and Daisy Greiner; Married Zelma Alma Ross; Father of Blayne M., Brenda. Education: Graduate, Briercrest Bible College 1952; Graduate with Honors and Q.A.A. Designation, Association of Administrative Assistants, 1966; Graduate of Personnel Management, I.C.S., 1960; Fire Engineers Degree, M.I.F.E., Institution of Fire Engineers, England, 1968; Diploma, American Management Association 1979, Safety Training Institute 1969; Numerous Short Courses in Training, Safety and Management Development. Career: Director of Training and Safety, J. R. Simplot Company. Organizational Memberships: Hazard Control Managers; American Society of Safety Engineers; Institution of Fire Engineers; National Fire Protection Association; Veterans of Safety International; National Fertilizer Solutions Association, Education Committee; Chairman of Safety and Health Committee, Fertilizer Institute, 1975 to present; Developer, Director/Coordinator, Intermountain Fertilizer Safety School, 1973 to present; Idaho Snake River Chapter, American Society of Safety Engineers; Internationally-Recognized Speaker and Lecturer to Fire and Police Departments; First President, Eastern Idaho Chapter of American Society for Training and Development. Community Activities: Idaho Society Sons of the American Revolution, State Vice President, Secretary-Treasurer of Old Fort Hall Chapter; Chaplain, Gideons International; Republican; Rotary International, Pocatello; Community Task Force on Geriatric Health Care, 1984 to present; Served on Faculty of Public Services Training Academy (Rockville, Maryland, May 1984) for Hazardous Materials Response Teams; Others. Religion: Church of the Nazarene. Honors and Awards: Honorary Life Member, Order of St. John; Distinguished Alumnus, Briercrest College; Honorary Member, American Association of Bible College's Honor Society Delta Epsilon Chi; National Service to Safety Award, Highest Award of National Safety Council; Listed in Numerous Biographical Reference Publications. Address: 21 Stanford, Pocatello, Idaho 83201.■

LINELLE C. GRIER

Retired Home Economist. Personal: Born September 15, 1917; Daughter of Mr. and Mrs. Chester Evans (deceased); Married Harold E. Grier, Son of Mr. and Mrs. Jefferson Grier (deceased); Mother of Prentis C. Nolan III. Education: B.S., Langston University, 1937; M.S., University of Wisconsin, 1949; Honorary Ph.D., Colorado State Christian College, 1973; M.S., Alcorn State University, 1978. Career: Retired Home Economist; Alcorn State University Supervisor of Off-Campus Teachers and Home Economics Teachers, State of Oklahoma; Home Management and Family Arts, Southern University; Chairperson, Head Teacher Education, Nutrition and Family Foods, Alcorn State University; Extension Officer, Alcorn State University. Organizational Memberships: Mississippi Consumer Association, Board Member 1964 to present; Mississippi Home Economics Association, Board Member 1980-82; American Home Economics Association; Kappa Omicron Phi, Organizer/Member 1982 to present. Community Activities: Alpha Kappa Alpha, Committee Member and Parliamentarian 1980-82, Member 1963 to present; Aimwell Federated Club, Secretary; Business and Professional Women's Club, Corresponding Secretary 1974; Natchez Social Civic Club, Organizer 1983; Kappa Omicron Phi, Donation 1983. Religion: First Baptist Church (Okmulgee, Oklahoma), 1925; Mt. Olive Baptist Church (Lorman, Mississippi), 1964 to present. Honors and Awards: Citation, Human Resources of U.S.A., 1973; Kappa Omicron Phi Award, 1979, 1982; Okmulgee County Award, 1937; Cooperative Extension Award, 1967; Research Grant, U.S.D.A., 1968; Retirement Awards, Alcorn State University and Alpha Kappa Alpha, 1982; Certificate of Merit for Service to Home Economics, 1972; Rust College Award, 1974; Listed in *Leaders in Education, Who's Who of American Women, World Who's Who of Women, Notable Americans of the Bicentennial Era, Two Thousand Women of Achievement.* Address: Box 224, Alcorn State University, Lorman, Mississippi 39096.■

LAURE ANNE ELISE DE BRANGES DE BOURCIA GROESBECK

Artist. Personal: Born January 31, 1936; Daughter of Vicomte Louis de Branges de Bourcia II and Diane McDonald de Branges de Bourcia; Mother of Gretchen Atlee, Genevieve de Branges. Education: Attended The Agnes Irwin School (Rosemont, Pennsylvania) 1954, The Philadelphia College of Art (Philadelphia, Pennsylvania) 1954-55. Career: Artist; One-Man Shows at The Agnes Irwin School (Rosemont, Pennsylvania) 1973, Philadelphia Cricket Club (Chestnut Hill, Pennsylvania) 1973. Religion: Episcopal. Honors and Awards: First Prize, Rehoboth Beach Art League, Rehoboth Beach, Delaware, 1944; Agnes Allen Art Prize, Agnes Irwin School, 1954. Address: 3204 Leigh Road, Pompano Beach, Florida 33062.■

GRATIA BAILEY GROVES

Education Specialist and Author. Personal: Born August 5, 1906, in West Virginia; Mother of Sue Ann Groves Armstrong. Education: Graduate, Charleston High

TWO THOUSAND NOTABLE AMERICANS

School, West Virginia; Degree, Morris Harvey College Extension; Graduate Degree, Columbia Teachers College. Career: Teacher of First Grade, 5 Years; Art Instructor; Director of Art Education, Kanawha County (245 Schools); Director of Instruction Levels 1-12; Supervisor of Elementary Schools, Fairfax County, Virginia, 1958-66; Coordinator of Education, University of Virginia, 1966-77; Lecturer, University of Virginia; Consultant, Encyclopaedia Britannica Educational Corporation; Writer and Lecturer, 1974 to present. Organizational Memberships: International Platform Association; Delta Kappa Gamma; National Education Association; American Association of School Administrators; National Safety Council; Palm Beach Writers Club; Vice-President, National League of American Pen Women, 2 Years; United States State Department Delegate, International Conference on Public Education, Geneva, Switzerland, 1955; Delegate by Invitation of King Gustav, International Art Congress, Lund, Sweden, 1955; Delegate to International Art Conference, The Hague 1957, Montreal (Canada) 1963; State of Virginia Delegate, Program to Study Education under Communism in Poland, U.S.S.R., Hungary, Romania, Czechoslovakia, Yugoslavia, East Germany; Study of Education of Aborigines, Australia, 1972; Study of History of Maoris, New Zealand; Visitor to Fiji Schools and Hawaii University; Studies of School Systems and Governments of France, Greece and Yugoslavia. Community Activities: Active in Home Town Government. Published Works: Author, *Glimpses Through the Curtain* and Two Other Books, One Educational and One Fiction; Contributor of Many Articles to Professional Journals. Honors and Awards: Fellow, Intercontinental Biographical Association, Cambridge, England; Honorary Member, Marshall University Kappa Pi; Grant for an Institute in Educational Media for Librarians, Department of Health, Education and Welfare, 1969; Listed in *Who's Who of American Women, Who's Who in the South and Southwest, Community Leaders of America, Creative People of the World, Dictionary of International Biography, World Who's Who of Women, International Who's Who of Intellectuals, Who's Who in the West and Southwest.* Address: 6830 Huntdale Street, Long Beach, California 90808.■

DAGFINN GUNNARSHAUG

Company President. Personal: Born February 21, 1933 in Haugesund, Norway; Son of Emma and Konrad (deceased); Married Anjel Isikli; Father of Oistein, Aagot, Tore, Inger-Elin. Education: Attended Okonomisk Gymnas, Business College, Haugesund, Norway, 1952; Course in Shipping, Industrikonsulent A/S, Oslo, Norway; Attended Military School, Heistadmoen, Kongsberg, Norway, 1953-54. Military: Served in the Norwegian Army, attaining rank of Second Lieutenant. Career: President, Consulmar Limited; Senior Vice President, Ugland Management Company; Former Positions include Vice President Viking Steamship Company, 1982; Vice President and Director of the Board, Merzario Maritime Agency Inc.; Director Job Security Program; A/S Haugesund Insurance Company, Norway, 1952-54; Northern State Power Company, 1955; Christian Haaland Shipping Company, Haugesund, Norway, 1956-68; Chairman of the Board and Chief Executive Officer, Boise-Griffin Steamship Company, 1969-83; Saudi Concordia Line, Jeddah, Saudi Arabia, Managing Director 1978-80, Director United States of America Division 1978-82; Chairman of the Board and President, Boise-Griffin Agencies, 1979-83. Organizational Memberships: President of the Board, Galleria Condominium, 1977-82; Director of the Board, Shipping Industry Mutual Assurance Association, 1981. Community Activities: American-Norwegian Chamber of Commerce, Director Security Bureau 1978, Director 1980. Honors and Awards: Honorary Member of the Norwegian Academic Association of the United States of America. Address: 35 86th Street, Brooklyn, New York 11709.■

VENU G. GUPTA

University Professor. Personal: Born April 3, 1934, in Hoshiarpur, Punjab, India; Married Sunita Gupta; Father of Sunil, Sanjiv. Education: B.A. with first class honors 1953, M.A. first class first 1955, M.Ed. first class first with highest academic distinction 1959, Punjab University; B.Ed., Central Institute of Education, Delhi University, 1958; Ph.D. with 4.0 Grade Point Average, Georgia State University, 1974. Career: Kutztown University of Pennsylvania, Professor of Counseling and Psychology 1977 to present, Associate Professor 1974-77; Teaching and Research Fellow, Georgia State University, 1972-74; Assistant Professor of Psychology and Counseling, Eastern Kentucky University, 1968-72; Assistant Professor of Psychology, University of Wisconsin-Stevens Point, 1966-68; Teaching and Research Fellow, University of Alberta, Canada, 1964-66; Lecturer, Colleges of Punjab and Kurukshetra Universities, India, 1955-63. Organizational Memberships: American Psychological Association; American Educational Research Association; American Personnel and Guidance Association; Association for Counselor Education and Supervision; American Mental Health Counselors Association; American Association for the Advancement of Science; American Association of University Professors; Phi Delta Kappa; International Council of Psychologists; International Association of Applied Psychology; International Association for Cross-Cultural Psychology; International Council on Education for Teaching. Community Activities: Radio and Television Appearances for Interviews; Lecturer on Hinduism to Various Interested Groups; World Travel; Languages and Literature. Religion: Hindu. Published Works: Author, "Intercorrelations of W.I.S.C.: Subtest-Scores of Seventy Children, Tested Two Years Apart," "Self-Actualization — East and West: A Counselor's Viewpoint," "Students' Perception of College Instructors Based on Faculty-Evaluation Ratings," "Piaget: A Human Learning Theory," "Effects of Varied Instruction on Student Ratings of University Faculty," and Research Studies Published and Presented at National and International Professional Conventions. Honors and Awards: Commendation Award, American Society of Distinguished Citizens, Beverly Hills, California, 1976; Diploma of Honor for Community Service, *International Who's Who in Community Service*, 1973; Creativity Recognition Award, International Personnel Research, Los Angeles, 1972; Outstanding Educator of America Award, Chicago, 1971; Award for Distinguished Service to the Teaching Profession, *Dictionary of International Biography*, 1970; Distinguished Achievement Award, London, 1970; Dean's Special Graduate Studies Scholarship, University of Alberta, Canada, 1963; Gold Medalist, Punjab University, India, 1959; Winner, Several Academic Prizes and Certificates of Merit; Listed in *Outstanding Educators of America, Dictionary of International Biography, Creative and Successful Personalities, Community Leaders of America, International Directory of Scholars Interested in Human Development in Cross-Cultural Perspective, Distinguished Citizens of America Directory, American Men and Women of Science, Social and Behavioral Sciences, Who's Who in the East, Who's Who in America, Who's Who in Education, The Seventies, International Who's Who of Intellectuals.* Address: 744 Highland Avenue, Kutztown, Pennsylvania 19530.■

LAWRENCE SIMPSON GUTHRIE, II

Circulation Librarian and Psychology Instructor. Personal: Born December 2, 1953; Son of Lawrence S. and Helen Janning Guthrie. Education: B.S., Georgetown University, 1976; M.A., University of Oklahoma, 1980. Career: Circulation Librarian at McFarlin Library, University of Tulsa; Psychology Instructor, Tulsa Junior College; Baseball Coach, Cascia Hall; Former Positions include Substitute Teacher, Baseball Coach, Information and Referred Librarian, Chemistry Tutor and Laboratory Assistant, Radiology Assistant, Psychiatric Technician and Assistant. Organizational Memberships: Elected Member, New York Academy of Sciences; Delta Phi Epsilon Foreign Service Fraternity. Community Activities: Initiator, "Today's Events" Column, *Tulsa World*; Presenter of Events on the Air, KXXO Radio; The Hunger Project; Coach, Junior High Baseball; Oklahoma Representative, An Comunn Gaidhealach (Scots Gaelic Society); Editor, *Oklahoma Collogue Literary Journal*, 1980. Religion: Roman Catholic; Knights of Columbus Baseball Coach. Honors and Awards: Academic Scholarship, Georgetown University, 1972-76; Research Assistant, Chestnut Lodge Sanitarium; Studied under Anna Freud, London; Listed in *Who's Who Among American High School Students, Community Leaders of the World, Personalities of the South.* Address: 1505½ East 19th Street, Tulsa, Oklahoma 74120.■

SALLY GROVER GUTIERREZ

Consultant. Personal: Born July 16, 1948; Daughter of Mrs. N. T. Grover; Married Thomas Andrew Gutierrez. Education: B.A. 1971, M.P.A. 1983, University of Southern California. Career: Consultant; Former Positions include Planning Analyst at The White House and Assistant Dean of the School of Public Administration, Director of Professional Development and Recruitment, and Assistant Director of the Civic Center Campus at the University of Southern California. Organizational Memberships: American Society for Public Administration, President Los Angeles Chapter 1983, Elected to National Council 1981, Chairperson of National Committee for Women 1979 and 1980; Municipal Management Assistants of Southern California, Board of Directors, 1977; California Women in Government, Founder 1975, Vice-Chairperson 1967, Chairperson 1977. Community Activities: Young Women's Christian Association of Santa Monica, Board of Directors 1980, Treasurer 1981, Vice-President of Fund Development 1982. Honors and Awards: Thomas Bradley Affirmative Action Award, Los Angeles Chapter of the American Society for Public Administration, 1980; Women's Achievement Award, TELACU, 1977; Henry Reining Award for Outstanding Contribution to the Los Angeles Metropolitan Area, American Society for Public Administration, 1976 and 1977; Listed in *Personalities of America, Outstanding Young Women of America.* Address: 965 Calle Miramar, Redondo Beach, California 90277.■

EDWARD LEE GUY

Real Estate Investments. Personal: Born October 28, 1937; Son of Lee Livingston Guy; Father of Stacy Lee. Education: B.A., Catawba College, 1969. Military: Served in the United States Army, 1960-62. Career: President, Super Chek Systems Inc., 1977 to present; President and General Manager, Multi-Chek Systems Inc., 1972-77; Owner of Inventory Service Company, 1970-72; Administrative Assistant, Consultants Services Company, Inc., 1969-70. Community Activities: American Mensa Ltd.; Tampa Bay Mensa; The International Legion of Intelligence (Intertel). Honors and Awards: F. M. Knetsche Award, 1967. Address: 7546 Armand Circle, Tampa, Florida 33614.■

MERRILL WILBER HAAS

Petroleum Consultant. Personal: Born July 9, 1910; Married Maria Haas; Father of Mariella Allard, Merrill Jr., Maria Cecilia, Frederick. Education: Attended the University of Kansas, 1928-31; B.A., University of Michigan, 1932; Undertook Postgraduate Studies, Harvard University, 1932-33. Career: Paleontologist, Humble Oil and Refining Company; District Geologist and Director of Paleontological Laboratory, Lago Petroleum Corporation, Venezuela; Division Geologist, Creole Petroleum Corporation, Venzuela; Area Geologist, Standard Oil Company, New Jersey, New York; Chief Geologist, Exploration Manager, Vice President, Director, The Carter Oil Company, Tulsa; Vice President for Exploration, Exxon, U.S.A. Organizational Memberships: Geological Society of America, Fellow; Houston Geological Society; Tulsa Geological Society; American Association of Petroleum Geologists, President 1974-75; Paleontological Research Institute, Trustee, President 1970-75; American Association of Petroleum Geologists Foundation, Trustee. Community Activities: American Geological Institute, Chairman Manpower Committee 1967-69; American Petroleum Institute, Chairman Reserves and Productive Capacity Committee, 1971-73; University of Kansas Geology Associates and Advisory Board, University of Kansas, 1961; Erasmus Haworth Distinguished Alumni Award; University of Kansas Distinguished Service Citation, 1966; The Merrill W. Haas Distinguished Visiting Professorship in Geology, University of Kansas, 1973; Honorary Member, American Association of Petroleum Geologists, 1979; Honorary Member, Houston Geological Society, 1980; Outstanding Achievement Award, University of Michigan, 1981. Address: 10910 Wickwild, Houston, Texas 77024. ∎

NORMAN HACKERMAN

College President, Professor. Personal: Born March 2, 1912, in Baltimore, Maryland; Son of Jacob and Anna Raffel Hackerman (both deceased); Married Gene Allison Coulbourn, August 25, 1940, Baltimore, Maryland; Father of Patricia Gale, Stephen Miles, Sally Griffith, Katherine Elizabeth. Education: A.B. 1932, Ph.D. 1935, Johns Hopkins University; LL.D. (honorary), Abilene Christian University, 1978; D.Sc. (honorary), Texas Christian University, 1978; D.Sc. (honorary), Austin College, 1975; LL.D. (honorary), St. Edward's University, 1972. Career: Rice University, President 1970 to present, Professor of Chemistry 1970 to present; The University of Texas at Austin, President 1967-70, Vice Chancellor for Academic Affairs 1963-67, Vice President and Provost 1961-63, Dean of Research and Sponsored Programs 1960-61, Director of the Corrosion Research Laboratory 1948-61, Chairman of Chemistry Department 1952-61, Professor of Chemistry 1950-70, Associate Professor of Chemistry 1946-50, Assistant Professor of Chemistry 1945-46; Research Chemist, Kellex Corporation, 1944-45; Assistant Professor of Chemistry, Virginia Polytechnic Institute, 1941-43; Assistant Chemist, United States Coast Guard, 1939-41; Research Chemist, Colloid Corporation, 1936-40; Assistant Professor of Chemistry, Loyola College, 1935-39. Organizational Memberships: American Academy of Arts and Sciences, Fellow 1978; American Philosophical Society, 1972; National Academy of Sciences, 1971; American Chemical Society, Executive Committee, Colloid Division 1955-58, Board of Editors, *American Chemical Society Monograph Series* 1956-62, Honorary Member 1975; National Association of Corrosion Engineers, Board of Directors 1952-55, Chairman A. B. Campbell Young Authors Award Committee 1960-78; Electrochemical Society, Chairman Corrosion Division 1951, Vice President 1954-57, President 1957-58, Interim Editor *Electrochemical Technology* 1965-68, Technical Editor *Journal of the Electrochemical Society* 1950-68, Editor 1969 to present, Honorary Member 1973; American Association for the Advancement of Science, Fellow; New York Academy of Sciences, Fellow; International Society of Electrochemistry. Community Activities: Solar Advisory Committee, State of Texas, 1980 to present; American Chemical Society Joint Board, Council Committee on Chemistry and Public Affairs 1980 to present; CO_2 Study Group, Department of Energy, 1977-80; University of California-Berkeley, Lawrence Berkeley Laboratory, Scientific and Educational Advisory Committee 1977-81; MITRE Corporation, Board of Trustees 1980 to present; American Council on Education, Board of Directors 1980-83; Oak Ridge Associated Universities, Board of Directors 1975-81; Independent Colleges and Universities of Texas, President 1974-81, Chairman of the Board 1982 to present; National Board of Graduate Education, 1971-75; Board on Energy Studies, National Academy of Sciences/National Research Council, Chairman 1974-77; National Science Board, Member 1968-80, Chairman 1974-80; Chairman Scientific Advisory Board, Robert A. Welch Foundation, 1982 to present; Environmental Pollution Panel, President's Science Advisory Committee 1965-66; Association of Universities for Research in Astronomy, Consultant 1964-78; Argonne National Laboratory, Chemical Engineering Division Review Committee, 1963-69, Chairman Board of Trustees 1969-73; Intersociety Corrosion Committee, Chairman 1956-58. Published Works: Author/Co-Author 203 Publications. Honors and Awards: American Institute Chemists Gold Medal, 1978; Honor Scroll, Texas Institute of Chemists, 1975; Palladium Medalist of the Electrochemical Society, 1965; Southwest Regional Award, American Chemical Society, 1965; Joseph L. Mattiello Award, 1964; Whitney Award of National Association of Corrosion Engineers, 1956; Mirabeau B. Lamar Award, Association of Texas Colleges and Universities, 1981; Distinguished Alumnus Award, Johns Hopkins University, 1982; Alpha Chi Sigma; Phi Kappa Phi; Phi Lambda Upsilon; Sigma Xi. Address: President's House, Rice University, Houston, Texas 77001. ∎

HOWARD SMITH HACKNEY

Farmer and Executive Director. Personal: Born May 20, 1910; Son of V. M. and Gusta Hackney (deceased); Married Lucille Morrow, Daughter of Harry and Lavina Morrow (deceased); Father of Albert Morrow, Roderick Allen, Katherine Ann Hackney Becker. Education: Graduate, Chester Township High School, 1928; B.S. cum laude, Wilmington College, 1928-32. Career: Farmer and Livestock Breeder, Duroc Swine 1921 to present, Southdown Sheep 1933 to present; Federal Farm Programmes, County Committee Member (elected 1938), Chairman of County Committee 1945-52, Manager 1952, County Executive Director (currently). Organizational Memberships: President and Director, Ohio Duroc Breeders Association; Member, United Duroc Swine Registry; American Southdown Breeders Association; Ohio Southdown Breeders Association; Secretary, Treasurer and Director, Farm Bureau; Treasurer and Director, Clinton County Agricultural Society; Helped Organize the Farmers Union Locally. Community Activities: Clinton County Community Action Council; Treasurer of Regional Planning Commission, NASCOE; Soil Conservation Society of America; American Association for the Advancement of Science; County, Regional and State Historical Societies; Member Board of Trustees, Wilmington College; Trustee, Clinton County Historical Society. Religion: Quaker, Sunday School Teacher and Superintendent, Clerk of Chester Friends Meeting, Member of Ministry and Council, on the Permanent Board of Wilmington Yearly Meeting, Helped Organize and was Chairman of the American Young Friends Fellowship, Board Member of the American Friends Service Committee. Honors and Awards: Recipient of Numerous Awards for Duroc Swine and Southdown Sheep, Breeder of Champions; Recipient of County and State Awards for Livestock Judging; Presented with Ohio and Midwest Area Award for Outstanding Service to Agriculture, 1970; Clinton County Award for Service to Agriculture and 4-H Clubs, 1975; NASCOE State Award for Community Service, 1981; State President's Award for Service to NASCOE, Soil Conservation Society of America, American Association for the Advancement of Science, and the County, Regional and State Historical Societies; Awarded Scholarship to Wilmington College; Chi Beta Phi Science Award for Outstanding Student, Wilmington College; Inducted into Ohio State Fair Hall of Fame, 1983; Listed in *Who's Who in Religion, Personalities of America, Personalities of the South, Personalities of the West and Midwest, Community Leaders and Noteworthy Americans, Book of Honor, Notable Americans, International Who's Who in Community Service, Dictionary of International Biography, International Register of Profiles, Men of Achievement, The Directory of Distinguished Americans, Men and Women of Distinction, The American Registry, American Patriots of 1980, Who's Who in the Midwest, Farmland Trust*. Address: 2003 Inwood Road, Wilmington, Ohio 45177. ∎

BRUCE CHARLES HALL

Sports Consultant. Personal: Born August 5, 1951; Son of Chuck Hall; Married Wanda Marie Brown, Daughter of Morris Brown; Father of Kimberly Marie, Ryan Todd. Education: Graduate, Edgewood High School, 1970; B.S. Physical Education 1974, M.B.A. Business Administration 1975, California State Polytechnic University. Military: Served with the California Army National Guard, Spec 6, 1971-77. Career: Sports Consultant, Professional Sports; Professional Sales, MacGregor Athletic; President, Chairman of the Board, Mueller-Hall, Inc.; Sales Representative, Sports West Sales. Organizational Memberships: Far West Ski Association, Vice President 1980; American Bowling Congress, President 1977; Mountain Meadows Golf Club, Treasurer 1981. Community Activities: American League of Professional Baseball Clubs, 1982; The National League of Professional Baseball Clubs, 1982; American Athletic Trainer Association, 1979; United States Golf Association, 1982; American National Red Cross, 1973; National Baseball Congress, 1981; United States Baseball Federation, 1980; National Athletic Trainers Association, 1979; National Sporting Goods Association, 1979; The Sports Foundation, 1979; Southern California Sports, 1982; Amateur Hockey Association of the United States, 1976; Sporting Goods Agents Association, 1979; The Athletic Institute. Honors and Awards: Top Salesman of the Year, 1976, 1977, 1978, 1979, 1980, 1981; Listed in *Who's Who in the West, Who's Who in America, Personalities of America, The Directory of Distinguished Americans, Community Leaders of America, Men of Achievement*. Address: 1450 South Cypress, Ontario, California 91761.■

WILFRED MCGREGOR HALL

Chairman and Chief Executive Officer. Personal: Born June 12, 1894; Son of Frederick F. and Annie Hall (deceased); Married Louise Thompson, Daughter of Lucien and Lizzie Thompson; Father of Frederick Folsom. Education: B.S., University of Colorado; Honorary Doctorate in Engineering, Tufts University. Military: Served with the United States Army, 1918. Career: Charles T. Main Company, Engineer Hydroelectric Construction 1916-17, Engineer Hydroelectric Investigation and Design 1920-22; Engineer, Chrisfield Contracting Company, 1919; Superintendent, Construction Engineering, UGI Contracting Company, 1922-28; Superintendent, Construction-Electric Bond and Share Company, 1929-31; Consulting Construction Engineer, 1932-33; Engineer in Charge of Construction, TVA, 1922-37; Manager, Engineer and Construction, P.R., 1937-41; with Charles T. Main, Inc. 1941 to present, Director 1943 to present, Chairman of the Board and Chief Executive Officer 1972 to present; Chairman and Chief Executive Officer, MAIN Constructors, Inc., 1981 to present; Chairman and Chief Executive Officer, The C. T. Main Corporation, 1981 to present. Organizational Memberships: Past Director, United States Commission of Large Dams; Fellow, American Society of Civil Engineers; Member, A.I.M., Fellow President's Council 1966; American Institute of Consulting Engineers, Past President Northeast Section; Past Director, Consulting Engineers Council of Northeast; Society of American Military Engineers; Newcomen Society in North America, Chairman Massachusetts Committee, Member of the Board; Member of the Board of Governors, Engineers Club of Boston; Boston Rotary Club, Past Director; Hamilton Trust, Past President; Director, Arkwright-Boston Manufacturers Insurance Company. Honors and Awards: Elected to Sigma Nu and Tau Beta Pi, University of Colorado; Distinguished Engineering Alumnus Award, University of Colorado; American Institute of Management's Marquis Award, 1965; American Society of Mechanical Engineers' George Westinghouse Gold Medal, 1971; George Norlin Silver Medal from the University of Colorado, 1972; Engineers Club of Boston, Engineer of the Year Award, 1977; Morgan Memorial Goodwill Industry's Distinguished Service Award, 1969. Address: 790 Boylston Street, The Fairfield, Boston, Massachusetts 02199.■

ROSEMARY N. HALLUM

Teacher, Writer, Consultant. Personal: Born October 2; Daughter of Fred F. Hallum. Education: B.A., University of California at Berkeley; M.A., San Jose State University; Ph.D., Walden University. Career: Teacher, Writer, Workshop Leader, Consultant, Piano Teacher; Former Positions include Dance and Exercise Teacher; Book Company Consultant; Teaching Assistant, Department of English, University of California at Berkeley; Summer Faculty/Extension Faculty, Boston University, University of Miami, Ottawa University, California State University-Hayward; Professional Pianist; Conducted Workshops in Early Childhood, Music, Movement, Language, Perceptual Motor Training, Social Dance, Creativity at Colleges and Universities, School Districts, Various Associations. Organizational Memberships: Phi Beta Kappa; Delta Kappa Gamma; Phi Delta Kappa; American Society of Composers, Authors and Publishers. Published Works: Author of *I Like to Read* series, *Action Reading Kit, Dr. Marcus Foster, a Man for all People, Beginnings, New Dimensions in Music*, and others; Composer of 24 records on Dance, Exercise and Movement; Producer of 6 Filmstrips; Author of Monthly Early Childhood Articles in *Teacher Magazine*, Contributor to *Childhood Education, California Magazine*. Honors and Awards: Scholarship, Delta Kappa Gamma, l981; Finalist Award, National Educational Film Festival, l974; Honorary Service Award, Parent-Teacher Association, l974; Best of the Year Filmstrip Award, *Previews*, 1975; Listed in *Who's Who in America, Who's Who in the West, Who's Who in California, World Who's Who of Women, Who's Who of American Women, International Who's Who in Community Service, International Who' Who of Intellectuals, Dictionary of International Biography, International Register of Profiles, American Registry, Community Leaders of America, Personalities of America, Personalities of the West and Midwest, Community Leaders and Noteworthy Americans, Notable Americans of the Bicentennial Era, Book of Honor, Men and Women of Distinction, International Book of Honor*. Address: l02l Otis Drive, Alameda, California 9450l.■

ROBERT D. HALVERSTADT

Senior Staff Vice President. Personal: Born January 25, 1920; Son of Roscoe B. and Dorothy Grubbs Halverstadt (both deceased); Father of Marta J. Carmen, Linda A. Orelup, Sally J. Education: Marine Officer Training, United States Coast Guard Academy, 1943; B.S.M.E., Case Institute of Technology, 1951; Apprentice Course Graduate, Republic Steel Corporation, 1945. Military: Served in the United States Coast Guard, 1943-45, attaining the rank of Lieutenant (jg). Career: Allegheny International, Senior Staff Vice President, President of Materials Technology Group, President and Board Member Special Metals Corporation; Co-chairman, Board Member, Titanium Metals Corporation of America; Vice President of Technology, Singer Company, 1973-74; Booz. Allen and Hamilton Inc., Group Vice President of Product and Process Design Group, Chief Executive Officer of Foster D. Snell Inc., President of Design and Development Inc., 1964-73; General Manager Operations Engineering, Continental Can Company, 1963-64; General Electric Company, Manager of Thomson Engineering Laboratory, Supervisor of Metal Working Research Laboratory, Engineer in Turbojet Engine Development, 1951-63; Republic Steel Corporation, Journeyman Machinist, Apprentice Machinist, 1940-51. Organizational Memberships: American Society of Mechanical Engineers; American Society for Metals, Fellow, Board of Trustees; American Institute for Chemical Engineers; Toastmasters International; Water Resources Association; Regional Plan Association; Chemists Club of New York; Oneida National Bank, Board Member; Centrex Laboratories, Board Member; Editorial Board, *International Journal of Turbo and Jet Engine Technology*. Community Activities: Utica Chamber of Commerce; Utica Industrial Development Council, Director; Industry Labor Education Council, Director, President; National Alliance of Business, Chairman; University Club of New York; Yahandasis Golf Club; Fort Schuyler Club; New York Academy of Science. Religion: United Church of Christ, Church School Teacher, Church School Superintendent. Honors and Awards: Commendation, President of the United States, 1976; Registered Professional Engineer, Ohio 1953, New York 1963; Three Patent Awards, General Electric Company, 1958; Fellow, A.S.M., 1977; Silver Anniversary Award, A.S.M., 1981; Tau Beta Pi; Sigma Xi; Listed in *Who's Who in Finance and Industry, Who's Who in the East, Who's Who in Technology Today, Who's Who in the World, Who's Who in Engineering*. Address: 333 Oenoke Ridge Road, New Canaan, Connecticut 06840.■

DOROTHY J. HAMAN

Marriage and Family Therapist. Personal: Born September 21, 1928; Daughter of F. W. Hensolt; Mother of Susan Haman Schubert, John H., Mark V., Frederick W. Education: B.S. Psychology/Sociology 1972, M.S.Ed. Guidance/Counseling 1974, University of Wisconsin-Platteville. Career: Marriage and Family Therapist. Community Activities: Founder, Galena Art Theatre, 1962; Regional Legislation Chairman, Parent and Teacher Association, 1963; Galena Citizens Advisory Committee, 1964; President, Galena Hospital Auxiliary, 1965; Director, Jo Daviess Cty Head Start, 1966; Board Member, Jo Daviess Cty Sheltered Workshop, 1975; Business and Professional Women's Association, 1980; Sedona Arts Center, 1982; Clinical Member, American Association of Marriage and Family Therapists, 1980; International Transactional Analysis Association, 1975. Honors and Awards: B.S. Degree with Honors. Address: P.O. Box 2295, Cottonwood, Arizona 86326.■

CALVIN S. HAMILTON

Planning Director. Personal: Born December 12, 1924; Married Glenda, Daughter of Mildred Padgett. Father of Seven Children. Education: Bachelor of Fine Arts in Landscape Architecture, University of Illinois, 1949; Master of City Planning, Harvard University Graduate School of Design, 1952; Research Associate, University College, Department of Town Planning, University of London, 1953. Military: Served with the United States Air Force, Radio Intelligence, 1943-46, Principal Duty

United States and Pacific Theatre. Career: Planning Director, City of Los Angeles; Former Executive Director of Planning in Indianapolis; Former Planning Consultant, Harland Bartholomew and Associates; Former Executive Director, Pittsburgh, Pennsylvania. Organizational Memberships: American Society of Landscape Architects, Fellow; Honorary Associate Member of American Institute of Architects; Member Executive Committee of Consultative Council, National Institute of Building Sciences; Member Council of Planning, Southern California Association of Governments; Civic Cen. Authority. Community Activities: Consultant, World Council of Churches, 1967; Former Member, Building Research Advisory Board, National Academy of Sciences, National Academy of Engineering, Executive Committee Co-Chairman, Technical Committee on Societal and Environmental Objectives; Chairman, United Way, 1982; Member Merced Theatre Consultant Committee; Member Board of Directors, Los Angeles Conservancy; Member Board of Directors, California Shore and Beach Preservation Association; Member Advisory Board, University of California at Los Angeles Extension School of Landscape Architecture; Member Board of Elders, Wilshire Presbyterian Church; Member Advisory Council, Los Angeles District Boy Scouts of America. Religion: Former Member General Board and Former Vice President, National Council of Churches of Christ, 1963-70; Former Member Board of Directors, Department of Urban Churches and Division of Home Missions, National Council of Churches, 1963-70. Honors and Awards: Bradford-Williams Award, American Society of Landscape Architects, 1973; Rotary International Foundation Fellowship for Advanced Study at the University of London, 1952-53; Selected by German Government for 4-Week Study Tour of Planning in German Cities, 1971; French Government for Study of New Innovative Transportation Technologies, 1972; Listed in *Who's Who in the West, Dictionary of International Biography, Community Leaders and Noteworthy Americans.* Address: 6298 Warner Drive, Los Angeles, California 90048.■

MADRID TURNER HAMILTON

Corporate President. Personal: Daughter of Paul (deceased) and Mary Hubert Turner; Married Norman Woodrow Hamilton (deceased); Mother of Alexander Turner. Education: B.A., Spelman College; M.S.W., Atlanta University; Ph.D., Union for Experimenting Colleges and Universities, 1979. Career: President, The M.T. Hamilton Enterpriese, Inc.; Licensed Realtor; Former Positions include Assistant Professor of Sociology, Morehouse College; Associate Professor of Social Work Education, San Francisco State University; Associate Professor of Sociology, University of Redlands; Social Worker, Bureau of Child Guidance, New York City Board of Education; Western Regional Director, Planned Parenthood Federation of America; Western Regional Representative, Family Service Association of America; Social Work Consultant, New York City Department of Public Health. Organizational Memberships: National Association of Social Workers; A.A.P.S.S. (formerly American Public Health Association); A.S.A.; A.K.D.-Sociology; Former Altrusan; Urban Bankers Association, 1983. Community Activities: Spelman College Alumnae Association, 1978; American Heritage Foundation, 1976; Founding Program Director, Columbia Area Young Women's Christian Association; Vice President, National Board of Young Women's Christian Association of United States of America; Young Women's Christian Association of San Francisco, Member, Vice President, Treasurer, Chairman Program Committee 1966-82; Young Women's Christian Association of Redlands, Treasurer, Chairman Finance Committee; Boards, United Way, White Plains (New York), Redlands; Volunteer, Urban League, New York, Bronx, San Francisco, Inland Empire; Spelman College Alumnae Association, Chairman Community Service Committee, Regional Coordinator; Founding President, Northern California Coalition of 100 Black Women, Former Positions include San Francisco President, Founder, California Coordinator, Population Study Commission; News Editor, San Francisco Democratic Women's Forum. Religion: Member of Presbyterian Church; Women's Day Speaker; Forums. Address: 136 Geneva Avenue, San Francisco, California 94112.■

FREDERICK GNICHTEL HAMMITT

Nuclear Engineer. Personal: Born September 25, 1923, in Trenton, New Jersey; Son of Andrew Baker and Julia (Stevenson Gnichtel) H.; Married Barbara Ann Hill on June 11, 1949; Father of Frederick, Harry, Jane. Education: B.S. Mechanical Engineering, Princeton University, 1944; M.S., University of Pennsylvania, 1949; M.S. Applied Mechanics, Stevens Institute, 1956; Ph.D. Nuclear Engineering, University of Michigan, 1958. Military: Served with the United States Navy, 1943-46. Career: Engineer, John A. Roebling Sons Company, Trenton 1946-68, Power Generators Ltd., Trenton 1948-50; Project Engineer, Reaction Motors Inc., Rockaway, New Jersey 1950-53, Worthington Corporation, Harrison, New Jersey 1953-55; Research Associate, University of Michigan, Ann Arbor 1955-57, Associate Research Engineer 1957-59, Associate Professor 1959-61, Professor Nuclear Engineering 1961 to present, Mechanical Engineering 1965 to present, Professor in Charge Cavitation and Multiphase Flow Laboratory 1967 to present; Consultant Government and Industry; Visiting Scholar Electricite de France, Paris, 1967, Societe Grenobloise Hydrauliques, Grenoble, France, 1971; Fulbright Senior Lecturer, French Nuclear Laboratory, Grenoble, 1974; Polish Academy Science Lecturer Institute Fluid Mechanics, Gdansk, 1976. Organizational Memberships: Registered Professional Engineer, New Jersey, Michigan, Fellow Institute Mechanical Engineers (U.K.); American Society of Mechanical Engineers, Past Chairman Cavitation Committee Fluids Division; A.S.T.M., Past Chairman Cavitation and Liquid Impingement; American Nuclear Society, Past Chairman Southeast Michigan Section; International Association Hydraulic Research, Chairman Cavitation Scale Effects Committee; Phi Beta Kappa; Sigma Xi; Tau Beta Pi. Religion: Presbyterian, Elder. Published Works: Author (with R. T. Knapp, J. W. Daily) *Cavitation* 1970, *Cavitation and Multiphase Flow Phenomena* 1980; Contributor 400 Articles to Professional Journals, 2 Chapters in Books; Patentee in Field. Address: 1306 Olivia Street, Ann Arbor, Michigan 48104.■

MARGARET FRANCES HAMPTON-KAUFFMAN

Bank Executive. Personal: Born May 12, 1947; Daughter of Mr. and Mrs. William Wade Hampton III; Married Kenneth Lee Kauffman, Son of LeRoy M. Kauffman. Education: M.B.A. Finance, Columbia University Graduate School of Business, 1973; Cours Superieur in French Language and Civilization, University of Nice, France, Summer 1969; B.A. summa cum laude with honors in French, Florida State University, 1969. Military: Served with AFROTC Auxiliary Drill Team and Service Organization, Angel Flight; Liaison Officer 1966-67, Comptroller 1967-68. Career: Senior Vice President, Corporate Planning, Bank South Corporation, Atlanta, Georgia, present; Vice President, Corporate Finance and Planning, National Bank of Georgia, Atlanta, 1976-81; A.V.P., Corporate Finance, Banking Industry Specialist, Manufacturer Hanover Trust Company, New York, 1975-76; Financial Analyst and Economist, Federal Reserve Board of Governors, Washington, D.C., 1973-74; Georgia Executive Women's Network Secretary, 1982-83. Organizational Memberships: Women's Forum, 1980 to present; Women's Commerce Club, 1981 to present; Planning Executives Institute, 1978 to present; American Institute of Banking, 1975 to present; The Institute of Management Sciences, 1978-79; The Institute of Financial Education, 1974-75; American Finance Association, 1973-74. Community Activities: Board of Trustees, Georgia Chapter Leukemia Society of America, 1980 to present, Vice President 1982-84, Treasurer 1981-82; Director of Atlanta Professional Women's Directory, 1981-83; Director of Accent Enterprises (Accent in Tango Restaurant, 1979-83); Member, High Technology Task Force, Atlanta Chamber of Commerce, 1982-83; Member, Government Affairs Subcommittee, Downtown Atlanta Chamber of Commerce, 1975-76; Guest Lecturer to Outside Groups at Small Business Seminars Sposored by SBA, Georgia State University, Emory University, DeKalb Chamber of Commerce and a Class on Project Feasibility Analysis at Georgia Institute of Technology; Alpha Delta Pi Sorority, 1965-69; Scholarship Chairman, Efficiency Chairman, Executive Board; Kappa Sigma Fraternity Little Sisters, 1966-69; President, Treasurer, Sweetheart, Snow Ball Queen. Religion: Episcopalian. Honors and Awards: An Outstanding Young Woman in America, 1978; Alcoa Foundation Fellow, 1973-74; Florida State University Hall of Fame, 1969; Phi Beta Kappa; Mortar Board; Garnet Key; Phi Kappa Phi; Beta Gamma Sigma; Gymnastica, Treasurer 1965-66; Pi Delta Phi, French, Vice President 1968-69; Outstanding Angel Merit Award, 1968; Listed in *International Who's Who of Intellectuals, Who's Who in Finance and Industry, Who's Who in the South and Southwest, Who's Who of American Women.* Address: 1065 West Paces Ferry Road, N.W., Atlanta, Georgia 30327.■

KENT R. HANCE

Congressman. Personal: Born November 14, 1942; Married Carol Hays; Father of Ron, Susan. Education: B.B.A., Texas Tech University, 1965; LL.B., University of Texas, 1968. Career: Member, United States House or Representatives, 1979 to present; Member, Texas Senate, 1974-78; Faculty, Texas Tech University, 1968-73; Law Practice in Lubbock, Texas, 1968-78. Organizational Memberships: 96th New Members Caucus, Chairman 1979 House Committee on Agriculture, Subcommittees on Cotton, Livestock and Grains, Conservation and Credit 1979-80; Science and Technology Committee, 1979-80; Consent Calendar Committee, 1979 to present; Committee on Ways and Means, Subcommittees on Trade and Public Assistance and Unemployment Compensation, 1981 to present; Texas Bar Association; American Bar Association. Community Activities: West Texas State University, Board of Regents 1972-74; Texas Boys' Ranch, Lubbock, Texas, Original Incorporator; Texas Tech Century Club; March of Dimes, Texas Chairman 1972-73; Water, Inc.; Southwest Lubbock Rotary Club; Lions Club; Chamber of Commerce. Religion: First Baptist Church. Honors and Awards: Best Freshman Congressman, *Texas Business Magazine*, 1980; Coalition for Peace throughStrength Leadership Award; Outstanding Professor, Texas Tech University. Address: P.O. Box 1, Lubbock, Texas 79401.■

JAMES ALPHONSO HANF

Naval Architect Technician, Poet. Personal: Born February 3, 1923; Married Ruth G.; Father of Maureen R. Career: Naval Architect Technician, Puget Sound Naval Shipyard, Bremerton; Lecturer on Writing Poetry for Clubs and Organizations. Organizational Memberships: New York Poetry Forum, Inc.; Stella Woodall Poetry

Society; Literarische Union (Germany); California Federation of Chaparral Poets; Ina Coolbrith Circle; International Academy of Poets; National Poetry Day Committee, Inc.; World Poetry Society; Kitsap County Wirters Club, President; Illinois State Poetry Society; Western World Haiku Society; International Biographical Association; International Platform Association. Religion: Baptist. Published Works: Poet, Specializing in Haiku (pseudonyms: James Alfred Wildwood, James Allen Wordsmith); Former Poetry Editor, *Coffee Break*; Author of Over 500 Poems Published in Books, Magazines and Anthologies, including *Washington Verse, Quickenings, Inky Trails, A.B.I.R.A. Digest, Poem, Adventures in Poetry*, and Others Published in Japan, Brazil, Argentine, Italy, India; Author of Journal Articles on Writing Poetry. Honors and Awards: Honorary Doctor of Literature, 1980; Poet Laureate, *Idaho* Magazine, 1978; Various Commendations, Awards and Prizes for Poetry; Diploma di Marito, Universita Delle Arti, Italy, 1982; Award of Recognition, *Inky Trails* Magazine, 1982; Special Honorary Memberships, Stella Woodall Poetry Society, 1982-83; Doctor of Literature, World University (expected 1983); Nominated Poet Laureate of Washington by International Poetry Society, 1981; Special Poetry Books given to him by Government of Sweden, 1982; Recipient of 1981 Testimonial of Outstanding Memberships in Annual Associate Category from A.B.I.R.A.; Listed in *Community Leaders of America, Community Leaders and Noteworthy Americans, International Who's Who of Intellectuals, Personalities of the West and Midwest, Who's Who in the West, Men of Achievement, International Who's Who in Poetry*. Address: P.O. Box 374, Bremerton, Washington 98310.■

EUGENE RALPH HANKS

Land Developer, Rancher, Forester. Personal: Born December 11, 1918; Married Frances Herrick; Father of Herrick, Russell, Stephen, Nina. Education: Attended California State Polytechnic University, 1939-40; Naval Aviation Cadet, Pensacola, 1942; University of Southern California, 1949-50; American University, 1958; Graduate, Armed Forces Command and Staff College, 1960; Naval Line School; Various Executive Short Courses. Military: Served with the United States Navy, Naval Aviator, rose through the ranks from Ensign to Captain, 1941-69. Career: Land Developer, Rancher, Forester; Naval Officer, 28 Years; Fighter Pilot (Ace), Test Pilot, Demonstration Pilot, "Blue Angel," First Operations Officer *USS Constellation* CVA64, Operations Director, Test Director. Organizational Memberships: American Fighter Aces Association; Combat Pilots Association; Blue Angels Association; Retired Officers Association; Naval Aviation Association; Naval Aviation Museum Foundation; National Rifle Association; National Foresters Association; Dun and Bradstreet Million Dollar Directory. Religion: Protestant. Honors and Awards: Navy Cross, 1943; Legion of Merit, 1968; Distinguished Flying Cross (2); Air Medal (7); Presidential Unit Citation; Various Campaign Medals. Address: Box 239, Mora, New Mexico 87732.■

BRADFORD CHARLES HANSON

Research Geologist. Personal: Born June 1, 1945; Son of Claude A. and Lucille M. Hanson. Education: B.S. Geology, University of Maryland, 1970; M.S. Geology, University of Arkansas, 1973; Postgraduate Studies in Geology, University of Kansas. Career: Senior Research Geologist, Louisiana Geological Survey, Baton Rouge, Louisiana; Consulting Geologist, 1979-80; Assistant Professor, West Texas State University, Western Michigan University, 1977-79; Research Scientist, University of Kansas Center for Research, Remote Sensing Laboratory, 1972-77. Organizational Memberships: Sigma Xi; American Association of Petroleum Geologists; Baton Rouge Geological Society, Charter Member, Society Sponsor A.A.P.G. Student Chapter, Louisiana State University 1982-83; National Water Well Association; Sigma Gamma Epsilon, Alpha Psi Chapter, Vice President 1971-72, University of Arkansas; Sigma Gamma Epsilon, Alpha Chapter, President 1973-74, University of Kansas. Community Activities: American Jaycees, 1979 to present; Advisory Committee, Research and Development, State of Louisiana Board of Regents, 1982 to present; Lecturer/Educator, Ground Water Workshops in Louisiana; Guest Speaker, Area Schools; Volunteer, Special Olympics. Honors and Awards: Listed in *Who's Who in the South and Southwest, Personalities of America, Men of Achievement, Biographical Roll of Honor, Directory of Distinguished Americans, International Book of Honor*. Address: 1680 O'Neal Lane, E-237, Baton Rouge, Louisiana 70816.■

ROBERT F. HARBRANT

Executive. Personal: Born October 6, 1942; Son of Berthol J. and Helen (Hankinson) Harbrant; Married Anne Pekala; Father of Christopher John, Mary Jeanne, Kathleen Marie, Julia Ann. Career: Food and Allied Service Trades Department, AFL-CIO, Executive Director 1977, Secretary-Treasurer 1977-79, President 1979 to present; Union Label and Service Trades Department, AFL-CIO, Public Relations Director 1967, Assistant to the Secretary 1972, Treasurer 1972, Established Consumer Boycott Division 1972, Executive Assistant 1974. Organizational Memberships: AFL-CIO Executive Council Ad Hoc Committees on Evolution of Work and Its Implications; Pension Investment; AFL-CIO Standing Committee on Community Services; AFL-CIO Standing Committee on Organization and Field Services; Coalition of Labor Union Women; Labor and Religion Conference Board of Directors; Labor Advisory Council, Center for Labor Research/Studies, Florida International University; Center for Labor and Industrial Relations, New York Institute of Technology; Executive Board, Consumer Federation of America. Community Activities: Boys Scouts of America, National Advisory Council, Chairman Labor Advisory Committee, National Catholic Committee on Scouting; American Civil Liberties Union; National Association for the Advancement of Colored People; Senior Advisory Board, Foundation on Violence in America; City of Hope National Labor Council; Claims Adjudication Board 58, United States Selective Service of Maryland; Sierra Club. Address: 815 Sixteenth Street, Northwest, Suite 408, Washington, District of Columbia 20006.■

EVELYN RENEE HARDAWAY

Data Processing Manager. Personal: Born December 19, 1948; Daughter of Mrs. Vesta M. Hardaway. Education: Attended the American Institute of Banking, Columbus, Georgia, 1969-70; Johnson C. Smith University, Charlotte, North Carolina, 1967-68. Career: Data Processing Manager, Katy Community Hospital, present; Manager/Operations Consultant, American Management Services; Account Executive, Flair Personnel Services; Office Manager, Cagle, Inc.; Auditing Clerk, First National Bank of Columbus. Organizational Memberships: National Association of Female Executives; International Platform Association. Community Activities: Blood Donor, 1976 to present; Big Sisters of Houston, 1978-79. Religion: Baptist. Honors and Awards: Operations Excellence Award, Houston District, 1st Quarter, 1979; Listed in *Who's Who of American Women, Personalities of the South, Personalities of America, Personalities of the World, The World Who's Who of Women, International Who's Who of Intellectuals, Biographical Roll of Honor*. Address: c/o Mrs. Vesta M. Hardaway, 5118 15th Avenue, Columbus, Georgia 31904.■

CAROLE MORGAN HARDY

Criminal Justice Consultant. Personal: Born July 26, 1946; Daughter of Sophia Hasty; Married Joseph Carl, Son of Mary Orloff. Education: B.A. 1969, M.A. Candidate, Wayne State University, Detroit, Michigan; M.A., Metropolitan Collegiate Institute, London, England, 1973; Postgraduate Studies, Oxford University, Oxford, England, 1977. Career: Criminal Justice Consultant; University Instructor; Management Consultant/Trainer; Administrator (public and private sectors). Organizational Memberships: American Jail Association, Chairperson Grants Committee 1983-84; National Association of Female Executives, Network Director; Entrepreneur's Alliance; Society for Marketing Professional Services; American Correctional Association; Graduate Association in Political Science, Chairperson 1972. Community Activities; San Jose Chamber of Commerce, 1981-83; Coalition of Human Services, Chairperson; "Our House," Drug and Alcohol Therapeutic Residence, Board of Directors; Colorado Governor's Task Force Appointment "Confidentiality and Access of Criminal Records", 1976-77; Law Enforcement Assistance Administration, 1978-79; National Institute of Mental Health; National Institute of Corrections Special Workshop/Task Force "Mental Health and Jails", 1973; Michigan Public Health Association Comprehensive Planning Council Task Force; 1971 Michigan Governor's Task Force "Crime Prevention and Community Relations." Honors and Awards: Pi Sigma Alpha, 1972; Listed in *Personalities of America, International Who's Who of Intellectuals, World Who's Who of Women, Who's Who of American Women, Outstanding Young Women in America*. Address: 1033 Rockcrest Drive, Marietta, Georgia 30062.■

TWO THOUSAND NOTABLE AMERICANS

Vicki Shell Hargrove

Personnel and Training Manager. Personal: Born July 4, 1947; Mother of One Son. Education: B.S. cum laude 1968, M.A. 1969, M.A. (plus 30 hours) 1972, Murray State University; Ph.D., The Ohio State University, 1979. Career: Personnel and Training Manager, Ohio River Steel Corporation, Calvert City, Kentucky, 1983 to present; Training Director, Airco Carbide, Louisville, Kentucky, 1982-83; Safety and Training Manager, Airco Carbide, Calvert City, Kentucky, 1981-82; Coordinator of Special Activities, Department of Industrial Education, Murray State University, 1978-81; Research Association, Interstate Curriculum Consortium, The Ohio State University, 1976-78; Distributive Education Coordinator and D.E.C.A. Advisor, Murray Area Vocational Education Center, 1972-76; Distributive Education Coordinator and D.E.C.A. Advisor, North Marshall High School, 1969-71; Teaching Assistant, Murray State University, 1968-69. Organizational Memberships: American Industrial Arts Association, Convention Exhibitor; American Council in Industrial Arts Teacher Education; Kentucky Industrial Education Association; Epsilon Pi Tau; National Association of Distributive Education Teachers, Past National Secretary-Treasurer, Past Member National Public Relations Committee, Past Chairman National Nominating Committee, Past State Membership Chairman, Life Member; American Vocational Association, Member House of Delegates, Presenter for Distributive Education Sessions, Past Member Advisory Committee for Member Benefits, Member and Recorder for Diatributive Education Sessions, Past Member Advisory Committee for Member Benefits, Member and Recorder for Distributive Education Policy and Planning Committee 1976-78; Kentucky Vocational Association, Past Vice President, Past Member State Nominating Committee, Past Distributive Education Memberships Chairman, Presenter at Distributive Education Sessions; Distributive Education Clubs of America, Central Regional Conference Consultant, Kentucky D.E.C.A. Board of Dirctors, Kentucky Constitution Committee, Kentucky Summer Camp Instructor, Chief Advisor for National Conference Area of Distribution Event, Ohio Fall Delegates Conference Judge, Ohio State Conference Judge; Council for Distributive Teacher Educators; Kentucky Association of Distributive Education Teachers, Past State President, Regional Secretary, Vice President; Phi Delta Kappa; American Vocational Education Research Association; American Educational Research Association. Community Activities: Parent-Teacher Association, Field Day Comittee Chairman, President Murray (Kentucky); Murray Woman's Club, Kappa Department Past Treasurer and Parliamentarian; Murray Swim Team, Swim Meet Timer and Line Judge; Charity Ball, Murray (Kentucky), Past Member Decorations, Publicity and Food Committees; Murray Country Club, Past Social Chairman; Children's Hospital Fund Drive, Volunteer for Muirfield Golf Tournament; Murray-Calloway County Swim Team Board, 1981-84; Chairperson, First District Parent-Teacher Association Committee, 1981-82. Religion: First United Methodist Church, Hannah Circle, Past Tresurer, Bible School Teacher. Published Works: Machine Shop State-of-the-Art Report, 1981; Number of Reports and Articles. Hoors and Awards: Outstanding Young Woman of Kentucky, 1980; Kentucky Board of Occupational Education Appointed Member of Advisory Committee to Area Vocational Education; Selected as Member of Advisory Committee on Eligibility and Accreditation for United States Department of Health, Education and Welfare, 1975-78; Outstanding Distributive Education Teacher of Kentucky, 1975; Favorite Teacher of North Marshall High School, 1971; Listed in *Outstanding Young Women of America, Personalities of the South, Who's Who Among Students in American Universities and Colleges, Community Leaders of America.* Address: 1528 Oxford Drive, Murray, Kentucky 42071.∎

Louise Harris

Researcher, Writer. Personal; Daughter of Samuel P. and Faustine M. Borden Harris (both deceased). Education: A.B., Economics, Brown University, 1926; Private Study in Organ with T. Tertius Noble, New York, 1938-42. Career: Researcher and Writer; Former Teacher and Recitalist of Piano and Organ. Organizational Memberships: American Guild of Organists, Life Member; American Historical Association; American Heritage Association; National Historical Society; National Archives; American Historical Association. Community Activities: Rhode Island Hospital, Children's Department; Brown University Medical School. Religion: Church Organist, 1929-50. Honors and Awards: Library of Human Resources in American Research Institute and American Heritage Association; Fellow, American Biographical Institute; Life Patron, A.B.I. Research Association; Life Fellow, Intercontinental Biographical Association; Life Fellow, Life Patron, International Institute of Community Service (now International Biographical Association); Honorary Fellow, Anglo-American Academy, England; Award of Statue of Victory "Personality of the Year" for 1974; Numerous Diplomas, Certificates, Desk and Wall Plaques; 3 Medals Minted in Royal Mint, London; Two Articles on the Pledge of Allegiance Published in Congressional Record; Listed in *Anglo-American Who's Who, International Book of Honor, Biographical Roll of Honor,* Numerous Other Biographical Listings. Address: 15 Jay Street, Rumford, Rhode Island 02916.∎

Paulette Proctor Harris

Faculty Member. Personal: Born October 5, 1949; Daughter of Mrs. Paul E. Proctor; Married Kenneth Lamar, Son of Lester M. Harris. Education: B.A. 1971, M.Ed. 1974, Augusta College; Doctoral Candidate, University of South Carolina, Columbia. Career: Faculty Member, School of Education, Augusta College; Former Teacher, Remedial Reading Instructor, Lead Teacher, Richmond County Public Schools, Augusta, Georgia. Community Activities: C.S.R.A. Reading Council, Membership Chairman 1982-83; C.S.R.A. Phi Delta Kappa, Research Representative, 1981-82; Rho Chapter Delta Kappa Gamma, Corresponding Secretary 1980 to present. Religion: Protestant. Honors and Awards: Houghton Elementary Teacher of the Year, 1974. Address: 2707 West Terrace Drive, Augusta, Georgia 30909.∎

Fred Joseph Harsaghy, Jr.

Educator. Personal: Born September 17, 1916; Married Helen Krusko; Father of Andrea Joan, Paula Jean, Beth Hope. Education: B.A. 1948, M.P.A. 1953, Ph.D. 1965, New York University; M.S. Library Science, Columbia University, 1954. Military: Served in the United States Army, 1943. Career: Assistant Reference Department, New York Public Library, 1930-37; Editorial Assistant, *Newsweek Magazine,* 1937-44; Supervisor, Reference Section, Department of State, Office of War Information/Voice of America, 1945-49; Director of American Information Centers in Nagoya, Kanazawa, Harodate, Japan, 1949-52; Reviews Editor, Institute Aeronautical Sciences, 1952-56; Chief Field Librarian, Arabian-American Oil Company, Dhahran, Saudi Arabia, 1956-60; Teacher of Social Studies, Danbury (Connecticut) High School, 1961-65; Professor of Political Science and American Civilization, Danbury State College, 1962-65; Lecturer in International Relations, 1974; College of Petroleum and Minerals, Dhahran, Saudi Arabia, Director Library Services, Professor 1965-69; Inter-American University, Puerto Rico, Area Director Libraries, Professor 1969-72; Chief Librarian/Professor, York College, City University of New York, 1972-74; Teacher of Special and Adult Education, Danbury Schools, 1975-84; Lecturer in Management and Political Science, University of New Haven, 1977-79; Consultant Developing School Facilities. Organizational Memberships: American Association of University Professors; American Society for Public Administration; American Association for the Advancement of Science; National Education Association; Special Libraries Association; American Library Association; American Management Association; American Academy of Political and Social Sciences; Association of Caribbean Universities and Research Institutes. Community Activities: Danbury Community Chorus; Renaissance Singers; Candlewood Choral Society. Religion: Member of Roman Catholic Church. Honors and Awards: New York State Scholar, 1944-48; Founder's Day Award, New York University, 1966. Address: P.O. Box 8897, Candlewood Hills, New Fairfield, Connecticut 06812.∎

Lawrence Clifford Hartge, Jr.

Marketing Manager. Personal: Born August 1, 1948, in Kearney, Nebraska; Son of Lawrence C. Hartge Sr. and Henrietta E. Hartge (Jurgens); Married Margaret L. Berge on June 9, 1980, in Montpellier, France. Education: B.S. Industrial Management and Computer Science, Purdue University, 1971; M.S. Management Information Systems, Krannert Graduate School of Management, Purdue University, 1972. Career: Marketing Manager, 3Com Corporation, Mt. View, California, 1981 to present; Manager Strategic Market Planning and Services of Business Computer Group 1980-81, Manager Data Communications Product Marketing 1977-80, Product Manager of Systems Communications 1976-77, Sales Development Manager for Canada and Western United States 1976, Regional Sales Support Engineer 1974-76, Project Manager 1972-74, Hewlett-Packard Company, Cupertino, California; Proprietor of Consulting and Contract-Software Firm, Software Dynamics, West Lafayette, Indiana, 1971-72; with Thermophysical Properties Research Center, West Lafayette, Indiana, 1970-71; Systems Analyst/Programmer, Eli Lilly and Company, Summer 1968; Applications Programmer, Flick-Reedy Corporation, Bensenville, Illinois, Summer 1968; Applications Programmer, Systems Science Corporation, Silver Spring, Maryland, Summer 1967; Programmer and Consultant in Game Theory and Geographic Data Mapping, University of Omaha, Omaha, Nebraska, Summer 1966. Organizational Memberships: Active Lecturer/Speaker, American Institute of Industrial Engineers, American Production and Inventory Control Society, Association for Computing Machinery, Australian Computer Society, Canadian Information Processing Society, Data Processing Management Association, Institute of Electrical and Electronic Engineers. Published Works: Author "Ethernet Arrives for Micros" *Interface Age* 1982, "Current Trends in On-line Business Systems" *Boeltin Technico del Centro de Informatica de la Facultad de Contabilidad y Administracion de la Universidad Nacional Autonoma de Mexico* 1980, "Is DDP Right for You?" *Computerworld* 1980, "Success with Distributed Data Processing Today and Its Future Direction" *Sixth International Congress — Data Processing in Europe* 1980, "HP's Network Concept Stresses Resource Sharing and Flexibility, *Data Communications* 1979, "Shop Floor Systems Sensitive to Workers' Habits" *Computerworld* 1977, "How to Tame the Data Monster that Electronic Technology Helped Create" *Maecon* 1976, "Computerized Manufacturing in the Job Shop" *Manufacturing Engineers* 1976, "Evaluation of Direct Heating Methods of Measuring Thermal Conductivity of Solids at High Temperatures," R. E. Taylor and L. C. Hartge Jr., *High Temperature-High Pressure* 1971. Honors and Awards: Listed in *Dictionary of International Biography, International Who's Who in Community Service, Who's Who in*

TWO THOUSAND NOTABLE AMERICANS

America, Notable Americans, Men of Achievement, Who's Who in Finance and Industry, Personalities of America, Book of Honor, Men and Women of Distinction, Directory of Distinguished Americans, Notable Personalities of America, Who's Who in the West, Who's Who in California, Who's Who in California Business and Finance, Personalities of the West and Midwest, The American Business Registry, Community Leaders and Noteworthy Americans, The American Education Registry, American Patriots of the 1980's. Address: 33218 Falcon Drive, Fremont, California 94536.■

NANCY LEE HARTMAN

Physician. Personal: Born July 29, 1951; Daughter of Mr. and Mrs. Richard Hartman. Education: Graduate, Barbizon School of Modeling, 1970; A.A. Medical Technology, Harcum Junior College, 1971; B.A. Biology, Lycoming College, 1974; M.S. Medical Biology, Long Island University, 1977; M.D. Medicine, American University of Caribbean, 1981; Intern, Williamsport Hospital School of Medical Technology; Certified as Medical Technologist by American Society of Clinical Pathologists; ECFMG Certification. Career: Second Year Resident in Internal Medicine; Former Positions include Technologist Microbiology Laboratory, North Shore Hospital; Paramedic, Porta Medic; Laboratory Supervisor, CLI Labs; Laboratory Technician, National Health Labs Inc., 1982; Developer Microbiology Department, North Shore Laboratories, Inc., 1976-78; Laboratory Technician, Drekter and Heisler Laboratories, 1975; Microbiology Department, New York Hospital and Cornell Medical Center, 1974-75; Director Microbiology Department, Jersey Shore Hospital, 1974; Clinical Laboratory Technician, Renovo Hospital, 1974; Intern, Williamsport Hospital, 1972-73; Clinical Laboratory Technician, Lock Haven Hospital, 1971-72. Organizational Memberships: New York Academy of Sciences, 1983; American Society for Microbiology, 1976; American Society of Clinical Pathologists, 1974. Honors and Awards: Allied Health Professions Traineeship Grant, 1975-77; Listed in *Five Thousand Personalities of the World, World Who's Who of Women, International Who's Who of Intellectuals, International Book of Honor, Directory of Distinguished Americans, Personalities of America, Who's Who of American Women.* Address: P.O. Box 98, Roslyn, New York 11576.■

CHERYL DELK HARTZOG

Animal Care Specialist. Personal: Born February 14, 1944; Daughter of W. R. (deceased) and Bertie Lee Delk; Married Daniel Edward Hartzog; Mother of Wendy Virginia, George Terrance, Daniel Jefferson. Education: Certified in Basic Banking by American Institute of Banking, Orangeburg Calhoun Technical College, 1972; Attended South Carolina Bankers School, University of South Carolina, 1973; Certified in Firefighting Technology by South Carolina Fire School, 1975; Certified in First Aid to the Injured by American National Red Cross, 1978; Certified Graphologist by Institute of Graphology, 1980; Certified as Animal Care Specialist/Veterinarian Assistant by North American Student of Animal Sciences Association; Certified in Radiological Monitoring by Department of Defense, Defense Civil Preparedness Agency. Career: Animal Care Specialist, Graphologist, Genealogist, Notary Public for South Carolina; Head Teller, Secretary and Supervisor of Operations, American Bank and Trust, 1965-74; Cashier, Sweden Gin Company, 1965; Cashier/Secretary, State Realty and Insurance Company, 1962-64. Community Activities: Secretary/Treasury, Hilda Volunteer Fire Department, 1973-84; Hilda Firemen's Fun Festival, Chairman, Beauty Contest Co-Chairman, Ticket Chairman, Novelty Chairman, King/Queen Contest Chairman, Finance Chairman 1975-84; Hilda Firemen's Spring Fair, Ticket Chairman, Treasurer; Oakland Quartet Concert, Chairman, Ticket Chairman, Advance Ticket Chairman, Entertainment Chairman; Secretary/Treasurer, Hilda Transportation Company, Inc. (School Bus); Secretary/Treasurer, Hilda Fellowship Club, 1975-84; Director, Hilda Community Drama Club; Woodmen of the World Woodcraft, 1981-84; Chairman Hilda Section, American Cancer Society, 1978-84; Chairman, Hilda Community Senior Citizen's Annual Social; Delegate, South Carolina Democratic Party Convention, Barnwell County, 1980-84; Hilda Firecracker Lawn-Mower Race Planning Committee, Advance Ticket Chairman 1983, Registration Chairman 1983; South Carolina Historical Society; *South Carolina Historical Magazine; South Carolina Magazine of Ancestral Research.* Religion: W.M.U. Director, Secretary; Director of Library Service; Choir Member, Officer, Soloist, Quartet Member; Sunday School Class Officer; Circle Member; Acteens Leader; Assistant Teacher Junior Girls; Vacation Bible School Teacher, Secretary; Church Council; Director, Church Drama Club; Founder, Baptist Young Women's Circle. Honors and Awards: Outstanding Service and Dedication Award, Hilda Volunteer Fire Department, 1977; I-Dare-You Honor Roll, Danforth Foundation, 1958; Listed in *Personalities of the South, Community Leaders of America, Personalities of America, Directory of Distinguished Americans, Biographical Roll of Honor, International Book of Honor, Notable Americans, Community Leaders of the World, World Who's Who of Women, Dictionary of International Biography.* Address: 120 Old Salem Road, P.O. Box 127, Hilda, South Carolina 29813.■

DANIEL EDWARD HARTZOG

Construction Project Manager. Personal: Born May 9, 1942; Son of Mr. and Mrs. George E. Hartzog; Married Cheryl Delk, Daughter of W. R. (deceased) and Bertie H. Delk; Father of Wendy Virginia, George Terrance, Daniel Jefferson. Education: Drafting I Certificate, Orangebrug-Calhoun Technical College; Teachers Certificate, State of South Carolina Department of Education; Jobsite Supervision Certificate, Associated General Contractors of America Inc.; Construction Motivation Seminar Certificate, Management Analysis Institute (Orlando, Florida); Certificate, South Carolina Firefighter School; Multimedia System Instruction First Aid to the Injured Certificate, American National Red Cross; Radiological Monitoring Certificate, Defense Civil Preparedness Agency. Military: Served in the United States Army National Guard of South Carolina, 1960-68 and 1973-77, attaining the rank of Sergeant. Career: Construction Project Manager, C.M.A. Construction Engineers Inc., 1979 to present; Job Superintendent, Perry M. Hartley Company Inc., 1976-79; Supervisor, Hartzog Construction Company, 1969-76; Supervisor, Hartley and Dicks Construction Company, 1967-69; Finish Carpenter 1965-67, Carpenter's Helper 1963-65, Hartzog Construction Company; Supervisor Assistant, Bud Berma Inc., 1961-63; Laborer, Hartzog Construction Company, 1957-60. Community Activities: Councilman 1971-79, Building Inspector 1971-79, Fire Inspector 1971-79, Town of Hilda; Trustee, Firemen's Insurance & Inspection Fund, 1973-79; Town of Hilda Councilman in Charge of Fire Department, 1971-79; Hilda Volunteer Fire Department, Lieutenant, 1973-83, 1984; Hilda Firemen's Spring Fair, Labor Chairman 1974-75, 1976, 1977; Oakland Quartet Concert, Seating Chairman 1974 & 1975, Concession Chairman 1976, Master of Ceremonies 1976; Hilda Firemen's Fun Festival, Chairman 1975 and 1976, Co-Chairman 1977 & 1978, Labor Chairman 1979, 1980, 1981, 1982, 1983, 1984; Hilda Firecracker Lawn-Mower Race, Inspector and Rules 1983; Hilda Transportation President, 1971-75; Hilda Community Center Committee, 1963-70; Cub Scout Leader, 1979, 1980; Hilda Fellowship Club, President 1975, 1976, 1980, 1981, Treasurer 1977 and 1978, Membership Committee Chairman 1978, 1979, Vice President 1982 and 1983; Hilda Community Senior Citizens Annual Social, Seating and Picture Chairman 1977-83; George Hartzog Family Reunion, Vice President 1977-78, President 1978-79; Charlie Hartzog Family Reunion, 1960-83; Jame L. Still Family Reunion, Vice President 1980; James W. Collins Family Reunion, 1982, 1983; Jacob Delk Family Reunion, 1981-83; Woodmen of the World; Harmony Masonic Lodge; U.S. Army National Guard Non-Commissioned Officers Club, 1976-77; Barnwell County Area Vocational School Carpentry Advisory Board, 1979-83; Barnwell County Advisory Committee, 1982, 1983. Religion: Double Pond Baptist Church. Honors and Awards: Outstanding Service Award 1979, for Service as Councilman for Town of Hilda 1971-79; Outstanding Service Award 1979, for Service as Lieutenant on Hilda Volunteer Fire Department 1973-79; Listed in *Who's Who in South Carolina, Personalities of the South, Community Leaders of America, Personalities of America, Directory of Distinguished Americans, Biographical Roll of Honor, International Book of Honor, Community Leaders of the World, Dictionary of International Biography.* Address: P.O. Box 127, Hilda, South Carolina 29813.■

FRANK JOSEPH HATAJACK

Commercial Oil Field Diver/Welder. Personal: Born July 1, 1945, in Port Jefferson, New York; Son of Frank Joseph (deceased) and Helen Lucy Hatajack; Married Susan N. Gray on February 18, 1979. Education: Graduate, Sayville High School, New York, 1959-63; B.S. Geological Engineering, Michigan Technological University, 1963-68; Attended Divers Institute of Technology, Washington, 1972; Welder Certificate, Diver Industrial Welding School, 1975; First Class FCC Radio Telephone Update License/Radar Endorsement, RETS, LA, 1980; Taylor Diving "In House" Training, Update on Diving Techniques, 1973 to present. Military: Served with the United States Navy, Aviation Electronic Technology, E-5, 1968-72; Stationed NAS Whidbey Island and *U.S.S. Constellation.* Religion: Seventh Day Adventist. Honors and Awards: First Eagle Scout of Troop 91, Boy Scouts of America, New York, 1960; VA-165 United States Navy Sailor of the Month, 1972; United States Navy Commendation for Activities in Vietnam, 1972; Listed in *Who's Who in the South and Southwest, Personalities of the South, Personalities of America, Distinguished Americans, Men of Achievement, Distinguished Americans, Men of Achievement, Biographical Roll of Honor, International Book of Honor.* Address: 78 Schill Avenue, Kenner, Louisiana 70065.■

RICHARD HENRY HAUCK

Educator. Personal: Born April 19, 1930; Son of George W. and Kathryn D. Hauck; Married Gilda T., Daughter of Francisco and Gregoria Tan; Father of Richard

Daniels. Education: B.Sc., Shippensburg University, 1957; Graduate Work in Instructional Media 1972, M.Sc. 1983, University of Bridgeport, Connecticut. Military: Served with the United States Air Force-ANG 1947-56, Active Duty 1952-53, AP, Class Instructor Photography, PIO HQ Officer, Honorable Discharge. Career: Chemistry and Physics Instructor, US-NDCC, Carson Long Institute, New Bloomfield, Pennsylvania, 1982 to present; Science Teacher, Morgan City Junior High School, Morgan City, Louisiana, 1979-82; Photographer, Graphic Artist, Prop Mechanic, Essex Machine Works, Essex, Connecticut, 1976-79; Editor, *Raintree Illustrated Science Encyclopedia)*, L. Urdang, Inc., 1978; Technical and Educational Consultant, Liaison Work with International Systems of Education and Economics, Originator of Bicentennial Commemorative Note Issue, Development of Curricula for Public Schools and Industrial Activity, Consultant for Projects "Learn" and "Polarity," Foreign Education Advisor and Manager for Banking, Project Work for Federal Funding, Full and Part-time, Educational Research Associates, Inc., Saybrook, Connecticut, 1969-77; Science Teacher and Curriculum Development for Board of Education, Milford, Connecticut, 1967-74; Science Teacher and AV Director for Board of Education, Montville, Connecticut, 1965-67; Water Chemist for Nuclear Powered Systems, Electric Boat Division, General Dynamics, Groton, Connecticut, 1964-65; Teacher of Chemistry, Physics, Science and Math, English in Various School Systems in California, Louisiana, Pennsylvania and Connecticut, Reporting and Photography for News Media, Manager of CCTV, 1957-64. Organizational Memberships: American Association for the Advancement of Science, 1963 to present; National Science Teachers Association, 1961 to present; New York Academy of Science, 1981 to present; Educational Research Association, 1969 to present, Consultant and President. Community Activities: Washington Fire Company, Mechanicsburg, Pennsylvania, 1947 to present; American Legion, 1953 to present; MD for Paper Money Club 1959-75, Charter Member; AF&AM 1963-77, Master 1971-72; Lions International 1963 to present, Secretary, Charter Member, Delegate; New England Numismatic Association, 1963-75; Great Eastern Numismatic Association 1963-77, Board of Governors; Education Research Association 1969 to present, Consultant, President, Member Board of Directors; Foreign Education Manager, Clinton National Bank, 1970-72; Connecticut Educational Media Association 1970, Founding Member; World Monies Museum, Director, 1973-76; Benefactor, University of Bohol, 1981. Honors and Awards: Episcopal Church Award for Sunday School Teacher, 1973; United States Navy Award for IBM Numbering Systems in Stock Control, 1951; Commemorative Pennsylvania Recogition for Teacher Promotion Student Interest in Science, 1959; Connecticut State Science Teachers Journal for Curriculum Development, 1962; Electric Boat Award for Revision of Winkler Test for Oxygen, 1965; Episcopal Church Award for Sunday School Teaching, 1973; Lions Club Special Award, 1975; University Bohol, P.I. Awards for Assistance in Educational Materials, Deemed Benefactor of the University, 1977; Charter Member Tiger Island Lions Club, 1981; American Biographical Institute, 1983; Listed in *Who's Who in America*. Address: 112 South Market Street, Mechanicsburg, Pennsylvania 17055.■

WERNER KARL HAUSMANN

Director of Quality Assurance. Personal: Born March 9, 1921; Married Helen Margaret; Father of Gregory Gustav. Education: M.S. Chemical Engineering 1945, D.Sc. 1947, Swiss Federation Institute of Technology; Postdoctoral Fellow, University of London, England, 1947-48. Military: Served in the Swiss Army, First Lieutenant, 1939-46. Career: Director Quality Assurance, Adria Laboratories, Inc.; Medical Research, New York City; Research Group Leader, Lederle Laboratories, Pearl River, New York; Associate Director Quality Control, Ayerst Laboratories, Rouses, Point, New York; Director Quality Control, Stuart Pharmaceutical Company, Pasadena, California. Organizational Memberships: American Society Quality Control, Certified Quality Engineer; Senior Member, Vice Chairman 1981, Chairman of Columbus Section 1982-83; New York Academy of Sciences, Fellow; American Association for the Advancement of Science, Fellow; Educational Television Association, President 1970-71; Civil Defense Radiation Officer, 1962-66; American Management Association, Taught Courses in Quality Control. Religion: Presbyterian. Honors and Awards: Postdoctoral Fellow, University of London, England, 1947-48; Fellow, New York Academy of Sciences, 1959; Fellow, American Association for the Advancement of Science, 1966. Address: 4610 Sandringham Drive, Columbus, Ohio 43220.■

TEDDIE NARVER HAYES

Technical Instructor. Personal: Born January 24, 1942; Son of Jake Hayes; Married Addie Adams; Father of Teddie Narver II. Education: Graduate of Carver High School, 1961; Attended North Carolina College, 1961-64; Diploma, United States Army Signal School, 1965; Associate Degree in Aviation Instrument/Electronics 1979, Airframe and Powerplant 1981, Spartan School of Aeronautics. Military: Served in the United States Army, 1964-78, attaining the rank of SSG; Served in the United States Army National Guard and Army Reserve. Career: Technical Instructor of International Students; Avionics Instructor, Pilot and A&P Mechanic. Organizational Memberships: Civil Air Patrol, Second Lieutenant, Command Pilot and Training Officer; Negro Airmen International; Aircraft Owners and Pilots Association. Community Activities: U.S.O. Service, Volunteer 1968; Church Brotherhood, President. Religion: Asbury Mt. Olive United Methodist Church. Honors and Awards: U.S.O. Serviceman of the Year, 1972; Commander's Award, Civil Air Patrol, 1975; Honor Graduate, Spartan School of Aeronautics, 1979. Address: 7221 S.W. Greenview Terrace, Topeka, Kansas 66619.■

WILLIAM IVERSON HEAD, SR.

Superintendent. Personal: Born April 4, 1925; Son of Mrs. D. R. Howard; Father of William I. Jr., Connie Suzanne, Alan David. Education: B.S. Textile Engineering, Georgia Institute of Technology, 1950. Military: Served with the United States Navy, World War II 3 Years, Pacific Theater, Aviation Radioman/Gunner in Dive Bombers; Reserve 40 Years, Captain. Career: Superintendent, Acetate Yarn Department, Fibers Division, Tennessee Eastman (Kodak), present; Superintendent, Various Departments, Acetate Yarn Division, Tennessee Eastman, 1966-76; Senior Textile Engineer in Charge of Acetate Quality Control, 1957-66; Textile Engineering, R&D and Quality Control, 1949-56. Organizational Memberships: American Association for Textile Technology; American Chemical Society; American Society for Quality Control. Community Activities: Kiwanis; Elks; Moose; Consultant, Radiological Unit, Sullivan County Civil Defense; Reserve Officers Association, Tennessee Vice President 1978-81, Tennessee President 1981-82; Naval Reserve Association; VFW; Military Order of World Wars; Retired Officers Association; International Platform Association; Mensa, East Tennessee President 1977-80; Intertel; The International Society for Philosophical Enquiry ("The Thousand"), Elected Fellow and Personnel Consultant 1978, International Vice President 1979, Senior Research Fellow and International President 1980 to present. Honors and Awards: Issued Five United States Patents of Significant Commercial Importance (mostly related to textured yarns); Three British Patents; Several French, German and Japanese Patents; Decorated Commendation Medal and Selected Service Meritorious Service Medal; Listed in *Who's Who in the South and Southwest*, *International Who's Who of Intellectuals*, *Directory of Distinguished Americans, Men of Achievement*. Address: 2026 Bruce Street, Kingsport, Tennessee 37664.■

CHARLES VIRGIL HEARN

Clergyman, Behavioral Scientist. Personal: Born September 4, 1930, in Westport, Indiana; Son of Forrest V. and Emma F. Hearn; Married Linda Elmendorf; Father of Debra Lynn, Charles Gregory, Martin Curtis. Education: Ph.D., Thomas A. Edison University, 1972; D.D., Trinity Hall College and Seminary, 1977; Diploma, Palm Beach Psychotherapy Training Center, 1976. Military: Served in the United States Army, 1951-53, attaining the rank of S.F.C. Career: Ordained to Ministry, Methodist Church, 1958; Pastor, Various Methodist Churches, Indiana, Texas, Wyoming, California, 1958-70; Interpersonal Minister, St. Albans Church of the Way, San Francisco, 1974 to present; Clergyman and Counselor, Green Oak Ranch Boys Camp, California, 1969-70; Director of Rehabilitation, Mary-Lind Foundation, Los Angeles, 1970-71; Medical Assistant, Fireside Hospital, Santa Monica, California, 1971-72; Director, Alcoholism Program, Patrician Hospital, Santa Monica, 1972-74; Proprietor, Executive Director, Consultation, Mediation, Referral, Santa Monica, 1974 to present; Vice Chairman, Western Los Angeles Alcoholism Coalition, 1974-78. Organizational Memberships: American Ministerial Association, President; American Board of Examiners in Psychotherapy, Diplomate; American Academy of Behavioral Science, Fellow; Association for Social Psychology; Western Association of Christians for Psychological Studies; National Council on Family Relations; American College of Clinic Administrators; Association of Labor-Management Administrators; Fellow, the International Council of Sex Education and Parenthood of the American University, Washington D.C. Community Activities: Western Los Angeles Alcoholism Alliance, Various Offices; Coastal Region Health Services, Proposal Review Committee; Special Advisor to Various Private/Non-Profit Programs; Democrat. Published Works: Contributor of Numerous Articles on Psychotherapy to Professional Publications. Honors and Awards: Bronze Star, United States Army; Listed in *Who's Who in the West*. Address: 1248 11th Street, Suite B, Santa Monica, California 90401.■

TWO THOUSAND NOTABLE AMERICANS

MARK HEATH

Dominican House of Studies President. Personal: Born April 20, 1918; Son of Leslie and Genevive Stapleton Heath. Education: B.S. United States Naval Academy, 1940; B.A., Providence College, 1943; S.T.L. Dominican House of Studies, 1948; Ph.D., University of St. Thomas, Rome, 1952; LL.D., La Salle College, 1965. Military: Graduate, United States Naval Academy, 1936-40. Career: President, Dominican House of Studies, 1976 to present; Director, Washington Theological Consortium, 1973-76; Chairman Graduate Departments Religious Studies and Religious Education, La Salle College 1965-68, Providence College 1967-73. Organizational Memberships: College Theology Society, President 1968-70; Association Professors Researchers Religious Education, Executive Committee 1974-76. Community Activities: Liturgical Committee Archdiocese of Philadelphia; Ecumenical Commission Diocese of Providence; Roman Catholic/Southern Baptist Dialogue; Director, Theological Colloquium Conference of Catholic Learned Societies. Religion: Ordained Roman Catholic Priest, 1947. Honors and Awards: LL.D., La Salle College, 1963. Address: 487 Michigan Avenue Northeast, Washington, D.C. 20017.■

GARRETT THOMAS HEBERLEIN

Graduate College Dean, Vice Provost for Research. Personal: Born April 11, 1939; Son of Edward Garrett and Ruth Andrus Heberlein; Married Donna Lee Frohm; Father of Wendy Ann, Edward Garrett. Education: Graduate, New Canaan High School, 1957; A.B., Ohio Wesleyan University, 1961; M.S., Northwestern University, 1963; Ph.D., State University of Ghent (Belgium), 1966; Postdoctoral Studies, 1967. Career: Dean of the Graduate College, Vice Provost for Research, Bowling Green State University; Assistant Professor, New York University, 1967-70; Associate Professor and Chair of Department of Biology, New York University, 1970-72; Associate Professor and Chair of Biological Sciences, University of Missouri, St. Louis, 1972-75; Professor and Chair of Department of Biological Sciences, Bowling Green State University, 1976-80. Organizational Memberships: Sigma Xi Science Honorary 1965 to present, Chapter President 1975; Beta Beta Beta Science Honorary, 1980 to present; New York Academy of Sciences; American Association for Advancement of Science; American Society for Microbiology; American Society of Plant Physiologists; Ohio Academy of Science National Council of University Research Administrators. Community Activities: Kiwanis International, 1978 to present; Phi Gamma Delta, 1957; Junto Philosophical Society, 1979, Chair Executive Committee 1981, President 1982; Planning Committee and Trustee University Heights Day Care Center, 1970-72; Metropolitan St. Louis Planning Board, 1973-76; Fund Raising Committees for League of Women Voters; American Cancer Society and United Way; Bowling Green City School Tax Levy Committee, 1981. Religion: Trustee and Elder, University Heights Presbyterian Church, New York, 1969-72; Elder, First Presbyterian Church, Bowling Green, Ohio 1979 to present, Chair Stewardship Committee 1981-82. Honors and Awards: Sigma Xi Young Scientist Award for Distinguished Research, 1970; St. Louis Business Leader of the Day Award, 1974; Research Grants from American Cancer Society 1967-69, National Institutes of Health 1963-82, Jane Coffin Child Memorial Fund for Medical Research 1966-72, Food and Drug Administration 1976-77, National Science Foundation 1976-80; N.I.G. Predoctoral Fellowship, 1962-65; Jane Coffin Childician Memorial Fund for Medical Research Postdoctoral Fellowship, 1965-67. Address: 1111 Bourgogne, Bowling Green, Ohio 43402.■

FREDERICK HECHT

Physician/Scientist, Institute President and Director. Personal: Born July 11, 1930; Son of Malcolm and Lucile Hecht; Married Dr. Barbara Kaiser-McCaw Hecht; Father of Frederick Malcolm, Matthew Winchester, Maude Bancroft, Tobias Orchs, Karrie McCaw (stepchild), Brian S. McCaw (stepchild). Education: B.A., Dartmouth College, 1952; Attended University of Paris, 1950-51; Middlebury College, 1952; Boston University, 1955-56; University of Rochester, Maryland, 1960. Military: Served with the United States Army, Sergeant, 1952-55, Interpreter-Translator of Russian, German, French. Career: Physician/Scientist; President and Director, Southwest Biomedical Research Institute; Professor of Pediatrics and Perinatal Medicine, University of Oregon Medical School, 1965-78; Postdoctoral Research Fellow in Medical Genetics and Pediatrics, University of Washington, 1962-65. Organizational Memberships: President and Director, The Genetics Center of Southwest Biomedical Research Institute, 1978 to present; Editorial Boards of the *American Journal of Human Genetics* 1977 to present, and *Cancer Genetics and Cytogenetics* 1980 to present. Community Activities: Boards of Directors, Youth Law Center (San Francisco), Hemophilia Association (Phoenix), Pilot Parents (Arizona), and the Arizona Center for Law in the Public Interest; Chairman of the Board, Southwest Biomedical Research Institute, 1978 to present. Religion: Director of the Jewish Genetic Disease Center (Arizona), 1980 to present. Honors and Awards: B.A. with honors, Dartmouth College, 1952; M.S. with distinction, University of Rochester, 1960; Alpha Omega Alpha Medical Honor Society, 1960; Ross Pediatric Research Award, 1970; Travelling Fellow of the Royal Society of Medicine, 1970-72; Various Scientific and Medical Honors. Address: The Genetics Center of Southwest Biomedical Research Institute, 123 East University Drive, Tampa, Arizona 85281.■

ROBERT H. HECKART

Clergyman, Lecturer, Educator, Author. Personal: Married Alice Pearl; Father of Paul R., Ruth E., Esther M., James R. Education: Pastor, 1922-48, 1957-58, 1973-76; District Superintendent, 1937-39; Commissioned General Evangelist, 1968-73, 1976 to present; College President, 1948-57; Camp Meeting Board Secretary 5 Years, President 16 Years; Served on Various Church Councils, Boards and Commissions Many Years; Elected Delegate to 5 Quadrennial General Conferences of His Denomination; Conducted 4 Missionary, Education, Evangelistic Missions to Numerous Countries in Latin America and West Indies, 3 to Mexico; Conducted 9 Study Tours to Europe, Asia, Africa, Mid-East and Israeli; Conducted Numerous Prophetic Conventions throughout the United States and Abroad; Conducted Prophetic Seminars in Bible Colleges; Radio Speaker; Member and Officer, President, Secretary, Treasurer in Ministerial Alliances in Various Cities; Air Raid Warden, World War II. Organizational Memberships: Delta Epsilon Chi Society. Published Works: Author, *Behold the Lamb of God*, *The Shepherd Psalm*, *Book on the Revelation* (in progress); Numerous Sermons and Articles for Religious Journals and for Ministerial Conventions. Honors and Awards: Recipient of Several Awards in Sermon Writing Contests; Citation and Bronze Plaque for 50 Years Meritorious Service to His Denomination. Address: 2022 Condor Street, Colorado Springs, Colorado 80909.■

MARILYN PATTON MANGUM HEILMAN

Retired. Personal: Born August 31, 1925; Daughter of Frank Mangum and Juanita Emerson; Married Walter Ritter Heilman, Jr. (deceased); Mother of Walter Ritter III. Education: B.A., Lindenwood College, 1947; M.A., East Tennessee State University, 1970. Career: Special Instructor in Modern Dance, Wake Forest College, 1957; Visiting Instructor in Art Education, East Tennessee State University, Summer 1971; Teacher, Art, History and Humanities, Bearden High School, Knoxville, Tennessee, 1958-81; Art Work Exhibited at E. G. Fisher Library, Lindenwood College, Hyatt Regency Hotel, Slocumb Gallery of East Tennessee State University, Offices of Volunteer Knoxville, West Town Mall (Knoxville). Organizational Memberships: National Art Education Association, Life Member, Vice President 1982-84, Director of Secondary Division 1977-79; National Art Honor Society and High School Students, National Director; Tennessee Art Education Association, President 1971-73; East Tennessee Art Education Association, Chairman 1964-67; American Crafts Council, 1961-81; International Society for Education through Art, 1965-84; United States Society for Education through Art, 1974-84; National Education Association, 1958-81; Tennessee Education Association, 1958-81; East Tennessee Education Association, 1958-81; American Associaton of University Women,~1948-81; Tennessee Arts Alliance, 1980-82; International Biographical Association. Community Activities: Member Board of Directors, Green County Heritage Trust, Greeneville Arts Guild; Chairperson, Greeneville/Greene County Bicentennial Weekend, April 23-26. Religion: Sunday School Teacher for Men and Women's Lancaster Class, Circle Co-Chairperson and Bible Study Teacher, Reporter for Tuesday Book Club. Published Works: "Report of the Secondary Division Sessions" *Career Education and the Art Teaching Profession*. Honors and Awards: Award for Outstanding Contributions to the Profession of Art Education, Eastern Regional N.A.E.A.; Significant Contribution to American Education Award, National Study of School Evaluations; Outstanding Contributions to the Profession of Art Education Award, Southeastern Regional N.A.E.A.; Award in Appreciation for Dedicated Service as a Member of the Board of Directors of the National Art Association, 1979; Listed in *Outstanding Secondary Educators, International Who's Who of Intellectuals, World Who's Who of Women, Dictionary of International Biography, International Register of Profiles, Men and Women of Distinction, Notable Americans*. Address: Apt. 18, Box 451-A, Greeneville, Tennessee 37743.■

DONALD CAIRNEY HELM

Research Geohydrologist, Group Leader. Personal: Born March 26, 1937; Son of Rev. Dr. Nathan T. and Rebecca C. Helm; Married Karen Reed, Daughter of Carl Reed (deceased) and Vera Dexter; Father of Rebecca Bernice. Education: B.A. cum laude, Amherst College, Amherst, Massachusetts, 1959; M.Div., Hartford Theological Seminary, Hartford, Connecticut, 1962; Attended Colorado School of Mines, Golden, Colorado, 1962-63, 1964-65; M.S. 1970, Ph.D. 1974, University of California at Berkeley. Career: Research Geohydrologist, University of California, Lawrence Livermore National Laboratory; Group Leader, Geohydrology and

Environmental Studies Group, 1981-82; Youth Advisor, Avon Congregational Church, Avon, Connecticut, 1959-62; Village Development Volunteer, Mitraniketan, India, 1963-64; Ground-Water Hydrologist, United States Geological Survey, 1965-78; Visiting Research Hydrologist, State Electricity Commission of Victoria, Melbourne, Australia, 1982-83. Organizational Memberships: National Water Well Association, 1966-69; American Society of Civil Engineers, 1972-77; Association of Engineering Geologists, 1972-77; American Geophysical Union, 1972 to present; Association of Geoscientists for International Development, 1975 to present; American Society for Testing and Materials, Committee on Waste Disposal, 1981 to present. Community Activities: President, Student Body, 1960-61; Instructor, Advanced Ground Water School, U.S.G.S., 1972-78; Instructor, UNESCO International Seminar on Land Subsidence, 1978; Advisor, United States Department of Energy, Subsidence Research Program, 1976-81; Summer Student Advisor, Office of Economic Opportunity, University of California, Livermore, 1981; Member High School Committee, American Friends Service Committee, 1966-68; Berkeley City Club, 1981 to present; Outlook Club, 1981 to present. Religion: Co-Chairman, New England Student Christian Movement, 1958-59; Member Board of Directors, Ecumenical Division, National Student Christian Federation, 1956-59; Founding Member, Board of Directors, Center for Theology and the Natural Sciences, Graduate Theological Union, Berkeley, 1981 to present. Honors and Awards: Amherst Alumni Scholarship, 4-Year, 1955-59; Hartford Prize Fellowship, 3-Year, 1959-62; Phillips Petroleum Fellow, 1962-63; Pan American Petroleum Fellow, 1964-65; United States Geological Survey Fellow, 1968-69; Bennet-Tyler Award in Systematic Theology, 1962; Invited Participant to NATO's Advanced Institute of Fluids in Porous Media, 1982. Address: One Acton Circle, Berkeley, California 94702. ■

DOROTHY LAVONNE HEMENWAY

Corporate Executive. Personal: Born February 26, 1934, in Boston, Massachusetts; Daughter of Stephen Oliver and Dorothy Esther Louise (Hill); Mother of Hiram Rodney Thompson III, Shyrll Ann Thompson, William Nathaniel Surrey III, Stephen Walter Surrey Sr. Education: Attended Boston Clerical Business School, 1953; B.A., New England School of Art, 1959; Professional Model Graduate, Fashion Signatures of Brookline, 1961; Advanced Mathematics and Statistics, Ft. Benjamin Harrison, Indiana, 1960-63; Massachusetts Institute of Technology, 1963-66; Certificated, Recreation Director, M.A. 1974, Northeastern University; Certificated, Environmentalist, Warren Center and University of Massachusetts, 1973; Certificated, Social Science, Simmons College and Boston University, 1974; Postgraduate, Pasadena City College, 1980. Career: President, Financial World International Corporation (Tax, Financial, Real Estate and Arts Management Consultant Firm), Las Vegas, Nevada; Pasadena, California; Dorchester, Massachusetts; President, Brackin Enterprises, Inc., Las Vegas, Nevada; Buena Park, California; Founder/President, Hemenway Foundation, Inc., Church of Realism, Henenway's College, CBM & SOHL Nutritional Center, Pasadena, California; Dorchester, Massachusetts; Producer, Technical Director, People's Theatre, Cambridge, Massachusetts, 1974-76; Producer, Director, Writer Television Series, Pasadena Unified School District 1977-78; Stage Manager, Technical Director, Costume Designer, Black Repertory Company, Boston, 1974-76; Accountant, Tax Consultant, Hill Realty, Dorchester, Massachusetts, and Mattapan Bowl-A-Drome, Mattapan, Massachusetts, 1975-80; Business Manager, Tax Consultant, People's Theatre, Cambridge, Massachusetts, 1975-79; Program Director, Robert Gould Shawhouse, Dorchester, 1972-76; Accountant Technician 1960-63, Statistician 1963-70, United States Government. Organizational Memberships: Jewelry Design Center Association; International Gem Finders Society; International Entrepreneurs Association; Society of California Accountants, Pasadena, California. Community Activities: Board of Directors, Children in Crisis, Boston, Massachusetts; Corporate Member, Family Services, Inc., Boston, Massachusetts; Executive Committee, People's Theatre, Cambridge, Massachusetts. Honors and Awards: Mary J. Mohan Book Award, 1951; Fran Meyers Award, 1980; Listed in *Who's Who in the West, Who's Who in America, Personalities of the West and Midwest, World Who's Who of Women, Book of Honor, Personalities of America.* Address: P.O. Box 40729, Pasadena, California 91104-7729. ■

WILLIAM R. HENDEE

Radiologist. Personal: Born January 1, 1938; Son of C. L. and A. M. Hendee; Married Hilda Jean Wesley; Father of Mikal, Shonn, Eric, Gareth, Gregory, Lara, Karel. Education: Attended Tulane University, New Orleans, Louisiana, 1955-57; B.A., Millsaps College, Jackson, Mississippi, 1957-59; Vanderbilt University, Nashville, Tennessee, 1959-60; Ph.D., University of Texas, Austin and Dallas, Texas, 1960-62. Career: AEC Fellow, National Reactor Testing Station, Idaho Falls, Idaho, 1960; Assistant Professor of Physics, Millsaps College, 1962-63; Associate Professor Physics, Millsaps College, 1963-64; Instructor of Modern Physics, Mississippi State University Extension, 1963; Associate Professor and Chairman, Department of Physics and Astronomy, Millsaps College, 1964-65; Assistant Professor of Radiology (Medical Physics) 1965-69, Associate Professor of Radiology (Medical Physics) 1969-73, Professor of Radiology (Medical Physics) 1974 to present, University of Colorado School of Medicine; Chairman, Department of Radiology, School of Medicine, University of Colorado Health Sciences Center, 1978 to present, Acting Chairman 1977-78; Staff of Veterans Administration Hospital, Denver, 1970 to present; Staff of Mercy Hospital, Denver, 1971 to present; Staff of Denver General Hospital, Denver, 1971 to present; Staff of Beth Israel Hospital, Denver, 1974 to present. Organizational Memberships: Member of or Holder of Offices and Committee Memberships in the American Association for Physics Teachers 1962 to present, Health Physics Society 1962 to present, Mississippi Academy of Sciences 1962-65, Southeastern Section of American Physical Society 1962-65, American Meteorological Society 1963-65, Central Mississippi Meteorological Chapter 1963-65, Omicron Delta Kappa 1963, American Association for the Advancement of Science 1963 to present, American Physical Society 1963 to present, American Association of Physicists in Medicine 1965 to present, Society of Nuclear Medicine Rocky Mountain Chapter 1967 to present, Society of Nuclear Medicine 1967 to present, American College of Radiology 1968 to present, American College of Radiology 1968 to present, International Radiation Protection Association 1971 to present, Society of Photo-Optical Instrumentation Engineers 1973 to present, American Nuclear Society Colorado Section 1974 to present, Radiological Society of North American Inc. 1976 to present, Society for Radiologic Engineers 1976-81, Alliance for Engineering in Medicine and Biology 1979 to present, World Federation of Nuclear Medicine and Biology International Advisory Council 1980, Colorado Medical Society 1981 to present, Colorado Radiological Society 1981 to present; Numerous Other Committee Memberships and Appointments; Serves on Many Editorial Boards of Journals including Honorary Editorial Advisory Board *Applied Radiology* 1972 to present, Editorial Board *Journal of Clinical Ultrasound* 1972-78, Consulting Editor *Journal of Nuclear Medicine Technology* 1973 to present, Others. Published Works: Author Approximately 115 Articles to Professional Journals and 18 Books. Honors and Awards: Theta Nu Sigma Award for Outstanding Science Major; A.E.C. Fellow in Radiological Physics; Gilbert X-Ray Fellow in Radiation Physics and Radiation Biology; N.S.F. Summer Research Fellowship, New Mexico Highlands University; A.E.C. Summer Research Fellowship, Radiation Dosimetry Section, Health Physics Division, Oak Ridge National Laboratory; Campus Associate, Danforth Foundation; Visiting Lecturer, Oak Ridge Associated Universities; Certified in Radiological Physics, American Board of Radiology; Certified in Landauer Memorial Award, Chicago, 1977; Fellow, American College of Radiology; Listed in *American Men of Science, Leaders in American Science, Dictionary of International Biography, Men of Achievement, Who's Who in Engineering, Community Leaders of America, Anglo-American Who's Who, Directory of Distinguished Americans, Who's Who in Technology Today, Personalities of the West and Midwest, Men of Achievement, Who's Who in Health Care, Who's Who in the West, Who's Who in America, Butterworth's Directory of Nuclear Medicine, International Who's Who in Engineering, American Men and Women of Science.* Address: 4248 North 109th Road, Lafayette, Colorado 80026. ■

DOUGLAS JAMES HENDERSON

Theoretical Physicist. Personal: Born July 28, 1934, in Calgary, Alberta, Canada; Son of Evelyn L. Henderson; Married Rose-Marie Steen-Nielssen; Father of Barbara, Dianne, Sharon. Education: B.A., 1st Class Honors, University of British Columbia, 1956; Ph.D., University of Utah, 1961. Career: Teaching Assistant, Department of Physics, University of Utah, 1956-57; Instructor, Department of Mathematics, University of Utah, 1960-61; Assistant Professor of Physics, University of Idaho, 1961-62; Assistant Professor Physics, Arizona State University, 1962-64; Associate Professor of Physics, University of Waterloo, Canada, 1964-67; Professor of Applied Mathematics and Physics, University of Waterloo, 1967-69; Research Scientist, I.B.M. Research Laboratory, San Jose, California, 1969 to present. Organizational Memberships: American Chemical Society; American Institute of Chemists, Fellow; American Physical Society, Fellow; Institute of Physics, Fellow; Canadian Association of Physicists; New York Academy of Science; Mathematical Association of America; Sigma Xi; Phi Kappa Phi; Sigma Pi Sigma. Religion: Missionary to South Africa, Church of Jesus Christ of Latter Day Saints, 1957-59. Published Works: Author of More than 150 Research Papers in Physics, Chemistry and Mathematics; Co-Author, Statistical Mechanics and Dynamics; Co-Editor of 15 Volume *Advanced Treatise on Physical Chemistry* and 6 Volume *Theoretical Chemistry: Advances and Perspectives*; Board of Editors, *Utilitas Mathematica*; Reviewer, *Mathematical Reviews*; Associate Editor, *Journal of Chemical Physics*; Advisory Board, Chemical Abstracts Service, 1981-83; Editorial Board, *Journal of Physical Chemistry*, 1984 to present. Honors and Awards: University of Great War Scholarship, 1953; Johnathan Rodgers Award, 1954; Province of British Columbia Bursary, 1954; Daniel Buchanan Scholarship for Highest Standing in Mathematics, 1955; Burbridge Scholarship for Highes Standing in Physics, 1955; National Research Council of Canada Bursary, 1956; Corning Glass Foundation Fellowship, 1959; Arizona State University Faculty Award, 1963; Alfred P. Sloan Foundation Fellowship, 1964, 1966; Ian Potter Foundation Fellowship, 1966; C.S.I.R.O. Research Fellowship, 1966; Visiting Scientist, C.S.I.R.O. Chemical Research Laboratories, Melbourne, Australia, 1966-67; Visiting Professor of Physics, National University of La Plata, Argentina, 1973; I.B.M. Outstanding Research Contribution Award, 1973; Visiting Professor of Physics, National University of La Plata, Argentina, 1973; I.M.B. Outstanding Research Contribution Award, 1973; Visiting Scientist, Institute of Physical Chemistry, Polish Academy of Science, 1973; Sabatical Visitor, I.B.M. Thomas J. Watson Research Center, Yorktown Heights, New York, 1973-74; Visiting Scientist, Korea Advanced Institute of Science, Seoul, Korea, 1974. Address: 2354 Skyview Terrace, Los Gatos, California 95030. ■

NELSON HOWARD HENDLER

Psychiatrist. Personal: Born August 15, 1944; Son of Albert and Winifred Hendler; Married Lee Meyerhoff, Daughter of Harvey and Lyn Meyerhoff; Father of Samuel M., Alexander M., Lindsay M. Education: B.A. cum laude, Princeton University, 1966; M.D. 1972, M.S. Physiology 1974, University of Maryland; Residency, Johns Hopkins University School of Medicine, 1972-75. Career: Psychiatrist Specializing in Chronic Pain; Clinical Psychopharmacology, Headache Treatment and Psychosomatic Medicine. Organizational Memberships: American Psychiatric Society; American Medical Association; American Society for Study of Headaches; Society of Biological Psychiatry; International Society for the Study of Pain; Psychosomatic Society of America. Community Activities: Board of Directors, Maryland Mental Health Association 1976-78, Baltimore Zoological Society 1977-79, Park School 1974-77, Technion University Baltimore Board, Ben Gurion University Baltimore Board, O.R.T. National and Baltimore Boards. Published Works: Author, *Coping with Chronic Pain* 1979, *Diagnosis and Non-Surgical Management of Chronic Pain* 1981, *Diagnosis and Treatment of Chronic Pain* 1982. Honors and Awards: Merit Scholarship Finalist, 1961; Graduate Cum Laude, Psychology, Princeton University, 1966; Sigma Xi, 1966; President, House Staff Society Council, Johns Hopkins Hospital, 1974-75; William Menenger Award, Honorable Mention, 1975; Falk Fellow, American Psychiatric Association, 1974-75. Address: Mensana Clinic, Greenspring Valley Road, Stevenson, Maryland 21153. ∎

ROBERT MICHAEL HENDRICKS

President and Chief Executive Officer, Director. Personal: Born August 23, 1943; Son of Chester Eugene Hendricks and Reba Eileen (Leake) Hendricks; Married Yvonne Sharon McAnally; Father of Robert Christian Hendricks. Education: B.A., University of California at Berkeley. Career: President, Chief Executive Officer, ADCO Re Life Assurance Company; Member Board of Directors, Assurance Distribution Company, Inc.; Director, Share Insurance, Inc.; Director, First Commerce Trust Company. Organizational Memberships: Chartered Life Underwriters; National Association of Life Underwriters; Orange County Association of Life Underwriters; Life Underwriters Training Council. Community Activities: Rotary Club International; 32nd Degree Mason; Scottish Rite; Al Malaikah Shrine; Chamber of Commerce; California Young Republicans; Council, Boy Scouts of America; Republican National Committee; American Biographical Institute Research Association; United States Senate Business Advisory Board; International Platform Association. Religion: Member, Trinity United Presbyterian Church. Honors and Awards: Recipient of Numerous Company and Civic Awards, including Company Leader, Man of the Year, Speaking Engagements Nationwide, CLU, LUTC I & II, Distinguished Service Award, Republican Party (thrice honored), Presidents Club, Century Club, Boy Scouts of America. Address: 1611 LaLoma Drive, Santa Ana, California 92705. ∎

RUTH OELKE HENDRIX

Educator. Personal: Born December 21, 1894; Daughter of William and Mary Oelke (deceased); Married Dr. H. E. Hendrix, Son of Mr. and Mrs. E. Hendrix (deceased). Education: Graduate, Blue Earth, Minnesota High School, 1913; B.S. Home Economics, North Central College, Naperville, Illinois, 1919; Attended Summer Session, Columbia University, 1927; M.S. Home Economics Education, Iowa State University, Ames, Iowa, 1932. Career: Educator. Organizational Memberships: Iowa Education Association; Minnesota Education Association; Arizona Education Association, 1929-40; Home Economics Education Association, 1932-40; Vocation Education Association, 1932-40; Delta Kappa Gamma, 1935-38. Community Activities: Mesa Lutheran Hospital ($1000.00 donation to furnish a room); Mesa Salvation Army ($1000.00 toward new building); Sunshine Acres Children' Home Northeast Mesa ($2500.00 to boy's dormitory); First Presbyterian Church Mesa (Conn electric organ in memory of husband, stage curtain, chancel carpet, dishes, kitchen cabinets); State Supervisor Home Economic in Arizona, 1934-40 (appointed); Member, American Business Women, Charter Member in Mesa, Arizona, President of Mesa Charter Chapter 1932 to present, Woman of the Year 1932; Charter Member, Soroptimist International, President (in early 1950's). Religion: Member, First Presbyterian Church, 1952 to present; First Woman on Session 3 Years, President of U.P.W. 2 Years, State President of Church Women United 1957. Honors and Awards: American Business Woman of the Year, 1932; Listed in *Who's Who in American Women*, *Who's Who in the West*, *Who's Who in the West and Midwest*, *International Who's Who of Intellectuals*, *Two Thousand Notable Americans*. Address: 255 West Brown Road, Mesa Christian Home, Mesa, Arizona 85201. ∎

EDWARD FRANK HENRY

Executive. Personal: Born March 18, 1923, in East Cleveland, Ohio; Son of Edward Emerson Henry and Mildred Adella (Kulow) Henry (dec); Married Nicole Annette Peth on June 18, 1977. Education: B.B.A. Accounting/Business Management, Dyke College, Cleveland, Ohio, 1948; Courses in Communications, Problem Solving Methods for Accountants and Administrators, How to Buy and Use Small Business Computers, Data Processing Concepts and Information, System Design, National Association of Accountants; Developing Computer-Based General Ledger Systems, Planning Cash Flow, Reading and Interpreting Financial Statements, Computer Fundamentals for Managers, American Management Association; Graduate, Modern School of Photography, New York, 1965; Microcomputer Literacy Program, McGraw Hill; Descriptive Geometry, Case University; Student, Cleveland Institute of Music, 1972; Studied Music Privately, 1931-43. Military: Served with the United States Air Force, 1st Lieutenant, 1943-46; United States Air Force Reserve, Information Officer, 9523rd VART, 1946-57. Career: President, Professional Managment Computer Systems, Cleveland, Ohio, 1970 to present; Vice President, Auto Data Systems Inc., Cleveland, Ohio, 1968-70; National Manager, Auto Accounting Division, United Data Processing, Cleveland, Ohio, 1966-68; Treasurer, Commerce Ford Sales Inc., Cleveland, Ohio, 1955-65; Office Manager, Frank C. Grismer Company and Broadway Buick Company, Cleveland, Ohio, 1951-55; Internal Auditor, E. F. Hauserman Company, Cleveland, Ohio, 1948-51; Account Executive/Announcer, WSRS Radio, Cleveland Heights, Ohio, 1943-48; Advertising/Graphics/Layout, Pesco Products Company, Cleveland, Ohio, 1942-43. Organizational Memberships: Data Processing Managers' Association; National Association of Professional Consultants; American Society of Professional Consultants; National Association of Accountants; American Management Association; International Platform Association. Community Activities: Military Order of World Wars; National Society of Literature and Arts; Metropolitan Museum of Art; American Horticultural Society; Cleveland Junior Chamber of Commerce; Euclid Junior Chamber of Commerce; National Geographic Society; Cleveland Grays; Smithsonian Institution; The Cousteau Society; Acacia Country Club; The Hermit Club; Junior Achievement, Chief Advisor 1948-49; Phi Kappa Gamma, Charter President of Gamma Chapter, National Vice President; Red Feather Community Chest, Member of Speaker's Division; Cleveland Philharmonic Orchestra, Past Board Member; DeMolay, Past Master Councillor, Cleveland Chapter 1942; Active in Masons, 33rd Degree; Northern Ohio Council of Little Theatres, Charter President 1954-56; Experimental Theatre Cleveland, Founder and Managing/Artistic Director 1959-63; Cleveland Playhouse, Rabbit Run Theatre, Jewish Community Theatre, Euclid Little Theatre, Others, Actor and Director 1950-65; Hermit Club, Cleveland, Ohio, Dramatic Director/Actor; Al Koran Shrine, Director (Search for Stars); American National Theatre and Academy, Local Liaison/Membership Committee Member; American Educational Theatre Association; American Community Theatre Association; American Theatre Association. Published Works: Author, "Internal Control Practices" 1976, "Computerized Accounting and Asset Accounting System" 1980, "Factomathics" (a simplified basic recordkeeping guideline) 1980. Honors and Awards: Decorated American Theatre, Asiatic Pacific Theatre with Two Bronze Stars; Philippine Liberation with One Bronze Star; Good Conduct and Victory Medals; Certificate of Appreciation from A.A.S.R. (Cleveland), 1982; Man of Achievement, 1981; National President's Award from National Sojourners, 1976; 33rd Degree Mason, 1978; DeMolay Legion of Honor, 1970; Honorary Order of Kentucky Colonels, 1967; Top Accountant (Cleveland District), Ford Division of Ford Motor Company, 1958; Ford Accountants' Certificate of Merit, 1956-65; Best Actor Award, Euclid Little Theatre, 1954-55; Cultural Doctorate in Computer Science from the World University Roundtable, 1983; Listed in *Directory of Distinguished Americans*, *Who's Who in Finance and Industry*, *Who's Who in the Midwest*, *Book of Honor*, *Personalities of the West and Midwest*. Address: 666 Echo Drive, Gates Mills, Ohio 44040. ∎

ZACHARY ADOLPHUS HENRY

Professor. Personal: Born April 25, 1930; Son of Walter R. and Annie L. Henry (deceased); Married Norma Ray Taylor, Daughter of Leander Taylor (deceased); Father of Zachary A. Jr., Lydia Carol, Vera Lynn, Nathan Lee, Stephen Taylor. Education: B.S. Agricultural Engineering, University of Georgia, 1951; M.S. Agricultural Engineering, Clemson University, 1957; Ph.D., North Carolina State University, 1962. Military: United States Navy, Lieutenant, 1952-55. Career: Professor, University of Tennessee, Knoxville, Tennessee; Construction Engineer, E. I. DuPont de Nemours, 1951-52; Irrigation Engineer, Tri-State Culvert and Manufacturing Corporation, 1955-57. Organizational Memberships: American Society of Agricultural Engineers; Chairman, Electric Power and Processing Division, 1981; American Society for Engineering Education; American Physical Society; American Society of Naval Engineers; American Association for the Advancement of Science; American Society of University Professors. Community Activities: Chairman of the Board, West End Learning Center and West End Academy (special education school program), 1970 to present; Sponsor of the University of Tennessee Chinese Student Program, 1965-75; Parents and Teachers Association, President Knox County, 1965-70. Religion: Member Corryton Baptist Church 1961 to present, Deacon, Youth Leader, Bible Teacher. Honors and Awards: Fellow of the Foundation for Cotton Research and Education, 1957-58; Gamma Sigma Delta, The Honor Society of Agriculture; Sigma Xi, The Scientific Honor Society; Phi Kappa Phi; Registered Professional Engineer, Tennessee, 05020. Address: 6300 Childs Road, Corryton, Tennessee 37721. ∎

RICHARD MURLEN HERD

Oral Maxillofacial Surgeon. Personal: Born September 16, 1918; Married Harriet Jean; Father of Richard M. Jr., Eric Alan, Dorothy Jean. Education: A.B. Chemistry, Indiana University, 1941; D.D.S., St. Louis University, 1945; University Oregeon Medical Schools, Hospitals and Clinics, 1948. Military: Served with the United States Navy, Lieutenant, 1945-47; United States Army, PFC, 1942-43. Career: Oral Maxillofacial Surgeon; Chief Oral Maxillofacial Surgeon, Louisville General Hospital; Assistant Professor, University of Louisville School of Dentistry; Consultant, Indiana University School of Dentistry. Organizational Memberships: Xi Psi Phi, President 1960-61; Kentucky Society Anesthesiologists, President 1957-58; American Society Oral Maxillofacial Surgeons; American Dental Association; International Dental Association; Great Lakes Society Oral Surgery; American Society Anesthesiologists; Research Society. Community Activities: Commander Paul Coble Post American Legion, 1961-62. Religion: Lutheran Cross Crown Church, 1960-62; Trustee, First Baptist Church, Indianapolis, 1963-64. Honors and Awards: Omicron Kappa Upsilon, 1952; Citizen for Day, Indianapolis, 1966; Boy Scouts Award, 1963; American Dental Leaders, 1965. Address: 6825 Creekside Lane, Indianapolis, Indiana 46220.■

CRAIG MAYNARD HERRING

Manager Microbiology/Sterility Assurance. Personal: Born June 25, 1945; Son of Mr. and Mrs. Robert Crosby; Married Nancy Ann Donald, Daughter of Mr. and Mrs. J. Steve Donald; Father of Brian Kenneth, Kevin Michael (both children from previous marriage). Education: B.S. Microbiology 1968, M.S. Microbiology 1970, University of Arizona. Career: Manager Microbiology/Sterility Assurance; Research Microbiologist; Vice President Manufacturing-Diagnostics. Organizational Memberships: American Society for Microbiology; Society for Industrial Microbiology; A.A.A.S.; Sigma Xi; American Society for Quality Control; New York Academy of Sciences. Community Activities: Rotary International, El Paso Lower Valley Club, Secretary; 32nd Degree Mason; Shriner. Honors and Awards: Listed in *Who's Who in the South and Southwest, Personalities of the South, Personalities of America*. Address: 11252 Ivanhoe Drive, El Paso, Texas 79936.■

KAYE ANN HERTH

Assistant Professor of Nursing. Personal: Born September 9, 1945; Married Leonard Alvin Herth; Mother of Wendy Joye, Randy Scott. Education: Diploma, St. Luke's Hospital School for Nursing, 1966; B.S., Northern Illinois University, 1968; M.S., University of Minnesota, 1973. Career: Team Leader, Medical-Surgical, Trinity Memorial Hospital, Cudahy, Wisconsin, 1966-67; Staff Nurse, Pediatrics, Geneva Community Hospital, Geneva, Illinois, 1967-68; Fundamental's Instructor, Milwaukee County Hospital, Wisconsin, 1968-69; Nursing Coordinator Medical-Surgical, United Hospital-Miller Division, St. Paul, Minnesota, 1969-71; Medical-Surgical Instructor, Lutheran Deaconess Hospital School of Nursing, Minneapolis, Minnesota, 1971-73; Assistant Professor of Nursing, East Tennessee State University, 1973-77; Assistant Professor of Nursing, University of Tennessee, Memphis, 1977-78; Assistant Professor of Nursing, University of Texas-Houston, 1978 to present. Organizational Memberships: Texas Nurses Association; American Nurses Association; Tennessee Nurses Association, Past Member Executive Board, District 5; American Association for the Advancement of Science, Resource Group; Nurses Christian Fellowship. Community Activities: Volunteer Speaker, Hear-Say-Organization for Hearing Impaired, 1982-83; Group Facilitator for Support Group of Cancer Patients and Their Families, American Cancer Society; Memphis Chapter, Make Today Count, Advisor, Member, 1977-78; Advisor to Senior Citizens Group Dealing with Problems Relating to Aging, Memphis, 1977-78; Counselor, Prospective Parents of Adopted Children, Memphis, 1978; Alexander Graham Bell Association, O.D.A.S. Executive Board; Red Cross, Coordinator and Teacher "Preparation for Parenthood" 1974-76; Consultant to the Department of Special Education, East Tennessee State University, Working with Parents and Deaf Children, 1973-77; Women's Division of Johnson City Chamber of Commerce, 1974-77. Published Works: "Beyond the Curtain of Silence," "Please Reach Out to Me Your Elderly Patient," "Early Recovery," "The Therapeutic Use of Music"; Manuscript, "Dealing with Loneliness"; Chapter in Nursing Text *Introduction to Nursing Practice*. Honors and Awards: Sigma Theta Tau; Nominated for Tennessee Nurse in Action, 1975; Outstanding Graduate Nurse for the State of Wisconsin, 1969; Outstanding Graduating Senior Northern Illinois University, 1968; Listed in *The Biographical Roll of Honor, International Who's Who in Education, World Who's Who of Women in Education*. Address: 3215 Laverne, Houston, Texas 77080.■

DEAN R. HESS

Educator. Personal: Born September 23, 1950; Son of Paul S. and Edith A. Hess; Married Susan S.; Father of Terri Anne. Education: Diploma in Respiratory Therapy, Saint Joseph Hospital, 1974; B.A. cum laude Chemistry, Messiah College, 1972; M.Ed., Millersville University, 1980. Career: Educator, Respiratory Therapy; Registered Respiratory Therapist, 1976 to present; Certified Respiratory Therapy Technician, 1977 to present. Organizational Memberships: American Association for Respiratory Therapy; American Association of Allied Health Professionals; Pennsylvania Society for Respiratory Therapy; American Institute of Biological Sciences; American Association for the Advancement of Science. Community Activities: American Heart Association, York Adams Pennsylvania Chapter, Board of Directors, Central Program Committee, Chairman of Emergency Cardiac Care Task Force 1983; South York Neighborhood Organization, Board of Directors, President 1983; Mayor's Neighborhood Advisory Council, City of New York; Chairman, York City Parking Task Force, 1983. Honors and Awards: Volunteer of the Year, American Heart Association, 1982; Listed in *Outstanding Young Men of America*. Address: 273 West Springettsbury Avenue, York, Pennsylvania 17403.■

PAUL ARMOUR HESSELGRAVE, JR.

Research Specialist. Personal: Born June 19, 1939, in Sparta, Wisconsin; Son of Mrs. Lillian M. Hesselgrave, Campbell, California; Married Patricia Ann, Daughter of Mr. and Mrs. Robert Meier. Education: B.S. Chemistry, San Jose State University, 1962; Additional Postgraduate Studies. Career: Research Specialist 1979 to present, Senior Manufacturing Research Engineer 1973-79, Materials and Process Engineer 1967-73, Associate Engineer 1962-67, Lockheed Missiles and Space Company; Certified Manufacturing Engineer; Certified Professional Chemist; Certified Electroplater-Finisher. Organizational Memberships: American Chemical Society; American Defense Preparedness Association; Society of Manufacturing Engineers. Religion: Roman Catholic, Confraternity of Christian Doctrine Religion High School Teacher 1964 to present. Honors and Awards: Vice President, Acting President of College Chemistry Fraternity, Phi Upsilon Pi, 1961-62. Address: 2462 Gallup Drive, Santa Clara, California 95051.■

GEORGE ALAN KARNES WALLIS HICKROD

Distinguished Professor. Personal: Born May 16, 1930, in Fort Branch, Indiana; Son of Hershell Roy and Bernice Ethel Wallis Karnes Hickrod; Married Lucy Jen Huang, June 17, 1954. Education: Attended Wabash College, Harvard University; Graduate Studies, University of Wisconsin. Military: Served with the Tenth Marine Regiment during the Korean War. Career: Teaching Positions at Muskingum College, Boston University, Lake Erie College, Illinois State University; Established Centre for the Study of Educational Finance, Illinois State University, 1975 (with Professor Emeritus Ben C. Hubbard); Distinguished Professor, University of Illinois, 1983 to present. Organizational Memberships: Phi Beta Kappa; Member First Board of Directors, American Education Finance Association; Editorial Board, *Journal of Education Finance*. Community Activities: Seneschal, Scottish-American Society of Central Illionis; Scottish and York Rite Mason; Benevolent and Protective Order of Elks; American Legion; Victorian Society of America; Life-Long Member, Democratic Party. Address: Center for the Study of Educational Finance, DeGarmo Hall, Illinois State University, Normal, Illinois 61761.■

W. B. (DUB) HICKS

Free Lance Writer, Playwright, Columnist, Actor. Personal: Born July 18, 1911; Father of Bonnie McAlister, Jim Hicks, Linda Humphrey, Jerry, W. B. Jr. (deceased). Education: Graduate, Sam Houston High School; United States Navy AMPHIB; Newspaper Institute of America, 1977. Military: Served with the United States Navy, 1941-45. Career: Free Lance Writer; Playwright Several Plays including *Condomania*; Columnist; Television and Stage Actor; Intelligence Operations for United States Services; Producer, Director, "The Great Debate" (a weekly cable television production); Feature Editor of *Ahora — Now* (a weekly publication serving the Mexican-American readers of Southern California). Organizational Memberships: President, Association of Former Intelligence Officers, 1980-81. Community Activities: Member Board of Directors, Southeast Community Theaters of San Diego; Board Member, Pathfinders; President, PACE Organization, 1970 to present; Instructor, Coping with Government, 1978, 1979, 1980; Instructor, Television, Movie Script Writing, 1980-81; Lectures Schools, Groups; Intelligence Operations, Government

Operations, Others; Television Productions for Public, Director and Producer; Stage and Television Actor; Producer of Musical Variety Play, 1982. Published Works: Author of Two Novels, 3 Stage Plays. Honors and Awards: Presidential Unit Citation, 1943; Good Conduct Award, United States Navy; Asiatic Pacific Service Award, United States Navy; Meritorious Service Award, 1945. Address: 161-4th Avenue A, Chula Vista, California 92010.■

BETTINA PEARSON HIGDON

Library Region Director. Personal: Born March 9, 1920; Daughter of Arthur and Mildred Bradley Pearson (deceased); Married Raymond Earl, Son of Ben and Emily (Wildman) Higdon (deceased). Education: A.B. 1941, M.A. 1961, Alabama College Montivallo; 6-Year Teacher's Certificate in Counseling and Guidance, University of Alabama at Tuscaloosa, 1971; Additional Studies, Auburn University, Birmingham-Southern College, Samford University, Wallace Community College. Career: Director, Cullman County Public Library Region, 1974 to present; Teacher, 1941-73; Guidance Counselor, 1962-65; World Book District Sales Manager, 1960-62; Guidance Supervisor, Cullman Country, Alabama, 1966-71; Broker for Investor Diversified Services, 1973-74. Organizational Memberships: National Education Association; A.E.A.; C.E.A.; American Association Women Deans and Counselors; Others. Community Activities: Organizing Regent, Dripping Springs Chapter, Daughters of the American Revolution, 1970-72, Regent 1982-84; Organizing Member, Nathen B. Fonnert United Daughers Confederacy, 1975; Organizing Member, North Central Alabama Genealogical Society, 1979; Treasurer, Kappa Mu Epsilon, Alabama College, 1940; Cullivan County Chamber of Commerce, 1977 to present. Religion: Chair, First United Methodist Church, 1944-82; Song Director, Bob Sapp Sunday School Class, 1970-82; Class Instructor (intermittently). Published Works: Author of Four Books. Honors and Awards: Woman of Achievement for Cullman Business and Professional Women's Association; Valedictorian, Bess High School, 1938; Listed in *Who's Who of American Women, Who's Who in Alabama, Who's Who in Genealogy*. Address: P.O. Box 325, Cullman, Alabama 35855.■

JERRY GLYNN MATTHEWS HILL

College Faculty Member. Personal: Born August 28, 1940; Son of Mr. and Mrs. Hozyter Matthews: Father of Jaree Lynn Hill. Education: B.S., Lamar University, 1961; M.Ed., Stephen F. Austin State University, 1963; Ed.D., McNeese State University, 1973. Career: College Faculty, Central State University; Classroom Teacher, Public Schools, Port Arthur, Texas Independent School District, Springdale, Arkansas School District, Pasadena, Texas Independent School District. Organizational Memberships: Higher Education Reading Council; Edmond Reading Council; Oklahoma City Reading Council; Oklahoma Reading Council; State Parliamentarian; International Reading Association; Association for Supervision and Curriculum Development, National Board Member; Oklahoma Association for Supervision and Curriculum Development, Secretary, State President; Delta Kappa Gamma, First Vice President of Chapter, State Committee; Phi Delta Kappa, Secretary. Community Activities: Daughters of the American Revolution; Delta Theta Chi, Education Director. Honors and Awards: Central State University Outstanding Faculty Women, 1976; Charter Member, Mortar Board. Address: 504 Pepperdine, Edmond, California 73034.■

RUTH BEEBE HILL

Writer, Lecturer. Personal: Born April 26, 1913; Daughter of Hermann and Flora Beebe (both deceased); Married; Mother of Reid. Education: Attended Oberlin College, 1931-32; B.S., Western Reserve University, 1935; Further Study at the University of Colorado, 1939-40. Career: Bridal Consultant, Denver, Colorado, and Boston, Massachusetts, 1941-43; Assistant, Department of Geology, Western Reserve University, 1935-37; Book Dramatist, 1947-52; Founder, Gull Hill (Private) Children's School, New Orleans, 1947; Assistant, Books and Authors, Los Angeles, 1950-54; Writer, Lecturer. Organizational Memberships: National League of American Pen Women, 1979 to present; National Writers, 1979 to present; American Academy Achievement Council, 1980 to present; Ohioana Library Association, 1980 to present. Community Activities: California Institute of Cancer Research, Los Angeles, Ways and Means Chairman, 1951-55; American Association of University Women, 1945-49; San Juan Island Historical Society, Friday Harbor, Washington, 1970 to present; Daughters of the American Revolution, San Juan Island Chapter, Member 1979 to present, American Indians Chairman 1979 to present. Published Works: Author *Hanto Yo*, Documentary Novel, 1979. Honors and Awards: Pulitzer Nomination, Books Across the Sea Award 1979, Cowboy Hall of Fame and Western Heritage Award 1980, American Academy of Achievement Honoree 1979, Northwest Booksellers Association Excellence in Writing Award 1980, Ohioana Book Award 1980, all for *Hanta Yo*. Address: Watershed Acres, Friday Harbor, Washington 98250.■

THOMAS BOWEN HILL, JR.

Lawyer, Personal: Born November 11, 1903; Son of Thomas Bowen Hill and Lida Tunstall (Inge) (both deceased); Married Mildred Ellen Abrams on September 22, 1925, Daughter of Alonzo Abrams and Mary Wood (Paul) Abrams (both deceased); Father of Thomas Bowen III, Mildred Inge Hill Hickson, Luther Abrams, William Inge II. Education: Graduate, Barnes School, Montgomery, Alabama, 1919; A.B. 1922, LL.B. 1924, University of Alabama; English Fellowship, University of Alabama, 1922-23 Session. Career: Associate Professor of German, University of Alabama, 1923-24 Session; Lawyer, Senior Member Firm of Hill, Hill, Carter, Franco, Cole and Black; Practiced Law in Montgomery, Alabama, 1924 to present. Organizational Memberships: Member, Montgomery County, Alabama State and American Bar Associations; President, Montgomery Bar Association, 1933; Vice President 1951-52, President 1952-53, Alabama State Bar Association; Member, Board of Commissioners of Alabama State Bar, 1953 to present; Chairman, Committee on Continuing Legal Education of Alabama State Bar Association, 1953-55; Special Chief Justice, Supreme Court of Alabama, 1968; Special Judge, Circuit Court of Montgomery County, Alabama, 1938; Delgate, Alabama State Bar to Judicial Conference of Fifth Circuit; Member, American College of Trial Lawyers, 1955 to present; Alabama Judicial Council, 1953; State Bar Delegate, House of Delegates, American Bar Association, 1959 to present; Member, American Judicature Society, 1948 to present; Life Fellow, American Bar Foundation, 1956 to present; Director, University of Alabama Law School Foundation; Charter Member, Farrah Law Society, 1969 to present; Chairman, Board of Directors, Union Bank and Trust Company, Montgomery, Alabama, 1955-76; Chairman Emeritus for Life, Board of Directors, Union Bank and Trust Company; Phi Beta Kappa; Phi Alpha Delta. Community Activities: Portrayed President Jefferson Davis in Centennial Re-enacment of Inauguration of President Davis as President of Confederacy, February 18, 1961; Member Board of Directors, Alabama State Chamber of Commerce, 1966 to present; Board of Directors, Chamber of Commerce of Montgomery, 1948-74; Member State Board of Directors, Alabama Motorists Association; Member Board of Directors, Alabama Bible Society; King Montala VII, Krewe of Phantom Host, 1968; Life Membership, Young Women's Christian Organization; Kiwanis International, President Montgomery Club 1933; Chapter Chairman, Montgomery Chapter of American Red Cross, 1945; Potentate, Alcazar Temple, A.A.O.N.M.S. (Shrine) 1948; Board of Directors, Children's Protective Home of Montgomery 1954-56; Former Member, Board of Directors of Montgomery Young Men's Christian Association; Former Member, Board of Directors, Montgomery Country Club. Religion: Episcopal, Member of Vestry, Senior Warden (2 terms), Church of Ascension, Montgomery, Alabama. Honors and Awards: Awarded Honorary LL.B. Degree, University of Alabama, 1978; Daniel J. Meador Outstanding Alumnus Award, University of Alabama School of Law, 1975; Dean's Award, University of Alabama School of Law, 1972; Elected to Membership, Alabama Academy of Honor, 1977; Freedoms Foundation at Valley Forge Award for Public Address Entitled "This Land We Love," 1971; Listed in *Who's Who in America, Who's Who in American Law*. Address: 1831 Hillwood Drive, Montgomery, Alabama 36106 ■

RITA KATHRYN HILLE

Financial Consultant. Personal: Born October 26, 1933; Married Paul Keith Bond December 28, 1953; Married Peter Felix Hille September 4, 1959; Mother of Four Daughters. Education: Enrolled M.B.A. Financial Planning Program, Golden Gate College; A.A., Social Service, San Jose City College, 1972; B.S., Business Management, San Jose State, 1974; Graduate of Realtors Institute, 1978; Certified Residential Broker Specialist, 1981; Licensed Securities Broker. Career: RKH Realty, 1977 to present; Securities Broker, Judy and Robinson; Sales Associate, Bell Inc. Realtors, 1975-77; Mortgage Loan Broker, Refinance Counselors, Inc., 1982-84. Organizational Memberships: National Association of Realtors, 1975 to present; San Jose Real Estate Board, 1975 to present; Los Altos Real Estate Board, 1975 to present; Palo Alto Real Estate Board, 1979-82; Menlo Park Real Estate Board, 1979-82; Sunnyvale Real Estate Board, 1980-82. Community Activities: League of Women Voters, 1974 to present; Los Altos Equal Opportunity Committee, 1978-79; Chairman MLS Program Committee, 1979-80. Published Works: Author of *The Creekside Chronicle* 1969, *Rita's Rap Sheet* 1978, *The Hille Chronicle* 1983. Address: 1963 Rock Street, Mountain View, California.■

BONNIE A. HILTON

Regional Marketing Director. Personal: Born December 18, 1945; Daughter of Allen A. and Yvonne Auerr. Education: B.A. magna cum laude in History, State College, Framingham, Massachusetts; M.S. Home Economics, Ohio State University, 1976; Ph.D. Family Management, Ohio State University, 1977. Career: Regional Marketing Director, Eastern Region, United Van Lines, 1982 to present; Director, Consumer Affairs at United Van Lines, 1980-82; Consumer Services, United Van Lines, 1977-80; Graduate Research, Ohio State University, 1975-76; Graduate Teaching Associate, Ohio State University, 1972-75; Social Science Teacher, Fremont, California, 1967-70. Organizational Memberships: Vice President, Central Midwest Chapter, Society of Consumer Affairs Professionals, 1981; President 1982, Director National Board 1982 to present; Career Competence Committee, American Council on Consumer Interests, 1981 to present. Community Activities: Home Economists in Business, St. Louis Executive Board, 1978-79 and 1980-81; American Home Economists in Business; Missouri H.E.A.; American Women in Radio and Television; National Council on Family Relations; Ministry to the Sick 1975-77, Coordinator Liturgical Council, Eucharistic Minister, Lector, Liturgical Dancer. Honors and Awards: Young Professional Award, Ohio State University, 1980; Listed in *Who's Who in American Women*. Address: 418 East Madison Avenue, Kirkwood, Missouri 63122.■

RONALD WILLARD HILWIG

Associate Professor. Personal: Born May 24, 1935; Son of Willard (deceased) and Virginia Hilwig-Ransom; Married Kay Thurston, Daughter of William and Alice Thurston; Father of Tona DeAune, Kara DeLana. Education: Preveterinary Studies, University of Arizona, 1963-65; D.V.M., College of Veterinary Medicine, Washington State University, 1969; M.Sc., Ohio State University, 1970; Ph.D., Ohio State University, 1972. Military: Served with the United States Army, Signal Corps, sp/5, 1957-60. Career: Associate Professor of Veterinary Science, Associate Research Scientist, University of Arizona, present; Assistant Professor of Clinical Science, Ohio State University, College of Veterinary Medicine, 1969-74. Organizational Memberships: American Veterinary Medical Associatioan; Academy of Veterinary Cardiology; National Association of Colleges and Teachers of Agriculture; New York Medical Association; Academy of Veterinary Cardiology; National Association of Colleges and Teachers of Agriculture; New York Academy of Science; Society of Phi Zeta; Gamma Sigma Delta, National Honor Society of Agriculture; Society of Sigma Xi; International Congress of Individualized Instruction. Community Activities: American Heart Association, 1969 to present; Saguaro Girl Scout Council, 1977 to present; Oracle Heights Recreation Association Competitive Swim Team, 1977 to present; Preveterinary Club, University of Arizona, 1975 to present. Religion: St. Marks United Methodist Church. Honors and Awards: Babe Ruth Award, Readers Digest Award, Danforth Foundational Award, Valedictorian, 1953; Erikson Award, Washington State University, College of Veterinary Medicine, 1969; Professor of the Year, College of Agriculture, University of Arizona, 1979; Teacher Fellow, National Association of Colleges and Teachers of Agriculture (N.A.C.T.A.), 1981; Western Regional Outstanding Teacher Award, N.A.C.T.A., 1981. Address: 7250 San Anna Drive, Tucson, Arizona 85704.■

EUGENE BRYSON HIMELICK

Plant Pathologist, Professor. Personal: Born Feburary 11, 1926; Son of Virgil B. Himelick; Married; Father of David E., Kirk J., Douglas N. Education: B.S., Ball State University, 1949; M.S., Purdue University, 1952; Ph.D., University of Illinois, 1959. Military: Served in the United States Navy as an Electronics Technician, 1945-50. Career: Plant Pathologist, Professor of Plant Pathology, Illinois National History Survey and University of Illinois. Organizational Memberships: International Society of Arboriculture, Executive Director 1969-79; Midwestern Chapter, International Society of Aboriculture, President 1969. Community Activities: Scoutmaster, Troop 10, 1961-75; Urbana Tree Commission, Chairman 1976 to present; Champaign County Development Council, 1973-77. Religion: First United Methodist Church, Urbana, Illinois, Board of Trustees, 1976; Administrative Board, 1980 to present; Chairman, Parsonage Committee, 1980 to present. Honors and Awards: Scouters Key, Ken Fredricks Award, Vigil Honor, Silver Beaver, Boy Scouts of America; Authors Citation, Honorary Life Award, Past Presidents Award, International Society of Arboriculture. Address: 601 Burkwood Court East, Urbana, Illinois 61801.■

CLARA S. HIRES

Author. Personal: Born April 8, 1897; Daughter of Charles E. Hires and Clara K. (Smith) Hires (both deceased). Education: Attended Wellesley College, 1916-19; B.A., Cornell University, 1928; Additional Studies at Teachers College, Columbia University, Rutgers University, Montclair Teachers College, University of Pennsylvania. Career: Science Teacher 1920-34, Edgewood School, Greenwich, Connecticut 1920-25, Buxton Country Day School, Short Hills, New Jersey 1929-32, Shore Road Academy, Brooklyn, New York 1932-34; Currently Selling Her Books, *Spores. Ferns. Microscopic Illusions Analyzed* Volume I 1965, Volume II 1978; Owner of Mistaire Laboratories, 1929 to present; Seeds and Spores were Germinated and Raised on Nutrient Media (jellied chemicals), Enclosed in Glass Containers (tubes and flasks), for Growers, Biological Supply Houses, Schools and Colleges World-Wide, Some Completely Sealed and Sold to Florists; Engaged in Original Scientific Research, 1930 to present. Organizational Memberships: Life Member of American Association for the Advancement of Science, New York Academy of Science New York Chapter, American Fern Society; Member, New Jersey Academy of Science; Botanical Society of America, Paleobotanical, Pteridological and Structural Sections; Paelontological Society; American Geological Institute; Torrey Botanical Club; New York Botanical Garden; New York Microscopal Society; American and New York Horticultural Societies; International Society of Stereology; Los Angeles International Fern Society; British Pteridological Society; International Biographical Association; Sigma Delta Epsilon, Kappa Chapter, Formerly Held Local and National Offices; American Museum of Natural History. Community Activities: Maplewood Garden Club; Summit Nature Club, National Audubon Society Chapter; American Association of University Women; Summit College Club; Wellesley and Cornell Clubs; League of Women Voters, Millburn, New Jersey; Wyoming Association, Millburn, New Jersey; Volunteer, Trustee on Management Board, Overlook Hospital, Summit, New Jersey, 1938-42. Published Works: Author of *Spores. Ferns. Microscopic Illusions Analyzed* Volumes I and II, as well as Numerous Articles for Scientific Journals, including Hundreds of Illustrations, Drawings, Photographs, and Photomicrographs. Honors and Awards: Keynote Speaker, Stereology Proceedings of Second International Congress, Chicago, 1967; Awards from Orchid and Horticultural Societies; Listed in *American Men of Science, Leaders in American Science, Who's Who of American Women, Who's Who in the East, The World Who's Who of Women, Two Thousand Women of Achievement, Dictionary of International Biography, International Authors and Writers Who's Who, Who's Who in America, International Who's Who of Intellectuals*. Address: 152 Glen Avenue, Millburn, New Jersey 07041.■

DWIGHT LEMOND HITE

Youth Service Staff Member. Personal: Born October 28, 1951; Son of Mr. and Mrs. Henry Hite; Married Cheryl Evans, Daughter of Mr. and Mrs. Evanda Evans; Father of Nacarra A. (Nikki). Education: Attended St. Bartholomew School, Catholic High Boys Academy, 1965-67; Central High School, 1967-70; AM&N College, 1970-71; University of Arkansas at Little Rock, 1972-74, 1979-80. Career: Staff Member, Alexander Youth Service, present; Marketing Representative, Siemens/Allis, Small Motor Division; Junior Accountant, Arkla Gas Company. Community Activities: Greater Little Rock Jaycees, Member Board of Directors 1976-77; Auxiliary Deputy Sheriff, 1979 to present; National Association for the Advancement of Colored People, 1982 to present; Trinity Lodge #33, Recording Secretary; Royal Arch, Knight Templar, 32nd Degree; Mason, Shriner, Council on Aging Volunteer, 1981 to present; Jaycees, Work with Youth, 1982 to present; Cancer Crusade, Volunteer 1976; United Way, Volunteer 1976; Art and Craft Design Ticket Chairman, Volunteer 1981. Religion: Mt. Zion Baptist Church, 1960 to present. Honors and Awards: Outstanding Service Award, Knight Templary, 1981; Outstanding Service Award, Freemasonry and Mankind in General, 1981; Listed in *Personalities of the South, Biographical Roll of Honor*. Address: 1704 High Street, Little Rock, Arkansas 72202.■

DONALD LEWIS HOBSON

Recorder's Court Judge. Personal: Born January 11, 1935; Son of Theresa and Oscar Hobson; Father of Donna Lynne. Education: Attended Ohio State University;

B.S. History, Eastern Michigan University; M.A., Michigan State University; J.D., Detroit College of Law; Postgraduate Work, University of Michigan, Wayne State University Law School, Hampton Institute, United States Naval Academy, University of Nevada. Military: Served an Active Tour of Duty in the United States Army, Honorable Discharge; Serves in the United States Naval Reserves, Judge Advocate General's Corps, rank of Lieutenant Commander. Career: Social Sciences Teacher, Detroit Public School System, 1957-64; Coordinator, Detroit Board of Education's Job Upgrading Program; Admitted to the Bar, 1965; Position with United States Attorneys Office, Washington, D.C.; Associate Partner, Goodman, Eden, Millender, Goodman and Bedrosian, Detroit, Michigan, 1965-72; Elected to Serve on the Bench of Common Pleas Court for City of Detroit, 1972; Clerk, Detroit Housing Commission; Clerk, Detroit Receiving Hospital, Counselor at Detroit Urban League's Green Pastures Camp (summers while attending college); Appointed by Governor William G. Milliken to Recorder's Court of Detroit in 1977, Subsequently Elected to Six-Year Term, 1978; Associate Professor, Detroit College of Law; Adjunct Lecturer, Law Department, Walsh College of Accounting and Business Administration. Organizational Memberships: Bar Memberships include Supreme Court of the United States, United States Court of Appeals (Sixth Circuit), District of Columbia Court of Appeals, State Bar of Michigan, State Bar of Wisconsin (inactive), District of Columbia (Washington) Unified Bar, Tax Court of the United States, United States District Court (Eastern District of Wisconsin); Arbitration Panelist and Member of Detroit Regional Advisory Council; American Arbitration Association; National Executive Board, National Lawyers Guild; Executive Board, American Trial Lawyers Association, Detroit Chapter; National Board, Council on Legal Educational Opportunities; Hearing Referee, Michigan Civil Rights Commission; Secretary, Income Tax Review Board, City of Detroit; Michigan Supreme Court's Special Committee on Landlord-Tenant Problems; National Board, National Bar Association; State Bar of Michigan Representative Assembly; Counsel, Grievance Board; Wolverine Bar Association, Treasurer, Vice President, President-Elect, President and Board of Directors; National Association for Equal Opportunity in Higher Education; National Board of Directors, National Bar Association Judicial Council; State Bar of Michigan's Special Committee on Professional and Judicial Ethics; State Bar Representative Assembly; National Association of Criminal Defense Lawyers, Honorary Member; Michigan Association of Criminal Defense Lawyers; Trustee, Black Law Student Scholarship Fund. Community Activities: Visiting Lecturer, Shaw College at Detroit; Chairman of Board of Trustees, Shaw College at Detroit; Serves on Boards of the Michigan Youth Foundation and Police Athletic League; Member, Urban Alliance; Co-Chairman, Concerned Citizens for Mental Health; Executive Board, Vice President, Detroit Branch National Association for the Advancement of Colored People. Honors and Awards: Eastern Michigan University Alumni Honors Award for Distinguished Service to Mankind and Continuing Interest in the University, 1974; Honorary Doctor of Humane Letters, Shaw College at Detroit for Distinguished Service to Mankind and his Continuing Interest in Educational Endeavors, 1977; Listed in *Who's Who in Michigan*, *Who's Who in American Law*, *Who's Who Among Black Americans*, *Community Leaders and Noteworthy Americans*, *Personalities of the West and Midwest*. Address: 2136 Bryanston Crescent, Detroit, Michigan 48207.■

HARLAN DAVID HOCKENBERG

Attorney at Law. Personal: Born July 1, 1927; Son of Mrs. Leonard Hockenberg; Married Dorothy A.; Father of Marni Lynn, Thomas Leonard, Edward Arkin. Education: B.A., University of Iowa, 1949; J.D., University of Iowa, 1952. Military: Served with the United States Navy, 1945. Career: Attorney at Law. Organizational Memberships: Honorary Fraternities; Delta Sigma Rho; Omicron Delta Kappa; Member, Board of Editors, *University of Iowa Law Review*, 1951-52. Community Activities: Member Board of Directors and Executive Committee, Greater Des Moines Chamber of Commerce; Second Vice President, Des Moines Chamber of Commerce; Past Chairman Bureau of Economic Development of Greater Des Moines Chamber of Commerce; Member, Pioneer Club; Des Moines Club; Wakonda Club; Member Board of Directors, West Des Moines State Bank, and the Aliber Foundation; Member Board of Directors, Jewish Institute of National Security Affairs; Member Board of Directors, Friends of the Israeli Institute for Economic Freedom; Regional Vice President and Member Executive Committee, American Public Affairs Committee; Past President, Des Moines Jewish Welfare Federation, 1973-74; Member Board of Directors, Council of Jewish Federations, 1969-73; President, Barrister's Inne, Des Moines, Iowa, 1960-61. Religion: Member Board of Trustees and President, Tifereth Israel Synagogue of Des Moines, Iowa, 1981-82. Honors and Awards: Co-Honoree, 1980, 1981 and 1982, 1979 Iowa Region, National Conference of Christians and Jews, Co-Chairman Iowa Region 1968-70; Listed in *Who's Who in the Midwest*. Address: 2880 Grand Avenue, Des Moines, Iowa 50312.■

JAMES DAY HODGSON

Professional Corporation Director, International Business Consultant. Personal: Born December 3, 1915; Married Maria Denend; Father of Nancy Ruth, Fredric Jesse. Education: A.B., University of Minnesota, 1938; Graduate Work at the University of Minnesota 1940, University of California Los Angeles 1946-47. Military: Served with the United States Navy as Air Officer, Carrier Pacific Duty, Air Combat Intelligence, 3 Years. Career: United States Ambassador to Japan, 1974-77; United States Secretary of Labor, 1970-73; United States Undersecretary of Labor, 1969-70; Chairman, President's Committee on Health Cost and Policy, 1973; Chairman, President's Committee on Construction Industry Collective Bargaining, 1970-72; Co-Chairman, Presidential Productivity Commission, 1971-72; Member, Cabinet Committee on International Economic Policy, 1970-73; Member, Cost of Living Council, 1970-73; 25 Years Corporation Executive and Supervisory Service with Principal Positions as Senior Vice President of Corporation Relations, and Vice President Industrial Relations at Lockheed Aircraft Corporation, 1941-68; 5 Years Service as Professional Corporation Director and International Business Consultant, 1977-82; University of California at Los Angeles, Part-Time Instructor of Industrial Relations (4 years), Community Relations Advisor (10 years), Adjunct Professor (4 years), Senior Advisor Pacific Basin Economic Study Center Graduate School of Management (3 years); Occasional Lecturer at University of California at Los Angeles, Temple University, University of Cincinnati, University of Minnesota, University of Colorado, University of Pennsylvania, University of Hawaii, Stanford University, Hoover Institute, United States Navy-Monterey, Baruch College (New York City); Director of Hewlett-Packard Company (Palo Alto, California), American Standard Inc. (New York City), ARA Services Inc. (Philadelphia, Pennsylvania), Calvin Bullock Ltd. (New York City), Ticor and Ticor Foundation (Los Angeles, California), California Federal Savings and Loan (Los Angeles), Pacific Scientific Corporation (Anaheim, California), United Television, Inc. (Minneapolis, Minnesota); Advisory Board, C. Itoh Company, Los Angeles, California; Senior Advisor, Mitsui Manufacturers Bank, Los Angeles, California; Advisor, Daini Seikosh Company Ltd., Tokyo, Japan (Seiko Watch Manufacturing Company); Advisor, Tokyo Consulting Group, Tokyo, Japan; Consultant, Ernst and Whinney, Los Angeles, California; Advisor, Gibson, Dunn and Crutcher, Los Angeles. Community Activities: Vice Chairman, National Committee, Pacific Basin Economic Council, Secretariat Stanford Research Institute; Director, Japan Society, New York City; Director, Pacific Forum, Honolulu, Hawaii; Director, Pacific Basin Institute, Santa Barbara, California; Director, Pan Pacific Association, Washington D.C.; Director, National Executive Service Corps, La Jolla, California; Adjunct Scholar, American Enterprise Institute, Washington D.C.; Chairman, Japan America Society of Southern California; Chairman, United States/Japan Business Education Project Japan Society, New York City; Advisor, Japanese Community and Cultural Center, Los Angeles, California; Advisor, Overseas Private Investment Corporation, Washington D.C.; Member, Council of Foreign Relations, New York City; Pepperdine University Board of Directors, Pepperdine Associates, Malibu, California; Board of Councilors, University of Southern California, School of Business Administration, Los Angeles, California; National Red Cross, Board of Governors, 1970-72; National Symphony Orchestra, Board of Directors, 1970-73; United Fund Campaign, United States Government Chairman, Washington D.C., 1972; Los Angeles Chamber of Commerce, Director 1977-80; Economic Resources Corporation, Los Angeles, Director 1973, 1974; National Alliance of Businessmen, Los Angeles, Director 1980; Orthopaedic Hospital, Los Angeles, Director 1981 to present; Member National Academy of Public Administration Panel, Study of "A Presidency for the 1980's," 1979-80; Burning Tree Club; Capitol Hill Club, Washington D.C.; Los Angeles Country Club; University Club, New York City. Published Works: Author Numerous Publications in his Field. Honors and Awards: Honorary Degrees from the University of Cincinnati 1972, Temple University 1971; Achievement Awards from the University of Minnesota 1969 and 1978. Address: 10132 Hillgrove Drive, Beverly Hills, California 90210.■

GLORIA THELMA ALBUERNE HOFF

Physicist, Educator. Personal: Born May 10, 1930, in Cienfuegos, Cuba; Naturalized United States Citizen, 1974; Daughter of Severiaxo Tranquilino Albuerne (deceased); Married Ramon Brewster Hoff; Mother of Erich Julian (deceased), Kevin Glade, Sharon Olivia. Education: Bachelor of Letters and Sciences, Our Lady of the Rosary Academy (American Dominican Academy), 1947; D.Sc., University of Havana, 1954; M.S., University of Chicago, 1957; Ph.D., University of Chicago, 1965. Career: Physicist, Associate Professor of Physics, University of Chicago, 1968 to present; Resident Research Associate, Argonne National Laboratory, 1966; Instructor in Physics, University of Illinois at Chicago, 1964-65; Assistant Professor of Physics, University of St. Thomas of Villanueva (Havana) 1957-58, Institute of Secondary Education (Havana) 1957-58, Institute of Secondary Education (Cienfuegos, Cuba) 1951-54. Organizational Memberships: Cuban Society of Doctors in Science and Philosophy, 1951-58; American Physical Society; American Association for the Advancement of Science; Sigma Xi, Elected Associate Member University of Chicago Chapter; New York Academy of Sciences. Community Activities: St. Thomas the Apostle Home and School Association, Executive Committee, Secretary 1977; Merit Program Parents Council, 1984; International House Council, 1956-57; Crossroads Student Center Council, 1956-57; Reviewer for *American Journal of Physics*, 1975-77. Religion: St. Thomas the Apostle Church (Chicago), Auxiliary Communion 1978 to present; Choir Member 1982 to present. Honors and Awards: 12 Prizes in Various Mathematics and Physics Courses, University of Havana, 1947-51; Fellowship, University of Havana, 1956-57; Summer Faculty Fellowship,

University of Illinois at Chicago Circle, 1965; Summer Faculty Fellowship, University of Illinois at Chicago Circle, 1973; Grant, University of Illinois at Chicago Circle Research Board, 1965-66. Address: 5634 South Blackstone Avenue, Chicago, Illinois 60637.■

HOWARD TORRENS HOFFMAN

Multi-Industry Executive. Personal: Born December 30, 1923, East St. Louis, Illinois; Son of Mrs B. E. Hoffman; Married Ruth Ann Gisela Koch; Father of Howard T., Jean Gisele, Glenn Kevin. Education: B.S.E.E., Iowa State University, 1950; M.S.E.E. 1972, Ph.D. 1977, Thomas University; Registered Professional Engineer. Military: Served in the Office of Military Government, United States Zone, Berlin, Germany, 1943-46. Career: President, Chief Executive Officer, Hoffman Associates; Board Chairman, Executive Director, H&R Associates; Division Manager, Teledyne-Ryan, San Diego, California, 1960-66; Manager, Missile Systems, Litton Industries, College Park, Maryland, 1959-60; Executive Engineer, I.T.T. Labs, Fort Wayne, Indiana, 1957-59; Missile Systems Engineer, McDonnell Aircraft Corporation, St. Louis, Missouri, 1955-57; Engineering Section Head, Joy Manufacturing Company, St. Louis, Missouri, 1950-55. Organizational Memberships: Institute of Electrical and Electronic Engineers; American Institute of Aeronautics and Astronautics; National Society of Professional Engineers; American Management Association; National Management Association; Armed Forces Communications and Electronic Association; International Platform Association. Community Activities: Association of the United States Army; Disabled American Veterans; University City Civic Association; Boy Scouts of America; United Crusade. Published Works: Articles on DC Amplifiers, Intrinsic Safety, Lunar Landing Radars, Space Radars and Program Control. Honors and Awards: Bronze Star Medal, 1945; Combat (Medical) Badge, 1945; United Crusade Community Service Award, 1972; Community Leaders Award, 1975; Listed in *Who's Who in America, Who's Who in the West, Who's Who in Finance and Industry, Who's Who in Aviation, Dictionary of International Biography, Personalities of America, Notable Americans, Personalities of the West and Midwest, Community Leaders and Noteworthy Americans, International Who's Who in Community Service, Men of Achievement, Who's Who in Aviation and Aerospace, Jane's Directory of Aviation and Aerospace, International Who's Who in Community Service, Dictionary of Distinguished Americans, Who's Who in California, Who's Who in California Finance and Industry*. Address: 5545 Stresemann Street, San Diego, California 92122.■

JULIUS J. HOFFMAN

United States District Judge. Personal: Born July 7, 1895, in Chicago, Illinois. Education: LL.B. 1915; LL.D. (honorary), Northwestern University School of Law. Career: Faculty Member, Northwestern University School of Law; Vice President and General Counsel, Brunswick Corporation. Organizational Memberships: Fellow, American Bar Association, 1956. Published Works: Many Public Addresses Delivered throughout the United States; Numerous Papers in Various Law Journals in the United States. Honors and Awards: Service Award, Award of Merit, Northwestern University School of Law; Award of Merit, Patent Law Association, Chicago, 1970; Plaque with Tribute from all his Colleagues on United States District Court; Plaque as Tribute to "A Lifetime of Public Service from Federal Bar Association," 1972. Address: Everett McKinley Dirksen Building, 219 South Dearborn Street, Chicago, Illinois 60604.■

AUDREY SONIA HOFFNUNG

Associate Professor. Personal: Born March 15, 1928; Daughter of Nathan and Gussie Karp Smith (both deceased); Married Joseph Hoffnung; Mother of Bonnie Fern Hoffnung Loewenstein, Tami Lynn Hoffnung Schwartzman. Education: B.A., Brooklyn College, 1949; M.A., Teachers College, Columbia University, 1950; Ph.D., City University of New York, 1974. Career: Associate Professor of Speech-Language Pathology, St. John's University; Adjunct Lecturer, Brooklyn College, 1973-77; Lecturer, Queens College, 1970-72; Consultant and Therapist, South Nassau Communities Hospital, 1964-65; Diagnostician and Therapist, Brooklyn College, 1958-62, 1963-64; Diagnostician, Consultant, Therapist, Morris J. Colomon Clinic for Mentally Retarded and Emotionally Disturbed, Brooklyn Jewish Hospital; Director of Speech-Language Therapy, Kingsbrook Medical Center, 1950-55; Speech Therapist, Ridgewood Cerebral Palsy Center, 1949-50. Organizational Memberships: Aphasia Study Group; American Speech-Language-Hearing Association; Long Island Speech-Language-Hearing Association; New York State Speech-Language-Hearing Association; New York City Speech-Language-Hearing Association; New York State English as a Second Language-Bilingual Education Association. Honors and Awards: Vocational Rehabilitation Administration Traineeship, 1971; Listed in *Who's Who of American Women*. Address: 3282 Woodward Street, Oceanside, New York 11572.■

FRANCIS LAFAYETTE HOLLOWAY, SR.

Construction Consultant. Personal: Born January 23, 1911; Son of Alexander M. and Alberta K. Holloway (deceased); Married Bessie Cheatham, Daughter of Archibald and Ethel Cheatham (deceased); Father of Francis L. Jr., Ethel H. Law. Education: B.S. Civil Engineering, University of Maryland, 1931. Career: Construction Consultant; Engineering and Geological Studies and Supervisory as well as Management Operations related to Highways, Airfields, Dams, and Foundations for Large Buildings (work has involved effort in 36 states and 24 foreign countries); Involved in Preparation of Claims. Community Activities: Aided in Scout Activities, Salvation Army, Young Men's Christian Association (including work effort and donations). Honors and Awards: Paul Harris Fellow, Citation, Rotary, 1981; Magna Charta Barons, Sons of the American Revolution; Listed in *Who's Who in the East, Personalities of America, Men of Achievement, International Who's Who of Intellectuals*. Address: 513 North Pinehurst Avenue, Salisbury, Maryland 21801.■

BRANTON KIETH HOLMBERG

Executive. Personal: Born March 6, 1936; Son of Victor August Holmberg; Married Margaret A., Daughter of Jessie Nelson; Father of James Michael, Ann Marie, Nelson John. Education: B.A. 1962, M.Ed. 1964, Central Washington University; Ed.D., University of Idaho, 1970. Military: Served in the United States Air Force as a Medical Service Specialist, Honorable Discharge 1963. Career: President, Northwest Horticulture Inc., International Highpoint Corporation, Holmberg Associates; Former President, Northpoint Corporation (Geriatric Care Centers); General Manager, Shuksan Convalescent Center; Director, U.S. International University, McChord AFB Program; Managing Partner, Holmberg, Jorgenson & Associate; Associate Director, Organization Development Center, Central Washington University. Organizational Memberships: American Management Association; International Registry of Organization Development Consultants; American Psychological Association; Organization Development Network; American Personnel and Guidance Association; American Association of University Professors; Certified Consultants International. Community Activities: Ellensburg Criminal Law and Justice Planning Committee; Professional Resource Person to Washington State Sub-committee on Corrections; Steering Committtee, U.S. Senatorial Business Advisory Board; Bellingham Chamber of Commerce; National Federation of Independent Businesses. Honors and Awards: Listed in *Who's Who in the West, American Men and Women of Science, Who's Who in Finance and Industry, Community Leaders of America*. Address: 910 Yew Street, Bellingham, Washington 98226.■

KENNETH MERTON HOLTZCLAW

Analytical Chemist. Personal: Born September 2, 1929; Son of Alvin Raymond and Esther Josephine (Mearkens); Married Margaret Bess Gould, Daughter of C. J. and E. Gould (deceased); Father of Kenneth Kelly, Brenda Bea, Brian Lee. Education: B.S. Chemistry, Loma Linda University, 1963. Military: Served with the United States Navy, 1950-54. Career: Analytical Chemist, Department of Soil and Environmental Science, University of California, Riverside; Research Assistant, B. F. Goodrich Aerospace, Rialto, California; Research Associate, Lockheed Propulsion, Mentone, California. Organizational Memberships: Soil Science Society of America; American Society of Agronomy. Honors and Awards: Recipient of Special Performance Award, University of California at Riverside, 1980. Address: 13812 Day Street, Riverside, California 92508.■

HARRY C. HONG

College Professor and Department Chairman. Personal: Born March 27, 1932; Married Doris; Son of Thomas and Benjamin. Education: Ph.D. 1965, M.A. 1961, both in History, University of Iowa; Attended Hillsdale College (Hillsdale, Michigan) 1959, Dankook University (Seoul, Korea) 1956. Career: Chairman and Professor of Political Science, Jamestown College, Jamestown, North Dakota. Organizational Memberships: North Dakota Social Science Association, Secretary-Treasurer 1967-68, President 1969-70, Board of Directors 1971-73; American Political Science Association; Association for Asian Studies. Community Activities: Advisory Board, American Security Council, 1971 to present; United States Congressional Advisory Board, 1981 to present; Presidential Advisory Board, 1981 to present; Jamestown Citizens Advisory Committee on Urban and Community Development, 1974-75; Jamestown Rotary Club, Board of Directors 1974-76, Chairman International Service Committee 1974-80. Honors and Awards: Presidential Achievement Award, 1981; Outstanding Educators of America Citation, 1971, 1972, 1973; Professor of the Year, Jamestown College, 1979; Listed in *Who's Who in the Midwest, International Who's Who in Education, International Book of Honor, Directory of Distinguished Americans.* Address: 250 - 18th Avenue, Jamestown, North Dakota 58401.■

DAVID LORNE HOOF

Physical Scientist. Personal: Born December 2, 1945; Son of Wayne and Mary Hoof; Married Bethea L. Giedhill; Father of Laura Louise, Emily Joy. Education: A.B. Chemistry, Cornell University, 1969; M.S. Chemistry 1971, Ph.D. Inorganic Chemistry 1974, Purdue University. Career: Physical Scientist, Office of Spent Fuel Management and Reprocessing Systems, United States Department of Energy; Previous Positions include Chemist, Chemical Engineer, Lecturer in Chemistry, N.S.F. Postdoctoral Fellow in Research Chemisry. Organizational Memberships: American Chemical Society, 1972-76; American Nuclear Society, 1978-80; Sigma Xi; American Association for the Advancement of Science, 1978-80; New York Academy of Sciences, 1978-80; Planetary Society, 1981-82. Community Activities: Episcopal Youth Fellowship Program, Leader 1975-76; District Architectural Review Committee, 1979-80. Religion: Saint Mary Magdelene Episcopal Church, 1974-82; Christ Church Episcopal, 1982 to present. Honors and Awards: All-American Interscholastic Swimming Team, 1962-64; N.S.F. Postdoctoral Fellowship, 1974-75; Sigma Xi, Research Society of North America, 1974; Listed in *Who's Who in the East, Community Leaders of America, Dictionary of International Biography, Who's Who in Technology Today.* Address: 11604 Silent Valley Lane, Gaithersburg, Maryland 20878.■

LARRY ALLAN HOOVER

Information Systems Manager and Marketing Executive. Personal: Born June 13, 1940; Son of Mr. and Mrs. Robert Paul Hoover; Married Frances Mango Hoover; Father of William Christopher. Education: A.A. Electrical Engineering, Charlotte College, 1961; B.S. Experimental Statistics, North Carolina State University; M.S. Management of Technology, American University, 1979. Career: Information Systems Manager and Automated Data Processing (ADP) Consultant; Deputy Direcotr, Advanced Programs, Planning Research Corporation, 1982 to present; Director, Systems Policy, CRC Systems Inc., 1980-82; Project Manager/Senior Consultant, Boeing Computer Services, 1974-80; Project Manager, Synergistics Cybernetics Inc., 1969-74; Member of Technical Staff, Computer Sciences Corporation, 1967-69; Analyst/Programmer, Lane Furniture Company, 1965-67. Organizational Memberships: Association for Science, Technology and Innovation, Membership Chairman 1979-82; American Management Association; World Futures Society; American Association for the Advancement of Science. Community Activities: Pinoca Volunteer Fire Department, Member 1960-61, Secretary 1961; Charlotte Life Saving and Rescue Squad, 1960-61; Jaycees-Junior Chamber of Commerce, Altavista Chapter, Secretary and Member of Board of Directors 1965-67. Religion: Member of Episcopalian Church, Property Committee 1983, Elected Vestry Member 1983-84. Honors and Awards: Statistics Delegate, Science Council, North Carolina State University, 1964-65; Pi Alpha Alpha National Honors Society, American University, Member 1979, Vice President 1982-83, Councilman 1983-84; Elected to Washington Academy of Sciences, 1981. Address: 801 Croydon Street, Sterling, Virginia 22170.■

REUBEN ARTHUR HOUSEAL

Clergyman, Educator, Writer. Personal: Born January 6, 1910, in York, Pennsylvania; Son of John Franklin and Beatrice Vervean Dellinger Houseal; Married First Wife, Jennie Belle Hinkle, June 1, 1929; Married Second Wife, Marguerite Edna Ruth Arnold, on November 26, 1964; Father of Reuben John, Elisabeth H. Honecker, Lawrence Garrison, (Stepfather of) John A. Johnson, Marguerite Johnson Redmond. Education: Graduate of Philadelphia College of Bible, 1932; B.A., M.A., University of Pennsylvania; Undertook Postgraduate Studies, Reformed Episcopal Theological Seminary, 1934-37; Th.D. 1973, Ph.D. 1977, L.L.D. (honorary), Clarksville School of Theology, Clarksville, Tennessee. Career; Pastor, Several Churches, including Bethany Community Church (Dayton, Ohio), Olive Branch Congregational Church (St. Louis, Missouri), Central Baptist Church (Erie, Pennsylvania), 1937-57; Founder, Director, GospeLiteHouse of the Air (a broadcast ministry in Pennsylvania, Ohio, Illinois, Missouri and Michigan), 1942 to present; Executive Board, Faculty, Greensburg Bible Institute, Pennsylvania, 1960-71; Institutional Chaplain, Mercer County, Pennsylvania, 1967 to present; Bible Conference/Evangelistic Ministry, Mercer County, Pennsylvania, 1967 to present. Organizational Memberships: Independent Fundamental Churches of America, Member 1938 to present, Chairman National Commission on Institutional Chaplains 1972 to present; Calvary School of Theology, Mercer, Pennsylvania, Co-Founder, Vice President, Academic Dean, 1974 to present; York Gospel Center, York, Pennsylvania, Constituent Member 1937 to present. Honors and Awards: Life Member, Mercer County Historical Society; Life Fellow, International Biographical Association; Life Patron, American Biographical Institute Research Association; Outstanding Alumnus Award, Philadelphia College of Bible; Honorary M.S., Conferred by the *Encyclopaedia Britannica*; Commissioned a Kentucky Colonel by that State's Governor, October 1977; Listed in *Who's Who in Religion, International Register of Profiles, International Men of Achievement, International Who's Who of Intellectuals, International Who's Who in Community Service, International Men and Women of Distinction, Dictionary of International Biography, Book of Honor, Notable Americans, Personalities of America, Community Leaders and Noteworthy Americans, American Registry Series, Community Leaders of America, Directory of Distinguished Americans, Personalities of the East, Biographical Roll of Honor, Who's Who in the East, Encyclopaedia of Contemporary Personalities, Who is Who, International Book of Honor, Five Thousand Personalities of the World, The World Biographical Hall of Fame.* Address: 132 South Erie Street, P.O. Box 132, Mercer, Pennsylvania 16137.■

RUTH ARNOLD HOUSEAL

Retired Educator. Personal: Born November 23, 1904, in Mercer, Pennsylvania; Daughter of Samuel B. McAle and Mary Edna Williams Arnold; Married First Husband, 1932; Married Second Husband, Rev. Dr. Reuben Arthur Houseal, November 26, 1964; Mother of John A. Johnson, Marguerite Johnson Redmond. Education: B.S., Slippery Rock State College, Pennsylvania, 1958; M.S.Ed., Westminster College, New Wilmington, Pennsylvania, 1963; Diploma for completing the Scofield Bible Course, Moody Bible Institute, 1966; D.R.E. 1973, L.H.D. (honorary) 1974, Clarksville School of Theology, Clarksville, Tennessee. Career: Teacher, Building Principal, Art Supervisor on Elementary Level, 27 Years; Worked with and Successfully Educated Exceptional Children 15 Years, Trained Student Teachers in that Field; Conducted Teacher Training Courses for Church Schools; Presently Active in The Cause-of-Christ and with the Independent Fundamental Churches of America. Organizational Memberships: National Education Association, Life Member; Pennsylvania State Education Association, Life Member; Mercer County Historical Society, Life Member; International Biographical Association, Life Fellow. Published Works: Textbook *A Survey of Christian Education.* Honors and Awards: Certificate of Merit and Distinguished Achievement for Meritorious Work and Citizenship, International Biographical Association; Life Patron, A.B.I.R.A.; Listed in *Who's Who in Religion, Dictionary of International Biography, International Register of Profiles, International Who's Who in Community Service, Book of Honor, Notable Americans, American Registry Series, Personalities of America, Community Leaders and Noteworthy Americans, Notable Personalities of America, International Men and Women of Achievement, World Who's Who of Women, Who's Who in Community Service, Who's Who of American Women, International Men and Women of Distinction, International Who's Who of Intellectuals, Who's Who in the East, Encyclopaedia of Contemporary Personalities, Who is Who, International Book of Honor, Community Leaders of America, The Directory of Distinguished Americans, Five Thousand Personalities of the World, The World Biographical Hall of Fame, The Biographical Roll of Honor.* Address: 132 South Erie Street, P.O. Box 132, Mercer, Pennsylvania 16137.■

NEAL PETER HOUSLANGER

Podiatrist. Personal: Born April 20, 1949; Son of William and Rhoda Houslanger; Married Bonnie; Father of Lisa, Stacy, Karen. Career: Podiatrist. Organizational Memberships: American Podiatry Association; Podiatry Society of New York; Executive Board, Nassau County Podiatry Society, 1979 to present; American College of Sports Medicine; Fellow, American Society of Podiatric Dermatology; International Academy for Standing and Walking Fitness; American Society of Computers in Medicine and Dentistry; American Academy of Podiatric Laser Surgery; Fellow, Academy of Ambulatory Foot Surgery; Board Eligible, American Board of Podiatric Surgery, Ambulatory Division. Community Activities: March of Dimes Birth Defects Foundation, Long Island Chapter, Director of Podiatric Medicine, Board of Directors 1981 to present; Kiwanis Club of Mineola, 1979 to present; Foot Health Screening, Local High School, 1979 to present; Lecturer to Senior Citizens Groups, Grammar and High Schools, 1979 to present. Honors and Awards: Podiatrist of the Year, Nassau County, 1981; Diplomate National Board of Podiatric Examiners, 1976; Listed in *Who's Who in the East, Community Leaders of the World, Personalities in America, Men of Achievement, Biographical Directory of the American Podiatry Association, The International Who's Who of Intellectuals, The Directory of Distinguished Americans.* Address: 24 Bruno Lane, Dix Hills, New York 11746.■

TWO THOUSAND NOTABLE AMERICANS

ADELINE B. HOWARD

Agriculture Owner/Manager. Personal: Born July 19, 1916; Daughter of William M. and Emma (Lienhard) Boller (both deceased); Married Alfred R. Howard, Son of William T. and Emaline (Johnson) Howard (both deceased); Mother of Jerry A., John A., Julian A. Education: Graduate, Potlatch High School, 1934; Secretarial, Kinman Business University, 1937. Career: Agriculture Owner/Manager; Secretary-Treasurer, Freeze Cemetery Maintenance District; Bookkeeping Services and Notary Public; Cashier, Potlatch Mercantile Company, 1936-42; Bookkeeper-Teller, Idaho First National Bank, Potlatch, 1959-61; Bookkeeper-Typist, University of Idaho, 1962-64; Senior Teller-Clerk, Idaho First National Bank, 1966-71; Secretary, 1971-77; Loan Assistant, 1977-79; Loan Officer and Operations Officer, 1979-81; Retired, 1981. Organizational Memberships: Idaho Federation Business and Professional Women's Clubs Inc., President 1981-82, President Elect 1980-81, First Vice President, 1979-80, Second Vice President 1978-79, Recording Secretary 1977-79, General Chairman Idaho State Convention in Moscow 1979, Chairman Idaho Reception at National Convention in Puerto Rico 1978, Chairman Idaho Breakfast at National Convention in Boston 1979, Delegate to National B.P.W. Conventions in Denver 1977, Puerto Rico 1978, Boston 1979, San Francisco 1981, San Antonio 1982; Potlatch Club, Business and Professional Women's Clubs Inc., Organized Potlatch Club 1974, President 1976-78, President Elect 1975-76, Treasurer 1979 to present; National Association of Bank Women, Active Member 1979 to present; Credit Women International, Active Member, Moscow Club 1970 to present; American Business Women's Association, Member Hell's Canyon Club at Lewiston, 1973 to present; Princeton Grange #426, Member 1945 to present, Worthy Master 1967-68 (only woman to serve Princeton Grange as Worthy Master since instituted), Member National Grange 1954, Member Centennial Club National Grange 1968; Idaho Women for Agriculture, Member Latah #1, 1982. Community Activities: University of Idaho, Moscow, Member of Selection Committee for University of Idaho County Honor Award 1967 to present; Crane Creek 4-H Club, Organizational Leader 1964-68; Potlatch Parent Teacher Association, Charter Member, President 1956 and 1957, Life Member Idaho Congress Parent Association 1958, District 2 Vice President of Idaho Congress Parent Teacher Association; Campfire Girls, Leader of Horizon Club, 1975; Potlatch Junior Miss Pageant, Auditor, 1979-83; Latah County Free Library Board, Board Member 1965 and 1966; Idaho Cystic Fibrosis Foundation, Potlatch Chairman 1981, 1983; Democratic Committee Chairperson, Idaho Precinct #27, 1982; Order of Eastern Star, Potlatch Chapter #48, Member 1942 to present, Worthy Matron 1953 and 1966-67, Current Secretary (past 14 years), Grand Representative of Kentucky 1953, Grand Representative of Washington 1976 and 1977, Member Potlatch Past Matrons 1951 to present, Secretary Past Matron's Club 1974 to present; Mistletoe Rebekah Lodge #85, International Order of the Odd Fellows, Active Member 1945 to present, Noble Grant 1951 and 1953, Lodge Deputy (3 terms), District Deputy President (3 terms), Staff Captain 1962 to present, Trustee 1970 and 1982, Militants, IOOF, Active Member Royal #5 Moscow 1954 to present, President Royal #5 (5 terms), Inspecting Officer, President of Department Association of Ladies Auxiliaries Patriarch Militants of Idaho, IOOF 1965-66; Theta Rho Girl's Clubs, IOOF, Advisor to Potlatch Theta Rho Girl's Club 1962 and 1963, Chairman of Theta Rho Girl's Clubs of Idaho, 1964; Daughters of the Nile, Member Malac Temple No. 55, Lewiston, 1952 to present; Ladies Encampment Auxiliary, IOOF, Member Clearwater Valley LEA #27, 1964 to present; Royal Neighbors of America, Member Camp #4266, Potlatch, 1973 to present; Senior Citizens Club; Member Potlatch Senior Citizens Club, 1980 to present; The Smithsonian Associates, National Member, 1983. Religion: Community Presbyterian Church, Potlatch, Sunday School Teacher 1946 and 1947, Elder 1978 and 1979, Current Treasurer (served past 10 years), Served on National Presbyterian Church Panel 1979, 1980, 1981. Honors and Awards: Decoration of Chivalry, 1961; Pi Rho Zeta Business Honorary, 1935; Girls' League Outstanding Girl Award, Potlatch High School, 1934; Plaque and Certificate for Outstanding Performance, Idaho Cystic Fibrosis Foundation, 1981 and 1982; Woman of Progress, North Central District, Business and Professional Women's Clubs Inc., 1982; Named First Lady of the Year by Beta Sigma Phi International, 1982; Listed in *Personalities of America, Personalities of the West and Midwest, Community Leaders of America, Biographical Roll of Honor, Notable Americans.* Address: Rt. 1, Box 213, Potlatch, Idaho 83855.■

DAVID M. HOWARD

General Director. Personal: Born January 28, 1928; Son of Dr. and Mrs. P. E. Howard; Married Phyllis G., Daughter of Lowell C. Gibson; Father of David M. Jr., Stephen G., Karen Elisabeth, Michael E. Education: B.A. Liberal Arts, Wheaton College, Illinois, 1949; M.A. Theology, Wheaton College Graduate School of Theology, 1952. Career: General Director, World Evangelical Fellowship Latin America Mission, 1953-68; Assistant General Director, Latin America Mission, 1958-68; Missions Director, Inter-Varsity Christian Fellowship, 1968-77; Director of Inter-Varsity Student Missionary Conventions, URBANA, 1973 and 1976; Director, Consultation on World Evangelization, Pattaya, Thailand, 1980. Community Activities: Board of Trustees, Wheaton College, Illinois, 1975 to present; Board of Trustees, Latin America Mission, 1965-80; Board of Directors, Overseas Counseling Service, 1982 to present; Board of Directors, Serve International, 1982 to present; Board of Directors, Deerfoot Lodge (Christian Camp), 1982 to present. Published Works: Author of Numerous Articles published in Magazines such as *Christianity Today, Eternity, HIS, Moody Monthly, United Evangelical Action, Evangelical Missions Quarterly, Pensamiento Cristiano,* Others; Author *Student Power in World Missions* 1979, *The Great Commission for Today* 1976, *Words of Fire, Rivers of Tears* 1976, *By the Power of the Holy Spirit* 1973, *How Come, God?* 1972, *The Costly Harvest* (formerly entitled *Hammered as Gold*) 1975. Honors and Awards: Doctor of Laws, Geneva College, 1974; Doctor of Humane Letters, Taylor University, 1978; Alumnus of the Year, Wheaton College, 1977; Crusader Club Christian Contribution Award, 1979. Address: 823 Anchor Court, Bartlett, Illinois 60103.■

GENE C. HOWARD

Attorney, State Senator. Personal: Born September 26, 1926, Son of Joe W. and Nell Howard; Married Belva J. Prestidge; Father of Belinda Janice, Joe Ted, Jean Ann Peterson. Education: LL.B., University of Oklahoma, 1951. Military: Served in the United States Air Force, 1944-46, 1961-62, attaining the rank of Lieutenant Colonel. Career: Attorney; Senator, State of Oklahoma, 1964 to present; Representative, State of Oklahoma, 1958-62. Organizational Memberships: Tulsa Bar Association; Oklahoma Bar Association; Phi Delta Phi. Community Activities: Oklahoma Senate, President pro tem 1975-81. Religion: Disciples of Christ. Honors and Awards: Outstanding Young Attorney for 1953, Tulsa County Bar Association; Honorary Member, O.C.U. Law School Alumni Association, 1977. Address: 4816 South Yorktown, Tulsa, Oklahoma 74105.■

JOHN WILFRED HOWARD

Commercial Artist. Personal: Born August 20, 1924; Son of John D. and Veral K. Howard; Married Leona Belle Thompson, Daughter of Fordie and Maude Thompson; Father of Bonnie D., Connie M., Sharon K., Teressa L., Sandra L. Education: College Credits in Art (2 years), Art Instruction Inc., Minneapolis, Minnesota, Graduated 1981. Military: Served with the United States Army Infantry, 1945-47. Career: Commercial Artist; Self-Employed Farmer; Life and Health Insurance Agent; General Agent, 1972-79. Organizational Memberships: Creative World Inc., 1982-83; International Platform Association. Religion: Member, Baptist Church, 1947-83. Honors and Awards: Competed with Artists throughout the United States and in Canada, Won the President's Top Award; Work Appears in *Artists U.S.A.* (internationally distributed book); Listed in *Men of Achievement, Personalities of the South, Personalities of America, Who's Who in the South and Southwest, Biographical Roll of Honor, Directory of Distinguished Americans, The International Who's Who of Intellectuals, International Register of Profiles.* Address: RR #2, Corinth, Kentucky 41010.■

COLLEEN JANET HOWE

Executive. Personal: Born February 17, 1933, in Detroit, Michigan; Married Gordon Howe; Mother of Marty Gordon, Mark Steven, Cathleen Jill, Murray Albert. Education: Graduate, Mackenzie High School, Detroit, Michigan, 1950. Career: President, Howe Enterprises, 1954 to present; Consultant, Hartford Whalers Hockey Club, Hartford, Connecticut, 1977 to present; President, Howe International Marketing; Investor/Manager; Licensed Life Insurance Agent, Connecticut; Consultant, Houston Aeros Hockey Club, Inc., Houston, Texas, 1973-77; Director, Howe Travel, Inc., Southfield, Michigan, 1975-79; Receptionist, Secretary, Ferd Prucher Art Studios, Detroit, Michigan, 1952-53; File Clerk, Receptionist, Recorder, Bethlehem Steel Company, Detroit, Michigan, 1950-52. Organizational Memberships: Hartford Life Underwriters Association; A.D.A.U.S.; Advertising Club of Greater Hartford; Convention and Visitors Bureau. Community Activities; Republican Candidate for First District Nomination for Congress; March of Dimes, Northern Connecticut Chapter, Executive Committee; Newington Children's

Hospital, Director; Sports Medicine Council, University of Connecticut; Organizer, Director, Benzie National Bank; Colonial Bank Advisory Board; Michigan 4-H Foundation, Board Member; Detroit Junior Wings, Michigan Amateur Hockey Program, Board Member, Spearheaded the Formulation of and Managed this First Successful Junior A Hockey Club in the United States. Published Works: Book *My Three Hockey Players*; Articles in Face-Off Hockey Publication and *The New York Times*. Religion: First Church of Christ Congregational. Honors and Awards: Honored for Outstanding Achievements in Insurance Field, Aetna Life Insurance Company; Voted Sportswoman of the Year, Sportcasters/Sportwriters of Detroit, 1972; Charter Oak Medal for Outstanding Community Achievement, Hartford Chamber of Commerce, 1979; Executive of the Year, *Connecticut Journal*; Listed in *Who's Who of American Women*. Address: 32 Plank Lane, Glastonbury, Connecticut 06033.■

JONATHAN (JON) THOMAS HOWE

Attorney at Law. Personal: Born December 16, 1940, in Evanston, Illinois; Married Lois H. Braun; Father of Heather, Jonathan T. Jr., Sara. Education: B.A. with honors in History, Northwestern University, Evanston, Illinois, 1963; J.D. with distinction, Duke University, Durham, North Carolina, 1966. Career: Partner, Jenner & Block, Chicago, Illinois; Engaged in General Practice, 1966 to present; Member, Firm Executive and Management Committee, 1975 to present; Senior Partner in Charge of Association and Administrative Law Department, 1978 to present; Admitted to Practice, Supreme Court of Illinois, 1966 to present; United States Tax Court, 1968 to present; United States District Court, Northern District of Illinois, 1966 to present; United States District Court, District of Columbia, 1976 to present; United States Court of Appeals, 7th Circuit, 1967 to present; United States Court of Appeals, 9th Circuit, 1980 to present; District Court of Columbia Court of Appeals, 1976 to present; United States Supreme Court, 1970 to present. Organizational Memberships: American Bar Association 1966 to present, Chairman Young Lawyers Section of Memberships Committee in Illinois 1967-71, Chairman Young Lawyers Section of Environmental Law Committee in Illinois 1970-73, Regional Director 1972-74, Member Antitrust Section 1967 to present, National Institute Committee 1973 to present, Corporate Banking and Business Law Section 1967 to present, Section on Litigation 1974 to present, Council Member for Educational Programs 1974-78, Administrative Law Section 1969 to present, International Law Committee 1977 to present, Continuing Education Committee 1977 to present; Illinois State Bar Association 1966 to present, Member Antitrust Section 1966 to present, Section Council 1980-81, Civil Practice Section 1966 to present, School Law Section 1969 to present, Environmental Law Section 1970 to present, Co-Editor of *Antitrust Newsletter* 1968-70; Chicago Bar Association 1966 to present, Chairman Judiciary and Bench Bar Relations Committee 1971-72, Executive Committee of Young Lawyers Section 1971-72, Defense of Prisoners Committee 1966 to present, Antitrust Law Committee 1971 to present, Continuing Education Committee 1977 to present; District of Columbia Bar Association, 1976 to present; American Judicature Society, 1966 to present; Legal Club of Chicago, 1974 to present; The Law Club, 1981 to present; Contributing Editor, Illinois Institute for Continuing Legal Education, 1973 to present. Community Activities: Board of Education, District #27, Northbrook, Illinois 1969 to present, Secretary 1969-72, President 1973 to present; Illinois Association of School Boards 1969 to present, President 1977-79, Vice President 1976-77, Director-at-Large 1972-76, Board of Directors 1971 to present, Chairman North Subdivision 1971-72, Member Advisory Council 1970-71, Chairman of Executive Committee and Board of Directors of Tri-County Division 1971-76; Chairman Board of Trustees, School Employee Benefit Trust, 1979 to present; President and Founding Member Board of Directors, School Management Foundation of Illinois, 1976 to present; National School Boards Association 1969 to present, NSBA National Board of Directors 1979 to present, NSBA Executive Committee 1981 to present, Chairman Resolutions and Policy Committee 1979-80, Vice Chairman 1980-81, Chairman Constitution and Bylaws Committee 1981 to present, Direct Affiliate Committee 1980 to present, NSBA Building Committee 1980 to present, Chairman Task Force on Global Education 1980-81, Chairperson Central Region 1979-80, Delegate NSBA Delegate Assembly 1976-79, Lecturer 1973 to present, Representative to Advisory Commission on Intergovernmental Affairs in Washington D.C. 1975, NSBA Representative to American Association of School Administrators Committee for the Advancement of School Administration, National Association of State Boards of Education and Council of Chief State School Officials 1978 to present, Federal Relations Network 1977 to present, AASA Committee on the Advancement of School Administration 1977-79, NSBA Delegate to American Medical Association Medical Education Committee 1979 to present; Executive Committee, Northfield Township Republican Organization, 1967-71; Congressional Campaign Manager, 13th Congressional District, Illinois, 1969; Northwestern University Alumni Association, Steering Committee 1967-68, Young Alumni Steering Committee 1971-72, Northwestern Club of Chicago 1967 to present, Alumni Fraternity Board 1973-76; Executives' Club of Chicago, 1980 to present; Duke University Alumni Association, Decade Program 1975 to present, Barristers Club 1976 to present; Lyric Opera Guild of Chicago, 1972 to present; Chicago Athletic Association 1975 to present, Chicago Council on Foreign Relations 1977 to present, Plaza Club Chicago 1976 to present, Sunset Ridge Country Club 1978 to present, Mid-America Club of Chicago 1980 to present. Religion: Member Board of Deacons 1975-78, Board of Trustees 1981 to present, Village Presbyterian Church of Northbrook, Illinois. Published Works: Author Numerous Publications in his Field, Lecturer and Author for Various Professional Societies, Trade Associations, Civic Organizations and Others. Honors and Awards: Order of the Coif, First in Graduating Class, Phi Alpha Delta Outstanding Scholastic Achievement Award, all while attending Duke University, Durham, North Carolina; Listed in *Who's Who in American Law, Who's Who in the Midwest, Notable Americans, Who's Who in America*. Address: 3845 Normandy Lane, Northbrook, Illinois 60062.■

CHING-YU HSU

State Advisor. Personal: Born December 25, 1898; Came to the United States December 1958, Naturalized 1964; Son of Shih-kang and Shu-yi (deceased); Married Anna; Father of Yu-kuan, Yin-po, Yin-show, Stephen, Peggy, Victor. Education: Graduate, Hunan College of Law, China, 1917-21; Postgraduate Research, Oxford University, England, 1922-25. Career: Instructor of Philosophy, Kwan Hwa University, Shanghai, 1926-27; Served in the Nationalist Government as Deputy Director of Editing and Translating Bureau, Concurrently Director of Association for Scientific Studies in Nanking 1928-30; Professor of Philosophy at Hunan University, 1930-32; Served in the Central Government as Acting Chairman of National Committee for Planning, 1932-34; Commissioner of Interior of Central Political Council, 1936-39; Headed Academic Lecture Corps and Led Inspection Group of New Life Movement, 1937; Appointed Special Administrator and Concurrently Commander of Peace Preservation Force in Hunan 1938-44; Instructor of Philosophy, Chun Chi College, Research Fellow at Institute of Oriental Studies of the University of Honkong, 1953-58; Instructor or Chinese History, Baptist College at Kowloon. Community Activities: Founded (in cooperation with a number of scholars) "China Rebuilding Federation," 1964; Sustaining Member, Republican National Committee; Member Advisory Board of American National Security Council; State Advisor, United States Congressional Advisory Board. Religion: Itinerant Speaker of the Methodist Church in Wilmington, Delaware, 1960. Published Works: Author *Philosophy of Love* (Changsha), *Philosophy of Confucius* (London), *Philosophy of the Beautiful, Critique on Marxism, Contemporary Political Thought of the West* (Shanghai), *On Chinese Culture, The Problem of China* (Hongkong), *Co-Wealthism and the New Age* (New York). Honors and Awards: Recipient of Medal of Merit awarded by President Reagan, 1982; Listed in *Who's Who in the World, Marquis Who's Who*. Address: 21-20 21st Street, Long Island City, New York 11105.■

JOSEPH JEN-YUAN HSU

Scientist, Technical Consultant, International Financial Consultant. Personal: Born March 25, 1928; Son of William Wang-Chih and Ping-Heng Ling; Married Helen Lu-sheng Wang, Daughter of Mr. and Mrs. L. C. Wang; Father of Ava, Hank, Bond, Lisa. Education: B.S. Physics, Monmouth, Illinois, 1954; M.S. Physics, University of Massachusetts, Amherst, Massachusetts, 1962; Ph.D. Candidate in Physics, University of Chicago, Chicago, Illinois, 1962-64; Ph.D. Biology, New York University, New York, New York, 1975. Career: Scientist, Technical Consultant, International Financial Consultant; Board Chairman, West-East Educational and Cultural Institute, Brooklyn, New York, Founder 1979 to present; Consultant, United States-China Commerce Council, New York, 1975 to present; Association Research Scientist, N.Y.U.M.C., 1967-74; Assistant Physicist, Argonne National Laboratory, Argonne, Illinois, 1962-67; Instructor in Atomic and Nuclear Physics, University of Massachusetts, Amherst, Massachusetts, 1958-62; Research Assistant in Chemistry, Monmouth College, Monmouth, Illinois, 1952-54; Translator and Budget Clerk, Joint Commission on Rural Reconstruction, Taipei, Taiwan, 1951-52. Organizational Memberships: Honorary Member, National Board of Advisors, American Biographical Institute, 1981 to present; American Venereal Disease Association, New York, 1981 to present; New York Academy of Sciences, 1980 to present; American Association for the Advancement of Science, 1981 to present. Community Activities: International Platform Association, 1979 to present; American Association of University Professors, 1958 to present. Religion: Christian. Published Works: Contributor Articles to Professional Journals. Honors and Awards: Listed in *Who's Who in Technology Today, Industry's Directory of Technical Consultants, International Who's Who of Intellectuals, Men and Women of Distinction, Notable Americans, Dictionary of International Biography, Personalities of America*, Others. Address: 1500 Hornell Loop, Spring Creek, Brooklyn, New York 11239.■

JOHN CHIH-AN HU

Specialist Engineer, Certified Professional Chemist. Personal: Born July 12, 1922, in Nanchang, Hupeh, China; Married Betty Siao-Yung Ho; Father of Arthur, Benjamin, Carl, David, Eileen, Franklin, George. Education: Graduate, National Central University, 1946; Passed High-Level Examinations, 1947; M.S. Organic Chemistry 1957, Postgraduate Studies 1957-61, University of Southern California. Career: Factory #1, Taiwan Fertilizer Manufacturing Company, Appointed Chemical Engineer 1947, Director of Research Department; Joined Chem Seal Corporation, 1961; Research and Development for Products Research and Chemical Corporation, 1962; The Boeing Company, Staff Member Materials and Technology Unit of Boeing Commercial Airplane Company 1971, Quality Assurance Laboratories of Boeing Aerospace Company 1971 to present; Invented Chromatopyrography, Patented 1979; Lecturer and Writer on Invention. Organizational

Memberships: American Chemical Society; Phi Lambda Upsilon. Published Works: Contributor to Articles to Professional Journals; Contributing Author to Two Books; Referee for Reviewing Manuscripts from Analytical Chemistry and Outlines of Short Course Offered by American Chemical Society. Address: 16212 122 Southeast, Renton, Washington 98055.■

L. RON HUBBARD

Author. Career: Author of Aviation Articles, Westerns, Sports Stories, Sea Stories, Detective Thrillers, Military Intrigues, and Adventure Stories; Aviation Articles and Photographs Published in *The Sportsman Pilot* (one of the first journals to regularly publish his work); Wrote Script for Columbia Motion Pictures, a 15-Part Serial called "The Secret of Treasure Island," 1937; Helped Launch (with John W. Cambell Jr.) "The Golden Age of Science Fiction" (as later called); Author of Best Seller, *Dianetics: The Modern Science of Mental Health*; Developed and Implemented a Simple Administrative Technology in Books such as *How to Live Though an Executive* and *Problems of Work*; Author *Science of Survival* 1951 (contained the foundations for the religion of Scientology); Trained Up and Formed Church Management Structure, Resigned all Boards in the Fall of 1966; Developed the Purification Program (a regimen of exercise, vitamins and sauna to rid the body of harmful effects of drugs, thus making spiritual advancement possible); Author of *Battlefield Earth: A Saga of the Year 3000* 1982 and 1983. Address: c/o LRH Personal Secretary, P.O. Box 29950, Los Angeles, California 90029.■

WILLIAM ROBERT HUDGINS

Neurosurgeon. Personal: Born March 10, 1939; Son of Rev. and Mrs. W. Douglas Hudgins; Married Cynthia Kite; Father of Catherine, David, Anne, Lauren. Education: Studies in Pre-Med, University of Oklahoma, 1957-60; M.D., University of Mississippi School of Medicine, 1964; Surgery Internship, Duke University Hospital, 1964-65; Neurosurgery, University of Tennessee, 1964-68. Military: Served in the United States Navy as a Neurosurgeon for Hospital Ship *U.S.S. Sanctuary* in Vietnam, 1969-71, attaining the rank of Lieutenant Commander, M.C. Career: Neurosurgeon in Private Practice; Former Staff Neurosurgeon, Scott and White Clinic, Temple, Texas. Organizational Memberships: Congress of Neurological Surgeons; American Association of Neurosurgeons; Society of Military Surgeons; American College of Angiology; American Geriatrics Society. Community Activities: Chairman of Neuroscience Section, St. Paul Hospital, 1980-84; American Heart Association Stroke Council, 1978 to present; Dallas Neuroscience Foundation, Board Member 1980 to present; Dallas Epilepsy Association, 1977 to present; Dallas Symphony Orchestra Guild, 1979-80; Course Director of Laser Neurosurgery Workshops in Dallas, Quarterly, 1980 to present; Developed Computer Program for Diagnosis of Back Pain, Appeared on Panel to Discuss "Artificial Intelligence," National Computer Conference, 1981. Religion: Ordained Deacon, Baptist Church, 1973. Published Works: "Lasers in Neurosurgery", Chapter 20 in Rand's *Microneurosurgery* Textbook, 1984; Author of 29 Articles in Medical Journals. Honors and Awards: Dean's Scholarship, University of Mississippi School of Medicine, 1960; Alpha Omega Alpha Medical Scholarship Society, 1964; Vietnamese Cross of Gallantry with Bronze Star, 1970; Diplomate, America Board of Neurological Surgery, 1972. Address: 4208 Edmondson, Dallas, Texas 75220.■

EUGENE CARL HUEBSCHMAN

College President. Personal: Born October 31, 1919, in Evanston, Indiana; Married Edna Arldt; Father of Donald, Mike, Ruth, Jo Anna. Education: B.S. Philosophy, Concordia Teachers College, Illinois, 1941; M.S., Physical Chemistry, Purdue University, 1946; Ph.D., Theoretical Physics, University of Texas, 1957. Career: President, Nathaniel Hawthorne College, Antrim, New Hampshire; Professor of Electrical Engineering, University of Tennesssee; Previous Positions include Coach, Football, River Forest College; Science Professor 10 Years, Head of Science Department and Athletic Director, Concordia College, Austin, Texas; Air Force Missile Development Center, Holloman Air Force Base, New Mexico; Technical Advisor to the Guidance Division, Wright Field, Dayton, Ohio; Has Made Over 20 Patent Proposals in Inertial Guidance; Teacher, Purdue University 1942-44, University of Texas 1946-54, University of New Mexico 1956-58, Sinclair College 1958-59, San Diego State University 1960, University of California 1961, University of Tennessee 1965-71; Chairman, Brevard Engineering College's Graduate Physics Department. Organizational Memberships: American Physical Society; Institute of Electrical and Electronic Engineers; American Institite of Aeronautics and Astronautics; Sigma Pi Sigma; Gamma Delta; Beta Sigma Psi; Southwest Basketball Officials Association; Southwest Football Officials Association. Community Activities: American Cancer Society, Educational Committee; Boy Scouts of America, Board Member; University of Tennessee Senate; Southwest Academic League, President; Oceanography and Pollution Corporation, Board Member, Founder; Comtel, Advanced Research, Computer Science and Mineiva Electronics, Board Member; International Platform Association. Religion: Christ Lutheran Church. Honors and Awards: Certificate of Accomplishment, Air Research and Development Command, Conferring upon him the Honorary Title of Outstanding Inventor; Solicited by Library of Congress to serve as Physical Science Advisor to Congress; Fellow, Explorer's Club, 1979; Listed in *International Scholars Directory*, *Silver Wings Fraternity*, *Creative and Successful Personalities*, *Dictionary of International Biography*, *International Register of Profiles*. Address: Nathaniel Hawthorne College, Antrim, New Hampshire 03440.■

CHERRY I. HUFF

Retired Medical Secretary. Personal: Born March 23, 1924; Daughter of Raymond Guerry and Lila Godwin (deceased) Irby; Married William BeauSegneiur Huff; Mother of William Godwin. Education: Graduate of Eufaula High School, 1944; Graduate in Journalism of Columbia University, 1948; Graduate in Spanish of City College of New York; Graduate of Medical Terminology Course, 1971; Graduate of Medical Secretarial Skills Course, 1972. Career: Medical Secretary. Organizational Memberships: Vice President, American Business Women's Association, 1966. Community Activities: Bethania Hospital Auxiliary, Coordinator of Volunteer Services. American Cancer Society, Texas Division Vice President, Secretary, Chairman of Public Education Committee, Local Unit District Public Education Chairman, Lay Director 1979-81; State Helping Smokers Quit Committee, State Board of Directors, Director at Large 1981-83; Executive Committee, Special Olympics, 1974-78; Advisor, Teens Aid the Retarded, 1975-77; Secretary, Wichita County Association Retarded Citizens, 1975-76; Executive Committee, Denton State School Parents Group, 1981-82; Parents of Retarded in State Schools; Human Relations Commission, City of Wichita Falls, 1982-83; Veterans of Foreign Wars, 1983-84; Ladies Auxiliary, Brookwood Medical Center, 1983-84; Charter Member, Eufaula Little Theatre, 1983-84; Newcomer's Club, 1983-84; American Biographical Institute Research Association, Life Patron and National Advisor, Nominating Committee 1983; President, Veterans of Foreign Wars Auxiliary, 1984-85. Religion: Baptist. Honors and Awards: Woman of the Year, American Business Women's Association, 1968-69; Volunteer of the Year, American Cancer Society, 1976; Outstanding Member of the Year, Wichita County Association for Retarded Citizens, 1976; Distinguished Service Award, American Cancer Society, 1982; Listed in *Personalities of America*, *Two Thousand Notable Americans*, *Five Thousand Personalities of the World*, *World Who's Who of Women*, *Community Leaders of America*, *International Book of Honor*, *Dictionary of International Biography*. Address: Route 5, Box 100, Eufaula, Alabama 36027.■

BRADLEY RICHARD HUGHES

Marketing Administrator. Personal: Born October 8, 1954; Son of Nancy Middleton; Married Linda W., Daughter of Velma McCants; Father of Bradley Richard Jr. Education: Associate of Arts, Oakland Community College; B.S. Journalism, B.S. Business, M.B.A. (double major), University of Colorado. Career: Marketing Administrator; Former Buyer and Salesman. Organizational Memberships: A.M.B.A. Executives. Community Activities: Brandychase, Board of Directors; Young Republicans; County and State Delegate; Republican Precinct Committeeman; Volunteer, National Jewish Hospital. Religion: Protestant. Honors and Awards: Member Mensa; Member Intertel; Listed in *Who's Who in the West*, *Personalities of America*. Address: 14453 East Jewell Avenue #204, Aurora, Colorado 80012.■

JOYCE MAY HUGHITT

Piano Instructor, Pianist. Personal: Born August 8, 1931; Daughter of Mrs. Rose A. Holmes; Married Robert A., Son of Mr. and Mrs. C. D. Nadeau; Mother of William D., Patricia M., Julie A. and Joyce A. Education: Special Student in University of Oregon Music School, 1941-49; B.A. Music, University of Portland, 1953; Graduate Studies at University of Portland, University of Oregon, Marylhurst College, Lewis and Clark College of Music; 12 Years Piano Performance Study with Pianist/Teacher Aurora Underwood, 6 Years Study with Pianist/Composer Robert Stoltze. Career: Teacher of Piano and Theory, Pianist, Piano Instructor at University of Portland, Portland, Oregon; Piano Instructor, Providence Academy, Vancouver, Washington; Oregon State Public School Certified Teacher; Adjunct Piano Instructor, Portland State College, Portland Community College, Portland State University; Class Piano Teacher, Portland Community College; Teacher of Piano in Portland Area since 1950; State Certified since 1953; Nationally Certified since 1963. Organizational Memberships: Oregon Music Teachers Association 1954 to present, Secretary Portland District 1961-63, State Merit Certificate Chairman 1966-68, Various Other Chairmanships over the Years; National Music Teachers Association 1954 to present; Oregon Federation of Music Clubs and National Federation of Music Clubs; Progressive Music Clubs, Courtesy Chairman, 3rd Vice President (presently). Community Activities: Active Parent in Parent Teacher Association, 1963-78; Served as Room Mother (while children were in grade school);

Secretary 4 Years, Neighborhood School; Phoned for City Telephoning for Parent Teacher Association for West Area; Campaigned for Tryon Creek State Park to be placed between Portland and Lake Oswego (park formed and is Nature Study Park in Southwest Portland and Lake Oswego); Donates Talents in Music for many things including Artist-Teacher Recital for Oregon Music Teachers Association at Marylhurst College (proceeds going towards young student scholarships, both state and national), Pianist at Scholarship Teas for Oregon Federation of Music Clubs and National. Religion: Aided in the Formation of a New Chapel (Riverview Chapel) for First Baptist Church of Eugene, Orgeon 1943, Served as Musician for Chapel and Secretary 1943-49, Taught Sunday School Classes; Sunday School Teacher, North Baptist Church in Portland. Honors and Awards: 1 of 1500 in the West and Midwest in 1982; Maintains 1 of 3 Hughitt Studios (other 2 maintained by husband in Portland and son in The Dalles, Oregon); Awarded 4-Year Stipend at the End of Sophomore Year in College, Became Instructor of Piano in the University's School of Music at the University of Portland; Became the First Non-Catholic Teacher to Teach at Providence Academy for Sisters of Charity of Providence. Address: 10010 Southwest Terwilliger Boulevard, Portland, Oregon 97219. ■

EDWARD HATCHER HUNT

Retired Extension Director. Personal: Born March 5, 1923; Son of Mr. and Mrs. James Daniel Hunt; Married Daisy Broadhurst, Daughter of Mr. and Mrs. George Marion Broadhurst; Father of Susan Elizabeth, Jane Marie, John Edward. Education: Diploma, Harlem High School, Harlem, Georgia, 1941; B.S.A. 1949, M.S.A. 1950, University of Georgia; Regional Extension Summer School, University of Arkansas, 1956. Military: Served with the United States Army, Corporal Technician 5th Grade, 1943-45. Career: Retired, 1983; Newton County Extension Director, 1958-83; Teaching Assistant, University of Georgia, 1949-50; Staff Member, Berry College, Mt. Berry, Georgia, 1950-55; Assistant County Agent, Polk County, Cedartown, Georgia; Assistant County Agent, Meriwether County, Greenville, Georgia. Organizational Memberships: Georgia Master 4-H Club 1971, Director 1972-78; Charter Member, ETERNA Club, College of Agriculture, University of Georgia; Piedmont and Georgia Cattleman's Association, 1966-82; Georgia and National Association of County Agricultural Agents, 1955-84; Director of Georgia Association of County Agricultural Agents, 1961-63; Epsilon Sigma Phi, Alpha Beta Chapter, National Honorary Fraternity, President 1980-81; Georgia and National Associations of Extension 4-H Agents, 1975-84; Atlanta Farmers Club; Atlanta Metro Agribusiness Council, 1970 to present; Newton County, Georgia, and National Farm Bureaus, 1958-84; Georgia Agribusiness Council, 1970-84; Georgia Agricultural Alumni Association, 1950-84; University of Georgia Alumni Society, 1950-84; Newton County Dairy Association, 1958-84. Community Activities: Secretary, Piedmont Cattlemen's Association, 1966 to present; Kiwanis Club of Covington 1958-84, Kiwanis Board of Directors 10 Terms, Distinguished Kiwanis Club President 1974-75, Georgia 12th Division Lieutenant Governor 1976-77, Georgia Kiwanis District Chairman of Administration 1977-78, Georgia District of Kiwanis Youth Services Chairman 1978-79, Georgia District of Kiwanis Inter-Club Chairman 1979-80, Georgia District of Kiwanis Chairman of Public Relations 1980-84, Georgia District of Kiwanis Chairman of Finance and Fund Raising, Elected to Life Membership #899 1977, Kiwanis Perfect Attendance 25 Years, Trustee of Georgia Kiwanis Foundation 1976-79; Charter Member, American Post Legion Post of Harlem, Georgia; Member of American Legion Post 32 of Covington 1958-84, Fair Chairman of Legion Sponsored Fair 26 Years; V.F.W. Post #2933, Member 1980-84; Cousins School Band Parents Organization 1978-79; Charter Member, Vice President 1983-84, President 1984-85, Chapter 1829 of National Association of Retired Federal Employees; President, Georgia Old Timers Association of Country Agricultural Agents, 1983-86; Director, Newton County Chapter #2265, American Association of Retired Persons, 1984; Organizer and Chairman, Reunion for 40th Cavalry Reconnaissance Troop World War II, (biennially) 1976 to present. Religion: First Baptist Church, Athens, Georgia 1948-50; First Baptist Church, Rome, Georgia, 1950-53; Mt. Lavender Baptist Church, Mt. Berry, Georgia, 1951-53; West Rome Baptist Church, 1953-55; First Baptist Church, Cedartown, Georgia, 1955-56; First Baptist Church, Warm Springs, Georgia, 1956-58; First Baptist Church Covington, Georgia 1968 to present, Deacon 1951 to present, Training Union Director 1964-66, Sunday School Teacher 16 Years, Deacon Chairman 1968, 1972-73, 1976-77. Honors and Awards: Life Member, Georgia Association of County Agricultural Agents, National Association of County Agricultural Agents, Georgia Association of Extension 4-H Agents, National Association of Extension 4-H Agents, Epsilon Sigma Phi (Alpha Beta Chapter); 24-Year Appreciation Award, Covington Rotary Club, 1982; Kiwanis Achievement Award for Untiring Efforts of Promoting Kiwanis from Covington Club, 1983; 25-Year Professional Assistance Award, Upper Ocmulgee River Soil and Water Conservation District, 1982; Newton County Chamber of Commerce Robert O. Arnold Award; Named a Master 4-H Club Member, 1971; Distinguished Service Award from Georgia and National Association of County Agricultural Agents, 1966; Farmers Club of Atlanta Metro Agribusiness Council Outstanding Government Employee Award, 1976; Distinguished Service to National 4-H Agents Association Award, 1981; State Distinguished Service to National 4-H Agents Association Award, 1981; State Distinguished Service Award, Epsilon Sigma Phi, 1980; Distinguished Service Award to Newton County Agriculture, 1981; District Award in Leadership and Georgia Agribusiness Development, 1981; 25-Year Service Award to 4-H Club, 1978; County Agent of the Year Award to Commercial Cattleman in County, 1980; Joint Man of the Year Award from Georgia Association of County Commissioners, 1970; U.S.D.A. Service Awards at 5-Year Intervals beginning in 1959 (5, 10, 15, 20, 25 years); Life Member #899 of Kiwanis International Award, 1977. Address: P.O. Box 68, Covington, Georgia 30209. ■

NANCY ELIZABETH BOTHMAN HUNT

Pianist, Educator, Adjucator. Personal: Born May 29, 1926; Daughter of Fred W. Sr. and Kathryn E. Bothman; Married Kenneth J. (deceased); Mother of Susan Nelson, Rebecca Robinson, Madeline Isley. Education: Honors Graduate, Jefferson High School, Portland, Oregon, 1943; Attended Wheaton College, Wheaton, Illinois, 1943-44; Advanced Piano Study with Lillian Pettibone, Portland, Oregon, 1957-71. Career: Pianist, Teacher, Adjudicator; Secretary, Part-Time 1942-44, Full-Time 1945-46, Part-Time 1948-51. Organizational Memberships: Oregon Music Teachers Association; Music Teachers National Association, President of Salem District 1962-64 and 1982 to present, President Eugene District 1975-77; Secretary, Oregon Music Teachers Association Executive Board 4 Years, and in many other Capacities on the Board over a 22-Year Period. Community Activities: President, Salem Community Concert Association, 1970-72; Chairman of Worker's Group in Community Concert Association, 1960-70. Religion: Church Organist and Pianist, 1946-72; Pianist at First Baptist Church, Eugene 1972-77, and First Baptist Church, Salem 1977 to present. Honors and Awards: Daughters of the American Revolution Good Citizenship Award, Jefferson High School Graduating Class of 1943, Portland, Oregon; Permanent Certificate of Professional Advancement for Distinction in Teaching of Music, 1965 to present, Oregon Music Teachers Association; Certified Teacher of Piano 1972 to present, Music Teachers National Association (having met their highest professional standards); Appointed Adjudicator for Oregon Music Teachers Association, 1974 to present. Address: 4470 Camellia Drive South, Salem, Oregon 97302. ■

JOHN B. HUNTER III

Microbiologist. Personal: Born November 20, 1922; Son of Sopha Marie and Johnny Booker; Married; Father of Steven John, Andrea Allan, Jackgyln Marie. Education: Attended Tennessee State University; B.S. Science, Ball State University, 1948; Olivet College. Military: Served with Company A 784th Tank Br., Att. 26th Division, 29th Division, 35th Division. Career: CH Microbiologist III. Community Activities: EMP, St. Mary's Hospital, Hillmans Memorial Hospital. Religion: Amezion Methodist Church 1964, Usher, Baord President. Honors and Awards: Dairy License #175, Illinois Society Microbiolgy; AMT #8454, American Public Health Assocation; Illinois Society of Technology; American Lung Association of Mid-Eastern Illinois; Executive Committee of American Lung Association of Illinois. ■

MARY FRANCES HUNTER

Assistant Professor. Personal: Born December 12, 1942; Daughter of Mr. and Mrs. Hasten Carter; Married Walter Earl, Son of Mr. and Mrs. Bam Hunter; Mother of Darrell Lynn, Velda Ann. Education: B.S. Home Economics, Philander Smith College, 1965; M.S. Vocation, Technical and Career Education, Oklahoma State University, 1975; Secondary Permanent Certificate, University of Michigan, 1972; Middle School Reading Certificate, Wayne State University, 1975; Home Economics, University of Central Arkansas, 1979. Career: Assistant Professor of Home Economics, Department Head, 1978 to present; Career Education Consultant, Coordinator and Teacher, Trainer, Detroit Public Schools, 1977-78; Home Economics and Career Education Teacher, 1969-70; Nutritionist, Archdiocesan Opportunity Program Project Head Start, Detroit, Michigan, 1970-77; Home Economics and Science Teacher, Village School District, Village, Arkansas, 1968-69; Home Economics Teacher, Alexander Hamilton Junior High School, Cleveland, Ohio, 1965-67. Organizational Memberships: National Council of Home Economics Administrators; American Home Economics Association; Council for Basic Education. Community Activities: Cub Scouts Pack 419, Den Mother 1976-78; Bi-Racial Advisory Committee, Little Rock Public Schools, 1982-85; Thrasher Boy's Club, Parent Advisory Council, 1982-85; Provident Relief Federated Club of American Association of Colored Women's Clubs, In Charge of Local Youth Program; Hansel and Gretel Interest Group of Jack and Jill of America, Inc., President 1982-84; Advocator for Battered Women Advisory Board, 1983-86; National Association for the Advancement of Colored People, 1978-79; Speaker, State Meeting, Arkansas Association of Colored Women's Clubs; American Association of University Women, Publicity Co-Chairperson Local Chapter 1979; Wrote Units in Child Development included in the Teaching Manuals for Oklahoma's Vocational High School Teachers, 1973; Faculty Representative, Board of Trustees, Philander Smith College, Serve on Academic Services and Development and Church Relations Committees 1982-84; Television Appearance, Stillwater, Oklahoma, 1974; Numerous Speaking Engagements and Consultant Work, "The Values of an Internship," "Interpersonal Relationships," "Values Clarification," "Career Education," "Neglected Areas of Home Economics"; Miss PSC and Coronation Ball Committees; Recruitment and Retention Committee. Religion: Canaan

Missionary Baptist Church; Membership Church of the New Covenant Baptist, Detroit, Michigan; Organizer of Usher Board 1972, Choir Member, Taught Vacation Bible School. Honors and Awards: Appointed by Arkansas Area Bishop of the United Methodist Church, Chairman of Philander Smith Colleges Board of Trustees to Serve on the Committee for the Selection of a New President for the College, 1983; Outstanding Young Woman of America, 1979; Female Faculty of the Year, Philander Smith College, 1980; Phi Kappa Phi National Honor Society, 1974; Department of H.E.W. Division of Vocational and Technical Education, EPDA-552 Awardee, Educational Fellowship, 1973; Exchange Student, Luther College, Decorah, Iowa, 1964; Miss United Negro College Fund, 1963; Listed in *Who's Who Among Students in American Universities and Colleges.* Address: 1813 South Monroe Street, Little Rock, Arkansas 72204. ■

FANNIE MAE HUTCHISON

Special Education Resource Specialist. Personal: Born November 11, 1929; Daughter of Mr. and Mrs. Lewis Hutchison. Education: B.S., Muskingum College, 1952; M.A., Chapman College, 1974; M.S., University of Southern California, 1975; Doctoral Candidate, University of Southern California, 1980. Career: Special Education Resource Specialist; Former Elementary Classroom Teacher, Teacher of Learning Handicapped, Administrator of Special Education Extended Year Program. Community Activities: Ventura Unified Education Association, President 1972-73; School Resource Network, Director 1977-78, Phi Delta Kappa, 1980 to present; Presenter California Council for Exceptional Children, 1981. Address: 956 Sharon Lane, Ventura, California 93001. ■

JANET KERN HUTSON

Educator. Personal: Born November 27, 1924; Daughter of Clarence and Mildred Kern (deceased); Married Wallace E. Hutson; Mother of Wallace Edward Jr., Janet Kaye (Hutson) Magaha. Education: Graduate of Caroline County High School, 1941; Graduate of Georgia Maude Beauty School, 1942; Master's Equivalency, University of Maryland, 1977. Career: Vocational Cosmetology Teacher; Former Positions include Owner/Operator Beauty Salon (Goldsboro and Denton, Maryland). Organizational Memberships: National Education Association; President, State of Maryland Education Association, 1977-78; Charter Member, Cosmetologists Association. Community Activities: Mayor of Denton, Maryland; Former State President, Professional Women's Clubs; Former President, Maryland Association of Technical Trade and Industrial Educators; Charter President, Bethany House Auxiliary, 1964-65; State Chaplain, Business and Professional Women's Club, 1983-84; Worthy Matron, Order of the Eastern Star, Caroline Chapter #62, 1983; Chairman, Caroline County Commission on Aging, 1972-74; Treasurer, Denton Chamber of Commerce, 1981; Iota Lambda Sigma. Religion: Member of Saint Luke's United Methodist Church; Former President, Saint Luke's United Methodist Women; Choir Member. Honors and Awards: Citation for Woman of the Year, Governor Hughes, 1980; Listed in *Who's Who in the East, World Who's Who of Women, Who's Who in America.* Address: 215 South Sixth Street, Denton, Maryland 21629. ■

HAZEL MORTIMER HYDE

Retired Educator. Personal: Born May 29, 1908; Daughter of Wilson Shannon and Ida Martha Powell Mortimer (both deceased); Married Harold Beardslee Hyde, Son of Mr. and Mrs. Leroy Hyde (both deceased). Education: B.S., Pittsburg State University, 1933; Graduate Studies undertaken at Michigan University, 1937; M.A., Northwestern University, 1946; Further Studies undertaken at Rockford College (Illinois) and Georgia University. Career: Head Social Studies Department, Washington Junior High School (Rockford, Illinois), 1956-68; with Rockford Public Schools, 1936-68; Summer Session Teaching United States History at Rockford College, 1950; Inter-Session Consultant in Social Studies at Rockford College, 1960-62. Organizational Memberships: Life Member, Illinois State Historical Society; Life Member, National Education Association; Phi Alpha Theta History Fraternity; Associate Member, Historic Preservation Society. Community Activities: Rockford Historical Society, Charter Board Member, Vice President in Charge of Programs, Recording Secretary 1983-84, Associate Editor *Nuggets of History*; Past Program Chairman for Education Department, Rockford Women's Club; Wing of New American Theatre; Rockford Contributor to Metropolitan Opera, Metropolitan Opera of Upper Midwest (Minneapolis, Minnesota), Florentine Opera (Milwaukee, Wisconsin), Lyric Opera (Chicago); Daughters of the American Revolution, Chaplain Rockford Chapter 1977-78, 1982-83, 1983-84. Religion: Member Court Street Methodist Church. Honors and Awards: Freedoms Foundation Teachers Award, 1961; Rockford's Lady of Distinction, Credo Club, 1962; Farr Teacher of the Year, Illinois State Historical Society, 1967; National Award as Illinios State Junior American Citizen Chairman, N.S.D.A.R., 1963; Honored during Woman's History Week for Local History Work, 1983. Address: 1518 Comanche Drive, Rockford, Illinois 61107. ■

J

BARBARA KAUTZ ILVENTO

Company Executive. Personal: Born September 6, 1941; Daughter of Palmy Kautz; Mother of Lauren, Charles II. Education: B.A., Florida International University, Miami, Florida; M.Ed., University of Miami. Career: Vice President of Sales, Bengis Associates, Inc.; Vice President, International Research Institute of America; Owner/Operator, Appleby's Eatery; Office Manager, Penta and Ilvento, C.P.A.'s; Executive Secretary, Beech-Nut Life Savers, Inc.; Medical Assistant, L. Melvin Elting Diagnostic Center, Allen B. Kendall M.D., F.A.C.S. Organizational Memberships: Monmouth County Medical Assistants Association, Founder, Charter Member 1962-68, President; New Jersey Medical Assistants Association, Chairperson, State Convention, 1964; Mental Health Task Force on Child Abuse, Assistant to Chairman 1975. Community Activities: Progress Club of Miami, Florida, Member 1978-81, First Woman Board Member 1979; South Dade Chamber of Commerce, Board of Directors, Chairperson of Membership Committee. Honors and Awards: Psi Chi Psychology National Honor Society; Charter Member, Certificate of Distinction, Psychology Department, Florida International University. Address: 16923 Southwest 87th Avenue, Miami, Florida 33157. ■

JORGE GARRON IMANA

Artist, Educator. Personal: Born September 20, 1930; Naturalized United States Citizen, 1976; Son of Juan and Lola Imana (both deceased); Married Cristina Garcia, Daughter of Daniel and Maria Luisa Garcia; Father of George, Ivan. Education: M.A., Academy Benavidez, University of San Francisco Xavier, Sucre, Bolivia, 1952; M.A. Biology, Normal School of Sucre, 1952. Military: Served in the Bolivian Army, 1953, attaining the rank of Lieutenant. Career: Artist; Owner of The Artists Showroom, San Diego; 89 One-man Shows in Latin America, the United States and Europe. Organizational Memberships: Art Director, Instituto Normal; Superior, La Paz, Bolivia, 1959-62; San Diego Watercolor Society; San Diego Art Institute; La Jolla Art Association, President 1977; Accademia Italia delle Arti e del Laburo. Community Activities: Consul of Bolivia for Southern California, 1969-74. Honors and Awards: Municipal Award, Sucre, Bolivia, 1958; Awards in Watercolor National Show, Lima, Peru, 1960 and 1962; First Award, Salon Nacional de Abril, La Paz, Bolivia, 1962; Purchase Award, Annual Show, San Diego Art Institute, 1965-67; Listed in *Who's Who in American Art, Who's Who in the West, Dictionary of International Biography.* Address: 3357 Caminito Gandara, La Jolla, California 92037. ■

LILLIAN LOUISE IMPERI

Forensic Psychiatrist. Personal: Born January 16, 1924; Mother of William John Rumbos, Jr. Education: B.S., Marygrove College, 1950; M.D., University of Michigan, 1955. Career: Forensic Psychiatrist; Former Psychiatrist. Organizational Memberships: American College of Forensic Psychiatry; American Academy of Child Psychiatry; American Medical Association; Kappa Gamma Pi; American Medical Women's Association; National Forensic Center; International Platform Association. Community Activities: Free Services to the Public, Center for Creative Living. Honors and Awards: Listed in *Two Thousand Women of Achievement, Who's Who of American Women, World Who's Who of Women, Five Thousand Personalities of the World, Who's Who of Intellectuals.* Address: 1520 Rodney Drive, #405, Los Angeles, California 90027. ■

GLADYS LORENE INGRAM

Retired. Personal: Born April 8, 1891; Widow; Mother of Viola M. Hoxie. Education: Graduate of Palmer School of Chiropractic, 1915; Postgraduate Study undertaken at Lincoln College of Chiropractic; Attended Numerous Other Seminars. Career: Chiropractic Practice in Missouri and Iowa, 59 Years; Speaker at National Chiropractic Association Annual Convention, 7 Years; Lobbyist at Jefferson City, Missouri, Helped to Defeat Bill Sponsored by Missouri Medical Association. Organizational Memberships: Charter Member, Tenton (Missouri) Business and Professional Club, 1927; President, Chillicothe (Missouri) Business and Professional Women's Club, 1934-35, 1935-36; Member Federation of Business and Professional Women's Club, 47 Years; Organized Business and Professional Women's Roundtable Club, Chillicothe; Program Director, Livingston County C.D. Program during World War II. Community Activities: Teacher of First Aid Classes; Board Secretary, Lincoln College of Chiropractic; First President, W.C.A., Honored by the Women's Council, National Chiropractic Association (now American Chiropractic Association); Life Member, Fellow, International College of Chiropractic. Religion: President, Christian Church of Chili; Teacher of Bible Class, Community Christian Church. Published Works: Author *Traveling an Uncharted Road,* Articles for the *National Chiropractic Journal* 1936-40. Honors and Awards: Invitation from President Harry Truman to attend the Highway Safety Conference, 1951 (63 Countries Represented); Invited to attend United Nations Club Reception; Honored for 2000 Hours of Volunteer Work during World War II; Honored by Palmer College of Chiropractic for Half Century of Practice; Listed in *Personalities of the West and Midwest, World Who's Who of Women.* Address: Chatham Hotel, 3701 Broadway, Kansas City, Missouri 64111. ■

R. GERALD IRVINE

Electrical Senior Engineer. Personal: Born March 31, 1937; Son of Raymond G. and Jane T. Irvine (both deceased); Married Elizabeth Ann Williams, Daughter of I. C. (deceased) and Flora Williams; Mother of Mrs. Juanita Birch, Edward Bruce, Mrs. Terri DeMers, Wendy Lynn. Education: B.S.E.E. with honors, Norwich University, 1959; Graduate Studies undertaken at the University of Vermont 1959-60, Union College 1970-73; M.B.A. with distinction, Long Island University, 1983. Military: Served in the United States Army Signal Corps, 1960-63, attaining the rank of First Lieutenant. Career: Electrical Senior Engineer, AT&T Technologies, Inc., 1978 to present; Staff Engineer, I.B.M.-Sterling Forest, 1974-78; Staff Engineer, Department of Public Service, State of New York, 1969-74; Electrical Engineer, Federal Power Commission, 1968-69; Engineer, Electrical Division, Stone & Webster Engineering Corporation, 1964-68; Associate Design Engineer, Union Carbide Nuclear Division, Y-12 Plant, 1963-64. Organizational Memberships: National Society of Professional Engineers, Energy Committee 1976-77; American Society of Heating, Refrigerating and Air Conditioning Engineers; Association of Energy Engineers, Certified Energy Manager, Charter Member; Illuminating Engineering Society, Associate Member, Industrial Lighting Committee, Electronic Manufacturing Facilities Lighting Committee Chairman; International Association of Electrical Inspectors, Associate Member; Institute of Electrical and Electronic Engineers; National Electrical Testing Association, Affiliate Member; National Fire Protection Association; National Society of Professional Engineers; Norwich Engineers Society; Volunteers in Technical Assistance, Consultant; New York State Society of Professional Engineers, Capital District, Treasurer 1973, Environmental Committee Chairman, President 1974; National Society of Professional Engineers, Energy Committee 1976-77. Community Activities: Consultant, Volunteers in Technical Service; Contributor to Reports for The Mayors Council on the Environment of the City of New York. Honors and Awards: Tau Beta Pi; Distinguished Service Award, Capital District Chapter, New York State Society of Professional Engineers, 1974. Address: 77 Mile Road, P.O. Box 246, Suffern, New York 10901. ■

THOMAS KORYU ISHII

Professor of Electrical Engineering. Personal: Born March 18, 1927; Son of Yoshitada Ishii; Married Eiko Bernadette Ishida; Father of Mutsum Michael, Naomi Bernadette, Megumi Margaret, Mayumi Mary. Education: B.S., Nihon University, Tokyo, 1950; M.S. 1957, Ph.D. 1959, University of Wisconsin at Madison; D.Eng., Nihon University, 1961. Career: Professor of Electrical Engineering, Marquette University, 1959 to present; Instructor, Nihon University, Tokyo, 1950-56. Organizational Memberships: Institute of Electrical and Electronic Engineers, Chairman Milwaukee Section 1972-73; Society of Sigma Xi, President Marquette University Chapter 1967-68; American Association of University Professors, President Marquette University Chapter 1972-73. Community Activities: Volunteer Catechism Teacher, St. Catherine Religious Education Program, 1970-83. Religion: Prefect, Marquette University Faculty Sodalty, 1967-68; Organizer, Pere Marquette Society, 1970; Alpha Sigma Nu. Honors and Awards: Institute of Electrical and Electronic Engineers Milwaukee Section Memorial Award, 1969. Address: 6601 West Carolann Drive, Brown Deer, Wisconsin 53223.■

M. ALI ISSARI

Educator, Filmmaker, Administrator. Personal: Born August 13, 1924, in Esfahan, Iran; Son of Mrs. Qamar Issari; Married Joan A.; Father of Scheherezade, Katayoun, Roxana. Education: B.A., University of Tehran, 1963; M.A. 1968, Ph.D. 1979, University of Southern California. Career: Professor of Cinema, Department of Telecommunication, College of Communication Arts and Sciences, Michigan State University, 1978-81; Director of Instructional Film and Multimedia Production Service and Professor, 1975-78; Co-director, N.I.R.T. (National Iranian Radio Television) Staff Training Project, Michigan State University, 1975-78; Project Director and Executive Producer, Iran Film Series Project, 1975-78; Director, M.S.U.-N.I.R.T. Program Coordinating Office, 1975-78; Head of Film Production Division and Associate Professor, Michigan State University, 1969-75; Presented Special Film Production Workshops in Cranbrook Institutions, Detroit 1973-74; Helped Organize and Present Various Local and International Film Festivals at M.S.U., 1970-73; Served as Judge for Midwest Film Festival (First International Film Festival Organized and Run by Students), 1972-73; Served as Special Consultant on Educational Television with the Saudi Arabian Ministry of Information, 1972; Assistant Motion Picture Officer (Production), United States Information Service, Tehran, Iran, 1955-65 (Distribution 1950-55); Acted as Liaison Officer and Interpreter between American and Iranian Government Officials, 1950-65; Official Cinematographer to the Iranian Royal Court, 1956-65; Motion Pictures and Public Relations Advisor to Iranian Oil Operating Companies, 1963-65; Free-lance Cinematographer and Reporter in Iran for Telenews and Visnews (B.C.I.N.A.) and United Press International, 1959-63; Initiated and Presented the First American Film Festival in Iran under the auspices of U.S.I.S.-Tehran, 1951; Films Officer, British Council in Tehran, 1945-50; Produced a Number of Stage Plays in English and Persian (Performed in Some of These); Translator and Interpeter, British Embassy in Tehran, 1943-45. Organizational Memberships: Michigan Film Association, Co-Founder and Member of First Board of Directors, 1974-75; Iran-America Society, Served on Various Cultural and Entertainment Committees 1950-64; Audio-Visual Society of Iran, Founder and Member of Board of Directors 1953; Anglo-Iranian Dramatic Society, Board of Directors 1945-49; Association for Educational Communication and Technology, 1966 to present; Society of Motion Picture and Television Engineers, Progress Committee 1960-65; Middle East Studies Association of North America, 1976 to preent; Society for Cinema Study, 1977 to present; The American Academy of Political and Social Sciences, 1976-82; Delta Kappa Alpha, Vice President 1967, Member 1966-69; University Film Association, 1959 to present. Community Activities: Youth Organization of Iran, Founder 1951; Introduced Rugby Football to Iran and Organized Rugby Football Federation, 1949, Secretary, Vice President and President 1949-52. Published Works: Co-Author (with Doris A. Paul) *What is Cinema Verite?*, *A Picture of Persia*; Contributor to Professional Journals, including *Audio Visual Instruction*, *Journal of the University Film Association*; Has designed, Written, Produced, Directed, Photographed and Edited over 1000 Documentaries, Slide Tapes and Multi-Image Presentation. Honors and Awards: Received the Cine Eagle Award, 1976; University Film Association/McGraw-Hill Scholarship Award, 1968; Meritorious Honor Award, U.S. Information Agency, 1965; Order of Mahnum Cap. Ord.: S. R. Daniae M. Sigillum, Denmark, 1960; Order of Esteghlal, Hashemite Jordan, 1959; Order of Oranje Nassau, Holland, 1959; Order of Ordinis Sancti Silvestri Papae, Pope John 23rd, Vatican, 1959; Order of Cavalieres, Italy, 1958; Orders of Pas and Kooshesh, Iran, 1957 and 1951; Listed in *Who's Who in America*, *Who's Who in the Midwest*, *Notable Americans*, *Men of Achievement*, *Dictionary of International Biography*, *Leaders in Education*. Address: 4454 Seneca Drive, Okemos, Michigan 48864.■

ROBERT ALLISON IVEY

Southern Baptist Minister. Personal: Born January 5, 1933; Son of Roy Simpson and Fannie Godfrey Ivey; Married Elizabeth Reeves, Daughter of Charles Lester Reeves, Jr. and Louise Bailey Reeves; Father of Timothy Reeves, John Brent, Mary Elizabeth. Education: Graduate of Woodruff High School, 1951; B.A., Furman University, 1955; B.D., Southeastern Baptist Theological Seminary, 1958; Th.D., Pioneer Theological Seminary, 1959. Military: Commissioned First Lieutenant in Reserves, 1965; Chaplain 51 QM Bn., South Carolina Army Reserve National Guard, 1964-66. Career: Pastor, Draytonville Baptist Church, Gaffney, South Carolina; Educational Director, David Street Baptist Church, Greenville, South Carolina, 1952; Music and Youth Director, Whitney Baptist Church, Whitney, South Carolina, 1952-53; Employee, Ballentine Super Markets, Woodruff, South Carolina, 1949. Organizational Memberships: President, Pacolet-Glendale Ministerial Association, 1960-61; Spartanburg Baptist Missions Committee 1956, 1960-62, 1964-65; Historian, Spartan Baptist Association, Spartanburg County, South Carolina, 1960-65; President, Spartan Baptist Pastor's Conference, 1964; Moderator, Concord Baptist Association, Virginia, 1968-70; General Board, Baptist General Association, Virginia, 1972-74; General Board, South Carolina Baptist Association, 1980-84; Moderator, Broad River Baptist Association, 1981-83. Community Activities: Pacolet Ruritan Club (Pacolet, South Carolina), Vice President 1964, President 1965; Lieutenant Governor for Ruritan in Spartan District, South Carolina, 1965-66; Ruritan Club Appomattox District, District Secretary 1967, Zone Governor 1968; South Hill Ruritan Club, Vice President 1969, President 1970-71; Friends of the Library of Cherokee County, South Carolina, Vice President 1981-84. Religion: Trip to Bible Lands, 1973; Preached in Cairo (Egypt), Jerusalem (Israel), Ramallah (West Bank); Trip to Zimbabwe, Africa, 1981; Preached Revivals at Bulawayo and Gwelo. Honors and Awards: National Beta Club, 1949-51; Curtis Vocational Certificate of Achievement, 1950; First Place, Story of the Month Contest, Winthrop College, 1951; Ruritan of the Year Award, Pacolet Ruritan Clubv 1965, South Hill Ruritan Club 1971. Address: Route 8 Box 355, Gaffney, South Carolina 29340.■

GARY DEAN JACKSON

Attorney. Personal: Born September 13, 1935, in Dallas, Texas; Married Gloria Ann Galouye, December 11, 1957; Father of David MacArthur, Daniel Marshall. Education: Graduate, Lindale High School, Lindale, Texas, 1953; B.A. Government, Southern Methodist University, 1957; Graduate Study in Government undertaken at Texas University-Austin 1958, Southern Methodist University 1958; LL.B., Baylor University, 1961; J.D., Baylor University, 1969. Military: Served in the United States Army, 1953 to present, attaining the rank of Colonel; Division Chief of 95th Manuever Training Command 1982 to present; Adjunct Faculty Member, U.S. Army Command and General Staff College, 1979 to present. Career: Admitted to Practice Before Supreme Court of Texas, United States District Courts (Northern District of Texas, Eastern District of Texas, Western District of Texas, Southern District of Texas, Northern District of Alabama), United States Courts of Appeal (First Circuit Boston, Third Circuit Philadelphia, Fourth Circuit Richmond, Fifth Circuit New Orleans, Seventh Circuit Chicago, Ninth Circuit San Francisco, Tenth Circuit Denver, Federal Circuit), United States Army Court of Review, United States Court of Military Appeals, United States Court of Claims, Supreme Court of the United States, Various Special Admissions; Partner, Jackson, Jackson & Loving, 1983 to present; Partner, Jackson & Jackson, 1982; Partner, Jackson & Almquist, 1980-81; Attorney in Private Practice, 1979-80; Partner, Jackson, Jenkins & Rowton, 1978-79; Partner, Colvin & Jackson, 1974-78; Attorney, Fraud Section, Criminal Division, United States Department of Justice, 1969-74; Judge of Municipal Court, Arlington, Texas, 1966-69; Partner, Pace, Jarvis & Jackson, 1961-66; Instructor, Tyler Junior College, 1962-65; Budget Examiner, Texas Legislative Budget Board, Texas, 1957-59. Organizational Memberships: Delta Theta Phi Law Fraternity; Dallas Bar Association; Dallas County Criminal Bar Association; Richardson Bar Association; Texas Criminal Defense Lawyers Association; State Bar of Texas; Federal Bar Association; National Association of Criminal Defense Attorneys; Association of Trial Lawyers of America; American Bar Association; Civil Affairs Association; Reserve Officers Association, Texas, Louisiana and Oklahoma, Life Member; Association of the United States Army; Military Order of World Wars; United States Army War College Alumni Association; Senior Army Reserve Commanders Association. Community Activities: Tyler Masonic Lodge #1233; Scottish Rite Bodies; Sharon Temple, Ancient Arabic Order Nobles of the Mystic Shrine; Rotary Club; Junior Chamber of Commerce, Past Director; Scoutmaster, Austin Capitol Area Council, Boy Scouts of America; East Texas Heart Association, Past Board Member; Smith County March of Dimes, Past Board Chairman; March of Dimes Telethons, Master of Ceremonies 1962-66; Smith County Republican Men's Club, Past President; Tyler Southern Methodist University Alumni Club, President 1964; Arlington Texas Baylor Alumni Club, President 1968; Arlington Boys Club, Past Board Member; Texas Council for Input on Crimes, Rehabilitation and Prevention, 1976; Editorial Board, *Baylor Law Review*; Former Editors of the *Baylor Law Review*, President 1978. Published Works: "Extraterritorial Jurisdiction and Appliation of the First-Found of First-Brought Statute" (an individual study project written for the U.S. Army War College) 1979, "Allied and Axis Host Nation Support in Europe during World War II: A Program for Preparation" (special study for the Military Studies Program, U.S. Army War College, co-authored with Colonel Dennis A. Wilkie) 1979, "Assignment of an Army Officer as an Advisor to a Reserve Component" (special study for the Advanced Course in Civil-Military Relations, U.S. Army War College) 1979, "White Collar Crimes in the United States" 1979, "Constitutional Provisions Concerning the Form and Procedure for the Enactment of Legislative Bills in Texas" 1961, "History of the Constitutionality of Local Laws in Texas" 1961. Honors and Awards: Meritorious Service Medal, 1982; Armed Forces Reserve Medal, 1972; Army Reserve Components Achievement Medal, 1973; Army Service Ribbon, 1982; Rifle M-16 Expert Qualification Badge, 1982; Pistol Caliber .45 Expert Qualification Badge, 1982; Carbine Caliber .30 Sharpshooter Qualification Badge, 1957; Rifle M-1 Sharpshooter Qualification Badge, 1964; Appreciation Resolution, Legislative Budget Office, 1959; Appreciation Award, March of Dimes, 1963; Appreciation Award, Arlington Bar Association, 1969; Commendation, Director, Federal Bureau of Investigation, 1971, 1972; Special Achievement Award, United States Attorney General, Department of Juctice, 1971; Appreciation Plaque, United States Department of Justice, 1974; Certificate of Appointment, Counsellor of Baylor University Law School, 1974; Certificate of Appreciation, Texas Criminal Defense Lawyers Project, State Bar of Texas and Texas Criminal Justice Council, 1975; Certificate of Appreciation, 4162nd U.S. Army Reserve School, 1980; Letter of Commendation, U.S. Army Third R.O.T.C. Region, Senior Program, Northeast Louisiana University, 1981; Appreciation Plaque from Officers and Enlisted Personnel, 4th Brigade, 95th Division, 1982; Listed in *Who's Who in America, Who's Who in American Law, Personalities of the South*. Address: 5534 Williamstown Road, Dallas, Texas 75230.■

JAMES AVELON JACKSON

Educational Administrator. Personal: Born June 5, 1942; Father of James III, Jay. Education: B.S. Education/Psychology, Southern Illinois University; M.A. Higher Education Administration/Law Enforcement, Sangamon State University; Currently Enrolled in Ed.D. Program in Higher Education Administration, Saint Louis University. Career: Chairman, Department of Criminal Justice, Saint Louis Community College, 1981 to present; Coordinator of Criminal Justice Community Service Programs, Southeastern Community College, 1979-81; Director, Institute for Administration of Justice, McKendree College, 1976-78; Assistant Professor, Minot State College, 1975-76; Director/Instructor Law Enforcement Program, Muscatine Community College, 1973-75; Juvenile Officer, Madison County Sheriff's Office, 1970-73. Organizational Memberships: American Association of University Administrators; Academy of Criminal Justice Sciences; President, Iowa Criminal Justice Educators Association, 1981; Illinois Association of Criminal Justice Scientists, State Curriculum Coordination Comittee 1978, Former Member; Midwestern Association of Criminal Justice Educators, Constitution Revision Committee, Executive Committee; Founder, Southern Illinois Criminal Justice Educators Association; Constitution Review Committee, Illinois Community Education Association; American Society of Criminologists; Lambda Alpha Epsilon; Anglo-American Academy. Honors and Awards: Teacher of the Year, Muscatine Community College, 1975; Jefferson's Community Service Award, Saint Louis, Missouri, 1979; Teacher of the Year, St. Louis Community College at Forest Park, 1982; Listed in *Community Leaders and Noteworthy Americans, Men of Achievement, Anglo-American Who's Who, Directory of Distinguished Americans, Who's Who in the Midwest*. Address: 327 East Schuetz, Lebanon, Illinois 62254.■

WILMA JACKSON (DARCY DEMILLE)

Writer, Columnist. Education: Baccalaureate Degree, University of Michigan, 1977; Certificate in Urban Studies-Substance Abuse, Michigan State University, 1976; Advanced Study, Creative Writing, Oakland University, 1974-75, 1976-77. Career: Feature Writer and Columnist, *Sepia* Magazine, 1961 to present; Columnist, *Hep* Magazine, 1963 to present; Columnist, *Soul-Teen* Magazine, 1973 to present; Feature Writer, Columnist, *Bronze Thrills Magazine*, 1957 to present; News Reporter, *Chicago Daily Defender*, 1956-59; Columnist, National Editions and Chicago Edition, *Daily Defender*, 1956-59; Women's Editor, Associated Negro Press, 1959-61; Syndicated Columnist, 1973 Newspapers, United States, Virgin Islands, Ghana, Kenya, Jamaica, Bahamas, 1959-64; Reporter, Feature Writer, Negro Press International, 1964-65; Executive Editor, *The Circle*, Urban League Newspaper, 1960-61; Market Research Interviewer, Barlow Survey Service, Chicago, 1958-59; Promotions/Publicity, Holiday Inn, Flint, Michigan, 1976; Guest Lecturer, Creative Writing, University of Michigan, Flint Campus, 1977-78; Coordinated Writers and Composers Day at the Artrain, Flint, Michigan, 1978; Moderator/Writing Seminar, Howard University, Communication Conference, 1979; Working Press, President Carter's Inauguration; Working Press, International Women's Year Confab, Houston, Texas, 1977; Counselor, State of Michigan, Case Aide, 1976-78; Advisor, Black Fashion Museum, New York City, 1979 to present; Recruiter, Manufacturers Life Insurance Company, 1979 to present; Evaluation Specialist, Instructor, The Kennedy Center, 1979 to present; Instructor, Creative Writing, Mass Communications, Job Seeking Skills, MOIS Computer, The Kennedy Center, Flint, Michigan; Entertainment Writer, *The Flint Journal*, 1981 to present; Consultant, TimeShares Inc.; Instructor, Psychology, Counseling, Jordan College, 1982-83; Columnist, "Dear Wilma," *The Flint Journal*, 1982-83. Organizational Memberships: Phi Delta Kappa Educational Fraternity; National Association of Media Women,

Founder, Past President, Public Relations 1981-82; The Links Inc., Membership Chairman 1981-82; Nominating Panels, Michigan Women's Hall of Fame. Published Works: Column "Confidentially Speaking" in *Hep* Magaine, 1957-60; Article "Ten Things I'll Always Remember" (series), *Ebony* Magaine, 1958; Columns "Just Ask Me," "Darcy DeMille's Data 'n Chatter," "Dear Soul Sister," "Star-O'Scope"; Article "New Champion of Black Brainpower/M.S.U.'s President Wharton," *Sepia* Magazine, 1976. Honors and Awards: Listed in *Contemporary Authors, Who's Who Among Black Americans, Who's Who of Intellectuals, Index to Periodical Articles, International Who's Who in Community Service, Who's Who of American Women, Who's Who in the Midwest.* Address: 2018 Whittlesey Street, Flint, Michigan 48503.■

GLORIA MARGARET JACOBS

Community Program Developer. Personal: Born July 28, 1924; Daughter of Merle Haley Price; Mother of David B. VandeMark, Cassandra V. Lown, William N. VandeMark, Kathryn V. Binkley, Lois Jacobs McKee, Alice Jacobs Baxter, Mildred Jacobs Baxter, George Jacobs Jr. Education: A.A., Western Washington University, 1972. Career: Community Program Developer; Former Community Affairs Consultant, Photo Checker. Organizational Memberships: National Council on Aging. Community Activities: Washington Foundation for the Blind, Secretary 1969. Religion: Tacoma (Washington) Baha'i Community, Secretary 1965-67. Honors and Awards: Certificate for Service, Benton/Franklin Community Action Committee, 1977; Plaque for Outstanding Service, Okanogan County Community Action Council, 1980. Address: P.O. Box 5459, Lacey, Washington 98503.■

PATRICIA DIANNE JACOBS

Executive. Personal: Born January 27, 1950; Daughter of Elix and Helen Jacobs. Education: B.A. magna cum laude, Lincoln University, Pennsylvania, 1970; J.D., Harvard Law School, 1973. Career: President, K-Com Micrographics Inc., Washington, D.C., 1983 to present; President and Chief Executive Officer, The American Association of Minority Enterprise Small Business Investment Companies, Washington, D.C.; Congressional Liaison Officer, Secretary of the United States Commerce Department, 1977; Assistant Minority Counsel, Small Business Committee, United States Senate, 1975-77; Instructor, Federal City College, Institute of Gerontology, 1976; Assistant Professor and Director of Legal Services Counseling, John Jay College of Criminal Justice, New York, 1974-75; Adjunct Associate Professor, Borough of Manhattan Community College, Center for African and African-American Affairs, New York, 1973-75; Lecturer in Administrative and Legislative Law, Seton Hall Law School, 1974-75; Associate (Partner and Co-Founder), Pickett and Jennings, P.C., Newark, New Jersey, 1975-76; Associate, Tax Department, Exxon Corporation, New York, 1973-75; Legal Clerk, General Motors Corporation, New York, 1972; Legal Intern, Walker, Kaplan and Mays, P.A., Little Rock, Arkansas, 1971-72; Assistant Director of Financial Aid, Lincoln University, Pennsylvania, 1970. Organizational Memberships: American Bar Association; National Bar Association; N.C.B.L.; Association of University and College Professors; Council of New York Law Associates; Potomac Fiscal Society; Lawyer's Study Group; Federal Bar Association; Harlem Lawyer's Association. Community Activities: Women's League of Voters; N.W.B.D.C.; Lincoln Alumni Club; Coalition of 100 Black Women of D.C.; Alpha Kappa Alpha. Honors and Awards: National Finalist, White House Fellows Program, 1975; Business Award, National Association of Black Manufacturers, 1976; Board of Directors, Winthroup Rockefeller Foundation 1976, Cooperative Assistant Fund 1976, Center for Youth Services 1976, Southwest Day Care Center 1976, Caribbean Capital Corporation 1976, Phoenix Service Corporation 1976, Council on Foundations 1976. Address: 5016 3rd Street, Northwest, Washington, D.C. 20011.■

PARLEY PARKER JACOBSEN

Certified Public Accountant, Financial Accountant. Personal: Born July 21, 1924, in Hou, Denmark; Son of Anders and Anna Jacobsen (deceased); Married Malia T. Luengthada; Father of Karen, Steven, Kathleen, Kelli, Kimberli. Education: Graduate of University of Wisconsin, 1942; Graduate of University of Utah, 1955. Military: Served in the United States Navy, 1942-46; Served in the United State Army Reserve, 1955-59. Career: Vice President Legal and Auditing 1978 to present, Vice President Finance 1963-78, Harman Management Corporation; Partner, Hansen, Jacobsen & Barnett, CPAs, Salt Lake and Predecessor Firms, 1955-63; Owner, Secretary-Treasurer, Abajo Petroleum and Kmoco Oil Company, 1957-59. Organizational Memberships: Board of Directors, Salt Lake City Chapter, E.D.P. Auditors, 1981, 1983; Institute of Certified Public Accountants; Auditing Committee, Utah Society of Certified Public Accountants, 1955; Institute of Internal Auditors; E.D.P. Auditors Association; American Management Association; National Management Association. Community Activities: Veterans of Foreign Wars; Taxation Committee, Chamber of Commerce, 1973. Religion: Finance Clerk, Blanding Ward, 1958. Honors and Awards: Certified Public Accountant, Certified Internal Auditor, Certified Information System Auditor, Statistician, C.M. Address: 7134 Turnagain Cove, Salt Lake City, Utah 84121.■

SHARON ANN JAEGER

Poet, Editor, Translator, Professor. Personal: Born January 15, 1945; Daughter of Paul Jaeger, Catherine S. Jaeger. Education: B.A. summa cum laude, University of Dayton, 1966; M.A. English, Boston College, 1971; D.A. English, State University of New York at Albany, 1982. Career: Co-Editor, Sachem Press; Director, INTERTEXT; Translator; Poet; Instructor, Writing Workshop, State University of New York at Albany; Instructor, Writing Center, Rensselaer Polytechnic Institute; Assistant to Editor-in-Chief, *Foundation* Magazine; Faculty Secretary and Records Specialist, School of Nursing, University of Alaska at Anchorage; Graduate Assistant, Department of English, Boston College; Graduate Assistant, Department of English, University of Dayton. Organizational Memberships: Poetry Society of America; Academy of American Poets; American Literary Translators Association; American Comparative Literature Association; Modern Language Association; Northeast Modern Language Association; Society for Textual Scholarship; Society for Critical Exchange; Mensa, 1969-70; International Society of the History of Rhetoric; International Association of Philosophy and Literature; Rhetoric Society of America; American Studies Association; Philological Association of the Pacific Coast; Philadelphia Writers Organization; Appalachian Writers Association; Cambridge Footnote Society, Co-Founder 1969-71. Community Activities: Community Volunteer, 1970-77; Volunteer Work with the Elderly, 1973-75; Save the Children, Sponsor 1980 to present; Sigma Tau Sigma, 1966. Published Works: Translation (in progress), *Methodologie der Literaturwissenschaft (Methods of Literary Scholarship)*, by Joseph P. Strelka. Honors and Awards: Research Fellowship, University of Pennsylvania, 1982-83; Fulbright Junior Lectureship to Portugal, 1983-84; Fulbright Nominee, Germany, 1982; President, C.L.A.S., University of Pennsylvania, 1982-83; Presidential Fellowship, 1979-82; First Place Award in Poetry, Graduate Division, McKinney Literary Competition, 1979; Austrian Government Scholarship for German Study, University of Salzburg, Summer 1966; Alpha Sigma Tau Honor Key, 1966; Chaminade Award for Excellence, 1966; Boston College Graduate Assistantship, 1969-70; University of Dayton Graduate Assistantship, 1966-67; Listed in *Outstanding Young Women of America, World Who's Who of Women, Dictionary of International Biography, International Authors and Writers Who's Who, Personalities of America, Personalities of the West and Midwest.* Address: P.O. Box 100014, Anchorage, Alaska 99510.■

MARY BERNADETTE JANNING

Administrator. Personal: Born May 20, 1917, in Custer City, Oklahoma; Daughter of Frank R. and Mary Kreizenbeck Janning (deceased). Education: Diploma in Nursing, St. Francis Hospital School of Nursing, Wichita, Kansas, 1942; B.S.N. 1951, M.S. 1972, Marquette University; Work toward Doctorate Degree, The George Washington University, 1970-72; Fellowship, National Endowment for the Humanities, University of Chicago, 1980. Career: Executive Director, Oklahoma Conference of Catholic Hospitals, 1980 to present; Executive Director, Franciscan Villa, Broken Arrow, Oklahoma, 1979-80; President and Chief Executive Officer 1973-79, Associate Administrator 1972-73, St. Francis Hospital, Wichita, Kansas; Administrative Resident, Georgetown University Hospital, Washington D.C., 1971-72; Provincial Administrator, Sisters of the Sorrowful Mother, 1965-70; Director of the School of Nursing, St. Francis Hospital, 1956-65; Associate Director of the School of Nursing, St. John's Hospital, Tulsa, Oklahoma, 1952-56; Director of Nursing Service, Holy Family Hospital, Estheville, Iowa, 1944-50; Various Nursing Positions, St. Francis Hospital, 1942-44. Organizational Memberships: National Nurses Association; State Nurses Association; District Nurses Association; National League for Nursing; Kansas Conference of Catholic Health Facilities, Board Member 1975-79, President 1977; Delegate to International Assemblies of the Sisters of the Sorrowful Mother, 1968, 1971, 1975; Delegate to Pronvincial Assemblies, Sisters of the Sorrowful Mother, 1971-83; American National Red Cross, Tulsa Chapter 1952-56, Midway Kansas Chapter 1972-79; American Diabetes Association. Community Activities: American Association of Nurse Anesthetists Council on Accreditation, 1975-78; Appointed to Oklahoma State Board of Nurse Registration and Nursing Education, President 1955, Member 1955-59; President, Wichita Medical Education Associates, 1977-79. Religion: Diocesan Council of Oklahoma, 1965-70; Tulsa Deanery Council, 1965-70; Catholic Hospital Association Council for Diploma Schools of Nursing, 1954-59; Board Member, Kansas Conference of Catholic Health Facilities, 1975-79. Published Works: "Our Students Lead the Way" 1955, "Nurses Change Too" 1958, "A Follow-up Study of Graduates of St. Francis School of Nursing, Wichita, Kansas, 1944-60"; *The Life of a Student Nurse*; Videocassette *Love Made Visible*. Honors and Awards: Outstanding Alumnus for Loyalty and Professional Achievement, St. Francis Hospital School of

Nursing, 1972; American Diabetes Association Citation Award for Service, 1976; American National Red Cross Award for Outstanding Volunteer Leadership, American Red Cross Midway Kansas Chapter, 1979; KRMG Radio 74 "Pat on the Back Service - Citizenship", 1979; Award for 22 Years of Service to St. Francis Hospital and the Wichita Community, 1979; Listed in *Who's Who in America, Dictionary of International Biography, Who's Who of American Women, Who's Who in Health Care Services, International Who's Who in Community Service, Notable Americans of the Bicentennial Era, American Catholic Who's Who, Notable Americans of 1978-79, Who's Who in Religion, Who's Who in the Southwest, Who's Who in the World*. Address: 17600 East 51st Street, Broken Arrow, Oklahoma 74012.■

DORINDA H. JAREST

Artist, Fine Arts Painter. Personal: Born December 13, 1912; Daughter of Everett H. and Elizabeth Hinckley (deceased); Married Joseph R. Jarest, Son of Rudolph and Angeline Jarest (deceased). Education: B.S. Architecture, University of New Hampshire, 1939; Summer Workshops with Eliot O'Hara, John Chetcutti, Paul Stryzick, Carl N. Schmalz, Claude Croney. Career: Artist and Fine Arts Painter (Illustrated *The Upper Ashuelot*, a History of Keene; Designed One Side of Keene Bicentennial Medal); Paintings Exhibited at Keene State College, Cheshire Hospital, 4 New Hampshire Banks, Others; Paintings in Number Private Collections in 48 States and 8 Foreign Countries; Former Positions include Teacher, Engineer Draftsman, Historic Building Surveyor, Architect, Graphic Artist/ Illustrator. Organizational Memberships: New Hampshire Art Association, 1945-52; Keene Art Association, Program Chairman, Exhibition Chairman; Southern Vermont Art Association; Newport Art Association; Jaffrey Art Association; Independent Artists, 1950-54. Community Activities: Donation of Paintings to Various Groups; Boy Scout and Girl Scout Work; Repaired Paintings for Cheshire Hospital. Honors and Awards: Popular Prize, New Hampshire Art Association, 1945; Numerous First and Second Prizes in Keene Art Association, 1960-72; Over 50 One-Man Shows. Address: Base Hill Road, Rural Route 2 Box 244, Keene, New Hampshire 03431.■

HUGH DONALD JASCOURT

Labor Law Counsel. Personal: Born March 25, 1935; Son of Jack and Gladys Jascourt (both deceased); Married Resa Zall; Father of Stephen D., Leigh R. Education: A.B. honors, University of Pennsylvania, 1956; J.D., Wayne State University Law School, 1960. Military: Served in the United States Army, 1956-57, attaining the rank of Lieutenant. Career: Labor Law Counsel, United States Department of Commerce; Assistant Solicitor, Labor Law, United States Department of Interior; Director, Public Employment Relations Research Institute; Professor, George Washington University Law School; House Counsel, American Federation of State, County and Municipal Employees; Labor Relations Counsel, Federal Reserve Board; Executive Director, Federal Bar Association; Attorney-Advisor, National Labor Relations Board; Assistant Director, Employee Management Relations, American Federation of Government Employees. Organizational Memberships: Industrial Relations Research Association, D.C. Chapter Board of Governors 1979-83; American Bar Association, Chairman Various Subcommittees; Society of Professionals in Dispute Resolution; Society of Federal Labor Relations Professionals; American Society for Public Administration; International Personnel Management Association. Community Activities: Chairman, Unfair Labor Practice Panel, Prince George's County P.E.R.B., 1973-81; Greenbelt Employee Relations Board, 1977 to present; National Jogging Association, Vice President 1980-83, Board of Directors 1969-83; Road Runners Club of America, President 1961-65; Maryland Public Sector Conference Board, 1973 to present; Prince George County Federation of Park and Recreation Councils, President 1969-71; Prince George County Parent-Teacher Association, Regional Vice President 1981; Maryland Congress of Parents and Teachers, Chairman Curriculum Committee. Religion: Religious School Committee of Congregation, 1974 to present. Published Works: Labor Relations Editor, *Journal of Law and Education*, 1973 to present; Author of Collective Bargaining Chapter, *Yearbook of School Law*, 1978-83; *Government Labor Relations* 1979, *Trends in Public Sector Labor Relations* 1974, *Public Sector Labor Relations* 1974. Honors and Awards: Coach/Manager, United States Team, International Cross Country Championship 1966, Southern Games (Trinidad) 1964; Maryland's Outstanding Volunteer Recreation Leader, 1968; Maryland's Outstanding Physical Fitness Leader, 1967; One of Five Maryland Outstanding Young Men of the Year, 1969; Editor-in-Chief, *Wayne Law Journal*, 1959-60; Robbins Award for Best Brief in Moot Court, 1960; Listed in *Who's Who in American Law, Who's Who in the East*. Address: 7 Maplewood Court, Greenbelt, Maryland 20770.■

DIANE MARTHA JASEK

Administrator. Personal: Born June 24, 1955; Daughter of Edward T. and Martha Rychlik Jasek. Education: B.A. Government and American Studies, University of Texas at Austin. Career: Director of C.I.C. Institutes; Former Positions include Legal Assistant to the Attorney General's Office (Prosecutor's Assistance Section), Staff Assistant on the State Pension Review Board, Meetings and Exhibits Coordinator of the State Bar of Texas, Personal Staff Assistant for Senator Chet Brooks. Organizational Memberships: Williamson County Democrats. Religion: Roman Catholic. Honors and Awards: Listed in *Outstanding Young Women of America, Who's Who in American Politics, World's Who's Who of Women, Personalities of the South, International Youth in Achievement, Personalities of America, Notable Americans*. Address: 915 Vance Street, Taylor, Texas 76574.■

JACOB K. JAVITS

Lawyer, Former United States Senator. Personal: Born May 18, 1904, in New York City, New York; Son of Morris and Ida Littman Javits; Married Marian Ann Borris, November 30, 1947; Father of Joy D., Joshua M., Carla. Education: LL.B., New York University, 1926; 37 Honorary Degrees. Military: Served in the United States Army, 1942-45, attaining the rank of Lieutenant Colonel. Career: Admitted to New York State Bar, 1927; Law Practice in New York City, 1927 to present; Attorney General of New York, 1955-57; Member 80th-83rd Congresses, 21st New York District; United States Senator from New York, 1957-81; Member Law Firm Javits, Trubin, Sillcocks and Edelman, 1958-71; Member Counsel Firm Trubin, Sillcocks, Edelman & Knapp, 1981 to present; Adjunct Professor, Political Science, State University of New York at Stony Brook, 1982 to present. Organizational Memberships: Chairman, North Atlantic Assembly's Political Committee, Committee of Nine, Parliamentarian's Committee for Less Developed Nations; United States Delegate to 25th Anniversary of United Nations General Assembly, 1970; National Commission Marijuana and Drug Abuse, 1971-73. Community Activities: American Legion; Veterans of Foreign Wars; Jewish War Veterans; City Athletic Club; Harmonie Club. Published Works: Author *A Proposal to Amend the Anti-Trust Laws* 1939, *Discrimination U.S.A.* 1960, *Order of Battle, A Republican's Call to Reason* 1964, *Who Makes War* 1973, *Javits: The Autobiography of a Public Man* 1981; Series of Articles on Political Philosophy for Republican Party, 1946. Honors and Awards: Legion of Merit; Commendation Ribbon; Civilian Award, Medal of Freedom, 1983. Address: 375 Park Avenue, New York, New York 10152.■

JAMES JOHN JELINEK

Emeritus Professor of Education. Personal: Born April 7, 1915; Married Elizabeth Louise; Father of Lawrence James. Education: B.S., University of Illinois, 1937; M.A., Northwestern University, 1940; Ph.D., Indiana University, 1951. Military: Served in the United States Naval Reserve, 1943-45, attaining the rank of Lieutenant. Career: Editor, Civil Service News of Illinois, 1937-38; Teacher, Kewanee (Illinois) High School, 1938-41; Assistant Professor in Journalism, University of Detroit, 1941-45; Research Director, The J. L. Hudson Company, Detroit, 1941-43; Associate Professor of Social Sciences, University of Missouri-Rolla, 1945-53; Professor of Education 1953-77, Emeritus Professor of Education 1977 to present, Arizona State University. Organizational Memberships: Association for Supervision and Curriculum Development, Board of Directors, Editor, Regional President; Far Western Philosophy of Education Society, Editor, President 1965 to present; Professors of Curriculum (International), Editor, Continuing Secretary 1974-81; American Educational Research Association, 1937 to present; American Philosophical Association, 1945 to present; American Educational Studies Association; American Association of University Professors; John Dewey Society, Factotum, Executive Committee 1945 to present; National Education Association, State Representative 1938 to present. Community Activities: National Citizens Commission for Public Schools, 1952-57; National Commission on the Education of Adolescents, 1961-62; Congress of Parents and Teachers, State Representative 1945-77; Council of Parent-Teacher Associations, President 1947-48; Arizona Council on Education, President 1968-70; National Scholastic Press Association, 1938-45; Quill and Scroll; United Nations Association of the United States of America, Congressional Liaison, Executive Board, State Division. Honors and Awards: Kappa Delta Pi; Alpha Kappa Psi; Kappa Phi Kappa; Pi Sigma Phi; All Writings included in the Archives of the Hoover Institution on War, Revolution and Peace; Awards in International Salons for Photographic Art. Address: 228 East Concorda Drive, Tempe, Arizona 85282.■

TWO THOUSAND NOTABLE AMERICANS

MAXWELL JOSEPH JEMMOTT-WILLIAMS

Teacher, Organist. Personal: Born October 30, 1953; Son of Inez Jemmott-Williams. Education: B.A. Communications, M.Sc. Marketing, Graduate Studies, University of California at Los Angeles. Career: Teacher; Organist; Choir Director; Former Banker. Address: 803 Ardilla Avenie, La Puente, California 91746.■

ROGER LANE JENKINS

Administrator. Personal: Born June 16, 1946; Son of Mr. and Mrs. Robert L. Jenkins; Married Basia M., Daughter of Drs. Jan and Janina Matthews; Father of Sean Kirk, Sasha Nicole. Education: B.S. Business Administration, Berea College, 1968; M.B.A, East Tennessee State University, 1970; Ph.D. Business Administration, The Ohio State University, 1976. Career: Dean for Graduate Business Programs, University of Tennessee; Former Marketing Professor, Accountant. Organizational Memberships: American Marketing Association; Association for Consumer Research; Academy for Marketing Science; Institute for Decision Sciences; Academy of International Business. Community Activities: Tennessee Chairman of Coalition to Prevent Shoplifting; National Board Member, Graduate Management Admissions Council; Board of Governors, Warren Wilson Alumni Association. Honors and Awards: Outstanding Professor, College of Business, 1978, 1979; Outstanding Professor, University of Tennessee, 1981; Governor's Merit Award for Outstanding Contributions to Higher Education in Tennessee, 1973; Outstanding Educator of the Year, National Jaycees, 1977; Maynard Award, American Marketing Association, 1977 (for outstanding research articles appearing in *Journal of Marketing*); Listed in *Who's Who in Education*, Others. Address: 3393 Topside Road, Knoxville, Tennessee 37920.■

MARY ELLEN JENKS-JORDAL

Executive. Personal: Born October 4, 1933; Daughter of Mrs. Emma Jenks; Married Douglas R. Jordal; Mother of Joyellyn Jenks, Jared Brent, Juliette Leslie. Education: B.S.Ed. 1956, M.S. 1957, University of Wisconsin-Madison. Career: Vice President, Consumer Affairs, The Pillsbury Company; Vice President 1979, Director of Consumer Services and Affairs 1976-79, Director of Consumer Services 1962-76, Green Giant Company; Editorial Writer, American Dairy Association, 1961; Director, Consumer Services, Salada Foods, 1957-61; Director, Speech Department, Monona Grove High School, 1956-57. Organizational Memberships: American Women in Radio and Television; Society for Nutrition Education; Society of Consumer Affairs Professionals in Business; Grocery Manufacturers of America; American Frozen Foods Institute, Chairperson of Program Planning Committee; Home Economists in Business. Community Activities: Better Business Bureau of Minnesota, Board of Directors. Honors and Awards: Publicity Chairperson, American Women in Radio and Television National Convention, 1977; Publicity Chairperson, American Home Economics Association National Convention, 1968; Publicity Chairperson, Home Economists in Business Microwave Seminar, 1975; Chairperson, Professional Women's Seminar, 1974. Address: 6624 Dovre Drive, Edina, Minnesota 55436.■

CLAYNE R. JENSEN

College Administrator. Personal: Born March 17, 1930 in Gunnison, Utah; Son of Alton H. and Arvilla R. Jensen; Married Elouise Henrie; Father of Craig, Mike, Blake, Chris. Education: B.A. 1952, M.A. 1956, University of Utah; Ph.D., Indiana University, 1963. Military: Served in United States Marine Corps, 1953-55, attaining the rank of Captain. Career: Teaching Assistant, Indiana University, 1961-62; Instructor to Associate Professor of Physical Education and Coach, Utah State University, 1956-64; Brigham Young University (Provo, Utah), Associate Professor and Coordinator College Programs 1965-67, Professor 1968-74, Assistant Dean College of Physical Education 1968-74, Dean 1974 to present; Visiting Professor, Northern Illinois University, DeKalb, 1969; Executive Director, Utah Inter-Agency Council for Recreation and Parks, 1962-65; Chairman, National Conference on Inter-Agency Planning for Parks and Recreation, 1963-64. Organizational Memberships: American Association for the Advancement of Science; International Platform Association; United States Olympic Academy, 1979; Brigham Young University Faculty Athletic Representative, 1974 to present; Executive Director and Governor, Utah Recreation and Parks Association, 1958-63; President, Utah Association for Health, Physical Education, Recreation and Athletics, 1970; Executive Council, American Association for Health, Physical Education, Recreation and Athletics, 1965-66 and 1966-67; Board of Governors, National Recreation and Parks Association, 1965-69; Utah Education Association. Community Activities: Editor, *Utah Journal of Health, Physical Education, and Recreation*, 1970-73; Steering Committee, Western College Men's Physical Education Society, 1963-64; Alumni, Intermountain Olympic Academy; Kiwanis International; Former Member Lions Club. Religion: Mormon. Published Works: Author of *Manual of Kinesiology* 1966, *Scientific Basis of Athletic Conditioning* 2nd 1978, *Conditioning Exercises to Improve Body Form and Function* 3rd 1972, *Square Dance* 1973, *Folk Dance* 1973, *Modern Track and Field Coaching Technique* 1974, *Recreation and Leisure Time Careers* 2nd 1982, *Winter Touring : Cross Country Skiing* 1977, *Leisure and Recreation in America: A Guide and Overview* 1977, *Issues in Outdoor Recreation* 1977, *Skiing* 4th 1983, *Outdoor Recreation in America* 4th 1983, *Applied Kinesiology: The Science of Human Performance* 3rd 1983, *Administrative Management of Physical Education and Athletic Program* 1983, *Backpacking for Fun and Fitness* 1982, *Measurement and Statistics in Physical Education* 1972, *Measurement and Evaluation in Physical Education and Athletics* 1980; Contributor of Articles to Professional Journals. Honors and Awards: Phi Kappa Phi; Service Award, Utah Chapter of American Association for Health, Physical Education, Recreation and Dance; Breitbard Foundation Athletic Excellence Award, 1955; Special Citation for Outstanding Contributions to Recreation and Park Development, State of Utah, 1965; Listed in *Biographical Roll of Honor, Who's Who in the World, Who's Who in America, Directory of Distinguished Americans, Who's Who in American Education, International Authors and Writers Who's Who, Dictionary of International Biography, Who's Who in the West, Outstanding Educators of America, Creative Personalities of the World, Leaders in Education, Contemporary Authors, Writer's Directory, Men of Achievement, Personalities of the West and Midwest, Community Leaders and Noteworthy Americans*. Address: 1900 Oak Lane, Provo, Utah 84601.■

ARACELI JIMENEZ

Student. Personal: Born November 22, 1960; Son of Eduardo and Hortensia M. de Jimenez. Education: A.A., Laredo Junior College, 1979; B.S. Secondary Education, Laredo State University, expected August 1984; Career: Student of Secondary Education. Community Activities: Future Homemakers of America, 1979 to present; Phi Theta Kappa, 1980 to present; Sigma Delta Mu, 1980 to present. Honors and Awards: National Honor Society, 1978 to present; Spanish National Honor Society, 1978 to present; Certificate of Achievement, Talent Roster of Minority Students, 1981; L.I.S.D. Award First Place Certamen "Carta A Mi Madre", 1978; Academic Excellence Award, Laredo Junior College, 1979; Certificate of Congratulation, State Representative Billy Hall, 1979; Outstanding Young Leadership Award, 1982; Society of Distinguished American High School Students, 1979; Listed in *Who's Who Among American High School Students, National Register of Outstanding Junior and Community College Students, Who's Who Among Students in American Junior Colleges, International Youth in Achievement, Personalities of America, Personalities of the South, Community Leaders of America, World Who's Who of Women, Community Leaders of the World, Biographical Roll of Honor, Dictionary of International Biography, Directory of Distinguished Americans, Personalites of the South*. Address: 3005 Salinas, Laredo, Texas 78040.■

CHARLES FOREMAN JOHNSON

Architect, Graphic Designer, Teacher, Architectural Photographer, Systems Engineer, Consultant. Personal: Born May 28, 1929, in Plainfield, New Jersey; Son of Charles E. and E. Lucile Casner Johnson; Father of Kevin, David. Education: Attended Union Junior College, 1947-48; B.Arch., University of Southern California, 1958; Postgraduate Studies in Systems Engineering, University of California at Los Angeles, 1959-60. Career: Blueprint Operator and Draftsman, Wigton Abbott, Plainfield, New Jersey, 1945-52; Designer, Draftsman, H. W. Underhill, Architect, Los Angeles, California, 1953-55; Designer, Carrington H. Lewis, Architect, Palos Verdes, California, 1954-56; Interiors and Window Displays, Crenshaw Hi Fi, Los Angeles, 1955-60; Graduate Architect, Ramo Wooldridge Corporation, Los Angeles, 1956-58; Technical Staff, Space Technology Laboratories, Los Angeles, 1958-60; Systems Engineer, Atlas Weapon System, Space Technology Labs, Los Angeles, 1960-62; Advanced Planner and Systems Engineer, Minuteman Weapon System, TRW Systems, Los Angeles, 1962-64; Director of Operations and Facility Planning, Systems Engineering and Integration Division, TRW Systems, 1964-68; Consultant, New Mexico Regional Medical Program, New Mexico State Department of Hospitals and Institutions and New Mexico State Planning Office, 1968-70; Charles F. Johnson, Principal, Private Practice in Architecture, Interiors, Color and Graphic Design, Los Angeles 1953-68, Santa Fe (New Mexico) 1968 to present; Consultant, Stereo, Video Systems Planning and Equipment Review, 1960 to present; Free-lance Architectural Photographer, 1971 to present; Apprentice Program for Architecture Students, 1980 to present; Creative Works include Empie Home "Whispering Boulders" (Carefree, Arizona) 1982, Private Home in Dillon (Colorado) 1981, Elias House (Santa Fe, New Mexico) 1976, Casa Largo (Santa Fe) 1975, Major Homes in Santa Fe 1970 to present, Others. Community Activities: Delta Sigma Phi; El Gancho Tennis Club; Santa Fe Coalition for the Arts, President 1974; Santa Fe Fiesta Melodrama, Set Designer 1969, 1971, 1974, 1977, 1978, 1981; Fiesta Parade, Designed Floats that won 2 Grand Prizes and 13 Hysterical First Prizes 1970-83. Published Works: Articles on Facility Management and Planning, Information Systems and General Organization; Architectural Articles;

Architectural Photographs Published in United States, France and Japan. Honors and Awards: Listed in *Who's Who in the West*, *Men of Achievement*, *Biographical Roll of Honor*, *Personalities of the West and Midwest*. Address: 14 General Sage Drive, Santa Fe, New Mexico 87505.■

JORENE K. JOHNSON

Urbanist. Personal: Born January 6, 1931; Daughter of Adam and Kathryn Freitag (deceased); Married Roland E. Johnson; Mother of Lorin I., Melissa K. Education: B.F.A., Pratt Institute, 1952; M.P.A., University of Cincinnati, 1975. Career: Urbanist; Former Interior Designer, Furniture Designer. Organizational Memberships: Cincinnati Chapter, National Society Fund Raisers, 1984; American Planners Association, 1983-84. Community Activities: Member Leadership Cincinnati Alumni, Class III, 1979-80; Ad Hoc Committees for Residential Care Facilities, City of Cincinnati, 1983; Mayor's Energy Commission, 1972; City Manager's C.O.P.E. Task Force; Co-Convenor, Parks, Recreation and Open Space Subcommittee; Board Member, Hamilton County Association Retarded Citizens, 1984; Community Chest Planning Board; Congress of Neighborhood Groups; Program for Cincinnati; Monfort Heights Civic Association, Trustee, Former President, Vice President; League of Women Voters, Cincinnati Area, Vice President 1971, Board Member 1969-72. Religion: Member of First Unitarian Church of Cincinnati; Recorder Endowment Trustees, 1983-84; Treasurer, 1977-83; Member Finance Committee, 1977-83; Secretary Board of Trustees, 1967, Member 1966-68; Newsletter Editor, 1965-67; Member Decorating, Day Care, Office, New Membership Committees; Treasurer Women's Alliance, 1970-72. Address: 5200 Race Road, Cincinnati, Ohio 45247.■

SAM D. JOHNSON

United States Circuit Judge. Personal: Born November 17, 1920; Son of Samuel Dodson and Flora Johnson (deceased); Married June Page, Daughter of Mr. and Mrs. Ira Page; Father of Page Johnson Harris, Janet Johnson Clements, Samuel James. Education: B.B.A., Baylor University, 1946; LL.B., University of Texas, 1949. Military: Served in the United States Army 95th Infantry during World War II. Career: United States Circuit Judge; Former Attorney at Law, County Attorney (Hill County), District Attorney (Hill County), District Judge (Hill County), Director of the Houston Legal Foundation, Appellate Judge of the 14th Court of Civil Appeals, Associate Justice of the Supreme Court of the State of Texas. Organizational Memberships: Texas Bar Association, Chairman Legal Services to the Poor in Civil Matters Committee 1973-74; Hill County Bar Association, President 1964-65; Central Texas Bar Association, President 1963-64; District and County Attorney's Association; Houston Bar Association; Travis County Bar Association; State Bar of Texas, Judicial Section, Executive Committee 1976 to present, Chairman Elect 1978-79, Secretary-Treasurer 1964-65; Fellow, Texas Bar Foundation; American Bar Association, Appellate Judges Conference Chairman 1976-77, Continuing Education Committee 1974-76, Executive Committee 1973-79, Board of Governors 1979-81; Judicial Administration Division of the American Bar Association, Member of the Council 1976-78; National Legal Aid and Defender Association, Board of Directors 1971 to present; Fellow, American Bar Foundation; Institute of Judicial Administration; American Judicature Society. Religion: Presbyterian. Published Works: *A Case for Automated Assignment*, *The Houston Legal Foundation: Excellence for Indigents*, *The Houston Legal Foundation: Advocate for the Indigent*, *Proving Motorist Uninsured*; Other Books and Articles. Honors and Awards: Designated One of Three Distinguished Alumni of Baylor University, 1978; President, Baylor Alumni Association, 1973-74; Honorary Order of the Coif, University of Texas School of Law, 1977; Honorary Membership, International Legal Fraternity of Phi Delta Phi; National Legal Aid and Defender Association's 1978 Arthur von Briesen Award, 1978; Chairman, Appellate Judge's Conference, Judicial Administration Division, American Bar Association, 1976-77; Board of Governors, American Bar Association, 1979-81. Address: 1811 Exposition, Austin, Texas 78703.■

WILLIAM PAGE JOHNSON

School Superintendent. Personal: Born September 25, 1942; Son of Mr. and Mrs. E. W. Johnson; Married Vivian, Daughter of Mr. and Mrs. Euell Casteel; Father of Krista, Trent. Education: B.A., University of Denver, 1964; M.A. 1972, Ph.D. 1974, University of Iowa. Career: Superintendent, Illinois School for the Deaf; Director of Special Education, A.E.A. #16, Mt. Pleasant, Iowa, 1974-77; Assistant Director of Special Education, Minneapolis Public Schools, 1973-74; High School Mathematics Instructor, Iowa School for the Deaf, Council Bluffs, Iowa, 1969-71; High School Mathematics Instructor, Portland, Oregon, 1968-69; Junior High School Mathematics Instructor, Council Bluffs Community School, 1964-68. Organizational Memberships: C.E.A.S.D., Executive Board Secretary; C.A.I.D.; Council of Exceptional Children; I.A.D.; Advisory Board, Builders of Skills; Advisory Council, Graduate Programs for Hearing Improvement, Northern Illinois University; Consultant in Special Education, MacMurray College. Community Activities: Executive Board Secretary, Conference of Educational Administrators Serving the Deaf, 1982-83; Rotary International; North Central Association Participant Reviewer of Special Function Schools, 1978 to present; Chairperson, Illinois State Board of Education, Steering Committee for the Development of Programmatic Guidelines for Hearing Improvement; Interpreter for the Deaf, 1960 to present. Religion: Trustee, First Presbyterian Church, 1981 to present; Board of Directors, Presbyterian Day Care Center; Ordained Deacon and Ordained Elder, United Presbyterian Church. Honors and Awards: Boss of the Year, American Business Women's Association, Jacksonville, 1978; Outstanding Young Teacher Award, Council Bluffs Jaycees, 1968; Finalist, Outstanding Young Man Award, Council Bluffs Jaycees; National Science Foundation Graduate Fellow, Oregon State University, 1967-68; National Science Foundation Graduate Fellow, University of Nebraska, 1965-66. Address: 928 West State, Jacksonville, Illinois 62650.■

RUTH LE ROY JOHNSTON

Retired Nosologist, Medical Record Administrator. Personal: Born June 19, 1915, in Elizabeth, New Jersey; Daughter of James Archibald and Frances Ione Davis Austin Le Roy; Married Earl B. Johnston (deceased); Mother of Jonathan Bruce Johnston (deceased). Education: Graduate, Battin High School, Elizabeth, New Jersey, 1934; B.A., Bob Jones University, 1945; R.R.A., Emory University, 1953; I.B.M. Computer Systems and FORTRAN, 1962-65; D.H.E.W., S.S.A. and Various I.D.C. Disease Nomenclature Workshops through 1979. Career: Assistant to Chief Medical Record Librarian, Grady Memorial Hospital, Atlanta, Georgia, 1948-53; Chief Medical Record Librarian, Georgia Baptist Hospital 1953-54, Memorial Mission Hospital (Asheville, North Carolina) 1954-55, Veterans Administration Hospital (Richmond, Virginia) 1955-60, Veterans Administration Center (Wood, Wisconsin) 1960, Veterans Administration Hospital (Hines, Illinois) 1960-62; Supervisory Medical Classification Specialist, Nosologist, Research and Statistics, Social Security Administration, Department of Health, Education and Welfare, Baltimore, Maryland, 1962-68; Consultant, Medical Records, Prince George's Hospital, Cheverly, Maryland, 1965-67; Medical Record Consultant, Health Data Service, Maryland Blue Cross/Blue Shield, Baltimore, 1969-71; Chief Medical Record Administrator, Good Samaritan Hospital, West Palm Beach, Florida, 1971-74; Chief Medical Record Administrator, Gorgas Hospital, United States Canal Zone, Panama, 1974-77; Consultant to Coco Solo Hospital, 1974-77; Retired, Working Part-time in Office of Arthur W. Young, M.D., P.A., North Palm Beach, Florida. Organizational Memberships: American Medical Record Association; Maryland Medical Record Association, Chairman Education Committee, Past Vice President; Virginia Medical Record Association, President, Treasurer; Veterans Administration, Area Medical Record Consultant, Speaker at National Conference; Member Various Other State Medical Record Associations. Community Activities: International Platform Association; National Audubon Society; National Republican Congressional Committee; Congressional V.I.P. Memberships; Republican National Committee; Republic Presidential Task Force, Charter Member; United States Senatorial Club; Panama Canal Club; National Association of Federal Retired Employees; American Association of Retired Persons. Religion: First Baptist Church, West Palm Beach, Florida, Adult Jubilee Choir. Published Works: Contributor to Professional Journals. Honors and Awards: Various Veterans Adminstration and Civil Service Awards, 1960-68; Life Fellow, American Biographical Institute Research Association; Listed in *Notable Americans*, *Who's Who*, *American Registry Series*, *World Who's Who of Women*, *Marquis Who's Who*, *Dictionary of International Biography*, *International Who's Who of Intellectuals*. Address: 100 Paradise Harbour Blvd., North Palm Beach, Florida 33408.■

THOMAS M. JOHNSTON

Executive. Personal: Born December 8, 1921; Married Betty Logan; Father of Thomas G (deceased), Robert Alexander, Hugh Samuel, Ann Johnston Taubel. Education: B.S., United States Military Academy, 1943; M.Eng., New York University, 1949; Completed all requirements for D.Eng.Sc. except Thesis, New York University, 1962. Military: Served in the United States Army Corps of Engineers, 1943-58, advancing through the ranks from Second Lieutenant to Major; United States Army Reserves Corps of Engineers, 1958-81, Major to Colonel. Career: President, Enreal Enterprises, Inc.; Former Positions include Engineering Executive with Westinghouse Electric Corporation, Chief of Technical Programs for the Federal Aviation Administration, United States Government, Manager of Systems Engineering, Missile Systems for the Raytheon Corporation, and Manager of Systems Analysis, Defense Electronics, R.C.A. Inc. Organizational Memberships: Operations Research Society of America; Registered Professional Engineer, Massachusetts. Community Activities: President, West Point Society of New England, 1969-71; Official Board, First Methodist Church, Moorestown, New Jersey, 1961-67; Fairfax County Democratic Committee, 1981 to present. Religion: Methodist. Honors and Awards: Instructor of Mathematics, United States Military Academy, 1949-52; Lecturer in Mathematics, University of California 1954-55, University of Maryland 1956-58, American University 1956-58; Adjunct Professor of Mathematics, United States Military Academy, 1968-70. Address: 3720 Carriage House Court, Alexandria, Virginia 22309.■

TWO THOUSAND NOTABLE AMERICANS

ERNST F. JOKL

Professor of Neurology and Sports Medicine. Personal: Born August 3, 1907; Married; Father of Marion Jokl Ball, Peter Jokl. Education: M.D., Breslau, Germany, 1930; M.B., B.Ch., Witwatersrand University, Johannesburg, South Africa, 1936. Military: Served as Consultant to Director General of Medical Services and Lecturer on Aviation Medicine, South African Armed Forces and Royal Air Force, South African Division, 1939-45. Career: Professor of Neurology, University of Kentucky School of Medicine (Lexington, Kentucky); Professor of Sports Medicine, University of Breslau; Professor of Physical Education, University of Stellenbosch, South Africa. Organizational Memberships: Fellow, American College of Cardiology; Honorary Fellow, International Federation of Sports Medicine; President, Research Committee, U.N.E.S.C.O.; International Council of Sport and Physical Education. Community Activities: Consultant to Senator Hubert Humphrey, 1958-66; Honorary Professor of Sports Medicine, Free University of West Berlin and University of Frankfurt, 1969 to present; Distinguished Professor, University of Kentucky, 1970; Founder, American College of Sports Medicine, 1956. Honors and Awards: Grand Cross of Merit of Federal Republic of Germany, 1972; Buckston Browne Prize of Harveian Society of London, 1942; Honorary Member, Rotary International, 1974; Prince Philip Lecturer, House of Lords, London, 1983. Address: 340 Kingsway, Lexington, Kentucky 40502. ∎

LEON JONES

Professor of Education. Personal: Born December 26, 1936; Son of Lander Corbin (deceased) and Una Bell Jones; Married Bobbie Jean; Father of Stephanie Ruth, Gloria Jean. Education: B.S., University of Arkansas at Pine Bluff, 1963; Ed.D., University of Massachusetts-Amherst, 1971; J.D., The Catholic University of America, 1981. Military: Served in the United States Navy, 1958-61, as a Petty Officer Second Class. Career: Mathematical Statistician, Army Procurement and Supply Agency, Joliet, Illinois, 1963-64; Timestudy Engineer, International Harvester Company, Memphis, Tennessee, 1966-68; Lecturer, School of Education, University of Massachusetts-Amherst, 1970-71; Coordinator, Research and Evaluation, Acting Associate Dean, College of Human Learning and Development, Governors State University, Park Forest South, Illinois, 1971-72; Full-time Faculty Member of the School of Education 1973 to present, Director of the Center for Research and Development 1974-76, Howard University; Special Research Assistant, Deputy Majority Whip, 97th Congress, United States House of Representatives, 1982. Organizational Memberships: American Institute of Parliamentarians, 1982 to present; International Platform Association; National Lawyers Guild; National Conference of Black Lawyers; National Association for the Advancement of Colored People; American Association of University Professors; Evaluation Research Society. Community Activities: Executive Officer, Parent-Teacher Association, Galway Elementary School, Montgomery County, Maryland, 1975 to present; Legal Intern, United States Senate, 1978; Legal Intern, United States House of Representatives, 1979; Officer, Calverton Citizens Association, Prince Georges County, Beltsville, Maryland, 1983. Religion: Baha'i Faith, Baha'is of the United States; Officer, Local Spiritual Assembly of the Baha'is of Montgomery County East, Silver Spring, Maryland. Honors and Awards: Fellow, United States Office of Education, Department of Health, Education and Welfare, 1969-71; Howard University Grant, 1973-75; Ford Foundation Award, 1975-76 (for School Desegregation Research). Address: 3104 Castleleigh Road, Silver Spring, Maryland 20904. ∎

MALLORY MILLETT JONES

Actress. Personal: Born in St. Paul, Minnesota; Daughter of James and Helen Millett; Mother of Kristen Vigard. Education: B.A., University of Minnesota; Specialized Language Studies at the University of Mexico, Mexico City; Studies with Charles Conrad in Los Angeles, Frank Corsaro and Lee Strasburg in New York City. Career: Active in New York Theatre for 10 Years, Working in Plays at LaMama, Theatre for the New City, W.P.A., Theatre Genesis; Appeared on Television in the United States and Europe; Appeared with the Living Theatre in America; Toured Europe with John Vaccaro's Playhouse of the Ridiculous; Member of Original Companies of "Annie" and "The Best Little Whorehouse in Texas"; Portrayed Roles of Hedda Gabler, Carla in "Kennedy's Children," Daughter of Jan Sterling and John McMartin in Berkshire Theatre Festival's "Dodsworth," Corinna Stroller in "The House of Blue Leaves"; Played Role of Kathy Smith on C.B.S. Daytime Drama "Love of Life" and Gena Venucci on N.B.C.'s "Another World"; Role of Louise Schiflin in "Only the Pretty Girls Die," an Eischied Movie of the Week for NBC; Roles in Films *Alone in the Dark* and *Tootsie*; Five One-Woman Photography Shows, New York City (St. Clements Gallery, Third Eye Gallery, Modernage Discovery Gallery); With Lisa Shreve, Has Written and Photographed Four Film Strips on Infant Care and Development and Co-Author Screenplay "Canberra." Published Works: Currently Working on Novel *A Leap of Faith*. Address: 484 West 43rd Street, New York, New York 10036. ∎

RUTH ELIZABETH JONES

Contract Services Coordinator. Personal: Born October 5, 1943, in Houston, Texas; Widow; Mother of Thaddies III. Education: Graduate, Phillis Wheatley High School, 1962; B.A. History, Texas Southern University, 1967. Career: Government Claims Representative, Aetna Life Insurance Company, 1968-70; Nutrition Coordinator, Senior Opportunity Services, 1974; Field Probation Officer 1975-77, Intake Probation Officer 1977-80, Community Assistance Program Coordinator 1980-82, Texas Juvenile Probation Commission Coordinator 1982, Contract Services Coordinator 1983, Bexar County Juvenile Probation Department. Organizational Memberships: Texas Corrections Association; Texas Probation Association. Community Activities: Ella Austin Community Center, Board of Directors 1974-82, President 1968-81; United Way Board of Contributors, 1975-79; Young Women's Christian Association, Board of Directors 1973-79, Vice President, 1977; Myra D. Hemmings Resource Center, Board of Directors 1981 to present; Economic Opportunities Development Corporation, Board of Directors 1974-77; San Antonio State Hospital Volunteer Council, 1973-75; Community Chest, Board of Directors 1972; Family Life Commission, Board of Directors 1983; Governor Mark White Transition Team, 1982-83; Democratic Women of Bexar County, President 1974-75; City of San Antonio Planning Commission, Member 1978 to present, Vice Chairman 1981; State Democratic Executive Committee, 1980 to present; Delta Sigma Theta; San Antonio Chapter, Texas Coalition of Black Democrats, Member 1980 to present, President 1983. Religion: Member, Holy Redeemer Catholic Church, Member of Choir, Lector. Honors and Awards: Outstanding Community Service Citation, City of San Antonio, 1980, 1983; Distinguished Public Service Award, Texas House of Representatives, 1974; Outstanding Contribution toward Good Government Award, Texas State Senate, 1975; Commissioned Yellow Rose of Texas, 1978; Appreciation Award, Young Women's Christian Association, 1978; Numerous Certificates of Appreciation from Various Social and Civic Organizations; Listed in *Who's Who of American Women*, *World Who's Who of Women*, *Who's Who in American Politics*, *Who's Who in Politics in the South and Southwest*, *Personalities of America*. Address: 4226 Redstone, San Antonio, Texas 78219. ∎

GARY BLAKE JORDAN

Electronic Warfare Engineer. Personal: Born February 3, 1939; Son of Lt. Col Robert Leslie and Lois Evelyn Jordan; Married Gloria Jean Heppler; Father of Gareth Kylae, Glynis Jerelle. Education: B.S.E.E., College of Applied Science, Ohio University, 1961; Ph.D. (honoris causa), Electrical Engineering, Sussex College of Technology, England, 1977; Doctor of Electrical Engineering, Pacific Southern University, 1977. Career: Director, National Intelligence Agency; Former Executive Vice President, The Electronic Warfare Organization. Organizational Memberships: Institute of Electrical and Electronic Engineers; American Defense Preparedness Association; Armed Forces Communications and Electronics Association; United States Naval Institute. Community Activities: Society for Technical Communication, Senior Member; Society for Scholarly Publishing, Charter Member; Radio Society of Great Britain, Corporate Member; American Radio Relay League, Full Member; Washington Academy of Science, Member-at-Large; Northern California DX Foundation; International Amateur Radio Club, Geneva, Switzerland; Association of Old Crows, Life Member; American Association for the Advancement of Science; Professional Association of Diving Instructors. Honors and Awards: Life Fellow, Lambda Xi Pi, 1961; Fellow, American Biographical Institute, 1980. Address: P.O. Box 3689, Stanford, California 94305. ∎

LUCILLE GALLOWAY JORDAN

Associate State Superintendent. Personal: Daughter of Mr. and Mrs. T. P. Galloway; Married F. L. S. Jordan; Mother of Noelle Jordan. Education: Undergraduate Studies at Asheville College, University of Tennessee; Master's Degree, University of Georgia; Ed.D., University of Georgia. Career: Associate State Superintendent of Schools, Office of Instructional Services, Georgia Department of Education; Directed Following Programs in Atlanta Public Schools, Title III, Teacher Corps Consortium of Eight Colleges and Universities, Elementary Curriculum and Program Development (1966-78); Classroom Teacher for 15 Years, North Carolina, Tennessee, Georgia. Organizational Memberships: National Association for Supervision and Curriculum Development, President; Phi Kappa Phi Honorary

Scholastic Society; Phi Kappa Delta Honorary, President; Georgia Association of Educational Leaders; American Association of University Women. Community Activities: Advisory Board, C.B.S. Television Specials; Teacher's Guide to Television, Advisory Board; Atlanta Teacher Educational Teacher's Guides to Television, Advisory Board; Atlanta Teacher Educational Services, Advisory Board; Atlanta Journal and Constitution Educational Advisory Board. Religion: Member Sandy Springs First Baptist Church. Honors and Awards: National Science Foundation Fellow, 1973; Listed in *Who's Who of American Educators, Who's Who of American Women, World Who's Who of Women, Two Thousand Women of Achievement.* Address: 2310 North Peachtree Way, Dunwoody, Georgia 30338.■

KAY S. JORGENSEN

Museum Administrator, State Representative. Personal: Born March 25, 1951; Daughter of Arnold and Twyla Jorgensen; Married Michael R. Pangburn; Mother of Merideth Kay Pangburn. Education: B.S.Ed., Black Hills State College, 1974; One Semester of Study, World Campus Afloat, Chapmon College; Auctioneer, Fort Smith Auction School. Career: Executive Director of Museum; South Dakota Legislator, House of Representatives; Former Positions include Auctioneer, Educator. Organizational Memberships: State History Association; Local History Association; Le Case Library Association; American Legislative Exchange Council; National Council of State Legislators. Community Activities: Select Committee on Mining, 1981-82; Governor's Ad Hoc Water Committee, 1981; High Plains Heritage Society, 1976 to present; Business and Professional Women; American Association of University Women; National Federation of Independent Business. Honors and Awards: Outstanding Alumnus, 1981. Address: 1314 Cardinal Court, Spearfish, South Dakota 57783.■

SANDRA THOMAS JOWERS

Executive. Personal: Born October 4, 1950; Daughter of Carl Dexter and Anita Lorraine (Garver) Thomas; Married Joseph Jacob Jowers. Education: B.S. Sociology, B.S. Business Education, East Texas State University, 1972. Career: Thomas Van and Storage, Inc., Office Manager 1972-74, President 1974 to present. Organizational Memberships: Business and Professional Women's Clubs, Member, Convention Delegate, Young Careerist Chairman 1980; Southwestern Warehouse and Transfer Association, Director 1979 to present, Vice President 1981; Movers Association, Director 1974 to present, President 1979; Alpha Chi. Religion: Member of Methodist Church. Honors and Awards: Outstanding Young Woman of America Award; Listed in *Who's Who in Finance and Industry.* Address: 3408 Lakeside Drive, Rockwall, Texas 75087.■

EDWIN ANTHONY JOYCE, JR.

Administrator. Personal: Born February 23, 1937, in Hampton, Virginia; Son of Edwin Anthony (deceased) and Leah Bell Gates Joyce; Married Mary Dale Smith; Father of Edwin Anthony, William Christopher, Kathy Smith, Kim Smith, Beth Smith, Kelly Smith, Carson Smith. Education: Graduate, Broadripple High School, Indianapolis, Indiana; B.A. Botany, Butler University, 1959; Graduate Level Course in Marine Invertebrate Zoology, Duke University, Summer 1958; M.S. Marine Biology, University of Florida, 1961; Graduate Level Course in Marine Algology, University of South Florida, 1966. Career: Director, Division of Marine Resources, Florida Department of Natural Resources, 1975 to present; Chief, Bureau of Marine Science and Technology, 1972-75; Supervisor, Marine Research Laboratory, 1968-72; Senior Fisheries Biologist, 1967-68; Other Former Positions. Organizational Memberships: National Shellfisheries Association; Gulf and Caribbean Fisheries Institute, Board of Directors; South Atlantic State-Federal Fisheries Management Board; Atlantic States Marine Fisheries Commission, Scientific Advisory Committee; Gulf States Marine Fisheries Commission, Technical Coordinating Committee; Capital City Kiwanis Club of Tallahassee; Gulf of Mexico and South Atlantic Fishery Management Councils, Designee for Executive Director; American Institute of Fishery Research Biologists; Sigma Xi; American Fisheries Society; Certified Fishery Scientist. Honors and Awards: Listed in *American Men of Science, Who's Who, Who's Who in the South and Southwest, Dictionary of International Biography, American Malacologists.* Address: Route 1 Box 180-H, Tallahassee, Florida 32312.■

RODDIE REAGAN JUDKINS

Development Engineer. Personal: Born December 31, 1941; Son of Ammon (deceased) and Hazel Judkins; Married Teressa Ward, Daughter of William H. and Lorene Ward; Father of Bridget Renee, Lisa Suzanne, Emily Robin. Education: B.S. 1963, M.S. 1965, Tennessee Polytechnic Institute; Ph.D., Georgia Institute of Technology, 1970. Career: Development Engineer, Oak Ridge National Laboratory; Technical Associate, E. R. Johnson Associates, Inc.; Vice President, Nuclear Audit and Testing Company, Inc.; Plant Manager and Vice President, Nuclear Chemicals and Metals Corporation; Instructor of Chemistry, Georgia Institute of Technology. Organizational Memberships: American Chemical Society; Society of Sigma Xi. Religion: Member, Concord United Methodist Church, 1978 to present; Member Church Administrative Board, 1982, 1983, 1984. Honors and Awards: Registered Professional Engineer; Honorary Lieutenant Colonel, Georgia Militia; Listed in *American Men and Women of Science, Who's Who in the South and Southwest.* Address: 9917 Rainbow Drive, Knoxville, Tennessee 37922.■

BOBBY MAC JUNKINS

Library Administrator, State Representative. Personal: Born November 1, 1946; Son of Rev. and Mrs. L. D. Junkins; Married Susie Junkins; Father of Jason Clay, Annie Blair. Education: Graduate, Hokes Bluff High School, 1965; Attended Gadsden State Junior College, 1967; B.S. 1969, M.S. Education 1972, Jacksonville State University; Advanced Graduate Work, University of Alabama. Career: Director, Gadsden Public Library, 1976 to present; Representative, Alabama Legislature, 1982-86; Assistant Director, Gadsden Public Library 1973-76; Teacher, Cherokee County High School, 1969-73; Audio-Visual Instructor, Jacksonville Elementary Media Center, 1968-69; Student Page, Gadsden Public Library, 1965-68. Organizational Memberships: Alabama Library Association, Chairman Federal Legislative Development; Southeastern Library Association; American Library Association. Community Activities: Gadsden Kiwanis Club, President 1982-83; Gadsden Metro Chamber of Commerce, Vice President 1977-80; Etowah County Resources Council, President 1981; State Democratic Executive Committee, District #30, 1978-82; Etowah County Council of Community Services; Gadsden Jaycees. Religion: Baptist. Honors and Awards: National Rules Committee, Democratic Convention, 1980; One of Alabama's Four Outstanding Young Men, 1979; Distingiushed Service Award, Gadsden Jaycees, 1979; Outstanding Young Man of Etowah County, 1978; Gadsden's Key Man Award, 1978. Address: 254 College Street, Gadsden, Alabama 35999.■

F. EILEEN KAGEY

Educator. Personal: Born July 29, 1925; Daughter of Joseph Leonard and Florida E. Niles Kagey (deceased). Education: B.S. Education, Ball State University, 1952; M.S. Education, Indiana University, Bloomington, 1955. Career: Educator (has taught kindergarten through sixth grade); Former Private Secretary. Organizational Memberships: American Federation of Teachers, Local #4, Building Representative 1966 to present; Indiana State Teachers Association; Life Member, National Education Association; Indiana Association for Supervision and Curriculum Development; National Association for Supervision and Curriculum Development. Community Activities: Fort Wayne Symphony Orchestra, Viola, 1942-44; Indianapolis Symphonic Choir, Alto, 1958-61; Illiana Community Players, 1982; Vice President in charge of Programs (Areas of Study), American Association of University Women, Hobart, Indiana, 1962-64; Calumet Corner Chapter, Sweet Adelines, Inc., Member 1977 to present, Public Relations Chairman 1980 to present, Board of Directors 1981 to present, Recording Secretary 1982-83. Religion: Roman Catholic. Published Works: Author *Jeremy: The People-Dog* (a children's science story, 1974). Honors and Awards: National Honor Society; Elected to Kappa Delta Pi National Education Honorary; Member American Biographical Institute Research Association; Listed in *Who's Who in the Midwest, Personalities of America, Biographical Roll of Honor.* Address: 3040 West 39th Place, Gary, Indiana 46408.■

EDWARD KAHN

Gynecologist, Obstetrician, Researcher, Inventor. Personal: Born September 16, 1913; Son of Emile Kahn and Pauline Andorn (both deceased); Married Faith-Hope Green; Father of Ellen, Faith Hope II, Paula Amy. Education: B.S., University College of Arts and Pure Science, New York University, 1934; M.D., Long Island College of Medicine, 1939; Assistant, Pathology, Long Island College of Medicine, Kings County Hospital Division, Brooklyn, New York, 1939-40; Internship and Residency, Knickerbocker Hospital, New York, New York, 1940-42. Military: Served in the United States Army, 1942-44, achieving the rank of First Lieutenant. Career: Sydenham Hospital (New York), Consultant in Obstetrics and Gynecology 1974 to present, Coordinator of Hysterography for Hysterosalpingography Clinics 1950 to present, Culdoscopist for Gynecological Services 1954 to present, Associate Visiting Obstetrician and Gynecologist 1955, Assistant Adjunct in Obstetrics and Gynecology 1944-47; Chief Female Gynecologist, Specialty Clinics, 1950 to present; Assistant Visiting Obstetrician and Gynecologist, Department of Hospitals, Sydenham, New York, 1949-55. Organizational Memberships: American College of Obstetricians and Gynecologists, Founding Fellow; International College of Surgeons, Fellow, Examiner in Obstetrics and Gynecology 1964, North American Federation Lecturer in Instructional Courses on Female Sterility 1962, New York State Surgical Section Lecturer 1957; Medical Jurisprudence Society, 1963, 1965; International Fertility Association, Teaching Clinics 1953; New York State Medical Society; Queens County Medical Society. Community Activities: Kings County Hospital (New York), Volunteer Assistant for Long Island College of Medicine Division of Pathology 1939-40; American National Red Cross, Instructor of Junior, Standard and Advanced Courses in Emergency Medical Service 1942; Knickerbocker Hospital Disaster Casualty Station, Originator, Designer, Chief of Mobile Emergency Units 1942; Sydenham Hospital Hysterography and Hysterosalpingography Services, Director of Teaching Program for Residents and Interns, 1950 to present; C.B.S. *Coast-to-Coast Calendar Show*, Panelist on Female Infertility and Sterility 1963. Religion: Lecturer, Invitational, All Denominations, Professional and Lay Groups. Honors and Awards: Special Recognition for Knickerbocker Hospital Disaster Mobile Units, 1942; Inventor, Traction Holder, Kahn Self-Retaining Uterine Trigger Cannula 1949, Kahn-Graves Open Side Vaginal Speculums 1957; Inventor, Traction Tenaculum with Offset Teeth and Curved Shaft 1949, Cannula Stand 1946, Kahn Giant Rubbert Cervical Acorn and Kahn Surgical Dissecting Scissors, Curved and Straight 1952, Kahn One-Piece Office Model Cannula 1954; Listed in *Leaders in American Science, Two Thousand Men of Achievement, Dictionary of International Biography, Community Leaders and Noteworthy Americans, Who's Who in the East, Wisdom Hall of Fame.* Address: 213-16-85th Avenue, Queens Village, New York 11427.■

FAITH-HOPE KAHN

Registered Nurse, Educator, Lecturer, Author, Inventor, Researcher, Administrator. Personal: Born April 25, 1921; Married Edward Kahn; Mother of Ellen-Leora, Faith-Hope II, Paula Amy. Education: Graduate, Beth Israel School of Nursing, 1942; Attended New York University, I.T.T. Education Services; Special Courses and Continued Education, 1943 to present. Military: Served in the Civil Defense Emergency Medical Service, 1942 to present; Served in the American Red Cross Disaster Service in the Field as Supervisor of Nurses and Set-Ups and as Operating Room Supervisor, Phoenixville General Hospital, Pennsylvania, 1942-43. Career: Manager, Team Coordinator and Registered Nurse, Dr. Edward Kahn, 1945 to present; Researcher, Obstetric and Gynecological Reconstruction Procedures, 1945 to present; Visiting Instructor for Upjohn and Rehabilitation 1977-78, Disaster Field Hospital Supervisor 1950, American Red Cross; Executive Director of Publicity and Applied Arts, St. John's Hospital, Smithtown, New York, 1942; Operating Room First Scrub Nurse, Beth Israel Hospital, 1942. Organizational Memberships: National Association of Physician Nurses Association; American Society of Abdominal Surgeons; National Critical Care Institute of Education; National League of Nurses; American League of Nurses; American Academy of Ambulatory Nursing Administration; Advisory Panel, *American Journal of Nursing*; New York Academy of Sciences; National Medical Society; American Law Enforcement Association; American Police Academy; National Association of Female Executives; International Platform Association; Nurses Association American College of Obstetrics and Gynecology; American Organization of Registered Nurses, Lecturer and Scientific Exhibitor 1943, Women's Convention Committee, First World Congress on Fertility and Sterility 1953. Community Activities: Woodhull Schools, Past President Parent-Teacher Association, Director and Coordinator of Advisory Education 1950-64, Past Executive Director of Publicity; American Security Council, Educator and Founder of Center for International Studies, National Advisory Board Member; Smithtown Historical Society; American Red Cross, Disaster Service; Civil Defense (Queens, New York), Chairman and Lecturer of Health Education Classes 1951, Director and Coordinator of Sterlingshire Sector 1951; Paul Revere Club, Washington, D.C., 1980; The American Shooter, International Development Fund Gold Club, 1979; American Law Enforcement Officers Association; American Police Academy, 1970 to present. Religion: St. Gabriels Episcopal Church of Holis, Building Fund Committee 1959; Contributor of Religious Crossword Puzzles, Lutheran School Chapel of the Redeemer, St. Gabriels Episcopal Church of Hollis. Honors and Awards: Patent Holder, Kahn Surgicap for Operating Room and Applied Fields; Poet Laureate, Sterlingshire Women's Club, 1951; Honored Operating Room Supervisor, Sydenham Hospital, 1942; Memorial Place, 1976; American Security Council Education Foundation and the Pentagon Education Center, 1979; Special Recognition Award, Center for International Studies, 1979. Address: 213-16-85th Avenue, Hollis Hills, New York 11427.■

TWO THOUSAND NOTABLE AMERICANS

ARAM H. KAILIAN

Architect, Builder, Developer. Personal: Born October 23, 1949; Son of Harry G. (deceased) and Louise Caily Kailian; Married Kathryn Zakian; Father of Arsine K., Aram E. Education: Attended Temple University 1967-69, Drexel University 1967-70; B.S. Architecture, Temple University College of Engineering, 1973. Career: Architect, Builder, Developer; Draftsman; Designer; Planner. Organizational Memberships: American Institute of Architects; Pennsylvania Society of Aritects; International Solar Energy Society, American Section; Construction Specifications Institute; American Arbitration Association; National Academy of Conciliators; National Trust for Historic Preservation; Urban Planning Institute; Solar Lobby; Grass Roots Alliance for Solar Power; Temple University Alumni; Registered Architect, Pennsylvania, New Jersey, New York; N.C.A.R.B. Certification. Community Activities: Armenian National Committee (Boston, Massachusetts), National Steering Committee 1978 to present; Armenian National Committee, Chairman 1982 to present; Armenian Assembly (Washington, D.C.), Executive Member 1979-81; A.R.F., Central Committee Member 1982 to present; Democratic Nationalities Council, 1976 to present; Armenian Sisters Academy (Radnor, Pennsylvania), Board Member 1981 to present, Service Volunteer 1974; National Republican Heritage Groups Council, 1976 to present; St. Gregory's Armenian Apostolic Church (Philadelphia, Pennsylvania), Donation of Master Plan and Community Center 1979-81; Senior Citizens Housing (Watertown, Massachusetts), Service Volunteer 1981; Armenian Community Center (Toms River, New Jersey), Donation of Master Plan and Community Center 1981. Honors and Awards: Listed in *Who's Who in the East, Who's Who in Real Estate, Personalities of America, World Leaders.* Address: 2249 Menlo Avenue, Glenside, Pennsylvania 19038.■

ROLAND J. KALB

Management Consultant. Personal: Born June 16, 1916; Married Lore; Father of Linda Susan, Richard Oskar. Education: Degree in Electrical Engineering, Tec. Lehranstalt, Vienna, 1938; Postgraduate Studies undertaken at the Ecole Radio Technique, Paris, France, 1938-1939. Career: Manager, Quality Control, Minerva Radio, Vienna, 1937-38; Chief Engineer, Minerva Radio, Paris, 1938-39; Plant Manager, Air King Products, New York City, 1941-47; General Manager, Teletone Radio, New York City, 1947-50; Chairman of the Board, Herold Radio and Electronics, Yonkers, New York, 1950-61; President, Roland Radio Corporation, 1950-61; Group Vice President, Fairbanks Morse and Company , Yonkers, 1961-63; Chief Executive, Pilot Radio Corporation, 1963-64; Group Vice President, Harmon Kardon and Jerrold Corporation 1963-65; President, Roland Electronics Corportion, New York City, 1965 to present; Management Consultant, Roland J. Kalb Associates, Inc., 1965 to present; Center for Preventive Psychiatry, Vice Chairman, Board of Trustees, 1968-72, Chairman 1972-79, Honorary Chairman 1979 to present; President, Oskar Kalb Memorial Foundation, 1964 to present. Organizational Memberships: International Consulting Association; American Management Association; American Hospital Association; American Public Health Association; Weitzman Institute of Science. Honors and Awards: Numerous Leadership and Appreciation Awards; Congressional Record, 1964, Pilot Record Corporation, Pioneering Free Enterprise. Address: 2 Eaton Lane, Scarsdale, New York 10583.■

ROBERT GRAY KALES

Industrialist. Personal: Born March 14, 1904; Son of William and Alice Kales (deceased); Married; Father of Jane K. Ryan, Robert Gray Jr., William Robert, Ann Howson, David Wallin, John Gray, Nancy Davis. Education: B.Sc. Civil Engineering, Massachusetts Institute of Technology; M.B.A., Harvard Graduate School of Business Administration. Military: Served in the United States Navy, 1942-66, rising through the ranks from Lieutenant to Captain. Career: President and Director, Kales Kramer Investment Company, 1935 to present; Director, Automotive Bin Service Company, Inc., of Michigan, 1967-79; Director, W.C. DuComb Company, Inc., 1979 to present; Vice President and Director, Basin Oil Company, 1947-74; Chairman of the Board, General Discount Corporation, 1951-62; Director, Independent Liberty Life Insurance Company, 1966 to present; President and Director, Industrial Resources, Inc., 1950-70; Chairman of the Board, Jefferson Terminal Warehouse, 1934-80; President and Director, Kales Realty Company, 1934-74; Director, Liberty Life and Accident Insurance Company, 1952-66; President and Director, Midwest Underwriters, Inc., 1938 to present; President and Director, Modern Construction, Inc., 1938-60; Chairman of the Board, Whitehead and Kales Company, 1928-76; Board of Directors, Atlas Energy, 1978 to present. Organizational Memberships: Military Order of World Wars, Detroit Chapter, Finance Officer 1946-47, Adjutant 1947-48; Senior Vice President 1948-49, Commander 1949-50, Michigan State Commander 1950-52; National Chapter, Military Order of World Wars, Member of the General Staff 1952-55, Junior Vice Commander-in-Chief 1956-57, Senior Vice Commander-in-Chief 1957-58, Commander-in-Chief 1958-59, Member of General Staff and/or Committees 1959 to present; Navy League of the United States, Southeastern Michigan Council, President and Director 1963-65, Secretary and Directory 1965-66, Treasurer and Director 1966-68, United States Naval Sea Cadets, United States Naval Reserve Training Center, Chairman Sea Cadet Committee 1965; Detroit Power Squadron, Instructor 1966. Honors and Awards: Naval Reserve Medal, 1942; American Campaign Medal, 1945; World War II Victory Medal, 1945; Navy and Marine Corps Medal, 1951; Naval Reserve Medal with Star, 1952; Armed Forces Reserve Medal, 1964; Order of the Croix de Guerre, France, 1959; Order of Lafayette, France, 1965. Address: 87 Cloverly Road, Grosse Pointe Farms, Michigan 48236.■

JOSEPH KAPACINSKAS

Engineer, Author. Personal. Born October 1920, 1907, in Mazuciai, Kybartai, Lithuania; Son of George and Teofile Baskeviciute Kapacinskas; Married Marie Kulikauskas, December 27, 1952; Father of Joseph Vytautas; Came to United States in 1949, Naturalized Citizen 1956. Education: Graduate, Technical College, Augsburg, Germany, 1948; Bachelor's Degree, Industrial Engineering, Allied Institute of Technology, Chicago, Illinois, 1960. Career: Administrator, City of Kaunas Transit Authority, Lithuania, 1929-40; Kaunas Electrical Power Station, Operated by National Railroad and Section; National Railroad, Treuchtlingen, Germany, 1944-45; Instructor and Chief Electrician, United Nations Relief and Rehabilitation Administration, Weissenburg, Germany, 1946-47; Burlington Northern Railroad, Inc., Chicago, 1951-72; Editor, *Sandara*, Weekly Lithuanian Newspaper, Chicago, 1973-76. Organizational Memberships: Lithuanian Engineers and Architects Association; Lithuanian Journalists Association, Secretary Chicago Chapter; American Society of Tool and Manufacturing Engineers. Community Activities: Lithuanian-American Council of Chicago; Lithuanian Alliance of America; Lithuanian World Community. Published Works: Contributor of Articles to *Lithuanian Daily News* and Other Lithuanian Newspapers in the United States. Author Three Books, *Siaubingos Dienos (Horrifying Days)* 1965, *Iseivio Dalia (Emigrant's Fate)* 1974, *Spaudos Baruose (Within the Press)* 1979. Honors and Awards: Listed in *Leaders in American Science, Dictionary of International Biography, Notable Americans of the Bicentennial Era, International Register of Profiles, Lithuanian Encyclopedia, History of Chicago Lithuanians, International Who's Who of Intellectuals, Who's Who in the Midwest.* Address: 6811 South Maplewood Avenue, Chicago, Illinois 60629.■

GARY KARLIN

Insurance Company Executive. Personal: Born January 18, 1934, in Chicago, Illinois; Son of Jack and Pearl Malin Karlin; Married Cheryl Daneman; Father of David, Paige. Education: Attended the University of Illinois 1951-52, Roosevelt University 1952. Career: with Mutual of New York, 1956-62, Sales Manager (Chicago) 1958-62, Regional Trainer 1962-63; President, Executive Motivation Inc., 1964 to present; Consultant in Field. Organizational Memberships: Chicago Association of Life Underwriters, Past Director; Past President, Illinois Leaders Round Table; International Association of Financial Planners; National Association of Life Underwriters, Life Member Million Dollar Round Table (Top of Table); MONY, Past Chairman Field Advisory Committee, Standing Chairman Field Underwriters Benefit/Contract Committee. Published Works: Contributing Editor, *Professional Management Magazine*, 1965-77; Contributor of Articles to Professional Journals; Narrator, Award-Winning Insurance Film, "Impressions of Life. . .Insurance." Honors and Awards: Twice Recognized in the Gold Book of Life Insurance; Annual Recipient of National Life and Health Quality Awards and N.S.A.A. (more than 20 years); Three-Time Vice President MONY's Mid-America Region; Chicago Area Man of the Decade, MONY; National President's Award, MONY; Listed in *Who's Who in the Midwest.* Address: 1497 Lake Shore Court, Barrington, Illinois 60010.■

FLORENCE W. KASLOW

Family Therapist and Psychologist. Personal: Born January 6; Daughter of Mr. and Mrs. Irving Whiteman; Married Solis Kaslow; Mother of Nadine Joy, Howard Ian. Education: A.B., Temple University, 1952; M.A., Ohio State University, 1954; Ph.D., Bryn Mawr College, 1969; Licensed Psychologist, Pennsylvania,

TWO THOUSAND NOTABLE AMERICANS

1973 to present; Licensed Psychologist, Florida, 1982 to present; Licensed Marriage and Family Therapist, Florida, 1982 to present; Registered, National Registry of Health Service Providers in Psychology 1975 to present, National Register of Providers in Marital and Family Therapy 1978 to present; Diplomate, Forensic Psychology and Family Psychology, American Board of Forensic Psychology and Amerian Board of Family Psychology; Diplomate, Clinical Psychology, American Board of Professional Psychology. Career: Consultant, Forensic Psychology Associates, Inc., 1981 to present; Family Therapy Principal Workshop Leader, Psychological Seminars, Inc., 1980 to present; Consultant in Family Therapy, Center Psychiatrists, 1980-81; Consultant in Marital and Family Therapy, Naval Regional Medical Center Departments of Psychiatry, Philadelphia, Pennsylvania, Portsmouth, Virginia and San Diego, California, 1976 to present; Visiting Professor and Board Member, Wisconsin Family Studies Institute, 1980 to present; Visiting Professor, Southwest Family Institute of Dallas, Texas, 1979 to present; Galveston Family Institute, 1979 to present; Editor, *Journal of Marital and Family Therapy*, 1976-81; Private Practice Individual, Marital, Family and Sex Therapist, 1964 to present. Organizational Memberships: American Board of Forensic Psychology, President 1978-80, Board Member 1978-81, Mid-Atlantic Regional Examination Chair 1979-80, Florida Regional Examination Chair 1981 to present; American Psychological Association; Member 1974 to present, Fellow 1981, Division of Industrial and Organizational Psychology, Division of Psychotherapy, Division of Psychoanalysis, Division of Psychology and Law, Division of Independent Practice, American Association for Marital and Family Therapy, Clinical Member 1971 to present, Approved Training Supervisor 1973 to present, National Legislation and Licensing Committee 1976-1979, Fellow 1976 to present, Judicial Council 1982-84; Charter Member, American Family Therapy Association, 1978; Pennsylvania Association of Marriage and Family Therapists, Member 1973-80, Chair Licensing Committee 1974-76, Treasurer 1974-75, Vice President 1976-77; Pennsylvania Psychological Association, Member 1974 to present, Fellow, Chair Program Committee Fall Conference 1975, Chair Awards Committee 1976, Chair Academic Division Program Spring Conference 1978, President Academic Division 1978-79; Philadelphia Society of Clinical Psychologists, Member 1974 to present, Fellow, Program Chair 1975-78, Executive Board 1975-78, Member at Large, Board 1976-78; Family Institute of Philadelphia, Member 1974 to present, Faculty of Training Program, Annual Conference Committee 1972-75; Eastern Psychological Association 1973-80; American Psychology-Law Society, Member 1975 to present, Chair Certification Committee 1977-78; Philadelphia Community Service Institute, 1976-80; American Association of Sex Educators, Counselors and Therapists, 1977 to present; Florida Association of Marital and Family Therapists, 1981 to present; Southeastern Psychological Association, 1981 to present; Florida Psychological Association, 1981 to present. Community Activities: Philadelphia Business and Professional Women's Group of Federation of Jewish Agencies, Steering Committee 1979-80. Religion: Member of Keneseth Israel Synagogue, Elkins Park, Pennsylvania; Teacher of Confirmation and Post-Confirmation Classes 1972-76. Honors and Awards: Order of the Owl Award, Temple University Montgomery Country Club, 1979; Outstanding Liberal Arts Alumnus of Temple University, 1966; Pi Gamma Mu National Social Science Honorary Society; Phi Alpha Theta National History Honorary Society; Temple University English Honorary Society; Traineeship, National Institute of Mental Health, Bryn Mawr; Fellowship, Ohio State Graduate School; Women's Club Scholarship, Alumni Prize for Outstanding Senior, Graduation with Distinction in Sociology, Temple University; Listed in *Men and Women of American Science, Compendium, Community Leaders and Noteworthy Americans, Outstanding Professionals in Human Services, Contemporary Authors, International Who's Who in Community Service, World Who's Who of Authors, World Who's Who of Women, Notable Americans of the Bicentennial Era, Who's Who of American Women, Dictionary of International Biography, International Register of Profiles, International Who's Who of Intellectuals, Who's Who in the East, Personalities of America, Men and Women of Distinction, Contemporary Personalities.* Address: 1900 Consulate Place, Apartment 1903, West Palm Beach, Florida 33401.■

RAYMOND EDWARD KASSAR

Executive. Personal: Born January 2, 1928; Son of Elizabeth Kassar. Education: B.A., Brown University, 1948; M.B.A., Harvard Univerity, 1952. Military: Served in the United States Naval Reserve, 1948-52; Served in the United States Air Force, 1952-53. Career: Private Investment; Chief Executive Officer and Chairman, Atari Inc; President, R.E. Kassar Corporation, 1974-78; Executive Vice President, Group Vice President, President of Three Divisions, Burlington Industries, 1948-74. Community Activities: Board of Directors, San Francisco Ballet, San Francisco Opera, San Francisco Museum Society, Martha Graham Company, San Francisco Symphony; Director, American Cancer Society. Address: 163 Chestnut Street, San Francisco, California 94133.■

ABBA J. KASTIN

Physician, Endocrinologist. Personal: Born December 24, 1934; Son of Isadore I. and Ruth Urdang Kastin (mother deceased). Education: A.B., Harvard College, 1956; M.D., Harvard Medical School, 1960. Career: Intern, Vanderbilt University Hospital, 1960-61; Resident in Medicine, Vanderbilt University Hospital, 1961-62; Clinical Associate, United States Public Health Service, National Institutes of Health, 1962-64; Clinical Investigator, Veterans Administration Hospital, New Orleans, 1965-68; Chief of Endocrinology Service, Veterans Administration Medical Center, New Orleans, 1968 to present; Professor, Department of Medicine, Tulane University School of Medicine, 1974 to present. Organizational Memberships: American Federation for Clinical Research; The Endocrine Society; American Association for the Advancement of Science; American Physiological Society; Society for Experimental Biology and Medicine; Society for Neuroscience; International Society of Psychoneuroendocrinology; International Society of Neuroendocrinology, Charter Member; International Pigment Cell Society, Charter Member; Honorary Member, La Societe de Dermo-Chimie, Chilean Society of Endocrinology, Philippine Society of Endocrinology and Metabolism, Peruvian Ob/Gyn Society, Polish Endocrine Society. Community Activities: Civic Symphony Orchestra, Viola; Medical Advisory Board, National Pituitary Agency, 1974-77; Editorial Board, *Journal of Clinical Endocrinolgy and Metabolism*, 1976-80; Editorial Bord, *Brain Research Bulletin* (Regional Editor), 1976 to present; Editorial Board, *Neuroscience and Biobehavioral Review* (Regional Editor), 1977 to present; Research Advisory Commission, National Association for Retarded Citizens, 1978-81; Consultant, F.D.A., 1979-80; Editor-in-Chief, *Peptides*, 1980 to present. Religion: Jewish; Board of Directors, Jewish Federation of Greater New Orleans. Honors and Awards: Doctorate (honoris causa), Universidad Nacionale Federico Vallarreal, Lima, Peru, 1980; Copernicus Medal of Medical Faculty of Krakow, Poland, 1979; Listed Among 300 Most Cited Authors 1961-76, Institute for Scientific Information (currently in top 100); Edward T. Tyler Fertility Award, 1975; Federal Business Association Eagle Award, 1975; William S. Middleton Award, 1982. Address: 4400 Morales Street, Metairie, Louisiana 70146.■

ABRAHAM I. KATSH

University President Emeritus, Professor Emeritus. Personal: Born August 10, 1908, in Poland; Came to the United States 1925; Son of Chief Rabbi of Petah Tikva (deceased); Married Estelle Wachtell; Father of Maskell Ethan, Salem Michael, Rochelle Senna. Education: B.S. 1931, M.A. 1932, J.D. 1936, New York University; Graduate Studies (Scholarship) undertaken at the Islamic Institute, Princeton University, 1941; Ph.D., Dropsie College, 1944; Honorary Doctorate of Hebrew Letters, Hebrew Union College-Jewish Institute of Religion, 1964; Honorary D.D., Spertus College, 1970; Honorary D.D., University of Dubuque, 1971; Honoary LL.D., Lebanon Valley College, 1971; Honorary LL.D., The Dropsie University, 1976; Honorary D.H.L., Villanova University, 1977. Career: President Emeritus 1976 to present, Professor, Dropsie University; Instructor 1933, Founded Jewish Center Foundation 1937, Established Library of Judaica and Hebraica 1942, Directed American Isreal Student and Professional Workshop in Israel 1949-67, Lecturer, Professor of Hebrew Culture and Education, Professor of Hebrew and Near Eastern Studies, Distinguished Professor of Research, Director Institute of Hebrew Studies, Professor Emeritus of Hebrew Culture and Education 1976 to present, New York University; Assistant Editor in Charge of Hebrew, *Modern Language Journal*, 1954-75. Organizational Memberships: Founder, National Association of Professors of Hebrew, First President; Modern Language Association, Chairman Committee for the Evaluation of Modern Hebrew Materials; Commission on Jewish Life and Culture, American Jewish Congress; Advisory Committee Hadassah; American School of Oriental Research (Jerusalem), Associate Trustee 1969-75; Jewish Academy of Arts and Sciences, President; Board of Directors, Histadruth Ivrit; Board of Directors, Jewish National Fund; Society for Biblical Literature; Phi Delta Kappa; Middle East Studies Association of North America, Fellow; Others. Published Works: Author Twenty Books, including *Torat Hayahasut Shel Einstein* 1936, *Hebrew in American Higher Education* 1941, *Hebraic Foundations of American Democracy* 1951, *Judaism in Islam* 1954, *Hayhuduth Ba-Islam* 1958, *Judaism and the Koran* 1962, *The Antonin Genizah Collection in the Saltykov-Schedrin Public Library in Leningrad* 1963, *Midrash David Hanagid* (translated from rare 13th century Judeo-Arabic manuscript on Bereshit [Genesis]) 1964, *Shemot* (Exodus) 1967, *Lamentations* 1971, *Scroll of Agony* — The Ch. A. Kaplan Diary of the Warsaw Ghetto (English Edition); Over 300 Articles for Learned and Professional Publications; Editor-in-Chief, *Jewish Quarterly Review*; Chairman of Editorial Board, *Jewish Apocryphal Literature*; Chairman of Board of Editors, Editor, *Hebrew Abstracts* (now *Hebrew Studies*). Honors and Awards: First Jewish Man to receive Honorary D.D. from Dubuque University; Private Audience with Pope Pius XII, 1953; Creation of "The Abraham I. Katsh Professorship of Hebrew Culture and Education," New York University Board of Trustees, 1957; Presidential Citation, New York University, 1965; Conducted First and Only Successful Cultural Undertaking in U.S.S.R. dealing with Hebraica and Judaica by a Western Scholar, 1956 (college now housed at Dropsie University);

Scroll of Agony — The Ch. A. Kaplan Diary of the Warsaw Ghetto selected in 1965 by *Book Week* as One of Best 13 Books of Autobiography; Received First National Board of License Scroll of Honor, 1979; National Association of Professors of Hebrew Published the Abraham I. Katsh Festschrift in Honor of Contribution to Hebrew Studies in American Universities, 1950; Presented Festschrift in Hebrew from Former New York University Students on 60th Birthday, 1969; Former Student Wrote Book in Hebrew about Professor Katsh, *Cholem v'Lochem (The Dreamer and the Accomplisher)* 1982; First Brith Abraham Gold Medal for Hebrew Scholarship and Learning; Tercentary Citation, Jewish Book Council of America (for contribution to literature on American Jewish History); Earnest O. Melby Award for Human Relations; National Association of Negro Business and Professional Women's Club Citation; First Schneiderman Prize; Washington Square College Meritorius Alumni Achievement Award (for outstanding Hebrew thought and original scholarship); Mayor's Citation, City of New York, 1965; Honored by State of Kentucky, Israeli Government; Brotherhood Award, Chapel of the Four Chaplains, 1967; Spiritual Leadership Award, Chapel of Four Chaplains, 1975; Mechayil el Chayil Award, Board of Rabbis of Greater Philadelphia, 1977; Morris J. Kaplum Prize for Distinguished Research, 1977; Visiting Scholar, Mishkenot Shaananim, Jerusalem, 1978; Municipality of Haifa Prize for Distinguished Achievements in Connection with Research and Publication of *Ginze Mishnah* and *Ginze Talmud;* Former Students and Friends Established Annual Prize in Name of Abraham Katsh at Hebrew University in Jerusalem, 1980; Avodah Award, Jewish Teachers Association of New York, 1980; First Charles Kramer Research Fellow of the Institute of Jewish Policy Planning and Research of the Synagogue Council of America, 1980; Grants from American Council of Learned Societies, Rockefeller Foundation, Lucius N. Littauer Foundation, Matz Foundation, Hebrew Academy of America, Many Others. Address: 45 East 89th Street, New York, New York 10028. ∎

GEORGE BERNARD KAUFFMAN

Professor of Chemistry. Personal: Born September 4, 1930; Son of Philip J. and Laura Fisher Kauffman; Married Laurie Papazian, Daughter of Mrs. Henry Fries; Father of Ruth Deborah, Judith Miriam, (Stepchildren:) Stanley Robert Papazian, Teresa Lynn Papazian. Education: B.A. with honors in Chemistry, University of Pennsylvania, 1951; Ph.D. Chemistry, University of Florida, 1956. Career: Professor of Chemistry, California State University, Fresno; Research Chemist, General Electric Company, 1957, 1959; Research Chemist, Humble Oil and Refining Company, 1956; Instructor in Chemistry, University of Texas, 1955-56; Research Participant, Oak Ridge National Laboratory, 1955; Graduate Assistant, University of Florida, 1951-55. Organizational Memberships: American Chemical Society, Division of History of Chemistry Chairman 1969-70, Symposium Chairman 1966, 1968 1970, Program Chairman 1967-69, Guest Lecturer on Cooperative Lecture Tours 1971, Executive Committee 1970-73, Councilor 1976-78, Oral History Committee 1978 to present, Nominating Committee 1979-80 and 1982-83, Dexter Award Committee 1978-81; History of Science Society; Society for the History of Alchemy and Chemistry; American Association for the Advancement of Science; Strinobergssallskapet (The Strindberg Society); Alpha Chi Sigma; Association of University of Pennsylvania Chemists; Gamma Sigma Epsilon; Hellenic Professional Association International; Mensa; Phi Kappa Phi; Phi Lambda Upsilon; Sigma Xi; United Professors of California; Union of Concerned Scientists. Published Works: Author of Eleven Books and More Than 500 Papers, Reviews and Encyclopedia Articles on Chemistry, Chemical Education and History of Science; Editor, *Topics in the History of Chemistry,* American Chemical Society Lectures on Tape Series, 1975-81; Contributing Editor, *Journal of College Science Teaching* 1973 to present, *The Hexagon* 1981 to present, *Polyhedron* 1982 to present. Honors and Awards: Recipient of 37 Research Grants, National Science Foundation, Research Corporation, American Chemical Society, Petroleum Research Fund, American Philosophical Society, National Academy of Science, National Research Council, National Endowment for the Humanities; John Simon Guggenheim Foundation, Fellow 1972-73, Grantee 1975; Outstanding Professor, California State University and Colleges System, 1973; Maufcturing Chemists Association College Chemistry Award for Excellence in Teaching, 1976; Lev Aleksandrovich Chugaev Memorial Diploma and Bronze Medal, U.S.S.R. Academy of Sciences, 1976; Visiting Scholar, University of California at Berkeley, 1976; Visiting Scholar, University of Puget Sound, 1978; Dexter International Award in the History of Chemistry, 1978; Westinghouse Science Talent Search Winner, 1948. Address: 3881 East Pico Avenue, Fresno, California 93726. ∎

JOYCE J. KAUFMAN

Chemist. Personal: Born June 21, 1929; Daughter of Abraham and Sarah (deceased) Deutch; Married Stanley Kaufman; Mother of Jan Caryl. Education: B.S. with honors 1949, M.A. 1959, Ph.D. Chemistry 1960, Johns Hopkins University; D.E.S. (tres honorable) Theoretical Physics, Sorbonne, Paris, 1963. Career: Chemist, Quantum Chemistry and Experimental Chemical Physics, Johns Hopkins University. Organizational Memberships: American Chemical Society, Chairman Maryland Section 1972, Councilor for Physical Chemistry Division 1971, 1973, 1976, 1979, 1982, Council Committee on Program Review 1974-77, Committee on Budget and Finacne 1981 to present, Chairman Subdivision of Theoretical Chemistry of the Division of Physical Chemsitry 1979-80 (chairman-elect 1978-79, vice chairman 1977-78); Appointed to Committee on International Membership, Sigma Xi, 1981; Appointed to Committee on Women in Pharmacology and Experimental Therapeutics, American Society for Pharmcology adn Experimental Therpeutics, 1981; Advisory in Theoretical Chemistry and Chemical Physics, Editorial Advisory Board, John Wiley and Interscience Publishers, 1965 to present; Advisory Editorial Board, *International Journal of Quantum Chemistry,* Appointed to Three-Year Term 1967, 1970, 1973, 1976, 1979, 1982; Advisory Editorial Board, *Molecular Pharmacology,* Appointed to Three Year Term 1967, 1970, 1973, 1976, 1979, 1982; Editor of the Benchmark Book Series in Phsycial Chemistry/Chemical Physics, 1975 (Appointed Overall Chemistry Editor, 1977); Consultant to the National Institute of Health on Site Visits in Field of Quantum Chemical Calculations in Molecules of Pharmacological and Biology Significance and the Field of Computers, 1970 to present, National Academy of Science, Committee on Nuclear Science, Ad Hoc Panel on Heavy Ion Sources, 1973; Consultant to United States Army Research Office in Development of Gaseous Lasers, 1973; Member of International Organizing Committee for Heavy Ion Source Conference, Gatlinburg, Tennessee, 1975; National Science Foundation Review Panel for Undergraduate Chemistry Education, 1977; Fogarty International Individual Exchange Specialist, United States National Institutes of Health-U.S.S.R. Ministry of Health (to set up joint research programs in areas of expertise in the biomedical research field), 1978; International Organizing Committee, International Conference on Theoretical Biophysics and Biochemistry, Tata Institute for Fundamental Research, Bombay, India, 1981; Committee for Congressional Task Force on Evnironmental Cancer and Heart and Lung Diseases; Workshop on Exposure, Metabolism and Mechanisms of Toxicity, 1981. Honors and Awards: Member Correspondant de L'Academie Europeenne des Sciences, des Arts et des Lettres, 1981; Garvan Medal, American Chemical Society (as outstanding woman chemist in the United States), 1974; Maryland Chemist Award, 1974; One of Ten Outstanding Women in the State of Maryland, 1974; Une Dame Chevalier, France Chapitre Centre National de la Recherche Scientifique, 1969; Martin Company Gold Medals in Honor of Soutstanding Scientific Accomplishemtns, 1964, 1965, 1966; Fellow, American Physical Society, 1966; Fellow, American Institute of Chemists, 1965; Phi Beta Kappa; Society of Sigma Xi. Address: 2424 Brambleton Road, Baltimore, Maryland 21209. ∎

STANLEY ROBERT KAY

Clinical Psychologist. Personal: Born June 7, 1946; Son of Leslie L. Kay; Married Theresa Maria de Monte, Daughter of Arthur and Mary de Monte; Father of Lisa Paula, Stacy Lynn. Education: B.A. Psychology, New York University, 1968; M.A. cum laude Psychology, Fairleigh Dickinson University, 1970; Attended the New School for Social Research 1971-73; Ph.D. Psychology, State University of New York at Stony Brook, 1980. Career: Clinical Psychologist, Bronx Psychiatric Center 1970 to present, Albert Einstein College of Medicine 1980 to present; Psychotherapist in Private Practice, Mahopac, New York, 1975 to present; Consulting Psychologist, Green Chimney's Children's Services, Brewster, New York, 1980-81; Psychometrist, The Klein Institute for Aptitude Testing, New York, New York, 1970. Organizational Memberships: American Psychological Association; Eastern Psychological Association; New York Psychologists in Public Service. Published Works: Author of Over 50 Publications in Scientific Journals, Several Monographs and Book Chapters, and 20 Professional Conference Papers; Author *The Cognitive Diagnostic Battery: Evaluation of Intellectual Disorders* 1982 and Five Psychological Tests (Span of Attention Test 1974, Color-Form Preference Test 1975, Color Form Representation Test 1975, Egocentricity of Thought Test 1975, Progressive Figure Drawing Test 1980); Editorial Consultant, *Perceptual and Motor Skills* 1979, *Psychological Reports* 1979, *The Journal of Nervous and Mental Disease* 1980-83, *Psychiatry Research* 1980, *Child Development* 1981, *Behavioral and Brain Sciences* 1982, and *Archives of General Psychiatry* 1983. Honors and Awards: Honorary Member, New York University Coat of Arms Society, 1968; Master of Arts in Psychology with Honors, 1970; Honorary Member, American Society of Distinguished Citizens, 1977; Certificate as Outstanding Employee of the Bronx Psychiatric Center, 1978; American Biographical Institute Citation for Distinguished Contribution to Psychology, 1981. Address: Kirkwood Road, R.F.D. 2, Mahopac, New York 10541. ∎

TWO THOUSAND NOTABLE AMERICANS

MICHAEL JOHN KEARNEY

Bank Executive. Personal: Born January 2, 1940; Son of Vincent Joseph and Evelyn Lynch Kearney; Married Lisa von Kaenel, Daughter of Joseph E. and Jane Sheehan von Kaenel; Father of Bridget Katherine Lynch, Andrew von Kaenel, Patrick Edward. Education: B.S.E.E. Electrical Engineering, Washington University (St. Louis), 1962; M.B.A, Wharton Graduate Division, University of Pennsylvania, 1964; Additional Studies at Goethe Institut Murnau (Bavaria), Volksbildungsheim Frankfurt (Germany), University of Maryland (Frankfurt, Germany), University of Missouri, Alliance Francaise (Guatemala City, Guatemala), Institute Mexicano Norte Americano de Relaciones Culturales (Mexico City, Mexico). Military: Served in the United States Army, 1964-66, attaining the rank of First Lieutenant. Career: Vice President, Manager of Relationship Profitability Support Systems, The First National Bank of Chicago, 1982 to present; Assistant Vice President to Vice President, Transportation Group, The First National Bank of Chicago, 1977-82; Assistant Manager, International Corporate Group and Mexico City Representative Office, The First National Bank of Chicago, 1973-76; Assistant to Officers, North American Marketing Group, The First National Bank of Chicago, 1972-73; International Sales Manager, Hussmann Refrigerator Company, St. Louis, Missouri, 1967-72; Assistant to Engineering Design Team, Alfred E. Teves K. G., Frankfurt, Germany, 1966-67; International Corporate Group, 1976-77; Omicron Delta Kappa; Beta Theta Pi. Community Activities: Iowa Genealogical Society; Scott County (Iowa) Genealogical Society; President, St. Stephen's Green Property Owners Association. Published Works: Co-Author (with Lisa von Kaenel) *Midwest Families*; Presently Researching the British-Swiss Legion in the Crimean War to Identify One N.C.O. Who Participated. Address: 2515 Peachtree Lane, Northbrook, Illinois 60062.■

RUTH FRANCES KEENE

Supply Systems Analyst. Personal: Born October 7, 1948; Daughter of Seymour and Sally Keene. Education: B.S. Mathematics, Arizona State University, 1970; M.S. Management Science, Fairleigh Dickinson University, 1978. Career: Inventory Management Specialist, United States Army Electronics Command, Philadelphia, Pennsylvania, 1970-74; Inventory Management Specialist, United States Army Communications and Electronics Materiel Readiness Command, Fort Monmouth, New Jersey, 1974-79; Chief, Inventory Management Division with the Crane Army Ammunition Activity, Crane, Indiana, 1979-80; Supply Systems Analyst, Headquarters, 60th Ordnance Group, Zweibruecken, West Germany, 1980 to present. Organizational Memberships: Association for Computing Machinery; Federally Employed Women, Chapter President 1977-78 and 1979-80, Chapter Vice President 1976-77, Chapter Program Chairman 1976-77, Chapter Recording Secretary 1975-76, Chapter Newsletter Editor 1974-77; Society of Logistics Engineers, Chapter Bylaws Chairman 1978, Chapter Program Chairman 1976-77; American Association for the Advancement of Science; National Association for Female Executives; Society of Professional and Executive Women; American Society for Public Administration; Association of Information Systems Professionals. Community Activities: National Organization for Women; Fort Monmouth Commanding General's Equal Employment Opportunity Advisory Committee, 1977-78; American Association of University Women. Honors and Awards: Outstanding Performance Award, United States Army Electronics Command, 1973; Letter of Appreciation, United States Army Communications and Electronics Materiel Readiness Command, 1978; Letter of Commendation, Crane Army Ammunition Activity, 1980; Listed in *Who's Who of American Women, Who's Who in the West, Directory of Distinguished Americans, Book of Honor, Who's Who of American Women*. Address: 4916 West Pinchot Avenue, Phoenix, Arizona 85031.■

PANAYOTIS P. KELALIS

Professor and Department Chairman. Personal: Born January 17, 1932; Son of Peter and Julia Kelalis; Married Barbara, Daughter of R. and J. Peoples. Education: Attended Heriot-Watt, University of Edinburgh (Scotland) 1950-51, Trinity College of the University of Dublin (Ireland) 1951-57; B.M., B.Ch., University of Dublin, 1957; M.S. Urology, University of Minnesota, 1963. Career: Professor of Urology and Chairman of the Department of Urology, Mayo Clinic, Rochester, Minnesota. Organizational Memberships: American Association of Genito-Urinary Surgeons; International Society of Urology; American Urological Association; Society for Pediatric Urology; American Academy of Pediatrics, Chairman Section on Urology. Honors and Awards: Honorary Member, Greek Urological Association; Edward J. Noble Foundation Award, 1964; Honorary Member, Sociedad Argentina de Urologia, Association Francaise D'Urologie, Sociedad Latino Americana de Urologia Infantile. Address: 1336 Camelback Court N.E., Rochester, Minnesota 55901.■

VINCENT CHARLES KELLEY

Professor and Division Head. Personal: Born January 23, 1916; Son of Charles Enoch and Stella May Ross Kelley (both deceased); Married Dorothy Jean MacArthur; Father of Nancy Jean, Thomas Vincent, Richard Charles, William MacArthur, Robert Kenneth, Jean Elizabeth, James Joseph. Education: B.A. Chemistry 1934, M.S. Physical Chemistry 1935, University of North Dakota; B.S. Education 1936, Ph.D. Biochemistry 1942, B.S. Medicine 1944, M.B. Medicine 1945, M.D. 1946, University of Minnesota. Military: Served in the United States Army as Private First Class A.S.T.P. 1943-45 and rising from First Lieutenant to Captain 1946-48; Served Successively as Chief of Department of Biophysics, Assistant Chief of Department of Biochemistry and Chief of Research Medicine. Career: Head of Division of Endocrinology, Metabolism and Renal Disease 1958 to present, Professor of Pediatrics 1958 to present, University of Washington-Seattle; Director of Research 1959-65, Associate Director of Medical Education 1958-63, Children's Orthopedic Hospital and Medical Center, Seattle, Washington; Consultant in Pediatrics, Madigan Army Hospital, Tacoma, Washington, 1958-69; Visiting Professor in Pediatrics, Kauikeolani Children's Hospital, Honolulu, Hawaii, 1958; Director, Utah State Department of Health, 1953-58; Associate Professor of Pediatrics 1952-58, Assistant Professor of Pediatrics 1950-52, University of Utah; Instructor in Pediatrics 1949-50, Swift Fellow in Pediatrics 1948-50, Rockefeller Research Fellow in Physiological Chemistry 1941-42, Teaching Assistant in Biochemistry 1940-41, University of Minnesota; Chief of Department of Biophysics, Assistant Chief of Department of Biochemistry, Chief of Research Medicine, (successively) 1946-48, A.A.F. School of Aviation Medicine; Assistant Resident in Pediatrics 1946, Intern in Pediatrics 1945-46, University of Minnesota Hospitals; Assistant Professor of Organic Chemistry, College of St. Thomas, St. Paul, Minnesota, 1942-43; Professor of Chemistry, Emory and Henry College, Emory, Virginia, 1941; Graduate Assistant in Chemistry 1934-35, Undergraduate Assistant in Chemistry 1933-34, University of North Dakota. Organizational Memberships: American Academy of Pediatrics; American Association for the Advancement of Science; American Association of University Professors; American Chemical Society; American College of Clinical Pharmacology and Chemotherapy; American Heart Association; American Institute of Biological Sciences; American Medical Association; American Pediatric Society; American Rheumatism Association; American Society of Nephrology; American Therapeutic Society; King County Medical Society; Lawson Wilkins Pediatric Endocrine Society; New York Academy of Sciences; North Pacific Pediatric Society; Pan-American Medical Association; Puget Sound Endocrine Society; Seattle Pediatric Society; Society for Experimental Biology and Medicine; The Endocrine Society; The Society for Pediatric Research; Washington Heart Association; Washington State Medical Association; Washington State Pediatric Society; Western Society for Clinical Research; Western Society for Pediatric Research, Past President. Published Works: Editor-in-Chief, *Practice of Pediatrics* (10 volumes with annual revisions), 1960 to present; Editor, *Metabolic, Endocrine and Genetic Disorders of Children*, (3 volumes), 1974; Chief Editor, *Pediatrics: International Medical Digest*, 1960-71; Editor, *American Journal of Diseases of Children*, 1958-68; Consultant Editor, *Pediatrics Medical Digest*, 1956-75; Editor and Advisory Board Member, *Audio-Digest*, 1956-72; Author and Contributor of Over 200 Articles and Book Chapters. Honors and Awards: Phi Beta Kappa; Sigma Xi; Phi Lambda Upsilon; Phi Eta Sigma; Kappa Kappa Psi; L. Mead Johnson Award for Pediatric Research, 1954; Ross Pediatric Education Award of the Western Society for Pediatric Reserach, 1971; Listed in *Who's Who in America, Who's Who in the West, Who's Who in the World, American Men and Women of Science*. Address: 8611 45th Avenue Northeast, Seattle, Washington 98115.■

H. HAROLD KELSO

Television Advertising Executive. Personal: Born September 12, 1931, in Davenport, Iowa; Son of Albia E. (deceased) and Victoria R. Nadolski Kelso; Married Marjorie Joann Wacker, June 27, 1952; Father of James Harold, Jodi Dianne. Education: Student in Public and Parochial Schools in Davenport (Iowa) and Billings (Montana). Career: Field Agent, Knights of Columbus Insurance Department, 1984 to present; Sales Manager, KOUS-TV (Harding/Billings, Montana), 1982-84; President, CoADS, Co-op Advertising Service Company, 1982; Advertising Manager 1976-82, Classified Advertising Manager 1975-76, Classified Sales Supervisor 1967-75, Classified Salesperson 1966-67, *The Billings Gazette*; Salesman, M. L. Schuman Specialty Advertising Company, 1965-66; Draftsman, Shell Oil Company, 1953-65; Chainman, Montana Highway Department, 1952-53; Door-to-Door Salesman, Fuller Brushes, Kirby Vacuums and Insurance, 1950-52. Organizational Memberships: President, Billings Advertising and Marketing Association, 1975-77. Community Activities: Consultant and Speaker at Area Schools, Colleges and Industry Association in Sales and Marketing, 1970-82; Commandant of Cadets and/or Squadron Commander, Billings Civil Air Patrol, 1959-64; United Way Campaign Team, 1976; United Way Commercial Division Leader, 1981; Billings Chamber of Commerce, Retail Merchants Committee 1977-81, Annual Meeting Committee 1977-80; Director, Billings Downtown Merchants Association, 1979-82; Past Grand Knight Third Degree, Past Faithful Navigator Fourth Degree, Former District Deputy, Editor State Newspaper 1977-80, State Warden 1982-83, State Ceremonials Director 1983-84, Knights of Columbus; Republican. Religion: Lector, Catholic Church, 1970-84; Member and/or Officer, Parish Council, St. Pius X Catholic Church, 1980-84. Published Works: *Classified Advertising Instruction*

Manual, Conversion to Electronic Typesetting, 1976; *The Art of Communication — Gateway to Success*, 1978. Honors and Awards: BAMA Community Citizen of the Year Award, 1977; Outstanding District Deputy for Montana 1982, Montana Knight of the Year 1974, Knights of Columbus; Billings Sertoma International Service to Mankind Award, 1980; Boss of the Year, American Business Women, Billings Chapter, 1979; Listed in *Who's Who in the West, International Men of Achievement, Community Leaders of America, Who's Who in America, Personalities of the West and Midwest, Biographical Roll of Honor*. Address: 1436 St. Johns, Billings, Montana 59102.■

DOROTHY ELIZABETH WALTER KEMP

Teacher. Personal: Born November 23, 1926, in Cincinnati, Ohio; Daughter of Frederick and Lula Walter; Married David Kemp. Education: Attended the College of Music of Cincinnati and the University of Cincinnati Teachers College; B.S., 1948; Attended Summer Courses at the University of Music of Cincinnati, Received a Certificate in French Horn in 1946; M.A., Eastern Kentucky University, 1949-50; Three Teaching Certificates, Miami University of Ohio; Studied Jazz with Saul Striks. Career: Professor of Music Theory, Music Education Methods, Arranging, Brass Instruments and Beginning Piano, Appalachian State University (Boone, North Carolina), 1950-54; Teacher of First Grade and Kindergarten, Cincinnati Public Schools, 1954-59; Assistant to the Publishing Department Editor, Willis Music Company (Cincinnati), 1959-62; Teacher of First Grade, Mount Health Public Schools (Ohio), 1963-67; Staff Member (Teacher of First Grade and Kindergarten, Music in Grades One to Six and Special Education), Newport Public Schools (Kentucky), 1967 to present; Free-lance Musician (French Horn, Accordian and Piano) and Arranger/Composer, 1950 to present; Conductor, Powel Crosley Junior Young Men's Christian Association Adult Symphonic Concert Band, 1972-79; Conductor, Founder, Librarian, Queen City Concert Band, 1979 to present. Organizational Memberships: American Federation of Musicians (Local 1 Cincinnati); Phi Beta National Music Fraternity. Published Works: "Christmas in Brass" (1959), "Four Brass for Christmas" (1960), "Easter in Brass" (with two original fanfares, 1962), "The Ground Hog Rock" (1977), "French Horn Finesse I, II, III" (Horn Quartets, 1981), "Northern and Southern Brass" (Brass Quartets, 1982). Honors and Awards: Listed in *International Who's Who of Intellectuals, International Who's Who of Musicians, Dictionary of International Biography, Western Biographical Dictionary, Personalities of America, Community Leaders and Noteworthy Americans, Personalities of the West and Midwest, Men and Women of Distinction, International Register of Profiles*, Others. Address: 4559 Hamilton Avenue, Cincinnati, Ohio 45223.■

WALTER KEMPNER

Physician, Professor Emeritus. Personal: Born January 25, 1903; Son of Walter and Lydia Rabinowitsch Kempner. Education: M.D., University of Heidelberg Medical School (Germany), 1926. Career: Physician; Professor Emeritus of Medicine 1972 to present, Professor of Medicine 1952-72, Associate Professor of Medicine 1947-52, Assistant Professor of Medicine 1941-47, Associate in Medicine 1934-41, Duke University; Assistant Physician, University Hospital, Berlin, 1928-33; Research Associate and Assistant to Professor O. Warburg, Kaiser Wilhelm Institut fuer Zellphysiologie, Berlin-Dahlem, 1927-28, 1933-34; Originator of Rice Diet in Treatment of Hypertensive and Arteriosclerotic Vascular Disease, Heart and Kidney Disease, Vascular Retinopathy, Diabetes Mellitus and Obesity. Organizational Memberships: Diplomate, American Board of Internal Medicine; Fellow, American College of Physicians; American Society of Internal Medicine; American Physiological Society; American Medical Association; Trustee, Walter Kempner Foundation. Honors and Awards: Walter Kempner Professorship of Medicine, Duke University, 1972; Kempner Symposium, Archives of Internal Medicine, 1974; Ciba Award, American Heart Association, 1975. Address: Box 3099, Duke University Medical Center, Durham, North Carolina 27710.■

BUDD LEROY KENDRICK

Licensed Psychologist. Personal: Born April 19, 1944; Son of Oscar F. Kendrick (deceased) and Miriam S. Stewart; Married Beverly A., Daughter of Robert and Erna Dockter; Father of Aaron Matthew, Edgar Seth, Cassandra Rachelle. Education: B.A. 1967, M.Ed. 1969, Ed.D. 1974, Idaho State University. Career: Licensed Psychologist, Adult/Child Development Center, Boise, Idaho, 1975 to present; Senior Rehabilitation Counselor, Vocational Rehabilitation Service, Pocatello, Idaho, 1970-73 and 1974-75; Psychologist, Counseling and Testing Center, Idaho State University, Pocatello, 1973-74; Director of Counseling and Testing, Midwestern College, Denison, Iowa, 1969-70; Psychology Teacher, Pocatello High School, 1967-69. Organizational Memberships: American Psychological Association; American Personnel and Guidance Association; Idaho Psychological Association, Secretary 1982-84; Idaho Personnel and Guidance Association, Leadership Council 1977-78, State Licensure Representative to American Personnel and Guidance Association 1977-78. Community Activities: Idaho Counselor Licensing Board, Chairman 1982-86; Idaho Psychological Association, Secretary 1982-84; Idaho Mental Health Association, Treasurer 1980-81; Idaho State School and Hospital, Human Rights Committee 1977; Trio Advisory Board, Idaho State University, 1975-76; Civil War Round Table of Southwest Idaho, Corresponding Secretary 1981-82. Honors and Awards: Distinguished Service Award, Granted by Idaho Personnel and Guidance Association, 1978. Address: 3125 Maywood Avenue, Boise, Idaho 83704.■

WILLIAM S. KENNEDY

Editor. Personal: Born January 23, 1926, in South Norfolk, Virginia; Son of William S. and Alice W. Kennedy. Education: Attended William and Mary College. Military: Served in the United States Navy, 1944-46. Career: Musical Career, Playing Saxaphone or Guitar under Locally and Nationally Known Band Leaders, until 1979; Publisher of Literary Magazine *Reflect*, 1979 to present. Community Activities: Promoter of Back-to-Beauty Poetry Movement, Nationally through the Magazine. Honors and Awards: Listed in *Directory of Distinguished Americans, Personalities of the South, Personalities of America*. Address: 3306 Argonne Avenue, Norfolk, Virginia 23509.■

DAVID L. KENT

Genealogical Research Consultant, Author. Personal: Born July 1, 1940; Son of Edith Tomlinson; Married Carol Joy Miller, Daughter of C. E. Miller; Father of Robert Lloyd, Susannah Mary, Zachary Miller, David Clark. Education: B.A. cum laude, Russian Studies, Brigham Young University, 1966. Career: Genealogical Record Searching and Transcribing in England, Ireland, Wales, United States, 1968-80. Organizational Memberships: Certified by Board of Certification of Genealogists, 1974 to present; Life Member, General Society of Mayflower Descendants; Society of Genealogists, London. Community Activities: National Genealogical Society's War of 1812, Pension Indexing Project Volunteer 1980 to present; Co-Founder, Erespin Press, 1979; Volunteer Reader for R. L. Chapman, Editor of *New Dictionary of American Slang*, 1982-83; Founder, Kent Research Foundation, Resource Center for Home Birth, Home Schooling, Pacifism Research and Support, 1976. Religion: Ordained Minister, Universal Life Church, 1980. Published Works: *Barbados and America* 1980, *Foreign Origins* 1981; Genealogical and Demographic Sourcebooks and Research Guides; Contributor of Book Reviews and Articles to Genealogical Periodicals, 1976 to present. Honors and Awards: Phi Eta Sigma; Phi Sigma Alpha; Life Member, Virginia Chapter, Society of Separationists; Listed in *Who's Who in Genealogy and Heraldry, Personalities of America*. Address: 115 West Koenig Lane 208, Austin, Texas 78751.■

ODIS W. KENTON

Systems Analyst. Military: Served in the United States Air Froce, 1961-69, attaining the rank of Staff Sergeant; Served in the New Jersey National Guard, 1976-78. Career: Systems Analyst, System Integration and Support Department, Automation Industries, Inc., Vitro Laboratories Division, 1982 to present; Consultant, Research Analyst, Ship Acquisition Integrated Logistics Support, Presearch Inc., 1981-82; Logistics Specialist/Assistant Office Manager, Lockheed Electronics Company, Inc., Product Support Division, 1980-81; Senior ILS Engineer, Taurio Corporation, 1979-80; Lead Systems Engineer, American

Communications Corporation, 1978-79; Electronics Technician, Port Authority Transit Corporation, 1974-78; Manager, Field Service and Customer Relations Department, Applied Metro Technology, Inc., 1970-74; Owner/Consultant, ODO Enterprises, 1970; Radio Communications Systems Field Installation Engineer, Melpar Inc., 1970; Engineering Associate, Westinghouse DECO, 1969-70. Organizational Memberships: Society of Logistics Engineers; American Society of Certified Engineering Technicians; Rutgers University Alumni Association. Honors and Awards: Dean's List, Rutgers University, 1976; Honor Student, United States Air Force Technical Schools, 1961, 1962, 1964, 1965; Honor Graduate, 210th FTD, 1964; Airman of the Month, 380th FMS 1962, 380th Bomb Wing 1962, 820th Air Division 1962; Achievement Award, SAC, 1965; Certificate of Achievement, KTTC-United States Air Force, 1965; Cost Reduction Award, Headquarters United States Air Force 1968, AFCS-USAF, 1968; Air Force Commendation Medal, Department of the Air Force, 1967; Presidential Unit Citation; Good Conduct Medal; National Defense Medal; Vietnam Campaign Medal with 3CC; Air Force Longevity Ribbon; Expert Marksman Medal; Vietnam Service Medal; 25 Membership Award, South Camden Branch Young Men's Christian Association, 1971; Merit Award, Howard W. Brown Y's Mens Club CG-YMCA, 1978; Recognition by Marquis Who's Who, 1980-81, 1982-83. Address: River Place East 1104, 1021 Arlington Blvd., Arlington, Virginia 22209.■

MICHAEL LEE KENYON

Executive. Personal: Born March 15, 1943; Son of Lester Kenyon; Married Eve Drew, Daughter of Mr. and Mrs. Arnold Drew; Father of Kim, Oliver Hewlitt, (Stepfather of:) Benjamin. Education: B.S. Marketing and Advertising, Northeastern University, 1966; Attended American Management Association Seminars. Career: President, Projections Marketing Research and Counsel; Former Positions include Vice President and Group Director of Aulino Baen Inc., Vice President and Director of Client Services of Herbert Epstein Inc., Vice President of Decisions Center Inc., Senior Study Director of Market Facts Inc., Research Analyst for Cunningham and Walsh Advertising Inc. Organizational Memberships: Monadnock Ad Club, President 1979-80; New Hampshire Ad Club, Board of Directors 1981 to present; Vermont Ad Club; Keene Area Chamber of Commerce. Community Activities: Board of Directors, Grand Monadnock Arts Council, Chairman 1980-81; Keene Family Young Men's Christian Association; Monadnock United Way; Incorporator, Keene Pops Choir. Address: 47 Marlboro Street, Keene, New Hampshire 03431.■

GRACE CABLE KEROHER

Geologist. Personal: Born February 8, 1901, in a Rural Area near Shenandoah, Iowa; Daughter of Edward Manker and Lucille (Trego) Cable; Married Raymond Keroher (deceased); Mother of Raymond Jr., Avarell (deceased). Education: B.A. 1936, M.S. 1969, University of Kansas, Lawrence. Career: United States Geological Survey, Washington D.C., 20 Years; Research Assistant, Museum of Northern Arizona, Flagstaff, 1972-76; Director of Public Information, Los Angeles Church Federation, 1947-51; Research Librarian, Aerojet Engineering Corporation, Azusa, California, 1945-46; Chemist, Government Ordinance Laboratory, Sunflower Ordinance Plant, Lawrence, Kansas, 1942-43. Organizational Memberships: Fellow, Geological Society of America. Community Activities: Worthy Matron, Trona Chapter, Order of the Eastern Star; President, Women's Society of Christian Service, 4 Years; Co-Organizer, Treasurer, Searles Valley Historical Society; Phi Beta Kappa; Sigma Xi; President, Flagstaff Woman's Club. Religion: Methodist; Member Ryland Methodist Church. Published Works: Free-lance Writings include Contributions to Pictorial History Books and Magazine Articles on Kansas and California History; Author of Numerous Scientific Publications. Honors and Awards: Haworth Distinguished Alumni Award, Kansas University; Meritorious Service Award, Department of the Interior; Listed in *The Biographical Roll of Honor, American Men of Science, Who's Who of American Women, Community Leaders and Noteworthy Americans, Personalities of the West and Midwest, World Who's Who of Women, Directory of Distinguished Americans.* Address: Box 215, Trona, California 93562.■

WILLIAM HENRY KIELMEYER

Senior Research Engineer. Personal: Born January 6, 1943; Son of P. H. Kielmeyer; Married Marjorie E., Daughter of E. G. Kaufman; Father of Cheryl A., Thomas W. Education: Bachelor of Ceramic Engineering, Ohio State University, 1966; M.Sc., Ceramic Engineering, Ohio State University, 1973. Career: Senior Research Engineer, Manville Corporation; Project Engineer, Owens-Corning Fiberglas. Organizational Memberships: American Ceramic Society; Mineral Insulation Manufacturers Association. Honors and Awards: Research Project Leader and Co-Patentee of Process for Making Insulating Fiber for Space Shuttle External Insulating System (Reusable Tile and Blankets). Address: 3374 West Chenango Avenue, Englewood, Colorado 80110.■

HULDA DARLYNE ATKINSON KILLIAN

Art Resource Teacher. Personal: Born October 9, 1928; Daughter of Joseph Donahue Sr. (deceased) and Gladys Peyton Atkinson; Married William Herty Killian Jr., Son of Mr. and Mrs. William H. Killian Sr.; Mother of William Herty III, Michael Anthony, Darnita Ruth. Education: Graduate, Pickard High School, Brenham, Texas, 1944; A.B., Spelman College, 1948; Studied at Atlanta University, Emory University, Atlanta College of Art; M.A.Ed., University of Georgia, 1968; Ed.S., University of Georgia, 1978; Postgraduate Study undertaken at the University of Georgia, 1981-82. Career: Art Resource Teacher (Supervisor), Atlanta Public Schools Area II; Kindergarten Teacher, Spelman College Nursery, Wheat Street Baptist Church Nursery School, Atlanta Public Schools; Elementary School Teacher; Art Teacher on Elementary, Middle and Secondary Levels; Art Teacher and Curriculum Developer, Sammye E. Coan Middle School (pilot middle school for state of Georgia); Teacher Representative, Revision Art Curriculum Guide, 1969. Organizational Memberships: United Teaching Profession; A.A.E.; Georgia Education Association; National Education Association; State and National Art Education Associations; Georgia Association of Middle School Principals; World Future Society; African American Family History Association; Black Artists Atlanta; National Conference of Artists. Community Activities: Atlanta 2000; National Alumni Association of Spelman College; University of Georgia Alumni Association; Atlanta Urban League Guild; Board Member, African American Family History Association (group presented "Homecoming" documentary exhibit on Black Georgians at Atlanta Public Library, 1982); Den Mother, Cub Scouts, 1950's; Girl Scout Leader, San Antonio, Texas. Religion: St. Paul of the Cross Catholic Church, Altar Rosary Society. Honors and Awards: Copper Repousse Exhibit, 1965 Witte Museum, San Antonio, Texas; Batiks by Darlyne, Atlanta, Georgia, 19657; Painting and Sculpture Exhibit, University of Tennessee, 1977; Presented First Education Section Conference of the World Future Society, University of Houston, Clear Lake City, 1978; Presenter, Genesa Conference, Mt. Gilead, North Carolina, 1982. Address: 1474 Ezra Church Drive Northwest, Atlanta, Georgia 30314.■

HARRY HYUNKIL KIM

Federal Administrator. Personal: Born January 17, 1938; Son of Hoonha Kim and Saengkun Chong; Married Jiyon Kyungja, Daughter of Kyuchong Kim and Ockyup Kim; Father of Peter Hyojin, Hanna Hyosun. Education: Graduate, Kyung Gi Junior and Senior High School, Seoul, 1957; B.A. Political Science, Kyung Hee University, 1961; M.A. International Relations, Sung Kyun Kwan University, 1963; M.A. Regional Studies, University of Washington-Seattle, 1967; Ph.D. Geography, University of Washington-Seattle, 1971. Military: Served in the Korean Army, 1961. Career: Federal Administrator, United States Department of Housing and Urban Development; Professor of Geography, University of South Florida, 1974-78; United States Department of Commerce and United States Department of Energy; Urban Planner, Department of Community and Environmental Development, King County, Seattle. Organizational Memberships: Association of American Geographers; National Geographic Society. Community Activities: President, Presbyterian Housing Association, 1983; Fellow, Seattle Pacific University; Chairman of the Board of Directors, Seattle-Washington Korean Association, 1981; President, Tampa Korean Association, Tampa, Florida, 1976; Board Member, Tampa Rotary Club, 1976-78. Religion: Ruling Elder Ordination and Installation, Forest Hills Presbyterian Church, Tampa, Florida 1975, and University Presbyterian Church, Seattle, Washington 1982; Board Member of Program Agency, General Assembly of Presbyterian Church U.S.A. 1983 to present, and General Assembly of Presbyterian Church of the United States 1976-79; Board Member of Presbyterian Ministry, Inc. of Alaska-Northwest Synod, 1983 to present; Committee Member of Seattle Presbytery, 1979 to present; President, Korean-American Soccer League, 1983 to present. Honors and Awards: Outstanding Professor Award by Senior Class, University of South Florida, Tampa, Florida, 1976; Fulbright Exchange Scholar to India, 1977. Address: 4239 Northeast 74th Street, Seattle, Washington 98115.■

ALICE MAE KIMBER

Retired Educator and Social Worker. Personal: Born March 24, 1921; Daughter of James Dee and Buena New Perkins; Married Victor Daniel Kimber; Mother of Betty Simpson. Education: B.A., Southern Missionary College, 1947; Attended Louisiana State University, Tulane University (taking social work courses). Career: Former Social Worker and Missionary Teacher, Social Worker in Mississippi and Florida for 15 Years; Home Economics Teacher in Rhodesia 1951-55; Volunteer Bible Missionary Teacher, Bethel College of Seventh-day Adventists, 1978-80 (in the Transkei of Africa); Dietician, Florida Hospital, Seventh-day Adventists, 4 Years; Taught Home Economics to Indians, Holbrook, Arizona, Seventh-day Adventist Mission. Organizational Memberships: Home Economics Club, President 1946; Social Workers Organization, 1947-51; Head State Committee, 1970. Religion: Seventh-day Adventist; Sabbath School Secretary for Seventh-day Adventist Church; Young People's Leader 1938; Health and Welfare Leader for Seventh-day Adventist Church in Florida, 1971; Church Treasurer, 1978. Honors and Awards: Listed in *Personalities of the South*. Address: 1421 Valencia Street, Sanford, Florida 32771.∎

FREDERIC WAYNE KING

Museum Administrator. Personal: Born May 20, 1936, in West Palm Beach, Florida; Son of Vera Hilda King; Married Sharon Ray Frances, Daughter of Ray and Barbara Ryther; Father of Jeffrey Craig. Education: B.S. 1957, M.S. 1961, University of Florida at Gainesville; Ph.D., University of Miami, 1966. Career: Director, Joint Curator of Herpetology, Florida State Museum; Joint Professor of Zoology, University of Florida; Affiliate Professor of Latin-American Studies, University of Florida; Affiliate Professor of School of Forest Resources and Conservation, University of Florida; University of Florida Council of Academic Deans Representative on the Board of Directors of the Division of Sponsored Research, 1980-82; Director of Zoology and Conservation 1975-79, Director of Conservation and Environmental Education 1973-75, Chairman of Educational Programs 1971-73, Scientific Editor of *Zoologica* 1971-79, Curator of Herpetology 1968-75, Associate Curator of Herpetology 1967-68, New York Zoological Society; Graduate Research Assistant in Herpetology, Florida State Museum, University of Florida, 1966-67; Assistant Professor, Santa Fe Junior College, Gainesville, Florida, 1966; Teaching Assistant in Zoology, University of Miami, 1963-66; John Prather Fellow, University of Chicago and Field Museum of Natural History, Chicago, 1961-62; Graduate Assistant in Zoology, University of Florida, Gainesville, 1959-61; Graduate Assistant in Herpetology, Florida State Museum, University of Florida, 1957-59. American Alligator Council, Founding Member (dissolved 1974); American Association of Museums/International Council of Museums; American Association of Zoological Parks and Aquariums, Professional Fellow 1970-79, Chairman Wildlife Conservation Committee 1972-74; American Committee for International Conservation, Elected to Executive Board 1975, Vice Chairman 1976-78, Chairman 1978-81; American Society of Ichthyologists and Herpetologists, Committee on Environmental Quality 1971-78, Chairman 1973-75, Committee on Traffic in Animals for Scientific Research 1972-78, Board of Governors 1975-77 and 1979-83, Representative to I.U.C.N./S.S.C. 1979 to present; Association of Systematics Collections, Council on Systematics Collections and the Law 1976-78, Chairman Committee on Long-Term Financial Stability 1981, Treasurer 1981 to present; Caribbean Conservation Corporation, Chairman of Conservation Committee 1973 to present; Center for Short-Lived Phenomena, Endangered Species Monitoring Program Advisory Panel 1973 to present; Herpetologists League, Fellow 1971; International Crocodilian Society (until dissolution in 1973-74); International Turtle and Tortoise Society (until dissolution in 1973); International Union for the Conservation of Nature and Natural Resources/Species Survival Commission, Deputy Chairman 1978 to present, Represents S.S.C. on I.U.C.N. Governing Council and on Program Planning Advisory Group 1978 to present, Serves on I.U.C.N./S.S.C. Steering Committee 1973 to present, Crocodile Specialist Group 1971 to present (Chairman 1973-79 and 1981 to present), Reptile/Amphibian Specialist Group 1973-78, TRAFFIC Group 1972 to present, Critical Marine Habitats Group 1976-77, Marine Turtle Task Force 1975, Marine Steering Committee 1978-79; International Zoo Yearbook Advisory Panel, 1972-79; Island Resources Foundation, Program Advisory Board 1977 to present; New York Zoological Society, Scientific Fellow 1970 to present, Conservation Fellow 1979 to present; Rare Animal Relief Effort Inc., Elected Trustee 1979-81; Sierra Club, International Earthcare Center Advisory Committee 1977 to present, Tropical Forest Advisory Committee 1977 to present; Society for the Study of Amphibians and Reptiles, Conservation Committee 1974-78. Honors and Awards: Order of the Golden Ark, 1981; Diploma de Reconocimiento, Universidad Autonoma de Santo Domingo, Dominican Republic, 1978; American Motors Corporation Conservation Award, Professional Category, 1975; President's Award, American Association of Zoological Parks and Aquariums, 1972, 1973. Address: 3420 Northwest 71 Street, Gainesville, Florida 32606.∎

JOSEPH JERONE KING

Executive, Consultant. Personal: Born September 27, 1910, in Spokane, Washington; Son of Joseph J. Sr. and Alice E. Halferty King (both deceased); Married Irma Kathleen Martin in 1937; Father of Sally Jo Thompson, Nikki Sue Ring, Cindy Lou Mullen. Education: Graduate of Salem (Oregon) High School; A.B. Economics/Sociology (with great distinction), Stanford University, 1935; M.A. Economics/Sociology, Duke University, 1937; Research Fellowship on Doctoral Thesis, Brookings Institution, 1938-39. Career: Instructor in Economics, Black Mountain (North Carolina) College, 1937-38; Chief of Regional Migratory Farm Labor Program, Chief of Regional Community Services and Co-operative Program, Regional Personnel Officer, Regional Administrative Management Officer, National Administrator's Representative on the U.S.D.A. Field Committee of the Columbia River Basin, United States Department of Agriculture (Portland, Oregon, Headquarters), 1939-51; Oregon State Director, Christian Rural Overseas Program, Sponsored Jointly by Catholic Relief Life, Church World Service, Lutheran World Relief, late 1940's; Senior Civilian in charge of Industrial Relations, Puget Sound Naval Shipyard (Bremerton, Washington), 1951; Public Affairs Director, Executive Vice President, Association of Washington Industries (Olympia, Washingtn), 1958; Association of Washington Business (Olympia), 1966; President, King's Public Affairs, Ltd. (Silverdale, Washington), 1978. Organizational Memberships: Governor's Committee for State Government Organization, 1950's; American Society for Public Administration, Past President Oregon State Chapter, President Washington State Chapter (2 terms); Chairman of Panels on Personnel Administration Leadership and Labor Relations for the Public Service; Society for Personnel Administration, Past President Puget Sound Chapter; Governor's Council for Reorganization of Washington State Government, 1960's; State-wide Public Education Management Survey, Director of Manpower 1970's; Tuition in Higher Education Select Legislative Committee; National Association of Secondary School Principals, Century III Leaders Scholarship Program Selection Committee; State Department of Public Instruction, Served on Several Advisory Committees (including Professional Education, Title IV, Urban, Rural, Racial and Disadvantaged); Washington State Council on Economic Education, Board of Directors. Community Activities: Governor's Committee on Employing the Physically Handicapped; Founder with President of Central Washington University Project for High School Youth Business Week; The American Red Cross, Chairman Kitsap County Chapter; Visiting Nurse Association, Chairman Citizen County Advisory Committee; Bremerton Aquatics Show, Inc., President; American Legion, Honorary 40/8, Post Mortem Club; Elks Lodge; Masons; Scottish Rite; Shrine; Rotary; Kitsap Golf and Country Club; Washington Athletic Club; Washington Generals; Washington Admirals. Religion: Protestant; Served on Oregon Council of Churches to Several Annual National Rural Life Conferneces. Published Works: Number of Articles including "F.S.A. Group Services in the Pacific Northwest," *Harvard Business Review*, 1944; "Cooperatives and Cutover Lands," *Sociology and Social Research*, 1944; "Rural Co-operative Self-Help Activities in the Pacific Northwest," *American Sociological Review*, 1943; "Back to the Land Movements," *Rural Sociology*, 1945; Guest Editorial Writer on Various Subjects including "Share the Tools," "Employees Plans Boost Efficiency," *Portland Oregon Journal*; Book Winning Reprinted 7 Times by the Association of Washington Industries. Honors and Awards: Phi Beta Kappa; A.B. with Great Distinction, Stanford University, 1935; *The Bremerton Sun* (daily) Featured an Editorial "Well Said" which Commended Development of a Code of Ethics for Public Servants; Award for Services Rendered in Promoting (and prompting of) Public Administration in State, American Society for Public Administration; Honorary Chief Journalist, 13th United States Naval District. Address: Ioka Beach, Hood Canal, 11655 Ioka Way N.W., Silverdale, Washington 98383.∎

SHARON FLORENCE KISSANE

Communications Consultant, Writer. Personal: Born July 2, 1940; Daughter of William and Agnes Mrotek; Married James Q. Kissane; Mother of Laura Janine, Elaine Marie. Education: B.A., De Paul University, 1962; M.A., Northwestern University, 1962; Ph.D., Loyola University, 1970. Career: President, Kissane Communications, Ltd.; Communications Consultant and Writer; Teacher; Editor. Organizational Memberships: Executive Club of Chicago; National Association of Women Business Owners, Board Member, Public Relations Officer 1980-81; League of Women Voters; Barrington Area Arts Concil, Founder of Writers Group. Community Activities: District 220 Gifted Program Task Force, 1979 to present; Barrington High School Curriculum Committee, Parents Representative 1981 to present; Crusade of Mercy, Block Chairman 1966; South Barrington Annual Art Fair, Founder 1979; Northwestern University Alumni Association Telethon, 1979-80; League of Women Voters Fund Drive, 1980-81. Honors and Awards: Honorary Citizen of Korea, 1965; Prix de Paris Art Award, 1974; Chicago Sketch Club Honorary Award, 1973; Northwestern University Alumni Achievement Award, 1979; Illinois Arts Council Artist-in-Residence Grant, 1978; Listed in *Who's Who Among American Women, International Who's Who of Women, National Social Register, Who's Who in Education, Who's Who in Community Service, Who's Who in Education*. Address: 15 Turning Shore Drive, Barrington, Illinois 60010.∎

SHINICHI KITADA

Research Biochemist. Personal: Born December 9, 1948; Son of Koichi and Asako Kitada. Education: M.D., Kyoto University Medical School, 1973; M.S. Biological Chemistry 1977, Ph.D. Biological Chemistry 1979, University of California at Los Angeles. Career: Research Biochemist; Resident Physician in Chest Disease Research Institute, Kyoto University, 1974-75; Intern, Kyoto University Hospital, 1973-74. Organizational Memberships: American Oil Chemists Society; Sigma Xi; New York Academy of Sciences; American Association for the Advancement of Science. Community Activities: Town Hall of California;

TWO THOUSAND NOTABLE AMERICANS

Dean's Council, College of Letters and Science, University of California at Los Angeles; International Platform Association. Religion: Member, Bel Air Presbyterian Church. Honors and Awards: Japan Society for the Promotion of Science Fellow, 1975-76; Edna Lievre Fellow, American Cancer Society, 1981-82. Address: 478 Landfair Avenue #5, Los Angeles, California 90024.■

SABRA CORBIN KITTNER

Supervisor of Media Services, Professor. Personal: Born November 1, 1922; Daughter of George E. and Hilda C. MacDorman (deceased); Mother of Sabra Corbin, Jo Corbin. Education: B.A., M.Ed., Western Maryland College; Graduate Studies undertaken at Catholic University and Johns Hopkins University. Career: Supervisor of Media Services, Carroll County Board of Education; Professor, Western Maryland College Graduate School. Organizational Memberships: A.E.C.T.; Association of Supervisors for Curriculum Development; Association of Supervisors and Administrators of Carroll County; Maryland Educational Media Organization. Religion: Member, Westminster United Methodist Church. Honors and Awards: Listed in *Who's Who of American Women, Two Thousand Women of Achievement, World Who's Who of Women, Dictionary of International Biography, National Register of Prominent Americans, Notable Americans of the Bicentennial Era, Community Leaders and Noteworthy Americans, Personalities of the South.* Address: 94 Willis Street, Westminster, Maryland 21157.■

BERNICE LICHTY KIZER

Chancery and Probate Judge. Personal: Born August 14, 1915, in Fort Smith, Arkansas; Daughter of Ernest and Opal C. Lichty; Married Harlan D. Kizer; Mother of J. Mayne Parker, Shirley Parker Wilhite, Karolyn Parker Sparkman, Mary K. Holt. Education: Graduate, Fort Smith High School; Attended Fort Smith Junior College (now Westark Community College) and Stephens College; LL.B. 1947, J.D. 1969, University of Arkansas. Career: Judge, Twelfth Judicial District Chancery and Probate Courts, 1975 to present; State Representative, House of Representatives, Arkansas State Legislature, 1961-74. Organizational Memberships: Sebastian County Bar Association; Crawford County Bar Association; Arkansas State Bar Association; Licensed to Practice before all Arkansas Courts, the United States Eighth Circuit Court of Appeals, United States Supreme Court. Community Activities: United Fund, Women's Division Chairman; Governor's Commission for the Aging; Library Week, State Chairman; Christmas Seals for Tuberculosis, State Chairman; Mental Health Association, State Chairman; Western Arkansas Counseling and Guidance Center, Board of Directors; City National Bank of Fort Smith, Board of Directors; Cottey College, Nevada, Missouri, Board of Directors; Western Arkansas Planning and Development District Inc., Board of Directors; Young Women's Christian Association; League of Women Voters; American Association of University Women; P.E.O.; Soroptimists; Business and Professional Women's Club. Honors and Awards: First Recipient, *Southwest Times Record* Woman Achiever Award; 1980 Horizons 100 Arkansas Women of Achievement, Arkansas Press Women; Outstanding Alumnae, School of Law, University of Arkansas; Listed in *Who's Who in America, Who's Who of American Women, Who's Who in Government, Who's Who in the South and Southwest, Personalities of the South, Who's Who in American Law.* Address: 1235 58 Terrace, Fort Smith, Arkansas 72904.■

BENTE KJOSS-HANSEN

Director of Scripps Hospital Center for Executive Health. Personal: Born March 9, 1948; Son of Consul Allen and Aase Kjos-Hansen. Education: B.S. English, University of Maine, 1970; M.A. Psychological Kinesiology, University of Northern Colorado, 1976; Ed.D. Psychological Kinesiology, University of Northern Colorado, 1982. Career: Director of Executive Health Program, Scripps Memorial Hospital; Teacher of Applied Anatomy and Kinesiology, San Diego State University, 1980-81; Teacher and Coach, Washington State University, 1976-78; Teacher, Mary C. Wheeler, Brown University, Providence, Rhode Island, 1970-73. Organizational Memberships: North American Society for Psychology of Sport and Physical Activitiy; Northwest Collegiate Women's Sport Association; American Biographical Institute Research Association. Honors and Awards: Presentation of Various Seminars; Listed in *Directory of Distinguished Americans, Personalities of America, Personalities of the West, Community Leaders of America, Who's Who Among San Diego Women, Who's Who in California.* Address: 10150 Campo Road, Spring Valley, California 92077.■

CARL FREDERICK KLEIN

Manager of Systems and Electronics Research. Personal: Born June 20, 1942; Son of Rose R. Klein; Married Mary Jean, Daughter of Elizabeth Uschan; Father of Christine, Mathew, John, James. Education: B.S.E.E. 1965, M.S.E.E. 1967, University of Wisconsin. Career: Manager of Systems and Electronics Research 1981 to present, Manager of Technological Forecasting 1980-81, Research Scientist 1979-80, Johnson Controls Inc.; Senior Research Engineer 1971-79, Research Engineer 1966, 1967-71, Johnson Service Company; Teacher of the Physics of Semiconductors and Electronic Circuit Design, Marquette University Evening Division, 1967-72; Development Engineer, Power Electronics Division, Louis Allis Company, 1965; Research and Development Technician in Digital Pulse Totalizer Lab, A. O. Smith Corporation, 1964; Application Engineer in Voltage Regulator Department, Allis Chalmers Manufacturing Company, 1963; Engineering Trainee, Falk Corporation, 1962. Organizational Memberships: Institute of Electrical and Electronic Engineering; World Future Society; American Association for the Advancement of Science. Religion: Administrative Board, Galena Street United Methodist Church, 1968-73; Church School Teacher, Salem United Methodist Church, 1981. Honors and Awards: National Honor Society, 1961; Eta Kappa Nu, 1965; Johnson Controls Inc. Scholarship; U.S. Patent Holder; Listed in *Who's Who in the Midwest.* Address: 5740 South Lochleven Lane, New Berlin, Wisconsin 53151.■

CORNELIS KLEIN

Professor of Mineralogy. Personal: Born September 4, 1937; Son of Dr. and Mrs. Cornelis Klein; Married Angela Mary Nobbs, Daughter of Mr. and Mrs. George Nobbs; Father of Marc Alexander, Stephanie Wilhelmina. Education: B.Sc. honors Geology 1958, M.Sc. 1960, McGill University, Montreal, Canada; Ph.D., Harvard University, 1965. Career: Professor of Mineralogy, Department of Geology, Indiana University, Bloomington; Member Precambrian Paleobiology Research Group, University of California at Los Angeles, 1979-84; Allston Burr Senior Tutor, Leverett House, Harvard College (Assistant Dean, Harvard College), 1966-70; Associate Professor of Mineralogy, Harvard University, 1969-72; Lecturer in Mineralogy, Harvard University, 1965-69; Associate in Research, Harvard University, 1963-65. Organizational Memberships: Associate Editor, *The American Mineralogist*, 1977-82; Executive Committee, Mineralogical Society of Canada, 1980, 1981; Fellow, Mineralogical Society of America; Fellow, Geological Society of America; Fellow, American Association for the Advancement of Science; Society of Economic Geologists and Mineralogical Associates of Canada. Honors and Awards: John Simon Guggenheim Memorial Fellowship, 1978. Address: 4521 Cambridge Court, Bloomington, Indiana 47401.■

JOHN A. KLINE

Educational Advisor, Chief Academic Officer. Personal: Born July 24, 1939; Son of L. A. Kline; Married Ann Louise, Daughter of Mrs. Forrest Henry; Father of Theresa Ann, William Marc, David Laurence, Nanette Louise, Melissa Ann. Education: B.S. English and Speech, Iowa State University, 1967; M.S. Interpersonal Community 1968, Ph.D. Interpersonal Communication 1970, University of Iowa. Career: Education Advisor and Chief Academic Officer, United States Air

Force Air University; Dean of Communication, Academic Instructor and Foreign Officer School, Air University, 1975-82; Associate Professor and Director of Graduate Studies in Speech and Dramatic Art, University of Missouri-Columbia, 1971-75; Assistant Professor in Speech Communication, University of New Mexico, 1970-71. Organizational Memberships: Phi Delta Kappa; Speech Communication Association, President of Applied Communication Section 1982-83; International Communication Association; Southern Speech Communication Association; Supporting Member, Women in Communication. Community Activities: Alabama Consortium for Development of Higher Education, 1975 to present; Narrative Review Board for the Blind, 1977 to present; Civil Air Patrol National Aerospace Education Advisory Committee, 1982-83; Presentation of Over 50 Speeches Annually to Civic and Religious Organizations. Religion: Member, Frazer Memorial United Methodist Church. Honors and Awards: Full N.D.E.A. Fellowship, University of Iowa, 1967-70; Central States Speech Association Outstanding Teacher, 1972; Phi Kappa Phi; Federal Employee of the Year, Montgomery, Alabama, 1979. Address: 3415 North Watermill Road, Montgomery, Alabama 36116. ∎

JEROME M. KLOSOWSKI

Scientific Consultant. Personal: Born March 30, 1940; Son of Rufus and Theola Klosowski; Married Ruth Ann, Daughter of Floyd and Lillian Jacobs; Father of Pamela, Patricia, Matthew. Education: B.S., Central Michigan University, 1961; M.A. Mathematics, Central Michigan University, 1965; M.S. Chemistry, Wayne State University, 1966. Career: Scientific Consultant, Dow Corning Corporation; Mathematics and Chemistry Teacher, Bay City Schools, Delta College, Bay City, Michigan. Organizational Memberships: American Society of Testing and Materials, Executive Committee 1980 to present, Chairman C24.40, C24.32 on Building Sealants, D-4 on Highway Materials, D-14 on Adhesives, L-6 on Buildings; Sealants and Waterproofs Institute; Construction Specification Institute; American Chemical Society; Sigma Xi; Society of Manufacturing Engineers. Religion: Youth Teacher, Parish Catholic School, 1976 to present; Active in Church Choir, 1957 to present. Published Works: Author of 18 Articles in Silicones used in Construction and Silicone Chemistry. Honors and Awards: 11 United States Patents and 46 Foreign Patents in Field of Silicone and Silane Chemistry. Address: 2029 Briar Drive, Bay City, Michigan 48706. ∎

FRANCES E. KNOCK

Surgeon, Chemist. Personal: Daughter of William Fred and Frances Tietze Engelmann; Married Theodre Knock, 1943. Education: B.S., University of Chicago; Ph.D. Organic Chemistry, 1943; M.D., University of Illinois. Career: Organic and Consulting Chemist, Armour Research Foundation, 1943-52; Consultant, Armour Research Foundation, Merck Sharpe and Dohme, E. R. Squibb and Sons; Intern, Evanston Hospital; Resident in General Surgery, Presbyterian Hospital, Chicago, 1959; Diplomate, American Board of Surgery, 1961 to present; Clinical Assistant Professor of Surgery, University of Illinois; Attending Surgeon, Augustana Hospital, Chicago; Director, Knock Research Foundation, 1955 to present (dedicated to conquer cancer by individualizing total patient care for each patient); American Pioneer in Chemical and Radioactive Tracer Studies of Drug Effects on Human Cancers to Individualize Chemotherapy for Each Patient in Accord with His Own Chemistry; Predicted that SH-bearing Nonhistone Chromosomal Proteins Played Major Role in Gene Regulation and Derangements underlying Cancer (Work now Corroborated in Other Laboratories); Research on Improving Drugs for Cancer Chemotherapy, Shielding Materials for Neutron Capture Therapy of Cancer, the Use of Antibodies as Peptizing Agents for Cytotoxic Colloids (expecially boron-10 and uranium-234) with Extrapolation of the Work now to Specific Monoclonal Antibodies as Peptizing Agents for Cytotoxic Colloids to Treat Cancer. Organizational Memberships: Fellow, International College of Surgeons, American Association for the Advancement of Science, American College of Angiology, International College of Angiology, American Geriatrics Society, American Institute of Chemists; American Medical Association; American Chemical Society. Religion: Holy Trinity Lutheran Church. Published Works: Author *Anticancer Agents*; Over 100 Papers in Medicinal and Organic, Surgery, High Polymers, Biophysics, Hypnotherapy and Ethical Principles in Medicine. Address: 416 Country Lane, Glenview, Illinois 60025. ∎

JEANNE KNOERLE

College Chancellor and Program Director. Personal: Born February 24, 1928. Education: B.A. Drama-Journalism, Saint Mary-of-the-Woods College, 1949; M.A. Journalism 1961, Ph.D. Comparative Literature/Asian 1966, Indiana University; Further Studies undertaken at Catholic University of America, Georgetown University. Career: Chancellor and Director of Endowment Program 1983 to present, President 1968-83, Assistant to President and Associate Professor of Asian Studies 1967-68, Chairman of Department of Journalism 1954-63, Saint Mary-of-the-Woods College; Visiting Professor, Providence College, Taichung, Taiwan, 1966-67; Summer Seminar in Art, Culture and Society, Taiwan, Summer 1966; Teacher, Immaculata High School, Washington, D.C., 1953-54; Teacher, Central Catholic High School, Fort Wayne, Indiana, 1952-53; Teacher, Providence High School, Chicago, Illinois, 1952; Teacher, St. Columbkille High School, Chicago, Illinois, 1952. Organizational Memberships: Association of Catholic Colleges and Universities, Chairwoman 1978-80, Board Member 1974-82; Association of American Colleges, Board Member 1976-80; American Council on Education, Board Member 1978-80, Commission on Women in Higher Education 1976-79; Council of Independent Colleges, Board Member 1980-83; International Association of University Presidents, Advisory Council, North American Council 1977-79; National Catholic Educational Association, Executive Committee 1978-80; Indiana Conference of Higher Education, President 1973-74; Associated Colleges of Indiana, President 1982-84, Vice President 1980-82; Independent Colleges and Universities of Indiana, Secretary-Treasurer 1979-80, Executive Board 1976-82; Fund for the Improvement of Postsecondary Education, 1982 to present; Federal Home Loan Bank of Indianapolis, Board Member 1976 to present; Grow Terre Haute, Executive Committee 1982 to present; Aquinas College, Board Member 1978-80; Mental Health Association of Vigo County, Board Member 1971-78; Indiana Academy in the Public Service, Board Member 1980-82; Center for Constitutional Studies of Mercer University Law School, Board Member 1980 to present; International Women's Year, Indiana Coordinating Commission 1970; National Institutes of Health, Division of Research Resources Advisory Council 1975-79; Women's College Coalition, Executive Committee 1973-77; Lilly-Poynter Project on "American Institutions and the Crisis of Confidence," Indiana University, Regional Chairperson 1974-77; Series of Seminars on "The President as Creative Leader," Association of American Colleges, Speaker 1974-75; N.B.C. *Today Show*, Participant 1971, 1980; President, Alliance for Growth and Progress, Economic Development Group, Terre Haute, Indiana, 1983 to present; Board Member, federal Home Loan Bank of Indianapolis, 1974 to present; Board Member, Union Hospital, Terre Haute, 1973 to present; Member Governor's committee for Indiana's Utility Future, 1984; Symposium on "Evangelization in the American Context: The Pastoral Presence in an Open Society," Center for Continuing Education, University of Notre Dame Participant, 1976; *Good Housekeeping* Women in Passage Program, Participant 1976-77; Symposium on "Evangelization in the American Context: The Pastoral Presence in an Open Society," Center for Continuing Education, University of Notre Dame, Participant 1976. Religion: Roman Catholic; Member Congregation of Sisters of Providence, July 22, 1949 to present. Published Works: *The Dream of the Red Chamber, a Critical Study*, 1972; "The Poetic Theories of Lu-Chi — With a Brief Comparison with Horace's Ars Poetica," *Journal of Aesthetics and Art Ctriticism*, 1966; "Ezra Pound and the Literature of China," *Tamkang Review*, Tamkung College of Arts and Sciences, Taipei, 1973; "The Chinese College Woman," *Indiana University Alumni* Magazine, 1967; *Pius XII and Modern Communications Theory*, M.A. Thesis; Frequent Speaker, Service Clubs, Professional Organizations, Church and Educational Groups. Honors and Awards: Honorary Doctor of Letters Degree, Rose-Hulman Institute of Technology, 1971; Honorary Doctor of Laws Degree, Indiana State University 1972, Indiana University 1975, Saint Mary's College (Notre Dame) 1981; Honorary Doctor of Divinity Degree, Indiana Central University, 1978; Summer Seminar in Art, Culture and Society, Taipei, Taiwan, Fulbright Award, 1966; Educational Counselor, Purdue University's Old Masters Program, 1970; Advisor of the Year Award, Catholic School Press Association, 1960; Mother Theodore Guerin Medallion for Outstanding Alumna, Saint Mary-of-the-Woods College, 1975; Listed in *Who's Who of American Women, Who's Who Among Authors and Journalists, Who's Who in Religion, Who's Who of Women, Who's Who in the Midwest, Who's Who of Women in Education, American Catholic Who's Who, Dictionary of International Biography, Leaders in Education, Directory of American Scholars, Terre Haute's People of Progress.* Address: Saint Mary-of-the-Woods College, Saint Mary-of-the-Woods, Indiana 47876. ∎

DORIS KOCHANOWSKY

Professor Emeritus of Mineral Engineering Management, Consultant. Personal: Born 1905, in Krasnojarsk, Siberia; Son of Julius and Maria Kochanowsky (deceased); Father of Vera. Education: Diplom Ingenieur Mine Surveying 1927, Mining Engineering 1929, Bergakademie at Freiberg; Undertook Graduate Studies at the Universities of Jena, Kothen, Clausthal (Germany), Federal Institute of Technology (Zurich, Switzerland); Dr.Ingenieur, University of Clausthal, 1955. Career: Research Associate, Bergbauverein, Essen, Germany and Bergakademie at Freiberg, 1930-33; Assistant to the President and Manager of Operations, Development and Research, Rheinische Kalksteinwerke GmbH (world's largest lime producer), 1933; Consultant to Mining and Equipment Firms in U.S.

and Abroad (including Joy Manufacturing, Dravo, Amax, Peabody Coal, Hercules Powder and Linzer Baslat); Manager, Asphaltite Mine "Minacar"; Professor of Mining Engineer and Economics, University of Cuyo, San Juan and Mendoza, Argentina, 1948-53; Faculty Member, Chairman Mineral Engineering Management Program, Pennsylvania State University; Retired 1970; Developed Theory of Blasting, Propositions of "Dynamic Coast Analysis" Methods, Postulation of Theories of Inclined Drilling and Promotion of This Method, Introduction of Idea of Mobile Crusher for Surface Mining. Organizational Memberships: American Institute of Mining Engineering; American Society for Engineering Education. Published Works: Co-author Three Textbooks on Open-Pit Minings; 66 Papers in 14 American and 16 Foreign Journals; Presentation of Invited Papers at 9 International Congresses, 1961 to present. Honors and Awards: *Who's Who in the East, American Men of Science, Leaders in American Science, National Register of Prominent Americans, Dictionary of International Biography, International Who's Who of Intellectuals, International Register of Profiles, Who's Who in America, Who's Who in the World.* Address: 426 Homan Avenue, State College, Pennsylvania 16801.■

MAHENDR SINGH KOCHAR

Medical Administrator. Personal: Born November 30, 1943; Son of Harnam Singh and Chanan Kaur Kochar; Married Arvind Kaur; Father of Baltej S., Ajay S. Education: M.B.B.S., All India Institute of Medical Sciences, New Delhi, India, 1965; M.S., Medical College of Wisconsin, Milwaukee, 1972. Career: Associate Chief of Staff for Education, Chief of Hypertension Section, Wood Veterans Administration Medical Center; Associate Professor of Medicine and Pharmacology, The Medical College of Wisconsin. Organizational Memberships: Fellow, American College of Physicians, Royal College of Physicians and Surgeons of Canada, American College of Clinical Pharmacology, American Academy of Family Practice; Royal College of Physicians of London; American College of Cardiology. Community Activities: Director, Milwaukee Blood Pressure Program, 1975-78; Wisconsin State High Blood Pressure Committee, 1978-81; American Heart Association of Wisconsin Affiliated Research Committee, 1980. Published Works: Author *Hypertension Control*, 1978; Editor, *Textbook of General Medicine*, 1983. Address: 18630 LeChateau Drive, Brookfield, Wisconsin 53005.■

CHRISTA A. KOCHENASH

Food Services Administrator. Personal: Born September 19, 1927; Daughter of Jacob and Hedwig Ammann; Married; Mother of Karl, Michael Anthony. Education: Completion of Secondary Education, Cologne, Germany, 1947; Completed Dental Assistant Program, University of Cologne, 1951; B.S. Vocational Education, Teaching Certification in Health Occupations Education, Colorado State University, 1972; M.A. Curriculum and Instruction/Health Occupations Administration, University of Northern Colorado, 1973; Certificate in Educational Administration, Colorado State University, 1977; Ed.D. Management of Native American Education, University of Northern Colorado, 1980. Career: Manager of Food Services, Administrator of Culinary Arts Program, Homestead Food Services, Pine Ridge Job Corps, Chadron, Nebraska; 1982 to present; Educational Consultant, Specializing in Indian Education and Special Education, 1979-82; Owner, Parkway Cabins, Chadron, 1977 to present; Vocational Planner, Coordinator, Teacher, Health Occupation Education, Oglala Sioux Community College, 1977-79; Intern, Assistant to the Director of Health Planning, Council of Government, Regional Development and Planning Commission, 1976; Consultant/Teacher, Monte Vista Consolidated Public School District, 1975-76; Health Occupations Coordinator/Teacher, Minndak Vocational Career Center, Wahpeton, North Dakota, 1973-75; Student Teacher, Community College of Denver, North Campus, 1972; Substitute Language Teacher, French and German, Colleges in Bethlehem and Allentown (Pennsylvania) Area, 1964-69; Certified Dental Assistant/Instructor, Drs. Gripp, Mehren, Korfhagen and Dental State Board of Nord Rhein Westfalen, 1949-58. Organizational Memberships: American Vocational Association; Phi Kappa Phi; Kappa Delta Pi; Colorado State University Alumni Association; University of Northern Colorado Alumni Association; Vocational Industrial Clubs of America; Allied Health Association; American Association of University Women; National Indian Education Association; National Association of Vocational Special Needs Personnel; National Association for the Self-Employed. Honors and Awards: Certificate of Honor, Dental State Board, Nord Rhein Westfalen, Cologne, Germany; B.S. with highest distinction, Colorado State University; Honor Member, Faculty Club, Colorado State University; Selected to Participate in Planning Workshop from Allied Health Association, Washington, D.C.; Served as Professional Advisor in Organizing North Dakota State Association of V.I.C.A., 1973-74; Served as Chapter Advisor for North Dakota's First V.I.C.A. Chapter at Minndak Vocational Career Center, 1973-74; Service Award, Saint Francis Nursing Home, for Volunteer Services to the Home and Aged, 1974; Awardee of Graduate Leadeship Development Fellowship for Nebraska, U.S.O.E., Washington, D.C.; Listed in *Biographical Roll of Honor, Who's Who in the Midwest, Women of the World.* Address: Route 1 Box 39A, Chadron, Nebraska 69337.■

ALEXANDER SANDOR KOCSIS

Engineer, Professor. Personal: Born February 26, 1921; Came to Canada, 1957; Married F. Toth Ottilia; Father of Suzanne, Kateline. Education: B.A., Cluj, Rumania, 1940; Dipl.Ing., Budapest, 1945; Doctor Ing., Technical University, Budapest, 1979. Military: Served in the Royal Hungarian Army, 1940-45, achieving the rank of Lieutenant; Served as a Colonel in the Hungarian Police, 1945-56. Career: Vice President, General Manager, Electro-Materials Corporation of America, Mamaroneck, New York, 1974-76; Vice President, Cummins Machinery Corporation, Patterson, New Jersey, 1976-82; Vice President, Technical Manager, Pulsonar Inc., Sherbrooke, Quebec, 1978-82; Vice President, Pima Inc., Englewood Cliffs, New Jersey, 1982 to present; Professor, University of Sherbrooke, 1959 to present; Electronics Engineer, Hungarian Ministry of Interior, 1945-56. Organizational Memberships: Senior Member, I.S.A.; Institute of Electrical and Electronic Engineers; I.S.H.M.; Canadian Engineering Institute; Ordre des Ingenieurs du Quebec. Honors and Awards: Various World War II Decorations; Citations for Excellence from President of Republic of Hungary and Citations for Excellence from Interior Ministry of Hungary, 1948-56; Various Awards for Conference Papers, 1974-82. Address: 1382 Laterriere, Sherbrooke, Quebec, Canada J1K 2R2.■

STANLEY E. KOLBE, JR.

Director of Government Affairs. Personal: Born February 1, 1953; Son of Mr. and Mrs. Stanley E. Kolbe, Sr. Education: B.S. Management and Labor Relations/Government Policy, Cornell University, 1976; M.A. with honors Government Policy/Legislative and Public Policy Analysis, George Washington University Graduate School, 1978; M.B.A. Business Financial Management/Governmental Relations, George Washington University School of Business, 1983. Career: Director of A.I.A./P.A.C. and Government Affairs, The American Institute of Architects, 1979 to present; Research Analyst in Federal Relations, United States Conference on Mayors, 1978-79; Analyst and Writer on Federal Affairs, National League of Cities/United States Conference of Mayors, 1977-78; United States Senate Legislative Aide, Office of Senator John C. Culver (Democrat-Iowa), 1976; New York State Senate Legislative Assistant, Office of Senator Linda Winikow (Democrat-38th District), 1976; Cornell University Teaching Assistant, Business and Occupational Sociology, 1975. Organizational Memberships: American Political Science Association. Community Activities: Campaign Manager, Iowa 3rd Congressional Race, 1978; Political Writer for Iowa Newspapers; Phi Delta Theta, Chairman Fund Raising, President Alumni Corporation; Kennedy Presidential Campaign, 1980; Culver for Senate Campaign, Iowa, 1980. Honors and Awards: National Honor Society of Academics; Cornell University Academic Award; Judge M. D. Tolles Academic Scholarship; Cornell University Academic Integrity Board; Listed in *Who's Who in America.* Address: 402 Constitution Avenue Northeast, Washington, D.C. 20002.■

LAURENCE KOLMAN

Filtration Executive. Personal: Born November 24, 1940; Son of Sol (deceased) and Sylvia Kolman; Married Elaine Susan Siegel (deceased); Father of Michele Blaine, Geoffrey Scott. Education: B.A. Sociology/Psychology, Hofstra, 1961; M.A.L.S. Business/Ecology, State University of New York at Stony Brook. Military: Served in the United States Air Force, 1962-67, attaining the rank of Captain. Career: Filtration Executive; Former Meat/Food Processing Executive, Computer Sales Executive, Registered Representative. Organizational Memberships: American Institute of Chemical Engineers, 1982-84; American Association for the Advancement of Science, 1981-84. Community Activities: Kiwanis Club, Elwood Chapter 1970-72, Chairman Youth Services (Suffolk West) 1972-73; Harbofields-Elwood Youth Development Association, President 1967-71; Friends of the Library, 1972-74; S.P.A.C.E.; Sierra Club; Planetary Society; American Museum of Natural History; Roberson Center for Cultural Arts; National Arbor Day Foundation. Religion: Jewish. Honors and Awards: United States Air Force Commendation Medal; Hofstra Alumni's George M. Estabrook Distinguished Service Award, 1968; Freedom Foundation at Valley Forge George Washington Honor Medal, 1965; Life Fellow, American Biographical Institute; Listed in *Who's Who in Finance and Industry, Who's Who in the World, Personalities of America, Biographical Roll of Honor, International Book of Honor, Directory of Distinguished Americans.* Address: 3 Lodi Lane, Monsey, New York 10952.■

TWO THOUSAND NOTABLE AMERICANS

ERIC SIU-WAI KONG

Research Scientist. Personal: Born January 14, 1953; Son of Woon-Man Kong; Married Susanna Lee, Daughter of Chiu-lin Lee. Education: B.A., University of California at Berkeley, 1974; M.Sc. 1976, Ph.D. 1978, Rensselaer Polytechnic Institute. Career: Research Scientist, N.A.S.A./Stanford University Joint Institute, Ames Research Center, Materials Sciences and Applications Office; Former Research Fellow. Organizational Memberships: Society of Plastics Engineers, Golden Gate Chapter, Chairman-Elect of Plastics Analysis Division 1982; New York Academy of Sciences; Society of Polymer Science, Japan. Honors and Awards: N.A.S.A. Grantee, 1979 to present; Research Fellowship, Japan Society for the Promotion of Science.■

MARY SCHROLLER KORDISCH

Associate Professor of Zoology. Personal: Born January 23, 1921; Daughter of Rudolph and Ida Schroller (deceased); Mother of Sherry K. Bourgeois, Terry M. Herbert, Foster C. Jr., Stanley R., Steven. Education: Graduate, Marysville High School, Marysville, Kansas, 1937; B.S. 1943, M.S. 1944, Kansas State University; Ph.D. Coursework, Louisiana State University. Career: Associate Professor of Zoology, Department of Biology, Mississippi State University, 1957 to present; Realtor, 1975 to present; Notary Public, 1980 to present; Teacher, Elementary School (La Crosse, Kansas) 1956-57, Rural School (La Crosse) 1954-55, Maplewood Elementary School (Maplewood, Louisiana) 1953-55, Rural Schools (Oketo, Kansas) 1937-40; Veterinarian Assistant, 1944-68; Instructor, Kansas State University, 1944; Undergraduate/Graduate Assistant, Kansas State University, 1940-44. Organizational Memberships: Mississippi State University Faculty Senate; Sponsor, Pred Med Society; Med Tech Advisor; Sponsor, Epsilon Alpha Epsilon; Sigma Xi; Kansas Academy of Science, 1944-54; Louisiana Academy of Science, 1956-74; Phi Alpha Mu; LaVerne Nayes American Legion. Community Activities: Boy Scout Den Mother; Girl Scout Leader; Campfire Girls Leader; Boy Scout Advisor; Board of Directors, Recording Secretary, California Women's Shelter; Teacher at Scoring School, Little League, American Legion; Recording Secretary, CLEAN (anti-pollution group); Education Chairman, Recording Secretary, American Business Women's Association; Neighborhood Drives for Heart, Polio, Cancer; Science Fair Judge, State and Local Levels; Diggers and Weeders Garden Club; Quota Club, Publicity Chairman. Religion: Former Member Oak Park Methodist Church; Present Member First Christian Church. Published Works: Co-Author, *Basic Human Anatomy* (with Sylvia Dickson), *Introduction to Zoology* (with Mississippi State University Biology Faculty); Author, *Genetics Manual*, Mississippi State University. Honors and Awards: Woman of the Year, American Business Women's Association, 1981-82; Phi Lambda Phi; Phi Alpha Mu; Sigma Xi; Listed in *Who's Who in America*, *Personalities of the South*. Address: Rural Route 12 Box 469, Lake Charles, Louisiana 70605.■

ANDRAS LEVENTE KORENYI-BOTH

Physician. Personal: Born March 30, 1937; Son of Erno Korenyi-Both (deceased) and Maria Korody Katona; Married Ildiko; Father of Andras, Gyorgy, Adam. Education: M.D., 1962; C.Sc. (Med.), 1972. Career: Extensive Research in Muscle Disease. Religion: Roman Catholic. Honors and Awards: American Medical Association for Continuing Medical Education. Address: 202 Wickford Road, Havertown, Pennsylvania 19083.■

EMMANUEL MARTIN KRAMER

Personal: Born in 1928, in Philadelphia, Pennsylvania; Married Judith Levine, December 1966; Father of Henry and Gary, Benjamin. Education: Graduate of Central High School, 1945; Graduate with Honors, Temple University, 1950; Master's Degree in Psychology, Temple University, 1952; Studied Architecture and History, University of London and University of Paris. Military: Served with the First Engineer Combat Battalion, First United States Infantry Division, Germany, 1946-47; Selected for Detached Service with Allied Military Government to Reorganize the School System in Bavaria. Career: Secondary Teacher, Cheltenham High School, Wyncote, Pennsylvania, 1956-84; College and University Teaching Position, Temple University, Philadelphia College for the Performing Arts, Harvard University, Beaver College for the Performing Arts, Harvard University, Beaver College, Philadelphia College of Art. Organizational Memberships: National Trust for Historic Preservation; Historical Commission of Cheltenham Township; Society for Historical Archaeology; Archaeological Institute of America. Community Activities: Radio and Television Interviews on Matters of History, Education and Archaeology; Selected by National Council of English Teachers as Speaker in John F. Kennedy Memorial Lecture Series; Presented Paper on Education at Convention of National Council of Social Studies Teachers, Cincinnati, Ohio, 1977; Presented Six Lectures on Maya Civilization in Yucatan, Mexico, 1977; Presented Paper at Conference for Historical Archaeology in San Antonio, Texas, 1978; Lectured on Art and Archaeology in Italy, Greece, Egypt and Mexico. Published Works: Book *Observations Concerning Aspects of Religious Architecture in Western Europe*, 1961; Articles, "The Archaeology of Local History of Glenside, Pennsylvania" 1979, "Treasures in the Trash" 1980, "The Glass Bottle Container, an Archaeological Point of View" 1981, "Archaeology on the William Penn House Site" 1982. Honors and Awards: Pi Gamma Mu, Alpha Sigma Pi, Kappa Phi Kappa, Psi Chi; Received Grants for Archaeological Work from William Penn Foundation, 1982, 1983, 1984; Listed in *Who's Who in the East*, *Community Leaders of the World*, *Personalities of America*, *Directory of Distinguished Americans*, *Men of Achievement*, *International Register of Profiles*, *International Who's Who of Intellectuals*. Address: 503 Laverock Road, Glenside, Pennsylvania 19038.■

JUANITA MORRIS KREPS

Economist. Personal: Born January 11, 1921; Married Clifton H. Kreps, Jr.; Mother of Sarah, Laura, Clifton III. Education: A.B., Berea College, 1942; M.A. 1944, Ph.D. 1948, Duke University. Career: Instructor in Economics 1945-46, Assistant Professor 1948-50, Denison University; Faculty Member 1955-57, Associate Professor 1962-68, Professor of Economics 1968-77, James B. Duke Professor 1972-77, Assistant Provost 1969-72, Vice President 1973-77, Duke University; United States Secretary of Commerce, 1977-79; Economist, Duke University; Former Member Board of Directors, New York Stock Exchange, R. J. Reynolds Industries Inc., J. C. Penney Company Inc., Eastman Kodak Company, North Carolina National Bank, Teachers Insurance and Annuity Association, College Retirement Equities Fund, Western Electric, North Carolina Blue Cross-Blue Shield; Present Member Board of Directors, R. J. Reynolds Industries Inc., J. C. Penney Company Inc., U.A.L. Inc., Citicorp, Eastman Kodak Company, American Telephone and Telegraph, Armco Inc. Deere and Company, Chrysler Corporation, Zurn Industries Inc.; Trustee, Duke Endowment. Organizational Memberships: Southern Economic Association, President 1975-76; Former Chairman of the Commission on Academic Affairs, American Council of Education; Former Council Member, American Association of University Professors; President-Elect, American Association for Higher Education When Designated Secretary of Commerce; Past Chairman of the Board of Trustees, Educational Testing Service; Past Vice President, Gerontological Society; Trilateral Commission; Council on Foreign Relations; Vice President, American Economic Association. Honors and Awards: Phi Beta Kappa; Numerous Honorary Degrees from Colleges and Universities; North Carolina Public Service Award, 1976; American Association of University Women Achievement Award, 1981; North Carolina Citizens Association's Public Service Award, 1982. Address: 1407 West Pettigrew Street, Durham, North Carolina 27705.■

KUMAR KRISHEN

Research and Development Manager. Personal: Born June 22, 1939; Son of Sri Kanth Bhat and Chandpora Dhanwati; Married Vijay Lakshmi; Father of Lovely, Sweetie, Anjala Selena. Education: B.S., Jammu and Kashmir University, 1959; Bachelors of Technology 1962, Masters of Technology 1963, Calcutta University; M.S. 1966, Ph.D. 1969, Kansas State University. Career: Manager, Research and Development; Communications and Tracking Programs Staff Scientist and Staff Engineer, Lockheed Electronics Company, 1969-75; Assistant Professor, Kansas State University, 1968-69. Organizational Memberships: Institute of Electrical and Electronic Engineers, Senior Member, Board Member Galveston Section. Community Activities: Chairman of Board, Krishen Foundation for Arts and Sciences. Religion: Past President and Cofounder, Hindu Worship Society. Honors and Awards: Highest Merit, Jammu and Kashmir University, 1959; Gold and Silver Medals, Calcutta University, 1962 and 1963; Kansas State University, Phi Kappa Phi, Eta Kappa Nu, 1966 and 1968; Outstanding Performance, N.A.S.A./Johnson Space Center, 1979.■

TWO THOUSAND NOTABLE AMERICANS

KARL ERIC KRISTOFFERSON

Author and Writer/Editor. Personal: Born March 3, 1929; Son of Edward and Oma Kristofferson; Married Barbara Elaine Dalton; Father of Karol, Paul, Scott. Education: A.A. with honors, Jacksonville University, 1961; B.S. with honors Journalism, University of Florida, 1963. Military: Served in the United States Air Force, 1950-53, attaining the rank of Staff Sergeant. Career: Chief Writer/Editor, N.A.S.A. Kennedy Space Center (Florida), 1974 to present (N.A.S.A. special assignment as executive speech writer for N.A.S.A. Administrator and Deputy Adminstrator, President of the United States on space-related subjects and the Director of Kennedy Space Center); Public Affairs Officer, I.R.S. District Office, Greensboro, North Carolina, 1972-74; Publications Supervisor, RCA, Ling-Temco-Vought and Boeing Company, Kennedy Space Center, 1964-72; Motion Picture Booker, Salesman, Paramount Pictures, Warner Brothers and United Artists, Jacksonville, 1953-61; Instructor, Creative Writing, Brevard Community College, Cocoa, Florida, 1968-77 (at various times); Free-lance Writer with Publication Credit in Most Major National Magazines, 1963 to present; Regular Assignment Writer for *Reader's Digest*. Organizational Memberships: Sigma Delta Chi; Cape Canaveral Press Club. Religion: Lutheran. Honors and Awards: Phi Kappa Phi; Kappa Tau Alpha; University of Florida Merit Achievement Award for Journalism, 1963; Citation for Magazine Writing, Aviation Space Writers Association, 1974; Apollo Achievement Award, N.A.S.A., 1969; Numerous N.A.S.A. Awards for Skylab Program, Apollo for Skylab Program, Apollo-Soyuz Project and Space Shuttle. Address: 3500 Melrose Avenue, Titusville, Florida 32780.■

WILLIAM A. KRIVOY

Pharmacologist. Personal: Born January 2, 1928, in Newark, New Jersey; Son of Rose Shafferman. Education: B.S. Chemistry and Biology, Georgetown University, 1948; M.S. Physiology 1949, Ph.D. Pharmacology, George Washington University School of Medicine; United States Public Health Service Postdoctoral Research Fellow, Department of Pharmacology, University of Pennsylvania School of Medicine, 1954-55; Fellow, Department of Pharmacology, University of Edinburgh School of Medicine, Edinburgh, Scotland, 1955-57. Career: Pharmacologist, Chemical Corps Medical Laboratories, Army Chemical Center, Maryland, 1950-54; Instructor, Department of Pharmacology, Tulane University School of Medicine, 1957-59; Assistant Professor 1959-63, Associate Professor 1963-68, Department of Pharmacology, Baylor University College of Medicine; Pharmacologist, National Institute on Drug Abuse, Addiction Research Center, Lexington, Kentucky, 1968 to present. Organizational Memberships: American College of Neuropsychopharmacology; American Society for Clinical Pharmacology and Therapeutics; American Society for Pharmacology and Experimental Therapeutics; Biophysical Society; British Pharmacological Society; International Society for Biochemical Pharmacology; International Society for Psychoneuroendocrinology; New York Academy of Sciences; Sociedade Brasileira de Farmacologia e de Terapeutica Experimental; Society for Experimental Biology and Medicine; Society of Sigma Xi; Texas Academy of Science. Published Works: Author/Co-Author Numerous Professional Publications. Address: 3100 Kirklevington Drive, Unit 3, Lexington, Kentucky 40502.■

DANIEL JAMES KUBIAK

State Representative. Personal: Born March 19, 1938, in Reagan, Texas; Son of Mr. and Mrs. John T. Kubiak; Married Zona Bassler; Father of Kelly Dan, Alyssa Lea, Kody Earl. Education: Graduate, Marlin High School, Marlin, Texas, 1957; A.A., Blinn College, 1959; B.B.A. 1962, Ph.D. Education, University of Texas at Austin; M.Ed., Midwestern University, 1968; Graduate Work, Georgetown University. Career: Texas State Representative, 27th District 1968-72, 36th District 1972 to present (Member Legislature Committees on Education, Agriculture, Parks and Wildlife, Penitentiaries, Special Committee on 4-quarter School Plan, 1970-72; Legislature Committee on Energy, Chairman of Agriculture Committee, 1976-78; Chairman, Joint Interim Committee to Study Ad Valorem Tax and Effect on Agricultural Land, 1977; Vice Chairman for Appropriations Committee, 1978-80; Agriculture and Rural Development Committee of Southern Legislative Conference, Appointed by Speaker of the House, 1979; Chairman for Budget and Oversight, Legislature Committees on Agriculture and Livestock, Appropriations and Rules, 1980 to present); Teacher of Government, Economics and Mathematics, Coach, Cypress-Fairbanks High School, Houston (Texas) and Vernon High School (Texas); Semi-Professional Football Player, Vernon Vikings, Texas; Operator, Construction Business, Rockdale, Texas. Published Works: Author, *Ten Tall Texans* 1967, *Monument to a Black Man* 1972; "Youth and Their Vote: A New Day is Coming," *Theory iinto Practice* Magazine, National Education Association, 1970. Honors and Awards: Man of the Year, Agriculture, Texas County Agricultural Agents Association, 1981; Honorary Member, Limestone Company Union, 1980; Appointed Department Member of Southwest Regional Energy Council by Speaker of the House Bill Clayton, 1980; Acknowledgement of Energy, Time and Interest as Member of Board of Directors, The University Cooperative Society, Inc.; Award of Appreciation, Central Texas Sports Center (Temple) and Westphalia Public Schools; Certificate of Appreciation for Participation in Gasohol Know-How Conference 11; Special Award, Texas Chiropractic Association; Certificate of Recognition for Support during 66th Legislative Session, Good Neighbor Commission of Texas; 1979; Award of Appreciation for Outstanding Contribution to Compensatory Education in Texas, 1979; Special Award for Outstanding Service and Support, Texans for Equitable Taxation, 1978-79; Special Award, Texas Industrial Vocational Association, 1976; T.I.V.A. Legislative Award, 1976; Award of Appreciation, Citizens of Buckholts, Texas, 1976; Special Award, Round Rock Lions Club, 1976; Certificate of Appreciation, Modernistic Social Club, 1976; Certificate of Appreciation, Dioceses of Austin Catholic Youth Organization, 1975; Certificate for Outstanding Service, 1975; Certificate of Appreciation, Lee County T.S.T.A. Local Association; South Central Texas District Outstanding Service Award, Optimist Club of Rockdale, 1974; Citation for Contributions in Communications in Texas, Texas Council of Teachers of English, 1974; One of the Best Legislators and Best-Educated Education Chairman in Modern Times, *Texas Monthly* Magazine, 1973; Special Award, Texas Personnel and Guidance Association, 1973; Certificate of Appreciation, Calvert (Texas) Chamber of Commerce, 1971; Honorary Appointment as Lifetime Member, 147th Fighter Group, Texas Air National Guard, 1970; Distinguished Service Award, 1970; Award for Excellence for Portraying Texas and its Past, Texas State Teachers Association, 1967; John T. Burton Scholarship Award for Young Education, 1963; Numerous Collegiate Elected Offices and Honors; Friend of Education Award, State of Texas, T.C.T.A., 1983; Legislator of the Decade Award, 36th Legislative District, 1984. Address: 135 Champions Drive, Rockdale, Texas 76567.■

CATHERINE (KAY) E. KRUSE

Corporation Executive. Personal: Born May 5, 1915, in Lawrence, Kansas; Married Robert R. Kruse; Mother of Philip R., David V., Stephen D., Barbara Claire Todd (Mrs. Michael C.). Education: A.B. Journalism, University of Kansas, 1936. Career: Secretary-Treasurer, Brock Hotel Corporation (with Corporation 23 years). Organizational Memberships: Security Equity Fund and Security Investment Funds, Director 1973 to present; Menninger Foundation Fellow; Projects with Industry Commission, Topeka, Kansas; Convention-Tourism Board, City of Topeka, 1977 to present. Community Activities: President, Native Daughters of Kansas, 1973; Chairman of Advisory Board, St. Francis Hospital, 1970-72; Chairman, Kansas Civil Service Board of Appeals, 1970; Chairman, Advisory Board, Young Women's Christian Association, 1976-82; Chairman, Women's Division, The Greater Topeka Chamber of Commerce, 1968; Board of Directors, United Way of Topeka, 1977-82. Religion: First Woman Moderator, The First Congregational Church of Topeka, 1975-77; President, Kansas Chapter, P.E.O., 1978-79. Honors and Awards: Listed in *World Who's Who of Women*, *Dictionary of International Biography*, *The National Register of Prominent Americans and International Notables*, *Community Leaders and Noteworthy Americans*, *Who's Who of American Women*, *Who's Who in Finance and Industry*. Address: 8010 Glen Albens Circle, Dallas, Texas 75225.■

ALEXANDER KUROSKY

Professor of Human Genetics and Biochemistry. Personal: Born September 12; Son of Peter and Stella Kurosky (deceased); Married Anna Kinik, Daughter of John (deceased) and Mary Kinik; Father of Lisa Kathryn, Tanya Kristine, Stephanie Ann. Education: B.Sc., University of British Columbia, Vancouver, Canada, 1965; M.Sc. 1969, Ph.D. 1972, University of Toronto, Toronto, Canada. Career: Research Technician, Canada Department of Agriculture, Harrow, Ontario and Vancouver, British Columbia, 1959-64; Research and Development Chemist, Canadian Breweries, Ltd., Toronto, 1965-67; Assistant Professor 1975-78, Associate Professor 1978-82, Professor 1982 to present, University of Texas Medical Branch. Organizational Memberships: American Society of Biological Chemists; American Chemical Society; Canadian Biochemical Society; American Association for the Advancement of Science; Society of Sigma Xi; American Society of Human Genetics. Honors and Awards: Province of Ontario Graduate Fellowship, 1968-71; Distinguished Teaching Award, Graduate School of Biomedical Sciences, Galveston, 1981; Listed in *Who's Who in the South and Southwest*. Address: 6605 Golfcrest Drive, Galveston, Texas 77551.■

JOHN FRANCIS KURTZKE, SR.

Neurologist, Epidemiologist. Personal: Born September 14, 1926, in Brooklyn, New York; Son of John Ambrose and Teresa Rose Knipper Kurtzke; Married

Margaret Mary Nevin, June 30, 1950; Father of John Francis Jr., Catherine Kurtzke Brown, Elizabeth Kurtzke Siebert, Joan Kurtzke Brennan, Robert, James, Christine. Education: B.S. summa cum laude, St. John's University, 1948; M.D., Cornell University, 1952; Diplomate in Neurology, American Board of Psychiatry and Neurology, 1958; Intern, King's County Hospital, Brooklyn, 1952-53; Resident in Neurology, Veteran's Administration Hospital, Bronx, New York, 1953-56. Military: Served with the United States Naval Reserve, 1944-46; Rear Admiral, M.C. Reserves; Liaison Officer, United States Navy Medical School, 1979 to present. Career: Chief of Neurology Service, Veterans Administration Hospitals, Coatesville (Pennsylvania) 1956-63, Washington 1963 to present; Member of Faculty 1958-63, Assistant Professor of Clinical Neurology 1963, Jefferson Medical College; Faculty Member 1963 to present, Professor of Neurology 1968 to present, Professor of Community Medicine 1968 to present, Vice Chairman of Department of Neurology 1976 to present, Georgetown Medical School; Consultant in Neurology, United States Naval Hospital, 1966 to present; Surgeon General of the Navy, 1970 to present. Organizational Memberships: National Institutes of Health Epilepsy Advisory Committee, Chairman Epidemiology Section 1973-76, VACO Advisory Group on Neurology 1974 to present, Chairman Work Group on Epidemiology, D.H.E.W. Commission for Control of Huntington's Disease 1976-78, A.A.N. Committee on National Needs in Neurology 1979 to present (chairman 1981 to present), A.A.N. Representative Council of Medical Specialty Societies 1979 to present, Naval Examining Board of Naval Medical Command 1980 to present; Medical Research Program Specialist for Neurology and Neurobiology, Veterans Administration Reserach Service, 1977-80; Member Committee on Multiple Sclerosis 1967 to present, Committee on Neuroepidemiology 1977 to present, World Federation of Neurology; Fellow, American Academy of Neurology, Chairman Section on Neuro-epidemiology 1971-75; Fellow, American Association for the Advancement of Science; Fellow, New York Academy of Science; Pan American Medical Association, Council Member, Section on Neurology; Fellow, American College of Epidemiology; Fellow, American College of Neurology; Fellow, American College of Epidemiology; Fellow, American College of Preventive Medicine; Fellow, American College of Physicians; Southern Medical Association; Association of Military Surgeons; American Neurological Associatoin; American Medical Association; American Association of University Professors; American Epidemiological Association; Association for Research in Nervous and Mental Disease; American Public Health Association; Society for Epidemiological Research; American Epilepsy Society; Society of Medical Consultants to Armed Forces, Committee on Research Affairs 1980 to present; Life Member, Naval Reserve Association, Naval Order of the United States, Reserve Officers Association; Naval Institute; Navy League; Fellow, A.C.P. Community Activities: Medical Advisory Board, National Multiple Sclerosis Society, 1966 to present; Working Group on Design of Clinical Studies in Multiple Sclerosis, 1976 to present; Advisory Board, International Federation of Multiple Sclerosis Societies, 1972 to present. Published Works: Author/Co-Author, *Epidemiology of Multiple Sclerosis* 1968, *Epidemiology of Cerebrovascular Disease* 1969, *Epidemiology of Neurologic and Sense Organ Disorders* 1973; Contributor of Chapters to Textbooks, Over 290 Articles to Professional Journals. Honors and Awards: Certificate of Merit, Surgeon General of the Navy, 1969; Navy Commendation Medal, 1974; Listed in *Who's Who in America.* Address: 7509 Salem Road, Falls Church, Virginia 22043.■

LOUANNA DICKERSON KUTSCHER

State Representative. Personal: Born April 2, 1935; Daughter of Lawrence and Beulah Dickerson; Married Gordon R. Kutscher, Son of Richard and Emilie Kutscher; Mother of Richard Gordon, Randy Keith, Robert Clark. Education: Graduate, Jackson High School, Jackson, Missouri, 1953. Career: Member of Missouri House of Representatives; Former Member of Missouri Senate. Community Activities: Missouri Federation of Women's Clubs, President 1978-80, Past Treasurer, Secretary, Vice President, Junior Director; Missouri Girls Town Foundation, Corresponding Secretary 1982; Conservation Federation of Missouri, Board of Directors 1978-82; General Federation of Women's Clubs Blueprint-21st Century Committee 1980-82; Vice President, Mid-Missouri Chapter, Conservation Federation, 1978-82. Religion: Trinity Lutheran Church (Jefferson City, Missouri), Women Missionary Society President 1968-70. Honors and Awards: General Federation of Women's Clubs Missouri Outstanding Junior Clubwoman, 1967; American Association of University Women Community Service Award, Jefferson City Branch, 1972. Address: 1815 Swifts Highway, Jefferson City, Missouri 65101.■

JACQUELYN PATTI KUTSKO

Author, Teacher. Personal: Born March 27, 1945; Daughter of Pete and Carolyn Patti; Married James Andrew Kutsko Sr., Son of Mary Kutsko; Mother of James Andrew Jr. Education: B.A. Comprehensive Business Education, University of Akron, 1967; Studies toward Master's Degree, Colorado State University. Career: Teacher in Private and Public High Schools, Private Business Colleges, Community College; Owner of Interior Decorating Studio; Former Executive Secretary. Organizational Memberships: National Business Education Association; Mountain Plains Business Education Association; Colordo Educators For and About Business; American Vocational Association; Colorado Vocational Association. Community Activities: Medical Office Assistant's Advisory Board, Community College of Denver; Business Program Advisory Board, Smoky Hill High School, Aurora, Colorado; Featured Speaker, Fall Yearbook Workshop, Colorado Springs, Colorado; Yearbook Advisor, Smoky Hill High School (won first place rating with two marks of distinction from Columbia Scholastic Press Association, first place ratings with distinction from National Scholastic Press Association). Honors and Awards: John Andrews Memorial Scholarship, 1965-67; 1981 Colordo Figure Skating Championships, Second Place in Bronze Dance; Listed in *Who's Who in the West, World Who's Who of Women, Personalities of America, Community Leaders of America.* Address: 8378 East Jamison Circle South, Englewood, Colorado 80112.■

CARL MARTIN KUTTLER, JR.

Junior College President. Personal: Born January 31, 1940; Son of Carl M. and Winona Kuttler; Married Evelyn Flathmann, Daughter of Edward and Erna Flathmann; Father of Carl Martin III, Cindy, Erika. Education: A.A. Management, St. Petersburg Junior College, 1960; B.S. Management, Florida State University, 1962; J.D., Stetson College of Law, 1965. Career: Instructor, Assistant to Vice President for Administration, Dean of Administrative Affairs, President, St. Petersburg Junior College, 1965 to present; Counsel to Pinellas County Legislative Delegation, April and May 1974; 2nd District Court of Appeals, Lakeland, Florida. Organizational Memberships: Appointed by Governor to Chair Florida Student Financial Assistance Commission, 1977; Florida Association of Community Colleges; Pinellas County Secondary School Administrators; Florida Bar Association; National Organization of Legal Problems in Education. Community Activities: Chamber of Commerce; Campaign Worker for Several United States Presidents; Candidate for Commissioner of Education, State of Florida, 1974. Religion: St. Luke's Methodist Church, Building Committee 1975, Secretary of Methodist Men 1976-78; Presider for Annual Fall Retreat Convention, Leeburg, Florida, 1976, 1977. Honors and Awards: Most Distinguished Alumnus, Stetson University Alumni Association, 1978; Outstanding Young Man of America, Jaycees of America, 1977; Resolution of Appreciation, Board of Overseers, Building Committee, Stetson College of Law (for serving as chairman during construction of new courtroom), 1977; Resolution of Appreciation, St. Luke's Methodist Church, 1975. Address: 8336 40th Avenue North, St. Petersburg, Florida 33709.■

JOON TAEK KWON

Principal Research Chemist. Personal: Born March 10, 1935; Son of Mr. and Mrs. Young Tae Kwon; Married Moon Ja Kwon; Father of Howard Albert, Daphne Elsa. Education: B.S. Chemistry Curriculum, University of Illinois, 1957; M.S. 1959, Ph.D. 1962, Inorganic Chemistry, Cornell University. Career: Principal Research Chemist, C-E Luminius, 1970 to present; Senior Research Chemist, Celanese Research Company, 1967-70; Research Chemist, Chamcell Limited, Edmonton, Alberta, Canada, 1965-67; Instructor II, Department of Chemistry, University of British Columbia, Vancouver, Canada, 1964-65; Postdoctoral Research and Teaching Fellow, Department of Chemistry, University of British Columbia, 1962-64. Organizational Memberships: American Chemical Society; Catalysis Society of New York; North American Thermal Analysis Society; The Royal Chemical Society, London; The Society of Chemical Industry, London; The Korean Chemical Society; Korean Scientists and Engineers in North America. Community Activities: Illini Alumni Association, Life Member; Cornell Club of Monmouth County, Cornell Alumni Association; Boy Scouts of America, Scoutmaster. Honors and Awards: Boy Scouts of America, Order of the Arrow, Scouters Award, District Award of Merit, Veterans Award; Research Grants, National Council of Canada, 1964-67; Industrial Grants in Aid, National Research Council of Canada, 1965-67. Address: 142 Derby Drive, Freehold Township, New Jersey 07728.■

CARL LA CAVA

Professor. Personal: Born March 20, 1932; Son of Albert La Cava (deceased); Married Dorothy L. Graziano (deceased); Father of Sandra, Jude. Education: B.B.A., Dyke College, 1950; Two M.B.A. Programs, Temple University of Philadelphia; Two Certification Courses at Penn State University; M.B.A., Baldwin-Wallace College, 1978. Military: Served in the United States Army, 1950, attaining a field promotion to Lieutenant, Army Corps of Engineers; United States Army Reserve. Career: Professor of Marketing, Dyke College, Cleveland, Ohio; Loan Executive, City of Cleveland; Growth Association, Jobs Council, National Alliance of Business; President, Custom Leasing Corporation. Organizational Memberships: Society of Automotive Engineers; American Management Association; Sales and Marketing Executives; Delta Mu Delta Honor Society for Academic Achievement. Community Activities: President, Baldwin-Wallace College M.B.A. Graduate Alumni Association, 1983; Head, Task Force Group to Aid Blacks, Hispanics, Ex-Offenders, Vietnam Veterans; Volunteer, Over 40 Unemployment, Handicapped, Youth Jobs Programs and Programs to Aid All Other Less Fortunate of the Community. Religion: Roman Catholic. Address: P.O. Box 741, Edgewater, Cleveland, Ohio 44107.■

CARMELA G. LACAYO

Executive. Personal: Born June 28, 1943; Daughter of Enrique Luis Lacayo, Mary Louise Velasquez. Education: B.A., Immaculate Heart College; B.A., Regina Mundi International University; Graduate Work in Public Administration, University of California-Los Angeles. Career: President/Executive Director, A.N.P.P.M./ N.A.H.E.-N.H.I.P.P.; Professor of Urban Development and Sociology, University of San Buenaventura, Colombia, 1973-74; Administrative Coordinator, Office of Mayor, Los Angeles, 1974-75. Organizational Memberships: National Council on Aging, Board of Directors; Gerontological Society of America W.G.S.; Continental Baking Company, I.T.T., Advisory Panel for Nutrition Education for Older Americans; European Values Systems Study, Center for Applied Research in the Apostolate, International Advisory Board for the Americas; National Policy Center on Housing and Living Arrangement for Older Americans, University of Michigan, Advisory Board; University of Southern California National Policy Center on Employment and Retirement; University of California-San Francisco Aging Health Policy Study Center, Advisory Board; Catholic Coordinating Committee for the White House Conference on Aging, United States Catholic Conference; Chairperson, Forum of National Hispanic Organizations, 1983. Honors and Awards: Latina Woman of the Year, Los Angeles, 1976; National Woman of the Year, Latin American Professional Women's Association, 1977. Address: 1730 West Olympic Boulevard, Los Angeles, California 90015-1964.■

ELSIE H. LACY

Poet, Author. Personal: Born in 1897; Married William Paris; Mother of Gertrude, Randolph (deceased), Waldo. Career: Poet and Author, 1952 to present; Teacher, Morgan County, Halsey Fork School 1919-24, Centerville School 1924-28, Bethel Chapel School 1929-33, Sycamore Grove School 1935. Organizational Memberships: American Composers, Authors and Publishers; Virginia Poetry Society; International Union; Life Member, International Clover Poetry Association. Religion: Member of the Grassy Lick Baptist Church. Published Works: Poems "Evening", *Scimitar and Song* 1955, "A Friend", *Christian Writers' Poetry* 1968, "Driftwood", *Poet* 1974, "Shadow Light", *South and West* 1978-79; Author of Books *Kentucky Verseland* 1956, *Characteristic Traits of Kentuckians* 1961, *From Kentucky Hills* 1962, *A Lacy Sampler* 1963, *From Cumberland Hills* 1962, *Poetized Musings* 1977, *Kentucky Themes and Scenes* 1977, *Peaceful as a Dove* 1978, *Voice of a Poet* 1978, *My America* 1975, *Our Kentucky* 1979, *Pastoral Themes* 1980, *Unfolded Themes* 1980, *Contemporized Themes* 1981, *Essays of Yesterday and Poems of Today* 1981, *Healthy Seeds* 1981, *Success* 1983. Honors and Awards: Certificates of Recognition, West Virginia Poetry Society, Flatwood Poetry Society, National Society of Poets; Listed in *International Register of Profiles, International Who's Who of Intellectuals, Who's Who of American Women, Who's Who of Women, Dictionary of International Biography, Poet's Hall of Fame, Personalities of the South.* Address: Route l, Box 241, Grassy Creek, Kentucky 41435.■

MICHAEL M. LAKS

Physician, Professor, Administrator. Personal: Born July 25, 1928; Married Sandra Beller, Daughter of Mat and Lillian Beller; Father of Helaina, Alexander. Education: B.A. 1951, Further Studies 1951-52, University of California at Los Angeles; M.D., University of Southern California, 1956; Intern 1956-57, Resident 1957-59, Chief Medical Resident 1959-60, Cedars of Lebanon Hospital (Los Angeles); Research Fellow in Medicine, Cedars of Lebanon Hospital, 1960-61; Special Cardiac Fellow, National Institutes of Health, 1965-67. Military: Served in the United States Naval Reserves. Career: Assistant Director, Department of Medicine, Cedars of Lebanon Hospital, 1961-64; Research Associate, Cedars-Sinai Medical Center, 1962-69; Director, Department of Medicine, Cedars of Lebanon Hospital, 1964-65; Physician in Charge of Cardiovascular Research Laboratory, Cedars of Lebanon Hospital, 1965-71; Senior Research Scientist, Cedars-Sinai Medical Center, 1969 to present; Director, Heart Station and Cardiovascular Research Laboratory, Harbor-University of California at Los Angeles Medical Center, 1971 to present; Cardiovascular Consultant, Wadsworth Veterans Administration Hospital, 1971 to present; Electrocardiographic Research Consultant, Hewlett-Packard, 1973 to present; Associate Chief, Division of Cardiology, Harbor-University of California at Los Angeles Medical Center, 1975 to present; Attending Physician, Cedars-Sinai Medical Center, 1965 to present; Assistant Professor of Medicine, University of California at Los Angeles, 1969-71; Consultant in Cardiology, Wadsworth Veterans Administration Hospital, 1971 to present; Associate Professor of Medicine, University of California at Los Angeles School of Medicine, 1972-75; Professor of Medicine, University of California at Los Angeles, 1975 to present; Visiting Internist, University of California at Los Angeles Hospital and Clinics, 1975 to present. Organizational Memberships: American Medical Association; American Federation for Clinical Research; American Association for the Advancement of Science; Diplomat, American Board of Internal Medicine; Fellow, American College of Cardiology; Fellow, American College of Physicians; American Physiology Society; Pan American Medical Association; Founding Fellow, American Geriatrics Society; Western Society for Clinical Research; Los Angeles County Heart Association; California Medical Association; Fellow, American College of Chest Physicians; Diplomat, American Board of Internal Medicine/Subspecialist in Cardiovascular Disorders; National Association of Para-Cardiac Specialists, Chairman Medical Advisory Committee; International Study for Research in Cardiac Metabolism; Fellow, Council on Clinical Cardiology; American Institute of Biology Sciences;

Fellow, The Royal Society of Medicine; California Thoracic Society; The New York Academy of Sciences; Western Association of Physicians. Honors and Awards: Honorary Scholastic Competitive Scholarship Award, American Chemical Society, 1947; Phi Beta Kappa; Alpha Omega Alpha; Phi Kappa Phi; Prize for Research Paper, American College of Physicians, 1961; Listed in *Dictionary of International Biography, Notable Americans, Who's Who in the West, Personalities of the West and Midwest, International Who's Who in Community Service, Men of Achievement.* Address: 1939 North Edgemont, Los Angeles, California 90027.

SHANKER LAL

Ophthalmologist. Personal: Born June 24, 1917; Son of Atmaram and Jekoreben Lal (both deceased); Married Kapilaben, Daughter of Gulabdas and Jivkoreben (both deceased); Father of Eight Children. Education: M.B.B.S., Medical College of Rangoon, Burma, 1942; Diploma of Ophthalmology, University of Bombay, 1944; Diploma of Ophthalmology, London, 1961; M.R.C.P., Royal College of Physicians and Surgeons, Glasgow, 1962; Diploma, American Board of Ophthalmology, 1976; Internship, Rangoon, 1939-41; Residency, Rangoon and Bombay, 1941-44. Career: Staff Physician, Veterans Administration Medical Center, Cheyenne, Wyoming, 1980 to present; Chief of Department of Ophthalmology, Noble Army Hospital, Fort McClellan, Alabama, 1979-80; Staff Physician, Veterans Administration Hospital, Montgomery, Alabama, 1976-79; Staff Physician and Chief of Medical Service, Mental Health Institute, Clarinda, Iowa, 1972-76; Fellowships, Moorfields Eye Hospital, London and Crossley Hospital, Liverpool, 1960-62; Consultant, Gandhi Hospital, Mandalay, 1950-58 and 1962-65. Organizational Memberships: Fellow, American Academy of Ophthalmology, 1974; Fellow, Royal College of Physicians and Surgeons, Glasgow, 1976. Community Activities: Rotary Club; Lions Club; Masons. Religion: Hindu; President, Sanatan Dharam Sabha, Mandalay, Burma, 1968-72. Honors and Awards: Physicians Recognition Awards, American Medical Association, 1973-76, 1976-79, 1979-82, 1982-85.■

LEANNE KAY LAMKE

Assistant Professor of Child Development and Family Relations. Personal: Born March 18, 1954; Daughter of Wayne E. and Edith E. Lamke. Education: B.A. Psychology summa cum laude, University of North Dakota, 1975; M.S. Family Studies 1978, Ph.D. Family Studies 1979, Texas Tech University. Career: Assistant Professor of Child Development and Family Relations, University of Arizona, 1982 to present; Assistant Professor of Family Studies, Arizona State University, 1979-82; Instructor of Department of Child Development and Family Relations 1978-79, Predoctoral Internship for Counseling Center 1977-78, Texas Tech University. Organizational Memberships: American Psychological Association; National Council on Family Relations; American Association for Marriage and Family Therapy; American Home Economics Association. Career: State Advisor of Student Member Section 1979-82, Board Member 1981-82, Arizona Home Economics Association; Consultant to Business and Industry in Communication Skills and Personnel Management. Honors and Awards: Certified Instructor, Minnesota Couples Communicaion Program; Clinical Member, American Association for Marriage and Family Therapy; Research Grants, Arizona State University 1979-82, Texas Tech University 1978. Address: 6462 North Oracle #4, Tucson, Arizona 85704.■

SELMA H. LAMKIN

Accountant, Publisher and Educator. Personal: Born March 29, 1925; Daughter of Julia Hoffman; Married Sherman A. Lamkin (deceased); Mother of Barry D., Deborah L. Leonard. Education: Attended Hebrew Teachers College 1943; Degree, Bentley College 1967; C.P.A. Career: Owner, Nikmal Publishing; Former Positions include Teaching Posts at Graham Junior College, Northeastern University and the Cambridge Young Women's Christian Association, Financial Manager of Group Dental Practice, Public Accountant, Supervisor of a War Plant; Author; Prepared Small Business Development Program for Roxbury Community College; Seminar on the Shoebox Syndrome, Boston. Organizational Memberships: Feminist Writers Guild, Steering Committee of National Women's Study. Community Activities: Treasurer, Mass Women's Political Caucus; Treasurer, League of Women Voters, 1980; Chair, Association of Women in Government Contractors; Legislative Chair and Treasurer, Fanueil Business and Professional Women. Published Works: Author of *A Small Business Survival Manual, The Shoebox Syndrome, Self-Instruction Accounting Course, Money Management and Investing.* Honors and Awards: Listed in *Who's Who of American Women, Personalities of America, International Who's Who.* Address: 698 River Street, Boston, Massachusetts 02126.■

SYLVIA M. LAMOUTTE

Symphony Orchestra Executive Director. Personal: Born November 29, 1935; Daughter of Roberto Lamoutte and Silvia Caro de Lamoutte. Education: Completed Basic Course with honors, University of Puerto Rico, 1954; Bachelor's Degree with honors 1958, Master's Degree with honors 1960, New England Conservatory of Music; Piano Studies with Elisa Tavarez and Miklos Schwalb; Duo Piano Studies with Luboschutz and Nemenoff; Early Music Studies with Daniel Pinkham; Ensemble Studies with Francis J. Cooke; Other Studies in Electronic Class Piano, Wurlitzer Method, and Baldwin Method. Career: Executive Director, Corporation of the Puerto Rico Symphony Orchestra, 1981 to present; Hostess on Weekly Radio Program on WRTV-FM; Private Music Teacher, Puerto Rico, 1960-80; Panelist and Music Critic on "Mirador Puertorriqueno" Television Program; Author and Publisher of 25 Music Books, 1964-80; Public Junior High School Instructor; Piano Teacher, New England Conservatory of Music, 1959-60; Performances in Puerto Rico, Massachusetts, and Dominican Republic; Lecturer on Music as a Career and on The Puertorian Danza. Organizational Memberships: American Musicological Society New England Chapter; Faculty Member, National Guild of Piano Teachers; American Music Scholarship Association; The University Society; President, New England Conservatory of Music Alumni Club of Puerto Rico, 1975-77; Board, Pro Arte Musical Inc., 1976-77; Board, Sociedad Musical de Puerto Rico, 1976-77; Vice President 1978, President 1978-81, Asociacion Pro Orquesta Sinfonica de Puerto Rico. Community Activities: National Board of Advisors, American Biographical Institute, 1982. Published Works: Author of Compilations, Adaptations and Arrangements of Puerto Rican Folk Music and Traditional Music for Piano from Preparatory Level to Grade 4 Published for the First Time in Puerto Rico or Elsewhere; Author of Danzas, "Amor Ausente," "Brisas de Borinquen," "Olas del Caribe." Honors and Awards: Walter W. Naumburg Scholarship, 1959-60; Pro Arte Musical Medal; Honorary Member, Pi Kappa Lambda; Listed in Education: *International Who's Who in Music.* Address: 267 San Jorge Street Apartment 12C, Santurce, Puerto Rico 00912.■

BARBARA JEANETTE LANCASTER

Educator. Personal: Born November 3, 1944; Daughter of James H. Miller; Married Ivie Wade Lancaster III, Son of I. W. Lancaster; Mother of Melinda Leigh, Jennifer Denise. Education: B.S.N., University of Tennessee, 1966; M.S.N., Case Western Reserve University, 1969; Ph.D., University of Oklahoma, 1977. Career: Appointed Dean, School of Nursing, Wright State University, 1984; Former Positions include Professor and Chairman of the M.S.N. Degree Program at the University of Alabama at Birmingham, Associate Professor at Texas Christian University, Nurse Clinician at the University Hospitals of Cleveland (Ohio), Staff Nurse at Mt. Sinai Hospital of Cleveland. Organizational Memberships: American Nurses Association; National League for Nursing, Member 1970 to present, Public Affairs Committee 1983, Chairman Regional Program Committee 1980; Alabama League for Nursing, President-Elect 1981-83, President 1983-85. Community Activities: Health Committee, Birmingham Women's Center, 1979; Health Goals Committee for the 1980's, Birmingham Chamber of Commerce, 1979; Board Member, Visiting Nurse Association, 1979 to present; Board Member, Jefferson-Shelby Lung Association, 1979 to present; Board Member, American Lung Association, 1981 to present; Chairman, Professional Advisory Committee, Visiting Nurses Association, 1979; Chairman, Smoking and Health Committee, Alabama Lung Association, 1981 to present; Health Screening, Cahaba Heights Elementary School, 1980; Professional Advisory Comittee, Jefferson County Health Department, 1980 to present; Prevention Volunteer, Birmingham Women's Center, 1981 to present. Religion: Family Life Committee 1981, Adult Church School Teacher 1981-82, Brookwood Baptist Church. Honors and Awards: Outstanding Clinical Paper, Ohio Nurses Association, 1969; Excellence in Writing Award, American Nurses Association, Texas Nurses Association, 1976; Book of the Year Award, *American Journal of Nursing,* 1981; Outstanding Media Award, Region 2, Sigma Theta Tau (for *Concepts of Advanced Nursing Practice: The Nurse as a Charge Agent*), 1982; Distinguished Alumnus Award, Frances Payne Bolton School of Nursing, Case Western Reserve University; Nominated to *Community Leaders of the World;* Listed in *International Who's Who in Education, Who's Who of American Women.* Address: 3916 River View Drive, Birmingham, Alabama 35243.■

TWO THOUSAND NOTABLE AMERICANS

JAMES TERRY LANCASTER

Director of Research and Development. Personal: Born February 9, 1933; Son of T.A. Lancaster Sr.; Married Patricia Philpot; Father of Michael Sean, Terry Elisabeth. Education: B.S.E.E. Tennessee Polytechnic Institute, 1958; M.S.E.E. 1965, Ph.D. 1971, Virginia Polytechnic Institute. Military: Served in the United States Army, 1953-55, attaining the rank of Sergeant, Army Security Agency. Career: Director of Research and Development, T.V.P.P.A., 1980 to present; Associate Professor of Electrical Engineering, Tennessee Tech University, 1961-80; Director and Founder of Engineering and Technology Department, Ferrum Junior College, 1967-68; Junior Engineer, Nashville Electric Service, 1958-61. Organizational Memberships: Institute of Electrical and Electronics Engineers; Chattanooga Engineers Club; Order of the Engineer. Community Activities: Rotary Club, Rocky Mount (Virginia) 1967-69, Cookeville (Tennessee) 1970-79. Religion: Presbyterian Church of the Red Bank-Cumberland, Sunday School Teacher 1979 to present; United Presbyterian Church of Cookeville, Tennessee, Sunday School Teacher and Deacon prior to 1979. Honors and Awards: Tau Beta Pi National Engineering Honor Fraternity; Eta Kappa Nu National Electrical Engineering Honor Fraternity; Kappa Mu Epsilon National Mathematics Honor Fraternity; Eta Epsilon Sigma Local Engineering Honor Fraternity; Ford Foundation Grant and Tennessee State Grant, 1964-67. Address: 411 Paragon Drive, Red Bank, Tennessee 37415.■

MING HUEY LAND

Professor of Architecture. Personal: Born July 10, 1940; Son of Chin-tu Land; Married Whei-ing, Daughter of Jin-Long Yang; Father of Judy Karen, Michael Henry. Education: B.S., National Taiwan Normal University, 1963; M.S., Northern Illinois University, 1968; Ed.D., Utah State University, 1970. Career: Professor of Architecture, Former Professor of Industrial Education, Miami University; Fulbright Visiting Profesor, Chungnam National University of Korea, Taejon; Assistant Professor, Eastern Illinois University. Organizational Memberships: American Society for Engineering Education; American Industrial Arts Association; Phi Delta Kappa; Epsilon Pi Tau; International Graphics, Inc. Community Activities: International Relations Committee, American Industrial Arts Association, 1975-77; Community Service Organization for Foreign Students, Oxford, Ohio. Honors and Awards: Fulbright Senior Fellowship, Council for International Exchange of Scholars, 1981; Major Research Grant, Ohio Advisory Council for Vocational Education, Columbus, Ohio, 1980. Address: 216 McKee Avenue, Oxford, Ohio 45056.■

NEWLIN JEWEL LANDERS

Contractor. Personal: Born July 10, 1906; Son of DeLoy Landers (deceased); Married Vernette Trosper Landers; Father of Larry, Marlin. Education: Attended Contractors School. Career: Positions with Howard Hughes Multi-Color Laboratory, Hughes Development Company, Paramount Motion Pictures Studios; Owner, Landers Machine Shop; Co-Owner, Selwyn-Landers Valve Company, Los Angeles, California; Inventor, Developer, Tester, Patentee and Manufacturer of High Pressure Valves; Bought and Improved Havasu Landing, Needles, California; Owner, Navajo Tract, Apple Valleys, 1950; Founder, Community of Landers and Landers Air Strip; Donor of Land and Building to Landers Volunteer Fire Department; Donor of Land to Homestead Valley Women's Club; Former Owner and Operator, Landers Gas Station and Water Delivery; Owner, Landers Septic Tanks and Water Systems. Organizational Memberships: American Biographical Institute, Life Fellow; International Biographical Association, Life Member. Community Activities: Landers Volunteer Fire Department, Honorary Member; Landers Garden Club; Moose Lodge. Honors and Awards: Businessman of the Week, KSST Radio Station, 1969; Plaque and Badge for 13 Years of Search and Rescue Work with Yucca Valley Sheriff Rangers; International Diploma of Honors for Community Service; Landers Community Dinner honoring Newlin as its Founding Father on 75th Birthday, 1981; Plaque in Appreciation of his Contributions, Landers Volunteer Fire Department Board of Directors, 1981. Address: 905 Landers Lane, Landers, California 92284.■

VERNETTE TROSPER LANDERS

Author, Retired School Counselor, Volunteer, Post Office Clerk. Personal: Born May 3, 1912; Daughter of LaVerne Trosper; Married Newlin J. Landers; Mother of Larry, Marlin. Education: A.B. with honors; M.A., 1935; Ed.D., 1953; Four Educational Credentials from the State of California (two of which are life-diplomas). Career: Author, Nine Books of Poetry; Volunteer 22 Years, Clerk-in-Charge, Landers Community Post Office; Guidance Project Director, 1967; Coordinator, Adult Education, 1965-67; District Counselor, Morongo Unified School District (California), 1965-72; Dean of Girls, 29 Palm High School, 1960-65; Assistant Professor, Los Angeles State College, 1950; Professor, Long Beach City College, 1946-47; Teacher, Secondary Schools, Motebello, California, 1935-45, 1948-50, 1951-59. Organizational Memberships: International Studies and Exchanges, Leonardo Da Vinci International Academy, Rome, Titular Member International Committee 1981 and 1984; International Academy of Poets (London), Life Fellow 191; International Biographical Association, Life Fellow 1984; National League of American Pen Women; International Platform Association; N.R.T.A.; C.T.A.; American and California Personnel and Guidance Associations; Phi Beta Kappa; Pi Lambda Theta; Sigma Delta Pi; Mortar Board; Prytanean; Spurs. Community Activities: Montebello Business and Professional Women's Club, President 1940; Soroptimist Club (29 Palms, California) Secretary 1962, Life Member 1983; Landers Association Inc., Vice President, Secretary, 1965-77; Landers Volunteer Fire Department, Secretary 1972-75; Desert Emergency Radio Service, Secretary; Hi Desert Playhouse Guild, Life Member; Hi Desert Memorial Hospital Guild, Life Member; Hi Desert Nature Museum, Life Member; Homestead Valley Women's Club, Life Member; Landers Area Chamber of Commerce; Landers Garden Club. Religion: Landers Community Church, Bible School Lecturer 4 Years. Honors and Awards: C.S.S.I. Poet Laureate, February 1981, Rome, Italy; International Diploma of Honor for Community Service, 1973; Certificate of Merit for Distinguished Service to Education, 1973; Creativity Award, International Personnel Research Association, 1972; Soroptimist of the Year, 29 Palms Soroptimist Club, 1969; International Winged Glory Diploma of Honors of Letters, Leonardo Da Vinci International Academy, Rome, Italy, 1982; Diploma of Merit in Letters, University of Arts, Parma, Italy, 1982; Statue of Victory "Personality of the Year 1984." World Culture Prize, National Center for Studies and Research Italian Academy; Golden Palm Diploma of Honor in Poetry, Leonardo Da Vinci Academy, 1984. Address: 905 Landers Lane, Landers, California 92284.■

HARVEY J. LANDRESS

Social Agency Executive. Personal: Born December 6, 1946; Son of Jack and Anne Landress; Married Susan S.; Father of Joshua. Education: B.A. Political Science, 1968, M.A. Political Science 1973, State University of New York-Binghamton; M.S.W., University of Louisville, 1975; Postgraduate Work, Gujarat University, Ahmedabad, India, 1971. Career: Director of Planning and Development, P.A.R. Comprehensive Drug Abuse Programs, 1979 to present; Assistant Professor of Social Work, St. Leo College, 1976-79; Adjunct Instructor, University of South Florida Department of Criminal Justice, St. Petersburg, 1980 to present; Social Worker, Elizabethtown, Kentucky, 1975-76; Social Worker, Ireland Army Hospital, Ft. Knox, Kentucky, 1975; Juvenile Counselor, Hodgenville, Kentucky, 1973-74; Adjunct Instructor, University of Kentucky-Ft. Knox Department of Political Science, 1973-76. Organizational Memberships: National Association of Social Workers, State Secretary 1979-81; United Faculty of Florida, First Vice President of St. Leo Chapter 1977-79; Florida Drug and Alcohol Abuse Association; Academy of Certified Social Workers; Numerous Other Professional and Civic Organizations. Community Activities: Chairman, Boys Village of San Antonio, Inc., 1982 to present; Chairman, Florida Coalition on Migrant Action, 1978-79; Chairman of 5th Congressional District of Kentucky, Common Cause, 1973-75; Experiment in International Living, Brattleboro, Vermont, 1979 to present; United States Peace Corps Volunteer, Kangavar, Iran, 1968-70. Published Works: Author of Professional Publications, 1968, 1980 and 1983. Honors and Awards: Fulbright-Hayes Fellowship, 1971; Outstanding Faculty Memgber, St. Leo College, 1979; Humanitarian Award, Pasco County (Florida) Community Action Agency, 1979; State and National Debating Awards, 1967-68; Listed in *Who's Who Among Students in American Universities and Colleges, Who's Who in the South and Southwest, International Who's Who of Contemporary Achievement, Five Thousand Personalities of the World, Dictionary of Distinguished Americans, Dictionary of International Biography, Men of Achievement.* Address: 1301 West Missouri Avenue, Dade City, Florida 33525.■

TWO THOUSAND NOTABLE AMERICANS

JOSEPH MICHAEL LANE

Orthopaedic Surgeon, Professor. Personal: Born October 27, 1939; Son of Mr. and Mrs. Frederick Lane; Married Barbara, Daughter of Ethel Greenhouse; Father of Debra, Jennifer. Education: Graduate, Great Neck Senior High School, 1957; A.B. (Chemistry), Columbia University, 1961; M.D., Harvard University, 1965. Military: Served in the United States Public Health Service at the National Institute of Dental Research of the National Institutes of Health, Bethesda, Maryland, 1967-69, as Research Associate. Career: Professor of Orthopaedic Surgery, Cornell University Medical School; Chief, Division of Orthopaedic Surgery, Memorial Sloan-Kettering Cancer Center; Chief, Metabolic Bone Disease Service, Hospital for Special Surgery. Organizational Memberships: New York Medical Society; American Academy of Orthopaedic Surgeons; Secretary, Committee of Educational Content, 1980 to present; President, Orthopaedic Research Society; Ewing's Surgical Oncology Society; National Institutes of Health, Musculoskeletal Study Section. Honors and Awards: Career Research Development Award, National Institutes of Health, 1977-82; Butz Frame Development Award, 1973-76; Resident Guest, American Orthopaedic Association, 1973; Carl Berg Travelling Fellowship, O.R.E.F., 1973; Kappa Delta Award, A.A.O.S., 1971; A.B. magna cum laude, Columbia University, 1961; Phi Beta Kappa, Columbia University, 1961; Charles Bjorkwall Prize, Columbia University, 1961. Address: 180 East End Avenue, New York, New York 10128.■

ANTON LANG

Professor Emeritus. Personal: Born January 18, 1913; Son of George Lang; Married Lydia Kamendrowsky; Father of Peter, Michael, Irene Lang Kleiman. Education: Attended Labes (Pomerania, then Germany) and Berlin (Germany) High Schools, Graduated 1932; Dr.Nat.Sci (Ph.D. equivalent), University of Berlin, 1939. Career: Visiting Professor, Department of Botany and Plant Sciences, University of California-Riverside; Professor Emeritus 1983 to present, Professor 1978-83, Director of Plant Research Laboratory (Michigan State University — Atomic Energy Commission) and Professor of Botany and Plant Pathology 1965-78, Michigan State University, East Lansing; Professor of Biology in Charge of Earhart-Campbell Plant Research Laboratories, California Institute of Technology, 1959-65; Assistant and Associate Professor, University of California-Los Angeles Department of Botany, 1952-59; Research Fellow and Senior Research Fellow, California Institute of Technology Division of Biology, Pasadena, 1950-52; Visiting Professor, Texas A. & M. College Department of Genetics, College Station, 1950; Research Associate, McGill University, Montreal, Quebec, Canada, 1949; Scientific Assistant, Kaiser Wilhelm (later Max Planck) Institute of Biology, Berlin (later Tubingen), Germany, 1939-49. Organizational Memberships: American Association for the Advancement of Science, Fellow, 1952 to present; American Society of Plant Physiologists, President 1970-71, Member 1953 to present; Society for Developmental Biology, President 1968-69, Member 1966 to present; German Botanical Society, 1955 to present; National Academy of Science National Research Council; Advisory Committee on the U.S.S.R. and Eastern Europe 1964-67, 1977-78; Committee on the Effects of Herbicides in Viet Nam Chairman 1971-75; National Science Foundation, Advisory Committee for Biology and Medicine, 1968-71; President's Committee on the National Medal of Science, 1976-79; Board of Trustees, Argonne Universities Association, 1965-71. Published Works: Editorial Board, *Encyclopedia of Plant Physiology* 1950-67, *Annual Review of Plant Physiology* 1958-62, *Plant Physiology* 1961-66, *American Journal of Botany* 1966-68; Consulting Editor, *Developmental Biology*, 1968-71; Co-Managing Editor, *Planta, An International Journal of Plant Biology*, 1967 to present; Board of Advisors, *Great Soviet Encyclopedia* American Edition, 1976-82. Honors and Awards: Senior Postdoctoral Fellowship, National Science Foundation, 1958; Leopoldina German Academy of Naturalists, Elected 1965; National Academy of Sciences, Elected 1967 (Chairman, Botany Section, 1983 to present); American Academy of Arts and Sciences, Elected 1968; Senior Scientist Award, Sigma Xi, Michigan State University Chapter, 1969; Honorary Vice President, XII International Botanical Congress, Leningrad, 1975; Distinguished Faculty Award, Michigan State University, 1976; Charles Reid Barnes Life Membership Award and Stephen Hales Prize, American Society of Plant Physiologists, 1976; Certificate of Merit, Botanical Society of America, 1979; Silver Medal, Massachusetts Horticultural Society, 1980; Honorary Doctor of Laws, University of Glasgow, United Kingdom, 1981; Honorary Member, German Botanical Society, 1983. Address: 1538 Cahill Drive, East Lansing, Michigan 48823.■

WALTER CONSUELO LANGSAM

University President Emeritus. Personal: Born January 2, 1906; Married Julia Elizabeth Stubblefield; Father of Walter Eaton, Geoffrey Hardinge. Education: B.S., City College of New York, 1925; M.A. 1926, Ph.D. 1930, Columbia University. Military: Office of Strategic Services 1944-45; Civilian Aide to Secretary of the Army, 1962-66; Chairman, Department of Army Historical Advisory Committee, 1968-72; Board of Consultants, National War College, 1972-76. Career: Columbia University, Instructor in History 1927-35, Assistant Professor of History 1935-38; Professor of History, Union College, 1938-45; President, Wagner College, 1945-52; President, Gettysburg College, 1952-55; President, University of Cincinnati, 1955-71; President Emeritus and Distinguished Service Professor, University of Cincinnati, 1971 to present. Organizational Memberships: North Central Association of Colleges and Secondary Schools Commission on Colleges and Universities, Member 1957-70, Executive Committee 1963-70, Vice Chairman 1966-68, Chairman 1968-70; Ohio College Association, President 1965-66. Community Activities: Endicott College (Beverly, Massachusetts), Trustee 1949 to present; Hamma School of Theology (Springfield, Ohio), Trustee 1967-70; University of Cincinnati Foundation, Trustee 1978 to present; Cincinnati Institute of Fine Arts, Trustee 1955 to present; Cincinnati Historical Society, Trustee 1972-82, Trustee Emeritus 1982 to present; Honorary Consul of Finland to Cincinnati, 1967-76; Cincinnati Branch, Federal Reserve Bank of Cleveland, Director 1961-66, Chairman of the Board 1964-66; Greater Cincinnati Chamber of Commerce, Board Member 1965-70, Senior Council Member 1972-76; Boy Scouts of America, Region Four Executive Committee 1965-70, East Central Region Advisory Council 1970-78, National Council 1967-75. Religion: Lutheran Church of America, Vice President of the Board of Theological Education, 1962-72. Published Works: Author of 14 Volumes of History. Honors and Awards: Townsend Harris Medal as Outstanding Alumnus, City College of New York, 1952; George Washington Honor Medal, Freedoms Foundation, 1956, 1958, 1973; Governor's Award for Outstanding Service to the State of Ohio, 1968; Silver Antelope Award, Boy Scouts of America, 1970; Outstanding Civilian Service Medal 1968, with Laurel Leaf Cluster 1971, with Second Laurel Leaf Cluster 1972, Department of Army; Commander's Cross, Order of Merit, West Germany, 1970; First Appreciation Medal, Wagner College, 1971; City College of New York's 125th Anniversary Medal, 1972; "Great Living Cincinnatian" Award, Greater Cincinnati Chamber of Commerce, 1972; Good Neighbor Award, Isaac M. Wise Temple, 1972; Silver Beaver, Boy Scouts of America, 1973; Americanism Medal, Daughters of the American Revolution, 1975; 12 Honorary Doctorate Degrees. Address: 1071 Celestial Street, Cincinnati, Ohio 45202.■

DEWEY FRANCIS LANGSTON

Professor, Graduate Coordinator. Personal: Born July 17, 1920; Married Dessie D. Rierson; Father of Jackie Frances, Judy Kaye. Education: Graduate of Wink High School, Wink, Texas, 1939; B.A., Eastern New Mexico University, 1943; M.Ed., Springfield College, Massachusetts, 1948; Director of Physical Education Degree, Indiana University, 1950; Doctor of Physical Education, Indiana University, 1951; Postdoctoral Studies, Stanford University, 1956. Military: Served in the New Mexico State Guard, 1942; Served in the United States Marine Corps Reserve, retiring as Captain in 1962 (wounded in Okinawa, 1945); United States Army Reserve, retiring as Lieutenant Colonel in 1971. Career: Graduate Assistant in History, Springfield College, 1946-47; Graduate Fellow, Physical Education, Indiana University, 1949-50; Assistant Professor, University of Arkansas, 1950-51; Assistant Professor of Physical Education, Eastern New Mexico University, 1951-53; Associate Professor of Physical Education, Eastern New Mexico University, 1953-57; Professor of Health and Physical Education, Eastern New Mexico, 1957 to present; Other Positions at Eastern New Mexico University include Head of Professional Education Program 1967-71, Varsity Track Coach 1951-56, Assistant Football Coach 1952-56, Chairman of the Division of Health, Physical Education and Recreation 1970-75; Director of Intercollegiate Athletics 1970-75, Assistant to the Dean of Admissions 1977-79, Affirmative Action Officer 1977-79, Professor and Graduate Coordinator, School of Health, Physical Education and Recreation 1979 to present; Instructor, Albuquerque United States Army Reserve and Other Military Schools, 1962-71. Organizational Memberships: New Mexico American Association of Health, Physical Education and Recreation, Chairman of Student Section 2 Years, Chairman of Honor Award 1961 and 1964, Representative to Southwest District Representative Assembly, Constitutional Revision Committee 1966-67, Chairman of College Section 1962-63, Vice President 1965-67, President 1967-68, Past Chairman of Research Section, President of N.M.C.Y.F. 2 Terms; Southwest District American Alliance of Health, Physical Education and Recreation, Chairman of Honors Awards 1958, Executive Committee, Honors Awards Committee 1959-71, Chairman of Professional Education Section 1961, Chairman of Boys' and Men's Athletic Section 1957, Chairman of Safety Section 1983; American Alliance of Health,

Physical Education and Recreation, Representative Assembly, Chairman of Safety Section 1963, College Physical Education Position Paper 1968-69, Safety Education Council 1969-70 and 1977-78, Graduate/Professional Preparation Committee 1966, Vice President A.S.C.S.A. 1977-78, President A.S.C.S.A. 1978-79, Board of Governors 1978-79, Chairman of Committee to Study National Convention 1978-79, Board of Directors A.S.C.S.A. 1968-74 and 1977-80. Community Activities: Chamber of Commerce of Roosevelt County; Portales Rotary Club, President, 1958-59; Rotary International, District Governor 1963-64; Roosevelt County Oral Vaccine Drive, Chairman 1957; Portales Armory Board, Chairman 1965-83; Roosevelt County United Fund, Board Member and General Fund Chairman 1968-74; Chairman of the Military Academy Review Board, Senator Schmidt, 1978-82. Religion: First Baptist Church (Portales, New Mexico), Member 1939 to present, Deacon 1976, Sunday School Teacher 1953-81. Published Works: Author of a Number of Professional Articles including "Sports on Stamps," "Do You Gamble in Physical Education?", "Postage Stamps That Save Lives" and "History of New Mexico on Postage Stamps"; Author, *Articles of Administration, District Policies and Procedures* for Rotary International, *Brief History of the Portales Rotary Club*. Honors and Awards: Military Decorations include Asiatic-Pacific Theatre, American Theatre, American Defense, WWII Victory, Occupation of Japan, China Defense, Purple Heart, Recommended for Silver Star; Phi Delta Kappa Service Key, 1964; Alpha Phi Omega Service Key, 1958; Paul Harris Award, Portales Rotary Club, 1976; Phi Delta Kappa Distinguished Service Award, 1973, 1978; Distinguished Service Award, Eastern New Mexico University, 1973; Phi Epsilon Kappa Honor Key, 1958; Sigma Delta Psi; Honor Award, Southwest District, American Alliance of Health, Physical Education and Recreation, 1968; Colonel Aide-de-Camp, Three Governors of New Mexico; Phi Kappa Phi; Professional Service Award, American School and Community Safety Association, 1980; Listed in *International Who's Who in Education, Personalities of America, International Who's Who of Intellectuals, Who's Who in the West, Who's Who in American Education, Who's Who in American Higher Education, Notable Americans, Dictionary of International Biography, National Social Directory, Book of Honor, Outstanding Educators of America, Personalities of the West and Midwest, Community Leaders of America, Men of Achievement, International Platform Association, Community Leaders and Noteworthy Americans, Notable Americans of the Bicentennial Era, American Society of Distinguished Citizens, Who's Who in Community Service*. Address: 1500 West 17th Lane, Portales, New Mexico 88130.■

GENE DANIEL LANIER

Professor of Library Science. Personal: Born March 13, 1934, in Conway, North Carolina; Son of Mrs. J. D. Lanier; Married Susan Roberts; Father of Leigh Katherine, Nicole McLean. Education: B.S., East Carolina University, 1955; M.S.L.S. 1957, Ph.D. 1968, University of North Carolina at Chapel Hill. Career: Teacher, Hillsborough (North Carolina) High School, 1956-57; Counterintelligence Specialist, Western Europe, 1957-59; East Carolina University, Assistant Librarian 1959-60, Head of the Acquisitions Department (Library) 1960-63, Associate Professor in the Department of Library Science 1963-64, Chairman and Professor of the Department of Library Science 1966-81, Professor 1981 to present; Visiting Professor, School of Library Science, University of North Carolina-Chapel Hill, Summer 1982; Part-time Instructor, School of Education, University of North Carolina-Chapel Hill, 1964-66. Organizational Memberships: American Library Association, White House Conference State Contact 1974-77; Southeastern Library Association, Committee on Librarianship as a Career 1969-71, Implementation Committee of Southeastern States Cooperative Library Survey 1974-76, Intellectual Freedom Committee 1983 to present; North Carolina Library Association, Education for Librarianship Committee Member 1965-66 and Chairman 1967-68, First Vice President 1971-73, President 1973-75, Chairman of Grievance Committee 1973-75, Executive Board 1975-77, Chairman of Nominating Committee 1978-79, Parliamentarian 1979, 1981, Chairman of Intellectual Freedom Committee 1980-84, Governmental Relations Committee 1980-82; North Carolina Learning Resources Association, Program Committee 1979-80, District II Director 1980-81; *North Carolina Libraries*, Director of Southeastern Student Manuscript Project, Editorial Board 1975-79; Association of American Library Schools; Alpha Beta Alpha; Phi Sigma Pi; Phi Delta Kappa; Beta Phi Mu; Greenville/Pitt County Media Society. Community Activities: Benevolent and Protective Order of the Elks, Lecturing Knight 1973-74; South Greenville Elementary School Parent-Teacher Association, Nominating Committee 1978-79. Religion: St. Paul's Episcopal Church; First Christian Church, Pastoral Oversight Committee 1971-73, Pulpit Committee 1974, Deacon 1976-79, Executive Board 1976-79, Music Committee 1978-79. Published Works: *The Library and Television: A Study of the Role of Television in Modern Library Service, The Transformation of School Libraries into Instructional Materials Centers*; Author of Articles, "Curricular Aids and the Materials Center," "The Textbook-Major Curriculum Problem," "Library Technical Assistants Bibliography," "A Bibliographical Primer to Intellectual Freedom." Honors and Awards: Hugh M. Hefner First Amendment Award in Education, Chicago, The Playboy Foundation, 1982; Mary Peacock Douglas Award, Winston-Salem, North Carolina, Association of School Librarians, 1982; American Library Association John Phillip Immroth Memorial Award in Intellectual Freedom, 1984; Listed in *Who's Who in Library Service, Who's Who in the South and Southwest, Biographical Directory of Librarians in the United States and Canada, Personalities of the South, International Scholars Directory, Men of Achievement, Adult and Community Education Directory, Notable Americans of 1976-77, Who's Who in Library and Information Services, Directory of Distinguished Americans*. Address: 526 Westchester Drive, Greenville, North Carolina 27834.■

WILLIAM JOSEPH LANNES, III

Electrical Engineer. Personal: Born October 12, 1937; Son of Mr. and Mrs. W. J. Lannes, Jr.; Married Patricia Anne Didier, Daughter of Mr. and Mrs. F. J. Didier; Father of David, Kenneth, Jennifer. Education: B.S.E.E., Tulane University, New Orleans, Louisiana, 1959; M.S.E.E., United States Naval Postgraduate School, Monterey, California, 1966; Registered Professional Engineer, State of Louisiana. Military: Served in the United States Marine Corps, 1959-70, advancing through the ranks from Second Lieutenant to Major, in Infantry and Communications-Electronics, Most Recently Operations Officer of Combined Action Group in Viet Nam. Career: Electrical Engineer; Director, Fifth District Savings and Loan Association, 1982 to present; Instructor of Electrical Engineering, University of New Orleans 1977-80, Delgado Junior College 1973-74. Organizational Memberships: Institute of Electrical and Electronics Engineers, Chairman New Orleans Section 1981-82, Vice-Chairman 1980-81, Secretary 1979-80, Director 1978-79, Seminar Chairman 1975-76, Student Activities Chairman 1973-74, Program Chairman 1977-78, Membership Chairman 1972-73; Society of Tulane Engineers, 1982 to present; Industry Advisor, E.P.R.I., 1980 to present; System and Equipment Committee, E.E.I., 1977 to present. Community Activities: Industry Advisory Board, Holy Cross College, New Orleans; Vice-Chairman, University of New Orleans Engineering Advisory Council, 1982-83; Committee, New Orleans Area Council, 1972-76; Volunteer, United Way, 1975, 1976, 1981; Treasurer, Parent-Teacher Association, 1971; Volunteer Coach, New Orleans Recreation Department, 1973; Louisiana Employees Committee on Political Action. Religion: Holy Spirit Church, Eucharist Lay Minister 1981 to present; Director of New Life, New Orleans Area, 1982; Volunteer Teacher, Confraternity of Christian Doctrine, 1972. Honors and Awards: Bronze Star with Combat 'V' for Service in Viet Nam, 1970; Cross of Gallantry, R.V.N., 1970; Outstanding Service Award, New Orleans Section Institute of Electrical and Electronics Engineers, 1976; Certificate of Merit, Mayor of New Orleans, 1964; Society of Sigma Xi, 1966; Eta Kappa Nu, 1977; Certificate of Appreciation for Participation in Exercises in Bangkok, Thailand, S.E.A.T.O., 1967; Letter of Appreciation 1962, Letter of Recognition 1960, United States Marine Corps; Listed in *Who's Who in the South and Southwest, Personalities of the South, Personalities of America, Men of Achievement*. Address: 7 Kings Canyon Drive, New Orleans, Louisiana 70114.■

JEFFREY LADD LANT

Writer and Management Consultant. Personal: Born February 16, 1947. Education: B.A. summa cum laude, University of California at Santa Barbara, 1969; M.A. 1970, Ph.D. 1975, Harvard University; Certificate of Advanced Graduate Studies in Higher Education Administration, Northeastern University, 1976. Career: President, Treasurer, Director, Jeffrey Lant Associates, Inc., 1979 to present; Assistant to President, Radcliffe College, Harvard University, 1978-79; Coordinator of Student Services, Boston College Evening College, 1976-78. Published Works: Author of *The Unabashed Self-Promoter's Guide: What Every Man, Woman, Child and Organization in America Needs to Know About Getting Ahead by Exploiting the Media* 1983, *The Consultant's Kit: Establishing and Operating Your Successful Consulting Business* 1981 (6th printing 1983), *Development Today: A Guide for Nonprofit Organizations* 1980 (revised second edition 1983), *Insubstantial Pageant: Ceremony and Confusion at Queen Victoria's Court* 1979 (United Kingdom edition) and 1980 (United States edition); Editor, *Our Harvard: Reflections on College Life by Twenty-Two Distinguished Americans*, 1982; General Editor, J.L.A. Nonprofit Technical Assistance Series; Featured in *Maverick: Succeeding as a Free-Lance Entrepreneur*, 1982; Author of More than 500 Articles. Honors and Awards: Official Citation, City of Cambridge, Massachusetts, 1983; Official Citation, Governor of Massachusetts, 1978, 1982; Official Citation, City of Boston, 1978; Official Citation, Massachusetts House of Representatives, 1978 and 1984; Harvard College Master's Award, 1975; Woodrow Wilson Fellow, 1969; Harvard Prize Fellow, 1969; Harvard Traveling Fellow, 1972-73; Listed in *Who's Who in the East, Book of Honor, Who's Who in Business and Finance, International Who's Who of Intellectuals, Men and Women of Distinction*. Address: 50 Follen Street, Suite 507, Cambridge, Massachusetts 02138.■

TWO THOUSAND NOTABLE AMERICANS

GERTIE MAE LARKIN

Registered Nurse. Personal: Born October 1, 1930, in Tipton, Oklahoma; Daughter of Urbane Aaron Sr. (deceased) and Willie Mae Linkous; Married William Clayton Larkin, Jr. (deceased 1970), Son of William Clayton Larkin, Sr. (deceased) and Ethel Maurine Jackson, on August 14, 1949; Mother of Sue Ann. Education: Graduate, Temple (Texas) High School, 1947; Temporary Teaching Certificate 1949, B.S.N. Studies 1970, Temple Junior College, 1949; Temporary Teaching Certificate, Hampton, Virginia, 1952; B.S.N., University of Mary Hardin-Baylor, Belton, Texas, 1975; Postgraduate Study, Texas Woman's University, Temple Campus, Texas, 1975-78. Career: Charge Nurse of Three to Eleven Shift and Registered Nurse, Cameron Community Hospital, Texas, 1980 to present; Staff Nurse, Santa Fe Memorial Hospital, Temple, Texas, 1976-80; Private Secretary, First National Bank of Temple, 1956-58; First Grade Teacher, Sinclair Elementary School, 1954-55; EKG Technician, Scott and White Memorial Hospital, 1951-52. Organizational Memberships: American Nursing Association; Texas Nursing Association; District 7 Nursing Association; Scott and White Memorial Hospital School of Nursing Alumnae Association. Community Activities: Volunteer Worker with Such Groups as Harvest House (senior citizens center), Parent-Teacher Association, Brownie Scout Troop (organizer 1966), 1958-70; Room Mother, Vandiver Elementary School, 1964-70; Annual Associate Member 1982 to present, Contributing Member to National Board of Advisors 1982 to present, American Biographical Institute. Religion: First Baptist Church, Temple, Texas, Attended since 1939; Baptized 1943, Sunday School Teacher 1958-60, Superintendent of 3-Year-Old Class 1960-73, Vacation Bible School Teacher, Visitor to Non-Christian Families with Small Children; Attended Glorieta Baptist Assembly to Learn to Teach Other Adults to Work with Toddlers and 3-Year-Olds, New Mexico, Summers 1960 and 1965. Honors and Awards: Listed in *Who's Who of American Women, World Who's Who of Women, Who's Who in the South and Southwest, Personalities of America, Directory of Distinguished Americans, Personalities of the South, Community Leaders of America, Book of Honor,* Address: 3716 Robinhood Drive, Temple, Texas 17502. ■

LAWRENCE LA ROCCO

Tool and Die Maker and Automated Machine Builder. Personal: Born April 18, 1926; Son of Joseph and Frances LaRocco (deceased); Married Jeanne C., Daughter of Jennie Lullo (deceased); Father of Linda Jacevich, Joseph, Sandra Shultz, Tom. Military: Served in the United States Army, 1944-46. Career: Tool and Die Maker, Catalina Tool and Mold (Tucson, Arizona) 1983 to present, D. Gottlieb Company (North Lake and Rockford, Illinois) 1974 to present; Automated Machine Builder; Tool Maker for Aircraft Missiles Division, Howard Hughes Aircraft Company, Tucson, Arizona, 1951-64; Owner, Job Shop, Addison, Illinois. Community Activities: Harlem and Winsor School Special Olympics, 1981-82; Special Education Volunteer with Donations and Machines, 198-82. Religion: Christian. Honors and Awards: Holder of Two Patents for Super Wee Block; Listed in *Who's Who in the Midwest, Who's Who in Technology Today, Personalities of America.* Address: 6230 South Country Club, Tucson, Arizona 85706. ■

CARL JACOB LARSON

Financial Consultant, Genealogist, Translator of Swedish. Personal: Born January 31, 1913; Son of Mr. and Mrs. Peter Larson (both deceased); Married Eva Lorene Anderson, Daughter of Mr. and Mrs. David P. Anderson (both deceased). Education: Accounting-Finance Diploma, Bay Path Institute, Springfield, Massachusetts, 1932; LL.B., Northeastern University School of Law, 1942; Graduate Studies at University of Missouri and University of Dayton. Military: Served in the Massachusetts National Guard, 104th Infantry, 1930-40, attaining the rank of Second Lieutenant; Served in the Massachusetts State Guard, 1941-46, attaining the rank of Major (retired). Career: Financial Consultant; Genealogist; Translator of Swedish; Appointments include Chief Auditor 1962-64 and Chief Plant Accountant 1964-66 and Contractor Audits Supervisor 1966-78 for Monsanto Research Corporation (Miamisburg, Ohio). Organizational Memberships: National Association of Accountants, Member 1950 to present, Vice-President of St. Louis Chapter 1960-62, Emeritus Life Member; American Accounting Association, Member 1950 to present, Emeritus Life Member. Community Activities: Consultant on Financial Matters for Local Social Service Agency; Trustee, Far Hills Temple Association, 1974 to present; Assistant in Organizing Massachusetts State Guard, 1941; Rock Moriah Lodge #740, Free and Accepted Masons, Centerville, Ohio; Scottish Rite, 32° Mason; Antioch Temple Shrine, Dayton, Ohio. Religion: Southminster Presbyterian Church, Centerville, Ohio, Member 1963 to present, Treasurer of Building Fund. Honors and Awards: Achievement Awards for Meritorious Service, Instituting Cost Savings and Procedure Manuals, Monsanto Company. Address: 248 Napoleon Drive, Kettering, Ohio 45429. ■

VERA ORAVEC LASKA

Professor, Author, Lecturer, Columnist. Personal: Born July 21, 1928; Married Andrew J. Laska; Mother of Thomas Vaclav, Paul Andrew. Education: M.A. Philosophy, M.A. History, Charles University, Prague; Ph.D. American History, University of Chicago, 1959. Career: Professor of History, Regis College; Author; Lecturer; Columnist; Foreign Student Counselor, University of Chicago, 1954-59; Consultant, Institute of International Education, New York, 1964-66; Fulbright Committee, Evaluator, Sao Paulo, Brazil, 1960-64. Organizational Memberships: American History Association; National Association of Foreign Student Affairs; Pan American Society; Czechoslovak Society of Arts and Sciences in America; New England History Teachers Association; Others. Community Activities: Advisory Board, Massachusetts Bicentennial Commission; Weston Bicentennial Commission; Weston Historical Commission; Weston Library Trustee; Lecturer on Queen Elisabeth 2, Royal Viking Line Ships, to Church, Historical and Women's Organizations. Published Works: Author of Over 100 Articles in Her Own Column in Local Newspapers and Book Reviews in Professional Journals; Author, "Remember the Ladies" in *Outstanding Women of American Revolution* 1976, *Czechs in America, 1633-1977* 1978, *Franklin and Women* 1979, *Benjamin Franklin, Diplomat* 1982, *Women in the Resistance and Holocaust* 1983, *Nazism, Resistance & Holocaust in World War II: A Bibliography* 1984. Honors and Awards: Masaryk Scholar, 1945, 1946; Outstanding Educator of America, 1972; Institute of International Education Fellow, 1947; International House Fellow, University of Chicago, 1948, 1949; National Endowment for the Humanities Grantee, 1974; Kidger Service Award in History, 1984. Address: 50 Woodchester Drive, Weston, Massachusetts 02193. ■

AGNES DOLORES LATTIMER

Pediatrician. Personal: Born May 13, 1928; Daughter of Hortense Lattimer; Married Frank Daniel Bethel; Mother of Bernard Cassell Goss. Education: Graduate, Booker T. Washington High School, Memphis, Tennessee, 1945; A.B., Fisk University, Nashville, 1949; M.D., The Chicago Medical School, Chicago, 1954; Intern, Cook County Hospital, Chicago, 1954-56; Resident, Pediatrics, Michael Reese Hospital, Chicago, 1956-58. Career: Pediatrician. Organizational Memberships: National Board of Medical Examiners, Diplomate; Ambulatory Pediatric Association; American Association for the Advancement of Science; American Institute of Hypnosis; Chicago Pediatric Society; American Academy of Pediatrics, Fellow, Secretary/Treasurer, President-Elect 1980-81, President of Illinois Chapter 1983-86; International College of Applied Nutrition, Fellow. Community Activities: Chicago Committee Against Lead Poisoning; Medical Consultant, Region V, Job Corps. Honors and Awards: Professor of the Year, The Chicago Medical School, 1968; Distinguished Alumnus Award, Chicago Medical School Alumni Association, 1971; Elected Membership to Alpha Gamma Pi Honorary Sorority for Excellence in Community Service, 1969; Image Award, League of Black Women, 1974; Listed in *Men and Women of Distinction, International Register of Profiles, World Who's Who of Women, Book of Honor, Who's Who of American Women.* Address: 2138 East 75th Street, Chicago, Illinois 60649. ■

DONALD PAUL LAUDA

Dean of University School of Technology. Personal: Born August 7, 1937; Son of Libbie Lauda; Married Sheila H., Daughter of Monica Henderson; Father of Thomas, Daren, Tanya. Education: B.A.E. 1963, M.S. 1964, Wayne State College; Ph.D., Iowa State University, 1966. Military: Served in the United

States Army, 1957-59, attaining the rank of Specialist 5. Career: Dean, Eastern Illinois University School of Technology; Former Positions include Time and Motion Study Engineer, University Faculty Member, Associate Director of Communications Center of the University of Hawaii. Organizational Memberships: A.C.I.A.T.E., Vice President; American Institute of Aeronautics and Astronautics; World Future Society; A.V.A.; I.I.E.A.; Epsilon Pi Tau. Community Activities: Board Member and Chairman of Vocational Committee, Rotary; Chairman of Accreditation (Organization) Committee and Director of Charleston 2000 Futures Project, Chamber of Commerce; Membership Committee, Tarble Arts Center; Task Force on Illinois 2000, Illinois State Chamber of Commerce. Honors and Awards: Industrial Teacher Educator of the Year, American Council for Industrial Arts Teacher Education, 1979; Laureate Citation, Epsilon Pi Tau, 1982; Postdoctoral Fellow, West Virginia University, 1969-70. ■

JUAN A. LAUREANO-COLON

Executive Director and Founder. Personal: Born December 11, 1946; Son of Juan and Dolores C. Laureano; Married Ana L. Sánchez, Daughter of José and Francisca Sanchez; Father of Enid, Viviana Janetza, Rosa Isela, José Antonio, Milagros Grisselle, Nancy, Yajaira. Education: A.A., Kansas Community College, 1977; B.S., Kansas Newman College, 1979; B.Min., International Bible Institute and Seminary, 1979; M.Th., International Bible Institute and Seminary, 1982; Bachelor of Management, Columbia Pacific University, 1983; D.D. (honoris causa), Church of Gospel Ministry, 1983. Military: Served in the United States Army, 1964-80, attaining the rank of Staff Sergeant. Career: Executive Director and Founder, The Christian Homes and Centers of Puerto Rico and Latin America, Inc. (offering free assistance and care for the elderly, orphans, alcoholics, drug addicts, and runaways, and ministry for prison inmates), 1980 to present. Organizational Memberships: Biblical Archeology Society; Smithsonian Institution; American Association for the Advancement of Science; Alumni Association of International Bible Institute and Seminary; Latin Studies. Community Activities: Lions Club; Jaycees. Religion: Interdenominational Christian. Honors and Awards: Decorated with Silver Star Medal, Bronze Star Medal, Air Medal, Army Commendation Medal, Republic of Viet Nam Gallantry Cross, Good Conduct Medal (4th Award), Purple Heart, The Republic of Viet Nam Civic Actions Honor Medal, Presidential Unit Citation, Meritious Unit Emblem, National Defense Medal, Viet Nam Service Medal, and Republic of Viet Nam Campaign Ribbon, United States Army. Address: Urb. Jard. de San Lorenzo, 2, A-15, San Lorenzo, Puerto Rico 00754. ■

ANTHONY JOSEPH LAUS

Educator. Personal: Born February 27, 1922; Son of Michael Laus and Mary Dileo; Married Lillian Marlene Peck; Father of Joseph, Thomas, Therese, Mary, John, Barbara, Paul, Michael, Christine. Education: B.S. Industrial and Vocational Mathematics, M.A. Secondary School Administration, University of San Francisco; Graduate Study in Mathematics at Villanova University, Psychological Testing at Duquesne University, Philosophy and Education at University of Pittsburgh, Aviation Science at San Mateo College, Engineering Materials at Stevens Institute, Engineering at Pennsylvania Military College. Military: Served in Army Air Force as Air Cadet. Career: Teacher of Mathematics and Engineering, Foothill College District; Former Positions Include Junior High and Senior High School Teacher; Senior Manufacturing Engineer, Lockheed Missile Corporation; Chairman, Engineering Division, San Jose College; Mathematics and Industrial Teacher, Pennsylvania State College; Teacher of Engineering Graphics, University of Delaware; Teacher of Engineering, Pennsylvania State University. Organizational Memberships: Member of Engineering, Vocational, and Industrial Associations. Community Activities: Right to Life; Boy Scouts of America; Right to Work. Religion: Teacher of Religion. Published Works: Author of *Descriptive Geometry, Spatial Relationship, Transition and Development of Surfaces.* Honors and Awards: Grants from National Science Foundation to Study Engineering Graphics at University of California, Engineering Materials at Stevens Institute and Graduate Mathematics at San Jose University. Address: 617 Oak Drive, Capitola, California 95010. ■

S. KENT LAUSON

Orthodontist, Real Estate Syndicator and Renovator. Personal: Born February 16, 1945; Son of Spencer and Marjorie Lauson. Education: Pre-Dental Studies, University of Wyoming, 1963-67; D.D.S., University of Iowa, 1971; Certificate in Periodontics, Wilford Medical Center, United States Air Force, 1972; M.S. Orthodontics, St. Louis University Medical Center, 1975. Military: Served in the United States Dental Corps, 1971-73, attaining the rank of Captain. Career: Orthodontist; Former Chief Executive Officer of Renewable Energy Company and Magazine Publisher. Organizational Memberships: Denver Investors Group; Colorado Apartment Association; Rocky Mountain Dental Study Group; Metropolitan Denver Dental Society; Colorado Dental Association; American Dental Association; American Association of Orthodontics; Orthodontic Research Foundation. Community Activities: American Cancer Society, Metro Denver Dental Committee 1978-79; Guest Lecturer, University of Colorado Dental School, 1977. Religion: Instructor, "I Can" Course, Mile Hi Church of Religious Science, 1983; Associate Degree in Religious Science, 1981. Honors and Awards: Certificate of Recognition, Colorado Department of Health, 1980; Honorary Alumnus, University of Colorado Dental School; Distinguished Alumni, Billings Senior High School National Belimi Award Ceremonies, 1977; Vocational Educational Award, Columbine High School, 1980; Certificate of Appreciation, Metro Denver Dental Society, 1977; Number of State and Local Tennis Championships, 1960-75; Listed in Eleven Biographical Reference Works. Address: 4282 B South Fairplay Circle, Aurora, California 80014. ■

KATHRYN HYDE LAUTERBACH

School Administrator. Personal: Born March 30, 1944; Daughter of Henry S. and Wilma H. Lauterbach. Education: Attended Rollins College 1962-64, Ambassador University Seven Seas 1965-66; B.S., Southern Connecticut State College, 1970; M.A. with honors, Fairfield University, 1972. Career: President, Executive Director, Chairman of the Board, Model Program for Learning Disabled Adolescents, Newbrook Academy, 1979 to present; Co-Author of Title III Grant for Model for Pre-School Handicapped Children, 1976-78; Special Education Teacher, Newtown Middle School 1973-76, Danbury (Connecticut) 1972-73. Organizational Memberships: Danbury Association to Aid the Handicapped and Retarded, 1978-80; Co-Chapter Founder, Council for Exceptional Children, Danbury, Connecticut, 1973; Council of Administrators of Special Education; Association for Supervision and Curriculum Development; Parent Advocate, 1979 to present. Honors and Awards: Students' Teacher of the Year Award, 1976, 1979. Address: Hydeaway, Bethel, Connecticut 06801. ■

EULA MAE TAYLOR LAVENDER

Real Estate Agent, Blueprint Maker, Artist and Artisan. Personal: Born April 14, 1923; Daughter of John Randolph and Ida Oma Marlowe Taylor (both deceased); Married First Husband (deceased 1958), in 1939; Married Second Husband Howard H. Lavender, 1964; Mother of William Randolph Morris, Gerald Lee Morris, David Andrew Morris (deceased 1982), H. Taylor Morris (deceased). Education: Attended Black Mountain High School, 2 Years. Career: Real Estate Agent; Blueprint Maker; Artist; Master Artisan of Afghans, Quilts, Rock Crafts, and Other Items (confined to wheelchair since 1976 with arthritis and non-articular rhumatism), Sold in United States, Japan, Canada, Mexico, Brazil, Taiwan, Republic of China, England, Khartoum, the Sudan, and Kenya; Producer of 49 Full-Sized Afghans, Three Bedspreads (one queen-sized), Six Capes, 26 Vests, 400 Doll Dresses and Hats, 6 Pairs Bedroom Shoes, and 3 pairs Baby Bootees in One Year; Opened Craftshop "Handcrafts by Lavender" in Her Home, 1979; Exhibitions of Craftwork throughout United States; Former Positions include Cafeteria Cook, Electronics Worker at Kearfott and at C. P. Clare, Census Enumerator, Seamstress and Tailor, Farmer, Carpenter, Mason, Electrian, Plumber, Dry Wall Finisher, Painter, Molasses Maker, Landscaper. Community Activities: Instrumental in Organizing Church of Her Faith in West Palm Beach, Florida, 1956. Religion: Sunday School Teacher, 30 Years; Singer, Pianist and Guitarist, Gospel Groups; President, P.H.Y.S. Honors and Awards: Ribbons and Honors for Afghans. Address: 1930 Highway 9, Black Mountain, North Carolina 28711. ■

DANIEL EDWARD LEACH

Attorney. Personal: Born April 2, 1937; Son of Mr. and Mrs. Vincent G. Leach; Married Jean Carter, Daughter of Dr. and Mrs. Leland F. Carter; Father of Robin Ann, Jennifer, Carter Vincent. Education: A.B., Colgate University, 1958; LL.B., Univerity of Detroit, 1961; LL.M., Georgetown University, 1963. Career: Partner in Law Firm; Former Positions include United States Department of Justice, Private Practice, and General Counsel (Presidential appointee) and Vice-Chairman of Federal Committee for the United States Senate Committee. Organizational Memberships: American Bar Association, Committee Co-

TWO THOUSAND NOTABLE AMERICANS

Chairman 1981; Maritime Law Association; National Lawyers Club; University Club. Community Activities: Presidential Appointee, National Commission on Employment Policy 1977-81, Administrative Conference of the United States 1977-81, President's Task Force on Youth Unemployment 1977-81; Delegate, Conference on Security and Cooperation in Europe, Madrid, Spain, 1980-81. Religion: Episcopal Church, Active Member and Committee Member. Honors and Awards: Various Awards and Citations for Government Service including Keys to Cities and Honors from Public Service Organizations and Busisness Groups, 1976-81. Address: 3419 Woodside Road, Alexandria, Virginia 22310.■

PRESTON HILDEBRAND LEAKE

Assistant Research and Development Director. Personal: Born August 8, 1929; Son of Perry H. (deceased) and Lydia C. Leake; Married Elizabeth Ann Kelly, Daughter of Mr. and Mrs. Paul Kelly; Father of Luther, Lawrence. Education: B.S., University of Virginia, 1950; M.A. 1953, Ph.D. 1954, Duke University. Career: Assistant Research and Development Director, Former Assistant Managing Director and Assistant to Managing Director, The American Tobacco Company; Former Positions include Assistant Research and Development Director for Albemarle Paper Company and Research Supervisor for Allied Chemical Corporation. Organizational Memberships: American Chemical Society, Chemical Health and Safety Division, Chemistry and the Law Division; American Institute of Chemists, Chairman of Virginia Chapter 1962, National Council Representative 1962-64; Technical Association of Pulp and Paper, Program Chairman of Virginia-Carolina Chapter 1963; Virginia Academy of Science, 1965 to present; American Chemical Society Virginia Section, Chairman of Radio and Television Committee 1964, Chairman of Publications Board 1965, Treasurer 1966, Secretary 1967, Vice-Chairman 1968, Chairman-Elect 1969, Program Chairman for Southeastern Regional Meeting 1969, Chairman 1970, Chairman of Nominating Committee 1971, Executive Committee 1971 to present, Alternate Councilor 1975-76, Councilor 1976 to present, Membership Affairs Committee Member 1976 to present and Member of Subcommittees 1977-79, Board of Trustees for Group Insurance Plans for Members 1979-82, Congressional Science Counselor to Dan Daniel (Representative 5th District, Virginia) 1974 to present, Member of Professional Relations Division, Chemical Information Division, Agricultural and Food Chemistry Division, Pesticide Chemistry Division, Chairman of Local Arrangements Committee and "Chemical, Physical and Production Aspects of Tobacco and Smoke" Symposium Chairman for Tobacco Chemists Research Conference (Richmond, Virginia) 1980. Community Activities: Chairman, Parent-Teacher Association, 1968-69; Chesterfield County School Advisory Committee, 1969-70; Ruritan Club; Chairman of Library Board, Chesterfield County, 1974-77. Honors and Awards: Sigma Xi, 1950; Phi Lambda Upsilon, 1954; Selected by Executive Vice-President to Participate in 3-Week Technical People-to-People Tour to London, Oslo, Leningrad, Moscow, Prague, Berlin and Frankfurt, American Chemical Society, 1971; Distingiushed Service Award, American Chemical Society Virginia Section, 1976. Address: 5400 Tomahawk Drive, Midlothian, Virginia 23113.■

JAMES MICHAEL LEARNARD

Insurance Agent. Personal: Born June 13, 1947, in Worcester, Massachusetts; Son of James F. Learnard and Katherine Learnard; Father of Sean Patrick. Education: Graduate, Terry Parker High School, 1966; A.A., Florida Junior College, 1968; Attended University of Florida at Gainesville 1969-70, University of North Florida 1973. Career: Insurance Agent, United Insurance Company of America, 1982 to present; Agent, V. P. National Auto Finance Corporation (Aiken, South Carolina), 1976-81; Correctional Officer, South Carolina Department of Corrections, 1975-76; Credit Collector, 1973-75; Epidemiologist, United States Department of Health, Center for Disease Control, 1972. Community Activities: Assistant Scoutmaster and Assistant Explorer Post Advisor, Boy Scouts of America, Jacksonville, Florida, 1966-70; Cub Scout Den Leader, Aiken, South Carolina, 1980-81; Umpire, Aiken Dixie Youth Baseball, 1983; Sponsor of Little League Baseball Team, 1983; Patron, Rose Hill Art Center, Aiken, South Carolina, 1981-83; Patron, Aiken Choral Society, Aiken, South Carolina, 1981-83. Religion: Roman Catholic; Knights of Columbus (4th degree), Aiken, South Carolina, 1978 to present. Published Works: Over 40 Poems in Print, Composer of Eight Songs, Six of Which Appear on His Album "Love Songs" (1983); Contributor of Poetry to Major Anthologies such as *A Time to Be Free* 1982, *Our Twentieth Century's Greatest Poems* 1982, *Contemporary Poets of America* 1982 and 1983, *P.S. I Love You* 1982, *Earth Shine* 1983, *New Poets Two* 1983. Honors and Awards: Poem "Epcot 1982" on Display at Walt Disney World, Orlando, Florida; Eagle Scout with Bronze Palm 1963, Outstanding Scout 1963, Boy Scouts of America; Listed in *Personalities of the South, Biographical Roll of Honor, Directory of Distinguished Americans, Personalities of America, Five Thousand Personalities of the World*. Address: Route 1 Box 117, Green Street, Graniteville, South Carolina 29829.■

PEGGY JEAN LEDBETTER

Dean of College of Nursing. Personal: Born January 3, 1939; Daughter of Rev. and Mrs. Smith Ledbetter. Education: Diploma Degree in Nursing, Baptist Hospital, Birmingham, Alabama, 1960; B.S., Samford University, Birmingham, Alabama, 1961; B.S.N., University of Alabama at Tuscaloosa, 1962; M.S.N., 1964; Ed.D., 1968. Career: Dean of College of Nursing; Psychiatric Nursing Instructor, University of Alabama, 1966-68; Assistant Professor of Medical-Surgical Nursing, University of Mississippi, 1964-66; Nurse Consultant on Chronic Disease and Aging Program, Alabama State Health Department, 1962-63; Staff Nurse, Birmingham Baptist Hospital, 1960-61. Organizational Memberships: Council of Nurse Researchers, American Nurses Association; National League for Nursing; Fellow, American Association of Colleges of Nursing; Fellow, Royal Society of Health; American Association for Higher Education; American Association of University Administrators; Sigma Theta Tau, Beta Chi Chapter. Community Activities: Shreveport Chamber of Commerce, Military Affairs Committee, 1974-78; Legislative Task Force Committee, 1979 to present; Air Force Association, 1975 to present; Upjohn Health Care Services, Committee Member, 1980; Southern University-Shreveport's Health Occupation Advisory Committee, 1980 to present; Shreveport Society for Nature Study, 1982 to present; Shreveport Regional Arts Council, 1981 to present; Shreveport Community Concert Association, 1982 to present; Shreveport Symphony, 1981 to present; Patron, Shreveport Little Theatre, 1980 to present; Patron, Shreveport Opera, 1981. Religion: Kelley Memorial Baptist Church, Personnel Committee. Honors and Awards: Secretary of Defense Appointment, Defense Advisory Committee on Women in the Service, 1972-74; Nurse Consultant 1976-80 and Emeritus 1980 to the Surgeon General of the United States Air Force; Louisiana State Board of Nurse Examiners, Gubernatorial Appointment 1971-74, President 1972-73; Nurse Member of Adivsory Board of Louisiana Department of Health and Human Resources; Gubernatorial Appointment, 1973 to present; Certificate in Recognition of Consistent and Devoted Service in Assisting the United States Air Force Recruiting Service and in Appreciation of Conscientious Efforts towards the Advancement of Peace through Air Power, Colonel William E. Reid (United States Air Force Commander), 1970. Address: P.O. Box 36974, Shreveport, Louisiana 71103.■

JAMES WIDNER LEE

Senior Group Supervisor of Advanced Design. Personal: Born November 9, 1935; Son of Robert E. and Pearlie M. Lee; Married Ola Ann, Daughter of George O. and Annie L. Sims; Father of James Edward, David Alan, Gary Richard. Education: Bachelor of Aeronautical Engineering, Auburn University, 1957; Graduate Study (Certificate) in Archaeology, University of Alabama, 1979-82. Career: Senior Group Supervisor, Advanced Design (rocket propulsion), Morton Thiokol, Inc. Organizational Memberships: Associate Fellow, Administrative Chairman A.I.A.A. Aerospace Sciences Meeting 1978, Chairman of Solid Rocket Session A.I.A.A./S.A.E./A.S.M.E. 18th Joint Propulsion Conference 1982, Solid Rocket Technical Committee 1980-82, Various Alabama/Mississippi Section Offices 1958 to present including Chairman 1971-72 and Advisory Board 1972-74, American Institute of Aeronautics and Astronautics; Joint Army, Navy, N.A.S.A., Air Force Ramjet Subcommittee, 1968 to present; Various Offices including President 1977-78 and Board of Directors 1975-79, Huntsville Association of Technical Societies; President, Thiokol Management Club, 1969; Registered Professional Engineer, Alabama. Community Activities: President 1984, Huntsville Chapter President 1981, Alabama Archaeological Society; President, Huntsville Athletic Booster Council, 1980-81; President, Huntsville High School Football Booster Club, 1980; President, Huntsville High School Wrestling Booster Club, 1978-79; Vice-President, Whitesburg Middle School Booster Club, 1976-77; Treasurer, Greenwyche Club (Recreational Association), 1976; President, Huntsville International Little, League, 1974-75; Committee Chairman, Boy Scouts of America, 1967-71; Pi Kappa Alpha Fraternity. Religion: Baptist Church. Honors and Awards: Martin Schilling Award for Outstanding Services to Alabama Section, American Institute of Aeronautics and Astronautics, 1960. Address: 1004 Appalachee Road, Huntsville, Alabama 35801.■

TWO THOUSAND NOTABLE AMERICANS

PAUL PO LO LEE

Tour Agency Executive. Personal: Born April 18, 1919; Son of Kuo Yuien and Lee Wu Mei Lan; Married Nancy Chan Wang, Daughter of W. C. Wang and Wang Bob Chu; Father of Spencer B., Linda W. C., Edsion B. C., Lanna W. C. Education: Graduate, Nanking University 1936, Chinese Military Academy. Career: President, Golden Horse Tours Inc., Stellar Tour Inc., 1979 to present; Manager, C.C.L.G. Travel Inc., New York City, 1978; Representative of Taiwan, Young Star Enterprise (U.S.A.) Inc.; Manager, Hong Kong Uzion International Ltd., Hong Kong; Manager, Yu Fong Trading Company, 1967-71; Manager, Sky Sea Travel and Trading Company, Ltd, Hong Kong, 1962-66; Manager, United China Cinema Enterprises Inc., 1959-62; Association Manager, Columbia Films of China Ltd., 1959-62. Organizational Memberships: Director, American Overseas Chinese Import-Export Association, 1977; Chairman, Chinese Military Academy Alumni Association in U.S.A., 1981; World Chinese Tourism Amity Conference Representative of New York, U.S.A.; World Chinese Traders Convention, Advisor; Asian American Affairs Study Association, Advisor. Community Activities: Republican Party; Charter Member, Republican President's Task Force; Board, New York City China Town Community Club Chairman, Asian American Republican National Federation; New York Lee Family Association, Director, 1979. Honors and Awards: Victory Medal, Chinese Army, 1945; Award, American Oversea Chinese Import-Export Association, 1978. Address: 25 Woodruff Avenue, Brooklyn, New York 11226.■

SIDNEY PHILLIP LEE

Senator of the United States Virgin Islands. Personal: Born April 20, 1920; Son of Samuel and Mollie Lee (deceased); Father of Phillip (Skipper), Candy. Education: Attended Wenonah Academy, 1931-35; B.S. Chemical Engineering, University of Pennsylvania, 1939; M.S. Chemical Engineering, Cornell University, 1940. Career: Senator of the United States Virgin Islands, Democratic House and Senate Council, 1979 to present; Chairman, Associated Dallas Laboratories, Dallas, Texas, 1940 to present; President, West Indies Investment Company, St. Croix, 1955 to present; Director and Executive Committee Member, American Shipbuilding, 1939-42; Senior Chemical Engineer, Atlantic Richfield, 1939-42. Organizational Memberships: Democratic National Committee Committee, 1970-76. Community Activities: Virgin Islands State Board of Education, 1970-76; President, Rotary Club Virgin Islands; Board of Directors, St. Croix Country Day School; Board of Directors, Good Hope School; Chairman, First Israel Bond Drive J.W.F., Dallas, Texas; Founding President, Jewish Community of St. Croix; Board of Directors, Temple Emmanuel, Dallas, Texas; President, Dallas Junior Chamber of Commerce; President, Dallas Lions Club. Honors and Awards: Tau Beta Pi; Sigma Xi; Mullin Fellow and Westinghouse Research Grant, 1940-43; Man of the Year, Builders and Contractors Association of St. Croix; One of Five Outstanding Young Texans, Texas Junior Chamber of Commerce; One of Ten Outstanding Young Men of America, 1951. Address: Chateau Pierre, Christiansted, St. Croix, United States Virgin Islands.■

WILLIAM JOHNSON LEE

Attorney and Administrator. Personal: Born January 13, 1924; Son of William J. Sr. (deceased) and Arah A. Lee; Married Marjorie Young, Daughter of Niles E. and Rosina Young (both deceased), on August 20, 1949; Father of David William, James Alan. Education: Attended Akron University, Denison University, Harvard University Graduate School and Ohio State University Law School; Admitted to Bar, State of Florida, 1962. Military: Served in the United States Army Air Corps, 1943-46, in the 28th Combat Weather Squadron. Career: Administrator, State Medical Board of Ohio, 1970 to present; Assistant Attorney General, Office of the Attorney General, State of Ohio, 1966-70; Private Practice of Law, Fort Lauderdale, Florida, 1965-66; Special Counsel, City Attorney's Office, Fort Lauderdale, Florida, 1963-65; Employed by Papy and Carruthers Law Firm, 1962-63; Lawyer in General Practice, 1959-62; Part-time Instructor, College of Business Administration, Kent State University, 1961-62; Assistant Counsel on Staff of Hupp Corporation, 1957-58; Ohio's Assistant State Liquor Control Director and Chief of Liquor Purchases, 1951-57; Mathematical, Pre-Meteorological and Electrical Engineering Education and Experience, United States Air Force; Research Assistant, Ohio State University Law School, 1948-49. Organizational Memberships: Broward County Bar Association; Akron Bar Association; Columbus Bar Association; American Legion; Pi Kappa Delta Honorary Forensic; Delta Theta Phi Legal Fraternity; Appointee, Federation of State Medical Board's National Commission for the Evaluation of Foreign Medical Schools. Religion: Church of the Messiah United Methodist Church, Westerville, Ohio; Melrose Park Methodist Church, Melrose Park, Florida, Church Board, Boy Scout Award Chairman for Church Troop 1963-65; Epworth Methodist Church, Columbus, Ohio, Pastoral Relations Committee, 1976. Honors and Awards: Listed in *Who is Who in Ohio, Who's Who in Health Care, Who's Who in American Law, Who's Who in the Midwest, Dictionary of International Biography, Men of Achievement, International Register of Profiles, International Who's Who of Intellectuals.* Address: 4893 Brittany Court West, Columbus, Ohio 43229.■

WILLIS LEGRAND LEE

Physicist and Executive. Personal: Born April 9, 1923, in Salt Lake City, Utah; Son of Benjamin Franklin and Edith Amelia Lindsay Lee; Married Jane Grace Olson, Daughter of Isabel M. Olson, on June 10, 1945; Father of Karen Jane Lee Smith, David Allen, Isabel Ann Lee Irwin, Willis LeGrand, Brenda Kay Lee Hall. Education: B.S. Physics 1950, M.S. Physics 1951, University of Utah; Ph.D. Electrical Engineering 1977, D.Sc. Physics 1978, Kensington University. Career: Corporate Scientist, Vice-President and Director, Survice Tomorrow, Inc., Laverkin, Utah; President and Chairman of the Board, International Geophysical Institute, Thousand Oaks, California; Consulting Physicist, 1970 to present; Educator, Moorpark College Simi Adult Education; President and Director, Galaxy Labs, Inc., 1960-63; Research Positions, Cook Electric Company, General Dynamics/Astronautics Company, Tektronix Inc., Northrop Corporation, Navy Electronics Laboratory Center 1952-70; Senior Engineer, Hughes Research and Development Laboratories, 1951-52. Organizational Memberships: Fellow, Institute for the Advancement of Engineering, 1981-82, 1982 to present; Senior Member, Chairman of Buenaventura Section 1978-79, Institute of Electrical and Electronics Engineers; American Association for the Advancement of Science; Laser Institute of America; American Ordnance Association; American Society of Engineering Education; American Radio Relay League. Community Activities: Board of Advisors, Kensington University; Life Fellow, International Biographical Association. Published Works: Patentee in His Field. Honors and Awards: Listed in *Book of Honor.* Address: 1879 North Marlowe Street, Thousand Oaks, California 91360.■

DWIGHT ADRIAN LEEDY

Association Administrator. Personal: Born April 7, 1947, in Greenfield, Ohio; Son of William and Emily Leedy. Education: B.S. Biology, Baldwin-Wallace College, 1969; M.S. Botany/Forest Ecology, University of Vermont, 1971. Career: Coordinator, Ohio Technology Transfer Organization; Extension Agent, Special Projects, Cooperative Extension Service, Ohio State University, Fremont Area Extension Center, 1982-83; County Extension Agent, 4-H, Cooperative Extension Service, Ohio State University, Seneca County (Ohio), 1979-82; Grade 9 General Science Teacher, Berlin (New Hampshire) Public Schools, 1973-79; Teaching Assistant, Plant Taxonomy, Botany Department, University of Vermont, Summer 1973; Grade 7 and 8 General Science Teacher, Berlin Public Schools, 1971-73; Teaching Fellow, Biology, University of Vermont, 1969-71; Undergraduate Laboratory Assistant, Introductory Biology, Baldwin-Wallace College, 1969; Director of Nature-Conservation Activities, Camp Kootaga, Kootaga Area Council, Boy Scouts of America, Summers 1962-66. Organizational Memberships: Ohio Forestry Association. Community Activities: Ohio Farm Bureau; The Nature Conservancy; National Wildlife Federation; Boy Scouts of America, Assistant Scoutmaster 1965-67, Scoutmaster 1968-69 & 1983, Merit Badge Counselor 1971 to present; Alpha Phi Omega. Published Works: Co-Author, "Precipitation from Fog Moisture in the Green Mountains of Vermont" 1968. Honors and Awards: 4-H County Forestry Award; Eagle Scout with 4 Palms, Boy Scouts of America; Vigil Honor, Order of the Arrow, Boy Scouts of America; William T. Hornaday Award for Distinguished Service to Conservation, Individual Medal, Boy Scouts of America; Junior Conservationist of Ohio for 1965, Ohio Forestry Association, Ohio Conservation Hall of Fame; Garden Clubs of Ohio Inc. Fellowship to Attend National Audubon Society Training Camp; Science Seminar (Science Honorary at Baldwin-Wallace College); National Science Foundation Undergraduate Research Participation Fellowship in Forest Ecology, University of Vermont, Summers 1967, 1968; Graduate Teaching

TWO THOUSAND NOTABLE AMERICANS

Fellowship, Botany Department, University of Vermont, 1969-71; District Achievement Award, Agriculture, Ohio Cooperative Extension Agents Association, 1981; Listed in *Who's Who Among Students in American Universities and Colleges, Community Leaders and Noteworthy Americans, Book of Honor, Dictionary of International Biography, International Who's Who in Community Service, Men of Achievement.* Address: 699 Rocky Road, Chillicothe, Ohio 45601.■

JANET CAROLINE LEESON

Corporate Executive. Personal: Born May 23, 1933; Daughter of Harold Arnold Tollefson and Sylvia Aino Makikangas (both parents deceased); Married Raymond Harry Leeson, Son of Stanley Raymond (deceased) and Nora MacMaster Leeson; Mother of Warren Scott, Debra Dolores, Barry Raymond. Education: Educational Training in Areas of Business, Accounting, Oil Painting; Attended Prairie State College and Cosmopolitan School of Business; Wilton Master School of Cake Decorating, 1973; Many Seminars and Workshops in Business; Degree in Leadership Training. Career: President, Leeson's Party Cakes, Inc.; Teacher of Cake Decorating, J. C. Penney, 1974-76; Office Manager, Pat Carpenter Associates, 1975; Head of Foreign Trade Department, Wilton Enterprises, Inc., 1970-75; Co-Owner, Ra-Ja-Lee T.V., 1962-68; Manager, Peak Service Cleaners, 1959-60. Organizational Memberships: American Business Women's Association, Genesis Charter Chapter, Public Relations Chairperson. Community Activities: Bremen Township Republican Organization; Den Mother, Boy Scouts of America, 1958-62; Den Mother, Girl Scouts of America, 1961-63; Bennett Parent-Teacher Association, 1956; Bremen Parent-Teacher Association, 1957-61; Board Member, Whittier Parent-Teacher Association, 1962-70; Room Mother and Other Volunteer Duties at Whittier; Mother's Club, Little League, 1961, 1964; Mother's Club, Babe Ruth League, 1964-65; Volunteer, Ingalls Memorial Hospital, 1963 to present; Decorator of Specialty Cakes for Special Events, Governor Thompson 1979-80, United States Navy 1979-81, 25th Anniversity of Tinley Park Chamber of Commerce 1980, Crestwood Nursing Home Occasions, 1979-80; Participant, Regional Level, Wade House Conference for Small Business; Attended State Hearings and Participated in Legislative Work, Springfield, Illinois, 1980; Testified at Federal Level on Regulatory Report. Religion: First Lutheran Church of Harvey, Member, Altar Guild, Lutheran Church Women. Honors and Awards: Donor of Specialty Cakes for A.M. Chicago Christmas Special, 1979; Plaques and Citations, United States Navy, 1979-81; First and Third Places, 1978, First Place 1980, Wedding Cake Division of Chicago Area Retail Bakers Convention Competition; Reed Citation for Participating in Work Release Program, Andrew High School, 1980; First Place for Two Charcoal and Pencil Portraits; First Place for Adult Wool Ensemble; Third Place for Child's Dress, Coat and Bonnet, 1957; Merit Badge of Counselor, Boy Scouts of America, 1974 to present. Address: 6713 West 163rd Place, Tinley Park, Illinois 60477.■

RENE-YVON MARIE MARC LEFEBVRE D'ARGENCE

Museum Director and Chief Curator. Personal: Born August 21, 1928; Son of Marc Lefebvre d'Argencé (deceased) and Andrée Thierry (deceased); Married Ritva Anneli Pelanne, Daughter of Mr. and Mrs. Pentti Pelanne; Father of Chantal, Yann, Luc. Education: Attended Collège St. Aspais (Fontainebleau), Lycee Albert Sarraut (Hanoi), Pembroke College (Cambridge, England); Licencié-es Lettres, Ecole Libre des Sciences Politiques, Sorbonne, 1952; Chinese 1950, Japanese 1951, Finnish 1952, Breveté de l'Ecole Nationale des Langues Orientales Vivantes. Military: Served with the Free French Forces in World War II. Career: Director and Chief Curator, Asian Art Museum of San Francisco, 1969 to present; Director, Avery Brundage Collection, 1965-68; Curator of Asiatic Collections, M. H. de Young Memorial Museum, San Francisco, 1964; Professor of Art History, University of California at Berkeley, 1962-65; Quai d'Orsay Grant, Taiwan, 1959; Curator, Blanchard de la Brosse Museum, Saigon, and Louis Finot Museum, Hanoi, 1954-58; Member, Ecole Française d'Extrême-Orient, 1954; Curator, Musee Cernuschi, Paris, 1953. Organizational Memberships: Trustee, Asian Art Foundation, 1979 to present; Advisory Committee, Society for Asian Art, 1964; Corresponding Member, Sociedad Asiatica de la Argentina. Community Activities: Vice President, Chinese-American Bilingual School of San Francisco, 1981 to present; Board Member, Institute of Sino-American Studies, 1981 to present; San Francisco-Osaka Sister City Committee, 1980 to present; San Francisco-Seoul Sister City Committee, 1980 to present; San Francisco-Shanghai Sister City Committee, 1980 to present; Trustee, Beaudry Foundation, 1977 to present; President 1976-79, Executive Vice-President 1979 to present, French-American Bilingual School, San Francisco; Founder, Ecole Française of San Francisco, 1967. Honors and Awards: Médaille de la Reconnaissance Française, 1957; Chevalier de l'Etoile du Nord (Sweden), 1968; Order of Merit, Avery Brundage Foundation, 1968; Honorary Doctor's Degree, Chinese Academy, Taiwan, 1969; Chevalier de l'Ordre du Merite (France), 1970; Officer of Culture Merit Order, Korea, 1982. Address: 16 Midhill Drive, Mill Valley, California 94941.■

ALBERTA ALANE LEGRAND

Real Estate Executive Sales Associate. Personal: Born March 29, 1952; Daughter of Dr. and Mrs. F. E. LeGrand. Education: B.S., Oklahoma State University, 1974; M.A. 1975, Ph.D. 1982, University of Southern California; Pilot License. Career: Executive Sales Associate, Century 21, present; Co-Director Kamp III Summer 1983, Head Counselor Summers 1970 to present, Kanakuk Kamps, Branson, Missouri; Women's Athletic Director, Associate Professor, Women's Head Volleyball Coach, Azusa Pacific University, 1976-81; Instructor and Volleyball Coach, Biola University, 1975-76; Graduate Assistant, Assistant Basketball and Assistant Track Coach, University of Southern California, 1974-75. Organizational Memberships: Women's Council of Realtors, Vice President and Program Chairman 1983-84, National Referral Network Committee 1984; National Association of Intercollegiate Athletics, Vice-President, of Women's National Volleyball Committee, 1980-81; Association for Intercollegiate Athletics for Women, Division III, Chairman of Women's All-American Volleyball Committee, 1980-81; California Collegiate Athletic Conference, President 1979-81, Secretary 1978-79; Azusa Pacific University, Faculty Athletic Council 1979-81, Rank and Salary Committee 1978-79; Chairperson, Oklahoma Board of Officials, 1982-83; Stillwater Board of Realtors, Banquet Committee Chairperson, 1982; HUD Liaison Chairperson, 1984. Community Activities: Youth Enterprises, Inc., Head Volleyball Coach for 3-Week Outreach Tours to Mexico; La Mirada Volleyball Club, President and Head Volleyball Coach, 1975-77; Kappa Delta Alumni Club, Co-Director of Pledge Class 1982-84, Chapter Advisor 1984 to present; Payne County 4-H Clubs, Sponsor of Bi-Annual LeGrand Trophy at State Livestock Judging Contests; California Interscholastic Federation, Clinician Director of Volleyball and Softball Officials in West Covina Area of Southern Caliofrnia; Easter Seals Campaign, Garage Sale and Auction Committee, 1981. Religion: Stillwater Christian Women's Club, 1981 to present; Athletes in Action, Women's Head Volleyball Coach, 1978-79; Evangelical Free Church, Fullerton, California, 1979; "I Found It" Campaign, Campus Crusade for Christ, Action Leaders Training, 1972-74, 1978; Sponsor Leaders on Campus. Honors and Awards: National N.A.I.A. Women's Volleyball Coach of the Year, 1980; N.A.I.A. National Championship Volleyball Team, Head Coach, 1980; A.I.A.W. Division III National Championship Volleyball Team, Head Coach, 1980; Top Six Outstanding Professors of Azusa Pacific University, 1981; Sigma Sigma Psi; Kappa Delta Pi; Oklahoma Member of Kappa Delta Sorority, 1974; Gamma Gamma; Mary Ann Stewart Award for Outstanding Leadership and Service to Oklahoma State University, 1973; Century 21 Million Dollar Producer; Listed in *World Who's Who of Women, Personalities of America, International Youth in Achievement, Directory of Distinguished Americans, Who's Who in California, Book of Honor, Outstanding Young Women in America, Personalities of the West and Midwest, Dictionary of International Biography.* Address: Route 5 Box 164, Stillwater, Oklahoma 74074.■

PAUL LOUIS LEHMANN

Professor Emeritus. Personal: Born September 10, 1906; Married Marion N. Lucks; Father of Peter Michael (deceased). Education: B.A., B.Sc. Education, Ohio State University, 1927; B.D., Union Theological Seminary, New York City, 1930; Honorary D.D., Lawrence College, Wisconsin, 1949; Honorary M.A., Harvard University, 1957; Honorary Litt.D., Elmhurst College, Illinois, 1967; D.Theol, University of Tuebingen, 1971; LL.D., Colorado College, 1973. Career: Charles A. Briggs Professor Emeritus 1974 to present, Charles A. Briggs Professor of Systematic Theology 1968-74, Auburn Professor of Systematic Theology 1963-67, Union Theological Seminary, New York; Florence Corliss Lamont Professor of Divinity 1957-63, Parkman Professor of Divinity 1956-57, Harvard University; Director of Graduate Studies 1952-56, Stephen Colwell Professor of Applied Christianity 1949-56, Associate Professor of Applied Christianity 1947-49, Princeton Theological Seminary; Associate Religious Editor, Westminster Press, 1946-47; Assistant Professor to Associate Professor of Biblical History, Literature and Interpretation, Wellesley College, 1941-46; Associate Professor of Biblical and Systematic Theology, Eden Theological Seminary, Webster Groves, Missouri, 1940-41; Professor of Religion and Philosophy, Elmhurst College, 1933-40; Visiting Professor of Systematic Theology and Ethics, Union Theological Seminary (Richmond, Virginia) 1974-76, San Francisco Theological Seminary (San Anselmo, California) 1976-77, Graduate Theological Union of University of California at Berkeley 1976 and 1977, Moravian Theological Seminary (Bethlehem, Pennsylvania) 1977; Roian-Fleck Lecturer in Religion, Bryn Mawr College, Pennsylvania, 1976; Visiting Professor of Christian Ethics, The Divinity School of Vanderbilt University, Nashville, Tennessee, 1982. Organizational

178

Memberships: Epsilon of Ohio Chapter, Phi Beta Kappa; American Theological Society, President 1969-70; Duodecim Theological Society; American Society of Christian Ethics; International Bonhoeffer Society; International Karl Barth Society. Community Activities: Founder and First Chairman, National Emergency Civil Liberties Committee; National Council of Churches, Council on the Churches and the Economic Order 1950-60, Council of the Churches and International Affairs 1950-60; Delegate, General Council, World Alliance of Reformed Churches, Sao Paulo 1949, Willingen (Germany) 1964; World Council of Churches, Lund, Sweden, 1964; Delegate, World Christian Peace Assembly, Prague 1966, Bucharest 1971. Religion: North Illinois Synod of the then Evangelical and Reformed Church, Ordained as Minister, 1937; United Presbyterian Church in the U.S.A., Received into the Presbytery of Boston 1946, Retired Member 1974. Published Works: Author of *Forgiveness: Decisive Issue in Protestant Thought* 1930, *Ethics in a Christian Context* 1963 (paper 1976), *The Transfiguration of Politics* 1974; Translator of *Re-educating Germany 1945* (by Werner Richter); Contributor of Over 200 Articles and Reviews to Religious Journals and 11 Essays to Symposia. Honors and Awards: "A Paul Lehmann Festschrift" in *Theology Today*, 1972; *The Context of Contemporary Theology: Essays in Honor of Paul Lehmann* edited by Alexander McKelway and E. David Willis, 1974; "Essays in Honor of Paul Lehmann" in *Union Seminary Quarterly Review*, 1974. Address: Apartment 6F, 176 East 77th Street, New York, New York 10021.■

PAUL MICHAEL LEHNER

Director and Executive. Personal: Born December 5, 1941; Son of Mr. and Mrs. Paul M. Lehner, Jr.; Married Linda Smith; Father of Suzanne Michelle, Paulyn Marie Lehner. Education: B.B.A. summa cum laude, University of Notre Dame, 1963; M.B.A. with distinction, Harvard Graduate School of Business Administration, 1969. Military: Served in the United States Navy, 1963-67, attaining the rank of Lieutenant, Supply Corps. Career: Director and Executive Vice-President, Tipton Lakes Company; President and Director, Tipton Lakes Community Association; President and Director, Nashville International Trading Company, Ind., 1977-81; Vice—President of Real Estate 1977 to present, Real Estate Projects Coordinator 1970-76, Consulting Group Member 1969, Irwin Management Company. Organizational Memberships: International Council of Shopping Centers, 1972-80; National Association of Home Builders, 1977 to present; National Association of Realtors, 1982 to present; Columbus Board of Realtors, 1973 to present; Director and President, Bartholomew County Homebuilders Association, 1984; Director, Indiana Homebuilders Association, 1984. Community Activities: Brown County Board of Zoning Appeals, President, 1976; Brown County Planning Commission, Vice-Chairman, 1975; Trustee, Town of Nashville, Indiana, 1977-81; County Representative, Senator Richard Lugar, 1976 to present; Region XI Area Development Commission, Executive Committee, 1977-81; Knights of Columbus, 1st, 2nd and 3rd Degrees, 1984; Director, Columbus Economic Development Board, 1983 to present; Rotary Club, 1984 to present; Campaign Treasurer for Indiana President Pro-tem Reobert Garton, 1983 to present. Religion: St. Agnes Parish Council, Vice-President, 1980-81. Honors and Awards: Beta Gamma Sigma, 1962-63; Beta Alpha Psi, 1963; Haskins and Sells Accounting Excellence, 1962; Harvard Fellowship, 1967; National Merit Letter of Commendation, 1959; Summa Cum Laude Graduate, University of Notre Dame, 1963; M.B.A. with distinction, Harvard University, 1969; Listed in *Who's Who in the Midwest*, *Men of Achievement*, *Who's Who in Finance and Industry*, *International Businessmen's Who's Who*, *Personalities of America*, *Men and Women of Distinction*. Address: 2265 West Carr Hill Road, Columbus, Indiana 47201.■

IRWIN LEHRHOFF

Psychologist, Speech Pathologist. Personal: Born June 4, 1929; Married Barbara; Father of Debra, Terri, Howard, Steven. Education: M.A. 1949, Ph.D. 1954, University of Southern California; Postdoctoral Training, Columbia University, New York; Studies at Rutgers and Princeton Universities; Nine Years Training in Psychology and Communicative Disorders; Certification as Marriage, Family and Child Counselor 1964, Psychologist 1967, Speech Pathologist 1974, State of California Board of Medical Examiners and Board of Quality Assurance; Certificate of Clinical Competence, American Speech and Hearing Association; Certified and Licensed in Speech Pathology, Psychology, and Marriage and Family Counseling. Career: Private Practice, President of Irwin Lehrhoff and Associates, Practice Accredited by Board of Examiners of Speech, Pathology and Audiology, 1954 to present; Director, Department of Communicative Disorders, Harbor General Hospital, Torrance, California, 1955-58. Organizational Memberships: American Academy of Private Practice in Speech Pathology and Audiology, Director and National President, 1974-78; American Association of Marriage and Family Counselors; American Orthopsychiatric Association, Fellow; American Association for the Advancement of Science; American Psychological Association, Member of Four Divisions; American Speech and Hearing Association; California Psychological Association; California Speech and Hearing Association; California Speech Pathologists and Audiologists in Private Practice, Director and President, 1973-77; International Society of Mental Health; Los Angeles County Psychological Association; New York Academy of Science. Community Activities: American Academy of Child Psychiatry, Advisory Board; Reiss-Davis Child Study Center, Board of Trustees 12 Years, Former Chairman of Budget, Personnel and Development Committees, Founder of Women's Division, Former Chairman of President's Committee; Thalians Community Mental Health Center, Cedar-Sinai Medical Center, Board of Directors, First Vice-President, Executive Committee, Executive Vice-Chairman, Chairman of Nominating Committee, Chairman of Hospital Liaison Committee; Thalians Presidents Club, Founder, Chairman; District Attorneys Advisory Council; President's Circle, Cardinal and Gold, University of Southern California. Published Works: Contributor, "Speech Problems in Children" 1958, "An Experimental Study of Auditory Threshold Acuity in Children with Cerebral Palsy by PGSR and Other Techniques" 1958, "A Study of PGSR Testing of RH Athetoids" 1961, "Parthogenesis and Treatment of Vocal Nodules" 1962, "Speech Problems in Children", and Numerous Other Articles to Speech, Psychology and Medical Journals. Honors and Awards: Listed in *American Men of Science*, *Who's Who in American Education*, *Who's Who in the West*, *Leaders in American Science*, *National Register of Prominent Americans and International Notables*, *Personalities of the West and Midwest*. Address: One Roxbury Plaza Suite 1200, 9701 Wilshire Boulevard, Beverly Hills, California 90212.■

JAMES HENRY LEIGH

Educator. Personal: Born February 6, 1952; Son of Mrs. John R. Davis; Married Jane Hudson, Daughter of Richard B. Hudson; Father of Daniel. Education: B.B.A. with honors 1974, M.B.A. 1976, University of Texas at Austin; Ph.D. Business Administration, University of Michigan at Ann Arbor, 1981. Career: Assistant Professor, Texas A. & M. University Department of Marketing; Former Positions include Research Associate in the Division of Research of the University of Michigan Graduate School of Business and Administrative Assistant in the Office of the President of University of Texas at Austin. Organizational Memberships: Academy of Marketing Science; American Academy of Advertising; American Institute for Decision Sciences; American Marketing Association; Association for Consumer Research; Southern Marketing Association; Southwestern Marketing Association; Institute of Management Sciences. Community Activities: Volunteer, Big Brother/Little Brother Program, 1974-76; Co-Coordinator and Panelist of Student Career Fair, Detroit Chapter of American Marketing Association, 1980; Junior Manager 1971, Senior Manager 1971-72, University of Texas at Austin Intramural Program. Honors and Awards: National Honor Society, 1969; Phi Eta Sigma, 1971; Beta Gamma Sigma, 1976; C.E. Griffin Scholarship in Marketing and Business Economics, 1976; General Electric Fellowship, 1976; Doctoral Consortium Fellow, American Marketing Association, 1978; Winner, Research Grant Competition, American Academy of Advertising, 1982. Address: 2809 Hillside Drive, Bryan, Texas 77802.■

HAROLD V. LEININGER

Consultant in Microbiology and Science Writer. Personal: Born June 18, 1925; Son of Wilfred C. Leininger (deceased) and Georgia Carpenter Phillips; Married; Father of Harold V., Jr. Education: B.S. 1948, M.S. 1950, Louisiana State University. Military: Served in the United States Navy, 1943-46, attaining the rank of Torpedoman Second Class. Career: Consultant in Microbiology; Science Writer on Microbiology, Food, Drugs, Cosmetics, Water, Effect of Nuclear Radiation on Food and Drugs, Sterilization Techniques, Decontamination Procedures, Laboratory Analysis; Director of National Center for Microbiology, Minneapolis, Minnesota, 1969-80; Liaison Microbiologist, 1957-63; Microbiologist, United States Food and Drug Administration, Washington, D.C., 1951-57; United States Food and Drug Inspector, New Orleans State Center, Louisiana, 1950-51; Lab Technician for Dairy Improvement, 1949-50. Organizational Memberships: Lecturer, University of Wisconsin at Madison, University of Wisconsin at River Falls, Univesity of Minnesota at Minneapolis; American Society of Microbiology; Institute of Food Technology; Association of Milk, Food and Environmental Sanitarians; Association of Food and Crug Officials, Vice-Chairman of Research Committee, 1979-80; Association of Official Analytical Chemists, General Referee, 1965-70; Minnesota Sanitarians Association; Central States Association of Food and Drug Officials. Community Activities: Writer, United States Public Health Service; Past President, Ruritans; Shriner; Mason; Voluntary Military Affiliate Radio Station Operator; Deputy Zone Director, New Mexico M.A.R.S.; Chairman, Hunting and Fishing, El Paso Coalition of Sportsmen; Sun City Amateur Radio Club. Religion: Episcopal, Vestryman,

1965. Published Works: Contributor of Over 30 Articles to Scientific Journals; Contributor of Chapter, *Compendium of Methods for Microbiological Examination of Foods*, 1976 and Current Edition; Author, Civil Defense Information for Food and Drug Officials; Contributor of Chapter to Handbook for Hospital Nurses. Honors and Awards: Award of Merit, United States Food and Drug Administration, 1977; Equal Opportunity Achievement Award, United States Food and Drug Administration, 1981; Certificate of Appreciation, National Rifle Association, 1983; Doctoral Degree, Phoenix, Arizona, 1956; W.A.E. Award, El Paso, 1983; Amigo Award, El Paso, 1981; Certificate of Loyal Service, United States Department of H.H.S., 1980; Junior Engineer in Radiological Knowledge, United States Public Health Service, 1955; Certificate of Honor, District of Columbia Chapter of American Red Cross, 1955. Address: 3200 Voss Drive, El Paso, Texas 79936.■

HORST H. E. LEIPHOLZ

Professor and Department Chairman. Personal: Born September 26, 1919; Married Ursula Schlag; Father of Barbara, Gunthara. Education: Dr. Ing. 1959, Docent 1962, Technical University of Stuttgart; Professor of Mechanics, Technical University of Karslruhe, 1963; Professor of Civil Engineering, University of Waterloo, 1969. Career: Professor and Chairman, Former Solid Mechanics Division Chairman, Dean of Graduate Studies, Associate Dean and Associate Chairman, University of Waterloo (Ontario, Canada) Department of Civil Engineering, 1969 to present; Professor, University of Karlsruhe, 1963-69; Assistant, Docent, Professor, University of Stuttgart, 1958-63; Structural Design Engineer, K. Elsasser (Consultant), Stuttgart, 1950-58. Organizational Memberships: Fellow and Director of Region II, American Academy of Mechanical Engineering, 1974-77; Fellow, Engineering Institute of Canada (E.I.C.); Chairman of Research and Development Division, Canadian Society for Mechanical Engineering, 1978-81; Gesellschaft für Augewendte Mathematik und Mechanik (G.A.M.M.), Executive Committee, 1978-82; International Society for Interaction of Mechanics and Mathematics; American Society of Mechanical Engineers; American Mathematics Society; Society of Engineering Science; S.C.I.T.E.C.; Association of Professional Engineers of the Province of Ontario (A.P.E.O.); Chairman, International Union of Theoretical and Applied Mechanics (I.U.T.A.M.) Symposium, 1969, 1978; Co-Chairman, International Symposium on Experimental Mechanics, Waterloo, 1974; Treasurer, Fourth International Conference on Fracture, Waterloo, 1977; Chairman, Canadian National Council for International Union of Theoretical and Applied Mechanics (I.U.T.A.M.); Paper Council, 15th International Congress of Theoretical and Applied Mechanics, Toronto, 1980. Published Works: Editor, Noordhoff Series on Mechanics of Elastic Stability; Regional Editor, Mechanical Research Communications; Editor, Canadian Society of Mechanical Engineering (C.S.M.E.) Transactions; Board of Editors, Solid Mechanics Archives, *Journal for Incorporating Mathematics in Applied Mechanics and Engineering*; Reviewer for Eight International Scientific Journals. Honors and Awards: Fellow, American Academy of Mechanics, 1972; Canadian Conference for Applied Mechanics (C.A.N.C.A.M.) Award for Outstanding Contribution to the Area of Applied Mechanics, 1975; Distinguished Teacher Award, University of Waterloo, 1976; Honorary Member, Canadian Fracture Mechanics Corporation, 1978; Fellow, Engineering Institute of Canada, 1980; Listed in Various Biographical Reference Publications. Address: 401 Warrington Drive, Waterloo, Ontario N2L 2P7, Canada.■

SHERRY LeMASTER

College Administrator. Personal: Born June 25, 1953; Daughter of John W. and Mary T. LeMaster. Education: B.S. Food Science and Technology 1975, M.S. Higher Education Administration 1983, University of Kentucky; Attended Bryn Mawr College and Higher Education Resource Services, Mid-Atlantic, Summer Institute for Women in Higher Education Administration, 1983. Career: Vice-President for Development 1981 to present, Dean of Students 1980-81, Midway College; Residence Hall Program Coordinator, Murray State University, 1978-80; Grant Specialist and Environmental Specialist, Commonwealth of Kentucky, 1977-78; Laboratory Technician, Central Kentucky Animal Disease Diagnostic Laboratory, 1976-77. Organizational Memberships: National Society of Fund Raising Executives, 1983 to present; National Association for Female Executives, 1983 to present; National Disciples Development Executive Conference Planning Committee, Appointed 1984; Kentucky Conference Chairman, Council for the Advancement and Support of Education, 1982; Accreditation Committee, Greater Lexington Area Chamber of Commerce, 1982; Institutional Representative for Midway College, National Identification Program for the Advancement of Women in Higher Eduation, 1980 to present; Newsletter Editor, Kentucky Association of Women Deans, Administrators and Counselors, 1981; National Association for Student Personnel Administrators; American Association of University Professors; Southern College Personnel Association. Community Activities: The Ninety-Nines, International Women Pilots, Kentucky-Bluegrass, 1983 to present; General Federation of Women's Clubs, Midway, Kentucky Chapter, 1982 to present; American Heart Association, Co-chairman of Woodford County 1983, Chairman of Midway (Kentucky) 1981; Zonta International Lexington (Kentucky) Chapter, Keeneland Chairman 1983, Board of Directors 1983-85, Amelia Earhart Committee Chairman 1983; Phi Beta Phi National Alumnae Association, Alumnae Province President, 1980-81; Kentucky Beta Chapter Pi Beta Phi House Association, Secretary of Board of Directors, 1982 to present; Alpha Kappa Psi Professional Business Fraternity Alumnae Association, Charter Member for Murray (Kentucky) Chapter; Lexington Pi Beta Phi Alumnae Club, Recording Secretary 1978, Arrowcraft Chairman 1977, Recommendation Committee Chairman 1976, Founders Day Chairman 1977; Ambassador, University of Kentucky College of Agriculture; Life Member, University of Kentucky Alumni Association; Honorable Order of Kentucky Colonels, Appointee 1978, Reappointed 1982; Aircraft Owners and Pilots Association. Religion: First United Methodist Church, Administrative Board, 1982 to present. Honors and Awards: Honorary Secretary of State, Commonwealth of Kentucky, Appointed 1983; Pilot Proficiency Wings Phase I, U.S. Department of Transportation Federal Aviation Administration, 1982; Young Career Women of Frankfort (Kentucky) 1981, Women of the Year Nominee for Lexington (Kentucky) 1982, National Federation of Business and Professional Women's Clubs; Outstanding Young Women Nominee, Bluegrass Junior Women's Club, Lexington, Kentucky, 1982 and 1983; Outstanding Woman in the Bluegrass Area Nominee, American Association of University Women, Lexington, Kentucky, 1983; Keynote Speaker, Hugh O'Brian Youth Foundation Kentucky Youth Leadership Seminar, 1983; Listed in *Dictionary of International Biography*, *Personalities of America*, *Personalities of the South*, the *Biographical Roll of Honor*, *Outstanding Young Women of America*, the *Directory of Distinguished Americans*, the *International Book of Honor*, *The Society Registry Bluegrass Blue Book*, *Who's Who of American Women*, *Who's Who in the South and Southwest*, *World Who's Who of Women*. Address: Midway College, Midway, Kentucky 40347.■

LAWRENCE LE ROY LEONARD, JR.

Family Counselor and Executive. Personal: Born November 28, 1943; Son of Lawrence L. and Elizabeth Leonard. Education: B.A., Pacific College, 1972; Postgraduate Work, Columbia University, 1975; D.D. 1979, Ph.D. 1980, Ms.D. 1981, Universal Life Church. Military: Served in the United States Marine Corps, 1963-69, attaining the rank of E5 Sergeant. Career: Family Counselor, Private Practice; President, Paper Talk; Chairman of Board of Trustees, Universal Life Church of St. Albans; President, Leonard Associates; Paintings Exhibited, Southwestern College (California) 1970, Lynn Kottler Galleries (New York City) 1971; Inventor of Painting Instrument, 1974; Creator of Portfolios for Actors and Models; Designer of Cover for *Feet* Magazine, New York City; Producer/Director, Actors Quarters, San Diego, California; Promoter/Coordinator for Performing Artists; Flautist, Early Morning Blues Band; Flautist/Percussionist, Ivanhoes; Flautist, Larry Leonard Experience (trio); Coordinator and Master of Ceremonies, U.S.O. Show, Marseilles, France, 1965. Community Activities: Southeast Queens Citizens Against Crime, 1978; Chairman, Counselor's Action Committee, Agency for Child Development, 1976; Community Liaison, Southeast Queens, New York, 1974-76; Supervisor, Parents Activity Committee, Amistad Child Care Center, 1974-76; Producer, Creative Arts Festival, Amistad, 1975; Scoutmaster, Boy Scouts of America, 1974; Consultant, Fordham Univerity Student Union, 1973-74; Producer, Community Music Festival, Neighborhood Services, 1973; Village Leader, Camp Hayden Marks, Fresh Air Fund, 1973; Counselor/Baseball Coach, Bill Dave Club, 1972-73; Campus Mediator, San Diego City College, 1968; City Marshall, Civilian Volunteer Patrol Program, New York City, 1974; Coach, Flippers Tumbling Team, 1974; Recreational Park Director, Neighborhood Services, 1974; Youth Director, Neighborhood Services Economic Development Program, 1973-74. Honors and Awards: Commendation, District Attorney, Queens County, New York, 1981; Commendation, Special Projects Coordinator, Day Care Council, New York, 1978; Commendation, Board of Directors, Amistad C.C.C., 1976; Commendation, Chance Program, Department of Social Services, New York City, 1975; Honorable Discharge, United States

Marine Corps, 1969; Certificate of Appreciation, Disabled American Veterans, 1967; Recipient of Honors for Work with the U.S.O. Show, French Consul, Marseilles, France, 1965; Tarawa Award for Excellence in Leadership, United States Marine Corps, 1964. Address: 179-71 Anderson Road, St. Albans, New York 11434.■

STANLEY CURTIS LEONBERG, JR.

Neurologist and Electroencephalographer. Born December 25, 1926; Son of Stanley Curtis (deceased) and Ethel M. Leonberg; Married Mildred Jane; Father of Barbara, Curtis, Gregory, Beth. Education: B.S., Ursinus College, 1949; M.D., Hahnemann Medical College, 1954. Career: Associate Professor of Clinical Neurology, Rutgers Medical School/University of Medicine and Dentistry of New Jersey; Neurologist and Electroencephalographer, South Jersey Medical Center, Cherry Hill, New Jersey; Former Doctor in Family Medical Practice. Organizational Memberships: Fellow, American College of Physicians, American Academy of Neurology, Royal Society of Medicine (England), American Heart Association (stroke council), New Jersey Academy of Medicine, American Academy of Clinical Electroencephalographers; American Medical Association; New Jersey and Camden County Medical Societies; American Medical Electroencephalograph Association; Fellow, American Electroencephalograph Society; American Medical Writers Association; American Epilepsy Society; Philadelphia Neurological Society; Neurological Association of New Jersey; Board of Managers, Cooper Medical Center, Camden, New Jersey, 1976 to present; Board of Trustees, American Medical Electroencephalograph Association, 1978 to present; Board of Directors, American Board of Electroencephalography, 1979 to present; Medical Advisory Board, Delaware Valley Chapter, National Multiple Sclerosis Society; Medical Advisory Board, New Jersey Society, American Epilepsy Society; Member Editorial Board, *Journal of the Medical Society of New Jersey*; President, Neurological Association of New Jersey, 1981-82; President, American Academy of Clinical Electroencephalographers, 1981-82. Religion: Methodist. Honors and Awards: Certificate of Merit for Best Scientific Exhibit in Neurology, American Medical Association, 1970 and 1973; First Award 1970 and Honorable Mention 1974 for Best Scientific Exhibit, New Jersey Medical Society. Address: 232 East Main Street, Moorestown, New Jersey 08057.■

ARNOLD FRED LESSARD

Banking Executive. Personal: Born October 9, 1983; Son of Mrs. Fred Lessard; Married Francine Treutenaere; Father of Arnaud Alfred. Education: Diploma in Accounting, Burdett College, Boston, Massachusetts, 1943; B.S. with honors, Boston University, 1949; M.A., Columbia University, New York, 1951; Postgraduate Studies in Business and Economics, Columbia University, Georgetown University, George Washington University. Military: Served in the United States Air Force, 1943-46, attaining the rank of First Lieutenant and serving as Bombardier/Navigator in the 5th Air Force and, 1951-53, attaining the rank of Captain and serving as Radar Observer Intelligence Officer in the Air Force Security Service. Career: Vice-President of Strategic Planning and Trade Banking, Chase Manhattan Bank, New York, New York, 1978 to present; Founding Chairman of Resources Engineering and Management International, London and Denver, 1971-78; Regional Vice-President, Vice-President, Associate and Consultant, Booz Allen and Hamilton, 1956-71; Director of Training, National Security Agency, 1953-56. Organizational Memberships: Founding Member, Regional Vice-President for Europe, Membership Review Committee, Institute of Management Consultants, 1965 to present. Community Activities: Director, Iran America Society, Tehran, Iran, 1959-62; Chairman of Management Development, Society for Personnel Administration, Washington, D.C., 1953-56. Honors and Awards: Pi Gamma Mu; Kappa Delta Pi; Phi Delta Kappa, 1949-50; Outstanding Performance Award, National Security Agency, 1955. Address: 702 Boulevard East, Guttenberg, New Jersey 07093.■

JAMES LUTHER LESTER

State Senator and Attorney at Law. Personal: Born January 12, 1932; Son of William M. and Elizabeth Miles (deceased) Lester; Married Gwendolyn Gleason; Father of James L., Jr., Frank G. Education: A.B., The Citadel, 1952; LL.B. (J.D.), University of Georgia Law School, 1957. Military: Served in the United States Army, 1952-58, rising through the ranks from Second Lieutenant to Captain. Career: State Senator, Georgia General Assembly, 1971 to present; Banking, Finance and Insurance Committee Chairman, Appropriations Committee Member, Human Resources Committee Member, Senate Policy Committee Member, Legislative Services Committee Member, Georgia General Assembly Session, 1976-84; Partner, Lester, Lester and Flynt Law Firm. Organizational Memberships: American Bar Association; Georgia Bar Association; Auugusta Bar Association; Association of Trial Lawyers in America. Community Activities: Chairman, Richmond County Democratic Executive Committee, 1966-70; Metropolitan Young Men's Christian Association, Board of Directors; Advisory Committee, Georgia-Carolina District Boy Scouts of America; Governor's Advisory Council on Mental Health and Mental Retardation; Committee on Constitutional Revision, Taxation Article, 1980-82; Chairman, Georgia Tax Reform Commission, 1978-81. Religion: Aldersgate Methodist Church, Augusta, Georgia, Member. Honors and Awards: Outstanding Service to Mentally Retarded Award, Augusta Association for Retarded Children, 1973; Public Affairs Award for Service to Mental Health, Mental Health Association of Metropolitan Atlanta, 1976; Outstanding Service to Education Award, Richmond County Educators Association, 1977; Distinguished Service Award, Georgia Association for Mental Health, 1977; Outstanding Service to Mental Health Award, Mental Health Association for Greater Augusta, 1978; Citation for Legislative Service, Georgia Municipal Association, 1979, 1983; Service Award for Outstanding Service, Georgia Hospital Association, 1979; Herman Haas Award for Outstanding Service to the Insurance Industry of Georgia, Independent Insurance Agents of Georgia, 1981; Senator of the Year Award, Georgia Association of Mental Health, 1983. Address: 770 Camellia Road, Augusta, Georgia 30909.■

W. BERNARD LESTER

Executive Director. Personal: Born January 9, 1939; Son of William D. Lester; Married; Father of Mark Allan. Education: B.S. Agriculture, University of Florida, 1961; M.S. Agricultural Economics, University of Florida, 1962; Ph.D. Agricultural Economics, Texas A&M University, 1965. Military: Served in the United States Army, 1965. Career: Executive Director (Lakeland, Florida), Former Deputy Director (Lakeland, Florida), Former Director of Economic Research Department (Gainesville, Florida), Former Research Economist (Gainesville, Florida), Florida Department of Citrus. Organizational Memberships: Citrus Advisory Committee, Florida Farm Bureau, 1981-82; Governing Council, Florida Future Farmers Foundation; Blue Key; Phi Kappa Phi; Gamma Sigma Delta; Alpha Zeta; Alpha Gamma Rho, Chairman of Undergraduate Awards Committee of Education Foundation 1981, Criteria Selection Committee of National Headquarters Project, Board of National Education Foundation. Community Activities: Committee Chairman, Kiwanis Club, College Station, Texas, 1967. Religion: First Methodist Church, Lakeland, Administrative Board, 1982. Honors and Awards: Listed in *Prominent People in Florida Government, Who's Who in the South and Southwest, Who's Who in Finance and Industry, Personalities of America, Directory of Distinguished Americans, Men of Achievement, Personalities of the South*. Address: 1420 Miller Lane, Lakeland, Florida 33801.■

ROBERT ERNEST LEVINE

Ophthalmologist and Ophthalmic Plastic Surgeon. Personal: Born August 28, 1939; Son of Irving Levine; Married Judith Yarmish; Father of Mark, David, Joseph. Education: A.B., Columbia College, 1960; M.D., New York University Medical School, 1964; Attended Mt. Sinai Hospital (New York) 1965, New York University-Bellevue Medical Center 1968; Heed Fellow, 1969; Certification, American Board of Ophthalmology, 1970. Military: Served in the United States Army Reserves, attaining the rank of Captain (inactive). Career: Ophthalmologist and Ophthalmic Plastic Surgeon; Associate Clinical Professor of Ophthalmology, University of Southern California; Chairman, Eye Section, St. Vincent Medical Centre. Organizational Memberships: American Medical Association; California Medical Association; American Academy of Ophthalmology; P.C.O.O.S.; Los Angeles County Medical Association; Los Angeles Society of Ophthalmology; Society of Heed Fellows; American Society of Ophthalmologic Plastic and Reconstructive Surgery, Inc.; Institute of Electrical and Electronics Engineers. Community Activities: Executive Vice-President, Hillel Hebrew Academy, Beverly Hills, 1976 to present. Religion: Beth Jacob Congregation, Beverly Hills, Former Member of Board of Directors and Chairman of Adult Education Institute. Honors and Awards: Heed Fellow, Postdoctorate in Ophthalmic Pathology, Estelle Doheny Eye Foundation, Los Angeles. Address: 3875 Wilshire Boulevard, Suite 301, Los Angeles, California 90010.■

SUZANNE LEVINE

Managing Editor. Personal: Native New Yorker. Education: Graduate summa cum laude, Radcliffe College, 1963. Career: Managing Editor, *Ms.* Magazine,

TWO THOUSAND NOTABLE AMERICANS

1972 to present; Managing Editor, *Sexual Behavior* Magazine, 1971; Free-lance Writer, Published in *Ladies Home Journal, Cosmopolitan, Today's Health,* 1970; Associate Articles Editor, *McCall's,* 1969; Feature Editor, *Mademoiselle* Magazine, 1966; Reporter, Time/Life Books, 1965; Editor and Writer, *Seattle* Magazine, 1963; Teaching Appointments include Poynter Fellowship at Yale University, Faculty Membership at New York University, and Woodrow Wilson Fellowship at Pomona College. Organizational Memberships: American Society of Magazine Editors, Executive Committee; Women in Communications, Consultant for "A National Certificate Program"; Women's Media Group, Board of Directors; Women's Action Alliance, Executive Committee. Published Works: Co-Editor, *The Decade of Women: A Ms. History of the Seventies in Words and Pictures,* February 1980; Editor, *She's Nobody's Baby,* 1983; Executive Producer, One-Hour Documentary "She's Nobody's Baby: American Women in the Twentieth Century." Honors and Awards: Listed in *Outstanding Women in Communications, Who's Who in America.* Address: 119 West 40th Street, New York, New York 10018.■

NORMA U. LEVITT

Professional Volunteer and Writer. Personal: Daughter of Henry and Anna Uttal (both deceased); Married; Mother of Sally Steinberg, Nancy Hoffman, Andrew. Education: B.A., Wellesley College. Career: Professional Volunteer and Writer. Community Activities: National Federation of Temple Sisterhood, President, 1967-73; Union of American Hebrew Congregations, Vice-Chairperson, 1977-79, 1981-83; World Union for Progressive Judaism, Chairperson of Executive Committee, 1974 to present; Synagogue Council of America, Vice-President, 1979 to present; Jewish Braille Institute, President, 1974-80; Religious Non-Governmental Organizations of the United Nations, President, 1980-82; United Nations and United States Mission to the United Nations, Non-Governmental Organization Representative; Leadership Conference of National Jewish Women's Organizations, Chairperson, 1976-79; Religion in American Life, Board Member; Others. Religion: Jewish. Honors and Awards: Phi Beta Kappa, 1937; Eleanor Roosevelt Award, American Jewish Congress; First Woman Officer, Union of American Hebrew Congregations, 1977; Honorary President, National Federation of Temple Sisterhood. Address: 15 East 64 Street, New York, New York 10021.■

KAREN LESLIE LEW

Information Officer. Personal: Born February 19, 1942; Mother of Kent Charles, Danika Leslie, Mark Daren; Daughter of Lyman and Betsy Woodman. Education: Attended San Francisco State College 1960-61, El Camino Junior College 1966, University of California at Los Angeles 1967, University of Alaska at Anchorage 1971, 1975, 1977, Sheldon Jackson College 1979, Anchorage Community College 1980, 1981, 1982. Career: Information Officer, State of Alaska Department of Fish and Game, 1983 to present; Information Officer, State of Alaska Department of National Resources 1979-83; Advertising Representative/Writer, *Alaskafest* Magazine, 1979; Advertising Manager, *Alaska Advocate,* 1977-78; Copywriter/Continuity Director, KYAK/KGOT-FM, 1976-77; Media Specialist, Alaska Native Commission on Alcoholism and Drug Abuse, 1974-75; Classified Advertising Manager, *Anchorage Daily News,* 1973-74; Copywriter/Media Buyer, Graphix West, 1972-73; Copywriter/Continuity Director, KYAK Radio, 1971-72; Administrative Assistant, Mike Ellis Advertising, 1971; Information Specialist, ITT Arctic Services, Inc., 1969-71. Organizational Memberships: Alaska Press Women, Member 1971 to present, Past Vice-President, Recording Secretary; National Federation of Press Women, 1971 to present; Public Relations Society of America, 1979 to present. Community Activities: LaLeche League, Instructor, 1962-68; Citizens' Advisory Educational Concerns Committee, 1980-82; Language Arts Curriculum Committee, 1980-82; Anchorage School District Community Resources Speaker, 1977-78; Anchorage Chess Club, Publicity Chairperson, 1976; United States Chess Federation, 1975 to present; Anchorage Council on Alcoholism, Second Vice-President, 1976; Anchorage Community Chorus; Theatre Guild, Inc.; Volunteer Publicity Worker, Anchorage Community Theatre, Theatre Guild Inc.; Anchorage Civic Opera, University of Alaska Theatre Department, Alaska Zoo (donor). Religion: Unitarian, Coordinator of Anchorage Liberal Religious Youth, 1976. Honors and Awards: Writing Awards, Alaska Press Women, Alaska Press Club, Public Relations Society of America (Alaska Chapter); One of Top Ten Writers in Nation, Federation of Press Women, 1972; Listed in *Who's Who of American Women, Who's Who in the West.* Address: 3120 West 79th Avenue, Anchorage, Alaska 99502.■

CHARLES BADY LEWIS

Baptist Seminary Administrator. Personal: Born September 20, 1913; Son of J. J. and Lizzie Lewis. Education: A.B., Leland College; B.D., Th.M., D.Min. Candidate, Mississippi Baptist Seminary. Career: Dean, Natchez Center of Mississippi Baptist Seminary; Dean of Religion and College Pastor, Natchez Junior College. Organizational Memberships: National Association of Baptist Professors of Religion; National Association of Adult Education; Philosophy Association. Community Activities: International B.S.U. Pastor Advisor; Mississippi B.S.U. Pastor Advisor; Men of Action of the World; Black America Business and Civic Association; King Denis A.F.& A.M., 1950-68. Honors and Awards: Listed in *Who's Who in Education, Who's Who in Religion, Who's Who in the B.S.U., Personalities of the South, Who's Who in Community Service, Notable Americans.* Address: 908 North Union, P.O. Box 53, Natchez, Mississippi 39120.■

CLAUDIA MAE JONES LEWIS

Appraisal, Advertising and Public Relations. Personal: Born January 19, 1928; Daughter of Earnest Jones (deceased) and Gertrude Chaney (Jones) Holtz; Married Henry Lewis Jr. Education: Attended Southern University; B.A., Texas Southern University, 1949; LVN, Graduate School of Nursing, 1950; Property Appraisal Degree, 1982. Career: Appraisal, Advertising and Public Relations; Former Positions as a Nurse. Organizational Memberships: Gulf Coast Texas Association of Assessing Officers; International Association of Assessing Officers. Community Activities: Notary Public of Texas; President, Southwood Civic Club; Past Grand Lady, Knights of St. Peter Claver Auxiliary, 1980; Big Sister, Inc.; Catholic Daughters of America; President, Ethel Ransom Art & Literary Club of Houston, 1978-86; Founder, El Puente Poco Bridge Club. Religion: Community Affairs Chairman, Sacred Heart Cathedral, 1982-83. Honors and Awards: Certificate of Appreciation from City of Houston, 1979; Proclamation from Commissioner Court, Phi Theta Kappa National Honor Society; Appreciation Award, Texas Association of Women Clubs, 1960; First Place Trophy in Bridge, National and Local Trophies, 1971; Trophies in Bowling, 1974-76. Address: 5215 Hancock Street, Houston, Texas 77004.■

ERV LEWIS

Purchasing Manager. Personal: Born August 19, 1936; Son of Mr. and Mrs. Henry J. Lewis; Married Barbara, Daughter of Mr. and Mrs. Ernest Green; Father of Hal, Pam, Steve, Cindy. Education: Political Science Degree, The Citadel, 1956; Graduate, Officer Candidates School, 1959; Certified Purshasing Manager. Military: Served in the United States Naval Reserves 1953-56, United States Army National Guard 1956-59, United States Army Reserves 1959-61. Career: Purshasing Manager, Wellman Industries, Inc.; Former Photographer, Singer/Guitarist, and Phonograph Record Producer. Organizational Memberships: Purchasing Management Association of the Carolinas and Virginia, Board of Directors, Chairman of Professional Development; National Association of Purchasing Management, Chairman of 5th District Professional Development. Community Activities: Parent-Teacher Association, President, 1961; Junior Chamber of Commerce, 1959-61; Boy Scouts of America, Leader 1961, Fund Raising Director 1970-71; Golden Gloves Boxing Coach, 1960-63; Teen Crusade, Inc., Director, 1975-78; Arhelger Evangelistic Association, Director, 1980 to present; Albert Long Happenings, Inc., Board of Advisors, 1978 to present; Canadian-American Folk Festival, Director, 1965-76; United Fund, Director, 1975; Gospel Music Association; Fellowship of Christian Athletes; Fellowship of Contemporary Christian Ministries; Fellowship of Christians in the Arts, Media and Entertainment. Religion: President, Erv Lewis Christian Outreach, Inc.; President, Herald Association, Inc.; Active Christian Singer, Songwriter and Recording Artist, Herald Records, United States and United Kingdom. Honors and Awards: Citations for Outstanding Purpose in Life, City of Tampa, Florida; National Communications Award for Promotion of Basic Human Understanding through Music;

TWO THOUSAND NOTABLE AMERICANS

Key to City of Florence, South Carolina; Honorary Citizenship, City of Myrtle Beach, South Carolina; Listed in *Personalities of the South, International Who's Who of Intellectuals, Dictionary of International Biography, Men of Achievement, Personalities of America, Community Leaders of America, Two Thousand Notable Americans.* Address: P.O. Box 218, Johnsonville, South Carolina 29555.■

CHOH-LUH LI

Professor. Personal: Born September 19, 1919, in Kwangchow, China; Married Julia Y. R.; Father of Claire Ming, David Yuan, Anne Ling. Education: M.D., National Medical College of Shanghai, China, 1942; M.S. Neuroanatomy 1950, Ph.D. Neurophysiology 1954, McGill University, Canada. Career: Clinical Professor in Department of Neurosurgery, George Washington University School of Medicine, 1974 to present; Medical Officer in Neurosurgery, National Institutes of Health, N.I.N.C.D.S., Department of Health, Education and Welfare, 1978 to present; Associate Neurosurgeon, National Institutes of Health, N.I.N.C.D.S., 1955-78; Chief of Section of Experimental Neurosurgery, National Institutes of Neurological Diseases and Blindness, National Institutes of Health, Bethesda, Maryland, 1954-55; Research Fellow in Neuroanatomy, Senior Resident in Neurosurgery, Resident in Neurology, Electroencephalography and Electromyography, Research Fellow in Neurophysiology and Instructor in Neuroanatomy, Montreal Neurological Institute, Montreal, Canada, 1947-54; Assistant Resident in Medicine, Resident and Instructor in Surgery, National Medical College of Shanghai, China, 1942-47. Organizational Memberships: New York Academy of Sciences; American Academy of Neurology; Washington Academy of Neurosurgery; American Association for the Advancement of Science; American Electroencephalograph Society; American Society for Electromyography of Electrodiagnosis; American Society for Experimental Biology; American Society for Physiology; Chinese Medical Society in the U.S.A.; Society for Neuroscience; International Association for the Study of Pain; American Epilepsy Society. International Brain Research Organization, 1962 to present; Research Society, American Neurological Surgeons, 1963 to present; American Center of Chinese Medicine, Board Director 1977-79. Published Works: Contributor of 81 Papers to Scientific Journals and Four Chapters to Neuroscientific Books; Editorial Board, *Journal of Electroencephalography and Clinical Neurophysiology* 1959-70 and 1979 to present, *Life Sciences* 1963-64, *International Journal of Neuropharmacology* 1963-64, *American Journal of Chinese Medicine* 1972 to present. Honors and Awards: Fellow, American Bureau of Medical Aid to China; Sigma Xi; Project Officer, Institute "Ruder Boskovic," Zagreb, Yugoslavia, 1970-73; Award for Distinguished Scientific Achievement, American-Chinese Medical and Health Association, 1978; Listed in *Personalities of the South, Who's Who in the East, American Men of Science, World Who's Who in Sciences, American Men and Women of Science, Men of Achievement, Book of Honor.* Address: 7001 Buxton Terrace, Bethesda, Maryland 20817.■

CHOH-MING LI

Professor Emeritus. Personal: Born February 17, 1912; Married Sylvia Lu; Father of Winston, Jean, Tony. Education: B.A. 1932, M.A. 1933, Ph.D. 1936, University of California at Berkeley. Career: Chairman, Board of Governors, The Hong Kong Arts Centre, 1974-77; President, The First Aisan Workshop on Higher Education, 1969; President, The Association of Southeast Asian Institution of Higher Learning, 1969-70; Council of the Association of Commonwealth Universities, 1964-65, 1966-67, 1972-74, 1976-77; Founding Vice Chancellor, The Chinese University of Hong Kong, 1963-78; Lecturer, Associate Professor, Professor of Business Administration, Director of Center for Chinese Studies, Professor Emeritus 1974 to present, University of California at Berkeley; Expert on the United Nations Population Commission and Statistical Commission, 1952-57; Chairman, Board of Trustees for Rehabilitation Affairs, National Government of China, 1949-50; Chief Delegate of the Republic of China to the United Nations Relief and Rehabilitation Conferences and to the United Nations Economic Commission for Asian and the Far East, 1947-49; Deputy Director-general, Chinese National Relief and Rehabilitation Adminstration, 1945-47; Member of China's Special Mission to U.S.A., Canada and United Kingdom, 1943-45; Professor of Economics, Nankai and Southwest Associated and Central Universities, China, 1937-43. Organizational Memberships: Council of the Association of Commonwealth Universities, 1964-65, 1966-67, 1972-74, 1976-77; President, The Association of Southeast Asian Institutions of Higher Learning, 1969-70; President, The First Asian Workshop on Higher Education, 1969; Chairman, Board of Governors, The Hong Kong Arts Centre, 1974-77; Board of Trustees, Asian Institute of Technology, Bangkok; Council of the World University of the World Academy of Art and Science; Editorial Board, *Asian Economic Review*, Indian Institute of Economics; Editorial Board, *Asian Survey*, University of California at Berkeley; Editorial Advisory Board, *Modern Asian Studies*; Editorial Advisory Board, *Tsing Hua Journal of Chinese Studies*; Life Fellow, Royal Economic Society; Life Fellow, Royal Society of Arts; American Economic Association; Association for Asian Studies; Fellow Member, World Academy of Art and Science; Associate Fellow, Silliman College, Yale University; Beta Gamma Sigma; Honorary Member, International Mark Twain Society. Honors and Awards: Commander of the Most Excellent Order of the British Empire, 1967; LL.D. honoris causa, University of Hong Kong 1967, University of Michigan 1967, Marquette University 1969, University of Western Ontario 1970, The Chinese University of Hong Kong 1978; Doctor of Social Science honoris causa, University of Pittsburgh, 1969; Knight Commander of the Order of the British Empire, 1973; The Elise and Walter A. Haas International Award of the University of California, 1974; The Clark Kerr Award of the University of California, 1979; Soong Foundation Hall of Fame Award, 1980; Fellow, The Society of The Berkeley Fellows, 1981; Honorary Professorship, Zhonfgshan University (Canton), Tsinghua University (Peking), Nankai University (Tientsin), 1983 to present. Address: 81 Northampton Avenue, Berkeley, California 94707.■

ALICE R. LIEBSON

Special Assistant. Personal: Born October 2, 1950; Daughter of Sidney H. and Jeannette B. Liebson. Education: B.A. Journalism, Western Connecticut State University, 1973. Career: Special Assistant to Connecticut Commissioner of Housing; Former Positions include Chief Aide to Ella Grasso for Re-Election Committee; A.B.C. News Political Consultant. Organizational Memberships: International Association of Business Communicators; Hartford Women's Network; Charter Member, Connecticut Women in Policy and Development; American Association of University Women, First Vice-President, 1980-82. Community Activities: Young Democrats of Stamford, President, 1976; Connecticut Women's Political Caucus, State Board, 1980 to present; Common Cause, State Board, 1980-81; Democratic National Party Conference, Delegate, 1978, 1982; United Way, Allocations Committee; Capitol Region Forum, Mayor's Appointee, 1979 to present; Red Cross Blood Drive, Chairman, 1976; Youth Division, United Jewish Appeal, Chairman, 1977; Women for Carter/Mondale, State Chairman, 1980; Democratic Women's Federation, Executive Committee, 1981 to present; Justice of the Peace, 1977 to present; West Hartford Economic Development Commission, 1983 to present; Steering committee, National Women's Political Caucus, 1983 to present; Affirmative Action Committee, Democratic State Party of Connecticut; Delegate, First Women's Leadership Conference, 1983. Honors and Awards: President Carter's Talent Bank of Women; Kentucky Colonel, 1976; Honored Twice by Connecticut General Assembly for Public Service; Special Community Service Award, G.E.C.C.; Y.W.C.A. Women in Leadership Recognition Award for Government Service, 1983; Listed in *Outstanding Young Women of America.* Address: 712 Farmington Avenue, West Hartford, Connecticut 06119.■

JOHN LIEU

Physician. Personal: Born August 15, 1904; Son of Rev. and Mrs. F. H. Lieu (both deceased); Married Dorothy A. Irwin; Father of Jon, Gladys. Education: M.D., St. John's University, Shanghai, China, 1926; D.T.M., Liverpool University, Liverpool, England, 1939. Career: Superintendent, Works and Mine Hospital, Hupeh, China, 1929-36; Assistant Medical Officer, Shanghai Municipal Council, Shanghai, China, 1929-36; Doctor-in-Charge, Municipal Hospital, Shanghai, 1936-45; Chief of Surgical Department, Municipal 6th Hospital, Shanghai, 1945-57; Assistant Port Health Officer, Hong Kong, 1957-59; Now Practicing in United States. Organizational Memberships: Academy of Medicine of Columbus; Ohio Medical Association; American Medical Association; American Association for the Advancement of Science; Ohio Academy of Science. Community Activities: Columbus Symphonic Orchestra, Sponsor; Friends of the Ohio State University; Smithsonian Institute; Geographic Society; National Historical Society; Columbus Association for the Performing Arts. Religion: Broad Street Presbyterian Church, Columbus, Ohio, Deacon 1968. Honors and Awards: Citation from the Chairman of Municipal Council, Shanghai, 1937; Citation from the Superintendent of Municipal Hospital, Shanghai, 1939; Rockefeller Scholarship, Rockefeller Foundation, U.S.A., 1940; Citation from the Commissioner of Public Health Department, Shanghai, 1945; Fellow, Royal Society of Health of Great Britain, 1972; Listed in *Who's Who in the Midwest, Dictionary of International Biography, National Society Directory, International Who's Who of Intellectuals.* Address: 645 Neil Avenue, Apartment 1011, Columbus, Ohio 43215.■

ALICE LEE LAN LIN

Physicist. Personal: Born October 28, 1937; Daughter of Tsing Tsing Wang; Married 1962; Mother of Peter A. Lin-Marcus. Education: A.B. Physics, University of California at Berkeley, 1963; M.A., George Washington University, Washington, D.C., 1974. Career: Physicist, Army Materials and Mechanics Research Center (Watertown, Massachusetts), Nondestructive Evaluation Branch 1980-82, Mechanics of Materials Division 1982 to present; Former Positions include

Physicist at N.A.S.A./Goddard Space Flight Center (Greenbelt, Maryland) 1975-80, Physics Teaching and Research Fellow at George Washington University and Catholic University (Washington, D.C.), Information Analysis Specialist at National Academy of Sciences (Washington, D.C.), Research Assistant at Cavendish Lab of University of Cambridge (England). Organizational Memberships: American Physical Society, 1971 to present; American Society for Non-Destructive Testing, 1980 to present; Acoustical Society of America, 1974-76; Optical Society of America, 1977-79; Society for Experimental Stress Analysis. Religion: Catholic. Published Works: "Deep Inelastic Electron-Nucleon Scattering" written at the Cavendish Laboratory with C. P. Wang and Other Articles on Electron Scattering published in *Nuovo Cimento, Nuclear Physics Journal* and *Journal of Physics* (U.K.); "Visualization of the Keller Edge Wave" with R. New, presented at the 1974 Acoustical Society Meeting, New York, 1974; Other Publications include "A New Ultrasonic Calibration Technique & Instrumentation," "A Bibliography on the Calibration & Characterization of Ultrasonic Transducers" and "Strength Comparisons of Two Slip-Cast, Reaction-Bonded Silicon Nitride Materials at Room Temperature, 2200° and 2500°" with J. R. Peters. Honors and Awards: Mencius Educational Foundation Grant, 1959-60; Teaching and Research Fellow, George Washington University, 1971-74; Listed in *Personalities of America, International Book of Honor, World Who's Who of Women*. Address: 28 Hallett Hill Road, Weston, Massachusetts 02193.■

HO-MU LIN

Laboratory Technical Director and Senior Research Fellow. Personal: Born July 12, 1938; Married Su-Jung; Father of Eugene, Jeffrey. Education: B.S. Chemical Engineering, National Taiwan University, 1962; Postgraduate Diploma, Tokyo Institute of Technology, Japan, 1966; Ph.D., Oklahoma State University, 1970. Military: Served in the Taiwanese Army (R.O.T.C.), 1962-63, attaining the rank of Second Lieutenant. Career: Technical Director and Senior Research Fellow, Thermodynamics Research Laboratory, Purdue University; Staff Member, National Taiwan University 1963-65, Tokyo Institute of Technology 1965-66, Oklahoma State University 1971-72, Purdue University 1973, Rice University 1974-75, Purdue University 1975 to present. Organizational Memberships: Full Member, American Institute of Chemical Engineers, American Chemical Society, Sigma Xi, Omega Xi Epsilon; Fellow, International Biographical Association. Published Works: Author or Co-Author of Over Fifty Technical Publications in Last Five Years. Honors and Awards: Fellowship, United Nations Educational, Scientific and Cultural Organization, 1965-66; American Petroleum Research Fund Award, 1968. Address: 400 North River Road No. 816, West Lafayette, Indiana 47906.■

MING-CHANG LIN

Research Chemist and Professor. Personal: Born October 24, 1936; Married; Father of Karen, Linus H., Ellena J. Education: B.Sc., Taiwan Normal University, 1960; Ph.D., University of Ottawa, Canada, 1966. Career: Supervisory Research Chemist, Naval Research Laboratory; Adjunct Professor of Chemistry, Catholic University, Washington, D.C.; Postdoctoral Research Associate, Cornell University, 1967-69; Postdoctoral Fellow, University of Ottawa, 1965-67; Graduate Student, University of Ottawa, 1962-65; Teaching Assistant, Taiwan Normal University, 1959-60, 1961-62. Military: Served in the Reserve Officers Training Corps, 1960-62, attaining the rank of Second Lieutenant. Organizational Memberships: American Chemical Society, 1971 to present; Combusion Institute, 1977 to present; Sigma Xi, 1975 to present; Fellow, Washington Academy of Sciences, 1975 to present. Honors and Awards: Hillebrand Prize, Chemical Society of Washington, 1975; Physical Sciences Award, Washington Academy of Sciences, 1976; Pure Science Award, Sigma Xi, Naval Research Lab, 1978; Navy Civilian Meritorious Service Award, 1979; Guggenheim Fellow, 1982-83; Humboldt Award. Address: 8897 McNair Drive, Alexandria, Virginia 22309.■

ELAYNE VERNA LINDBERG

Art Gallery Owner, Certified Graphoanalyst. Personal: Born April 27, in Browerville, Minnesota; Daughter of Leslie and Velma Breighhaupt Averill (both deceased); Married Russell Lindberg, Son of Harry and Victoria Lindberg; Mother of Gary, Bonnie Lindberg-Carlson. Education: Degree in Social Sciences, University of Minnesota. Career: President, Owner and Manager, Elayne Galleries, Inc., Minneapolis, 1971 to present; Appraiser and Restorer of Paintings; With Security Division, Dayton Department Store, Minneapolis, Minnesota, 1965-71. Organizational Memberships: Associate Member, American Society of Appraisers; National Home Fashions League; Charter Member, World Association of Questioned Document Examiners; International Grapho Analysis Society; Fine Arts Guild (London, England); National Association of Certified Antique Art Appraisers; International Society of Appraisers (Chicago, Illinois). Community Activities: Calhoun Beach, Minneapolis; Expert Witness in Handwriting Analysis for Attorney General's Office, Police Departments, Attorneys, and Individuals, 15 Years. Published Works: Co-Author and Composer of Verse and Sacred Music including "A Broken Heart I Gave" and "There Are Times." Honors and Awards: Life Fellow, American Biographical Institute; Listed in *Personalities of the West and Midwest, Book of Honor, International Who's Who of Intellectuals, Who's Who of American Women, Who's Who Upper Midwest*. Address: 2950 Dean Boulevard, Minneapolis, Minnesota 55416.■

RONALD AARON LINDSAY

Senior Accountant. Personal: Born September 27, 1957; Son of Shirley R. Lindsay. Education: Graduate, George Washington High School, 1975; B.B.A., Tennessee State University, 1981. Career: Senior Accountant, City of Indianapolis, 1982 to present; Substitute Teacher, Indianapolis Public Schools, 1981; Radial Drill Operator, Detroit Diesel Allison Division of General Motors Corporation, 1979; Production Grinder/General Inspector, Ford Motor Company, 1977-78; Bank Teller, Merchants National Bank and Trust Company, 1976. Organizational Memberships: National Association of Black Accountants, 1982. Community Activities: Student Union Board of Governors, Chairman, 1978-79; Student Election Commission, Co-Chairman 1977-78; Student Faculty Advisory Board, 1978-80; Tennessee State University, Peer Counselor, 1979-80; University Food Services Committee, 1978-80; Marion County Board of Voters Registration, Deputy Registrar, 1982. Honors and Awards: Student Leadership Scholarship, 1978-79; Student Union Board of Governors Award, 1979; Student Faculty Advisory Board Award, 1978; Listed in *Outstanding Young Men of America, Men of Achievement, International Youth in Achievement, Directory of Distinguished Americans*. Address: 3949 Cornelius Avenue, Indianapolis, Indiana 46208.■

FELICE M. LIPPERT

Food Research Consultant. Personal: Born February 9, 1930; Daughter of Mollie Mark; Married Albert; Mother of Keith L., Randy S. Education: B.A. Home Economics, Master's Degree Work, Hunter College, New York; Fundamentals of Management and Organizational Behavior for Women Seminar, Wharton School, 1976; Tribute to Women in International Industry Seminar, 1978. Career: Consultant to Weight Watchers International, Inc., 1981 to present; Vice-President of Food Research 1976-81, Director of Food Research 1963-76, Corporate Secretary 1971-76, Secretary/Director 1968-71, Treasurer 1963-68, Weight Watchers International, Inc.; Elementary School Teacher, Tuckahoe, New York, 1951-56; Assisting in the Publication of *Weight Watchers* Magazine and Weight Watchers Cookbooks and Instrumental in Developing the Weight Watchers Weight Reduction Program. Organizational Memberships: Home Economics in Business, New York City; American Home Economics Association; National Home Economics Society. Community Activities: Fund Raising Chairman, Mr./Mrs. League, City of Hope, New York City; American Parkinson's Disease Association; Trustee, North Shore University Hospital, 1979 to present; Chi Omicron; Fellow, Baruch College, 1979 to present. Religion: Hadassah, Life Member. Honors and Awards: City of Hope Spirit of Life Award, 1974; Tribute to Women in International Industry Award, National Board Young Women's Christian Association U.S.A., 1978; Listed in *Who's Who of American Women, Who's Who in Finance and Industry, World Who's Who of Women, Standard and Poor's Register of Corporations, Directors and Executives, Who's Who in the East, Who's Who in America, Personalities of America, Women in Business, Who's Who in World Jewry*. Address: Sousa Drive, Sands Point, New York 11050.■

IRVIN C. LISTER

Chiropractic Physician. Personal: Born October 18, 1933, in Birmingham, Alabama; Son of Robert Hood Lister (deceased); Married Dorothy Elizabeth Clevenger, October 18, 1956; Father of Elizabeth Ann, Linda Dianne, David Canon. Education: Attended University of Tuscaloosa (Tuscaloosa, Alabama) 1951-52, Del Mar College (Corpus Christi, Texas) 1953-54, Tulane University (New Orleans, Louisiana) 1954-55, William and Mary College (Norfolk, Virginia) 1955-57; D.C., Logan Chiropractic College (St. Louis, Missouri), 1961; Postgraduate Work, Louisiana State University (Baton Rouge), 1961; X-Ray Interpretation,

TWO THOUSAND NOTABLE AMERICANS

Erhardt Seminars, New Orleans, Louisiana, 1974-75; Postgraduate Work in X-Ray Technique, Physical Diagnosis, Hygiene and Laboratory Technique, Palmer College (Baton Rouge, Louisiana), 1974; Attending Texas Chiropractic College, Pasadena, Texas. Military: Served in the United States Navy Hospital Corps, 1952-56. Career: Private Practice Chiropractic Physician, Lafayette, Louisiana, 1961 to present. Organizational Memberships: Licensed in Florida and Louisiana; Lecturer on X-Ray Interpretation 1971, President 1964-65, President of District III 1961-63, Board of Directors 1963-64 and 1965-66, Chairman 1971, Chiropractic Association of Louisiana; Lecturer on Chiropractic throughout Southwestern Louisiana, 1975-76; Speakers Bureau, 1966-70; International Chiropractors Association; American Chiropractic Association; Parker Chiropractic Research Foundation. Community Activities: Lafayette Lions Club. Religion: Baptist. Honors and Awards: Lion of the Year, 1961. Address: 113 Longview Drive, Lafayette, Louisiana 70506.■

FRANK-FOTIOS K. LITSAS

Professor of Classics. Personal: Born in 1943; Son of Constantine and Georgia Litsas. Education: License in Philosophy, University of Athens, Greece, 1966; Officer's Degree for Greek Army, School of Reserve Army, 1969; M.A., University of East Michigan, 1974; Ph.D., University of Chicago, 1980. Military: Served in the Greek Army, 1969-71, attaining the rank of Lieutenant Captain. Career: Professor of Classics, University of Illinois at Chicago, 1978 to present; Instructor, Northeastern Illinois University, 1976-78; Research Assistant, University of Chicago, 1975-76; Consultant, Ann Arbor Public Schools, Michigan, 1972-74; Director, Greek Community School, Ann Arbor, Michigan, 1971-74; High School Teacher, Ministry of Education of Greece, 1966-71. Organizational Memberships: American Historical Association; Modern Language Association; Association of American Byzantinists; Modern Greek Studies Association; Hellenic Professional Society of Illinois, President, 1982-83. Community Activities: Board Member, Greek Education Committee, Parochial Greek Schools of Chicago Area, 1977 to present; Lecturer-Translator, Hellenic Foundation of Chicago, 1976 to present; Committee Member, Greek Ethnic Parade of Chicago, 1977 to present; Faculty Advisor, Hellenic Students Club of Chicago, 1978 to present; Proficiency Writer and Examiner, City of Chicago Board of Education, 1976-82; Life Member, Hellenic Voters of America, 1980 to present. Religion: Greek Orthodox Diocese of Chicago, Religious Education Commission, Director of Seminar on Greek Orthodox Studies 1977-80, Moderator of "Greek Orthodox Hour" Radio Program 1976 to present. Published Works: Author of Numerus Books and Articles in his Professional Field. Honors and Awards: Certificate of Merit, Greek Army, 1971; Research Award, Academy of Athens, Greece, 1972; Citation, City of Ann Arbor Board of Education, 1974; Citation of Merit, Northeastern Illinois University, 1977; Outstanding Citizen, Citizenship Council of Metropolitan Chicago, 1979; Archon-Knight of Patriarchate of Constantinople, 1980; Citations and Honorary Membership in Numerous Ethnic and Religious Organizations. Address: 5700 North Sheridan Road #1110, Chicago, Illinois 60660.■

NORMAN MATHER LITTELL

Retired Attorney and Claims Consultant. Personal: Son of Rev. and Mrs. Joseph Littell (both deceased); Married Katherine Maher (deceased); Father of Katharine Mather, Norman Mather. Education: Graduate, Wabash College, Crawfordsville, Indiana, 1921; Attended Christ Church College, Oxford University, 1922-23; B.A., Oxford University. Military: Served in the Student Army Training Corps, Wabash College, attaining the rank of Private. Career: Partner, Evans McClaren and Littell, South Washington; Appointed Assistant United States Attorney General, 1939-44; Private Practice, Washington, D.C., 1944-81; Consultant Drafting Foreign Investment Encouragement Law, with President Eisenhower; First Foreigner Invited to Speak before Legislation, Yuan; General Consultant and Claims Attorney for Navajo Tribe, Retiring in 1981. Organizational Memberships: International Bar Association, Organizer and Chairman of Committee on Foreign Investment Encouragement Laws; American Bar Association. Religion: St. James Episcopal Church, Lothian, Maryland, 1962 to present. Published Works: *Trails of the Sea*, 1982. Honors and Awards: State, Interstate, Intercollegiate Oratorical Contests, Indiana, 1920; Rhodes Scholarship to Attend Oxford University, 1922-23; Listed in *Community Leaders and Noteworthy Americans*, *Personalities of the South*, *Who's Who*. Address: 855 Mason Avenue, Deale, Maryland 20751.■

FLORENCE ELIZABETH HERBERT LITTLE

Educator. Personal: Born July 7, 1911; Daughter of Charles and Bertha Schlechter Herbert (both deceased); Married Alfred Lamon (decease), Son of Frank and Ina Little (both deceased); Mother of Alan Rush, Barbara Jean Little Votaw. Education: B.A., Michigan State University, 1932; M.S.E., Drake University, 1962; Graduate Work, Western State College of Gunnison (Colorado) 1959, Denver University 1962. Career: Tutor and Substitute Teacher; Retired Educator, Des Moines (Iowa) Public Schools, 20 Years Service; Teacher and Accompanist, instituting music programs in Bridgeport (Illinois) 1945, Holt (Michigan) 1945-46, Hanover (Michigan) 1949-50, Pittsford (Michigan) 1950-53. Organizational Memberships: Mu Phi Epsilon, Corresponding Secretary; Kappa Kappa Iota, Chapter President, Secretary, Treasurer, State Vice-President; National Education Association; Iowa State Education Association; Des Moines Education Association. Community Activities: CB Clubs; Volunteer for Money Raising Events, Restoration of Destrehan Manor, 1978-82; St. John the Baptist Parish Civil Defense. Religion: Sunday School Teacher, 1926-28, 1932-33; Church Choir, 1927-28, 1936; Director of Children's Church, Holt, Michigan, 1947-49. Honors and Awards: National Science Foundation Award, 1963-64; Patriarch, Michigan State University, 1982; A.B.I.R.A.; Listed in *Who's Who of American Women*. Address: 333 Lee Drive, Apt. 327, Baton Rouge, Louisiana 70808.■

CAMERON BRUCE LITTLEJOHN

Chief Justice of State Court. Personal: Born July 22, 1913; Son of Cameron and Lady Sara Warmoth Littlejohn (both deceased); Married Inell Smith (deceased); Father of Inell Littlejohn Allen, Cameron Bruce Jr. Education: A.B. 1935, LL.D. 1968, Wofford College; LL.B. 1936, J.D. 1970, University of South Carolina. Military: Served in the United States Army, 1943-46, attaining the rank of First Lieutenant, Prosecutor of Japanese War Criminals in Philippine Islands. Career: Chief Justice, Supreme Court of South Carolina, March 1984 to present; Former Associate Justice, Supreme Court of South Carolina; Private Practice Attorney, Spartanburg, South Carolina, 1936-43 and 1946-49. Community Activities: South Carolina House of Representatives, Member 1937-43 and 1947-49, Speaker 1947-49; Circuit Court Trial Judge, 1949-67; Delegate to Several County and State and Two National Democratic Conventions; American Legion; Veterans of Foreign Wars; 40 and 8. Religion: Baptist. Published Works: Author, *A Laugh with the Judge*, a collection of court-oriented anecdotes. Honors and Awards: Spartanburg Kiwanis Club Man of the Year, 1975; Occasional Lecturer, University of South Carolina School of Law; Board of Trustees, North Greenville College, 1962-67; Wofford Associates, 1977 to present; Wofford College Alumni Board of Directors, 1966-68. Address: 450 Connecticut Avenue, Spartanburg, South Carolina 29302.■

RAYMOND LEROY LIVINGSTON, SR.

Retired Consultant on Fruit and Pecan Production. Personal: Born December 28, 1919; Son of Mr. and Mrs. W. G. Livingston (both deceased); Married Christine C., Daughter of Mr. and Mrs. Marvin Catter (both deceased); Father of Raymond Leroy, Jr., William Marvin, Robert Warner. Education: B.S. Agricultural Science, Auburn University, 1943; M.S. Pomology, University of California, 1949. Military: Served in the United States Navy, 1943-46, attaining the rank of Lieutenant Senior Grade. Career: Retired Professional Consultant on Pecan and Fruit Production; Head of Extension Horticulture Department 1957-81, Horticulturist for Fruits and Nuts with Cooperative Extension Service 1957-58, University of Georgia; Assistant Horticulturist, Auburn University Horticulture Department, 1956-57; Horticulturist and Field Station Superintendent, Southeast Alabama Horticulture Field Station, Houston, County, Alabama, 1950-55; Vocational Agriculture Teacher, Redding High School, California, 1949-50; Graduate Assistant, University of California Pomology Department, 1947-48; Assistant County Agent, Dothan, Alabama, 1946-47; Assistant Instructor, Auburn University Department of Horticulture, 1943. Organizational Memberships: American Society of Horticultural Sciences, Chairman of Southern Region Extension Horticulture Section 1969-71, Youth Committee 1972-74; Special Vice President, Georgia Horticultural Society, 1966-71; Organizer, Georgia Pecan Grower Association, 1964; Southeastern Pecan Growers Association; National Pecan Council; Epsilon Sigma Phi; Sigma Xi; Alpha Zeta; Gamma Sigma Delta; Alpha Gamma Rho. Community Activities: Organizer, First 4-H Pecan Project; Director, National Junior Horticultural Association, 1958 to present. Published Works: Author of "Pecans in Georgia" Bulletin and First Pecan Spray Schedule. Honors and Awards: National Gold Pecan Award for Educational Leadership, 1961; Distinguished Service Award and Diamond Pin, National Junior Horticultural Association, 1968. Address: Route 3 Box 222, Goodwater, Alabama 35072.■

185

TWO THOUSAND NOTABLE AMERICANS

CHARLES WILLIAM LOBB

Electronics Company Executive. Personal: Born December 10, 1932; Son of Lloyd W. and Urazelle Huhn Lobb; Married Charlotte Carter, Daughter of Edwin M. and Valrie Moore (deceased) Carter; Father of Carolyn Jane, Patricia Ann. Education: B.E.E., University of Minnesota, 1955; M.S.E.E., University of Southern California, 1968. Military: Served in the United States Air Force, 1956-58, attaining the rank of Captain. Career: Assistant Director of Technical Education Center 1980 to present, Department Manager 1978-80, Section Head 1971-78, Group Head 1968-71, Technical Staff 1958-68, Hughes Aircraft Company; Lecturer, University of California at Los Angeles; Consultant to California Commission on Industrial Innovation, 1982; Instructor, Hughes ATEP Program, 1967-78; Technical Staff in Engineering Research and Development, General Mills, Inc., 1955-56. Organizational Memberships: Institute of Electrical and Electronics Engineers; Panelist, Association for Computing Machinery, 1981; American Radio Relay League; California Engineering Foundation; American Society of Engineering Education. Community Activities: Touring Lecturer, Various Amateur Radio Clubs, 1981-82. Published Works: Contributor of Articles on Computers to Various Professional Publications. Honors and Awards: Air Defense Command Commendation, 1964; Hughes Masters Fellow, 1966-68; Listed in *Who's Who in the West, Who's Who in California, Men of Achievement*. Address: 1843 244th Street, Lomita, California 90717.∎

SARAH LARKIN LOENING

Author. Personal: Widow; Mother of One Son. Career: Author. Community Activities: Founder and Chairman, Biblical Garden at Cathedral St. John the Divine; Past Chairman, Arts and Skill Corps, American Red Cross at Camp Upton; Hroswittia Club; Colony Club. Published Works: Author, *Three Rivers, Joan of Arc, Mountain in the Field, Dimo, The Gift of Life, Vignettes of a Life*, Others. Honors and Awards: Dame, American Order of St. John of Jerusalem; Medaille de la Reconnaissance par le Gouvernement Francais; Horticulture Award, Garden Club of American Zone III, 1981; Citation of Appreciation for Biblical Garden to Both Cathedral St. John the Divine and Sarah Larkin Loening, Layman's National Bible Committee. Address: P.O. Box 905, Southampton, New York 11968.∎

LEWIS M. K. LONG

Private Practice Psychologist. Personal: Born November 19, 1922; Married Alice Deaton; Father of Mark, Susan, David, Stephen. Education: B.A. 1947, M.S. 1949, B.S. 1950, University of Oklahoma; M.A. 1953, Ph.D. 1956, Harvard University; M.B.P.A., Southeastern University, 1981. Military: Served in the United States Naval Reserve, 1943-46, attaining the rank of Lieutenant Junior Grade. Career: Private Practice Psychologist; Former Positions include Staff Psychologist for National Institutes of Mental Health, Director of Selection for North Africa, Near East and Asia for the Peace Corps, Research and Evaluation Director for the Teacher Corps, Director of Selection for V.I.S.T.A. Organizational Memberships: American Psychology Association; District of Columbia Psychology Association; Northern Virginia Society of Clinical Psychology; American Sociology Association. Community Activities: Vice-Chairman, Mount Vernon Community Mental Health Clinic, 1976-78; Board, United Community Ministries, 1974-76; Various Positions, Boy Scouts of America Troop 781; President, Stephen Foster Parent-Teacher Association, 1969-70; Committee Member, Ft. Hunt Parent-Teacher Association, 1972-74; Chairman, Mt. Vernon Dads League, Basketball. Religion: Mt. Vernon Unitarian Church, Board, 1972-74. Published Works: Co-Author, *Staffing for Better Schools*, U.S.G.P.O., 1967; Numerous Other Publications. Honors and Awards: Charles Smith Award, Howard University, 1951-52; United States State Department Scholarship to Brazil and Venezuela, 1953 (declined); S.S.R.C. Research Award, 1954. Address: 213 South Alfred, Alexandria, Virginia 22314.∎

LUCY ENID LOPEZ-ROIG

Clinical, Industrial Psychologist. Personal: Born November 23, 1936 in Rio Piedras, Puerto Rico; Daughter of Jose Antonio and Victoria Luisa Roig Lopez-Puig. Education: B.A., Seton Hall College, 1958; M.S., Caribbean Center for Advanced Studies, 1969; Ph.D., Purdue University, 1972. Career: Director of Training, Psychological Services, Puerto Rico Medical Center, Rio Piedras, 1966-67; Chief of Psychological Services, Puerto Rico Police Department, Hato Rey, 1961-66; Chief of Psychological Services for Chief Selection Program 1967-69, Chief of Office of Motivation 1972-74, Chief of Division of Personnel 1974-75, Assistant Executive Director for Human Relations 1975-78, Puerto Rico Water Resources Authority, Santurce; Consultant to President and Associate Professor, Interamerican University, Hato Rey, Puerto Rico, 1978 to present; Private Practice in Clinical Psychology, Hato Rey, 1972 to present; President, Lucy Lopez-Roig and Associates, 1978 to present; Professor 1975 to present, Director of Industrial-Organizational Psychology Program 1978 to present, Caribbean Center for Advanced Studies, Santurce; Consultant to Puerto Rico Department of Education, 1967-68; Consultant, Colegio Puertorriqueno de Ninas, Puerto Rican Association of Private Schools, 1974-78; Board of Directors, Instituto Psicologico de Puerto Rico, 1975-76; President, Quality of Life Committee, Chamber of Commerce of Puerto Rico, 1982 to present. Organizational Memberships: American Psychological Association, Division 14; Puerto Rican Psychological Association; Asociación de Personal Público; Sigma Xi. Published Works: Author, *An Approach to the Empathic Process* 1972, *A Critical Review and Research Proposal for the Selection and Training of Paraprofessionals* 1971, *Development of a Locus Scale for Managers* 1972; Co-Author, *Helping Supervisors to Cope* 1977, *Source of Stress in Six Occupational Groups in Puerto Rico* 1982. Honors and Awards: Award for Contribution to Human Relations, Puerto Rico Water Resources Authority, 1976; Award for Contributions in Education, Puerto Rican Association of Private Schools, 1974; Outstanding Woman of the Year in Public Administration, Blue Cross of Puerto Rico, 1975; Outstanding Professional Woman of the Year, Chamber of Commerce of Puerto Rico, 1982; Nominee for Psychologist of the Year, Puerto Rican Psychological Association, 1983. Address: 70 King's Court, Santurce, Puerto Rico 00911.∎

GERALD D. LORGE

State Senator. Personal: Born July 9, 1922, in Bear Creek, Wisconsin; Son of Joseph J. Lorge; Married Christina C. Ziegler; Father of Robert, William, Anna, Julie, Christina. Education: Graduate, Bear Creek Public High School; J.D., Marquette University Law School, 1952. Military: Served in the United States Marine Corps, 1942-45, attaining the rank of Technical Sergeant. Career: Senator for 14th District 1955-79 and 1980-85, Senate Committee on Insurance and Utilities, Joint Legislative Council, Joint Committee on Revisions, Repeals and Uniform Laws, Special Committee on Adoption Laws, Wisconsin State Senate; Assemblyman, Outagamie 2nd District, 1951-55. Organizational Memberships: Outagamie Bar Association; Wisconsin Bar Association; American Bar Association; Past Chairman of Justice and Law Enforcement Committee, Midwestern Council of State Governments, 1970-72; President 1973-74, Vice-President 1972-73, Executive Committee 1971-79, National Conference of Insurance Legislators of the United States. Community Activities: Life Member, Republican Party; Chairman, Marquette University Young G.O.P. Law School Club, 1949-50; Milwaukee County Republican Committee 4th Ward; Outagamie and Waupaca County Republican Units; Moose; Boy Scouts of America; Veterans of Foreign Wars; Disabled American Veterans; American Legion; Knights of Columbus; Marquette University Alumni Association; Local Conservation Clubs; Young Men's Christian Association-B.M.C. Health Club. Address: P.O. Box 47, Bear Creek, Wisconsin 54922.∎

CORNELIS A. LOS

Econometrician. Personal: Born December 14, 1951; Son of Klaas Los and Adriaantje Nieuwland-Los; Father of Francesca Rose Eloise. Education: Candidatus Cum Laude 1974, Doctorandus 1976, Groningen University, The Netherlands; London School of Economics, 1975-76; Postgraduate Diploma, Institute of Social Studies, The Hague, 1977; M.Phil. Economics 1980, Ph.D. Economics 1984, Columbia University. Career: Economist, Federal Reserve Bank of New York, 1981 to present; Instructor 1980-81, Preceptor 1979-81, Teaching Assistant 1978-80, Columbia University; Adjunct Lecturer, Hunter College 1980,

City College of New York 1980. Organizational Memberships: The Econometric Society, 1979 to present; American Economic Association, 1980 to present; American Statistical Association, 1981 to present; Time Series Analysis and Forecasting Society, 1982 to present; Institute of Electrical and Electronics Engineers Control Systems Society, 1979 to present; New York Academy of Sciences, 1981 to present; International Institute of Forecasters, 1983; Metropolitan Economic Association, 1982 to present. Community Activities: Certified Yoga Instructor, Young Men's Christian Association, 1980; Physical Fitness Instructor, International House, New York, 1978-79; Student Rowing Crews, Groningen University and London School of Economics, 1974-76; Editor, Department of Economics Student Bulletin, Groningen University, 1970-72. Religion: Greek Orthodox Church, 1981 to present. Honors and Awards: Fulbright-Hays Travel Grant, 1977; Fellowship, Groningen University, 1975-76; Cum Laude Graduate, 1974; Scholten Cordes Fund, 2 Awards; M.A.O.C. Countess Van Bylandt Foundation (The Hague) 1976; Lady Van Renswoude of the Hague Foundation, 4 Awards, 1974-75; Commercial Club of Groningen, 1 Book Award, 1970. Address: 108 Erie Street Apartment 1, Jersey City, New Jersey 07302.∎

MARY ANNE ELIZABETH LOUGHLIN

Television News Anchor and Producer. Personal: Born July 30, 1956; Daughter of Dr. and Mrs. John F. Loughlin. Education: B.S. Communications, Florida State University, 1977. Career: News Anchor and Producer, Cable News Network; Former Positions include Television Show Producer and Host for WTBS (Atlanta, Georgia), Television News Anchorwoman and Producer for WECA (Tallahassee, Florida) and Radio News Reporter for WFSU-FM (Tallahassee). Organizational Memberships: Women in Communications; Women in Cable; American Women in Radio and Television. Religion: Roman Catholic. Honors and Awards: Women at Work Broadcast Award, National Commission on Working Women, 1982; Woman of Achievement, American Women in Radio and Television, 1982; Two Georgia Emmy Award Nominations, 1982; Talent Nomination, *On Cable* Magazine, 1982; Achievement Award Nomination, American Women in Radio and Television, 1983; Listed in *Who's Who in the South and Southwest, Personalities of the South, Personalities of America, International Who's Who of Women, Directory of Distinguished Americans, Dictionary of International Biography, International Book of Honor*. Address: 195 Triumph Drive Northwest, Atlanta, Georgia 30327.∎

THOMAS DARRYL LOVE

Human Resources Development Specialist. Personal: Born February 28, 1935, in Refugio, Texas. Education: B.A. English, Baylor University, Waco, Texas; M.A. Human Resources Management, Pepperdine University, Los Angeles, California, 1977. Military: Served in the United States Marine Corps, 1968-78, advancing through the ranks from Second Lieutenant to Major (retired). Career: Senior Personnel Representative for Human Resources Development, Data General Corporation, Austin, Texas, 1981 to present; Management Development Specialist, Texas Instruments, Houston, 1980-81; Training Specialist, The University of Texas at Austin, 1978-80. Organizational Memberships: American Society for Training and Development; Private Industry Council, Vice-Chairman, 1980; Advisory Board for Human Resources Development, University of Texas at Austin Graduate School of Education; Advisory Board for Business and Industry, Austin Community College, Austin, Texas; Kappa Delta Pi. Honors and Awards: Bronze Star with Combat 'V'; Joint Services Commendation Medal for Meritorious Service. Address: 11508 Sweetwater Trail, Austin, Texas 78750.∎

DENNIS JOSEPH LOVELACE (DECEASED)

Management Services Consultant. Personal: Born June 18, 1940; Son of Marcus and Joyce C. Lovelace; Married to Connie Lynn Han Soon Chung; Father of Deborah Ann, Darlene Ann. Education: A.A. 1976, B.A. 1977, University of Maryland; M.S., University of Southern California, 1979. Military: Served in the United States Army, 1958-78, attaining the rank of Master Sergeant. Career: Management Services Consultant, Reno, Nevada; Former Personnel Manager. Organizational Memberships: Association for Systems Management, Editor of Newsletter, 1980; American Management Association; American Planning Association; International Platform Association; American Society of Professional Consultants. Community Activities: Fellow, American Biographical Association, 1981; University of Southern California Alumni Association, 1979; California Community College Lifetime Instructor in Business and Industrial Management, 1979. Honors and Awards: Meritorious Service Medal 1978, Commendation Medal 1965, Commendation Medal with First Oak Leaf Cluster 1968, Commendation Medal with Second Oak Leaf Cluster 1970, United States Army. Address: P.O. Box 6475, Reno, Nevada 89503.∎

BARBARA SAWYER LOWRY

Medical Research Investigator. Personal: Born March 31, 1924; Married John B., Jr.; Mother of Arthur Samuel, John B., III, Peter Alfred, Charles Warren. Education: A.B., Bryn Mawr College, 1946; M.D., Temple University School of Medicine, 1954; M.S. Clinical Microbiology, The Thomas Jefferson University School of Graduate Studies, 1977. Military: Service in the United States Army, 1978 to present, holding the rank of Colonel (P). Career: Research Investigator, United States Army Medical Institute of Infectious Diseases; Former Positions include Assistant Pathologist through Laboratory Director in Various Hospitals in New York and Pennsylvania, Visiting Assistant Professor of Pathology at the Woman's Medical College of Pennsylvania (Philadelphia, Pennsylvania) 1968-78, Instructor in Pathology at Jefferson Medical College (Philadelphia, Pennsylvania) 1974-78. Organizational Memberships: American Society of Clinical Pathologists, Fellow; College of American Pathologists, Fellow; International Academy of Pathology; Association of Clinical Scientists; New York Academy of Sciences; American Society of Microbiology; American Medical Women's Association Branch #25 (Philadelphia), Secretary 1978, President-Elect 1979-80, President 1981-82, Delegate to National Meeting 1981 and 1983, State Director for Pennsylvania 1982-83, Governor for Region III 1983 to present. Community Activities: Coatesville Hospital, Secretary of Staff, Executive Committee of the Staff, 1967-70; American Cancer Society, Chester County Unit Board, 1970-76; Temple Univesity Medical Alumni Association, Board of Directors 1970-76, Alumni Congress 1974-78; Boy Scouts of America, Den Mother to Explorer Advisor (wood badge and wood bead training), 15 Years. Religion: Society of Friends. Published Works: Contributor of Articles to *American Journal of Clinical Pathology, Annals of Clinical and Laboratory Science, Journal of Laboratory Investigation, Proceddings of the 2nd International Symposium on Legionella*. Honors and Awards: Legion of Honor, Chapel of Four Chaplains, Philadelphia, Pennsylvania. Address: 5641D Etzler Road, Frederick, Maryland 21701.∎

AUBREY KEITH LUCAS

University President. Personal: Born July 12, 1934, in State Line, Mississippi; Son of Keith C. (deceased) and Audell Robertson Lucas; Married Ella F. Ginn, Daughter of Baxter H. (deceased) and Fannie Godbold Ginn; Father of Frances, Carol, Alan, Mark. Education: Graduate, State Line High School, 1952; B.S. with honors Education and History 1955, M.A. Psychology of Reading 1956, University of Southern Mississippi; Ph.D. Administration of Higher Education, Florida State University, 1966. Career: President 1975 to present, Dean of Graduate School, Coordinator of Research and Professor of Higher Education 1970-71, Registrar and Associate Professor of Educational Administration 1963-70, Director of Admissions and Associate Professor of Education 1957-61, Assistant Director of Reading Clinic 1955-56, University of Southern Mississippi; Consultant to Junior and Senior Colleges in Curriculum, Admissions and Records, and Organization and Administration; President, Delta State University, 1970-75; Research Assistant in Computer Center and Office of Institutional Research and Service, Florida State University, 1961-63; Instructor, Hinds Junior College, 1956-57. Organizational Memberships: Former Member, State Commission on Postsecondary Education; Mississippi Representative, Southern Regional Education Board; Committee on Policies and Purposes, American

Association of State Colleges and Universities; Past President, Mississippi Association of Colleges; Commission on National Development in Postsecondary Education; Faculty Representative, Committee of the Football Association, 1981; Board of Directors, American Association of State Colleges and Universities, 1983-85; Omicron Delta Kappa; Phi Kappa Phi; Pi Kappa Pi; Pi Gamma Mu; Pi Tau Chi; Kapa Delta Pi; Phi Delta Kappa; Red Red Rose; Newcomen Society of North America; Kappa Pi; Pi Kappa Delta; Mississippi Arts Commission, Chairman, 1982-83; Mississippi Committee for the Humanities; Phi Theta Kappa, Honorary Member, National Board of Directors, 1980 to present. Community Activities: Hub City Kiwanis Club; Mississippi Economic Council; Hattiesburg Chamber of Commerce; Past President, Forrest-Lamar United Way, Board of Directors; Past Mississippi Crusade Chairman, American Cancer Society. Religion: Parkway Heights United Methodist Church of Hattiesburg; University of Southern Mississippi Wesley Foundation, Board of Directors; Conference Lay Leader of the Mississippi Conference of United Methodist Church, 1980 to present. Published Works: Author, *The Mississippi Legislature and Mississippi Public Higher Education: 1980-1960*; Contributing Author to *History of Mississippi*; Author of Consultative Studies and Reports. Honors and Awards: Listed in *Who's Who in America, Who's Who in the South and Southwest, Who's Who Among Students in American Universities and Colleges; Dictionary of International Biography, Leaders in Education.*■

MAURICE H. LUNTZ

Professor of Ophthalmology. Personal: Born July 27, 1930; Son of Montague Luntz; Married Angela June Rose; Father of Melvyn H. B., Caryn Susan, David Sean. Education: M.B.Ch.B., Cape Town University, 1952; F.R.C.S. Education, 1957; M.D., Witwatersrand University, 1974; Diplomate, American Board of Ophthalmology, 1979; F.A.C.S., 1979. Career: Professor of Ophthalmology, New York City; Professor of Ophthalmology, Witwatersrand University. Organizational Memberships: International Council of Ophthalmology, 1972 to present; Academia Ophthalmologica Internationalis, 1974 to present. Community Activities: Officer, Order of St. John of Jerusalem, 1976 to present. Honors and Awards: Lewis Memorial Scholarship, 1950-52; Elected to Academia Ophthalmologica Internationalis, 1974; Invited Speaker, Over 100 Congresses, National and International. Address: 180 East End Avenue, New York, New York 10028.■

DOMINGO VALENTIN LUGO

Company Executive. Personal: Born September 18, 1935; Son of Domingo Lugo Ruiz (deceased); Married Angela Soto, Daughter of Patrio Soto (deceased); Father of Elvin, Alvin D, Alberto, Raul D. Education: Graduate, Dr. Perea School, 1955; Associate's Degree in Electronics Engineering, University of Puerto Rico, 1977. Career: Vice-President, Former Field Service Engineer, Ortiz Music and Vending; Owner, Doluva Electronics; Vice-President, Ramos and Lugo Music Corporation. Organizational Memberships: Institute of Electrical and Electronics Engineers, 1976; President, Radio and Television Technical Association, 1978-79; Counselor, Western Amateur Radio Club, 1980. Community Activities: Guanajibo Sertoma Club, Charter Member 1971, President 1978-79, Lieutenant Governor 1979, Treasurer 1974-77, Sertoma Heart Campaign 1978, National Campaign Crippled Boys and Adults 1973. Religion: Catholic Church, Active Member. Honors and Awards: Gem Award 1972, Tribune Award 1976, Senator Award 1977-78, Award of Merit 1978-79, Life Member 1980, Sertoma International. Address: P.O. Box 656, Moca, Puerto Rico 00716.■

E. RALPH LUPIN

Physician and Business Consultant. Personal: Born April 1, 1931; Son of Yetta Lupin; Married Freda Merlin; Father of Jay Stephen. Education: B.S.Pharm., Loyola University of the South; M.D., Louisiana State University, 1956. Military: Served in the United States Air Force Reserve, 1958-60, attaining the rank of Captain. Career: Physician; Business Consultant to National Medical Enterprise, Inc.; Former Positions include Medical Director for Home Health Services of Louisiana, President and Chairman of the Board for Unihealth Services Corporation, and President and Chairman of the Board of Datamedics Corporation. Organizational Memberships: Diplomate, American College of Obstetrics and Gynecology; Board Certification, American Board of Obstetrics and Gynecology; American Medical Association; Louisiana State Medical Society; Jefferson Parish Medical Society; New Orleans Gynecological and Obstetrical Society; Gynecological Laser Society; American Fertility Society. Community Activities: Elected Member, Orleans Parish Democratic Executive Committee, 1982; Chief Deputy Coroner, Orleans Parish, 1972-82; Elected Member, Human Relations Committee, City of New Orleans, 1976-78; Board of Directors, American Red Cross, New Orleans Chapter; Rotary Club, Member and Board of Directors, 1965 to present; Board of Directors, Leukemia Society of America, 1970; Board of Trustees, New Orleans Symphony Society, 1980-82; Trustee, Louisiana State Museum, 1982; Chairman, Upper Pontabla Commission, 1976-80; Board of Directors, Repertory Theater of New Orleans, 1981 to present; Board of Trustees, Physicians New Orleans Foundation, 1981 to present; Board of Directors, St. Charles General Hospital, 1981 to present. Religion: Conservative Congregation of New Orleans, Vice-President of Board of Directors, 1962 to present. Address: 1021 Chartres Street, New Orleans, Louisiana 70116.■

ALFRED C. LUTZ

Company Co-Owner and Manager. Personal: Born September 27, 1940; Son of Ralph and Anna Lutz; Married Carol Richards, Daughter of Charles and Laura Richards; Father of John C., James C., Lawrence L. Education: A.A. with high honors, Oakton Community College, Morton Grove, Illinois, 1973; B.A. 1976, M.B.A. 1981, DePaul University, Chicago, Illinois. Military: Served in the United States Naval Reserve, attaining the rank of Ensign. Career: Co-Owner and Manager, A & C Services, Park Ridge, Illinois; Former Positions include Regional Service Manager for General Instruments Corporation (Park Ridge, Illinois) and National Service Manager for Robert Bosch Corporation Blaupunkt Division (Broadview, Illinois). Community Activities: Park Ridge Fine Arts Society, Treasurer, 1980 to present; Oakton Community College Alumni Association, 1980 to present; DePaul Alumni Association, 1980 to present. Address: 233 East Avenue, Park Ridge, Illinois 60068.■

CAROL RICHARDS LUTZ

Attorney. Personal: Born March 4, 1937; Daughter of Charles and Laura Richards; Married Alfred C., Son of Ralph and Anna Lutz; Mother of Alan K., Kelly J., Ken R., Kitch G. Lark. Education: A.A. with high honors, Oakton Community College, Morton Grove, Illinois, 1972; B.A., DePaul University, Chicago, Illinois, 1976; J.D. with Honors, I.I.T.-Chicago-Kent College of Law, 1978. Career: Private Practice Attorney; Railroad Attorney, CMStP&P Railroad, 1978-81; Admitted to United States District Court of Illinois Bar 1978, Northern District of Illinois Bar 1978, 7th Circuit Court of Appeals Bar 1978, United States Supreme Court Bar 1981, United States Claims Court Bar 1982; Associate Realtor, 1969-73; Dance Teacher, 1959-67. Organizational Memberships: Illinois State Bar Association; American Bar Association; Chicago Bar Association; Women's Bar Association of Illinois; Park Ridge Women Entrepreneurs, Founder; American Association of University Women; League of Women Voters. Community Activities: Park Ridge Public Library, Executive Secretary of Board of Directors, 1980-83; Park Ridge United Way, Legal Counsel, 1983 to present; Park Ridge Fine Arts Society, Board of Directors, 1980 to present; Women Helping Women, 1981 to present; DePaul University Alumni Association, 1980-83; Oakton Community College Alumni Association, 1980 to present; Phi Alpha Delta Law Fraternity International, Member 1975 to present, First Woman Justice of Chicago Alumni Chapter 1982, Executive Secretary 1983. Honors and Awards: Distinguished Alumni Award, Oakton Community College, 1982; Chicago Young Women's Christian Association Certificate of Leadership, 1979. Address: 233 East Avenue, Park Ridge, Illinois 60068.■

JAMES E. LYONS

International Business Consultant. Personal: Born October 21, 1928; Son of Lacey and Janie Louise Lyons; Married Ollie M.; Father of James E., Jr., Katherine Brown Lyons. Education: B.S. and D.Sc. 1960, M.B.A. 1962, The National College; Ph.D., Clayton University, 1972. Military: Served in the United States Air Force, 1944-50. Career: International Business Consultant; Chairman of the Board and Chief Executive, Leasetran Corporation 1968-82; Central Industries 1964-68. Organizational Memberships: Florida Council of 100, Member 1971 to present, Board of Directors 1975-77; Air Force Association, Member 1955 to present, Air Council 1981 to present, Chapter President, 1982-83. Community Activities: Florida Institute of Technology, Instrumental in Founding 1958, Chairman of Board of Trustees 1975 to present, Lecturer and First Chairman of Steering Committee; Chairman, Alliance with the Republic of Colombia, South America, 1971-75; Federal Reserve Bank, Chairman Jacksonville Branch, Board 1971-78. Religion: First Baptist Church, Finance Committee, Personnel Committee. Honors and Awards: CHIEF Award for Champion of Higher Education in Florida, Presented by Seventeen University Presidents in Florida, 1978; Honorary Doctor of Science Degree, Florida Institute of Technology, 1978; Honorary Doctor of Humane Letters, Nathaniel Hawthorne College, Antrim, New Hampshire, 1982; Honorary Doctor of Aeronautical Science, Southwestern University, 1982. Address: 1824 East Lake Cannon Drive, Winter Haven, Florida 33880.■

TWO THOUSAND NOTABLE AMERICANS

MICHAEL ALLEN LYTLE

Assistant to University System Chancellor. Personal: Born October 22, 1946; Son of Milton E. and Geraldine Young Lytle; Married. Education: A.B., Indiana University, 1973; Certificate of Advanced Graduate Study, Sam Houston State University, 1977; M.Ed. 1978, Postgraduate Doctoral Study, Texas A. & M. University. Military: Served in the United States Army Reserve, 1969-70 and 1972 to present; Served in the United States Army, 1970-72, rising through the ranks from First Lieutenant to Major, serving as Platoon Leader and Provost Marshal in Vietnam. Career: Assistant to the Chancellor, Texas A. & M. University System; Former Positions include Instructor of Criminal Justice, Military Officer. Organizational Memberships: Academy of Criminal Justice Sciences; American Association for Higher Education; American Judicature Society; American Society for Public Administration; Fellow, Inter-University Seminar on Armed Forces and Society; Policy Studies Organization. Community Activities: American Defense Preparedness Association; Reserve Officers Association; Association of the United States Army; Special Contributor, Atlantic Council of the United States; Executive Director, Texas Committee for Employer Support of the Guard and Reserve; Bryan-College Station Chamber of Commerce. Religion: St. Thomas Episcopal Church, College Station, Texas. Honors and Awards: Bronze Star Medal; Army Commendation Medal with Second Oak Leaf Cluster; Staff Service Honor Medal First Class of the Republic of Viet Nam; Named Fellow, Inter-University Seminar on Armed Forces and Society, 1979; Phi Delta Kappa, 1981; Listed in *Who's Who in the South and Southwest, Personalities of the South, Personalities of America, Men of Achievement, Biographical Roll of Honor.* Address: 1806 Langford Street, College Station, Texas 77840.■

PEARL MA

Microbiologist. Personal: Born August 10, 1928; Daughter of Chiu-Ki and Yee Mui Lum Ma. Education: Graduate, St. Stephen's Girls College, Hong Kong (with degree of London Matriculation), 1946; B.A. Biology, Rosemont College, Pennsylvania, 1950; M.S. Microbiology, University of Pennsylvania Graduate School of Liberal Arts and Sciences, Philadelphia, 1955; Ph.D. Microbiology, Jefferson University, Philadelphia, 1951. Career: Coordinator of Intercity Infectious Disease Rounds, St. Vincent's Hospital and Medical Center of New York, 1980 to present; Lecturer in Virology, Department of Public Health and Bacteriology, Wagner College, Staten Island, New York, 1972-73; Assistant Professor, Clinical Pathology, New York University School of Medicine, 1971 to present; Chief of Microbiology, St. Vincent's Hospital and Medical Center of New York, 1970 to present; Chief of Microbiology and Cytogenetics, Department of Clinical Pathology, Akron City Hospital, Akron, Ohio, 1965-69; Research Associate, Department of Pathology, Medical College of Virginia (Richmond), 1964-65; Associate in Medicine 1963-64, Adjunct Research Associate 1961-62, Research Associate in Public Health/Infectious Diseases 1961-62, Hehnemann Medical College and Hospital (Philadelphia); Chief of Microbiology, Oncologic Hospital, Philadelphia, 1961-62; Consultant in Microbiology, Woman's Hospital of Philadelphia, 1961-62; Consultant in Microbiology and Hematology, Toxicology Laboratory, Philadelphia, 1961; Consultant in Microbiology, Salem County Hospital, New Jersey, 1961; Instructor of Nursing Microbiology, School of Nursing, Jefferson Hospital, Philadelphia; Consultant in Mycology and Clinical Microbiology 1959-61, Chief of Mycology and Assistant Bacteriologist 1954-59, Jefferson University, Philadelphia. Organizational Memberships: Association for Women in Science; New York Academy of Sciences, Advisory Committee of Microbiology Section 1976 to present; Public Health and Medical Laboratory Microbiology, Registered Specialist 1973; Medical Mycology Society of New York, 1972; New York City Branch of the American Society for Microbiology; Mid-West Society for Electron Microscopists; American Association for the Advancement of Science; Women's American Medical Association; Eastern Pennsylvania Branch, American Society for Microbiology; National-American Society for Microbiology; Association of Clinical Scientists. Published Works: Numerous Professional Articles including "A Case of Acanthamoeba Keratitis in New York City and a Review of Ten Cases" (with E. Willaert, K. B. Juechter and A. R. Stevens) 1982, "Three-Step Stool Examination for Cryptosporidiosis in Ten Homosexual Men with Protracted Watery Diarrhea" (with Rosemary Soave) 1982, "A Sudden Fall in Ampicillin Resistance in Salmonella Typhimurium" (with C. E. Cherubin, G. F. Timoney, M. F. Sierra and J. Marr) 1980, "The Microbiology Laboratory in Diagnosis and Therapy" 1980; Other Technical Publications and Professional Presentations, 1962 to present; Reviewer for *New England Journal of Medicine* on Cryptosporidiosis, 1983. Honors and Awards: Elected Member, Infectious Diseases Society of America, 1981; Coordinator of Inter-City Infectious Disease Rounds, St. Vincent's Hospital and Medical Center of New York, 1980 to present; Antimicrobial Tests of New Antibiotics on Clinical Isolates, 1978 to present; Biomedical Research Support Grant, St. Vincent's Hospital, 1977; Fellow, New York Academy of Sciences, 1977 to present; General Research Fund Award, United States National Institute of Health, Most Successful Alumnus of the Year, Rosemont College Alumni Association, 1965; Candidate, *Young Women of America*, 1965; Research Grant on Heat Shock Method of Phage Typing Non-Typable Staphylococcus Aureus, National Institute of Allergy and Infectious Diseases, National Institute of Health, 1965-68; Graduate with Distinction in Biology, Rosemont College, Pennsylvania; Kistler's Honor Society, Rosemont College; Listed in *Who's Who of American Women, Two Thousand Women of Achievement, Dictionary of International Biography, National Register of Prominent Americans, Who's Who in the Midwest, Who's Who in the East, International Who's Who in Community Service, World Who's Who of Women, Who's Who Directory, Who's Who in America, International Who's Who of Intellectuals, Notable Americans, Community Leaders of America, Men and Women of Distinction, Who's Who in Technology Today*. Address: 531 Main Street North, New York, New York 10044.■

ALBERTO J. L. MACARIO

Research Physician, Administrator. Personal: Born December 1, 1935; Son of Alberto C. and Maria E. Giraudi Macario; Married Everly Conway; Father of Alex, Everly. Education: M.D., University of Buenos Aires School of Medicine. Career: Research Physician, Center for Laboratories and Research, New York State Department of Health, 1981 to present; Director of the Clinical and Experimental Immunology Section, Laboratory Medicine Institute, Center for Laboratories and Research, New York State Department of Health, 1981-83; Chief of Hematology, Clinical Laboratory Center, New York State Department of Health, 1979-81; Research Scientist, Division of Laboratories and Research, New York State Department of Health 1976-79; Brown University (Providence, Rhode Island) 1974-76; Head of the Laboratory of Immunology, International Agency for Research on Cancer, World Health Organization, Lyons, France, 1973-74; Member of Scientific Staff, Laboratory of Cell Biology, National Research Council of Italy (Rome), 1971-73; Eleanor Roosevelt Fellow, International Union Against Cancer, Department of Tumorbiology, Karolinska Institute, Stockholm, Sweden, 1969-71; Head of the Department of Radioactive Isotopes, Institute for Hematological Investigations, National Academy of Medicine of Argentina, 1967-69; Fellow, National Research Council of Argentina, 1964-69; Physician/Hematologist, Rivadavia Hospital, Buenos Aires, 1962-64. Organizational Memberships: Scandinavian Society for Immunology; Italian Association of Immunologists; French Society for Immunology; American Association of Immunologists; American Society for Microbiology; American Association of Pathologists. Community Activities: Coordinator of Research on Immunology of Cancer, International Agency for Research on Cancer, World Health Organization, Lyons, France, 1973-74; Sponsor, Supervisor, Postdoctoral Fellows from Several Countries, 1970 to present; Consultant to Number of Ad Hoc Committees, 1961 to present; Grant Proposals Reviewer for Study Section, National Institutes of Health, 1976-79; Supervisor of Cytohematology Segment, Hematology Proficiency Testing Program, State of New York, 1976-79; Director of Hematology Proficiency Testing Program, State of New York, 1979-81; Reference for Cell Identification, Center for Disease Control, Department of Health, Education, and Welfare, Atlanta, 1978-81; Co-Organizer of Hybridoma Unit, Center for Laboratories and Research, New York State Department of Health, Albany, New York, 1981-83; Volunteer Tennis Coach for Teen-agers, 1979 to present; Contributions and Donations to Several Organizations, including Cohoes Music Hall (1978), Church, Diocesan Development Program (1981-82); Free Medical Assistance to Poor in Developing Countries during Vacations, 1957 to present. Honors and Awards: Diploma de Honor, National University of Buenos Aires, 1961; Bernardino Rivadavia Prize, National Academy of Medicine of Argentina, 1967; Ciencia e Investigacion Prize, Argentinian Society for the Advancement of Science, 1967; Travel Fellowship, Ford Foundation/National Academy of Sciences, 1968; Eleanor Roosevelt Fellowship, International Union against Cancer/ American Cancer Society, 1969; Reviewer of Grant Proposals for National Institutes of Health, 1976-79; Invited Speaker, Convener, Chairman, Workshops, Symposia and Round Tables; Lecturer at Numerous Scientific Congresses and Meetings, Seminar Series, International Courses, 1962 to present; Awarded Numerous Fellowship, Grants, Contracts, by National and International Agencies. Address: 18 Carriage Road, Delmar, New York 12054.■

SHARON ELIZABETH MACE

Physician, Administrator. Personal: Born October 30, 1949; Daughter of James and Leona Mace. Education: B.S., Syracuse University, 1971; M.D., Upstate Medical Center, 1975. Career: Assistant Director, Staff Physician, Department of Emergency Medicine Residency Coordinator, Emergency Medicine Residency Program, Mt. Sinai Medical Center; Helicoptor Flight Physician, Department of Emergency Medicine, Cleveland Metropolitan General Hospital, 1982-83; Research Associate, Department of Investigative Medicine, Mt. Sinai Medical Center, 1979-80: Cardiology Fellowship, Case Western Reserve University Hospitals, 1977-79; Pediatric Internship and Residency, Case Western Reserve University Hospitals, 1975-77. Organizational Memberships: American College of Emergency

Physicians, National and Ohio Chapters; Society of Teachers of Emergency Medicine; University Association of Emergency Medicine; Faculty, Case Western Reserve University, Department of Medicine and Pediatrics. Community Activities: Education and Membership Committees, Ohio Chapter, American College of Emergency Physicians. Religion: Congregationalist. Honors and Awards: Presentations before the American College of Emergency Physicians, American Academy of Pediatrics, Society for Pediatric Research; Residency Science Day Award; Listed in *Who's Who of American Women, World Who's Who of Women, Biographical Roll of Honor, Personalities of America*. Address: 8243 Merrie Lane, Chesterland, Ohio 44026.■

SANDY MACEBUH

Writer and Consultant. Education: Bachelor's Degree in Psychology and Theatre, University of Minnesota; Master's Degree in Communications, Theatre and Consumer Behavior, Wayne State University; Ph.D., University of Toledo; Ph.D., New York University. Career: Communications Consultant and Free-lance Writer, 1981 to present; Poet; Analyst and Communications Coordinator, Kemper Insurance, 1980-81; Instructor and Community Liaison, Stautzenberger College (Learning Achievements), Toledo, Ohio, 1979-80; Instructor and Community Liaison, Bowling Green State University (Upward Bound Program) and Toledo University, 1977-79; Owner, Manager, Coordinator, "Black Inspiration" (Detroit); Graduate Laboratory Assistant and Assistant Editor, Wayne State University; Communications Consultant, KDIA Radio, Oakland, California; Tutor, University of Minnesota. Organizational Memberships: Dramatists Guild; Authors League of America; American Theatre Association; Women in Communications, Associate Member; American Management Association, 1981; Black Writers Conference Association; International Writers Women's Guild. Community Activities: Young Women's Christian Association; Volunteer during Political Campaign of Betty Forness. Honors and Awards: Poet Laureate, University of Montana; Listed in *International Who's Who of Intellectuals, Directory of Distinguished Americans, Personalities of America, Notable Americans*. Address: 251 Tyler Street, Trenton, New Jersey 08609.■

JAMES THOMAS MACGREGOR

Toxicologist, Educator. Personal: Born January 14, 1944; Son of James MacGregor, Phyllis Bowman MacGregor; Married Judith Anne Anello, Daughter of John and Phyllis Anello; Father of Jennifer Lee. Education: B.S. Chemistry, Union College, 1965; Ph.D. Toxicology, University of Rochester School of Medicine and Dentistry, 1970. Career: Toxicologist, United States Department of Agriculture, Western Regional Research Center, 1972 to present; Postdoctoral Fellow, Department of Pharmacology and Toxicology, University of California at San Francisco, 1970-72; Adjunct Associate Professor, Department of Biomedical and Environmental Health Sciences, School of Public Health, University of California at Berkeley, 1982 to present; Lecturer, Department of Biomedical and Environmental Health Sciences, School of Public Health, University of California at Berkeley, 1978-81; Adjunct Faculty, Department of Continuing Education, University of San Francisco, 1980; Lecturer in Food Science, Department of Nutritional Sciences, University of California at Berkeley, 1972-78. Organizational Memberships: Environmental Mutagen Society; Society of Toxicology; American Association for the Advancement of Science; New York Academy of Sciences; Genetic and Environmental Toxicology Association of Northern California, President 1982, Program Chairman and President-Elect 1981-82; United States Environmental Protection Agency Gene-Tox Program, Micronucleus Panel 1979-80; Northern California Association for Environmental and Genetic Toxicology, Nominating Committee 1979; Consultant, Program on Genetic Effects of Fluoride, Department of Pharmacology and Toxicology, University of California at San Francisco, 1978; United States Department of Agriculture Work Conference on the Safety of Dimilin, 1976-77; United States Department of Agriculture-State Agricultural Experiment Station Western Regional Planning Committee, Task Force on Quality of Food, 1975-77. Published Works: Numerous Professional Journal Articles or Book Chapters, including "Persistence of Micronuclei in Peripheral Blood Erythrocytes: Detection of Chronic Chromosome Breakage in Mice" (with R. Schlegel) 1982, "The *B. subtilis* Multi-gene Sporulation Test for Mutagens: Detection of Mutagens inactive in the *Salmonella his* Reversion Test" (with L. E. Sacks, in press), "Fluoride in Pregnancy" (with F. A. Smith and H. C. Hodge) 1982. Honors and Awards: Diplomate, American Board of Toxicology, 1980; Postdoctoral Fellowship 1970-72, Predoctoral Fellowship 1965-70, National Institutes of Health; Associate Member, Sigma Xi; New York State Regents Scholarship; Cummulative Dean's List Academic Index, 1961-65; Bausch and Lomb Science Award, Outstanding Potential in Science, 1961; High School Valedictorian; Listed in *Who's Who in the West, Men of Achievement, Personalities of the West and Midwest, Directory of Distinguished Americans*. Address: 2636 Carmelita Way, Pinole, California 94564.■

JERZY (GEORGE) J. MACIUSZKO

Professor and Library Director. Personal: Born July 15, 1913; Son of Bonifacy and Aleksandra Maciuszko (deceased); Married Kathleen Lynn Mart; Father of Christina Aleksandra. Education: M.A. English Language and Literature, University of Warsaw, Poland, 1936; M.S.L.S. Library Science, Western Reserve University, 1953; Ph.D. Library Science, Case Western Reserve University, 1962. Military: Served with the United States Army, 1945-46 as Polish Liaison Officer in Heidelberg, Germany, attaining the rank of Acting Captain. Career: Professor and Retired Library Director; Baldwin-Wallace College, Professor Emeritus 1978 to present, Professor and Library Director 1974-78; Consultant, Cleveland State University 1979; Alliance College, Chairman Division of Slavic and Modern Languages 1973-74, Chairman Year Abroad Committee and Director of Program at Jagellonian University, Cracow, Poland 1969-74, Chairman Department of Slavic Studies 1969-73, Teacher Polish Language and Literature 1951-52; Lecturer Polish Language and Literature, Case Western Reserve University, 1964-69; Cleveland Public Library, Head John G. White Department 1963-69, Assistant Head Foreign Literature Department 1953-63; Inspector, British Ministry of Education, Polish Secondary Schools in England, 1946-51; Teacher, Warsaw Model Secondary School, 1936-37, 1938-39. Organizational Memberships: American Library Association, Chairman Slavic Subsection Division of College and Research Libraries 1968-69; American Association for the Advancement of Slavic Studies; American Association of Teachers of Slavic and East European Languages, Chapter President 1965-66; Charter Member, Association for the Advancement of Polish Studies; Association of Polish Writers in Exile; Polish Society of Arts and Sciences; Polish Institute of Arts and Sciences in America; The Kosciuszko Foundation; Polish American Historical Association; Cleveland Public Library Staff Association, President 1964-65; Case Western Reserve University Library School Alumni Association, President 1970-71; Modern Language Association. Published Works: Author of *The Polish Short Story in English: A Guide and Critical Bibliography* 1968; Author of "Polish Letters in America," a Chapter in *Poles in America* 1978; "Polish-American Literature," a Chapter in *Ethnic Perspectives in American Literature* 1983; Reviewer of Polish Books for *World Literature Today*; Translator of Short Story "A Turban" in *Ten Contemporary Polish Stories* 1958; Contributor to *Encyclopedia of World Literature in the Twentieth Century* 1975. Honors and Awards: Doctoral Dissertation Award, Kosciuszko Foundation, 1967; Hilbert T. Ficken Award, Baldwin-Wallace College, 1973. Address: 133 Sunset Drive, Berea, Ohio 44017.■

WARREN FREDERICK MACKARA

Educator. Personal: Born July 6, 1947; Son of A. W. and Eleanor F. Mackara. Education: A.B. Economics, Rutgers University, 1969; Ph.D. Economics, Texas A. & M. University, 1976. Career: Associate Professor of Economics and Director of the Center for Economic Education, East Tennessee State University, 1975 to present; Financial Economist, Federal Reserve Bank of America, 1973-75. Organizational Memberships: American Economic Association; Southern Economic Association; Western Economic Association; Tennessee Council on Economic Education, Board of Directors; National Association of Economic Educators; Executive Board, State of Franklin Council for the Social Studies (Coordinating Editor); Tennessee Council for the Social Studies. Religion: St. John's Episcopal Church (Johnson City, Tennessee), Lay Reader. Honors and Awards: Henry Rutgers Scholar with High Distinction in Economics, 1969; Listed in *Outstanding Young Men of America, Who's Who in the South and Southwest, Personalities of the South, Men of Achievement*. Address: 1026 Pagel Court, Johnson City, Tennessee 37601.■

KENNETH DONALD MACKENZIE

Professor, Management Consulting Executive. Personal: Born December 20, 1937; Son of Kenneth V. Mackenzie; Married Sally McHenry, Daughter of Dean

E. McHenry; Father of Dorothy Jane Rivette, Carolyn Beta, Susan Gamma, Nancy Delta. Education: A.B. Mathematics, University of California at Berkeley, 1960; Ph.D. Business Administration, University of California at Berkeley, 1964. Military: Served in the United States Marine Corps Reserve, 1956-60; Served in the United States Army National Guard, 1960-64, attaining the rank of Lieutenant. Career: Management Consulting Executive, Organizational Systems Inc.; Professor, School of Business, University of Kansas, 1972 to present; Professor, University of Waterloo 1960-72, University of Pennsylvania 1967-71, Carnegie-Mellon 1964-67. Organizational Memberships: Associate Editor, *Management Science*; Editorial Board, *Human Systems Management*; Operations Research Society of America; International Communication Association; American Psychological Association; Institute of Management Sciences; Academy of Management; American Management Association; American Association for the Advancement of Science; New York Academy of Sciences. Honors and Awards: Edmund P. Learned Distinguished Professor, 1972; Canpark Award for Best Theoretical Paper, 1980; Fellow, American Association for the Advancement of Science, 1972; Undergraduate and Graduate Fellowship and Scholarships; Numerous Research Grants. Address: 502 Millstone Drive, Lawrence, Kansas 66044.■

WILLIAM AUGUST MAESEN

President of Educational Institution. Personal: Born May 18, 1939; Son of August and Wilhelmina Maesen; Married Sherry Jaeger; Father of Ryan and Betsy, Steven. Education: B.A., B.S.B., Oklahoma City University; M.A., Indiana State University; Ph.D., University of Illinois-Chicago; Postdoctoral Studies, Michigan State University, University of Illinois-Chicago. Military: Served in the United States Air Force Reserves, rising through the grades to the rank of Staff Sergeant. Career: President, Chicago Institute for Advanced Studies; Former Positions include Associate Professor, School of Social Work, Grand Valley State College; Associate Professor of Behavioral Sciences, College of St. Francis, Joliet, Illinois. Organizational Memberships: American Sociological Association; National Association of Social Workers; Community Development Society. Community Activities: Retired Senior Volunteer Program, Joliet, Illinois (advisory board); Cathedral Shelter of Chicago (consultant). Religion: Christ Episcopal Church, Joliet, Illinois; Lay Reader; Vestryman; Senior Warden. Honors and Awards: Beta Gamma; Alpha Kappa Delta; Listed in Several Biographical References. Address: P.O. Box 4380, Chicago, Illinois 60680.■

LARRY ELLIOT MAGARGAL

Ophthalmologist. Personal: Born June 14, 1941; Married Helga Olsen; Father of Lauren Elizabeth, Larry Elliot Jr., Geoffrey Robb. Education: A.B. honors Biology, Temple University, 1965; M.D. honors, Temple Medical School, 1969; Fellow, American College of Surgeons, 1977. Military: Served in the United States Army, 1972-73, attaining the rank of Captain. Career: Ophthalmologist. Organizational Memberships: American Diabetes Association, Philadelphia Chapter Board of Directors 1981 to present; Co-Director, Retina Vascular Unit, Wills Eye Hospital, 1975 to present; Member of 15 Medical Societies. Community Activities: Torresdale Civic Association, 1978 to present; Pen Ryn School Association, 1977 to present; Philadelphia Art Museum, Patron 1980 to present. Religion: Men of Nazareth, 1981 to present. Published Works: Co-Author, 5 Chapters in Ophthalmic Texts, 45 Ophthalmic Papers. Honors and Awards: Philadelphia Medical Society Scholarship, 1963-65; Pharmaceutical Manufacturers Fellowship, 1968-69; Wills Eye Hospital Retina Fellowship, 1975-76; Eli Lilly Award for Excellence in Pharmacology, 1969. Address: 9601 Milnor Street, Philadelphia, Pennsylvania 19114.■

JOHN ANTHONY MAGLIANA

Executive. Personal: Born July 2, 1935; Married. Education: B.S.E.E., St. Louis University, 1956; Master's Degree, Engineering Executive Program, University of California at Los Angeles, 1968. Career: President and Chief Executive Officer, Acctran Systems; Former President and Chief Executive Officer, Datasaab Systems; Director, TRW; Vice President, International Trivex. Organizational Memberships: Presidents Association; Director, Datasaab 1973-81, Saab-Totem 1973-81, Acctran Systems 1982. Community Activities: Confrerie des Tastevin. Religion: Roman Catholic. Address: 45 Binney Lane, Old Greenwich, Connecticut 06870.■

GERALD DONALD MAGNES

Dentist, Educator. Personal: Born September 27, 1933; Son of H. Magnes; Married Loretta Bass; Father of Scott Alan, Craig Neil. Education: B.S. 1956, D.D.S. 1958, University of Illinois. Career: Individual Practice in Dentistry; Instructor, University of Illinois College of Dentistry; Consultant, Warner-Chilcott Laboratories, Morris Plains, New Jersey, 1964. Organizational Memberships: American Dental Association; Chicago Dental Society; American Cancer Society; University of Illinois Alumni Association; Alpha Omega; International Association for Dental Research; American Association for Dental Research. Community Activities: Speaker, American Cancer Society, 1969-70; Donator of Scientific Exhibit to University of Illinois Medical School, 1968. Religion: Temple Beth Israel. Published Works: Contributor of Articles to Professional Journals, "Proteolytic Enzymes in Oral Surgery," "Intraosseous Anesthesia," "Use of Modified Expander in Correcting Crossbite." Honors and Awards: Certificate of Recognition, American Dental Association, 1967; Award Winning Exhibit, National American Dental Association, 1967; Fellowship, The Royal Society of Health. Address: 4625 Grove Street, Skokie, Illinois 60076.■

JOAN MAHAFFEY

Registry Director. Personal: Born February 7, 1926; Daughter of Annie Christofferson Mills. Education: R.N., Methodist Hospital of Southern California, 1950; B.S.N. Health Science 1971, M.P.H. 1976, California State University-Northridge. Career: Registry Director, Epicenter Professional Registry, Inc.; Consultant and Speaker in Field; Regional Director, Epicenter Region 3 of California Nurses Association, 1974-81; Coordinator Nursing Education, 1972; Office Nurse for Henry L. Lopez, M.D., 1957-72; Office Nurse for Robert K. Kerland, M.D., 1951-55; Staff Nurse, Methodist Hospital, 1950. Organizational Memberships: American Biographical Institute Research Association; National Association of Female Executives, Inc.; National League for Nursing; American Nurses Association; School Nurses Organization; Valley Nursing Education Council; Appointee Supervisor, Baxter Ward Task Force on Health Systems Age, 1975; American Chemical Society, San Fernando Valley Unit, Board of Directors, Vice President Fund Raising. Community Activities: Director, Verdugo Hills Visiting Nurses Association, 1972-80; Soroptimist International, San Fernando Valley Club, Member 1979 to present, Recording and Corresponding Secretary, President-Elect 1983-84; San Fernando Valley Emblem Club #37, Corresponding Secretary 1962 to present, Marshall, Assistant Marshall, Chaplain; Volunteer Fund Raiser, American Chemical Society, 1982. Honors and Awards: Twenty Year Pin, Emblem Club of San Fernando; Listed in *Biographical Roll of Honor, Who's Who of American Women, Five Thousand Personalities of the World, World Who's Who of Women*. Address: 6620 Glade Avenue, Canoga Park, California 91303.■

EDWARD PATRICK MAHER

Management Consultant, Therapist. Personal: Born May 22, 1937; Married Constance Catherine Schorr, Daughter of Orpha Sandall; Father of Heather Siobhan, Maura Helene. Education: B.A./B.S. Political Science/Education, University of Minnesota, 1960; M.Ed. Educational Psychology, University of Minnesota, 1965. Career: Teacher and Coach, Public and Private Schools, Excelsior, Minnesota, 1961-66; Coordinator, Training Programs for Adult Volunteers, Knights of Columbus, Youth Department, New Haven, Connecticut, 1966-70; Executive Vice President, Sales Recruitment and Training, Action Display Inc., Minneapolis, Minnesota, 1970-72; Manager, Sales Staff, Sanford Rose Associates, Minneapolis, 1972-73; Vice President Sales and Marketing, Progress Associates Inc., Minneapolis, 1973-77; Owner, Power Action Training, Human Resource Development and Management Consulting, La Mesa, California, 1977 to present; Director, HOPE Unlimited Inc., Private Agency, Marriage/Family Therapists (specializing in alcohol and chemical dependency), 1978 to present; Instructor, University of California at San Diego, 1979 to present. Organizational Memberships: National Association of Alcohol Counselors; California Association of Alcohol Counselors; California Association of Marriage and Family Therapists, Chairman of Professional Education 1979 to present, Chairman of Commission on Corporate Planning 1980 to present; American Society for Training and Development; International Transactional Analysis Association. Community Activities:

TWO THOUSAND NOTABLE AMERICANS

Active in San Diego Politics. Honors and Awards: Listed in *Who's Who in the West, Who's Who in California.* Address: 4383 Rous Street, San Diego, California 92122.■

BENJAMIN COMAWAS MAHILUM

Teaching and Research. Personal: Born September 9, 1931; Married Paulita R. Melchor, Daughter of Claudia R. Melchor; Father of David, Lourdes, Ma. Junever, Lyman, Jorge, Don. Education: M.S. Soil Science, University of Hawaii at Manoa; Ph.D. Soil Science, Oklahoma State University; Postgraduate Training, United States Salinity Laboratory, Riverside, California. Career: Assistant Professor of Soil Science, College of Agriculture, University of Hawaii at Hilo, 1979 to present; Technical Professional, Department of Agronomy, Oklahoma State University, 1980; Visiting Assistant Professor, Department of Agronomy, Oklahoma State University, 1977-79; Consultant, Bill's Coal Company, Inc., Pittsburgh, Kansas, 1978; Science Research Chief, Forest Research Institute, University of the Philippines at Los Banos, 1977; Consultant, INCO Mining Corporation, Tolosa, Leyte, Philippines, 1977; Director, Regional Coconut Research Center, Visayas State College of Agriculture, Baybay, Leyte, Philippines, 1974-77; Associate Professor and Chairman, Department of Agronomy and Soils, Visayas State College of Agriculture, 1974-77; Chairman, Agronomy and Soils Committee, College Task Force which prepared an Institution Building Program for Visayas State College of Agriculture, 1975-77; National Research Committee for Industrial Oil Crops and Spices, Philippine Council for Agriculture and Resources Research, Los Banos, Laguna, Philippines, 1974-75; Ad hoc National Research Committee to Integrate National Researches on *Leucaena laucocephala* (ipil-ipil), National Science Development Board, Bicutan, Taguig, Rizal, Philippines, 1977; National Research Committee for Coconuts and Other Industrial Oil Crops, Philippine Council for Agriculture and Resources Research, 1975-77; Associate Professor III and Research Coordinator, University of Eastern Philippines, 1974; Associate Professor II and Research Coordinator, University of Eastern Philippines, 1973-74; Assistant Professor III, University of Southern Mindanao, Kabacan, North Cotabato, Philippines, 1971-73. Organizational Memberships: List of Consultants on Soils and Crops, A.R.C.P.A.C.S.; International Soil Science Society; American Association for the Advancement of Science; Society of Sigma Xi; Soil Science Society of America; America Society of Agronomy. Published Works: Author Numerous Technical Papers (including) "Effects of Liming and Fertilization on Yield and P Uptake of Crops Grown in Highly Weathered Tropical Soils" (1981), "Sorption, Movement, Degradation and Persistence of Organic Compounds in Soils" (with L. G. Morrill and S.H. Mohiuddin), "Current Status and Problems of the Coconut Industry in the Philippines" (1976). Honors and Awards: National Science Development Board Scholarship for Ph.D., 1967-71; East-West Center Scholarship for M.S., 1963-65; Presidential Honor Award, Oklahoma State University, 1971; Listed in *American Men and Women of Science, Who's Who in the West, Personalities of the West and Midwest, Men of Achievement, International Who's Who of Intellectuals.* Address: Ohia Street, Honokaa, Hawaii 96727.■

EDNA JUNE MAIN

Educator. Personal: Born September 1, 1940; Daughter of Mrs. Edna Dewey; Married Donald John Main, Son of Mrs. Barbara Main; Father of Alison Teresa, Susan Christine, Steven Donald. Education: Two-Year Degree, Merchandising, Tobe-Corburn School, New York City, 1960; B.A. Elementary Education 1974, Master's Degree in Elementary Education 1979, Master's Degree in Administration and Supervision 1983, University of North Florida. Career: Teacher, Third Grade, Holiday Hill Elementary School, Jacksonville, Florida. Organizational Memberships: United Way Representative, 1981-83; National Science Teachers Association, Representative 1982-83; National Council of Teacher of English, Representative 1982-83; Phi Delta Kappa; Delta Kappa Gamma Society International; Educational Community Credit Union Representative, 1976-81; Duval County Reading Council; Council for Elementary Science International; Association for Supervision and Curriculum Development; Florida Association of Science Teachers; National Society for the Study of Education; Florida State Reading Council. Community Activities: Presenter, Seminar for Interns in Elementary Education, University of North Florida, 1982; College of Education Field Services Advisory Council, University of North Florida, 1982-83; Courtesy Appointment as Instructor, University of South Florida, 1980-81. Honors and Awards: National Science Teachers Association Science Teachers Achievement Recognition Award, 1983; Nominee for Duval County Teacher of the Year, 1979, 1980, 1981, 1983; Semi-Finalist, Duval County Teacher of the Year, 1983; Phi Kappa Phi Honor Society; Master's in Elementary Education with 4.0 Average, 1979; B.A. with Highest Distinction, University of North Florida, 1974; Academic Scholarship, University of North Florida, 1973-74; Academic Scholarship, Tobe-Corburn School, 1958-60; Listed in *Personalities of the South, Who's Who Among Students in American Universities and Colleges.* Address: 6829 Clifton Forge Road, Jacksonville, Florida 32211.■

DOLORES A. SVACIK MAITZEN

Assistant Professor. Personal: Born November 2, 1952; Married Robert H. Maitzen, Jr. Education: B.S. Education, Illinois State University, 1973; M.S. Education, Chicago State University, 1976. Career: Assistant Professor, Home Economics Department, Arizona State University; Occupational In-Service Teacher; Educator, State of Arizona. Organizational Memberships: Arizona Vocational Association, Board of Directors and Executive Board; American Vocational Association; Arizona Association of Vocational Home Economics Educators, Membership Chairman 1981-83; American Home Economics Association; Arizona Home Economics Executive Board Association, Professional Awards Chairman 1982-84; State Home Economics Advisory Council, 1981-82; State Consumer/In-service Advisory Board, Valley H.E.R.O., 1981 to present; National Education Association; Arizona Home Economics Teacher Education Council; Women's Recreation Association, President; Alpha Gamma Delta; Lambda Upsilon Sigma. Religion: St. Joseph Catholic Parish, Religious Education Instructor, Executive Committee, Retreat Search Team. Honors and Awards: Professional Recognition Award, Arizona Home Economics Association (in Elementary, Secondary and Adult Education), 1982; National Poetry Association Award. Address: 3702 East Dahlia Drive, Phoenix, Arizona 85032.■

BEN B. M. MAK

Executive. Personal: Born June 11, 1926; Father of Loreta, Andrey, Donald. Education: M.S.M.E., M.A.B.A.; Studied in Cracaw, Frieburg, Regensburg, Miami, Washington; United States Army, Postgrduate Studies in Propellant and Explosives 1962, Administration D.O.D. 1963, Value Engineering D.O.D. 1965, Logistics D.O.D. War College 1965. Career: Engineering Manager; Business Executive; D.O.D. Project Manager Office; C.B.U., Rockets, Ammunition, 1962-69; Curtis Wright Corporation-Subsidiary, Engineering Manager, General Manager 1969-74; Valian Metal Products Corporation, Vice President 1974-79; Engineering Manager, College of Medicine and Dentistry of New Jersey, 1980. Organizational Memberships: American Society of Mechanical Engineers; Association of Energy Engineers; American Society of Metals; Value Engineering Society; U.E.S.A., Inc.; Association of Physical Plant Administrators; Association of College and University Business Officers. Community Activities: Irvington Planning Board, 1976-78; President New Jersey Chapter, U.E.S.A., Inc., 1966-68, 1976-82, 1984 to present; Veterans, 1962 to present. Religion: Church Member Serving on Various Committees. Published Works: Author of Books on Value Analysis, Bomb Fragmentation, Value Engineering; Author of Numerous Research Papers on Double Base Propellants, Cyclothol Explosives, Value Engineering. Honors and Awards: Awards and Citations of Merit from United States Army, Air Force, Navy, D.O.D. Department, D.O.D. V.E.S.O., Industry, Colleges. Address: South Orange, New Jersey 07079.■

AMERICO IMRE MAKK

Artist (Painter). Personal: Born August 24, 1927, in Hungary; Son of Pal and Katalin Samoday Makk; Married Eva Holusa; Father of A. B. Education: Graduate, Saint Benedictin Gimnasium, Gyor, Hungary; Hungarian National Academy of Fine Arts, Budapest; Academy of Fine Arts Scholarship Student, Rome, Italy. Career: Co-Chairman, Hawaii Heart Association Art for Heart Exhibition; Co-Chairman, Cerebral Palsey/Carnegie International Center Exhibition; Chairman, World Federation of Hungarian Artists, New York; Vice President, American Hungarian Art Association, New York; Official Artist of the Brazilian Government; Professoro de Bela Artes de Associacao Paulista de Belas Artes; Professor of Fine Arts, Academia de Belas Artes, Sao Paulo, Brazil. Organizational Memberships: American Professional Art League, New York; The Fifty American Artists Association, New York; Associacao Paulista de Belas Artes, Sao Paulo, Brazil; Associacao dos Professionais de Imprensa de Sao Paulo, Brazil; International Art Exchange, New York, Paris, Monaco; Two/Ten Association, U.S.A.; Metropolitan Museum of Art, New York; National Geographic Society, Washington, D.C.; Arpad Academy, U.S.A.; Accademia Italia delle Arti; Major Exhibitions with Wife in Lafayette (Louisiana) 1981, Vancouver (British Columbia) 1980, Scottsdale (Arizona) 1980, Wichita (Kansas) 1979-80, San Francisco (California) 1978-80, Chicago (Illinois) 1979, Honolulu (Hawaii) 1976-77 and 1981, San Antonio (Texas) 1972-78 and 1981, El Paso (Texas) 1971-80, Austin (Texas) 1971-79, Los Angeles (California) 1970-78, Amarillo (Texas) 1969-76, Charleston (West Virginia) 1972 and 1975, Miami (Florida) 1968-78, Washington D.C. 1966 and 1969, New Jersey 1963-65, Dayton (Ohio) 1963 and 1970, New York World's Fair 1963-64, New York 1963-67, Ponta Grossa 1962, Sao Carlos 1961, Rio de Janeiro, Sao Paulo, Joao Pessoa and Areia 1959, Manaus 1958, Sobral 1956-57, Victoria, Salvador, Recife, Natal and Fortaleza 1956, Rio de Janeiro 1956; Major Works (individual and in conjunction with Eva Makk) include Murals for Chapel of the Immaculate Conception (Cornwall, New York), "The

Ascension" (Mural for Memorial United Church of Christ, Dayton, Ohio), Portraits of President Carter (1979) and President Reagan (1983), Protrait of Archbishop Scalabrini for Archdiocese of New York, Cupola and Murals for Basilica Nostra Senhora do Rosario (Ponta Grossa), Ceiling and Murals depicting the Life of St. Charles and Portrait of the Bishop, Palacio do Bispo (San Carlos), Murals depicting the Life of St. Sebastian, Igreja Matris, Taquaritinga (Sao Paulo), "La Via Sacra" (Fourteen Stations of the Cross in Large, Modern Compositions), Nostra Senhora do Carmo, Araraquara (Sao Paulo), Murals and Ceiling Igreja Nostra Senhora dos Remedios, Sousa, Paraiba and Others. Published Works: Works Published or Reviewed in Many Art Publications and Periodicals Internationally. Honors and Awards: Gold Medal, Arpad Academy, 1981; Gold Medal, World Fair First Prize for Painting, Italian Academy of Art, 1980; Merit Award, *Notable Americans of the Bicentennial Era*, 1976; Merit Award, *International Who's Who in Art*, Cambridge, 1973; Diploma Award of Achievement, London, England, 1972; Certificates of Merit, London, England, 1970-72; Annual Masters of Contemporary Painters Salon Award, Miami, 1969; International Art Exchange Directors First Prize, New York/Paris, 1967; American Ecclesiastical Award for Achievement, New York, 1962; Merit Awards in Recognition of Outstanding Accomplishment, Rio de Janeiro, Sao Paulo, Manaus, Ceara, Paraiba, Bahia, Pernambuco, Parana, Joao Pessoa, Areia, Sao Carlos, Ponta Grossa, 1958-62; Metropolitan Honorable Mention, 1958; Special Merit Award, 1955; First Prize Eldorado (Gold Medal), Sao Paulo, Brazil, 1953; Vatican Portrait Award for Portrait of Cardinal Mindzhenty, 1948; Academy Italian Scholarship, Budapest, 1948; Centenarium Prize, Budapest, 1948. Address: 1515 Laukahi Street, Honolulu, Hawaii 96821.■

EVA MAKK

Artist, Painter. Personal: Born December 1, 1933, in Hawas, Ethiopia, Africa; Daughter of Dr. Bert and Julia Ribenyi Holusa; Married Americo Imre Makk; Mother of A. B. Education: Studied at the Academy of Fine Arts (Paris, France) and the Academy of Fine Arts summa cum laude (Rome, Italy). Career: Professor of Fine Arts, Academia de Belas Artes, Sao Paulo, Brazil; Professora de Belas Artes de Associacao Paulista de Belas Artes; Official Artist of the Brazilian Government; Director, American Hungarian Art Association; Director, World Federation of Hungarian Artists; Co-Chairman, Cerebral Palsy/Carnegie International Center Exhibition; Co-Chairman, Hawaii Heart Association Art for Heart Exhibition; Major Works include Ingreja Sagrada Familia (tinted glass), Ingreja Santa Barbara (murals and ceiling), Ingreja San Jose (mural), Chapel of the Immaculate Conception (murals, Cornwell, New York), Memorial United Church of Christ (mural "The Ascension" in Dayton, Ohio), Others; Major Exhibitions include Lafayette (Louisiana) 1981, Vancouver (British Columbia, Canada) 1980, San Francisco (California) 1979-80, Many Others since 1950; Television Appearances Annually since 1963 in Conjunction with Major Exhibitions and Major Works in the United States. Organizational Memberships: American Professional Art League, New York; The Fifty American Artists Association, New York; Associacao Paulistas de Belas Artes, Sao Paulo, Brazil; Associacao Dos Professionaais de Impresna de Sao Paulo, Brazil; International Art Exchange, New York, Paris, Monaco; Metropolitan Museum of Art, New York; National Geographic Society, Washington D.C.; Arpad Academy, U.S.A.; Accademia Italia delle Arti. Published Works: Works Published or Reviewed in National and International Periodicals and Newspapers. Honors and Awards: Silver Medal, Sao Paulo, 1953; First Prize, San Bernardo, 1954; Gold Medal, Sobral Museum, Sobral, Brazil, 1956; Academy First Prize, Sao Paulo, 1958; Metroplitan Honorable Mention, 1958; Merit Awards in Recognition of Outstanding Accomplishment, 1958-62; American Ecclesiastical Award of Achievement, New York, 1962; Mention of Merit, Carnegie Exhibition, 1966; Annual Masters and Contemporary Painters Salon Award, Miami, 1969; Certificates of Merit, London, England, 1970, 1971, 1972; Diploma Award of Achievement, London, 1972; Merit Award, Cambridge, 1973; Merit Award, *Notable Americans of the Bicentennial Era*, 1976; Gold Medal World First Prize for Painting, Italian Academy of Art, 1979; Gold Medal, Arpad Academy, U.S.A., 1981. Address: 1515 Laukahi Street, Honolulu, Hawaii 96821.■

HOWARD GERALD MALIN

Podiatrist, Journalist, Educator, Lecturer. Personal: Born December 2, 1941; Son of Leon Nathan and Rena Rose Malin. Education: A.B. Biology, University of Rhode Island, 1964; Certificat d'Etudes Francaises, Universite de Poitiers, Institut d'Etudes Francaises de Touraine, 1965; Certificate in Cytotechnology, Our Lady of Fatima Hospital, Institute of Pathology, 1965; Stage Hospitalier en Cytologie, Universite de Tours, 1967; M.A., Brigham Young University, 1969; B.Sc. 1972, D.P.M. 1972, California College of Podiatric Medicine; Certificate in First Year of Medical and Surgical Podiatric Residency 1973, Certificate in Second Year of Medical and Surgical Podiatric Medicine Residency 1974, New York College of Podiatric Medicine; Certificate, Instructor, Advanced Cardiac Life Support, American Heart Association, 1978; M.Sc., Pepperdine University, 1978. Military: Served in the United States Air Force, 1977-80, attaining the rank of Captain; Service in the United States Air Force Reserves, 1980 to present. Career: Undergraduate Assistant for Botany Department, University of Rhode Island, Kingston, 1961-64; Teaching Assistant, Basic Sciences, California College of Podiatric Medicine, San Francisco, 1969-72; Research Assistant, Basic Sciences, California College of Podiatric Medicine, 1970-72; Podiatry Extern, Veterans Administration Medical Center, Wadsworth, Kansas, 1971-72; Podiatry Extern, Marine Corps Reserve Depot, San Diego, 1972; Instructor, Podiatric Surgery, New York College of Podiatric Medicine, 1973-74; Private Practitioner, Podiatric Medicine and Surgery, Brooklyn, New York, 1974-77; Hospital Staff (Podiatrist), Prospect Hospital, Bronx, New York, 1974-77; Chief, Podiatry Service, David Grant United States Air Force Medical Center, Travis Air Force Base, California, 1977-80; Hospital Staff (Podiatrist), David Grant United States Air Force Medical Center, 1977; Chief, Podiatric Service, Veterans Administration Medical Center, Martinsburg, West Virginia, 1980 to present. Organizational Memberships: American Podiatry Students Association, 1968-72; American Public Health Association, 1972 to present; American Podiatry Association, 1973 to present; The New York Academy of Sciences, 1973 to present; Academy of Podiatric Medicine, 1973 to present; American Chemical Society; American Association for the Advancement of Science; Nassau County Podiatry Society of New York; Association of Podiatrists in Federal Service; California College of Podiatric Medicine Alumni Association; Mediaeval Academy of America; American College of Foot Orthopedics; American Diabetes Association; American Lung Association; American Academy of Podiatric Sports Medicine; American Society of Podiatric Medicine; American Society of Podiatric Dermatology; The Association of Military Surgeons of The United States; Phi Delta Kappa International Honorary Educational Fraternity. Community Activities: Operation Hand-to-Hand, California College of Podiatric Medicine, Member 1969-72, Co-Director 1971-72; Podiatry Toastmasters Club, California College of Podiatric Medicine, Member 1970-72, Educational Vice President 1971, President 1972; American Red Cross, Volunteer Podiatrist, David Grant United States Air Force Medical Center, Travis Air Force Base, California, 1977-80; Benevolent and Protective Order of Elks, Fairfield #1976, (Fairfield, California), Americanism Chairman 1978-80, Inner Guard 1979, Chaplain 1979-80, Esteemed Lecturing Knight 1980; Loyal Order of Moose, Fairfield Lodge #861, 1978 to present; Blood Drive Representative, Orthopedic Department, David Grant U.S.A.F. Medical Center, 1978-79; American Red Corss Volunteer, Veterans Administration Medical Center, Martinsburg, West Virginia, 1980 to present; Veterans Administration Voluntary Service Volunteer, Veterans Administration Medical Center, Martinsburg, 1980 to present; Kiwanis Club, Martinsburg, 1981 to present; Instructor, Berkeley County Adult and Community Education, Martinsburg, 1980 to present; Instructor, Educational Development Program, Veterans Administration Medical Center, Martinsburg, 1981 to present; Lions Club (Inwood-Bunker Hill, West Virginia), Member 1982 to present, Lion Tamer 1982-83; American Legion, Hampshire Post 91 (Romney, West Virginia), Life Member 1982 to present; Disabled American Veterans, Eastern Panhandle 8, Life Member, 1981 to present. Religion: Pulpit Committee 1980-81, Lay Rabbi 1980 to present, Pulpit Co-Chairman 1982 to present, Beth Jacob Congregation, Martinsburg, West Virginia. Honors and Awards: Certificate of Volunteer Service, Miriam Hospital, Providence, Rhode Island, 1960; Certificate of Achievement, Region Four, Foreign Language Fair, Brigham Young University, 1968; Brigham Young University Graduate Student Scholarship Award, 1969; National Health Professions Scholarship Award, California College of Podiatric Medicine, 1971; Toastmasters Well-Informed Speakers Award in Literature/Philosophy 1971, in History/Law 1972; Continual Higher Education Award, California College of Podiatric Medicine, 1972; Basic Sciences Award, California College of Podiatric Medicine, 1972; Pi Omega Delta's Clemenson Award, 1972; Podiatry Toastmasters Club Service Award, 1972; California Podiatry Students Association Service Award, Literary Editor of Yearbook, 1972; Presented Key to the City of Marseilles, France, 1973; The Dr. Marvin D. Steinberg Book Award, New York College of Podiatric Medicine, 1973, 1974; Outstanding Professional in Human Sevices, The American Academy of Human Services, 1974-75; American Red Cross Three-Year Service Award Pin, David Grant U.S.A.F. Medical Center, 1979; Certificate of Appreciation, Society of Air Force Physcian Assistants, 1979; Presidential Sports Award, Fitness Walking, 1979; American Red Cross Four-Year Service Award Pin, 1980; American Red Cross Meritorious Award, 1980; American Red Cross Five-Year Service Award Pin, 1981; Distinguished Achievement Awrd, Cambridge, England, 1981; Veterans Administration Voluntary Service Award, 100 Hours 1981, 300 Hours 1981, 500 Hours 1982, 1000 Hours 1982; Fellowships from the American College of Foot Orthopedics, American Society of Podiatric Medicine, American Society of Podiatric Dermatology, International Biographical Association; Listed in *International Register of Profiles, International Who's Who of Intellectuals, Who's Who in the South and Southwest*. Address: 210 Shenandoah Road, Apt. 2-D, Martinsburg, West Virginia 25401.■

THOMAS F. MALLON

Foreign Exchange Broker. Personal: Born January 2, 1944, in New York City, New York; Son of Thomas Francis and Rose Marie McDonnell Mallon; Married

Elizabeth Ann Kiely, June 4, 1966; Father of Eileen Elizabeth, Erin Cristin. Education: B.B.A., Manhattan College, 1966; Postgraduate Study undertaken at Hofstra University, 1966-71. Career: Accounting Clerk, Exxon, New York City, 1965-66; Foreign Exchange Clerk, Dealer, Brown Brothers, Harriman & Company, New York City, 1966-69; Chief Foreign Exchange Dealer, Banca Nazionale dei Lavoro, New York City, 1969-70; Assistant Cashier, Foreign Exchange Dealer, Security Pacific International Bank, 1970-71; Owner and President, Thomas F. Mallon Associates, New York City, 1971-72; President and Director, Kirkland, Whittaker and Mallon, 1972-75; Secretary, Treasurer, Director, Mallon & Dorney Company Ltd., 1975 to present; Secretary, Treasurer and Director, Mallon & Dorney Company (Canada) Ltd., Toronto, 1979 to present; Lecturer, American Institute of Banking, New York City; Vice President, Secretary/Treasurer, Director, Harlow Meyer Savage Inc., New York 1981-82; Vice President, Secretary/Treasurer, Director, EuroBrokers Harlow Inc., Toronto, 1981-82; President, Thomas F. Mallon Associates Inc., 1982 to present; Director, Tullett & Riley Futures Inc., 1982 to present. Organizational Memberships: Foreign Exchange Brokers Association, Past Secretary; Association Cambiste International. Community Activities: Downtown Athletic Club; Strathmore Civic Association; International Platform Association. Religion: Roman Catholic. Published Works: Editor and Contributing Author, "Roche Currency Survey." Honors and Awards: Certificate of Appreciation, University of South Carolina. Address: 22 Bagatelle Road, Dix Hills, New York 11746.■

RICHARD ALLAN MANAHAN

Educator, Administrator. Personal: Born April 26, 1939; Son of Mrs. Edith Manahan; Married Lois Ann, Daughter of Mr. and Mrs. W. C. Smith; Father of Jennifer DeAnn, Eric Richard. Education: B.S. Business Education and Economics 1965, M.S. Business Administration 1971, Ed.D. Educational Administration 1975, Illinois State University. Military: Served in the United States Army, 1958-60. Career: Vice President for Finance and Administration, Professor of Accountancy, East Tennessee State University; Vice President for Business Affairs and Associate Professor of Business, Radford University, Radford, Virginia; Systems Auditor, Illinois Board of Regents, Springfield, Illinois; Administrative Services Coordinator, Illinois State University, Normal, Illinois; Staff Auditor and Accountant, Alexander Grant & Company, Bloomington, Illinois; Auditing Assistant, Springfield Marine Bank, Springfield, Illinois. Organizational Memberships: Delta Mu Delta; Kappa Delta Pi; Association of American Medical Colleges; American Association of Higher Education; Association for Institutional Research; American Institute of Certified Public Accountants; Southern Association for Institutional Research; American Accounting Association; Institute of Internal Auditors; Tennessee Society of Certified Public Accountants. Community Activities: President, Parent Teacher Organization, Centennial School, Bloomington, Illinois; Citizens Advisory Council, Bloomington Public Schools; Treasurer, Jaycees, Springfield, Illinois; Treasurer, Springfield Flag Football League, Inc.; United Fund Campaign Drive, Bloomington; Young Men's Christian Association Fund Drive, Bloomington; Ancient Free and Accepted Masons of Illinois; Bloomington Consistory; Shrine, Mohammed Temple, Peoria, Illinois. Honors and Awards: Spoke Award, Presidential Award of Honor, Ambassador State Award, Jaycees; Testimonial Resolution Passed by Radford University Board of Visitors, 1981; Kappa Delta Pi; Delta Mu Delta, Beta Chi Chapter. Address: 2900 James Drive, Johnson City, Tennessee 37601.■

BETTY MANALATOS

Civic Leader. Personal: Born 1898 in Pennsylvania; Daughter of Charles and Joan Simpson Stein; Married Paul Manalatos (deceased); Mother of Paul. Education: Graduate, Saint Lukes High School, Scranton, Pennsylvania; Graduated as Surgical Nurse, Westside Hospital, Scranton, Pennsylvania, 1926. Community Activities: Volunteer, Veterans Hospital, Crippled Children's Hospital, Retarded Children's Schools; American Red Cross, 7½ Gallon Blood Donor; Senior Citizens Volunteer; Volunteer for the Blind; Order of the Rose Women's Advertising Club, Portland, Oregon; International Association of Turtles, Life Member; Mokattam Temple #12 Daughters of the Nile, Los Angeles, California; Triangle Chapter #456, Order of the Eastern Star, 25 Years; Order of the White Shrine of Jerusalem #23; Degree of Pocahontas of Triuma Council #273, Santa Monica, California, 25 Years; Ladies of the Grand Army of the Republic, Department of California Past President, Past National President, Life Member, Memorial Home Chairman, Board of Directors 15 years; Sons of Civil War Veterans Auxiliary, Los Angeles, President; Steven Jackson Relief Corps #124, President; Venice (California) Women's Club; International Platform Association, Honored Member. Honors and Awards: Keys to the Cities of Boston (Massachusetts), Scranton (Pennsylvania), Wilmington (Delaware), Oklahoma City (Oklahoma), San Francisco, Los Angeles, Palm Springs, Monterey and Santa Monica (California), New York (New York); Attendance of Commissioning Ceremonies of U.S.S. John F. Kennedy, Newport News, Virginia, 1968; Numerous Awards and Citations; Listed in Notable Americans, International Register of Profiles, International Who's Who of Intellectuals, International Book of Honor. Address: 10731 Oregon Avenue, Culver City, California 90230.■

MYRNA P. MANDELL

University Professor. Personal: Born January 4, 1941; daughter of Harry (deceased) and Ceil Mandell. Education: B.A. Sociology, Brooklyn College, 1961; M.P.A., New York University, 1978; M.P.A. 1980, Ph.D. 1981, University of Southern California. Career: Professor, Department of Management, California State University-Northridge; Former Housing Coordinator, Training Coordinator, Public Relations Coordinator, Department of Housing and Urban Development; Housing Consultant, Public Housing Authority; Research Assistant, Los Angeles County Commission. Organizational Memberships: American Management Association; American Society for Public Administration, Student Council Program Committee; American Society for Training Development; National Association of Housing and Development Officials; Western Government Regional Association, Program Committee. Community Activities: Public Administration Graduate Association Network (PAGAN); Co-Founder/Chairman, American Association of University Women; Corporate Relations Officer, California Women in Government. Honors and Awards: Certificate of Appreciation, A.S.P.A. Student Board; Various Awards of Appreciation, Department of Housing and Urban Development. Address: 4549 Keever Avenue, Long Beach, California 90807.■

KARL LEE MANDERS

Neurological Surgeon. Personal: Born January 21, 1927; Son of Frances Edna Cohan; Married Ann Lorrain Laprell; Father of Karlanna, Maidena. Education: Attended Cornell University 1944-46; M.D., University of Buffalo School of Medicine, 1950; Resident in Neurological Surgery, University of Virginia Hospital 1950-52, Henry Ford Hospital 1954-56. Military: Served in the United States Navy, 1952-54, attaining the rank of Lieutenant. Career: Coroner, Marion County, Indianapolis, Indiana, 1977 to present; Neurological Surgeon, 1956 to present; Medical Director, Community Hospital Rehabilitation Center for Pain; Chairman of Baromedical Department, Community Hospital. Community Activities: Crossroads Rehabilitation Center, Medical Board; Indiana Multiple Sclerosis Society, Medical Board. Religion: Guest Lecturer, Unitarian All Souls Church, 1979-80. Honors and Awards: Certificate of Achievement, United States Army, 1969; James Gibson Anatomical Society Award, 1946. Address: 5845 Highfall Road, Indianapolis, Indiana 46226.■

RONALD WILLIAM MANDERSCHEID

Educator, Administrator. Personal: Born September 28, 1943, in LaCrosse, Wisconsin; Son of Norene E. Manderscheid; Married Frances Elizabeth, Daughter of Dr. and Mrs. John Fedkin. Education: B.A. Loras College, 1965; M.A., Marquette University, 1967; Ph.D., University of Maryland, 1975. Military: Served in the United States Army, 1967-69. Career: Teaching Assistant 1956-66, Lecturer Summer 1967, Marquette University; Lecturer, University of Maryland, 1968-69; Language Instructor, United States Army, Republic of Vietnam, 1969; Teaching Assistant 1970-71, Instructor 1973-75, Assistant Professor 1975-81, Associate Professor 1981 to present, University of Maryland; Research Associate Summer 1966, Research Assistant 1966-67, Marquette University; Research Assistant 1971-72, Computer Consultant Fall 1973, Research Assistant 1973-74, University of Maryland; Research Associate 1972-74, Contract Researcher 1974-75, Research Sociologist 1975-77, Senior Research Sociologist 1977-79, Senior Team Leader and Research Sociologist 1979-80, Chief of Evaluation and Needs Assessment Section 1980 to present, Acting Chief of Survey and Reports Branch 1981 to present, National Institute of Mental Health; Consultant, State of Virginia, Spring 1976; Consultant in Research, George Washington University, 1978 to present; Dissertation Director, New York University, 1981; Director of Research for Ph.D. Dissertation in Sociology, Department of Sociology, George Washington University, 1978 to present. Organizational Memberships: American Association for the Advancement of Science, Collaborating Reviewer for Science Books and Films 1978 to present; American Association of University Professors; American Public Health Association; American Sociological Association, Ad Hoc Committee on Housing and the Physical Environment 1975-76, Steering Committee 1976 to present; Austrian Society for Cybernetic Studies; District of Columbia Sociological Society; Eastern Sociological Society, Co-Chairman Committee on the Profession 1979-80, Executive Committee 1980-81; Eastern Sociological Society, Job Placement Committee 1976-77, 1977-78, Chairman 1978-79; International Sociological Association; New York Academy of Sciences; Society for Applied Sociology; Society for General Systems

Research, Chairman Executive Committee of Metropolitan Washington Chapter 1975 to present, Board of Managers and Delegate of Washington Academy of Sciences 1977 to present; Fellow, Washington Academy of Sciences; Alpha Kappa Delta; Delta Epsilon Sigma; Phi Kappa Phi; Pi Gamma Mu; Scientific Correspondent, *International Cybernetics Newsletter*, 1976 to present. Published Works: Corresponding Editor, *Alienation Theory and Research: An International Multidisciplinary Journal*, 1981 to present; Editor, *Systems Science and the Future of Health*, 1976; Author of Numerous Professional Articles (including) "The Child Becomes a Person: Some Theoretical Considerations" 1971, "Mental Health and the Future" 1976, "Dimensions of Classroom Psychosocioal Environment" 1977, "Review of Stress and Old Age" 1981. Honors and Awards: Kerndt Scholarship, Loras College, 1961-65; O'Malley Scholarship, Loras College, 1964-65; National Science Foundation Traineeship, 1967; National Institute of Mental Health Traineeship, 1967; Listed in *American Men and Women of Science, The American Registry, Community Leaders and Noteworthy Americans, Community Leaders of America, Dictionary of International Biography, International Who's Who in Community Service, Men and Women of Distinction, Men of Achievement, Notable Americans, Personalities of America, Personalities of the West and Midwest, Who's Who in the East.* Address: 6 Monument Court, Rockville, Maryland 20850.■

CLAUDE THOMAS MANGRUM, JR.

Probation Officer. Personal: Born December 10, 1930; Son of C. T. and Lillian Mangrum; Married Elaine Marie Carter, Daughter of Churchill and Julia Carter; Father of Dianna Lynn, Liza Michelle, Robert Anthony. Education: Th.B. Theology, Malone College, 1952; B.A. Social Science, Youngstown University, 1956; M.A. Sociology, Kent State University, 1958; M.P.A., University of Southern California, 1972. Career: Assistant Chief Probation Officer; Probation Officer, Supervisor and Director, San Bernardino, 1962-79; Probation Officer, Cleveland, Ohio, 1959-61; Minister, Friends Church, North Carolina and Ohio, 1952-59. Organizational Memberships: California Probation, Parole and Correctional Association, President 1977-78 and 1979-80; Western Correctional Association, Treasurer 1980-81; American Probation and Parole Association, Secretary 1981-83; American Bar Association; American Correctional Association; American Society of Public Administration; American Society of Criminology; American Management Association. Community Activities: Family Service Agency of San Bernardino, President 1974-77; Exchange Club of Uptown San Bernardino, President 1980-81; San Bernardino County Peace Officers Association, President 1968; Arrowhead United Way, Allocations Committee 1978-83. Honors and Awards: Pepperdine Award in Correction, Western Correctional Association, 1980; Haye Award for Writing in Corrections, California Probation, Parole and Correctional Association, 1981. Address: 2332 Arrowhead Avenue, San Bernardino, California 92405.■

ROBERT E. MANLEY

Attorney, Economist. Personal: Born November 24, 1935; Son of John M. and Helen M. Manley; Father of Robert E. Jr. Education: Sc.B., Xavier University, 1956; A.M., University of Cincinnati, 1957; J.D., Harvard University, 1960; Postgraduate Study, London School of Economics and Political Science 1960, Massachusetts Institute of Technology 1972. Career: Adjunct Associate Professor of Economics, Xavier University, 1962-72; Lecturer on Law of Municipal Corporations and on Law of Land Use Planning, Salmon P. Chase College of Law, Northern Kentucky State University, 1965-72; Visiting Lecturer on Community Planning Law, College of Design, Architecture and Art, University of Cincinnati, 1967-73; Adjunct Associate Professor of Urban Planning, College of Design, Architecture and Art, University of Cincinnati, 1972-82; Lecturer on Law, College of Law, University of Cincinnati, 1977-80; Taft Teaching Fellow of Economics, University of Cincinnati, 1956-67; Adjunct Professor of Education, University of Cincinnati; Adjunct Professor of Law, University of Cincinnati, 1980 to present; Adjunct Professor of Planning, University of Cincinnati, 1982 to present; Partner, Manley, Jordan & Fischer, A Legal Professional Association. Organizational Memberships: Lecturer, Seminar on Financing Local Government, Section of Local Government Law, Annual Meeting, American Bar Association, 1973; Lecturer, American Bar Association National Institute on Housing, St. Louis, Missouri, 1971; Chairman Committee on Government Tort Liability 1972, Chairman Subcommittee on Computer and Right of Privacy 1972-73, Council Member of Section of Local Government Law 1976 to present, American Bar Association; Chairman Committee on Housing, Urban Development and Land Planning Law 1973-76, Chairman Committee on Antitrust Law 1967-68, Chairman Coordinating Committee on Explorer Scout Post 1973-75, Chairman Law Day Committee 1973-74, Cincinnati Bar Association; Lecturer, Council of School Attorneys (Miami, Florida) 1975, Large School Systems Conference on Measurement in Education (Tampa, Florida) 1975, Symposium on Myelomenigocele (College of Medicine, University of Cincinnati) 1976, Interdisciplinary Seminar on Urban Preservation (University of Cincinnati and the Miami Purchase Association) 1977, "Magnet Schools and Metropolitanism: No Other Way to Go" (Annual International Conference on Magnet Schools, San Diego) 1979, "Judicial Mismanagement of Public Schools (Dartmouth College) 1979, "Schools and Cities in Crisis" (Ohio Educational Seminar) 1979, "Aspectos Legales de la Ecologia Urbana" (Universidad Javeriana, Bogota, Colombia) 1979, "Legal Problems of Greek Organizations" (National Panhellenic Conference Annual Meeting) 1979, "Current Legal Mileau of Fraternities" (Edgewater Conference) 1981, Others; Chairman, Conference on State and Local Administration of Federal Policies: A Strain on American Federalism Section of Urban, State and Local Government Law, Annual Meeting, American Bar Association, Honolulu, Hawaii, 1980. Published Works: Author *The Effect of Aesthetic Considerations on the Validity of Zoning Ordinances* (1974), *Environmental Quality Protection Regulation for the City of Cincinnati: A Preliminary Strategy Report* (1974), *Outline of a System of Environmental Protection Zoning Ordinances for the City of Cincinnati* (1974), *Metropolitan School Desegregation* (1978); Author/Co-Author Various Professional Articles. Address: 1861 Dexter Avenue, Cincinnati, Ohio 45206.■

FELIX NORMAN MANSAGER

Professor. Personal: Born January 30, 1911, in Dell Rapids, South Dakota; Married Geraldine Larson; Father of Donna M. Hogsven (Mrs. Harlan), Eva Kay Sieverts (Mrs. Walter), Douglas Norman. Education: Graduate, Colton High School, 1928. Career: The Hoover Company, Salesman (Green Bay, Wisconsin) 1929, Field Representative (Minneapolis, Minnesota) 1931, Salesman (St. Paul, Minnesota) 1931, Salesman (Sioux Falls, South Dakota) 1935, Territory Manager (Denver, Colorado) 1936, Campaign Manager (Tacoma, Washington) 1936, Service Salesman (Bellingham, Washington) 1937, Campaign Manager (Sioux Falls) 1938, District Manager (Sioux Falls) 1940, District Manager (Milwaukee, Wisconsin) 1950, Branch Manager (Minneapolis) 1952, Division Manager (Chicago, Illinois) 1953, Field Sales Manager (North Canton, Ohio) 1955, General Sales Manager 1959, Vice President of Sales 1959, Executive Vice President and Director 1961, Executive Vice President and Director (The Hoover Group) 1963, Chairman/President 1966; Chairman/President, Hoover Worldwide Corporation, 1966; President, The Hoover Company Ltd., Canada, 1966; Chairman, Hoover Ltd., United Kingdom, 1966; President, Director General, S. A. Hoover, Dijon, France, 1967; Honorary President, S.A. Hoover, Dijon, France, 1972; Retired (Remaining Director of The Hoover Company) 1975; Honorary Director, The Hoover Company, 1981; Professor, (Goodyear Chair), School of Business Administration, University of Akron, 1978-84. Organizational Memberships: Council on Foreign Relations; British Institute of Management, Fellow. Community Activities: The Newcomen Society of North America; Pilgrims of the United States; The Ditchley Foundation, Governor; Honorary Member, World League of Norsemen; Honorary Member, Torske Klubben; Masonic Shrine, 32nd Degree Mason; Association of Ohio Commodores; Metropolitan Club, New York, New York; Chevaliers du Tastevin, Dijon, France; Congress Lake Country Club, Hartville, Ohio; Oakwood Country Club, Canton, Ohio; The Canton Club, Canton, Ohio; Trustee-at-Large, Independent College Funds of America; Board of Trustees, Ohio Foundation of Independent Colleges, Graduate Theological Union. Honors and Awards: Honorary LL.D., Capital University, 1967; Grand Officer, Order of Grand Ducs d'Occident, 1968; Chevalier of the Order of Leopold (Belgium), 1969; Honorary LL.D., Strathclyde University (Scotland), 1970; Order of St. Olav, Knight First Class (Norway), 1971; Marketing Award, British Institute of Marketing, 1971; Medal of Honor, Vaasa University (Finland), 1972; Honorary L.H.D., Malone College, 1972; Chevalier of the Legion of Honor (France), 1973; Fellow, University College, Cardiff, Wales, 1973; Honorary PD.D., Walsh College, 1974; Honorary Member, Beta Sigma Gamma, The University of Akron, 1974; Grand Ufficiale, Order Al Merito Della Republica Italiana, 1975; Honorary Knight of the Most Excellent Order of the British Empire, 1976; Wartburg College Honorary HH.D., 1976; Person of the Year, Capital University Chapter Tau Pi Phi, 1981. Address: 3421 Lindel Court, N.W., Canton, Ohio 44718.■

SEYMOUR ZACHARY MANSDORF

Executive. Personal: Born June 6, 1947; Married Marsha D.; Father of Brett, Bart. Education: B.A. Biology/Earth Science, University of Akron, 1969; M.S. Industrial and Environmental Health, School of Public Health, University of Michigan, 1972; Graduate Studies in Toxicology and Environmental Management, University of Michigan 1972-73, Drexel University 1974-75; M.S. Industrial Safety, Central Missouri State University, 1980; Ph.D. (in progress), Environmental Health, University of Kansas; Numerous Short Courses and Specialized Training Programs. Military: Service in the United States Army Reserves Medical Service Corps, 1973 to present, holding the rank of Captain. Career: Certified Industrial Hygienist 1978; Registered Sanitarian 1973; President, S. Z. Mansdorf and Associates, 1981 to present; Principal Industrial Hygienist 1980-81, Program Manager for Industrial Hygiene 1979-81, Senior Scientist 1979-80, Environmental Systems Department, Midwest Research Institute, 1979-81; Corporate Industrial Hygienist and Radiation Protection Officer, Goodyear Tire and Rubber Company, 1977-79; Industrial Hygienist, Office of Training and Development, Occupational Safety and Health Administration, 1976-77; Scientist, Creative Biology Laboratory, Inc., 1976; Computer Programmer II, School of Public Health, University of Michigan, 1972-73; Operations Manager, Creative Biology Laboratory, Inc., 1969-71; Group Leader, Environmental Management Laboratory, University of Akron, 1968-69; Instructor, Radiation Protection and Particulate Sampling, Midwest Center for Occupational Health and Safety; Lecturer III, Physics, University of Akron, Visiting Lecturer, Carcinogens and Carcinogenesis, O.S.H.A. Training Institute; Adjunct Instructor, Burlington County College; Instructor, Biology, University of Maryland (Extension); Instructor, Ecology, Los Angeles Community College (Korea Extension). Organizational Memberships: American Industrial Hygiene Association, Chairperson Ionizing Radiation Committee 1981, Editorial Advisor *AIHA Journal* 1981-83, Personal Protective Equipment Committee 1982-83; American Society for Testing and Meterials, Subtask Chairman F-23 Personal Protective Clothing; American Academy of Industrial Hygiene; American Academy of Sanitarians; National Environmental Health Association; Air Pollution Control Association; American Society of Safety Engineers, Professional Member; American Association for the Advancement of Science; American Chemical Society; Controlled Release Society, Secretary 1980-82, Vice President 1982-83; Panelist, Controlled Release Symposium (Occupation Hazards), National Bureau of Standards, Gaithersburg, Maryland, 1978; M.R.I. Council of Principal Scientists, Director 1980-81. Published Works: *Controlled Release Delivery Systems*, 1982; Numerous Articles, Papers and Reports including, "An Industrial Hygiene Alert System" (with R. Modrell) 1981, "Environmental Health and Occupational Safety Aspects of Resource Recovery" (with M.A. Golembiewski, C. Reaux and S. Berardinelli) 1980, "Evaluation of Controlled Release Aquatic Herbicides" (with G. A. Janes) 1980, "Controlled Release: Providing for Environmental Data" 1978. Honors and Awards: Public Health Service Fellowship, University of Michigan, 1971-72; Phi Sigma, President Akron University Chapter 1969; Listed in *Who's Who in Technology Today, Who's Who in the Midwest, Men of Achievement.*■

CARL RICHARD MAPPES

Interpreter. Personal: Born February 17, 1935, in Saint Louis, Missouri; Son of Theodore Roosevelt and Elsie Day Brown Mappes. Education: Graduate, Washington-Lee Senior High School, 1953; Studies at the Leadership Training Institute 1959, Paul Smiths College 1959-60; B.A., University of Montana, 1965; Attended the University of Missouri, 1972-74; Ph.D. Awarded by Six Accredited American Universities, 1979; Completed Ten Other Schools. Military: Served in the United States Navy, 1953-61, with the rank of Quartermaster; Served in N.A.T.O. Operations and Protection of American Oil Rights in Iran. Career: Public Relations Representative, Association of American Railroads, Washington D.C., 1953-54; Design Engineer, Kendrick and Redinger, Counts and Lawrence, William H. Singelton Company (all in Washington, D.C. Area), 1954-59; Customer Services Representative, Eastern Airlines, Washington, D.C., 1960-61; Resource Manager, U.S. Department of Agriculture/U.S. Forest Service, Montana, 1966; Resource Manager, U.S. Department of Interior/National Park Service, Yellowstone and Grand Canyon, 1966; Staff Photographer, U.S. Department of Agriculture/Office of Assistant Director, Washington D.C., 1969; Researcher/Information Specialist for the Secretary of the Interior, Resource Manager, U.S. Department of the Interior/National Park Service, Everglades, 1969; Statistics Researcher, U.S. Department of Commerce/Social and Economic Statistics Administration, 1980; Interpreter, U.S. Department of Interior/National Park Service, Grand Canyon, 1981 to present. Organizational Memberships: American Geographical Society; Ecological Society of America; Geological Society of America; International Platform Association; National Defense Transportation Association; Royal Geographical Society; Many Others. Religion: United Methodist. Published Works: Work has gone into an estimated 12,500 publications since 1947 (from assignments in 48 states and 38 foreign countries); Included in *Working Press of the Nation.* Honors and Awards: Speaker before Numerous Small-to-Large Government, Business and General Public Audiences throughout the Country since 1958; Numerous Awards for Professional Services in Engineering, Writing, Speaking, Research and Public Affairs (for work resulting in passage of landmark legislation). Address: P.O. Box 759, Kimberling City, Missouri 65686.■

SIMEON-DAVID MARABLE

Art Teacher. Personal: Born May 10, 1948; Son of Daniel Berry and Marsima Marable; Married Pamela Joyce Sorenson; Father of Simeon-David de Paul, Daniel-Dale, Christophere, Jason-Andrew, Bertley, Joanna Lee. Education: B.A. English and Art, Lea College (Albert Lea, Minnesota), 1970; Postgraduate Study undertaken at Tyler School of Art (Philadelphia, Pennsylvania). Military: Served in the United States Army, 1970. Career: Art Teacher, Grades 6, 7, and 8, William Penn School, Pennsbury School System. Organizational Memberships: Bucks County Art Educators, President, 1973-74; Middletown Historical Association, Resident Artist 1976-1977; Three Arches Corporation, Resident Artist 1975-1981. Community Activities: Delta Sigma Phi Fraternity; Levittown Artists Association, Teacher; Pennsbury Adult Education; Neshaminy Adult Education; Middletown Athletic Association, Baseball and Soccer Coach. Religion: Roman Catholic. Honors and Awards: Artist of the Year, Albert Lea Lions Club; Painting in Chapel at Fort Dix, New Jersey, 1970; National Society of Arts and Literature, Nominated for Membership by Author James A. Michener; Creator and Copyrighter, Philadelphia City of Champs Logo; Listed in *Who's Who in America, Men of Achievement, Community Leaders of America, International Platform Association, Directory of Distinguished Americans, International Who's Who of Contemporary Achievement, Dictionary of International Biography, Personalities of America, Who's Who in the East.* Address: 18 Spindle Tree Road, Levittown, Pennsylvania 19056.■

CAROL DOLORES MARDELL-CZUDNOWSKI

Psychologist, Educator, Author. Personal: Born November 30, 1935; Daughter of Albert and Lee Goldstein; Married Moshe Czudnowski; Mother of Benjamin, Dina, Ruth. Education: B.S. Elementary Education, University of Illinois, 1956; M.A. Educational Psychology, University of Chicago, 1958; Ph.D. Communicative Disorders, Northwestern University, 1972. Career: Associate Professor, Northern Illinois University, 1978 to present; Associate Professor, Northeastern Illinois University, 1974-78; Assistant Professor, Northwestern University, 1973-74; Research Project Director, Illinois Office of Education, Chicago, 1971-73; Learning Disabilities Consultant, 1970-71; Learning Disabilities Teacher, Highland Park, Illinois, 1969-70; Tutor, Skokie, Illinois, 1965-68; Private Practice Psychologist, Skokie, 1962-68; School Psychometrist, 1959-60; Classroom Teacher, 1956-59. Organizational Memberships: American Psychological Association; Council for Exceptional Children; Association for Children and Adults with Learning Disabilities; Midwestern Educational Research Association; Society for Learning Disablties and Remedical Education; Foundation for Exceptional Children. Community Activities: Illinois Early Childhood Task Force, 1972-73; Fund for Perceptually Handicapped Children, Board Member 1973-78; Illinois State Task Force for Child Care Training, 1973-75; Kappa Delta Pi, Faculty Sponsor, 1980-82. Published Works: Editorial Board, *Journal of Learning Disabilities* 1976 to present, *Journal for Division for Early Children* 1981 to present; Author (with Janet Lerner and Dorothea Goldenberg) *Special Education for Early Childhood Years,* (with Dorothea Goldenberg) *Development Indicators for the Assessment of Learning;* Numerous Articles. Honors and Awards: Alpha Lambda Delta; Kappa Delta Pi; Phi Kappa Phi; Phi Delta Kappa. Address: 6 Jennifer Lane, DeKalb, Illinois 60113.■

FRANK MARES

Manager. Personal: Born November 1, 1932; Son of Antonin and Anna Mares; Married Jirina, Daughter of Karel and Jirina Chocholous; Father of Peter John, Marie Pauline. Education: B.S., Technical University, Prague, Czechoslovakia, 1957; Ph.D., Czechoslovak Academy of Sciences, 1960; Postdoctoral Fellow, University of California at Berkeley, 1965-67. Career: Senior Research Chemist, Group Leader, Technical Research Supervisor, Senior Research Associate, Research Scientist, Manager, Allied Corporation, Corporate Research and Development, 1970 to present; Lecturer, University of California at Berkeley Department of Chemistry, 1969-70; Scientific Assistant, University of Tubingen, Institut for Organische Chemie, Tubingen, West Germany, 1968-69; Leader of Research Group 1967-68, Staff Member 1960-65, Editor of Collection of Czechoslovak Chemical Communication 1961-68, Member of Committee for Preparation of First International I.U.P.A.C. Meeting on Organosilicon Compounds 1965, Academy of Sciences, Prague, Czechoslovakia. Organizational Memberships: American Chemical Society. Published Works: 60 Published Papers; 20 Patents. Honors and Awards: Chairman's Award for Outstanding Technical and Business Contribution, Allied Corporation, 1981. Address: 32 Valley Forge Drive, Whippany, New Jersey 07981.■

RAYMOND P. MARIELLA, JR.

Research Associate. Personal: Born July 12, 1947; Married Nancy A. Education: B.A. magna cum laude, Rice University, 1969; A.M., Harvard University, 1970; Ph.D, Harvard University, 1973. Career: Research Associate, Allied Corporation; Former Lecturer on Chemistry, Harvard University. Organizational Memberships: American Chemical Society; American Association for the Advancement of Science; Materials Research Society. Published Works: Author/ Co-Author, Numerous Scientific Articles; Sole Inventor, U.S. Patent 4,320,300 (on Solar Driven Isotope Separation). Honors and Awards: American Chemical Society Award in Analytical Chemistry, 1968; Texas Society of Professional Engineers Award in Mathematics, 1968; Woodrow Wilson Fellow, 1969; National Science Foundation Graduate Fellowship, 1969-72; Listed in New York Academy of Science; *Who's Who in Technology Today, Who's Who in Lasers and Quantum Electronics, Directory of World Researchers, Men of Achievement, International Who's Who in Engineering, American Men and Women of Science.* Address: 13 Arrowhead Road, Convent Station, New Jersey 07961.■

CLYDE LOCKWOOD MARINE

Executive. Personal: Born December 25, 1936; Son of Harry and Idelle Marine; Married; Father of Cathleen, Sharon. Education: B.S. Agriculture, University of Tennessee, 1958; M.S. Agricultural Economics, University of Illinois, 1959; Ph.D. Agricultural Economics, Michigan State University, 1963. Military: Served in the United States Army, 1959-60. Career: Group Vice President, Central Soya Company, Inc., 1975 to present; Vice President, Ingredient Purchasing Company, 1973-75; Manager of Ingredient Purchasing, Central Soya Company, Inc., 1970-73; Corporate Economist, Central Soya Company, Inc., 1967-70; Manager of Market Planning, Agricultural Chemicals Division, Mobil Chemical Company, 1964-67; Senior Market Analyst, Pet Milk Company, St. Louis, Missouri, 1963-64. Organizational Memberships: Chairman, National Soybean Processors Association; Chairman of Purchasing Council, Member Market and Economic Advisory Committees, American Feed Manufacturers Association; Iced Broilers Committee, The Chicago Board of Trade; Food and Agriculture Committee, United States Chamber of Commerce; Agricultural Technical Advisory Committee on Oilseeds, Products, United States Department of Agriculture. Community Activities: Board of Directors, Fort Wayne Public Transportation Corporation; Limberlost Girl Scout Council, Board of Directors; Fort Wayne Fine Arts Foundation, Board of Directors; Finance Vice President and Treasurer, Fort Wayne Philharmonic Orchestra; American Agriculture Economics Association; Chicago Board of Trade; Chicago Mercantile Exchange. Address: 3408 North Washington Road, Fort Wayne, Indiana 46804.■

PETER MARK

Opera Association Administrator/Conductor, Educator. Personal: Born October 31, 1940; Son of Irving and Edna Mark; Married Thea Musgrave, Daughter of Joan Musgrave. Education: B.A. (Woodrow Wilson Fellow), Columbia University, 1961; M.S., Juilliard School of Music, 1963. Career: General Director and Conductor, Virginia Opera Association, 1975 to present; Professor of Music and Dramatic Art, University of California at Santa Barbara, 1965 to present; Concert Violist, United States, South America, U.S.S.R., Europe, 1961-67; Boy Soprano, Boys Chorus and Soloist, New York City Opera and Metropolitan Opera, 1953-57. Organizational Memberships: Musicians Union, New York City, Los Angeles, London, Norfolk (Virginia). Community Activities: Conducted American Premiere of Musgrave's *Mary, Queen of Scots* 1978, World Premiere of Musgrave's *A Christmas Carol* 1979, British Premiere of Musgrave's *A Christmas Carol* 1981. Honors and Awards: Phi Beta Kappa; Woodrow Wilson Fellowship; Elias Lifchey Award, 1962-63; Honorary Citizen of Norfolk, Virginia, 1978; Fellow, Creative Arts Institute, University of California, 1968-69. Address: c/o Virginia Opera Association, P.O. Box 625, Norfolk Virginia 23501.■

ALAN JOHN MARKWORTH

Senior Research Scientist. Personal: Born July 13, 1937; Son of Eleanore Markworth; Married Margaret G. Raines; Father (by previous marriage) of Sharon Marie, David John, Caroline Marie. Education: B.Sc. honors Physics, Case Institute of Technology, 1959; M.Sc. Physics 1961, Ph.D. Physics 1969, The Ohio State University. Career: Senior Research Scientist, Physical Metallurgy Section, Battelle, Columbus (Ohio) Laboratories (employed at Battelle since 1966). Organizational Memberships: American Society of Metals; American Institute of Mining, Metallurgical and Petroleum Engineers; American Association of Physics Teachers, Ohio Section/American Physical Society. Community Activities: Big Brothers/Big Sisters of Columbus and Franklin County Inc., 1982 to present; Franklin County Children's Services, Foster Parent 1967-70. Religion: First Community Church, Columbus, Ohio. Honors and Awards: Sigma Pi Sigma; Sigma Xi; American Society for Metals "Computer Simulation in Materials Science" Technical Activity. Address: 1679 Cambridge Boulevard, Columbus, Ohio 43212.■

WILLIAM WEI-YI MARR

Research Engineer. Personal: Born September 3, 1936; Son of Chieh-Ying Marr; Married Jane; Father of Dennis, Alvin. Education: Attended the Taipei Institute of Technology, 1957; M.S., Marquette University, 1963; Ph.D., University of Wisconsin-Madison, 1969. Career: Research Engineer, Argonne National Laboratory; Senior Engineering Analyst, Allis-Chalmers Manufacturing Company, Milwaukee, Wisconsin, 1963-67. Community Activities: Chicago Cooperative Chinese Language School, Principal 1980-82. Honors and Awards: Outstanding New Citizen Award, Chicago, 1972; Creative Modern Poetry Award, Taiwan, 1981; Poetry Translation Award, Taiwan, 1982. Address: 737 Ridgeview Street, Downers Grove, Illinois 60516.■

PATRICIA ANN MARSHALL

Assistant Director of Appraisal. Personal: Born December 21, 1941; Daughter of Warren Vernon and Charlene Stafford; Mother of Robin Christine, Sherry Lynn. Education: Attended Texas Women's University, 1960-61; B.S. 1972, M.Ed. 1976, University of Houston; Postgraduate Studies, Houston Baptist University, 1981 to present. Career: Assistant Director of Appraisal; Educational Diagnostician; Teacher, Spring Branch Independent School District; Teacher, Adult Continuing Education; Tutor, Grade School through Senior High School Students; Doctor's Assistant and Nurse; Nurse Aide; Secretary. Organizational Memberships: Hou-Met Diagnosticians; Council for Exceptional Children; Texas Educational Diagnostician Association; Texas State Teachers Association, Life Member; National Education Association; Association for Children with Learning Disabilities; Spring Branch Education Association; Association for Retarded Children; Registered Educational Diagnostician. Community Activities: Program Chairman, Hou-Met Conference, 1982; Country Playhouse, 1972 to present; Order of the Rainbow for Girls, Worthy Advisor 1958, Grand Cross of Color 1958. Phi Kappa Phi Honor Society, 1976 to present; Listed in *Who's Who of American Women, Five Thousand Personalities of the World, Personalities of America, Personalities of the South.* Address: 5523 Maywood, Houston, Texas 77053.■

STEPHANIE P. MARSHALL

Assistant Superintendent of Schools, Assistant Professor, Consultant. Personal: Born July 19, 1945; Daughter of Anne Pace; Married Robert Dean Marshall, Son of Margaret Marshall. Education: Attended Muhlenberg College, 1965-67; B.A., Queens College, 1967; M.A., University of Chicago, 1971; Ph.D., Loyola University of Chicago, 1983. Career: Assistant Superintendent of Schools, Assistant Professor, Consultant; Former Positions include Curriculum Administrator,

National Consultant, Graduate Faculty Member, Elementary and Junior High School Teacher. Organizational Memberships: American Association of School Administrators; Association of Supervision and Curriculum Development; Illinois Association of Supervision and Curriculum Development, Board of Directors 1980-83; West Suburban Association of Supervision and Curriculum Development, President 1981-83; National Council of Gifted Education; Illinois Council of Gifted. Community Activities: Naperville Chamber of Commerce Education Committee, 1974-76; Naperville Adult Education Coordinating Council, 1974-76; Batavia Sesquicentennial Committee, 1982 to present; Batavia Parent Teacher Organization Executive Board, 1976 to present; Board of Directors, Batavia Social Services Corporation, 1980 to present. Religion: Member Fourth Presbyterian Church, Chicago, 1976 to present. Honors and Awards: Pi Lambda Theta; Phi Delta Kappa; Appointed Member, Illinois Advisory Committee on Gifted Education 1980, Illinois Advisory Committee on Textbooks; Listed in *Who's Who in the Midwest, Personalities of the West and Midwest.* Address: 1145 Wheaton Oaks Drive, Wheaton, Illinois 60187.■

JESSE L. MARTIN

Manager of Engineering Methods. Personal: Born October 20, 1939; Son of Willie and Rosa Bailey Martin. Education: Graduate of Lynn High School, 1958; Attended Walker Junior College; B.E.E 1963, B.I.E. 1968, M.S. 1973, Auburn University. Career: Southern Electric System, Employee 1964 to present, Manager of Engineering Methods 1976 to present. Organizational Memberships: Institute of Industrial Engineers, Senior Member, Region VII Vice President 1983-85, Board of Directors 1983-85, President Birmingham Chapter 1983, First Vice President 1982, Second Vice President 1981, Treasurer 1980, Secretary 1979, Chairman Region VII Chapter Development 1983, Regional Chairman Coordinator Utilities Division 1981, Program Chairman-Elect 1982, Program Chairman 1983; Visitor for the Accreditation Board for Engineering and Technology (A.B.E.T.); Auburn Engineering Alumni Council, 1976-80; Drafting Advisory Board, Bessemer State Technical College, 1972-77; Senior Member, Institute of Electrical and Electronic Engineers. Religion: Union Baptist Church, Sunday School Teacher, 1973-78; Shades Mountain Baptist Church, Singles Sunday School Council. Honors and Awards: President of the Student Body, Lynn High School, 1958; Honor Student, Lynn High School; Elected Mr. Lynn High School, 1957; Freshman Class Representative to the Student Council, Walker Junior College; Outstanding Senator, Student Dormitory Council, Auburn University, 1962; Listed in *Personalities of the South.* Address: 2688 Buckboard Road, Birmingham, Alabama 35244.■

JOSEPH J. B. MARTIN

Telecommunications Systems Consultant. Personal: Born August 19, 1943; Son of Joseph J. and Merrlyn Baxter Martin; Married Giselle Paris, Daughter of Mario and Flora Paris. Education: B.A. Political Science, DePauw University, 1965; M.A. Political Science, Monterey Institute of International Studies, 1971; M.B.A. International Business, Golden Gate University, 1980; M.B.A. Telecommunications Management, Golden Gate University, 1980. Career: Telecommunications Systems Consultant, 1982 to present; Telecommunications Manager, 1978-82; Insurance Broker/Consultant/Manager, 1972-78; Teacher, 1967-69. Organizational Memberships: Telecommunications Association; World Affairs Council; Oakland World Trade Club; Association of M.B.A.'s. Community Activities: U.S.G./G.S.A./A.D.T.S. (Telecommunications, Federal Government), 1978-82; Monterey Institute of International Studies Alumni Association, Vice President of Board 1980 to present; United Nations Association, Representative 1970-71, Council on International Relations 1970-71; California Association of the Deaf. Religion: Valley Christian Center, Dublin, California; Methodist Church, Ann Arbor, Michigan; Christian Broadcast Network; TransWorld Radio; Rex Humbard Ministries. Honors and Awards: Scholarship, Monterey Institute of Foreign/International Studies, 1970-71; Representative to Council of International Relations, United Nations Affairs in Elsinor, Denmark, 1970-71; Bing Crosby Pebble Beach Scholarship Finance Award, 1971.■

WILLIAM COLLIER MARTIN

Health Care Administrator. Personal: Born August 16, 1926; Son of William Henry Martin (deceased); Married Alice Elizabeth Nickle, Daughter of Edgar Ralph Nickle, Alice W. Nickle; Father of Mary Anne, Patricia Jean, William Collier Jr., Nancy Lee. Education: B.S., University of Georgia, 1950; Graduate Program in Hospital Administration, Charlotte Memorial Hospital (Charlotte, North Carolina), 1950-52; Attended the University of Oklahoma, 1970; Graduate, United States Army Command and General Staff College, 1971; Graduate, United States Civil Defense Staff College, 1972. Military: Served in the United States Navy, 1944-46; Served in the United States Naval Reserves, 1946-52; Served in the United States Army, 1959-77, retiring with the rank of Lieutenant Colonel. Career: Administrator, Rockmart-Aragon Hospital, Rockmart, Georgia, 1951-54; Assistant Administrator/Administrator, Saint Agnes Hospital, Raleigh, North Carolina, 1954-56; Administrator, Florence-Darlington Tuberculosis Sanitorium, Florence, South Carolina, 1956-58; Executive Director, Thom's Rehabilitation Hospital, Asheville, North Carolina, 1977-78; Member Board of Trustees, Chairman 1979-82, Secretary 1982-83, Public Health Trust of Escambia County, Pensacola, Florida, 1979 to present; Chairman Corporate Organization Committee, Hospice Steering Committee, Pensacola, 1980-81; Executive Director 1983 to present, Board of Directors (Chairman 1981, 1982, 1983), Hospice of Northwest Florida, Inc., Pensacola, 1981 to present. Organizational Memberships: North Carolina Hospital Association, 1954-56, 1977-78; American Hospital Association; American Association of Hospital Accountants, 1954-64; South Carolina Hospital Association, Member 1956-59, Chairman Disaster Planning Committee 1957 and 1958; Association of the United States Army, Member 1964 to present, Board Member of Denver-Centennial Chapter 1974-77, Board Member of Greater Gulf Coast Chapter 1979-82; Association of Military Surgeons of the United States; American Society for Training and Development, Member 1977-82, Board of Directors of Western North Carolina Chapter 1977-80, Board of Directors of Gulf Coast Chapter 1979-82; American Academy of Medical Administrators, Advanced to Fellowship Status 1983; National Hospice Organization. Community Activities: Boy Scouts of America, Sea Explorer Leader (Ship 475, Florence, South Carolina) 1956-58, Sea Explorer Leader (Ship 535, Fort Campbell, Kentucky) 1959-61, Sea Explorer Leader (Ship 9, Coco Solo, Canal Zone) 1961-64, Commissioner for Exploring (Ryukyu Islands) 1968-69, Explorer Advisor (Far East Council, Ryukyu Islands) 1969-71; United States Power Squadrons, Member 1961 to present, Safe Boating Instructor 1962-63; Community Health Education Programs Designed, Directed and Presented in Canal Zone, Fort Bragg (North Carolina), Denver (Colorado), Ryukyu Islands, Stuttgart (West Germany), Asheville (North Carolina), Northwest Florida, 1962 to present; DeMolay Advisor, (Okinawa, Ryukyu Islands) 1969-71, DeMolay Advisor (Stuttgart, West Germany) 1971-73, DeMolay Advisor (Heidelberg, West Germany) 1973-74; Stuttgart Model Railroad Association (a German/American Organization), Member 1971-73, Vice President 1972, President 1973; Colonial Army Color Guard and Patriotic Programs, Denver, Colorado, 1975, 1976; American Society for Training and Development, Member 1977-82, Board of Directors 1977-82; Emergency Preparedness Advisor, Colorado-Wyoming Planning Commission 1974-77, Emergency Preparedness Office Metro Denver 1974-77, State Disaster Nursing Coordinating Committee (Denver) 1975-77; White House Committee on Disaster Planning, 1975-77; North Carolina Governor's Advisory Committee on Rehabilitation Centers, 1977-78; The President's Committee on Employment of the Handicapped, 1977-78; Health and Human Services Task Force of Citizens Goals for Pensacola and Escambia County, 1981 to present; Guest Lecturer, Colleges, Universities, Civic Clubs, Hospitals, United States, Republic of Panama, Ryukyu Islands, West Germany. Religion: Usher 1971-73, Chapel Advisory Committee 1972-73, Chapel Finance Committee 1972-73, President of Protestant Men of the Chapel 1972-73, Kelley Barracks, Moeringen, West Germany; Usher 1973-74, Chapel Advisory Committee 1973-74, Protestant Men of the Chapel 1973-74, Mark Twain Village Chapel, Heidelberg, West Germany; Usher, Burns United Methodist Church, Aurora, Colorado, 1974-75; Usher 1979 to present, Team Captain 1980 to present, Assistant Chief Usher 1982 to present, Administrative Board 1979 to present (vice chairman 1979-80), Finance Committee 1979 to present, Methodist Men's Club Vice President 1979 and President 1980, Pine Forest United Methodist Church, Pensacola, Florida; Certified Lay Speaker, United Methodist Church, 1980 to present. Published Works: Articles Written on Disaster Planning, Conducting Mass Casualty Exercises, Field Medical Service, Training Methods, Use of Audio-Visuals, Speakers Bureau Development, Health Care Planning, Community Health Education. Honors and Awards: Legion of Merit, 1977; Bronze Star Medal, 1967; Meritorious Service Medal with Oak Leaf Cluster, 1971, 1974; American Defense Service Medal, 1944; Asiatic-Pacific Service Medal, 1945; World War II Victory Medal, 1945; Navy Occupation Medal, Asia, 1945; China Service Medal, 1947; National Defense Service Medal with Oak Leaf Cluster, 1950, 1964; Vietnam Service Medal, 1967; Armed Forces Reserve Medal, 1967; Armed Forces Reserve Medal with Hourglass Devise 1977; Overseas Service Medal with Number 2, 1981; Army Service Medal, 1981; Vietnam Royal Cross of Gallantry with Bronze Palm, 1969; Vietnam Campaign Medal, 1967; Expert Field Medical Badge, 1968; Overseas Combat Bars; Scouter of the Year, Fort Campbell, Kentucky, 1961; Scouter's Key, Okinawa, Ryukyu Islands, 1970; Certificate of Appreciation, United States Army Southern Command, 1964; Certificate of Appreciation, Kelley Barracks Chapel, 1973; Listed in *Who's Who in the South and Southwest, Who's Who in Finance and Industry, Men of Achievement, Personalities of the South, Biographical Roll of Honor.* Address: 3225 Pursell Drive, Pensacola, Florida 32506.■

JULIO ANTONIO MARTINEZ GANDARA

Associate Librarian. Personal: Born October 4, 1931. Education: M.A.L.S., University of Michigan, 1967; M.A., University of Minnesota, 1971; Ph.D., University of California at Riverside, 1980. Career: Associate Librarian, San Diego State University Library. Organizational Memberships: National Librarians Association, Executive Board 1978-80, Chairman Professional Welfare Committee 1975-80. Religion: Unitarian Church, 1973 to present. Published Works: Assistant Editor, *Cognition and Brain Theory*, 1979 to present; Author, *Chicano Scholars: A Bio-Bibliographical Directory*, 1979; Editor and Contributor, *Chicano Literature: A Reader's Encyclopedia*, 1983; Numerous Scholarly Articles and Book Reviews. Honors and Awards: Southern Illinois University Tuition and Activity Award, 1960-63; University of California Regents Fellow, 1975-76. Address: 5642 Hamill Avenue, San Diego, California 92120.■

JOHN D. MARVELLE

Microcomputer and Educational Consultant. Personal: Born November 22, 1950; Son of John and Hazel Marvelle; Married Elise Manning, Daughter of John and Marie Manning; Father of Jared Manning. Education: B.A., Bridgewater State College, 1972; M.Ed., Bridgewater State College, 1976; Ed.D. Candidate, University of Massachusetts-Amherst. Career: Microcomputer and Educational Consultant; Project Director, Project IMPACT 1976-80, Project Life 1980-83 (E.S.E.A. Title IV-C Projects, Innovative Educational Curriculum Development Projects); Teacher of Young Children with Special Needs, Mansfield Public Schools, 1973-76. Organizational Memberships: Boston Computer Society, 1982 to present; A.S.T.D., 1979 to present. Community Activities: President, Attleboro Area Department of Social Services Citizens Board, 1981 to present; Statewide Advisory Council, Massachusetts Office for Children, 1973-75; Brockton Area Headstart Policy Board, 1973-75; Foster Parent. Honors and Awards: Phi Delta Kappa Educational Honor Society; Massachusetts Validation Award as Director of Project IMPACT, 1978; Distinguished Educator Award, Charles F. Kettering Foundation. Address: 8 Kingsley Road, Norton, Massachusetts 02766.■

GARY D. MARX

Association Executive. Personal: Born November 28, 1938; Son of Harvey and Lucille Marx; Married Judy R., Daughter of Ray and Lucille Goebel; Father of John, Daniel. Education: B.A., University of South Dakota, Vermillion. Career: Associate Executive Director, American Association of School Administrators; Executive Director of Communications, Jefferson County Public Schools, Colorado; Director of Communications, Westside Community Schools, Omaha, Nebraska; Announcer, Newscaster, Producer, WOW Radio-TV (Omaha) and KSOO Radio-TV (Sioux Falls); Professional Narrator/Announcer, Vice President, Owner, KOAK AM-FM, Red Oak, Iowa; Former Vice President, Communications Development, Inc. Organizational Memberships: P.R.S.A., Accredited-Executive Commission of Association Section; N.S.P.R.A., Accredited; A.S.A.E.; A.F.T.R.A.; A.A.S.A. Community Activities: Ad Hoc Committee on Copyright; Joint Council on Educational Telecommunications; Omaha Parks and Recreation Board; Omaha Urban Growth Policy Committee; Chairman, Keystone Community Task Force; National Teacher of the Year Committee; Volunteer Bureau Board of Directors, Equilibria Medical Center Board of Directors; Community Health Forum Board of Directors; American Cancer Society Board of Directors, Nebraska, Colorado; United Way Campaigns; Others. Religion: United Church of Christ; World Hunger Task Force Chairman, Nebraska; Board of Trustees, Board of Deacons (Chairman), First Central Congregational Church, Omaha. Honors and Awards: Outstanding Young Man of Omaha, 1970, 1971; National Radio Advertising Bureau Commercials Award; United Way Awards, National Capital Area; Nebraska Leadership Award; King of Keystone; District Service Award, American Cancer Society; Other Awards; Listed in *Outstanding Young Men of America*. Address: 1831 Toyon Way, Vienna, Virginia 22180.■

UNA M. MASTERSON

Citizen Advocate for the Mentally Retarded, Community Companion for the Blind. Personal: Born August 23, 1918; Daughter of William E. and Kathryn M. Myers (deceased), Homestead, Florida; Married Fred A.; Mother of Fred A. Jr., William E., Thomas L. (deceased), Jr. Walker, Gary McCarty. Education: University of Miami, 1936-37; University of Texas, 1961-63; Miami-Dade Junior College, 1966-67; Mechanical Engineer, Business Administration, A.D.P. Military: Instructor, Aircraft Fab Air Search and Rescue, Commander Cadets and Groups, Civil Air Patrol, 1947-49; Auxiliary Air Force Captain. Career: Citizen Advocate, Mentally Retarded; Community Companion, Blind; Former Positions include Accountable Property Officer in Data Processing Office, National Item Commodity Manager for Early Space Flight Programs. Organizational Memberships: Data Processing Management Association, Vice President Education 1961-78, Editor Newsletter; American Business Women Association; Federally Employed Women, 1972-75. Community Activities: Instructor, A.D.P., High School, Business Managers, 1961-64; Disaster Committee Coordinator, Japan, Texas, New Mexico, 1955-56, 1963-65; Area Warden, Civil Defense, Texas 1962-63, Florida 1932-45; Volunteer Auditor, Federal Credit Union, 1963-64; Colonel, Governor's Staff, State of Mississippi, 1976-80; Religion: Secretary-Treasurer, Baptist Missionary Society, Japan, 1954-56; Women's Auxiliary, Shriners Crippled Children, Japan, 1954-57; Mother Advisor, International Rainbow Girls, Japan, 1954-57; Teacher, Choir Member. Honors and Awards: Allison Aircraft and Engineering Tool, 1944; Grand Cross of Color, 1955; Train Equipment Management, Air Force Computer, 1967; President, A.F.G.E., A.F.L.-C.I.O., 1971-78; Vultee Aircraft Ribsling, 1942; Rehabilitation Iow Jima, 1956; Judge Advocate, American Legion Post, 1977-79; Listed in *Who's Who in Labor, World Who's Who of Women, Marquis Who's Who in the East*. Address: 224 Grove Avenue, Thorofare, New Jersey 08086.■

TOM HARRELL MATHENY

Lawyer. Personal: Born in Houston, Texas; Son of Whitman and Lorene Harrell Matheny. Education: B.A., Southeastern Louisiana University, 1954; J.D., Tulane University, 1957. Career: Admitted to Louisiana Bar, 1957; Partner, Pittman, Matheny, Lewis and Moody, Hammond, Louisiana; Chairman of Board, First Guaranty Bank, Hammond; Vice President, Edwards & Associates, Southern Brick Supply, Inc.; Chairman of the Board, WTGI, Inc.; General Counsel, First Guaranty Bank; Faculty, Southeastern Louisiana University, Holy Cross College of New Orleans. Organizational Memberships: American Bar Association, Committee on Probate; Louisiana Bar Association, Chairman Committee on Legal Aid, Committee on Prison Reform; 21st Judicial District Bar Association, Past Secretary-Treasurer, Vice President 1967-68 and 1971; Commercial Law League of America, Past Member Committee on Ethics; Louisiana Alumni Council, President 1963-65; Academy of Religion and Mental Health; International Platform Association; Louisiana Association; Louisiana Association Claimant's Compensation Attorneys; Southeastern Louisiana College Alumni Association, Director, President 1961-62, Board for Special Fund 1959-62, Director Tangipahoa Chapter; Tulane Alumni Association; U.N. Association; American Trial Lawyers Association; American Judicature Society; Law-Science Institute; World Peace Through Law Academy, Committee on Conciliation; American Academy of Political and Social Science; American Academy of Law and Science; Law Science Institute; Hammond Association of Commerce, Director 1960-65; Phi Delta Phi; Phi Delta, Phi Alpha Delta. Community Activities: Board of Trustees, Scarritt College, 1975-81; Honorary Secretary, United States Committee for the Audenshaw Foundation; Chairman of Advancement Committee of Hammond 1960-64, District Council 1957-66, Executive Board of Istrouma Area Council 1966 to present, Boy Scouts of America; Campaign Manager, Democratic Candidate for Governor of Louisiana, 1959-60, 1963-64; Board of Directors, Tangipahoa Parish Association of Retarded Citizens 1957-67, Hammond United Givers Fund 1957-68, Louisiana Council of Churches, Louisiana Interchurch Conference; Trustee, Centenary College; Honorary Trustee, John F. Kennedy College; Chairman of the Board, Wesley Foundation; Mason (Shriner); K.C.C.H.; DeMolay, District Deputy of Supreme Court 1964 to present, Legion of Honor; Kiwanian, Vice President, Director; Rotarian; International Society of Barristers; International Association of Valuers. Religion: President Judicial Council, United Methodist Church (Supreme Court of the Denomination), 1976 to present; President, National Association of Conference Lay Leaders, United Methodist Church, 1966-82; Board of Trustees, Louisiana Annual Conference, United Methodist Church; World United Methodist Conference, London 1966, Denver 1971, Dublin 1976, Hawaii 1981; Delegate to General Conference, United Methodist Church, 1968, 1970, 1972. Honors and Awards: Man of the Year, Hammond, 1961, 1964; Man of the Year, Louisiana State Junior Chamber of Commerce. Address: P.O. Box 221, Hammond, Louisiana 70404.■

JEAN HUMPHRIES MAULDIN

Aviation Company Executive. Personal: Born August 16, 1923, in Gordonville, Texas; Daughter of James Wiley and Lena Leota Neol-Crain Humphries; Married William Henry Mauldin, February 28, 1942; Mother of Bruce Patrick, William Timothy III. Education: B.S., Hardin Simmons University, 1943; M.S.,

University of Southern California, 1961; Postgraduate Studies undertaken at Westfield College, University of London 1977-78, Warnborough College (Oxford) 1977-78. Career: President, Stardust Aviation Inc., Santa Ana, California, 1962 to present; President, Mauldin and Staff, Public Relations, Los Angeles, 1957-78; Psychological Counselor, First Baptist Church Social Services, 1953-57. Organizational Memberships: American Management Association; Experimental Aircraft and Pilots Association; National Women Pilots; Women for Experimental Aircraft and Pilots Association; International Platform Association. Community Activities: California Democratic Central Committee, Executive Board; Orange County Democratic Central Committee, Executive Board; California Democratic Council, 1953-70; California Democratic Central Committee, 1957 to present; Orange County Democratic Central Committee, 1960 to present; Democratic National Convention, Delegate 1974-78; United States Congressional Advisory Board; Santa Ana Friends of the Public Library, President 1973-76; McFadden Friends of the Library, Santa Ana, 1976-80; American Cancer Society, Orange County Cancer Crusade Chairman 1974; Historical Preservation Society, Executive Board Member 1970 to present; Business and Professional Women's Clubs of America; National Women's Political Caucus; Democratic Coalition Central Committees; California Friends of the Library, Life Member; League of Women Voters; National Federation of Democratic Women; California Federation of County Central Committee Members; Jefferson Club; Democratic Alliance; American Security Council; Peace Through Strength; National Audubon Society; Sea and Sage; Town Hall of California; Los Angeles World Affairs Council; World Wildlife Federation; Amnesty International; Fellow, International Biographical Institute; Executive Council, Foundation for the Creative Arts and the Performing Arts. Religion: Trinity Episcopal Church, Tustin, California; Protestant Episcopal Church of America, Lay Leader; Women's Missionary Society, Chairman. Published Works: Author *Winters, The Pilot, The Man* 1961, *The Consummate Barnstormer* 1962, *The Daredevil Clown* 1965; Advisory Producer of Television Film, "Attack on the Americas." Honors and Awards: Woman of the Year, Key Woman in Politics, California Democratic Party, 1960-80; Listed in *Who's Who in Finance and Industry, Who's Who of American Women, Who's Who in Politics, Who's Who in American Politics, International Who's Who of Intellectuals, International Who's Who in the World.* Address: 1013 West Elliott Place, Santa Ana, California 92704.■

MAURICE MAURIN

Artist (Painter). Personal: Born June 23, 1939. Education: Fine Arts School, Quebec City, Canada; Academy San Fernando, Madrid; Instituto Cultura Hispanica, Madrid; Bienal Hispano Americana, Madrid; University of Madrid. Career: Expressionist, Painting Mostly Landscapes and Portraits; Exhibits in Madrid, Quebec City, Ottawa, Buenos Aires, Caracas, Lisbon, Rio de Janeiro, Stockholm; Teacher of Drawing, Oil Painting, Anatomy (Spain and Canada); Paintings in Several Private and Public Collections. Organizational Memberships: Mensa International, International Fine Arts Guild. Honors and Awards: Gold Medal, Accademia Italia delle Arti; Grants, Canada Council, Government of Canada, Government of Spain; Listed in *Who's Who, Contemporary Personalities, International Who's Who of Intellectuals, Men of Achievement, Personalities of America.* Address: P.O. Box 506, Haute-ville, Quebec City, Province of Quebec, Canada G1R 4R8.■

THAMES LeRoy MAUZY

State Representative, Businessman. Personal: Born November 13, 1908; Son of Charles Mauzy (deceased); Married Helen, Daughter of Carl O. Nelson (deceased); Father of Landon, Sharon M. Shaver. Education: Graduate, Warsaw High School, Warsaw, Indiana; Graduate in Business Administration, Anthony Wayne College of Commerce. Career: State Representative, 1966-82; Owner, Home Furniture Mart, Warsaw, Indiana. Community Activities: Winona Lake Town Board, Indiana, 1948-56; Honorary Rotarian; Elk; Mason; Scottish Rite; Past Director, Warsaw Chamber of Commerce; Salvation Army, Board Member; Reagan Presidential Task Force. Religion: Presbyterian. Honors and Awards: Soil and Conservation Award, 1972; J.C.C. Safe Driving Award, 1974; Kosco Skeet Champion, 1947; A.C.I. Award for Retain Excellence, 1962. Address: 1025 Country Club Lane, Warsaw, Indiana 46580.■

THOMAS JAMES MAXWELL

Anthropologist, Professor. Personal: Born June 22, 1924; Son of Rev. T. J. Maxwell; Married Ruth Lautzenheiser, Daughter of Russ Lautzenheiser; Father of Linda, Susan, David. Education: B.A., College of Wooster, 1947; B.S.H., University of San Marcos (Lima, Peru), 1949; M.A., University of Missouri, 1953; Ph.D., Indiana University, 1962. Military: Served in the United States Army Air Force, 1942-45, attaining the rank of Second Lieutenant. Career: Professor, California Lutheran College, 1965 to present; Interamerican University, San German, Puerto Rico, Faculty Member 1956-65, Department Chairman 1956-63, Academic Dean 1963-65. Community Activities: City of Thousand Oaks Archaeological Consultant, 1973-74; County of Ventura Archaeological Consultant, 1975 to present; Campaign Worker; El Hogar Colonia Drug Program, Consultant 1976; Coneso Valley Days, Grand Marshall Candidate 1976; Coneso Future, Canyons Task Force 1973-74. Religion: Ventura County Council of Churches, Board Member 1970 to present; United Methodist Church, Lay Leader 1968-72, Conference Delegate 1970. Honors and Awards: Fulbright Scholar, Mysore, India, 1964; Lisle Fellowship, Cali, Colombia, 1966. Address: 3268 Luther Avenue, Thousand Oaks, California 93160.■

JUDE THOMAS MAY

Full Professor. Personal: Born June 7, 1936; Son of James A. (deceased) and Frances C. Temple May; Married Anita Rasi, Daughter of Peter J. (deceased) and Rose Rotundo Rasi; Father of Rose Marie, Thomas Garvey. Education: B.A., B.S., St. Mary's University, 1958; M.S., University of Pittsburgh, 1962; Ph.D., Tulane University, 1969. Military: Served in the United States Army Infantry, 1960-61, with the rank of Private First Class. Career: Assistant to Full Professor, College of Public Health, University of Oklahoma Health Sciences Center, 1968 to present; Adjunct Assistant to Adjunct Full Professor, Department of Sociology, University of Oklahoma, 1973 to present; Adjunct Professor, Department of Anthropology, Southern Methodist University, 1980 to present. Organizational Memberships: Society for Applied Anthropology, Fellow 1976 to present, Treasurer 1982 to present; American Public Health Association; International Society for History of Medicine; American Sociological Association. Published Works: *The Neighborhood Health Center Program: Its Growth and Problems, An Introduction,* 1976; Various Chapters in Books, Articles and Reports. Honors and Awards: Graduate Assistant, Department of History, University of Pittsburgh, 1961-62; Josiah Macy Jr. Predoctoral Fellowship, Tulane University, 1965-68; Summer Community of Scholars, Miner Foundation, New York, 1968; Grant-in-Aid, American Philosophical Society, 1971; Travel Grant, American Council of Learned Societies, Denmark, 1974; Travel Grant, National Science Foundation, Scotland, 1981. Address: 733 Northeast 18th Street, Oklahoma City, Oklahoma 73105.■

OLIVIA L. MAY

Bookkeeper. Personal: Born December 20, 1912; Daughter of Rev. F. W. and Marie H. Lammert (deceased); Married Vernon May (deceased), Son of William Byrd and Rosells May (deceased); Mother of Curtis L. Education: Self Employed, Bookkeeping and Tax Service; Senior Administrator, Exxon Company, U.S.A., 1944-77 (retired); Bookkeeper and Office Manager, Miller Motor Company, Katy, Texas, 1934-44. Organizational Memberships: American Society of Women Accountants, Treasurer, Recording Secretary, Corresponding Secretary, Second Vice President, Director 1960 to present; Desk and Derrick Club of Houston, Treasurer 1951 to present. Community Activities: Accountant for City of Katy, 1944-49; Auditor, City of Katy, 1949-61; Chairman of Supervisory Committee for Exxon, Katy Federal Credit Union, 1948 to present; Treasurer, Texas Wendish Heritage Society, 1981-82; German-Texas Heritage Society. Religion: Sunday School Teacher, 1940-76; Assistant Organist, 1946-56. Honors and Awards: Listed in *Who's Who of American Women.* Address: 1610 East Avenue, Katy, Texas 77449.■

JEROME STEPHEN MAYERSAK

Physician. Personal: Born July 4, 1938; Son of Joseph and Libby Mayersak (mother deceased); Married Priscilla M.; Father of Kathlyne M. Mayersak Evans, Priscilla K., Tzena L. Education: B.A., Johns Hopkins University, 1960; M.D., George Washington University, 1964. Career: Physician, Specializing in Urology, J. S. Mayersak, M.D., Service Corporation; Formerly with Medical Arts Group, Wisconsin Rapids, Wisconsin. Organizational Memberships: American Medical Association; International College of Surgeons in Urology; American Mensa Society; American Association of Physicians and Surgeons; Wisconsin State Medical Society; Aerospace Medical Society; Society of Sigma Xi; Renal Physicians Association. Community Activities: Chairman, Merrill Airport Commission, Merrill, Wisconsin. Honors and Awards: Physician's Recognition Award, American Medical Association, 1978-84; Honorary Member, Asociacion Medica Panamericana Capitulo Ecuatoriana (The Pan-American Medical Association), 1970; Honorary Member, Sociedad Ecuatoriana de Urologia (Ecuadorian Urological Society), 1970. Address: 717 Tee Lane Drive, Merrill, Wisconsin 54452.■

ROSEMARIE LEANDRI MAYNES

Physician. Personal: Born September 1, 1941; Daughter of Daniel J. (deceased) and Mary Skovronsky Leandri; Married James Francis Maynes; Mother of Michelle Marie, James Francis Jr. Education: B.S., College Misericordia; Graduate Study undertaken at Rutgers University, Temple University, Rosemont College; D.O., Philadelphia College of Osteopathic Medicine. Career: Physician, Maynes Medical-Dental Center; Chief School Physician, Wissahickon District; Staff Member, Chestnut Hill Hospital, Suburban General Hospital; Medical Consultant, The Pilling Corporation; Preceptor in Family Medicine, Jefferson University School of Medicine, Philadelphia College of Osteopathic Medicine, University of Pennsylvania Medical College, Chestnut Hill Hospital, Suburban General Hospital; Cardiopulmonary Physiologist, Mt. Zion Hospital and Medical Center, San Francisco, 1967-68; Research Pharmacologist, Smith-Kline-French, 1963-67. Organizational Memberships: American Osteopathic Association; American College of General Practitioners in Osteopathic Medicine and Surgery; American Academy of Osteopathy; Pennsylvania Osteopathic Medical Association, District X Delegate; Pennsylvania Osteopathic General Practitioners Society; American Medical Women's Association; Philadelphia College of Osteopathic Medicine Alumni Association; College Misericordia Alumni Association; American Professional Practice Association; International College of General Practitioners; Lamda Omicron Gamma National Medical Fraternity; Diplomate, National Board of Medical Examiners. Community Activities: Bucks-Mont Dance Theater Company, Board of Directors; Budzynski School of Ballet; Montgomery-Bucks Dental Wives Association; Business and Professional Women's Association; Utilization Committee Chairman, Desher Hill Nursing Home. Religion: Roman Catholic. Honors and Awards: Continuing Education Award, American Osteopathic Association; Physicians Recognition Award, American Medical Association; Karr Fellowship Award, Smith-Kline-French; Recognition Award, American Academy of Family Physicians; Grant, Northeastern Pennsylvania Society of Medical Technology and Clinical Pathology; Honors Scholarship, College Misericordia. Listed in *Who's Who in the East, Outstanding Young Women of America.* Address: 1504 Temple Drive, Maple Glen, Pennsylvania 19002.■

DON McANALLY

Editor, Publisher. Personal: Born October 27, 1913, in Sewell, New Jersey; Son of James C. and Ina MacLeod McAnally; Married Edith P. McKinney, December 11, 1934; Father of Shirley Ann English. Education: Graduate, High School, Woodbury, New Jersey; John Wanamaker Cadet Institute, Philadelphia; Sales Analysis Institute, Chicago. Career: Editor/Publisher, O & A Marketing News 1966 to present, *California Senior Citizen News* 1977 to present, *The Automotive Booster of California* 1974 to present; Publisher, *California Businesswoman*, 1978; 1975-76; Owner, Hovercraft of Southern California, 1975-76; Editor, *Pacific Oil Marketer*, Los Angeles, 1960-66; Sales Promotion Manager and Product Sales Manager, LOF Glass Fibers Company, Toledo, 1953-59; Assistant Advertising Manager, Libbey-Owens-Ford Glass Company, Toledo, 1947-53; Editor, Owens-Illinois Company Publications, New Jersey and Ohio, 1945-47; Reporter and Editor, *Woodbury Daily Times*, New Jersey, 1932-45. Community Activities: Lions Club, Montrose, California; California Independent Oil Marketers Association; Masquers, Hollywood, California; Silver Dollar Club, San Fernando Valley, California; Roorag, Los Angeles; Automotive Booster Club of Greater Los Angeles; OX 5 Aviation Pioneers, National and Southern California Wing; Greater Los Angeles Press Club. Honors and Awards: Man of the Year, Pacific Oil Confernece, 1977; Special Award, Automotive Affiliated Representative, 1979; Appreciation Award, Western Oil Industry TBA Group, 1971; Appreciation Plaque, Douglas Oil Ex-Employees, 1980; Award Winning Editor, Toledo Club of Printing House Craftsmen, 1950; Good Neighbor Award, Toledo, Ohio, 1948. Address: 4409 Indiana Avenue, La Canada, California 91011.■

JOE DAVID McBEE

University Library Department Head. Personal: Born August 22, 1947, in Sewanee, Tennessee; Son of Ernest and Lucille McBee (both. deceased). Education: B.B.A., Florida State Christian University, Fort Lauderdale, Florida, 1966-71; Postgraduate Studies, Middle Tennessee State University, Murfreesboro, Tennessee, Summer 1975; Master's Degrees in Educational Administration and Supervision, Tennessee State University, 1981-83. Career: Jessie Ball duPont Library, University of the South, Sewanee, Tennessee, Circulation Assistant (part-time) Summers (and vacations) 1965-70, Circulation Supervisor 1971-72, Head of Serials and Binding Department 1972 to present; Elected Road Commissioner, First Road District of Franklin County, 1974 to present, Secretary 1978-82, Chairman 1982 to present; Periodical Committee, 1976 to present; Waterloo Union List Project, 1982; Committee on Library Pick-ups, 1982; Tennessee Library Association; Mid-State Library Association; Franklin County Historical Society; Employee's Committee on the University of the South, 1977-80; Sewanee Community Council; Serials Online by Ebsco Subscription Service, Knoxville, 1982; Tennessee Library Association Conference, Serials Online by F W Faxon Company, Nashville, 1982; Southern College and University Union Library Workshop in Sewanee, 1982; Attended Various Workshops; Member Tennessee and Sewanee Chapter of American Association of University Professors; Supervised Move of Journals from School of Theology Library to DuPont, Summer 1982. Community Activities: Franklin County Democratic Executive Committee, 1980 to present; Precinct Chairman of Democratic Party of Sewanee, 1974 to present; Sewanee Community Action, Member Board of Directors, 1978 to present; Sewanee Youth Center, Member Board of Directors 1981 to present, President 1982; Sewanee Civic Association, Member Board of Directors 1977-81, Member 1975 to present, President 1979-80; Sewanee Community Memorial Association, Member Board of Directors 1975-82, Member 1975 to present, Secretary 1975-82; Member E.Q.B. of Sewanee, 1979-80; Member Board of Directors, Franklin County Historical Society, 1983 to present; Franklin County Chamber of Commerce, Member Board of Directors 1980-81, Member 1980 to present, Member Community Relations Communications Committee 1980-81, Chairman Membership Retention Committee 1981, Chairman Banquet Committee 1981, Adult Education Committee of Franklin County, 1981 to present; Grace Fellowship Church, Trustee 1974 to present, Secretary-Treasurer 1968 to present, Chairman of the Board of Trustees 1975 to present. Honors and Awards: Named Outstanding Young Man of the Year, Franklin County Jaycees for 1980; Appointed Aid to State Senator Ernest Crouch's Office for Franklin County, 1981 to present; Honored with a Senate Joint Resolution No. 192 on January 15, 1982, by the State of Tennessee; Listed in *Who's Who in the South and Southwest, Personalities of America, Personalities of the South, Men of Achievement, Community Leaders of the World, Directory of Distinguished Americans, International Who's Who of Contemporary Achievement, International Who's Who of Intellectuals.* Address: P.O. Box 27, Sewanee, Tennessee 37375.■

WENDELL F. McBURNEY

Research Administrator. Personal: Born February 2, 1933, in Spring Valley, New York; Married Jean W., in 1933; Father of Cynthia Jean, Willson Stuart, Laurie Kay. Education: B.S. Biological Sciences, Geneva College, 1955; M.A. General Science 1966, Ed.D. Science Education 1967, Indiana University. Military: Served in the United States Army Chemical Corps, 1956-58. Career: Assistant Dean 1973-76, Associate Dean 1976-78, Acting Dean 1978-79, Dean 1979 to present, Research and Sponsored Programs, Indiana University-Purdue University at Indianapolis; Assistant Professor 1966-73, Associate Professor 1973 to present, Science Education, School of Education, Indiana University; Academic Analyst, Indianapolis Center for Advanced Research, Indianapolis, Indiana, 1973-77; Executive Director, Indianapolis Scientific and Engineering Foundation, Inc., 1973-75; Coordinator for School Science, College of Arts and Sciences, Indiana University, Bloomington, 1967-73; Director, Numerous Institutes and Seminars for Teachers and Students of Science, 1967-77; Teacher, Biology, Advanced Biology, General Science, Beaver Area Schools, Beaver, Pennsylvania, 1955-64. Organizational Memberships: Association of Governing Board of Universities and Colleges, Institutional Membership; Association of Midwestern College Biology Teachers; Hoosier Association of Science Teachers; Indiana Academy of Science; Indiana University Alumni Association, Life Member; National Association of Biology Teachers; National Council of University Research Administrators; National Science Teachers Association; Phi Delta Kappa; Society of Sigma Xi. Community Activities: Eagle-Union Community School Board of Trustees, Zionsville, Indiana, 1982 to present; Board of Trustees 1969 to present, Chairman Education Committee 1980 to present, Geneva College;

Superintendent, Poultry Division, Boone County 4-H Fair, Lebanon, Indiana, 1977 to present; Chairman, Eagle Township 4-H Advisory Council, Boone County, Indiana, 1979; Boone County 4-H Council, Lebanon, Indiana, Member 1978-79. Religion: Member and Chairman of Board of Education and Publication 1969-71, Elder 1968 to present, Reformed Presbyterian Church of North America. Honors and Awards: Honorable Order of Kentucky Colonels, 1969 to present; Life Science Award, March of Dimes, Central Indiana Chapter, 1977; Phi Delta Kappa; Listed in *Who's Who in the Midwest, American Men and Women of Science, Outstanding Educators of America, Leaders in Education.* Address: 11750 Greenfield Road, Zionsville, Indiana 46077.∎

ROBERT B. McCALL

Senior Scientist, Science Writer. Personal: Born June 21, 1940; Son of Blance B. McCall; Married Rozanne, Daughter of Eugene Allison; Father of Darin, Stacey. Education: B.A. Psychology, DePauw University, 1962; M.A. Psychology 1964, Ph.D. Psychology 1965, University of Illinois at Urbana. Career: Senior Scientist and Science Writer, Boys Town; Contributing Editor and Monthly Columnist, *Parents*; Senior Scientist and Chief, Perceptual Cognitive Development Section, Fels Research Institute, Yellow Springs, Ohio, 1968-77; Associate Professor of Psychology, Antioch College; Assistant Professor of Psychology, University of North Carolina at Chapel Hill, 1966-68. Organizational Memberships: American Psychological Association, Continuing Commission on Public Information 1979-80, 1982-84; Society for Research in Child Development, Social Policy Committee 1981 to present. Published Works: 20 News Features on Children, Youth, Families; Author 11 Books and Monographs, 80 Articles for Professional Audiences; 2 Books and 20 Articles for General Audiences. Honors and Awards: Media Award for Science/Families, American Psychological Foundation, American Academy of Physicians. Address: 21920 Skyline Drive, Elkhorn, Nebraska 68022.∎

EVA KARIN McCLINTOCK

Corporate Executive. Personal: Born March 23, 1938; Married Ronald, Son of John H. McClintock, Sr; Mother of Kurt, Jim, Scott. Education: Graduate, High School in West Germany, 1953; Graduate, Business School, 1957. Career: Corporate Vice President, Vice President of Sales, Director of Marketing 1979 to present, Concept Now Cosmetics; Director of Sales Training, Pola U.S.A., 1977-79; Divisional Sales Manager, Luzier Cosmetics, 1976-77; District Sales, Avon Products, 1966-76. Organizational Memberships: American Business Women's Association; We Can Women's Network; National Association of Female Executive. Community Activities: Den Mother, Cub Scouts of America, 1966-68. Religion: Christ Lutheran Church, Long Beach, California. Honors and Awards: Management Excellence Award, Avon, 1968; Avon Circle of Excellence, 1972, 1975; Listed in *Who's Who of American Women, Personalities of America, Personalities of the West and Midwest, Who's Who in the West, World Who's Who of Women.* Address: 5183 Melbourne Drive, Cypress, California 90630.∎

J. DOUGLAS McCLUSKIE

Administrator. Personal: Born March 1, 1923; Son of Mr. and Mrs. J. S. McCluskie (deceased); Married Dorothy B., Daughter of Mr. and Mrs. N. Ray Bogart (father deceased); Father of Craig S., Jody R. McLean, James D. Education: D.V.M., Michigan State University, 1946; Studies in Public Health and Medical Statistics, University of Colorado Medical Center, 1955-56; M.P.H., University of Michigan, 1957. Military: Served in the United States Army Veterinary Corps, 1951-53, attaining the rank of Captain. Career: Director, Environmental Health Service, Denver Department of Health and Hospitals; Assistant Professor of Clinical Preventive Medicine, University of Colorado Medical Center, 1972; Chief 1956-60, Assistant Chief 1953-56, Veterinary Public Health Section, Environmental Health Service, Denver Department of Health and Hospitals, 1956-60; Senior Veterinarian, Detroit Department of Health, 1947-51. Organizational Memberships: Denver General Hospital, Infection Control Committee, Chairman 1967-78, Vice Chairman and Secretary 1979 to present; American Veterinary Medical Association; National Environmental Health Association; Colorado Environmental Health Association; American Board of Veterinary Public Health, Vice President 1963-65. Religion: Member Wellshire Presbyterian Church, Denver. Honors and Awards: Delta Omega; Phi Kappa Phi. Address: 35 Viking Drive, Englewood, Colorado 80110.∎

JOHN MACK McCOIN

Social Worker. Personal: Born January 21, 1931, in Sparta, North Carolina. Education: A.A., Wingate Junior College, 1955; B.S., Appalachian State Teachers College, 1957; M.S.S.W., Richmond Professional Institute, 1962; Ph.D., University of Minnesota, 1977; Attended the University of North Carolina, 1959-60; New York University, 1969; Postgraduate Center for Mental Health, 1970; Academy of Health Sciences, United States Army, 1975-76, 1977-78; University of Chicago, 1978. Military: Served with the United States Army Reserve, 1972 to present; United States Marine Corps, 1948-52; United States Marine Corps Reserve, 1957-72. Career: Supervisory Social Worker, Veterans Administration Medical Center, Leavenworth, Kansas, 1983 to present; Social Worker, Veterans Administration Medical Center, Battle Creek, Michigan, 1981-83; Associate Professor, School of Social Work, Grand Valley State Colleges, Allendale, Michigan, 1979-81; Assistant Professor, Social Work Department, University of Wisconsin, Oshkosh, 1977-79; Social Worker, F.D.R. Veterans Administration Health Care Facility, Montrose, New York, 1975-77; Social Worker, Veterans Administration Hospital, Montrose, 1968-73; Senior Psychiatric Social Worker, Cornell University Medical Center, White Plains, New York, 1966-68; Social Worker, Wake County Welfare Department, Raleigh, North Carolina, 1963-64; Clinical Social Worker, Dorothea Dix State Hospital, Raleigh, 1962-63; High School Teacher, Brevard County Board of Education, Titusville, Florida, 1956-57. Organizational Memberships: Academy of Certified Social Workers; American Society for Public Administration; Certified Social Worker, New York; Council on Social Work Education; National Association of Social Workers; Register of Clinical Social Workers; Reserve Officers Association of the United States; Alpha Delta Mu; American Biographical Research Association. Published Works: Author, *Adult Foster Homes: Their Managers and Residents*, 1983; Contributor of Numerous Articles and Letters to Professional Journals, City and County Newspapers, Military Newspapers, and Local Hospital Publications. Honors and Awards: Outstanding Performance Award, F.D.R. Veterans Administration Hospital, 1971; Education Grant, National Institute on Mental Health: Educational Grant, University of Wisconsin, 1978; Listed in *Book of Honor, Community Leaders of America, Dictionary of International Biography, Directory of Distinguished Americans, International Who's Who of Intellectuals, Men of Achievement, Personalities of America, Personalities of the West and Midwest, Two Thousand Notable Americans, Who's Who in the Midwest.* Address: 310-B Kiowa Street, Leavenworth, Kansas 66048.∎

LEN GARDNER McCORMICK

Corporate Executive. Personal: Born October 28, 1922; Son of Van and Jimmie McCormick (both deceased); Married Vera Lu Sumner; Father of Kathryn Blanton Bettis, Charles V. Blanton Jr., Daniel T. Blanton, Gail S. Blanton, Van B. McCormick. Education: B.B.A. 1947, LL.B. 1950, J.D. 1969, Baylor University. Military: Served in the United States Marine Corp, 1942-45, 1950-52. Career: City Attorney, City of Midland, 1952-53; Private Law Practice, McCormick, Branum, Cason and Jennings, 1953-57; Oil Operator, Len G. McCormick and Associates, 1957-60; President and Chairman of the Board, Santiago Oil and

TWO THOUSAND NOTABLE AMERICANS

and Gas Company, 1960-62; Chairman of the Board, Big Bend Ranch Company, 1960-62; President and Chairman of the Board, Santana Petroleum Company, 1962 to present; President and Chairman of the Board, Gold Metals Consolidation Mining Company, 1963-67; President, Pasto Neuva Oil Company, 1963-67; Consultant to Chilocote Land Company, 1969-70; Beacon Hill Farms, Inc., President 1970 to present, Chairman of the Board 1975 to present. Organizational Memberships: American Association of Petroleum Landmen; Independent Petroleum Association of America; Texas Independent Producers and Royalty Association; Phi Alpha Delta; Petroleum Club of Houston, Petroleum Club of Midland. Community Activities: Houston Chamber of Commerce. Religion: Methodist. Address: 603 Rebecca Pines Court, Houston, Texas 77024.■

GENEVIEVE BELL McDANIEL

Retired Educator. Personal: Born October 14, 1915; Daughter of Romie C. (deceased) and Ida Russell Bell; Married Edgar N. (deceased); Mother of Joseph Starrett, Rebecca McDaniel Thompson. Education: B.A. English 1960, M.A. English 1964, Marshall University; Forty Semester Hours Post Graduate Study, Marshall University. Career: Retired Educator, 1979 to present; Former Positions Include Teacher, Beverly Hills Junior High School, Cabell County, West Virginia; Student Teacher, Ona Junior High School, 1964-67; Part-time Instructor, Marshall University, 1964-67; Glenville (West Virginia) State College, Assistant Professor of English 1968-74, Associate Professor 1974-76; Classroom Teacher, Hurricane, Putnam County, West Virginia, 1976-79; Organizational Memberships: Modern Language Association, 1963 to present; National Council of Teachers of English, 1958 to present; Conference on English Education, 1964; Association for Teacher Education, 1974 to present; Association for Student Teaching, 1960-69; Organizer and President, Cabel County (West Virginia) Teachers of English, 1963; Faculty-Administration Organization, Glenville State College, 1968-76; Kappa Delta Pi, 1957 to present. Community Activities: Organizer and President, Altizer Elementary School Parent-Teacher Association, 1946-47; Ways and Means Chairman, Gallaher Elementary School, 1948-51; Beverly Hills Woman's Club, 1948-58; Group Leader, Camp Fire Girls, 1949-59; Organizer, Beverly Hills Junior High School Parent-Teacher Association, 1955; Vice-President and President, West Virginia Council of Teachers of English, 1962-67; American Association of University Women, Secretary Modern Literature Group 1964-67, Education Chairman 1972-76; Board of Directors, National Council of Teachers of English, 1967-68; Vice-President and President, Alpha Zeta Chapter, Delta Kappa Gamma, 1972-76; Treasurer, West Virginia College English Teachers, 1972-74; Vice-President, Putnam Teachers of English, 1977-80; Kanawha Valley Genealogical Society, Treasurer 1977-80, President 1980-82, Board of Directors 1977 to present, Editor of Journal 1980-82; Co-Founder and Volunteer, Genealogical Library, Dunbar, West Virginia, 1980 to present; Vice-President, West Virginia Historical Society; Secretary, Putnam County (West Virginia) Retired Teachers; Editor Bell Family Newsletter 1980 to present, Russell Family Newsletter 1980 to present, Oxley Family Newsletter 1980 to present. Religion: Member of Presbyterian Church. Honors and Awards: Daughters of American Republic Citizenship Medal, 1931 and 1934; Science and Latin Awards, 1931; Delta Kappa Gamma Scholarship, West Virginia, 1968 and 1971; Certificate for Twenty Years Service to Students in West Virginia, 1979; Distinguished West Virginian, 1980; Outstanding Citizen of West Virginia, 1982. Address: Route 2, Box 22, Cherry Street, Hurricane, West Virginia 25526.■

JOHN H. McDONALD

Chiropractice and Naturopathic Physician. Personal: Born July 30, 1924; Son of Dr. and Mrs. Chester B. McDonald; Married Lois; Father of John C. B., Sharon Marsh, Rebecca. Education: Attended Western Michigan University, Wayne State University, University of Detroit; Graduate, cum laude, of National College of Chiropractic and Drugless Physicians, 1948; Post Graduate Study in Chiropractic Orthopedics; Board Eligible, American Board of Chiropractic Orthopedics; Diplomate, National Board of Physical Therapists; Licensed Naturopathic Physician; Doctor of Drugless Therapy. Career: Chiropractioner, Nurtritionist, Drugless Practitioner, 1948 to present. Organizational Memberships: Michigan Chiropractic Association, President 1964-65, Vice President 1963, Board of Directors 1962-66 and 1969-71, Treasurer 1970-71; President, District #2, Michigan Chiropractic Association, 1957-62; Vice President and Board of Directors, Southwestern Michigan Chiropractors; House of Delegates, Michigan State Chiropractic Society; American Council on Chiropractic Orthopedics; Michigan Society of Chiropractic Orthopedics; American Chiropractic Association, Charter Member, Council on Nutrition; World Christian Chiropractors Association; National Association of Physical Therapists; National Council of Chiropractic Roentgenologist; American Council on Chiropractic Physiotherapy; National Association of Naturopathic Physicians; Parker Chiropractic Research Foundation; National College of Chiropractic Alumni Association; Spears Chiropractice Hospital, Associate Staff Member, Field Research Council; Educational Research Society of California; Rockley Research Academy; Fellow, Congress on Research for Chiropractors; National Academy of Acupuncture; Hahnemann Medical Society of America; Inter-American Congress of Physicians; Honorary Fellow, Florida Academy of Naturopathic Medicine; Florida Chiropractic Association; Arizona Association of Naturopathic Medicine; National Health Federation; International Academy of Preventive Medicine. Community Activities: Past Precinct Representative, Berrien County Republicans; Past Chairman Professional Division, Community Chest; Twin Cities Chamber of Commerce, 1948 to present; Past President, Northeast Fairplain Elementary Parent-Teacher Association; Past Chairman, Five Fairplain Schools Parent-Teacher Association Coordinating Council; Past Director, Benton Harbor Kiwanis Club; Berrien County Sportsman Club. Religion: Napier Parkview Baptist Church; Past Member of Church Board; Past Chairman Christian Education Committee; Past Sunday School Superintendant and Teacher; Gideons International; Co-Founder and Former Member of Board of Directors of Berrien County Youth for Christ. Honors and Awards: Certificate of Merit for Civic and Professional Services, Michigan Chiropractic Association, Four Sucessive Years, 1959-62; Listed in *Who's Who in Chiropractic International*. Address: 1533 Oak Terrace, St. Joseph, Michigan 49022.■

MARIANNE MORI McDONALD

Researcher. Personal: Born January 2, 1937; Daughter of Eugene Francis McDonald (deceased); Married Torajiro Mori, Son of Hajime Mori; Mother of Eugene, Conrad, Bryan, Bridget, Kirstie, Hiroshi. Education: B.A., Bryn Mawr, 1958; M.A., University of Chicago, 1960; Ph.D., University of California at Irvine, 1975. Career: Research Appointment with Thesaurus Linguae Graecae Project, University of California at Irvine; Teaching Assistant and Instructor in Classics, University of California, 1972-79. Organizational Memberships: American Philological Association; American Association of University Professors; Hellenic Society; American Classical League; American Comparative Literature Association; California Foreign Language Teacher's Association. Community Activities: La Jolla Country Day School Board, 1971-73; American College of Greece, Board Member 1981 to present; Advisory Board, Scripps Hospital, 1982 to present; National Board of Advisors, American Biographical Institute, 1982 to present; Board Member, Centrum, 1982 to present; Board Member, Thesaurus Linguae Graecae, 1982 to present; Board Member, Hellenic University Club of Southern California, 1982 to present. Religion: Member, Buddhist Temple of Vista, 1980 to present; Greek Orthodox Church, Saints Constantine and Helen, 1982 to present. Published Works: Numerous Books and Articles in Classics (including) *Terms for Happiness in Euripides*, *Euripides in Cinema: The Heart Made Visible*. Honors and Awards: Distinguished Service Award, University of California at Irvine, 1982; Listed in *World Who's Who of Women*, *Dictionary of International Biography*, *International Who's Who in Education*, *Personalities of America*, *Community Leaders of America*, *Personalities of the West and Midwest*, *Community Leaders and Noteworthy Americans*, *American Registry Series*, *Book of Honor*. Address: Box 929 El Arco Iris, Rancho Santa Fe, California 92067.■

LOU ANN McELYEA

Executive. Personal: Born September 10, 1946; Daughter of Hazel McElyea. Education: B.S. Business Administration, Washington University (St. Louis); M.B.A., Lindenwood College. Career: President, Information Systems, Inc., 1980 to present; Consultant, Automated Systems; Created and Managed Office Systems Department, Mallinckrodt Inc., 1978-80; Stock Broker, Registered Representative, Bache Halsey Stuart Shields, Inc., 1977-78; Director, Administrative

Services, School of Engineering, Washington University, 1972-77; Educational Training Coordinator, Missouri Pacific Railroad, 1970-72. Organizational Memberships: International Information/Word Processing Association, National Consultants Advisory Committee, National Speakers Bureau; I.W.P., Vice President 1980-81, National Consultants Council 1980 to present; Administrative Management Society; Independent Computer Consultants Association. Community Activities: Campbell Chamber of Commerce. Religion: Baptist. Honors and Awards: Alpha Sigma Lambda; Listed in *Who's Who in the Midwest.* Address: 806 Bailey Street, Campbell, Missouri 63376.■

MARGUERITE VIRGINIA FRENCH McFANN

Real Estate Broker. Personal: Born November 8, 1926; Daughter of Ernest Harold French and Leila Ellen Bishop Roberts; Married Virgil Lewis McFann, Son of Demetrius McFann; Mother of Wayne, Judith, Linda K. (deceased). Education: Attended Miami Jacobs Business College, Dayton University; B.A., Antelope Valley College; Studies in Real Estate, University of California at Los Angeles. Career: Real Estate Broker, 1971 to present; Owner/Director, Teen Screen Modeling and Magazine Agency, 1961-65; Secretary, N.A.S.A., Edwards Air Force Base, 1959-61. Organizational Memberships: Executive Female Association, California Director. Community Activities: Republican Women's Club; Quartz Hill Christian Women's Club; Rebekkahs; Royal Neighbors of America; Board of Trade; Director, Palmdale International Airport, 1983 to present. Honors and Awards: Listed in *Who's Who of American Women, Worlds Who's Who of Women, Personalities of West.* Address: 1450 Boyden Avenue, Lancaster, California 93534.■

JAMES WILLIAM McFARLAND

Director of Real Estate. Personal: Born September 7, 1948; Son of Frances McFarland Johnson; Married Miriam Webster; Father of James William Jr., Mimi Morrow. Education: B.S., University of Alabama. Career: Vice President, Ward McFarland, Inc.; Director of Real Estate, Winn-Dixie Stores, Louisville, Kentucky, 1970-73. Organizational Memberships: Chamber of Commerce; Delta Sigma Pi; Chairman, State of Alabama Rapid Rail Transit Commission, 1982 to present; President, Alabama Association of Railroad Passengers; Vice Chairman, Louisiana Mississippi Alabama Rapid Rail Transit Commission, 1983 to present; Kiwanis Club of Greater Tuscaloosa, 1978 to present; Board of Directors, Tuscaloosa Kidney Foundation, 1977; National Association of Railroad Passengers, 1979 to present. Religion: Member Episcopal Church, Episcopal Young Churchman Advisor 1976-79, Vestry of Christ Episcopal Church 1978 to present. Honors and Awards: Honorary Citizen of New Orleans, 1983; Outstanding Real Estate Graduate, University of Alabama, 1970; Listed in *Who's Who in the South, Personalities of the South, Outstanding Young Men of America, Who's Who in Finance and Industry, Dictionary of International Biography.* Address: 4714 7th Court East, Tuscaloosa, Alabama 35405.■

ROBERT C. McGEE, JR.

Corporate Executive. Personal: Born May 24, 1936; Married Ann Peterson; Father of Marjorie Ann, Robert Matthew, Mary Katherine, Lauren Paige. Education: B.S. Aeronautical Engineering, University of Virginia, 1960. Military: Served in the United States Army, 1960-62, achieving the rank of First Lieutenant. Career: President, Swan, Inc.; President, Forge Aerospace, Inc.; Vice President, All American Industries; Director of Marketing, Fairchild Hiller Corporation; Washington Representative, Hiller Aircraft Corporation; Sales Engineer, Sikorsky Aircraft Company; Director of Spectrographic Analysis Laboratory, United States Army; Project Manager, United States Army Light Observation Helicopter Project. Organizational Memberships: American Management Association; American Helicopter Society; National Security Industrial Association; United States Army Association; Aviation Association of America; National Aviation Club; Institute of Aeronautics and Astronautics. Community Activities: Young Men's Christian Association, Director 1978-79; Governors Small Business Advisory Council, Council Executive Committee, Taxation Committee; Virginia Manufacturers Association, Chairman; Small Business Council, Virginia Chamber of Commerce; Small Business Council, Richmond Metropolitan Chamber of Commerce; Chairman of the Board, Virginia Small Business Finance Authority; Director, Virginia Center for Innnovative Technology; Member Advisory Board, School of Business, University of Richmond; Member Parents Council, Hampden Sydney College. Honors and Awards: Meritorious Achievement Award, National Aviation Club; United States Army Commendation Award. Address: Route 2 Box 396, River Road, Richmond, Virginia 23233.■

SCOTT DOUGLAS McGILL

City Administrator. Personal: Born September 24, 1946; Son of Gaylord A. McGill; Married Cathleen Ann, Daughter of Bernese Chaffin; Father of Kelly Meghan, Kerry Shannon. Education: B.S. Mathematics, Allegheny College, 1968; B.S. Meteorology, New York University, 1971; M.A. Management, University of Nebraska, 1972; D.P.A. Candidate, University of Colorado. Military: Served in the United States Air Force, 1968-72, attaining the rank of Captain. Career: Director of Data Processing, City of Colorado Springs (Colorado); Manager of Programming and Design, City of Colorado Springs, 1975-76; Senior Systems Analyst, Sperry Univac, 1972-75; Programmer, United States Air Force, 1970-72. Organizational Memberships: D.P.M.A., Past President 1978; A.C.M., Past Chairman 1977-78; Colorado Intergovernmental A.D.P. Council; Rocky Mountain Association of Local Governmental Computer Users, Past Chairman 1981; S.M.I.S., Director 1983; American Management Association, 6190 Continuing Seminar on Management Information Systems. Community Activities: Chins-Up, Treasurer 1981-82; Pikes Peak Council, Boy Scouts of America, Board of Directors 1979 to present; Goodwill Industries of Colorado Springs, Inc., Board of Directors 1982; University of Colordo at Colorado Springs College of Business Advisory Council, 1978 to present; Pikes Peak Kiwanis, President 1984; Colorado Springs Symphony Council, 1982. Religion: Chairperson, Administrative Board, Calvary United Methodist Church. Honors and Awards: Greater Colorado Service Award, Denver Federal Executive Board, 1980; Award for Outstanding Contributions to Data Processing on Local Government, Colorado Intergovernmental A.D.P. Council, 1978; Individual Performance Award, D.P.M.A., 1978; Certificate of Data Processing, Institute for Certification of Computer Professionals, 1975. Address: 4529 Misty Drive, Colorado Springs, Colorado 80907.■

VERN JAMES McGINNIS

Executive Director of Corporate Communications. Personal: Born May 19, 1941; Son of George H. and Margaret R. McGinnis; Married Jackquine Janiece, Daughter of Leora M. Kirby; Father of Debra Colleen, Curt Bradley. Education: Attended Illinois State University, 1959-61: B.S. Agricultural Industries 1963, M.S. Agricultural Economics 1965, University of Illinois. Military: Served in the United States Army Reserves, 1967-73, with rank of SP5. Career: Executive Director Corporate Communications, Growmark, Inc., 1980 to present; Field Services Administrative Director, Growmark, Inc., 1980; Director of Market Development 1975-80, Director of Planning Services 1971-75, Marketing Research Manager 1967-71, Marketing Research Analyst 1965-67, FS Services, Inc. Organizational Memberships: American Marketing Association, National President 1978-79; Public Relations Society of America; International Association of Business Communicators. Community Activities: Bloomington Chamber of Commerce, 1981 to present. Honors and Awards: Metzger Award, American Institute of Cooperatives, 1965; Doane Award, Illinois Farmhouse Fraternity, 1963; Alpha Zeta Agricultural Honorary Fraternity, 1962; Listed in *Who's Who in the Midwest, Who's Who in Business and Finance.* Address: 209A South Towanda Avenue, Normal, Illinois 61761.■

STERLING FISHER McILHANY

Company President. Personal: Born April 12, 1930. Education: B.F.A. with high honors, University of Texas, 1953; Graduate Studies undertaken at the University of California at Los Angeles 1953-56, Universita per Stranieri (Perugia, Italy) 1957; Certificate, Accademia delle Belle Arti (Rome, Italy), 1957-58. Career: Editor, *Art Horizons* Magazine; President, I.F.O.T.A., Inc.; Senior Editor, *American Artist* Magazine 1969-71, Litton Educational Publishing 1969-70, Reinhold Book Corporation 1961-69, Watson-Guptill Publications 1959-61; Instructor, School of Visual Arts, 1961-69; Host, "Books and the Artist" WRVR

Radio Series, 1960-61; Teaching Assistant, University of California at Los Angeles, 1953-56. Organizational Memberships: National Society of Literature and the Arts. Community Activities: St. Luke's in the Fields Outreach (New York City), Community Service Chairman 1979 to present; Christ College Fellow (Cambridge); Human Resources of the United States of America (Washington, D.C.), 1976 to present; International Platform Association; International Biographical Centre; Rotary International, Fellow; The Smithsonian Associates; American Museum of Natural History; Free Theatre, Fellow, Executive Board. Religion: Roman Catholic. Honors and Awards: First Place National Award, Students International Travel Association Free Tour of European Art Centers, 1952; American Patriot of the Bicentennial, *Profiles of Freedom - A Cross Section of Proud Bicentennial Americans*; Listed in *The National Register of Prominent Americans and International Notables, Men and Women of Distinction, Book of Honor.* Address: P.O. Box 473, New York, New York 10014.■

DANIEL LEE McIVOR

Licensed Clinical Psychologist. Personal: Born August 23, 1940; Son of Beryl McIvor; Married Barbara Joan Engbrecht, February 4, 1984; Father of Lisa Marie. Education: B.S., University of Washington, 1965; M.S., Central Washington State College, 1967; M.A., University of Iowa, 1969; Ph.D., University of Manitoba (Winnipeg, Canada), 1976. Military: Served in the United States Army Ordnance Corps, 1958-61, with the rank of SP/4. Career: Private Practice, Psychotherapy, Psychology, Assessment, Consultant, 1981 to present; President, Board of Directors, Benton-Franklin Elders Services, 1983; Consultant, Hanford Environmental Health Foundation, Richland, Washington, 1983; Consultant, Mid-Columbia Mental Health Center, Richland, Washington, 1983; Manager, Outpatient Department, Mid-Columbia Mental Health Center, Richland, Washington, 1981; Manager, Franklin County Mental Health, Pasco, Washington, 1981; Half-time Clinical Psychologist, Half-time Consultant to Corporate Development Planning Team, Mid-Columbia Mental Health Center, 1981; Psychologist, Mid-Columbia Mental Health Center, 1978-81; Psychologist III, Province of Manitoba, Ministry of Corrective and Rehabilitative Services, Winnipeg, 1975-76 (part-time) and 1976-78; Consulting Psychologist, Child Guidance Clinic, Winnipeg, 1975-76; Clinical Psychology Intern, University of Washington Medical School, 1973-74; Chief Psychologist, Province of Manitoba Forensic Services, 1973; Consultant Psychologist, Province of Manitoba, 1972-73; New Careers Trainer, Province of Manitoba, 1972-73; Relief Guard and Consultant, Headingley Correctional Institution, Headingley, Manitoba, 1972; Consultant, Psychologist, Victoria Order of Nurses, Winnipeg, 1971-782; Staff Psychologist, Pontiac State Hospital, Pontiac, Michigan, 1969-71; Consultant Psychologist, Local Elementary School, Iowa City, Iowa, 1968-69; Clinical Psychology Extern, Marshfield Clinic, Marshfield, Wisconsin, 1968; Cottage Parent, Fort Worden Treatment Center, Port Townsend, Washington, 1964; Lecturer, Department of Psychology, University of Manitoba, 1974-75; Teaching Assistant, Department of Psychology, University of Manitoba, 1971-72; Teaching Assistant, Department of Psychology, University of Iowa, 1967-69; Teaching Assistant, Department of Psychology, Central Washington State College, 1965-67. Organizational Memberships: American Psychological Association; Canadian Psychological Association; Registered Psychologist, Michigan, 1971 to present; Licensed Psychologist, Washington, 1978 to present; Washington State Psychological Association, President Nine-County Regional Chapter 1979; Registered Psychologist, Manitoba, 1977 to present; Manitoba Psychological Society, Vice President 1975 to present; Board of Directors, Benton-Franklin Elders Services, Pasco, Washington, 1982 to present; Advisory Board, CONTACT Teleministries, Richland, Washington, 1982 to present; Consultant Psychologist, Tri-City Chaplaincy, Kennewick, Washington, 1982 to present; Listed in *National Register of Health Providers in Psychology,* 1980 to present. Community Activities: Board of Directors, Goodwill Industries. Published Works: Co-Author, "Working with Incest Victims: The Children" (with Elaine Adolf, M.S.W.) in *Canadian Journal of Psychiatric Nursing* 1983, "Working with Incest Victims: The Adults" (with Deena Evans, M.S.W.) in *Canadian Journal of Psychiatric Nursing* 1983, "Assisting Adult Children Understand Their Aging Parents" (with L. Allen) 1981, "Preliminary Results from a Community Release Centre" (with B. Horner and R. Boittiaux) 1979, "Group Therapy for Women Going Through Divorce" (with A. Rosario) 1979; "Raising Pigeons as a Therapeutic Agent in the Adjustment to Retirement" (with M. Crawford) 1977, "The Behaviorist Hockey Consultant" (with M. Crawford) 1976, "The Canadian-American Internship Dilemma" (with A. Herscovitch) 1973; Author, "Stepping-Out: Planning the First Date" in *Singles Northwest Magazine* 1983, "Working with Incest Offenders" in *The Gavel and Blot* 1984, "Psychiatric Nurses Provide Leadership" 1975, "Myopia, Hallucinations and Delusions" (1976), "The Application of Behavior Modification Procedures in a Special Education Classroom" 1977, "Diagnostic Pitfalls in Parkinson's Disease" 1977, "The Role of a Clinical Psychologist in a Nursing Home" 1977. Honors and Awards: Listed in *Men of Achievement, Two Thousand Notable Americans, Who's Who in the West.* Address: 2205 Camden, Richland, Washington 99352.■

JOHN DENNIS McKENNA

Executive. Personal: Born April 1, 1940; Son of Mr. and Mrs. Hubert Guy McKenna; Married Christel Klages; Father of Marc, Michelle. Education: B.S. Chemical Engineering, Manhattan College, 1961; M.S. Chemical Engineering, Newark College of Engineering, 1968; M.B.A., Rider College, 1974. Career: President, ETS, Inc.; President, Enviro-Systems & Research (Roanoke, Virginia), 1978-79; Vice President, ES&R (Roanoke), 1972-78; Project Director, Research Cottrell (Bound Brook, New Jersey), 1968-72; Project Leader, Princeton Chemical Research (Princeton, New Jersey), 1967-68; Technical Assistant to President, Eldib Engineering and Research, Inc. (Newark, New Jersey), 1964-67. Organizational Memberships: American Institute of Chemical Engineering, Central Virginia Section Chairman 1980-81: Air Pollution Control Association. Religion: Roman Catholic. Honors and Awards: National Science Foundation Consultant for the College Faculty Workshop Program, Grant 1978-79; Environmental Protection Agency Fabric Filter Workshop Lecturer, 1978-79; Scientific Reviewer for E.P.A. Publications, 1977-78; Listed in *Who's Who in Engineering.* Address: 4118 Chaparral Drive, Southwest, Roanoke, Virginia 24018.■

JOHN H. McKENNA

Roman Catholic Priest, Professor. Personal: Born May 25, 1936; Son of William E. and Virginia Holcomb McKenna. Education: B.A., Mary Immaculate Seminary and College, 1960; M.Div., Mary Immaculate Seminary and College, 1974; S.T.L., Theological Faculty of Trier (Germany), 1968; S.T.D., Theological Faculty of Trier, 1971; Diploma in Sacred Liturgy, Liturgical Institute, Trier, 1971. Career: Roman Catholic Priest; Professor, St. John's University; Member Board of Directors, Pastoral Institute of Archdiocese of Brooklyn, 1975; Advisor, American Bishops Committee on the Liturgy, 1975; Assistant Professor of Systematics and Liturgy, St. John's University, 1972-75; Assistant Professor of Systematics and Liturgy, Seminary of Our Lady of Angels, 1971-72. Organizational Memberships: North American Academy of Liturgists, Governing Committee 1978; Catholic Theological Society of America; Society for the Scientific Study of Religion; National Liturgical Conference of America. Published Works: "The Eucharistic Epiclesis: Myopia or Microcosm" 1975, *Eucharist and Holy Spirit* 1975, "Ritual Activity" 1976, "The Eucharistic Epiclesis in 20th Century Theology" 1976, "The Eucharist, the Resurrection and the Future" 1978, *Be What You Celebrate: An Audio Visual History of the Eucharist* (5-part Filmstrip) 1982. Honors and Awards: *Eucharist and Holy Spirit* Selected as Alcuin Club's 1975 Publication; President of North American Academy of Liturgy. Address: Vincentian Residence, St. John's University, Grand Central and Utopia Parkways, Jamaica, New York 11439.■

NANCY JANE McLEOD

City Administrator. Personal: Born June 19, 1946; Daughter of Kenneth L. McLeod. Education: B.A. 1967, M.B.A. 1970, University of Arizona; D.P.A. Candidate, Arizona State University. Career: Assistant Director, Former Planning Coordinator, Chief Program Planner, Planning Assistant and Administrative Aide to Director, City of Phoenix Human Resources Department. Organizational Memberships: American Society for Public Administration; American Management Association; Business and Professional Women of Phoenix, President 1980-82, First Vice President 1978-80; American Planning Association; Academy of Political Science. Community Activities: Society for the Advancement of Management, Board of Directors, Vice President of Finance; Appointed to Governor's Energy Awareness Special Events Committee; Chairman, Data Elements Committee for Community Information Systems, Maricopa Association of Governments; National Association of Female Executives; Toastmasters International, Chapter Vice President of Administration 1981, Certified as Competent Toastmaster 1981; Central Arizona Museum; Arizona Historical Society; Phoenix Zoological Society. Honors and Awards: Woman of the Year 1983, Outstanding Member 1980-81, Young Career Woman of the Year 1974, Phoenix Business and Professional Women; Young Career Woman of the Year Runner-up, State of Arizona Business and Professional Women, 1974; Listed in *Who's Who of American Women, Who's Who in the West, Personalities of America, Personalities of the West and Midwest, World Who's Who of Women, Community Leaders of the World.* Address: 3753 East Bloomfield, Phoenix, Arizona 85032.■

EDWARD JOSEPH McMANUS

District Court Judge. Personal: Born February 9, 1920; Son of Edward W. and Kathleen McManus; Married Sally H., Daughter of David L. and Marybel

Joyce Hassett; Father of David P., Edward W., John N., Thomas J., Dennis Q. Education: Attended St. Ambrose College, 1936-38; B.A. 1940, J.D. 1942, University of Iowa. Military: Served in the United States Naval Reserves, 1942-46, attaining the rank of Lieutenant. Career: Chief Judge, United States District Court, Northern District of Iowa; Lieutenant Governor of Iowa, 1959-62; General Practice in Law, 1946-62; Member of Iowa Senate, 1955-59; City Attorney, Keokuk, Iowa, 1946-55; Delegate to Democratic National Convention, 1956, 1960. Address: P.O. Box 4815, Cedar Rapids, Iowa 52407.■

LOIS I. D. MCNAIR.

Speech-Language Pathologist. Education: B.S., Emerson College, 1967; M.Ed., Boston State College, 1969; Graduate Study undertaken at Boston University, 1970-75; Ph.D., Heed University, 1982. Career: Speech-Language Pathologist; Former X-Ray Technician, Teacher. Organizational Memberships: American Speech-Hearing-Language Association; A.G. Bell; American Personnel and Guidance Association; National Education Association; Maine Teachers Association; Maine Speech and Hearing Association; Maine Personnel and Guidance Association; American Public Health Association; Royal Society of Health; Others. Address: P.O. Box 393, Houlton, Maine 04730.■

MYRON JAMES MEDIN, JR.

City Manager. Personal: Born July 8, 1931; Son of Rev. and Mrs. Myron J. Medin; Married Alice Louise; Father of John, Kären, Anne. Education: B.A., St. Olaf College, 1954; M.P.A., University of Michigan, 1959. Military: Served in the United States Air Force, 1955-57, attaining the rank of First Lieutenant. Career: City Manager, Fond du Lac, Wisconsin, 1967 to present; City Manager, New Ulm, Michigan, 1963-67; Administrative Assistant to City Manager, Fond du Lac, 1959-63. Organizational Memberships: International City Management Association, Committee on Local Government Personnel 1977-78; International Council of Academy Advisors, Member 1978-79, Policy Advisory Network 1974-75; American Society of Public Administrators; Wisconsin Coalition for Action on Shared Taxes, Executive Committee 1971. Community Activities: Governor's Regionalism Task Force Advisory Committee, 1969-70; Wisconsin Coalition on Human Needs and Budget Priorities, 1973; Wisconsin City Management Association, President 1975-76; Wisconsin Alliance of Cities, Vice President 1972-73; League of Wisconsin Municipalities, Executive Committee 1978-80, District Vice President 1973-75, Legislative Committee 1978-80, Chairman Resolutions Committee 1975; National League of Cities, Committee on Human Resource Development 1974-80, Committee on Intergovernmental Relations 1971-73. Honors and Awards: Special Award for Outstanding and Dedicated Service in Community Leadership, Fond du Lac Association of Commerce, 1978. Address: 528 Highland Court, Fond du Lac, Wisconsin 54935.■

JOHN A. MEDINA

Administrator. Personal: Born January 27, 1942; Son of Mr. and Mrs. Vincent Medina; Father of Michelle Lillian, Tino Marcellus. Education: Graduate, Notre Dame High School (Price, Utah); Attended Big Bend Community College; A.S., College of Eastern Utah, 1968; B.S., Weber State College, 1969; Further Studies undertaken at University of California Extension, 1971; M.S., University of Utah, 1978; Various Military Schools and Courses, 1962-66. Military: Served in the United States Air Force, 1962-66, attaining the rank of Sergeant. Career: Director, Utah Anti-Discrimination Division, State of Utah, Industrial Commission, 1979 to present; Director, Mobile Homes and Recreational Vehicles Division, State of Utah, Department of Business Regulation, 1978-79; Ombudsman, Office of the Governor, State of Utah, 1975-78; Acting Project Director, SOCIO/MACCSP, 1974-75; Associate Director, Uplands Inc., 1970-74; Insurance Consultant, Metropolitan Life Insurance Company, 1969-70. Organizational Memberships: American Marketing Association. Community Activities: Carbon County Jaycees, Director, Organizational Vice President, Chairman Ways and Means Committee; Board Member, Community Action Program; Board Member, Southeastern Utah Economics Development; One of Founders, Organizer, Carbon County Boys Club; Vice President/President of Carbon County Chapter, State Vice President, Central Action Board, Executive Council, Spanish Speaking Organization for Community, Integrity and Opportunity; Chairman, Governor's Policy/Advisory Council on Hispanic Affairs; Chairman, Rocky Mountain Institute on Law Enforcement; Member, First Statewide Chicano Economics Development Conference in Utah; Region VII H.E.W. Task Force; College of Eastern Utah Booster Club; Weber State Alumni Association; University of Utah Alumni Association; Utah Ballet Folkolorico Board; Chairman, Minority Economic Development Coalition of Utah; IMAGE, President 1979-80; LULAC; Board of Governor's, Financial Counseling Center, Ogden, Utah; Hill AFB-EEO Advisory Council; Site Reviewers for State Mental Health; State Affirmative Action Review Committee; State Central Democratic Committee; Veterans of Foreign Wars; KTVX News Advisory Board; Chairman, Unity Conference, 1979; Commissioner, Davis County Housing Authority. Honors and Awards: Airman of the Month, June and August, 1963; Airman of the Quarter, 1965; Chairman of Airman's Council, 1965; Presidential Unit Citation, 463 Aerospace Wing, 1966; Director of Minority Airman's Program, 1966; SPOKE Award, 1967; Key Man Award, 1968; Outstanding Young Man of America, 1969; Distinguished Service Nominee, 1972; Spanish Speaking Organization for Community, Integrity and Opportunity Achievement Award, 1974, 1975; Spanish Achievement Award, 1976; Chicano of the Year Award, 1977; Grant/San Juan County Community Award, 1978; Salt Lake City Community Award, 1978; KTVX Media Award, 1979. Address: 4283 Phillips Lane, Salt Lake City, Utah 84107.■

DENISE L. MEDVED

Executive. Personal: Born May 21, 1952; Daughter of Martin and Doris William Medved. Education: B.S., University of Tennessee, 1974; Also Attended Wesleyan College. Career: Vice President (First Woman, Youngest in Agency's History) and Creative Director 1981 to present, Creative Director 1979-81, Associate Creative Director 1977-79, Copy Supervisor 1976-77, Copy Writer 1975-76, The Direct Marketing Agency, Inc.; Editor, Founder, Creator, National Publication *Businesswoman*, 1976 to present; Promotion Coordinator, The Direct Marketing Association, 1974-75; Copywriter, John M. Rose Advertising Agency, Knoxville, Tennessee, 1973-74; Division Sales Assistant, Sears, Roebuck & Company, Knoxville, 1969-74. Organizational Memberships: New York Women in Communications, Committee Member; Direct Marketing Association, Speaker; Direct Marketing Educational Foundation, Speaker; National Association of Female Executives; Delta Delta Delta; Phi Kappa Phi. Community Activities: Actress, Singer, Performer, Number of New York Area Theatres, Cabarets; River Hills Ski Club, Officer; Greenwich Democratic Women, Officer. Honors and Awards: Outstanding Woman in Communications, American Association of University Women; Listed in *Who's Who of American Women, Who's Who in Advertising, Who's Who in Business and Industry*. Address: 88 Davenport Ridge Road, Stamford, Connecticut 06903.■

LEWIS EUGENE MEHL

Psychotherapist, Scientist, Physician. Personal: Born January 26, 1954; Son of J. and E. Mehl; Married Gayle H. Peterson, Daughter of Jessie Peterson; Father of R. Sorrel Madrona, A. Yarrow Madrona. Education: B.A., Indiana University, 1972; M.D., Stanford University, 1975; Ph.D., Psychological Studies Institute (Palo Alto, California). Career: Psychotherapist, Scientist, Physician; Clinical Assistant Professor, Stanford University School of Medicine; Instructor, Psychological Studies Institute; Private Practice, Holistic Psychotherapy and Medical Group, Berkeley; Workshop Leader, Psychophysiological Associates. Organizational Memberships: American Psychiatric Association; Association of American Indian Physicians. Published Works: Author Over 40 Scientific Papers in Psychophysiology, Birth Psychology; Author, *Mind and Matter, Foundations for Holistic Health* (Volumes 1 and 2). Address: 1749 Vine Street, Berkeley, California 94703.■

VED PARKASH MEHTA

Writer. Personal: Born March 21, 1934; Naturalized United States Citizen; Son of Dr. and Mrs. A. R. Mehta. Education: Attended the Arkansas School for the Blind; B.A., Pomona College, 1956; B.A. honors in Modern History, Oxford University, 1959; M.A., Harvard University, 1961; M.A., Oxford, 1962. Career: Staff Writer, *The New Yorker*, 1961 to present. Community Activities: Council on Foreign Relations, 1979. Published Works: *Face to Face* 1957 (Secondary Education Annual Book Award 1958), *BBC Dramatization on Home Program and Serial Reading on Light Program* 1958, *Walking the Indian Streets* 1960, *Fly and the Fly-Bottle* 1963, *The New Theologian* 1966, *Delinquent Chacha* 1967, *Portrait of India* 1970, *John is Easy to Please* 1971, *Daddyji* 1972, *Mahatma Gandhi & His Apostles* 1977, *The New India* 1978, *Mamaji* 1979; Number of Translations, Articles and Stories in U.S. British and Indian Papers and Magazines, 1957 to present; Writer and Commentator of TV Documentary Film *Chaachaji: My Poor Relations* (PBS 1978, BBC 1980). Honors and Awards: Hazen Fellow, 1956-59; Harvard Prize Fellow, 1959-60; Guggenheim Fellow, 1971-72, 1977-78; Ford Foundation, Travel and Study Grantee 1971-76, Public Policy Grant 1979-82; Association of Indians of America Award, 1978; Visiting Scholar, Case Western Reserve University, 1974; Beatty Lecturer, McGill University, 1979; Honorary D.Litt., Pomona College 1972, Bard College 1982. Address: 1035 Fifth Avenue, New York, New York 10028.■

TWO THOUSAND NOTABLE AMERICANS

WILBUR L. MEIER, JR.

College Dean. Personal: Born January 3, 1939; Son of Wilbur L. Meier, Sr.; Married Judy Lee Longbotham; Father of Melynn, Marla, Melissa. Education: B.S. 1962, M.S. 1964, Ph.D. 1967, University of Texas at Austin. Career: Dean, College of Engineering, The Pennsylvania State University; Former Positions include Head of School of Industrial Engineering at Purdue University, Professor and Chairman of the Department of Industrial Engineering at Iowa State University, Assistant Head of the Department of Industrial Engineering at Texas A. & M. University, Professor, Associate Professor and Assistant Professor of Industrial Engineering at Texas A. & M. University. Organizational Memberships: Institute of Industrial Engineers, Executive Vice President of Chapter Operations 1981 to present, Chairman of Productivity Mission Review Committee 1980, Vice President of Region VIII 1978-80, Director of Operations Research Division 1975-76, President/Vice President Central Indiana Chapter 1975-77; Alpha Pi Mu, President 1980-81, Executive Vice President 1978-80, Regional Director (Region IV) 1976-78, Associate Editor *Cogwheel* 1970-76, Faculty Advisor of Purdue and Texas A. & M. Chapters; American Society of Civil Engineers, Secretary/Treasurer Austin Branch 1965-66, Chairman of Research Committee of Water Resources Planning and Management Division 1974-75; National Society of Professional Engineers; Indiana Society of Professional Engineers, Potter Chapter Director 1976-78, Travis Chapter Director 1964; American Society for Engineering Education, Vice Chairman and Chairman of Industrial Engineering Division 1977-79; Society of Manufacturing Engineers, Accreditation Committee, Accreditation Board for Engineering and Technology. Community Activities: Rotary International, Ames Club 1973-74, Lafayette Club 1974-81, State College Club 1981 to present. Religion: Calvary Baptist Church (Lafayette, Indiana), Deacon 1976-79, Teacher of Adult and Young Adult Bible Classes, Chairman Finance Committee 1980-81. Honors and Awards: Tau Beta Pi; Alpha Pi Mu; Phi Kappa Phi; Chi Epsilon; Sigma Xi; Omicron Delta Kappa; Outstanding Young Engineer for 1966, Travis Chapter, Texas Society of Professional Engineers; United States Public Health Service Fellowship, University of Texas-Austin, 1966. Address: 596 Shadow Lane, State College, Pennsylvania 16801.■

CAROLYN LOUISE MEIN

Exponent of Humanetics. Personal: Born November 10, 1950; Daughter of Orville E. (deceased) and Nadine Mein. Education: A.A., Metropolitan Community College, 1973; Diplomate, National Board of Chiropractic Examiners, 1973; D.C., Cleveland Chiropractic College, 1974; Acupuncture Certification, Texas Chiropractic College, 1975; Fellow, American Council of Applied Clinical Nutrition, 1976; B.A. Individual Studies, Bio-nutrition, Columbia College, 1977; Diplomate, International Board of Applied Kinesiology, 1978; Exponent of Humanetics, 1979. Career: Individual Practice in Humanetics, Rancho Santa Fe (California) 1979 to present, Independence (Missouri) 1977-79; Chiropractic Practice, Independence, 1974-77. Organizational Memberships: International College of Applied Kinesiology, Charter Member 1976 to present; National I-Grow Club of America, Health Services Consultant 1976 to present; Tri-Life Educational Foundation, Consultant and Advisor 1981 to present; American Chiropractic Association; Missouri State Chiropractic Association; Cleveland Chiropractic College Alumni Association. Published Works: Author Research Papers "Hand Acupuncture and Special Effect Points" and "The Sacrotuberous Ligament in the Correction of Structural Faults" (Published in *Collected Papers of the Diplomates of the International College of Applied Kinesiology*). Honors and Awards: Cleveland Chiropractic College Outstanding Student Award, 1971, 1973; Listed in *Who's Who in Chiropractic, World Who's Who of Women, Who's Who Among San Diego Women, Directory of Distinguished Americans*. Address: 12941 Caminito En Flor, Del Mar, California 92014.■

JOSEPHINE WEAVER MELLICHAMP

Writer, Historian. Personal: Born September 30, 1923, in Helton, North Carolina; Daughter of James Thomas Hampton and Bonnie Clyde Bauguess Weaver (both deceased); Married Stiles A. Mellichamp, Sr., Son of Joseph Capers Sr. and Annie Pearce Mellichamp (both deceased); Stepmother of Stiles A. Jr., Joseph Capers III. Education: Graduate, Lansing High School (Lansing, North Carolina), 1940; A.B. cum laude, Emory and Henry College, 1943; Graduate Studies, Division of Journalism, Emory University, 1950-51. Career: Newspaper Librarian 12 Years, Assistant Head Librarian 1957-79, *The Atlanta Journal* and *The Atlanta Constitution* (Atlanta, Georgia); Editorial Assistant, Emory University Office of Public Information, 1951-53; Free-lance Writer, 1953-75; High School English Teacher, Lansing and Jefferson High Schools, Ashe County, North Carolina, 1943-50; Price Comparer, Macy's, New York City, Summer 1944; Office Worker, E. I. du Pont de Nemours, Wilmington, Delaware, 1944. Organizational Memberships: Fellow, International Biographical Association; International Platform Association; National League of American Pen Women, Inc.; Dixie Council of Authors and Journalists, Inc.; Southeastern Writers Association, Inc.; Atlanta Writers Club; Village Writers Group, Inc.; Atlanta Historical Society. Community Activities: Reference Department Captain, *Atlanta Journal-Constitution* Employee's One-Pledge Plan Campaign (for United Way), 1971; Four-Member *Atlanta Journal-Constitution* Employee's One-Pledge Plan Fund, Inc., Board of Trustees 1974, Board Vice Chairman 1976; Annual Contributor to Emory and Henry College, Emory University, Mercer University, Oglethorpe University, University of Georgia, Woodruff Medical Center of Emory University; Sponsor, Josephine Mellichamp Journalism Award, Dixie Council of Authors and Journalists Annual Creative Writing and Inspirational Workshop, 1979 to present. Religion: Hill-Wade Bible Class, St. Mark United Methodist Church, Atlanta, 1972 to present. Published Works: *Senators from Georgia* (containing biographies of all 53 United States Senators from Georgia from 1789 to 1980); *Georgia Heritage*; Author Historical Feature Articles and Children's Fantasy Stories in National and Regional Periodicals. Honors and Awards: Dixie Council of Authors and Journalists 1976 Award to the Georgia Author of the Year in Non-Fiction (for *Senators from Georgia*, (model book in a political series), 1977; Listed in *Contemporary Authors, International Authors and Writers Who's Who, World Who's Who of Women, International Who's Who of Intellectuals, International Register of Profiles, Dictionary of International Biography, Directory of Professional Creative Women of the National League of American Pen Women*. Address: 1124 Reeder Circle, N.E., Atlanta, Georgia 30306.■

MICHAEL VANCE MELLINGER

Ecologist, Project Manager. Personal: Born December 21, 1945; Son of Vance C. and Arlene F. Mellinger; Married Karen Jane Solliday, Daughter of Joseph P. and Ruth M. Solliday; Father of Scott Michael, Christopher Joseph. Education: B.A., Bloomsburg State College, 1967; Ph.D., Syracuse University, 1972. Military: Served in the United States Army Reserves, 1969-75, attaining the rank of Sergeant. Career: Ecologist and Project Manager, Roy F. Weston, Inc.; Former Terrestrial Ecologist and Project Coordinator. Organizational Memberships: Ecological Society of America; American Association for the Advancement of Science; American Institute of Biological Sciences; British Ecological Society; Sigma Xi; Environmental Defense Fund. Community Activities: Young Men's Christian Association Indian Guides, Officer 1981 to present; Lionville Youth Association, Coach 1980 to present. Honors and Awards: N.D.E.A. Fellow, 1970-72; Bloomsburg State College Service Key, 1967; Lifetime Athletic Pass, 1967; Listed in *Who's Who in the East, Who's Who Among Students in American Universities and Colleges, American Men and Women of Science*. Address: 122 Baker Drive, Exton, Pennsylvania 19341.■

HENRY GOULART MELLO

Personal: Born December 25, 1908, in East Oakland, California; Son of Manuel D. and Marie G. Mellow; Married Georgina L., 1941 (deceased 1974); Second Wife, Mamie Anita; Father of Georgina Marie, Henrietta. Education: A.B., St. Mary's College, 1931; Certificate of Public Health, Harvard School of Public Health Administration; Studies at the Marquette Medical School, 1931-36; Internship, St. Mary's Hospital (San Francisco) 1935-36; Licensed in State of California, 1936; M.P.H., 1949. Military: Served in the United States Army Reserves, 1941-45, achieving the rank of Lieutenant Colonel. Career: Teacher-in-Training, Civilian Conservation Corporation, Northern California, 1936-37; Resident Physician and Doctor, Enloe Hospital (Chico, California), 1937-38; General Private Practice (Alameda, California), City Physician and City of Alameda Public Health Doctor 1938-40; Solano County Health Officer, retiring after 22½ Years. Organizational Memberships: Life Member, Royal Society of Health (England); American Public Health Association; California Public Health Association; Bay Area Health Officers; California Academy of General Practice; Academy of Administration of the U.S.A.; Marquette Medical School Outstanding Alumnus.

Community Activities: President, Senior Citizens in Vallejo; Men and Women of Portuguese Lodges; Eagles Lodges; President, Cabrillo Club; St. Mary's Alumni Association of East Bay; Holy Name Society, St. Basil's Church. Honors and Awards: Legion of Merit; Three Combat Stars; Outstanding Health Officer in U.S.A.; Certificate for Outstanding Military Service from Queen of England, 1945. Address: 33 Balboa Avenue, Vallejo, California 94590.■

IRA B. MELTON, SR.

Personal: Born December 21, 1918, in Nashville, Tennessee; son of Ira H. and Floy Dodgen Melton; Married Mildred Drumond; Father of Ira B. Jr., Donna Sue Benson, Timothy LaRue, Charles Alan, Kathleen Ruth Stephens. Military: Served in the United States Infantry during World War II. Career: Vice President and Director, Consolidated Consultants Inc., C.C.I. Funds Inc., C.C.I. Realty Inc.; Owner, Ira B. Melton Enterprises; President, Melton-McKinney Inc.; Vice President, Mortgage Investment Inc.; Vice President/Treasurer, Specialized Training Institute Inc.; Vice President/Director Peachstone Development Corporation; Director, Shallowford Arms Inc.; Member, Austin Realty Company; Partner, Warren 1-20 Association; Licensed Securities and Real Estate Representative. Community Activities: Former Judge of Municipal Court, Councilman, Mayor, Pine Lake, Georgia; Former Civil Defense Commander, Pine Lake; Director, DeKalb Chamber of Commerce; Director, DeKalb Young Men's Christian Association; Post Commander, American Legion; Past Governor, Loyal Order of Moose, Decatur Lodge #902; Chef de Gare of Fulton County Voiture 217, 40 and 8 Society; Former Member, Elks; Chairman, DeKalb County Zoning Appeals Board; DeKalb Municipal Association; DeKalb County Board of Registrars; Past President, Atlanta Metro Master Plumbers Association; Past Scoutmaster of Troop 202, Boy Scouts of America; President, Pine Lake Lions Club; President, Pine Lake Civic Club; DeKalb Grand Jury Association; Georgia Peace Officers Association; International Platform Association; Board of Policy, Liberty Lobby (Washington, D.C.); North Georgia Coon Hunters Association; Honorary Member, Plumbing Inspectors Association; Former Deputy Sheriff, DeKalb County; Governor's Staff, Governor Marvin Griffin, Governor Jimmy Carter, Governor George Busbee. Religion: Pine Lake Baptist Church, Former Choir Director, Former Chairman Board of Trustees, Deacon; Baptist Witnessing Foundation (Jacksonville, Florida); Property Committee, Atlanta Baptist Association. Honors and Awards: Two Bronze Battle Stars; Fellow, Intercontinental Biographical Association; Honorary Fellow, Anglo-American Academy; Listed in *Who's Who in Georgia, Who's Who in the National Council for Individual Excellence, Outstanding Americans in the South, Dictionary of International Biography, International Who's Who of Intellectuals, Personalities of the South, Men of Achievement, International Who's Who in Community Service, Book of Honor, Personalities of America, Notable Americans, Community Leaders and Noteworthy Americans, Men and Women of Distinction, Anglo-American Who's Who, Community Leaders of America, Contemporary Personalities, International Book of Honor.* Address: 613 Dogwood Road, Pine Lake, Georgia 30072.■

WERNER MAX MENDEL

Captain of Sailing Vessel, Professor. Personal: Born June 11, 1927; Father of Carl M. and Dirk B. Education: B.A. Psychology, University of California-Los Angeles, 1948; M.A. Psychology, Stanford University, 1949; M.D., Stanford School of Medicine, 1953; Intern, Los Angeles County General Hospital, 1953-54; Residency in Psychiatry, St. Elizabeth Hospital 1954-55, Winter Veterans Administration Hospital 1955-57; Licensed in California and Washington, D.C.; Certified in Psychiatry and Medicine, National Boards of Medical Examiners 1954, American Board of Psychiatry and Neurology, American Psychoanalytic Association 1968. Career: University of Southern California School of Medicine, Instructor in Psychiatry 1958-60, Assistant Professor 1960-64, Associate Professor 1964-67, Professor 1967 to present; Visiting Faculty, Chicago Ontoanalytic Institute, 1962-73; Instructor, Southern California Psychoanalytic Institute, 1965-81; Metropolitan State Hospital, Norwalk, California, Staff Psychiatrist 1957-58, Director of Outpatient Services 1958-60; Chief Senior Clerkship in Psychiatry, University of Southern California School of Medicine, 1960-62; Los Angeles County-University of Southern California Medical Center Psychiatric Hospital, Attending Staff 1960-82, Chief Teaching Service 1962-65, Clinical Director Adult Inpatient Services 1965-67, Director Work Rehabilitation Project 1973-76, Director Emergency Psychiatric Services 1976-77; Director, University of Southern California Department of Psychiatry, 1968-82; Organizational Memberships: American Medical Association, 1959-76; American Association of Medical Colleges, 1959-67; American Ontoanalytic Association, 1962-73; American Academy of Psychoanalysis, 1966-82; American Psychoanalytic Association, 1968-76; Los Angeles County Medical Association, 1959-76; Southern California Psychoanalytic Institute, 1965-81; Southern California Psychiatric Society, 1959-81; International Psychoanalytic Association, 1968-76; Caribbean Psychiatric Association, 1979-82; American Association for Partial Hospitalization Inc, 1981-82; International Association of Gerontology, 1981-82; National Committee on Psychiatry and Medical Practice, American Psychiatric Association; American Academy of General Practice, Mental Health Committee, Consultant, 1963-66; California Medical Association, Secretary Section on Psychiatry and Neurology 1964-66, Chairman 1966-67; Experimental and Special Training Review Committee, National Institute of Mental Health, 1968-72; Examiner, American Board of Neurology and Psychiatry, 1964-82; Editoral Board, *Voices* 1966-70, *Existential Psychiatry* 1966-74, *International Journal of Partial Hospitalization* 1980-82; Book and Article Review Staff, *American Journal of Psychotherapy*, 1975-82; Reviewer, *Hospital and Community Psychiatry*, 1980-82. Community Activities: Advisory Board, Westside and Coastal Friends Inc., 1980-82; Department of Mental Hygiene, State of California, Consultant 1960-74, Member Special Residency Training Review Board 1965-74, Member Research Advisory Committee 1970-74; Chairman, Medical Advisory Board, Human Resource Institute Inc., 1970-75; Chairman, Advisory Board on State Hospitals, State Department of Health, 1976-78; Chairman, Governor's Medical Advisory Board, California State Department of Corrections, 1976-79; Consultant, California State Board of Medical Quality Assurance, 1976-82; Ad Hoc Committee on AB 717, State of California/University of Southern California School of Pharmacy, 1977-79; Mental Health Clinical Research Advisory Panel, State of California, 1979-82; Los Angeles City Unified School District, Consultant on Teacher Competency 1979-82, Consultant on Staff Development Programs 1979-82; Ad Hoc Committee on AB 345, State Hospital Planning, State of California, 1979-81; Board of Directors, Transitional Living Centers of Los Angeles County, Member 1980-82, Chairman 1981-82; Special Projects Editor, Basic Books, Inc., 1966-69; Editor-in-Chief, Mara Books, Los Angeles, 1969-82; Advisory Board, International Encyclopedia of Psychiatry, Psychoanalysis and Psychology, 1974-82. Published Works: Author of Numerous Books, Reviews, Papers and Articles, Including Most Currently "The Concept of Responsibility as a Variable in the Clinical Transaction," *Journal of Operational Psychiatry* 1981, "Mainstreaming: An Approach to the Treatment of the Chronically and Severely Mentally Ill Patients in the Community," *The Hillside Journal of Clinical Psychiatry* 1980, "Staff Burn-out: Diagnosis, Treatment and Prevention," *New Directions for Mental Health Services* 1979. Honors and Awards: Fellow, American Psychiatric Association, 1964; Scholar-in-Residence, Rockefeller Foundation, Bellagio, Italy, 1980; Bronze Medal, University of Helsinki, Finland, 1980; Listed in *Dictionary of International Biography, Biographical Directory, Directory of Medical Specialists, Who's Who in the West, American Men of Science Directory, International Scholars Directory, Contemporary Authors, Who's Who in America, Who's Who in the World.* Address: P.O. Box 2870, Estes Park, Colorado 80517.■

MAKRAM H. MESHREKI

Research Chemist. Personal: Born October 27, 1936; Son of Habib and Wadida Meshreki; Married Yvonne L., Daughter of Habib and Aziza Mitry; Father of Samer M., Lotus M. Education: B.Sc. honors 1958, M.Sc. 1962, Ph.D. 1965, Faculty of Science, Alexandria University (Egypt). Career: Research Chemist, ICI Americas, Inc.; Senior Research Chemist, G. D. Searle & Company, Chicago, 1973-76; Postdoctoral Fellow, Research Associate, Biochemistry, Purdue University, 1972-73; University of Montana, 1971-72; Ohio State University, 1968-71; Assistant Professor, Alexandria University, 1966-68. Organizational Memberships: American Chemical Society; Sigma Xi; Institute of Food Technologists. Religion: Treasurer, Board of Deacons, St. Mary Coptic Orthodox Church of Delaware, 1980 to present. Honors and Awards: Listed in *Who's Who in the East, Men of Achievement.* Address: 2524 Channin Drive, Wilmington, Delaware, 19810.■

ROGER DALE METCALF

Dentist. Personal: Born July 24, 1950; Son of Frank D. Metcalf; Married Linda Susan; Father of Roger Dale, Jr., Kelli Anne. Education: Graduate of Castleberry High School, 1968; B.S. 1973, D.D.S. 1977, Baylor University. Attending M.B.A. Program at Dallas Baptist College. Career: Dentist. Organizational Memberships: American Dental Association; Texas Dental Association; Fort Worth District Dental Society; Academy of General Dentistry; Academy of Gold for Operators; Alumni Association of Student Clinicians of American Dentistry; Arlington Dental Study Club. Community Activities: Rotary Club International, 1982; American Cancer Society, Arlington Unit, Board of Directors 1980, Vice President 1982, President and Chairman of the Board 1983. Religion: Member of Tate Springs Baptist Church, Arlington, Texas. Honors and Awards: M.E.N.S.A., 1980; Outstanding Young Men of America, Jaycees, 1983; Beta Beta Beta Biology Honor Fraternity, 1972; Alpha Epsilon Delta Pre-medical Honor Fraternity, 1972; Graduation Award of Dental School, American Dental Society of Anesthesiology; Founding Brother, Sigma Phi Upsilon Fraternity. Listed in *Who's Who in the South and Southwest.* Address: 5126 Bridgewater, Arlington, Texas 6017.■

TWO THOUSAND NOTABLE AMERICANS

GEORGE MICHAEL MEYER

Executive, Mechanical and Chemical Engineer. Personal: Born March 28, 1935; Son of Hans and Marie Henriette Meyer (mother deceased); Married Ruth Elizabeth. Education: B.S.E.; M.S.M.E. Career: President, Engineers and Energy Investments. Organizational Memberships: Society of Naval Architecture and Marine Engineering. Community Activities: Sponsor, S.O.S. Children's Village Association, Austria/Philippines. Religion: Lutheran. Honors and Awards: Bronze Medal, German Medical Society, 1969; Member Various Gas, Petroleum and Chemical Committees. Address: Marble Hill, New Preston, Connecticut 06777.■

J. THEODORE MEYER

Illinois General Assemblyman, Attorney. Personal: Born April 13, 1936; Son of Joseph T. (deceased) and Mary Meyer; Married Marilu Bartholomew; Father of Jean, Joseph. Education: Graduate of St. Ignatius High School; B.S., John Carroll University; Attended the University of Chicago; J.D., De Paul University College of Law. Career: Member, Illinois General Assembly, 1966-72, 1974 to present; Attorney at Law. Organizational Memberships: American Bar Association; Illinois Bar Association; Southwest Bar Association. Community Activities: Energy and Environment Committee, Chairman; Natural Resource Committee, National Conference of State Legislature; Federal/State Task Force on Energy; Environment, Energy and Natural Resources Committee, Past Minority Spokesman; Public Health Survey Study Commission; Lake Michigan and Adjoining Lands Commission; State Parks and Recreation Commission; House Environmental Study Committee, Past Chairman; Midwest Legislative Council on Environment, Chairman, Founder; Joint House/Senate Subcommittee to Review Statewide Air and Water Plans, Chairman. Honors and Awards: Distinguished Legislator, Chicago Bar Association; Illinois Wildlife Federation; Illinois League of Conservative Voters; United States Environmental Protection Agency and Self-Help Center; Environmental Legislator of the Year Award, Committee on Courts and Justice; Legislator Appreciation Award, Veterans of Foreign Wars; Ten Years Outstanding Legislative Leadership Award, Chicago Lund Association. Address: 9007 South Leavitt, Chicago, Illinois 60620.■

MARY JUSTINA GRATTAN MILAM

Sociologist, Linguist, Free-lance Writer. Personal: Born May 10, 1930; Daughter of F. P. Grattan (deceased) and Catherine Lyons Grattan Byrnes; Married David Leake Milam, Son of David Walker and Mary Milam (both deceased); Father of David Leake Jr., Barnaby Walker, Melinda Sue. Education: Attended Kansas City University (now the University of Missouri at Kansas City), 1947-50; B.A. with honors 1969, M.A. 1971, North Texas State University; Ph.D., The Texas Women's University, 1977; Research Scholar, London School of Economics and Political Science, 1983-84. Career: Sociologist/Linguist; Free-lance Writer; Former Positions include Reporter, Newscaster/Broadcaster, Columnist. Organizational Memberships: International Sociological Association; American Sociological Association; Society for the Study of Social Problems; Mid-South Sociological Association; Southwest Sociological Association; Alpha Kappa Delta, Treasurer 1970-71. Community Activities: Girl Scouts of America, Troop Leader and Leader Trainer in Campcraft, Day Camp Director 1965-66; Boy Scouts of America, Cub Scout Leader and Leader Trainer. Religion: Altar Society, Mother's Club, St. Thomas Aquinas Parish (Dallas, Texas), 1961-64. Honors and Awards: Girl Scout Award, 1966, 1967; Cub Scout Award, 1964; First Prize, Short Story Contest, North Texas State University, 1970; B.A. with honors, 1969; Alpha Kappa Delta; Best Student Paper, S.W.S.A., 1974; Listed in *Who's Who in the South and Southwest*, *World Who's Who of Women*, *Personalities of America*, *Personalities of the South*, *Biographical Roll of Honor*. Address: 6222 Malcolm Drive, Dallas, Texas 75214.■

CHARLES P. MILLER

Doctor of Chiropractic, State Senator. Personal: Born April 29, 1918; Son of William and Anna Victoria Miller (deceased); Married Virginia M., Daughter of W. Chester and Mabel Ferrington; Father of Charles Paul, David Alan, Steven Edward, Dennis Jon, Evelyn Marie, Scot Allen. Education: Graduate, St. Stephens High School (Port Huron, Michigan); Attended Burlington (Iowa) Community College and Palmer College of Chiropractic. Military: Served as Chief Petty Officer in the United States Navy 1940-46; Served in the United States Naval Reserves, 1946-52. Career: Doctor of Chiropractic; State Senator. Organizational Memberships: Chiropractic Society of Iowa, Past President; International Chiropractors Association, First Vice President 1970-74; State and Federal Assembly of National Council of State Legislators, 1974 to present. Community Activities: Boy Scouts of America; American Legion; Veterans of Foreign Wars; Fraternal Order of Eagles; Benevolent and Protective Order of Elks; Knights of Columbus; Knights of Columbus, 4th Degree. Religion: Catholic. Honors and Awards: Silver Beaver Scouting Award, 1958; Speaker Pro-tem, House of Representatives, Iowa General Assembly, 1965-66; President Pro-tem, Iowa Senate, 1983-85; Fellow Award, Palmer Academy of Chiropractic, 1966; Fellowship Award, International Chiropractors Association, 1969. Address: 801 High Street, Burlington, Iowa 52601.■

FRANK G. MILLER

Computer Applications Software Manager. Personal: Born April 8, 1930; Son of O. R. Miller; Father of Michael F., Janet M. Susan A. Education: B.A. Business, San Angelo Junior College, San Angelo, Texas, 1956; B.B.A. Accounting, University of Texas, Austin, Texas, 1958. Served with the United States Army Signal Corps, 1951-53. Career: Manager, Computer Applications Software; Former Systems Analyst, Computers. Organizational Memberships: Association Systems Management, Treasurer 1976-77 and 1977-78, Secretary 1975-76. Community Activities: Knights of Columbus, Council 799, Dallas; The Alhambra Order of Brothers. Religion: Catholic. Address: 9415 Shady Valley Drive, Dallas, Texas 75238.■

GEORGE J. MILLER

Paleontologist, Educator. Personal: Born November 15, 1921; Son of Mrs. Jacob Miller; Married Patricia Klar. Education: B.S., California State University at Long Beach, 1967; M.S., Idaho State University at Pocatello, 1975. Military: Served in the United States Navy, 1943-45. Career: Paleontologist, Educator; Former Paleontologist in Field and Research. Organizational Memberships: Society of Vertebrate Paleontologists; Paleontological Society; Western Association of Vertebrate Paleontologists; Society for the Study of Evolution; Others. Community Activities: Director of Volunteers and Senior Citizens in Paleontological Work in Field and Museum at Rancho La Brea Project, 1969-72; Director of Volunteers and Senior Citizens in Paleontological Work at Imperial Valley College Museum, 1972 to present. Address: B.S.R. 762, Julian, California 92036.■

IRMA GANZ MILLER

Publishing Company Executive. Personal: Born December 25, 1916; Daughter of Jacob Ganz (deceased) and Dora Weinberger Ganz; Married Milton Miller; Mother of Jeffrey Harold, Lee James. Education: B.A., Pennsylvania State University, 1938. Career: Managing Director, Soccer Associates, 1948 to present; Business Manager, Jeffrey Lee Syndicate, 1953-80; President, Sportshelf Publishing, 1953 to present; Managing Editor, *Soccer News*, 1968-77; Columnist, Long Island Press, 1969-73; Soccer Journalist, *Reuter's*, 1967-77; Director, Wide World Book Centre, Ltd., 1966-80. Organizational Memberships: Soccer Writers Association, President 1969-77; National Sportscasters and Sportswriters Association; International Platform Association; National Recreation Association; American Alliance of Health, Physical Education and Recreation; National Parks and Recreation Association; American Booksellers Association; Pennsylvania State Alumni Association. Community Activities: Donation of Personal Library to Pattee Library, Pennsylvania State University, 1980, 1981. Honors and Awards: First Female Journalist, Accredited by Federation International for Football, 1966. Address: P.O. Box 634, New Rochelle, New York 10802.■

ROBERT J. MILLER

Author. Personal: Born June 12, 1918, in Plainview, Arkansas; Son of Homer Cleo Miller and Matilda Alice Dalton (both deceased). Education: A.A., Hendrix College; B.S., State Teachers College (now University of Central Arkansas), 1941. Military: Served in the United States General Army. Career: Author;

Resident Poet, McDowell Colony, Peterborough, New Hampshire, 1941. Organizational Memberships: American Poets Fellowship Society; Florida State Poetry Society Inc.; National Society of Poets Inc. Community Activities: Cousteau Society; National Historical Society; Arkansas Sheriffs Association. Published Works: *To Span the Seasons* 1977, *Freely Remembered* 1972, *Weird Balk* 1964, *Rustique* 1947; Contributor to Anthologies (including) *The Family Treasury of Great Poems* and *Our Twentieth Century's Greatest Poems*, *Our World's Best Loved Poems* (all three published by the World of Poetry Press); An Anthology *Lyrical Treasures*, *Classic and Modern* 1983; *A Burst of Trumpets*, *Yearbook of Modern Poetry*, *Versatility in Verse*, *Phytography Sketch Manual* (unpublished), *Poetry Parade*, *Melody of the Muse*, *Lyrical Voices*; *Outstanding Contemporary Poetry*, Sandwich, Il., 1972; Contributor to Periodicals (including) *United Poets*, *American Poet*, *Modern Images*. Honors and Awards: Distinguished Achievement Citation, International Biographical Centre, Cambridge, 1975; Diploma di Merito, Terme[1], Italy 1982, Statue of Victory 1984; Listed in *Personalities of the South*, *Notable Americans*, *International Register of Profiles*, *International Who's Who in Poetry*, *Men of Achievement*, *Personalities of America*. Address: Highway 80 West, Box 17, Danville, Arkansas 72833.■

JAY EDISON MINTON

Attorney, Insurance Executive. Personal: Born September 13, 1893; Married Elizabeth S.; Father of Jay E., Jr. Education: A.B., LL.B., J.D., Missouri University. Military: Served in the United States Army, 1918, attaining the rank of Second Lieutenant. Career: Vice President, Universal Underwriters Insurance Company, Kansas City, Missouri, 1935; Executive Vice President, Automobile Dealers Mutual Insurance Company, 1945; Chairman of Board, President, Indemnity Underwriters Insurance Company, 1977; Chairman of Board, Commercial Life and Accident Insurance Company, 1981. Organizational Memberships: Sigma Chi (initiated 1914), Life Member, Order of Constantine Vice President 1973, Committee of Trustees 1978-83, Dallas Chapter Alumni Association President 1973-74; Life Member, Phi Delta Phi Legal Fraternity; Mason, 32nd Degree in Scottish and York Rites, Shriner; Knights of Malta, Former Knight of Honor, Knight of Grace, Order of St. John of Jerusalem, Knights of Malta, Hospitalers, Commander of the Commandery of the Red River; Military Order of World Wars, Chapter Commander 1973, State Commander 1974, Regional Commander 1975-76, General Staff-at-Large (Emeritus); Retired Officers Association, President of Dallas Chapter 1972; Reserve Officers Association; Sons of the American Revolution, Vice President of Dallas Chapter 1973; Navy League; American Legion, Past Vice President of Dallas Chapter (Post 58) 9173; Association of the United States Army, Board of Directors 1973; Missouri University Alumni Association, President Dallas Alumni Association 1973-74; Second Amendment Foundation; National Tax Limitation Committee; Congressional VIP Card; American Cause, Charter Sponsoring Member; National Association of Concerned Veterans; American Security Council, National Advisory Board; United States Senatorial Club; Braniff International Council; National Federation for Decency; American Conservative Union; Sustaining Member, Republican National Committee; Lancers Club; Admirals Club; American Association of Retired Persons; National Sojourners Association; Charter Member, Pershing Memorial Foundation Fund; Vice President, Kiwanis Club of Addison. Published Works: Author Book of Poetry, *Poetry Per Se*; Composer of Six Songs, "Bedtime Lullaby," "Nearly All the Time," "I Want You, I Need You, I Love You," "Traveling Man's Lament," "Always Chasing the Blues," "Sigma Chi Serenade". Religion: Lovers Lane Methodist Church (third largest Methodist Church in Christendom), Lay Leader 1972, President Men's Club 1974. Honors and Awards: Sigma Chi, Two Grand Consul Citations, Three Certificates of Appreciation; Listed in *Who's Who in the South and Southwest*, *Who's Who in Commerce and Industry*, *Personalities of the South*, *Dictionary of International Biography*, *Notable Americans of the Bicentennial Era*, *International Who's Who of Intellectuals*, *Directory of Distinguished Americans*. Address: P.O. Box 12007, Dallas, Texas 75225.■

RUSSELL HARRY MITCHELL

Dermatologist. Personal: Born October 19, 1925; Son of William John and Anna Lillian Mitchell (deceased); Married Judith Lawes, May 24, 1968; Father of Kathy Ellen, Gregory Alan, Jill Elaine, Crystal Anne. Education: Attended St. Ambrose College 1944-45, Notre Dame University 1945-46; B.S., B.A., University of Minnesota, 1947; B.M., M.D., University of Minnesota, 1951; Postgraduate Studies in Dermatology and Basic Science, University of Pennsylvania, 1968-69; Intern, Gorgas Hospital, Canal Zone, 1951-52; Resident in Dermatology, Naval Hospital, Philadelphia, 1967-68, 1968-70; Certified, American Board of Dermatology, 1972. Military: Served in the United States Navy, 1943-46, 1943-44, 1964-80, attaining the rank of Captain. Career: Assistant Chief, Out-Patient Department, Gorgas Hospital, 1955-64; Chief of Medical and Surgery Wards, Arizona State Hospital, Phoenix, Arizona, 1965; Commander Officer of First Medical Battalion and Assistant Division Surgeon, First Marine Division, 1965-67; Residency Training, Naval Hospital (Philadelphia) and University of Pennsylvania, 1967-70; Chief of Dermatology, Pensacola Naval Hospital, 1970-73; Chief, Out-patient Service, Pensacola Naval Hospital, 1972-73; Dermatologist (Instructor of Medical Students, Physician Assistants, Interns, Residents and Paramedical Personnel), National Naval Medical Center, Bethesda, Maryland, 1973 to present; Lecturer in Dermatology to Student Flight Surgeons, NAMC, 1970-73; Assistant Professor, Department of Medicine (Dermatology), Georgetown University Medical School, 1975 to present; Consultant Dermatologist, Prince William Hospital, 1974 to present; Staff Member, Loudoun Memorial Hospital, 1978 to present; Licensed to Practice in Minnesota, Canal Zone, Arizona, Virginia, New Mexico. Organizational Memberships: Fellow, American Academy of Dermatology; Fellow, American College of Physicians; American Medical Association; Association of Military Surgeons; Association of Military Dermatologists, Life Member; Naval Institute; Society for American Archaeology; Phi Chi Medical Fraternity; Diplomate, American Board of Dermatology; Fellow, Explorers Club; Prince William County Medical Society; Diplomate, Pan American Medical Association; Associate Member, Marine's Memorial Club; Loudoun County Medical Society; Dermatology Foundation; Royal Society of Medicine; Archaeological Society of Panama, Secretary 1959-60, President 1961-64. Honors and Awards: Bronze Star with Combat V; Presidential Unit Citation with Bronze Star; Naval Unit Citation with Bronze Star; Condecoracion Nacional de la Order de Vasco Nuñez de Balboa en el grado de Caballero; Combat Action Ribbon; Vietnam Gallantry Cross with Palm and Clasp; North American Defense Medal; Victory Medal (WWII); National Defense Medal with Star; Naval Reserve Medal; Vietnam Campaign Medal with Date Bar; Vietnam Service Medal with Marine Corps Combat Insignia and Two Stars. Address: Rural Route #2, Box 99, Leesburg, Virginia 22075.■

YAR WASYL MOCIUK

Executive. Personal: Born January 16, 1927 in Mylovania, Ukraine; Came to United States 1950, Naturalized 1956; Son of Mykola and Evdochia Mociuk; Married Irene Groch; Father of Daria, Natalia. Education: Attended University of Erlangen (Germany), Ukranian Free University, Munich (Germany) 1947-50; B.A. Dramatic Literature and Film, City College of New York, 1957; M.A. Educational Psychology, Jackson State University, 1968; M.S.M.S. Audio Visual Education 1971, Ph.D. Cinema Arts and Sciences, World University, Arizona. Career: President, Filmtreat International Corp.; Former Positions Include Assistant Dean of Communication, Peoples University of the Americas, New York; Organizer, C & M Film Service Inc. Organizational Memberships: President, Ukrainian Cinema Association of America; Society of Motion Picture and Television Engineers; University Film Association; Member of University Professor's Association. Community Activities: Treasurer, Ukrainian Free University Foundation; Branch President, Ukrainian Fraternal Association; Slavonic League; Republican Party; State Advisor, United States Congresional Advisory Board; Appeared as Lecturer and Speaker, Many Schools and Organizations. Honors and Awards: Author of History of Ukrainian Cinema and History of School of Ukrainian Studies; Received United States Patent for Method and Apparatus for Treating Motion Picture Film, 1971; Awarded Doctor of Humane Letters, Peoples University, San Juan, Puerto Rico, 1973; Listed in *Who's Who in the East*, *Who's Who in Finance and Industry*, *Who's Who in America*, *Who's Who in the World*, *International Motion Picture and Television Almanac*, *Ukrainians in North America*, *Community Leaders and Noteworthy Americans*, *Men of Achievement*, *Men and Women of Distinction*, *International Who's Who of Intellectuals*, *Dictionary of International Biography*, *International Register of Profiles*. Address: 2 Essex Place, Bronxville, New York 10708.■

BERNHARD MOLLENHAUER

Writer and Philosopher. Personal: Born 1902 in California; Son of Bernhard Mollenhauer, Sr. (deceased); Married Tekla Van Norman. Education: Studies at the Isis Conservatory of Music, Point Loma, California, 1923-26. Career: Author; Philosopher; Musician, Raja Yoga Orchestra, 1924-46; Clerk in Local

Stores. Organizational Memberships: Life Member, India Academy of Philosophy at Calcutta University; American Society of Psychical Research; Psychic Research Society of London, England; Metaphysical Society of America; Hegel Society of America; Royal Philosophical Society of Glasgow; Canadian Philosophical Society; Canadian Maritain Association; Life Fellow, International Institute of Arts and Letters, Switzerland; Secretary, San Diego Browning Society. Published Works: Author, "Horizons of the Western Mind," *Hibbert Journal*, 1952; "Lutoslawski and the Knight Among Nations," *American Slavic and East European Review*, 1954; "The Political Philosophy of William E. Hocking," *Journal of the Royal Philosophical Society of Glasgow*, 1971; Essay on Spinoza as Contribution to the Radhakrishnan Souvenir Volume presented to Dr. Radhakrishna, President of India; Contributor to B. L. Atreya Souvenir Volume; *The Quest for Lasting Peace*, 1980; *The Quest for Truth*, 1981; Philosophy and Poetry (co-authored with wife, Tekla Van Norman); Contributor of Articles to Scholarly Journals. Honors and Awards: Honorary Ph.D.; Listed in *Directory of American Scholars, Dictionary of International Biography, Men of Achievement, Who's Who in America*. Address: 3614 Third Avenue, San Diego, California 92103.■

RICHARD MATTERN MONTGOMERY

Retired United States Air Force Officer. Personal: Born December 15, 1911, Hollidaysburg, Pennsylvania; Son of Charles Wesley and Eve (Mattern) Montgomery; Father of Nancy M. Hunter, Richard M. Jr., Thomas C. Education: B.S., United States Military Academy, 1933; Graduate, Air War College, 47; Graduate, United States Air Corps Flying Training Center, San Antonio, Texas, 1934; Graduate, United States Air Corps Technical Training School, Rantoul, Illinois, 1938. Military: Served in the United States Air Force, advancing through the grades to Lieutenant General, 1962; Held assignments at Various Army Air Fields in Panama, Texas and Oklahoma as Chief Inspector, Test Pilot, Flying Instructor, Flight and Stage Commander and Director of Flying Training; Built and Commanded Army Air Field, Independence, Kansas; Chief of Individual Training Division, Office, 1943; Assistant-Chief of Air Staff Training at the Pentagon, Washington, D.C., 1943-44; Commanded 383rd Bomb Wing (B-29), 1944-45; Assignment at Headquarters Far East Command (under General MacArthur), Tokyo, 1947-48; Commander, 51st Jet Fighter Wing, Naha Air Force Base, Okinawa, 1948-49; Deputy Commander, 97th Bomb Wing, Biggs Air Force Base, El Paso, Texas, 1949-51; Chief of Staff, Strategic Air Command (under General Burtis E. LeMay), 1952-56; Deputy Commander, Second Air Force, Barksdale Air Force Base, Louisiana, 1956-58; Commander, Third Air Division, Strategic Air Command, Anderson Air Force Base, Guam, M.I., 1958-59; Assistant Vice Chief of the Air Staff, Headquarters United States Air Force, Pentagon, Washington D.C., 1959-62; Vice Commander-in-Chief (VCINC), U.S. Air Forces, Europe, 1962-66. Career: Since Retirement from United States Air Force, Executive Vice President, Freedoms Foundation at Valley Force, Pennsylvania, 1967-68, Regional Vice President 1968-76, National Trustee 1976 to present; Director, General Services Life Insurance, 1968-82; Town Commissioner, Longboat Key, Florida, 1971-73. Community Activities: 32nd Degree Mason, Scottish Rite; Shriner; Order of Daedalian; West Point Society; Retired Officers Association; Air Force Association; Army and Navy Club, Washington D.C. Honors and Awards: Honored by Boy Scouts of America with Silver Beaver and Silver Antelope, and by Pennsylvania State University with Gold Medal for Service to Humanity; Decorated: Distinguished Service Medal with Oak Leaf Cluster, Legion of Merit with Oak Leaf Cluster, Army Commendation Medal with Two Oak Leaf Clusters. Address: P.O. Box 93, Longboat Key, Florida 33548.■

JOHN ALLEN MOONEY

Executive. Personal: Born May 17, 1918; Son of Harry Edmon and Maybelle Mooney; Married Nettie, Cyrus and Anna Hayes; Father of John Allen Jr., Suzann, Jean, Nancy. Education: Attended River Falls College (Pre-Med Courses). Career: President and Chief Executive Officer, Western Dressing, Inc.; President and Chief Executive Officer, M & R Sales Corporation (Monarch and Richelieu); National Sales Manager, Western Dressing, Inc., 1970-78; National Sales Manager and Vice President, M & R Sales Corporation, 1969-78; Salesman, Consolidated Foods Corporation 1945-69, Reid Murdock & Company 1940-45. Community Activities: Elected to National Election Council, Boy Scouts of America; National Representative, Boy Scouts of America, LaCrosse Chapter; Treasurer, Shriners Hospitals for Crippled Children, Chicago, 1983; Co-Chairman, Several Zor Shrine Temple Ceremonials, LaCrosse, Wisconsin; Member Rebild National Park Society, Inc., Aalborg, Denmark; Sons of Norway, LaCrosse, Wisconsin; Director, First National Bank of LaGrange (LaGrange, Illinois); Director, Waunakee Alloy Casting Corporation (Waunakee, Wisconsin); Board of Trustees and Vice President, Gundersen Medical Foundation (LaCrosse, Wisconsin); Board of Governors, National Fishing Hall of Fame (Hayward, Wisconsin); La Crosse Elks Club; LaCrosse Plugs; LaCrosse Country Club; The La Crosse Club; La Crosse Moose Club; Past Potentate, Zor Shrine Temple, 1962; Honorary Past Potentate, Medinah Shrine Temple; Elected Emeritus Status Board of Governors, Shriners Hospitals for Crippled Children, Chicago Unit; Chairman, Shrine Hospital Day 1982; Board of Governors, Shriners Hospitals for Crippled Children, Minneapolis and St. Paul (Minnesota), 1952-69; LaCrosse Lutheran Hospital Corporation; Associate Board of Governors, LaGrange Memorial Hospital; Support Committee, Heritage Club, LaCrosse Lutheran Hospital; John Allen Mooney Amery Masonic Lodge (Amery, Wisconsin); Parade Marshal, Amery Fall Festival, 1962; Parade Marshal, River Falls Shrine Hospital Benefit Football Parade, 1962; Honorary Member, LaCrosse Boy's Choir; Honorary Kentucky Colonel; Life Member, American Biographical Institute Research Association. Honors and Awards: Order of the Arrow, Boy Scouts of America; Community and Leadership Award for Outstanding Community Leadership Dedication and Service, LaCrosse, Wisconsin, 1984; Pope John XXIII Award for Distinguished Service from Viterbo College, LaCrosse, Wisconsin; Festmaster, Oktoberfest U.S.A., LaCrosse, 1982-83; Man of the Year, LaCrosse Chamber of Commerce, 1983; Executive Board, Boy Scouts of America, Gateway Area Council; Listed in *Who's Who in America, Who's Who in the World, Who's Who in the Midwest, Who's Who in Finance and Industry, Directory of Distinguished Americans, Personalities of the West and Midwest, International Register of Profiles, Men of Achievement, International Book of Honor, Personalities of America, Biographical Roll of Honor*. Address: 1515 North Harlem Avenue, Oak Park, Illinois 60302.■

DALTON MOORE, JR.

Consulting Geologist, Scientist and Petroleum Engineer. Personal: Born March 25, 1918; Son of Dalton and Anne Yonge Moore (deceased). Education: Graduate, Tarleton University, 1938; Graduate, Texas A&M University, 1942; Graduate, Army War College, Command and General Staff College of the United States Army, 1945. Military: 2nd Lieutenant Commission in United States Army, 1940; Major, Coast Artillery Corp, 1947; Aide-de-Camp to 5 Generals during World War II. Career: Consulting Geologist, Scientist, Petroleum Engineer; Oil Field Pulling Unit Operator, 1939; Research Engineer, U.S. Engineer at Galveston, Texas, 1940; District Engineer for Oil Company, 1946, 1947; Chief Reservoir for 2 Oil Companies, 1948, 1949; Manager of Oil Company, 1950, 1951, 1952; Manager of Large Water Flood, 1953, 1954, 1955; President, Part Owner, Several Oil Companies. Organizational Memberships: West Central Texas Section A.I.M.E., Chairman 1954; Registered Professional Engineer, Texas, 1951 to present. Community Activities: American Red Cross, Taylor County Chapter, Director 1956, 1957, 1958, 1960, Member 1963-66; Boy Scouts of America, Eagle Scout 1932; Sweetwater (Texas) Junior Chamber of Commerce, Organizer and 1st President 1940; Taylor County Democratic Committee, Secretary 1965, 1966, 1967; Texas Democratic Convention, Appointed Representative 1960, 1962, 1964; Wrote Oil Reports for Most National Banks, 1958-66. Honors and Awards: Served as Scientist Advisor to U.S. Military Board during World War II; Recipient Numerous Military Medals, Awards and Letters for Accomplishments; Certificate as 25-Year Member of A.I.M.E. in 1965; Senior Membership Status in American Institute of Mining, Metallurgical and Petroleum Engineers in 1983. Address: 4065 Waldemar Drive, Abilene, Texas 79605.■

LAWRENCE GLEN MOREHOUSE

Professor of Pathology, Laboratory Administrator. Personal: Born July 21, 1925; Married; Father of Timothy, Glenn Ellen. Education: B.S. Biological Science 1952, D.V.M. 1952, Kansas State University; M.S. Animal Pathology 1956, Ph.D. Animal Pathology 1960, Purdue University. Military: Served in the United States Navy, 1943-46; Served in the United States Army, 1952-56, attaining the rank of 2nd Lieutenant. Career: Professor of Pathology and Director of Veterinary Medical Diagnostic Laboratory, College of Veterinary Medicine, University of Missouri; Chairman, Department of Veterinary Pathology, University of Missouri, 1964-70; Discipline Leader, Pathology and Toxicology, Animal Health Division, U.S.D.A. National Animal Disease Laboratory, 1960-64. Organizational Memberships: American Association of Veterinary Laboratory Diagnosticians, President 1978-79, Secretary/Treasurer 1980 to present; Fellow, Royal Society of Health, London; American Veterinary Medicine Association; Conference of Research Workers in Animal Disease in North America; New York Academy of Sciences; United States Animal Health Association; American Association for Laboratory Animal Sciences. Religion: Presbyterian Church (Columbia, Missouri), Deacon, Elder and Clerk of Session. Honors and Awards: Phi Zeta; Gamma Sigma Delta; Sigma Xi; Three Certificates of Merit, United States Department of Agriculture; E. P. Pope Memorial Award for Outstanding Contributions to Diagnostic Veterinary Medicine, American Association of Veterinary Laboratory Diagnosticians. Address: 916 Danforth Drive, Columbia, Missouri 65201.■

SHARON YURIKO MORIWAKI

Program Administrator. Personal: Born December 29, 1945; Daughter of Mr. and Mrs. Yutaka Moriwaki. Education: B.A. 1967, M.A. 1969, Ph.D. 1972, University of Southern California; J.D., Loyola Law School, 1984. Career: Department of Labor and Industrial Relations, State of Hawaii; Associate Director, Hawaii Gerontology Center; Evaluation Branch Chief/Training Director, California Department of Aging; Research Project Director at Andrus Gerontology Center, Assistant Professor, University of Southern California. Organizational Memberships: American Psychological Association; Gerontological Society; Western Gerontology Society; White House Conference on Aging, Technical Committee 1981; Hawaii Senior Companion Advisory Council, Vice Chairman 1978-82. Community Activities: Governor's Commission on the Status of Women, Member 1978 to present, Secretary 1979-82, Statewide Conference Chairman 1979; Honolulu City and County Neighborhood Board, 1981-82; Governor's White House Conference on Aging, Delegate, Technical Issue Chairman 1980-82; State of Hawaii Policy Advisory Board for Elderly Affairs, 1980-82; St. Louis Heights Community Association, Secretary 1978-80, President 1981-82; Democratic Party of Hawaii, Precinct Secretary 1978-82; Hawaii Public Broadcasting Authority Community Advisory Board, 1980-82. Honors and Awards: Loyola Law School Dean's Scholarship 1983, Dean's List 1982-84, Loyola Law Review 1982; National Retired Teachers Association Scholarship, 1971; Biomedical Support Grant, National Institutes of Health, 1970-71; National Institute of Child Health and Human Development Fellowship, 1967-71; Phi Beta Kappa, 1967; Listed in *Who's Who of American Women, Who's Who in the West, World Who's Who of Women, Who's Who of Women. Who's Who Among American Law Students.* Address: 1812 St. Louis Drive, Honolulu, Hawaii 96816.■

JOHN VINCENT MORLINO

Resident in Family Medicine. Personal: Born May 7, 1946; Son of Mr. and Mrs. Vincent Morlino; Married Melanie, Daughter of Mr. and Mrs. Larry Palmgren; Father of Rachel Amy, Priscilla April, Brad Skipper. Education: B.S. Biology cum laude, Upsala College, 1975; D.O., Philadelphia College of Osteopathic Medicine, 1979; Intern, Memorial General Hospital, Union, New Jersey, 1979-80. Career: Resident in Family Medicine, Memorial General Hospital, Union, New Jersey; Medical Staff, Point Pleasant Hospital. Pharmaceutical Research Assistant, Hoffmann-La Roche, Inc., Nutley, New Jersey, 1969-75. Organizational Memberships: Philadelphia College of Osteopathic Medicine Alumni Association; American Osteopathic Physicians and Surgeons; Ocean County Medical Society; American College of Emergency Physicians. Community Activities: St. Benedict's Prep Alumni Association; Mensa, New York Chapter; Bricktown Jaycees. Religion: J.D.L. 1980; St. Francis Xavier Parish Council. Honors and Awards: Tri-Beta Biological Honor Society; Listed in *Who's Who in Finance and Industry.* Address: 616 Hill Drive, Herbertsville, New Jersey 08723.■

ALVIN L. MORRIS

Consulting Meteorologist, Executive. Personal: Born June 7, 1920; Son of Roy and Eva Morris (deceased); Married Nadean Davidson, Daughter of Jessie M. and Esther W. Davidson (deceased); Father of Andrew N., Nancy L., Mildred M., Ann E., Jane C. Education: Attended Western State College (Gunnison, Colorado) 1938-41; B.S., University of Chicago, 1942; M.S., United States Naval Postgraduate School, 1953. Military: Served in the United States Navy, 1942-46, 1950-58, attaining the rank of Commander; Promoted to rank of Captain in United States Naval Reserves, 1962. Career: Consulting Meteorologist, President, Ambient Analysis, Inc.; Science Administrator, National Center for Atmospheric Research, 1963-75; Director of Research, United States Navy Weather Research Facility (Norfolk, Virginia), 1958-62; Meteorologist, Pacific Gas & Electric Company (San Francisco), 1947-50. Organizational Memberships: American Meteorological Society, Chairman Committee for Atmospheric Measurement 1978-81; American Society for Testing and Materials, Chairman Meteorology Committee 1973-77; American Geophysical Union. Community Activities: Home Hospitality for Foreign Students, University of Colorado, Treasurer 1969-70; Convened Conference "Air Quality Meteorology and Atmospheric Ozone" and Edited Proceedings for American Society for Testing and Materials, University of Colorado, 1977. Honors and Awards: Civil Aeronautics Administration Weather Bureau Fellowship to University of Chicago, 1941; Certified as Consulting Meteorologist, American Meteorological Society, 1979; Listed in *Who's Who in the West, Leaders in American Science.* Address: 15759 Sunshine Canyon, Boulder, Colorado 80302.■

RICHARD MORRIS

Psychotherapist and Hypno-Analyst. Personal: Born January 26; Son of Robert and Molly Morris; Married Dr. Margaret Morris. Education: B.S. Psychology, Dickinson (Penn State), Carlisle, Pennsylvania; M.A. Social Sciences and Humanities/Counseling the Urban Disadvantaged 1969, Ph.D. Program in Clinical Psychology 1970-72, New York University; Trained and Certified as Director, Mount Vernon Crisis Hotline, Westchester County Narcotics Council; Permanent Certification as Counselor in New York State, Long Island University, 1977; M.A. Psychology, Clinical Mental Health Sciences and Psychotherapy, New School for Social Research, 1977; N.D., American College of Nutripathy; Ph.D. Clinical Psychology, School of Professional Psychology, F.I.T., 1981; R.H.D., American Association of Professional Hypnologists; Full Clinical Member, American Association of Marriage and Family Therapists; Clinical Member, American Association of Nutritional and Dietary Consultants; Consultant to American Association of Professional Hypnotherapists. Military: Officer in the United States Army Special Forces Division, 1966-67; Training at U.S.A.T.S.C.H., Fort Eustis, Virginia; Decorated as a Vietnam Era Veteran. Career: Founder, Director and Senior Staff Psychotherapist of Central Westchester Psychotherapy and Family Counseling Service; Lecturer, Adjunct Faculty in Psychology, Behavioral Sciences and Humanities Departments, Mercy College (Dobbs Ferry, New York); Psychological Sports Consultant for Several Professional and Collegiate Athletic Teams and Individual Athletes; Psycho-nutritional Consultant (Sports Psychologist) to the 1984 U.S. Olympic Teams (Winter and Summer); Past Positions include Guidance Counselor, Crisis Counselor, Recreation Counselor, Rehabilitation Counselor for United States Army, New York Board of Education, Odessey House Group, Family Life Institute and Other Organizations; Teacher at All Levels and Subjects in Public Schools and Colleges; Karate Instructor of 16 Years (3rd Degree Black Belt), Privately and in the United States. Organizational Memberships: Permanently Certified Counselor and Teacher, Secondary Level Personnel Counseling and Secondary Level Social Sciences, New York State and New York City; Certified Third Degree Black Belt Karate Master. Community Activities: Worked in Day Camps, Swimming Programs, Karate and Physical Fitness Training (summers); White Plains Young Men's Christian Association Weightlifting Teams, Founder, Captain; City of Yonkers Neighborhood Council, Director 1979; New York Metropolitan A.A.U. Powerlifting Committee, President 1978-81; Psycho-nutritional Consultant to General Health Management Corporation, Bloomfield, Connecticut; Consultant, V.P.S. Health Corporation (Middletown, New York); National Board of Advisors, American Biographical Institute; International Academy of Nutritional Consultants; World Congress of Professional Hypnotists, Advisory Member. Honors and Awards: Powerlifting, Weightlifting and Wrestling Champion; Captain of Championship Teams, Eastern States Powerlifting Championships, 1969, 1970, 1974, 1975; Winner of Over 300 Trophies and Titles, Holder of Numerous State, National, U.S. Army and Regional Records for Football, Wrestling, Karate and Weightlifting; Outstanding Teacher in Harrison, 1969; Several Military Meritorious Service Medals during Vietnam Era; Most Valuable Wrestling Coach, Westchester County, 1975; Athlete of the Year, New York Metropolitan American Association of Universities, 1977; Man of the Year Award, Yonkers City Youth Council, 1978; Athletic Scholarship to College; Recipient of 2 Presidential Sports Awards by President Jimmy Carter (one in Karate 1977, one in Jogging 1978); Certificate of Participation, United States Olympic Committee; Certificate of Merit, United States Olympic Society; Football Centennial Certificate, National Federation of State High School Athletic Association, 1962. Address: P.O. Box 75, Ardsley, New York 10502.■

CAROL L. MORROW

Insurance Administrator. Personal: Born May 7, 1943; Daughter of Mr. and Mrs. E. C. Kline; Mother of Quinn A. Stowe, William E. Stowe. Education: B.A., Southwest Texas State University, 1966; J.D., South Texas College of Law, 1977. Career: Associate General Counsel and Assistant Secretary, Government Personnel Mutual Life Insurance Company; Former Assistant General Counsel and Assistant Secretary, Government Personnel Mutual Life Insurance Company.

Organizational Memberships: American Bar Association; State Bar Association; San Antonio Bar Association; Association of Life Insurance Counsel; American Corporate Counsel Association; League of Women Voters. Community Activities: Texas Women's Legal Rights Committee, 1979; Law Day Committee, 1983; GPM Federal Credit Union, Board of Directors 1979 to present; GPM Political Action Committee, Treasurer 1979 to present. Religion: Church of Today Divine Science. Honors and Awards: Listed in *Who's Who in American Law, Who's Who in the Southwest, World Who's Who of Women, Personalities of the South.* Address: 719 President, San Antonio, Texas 78216.■

LAURICE CULP MOSELEY

Music Entrepreneur. Personal: Born February 15, 1927; Daughter of John C. and Alma Roma Hand Foshee (deceased); Married Charles W. Culp (deceased); Second Husband Ernest B. Moseley Jr., Son of Ernest B. and Ida Moseley. Career: Founder, Chairman of the Board, Culp Piano and Organ Company, 1955 to present (Music Entrepreneur, Hammond Organs, Kawai Pianos and Organs, Kimball Pianos and Organs, Bosendorfer Pianos, Conn Pianos and Organs, Music Computers, Others); Producer, Local Network Variety Television Show; Former Positions include Auditor for Naval Air Station (Pensacola, Florida), Personnel Clerk at Maxwell Air Force Base (Montgomery, Alabama), Payroll Clerk for the Selective Service System in the State of Alabama. Organizational Memberships: National Association of Music Merchants; National Association for Female Executives; Advisory Committee to Manufacturers, 1983-84. Community Activities: Presidential Task Force, 1982 to present; Notary Public, State of Alabama. Religion: McGeehee Road Baptist Church, Montgomery. Published Works: Author *Six Lessons Toward Keyboard Mastery.* Honors and Awards: Achieved #1 Rating in World in Retail Sales for Kimball, 1978; Listed in *Who's Who of American Women, Personalities of the South, World Who's Who of Women, Five Thousand Personalities of the World, Community Leaders of the World, International Book of Honor, Who's Who in the South and Southwest, Directory of Distinguished Americans, International Register of Profiles.* Address: 2543 Wildwood Drive, Montgomery, Alabama 36111.■

ELBERT RAYMOND MOSES, JR.

Professor Emeritus. Personal: Born March 31, 1908, New Concord, Ohio; Son of Elbert Raymond Sr. and Helen Martha Miller Moses (both deceased); Married Mary Miller Sterrett; Father of James Elbert (deceased). Education: A.B., University of Pittsburgh, 1932; M.Sc. 1934, Ph.D. 1936, University of Michigan. Career: Professor Emeritus; Chairman, Department of Speech and Dramatic Arts, Clarion State College, Pennsylvania, 1959-71; Associate Professor, Michigan State University, 1956-59; Associate Professor, Eastern Illinois State University, 1946-56; Fulbright Lecturer, Philippines, 1955-56; Assistant Professor, Ohio State University, 1938-46; Woman's College, University of North Carolina, 1936-38. Community Activities: Foreign Students and Teachers, Department of Health, Education and Welfare, 1964-65; Liaison Representative, Peace Corps, Clarion State College, 1961-65; President, Clarion County Library Board, 1968-71; 1st Executive Director, United Way, Clarion County, 1972-74; Commissioner, Boy Scouts of America, French Creek Council, Indian Trails District, 1975-78; President, Clarion County Historical Society, 1976-78; President, Clarion Rotary Club, 1966-67; District Governor, Rotary No. 728, 1973-74; Commander, VFW Parker D. Cramer Post No. 2145, 1963; Commander, American Legion, Craig E. Fleming Post No. 66, 1966; Worthy Patron, Eastern Star, Clarion Chapter 267, 1964-74; Worthy Patron, Order of Eastern Star, East Brady Chapter No. 311, 1975-80; Order of the White Shrine of Jerusalem, Joppa Shrine No. 48, New Betheleem, Pennsylvania, Watchman of Shepherds 1979-80; Most Excellent High Priest, Eden Royal Arch Chapter No. 259, Clarion, Pennsylvania, 1967; Member Northwest District Training Advisory Council of Pennsylvania, Department of Aging, 1980-81; Selected as Alternate Delegate from Pennsylvania to 1981 White House Conference on Aging; President, Venango County Advisory Council on Aging, 1978-79; Sons of the American Revolution, Chapter President, Member of State Board of Management, 1965-68, 1978-82. Published Works: Author Numerous Articles in National and International Journals of Phonetics and Speech including *A Guide to Effective Speaking* (Alemars, Manila, 1956; Vantage Press, 1957); *Phonetics: History and Interpretation* (Prentice Hall, 1964); *Three Attributes of God* (Apollo Book Company, Inc., 1983). Honors and Awards: Commanding General's Commendation, Signal School, Ft. Monmouth, New Jersey, 1953; Certificate of Appreciation, Nicaraguan Government Department of Public Health, 1974; Silver Beaver Award, Boy Scouts of America, 1978; Phi Delta Kappa Service Key 1978, and Certificate of Recognition for Distinguished Service to Education 1981; Citizen of the Year, Clarion Chamber of Commerce, 1976; Citation by the House of Representatives, Commonwealth of Pennsylvania, December 8, 1981, for Total Involvement in Concerns and Well-being of Fellow Men; Appointed Honorary, Secretary's Advocate, Department of Aging, Pennsylvania, 1980; Listed in *Who's Who in the East, Directory of American Scholars, Who's Who in American Education, National Social Directory, Contemporary Authors, Who's Who in the Methodist Church, Who's Who in Religion, Creative and Successful Personalities of the World, International Biographical Association Yearbook and Biographical Directory 1974-80, International Authors and Writers Who's Who 1976-77, Five Hundred First Families of America, The Hereditary Register of the United States of America, The Royal Blue Book, International Who's Who in Community Service, The National Register of Prominent Americans and International Notables 1976-77, Community Leaders and Noteworthy Americans, International Register of Profiles North American Edition, The Writer's Directory 1974-76, Biographical Dictionary of Phonetic Sciences, International Scholars Directory 1972* (Strasbourg, France), *Lexicon De Comunicologia* (ed. Jorge Perello, Barcelona, Spain, 1977), *Two Thousand Men of Achievement, Who's Who in Chicago and Illinois 1950, Who's Who in America* (monthly supplement) 1946, *Directory of Educational Specialists 1972-73, Who's Who in America 1974-75, Regional Listings East, Men of Achievement 1974, Directory of International Biography* 1967, 1973-74, the *Biographical Roll of Honor.* Address: 4717 North Columbine Drive, Prescott Valley, Arizona 86312.■

JAMES ANTHONY MOSES, JR.

Clinical and Research Neuropsychologist. Personal: Born February 25, 1947; Son of James A. Sr. and Lucille M. Moses. Education: B.A. magna cum laude, San Francisco State University, 1968; M.S., San Jose State University, 1970; M.A. 1971, Ph.D. 1974, University of Colorado at Boulder. Career: Clinical and Research Neuropsychologist; School Psychologist, Group Counselor and Consultant, Campbell Union High School District. Organizational Memberships: American Psychological Association; Western Psychological Association; International Neuropsychological Society; National Academy of Neuropsychologists; Society for Personality Assessment; Stanford University Clinical Faculty Association. Community Activities: Islam Temple Shriners, Clown Unit 1969-75, Stanford University, Volunteer Member, Clinical Faculty 1975 to present, Chief Instructor of Self-Defense Class 1981 to present; Zen Budokai Self-Defense Academy, Uncompensated Instructor 1968 to present; Order of DeMolay, Past Master Councilor of Islam Chapter 1964-65, Member 1962-68. Honors and Awards: Outstanding Volunteer Service Award, Veterans Administration, 1974; Superior Performance Awards, Veterans Administration, 1978, 1980; Multiple Awards for Public Service, Order of DeMolay; Life Membership, California Scholarship Federation, 1964; Magna Cum Laude Graduate, San Francisco State University, 1968; Psi Chi National Psychology Honor Society, 1968; Karate Champion, Zen Budokai Society, 1968; George Hendry Memorial Scholarship, 1969-73; U.S.P.H.S. Intermediate Level Fellow in Clinical Psychology, 1970-71. Address: 177 Westlawn Avenue, Daly City, California 94015.■

MARY MILLER STERRETT MOSES

Retired Educator. Personal: Born November 19, 1906; Daughter of Harry and Lottie Sterrett (deceased); Married Elbert R. Moses Jr., Son of E. R. and Helen Martha Moses (deceased); Mother of James Elbert (deceased). Education: A.B. 1928, M.A. 1931, University of Pittsburgh; Further Graduate Study undertaken at the University of Michigan. Career: Teacher, Sewichley High School 1928-29, Greentree Public School 1929-30; Substitute Teacher, Pittsburgh Public School 1931-33; Research Analyst, Cryptanalytic War Department, 1942-46; Instructor in English, Ohio State University 1946, Eastern Illinois State University 1953-54 and 1955, Cebu American School (Philippines) 1955-56, Okemos High School (Okemos, Michigan) 1958-59; Speech Therapist, Clarion County Public Schools (Clarion, Pensylvania) 1959-61. Organizational Memberships: Quill Club, Secretary; Phi Alpha Theta, Beta Chapter President; Pi Lambda Theta. Community Activities: Clarion Woman's Club, President 1966-67; Daughters of the American Revolution, First Vice Regent (Clarion); Worthy Matron, Clarion Chapter, Order of the Eastern Star, 1973-74; Worthy High Priestess, White Shrine, Joppa Shrine, North Bethlehem, Pennsylvania, 1979-80; Appointed Grand Chapter Committee Member, Order of the Eastern Star, 1974-75; Supreme Instructor, White Shrine, Joppa Shrine, 1980-81. Religion: United Methodist. Honors and Awards: Martha Washington Medal, Sons of the American Revolution, 1981; Phi Alpha Theta; Pi Lambda Theta. Address: 4717 North Columbine Drive, Prescott Valley, Arizona 86312.■

RUTH MAE MOSLEY

Minister. Personal: Born March 10, 1930; Daughter of Les and Versie M. Newborn; Mother of William J., Richard, Pearl Scott. Education: A.A., 1982; Ordained Unity Minister, 1966; Church Management Consultant, 1977 to present. Career: Minister. Organizational Memberships: Association of Unity Churches, President 1981, Vice President 1980-81, Board of Trustees 1976-81, By-Laws Committee; Director and Founder, Association of Unity Churches Urban Ministrial School, 1979 to present. Community Activities: Chaplain, Rosa L. Grags Civic and Education Club, 1978 to present; Chairperson, City of Detroit Council

Damiani. Education: Bachelor's Degree in Education with Concentration in Psychology and History, University of Puerto Rico, Río Piedras Campus; Yoga Preparation and Training under instructors in Puerto Rico, Santo Domingo, Mexico, Venezuela, United States, Brazil, Japan, India, China. Career: Yoga Experience, 15 Years Practice and Service; Lecturer, Carnegie Library (San Juan, Puerto Rico), University of Puerto Rico (Río Piedras Campus), Catholic University (Ponce, Puerto Rico), Interamerican University (Hato Rey and Bayamón Campus), Seminary of Supervisors Project Head Start in Puerto Rico, Model City (Municipal Government of San Juan), Seminary of Elementary School Teachers of San Louis Rey Catholic College (San Juan), Organization of Civic Ladies of Puerto Rico, Seminary of Rural Teachers (San Juan), Labor Department Employees (San Juan), Chemists of Puerto Rico, Department of Agriculture, Seminary Rosa Bell College, Seminary Abelardo, Modeling Academy "Polyana" (San Juan), Association of Professional Esthetician and Beauty Counselor of Puerto Rico and the Caribbean Area (San Juan), Cultural Center (Santo Domingo); Karma Yoga Centers in Condado (Santurce), San Francisco (Río Piedras), Magnolia Bayamón, Villa Blanca Caguas. Organizational Memberships: International Yoga Teachers Association, Puerto Rico Representative; International Yoga Coordination Center, Puerto Rico Representative; International Yoga Fellowship, Affiliated Member. Published Works: *Karmic Discipline, Perfiles del Karma*; Recordings, "Relajación Dinámica" (LP), "Dinámica Relajación" (Cassette); Articles include "International Light" and "Yoga Awareness"; Columnist (2 Years) for *Angela Luisa* Magazine; Various Press Activities. Honors and Awards: Acknowledgement for International Work and Yogui Dedication by Yogui Bhajan, Swami Pranavananda, Swami Satyananda; Nominated as Yoguini Internationally Recognized; Acquired Power of Shakti by using a secret Mantra, 1982; Initiation as Yoguini with Tibetan Monks, 1982. Address: Siena 307 College Park, Puerto Rico 00921.■

EMIL M. MRAK

Chancellor Emeritus. Personal: Born October 27, 1901, in San Francisco, California; Married Vera Dudley Greaves, November 16, 1945; Father of Robert Emil, Antoinette Vera Hodapp. Education: B.S. 1926, M.S. 1928, Ph.D. 1936, University of California at Berkeley. Career: Research Assistant 1926-37, Instructor and Junior Mycologist (Agricultural Experimental Station) 1939-41, Assistant Professor and Associate Mycologist 1941-44, Associate Professor and Associate Mycologist 1945-48, Professor/Food Technologist/Department Chairman/Mycologist 1948-55, Professor/Food Technologist/Department Chairman 1955-59, Chancellor 1959-69, Chancellor Emeritus/Professor Emeritus/Food Technologist Emeritus 1969 to present, University of California at Davis; Food Technologist, Chairman of Committee on Food Research, War Department, Office of the Quarter Master General, 1944-45. Organizational Memberships: American Academy of Microbiology; Director-at-Large, California Aggie Alumni Association; Director, California Aggie Alumni Foundation; California State Advisory Board on Alcohol and Related Problems; Institute of Food Technologists; Past President, International Congress of Food and Science Technology; I.R.I. Research Institute, Trustee; Chairman, National Research Council, General Committee on DoD Program; Trustee Emeritus, Nestle Foundation; Chairman of the Board, Nutrition Foundation; Sacramento Safety Council; Society of American Microbiologists; Chairman, Board of Governors, The Refrigeration Research Foundation; Fellow, American Academy of Arts and Sciences; Society for Ecotoxicology and Environmental Safety; Alpha Gamma Rho; Alpha Zeta; Bohemian Club; Cosmos Club; Gamma Alpha Graduate Scientific Society; Phi Sigma; Phi Tau Sigma; Sigma Xi; Phi Kappa Phi. Honors and Awards: Honorary Fellow from the Institute of Food Science and Technology from the United Kingdom, 1983; Honorary LL.D., University of California at Davis, 1969; Honorary Ds.C., Michigan State University, 1970; Doctor Honoris Causa, Swiss Federal Institute of Technology, 1971; Nicholas Appert Medal 1957, Babcock-Hart Medal 1961, International Award 1963, Institute of Food Technologists; Underwood-Prescott Award, 1964; Tanner Lecturer, 1969; Diploma de Honor by the Association of Food Technologists Mexico, 1969; Outstanding Civilian Service Award, Department of the Army, 1969; Administration Building on University of California-Davis Campus Named Mrak Hall, 1969; Outstanding Alumnus of the Year, California Aggie Association, 1970; Fellow, Institute of Food Technologists, 1970; Distinguished Food Scientist of the Year, New York Section, Institute of Food Technologists, 1970; Honorary Fellow, Institute of Food Science and Technology of Great Britain, 1970; Honorary Life Member, California Agricultural Commissioners, 1971; California Canners League Hall of Fame, 1972; Distinguished Service Award, School of Medicine, University of California at Davis, 1972; Forty Niners Service Award, National Canners Association, 1973; Spencer Award, American Chemical Society, 1973; American Society of Quality Control Testimonial Award, 1973; Honorary Recognition for Communicative Skills, 1973; First Honorary Member, University of California at Davis Law Alumni Association, 1974; First Recipient, Philadelphia Society Section Award, Institute of Food Technologists, 1975; Honorary Member, Earl F. Wolfman, Jr., Surgical Society, 1976; Atwater Memorial Lecturer Award, U.S.D.A., 1976; Fellow, American Academy of Arts and Sciences, 1977; Alpha Gamma Rho Hall of Fame, 1980. Address: 602 Cordova Place, Davis, California 95616.■

MAKIO MURAYAMA

Research Biochemist. Personal: Married Sonoko Soga (deceased); Father of Gibbs Soga, Alice Myra. Education: A.B. 1938, M.A. 1940, University of California at Berkeley; Ph.D., University of Michigan, 1953. Career: Research Biochemist, National Institutes of Health, Bethesda, Maryland; Former Positions include Special Research Fellow to Cavendish Laboratory (Cambridge University, England), Research Fellow in Chemistry with Professor Linus Pauling (Caltech), Research Biochemist at Harper Hospital (Detroit, Michigan), Research Biochemist at Bellevue Hospital (New York City). Organizational Memberships: American Chemical Society; American Society of Biological Chemists; American Association for the Advancement of Science; Association of Clinical Chemists; Sigma Xi; New York Academy of Sciences. Community Activities: American Friends Service Committee, Chicago 1942-43, Detroit 1943-48, Pasadena 1954-56. Honors and Awards: Martin Luther King Jr. Medical Achievement Award, 1972; Award in Research, Association for Sickle Cell Anemia, New York, 1969; Nisei of the Biennium Honoree, Japanese American Citizens League (National Recognition Award), 1971-72. Address: 5010 Benton Avenue, Bethesda, Maryland 20814.■

HAZEL STEWARD MURDOCK

Retired Administrator. Personal: Born January 10, 1909; Daughter of Earl and Amanda (Simpson) Steward (both deceased); Married James H. Murdock (divorced); Mother of Jane Ann, Bonny Lou (Murdock) Thrower. Education: A.B., Culver-Stockton College, Canton, Missouri, 1929; A.M., University of Missouri, Columbia, 1938. Military: Served with the United States Navy WAVES, Lieutenant (j.g.), 1943-44. Career: Secretary to Administrator, Christian College, Columbia, Missouri, 1929-34; Secretary to Dean of Education 1934-43, Administrative Assistant to Vice President of Business Operations 1950-52, Administrative Assistant to Dean of School of Journalism 1952-78, University of Missouri, Columbia. Organizational Memberships: National Society of Published Poets. Community Activities: Columbia Business and Professional Women's Club, President 1942 and 1963; Member Boone County Mental Health Association Board, 1976-84; Volunteer, Harry S. Truman Veterans Hospital 1981-82, Volunteer in Corrections (Missouri Prisons) 1982 to present. Published Works: Contributor Articles to Professional Journals; Several Published Poems. Honors and Awards: First Prizes for One-Act Plays, University of Missouri-Columbia Writing Contests; Beta Beta Beta; Kappa Tau Alpha; Sigma Delta Chi. Address: 413 Hitt Street, Apartment 103, Columbia, Missouri 65201.■

ILDAURA MURILLO-ROHDE

Family Therapist, Educator. Personal: Daughter of Amalio and Ana Diaz de Murillo (deceased); Married Erling Rohde, Son of Erling and Esther White Rohde (both deceased). Education: B.S. 1951, M.A. 1953, M.Ed. 1961, Teachers College, Columbia University; Ph.D., New York University, 1971; Further Studies in Psychotherapy and Urban Sociology. Career: Professor and Dean, College of Nursing; Family Therapist, State University of New York, Brooklyn; Mental Health/Psychiatric Nurse, Associate Dean and Professor of Psychosocial Nursing, University of Washington, Seattle, 1976-82; Associate Professor and Psychiatric Coordinator, Hostos College, City University of New York, 1972-76; Assistant Professor and Director of Undergraduate Mental Health Integration Program, New York University, 1970-72; Associate Professor and Chairman, Department of Mental Health, Psychiatric Nursing Department, Graduate School of Nursing, New York Medical Center, 1964-69; Psychiatric Consultant, Guatemalan Government, 1963-64; Chief Psychiatric Nurse, Psychiatric Division, Metropolitan Hospital, New York City, 1961-63. Organizational Memberships: New York Association of Marriage and Family Therapy, President 1973-75; National Association of Hispanic Nurses, Founder and President 1976-80; American Nurses Association, Commissioner on Human Rights, Member Cabinet on Human Rights 1982-86; National Coalition on Hispanic Mental Health and Human Service Organization, Chairwoman Board of Directors 1976-82; American Orthopsychiatric

TWO THOUSAND NOTABLE AMERICANS

Association, Board of Directors 1976-79; National Advisory Committee, White House Conference on Families, 1979-81. Community Activities: King County Health Planning Council, Board of Directors 1977-79, Council President and Chairwoman of Board of Directors 1980-81; Board of Directors, Puget Sound H.S.A., 1979-81; Washington State Advisory Committee, United States Commission on Civil Rights, 1977-82; National Advisory Committee, White House Conference on Families, 1979-81; Held Hearings for United States Commission on Civil Rights on Administration of Justice for Women and Minorities in Washington State, 1979; Held Hearings to Investigate Health Care to Hispanics and Indians, Human Rights Commission, American Nurses Association, 1979; Selected to Participate in Washington State Conference on Children and Youth White House Conference, 1981; Dr. Ildaura Murillo-Rohde Scholarship Created by National Association of Hispanic Nurses for Outstanding Contribution and as Founder, 1980. Honors and Awards: Fellow, American Association of Marriage and Family Therapy; Fellow, American Academy of Nursing; Fellow, International Institute of Community Service; University Honors Scholar, New York University, 1972; Life Member, Sigma Theta Tau, Upsilon Chapter; Citizen of the Day, XIXI Radio Station, Seattle, May 10, 1979; Listed in *Who's Who of American Women, Outstanding Professionals in Human Services, World Who's Who of Women, National Register of Prominent Americans and International Notables, Notable Americans of the Bicentennial Era, Who's Who in Health Care, International Who's Who of Intellectuals, Personalities of America, Men and Women of Distinction.* Address: 300 West 108 Street, New York, New York 10025.■

KAREN JANE MURRAY

Author. Personal: Born March 19, 1928. Education: B.A., St. Olaf College (Northfield, Minnesota), 1949; Coursework Completed for Ph.D. in American Studies, University of Minnesota, 1952; M.S.W., University of Minnesota, 1959. Career: Author, Director, Downtown Mental Health Center, San Jose, California; Director, Children's Services, Santa Clara County, San Jose; Director, Psychiatric Social Workers, Santa Clara County, San Jose; Lecturer in Administration, Graduate School of Social Work, San Jose State University. Organizational Memberships: National Association of Social Workers, Chairman Santa Clara Chapter 1964-67, Delegate to Delegate Assembly 6 Years, National Committee on Inquiry 1975-81; Clinical Society of Social Workers, Charter Founder 1969. Community Activities: Mental Health Consultant to California State Legislature/Social Work, 1970; State of California Department of Mental Hygiene, Staffing Project 1971; Mental Health Task Force, State Committee Program Chief 1969; American Orthopsychiatric Association; Zonta Professional Women's Organization, Vice President 1969-70. Honors and Awards: Listed in *Who's Who of American Women, Who's Who in the Far West, Who's Who of World Women, Who's Who in the West and Midwest.* Address: Route 6 Box 447 H, Fairview, North Carolina 28730.■

SAM E. MURRELL, JR.

Attorney. Personal: Born September 28, 1927; Son of Sam E. Murrell; Married Mercerdees L.; Father of Joan M., Katherine Jean, Sarah Elizabeth, Sam E. III. Education: A.A. 1946, J.D. 1948, University of Florida. Military: Served in the United States Army, 1951-52, achieving the rank of First Lieutenant. Career: Attorney. Organizational Memberships: The Florida Bar Association; District of Columbia Bar Association; New York Bar Association; Pennsylvania Bar Association; Wisconsin Bar Association; American Bar Association; American Trial Lawyers Association; Association of Trial Lawyers of America; National Association of Criminal Defense Lawyers; Academy of Florida Trial Lawyers; Federal Bar Association; Inter-American Bar Association; National Lawyers Club; American Immigration Lawyers Association; American Arbitration Association; International Bar Association; Customs Bar Association; Federal Communications Bar Association; Association of Interstate Commerce Commission Practitioners. Community Activities: President, Orlando Rowing Association; New York Cotton Exchange; New York Mercantile Exchange; New York Futures Exchange; Citrus Associates of New York Cotton Exchange; New Orleans Commodity Exchange; Mid-America Commodity Exchange; Florida Farm Bureau; North Carolina Farm Bureau; Loyal Order of the Moose; Benevolent and Protective Order of the Elks; National Eagle Scout Association; Alpha Phi Omega. Religion: Presbyterian. Address: 3041 Westchester, Orlando, Florida 32803.■

MELVIN L. MYERS

Educator. Personal: Born October 3, 1976; Son of Mr. and Mrs. Hannibal Myers; Father of Kerry Y., Melvin Jr. Education: B.S., Prairie View A&M University, 1959; M.Ed., University of Arizona, 1971; M.S.Ed., Monmouth College, New Jersey, 1983. Military: Served with the United States Army as Lieutenant Colonel, 1959-79, Retired. Career: Educator. Organizational Memberships: Council for Exceptional Children, 1979 to present; Association for Supervision and Curriculum Development, 1979 to present; National Education Association, 1979-83; New Jersey Education Association, 1979-83. Community Activities: National Association for the Advancement of Colored People, 1979 to present; Disabled American Veterans, 1979 to present; Retired Officers Association, 1979 to present; Kiwanis Club, 1978-83. Religion: Protestant Youth of the Chapel, Fort Monmouth, New Jersey, 1971-81. Honors and Awards: Bronze Star Medal, 1968; Meritorious Service Medals, 1972, 1979; Certificate of Achievement with Medallion, 1976; *Personalities of the South, Who's Who in the East.* Address: 1042 Creekmont, Houston, Texas 77091.■

SAMUEL L. MYERS

President of Education Association. Personal: Born April 18, 1919, in Baltimore, Maryland; Married Marion Myers; Father of Samuel L. Jr., Yvette M. May, Tama M. Clark. Education: A.B. summa cum laude in Social Science, Morgan State College, 1940; M.A. Economics, Boston University, 1942; M.A. Economics 1948, Ph.D. Economics 1949, Harvard University; Postdoctoral Study, Ford Foundation Faculty Fellow, University of Pennsylvania, 1960; Foreign Service Institute, United States Department of State, 1966. Military: Served in World War II, 1942-46, receiving the Pacific Theatre Ribbon and attaining the rank of Captain, United States Army. Career: National Association for Equal Opportunity in Higher Education, Past Executive Director, President 1977 to present; President, Bowie State College, 1967-77; Advisor, Regional Integration and Trade, Bureau of Inter-American Affairs, United States Department of State, 1963-67; Associate Professor, Professor and Chairman of the Division of Social Services, Morgan State College, 1950-63; Economist, Bureau of Labor Statistics, United States Department of Labor, 1950; Research Associate, Harvard University, 1949. Organizational Memberships: American Association of State Colleges and Universities, Member Board of Directors 1976-77, Representative of National Advisory Council on International Teacher Exchange 1972-77, Chairman Committee on International Programs 1972-75; Task Force on International Study Centers, 1973; Maryland Association of Higher Education, President 1971-72; Middle States Association of Colleges and School, Commission on Higher Education 1976-77. Community Activities: Maryland Tax Commission, 1958; Governor's Commission on Prevailing Wage Law in Maryland, 1962; Morgan State College, Leadership Role in Establishing Morgan State College Graduate School, 1962; Council on Consumer Information, National President 1963; State Scholarship Board of Maryland, 1968-77; Governor's Commission to Study Aid to Non-Public Schools, Vice Chairman 1969-70; Maryland Committee for the Humanities and Public Policy, Vice Chairman 1974-76; Governor's Task Force on Desegregation of Higher Education, 1974; Committee on the Future Desegregation of Higher Education, 1974; Committee on the Future of International Studies, Steering Committee 1973; Technical Assistance Consortium for Improved College Services, Vice Chairman 1974-77; National Education Advisory Committee of Consumers Union, 1976 to present; Delegation of College and University Presidents to India 1971, People's Republic of China 1975, Republic of China 1976; Chairperson, Delegation to India 1972, Delegation of Presidents to Pakistan 1973, Delegation of Educators to Nigeria 1973. Honors and Awards: Alpha Kappa Mu Honor Society; Graduate Assistant, Boston University; Research Fellow, Harvard University; Rosenwald Fellow, Harvard University; Outstanding Citizen of the Year, Bowie, Maryland, 1974; Alumnus of the Year, Morgan State University, 1976; Citation for Outstanding Community Service for Writing Series of Booklets Distributed by the Urban League to Help Low-Income Groups, Baltimore Urban League, 1964; President Emeritus, Bowie State College, 1977. Address: 2243 Wisconsin Avenue, Northwest, Washington, D.C. 20007.■

GOVINDASAMI NAADIMUTHU

Professor, Chairman. Personal: Born August 9, 1947; Son of G. Govindasami; Married Amirtha Doraiswamy; Father of Revathi. Education: B.E., Madras University, 1968; D.I.I.T., Indian Institute of Technology, 1969; M.S. 1971, Ph.D 1974, Kansas State University. Career: Fairleigh Dickinson University, Industrial Engineering and Management Science, Chairman 1982 to present, Associate Professor 1978-83, Assistant Professor 1974-78; Assistant Professor, Industrial Engineering, California Polytechnic State University, San Luis Obispo, 1973-74. Organizational Memberships: Senior Member, American Institute of Industrial Engineers, 1980; Registered Professional Engineer, New Jersey, Pennsylvania. Community Activities: Unpaid Consultant to Many Past and Present Students on the Professional Problems of Various Industries and Business Concerns in Which They Work; Faculty Advisor for A.I.I.E., Fairleigh Dickinson University, Chapter #839; Faculty on the Courses on "Desalination", Saint Croix, United States Virgin Islands, July and December 1977, December 1978, October 1982 and Singer Island, Florida, August 1978; Faculty on Continuing Education Programs in Industrial Engineering, Bendix Corporation 1975 and GAF Corporation 1976. Published Works: Co-Author "Stochastic Modeling and Optimization of Water Resource Systems", " Nonmetameric Color Matching", "Stochastic Maximum Principle in the Optimal Control of Water Resource Systems", "Water Resources Modeling and Optimization Based on Conservation and Flooding Pools", "Differential Quadrature and Partial Differential Equations: Some Numerical Results", "Application of Invariant Imbedding to the Estimation of Process Duration", "Piecewise Suboptimal Control Laws for Differential Games." Honors and Awards: Phi Kappa Phi; Alpha Pi Mu; Tau Beta Pi; 4.0 Grade Point Average for Ph.D. and M.S. Degrees; Awarded Medal for First Rank in the Graduating Class of D.I.I.T.; Listed in *Who's Who in Education, Directory of World Researchers.* Address: 631 Colonial Boulevard, Washington Township, Westwood, New Jersey 07675.■

BARBARA LEIGH NACOL

Administrator. Personal: Born February 2, 1948; Daughter of E. B. Hunt. Education: B.A. 1973, M.Ed. 1975, Ph.D. 1982; University of Houston; Teacher Corps, 1973-75. Career: President and Executive Administrator, Hyperbaric Medical Center; Former Business Manager, Law Offices of Mae Nacol and Associates; Teacher, Houston Independent School District; Teacher Corps, Harris County, Texas. Organizational Memberships: Environmental Education Association, Charter Member; Under Sea Medical Society; American Judicature Society. Community Activities: Deputy Constable, Harris County, Texas; Certified Peace Officer, TECLOSE; HBO Medical Center of Houston, Executive Director. Honors and Awards: Outstanding Scholastic Achievement Award, Texas A&M University; Community Service Award, City of Houston. Address: 6012 Memorial Drive, Houston, Texas 77007.■

KENNETH MASUHISA NAGATA

Resource Associate, Botanist. Personal: Born June 26, 1945; Son of Mr. and Mrs. Kanao Nagata (deceased); Married Linda M., Daughter of Mr. and Mrs. Charles Yamada; Father of Stefanie M., Sarah M. Education: B.A. 1968, M.A. 1980, University of Hawaii at Manoa. Career: Research Associate, Botanist; Instructor of Botany, University of Hawaii at Manoa, 1972-74; Instructor of Botany, Chaminade University of Honolulu, 1977-78; Instructor of Botany, Kapiolani Community College, 1978, 1981; Instructor of Botany, Leeward Community College, 1984; Former Research Assistant. Organizational Memberships: Sigma Xi; Society for Economic Botany; Smithsonian Associates; Hawaiian Botanical Society; Texas Academy of Science; Bernice P. Bishop Museum, Field Botanist 1978 to present. Community Activities: Botanist, State Animal Species Advisory Committee, 1979 to present; Judge, Senior Research Division, Hawaiian Science and Engineering Fair, 1982; Chairman, Outings Committee, Sierra Club, Hawaii Chapter 1974-76, Vice Chairman Executive Committee 1980-81, Secretary 1981-82. Honors and Awards: Hamilton Library Prize in Pacific Islands Research, 1980. Address: 1655 Makaloa Street, Honolulu, Hawaii 96814.■

JAMES ALLEN NALL, SR.

Professor of Mathematics. Personal: Born August 14, 1917; Father of James A. Jr., Joy Adronie. Education: B.S., Alabama State College, 1947; M.A., Columbia University, 1952; Studies in Mathematics, University of California-Los Angeles, 1958, 1962, New Mexico State University 1964, 1965, 1966, University of Florida, Gainesville; Graduate Studies toward Ph.D. in Mathematics Education. Military: Served in the United States Army, 1943-46, attaining the rank of Technician 4th Grade. Career: Professor of Mathematics, Central Florida Community College; Dean of the College, Hampton Junior College, Ocala, Florida; Instructor in Mathematics and Science, Stevenson Junior High School, Los Angeles, 1958-60; Mathematics Instructor, Parker High School, Birmingham, Alabama, 1952-57; Coordinator of Guidance for all Ninth Grade Faculty, Mathematics Instructor and Assistant Principal, Training School, Jasper, Alabama. Organizational Memberships: Alpha Kappa Mu, Charter Member Alabama State College, 1947; Phi Delta Kappa; National Council of Teachers of Mathematics. Community Activities: Community Development Block Grant Citizen Advisory Committee, 1978. Religion: Charter Member, Secretary of the Board of Directors, Twenty-Seventh Avenue Church of Christ, Inc., Ocala, 1979 to present. Honors and Awards: World War II Victory Medal; Bronze Star; Three Battle Stars; Listed in *Who's Who in American Education, International Who's Who in Education, Who's Who of Intellectuals* (Volume 5, 1983, International Biographical Centre, Cambridge, England). Address: P.O. Box 1047, Ocala, Florida 32678.■

BAHRAM NAMDARI

Physician. Personal: Born October 26, 1939; Son of Rostam and Sarvaar (Bondarian) Namdari; Married Kathleen Wilmore; Father of Three Children. Education: M.D., 1966; Resident General Surgery, Saint John's Mercy Medical Center, 1969-73; Fellowship Cardiovascular Surgery, Baylor College of Medicine, 1974; Certified by and Diplomate of American Board of Surgery. Career: Physician in Private Practice in General and Vascular Surgery and Surgical Treatment of Morbid Obesity; Staff Member at Saint Mary's Hospital, Saint Luke's Hospital, Saint Michael Hospital, Mount Sinai Hospital, Good Samaritan Hospital, Trinity Memorial Hospital, Saint Anthony Hospital, Family Hospital, Saint Francis Hospital; Frequent Lecturer; Presented a Continuing Medical Education Program About Obesity and Its Related Operations, Saint Luke's Hospital, 1983. Organizational Memberships: Medical Society of Milwaukee County; Milwaukee Academy of Surgery; Wisconsin Medical Society; Wisconsin Surgical Society; Affiliate Member, Royal Society of Medicine of England; American Medical Association; World Medical Association; Michael DeBakey International Cardiovascular Society; Fellow, American College of Surgeons; Fellow, International College of Surgeons. Published Works: Author of Articles "Untoward Effects: Vagotomy or Drainage Procedures," *Missouri Medicine* 1973; Presented Paper "Morbid Obesity and Its Related Operations, Pros and Cons" to Milwaukee Academy of Surgery and Wisconsin Surgical Society, 1982. Honors and Awards: Award for Invention of Opthalmologic Device, Physics Department of Faculty of Medicine; Award for Best Thesis, Medical School, 1966; Award for Published Research on New Method of Pylorplasty, Saint John's Mercy Medical Center; Research Grant for Invention of Electronic Medical Equipment; 3 Patents Received in 1984, Other Patents Pending. Address: 2315 North Lake Drive, Milwaukee, Wisconsin 53211.■

TWO THOUSAND NOTABLE AMERICANS

ANNA LOUISE NAPPER

Avon District Manager. Personal: Born April 22, 1937; Married Robert F.; Mother of Robert F. III, Catherine E. Education: Attended Cheyney State Teacher's College, 1955-59; Additional Studies. Career: Playground Instructor, Day Camp Director, City of Harrisburg, 1956-62; Group Worker, Methodist Center, 1962-66; Second Grade Instructor, Holy Family School, Harrisburg, 1966-67; Activities Representative for Halfway House, 1967-68; Director of Day Care, 1968-74. Community Activities: Uptown Civic Association, 1962-66; Program and Social Chairman, Lincoln Elementary P.T.A., 1962-63; Lancaster Area Association for Education of Young Children, 1969-73; Others. Religion: Episcopalian. Honors and Awards: Certificate in Child Care, Harrisburg Area Community College, 1972; Helped Form Harrisburg Area Association for Education of Young Children, 1974; Volunteer Award, Avon, 1979-80; Others. Address: 1734 Evergreen Road, Harrisburg, Pennsylvania 17109.■

FERNANDO M. NARCIANDI

Executive. Personal: Born May 30, 1947; Son of Mateo Narciandi; Married Consuelo; Father of Eric. Education: A.A. Accounting; B.S. Management/Finance. Military: Served in the United States Marine Corps, attaining the rank of Sergeant. Career: President, Fiesta Enterprises, Inc.; Former Positions Include President, YMC Corporation, California; Credit and Collection Manager, Penn General Agencies of California; Penn Life Corporation, General Manager and Controller, Employee Benefits Consultant, Internal Audit Manager. Organizational Memberships: Institute of Internal Auditors; Credit Managers Association; American Management Association. Community Activities: Republican Party; Zoological Society of Florida; Disabled American Veterans. Religion: Member of Catholic Church. Honors and Awards: Awarded Purple Heart. Address: 14803 Southwest 140 Court, Miami, Florida 33186.■

JOHN JOSEPH NATALINI

Professor. Personal: Born April 27, 1944; Son of Edward and Anna Natalini. Education: B.S. Biology, Villanova University, 1966; M.S. and Ph.D. Biology, Northwestern University, 1971; Continuing Education, University of Missouri-Columbia, Southern Illinois University School of Medicine. Career: College Professor, Chairperson of Biology Department, Quincy College. Organizational Memberships: American Association for the Advancement of Science; Sigma Xi; Danforth Associate; A.I.B.S.; Illinois State Academy of Science; International Academy of Science; International Academy of Chronobiology; National Science Teachers Association; Society of College Science Teachers; Association of Midwest Biology Teachers; National Association of Biology Teachers. Community Activities: Central Illinois Health Planning Committee, 1975-76; Director, Quinsippi Science Fair for High School Science Projects, 1976-77; Judge for Many High School Science Fairs; Organizer, Adams County Health Fair. Religion: Lector and Usher at Quincy College Chapel. Honors and Awards: Grants, Quincy College Faculty Development, 1975, 1978-81; Huck Award, 1976; Listed in *American Men and Women of Science, American Names and Faces, International Who's Who in Education, Who's Who in the Midwest, Outstanding Young Men of America, Who's Who in Technology Today, Personalities of America.* Address: 1860 Chestnut, Quincy, Illinois 62301.■

JOSE P. NAZARENO

Pathologist. Personal: Born November 29, 1925, in Naic, Cavite, Philippines; Son of Maximino Nazareno Sr.; Married Charlene Boardman; Father of Christopher. Education: A.A., National University, 1948; M.D., Manila Central University, Manila, Philippines, 1953; Intern, Mt. St. Mary Hospital, Niagara Falls, New York, 1954-55; House Staff, Our Lady of Lourdes Hospital, Binghamton, New York, 1955-56; Pathology Residency, Kilmer Memorial Laboratory, Binghamton General Hospital 1956-57, Roswell Park Memorial Institute, Buffalo 1957-59, Deaconess Hospital, Buffalo 1959-60. Career: Assistant Pathologist, Kilmer Memorial Laboratory, 1964-69; Director of Laboratories, Binghamton Psychiatric Center, 1969 to present; Owner, Director, Southern Tier Medical Laboratory, Inc., 1969-83; Acupuncturist, 240 Riverside Drive, Johnson City, New York, 1979 to present. Organizational Memberships: Certified in Pathology (AP), 1963; Pan American Medical Association, Diplomate in Pathology; New York State Office of Mental Hygiene Medical Staff President Organization, 1982 to present; Charter President, Southern Tier Chapter of Organization of New York State Management/Confidential Employees, Inc., 1983-84; Association of Fil-American Pathologists, President Board of Directors 1969-71, 1977-79, Secretary-Treasurer 1979-80; Association of Philippine Practicing Physicians in America, Board of Governors 1972, Life Member; Medical-Dental Staff, Binghamton Psychiatric Center, President 1980-84; Pan American Medical Association, Diplomate; College of American Pathologists, Fellow; American Society of Clinical Pathologists, Fellow; New York State Society of Pathologists; Private Practitioners of Pathology Foundation, Inc.; Broome County Medical Society; American Medical Association; New York State Society of Acupuncture for Physicians and Dentists; Occidental Institute of Chinese Studies Alumni Association, Supporting Member. Community Activities: Manila Central University Alumni Association of the United States and Canada, First President 1976-77, President-elect 1983-84; American Civic Association, Binghamton, New York, Board of Governors and Treasurer 1962-70; Honorary Advisor, Cavite Association, U.S.A., 1980-86; International Platform Association, Inducted 1982. Published Works: "Lipoma of the Pleura," "The Cholangiogram: Postmortem Study," "Pathology of Acute Salt Poisoning in Infants." Honors and Awards: American Medical Association Physician Recognition Award; Pathology Continuing Medical Education Award; Plaque of Honor, Manila Central University Medical Alumni Association, Philippines, 1978; Award for Devoted Service, American Civic Association, 1970; Founding Father Award, Association of Philippine Practicing Physicians in America, 1979; Award for Most Outstanding Filipino Professional in America, Pathology and Acupuncture, United Filipino American Lawyer's Association in America, 1982; Listed in *Community Leaders and Noteworthy Americans, Men of Achievement, Who's Who in the East, Book of Honor, Directory of Medical Specialists.* Address: 240 Riverside Drive, Johnson City, New York 13790.■

RALPH ARNOLD NEEPER

Computer Specialist. Personal: Born September 29, 1940; Son of Mrs. Guy E. Neeper; Married Nancy Diane Smith; Father of Rachel, Claudine, Jennifer Alice. Education: B.S. Psychology/Sociology, Purdue University, 1963; Student of Mathematics, University of Toledo, 1963-68; Student of Photogrammetry, Southern Illinois University, 1968-69; M.S. Photogrammetry, Purdue University, 1972. Career: Computer Specialist, Pentagon; Former Positions Include Surveyor; Mathematics Instructor; Mail Carrier; Cartographer; Mathematician. Organizational Memberships: American Society for Photogrammetry; American Congress on Surveying and Mapping; Mathematical Association of America; American Mathematical Society; Association of Computing Machines; American Defense Preparation Association; Air Force Association; American Library Association; American Association for the Advancement of Science. Community Activities: Volunteer Emergency Foster Care, Board Member 1983; Prince William County Mass Transportation Committee, 1983-84; Conductor of Commuter Bus, 1983-84; Keyworker, Combined Federal Campaign; Six Gallon Blood Donor, American Red Cross; Volunteer, American Heart Association, 1982-84; Notary Public for Commonwealth of Virginia, 1983-86. Religion: Gideon's Int., 1975 to present; Holy Trinity Lutheran Church of Saint Louis, Member 1968-77, Council 1975-77; Epiphany Lutheran Church of Dale City (Virginia), Member 1977 to present, Council Secretary 1981; Lorton Liturgical Committee, 1978-82; Prince William County Cooperative Council of Ministries, Member 1983 to present, Treasurer 1984. Honors and Awards: Dean's List; Pi Mu Epsilon; M.E.N.S.A., 1964; Listed in *Who's Who in the Midwest, Who's Who in the South and Southwest, International Who's Who in Community Service, Community Leaders of America, Community Leaders of the World, Anglo-American Who's Who, Personalities of America, Personalities of the West and Midwest, Personalities of the South, Who's Who in Aviation and Aerospace, Who's Who in Computers and Data Processing, Dictionary of International Biography, Men of Achievement, International Who's Who of Intellectuals.* Address: 13530 Delaney Road, Woodbridge, Virginia 22193.■

KALO EDWARD NEIDEERT

Professor. Personal: Born September 1, 1918; Son of Edward R. and Margaret Kinsey (deceased) Neidert; Married Stella Vest; Father of Edward, Karl, David, Wayne, Margaret. Education: B.S. 1949, M.S. 1950 Business Administration, Washington University; Post Graduate Studies University of Minnesota, 1950-

54. Career: Accounting Professor, University of Nevada; Former Positions Include Instructor, University of Minnesota; Assistant Professor, University of Mississippi; Assistant Professor, University of Texas; Assistant Professor, Gustavus Adolphus College. Organizational Memberships: American Institute of Certified Public Accountants; Nevada Society of Certified Public Accountants; American Accounting Association; Financial Management Association; American Finance Association; Western Finance Association; American Economics Association. Community Activities: Board of Directors and Treasurer, Tahoe Timber Trails Association, 1980 to present; Washoe State Employees Federal Credit Union, Auditor 1969-82, Board of Directors and Treasurer 1982 to present; Assistant Scoutmaster, Troop 10, Boy Scouts of America, 1972 to present. Religion: Member of Saint John's Presbyterian Church, Elder 1974 to present, Board of Directors Child Care Center 1982 to present; District Skipper, Presbyterian Mariners, 1978-80. Honors and Awards: B.S. Business Administration Received With Honors, 1949; Boy Scouts of America, Scouters Key 1972, District Award of Merit 1976. Address: 2300 Balsam Street, Reno, Nevada 89509.■

LARRY DEAN NELSON

Executive. Personal: Born August 5, 1937; Son of Mr. and Mrs. C. Aaron Nelson; Married Linda Hawkins. Education: B.A. Mathematics, Physics, Phillips University, 1959; M.S. Mathematics, Kansas State University, 1962; Ph.D. Mathematics (Computer Science), Ohio State University, 1965. Career: Battelle Memorial Institute and Ohio State Research Foundation, 1962-65; Supervisor, M.T.S., Mathematics, and M.I.S., Bellcomm, Inc., 1975-72; Supervisor, Management Information Systems, Bell Telephone Laboratories, 1972-77; Supervisor, Rate and Tariff, Division of Americn Telephone and Telegraph Company, 1977-79; Deputy Administrator, Research and Special Programs Administration, United States Department of Transportation, 1979-81; President, MCS, Inc., 1981 to present. Organizational Memberships: Institute of Electrical and Electronic Engineering, Secretary 1982-83; Systems, Man and Cybernetics Society, Vice President 1982-84; Computer Society; A.C.M.; American Mathematical Society; New York Academy of Sciences; Mathematical Programming Society; Sigma Xi. Community Activities: Research and Special Programs Administration of the United States Department of Transportation, Deputy Administrator 1979-81; Management Committee of the United States Transportation Test Center, 1979-81; American Delegation, Fifth Meeting of the U.S.-U.S.S.R. Joint Committee on Cooperation in the Field of Transportation and Head of American Delegation Working Group, Fifth Meeting of the United States-Soviet Working Group on "Transport of the Future," Moscow, U.S.S.R., June 1979; Odd Jobs Club, Organizer and Sponsor 1967-72. Religion: Member National Executive Committee, Interdenominational Ecumenical Movement, 1961-62. Published Works: Several Articles in the Computer and Applied Mathematics Field. Honors and Awards: Sigma Xi; Phi Kappa Phi; Pi Mu Epsilon; Apollo Achievement Award, 1973; I.E.E.E. Washington Section Certificates of Appreciation, 1969 and 1971; Listed in *Outstanding Young Men of America*. Address: 440 New Jersey Avenue, Southeast, Washington, D.C. 20003.■

RALPH E. NELSON

Executive. Personal: Born July 30, 1946; Son of Vernon and Astrid Nelson; Married Elarie M.; Father of Anne Marie. Education: B.S. Industrial Arts, McPherson College, 1971; M.B.A., Business Administration in Enterprise Management, University of Sarasota, 1980; M.F.M. Master of Financial Management in Financial Planning, University of Sarasota, 1981; Master of Human Services, The University of Sarasota, 1983; Ph.D. Financial Planning and Management, Columbia Pacific University, 1984; Registered Landscape Architect, State of Florida; Certified in Civil Engineering Technology, 1976. Career: President, R.E. Nelson and Associates, Planners, Architects, Landscape Architects and Engineers and Surveyors, Inc., 1978 to present; Vice President and Director of Planning, Dan Zoller Engineering, Inc., Engineers and Planners, 1976-78; Department Supervisor in Planning, Roberts and Zoller Inc., 1971 to 1976; Earlier Positions with Brethren Architectural Service and D.H. Lessig, Engineers. Organizational Memberships: Full Member, American Society of Landscape Architects; I.C.E.T.; American Planning Association (formerly American Institute of Planners), Associate Member, Member American Society Officals; Florida Planning and Zoning Association, Charter Member, President of Gulf Coast Chapter 1980-81, First Vice President of Gulf Coast Chapter 1979-80, Director of Gulf Coast Chapter 1978-79; Metropolitan Association of Urban Designers and Environmental Planners. Religion: Member of Southern Baptist Church. Honors and Awards: Listed in *Who's Who in the South and Southwest, Personalities of America, Personalities of the South, Dictionary of International Biography, Men of Achievement, International Register of Profiles, Men and Women of Distinction, Community Leaders of America, International Who's Who of Intellectuals, American Registry Series, Book of Honor, Directory of Distinguished Americans, International Who's Who in Community Service, International Who's Who in Engineering*. Address: P.O. Box 11255, Bradenton, Florida 33507.■

PHYLLIS SCHNEIDER NESBIT

District Judge. Personal: Born September 21, 1919; Daughter of Vernon and Irma Mae Schneider (deceased); Married Peter Nicholas Nesbit. Education: B.S. Chemistry 1948, B.S. Law 1958, Juris Doctor 1969, University of Alabama; American Judicial Academy, Certificates 1970 and 1972. Career: District Judge, Baldwin County, Alabama; Lawyer, 1958-76; Municipal Judge, 1964-76; City Attorney, 1975-76. Organizational Memberships: Phi Delta Delta; American Judicature Society; Alabama District Judges Association; Treasurer, Alabama Council Juvenile Court Judges, 1978-81; President, Alabama Municipal Judges Association, 1970-73; President, Alabama Women Lawyers Association, 1966-67; National Association of Women Lawyers; National Association of Women Judges; President, Bald County Bar Association, 1967-68. Community Activities: Vice President Women's Affairs, South Alabama Chapter National Safety Council, 1978-83; Baldwin Youth Services; President, Spanish Fort Business and Professional Women's Club, 1974-75; Secretary, Baldwin County Mental Health/Mental Retardation, 1972-74; Joint Legislative Council of Alabama, Treasurer 1972-73; Auditor 1971-72. Religion: Secretary-Treasurer Eastern Shore Wesley Bible Church, 1964 to present. Honors and Awards: Club and District I of Alabama Federation of Business and Professional Womens' Clubs, Women of Achievement Award 1978, State Runner-up 1979. Address: 302 Creek Drive, Fairhope, Alabama 36532.■

VERA C. NESMITH

Administrative and Medical Secretary. Personal: Born October 24, 1917; Daughter of Ernest H. and Edith E. Cox (both deceased); Married J. Vernon (now deceased); Mother of Patricia E., James E. and John S. (stepsons). Education: Graduate, Orlando, Florida Senior High School, 1936; Diploma, Orlando Secretarial School, 1937; Attended Orlando Junior College; Undertook Courses sponsored by the University of Tennessee, Florida State University; Attended Courses sponsored by the American Association of Medical Assistants. Career: Secretary, Department of Health and Rehabilitatvie Services, Orlando, Florida, 1976-80; Secretary, Vocational Rehabilitation, Orlando, 1938-76; Instructor and Secretary, Orlando Secretarial School, 1937-38; Retired, 1980; Currently Working Part-time with Kelly Services in Winter Park and Orlando; Instructor for Training Session at St. Petersburg, Florida, under Direction of University of Tennessee for Special Course, 1978; Former Lecturer to Secretarial Groups in Department of Health and Rehabilitative Services through Training Section. Organizational Memberships: American Medical Association of Medical Assistants, Secretary-Treasurer, Program Chairman for National Convention; Florida State Society of American Association of Medical Assistants, President, President-Elect, Parliamentarian, Membership Chairman, Board Member, Convention Chairman; Orange County Chapter of American Association of Medical Assistants, President 2 Terms, Parliamentarian, Chaplain; National Registry of Medical Secretaries, President 1958-59; National Association of Rehabilitation Secretaries, Member and Committee Member 1974-80; Southeastern Regional Association of Rehabilitation Secretaries, Chairman and Committee Member 1974-80, Wrote Handbook and 5-Year History; Orlando Association of Rehabilitation Secretaries, Charter Member, Parliamentarian and Committee Member 1974-80; Florida Association of Rehabilitation Secretaries, Charter Member, President-Elect, Parliamentarian, President, Installing Officer; Orange County Chapter Florida Rehabilitation Association, Charter Member. Community Activities: Life Fellow, American Biographical Institute; Participated in American Cancer Society Research Study, 1966-81; Participant in Projects to Aid Cancer Society, Tumor Clinic, Orange County Convalescent Home, Various Nursing Homes and Hospitals, 1960 to present; Fund Raiser for Cerebral Palsy, Heart Fund, Muscular Dystrophy; United Appeal Chairman, 1950-60; Collected and Packaged Artificial Limbs, Braces and Orthopedic Appliances for Overseas Handicapped, 1950-60; Chairman of Blood Bank Account for Vocational Rehabilitation, 1938-76. Religion: Member of Broadway United Methodist Church, Kindergarten Sunday School Teacher 1932-62, Choir Member 1932 to present, Member of Administrative Board and Council on Ministries 1970-80, Chairman of Evangelism Commission 1976-80, Leader and Member of Sonshiners Circle 1979 to present, Member of Women's Society 1979-82, Chairman of Publicity Committee for Women's Society 1980 and 1981, Member of Adult Friendship Sunday School Class 1962 to present, Staff/Pastor/Parish Committee Member 1982 and Chairman 1984, Member Missions

Committee. Published Works: Wrote Handbooks for Florida Association of Rehabilitation Secretaries, Florida State Society A.A.M.A., Orange County Chapter A.A.M.A. Honors and Awards: Citation, Florida Rehabilitation Association; Outstanding Member of the Year, Orange County Chapter of A.A.M.A, 1965; Medical Assistant of the Year, Florida State Society A.A.M.A., 1965; Plaque from State of Florida Vocational Rehabilitation Services for 35 Years of Service, 1973; Secretary of the Year, Florida Association of Rehabilitation Secretaries, 1976; Life Member, Orange County A.A.M.A. (first such award given); Plaque for Outstanding Service at State Convention, Florida State Society A.A.M.A., 1980; Member of International Biographical Association, Cambridge, England; Plaque for Outstanding Service, Florida Association of Rehabilitation Secretaries, 1977; Secretary of the Week, Orlando, Florida, 1974; Engraved Silver Bowl, Department of Health and Rehabilitative Services, 1978; Listed in *Who's Who of American Women, Who's Who in the South and Southwest, Dictionary of International Biography, Commmunity Leaders and Noteworthy Americans, Personalities of the South, Social Registry, World Who's Who of Women, Book of Honor, American Patriots of the 1980's, International Register of Profiles, The Directory of Distinguished Americans.* Address: 1912 Weber Street, Orlando, Florida 32803.■

HOWARD L. NESS

Professor. Personal: Born April 6, 1920; Married Joyce M.; Father of Carole S. Klein, Beverly J. Parke, Howard L. Jr., Kathryn J.. Education: B.B.A., University of Toledo, 1942; M.B.A., Northwestern University, 1946; J.D., University of Toledo, 1949. Military: Served in the United States Naval Reserves, 1942-44, attaining rank of Ensign. Career: Professor of Accounting, Arizona State University, College of Business Administration, 1949-50; Practicing Attorney, 1950-52; General Counsel, Martin Brother Box Company, 1952-54; Professor, Accounting Department, University of Toledo College of Business Administration, 1946-49 and 1954 to present. Organizational Memberships: Taxation Committee, Toledo Bar Association; Ohio Bar Association; Adjunct Closely-Held Corporations, American Bar Association; Continuing Professsional Education Committee Toledo Chapter, Ohio Society of Certified Public Accountants; Beta Alpha Psi; Beta Gamma Sigma; Phi Kappa Phi. Community Activities: President, University of Toledo Alumni Association, 1961. Religion: Member of Hope Lutheran Church, Immediate Past Financial Secretary; Board of Directors, Toledo Campus Ministry. Published Works: Editor and Writer for "The Employees Income Tax Guide" 1954 to present, "You and Your Congress" 1977 and l979, "Social Security" 1960; Revising Editor, "Merten's Law of Federal Income Taxation" 1958. Honors and Awards: A.I.C.A.P. Elijah Watts Sells Award; Listed in *International Who's Who in Education.* Address: 2365 Goddard Road, Toledo, Ohio 43606.■

JANET ELIZABETH NETHERCOTT

Author, Dramatist, Lecturer, Nursing Service Owner-Operator, Corporate Executive. Personal: Born July 27, 1919; Married John S. Education: Graduate, Traverse City High School, Traverse City, Michigan; Attended Ferris (State) Institute, Big Rapids, Michigan; Chicago School of Interior Decoration, Chicago, Illinois. Career: Author; Dramatist; Lecturer; Owner-Operator, Nethercott Nursing Service; President, Nethercott Ministries, Inc.; Owner, Nethercott Institute, Winter Haven, Florida; Co-Owner, Traverse City Paper Company, Traverse City, Michigan; Instructor, Polk Vocational Technical Center. Organizational Memberships: Life Member, Gideons International Auxiliary, State President Michigan Gideon Auxiliary, State Chaplain Michigan Gideon Auxiliary; American Society of Women Accountants; International Biographical Centre; Professional Member, National Writers Club; American Business Women's Association. Community Activities: President, Nethercott Ministries, Inc. (serves entirely gratis); Donates all Remuneration from her Writings to Help Those in Need regardless of Race of Color and without Discrimination; Provides through Nethercott Ministries Spanish Testaments for Migrants, Scholarships in Christian Education, Support Missionaries; Circulates Christian Literature to Help Needy and Discouraged; Holds Spiritual Retreats and Weekly Prayer Meetings for Public. Religion: Past State President, Auxiliary of Gideons International, Past State Chaplain; President Nethercott Ministries, Inc. (charitable, religious non-profit organization). Published Works: Author, "Christmas 365 Days a Year," "The Unexpected Bridegroom," "Poems from the Heart," "Two Loves." Honors and Awards: Certificate of Recognition in Honor, Florida State of the Arts; Wrote and Dedicated a Poem to Mr. Richard D. Pope, Founder of Cypress Gardens; Wrote and Dedicated a Poem to Dr. and Mrs. Vincent Peale; Wrote and Dramatized Skit, "The First Thanksgiving," to 1000 Persons at Foundation for Christian Living Thanksgiving Reunion in Bermuda. Address: 2411 Cypress Gardens Boulevard, Winter Haven, Florida 33880.■

JOHN L. NEUMEYER

Professor. Personal: Born July 19, 1930; Married Evelyn Friedman; Father of Ann Martha, David A., Elizabeth J. Education: Graduate of Bronx High School of Science, 1948; B.S., Columbia University, 1952; Ph.D., University of Wisconsin, 1961. Military: Served in the United States Army, 1953-55, attaining the rank of Corporal. Career: Professor of Chemistry and Medicinal Chemistry, Northeastern University; Chemist. Organizational Memberships: Chairman Medicinal Chemistry Division, American Chemical Society, 1982-83; Sigma Xi; Rho Chi; American Pharmaceutical Association; Chairman Medicinal Chemistry Group Northeastern Section, American Chemical Society, 1966; President Northeastern University Chapter, Phi Kappa Phi, 1979-80; American Association for the Advancement of Science. Community Activities: Chairman, Wayland Massachusetts Board of Health, 1969-75; Massachusetts Pesticides Committee, 1980 to present. Honors and Awards: Pfeiffer Scholarship, American Foundation for Pharmaceutical Education Fellowship; N.I.H. Predoctoral Fellowship; First Prize, Lunsford Richardson Award, 1961; Fellow, Academy of Pharmaceutical Sciences, 1975; Gustavus A. Pfeiffer Memorial Research Fellowship, 1975; Senior Hays-Fulbright Fellow, 1975-76; Faculty Lecturer, Northeastern University, 1978; Distinguished University Professor, 1980 to present; Research Achievement Award in Pharmaceutical/Medicinal Chemistry, Academy Pharmaceutical Sciences American Pharmaceutical Association, 1982; Fellow, American Association for the Advancement of Science, 1984. Address: 1 Holiday Road, Wayland, Massachusetts 01778.■

ROY NORMAN NEVANS

Executive. Personal: Born July 1, 1931; Son of Lillian Margolis; Married Virginia Place; Father of Lisa Ann, Laurel Sue, Judy Lynn. Education: B.S., University of Pennsylvania, 1953; M.B.A., Columbia University, 1957. Military: Served in the United States Navy, 1953-56 (Active Duty) and 1956-73 (Active Reserve Duty). Career: International Marketing Executive; Former Positions include Producer of Theatre, Television and Films. Organizational Memberships: National Academy of Television Arts and Sciences; British Film Institute. Community Activities: World Trade Club, Vice President, Director; International Trade Development Committee; Council for United States-China Trade. Address: 19 Sunnyridge Road, Harrison, New York 10528.■

JOHN MELVIN NEWBY

College President. Personal: Born January 31, 1928; Son of James Edwin and Mary Augusta Williams Newby (both deceased); Married Rebecca Jean Hall; Father of Sharon Jean Page, Karen Jane White, Becky Lynette Holton, John Melvin Jr. Education: Diploma, Union Bible Seminary, 1948; Marion College, 1950; A.B., La Verne College, 1952; M.S., University of Southern California, 1958; Ph.D., Michigan State University, 1972. Career: President, Central Wesleyan College, Central, South Carolina, 1979 to present; Formerly Vice President for Administrative Affairs, Acting Dean of Academic Affairs, Director of Research and Planning, Registrar, Spring Arbor College, Spring Arbor, Michigan; Director of Business Affairs, Registrar and Instructor, Owosso College, Owosso, Michigan. Organizational Memberships: American Association for Affirmative Action; Association for Institutional Research; American Association for Higher Education; Student Attrition Task Force and Student Learning Outcomes Task Force, Research and Management Projects, Chairman; Undergraduate Assessment Program; Council Educational Testing Service; Small College Consulting Network; North Central Association, Evaluator. Community Activities: Owosso Library Board, Secretary; Owosso and Jackson, Michigan, and Clemson, South Carolina Rotary Clubs, Board of Directors; Jackson Rotary Club, General Program Chairman; JHL Areawide Comprehensive Health Planning Association, Council Member; Michigan Heart Association, Board Member, Swim for Heart Fund-Raising Project Chairman. Religion: Ordained Minister of Pilgrim Holiness Church, 1951; Minister, Pilgrim Holiness Church, San Dimas and Pasadena, California, 1950-59; Instructor of Music, Upland California College, 1951-52; Manager of Schools, Pilgrim Holiness College, Zambia, Africa, 1959-63; Acting Field Supervisor and Educational Secretary, 1963-64; 1970-79, Ordained Elder of the Free Methodist Church; Currently, Ordained Elder of The Wesleyan Church, 1979. Honors and Awards: Phi Kappa Phi; Phi Delta Kappa; Listed in *Who's Who in the Midwest, Who's Who in America, Personalities of the South, American Registry Series, Men of Achievement,* Publications of the International Biographical Center and the American Biographical Institute. Address: Box 408, Central Wesleyan College, Central, South Carolina 29630.■

ANNETTE GOERLICH NEWMAN

Shopping Center Manager, CSM, Real Estate Developer, Registered Pharmacist. Personal: Born January 19, 1940; Daughter of David August and Mary

Eloise Simpson Goerlich; Mother of Anne Kristen, Mark David, Gregory Hartley. Education: Doctor of Pharmacy, University of California School of Pharmacy, San Francisco, 1963. Career: Pharmacist, Village Drug, 1963-69; Pharmaceutical Consultant, 1962-72; Store Manager, The Drug Store of Fig Garden Village, 1972-77; Manager, Fig Garden Village Shopping Center, Fresno, 1977 to present. Organizational Memberships: Fig Garden Village Merchants Association, Board of Directors; R. B. Bailey Inc., Secretary; Sundown Inc., Secretary; Fig Garden Village Inc., Secretary; Certified Shopping Center Manager, CSM. Community Activities: California Club Honorary Society, University of California-San Francisco; Blue Gold Club University of California School of Pharmacy; Fresno-Madera Pharmacy Association; Pharmacy Alumni Association, University of California; National Association of Female Executives; Junior League of Fresno; American Association of University Women; Women's Symphony League; Ladies Aide to Retarded Children; Executive Board of Directors, Fresno Arts Center; Foundation Board of Directors, Saint Agnes Hospital. Honors and Awards: Honors at Entrance, University of California; Nominee, Rosalie M. Stern Award, 1971-72; Listed in *Who's Who in the West, Who's Who of American Women, World Who's Who of Women*. Address: 3909 West Fir, Fresno, California 93711.■

MAXINE H. NEWTON

Educator. Personal: Born August 13, 1917; Daughter of Samuel Forest Hill (deceased) and Almena May Morriss; Married George A. Newton; Mother of George Fred, Merry Jayne. Education: Graduate of Cyprus High School, 1936; Upholstery Classes, Salt Lake County Recreation Center, 1953-54; Graduate cum laude of University of Utah, 1966; L.D.S., University of Utah Institute, 1966; M.Ed., University of Utah, 1975; Additional Studies at Brigham Young University, Utah State University. Career: Dressmaker for Mrs. J. C. Dodgson, 1936-43; Cashier, Salesgirl and Elevator Operator, ZCMI Company, Auerbach Company, Paris Company, J. C. Penney Company, Woolworth Company, Mode O. Day Clothing Manufacturer; Demonstrator and Sample Maker for Singer Sewing Machine Company; Stock Record Clerk, Kearns Army Base, 1943-45; Dressmaker, 1945-59; Manager School Lunch Program at Monroe Elementary School, 1959-62; Teacher, West Lake Junior High School, 1966-69; Teacher and Department Chairman, Granger High School, 1969 to present. Organizational Memberships: Sigma Delta Omicron, Member and Officer, 1964-66; Omicron Nu, Member and Officer, 1965-66; Utah Home Economics Association, District Chairman and Board Member, 1971-73; P.T.S.A. Faculty Representative, 1970-74; J.C. Penney Fashion Board, Member and Chairman, 1973-79; Study of Utah Student Activities Board, 1977-78; G.E.A. Faculty Representative, 1972-73; Resource Person, Brigham Young University Children's Clothing Workshop, 1972; Resource Person, Granite District Lingerie Workshop, 1973; Resource Person, Granite District Tailoring Workshop, 1974; Resource Person, Utah State University Clothing Services Workshop, 1972; Resource Person, Home Economics Student Teachers, University of Utah. Community Activities: Future Homemakers of America/H.E.R.O., Granger High Advisor 1969-84; Utah State Teacher of the Year, Home Economics for 1983; Brigham University Scholarship named for Maxine H. Newton, 1984; Utah State Advisor 1973-83, Region Chairman 1976, 1978, 1981-83, Utah State Advisor 1973-83, Region Chairman 1976, 1978, 1981-83, Chaperon; Forecast Magazine Advisory Board, 1981-83; Granger High School, Chaperon, Seamstress for School Activities, Coach for Students Entering "Make It With Wool" Contest; National Convention Delegate, Utah Vocational Association; National Convention Delegate, Utah Home Economics Association. Published Works: Producer of Filmstrips "Future Homemakers of America/H.E.R.O. in Action" and "Children's Clothing" Used in Utah Schools. Honors and Awards: Thirty-Three First Places at State Fair; First Runner Up, Mother of the Year, Cottonwood Mall, Salt Lake City, Utah, 1965; Four-Year Normal Scholarship to Attend University of Utah, 1962-66; Scholarship, Sterling W. Sill Leadership Award, 1965; Utah State Honorary Degree for Outstanding Service to Granger High School and State of Utah, Future Homemakers of America/H.E.R.O., 1975; Vocational Teacher of the Year, Utah State, 1979; Listed in *Who's Who in the West, Community Leaders of America, World Who's Who of Women, Dictionary of International Biography*. Address: 3694 South 6400 West, West Valley City, Utah 84120.■

ROGER GERHARD NEWTON

Professor. Personal: Born November 30, 1924, Landsberg/Warthe, Germany, Naturalized 1949; Son of Arthur and Margaret Newton; Married Ruth Gordon; Father of Julie, Rachel, Paul. Education: Attended University of Berlin, 1946; A.B. summa cum laude 1949, M.A. 1950, Ph.D. 1953, Harvard University. Military: Served in the United States Army, 1946-47, attaining the rank of Corporal. Career: Indiana University, Distinguished Professor of Physics 1978 to present, Chairman Physics Department 1973-80, Director, Indiana University Institute for Advanced Study, 1982 to present; Distinguished Chairman Mathematics Physics Program 1965 to present, Professor of Physics 1960-78; Associate Professor 1958-60, Assistant Professor 1955-58; Radiation Laboratory, Berkeley, 1955; Visiting Professor, Ohio State University, 1958; Visiting Professor, University of Geneva, 1972; Member Institute for Advanced Study, Princeton, 1953-55, 1979; University of Montpellier, France, 1971-72; University of Rome, 1962-63. Organizational Memberships: Fellow, American Physical Society; American Association for the Advancement of Science, Member, Nominations Committee of Physics Section, 1982-85; New York Academy of Science; Federation of American Scientists; Sigma Xi, American Association of University Professors; Phi Beta Kappa. Community Activities: President, Bloomington Chapter, American Civil Liberties Union, l968; Amnesty International. Published Works: Author of The Complex j-Plane 1964, Scattering Theory of Waves and Particles 1966, 2nd 1982; Author of Numerous Articles in Professional Journals. Honors and Awards: Bowdoin Prize, Harvard, 1948; National Science Foundation Senior Post Doctorate Fellow, 1962-63; Frank B. Jewett Fellow, 1953-55. Address: 1023 Ballantine, Bloomington, Indiana 4740l.■

ARTHUR MAGUTH NEZU

Clinical Assistant Professor, Project Associate Director, Major Advisor, Assistant Director and Coordinator of Training, Counseling Program Co-Director. Personal: Born November 24, 1952; Son of Tetsuo and Mary Nezu; Married Christine Maguth, Daughter of Frank and Alice Maguth; Father of (stepchildren) Frank, Alice, Linda. Education: B.A. Psychology 1974, M.A. Clinical Psychology 1976, Ph.D. Clinical Psychology 1979, State University of New York at Stony Brook. Career: Co-Director, Readjustment Counseling Program for Vietnam Veterans 1982 to present, Clinical Assistant Professor in Department of Psychology 1981 to present, Clinical Assistant Professor in Department of Community Dentistry School of Dentistry 1981 to present, Associate Director of Natural Setting Therapeutic Management Project 1980 to present, Major Advisor to Institute for Leadership Studies 1980 to present, Assistant Director and Coordinator of Training in Division of Psychological Services 1978 to present, Fairleigh Dickinson University; Adjunct Faculty, School of Metropolitan and Community Studies, Ramapo College of New Jersey, 1980; Intern in Clinical Psychology, Department of Psychological Services, Norwich Hospital, Connecticut, 1977-78; Instructor, Department of Psychology, State University of New York at Stony Brook, 1976-77; Teaching Assistant, Department of Psychology, State University of New York at Stony Brook, 1974-77. Organizational Memberships: American Psychological Association; Eastern Psychological Association; Association for the Advancement of Behavior Therapy; Phi Beta Kappa Association of New York; American Association of Dental Schools; Society for Behavioral Medicine; American Association on Mental Deficiency; American Association for the Advancement of Science. Community Activities: Public Speaker for Community Organizations, Schools and Parent-Teacher Associations; Active Member in Association for Children with Down's Syndrome; Volunteer in Psychiatric Hospitals; Consultant to Veteran's Organizations; Consultant to Alcoholism Rehabilitation Organizations. Honors and Awards: New York State Regents Scholarships, 1970-74; Phi Beta Kappa, 1974; Undergraduate Psychology Award, 1974; Research/Teaching Fellowships, 1974-77; Fairleigh Dickinson University Board of Trustees' Honor, 1982; Listed in *Who's Who in the East, International Men of Achievement, Personalities of America, Community Leaders of the World*. Address: 452 Churchill Road, Teaneck, New Jersey 07666.■

TOAN CAO NGUYEN

Engineer. Personal: Born May 20, 1952; Son of Tan V. Nguyen; Married Truc T. Tran. Education: B.S. Engineering, California State University-Long Beach, 1975; M.S. Mechanical Engineering, University of Southern California, 1977. Career: Engineer, International Telephone and Telegraph/Grinnell Corporation, 1981 to present; Lecturer, California State University-Long Beach, 1980-81; Engineer, Kobe, Inc., 1978-80; Engineer, C.F. Braun and Company, 1978; Engineer, Borg Warner Corporation, 1977-78; Engineer, American Safety Equipment Corporation, 1975-77. Organizational Memberships: American Society of Mechanical Engineers. Community Organizations: Vice President, Organization of Vietnamese Students, California State University-Long Beach, 1974-75. Honors and Awards: California State University-Long Beach, President's Honor List 1972-73; Graduate with Honors (cum laude) 1975; Registered as Professional Engineer (Mechanical Branch), State of California, 1978 to present. Address: 818 Gaviota Avenue, Long Beach, California 90813.■

ROSEMARY THOMAS NICHOLSON

Executive. Personal: Born February 10, 1941; Daughter of Roosevelt Ted and Mary Adeline Burt Thomas (deceased); Mother of Keith Wade, Sheila Kay, Glenn Alan. Education: Graduated with Honors, Meridian High School, 1958; Attended Georgia State University, 1976-77; Attended Edison Community College, 1981. Career: District Manager, Social Security Administration, Fort Myers, Florida, 1980 to present; Assistant District Manager, Social Security

Administration, Lakeland, Florida, 1979-80; Supervisor Regional Commissioner's Inquires Staff, Congressional Liaison, Atlanta Regional Office, Social Security, 1978-79; Assistant District Manager, East Point Georgia Social Security, 1974-78; Staff Assistant, Regional Office Sytems, Atlanta, Georgia, 1974; Operations Supervisor, Social Security, Nashville, Tennessee, 1973. Organizational Memberships: Vice President, Southwest Florida Chapter, Florida Association of Health and Human Services, 1981-84; Vice President, State Association, Florida Association of Health and Social Services, Atlanta Regional Management Association, 1979-84; Atlanta Regional Representative on the National Council of Social Security Management Association of the Management Committee; Corresponding Secretary, Fort Myers Club of Zonta International, 1983-84; Secretary, Zonta International, 1983-84; Board of Directors, Community Coordinating Council of Lee County, Florida, 1982-83; Recording Secretary Coordinating Council of Lee County, Florida, 1983-84; American Society of Professional and Executive Women, 1980-84; National Association of Female Executives 1980-84; Network, Fort Myers Chapter, 1982-84; American Business Women's Association, Hospitality Chairman Cape Coral Caloosa Chapter 1982-83; Vice President 1981-82, President Florida Gold Chapter 1979, President Southside Charter Chapter 1977, Vice President 1976, Recording Secretary 1974; Fort Myers Celebration of Women Member 1984; Child Advocacy Group Committee Member 1983-84; Citizens Advisory Committee of Lee County's Small Cities CDBG Program 1984. Religion: Finance Committee First Baptist Church, Cape Coral, Florida, 1982-84; Sunday School Teacher, Meridian, Mississippi. Honors and Awards: Woman of the Year Award, American Business Women's Association, Southside Charter Chapter, 1978; Various Departmental Awards for Superior Performance, High Quality Increase. Address: 1311 Southeast 34th Street, Cape Coral, Florida 33904.■

THEODORE ROOSEVELT NICHOLSON

Executive, Public Speaker, Consultant. Personal: Born April 14, 1947; son of James and Maywood; Father of Tasheea Theodora, Thema Ariel, Dennis Sinclair. Education: B.A. Political Science/Economics, Lincoln University, 1969; Legal Training, University of Cincinnati Law School, 1969; Legal Training, Dickinson School of Law, 1969-70; Marketing Courses, Wharton School, 1977; M.B.A. Management/Marketing, La Salle College, 1985; Certified in Management and Sales Management by American Telephone/Telegraph Company 1974; Real Estate License, Commonwealth of Pennsylvania, 1973; Certified in Executive Leadership/Management Training by Leadership Management Institute, 1975; Certified in Strategic Planning by American Management Association, 1976; Certified in Design and Evaluation of United States Development Programs in Less Developed Countries by United States Department of State, 1977; Training in BASIC Computer Language, La Salle College, 1979; Training in Military Intelligence, Logistics and Civil Affairs, U.S. Army School of Professional Development. Military: Serves as a Public Administration and Mobilization Office (Captain) in the United States Army Reserves. Career: National Account Executive, General Electric Corporation, 1983; Business Consultant, 1978-83; Project Design Officer, 1978-82, In-and-Out Trader, 1978-82; President and Chief Operating Officer, Business Services Company Inc., 1975-78; Vice President of Sales, Fifth Dimensions Inc., 1974-75; Bell of Pennsylvania, Business Operations Manager 1974, Sales Manager 1972-74, Special Task Force Coordinator 1972; Project Manager 1972; Senior Staff Associate Marketing Methods and Procedures, 1971-72, Account Executive 1971, Staff Associate 1970-71, Communications Consultant 1970; Management Trainee 1970, Training in Marketing Methods, Corporate Financing; Management Information Systems; Communication Planning, A.T.&T. Organizational Memberships: American Management Association: Society for the Advancement of Management; National Alliance of Businessmen; International Platform Association; International Investment Conference; United States Reserve Officers Association. Community Activities: Jaycees; Boy Scouts of America, District Executive, Fund Raiser; Board Member, Houston Drug Preventive Program; Block Captain, Ross Street Neighbors; Fund Raiser, United Way, Red Cross, Pride and Progress Youth Development Center. Honors and Awards: Featured in *Black Enterprise* Magazine, 1976; Boy Scouts of America, Distinguished Service Award, Century Award; Humanitarian Service and Army Achievement Awards, United States Army; Listed in *Who's Who in the East, Who's Who in Industry and Finance, Directory of Distinguished Americans, The Biographical Roll of Honor, Personalities of America, Men and Women of Distinction.* Address: P.O. Box 15726, Philadelphia, Pennsylvania 19103.■

HERMAN NICKERSON, JR.

Retired Officer. Personal: Born July 30, 1913; Son of Herman and Emma (Carver) Nickerson (deceased); Married Phyllis Anne Winters; Father of John Herman, Dennis Anne. Education: B.S. Business Administration, Boston University, 1935; Certified as Genealogist, 1978. Military: Served in the United States Marine Corps, 1935-70, attaining the rank of Lieutenant General and serving as President of the American Society of Military Comptrollers, Fiscal Director of Marine Corps, and Operations Officer of Truce Supervision in Palestine. Career: Retired Officer, United States Marine Corps; Administrator, National Credit Union Administration, 1970-76. Community Activities: Executive Secretary, National Society of Sons of American Revolution; Society of Colonial Wars; Descendants of the Mayflower; Sons of the Revolution; Sons of the American Revolution; Honorary Member, Society of the Cincinnati, State of New Hampshire; Honorary Member, Military Historical Society of Massachusetts; Mason, Shriner, Knight Templar; Honorary Member, International Supreme Council, Order of DeMolay; Legion of Valor of the United States of American; American Legion; Disabled American Veterans; Ancient and Honorable Artillery Company of Massachusetts; Registrar, District of Columbia Society of Founders and Patriots of America, 1978-80; First Vice President, National Genealogical Society; Colonial Clergy; Colonial Governors; Order of the Crown of Charlemagne, Order of Americans of Armorial Ancestry; Flagon and Trenchers; Secretary-Treasurer, Descendants of Illegitimate Sons and Daughters of the Kings of Britain; Past Governor General, Hereditary Order of Descendants of Loyalists and Patriots of American Revolution; Baronial Order of Magna Carta. Religion: Chairman, Trustees, Richlands United Methodist Church. Published Works: Author of Article Published in NGS Quarterly 1979. Honors and Awards: Army Distinguished Service Cross; Navy Distinguished Service Medal with Gold Star in Lieu of 2nd Award; Silver Star; Legion of Merit with Combat "V" with 2 Gold Stars in Lieu of 2nd and 3rd Awards: Bronze Star Medal; Air Medal. Address: 107 Lake Lane, Rock Creek, Jacksonville, North Carolina 28540.■

PAUL L. NICOLETTI

Professor. Personal: Born October 26, 1932; Son of Mr. Felix Nicoletti; Married Earlene; Father of Diana, Julie, Nancy. Education: B.S. 1956, D.V.M. 1956, University of Missouri; M.S., University of Wisconsin, 1962. Career: Professor, College of Veterinary Medicine, University of Florida, Gainesville, present; Former Epidemiologist, United States Department of Agriculture, 1972-78; Epizootiologist, Food and Agriculture, Organization United Nations, Teheran, Iran, 1968-72. Organizational Memberships: American Veterinary Medical Association; Florida Veterinary Medical Association; United States Health Association; American College Veterinary Preventive Medicine; American Association Bovine Practitioners; American Teachers of Preventive Medicine. Honors and Awards: Borden Award, 1979; Florida Cattlemens Association, 1978; Diary Farmers Inc., 1978; Gold Star Award, Florida Veterinary Medical Association, 1981; North Dairy Farmers Association, Puerto Rico, 1977. Address: 2552 Southwest 14th Drive, Gainesville, Florida 32608.■

CLAUDIO NICOLINI

Professor. Personal: Father of Two Children. Career: Professor of Biophysics, Temple University Health Science Center; Former Associate Professor of Physics, University of Bari; Research Associate, Massachusetts Institute of Technology, Brown University, Brookhaven National Laboratory; Consultant to North Atlantic Treaty Organization, National Institutes of Health, National Science Foundation, M.R.C. of Canada, C.N.R. of Italy. Organizational Memberships: New York Academy of Sciences; Biophysical Society; Founding Member, Analytical Cytology Society; Cell Kinetic Society, Founding Member, National Program Committee; President Student Sentate, University of Padua, Italy, 1964-66; National Security, University Students of Physics and Mathematics, Italy, 1966; Director, N.A.T.O.-A.S.I., 1978, 1980-81, 1983; Director, International School of Pure and Applied Biostructure, 1979 to present. Published Works: Contributor to Professional Periodicals; Editor, *Cell Biophysics*, An International Journal; Author of Books on Cell Growth, Chromatic Structure and Function, Chemical Carcinogenesis, Modeling and Analysis in Biomedicine. Honors and Awards: Research Grants, National Institutes of Health, National Science Foundation;

International Honorary Committee for Alfred Nobel and Gelileo Galilei Celebrations, 1983; Chairman, Nobel Symposium. Address: Department of Biophysics, Temple University Health Science Center, Philadelphia, Pennsylvania 19140.■

HENRY ZYGMUNT NIEDZIELSKI

Educator. Personal: Born March 30, 1931; Son of Sigismond Niedzielski; Married Krystyna; Father of Henry Jr., Daniel, Robert, Anna Pia. Education: Ph.D., Dijon, France, 1954; B.A. 1959, Ph.D. 1964, University of Connecticut. Military: Served in the French Armored Cavalry, 1951-53. Career: University of Massachusetts, Instructor 1962-64, Assistant Professor 1965-66; Freelance Interpreter, 1960-64, 1970 to present; Universite Laval, Quebec, Assistant Professor 1964-65, Associate Professor 1966-72; Professor 1972 to present, Chairman Division of French 1968-70, Linguistics Specialist 1963-69, N.D.E.A., E.P.D.A.; Fulbright-Hays Lecturer, Krakow, Poland 1972-74, Burundi 1980-81. Organizational Memberships: Director, American Council on the Teaching of French Language, 1971-72; President, Hawaiian Association of Language Teachers, 1968-69; Delegate, Northeastern Conference on the Teaching of Foreign Languages, 1966; National Representative, Association of International Method, 1973 to present; President, Association of American Teachers of French, Hawaii, 1980 to 1982; Founding President, Hawaii Association of Translators, 1982. Community Activities: Family Education Centers of Hawaii, University of Hawaii, President 1968-70, Chairman of the Board 1970-72; Alliance Francaise, Director 1969-70, President 1978-79; Scholarship Committee, Rotary International Waikiki; Director, Condominium Owners Association. Honors and Awards: National Defense Education Act Fellowship, 1959-62; Fulbright-Hays Lecturing Grants, 1972-74, 1980-81; Hawaii Community Service Award, 1971. Address: 419 Keoniana 904, Honolulu, Hawaii 96815.■

VERNON JAMES NIELSEN

Entrepreneur. Personal: Born February 28, 1949; Son of Mrs. Hilda Nielsen; Father of Candice, Gregory, Jennifer. Education: University of Calgary, B.Comm. 1971. Career: Entrepreneur; Salesman, Occidental Life Insurance Company; Sales Management, General Foods Ltd.; General Management, Barry Brokerage Ltd. Organizational Memberships: Chairman, Alberta Food Brokers Association, 1981; Director, Canadian Food Broker Association, 1980-83. Religion: Elder, United Church, 1975. Honors and Awards: Listed in Who's Who, Personalities of America, Who's Who in Finance & Industry, 1981-82; Who's Who in World, 1982-83. Address: 63 Lancaster Cres. St. Albert, Alberta, Canada T8N 2N9.■

VERNON LLOYD NIKKEL

Industrial Relations Executive. Personal: Born May 26, 1928; Son of Mrs. H. P. Nikkel; Married Lennea O.; Father of Greta Ann, Sanford Louis. Education: B.M.E., Bethany College, Lindsborg, Kansas, 1950; M.S., Kansas State College, Emporia, Kansas, 1961. Career: Vice President Director of Industrial Relations; Teacher of Music; Farmer. Organizational Memberships: American Society of Personnel Administrators 1965-, District Director of Kansas 1970-77, Regional Vice President 1971; Accredited Executive in Personnel, 1981. Community Activities: City Councilman, Hesston, 1961-63; Mayor, Hesston, 1967-69; President, Hesston Development Incorporated, 1972-76; Tri County Community Mental Health Board, Harvey County, 1965-71; Substance Abuse Board, Harvey County, 1976; Harvey County Orchestra Association, 1973; Chairman, Kansas Balance of State Private Industry Council, 1979; Harvey County Chamber of Commerce; Board of Directors of the Kansas Association of Commerce and Industry; Chairman, Human Resources Committee. Religion: Hesston United Methodist Church, Administrative Board, Lay Delegate to Annual Conference; Chairman, West Kansas Annual Conference Sessions Planning Committee of the United Methodist Church. Honors and Awards: Harvey County Community Mental Health Award, 1971; Citation Award, Kansas Department of Employment Security, 1976; Alumni Award of Merit, Bethany College, 1980. Address: Box 67, Hesston, Kansas 67062.■

DORIS KELL NILES

Extension Director. Personal: Born July 26, 1903; Father of Malcolm, Katey Niles Walker, James, Margaret Niles Rice. Education: A.B., Stanford University, 1926; M.A. 1927; Ph.D. 1931; Harvard University Research Fellow, 1930. Career: University Extension, University of California-Davis, 1960-; College of the Redwoods, 1977-; Executive Director of the Nature Discovery Volunteers, 1981-; Curator, Natural History Museum College of Redwoods, 1980-; Humboldt State University 1927, 1940, 1945, 1955, 1958. Associate Professor, Arizona State University, 1931-. Organizational Memberships: Nature Conservancy; Western Society Malacologists; Audubon Society; Phi Beta Kappa; New York Academy Sciences; California Academy of Sciences; International Oceanic Foundation; American Forestry Association; American Association for Advancement Science; California Native Plant Society. Community Activities: Executive Director, Nature Discovery Volunteers, 1981-83; Friends of the Clarke Museum 1983; Friends of the Dunes, 1983; Western Interpreters Association, 1981-83; Commonwealth Club of California, 1983; Council of California Growers, 1983; Humboldt Redwood Interpretive Association, 1981-83; Directed 9 Trips to the Hawaiian Islands; Flora, Fauna and Geology of Hawaiian Islands for University Extension 1969-80. Honors and Awards: Royall Victor Fellow, 1930; Awarded Science Trip to Baja California and nearby Pacific Islands, 1975; Award for Section in "As We Live and Breathe" by National Geographic, 1971; Grant from Humboldt Area Foundation, Publisher of 32 booklets by him on Natural History of North Coast California, 1982-83. Address: P.O. Box 307, Loleta, California 95551.■

RAYMOND NILSSON

Opera and Concert Singer, Professor of Voice and Opera. Personal: Born May 26, 1920; Son of Leslie and Annie Arleen Nilsson (both deceased); Married Mildred Hartle Stockslager; Father of Michael John, Mary Anne, Diana Elizabeth. Education: Studies at Brighton College and the University of London (both in the United Kingdom); B.A., University of Sydney, Australia. Military: Served in Army Intelligence in the Australian 9th Division in New Guinea, 1941-44, attaining the rank of Lieutenant. Career: Teacher, Sydney Church of England Grammar School, Sydney, Australia; Principal Tenor, Royal Opera House, Covent Garden, London, San Francisco Opera Company and Opera Houses in Europe and Australia; Professor of Voice and Opera, Department of Music, San Jose State University. Community Activities: Organized Menlo Park Concert Series, 1972; Director, City of Menlo Park Concert Series, 1972, 1973; Conducted and Directed Opera "Street Scene" by Kurt Weill for Palo Alto, California, Musical Repertory Theater, 1971; Directed "Lucia di Lammermoor" for El Camino Opera Company, San Jose, 1979; Prepared the Principals in Gilbert and Sullivan's "Iolanthe" for San Jose Gilbert and Sullivan Society, 1979. Honors and Awards: Phi Kappa Phi (with special award); Layman Martin Harrison Scholarship, New South Wales State Conservatorium of Music, Australia; Licentiate of Royal Schools of Music; Winner of Both Opera and Oratorio Sections, City of Sydney Eisteddfod, 1939, 1945; Burke's Peerage, 1982. Address: 1285 Middle Avenue, Menlo Park, Californa 94025.■

GERALD NIMBERG

Financial/Investment Counselor. Personal: Born June 19, 1943; Son of Mr. and Mrs. Theodore Nimberg; Married Ann Ruth, Daughter of Mr. David Holmes; Father of Jeffrey Martin, Stephanie Sharon. Education: Certificate of Financial Planning, University of Colorado, 1984; M.B.A., Finance, Wharton School of Finance, 1970; B.S., Mathematics, Worcester Polytechnic Institute, 1966. Career: Financial/Investment Counselor. Organizational Memberships: Institute for Certified Financial Planners, 1982-83; American Management Association, 1983; National Microfilm Association 1970-74. Community Activities: Republican

Party Committee; Cherry Hill Township; Mason Lodge, Senior Deacon, Maple Shade, New Jersey; Volunteer Fireman, Cherry Hill Township; Town Watch, Cherry Hill Township; Organizer/Fund Raiser, American Cancer Society; Public Donations to Federal and Local Government, as well as to Academic, Medical and Religious Organizations, presently. Religion: Jewish, Member Temple Beth El and Beth El Men's Club, 1977 to present. Honors and Awards: Dean's List, Wharton School, 1968, 1970; Dean's List, Worchester Polytechnic Institute, 1965; Massachusetts State Scholarship, 1961; Listed in *Who's Who in the East, Community Leaders of the World, Men of Achievement*. Address: 408 Queen Anne Road, Cherry Hill, New Jersey 08003. ■

WAI-KIT NIP

Associate Professor. Personal: Born May 5, 1941; Son of Mr. Chuck-Foon Nip (deceased) and Jean Sze Nip; Married Li, Daughter of Mr. and Mrs. C. C. Liu; Father of Jun-Yuh, Jaime. Education: M.S., Food Technology 1965, Ph.D., Food Technology 1969, Texas A&M University; B.S., Food Technology, National Chung-Hsing University, Taiwan, 1962. Career: Associate Professor of Food Science and Technology, University of Hawaii, present; Assistant Professor, University of Hawaii, 1976-82; Research Associate, University of Wisconsin, 1974-76; Associate Professor, National Chung-Hsing University, Taiwan, 1969-74. Organizational Memberships: Institute of Food Technologist, Professional Member, Chairman-Elect Hawaii Section 1983-84, Alternate Councilor 1979-83; World Mariculture Society; American Society Horticultural Science; American Association of Cereal Chemists. Community Activities: Hawaii Chinese Association, Board of Directors 1981-84, Vice President 1982-84. Honors and Awards: Phi Tau Sigma 1982; Listed in *American Men and Women of Science, Who's Who in the West, Who's Who in Technology Today, Personalities of America, Community Leaders of America, Directory of Distinguished Americans*. Address: 1615 Wilder Avenue #304, Honolulu, Hawaii 96822. ■

LEON D. NOBES

Professor. Personal: Born April 9, 1911. Education: B.A., magna cum laude 1964, M.A., 1966, Western Michigan University; Certified by United States Navy in Metallurgic Training, Navy Contract Law, Supervisory Development Training; Certified in Advanced Statistical Quality Control by American Society of Quality Control. Military: Served in the Michigan State Troops Infantry in World War II, Attaining the rank of Captain; Served in the United States Navy during Korean Conflict as a Supervisory Production Specialist and Production Engineering Division Supervisor. Career: Assistant Professor Emeritus, Western Michigan University; Former Positions Include Director of Priorities, Continental Aviation and Engineering Corporation. Organizational Memberships: National Advisory Board, American Security Council; The MacArthur Committee; United States Naval Institute. Community Activities: Republican Presidential Task Force; American Defense Preparedness Association; National Rifle Association; Fraternal Order of Eagles; Muskegon Pistol and Rifle Club; Life Member, Lovell Moore Masonic Lodge, 182 F.&A.M.; Ancient Accepted Scottish Rite, 32; Shrine; Royal Arch Masons; Council, Royal and Select Masters; Muskegon Commandery, Knights Templar. Published Works: Author of Numerous Articles and Poems including "Protracted Conflict with the Soviets and Our Alternatives" 1973, "Kentucky" 1980, "The Queen Mother" 1981, "Poland's Heroes" 1981; Author of a Volume of Poetry *Snow, Wind and Ice* 1979. Honors and Awards: Honored for Work in Education, Defense, and Community Affairs, State of Michigan Legislative Resolution, 1980; Honorable Order of Kentucky Colonels, Commonwealth of Kentucky, 1980; Sovereign Hospitaller Order of Saint John, 1982; Academic Honor Societies Phi Theta Kappa (scholastic), Phi Rho Pi (forensic), Delta Psi Omega (dramatic), Theta Alpha Phi (dramatic), Kappa Delta Pi (education), Pi Gamma Mu (social science), Alpha Kappa Psi (professional business); Listed in *Burke's Peerage, Contemporary Personalities, Community Leaders of America, Men of Achievement, Men and Women of Distinction, Community Leaders of America, International Who's Who of Intellectuals*. Address: 2033 Crozier Avenue, Muskegon, Michigan 49441. ■

WESTON HENRY NOBLE

Professor of Music. Personal: November 30, 1922; Son of Mr. and Mrs. Merwin Noble. Education: B.A., Luther College, 1943; M.M., University of Michigan, Ann Arbor, Michigan, 1953; Honorary Doctorate, Augustana College, Sioux Falls, South Dakota, 1971. Career: Professor of Music, Luther College. Organizational Memberships: Music Educators National Conference; Iowa Music Educators; Iowa Bandmasters Association; College and University Bandmasters Association, State Chairman for Iowa, 1961-63; Music Teachers National Association, State Vice-President, 1961-63; College Music Society; American Bandmasters Association; American Choral Directors Association, Charter Member 1958, State Chairman for Iowa 1961-63. Honors and Awards: Conducted the Luther College Nordic Choir, Luther College Concert Band, and/or festival groups in Orchestra Hall (Chicago), Town Hall, Carnegie Hall, Lincoln Center (all in New York), J. F. Kennedy Center (Washington, D.C.), Music Center (Los Angeles), and Orchestra Hall (Minneapolis); Four Concert tours of Europe from Norway to Rumania; Guest Director for Music Festivals in Forty-Two States (including Alaska and Hawaii), Canada and Europe; Guest Faculty Member at Twenty-Seven Colleges or Universities; Listed in *International Register of Profiles, Dictionary of International Biography, Intercontinental Biographical Association, Creative and Successful Personalities of the World* 1970, *Who's Who in Music, The World Who's Who of Musicians, Dictionary of Distinguished Americans, International Book of Honor, Encyclopaedie "Accademia Italia"*. Address: 602 Mound, Decorah, Iowa 52101. ■

EUGENE JORGEN NORDBY

Orthopaedic Surgeon. Personal: Born April 30, 1918; Son of Herman and Lucille Nordby (both deceased); Married Olive Marie Jensen; Father of Jon Jorgen. Education: B.A., Luther College, 1939; M.D., University of Wisconsin Medical School, 1943; Intern, Madison General Hospital, Wisconsin, 1943-44; Assistant in Orthopaedic Surgery, 1944-48. Military: Served in the United States Army Medical Corps, 1944-46, attaining the rank of Captain. Career: Consulting Orthopaedic Surgeon; Madison General Hospital, Orthopaedic Surgeon 1948-81, Chief of Staff 1957-63, Board of Directors 1957-76; Associate Clinical Professor, University of Wisconsin Medical School, 1961-81, Chief of Staff 1957-63, Board of Directors 1957-76; Associate Clinical Professor, University of Wisconsin Medical School, 1961-81. Organizational Memberships: Wisconsin Medical Society (councilor, 1961-76; chairman, 1968-76; treasurer, 1976-82); American Academy of Orthopaedic Surgery (board of directors, 1972-73; chairman, board of councilors, 1973; chairman, committee on the spine, 1975-81); Association of Bone and Joint Surgeons (president, 1973); Clinical Orthopaedic Society; International Society for Study of Lumbar Spine. Community Activities: Wisconsin Physicians Service (board of directors, 1958-81; chairman, 1979-); Wisconsin Regional Medical Program (director); Wiconsin Health Care Liability Plan; Norwegian American Museum (president of Board, 1968-82); Sunset Village (board member, 1952-54); Sister City Committee, Madison-Oslo. Religion: Bethel Lutheran Church, 1934-82; President, Church Council, 1956-58; Chairman, Call Committee, 1959. Honors and Awards: Distinguished Service Award, Luther College, 1964; Council Award, State Medical Society of Wisconsin, 1976; Knights Cross, 1st Class, Royal Order of St. Olav, Norway, 1979; Eagle Scout, 1934. Address: 6234 South Highlands, Madison, Wisconsin 53705. ■

WALLACE NORMAN

Company Executive. Personal: Born February 5, 1926; Son of Leland Fleming Norman (deceased) and Alma Lucile Brown Norman; Married Maurene Collums, Daughter of John Collums and Glennie Crocker Collums (both deceased). Education: Student, East Central Junior College 1942, University of Mississippi 1946, Millsaps College 1946; B.S., Oklahoma City, 1948. Military: Served with the United States Naval Reserves during World War II. Career: Owner, Manager, Wallace Norman Insurance Agency, Houston, Mississippi, 1949 to present; Norman Oil Company, 1956 to present; President, National Leasing Company, Houston, Mississippi, 1969 to present; President, U.S. Plastics, 1969 to present; President, Calhoun National Company, 1974 to present; President, Norman Trucking Company, 1975 to present; President, Plastics of America, 1982 to present. Organizational Memberships: Mississippi Association of Insurance Agents, 1949 to present; Mississippi Manufacturing Association; American Waterworks Association. Community Activities Disabled American Veterans; Veterans of Foreign Wars; American Legion; Chairman, Running Bear District Boy Scouts of America, 1971-73; Exchange Club; Mississippi Economic Council. Religion: Methodist, Member Gideons International. Address: Box 208, Houston, Mississippi 38851. ■

ALAN E. NORRIS

Judge. Personal: Born August 15, 1935, in Columbus, Ohio; Married Nancy Jeanne Myers; Father of Tom Edward Jackson, Tracy Elaine. Education: B.A., with honors, Otterbein College, 1957; Certificate, La Sorbonne, University of Paris, 1956; LL.B., (Root-Tilden Scholar), New York University School of Law, 1960. Career: Attorney at Law, Admitted to Practice 1960, Vorys, Sater, Seymour & Pease, Columbus, Ohio 1961-62; Metz, Bailey, Norris & Spicer, Westerville, Ohio 1962-80; Instructor of Business Law, Otterbein College, 1976-80; Judge, Tenth District Court of Appeals, 1981 to present; State Representative, 1967-80; House Minority Whip, 1973-78; City Prosecutor, City of Westerville, 1962-66; Law Clerk, Chief Justice Kingsley A. Taft, 1960-61. Organizational Memberships: Columbus Bar Association, Ad Hoc Committee 1976-78, Legislative Committee 1972-74, Committee on the Judiciary 1967-72, Chairman Committee on the Judiciary 1969 and 1970, Real Property Committee 1964-67, Professional Ethics Committee 1961-64; Ohio State Bar Association, Modern Courts Committee 1961-64, Electronics Reporting Committee 1970; American Bar Association; General Practice Section and Family Law Section 1976-80; Institute of Judicial Administration, 1981 to present; American Judicature Society, 1982 to present. Community Activities: Franklin County Republican Central Committee 1962-80, Chairman Rules Committee 1976-78; Ohio Republican Party, Special Finance Committee 1976-78, Federal Judiciary Task Force 1979-80; Westerville Zoning Board of Appeals 1962-66, Chairman 1966; Ohio American Revolution Bicentennial Commission 1970-80, Chairman 1975-80, Vice Chairman 1971-75; Ohio Constitutional Revision Commission 1971-77, Chairman Grand and Petit Jury Committee 1975-76; National Conference of State Legislatures, Committee on Ethics, Elections and Reapportionment 1976-80, Chairman Subcommittee on Voters, Candidates and Equipment 1979-80; Dangerous Offender Project (Academy for Contemporary Problems), Advisory Committee 1975-78; Federal Elections Commission Advisory Committee 1975-76; National Legislative Conference, Reapportionment Committee 1973-76, Chairman 1974-76; Council of State Governments, Committee on Suggested State Legislation 1967-76, Member Executive Subcommittee 1969-76; Ohio Comprehensive Health Planning Council 1971-72; Member of or Held Offices and Committee Memberships in Kiwanis, Masons, Boy Scouts of America, Central Ohio American Revolution Bicentennial Commission, Otterbein College, United Methodist Church, The Westerville Fund; Trustee, United Methodist Children's Home, Worthington, Ohio, 1970-82; Maryhaven Inc., Board of Directors 1975-78; Westerville Historical Society 1961 to present, President 1967-69; Columbus Area Council on Alcoholism, Research Committee; Young Men's Christian Association, North Branch, Advisory Board of Management; Emerson School Parent Teacher Association, President 1972-73; Ohio Historical Society, Westerville Area Council of Churches 1968-71, Sons of the American Revolution; Lecturer for Ohio State Bar Association Continuing Legal Education Seminars, Ohio Academy of Trial Lawyers Continuing Legal Education Seminars, Columbus Bar Association Noon Luncheon Series, Ohio Judicial Conference, Columbus Bar Association Continuing Legal Education Seminars, Buckeye Girls' State. Published Works: Contributor of Numerous Articles to Professional Journals. Honors and Awards: Jaycee Distinguished Service Award, "Outstanding Young Man Award," 1967; Public Service Resolution of Honor, Ohio Prosecuting Attorneys Association, 1971; Legislator of the Year, Ohio Academy of Trial Lawyers, 1972; Special Achievement Award, Otterbein College, 1973; Honorary Kentucky Colonel, Commission Granted 1971; Eagleton Institute (Rutgers University) Seminar for Outstanding State Legislators, 1969; Listed in Who's Who in Ohio, Who's Who in Government, Who's Who in American Politics, Who's Who in the Midwest, Outstanding Americans, Community Leaders and Noteworthy Americans, Who's Who Among Authors and Journalists, Notable Americans, Dictionary of International Biography, Who's Who in American Law, Who's Who in American Lawyers, Personalities of the West and Midwest, International Who's Who in Community Service, The Best Lawyers in America, Men of Achievement, Blue Book of Franklin County. Address: 58 West College Avenue, Westerville, Ohio 43081.■

WILLIAM CARLTON NORTHRUP

Accountant, Statistician. Personal: Born December 1, 1930; Son of Mr. and Mrs. L. L. Northrup; Married Sharon Joan Carlson; Father of Richard Carlton, Karen Frances. Education: B.S., 1953, M.B.A., 1974, University of Missouri; Attended Middle Management Seminars, 1970-73; Studies in Hospital Budgeting, H.F.M.A., 1980. Career: Accountant V/Statistician, Cost and Reimbursement Specialist, County of Cook/Cook County Hospital; Management Analyst III, Health and Hospital Governing Committee; Chief Accountant, National Congress of Parents and Teachers; Account Executive, London Commodity House; Supervisor, Research and Records, Missouri Crippled Childrens Service; Accountant II, Missouri Division of Health; Account Executive, Chief Estimator, Estimator, Cost Accountant, Assistant Product Manager, American Press Inc.; Production Planner, Production Scheduler/Merchandiser, Cut Editor, M.F.A. Publishing Division; Management Trainee, Thriftway Food Mart; Assistant Treasurer, M.F.A. Insurance; Research Associate, University of Missouri, Rural Sociology Department; Sales Representative, World Book International; Stock Broker. Organizational Memberships: H.F.M.A. (advanced status); A.I.C.P.A.; American Statistial Association; Mathematics Association of America; American Management Association; Association of M.B.A. Executives; Delta Sigma Pi (life member; chancellor, 1953; historian, 1952; reporter, Delta Sig Chatter, 1951); Fifth Street Syndicate Investment Club. Community Activities: Chicago Council on Foreign Relations, 1982, APHA 1982; IPHA 1982; Presidential Task Force, 1982; National Conservative Political Action Committee, 1982; National Tax Limitation Committee and Better Government Association; Republican National Committee; Illinois Parent-Teacher Association, 1977; United States Senatorial Club, 1978 to present; American Security Council (national advisory board); Twilight Optimist Club (president, 1st vice president, secretary-treasurer, board of directors, 1970-76); S.P.E.B.S.Q.S.A. (secretary-treasurer, board of directors, 1st vice president, 2nd vice president, 1972-76); Columbia Jaycees Secretary-Treasurer, 1964—; Teen Auto Club, Steering Committee, 1972; Camp Wannonoya, Steering Committee, 1976; Finance Study Commission, City of Columbia, 1974; Mizzou Employees Federal Credit Union, 1972-74; Boone County Juvenile Court Probation Officer, 1971-72; A.B.I.R.A. Life Member, 1979 to present; Republican Presidential Task Force, 1981; Cook County Republicans, Charter Member, 1981; Columbia Town Meeting Steering Committee, 1976; Stephens College Cultural Events Series House Manager, 1976; Cub Scout Pack Committee Chairman, 1965; Packyderm Club of Boone County, 1974-76; Advisory Council for Committee to Re-elect George Parker, 1974-76; American Mensa Selection Agency, 1970 to present; Columbia Little League Coach, 1976; International Platform Association; A.A.U.C.G., 1981; Missouri Public Health Association, 1979 to present. Religion: Bethel Baptist Church, Columbia, Missouri, Youth Director, 1972, Sunday School Teacher, 1972, Nominating Committee 1972-74, Choir Director, 1974, Editor Bethel Banner 1972-76; Boone County Pastoral Alliance, Executive Committee, 1974; Student, Religious Council, University of Missouri, 1952. Honors and Awards: First Runner-up, Open Competition Exam, Candidate for M.B.A., Finance, University of Missouri, 1974; Special Advisory to the Governor of the State of Missouri for Printing and Publishing, 1965; Nominated to National Honor Society, 1946, 1947, 1948; Quiz Kids of Missouri, 1940; Highest Score Ever Recorded on Engineering Applicant Exam, Westinghouse, Kansas City, 1953; William Greenleaf Eliot Society, Washington University. Address: 24 Williamsburg, Evanston, Illinois 60203.■

ALAN PAUL NORTON

Executive Management Consultant. Personal: February 22, 1943, Calgary, Alta., Canada; Son of Chester P. and Betty (Luxford) Norton; Married Lynda Diane Dunbar; Father of Alana Lea. Education: Certificate in Business Administration, Southern Alta. Institute of Technology, 1971. Career: Collection Supervisor, Calgary General Credit Ltd., 1964-66; Area Financial Manager, Massey-Ferguson Industries Ltd., Calgary, 1966-67; Retail Credit Analyst, Gulf Oil Canada Ltd., Calgary, 1968-70; Crew Training Officer Universal Ambulance Service Ltd., Calgary, 1970; Financial Correspondant, Allis-Chalmers Credit Corporation, Calgary, 1970-71; Instructional Administrator, St. John Ambulance, Calgary, 1972-73; Divisional Credit Manager, Neonex Shelter Ltd., Calgary, 1973-77; Credit Manager, Westburne Divisions Engineering and Plumbing Supplies Ltd., Calgary, 1978-79; Alta. Electric Supply Ltd., 1978-79; General Manager, The Marsh Group of Cosmetics, Calgary, 1979-; Western Regional Credit Manager, Gough Electric Ltd., Calgary, 1979-80; Vice President of Finance, Eastlake Development Corporation Ltd., 1980-81; President, Alan P. Norton & Associates, 1981-; Chairman of Area Advisory Committee, Creditel of Canada Ltd., 1978-81. Honors and Awards: Decorated Order of St. John; Recipient Provincial Shield, Alta. Provincial Council of St. John Ambulance, 1971; Priory Vote of Thanks of St. John Ambulance, Governor General Canada, 1974; Notary Public, Calgary, 1976-; Member Coalition for Life, Alliance for Life (Director, Vice President), Calgary Pro-Life Association; Right to Life. Religion: Mormon. Address: 59 Huntford Road, North East, Calgary AB T2K 3Y8 Canada.■

JOHN EDMONDSON NORVELL, III

Professor and Department Chairman. Personal: Born November 18, 1929, in Charleston, West Virginia; Son of John E. and Mathilde Wood Norvell (deceased); Married Rosemary Justice; Father of John Edmondson IV, Scott Justice. Education: B.S., cum laude Biology, University of Charleston, 1953; M.S., Zoology, West Virginia University, 1956; Ph.D., Anatomy, Ohio State University, 1966. Military: Served in the United States Naval Reserve, 1947-48. Career: Professor and Chairman, Department of Anatomy, Schools of Medicine and Dentistry, Oral Roberts University, 1976 to present; Visiting Professor, Department of Human Anatomy, University of Nairobi, Kenya, 1982; Associate Professor, Department of Anatomy, Medical College of Virginia (Health Sciences Division), Virginia Commonwealth University, 1966-76; Assistant Instructor of Anatomy, Ohio State University, 1962-65; Assistant Professor, Department of Biology, Otterbein College, 1960-62; Instructor, Department of Biology, Johnstown College, University of Pittsburgh, 1956-60; Member of Neuroanatomy Visiting

TWO THOUSAND NOTABLE AMERICANS

Scientists Program, National Institutes of Health; Anatomy Consultant, Department of Surgery, United States Naval Hospital, Portsmouth, Virginia; Coordinator, Neuroscience Program, Phillip Morris Company Research Center; Visiting Lecturer in Anatomy, University of Virginia (Department of Anatomy, School of Medicine). Organizational Memberships: American Association for the Advancement of Science; American Association of Anatomists; American Association of Dental Schools (Section on Anatomical Sciences), Chairman-elect 1978-79, Chairman 1979-80; Association of Anatomy Chairmen; Governor's Mini-Cabinet on Health and Human Resources (Oklahoma); Oklahoma State Anatomical Board, Chairman 1978 to present; Sigma Xi; Society for Neuroscience, Transplantation Society. Published Works: Author of Six Books including *Anatomia Humana*, *Atlas of Neuroanatomy, Atlas of Cross Sections on the Human Body*; Author/Co-Author Numerous Scientific Papers and Abstracts; Presented Paper on "Degeneration and regeneration of the intrinsic nerves of the heart after transplantation" at IX International Congress of Anatomists, Leningrad, 1970. Honors and Awards: Chi Beta Phi Scholarship Key; Ohio State University Graduate Fellowship; Outstanding Teacher of the Year, Medical College of Virginia, 1970, 1971, 1972, 1975; Invited Speaker on "Interaction between Harderian glands and pineal glands in rats and hamsters" at Department of Applied Pharmacology, Hadassah Medical School, The Hebrew University, Jerusalem, Israel, 1974; Member Anatomy Delegation to People's Republic of China, 1983; Listed in *Who's Who in the South and Southwest, Who's Who in Health Care, Men of Achievement, International Who's Who of Intellectuals, American Men and Women of Science*. Address: 9909 South Kingston Avenue, Tulsa, Oklahoma 74137.■

DARLENE MARIE NOSWORTHY

Dance Instructor, Choreographer. Personal: Born June 19, 1948; Daughter of Ray and Queenie Heylek; Married Duncan Keith; Mother of Jeffrey Wayne, and Brandon Keith. Education: B.A., Theater Arts, M.A., Dance and Theater Arts, California State University at Chico. Career: Dance Instructor, Choreographer. Organizational Memberships: National Dance Association; Dance Educators of America; Northern California Dance Council, Vice President 1982-84. Community Activities: Choreographer, Feather River Civic Light Opera, 1983-84; Numerous Dance Performances for Hospitals, Charities and Churches, 1966 to present; President, Vice President, Honorary Member, Sergeant-at-Arms, Prexy Council Chaplain, Representative, La Estrellita Tri-Hi-Y, 1960's; President, Vice President, Treasurer, Orchesis; Las Moras Service Club. Religion: Methodist. Honors and Awards: Numerous Dance Awards, 1960-83; Numerous Baton Twirling Awards, 1960's; Listed in *National Dean's List, International Youth in Achievement, Community Leaders of America, Personalities of America, World Who's Who of Women, Directory of Distinguished Americans, Community Leaders of the World, Biographical Roll of Honor*. Address: 14184 Creston Road, Magalia, California 95954.■

VIRGINIA SIMMONS NYABONGO

Author, Lecturer. Personal: Born March 20, 1913, in Baltimore, Maryland; Daughter of Vester and Mary Warren Simmons (both deceased). Education: B.A., French and History, Bennett College, 1934; M.A., French, University of Wisconsin, 1937; Ph.D., French, University of Wisconsin; M.A., Student Personnel Administration and Guidance, 1948; Professional Diploma, Dean of Students, Teachers College, Columbia University, 1962; Certificat d'Études Françaises, Certificat de Phonétique, Diplôme d'Études Avancées de Phonétique, University of Grenoble, France, 1939; Post-Doctoral Studies, Japan Program, Syracuse University. Career: Author/Lecturer; Professor of French, Research Professor, Director of Student Personnel and Guidance, 1944-58; Tennessee State University, 1944-78, Bennett College, 1934-36, 1941-42; Dean of Students, Acting Registrar, Instructor, Secretary; Assistant Professor of French, Wilberforce University, 1937-41. Organizational Memberships: American Association of Teachers of French, Tennessee Chapter, (President, 1972-73); Tennessee Philological Association (President, 1967-68); Tennessee Foreign Language Teaching Association (Board of Directors, 1969, 1970; Co-Editor, Newsletter, 1971); Modern Languages Association (French VIII Chairman); National Association of Dean's of Women Advisers Girls (President); National Association of Deans of Women, Administrators, Counselors (Committee on International Students). Community Activities: United Nations Association, U.S.A., Nashville Chapter (President, 1977); American Association of University Women (1st Vice President, 1970-72); Tennessee Division Area Representative, International Relations, Study Topics Chairman, Redefining the Goals of Education; Nashville Branch Delegate to National Conventions, Chicago, Albuquerque, and Centennial Convention in Boston, 1981); I.F.U.W., Tokyo and Kyoto, Japan (Discussion Group Leader, Interpreter in English and French, 1974); I.F.U.W. Karlsruhe, Philadelphia, Vancouver; National Education Association Delegate to World Confederation of Organizations of the Teaching Profession in Dublin, 1968, and Abidjan, Ivory Coast, 1969; Nashville Area Chamber of Commerce (Committee on Education, 1971; Metro Council Committee); Citizens Coordinating Committee, Model Cities Program, 1972-75; Davidson County Democratic Women's Club (Past Vice-President); Tennessee Federation of Democratic Women (Past Corresponding Secretary). Religion: First Baptist Church, Capitol Hill, Nashville, Former Youth Committee, Co-Chairman Centennial Committee 1965. Honors and Awards: Non-Resident Scholar, University Scholar, University of Wisconsin, 1936-37, 1942-44; Franco-American Fellow, Institute of International Education, Grenoble, France, 1938-39; Postdoctoral Research, Fulbright Program, Paris, 1952-53; Fellow, African Studies Association, International Institute of Arts and Letters, Postdoctoral Fellow, Society for Values in Higher Education; Tennessee State University Golden Anniversary Faculty Service Award, 1962; Tennessee State University Presidential Citation, 1978; Ministère de l'Éducation Nationale, République Française, Chevalier dans l'Ordre des Palmes Académiques, 1963, Officer 1968; Citations, N.A.W.D.A.C., A.A.U.W., 1981; Democratic National Committee, 1982. Address: 936 34th Avenue North, Nashville, Tennessee 37209.■

WILLIAM PRESTON NYE

Research Entomologist (Retired). Personal: Born January 10, 1917; Father of Pamela Quinnett (Mrs. Paul), James, Janet Anderson (Mrs. Rodney), Ted W., David P. Education: B.S., 1940, M.S., 1947, Utah State University. Military: Served in the United States Marine Corps, 1940-45, and in the Marine Corps Reserve 1945-62, retiring with the rank of Lieutenant Colonel. Career: Retired Research Entomologist/Apiculturist U.S.D.A., A.R.S. Organizational Memberships: Entomology Society of America, 1947-77; Emeritus; International Bee Research Association, 1962-77; Organization of Professional Employees, U.S.D.A., 1960 to present; Western Apicultural Society of America, 1978 to present. Religion: Church of Jesus Christ of Latter-Day Saints, High Priest Leadership Group, Member Hyrum Third Ward. Honors and Awards: Numerous Photographic Awards from Entomological Society of America and International Groups; U.S.D.A. Merit Award, 1968. Address: 459 Valley View Drive, Hyrum, Utah 84319.■

MARGUERITE E. O'BANION

Executive Secretary. Personal: Born February 18; Daughter of J. W. O'Banion (deceased). Education: Graduate of Swifton High School, Arkansas, 1935; B.A., Harding University, 1942; Graduate of Dale Carnegie Program, 1954; LL.D., Alabama Christian College, 1979. Career: Executive Secretary to Dr. George S. Benson, 38 Years. Organizational Memberships: Business and Professional Women's Club, Past President; American Association of University Women, Past Secretary Searcy Branch; Harding Business Women's Club, Founding President, Reporter; Associated Women for Harding, Charter Member, First Life Member, Secretary Searcy Chapter (1 Year); Arkansas Chapter, Freedoms Foundation of Valley Forge. Religion: Church of Christ. Honors and Awards: Distinguished Citizenship Award, National Education Program; LL.D., Alabama Christian College, 1979; First Woman Among Churches of Christ to Receive an LL.D. Degree. Address: Harding University, Box 751, Searcy, Arkansas 72143.■

SAMUEL EUGENE OBERMAN

Management Consulting Executive. Personal: Born September 8, 1933; Son of Max and Betty Oberman; Married Judith Meshberg; Father of Scott Evan, Amy Lisa. Education: B.S. Economics, Wharton School of Finance and Commerce, University of Pennsylvania, 1955; M.B.A., University of Michigan, 1958. Military: Served in the United States Navy, 1955-57, attaining the rank of SK2. Career: President, Dan Rowe Associates, Management Consultants; Director of Personnel, Methodist Hospital of Brooklyn; Wage and Salary Administrator, New York Hospital; Wage and Salary Analyst, Columbia Broadcasting System. Organizational Memberships: American Institute of Management, Presidents Council; American Society of Professional Consultants; American Society for Personnel Administration; American Society of Business and Management Consultants, Charter Member. Community Activities: American Jewish Committee, President Long Island Chapter 1977-79; Congressional Committee, 1980 to present; Greater Westbury Community Coalition, Co-Chairman 1970-76; Young Men's Christian Association of Long Island, Board of Directors 1976-80; Greater Westbury Arts Council, Board of Directors 1976-80; Community Conflict Resolution, Mediator and Arbitrator 1972 to present. Religion: Community Reform Temple, Board of Directors 1978-80. Honors and Awards: American Jewish Committee Human Relations Award, 1979; University of Wisconsin School of Banking Faculty, 1973-78; Listed in *Who's Who in Finance and Industry*, *Community Leaders of America*, *International Men of Achievement*. Address: 65 Chenango Drive, Jericho, New York 11753.■

THERESE DE STE. MARTHE O'BRIAN

Translator, Interpreter. Personal: Born December 30, 1942, in Philadelphia, Pennsylvania; Married Brian K. O'Brian Jr., June 18, 1964 (deceased); Mother of Brian K. III (deceased), Maureen Karen (deceased). Education: A.B. summa cum laude, Catholic University of America; M.A., Ed.D. summa cum laude, Columbia University Teachers College; M.S. Journalism, Columbia University; Ph.D. summa cum laude in Psychology, Harvard University; Ph.D. summa cum laude in Psychology, Sorbonne, Paris; Further Studies (Rhodes Scholar), Oxford University. Career: Teacher of English, Languages, and Journalism; Editor for Magazines and Publishing Houses; Teacher, Spanish and Journalism, Columbia University College of Physicians and Surgeons; Translator, Interpretor, United Nations; Teacher, Berlitz School of Languages; Consultant, New York State Department of Education. Organizational Memberships: American Society of Professional and Executive Women; American Association of University Women, New York State Teachers Union; National Organization of Women; National Education Association; American Association of Artists and Writers; Executive Women; United Federation of Teachers; Mensa; International Platform Association; Smithsonian Associates; Phi Beta Kappa; Kappa Tau Alpha; Delta Kappa Gamma. Community Activities: Democrat; Aspen Club; Lake Tahoe Club; Windham Mountain Club; Windham Country Club; Elmridge Bath and Tennis Club; Playboy Club; Lake Placid Club. Religion: Roman Catholic. Published Works: Author of Articles for Magazines, Newspapers. Address: Riverdale, New York 10471.■

WALTER GREGORY O'DONNELL

Educator. Personal: Born February 3, 1903; Married Angela M., Daughter of Salvatore Oriti; Father of Charles, Kathleen, Roger, Arleen. Education: B.A. Social Science and English, Western Reserve University, 1932; LL.B. Law, Cleveland-John Marshall Law School, 1930; M.A. Education Philosophy and Economics, Western Reserve University, 1944; Ph.D. Economics and Social-Economic Philosophy, Columbia University, 1959. Career: Visiting Professor of Management, School of Administrative Science, University of Alabama, Huntsville, 1983 to present; Professor of Management Emeritus, University of Massachusetts, Amherst, Massachusetts, present; Distinguished Visiting Professor of Management, Bowling Green State University, 1978-80; Practice of Law, State of Florida; Management Consultant, TWI Foundation; Institute Leader, National Association of Manufacturers; Institute Leader and Management Consultant, National Foreman's Institute; Member of Panel of Arbitrators, American Arbitration Association; Reorganized and Reactivated the College of Management Philosophy of the Institute of Management Sciences. Organizational Memberships: Member and Vice Chairman, COLPHIL-TIMS Executive Committee; Presented Monograph on "An Heuristic Analytical-Diagnostic Model for Problem/Opportunity Search and Detection," at National Meeting of Institute of Management Sciences in New York City, 1978; Presented Monograph on "Some Philosophical Issues in Management Sciences at COLPHIL-TIMS Session in Milwaukee, Wisconsin, 1979; Presented 4th of Series of Monographs on "Towards Unifying the Management Sciences" at COLPHIL Session of Institutes of Management Sciences in Washington D.C. 1980, Fifth of Series, "Pragmatic Managerial and Teleological Integrate Attributes" in Toronto TIMS Meetings, 1981; The Institute of Management Sciences, Founder of TIMS Sub-Unit, "College" of Management Philosophy, repeatedly Chairman or Vice Chairman and Executive Director, 1960 to present; American Association for the Advancement of Science; Academy of Management. Community Activities: Ohio Post-War Planning Commission, Beach and Shore Erosion Committee, 1945; Ohio Friends of Public Schools, Organizer and Director, 1946-47; Ohio World Federalists, Organized and Directed with President Holiday of SOHIO Inc., 1945-47; Elected to Cuyahoga County Planning Commission, 1935; Long-Range Planning Committee of Institute of Management Sciences; Chairman of Faculty Committee Planning Doctoral Program in the School of Business Administration, University of Massachusetts, Amherst, Massachusetts, 1970; National Planning Association's New England Planning Commission, Member Committees on Natural Resources and Management. Honors and Awards: Emeritus Professor of Management, University of Massachusetts, 1973 to present; Five Distinguished Visiting Professorships at Other Universities, 1973-82; Fulbright Lecturer's Award to Teach Innovative Courses, University of Madrid, 1963; Numerous Research Grants to Present Monographs on Decision Theory, Administrative Issues and Problems in Developing Countries, and Philosophy of Management, including Belgium, Austria, Italy, Mexico, and Peru, 1960-67; Numerous Biographical Listings including those in *Who's Who in America*, *Who's Who in the World*, *Book of Honor*. Address: P.O. Box 182, Ashfield, Massachusetts 01330.■

TWO THOUSAND NOTABLE AMERICANS

KARL LYNN OESTREICH

Management Consulting Executive. Personal: Born October 7, 1942; Son of Karl E. Oestreich; Married; Father of Karl Lynn, Nicole Marie. Education: B.S. Economics, University of Wisconsin, 1965; Computer Science, Akron University, 1967; APICS Certification, 1980. Career: Vice President Management Consulting; Former Positions include Associate Management Consulting with The Austin Company, Production Control Manager and Corporate Materials Manager with Rust-Oleum Corporation, General Manager of Production Materials and Inventory Control with Intercraft Industries, Supervisor Production Control with Baxter Laboratories, Systems Analyst Firestone Tire and Rubber Company. Organizational Memberships: Board of Directors, American Production and Inventory Control Society, Chicago Chapter President 1981; General Chairman of 1983 APICS Mid-America Seminar. Community Activities: Executive Board, Northeast Illinois Boy Scout Council, 1974-78; Village Trustee, Morton Grove 1973-76, Chairman Police and Fire Committee, Chairman Traffic and Safety and Civil Defense; Cubmaster, Pack 273, 1977-79; Executive Board of Directors, Association for the Protection of the Adopted Triangle. Honors and Awards: CPIM Certification, American Production and Inventory Control Society, 1980; Listed in *Marquis Who's Who in the West, Men of Achievement.* Address: 7409 Davis, Morton Grove, Illinois 60053.■

ROBERT LYNN OGDEN

Canadian Government Official. Personal: Born January 28, 1947; Son of Robert Wilson and Eva Ailene (Gay) Ogden; Married Arlene Gail, September 2, 1966; Father of Nathan Stuart, Aaron Matthew. Education: B.A. with honors, University Alta., 1970; M.A. 1971, Certificate in Computer Programming 1968, Certificate in Archival Principles and Administration 1971, Certificate in Collective Bargaining 1978, Carleton University. Career: Team Leader, Parks Canada Historic Sites Provincial Museums and Archives Alta., 1970; Coordinator, National Business Archives Program, Public Archives of Canada, 1971-73; City Archivist, Vancouver, B.C., Canada, 1973-75; Regional Director, Prairie Region Canadian Conservation Institute, Ottawa, Ontario, 1975-77; Regional Director, Atlantic Region Canadian Conservation Institute, Moncton, N.B., 1977-79; Executive Director, Canadian Museums Association, Ottawa, 1979-81; Assistant Deputy Minister, Department Cultural Affairs and Historic Resources, Province of Manitoba, Winnipeg, 1981-; Adjunct Professor, University B.C.; Instructor, Carleton University, Vancouver City College; Museum Consultant Secretary-Treasurer, Chairman Personnel Committee, Victorian Order of Nurses, Moncton; Special Advisor, Ottawa-Gloucester Family Enrichment Association. Organizational Memberships: International Council Museums; International Institute Conservation of Artistic and Historic Works; Canadian Museums Association; Association of Canadian Archivists; Canadian Historic Association; Royal Canadian Geographic Society; Le Cercle Molière, Alliance Fran£aise, Phi Alpha Theta. Address: 99 Briarcliff Bay, Winnipeg MB R3T Canada.■

ARTHUR CARLISLE OIEN

Educator. Personal: Born April 10, 1930; Son of Alfred Carl Oien, Mable Margaret Martinson (both deceased). Education: B.A. summa cum laude, Concordia College, Moorhead, Minnesota, 1952; M.A., University of Minnesota, 1954; Further Studies at the University of Minnesota, 1957-60. Military: Served in the United States Army Security Agency, 1954-57. Career: Associate Professor of History, Bridgewater State College, 1963 to present; Assistant Dean of Men, Luther College, Decorah, Iowa, 1960-62; Instructor, Bemidji State College, Bemidji, Minnesota, 1962-63. Organizational Memberships: Missouri Historical Society; National Education Association; Massachusetts Teachers Association; Bridgewater State College Association; American Association of University Professors; New England Historical Society; New England History Teachers Association; First Fellow, Confederate Historical Institute. Community Activities: Smithsonian Institution, Associate; American Museum of Natural History, Associate; National Audubon Society; University of Minnesota Alumni Association, Life Member; Concordia College Alumni Association. Religion: Lutheran, Former Sunday School Teacher, Luther League. Honors and Awards: Alpha Society; Zeta Sigma Phi; Phi Alpha Theta; Regional Honors for Debate and Discussion; High School Valedictorian, 1948; International Platform Association; National Defense Ribbon; Good Conduct Medal; Sharpshooters Medal; Life Fellow, American Biographical Institute; Listed in *International Who's Who in Education, Who's Who in the East, Personalities of America, Directory of Distinguished Americans, International Who's Who of Intellectuals, Men of Achievement, Dictionary of International Biography.* Address: Fox Run, 220 Bedford Street, Grayson Building #9, Bridgewater, Massachusetts 02324.■

RENEE LOLA OKOYE

Occupational Therapist. Personal: Born January 8, 1945; Daughter of Eleanor Fells; Mother of Amaogechukwu, Nkeiruka. Education: Attended the Ithaca College School of Music, 1962-63; B.S. 1966, Certificate in Occupational Therapy 1967, New York University School of Education; M.S., School of Allied Health Sciences, State University of New York at Stony Brook, 1978; New York State Licensed Occupational Therapist. Career: Clinical Instructor, School of Health Related Professions, University of Buffalo, 1972-74; Lecturer, World Health Organization Trainee Program, 1973; Clinical Assistant Professor, New York University, 1974-79; Consultant to Dean's Committee on Graduate Programs, Howard University College of Allied Health Sciences, 1977; Occupational Therapist, Medical Missionary, Children's Bible Fellowship of New York, 1979 to present; Occupational Therapist in Private Practice, 1975 to present; Clinical Assistant Professor, New York University Department of Occupational Therapy, 1974-78; Supervisor, Clinical Education, New York University Medical Center, Goldwater Memorial Hospital, 1970-74; Staff Therapist, St. Vincent's Hospital, 1967-69. Organizational Memberships: American Occupational Therapy Association; Long Island District, New York State Occupational Therapy Association; World Federation of Occupational Therapists. Published Works: Author, *An Eclectic Approach to Treatment of the Adult with Perceptual Motor Dysfunction* 1975, *Functional Evaluation of the Adult with Central Nervous System Dysfunction* 1976, *Neurosciences for the Practicing Clinician* (pending). Honors and Awards: Certificate of Appreciation, Long Island District, New York State Occupational Therapy Association, 1978; Certificate of Professional Achievement, State University of New York at Stony Brook, 1978; Certificate of Merit, Excellence in Practice in Physical Disabilities, New York State Occupational Therapy Association, 1979. Address: 59 Ford Drive West, Massapequa, New York 11758.■

CLIFTON OLIVER, JR.

Professor. Personal: Born December 3, 1915; Son of Clifton and Laura Peal Oliver. Education: B.A., M.A., Texas Tech University. Military: Served in the United States Army, attaining the rank of Second Lieutenant. Career: Retired Professor Emeritus, University of Florida; Associate Professor of Management, College of Business Administration, University of Florida; Consultant to a Number of Business Firms and Governmental Agencies. Organizational Memberships: American Arbitration Association; American Society of Training Directors; National Council of Small Business Management; American Society Personnel Association; American Education Association; American Arbitration Association; National Association of Purchasing Agents; National Football Foundation and Hall of Fame; Alpha Chi; Pi Sigma Alpha; Kappa Psi; Pi Gamma Mu; Alpha Kappa; Alpha Tau Omega. Community Activities: Florida Committee on Manpower; State of Florida Merit System, Chairman State Suggestion Committee; Industrial Communications Council, Director; F Club Athletic Association, University of Florida; Elks; Kiwanis; American Legion; Florida Blue Key. Religion: Baptist. Honors and Awards: Recognized for Contributions to Alpha Kappa Psi, Florida Banking Association, Florida Purchasing Association; Listed in *International Who's Who in Community Service, American Men and Women of Science, Dictionary of International Biography, Royal Blue Book, National Social Directory, Directory of Educational Specialists, Personalities of the South, Who's Who in the Southeast.* Address: P.O. Box 14505, Gainesville, Florida 32604.■

M. EUGENE OLSEN

Official Court Reporter. Personal: Born May 4, 1920, in Neola, Iowa; Son of Julius O. and Florence R. Olsen (both deceased). Education: Graduate, American Institute of Business, Des Moines, Iowa, 1940; Graduate, Stenotype Institute of Washington, Washington, D.C., 1957; B.S., The Creighton University, Omaha, Nebraska, 1949; B.S. (honorary), Jones College, Jacksonville, Florida, 1965. Career: Official Shorthand Reporter, Joint and Combined Chiefs of Staff, Washington, D.C., 1942-43; Reporter Assigned to a Special Presidential Mission to South American Countries, 1943-44; Reporter, United States Embassy, Ottawa, Canada, 1944-45; Official Court Reporter, International Military Tribunal for the Far East, Tokyo, 1945-47; Official Shorthand Reporter to Central Intelligence Agency Director Allen W. Dulles, Washington, D.C., 1952-57; Partner in Court Reporting Firm, 1957-72; Official Court Reporter, United States District Court, Washington D.C. (reported part of every Watergate trial, trials of Maryland United States Senator Brewster, United States Congressman Passman of Louisiana,

TWO THOUSAND NOTABLE AMERICANS

California Lieutenant Governor Reinecke, Texas Governor and United States Treasury Secretary John B. Connally; Served as Official Court Reporter at first international political assassination trial in United States; Served as Official Court Reporter at trial of John W. Hinckley, Jr.). Organizational Memberships: National Shorthand Reporters Association, Chairman National Seminar in Washington D.C. 1976, Member Board of Academy of Professional Reporters 1976-79, Served as Chairman or Member on Over 15 Boards and Committees including Chairmanship of National Speed Contest in Atlanta in 1980 and in San Francisco in 1981; Associated Stenotypists of America, President 1969-70; United States Court Reporters Association, Chairman Ethics Committee 1974-75, Board of Directors 1979-80; Pacific Northwest Court Reporters Association, Chairman Examining Committee 1967-71, President-elect 1971-72; Oregon Shorthand Reporters Association, Secretary-Treasurer 1965-67, Vice President 1967-69, President 1969-70, Chairman Oregon Seminar 1970, Executive Committee and Chairman Examining Committee 1970-72; Maryland Shorthand Reporters Association, Chairman Maryland Seminar 1975, Chairman Education Committee 1974-76; Virginia Shorthand Reporters Association, Chairman Education Committee 1977 to present; Louisiana Shorthand Reporters Association, Secretary-Treasurer 1963-64; Tennessee Court Reporters Association; Chartered Shorthand Reporters Association of Ontario, Canada, Fellow 1969; Honorary Lifetime Member of Oregon Shorthand Reporters Association 1972, North Dakota Shorthand Reporters Association 1974, West Virginia Shorthand Reporters Association 1975, Washington State Shorthand Reporters Association 1978; International Platform Association. Community Activities: Washington D.C. Performing Arts Society; Washington D.C. National Symphony Orchestra Association. Published Works: Author of Numerous Articles on Court Reporting Published in the National Shorthand Reporters Association's *National Shorthand Reporter*, the United States Court Reporters Association's *Circuit Rider*, and in Other National Professional Magazines, as well as Numerous State and Local Court Reporting Publications. Honors and Awards: Honorary B.S. Degree, Jones College, Jacksonville, Florida, 1965; National Shorthand Reporters Association, Certificate of Proficiency 1964, Certificate of Merit 1964, Top Recruiting Award 1969, Founding Fellow of the Academy of Professional Reporters 1975, Distinguished Service Award 1977 (presented on only 30 occasions in 90 years); Associated Stenotypists of America, Bronze Medal at 1965 National Shorthand Speed Contest for 280 Words per Minute, Master Reporter Award 1965, Expert Reporter Award 1965; Oregon Shorthand Reporters Association, Award of Excellence 1966, Tiger Award 1967, Certificate of Achievement 1967, Spark Plug Award 1968, Distinguished Service Award 1978; Washington State Shorthand Reporters Association, Certificate of Achievement, 1968; Pacific Northwest Court Reporters Association, Expert Reporter Certificate, 1969; Tennessee Court Reporters Association, Certificate of Accomplishment, 1965; Chartered Shorthand Reporters Association of Ontario, Canada, Fellow 1969; United States Army, Army Commendation Medal presented at American Embassy, Ottawa, Canada, 1945; Certified Shorthand Reporter Certificates include Certificates issued by California, Colorado, Florida, Iowa, Kansas, Maryland, New Hampshire, North Dakota, Ohio, Oklahoma, Tennessee, Utah, Virginia, Washington, West Virginia, Ontario Province. Address: 800 Fourth Street Southwest, Apartment 801, Washington, D.C. 20024.■

GERALD WALTER OLSON

Soil Technologist, Assistant Professor, Associate Professor. Personal: Born March 22, 1932, in Gothenburg, Nebraska; Married Mary Lee Gruber in 1961; Father of Bradford, David, Eric. Education: B.S. 1954, M.S. 1959, University of Nebraska; Ph.D. Soils, University of Wisconsin, 1962. Military: Served in the United States Army, 1954-56. Career: Worked with International Cooperation Administration in India, 1957-78; Party Chief of Soil Survey in Florence and Menominee Counties, Wisconsin; Soil Technologist, Assistant Professor, Associate Professor, Cornell University, Ithaca, New York, 1962 to present; Senior Soils Consultant, Food and Agriculture Organization of the United Nations, Rome and Iran, 1972; Visiting Soil Scientist to Environmental Geology Section of Kansas Geological Survey, 1973; Soils Consulting Work in New York State, the United States, Canada, Central America including Belize, Guatemala and Honduras, South American including Brazil and Venezuela, Europe including England and Italy, Asia including India, Iran, Japan, Philippines, Taiwan, Turkey, Thailand, Vietnam, the Pacific including Hawaii, New Zealand and Tahiti, Mexico, Puerto Rico, and Australia in the State of Victoria; Research, Teaching and Extension Work in Soil Survey Interpretations and Uses of Soil Information. Organizational Memberships: Epsilon Sigma Phi National Honorary Fraternity; Fellow, American Association for the Advancement of Science; Sigma Xi; Gamma Sigma Delta; American Society of Agronomy; Numerous Other Honorary and Professional Societies. Published Works: Author, *Field Guide to Soils and the Environment*, 1984. Honors and Awards: Received Special Recognition from Kansas Geological Survey. Address: 153 Emmerson Hall, Department of Agronomy (Soils), Cornell University, Ithaca, New York 14853.■

HARRY AXEL OLSON

Psychologist, Seminar Leader. Personal: Born December 5, 1944; Son of Axel and Mary Olson; Married Carol M.; Father of David Barclay. Education: Attended Philadelphia College of the Bible, 1962-64; Temple University, Philadelphia, A.B. 1966, Ed.M. 1968; Lutheran Theological Seminary, Philadelphia, 1966-67; Ph.D. Clinical Psychology, University of Tennessee, 1972. Career: Psychologist in Private Practice, Seminar Leader, 1978 to present; Director of Training, Walter P. Carter Center, Baltimore, 1974-78; Psychologist, Spring Grove Hospital Center, 1973-74; Director, Residential Treatment Services, Lutheran Social Services, Baltimore, 1972-73. Organizational Memberships: North American Society of Adlerian Psychology, Chairperson Region IV 1976-81; American Psychological Association; Maryland Psychological Association, Executive Committee Division 2 (Psychologists in Public Service) 1976-78; International Society of Hypnosis; Society for Clinical and Experimental Hypnosis; American Society of Clinical Hypnosis; National Speakers Association; International Platform Association; Baltimore Association of Consulting Psychologists. Community Activities: Kiwanis Club of Reisterstown; Baltimore County Chamber of Comerce, Membership Committee 1980 to present, Chairman 1980 to present, Speakers Bureau 1982 to present. Religion: Preaches at Various Churches and Religious Gatherings; Trinity Lutheran Church, Reisterstown, Senior High School Sunday School Teacher 1979 to present, Choir Member 1982 to present. Honors and Awards: University of Nonservice Fellowship, 1968-72; Listed in *Men of Achievement*, *Who's Who in the East*, *Community Leaders and Noteworthy Americans*. Address: 708 Church Road, Reisterstown, Maryland 21136.■

JAMES CLIFTON OLSON

Historian, Educator. Personal: Born January 23, 1917; Married Vera Blanche Farrington; Father of Elizabeth Goldring, Sarah Margaret. Education: A.B., Morningside College, 1938; M.A., University of Nebraska, 1939; Ph.D., University of Nebraska, 1942; LL.D., Morningside College, 1968; Litt.D., Chonnam National University, Korea, 1978; Litt.D., University of Nebraska, 1980. Military: Served with the United States Army Air Forces, 1942-46. Career: Instructor, Northwest Missouri State Teachers College, Maryville, Summers 1940-42; Director, Nebraska State Historical Society, Lincoln, Nebraska, 1954-56; Lecturer, University of Omaha, 1947-50; OAS Professor of American History, El Colegio De Mexico, Mexico City, 1962; Visiting Professor, University of Colorado, Boulder, Colorado, Summer 1965; University of Nebraska, Lecturer 1946-54, Associate Professor (part-time) 1954-56, Professor 1956-58, Bennett S. and Dorothy Martin Professor of History 1962-65, Chairman Department of History 1956-65, Associate Dean of Graduate College and Director of Graduate Program Development 1965-66, Dean of Graduate College and University Research Administrator 1966-68, Vice Chancellor for Graduate Studies and Research 1968; University of Missouri, Kansas City, Chancellor 1968-76, Interim President 1976-77, President 1977 to present. Organizational Memberships: Eastern National Park and Monument Association, Board of Directors 1983 to present; Joint Commission of the American Bar Association and Council on Post-Secondary Education, 1983 to present; American Association for State and Local History, Member of Council 1948-56, Regional Vice President 1956-62, President 1962-64, Member Editorial Committee 1958-62, Member Committee on Awards and Grants-in-Aide 1961-68, Chairman 1965-68; American Association of University Professors, Vice President University of Nebraska Chapter 1958-59, American Council on Education, Commission on Women 1978-81, Caucus on the Arts in Higher Education; American Historical Association, Member Committee on Committees 1965-68; Association of American Universities, Committee on Graduate Education Chairman 1979 to present; Association of Urban Universities, Vice President 1972-73, President 1973-75; Committee on Urban Public Universities; Coordinating Board for Higher Education, State of Missouri, Member Advisory Council, Chairman 1978-79, 1981-82, Secretary 1980-81; Council for Basic Education, Charter Member; Council on Post-Secondary Accreditation, Member of Board 1974-77, Task Force on Graduate Education Committee 1979 to present; Department of the Army, Historical Advisory Committee 1980 to present; Department of the Army, Historical Advisory Committee 1980 to present, Chairman 1981 to present; Inter-American Organization for Higher Education, Executive Committee for North America 1980 to present, Vice President 1981 to present; Kansas City Regional Council for Higher Education, Chairman of Board 1974-76, Honorary Director 1977-80; Mid-America State Universities Association, Chairman 1978-79; Mid-America Arts Alliance, Member Board of Directors 1974 to present, Chairman 1977-81; Midwest Research Institute, Member Board of Trustees 1976 to present; Mississippi Valley Historical Association, Secretary-Treasurer 1953-56; Missouri Council on Public Higher Education, President 1977-78; National Association of State Universities and Land-Grant Colleges, Commission on Fine Arts 1978 to present, Committee on International Affairs 1981 to present; National Research Council, Committee on Study of Research, Doctorate Programs in the United States; Nebraska History and Social Studies Teachers Association, President 1957-58; Nebraska State Historical Society, Member Executive Board 1957-68, President 1962-68, Honorary Life Member; Nebraska Writers Guild, President 1951-53; North Central Association, Evaluation and Review Committee, Commission on Higher Education; Organization of American Historians, Member Executive Committee 1963-66; Rotary Club of Columbia, Missouri; Saint Louis Symphony Society, Board of Directors 1977 to present; Standard Milling Company, Board of Directors 1975 to present; The Harry S. Truman Library Institute, Member Board of Directors, Chairman Grants-in-Aid Committee 1968-79, Vice President 1977-81, President 1981 to present; Western History Association. Community Activities: Morningside College, Board of Directors, 1972-81; Nelson Gallery Foundation and William R. Nelson Trust; United Telecommunications Inc., Board of Directors, 1977 to present; University of Mid-America, Board of Trustees, Chairman, 1979-82. Religion: Missouri United Methodist Church, Columbia, Missouri. Honors and Awards: Phi Beta Kappa; Omicron Delta Kappa; Phi Kappa Phi; Pi Gamma Mu; Montana Heritage Award, State Historical Society of Montana, 1958; Civic Service Award, Human Brand Hebrew Academy of Greater Kansas City, 1981. Address: 1900 South Providence Road, Columbia, Missouri 65201.■

JIM LEE OLSON

Director of Psychiatric Programs. Personal: Born January 3, 1941; Son of Mr. and Mrs. C. A. (Art) Olson; Married Eva Marie Marcinkowski, Daughter of Mrs. Mary Marcinkowski. Education: B.A. Psychology 1963, M.A. Psychology 1964, San Jose State University; Ph.D. Clinical Psychology, University of Kansas, 1968; Clinical Internship, Topeka V.A. Hospital and the Menninger Foundation, 1967-68. Military: Served with the United States Army, attaining the rank of Captain, Medical Service Corps, Ft. Sam Houston 1968-69, Ft. Leonard Wood 1969-70, Republic of Vietnam 1970-71. Career: Director of Psychiatric Programs, Hospital Corporation of America; Director of Psychological Services, Health Care Corporation, Chattanooga, Tennessee, 1978-81; Administrative Director and Supervising Psychologist, Mental Health Center of Milwaukee County, Milwaukee, Wisconsin, 1971-78; Private Practice of Clinical Psychology, Milwaukee, Wisconsin, 1971-78; Assistant Professor, Medical College of Wisconsin, Milwaukee, Wisconsin, 1973-78; Chief Psychologist, Inpatient Service, Letterman General Hospital, Presidio of San Francisco, California, 1971. Organizational Memberships: American Psychological Association; Tennessee Psychological Association; APA Divisions of Clinical, Consulting, and Psychotherapy; Psychologist in Independent Practice; Association of Psychology Internship Centers; Director of Internship Training in Clinical Psychology, Valley Psychiatric Hospital, Chattanooga, Tennessee, 1978-81; Nashville Area Mental Health Association. Community Activities: Board of Directors, Saint Vincent Home for Girls, Milwaukee, Wisconsin, 1973-76; Mental Health Planning Council of Milwaukee County, Milwaukee, Wisconsin, 1973-78; Alumni Association of Sigma Phi Epsilon Fraternity, 1963 to present; Board of Editors, *Neuropsychology Journal* 1978-81, Review Board 1981 to present. Honors and Awards: Bronze Star, Republic of Vietnam, United States Army, 1970; Society of the Sigma Xi, National Honorary Research Society, 1960 to present; Phi Kappa Phi, Honorary Scholastic Society, 1964 to present; Graduated with Distinction, Honors in Psychology, San Jose State University, 1963; Distinguished Military Graduate, 1963; Listed in *Who's Who in the South and Southwest, Personalities of the South and Southwest, Personalities of the South, Directory of Distinguished Americans, Men of Achievement.* Address: 3904 Trimble Road, Nashville, Tennesseee 37215.■

JOHN BENNET OLSON, JR.

Professor Emeritus. Personal: Born February 13, 1917; Son of John Bennet and Hedwig Christina Matthilda Munthe Olson (both deceased); Married Dorothy Daggett; Father of Christina Jane, Loren Leslie, Mary Carol. Education: B.S. cum laude, Beloit College, 1938; M.A. 1941, Ph.D. 1950, University of California at Los Angeles. Military: Served in the United States Army, 1945-46. Career: Research Assistant, Scripps Institution of Oceanography; Research Engineer, Douglas Aircraft Company; Research Associate, Cardiology, Children's Hospital, Los Angeles; Senior Research Fellow, Chemistry, California Institute of Technology; Chairman, Natural Sciences, Shimer College; Professor Emeritus, Purdue University. Organizational Memberships: New York Academy of Sciences; Indiana Academy of Sciences; Association of Midwest College Biology Teachers, Vice President 1963, President 1964; Indiana College Biology Teachers Association, President 1975; National Association for Research in Science Teaching; National Association of Biology Teachers; Member Number of Other Professional Organizations. Community Activities: Mental Health Association, Carroll County, Illinois, Vice President 1961-64; Friends Service Committee, Public Speaker 1957-58; Speakers Bureau, Indiana Academy of Science, 1965-70; National Science Foundation, Panelist 1963-72; National Institute for Campus Ministry, Workshop Leader 1979; Thomas Jefferson Gallery, Santa Monica, California, Director 1943-45; Watson's Crick Gallery, Purdue University, Director 1974-80. Religion: Christian Science Church, 1920-38; Unitarian-Universalist, 1950 to present; Board Member, University Church of Purdue, 1972-78; Volunteer, Lafayette Urban Ministry, 1967 to present. Honors and Awards: Professor of the Year, Association of Midwest College Biology Teachers, 1972; Distinguished Service Award, Beloit College Alumni Association, 1973; Best Painting in Show, First in Oils, First and Second in Enamels, Barnsdahl Park Gallery, Los Angeles, 1957. Address: 416 South Chauncey, West Lafayette, Indiana 47906.■

LAFEL EARL OMAN

District Judge Pro Tempore, Lawyer. Personal: Born May 7, 1912; Son of Mr. and Mrs. Earl A. Oman (both deceased); Married Arlie Giles; Father of Sharon O. Beck, Phyllis O. Bowman, Conrad LaFel, Kester LaFel. Education: J.D., University of Utah College of Law. Military: Served in the United States Navy, 1943-46, attaining the rank of Lieutenant. Career: District Judge Pro Tempore, Special Master; Lawyer; Former Positions include Justice and Chief Justice, New Mexico Supreme Court and Judge and Senior Judge, New Mexico Court of Appeals. Organizational Memberships: American Judicature Society, Director 1970-74; Continuing Legal Education of New Mexico; Conference of Chief Justices; American Bar Association; New Mexico Bar Association; New Mexico Bar Association; Utah Bar Association; Dona Ana County Bar Association, President 1952-53; First Judicial District Bar Association; Southwestern Legal Foundation, Local Representative; Law-Science Academy; Defense Research Institute; American Trial Lawyers Association; Phi Alpha Delta Fraternity; Institute of Judicial Administration; Section of Judicial Administration, American Bar Association, New Mexico Membership Chairman; Appellate Judges Conference; National Legal Aid and Defender Association; American Law Institute. Community Activities: Rotary Club of Las Cruces, Member 1948-66, President 1952-53; Rotary Club of Santa Fe, Member 1966 to present, Director 1973-74, Vice President 1975-76, Prsident 1976-77; New Mexico Historical Society; Historical Society of Santa Fe; Santa Fe Opera Guild; Visiting Nurse Service Inc., Director and Vice President 1980 to present; Assistant City Attorney, Las Cruces, 1958-59; City Attorney, Truth or Consequences, New Mexico, 1959-61; New Mexico Board of Bar Examiners, 1964-66; New Mexico Judicial Standards Commission, 1968-70, 1971-72; New Mexico Judicial Council, 1972-76; New Mexico Court of Appeals, 1966-70; New Mexico Supreme Court, 1971-77; Chief Justice, New Mexico Supreme Court, 1976-77. Religion: St. John's United Methodist Church, Santa Fe, Chairman of Administrative Board 1972-74, Board of Trustees, Pastor Parish Relations, Finance Committee, Sunday School Teacher. Honors and Awards: Herbert Harley Award, American Judicature Society; Judicial Service Award, Outstanding Service Award, New Mexico State Bar Association; Senate Memorial 35, 33rd Legislature of the State of New Mexico, Commendation for Outstanding Work and Great Contributions to the People of the State of New Mexico and the Administration of Justice; Testimonial of Gratitude and Respect, New Mexico Judicial Council, 1977; Credential in Recognition and Appreciation of Active Service on the Supreme Court of New Mexico, Judicial Conference of New Mexico. Address: 510 Camino Pinones, Santa Fe, New Mexico 87501.■

YOSHIAKI OMURA

Visiting Research Professor, Medical Administrator, Physician, Association Executive. Personal: Born March 28, 1934; Son of Tsunejiro and Minako Omura. Education: Pre-Medical Studies, Department of Electrical Engineering, Nihon University, 1952-54; B.Sc., Department of Applied Physics, Waseda University, 1947; M.D., School of Medicine, Yokohama City University, 1958; Graduate Studies in Experimental Physics, Columbia University, 1960-63; Sc.D., Departments of Pharmacology and Surgery, College of Physicians and Surgeons, Columbia University, 1965. Career: Rotating Intern, Tokyo University Hospital, 1958; Rotating Intern, Norwalk (Connecticut) Hospital, 1959; Research Fellow, Cardiovascular Surgery, Columbia University, 1960; Resident Physician in Surgery, Francis Delafield Hospital, Cancer Institute of Columbia University, 1961-65; Visiting Research Professor, Department of Electrical Engineering, Manhattan College, 1962 to present; Research Consultant, Orthopedic Surgery, Columbia University, 1965-66; Part-Time Emergency Room Physician, Englewood Hospital (New Jersey), 1965-66; Research Consultant, Pharamcology Department, New York Down State Medical Center, State University of New York, 1966; Assistant Professor of Pharmacology and Instructor in Surgery, New York Medical College, 1966-72; Director of Medical Research, Heart Disease Research Foundation, 1972 to present; Consultant, Lincoln Hospital Drug De-Toxification Program (by acupuncture), 1973-74; Visiting Professor, University of Paris, Summers of 1973-77; Editor-in-Chief, *Acupuncture and Electro-Therapeutics Research, The International Journal,* 1974 to present; Maitre de Recherche, Distinguished Foreign Scientist Program of INSERM (National Institute of Health and Medical Research) of the French Government, 1977; President, International College of Acupuncture and Electro-Therapeutics (Chartered College, New York State Department of Education), 1980 to present; Editorial Consultant, *Journal of Electrocardiology*, 1980 to present; Attending Physician, Department of Neuro-science, Long Island College Hospital, 1980 to present; Vice President, International Kirlian Research Association, 1981 to present; Adjunct Professor, Department of Pharmacology, Chicago Medical School, 1982 to present. Organizational Memberships: Fellow, New York Cardiological Society; Fellow, American College of Angiology; Fellow, American College of Acupuncture; Fellow, International College of Acupuncture and Electro-Therapeutics; New York Academy of Sciences; American Society of Artificial Internal Organs. Community Activities: Chairman, Science Division, Children's Art and Science Workshop, New York, 1971 to present; Chairman, Columbia University Affiliation and Community Medicine Committee Community Board, Francis Delafield Hospital, 1974-75; President, New York Japanese Medical Society, 1963-75. Honors and Awards: Research Fellow, Cardiovascular Surgery, Columbia University, 1960; Research Grant, American Cancer Institute, 1961-63; Faculty Grant, John Polacek Foundation, 1966-72; National Institutes of Health Research Grant, 1967-72; Research Grant, Heart Disease Research Foundation, 1972 to present; Matire de Recherche, Distinguished Foreign Scientist Program of INSERM, Research Unit #95, Nancy, France, 1977; Listed in Several International and U.S. Biographical Publications.■

JOANN C. ONDROVIK

Psychologist. Personal: Born February 13, 1944; Daughter of Mr. and Mrs. Frank Ondrovik; Married Nick Duren, Son of Mr. and Mrs. Buddy Duren; Mother of Jolie, Tad, Michael, Jeff. Education: Certificates in Speech and Hearing Therapy, Counseling, School Psychology; Bachelor's Degree in Speech and Hearing Therapy, Texas Women's University; Doctorate in Counseling and Guidance, Texas A&M University, 1973; Certified Trainer for Human Potential Seminar Group Processes and Masters and Johnson Sex Therapy. Career: Licensed by Texas State Board of Examiners; Registered National Health Service Provider in Psychology; Psychologist in Private Practice; Consultant on McCuistion Hospital Staff; Former Assistant Director of Psychological Services, Dallas Independent School District; Adjunct Professor, Psychology Department, East Texas State University Graduate School. Organizational Memberships: American Psychological Association; Red River Valley Association of Children with Learning Defects; Association for the Advancement of Psychology; Texas Psychotherapy Association; Association of Family Conciliation Courts; Association for Advancement of Behavior Therapy; Texas Speech and Hearing Association; New York Academy of Sciences; Northeast Texas Counselor's Association; American Society of Psychologists in Private Practice; Association for the Advancement of Psychotherapy; Dallas Psychological Association; Association for Women in Psychology; American Board of Forensic Psychology; Biofeedback Research Society of America; Texas Biofeedback Association; Southwest Psychological Association. Community Activities: Secretary, Airport Advisory Board, Paris City Council; Lamar County Young Women's Christian Association, Board Member 1977-83; Chamber of Commerce; Government Drug Abuse Council of Lamar County; Lamar County Human Resources Council; Lamar County League of Women Voters; Round Table; Northeast Texas Library Board; Family Haven, Shelter for Battered Women; American Cancer Society (Paris, Texas); Texas Lyceum Association, Inc. Honors and Awards: Certificate of Appreciation, Interfaith Disaster Services, 1983; Certificate of Recognition, Y.W.C.A. of Paris, 1983; Honored for Outstanding Support, Big Brothers/Big Sisters of America, 1978-79; Listed in *International Who's Who in Community Service, Personalities of the South, Who's Who of American Women*. Address: 3775 Leigh Drive, Paris, Texas 75460.■

JOHN JOSEPH O'NEIL

Art Administrator, Artist. Personal: Born April 20, 1932; Son of Elizabeth Grady O'Neil; Married Robin, Daughter of Sarah Harmon; Father of Virginia, Johnny, Tommy. Education: B.A., New York State University-Brooklyn, 1952; B.S., New York State University-Buffalo, 1960; Attended the University of Florence, 1959-60; M.A. 1962, M.F.A. 1967, Ed.D. 1973, Columbia University, New York City. Military: Served with the United States Army as Staff Photographer, Korea, 1952-54. Career: Art Administrator, Department of Art, University of South Carolina (Columbia); Artist; Graphic Designer, National Broadcasting, 1950-51; Display Artist, B. Altman (New York) 1951-52; Givandan Advertising 1954-55; Free-lance Work for Blue Cross/Blue Shield Insurance; Work has appeared in *Time, Life, Look, Fortune, U.S. News and World Report, New York Times, Bride's Magazine*, Others. Organizational Memberships: Southeastern Art Conference, 1963-83; Southern Graphic Council, Member 1972-83, President 1980-82; Artist's Guild of Columbia, Member 1963-83, Treasurer 1973-74, President 1966-67; South Carolina Craftsmen, Member 1963-83, Exhibition Chairman 1983; Sigma Epsilon; Kappa Delta Phi; South Carolina Art Education Association; Guild of South Carolina Artists, Chairman Nominating Committee; Columbia Museum of Art, Board of Directors 1983. Community Activities: Presidential Panel, Federal Graphic Design, National Endowment for the Arts, Member 1970-83; Telecommunications Instructions, Korean Culture Committee, University of South Carolina, 1979-83; Accessions Committee 1983, Membership Committee 1983, Committee on Animal Rights, Faculty Advisor 1982-83, Columbia Museum; World Print Council, 1980-83; Council on Child Abuse and Neglect-Graphic Design, 1977-83; Lyric Opera-Graphic Design, 1977-83; Museum Advisory Committee 1969-77, Member 1977-83, McKissick Museum, University of South Carolina. Religion: Roman Catholic. Honors and Awards: Art in Architecture, American Institute of Architects, 1979; Southeastern Invitational, University of Georgia, 1980; Irene Teache Memorial Exhibition, 1980; South Carolina Arts Collection, Presidential Panel on Graphic Design; National Endowment for the Arts. Address: 4225 Sequoia Road, Columbia, South Carolina 29206.■

RUTH O'NEAL

Associate Professor. Personal: Born June 7, 1915; Daughter of Mr. and Mrs. Joseph Bryan O'Neal (deceased). Education: A.B., Transylvania University, 1939; M.D., Medical College of Virginia, 1943; M.S. Pediatrics, Mayo Foundation Fellow in Pediatrics, 1948. Career: Assistant in Clinical Pediatrics 1948-51, Instructor in Clinical Pediatrics 1951-69, Assistant Professor of Pediatrics 1969-72, Bowman Gray School of Medicine; Associate Director of Pediatrics, Reynolds Memorial Hospital, 1969-72; Director of Pediatrics, Reynolds Health Center, 1972-77; Associate Professor of Pediatrics, Bowman Gray School of Medicine, 1972 to present. Organizational Memberships: Fellow, American Medical Association; Mayo Foundation Alumni Association; Society for Research in Child Development; Forsyth County Medical Society; Medical Society of the State of North Carolina; North Carolina Pediatric Society; North Carolina Mental Hygiene Society; Southern Medical Association; American Academy of Pediatrics; American Board of Pediatrics, Diplomate 1951; Ambulatory Pediatric Association; Southern Society for Pediatric Research; International College of Pediatrics; American Women's Medical Association; National Association of Child Abuse and/or Neglect; The International Society for the Prevention of Child Abuse and Neglect; Southern Medical Society. Community Activities: The Community Council, Welfare Division 1950-52; Soroptimist International, Board and Secretary 1952-54, Continuing Life Member; Girl Scouts of America, Co-Leader 1954-56, Girl Scout Board 1957-60 and 1961-64, Personnel Committee 1957-68, Camp Committee 1954-66, Selections Committee 1959-68, Personnel Committee 1969 to present; Young Women's Christian Association, Camp Committee 1966, Chairman of Camp Committee 1967-69, Board Member 1967-69; Citizens Planning Committee, Winston-Salem (North Carolina), 1963-64; Planned Parenthood Board, 1978 to present; Northwest Child Development Board, 1977 to present; Workshops on Child Abuse and Neglect, Bowman Gray School of Medicine, 1975; FACTS (Family and Child Treatment Systems), Organized Community and Hospital Groups for Child Abuse/Neglect 1975; SCAN; ESCAPE (Exchange Club) Board, 1980 to present; March of Dimes, Board of Directors 1972 to present, Medical Advisory Committee 1972 to present; Business and Professional Women's Club; Order of the Eastern Star; North Carolina State Art Society; North Carolina Society for the Preservation of Antiquities; North Carolina Literary and Historical Association; Photographic Society of America; Piedmont Craftsmen Inc.; Forsyth Country Club. Religion: First Christian Church, Finance Committee 1958, 1959, 1960, Church Board 1962-70, Committee for Nursery 1957-66, Committee for Kindergarten and Play School 1964-68, Committee for Christian Action and Community Service 1964-66 (Chairman 1968-70), Elder 1974-79, Santree Board 1978 to present, National Benevolent Board 1980 to present. Honors and Awards: Listed in *Who's Who in America, Who's Who Among American Women and North Carolina Lives, Who's Who in the South and Southwest, Personalities of the South*. Address: 445 Springdale Avenue, Winston-Salem, North Carolina 27104.■

MARIAN P. OPALA

Justice, Supreme Court of Oklahoma. Personal: Born January 20, 1921; Father of Joseph Anthony. Education: B.S. Economics, Oklahoma City University, 1957; J.D., Oklahoma City University School of Law, 1953; LL.M., New York University College of Law, 1968; LL.D. (honorary), Oklahoma City University School of Law, 1981. Career: Assistant County Attorney for Oklahoma County, 1953-56; Private Practice in Oklahoma City, 1956-60; Referee of the Supreme Court of Oklahoma, 1960-65; Private Practice in Oklahoma City, 1965-67; Professor of Law, Oklahoma City University of Law, 1965-69; Legal Assistant to Justice McInerney, Oklahoma Supreme Court, 1967-68; Administrative Director of the Courts of Oklahoma, 1968-77; Adjunct Profesor, University of Oklahoma College of Law, 1969 to present; Presiding Judge, State Industrial Court, 1977-78; Judge, Workers' Compensation Court, 1978; Justice, Supreme Court of Oklahoma, 1978 to present; Adjunct Professor, Oklahoma City University School of Law, 1983 to present. Organizational Memberships: Phi Delta Phi Legal Fraternity; Order of the Coif; American Society for Legal History, New York University Institute of Judicial Administration; Oklahoma Heritage

TWO THOUSAND NOTABLE AMERICANS

Association. Community Activities: Oklahoma Crime Commission, Member 1970-77; National Conference of State Court Administrators, Chairman 1976-77; Council on Juvenile Delinquency, Member of Executive Committee 1970 to present, Vice Chairman 1978 to present; American Association for Law School, Chairman Legal History Section 1976-77; New York University Summer Program for Law Teachers Alumni Association, President 1971; Oklahoma Commission to the National Conference of Commissioners on Uniform State Laws, 1982-86; Commission on Oklahoma Uniform Jury Instructions, Criminal Chairman 1971-81. Honors and Awards: Phi Alpha Delta/Oklahoma City University Alumni Award, 1962; Supreme Court's Oversight Committee, Award for Committment to the Improvement of Judicial Service to Youth of the State of Oklahoma and Assistance to the Oversight Committee; Court Related and Community Services Division DISRS, Award for Innovative Programs for Youth as Administrative Director of the Courts; Oklahoma Shorthand Reporters Association Award for Outstanding and Dedicated Service; Supreme Court of Oklahoma, Award in Appreciation for Lasting Contributions to the Oklahoma Judiciary and Distinguished Service as the First Administrative Director of the Courts, 1977; American Judicature Society's Herbert Harley Award for Outstanding Achievement in Court Improvement, 1977; Oklahoma Bar Association's Law and Citizenship Education Special Committee, Award for Exceptional Contribution to Law-Citizenship Education in Oklahoma; American Society for Public Administration's (ASPA) Award for Public Administrator for the Month of December, 1978; 1979 Oklahoma City University Distinguished Alumni Award; 1980 Valley Forge Honor Certificate, Freedoms Foundation at Valley Forge. Address: 5709 Northwest 64th, Oklahoma City, Oklahoma 73132. ■

KURT OPPELT

Corporate Executive, Private Practitioner Sport Analysis and Counseling. Personal: Born March 18, 1932; Son of Josef and Rosa Karl Oppelt; Married Cathleen Ellen Pavlis, Daughter of John and Kay Pavlis; Father of Kurt, Christopher Thomas. Education: Matura, Sportlehrer, Kaufmann, Vienna, Austria, 1953-60; Ph.D. (Education), California, 1979. Career: Private Practice, Sport Analysis, Sports Psychology; President, Success Systems Inc., Winter Park, Florida; Professor, The Pennsylvania State University, 1967-80; Specialist and Consultant, President J. F. Kennedy Physical Fitness Program, 1961-67; Coach, Royal Dutch Figure Skating Team, 1957-60; Director, JKO Packaging, Vienna, Austria, 1954-60. Organizational Memberships: American College of Sports Medicine; American Public Health Association; National Therapeutic Recreation Society; American Alliance for Health, Physical Education, Recreation and Dance; American Society of Professional Consultants. Community Activities: International Council on Therapeutic Ice Skating, 1974 to present, Executive Vice President; C.C.C. Pennsylvania Association of Retarded Citizens, Member 1976-80, Vice President, Member Various Comittees; Ice Skating Institute of America, 1972-76, Chairman Committee on Handicapped Programs; Founder, Ice Skating Therapy. Honors and Awards: Austrian, European, World Champion and Olympic Gold Medal Winner in Ice Skating, 1956; Sportsman of the Year; Olympic and Ice Skating Halls of Fame; Golden Honor Awards, Amateur and Olympic Committees, 1956; Key to the City of Charlotte, North Carolina, 1976. Address: P.O. Box 4541, Winter Park, Florida 32793. ■

HENRY ORLAND

Composer, Conductor, Professor, Writer. Personal: Born April 23, 1918; Son of Theodore and Hedwig (Weill) Orland (both deceased). Education: B.Mus. 1949, M.Mus. 1950, Ph.D. 1959, Northwestern University; Certificat d'Etudes, University of Strasbourg, 1947. Military: Served with the United States Army during World War II as Liaison Officer. Career: Composer, Conductor, Professor, Writer. Organizational Memberships: American Society of Composers, Authors and Publishers; American Musicological Society; American Federation of Musicians; American Society of University Composers; Bibliotheque Internationale de Musique Contemporaine. Community Activities: Amnesty International, Urgent Action Committee. Honors and Awards: Delius Prize for Composition, 1973; MacDowell Foundation Resident Composer Fellow; 1951 Chicago Music Critics Award for Composition; 1950 National Music Honorary Society, Phi Kappa Lambda; Decorated Purple Heart, 5 Battle Stars. Address: 21 Bon Price Terrace, St. Louis, Missouri 63132. ■

MARGARET ROBERTA ORLICH

University Administrator. Personal: Born February 27, 1917; Daughter of Mr. and Mrs. Henry John Carlson (deceased); Married Eli, Son of Mr. and Mrs. Peter Orlich (deceased). Education: Graduate, Duluth High School, 1935; B.S. 1939, M.A. 1955, Ed.D. 1983, University of Minnesota. Career: Administrator, University of Minnesota-Duluth; Former Positions include High School Teacher, High School Principal, Superintendent of Schools. Organizational Memberships: Alpha Delta Kappa, National and International President 1971-73, International Field Representative, Other Offices including North Central Regional Grand Vice President and President-Elect; Council of Presidents of National Organizations in the U.S.A., National President 1978-80, Vice President and Other Offices, Editor of *Communication Links* 1978-80; Minnesota Association of Women Highway Safety Leaders, First Vice President 1980-84, Editor *Minnesota Safe Ways* 1980 to present; National Association of Women Highway Safety Leaders, National Board Member 1978-80; National Education Association, Life Member, Curriculum Committee Member; Minnesota Education Association, Delegate-at-Large, President and Secretary of Local Units (during 1950's); American Federation of Teachers, President and Other Offices (during 1960's); National Council of Social Studies; Minnesota Council of Social Studies, Local Chairman of Social Studies Curriculum Committee in Duluth (several years); St. Louis County Historical Society; Friends of the Library, Duluth Committee (during 1960's); Duluth Business and Professional Women's Club, President (late 1960's) and Other Offices; Minnesota Business and Professional Women's Club, International Relations Chairperson 1970-72, Young Career Women Chairman 1972-74, Wrote International Newsletter 1970-72; National Federation of Business and Professional Women's Clubs; American Association of University Women, International Relations Chairperson 1960's and 1980-82, Other Committees; Parent-Teacher-Student Organization, Local President (during 1950's), Numerous Committees, Program Chairman 15 Years; League of Women Voters, Unit Leader on Local Level 8 Years, Numerous Clubs, District VIII President 1980-82, St. Louis County Federation Secretary, Minnesota Federation of Women's Club International World Affairs Representative, President of Local Affiliation, 20th Century Club of Duluth; Head of the Lakes United Nations Association, Founder, Treasurer 1980-84, Past President 1974-76, Served in all Offices and all Committees, Founded in 1962; Head of the Lakes World Affairs Council, Co-Founder 1970, Served as President 1974-76, All Offices and Committees; Young Men's Christian Association, International Relations Committee 1977 to present, Helped Sponsor "Know Your Government" Tour for High School Students to Washington D.C., New York, Boston and Many Historical Parts of the Eastern United States, Instructor and Leader, Helped Pay the Way for Several Poorer Students; Young Women's Christian Association, Life Member, Served on Various Committees for Past 15 Years; Duluth Woman's Club, Member, Donated Several Philanthropic Programs; Mayor's Committee on the United Nations 1962 to present, Chairman for Several Years; International Folk Festival, Served on Various Committees and Charge of United Nations Booth for Last 10 Years; Feast of Nations, Founder and Served on Many Committees 1965 to present; Model United Nations, Co-Founder in Establishing a Model General Assembly Among High School Students in Minnesota, Wisconsin, Michigan and Ontario (Canada); Arrowhead Model United Nations, Assistant 1975 to present; Order of the Eastern Star, White Shrine, Daughters of the Nile, Served in Various Offices and on Several Committees 1955 to present. Published Works: Contributor of Articles to Organizational and Professional Journals. Honors and Awards: UNESCO Scholarship, Studies UNESCO Around the World, 1970; United Nations Fellowship Award, International Business and Professional Women's Clubs, 1970; United Nations Peace Award, 1975; American Association of the United Nations, National Award 1964, National Membership Award; Young Men's Christian Association, Statesmanship Award 1971, Service to Youth Award 1974; Business and Professional Women's Club, State Award for Outstanding Service in International Relations, State Award for Helping Handicapped Students 1975; Finalist for Duluth's Hall of Fame 1972 and for Woman of the Year; Alpha Delta Kappa Award for Distinguished Service to Alpha Delta Kappa, 1975 (National and International Award); Duluth Civic Service Awards from 3 Different Mayors; Written up in *Ladies Home Journal*, July 1970; Numerous Biographical Listings. Address: 421 Anderson Road, Duluth, Minnesota 55811. ■

ARACELI ORTIZ

Professor. Personal: Born January 15, 1937, in Culebra Island, Puerto Rico; Daughter of Jesus M. Ortiz (deceased) and Pura Martinez; Married Jesus Latimer; Mother of Paul. Education: Graduate of Colegio San Antonio (High School); B.S., University of Puerto Rico, 1958; D.M.D., University of Puerto Rico, 1962; Resident in General Pathology, University District Hospital, Puerto Rico, 1962-65; M.S.D., Specialty in Oral Pathology, Indiana University, 1967. Career: McGill University, Montreal, Canada, 1967-73; Professor, School of Dentistry, University of Puerto Rico, 1973 to present Guest Lecturer, Forensic Odontology for the Interamerican University Law School, 1973 to present; Extensive Lecturer and Table Clinican in the United States, Canada, Puerto Rico and South America; Producer of 30-Minute Public Service Television Program "Sonrie Puerto Rico." Organizational Memberships: American Academy of Oral Pathology Diplomate; American Board of Medicine, Diplomate; American Board of Forensic Odontology, Diplomate; American Dental Association; College of Dental Surgeons, Puerto Rico; American Academy of Oral Medicine; Canadian Academy of Oral Pathology; Canadian Academy of Oral Medicine; American Society of Forensic Sciences; Canadian Society of Forensic Odontology; Puerto Rico Society of Periodontology; Beta Beta Beta; Association of Women Dentists of Puerto Rico; Association for Educational Communications and Technology; American Cancer Society. Community Activities: Zonta International, Area V Director, District XI 1980-82, President Club San Juan 1979-80; National Institute of Health, United States Department of Health, Education and Welfare, Clinical Care Training Committee 1972-73; Producer and Moderator for Public Service Television Program on Dental Health. Religion: Roman Catholic. Honors and Awards: Public Service Program "Sonrie Puerto Rico" Chosen as Best Public Service Program for the Year (Instructional), Tele Radial Institute of Ethics of Puerto Rico, 1978, 1980, 1981, and the Bronze Medal at the 25th International Film and Television Festival of New York, 1982; Distinguished Alumni, Colegio San Antonio, 1964; Distinguished Alumni, University of Puerto Rico School of Dentistry, 1965; Distinguished Alumni Association of Student Clinicians, American Dental Association, 1966; Outstanding Lady of 1976, Chamber of Commerce, Puerto Rico; Distinguished Lady of the Year, Federation of Journalists and Press Writers of Puerto Rico, 1977; 1980 Faculty Advisory Award, Alumni Association of Student Clinicians of the American Dental Association; Distinguished Woman Dentist, American Association of Women Dentists, 1979; Consultant in Oral Pathology and Oral Medicine, Veterans Administration Hospital, Puerto Rico, 1973 to present. Address: Condominio Sequovia Apartment 410, Hato Rey, Puerto Rico 00918.■

ROMAN SVIATOSLAV ORYSHKEVICH

Physician, Educator. Personal: Born August 5, 1928, in Olesko, Ukraine; Son of Simeon and Caroline Deneshchuk Oryshkevich; Married Oksana Lishchynsky, 1962; Father of Marta, Mark, Alexandra. Education: D.D.S. 1952, M.D. 1953, University of Heidelberg; West German Licensure to Practice Medicine and Surgery 1953, Dentistry 1954; Post-graduate Studies in Experimental Cancer, Research Institute of Rupert-Charles University, earing a Ph.D. cum laude 1955; Rotating Internship, Coney Island Hospital (Brooklyn, New York), 1955-56; Resident/Fellowship, New York University Hospital/Bellevue Medical Center (New York City) and Western Reserve University Affiliated Hospitals (Cleveland, Ohio). Career: Clinical Instructor 1962, Assistant Professor, Associate Clinical Professor 1975 to present, Director of University of Illinois Affiliated Hospitals Integrated Residency Training Program in Physical Medicine and Rehabilitation; Assistant Chief 1961, Acting Chief 1974, Chief of Rehabilitation Medicine Service 1975 to present, Veterans Administration West Side Medical Center; Certified in Electromyography and Electrodiagnosis, 1964; Diplomate, American Board of Physical Medicine and Rehabilitation, 1966. Organizational Memberships: Ukrainian Medical Association of North America, Illinois Chapter, Secretary 1971-75, President-Elect 1975-77, President 1977-79; Illinois Society of Physical Medicine and Rehabilitation, Secretary-Treasurer 1977-78, Vice President and President-Elect 1978-79, President 1979-80; World Federation of Ukrainian Medical Association, Elected First Executive Secretary of Science and Research 1977-79; Ukrainian World Medical Museum in Chicago, Founder 1977, Elected First President 1979; Chicago Society of Physical Medicine and Rehabilitation, Elected First President 1978; Ukrainian Academy of Medical Sciences, Founder 1979, Elected First President 1979-80; Specialty Consultant to Editorial Board in Physical Medicine and Rehabilitation, *Chicago Medical Journal*, 1978 to present; American Museum of Physical Medicine and Rehabilitation, Founder 1980, First President 1980; American Academy of Physical Medicine and Rehabilitation, Fellow; Association of Academic Psychiatrists; American Association of University Professors; American Congress of Rehabilitation Medicine; American Association of Electromyography and Electrodiagnosis; American Medical Writers Association; Association of Medical Rehabilitation Directors and Coordinators; Biofeedback Research Society of America; Illinois Society of Physical Medicine and Rehabilitation; Chicago Society of Physical Medicine and Rehabilitation; National Association of Veterans Administration Physicians; International Rehabilitation Medicine Association; International Society of Electrophysiological Kinesiology; Federation of American Scientists. Religion: Ukrainian Catholic Church. Honors and Awards: Listed in *International Who's Who in Community Service, Notable Americans, International Who's Who of Intellectuals, Men of Achievement*, Others. Address: 1819 North 78 Court, Elmwood Park, Illinois 60635.■

OSAYIMWENSE OSA

Educator. Personal: Born June 27, 1951; Son of Mr. and Mrs. J. N. Osa; Married Justina O. Idemudia; Father of Osaguona, Osazuwa, Ewere. Education: B.A. (Hons), Certificate in Education 1973, Ahmadu Bello University; M.A. English, University of New Brunswick, 1978; Ed.D. English Language and Arts Education, Uniersity of Houston, 1981. Career: Professor, Bendel State University, Nigeria; Former Positions include High School/Advanced Level Instructor, Examiner in English for the West African Examinations Council, Team Leader/Examiner for the National Teachers Institute (Kaduna, Nigeria), Professor at the University of Houston (Central Campus), Acting Director of African and Afro-American Studies Program at the University of Houston (University Park). Organizational Memberships: National Society for the Study of Education, 1980 to present; Arizona English Teachers Association, 1983; American Library Association, 1982-83; African Literature Association, 1979; Comparative and International Education Society, 1979; National Council of Teachers of English, 1978-79; Nigeria English Studies Association, 1982-83; Texas Association of Africanists, 1979; Association for Supervision and Curriculum Development, 1979-80. Community Activities: University of Houston Faculty Expert on African Religions and Philosophy/Culture, Discussing African Religions, Philosophy, Culture and Education in Houston and for U.S. National News Media, 1979-82; Guest Speaker on African Education/ Affairs, KYOK Radio and KTSU Radio, Houston, 1980-81. Religion: Christian. Published Works: Scholarly Contributions (Published Articles) to *World Literature Written in English* 1981 and 1983, *English Journal* 1983, *Arizona English Bulletin* 1980, 1982, 1983, *Research in African Literatures* 1983. Honors and Awards: University of New Brunswick (Canada) Summer Research Grant, 1977; Federal Nigeria Postgraduate Award, 1976, 1980; Nominated to *Who's Who in the South and Southwest*. Address: P.O. Box 5484, Benin City, Nigeria.■

GEORGE COLEMAN OSBORN

Retired University Professor. Personal: Born May 15, 1904; Married Margaret McMillen; Father of Margaret Elizabeth, Alice Jean Osborn Polk. Education: A.B., Mississippi College, 1927; A.M. 1932, Ph.D. 1938, Indiana University; Post-doctoral Study undertaken at Harvard University. Career: Retired Professor of History and Political Science; Former Positions include Head of History Department at Berry College, Research Expert on Taxation for the Finance Committee of the United States Senate, Associate Professor of History at the University of Mississippi, Head of the History Department at Memphis State University and Professor of History and Social Studies at the University of Florida (27 Years). Organizational Memberships: American Historical Association; Organization of American Historians; American Association of University Professors; Southern Historical Association; American Academy of Political and Social Sciences. Published Works: Author of Numerous Research Articles and Book Reviews and of Books: *John Sharp Williams: Planter Statesman of the Deep South, Woodrow Wilson Early Years, 1856-1902, First Baptist Church, Gainesville, Florida, 1870-1970: A History, John James Tigert: American Educator, Woodrow Wilson in British Opinion and Thought, James Kimble Vardaman: Southern Commoner, Role of the British Press in the 1976 Presidential Election*. Honors and Awards: Research Grants from the American Philosophical Society, the Woodrow Wilson Foundation and the University of Florida; Florida Blue Key Distinguished Faculty Award, 1969; Phi Kappa Phi National Academic Honor Society, 1976; Mississippi College Service to Humanity Award, 1976. Address: 1714 N.W. 7th Avenue, Gainesville, Florida 32603.■

JOSEPH PATRICK OSBORN

Coach. Personal: Born April 18, 1947; Son of John T. and Lillian T. Osborn. Education: Graduate of Father Judge High School, 1965; Attended Bergen Community College, 1978-80. Military: Served in the United States Army, 1966-69, attaining the rank of SP/4. Career: Coach, Bergen Vocational Schools; Former Assistant Athletic Director for the Lodi Boys Club and Social Worker. Community Activities: Assistant Director, The Lodi Heart Fund; Lodi Old Timers Little League; Baseball Coach, Lodi Yankees (3 Years in Lodi Recreation and 1 Year in Lodi Little League); Coach, American League Western Champions (Lodi Yankees), 1982; Big Brother, Town of Lodi, 1978 to present; Drug and Alcohol Education, DeVries Park Housing Project, 1980; Volunteer to Friends Hospital and the Philadelphia Byberry Hospital, 1975-77; Hospice Program Volunteer, Hackensack Hospital, 1982; Active Supporter of the International Year of the Child Campaign, 1980. Published Works: Author of Book *Poems for Christ*. Honors and Awards: Coach of the Year, County of Bergen, Hackensack Baseball League, 1981; Coach of Championship Costello Cubs in the Stick Ball League at Lodi Boys Club, 1979; National Defense Service Medal, 1967-69; Vietnam Campaign Medal, 1967-69; Vietnam Service Medal, 1967-69; Bergen Community College Dean's List and Honor List, 1979; City of Philadelphia Basketball Foul Shooting Champion, 1963; General Assembly Resolution from the State of New Jersey by Assemblyman Burns for Coaching the Lodi Boys

Club Softball Team to the State Championship in 1979; Coach of the State of New Jersey Softball Champions, Lodi Boys Club; Certificate of Service, National Council on Alcoholism (for invaluable contributions counselling and conducting public health fairs), 1978; Certificate from the New Jersey State Department of Health for work with Young People and Women Afflicted with Drug and Alcohol Abuse, 1978; Certificate of Achievement in Behavior Modification, State of New Jersey Drug and Alcohol Training Center (Princeton), 1978; Certificate of Outstanding Service to the National Council on Alcoholism, 1979. Address: P.O. Box 31, Rochelle Park, New Jersey 07662.■

PRIME F. OSBORN, III

Corporate Chairman. Personal: Born July 31, 1915, in Greensboro, Alabama; Married Grace Hambrick; Father of Prime F. IV, Mary Anne. Education: J.D. 1939, LL.D. (honorary) 1970, University of Alabama at Tuscaloosa. Military: Served with the United States Army, advancing from Second Lieutenant to Lieutenant Colonel of Artillery, Pacific Theatre including Hawaii, Guam, Saipan and Iwo Jima; Graduate of Command and General Staff School, United States Army, 1942; Executive Reservist, Office of Emergency Transportation, Department of Transportation of the United States. Career: Assistant Attorney General, State of Alabama (Montgomery), 1939-41; Commerce Attorney, Gulf, Mobile and Ohio Railroad (Mobile, Alabama), 1946-51; General Solicitor, Louisville and Nashville Railroad (Louisville, Kentucky), 1951-57; Vice President and General Counsel, Atlantic Coast Line Railroad Company (Wilmington, North Carolina and Jacksonville, Florida), 1970-78; President and Chief Executive Officer, Louisville and Nashville Railroad Company (Louisville, Kentucky), 1972-74; President and Chief Executive Officer, Seaboard Coast Line Industries, Inc. (Jacksonville, Florida), Seaboard Coast Line Railroad and Louisville and Nashville Railroad, 1978-80; Chairman, CSX Corporation, 1980 to present. Community Activities: Boy Scouts of America, President North Florida Council 1962-66, Chairman Region Six 1965-69, Member Regional Executive Committee Southeastern Region, National Executive Board National Railroad Committee on Scouting, National Exploring Committee Chairman Executive Board (Old Kentucky Home Council); United Fund of Jacksonville (Florida), Director 1962-70, Senior Vice President 1971; Duval County Taxpayers Association, President 1963-66; Greater Jacksonville Area Chamber of Commerce, President 1970-71; United Fund of Louisville (Kentucky), Director 1972-74; Greater Louisville Area Chamber of Commerce, Director 1972-74; University of Alabama National Alumni Association, Executive Committee, National Vice President 1974-75; Jacksonville University Board of Trustees, 1963-77; Trustee, Protestant Episcopal Theological Seminary of Virginia, 1963-68; Board of Overseers and Directors, Sweet Briar College (Sweet Briar, Virginia), 1968-77; Director and Trustee, Jacksonville Episcopal High School, 1969-72; Board of Directors, Berry College (Mt. Berry, Georgia, 1972-77; Dean's Advisory Council, Purdue University; Executive in Residence, Auburn University, 1979; Honorary President, Troy State University, 1981; Board of Advisors, Jacksonville Salvation Army, 1965-71; Board of Advisors, Louisville Salvation Army, 1972-74; National Advisory Council Chairman, Salvation Army, 1978 to present; Young Americans for Freedom, National Advisory Council; Southern States Industrial Council, Executive Committee, Vice President; Advisory Council, Spirit of '76 Foundation; Advisory Committee, Young Life; State of Florida Governor's Advisory Council on Economic Development, Commission on Transportation; Florida Council of 100; Saint Vincent's Medical Center, Lay Advisory Board, Executive Committee; Trustee, Freedoms Foundation at Valley Forge; National Advisory Board, American Security Council; Trustee, Florida Independent College Fund; Sigma Alpha Epsilon Fraternity, President Alabama Mu Chapter; Omicron Delta Kappa; Beta Gamma Sigma Honorary, University of Florida; Scabbard and Blade; Masons; American Legion; Huguenot Society; Military Order of the Stars and Bars; Military Order of the World Wars; Rotary Club of Jacksonville; Society of Colonial Wars; Sons of the American Revolution; Sons of Confederate Veterans, Kirby Smith Chapter; The Southern Academy of Letters, Arts and Sciences, Director General; Veterans of Foreign Wars; Florida Yacht Club (Jacksonville); Timuquana Country Club (Jacksonville); Deerwood Country Club (Jacksonville); River Club (Jacksonville); Ponte Vedra Club (Ponte Vedra Beach, Florida); Tournament Players Club (Ponte Vedra Beach); Sawgrass (Ponte Vedra Beach); Augusta National (Augusta, Georgia); Commonwealth Club (Richmond, Virginia); Laurel Valley Country Club (Ligonier, Pennsylvania); Louisville Country Club (Louisville, Kentucky); Pendennis Club (Louisville); Army and Navy Club (Washington, D.C.); Metropolitan Club (Washington, D.C.); Union League Club (New York, New York). Religion: Member Protestant Episcopal Church in the United States; Member National Executive Council of the Episcopal Church, 1963-70; Member House of Deputies, General Convention from Diocese of Alabama, 1948-50, Diocese of Kentucky 1956-58, Diocese of East Carolina 1958-58, Diocese of Florida 1965-67 and 1968-70; Chairman, Laymen's Work from Diocese of Alabama 1947-51, Diocese of Kentucky 1952-56; Provincial Chairman, Laymen's Work, Fourth Province, 1952-58; Member Urban Industrial Division, National Executive Council, 1955-59; Member Executive Committee, Provincial Synod, Fourth Province, 1961-70; Vestry, St. Paul's Episcopal Church (Louisville, Kentucky) 1952-56, St. John's Episcopal Church (Wilmington, North Carolina) 1957-60, St. Mark's Episcopal Church (Jacksonville, Florida) 1963-66, 1976-79 and 1980. Honors and Awards: Decorated American Theatre Medal, American Defense Medal, Pacific Theatre Medal with 2 Campaign Stars, Army Commendation Medal, Bronze Star; Man of the Year Award, Jacksonville, Florida, 1962; Silver Beaver Award, Boy Scouts of America, 1965; Silver Antelope Award, Boy Scouts of America, 1967; Management Award, Sales and Marketing Executives Association, 1970; Silver Buffalo Aawrd, Boy Scouts of America, 1972; Religious Heritage of America Award, 1973; Bicentennial Brotherhood Award, National Conference of Christians and Jews, 1976; Award of Merit, Alabama State Bar, 1977; Man of the South, 1978; Executive of the Day, University of North Florida, 1978; Transportation Man of the Year, National Defense Transportation Association, 1981; William Booth Award, The Salvation Army, 1981; Americanism Award, Anti-Defamation League, 1981; Listed in *Book of Honor, Community Leaders of America, Dictionary of International Biography, Executive and Professional Hall of Fame, Florida Lives, International Register of Profiles, Men of Achievement, National Register of Prominent Americans, Personalities of the South, Who's Who in America, Who's Who in Commerce and Industry, Who's Who in Florida, Who's Who in Railroading, Who's Who in Religion, Who's Who in the Southeast, Who's Who in the South and Southwest, Who's Who in the World*. Address: 5005 Yacht Club Road, Jacksonville, Florida 32210.■

CHARLES E. OSBORNE

Assistant Dean, Professor. Personal: Born February 4, 1947; Son of Mr. and Mrs. Charles W. Osborne; Married Janice Marie, Daughter of Mr. and Mrs. Earl Philips; Father of Ashley Michelle, Courtney Elizabeth. Education: B.S. 1969, M.S.Ed. 1970, Ed.D. 1972, Northern Illinois University (DeKalb, Illinois). Career: Assistant Dean for Continuing Medical Education, Professor of Medical Education, Southern Illinois University School of Medicine (Springfield, Illinois), 1977 to present; Director of Research, Commission on Professional and Hospital Activities, 1975-77; Director, Office of Evaluation, American Academy of Pediatrics, 1971-75. Organizational Memberships: Board of Directors 1978 to present, Secretary 1982, Illinois Council on Continuing Medical Education; Co-Chairman 1979 to present, Continuing Medical Education Advisory Committee, Illinois Cancer Council; Nursing Education Committee 1978 to present, Lincoln Land Community College; American Public Health Association; American Educational Research Association; Association of American Medical Colleges; Board of Trustees 1974-75, Children's Hospital Automated Medical Program (CHAMP); Board of Directors 1977-79, Human Services Education Council; Board of Governors, Southern Illinois University School of Medicine; Alumni Association, Southern Illinois University School of Medicine, 1979-85; President, Dale Carnegie Program in Effective Speaking and Human Relations. Community Activities: Society of Medical College Directors of Continuing Medical Education Research Committee 1984; Illinois Council in Continuing Medical Education, Workshop Committee 1978 to present, Research Committee 1979 to present (Chairman 1983), Congress Committee Member 1982, Chairman of Committee 1983; Illinois Heart Association Education Committee, 1979 to present; Central Illinois Consortium for Health Manpower Education Chairman, Faculty Development Task Force; Editorial Reviewer for *The Journal of Pediatrics, Medical Care, Illinois Medical Journal*; Site Visitor for Accreditation Council for Continuing Medical Education and the Illinois Council on Continuing Medical Education. Honors and Awards: Certificate of Appreciation, Southern Illinois University School of Medicine, 1978; Award of Merit, American Academy of Family Physicians, 1975; Citation for Outstanding Service Rendered, American Academy of Psychiatrics, 1975; Certificate of Appreciation, Project Head Start, 1975; Certificate of Achievement, American Association of Medical Society Executives, 1972; Listed in *International Book of Honor, Directory of Distinguished Americans, Who's Who in the Midwest, Men of Achievement, Who's Who in Health Care, International Who's Who of Intellectuals*. Address: 2505 Manchester Drive, Springfield, Illinois 62704.■

WALTER WYATT OSBORNE

Agricultural Consultant and Author. Personal: Born October 31, 1925; Son of Garnette E. Osborne; Married Flora Drewry Bethell; Father of Walter Wyatt Jr., Bethell Anne, Alease Drewry, Anders Osborne Gonzalez. Education: B.S. Agronomy 1951, M.S. Plant Pathology and Physiology 1958, Virginia Polytechnic Institute and State University; Ph.D. Plant Pathology and Nematology, Rutgers University. Career: Consultant, International Agricultural Institute, Inc.,

TWO THOUSAND NOTABLE AMERICANS

1979 to present; Consultant, Agri-Tech Laboratories, Inc., 1977-79; Virginia Polytechnic Institute and State University, Retired Professor, Professor of Plant Pathology 1967-77, Associate Professor of Plant Pathology 1958-67, Assistant Professor of Plant Pathology 1956-58; Assistant Manager, Bethell Pontiac Company, Inc., 1951-53. Organizational Memberships: Southern Soybean Disease Workers' Council, Chairman Organizational Steering Committee, First President, Member Board of Directors, Chairman Publications Committee, Chairman Nominating Committee; Chairman Tobacco Disease Council, Annual Tobacco Workers Conference; Sigma Xi, Rutgers and Virginia Polytechnic Institute and State University Chapters; Society of Nematologists, Co-Chairman SON/ASTM ad hoc Committee; European Society of Nematologists; American Phytopathological Society, Potomac Division, Southern Division; American Society of Agronomy Industry Peanut Disease Workers Council, Past President National Extension, Organizational Chairman, Member Board of Directors, Chairman Aflatoxin Disease Control Committee, Chairman Nominating Committee, Chairman Publications and Publicity Committee, Chairman Committee on Regional Projects; Tobacco Workers Council, Chairman Tobacco Disease Council—Nematode Control Agents, Chairman Tobacco Disease Loss Estimates (Virginia); American Standards for Testing and Materials, Co-Chairman of E35-15 Nematode Control Agents Committee, Chairman ASTM Nematology Terminology Committee; Virginia Academy of Science; Virginia Pesticide Association, Charter Member and Member Board of Directors 8 Years; Virginia Plant Protection Conference Organizational Chairman; American Association for the Advancement of Science. Published Works: Author Numerous National and International Scientific Papers and Magazine Articles on the Identification and Control of Nematodes and Plant Diseases. Honors and Awards: Recognized Internationally for Original Research in Agriculture and has Conducted Lectures, Seminars and Consultations in South America, Central America, Europe, Africa, the Middle East, and Asia; Inducted into Sigma Xi, 1958; Developed Centrifucation-Flotation Method to Extract Soil Borne Nematodes, Eggs, Cysts, and Microsclerotia from Samples of Soil, Shortening Extraction Time from Two Days to Ten Minutes, 1960; Discovered a Cyst Nematode on Tobacco in Amelia County, Virginia Which was Later Named the "Osborne Cyst Nematode" by Dr. L. I. Miller, 1962; Designed and Constructed Self-Contained Mobile Nematode Diagnostic and Control Laboratory (first mobile laboratory in the U.S.A.), 1965; Initiated Extensive Greenhouse and Field Plot Research to Determine Optimum Chemical Methods of Application and Rates for the Most Economical Pest Management on Tobacco, Peanuts, and Soybeans, also Appointed Research and Extension Directorship of this Program, 1967; Appointed Virginia Coordinator of Regional Peanut Podrot Diseases Control and Applied Control of Other Peanut Diseases in Combined Regional Program with North Carolina State University, 1970; Man of the Year in Agriculture, Colombia, South America, 1972; National Co-Chairman of Society of Nematologists/American Standards for Testing and Materials Committee Which Developed and Published Guidelines for Evaluation of Nematocides, 1973; Award of Excellence, Southern Soybean Disease Workers' Council, 1974; Leadership Award, Southern Soybean Disease Workers, 1980; Listed in *International Who's Who in Education*. Address: Winter, 4209 Saltwater Blvd., Tampa, Florida 33615; Summer, 1319 Main Street, South Boston, Virginia 24592.■

ROY OSWALD

Owner and Manager Rental Property. Personal: Born July 20, 1944. Education: B.S. Business Administration, Troy State University, 1969; Diploma in Graphic Arts, John Patterson Technical College, 1978. Military: Served in the United States Army Infantry, Vietnam/Cambodia, 1969-71. Career: Owner and Manager of Rental Property; Former Positions include Sanitarian, Salesman, Buyer, Social Worker. Organizational Memberships: International Academy of Poets; Academy of American Poets; American Poets Fellowship Society; P.O.E.T.S.; Western World Haiku Society; Society of Christian Poets; American Biographical Institute; International Biographical Association. Honors and Awards: Listed in *International Authors and Writers Who's Who, Men of Achievement, Personalities of the South, Directory of Distinguished Americans, Two Thousand Notable Americans, International Book of Honor, Dictionary of International Biography, Five Thousand Personalities of the World*. Address: 1136 Lombard Drive, Montgomery, Alabama 36109.■

RAYMOND B. OTERO

Professor, Consultant. Personal: Born May 8, 1938; Married Tamara Ann; Father of Raymond Jr., Bryan C. Education: B.S., University of Dayton, 1960; M.S., University of Rochester, 1963; Ph.D., University of Maryland, 1968. Career: Professor/Consultant, Eastern Kentucky University. Organizational Memberships: A.S.M.; New York Academy of Sciences; A.P.I.C.; K.A.S.; A.T.S.; S.C.A.C.M. Community Activities: President, South Central Association for Clinical Micro., 1974. Honors and Awards: Excellence in Teaching, Eastern Kentucky University, 1980. Address: 3410 Merrick, Lexington, Kentucky 40502.■

MURRAY EADE OTHMER

Consulting Chemical Engineer. Personal: Born August 6, 1907; Son of Harry R. Othmer (deceased); Married Mary M.; Father of David A. Education: B.S., Grinnell College, Grinnell, Iowa, 1929; Graduate Studies, University of Rochester, 1930, 1931; M.S. Engineering, University of Michigan, 1933. Career: Chemical Engineer, Eastman Kodak and American Cyanamid; Professor of Chemical Engineering, Tufts University and University of Puerto Rico; Technical Director, Valores Guatemaltecos, Guatemala City; South American Production Supervisor, Sterling Drug; Director, C.A.I. Productora de Grasas and Tresco, Caracas. Organizational Memberships: American Institute of Chemical Engineering; American Chemical Society; American Oil Chem. Society; A.A.A.S., Fellow 1964; National Institute Oilseed Processors, Quality Control Committee. Community Activities: Triangle Memorial Society, Director 1974 to date; International Executive Service Corps, Volunteer 1982. Honors and Awards: Fellow, A.A.A.S., 1964; Society of Sigma Xi, 1942 to present; Registered Professional Engineer, Com. of Massachusetts, 1943 to present; International Executive Service Corps, Malaysia Selagor and Silver Plaques; Listed in *Who's Who in the South and Southwest, American Men and Women of Science*. Address: 1087 Burning Tree Drive, Chapel Hill, North Carolina 27514.■

EDWARD THOMAS O'TOOLE, JR.

Microbiologist and Educator. Personal: Born July 7, 1933, in Frederick, Maryland; Married Edith Helen Stimson, April 19, 1958; Father of Shirley Hope, Edward Thomas III, Eugene Stanley. Education: B.S., University of Maryland at College Park, 1958; Sc.M., Johns Hopkins School of Hygiene and Public Health, Baltimore (Maryland), 1971; Ph.D., Union Graduate School (Cincinnati, Ohio), 1977; Additional Studies undertaken at the University of Maryland Dental School, Johns Hopkins Medical School, Loyola College (Baltimore), the United States Army Medical Technology School, the United States Army Laboratory Technology School, the United States Army Blood Bank School; Registered Microbiologist in the Areas of General Microbiology, Pathologic Microbiology and Parisitology, National Registry of Microbiologists of the American Academy of Microbiology; Microbiology Specialist in Areas of Public Health and Medical Laboratory Microbiology, Registry Numbers 731 and 198 (1971); National Registry of Scientific and Technical Personnel; American Society of Clinical Pathology Registry Number 852 in the Area of Cytology, 1964; Advanced Professional Certification in Teaching, State of Maryland, 1960; Certification in Cytology, Johns Hopkins Hospital, 1962; Certification in Mycology and Parasitology, Maryland State Health Department, 1963; Certification in Fluorescence Microscopy, C.I.S.I., 1974; Numerous Workshops. Military: Served in the United States Army Medical Service, 1956-58. Career: Teacher, Baltimore County Board of Education, 1958-60; Chief Microbiologist, Saint Joseph Hospital, Baltimore (Maryland), 1960-64; Cytopathologist and Microbiolgy Consultant, Hospital for the Women of Maryland (now Greater Baltimore Medical Center), 1964-65; Chief Microbiologist, Becton Dickinson and Company, Hunt Valley (Maryland), 1964-68; Director, Sterility Services and Clinical Laboratory, Huntingdon Research Center Inc., Brooklynville (Maryland), 1968-72; Teacher, Baltimore City Schools, 1972 to present; Microbiologist, Food and Drug Administration, Washington D.C., 1978 to present; Senior Partner, E²+3, Microbiology, Parasitology and Cytology, Riderwood (Maryland), 1964 to present. Organizational Memberships: American Society for Microbiology, National Level and Maryland Branch; Secretary-

Treasurer, Member Archives Committee, Member Program Committee, Social Committee, American Institute for Biological Sciences; American Association for the Advancement of Science; American Society of Clinical Pathologists; American Society of Medical Technologists; Maryland Society of Medical Technologists; Central Atlantic States Association of Food and Drug Officials; Institute of Food Technology; National Science Teachers Association; Past Member, American Association for Contamination Control, American Chemical Society, Society for Cosmetic Chemists, Soap and Detergent Association, The Royal Society of Health (London, England), Maryland State Teachers Association. Community Activities: Boy Scout Testing Counselor; Firearms Safety Instructor; Hunter Safety Instructor; Leader, Junior's Rifle and Pistol Club; CPR Instructor; Boating Safety Instructor. Religion: Roman Catholic. Honors and Awards: Kappa Kappa Psi (Music). Address: P.O. Box 303, Riderwood, Maryland 21139. ■

CARL-OLOF NILS STEN OVENFORS

Professor of Radiological Sciences. Personal: Born September 26, 1923; Son of Carl (deceased) and Signe Olson; Married Aimee; Father of Claes Olof, Aimee. Education: Graduate of Norra Latin College, 1941; M.S. 1951, Ph.D. 1964, Docent 1964, Karolinska Institute Medical School (Stockholm, Sweden). Military: Served in the Swedish Navy as a Medical Officer, 1951-52, attaining the rank of Captain. Career: Chief of Department of Thoracic Radiology, Karolinska Institute, Stockholm, 1968-70; Chief of Radiology, Veterans Administration Center, San Francisco, 1970-77; Professor of Radiology, University of California Medical Center at San Francisco; Professor of Radiological Sciences, University of California at Los Angeles. Organizational Memberships: The Fleischmer Society, Member 1969 to present, Chairman of Rules Committee 1981 to present; North American Society for Cardiac Radiology; Radiology Society of North America; Society for Thoracic Radiology, Founding Member 1982. Community Activities: University of California Medical Center, San Francisco, Teaching and Executive Committees 1970-77. Honors and Awards: Picker Research Fellow 1962-63 and 1966-68; Picker Scholar 1961-62, The James Picker Foundation for Radiology Research. Address: 4300 Empress Avenue, Encino, California 91436. ■

J. HOMER HAROLD OVERHOLSER

Executive. Personal: Born June 18, 1914; Son of Alden Earl Overholser (deceased); Married Lee, Daughter of Allalee Whelan (deceased); Father of James Alan, Sharyl Ann. Education: Studies in Mechanical Engineering, Wittenberg College, 1935; Studies in Aerospace Engineering 1939, Business Administration 1955, University of California at Los Angeles. Career: Design Engineer, National Supply Company, 1935-36; Development Engineer, Chrysler Airtemp Division, 1936-38; Project Engineer, Vultee Aircraft Corporation, 1938-39; Engineering Supervisor, Northrop Aircraft Corporation, 1939-43; Chief Engineer 1943-46, Executive Vice President and Director 1946-53, Hydro-Aire Inc.; Vice President and Board Chairman, Skyline Catering Corporation 1952-59, K&S Building Corporation 1952-56; Assistant General Manager, Pacific Division, Bendix Corporation, 1953-58; President and Chairman of the Board, Hydrodyne Corporation, 1958-59; Vice President and Director, Poly Industries, Inc., 1959-60; President and Chairman of the Board, Dynamatics Inc., 1960-61; Executive Vice President and Director, U.S. Sytems Inc., 1961-62; President and Chairman of the Board, Solar Systems Inc., 1961-62; Vice President and Director, Buckingham Palace Corporation, 1961-63; President and Chairman of the Board, Woodland Savings and Loan, 1961-63; Director, Casa Electronics Corporation, 1961-62; President and Board Chairman, Corporation Service Inc., 1961-63, Precision Dipbraze Inc. 1961-67; Director, Southwest Bank, 1961-63; Vice President and Board Chairman, National Post-Pak Systems Inc., 1961-63; Vice President and Director, Woodlake Realty Inc., 1962 to present; President and Board Chairman, Mio Dio Uranium Corporation, 1962-65; President, American Investment Company, 1962-63; Executive Vice President and Director, American Hydrocarbon Corporation, 1963-64; President and Director, Basic Industries Inc., 1963-64; Vice President and Director, Intercontinental Engineering and Manufacturing Corporation, 1963-64; President and Board Chairman, Aero Spacelines Inc., 1963-65; Founder and Director, Independence Bank, 1963-68; President, Jaco Management Company, 1963-69; Vice President and Director, E.M.C. Instrumentation Inc., 1964-65; Vice President and Director, S.O.M. Corporation, 1964 to present; Chairman of the Board, Saalfield Aircraft Corporation, 1965-68; President and Director, California Time Airlines, 1965-66; Chairman of the Board and Secretary, Varadyne Inc., 1966-69; Secretary and Director, Interdyne Inc., 1967-70; Chairman of the Board and Vice President, Zolomatics Inc., 1967-70; President and Director, Palm Springs Mobile Country Club, 1967-70; President and Director, Microwave Sensor Systems Inc., 1968-70; Chairman of the Board and Director, United Optical Systems Inc., 1968-70; Chairman of the Board, Clerke Technicorp Inc. 1968-75, Clerke Recreation Products Inc. 1968-74; President and Chairman of the Board, Aqua Systems Inc., 1968-70; Vice President and Director, Blue Haven Pools Inc., 1968-70; Director, S.D.L. Optical Corporation, 1968-70; President, The Overholser Foundation, 1968 to present; President and Chairman of the Board, Sierra Pacific Financial Corporation 1969-71, Sierra Western Life Insurance Company 1969-72; Director, Electromask Inc., 1969-70; Secretary, Director and Chairman of Finance Committee, Varadyne Industries, Inc., 1969 to present; Chairman of the Board, J.Y.S. Corporation 1969-71, Spectran International Ltd. 1971-74, Royal Catfish Industries Inc. 1970-72, International Houseboats and Recreation Inc. 1970-75; Chairman of the Board and President, Western-Pacific Resources Inc. 1970-72, Royal Pacific Financial Corporation 1970-73; Chairman of the Board, World Finance and Mortgage Corporation 1970-71, Sierra Pacific Development Corporation 1970-72, Georgetown Associates Inc. 1970-72; Chairman of the Board and President, Hotel Development Corporation 1970-73, Karr Publications 1971-72, Foreign Commerce Corporation 1971-73, Consolidated Recreation Corporation 1972-77; Chairman of the Board, Los Cocos Development Corporation, 1972-74; Chairman of the Board and President, Highland Associate Inc., 1973-74; Chairman of the Board, Southern California Hotel Corporation 1973-74, Highland Park Ford Inc. 1973-74; President and Director, Brush Award Vending Corporation, 1976-77; Chairman of the Board and President, Alphatec International Inc. 1977-79, National Golf Products Inc. 1977 to present, National Golf Media Inc. 1977 to present; Chairman of the Board and Executive Vice President, Franchise Associates Inc., 1979 to present; Chairman of the Board and Secretary/Treasurer, Pusser's Inc., 1979 to present; Vice President and Chief Financial Officer, Vital Communications Inc., 1979 to present; Number of Former Business Partnerships. Organizational Memberships: Institute of Aero Sciences; American Ordnance Association; American Society of Mechanical Engineers; American Institute of Management; American Helicopter Society; Air Force Association; Association of the United States Army; Registered California Professional Engineer; Chairman, S.A.E. Fuel Valve Committee; American Society of Air Affairs. Community Activities: International Platform Association; Republican Party; North Hollywood Chamber of Commerce; Aviation Committee, Los Angeles Chamber of Commerce; Industry Chairman, Los Angeles County March of Dimes; Hollywood Chamber of Commerce; Lakeside Golf Club; Braemar Golf Club; Free and Accepted Masons; Lodge of Perfection (32nd Degree); Al Malaikah Shrine; Woodland Hills Shrine Club; Patron Member, Los Angeles County Museum of Art; Chairman of the Board of Governors, San Fernando Wine and Food Society; National Voter Advisory Board, American Security Council; Los Angeles World Affairs Council; Sons of the American Revolution. Religion: Church of God of Abrahamic Faith. Published Works: Articles "Diversification in Business," "Anti-Skid Braking System," "Bendix-Decca Navigation System Applied to Helicopter Operations." Honors and Awards: Designed and Developed First Wing Folding Method for U.S. Navy Airplanes (1941); Developed and Put into Operation, HYTROL (first and most widely used aircraft anti-skid braking system); Pioneered Construction of Pregnant Guppy (world's first outsized cargo airplane); Developed First Sonic Altimeter (1957); Pioneered the Adoption of Decca Navigation System in Canada (1959); Designed a Pure Hydraulic Drive for Cars (1947); Designed First Self-Contained Room Air Conditioner in U.S. (1938); Developed and Marketed First Successful Solar Heating System for Swimming Pools (1961); Holds Patents on Hydraulic Valves, Fuel Valves, Micronic Filters, Hydraulic Drive System, Tire Warning Device; Certificate of Appreciation, The National Foundation of Infantile Paralysis; The Honorable Order of Kentucky Colonels; Freedom Season Pioneer Award, Woodland Hills Chamber of Commerce; Certificate of Appreciation, Young Americans for Freedom; 2,000,000 Mile Club, United Airlines, 1957; Certificate of Merit for Distinguished Service in Business Development; Listed in *Who's Who in the World, Who's Who in America, Who's Who in California, Who's Who in the United States, Who's Who in Finance and Industry, Who's Who in the West, Who's Who in Business and Finance, Who's Who in Steel and Metals, Who's Who in California Business and Finance, World Who's Who in Commerce and Industry, International Businessmen's Who's Who, International Who's Who in Community Service, International Who's Who of Intellectuals, Dictionary of International Biography, International Year Book and Statesmen's Who's Who, International Register of Profiles, International Book of Honor, Men of Achievement, Directory of Distinguished Americans, Community Leaders and Noteworthy Americans, Community Leaders of America, Personalities of the West and Midwest, The Social Register, National Social Directory, Royal Blue Book, The California Register, The Blue Book, Los Angeles Blue Book, Notable Americans of the Bicentennial Era, Men and Women of Distinction, Personalities of America*, Others. Address: 4961 Palomar Drive, Tarzana, California 91356. ■

NORMAN LLOYD OWEN

Educational Administrator. Personal: Born January 13, 1937; Married Muriel L.; Father of Paul, Sharene. Education: Master's Degree in Educational Administration, University of California, 1978; Doctorate in Education, Stanford University, 1970. Career: President, Learning Horizons; Former Professor of Music; Creator of Unique Instructional Design Used in Software Program for the Apple II entitled "Learning to Read: Letters, Words, Sentences," (Edu-Ware-Peachtree, Inc.). Organizational Memberships: La Mesa Chamber of Commerce; American Curriculum and Supervision Committee; California Curriculum Committee. Community Activities: President, Greenville Orpheus Society, 1970-72; President, First Marianas Fellowship, 1974. Religion: Organist for Various Churches. Honors and Awards: Stanford Allyne Fellowship, 1968; Listed in Twelve Biographical Works. Address: 5924 Highplace Drive, San Diego, California 92120. ■

TWO THOUSAND NOTABLE AMERICANS

WILLIE P. OWENS

Retired Educator. Personal: Daughter of Richard and Annie B. Perry (both deceased); Mother of One Daughter. Education: B.S., Winston-Salem Teacher's College; Further Studies at Bennett's College, J. C. Smith University, University of North Carolina at Chapel Hill, University of North Carolina at Charlotte, 1940-60. Career: Elementary School Teacher in Mecklenburg County and in the Charlotte City School System, 1937-71; In Charge of Music Programs, 1937-63; Head of First Head Start Program at Anna Jones Elementary School. Community Activities: American Association of Retired Persons. Religion: Greenville Memorial African Methodist Episcopal Church, Member Over 40 Years, Organized First Youth Choir, Superintendent of Buds of Promise, Sunday School Superintendent, Adult Sunday School Teacher, Played for and Sang in Senior Choir, Member of State Board #3 and Missionary Circle #3, Chairperson for Mortgage Burning of Greenville Tabernacle Church 1968. Honors and Awards: Honored by Laymen's Council of African Methodist Episcopal Zionist Church with Banquet at J. D. Smith University; Certificate of Honor from Presiding Elder of Church, 1976; Youth Day Program Dedicated to Her, 1981; Plaque, Board of Christian Education. Address: 1909 Taylor Avenue, Charlotte, North Carolina 28216.■

EARL W. OYLER

Vocal and Instrumental Supervisor. Personal: Son of Walter and Ethel Oyler (both deceased); Married Janet Marie; Father of Leiann. Education: B.M., James Millikin University, 1952; M.M., Illinois State University, 1956; Advanced Graduate Work, University of Illinois; Attending Lincoln Land Community College. Military: Served with the United States Army, Member and Vocalist of the United States Artillery Band in Japan and Korea. Career: Teacher of Vocal and Instrumental Music in Public Schools, 17 Years; Band and Vocal Director, Tovey School, Tovey, Illinois; Formerly Vocal Director, Assumption Elementary and Junior High School, Assumption, Illinois; Vocal Supervisor, Elementary and High School Choral Director, Nokomis Community Unit School, Nokomis, Illinois; Vocal Director, Piper City School, Piper City, Illinois; Student of Computer Science, Electronic Data Processing and Business (Lincoln Land), Computer Languages of Cobol, Fortran, R.P.G. I and II, Basic, J.C.L. and Assembler. Organizational Memberships: Phi Theta Kappa; Alpha Beta Gamma, President 1982-83, Vocalist, Pianist, Delgate National Convention 1983; Decatur Area Music Teachers Association, President 1976-79, Organ Syllabus Chairman 1983-84; Nokomis Teachers Association, President 1960-63; Illinois Education Association, Representative of the General Assembly 3 Years, Vocalist 2 Years; Superintendent of the State of Illinois, Vocalist; Illinois State Music Teachers Association, Member, Former Chairman, Voice Syllabus Committee. Community Activities; Senior Olympics of the State of Illinois, Vocalist; National Oratorical Society, Vocalist; Taylorville Municipal Band, Soloist; Springfield Municipal Band; Springfield Municipal Opera, Vocal Director, Soloist "1776," Vocalist 1981 Season of "Camelot," Vocal and Dramatic Lead as Mr. Bumble in "Oliver," Vocal and Dramatic Lead as Dr. Engel in "Student Prince"; Oyler Family Historian, Family Farm Manager. Religion: First Baptist Church of Taylorville, Deacon, Past Director of Music, Choir Director. Published Works: Words and Music for Bicentennial Song "1776 History"; Words and Music for Original Musical "The Tempo of the Times"; Official State Fair Song for the State of Illinois, "Our Illinois, Our Land of Lincoln." Honors and Awards: Honorable Mention, American Song Festival, for "Off in the Distance," (a Christmas selection); Alpha Beta Gamma; Phi Theta Kappa; Music Scholarship to James Millikin University, 1948; State Certification in Organ and Piano; National Certification in Voice, Piano, Music Theory and Organ; Listed in the *International Who's Who in Music* and *Musicians Directory*, the *Directory of Distinguished Americans*, the *International Book of Honor*. Address: 620 Pauline Street, Taylorville, Illinois 62568.■

ARNOLD DANIEL PALMER

Professional Golfer, Business Executive, Author. Personal: Born September 10, 1929, in Pennsylvania; Son of Milfred J. Deacon and Doris M. Palmer (both deceased); Married Winifred Walzer, 1954; Father of Margaret Ann Reintgen, Amy Lyn Saunders. Education: Attended Wake Forest University. Military: Served in the United States Coast Guard, 3 Years. Career: Professional Golfer; President, Arnold Palmer Enterprises; President, Major Owner, Arnold Palmer Cadillac, Charlotte, North Carolina, and Arnold Palmer Motors, Latrobe, Pennsylvania; President, Whole Owner, Latrobe Country Club, 1971 to present; President, Principal Owner, Bay Hill Club and Lodge, Orlando, Florida, 1969 to present; Major Stockholder, Member of Board of Directors, ProGroup Inc., Sporting Goods Manufacturer; Palmer Course Design; Arnold Palmer Aviation Charter Service. Organizational Memberships: Laurel Valley Golf Club; Ironwood Country Club, Palm Desert, California, Business Associate; Westmoreland County, Pennsylvania, Airport Authority; United States Golf Association, National Chairman, Associates Program, Museum Committee; Professional Golfers Association of America; Rolling Rock Club, Ligonier, Pennsylvania; Duquesne Club, Pittsburgh; Oakmont Country Club, Pennsylvania; Quail Hollow Country Club, Charlotte, North Carolina; Cherry Hills Country Club, Denver, Colorado; Lakeside Country Club, Hollywood, California; Wilshire Country Club, Los Angeles, California; Indian Wells Country Club, Palm Desert, California; Certified Business Jet Pilot. Community Activities: National Foundation of the March of Dimes, Board of Trustees, Honorary National Chairman 1970-; Latrobe Area Hospital, Pennsylvania, Board of Directors. Published Works: Author, *Arnold Palmer Golf Book, Portrait of a Professional Golfer, My Game and Yours, Situation Golf, Go for Broke, Arnold Palmer's Best 54 Golf Holes.* Honors and Awards: Athlete of the Decade, Associated Press Poll, 1960's; Winner, United State Amateur Championship, 1954; Hickok Athlete of the Year, 1960; Sportsman of the Year Trophy, *Sports Illustrated,* 1960; Charter Member, World Golf Hall of Fame, Pinehurst, North Carolina; American Golf Hall of Fame, Foxburg, Pennsylvania; Winner, Five West Penn Amateur Championships; Honorary Doctor of Laws Degree, Wake Forest University, National College of Education; Honorary Doctor of Humanities Degree, Thiel College; Honorary Doctor of Human Letters, Florida Southern College; Professional Golfers of America Hall of Fame; Bob Jones Award, United States Golf Association; William D. Richardson and Charles Bartlett Awards, Golf Writers Association of America; Herb Graffis Award, National Golf Foundation; Gold Tee Award, Metropolitan Golf Writers Association; Man of Silver Era, *Golf Digest;* Partner in Science Award, March of Dimes Birth Defects Foundation; Player of the Year, Professional Golfers Association, 1960, 1962; Vardon Trophy, 1961, 1962, 1964, 1967; United States Ryder Cup Team, Member 1961, 1963, 1965, 1967, 1971, 1973, and Team Captain 1963, 1975; Pennsylvania Sports Hall of Fame; Western Pennsylvania Sports Hall of Fame; Arthur J. Rooney Award, Catholic Youth Association, Pittsburgh; Lowman Humanitarian Award, Los Angeles; Theodore Roosevelt Award, National Collegiate Athletic Association; Old Tom Morris Award, Golf Course Superintendents of America; Distinguished Pennsylvanian, 1980; Winner, Canadian Open 1955, Panama Open 1956, Columbia Open 1956, Eastern Open 1956, Insurance City Open 1956, 1960, Houston Open 1957, Azalea Open 1957, Rubber City Open 1957, San Diego Open 1957, 1961, St. Petersburg Open 1958, Pepsi Open 1958, Masters Championship 1958, 1960, 1962, 1964, Okalhoma City Open 1959, 1964, United States Open Championship 1960, Mobile Open 1960, Baton Rouge Open 1960, 1961, Texas Open 1960, 1961, 1962, Canada Cup (with partner Sam Snead) 1960, 1962, Pensacola Open 1960, 1963, Bob Hope Desert Classic 1960, 1962, 1968, 1971, 1973, Colonial National Invitational 1962, British Open Championship 1961, 1962, Tournament of Champions 1962, 1965, 1966, American Golf Classic 1962, 1967, Phoenix Open 1961, 1962, 1963, Cleveland Open 1963, Whitemarsh Open 1963, Australian Wills Masters 1963, Canada Cup (partner Jack Nicklaus) 1963, 1964, 1966, Los Angeles Open 1963, 1966, 1967, Thunderbird Classic 1963, 1967, World Cup (partner Jack Nicklaus) 1964, 1967, Australian Open 1966, Houston Champions International 1966, Professional Golfers Association Team Championship (partner Jack Nicklaus), 1970, 1971, Tucson Open 1967, World Cup International Trophy 1967, Kemper Open 1968, Heritage Classic 1969, Danny Thomas Diplomat Classic 1969, Citrus Open 1971, Westchester Classic 1971, Lancome Trophy (France) 1971, Spanish Open 1975, British Professional Golfers Association Championship 1975, Canadian Professional Golfers Association 1980, Professional Golfers Association Seniors 1980, 1984 United States Golf Association Senior Open 1981, Marlboro Classic 1982, *Denver Post* Champions of Golf 1982, Boca Grove Seniors 1983. Address: P.O. Box 52, Youngstown, Pennsylvania 15696-0052.■

CLAUDE FUNSTON PALMER

Retired Photographer. Personal: Born May 16, 1899; Son of Mr. and Mrs. Thomas E. Palmer (both deceased); Married Helen Gail, Daughter of Mr. and Mrs. Jonathan Mattley (both deceased); Father of Elizabeth Jean (Mrs. Ian) McBride. Education: B.S., Oregon State University, 1922; M.Photog., Professional Photographers Association of America, 1967. Military: Served in the Reserve Officers Training Corps, 1918-22, advancing through the ranks from Private (Infantry) to Lieutenant Colonel; Served in the O.R.C., 1922-27, attaining the rank of Second Lieutenant, Field Artillery. Career: Retired; Commercial Photographer, 1925-78; Salesman, Photographic Supply, 1919-22. Community Activities: Director, Portland Chamber of Commerce, 1950; President, Oregon Advertising Club, 1945; President, Oregon Chapter National Federation of Sales Executives, 1948; President, Oregon State University Alumni Association, 1947; President, Oregon State University Dads Club, 1946; President, Oregon State University Foundation, 1950; National President, Professional Photographers of America. Religion: First Presbyterian Church of Portland, 1925 to present; Chairman of Board, Salvation Army, 1975. Honors and Awards: Honorary Master of Photography, Professional Photographers of America, 1967; Legion of Honor, Kiwanis International, 1957; Life Member of Board, Salvation Army, 1975. Address: 1000 Southwest Vista Avenue, Portland, Oregon 97205.■

ROSEYLEE KATHRYN PALMER

Artist, College Administrator. Personal: Born September 27, 1923; Daughter of J. M. and Arizona Steen (deceased); Married Everett S. Palmer Jr.; Mother of Jerry Everett. Education: Graduate, Henryetta (Oklahoma) High School; Attended Odessa College; A.A., Frank Phillips College; B.S. Art Education, M.A., Postgraduate Study, West Texas State University; Postgraduate Study, North Texas State University; Private Study with Professional Artists. Career: Chairman of the Fine Arts Division, Frank Phillips College; Major Exhibitions at West Texas State University, Odessa College, Frank Phillips College, Texas State Capitol, The National Cowgirl Hall of Fame, Carson County Square House Museum, The Lake Meredith Aquatic and Wildlife Museum, The Layland Museum, Texas Women Western Artist Exhibits, Texas Fine Arts Association Exhibits, New Mexico Wildlife Federation Convention (Solo Exhibit), Juried Art Exhibits on Local, State and National Levels. Organizational Memberships: Texas Fine Art Association; Texas Junior College Teacher's Association; Artists Studio, Inc.; Amarillo Art Alliance, Amarillo Art Center; Southwestern Watercolor Society; The Cowgirl Hall of Fame; Magic Plains Arts Council; International Society of Artists; New Mexico Wildlife Federation; National Wildlife Federation. Published Works: *A Study of Synthetic Paints and Painting Methods.* Honors and Awards: Local, State and National Art Exhibits Awards; Awards for Community Service; Award of Excellence in Fine Arts, Artist Studio, Inc., 1978; Nominee for Texas Panhandle Distinguished Women Award, 1976, 1978, 1980, 1981; Listed in *Who's Who in Texas, Blue Book of the Texas Panhandle, American Artists of Renown, World Who's Who of Women, Personalities of the South.* Address: 1409 Marigold, Borger, Texas 79007.■

WILLIAM JOSEPH PALMER

Construction Industry Group Executive. Personal: Born September 3, 1934; Son of Harold L. and Henrietta (Yagerman) Palmer; Married Judith Pollock;

Father of William, Kathryn, Leslie, Emily. Education: B.S., University of California-Berkeley, 1962. Military: Served in the United States Navy, Lieutenant. Career: Partner/Chairman, Construction Industry Group, present; Coopers & Lybrand, Chairman of Construction Industry Division 1973-80, Managing Partner, Sacramento 1976-80, Partner, San Francisco 1972-76, Staff Certified Public Accountant 1963-72. Organizational Memberships: American Institute of Certified Public Accountants, Vice-Chairman of Construction Accounting Committee 1975-80; California Society of Certified Public Accountants, Chairman Annual Construction Industry Conference 1979; National Association of Accountants, President Oakland-East Bay Chapter 1972-73; Associated General Contractors of California, Member San Francisco District Board of Directors 1974-76, Construction Education Committee 1976-77, Tax and Finance Committee 1977 to present, State Board of Directors 1978-79; National Tax Limitation Committee, Director 1981 to present. Community Activities: Assistant California Finance Chairman 1980 Presidential Campaign; Treasurer of 1972 Presidential Primary Campaign; Treasurer of County Committee in 1974 California Gubernatorial Campaign; Candidate for 1972 High School District Board Elections; Board of Directors, Booth Home for Unwed Mothers (Salvation Army); Finance Committee, League of Women Voters of Sacramento; Chairman, Membership Committee, Director, Comstock Club; Board of Trustees, Superior California Symphony Foundation; Board of Directors and Vice President, Metropolitan Sacramento Young Men's Christian Association; Sacramento Metropolitan Chamber of Commerce International Committee; Chairman, 1978 Fund Raising Drive, Sacramento Society for the Prevention of Cruelty to Animals; Chairman, Fund Raising Drive, 1979 United Way Campaign Professional Division; Board of Directors, KXPR National Public Radio. Religion: Presbyterian. Published Works: Author of Several Books including *Construction Accounting and Financial Management* 1977, *The Construction Business Handbook* 1978, *Audit and Accounting Guide for Construction Contractors* 1980. Honors and Awards: Man of the Year, National Association of Accountants, 1968. Address: 34 Riverbank Place, Carmichael, California 95608.■

HARRY A. PALMITER

Publisher, Senior Editor. Personal: Born December 14, 1922; Son of Louis O. and Carrie T. Palmiter (both deceased); Married Marjory R.; Father of Lynn E., Steven J. Education: B.S., College of Agriculture, University of Wisconsin, 1950. Military: Served in the United States Army, 1943-46. Career: Assistant Editor 1950-54, Manager Merchandising Development Division 1954-58, Olsen Publishing Company, Inc.; Promotion Chief, Markets Division, Wisconsin Department of Agriculture, 1958-62; Editor 1962-78, Publisher/Senior Editor 1978 to present, The Cheese Reporter Publishing Company. Organizational Memberships: Alpha Gamma Rho; International Milk and Food Sanitarians; Wisconsin Marketing Advisory Council; International Cheese and Deli Seminar; Wisconsin Cheesemakers' Association, Life Member; Northeast Wisconsin Cheesemakers' and Buttermakers' Association, Life Member; Wisconsin Dairy Technology Society; Society of Dairy Technology, United Kingdom. Community Activities: Soutmaster 1973-76, Committee Chairman 1976 to present, District Committee 1976 to present, Boy Scouts of America; Young Men's Christian Association of Metro Madison; Madison Lapidary & Mineral Club; Midwest Federation of Minerology & Geological Society. Religion: United Presbyterian Church of United States, Elder 1966 to present. Honors and Awards: Wisconsin Cheese Seminar Service Award, 1973; Northeast Wisconsin Cheesemakers' and Buttermakers' Association, Life Membership, Service Award 1978; District Award of Merit 1978, Leader of Distinction 1975, 1976, 1977, Order of the Arrow 1975, Brotherhood 1976, Boy Scouts of America. Address: 917 Lorraine Drive, Madison, Wisconsin 53706.■

JULIAN IVANHOE PALMORE, III

Mathematics Professor. Personal: Born September 26, 1938; Son of Keith S. Smith; Married Barbara Bland Hawkins; Father of Andrew Handson, Rebecca Keith. Education: B.E.P., Cornell University, 1961; M.S.E., Princeton University, 1965; Ph.D. Astronomy, Yale University, 1967; Ph.D. Mathematics, University of California at Berkeley, 1973. Military: Served in the United States Navy, 1961-64, attaining the rank of Lieutenant (j.g.). Career: Research Engineer, National Aeronautics and Space Administration (Huntsville, Alabama), 1961-64; Research Associate, University of Minnesota (Minneapolis), 1967-68; Visiting Appointments at the University of Michigan 1975-77, Massachusetts Institute of Technology 1973-75; Mathematics Professor, University of Illinois. Organizational Memberships: American Mathematical Society; Royal Astronomical Society; The Planetary Society; Sigma Xi. Community Activities: Panel of Judges, Lilly Faculty Open Fellowships, 1979-83. Honors and Awards: American Rocket Society Award, 1960; National Science Foundation Research Grantee, 1974-84 (Principal Investigator); Lilly Postdoctoral Fellow, Massachusetts Institute of Technology, 1974-75; Center for Advanced Study, University of Illinois, 1979. Address: 402 West Vermont Street, Urbana, Illinois 61801.■

LOUIS ALEXANDER PALUMBO, JR.

Clergyman, Scientist, Educator, Theologian, Humanitarian, Researcher. Personal: Born November 24, 1919, in Johnston, Rhode Island; Son of Louis Albino and Michelina (Margaret) Albano Palumbo (both deceased). Education: B.D.; S.T.L. (Rome); Th.D. (Naples); D.R.S.; L.L.D.; B.S.; M.S.; Sc.D.; M.D.; N.D.; Dr.Hom.Med.; A.B.; M.A.; Ph.D.; Ed.D.; Graduate of New England Institute of Anatomy, Sanitary Sciences and Embalming (Boston); Licensed Clinical Psychotherapist; Diplomate, P.B.P.T.C.; More than One Hundred Earned Doctorates, all maxima cum laude. Career: Registered Embalmer, 1946; President, Evangelical Bible Seminary and College, Italian Branch; Vice President, Academic Department, Fundamental Bible Seminary, Italian Branch, O.M.C.; Vice Dean, Thomas Alva Edison College, Palm Beach, Florida; Researcher, Various Fields of Science, Natural, Supernatural, Ecology, Nursing Education. Organizational Memberships: International Platform Association; National Society of Psychological Counsellors; Gamma Pi Epsilon; International Board of Directors, Ohio Christian College; President, All Commissions, Boards, Otay Mesa College (San Diego, California). Religion: Catholic. Published Works: Author Numerous Publications in the Fields of Theology, Philosophy, Supernatural and Natural Sciences. Honors and Awards: Cavalier of Justice, Delegate to Canada, Grand Official, Military Order of Sweden, Saint Bridget's; Knight of the Grand Cross, Order of Saint John of Jerusalem; Knight Commander, Thomas Alva Edison College; Honorary Pin for Free Humanitarian Service, 1944-46, Rhode Island Hospital (Providence, Rhode Island); Listed in *Book of Honor, Notable Americans, Directory of Distinguished Americans, Community Leaders and Noteworthy Americans, Community Leaders of America, American Registry, Personalities of America.* Address: c/o 5 Beckwith Street, Cranston, Rhode Island 02910.■

HAGOP SARKIS PAMBOOKIAN

Professor. Personal: Born December 18, 1932; Son of Sarkis (deceased) and Tamom Pambookian of Beirut, Lebanon. Education: B.A. Psychology, American University of Beirut, Lebanon, 1957; M.A. Educational Psychology, Columbia University, 1963; Ph.D. Educational Psychology, University of Michigan, 1972. Career: Associate Professor of Psychology, Elizabeth City State University, Elizabeth City, North Carolina; Senior Fulbright Fellow, Yerevan State University, Armenia, U.S.S.R., 1978-79; Assistant Professor of Educational Psychology, Marquette University, 1974-78; University of Michigan, Research Associate Center for Research on Learning and Teaching 1971-74, Teaching Fellow 1971-72; Assistant Professor of Psychology, State University of New York College-Potsdam, 1966-70; Instructor in Psychology, Adirondack Community College, Hudson Falls, New York, 1964-66; Teacher, Melkonian Educational Institute, Nicosia, Cyprus, 1960-61; Teacher, Armenian Evangelical College, Beirut, Lebanon, 1957-60; Teacher, Armenian Evangelical High School, Beirut, Lebanon, 1956-57. Organizatinal Memberships: American Psychological Association; International Council of Psychologists; National Association for Armenian Studies and Research; National Association for the Education of Young Children; Society for Cross-Cultural Research; Southeastern Psychological Association; Phi Delta Kappa. Community Activities: General Secretary, Armenian Evangelical Teachers Association, Beirut, Lebanon, 1957-60; Armenian General Benevolent Union, Correspondence Secretary Junior League New York 1962, President 1975-78; The International Club, Columbia University, Milwaukee Chapter, Secretary General 1962-63, President 1962-63; Vice-President, Tri-County Psychological Association, Glens Falls, New York, 1966; Executive Committee Member, Tekeyan Cultural Association, Detroit, Michigan, 1972-74; Chairman VIP Reception Committee, International Platform Association, 1974-80; Chairman, The Armenian Genocide Committee of Wisconsin, 1975; Director, National Opinion Survey of the Armenian General Benevolent Union, 1975-76; Chairman, Task Force, Milwaukee Educational Resources Coordinating Committee, 1975-76; Member Program Committee, International Institute, Milwaukee, Wisconsin, 1975-78; Chairman of Committee to Raise Money for Victims/Families of Civil War in Lebanon, Wisconsin, 1976; Radio and Television Interviews and Numerous Addresses/Illustrated Talks to Various Professional, Civic, Church, Senior Citizen, Student and Teacher Groups. Religion: Member of the Armenian Apostolic (Orthodox) Church. Honors and Awards: Certificate of Merit,

Kappa Delta Pi, Iota Alpha Chapter, 1964; Certificate of Appreciation, Kiwanis International of Hudson Falls, New York 1965, of Clarksville, Indiana 1980, of Elizabeth City, North Carolina 1982; Member Board of Governors, International Platform Association, 1976-80; Citation for Distinguished Career and Community Service, Board of Supervisors of Milwaukee County, 1978; Fulbright Fellowship/Lectureship, 1978; Oliver Max Gardner Award Nominee, Elizabeth City State University, 1982; Listed in *Who's Who in the East, Dictionary of International Biography, Community Leaders of America, Community Leaders and Noteworthy Americans, Men of Achievement, Personalities of the West and Midwest, Who's Who in the Midwest, International Who's Who in Education, International Who's Who in Community Service.* Address: P.O. Box 2113, Elizabeth City, North Carolina 27909.∎

LINDA DIANA PAPPAS HALE

Consultant. Personal: Born February 5, 1942; Daughter of Mr. and Mrs. Joseph Saffranko; Married Thomas Morgan Hale; Stepmother of Rodney Hale, Kenneth Hale, Timothy Hale, Marilee Hale. Education: B.A. Sociology 1963, M.A. Sociology 1973, Graduate Study Math 1966, Southern Illinois University. Career: Principal Management Consultant, Hay Associates, 1974-77; Associate Director, President's Commission on Military Compensation, 1977-78; Director, Social Systems Research Department, General Research Corporation, 1977-80; Senior Consultant, Hay Associates, 1981 to present. Organizational Memberships: American Compensation Association; American Sociological Association. Community Activities: Counselor, Offender Aid and Restoration Program, 1979-84; Red Cross CPR Instructor, 1978-80; Developed and Implemented Local Casualty Assistance Program, Navy Relief Counselor, 1967-69; Speaker Federal Women's Program, Nuclear Regulatory Commission, 1977. Religion: United Methodist Church, Finance Committee 1980-84, Administrative Board 1981-84. Honor and Awards: Southern Illinois University, Undergraduate Assistantship 1961-63, Graduate Fellowship 1968, Graduate Assistantship 1969-70; Letter of Commendation, Navy Relief Executive Secretary/Vice President, 1968. Address: 9804 Ward Court, Fairfax, Virginia 22032.∎

EMANUEL MARTIN PAPPER

Educator. Personal: Born July 12, 1915; Son of Lillian Weitzner Papper; Married Patricia Meyer; Father of Richard Nelson, Barbara Ellen Papper Lupatkin. Education: Graduate of Boys High School, 1931; A.B., Columbia University, 1935; M.D., New York University, 1938; Intern 1939, Resident 1940-42, Bellevue Hospital; Certification, American Board of Anesthesiology, 1943; F.F.A.R.C.S., England, 1964; F.A.C.P., 1968. Military: Served in the United States Army Medical Corps as Chief, Section of Anesthesiology, Tourney Dibble and Walter Reed Hospitals, 1942-46, attaining the rank of Major. Career: Licensed in New York, California, Florida, Colorado; New York University, Fellow in Medicine, 1938, Fellow in Physiology 1940, Instructor in Anesthesiology 1942, Assistant Professor 1946-49, Associate Professor 1949; Columbia University, Professor of Anesthesiology, Chairman of the Department of Anesthesiology 1949-69; Director of Anesthesiology Service, Presbyterian Hospital, 1949-69; Director of Anesthesiology and Visiting Anesthesiologist, Francis Delafield Hospital, 1951-69; Vice President of Medical Affairs, Dean, University of Miami School of Medicine, 1969-81; University of Miami, Professor of Anesthesiology 1969 to present, Professor of Pharmacology 1974 to present; Numerous Visiting Professorships and Named Lectures, including Rovenstine Lecture (New York State Society of Anesthesiologists) and Shields Lecture (Toronto, Canada), 1955 to present; Number of Consulting Positions. Organizational Memberships: Alpha Omega Alpha; American Association for the Advancement of Science; American Association for Thoracic Surgery; American Board of Anesthesiology; American College of Anesthesiologists; American College of Physicians; American Heart Association; American Medical Association; American Pain Society; American Physicians Fellowship, Inc.; American Society of Anesthesiologists; Amerian Society for Biographical Research; American Society for Clinical Investigation; Life Member, American Society for Pharmacology and Experimental Therapeutics; Division of Drug Metabolism; American Surgical Association; American Thoracic Society; American Trudeau Society; Association for Academic Health Center; Association of American Medical Colleges; Association of Anaesthetics of Great Britain and Ireland; Association of University Anesthetists; Australian Society of Anesthesiologists; Cuban Medical Association in Exile; Eastern Pain Association; European Academy of Anesthesiology; California Society of Anesthesiologists; Finnish Society of Anesthesiologists; Florida Medical Association; Florida Society of Anesthesiologists; Florida Thoracic Society; German Society of Anesthesiologists; Halstead Society; Harvey Society; International Association for the Study of Pain; Israel Society of Anesthesiologists; Latin American Association of Toxicology; Maryland-District of Columbia Society of Anesthesiologists; Medical Society of the County of New York; United States-China Physicians Friendship Association; Venezuelan Society of Anesthesiology; World Federation Societies of Anesthesiologists. Community Activities: Century Association; Cosmos Club; Grove Island Club; Miami Club; Palm Bay Club; Rotary Club; Standard Club. Published Works: Author, 236 Scientific Papers Published in Various Medical and Scientific Journals; Author, 4 Books; Editor, 3 Books. Honors and Awards: Honorary President, French Society of Anesthesiology and Resuscitation; Wisdom Award, Wisdom Hall of Fame; Distinguished Service Award, American Society of Anesthesiologists; Medal of Honor, City of Paris; Honorary Professor, Silver Medal, Universidad Catolics de Santiago de Guayaquil, University of Madrid School of Medicine; Distinguished Alumnus Award in the Health Sciences, New York University School of Medicine; Several Honorary Alumnus and Professor Positions; Man of the Year, Boys High School; Outstanding Educator in America; Meritorious Service Award, A.A.M.C.M.; E.M. Papper Honorary Lectureships in Anesthesiology, Columbia University, University of California-Los Angeles; Honorary President V, European Congress of Anesthesiology; Honorary Member, European Academy of Anesthesiology; Honorary Professor, University of Santiago de Chile; Tel Aviv University's Board of Governors; Honorary Fellow, Faculty of Anaesthetics, Royal College of Surgeons; Honorary Member, Panamanian Society of Anesthesiologists, Latin American Society of Anesthesiologists; John Jay Award, Columbia College, 1984; Listed in *Who's Who in America, Who's Who in the East, Who's Who in World Jewry, American Men of Science, American Men of Medicine, Modern Medicine Contemporaries, Blue Book, Dictionary of International Biography, Community Leaders of America, Directory of Educational Specialists, National Register of Prominent Americans and International Notables, Who's Who in Health Care, International Who's Who in Education,* and Others. Address: 1 Grove Isle Drive, Apartment 1501, Miami, Florida 33133.∎

MICHAEL E. PARADISE

University Chancellor. Personal: Born March 26, 1928; Married Ann Ramos; Father of Maria, George, Andrew. Education: B.Sc., Morningside College, 1955; M.A. 1958, Ed.D. 1962, University of Northern Colorado. Military: Served in the Greek Air Force. Career: Chancellor, University of Alaska, Juneau, present; Former Positions include President of Northeastern Nebraska College, President of Central Technical Community College, President of Nebraska Association of Colleges and Universities, President of Kansas-Nebraska Educational Consortium, President of Nebraska Association of Technical Community Colleges; President of Nebraska Association of Junior Colleges; President of the Faculty Senate of Chadron State College. Organizational Memberships: American Association for the Advancement of Science; American Association of Community and Junior Collges; American Association of Higher Education; American Association of State Colleges and Universities; American Management Association; American Mathematical Society; American Technical Education Association; American Vocational Association; Association for the Study of Higher Education; Mathematical Association of America. Community Activities: Past Presidents of Hastings Area Chamber of Commerce; Hastings United Way; Norfolk Noon Toastmasters Club; Chadron Kiwanis Club; Chadron Toastmasters Club; Executive Board, Greater Juneau Chamber of Commerce, Board of Directors, Hastings Economic Development Corporation; Goldenrod Girl Scout Council's Board of Directors; We-So-Braska Girl Scout Council's Board of Directors; Hastings Rotary Club Board of Directors; Hastings and Adams County Planning and Zone Commission; Chadron Planning Commission. Religion: Holy Trinity Orthodox Church Council. Honors and Awards: Recipients Military Citations; Citations of Appreciation from Students; Commendations from Faculty, Chadron State College Faculty Senate; Northeastern Nebraska College Faculty Senate; Central Technical Community College Faculty Senate and Association; Citations from Chadron Toastmasters Club; Chadron Kiwanis Club; Norfolk Chamber of Commerce; Hastings Area Chamber of Commerce; Hastings United Way. Address: 8309 Gladstone Street, Juneau, Alaska 99801.∎

C. ALAN PARBURY

Management Consultant. Personal: Born August 13, 1947; Son of Charles B. and Ethel N. Parbury; Married Sandra W., Daughter of Theodore and Shirley Wanderer; Father of (stepchildren) Cynthia, Holly. Education: B.Sc., University of Santa Clara, 1970; College of San Mateo, 1972; Security Pacific Financial Management, 1980. Military: Served in the Reserve Officers Training Corp, 2 Years. Career: Management Consultant and Vice President, TWA Management Corporation; Vice President, Cypress Capital Corporation; Former Positions include Sales and Operations Manager for Giantree Corporation, Broker for

Merrill Lynch, Management Consultant for G. J. May International, General Manager for B.W.A. Dairy Products, Area Manager for American Business Systems. Organizational Memberships: American Management Association; International Platform Association; United States Golf Association. Community Activities: President, Kiwanis Club, 1980; Elks Club; Republican National Committee; Volunteer for United Cerebral Palsey, Special Olympics, Big Brothers of America, Little League (coach); Funding Director, Women's Professional Golf Tour. Honors and Awards: University of Santa Clara Bronco Bench, 1981; Listed in *Who's Who in American Universities, Who's Who in Finance and Industry, Who's Who in the West, Who's Who in America.* Address: 178 Joaquin Circle, San Ramon, California 94583.■

PHILLIP (FELIPE) SANCHEZ PARIS

Educational Consultant. Personal: Born September 29, 1941; Son of Juan and Maria Paris (deceased); Married Paula Ledgerwood Chinn, Daughter of James and Pauline Ledgerwood; Father of Jacqueline Janine, Phillip II, David Anthony, Paul James. Education: B.S.F.S., Edmund A. Walsh School of Foreign Service, Georgetown University, 1963; M.A. International Relations 1967, Ph.D. Political Science 1973, University of Southern California. Career: Educational Consultant, Bilingual/Multi-Cultural Education, Northwest Regional Educational Laboratory, present; Coordinator, TITLE I, Community Service and Continuing Education, California, 1972-75; Assistant Professor of Political Science and Latin American Studies, California Lutheran College, University of Southern California, 1967-72; Director (Acting), Hispanic Research Institute, Colegio Cesar Chavez, 1980-81. Organizational Memberships: American Society for Public Administration; American Educational Research Association; National Association of Bilingual Educators; Oregon Association of Researchers. Community Activities: Committee of Spanish-Speaking People of Oregon, Board Member; Colegio Cesar Chavez, Chairperson Board of Trustees; Environmental Planning Commission, City of Davis, California; N.I.E. Task Force on Increasing Participation of Women and Minorities; C.E.D.A.R. Educational Equity Task Force; Governors Commission (California) on Women's Equity; University Task Force on Chicanos at University of California; Mid-Willamette Valley Racial Consortium; National Council of La Raza; Oregon Bilingual Education Task Force. Religion: St. James Early Childhood Committee, St. James Parish Council, Marianist Missionary Society. Honors and Awards: Harris Fellowship to Argentina, 1967; Honorary Award for Services, Colegio Cesar Chavez, 1977; N.D.E.A. Teaching Fellow, 1967-68; Certificate of Appreciation, City of Davis; Phi Alpha Theta; Listed in *International Who's Who of Intellectuals, Community Leaders and Noteworthy Americans, Who's Who in America, Dictionary of International Biography.* Address: 17620 Blue Heron Road, Lake Oswego, Oregon 97034.■

BARRETT PARKER

Lecturer, Writer. Personal: Born October 12, 1908; Son of William Belmont Parker (deceased); Married Pamela Mary Smeeton; Father of Hugh Anthony Smeeton. Education: Roxbury Latin School, 1921-26; A.B., Haverford College, 1932; A.M., Harvard University, 1935; Attended University of London, Studied International Law, Economics, History, 1949-50. Military: Served in the United States Army Air Force, 1942-46, attaining the rank of Major. Career: Teaching and Publishing, 1935-42; United States Foreign Service, 1947-70, Retired; Lecturer in English Literature, American University, 1970-73. Organizational Memberships: Council on Foreign Relations, 1952-72; Atlantic Council, 1966-76; United Nations Associate, 1968-78; English Speaking Union, 1942-72; World Affair Council, 1980- to present. Community Activities: Bicentennial Committee, Brunswick, 1976; Joshua L. Chamberlain Sesqui Centennial Celebration, Vice Chairman, Chairman 1978; Brunswick Urban Development Committee, 1977-78; Central Senior Citizens Association, Board Member 1978-80, PRO 1980-81; Brunswick Voter Registration Board, 1979-80; Pejepscot Historical Society Board Member, 1981-84; American Cancer Society, Maine Division, Board Member, 1980-81. Religion: Brunswick Area Church Council, 1975-84; Delegate Maine Episcopalian Diocesan Convention, 1982-83; Chairman, Diocesan Commission on World Peace and Social Justice, 1982-84. Honors and Awards: Commendation Medal, United States Army, 1946; Chevalier Legion d'Honneur, France, 1947; Coronation Medal, Great Britain, 1953. Address: 57 McKeen Street, Brunswick, Maine 04011.■

CAMILLE KILLIAN PARKER

Ophthalmology. Personal: Born June 28, 1918; Married Francis W. Parker, Jr.; Mother of Paul Wesley Killian, Clyde Bernard Killian. Education: Premedical Courses, University of Chicago, 1942-43; B.S. 1945, M.D. 1946, University of Illinois; Intern, Wesley Memorial Hospital, 1946-47; Postgraduate in Ophthalmology, Northwestern University, 1947-48; Resident in Opthalmology, Illinois Eye and Ear Infirmary, 1949-50. Career: Ophthalmology. Organizational Memberships: Diplomate, American Board of Ophthalmology, 1952; Medical Staff Secretary, Memorial Hosptal, 1959; Medical Staff President, Saint Joseph Hospital, 1965; President, Cass County Medical Society, 1971; Fellow, American Academy of Ophthalmology and Otolaryngology, 1952; Charter Member, Society of Eye Surgeons, 1969; Indiana State Medical Association; Indiana Academy of Ophthalmology and Otolaryngology; American Medical Association; Mental Guidance Board, 1967-69; President, Indiana Academy of Ophthalmology, 1979-80. Community Activities: Vice President, Altrusa Club, 1967-69; President, Culver Mothers Club, 1968-69; President, Logansport Council for Public Schools, 1961-62; Legislative Affairs Committee, Chamber of Commerce; Republican Women's Club. Religion: Methodist Chairman, Social Concerns 1963-65, Official Board 1961-65. Honors and Awards: Service Award, Culver Military Academy, 1969; Physicians Recognition Award, 1971, 1976, 1979, 1984. Address: 2500 East Broadway, Logansport, Indiana 46947.■

LUCY THIMANN PARKER

Psychologist, Clinical Director. Personal: Born January 21, 1933, in Vienna, Austria; Daughter of Dr. and Mrs. Joseph Thimann (both deceased); Married Dr. Robert Alan Parker; Mother of Karen Sue, Janet Lee, Geoffrey Samuel, Linda Ann. Education: B.S. Elementary Education 1958, Ed.M. Counselor Education 1965, Ed.D. Education and Counseling 1974, Boston University; Ph.D. Clinical Psychology, Heed University, 1973; Leadership Training Institute, 1967; Newton Mental Health Center Teaching Conference, 1965-67. Career: Clinical Director, Senior Staff Psychologist, Chestnut Hill Psychotherapy Associates, Chestnut Hill Medical Center, Massachusetts, 1970 to present; Senior Consultant, The Parker Associates, 1977-; Senior Consultant, Massachusetts Teachers Association, 1974-78; Senior Counseling Psychologist, Leslie B. Cutler Child Guidance Clinic, Massachusetts, 1967-70; Consulting Psychologist, Walker Home for Children, Massachusetts, 1968-72; School Adjustment Counselor, Needham Public Schools, Massachusetts, 1964-67; Psychological Consultant, Camp Baird, Boston Children's Services Association Residential Camp, Massachusetts, 1966-68; Private Practice in Psychotherapy and Crisis Intervention, Massachusetts, 1965-72; Heed University, Professor in Psychology and Education 1972-78, Associate Professor in Psychology and Education, New England Coordinator 1972-74; Associate Professor in Education, Newton College, 1972-75; Research Associate in Behavioral Sciences, Massachusetts College of Optometry, 1973-75; Assistant Professor in Education, Lesley College, 1967-72; Northeastern University Graduate School of Education, Lecturer in Psychology 1966-67; Field Work Supervisor, Needham Public Schools, Boston University Graduate School of Education, 1965-67; Educational Therapist, Department of Special Education, Newton Public Schools 1960-65, Brockton Public Schools 1959-62; Junior High School Teacher, Temple Shalom, 1962-64; Elementary School Teacher, Bellingham Public Schools, 1958-59; Guest Lecturer, University of Massachusetts School of Education 1972-78, Framingham State College Psychology Department 1973-78, Bridgewater State College Psychology Department 1973-78, Boston University Graduate School of Education 1966-72, Northeastern University Graduate School of Education 1966-72, Rhode Island College Graduate School of Education 1966-72; Senior Consultant, The Parker Associates, 1977 to present. Organizational Memberships: American Psychological Association; American Association of University Professors; American Society of Clinical Hypnosis; American Association of Sex Educators, Counselors and Therapists; American Group Psychotherapy Association; American Personnel and Guidance Association; International Association of Group Psychotherapy; International Society for Clinical and Experimental Hypnosis; Society for Clinical and Experimental Hypnosis; Massachusetts Psychological Association; American Orthopsychiatric Association; Boston Area Personnel and Guidance Association; Association for Humanistic Psychology; American Association of Marriage and Family Therapy, Co-Chairperson Regional Screening Board 1981; Massachusetts Association of Marriage and Family Therapy, Regional Board 1981-82; Psychologist License, Elementary Teacher's Certificate, Guidance Counselor's Certificate, School Adjustment Counselor's Certificate, Director of Guidance Certificate, State of Massachusetts. Community Activities: Sensitivity Group Trainer, Human Relations Consultant, National Training Laboratories, 1968-73; Project Lighthouse, Title III, 1968-72; Crisis Intervention Work, Police Departments, Fire Departments, Community. Published Works; Numerous Articles in Professional Publications including "The Management of Behavior in a Pediatric Clinical Setting," "Behavior: The

Neglected Aspect of Eye Safety," "A Study of Vision Screening Programs in Massachusetts Public Schools"; Textbook Pending Publication, *Manual for Teachers Working with Problem Children in the Classroom.* Honors and Awards: Fellow, American Academy of Optometry 1974, International Council of Sex Education and Parenthood 1980, American Academy of Science, International Biographical Association, International Hypnotherapy Society 1983; Diplomate, American Academy of Behavioral Medicine, 1982; Diplomate, International Association of Professional Counseling and Psychotherapy, 1983; Listed in *Who's Who of American Women, Who's Who in the East, Dictionary of International Biography, World Who's Who of Women, Community Leaders and Noteworthy Americans, International Register of Profiles, National Register of Health Service Providers in Psychology, Men and Women of Distinction, The Directory of Distinguished Americans, Personalities of America, The American Registry Series, The Anglo-American Who's Who, Notable Personalities of America, Personalities of the East, International Book of Honor, Community Leaders of the World, Personalities of the East, International Who's Who of Contemporary Achievement, Five Thousand Personalities of the World.* Address: Suite 108, 25 Boylston Street, Chestnut Hill, Massachusetts 02167. ■

ROBERT A. PARKER

Financial Planner. Personal: Born June 3, 1935; Son of Mr. and Mrs. Ira C. Parker; Father of Natasha Chiu. Education: B.S., Arkansas State University, 1958; M.P.H., University of North Carolina, 1962. Military: Served in the United States Army, Captain, 1958-62. Career: Financial Planner, present; Former Positions as Health Planner, Faculty Member of Washington University (St. Louis, Missouri), Visiting Member of the Faculty of the University of Oklahoma. Organizational Memberships: Board of Directors, Family Planning Council; Founder Member, American Association of Comprehensive Health Planning; Chairman of Various Sub-Committees, American Public Health Association, St. Louis Society of Association Executives, National Association of Life Underwriters. Community Activities: Committee on Environmental Impact; East West Gateway Coordinating Council, St. Louis, Missouri; Meals on Wheels, East Orange, New Jersey, Treasurer; Advisory Committee, St. Louis University, School of Nursing. Honors and Awards: Listed in *Who's Who in American Colleges and Universities, Who's Who in Health Care, Who's Who in Finance and Industry, Who's Who in the Midwest, International Men of Achievement, Personalities of America.* Address: 1971 Beacon Grove Drive, St. Louis, Missouri 63141. ■

W. DALE PARKER

Political Advisor. Personal: Born April 13, 1925; Son of Otis and Eva Parker (both deceased); Married Boots Farthing, Daughter of Joe and Ida Farthing; Father of Jacqueline Susan. Education: Graduate, College of William and Mary; Attended the University of Virginia, University of Delaware, California Western University, University of California and Stetson University; Certified Conference Leader in All States. Military: Served with the United States Coast Guard and Navy during World War II. Career: Held Several Engineering Positions Prior to Becoming the Assistant Director of Salaried Personnel in Charge of Public Relations and Counseling, General Motors Corporation, 11 Years; Engineer and Member of Speaker's Staff, Space Program with General Dynamics; Aerospace Scientist and Management Specialist, NASA, Houston, Texas; Helped Form the International Institute of Human Relations; Former Vice President, Travel International Inc.; Former Vice President, Spangler Television, Inc., New York City; Columnist, "Personalities in the News" (appeared in seven newspapers on the West Coast during the 1960's); Magazine Editor; Management Consultant to Various Corporations. Community Activities: Has Contributed Time, Effort, and Resources to Many Charitable Oganizations and Individuals for Over 30 Years; Has Worked with Republican and Democratic Party Members on Many Campaigns and on Getting Legislation Passed at All Levels of Government; Candidate for Governor of Florida, 1976. Published Works: Author, *Philosophy of Genius, Gutless America.* Honors and Awards: Holder of Several Copyrights and Patents, including Those for Medallions in the Field of Sports and the Astronaut Celestial Navigation Training Center at the University of North Carolina. Address: P.O. Box 1441, Titusville, Florida 32780. ■

MUKUND R. PARKHIE

Toxicologist. Personal: Born August 4, 1933; Son of Dr. and Mrs. R. S. Parkhie; Married Barbara Helene, Daughter of Mr. and Mrs. Maurice L. Tyler; Father of Ravi, Meera, Ram, Shyam. Education: Ph.D., University of Missouri, Columbia, 1970; M.Sc., University of Saskatchewan, Saskatoon, Canada, 1963; M.V.Sc., Agra University, Agra, India, 1960; D.V.M., University of Jabalpur, India, 1957; E.C.F.V.G. Certificate, American Veterinary Medical Association, Chicago, 1972. Career: Veterinary Toxicologist, 1977 to present; Health Science Advisor (Medicine), 1982; Senior Visiting Scientist in Teratology, Medical Research Council, England, 1980-81; Toxicologist, 1977-80; Pharmacologist, 1974-77; Veterinary Pathologist, 1973-74; Staff Scientist, 1972-73; Cardiovascular Physiologist, 1970-72; Research Assistant in Endocrinology, 1965-70; Research Assistant in Biochemical Genetics, 1963-65; Research Fellow, Reproductive Physiology, 1961-63; Assistant Professor, Preventive Medicine, 1960-61; Research Fellow in Genetics, 1958-60, Veterinarian, 1957-58. Organizational Memberships: Chairman, General Technical Session, First World Congress on Toxicology and Environmental Health, 1982; Chairman, Admission Committee, Food and Drug Administration; Sigma Xi Honor Society, 1978-79; Fellow, American College of Veterinary Toxicologists; Panel Member, Fourth International Congress on Controlled Release Technology; Society of Toxicology; American Society of Veterinary Physiologists and Pharmacologists; American Physiological Society; Endocrine Society; Society for the Study of Reproduction; Council Member, Basic Science, American Heart Association; International Health, American Public Health Association; Drug Metabolism Diss. Group. Community Activities: Judge, Montgomery and Prince George County Schools Science Fairs, 1978-80 and 1982; Vice President, Indo-American Cultural Association, 1979-80; Toastmaster International; Judge, National Science Teachers Association/National Aeronautics and Space Administration Science Projects, 1970-72. Honors and Awards: Quality Award, Food and Drug Administration, 1979; United States National Academy of Sciences Fellowship, 1970-72; Worcester Foundation Fellow in Reproduction, 1970; National Research Council of Canada Fellow, 1962-63; World University Service of Canada Scholar, 1961-62; Senior Research Fellow, Government of India, 1960; Junior Research Fellow, Government of India, 1958-60; Listed in *Men of Achievement, American Men and Women of Science, Who's Who in Washington.* Address: 790 West Side Drive, Gaithersburg, Maryland 20878. ■

FRED PARKS

Attorney-at-Law. Personal: Born July 9, 1906; Son of John and Nora Soden Parks (both deceased); Married Mabel Roberson; Father of Judith Stauffer. Education: Preparatory Education, Rice University; LL.B., South Texas School of Law, 1937. Military: Served in the United States Army Air Corps; Honorable Discharge, 1945. Career: Instructor, South Texas School of Law, Houston, 1949, 1951-55; Attorney-at-Law. Organizational Memberships: Southeastern Legal Foundation, Research Fellow; Houston Junior Bar Association, President 1940; Texas Junior Bar Association, President 1942; Houston Bar Association, Director 1941-42, 1946-47; American Bar Association; International Bar Association; State Bar of Texas, Grievance Committee 1941, 1947-49, Director 8th District 1954-57, Vice President 1957-58; American Judicature Society; Maritime Law Association of the United States of America; Selden Society. Community Activities: Lecturer, "Some Practical Aspects of the Preparation and Trial of Damage Suits in Texas," University of Houston Law School, 1955, University of Texas School of Law 1956, South Texas School of Law, 1954, Before State Bar of Texas Institute 1956, "Effective Utilization of Medical Evidence," Southwestern Legal Foundation, Southern Methodist University, 1957. Published Works: Author, "Legal Aspects of Medical Records," *Texas Association of Medical Records Librarians Bulletin,* 1958. Honors and Awards: Bronze Star, Numerous Battle Stars, Numerous Unit and Group Citations, United States Army Air Corps. Address: 3385 Del Monte Drive, Houston, Texas 77019. ■

ROBERTA ARLENE PARSONS

Executive. Personal: Born November 19, 1934; Daughter of George Lester (deceased) and Audrey Velma Buzzard; Married Jack J. Parsons; Mother of Monte Jay, Russell Joe. Education: Graduate Grand Island High School, 1951; Attended Valley Junior College, 1971-74; Attended Harbor Junior College, 1977-80; Attended University of California-Los Angeles, 1980-81. Career: Vice President, Corporate Administrator and Assistant to the President, Keenan and Associates, 1981 to present; Secretary, Fred S. James, 1972-75; Administrative Assistant, Frank B. Hall, 1975; Accounts Administrator, Emett and Chandler, 1975-76; Executive Secretary, Hoyne Industries, 1976-77; Assistant Vice President, Personnel, Keenan and Associates, Inc. Organizational Memberships: Past President, Torrance Del Amo Chapter of Professional Secretaries International, 1972-79; Past Member, Personnel and Industrial Relations Association. Community Activities: South Bay Center Cerebral Palsy Telethon, Director 1975-81, Former Assistant Director, Former Supervisor; Past Board Member, Fre-Way Little League, 1977-78. Honors and Awards: Certified Professional Secretary, 1973; Notary Public, 1971 to present. Address: 23768 Sandhurst Lane, Harbor City, California 90710. ■

TWO THOUSAND NOTABLE AMERICANS

TARLTON FLEMING PARSONS II

Executive. Personal: Born December 5, 1927; Married Joan Norwood Ferguson; Father of Tarlton Fleming Parsons III, Aileen-Elinor; Dawn Fleming Parsons Kearnes. Education: Diploma, Woodberry Forest School, 1945; Attended University of Delaware, 1945; Attended Amherst College, 1946; B.S., United States Military Academy, West Point, 1950; M.B.A., Babson College, 1965. Military: Served in the United States Army, 1945-73, attaining the rank of Lieutenant Colonel. Career: Chairman and President, Cumberland Limited; Former Positions Include Vice Chairman and Chief Executive Officer, International Equity Corporation; Property Manager, Tysons Realty; Property Manager, Star Realty; United States Army, Lieutenant Colonel, Infantry, Ordnance, General Staff. Organizational Memberships: Association of the United States Army; American Defense Preparedness Association. Honors and Awards: Bronze Star Medal with Oak Leaf Clusters; Meritorious Service Medal; Army Commendations Medal with Three Oak Leaf Clusters; New York Conspicuous Service Cross; French Legion of Honor; French Croix de Guerre; American Legion Citizenship Medal; Knight Commander of Justice and Grand Cross; Sovereign Order of Saint John of Jerusalem; Knight, Greek Order of Saint Dennis of Zante; Grand Exarch and Grand Officer; Ordo Constantini Magni; Knight of Grace, Order of Saint Lazarus; Member, Order of the Crown of Charlemagne; Royal Yugoslav Commemorative War Cross; American Ordnance Association Medal; Augustan Society Medal; Fellow, Augustan Society; Fellow, Society of Antiquarians of Scotland; Fellow, Royal Society of Arts; Honorary Doctorate of Science; Honorary D.D., and others. Address: Swansholm, 2500 Culpeper Road, Alexandria, Virginia 22308. ■

AMY KING PASCHALL

Public Relations. Personal: Born February 9, 1951; Daughter of Eliza K. Paschall. Education: Diploma, Druid Hills High School, 1965-69; B.A. Communications, Grinnell College, 1969-73; Advanced Communication Seminar, United States Department of Labor, 1978; Certificate, Public Information Officers Workshop, United States Department of Labor, 1978; Advanced Communications Seminar, United States Department of Labor, 1979; Stress Management, Georgia Department of Labor, 1980; Career Development, Georgia Department of Labor, 1981; Basic Accounting, DeKalb Vo-Tech School, 1982-83. Career: Public Relations. Organizational Memberships: International Association of Personnel in Employment Security, Joined 1973, Chairman of Public Relations Committee 1978, 1979, 1982, 1983; Georgia Chapter, Co-Chairman Legislative and Historical Projects Committees, 1982, 1983; International Public Relations Committee, 1980-84; Editor, Georgia I.A.P.E.S. Newsletter, 1979 to present; Women in Communications, Inc., 1972 to present, Secretary Grinnell College Chapter. Community Activities: State Governor's Council on the Deaf (appointed to represent Labor Department), 1979-82; Metro Atlanta Task Committee on the Handicapped (MATCH), 1976 to present, Chairman Public Relations Committee 1981-82; Panel Consultant, Seminar on Section 504, by Planning and Human Systems, Inc., 1979; Panelist, 4th Kiwanis Institute on Deafness, 1984; Leader, Public Relations Section, 14th Regional Institute on Deafness, 1984. Religion: Member, Christian Science Branch Church. Honors and Awards: Francis K. Harris Internship, Grinnel College Magazine, 1973; Second Place, Excellence in I.A.P.E.S. Publications, 1978, 1979; First Place, Excellence in I.A.P.E.S. Publications, 1981, 1982, 1983; Outstanding Disabled Woman of the Year, Decatur, Georgia's Pilot Club, 1982. Address: 3803-E North Decatur Road, Decatur, Georgia 30032. ■

JAMES ERNEST PASCHALL

Retired United States Air Force Major General. Personal: Born March 31, 1923; Son of Joshua Ernest and Claire Hodges Paschall (both deceased); Married Lelia Atkinson; Father of Anne P. Weinheimer, Julia P. Munkvold. Education: B.S., United States Military Academy, 1946; B.S. Aeronautical Engineering, United States Air Force Institute of Technology, 1951; M.B.A. Advanced Management, George Washington University, 1961; Graduate, Industrial College of the Armed Forces, 1965; Attended Brookings Institute Seminar for Federal Science Executives, 1966; University of California at Berkeley, Executive Development Program, 1968. Career: Vice Commander, Air Force Special Weapons Center, Kirtland Air Force Base, New Mexico, 1969-70, Commander 1969-70; Deputy Commander, 22nd North American Air Defense Command (NORAD) Region, North Bay, Ontario, Canada, 1970-71; Commander, 26th North American Air Defense Command/Continental Air Defense Command (NORAD/CONAD) Region, with additional duty as Commander, 26th Air Division, Aerospace Defense Command, Luke Air Force Base, Arizona, 1971-73; Deputy Chief of Staff, Plans and Programs, NORAD/CONAD, with additional position as Deputy Chief of Staff, Plans and Programs, Aerospace Defense Command (ADC), Ent Air Force Base, Colorado, 1973-74; Commander, Fourteenth Aerospace Force, ADC, Ent Air Force Base, Colorado, 1974-75; Vice Commander in Chief, Aerospace Defense Command (ADCOM), Ent Air Force Base, Colorado, 1975-76; Retired, Major General, United States Air Force, 1976; Involved in Farm and Forestry Management and Personal Investments; Elected Member of Walnut Creek Town Council; Mayor Pro Tem of the Town of Walnut Creek; Member of Goldsboro, North Carolina Board of Directors, Branch Banking and Trust Company. Organizational Memberships: Scientific Research Society of America; Order of Daedalians; Air Force Association; Association of Graduates of United States Military Academy; Association of Graduates Industrial College of the Armed Forces; Retired Officers' Association; American Forestry Association; North Carolina Forestry Association. Community Activities: Member Board of Directors, Albuquerque, New Mexico, Chamber of Commerce, 1969-70; Member Regional Advisory Group on Public Science and Administration for the University of New Mexico, 1968-76; Member Board of Directors, Albuquerque, New Mexico, United Community Fund, 1969-70; Albuquerque Airport Industrial Advisory Board, 1970; Albuquerque Armed Forces Advisory Committee, 1968-70; Albuquerque Region Federal Executive Board, 1968-70; Albuquerque Interagency Board of the United States Civil Service, 1969-70; Albuquerque Federal Executive Association, 1968-70; Member Board of Directors, Phoenix, Arizona, Metropolitan Chamber of Commerce, 1972-73; Arizona Governor's Aerospace Education Advisory Council, 1972-73; Phoenix Armed Forces Advisory Committee, 1972-73; Member Board of Directors, Pikes Peak United Way, Colorado Springs, Colorado, 1974-75; Colorado Governor's Armed Forces Advisory Council 1975-76; Executive Board of Tuscarora Council Boy Scouts of America, 1977 to present; Vice President, Tuscarora Council Boy Scouts of America, Goldsboro, North Carolina, 1980 to present; President, Scott-Berkeley Chapter Air Force Association, 1978-79; Goldsboro, North Carolina, Chamber of Commerce Military Advisory Committee, 1978 to present; Member Board of Directors, Wayne County Chapter of the American Red Cross, 1978 to present; North Carolina Governor's Advisory Commission on Military Affairs, 1982 to present. Religion: Member Board of Directors, Springfield Christian Church, 1957-68; Chairman Board of Directors, Springfield Christian Church, 1964-65. Honors and Awards: Decorated Distinguished Service Medal, Legion of Merit, Air Force Commendation Medal, Army Commendation Medal; Listed in *Who's Who in America, Who's Who in the South and Southwest, Dictionary of International Biography, Personalities of the West and Midwest, Community Leaders and Noteworthy Americans, Who's Who in the South and Southwest, Personalities of America, Personalities of the South*. Address: 416 Walnut Creek Drive, Goldsboro, North Carolina 27530. ■

WILLIAM R. PASEWARK, JR.

Regulatory Compliance Accountant. Personal: Born December 17, 1956; Son of W. R. Pasewark and M. J. Pasewark. Education: B.B.A. Finance, University of Texas at Austin, 1979; M.B.A. Accounting, Texas A&M University, 1981. Career: Regulatory Compliance Accountant, present; Graduate Assistant, Texas A&M University, 1980-81; Credit Analyst, Frost National Bank, San Antonio, Texas, 1979-80; Assistant Sergeant-at-Arms, Texas State Senate, Austin, Texas, 1977-78. Organizational Memberships: Council of Petroleum Accountants of The Permian Basin, 1981 to present; M.B.A. Association, Social Chairman 1980-81; Exxon Club of Midland, Treasurer 1982-83; American Institute of Banking, 1979-80; University Finance Association, 1978-79. Community Activities: Instructor of Fundamentals of Accounting, Night Faculty, Midland College, 1983; Advisor, Explorer Post 138, Buffalo Trail Council, Midland, Texas, 1981-82; Area Fund Raiser, United Way, 1982; San Antonio Chamber of Commerce, 1979-80; Department Chairman for Multiple Sclerosis Campaign, 1980. Religion: Member First Methodist Church in Midland, Texas, Member Singles Class. Honors and Awards: Eagle Scout, 1973; Fourth Place, American Institute of Banking Paperwriting Contest, "Lending to Food and Fiber Producing Entities, The Role of the Large Urban Bank," 1980; Listed in *Outstanding Young Men of America, Personalities of the South*. Address: 1304 College, Midland, Texas 79701. ■

JULIET JORGE PATAWARAN

Specialized Office Technician. Personal: Born August 12, 1938; Daughter of Nicanor Galvez Jorge and Luz (Butalid) Fortich Jorge; Married Benjamin Lising, Son of Estanislao Patawaran and Felisa Lising Patawaran (both deceased), on March 31, 1932; Mother of Nic Rizaldy, Lizette, Benjamin Jr. Education: B.S. Foreign Service, University of the Philippines; Secretarial Course, Philippines; Office Skills, Seattle Opportunities and Industrialization Center. Career: Specialized Office Technician, present; Former Positions as Transportation Clerk, Secretary, Senior Clerk, Supervisor, Information Writer, Radio-Producer-Announcer, Executive Secretary of Rural Broadcasting Council in the Philippines, Scriptwriter. Community Activities: Port of Seattle Toastmasters Club, Vice President;

TWO THOUSAND NOTABLE AMERICANS

University of the Philippines Alumni Association of the Northwest, Treasurer; Filipino Community of Seattle; Filipino-American Political Action Group; Circulo Ponpargueno; Togalog Circle; Tomorrow Club. Religion: Roman Catholic; Helps in Religious Activities in St. Edward, St. George and St. Paul Churches. Honors and Awards: Recipient of Seattle/OIC Edwin W. Stallworth Employee Award for Outstanding Achievement; Colombo Plan Scholarship, London, England; Awarded by Philippine Government; Medals, Plaque, Certificates of Recognition, Gold Bracelets and Other Scholarships; Competent Toastmaster Certificate. Address: 3026 South Portland Street, Seattle, Washington 98108.■

CLARE S. PATAWY

Aerospace Engineer. Personal: Born June 26, 1957; Daughter of Sherwood and Lorraine Scaly; Married Lawrence Harold Patawy, Son of Brent and Sarah Patawy; Mother of Sean, Sharon. Education: B.S. Aerospace Engineering, Rensselaer Polytechnic Institute, 1979; M.S. Aerospace Engineering, University of California, 1981; Additional Studies. Career: Aerospace Engineer, TRW Corporation, San Bernardino, California, 1979-82; Aerospace Engineer, Pratt-Whitney, West Palm Beach, Florida, 1982 to present. Organizational Memberships: American Association for the Advancement of Science; American Institute of Aeronautics and Astronautics; National Association for the Advancement of Science; National Science Foundation. Community Activities: Boys Scouts of America, Cub Scout Den Mother, Webelo Den Mother; Volunteer, American Red Cross; Girl Scouts of America, Brownie Troop Leader, Girl Scout Leader, Outing Director; Daughters of the American Revolution; Fund Raiser, March of Dimes, American Cancer Society, American Heart Association; Business and Professional Women's Clubs; Order of Eastern Star; Phi Beta Kappa; Alpha Delta Pi. Religion: Presbyterian; Sunday School Teacher; Chairman, Budget Committee. Honors and Awards: Thank You Award, Boy Scouts of America; Den Mother of the Year, Boy Scouts of America; Graduate with Honors, University of California, Rensselaer Polytechnic Institute. Address: 1830 Embassy Drive, Apartment 508, West Palm Beach, Florida 33401.■

NORMAN PATAYER

Civil Engineer. Personal: Born 21 January 1939; Son of Herald and Lila Patayer; Married Carol F.; Father of Ronald and Marla. Education: B.S., Newark College of Engineering, 1961; Post-graduate Studies, Princeton University, 1965. Military: Served in United States Army Reserve, (Army Corps of Engineers Branch), 1965-72, attaining rank of Captain. Career: Civil Engineering Supervisor, Trenton Municipal Waterworks, Trenton, New Jersey, 1966 to present; Water and Drainage Engineering Technician, Elizabeth, New Jersey, 1962-1966. Organizational Memberships: American Society of Civil Engineers, Member 1967 to present, Vice-President Trenton Chapter 1975, President Trenton Chapter 1978. Community Activities: Benevolent and Protective Order of Elks, 1970 to present; Sons of the American Revolution, Chairman Membership Committee Newark Chapter 1965, Vice-President Trenton Chapter 1978; Boy Scouts of America, Cub Scout Master, District Chairman Wood Badge Committee, President Local Executive Committee. Religion: Member of United Methodist Church, Trenton, New Jersey, 1968 to present; Lay Pastor, 1980; Chairman, Sunday School Attendence Committee, 1982. Honors and Awards: Brother of the Month, Benevolent and Protective Order of Elks, 1980; Certificate of Recognition, Sons of the American Revolution, Trenton Chapter, 1979; Distinguished Alumni Club, Newark College of Engineering, 1983.■

JOSEPH PATBALD

Psychologist. Personal: Born March 15, 1938; Son of Samuel J. and Margaret M. Patbald. Education: B.A. Psychology, Slippery Rock State College, 1959; M.A. Guidance and Counseling, University of Rochester, 1961; Ph.D., University of Pennsylvania, 1964. Military: United States Army, 1964-68, Captain. Career: Staff Member 1968-70, Director Suicide Crisis Hotline 1970-74, Freedom Mental Health Center, Philadelphia, Pennsylvania; Associate Psychologist Student Counseling Services 1974-78, Director and Chief Psychologist Student Counseling Services and Crisis Prevention Center 1978 to present, Temple University, Philadelphia, Pennsylvania. Organizational Memberships: American Psychological Association; Pennsylvania Psychological Association; Eastern Psychological Association; Philadelphia Psychology Society; American Personnel and Guidance Association, 1970 to present; Association of Mental Health Directors, 1971 to present. Community Activities: Big Brothers; Save the Whale Society. Religion: Member of St Paul's Catholic Church, Philadelphia, Pennsylvania. Published Works: Author of "I'm Down and You're Up," *Psychology Today*, 1982; Various Articles in Association Journals. Honors and Awards: Certificate of Appreciation for Outstanding Service, Freedom Mental Health Center, 1972; Listed in *Who's Who in America, Who's Who in the East.*■

MARION PATBY

Office Manager. Personal: Born January 25, 1961; Daughter of Larry and Linda Patby. Education: B.A. English, Clemson University, Clemson, South Carolina, 1983; Additional Studies. Career: Secretary 1981-82, Office Manager 1982 to present, Glickly and Acklen Architectural Firm, Oswego, New York. Organizational Memberships: New York Managerial Association. Community Activities: Girl Scouts of America. Honors and Awards: B.A. cum laude, Clemson University, Clemson, South Carolina, 1983.■

RONDA LYSETTE PATCAIRN

Educator. Personal: Born December 5, 1949, in Shreveport, Louisiana; Daughter of T. H. and Marie Thibidaux; Married Louis Patcairn; Mother of Amber, Thomas. Education: B.A., 1970, M.A. Education 1972, Louisiana State University. Career: Teacher, Saint Mary's Elementary School, Shreveport, Louisiana, 1972-78; Instructor Elementary Education, Spokane Falls Community College, Spokane, Washington, 1978 to present. Organizational Memberships: National Education Association. Religion: Member of Gonzaga Catholic Church, 1978 to present. Address: West 1621 9th Avenue, Spokane, Washington 99204.■

MARLENA B. PATCH

Corporate Executive Vice-President. Personal: Born July 7, 1945; Daughter of Joseph and Angela Zifeller; Married Henry Patch; Mother of Carl, Carolyn. Education: B.A., University of California, 1967; Attended Executive Seminars (Travel Industry), 1976, 1980, 1983. Career: Executive Vice-President and Partner, Patch Associates, Baltimore, Maryland, 1982 to present; Executive Secretary, DuPont Chemical, Los Angeles, California, 1969-72; Assistant to Vice-President, Marion Travel Agency, 1975-80. Organizational Memberships: Maryland Society of Organizational Executives, 1970-72. Community Activities: Baltimore County Recreational League, 1978 to present; Parent-Teacher Association, 1977 to present. Religion: Member of First United Presbyterian Church in Waldorf, Maryland, 1982 to present; United Women Church League, Vice-President 1983, Chairman 1982, Secretary 1982; Sunday School Teacher, Elementary and Junior High Levels, 1982 to present; Budget Committee. Published Works: Travel Articles for Local Newspapers; Author of Books *Planning Travel for Corporate Executives, The Role of Consulting in Travel Planning*; Co-author of *Agenda Decision-Making: Travel and Accomodation Factors*. Honors and Awards: DuPont Chemical, Certificate of Appreciation 1970, Executive Secretary of the Year 1971; Planner of the Year, Maryland Society of Organization Executive's, 1984; Listed in *Personalities of America, Community Leaders of America, Who's Who of American Women*. Address: c/o Route 2, Box 239-T, Waldorf, Maryland 20601.■

TWO THOUSAND NOTABLE AMERICANS

LLOYD PATCHOWSKI

Marriage and Family Counselor. Personal: Born October 19, 1936; Son of George and Martha Patch (both deceased); Married Harriet Thurman, Daughter of Henry and Alice Thurman (both deceased); Father of Gregory, Keith, Melissa, Amanda, Carol, Joseph. Education: B.S. History, University of North Carolina at Chapel Hill, 1957; M.S. Marriage and Family Counseling, University of South Carolina, Columbia, South Carolina, 1960; Ph.D. Marriage and Family Counseling, University of California at Los Angeles, 1974. Career: Teaching Assistant, University of South Carolina, Columbia, South Carolina, 1957-60; Counselor, Forestgreen High School, Columbia, South Carolina, 1960-62; Marriage and Family Counselor, Marriage and Family Services Inc., Los Angeles, California, 1962-76; Marriage and Family Counselor, Private Practice, Raleigh, North Carolina, 1976 to present. Organizational Memberships: American Association for the Advancement of Science; American Association for Marriage and Family Therapists; American Businessmen's Association; American Medical Association; National Association for the Advancement of Science; National Education Association. Community Activities: Smithsonian Institution; Active in the Society for the Prevention of Cruelty to Animals; Sons of the American Revolution; Rotary International; Committee to Aid Immigrants; Chamber of Commerce, Raleigh, North Carolina; Jaycees; National Institutes of Health; Volunteer, March of Dimes, American Red Cross; Volunteer Marriage and Family Counselor, Local HELP Hotlines. Religion: First Methodist Church, Raleigh, North Carolina, Counselor, Sunday School Teacher; Republican Party, Active in Local Elections; Muscular Dystrophy Association; Coordinated Local Fund Raising Telethon. Published Works: Author Numerous Articles in Professional Journals; Book in Progress. Honors and Awards: Certificate for Volunteer Efforts, March of Dimes, 1981; Graduate with Honors, University of California; Employee of the Day, WQDR, 1982; Certificate of Appreciation, American Heart Association. Address: 6212-L North Hills Drive, Raleigh, North Carolina 27609.■

LARRY EUGENE PATE

University Professor. Personal: Born January 27, 1945; Son of Leslie (deceased) and Mildred Pate; Married Kathryn Anne Clyde, Daughter of Max and Connie Clyde, on July 9, 1979; Father of Benjamin David (from previous marriage to Pamela May Paton), Anna Kathryn, Lesley Elizabeth. Education: B.A. summa cum laude in Social Science 1971, M.S. Administration, University of California, Irvine; Ph.D. Organizational Behavior, University of Illinois, Urbana, 1979. Military: Served in the United States Army, Vietnam 1967-69, attaining the rank of Captain. Career: Associate Professor of Organizational Behavior, Board of Advisors Faculty Scholar 1981 to present, Assistant Professor of Organization and Administration, School of Business 1978-81, University of Kansas; Visiting Associate Professor of Psychology, Institute of Safety and Systems Management Summer 1982, Visiting Associate Professor of Organizational Behavior, School of Business Administration Summer 1981, University of Southern California; Visiting Assistant Professor of Management, Graduate School of Business, University of Wisconsin-Madison, 1977-78; Visiting Assistant Professor of Management, College of Business Administration, University of Nebraska-Lincoln, 1975-77; Research and Teaching Assistant, Department of Business Administration and Bureau of Economic and Business Research, University of Illinois at Urbana-Champaign, 1973-75; Engineer Schedules Analyst, Space Systems Center (Space Shuttle Project), McDonnell Douglas Astronautics, 1972-73; Research Assistant, Public Policy Research Organization (Land-Use Project), University of California System, 1972-73; Instructor in Leadership and Director of the Precommission Program, Southern California USAR School, 1970-73; Consultant to General Motors, Chrysler Motors, Lincoln Liberty Life Insurance, Westside Community Schools, Certain-Teed, Rockwell International. Organizational Memberships: Academy of Management, OD Division 1979 and 1981, OB Division 1980, Session Chairman 1979 and 1981, Occasional Reviewer for *Academy of Management Review*; Midwest Academy of Management, Program Committee 1980-82, Session Chairman 1980; Eastern Academy of Management, Program Committee 1981; American Association for the Advancement of Science; American Institute for Decision Sciences, Program Committee 1979-82, Session Chairman 1979-80; American Psychological Association; British Psychological Society; International Association of Applied Psychology; Agency for International Development Workshop, 1977; Occasional Reviewer for Professional Journals and Publishers. Published Works: Author Numerous Publications in His Field. Honors and Awards: Decorated Bronze Star, Air Medal, Purple Heart, Vietnamese Cross of Gallantry, Combat Infantryman's Badge, Vietnam Service and Campaign Medals, Good Conduct Medal, National Defense Medal, Distinguished Unit Citations; Honors Scholar, School of Social Sciences, Summa Cum Laude Graduate, University of California at Irvine; Listed in *Outstanding Young Men of America, Men of Achievement, International Who's Who of Intellectuals, Who's Who in Frontier Science and Technology, Dictionary of International Biography, Who's Who in the Midwest*. Address: 3217 Saddlehorn Drive, Lawrence, Kansas 66044.■

JACQUELYN NYE PATERNO

Educator. Personal: Born March 4, 1957; Daughter of Mr. and Mrs. Jack L. Nye; Married Charles F., Son of Dr. and Mrs. Charles Paterno; Mother of Charles Nye. Education: Teacher Certification, Baptist College of Charleston, 1980; B.S Microbiology, Clemson University, 1979. Career: Science Teacher, McCants Junior High School, present. Organizational Memberships: Palmetto State Teacher's Association, 1980 to present; National Education Association, 1980-81. Community Activities: Association for Retarded Citizens, 1975-82; Blue Key National Honor Fraternity 1977-79, First Woman President on Clemson University Campus 1978-79; Kappa Kappa Gamma Alumnae Club Secretary/Treasurer 1979-80, Treasurer 1982; Phi Kappa Phi, 1978 to present; Kappa Kappa Gamma Advisory Board, Clemson University, 1980 to present; Mortar Board, 1978-79; Microbiology Society, 1976-79; Alpha Epsilon Delta, 1977-79; Phi Eta Sigma, 1976 to present; Alpha Lambda Delta, 1975-76; Kappa Kappa Gamma, 1975 to present, First Vice President 1977-78, Panhellenic Delegate 1975-76; Alpha Tau Omega Little Sister 1976 to present, President 1978-79; Clemson Student Government Supreme Court Judge 1978-79, Student Government Trial Court Judge, Chairman 1977-78; Sigma Tau Epsilon, Volunteer Tutor 1977-79; MS Volleyball Marathon, 1975-78; MS Balloon Derby, 1979; American Lung Association Run 1979; Easter Egg Hunt for Underprivileged, 1982; Counselor Camp Funmore for Retarded Citizens, 1975; Daughters of the American Revolution, Barons of Runnemeade, 1978 to present; Old Plymouth Colony Descendants, 1978 to present; New England Women, 1976 to present; Daughters of Founders and Patriots of America, 1976 to present. Religion: Macedonia United Methodist Church Council on Ministries 1975, United Methodist Youth Fellowship President 1975; Clemson United Methodist Church Bible School Teacher 1979, Offertory Counter 1979. Honors and Awards: Baptist College of Charleston Most Outstanding Student Teacher Award, 1980; Clemson University Outstanding Greek Student Award, 1979; Alpha Tau Omega Sweetheart, 1979; Greek Goddess, 1978, 1979; Kappa Kappa Gamma Loyalty Key Recipient, 1979; Daughters of the American Revolution Good Citizen Award, 1975; Camp Funmore Outstanding Counselor Award, 1975; Mullins Jaycees, Miss Mullins Title, 1975-76; Listed in *Outstanding Young Women of America, International Youth in Achievement, Who's Who Among Students in American Universities and Colleges*. Address: 101 Hanover Way, Seneca, South Carolina 29678.■

PHILIP Y. PATERSON

Chairman and Guy and Anne Youmans Professor of Microbiology-Immunology. Personal: Born February 6, 1923; Married Virginia Bray, Daughter of Mrs. Virginia C. Bray; Father of Anne, Peter, Ben. Education: B.S. 1946, M.B. 1947, M.D. 1948, University of Minnesota. Military: Served in the United States Army Reserve, 1951-52, advancing through the grades from First Lieutenant to Captain MC. Career: Chairman and Guy Anne Youmans Professor of Microbiology-Immunology. Community Activities: Unitarian Church Forum Chairman, Staten Island, New York, New York (speakers included Norman Thomas, Patrick Murphy Malin, Lewis Thomas), 1958-60; North Shore Interfaith Housing Council, 1981. Religion: Trinity Church of North Shore, Education, Worship and Community Concerns Commissions, 1968-81. Address: 1025 Chestnut Avenue, Wilmette, Illinois 60091.■

GENNILLA ATKINS PATES

Private Piano Instructor. Personal: Born May 29, 1908; Daughter of Rev. and Mrs. Hampton Stuart Atkins (deceased); Married James Scott, Son of Mr. and Mrs. Ernest Orin Pates; Mother of Jacqueline Anne Henninger, James Morgan. Education: Attended Lee Baptist Institute, Pennington Gap, Virginia; Robbins Chapel High School, Keokee, Lee County, Virginia, 1922; Averett College, Danville, Virginia, 1923; Shenandoah College, Dayton, Virginia (now Winchester Virginia), 1925; Piano Graduate, 1927; B.S.Mus.Ed., Mary Washington College of the University of Virginia, Fredericksburg, Virginia, 1946. Career:

Private Piano Teacher, Fredericksburg, Virginia, present; Former Professional Occupations include Speech Teacher at City Schools in Cullman, Alabama, Piano and Drama Teacher at Pineland College, Salemburg, North Carolina, Stenographer for Brown Air Base, Marine Base, Quantico, Virginia; Clerk to the Superintendant of Schools and the County School Board, Spotsylvania, Virginia, 1945 to present. Organizational Memberships: National Federation of Music Clubs, Virginia Federation of Music Clubs, Former Virginia Branch Third Vice President; National Guild of Piano Teachers, Local Chairperson 11 Years. Community Activities: Aid in Mental Health Volunteer Department, 12 Years; Volunteer in Fish Organization, sponsored by St. George Episcopal Church, Several Years; 25 Years Volunteer Service to Mary Washington Hospital serving alternately in the capacities of Shop Helper, Supply Cart Visitor, Gray Lady, Emergency Lounge Hostess, Surgical Lounge Hostess (presently). Religion: Local Church World Day of Prayer, 1 Year; Superintenant of Sunday School of College, Pineland College (ca. 1952); Church One Missionary "Circle," 1979; Member Baraca Sunday School Class, Fredericksburg Baptist Church, Fredericksburg, Virginia. Honors and Awards: Elected to National Guild of Piano Teachers Hall of Fame, 1972; Member Carolina Playmakers, University of North Carolina, 1937; Inducted in to Alpha Psi Omega (Dramatic Fraternity), 1945. Address: 1500 Augustine Avenue, Fredericksburg, Virginia 22401.■

H. HUNTER PATRICK, JR.

Lawyer. Personal: Born August 19, 1939; Son of Hunter Patrick Sr.; Married Charlotte A., Daughter of Mr. and Mrs. C. B. Wilson; Father of Michael H., Colleen A. Education: Graduate, High School, Glendo, Wyoming, 1957; B.A. 1961, J.D. 1966, University of Wyoming. Career: Lawyer, present; Former Position as High School Teacher of English and Speech. Organizational Memberships: American Bar Association; Wyoming Bar Association; Colorado Bar Association; Park Count Bar Association, Past President; Wyoming Association of Judges, President 1973-79; American Judges Association; American Judicature Society. Community Activities: Justice of the Peace, Park County, Wyoming, 1970 to present; Wyoming Judicial Planning Committee, 1979-81; City Attorney, City of Powell, Wyoming, 1968 to present; Wyoming Delegate to Judicial Administration Division of American Bar Association, 1981 and 1982; Director of Court Session of Girls State, 1982, 1983, 1984; Presbyterian Church, Elder; Powell Rotary Club, President, 1973, 1974; Elks; Odd-Fellows. Religion: Member Presbyterian Church, Elder in Union Presbyterian Church of Powell, Wyoming. Address: P.O. Box 941, Powell, Wyoming 82435.■

RONALD JAMES PATTEN

University School of Business Administration Dean. Personal: Born July 17, 1935; Son of Rudolph and Cecelia Pataconi; Married Shirley Ann, Daughter of Mr. and Mrs. Frank Bierman; Father of Christine Marie, Cheryl Ann, Charlene Denise. Education: B.A. 1957, M.A. 1959, Michigan State University; Ph.D., University of Alabama, 1963. Military: Served with the United States Army Field Artillery as Second Lieutenant, 1958. Career: Dean, School of Business Administration, University of Connecticut, 1974 to present; Director of Research Financial Accounting Standards Board, 1973-74; Head, Department of Accounting 1966-73, Associate Professor of Accounting 1965-67, Virginia Polytechnic Institute and State University; Assistant Professor of Accounting, University of Colorado, 1963-65. Organizational Memberships: Delta Sigma Pi, District Director 1967-68; American Accounting Association, Screening Committee for Notable Contributions to Accounting Literature Award 1966-67, 1967-68, Educational Research Project Advisory Committee 1967-68, Committee on CPA Examinations 1968-69, 1969-70 (Chairman), 1970-71 (Chairman), Southeast Regional Group Committee 1968-69, 1969-70 (Chairman), 1970-71, 1971-72, 1972-73, Committee for Professional Development and Continuing Education 1971-72, 1972-73 (Chairman), 1973-74 (Chairman), Committee on Financial Accounting Standards 1974-75, Nominating Committee Northeast Regional Group 1975-76, Committee on Professional Examinations 1976-77 (Chairman), Committee on the Accounting Educator Award 1979-80, Deloitte, Haskins and Sells Wildman Medal Committee 1980-81; American Institute of Certified Public Accountants, Committee on Relations with Universities 1969-70, 1970-71, 1971-72, Committee on Educational Policy 1972-73, Committee on Relations with Educational Institutions 1975-76, 1976-77, 1977-78 (Chairman), 1978-79 (Chairman), 1979-80 (Chairman), Education Executive Committee, 1977-78, 1978-79, 1979-80, Grants-in-Aid Selection Task Force 1977-78 (Chairman), 1978-79 (Chairman), 1979-80 (Chairman), Task Force on Implementation Issues of Relevant Experience Requirement 1980 (Chairman); Virginia Society of Certified Public Accountants, Board of Editors of *The Virginia Accountant* 1967-68, Education Committee 1968-69 (Vice-Chairman), 1969-70 (Chairman), Director 1970-71, 1971-72, Ad hoc Committee of Professional Development Course Requirements 1971-72, 1972-73, Public Relations Committee 1972-73 (Chairman); National Association of Accountants, Committee on Socio-Economic Programs 1972-73, Committee on Research 1978-79, 1979-80, 1980-81, 1981-82, 1982-83, Committee on Academic Relations 1983-84; Connecticut Society of Certified Public Accountants, Ad hoc Committee on State Accountancy Act 1975-76, 1976-77, By-Laws Committee 1977, Committee on Cooperation with Bankers and Other Credit Grantors 1979-80; American Assembly of Collegiate Schools of Business, Visitation Committee 1975-76, 1976-77, 1977-78, Continuing Accreditation Committee 1975-76, 1976-77, 1977-78, 1979-80 (Chairman), 1980-81 (Chairman), Regional Representatives' Committee 1977-78, 1978-79, Committee of Academic Consultants 1977-78, 1978-79, 1979-80, 1980-81, 1981-82, Standards Committee 1978-79, Western Electric Awards Selection Committee 1979, Operations Committee 1979-80, Operations Management Committee 1979-80, Executive Committee of the Accreditation Council 1980-81, 1981-82, Board of Directors 1981-82, 1982-83, 1983-84, Accounting Accreditation Committee 1981-82 (Chairman), Accounting Standards Committee (Chairman) 1983-84; Beta Gamma Sigma, National Board of Governors 1976-77, 1977-78, 1978-79, 1979-80, National Communications Committee 1976-77, 1977-78, 1978-79 (Chairman), 1979-80 (Chairman), 1980-81 (Chairman), 1981-82 (Chairman), National Executive Committee, 1978-79, 1979-80, 1980-81, 1981-82, 1982-83, 1983-84, National Secretary-Treasurer 1980-81, 1981-82, National Vice President 1982-83, 1983-84, National President 1984; National Association of State Universities and Land-Grant Colleges, Commission on Education for the Business Professions 1979-80, 1980-81, 1981-82. Community Activities: Connecticut Joint Council on Economic Education, Board of Trustees 1976-77, 1977-78, 1979-80, 1980-81, 1981-82, 1982-83, 1983-84, Nominating Committee 1977-78 (Chairman), 1982-83 (Chairman), Blue Ribbon Advisory Committee 1979; Greater Hartford Chamber of Commerce, Judging Committee for Business Journalism Awards 1979-80 (Chairman), 1980-81 (Chairman), 1981-82 (Chairman). Religion: Member Church Council, Ebenezer Lutheran Church, Willimantic, Connecticut, 1980-81; Treasurer, University Lutheran Church, Tuscaloosa, Alabama, 1962-63. Honors and Awards: National Quartermaster Award, National Quartermaster Association, 1956. Address: 39 Storrs Heights Road, Storrs, Connecticut 06268.■

LUCY PHELPS PATTERSON

Educator. Personal: Born June 21, 1931; Daughter of John C. and Florence H. Phelps; Married Albert S.; Mother of Albert Harllee. Education: A.B., Howard University, 1950; M.S.W., University of Denver, 1963; Post-master's Study, University of Texas and University of Virginia. Career: Branham Professor and Director of Social Work Program, Bishop College, Dallas, Texas; Former Assistant Professor and Internship Coordinator for North Texas State University; Former Planning Director for Community Council of Greater Dallas; Former Social Agency Administrator and Executive Director, Dallas County Child Care Council and Inter-Agency Project; Former Social Worker and Supervisor, Dallas County Department of Public Welfare. Organizational Memberships: Texas Chapter of National Association of Social Workers, State Wide Secretary 1976-80, Board Member and Executive Committee Member 1976-80; Board Member, Texas Council of National Association of Social Workers, 1968-75; Dallas Chapter of National Association of Social Workers, Board Member 1968-80, Secretary 1960-61; Council on Social Work Education: Texas Association of College Teachers; Founder and First President, North Texas Association of Black Social Workers; Charter Member, National Association of Social Workers; Charter Member, Academy of Certified Social Workers. Community Activities: First Black Woman Elected City Councilwoman, City of Dallas, 1973-80; Region 13 of Texas Municipal League, First Black President 1975-76, Vice President 1974-75; Commissioner, Dallas Housing Authority; Board of Directors, Dallas/Fort Worth Regional Airport Board; Chairwoman, Human Development Committee for City of Dallas; Member, National League of Cities, Human Resources Committee, Steering and Policy Committee, Community Development Committee; President of John Neely Bryan Parent-Teacher Association, 1980-82; Black Adoption Advisory Board Member of Texas Department of Human Resources, 1979 to present; Honorary Chairwoman, Black Foster Family Recruitment Week, 1976; Regional Advisory Committee Member, Early Periodic Screening/Diagnosis and Treatment Project on Sickle Cell Anemia, 1976-80; Appointed by President Jimmy Carter, White House Committee on Hospital Cost Containment, 1979-80. Religion: Member of Saint Paul United Methodist Church; Member of Board of Church and Society, Northeast District United Methodist Church, 1974-81. Honors and Awards: "Black Women: Achievement Against the Odds," Women's Bureau, Department of Labor and East Oak Cliff District, 1980; Fair Housing Award, Greater Dallas Housing Opportunity; Galaxy of Stars Award for Achievement in Public Service, D.I.S.D.; Award of Appreciation, National Association of Social Workers; Leadership Commendation, City of Dallas, 1979; Received Ethel Carter Branham Endowed Chair in Social Work, Bishop College; National Sojourner Truth Meritorious Service Award from Business and Professional Women; Women Helping Women Award from Women's Center of

Dallas; State of Texas Legislative Commendation, 1975 and 1977; Mother of the Year, 1975-76, John Neely Bryan Elementary School; Outstanding Educator of America, 1975; Social Worker of the Year, National Association of Social Workers, 1976; Achievement Award from Henry W. Longfellow School, l976; Citizen of the Year, 1975; Woman of the Year, Zeta Phi Beta, 1975; Higher Education Achievement Award, 1980-81; Listed in Who's Who of Women. Address: 2779 Almeda Drive, Dallas, Texas 75216.■

ZELLA JUSTINA BLACK PATTERSON

Author, Researcher, Home Economist. Personal: Born May 20, 1909; Daughter of Thomas and Mary E. (Horst) Black (both deceased); Married George Washington Patterson (deceased). Education: Graduate of Secondary Laboratory School, Langston University, Received Normal Diploma, Life Certificate in Elementary Education, Home Economics Certificate, 1929; B.S. Home Economics, Langston University, 1937; Received Certificate in Vocational Home Economics, 1938; M.S. Home Economics Education, Colorado State University, 1941; Continued Studies at University of California-Berkeley Summers 1948 and 1952 and Oklahoma State University 1967-68. Career: Researcher, Author, Home Economist; Teacher, Excelsior School, Logan County, 1930-34; Teacher of Homemaking, Washington High School, Stillwater, Oklahoma; Teacher for Adults, Night School, Douglas High School; Langston University Vocational Homemaking Teacher, Resident Teacher Trainer, Supervising Teacher, 1937-46; Home Demonstration Agent, F.E.R.A. Program, Choctaw County and Seminole County, 1934-36; Supervisor, Canning Kitchen, Foods; Instructor, Clothing, Home Economics Methods; College Teaching as Instructor, Assistant and Associate Professor, Langston University, 1963-72; Family Living Specialist, Oklahoma State University, United States Department of Agriculture, 1972-74; Chairman, Department of Home Economics, Langston University, 1965-72; Developer Vocational Program, Langston City High School; Member Langston University Research Team, Project for Oklahoma State University Cooperative Experiment Station on Grant from United States Department of Agriculture Cooperative State Research Service. Organizational Memberships: Business and Professional Women's Club; Counselor Northwest District, National Homemakers Association; State Advisor, New Homemakers of America; Chairman, Home Economics Section, Northwest District Teachers Association; Reporter and Chairman Publicity Committee, Home Economics Section, Oklahoma Association of Negro Teachers; State Curriculum Revision Committee on Family Relations; American Home Economics Association; Oklahoma Home Economics Association; Life Member, Langston University Alumni Association; Life Member, Colorado State University Alumni Association; Langston University Home Economics Alumni Association; Logan County and National Retired Teachers Association; American Vocational Association; Oklahoma Vocational Home Economics Association. Community Activities: Oklahoma Historical Society, Life Member, Board of Directors 1983, State Chairman Black Heritage Committee 1984; Alpha Kappa Alpha, Alpha Upsilon Omega Chapter, Basileus, Tamiouchis 1953-59, Grammateus 1971; Honorary Board of Directors, American Biographical Institute; Smithsonian Associates; National Trust for Historic Preservation; Life Member, Member Board of Directors, Logan County Historical Society; Oklahoma Historical Society, Diamond Jubilee Commission, Board of Directors 1983-86, State Chairman of Black Heritage Committee; Past Worthy Matron, Order of the Eastern Star; 4-H Club Coach. Religion: Member of the New Hope Baptist Church, Building Fund Secretary 1972 to present. Published Works: Author of Articles "The Multigenerational Family History - A Case Study of a Black Family," "Nutrition, Family Commensality and Academic Performance Among High School Youth" (*Journal of Home Economics*, 1970); Author of Books *A Garden of Poems* 1976, *Langston University - A History* 1978, *Churches of Langston* 1982. Honors and Awards: Langston Federated Club, Woman of the Year 1959, Regional Federated Club Woman of the Year 1976, Regional and State Woman of the Year 1977; Grant to Attend Oklahoma State University, Title III of Higher Education Act, 1967-68; Honor Alumni, Colorado State University, 1976; Published Works Accepted for Inclusion in Library of Congress Collection. Address: P.O. Box 96, Langston, Oklahoma 73050.■

CAROL ANN PAUL

Administrator. Personal: Born December 17, 1936 in Brockton, Massachusetts; Daughter of Mr. and Mrs. J.W. Bjork; Married Dr. Robert D. Paul; Mother of Christine M., Dana J., Stephanie F., Robert Rea. Education: B.S., Pre-Medical, University of Massachusetts-Amherst, 1958; M.A.T., Rhode Island College, 1968; M.A.T., Brown University, 1970; Ed.D. Department of Systems, an Adaptation, School of Education, Boston University, 1978. Career: Assistant Vice President of Academic Planning, Fairleigh Dickinson University, Rutherford, New Jersey, 1980 to present; Master Planner, Department of Higher Education, State of New Jersey, Trenton, 1978-80; North Shore Community College, Beverly, Massachusetts, Assistant Dean, Assistant Professor 1969-80, Assistant Dean of Faculty 1974-78, Assistant Professor of Biology 1969-74; Biology Teacher, Attleboro High School, Massachusetts, 1965-68; Substitute Teacher, K-12, Groton Public Schools, Connecticut, 1964-65; Mathematics Teacher, Fitch Senior High School, Groton, Connecticut, 1959-60; Research, Characteristics of College and University Administrators. Organizational Memberships: National Council of Administrative Women in Education, 1977 to present; Pi Lambda Theta, 1977 to present; Professional and Organizational Development Network in Higher Education, Member 1976 to present, National Conference Planning Committee 1977, Professional Relations and Membership Committee 1978-79; National Council for Staff, Professional and Organizational Development, Member 1976 to present, National Executive Board 1979-80, Northeast Regional Representative 1979-80, Charter Member Northeast Region 1976, Northeast Conference Planning Committee 1978 to present, Chairperson Conference Planning Committee 1980 to present; Phi Delta Kappa, 1976 to present; Association for Supervision and Curriculum Development, 1975-78; Massachusetts Administrators in Community Colleges, 1974-78; National Association of Biology Teachers, 1966 to present. Community Activities: League of Women Voters of the United States, Member 1958 to present, Groton, Connecticut Chapter 1959-65, Attleboro Massachusetts Chapter 1965-69; Beverly Massachusetts Chapter 1969-77, Cranford New Jersey Chapter 1977 to present, Board of Directors 1960-63, 1967-69, 1970-74, 1981 to present, Vice President 1971-73, 1981-83; Brown University Alumni Representative, 1972 to present; College Club of Cranford, 1977-81; City of Salem, College Representative 1976-77, Advisory Council for Alternative Education; Policy Committee for Mayorality Candidate, Beverly, 1975; Board of Directors, Committee for Choice in the Beverly Schools, 1974-75; Mayor's Task Force for Economic Development, City of Beverly, 1974. Religion: Teacher, Grades 9-12, Confraternity of Christian Doctrine, Saint Mary's, Beverly, Massachusetts, 1976-77. Published Works: Author, Numerous Articles for Professional Publications, including "Personal, Educational and Career Characteristics of Male and Female College Administrators in Massachusetts" with Phyllis R. Sweet, Nancy Brigham, "Are Women Obtaining Faculty and Administrative Positions in Higher Education?" with Nancy Brigham, "Women's Place in Academia"; Editor, *Northeastern Regional Newsletter*, National Council for Staff, Program, and Organizational Development; *Study Guide for Introductory Biology, Instructor's Manual for Introductory Biology*, both with Michele Balcomb; *Minicourses for Principles of Biological Science, Laboratory Experiments of Biological Science*. Honors and Awards: Pi Lambda Theta, 1977; Phi Delta Kappa, 1976; Academic Year Fellowship to Brown University 1968-69, In-Service Institute, Organic and Biochemistry 1967-68, Special Material Workshop 1966, State College at Bridgewater, Intensive Training Workshop, Bowdoin College, Maine 1966, National Science Foundation; State of Massachusetts Scholarship to attend the University of Massachusetts, 1954-58; National Honor Society; Listed in *International Who's Who of Women, Notable Americans, International Who's Who in Education, International Who's Who of Intellectuals*. Address: 18 Central Avenue, Cranford, New Jersey 07016.■

DOUGLAS FRANK PAULSEN

Professor. Personal: Born October 7, 1952; Son of Mr. and Mrs. Douglas F. Paulsen, Sr. Education: B.A. Biology, Western Maryland College, 1974; Ph.D. Anatomy, Bowman Gray School of Medicine, Wake Forest University, 1979. Career: Assistant Professor of Anatomy, Morehouse School of Medicine; Former Positions include National Institutes of Health Individual Postdoctoral Fellow, California State University-Northridge; Instructor, Nurse Anesthetist Program at Bowman Gray School of Medicine; Teaching Assistant, Anatomy, Bowman Gray School of Medicine. Organizational Memberships: Current Society for Developmental Biology; American Association of Anatomists; Sigma Xi; New York Academy of Science; Pan American Association of Anatomy; Southern Society of Anatomists. Community Activities: Steering Committee, Network University of the Atlanta Network, 1981-82; Manager, Fund Raising Committee of the Atlanta Network, 1982. Honors and Awards: Scholarship (Fellowship) Bowman Gray School of Medicine, Wake Forest University, 1974-75; Four Consecutive Bowman Gray School of Medicine Teaching Assistantships, 1975-79; Recipient of American Heart Association Grant-in-Aid for Biomedical Research, 1981-82; NIH/MBRS Research Grant, 1983-87; Faculty Recognition for Outstanding Contributions in Research and Teaching at Morehouse School of Medicine, 1982. Address: 2192 Rhine Hill Road, Southeast, Atlanta, Georgia 30315.■

JOSEPH C. PAULSEN

Corporate Executive, Publishers Representative. Personal: Born November 30, 1925, in New York, New York; Married Ann D. Moore on September 17, 1949; Father of Bradly, Joann, Nancy, Amy. Education: Attended Birmingham Southern College, 1943-44; St. Johns University, 1945-48, City College of New York, 1949; Dale Carnegie. Career: President, J. Paulsen, Inc., Publishers Representative, New York, New York; Advertising Director and Representative,

TWA Ambassador Magazine, Northwest Passages, Frontier Magazine, KOA Handbook for Campers, Southern Pulp and Paper Manufacturing; Advertising Director 1965-67, Eastern Manager 1957-65, Oklahoma Publishing; Vice President, Austin Le Strange Company, 1952-57; Account Executive, Robert Bories Company, 1951-52; New York Journal American, 1949-51; Research, Hearst Advertising Service, 1949. Organizational Memberships: Farm Publication Men New York Treasurer, Past President; N.A.A.M.A.; Agricultural Published Association, Former Director; Farm Publication Reports, Director; State Farm Paper Advertising Bureau, Vice-Chairman, Director; N.A.A.M.A. Southwest, Vice President; Oklahoma City Press and Advertising Club. Community Activities: Hartsdale Republican Club; Civic Association; Knights of Columbus; Orienta YC, Vice Commander; Mensa; Community Chest, Chairman; Quail Creek Country Club; Beacon Club; Guest Speaker, Association Radio-TV Farm Directors. Address: 23 Woodland Place, Chappaqua, New York 10514.■

NORMA PAULUS

Oregon Secretary of State. Personal: Born March 13, 1933; Daughter of Paul Emil and Ella Marie (Hellbusch) Petersen (deceased); Married William G.; Mother of Elizabeth, William Frederick. Education: LL.B., Willamette Law School, 1962. Career: Oregon Secretary of State, present; Elected Oregon House of Representatives, 1970, 1972, 1974; Of Counsel, Paulus & Callaghan Attorneys, 1973-76; Self-Employed Appellate Lawyer, 1962 to present; Secretary of Chief Justice, Oregon Supreme Court, 1955-61; Legal Secretary, Salem, Oregon, 1953-55; Secretary to Harney County District Attorney, 1950-53. Organizational Memberships: Director, National Society of State Legislatures, 1971-72; Oregon State Bar Association; Marion County Bar Association; National Order of Women Legislators, 1973-76; Delta Kappa Gamma Society, International. Community Activities: Willamette University Board of Trustees; Director, Benedictine Foundation of Oregon; Oregon Delegate to First National Criminal Justice Conference, 1973; Governor's Task Force on Early Childhood Development; Zonta International; Business and Professional Women; Fellow, Eagleton Institute of Politics, 1971. Honors and Awards: Golden Torch Award, Business and Professional Women of Oregon, 1971; City of Salem's Distinguished Service Award, 1971; Women in Communications "Abigail Scott Duniway Award," 1979; Named One of the "Women of the Future" by *Ladies' Home Journal* Editorial Board, 1979; Honor Student at Willamette Law School; First in Moot Court Competition, Willamette Law School. Address: 136 State Capitol, Salem, Oregon 97310.■

ELAINE BLANCHE PAVELKA

Educator. Personal: Daughter of Mrs. Mildred Pavelka. Education: B.A., M.S., Northwestern University; Ph.D., University of Illinois. Career: Mathematics Professor, Morton College, present; Mathematics Instructor, Leyden Community High School; Mathematician, Northwestern University Aerial Measurements Laboratory. Organizational Memberships: American Educational Research Association; American Mathematical Association of Two-Year Colleges, Vice President; American Mathematical Society; Association for Women in Mathematics; Canadian Society for the History and Philosophy of Mathematics; Mathematics Association of America; Mathematics Action Group; Illinois Council of Teachers of Mathematics; Illinois Mathematics Association of Community Colleges; National Council of Teachers of Mathematics; School Science and Mathematics Association; Society for Industrial and Applied Mathematics; Pi Mu Epsilon; Sigma Delta Epsilon. Community Activities: Northwestern University Alumni Association; University of Illinois Alumni Association. Honors and Awards: Member, American Mensa Limited; Member, Intertel; Only Community College Professor Asked to Present a Paper before the Third International Congress on Mathematics Education, Karlsruhe, Germany, 1976; Listed in *Who's Who of American Women, Who's Who in the Midwest, World Who's Who of Women, International Who's Who in Education, International Who's Who in Intellectuals, International Who's Who in Community Service, International Register of Profiles, Dictionary of International Biography, Men and Women of Distinction, Personalities of America, Personalities of the West and Midwest, Notable Americans, Directory of Distinguished Americans, Community Leaders and Noteworthy Americans, Who's Who in Technology Today, The Registry of American Achievement, Leading Consultants in Technology, Contemporary Personalities, Five Thousand Personalities of the World.* Address: 1900 Euclid Avenue, Berwyn, Illinois 60402.■

MARGARET A. PAYNE

Assistant Commissioner. Personal: Born May 25, 1942; Daughter of Douglass and Jean Payne; Married John P. Clements. Education: B.S. Community Recreation, State University of New York at Cortland, 1964; M.A. Community Recreation Administration, New York University, New York, New York, 1970. Career: Assistant Commissioner, New York State Office of Parks, Recreation and Historic Preservation, 1976 to present; Commissioner of Parks, Recreation Youth Services, Town of Greenburgh, New York, 1975-76; Regional Park Supervisor, Nassau County, New York Department Recreation Parks, 1970-75; Park Director, Nassau County R&P, 1967-70; Assistant Park Director, Nassau County, 1966-67; Recreation Supervisor, Oceanside, New York, School District Recreation Department, 1964-66. Organizational Memberships: National Recreation and Park Association; New York State Recreation and Park Society, President-Elect 1975; National Park and Conservation Association; New York State Outdoor Education Association; Northeast Recreation and Park Association; World Leisure and Recreation Association. Community Activities: American Dance Guild Board of Directors, 1975-78; Metcalf Endowment Fund, Chairman 1981-82; Nassau County Girl Scout Council, 1973-75; Nassau County Boy Scout Career Exploration Project, 1970. Honors and Awards: Metropolitan New York Award of the Year, 1982; APRS Committee Chairman of the Year, 1979; Nassau County Recreation, Park and Conservation Association, Distinguished Professional Award, 1975. Address: 2 Chaucer Street, Hartsdale, New York 10530.■

RONALD E. PEAKE

Professor. Personal: Born September 16, 1935; Son of Dr. and Mrs. F. A. Peake; Married Ann Priestley; Father of Annette Peake Mead, Ronald Allen, Steven Priestley. Education: B.S., Howard College/Samford University, 1957; M.A. 1961, E.D.D. 1964, University of Alabama. Career: Professor, University of West Florida; Assistant Professor of Education, University of Southwestern Louisiana, 1965-68; Administrator Towers High School, Dekalb County, Georgia, 1964; Director, Curriculum Laboratory, University of Alabama, 1962-64; Teacher, Birmingham Public Schools, 1957-61. Organizational Memberships: Association for Supervision and Curriculum Development; F.A.S.C.D.; A.T.E.; F.A.T.E.; S.R.A.T.E.; F.A.S.D.; Omicron Delta Kappa, Phi Delta Kappa; Kappa Phi Kappa. Community Activities: Pensacola Arts Council, 1977 to present; West Florida Festival Chorus, 1977; Soloist with Pensacola Symphony, 1982; Musical Performer, Pensacola Arts Festival. Religion: Elder, First Presbyterian Church, Pensacola, 1970 to present. Honors and Awards: U.W.F. Distinguished Service Award, 1980; Distinguished Service Award, Florida Association of Teacher Educators, 1981; Outstanding Educators of America, 1974-75; Listed in *Personalities of the South, Who's Who in the South and Southwest, Community Leaders of America, International Biography, Who's Who in American Universities and Colleges.* Address: 2931 Swan Lane, Pensacola, Florida 32504.■

JANICE MARIE PEARL

Neurosurgeon, Restaurant Theatre Owner-Operator. Personal: Born May 24, 1932; Daughter of Dr. and Mrs. William A. Pearl (deceased); Mother of Cynthia Ann. Education: B.A. with honors, Indiana University, 1954; B.S., Columbia University, 1959; M.D., Ph.D. (in progress), John Hopkins University, 1963; Fellow and Resident, University of Minnesota, 1963-66; Resident and Chief Resident, Barrow Neurological Institute and Maricopa County General Hospital, Phoenix, Arizona, 1966-69. Career: Neurological Surgeon, 1969 to present; Owner/Operator, Restaurant Theatre; Former Professional Occupation as Singing Star of Opera, Musical Comedy, Concert Stage and Major Hotels. Organizational Memberships: Mu Phi Epsilon, Secretary 1954; Washington Players Guild, Secretary 1950; Johns Hopkins Medical and Surgical, Served on Many Hospital Committees. Community Activities: Volunteer, Hull House, Chicago, 1942-45; Member of Spurs, Pamarada and Mortar Board Service Honoraries during College (elected memberships); Muscular Dystrophy Benefit Concerts, Minneapolis,

1964-65; Active in LaConner Fund Drives for Historical Preservation through Free Concerts and Free Dinners for the Underprivileged; Offers Free Surgical Care to Medically Indigent. Religion: Soloist for Many Leading Churches including Fifth Avenue Presbyterian Church (New York, New York), Hanson Place Methodist Church (Brooklyn, New York), Temple Beth Emanuel (New York, New York), First Church of Christ Scientist (Seattle, Washington), 1953-59 (previous work with smaller churches, singing premiers of several religious cantatas and masses). Honors and Awards: Mu Phi Epsilon, Music Honorary, 1949; Spurs, Pamarada and Mortar Board, College Honoraries, 1949-55; American Legion Award for Citizenship, 1945; Gold Award, Indiana University, 1952; Winner of Many Musical Competitions including Portland Symphony (1956), Washington Music Teachers (1947), San Francisco Opera (1956); Scholarship Student, Indiana University; Geigy Pharmaceutical Summer Research Grant, 1961; Three-Time Winner American Medical Association Original Research Competitions, Two-Time Winner American College of Surgeons. Address: Box 757, LaConner, Washington 98257. ■

AGNES BRANCH PEARLMAN

Writer and Lecturer. Personal: Born November 22, 1922; Daughter of William Norwood Branch and Icy Maud Christian (both deceased); Married Carl Kenneth Pearlman, Son of Ike Pearlman and Ida Krellenstein (both deceased); Mother of Philip Branch, Nancy Sue. Education: B.S., Marshall University, Huntington, West Virginia, 1944; Certificate, New York School of Interior Design, 1945; M.A., University of Southern California, Los Angeles, 1966. Career: Writer and Lecturer, 1948 to present; Past Member of Faculty, Woodbury College, Los Angeles; Former Lecturer at Santa Ana College. Organizational Memberships: Auxiliary to Orange County Medical Association, Board of Directors, 1950's; Active in the American Association of University Women, Archaeological Survey Association, Photographic Society of America. Community Activities: Bowers Museum Foundation, Board of Directors and Vice President 1972-79; Traveling Shutterbugs, President 1978-80; Orange County Camera Club, Vice President 1980-82; Orange County Genealogical Society, Board of Directors 1973-78, Vice President 1973-75, Parliamentarian 1976-78; Daughters of the American Revolution, Past Genealogical Chairman; Active in League of Women Voters, Orange County Philharmonc Society (one of founders), Amateur Chamber Music Players, Idyllwild School of Music and the Arts Associates, Ecology Center of Southern California. Published Works: Editor, *Christian Family Chronicles*, 1979 to present; Author, "The White Families of Boone County, West Virginia" 1980, "Mitchell Lines in Southern West Virginia" 1980; Co-Editor, *Saddleback Ancestors — Rancho Families of Southern California* 1969; Editor, *Genealogical Index and Gazetteer for Bowman's Reference Book of Wyoming County History* 1977; Editor, *West Virginia's Southern Counties 1850 Census Surname Index* 1976; Columnist, "Family Pearls" in *The West Virginia Hillbilly*, 1969 to present; Other Publications. Honors and Awards: Bowers Museum Foundation, Commendation for Services, 1972-79; Young Women's Christian Association, Citation for Lectures, 1950's; Orange County Camera Club, Awards for Photographic Excellence; Commodore of the Ship of State by Secretary of State, West Virginia, for Legislative Efforts, 1979; Listed in *Who's Who in Genealogy and Heraldry*, *Who's Who in Orange County*. Address: 2001 North Westwood Avenue, Santa Ana, California 92706. ■

REGINALD A. PEARMAN

Educator. Personal: Born August 8, 1918; Father of Jocelyn R., Reginald A. Jr.. Education: B.S. Education 1942, Ed.M. 1949, Boston University; C.A.G.S., 1951; Advanced Study, Harvard University, Columbia University; Graduate, United States Athletic School, Chalons sur Marne, France. Military: Served in the United States Army Medical Branch, Grade T/5 in Europe during World War II, 1943-46. Career: Junior High School Teacher, Inkster, Michigan; Director of Health and Physical Education, Leland College, Baker, Louisiana; Director of Health and Physical Education, Morristown College, Tennessee; Bowie State College, Maryland, Health Education Specialist 30 Years, Professor Emeritus. Organizational Memberships: American Physical Health Association; American Association of Health, Physical Education and Recreation; A.S.A.; National Recreational and Parks Society. Community Activities: Omega Pi Phi Fraternity, Keeper of Records and Seals, Keeper of Finance, Gamma Chapter, Boston, Massachusetts; Saint Augustine's Camp, Foxboro, Massachusetts, Director, Senior Counselor; Leland College, Health and Physical Education Committee; Health and Physical Education Committee, Morristown College; Work with Democrat Club, Boston; Bel Air Boy's Club, Bowie, Maryland. Religion: Member of Shrine Catholic Immaculate Conception, Washington, D.C.; Saint Augustine's Church, Boston, Massachusetts; Men's Club; Boy's Club. Honors and Awards: Maryland Meritorious Service Plaque, 1981; Fellow, American Physical Health Association; Fellow, American Association of Health, Physical Education and Recreation; Fellow, National Parks and Recreation Society; Fellow, American School Health Association. Address: P.O. Box 375, Bowie, Maryland 20715. ■

NORMAN PEARSON

Business and Consulting Executive. Personal: Born October 24, 1928, in Stanley, County Durham, United Kingdom; Married Gerda Maria Josefine Riedl, 1972. Education: Professional Degree, B.A. with honors Town and Country Planning, University of Durham, 1951; Ph.D. Land Economics, International Institute for Advanced Studies, 1979; M.B.A. 1980, D.B.A. 1982, Pacific Western University. Military: Served in the Royal Air Force-N.A.T.O.-R.C.A.F. in the United Kingdom, Canada, Iceland and the United States 1952-53 and in Royal Air Force Volunteer Reserve 1953-58 as Flying Officer, G.D./Nav(Aircrew). Career: President, Norman Pearson & Associates Limited, 1976 to present; Planner, Professional Consulting Practice, 1962 to present; Planning Analyst, City of Toronto Planning Board, Commissioner of Planning, Town of Burlington, Ontario, 1959-62; Planner, Central Mortgage and Housing Corporation, Ottawa, 1954-55; Planning Assistant, London City Council, 1953-54; Administrative Assistant, Scottish Division, National Coal Board, Scotland, 1951-52; Planning Assistant, Messrs. Allen & Mattocks, Consulting Planners and Landscape Designers and Architects, United Kingdom, 1949-51; Planning Assistant, Accrington Town Plan and Bedford County Planning Survey, University of Durham Planning Team, United Kingdom, 1947-49; Consultant to Stanley Urban District Council, United Kingdom, 1946-47; Many Achievements as Planner, including Official Plans for Township of Chinagauacousy 1964-70, Georgian Bay Regional Plan 1968-72, Officials Plans for Welland Area Planning Board 1963-70, Research for Appraisal Institute of Canada, Land Banking Principles and Practice 1972-75, Study of Impact on Planning Bruce Nuclear Power Development, Kincardine and Several Related Municipalities 1974-75, Advisor to U.D.I. London, Parks and Recreation Policies, Official Plan; Adjunct Professor, International Institute for Advanced Studies, 1980 to present; Professor of Political Science, University of Western Ontario, Urban/Regional Program, 1972-77; Assistant Professor of Geography, Chairman, Director of Center for Resource Development, University of Guelph, 1967-72; Special Lecturer in Planning, McMaster University 1956-64, Waterloo Lutheran University 1961-63; Real Estate Professional Appraiser, Alpha Appraisal Association, 1976; Ontario Land Economist, 1963. Organizational Memberships: Royal Town Planning Institute, United Kingdom, Associate Member 1955, Fellow 1972; International Society of City and Regional Planners, 1972; Canadian Institute of Planners, Associate Member 1956, Member 1959; American Institute of Planners, 1973; American Institute of Certified Planners, Charter Member 1978; Canadian Association of Certified Planning Technicians, 1979; Royal Economic Society, Member 1952, Fellow 1955, Life Fellow 1966; Intercontinental Biographical Association, Fellow 1975, Life Fellow 1976; United States Committee for Monetary Research and Education, Member 1975, Life Member 1976; American Geographical Society, Life Fellow, 1976; Atlantic Economic Association, Life Fellow, 1978; International Fraternity of Lambda Alpha, Land Economics, 1969; British Sociological Association, Founder, Member 1953 to present; International Joint Commission, Canadian Universities Representative, Social Sciences, Economic and Legal Aspects Standing Committee, Research Advisory Board, 1972-76; International Association of Great Lakes Research, *Journal of Great Lakes Research*, Editorial Board 1973-80; Great Lakes Tomorrow, Canadian Vice-President, 1976-77; National Research Council of the United States, Committee A1BO3, Economic and Environmental Factors of Transportation, Transportation Research Board 1973-79, Corresponding Member 1979; New Communities and Large-Scale Development Council, Urban Land Institute, United States, 1979 to present. Community Activities: President/Chairman of the Board of Governors, Pacific Western University, Canada; Numerous Audio-Visual Presentations; Numerous Public Lectures. Published Works: Editor, *The Ontario Land Economist*, 1978 to present; Co-Author or Co-Editor, Four Books, including Editorship of *Regional and Resource Planning in Canada*; Contributor of 80 Articles to Refereed Academic and Professional Journals or Chapters to Books; Contributor of 200 Articles to Non-Referred Journals, Reports, Conference Papers or Abstracts; Author, 46 Newspaper Articles for Book Reviews. Honors and Awards: Knight of Malta, Chevalier; President's Prize, Bronze Medal; Royal Town Planning Institute, United Kingdom, 1957; Honorary Member, Bruce Trail Association, 1960 to present; Listed in *Dictionary of International Biography*, *American Men and Women of Science*, *Who's Who in the Midwest*, *Men of Achievement*, *International Who's Who of Community Service*, *Internationl Register of Profiles* (World

TWO THOUSAND NOTABLE AMERICANS

Edition), *International Who's Who of Intellectuals, Men and Women of Distinction, Who's Who in the Commonwealth.* Address: P.O. Box 5362, Station A, London, Ontario N6A 4L6, Canada.■

GEORGE MERRILL PEAVY

Veterinarian. Personal: Born December 19, 1949; Son of Mr. and Mrs. Merrill A. Peavy; Married Lynn B., Daughter of Mr. and Mrs. Edwin Berhio. Education: B.S. 1972, D.V.M. 1974, University of California-Davis. Career: Veterinarian. Organizational Memberships: American Veterinary Medical Association, 1974 to present, Member AVMA-PAC Board of Directors 1982 to present; California Veterinary Medical Association, 1974 to present, Chairman CVMA Legislative Committee 1977-78, Chairman CVMA-PAC Board of Directors 1977 to present; American Association of Zoo Veterinarians, 1974 to present; American Animal Hospital Association, 1974 to present; Southern California Veterinary Medical Association, 1974 to present; American Association of Avian Veterinarians, 1980 to present; Sigma Xi, 1976 to present. Community Activities: Member Health Advisory Committee to United States Senator S. I. Hayakawa, 1977-82. Religion: San Clemente Presbyterian Church; Advisor to Several Evangelical Christian Organizations. Honors and Awards: Award of Merit, California Veterinary Medical Association. Address: 1833 South El Camino Real, San Clemente, California 92672.■

JOHN WESLEY PEAVY, JR.

Judge. Personal: Born April 28, 1943, in Houston, Texas; Married; Father of Three Children. Education: Graduate, Phyllis Wheatly Senior High School, 1960; A.B. Accounting, Howard University, 1964; Postgraduate Work at Howard University School of Law, 1964-67. Career: Judge, 246th District Court, appointed by Governor Briscoe, present; Judge-Justice of the Peace, Precinct 7 Position 2, appointed by the Harris Count Commissioner's Court, Houston, Texas, 1973; Associate Counsel for Project Home (pilot project funded by the Ford Foundation, Housing and Urban Development, Houston Housing and Development Corporation, Houston-Galveston Area Council), 1970-71; Executive Assistant to County Judge Bill Elliott, 1968-70; Associate Field Coordinator, Harris County Community Action Association, 1967-68; Practice of Law, Berry, Lott, Peavy & Williams, 1967-72; Administrative Assistant for President Lyndon Johnson, National Aeronautics and Space Council, the White House, Washington D.C., 1964-67; Accounting Clerk, National Aeronautics and Space Council, the White House, Washington D.C., 1961-64. Organizational Memberships: Houston Lawyers' Association, Political Action Committee; National Bar Foundation, Board of Directors; Houston Bar Association; National Bar Association; American Bar Association; Junior Bar Association of Houston; State Junior Bar Small Claims Court Handbook Committee, 1977; State Bar of Texas Court Reorganization Committee; Judicial Council; American Judges Association; National Council of Juvenile and Family Court Judges; Committee on Legal Services to Indigent in Civil Matters 1977, Courts of Original Jurisdiction 1978, State Bar of Texas. Community Activities: Family Chairman, W. L. Davis Division, Sam Houston Boy Scouts, 1976; Alpha Phi Alpha Fraternity; Urban League; Harris County Council of Organizations; Life Member, National Association for the Advancement of Colored People; Houston Business and Professional Men's Club, Nominating Committee; Young Men's Christian Association Century Club; Former Democratic Precinct Chairman of Precinct 292, Houston, Texas; Advisory Board, KYOK Radio Station; Legal Advisor, Riverside Lion's Club; Board of Directors, Mercy Hospital; A. Phillip Randolph Institute, Steering Committee; Board of Directors, Houston Citizens Chamber of Commerce; Project Pull; Eliza Johnson Center for the Aged; South Center Branch, Young Men's Christian Association; United Negro College Fund; Julia C. Hester House; St. Elizabeth Hospital, Houston Council of Human Relations, Volunteers of America; Appointed by Mayor of the City of Houston as Member of the Housing Assistance Technical Advisory Group, 1974; Honorary Co-Chairman, Citizens for Better Transit, 1978; Downtown Rotary Club of Houston; Urban Policy Task Force for the City of Houston, 1978; Board of Directors, Houston Grand Opera and Lyric Theater Foundation. Religion: Member Antioch Missionary Baptist Church. Honors and Awards: Chicago Tribune Award for Outstanding Military Student; Plaque from Young Men's Christian Association for Contributing Most to the Community; Academic Scholarship to Howard University School of Law; Eagle Scout, Member of Order of the Arrow, Boy Scouts of America, 1960; Distinguished Achievers Award, Young Men's Christian Association, 1973 and 1977; Honorary Member, I.L.A. Local #872; Who's Who Recipient of Young Men's Christian Association Award for Outstanding Service to the Community, 1974; National Judicial College Certificate, 1979; Phi Alpha Delta Law Fraternity; International Achievement Award; Houston Lawyers Association Achievement Award, 1980; Outstanding Young Business and Professional Men, Houston Young Adult Club, 1979; Kaleidoscope District, Exploring Division, Sam Houston Area Council Boy Scouts of America, Appreciation Award, 1979; Honorary Degree of Doctor of Humanities, National University of Graduate Studies, 1979; Listed in *Personalities of the South, Who's Who Among Black Americans, International Who's Who of Intellectuals, Notable Americans of the Bicentennial Era, Who's Who in Texas, Who's Who in America, Who's Who in the South, Outstanding Young Men in America, International Dictionary of Judges, Book of Honor, Community Leaders and Noteworthy Americans, Who's Who in American Law.* Address: 246th Judicial District Court, 1115 Congress Street, Houston, Texas 77002.■

DIANNE KAWECKI PECK

Architect. Personal: Born in 1945; Daughter of Thaddeus Walter and Harriet Ann Kawecki; Married Gerald Paul Peck; Mother of Samantha Gillian, Alexis Hilary. Education: Bachelor of Architecture, Carnegie-Mellon University, 1968; Certificate, Critical Path Construction; Three-Dimensional Vector Analysis, New York University. Organizational Memberships: Health Systems Agency of Northern Virginia; American Institute of Architects, 1970-78; Soroptimist International, 1977; Washington Professional Women's Cooperative, 1977; American Association of University Women, 1974-76; Community Activities: Vice President, Vocational Education Foundation, 1976; Chairwoman, Architect and Engineers United Way; Industrial Development Authority of Prince William, Chairwoman 1976, Vice Chairwoman 1977; Director, Prince William Chamber of Commerce, 1977. Published Works: Inner-City Rehabilitation Study, 1973. Honors and Awards: Prince William Board of Supervisors Commendation, 1976; Health Systems Agency Commendation, 1977; Listed in *Who's Who in the Southeast, Who's Who of American Women, Personalities of the South, World Who's Who of Women.* Address: 11510 Wildflower Court, Woodbridge, Virginia 22192.■

EVAN E. S. PEELLE

Management Consultant, Behavioral Scientist, Futurist. Personal: Born October 10, 1944; Daughter of William and Vivian Sallee; Mother of Rebecca Ann. Education: M.A. Education 1973, M.A. Psychology 1975, Ph.D. Behavioral Sciences 1980, University of Michigan; B.S. Education, Wayne State University, 1966. Career: President/Consultant, Consulting Associate, Evan Peelle & Associates, Emmons-Labus & Associates, Consulting Associate; President, Family Survival Inc.; Assistant Director, Panama Expedition, Ethnology and Change of Choco Indians, 1981; Participant, "Biocultural Odyssey," Smithsonian Institution, 1981; Writer, "Management Maxims" Column in *Computer Times*; Editor, "Terrorism and Crime, Practical Security Measures"; Director of Research and Development, Human Synergistics, Inc., 1978-81; Sales Manager, Worldwide Edugraphics Printing and Publishing Company, 1977-78; Consultant, Trainer, Program Director, University of Michigan, 1972-77; Instructor, University of Michigan, 1975; Editor, Consultant, Trainer, Administrator, Livingston and Washtenaw County Intermediate Schools, 1975-72. Organizational Memberships: Management Trainer for Business Education, Division of Dun and Bradstreet; President, International Survival Institute/Family Survival Inc., Services in Security, Survival, Educational Adventure Expeditions to Remote Regions of the World such as Rain Forests of Panama with Choco Indians and the Florida Everglades. Community Activities: Invited to Participate in the Smithsonian Institution's International Symposium on Human Adaptation, 1981; Archeological Surveys with Artifacts donated to Museums, Rain Forests of Central America and Unexplored Wild Caves of Southeastern United States, 1981; Training, Planning Assistance and Trade an Cultural Exchanges with North and Central and South American Indian Tribes; Presentations to Various Civic Clubs, Public Schools, Professional Organizations. Honors and Awards: One of the First Women Elected for Membership in the Explorers Club. Address: 3335 Burbank, Ann Arbor, Michigan 48105.■

ROBERT DONALD PEHLKE

Educator. Personal: Born February 11, 1933; Son of Robert William Pehlke (deceased) and Mrs. O.H. Perry; Married Julie Anne Kehoe; Father of Robert Donald Jr., Elizabeth Anne, David Richard. Education: B.S.E., University of Michigan, 1955; S.M. 1958, Sc.D. 1960, Massachusetts Institute of Technology; Attended Technological Institute, Aachen, Germany, 1956-57. Career: University of Michigan, Assistant Professor of Met. Engineering 1960, Professor 1968

TWO THOUSAND NOTABLE AMERICANS

to present, Chairman Department of Materials and Metallurgical Engineering 1968 to present. Organizational Memberships: American Society for Metals, Secretary Metals Academy Committee 1977, Technical Divisions Board 1982 to present; Director, A.I.M.E. Iron and Steel Society, 1976-77; A.I.M.E. Met. Society; American Foundrymen's Society; American Society of Engineering Education; German Iron and Steel Society; London Iron and Steel Society; Japan Iron and Steel Society; New York Academy of Science; Sigma Xi; Tau Beta Pi; National President, Alpha Sigma Mu, 1977-78; Registered Professional Engineer, Michigan. Community Activities: Ann Arbor Amateur Hockey Association, President 1977-79, Board of Directors 1976-8l. Honors and Awards: Fellow, American Society for Metals, 1977; Gold Medal Science of Extractive Metals, 1976; Howe Memorial Lecturer, 1980; Fellow, Met. Society, 1983; Distinguished Life Member, Iron and Steel Society, 1979, A.I.M.E.; National Science Foundation Fellow, 1955-56; Fulbright Scholar, 1956-57. Address: 9 Regent Drive, Ann Arbor, Michigan 48104.■

PATRICK R. PENLAND

Professor. Education: B.A., University of British Columbia, Vancouver, Canada, 1948; B.L.S., McGill University, Montreal, Canada, 1953; A.M.L.S. 1955, Ph.D. 1960, University of Michigan; Post Doctoral, Information Science, Yale University; Post Doctoral, Survey Research, Columbia University, 1976. Career: Professor, Education and Library Science, School of Library and Information Science, University of Pittsburgh, Pittsburgh, Pennsylvania; Other Professional Areas include Interviewing and Consultation, Workshops and Institutes, Meetings and Conferences, Survey and Community Research, Appraisal and Evaluation, Professional Consultation, Information Processing, Learning and Communications Behavior, Media and Audiovisual Studies, Organizational Communications, Guidance and Materials, Research Methods and Appraisal Evaluation. Published Works: Author of Books *Communication Science and Technology* 1974, *Interpersonal Communication* 1974, *Group Dynamics and Individual Development* 1974, and others; Author of Articles "Beyond the Formalities," *School Media Quarterly* 1973, "Alternate Learning Environments," *International Journal of Instructional Media* 1981-82, "Public Library as a Community Resource," *Community Education Journal* 1981, and others; Author of Monographs "Self Planned Learning in America" 1977, "Library as a Learning Service Center" 1978, and others. Honors and Awards: Listed in *Who's Who in American Education, Men of Achievement, Community Leaders of America, Leaders in Education, Biographical Directory of Librarians, Who's Who in Consulting*. Address: School of Library and Information Science, University of Pittsburgh, Pittsburgh, Pennsylvania 15260.■

RODNEY A. PERALA

Scientist. Personal: Born August 25, 1943; Son of Albert Perala; Married Nancy Johnson, Daughter of Wallace Johnson; Father of Tadd, Matt. Education: B.S. 1965, M.S.E.E. 1966, University of Minnesota; Ph.D., University of Denver, 1971. Career: Vice President, Electro-Magnetic Applications, Inc., 1978 to present; Leader of Electro-Magnetic Coupling Group, Mission Research Corporation, 1973-78; Assistant Professor of Electrical Engineering, University of Americas, Puebla, Mexico, 1972-73. Organizational Memberships: Institute of Electrical and Electronic Engineers; American Radio Relay League. Published Works: Author of Over 100 Technical Papers/Reports. Honors and Awards: Alpha Kappa Nu; Tau Beta Pi; N.A.S.A. Fellow; Listed in *Who's Who in the West*. Address: P.O. Box 125, Indian Hills, Colorado 80454.■

ROBERT L. PERDIUE

Podiatrist. Personal: Born April 10, 1945; Son of Raymond L. Perdiue; Married Mary Jane Leslie, Daughter of Mr. and Mrs. Stanley Leslie. Education: B.A. Physiology, Southern Illinois University, Carbondale, Illinois, 1967; M.S. Biology, Incarnate Word College, San Antonio, Texas, 1971; D.P.M. Podiatry, Illinois College of Podiatric Medicine, Chicago, Illinois, 1975. Military: Served in the United States Army, Active Duty 1967-70 and 1975-78, attaining the rank of Captain. Career: Chief, Podiatry Service, United States Reynolds Army Hospital, Fort Sill, Oklahoma, 1975-77; Director of Podiatric Education, United States Reynolds Army Hospital, Fort Sill, Oklahoma, 1977; Clinical Instructor, Department of Podiatric Medicine, California College of Podiatric Medicine, San Francisco, California, 1978; Clinical Assistant Professor, Department of Family Practice, University of Texas Health Science Center, Podiatry Residency Program, San Antonio, Texas, 1978 to present; Member Board of Directors, Alamo General Hospital, San Antonio, Texas, 1979. Organizational Memberships: American Association of Hospital Podiatrists, Fellow; American Board of Podiatric Surgery, Diplomate; American Society of Podiatric Dermatologists, Fellow; American Society of Podiatric Medicine, Fellow; American Podiatry Association; Beta Sigma Gamma National Health Science Honorary Fraternity; National Board of Podiatric Examiners, Diplomate; Texas Podiatry Association; Licensed in the State of Indiana 1975, Texas 1975. Affiliated with Reynolds Army Hospital, Fort Sill, Oklahoma 1975-77, Alamo General Hospital, San Antonio, Texas 1977 to present, Park North General Hospital, San Antonio, Texas 1977 to present, St. Benedict's Hospital, San Antonio, Texas 1977 to present. Community Activities: Daleville Lodge #730, Daleville, Indiana; Lawton Commandery #18 K. T., Lawton, Oklahoma, San Antonio, Texas; Scottish Rite, Alzafar Temple Shrine, San Antonio; Optimist Club; Committee Chairman, Boy Scout Troop #497. Religion: Ruling Elder, San Pedro Presbyterian Church, San Antonio, Texas. Published Works: Contributor Articles to Professional Journals. Address: 14102 Broken Tree, San Antonio, Texas 78247.■

CHARLES RUSSELL PERKINS

Extension Service Administrator. Personal: Born August 12, 1939; Son of Mr. and Mrs. Delma D. Perkins; Married Julia Blanche Ware; Father of Tracy Alison, Dana Lynn, Elizabeth Ware. Education: B.S., Virginia Polytechnic Institute and State University, 1963; M.Agr., North Carolina State University, 1966; Ed.D., Virginia Polytechnic Institute and State University, 1978. Career: Southeast District Chairman, Virginia Cooperative Extension Service; Former Positions include Director of Farm Management Records Department, South Carolina Farm Bureau. Organizational Memberships: Epsilon Sigma Phi; Phi Delta Kappa; Virginia Extension Service Association; Adult Education Association of the U.S.A. Community Activities: Appomattox County Economic Development Commission, President 1979; Holiday Lake 4-H Camp, Inc., Chairman of the Board of Directors 1971; Caroline County Jaycees, President 1967; Bowling Green Volunteer Fire Department, Secretary 1967; Ruritan National, President Oakville Club 1975, Social Services Chairman Windsor Club 1983; Chowan Challenge Committee; Virginia Market Hog Show and Sale Committee; Board of Directors, Southeast District 4-H Educational Center Inc.; Personnel Committee, Southeast District 4-H Educational Center Inc.; Coordinating Committee, Nansemond/Chuckatuck Rural Clean Water Project; Administrative Committee, Nansemond/Chuckatuck Rural Clean Water Project; Windsor Elementary School Parent-Teacher Association; Windsor Athletic Club. Religion: Chairman of Administrative Board, Memorial United Methodist Church (Appomattox, Virginia), 1979; Leader of Methodist Youth Fellowship, Memorial United Methodist Church, 1979; Windsor Congregational Christian Church, 1981 to present; Assistant Sunday School Superintendent, 1982, 1983. Honors and Awards: F.F.A. State Farmer Degree, 1958; Block and Bridle, 1961; Alpha Zeta, 1962; Agricultural Policy Institute Fellow, 1966; Farm Foundation Fellow, 1977; Virginia Polytechnic Institute and State University Graduate Honor Court, 1977; Epsilon Sigma Phi Outstanding Accomplishment Award, 1981; Listed in *Who's Who in the South and Southwest*. Address: P.O. Box 132, Windsor, Virginia 23487.■

DAN PERKINS

Clinical Psychologist, Professor, Consultant, Instructional Supervisor. Personal: Born April 28, 1939; Son of H. G. Perkins; Married Fredda, Daughter of Mr. and Mrs. Fred Moore; Father of Jennifer, Hope. Education: A.A., Canton Community College, 1962; B.S. 1965, M.A. 1966, Bradley University; Ph.D., North Texas State University, 1972; Postdoctoral Work, North Texas State University, The Hypnosis Institute, 1974. Military: Served in United States Army, Hawaii, 1958-61, Sp/4. Career: Clinical Psychologist, Professor of Psychology, Consultant, Instructional Supervisor, present; Former Professional Occupations include Intern Psychologist, Instructor of Psychology, and Staff Psychologist at Peoria State Hospital, Counselor at a Community College, Teacher's Assistant, and Consultant to Two Mental Health Programs, McKinney Job Corps and Richland College. Organizational Memberships: Member Four Regional Psychological Associations; Program Chairman Texas Psychological Association 1978; Executive Committee Dallas Psychological Association 1974; Association for the Advancement of Behavior Therapy, Division of Psychological Hypnosis; Metroplex Association of Behavior Therapists. Community Activities: Human Service Advisory Board, Richland College; Many Speaking Engagements for Civic Organizations including Texas Employment Commission, Parent Teacher Association, Rehabilitation Centers, Community College Workshops, Parents without Partners, Treasurer, Dallas Psychological Association. Honors and Awards: Distinguished Service Award, Richland College, Dallas, Texas Address: 523 West Hunt Street, McKinney, Texas 75069.■

ROBERT GREEN PERKINS, JR.

Educator. Personal: Born December 3, 1926; Son of Robert G. Perkins and Ester Wagner Perkins (deceased); Married Christine H., Daughter of Garfield

Hill and Nettie Hill Whitehead (deceased); Father of Helen Jane Sams. Education: Attended Steed College, Tri-City Technical Institute, State Technical Institute, and East Tennessee State University; Attending University of Tennessee. Military: Served in the United States Navy, 1944-46, F1C. Career: Instructor, Elizabethton State Area School; Former Position as Electrical Supervisor, Beaunit Fibers. Organizational Memberships: Instrument Society of America, 1967-71; A.V.A.; T.V.A., Local Representative; T.E.A. Community Activities: Foreman, Carter County Grand Jury, 1964; West End Citizens Organization 1967-68; Tiger Valley Parent Teacher Association 1956-64, President 1957-58, Vice President 1959-64; Tiger Valley Citizens Club 1959-60, Secretary 1960. Religion: Former Member Rock Springs Baptist Church, Johnson County; Member Little Doe Free Will Baptist Church, Hampton; Teacher, Director (1 term), Training Union, 1949-67; Attends Watauga Point United Methodist Church, Elizabethton. Address: Route 6, Linda Circle, Box 501, Elizabethton, Tennessee 37643.■

EILEEN E. PERLMAN

Investor, Volunteer Civic Worker. Personal: Born October 31, 1935; Daughter of Bennett V. Christensen and Eleanor Lucille Christensen; Married Clifford Seely Perlman; Mother of Jason, Clayton, Ivy. Education: Attended Northwestern University 1954, Patricia Stevens Modeling School, Liberty Baptist College 1978-80. Career: Co-Founder, Lum's Inc. (Restaurant Chain). Community Activities: Protect Our Children; Anti-ERA Campaign Worker; Board of Directors, Women for Responsible Legislature and Political Action, South Florida Chapter; Active in Floridians Against Casino Takeover; U.S. Lawn Tennis Association; Board of Directors, U.S. Figure Skating Association; American Bridge Club; American Security Council, National Advisory Board; Sustaining Member, Republican National Committee; Phil Crane for President; Financial Secretary-Treasurer, Christian Women's Club, 1973-75; Founding Charter Member, National Advisory Committee to Bring Back School Prayer, 1980; Founding Member, Moral Majority, 1978; American Red Cross; U.S. Interfaith Committee Against Blasphemy; American Biographical Institute; Westminster Christian School Transportation Committee, 1978-81; Christian Broadcasting Company; 700 Club; PTL Club; Prayer Chairman, Southern Florida District, Concerned Women for America, 1980 to present; Home District Congressional Liaison, 1984 to present; Old Time Gospel Hour Faith Partners; Sponsor, Republican Victory Fund, 1980; International Platform Association; National Federation of Republic Women; Century Club. Religion: Granada Presbyterian Church, Visitation Chairman 1973-75, Circle Chairman 1978-80, Prayer Committee Member 1980 to present. Honors and Awards: Various Certificates of Honor; Listed in *Who's Who of American Women, Who's Who of Women of the World, Who's Who in the South and Southwest, International Who's Who of Intellectuals, Directory of Distinguished Americans, Personalities of the South, Personalities of America, Community Leaders of the World, The World Biographical Hall of Fame, International Who's Who of Contemporary Achievement, International Book of Honor, International Register of Personalities, The American Registry, Five Thousand Personalities of the World, Progressive Personalities in Profile.* Address: 6401 Cellini, Coral Gables, Florida 33146.■

ROBERT GEORGE PERRIN

Associate Professor, Author. Personal: Born May 17, 1945; Son of Walter George Perrin Jr. and Pauline Shirley (Ross) Perrin; Married Diane Lynn Ochsenbein, Daughter of Robert Roy Ochsenbein (deceased) and Virginia Alice (Pease) Ochsenbein; Father of John Robert, Michael George. Education: A.B., California State University, Northridge, 1967; M.A., University of California, Riverside, 1969; Ph.D., University of British Columbia, Vancouver, Canada, 1974. Career: Associate Professor of Sociology; Author; Killam Predoctoral Fellow, University of British Columbia, 1970-72. Organizational Memberships: American Sociological Association; Southern Sociological Association; Research Committee on History of Sociology (under auspices of International Sociological Association); American Association of University Professors; Others. Community Activities: Editorial Consultant; Contributing Editor, *The Journal of the History of Sociology.* Published Works: Contributor Numerous Articles to Professional and Scholarly Journals; Co-Author (with Robert Nisbet) of *The Social Bond,* 2nd Edition, Knopf-Random House, 1977. Honors and Awards: College of Liberal Arts, University of Tennessee Award for Teaching Excellence, 1979 and 1980; Graduate School, The University of Tennessee Research Award, 1979. Address: 5405 Lance Drive, Knoxville, Tennessee 37919.■

REGINALD CARMAN PERRY

Retired Educator. Personal: Born August 15, 1903; Son of William and Mary (Harwood) Perry (both deceased). Education: Diploma, Methodist College, 1921; Diploma, Memorial University College, 1927; B.A., Mt. Allison University, 1930; B.D., Victoria University, 1935; M.A. 1936, Ph.D. 1945, Toronto University; Postdoctoral Studies, Harvard University, 1951-54. Career: Retired; Former School Principal, Newfoundland; Minister, United Church of Canada; Instructor, Syracuse University; Assistant Professor, Oklahoma A&M College (now Oklahoma State University); Associate Professor, AM&N College (now University of Arkansas-Pine Bluff); Professor of Humanities and Philosophy, University of Arkansas-Pine Bluff. Organizational Memberships: American Philosophical Association; Arkansas Philosophy Association; Arkansas Retired Teachers Association, Life Member; National Retired Teachers Association; American Association of University Professors, Former Member; International Platform Association, Former Member; Arkansas Sheriff's Association, Honorary Charter Member. Community Activities: Emmanuel College, Toronto, Dean of Men's Residence 1932-33; Donations to United Fund, United Way, CARE, Arkansas Sheriff's Boys and Girls Ranches, Inc., National Foundation for Cancer Research, National Humane Education Society, Talking Bible for Nursing Homes-Pine Bluff, Asian-American Lions Relief Fund, African Enterprise. Religion: Active in Sunday Schools of Methodist and United Church; Professional Duties 1933-34, 1936-41; Taught Philosphy of Religion, Oklahoma A&M College and World Religions, AM&N, U.A.P.B. Published Works: "Some Observations Concerning the Philosophy of Charles S. Peirce," "Professor Ayer's 'Freedom of Necessity,'" "Some Comments on Schlick's Ethical Theory," and Others. Honors and Awards: First in Physics and Honors Student, Methodist College; Honors Latin, Memorial University College; Bursary, Mt. Allison University; Plaque upon Retirement, International Club, U.A.P.B., 1976. Address: 110 Beech Street, Apartment 2, Pine Bluff, Arkansas 71601.■

M. RAY PERRYMAN

Herman Brown Professor of Economics, Author. Personal: Born December 25, 1952; Son of Mr. and Mrs. M. A. Perryman Jr.; Married Nancy Beth; Father of Skye Lynn. Education: B.S. Mathematics and Economics, Baylor University, 1974; Ph.D. Economics, Rice University, 1978. Career: Herman Brown Professor of Economics, Baylor University; Founder and Director, Center for the Advancement of Economic Analysis, Baylor University; Director, Baylor University Honors Program; Editor and Author, *Trends in the Texas Economy;* Director, Texas Econometric Model Project; Founder and Director, Baylor University Forecasting Service; Graduate Faculty, Baylor University; Editor, *Advances in Economic Analysis* Working Paper Series; Regular Contributor, *Texas Business* Magazine; Author, *The Texas Economy* (monthly column in *Texas Banker's Record*); Author, *Economic Outlook* (quarterly column in *Business Review*); Editor and Author, *The Texas Economic Update* (subscription newsletter); Co-Writer and Co-Host, *Money Facts* (weekly economic information program); Director, American Conference of the International Time Series Association, 1980 and 1981; Economic Consultant, Comptroller of Public Accounts, State of Texas; Senior Consultant, Center for Community Research and Development; Member, Intergovernmental Fiscal Relations Committee, National Tax Association, Tax Institute of America; Member, State Income and Business Taxation Committee, National Tax Association, Tax Institute of America; Developmental Consultant and Continuing Advisor, Lincoln Center for Economic Awareness, Houston Independent School District; Senior Consultant, Resource Economics and Management Associates; Publication Review Board, North American Economics and Finance Association; Secretary and Executive Committee Member, Time Series Interaction Committee of the United States; Member Economic Forecasting Panel, *Inside Texas;* Program Committee, 1983 Conference of the Allied Social Science Association; Chairman, Honors Program Committee (Colloquium Subcommittee, Curriculum Subcommittee, Awards Subcommittee, Research Subcommittee); Member United States

Congressional Advisory Board; Director of Economic Division, Inter-University Consortium for Political and Social Research, Baylor University; Editor, International Series in Economic Modeling; Developmental Editor, *International Journal of Econometric Modelling*; Director of North American Programs, Time Series Analysis and Forecasting European Interest Group; Member Publicaton Committee, *Baylor Business Studies*, Baylor University; Reviewer for Several Professional Journals. Organizational Memberships: American Academy of Arts and Sciences; American Association for the Advancement of Science; American Economic Association; American Finance Association; American Statistical Association; Association for Christian Economists, Founding Member; Association for Social Economics; Association for Evolutionary Economics; Atlantic Economic Society; Economic History Association; Econometric Society; Hastings Center, Institute for Society, Ethics and the Life Sciences; History of Economics Society; Institute for Socioeconomic Studies; Institute of Mathematical Statistics; International Association of Mathematical Modeling, Charter Member; International Institute of Forecasters; International Time Series Association, Charter Member; Mathematical Association of America; Midwest Economic Association; Missouri Valley Economic Association; National Association of Business Economists; National Tax Association, Tax Institute of America; North American Economics and Finance Association; Post-Keynesian Economic Association, Charter Member; Royal Economic Society, England; Society for Economic Analysis, England; Southern Economic Association; Southwestern Economic Association; Southwestern Federation of Administrative Disciplines; Southwestern Social Science Association; Southwestern Society for Economists; Time Series Interaction Committee of the United States, Founding Member; Western Economic Association; Baker Street Irregulars; Sherlock Holmes Society of London. Published Works: Author Numerous Publications in his Field. Honors and Awards: National Merit Scholar; Summa Cum Laude Graduate of the Baylor University Honors Program, 1974; Outstanding Student, Baylor University, 1974; Outstanding Mathematics Major and Outstanding Economics Major, Baylor University, 1974; First Southwest Bancorporation Scholarship; Alpha Chi Scholarship Award; Dean's Distinguished Honor List, 1971-74; Omicron Delta Epsilon Outstanding Paper in Economics Award, 1974; Rice University Graduate Fellowship, 1974-77; Baylor University Research Sabbatical, 1978-82; Distinguished Professor Award, Hankamer School of Business, 1979; Citation for Teaching Excellence, 1978-82; Citation for Research Excellence, 1978-82; Most Popular Professor, Hankamer School of Business, 1979; First Recipient, Outstanding Alumnus in Economics Research, Rice University, 1979; Outstanding Young Economist and Social Scientist in the United States, National Science Foundation; Alpha Chi; Omicron Delta Epsilon; Omicron Delta Kappa; Phi Eta Sigma; Beta Gamma Sigma; Listed in *Who's Who in the South and Southwest*, *Who's Who Among Writers*, *American Men and Women of Science*, *Personalities of the South*, *Heritage Foundation Public Policy Experts*, *Men of Achievement*, *World Who's Who of Men*, *International Who's Who in Education*, *International Authors and Writers Who's Who*. Address: 309 Brookwood Drive, Waco, Texas 76710.■

EMMA NANCY PERRY-OVERALL

Postal Employment Development Training Technician. Personal: Born December 15, 1937; Daughter of Mildred S. Overall; Mother of Michael Andre and Reginald Louis. Education: Diploma, Horace A. Mann High School, 1956; B.A. Business Education, Philander Smith College, 1975; Graduate, University of Arkansas, Management/Supervision, Division of Continuing Education, 3.3 CEU's, 1980-81; Teacher Certification, Arkansas State Board of Education. Career: Postal Employment Development Training Technician, Employee and Labor Relations Unit, present; Former Professional Occupations include Clerk, General Office, Little Rock Housing Authority; PTF Distribution Clerk Career, Job Instructor, Distribution-Secondary Registry Relief Clerk Career, MPLSM Distribution Clerk, Acting MPLSM Job Instructor, 104-B Detailed Acting Supervisor-Collections/Delivery Customer Services, Station, 204-B Detailed Acting Multi-Letter Sorting Machine Supervisor, all for the United States Postal Service for Functional Units of Mail Processing, Customer Services/Collections/Delivery. Organizational Memberships: Postmasters E.E.O. Advisory Committee, Chairperson 1982 to present; Publicity Manager 1981-82; Arkansas Teachers Association; National Teachers Association; American Association for University Women, New Life Member. Community Activities: Urban League of Arkansas, Chairperson Advisory Board 1982-83, Executive Board of Directors, Membership Committee 1983 to present; Arkansans for the Arts, Supportive Member; Reunion Class of "56" Chairperson 1976 to present; Volunteer Student Council Worker, Forest Heights JRH, 1975; Volunteer Room Parent, Lee Elementary School, 1965; Girls Training School Auxillary, Volunteer Girls Sponsor 1966-69; Volunteer Extra-Curricular Activities Chaperon for Little Rock Central High School, 1975-78. Religion: Allen Temple A.M.E. Sunday School Secretary 1954-56, Secretary Laymen's Organization 1959-60; Chairperson Masters-Debutane Organization A.M.E. Church, 1977; Member, Volunteer Speaker/Lecturer, Missionary Society, Allen Temple A.M.E. Church 1974 to present. Honors and Awards: First Place, Little Rock City Beautiful Essay, 1955; Recipient of Honors Scholarship to Lincoln University, Missouri, City Teachers Association, 1956; Quality Step Performance Award, United States Postal Service for PEDC Training, 1974; Advisory Board Member Recognition Award, Urban League of Arkansas, 1983; Listed in *Who's Who of Women in Business*, *Personalities of America*, *World Who's Who*. Address: 1123 Appianway Street, Little Rock, Arkansas 72204.■

ROLAND IRVING PERUSSE

Professor. Personal: Born May 18, 1921; Married Luz Amalia; Father of Clifford, Dawn, Nancy. Education: B.A. Journalism, University of Wisconsin, 1946; Ph.D. International Relations, American University, 1955. Military: Served in the United States Army, Military Intelligence, 1943-46, attaining the rank of First Lieutenant. Career: Professor of Political Science, Inter-American University; United States Foreign Service. Organizational Memberships: The Heritage Foundation; Caribbean Studies Association; International Studies Association; American Foreign Service Association; United States United Nations Association. Community Activities: Mayland Citizens Committee for Fair Congressional Redistricting, Founder and First Chairman 1962 to present; Americas Foundation, Member Board of Directors 1970 to present; National Advisory Council, Hampshire College, Amherst, Massachusetts, 1972 to present; Advisor on Rockefeller Presidential Mission to Latin America, 1969; Member Puerto Rico State Committee for the Election of George Bush as President, 1979-80. Religion: Lay Minister, First Unitarian Church, El Paso, Texas, 1964-66. Honors and Awards: Phi Kappa Phi Honorary Society; "W" Club, University of Wisconsin; Certificate of Merit signed by General Eisenhower; Legion of Merit, United States Army; Citation from United States United Nations Association; Citation from Bethesda-Chevy Chase (Maryland) Chamber of Commerce; Citation by Phi Kappa Phi; Citation from North-South Center of Puerto Rico; Citation from Caribbean Studies Association; Others. Address: Penthouse G, Condo El Monte North, Hato Rey, Puerto Rico 00918.■

PATRIC O. PESKE

Diagnostic Psychologist. Personal: Born September 21, 1942; Son of E. M. Bordeaux and R. W. Peske; Married; Father of Arthur Aleksandor. Education: B.A. 1968, M.A. 1972, University of Akron; Advanced Coursework at Temple University, Case Western Reserve, University of Chicago, Department of Continuing Education. Career: Diagnostic Psychologist, Children and Adults. Organizational Memberships: American Psychological Association; International Congress for Study of Art and Psychopathology; International Congress for Study of Rorschach Psychology; British Society for Study Projective Psychology; Society Personality Assessment; National Rorschach Society, President 1976 to present; National Association School Psychologists; International Platform Association. Community Activities: Lecturer to Numerous Civic and Other Organizations regarding Child Psychology and Adjustment. Published Works: Author of Over 50 Publications and Children's Rights Charter-International Distribution. Honors and Awards: United States Delegate, International Rorschach Congress, 1977; Member International Platform Association 1976 to present; President, National Rorschach Society, 1976 to present; Professional Research Awards, 1973, 1974, 1975, 1976, 1977, 1978; Listed in *Personalities of America*, *Notable Americans*. Address: P.O. Box 7149, Flint, Michigan 48507.■

MARGUERITE HARLESS PETERS

Office Manager. Personal: Born April 13, 1924; Daughter of G. R. Harless; Mother of Wayne H., Gary M., Clark L., Marilyn Peters Baltzley. Education: A.A., Kansas City Junior College, 1943. Career: Office Manager, Dallas Office, Bridgeport Brass Company; Former Positions include Executive Vice President of Walden International Search (Dallas) and Vice President of Professional Communications (Dallas). Organizational Memberships: Dallas Council on Foreign Affairs; International Trade Association; French-American Chamber of Commerce; Dallas Chamber of Commerce; American Society of Training and Development; Seminar Leader, Continuing Education Division, Texas Christian University and Fort Worth and Rickland College. Community Activities: Candidate for Mayor, Cape Coral, Florida, 1977; Vice Chairman, Lone Star Chapter, Mensa, 1978; Vice Chairman, Committee for WUSF-TV, University of South Florida Television Station, Tampa, Florida, 1975-78; Vice Chairman, Lt. Governors Conference on Ethics, State of Texas, 1973; Charter Board Member, KIDZ-TV (Educational Television), Wichita Falls, Texas, 1971-74; President, Society of Symphony Women, Fort Myers, Florida, 1975-77; Fort Myers Symphony Board, 1974-77; Delegate, National Conference on Government, Dallas, 1973; Chairman Fund Raising, North Texas Rehabilitation Center, 1973-74; Board Member, Daughters of the American Revolution, Lawrence Kearney Chapter, Cape Coral, Florida, 1975-77; Founding Board Member, MH/MR Center, Wichita Falls, 1970-74; Youth Volunteer Director, Burkburnett High School, Burkburnett, Texas, 1962-65; Campaign Manager for Barefoot Sanders Candidate for U.S. Senate, 1973; Life Member, Burkburnett Chapter of Parent-Teacher Association, Former President; Campaign Manager for Richard Stone for U.S. Senate, Florida, 1974. Address: 9450 Royal Lane #1051, Dallas, Texas 75243.■

TWO THOUSAND NOTABLE AMERICANS

GARY MICHAEL PETERSEN

Executive. Personal: Born November 23, 1947; Son of Kathleen Petersen; Married Alexandra; Father of Samantha Kate, Jesse Garett. Education: Attended College in Santa Monica, California. Career: Co-Owner, Vice President, Director of Sales, Disc Jockey, Radio Station KRCK-AM (Ridgecrest, California); Founder, President, Ecolo-Haul (Pacific Palisades, California), 1972 to present; President, Aluminum Recycling Corporation; National Science Foundation Consultant, Committee for National Recycling Policy; Advisor, United States Conference of Mayors, National Recycling Coalition; Consultant, Environmental Protection Agency. Organizational Memberships: California Waste Management Board, Steering Committee; California Resource Recovery Association, Founder, Board of Directors; California Industry Environmental Council; Governor's Resource Utilization Task Force. Community Activities: Citizen's Solid Waste Environmental Advisory Committee, County of Los Angeles; Cousteau Society, Founding Member; Wilderness Society; World Wildlife Fund; Defenders of Wildlife; Los Angeles Beautiful, Board of Directors; Santa Monica Beautification and Recycling Program. Honors and Aards: Numerous Honors and Awards from City, County and State Government and Civic Organizations; Recycling Award, California Committee for Resource Recovery; Nominated Seven Times for Tyler Ecology Award, included in *The Peter Plan* by Laurence Peter (author of *The Peter Principle*; Listed in *Who's Who in the World, Who's Who in Finance and Industry, Outstanding Young Men of America, Men of Achievement*. Address: P.O. Box 1263, Pacific Palisades, California 90272.■

ALBERT JON PETERSON

Architect, Planner. Personal: Born February 10, 1934; Son of Mr. and Mrs. Albert John Peterson; Father of Ingrid. Education: B.S. Pure Mathematics 1958, M.Arch. 1962, University of Oregon; Certified Fallout Shelter Analyst, Portland State University, 1969. Military: Served in the United States Air Force, 1958-60, attaining the rank of Captain. Career: Architect, Planner; Former Professor of Architecture, Portland State University, California Polytechnic State University, University of Idaho, University of North Carolina, University of Oregon. Organizational Memberships: American Institute of Architects; American Planning Association; Association of Collegiate Schools of Architecture; Society of Architectural Historians; American Arbitration Association; City Club of Portland, Chairman Port Study Committee 1973. Community Activities: Rogue Valley Art Association, Medford (Oregon) Gallery Manager 1967; Portland Art Association. Religion: Lutheran. Honors and Awards: Women's Architectural League of Portland Fellowships, 1960, 1961; Program Exhibitor, International Design Conference in Aspen (Colorado), 1976; Installation, University of Idaho Art Gallery, 1979; Various Papers, Monographs, Publications. Address: 173 Northeast Bridgeton Road, Boat 21, Portland, Oregon 97211.■

DANIEL LOREN PETERSON

Professor. Personal: Born December 28, 1937; Son of Lloyd William Peterson; Married Judith Palmquist, Daughter of Edward and Virginia Palmquist; Father of Lloyd William, Juli Anne. Education: A.B.A., Kansas City Junior College, 1958; B.S., Rockhurst College, 1959; M.A., University of Missouri at Kansas City, 1963; Ed.D., University of Missouri at Columbia, 1967. Career: Professor of Special Education, Northern Arizona University, present; Former Professional Occupations include Teacher, School Principal and School Psychologist. Organizational Memberships: Council for Exceptional Children, Chapter President, Columbia, Missouri, 1965; Coordinator, Council for Exceptional Children, Student Affairs, 1966-68; President, Children's Service Association, 1969. Community Activities: Chairman, Special Education Advisory Committee, 1974 and 1982; President, Cocino Association for Mentally Retarded, 1973; President, Flagstaff Association for Children with Learning Disabilities, 1974; Chairman, Flagstaff Emergency Medical Services, 1981-82; Coordinator, Association for Children with Learning Disabilities, Northern Region, 1978-81. Religion: Teacher 1959-62, President 1963, Legion of Mary; President, Board of Directors, Newman Center, Athens, Ohio, 1971. Honors and Awards: Outstanding Young Man, Athens, Ohio, 1968; Certificate of Merit, National Foundation, 1969; Leaders in American Education, 1972; Outstanding Educators of America, 1975; Outstanding Faculty Member, N.A.U., 1975 to present; Outstanding Service, A.A.C.L.D., 1977; Outstanding Teacher of Exceptional Children, 1975; Listed in *Who's Who in International Education, Men of Achievement, International Who's Who of Intellectuals*. Address: 1351 North LaCosta, Flagstaff, Arizona 86001.■

FRANK DEWEY PETERSON

Business Executive, School Administrator. Personal: Born September 1, 1899, in Taylor County, Kentucky; Son of John Artibury and Lou Vinie (Sinclair) Peterson; Married Audrey Whitlock (deceased), Second Marriage to Jewell C. Callison. Education: A.B., Centre College, 1924; Attended Bowling Green Business College 1924, University of Chicago 1932, University of Kentucky 1934; LL.D., Georgetown College, 1953. Career: Director of School Finance, Kentucky Department of Education, 1925-36; Administrator of Kentucky, N.Y.A., 1935-36; Deputy Commissioner of Finance, Comptroller, State of Kentucky, 1936-41; Comptroller 1941-55, Secretary Board of Trustees 1942-63, University Treasurer 1944-63, Vice President of Business Administration 1955-64, Founder College Business Management Institute 1953, University of Kentucky; Secretary, Treasurer, Director, Southeastern States Securities Inc. 1963, Royce Blevins Construction Inc. 1963-79; Treasurer, Secretary, R. L. Saunders Company, 1968-83; President, 7-Kings Inc. Franchise (Jiffy Francise System) and Salty Bay Oyster House, 1969-71; Treasurer, Director, Town and Country Realty Company, General Tire Service; Director, Spindletop Research Inc., Kentucky Family Security Insurance Company Inc., 1961-83; Director, Secretary, Lexington Fire Protection Corporation 1975-, Saylor's Corporation 1976-79, Bellaire Enterprises General Partnership 1977-; Financial Consultant, Representative for Rural States before N.Y.A., 1936; Chairman Kentucky Fair Wage Scale Commission, 1937; Member National Committee on Uniform Distribution of Federal Aid to Distressed School Districts in the United States, 1934-35; President, International Book Project, 1969; Member City-Fayette County Merger Committee, 1972-73; Member State Advisory Council, S.B.A.; President Board of Trustees, Central Baptist Hospital (Lexington, Kentucky), 1955-64; President, Carnhan House, University of Kentucky, 1956-61; President, United Community Fund (Lexington), 1959-62; Member Baptist Hospital Commission, Kentucky, 1955-64; Board of Overseers, Centre College, 1944; Board Member, American Family Security Foundation; Secretary, Treasurer, Kentucky Research Foundation, 1949-63; Treasurer, Thomas P. Cooper Agricultural Foundation, 1952-63; President Board of Directors, International Book Project, 1966-79; Board of Directors, College Business Management Institute, University of Kentucky, 1952-63. Organizational Memberships: Southern Association of College and University Business Officers, President 1952; Kentucky Education Association; Central Association College and University Business Association; Phi Delta Kappa; Omicron Delta Kappa; Beta Gamma Sigma; Kappa Sigma. Community Activities: Civil War Round Table; Chamberlain Literary Society; Thoroughbred Club of America; Life Member, President's Club, Georgetown College; Spindletop Club; Lafayette Club; Mason; Shriner; Kiwanis Club, President, District Lieutenant Governor 1975-76; Lexington Country Club. Religion: Baptist, Deacon, Trustee. Published Works: Author *Uniform Financial Accounting System for County, City and Graded School Districts for Kentucky*, Various Articles; Editorial Consultant, College and University Business Magazine. Honors and Awards: Certificate of Appreciation, Southern Association of College and University Business Officers 1956, Campbellsville College 1953, City of Louisville 1937, Taylor County (Kentucky) 1958; Distinguished Service Award, University of Kentucky, 1974; Named Kentucky Colonel, 1938; Distinguished Alumni of Centre College, 1980; Frank D. Peterson Service Building at University of Kentucky Named in His Honor, 1978; Distinguished Service Award, Kiwanis Club. Address: 766 Chinoe Road, Lexington, Kentucky 40502.■

MARGARET MARY PETERSON

Locum Tenens Radiotherapy Technologist. Personal: Born July 25, 1948; Daughter of Margaret and Andrew Peterson. Education: B.S. Business Administration, University of Phoenix, 1982; R.T.T. Radiation Therapy Technology, University of Southern California, 1970; R.T. Diagnostic Radiology, United States Public Health Service Hospital, New York, 1968; Vocational Teaching Credentials, University of California-San Francisco, 1980. Career: Locum Tenens Radiotherapy Technologist, present; Former Professional Occupations include Clinical Consultant in ATC Medical Technology, Department Head of Radiation Therapy at Peninsula Hospital and Medical CTR, and Chief Technologist at South Bay Hospital, Redondo Beach, California. Organizational Memberships: Past President, American Association of Medical Dosimetrists, 1979-81; Past Vice President, North California Society of Radiation Therapy Technologists, 1980; President-Elect N.C.S.R.H., 1981; Member A.A.M.D., N.C.S.R.H., J.R.C., A.A.P.M., C.S.R.T., A.U.R.T. Community Activities: Co-Chairperson, Management Steering Committee, Peninsula Hospital and Medical Center, 1980-81; Secretary, Supervisory Committee of Credit Union for Peninsula Hospital and Medical Center, 1980-83. Honors and Awards: Outstanding Student, Los Angeles County, University of Southern California Radiation Therapy Technology School, 1970.■

GEORGE J. PETRELLO

University Administrator. Personal: Born April 30, 1938; Son of Mrs. Rose Araneo; Married Barbara. Education: B.A., Montclair State College; M.B.A., Seton Hall University; Ph.D., New York University. Career: Dean, School of Business, St. Mary's University (San Antonio, Texas); Former Positions as Professor of Economics and Business Administration, Public Accountant, Assistant Personnel Director, Private and Governmental Management Consultant. Organizational

TWO THOUSAND NOTABLE AMERICANS

Membership Academy of Management; National Business Education Association; Southwest Federation of Academic Disciplines; Southwestern Business Administration Association; Representative to the American Assembly of Collegiate Schools of Business. Community Activities: Board of Directors, San Antonio Federation for Free Enterprise, Unit Campaign Director, United Way, 1982; Member and Program Director, Optimist International, 1968; Commissioner of the Accreditation Commission for Independent Schools and Colleges, Washington D.C., 1983-86; Education Task Force Chairman, San Antonio Chamber of Commerce, 1979-80; Convention Program Committee, American Council of Education, 1981. Honors and Awards: Pi Omega Pi; Honorary Fellow, Anglo-American Academy, 1980; Founders Day Award, New York University, 1969; Delta Pi Epsilon; Delta Pi Epsilon Alumni Award for Outstanding Research, New York University, 1974; Phi Delta Kappa; Listed in *Men and Women of Science*. Address: 5514 Ben Hur, San Antonio, Texas 78229.■

ELIJAH EDWARD PETTY

Chemical Engineer. Personal: Born June 12, 1920; Son of Mr. and Mrs. Curtis Petty (both deceased); Married Nelda Morris; Father of Montie Curtis, Vicki A. Education: B.S.Ch.E., University of Oklahoma, 1948; A.S.T.P., Mechanical Engineering, University of Arizona, 1944. Military: Served in the United States Army, attaining the rank of Technical Sergeant. Career: Chemical Engineer, Edible Oils/Protein Industry; Chemical Engineer, Chemical Agricultural Processes. Organizational Memberships: American Oil Chemists Society; American Institute of Chemical Engineers; Professional Engineer, State of Texas. Community Activities: Advisory Committee, Jacksonville (Illinois) School Board; Chairman, Jacksonville Community Chest; Advisory Engineer, São Paulo, Brazil, School Board. Religion: Represenative to C.O.D.A., 1980; Board of Directors, David Hulse Evangelistic Association, Inc., 1981; Outreach Chairman, Lost Coin Body of Christ, 1981. Honors and Awards: Recognition Certificate of Professional Achievement, American Institute of Chemical Engineers, 1979; Listed in *Community Leaders of America, American Registry, Biographical Roll of Honor, Book of Honor, Directory of Distinguished Americans, Five Thousand Personalities of the World, International Book of Honor, Personalities of America, Personalities of the West and Midwest, Two Thousand Notable Americans, Who's Who in Technology Today, Who's Who in Finance and Industry, Who's Who in the Midwest, Who's Who in the World, Who's Who in Technology Today, Dictionary of International Biography, International Register of Profiles, International Who's Who in Community Service, International Who's Who in Engineering, International Who's Who of Intellectuals, Men and Women of Distinction, Men of Achievement, Contemporary Personalities*. Address: #1 Curtis Court, Mount Zion, Illinois 62549.■

JOHN WILLIAM PFEIFFER

Publisher, Writer, Economist and Management Consultant. Personal: Born July 10, 1937; Son of Mr. and Mrs. J. W. Pfeiffer; Married to Judith; Father of Heidi, Wilson. Education: B.A., University of Maryland, 1962; Ph.D., University of Iowa, 1968; J.D., Western State University, 1982. Military: Served in the United States Army, 1958-62. Published Works: Author of *Instrumentation in Human Relations Training* (1973, 2nd edition 1976), *Reference Guide to Handbooks and Annuals* (1975, 1977, 1981); Editor of *A Handbook of Structured Experiences for Human Relations Training* (8 Volumes, 1969-80), *The Annual Handbook for Group Facilitators* (10 Volumes, 1972-81), *The 1983 Annual for Facilitators, Trainers and Consultants, The 1982 Annual for Facilitators, Trainers and Consultants, Group and Organization Studies: International Journal for Group Facilitators* (1976-80). Honors and Awards: Received Honorary Doctor of Applied Behavioral Science, California American University, 1980. Address: 369 Mesa Way, La Jolla, California 92037.■

HARVEY WILLIAM PHELPS

Consultant, College Administrator. Personal: Born June 27, 1922; Son of Harvey Jay Phelps (deceased); Married; Father of Castle Wright, Stuart Harvey, Martha Gail Phelps DeMers. Education: B.S., University of Idaho-Southern Branch (now Idaho State University), 1946; M.D., St. Louis University, 1949; Intern, Brooke General Hospital, Fort Sam Houston, Texas, 1949-50; Resident in Internal Medicine, Fitzsimmons General Hospital, Denver, Colorado, 1951-54; Basic Science Course, Walter Reed Army Institute of Research, 1954-55. Military: Served in the United States Medical Corps, 1949-66, Retired Lieutenant Colonel. Career: Chief, Medical Service, United States Army Hospital, Fort MacArthur, California, 1955-57; Resident in Pulmonary Diseases, Fitzsimmons General Hospital, Denver, Colorado, 1957-58; Assistant Chief of Pulmonary Disease Service, Fitzsimmons General Hospital, 1958-59; Chief, Department of Medicine, United States Army Medical Center, Japan, 1959-62; Consultant in Internal Medicine to the Surgeon, United States Army, Japan, 1959-62; Consultant in Pulmonary Disease, Tri-Service (Army, Air Force, Navy) in Japan, 1959-62; United States Command and General Staff College, 1962-63; Chief, Department of Medicine, DeWitt Army Hospital, Fort Belvoir, Virginia, 1963-65; Chief, Pulmonary Disease Service, Valley Forge General Hospital, Phoenixville, Pennsylvania, 1965-66; Director of Inhalation Therapy and Pulmonary Function Laboratories, St. Mary-Corwin Hospital and Parkview Episcopal Hospital, Pueblo, Colorado, 1966-78; Chief of Staff, Parkview Episcopal Hospital, 1970-72; Clinical Associate in Medicine, Women's Medical Center, Philadelphia, Pennsylvania, 1965-66; Consultant in Disease of the Chest, Colorado State Hospital, 1966 to present; Director, Southern Colorado State College Associate Degree Program (Respiratory Therapy), 1971 to present. Organizational Memberships: Fellow, American College of Chest Physicians; Committee on Pulmonary Physiology, American College of Chest Physicians; American Thoracic Society; Fellow, American College of Physicians; Pueblo County Medical Society; Colorado Medical Society; American Medical Association; Air Pollution Variance Board, State of Colorado; House of Delegates, Colorado State Medical Society; President, Colorado Chapter, American College of Chest Physicians, 1974. Community Activities: Elected State Senator, District #25, 1976. Honors and Awards: James J. Waring Award in Chest Diseases, 1972; Colorado Medical Society Community Service Award, 1980. Address: 2424 North Greenwood, Pueblo, Colorado 81003.■

LEAL PHELPS

Music Educator. Personal: Born March 11, 1902; Daughter of Ogden Richart and Anna Johnston Richart (both deceased); Married James Edward Phelps; Mother of Dr. Robert, Wilma Karayan. Education: Graduate of Kansas City Conservatory of Music, 1930; Piano Study, Sir Carl Busch, Composer/Teacher, John Thompson, Sergie Tarnowsky, Maurice Zam, Helen Poole. Career: Piano Teacher. Organizational Memberships: Piano Guild, Member Over 30 Years; Music Teacher's Association, Member Over 30 Years. Community Activities: Teacher to Bonnel Nunez, Author/Composer, William Pearson, Music Arranger/Composer; Maurice Kenton Phelps Ch. #1022, City of Hope, Past President. Honors and Awards: Award, United States Veterans of Foreign Wars, Los Angeles City Hall Post 768, 1969. Address: 2585 Yardarm, Port Hueneme, California 93041.■

PHILIP MONFORD PHIBBS

University President. Personal: Born October 2, 1931; Son of Clifford and Dorothy (Wright) Phibbs; Married Gwen Willis, Daughter of Elizabeth Willis; Father of Kathy, Jennifer, Diana. Education: B.A. highest honors, Washington State University, 1953; Attended Cambridge University, England, 1953, 1954; M.A., University of Chicago, 1955; Ph.D., University of Chicago, 1957. Military: Served in the United States Air Force, 1958-61, attaining the rank of First Lieutenant. Career: President, University of Puget Sound, present; Government Intern, Navy Department, Washington D.C., 1955-57; Congressional Fellow, Washington D.C., 1957-58 Professor of Political Science, Wellesley College, 1961-73; Executive Vice President, Wellesley College, 1968-73. Organizational Memberships: Chairman Board of Directors, N.A.I.C.U., 1982 to present; Member Board of Directors, N.A.I.C.U., 1979-82; A.C.E. Committee on International Education Relations, 1978-80; Board of Directors, N.A.S.C.U.M.C. and Public Policy Committee, 1979 to present; U.M.C. University Senate, 1981-83; American Association of University Professors, 1965 to present; American Political Science Association, 1961 to present; Association for Asian Studies, 1965; Association A.B.A., 1976 to present; Association Danforth Foundation, 1963 to present. Community Activities: Member Board of Directors, Tac-Pierce County Chamber of Commerce; Member Pac Science Center Foundation, 1973 to present; Education Council of Seattle Opera; Seattle Committee on Foreign Relations; The Seattle Foundation, 1980-82; Tac Youth Symphony Advisory Board, 1981-82; Vice-Chairman, Washington Friends of Higher Education; Member Commonwealth

TWO THOUSAND NOTABLE AMERICANS

Club of California, 1975 to present; Washington State Council for Postsecondary Education, 1974-79; Trustee Tac Art Museum, 1975-81. Honors and Awards: Phi Beta Kappa, 1952; Phi Kappa Phi; Rotary Foundation Fellow, Cambridge University, England, 1953-54; Edward Hillman Fellowship, University of Chicago, 1954-57. Address: 3500 North 18th, Tacoma, Washington 98406.■

JAMES R. PHIFER

University Administrator. Personal: Born November 10, 1944; Son of John L. Phifer and Lynn Woodlock; Married Linnie Opal, Daughter of Eleanor Blegebron; Father of Trystan Nicole, Tamsyn Rene. Education: B.A. 1966, M.A. 1968, Ph.D. 1975, University of Colorado at Boulder. Career: Dean of Arts and Sciences, State University of New York at Utica; Head of Division of Social Science 1977-80, Associate Professor of History 1968-77, Wayne State College (Nebraska). Organizational Memberships: Conference on British Studies; American Historical Association; Historians of Early Modern Europe. Community Activities: Nebraska Committee for the Humanities, N.E.H. Affiliate, 1979-80; Danforth Associate, 1976 to present; Director, British Institute, Wayne State College, 1972-80; Area Moderator, Nebraska Arts Council, 1976. Honors and Awards: Academic Merit Scholarships, University of Colorado, 1964; Nebraska Council for the Humanities Research Grant, 1971; Nebraska State Board of Trustees Research Fellowships, 1971-72 and 1974-75; Outstanding Teaching Award, Wayne State College, 1980. Address: 18 Bonnie Brae, Utica, New York 13501.■

JOSEPH LAWRENCE PHILBRICK

University Professor, Therapist. Personal: Born September 27, 1927; Son of Ralph H. Philbrick; Married Wileeta F. Washburn, Daughter of William A. Washburn; Father of Joseph L. Jr., Jeana A. Jahier, Kellie C., Karen C. Education: B.A. 1949, M.A. 1950, Ph.D. Student Personnel Services 1955, Baylor University; Post-doctoral Studies undertaken at the University of Southern California, the University of California at Berkeley, the University of Michoacan (Mexico) and the University of Nairobi. Career: Professor, California State Polytechnic University; Former Pastoral Counselor/Minister, Genealogical Researcher/Consultant. Organizational Memberships: American Psychological Association; Western Psychological Association; California State Psychological Association; American Personnel and Guidance Association; California Personnel and Guidance Association. Community Activities: Adjunct Faculty, Newport-Mesa Public Schools; School Board Candidate; Faculty Senator, California State University; Resident Counselor, American Institute of Family Relations; Faculty, St. Andrews Presbyterian Church, Newport Beach; Group Consultant, East African Airways; Consultant, Orange County Genealogical Society; Life Member, Scituate Historical Society. Religion: Pastoral Counseling, Teaching, Speaking, Conference Speaker; Adult Teacher, St. Andrews Presbyterian Church. Honors and Awards: National Science Fellowship, Beloit College, 1964; National Science Fellowship in Psychology, University of California at Berkeley, 1965; Consultant, Pan-African Congress on Psychology, Nairobi; Extensive Cross-Cultural Psychology Research in Africa; President, Philbrick/Philbrook Family Organization International. Address: 1823 West Bay Avenue, Newport Beach, California 92663.■

JAMES LAWRENCE PHILLIPS

Physician, Hospital Administrator, Educator. Personal: Born March 1, 1932; Son of Daniel S. Phillips; Married Barbara Ann Eiserman, Daughter of Margaret Eiserman; Father of James L. Jr., Jeffrey S., Steven C. Education: B.A., Washington & Jefferson College, 1954; M.D., Case Western Reserve University School of Medicine, 1958; Advanced Management Program, Harvard University Graduate School of Business, 1979. Military: Served in the United States Naval Reserve, 1962-64, attaining the rank of Lieutenant Commander. Career: Physician-in-Chief, West of the Ohio Permanente Medical Group Inc., 1968 to present; Chief of Staff, Kaiser Foundation Hospital, Parma, Ohio, 1970 to present; Assistant Clinical Professor in Pediatrics, Case Western Reserve University School of Medicine, 1972 to present; Regional Chief, Department of Pediatrics, Ohio Permanente Medical Group Inc., 1964 to present. Organizational Memberships: Northern Ohio Pediatric Society; Cleveland Academy of Medicine; Ohio State Medical Association; Association for Ambulatory Pediatric Services; Fellow, American Academy of Pediatrics. Community Activities: President, Case Western Reserve University School of Medicine Alumni Association, 1981-82; President, General Alumni Association, Washington & Jefferson College, 1978-79; United Way Services Delegate Assembly, 1981 to present; United Way Services Health, Education, Advocacy & Research Panel, 1976 to present; President, Board of Trustees of Family Health Association, 1976 and 1977; Board of Trustees, Washington and Jefferson College, 1981-86. Religion: Board of Trustees, Mt. Pleasant Church of God, 1976 to present. Honors and Awards: Birch Scholarship Award, Washington and Jefferson College, 1954; Jesse Smith Noyes Scholarship, Washington and Jefferson College, 1954. Address: 2177 South Overlook Road, Cleveland Heights, Ohio 44106.■

RALPH WESLEY PHILLIPS

Retired. Personal: Born February 7, 1909; Son of Elijah and Margaret Phillips (deceased); Married Mary Pozzi, Daughter of John and Maddalena Pozzi (deceased); Married Ellen Dodds Herron, November 1, 1983, Daughter of Elbert Lee and Yvonne Simonet Dodds (deceased); Father of Maria Diana Phillips Yates (Mrs. Richard L. Yates). Education: B.S. Agriculture 1930, D.Sc. (honorary) 1952, Berea College; M.A. 1931, Ph.D. 1934, University of Missouri; D.Sc. (honorary) West Virginia University, 1970. Career: Retired; Deputy Director General, Food and Agriculture Organization of the United Nations, Rome, Italy, 1978-81; Executive Director, International Organization Affairs, United States Department of Agriculture, Washington D.C., 1957-78; Deputy Director, Agriculture Division, Food and Agriculture Organization of the United Nations, Washington D.C., and Rome, Italy, 1949-57; Chief, Animal Production and Health Branch, Food and Agriculture Organization of the United Nations (then in Washington, D.C.), 1946-49; Senior Animal Husbandman, In Charge Animal Genetics Investigations, United States Department of Agriculture, Beltsville, Maryland, 1941-46; Professor and Head, Department of Animal Husbandry, Utah State University, 1939-41; Associate Animal Husbandman, and Physiologist, United States Department of Agriculture, Beltsville, Maryland, 1936-39; Instructor and Assistant Animal Husbandman, University of Massachusetts, 1933-36; Research Assistant in Animal Husbandry, University of Missouri, 1930-33; Consultant on Animal Breeding to the Governments of China and India, for the United States Department of State, 1943-44; Scientific Secretary for Agriculture, United Nations Conference on Science and Technology for the Benefit of Less Developed Areas, Geneva, Switzerland, 1962-63. Organizational Memberships: Gamma Alpha Graduate Scientific Fraternity, Elected 1930; Gamma Sigma Delta, The Honor Society of Agriculture, Elected 1931; Society of Sigma Xi, Elected 1931; American Society of Animal Science, Founding Editor of *The Journal of Animal Science* 1942-49; American Genetic Association, Vice President 1966; President 1967. Published Works: Author or Co-Author of 240 Scientific, Technical and Review Papers, Chapters in Books, and Books on Various Aspects of the Physiology of Reproduction, Animal Climatology, Animal Genetics, Animal Production, and International Agriculture. Honors and Awards: Fellow, American Association for the Advancement of Science, 1940; Special Citation by Fifth International Congress of Physiology of Reproduction and Artificial Insemination, Trento, Italy, 1964; Fellow, American Society of Animal Science, 1965; Berea College Distinguished Alumnus Award, 1968; Officer in Government of Italy's Order of Merit, 1966; Superior Service Award, United States Department of Agriculture, 1960; Distinguished Service Award, United States Department of Agriculture, 1970; L. S. Klinck Memorial Lecturer, for Agricultural Institute of Canada, lecturing in 14 Cities during 1969-70; Recognition Award, Agricultural Institute of Canada, 1970; American Society of Animal Science's International Animal Agriculture Award, 1975; Honorary Member, American Home Economics Association, 1976; Elected to Cosmos Club, Washington D.C., 1960; Listed in *Who's Who in America, Who's Who in the World*. Address: The Representative, Apartment 810, 1101 South Arlington Ridge Road, Arlington, Virginia 22202.■

RANDY E. PHILLIPS

Marketing Researcher and Legislator. Personal: Born August 30, 1950. Education: B.A. Political Science and History, Alaska Methodist University, Anchorage, Alaska, 1973. Career: Marketing Researcher and Legislator; Member, Alaska House of Representatives, 1977 to present; Marketing Researcher, Gamel Homes, 1982-83; Contract Administrative Assistant, Quadrant Development, 1981; Contract Administrative Assistant, Bell, Herrin and Associates, 1980; Contract Administrative Assistant, Tryck, Nyman and Hayes, 1978-79; Partner, Alaska Information Services, 1977-79; Legislative Aide to the House Minority, 1975-

TWO THOUSAND NOTABLE AMERICANS

76; Engineer Technician, City of Anchorage, 1974; Engineer Technician, Tryck, Nyman and Hayes, 1970-74. Community Activities: Coach, Little League Team, Eagle River; Member, Kiwanis Club of Eagle River. Address: P.O. Box 142, Eagle River, Alaska 99577.■

RICHARD DEAN PHILLIPS

Manager of Biological Research. Personal: Born September 17, 1929; Son of Hazel Hallow; Married Elizabeth Anne, Daughter of Porter Evans. Education: B.A. Physiology 1958, Ph.D. Physiology 1966, University of California, Berkeley. Military: Served in the United States Air Force, A/1C, 1952-56. Career: Manager of Biological Research, present; Former Position as Physiologist. Organizational Memberships: American Physiological Society; I.E.E.E.; Bioelectromagnetics Society, Board of Directors; Editorial Board, *Bioelectromagnetic Journal*. Community Activities: C.O.M.A.R.-I.E.E.E. Committee on Man and Radiation, 1979-82; N.C.R.P., National Council on Radiation Protection and Measurement Committee 53, 1978-82; U.S./U.S.S.R. Scientific Exchange Program on Nonionizing Electromagnetic Radiation, 1977-82; U.S./Italy Scientific Exchange on High Voltage Transmission Systems, 1980-82. Religion: Presbyterian Church, 1974 to present. Honors and Awards: United States Navy Educational Fellowship, 1965-66.■

RONALD FRANK PHILLIPS

Dean and Professor of Law. Personal: Born November 25, 1934; Son of Frank J. Phillips (deceased) and Maudie E. Phillips; Married Jamie Bottoms, Daughter of Mr. and Mrs. Ray Bottoms; Father of Celeste Phillips Oliveira, Joel J., Phil E. Education: B.S., Abilene Christian University, 1955; J.D., University of Texas, 1965. Military: Texas National Guard, Reserve Status, 1952-58. Career: Dean and Professor of Law, Pepperdine University School of Law, present; Building Contractor, Phillips Homes Inc., Abilene, Texas, 1955-56; Salesman, Security Savings Stamps and Western National Life Insurance Company, Abilene, Texas, 1957; Business Branch Manager, Phillips Weatherstripping Company, Midland, Texas, 1958-62 and Austin, Texas, 1963-65; Corporate Staff Attorney, McWood Corporation, Abilene, Texas, 1965-67; Private Law Practice and Lecturer in Business Law in Department of Business Administration of Abilene Christian University, Abilene, 1967-70; Dean and Professor of Law, Pepperdine University School of Law, Santa Ana, California, 1970-72, Anaheim, California, 1972-78, and Malibu, California, 1978 to present. Organizational Memberships: State Bar of California; State Bar of Texas; American Bar Association; Los Angeles Bar Association; Orange County Bar Association; Committee on Law School Education, State Bar of California; American Law Institute; Chairman, Association of American Law Schools Section on the Administration of Law Schools, 1982; Pepperdine University Academic Council; Pepperdine University Strategic Planning Committee; Chancellor's Council, Pepperdine University; Phi Delta Phi Legal Fraternity. Community Activities: Pepperdine University Associates; Coaching in Various Youth Programs including A.Y.S.O. Soccer, Little League Baseball, Junior All-American Football, and City Recreational Basketball. Religion: Elder, University Church of Christ, Malibu, California, 1978 to present; Christian Legal Society. Honors and Awards: Outstanding Educators of America, 1972, 1975; Abilene Christian University Alumni Citation, 1974; Listed in *Notable Americans, Who's Who in American Law, Community Leaders and Noteworthy Americans, Dictionary of International Biography, Men of Achievement, International Who's Who in Education, Personalities of America, Who's Who in the West, Who's Who in California*. Address: 21804 Pacific Coast Highway, Malibu, California 90265.■

WILLIAM A. PHILLIPS

Executive. Personal: Born July 24, 1933; Son of Earl E. Phillips; Married Janet E. Quade, Daughter of Agnes E. Quade; Father of Kathryn, William A. Jr., Michael, Reynaldo. Education: B.S., Ball State University, 1957; M.A., Indiana State University, 1969; Ed.D., Oregon State University, 1973. Career: President, Phillips, Prickett, Quade, Inc.; Owner, Business and Professional Training Consultants, 1981 to present; Owner, Pots-and-Plants Garden Center, 1979-81; Director, Management Development, Northern Arizona University, 1975-81; Assistant Principal, Career Opportunities Center, Saginaw, Michigan, 1973-75; Distributive Education Teacher, Fort Wayne Public Schools, 1967-70; Mutual Fund Manager, Patterson Securities, 1965-67; District Manager, Investors Diversified, 1963-65; Store Supervisor 1962-63, Store Manager 1960-62, EF MacDonald Stamp Company; Assistant Buyer, LS Ayres & Company, 1958-60; Salesman, Prentice-Hall, Inc., 1957-68; State Agent Central Indiana, Prairie State Farmer Inc., 1956-57. Organizational Memberships: American Entrepreneur Association; American Society of Training and Development; Vice President, Indiana Vocational Association, 1969; President, Arizona Adult Vocational Education Teachers, 1979-81; President, Grand Canyon Chapter, American Society of Training and Development, 1982; International Council for Small Business; Center for Entrepreneural Management. Community Activities: Vice President, Flagstaff Industrial Development Authority, 1979 to present; Board of Directors, Flagstaff Chamber of Commerce; Northern Arizona Business Industry Education Council; Vocational/Career Education Advisory Council, Chairman 1976-80. Honors and Awards: E.P.D.A. Awardee, U.S.O.E. Doctoral Grant in Vocational Education, 1970-73; Listed in *Who's Who in America in Cooperative Education, Who's Who in the West*. Address: 801 West University Heights Drive South, Flagstaff, Arizona 86001.■

WILMA FRANCES PHILLIPS

School Psychologist. Personal: Born May 2, 1927; Daughter of Albert J. Fox and Anna Viola Fox; Married Doyle C., Son of Harvey and Myrlle Phillips (deceased); Mother of Lyndon D., Devaron Dae, Clayton C. Education: B.S. with highest honors, University of Southern Mississippi; M.A.E. 1972, Ed.D. 1976, Ball State University. Career: School Psychologist, Mireno Valley Unified School District, present; Associate Professor Curriculum and Instruction, Loma Linda University; Elementary School Teacher, Richmond Community Schools, Richmond, Indiana. Organizational Memberships: Chairman, Liaison Committee, Early Childhood Education, California Articulation Conference; 1980 Task Force on Special Education; General Conference Seventh-day Adventist Private School System; 1977 Chairman, Early Childhood Education, National Committee, General Conference Seventh-day Adventist; Phi Delta Kappa, Newsletter Editor. Community Activities: Riverside County Advisory Committee on Special Education, Representative, 1981-83; Riverside County Advisory Committee on Special Education, Member Legislative Committee, 1981-82; Parent Advisory Committee on Special Education for Moreno Valley, Member and Chairman of Legislative Committee, 1981-83. Honors and Awards: B.S. Degree with Highest Honors, 1963; Phi Delta Kappa, 1976 to present; Phi Lambda Theta, 1975 to present; Kappa Delta Phi, 1963 to present; Doctoral Fellowship, 1974-76; *Listed in Who's Who in the West*. Address: 5440 College, Riverside, California 92505.■

RAMESH CHANDER PHUTELA

Research Associate. Personal: Born December 23, 1951; Son of Mr. and Mrs. Mulkh Raj Phutela. Education: B.Sc., Panjab University (Chandigarh, India), 1972; M.Sc., Punjab Agricultural University (Ludhiana, India), 1975; Ph.D., University of Hull (Hull, England), 1978. Career: Research Associate in Chemistry Department and Lawrence Berkeley Laboratory, University of California at Berkeley, 1981 to present; Research Associate, James Franck Institute, University of Chicago, 1979-81; Postdoctoral Fellow, Chemistry Department, University of Otago (Dunedin, New Zealand), 1978-79. Organizational Memberships: American Chemical Society; North American Thermal Analysis Society. Honors and Awards: University of Hull Research Studentship, 1975-77; Published a Number of Research Papers in Different Areas of Thermodynamics. Address: 2732 Benvenue Avenue #1, Berkeley, California 94705.■

BRIAN ALAN PICKARD

Attorney at Law. Personal: Born June 10, 1952; Son of Dr. H. Pickard. Education: B.A. Economics, University of Western Ontario, 1974; M.A.M. Aviation Management, Embry-Riddle Aeronautical University, 1977; J.D., Western State University College of Law, 1980. Career: Management Consultant, Pearpic Management, Inc., present. Organizational Memberships: American Bar Association, 1981; Orange County Trial Lawyers Association, 1980; California Trial Lawyers Association, 1981; Association of Trial Lawyers of America, 1982; American Bar Association Government Litigation Section, 1982. Community

Activities: Alpha Eta Rho International Aviation Honor Society, Vice President 1976. Published Works: Contributor Articles to *Aviation Research Journal*, 1977. Honors and Awards: American Jurisprudence Award, 1979; National Dean's List, 1980-81; West Publishing Award for Trial Practice, 1980; Listed in *Who's Who in the West*, *Who's Who in America*. Address: 1907 Deerpark Drive #500, Fullerton, California 92631.■

VIOLA CRENSHAW FOGLE PICKERING

Retired Educator. Personal: Born April 3, 1899; Daughter of Joseph Martin Fogle and Dora Nancy Sturkie Fogle (both deceased); Married W. F. Crenshaw (deceased 1932); Married Second Husband Francis H. Pickering (deceased 1973); Mother of (stepmother of) Ten Children. Education: A.B., Anderson College, 1927; Additional Studies. Career: Teacher in the Lancaster City School System 32 Years, Retired 1966; Community Activities: Director, Vacation of Bible School for Over 30 Years; Director, Church Library; Choir Member; Youth Director; Member Senior Citizens Sunshine Club, Heath Springs, South Carolina. Religion: Member Heath Springs Baptist Church. Honors and Awards: Recipient Golden 50-Year Diploma from Anderson College; 50-Year State Award as an Extension Homemakers Club Council Member (promotes higher standards of living in homes and communities). Address: Stage Street, Box 23, Heath Springs, South Carolina 29058.■

JOE EUGENE PIERCE

Department Head. Personal: Born April 30, 1924; Son of Velner Campisi; Married Gwendolyn Marie Harris; Father of Carol Jean Pierce-Colfer, David Brian. Education: B.S., University of Oklahoma, 1949; M.A. 1951, Ph.D. 1957, Indiana University. Military: Served in the United States Army, 1942-46, 1950-51; Oklahoma National Guard, 45th Infantry Division, 1946-49. Career: Head of Department of Anthropology presently, Professor of Anthropology 1961-80, Portland State University; Assistant Professor, Georgetown University, 1955-61; Fulbright Senior Lectureship to the University of Education in Osaka, Japan; Fulbright Senior Lectureship at the SEAMEORELC, Singapore; Writer. Organizational Memberships: American Anthropological Association; Linguistic Society of America; New York Academy of Science; American Academy of Social and Political Science; Sigma Xi; Numerous Others. Community Activities: Board of Directors, Northwest American Indian Foundation and Center, 1961-65; Governor's Gold Medal Committee on Second Language Teaching in Oregon, 1979 to present. Religion: Deacon, First Congregational Church of Portland, Oregon, 1963-65. Honors and Awards: N.S.F. Research Grant ($50,000.00), 1964-69; Advisor to the Children's Language Project, Oregon Medical Center, 1965 to present; Elected to Sigma Xi; New York Academy of Science; American Academy of Social and Political Science; Others; Listed in *Who's Who in the West*, *Who's Who*, *Community Leaders and Noteworthy Americans*. Address: 512 Southwest Maplecrest Drive, Portland, Oregon 97219.■

LAWRENCE MICHAEL PIETRZAK

Research Engineer. Personal: Born June 27, 1942; Son of Eugene and Stella Pietrzak; Married Betty Jane; Father of Jeffrey, Michelle, Beth. Education: Attended Villanova University, 1960-62; B.S. summa cum laude, University of Detroit, 1965; M.S., Massachusetts Institute of Technology, 1967; Professional Engineer Degree, Massachusetts Institute of Technology, 1967. Career: Research Engineer and Director of Protection Technolgoy Systems Group, Mission Research Corporation. Organizational Memberships: American Association for the Advancement of Science; American Society of Civil Engineers; American Society for Industrial Security. Community Activities: Young Men's Christian Association Parent/Child Program, 1980-82. Religion: Roman Catholic. Honors and Awards: Award for Outstanding Services to the Fire Services and Community, Santa Barbara, 1979; National Science Foundation Fellow, 1965-66; A.I.S.C. Fellow, 1966-67; Tau Beta Pi; Chi Epsilon; Phi Sigma Tau; Sigma Xi; Theta Tau Award, First in Class, University of Detroit, 1965. Address: 5218 Parejo, Santa Barbara, California 93111.■

AUGUSTUS PIGNATARO

Optical Physicist. Personal: Born August 12, 1943; Son of Frank and Amelia Pignataro; Married Lynn Marie, Daughter of Robert and Winnie Kline; Father of Lisa Marie, Julie Marie, Jeffrey David. Education: B.S. Physics, California State University at Los Angeles, 1965; M.B.A. Management, California Lutheran College, Thousand Oaks, California, 1975. Career: Optical Physicist, 1967 to present; Engineer, Atlantic Research Corporation, Costa Mesa, California, 1965-67. Organizational Memberships: Infrared Information Symposium. Community Activities: California Notary Public, 1982 to present. Religion: Catholic, Marriage Encounter, 1974-80. Honors and Awards: United States Navy Award of Merit Group Achievement, 1979; Listed in *Who's Who in the West*, *American Men and Women of Science*. Address: 1094 Harris Avenue, Camarillo, California 93010.■

GORDON YEE KEAWE A HEULU PIIANAIA

Institute Director, Corporate Executive. Personal: Born May 7, 1940; Son of Abraham and Anne Piianaia; Married Billie Lea Tanson, Daughter of William and Eileen Tanson; Father of St. Chad Kalilioku, Christopher Kaliko. Education: Graduate, Kamehameha School for Boys, 1958; California Maritime Academy, 1964; B.S. Nautical Science 1969, M.A. Geography, University of Hawaii. Military: Served in the United States Navy, Lieutenant Commander, 1957-82 (Retired). Career: Director, Hawaiian Studies Institute, 1977 to present; President, NRG Hawaii Inc., 1980 to present; Program Specialist in Hawaiian Studies, Kamehameha Schools/Bishop Estate, 1972-76; Math/Science Instructor, Punahou Schools, 1969-71; University of Hawaii, Department of Geography/Continuing Education, 1969 to present; Military Sea Transportation Service Honolulu, 1965-69. Organizational Memberships: United States Naval Reserve Association; National Association of Asian and Pacific Educators; Pacific Association of Professional Archaeologists; Association of American Geographers; International Geographical Union. Community Activities: Elks Lodge, 1976 to present; American Youth Soccer Organization, 1975-79; Polynesian Voyaging Society, 1977 to present; Advisor, Co-Chairperson Education Committee; Captain, 1980 Non-instrumental Navigation Project; Director, Hokule'a State of Hawaii Bicentennial Project, 1976; Bishop Museum Association; Oceanic Society. Honors and Awards: Alumni Special Recognition Award, 1977; High Commissioner Award, Tahiti, 1980; House Res. Number 582 (10th Legislature), 1980; Office of the Mayor, Honolulu, 1976; City and County of Honolulu Proclamation, 1976; County of Maui Proclamation, 1976; County of Hawaii, 1976; Award from Governor, State of Hawaii, 1976; Cook Islands Government, 1980; Listed in *Men of Achievement*, 1981. Address: 570 Ka Awakea Road, Kailua, Hawaii 96734.■

LAURENCE OSCAR PILGERAM

Research Biochemist. Personal: Born June 23, 1924; Son of John and Bertha Pilgeram; Married Cynthia Ann, Daughter of J. and V. Moore; Father of Karl Erich, Kurt John. Education: A.A. 1948, B.A. 1949, Ph.D. 1953, University of California at Berkeley. Career: Research Biochemist, presently; Former Professional Occupations include Instructor at the University of Illinois College of Medicine, Assistant Professor at Stanford University College of Medicine, Director of the Arteriosclerosis Research Laboratory at the University of Minnesota School of Medicine, and Director of the Thrombosis Laboratory at the Baylor University College of Medicine. Community Activities: Delegate, Council on Thrombosis, American Heart Association; Delegate, Council on Stroke, American Heart Association; Study Section, National Institutes of Health. Honors and Awards: CIBA Award, London, 1959; Karl Thomae Award, Germany, 1973; Others. Address: 313 Moreton Bay Lane, Goleta, California 93117.■

MARC PILISUK

Professor. Personal: Born January 19, 1934; Son of Mr. and Mrs. Louis Pilisuk; Married; Father of Tammy and Jeffrey. Education: B.A., Queens College,

New York City, 1955; M.A. 1956, Ph.D. 1961, University of Michigan, Ann Arbor. Career: Professor of Applied Behavioral Sciences 1977 to present, Chairperson Department of Applied Behavioral Sciences 1977-82, Counseling Psychologist, University of California-Davis; Consultant, Pacific Children and Family Counseling Center, Oakland, California, and Consultant, Berkeley Community and Mental Health Consultation Services, Berkeley, California, 1975-77; Professor in Residence, School of Public Health, University of California-Berkeley, 1972-75; Director of Graduate Training Program in Youth Involvement, Alienation and Drug Abuse Program, Berkeley, California, 1970-75; Professor in Residence, School of Social Welfare 1968-72, Lecturer in Psychology 1968-69, Visiting Associate Professor of Psychology 1967-68, University of California-Berkeley; Associate Professor of Psychology and Administrative Sciences, Krannert Graduate School of Industrial Administration and Department of Psychology, Purdue University, West Lafayette, Indiana, 1965-67; Research Associate, Institute for Social Research, University of Michigan, Ann Arbor, 1964-65; Associate Research Psychologist, Mental Health Research Institute, Assistant Professor of Psychology in Nursing Graduate Programs in Psychiatric Nursing and Medical Surgical Nursing, Lecturer in the Department of Psychology, University of Michigan, Ann Arbor, 1961-65; Assistant Professor of Psychology, Oberlin College, Oberlin, Ohio, 1961; Assistant Research Psychologist, Mental Health Research Institute, University of Michigan, Ann Arbor, 1960; Diagnostics and Therapy, Children's Psychiatric Hospital, Ann Arbor, Michigan, 1950-60. Organizational Memberships: American Orthopsychiatric Association, Fellow, Member Committee on Mental Health Aspects of War, Violence and Aggression, Member Committee on Social Issues; American Psychological Association, Fellow; American Public Health Association; Society for the Psychological Study of Social Issues; Western Gerontological Association; Member Committee for Gordon Allport Essay Contest (SPSSI). Honors and Awards: Departmental Honors in Psychology, Queens College, 1955; Psi Chi Psychological Honor Society, 1955-56; United States Public Health Service Fellowship, 1955-56; National Science Foundation, Honorable Mention for Research Design, 1959; Society for Psychological Study of Social Issues Award for Essay (with Thomas Hayden) in Contest on Research Approaches to Potential Threats to Peace, 1965; National Institute of Mental Health, Predoctoral Research Fellowship, 1959-60; Sigma Xi, R.E.S.A. Grant-in-Aid for Pilot Study "Psychology of Arms Reduction," 1963-65, Renewed 1965-68; Society fo Psychological Study of Social Issues, Grant-in-Aid for Study of Vocational Commitments to a Defense-Oriented Social Study, 1964-65; Society for Psychological Study of Social Issues, Grant-in-Aid for Observatoin and Study of Resurrection City; University of California Office of Research Awards, Free Clinic Study 1970, Evaluation of Training in Youth Programs 1971, Consumer-Designed Evaluation of "Alternative" Student Services 1972, Study of Problems of Vietnam Veterans 1973, Study of Training of Professionals in Human Services 1974, University of California; Committee on Teaching Evaluation of Field Studies Education; Eagle Feather from University of California-Davis Native American Faculty; Listed in *Who's Who in California, Men of Achievement, American Men and Women of Science, Community Leaders and Noteworthy Americans, Contemporary Authors, Dictionary of International Biography, International Authors and Writers Who's Who, Outstanding Professionals in Human Services, The World Who's Who of Authors, Who's Who in the United States, Who's Who in the West*. Address: 494 Cragmont, Berkeley, California 94708.■

DAN R. PILKINGTON

Government Administrator. Personal: Born June 23, 1934; Son of John L. (deceased) and Ethel M. Pilkington; Married Alice Jensen Marler, Daughter of Alice Jensen; Father of Rodney, Jeanne (Mrs. Wayne Teachout), John Marler, Denise (Mrs. Brent Winslow), Larry Marler, Ken Marler. Education: A.A., North Idaho College, Coeur d'Alene, Idaho, 1958; B.S. Business, University of Idaho, Moscow, 1960. Military: Served in the United States Army, 1954-56. Career: Government Administrator, Director Department of General Services, presently; Former Professional Occupations include Purchasing Agent, Employment Counselor, and Company Manager. Organizational Memberships: Lifetime Member, National Association of State Purchasing Officials; Current Member, National Institute of Governmental Purchasing; Past Local Chapter President, National Association of Purchasing Management. Community Activities: Tuesday Mourner Toastmasters, A.T.M., Past President, 1978 to present; Idaho Jaycees, 1964-71; Board of Directors, Idaho Junior Miss Pageant, 1968-71; Past President, University of Idaho Federal Credit Union, 1970; Past Local and District President, Idaho Chapter of International Association of Personnel in Employment Security, 1964-65. Honors and Awards: "Outstanding Toastmaster," Tuesday Mourner Toastmasters, Las Vegas, Nevada, 1980; "Outstanding Jaycee Award," Moscow, Idaho, 1966; "Outstanding State Chairman Award," Idaho Jaycees, 1965; "Outstanding Young Men of America," 1967; Listed in *Who's Who in the West, Who's Who in Government*. Address: 3456 Monte Carlo Drive, Las Vegas, Nevada 89121.■

JERZY TADEUSZ PINDERA

Educator. Personal: Born 1914; Married Aleksandra Anna; Father of Marek-Jerzy, Maciej-Zenon. Education: Bachelor of Applied Science (equivalent), Warsaw Technical University, 1936; Master of Engineering in Aeronautical Engineering, Lodz Technical University, 1947; Doctor of Applied Science, Polish Academy of Sciences, 1959; Doctor hab., D.Sc., Technical University of Cracow, 1962. Military: Served in the Polish Army, 1939, as an Officer of the Artillery; Wounded at Warsaw, 1939; Taken Prisoner by the German Army. Career: Director Institute for Experimental Mechanics, Adjunct Professor, University of Waterloo, 1983 to present; Professor of Engineering, University of Waterloo, 1965-83; Visiting Professor, Michigan State University, 1963-65; Head of Experimental Mechanics Laboratory, Building Research Institute, Warsaw, 1959-62; Deputy Professor, Head of Experimental Mechanics Laboratory, Polish Academy of Sciences, 1954-59; Head of Laboratory, Aeronautical Institute, Warsaw, 1947-52; Assistant, Polish Airlines "Lot," 1947. Organizational Memberships: Chairman, Experimental Mechanics Sub-Division, Research and Development Division, Canadian Society for Mechanical Engineering, 1984 to present; Editorial Advisory Board, Mechanics Research Communications, 1974 to present; Society for Experimental Stress Analysis, Member Various Committees, Reviewer 1963 to present; Reviewer, *Applied Mechanics Review*, 1965 to present; International Symposium on Experimental Mechanics, University of Waterloo (Ontario, Canada), Organizer, Chairman 1972; Coordinator Session on "Advanced Topics of Experimental Mechanics," International Center for Mechanical Science (Udine, Italy), 1978; President, J. T. Pindera & Sons, Engineering Services, Inc. Community Activities: Resistance in the Concentration Camp Sachsenhausen in Oranienburg, 1940-45 (Prisoner #28862). Published Works: Author of 100 Research Papers and Review Papers, 5 Books, 6 Patents, 2 Patents Applied For. Honors and Awards: M. M. Frocht Award, Outstanding Achievements in Education of Experimental Mechanics, Society for Experimental Stress Analysis, 1978; Prize of the Polish Society for Theoretical and Applied Mechanics, for Paper "Investigations of Some Rheological Photoelastic Properties of Some Polyester Resins," 1960; Prize for Scientific and Organizational Achievement in the Field of Photoelasticity, Outline of Photoelasticity, Board of the State Technical Publishers, 1954; Military Decoration, Medal for Participation in the Defense War, 1939. Address: 310 Grant Crescent, Waterloo, Ontario N2K 3G1 Canada.■

RICHARD L. PINION

Chartered Life Underwriter, Insurance Company Administrator. Education: A.A. Business Administration, Hagerstown Junior College, 1968; B.S. Business Administration 1970, M.B.A. Marketing 1973, American University; Basic and Standard Certificates, American Institute of Banking, 1974; Chartered Life Underwriter; Agency Management Training Course, 1982; Management Orientation Student Course, 1977; Motivational Theories and Management Practices, 1983; Attended Home Office Schools for Pensions, Tax-Deferred Annuities, Deferred Compensation, Personal Lines; Enrolled in Chartered Financial Consultant Certification Course. Career: Superintendent, Washington Branch Office, Aetna Insurance Company. Organizational Memberships: General Agents and Management Association; National Association of Life Underwriters; Chartered Life Underwriter Society; American Marketing Association; International Management Personnel Association; Life Underwriters Political Action Committee; Association of M.B.A. Executives Inc. Community Activities: Wolf Trap Association; Washington Humane Society; Hagerstown Alumni Association; American University Alumni Association. Honors and Awards: Million Dollar Round Table; Sales Management Award; National Sales Achievement Award; National Quality Award; Corps of Regionnaires; #1 Manager with Aerna in Federal Government Market; Listed in *Who's Who in the South and Southwest*; Nominated to *Who's Who in Business and Finance, Outstanding Young Men of America*. Address: Park Place, P.O. Box 1690, 7926 Jones Branch Drive, Merrifield, Virginia 22116.■

KATHRYN T. PIPER

Executive. Personal: Born November 26; Daughter of Thelma Thomas; Mother of James, Jerrold, Sue. Education: B.A. English, Speech, Journalism, Communications, Marketing, Radio/Television, Public Relations, Advertising, Loretto Heights College (Denver, Colorado); Attended the University of Denver and the University of Colorado. Career: President, Piper & Associates, Ltd., Public Relations and Advertising, 1965 to present; Former Positions in Radio, Television, with Newspapers (Writer, Coorespondent). Organizational Memberships: National Federation of Press Women; Colorado Press Women; Public Relations Society of America; National Association of Female Executives. Community Activities: Denver Civic Ballet; Denver Debutante Ball; New York Debutante Ball; Catalyst Resource Board; Editor, *Denver Social Register and Record*; Vice President, Yuan Mongolian Barbecue; Vice President, Pacific International Trading Company. Honors and Awards: First Place Awards, Various Categories of Writing and Advertising, National Federation of Press Women, 1967-80; Colorado Women of Achievement, Colorado Press Women, 1976; National Woman of Achievement, National Federation of Press Women, 1978. Address: 120 South Marion Parkway, Denver, Colorado 80209.■

TWO THOUSAND NOTABLE AMERICANS

ESTUS W. PIRKLE

Pastor, Evangelist, Christian Film Producer. Personal: Born March 12, 1930; Son of Grover Washington Pirkle (deceased); Married Annie Catherine; Father of Letha Dianne, Gregory, Don. Education: Norman Junior College, Norman Park, Georgia, 1949; B.A., Mercer University, Macon, Georgia, 1951, Bachelor of Divinity, Master of Religious Education 1956, Master of Theology 1958, Southwestern Baptist Seminary, Fort Worth, Texas. Career: Pastor, Evangelist, present; Author of Christian Books; Producer, 60-Minute Color 16mm Film Full-Length Motion Pictures, "If Footmen Tire Your, What Will Horses Do?" 1972, "The Burning Hell" 1974, "The Believer's Heaven" 1977; Preacher, 40 Revivals, Conferences, Camp Meetings, Each Year. Religion: Over 2,000,000 Have Professed Faith in Jesus Christ at the Showing of his Films. Published Works: *Preachers in Space* 1969, *If Footmen Tire You Out, What Will Horses Do?"* 1969, *Book of Sermon Outlines* 1973, *Who Will Build Your House?* 1978. Honors and Awards: "The Burning Hell" has been Translated in Spanish and Portuguese and has been Distributed All Over the World; Valedictorian Norman Junior College, 1949; Cum Laude Graduate, Mercer University, 1957, Doctor of Divinity Degree by Covington Theological Seminary, Rossville, California, 1982. Address: P.O. Box 80, Myrtle, Mississippi 38650.■

JAMES EUGENE PITTMAN, JR.

Vermiculturist, Executive. Personal: Born May 28, 1948, in Long Beach, California; Son of James E. Pittman and Lenora Fern Hunsaker; Married Brenda June Petker, November 12, 1977; Father of Kerri Lynn, Michelle Nichole, Olivia Marie. Education: Graduate of Long Beach Polytechnic High School, 1966; Attended Long Beach City College 1967-68, Los Angeles Trade Technical College 1970; Extension Study, University of Iowa, Iowa State University; Additional Special Studies, University of Michigan, University of Missouri, 1977; Certification, Los Angeles County Health Department, Los Angeles City Department of Building and Safety, Long Beach City Department of Building and Safety, International Organic Growers Association, California Organic Growers Association. Career: Marketing Director, Jay-Fran Inc. (Iowa City) 1977, Invivo Inc. (Iowa City) 1977; Consultant, Consultant Services Associates Inc., P/C Enterprises (Indianapolis, Indiana); Marketing Consultant, Bio-Chemical Catalysts Inc. (Grand Rapids, Iowa), Bio-Eco Systems Inc. (Franklin, Indiana) 1976; Owner, Templeton Worm Ranch (Templeton, California), 1974-79; Owner, American Eco-Systems (Oceanside, California), 1977 to present; Seminars, Lectures, "Earthworms in Agriculture Today," "Earthworms and Their Relation to Feeding Mankind," "Microflora - What Is It?," "What Makes Things Grow?," "Earthworms and Crops," "Raising Earthworms for Profit," "Earthworms and Bacteria - Working Together." Organizational Memberships: California Farm Bureau; Western Organic Growers Association; Vermiculturists Trade Association; National Foundation of Independent Businesses. Community Activities: Rotary Club International, Board of Directors 1977, Chairman Local Club, World Community Services 1977-78; National S.B.A. Club; Benevolent and Protective Order of Elks; International Platform Association; Free Mason; Republican Presidential Task Force; National Rifle Association. Honors and Awards: Award of Appreciation, Rotary International 1977, Kiwanis Club 1977, Lions Club 1976, Chamber of Commerce (Atascadero, California) 1976, California State University at Cal Poly (San Luis Obispo) 1976, Madera Unified School District 1977, Fresno State University 1977; Listed in *Who's Who in Finance and Industry, Who's Who in the West, Who's Who in California, International Who's Who of Intellectuals, Biographical Roll of Honor.* Address: 368 East Broadway, Vista, California 92083.■

JULIAN GERARD PLANTE

Library Director and Research Professor. Personal: Son of Roland J. and Marion M. (Herold) Plante (both deceased). Education: B.A. Classics, St. John's University, Collegeville, Minnesota; M.A. Classical Philology, Ph.D. Classical and Medieval Philology, Fordham University, New York. Career: Director, Hill Monastic Manuscript Library, Research Professor of Classics at St. Johns' University, Collegeville, Minnesota, presently; Former Professional Occupations include Lecturer in Department of Classical Languages and Hebrew at City College of New York, Assistant to the President at Elmer R. Davis and Associates in New York, and Bibliographical Research Assistant at the Columbia-Presbyterian Medical Center in New York (working on the Tissue Culture Project). Organizational Memberships: Medieval Association of the Midwest, President 1982-83, Vice President 1981-82; Medieval Academy of America, Councilor 1982-85; American Philological Association; Stearn County Historical Society; Minnesota Historical Society; Benton County Historical Society. Honors and Awards: Lalibela Cross, 1973, Decorated by His Holiness Abuna Theophilos, Patriarch, Ethiopian Orthodox Church. Address: 1603 Cherry Lane, St. Cloud, Minnesota 56301.■

DAVID ANTHONY PLAWECKI

State Senator. Personal: Born November 8, 1947; Son of Ed and Lakadya Plawecki; Married; Father of Brent David. Education: B.S., General Motors Institute, 1970; M.B.A., University of Michigan, 1977. Career: State Senator. Community Activities: Treasurer and Executive Board Member, 15th Congressional Democratic Party 1970, Young Democrat 15th Congressional District 1968-69; Vice Chairman, Dearborn Heights Democratic Club, 1970-71; Board Member, Center for International Transportation Exchange; Board Member, Quality of Work Life Council Inc.; State Senator; Chairman, Senate Labor and Retirement Committee; Vice Chairman, Senate Transportation Committee; Member Senate Administration and Rules; Senate Majority Floor Leader; Jaycees; Goodfellows Polish Legion of American Veterans; Knights of Columbus; G.M.E. Alumni Association; Kingswood-Crestwood Civic Association; Polish American Congress; University of Michigan Alumni Association; Board Member, Michigan Quality of Work-Life Council, Wayne State University; Center for International Transportation Exchange, Michigan State University. Honors and Awards: Annual Legislator of the Year, Police Officers Association, 1979; Distinguished Service Award, Michigan Arson Committee, 1979; Legislative Service Award; Polish Legion of American Veterans, 1980; Dearborn Association of Retarded Children; Dearborn Heights Jaycees; Michigan School Boards and Administrators; Detroit Police Officers. Address: 1157 North John Daly, Dearborn Heights, Michigan 48127.■

DONALD LOVELLE PLUCKNETT

Scientific Advisor. Personal: Born September 9, 1931; Son of Mr. and Mrs. Donald Plucknett; Married Sue R., Daughter of Mrs. William Jay Richards; Father of Karen Starkweather, Roy, Duane. Education: B.A. General Agriculture 1953, M.S. Agronomy 1957, University of Nebraska; Ph.D. Tropical Soil Science, University of Hawaii, 1961. Military: Served in the United States Army, Korea and Hawaii, First Lieutenant, 1953-55. Career: Scientific Advisor, CGIAR, World Bank, 1980 to present; Chief, Agriculture and Rural Development Division, Bureau for Asia, Agency for International Development (AID), 1979-80; Deputy Executive Director, Board for International Food and Agriculture Development, 1978-79; Professor of Agronomy and Soil Science, University of Hawaii, 1970-80; Chief, Soil and Water Management Division, Office of Agriculture, Technical Assistance Bureau, Agency for International Development, 1973-76; Associate Professor of Agronomy 1965-70, Assistant Professor of Agronomy 1961-65, Instructor in Soil Science 1960-61, University of Hawaii. Organizational Memberships: American Society of Agronomy, Fellow 1980; American Association for the Advancement of Science, Fellow 1980; Crop Science Society of America; International Society for Tropical Root Crops, President 1976-83; Soil Science Society of America, Fellow 1980; Society for Economic Botany; National Academy of Sciences, Member Numerous Expert Panels. Published Works: Author or Editor of 12 Books on Tropical Agriculture, More Than 100 Other Professional Publications including Articles in *Agronomy Journal, Economic Botany, Experimental Agriculture, Field Crop Abstracts, Pacific Science, Plant and Soil, Soil Science Society of America Proceedings, Tropical Agriculture, Science and Weed Science.* Honors and Awards: Superior Honor Award, Agency for International Development, 1976; Chairman, National Academy of Sciences Vegetable Farming Systems Delegation to the People's Republic of China, 1977; Fellow, American Society of Agronomy, 1980; Fellow, Soil Science Society of America, 1980; Fellow, American Association for the Advancement of Science, 1982. Address: 4205 St. Jerome Drive, Annandale, Virginia 22003.■

BOB LEE PLYLER

Ladder Manufacturing Executive. Personal: Born December 20, 1936; Son of Lee Roy and Altha Cleo McSpadden Plyler; Married Paulette Durso; Father of Vonda Lynn, Pamela Lee, Bobby Lee, Joseph Lane, Rick Todd. Education: A.A., Arlington State, 1955; B.A., Texas A&M University, 1957; Honorary A.F.D., London Institute, 1972. Military: Served in the United States Air Force, 1955, Honorable Discharge 1956. Career: President, Acme Ladders, Inc., Houston, Texas, 1966 to present; Plant Manager, Lone Star Ladder Company, 1957-66. Community Activities: President, Gulf Meadow Civic Association; Former Special Advisor and Master of Ceremonies, Consular Ball of Houston; Master of Ceremonies, Noches Americas International Ball; Former Vice President, Greater Houston Civic Foundation; Former Protocol Representative to the Office of the Mayor; Houston Jaycees; Chairman, Galveston County Drainage District; Member Board of Directors, Houston-Taipia Sister City Committee; Master Mason and Shriner; Houston Chamber of Commerce; Life Member,

Houston Livestock Show and Rodeo Committee; Sustaining Member, National Republican Committee; Board Member, American Ladder Institute. Honors and Awards: Fellow, American Biographical Institute; Listed in *Personalities of the South, Notable Americans of the Bicentennial Era, Who's Who in Texas, Who's Who in the South and Southwest, Book of Honor, International Who's Who in Community Service, Who's Who in Finance and Industry.* Address: Box 26593, Houston, Texas 77207.■

RAYMOND GLENN POEHNER

Retired Banker, Retired Naval Officer. Personal: Born October 1, 1923; Son of Raymond Frank Poehner (deceased), Winnifred McCracken; Married Ella Frances; Father of David R., Diane M., Leslie, Rebecca G., Jon A., (Stepfather of) Bruce Gillespie, Tony Gillespie. Education: Attended Military Service School; Graduate of Dale Carnegie Course; Attended American Banking Institute. Military: Served in the United States Navy, 1941-65. Career: Security Pacific National Bank, 1966-78; Bank Speaking Group. Community Activities: March of Dimes Foundation; Optimist International Director; Veterans of Foreign Wars; Fleet Reserve Association; United States Naval Institute; Republican Senatorial Committee. Religion: Christian. Honors and Awards: Art Scholarship, Chicago Art Institute, 1937; Letters of Commendation, United States Navy, 1957, 1960, 1964; War Service Medal, World War II, Korean War, Vietnam; Letter of Appreciation, Security Pacific Bank; Listed in *Personalities of the West ant Midwest.* Address: Gulf Breeze, Florida.■

HERBERT ACKLAND POHL

Professor. Personal: Born February 17, 1916; Son of Lucien Charles and Emily May Pohl (deceased); Married Eleanor Kathleen Rich, Daughter of William and Leontine Rich (deceased); Father of Douglas, Particia (Mrs. Robert Langdon), Elaine (Mrs. Gene Oltmans), Charles, William. Education: A.B. magna cum laude with honors, Duke University, 1936; Ph.D. Physical Chemistry, Duke University, 1939; University of Heidelberg, 1936; Johns Hopkins Medical School, 1939; University of Delaware, 1946-47. Military: Served in the NDRC 1941-42, Naval Research Laboratory 1942-45. Career: Senior Chemist, United States Naval Research Laboratory, 1942-45; Research Associate, Textile Fibers Department, du Pont Company 1945-50, Atomic Energy Division 1950-56, Engineering Department E. I. du Pont de Nemours and Company 1957; Senior Research Asociate, Lecturer, School of Engineering Plastics Department, Princeton University, Princeton, New Jersey, 1957-62; Professor of Materials Science, Polytechnic Institute of Brooklyn, Department of Chemistry and Electrical Engineering, 1962-63; Professor of Physics, Oklahoma State University, 1964 to present; Visiting Professor, Quantum Chemistry Group, Uppsala University, Uppsala, Sweden, 1963-64. Community Activities: Editor, *Journal Biological Physics;* Co-Editor, *Digest on Dielectrics;* Past Regional Director, Oklahoma Laboratory for Cancer Research of National Foundation for Cancer Research; Vice President Sci-Tech Corp; President, Princeton Chapter, United World Federalists, 1959-61; Vice President, Stillwater Unitarian Church, 1978-79; President and Research Director, Pohl Cancer Research Laboratory, Inc., 1982 to present. Religion: Vice President, Stillwater Unitarian Church, 1978-79. Honors and Awards: Recipient Rensselaer Award in Science, 1933; Society Plastics Award, 1959; *Who's Who* Community Service Award; Stillwater Writer's Award; Harshaw Prize. Address: 515 Harned Avenue, Stillwater, Oklahoma 74074.■

SANDRA JEAN POKLUDA

School Administrator. Personal: Born December 25, 1940; Daughter of Mrs. Dorothy Whearley; Married James Alois Pokluda, Son of Mr. and Mrs. A. L. Pokluda; Mother of Jamie Ann, Brian James. Education: B.B.A. 1963, M.Ed. 1975, Sam Houston State University. Career: Director, Outreach Department, Mexia State School for the Retarded, 1981 to present; Education Specialist (Quality Assurance) 1977-78, Coordinator of Follow-up 1978-81, Mexia State School for the Retarded; Assistant Team Project Director, Mexia State School, 1976-77; Teacher, Mexia Independent School District, 1974-75; Teacher, LaMarque Independent School District, 1963-73. Organizational Memberships: Texas Public Employees Association; American Association on Metal Deficiency; Texas Association on Mental Deficiency. Community Activities: Sam Houston State University Alumni Association; Parent-Teacher Association; Band Boosters. Religion: Baptist. Honors and Awards: Parent-Teacher Association Appreciation Award, 1976. Address: 1102 North Red River, Mexia, Texas 76667.■

KAREN SAFER POLICH

Architectural Historian and Photographer. Personal: Born February 2, 1951; Daughter of Mr. and Mrs. Henry E. Safer; Married Frank A. Polich, Son of Mr. and Mrs. F. Polich. Education: A.A., Santa Monica College, 1972; B.A., University of California at Los Angeles, 1974; M.A., California State University at Long Beach. Career: Architectural Historian and Photographer; Former Executive in Sales Retail, Research Assistant, Assistant Slide Curator. Organizational Memberships: Historical Society of Long Beach, Vice President 1982-83; Los Angeles Historical Society; Los Angeles Conservancy; Theatre Historical Society; Society of Architectural Historians; Long Beach Cultural and Historical Society; Women in Photography; Los Angeles County Museum. Community Activities: Photographic Consultant, California State University at Long Beach Special Prints Collection, 1980; Guest Curator/Researcher, Long Beach Museum of Art; Long Beach Symphony Guild Design Homes; Theatre Historical Society, Contributing Author to Publication; University of California at Los Angeles Alumni Association; Smithsonian Institute. Honors and Awards: Graduated summa cum laude, California State University at Long Beach, 1981; Graduated cum laude, University of California at Los Angeles, 1974; Scholastic Honors, Phi Delta Kappa; Gallery Exhibitions of Photography; Listed in *Who's Who in the West.* Address: 1136 East Third Street, Long Beach, California 90802.■

ROBERT H. POLLACK

Educator. Personal: Born June 26, 1927; Son of Bertha Levy Pollack; Married Martha Katz; Father of Jonathan, Lance, Scott. Education: B.S. Psychology, City College of New York, 1948; M.A. Psychology, Ph.D. Psychology, Clark University, 1948-53. Military: Served in the United States Army, 1945-46, attaining the rank of Corporal. Career: Professor and Director, Graduate Training in Psychology, University of Georgia-Athens, 1969 to present; Deputy Director of Research, Department of Research, Institute for Juvenile Research, Chicago (Illinois), 1963-69; Lecturer, Department of Psychology, University of Sydney, New South Wales, Australia, 1953-61. Organizational Memberships: Fellow, American Association for the Advancement of Science; Fellow, American Psychological Association; American Association of Sex Educators, Counselors and Therapists; Gerontological Society; Society for the Scientific Study of Sex. Honors and Awards: University of Georgia's Award for Significant Research Contributions, 1978; N.I.M.H. Special Research Fellowship to Investigate Contour Interaction, Columbia University, 1961; N.I.C.H.D. Research Grant to Study "Intelligence and Perceptual Development in Childhood," 1965-76 (renewed 1967-71, 1972-75); N.I.H. Research Grant to Study "Sensory and Perceptual Processes in the Aged," 1975-78. Address: 190 Gatewood Place, Athens, Georgia 30606.■

STEPHEN J. POLLACK

Executive, Stockbroker. Personal: Born August 25, 1937, in New York City; Son of Harold S. and Gladys H. Pollack. Education: Graduate of the Hill School, Pottstown, Pennsylvania, 1956; B.S. Economics, Wharton School of Business and Finance, University of Pennsylvania, 1960. Military: Served in the United States Army, Honorably Discharged in 1966. Career: First Vice President, Investments, Dean Witter Reynolds Inc., 1977 to present; Vice President, Retail Sales Drexel Burnham Lambert, 1960-77. Organizational Memberships: International Association of Financial Planners; Association of Investment Brokers, Board Member. Community Activities: Yale Club; Town Club; Atrium Club; Young Men's Philanthropic Club, Board Member; Cosmopolitan League of City of Hope, Board Member; Whitney Museum, Vice President and Circle Member; Schuykill Country Club; Wharton School Club of New York; University of Pennsylvania Club; Ionosphere Club of Eastern Airlines; Clipper Club of Pan American Airlines; Admirals Club of American Airlines; Ambassador Club of Trans World Airlines; Eastside Young Republican Club; Knickerbocker Republican Club; East Side Tennis Club; Matterhorn Sports Club; Former Member, Fresh Meadow and Berkleigh Country Clubs; Amex Club of New York; Life Member, American Biographical Institute. Religion: Sutton Place Synagogue; Temple Emanu-El, New York; Gotham B'nai B'rith, Member of the Board. Address: 245 East 40th Street, Apartment 14 E, New York, New York 10016.■

TWO THOUSAND NOTABLE AMERICANS

GERTRUDE S. POLLITT

Psychotherapist, Consultant, Supervisor, Lecturer. Personal: Daughter of Julius and Sidonie Stein (both deceased); Married to Erwin P. (now deceased). Education: Social Service Course, British Council and London School of Economics, 1945; B.A., Roosevelt University, 1954; M.A., University of Chicago, 1956; Certificate, Chicago Institute for Psychoanalysis, 1963. Career: Psychotherapist and Clinical Social Worker; Lecturer, Institute for Psychoanalysis, University of Chicago, School of Social Service Administration, both Professional (1982) and Development (1984) Programs; Formerly Psychiatric Social Worker, Director of Therapeutic Play Center, Principal Welfare Officer and Deputy Director with the United Nations Relief and Rehabilitation Administration, International Refugee Organization, United States Zone in Germany 1945-49, Resident Social Worker with Anna Freud in Essex, England 1944-45. Organizational Memberships: National Association of Social Workers, Member 1955 to present, Membership Chairman 1956-58, Chairperson of Psychiatric and Mental Health Council 1960-64, Chairperson of Private Practice Committee 1969-72; World Federation of Mental Health, 1960 to present; American Orthospychiatric Association, 1960 to present; Academy of Certified Social Workers, 1981. Community Activities: Member, Menninger Foundation, 1960 to present; Member, Winnetka Women's Club, 1980 to present; Made Donations to Various Social Agencies. Honors and Awards: Licensed Clinical Social Worker, State of California, 1978 to present; Fellow, American Orthopsychiatric Association, 1967; Fellow 1977, Board Member of Illinois Society for Clinical Social Work, Glencoe Youth Service, Winnetka Women's Organization for Rehabilitation and Training; Case Record Exhibit, Child Welfare League of America, 1956 (record incorporated in permanent library of the league); Listed in *Registry of Health Care Providers in Clinical Social Work, Who's Who in the West and Midwest, Who's Who of American Women, The World Who's Who of Women, Personalities of the West and Midwest, Notable Americans*. Address: 481 Oakdale Avenue, Glencoe, Illinois 60022.■

JULIUS REID POOVEY

State Representative, Retired Accountant. Personal: Born September 24, 1902, in Hickory, North Carolina; Son of Lloyd Willard and Nancy Thomas Reid Poovey; Married Kathryn Violet Icard, April 7, 1928; Father of Mrs. Walter N. Young Jr., J. Reid Jr., William B., James N. Education: Attended Hickory City Schools, Weaver College; Commercial Graduate, Lenoir-Rhyne College, 1922. Military: Served in the United States Coast Guard, 1944-45. Career: Representative in General Assembly, 1967, 1977-78, 1979-80, 1981-82, 1983-84; Senator in General Assembly, 1969, 1973-74; Judge pro-tem, Hickory Municipal Court. Organizational Memberships: Member Catawba County Board of Elections; Member Board of Advisors, North Carolina Federation of College Republicans; State, County, Precinct Republican Executive Committees. Religion: Episcopalian. Address: 61 Twentieth Avenue Northwest, Hickory, North Carolina 28601.■

JACK POPE

Chief Justice, Supreme Court of the State of Texas. Personal: Born April 18, 1913, in Abilene, Texas; Married Allene Nichols. Education: B.A., Abilene Christian University, 1934; LL.B., The University of Texas School of Law, 1937; LL.D., Abilene Christian University, 1980; LL.D., Pepperdine University, 1981; LL.D., St. Mary's University, 1982. Military: Served in the United States Navy, Two Years. Career: Practiced Law in Corpus Christi, Texas, 1937-46; District Judge, 94th District Court, 1946-50; Justice, Court of Civil Appeals, 1950-65; Justice, Supreme Court of Texas, 1965-82; Chief Justice, Supreme Court of Texas, 1982 to present; Chairman 1961-62, Committee on Family Law 1952-55, Legislative Committee 1959, Chairman Ethics Committee 1972-73, Court Judicial Section; Chairman, Appellate Judges Section, 1972; Chairman, Board of Editors, *Appellate Procedure in Texas*; Rules Member, Supreme Court Advisory Committee; Chairman, State Law Library Board. Organizational Memberships: President, Nueces County Bar, 1946; Chairman, Citizenship Committee, State Bar, 1952-53; Chairman, State Bar Committee on Rules and Statutes, 1959-60; Committee on Administration of Justice, 1958-64, 1975 to present; Nueces County Bar; San Antonio Bar; Travis County Bar; Hill County Bar; American Judicature Society; American Bar Association; Law-Science Institute; American Society for Legal History. Community Activities: Trustee, Abilene Christian University, 1954 to present; President, Austin Knife and Fork, 1980. Published Works: Author of Nearly 1000 Published Opinions; Author of 70 Law Review and Other Law Related Articles. Honors and Awards: Law Review Award, Texas Bar Foundation, 1979, 1980, 1981; Rosewood Gavel Award, St. Mary's School of Law, 1962; St. Thomas More Award, St. Mary's University, 1982; Joe Greenhill Judicial Award, 1982; Phi Delta Phi; Order of the Coif; Silver Beaver Awrd, Alamo Council, Boy Scouts of America. Address: The Supreme Court of Texas, Capitol Station, Box 12248, Austin, Texas 78711.■

MARY MAUDE POPE (DECEASED)

Bishop. Personal: Born January 27, 1916; Deceased 1983; Daughter of Delia Smith (deceased); Married Roy (deceased). Education: Graduate, Riverdale High School; Attended North Carolina State University, University of North Carolina and American School of Chicago. Career: Bishop, Founder and Pastor of Mt. Sinai Churches Worldwide with Headquarters in Raleigh, North Carolina; Founder, Mt. Sinai Saints of God Holiness Churches of America, Inc., 1946; Established Churches in London, England, Ghana, West Africa, Nigeria, Germany and Other Parts of the World; Founder, Mt. Sinai Training Center and Orphanage School in Nigeria, West Africa; Established 100 Missions in Nigeria. Organizational Memberships: Raleigh Ministerial Alliance. Honors and Awards: Member, International Biographical Centre, Cambridge, England; Received Award from Shaw University, 1978; Received Award from Mayor J. J. Obot, Nto Akpan Village Council; Listed in *Who's Who in North Carolina, Who's Who Among Black Americans, Who's Who of American Women, Notable Americans, Dictionary of International Biography*. Address: 1220 Crosslink Road, Raleigh, North Carolina 27601.■

BLAINE ROBERT PORTER

University Professor. Personal: Born February 24, 1922; Son of Brigham Ernest and Edna Brough Porter (deceased); Married Elizabeth Taylor (deceased), 2nd Wife Barbara Duessler; Father of Claudia Porter Black, Robert B. Porter, David T. Porter, Patricia Porter Hintze, Corinna Porter. Education: B.S. 1947, M.A. 1949, Brigham Young University; Ph.D., Cornell University, 1952. Military: Served in the United States Army Air Force, 1942-45, attaining the rank of First Lieutenant. Career: Assistant Professor, Iowa State University, 1952-55; Chairman, Department of Home Development and Family Relations, Brigham Young University, 1955-65; Visiting Professor, University of London (Fulbright Research Scholar, London School of Economics and Political Science), 1965-66; Dean, College of Family Living, Brigham Young University, 1966-80; Visiting Professor, University of Wurzburg (German), 1980, 1981; University Professor (first to be given this honor), Brigham Young University, 1980 to present. Organizational Memberships: American Association of Marriage and Family Therapists; National Council on Family Relations, President 1963-64; American Sociological Association, Secretary 1963-66; Utah Council on Family Relations, President 1957-58; American Psychological Association; American Home Economics Association; American Association of University Professors; National Association for the Education of Young Children; Society for Research in Child Development; Omicron Nu; Phi Kappa Phi; Sigma Xi. Religion: Member of the Church of Jesus Christ of Latter-day Saints; Served as Bishop 1962-65, Numerous Ward, Stake and General Church Assignments. Honors and Awards: Fulbright

TWO THOUSAND NOTABLE AMERICANS

Research Scholar and Visiting Professor, University of London, 1965-66; University Professor, Brigham Young University, 1980 to present; Professor of the Year, Brigham Young University, 1963-64; Listed in *American Men and Women of Science, The Blue Book, Community Leaders and Noteworthy Americans, International Who's Who in Community Service, Men of Achievement, The National Register of Prominent Americans and International Notables, Outstanding Educators of America, Personalities of the West and Midwest, Who's Who in America, Who's Who in American College and University Administration, Who's Who in American Education, Who's Who in the West, Who's Who in the World.* Address: 1675 Pine Lane, Provo, Utah 84604.■

MICHAEL LEROY PORTER

Editorial Consultant, Historian, Columnist, Poet, Writer, Lecturer. Personal: Born November 23, 1947; Son of Leroy and Doretha Porter. Education: B.A., Virginia State University, 1969; M.A., Atlanta University, 1972; Ph.D., Emory University, 1974; Additional Studies, Kent State University, University of Hawaii, Georgia State University, University of Colorado, Stanford University, University of Virginia, Cambridge University (Queens College). Military: Served in the United States Army, PFC, Hospital Corpsman, 1969-71. Career: Editorial Consultant; Historian; Columnist; Lecturer; Poet; Writer; Fulbright Scholar; Visiting Lecturer, Spelman and Morehouse Colleges, Atlanta, Georgia, 1971-72; Assistant Professor of History, Washington State University, Pullman, Washington, 1974-75; Assistant Educational Coordinator, Target Projects Program, Newport News, Virginia, 1977; Assistant Professor of History, Hampton Institute, Hampton, Virginia, 1977-80; Insurance Executive, North Carolina Mutual Insurance Company, Newport News, Virginia, 1980; Security Officer, Old Dominion Security Inc., Hampton, Virginia, 1981-82. Organizational Memberships: National Writer's Association; The American Association for the Advancement of Humanities; The Poetry Society of America. Community Activities: International Platform Association; International Biographical Association; Republican Party; Associate Club International; British Airways Executives Club; National Audubon Society; National Historical Society; United States Defense Committee; Big Brothers/Big Sisters of America; The Peninsula, Educational Columnist, 1976-83; Peninsula Council of Clubs, Recording Secretary 1980-81; Book Donation to Hampton City Library, 1983; United States Presidential Task Force, 1982; Huntington High School Alumni Association; Editorial Consultant for the American Biographical Institute 1982 to present, International Biographical Centre 1980 to present, Who's Who Among Black Americans Inc. 1976 to present, Marquis Who's Who Inc. 1981-83, Bernard Harris Publishing Company 1982, Big Brothers/Big Sisters of America 1982, Gale Research Company 1982-83. Religion: Children's Choir Pianist 1957-60, Youth Choir Pianist 1960-65, Shalom Baptist Church; Peninsula Church Pianists' Association, 1960-65; Sunday School Pianist, 1960-65. Honors and Awards: Fulbright Scholar; Birthday Honors List, Hampton Roads Jaycees, 1980; United States Presidential Medal of Merit, 1982; United States Presidential Honor Roll, 1982; United States Congressional Special Achievement Award, 1982; United States Presidential Task Force, 1982; Fellow of the International Biographical Association, Cambridge, England, 1982-83; Honorary Editorial Advisory Board Member for American Biographical Institute, 1982-83. Address: 3 Adrian Circle, Hampton, Virginia 23669.■

(MRS.) COLLICE HENRY PORTNOFF

Educator. Personal: Born December 9, 1898; Married George Portnoff (deceased); Mother of Lisa Crehan. Education: A.B. 1921, M.A. 1922, University of California at Berkeley; Ph.D., Stanford University, 1927; Carter Memorial Fellow, Academic Fellow, American Academy of Rome, 1927-30; M.A., 1930. Career: Professor of English 1945-69, Department Chairman and Acting Head of the Division of Language and Literature 1957-58, Chairman of the English Department 1957-64, Professor Emeritus 1969 to present, Arizona State University. Organizational Memberships: National Society of Arts and Letters; National Council of Teachers of English; Alumni Association of the American Academy of Rome; Rocky Mountain Modern Language Association, President 1964; Centro Studie e Scambi Internationali; American Translation Association. Community Activities: Director 1960, General Chairman 1961, Pageant of Miracle of Roses, Scottsdale, Arizona; Board of Directors, Phoenix Chamber Music Society; Board of Directors, Valley Shakespeare Theatre. Honors and Awards: Recipient of Medal for Achievement in Drama, National Society for Arts and Letters; Distinguished Teacher Award, Arizona State University Alumni Association. Address: 6310 North Quail Run Road, Paradise Valley, Arizona 85253.■

CHARLES STERLING PORTWOOD, III

Computing Company Executive. Personal: Born February 18, 1942, in Memphis; Son of Charles S. and Mary Ruth (Cochran) Portwood. Education: B.S. in Chemical Engineering, University of Kansas, 1964; M.S. in Nuclear Engineering, University of California at Berkeley, 1969; Ph.D. Business Administration, 1972. Career: Teaching Assistant, Nuclear Physics and Thermodynamics, University of California at Berkeley, 1964-65; Computer Consultant Radiation Hazard, Manned Spacecraft Center, Houston, Summer 1966; Physicist, Lawrence Radiation Laboratory, Berkeley, 1965-67; Systems Analyst, Office Secretary of Defense, Pentagon, Washington, Summer 1967; Computer and Statistical Analysis Department City and Regional Planning, University of California at Berkeley, 1968-69; Systems Designer, Space Sciences Laboratory, Berkeley, 1967-70; Assistant Professor of Business Economics and Statistics, College Business Administration, University of Hawaii, Honolulu 1970-71, Visiting Assistant Professor of Sociology 1972-73, Consultant Program in Futures Research 1972-74, Assistant Professor Education College of Education 1972-78, Director Evaluation Curriculum Research Group 1972-74, Assistant Professor Public Health School of Public Health 1977-78; President Pan Pacific Computing Company, 1978; Consultant in Statistics, Economics, Research Methodology, Educational Evaluation, 1970 to present; Director, Research Consultants Inc., Honolulu, 1970 to present; Appeared on *Voices of Dissent* Program, Station KGMB-TV, 1973; Member Tutorial Faculty, International College, Los Angeles, 1973-78; Futures Research Consultant, Hawaii State Legislature, 1973-74; Management Consultant; Guest Lecturer, Thai Ministry of Education 1976, Various Educational Institutions. Organizational Memberships: Association Computing Machinery; American Institute Decision Sciences. Published Works: Contributor Articles on Data and Mathematical Analysis to Professional Journals. Honors and Awards: NSF Research Grantee, 1974-75, University of Hawaii Grantee, 1970-71; Charles A. Haskins Scholar, 1963-64. Address: 2600 South King Street, Ste. 207, Honolulu, Hawaii 96826.■

JAMES RONALD POSEY

Clinical Social Psychologist. Personal: Born May 27, 1932; Son of Jewell and Isabelle Posey; Father of Janice Lynn, John Mark, Jill Annette, Jennifer Denise. Education: B.A., University of Redlands, 1954; B.D., Berkeley Baptist Divinity School, 1957; M.A., California State University at Sacramento, 1965; Ph.D., United States International University, 1971. Career: Clinical Social Psychologist; Former Positions include American Baptist Minister, Marriage Counselor, College Faculty in Social Psychology, Consultant to Law Enforcement Agencies, Staff Psychologist for Department of Corrections (Michigan), Criminal Justice Faculty Member. Organizational Memberships: American Psychological Association; Association for Humanistic Society; American Academy of Science. Community Activities: Board of Managers, San Jaun Young Men's Christian Association, 1958-62; Citizens Committee on Family Life Education, 1965; Foothill Farms Improvement Association, 1957-59; Faculty Senate, 1973-76; Numerous Consultancies, Police Agencies, 1972-76, Trainer, Department of Correction, New Jersey, 1973-77; Civil Rights, Environmental Protection; Rotary Club, 1981-82. Religion: Minister, First Baptist Church of Foothill Farms, 1957-62; First Baptist Church of Carmichael, Sunday School Teacher, Organizing Committee on Counseling Center. Honors and Awards: Freedom Foundation, 1960; Outstanding Educator of America, 1973; Nominee, Outstanding Young Man of America, Jaycees, 1976; Received Tenure, 1975; California State License, 1981; California State Education Administration Service Credential, 1981; Superior Achievement, State of California, 1982. Address: 8288 Cottonfield Way, Sacramento, California 95825.■

EUGENE POTENTE, JR.

Interior Designer. Personal: Son of Mr. and Mrs. Eugene Potente, Sr.; Married Joan C.; Father of Eugene J., Peter M., John, Suzanne M. Education: Ph.B.,

TWO THOUSAND NOTABLE AMERICANS

Marquette University, 1943; Military Government, Foreign Affairs, Stanford University, 1944; New York School of Interior Design, 1948; Military: Served in the United States Army Military Government as Sergeant Investigator. Career: President, Studios of Potente Inc.; Architectural Services Associates, Inc.; Business Leasing Services of Wisconsin, Inc. Organizational Memberships: Interfaith Forum on Religion, Art and Architecture, President 1982-83; American Society for Church Architecture, Treasurer 1976-78; American Society of Interior Designers, Treasurer Wisconsin Chapter 1981-87; Institute of Business Designers; Interior Designer Member, Vice Chairman, Wisconsin State Capitol and Executive Mansion Board, 1981-87; Rotary International. Religion: Roman Catholic. Honors and Awards: Member, Alpha Sigma Nu; Member, Kappa Tau Alpha. Address: 6634 Third Avenue, Kenosha, Wisconsin 53140.■

J. W. POU

Educational Administrator. Personal: Born July 8, 1917; Son of Mr. and Mrs. W. C. Pou (deceased); Married; Father of John Jr., David, Connie. Education: B.S., North Carolina State University; M.S., University of Wisconsin; Ph.D., Cornell University. Military: Served in the United States Army, Pacific Ocean Areas Theatre, 1943-45, attaining the rank of Major; Retired Lieutenant Colonel, United States Army Reserve. Career: Assistant Director, Cooperative Extension Service, University of Georgia at Athens; Former Positions include Vice President of Wachovia Bank and Trust Company of North America, Director of Cooperative Extension Service of the University of Arizona at Tucson, Head of Animal Industry Department of North Carolina State University, Head of Dairy Department at University of Maryland. Organizational Memberships: President, Association of Agricultural Bankers; President, Coastal Plain Planning and Development Commission; President, North Carolina Society of Farm Managers and Rural Appraisers; Chairman, Agricultural Committee, North Carolina Bankers Association; Chairman, Western States Agricultural Extension Service Directors; Chairman, Southern Division, American Dairy Science Association. Community Activities: Board of Trustees, North Carolina State University; Board of Trustees, North Carolina Teachers and State Employees Retirement System; President, North Carolina State University Alumni Association; President, Greenville (North Carolina) Chamber of Commerce and Merchants Association; President, North Carolina 4-H Development Fund Inc.; President, Pitt County (North Carolina) United Fund; President, Pitt County Mental Health Association; Chairman, Committee on Honorary Degrees, North Carolina State University; Chairman, Long Range Planning Committee, School of Agriculture; Chairman, Board of Directors, North Carolina State University Young Men's Christian Association; Chairman, Eastern Lung Association Christmas Seal Campaign; Chairman, Bond Campaign for New Pitt County Memorial Hospital; Coach, National Champion 4-H Dairy Cattle Judging Team; Governor's Civil Defense Council, State of Arizona; Arizona Agricultural Conservation and Stabilization State Committee; U.S.D.A. Disaster Committee for State of Arizona; Rotary Club, President Greenville (North Carolina) Club 1969-70; Farm House; Alpha Zeta; Phi Kappa Phi; Gamma Sigma Delta; Epsilon Sigma Phi; Alpha Tau Alpha; Lambda Gamma Delta; Golden Chain; Blue Key; Georgia Land Development Association, Secretary. Religion: Chairman, Board of Deacons, Oakmont Baptist Church, Greenville, North Carolina, 1970. Honors and Awards: North Carolina 4-H Alumni Award, 1962; The University of Arizona Medallion Award of Merit, 1961; Pitt County United Fund Outstanding Citizenship Award, 1964; Future Farmers of America Outstanding Service Award, 1965; Exchange Club Book of Golden Deeds Award, 1968; President's Key Award, Greenville (North Carolina) Chamber of Commerce and Merchants Association, 1969; Greenville Citizen of the Year, 1970; Distinguished Alumni Award, North Carolina State University, 1977; Agricultural Spokesman of the Year, *Farm Chemicals Magazine*, 1974. Address: 379 Sandstone Drive, Athens, Georgia 30605.■

CLARA JEAN (HILL) POULOS

Registered Nutrition Specialist. Personal: Born January 1, 1941; Daughter of Clara G. Hill; Married Themis. Education: Ph.D. Nutrition, Donsbach University; Ph.D., Florida State University; B.Sc. Biology, Christian University; M.Sc. Biology, Florida State University; L.V.N., Cabrillo College Vocational Nursing Program; Attended Smith Business College; Clinical Hypnotherapist, College of Clinical Hypnosis, Hawaii. Career: Registered Nutrition Specialist; Director Research, Leapou Laboratory, Aptos, 1973-76; Monterey Bay Research Institute, Santa Cruz, California, 1976; Nutrition Specialist in Private Practice, Santa Cruz, 1975 to present; Instructor, Santa Cruz Extension University of California; Instructor, Stoddard Associates; Seminars Consultant to Biological-Medical Laboratory, Chicago-Nutra-Med Research Corporation, New York; Akor-Miller Pharmaceuticals; Chicago-Monterey Bay Aquaculture Farms; Ressurection Distribution, Dartell Laboratories. Organizational Memberships: Fellow, International College of Applied Nutrition; American Nutritionist Association; International Academy Nutritional Consultants; American Diabetes Association; American Association for the Advancement of Science; American Public Health Association; California Academy of Science; International Fishery Association. Community Activities: International Platform Society; International Toastmistress; American Federal Chess Association. Honors and Awards: NuJulander International Research Award, 1971; Wainwright Foundation Award, 1979; Various State and Local Awards. Address: 921 Brommer Street, Santa Cruz, California 95062.■

DWIGHT E. POWELL

University Educator, Administrator. Personal: Born February 6, 1948; Son of James C. Powell, Lyvonne O. Powell; Married; Father of Ryan Thomas. Education: Attended South City College 1966-69, University of Illinois-Chicago Circle Campus (Summer) 1968; Graduate, Roosevelt University, 1971; M.S.W., University of Illinois-Chicago Circle Campus, Jane Addams School of Social Work, 1975; Various Educational Certificates. Career: Assistant Specialist in Aging (Geriatrician), Mayor's Office for Senior Citizens, Chicago, 2 Years; Law Clerk, S. Ira Miller, Attorney at Law, 3 Years; Social Worker, Jane Addams School of Social Work, Miles Square Mental Health Center, 1 Year; Social Worker, Maywood (Illinois) Police Department, 1 Year; Adult Probation Officer, Cook County Adult Probation Department, Chicago, 18 Months; Social Worker II, Methodist Youth Service, Chicago, 1 Year; Social Worker II, United Charities of Chicago, 5 Years; Faculty Member, Coordinator of Adult and Family Services, Chicago State University, 1976 to present; Faculty Member, Malcolm X College, Chicago; Family Service and Mental Health Center of South Cook County, Harvey, Illinois/Chicago Height, Illinois, Supervising Student, Therapist. Organizational Memberships: Association of Retired Persons; National Association of Social Workers; National Registry of Health Care Providers for Psychiatric Social Workers; The Substance Abuse Service of Chicago, Board Member. Community Activities: Avalon Park-Chatham Community Youth Center, Youth Counselor, Director/ Sponsor; Illinois Probation Department, Parole and Correctional Association Member. Published Works: Articles "Crimes Against the Elderly" 1980, "The Joys of Aging" 1980, "Self-Acceptance" 1979, "Pluses and Minuses" 1979. Honors and Awards: Listed in *Who's Who in the Midwest, Personalities of the West and Midwest, Men of Achievement*. Address: 8231 Jeffery, Chicago, Illinois 60617.■

ANN POWELL-BROWN

Publicist and Educator. Personal: Born March 19, 1947; Daughter of Ethel B. Powell; Married Richard L. Brown. Education: B.S. Education 1969, M.S. Reading 1974, Central Missouri State University; Ph.D. Candidate, University of Missouri at Kansas City, 1982. Career: Co-Owner and Executive, American Media Escorts; Special Education Placement and Learning Disabilities Identification Teams, Kansas City School District, 1973-84; Adjunct Faculty, University of Missouri at Kansas City 1981, Ottawa University 1980, Providence College (Taichung, Taiwan) 1972; Classroom Teacher, Biloxi, Mississippi, 1969-71. Organizational Memberships: Council for Exceptional Children; Association for Children with Learning Disabilities; Pi Lambda Theta; International Reading Association, Secretary Kansas City Branch 1974; American Anthropological Association. Community Activities: Eggs and Issues; The Central Exchange; International Relations Council of Kansas City; Friends of Art, Nelson Museum; Friends of St. Mary's, Founder, Member Board of Directors 1982; American Association of University Women; Committee for Indochinese Development, Vice President 1977; Gray Panthers; Educational Council of Episcopal Diocese, Western Missouri, 1977; Public Affairs Committee, Jewish Community Center, 1978; Speaker, Various Organizations. Religion: St. Andrews Episcopal Church and Challinor Guild. Honors and Awards: Listed in *Outstanding Young Women of America, Who's Who in the Midwest*. Address: 501 Knickerbocker Place, Kansas City, Missouri 64111.■

PAUL W. POWERS

State Senator. Personal: Born September 13, 1942; Son of Phil and Martha Powers. Education: Degree in Economics-Marketing, University of Iowa, 1964-66; Public Policy, American University Graduate School, 1971-72; Graduate, Wahlert High School, Iowa. Military: Served in the United States Army and the Iowa National Guard. Career: Colorado State Senator; Cattle Ranch Owner and Operator, McCoy, Colorado; President and Founder, North American Construction Company. Organizational Memberships: Metro Denver Executive Club; Co-Chairman, Colorado Reagan for President Committee, 1980; Colorado State Senator, Republican, Denver District 6 Committee Assignments as Chairman of Judiciary, Member of Appropriations, Transportation, Finance, Legal Services and Statutory Revision Committees, 1978 to present; Boys Club of Denver, Member Board of Directors, Denver Regional Council of Governments, Regional Airport Advisory Committee, President and Founder of Denver Organization for Job Placement of Disadvantaged Youths, 1981 to present. Religion: Catholic. Honors and Awards: County Division of Disabled Board, Legislator of the Year, 1981; Listed in *Who's Who in the West*. Address: 333 Vine Street, Denver, Colorado 80206.■

DANIEL FRANK POYNTER

Author and Publisher. Personal: Born September 17, 1938; Son of William F. Poynter. Education: Graduate, Lowell High School, San Francisco, 1956; B.A. Social Science, California State University at Chico, 1960; Postgraduate Work, San Francisco Law School, 2 Years. Military: Served in the California National Guard and the United States Army Reserve, 1956-74. Career: Author/Publisher; Former Position as Parachute Design Specialist. Organizational Memberships: United States Parachute Association, Life Member 1962 to present, Secretary (2 terms), Chairman of the Board, Executive Committee (2 terms), Equipment Inspector at National Parachuting Championships (10 years), Member Competition Jury, Jury President, Training Judge, Competitor, Served with 3 United States Parachute Teams as Observer and Chief of Delegation in Bulgaria 1966, Germany 1975, Australia 1977, Chairman of Safety and Training Committee (3 terms), Chairman of Constitution and By-Laws Committee, Chairman Publications Committee, Member Awards and Other Committees, Testified at Numerous State and Federal Hearings on Behalf of Sport Parachuting, Served as USPA Delegate to National Sport Aviation Council, Past Alternate Delegate to Commission Internationale du Parachutism of the Federation Aeronautique Internationale in Paris, Instrumental in Establishing the USPA Jumpmaster and Instructor Programs; Parachute Equipment Industry Association, Member, Past Secretary, Past Chairman of FAA-SAE-USPA Parachute Technical Standard Order Committee, Past Editor of PEIA News-briefs; National Aeronautic Association, Member, Past USPA Delegate to Annual Meeting; Calistoga Skydivers, Past Secretary; Northern California Parachute Council, Past Delegate and Secretary; Northeast Sport Parachute Council, Past Delegate, Secretary and President, Past Editor *Spotter Newsmagazine*; Experimental Aircraft Association; Survival and Flight Equipment Association; Soaring Society of America; American Institute of Aeronautics and Astronautics, Served on Aerodynamic Decelerator (parachtues) and Balloon Technology Technical Committee, Session Chairman for 1979 Conference in Houston; United States Hang Gliding Association, Life Member, Past Director, Instrumental in Establishing the Instructor Program and Basic Board Organization (committee system), Chief of the United States Delegation to the World Hang Gliding Championships in Austria 1976; Commission Internationale de Vol Libre (Hang Gliding) of the Federation Aeronautique Internationale in Paris, United States Delegate, Two-Term Past President, Lifetime President d'Honneur; International Frisbee Association; United States Flying Tube Association, Founding Member; Aviation/Space Writers Association, Took Part in International News Conferences in Israel in 1978, Colombia 1979, Netherlands 1983; COSMEP, International Association of Independent Publishers, Two-Term Director, Established Several Programs including the Chapter Concept and the Book Exhibit Service, Served as Panelist at Conferences in Port Townsend, Washington in 1979, California, Pennsylvania in 1980, San Francisco in 1981, Contributed Articles to *The Independent Publisher*; Santa Barbara Chapter of COSMPE, President 1979-82; Association of American Publishers; Museum of Parachuting and Air Safety, Past Director; Book Publicists of Southern California. Published Works: Contributor Technical and Popular Articles and Numerous Photographs to Professional Journals; Author Numerous Books including *The Parachute Manual, Parachuting, The Skydivers' Handbook, Parachute Rigging Course, Parachuting Instructor/Examiner Course, Parachuting Manual with Log, Manual Basico de Paracaidismo* (Spanish), *Hang Gliding, Manned Kiting, Hang Gliding Manual with Log, Handbuch des Drachenfliegers* (German), *Hang Gliding* (Russian), *Frisbee Players' Handbook, Frisbee* (Japanese), *Toobee Players' Handbook, The Self-Publishing Manual, How To Write, Print and Sell Your Own Book, Publishing Short-Run Books, Book Fairs, Business Letters for Publishers, Computer Selection Guide, Word Processors and Information Processing*; Contributor Numerous Chapters to Books. Honors and Awards: Issued United States Patent for Parachute Pack Pop Top Container, 1975; Achievement Award, United States Parachute Association, 1981; 20-Year Certificate of Membership, United States Parachute Association, 1981; Diplome de Vol Libre, Federation Aeronautique Internationale, 1979; Gold Parachutists Wings, United States Parachute Association, 1972; Meritorious Achievement Award, Central Atlantic Sport Parachute Association; Numerous Certificates of Appreciation for Service in Various Events and Programs such as the One from Lake Placid, New York, Chamber of Commerce for Directing their Parachuting Competition for Seven Years; Listed in *The International Authors and Writers Who's Who, Who's Who in California, Contemporary Authors, Who's Who in the West, Jane's Who's Who in Aviation and Aerospace, Men of Achievement, Personalities of America, The Social Register*, Listed as an Expert Witness by the National Forensic Center, Technical Advisory Service for Attorneys, *The Lawyer's Guide to Legal Consultants, Expert Witnesses, Services, Books and Products*. Address: RR #1, Box P, Goleta, California.■

RICHARD A. POZNIAK

Public Relations Administrator. Personal: Born December 7, 1947; Son of Benjamin and Eleanor Pozniak; Married Sandra; Father of Alexa, Jonathan. Education: B.S. Business and Organizational Communications, Emerson College; Further Studies at the Executive Management Institute, Wharton School, University of Pennsylvania and New York University. Career: Public Relations Director, Massachusetts Hospital Association; Former Press Aide to President Jimmy Carter and Boston Mayor Kevin White, Public Relations Director at Babson College, Emerson College and Builders Association of Boston. Organizational Memberships: Public Relations Society of America; Publicity Club of Boston; International Association of Business Communicators. Community Activities: Board of Directors, Consumers Credit Counseling Service of Eastern Massachusetts. Honors and Awards: Gold Quill Award for Excellence in Public Affairs, International Association of Business Communicators, 1983; Bell Ringer Award for Excellence in Public Affairs, Publicity Club of Boston, 1981, 1983. Address: 11 Chester Road, Billerica, Massachusetts 01866.■

JUAN DE DIOS POZO-OLANO

Corporate Executive and Public Health Expert. Personal: Born March 8, 1947; Son of Máximo Pozo Cáceres; Married Teresita A., Daughter of Cristino F. Alfaro; Father of Juan de Dios Jr., Jean-Jacques. Education: D.Sc., University of Paris, La Sorbonne, 1967; Ph.D., San Marcos University, Lima, 1969; M.P.H., Harvard University, 1976. Career: Corporate Executive and Public Health Expert; Has Contributed Extensively to Biomedical Research, specifically to the Fields of Developmental and Clinical Neurology; Currently Involved in International Health Programs Promoting Better Health Care in Poorer Countries. Organizational Memberships: International Brain Research Organization, 1967 to present. Community Activities: Pugwash Conferences on Science and World Affairs, 1965 to present. Religion: Catholic. Published Works: Author Numerous Works on the Electric Activity of the Human Brain. Honors and Awards: Scholarship from the French Government and the Organization of American States to Pursue Studies at La Sorbonne in Paris; Scholarship from United States Public Health Service to Pursue Studies in Public Health at Harvard University, 1975-76; Fellow at Fletcher School of Law and Diplomacy Assigned in Residence to Mexico to Organize the University of Monterrey Medical School, 1974-75; First Latin American Invited to Become a Member of the Pugwash Conferences on Science and World Affairs. Address: 7021 Old Dominion Drive, McLean, Virginia 22101.■

GERALD DAVID PRAGER

Geologist. Personal: Born October 25, 1940; Son of Omar R. Prager; Married Brenda Gayle, Daughter of Sadie M. Stamm. Education: B.S., University of Kansas, 1962; C.A.G.S., Northeastern University, 1978; Ph.D., University of Cincinnati, 1971. Military: Served in the United States Navy, 1962-66, Lieutenant. Career: Geologist; Exploration Stratigrapher, Texaco, Inc.; Chief Geologist, Howard-Donley Associates, 1980-81; Professor, Ohio University, 1978-80; Professor, Northeastern University, 1973-78. Organizational Memberships: American Association of Petroleum Geologists; Geological Society of America; Society of Exploration Geophysicists; American Society of Photogrammetrists; Sigma Xi. Honors and Awards: National Merit Scholar, 1958; Haworth Award, 1962; W. A. Tarr Award, 1962; N.D.E.A. Fellowship, 1966-70. Address: 2027 St. Nick Drive, New Orleans, Louisiana 70114.■

OM PRAKASH

Psychiatrist. Personal: Born August 10, 1933; Son of Rameshwar Prasad Gupta; Father of Eva, Om II, Neal. Education: M.D., Patna Medical College, Patna University, Patna, India, 1959; House Officer in Surgery 1959, House Officer in Medicine 1960, Patna Medical College Hospital; Diploma in Tropical Diseases and Hygiene, London, England, 1961; Rotating Intern in Doctors Hospital, Toronto, Canada, 1961-62; Straight Intern in Pathology, Michael Reese Hospital, Chicago, Illinois, 1962-63; Residency in General Psychiatry, Illinois State University, Chicago, Illinois, 1963-65; Residency in Child Psychiatry, University of Iowa, Iowa City, Iowa, 1965-66; Residency in Child Psychiatry, University of Missouri (Kansas City General Hospital), Kansas City, Missouri, 1966-67; Attended Courses at University of California at Los Angeles 1967, Columbia University (New York) 1972-73, American Academy of Psychiatry and Law Tri-State Chapter (New York) 1981-82, Forensic Psychiatry Clinic of the Criminal and Supreme Courts of New York 1982-83, Training Program in RDC and SADS at the College of Physicians and Surgeons, Department of Psychiatry, Columbia University; Board Certified in General Psychiatry, 1978; Board Certified in Child Psychiatry, 1981. Career: Faculty Member, American Academy of Psychiatry and Law, Tri-State Chapter, New York, 1982-83; In Charge of Female Adolescent Unit, Youth Center, St. Louis State Hospital, St. Louis, Missouri, 1967; Medical Director, Day Care Center of Ingham County, Lansing, Michigan, 1968; In Charge of Youth Center, Rochester State Hospital, Rochester, New York, 1968; Chief Psychiatrist, Queensboro Rehabilitation Center, Office of Drug Abuse, State of New York, 1970-76; Administrative and Clinical Psychiatrist, Multiple Disability Units, Creedmoor Psychiatric Center, Queens Village, New York, 1976-78; Medical Administrator (half-time), Creedmoor Psychiatric Center (Elm York Adult Home), Queens, New York, 1980-83; Clinical Psychiatrist II (half-time), S.S.U., Creedmoor Psychiatric Center, Queens, New York, 1983 to present; Director, Department of Psychiatry, Wyckoff Heights Hospital, Brooklyn, New York, 1980 to present. Organizational Memberships: Active Fellow, American Psychiatric Association, American Academy of Child Psychiatry, American College of International Physicians, New York Medical Society, American Society of Law and Medicine, American Academy of Psychiatry and Law. Honors and Awards: Physician's Recognition Award, American Association for Continuing Medical Education, 1969, 1972, 1975, 1978, 1981, 1984. Address: 85-95 188th Street, Holliswood, New York 11423.■

JOHN WEBSTER PRAMBERG

Certified Public Accountant. Education: B.S. Organizational Behavior, Babson College, Babson Park, Massachusetts, 1976; M.S. Taxation, Bentley College Waltham, Massachusetts, 1979. Career: Certified Public Accountant. Organizational Memberships: Steering Committee, National Tax Limitation Committee, Washington, D.C.; National Taxpayer's Union, Washington, D.C.; American Association of Independent Investors, Chicago, Illinois; Sponsor, National Taxpayer's Legal Fund, Washington, D.C. Community Activities: Chairman, Ward 3 Newburyport Republican Committee; Commissioner, City of Newburyport Conservation Commission; Incorporator, Newburyport Health Center; National Advisory Board, American Security Council, Washington, D.C.; International Platform Association, Cleveland Heights, Ohio; Newburyport Republican City Committee; START-A Republican Campaign Organization, Boston; Committee to Elect a Republican Legislature, Boston; Citizens for Reagan, Washington, D.C.; Americans for Change, Washington, D.C.; American Conservative Union, Washington, D.C.; Essex County (Massachusetts) Conservative Club; Accuracy in Media, Washington D.C.; HALT-An Organization of Americans for Legal Reform, Washington, D.C.; U.S. Consumers Association, Washington D.C.; Bentley College Century Club, Waltham, Massachusetts; Bentley College Career Advising Network, Waltham, Massachusetts; Theta Chi Fraternity; Phi Delta Phi Fraternity; Merrimack River (Massachusetts) Watershed Council; Essex County (Massachusetts) Greenbelt Association; Earthwatch, Belmont, Massachusetts; Cousteau Society, New York City; National Audubon Society, New York City; International Crane Foundation, Baraboo, Wisconsin; Oceanic Society, Stamford, Connecticut; Wilderness Society, Washington, D.C.; The Nature Conservancy, Arlington, Virginia; WNEH-TV, New Hampshire Public Television; Sons and Daughters of the First Settlers of Olde Newbury, Massachusetts; Historical Society of Olde Newbury, Massachusetts; Newburyport Maritime Society; Essex Institute, Salem, Massachusetts; Museum of Fine Arts, Boston; Sustaining Member, Republican National Committee, Washington, D.C.; National Associate, Metropolitan Museum of Art, New York City; Smithsonian Institution, Washington, D.C. Honors and Awards: Member National Honorary Ronald Reagan Inaugural Committee; Recipient, City of Newburyport Fire Prevention Award; Veterans of Foreign Wars Voice of Democracy Public Speaking Award. Address: P.O. Box 455, Newburyport, Massachusetts 01950.■

GHILLEAN TOLMIE PRANCE

Senior Vice President for Science. Personal: Born July 13, 1937; Son of Basil Camden and Margaret Hope Prance (deceased); Married Anne E.; Father of Rachel Julia, Sarah Elizabeth. Education: Attended Malvern College, Worcestershire, England, 1952-56; B.A. with honors 1960, M.A. 1965, D.Ph. Botany 1963, Oxford University. Career: Research Assistant 1963-66, Associate Curator 1966-68, B. A. Krukoff Curator of Amazonian Botany 1968-75, Director Botanical Research 1975-81, Vice President 1977-81, Senior Vice President for Science 1981 to present, New York Botanical Garden; Director, New York Botanical Garden Institute of Economic Botany, 1981 to present; Adjunct Professor, Lehman College, City University of New York, 1968 to present, Member Graduate Faculty 1969 to present; Director of Graduate Training Program in Tropical Botany at Instituto Nacional de Pesquisas da Amazonia, Manaus, Brazil for its Initial 2 Years, 1973-75. Organizational Memberships: Fellow, Linnean Society of London; Fellow, Explorers Club, Elected 1978; American Society of Plant Taxonomists; American Institute of Biological Sciences; Botanical Society of the British Isles; Interciencia Association; Botanical Society of America; International Association for Plant Taxonomy; Sociedade Botanica de Brasil; Sociedade Brasileira para o Progresso da Ciencia; Society of Economic Botany; Society of Systematic Zoology; The Association for Tropical Biology; The Association pour l'etude Taxonomique de le Flore d'Afrique Tropicale; The Torrey Botanical Club; The New York Academy of Sciences; Editorial Advisor for Bulletin of the Torrey Botanical Club, 1969 to present; Editorial Advisory Board for *Acta Amazonica*, 1971 to present; Editorial Advisory Board, *Biotropica*, 1976 to present; Member Faculty Publications Committee of Columbia University Press, 1976-82; Botanical Editor of *Evolutionary Biology*, 1980 to present. Community Activities: Member Mayor's Cable Television Commission, White Plains, New York, 1981 to present. Published Works: Editor of "Extinction is Forever," Proceedings of a Symposium on the Status of Threatened and Endangered Plants of the Americas, The New York Botanical Garden, 1977 (co-editor T. S. Elias); "Biological Diversification in the Tropics," Proceedings of the 5th ATB Symposium Caracas, Venezuela, 1979, Columbia University Press, 1981. Honors and Awards: Recipient Several National Science Foundation Grants for Plant Survey of Brazilian Amazonia and Associate Monographic Studies; Boldero Natural History Prize, Malvern College, 1956; Diploma de Honra ao Mérito, Instituto Nacional de Pesquisas da Amazonia, 1978; Diploma de Honora ao Mérito, Instituto Nacional de Pesquisas da Amazonia, Herbarium 100,000th Specimen Commemoration, 1981; Fil. Dr. honoris causa. Address: 18 Midchester Avenue, White Plains, New York 10606.■

ANANDA S. PRASAD

Professor of Medicine, Division Director, Hospital Staff Member. Personal: Born January 1, 1928; Married Aryabala; Father of Rita, Sheila, Ashok, Audrey. Education: B.Sc., Patna Science College, 1946; M.B., B.S., Patna Medical College, 1951; Ph.D. Medicine, University of Minnesota, 1957. Career: Instructor, Department of Medicine, University Hospital, University of Minnesota, 1957-58; Visiting Associate Professor of Medicine, Shiraz Medical Faculty and Associate in Medicine, Nemazer Hospital, Shiraz, Iran, 1958-60; Visiting Professor and Chairman, Department of Medicine, Shiraz Medical Faculty, University of Shiraz and Associate in Medicine, Nemazee Hospital, Shiraz, Iran, 1960; Assistant Professor of Medicine in Nutrition, Vanderbilt University, Nashville, Tennessee; Director, Nutrition Program, United States Naval Medical Research Unit #3, Cairo, U.A.R., 1961-63; Assistant Professor of Medicine, Chief of Hematology Division 1963-64, Professor of Medicine and Director Division of Hematology 1968 to present, Wayne State University School of Medicine; Staff, Veterans Administration Hospital, Allen Park, Michigan, 1965 to present; Associate Chief of Staff for Research, Veterans Administration Hospital, Allen Park, Michigan, 1976-78. Organizational Memberships: American Board of Nutrition, Diplomate; Alpha Omega Alpha; American College of Physicians, Fellow; American Federation for Clinical Research; American Institute of Nutrition; American Medical Association; American Physiological Society; American Society for Clinical Investigation; American Society for Clinical Nutrition; American Society of Hematology; American Society of Internal Medicine; Association of America Physicians; Central Society for Clinical Research; Cosmos Club, Washington D.C.; Council of Biology Editors; International Society of Hematology, Fellow; Michigan State Medical Society; Minnesota Alumni Association; National Academy of Sciences, National Research Council, Food and Nutrition Board, Subcommittee on Trace Elements, 1965-68; Scientific Councils of the American Heart Association; Sigma Xi; Society for Experimental Biology and Medicine, Councillor Michigan Chapter 1967-71; Wayne County Medical Society; World-Wide Academy of Scholars; Certified by the American Board of Nutrition; Licensed in Michigan and Great Britain. Community Activities: Awards Committee, American Society of Clinical Nutrition, 1969-70; American Federation for Clinical Research, Ann Arbor, Detroit, Toledo, East Lansing Chapter, Councillor and Secretary-Treasurer 1966-68, President-elect 1968-69, President 1969-70, Chairman Zinc Session, F.A.S.E.B., Atlantic City, New Jersey, 1971; Chairman, Selenium Session, F.A.S.E.B., Atlantic, New Jersey, 1971; Chairman, Selenium Session, F.A.S.E.B., Atlantic City, 1972; Trace Elements Panel, American Institute of Nutrition; Co-Chairman, Zinc Session, F.A.S.E.B., Atlantic City, 1973; Chairman, Hematology Section, Central Society for Clinical Research, Chicago, Illinois, 1973; Chairman, International Symposium on Trace Elements in Human Health and Disease, Detroit, 1974; Chairman, Trace Metals and Their Blood Cell Effects Section of Fourth International Symposium on Red Cell Metabolism and Function, University of Michigan, Ann Arbor, 1974, 1977; Chairman, Zinc Session, F.A.S.E.B., Atlantic City 1975, Anaheim, California 1976; Co-Chairman,

Symposium on Zinc Metabolism, Meyer Laboratories Institute of Research, Fort Lauderdale, Florida, 1976; Chairman, Zinc Session, F.A.S.E.B., Dallas, Texas, 1979; Consultant, Ad Hoc Conference on Adverse Health Effects of Nutrients in Man, F.A.S.E.B., Bethesda, Maryland, 1979; Chairman, Committee 5, Trace Elements in Human Nutrition, of Commission IV, International Union of Nutritional Sciences (IUNS), 1979-81; Member Honorary Committee of the International Center for the Study of Trace Elements, Club UNESCO du Rhone, Lyon, 1982. Published Works: Author Over 200 Articles, Reports, and Chapters in Books on Subjects in his Field (combined). Honors and Awards: Caldwell Memorial Prize, 1944; Pfizer Resident Scholarship, 1955-56; Awarded Title of Honorary Professor of Medicine, University of Shiraz, Iran, 1960; Research Recognition Award, Wayne State University School of Medicine, 1964; Joseph Goldberger Award in Clinical Nutrition, American Medical Association, 1975; American College of Nutrition Award, Montreal, 1976; Elected Fellow of the American Association for the Advancement of Sciences; Robert H. Herman Award, American Society of Clinical Nutrition, 1984; Listed in *Who's Who in America, Who's Who in the World, Who's Who in World Science.* Address: 4710 Cove Road, Orchard Lake, Michigan 48033.■

Sartell Prentice, Jr.

Counselor on Incentive Employee Profit Participation Programs, Lecturer. Personal: Born December 28, 1903; Son of Rev. Sartell Prentice and Lydia Beekman Venderpoel Prentice; Married Marjorie Phelps Koop in 1930 (divorced); Married Second Wife Agnes L. Papekas (divorced); Married Third Wife Elinor L. Haight Buck (deceased, 1977); Married Fourth Wife Geraldine Eleanor Hoyt (deceased); Father of (from first marriage) Patricia Phelps, Adelaide Vanderpoel (both deceased), (from second marriage) Peter Sartell. Education: Taft School; Yale University; B.A., Stanford University, 1925; M.B.A., Harvard Business School, 1927; Attended Freedom School, Colorado, 1957; Courses at Free Enterprise Institute, Los Angeles, 1962 to present. Career: Security Salesman, National Cash Credit Association, New York, 1928-31; Training for Foreign Service, Socony Vacuum Oil Company, New York, 1931; Executive Assistant to the President, Vacuum Oil Company, S.A.I., Genoa, Italy, 1931-35; Marketing Assistant, Foreign Department, Socony Vacuum Oil Company, New York, 1935; Research, Script Writer, March of Time Movie and Radio, New York, 1935-37; Actor, Summer Stock, Barter Theatre, Abingdon, Virginia, 1938; Salesman, Automatic Canteen Company, New York, 1940-41; Public Relations, Advertising Representative, *Time* Magazine, New York and Boston, 1941-46; Administrative Secretary, Commission of the Churches on International Affairs, 1947-48; Field Secretary, Northeastern Chapter, Council on Profit Sharing Industries (now Profit Sharing Council of America), 1950-54; On Lecture Circuit, Associated Clubs of America (addressed dinner clubs throughout the country), 1956-58; New York State Chairman, National Committee for Economic Freedom, 1960; Counselor for Profit Sharing, 1954 to present. Organizational Memberships: International Platform Association; American Waldemsian Aid Society, Director 1944-61; Society of Professional Management Consultants, Inc., Charter Member; The Western Pension Conference; Town Hall of California; Toastmasters International; International Platform Association; Yale, Stanford, Harvard and Harvard Business School Clubs of Southern California. Religion: Protestant. Published Works: Articles have appeared in *Management Review, Stanford Review, Rampart Journal of Individualist Thought, Journal of Management,* as well as Many Others. Honors and Awards: Liberty Award, Congress of Freedom Inc., 1967, 1973, 1974, 1975, 1976, 1977; Twice Recognized by Having His Talks Published in *Vital Speeches of the Day;* Listed in *Two Thousand Men of Achievement, Men of Achievement, Who's Who in Finance and Industry, Who's Who in the West, Royal Blue Book, Blue Book, Dictionary of International Biography, Personalities of the West and Midwest, Community Leaders and Noteworthy Americans, Notable Americans, Register of Prominent Americans.* Address: 1404 Chamberlain Road, Pasadena, California 91103.■

Frederick Willard Preston

Surgeon and Director of Surgical Education. Personal: Born June 27, 1912; Father of Frederick Willard Jr., David Eldred, William Blackmore. Education: B.A., Yale University, 1935; M.D. 1940, M.S. Physiology 1942, Northwestern University; M.S. Surgery, University of Minnesota, 1947. Military: Served in the United States Army, Mediterranean and European Theaters, First Lieutenant to Major, 1943-45. Career: Associate Surgeon, Cook County Hospital, 1948-49; Attending Surgeon, Veterans Administration Hospital, Hines, Illinois, 1950-53; Assistant Attending Surgeon, Chicago Wesley Memorial Hospital, 1950-62; Associate Attending Surgeon, Chicago Wesley Memorial Hospital (now Northwestern Memorial Hospital), 1962-75; Staff, Veterans Administration Research Hospital, Chicago, 1953-72, Chief Surgical Service 1953-67; Senior Attending Surgeon, Henrotin and Skokie Valley Community Hospitals, 1967-75; Santa Barbara General Hospital, Chairman Department of Surgery and Director of Surgical Education 1975-78; Santa Barbara Cottage Hospital, Director of Surgical Education, 1975 to present; Clinical Assistant in Surgery, University of Illinois, 1948-49; Instructor in Surgery, 1950-52; Associate in Surgery, 1952-53; Assistant Professor of Surgery, 1953-58; Associate Professor of Surgery, 1958-60; Professor of Surgery, Northwestern University Medical School, 1960-75; Research Physiologist, University of California, Santa Barbara, 1976 to present. Organizational Memberships: American Association for Cancer Research, President Chicago Section 1963-64; American College of Surgeons, President Chicago Metropolitan Chapter 1965-66, Councilor Chicago Metropolitan Chapter 1965-66, Councilor Chicago Metropolitan Chapter 1967-70; American Federation of Clinical Research; American Geriatric Society; American Medical Association; American Surgical Association; American Trauma Society; Association for Clinical Surgery; Association of Surgeons of the Veterans Administration, Councilor 1967-69; Central Surgical Association; Chicago Academy of Sciences, Secretary 1961-67; Chicago Surgical Society, Secretary 1961-63, President 1968-69, Councilor 1969-72; Institute of Medicine of Chicago; Mayo Clinic Alumni Association; Pacific Coast Surgical Association; Pan-Pacific Surgeon Association; Priestly Society; Société Internationale de Chirurgie; Society for Surgery of the Alimentary Tract; Reticuloendothelial Society; Western Surgical Association, Recorder 1961-67. Community Activities: Village of Winnetka Caucus Committee, 1956; Board of Trustees, English Speaking Union, Chicago Chapter, 1960-65; Board of Trustees, Schweppe Foundation, 1958 to present; Advisory Committee on Arrangements, American College of Surgeons, 1958, 1961, Secretary 1958; Chicago Committee on Trauma, American College of Surgeons, 1962-75; Local Committee on Arrangements, Central Surgical Association, 1963, 1966, 1969, Chairman 1963; Nominating Committee, Central Surgical Association, 1964; Committee of Judges for Chicago Surgical Society, Prize Essay Award, Chairman 1964; Medical and Scientific Committee, Illinois Division, American Cancer Society, 1961 and 1971; Professional Education Committee, Illinois Division, American Cancer Society, 1971-75; Editorial Board, Lewis' Practice of Surgery, Hoeber Medical Division, Harper and Row, Publishers, Inc., Hagerstown, Maryland, 1961-76; MedicoTeam Serving in Algeria, Team Captain 1964; Twenty-fifth Annual Reunion Committee, Class of 1940, Northwestern University Medical School, Chairman; Supreme Academic Council, Official University of the Congo, Lubumbashi, Congo/L, 1965-71; Committee on Professional Fees, Institute of Medicine of Chicago, 1966-70; Reearch Grant Committee, Institute of Medicine of Chicago, 1967-69; Governing Member and Member of Planning Committee, Shedd Aquarium, Chicago, 1967-75; Aesculapian Institute and Foundation, Secretary and Member of Board of Directors; Editorial Board, *International Surgical Digest,* Consulting Editor 1969-70; Nominating Committee, Chicago Surgical Society, 1969-74; American College of Surgeons, Regional Committee on Trauma for Southern California, Chairman for Santa Barbara County. Published Works: Editor, *Transactions Western Surgical Association* 1961-67, *Textbook of Surgical Physiology* with J. M. Beal 1969, *Loose Leaf Text Book of General Surgery* (3 Volumes) 1961-76, *Manual of Ambulatory Surgery* 1982; Author 123 Articles on Various Subjects in the Field of Surgery, Surgical Research, Oncology, and Trauma; Surgical Motion Pictures approved by the American College of Surgeons. Honors and Awards: Life Member, Schweppe Foundation, Board of Directors; Listed in *American Men of Science, Who's Who in the Midwest, Who's Who in America, Who's Who in the World, Who's Who in the West, Who's Who in California, Directory of Medical Specialists.* Address: 755 Via Airosa, Santa Barbara, California 93110.■

Naima Wallenrod Prevots

Professor, Writer, Critic. Personal: Born May 27, 1935; Daughter of Rae Wallenrod; Married Martin Wallen; Mother of Becky, Aaron. Education: Attended Brandeis University, Brooklyn College; B.A., Juilliard School of Dance, 1955; M.S., University of Wisconsin, 1960; Ph.D., University of Southern California, 1983. Career: Performed with Merce Cunningham, Fred Berk, Marie Marchosky, Mont-Brooks, Pola Nirenska, 1953-69; Co-Founder, Washington Contemporary Dance Company, 1963-67; Guest Choreographer, Brooklyn College, St. Louis Opera, Princeton Regional Ballet, Washington Repertory Company, 1955-76; Curriculum Specialist, CAREL Office of Education, 1967-69; Founder, Wolf Trap Academy of Dance, 1971; Accreditation Teams, Commission of Higher Education, Middle States Association, 1975-82. Organizational Memberships: Congress on Research in Dance, Executive Committee 1976-78; American Dance Guild, National Executive Committee 1973-75; Joint Conference Committee, C.O.R.D. and A.D.G. 1981. Community Activities: National Endowment for the Arts, Panelist and Consultant 1979 to present; Dance Panel, California Arts Commission, 1979-81; Los Angeles Dance Alliance, Kaleidoscope Selection Committee 1979-81; Chairperson, Alliance for Arts Education, D.C. Chapter 1976-78; D.C. Arts Commission, Dance Panel 1973-74 and 1976-78; Kennedy Center, Committee on Programs for Youth, 1979; Board of Directors, Project Arts, Montgomery County, 1976-79; Guest Lecturer, U.S.I.A., Smithsonian Film Institute, American Theatre Association, Music Educators Association, California Institute for the Arts, 1967-79. Honors and Awards: Phi Beta Kappa; Phi Delta Kappa; Master Teachers Artists in Schools, National Endowment for the Arts, 1975 to present; Grant, National Endowment for the Humanities, Interdisciplinary Curriculum Project, 1974; Citation, White House Conference on Youth, for Direction and Production of Film "Children Dance," 1971; American University College of Arts and Sciences Award for Program Development, 1976; National Dance Association Plaudit Award, 1980; Visiting Scholar, University of California at Los Angeles, 1979-81. Address: 5219 Mass Avenue, Bethesda, Maryland 20816.■

TWO THOUSAND NOTABLE AMERICANS

HERBERT GENE PRICE

University Administrator. Personal: Born November 30, 1936; Son of Mrs. Mack Gaby. Education: B.S. 1957, M.Ed. 1961, North Texas State University. Career: Director of University Relations, University of Nebraska, 1976 to present; Public School Administrator, 1971-74; President, Public Relations and Advertising Firm, 1974-76; Magazine Editor; Tennis Professional; Television Producer and Product Manager; Teacher/Coach. Organizational Memberships: International Association of Business Communitors, Board of Directors (Omaha) 1983; Education Director (Omaha) 1983, Community Service and Awards Committee Chairperson (Miami) 1981; Public Relations Society of America, Publicity Chairman (Omaha) 1983, Program Chairman (Omaha) 1982, Board of Directors (Miami) 1980, Publicity Chairman (Miami) 1980; National Association of Vocational Technical Education Communicators, Board of Directors 1978-80, Vice President 1979-80, Convention Chairperson 1980; Florida Association of Community Colleges, Board of Directors 1981, Institutional Advancement Commission Chairperson 1981, Community College Week Chairman 1980; Southeast Florida Educational Consortium, Public Information Task Force Chairperson 1980-81; Council for the Advancement and Support of Education, 1978-83; Nebraska Community College Community Relations Committee Chairperson, 1977-78. Community Activities: American Heart Association, Douglas/Sarpy Counties, Nebraska, Board of Directors 1982-85, State Public Relations Committee 1983; Performing Artists, Omaha, Board of Directors 1982-83, Friends of Performing Artists President 1983; Metropolitan Arts Council, Omaha, Steering Committee, 1983; Combined Health Agencies Drive, Omaha, Honorary Chairman for Colleges and Universities, 1982; United Way of the Midlands, Planning and Allocation Committee 1982 and 1983, Loaned Executive 1978; United Way of Dade County, Allocation Panel, 1981; Greater Omaha Chamber of Commerce, Governmental Relations Committee 1983, Education Committeee 1978, 1979; River City Roundup, Omaha, Public Relations Committee, 1983; Association of Retarded Citizens, Advocacy Advisory Board (Miami), 1980-81; Performing Arts for Community and Education, Board of Directors 1980-81, Friends of PACE President 1981; Big Orange Festival, Miami, Planning Board, 1981; Asociacion Los Viejos Utiles, Miami, Board of Directors, 1980-81; Governor's Energy Commission, Florida, 1980, 1981. Honors and Awards: Honorary Life Member, Texas Council of Parent Teacher Association 1965; Dallas Jaycees Outstanding Contribution to Youth, 1964 and 1965; Association of Retarded Citizens, Miami, Citizen Advocacy Award, 1981; Performing Arts for Community and Education, Miami, Citation, 1980 and 1981; Florida Association of Community Colleges, Institutional Publications Award, 1980; Listed in *Who's Who in the South and Southwest*. Address: 5119 Davenport, Omaha, Nebraska 68132.■

JAMES HAROLD PRICE

Educator. Personal: Born February 5, 1943; Son of Dorothy Hults; Married Joy Ann, Daughter of Claude and Doris Pearsall. Education: B.S. 1966, M.S. 1968, Indiana State University; Ph.D., Western Michigan University, 1973; M.P.H., Health Sciences Center, University of Oklahoma, 1977. Career: Professor and Chairman, Department of Health Education, University of Toledo; Associate Professor, Health and Safety Education, Kent State University, 1977-80; Assistant Professor, Health Education, University of Wisconsin at Oshkosh, 1973-76; Space Science Lecturer, N.A.S.A., Lewis Research Center, 1969; Instructor in Science Education, Indiana State University, 1966-69. Organizational Memberships: American Association for the Advancmeent of Health Education; American Public Health Association; American School Health Association; Society of Public Health Educators; International Union of Health Educators; Eta Sigma Gamma. Community Activities: Board Member, American Cancer Society, American Red Cross; Life Member, Boys Clubs of America. Published Works: Textbook Reviewer for Professional Journals *Health Education, Health Values, Journal of School Health*; Contributing Editor, *Journal of Nursing Care*; Textbook Author *Human Sex and Sexuality* 1977, *Consumer Health Care* 1983. Honors and Awards: Vice President of United States Award for Footsteps on the Moon. Address: 4214 Herman, Toledo, Ohio 43623.■

PAUL BUFORD PRICE

Professor of Physics, Laboratory Director, Physicist. Personal: Born November 8, 1932, in Memphis, Tennessee; Son of Paul Buford and Eva (Dupuy) Price (both deceased); Married Jo Ann Baum, June 28, 1958; Father of Paul Buford III, Heather Alynn, Pamela Margaret, Alison Gaynor. Education: B.S. summa cum laude, Davidson College, 1954; M.S. 1956, Ph.D. 1958, University of Virginia. Career: Professor of Physics 1969 to present, Director of Space Science Laboratory 1979 to present, University of California at Berkeley; Board of Directors, Terradex Corporation; Consultant for N.A.S.A. on Lunar Sample Analysis Planning Team; Adjunct Professor of Physics, Rensselaer Polytechnic Institute, 1967-68; Visiting Professor, Tata Institute of Fundamental Research, Bombay, India, 1965-66; Physicist, General Electric Research Laboratory (Schenectady, New York), 1960-69; National Science Foundation Postdoctoral Fellow, Cambridge University, England, 1959-60; Fulbright Scholar, University of Bristol, England, 1958-59. Organizational Memberships: Fellow, Chairman Cosmic Physics Division, American Physical Society; Fellow, American Geophysical Union; American Astronomical Society; Space Science Board, National Academy of Science. Published Works: Author (with others), *Nuclear Tracks in Solids*; Contributor of Articles in Professional Journals; Patentee in Field; Research on Space and Astrophysics, Nuclear Physics, Particularly Developmental Solid State Track Detectors and their Applications to Geophysics, Space and Nuclear Physics Problems; Discovery of Fossil Particle Tracks and Fission Track Method of Dating; Discovery of Ultra-Heavy Cosmic Rays. Honors and Awards: Distinguished Service Award, American Nuclear Society, 1964; Industrial Research Awards, 1964 and 1965; Ernest O. Lawrence Memorial Award of A.E.C., 1971; Medal for Exceptional Scientific Achievement, N.A.S.A., 1973; Honorary Sc.D., Davidson College, 1973; Guggenheim Fellow, 1976-77; Elected to the National Academy of Sciences, 1975; Listed in *Who's Who in America*. Address: 1056 Overlook Road, Berkeley, California 94708.■

RICHARD LEE PRICE

Acting Justice of the Supreme Court, Civil Court Judge. Personal: Born September 19, 1940; Son of Saul and Claire Price; Married Carolyn; Father of Lisa, Howard. Education: B.A., Roanoke College, 1957; J.D., New York Law School, 1964. Career: Chief Law Assistant in Charge of Law Department, Civil Court; Law Secretary to Judge Harry David, Civil Court; Attorney, Harry L. Lipsig; Acting Justice of the Supreme Court, Bronx County, and Judge of Civil Court, Elected 1980. Organizational Memberships: American Bar Association; Association of the Bar of the City of New York; New York State Bar Association; Association of Trial Lawyers of America; New York State Trial Lawyers Association, Inc.; Jewish Lawyers Guild, Board of Directors; New York City Criminal and Civil Courts Bar Association, Vice President; Metropolitan Women's Bar Association, Board of Directors; American Judges Association, Assistant Treasurer; American Judges Foundation, Treasurer; Council of New York Law Associates; New York Women's Bar Association; National Association of Women Judges; New York County Lawyers Association, Chairman Law Related Education Committee. Community Activities: Lawyers Unit, B'nai B'rith, President 1979-80; Community School District 1, Elected Member 1973-74 and 1975-80, Elected Vice Chairman 1979-80; Arbitrators Association of the Small Claims Court, President 1979-80; Educational Alliance Alumni Association; Lawyers Lodge #2929, B'nai B'rith, 1976-78; Civil Court Law Secretaries Association, President 1973-75; 7th Precinct, Auxiliary Police, Executive Officer/Lieutenant until 1980; Grand Street Consumers Society, Board of Directors; East River Housing Corporation, Board Member; East Side Chamber of Commerce; National Organization of Women; Lower East Side Businessmen's Association, Board of Directors; New York Consumers Assembly. Religion: East Side Torah Center, Board of Directors. Honors and Awards: Honorary Doctor of Laws, Shaw University, Raleigh, North Carolina, 1980. Address: 577 Grand Street, New York, New York 10002.■

ROBERT WILLIAM PRINDLE

Geotechnical Engineer. Personal: Born November 19, 1950; Son of Robert E. and Margaret E. Prindle. Education: Attended St. John's College (Camarillo, California), 1968-70; B.S.C.E. summa cum laude, Loyola University of Los Angeles, 1974; M.S., California Institute of Technology, 1975. Career: Geotechnical Engineer, Sandia National Laboratories; Engineering Aide, Los Angeles County Sanitation Districts, 1973-74; Student Engineer, Los Angeles Department of Water and Power, 1974, 1975; Staff Engineer, Fugro Inc. (now Ertec, Inc.), Long Beach, California; Senior Staff Engineer, Woodward-Clyde Consultants, Santa Ana, California. Organizational Memberships: Registered Professional Engineer, California; American Society of Civil Engineers; National Society of Professional Engineers; International Society of Soil Mechanics and Foundation Engineering. Community Activities: Loyola University Men's Chorus, 1971-74, 1976-79; New Mexico Symphony Orchestra Chorus, 1981 to present. Religion: Roman Catholic; Scripture Reader, Eucharistic Minister 1980 to present. Honors and Awards: Tau Beta Pi, Chapter President 1973-74; Alpha Sigma Nu, Chapter President 1973-74; Alpha Sigma Nu Scholar of the Year Award, 1974; Gerome K. Doolan Engineering Award, Loyola University, 1974; Loyola University Men's Chorus Award, 1974; Presidential Citation for Service to the University Community, Loyola University, 1974; California State Graduate Fellow, 1974-75; Institute Fellow, California Institute of Technology, 1974-75. Address: 14335 Camino del Rey Northeast, Albuquerque, New Mexico 87123.■

TWO THOUSAND NOTABLE AMERICANS

PETER CHARLES HOWARD PRITCHARD

Association Executive. Personal: Born June 26, 1943; Son of Prof. J. J. and Mrs. M. R. Pritchard (father deceased); Married Sibille Hart, Daughter of Mr. and Mrs. J. B. Hart; Father of Sebastian, Dominic, Cameron. Education: B.A. with honors in Chemistry 1965, M.A. 1968, Oxford University, Magdalen College; Ph.D. Zoology, University of Florida, 1969. Career: Vice President for Science and Research, Florida Audubon Society; Former Position as Coordinator of Marine Turtle Programs for World Wildlife Fund/International Union for Conservation of Nature; Extensive Travel in Most Countries of Latin America and in Africa, Southeast Asia, Papua New Guinea, Micronesia, New Caledonia and Others. Organizational Memberships: American Society of Ichthyologists and Herpetologists; Society for the Study of Amphibians and Reptiles; Herpetologists League. Community Activities: Co-Chairman, Marine Turtle Recovery Team (U.S.D.I. and U.S.D.C.), Florida Panther Recovery Team, United States Department of Interior; Florida Panther Advisory Committee, Florida Game Commission; Technical Team, West Atlantic Turtle Symposium; I.U.C.N. Sea Turtle Specialist Group; Co-Chairman, Gopher Tortoise Council; Fellow, Explorers Club. Published Works: Author Three Books and Almost 100 Scientific Papers and Articles. Address: 401 South Central Avenue, Oviedo, Florida 32765.■

JOHN C. PRITZLAFF, JR.

Investment Manager, State Senator. Personal: Born May 10, 1925; Son of John C. and Elinor Gallum Pritzlaff, Sr. (deceased); Married Mary Dell Olin; Father of Ann, John, Barbara, Richard. Education: B.A., Princeton University, 1949. Military: Served in the United States Army Infantry, 1943-45, with the rank of TSGT/3. Career: Investment Manager; Arizona State Representative, 1963-69; U.S. Ambassador to Malta, 1969-72; Arizona State Senator 1975-82, Republican Whip 1977-78, Chairman Appropriations Committee 1979-82, Co-Chairman Joint Committee on Reapportionment and Redistricting, Chairman Joint Legislative Budget Committee 1980 and 1982. Organizational Memberships: National Council of State Legislators; Education Commission of the States; Republican National Finance Committee. Community Activities: Chamber of Commerce of Arizona; Rotary Club, Scottsdale and Phoenix; Republican Precinct Committeeman; Board Member, Heard Museum; Board of Trustees, St. Luke's Hospital; Board Member, American Graduate School of International Management; Board Member, Marshall & Ilsley Trust Company. Religion: Nashotah Seminary, Board of Directors; Vestry, St. Barnabas on the Desert (Scottsdale, Arizona), 1961-67. Address: 4954 East Rockridge Road, Phoenix, Arizona 85018.■

JAMES CHRISTIAN PRODAN

Educator, Administrator. Personal: Born January 4, 1947; Son of Muriel Prodan; Father of Christopher, Tana. Education: B.S. Education, Ohio State University, 1969; M.Mus., Catholic University of America, 1972; Doctor of Musical Arts, Ohio State University, 1976; Oboe Study under John Mack (Cleveland Orchestra), James Caldwell (National Symphony, Oberlin Conservatory), William Baker (Ohio State University), Marcel Moyse. Career: Associate Professor of Music, Associate Conductor of Wind Ensemble 1982, Oboe, Chamber Music Coach, Student Teacher Supervisor, Graduate Faculty 1979, University of North Carolina at Greensboro; Assistant Profesor of Music, Conductor of Wind Choir 1978-79, Summer Instrument Repair Seminar & Chamber Music Workshop 1977-79, Graduate Faculty 1975-79, The Oboe Camp (Kenyon College) 1975-79, University of Akron; Graduate Associate, Oboe Reedmaking 1973-75, The Oboe Camp 1973-75, Ohio State University; Part-time Instructor, Oboe, Bassoon, Clarinet, Otterbein College, 1972-74; Director Joseph Robinson Oboe Seminar 1981 & 1982, Woodwind Coordinator 1981-84, Director of Thomas Stacy International English Horn Seminar 1980-82, Director of Instrument Repair Seminar 1980 & 1981, Director of North Carolina Double Reed Camp 1980-84, University of North Carolina at Greensboro; Coordinator of Applied Music 1978-79, Director of Instrument Repair Seminar and Director of Chamber Music Workshop 1977-79, Resident and Touring Arts Director/Student Recital Administrator/Administrative Assistant 1976-79, University of Akron; Graduate Administrative Associate to the Assistant Director of the School of Music 1973-75, Coordinator of Oboe Camp 1973-79, Ohio State University; Numerous Solo, Concerto and Conducting Appearances; Numerous Professional Performances including Haiti National Philharmonic (Principal Oboe) 1982, Greensboro Symphony (Principal Oboe), Winston-Salem Symphony (Solo English Horn) 1980, Akron Symphony (Principal Oboe) 1975-79, Washington D.C. Baroque Arts Society (Principal Oboe) 1970-72, Others. Organizational Memberships: International Double Reed Society, Librarian, Executive Committee; Phi Mu Alpha Sinfonia, Faculty Advisor; Kappa Kappa Psi; American Federation of Musicians, Local 802; American Symphony Orchestra League; National Association of College Wind and Percussion Instructors; Music Educators National Conference; North Carolina Music Educators Association; Music Teachers National Association. Honors and Awards: Pi Kappa Lambda; Listed in *Who's Who in America*, *Men of Achievement*, *Personalities of America*, *International Who's Who of Intellectuals*, *Directory of Distinguished Americans*, *Who's Who in American Music*. Address: 1814 Dunleith Way, Greensboro, North Carolina 27408.■

NATHAN E. PROMISEL

Consulting Engineer. Personal: Born June 20, 1908; Father of David Mark, Larry Jay. Education: B.S. 1929, M.S. 1930, Massachusetts Institute of Technology; Doctoral Work, Yale University, 1932-33. Career: Assistant Laboratory Director, International Silver Company, 1930-40; Chief Materials Scientist and Engineer, Department of the United States Navy, Aeronautics and Weapons, 1940-66; Executive Director, National Materials Advisory Board, National Academy of Sciences, 1966-74; International Consultant, Materials and Policy, 1974 to present. Organizational Memberships: American Society of Metals, Fellow, Honorary Member, President 1972; Federation of Materials Societies, President 1972-73; British Institute of Metallurgists, Fellow; Society of Automotive Engineers, Chairman Aerospace Materials Division 1959-74; American Institute of Mining, Metallurgical and Petroleum Engineers, Honorary Member; American Society for Testing and Materials, Honorary Member; Alpha Sigma Mu Society, Honorary Member; Society for the Advancement of Materials and Process Engineering, Fellow. Community Activities: North Atlantic Treaty Organization, Chairman/Member Aerospace Panel 1959-71; Organization for Economic Cooperation and Development, United States Representative, Materials, 1967-70; United States/U.S.S.R. Scientific Exchange Program, Chairman Materials 1973-77; National Materials Advisory Board; Advisory Committees of Oak Ridge National Laboratory, Lehigh University, University of Pennsylvania, United States Navy Laboratories, United States Congress Office of Technology Assessment; International Conference on Materials Behavior, Permanent Honorary President. Published Works: Author of 65 Technical Articles; Contributor/Editor, Approximately 8 Books. Honors and Awards: Honorary Doctor of Engineering, Michigan Technological University, 1978; Elected Member, National Academy of Engineering, 1978; National Capitol Engineer of the Year, Council of Engineering and Architectural Societies, 1974; Outstanding Accomplishment Awards, United States Navy, 1955-64; Carnegie Honorary Lecture, 1961; Gillett Distinguished Lecture, 1965; Burgess Award, 1961; Distinguished Lecture, Electrochemical Society, 1970; First Decennial Award, Federation of Materials Societies, 1982; Honorary Guest, U.S.S.R. Academy of Sciences; Distinguished Lecture, American Institute of Mining, Metallurgical and Petroleum Engineers and American Society for Metals, 1984. Address: 12519 Davan Drive, Silver Spring, Maryland 20904.■

E. ALLEN PROPST

Pilot, Retired Educator. Personal: Born January 11, 1926, near Albany, Oregon; Son of Elmer E. and Eva Anna Propst; Father of Richard L. and Ronald D. Military: Served in Sensitive Security Area of the Military Police, 1945-46. Career: Aircraft Pilot; Flight and Ground Instructor; Teacher, Course in Airplanes and Their Instruments; Operator, Aerial Pesticide Applicator and Technical Field Advisory Service, 1951-69; Candidate for Governor of Oregon (3 Times). Community Activities: As Candidate for Office of Governor of Oregon, Called Attention of Alleged Secret United States Intelligence Agencies and Their Activities and/or Involvement on such Cases as the D. B. Cooper Airplane Hijacking; Has on File Pending Criminal Complaint on Alleged Secret Intelligence Agencies and has Pushed for a United States Senatorial Investigation on Involvement of These Agencies into American Politics; United States Congressional Advisory Board, Chairman's Advisor (Selected for Advisory Capacity on Matters of Internal and National Security). Religion: First Christian Church (Co-Founded by Great Grandfather). Published Works: Author of Documents and Memoranda Pertaining to Internal and National Security. Honors and Awards: Listed in *Personalities of the West and Midwest*, *Dictionary of International Biography*, *Men of Achievement*, *International Who's Who of Intellectuals*, *International Register of Profiles of North America*, *Personalities of America*, *Community Leaders and Noteworthy Americans*, *Book of Honor*, *Men and Women of Distinction*. Address: 253 Southeast Scravel Hill Road, Albany, Oregon 97321.■

TWO THOUSAND NOTABLE AMERICANS

HAROLD LEE PROSSER

Writer and Book Reviewer. Personal: Born December 31, 1944; Married Grace Eileen; Father of Rachael Maranda and Rebecca Dawn Prosser. Education: A.A. English, Santa Monica College, 1968; Attended California State University at Northridge, 1968-69; B.S. Sociology, Southwest Missouri State University, 1974; M.S.E.D. Social Science (Sociology), Southwest Missouri State University, 1982. Career: Writer and Book Reviewer, 1963 to present. Community Activities: English Tutor to Minority and Handicapped Persons, California, 1968-69. Religion: American Baptist. Honors and Awards: Author, *Robert Bloch, Charles Beaumont, Poul Anderson* (all three forthcoming sociological books); Manuscripts on Permanent File and Storage at Archives of Contemporary History, University of Wyoming. Address: 1313 South Jefferson Avenue, Springfield, Missouri 65807.■

LOIS MAHARAM PROVDA

Educational Therapist. Personal: Born March 19, 1942; Daughter of Arthur and Helen Maharam; Married Paul Irwin, Son of Raymond and Freida Schwartz; Mother of Asher, Alexander. Education: B.S., Boston University, 1962; M.A., New York University, 1964; Certificate of Advanced Study, New York University, 1976; Credential in School Psychology, California State University at Northridge; Ph.D., Kensington University (Glendale, California), 1983. Career: Educational Director, New York Hospital, Payne Whitney Psychiatric Clinic, New York, New York, 1964-68; Reading Director, Buckingham School, Brooklyn, New York, 1968-73; Instructor, City University of New York, Brooklyn College, 1973-76; Educational Therapist, Private Practice, Los Angeles, California, 1976 to present. Organizational Memberships: Fellow, American Orthopsychiatric Association; International Reading Association; Association for Children With Learning Disabilities; California Association of Psychologists and Psychometrists; California Association of Educational Therapists. Community Activities: Bureau of Jewish Education, Special Education Committee, Los Angeles, California, 1980 to present. Honors and Awards: Listed in *Who's Who of American Women, World Who's Who of Women, Men and Women of Distinction*. Address: 208 South Lasky Drive, Beverly Hills, California 90202.■

SHEPHERD GREEN PRYOR, III

Aerospace Engineer, Lawyer. Personal: Born June 27, 1919, in Fitzgerald, Ben Hill County, Georgia; Son of Shepherd Green Pryor Jr. and Jeffie Moore Persons Pryor (both deceased); Married Lenora Standifer on May 17, 1941; Father of Sandra Anita, Pryor Clarkson, Shepherd Green IV, Robert Stephen Pryor, Patty Jeanne Pryor Smith, Alan Persons Pryor, Susan Lenora Pryor. Education: B.S. Aerospace Engineering, Georgia Institute of Technology, 1947; J.D., Woodrow Wilson College of Law (Atlanta, Georgia), 1974. Military: Served in the United States Air Force as Captain and in the United States Air Force Reserve, 1942-46. Career: Engineer, Hartford Accident and Indemnity Company, 1947-56; Engineer with Lockheed Georgia Company, 1956 to present (Nuclear Engineer 1957-64, Research and Development Representative 1964 to present); Real Estate Sales, Cole Realty Company and Nelson Realty Company (Atlanta, Georgia), Valient Properties (Marietta, Georgia); Admitted to Practic Law in Georgia 1974, with State Bar of Georgia, Superior Court of Fulton County, Georgia Court of Appeals, Georgia Supreme Court, United States District Court (Northern District of Georgia), the Fifth District Court of Appeals (New Orleans, Louisiana), the Eleventh District Court of Appeals (Atlanta, Georgia) and the United States Supreme Court. Organizational Memberships: Registered Professional Engineer, Georgia; Licensed Pilot; American Bar Association; State Bar of Georgia; Sigma Delta Kappa; Pi Kappa Phi; Kappa Kappa Psi. Community Activities: Past President, Loring Heights Civic Association, Atlanta, Georgia; Sandy Springs Civic Association, Devonwood Division; Trustee, Masonic Children's Home, 1965-78; Mensa; Intertel; Mason; Shriner. Religion: Methodist. Address: 135 Spalding Drive Northeast, Atlanta, Georgia 30328.■

NORBERT PHILLIP PSUTY

Research Center Director, Distinguished Professor. Personal: Born June 13, 1937; Son of Phillip and Jessie Psuty; Married Sylvia Helen, Daughter of Walter and Helen Zurinsky; Father of Eric, Scott, Ross. Education: B.S. Geography and Geology, Wayne State University, 1959; M.S. Geography, Miami University (Oxford, Ohio), 1960; Ph.D. Geography, Louisiana State University, 1966. Career: Director, Center for Coastal and Environmental Studies; Associate Professor in Departments of Geology and Geography 1969-73, Director Marine Sciences Center 1972-76, Professor in Departments of Geography and Geology 1973-81, Distinguished Professor 1981 to present, Rutgers University; Assistant Professor, Department of Geography, University of Wisconsin-Madison, 1965-69; Instructor, Department of Geography and Geology, University of Miami (Florida), 1964-65. Organizational Memberships: Appointed Member, Oceans and Shoreline Committee, Sierra Club, 1972-74; Appointed Member 1973 to present, Elected Chairman 1976-79, Committee on Marine Geography, Association of American Geographers; Appointed United States Member, Committee on Geomorphology, Pan American Institute of Geography and History, Organization of American States, 1973-78; Appointed Member, Scientific-Technical Panel, Marine Environmental Systems Analysis Program, N.O.A.A., 1975-78; Appointed Member, Task Force on Water Management and Planning, New Jersey Pinelands, Department of Environmental Protection, 1976-77; Appointed Member 1977 to present, U.S. Member Executive Committee 1984-89, Commission on Coastal Environments, International Geographical Union; Appointed by Governor Byrne to Battleship New Jersey Study Commission, 1977-80; Appointed United States Member, Committee on Physical Geography, Pan American Institute of Geography and History, Organization of American States, 1978 to present; Barrier Islands Committee, National Park Service, Department of the Interior, 1979 to present; Appointed Member, Bureau of Land Management, Outer Continental Shelf Advisory Committee, North Atlantic Technical Working Group, 1979-84; Appointed Member, Bureau of Land Management, Outer Continental Shelf Advisory Committee, Mid-Atlantic Technical Working Group, 1979-84; President, The Coastal Society, 1980-82; Elected Chair, Coastal and Marine Geography Specialty Group, Association of American Geographers, 1981-82; Water Policy Advisory Committee, East Brunswick Township, New Jersey, 1981-84; Member Editorial Board, *Coastal Zone Management Journal*, 1981 to present; Chair, Geological Survey Review Committee, New Jersey Academy of Science, 1981-82; CEIP Steering Committee, East Brunswick Township, New Jersey, 1981-82; President, New Jersey Academy of Science; Member Editorial Board, *Annals*, Association of American Geographers, 1982. Honors and Awards: National Science Foundation Award to Participate in a Four-Week Remote Sensing Workshop, 1969; National Science Foundation Award to Participate in a Three-Week Conference on Geology of the Mississippi Sound (Coastal Ecology), 1966; Recipient of Research Grants Totaling in Excess of 1.5 Million Dollars from the National Aeronautical and Space Administration, National Science Foundation, Environmental Protection Agency, Office of Naval Research, National Park Service, New Jersey Department of Environmental Protection, New Jersey Department of Energy, National Sea Grant Program, New Jersey Office of Coastal Zone Management, National Oceanic and Atmospheric Administration, Soil Conservation Service, Housing and Urban Development, United States Office of Education, as well as In-House Support, 1965 to present. Address: Center for Coastal and Environmental Studies, Rutgers University, Busch Campus, New Brunswick, New Jersey 08903.■

RUBY PARKER PUCKETT

Administrator, Food and Nutrition Services Executive. Personal: Married Larry W. Puckett. Education: B.S. Food & Nutrition, Auburn University, 1954; Certificate, Dietetic Internship, Henry Ford Hospital, 1955; Certificate, Management by Objectives, Waterman Memorial Hospital, 1966; Vocational Education, Graduate School 1970-73, Postgraduate Work 1980, University of Florida; M.A. Education/Health Care, Central Michigan University, 1976; Numerous In-Service Classes, Seminars and Workshops. Career: Staff Dietitian, Hospital in Houston, Texas, 1955-56; Only Dietitian, Hospital in Meridian, Mississippi, 1957-58; Assistant Director, Hospital in Jackson, Mississippi, 1960-61; Director of Dietetics, Hospital in Knoxville (Tennessee) 1961-63, Eustis (Florida) 1963-68, Gainesville (Florida) 1968-74; Director of Food and Nutrition, J-325 Shands Hospital, University of Florida at Gainesville, 1974 to present; C.U.P.S. Program, University of Florida, 1974 to present; Instructor, Education, Community College of Gainesville, 1977-81; President, Square One, Inc., Consulting, Gainesville, 1979 to present; Numerous Positions in Education and Training, 1955 to present; Teacher of Dietetic Interns, Veterans Administration Hospital, Houston,

1955-56; Teacher of Nutrition and Diet Therapy, Meridian Junior College, Matty Hersee Hospital 1957-58, Fort Sanders Presbyterian 1961-63; Preceptor, Coordinator, Food Service Correspondence Course, Waterman Memorial Hospital, 1963-68; Developer, One-Year Training Course for Food Service Supervisors, J. Hillis Miller Health Center, 1968 to present; Coordinator of Food Service Supervisor Course, Instructor, Division of Independent Study, 1972; Clinical Instructor, Dietetic Students, 1975 to present. Organizational Memberships: International Platform Association; Numerous Committee Positions, American Dietetic Association, Gainesville Dietetic Association; Florida Dietetic Association; Field Agency Nutrition; Southeastern Hospital Conference for Dietitians; American Society of Hospital Food Service Administrators, Several Committee Positions; Florida Council on Aging, Nutrition Section; University of Florida Clinical and Community Coordinated Undergraduate Dietetic Program; North Central Florida Planning Council; Florida Department of Education; North Florida Regional Vocational School; Nutrition Advisory Committee; National Research Council Advisory Board on Military Personnel Supplies; Hospital, Institution and Educational Food Service Society, Competency Committee, Advisor to Organized Florida Chapter 1965-78. Community Activities: Pilot Club's Marquis Library Society, Inc.; Gainesville Campus Federal Credit Union, Chairperson of Board; United Way, Stokes Report; Consultant to Nursing Homes, 1965-67; Guest Speaker over 300 Times to Local, State, National Conventions or Annual Meetings, 1965-78; Advisor, Several Junior Colleges, Developing Programs, 1968-69; Chosen One of Eight Administrative Dietitians in Nation to Develop Educational Tapes for American Dietetic Association; Assisted Development, Dietetic Internship, J. Hillis Miller Health Center, 1968-69; Part-time Instructor, Santa Fe Community College, 1978 to present; Faculty of ADA-HEW Cost Containment Workshop, 1979-80. Religion: Church of Jesus Christ of the Latter-day Saints, Stake/Ward Activities. Published Works: Author Numerous Books and Manuals; Contributing Editor, Numerous Trade Magazines; Letters to the Editor. Honors and Awards: Education Leader in Florida Hospital, Institution, Education Food Service Society Scholarship in Food Service Education, 1970; Representative to Florida Hospital Dietitians, White House Conference of Food, Nutrition and Health, 1969; Assisted with Organization Implementation, Florida Conference on Food, Nutrition and Health, 1970; Fellow, Royal Society of Health, 1971; Outstanding Dietitian in Florida, 1972; Outstanding Community Leader, Radio Station WRUF, 1972; Pi Lambda Theta Educational Honor Society, 1971; Kappa Delta Pi Educational Honor Society; Florida Who is Who Advisory Board, 1974; National Nutritional Policy Study Hearings, Senate Select Committee on Nutrition and Human Needs, 1974; Who's Who Honorary Society of America, 1975; Scholarship Named in Honor, Given by Florida Hospital, Institution, Educational Food Service Society, 1975; One of 50 Women Who are Top Manager, 1977; I.F.M.A.'s Silver Plate Award, International Gold and Silver Plate Society, 1978; Ivy Award, Restauranteurs of Distinction, 1980; Hall of Fame, Woodlawn High School, 1982; Listed in *Who's Who of Women, World Who's Who of Women, Dictionary of International Biography, Who's Who in the South and Southwest, Florida Who's Who, National Register of Prominent Americans and International Notables, Community Leaders and Noteworthy Americans, Contemporary Authors, Who's Who in America.* Address: Route 3, Box 108-B2, Gainesville, Florida 32606.■

DONALD RAY PUDDY

Chief of Flight Operations Systems. Personal: Born May 31, 1937; Son of Mr. and Mrs. L. A. Puddy; Married Dana Carol Timberlake, Daughter of Mrs. M. D. Timberlake; Father of Michael R., Douglas A., Glenn L. Education: B.S. Mechanical Engineering, University of Oklahoma, 1960; M.B.A, University of Houston, Clear Lake City, 1978. Military: Served in the United States Air Force, Ellington Air Force Base, Houston, Texas, rising through the ranks from Second Lieutenant to Captain, 1960-64. Career: with N.A.S.A. Manned Spacecraft Center (now Johnson Space Center), Houston, Texas, 1964-66; Section Head, Lunar Module Systems Branch, Lunar Module (LM) Environmental and Electrical Engineer (EECOM) in Apollo 5 Mission, 1966-69; Assistant Branch Chief, Lunar Module Systems Branch, Served as LM EECOM in Apollo 9 and 10, and as LM EECOM Flight Controller during the Powered Descent and Ascent of the LM for Apollo 11, Served as LM Spacecraft Analysis Flight Controller during Apollo 12, 13, 14 and 15, Flight Director during Apollo 16, 1969-72; Assistant Branch Chief, Space Science and Technology Branch, Served as Command and Service Module Spacecraft Analysis Flight Controller during Apollo 17, Prime Flight Director for Unmanned Launch during Skylab, Flight Director for all Skylab Missions, 1972-74; Branch Chief, Mission Operations Branch, Flight Director of Apollo Soyuz Test Project, 1974-75; Flight Director for Approach and Landing Tests, 1976-77; Flight Director for STS-1, 1978-81; Division Chief, Systems Division and Flight Director for STS-2, 1981-82; Chief, Mission Operations Systems Division, 1982 to present. Organizational Memberships: Council Member, American Institute of Aeronautics and Astronautics; Pi Tau Sigma; Sigma Tau; Phi Kappa Phi. Community Activities: Past President, Ed White Elementary Parent Teacher Association. Honors and Awards: MSC Superior Achievement Award; Presidential Medal of Freedom, Apollo XII Mission Operations Team, 1970; MSC Group Achievement Award, Lunar Traverse Planning Team, 1971; N.A.S.A. Exceptional Service Medal, 1973 (Skylab); JSC Group Achievement Award, Lunar Landing Team, 1973; JSC Group Achievement Award, 1974; Outstanding Performance Rating, 1982; Senior Executive Service, 1982; Listed in *Who's Who in the South and Southwest, Who's Who in Government, Who's Who in Aviation and Aerospace, Who's Who in Houston.* Address: 221 Bayou View Drive, Seabrook, Texas 77586.■

GARY LAURENCE PUDNEY

Television Network Executive. Personal: Born July 20, 1934. Education: B.A., University of California at Los Angeles. Military: Served in the United States Air Force as Captain. Career: Vice President of Special Projects 1978 to present, Senior Executive in Charge of Talent 1979 to present, Various Positions in New York and on the West Coast 1966-74, ABC Television; Executive in Charge of Variety Television Department, International Famous Agency (agency merged with Creative Management Associates to become International Creative Management), 1974-76; Vice President and Executive Producer, Yongstreet International, 1976; Executive in Charge of West Coast Production for "ABC Stage 67," (on exclusive contract), Joined ABC as Director of Specials and Talent in New York 1968, Director of Nighttime Live and Tape Production on the West Coast 1969, Elected Vice President of Nighttime Tape Program Production for ABC Entertainment on the West Coast 1972, Named Vice President of Variety Programs 1973, Executive in Charge of Talent for ABC's 4-Hour 25th Anniversary Celebration Special 1977; Programming Executive at Compton Advertising and Young and Rubicam Advertising Agencies. Address: 2170 Century Park East, Century City, California 90067.■

PERRY ALAN PUGNO

Hospital Department Director. Personal: Born April 28, 1948; Son of Mr. and Mrs. Perry Pugno; Married Terry Gail, Daughter of Mr. and Mrs. Gerald Ren; Father of Andrew, Joseph, Benjamin. Education: B.A., University of California at Riverside, 1970; M.D., University of California at Davis, 1974; American Board of Family Practice, 1977; M.P.H., Loma Linda University, 1983. Military: Served in the United States Public Health Service, 1977-78, with the rank of Lieutenant Commander. Career: Director of Medical Education and Family Practice Department, Shasta General Hospital in Affiliation with the University of California at Davis, 1983 to present; Educational Director in Family Medicine, University of Connecticut, 1982-83; Emergency Department Director, Riverside Community Hospital, 1980-82; Residency Director, Family Practice, Loma Linda, California, 1978-80; Senior Surgeon, National Health Service Corps, 1977-78. Organizational Memberships: American Academy of Family Physicians; Society of Teachers of Family Medicine; American College of Emergency Physicians. Community Activities: Young Men's Christian Association, National Officer 1978-82; National Commission on Cancer, 1976-77; California Medical Quality Review Committee, 1980-82; American Cancer Society, Executive Board 1976-77. Religion: Roman Catholic. Honors and Awards: Phi Beta Kappa; Phi Kappa Phi, Lange Medical Publications Award, 1974; Meade Johnson Award for Graduate Medical Education, 1975; American Medical Association Physician Recognition Award, 1977, 1981. Address: 2615 Hospital Lane, Redding, California 96001.■

ROBERT ADRIAN PUGSLEY

Professor of Law. Personal: Born December 27, 1946; Son of Mary C. Pugsley; Married Cathleen Ruth Cox, Daughter of Mr. and Mrs. C. W. Cox. Education: Regents Diploma, Salesian Seminary (High School), New York, 1964; B.A. Sociology, State University of New York at Stony Brook, 1968; J.D. 1975, LL.M. Criminal Justice 1977, New York University School of Law. Career: Professor of Law, Southwestern University School of Law, 1981 to present; Associate Professor of Law, Southwestern University School of Law, 1978-81; Acting Deputy Director, Criminal Law Education and Research (CLEAR) Center, New York University School of Law, 1977-78; Adjunct Assistant Professor, Criminology and Criminal Justice, Southampton College, Long Island University, 1975-76; Coordinator of Peace Education Programs, The Christophers, New York City, 1971-78; Instructor in Sociology, The New School for Social Research, New York City, 1969-71. Organizational Memberships: American Society of Criminology; American Legal Studies Association; American Society for Political and Legal Philosophy; Institute for Study of Bioethics and Life Sciences, The Hastings Center. Community Activities: Consultant in Peace Education to National Catholic Educational Association, 1972-75; Creative Advisor to "Christopher Closeup," Nationally Syndicated Public Affairs Television Program, 1975-83; Executive Committee, N.G.O.'s at the United Nation, Office of Public Information, 1977; Board of Advisors, Center for Legal Education, City

College of New York/City University of New York, 1978 to present; Producer and Moderator, "Inside L.A.," Public Affairs Program on KPFK-FM Los Angeles, 1979 to present; Issues Task Force of Los Angeles Conservancy, 1980-81; Co-Convener, Southern California Coalition Against the Death Penalty, 1981-83; Convener 1983, Legal Panel, Los Angeles Area Committee for Conscientious Objectors, 1979-81; Member Death Penalty Committee, Lawyers' Support Group, Amnesty International U.S.A.; Moderator, "Earth Alert," Los Angeles Cable Television Program Series on Environmental Issues, 1983 to present; Founder and Coordinator, The Wednesday Evening Society, 1979 to present; Founding Member, Church-State Circle, Los Angeles, 1983 to present. Religion: Roman Catholic. Honors and Awards: Robert Marshall Fellowship in Civil Liberties, CLEAR Center, New York University School of Law, 1976-78; Outstanding Young Men of America, 1977; Selected Participant, National Endowment for the Humanities, 1979 Summer Seminar for Law Teachers, University of California at Los Angeles. Address: 675 So. West-Moreland Avenue, Los Angeles, California 90005.■

RAMAKRISHNA PULIGANDLA

Professor of Philosophy. Personal: Born September 8, 1930; Son of P. V. Raman; Married Janaki, Daughter of V. B. Sastry; Father of Balaram, Sita, Usha, Vijay, Russell. Education: B.Sc. 1949, M.Sc. 1951, Andhra University; M.S., Purdue University, 1960; A.M., University of South Dakota, 1962; Ph.D., Rice University, 1966. Career: Professor of Philosophy, The University of Toledo, 1966 to present; Visiting Lecturer in Philosophy, Knox College, 1965-66; Associate Professor of Mathematics, Texas Southern University, 1964-65; Fellow in Philosophy, Rice University, 1963-64; Associate Professor in Physics, Yankton College, 1960-63; Lecturer in Physics, R.V. College, Nellore, India, 1951-58. Organizational Memberships: American Philosophical Association; Association for Philosophy of Science; Society for Asian and Comparative Philosophy; American Association for the Advancement of Science. Honors and Awards: Phi Kappa Phi National Honor Society. Address: 4138 Beverly Drive, Toledo, Ohio 43614.■

PAUL EDISON PULLIAM

Electrical Engineer. Personal: Born June 6, 1912, in Nickerson, Kansas; Son of George Washington Pulliam; Married Ila M. Catrett; Father of Carol Ann Pulliam Rolls, Paula Ann Pulliam Bermingham. Education: Graduate of Hickman High School (Columbia, Missouri), 1932; Field Artillery R.O.T.C., University of Missouri, 1932-34 and 1935-37; B.S.E.E., University of Missouri-Columbia, 1951. Military: Served in the United States Army Air Force during World War II (3½ Years Active Duty); Presently Holds Rank of Retired Major. Career: Electrical Engineer. Organizational Memberships: Institute of Radio Engineers; American Institute of Electrical Engineers; Institute of Electrical and Electronic Engineers; Former Member, National Society of Professional Engineers; Society of American Military Engineers; Life Member, Reserve Officers Association of the U.S.A. Religion: Baptist. Honors and Awards: Received the Army Commendation Ribbon for Suggesting Use of SCR584 Radar by Field Artillery and Its Modification into SCR784; Was in First Guided Missile Regiment at Fort Bliss, 1948-49; Qualified as Guided Missile Officer; Named Polaris Weapon System, Redstone Arsenal; Compatriot, Sons of the American Revolution, 1982. Address: 7916 Grandstaff Drive, Sacramento, California 95823.■

CHARLES F. PULVARI

Educator. Personal: Born July 19, 1907, in Hungary. Education: Dipl.Ing., Royal Hungarian University of Technical Science, 1929. Career: Professor Emeritus, Catholic University of America, 1954 to present; President, Electrocristal Corporation, Inc., 1961 to present; Principal Investigator, United States Air Force and United States Navy, 1949-70; Owner, Pulvari Electrophysical Laboratory, 1943-49; Executive Director, Hungarian Radio and Communication Company, 1935-45; Lecturer, University of Technical Science, Budapest, 1943; Research Engineering Laboratory, Hungarian Tel. Manufacturing Company, Standard Company, Budapest, 1929-33; Director, Kenilcrest Corporation, 1969 to present. Organizational Memberships: New York Academy of Sciences, Life Member, Past Chairman of Crystal Committee; Sigma Xi, Past Chairman Catholic University Chapter; Tau Beta Pi. Published Works: Author, 60 Papers, Reports, Articles; Contributing Editor, *Computer Handbook*, 1960. Honors and Awards: Fellow, New York Academy of Science 1978, American Ceramic Society 1978, Institute of Electrical and Electronic Engineers 1970; Americanism Medal, Daughters of the American Revolution, 1975; IR 100 Award, *Indus Research* Magazine, 1963; Patents Held, 75 in Ferroelectrics, Electrostatics, Television, Radio, Sound Reproduction, including Apparatus for Electrostatic Recording and Reproduction (ferroelectric memory) 1950, Force Sensor 1966, Polar Vapor Sensing Means 1971; Invented Method, Established Studio for Postsynchronizing Movies into Hungarian, 1935-45; Developed First Light Valve-Operated CRT, 1936; Developed First Noise Eliminator for Radio Receivers, 1935; Developed First Solid State Light Valve; Honorary Doctoral Degree, Golden Diploma, Royal Hungarian University of Technical Sciences, 1981; Developed Patents on a More Effective Polymerisotion Process and on a Solar to Electrical Conversion "Thermal Detector." Address: 2014 Taylor Street, Northeast, Washington, D.C. 20018.■

MADAN L. PURI

Professor of Mathematics. Personal: Born February 20, 1929; Son of Mr. and Mrs. G. D. Puri; Married Uma S.; Father of Sandeep, Pradeep, Purnima. Education: B.S. 1948, M.A. 1950, D.Sc. 1975, Punjab University, India; Ph.D., University of California at Berkeley, 1962. Career: Professor of Mathematics, Indiana University at Bloomington; Visiting Professor, University of Washington at Seattle, 1978-79; The Alexander von Humboldt Guest Professor, University of Gottingen, 1974-75; Visiting Professor, University of Bern (Switzerland) 1982, University of California at Irvine 1978, University of Auckland (New Zealand) 1977, University of Goteburg (Sweden) 1976. Organizational Memberships: Fellow, Institute of Mathematical Statistics; Fellow, American Statistical Association; Elected Member, International Statistical Institute; Fellow, Royal Statistical Society; Mathematical Association of America. Community Activities: Chairman, Institute of Mathematical Statistics Committee on Summer Research Institutes, 1971-75; Participant, Visiting Lecturer Program in Statistics, 1967-70, 1977-83; Member Scientific Committee of the International Association for Statistics in Physical Sciences, 1973; Director, Summer Research Institute on "Statistical Inference for Stochastic Processes," National Science Foundation, 1975; Director, First International Symposium on Nonferametric Techniques in Statistical Inference, Sponsored by Air Force Office of Scientific Research, 1969. Honors and Awards: Elected Fellow, Royal Statistical Society 1967, Institute of Mathematical Statistice 1969, American Statistical Association 1970; Elected Member, International Statistical Association 1972, New York Academy of Sciences 1975; Award D.Sc. by Punjab University, India, 1975. Address: Department of Mathematics, Indiana University, Bloomington, Indiana 47405.■

ADA M. PURYEAR

Education Administrator. Personal: Born October 24; Mother of Paul Jr., Paula. Education: B.A. Mathematics, Talladega College, 1953; M.A. Reading, University of Chicago, 1958; A.B.D., Education Administration and Supervision K-12, Florida State University; Chicago State University; Florida A&M University; Fish University, Tuskegee Institute. Career: Administrator of Early Childhood and Elementary Education, Florida State Department of Education; Former Positions include Mathematics High School Teacher, Elementary Teacher and Audio-Visual Coordinator, Reading Center Founder/Director, Assistant Professor at Norfolk State University and Tuskegee Institute, Freshman Math Coordinator and Assistant Math Professor at Fisk University, Consultant and Tutor. Organizational Memberships: International Reading Association, EC Committee, Textbook Committee, Award Committee; IRA Concerned Educators of Black Students, Vice President; Florida Elementary School Principals; Florida Council on Elementary Education; Child Development Associates; Florida Association on Children Under Six; DOE Liaison; Leon Association on Children Under Six, President; National Council of Teachers of Math; N.A.E.Y.C.; State Consultant in Elementary Education. Community Activities: Alpha Kappa Alpha Sorority, Treasurer, Undergraduate Advisor, Secretary, Project AKA Director; Member, National Association for the Advancement of Colored People; National Urban League; Leon County 4C Advisory Board; Florida Center for Children and Youth Education Cluster; Interracial Women's Council, President; Jack and Jill of America, Teen Sponsor, President; Driftrs Inc., Tallahassee President, Vice President, Historian and National Membership Chairperson; International Voters League. Religion: Deacon, Presbyterian Church; Church School Teacher; Youth Committee. Honors and Awards: 1983 National NOW Black Woman Award; Phi Kappa Phi; Phi Delta Kappa; Pi Lambda Theta; Crown and Scepter Club; Listed in *Who's Who in Black America*, *Who's Who in the South and Southeast*, *Personalities of the South*, *World Who's Who*, Others. Address: 3228 Constellation Court, Tallahassee, Florida 32312.■

MICHAEL PUSKARICH

Mining Company Owner and General Manager. Personal: Born March 25, 1929; Son of Frank and Mary Puskarich; Married Mary Bell; Father of Lynn,

Michael, Matthew. Education: Self-educated in Construction, Mining, Farming. Career: Owner, General Manager, Mining Company; Former Occupations in Construction and Farming. Community Activities: Director, Ohio United Fund, 1961; Ohio Mining and Reclamation, 1963; MARC, 1978; Donated to Harrion Community Hospital; Land Theater, Trumpet; Ashland College; Oterbein College; 4-H of State of Ohio; 4-H Foundation; The Firemen of St. Clarisville, Piedmont, Freeport, Flushing, Cadiz, New Athens, Antrim, Hopedale, Ohio. Religion: Presbyterian; Active in Churches in Nothingham, New Athens, Scio, Jewett, Flushing, and St. Clarisville, Ohio. Honors and Awards: Outstanding Patriot Award, Flushing American Legion, 2 Years, 1979-80; Layman Award, Nothingham Presbyterian Church, 1980; Community Leaders Award, Piedmont, Ohio, 1980; Coal Man of the Year (with brothers), 1982. Address: Route #3, Cadiz, Ohio 43907.■

CAROLYN MOATE PUTNAM

Counseling Psychologist, Speech and Hearing Pathologist. Personal: Born November 20, 1913; Mother of Allison Stripling Fleming. Education: A.B., Wesleyan College for Women, Macon, Georgia, 1935; Master's Degree, Emory University, Atlanta, Georgia, 1953; Doctorate, East Texas University, Commerce, Texas, 1973; Attended Columbia, Eastern Michigan; University of Florida; University of Texas; Wesleyan Conservatory; Centenary College. Career: Counseling Psychologist; Speech and Hearing Pathologist; Former Positions as Elementary School Teacher, High School Teacher, School Supervisor, College Teacher, Speech and Hearing Therapist, Counselor and Therapist, Developer of Program for the Gifted, Director of Rehabilitation Clinic, Psychological Consultant, Program Director of Alcoholism Center. Organizational Memberships: C.E.C. 1955-56, Secretary 1955-56; Theater Guild, President 1938-40; Member and Consultant to Altanta, Georgia, Family Service, 1958-60; Georgia Gifted Children, Committee Member, 1958; A.C.E.S.; N.V.G.A.; S.P.A.T.E.; A.S.C.A.; Psi Chi National Scholastic Honor Society; A.R.C.A.; American Speech and Hearing Association. Community Activities: Member of Woman's Club; Junior Service League; Sunday School Teacher; P.T.A. Offices, President and Secretary; Red Cross Grey Lady; Consultant to Atlanta, Georgia, Family Service Organization; Member Nation-Wide Group on the Gifted Invited by Congressional Sub-Committee to Participate in Miami 1958 Conference; Others. Religion: Developed and Equipped Children's Center at Ephiphany Episcopal Church, Commerce, Texas; Offers Free Psychological, Speech and Hearing Therapy at Church. Honors and Awards: Scholastic Honor and Tuition to Undergraduate College (Wesleyan College, 1931) and Graduate School (Emory University, 1950); Special Invitation by Congressional Sub-Committee on Gifted as Result of Founding of First County School Program for Gifted in Sarasota County, Florida. Address: 220 Brookhaven Terrace, Commerce, Texas 75428.■

ROBERT BREWER PUYEAR

Company Section Manager. Personal: Born August 21, 1932; Son of Mr. and Mrs. H. G. Puyear; Married Donna G. Timmons, Daughter of Mr. and Mrs. A. R. Timmons (deceased); Father of Jill B., Timothy H., Sue E. Education: B.S. Chemical Engineering, University of Missouri, Rolla, 1954; M.S. Industrial Administration, Purdue University, 1967. Military: Served in the United States Army Corps of Engineering as Second Lieutenant 1955-56, First Lieutenant 1956-57, Active Reserves 1957-58. Career: Manager, Materials Technology Section, Monsanto Company; Union Carbide Corporation, Stellite Division, Kokomo, Indiana, Technology Department, Engineer 1954-55, 1957-61, Group Leader 1961-67, Materials Systems Division Product Manager, Bethel, Connecticut 1967-68, Indianapolis, Indiana, 1969; Monsanto Company, St. Louis, Missouri, Materials Specialist 1970-71, Superintendent 1971-74. Organizational Memberships: Materials Technology Institute of the Chemical Process Industries Inc., Co-Founder, First Chairman, Board of Directors (founded 1977, director 1977 to present); National Association of Corrosion Engineers, Chairman St. Louis Section 1976, Trustee 1982 to present; American Institute of Chemical Engineers; American Society of Metals; American Management Association. Community Activities: Boy Scouts of America, Explorer Advisor, Scoutmaster, Merit Badge Counselor, Eagle Scout, Order of the Arrow; River Bend Bath and Tennis Club, Director 1972-74; Parkway Central Association of Music Parents, Board Member 1982, Vice President 1983-84. Religion: United Methodist Church, Certified Lay Speaker, Lay Leader of Local Church 1967-68, 1971-74, Sunday School Teacher, Other Assignments and Activities. Honors and Awards: Issued United States Patents in 1963 (2), 1967, 1968; Registered Professional Engineer in California 1976, Missouri 1977; Accredited by National Association of Corrosion Engineers as "Corrosion Specialist." Address: 226 River Valley Drive, Chesterfield, Missouri 63017.■

STEVEN M. PYBRUM

Management Consultant, Author, Lecturer. Education: B.A., California State Polytechnic University San Luis Obispo; M.B.A. Taxation, Golden Gate University. Career: Cost Accountant, Wrigley's Jr.; Controller of Large Corporation with Four Wholly Owned Subsidiaries; Owner and Founder, Steven M. Pybrum and Associates Management Consulting Firm; Owner/Founder, Executive Management Service; Instructor of Taxation, California State Polytechnic University; Public Accountant in Santa Cruz County and San Joaquin Valley; Author of Newspaper and Magazine Article "Agri-Business Tax Tips," and Radio Program "Tax Tips." Organizational Memberships: California Certified Public Accountant Society; California Bar Association; California Cattlemen's Association; National Cattlemen's Association; Western Growers Association. Community Activities: Atascadero Chamber of Commerce, Treasurer; Controllers Roundtable of San Luis Obispo County, Founder, President; Lions International; Exchange Club; Elks Club. Honors and Awards: Listed in *Who's Who in America*, *Who's Who in Real Estate*, *Who's Who in California*. Address: 249 Vista Court, Los Osos, California 93402.■

JUNGJO PYUN

Laboratory Staff Member. Personal: Born October 12, 1942; Son of Muhrim and Bocksoon Pyun; Married Saelan Park, Daughter of Hojoon and Sung Sook Park; Father of Jennifer Insook, Evelyn Inhae. Education: B.S. magna cum laude, Seoul National University, 1965; M.S., State University of New York, 1970; Ph.D., University of Michigan, 1973. Career: Staff Member, Los Alamos National Laboratory, 1977 to present; Associate Nuclear Engineer, Brookhaven National Laboratory, 1976-77; Principal Investigator, Combustion Engineering, Inc., 1973-76. Organizational Memberships: American Nuclear Society; Sigma Xi; The Scientific Research Society. Honors and Awards: Recipient Distinguished Service Award, Brookhaven National Laboratory, 1977. Address: 232 Canada Way, Los Alamos, New Mexico 87544.■

ROBERT L. QUALLY

Corporate Executive. Personal: Born August 24, 1947; Son of Mr. and Mrs. E. M. Qually. Education: Advanced Study in Communications, Center for Humanistic Studies, Aspen, Colorado, 1972; B.F.A. Graphic Design, Colorado State University, 1972; A.A. Liberal Arts, Northeastern Colorado, 1970. Military: Served in the Colorado National Guard, 1968-74, attaining the rank of First Lieutenant. Career: President and Creative Director, Qually and Company, Inc., Chicago/Evanston, Illinois; Vice President and Creative Director, Lee King and Partners, Chicago, New York, Los Angeles; Design Director, Stephens, Biondi and DeCicco, Chicago; Senior Designer, Salesvertising, Denver, Colorado; Principal, Quill Images, Fort Collins, Colorado. Organizational Memberships: American Institute of Graphic Arts; Society of Typographic Arts; Council of Foreign Relations; Chicago Ad Club; Industrial Graphics International; Chicago Art Institute; Chicago Museum of Contemporary Arts; Chicago Athletic Association; Life Member, Colorado State University Alumni Association. Community Activities: National Center for Child Abuse, Denver, Colorado; American Cancer Society; Art Institute of Chicago; Museum of Contemporary Art, Chicago; Variety Club. Honors and Awards: Mr. Qually has been featured in 40 Books; Recipient 225 Local, National and International Awards for his Work in Graphic Design, Art Direction, Writing and Film Production, including the Clio Award in Each Area; His New Product Development Work has Successfully Introduced 52 New Products to the Marketplace; Holder of 4 Patents for New Products and Design; Work Part of Permanent Collection of Museum of Modern Art in New York and the Smithsonian Institute in Washington D.C. Address: 2238 Central Street, Evanston, Illinois 60201.■

DENNIS MICHAEL QUINN

Professor. Personal: Born March 26, 1944; Son of Donald Pena Quinn and Joyce C. Nye; Married Janice Darley, Daughter of Roy M. and Kathleen Darley; Father of Mary, Lisa, Adam, Paul-Moshe. Education: B.A. English, Brigham Young University, 1968; M.A. History, University of Utah, 1973; Ph.D. History, Yale University, 1976. Military: Served with United States Army Intelligence, Washington D.C., Munich, Germany, 1968-71. Career: Professor of History, History Department, Brigham Young University. Organizational Memberships: American Historical Association; Organization of American Historians; Western History Association; Utah State Historical Society; Mormon History Association; John Whitmer Historical Association; Program, Committee, Western History Association, 1981-82. Community Activities: Member Advisory Council, Charles Redd Center for Western Studies, 1980-83; Board of Editors, *Journal of Mormon History*, 1980-83; Board of Editors, *John Whitmer Historical Association Journal*, 1980-83; Board of Directors, Signature Books Inc., 1981 to present; Volunteer Worker for Democratic Party Campaigns, 1978, 1980, 1982. 1984. Religion: Active Member of Church of Jesus Christ of Latter-day Saints with Service in Local Administrative Offices as Branch President, Bishopric, High Council; Volunteer, Full-time Representative of Church of Jesus Christ of Latter-day Saints in England, 1963-65. Honors and Awards: Phi Kappa Phi Honor Fraternity, 1968; Brigham Young University Scholarships, 1966-68; Graduation with Honors, Brigham Young University, 1968; Yale University Fellowships, 1973-75; Samuel F. Bemis Prize from Yale University, 1975; Mrs. Giles Whiting Dissertation Fellowship, New York City, 1975-76; Egleston and Beinecke Prizes for Best Dissertation, Yale University, 1976; Stipend from National Endowment for the Humanities, 1977. Address: 923 Third Avenue, Salt Lake City, Utah 84103.■

JAMES TAYLOR QUINN

Fine Arts Center Director. Personal: Born December 23, 1942; Son of Mrs. Inez Quinn; Married Patricia Davis; Father of Endymion Selene. Education: B.F.A. 1964, M.F.A. 1966, Virginia Commonwealth University, Richmond, Virginia; Attended Arts Students League of New York, Summer 1968; Ph.D., Ohio University, Athens Ohio, 1972. Career: Director, Peninsular Fine Arts Centre, Hampton, Virginia; Professor, Chairman, Department of Art, University of Mississippi, Oxford, Mississippi; Associate Professor, Chairman, Department of Art, George Mason University, Fairfax, Virginia; Assistant Professor, Ohio University, Athens, Ohio; Instructor, Department of Art, Shepherd College, Shepherdstown, West Virginia; Instructor, Department of Art, Louisiana Tech University, Ruston, Louisiana. Organizational Memberships: Elected Fellow, Royal Society of Arts, London, England, 1972. Community Activities: Served on National Advisory Board, The Alliance for Arts Education, Washington D.C., 1971, 1974. Honors and Awards: Outstanding Young Man of America, United States Jaycees, 1978; Martin Luther King Tutorial Award, 1972; Listed in *Men of Achievement*. Address: 3750 Kecoughtan Road, Hampton, Virginia 23669.■

WILLIAM EDWARD QUIST

Metallurgical Engineer. Personal: Born May 13, 1935; Son of Mr. and Mrs. Edward J. Quist; Married Ruth Marie, Daughter of Mr. and Mrs. Richard L. Schiller; Father of Brooke William, Brittany Marie. Education: B.S. Metallurgical Engineering 1957, M.S. Metallurgical Engineering 1964, Ph.D. Metallurgical Engineering 1974, University of Washington. Military: Served with Air Force ROTC, 1953-55. Career: Metallurgical Engineer, The Boeing Company, present; Metallurgist and Chemist, Pacific Car and Foundry Company, 1958-59; Corrosive Engineer, Farwest Corrosion Control, 1957. Organizational Memberships: S.P.E.E.A., 1959 to present; American Society for Metals, 1955 to present; Alpha Sigma Mu, 1970 to present; Professional Engineer, State of Washington, 1976 to present; A.I.M.E., 1955-65. Community Activities: Chairman, Puget Sound Chapter of the American Society for Metals, 1974; Co-Chairman, Pacific Northwest Metals and Minerals Conference, 1977; Chairman, Pacific Northwest Materials Conference, 1983. Religion: Emmanuel Bible Church 1953-70, Sunday School Teacher, Superintendent, Board Member; Westminster Chapel 1970 to present, Various Teaching and Youth Organizational Responsibilities. Honors and Awards: Four Patents on Aluminum Alloy, 1965, 1981 (2), 1982; Execeptional Invention Award, The Boeing Company, 1980; Certificate of Recognition, A.I.A.A., 1981; Certificates of Recognition (2), The Boeing Company, 1981; Outstanding Paper Award, A.S.T.M., 1969. Address: 1821 Northeast 27th Street, Redmond, Washington 98052.■

JUSTO SONGAO QUITUGUA

Educator. Personal: Born February 19, 1950; Son of Grabiel R. Quitugua; Married Judymae D. Education: Saipan Teacher Trainee, Certificate, 1970-71; Community College of Micronesia, 1971-72; B.A., University of Guam, 1974-76; M.Ed., University of Hawaii, Manoa, 1978-80. Career: Language Arts and Mathematics Resource Teacher, presently; Former Positions include Elementary School Teacher, Mathematics Teacher, Science Teacher, Remedial Reading Teacher, Social Studies Teacher, Adult Basic Education Teacher, G.E.D. Examiner; Community College of Micronesia Off-Campus Darkroom Assistant Instructor. Organizational

TWO THOUSAND NOTABLE AMERICANS

Memberships: Title I School Level Council, 1980; International Reading Association, 1978; Saipan Teachers Union, 1970; Guam Federation of Teachers 1980, East Council for Basic Education 1981. Community Activities: Chalan Kanoa Elementary Parent Teacher Association, 1969; Hopwood Junior High School Parent Teacher Association, 1972; San Vicente Elementary Parent Teacher Association, 1976; Oleai Elementary Parent Teacher Association, 1977; J. P. Torres Elementary Parent Teacher Association, 1980; C. L. Taitano Elementary Parent Teacher Association, 1981. Honors and Awards: University of Guam Outstanding Scholastic Achievement and Academic Excellence, 1976; SAITEC Participant, 1970; Community College of Micronesia Scholarship Recipient, 1971; Marianas District Government Educational Leave, 1974; East-West Center Grantee, 1978; Graduated magna cum laude, 1976; Listed in *Who's Who in the West, Personalities of America*. Address: P.O. Box 10055, Sinajana, Guam 96910.■

MOHAMMED SAYEED QURAISHI

Entomologist/Toxicologist. Personal: Born June 23, 1924; Son of Mohammed Latif Quraishi (deceased) and Akhtar Jehan; Married Akhtar Imitaz, Daughter of Imtiaz Mohammed Khan and Nisar Begam (both deceased), Father of Rana, Naveed, Sabah. Education: B.Sc., Agra University, 1942; M.Sc., Aligarh Muslim University, 1944; Ph.D., University of Massachusetts, 1948. Career: Entomologist/Toxicologist, National Institutes of Health, present; Former Positions include Chief, Scientist, New York State Science Service; Professor, North Dakota State University; Senior Scientist, Central Treaty Organization, Institute of Nuclear Science, Tehran, Iran, 1960-64; Head, Interdepartmental Pesticide Residue Laboratory, North Dakota State University, 1966-72; Associate Professor, University of Manitaba, Winnipeg, Canada, 1964-66; Senior Member, United Nation WHO Malaria Team, 1949-51; Entomologist, Malaria Institute, Pakistan, 1951-55; Senior Research Officer, Pakistan Council of Scientific and Industrial Research, Senior Scientific Officer, Pakistan Atomic Energy Commission, Archaeology and History of Science. Organizational Memberships: American Chemical Society; Society of Environmental Toxicoogy and Chemistry; Entomological Society of America; Member Editorial Board of Society of Environmental Toxicology and Chemistry and Publications Committee in Charge of Special Publications; Delivered Invitational Lectures in Academic and Scientific Societies in the United States and Abroad; Invited to Attend International Conference on Science in Islamic Polity: Its Past, Present and Future, Islamabad, Pakistan, 1983. Community Activities: Active in Asian-American Cultural Activities; President, Tri-State Pakistan American Association, 1974-75; Chairman, National Institutes of Health Asian-American Cultural Association, 1980-81. Published Works: Contributed Paper, "A Holistic View of Muslim Science in the 13th and 14th Centuries A.D." (co-author with Mrs. Akhtar Imtiaz Quraishi); Author of 50 Scientific Papers in International Scientific Journals; Book, *Biochemical Insect Control: Its Impact on Economy, Environment, and Natural Selection*, Wiley-Interscience 1977. Honors and Awards: Merit Scholarship, 1942-44; Overseas Scholarship, 1946-49; Phi Kappa Phi, 1948; Sigma Xi, 1948; Delivered Invitational Lectures at Academic, Scientific and Cultural Societies' Meetings, 1970-82; Quality Increase, 1980; Listed in *Who's Who in the World, Who's Who in America, Personalities of America, American Men and Women of Science, Who's Who in the East*. Address: 19813 Cochrane Way, Gaithersburg, Maryland 20879.■

SHERRY SWETT RAATZ

Civic Leader. Personal: Born September 20, 1933; Daughter of Mr. and Mrs. L. L. Swett; Married First Husband John Swanson (divorced); Married Second Husband Charles F. Raatz Jr. in 1961, Son of Mrs. C. F. Raatz; Mother of Robin Elaine, Roger Lockwood, Rondee Doreen, Reneé Josette. Education: B.A. General Studies with a Major in Creative Dramatics and Drama, University of Washington, 1955. Career: Sang at Age 4 on "Uncle Frank's Children's Hour," KJR Radio, Seattle, Washington, also Started Career in Vaudeville at the Palomar (Pantages), Orpheum, and Paramount Theatres in Seattle, Washington; Solo Act in Vaudeville at Age 8, Palomar Theatre, "The Diminutive Sophie Tucker"; Played Vaudeville Houses throughout Washington State; Toured Canada with Major Bowes Unit; Sang with "Magic Circle Show"; Sang at Army, Navy, Marine Corps and Air Force Installations, Hospital Wards, Sick Bays, Open Fields, Mess Halls, Hangers, Aircraft Carriers throughout Washington State and Oregon, through the U.S.O., Civilian War Commission, Young Men's Christian Association, Washington Athletic Club, and Others during World War II; Professional Model during High School; Entertained Armed Forces during Korean War for the U.S.O., Elk's Club, U.W. Club Encore; Featured Performer in Stage Musical Revue, "Joy Ride," Huntington Hartford Theatre, Hollywood, and Schubert Theatre, Chicago, 1956; Leading Role in Television Series, "Sally"; Leading Role in Live Television Presentation, "Mrs. Moonlight," Matinee Theatre; Sang Several Engagements at Cabaret Concertheatre; Made Many Vocal Recording Demos for Songwriters; Secretary to City Librarian, Willard O. Youngs, Seattle Public Library, 1959; Professional Artist; Illustrated Article, "Piracy in Iceland," for *The American-Scandinavian Review*, Vol XLIX, September 1961. Organizational Memberships: American Guild of Variety Artists and Actors Equity (on honorary withdrawal). Community Activities: Rainier Chapter, National Society, Daughters of the American Revolution 1979 to present, First Vice-Regent, 1981 to present, Wrote "The N.S.D.A.R. March" 1982; Daughters of Founders and Patriots of America, Washington Chapter, 1982 to present; Freedoms Foundation at Valley Forge, Wrote "The Freedoms Foundation Song," 1982. Honors and Awards: Queen Anne High School, Honor Society, 4-Star Thespian in National Thespian Society, Masque and Gavel Award as Best Actress; Graduated from the University of Washington cum laude, 1955; Elected to Phi Beta Kappa, 1955; Recipient of High Scholarship Award in General Studies at the University of Washington, 1954; Creative Dramatics Award, University of Washington, 1955; Invited by Alpha of Theta Sigma Phi to 24th Annual Matrix Table honoring Seattle Women of Achievement, 1955; Certificate of Merit, Washington Athletic Club of Seattle, for "Entertaining Thousands of Servicemen during World War II as a Member of the W.A.C. Victory Show," 1945; Certificate of Appreciation, Seattle War Commission, for 5000 Hours of Volunteer Service, 1945; Certificate of Appreciation, Mayor William F. Devin and the City Council of the City of Seattle, Washington, in Recognition of Patriotic Volunteer Service through the Seattle Civilian War Commission during World War II, 1945; Thank You Letter from United States Treasury Department (War Savings Staff) for Singing and Selling Bonds for the War Effort during World War II at the Orpheum Theatre; Gold Locket with Wings from the Men of the B29 Flying Fortress Wing at Boeing Field for Entertaining Many Hours, 1943; Referred to as "Sweetheart of the Army," United States Army Circulars. Address: 7500 - 27th Northeast, Seattle, Washington 98115.■

GEORGE B. RABB

Zoological Park Director. Personal: Born January 2, 1930; Son of Joseph A. Rabb; Married Mary. S., Daughter of Mrs. John Sughrue Sr. Education: B.S. with honors, College of Charleston, 1951; M.A. 1952, Ph.D. 1957 Zoology, University of Michigan. Career: Currently Director, Curator and Coordinator of Research 1956-64, Associate Director 1964-75, Deputy Director 1969-75, Chicago Zoological Park. Organizational Memberships: Fellow, American Association for the Advancement of Science; American Society of Ichthyologists and Herpetologists, President 1978; Herpetologists League; Society of Systematic Zoology; Society of Mammalogists; Society for the Study of Evolution; Ecological Society of America, American Society of Zoologists; Society for the Study of Animal Behavior; American Association of Museums; American Society of Naturalists; American Association of Zoological Parks and Aquariums, Director 1979-80; International Union of Directors of Zoological Gardens. Address: 8500 Rockefeller, Brookfield, Illinois 60513.■

MICHAEL J. RABINS

Professor and Department Chairman. Personal: Born February 24, 1932; Son of Herman Rabins; Married Joan, Daughter of Rose Wrynn; Father of Andrew, Evan, Alexandra. Education: Graduate, Bronx High School of Science, Bronx, New York, 1949; B.S. Mechanical Engineering, Massachusetts Institute of Technology, Cambridge, Massachusetts, 1953; M.S. Mechanical Engineering, Carnegie Institute of Technology, Pittsburgh, Pennsylvania, 1954; Ph.D. Mechanical Engineering, University of Wisconsin, Madison, Wisconsin, 1959. Career: Professor and Chairman of Mechanical Engineering, present; Director of Office of University Research, Department of Transportation, 1975-77; Professor, Polytechnic Institute of New York; Associate Professor, New York University, 1954-70; Member of Technical Staff, Bell Telephone Laboratories at Murray Hill, New Jersey, Summers 1967, 1968, 1969. Organizational Memberships: American Society of Mechanical Engineers, D.S.C.D. Executive Committee and Vice President of Communications; Vice President, American Automatic Control Council; Accreditation Board for Engineering Education; American Society of Engineering Education. Community Activities: Chairman, United States Department of Energy Task Force, 1979-80; Chairman, Advisory Panel, United States Office of Technology Assessment, 1981-82; Chairman, 3 Center Transportation Committee of City of Detroit, 1980; Acting Director of Newly Formed Urban Transportation Institute at Wayne State University, present. Honors and Awards: Certificate of Appreciation from Mayor Coleman Young, Detroit, Michigan, 1980; Chosen as Member of Automatic Control Council/Exchange Visit Team to Visit the U.S.S.R., 1978; Department of Transportation Secretary's Silver Medal, 1977; Department of Transportation Secretary's Award, 1977; Department of Transportation Award for Superior Performance, 1976; Visiting Professor, Polytechnic Institute de Grenoble, France, Spring 1975. Address: 29988 Fernhill Drive, Farmington Hills, Michigan 48018.■

ARI RABL

Physicist and Engineer. Personal: Born February 21, 1942. Education: B.Sc. Mathematics and Physics, Beloit College, Wisconsin, 1963; M.A. 1936, Ph.D. Physics 1969, University of California, Berkeley. Career: Physicist and Engineer (solar energy and energy conservation), Princeton University, 1980 to present; Principal Scientist, Solar Energy Research Institute, Golden, Colorado, 1978-80; Physicist, Argonne National Laboratory, Argonne, Illinois, 1974-78; Research Associate, Ohio State University, Columbus, Ohio, 1972-74; Research Associate, Weizmann Institute, Israel, 1970-71. Organizational Memberships: American Physical Society; International Solar Energy Society; American Society Mechanical Engineering; Federation of American Scientists. Honors and Awards: Fulbright Scholarship, 1961-63; Phi Beta Kappa. Address: 21 Sayre Drive, Princeton, NJ 08540.■

WILLIAM J. RABON, JR.

Architect. Personal: Born February 7, 1931, in Marion, South Carolina; Son of William James and Beatrice Baker Rabon. Education: B.S. Architecture, Clemson

College, 1951; B.Arch. with honors, North Carolina State College, 1955; M.Arch., Massachusetts Institute of Technology, 1956. Military: Served in the United States Army, 1951-53, attaining the rank of First Lieutenant. Career: Designer with Architectural Firms in New York City and Birmingham (Michigan), 1958-61; Designer and Associate of Firm John Carl Warnecke and Associates, San Francisco, 1961-63 and 1963-66; Designer and Associate with Firm Keyes, Lethbridge and Condon, Architects, Washington, D.C., 1966-68; Principal Partner, A.M. Kinney and William J. Rabon Associates, Cincinnati, Ohio, 1968 to present; Vice President and Director of Architural Design, A.M. Kinney and William J. Rabon Associates, Cincinnati, Ohio, 1968 to present; Vice President and Director of Architectural Design, A.M. Kinney Inc, 1977 to present; Lecturer, University of California at Berkeley, 1963-65; Assistant Professor of Architectural Design, Catholic University, 1967-68; Principal Works include Kaiser Technical Center (Pleasanton, California), Clermont National Bank (Milford, Ohio), Pavilion Building of the Children's Hospital Medical Center (Cincinnati, Ohio), EG&G Hydrospace Inc. (Rockville, Maryland), Mead Johnson Park (Evansville, Indiana), Hamilton County (Ohio) Vocational Schools, Environmental Protection Agency Headquarters (Cincinnati, Ohio), Arapahoe Chemical Company Headquarters and Research Center (Boulder, Colorado), Proctor and Gamble Winton-Hill Tunnel (Cincinnati, Ohio), Children's Hospital Therapy Complex (Cincinnati, Ohio), Toyota Regional Center (Cincinnati, Ohio), NALCO Chemical Company Research Center (Naperville, Illinois). Organizational Memberships: American Institute of Architects. Honors and Awards: Industrial Research Lab of Year Award, 1970; American Institute of Architects Honor Award for Pavilion Building, 1973; American Institute of Architects Honor Award 1976, Concrete Reinforcing Steel Institute National Design Award 1976, All for Arapahoe Chemical Company Headquarters and Research Center; American Institute of Architects Honor Award for Proctor and Gamble Winton-Hill Tunnel, 1978; American Institue of Architects Honor Award 1978, American Wood Council Merit Award 1981, Both for Children's Hospital Therapy Complex; American Institute of Architects Honor Award for Toyota Regional Center, 1980; American Institute of Architects Honors Awards for NALCO Chemical Company Research Center, 1980 and 1981, Decorated with Presidential Unit Citation, Silver Star, Bronze Star with V for Valor, Bronze Star for Meritorious Service and Purple Heart; Massachusetts Institute of Technology Graduate School Scholarship, 1955-56, Fulbright Scholar to Italy, 1957-58. Biographical Listings: *Who's Who in the World, Who's Who in Finance and Industry, Who's Who in the Midwest, The Directory of Distinguished Americans, Notable Americans, International Who's Who in Community Service, Dictionary of International Biography*. Address: 2324 Madison Road, Cincinnati, Ohio 45208.■

FRED RADEWAGEN

Consultant. Personal: Born March 20, 1944; Son of Mr. and Mrs. H. F. Radewagen; Married Amata Coleman, Daughter of Governor and Mrs. Peter T. Coleman; Father of Erika Catherine, Mark Peter, Kirsten Alexandra. Education: B.A., Northwestern University, 1966; M.S.F.S., Georgetown University, 1968. Career: Consultant, Pacific Islands Washington Office, present; Director, State and Federation Relations, Republican Governors Association, 1979-82; Director Political and Governmental Participation Programs, United States Chamber of Commerce, 1976-79; Associate Director, 1975-76; Staff Coordinator, Territorial Affairs, United States Department of Interior, 1971-75; Washington Representative, High Commissioner Trust Territory of Pacific Islands, 1969-71; Republican President, Campaign and Inaugural Staff, 1968-69. Organizational Memberships: Delta Tau Delta Alumni, President 1971-75; National Capital Interfraternity Forum, President 1975-77; Capitol Hill Club, Life Member. Community Activities: Alexandria Republican City Committee, Member 1979-80; Delegate, Virginia Republican State Convention, 1981. Religion: Member Westminster Presbyterian Church 1970 to present, Member Christian Education Committee 1980-81. Honors and Awards: Delegate, Tenth Foreign Policy Conference, American Council of Young Political Leaders, 1982. Address: 103 East Luray Avenue, Alexandria, Virginia 22301.■

EDWARD JOHN RADLO

Patent Attorney. Personal: Born March 7, 1946; Son of Dr. Edward Z. Radlo; Married Virginia Judith; Father of Heather Sue. Education: B.S. Mathematics, Massachusetts Institute of Technology, Cambridge, Massachusetts, 1967; J.D., Harvard Law School, Cambridge, Massachusetts, 1972. Military: Served with the United States Public Health Service, Lieutenant (j.g.), 1967-69. Career: Patent Attorney, Ford Aerospace and Communications Corporation, Palo Alto, California, 1978 to present; Patent Attorney, Varian Associates, Inc., Palo Alto, California, 1974-78; Patent Attorney, Honeywell Information Systems, Inc., Waltham, Massachusetts, 1973-74; Law Clerk, Supreme Court of Rhode Island, Providence, Rhode Island, 1972-73; Staff Director, Massachusetts Attorney General's Advisory Commission on Juvenile Code Revision, Boston, Massachusetts, 1970-72; Lecturer in Intellectual Property Law at University of California-San Francisco, San Jose State University, University of Santa Clara Graduate School of Business and Administration. Organizational Memberships: Admitted to California (1972), Rhode Island (1973), United States Patent Office (1973), Canadian Patent Office (1974) Bars. Community Activities: Secretary, Associated Radio Amateurs of Southern New England, Inc., 1962-63; Southern Peninsula Emergency Communications System, 1979 to present; Environmental Defense Fund; Union of Concerned Scientists; Lawyers' Alliance for Nuclear Arms Control. Honors and Awards: Salutatorian, Tolman High School, 1963; High Dean's List, Massachusetts Institute of Technology, 1963-67; Elected to Sigma Xi, National Scientific Honorary, 1967; Nominated for Woodrow Wilson Fellowship, 1967; Letter of Commendation, United States Public Health Service, 1969; Rookie of the Year, Northern California Contest Club, 1979. Address: 897 Newell Road, Palo Alto, California 94303.■

HARKISAN D. RAJ

Professor. Personal: Born January 1, 1926; Son of Dunichand C. (deceased) and Moor D. Tejwani; Married Anita Devika Jhurani, Daughter of Hemraj (deceased) and Bhagwani H. Jhurani; Father of (sons) Robin, Arnaz. Education: B.S. with honors Medical Microbiology, University of Bombay, India, 1947; M.S. Biochemistry 1952, Ph.D. Biochemistry 1955, University of Poona, India; Postdoctoral Fellow, Texas A&M University of Texas, College Station, 1956. Career: Professor, California State University, Long Beach, California, 1962 to present; Bacteriologist, Public Health Service, Poona and Bombay, India, 1948-56; Instructor, Oregon State University, Corvallis, Oregon, 1957-58; Assistant Professor, University of Washington, Seattle, Washington, 1958-62. Organizational Memberships: Southern California Society for Electron Microscopy, 1963 to present; American Society for Microbiology, 1958 to present; Life Member, Sigma Xi, 1958 to present. Community Activities: Advisory Board Member of Advanced Medical Sciences, Inc., California, 1972; Consultant to Various Private Corporations, 1960 to present; Radiation Safety Committee, California State University, Long Beach, California, 1962 to present; Speakers Bureau, California State University, Long Beach, 1962 to present. Published Works: Author Over 50 Research Papers, Reviews and Reports concerning Bacterial Physiology, Metabolism, Taxonomy and Ultra-structure. Honors and Awards: Discovered Bacterial Species, *Microcyclus flavus* and *Cyclobacterium marinus*; Listed in *Bergey's Manual of Determinative Bacteriology, Specialty Expert Register of the FAO of the United Nations*, Rome, Italy 1967 to present. Address: 16251 Gentry Lane, Huntington Beach, California 92647.■

RENGA RAJAN

Senior Research Engineer. Personal: Born January 8, 1952; Son of Mr. and Mrs. R. Parthasarathy; Married Komal N., Daughter of Mr. and Mrs. N. Vijayaraghavachar; Father of Vikram. Education: B.S. Chemical Engineering, Regional Engineering College, Tiruchi, India, 1973; M.S. Chemical Engineering, Clarkson College of Technology, Potsdam, New York, 1976; Ph.D. Chemical Engineering, West Virginia University, Morgantown, West Virginia, 1978. Career: Senior Research Engineer in Oil and Gas Research and Development, Exxon Production Research, Houston, Texas, present. Organizational Memberships: American Institute Chemical Engineers; S.P.E. Honors and Awards: National Merit Scholarship, 1967-73; University (Madras) First Rank Gold Medalist, 1973; Jawaharlal Nehru Memorial Fund Award, 1973; Dr. Govinda Rao Memorial Award, 1973; Summa Cum Laude Graduate in B.S., M.S. and Ph.D., 1973-78; Listed in *Who's Who in the South and Southwest, Men of Achievement, Personalities of America, Personalities of the South, Directory of Distinguished Americans, Biographical Roll of Honor*. Address: 11822 North Fairhollow, Houston, Texas 77043.■

KUNWAR RAJENDRA

Urban Transportation Planner, Consultant Civil Engineer, Educator. Personal: Born September 10, 1938; Son of R. M. Pawsey; Married Shanno, Daughter of R. S. Tandon; Father of Archana, Rachana, Anuja. Education: B.S., Agra University, India, 1957; B.E. 1960, M.S. 1974, University of Roorkee, Roorkee, India; Ph.D., Michigan State University, East Lansing, 1980. Career: Consultant Civil Engineer, Urban Transportation Planner, Teacher at Michigan State

University, present; Former Positions as Civil Engineer. Organizational Memberships: American Society of Civil Engineers, Member Urban Transportation Economics Committee; Institute of Transportation Engineers, Chairman Sub-Committee, Member Several Committees; Transportation Research Board; Indian Roads Congress. Community Activities: Director and Chairman of Community Organizations for Cultural Activities and Children's Programs. Honors and Awards: First Prize Voice of America Contest, 1952; Mayor's Citation of Appreciation, 1978. Address: 5244 Bluehaven Drive, East Lansing, Michigan 48823.■

VANGIPURAM S. RAMACHANDRAN

Research Council Section Head. Personal: Born December 30, 1929, Bangalore, India; Son of V. V. Seshachari and V. Rangammal (both deceased); Married Vasundhara, Daughter of S. V. Raghavan and T. R. Sengammal; Father of Parkash, Jayanthi. Education: B.Sc., M.Sc.; D.Phil.; D.Sc.; C.Chem.; F.R.S.C.; F.I.Ceram.; F.A.C.S. Career: Senior Scientific Officer, Central Building Research Institute, Roorkee, India; Research Officer, Head Building Materials Section, Division of Building Research, National Research Council, Canada; Engaged in Research 32 Years in Catalysis, Clay Mineralogy, Lime, Gypsum, Cement Chemistry, Concrete Technology. Organizational Memberships: Royal Society of Chemistry and Ceramic Society, U.K., Fellow; American Ceramic Society, Fellow, Member Board of Abstractors 16 Years; Chemical Abstracts Service, Member Board of Abstractors 13 Years; American Society for Testing and Materials; International Confederation of Thermal Analysis; American Chemical Society, Chairman Various Committees, Chapter Contributor to Annual Publication *Cements Research Progress* 10 Years; Member Editorial Board, *Journal of Materials and Structures*, France; RILEM Organization, France, Full Member, Member Advisory Committee; Member Organizing Committees of Several International Conferences; Canadian Standards Association, Member 2 Steering Committees. Published Works: Author 4 Books (2 translated into Russian); Contributor Several Chapters to Books; Author 130 Research Papers; Editor, *Handbook of Concrete Admixtures*; Author *Silica Fume in Concrete* (in progress). Honors and Awards: Delivered Several Lectures by Invitation to Various Organizations in Denmark, Mexico, Switzerland, France, India, U.S.A., Sweden, China and Canada; United Nations Expert on Concrete, Delivered Series of Lectures in India (1981) and Invited to Visit China as Concrete Expert (1983); Plaque, Editoral Board of *Il Cemento*, Italy; Nominee, Mettler Award, International Confederation of Thermal Analysis; Listed in *Commonwealth Who's Who, Men of Achievement, Directory of Distinguished Americans, Personalities of America, International Book of Honor, International Who's Who of Contemporay Achievement, International Biography of Intellectuals*. Address: 1079 Elmlea Drive, Ottawa, Canada K1J 6W3.■

JOSE RAMIREZ-RIVERA

Professor, Medical Director. Personal: Born June 26, 1929; Son of Juan J. and María de las Nieves Ramírez; Married Leila Suñer; Father of Federico, Steven, Sally, Juliette, Natasha, Leila. Education: B.A., Johns Hopkins University, Baltimore, Maryland, 1949; M.D., Yale University School of Medicine, 1953; Intern, University of Maryland Hospital, 1953-54; Resident in Medicine, University Hospital, Baltimore, Maryland, 1954-55; Fellow in Hematology 1958-59, Resident 1959. Military: Served with the United States Public Health Service as Senior Assistant Surgeon, 1955-57. Career: Professor of Medicine, Medical Director, University of Medical Services, University of Puerto Rico, School of Medicine, 1983 to present; Associate Staff Physician, VA Hospital, Baltimore 1960-67, Associate Chief of Staff 1962-68; Assistant in Medicine, Johns Hopkins University 1960-67; Medicine Instructor 1967-68; Associate Professor, Duke University, Durham, North Carolina, 1968-70; Director Medical Education and Clinical Investigations, Western Region, Puerto Rico, 1970-80; Chief of Medicine, Mayaguezz Medical Center, Puerto Rico, 1971-82; Director, Rincon Rural Helth Initiative Project, Rincon, Puerto Rico, 1975-82; Professor of Medicine and Director, Western Educational Consortium, University of Puerto Rico, School of Medicine, 1974-83. Organizational Memberships: Fellow, American College of Physicians; Royal Society of Medicine; American Medical Association; American Federation Clinical Research; American Thoracic Society, Board of Directors Puerto Rico Lung Association, 1975-80. Community Activities: Evaluation Committee, Council of Higher Education for Cayey Medical School, President 1978 to present; Member *ex officio*, Advisory Committee, L.C.M.E. to Cayey Medical School, 1979; Evaluation Committee, C.H.E. for Medical School San Juan Bautista, 1979; Member Board of Directors, Southwestern Educational Society, Mayaguez, Puerto Rico, 1979-80; Special Consultant to the Board of Education of New York for the Evaluation of the Universidad del Noreste, Tampico, Mexico, March 1982. Honors and Awards: Blaine Brower Traveling Scholarship, American College of Physicians 1967, Swedish and French Institutions; Chosen Man of the Year in 1975, Western Section, Puerto Rico Medical Society; Chosen Man of the Year in 1981, Western Section, Puerto Rico Medical Society. Address: 700 Eucalipto Street, Caparra Heights, Río Piedras, Puerto Rico 00920.■

OSCAR ALBERTO RAMIREZ-SMITH

Corporate Executive. Personal: Born December 23, 1949; Son of Oscar Ramíriz (deceased) and Coralia de Ramíriz; Married Patricia Panzacchi, Daughter of Nino and Marisa Panzacchi; Father of Carla Beatriz and Claudia Patricia. Education: Area Comunes, Universidad Nacional de El Salvador, 1967-69; Instituto Tecnológico y de Estudios Superiores de Monterrey, Mexico, 1973; Postgraduate Work, Instituto Centroamericano de Administración de Empresas, Nicaragua, 1973-75; Catholic University José Simeón Cañas, El Salvador, 1975-76. Career: President and Chief Executive Officer, IIM Corporation, present; Executive Director, Compañia Azucarera Salvadoreña, S.A., El Salvadore, 1979-80; Assistant to the Chairman of the Board "ADOC," El Salvadore, 1978-79; General Manager, Delicia, S.A. de C.V., El Salvadore, 1977-78; Administrative Manager, Alcoa de Centroamerica, S.A., El Salvadore 1975-77, Special Projects Manager 1975. Organizational Memberships: M.B.A. Honors and Awards: Honorific Mention, (ITESM) Instituto Technológico y de Estudios Superiores de Monterrey, Mexico; Listed in *Who's Who in the World*. Address: 8460 Southwest 27th Place, Davie, Florida 33328.■

EDWARD SAMUEL RAMOV

Educator. Personal: Born July 16, 1936; Son of Leonard and Mamie Ramov. Education: B.S. Education 1958, M.S. Education 1961, Temple University. Career: Teacher of Mathematics, Public High School. Community Activities: Executive Director, Jewish Defense League. Religion: President Young Israel of Oxford Circle. Honors and Awards: Recipient National Science Foundation Grants, 1961, 1962; Legion of Merit Award, Chapel of Four Chaplains, for Work with the Poor and Community Relations. Address: 1321 Levick Street, Philadelphia, Pennsylvania 19111.■

JETTIE CECIL RAMSEY

Administrative Captain of County Jail. Personal: Born August 31, 1925; Son of Joseph James and Nonnie Bell (Mann) Ramsey (both deceased); Married Pauline Cordelia Thaden, Daughter of Herman Meigs and Angelena (Nickolas) Thaden (both deceased); Father of Joseph Cecil (deceased), Pauline Diana (deceased), Wilson Lujack. Education: B.B.A., Massey College, 1955; Postgraduate Work, Florida Junior College, 1968, 1973, 1982; Georgia University, 1972; Florida Technological University, 1972. Military: Served with the United States Naval Reserve, World War II, 1943-46. Career: Part-time Instructor, State Rules and Regulations, Florida Junior College, Police Academy; Engineer, Duval Engineering and Company, Jacksonville, Florida, 1946-66; with Office of Sheriff, Duval County 1966 to present, Warden Duval County Prison Rehabilitation Officer 1971-73, Superintendent of Jails 1973, Administrative Captain Duval County Jail 1976 to present. Organizational Memberships: Captain, Jacksonville Police Reserve, 1968-75; Florida Peace Officer Association; Fraternal Order of Police; Correctional Officers Association; Supervisors Union. Community Activities: Duval County Democratic Executive Committee, 1958 to present; 32nd Degree Mason, Worshipful Master, 1974; Shriner, Member Order of Eastern Star, Worthy Patron 1960 and 1981; Sons of Confederate Veterans; Troop Scoutmaster, Boy Scouts of America; Southern Geneologists' Exchange Society; Genealogist; V.F.W., Vice Commander 1975. Religion: Member Jacksonville Baptist Temple, 1953 to present. Published Works: Author, *The Road Back to the Mainline*. Honors and Awards: Appreciation Medal, Order of DeMolay for Boys, 1967; Grand Cross of Color, Rainbow Girls, 1969; Cross of Honor, DeMolay, 1970; American Automobile Association, Medals for Saving a Life. Address: 1039 Hood Avenue, Jacksonville, Florida 32205.■

ARVILLA C. RANK

Independent Living Coordinator for Hearing Impaired. Personal: Born April 4, 1984; Daughter of Peter and Agnes Rank. Education: B.S. Business Administration, St. Norbert College, De Pere, Wisconsin, 1958; M.S. Business Administration, University of Wisconsin-Madison, 1970; M.S. Special Education, University of Wisconsin-Milwaukee, 1978. Career: Independent Living Coordinator for Hearing Impaired; Former Teacher of the Deaf (High School Business Education), Hospital Accountant, Audit Reviewer for Insurance Company. Organizational Memberships: Convention of American Instructors of the Deaf; Delta Pi Epsilon; National Business Education Association. Community Activities: National Association of the Deaf, 1973 to present; Wisconsin Association of the Deaf, Member 1973 to present, President-elect 1983, President 1985; Wisconsin Registry of Interpreters for the Deaf, Member 1972 to present, Legislative Committee 1980 to present, Trustee 1982 to present, Treasurer 1973-77, Reverse Skills Certification 1979 to present, Interpreter Evaluation Team 1980 to present; Wisconsin Disability Coalition, Member 1978 to present, State Board 1978 to 1983, Member Southeast Region of Wisconsin Disability Coalition 1977 to present, Treasurer 1978-80; Wisconsin Division Vocational Rehabilitation Advisory Board, 1981-82. Religion: International Catholic Deaf Association, Member 1966 to present, President 1981 to present, Vice President 1980-81, Secretary 1977-79, Midwest Region I.C.D.A. First President 1977-79, Milwaukee Chapter 7 I.C.D.A. Secretary 1969-73, President 1973-75, Vice President 1975-79, Chairperson 190 ICDA Convention in Milwaukee. Honors and Awards: Quota International Deaf Woman of the Year for District 22, 1982; Greater Milwaukee Volunteer Action Center Recognition for Outstanding Community Service, 1983; Wisconsin Association of the Deaf Golden Hands Award, 1983; St. Norbert College Alma Mater Award, 1983; Wisconsin Registry of Interpeters for the Deaf Award of Appreciation for Outstanding and Dedicated Service, 1983; Milwaukee County Commission for Handicapped and Disabled Persons Recognition, 1983. Address: 6358 South 20th Street, Milwaukee, Wisconsin 53221.■

KELLY DAVID RANKIN

Supervisor of Physical Education, Health and Athletics. Personal: Born March 9, 1940; Son of Mr. and Mrs. Elmo C. Rankin; Married Janice Lynn; Father of John David, Rachael Lynn, Jennifer Diane. Education: B.S. Elementary Education, Kansas University, 1962; M.S. Administration, Washburn University, 1965; Education Specialist, Elementary Education, Emporia State University, 1970; Ed.D. Physical Education, Kansas University, 1975. Career: Sixth Grade Teacher, Elementary Principal, Coordinator Elementary Physical Education, Topeka, Kansas, 1962-69; Assistant Professor, Emporia Kansas University, 1969-72; Teaching Assistant Instructor, Kansas University, 1972-75; Assistant Professor, University of Oregon, 1975-80, Supervisor of Physical Education, Health and Athletics, Vancouver Schools, 1980 to present. Organizational Memberships: President-elect, President, Kansas Association of Health, Physical Education, Recreation, 1972-73; Oregon Association; H.P.E.R.; Washington A.H.P.E.R.; A.A.H.P.E.R.; Physical Educator. Community Activities: Eugene Sports Program, Eugene, Oregon; Young Men's Christian Association, Board of Directors; City Parks and Recreation, Board of Directors, Vancouver, Washington. Religion: Ruling Elder, Central Presbyterian Church, Eugene, Oregon; Member, First Presbyterian Church, Vancouver, Washington. Published Works: Contributor Numerous Articles and Papers to Professional Journals. Honors and Awards: Coach of the Year, Kansas Gymnastics Association, 1968; Eagle Scout; Kansas Gymnastics Judge of the Year, 1972-73; Judge, 1966-75; Track Starter, United States Olympic Trials 1976, 1980, United States Olympic Sports Festival II and III 1979-81; Selected to Start the 1984 Olympics in Los Angeles, California. Address: 6220 Montana Lane, Vancouver, Washington 98661.■

HONORA M. F. RANKINE-GALLOWAY

University Professor. Personal: Born July 9, 1947; Daughter of Catherine Feenan; Married Gerald P. F. Rankine-Galloway; Mother of Adrian J. T. Education: B.A., College of New Rochelle, 1969; M.A. 1970, Ph.D. 1973, University of Pennsylvania. Career: Assistant Professor, Department of English, and Director, Writing Center, Long Island University, C. W. Post Center, 1980-83; Lecturer in American Literature and Civilization, Institut d'etudes anglaises et nord-americaines, Universite de Caen, France, 1978-80; Fulbright Lecturer in American Literature, Universite de Caen, 1977-78; Assistant Professor, Department of English, Rutgers University, 1973-80; Instructor, University of Pennsylvania, College of General Studies, 1973; Instructor of English as a Foreign Language, Vacances Studieuses, Sutton, Surrey, England, Summer 1972; Lectrice, Universite de Provence, Department d'Americain, Aix-en-Provence, France, 1971-72; Teaching Fellow, Department of English, University of Pennsylvania, 1970-71, 1972; Substitute Teacher, Philadelphia Public Schools, 1970; Reader, Department of English, University of Pennsylvania, 1969-70; Book Reviewer, United States International Communication Agency, African Regional Services, Paris, France, 1979-80; Faculty Advisor for Study in the United States, Universite de Caen, 1977-80. Review Editor, McGraw Hill 1981, Houghton Mifflin 1983. Organizational Memberships: American Association of University Professors, Treasurer C. W. Post Chapter; Modern Language Association; American Studies Association; Association francaise d'etudes americaines; International Biographical Association; American Federation of Teachers. Community Activities: Fulbright Lecturer in American Literature, Universite de Caine, 1977-78; Lectures for U.S.I.C.A. in North and West Africa, 1979-80. Published Works: "Mythologies de Yeats: Les Cahiers du Poete," in Le Cahier De L'Herne 1981, "Review of The Life of John O'Hara by Frank MacShane" in PLA Review 1983, "Nikki Giovanni" and "Daniel Hoffman" in Critical Survey of Poetry 1982, "John Barth's Short Fiction: The Key to the Treasure is the Treasurer" in Hungarian Studies in English, "Henry Miller" in Critical Survey of Long Fiction 1983. Honors and Awards: Major Research Grant, Long Island University, 1981-82; Fulbright Lecturer in American Literature, Universite de Caen, 1977-78; Faculty Academic Study Program Award 1977, Rutgers Research Council Grant 1977-78, Rutgers University; Readership 1969-70, Teaching Fellowship 1970-71, 1972-73, Secretary of Graduate English Club 1971, University of Pennsylvania; Honors at Entrance and Full Tuition Scholarship, Dean's Scholar 1966-67, 1967-69, First Honors 1965-66, 1968-69, Departmental Honors in English 1969, College of New Rochelle; New York State Beginning Teaching Fellowship, 1969-71; Elks National Most Valuable Student Award, 1965-66; New York State Regents Scholarship, 1965-69. Address: 123 West 93 Street, Apartment 7C, New York, New York 10025.■

GUY HARVEY RANSON

Professor of Religion. Personal: Born November 26, 1916; Son of J. M. and Willie Ann Hardesty Ranson (both deceased); Married Rose Ellen Clark; Father of Kenneth Clark, Kelly Maurice, Diana Ranson Seklaoui. Education: B.A., Hardin-Simmons University, 1939; M.A., University of Kentucky, 1944; Ph.D., Yale University, 1956; Further Studies at the University of Cambridge, 1947-48. Career: Professor of Philosophy and Chairman of Department, William Jewell College, Missouri, 1948-52; Associate Professor of Christian Ethics, Southern Baptist Seminary, 1952-58; Research Scholar, Yale Divinity School, 1958-59; Associate Professor of Christian Ethics, Duke Divinity School, 1959-60; Associate Professor, Princeton Theological Seminary, 1960-61; chairman of the Department of Religion 1961-77, Professor of Religion 1961 to present, Trinity University, San Antonio, Texas. Organizational Memberships: American Academy of Religion; American Society of Christian Ethics; American Association of University Professors; American Philosophical Society; American Society of Church History. Community Activities: Inman Christian Center, San Antonio, Board of Directors 1966-69, Chairman 1968, 1969; San Antonio Council of Churches, Chairman Social Action Committee 1964-70; Social Welfare Council, San Antonio, 1979; Yale Club of San Antonio, Board of Directors 1977 to present, President 1978. Religion: Ordained Minister, United Presbyterian Church in the U.S.A.; Union Mission Presbytery; Ministerial Relations Committee, Ministerial Candidates Committee, Ecumenical Relations; Vice Moderator, 1972. Honors and Awards: Citation for Service to Yale Club, 1978; Research Grant to Undertake Archaeological Excavation at Hebron, 1966. Address: 115 Irvington Drive, San Antonio, Texas 78209.■

CARL S. RAPHAEL

Executive, Administrator. Personal: Born April 23, 1943, in Kew Gardens, New York; Son of Harold and Ruth Raphael; Married Ellen Gibson Muller, January 15, 1966; Father of Larissa, Heather. Education: B.S., Dalhousie University, 1965; M.A., Queens College, 1966; M.B.A., Fordham University, 1974. Career: Pharmaceutical Representative, Hoffmann-La Roche, Nutley, New Jersey, 1967-70; Medical Center Representative 1970-71, Marketing Research Assistant 1971-72, Marketing Research Analyst 1972-73, Senior Analyst, Coordinator of Health Economics 1973-75, Hoffmann-La Roche; Marketing Manager, Health Application Systems, Inc., Saddle Brook, New Jersey, 1975-76; Senior Marketing Analyst, Merck, Sharp and Dohme, West Point, Pennsylvania, 1976-78; Product Research Manager, and Manager of Marketing Analysis, E. R. Squibb and Sons, Inc., Lawrenceville, New Jersey, 1978-79; Vice President, Research Director 1979-80, Senior Vice President 1980 to present, Danis Research, Inc., Fairfield, New Jersey; Consultant in Health Care Administration. Organizational Memberships: Group Health Association of America; Association of M.B.A. Executives; Pharmaceutical Manufacturers Association; American Marketing Association; Tau Epsilon Phi. Community Activities: Union County Consumer Affairs Advisory Committee 1974, Vice Chairman 1975-76, Chairman 1976-

77; Warrington Community Ambulance Corps, Crew Chief and President; R.E.M.T.A.; E.M.T.-P.; Bucks County Emergency Health Council. Address: 1705 LaRue Lane, Warrington, Pennsylvania 18976.■

JAMES A. RAPP

Director of Marketing Services. Personal: Born December 30, 1946; Son of William and Catherine Rapp; Married. Education: B.A. English, Benedictine Colleges, Atchison, Kansas, 1969; Attended St. John's University, Collegeville, Minnesota. Career: Director of Marketing Services, Stewart Enterprises, New Orleans, Louisiana, 1978 to present; Director of Marketing and Development, WYES-TV, Channel 12, New Orleans, Louisiana, 1974-78; Managing Editor, *The Daily Record*, New Orleans, Louisiana, 1973; Managing Editor, *Apartment Living Magazine*, St. Louis, Missouri, 1972-73; Assistant Promotion Director, Hickey-Mitchell Company, St. Louis, Missouri, 1970-72. Organizational Memberships: Advertising Club of New Orleans; Public Relations Society of America. Community Activities: Louisiana State Historical Society; New Orleans Opera (Men's Club); Louisiana Landmarks Society, Inc.; United States Fencing Association, Inc.; New Orleans Museum of Art; Faubourg Marigny Improvement Association. Honors and Awards: Anvil Award of Excellence, Public Relations Society of America, 1983; Listed in *Who's Who in the South and Southwest*, *Personalities of America*, *Personalities of the South*, *Men of Achievement*, *International Who's Who of Contemporary Achievement*. Address: 509 Mandeville Street, New Orleans, Louisiana 70117.■

MANOHAR LAL RATHI

Hospital Administrator, Associate Professor. Personal: Born December 25, 1933; Son of B. M. Rathi; Married Kamla; Father of Sanjeev and Rajeev. Education: M.B.B.S. (M.D.), Rajasthan University, Jaipur, India, 1955-61; Board Certified in Pediatrics 1970 and Neonatal/Parinatal Medicine 1978. Career: Chairman, Department of Pediatrics, Christ Hospital, Oak Lawn, Illinois, 1980 to present; Director of Perinatal Medicine and Attending Pediatrician, Christ Hospital Perinatal Center, Oak Lawn, Illinois, 1974 to present; Associate Professor of Pediatrics, Rush Medical College, Chicago Illinois, 1979 to present; Consultant Obstetrician, Christ Hospital, Oak Lawn, 1976 to present; Consultant Neonatologist, Little Company of Mary Hospital, Evergreen Park, Illinois, 1972 to present; Consultant Neonatologist, Palos Community Hospital, Palos Heights, Illinois, 1978 to present; Consultant Neonatologist, St. Francis Hospital, Blue Island, Illinois, 1979 to present; Assistant Professor of Pediatrics, Rush Medical College, Chicago, Illinois, 1974-79; Director of Newborn Medicine, Little Company of Mary Hospital, Evergreen Park, Illinois, 1972-74; Coordinator-Pediatric Education, Assistant Director and Senior Attending in Division of Pediatrics, Little Company of Mary Hospital, Evergreen Park, 1972-74; Clinical Instructor, Department of Pediatrics, College of Medicine, Downstate Medical Center, State University of New York, Brooklyn, New York, 1971-72; Chief-Division of Neonatology and Assistant Attending of Department of Pediatrics 1971-72, Fellow in Neonatology 1970-71, Methodist Hospital of Brooklyn, New York; Registrar Physician-Internal Medicine, Ashington Hospital, Ashington, U.K., 1967-68; Registrar Physician-Pediatrics, United Newcastle Hospital, Newcastle on Tyne, U.K., 1965-67; Resident Senior House Physician-Pediatrics, General Hospital, Oldham, U.K., 1964-65; Resident House Physician, Internal Medicine, Memorial Hospital, Darlington, U.K., 1963-64; Resident House Physician, Internal Medicine, Friarage Hospital, Northallerton, U.K., 1963; Resident House Physician, Pediatrics, General Hospital, Middlesbrough, U.K., 1962-63; Casualty Medical Officer Emergency Room 1961-62, Resident House Physician 1961, Bombay Hospital, Bombay, India. Organizational Memberships: American Academy of Pediatrics, Fellow 1971 to present, Member Perinatal Section 1975 to present, Member Illinois Chapter Committee on the Fetus and Newborn 1976-81; Chicago Medical Society, 1973 to present; Illinois State Medical Society, 1973 to present; American Medical Association, 1973 to present; Chicago Pediatric Society, 1973 to present; Medical Society of the County of Kings, Brooklyn, New York, 1972; Medical Society of the State of New York, Lake Success, New York, 1972; Member Infections Control Committee, Illinois Chapter, American Academy of Pediatrics, 1973-74; New York Academy of Science, 1978; Thoracic Society, 1981 to present; Society of Critical Care Medicine, Anaheim, California, 1981; Member Executive Committee and Education Committee, Christ Hospital, 1980 to present. Religion: Past President, Hindu Temple of Greater Chicago, 1980-81. Published Works: Author Numerous Professional Publications. Honors and Awards: Outstanding New Citizen Award for the State of Illinois, 1978; Hummell Foundation Grant, 1976-77; American Medical Association Certificate, 1971, 1974; Recipient Grants from the Hummell Foundation and Wyeth Laboratories. Address: 9221 South Tripp, Oak Lawn, Illinois 60453.■

BYRON ALLEN RATLIFF

Engineering Design Consultant. Personal: Born February 13, 1938; Son of Mr. and Mrs. George M. Ratliff; Married Stella Wanell Standridge, Daughter of Mr. and Mrs. Horace Standridge; Father of Scott Allen, Angela Wanell. Education: Graduate, Decatur High School; Graduate, Decatur Iron and Steel Company Engineering Design Course, 1956; Attended University of Alabama, 2 Years; Graduate, Barnard and Burk, Inc. Power Engineering Design Course, 1974. Career: Engineering Design, Consultant, present; with Decatur Iron and Steel Company, Decatur, Alabama, 1956-58; Thiokol Chemical Company, Huntsville, Alabama, 1958-64; Brown Engineering Company, Huntsville, Alabama, 1964-68; Barnard and Burk, Inc., Baton Rouge, Louisiana, 1968-80; Imes and Associates, Inc., Baton Rouge, Louisiana, 1980 to present. Organizational Memberships: Senior Engineering Technician, National Institute for the Certification of Engineering Technicians, Certification #020267. Community Activities: Vice President and President, Barnard and Burk Recreation League. Religion: Board of Trustees, 6th Avenue Church of God, Decatur, Alabama; Sunday School Superintendent, Church Council, Youth Director, Chapelwood Church of God, Baton Rouge, Louisiana. Address: 9634 Glennsade Avenue, Baton Rouge, Louisiana 70814.■

DAVID WALTER RATLIFF

Oil Executive. Personal: Born July 3, 1949; Son of Mr. and Mrs. Arch Ratliff; Married Bonnie Jean, Daughter of Dr. and Mrs. William Fryer; Father of Tami, David Jr. Education: B.B.A., McMurry College, 1971. Career: Oil Executive. Community Activities: Director, Abilene Boys Ranch, 1981-82; Director, West Texas Rehabilitation Center, 1980-82. Religion: Member University Church of Christ. Honors and Awards: Listed in *Outstanding Young Men of America*. Address: 1298 Kingbury Road, Abilene, Texas 79602.■

GERALD L. RATLIFF

Associate Professor of Theatre. Personal: Born October 23, 1944; Son of Frank and Peggy Donisi. Education: B.A. magna cum laude, Georgetown University, 1967; M.A., University of Cincinnati, 1970; Ph.D., Bowling Green State University, 1975. Career: Feature Writer/Reporter, *Lexington Herald-Leader News*, 1967-68; Instructor, Glenville State College, 1970-72; Fellow, Bowling Green State University, 1972-75; Associate Professor, Deputy Chair/Graduate Advisor, Montclair State College, 1975 to present. Organizational Memberships: Theta Alpha Phi Honorary Drama Fraternity, National Council; Speech Communications Association, National Secretary, Theatre Interest Area, 1978-80, 1980 to present; International Arts Association, Vice President of Research 1975-78; Speech and Theatre Association of New Jersey, President 1978-80; Speech Communication Association, National Review Board, "Educational Resources in Communication" 1976 to present; Popular Culture Association Center for the Study of Popular Culture, Bowling Green State University, National Review Panel, "The State of the Study of Popular Culture Studies in Four-Year Colleges and Universities" 1978-79; National Eastern Regional Research Seminar, "A Homiletic on an Evaluation Assessment of Reader's Theatre in a 'Performance' Context," Director 1982; Speech and Theatre Association of New Jersey State Convention, Chairman 1980; Eastern Communication Association National Convention, Chairman 1980; American Theatre Association National Convention, Publicity Chairman 1979; Secondary School Theatre Association, Chairman of Publicity, Region II, 1979-80; Speech Communication Association, States Advisory Council 1975-77; Association Internationale du Theatre pour Lengance et la Jeunesse; American Studies Association; American Society for Theatre Research; College English Association; Edna St. Vincent Millay Society, Charter Member; International Platform Association; National Writers Club; New Jersey College English Association; Ibsen Society of America, Charter Member; National Council of Teachers of English; O'Neill Society, Charter Member; New York State Speech Association; Southeastern Theatre Conference. Published Works: Numerous Professional Papers and Presentations including (most recent) "Word Games: Verbal Gymnastics in Samuel Beckett's Waiting for Godot" 1979, "To Be Young, Gifted and Black: The 'Poetic Vision' of Lorraine Hansberry's 'American Women'" 1980, "The Theatrical Ingredient of 'Movement' in Readers Theatre" 1980, "The Performance Role of Reader's Theatre in the Secondary Classroom" 1981; Other Articles, Poems, Reviews and Critiques; Editorial Board, Communication Education, 1981 to present; Referee, *Quarterly Journal of Speech*, 1981 to present; National Editor, *The Cue*, 1979 to present; United States Poetry Editor, *Inscape*, 1976-78; Editor, "Reader's Theatre is Alive and Well," *Reader's Theatre News*, 1981 to present; Author of Several Textbooks, *Beginning Scene Study: Aristophanes to Albee*, *The Theatre Student: Speech and Drama Club Activities*, *Beginning Reader's Theatre: A Primer for Classroom Performance*. Honors and Awards: Fellow, International Academy of Poets; Fellow, American Film Institute; Poetry Congress Achievement Award, 1969; Listed in *Who's Who in Education*, *Dictionary of International Biography*, *International Who's Who of Poets*, *Directory of Distinguished Americans*, *Personalities of the East*. Address: 361 Crestmont Road, Cedar Grove, New Jersey 07043.■

TWO THOUSAND NOTABLE AMERICANS

LOUIS J. RATLIFF, JR.

Professor of Mathematics. Personal: Born September 1, 1931; Son of Mr. and Mrs. Earl S. McCracken. Education: B.A., State University of Iowa, 1953; University of Chicago, 1954; M.A. 1958, Ph.D. 1961, State University of Iowa. Military: Served in the United States Air Force, Second Lieutenant, First Lieutenant, Meteorologist, 1953-57. Career: Graduate Student and Teaching Assistant, State University of Iowa, 1957-61; Lecturer in Mathematics, Indiana University, 1961-63; Lecturer, Assistant Professor, Associate Professor, Professor of Mathematics, University of California at Riverside, 1963 to present. Organizational Memberships: Phi Beta Kappa; American Mathematical Society. Religion: Seventh Day Adventist. Honors and Awards: Graduated with Honors, State University of Iowa, 1953; National Science Foundation Cooperative Fellowship, 1960-62; National Science Foundation Research Contracts, 1965-68, 1970-82. Address: 3139 Newell Drive, Riverside, California 92507.■

MARSHALL ARTHUR RAUCH

Corporate Executive. Personal: Born February 2, 1923; Son of Nathan A. and Tillie P. Rauch; Married Jeanne Girard; Father of John, Ingrid, Marc, Peter, Stephanie. Education: Attended Duke University, Durham, North Carolina. Military: Served with the United States Army, Infantry, Overseas European Theater, World War II. Career: Chairman of the Board, President and Director, Rauch Industries, Inc., Gastonia, North Carolina; Director and Treasurer, The E. P. Press, Inc., Gastonia; Director, Majestic Insurance Financing Corporation, Gastonia; President and Director, P. D. R. Trucking, Inc., Gastonia; President and Director, Magic Limited, Gastonia. Community Activities: Mayor Pro Tem, City of Gastonia, 1952-54, 1961-63; City Councilman, City of Gastonia, 1952-54, 1961-65; North Carolina State Senator, 25th District, 1967-82; Governor's Good Neighbor Council, 1963-69; Chairman, Gastonia Human Relations Committee, 1964-67; Chairman, North Carolina Committee on Population and Family, 1968-69; North Carolina Jail Study Commission, 1968; Advisory Council, North Carolina Committee for Children and Youth, 1968-69; President, Duke University, Gaston Alumni Association, 1961-62; President, Associated Industries, 1964-65; Director, Gastonia Chamber of Commerce, 1965-66; Director, Gaston Skills, 1964-66; Director, Salvation Army Boys Club, 1963-71; Director United Fund, 1963-67; Director, Gaston Boys Club, 1964-71; Director, Carolina's A.A.U., 1951-53; Director, Gaston Museum of Natural History, 1963-64; Director, Holy Angels Nursery, Belmont, North Carolina, 1960-73; Director, Gaston Community Action, Inc., 1966; Director, Gaston-Cleveland Tuberculosis Association, 1968; Director, Gastonia Young Men's Christian Association 1969-70, President 1970-71; Chairman, Employ the Handicap Committee, 1964-65; Senior Advisor, Gastonia Boys Club, 1947-63; Big Brother, 1951-60; North Carolina Citizens Committee for Dental Health, 1968-73; Vice President and Director, Community Concert Association, 1960-61; Top Management Advisory Committee, Gaston County Industrial Management Club, 1963-65; Consulting Commission Pioneer Girl Scout Council, 1968-69; Board of Advisory, Gardner Webb College, 1969-77; Director, Planned Parenthood and World Population, New York, 1968-69; Trustee, University of North Carolina, 1969-73; Advisory Committee, North Carolina Vocational Textile School, 1970-71; North Carolina Advisory Budget Commission, 1973-74, 1977-80; North Carolina Senate Vice Chairman, Appropriations, 1969-70; North Carolina Senate Chairman, Intergovernment Relations, 1971-72; North Carolina Senate Chairman, State Government, 1973-74; North Carolina Senate Vice Chairman, Finance, 1973-74, 1980-82; North Carolina Senate Chairman, Law Enforcement and Crime Control, 1975-76; North Carolina Senate Chairman, Finance, 1977-80; North Carolina Senate Vice Chairman, Manufacturing, Labor and Commerce, 1977-82; Vice Chairman, Governmental Incentive Commission, 1977-79; Sports Facility Commission, 1977-80; Vice Chairman, Governmental Incentive Commission, 1977-79; Legislative Services Commission, 1977-82; Chairman, Building Committee, Legislative Services Commission, 1977-80; North Carolina Land Conservancy Board of Trustees, 1978-80; Intangibles Tax Study Commission, 1978; Chairman, Legislative Tax Study Commission, 1977-82; Chairman, Wildlife Tax Study Commission, 1979-80; Southern Legislative Conference, Fiscal Affairs and Steering Committee, 1980; Legislative Ethics Commission, 1981-82; Chairman, North Carolina Highway Study Commission, 1981; Chairman, Senate Legislative Redistricting Committee, 1981-82; Senate Committees, Utilities, Higher Education, Transportation, Appropriations, Ways and Means, Special Ways and Means, Finance, Manufacturing, Labor and Commerce. Honors and Awards: Listed in *Who's Who in World Jewry, Who's Who in the South and Southwest, Leading Men in the United States, Who's Who in Israel, Who's Who in American Politics, The National Register of Prominent Americans*. Address: 1121 Scotch Drive, Gastonia, North Carolina 20852.■

ROBERT RAUNIKAR

Professor of Agricultural Economics. Personal: Born June 13, 1931; Son of Mr. and Mrs. Ed Raunikar; Married Angelum L.; Father of Robert Austin, Jane Manning, Frank Edwin. Education: B.S. Agricultural Education 1956, M.S. Agricultural Economics 1958, Oklahoma State University; Ph.D. Agricultural Economics, North Carolina State University, 1963. Military: Served in the United States Air Force, Staff Sergeant, 1951-55. Career: Professor of Agricultural Economics, University of Georgia, 1962 to present. Organizational Memberships: A.A.E.A., Editorial Council, 1974-77; S.A.E.A., Vice President 1977-78, President 1982-83; Agricultural Economics Association of Georgia. Religion: First Baptist Church, Griffin, Georgia, Deacon 1980 to present, Chairman Music Committee 1982-83. Honors and Awards: Pi Gamma Mu; Gamma Sigma Delta; Listed in *Men of Achievement, Directory of Distinguished Americans, Personalities of America, Personalities of the South, American Men and Women of Science, Community Leaders and Noteworthy Americans, Who's Who in the South and Southwest, Who's Who in America*. Address: 937 Springer Drive, Griffin, Georgia 30223.■

CREAD L. RAY, JR.

State Supreme Court Justice. Personal: Born March 10, 1931; Son of Cread L. and Antonio Ray (both deceased); Married Janet Watson Keller; Father of Sue Ann Culver, Robert, Glenn, David Keller, Marcie, Anne Marie. Education: B.B.A., Texas A&M University, 1952; J.D., University of Texas, 1957; L.H.D., Wiley College, Marshall, Texas, 1980. Military: Served with the United States Air Force Reserve, attaining the rank of Lieutenant Colonel, 1978. Career: Justice, Supreme Court of Texas; Former Associate Justice, Court of Appeals (6th), Texarkana, Texas; State Representative, 1966-70; Harrison County Judge, 1959-61; Law Practice, Marshall, Texas, 1957-59, 1961-70. Organizational Memberships: Rotary Club of Austin, Texas, 1982 to present; Boy Scouts of America, Currently Holder of Various National, Regional, and Local Offices. Religion: Member First United Methodist Church, Austin, Texas; Lay Speaker for Methodist Church; United Methodist Scouters Association. Honors and Awards: Distinguished Eagle Award, 1982; Silver Antelope Award, 1980; Silver Beaver Award, 1975. Address: 4800 Wild Briar Pass, Austin, Texas 78746.■

JULE-KEYES RAY

Retired. Personal: Born August 16, 1912; Married Edward S.; Mother of Bonnie Ray Sey, Dr. Edward S. Jr., Dr. Gaylord W., William R., J. Enos. Education: R.N., St. Vincent's Charity Hospital School of Nursing, Cleveland, Ohio, 1933; Models Guild, Cleveland, Ohio, 1938; Attended Virginia Commonwealth University and University of Richmond. Career: Former Positions include Fashion and Photographic Model, Operating Room Supervisor at Mt. Royal Hospital in Ohio, Cleveland City Hospital in Ohio, State Park Hospital in South Carolina, Pine Camp Tuberculosis Hospital in Virginia, Superintendent of Nurses at Mt. Royal Hospital in Ohio, Pine Camp Hospital in Virginia. Community Activities: Volunteer, Elyria Settlement House, 1928; Disaster Chairman, North Royalton, Ohio, 1938; Member and Past President, Woman's Auxiliary, Richmond Academy of Medicine, 1943 to present; Member and Past Director, Woman's Auxiliary, Medical Society of Virginia, 1943 to present; Board, Sheltering Arms Hospital, 1950 to present; Member, Medical College of Virginia Auxiliary; Captain, Heart Fund Association, 9 Years; R.N. Volunteer, Tidewater Bloodmobile, 9 Years; Volunteer, American Red Cross, 9 Years; Volunteer, Chesterfield Red Cross, 9 Years; Volunteer, Women in Community Service, 3 Years; Volunteer Screener for Students, National Job Corps, 3 Years; In Charge of Volunteers, Richmond Tuberculosis Clinic, 3 Years; Chairman, Emergency Room Volunteers, Medical College of Virginia Hospital of Virginia Commonwealth University, 3 Years; Member, Virginia Museum of Fine Arts, 1972 to present; Artist-Member, Tuckahoe Artists Association, 1981 to present; Numerous Chairmanships for Philanthropic Fund-Raising for Sheltering Arms Hospital and Crippled Children's Hospital. Honors and Awards: First Jessie Richards Award, 1500 Hours Voluntary Services, Medical College of Virginia Hospital, 1974; Listed in *Dictionary of International Biography, Anglo-American Who's Who, Community Leaders of Virginia*. Address: 7604 Hampshire Road, Richmond, Virginia 23229.■

ROBERT DURANT RAY

Professor and Department Head. Personal: Born September 21, 1914; Married Genevieve Triau; Father of Frances Carol, Robert Triau, Esten Bernard, Gisele Antoinette, Charles Alexander. Education: B.A. cum laude in Zoology 1932-36, M.D. Anatomy 1937-40, Ph.D. Anatomy 1947-48, University of California; M.D., Harvard Medical School, 1941-43; University of California Medical School, 1936-37. Military: Served in the United States Army, Captain, Theater Consultant in Orthopaedic Surgery, MTO-USA, Head of Surgery, 61st Evacuation Hospital, 1945-47. Honors and Awards: Carnegie Research Fellowship,

University of California, 1938-40; Kappa Delta Annual National Award for Outstanding Research in Orthpaedic Surgery, 1954; "Research in Orthopaedics," Kappa Delta Annual National Award for Outstanding Research (in collaboration with Dr. Galente, Dr. Luck and Dr. Rostoker) "Sintered Fiber Metal Composites as a Basis for Attachment of Implant to Bone" 1970; Medical Doctor of Science Honoria Causa Degree, University of Umea, Sweden, 1972. Address: 227 Dempster Street, Evanston, Illinois 60201.■

GENE RAYMOND

Actor, Producer, Director, Composer. Personal: Born August 13, 1908, New York, New York; Son of LeRoy D. and Mary (Smith) Guion; Married (1st) Jeanette MacDonald, June 16, 1937 (deceased); Married (2nd) former Mrs. Nel Bentley Hees, September 8, 1974. Education: Student, Professional Children's School, New York, New York. Military: Served in the United States Air Force Reserves to Colonel, 1945-68. Career: Broadway Debut in *The Piper*, 1920; Other Broadway Appearances include *Eyvind of the Hills* 1921, *Why Not?* 1922, *The Potters* 1923, *Cradle Snatchers* 1925, *Take My Advice* 1927, *Mirrors* 1928, *Sherlock Holmes* 1928, *Say When* 1928, *The War Song* 1928, *Jonesy* 1929, *Young Sinners* 1929, *A Shadow of My Enemy* 1957; Other Theater Appearances include *The Man in Possession* (Dennis, Massachusetts) 1946, *The Guardsman* 1951, *The Voice of the Turtle* 1952, *Angel Street* (Richmond, Virginia) 1952, *Petrified Forest* 1952, *Call Me Madam* 1952, *Private Lives* 1953, *The Moon is Blue* 1953, *Be Quiet, My Love* 1953, *Detective Story* 1954, *The Devil's Disciple* 1954, *The Fifth Season* 1955, *Will Success Spoil Rock Hunter* (Los Angeles, San Francisco) 1956, *Romeo and Juliet* (Pasadena Playhouse) 1956, *The Seven Year Itch* 1948, *Holiday for Lovers* (Chicago) 1959; Appeared as Joseph Cantwell in National Touring Company, *The Best Man* 1960, *Majority of One* 1962, *Mr. Roberts* 1962, *Kiss Me Kate* 1962; Other Roles include *Candida* 1961, *The Moon is Blue* 1963, *Madly in Love* 1963, Film Appearances include *Personal Maid* 1931, *Stolen Heaven* 1931, *Ladies of the Big House* 1932, *The Night of June 13th, Forgotten Commandments* 1932, *If I Had a Million* 1932, *Red Dust* 1932, *Ex-Lady* 1933, *The House on 56th Street* 1933, *Zoo in Budapest* 1933, *Bried Moment* 1933, *Ann Carver's Profession* 1933, *Flying Down to Rio* 1933, *Sadie McKee* 1934, *I Am Suzanne Fox* 1934, *Coming Out Party* 1936, *Transatlantic Merry-Go-Round* 1934, *Behold My Wife* 1935, *The Woman in Red* 1935, *Seven Keys to Baldpate* 1935, *Hooray for Love* 1935, *Love Bet* 1936, *Walking on Air* 1936, *The Bride Walks Out* 1936, *The Smartest Girl in Town, Transient Lady* 1936, *There Goes My Girl* 1937, *Life of the Party* 1938, *Cross-Country Romance* 1940, *Mr. and Mrs. Smith* 1941, *The Locket* 1946, *Assigned to Danger* 1948, *Million-Dollar Weekend* 1948, *Sofia* 1948, *Hit the Deck* 1955, *Plunder Road* 1957, *The Best Man, I'd Rather Be Rich* 1964; TV Appearances include *Ed Sullivan's Toast the Town, Ken Murray Show, Robert Montgomery Presents, Tales of Tomorrow, Lux Video Theater, Pulitzer Prize Theater, Broadway TV Theatre, Schlitz Playhouse, Fireside Theater, TV Reader's Digest, Barbara Stanwyck Show, Sam Benedict, U.S. Steel Hour, Adamsburg, U.S.A., The Defenders, Outer Limits, Channing, The Loretta Young Show, Matinee Theater, Playhouse 90, Climax, Johnny Ringo, Ethel Barrymore Theater, F.B.I., Ironside, Apple Way, Judd for the Defense, Bold Ones, Name of the Game, The Interns, Mannix* and Others; Organizational Memberships: Screen Actors Guild, Director; Trustee, Academy TV Arts and Sciences. Community Activities: Past Vice President, Arthritis Foundation, Southern California; President, Motion Picture and TV Fund, 1980; Air Force Association, President Los Angeles Chapter; Players Club, New York, New York; New York Athletic Club; Bel Air Country Club, Los Angeles; Army and Navy Club, Washington; Order of Daedalians. Published Works: Author Teleplay "Prima Donna"; Composer Songs, "Will You?", "Let Me Always Sing," "Release." Honors and Awards: Decorated Legion of Merit and Others; Distinguished Service Award, Arthritis Foundation; Humanitarian Award, Air Force Association; Better World Award, VFW; Bronze Halo Award, Southern California Motion Picture Council. Address: 9570 Wilshire Boulevard, Beverly Hills, California 90212.■

WILLIAM D. READ

Media Specialist. Personal: Born December 10, 1951; Son of George D. Read. Education: A.A., Jones County Junior College, 1972; B.S. Library Science, Hattiesburg, Mississippi, 1973; Additional Graduate Work, Mississippi State University and University of Southern Mississippi. Career: Media Specialist, Memphis State University Campus School Media Center, Memphis, Tennessee; Part-time Librarian, Rutledge College, Memphis, Tennessee; Librarian, Rutledge College; Librarian, Meridian City Schools; Head Librarian, Purvis Public Library; Special Education Teacher, Bay Springs Middle School; Head Librarian, Nadi College, Nadi, Fiji Islands; Head Technical Librarian, Civil Aviation Technical Library; Teacher of English as a Second Language, Nadi College. Organizational Memberships: West Tennessee Library Association, Treasurer; American Library Association; Tennessee Library Association; Tennessee Education Association; Memphis Education Association; University of Southern Mississippi Library Science Alumni Association. Community Activities: Member Board of Directors, International Group of Memphis, 1982; Volunteer Language Translator and Tutor, Memphis Public Library; Volunteer Language Translator, American Red Cross, 1979 to present; United States Peace Corps, Librarian, 1976-78; Fiji Island, Volunteer Youth Court Counselor, 1976; Volunteer Adult Mental Health Counselor, 1976. Honors and Awards: Selected as Outstanding School Librarian Medical Specialist for the State of Mississippi, 1975; Selected as Outstanding Student, Ocean Springs Parent Teacher Association, 1970. Address: 3554 Dalebranch Number 2, Memphis, Tennessee 38116.■

CHARLES FALKINER READE, JR.

Chief Executive Officer/International Merchant of Metal and Mineral Powders. Personal: Born June 24, 1941, in Evanston, Illinois; Son of Charles Falkiner and Elizabeth Boomer Reade; Married Emily Schroeder, September 9, 1978; Father of Amanda Browning. Education: Graduate of the University of Miami, 1965; Harvard Business School, 1971; Continuing Courses at New York Graduate School of Business. Military; Served in the United States Army, 1966-69, attaining the rank of Captain. Career: Salesmen, Southern Bell Telephone and Telegraph Company, 1965-66; Institutional Salesman, Blyth Eastman Dillon and Company, 1973-77; Director of Metal Powder Division, General Manager of Chemical Division, General Manager of Reade Advertising Agency, Reade Manufacturing Company, Inc., Lakehurst, New Jersey, 1977 to present; President, Reade International Corporation, Rumson, New Jersey, 1983 to present; President, Reade Metals and Minerals Corporation, Rumson, New Jersey, 1983 to present; Management Consultant on Size Reduction and Separation Screening Technology and Safety. Organizational Memberships: The Metallurgical Society, American Institute of Metallurgical Engineers; American Society for Metals; American Welding Society; International Precious Metals Institute, Royal Society of Chemistry, United Kingdom; American Society for Testing Materials, Committee for International Standardization, Voting Member; American Institute of Mechanical Engineers; Air Force Association; American Defense Preparedness Association; American Foundrymen's Society; America Iron and Steel Institute; American Powder Metallurgy Institute; American Pyrotechnics Society; NAM; Navy League, Life Member; American Chemical Society; Royal Society of Chemistry. Community Activities: Director, Munson Geothermal Inc.; Guest Lecturer on World Trade and Particulate Manufacturing to Department of Commerce Seminars, Universities and Professional Associations; University Barge Club, Philadelphia; United Sates Army Special Warfare Museum, Trustee; Boy Scouts of America, Council Executive Board; Defender/Courageous 12-Meter Group, Area Finance Chairman; Friends for Reagan Committee, National Chairman, 1976; Businessmen for President Ford Committee, National Chairman 1976, New York City Urban Minority Consulting, Volunteer Consultant; Keep Rumson Safe Committee, Chairman; M.D.O.S.S. Volunteer Nursing Services, Finance Committee; Republican National Finance Committee; Republican Party County Committeeman; Rumson Volunteer Fire Department; United Way, Fund Raising Committee; Advertising Club of New York; Associate Clubs, Life Member; World Trade Club; Harvard Club of New York City and Philadelphia; Monmouth Boat Club; Navensink River Rod and Gun Club; New York Yacht Club; North Shewsbury Ice Boat and Yacht Club. Religion: Episcopalian. Published Works; Founder, *R.E.I.T. Quarterly Journal*, Blyth Eastman Dillon and Company, Inc.; Contributor of Articles to Business and Leisure Publications. Honors and Awards: Bronze Stars (3); Air Medal; Army Commendation Medals (2); Thailand Ranger Badge; Scabbard and Blade, National Military Honorary Society, 1964; Distinguished Military Graduate, 1965; Outstanding Salesman Award, Southern Bell Telephone and Telegraph, 1966; Top Ten Salesmen Award, Blyth Eastman Dillon and Company, Inc., 1972; Listed in *National Record of Prominent Americans and International Notables, Who's Who in Finance and Industry, Who's Who in the World, Directory of Distinguished Americans.* Address: 18 First Street, Rumson, New Jersey 07760.■

JOY PARTNEY REAGAN

Administrator. Personal: Born September 25, 1928; Daughter of Mr. and Mrs. Donald Partney; Married L. David Reagan; Mother of Cyndy R. Klinger, Bonnie, Eric. Education: Undergraduate Studies at Baylor University; B.A. Sociology, Lamar University; M.A. Criminal Justice, Sam Houston State University; Postgraduate Studies undertaken at the University of Houston, University of Chicago, University of Texas; Research undertaken in London, England. Career: Administrator, Buckner Children's Village and Family Care Center, Beaumont, Texas (formerly Beaumont Children's Home), 1967 to present; Researched and Assisted in Design of Multi-Service Campus for Children and Family Servies to Pine Woods Area of Southern Texas. Organizational Memberships: National Association of Homes for Children, Peer Review Chairman; Southwestern Association of Child Care Executives, Vice President; Texas Association of Licensed Children's Services, Public Relations Chairman, Legislative Committee; Executives of Texas Homes for Children, Secretary, Legislative Committee; American Association of Psychiatric Services for Children, Paper at Annual Meeting. Community Activities: Beaumont Chamber of Commerce; Beaumont Executive Roundtable; State Center for Human Development, Advisory Board. Honors and Awards: Social Work Contribution of the Year, Southeast Texas Social Welfare Association, 1973. Address: 5565 Hooks, Beaumont, Texas 77706.■

R. LEE REAVES

Educational Television Network Director. Personal: Born December 10, 1909; Son of Benjamin A. and Ellie Martin Reaves (both deceased); Father of Anne, Robin. Education: A.B.; M.A. Career: Director, Arkansas Educational Television Network; Former Positions include Secretary of State Senate, State Senator, Radio Broadcaster/Owner, Hospital Director, School Superintendent. Organizational Memberships: Board of Southern Educational Communication Association; National Association of Educational Broadcasters. Community Activities: Rotary Club; Phi Delta Kappa Fraternity. Religion: Methodist. Honors and Awards: Secretary of State Senate Emeritus; Honorary Doctorate Degree. Address: 400 North University, #713, Little Rock, Arkansas 72205.■

LESTER NICHOLAS RECKTENWALD

Author. Personal: Son of Peter Wende (deceased) and Catherine (Delsing) Recktenwald; Married Hilda Gertrude Markert; Father of John Francis. Education: Diploma, B.S. with distinction, M.A., University of Minnesota, Saint Cloud; Advanced Studies, University of Minnesota, University of Wisconsin, Columbia University; Ph.D., Sussex Tech. Career: Author Academic Productions, present; Teacher and Administrator in Minnesota, North Dakota, Wisconsin, New York and Tennessee (until 1944); Veterans Counselor and Unit Director, City College of New York City, Marquette University, Private in New York City, Loyola University of New Orleans; Organizer and Director, Psychology Department, Villanova University, Professor (until 1960); Counselor Educator, University of Scranton, 1960-61; Professor and Chairman, Graduate Testing Program, West Chester State College of Pennsylvania, 1962-73. Organizational Memberships: American Personnel and Guidance Association, Wisconsin, President 1939-40, Program Director; President, Association of Higher Education, West Chester State College, Editor; American, Eastern, Pennsylvania Psychological Associations; All Levels of Personnel and Guidance Association including Philadelphia Area; Various Educational Associations. Community Activities: Certified Counselor, Pennsylvania Professional Counselor Board, 1981-84; Research Work for Commission for Investigation of History and Social Studies, University of Minnesota, 1931; Lecturer WHAD in Milwaukee 1937-39, Lecturer at Breakfast Gatherings; Member Survey Team from Columbia University for Neward, New Jersey Schools, 1943. Published Works: Author of Two Books, Seven Monographs, Two Workbooks, Numerous Articles and Other Writings, 1934 to present. Honors and Awards: Honorary Memberships, Eugene Field Society and Mark Twain Society, 1945; Life Fellow International Institute Arts and Letters, 1960; Life Contributor Archives of History of American Psychology, University of Akron, 1968; Life Member, International Council of Psychologists, 1976; Honorary Board of Advisors, American Biographical Institute; Listed in *Who's Who in Community Service, International Authors and Writers Who's Who, Who's Who of Intellectuals, Men and Women of Distinction.* Address: 480 Quigley Road, Wayne (Strafford), Pennsylvania 19087.■

DORRIS HULL REED

Communications Consulting Firm Executive. Personal: Born September 7, 1924; Daughter of Claude Lewis (deceased) and Genevieve Marie (Turner) Hull; Married First Husband Willard James Musson (deceased); Married Second Husband John L. Jr., Son of John L. (deceased) and Eleanor Bell (Adams) Reed; Mother of Willard James Musson Jr., Julie Musson Booth, Scott Hull Musson; Stepchildren John L. III, James Robert, Allyson Gwynn. Education: Communications and Music Programs, Michigan State College; Radio Production Curriculum, University of Michigan Extension. Career: Vice President, Administrator and Secretary, Treasurer of Communications Consulting Firm of McHugh and Hoffman, Inc., 1969 to present; Traffic Manager, WWJ-TV, 1948-50; Radio Broadcaster, "Minute Parade," WWJ-AM Detroit, NBC Station, 1950-54. Organizational Memberships: American Women in Radio and Television, District of Columbia Chapter; Professional Women's Network of Fairfax, Virginia. Community Activities: City of Fairfax Chamber of Commerce, First Ways and Means Chair 1978, Board of Directors 1979-81, President-elect 1981, President 1982; American Red Cross, Special Gifts Committee, 1979-81; Recordings for the Blind, Reader of Textbooks; United Way of Capital Area, Nominating Committee, 1983; Public Information Advisory Board, City of Fairfax, Virginia, 1982-84; Cub Scout, Den Leader, Brownie/Scouts Den Mother. Religion: Episcopalian and Student of Unity, Choir Member, Unity Church, 1979-81. Honors and Awards: Certificate of Appreciation, Chamber of Commerce, 1980 and 1981; Resolution of Achievement as 1982 President City of Fairfax, Chamber of Commerce; Listed in *Who's Who in the South and Southwest.* Address: 3854 University Drive, Fairfax, Virginia 22030.■

MARIE CHRISTINA REEPMEYER

Assistant Librarian. Personal: Born October 4, 1947, Cohoes, New York; Daughter of Herman J. and Marion L. (Debien) Reepmeyer. Education: A.A. Humanities, Stephens College, Columbia, Missouri, 1967; B.A. Sociology, State University of New York at Buffalo, 1969; Master's Degree in Library and Information Science, State University of New York at Albany, 1974. Career: Assistant Librarian, New York State Department of Law, Albany, New York, 1979 to present; Head Legal Services Librarian, Legal Aid Society, Albany, New York, 1977-79; Receptionist and Librarian, Woodland Village Retirement Home, Troy, New York, 1977-80; Assistant Librarian, New York State Education Department, Albany, New York, 1979; Caseworker, Central Intake, Erie County Welfare Department, Buffalo, New York, 1969-70; Library Aide, Mark Skinner Public Library, Manchester, Vermont, 1976; Wholesale Director, We Care Mink Oil Products, 1971 to present; Librarian, Secular (Third) Order of Discalced Carmelites, Monastery, Schenectady, New York, 1982 to present (volunteer). Organizational Memberships: New York State Interagency Information Group, 1979 to present; American Association of Law Librarians, 1978, 1980 to present; American Association of University Women 1980 to present, Board of Directors of Albany, New York Branch 1980-82, Newsletter Editor and Typist, Corresponding Secretary, Delegate to Centennial Convention in Boston, Massachusetts 1981, Vice Chairman of Eastern Area Interbranch Council of Upstate New York 1981-82, Member Nominating Committee 1984, Alternate Delegate to New York State Division Convention in Jamestown, New York 1980; Teller, New York State Division Convention in Albany, New York, 1983. Community Activities: Organist, 1962-64; Young Woman's Christian Association, Albany, New York Branch Board of Directors 1982-83, Chairperson World Mutual Service Committee, Member Scholarship Committee, Gallery Committee and Arrangements Committee of Tribute for Women 1983, Clean-up Committee during Remodeling of Facility, Pricing Committee and Cashier for YWCA Flea Market 1983; Employee's Assistance Program, New York State Department of Law, 1981; President, Young Republican's Club, Stephens College, 1966-67; Chair, Miss Missouri Young Republican Queen Contest, 1967. Religion: Confirmed at St. Ambrose Church, Latham, New York, 1963; Member in Prayer for World Peace of the Blue Army of Our Lady of Fatima, 1982 to present; Perpetual Membership in Franciscan Missionary Union, Mt. Vernon, New York, 1968 to present; Member Missionary Association of Mary Immaculate, Oblate Missions; Member Cell Rosary, Albany, New York, 1983 to present; Pilgrimage to Fatima, Portugal, 1983; Pilgrimage to St. Anne de Beaupre, Canada, 1982; Member Formation in the Secular Order of Discalced Carmelites, Schenectady, New York, 1983 to present; Perpetual Adoration Society, St. Paul the Apostle Church, Troy, New York, 1983 to present; Perpetual Membership for Reepmeyer Family and Relatives, Carmelite High Mass Association, St. Antonio, Texas, 1983 to present; Sponsor, Mother Teresa and Concerned Women for America; Member St. Joan of Arc Parish, Menands, New York, 1979 to present; Contributions to Handicapped, American Indian and Catholic Near East Welfare Association; Attendance at Mariapolis, Fordham University, New York City, with Focolare, 1983; Study with Holy Family Catechetical Institute for Associate Degree in Theology, Baltic, Connecticut, 1983; Member Padre Pio Prayer Group, Siena College, Londonville, New York, 1982 to present; Participant at Rosary Celebration, Auriesville Shrine, New York, 1983; Perpetual Membership in The Confraternity of the Most Holy Rosary, Portland, Oregon, 1984. Honors and Awards: Elk's Youth Leadership Contest Winner, Colonie, New York, 1962-63; Listed in *Who's Who of American Women, Personalities of America, The Directory of Distinguished Americans.* Address: 12 MacDonald Circle, Menands, New York 12204.■

RONALD CROPPER REEVE, JR.

Corporation Executive. Personal: Born January 29, 1943; Son of Ronald and Aldus Reeve; Married Deborah Crooks, Daughter of Shirley R. Crooks; Father of Heather Renee, Michael Scott, Thomas Adam. Education: B.Sc. Physics, Ohio State University, 1967; M.B.A. Marketing, Xavier University, 1972. Military: Served with the Ohio Air National Guard, 1965-68; United States Air Force, 1968-69. Career: Chief Executive Officer, R. C. Reeve, Inc., 1983 to present; Chairman 1979-82, Advanced Robotics; General Manager 1977-79, Marketing Manager 1975-77, Product Manager 1974-75, Air Products and Chemicals;

TWO THOUSAND NOTABLE AMERICANS

Product Planner 1972-74, Product Engineer 1970-72, Project Engineer 1969-70, Development Engineer 1969, General Electric Company. Organizational Memberships: American Welding Society 1974 to present, Chairman Chapter 5 A.W.S. Handbook; American Society for Metals 1975 to present, Contributor to Handbook; Robotics International, 1980 to present; Robot Institute of America, 1979 to present; Society of Manufacturing Engineers, 1979 to present; Computer and Automated Systems Association, 1982 to present; Japan Industrial Robot Association, 1982 to present. Community Activities: Annehurst Village Civic Association, 1970-74; Hoover Yacht Club, 1976 to present; Thistle Fleet 126, 1976 to present, Treasurer, Chief Measurer; Spring Grove Civic Association, 1976 to present; American Welding Society Committee on Welding Automation, 1979 and 1980. Honors and Awards: Small Business Person of the Year, 1981; S.B.A. Small Businessman of the Year, 1980; Listed in *Who's Who in the World*. Address: 1131 Hempstead Court, Westerville, Ohio 43081.■

PATRICK ALOYSIUS REEVES

Corporate Executive. Personal: Born April 21, 1939; Father of Patricia P., Jennifer E. Education: B.B.A. Marketing, University of Cincinnati, 1963. Military: Served in the United States Army, E-5, 1956-64. Career: President and Creative Director, Reeves Advertising, Inc., 1971 to present; Copy Group Head, Ralph H. Jones, Inc., 1970; Copy Supervisor, Clinton E. Frank, Inc., 1968-70; Copywriter, Northlich, Stollye, Inc., 1966-68. Organizational Memberships: New York Art Directors Club; Music for Kids, President 1974-76; Queen City Council for the Performing Arts, Vice President 1979 to present. Community Activities: United Appeal; Businessmen for Xavier University; University of Cincinnati Committee of 100; Cincinnati Reverfront Paddlewheel Committee; Founder, The Cincinnati Competition. Religion: Full Gospel Businessmen's Fellowship, 1978 to present. Honors and Awards: 250 Awards for Creative Excellence, 1961 to present; One of Seven Outstanding Young Men of the Year, Greater Cincinnati; 1969 Chairman's Award, Cincinnati Art Directors Club. Address: 266 Mystic Avenue, Cincinnati, Ohio 45216.■

WILLIAM R. REEVY

Clinical Psychologist. Personal: Born February 3, 1922; Son of Stefan Jan and Marie Soltis Révay (both deceased); Married Carole May Jones; Father of Anthony William, Carolyn Upton and Gretchen Maria. Education: A.B., Stanford University, 1946; Ph.D. Clinical Psychology, Pennsylvania State University, 1954. Career: Chief Psychology Service 1974, Unit Psychologist 1977 to present, Federal Correctional Institution, Butner, North Carolina, 1976 to present; Staff Psychologist, Federal Reformatory, Petersburg, Virginia, 1975-76; Clinical Psychologist, Samaritan Hospital Unit, Rensselaer County Mental Health Center, Troy, New York, 1973-75; Professor of Psychology, 1971-73; Professor of Psychology and Head Department of Psychology and Education 1969-71, Associate Professor of Psychology and Head Department of Psychology and Education 1968-69, New Mexico Institute of Mining and Technology; Associate Professor of Psychology, State University of New York, Cortland, New York, 1964-68; Consultant, Department of Mental Hygiene, State of New York, Clinical Psychologist, Auburn State Prison, 1964-68; Associate Chief Psychologist, District of Columbia General Hospital, Washington D.C., 1962-64; Assistant Professor of Psychiatry, Georgetown University Medical School, 1962-64; Director of Clinical Studies, Northern Virginia Mental Health Project, Falls Church, Virginia, 1961-62; Associate Professor of Psychology, Texas Technological College, Lubbock, Texas, 1960-61; Assistant Professor of Psychology and Counselor, Sacramento State College, Sacramento, California, 1957-60; Instructor 1955, Assistant Professor 1956, DePaul University, Chicago, Illinois; Associate Professor of Psychology, Richmond Professional Institute of the College of William and Mary, Richmond, Virginia, 1954-55; Teaching Assistant 1952-53, Assistant to Dr. Clifford R. Adams 1951-52, The Pennsylvania State University; Teaching Assistant, New York University, Washington Square East, New York, New York, 1946-48. Organizational Memberships: Academy of Psychologists in Marital and Family Therapy, Chairman Nominating Committee 1963, Chairman Committee on Training and Standards 1964, Executive Committee 1964, President 1967-70, Chairman Constitution Committee 1970; American Association of Marriage and Family Therapy; American Psychological Association; Institute for Rational Living, Fellow; Academy of Political Science; American Society for Aesthetics; MacDowell Colony, Associate Fellow; New York Academy of Sciences, Active Member; Society for Applied Anthropology, Fellow; Society for Scientific Study of Sex, Fellow; Society for the Psychological Study of Social Issues. Published Works: Contributor Articles to Professional Journals, including "Petting Experience and Marital Success: A Review and Statement," in *Journal of Sex Research* February 1972; Author Chapters in professional Books. Honors and Awards: Phi Beta Kappa; Psi Chi; Sigma Xi; Certificate, Academy of Psychologists in Marital and Family Therapy; Certificate, American Association of Marital and Family Therapy; Diploma, Menninger Foundation, Marriage Counseling Training Program; Certified Psychologist, State of New York, 1966; Certified Psychologist, State of New Mexico, 1969 (not renewed); Certified Psychologist, State of California, 1967; Licensed Marriage, Family and Child Counselor, California, 1966; Listed in *American Men of Science, The Blue Book, Community Leaders of America, Dictionary of International Biography, Directory of Educational Specialists, International Scholars Directory, International Who's Who in Community Service, Leaders in American Science, Men of Achievement, National Register of Educational Researchers, Notable Americas of the Bicentennial Era, Personalities of the West and Midwest, Two Thousand Men of Achievement, Who's Who Among Authors and Journalists, Who's Who in the South and Southwest, Who's Who in the East, Who's Who in the West*. Address: 730 Crestview Drive, Durham, North Carolina 27712.■

EVERETT LEE REFIOR

Labor Economist, Emeritus Professor of Economics. Personal: Born January 23, 1919; Son of Fred C. and Daisy E. Refior; Married Marie E. Culp; Father of Gene Allan, Wendell Frederick, Paul Douglas, Donna Marie. Education: Graduate of Donnellson High School, Iowa, 1935; B.A. summa cum laude, Iowa Wesleyan College, 1942; Postgraduate Studies, University of Glasgow, Scotland, 1945; M.A., University of Chicago, 1955; Ph.D., University of Iowa, 1962. Military: Served in the Army of the United States, 1943-46, as a Medical Technician in the United States and England, with rank of Private First Class. Career: Instructor, Iowa Wesleyan College, 1947-50; Associate Professor, Simpson College, 1952-54; Professor of Economics, University of Wisconsin-Whitewater, 1955-83. Organizational Memberships: Industrial Relations Research Association, Academic Vice President, Wisconsin Chapter 1978-82; American Economic Association; Midwest Economics Association; Wisconsin Federation of Teachers; Federation of American Scientists. Community Activities: Governor's Commission on the United Nations, 1971 to present; United Nations Association, President Walworth County Chapter 1979-80; World Federalist Association, Founder Whitewater Chapter, President 1960-68, 1976-78, President Midwest Region, 1969-71, 1975 to present, National Board 1968-76, 1978 to present, United States Delegate to World Congresses at Ottowa 1970, Brussels 1972, Paris 1977, Tokyo 1980; World Citizens Assembly, Executive Committee 1980 to present; State Coordinator, Campaign for United Nations Reform, 1984 to present; Democratic Party, Precinct Committeeman 1966 to present, County Chairman 1968-72, District Vice Chairman 1975-78, State Platform Committee 1977 to present; Kiwanis; SANE; American Civil Liberties Union; Common Cause; Alcohol Problems Council of Wisconsin, Board of Directors 1975 to present. Religion: Methodist Lay Speaker, 1959 to present; Janesville District Director of Christian Social Concerns, 1961-67; Wisconsin Conference Board of Church and Society, 1970-76; Board of Directors, Wisconsin Protestant Legislative Council, 1965-69. Honors and Awards: Order of Artus (now Omicron Delta Epsilon), 1951; Ford Foundation Summer Faculty Fellowship, 1959; Listed in *Wisconsin Men of Achievement, Who's Who in the Midwest, Who's Who in America, Who's Who in the World*. Address: 205 North Fremont, Whitewater, Wisconsin 53190.■

CLAIRE N. REGNIER

Business Consultant. Personal: Born May 2, 1939. Education: B.S. cum laude, Journalism, Trinity University, 1961. Career: President, Metro Consultants; Established *Showboat*, a Monthly Newspaper, 1968, Editor 1968-80, Publisher's Representative; First Executive Director, San Antonio River Association, 1968-81. Organizational Memberships: Women in Communications, Inc.; Texas Public Relations Association; San Antonio Press Club; Texas Recreation and Parks Society; International Association of Business Communicators. Community Activities: Downtown Holiday River Festival, Originator; Centro 21 Downtown Revitalization Task Force, Chairman 1977-83; Parks and Recreation Advisory Board, 1978 to present; Representative to San Antonio River Corridor Committee; San Antonio Council, Girl Scouts of America, Board of Directors, Chairman; Fiesta San Antonio Commission, Commissioner; University Roundtable; Council on International Relations; Altrusa Club of San Antonio; Trinity University Alumni Association. Religion: St. Luke's Episcopal Church. Honors and Awards: Awards of Excellence for Editing Showboat, 1970-74; Trinity University Alumni Council President's Citation for Outstanding Services, 1974-76; Communicator

TWO THOUSAND NOTABLE AMERICANS

of the Year, 1977; Addressed Council on Urban Economic Development, 1980; Headliner Award for Public Endeavors, 1980; Southwest Region Banner Award, Excellence in Communication, 1981; Listed in *Outstanding Young Women of America, Notable Americans, Who's Who of American Women, World Who's Who of Women, Personalities of America, Who's Who of the South and Southwest.* Address: 7772 Woodridge Street, San Antonio, Texas 78209.■

JAMES R. REHAK

Orthodontist. Personal: Married Joann Marie Tabbert, October 15, 1969; Father of Suzanne Therese. Education: B.S. 1960, D.D.S. cum laude 1962, M.S. 1967, Certificate of Orthodontists 1965, University of Illinois. Military: Served in the United States Army Reserves, 1963-68, attaining the rank of Captain. Career: Private Practice in Orthodontics, 1965 to present; Associate Professor, University of Illinois; Orthodontic Consultant, 1966-68. Organizational Memberships: American Association of Orthodontists; Illinois Association of Orthodontists; Southern Society of Orthodontists; American Dental Association; Illinois Dental Association; Chicago Dental Society; Florida Dental Association; West Coast Dental Society; Royal Society of Health, Fellow; International Platform Association; Omicron Kappa Upsilon Honorary Dental Society; Federation Dentaire Internationale; International Biographical Association, Life Fellow. Published Works: Articles in Journal of Dental Research, Dental Clinics of North America, Journal of the American Medical Association. Honors and Awards: Listed in *Who's Who in the Midwest, Who's Who in the Southeast, Dictionary of International Biography, Men of Achievement, Notable Americans, Men of Distinction.* Address: 4115 Del Prado Boulevard, Cape Coral, Florida 33904.■

LYNN P. REHM

Professor of Psychology. Personal: Born May 20, 1941; Son of Stanley F. (deceased) and Bernice S. Rehm; Married Susan Higginbotham; Father of Elisabeth Susan, Sarah Ann. Education: B.A. Psychology, University of Southern California, 1963; M.A. Clinical Psychology 1966, Ph.D. Clinical Psychology 1970, University of Wisconsin-Madison. Career: Professor of Psychology, University of Houston; Associate Professor, Psychological Department, University of Pittsburgh; Assistant Professor, Neuropsychiatric Institute, University of California-Los Angeles. Organizational Memberships: American Psychological Association; Association for the Advancement of Behavioral Therapy; A.A.A.S.; Society for Psychotherapy Research. Honors and Awards: Phi Beta Kappa; Phi Eta Sigma. Address: 7906 Burning Hills Drive, Houston, Texas 77071.■

FREDERICK A. REICHLE

Professor of Surgery, Department Chairman. Born April 20, 1935, Neshaminy, Pennsylvania. Education: B.A. 1957, M.D. 1961, M.S. Biochemistry 1961, M.S. Surgery 1966, Temple University; Intern, Abington Memorial Hospital, 1962; Resident, Temple University Hospital, 1966. Career: Professor of Surgery, Chairman of Department of Surgery, Presbyterian-University of Pennsylvania Medical Center; Surgeon, Presbyterian-University of Pennsylvania Medical Center; Associate Attending Surgeon, Episcopal Hospital, St. Mary's Hospital, St. Christopher's Hospital for Children, Phoenixville Hospital; Consultant, Veterans Hospital, Wilkes-Barre, Pennsylvania; Consultant, The Germantown Dispensary and Hospital. Organizational Memberships: American Board of Surgery, Diplomate 1968; American Surgical Association; Society of University Surgeons; American Medical Association; Pennsylvania Medical Society; Phi Rho Sigma Medical Fraternity, 1959; Sigma Xi; Association for Academic Surgery; The New York Academy of Sciences; American Association for the Advancement of Science; American Biographical Institute, National Board of Advisors; Royal Society of Medicine; Delaware Valley Vascular Society; American College of Angiology; American Institute of Ultrasound in Medicine; American Physiological Society; The College of Physicians of Philadelphia, Fellow; American Society for Pharmacology and Experimental Therapeutics, Inc.; Surgical Historical Society; Societe Internationale de Chirurgie; Collequim Internationale Chirurgie Digestive; Society for Vascular Surgery; Society for Surgery of the Alimentary Tract; National Kidney Foundation, Professional Member; International Society on Thrombosis and Haemostatis; Philadelphia Academy of Surgery; American College of Surgeons, Fellow; American Gastroenterological Association; National Association of the Professions; American Federation for Clinical Research; Association of Program Directors in Surgery; Heart Association of Southeastern Pennsylvania; American Diabetes Association; American Association of Cancer Research; American Heart Association; American Society of Abdominal Surgeons; Surgical Biology Club; American Aging Association; American Geriatrics Society; American Society of Contemporary Medicine and Surgery; Board of Appeals in Accreditation Council for Graduate Medical Education. Community Activities: Site Visitor, Canadian Department of Health and Welfare, Programs Branch, 1977; Lectures and Forums Committee of the Medical Faculty Senate, 1976-79; Specialist Site Visitor, Residency Review Committee for Surgery, Liaison Committee on Graduate Medical Education, American Medical Association, 1979; Specialist Site Visitor, Inspection for Continuation of General Surgical Residency Training Program, 1980, the Society for Vascular Surgery. Honors and Awards: Temple University Full Tuition Competitive Scholarship, 1953; College of Liberal Arts Graduation Award, Temple University, 1957; Nathan Lane Award for the Highest Student Achievement in Chemistry, Temple University, 1957; Graduate summa cum laude, 1957; Fellowship in Nutrition, American Medical Association Summer of Medical School, 1961; Surgical Resident's Research Paper Award, Philadelphia Academy of Surgery, 1966, 1967; Gross Essay Prize of the Philadelphia Academy of Surgery; Recipient of Established Investigatorship Grant, American Heart Association, 1973; Omega Alpha; Honorary Member, Chilean Surgical Society; Listed in *Who's Who in the East, Who's Who in America, Who's Who in the World.* Address: 51 North 39th Street, Philadelphia, Pennsylvania 19104.■

DARCY TYSON REID

Attorney, Educator. Personal: Born March 3, 1946; Daughter of Mr. and Mrs. George D. Cremer; Mother of Stephen David. Education: B.A. Speech and History 1966, Postgraduate and Graduate Work 1966-67, 1972-73, San Diego State University; Elementary and Secondary California Teaching Credentials; J.D., University of California Hastings College of Law, 1967-70. Career: Lawyer, Fresno County Legal Services 1975-81, Richmond Legal Assistance 1974-75; Teacher, National Teacher Corp 1966-67, Other Teaching 1974-75. Organizational Memberships: Fresno County Bar Association, 1975-82; Fresno Young Lawyers, 1975-82; California Women Lawyers, 1978-81; Western Advisory Board for Law Students Civil Rights Research Council, 1974 to present; National Board of Law Students Civil Rights Research Council 1960-70, Chapter Chairman 1969-70, Curriculum Committee Chairman 1968-69; Health Committee of the Fresno Commission on the Status of Women, 1978-81; Subcommittee of the Fresno County Mental Health Advisory Board, 1979-80; Fresno Democratic Coalition 1977-82, Program Director 1978-79; San Francisco Federated Young Democrats 1967-70, 1971-72, Secretary 1968-69. Religion: United Methodist. Honors and Awards: Listed in *Who's Who in American Law, Who's Who in California, Who's Who in American Colleges and Universities, Dictionary of International Biography.* Address: 730 Fowler Avenue, Clovis, California 93612.■

HENRIETTA REIFLER

Librarian. Personal: Born July 29, 1917; Daughter of Mendel and Annie Brown (both deceased); Married Erwin Reifler (deceased); Mother of Victoria R. Bricker, Frank J. Reifler, Anna Irene Leepansen, Consuela Margaret Reveles, Michaela Thea Kaplowitz. Education: B.A. English Honors, University of London, 1941; B.A. 1950, M.A. 1959, M.L.S. 1969, all from the University of Washington-Seattle. Career: Teacher of English, Mary Farnham School for Girls, China, 1936-39; Teacher of English and Speech, St. Nicholas School Seattle, 1954-58; Instructor, Department of English, Everett Community College, Washington, 1959-61; Lecturer, Department of English, University of Washington-Seattle, 1961-68; Librarian, Washington State University-Pullman, 1969-82. Organizational Memberships: National Council of Teachers of English, Judge Achievement Awards 1961-65; Washington Library Association Women's Caucus, Chairman and Program Chairman 1976-80, Continuing Education Committee 1973-76, 1981-83; Washington State University Commission on the Status of Women, Secretary 1977-78; Pacific Northwest Library Association Quarterly, Indexer 1973-76; Phi Beta Kappa, Secretary Local Chapter 1972-75. Community Activities: Washington Women United, 1979 to present; Hadassah, 1971 to present; Donations to Local and National Charities such as United Way and Easter Seals, National Jewish and Israeli Loan Societies and Orphanages, Organizations for the Blind, Holocaust Studies, Ethiopian Jews, Tree Planting, Equal Rights Amendment, National Organization of Women; Political Contributions for the Democratic Party, 1971 to present; Committee of 100; Fortune Society; Klanwatch; National Association for the Advancement of Colored People. Religion: Member Herzl Conservative Congregation, 1948-57, 1961-69; Temple Beth Ann, 1957-61; Herzl-Ner Tamid Congregation, Mercer Island, 1948-69; Temple Beth Shalom, Spokane, 1970-82; Congregation Beth Shalom, Seattle, 1983 to present. Honors and Awards: Phi Beta Kappa, 1950; The Cum Laude Society, 1956. Address: 221 Northeast 94th Street, Seattle, Washington 98115.■

TWO THOUSAND NOTABLE AMERICANS

JEANETTE P. REILLY

Consulting Clinical Psychologist. Personal: Born October 19, 1908; Daughter of George Lindsey and Marie Bloedorn Parker (both deceased); Married Peter C. Reilly Jr.; Mother of Marie R. Heed, Sara Jean R. Wilhelm, Patricia Ann R. Davis. Education: A.B., University of Colorado, 1929; M.A. 1951, Ed.D. 1959, Columbia University; Postdoctoral Studies in Clinical Psychology, Larue Carter Hospital, Indianapolis, 1960-61; Post-doctoral Studies in Child Psychology, Riley Hospital, 1961. Career: Consulting Clinical Psychologist; Former Staff Member, St. Vincent's Hospital, Indianapolis; Lecturer, Butler University; Consultant, Christian Theological Seminary; Consulting Clinical Psychologist, Veterans Administration, Indianapolis; Cerebral Palsy Clinic, University Medical Center; Teacher, Speech and Drama, Denver, Colorado. Organizational Memberships: American Psychological Association; National Register of Health Service Providers in Psychology; Indiana Psychology Association; Central Indiana Psychology Association; American Personnel and Guidance Association; American Vocational Guidance Association. Community Activities: Community Hospital Foundation Board, 1978 to present; Hanover College, Board of Trustees 1975 to present; University of Notre Dame Women's Auxiliary Council, 1953 to present; Governor's Advisory Council on Division of Mental Retardation and Other Developmental Disabilities, 1975; Indiana State Board of Examiners in Psychology, Chairman 1969-70, Board Member 1969-75; St. Richards School, Indianapolis, Board Member 1967-73; Indianapolis Day Nursery Board, 1957-62; Indiana Mental Health Advocacy Board, 1981-83. Religion: Second Presbyterian Church, Indianapolis. Honors and Awards: Sagamore of the Wabash, 1980; Mayor's Citation, 1975; Governor's Citation, 1967, 1970; Mortar Board; Pi Lambda Theta; Kappa Delta Pi; Listed in *Who's Who of American Women, World Who's Who of Women, Who's Who in the Midwest*. Address: 1015 Stratford Hall, Indianapolis, Indiana 46260.■

HARRY CHARLES REINL

Economist. Personal: Born November 13, 1932; Son of Carl and Angela Plass Reinl (both deceased). Education: B.S., Fordham University, 1953; Certificate, United States Department Agriculture Graduate School, 1966; A.M., The George Washington University, 1968; Student Special Program, Applied Urban Economics, Massachusetts Institute of Technology, 1972; National Resident Associate Program Member, Smithsonian Institution, Washington D.C. Military: Served with the United States Army Ordnance C, First Lieutenant, 1953-55; Commissioner Officer in Reserves, 1955; Honorable Discharge as First Lieutenant, United States Army Reserve Ordnance Corps; Reserve Commissioner Officer, United States Army, 1962. Career: Economist; Labor Economist, Office of Personnel Management, Washington D.C., 1968 to present; Labor Economist, Office Manpower Administration, United States Department of Labor, Washington D.C., 1962-68; Junior Observer, Sperry Rand Corporation, New York City, 1958-62; Manager New York Branch, Wilmark Service System, 1971; Associate National Archives, 1976 to present; Federal Project, Appropriate Technology Small Grant Program, United States Department of Energy, Region III through Third Round 1981. Organizational Memberships: Appointed State Advisor (Virginia), United States Congressional Advisory Board, 1982 to present; Special Agent, IIOCIA, American Police Academy, 1982 to present; Member ex officio Board of Trustees, American Police Hall of Fame and Museum. Community Activities: Republican Party; Sustaining Member, Republican National Committee 1975 to present, Life Member 1979 to present; National Republican Congressional Committee 1978 to present; Fellow Member, RNC Ambassadors Club, 1981 to present; Contributed to the Execution of Programs with the Department of Labor 1968; Participated in the Formulation of the Republican Legislative Agenda for 1981; Contributed to the United States Senate Legislation Tar and Labor Programs; Worked through the American Security Council Education Foundation on "Fairness Doctrine"; International Biographical Centre, Acted in IBC Choir at 8th IBC Congress in Beverly Hills, California, 1981; Telethon Volunteer, The George Washington University, Resident Associate Program Member 1973, 1974, 1979; University Building Development Fund. Religion: Roman Catholic. Honors and Awards: Certificate of Appreciation, America Police Academy, 1979; National Defense Service Medal, 1955; Korean Service Medal and United Nations Service Medal, 1955; Certificate of Service, Department of Labor, 1968; Community Leader of the United States Award, 1979; Elected Honorary Fellow, Anglo-American Academy, 1980; New York Academy of Sciences, 1982; Life Member, Republican Party of the United States of America, 1979; Republican Certificate of Appreciation, 1982; Listed in *Book of Honor*. Address: 1111 Arlington Blvd, 109W, Arlington, Virginia 22209.■

ARNOLD REISMAN

Professor. Personal: Born August 2, 1934; Son of Rose and Isadore Reisman; Married Ellen Kronheim. Education: B.S. Engineering 1955, M.S. Engineering 1957, Ph.D. Engineering 1963, University of California-Los Angeles. Career: Professor of Operations Research, Case Western Reserve University; Visiting Professor, Hebrew University of Jerusalem, 1975; Visiting Professor, Japan-American Institute of Management Science, Honolulu, Hawaii, 1975; Visiting Professor of Business Economics and Quantitative Methods, University of Hawaii, 1971; Visiting Professor of Engineering and Acting Chairman, Department of Industrial and Operations Science, University of Wisconsin-Milwaukee, 1966-68; Assistant to Associate Professor of Engineering, California State University at Los Angeles, 1957-66. Organizational Memberships: Japan-American Institute of Management Science, Institutional Planning Committee, Board of Trustees 1975 to present; Operations Research Society of America, Chairman Education Sciences Section 1974, 1975; T.I.M.S.; American Institute of Industrial Engineers, Fellow, American Association for the Advancement of Science, Member of Council 1970; A.S.E.E.; A.A.U.P.; Omega Rho; Phi Delta Kappa. Community Activities: Jewish Community Federation, Delegate Assembly 1973-78; Hillel Foundation, Board of Trustees 1972-76; Shaker Heights Citizens Advisory Committee, 1972 and 1978; United Jewish Appeal and Israel Emergency Fund Drive, University Division, Coordinator; Cleveland Coalition of Health Care Cost Effectiveness, Founder and Member, Board of Directors 1978 to present. Published Works: Author of 11 Professional (Text) Books, One Non-Fiction Book *Welcome Tomorrow*, Co-Authored with Ellen Reisman, and Over 100 Articles in Professional Journals. Honors and Awards: Cleveland Engineer of the Year, 1973; Listed in *Who's Who in the World, Who's Who in America, Community Leaders and Noteworthy Americans, Who's Who in the Midwest, International Scholars Directory, Outstanding Educators in America, American Men and Women of Science*. Address: 18428 Parkland Drive, Shaker Heights, Ohio 44122.■

FREDERICKA K. REISMAN

Elementary Education Department Chairman. Personal: Born September 22, 1930; Daughter of Samuel Kauffman; Mother of Lisa Reisman Halterman. Education: B.A. 1952, M.S. 1963, Ph.D. 1968, Syracuse University. Career: Chairman Department of Elementary Education, Professor 1979 to present, Associate Professor 1974-79, Assistant Professor 1969-74, University of Georgia, Athens, Georgia. Organizational Memberships: American Psychological Association; American Education Research Association; National Council of Teachers of Mathematics; Council for Exceptional Children; National Association for Educators of Young Children; Association for Childhood Education International; Association of Teacher Educators; Georgia Council for Exceptional Children; Georgia Association for Young Children; Association for Supervision and Curriculum Development; American Association of University Professors; Association for Children with Learning Disabilities; Jean Piaget Society; National Middle School Association; The American Orthopsychiatric Association; The National Society for the Study of Education; Kappa Delta Pi; Society on Research in Child Development; Member Numerous Committees and Panels within the University of Georgia including Chairperson College of Education Promotions Review Committee 1982, Chairperson University of Georgia Tenure Committee 1982, Secretary Bicentennial Scholarship Committee 1982-85, Chairman Search Committee for Head of Division of Exceptional Children 1982, Representative to University Council 1980-83, Member and Committee Secretary Search Committee for Dean of College of Education 1981, Chairman Faculty Senate Committee on Graduate Courses and Program 1980. Community Activities: International Federation of Learning Disabilities, Amsterdam, Netherlands, Program Committee, Awards Committee; Selected to Present International Honors Award to Marianne Frostig at Awards Banquet, 1974; International Federation of Learning Disabilities, Brussels, Belgium, Sessions Chairman, Program Committee, Toastmistress of Awards Banquet, 1975; International Federation of Learning Disabilities, Montreal, Canada, Program Committee, Member Board of Directors, Member Professional Advisory Board; Taught First Mini-Course for Georgia Council of Teachers of Mathematics, 15th Annual Georgia Mathematics Conference (Participants earned University of Georgia Credit, Emory University Credit, and West Georgia College Credit); Program Chairman to Screen U.S. Paper Presenters, Early Childhood Conference, Tel Aviv, Israel, 1980; Main Speaker, College of Education Memorial Lecture, University of Washington, Seattle, Washington, 1982; Presentation at 1981 Annual Meeting of Eastern Educational Research Association, Philadelphia, Pennsylvania, 1981; Presentation at 1981 A.E.R.A. Annual Meeting in Los Angeles, California, 1981. Published Works: Author Several Textbooks and Journal Articles. Honors and Awards: Graduate Assistantship in Mathematics Education, Syracuse University, 1965-67; Awarded Teaching Lectureship in Mathematics Education, Syracuse University, 1967-68; Postdoctoral Lectureship in Mathematics Education by David Krathwohl, former Dean College of Education, Syracuse University, 1968-69; Association of Teacher Educators, Research Award, Third Place, "A Diagnostic Strategy Using Comparisons of Teacher's Stated Philosophy and Stated Practices Toward Discipline" (with Ron Goldenberg), 1974; Pi Lambda Theta; Phi Delta Kappa; Invited to Governor's Conference on Education, Atlanta, 1968; Received Summer Research Award, College of Education, University of Georiga, Summer 1978; Appointed to Graduate Faculty, University of Georgia, 1978; 1 of 3 Top Applicants out of 226 given Consideration for Position of Chairman of Department of Education, Villanova University, Villanova, Pennsylvania, 1978; Invited to Serve on Doctoral Committee at University of Pennsylvania joining Drs. Rydia Rose (Director of Teacher Education) and Ken George (Science Education) as 3rd Member of Advisory, Examining, and Reading Committee; Invited to Serve on Doctoral Committee, Northwestern University, Natchitoches, Louisiana; Planning Grant (with Dr. Andrew Shotick) from Southeast Regional Learning Resource Center Network to Develop Model Program for Training Leadership Personnel for Preparing Regular Classroom and Special Education Teachers for Teaching Children with Special Educational Needs; Listed in *Who's Who in the South and Southwest.* Address: 130 Cedar Circle, Athens, Georgia 30601.■

JUDITH REISMAN

Research Professor. Education: Bachelor's Degree (waived in lieu of professional mass media experience), Case Western Reserve University, 1975; Master's Degree, Speech Communication, Case Western Reserve University, 1976; Completed Doctoral Degree and Dissertation, Case Western Reserve University, 1980. Career: Research Professor (School of Education), Project Director and Principle Investigator (Office of Juvenile Justice and Delinquency Prevention), The American University, 1983 to present; Research in Media Sociology, Department of Anthropology/Sociology, 1981-83. Organizational Memberships: American Association for the Advancement of Science; American Association of Composers, Authors and Publishers; American Federation of Television and Recording Artists; International Communication Association; New York Academy of Sciences; Ohio Academy of Science; The Hastings Center/Institute of Society, Ethics and the Life Sciences; World Association of Infant Psychiatry. Published Works: Books Forthcoming, *317: A Scholarly Examination of the Kinsey Experiments on Child Sexuality* and *From Shirley Temple to Pretty Baby: The Journey of the Child;* Author/Co-Author Various Professional Articles; Composer Number of Original Songs/Media Material. Honors and Awards: Sound Filmstrip "Families" has received the Dukane Annual Award for Outstanding Creativity in Sound Filmstrip Production (1982), First Place Gold Camera Award for "Learning" at the Industrial Film Festival (1982), Second Place Silver Screen Award for "Learning" at the Industrial Film Festival (1982), Best Films and Filmstrip of the Year by *Learning* Magazine (1981-82) and Silver Plaque Award for "Making Rules" at the International Communication Family Video Competition (1982); Emmy Nominee for Public Service Spot, "Pride of Country," 1976; First Place for Local TV Services, 1974; "Best of 1965" Les Clayppol, KPFC Pacifica, Best Songs Written in 1965. Address: The American University, School of Education, 5010 Wisconsin Avenue, N.W., Washington D.C. 20016.■

ESTHER G. RENTERIA

Corporate Executive. Personal: Born May 1, 1939; Daughter of Oliver Jay and Violet Wellman Gatfield (both deceased); (raised by) Mr. and Mrs. Daryl Locey. Education: A.A., East Los Angeles College, 1958; B.A., California State University, Los Angeles, 1974. Career: President, Esther Renteria Public Relations, Inc.; Newspaper Reporter, Alhambra Post Advocate, 1959-61; Newspaper Editor, *East Los Angeles Tribune-Gazette,* 1962-68; Radio Assignment Editor/Newswriter, KNX Radio, 1968; Associate Producer/Program Moderator, "Ahora" (Now) Television Series, KCET (PBS) Channel 28, 1969-70; Associate Producer, "Siesta Is Over" and "Bienvenidos" Television Series, KNXT (CBS) Channel 2, 1970-74; Public Information Director, East Los Angeles College, 1970-83. Community Activities: Bilingual Foundation of the Arts; Plaza de la Raza Cultural Center; East Los Angeles Regional Occupational Center Advisory Board; California Committee College Association P.I.O.'s; East Los Angeles Service Center Advisory Council; Cleland House of Neighborly Service, Board of Directors; Publicity Director, 16th of September Festival; Public Relations Director, Los Angeles Street Scene Festival, co-sponsored by City of Los Angeles and Schlitz Brewing Company, in Los Angeles Civic Center, 1978 to present; Statewide Publicity Director, Governor's 1980 Chicana Issues Conference; Los Angeles County Commission on Police and Mexican American Community Relations; Future Broadcasting Corporation, Secretary Board of Directors. Published Works: Published Various Newspapers and Magazines. Honors and Awards: Outstanding Journalistic Achievement Award, East Los Angeles College, 1964; Silver Spur (Espuela de Plata), as an Outstanding Image Maker in the Spanish-Speaking Community for Weekly Television Series, "The Siesta Is Over," Awarded by "Nosotros" President Ricardo Montalban, 1972; "The Siesta Is Over" Nominated for Emmy Awards, 1970, 1972; Honored by Los Angeles County Probation Department, 1973; Named Professional Person of the Month, East Los Angeles Community Union, 1974; Honored by Los Angeles County Parks and Recreation Department for Assisting in Improvement of Programming in East Los Angeles Area, 1975; Recognized by Los Angeles Eastside Sports Association for Community Service, 1978; Honored for Outstanding Service, Sixteenth of September Festival Committee, 1979; Honorary Membership Award, Chicanos for Creative Medicine, 1980; Honored by East Los Angeles College Student Body for Service, 1981; Honored by Los Angeles City Bicentennial Committee for Contributions to the City, 1981; Presented with Plaque on "Anthony Quinn Day," Los Angeles County Library, 1981; Listed in *Who's Who of American Women, Who's Who in California.* Address: 301 Dochan Circle, Montebello, California 90640.■

ROSE ELEANOR REPLOGLE

Restorer. Personal: Born January 14, 1909; Widow; Mother of Ronald, Richard H., Charles M. Education: Graduate of Omaha Tech, 1927; Graduate of Faribault School of Christian Leadership, 1939. Career: Restorer of Oriental Carpets and Tapestries; Executive Secretary, Nebraska-Iowa Grain Company, Omaha, 1928-32. Organizational Memberships: Smithsonian Institution, 1982-83; The Honorary Directors Association of Rockhurst College, 1983; Friends of Art, Nelson-Adkins Gallery, 1978-84. Community Activities: Art Study Club, Nelson-Atkins Gallery, 1983-84; Women's Chamber of Commerce, Attendance Chairman, Board of Directors 1980-81; Soroptimist International, Hospitality Chairman 1979-80; Woman's City Club, Hospital Committee 1980-81, Hostess Committee 1982-84; King's Daughters and Sons International, First Vice President 1984; P.E.O. Sisterhood, Chapter J.I., Budget Chairman 1976-81; Red Mitten Writers Club, Member 21 Years, President 1977-79; Baptist Hospital Women's Auxiliary; Adult Friendship Club, Country Club Christian Church. Religion: Leader, Circle I, Country Club Christian Church, 1977-79; Corresponding Secretary Circle 19, 1984; Bible Study Group, 14 Years. Honors and Awards: Happiest Married Couple Citation, Minneapolis Aquatennial, 1948; State Winner National Chicken Cooking Competition, 1961, 1962, 1963, 1964, 1968; Chosen to Restore 18th Century Tapestries, University of Kansas Museum of Art, Lawrence, Kansas, 1977. Address: 6821 Brookside Road, Kansas City, Missouri 64113.■

CECIL R. REYNOLDS

Associate Professor and Program Director. Personal: Born February 7, 1952; Son of Mr. and Mrs. C. C. Reynolds; Married Brenda Cherry. Education: B.A. Psychology, University of North Carolina-Wilmington, 1975; M.Ed. Psychometrics 1976, Ed.S. School Psychology 1977, Ph.D. Educational Psychology 1978, University of Georgia. Career: Associate Professor and Director, School Psychology Training Program, Texas A&M University; Acting Director, Buros Institute of Mental Measurements, University of Nebraska 1979, Associate Director 1980-81; Assistant Professor, University of Nebraska-Lincoln, 1978-81; Psychologist, Rutland Center for Severely Emotionally Disturbed Children, 1976-78. Organizational Memberships: American Psychological Association; American Education Research Association; National Council on Measurement in Education; National Association of School Psychologists; National Association for Gifted Children; New York Academy of Science; National Academy of Neuropsychologists. Community Activities: Past President, S.S.H. Jaycees, 1975. Honors and Awards: Outstanding Young Man of America, 1980; Kappa Delta Pi Award of Excellence for Outstanding Contributions to Education, 1978; Paper of the Year, *Gifted Child Quarterly,* 1978; American Psychological Association, Division 16, Lightner Whitmer Award as Outstanding Young School Psychologist in the United States of America, 1980; American Psychological Association, Division 5, Outstanding Contributor in First 10 Postdoctoral Years, 1981. Address: 2714 Pierre Place, College Station, Texas 77840.■

CLAYTON REYNOLDS

Endocrinologist. Personal: Born December 9, 1943; Son of Olive Reynolds; Married Janet Marita; Father of Lorena Marlo, Juanita Joy. Education: B.S. and Pre-Medical Diploma, Memorial University, St. John's, Newfoundland, 1964; Rotating Internship, Royal Victoria Hospital, Montreal, 1968-69; Resident in Medicine, St. John's General Hospital, Newfoundland, 1969-70; Fellow in Medicine, Mayo Graduate School, Rochester, Minnesota, 1970-72; Advanced Clinical Resident in Endocrinology, Mayo Graduate School, 1972-74; M.D., C.M., McGill University, Montreal, Quebec, 1968; L.M.C.C., Licentiate of the Medical

Council of Canada, 1968; F.R.C.P.(C), Royal College of Physicians and Surgeons of Canada, 1973; M.S. Medicine, University of Minnesota, Minneapolis, Minnesota, 1974; F.A.C.P., American College of Physicians, 1976. Career: Teaching, Professional or Research Positions Held during Residency Training, Medical Seminars for Students, Interns and Residents, Royal Victoria Hospital, St. John's General Hospital, Mayo Graduate School; University of British Columbia, Faculty Member 1975, Assistant Professor of Medicine 1977, Associate Professor of Medicine 1982; Currently in Private Practice of Endocrinology, Valley Endocrine and Diabetes Treatment Center, Lancaster, California; Medical Staff Appointments at Antelope Valley Hospital Medical Center (Lancaster, California), Lancaster Community Hospital (Lancaster, California), Palmdale Hospital Medical Center (Palmdale, California), Mira Loma Hospital (Lancaster, California). Organizational Memberships: Canadian Diabetes Association, Clinical and Scientific Section; American Diabetes Association; Canadian Society for Endocrine and Metabolism; Vancouver Medical Association; B.C. Medical Association; Canadian Medical Association; Canadian Medical Association; Endocrine Society; B.C. Society for Internal Medicine; International Diabetes Federation; Canadian Society for Clinical Investigation; American Federation of Clinical Research; International Association for Medical Assistance to Travelers; American College of Physicians; Royal College of Physicians and Surgeons of Canada; Health Sciences Historical Society; Thyroid Foundation of Canada. Community Activities: Lifetime Fellow, International Biographical Association; Executive Funding Committee, Children's Liver Foundation, Inc., Antelope Valley Branch; Local Hospital Committees; Many Lectures to the Public on Diabetes; Numerous Other Community Activities. Published Works: Contributor Articles to Professional Journals including "Obesity and Diabetes," in *B.C. Medical Journal* 1983, "Hyperosmolar, Hyperglycemic, Nonketotic Coma—A Clinical Review," in *British Columbia Medical Journal* 1979; Other Professional Publications. Honors and Awards: E.W. Vaters Scholarship, Grade 9, 1958; Confederation Scholarship, Grade 10, 1959; Electoral Scholarship and Governor General's Bronze Medal, High School Graduation, 1960; Centenary of Responsible Government Scholarship, Memorial University, St. John's, Newfoundland, 1961; Dr. V. P. Burkes Scholarship, Memorial University, 1962; Encyclopedia Britannica Prize, Science Student Excelling also in Liberal Arts and Humanities, Memorial University, 1964; National Scholar, McGill University, Montreal, Quebec, 1964-65; National Scholar, McGill University, Montreal, Quebec, 1965-66; Quebec Inter-University CPC Competition Prize, 1967; Campbell-Howard Prize in Clinical Medicine, McGill University, 1968; Listed in *Who's Who in the World, Dictionary of International Biography, Men of Achievement, International Who's Who of Intellectuals, Personalities of America, Who's Who in Western Europe, International Who's Who in Community Service, Notable Americans, Biographical Directory of the American College of Physicians, Who's Who in the Commonwealth, British Columbia's Who's Who, International Register of Profiles, Men and Women of Distinction, The Encyclopedia of Newfoundland, Biographical Roll of Honor, Two Thousand Notable Americans, International Book of Honor, Men of Achievement*. Address: Valley Endocrine and Diabetes Treatment Center, 44421 Tenth Street West, Suite B, Lancaster, California 93534. ∎

RICHARD SAMUEL REYNOLDS III

Company Executive. Personal: Born August 8, 1934; Son of Mrs. Richard S. Reynolds Jr.; Married Pamela Coe, Daughter of Mrs. Dell Coe and Mr. Robert Coe; Father of Richard Samuel IV, Anne Brice, Katherine Louise. Education: Graduate magna cum laude, Woodberry Forest School, 1948-52; Attended Princeton University, 1952-56. Career: Vice President, Robertshaw Controls Company, Former Assistant to the Chairman and Assistant Vice President. Community Activities: Chairman, Richmond Area 1974 United Givers Fund Campaign; Fund Raising Chairman, Richmond Area Mental Health Association, 1972; Chairman, United Negro College Fund Campaign, 1982; Board of Directors, Boy Scouts of America, Robert E. Lee Council; Reynolds Homestead Advisory Committee; National Conference of Christians and Jews; Elected House of Delegates, State of Virginia, 1975. Religion: Second Presbyterian Church, Richmond, Virginia. Address: 309 Stockton Lane, Richmond, Virginia 23221. ∎

EUGENE EVANS RHEMANN

Coordinator of Music Education. Personal: Born July 19, 1941; Son of Mrs. C. A. Rhemann; Married JoAnn B., Daughter of I. W. Bailey; Father of Edward Eugene. Education: Bachelor of Music Education, University of Texas at Austin; Graduate Studies in Educational Administration and Curriculum and Instruction at University of Texas at Austin. Career: Coordinator of Music Education, Robstown I.S.D. Organizational Memberships: State Board Member, Texas Music Educators Association; President, Robstown Association of Texas Professional Educators; Member of Texas State Curriculum Committee; Kappa Kappa Psi. Community Activities: Appropriations Committee, United Way of Coastal Bend of Texas, 1982; Chairman, University of Texas Band Day Activities (145 participating bands), 1962; Chamber of Commerce, 1968; International Rotary Club Drug Prevention Committee of Robstown, 1981-82; State Curriculum Committee for Fine Arts, English, Mathematics and Other Languages, 1982. Religion: Lay Speaker, United Methodist Church, 19 Years; Chairman of Pastor-Parish Relations, Chairman Worship and Evangelism Committee, Church Choir Director, Sunday School Teacher. Honors and Awards: Outstanding Band, New Orleans Mardi Gras Parade, 1975; Honors Bands for Governor of Texas Inaugural Parades, 1972 and 1979; Robstown Band Played for Vice President of the United States, Walter Mondale, at Corpus Christi Naval Air Station; Listed in *International Who's Who in Music*. Address: 313 Ashburn, Robstown, Texas 78380. ∎

JOHNG SIK RHIM

Medical Researcher. Personal: Born July 24, 1930; Son of Hak Yoon and Moo Duk Rhim; Married Mary Lytle; Father of Jonathan, Christopher, Peter, Andrew, Michael. Education: B.S. 1953, M.D. 1957, Seoul National University. Career: Medical Research (Cancer), National Cancer Institute, National Institutes of Health, Bethesda, Maryland; Research Virologist at Various University Medical Schools (University of Cincinnati, Baylor Unversity, University of Pittsburgh Graduate School of Public Health). Organizational Memberships: American Association for the Advancement of Science; American Association for Cancer Research; American Association for Immunologists; American Medical Association; American Society of Microbiologists; Society of Experimental Biology and Medicine; New York Academy of Sciences; International Association of Comparative Leukemia Research. Community Activities: Winchester School, Silver Spring, Maryland, Board of Directors. Religion: Protestant. Address: 8309 Melody Court, Bethesda, Maryland 20817. ∎

JAMES RALPH RHODES

Director of Employee Relations. Personal: Born September 7, 1931; Son of E. F. Rhodes; Married Janet F., Daughter of Jewell W. Frederick; Father of Catherine, Michele, Brian, Christopher Decker (stepson); Stepsons Michael Decker, Paul Decker. Education: B.A., Elon College, 1953; M.F.A., Ohio University, 1954; Ed.D. Candidate, University of North Carolina-Greensboro. Career: Director of Employee Relations/Human Resources Development, Guilford County; Former Positions include Deputy Director, Housing and Urban Development Area Office, North Carolina; Director of Employee Development and Training, FHA, Washington D.C.; Educational Specialist, United States Army Engineer School, Ft. Belvoir, Virginia; Teacher, Public Schools in Ohio, Virginia and Maryland. Organizational Memberships: American Society for Training and Development; International Personnel Management Association, North Carolina Chapter; Former Member, American Society for Personnel Administration. Community Activities: Volunteer Fireman, Manassas, Virginia, 1962-71; Volunteer Rescue Squad, Manassas, Virginia, 1963-71; Director, Barbershop Chorus (SPEBQSA), Manassas, Virginia, 1957-61; Director, Sweet Adelines Chorus, Manassas, Virginia, 1964-66; Board of Zoning Appeals, Manassas, Virginia, 1967-71; Member Barbershop Chorus (SPEBSQSA), Greensboro, North Carolina, 1971-76; Director, Sweet Adelines Chorus, Greensboro, North Carolina, 1973-74. Religion: Church Council, Lutheran Church, Manassas, Virginia, 1964-68; Director of Music, Methodist Church, Manassas, Virginia, 1960-62; Director of Music, Lutheran Church, Manassas, Virginia, 1966-71. Honors and Awards: Fireman of the Year, Manassas, Virginia, 1965; Sigma Mu Sigma, National Honorary Fraternity, Elon College, 1951; Phi Mu Alpha Sinfonia, National Honorary Music Fraternity, Ohio University, 1954; National Honor Society, Burlington High School, Burlington, North Carolina, 1948; Quill and Scroll, National High School Journalism Society, Burlington, North Carolina, 1948. Address: 1414 Gracewood Drive, Greensboro, North Carolina 27408. ∎

FRANCES DODSON RHOME

College Professor and Administrator. Personal: Born April 15, 1916; Daughter of May Howell Dodson; Married Lt. Colonel H. Stanton Rhome (deceased); Mother of Major Robert C. Education: A.A., Glendale College; B.A., University of California at Los Angeles; M.A., New Mexico State University; Ph.D., Indiana University. Career: Director, Institute of Humanities Research; Member, National Council of Humanities; Director, Affirmative Action Affairs, Indiana University System; Professor of English (tenured), Indiana University; Freelance Reader and Sub-Editor; Co-Publisher, *Montrose Herald-Tribune*; Executive Director, Chamber of Commerce; College Counselor and Student Personnel Administrator; Secondary School Teacher; Lecturer; Writer; Research Scholar; Contributor

TWO THOUSAND NOTABLE AMERICANS

to Journals; Consultant. Honors and Awards: Distinguished Indiana Citizen, 1978; Scholarship, Indiana University, 1965; Fellowship, New Mexico Highlands University, 1965; National Award for Outstanding Dramatics Program in Secondary School, 1963; American Legion "Teacher of the Year" Award, 1962; Listed in *Dictionary of International Biography, Notable Americans of the Bicentennial Era*. Address: 9313 S. Pointe-LaSalle Drive, Bloomington, Indiana 47401.■

EDWARD PETER RICCARDO

Professor, Program Director. Personal: Born December 15, 1943; Father of Patricia Eileen, Katherine Ann. Education: B.A., Old Dominion University, 1966; M.A. 1967, Ph.C. 1969, Northwestern University. Career: Professor of Philosophy, Director Honors Program, Triton College, River Grove, Illinois; Former Regional Director of "Energy and the Way We Live" Forum. Organizational Memberships: American Philosophical Association, 1982; American Humanistic Philosophical Association, President, 1978; Illinois Institute of Psychology, Board Member 1978. Community Activities: Washington Irving Parent Teachers Organization, President 1982, Secretary 1981, Vice President 1980; Girl Scout Leader, Troop #1; National Organization for Women. Religion: Confraternity of Christian Doctrine, Instructor. Honors and Awards: Faculty Member of the Year Award, 1978; Triton Special Recognition Award, 1980; Woodrow Wilson Fellow, 1966; Northwestern University Fellow, 1967-69. Address: 1034 South Humphrey Avenue, Oak Park, Illinois 60304.■

BILLIE ANN RICE

Director of Academic Computing. Personal: Born February 16, 1937; Daughter of Kathleen H. Perrin; Married Kenneth E.; Mother of Kathleen, Annette. Education: B.S. Mathematics 1959, M.S. Mathematics 1961, Auburn University; Ph.D. Mathematics, Georgia State University, 1973; Computer Science, Georgia Institute of Technology, 1983. Career: Director of Academic Computing, present; Former Positions include Teacher at Auburn University 1961-62, State University of New York at Buffalo 1962-64, Georgia State University 1965-73, DeKalb Community College 1974-80. Organizational Memberships: Steering Committee, C.I.M.S.E., 1981 to present; Advisory Board, Clark College, 1982 to present; Associate Editor, M.A.A. 2-Year College Journal, 1983; Committee on Placement Exams, M.A.A., 1981 to present. Religion: North Avenue Presbyterian Church. Honors and Awards: N.S.F. Science Faculty Fellowship, 1966-67; Local Assessment on Science Education in 2-Year Colleges (N.S.F. grant), 1978; N.S.F. Cause Grant ($250,000), 1980; Director of Grants (aforementioned). Address: 4970 Peachtree Dunwoody, Atlanta, Georgia 30342.■

PATRICIA BRITTINGHAM RICE

Executive. Personal: Born July 14, 1941; Daughter of Kenneth L. Brittingham, Faye McClelland Brittingham; Mother of Philip Charles, Debora Faye, Jeffrey Allan. Education: Graduate of Chamblee High School, 1959; College Courses in Business Management and Accounting. Career: President, Property Management Firm; Former Accountant. Organizational Memberships: National Association of Female Executives; National Association of Women in Construction, 1973-78. Community Activities: Parent-Teacher Association, Secretary. Honors and Awards: Listed in *Who's Who in American Women, Who's Who in Finance and Industry, Personalities of America*. Address: 155 Teepee Lane, Lavonia, Georgia 30553.■

WILLIAM DAVID RICE

Executive. Personal: Born January 30, 1920; Married JoAnne Twelves; Father of William E., Robert G., Taylor D., James A. Education: B.S. in Chemistry, University of Utah, 1942. Military: Served with the United States Navy, 1941-46; Commanding Officer, Minesweeper, 1945-46; Retired Commander, United States Naval Reserve, 1965. Career: President, Advertising Research Associates, Salt Lake City, 1946-47; Vice President, Cooper & Crowe Inc., 1947-53; President, Demiris, Rice and Associates, 1953 to present. Organizational Memberships: American Institute of Management, President's Council 1971-72; Utah Association of Advertising Agencies; International Platform Association; Utah Advertising Federation; University Club of Salt Lake City, President 1982-83. Community Activities: Utah Travelers Aide Society, President 1972-73, Member of the Board; Salt Lake Mental Health Association, President 1961-62; Utah Association of Mental Health, President 1964-66, Member of the Board; National Association of Mental Health, Vice President of Communications 1973-75; Utah Mental Health Advisory Council, Chairman 1978-80, Member of the Council; Hospice of Salt Lake City, Board of Directors 1978 to present; Committee for the Severly Mentally Impaired in Utah, Chairman 1979-81; American Mensa for Utah, Proctor 1970 to present. Honors and Awards: Distinguished Service Award, Utah Medical Association, 1975; Honored by the National Association of Mental Health, 1975. Address: 1435 Military Way, Salt Lake City, Utah 84103.■

WILLIAM YNGVE RICE

Bank Executive. Personal: Born June 22, 1930; Son of Mrs. J. H. Rice; Married Rachel Gallenkamp; Father of William Y. III, John Robin, Drew M. Education: B.B.A. Management, Baylor University, 1951; Career: Chairman of the Board, Investments, Town North National Bank. Organizational Memberships: Director, American Bancorporation. Community Activities: Longview City Councilman, Mayor, 1969-80; Vice Chairman, East Texas Council of Governments, 1970-71; Vice President and Director, Sabin River Authority of Texas, 1980 to present; Director, East Texas Chamber of Commerce; Director, Longview Chamber of Commerce; Trustee, LeTouneau College. Religion: Chairman of Deacons, First Baptist Church of Longview. Honors and Awards: Longview Citizen of the Year, 1971; Phillips Petroleum Company Community Service Award. Address: 1308 Inverness, Longview, Texas 75601.■

EARL F. RICHARDS

Professor of Electrical Engineering. Personal: Born March 11, 1923; Son of Mrs. Esther Stancer; Married Marjorie Holt; Father of Dennis Lee, Laura Lee. Education: B.S.E.E., Wayne State University, 1951; M.S.E.E., Missouri School of Mines and Metallurgy, 1961; Ph.D., University of Missouri, 1971. Military: Served in the United States Army, Office of Strategic Services, 1942-46. Career: Professor of Electrical Engineering 1978 to present, Associate Professor of Electrical Engineering 1976-78, Assistant Professor of Electrical Engineering 1971-76, 1962-63, Instructor 1964-71, 1958-62, University of Missouri-Rolla; Part-time Lecturer in Electrical Engineering, University of Detroit, 1956-58; Instructor, United States Army Radio School, 1945; Consultant, Missouri Public Service Commission, Jefferson City, Missouri, 1981; Consultant, Wanlass Corporation, Anaheim, California, 1980-81; Consultant, Magnetic Peripherals, Inc., Oklahoma City, 1980; Consultant, Emerson Electric Corporation, St. Louis, Missouri, 1978-80; Consultant, Wisconsin Electric Power Company, Milwaukee, Wisconsin, 1978; Consultant, Detroit Tool, Lebanon, Missouri, 1973-74; Control Systems Design for Nuclear Reactors and Systems Modeling, Argonne National Laboratory, Argonne, Illinois, Summer 1963; Consultant to Revere Copper and Brass, Development of Maintenance Manuals for Servicing Control Systems for Copper and Brass Rollin Mills, Detroit, Michigan, Summer 1959; Design and Control Systems for Various Rolling, Shaping and Extrusion Mills and Power Distribution Associated with Plant Operation, 1954-58; Design of Process Control Equipment and Plant Power Distribution Systems, Pennsylvania Salt Manufacturing Company, Wyandotte, Michigan, 1952-53; Design of Plant Power Distribution Systems, Electronic Control Corporation, Detroit, Michigan, 1951-52; Maintenance of Central Office Telephone Equipment, Michigan Bell Telephone, Detroit, Michigan, 1941-42, 1946-47; Registered Professional Engineer, Missouri and Michigan. Published Works: Contributor Articles to Professional Journals including "Construction of Liapunov Functions by the Analog Computer" in *I.E.E.E. Transactions on Education* June 1966, "Root Determination by Means of an S Plane Transformation on an Iterative Analog Computer," in *I.E.E.E Transactions on Education* 1966, "A Two-Way Automatic Communications System for Use on an Electrical Power Distribution System" in *21st Midwest Syposium on Circuits and Systems* (Iowa State University) 1978. Honors and Awards: Eta Kappa Nu; Sigma Xi; Outstanding Faculty Advisor, Student Branch, University of Missouri-Rolla American Institute of Aeronautics, 1966, 1967; "International Yearbook on Analog and Digital Processing," International Computation Center, Rome, Italy, 1967; Tau Beta Pi; Institute of Electrical and Electronic Engineering Power Engineering Society Award for Chairman of 1974 Midwest Power Symposium; Recipient Grants and Awards from Emerson Electric Two-Way Automatic Communication System and Missouri Public Service Commission; Listed in *Who's Who in Missouri Education, Who's Who in the Midwest, Who's Who in Technology Today, Dictionary of International Biography, Men of Achievement, Personalities of the West and Midwest, The Directory of Distinguished Americans, Personalities of America, Directory of World Researchers, Who's Who in Engineering, International Who's Who in Engineering, American Men and Women of Science*. Address: 8 Hyer Court, Rolla, Missouri 65401.■

TWO THOUSAND NOTABLE AMERICANS

NOVELLE HAMILTON RICHARDS

Editor. Personal: Born November 24, 1917; Married Ruby Viola; Father of Five Children. Education: Diploma in Journalism, London Polytechnic Institute, London, England, 1951. Career: Editor, *Worker's Voice* Newspaper, Antigua, West Indies. Organizational Memberships: Member Board of Directors, Caribbean Press Association, 1952-58. Community Activities: Chairman, Antigua Housing and Planning Authority, 1952-58; Member Antigua Legislative Council, 1951-58; Elected to Federal Parliament of West Indies, 1958-62; Cabinet Minister Federal Parliament, West Indies, 1958-62; President Antigua Senate, 1967; Diplomatic Commissioner to Canada for West Indies Associate States, 1967-72; Director Tourism and Trade in Canada for Antigua and Barbuda, Governor General's Deputy for Antigua and Barbuda, present. Address: 1 Oriole Road, Apartment 310, Toronto, Ontario, Canada M4V2E6.■

EMANUEL ROSS RICHARDSON

Foreign Military Sales Manager. Personal: Born December 23, 1924; Son of Mr. and Mrs. George C. (Lelia A.) Richardson (both deceased); Married Irene B., Daughter of Mr. and Mrs. Albert Burnette (both deceased); Father of Angela Dawn, Eric Bernard. Education: B.S. Social Science, Hampton Institute, Hampton, Virginia, 1950; M.A. Public Administration, Central Michigan University, Mt. Pleasant, Michigan, 1973; Attended Cornell University Law School, 1950-53; Diploma, Air Command and Staff College, 1974. Military: Served with the United States Army, 1943-46. Career: Foreign Military Sales Manager, present; Former Positions include Air Force Executive Agent for Retail Agreements, Supply Systems Analyst, Recreation Director, Substitute Secondary Education School Teacher; Proprietor, A to Z Rental Center, Xenia, Ohio, 1969-72. Organizational Memberships: Society of Logistics Engineers; Air Force Association; American Defense Preparedness Association; Phi Alpha Delta Law Fraternity. Community Activities: President, Wilberforce Community Property Owners and Voters Association, 1964-67; Chairman, Xenia, Ohio Area Human Relations Council, 1969-72; Secretary-Treasurer, Greene County Health and Welfare Planning Council, 1967-75; Secretary, Xenia Toastmasters 1972-75; Dayton, Ohio Council on World Affairs, 1966 to present; Board of Trustees, Greene City Historical Society, 1982 to present; Xenia Area Chamber of Commerce, 1970 to present; President, Town and Country Club of Greene City, 1972-74, 1981 to present; State Secretary, Association for Afro-American Life and History, President; Committee Against Discrimination in Housing, 1964 to present; Special Events Chairman, Kiwanis Club of Xenia; Secretary, Form City Tour Committee, 1978-79; International Platform Association; International Biographical Association. Religion: Vestry, Finance Committee, Episcopal Church, Dayton, 1980-81; President, Men's Club, St. George Episcopal Church, 1982 to present; Hobson Fellow, Episcopal Church 2nd Diocese of Ohio; Chairman Ways and Means Committee, 1982 to present; Lay Reader, St. George Episcopal Church, 1965 to present. Honors and Awards: Outstanding Performance Award, 1976; Proprietor of the Month by Radio Station WGIC, 1971; Listed in *Who's Who in the Midwest, Who's Who in Aviation, International Who's Who of Community Leaders, Men of Achievement, International Book of Honor, Who's Who in the West and Midwest*. Address: P.O. Box 512, Wilberforce, Ohio 45384.■

GILBERT PAYTON RICHARDSON, SR.

Association Executive. Personal: Born November 4, 1926; Son of Mrs. Claude B. (Doris) Richardson; Married Lee Ann Gillen; Father of Amy L., Gilbert P. Jr., Susan L. Education: Attended Mexico City College, 1948; B.A. History-Political Science, David Lipscomb College, 1949; M.A. Diplomatic History, George Peabody College of Vanderbilt University, 1951; Residence and Languages toward Ph.D., American University, Washington D.C.; Graduate, United States Air University, Allied Officers School, 1967. Military: Served in the United States Army, 1945-47, attaining the rank of Corporal, Served in Italy 5th Army, Repatriation of German Prisoners of War, Crimes. Career: President, American Association for Study of the United States in World Affairs, present; Former Positions include Senior Civilian Professor, Graduate School United States Defense Intelligence Agency lecturing to United States Military Attaches; Professor, United States Department of Agriculture Graduate School; Assistant Professor of International Relations, Pepperdine University, Los Angeles; Instructor, Assistant Professor, History and Political Science, previously Director of Admissions, Florida Southern College, Lakeland, Florida. Organizational Memberships: Florida Historical Society, Board of Directors, 1957-59; President, Chairman of the Board of Lake Region Executive Club, 1958-61; American Association of University Professors; International Platform Association; Executive Director, American Association for the Study of United States in World Affairs, 1978-82. Community Activities: Vice Commander, American Legion Posts 4 & 8 Winter Haven, Lakeland, Florida; President, Republican Men's Club, Winter Haven and Polk County, Lakeland, Florida; Chairman, Americanism in School Affairs, American Legion, Department of Florida; Alternate and Delegate, Republican National Convention, Chicago, 1960; Nominee, State Superintendent of Public Instruction, State of Florida Veterans of Foreign Wars; AMVETS, Winter Haven and Lakeland, Florida; Annandale Road Defense Association, Virginia. Religion: Church of Christ, 1940 to present; Founded First Spanish Language Service for Church of Christ Congregation in Washington Area; Deacon, Redondo Beach, California, 1965; Deacon, McLean, Virginia 1968, Bond Trustee. Honors and Awards: Pi Gamma Mu, International Social Science Honor Fraternity; Sigma Tau Delta; United States Junior Chamber of Commerce Award, 1961; Honorary Degrees from School of the Americas, Panama 1970, Panama's Inter-American Air Force Academy 1970. Listed in *Who's Who in the South and Southwest, Men of Achievement, Who's Who in Washington D.C.* Address: 90 Lake Hunter Drive, Lakeland, Florida 33802.■

LEE A. RICHMAN

Health Educator, Chief of Health Research. Personal: Born May 24, 1947; Son of Morris and Madeline Richman; Married Karen M. Gonzalez-Richman, Daughter of Peter and Lucy Gonzalez. Education: B.A. 1969, M.S.P.H. 1971, University of California at Los Angeles; Dr.P.H., University of California at Berkeley, 1976. Career: Health Educator, Chief of Health Research, Ebon Research Systems, present; Former Positions include Consultant, Project Hope in Jamaica; Chief of Vasectomy Services, Planned Parenthood, Los Angeles; Research Consultant, Tracor Jitco, Rockville, Maryland; Assistant Coordinating Editor, Barrington Publishing Corporation; Lab Technologist, Department of Biological Chemistry, University of California at Los Angeles. Organizational Memberships: American Public Health Association; Maryland Public Health Association; Society for Public Health Education; University of California at Los Angeles Alumni Association; University of California at Berkeley Public Health Alumni Association; University of California at Los Angeles Public Health Alumni Association. Community Activities: Consultant, California State Department of Education, 1974-76; Lecturer, Planned Parenthood, Oakland, California, 1972-75; Project Evaluator, Television Health Information Project, University of California at San Francisco, 1973; Clinic Coordinator, Counselor, Planned Parenthood, Los Angeles, 1970-72; Counselor, Committee for the Eradication of Syphilis, Los Angeles, 1970-72; Special Health Officer, Venice Youth Clinic, Los Angeles, 1970 and 1971; Psychiatric Worker, Los Angeles Veterans Administration. Honors and Awards: Delta Omega, Public Health Honorary, 1971; Veterans Administration Voluntary Service Certificate; American National Red Cross Certificate of Merit; Los Angeles City Schools Volunteer Service Award; Scholarship in Public Health Education, California Congress of Parents and Teachers, 1975; Predoctoral Research Fellowships, California Department of Health, United States Public Health Service. Address: 603 Southlawn Lane, Rockville, Maryland 20850.■

JOHN RICHMOND

Attorney at Law. Personal: Born December 10, 1907. Education: B.S. 1928, M.S. 1934, University of California at Berkeley; LL.B., Oakland College of Law, 1942; Honorary Ph.D., Hamilton State University, 1973. Military: Served in the United States Army Air Force, 1942-45. Career: President, Richmond Enterprises, 1928 to present; Attorney, Richmond Enterprises, 1946 to present; Attorney at Law, Private Practice, 1946 to present. Organizational Memberships: California State Bar Association; Alameda County Bar Association; Berkeley-Albany Bar Association; American Bar Association; Federal Bar Association; Supreme Court Historical Society. Community Activities: Henry Morse Stephens Lodge #541, Free and Accepted Masons, Master 1958; Ancient and Accepted Scottish Rite of Freemasonry Southern Jurisdiction of U.S.A.; Aahmes Temple A.A.O.N.M.S.; Masters and Past Masters Association, Masons; National Lawyers Club, Founder Member 1952; University of California at Berkeley Alumni Association; International Platform Association; American Association for the Advancement

of Science; Intercontinental Biographical Association; American Biographical Institute Research Association; National Historical Society; Pan Xenia; Veterans of Foreign Wars, Berkeley Post #703, Commander 1962; United Veterans Council of Berkeley, President 1963; City of Berkeley Lincoln and Washington Patriotic Program, Co-Chairman 1962; City of Berkeley Memorial Services, General Chairman 1963; City of Berkeley Marin Point Aquatic Park Memorial Services, General Chairman 1963; Grand Lodge of Free and Accepted Masons of California Sojourners Committee, Member 1958-66; Veterans of Foreign Wars of the United States National Membership Committee of 1980 and 1981; Supreme Court Historical Society, Founder Member, 1976; National Lawyers Club, Founder Member, 1952. Honors and Awards: Listed in *National Register of Prominent Americans, Two Thousand Men of Achievement, Dictionary of International Biography, Who's Who in California, National Register of Prominent Americans and International Notables, Men of Achievement, International Who's Who in Community Service, Community Leaders and Noteworthy Americans, American Heritage Research Association, Who's Who in the World, Who's Who in California, World Who's Who in Finance and Industry, Personalities of the West and Midwest, Community Leaders and Noteworthy Americans, Who's Who in American Law, Book of Honor, Personalities of America, Who's Who in the World, Who's Who in the West, American Registry Series, Directory of Distinguished Americans, Men and Women of Distinction, Who's Who in Finance and Industry, International Who's Who of Intellectuals.* Address: 1611 Bonita Avenue, Berkeley, California 94709.■

ANTHONY RALPH RICIGLIANO

Assistant Director. Personal: Born August 2, 1929; Son of Mrs. A. Ricigliano; Married Isabell P., Daughter of Mrs. M. Grieco; Father of Mark A., Robert S., Lisa M. Education: B.S. Civil Engineering, New Jersey Institute of Technology, 1958; M.S. Environmental Science, Rutgers University, 1959. Military: Served in the United States Army Corps of Engineers, 1951-53, attaining the rank of Sergeant First Class (Platoon Sergeant of Combat Engineer Platoon, 116th Engineer Combat Battalion). Career: Assistant Director, Division of Water Resources, New Jersey Department of Environmental Protection, present; Former Occupations include Various Engineering and Administrative Positions in the New Jersey Department of Environmental Protection. Organizational Memberships: New Jersey Water Pollution Control Association, Member 1959 to present; Former Occupations include Various Engineering and Administrative Positions in the New Jersey Department of Environmental Protection. Organizational Memberships: New Jersey Water Pollution Control Association, Member 1959 to present, President 1979 and 1980; Water Pollution Control Federation, Served on Executive Committee 1980-81, Board of Directors 1980-83; Authorities Association of New Jersey; Inter-American Society of Sanitary and Environmental Engineers; Diplomate, American Academy of Environmental Engineers; National Society of Professional Engineers; Licensed Professional Engineer by the States of New Jersey and Florida. Community Activities: Active in Youth Baseball Programs, 1972-81; President, Lawrence Township Junior Baseball Association, 1977-79; Organized and Supervised a Youth Instructional Baseball Clinic Program, 1980-81; Member and Vice Chairman, Lawrence Township Recreation Advisory Committee, 1981-84. Honors and Awards: Award by Utility Contractors Association of New Jersey for Recognition of Efforts to Combat Water Pollution in New Jersey, 1975; Award by Authorities Association of New Jersey for Outstanding Civic Service, 1978; Award by Water Pollution Federation for Outstanding Service. Address: 4020 Quakerbridge Road, Trenton, New Jersey 08619.■

ROBERT LYLE RIDGWAY

United States Army Veterinarian. Personal: Born October 3, 1938; Son of Mr. and Mrs. Harmon Ridgway; Married Carolyn June Ridgway, Daughter of Donald Johnson; Father of Joan Amy. Education: A.A., Dodge City Junior College, 1959; B.S., Fort Hays Kansas City College, 1962; D.V.M. 1971, Kansas State University. Military: United States Army Veterinary Corps. Career: United States Army Veterinarian; Former Professional Scouter, Boy Scouts of America. Organizational Memberships: American Veterinary Medical Association; American Association of Veterinary Food Hygiene. Community Activities: Rotary Club, Vice President, 1963 to present; Boy Scouts of America, Council Commissioner 1959, District Commissioner 1975, District Chairman 1981, Wood Badge Course Director 1979. Religion: Lay Speaker Methodist Church; Member of Official Board, Methodist Church Gaithersburg. Honors and Awards: District Award of Merit, 1981; Legion of Merit, 1982; Commendation from Governor of State of Kansas, 1965; Golden Carabao, Boy Scouts of America. Address: Kuala Lumpur, Department of State, Washington, D.C. 20520.■

GREGORY FRANK RIEDE

Director of Psychological Services. Personal: Born January 13, 1948; Son of Ann Feduniszyn; Married Karen Anne; Father of Meredith Rene, Allison Michelle. Education: B.A. Psychology, University of Missouri, 1970; M.S. Clinical Psychology, Central Missouri State University, 1972; Ph.D. Counseling Psychology, University of Missouri, 1975. Career: Director of Psychological Services, present; Internship, Fulton State Hospital, 1971; Professor, Central Missouri State University, 1972-74; Texas Criminal Justice Center, 1974-79; Houston Police Department, 1979 to present. Organizational Memberships: American Psychological Association, 1974 to present; Criminal Justice Research Society, Vice President, 1974-79. Community Activities: Member of Advisory Board for the Treatment of Alcoholics in Houston, 1979; Member of Advisory Committee, Labor/Management Employee Assistance Program, 1982 to present; Met with State Representative to Discuss Child Sexual Abuse, 1979; Guest Speaker for Houston Psychological Association, 1979; Made Presentation to Children's Mental Health Services on the Subject of Battered Wives, 1979; Guest Speaker at Luncheon given by Chamber of Commerce, Crime Control Committee, 1979; Made Presentation to Parents of Retarded Children in Houston, 1979; Participates in S.T.A.R. Program in Austin (Systems Training and Analysis Requirements for Criminal Justice Participants), 1979 to present. Honors and Awards: Psi Chi in Psychology, 1971; Kappa Delta Pi in Education, 1973; Phi Delta Kappa in Education, 1973. Address: 5335 Brownlee Lane, Houston, Texas 77373.■

STEVEN D. RIEDEL

Corporate Executive. Personal: Born June 2, 1943; Son of Harold and Lucy Riedel; Married Fern Margeret; Father of Phillip, Mark. Education: B.S., University of Wisconsin-Eau Claire, 1965. Career: President, Betacom Corporation, 1983 to present; Vice President Product Marketing, Burroughs Corporation, 1979; Vice President Distributor Sales 1982, Regional Sales Manager 1977, Product Manager 1975, Milwaukee Branch Manager 1973, Madison Branch Manager 1971, Zone Manager-Minneapolis 1969, Senior Account Manager 1968, Northern Telecom. Organizational Memberships: American Association Individual Investors, 1982; National Association of Accountants, 1967. Community Activities: National Tax Limitation Committee, 1980 to present; Republican Party, 1978 to present, World Mission 1982. Religion: Parish Council Secretary 1977, Parish Council President St. Clares, Member Pax Christie (currently). Honors and Awards: Legion of Honor, Burroughs, 1966-72; President's Club, 1966-72; Outstanding Marketing Award, 1968; Training Award, 1972; Director BetaCom Corporation (1982), and Retail Sales Network (1982); Listed in *Who's Who in the Midwest, Who's Who in Industry*. Address: 9299 Talus Circle, Eden Prairie, Minnesota 55344.■

HERMAN E. RIES, JR.

Research Associate. Personal: Born May 6, 1911, in Scranton, Pennsylvania; Son of Herman and Henrietta Ries; Married Elizabeth Hamburger (deceased), Second Wife Mildred Small Allen; Father of Walter E., Richard A. Education: B.S., University of Chicago, 1933; Ph.D. Physical Chemistry, University of Chicago, 1936. Career: Head of Physical Chemistry Section, Associate Director of Catalysis Division, Sinclair Research Laboratories, 1936-51; Research Associate, Standard Oil Company, 1951-72; Visiting Scientist, Cavendish Laboratory, University of Cambridge, England, 1964; Visiting Professor, Institute for Chemical Research, Kyoto University, Japan, 1972-74; Research Associate, Department of Biology, University of Chicago, 1974 to present; Consultant, Argonne National Laboratory, 1977 to present; Visiting Scientist, Summer 1978; Robert A. Welch Foundation Lecturer, University of Texas, 1978-79; Research Associate, University of Paris, 1984. Organizational Memberships: Gordon Research Conference on Chemistry at Interfaces, Chairman 1960; International Congresses on Surface Activity, London 1957, Brussels 1964, Barcelona 1968, Zurich 1972, Moscow 1978, Jerusalem 1981, Paris 1983; A.C.S. Divisions of Colloid and Surface Chemistry, Petroleum Chemistry, Physical Chemistry, Polymer Chemistry and Water, Air and Waste Chemistry; American Association for the Advancement of Science; A.S.L.E.; A.I.C.; Chemical Society, London; Chemical Society of Japan; Catalysis Club of Chicago; Coordinator of Critical Tables on Monolayers; Advisory Editorial Boards of Several Chemical Journals. Community Activities: University of Chicago String Quartette and Symphony. Honors and Awards: Phi Beta

Kappa; Sigma Xi; Ipatieff Prize, American Chemical Society, 1950; Certificate of Merit Award, Division of Colloid and Surface Chemistry, American Chemical Society, 1975-76; Listed in *Who's Who in America, World Who's Who in Science, Who's Who in the World*. Address: 5660 Blackstone Avenue, Chicago, Illinois 60637.■

FRED W. RIGGS

Professor of Political Science. Personal: Born July 3, 1917; Son of Grace Riggs; Married Clara-Louise Mather; Father of Gwendolyn Riggs Cook. Education: B.A., University of Illinois, 1938; M.A., Fletcher School of Law and Diplomacy, 1941; Ph.D., Columbia University, 1948. Career: Professor of Political Science, University of Hawaii, 1967 to present; Arthur F. Bentley Professor, Indiana University, 1956-67; Public Administration Clearing House, New York, 1951-55; Foreign Policy Association, 1948-51; Visiting Professor, Massachusetts Institute of Technology, 1956-66; Senior Scholar, East-West Center, Hawaii, 1962-63. Organizational Memberships: Fellow, Center for Advanced Study, Stanford, 1966-67; Chairman, Committee on Conceptual and Terminological Analysis, International Social Science Council; Co-opted Member, International Social Science Council; International Council, International Association of Terminology; Chairman, Comparative Administration Group, American Society for Public Administration, 1960-71; International Political Science Association; International Studies Association; American Society for Information Science; American Political Science Association; Association for Asian Studies; International Sociological Association. Community Activities: Fellow, Social Science Research Council, 1957-58; Chairman, International Ad Hoc Committee, Interconcept, U.N.E.S.C.O., 1977-79. Honors and Awards: Phi Beta Kappa, Graduate with High Honors, University of Illinois, 1938; University and Gilder Fellowships, Columbia University, 1942, 1947. Address: 3920 Lurline Drive, Honolulu, Hawaii 96816.■

JOSEPH N. RIGGS

Association Executive. Personal: Born January 1, 1916, in Louisville, Kentucky; Married Mary Aline Ratterman; Father of Joseph C., Charles D., Patrick X., Theresa L., Michael A., Angela L., Nicholas W. Education: Attended University of Kentucky, Lexington, Kentucky, 1938; D.C., Palmer College of Chiropractic, Davenport, Iowa, 1947. Career: Member Credit Committee, Kentucky Chiropractic Credit Union, 1958 to present; Chairman, Kentucky Chiropractic Society, President's Advisory Committee, 1969 to present; Director, Kentucky Chiropractic Society, 1969 to present; Board Member, Louisville-Jefferson County Commission for the Natural History Museum, 1981 to present; President, Kentucky Association of Chiropractors, 3rd District, 1949-50; Member, 12th Ward Democratic Club, 1952-60; District Director, Kentucky Association of Chiropractors, 1954-59; President, Flaget High School, Parent Teacher Association, 1958; Board Chairman, Kentucky Association of Chiropractors, 1959-60; Member Kentuckiana Children's Center Advisory Board, 1959-60; Executive Secretary, Kentucky State Board of Chiropractic Examiners, 1959-76; Kentucky Delegate, Federation of State Chiropractic Licensing Boards, 1960-75; Chairman, Kentucky Association of Chiropractors' Budget Committee, 1961-65; Member, Kentucky Association of Chiropractors' Legal Action Committee, 1964-72; Director, Federation of State Chiropractic Licensing Boards, 1965-71; President, St. Raphael's Holy Name Society, 1969; Director, National Board of Chiropractic Examiners, 1971-80; Vice President, National Board of Chiropractic Examiners, 1971-80; Vice President, National Board of Chiropractic Examiners, 1973-75; Member, Accrediting Committee, Association of Chiropractic Colleges, 1974-75; Treasurer, United Chiropractic Commission, 1974; President, National Board Chiropractic Examiners, 1976-77. Organizational Memberships: Kentucky State Chiropractic Society; International Chiropractors' Association; Palmer College of Chiropractic Alumni Association. Honors and Awards: Honorary Positions on Bellarmine College Civic Council and Bellarmine College Founders' Circle; Kentucky Association of Chiropractors' President's Award, 1956; Fellow, Kentucky Association of Chiropractors, 1957; Colonel, Honorable Order of Kentucky Colonels, 1960; Fellow, International Chiropractors' Association, 1970; Chiropractor of the Year, Kentucky Chiropractic Society, 1974; Chiropractor of the Year, Kentucky Chiropractic Society, 1975. Address: 1701 Gardiner Lane, Louisville, Kentucky 40205.■

KARL ALTON RIGGS, JR.

Geologic Consultant and Educator. Personal: Born August 12, 1929; Son of Karl A. Riggs and Marjorie Elizabeth (Urquhart) Riggs; Married Patricia Ann (Hartrick); Father of George Hartrick, Mrs. Kathryn Ann (Riggs) Keen, Linda Kay. Education: Ph.D., Iowa State University, Ames, Iowa, 1956; M.S. Geology 1952, B.S. with honors in Geology, Michigan State University. Military: R.O.T.C., Two Years, Michigan State University. Career: Geologic Consultant and Educator; Part-time Tree Surgeon, 1941-50; Half-time Instructor 1952-56, Half-time Research Associate 1953-56, Iowa State University; Senior Research Technologist, Mobil Research and Development, Dallas, Texas, 1956-59; Part-time Chief Geologist and Director, Nortex Oil and Gas, Dallas, 1959-62; Part-time Civil Engineer, Forrest and Cotton Civil Engineers, Dallas, Texas, 1962; Assistant Professor, Western Michigan University, Kalamazoo, 1966-68; Assistant Professor 1968-73, Associate Professor, Mississippi State University; Geological Consultant in Petroleum, Mining and Engineering Geology, 1952 to present; Part-time Vice President and Director, ConOil Drilling Programs, Inc., New York City, 1982. Organizational Memberships: Organizer for American Mineralogical Abstracts, 1978 to present; Certified, American Institute of Professional Geologists; Fellow, Geological Society of America; American Association of Petroleum Geologists; National Military Intelligence Association; Society of Economic Paleontologists and Mineralogists; Mineralogical Society of America; Mississippi Academy of Science. Community Activities: Consultant to the Board of Higher Education and Ministry of the National United Methodist Church, 1983 to present; Precinct Chairman 1960-62, District Chairman and Executive Committee 1962, Dallas County Republicans, Dallas, Texas; Numerous Leadership Positions in Junior Chamber of Commerce, Chamber of Commerce, and Kiwanis Club; Volunteer Messenger, Civil Defense Service, World War II, 1942-45. Religion: Lay Preacher for United Methodist Church and Gideons; Many Leadership Roles in the United Methodist Church. Address: 109 Grand Ridge Drive, Starkville, Mississippi 39759.■

DONALD CROSBY RILEY

Business Consultant and Independent Real Estate Broker. Personal: Born September 27, 1925; Son of Leila C. Shaw. Education: B.B.A., University of Wisconsin and Ohio State University, 1945; M.B.A., Metropolitan Collegiate Institute of London, 1947; Ph.D., Pacific Northwestern University, 1949. Career: Business Consultant and Independent Real Estate Broker, present; Former Position as Marketing Executive. Organizational Memberships: Sales Executives Club of New York, 1960 to present; Sales and Marketing Executives International, 1960 to present; Data Processing Management Association International, Member Executive Committee 1980-81; New York Academy of Sciences, 1970-80; American Chemical Society, 1978 to present; Real Estate Board of New York, 1978 to present; National Realty Club, 1978 to present. Community Activities: Republican Presidential Task Force, Charter Member 1982; Joint Presidential Congressional Steering Committee, 1982; United States Defense Committee, 1982; National Committee on American Foreign Policy, 1981 to present; Asia Society, 1980 to present; Aviation Hall of Fame, Charter Member 1979-81. Address: 40 Central Park South, New York, New York 10019.■

WARREN MARSHALL RINGSDORF, JR.

Professor. Personal: Born May 2, 1930; Son of Dr. Warren M. and Mrs. Mary F. Ringsdorf; Married Doris Lemerle Carpenter; Father of Warren Marshall III, Valerie Ann. Education: B.A., Asbury College, 1951; M.S., University of Alabama Graduate School, 1956; D.M.D., University of Alabama School of Dentistry, 1956; Fellow in Oral Medicine, University of Alabama School of Dentistry, 1962. Military: Served in the United States Air Force, 1956-58, attaining the rank of Captain. Career: Dentist in the United States Air Force, 1956-58; Private Dental Practice, 1958-59; Assistant Professor in Dentistry, 1959-64, Associate

Professor of Dentistry 1964-81, Professor of Dentistry 1982 to present, University of Alabama School of Dentistry; Private Practice in Nutritional Counseling. Organizational Memberships: Seventh District Dental Society; Alabama Dental Association; American Dental Association; American Academy of Oral Medicine; Academy of Orthomolecular Psychiatry; Nutrition Today Society. Community Activities: Teen Challenge of Birmingham, Board of Directors; Saint Anne's Home, Inc., Board of Directors; Jefferson County Mental Health Society, Committee on Alcoholism, Board of Directors; Martha R. Jones Foundation for Health Education, Inc., Board of Directors. Published Works: Author of 375 Articles in the Health Services, Six Books, most recently *Psychodietetics* and *The Vitamin C Connection*. Honors and Awards: Research Award, Chicago Dental Society, 1966, 1968; Honors and Achievement Award, Angiology Research Foundation, 1968; Scientific Fellow, Academy of Orthomolecular Psychiatry, 1981. Address: 728 Sussex Drive, Birmingham, Alabama 35226.■

JOHN RITCHIE

Scholar-in-Residence. Personal: Born March 19, 1904; Married Sarah Wallace; Father of John Jr., Albert. Education: B.A. 1925, LL.B. 1927, University of Virginia; J.S.D., Yale University, 1931; LL.D. (honorary), College of William and Mary, 1979; Sterling Fellow, Yale University, 1930-31. Military: Served as the Judge Advocate 65th Infantry Division of the United States Army, 1942-46, attaining the rank of Colonel. Career: With Ritchie, Chase, Canady and Swenson, 1927-28; Assistant Professor, Furman University, 1928-30; Assistant Professor, University of Washington, 1931-36; Professor, University of Maryland, 1936-37; Professor, University of Virginia, 1937-52 and 1972-74; Dean of Law School and Kirby Professor, Washington University, 1952-53; Dean of Law School and Professor, University of Wisconsin, 1953-57; Dean of Law School and Wigmore Professor, Northwestern University, 1957-72; Dean and Wigmore Professor Emeritus, 1972 to present; Scholar-in-Residence, University of Virginia Law School since 1974. Organizational Memberships: Association of American Law Schools, President 1964; Judge Advocates Association, President 1952; Order of the Coif, National President 1952-55; American Bar Association; Virginia Bar Association; Law Club of Chicago. Community Activities: American Council on Education, Director 1965-68, United Charities of Chicago, Director 1966-72; American Bar Foundation, Life Fellow 1970 to present; Illinois Judicial Advisory Council, 1964-68; House of Delegates, American Bar Association, 1952-72; Editorial Board, Foundation Press, 1960 to present; Committee to Draft Code of Professional Responsibility, American Bar Association, 1964-69; Member Advisory Board, Center for Law and National Security, 1982 to present. Religion: Episcopalian. Published Works: Co-Author with Alford and Effland *Cases and Materials on Decedents' Estates and Trusts* (6th Edition) 1982; Author *A History of the University of Virginia Law School 1826-1926* 1978; Contributor Articles to Various Legal Publications. Honors and Awards: Phi Beta Kappa; Order of the Coif; Raven Society; Omicron Delta Kappa; Tucker Lecturer, Washington and Lee University, 1964; De Tocqueville Lecturer, Marquette University, 1967. Address: 1848 Westview Road, Charlottesville, Virginia 22903.■

ROY E. RITTS, JR.

Professor, Consultant. Personal: Born January 16, 1929, in St. Petersburg, Florida. Education: A.B., University Scholar, George Washington University, 1948; M.D., George Washington University School of Medicine, 1951; Intern, District of Columbia General Hospital, 1951-52; Fellow in Medicine (Infectious Diseases), George Washington University School of Medicine at the District of Columbia General Hospital, 1952-53; Research Fellow in Medicine, Harvard Medical School, 1954-55; Certified by the National Board of Medical Examiners 1952, American Board of Medical Microbiology, 1962; Licensed in District of Columbia and Minnesota. Military: Served in the United States Naval Reserve, Ensign 1948-51, Lieutenant (j.g.) 1951-56. Career: Assistant in Medicine, Peter Bent Brigham Hospital, 1954-55; Visiting Investigator, Rockefeller Institute, 1955-57; Research Associate, Rockefeller Institute, 1957-58; Associate Professor of Microbiology 1958-61, Chairman of the Department of Microbiology 1959-64, Professorial Lecturer in Medicine 1961-64, Professor of Microbiology 1961-64, Georgetown University School of Medicine; Professorial Lecturer in Immunology, University of Chicago School of Medicine, 1964-68; Director, A.M.A.-E.R.F. Institute for Biomedical Research, 1964-68; Director of Medical Research, American Medical Association, 1966-68; Chairman and Consultant, Department of Microbiology, Mayo Clinic, 1968-79; Professor of Microbiology, Mayo Graduate School of Medicine, University of Minnesota, 1968 to present; Professor of Oncology, Mayo Medical School, 1979 to present; Consultant and Merit Grant Reviewer, Veterans Administration Central Office, Immunology of Cancer, 1972-78, 1980-82. Organizational Memberships: American Academy of Microbiology, Fellow; American College of Physicians, Fellow; American College of Chest Physicians, Fellow; Association of Clinical Scientists, Fellow; Infectious Disease Association of Clinical Scientists, Fellow; Infectious Disease Society of America, Fellow; Royal Society of Health, Fellow; Association of Clinical Scientists, Fellow; American Association of Immunologists; American Association For Cancer Research; American Federation for Clinical Research; American Rheumatism Association; American Society for Clinical Oncology; American Society for Microbiology, Vice President Washington-Maryland Branch 1963, Vice President 1969, President North Central Branch 1970; American Society of Surgical Oncology (Ewing Society); British Society of Immunologists; International Association for the Study of Lung Cancer. Board of Directors 1974-76, Secretary General 1976-78; Reticuloendothelial Society; Society for Experimental Medicine and Biology; Society for General Microbiology, England; Gesellschaft fur Immunologie; Alpha Chi Sigma; Phi Chi; Society of Sigma Xi; International Study Group on Cardiac Transplantation, Registry Committee, Immunology Committee 1980 to present; American Board of Medical Laboratory Immunology, Member 1976-83, Committee on Oral Examinations 1978 to present, Chairman 1980-83; Committee on Allergy and Clinical Immunology, American College of Chest Physicians, Member 1976-78, Executive Committee 1978-79; Federation of American Societies for Experimental Biology, National Correspondent 1974 to present; International Union of Immunology Societies, Standards Executive Committee Chairman 1973 to present, Council 1974 to present; WHO Expert Committee on Standardization 1973 to present, WHO Expert Panel on Immunology 1983 to present; Board of Directors, KMS Industries, Inc., Ann Arbor, MI, 1983 to present; Section Editor, *Journal of Immunology*, 1982 to present. Community Activities: Sigma Chi; Cosmos Club, Washington D.C., 1964-78; University Club of Rochester, Board of Directors 1971-75, President 1975. Honors and Awards: Gate and Key; Alpha Theta Nu; William Beaumont Medical Society; Alpha Omega Alpha; Listed in *American Men and Women of Science, American Men of Medicine, Dictionary of International Biography, The Blue Book, Who's Who in the World, Who's Who in the World of Medicine, World Who's Who in Science, Who's Who in America*. Address: Microbiology Research Laboratory, Mayo Foundation, Rochester, Minnesota 55901.■

HARRIETTE FRANCES SMITH RITZ

Administrative Assistant. Personal: Born March 8, 1909; Daughter of Charlotte J. and Harry F. Smith (deceased); Married Gale, Son of Frank and Elsie Ritz (deceased). Education: B.S. Business 1934, M.S. Education 1936, Indiana University; M.Div., Winebrenner Theological Seminary, 1971. Career: Administrative Assistant Community Education, Professor Emeritus, Associate Professor of Business, Chairman Division of Business, Findlay College; Other Former Positions include Professor of Business, Ohio Northern University, Chairman Department of Business; Professor of Business, Bloomsburg State College; Chairman Department of Business, Findlay College; Faculty Naval Training Staff, Indiana University, Beaver College. Organizational Memberships: National Association of Tax Accountants (until 1975); American Accounting Association, 1934-75; National Business Teachers Association; United Business Teachers Association; Ohio Business Teachers Association; Midwest Business Teachers Association; Phi Beta Lambda; Future Business Leaders of America; Ohio Community Education Association, 1978-83; Delta Kappa Gamma; Delta Pi Epsilon; Kappa Delta Pi. Community Activities: Examining Committee of National Association of Business Colleges, 1954-57; Auditor, Allen County Red Cross, 1956-60; Auditor, Hancock County United Way Campaigns, 1962-81; Income Tax Consultant, Center for Migrant Workers, 1962-64; RSVP, Mobile Meals, 1974 to present; Winebrenner Village Auxiliary, 1962 to present; County Home Auxiliary; Business and Professional Women's Clubs; Altrusa International Women. Religion: Member National Religious Education Association, 1971 to present; Recorder of Church Board, Christian Church, Findlay, Ohio, Chairman Board of Elders 1981-82, Faculty Christian Fellowship State Secretary 1955-65, District President 1955-65, W.C.S.C.; Trustee, Winebrenner Theological Seminary. Honors and Awards: Delta Pi Epsilon, 1944; Kappa Delta Pi, 1946; Delta Kappa Gamma, 1947; Advisor Panhellenic, 1963-69; Phi Beta Lambda, Unlimited Service Awards; Findlay College Distinguished Association, 1976; Findlay College Named Newly Decorated Auditorium in Her and Her Husband's Honor, January 1982; Distinguished Alumnus Winebrenner Theological Seminary, 1982. Address: 1500 Tiffin Avenue, Findlay, Ohio 45840.■

TWO THOUSAND NOTABLE AMERICANS

LESLIE ANN RIVERA

Museum Coordinator. Personal: Born March 7, 1947; Daughter of Dr. and Mrs. Luis Rivera. Education: Attended Gulf Park Junior College, 1965; University of Colorado, Boulder, Colorado, 1967; University of Miami, 1970; M.A. European History 1977, M.A. British Literature 1978, Wroxton College of Fairleigh Dickinson University. Career: Teacher of History, English and Social Studies; Volunteer Coordinator, Historical Association of Southern Florida; Volunteer Coordinator, Historical Museum. Organizational Memberships: Florida Directors of Volunteers in Agencies; Association of Volunteer Administration, Corresponding Secretary, 1981-83. Community Activities: National Association for Female Executives, 1980-83; Corresponding Secretary, Friends of Mental Health, Dade County Branch of the Mental Health Association, 1980-81; Barton Ravlin Chapter, Women's Cancer Association, 1979-82, Memorials, Wills and Legacies; Founding Member 1980-81, Florida Trust for Historical Preservaton; LaLega dei Viscayani President, Vizcaya Museum 1981-82, Vizcaya Board Member 1982-83, Vizcaya Ball Committee Member 1983; Board of Directors, Coconut Grove Republican Woman's Club; Member Dade Heritage Trust, 1978-83; Villagers Preservation, 1981-83; English Speaking Union, 1979-83; American Association of University Women, 1983; Junior League Staff Writer 1981-83, Member Junior League of Miami Inc. 1981 to present; Tester Jewels, South Florida Theatre Company, Shakespeare Festival, 1981 to present; 1982 Columbus Exposition, Board of Trustees, 1983. Religion: First Presbyterian Church, Miami, Florida, Sunday School Teacher, 1975. Honors and Awards: *Who's Who of American Women, World Who's Who of Women, Personalities of America, Biographical Roll of Honor*. Address: 73 Edgewater Drive, Coral Gables, Florida 33133.■

JOSEPH PADULA RIZZA

Academy President. Personal: Born January 30, 1915; Son of Paul and Conetta Rizza (deceased); Married Marie Antoinette Follin; Father of Barbara Schwaner. Education: Attended Pennsylvania Maritime Academy, 1936; B.A., University of Washington, 1951; M.A., Boston University, 1958; Graduate, Naval War College, 1957; Graduate, National War College, 1971. Career: President, California Maritime Academy, present; Retired from United States Navy, 1942-72; Commissioned Officer through rank Captain, United States Navy; Officer through Master in United States Merchant Marine, 1936-42; Commanding Officer of Destroyers and Attack Transports, United States Navy; Commanded Destroyer Squadron Atlantic Fleet; Commanded United States Naval Advisory Group Republic of Korea; Served on Staff of Joint Chiefs of Staff; Director of Education and Chairman, Department of Curriculum Development at the National War College, Washington D.C.; Chief of Staff Commander of Naval Forces in Vietnam. Organizational Memberships: American Society of International Law; National Association of Industrial Technology. Community Activities: Council of American Master Mariners; Past President, Vallejo Rotary Club, 1981-82; Board of Directors, Vallejo Chamber of Commerce, 1979-83; Vice President, Silverado Council Boy Scouts of America; Licensed Master Mariners Unlimited Tonnage. Religion: Presbyterian. Honors and Awards: Phi Beta Kappa, University of Washington, 1951; Two Legion of Merits, Vietnam National War College; Joint Service Commendation Medal, Staff Joint Chiefs of Staff; Navy Commendation Medal; California Medal of Merit; Numerous Commendations for Outstanding Leadership; U.S. Department of Transportation Award for Exceptional Public Service, 1983; Made President Emeritus of California Maritime Academy upon Retirement in 1984. Address: California Maritime Academy, P.O. Box 1392, Vallejo, California 94590.■

ARLISS LLOYD ROADEN

University President. Personal: Born September 27, 1930; Son of Mr. and Mrs. Johnie Samuel Roaden; Married Mary Etta Mitchell; Father of Janice (Mrs. John) Skelton, Sharon (Mrs. Walter) Hagen. Education: Diploma, Cumberland College, Kentucky, 1949; A.B., Carson Newman College, Tennessee, 1951; M.S. 1958, Ed.D. 1961, University of Tennessee. Military: Served with the United States Army Signal Corps, 1951-53. Career: President, Tennessee Technological University, present; Former Positions include Vice Provost for Research and Dean of the Graduate School, The Ohio State University; Director of Graduate Studies in Education, Associate Dean College of Education, Acting Dean College of Education, Ohio State Faculty, Auburn University; Staff Assistant, Oak Ridge Institute of Nuclear Studies; Management Aid, Paducah Municipal Housing Commission; Interview Examiner, Kentucky Department of Employment Security; Cryptographer, United States Army. Organizational Memberships: Past President, Tennessee College Association; State Representative, American Association of State Colleges and Universities; Phi Delta Kappa Education Foundation Board of Governors; Member N.C.A.A. Council, Division I-AA/Central, 1983-85. Community Activities: Teen Challenge, Board of Directors; United Way, Board of Directors; Boy Scouts of America, S.M.E. Chairman; Rotary Club; Lions Club; Cookeville Planning Commission; Upper Cumberland Broadcast Council. Religion: Member and Sunday School Teacher, Baptist Church. Honors and Awards: Centennial Medallion for Distinguished Faculty, Ohio State University, 1970; Distinguished Alumnus, Cumberland College, Kentucky, 1975; Silver Beaver Award, 1983; Rotarian of the Year, 1984. Address: Box 5007, Tennessee Technological University, Cookeville, Tennessee 38505.■

SUSAN P. ROBBINS

Assistant Professor of Social Work. Personal: Born August 15, 1948; Daughter of Harold J. and Rose Robbins (both deceased). Education: A.A., Manhattan Community College, 1972; B.A., Hamline University, 1974; M.S.W., University of Minnesota, 1976; D.S.W., Tulane University, 1979. Career: Assistant Professor of Social Work, University of Houston Graduate School of Social Work; Coordinator, Criminal Justice/Corrections Program, Dominican College; Program Planning and Research Consultant, Seminole Tribe of Florida; Therapist, Private Practice; Guitar Instructor. Organizational Memberships: National Association of Social Workers; Council on Social Work Education; Southern Sociological Society; National Council on Crime and Delinquency; American Academy of Political and Social Science. Community Activities: Treasurer, Cherryhurst Civic Club, 1981-83; Judge, Tulane University Law School Moot Court Client Counseling, 1979; Social Work Member, National Association for Patients on Hemodialysis and Transplantation, 1978-80; Teaching Assistant Conservation of Human Resources Program, Augsburg College, 1973-75; Member Nation Indian Youth Council, 1968-69. Honors and Awards: Manhattan Community College, Valedictorian, Dean's Award, Liberal Arts Award, Phi Beta Kappa Award, Phi Theta Kappa, all in 1974; University of Minnesota, Phi Kappa Phi, 1976; Fellowship in Women's Club of Minneapolis 1974-75; Fellowship in National Institute of Mental Health, 1976-78; Listed in *Outstanding Young Women of America, Who's Who in the South and Southwest, Directory of Distinguished Americans*. Address: Graduate School of Social Work, University of Houston, 4800 Calhoun Road, Houston, Texas 77004.■

GERTRUD K. ROBERTS

Concert Harpsichordist, Composer. Personal: Born August 23, 1906, in Hastings, Minnesota; Daughter of Adolph Gustav and Anna Marie Kloetzer Kuenzel (both deceased); Married Joyce O. Roberts, June 4, 1934; Mother of Michael Stefan, Marcia Roberts Morse. Education: B.A., University of Minnesota, 1928; Attended the Leipzig Conservatory of Music, 1930-31; Private Study with Madame Julia Elbogen, Vienna, Austria, 1935-36; Studied Art History under Dr. Gustav Ecke and Dr. Jean Charlot. Career: Recitals and Concerts in America and Europe since Age 12; Harpsichord Concerts throughout United States and Hawaii since 1936; First Public Performance on Harpsichord, including Own Composition, Women's City Club, St. Paul, Minnesota, 1936; Traveled Coast to Coast and all Hawaiian Islands (except Molokai) with Harpsichords; Sponsored by State Foundation of Culture and the Arts to Introduce Harpsichord Concerts to Outer Islands of Kauai, Maui, Hawaii, 1968; Commissioned to Compose Music for Honolulu Community Theatre's Production of Jean Anouilh's "Thieves Carnival" and Shakespeare's "Tempest," Honolulu Youth Theatre's Production of Eva Le Gallienne's "Alice in Wonderland,' University of Hawaii's Theatre Development's Production of Lorca's "Yerma," Pineapple Companies of Hawaii Documentary Film Music for "Pineapple Country Hawaii"; Compositions include "Triptych" 1961, "Petite Suite" 1955, "Pasacaille" 1956, "In a Secret Garden" 1954, "Elegy for John F. Kennedy" 1965, "Das Kleine Buch der Bilder," "Fantasy after Psalm 150," "Double Concerto"; Number of Short Compositions for Children. Organizational Memberships: National Society of Arts and Letters, President 1971-74; National Association of Composers and Conductors; American Music Center, Composer Member; National Guild of Piano Teachers, National Judge, Hall of Fame; National League of American Pen Women, Composer Member, President Honolulu Chapter 1974-76; American Association of University Women; Sigma Alpha Iota; Alpha Gamma Delta. Community Activities: Honolulu Piano Teachers Association, President 1970-72; Honolulu Chamber Music Society, Founder, Patron; Honolulu Morning Music Club; Honolulu Academy of Arts; Honolulu Museum, Polynesian Artifacts; Fritz Hart Foundation, Founder, President; Jean Charlot Foundation, Founder, President. Published Works: *Chaconne for Harpsichord, Rondo-Hommage to Couperin*, "Twelve Time-Gardens." Honors and Awards: Honorary Life Member, Honolulu Community Theatre; Honorary Citizen, Home-town of Hastings, Minnesota; Most Distinguished Citizen for 1975 in the Arts, Alpha Gamma Delta; Listed in *Men and Women of Hawaii, Personalities of the West and Midwest, Who's Who of American Women, Who's Who in the West, International*

TWO THOUSAND NOTABLE AMERICANS

Who's Who in Community Service, Two Thousand Women of Achievement, World Who's Who of Musicians, World Who's Who of Women, International Harpsichord Blue Book, National Register of Prominent Americans and International Notables, Dictionary of International Biography, Women Composers of America, International Who's Who in Music and Musicians Directory. Address: 4723 Moa Street, Hawaii 96816.■

KATHLEEN JOY DOTY ROBERTS

Educator. Personal: Born April 19, 1951, in Jamaica, New York; Daughter of Alfred Arthur and Helen Carolina (Sohl) Doty; Married Robert Louis on November 24, 1974; Mother of Robert Louis, Michael Sean. Education: B.A. Education, Queens College, 1972; M.S. Special Education, 1974; Certificate of Advanced Study in Educational Administration, Hofstra University, 1982. Career: Health Conservation Teacher, Woodside Junior High School, Woodside, New York, 1973-77; Health Conservation Teacher, Ridgewood (New York) Junior High School 1977-78, Educational Consultant 1978-79, Teacher Coordinator 1979-81; Resource Room Teacher, Grover Cleveland High School, Ridgewood, 1981 to present; Certified New York State Department Mental Hygiene; Certified New York State School District Administrator, Educational Administrator, Educational Supervisor; Licensed New York City Supervisor of Special Education, New York City Educational Administrator. Organizational Memberships: National Education Association; New York State Teachers Association; National Educators Fellowship; Council for Exceptional Children. Community Activities: National Society Daughters of the American Revolution; Colonial Daughters of the Seventeenth Century; Society Mayflower Descendants; Grand Cross of Color State New York; American Association of University Women; Phi Delta Kappa; Republican Party. Religion: Baptist. Published Works: Author *Closed Circuit Television and Other Devices for the Partially Sighted*, 1971. Address: 52 Hicksville Road, Massapequa, New York 11758.■

SUSAN C. ROBERTS

Associate Professor of Education. Personal: Born June 20, 1945; Daughter of Dr. and Mrs. Bruno Grossman (both deceased); Married Norman T. Education: B.A. French, Rollins College, 1966; M.A. Mental Retardation, University of South Florida, 1969; Ph.D. Emotional Disturbance, University of Florida, 1972. Career: Associate Professor of Education, Barry University, 1976 to present; Assistant Professor of Education, Barry College, 1973-76; Assistant Professor of Education, University of Miami, 1972-73; Curriculum Coordinator for Exceptional Education, Brevard County, Florida, 1968-70; Teacher of Trainable Mentally Retarded Children, Brevard County, Florida, 1966-68; Teacher of Emotionally Disturbed Children, Children's Mental Health Unit, Gainesville, Florida; Supervisor of Interns, Emotionally Disturbed and Learning Disabled Children, Alachua County, Florida; Teaching Assistant, Introductory Course to Emotionally Disturbed and Learning Disabled Children, Alachua County, Florida; Teaching Assistant, Introductory Course to Emotional Disturbance, University of Florida; Consultant, University of Miami Special Education Department 1974, and for Seven Weeks of Inservice Training for Teachers in Miami, Florida 1979. Organizational Memberships: Council for Exceptional Children, Regular Member and Student C.E.C. Faculty Advisor, Barry College, 1974 to present; Kappa Delta Pi. Religion: National Council of Jewish Women, 1973 to present. Published Works: Author Numerous Professional Publications including "The Effect of the Mentally Retarded Child on Other Siblings" (with J. Fisher) in *Education*, "An Improvement in Special Education Majors, Ability to Identify Children's Learning Problems: What Made the Difference?" in *Reading Improvement*, "College Student Organizations: Are They a Waste of Time?" in *College Student Journal* 1982, "Off-Campus College Courses: Pros and Cons" in *College Student Journal* 1982, "Faculty Promotions in Higher Education and Diminishing Resources" in *College Student Journal* 1982. Honors and Awards: Recipient Doctoral Fellowships, 1970 and 1971; Summer Traineeships, 1968 and 1969; Member Editorial Board, *College Student Journal*, 1982 to present; Outstanding Woman of the Year Nominee, Barry College, 1977; Phi Kappa Phi, 1972; Listed in *Who's Who in the South and Southwest, International Who's Who of Women, Personalities of the South, Directory of Distinguished Americans*. Address: 1121 Crandon Boulevard, Key Biscayne, Florida 33149.■

CORINE ROBERTSON

Association Executive. Personal: Born March 15, 1953; Daughter of Mr. and Mrs. Ben Medina; Married E. Dale, Son of Ed Robertson; Mother of Christopher, Courtney. Education: Attended the University of Texas at Austin; Georgetown University, Washington, D.C. Career: Executive Director, Big Brothers/Big Sisters of Rio Grande Valley, 5 Years. Community Activities: Big Brothers/Big Sisters of America, Treasurer National Professional Staff Council 1982, Secretary National Professional Staff Council 1981, Peer Evaluator 1981-82, Co-Leader Citizen's Board Development Program 1980 to present, Chairman Region X Professional Staff Council; President, Zonta Club of Brownsville, 1982; Chairman, Cameron County Housing Authority, 1981-82; Co-Founder, Battered Women's Shelter, 1977; Cameron County Democratic Women; Cameron County Bar Auxiliary; Consultant, Texas Conference of Churches on Publication *A Convenant to Care*. Honors and Awards: Outstanding Volunteer Award, Cameron County Bar Auxiliary, 1977; Outstanding Young Woman of America, 1980 and 1981; Corina Robertson Home for Battered Women and Children, 1982; Listed in *Personalities of America, Personalities of the Southwest, Community Leaders of America*. Address: 13 Casa de Palmas, Brownsville, Texas 78520.■

HAROLD F. ROBERTSON, JR.

Associate Professor of Education. Personal: Born May 29, 1937; Son of Harold F. Robertson, Sr. (deceased) and J. Elizabeth Robertson; Married Bette Mae; Father of Stacey Lynn, Harold Frederick III, Marcia Elizabeth, David Thomas. Education: B.S. 1950-54, M.Ed. 1958-61, St. Lawrence University; M.S.Ed. 1961-64, Ed.D. 1964-72, Temple University. Career: Science Teacher, Clifton-Fine Central, 1958-59; Science Teacher, Canton Central School, Summer 1962; Science Teacher, Madrid-Waddington Central, 1959-64; Camp Director, Boy Scouts of America, 1968-70; Coordinator of Teacher Education and Assistant Professor of Education, St. Lawrence University, 1968-76; Director of A.I.D.P. Project on Competency Based Teacher Education, 1976-79, Canisius College; Associate Professor of Education, Hendrix College, 1979 to present; Director, 3 National Science Foundation Summer Workshops. Organizational Memberships: Phi Delta Kappa; American Association of Colleges of Teacher Education; National Indian Education Association; Association of Teacher Education; Science Teachers Association; Association for Supervision and Curriculum Development; Association for Education of Teachers in Science. Religion: Baptist. Published Works: Editor, *C.O.T.E. Journal*, Buffalo Teachers Center Council Achievements, 1977-79; Manuscript Reviewer, *Journal of Teacher Education*. Honors and Awards: National Science Foundation Academic Year Institute, Temple University, 1963-64; Teaching Associate, Temple University, 1964-67; Boy Scouts of America Vigil Award; State Presidential Award, A.A.C.T.E.; Listed in *Who's Who in South and Southwest*. Address: 13 Sandstone, Conway, Arkansas 72032.■

MARGARET E. ROBERTSON

City Council Official. Personal: Born September 8, 1917; Married J. P. Robertson; Mother of Bonnie Sue White. Education: Attended the University

of Alabama, Mobile, Alabama; Massey Business College. Career: Development Assistant 1983, Counselor 1978-82, Rice Realty Company, Birmingham, Alabama; Property Manager, Southern Division, Hillmark Corporation, Ltd., Birmingham, Alabama, 1973-77; Vice President and General Manager, Mountain Brook Realty Company, Birmingham, Alabama, 1949-73; Resident Manager Snug Harbor Homes, Prichard, Alambama, Julius E. Marx, Realtor, Mobile, Alabama, 1944-48; Procurement and Cost Accounting, Brookley Air Force Base, Mobile, Alabama, 1942-44. Community Activities: Home City Council, Served Two Terms, 1976-84; Jefferson County Transportation Citizens Committee; Council Representative, Library Board, School Board; Citizens Committee, Regional Planning; Advisory Counselor, R.S.V.P. Program of Jefferson County, Retired Senior Volunteer; American Cancer Society; Alabama Division, Board of Directors, Homewood, Alabama. Honors and Awards: Homewood City Council Elected Official Two Terms; Listed in *Who's Who of American Women, Who's Who in the South and Southwest*.■

FRED SMITH ROBIE

College President. Personal: Born March 7, 1920; Son of George and Blanche Robie; Married Mary Louise Kent; Father of William Randolph, Nancy Ann, Fred Kent. Education: B.A., University of Pittsburgh, 1941; M.A., University of Michigan, 1949; Ph.D., University of Pittsburgh, 1970. Military: Served with the United States Field Artillery as Captain, 1942-46. Career: President, Jefferson Technical College, 1970 to present; Instructor, Speech, West Virginia University, 1946-47; Assistant Professor, University of Pittsburgh, 1947-51; Special Agent, F.B.I., 1951-60; Alumni Director, University of Pittsburgh, 1960-67; Assistant Director, Director of Admissions, University of Pittsburgh, 1967-70. Organizational Memberships: Executive Secretary, Debating Association of Pennsylvania Colleges, 1950-51; President, Ohio Association Technical Collges, 1974; Member National Committees on Alumni Programs Research Two-Year College Alumni Programs; Consultant Evaluator, Committee of Higher Education, North Central Association of Colleges and Schools, Commissioner 1981-85. Community Activities: Steubenville Area Chamber of Commerce, Vice President, 1977-78; Rotary Club of Steubenville, President 1976-77; Steubenville Area United Way, President 1977; Executive Committee, Ohio Affiliate, Inc., American Heart Association; Jefferson County Heart Association, Campaign Chairman 1974-77; Fort Steuben Boy Scout Council Board of Directors; Jefferson County Heart Association, President 1980-81. Honors and Awards: Ford Foundation Grantee, 1968-69. Address: 1718 Williams Place, Steubenille, Ohio 43952.■

ELI ROBINS

Psychiatrist. Personal: Born February 22, 1921, Houston, Texas; Married Lee Nelken; Father of Four Children. Education: B.A., Rice University, Houston, Texas, 1940; M.D., Harvard Medical School, 1943; Rotating Internship, Mt. Sinai Hospital, New York City, 1944; Assistant Resident in Psychiatry, Massachusetts General Hospital, 1944-45; Resident in Psychiatry, McLean Hospital, Waverly, Massachusetts, 1945-46; Resident in Neurology, Pratt Diagnostic Hospital, 1948-49; Fellow in Psychiatry, Pratt Diagnostic Hospital, Boston, 1948; United States Public Health Fellow in Pharmacology and Neuropsychiatry, Washington University Medical School, St. Louis, Missouri, 1949-51; Fellow in Psychiatry, Barnes Hospital, St. Louis, Missouri, 1949-51. Career: Psychiatrist, Barnes and Allied Hospitals, St. Louis, 1975 to present; Psychiatrist-in-Chief 1963-75, Assistant Psychiatrist 1951-63, Assistant Psychiatrist 1951-53, Barnes and Allied Hospitals, St. Louis; Attending Psychiatrist, St. Louis City Hospital, 1951 to present; Visiting Psychiatrist, St. Louis State Hospital, 1958 to present; Chief, Neurologic and Psychiatric Services, United States Army, Murphy General Hospital, Waltham, Massachusetts, 1947-48; Assistant in Psychiatry, Harvard Medical School, 1944-45; Assistant in Neurology, Boston University School of Medicine, 1948; Washington University School of Medicine, Instructor in Neuropsychiatry 1951-53, Assistant Professor of Psychiatry 1953-56, Associate Professor of Psychiatry 1956-58, Professor of Psychiatry 1958-66, Head Department of Psychiatry 1963-75, Wallace Renard Professor of Psychiatry 1966 to present. Organizational Memberships: American Academy of Neurology; American Association for the Advancement of Science, Fellow; American College of Neuropsychopharmacology, Honorary Fellow; American Federation for Clinical Research; American Psychiatric Association, Life Fellow; American Psychopathological Association; American Society of Biological Chemists; American Society for Clinical Investigation; American Society for Neurochemistry; Association for Research in Nervous and Mental Diseases, Vice President 1960; Histochemical Society; International Brain Research Organization; International Psychiatric Association for Advancement of Electrotherapy; International Society of Psychoneuroendocrinology; New York Academy of Sciences, Fellow; Psychiatric Research Society; Royal College of Psychiatrists, Fellow; Society of Biological Psychiatry; Society for Enurosciences; The Classification Society, North American Branch; Editorial Board, *Journal of Neurochemistry*, 1968-74; Advisory Editorial Board, *Biological Psychiatry*, 1970-75; Editorial Board, *Biological Psychiatry* 1975-77; Editorial Board, *Medical World News*, 1970-79; Editorial Board, *Communications in Psychopharmacology*, 1975 to present; Member Editorial Committee, *Biological Psychiatry*, 1977 to present; Editorial Advisory Board, *Neurochemistry International*, 1980 to present. Honors and Awards: Vice President, Association for Research in Nervous and Mental Disease, 1960; Gold Medal Award, Society of Biological Psychiatry, 1974; President, Society to Conquer Mental Illness, 1974 to present; Sigma Xi; Phi Beta Kappa; Alpha Omega Alpha; Heinrich Waelsch Lecturer in Neuroscience, Columbia University, 1976; Paul H. Hoch Award, American Psychopathological Association, 1977; Award of Merit, St. Louis Medical Society, 1978; Salmon Medalist, The Salmon Committee on Psychiatry and Mental Hygiene, New York Academy of Medicine; A.P.A. Foundations' Fund Prize for Research in Psychiatry, 1982; Distinguished Service Award, National Alliance for the Mentally Ill, 1983; Certificate of Honor Membership, St. Louis, Medical Society, 1984; Honorary Doctor of Science Degree, Washington University, St. Louis, Missouri, 1984. Address: No. 1 Forest Ridge, St. Louis, Missouri 63105.■

ROLAND KENITH ROBINS

Professor and Research Center Director. Personal: Born December 13, 1926; Son of Kenith R. (deceased) and Florence Cropper Robins; Married Lessa Rasmussen, Daughter of Grand (deceased) and Celestia Batty Rasmussen; Father of Corinne Robins Arrington, Kenith Leon, Renee Robins Tannahill, Rhonda Robins Cooper, Rochelle Robins Jarmin, Roy Lynn. Education: B.A. Chemistry 1948, M.A. Chemistry 1949, Brigham Young University, Provo, Utah; Ph.D. Organic Chemistry, Oregon State University, Corvallis, Oregon, 1952; Postdoctoral Fellowship in Medicinal Chemistry, Sloan-Kettering Institute of Cancer Research at Wellcome Research Laboratories, Tuckahoe, New York, 1952-53. Military: Served in the United States Medical Corp as Corporal, 1944-45. Career: Professor of Chemistry and Biochemistry and Director of the Cancer Research Center, Brigham Young University, Provo, Utah, 1977 to present; Vice President Research and Development, ICN Pharmaceuticals, Inc., Irvine, California 1969-73, Senior Vice President 1973-77; Director, ICN Nucleic Acid Research Institute, Irvine, California, 1969-73; Professor of Chemistry, University of Utah, Salt Lake City, Utah 1964-69, Professor of Medicinal Chemistry and Chairman Graduate Program Medicinal Chemistry and Graduate Program Chemistry 1966-69; Associate Professor of Chemistry, Arizona State University, Tucson, Arizona 1957-60, Professor of Chemistry 1960-63; Assistant Professor, New Mexico Highland University, Las Vegas, New Mexico 1953-54, Associate Professor 1954-57. Organizational Memberships: American Chemical Society; American Association for Cancer Research. Community Activities: Consultant, National Cancer Institute, 1959-69; National Institutes of Health, Medicinal Chemistry "A" Study Section, Consultant 1967-69; National Institutes of Health, Member Advisory Committee on Clinical Investigations 1971-74, Consultant for Formulations of United States National Cancer Plan, January 1972; Advisor to World Health Organization Secretariat, Steering Committee on Chemotherapy and Parasitology of Chagas Disease, September 1978. Honors and Awards: Utah Award, Utah Division, American Chemical Society, 1981.■

MARIE J. ROBINSON

Professor of Speech. Personal: Born January 21, 1915; Daughter of Harry and Marie J. V. Robinson (both deceased). Education: B.L.I. with honors, Emerson College, Boston, Massachusetts, 1935; M.A. with honors, Michigan State University, East Lansing, Michigan, 1944; Ph.D., Northwestern University, Evanston, Illinois, 1960. Career: Teacher Speech, Drama, Director of Plays, Contests, Lockport Senior High School, Lockport, New York, 1935-43; Head, Department of Speech and Drama, State Teachers College, Bemidji, Minnesota, 1944-45; Instructor, School of Speech, Syracuse University, Syracuse, New York, 1945-49; Head, Department of Speech 1953-73, Professor of Speech 1950-80, Illinois Wesleyan University, Bloomington, Illinois. Organizational Memberships: New York State Speech Association, Charter Member, Secretary; Illinois Speech and Theatre Association, Vice President 1961-62; I.W.U. Chapter, Phi Kappa Phi, Secretary 1960-61, President 1963-64, 1964-65, 1969-70; Central States Speech Association, Advisory Committee 1961-62, 1962-63; C.S.C.A., President Speech and Drama, 1966-67, 1967-68; Chairman Oral Interpretation Pi Kappa Delta Bi-Province Tournament 1972, Chairman Individual Events Pi Kappa Delta Bi-Province Tournament 1974; Chairman, High School and College Interpretation Regulations, Speech Communication Association, 1972; Chairman, Festival and Tournament Committee, 1973; Lieutenant Governor, Province of Illinois, Pi Kappa Delta, 1972-74; Governor, Province of Illinois, Pi Kappa Delta, 1974-76; Director of Forensics, I.W.U., 1951-72; Director of Community Players, Bloomington, Illinois, Readings, Interpretation Programs, 1951 to present; Visiting Artist, Carthage College, Wisconsin, 1966, 1968; Visiting Lecturer in Speech, General Beadle State College, South Dakota, 1969; Visiting Lecturer at Interpretation Contest Ottawa, Illinois, 1969; Visiting Lecturer at 2-Day Symposium, Dakota State College, South Dakota, 1970-71; Visiting Lecturer in Interpretation at 2-Day Session, Carthage College, Wisconsin, 1970; Visiting Lecturer in Interpretation at 2-Day Session, Bowling Green State University, Ohio, 1971; Speaker to Professional Organizations; Speech Communication Association, Life Emeritus, 1980; Central States Speech Association, Advisory Committee, 1961-63; Illinois Speech and Theatre Association, Life Emeritus, 1980; American Theatre Association; American Forensic Association, Life Emeritus 1980, American Association of University Professors; Illinois Inter-Collegiate Oratorical Association; Illinois Interpretation Workshop; International Platform Association; Alpha Epsilon Rho; Alpha Lambda Delta; Kappa Delta Pi; Phi Kappa Phi; Pi Kappa Delta; Theta Alpha Phi. Honors and Awards: Teacher of the Year Award, I.W.U., 1966-67; I.S.T.A. Presidential Award, 1980; Listed in *Book of Honor, Community Leaders and Noteworthy Americans, Creative and Successful Personalities of the World, Dictionary of International Biography, Directory of American Scholars, Directory of International Biography, Illinois Lives, International Book of Honor, International Scholars Directory, International Platform Artists, International Who's Who in Community Service, International Who's Who in Education, International Who's Who of Intellectuals, Men and Women of Distinction, Personalities of America, Notable Americans of the Bicentennial Era, Personalities of the West and Midwest, Who's Who in America, Who's Who of American Women, Who's Who Among Authors and Journalists, Who's Who in Education, Who's Who in the Midwest, World Who's Who of Women, World Who's Who of Women in Education.* Address: 2205 Lamon Drive, Bloomington, Illinois 61701.■

RALPH ROLLIN ROBINSON

Gynecologist-Obstetrician. Personal: Born July 7, 1913, in Nashville, Kansas; Son of Walter S. Sr. (deceased) and Mary Emma Inslee; Father of Mark Stuart, Kim Ella, Nancy Harriett, Ralph R. Jr., Rachel Catherine. Education: Engineering Degree, Oklahoma State University, 1935; Medical Degree, University of Washington School of Medicine, Seattle, 1951; Intern 1951-52, Resident in Obstetric-Gynecology 1952-55, University of Oklahoma; Certified by the American Board of Obstetrics-Gynecology, 1962; Postgraduate Course in Laparoscopy, Virginia Mason Medical Center, Washington, 1972. Career: Miners Memorial Hospital, Middlesboro, Kentucky, 1955-59; Swedish Hospital, Seattle, Washington, 1959-63; Middlesboro Community Hospital, Staff Member 1963 to present, Chief of Staff 1974-75; Clairborne County Hospital, Tazewell, Tennessee, 1963 to present; Pineville Community Hospital, 1963 to present; Holds Medical Licenses to Practice in West Virginia, Washington, Missouri, Mississippi, Ohio, Kentucky, Tennessee, Texas, North Carolina, South Carolina, Alabama, California, Virginia; Private Practice, Middlesboro, Kentucky; Medical Clinics, Birmingham Women's Medical Clinic, Mobile Medical Clinic (both in Alabama), Volunteer Medical Clinic (Tennessee), Jackson Women's Medical Clinic (Mississippi); Consultant, Battelle Pacific Northwest Laboratories, Wyeth Laboratories, World Population Council, Abbott Laboratories, Julius Schmid Inc.; Number of Inventions, including Intra-Uterine Birth Control Devices known as Saf-T-Coil, Currette Device, Intra-Uterine U Stem Pessary, Disposal Shoe Cover, Intra-Uterine Inserter, Rotating Wing Aircraft, Shielded Intrauterine Device. Organizational Memberships: American Board of Obstetrics-Gynecology (diplomate); American College of Surgeons; American College of Obestetrics-Gynecology; Washington State Obstetrical Society; Seattle Professional Engineers Society; Southern Medical Association; Bell County Medical Society. Community Activities: World Population Council; Maternal and Infant Care Project, Bell County, Kentucky; M&I Clinics. Religion: First Presbyterian Church of Middlesboro, Deacon. Honors and Awards: Invitation to Scientific Sessions of the Fifth National Congress of Iranian Gynecologists and Obstetricians in Tehran, Iran; Participant, Pan American Medical Association 42nd Annual Congress, Buenos Aires; Attended First International Congress of Gynecological Laparoscopy, November 1973; Listed in *Who's Who in Community Service*, Others. Address: 322 Englewood Road, Middlesboro, Kentucky 40965.■

RENAULT A. ROBINSON

Housing Authority Commissioner, Community Leader. Personal: Born September 8, 1942, in Chicago, Illinois; Married; Mother of Four Children. Education: B.A. 1970, M.A. 1971, Roosevelt University, Chicago, Illinois; Urban Fellow, School of Psychology, Northwestern University, 1972-73. Career: Chicago Police Department (Active), 1964-73; Chicago Police Department (Inactive), Chicago, Illinois, 1973 to present; Secretary-Treasurer, League to Improve the Community, 1978 to present; Appointed Commissioner of Chicago Housing Authority, 1979 to present. Organizational Memberships: National Information Officer, National Black Police Association; American Society of Criminology; American Society of Association Executives. Community Activities: International Platform Association; President, Afro-American Police League, Chicago, Illinois; Secretary/Treasurer, Positive Anti-Crime Thrust; City Club of Chicago; Meeting Planners International. Honors and Awards: Recognition Award, Catholic Interracial Council of Chicago, 1969; Civil Liberties Award, The Illinois Division of the American Civil Liberties Union, 1969; One of the Top Men of the Year, Chicago Jaycees, 1970; Recognition Award, N.I.U. Black Arts Festival, 1971; Certificate of Brotherhood, Malcolm X College, 1972; Certificate of Merit, Malcolm X College, 1973; Humanitarian Award, The Youth for Christ Choir, 1973; Black Olympics Committee Award, 1973; Certificate of Award from Search for Truth, 1973; National Association of Black Social Workers Award, 1974; Award of Achievement, Malcolm X College, Phi Beta Lambda, 1974; Outstanding and Dedicated Service Award, Westside Christian Parish, 1974; Recognition of Community Services, League of Martin, Milwaukee, Wisconsin, 1974; Black S.P.E.A.R. for Serving the Masses, Farragut High School, 1974; Achievement Award, Charles Douglas and Company, 1974; Certificate of Appreciation for Outstanding and Dedicated Service, B.S.P.A., 1975; In Appreciation of Dedication to the People Award, Paul J. Hall Boys Club, 1975; Third Annual Dr. Martin Luther King Jr. Award S.C.L.C., Suburban Chapter, 1975; Award of Merit, Eternal Flames Production, Inc., 1975; National Association of Black Social Workers Service Award for Outstanding Contribution to the Black Community, 1975; I Am My Brother's Keeper Award, Policeman for a Better Gary, Indiana, 1975; Award for Outstanding Achievement, Minority Alliance Group, Cook County, Illinois, 1975; Outstanding Achievement Award, Black Students Psychological Association, 1975; Appreciation Award, The Guardians, 1975; AABS Award for Excellence, 1976; Service to the Community, Newspaper Guild, 1976; Humanitarian Service Award, Centers for New Horizons, Inc., 1976; Gratitude and Appreciation Award, The Kiwanis Club of Roseland, 1976; Breadbasket Commercial Association, 1976 Affirmative Action Award, 1976; Public Service Award, Cook County Bar Association, 1976; The Order of Companions of Honor of the African Methodist Episcopal Church, 1978; The Nation of Islam, The Distinguished Service Award, 1979; John D. Rockefeller II Youth Award for 1978, 1979; Listed in *Who's Who in the Midwest, Outstanding Young Men of America, Who's Who Among Black Americans, International Who's Who in Community Service, Contemporary Notables,* The Library of Congress Science and Technology Division, *The International Register of Profiles, Directory of Special Libraries and Information Centers.* Address: 4739 South Greenwood, Chicago, Illinois 60628.■

PETER GEORGE ROCHE DE COPPENS

Professor, Writer, Lecturer, Psychotherapist, Financial Consultant. Personal: Born May 24, 1938; Son of Alice de Coppens via Finocchiaro, Milano, Italy. Education: B.S., Columbia University, 1965; M.A. Cultural Anthropology, Fordham University, 1966; M.S.W. Psychiatric Casework/Psychotherapy, University of Montreal, 1978. Career: Teaching Assistant 1965-66, Teaching Fellow 1966-68, Instructor of Sociology 1968-69, Fordham University; Assistant Professor of Sociology/Anthropology 1970-71, Associate Professor of Sociology/Anthropology 1971-76, Full Professor of Sociology/Anthropology 1976-81, Senior and Tenured Member of Sociology/Anthropology Department at present, East Stroudsburg University; Tutor of Foreign Languages, Columbia University, 1958-65; Tutor of Recreational Skills including Skiing, Tennis, Sailing, and Flying; Education Consultant, Regina Laudis Monastery, Bethlehem, Connecticut, 1968-70; Education Consultant, Montfort Fathers, Ozone Park, New York, 1968-71; Field Faculty Member (Associate Professor of Psychology), Humanistic Psychology Institute, San Francisco, California, 1975-79; Chairman of the Educational Development Committee and Dean of Arts and Sciences, International Institute of Integral Human Sciences, Montreal, Canada, 1976-79; Private Practice of Psychosynthesis and Spiritual Growth, 1975-81; Foreign Correspondent 1961-63, Financial Consultant 1961-63, Gottardo Ruffoni, Milano, Italy, 1961-63; Investment Consultant and Limited Partner, Investment Brokers Corporation, New York, New York, 1973-77. Organizational Memberships: American Sociological Association; American Association for the Advancement of Science; American Orthopsychiatric Association; Society for the Psychological Study of Social Issues; International Institute of Integral Human Sciences, Montreal; Dean of Arts and Sciences, 1977-78 and present. Community Activities: Lecturer at Various Universities, Colleges, and Institutes for Human and Spiritual Growth. Published Works: Author, *Ideal Man in Classical Sociology* 1976, *Spiritual Man in the Modern World* 1976, *The Nature and Use of Ritual* 1977 and 1979, *Spiritual Perspective* 1980,

Spiritual Perspective II 1982, Others. Religion: Member and Reader in Eastern Orthodox Church. Honors and Awards: B.S. with honors in Sociology, Columbia University; Phi Beta Kappa, Columbia University; Alpha Kappa Delta, Honor Sociological Society; Woodrow Wilson Fellow, 1969-70; Woodrow Wilson Intern, 1970-71; East Stroudsburg College Professional Development Award, 1979; Knighted "Knight Commander of Malta," on July 12, 1980; Listed in *American Men and Women of Science, Who's Who in the East, Dictionary of International Biography, Men of Achievement.* Address: 244 Analomink Street, East Stroudsburg, Pennsylvania 18301.■

MARY COLUMBRO RODGERS

Professor of English and Chancellor. Personal: Born April 17, 1925; Daughter of Nicola and Nancy Columbro; Mother of Daniel Robert III, Mary Patricia, Mary Kristine. Education: B.A., Notre Dame College, Cleveland, 1957; M.A., Western Reserve University, 1962; Ph.D., Ohio State University, 1964; Fulbright Postdoctoral Research, University of Rome, Italy, 1964-65; Ed.D., California National Open University, 1975; D.Litt., California National Open University, 1978. Career: Language Arts Teacher, Cleveland Elementary Schools, 1945-51; English Teacher, Cleveland Secondary Schools, 1945-51; English Supervisor, Ohio State University, 1962-64; Chancellor, The Open University of America, 1965 to present; Assistant Professor of English, University of Maryland, 1965-67; Associate Professor of English, Trinity College, Washington, D.C., 1967-68; Professor of English, University of the District of Columbia, 1968 to present. Organizational Memberships: American Open University Academy, Dean 1965 to present; National Council of Teachers of English; Fellowship of Catholic Scholars; Poetry Society of America; American Educational Research Association; Pi Lambda Theta; Linguistic Society of America. Community Activities: Founder (with Daniel Richard Rodgers and Emma Kuhlwein Rodgers), The Open University of America, The American Open University, 1965; President, Maryland Open University, 1972; President, National Open University, Washington, D.C., 1973; President, California National Open University, Sacramento, 1975; President, Nevada National Open University, Carson City, 1978; Founder, American Open University Creditbank, 1965; Founder, American Open University Library, 1965; Founder, American Open University Press, 1965; Founder, Catholic Open University Missionaries, 1965; Founder, Catholic Open University, 1965. Published Works: Author of 52 Published Books and Monographs including *Open University Structures and Adult Learning* (with David Horgan and Venetia Terrell) 1982, *Modes and Models: Four Lessons for Young Writers* 1981, *Open University of America System Source Book, Ten Years, 1968-78* (with Daniel R. Rodgers) 1980, *Essays and Poems on Life and Literature* 1979, *Chapbook of Children's Literature* 1977, *Analysis and Synthesis of Teaching Methods* (with Frederick S. Turk) 1917, *Catalogue of the Open University of America* 1971, *New Design in the Teaching of English* 1972, *Catalogue of Concepts for the Open University of America System* 1968, *State Supervision of English and Reading Instruction* 1967. Honors and Awards: Listed in *Directory of American Scholars, Personalities of the South, American Authors of Today, Two Thousand Women of Achievement, Contemporary Authors, Dictionary of International Biography, World Who's Who of Women, International Scholars Directory, Who's Who of American Women, Community Leaders of America, Who's Who in Washington.* Address: 3916 Commander Drive, College Heights Estates, Hyattsville, Maryland.■

WILLIAM H. RODGERS, SR.

Certified Hospital Engineer. Personal: Born April 11, 1916; Son of William Thomas Rodgers and Mary Melvina (Drake) Rodgers (both deceased); Married First Wife Joy M. Echerd in 1941 (divorced 1945); Married Second Wife Annie Kathryn Dilley in December 1945; Father of Mrs. Melvina Grace (Rodgers) Peterson, William Harry Rodgers Jr. Education: Attended School of Electrical Engineering, University of Arkansas at Fayetteville, Arkansas, 1935-37; Joplin Business College, Joplin, Missouri, 1937-38; Graduate, Air Conditioning Training Corporation at Youngstown, Ohio, 1950; Graduate, Trane Air Conditioning School, 1978. Career: Shipping Clerk, Wilkerson Shoe Company, St. Louis, Missouri, 1938-39; Plumber, Knost Construction Company, Webb City, Missouri, 1939-40; Supervisor of Production and Maintenance, Atlas Powder Company, Joplin, Missouri and Paducah, Kentucky, 1940-45; Brakeman, Illinois Central Railroad, Paducah, Kentucky, 1946-47; Plumber, Graves and Morrow Plumbing Company, Paducah, Kentucky, 1947-49; Owner and Operator, W. H. Rodgers Plumbing and Heating Company, Glasgow, Kentucky, 1949-65; Hospital Engineer, District Six State Tuberculosis and Respiratory Disease Hospital, 1965-76; Facility Engineer, Glasgow State Intermediate Care Facility, Glasgow, Kentucky, 1976-82. Organizational Memberships: Chairman, Safety Committee, Glasgow Department of Human Resources, 1965-82; Member Administration and Operations Committee, 1965-82; District Maintenance Hospital Director, 1965-82; Certified Master and Journeyman Plumber, 1960-81; Certified as Hospital Engineer (first in world), 1972; American Society for Hospital Engineers, 1965-82; Kentucky Society for Hospital Engineers 1965-82, President 1977-78, Secretary 1971-74, 1978-82; National Society for Hospital Engineers 1977-82, Treasurer 1977-82, Secretary and Treasurer 1982-84; Southeastern Society for Hospital Engineers, 1976-82; Refrigeration Service Engineers 1972-78, President 1975-78; Human Resources Maintenance Advisory Committee, 1970-82; Certified Non-Commercial Insecticide Applicator, 1977-82. Community Activities: Boy Scouts of America, 1922-84; Rotary Club, 32 Years; Charter Member, Barren County Wildlife Conservation Club, President 1961; Charter Member, Barren River Rod and Gun Club; National Rifle Association, Glasgow Band Boosters, 1956-67; Glasgow Quarterback Club, 1960-82; Charter Member, Glasgow Auxiliary Police, 1960-80; Mason, 32nd Degree Scottish Rite, Master of Blue Lodge 1961; Shriner-Kosair Temple; Royal and Select Master 1952-82, Illustrious Master 1958 to present, 1969-82 (consecutively); Royal Arch Mason 1952-82, High Priest 1958, 1968-69, 1971, 1972, 1973, 1974, 1975, 1977, 1978, 1979, Deputy Grand High Priest of Royal Arch Chapter 1971, 1972, 1973, 1975, 1976, 1977, Grand Coordinator of Royal Arch Chapter 1977, 1978, 1979, Knight Templar, Commander 1959, Prelate 1960-82; Order of Eastern Star, Past Patron (5 times); White Shrine of Jerusalem, Past Watchman of Shepherds (5 times); Deputy Supreme Watchman of Shepherds, White Shrine of Jerusalem, 1976, 1977, 1978, 1979, 1980; Supreme Arbituary Committee of White Shrine of Jerusalem, 1981-82; Supreme Fraternal Relations Committee of White Shrine of Jerusalem, 1982-83; Order of Amarath; Charter Member South Central Kentucky York Rite Association, 1956-82; Past Masters in South Central Kentucky, 1962-82; Kosair Past Masters Club, 1965-82; Charter Member Glasgow Shrine Club; Charter Member Glasgow Scottish Rite Club; Certified Hunters Safety Instructor; Certified Red Cross First Aid Instructor; Boy Scouts of America Scouters Association; Scout Life Guard and Swimming Instructor; Registered Democrat; Member Baden Powell Rover Crew, Boy Scouts of America; Contingent Leader, Tophilmont Scout Ranch, 1968, 1970, 1972; Member Ceremonial Staff, National Jamboree, Boy Scouts of America, 1981; Scoutamster, Troop 113, Glasgow, Kentucky, 28 years; Sponsor and Coordinator Cub Scout Pack 113, Glasgow, Kentucky, 1979-82; Camping and Activities Committee, 1964-82; Barren County Disaster and Emergency Services. Honors and Awards: Eagle Scout Award, 1933; Kentucky Colonel, 1969; Kentucky Admiral, 1967; Silver Beaver, Boy Scouts of America, 1974; York Cross of Honor; Order of Silver Trowel; Order of High Priesthood; God and Country Award, Medal of Merit, Medal of Honor, Vigil Member of Order of Arrow 1932-82, Chief of Fire Builders, Recipient Scouters Award, Scoutmasters Key, Cal Rogers Award, Boy Scouts of America; Sportsman of the Year Award; Numerous Biographical Listings. Address: 716 East Main, Glasgow, Kentucky 42141.■

MARCIA V. ROEBUCK-HOARD

Managing Editor. Personal: Born January 18, 1950; Daughter of Mr. and Mrs. A. L. Rowe; Married Charles M. Jr.; Mother of Turia P. Education: M.Ed., B.S. Education, National College of Education. Career: Managing Editor, *Ebony Junior*; Former Editor with Scott Foresman and Company. Community Activities: Board of Directors, Chicago U.N.I.C.E.F.; Literacy Volunteers of Chicago; Reading is Fundamental; Executive Council, Friends of WTTW; Alpha Kappa Alpha. Religion: Catholic. Honors and Awards: Outstanding Young Woman of America, 1981; Listed in *Who's Who in the Midwest, Personalities of the West and Midwest, World Who's Who of Women, Directory of Distinguished Americans.* Address: 9124 MacArthur Court, Des Plaines, Illinois 60016.■

DOROTHY MARY ROELS

Department of Health Deputy Director. Personal: Born June 28, 1925; Daughter of Harold and Phyllis Broadhurst (deceased); Married Oswald A. Roels, Son of Ghisleau and Elvira Roels (deceased); Mother of Margaret Ann Roels Talarico. Education: M.B.Ch.B., Liverpool University Medical School, England, 1949; D.T.M.&H., Liverpool School of Tropical Medicine, England. Career: Deputy Director, Region 8, Texas Department of Health, 1976 to present. Organizational Memberships: British Medical Association, 1950-62; Royal Society Tropical Medicine, 1953-62; New York County Medical Association, 1968 to present; International Health Association, 1978 to present; United States Mexico-Border Health Association, 1978 to present; Texas Public Health Association, 1976 to present; Texas Parinatal Association, 1979 to present. Community Activities: Coastal Bend Council of Governments, Texas, 1977 to present; Health Council, Chairman 1981-82; Human Resources Committee, Emergency Medical Services Committee. Honors and Awards: Warrington-Yorke Medal, Liverpool School of Tropical Medicine, 1953; Recognition Award, Coastal Bend Council of Governments, 1979, 1983. Address: 28 Hewit Drive, Corpus Christi, Texas 78404.■

JAMES A. ROLLINS

Professor of Psychology. Personal: Born September 16, 1931; Son of Virginia Smith Rollins Seeger; Married Nanette Patchell; Father of Elizabeth Dawn. Education: B.S. Botany and Chemistry 1954, M.A. History 1956, University of Arkansas; Ed.D. Counseling Psychology, Boston University, 1968. Career: Professor of Psychology 1973 to present, Associate Professor of Psychology 1968-73, Department of Psychology and Counseling, University of Central Arkansas, Conway; Assistant Professor, Counseling Psychologist, Rhode Island College, Providence, Rhode Island, 1966-68; Guest Professor, Department of Education, Psychology and Guidance, University of Tennessee, Knoxville, Tennessee, Summer Quarter 1966; Psychologist, North Suffolk Mental Health Clinic, Boston, Massachusetts, Spring 1966; Coordinator Psycho-Educational Clinic, Department of Counselor Education, Boston University, Boston, Massachusetts, 1965-66; Consulting Psychologist, North Shore Mental Health Clinic, Quincy, Massachusetts, 1965; Administrative Assistant to the Director of Pupil Personnel Services, Lexington Public Schools, Lexington, Massachusetts, 1964-65; Teaching Fellow, Department of Counselor Education, Boston University, Boston, Massachusetts, 1974-75; Training Supervisor, Project C.A.U.S.E. (Federal Anti-Poverty Program), Boston University, Boston, Massachusetts, Summer 1964; National Defense Education Act Advanced Counseling and Guidance Institute, Boston University, Boston, Massachusetts, 1963-64; Educational Counselor, Vandenberg Air Force Base, Vandenberg, California, Summer 1963; Counselor, Lompoc Unified School District, Lompoc, California, 1962-63; School Psychologist, Canal Zone Government, Balboa, Canal Zone Czechoslavakia, 1961-62; Teacher, Cristobal Junior Senior High School, Coco Solo, Canal Zone Czechoslovakia, 1960-61; Head Resident Counselor, University of Denver, Denver, Colorado, 1958-59; Men's Counselor, Arkansas State College, State College, Arkansas, 1956-58; Teacher, Hoxie Junior-Senior High School, Hoxie, Arkansas, 1955-56; Head Counselor, Freshman Program, University of Arkansas, Fayetteville, Arkansas, 1954-55. Organizational Memberships: American Psychological Association; American Personnel and Guidance Association; American College Personnel Association; American Association for Counselor Educators and Supervisors; Southern Association for Counselor Education and Supervision; Arkansas Association for Counselor Educators and Supervisors; Arkansas Personnel and Guidance Association; Arkansas Psychological Association; American Association of University Professors. Religion: Board of Education, Methodist Church, 1975-80. Honors and Awards: Licensed Psychologist, State of Arkansas; Licensed for Private Practice as Counselor, State of Arkansas; Listed in *National Health Service Providers in Psychology, Who's Who in Education in the South and Southwest.* Address: 3 Rosewood Drive-Westgate, Conway, Arkansas 72032.■

STEPHEN FRANK ROLLISON

Television News Director. Personal: Born July 19, 1948; Son of Mr. Ellie Frank Rollison and Mrs. Ruth Brogden Rollison. Education: A.B.J., University of Georgia, 1973; M.Ed., Columbus College, 1975; Residency for Ph.D., Auburn University, 1976-77. Military: Served in the United States Army as First Lieutenant, 1968-71; United States Army Reserve, Captain, 1971-77. Career: Television News Director, KAAL-TV, Inc., Austin, Minnesota, 1981 to present; Assignment Editor, WQAD-TV, Moline, Illinois, 1979-81; Distributorship Operator, Atlanta *Journal*, Atlanta, Georgia, 1978-79; Sales Representative, Prudential Insurance, Albany, Georgia, 1978; Broadcast Journalist, WRBL-TV, Columbus, Georgia, 1977-78; Postgraduate Study, Teaching Assistant while Doctoral Student, 1975-77; Broadcast Journalist, WTVM-TV, Columbus, Georgia, 1973-75. Organizational Memberships: Sigma Delta Chi, Society of Professional Journalists, Radio-Television News Directors Association; Mississippi Valley Press Club, Davenport, Iowa, 1980-81; Georgia Association of Newscasters, 1973-75; Columbus, Georgia, Press Club, Treasurer 1974-75. Community Activities: University of Georgia Alumni Society; Columbus College Alumni Association; Reserve Officers Association; American Historical Association; Association of the United States Army; Albany, Georgia, Chamber of Commerce, 1978; Albany, Georgia, Chamber of Commerce Memberships Drive, 1978; National Association of Life Underwriters, 1978; Muscular Dystrophy Association Telethon, Television Personality Volunteer at CBS and ABC Affiliated Stations, 1977, 1980-82; Cerebral Palsy Telethon, Television Personality Volunteer at ABC Affiliate Station, 1981; Writer/Producer/Editor of Television News Programs, "The Vietnam Legacy: Agent Orange," "The Vietnam Legacy: Post-Vietnam Syndrome," "Fort McCoy Wisconsin: The Cuban Refugees" (all copyright 1980-81, WQAD-TV). Religion: Roman Catholic; Coordinated United States Agency for International Development (USAID) Aid Progrms for District Level Religious Leaders, Republic of Vietnam, 1970-71; Religious Affiliations include Catholic Parishes in United States and Europe; Pilgrimages to the Vatican and Lourdes. Honors and Awards: Phi Alpha Theta, International Honor Society in History; Associated Press Broadcast Journalism Award (news film), 1973; Associated Press Broadcast Journalism Award (news coverage), 1973; Decorated Bronze Star (United States) 1971, Cross of Gallantry with Bronze Star (Republic of Vietnam) 1971, Cross of Gallantry with Silver Star (Republic of Vietnam) 1971; Listed in *Who's Who in the Midwest, Personalities of America, The Directory of Distinguished Americans, Men of Achievement, Who's Who in Finance and Industry, Personalities of the West and Midwest.* Address: KAAL-TV, Inc., P.O. Box 577, Austin, Minnesota 55912.■

DANIEL DAVID ROMAN

Professor. Personal: Born November 9, 1921; Son of Augusta Schriar; Married Rosalyn G.; Father of Harlon Scott, JoDy Coleen. Education: B.S. Business and Law 1949, M.A. Economics 1953, Ph.D. 1956, University of Southern California. Military: Served in the United States Naval Reserve, 1942-46. Career: Professor of Management Science, George Washington University, Washington D.C., present; Former Positions include Consultant, Manager of the Master Planning Division of The Marguardt Corporation, and Professor at California State University at San Fernando, Florida State University, American University. Organizational Memberships: American Academy of Management, Vice President Eastern Region 1967-69; American Association for the Advancement of Science; National Association of Purchasing Management, Chairman Academic Advisory Committee 1972-77, Director Certification Program 1973-75; World Future Society. Published Works: Author *The Administration and Economics of Technology* 1968, *Certification Study Guide* (Ed.) Second Edition 1977, *Science, Technology and Innovation: A Systems Approach* 1979, *International Business and Technological Innovator* (Co-Author with J. Puett Jr.) 1983; Contributor of Approximately 60 Articles to Professional Journals. Honors and Awards: Fellowships from Foundation for Economic Education, 1961; Omicron Delta Epsilon, Economics Honor Fraternity, 1952-56; Ford Foundation Faculty Workshop, Carnegie Institute of Technology, 1965; Ford Research Grant, 1967; National Association of Purchasing Management Faculty Internship, 1966; National Science Foundation Travel Grant, 1973; NAPM District 5 Professional Development Man of the Year, 1976-77. Address: 5905 Tudor Lane, Rockville, Maryland 20852.■

MARJORIE REINWALD ROMANOFF

Adjunct Professor. Personal: Born September 29, 1923; Daughter of David E. and Gertrude R. Reinwald; Married Milford M. Romanoff; Mother of Dr. Bennett S., Lawrence M., Janet Beth (deceased). Education: B.Ed. 1947, M.Ed. 1968, Ed.D. 1976, University of Toledo, 1947-48; Substitute Teacher, Toledo Public Schools, 4 Years; Tutored Children in Reading, 10 Years; Teacher, McKinley School, Toledo, 1964-65; Conducted Seminars in New Math for Faculty at McKinley School, 1964-65; Conducted Seminars in New Math for Faculty at McKinley School, 1964-65; Consultant to Curriculum Revision in Language Arts, Toledo Public Schools, 1966; Conducted Workshops in Creative Writing for International Reading Association, 1972; Supervisor of Student Teachers, The University of Toledo, 1968-73; Chairperson, Long Range Planning Committee, National Pi Lambda Theta, 1979-84; Speaker, Toledo Association of Student Teachers, 1971; Speaker, Future Teachers of America, De Vilbiss High School, 1971; Demonstration, Beta Eta, Pi Lambda Theta, "Social Interaction Techniques," 1973; Consultant to Education Planning Committee, Toledo Public Schools, for Curriculum Revisions in Reading Instruction, 1973; Consultant to Toledo Hebrew Academy Elementary School, 1969-75, 1976-85; Instructor, Mary Manse College, Toledo, 1974; Consultant, Toledo Hospital Nursing Educators, 1975; Consultant, Toledo Board of Education, Middle East Studies, 1975-76; Teacher, The Temple Religious School, 1947-73; Conducted Teacher Education Workshop, Ryder Elementary School, 1975; Teacher Education Workshops, Hebrew Academy Elementary, 1975-76 and 1982-84; Consultant, Toledo Public Schools, Ethnic Studies Program, 1976-77; Instructor, Adult Education, Children's Literature, Sylvania Public Schools, 1977; Workshop, Great Book Leaders, 1977; Attended National Conference, International Reading Association, 1977; Instructor, The University of Toledo Community and Technical College, 1977; Adjunct Assistant Professor, Bowling Green State University, Elementary Education, 1978 to present; Instructor, American Language Institute, The University of Toledo, 1978 to present; Assistant to the Director, American Language Institute, 1979; Speaker, Temple Shomer Emunim, Sylvania, 1979; Conducted Workship, Hadassah, 1980; Ethnic Studies Committee History Department, The University of Toledo, 1980. Organizational Memberships: American Educational Research Association; International Reading Association, National, State, and Local Groups; American Association of Colleges of Teacher Education; National Society for the Study of Education; Association for Supervision and Curriculum Development; Toledo Association of Children's Literature; Teachers of English to Speakers of

Other Languages. Community Activities: Lucas County Children's Services Board, Board of Trustees 1974-76; Cummings Treatment Center for Adolescents, Board of Trustees 1976-79, President, Liaison to Community Chest 1978-80; Toledo Bureau of Jewish Education, Board of Trustees 1976-85; Vice President, President 1982-84; Citizens Advisory Commitee to Crosby Gardens 1976-79, 1979-82; Big Sisters, Board of Trustees 1978-80; Big Brothers, Board of Trustees 1980; Jewish Family Service, Vice President 1981-85, Board of Trustees 1978-85; Jewish Welfare Federation, Budget and Planning Committee 1979-80; Juvenile Court, Citizens Review Board, Board Member 1979-84; Community Planning Council, Board Member 1980-85; Americans for Democratic Action, Former Board Member; Common Cause; C.A.R.I.H. (asthma research); Council for Jewish Women; American Civil Liberties Union; Darlington House Home for the Aged; Great Books Group, Founder of Toledo Group; Hadassah, Past President Toledo Chapter, Former Board Member of Central States Region; Northwestern University Alumni Association; Planned Parenthood; Organization for Rehabilitation through Training; Toledo Museum of Art; Professor of Record, University of Toledo, College of Education; Course for Great Books Leaders, 1983-84; Toledo Symphony Orchestra Association; Toledo Modern Art Group; Toledo Zoological Society; The Temple Congregation Chomer Emunin, Former Sisterhod Board Member; Jewish Welfare Federation Speakers Bureau, Former Executive Board Member of Women's Division, Vice President 1984-86, The University of Toledo Alumni Association; Women's International League for Peace and Freedom; Board of Jewish Education; Cummings, Crosby Gardens; Board of Trustees, Family Life Education, 1984-87; Children's Literature Workshop for Children and Teachers, Elmhurst Elementary School, 1984; Conducted Series of Lectures/Discussions, Social Studies Seminars, University of Toledo, on "Religion in the Public Schools," 1984. Honors and Awards: Phi Kappa Phi; Kappa Delta Pi; Pi Lambda Theta; Phi Delta Kappa; Fellow, International Biographical Association, 1979; Listed in *World Who's Who of Women, Community Leaders and Noteworthy Americans, International Register of Profiles, Who's Who of American Women, Who's Who in Midwest America.* Address: 2514 Bexford Place, Toledo, Ohio 43606.■

CARLOS ANTONIO ROMERO-BARCELO

Governor of Puerto Rico. Personal: Born September 4, 1932; Son of Josefina Barceló de Romero, Antonio Romero-Moreno (both deceased); Married Kathleen Donnelly de Romero; Father of Carlos, Andrés, Juan Carlos, Melinda. Education: Graduate of Phillips Exeter Academy, Exeter, New Hampshire, 1949; B.A., Yale University, 1953; LL.B., University of Puerto Rico, 1956. Career: Attorney in Private Practice, San Juan, Puerto Rico, 1956-58; Mayor of San Juan, 1969-77; Governor of Puerto Rico, 1977 to present. Organizational Memberships: National League of Cities, Former Member, President 1975; Southern Governors Association, Chairman 1980-81; National Governors Association; New Progressive Party of Puerto Rico, President 1974 to present. Community Activities: National Advisory Council for Disadvantaged Children, 1976. Religion: Roman Catholic. Honors and Awards: Honorary LL.D., University of Bridgeport, 1977; Outstanding Young Man of the Year, Jaycees Award, 1968; James J. and Jane Hoey Award for Interracial Justice, Catholic Interracial Council of New York City, 1977; Special Gold Medal Award for Achievement in Bilingual Education, The Spanish Institute, New York City, 1979; Attorney General's Medal for Eminent Public Service, United States Department of Justice, 1981. Address: La Fortaleza, San Juan, Puerto Rico 00901.■

DAVID LEIGH ROOT

Corporate Executive. Personal: Born August 14, 1950; Son of Robert William and Mary Josephine Root; Married Kay Furhman, Daughter of James and Charlene Fuhrman; Father of Whitney Gardner, Jay Fuhrman. Education: B.A., Hillsdale College. Career: President, Executive Vice President, Vice President/Real Estate, Real Estate/Regional Manager, Root Outdoor Advertising, Inc. Organizational Memberships: President, Pima Investment Group, 1979; Vice President, R&B Investments, Inc., 1976; Vice President, Root Parking Systems, 1976; Treasurer, Toledo Media, Inc., 1980; Advisory Board, Mid-American National Bank and Trust, 1980; Board of Directors, Traffic Audit Bureau, Inc., 1980; Institute of Outdoor Advertising; Outdoor Advertising Association of America; Outdoor Advertising Association of Ohio; Small Businessmen's Association; Tobacco Institute; National Federation of Independent Business. Community Activities: Advertising Club of Toledo; Downtown Toledo Associates; Highway Users Federation; Press Club of Toledo; Toledo Museum of Art, President's Council 1979; Toledo Zoological Society; Better Business Bureau; Crosby Gardens; National Trust for Historic Preservation; Smithsonian Associates; Delta Tau Delta Fraternity; Medical College of Ohio Foundation; National Wildlife Federation; American Red Cross, Public Relations Committee, 1982. Honors and Awards: Outstanding Alumni of the Year, Delta Tau Delta Fraternity; National Training and Development Award, Distributive Education Clubs of America; Silver Award for Advertising Excellence from Advertising Club of Toledo; Communications Award for 1979, American Red Cross; Outstanding Recruiting Service and Support Award, United States Army. Address: 333 East Front Street, Perrysburg, OH 43551.■

WILLIAM E. ROPER

Federal Government Executive, Engineer. Personal: Born May 31, 1942, in Baraboo, Wisconsin; Son of William Laverne and Gladys Rose (Kingsley) Roper; Married Kathy Jean Widdows on September 3, 1967, Daughter of Mr. and Mrs. W. Widdows; Father of Jeannie Marie, Christina Danielle, Renee Elizabeth. Education: B.S. 1965, M.S. 1966, University of Wisconsin; Ph.D., Michigan State University, 1969; Graduate, Federal Executive Institute, 1979; Graduate, Federal Executive Development Program, 1980. Military: Served in the United States Army Corp of Engineers as Captain, 1970-72; Distinguished Military Graduate of the University of Wisconsin ROTC Program, 1965; Major in the United States Army Reserves, 1975 to present; Graduate of the United States Army Corp of Engineers Advanced Officers Program and Present Apendee in the Commander General Staff College. Career: Farm Manager, Madison, Wisconsin, 1957-65; Member of Faculty, University of Wisconsin, Madison, 1965-66; Member of Faculty, Michigan State University, 1966-69; Member of Faculty, North Carolina State University, 1969-70; Chief Industrial and Agricultural Waste Section, Office of Solid Waste Management, Environmental Protection Agency (EPA), Washington D.C., 1972-73; Chief, Surface Transportation Regulatory Programs, Office of Noise Abatement and Control (EPA), 1973-74; Chief Engineer Advisor, Standards and Regulations Division (EPA), 1974-75; Chief, Surface Transportation Branch (EPA), 1975-80; Director, Plans and Programs Staff (EPA), 1980-81; Director, Research and Development for Civil Works Programs, United States Corp of Engineers, Washingon D.C., 1981 to present. Organizational Memberships: Registered Professional Engineer, Wisconsin; A.A.A.S. Community Activities: Board Member, A&P Corporation, 1979 to present; President, B&K Associates, 1981 to present; Board Member, Carl-Chris Corporation, 1981 to present; Policy Issues Committee, Federal Executive Institute Alumni Association, 1980 to present; Chairman, Emergency Preparedness Committee, Crystal Mall #2, 1980-81; Deputy Chairman, Interagency Task Force on Pesticide Container Disposal, 1972-73; Presidential Committee on Forest Resources, 1972 to present; Secretary of Transportation Task Force on Automotive Designs for the 1980's, 1977-78; Executive Board Member, Sunny View Citizen Association, 1970-72; National Wildlife Federation; National Trust for Historic Preservation; National Academy of Science Transportation and Research Board; Smithsonian Institution Foundation, Resident Associate. Address: 9339 Boothe Street, Alexandria, Virginia 22309.■

DONALD THOMAS RORABAUGH

Metallurgist, Project Engineer. Personal: Born September 8, 1944; Son of Mr. and Mrs. D. Rorabaugh; Married Joan Lorraine Hoff; Father of Dennis Allen. Education: B.S. 1967, M.S. Drexel University, Philadelphia, Pennsylvania; Postgraduate Studies in Business and Management, Drexel University and Florida Institute of Technology, 1970 to present; Number of Job-Related College and Governnment Short Courses, 1970 to present. Career: Matallurgist/Project Engineer, R&D Studies; Former Metallurgist/Project Associate and Quality Control Manager. Organizational Memberships: Research Society of North America; New York Academy of Sciences; American Society for Metals; American Institute of Metallurgical Mining and Petroleum Engineers; American Defense Preparedness Association. Community Activities: Young Men's Christian Association, Sports and Building Committee, Judo Instructor, Self-Defense and Exercise Instructor; Amateur Athletic Union, Sports Committee, Official, Referee; Boy Scouts of America, Eagle Scout with Gold Palm, Assistant Scoutmaster, Assistant Explorer Leader. Religion: Usher, Holy Name Society. Honors and Awards: Number of Outstanding Performance Awards; Over 100 Suggestion Awards; Number of Letters of Commendation and Special Act Awards for Significant R&D Activities; Y.M.C.A. Award for Dedicated Service to the Community; Listed in Several Biographical Publications. Address: P.O. Box 477, Netcong, New Jersey 07857.■

MARTIN J. ROSEN

Attorney and Organization Executive. Personal: Born September 9, 1931; Son of Mrs. Sylvia Rosen; Married Joan, Daughter of Mrs. Mary Meyersieck; Father of Dirk, Marika. Education: A.B. with honors, University of California at Los Angeles, 1953; J.D., School of Law, University of California at Berkeley, 1956; Attended the Institute of Social Studies, The Hague, Netherlands. Military: Served in the United States Air Force Strategic Air Command as Staff Judge Advocate, Castle Air Force Base, 1958-60. Career: Attorney, President of The Trust for Public Land, present. Organizational Memberships: California

TWO THOUSAND NOTABLE AMERICANS

State Bar Association; American Bar Association; Association of Interstate Commerce Commission Practitioners; Conference of California Public Utility Counsel; Motor Carrier Lawyers Association. Honors and Awards: Law School Association Scholar in Law, 1953-54; Walter Perry Johnson Scholar in Law, 1954-55; Frank Wehe Scholar in Law, 1955-56; Order of the Coif. Address: 61 Lee Street, Mill Valley, California 94941. ■

ALEX ROSENBERG

Company Executive. Education: Attended Albright School, 1935-37; School of the Philadelphia Museum of Art, 1937-40. Military: Served in the United States Army Air Force as Second Lieutenant, 1943-45. Career: President, Anserphone, 1959-66; Assistant Secretary and Director, Noreste Corporation (Puerto Rico) Real Estate; Secretary and Director, General Cablevision of Texas, 1968-72; Vice President and Director, Communicable, Inc. (Florida), 1967-71; Vice President and Director, Five Beaches C.A.T.V. Corporation (Florida), 1967-71; Vice President and Director, General Cablevision of Palatca (Florida), 1967-71; Vice President and Director, Beacon Cable Corporation, 1966-71; President and Director, Modern Cable Corporation, 1966-71; President and Director B.F.C.-C.A.T.V. Corporation, 1966-71; Vice President and Director, Starfax Corporation Real Estate, 1968-70; General Partner Lakewood Plaza Associates, Lakewood, New Jersey, 1973 to present; General Partner, Rostin Associates, Austin, Texas, 1970 to present; President, Transworld Art Inc., Alex Rosenberg Gallery and Alba Editions, 1968 to present. Organizational Memberships: Member Print and Drawing Council Israel Museum, 1980; Lecturer, Parsons School of Design (New School), 1979 to present; Recognized Art Appraiser with Special Emphasis on Graphic Art (has appraised over 100 editions for tax purposes during last two years); Participant, 1980, 1982 World Art Market Conference sponsored by *Art News, Antiques World* and the *Art Newsletter*, New York City; Member All Major Local Museums; Artists' Rights Today, Board Member; Visual Artists and Galleries Association, Board Member; International Meeting of Fine Arts Dealers, Board Member; Association of Artist-Run Galleries, Board Member; Fine Art Publishers Association, Vice President and Board Member. Community Activities: Trustee, Guttman Institute 1979, Acting Co-Chairman 1980; Treasurer, National Emergency Civil Liberties Commission; Director, National Board of S.A.N.E.; Director, New York Council of S.A.N.E.; Vice President, Director and Member of Executive Committee of West Side Chamber of Commerce, 1968-74; Trustee and Treasurer of Board of the New Lincoln School, 1968-71; Trustee, Givat Haviva, Hadera, Israel; Delegate, 28th World Zionist Congress, Jerusalem, 1972; Trustee, Stephen Wise Free Synagogue, 1967-70, 1973-76; Member Community Planning Board #7, 1965-67, 1970-72; Director, Lower West Side Anti-Poverty Board, 1965-66; Member Lincoln Center Community Council, 1968-74; Southern Elections Fund; Friends of Welfare Rights Organization; Steering Committee of "EQUAL" Committee for Integrated, Quality Education, 1965-68; Committee for an Independent Civilian Police Review Board 1967 Steering Committee "PEARL" Committee on Public Education and Religious Liberty; Democratic District Leader 67 A.D. New York, 1964-74; Democratic State Committeeman 67 A.D., 1970-73; New York County Democratic Executive Committee, 1964-74; Elected Delegate (19 C.D. New York) 1968 Democratic National Convention; Elected Delegate (19 C.D. New York) 1972 Democratic National Convention; N.D.C. Coordinator of New Your County, Lindsay for Mayor, 1969; Manager, New York County O'Dwyer for Senate, 1968; Delegate Committee for a Democratic Alternative (CDA), 1967-68; Delegate Committee for Democratic Voters (CDV), 1960-68; Steering Committee, Democratic Foreign Policy Committee, New York, 1967-68; Member New York County Democratic Party Committee on Human Relations, 1963-65. Religion: Stephen Wise Free Synagogue. Published Works: Author "Homage to Tobey," 1974; Contributor Articles to Professional Journals. Honors and Awards: Special Prize Winner, Best Graphic Publisher 1976. Grenchan (Switzerland) Triennial; Israel Prize to Reuven Rubin for Transworld Art Publication of "The Prophets" for Israel's 25th Anniversary, 1974. Address: Transworld Art Inc., Alex Rosenberg Gallery, 20 West 57th Street, New York, New York 10019. ■

CLAIRE FREHLING ROSENBERG

Associate Professor. Personal: Born August 20, 1926; Daughter of Dr. Joseph Frehling and Lillian M. Frehling (deceased); Married Samuel I., Son of Mr. and Mrs. Nathan Rosenberg (deceased); Mother of Ann, Robert. Education: Doctor of Education Degree in Curriculum and Instruction 1977, Master of Education Degree in Curriculum and Instruction 1973, Bachelor of Science Degree in Business Education 1967, University of New Orleans. Career: Associate Professor, Business Communication and Office Systems (specialty in teaching physically handicapped); Associate Professor 1981, Assistant Professor 1977, Instructor 1974-76, Special Lecturer for College of Education 1969-79, University of New Orleans; Orleans Parish School Board and System, 1967-73. Organizational Memberships: American Association of University Professors; Association for Supervision and Curriculum Development; American Vocational Association; Louisiana Association of Educators; Louisiana Association for Higher Education; Louisiana Association for Supervision and Curriculum Development; Louisiana Business Education Association; Louisiana Vocational Association; National Business Education Association; National Education Association; Office Systems Research Association, Charter Member 1980; Southern Business Education Association; Association of Teacher Educators; Association of Records Managers and Administrators, Inc.; American Business Communications Association. Community Activities: American Cancer Society, Block Chairman; City of Hope Foundation; Children's Hospital Women's Auxiliary; Contemporary Arts Center; Friends of the Cabildo; Friends of the Audubon Zoo; Heart Association, Block Chairman; Mother's March for Cancer Society, Block Chairman; Multiple Sclerosis Foundation; Registry of Interpreters for the Deaf; Touro Infirmary Women's Auxiliary; Tulane Medical Center Women's Auxiliary; Tuberculosis Association; United Way, Block Chairman; American Red Cross, Chairman Motor Corporation and Disaster Unit, 1956-63. Religion: Brandeis University Women's Committee, Fund Raising Chairman 1954; Jewish Welfare Fund, Special Donor Unit; National Council of Jewish Women; Touro Synagogue Sisterhood, Secretary 1962, Vice President 1965. Honors and Awards: Phi Chi Theta, Business Honor Fraternity, Vice President 1967-68; WTIX Public Service Award, 1968; City of New Orleans Mayor's Commendation, 1970; Graduate Assistantship, University of New Orleans, 1973; Phi Delta Kappa, Educational Honor Society, 1975; Kappa Delta Pi, Educational Honor Society, Secretary 1976, 1977, 1977-78; Alpha Theta Epsilon, Scholastic Honor Society, 1977; Phi Kappa Phi, National Honor Society, 1977, Vice President 1978-80, President 1980-83; UNO-Carver Complex of Schools Partnership Program Certificate of Appreciation, 1980; "Real Pro Award," Future Business Leaders of America, Phi Beta Lambda, 1980; Omicron Delta Kappa, National Leadership Honor Society, 1981; Beta Gamma Sigma, National Business Honor Society, 1981; Listed in *The World Who's Who of Women, Who's Who in the South and Southwest, The International Register of Profiles, Who's Who of American Women, The International Who's Who of Intellectuals, Personalities of the South, Personalities of America, Biographical Roll of Honor, Directory of Distinguished Americans. Address: 4915 Bancroft Drive, New Orleans, Louisiana 70122.*

LEONARD H. ROSENBERG

Insurance Company Executive. Personal: Born December 1, 1912, in Baltimore, Maryland; Son of Henry I. and Laura Hollander Rosenberg (both deceased); Married Edna Mazer, November 20, 1936; Father of Theodore, Victor, Laurie, Leonard Jr. Education: Graduate, Forest Park High School, 1930; B.S.M.S., Carnegie Institute of Technology, 1934; Graduate of the Air Force Navigation School, Central Instructors School; Courses in Philosophy, Loyola College; Life Insurance Marketing, S.M.U.; Courses in Insurance Management, University of Maryland; United States Air Force Command and General Staff School. Military: Served in the United States Air Force, Education Staff Specialty Rating, 1956 to present; Rank of Lieutenant Colonel, Retired. Career: The Chesapeake Life Insurance Company, President and Founder 1956-73, Chairman of the Board 1973-83, Retired 1983; Strasco Insurance Agency Inc., Insurance Salesman, Underwriter and General Manager 1935 to present, Vice President (retired 1983); Director, Bayshore Industries, 1949-61; The Chesapeake Fund, Inc., Vice President 1961-68, President 1968-74; The Chesapeake Investment Corporation, Vice President 1963-68, President 1968-74; Columbus Mutual Life Insurance Company, State Agent 1939-55; Director, Green Associates, 1960-73; Mid-Atlantic Real Estate Investment Trust Board, Treasurer 1971-75; National City Bank of Maryland, Director, Chairman of the Finance Committee and Member of Executive Committee 1967-70; Preferred Equity Insurance Company, President 1968-70, Chairman of the Board 1970-71; Reliance Life Insurance Company of Pittsburgh, District Manager 1935-39; Suburban Trust Company, Special Advisory Board 1970-73; Instructor, Civilian Pilot Training Program, The Johns Hopkins University and University of Baltimore, 1939-42; Instructor, Life Office Management Association Courses, 1957 to present; Math and Physics Instructor, Baltimore City College Night School 1935-39. Organizational Memberships: Insurance Hall of Fame, Board of Governors 1970 to present; International Insurance Seminars, Board of Directors and Board of Governors 1970 to present, Chairman Finance Directorate 1972 to present; Maryland Life and Health Insurance Guaranty Association, Assistant Secretary and Treasurer 1972-81, Secretary/Treasurer 1981-83; Maryland Public Broadcasting Commission, Chairman 1971 to present, Commissioner 1967-71; National Association of Life Companies, Board of Directors 1965 to present, President 1968-70; American Institute of Astronautics and Aeronautics. Community Activities: Center Stage, Board of Directors 1977 to present; Community College of Baltimore, Board of Trustees 1976 to present; The Humanities Institute, Inc., Board of Advisors 1979 to present; Baltimore Museum of Art; Baltimore Symphony Orchestra Association; Carnegie-Mellon University, Baltimore Area Advisory; Institute of Navigation; Walters Art Gallery. Published Works: *Development of Modern Merchandising in the Life Insurance Industry* 1972, *Pointers* 1949-56, *Pattern Selling* 1950; Number of Professional Articles, including " Adjunsting Life Company Earnings: A Brief Survey of Alternatives," "Advancement Through Training," and "Average Income Families Are Our Average Sale." Honors and Awards: Career Development Award, B'nai B'rith Career and Counseling Services, 1975; Outstanding Contribution to the Field of Occupational Education, State University of New York at Buffalo; Executive Leadership in Training, American Society for Training and Development, 1970; Outstanding Alumni, Carnegie-Mellon University, 1967; Outstanding Alumni, Tau Delta Phi Fraternity, 1967; Outstanding Service to the Insurance Industry, William P. White Award, 1967; Listed in *Leading Men in the United States of America, Who's Who in Aviation, Who's*

TWO THOUSAND NOTABLE AMERICANS

Who in Commerce and Industry, Who's Who in Community Service, Who's Who in the East, Who's Who in Government, Who's Who in Insurance, Who's Who in World Jewry, Dictionary of International Biography, Men of Achievement, Men and Women of Distinction, Community Leaders and Noteworthy Americans, Personalities of the South, Personalities of America. Address: 22 Bouton Green, Baltimore, Maryland 21210. ■

HAROLD ROSENBLUM

Senior Staff Consultant. Personal: Born March 30, 1918; Son of Sadie Rosenblum; Married Hannah B. Wrubel; Father of Lawrence J., Susan L. Shevitz, Ira F. Education: B.Ch.E., The Cooper Union, 1943; Attended the City University of New York, 1943-44; M.E.E., New York University, 1951; Polytechnic Institute of Brooklyn, 1957; Postgraduate Studies in Electrical Engineering, New York University, 1958; Graduate Studies, University of Florida, Gainesville, 1968-71; Graduate Studies in Education, University of Central Florida, 1973-74. Military: Served in the United States Navy as Electronics Technician 1/C, 1945-46. Career: Senior Staff Consultant, Singer Company, Link Simulation Systems Division; Self-Employed Management Engineering Consultant; Director of Technical Sales, Applied Devices Corporation; Deputy Director of Engineering, Head of Systems Engineering Division, Assistant Technical Director, Head of Aerospace Systems Trainers Department, Head of Air Tactics Branch, Naval Training Equipment Center; Head Radar Systems Design Group, New York Naval Shipyard. Organizational Memberships: Senior Member, Institute of Electrical and Electronic Engineers; New York Academy of Sciences; Sigma Xi. Community Activities: Greater Orlando Catholic/Jewish Dialogue, Steering Committee 1974-76, Co-Chairman 1976-78; Jewish Federation of Greater Orlando, Maitland, Florida, Chairman Speakers Bureau 1976-77; Judaica High School, Orlando, Florida, Governing Committee 1975-76, Volunteer Teacher 1977-79; Orange County, Florida, School Board, Additions Program Resource Volunteer, 1975 to present; Toastmasters Club, Naval Training Center President 1966-67; Solomon Schechter School of Queens, Rego Park, New York, Board of Governors 1962-65. Religion: Jewish; Congregation Ohev Shalom, Orlando, Florida 1969 to present, Volunteer Teacher Elementary and Adult Divisions 1970-81, Chairman Religious Committee 1972, 1976-77, Chairman Education Committee 1973-75, Board of Directors 1970-77; Temple Israel, Orlando, Florida 1965-69, 1979 to present, Board of Directors 1966-69; Marathon Jewish Center, Douglastown, New York 1954-65, Board of Directors 1966-69, Chairman Adult Education Committee 1962-63. Honors and Awards: United States Navy, Outstanding Performance Award 1970, Letter of Congratulations 1966, Award in Merit in Group Achievement 1963, 1965, Commendation 1950, 1961, 1965, Sustained Superior Performance Award 1964, Superior Achievement Award 1963, Superior Accomplishment Award 1960, Beneficial Suggestion Award 1949, 1957, Letter of Appreciation 1953, 1957. Address: 1310 Webster Street, Orlando, Florida 32804. ■

MARTIN JACK ROSENBLUM

Admissions Specialist and Academic Advisor. Personal: Born August 19, 1946; Son of Sander and Esther Rosenblum; Married Maureen; Father of Sarah Terez. Education: B.S. English, University of Wisconsin-Madison, 1969; M.A. Literature and Creative Writing 1971, Ph.D. American Literature 1980, University of Wisconsin-Milwaukee. Career: Lecturer in Creative Writing, Literature and Composition, University of Wisconsin-Milwaukee; Director/Instructor of Literature and Writing Seminars, Marquette University, Continuing Education Division; Teaching Assistant for Literature, Composition and Creative Writing Courses, Research Project Assistant in Department of English, University of Wisconsin-Milwaukee; Counselor, Bread and Roses Women's Health Center, Milwaukee, Wisconsin, Family Health Program; Executive Director, Lawyers for the Creative Arts, Chicago, Illinois. Organizational Memberships: Modern Language Association. Community Activities: Vice President and Founding Board Member, Legal Aid for Artists; Founding Board Member, Word City; Vice President and Consultant for Arts Programs, Management Support Associates of Milwaukee. Published Works: Author Numerous Publications including *The Werewolf Sequence* 1974, *Home* 1971, *Divisions/One* 1978, *Brewing: 20 Milwaukee Poets* 1972, *Carl Rakosi: Critical Biography* 1983. Honors and Awards: Recipient of Two Knapp Fellowships, University of Wisconsin-Milwaukee, 1977; Honorary Guest Lecturer, School of American Studies, University of East Anglia, Norwich, England, 1977; Selected by Yale Poetry Collection as One of America's Important Young Poets and All Published Works are Permanently Collected at Sterling Memorial Library, Yale University, 1976; Guest Lecturer, Institute of World Affairs, University of Wisconsin-Milwaukee, 1972; Academy of American Poets Award, 1971; Selected by Center for Contemporary Poetry as One of Wisconsin's Leading Poets and Permanent Collection of All Manuscripts, Publications and Related Documents Established at Murphy Library, University of Wisconsin-LaCrosse, 1970. Address: 2521 East Stratford Court, Shorewood, Wisconsin 53211. ■

MAYDIE FAY ROSS

Reading Specialist. Personal: Born April 14, 1945; Daughter of Willis Louis Ross Jr. (deceased) and Hazel Fay Long Ross. Education: Graduate, Istrouma High School, Baton Rouge, Louisiana, 1963; B.S., Southeastern Louisiana University, 1971; M.Ed., Loyola University of the South, 1980. Career: Reading Specialist, Vic A. Pitre Elementary; Adult Education Teacher (part-time), Jefferson Parish School Board, present, Former Positions include Resource Teacher for Slow Learners, Reading Lab Teacher, J. L. Butler Elementary School, Jefferson Parish School Board; Special Education Resource Teacher for Learning Disabled, Gretna Middle, Jefferson Parish School Board. Organizational Memberships: International Reading Association; Louisiana State International Reading Association; Jefferson Parish Council of International Reading Association, Past Secretary; American Association of University Women, Metairie, Gretna Branch; Delta Kappa Gamma, Beta Lambda Chapter; Louisiana Association for Public Community and Adult Education. Community Activities: National Society of Magna Charta Dames; Clan Ross Association of the United States, Inc.; The Caledonian Society of New Orleans, Louisiana; Vice Regent of the Vieux Carré Chapter of National Society of the Daughters of the American Revolution, Past Secretary (descendant of John Penick of Virginia). Religion: Methodist. Honors and Awards: Outstanding Home Economics Student for 1971 at Southeastern Louisiana University; Reading Teacher of the Year for 1981-82, presented by the Jefferson Parish Council of the International Reading Association; Listed in *Personalities of the South*. Address: 548-B Terry Parkway, Gretna, Louisiana 70053. ■

RICHARD ROSS

Consulting Engineer. Personal: Born January 14, 1933; Son of Fay Preston Ross; Married Leah May Vaughan, Daughter of Everett Johnson Vaughan and Mildred McKibben Vaughan Newton; Father of Charles, Lynn, George. Education: B.S.A.E., Wichita University; M.S.A.E., University of Southern California; Ph.D. Candidate, Stanford University. Military: Served in the United States Air Force Reserves, 1958-61, attaining the rank of Captain. Career: Director, Ross Aviation Associates, 1977 to present; Visiting Associate Professor, University of Kansas, 1976-77; Chief, Aerodynamics and Propulsion, Gates Learjet Corporation, 1971-77 (leave of absence 1976-77); Senior Technical Engineer, Lear Jet Company, 1968 (summer); Assistant Professor of Aeronautical Engineering, Wichita State University, 1965-68; Faculty Fellow, NASA Ames Research Center, 1967 (summer); Senior Aerodynamics Engineer, 1960-65; Aeronautical Engineer, United States Air Force, 1958-60; Aerodynamist, Lockheed-California Company, 1956-58; Student Engineer, University of Wichita Engineering Research Department, 1955-56. Organizational Memberships: American Institute of Aeronatics and Astronautics, Associate Fellow, Faculty Advisor to Wichita State University Student Chapter 1966-68, Wichita Section Program Chairman 1973-74, Treasurer 1974-75, Vice Chairman 1975-76, Chairman 1976-77, Faculty Advisor to University of Kansas Student Chapter 1976-77, Member General Aviation Systems Technology Committee 1976 to present, Member Turboject Engine Testing Working Group 1972 to present; Society of Automotive Engineers, Organizer and Chairman of Session on Aerodynamics for the 1976 National Business Aircraft Meeting; National Society of Professional Engineers, Secretary-Treasurer of Engineers in Education Section 1968-69; Wichita Professional Engineers Society, Chairman of Young Engineers Committee 1968-69. Community Activities: Boy Scouts of America, Scoutmaster 1973-77, Assistant Scoutmaster 1977-82, School District Board of Education 1976-82, President 1980-82. Religion: Methodist 1945-82, Lay Leader, Chairman Church Council, Chairman Administrative Board, Chairman Council on Ministries, Lay Speaker. Honors and Awards: American Society for Engineering Education, National Aeronautics and Space Administration, Summer Faculty Fellowship, Stanford University, Ames Research Center, Fluid Mechanics, Summer 1967, Invited to Return 1968 (unable to attend); National Science Foundation Traineeship, Stanford University, 1968-70 (supplemented by additional grant from Department of Aeronautics and Astronautics); National Science Foundation, Science Faculty Fellowship, Stanford University, Fluid Mechanics, 1970-71; American Institute of Aeronautics and Astronautics, Outstanding Faculty Advisor Citation, Wichita State University 1968, Certificate of Appreciation 1976, Section Chairman Citation 1977; Wichita, Kansas, Professional Engineers Society, Outstanding Young Engineer in 1968; Colorado State University Summer Fellowship, Fluid Mechanics, Summer 1966 (unable to attend); Sigma Gamma Tau, National Aeronautical Engineering Honor Society, 1954 to present; Tau Beta Pi, National Engineering Honor Society, 1967 to present; Boy Scouts of America, Quivira Council, Distinguished Service Award; Chairman of Board of Directors, 1976 to present; Listed in *Who's Who in the Midwest, Who's Who in Aviation, Who's Who in America, Who's Who in Technology Today, Community Leaders and Noteworthy Americans, Who's Who in Aviation and Aerospace, Men of Achievement, Notable Americans, International Who's Who in Community Service, Personalities of the West and Midwest, International Who's Who of Intellectuals, Dictionary of International Biography, Personalities of America, Who's Who in the Methodist Church.* Address: RFD 1, Sedgwick, Kansas 67135. ■

TWO THOUSAND NOTABLE AMERICANS

RUSSELL ROSS

Professor of Pathology. Personal: Born May 25, 1929; Married Jean Long Teller; Father of Valerie, Douglas. Education: Graduate of R. E. Lee High School, 1947; A.B. Chemistry, Cornell University, 1951; D.D.S., Columbia University, 1955; Ph.D., University of Washington, 1962. Career: Professor and Chairman of Pathology, Adjunct Professor of Biochemistry, University of Washington. Organizational Memberships: American Society for Cell Biology; Histochemical Society; Sigma Xi, Secretary University of Washington Chapter; American Association for the Advancement of Science; Royal Microscopical Society, Fellow; International Academy of Pathology; Electron Microscope Society of America; American Society for Experimental Pathology; American Association of University Professors; International Society for Cell Biology; American Association of Pathologists and Bacteriologists; American Heart Association, Fellow, Council on Arteriosclerosis; Gerontological Society; The Tissue Culture Association, Foundation Cardiologique Princess Liliane, Brussels, Belgium, Advisory Board 1977-82; Northwest-Rocky Mountain Regional Research Review and Advisory Committee, American Heart Association, 1979-83; American Longevity Association, Scientific Board 1980 to present; National Diabetes Research Interchange, Steering Committee 1980-82; Member National Advisory Heart, Lung and Blood Council, National Institutes of Health, 1978-82. Published Works: Editorial Board, Proceedings of the Society for Experimental Biology and Medicine, 1971 to present, *Connective Tissue Research* and *International Journal* 1971 to present, *Blood Vessels* (Field Editor) 1973, *Experimental and Molecular Pathology* 1974 to present, *Cell Biology International Reports* 1976 to present, *Journal of Supramolecular Structure* 1980 to present, *American Journal of Pathology* 1980 to present; Associate Editor, *Arteriosclerosis: A Journal of Vascular Biology and Diseases*, 1980 to present; Associate Editor, *Journal of Cellular Physiology*, 1979 to present; Other Former Editorial Positions. Honors and Awards: Bausch and Lomb Science Award, 1947; Westinghouse Science Talent Search Award, Honorable Mention, 1947; Alpha Epsilon Delta; William Jarvie Society for Dental Research, 1953; Special Research Fellowship, National Institute of Dental Research, N.I.G., 1958; Career Development Research Award, National Institute Dental Research, 1962-67; Eleanor Roosevelt Fellowship, International Union Against Cancer (declined), 1966; John Simon Guggenheim Fellowship, 1966-67; Visiting Fellow, Clare Hall, Cambridge University, 1966-68; Visiting Scientist, Strangeways Research Laboratory, Cambridge, England, 1966-68; Birnberg Research Medal, Columbia University School of Dental and Oral Surgery, 1975; Tenth Geiger Memorial Lecturer, University of Southern California, 1976; Seventeenth Annual Herman Beerman Lecturer, Society for Investigative Dermatology, Washington, D.C., 1977; Sarnoff Professor of Cardiology, Duke University Medical Center, Durham, North Carolina, 1977; Organizer, Symposium to Celebrate 500th Anniversary, University of Uppsala, Sweden, 1977; Foreign Corresponding Member, Royal Belgium Academy of Sciences-Medicine, 1979 to present; George Lyman Duff Memorial Lecturer, American Heart Association Annual Scientific Sessions, Miami, Florida, 1980; Fourth International Postgraduate Course on Myocardial Infraction and Agina Pectoris, Lecturer, Davos, Switzerland, 1981; Fourth I. H. Page Lecturer, Cleveland Clinic Foundation and Research Division, Cleveland, Ohio, 1981; Harvey Society, Harvey Lecturer, 1982; Gordon Wilson Medal, American Clinical and Climatological Association, 1981. Address: 4811 Northeast 42nd Street, Seattle, Washington 98105.■

WESLEY FREDERICK ROSS

Clinical and Research Psychologist. Personal: Born February 23, 1941; Son of Welsey K. Ross; Married Shirley Ann Cody, Daughter of Charles and Ina Cody; Father of Wesley Charles. Education: A.B. 1962, M.A. 1964, Ph.D. 1969, University of Kentucky. Military: Served in the United States Public Health Service as Scientist Director, 1966 to present. Career: Clinical and Research Psychologist, present; Educator. Organizational Memberships: Kappa Delta Pi 1961-68, President 1963-64; Phi Delta Kappa, 1963-75; Central Kentucky Psychological Association, Vice President 1966, Secretary 1965; American Psychological Association, 1969 to present; Psychologists in Public Service, 1972 to present. Community Activities: Young Men's Christian Association, Indian Guides Program, Held Various Offices at the Local, Regional and National Levels (most recently National Sachem and National Talley Keeper), 1975 to present; Young Men's Christian Association, Chairman of National Long House in Lexington, Kentucky 1981, Member Board of Directors of YMCA of Metropolitan Lexington 1980 to present, Secretary of Board 1983; Bluegrass Council, Boy Scouts of America 1976-79; Board of Directors and Coach, Dixie Baseball League, 1975-80, President of League 1981; Governor's Commission on Drug Abuse, 1976; United Way of the Bluegrass 1981-83, Campaign Cabinet 1982-83, Chairman of Combined Federal Campaign for the Eight-County Area 1982-83; Bluegrass Railroad Club 1972 to present, President 1975 and 1982, Secretary 1974. Religion: Member Lutheran Church. Honors and Awards: Superior Performance Award, Department of Health, Education and Welfare, 1962; Traineeship, United States Vocational Rehabilitation Administration, 1962-64; Letter of Commendation, Federal Correctional Institution, Lexington, Kentucky, 1983. Address: 1749 Bahama Road, Lexington, Kentucky 40511.■

ALAIN BENJAMIN ROSSIER

Paraplegist and Professor. Personal: Born November 29, 1930; Son of Guy Henri Rossier (deceased) and Madame Guy Rossier; Married Birte Andersen. Education: Federal Diploma 1957, M.D. 1958, Medical School, University of Lausanne. Career: Paraplegist, Chief Spinal Cord Service, Professor of Spinal Cord Injury Rehabilitation, Department of Orthopedics, Harvard Medical School; Consultant in S.C.I. at Massachusetts Rehabilitation and Braintree Hospitals; Consultant in Neurosurgery and Orthopedic Surgery at Children's Hospital Medical Center, Boston. Organizational Memberships: President-elect, International Medical Society of Paraplegia; Founding Member, International Continuence Society; American Urological Association; American Association of Orthopedic Surgeons; American Spinal Injury Association; American Congress of Rehabilitation; American Association of Neurological Surgeons. Honors and Awards: Premio Missions del Medico, Carlo Erba Foundation, 1973; Laureate of the Julius Adams Stratton Prize, 1976; Speedy Award, P.V.A., 1982. Address: 866 West Roxbury Parkway, Chestnut Hill, Massachusetts 02167.■

FREDERIC HULL ROTH

Certified Public Accountant. Personal: Born February 20, 1914, in Cleveland, Ohio; Son of Stanley E. and Myrtle Hull Roth (both deceased); Married Emmy Alice; Father of Frederic Hull Jr., Robert Allan Roth (deceased). Education: A.B., Wooster College, 1935; M.B.A., Harvard Graduate School of Business Administration, 1937. Career: Certified Public Accountant in Ohio 1942, Louisiana 1963, Virginia 1968, North Carolina 1971; Partner with Scovell, Wellington and Company in 1939, Scovall merged with Lybrand, Ross Brothers and Montgomery in 1962, Lybrand became Coopers and Lybrand in 1973. Organizational Memberships: National Association of Accountants; Tax Club of Cleveland; Institute of Internal Auditors, Cleveland Chapter, Board of Governors 1972-75; American Institute of Management; Ohio Society of Certified Public Accountants, Director 1961-62, Vice President 1962-63, Chairman of Various Committees, President-Elect 1966-67, President 1967-68; Ohio Society of Certified Public Accountants, Cleveland Chapter, Treasurer, Vice President, President 1960-61, Director, Chairman of Various Committees; American Institute of Certified Public Accountants, Member of Council 1968-70. Community Activities: Lake Erie Lodge; Al Sirat Grotto; Lake Erie Consistory; Al Koran Shrine; Grotto Big Six; Museum of National Heritage; Newcomen Society of North America; International Platform Association; Mid-Day; Chamber of Commerce; Harvard Business School; City Club; Board of Directors, Magnetics International Inc., Shaker Medical Center Hospital; Rotary Club of Cleveland, 1951 to present, Chairperson Various Committees; University Club; Union Club; Westwood Country Club; Clifton Club; Cleveland Yacht Club, Treasurer 1961-65, Director and Fleet Captain 1966, Rear Commander 1967, Vice Commander 1968, Commodore 1969, Beaver Creek Hunt Club; Catawba Island Club; Play House; Forty Club, Chairperson 1965; Al Koran Mariners; International Order of the Blue Gavel, Past Commodores Association, C.Y.C. Chapter, Secretary-Treasurer 1972, President 1973; District 9 of I.O.B.G., Eastern Vice President 1976, Third Vice President 1977, Second Vice President 1978, First Vice President 1979, President 1980; Cleveland Play House, Director and Treasurer 1964-66, Director 1967-76, Finance Committee 1968-72, Served in Other Capacities, Charter Member, *USS Constitution* Museum; Friends of Crawford Auto Museum, Donor of Classic 1957 Eldorado Brougham Cadillac in 1979; Cheshire Cheese Club; Smithsonian Institution; National Advisory Board of American Security Council; Honorary Knight of Royal Rosarians; Navy League, Advisory Congressional Board; N.R.A.; Western Research Historical Society; Ohio Historical Society; Great Lakes Historical Society; Society for British Genealogy and Family History; American Farmland Trust; Society of Colonial Wars; F&P of America; Sons of American Colonists; Sons of the Revolution; Sons of the American Revolution; Military Order of the Stars and Bars; Sons of Confederate Veterans; Sons of Union Veterans; Colonial Order of Acorn; Order of Descendants of Colonial Physicians; Descendant of Colonial Clergy; Society War of 1812; S&D of Pilgrims; Republican Party; President's Associates, Wooster College; Century Fund, Harvard Finance Committee, Antioch 1976-79; Center for International Security Studies. Honors and Awards: Patriot's Award and George Washington Award, Museum of National Heritage; S.I.R. Award, 1976; Paul Harris Fellow, 1979; Listed in *Who's Who in America, Who is Who in Ohio, Who's Who in Ohio, Who's Who in the Midwest, Who's Who in Finance and Industry, Ohio Lives, National Register of Prominent Americans and International Notables, Community Leaders of America, Biographical Roll of Honor, The International Yearbook and Statesmen's Who's Who, Two Thousand Men of Achievement, The National Cyclopedia of American Biography, Dictionary of International Biography, International Who's Who in Community Service, Who's Who in the World, Men of Achievement, International Registry of Who's Who, United States Who is Who, Outstanding Americans, The International Register of Profiles, Notable Americans of the Bicentennial Era, Library of Human Resources, Quest Who's Who, Who's Who of Intellectuals, Personalities of the West and Midwest, Book of Honor, Personalities of America, Men and Women of Distinction, Directory of Distinguished Americans, The American Registry Series, Cleveland Blue Book, The Blue Book, Royal Blue Book, National Social Directory, Social Register.* Address: 20661 Avalon Drive, Rocky River, Ohio 44116.■

BARRY KENNETH ROTHMAN

Entertainment Lawyer. Personal: Born June 12, 1942; Son of Abraham Rothman and Lillian Rothman; Married Joanne; Father of Joshua. Education: B.A., University of California at Los Angeles, 1965; J.D., Southwestern University, 1970. Career: Entertainment Lawyer. Organizational Memberships: International Platform Association. Honors and Awards: Awarded Year of the Child from United Artists. Address: 9200 Sunset Boulevard, Suite 509, Los Angeles, California 90069.■

ROGE ROUSH

Director, Writer, Teacher. Personal: Born April 20, 1944; Son of Roger R. Roush. Education: M.A. with honors in Drama, California State University, Los Angeles, California, 1982; M.F.A. Candidate, California Institute of the Arts, Valencia, California, 1978-79; Cinema Program, Columbia College, Hollywood, California, 1977; A.A. with honors in Drama, Lake Tahoe Community College, South Lake Tahoe, California, 1977; Diploma with honors, Fashion Institute of Design and Merchandising, Los Angeles, California, 1972; B.A. German and Economics, Western Washington State University, Bellingham, Washington, 1971; Diploma with honors in German, Defense Language Institute, Monterey, California, 1963; Certificate in French, Institut D'Études Françaises de Touraine, Université de Poitiers, France, 1963; Zeugnis in German with honors, Wiener Internationale Hochschulkurse, University of Vienna, Austria, 1963; Diploma in Languages and Mathematics, Clover Park High School, Tacoma, Washington, 1962. Military: Served with the United States Army Security Agency, 1964-68, German Interpreter and Voice Interceptor. Career: Director, Writer, Teacher, Truckee Meadows Community College. Organizational Memberships: American Theatre Association; Academy of Television Arts and Sciences; Society for Cinema Studies; Society of Motion Picture and Television Engineers; University Film and Video Association. Community Activities: Patron of the American Film Institute, Filmex of Los Angeles, Oregon Shakespearean Festival, San Francisco Museum of Modern Art, Sierra Arts Foundation; International Biographical Association; Sons of the American Revolution; Toastmasters International; Roush and Allied Families Association of America; Veterans of Foreign Wars. Honors and Awards: Decorated Army of Occupation Medal (Berlin), Good Conduct Medal, National Defense Service Medal, Expert Badges in Rifle and Bayonet; Certificate of Achievement, Defense Language Institute; Mu Alpha Theta (math honorary), 1958; Alonzo Stagg Medal for Athletics, 1963; Listed in *Men of Achievement, International Register of Profiles, History of the Roush Family in America*. Address: P.O. Box 20884, Reno, Nevada 89515.■

HERBERT J. ROWE

Association Executive. Personal: Born March 25, 1924; Married Ann Muter; Father of Edith L., Douglas H., Stephen F., James D. Education: Studies at the University of Texas, Purdue University, University of Illinois; Bachelor's Degree in Marketing and Management. Military: Served in the United States Marine Corps 1942-46, 1950-52, Captain in the United States Marine Corps Reserve. Career: Vice President 1978 to present, Board of Governors 1969-75, Electronic Industries Association; Former Associate Administrator, External Affairs, N.A.S.A. Headquarters, Washington, D.C.; Chairman of the Board, PEMCOR, Inc., Illinois; President, Chairman of the Board, The Muter Company. Organizational Memberships: American Loudspeaker Manufacturers Association; University of Illinois Foundation; Electronic Industries Foundation; Kappa Kappa Corporation of Sigma Xi Fraternity; Association of Electronic Manufacturers. Community Activities: Beta Gamma Sigma; Alpha Phi Omega; Sigma Chi; Ancient Free and Accepted Masons of Illinois; Ancient Accepted Scottish Rite; Medinah Temple; Ancient Arabic Order of Nobles of the Mystic Shrine; Flossmor Country Club; Field Museum of Natural History; Chicago Art Institute; American Management Association; National Space Institute; National Association of Government Communicators; American Institute of Aeronautics and Astronautics; National Air and Space Museum of the Smithsonian Institute, Advisory Board; Boy Scouts of America, Several National Committees. Religion: Flossmoor Community Church. Honors and Awards: Boy Scouts of America, Distinguished Eagle Scout Award 1971, Silver Beaver, Silver Antelope. Address: 1451 Highwood Drive, McLean, Virginia 22101.■

JACK IRVING ROZENE

Advertising Agency Executive. Personal: Born October 18, 1904, in Belfast, Ireland; Son of Saul and Rose (Leah) Rozene; Came to the United States in 1908; Married Florence Haniwitz on May 31, 1931; Father of Beverly Tootell. Education: Student, University of Bridgeport, Connecticut, 1943, Columbia. Career: Account Executive, Bridgeport Post Telegram, 1925-31, 1933-35; Advertising Manager, Retail Store, Bridgeport, 1931-33; President, Rozene Advertising Agency Inc., Bridgeport, 1935-82; Instructor, University of Bridgeport, 1952. Community Activities: Advertising Club Bridgeport, Past President; Mill River Chamber of Commerce; Mason (Shriner); Order of Golden Chain, Past Grand Patron; Order of Girls of Golden Court, Founder, Supreme Advisory Councilor, Past Dad Advisor; Probus Club, Past President, Bridgeport; President and Founder, Fountains Square Club, Lake Worth, Florida; Founder and President, Fountains Chamber Orchestra, Lake Worth, Florida. Religion: Member Rodeph Sholom Synagogue, Bridgeport. Honors and Awards: Legion of Honor, Order de Molay, 1968; Named Alumni Man of the Year, University School, Bridgeport; Man of the Year, Advertising Club Bridgeport; Pierpont Edward Medal of Honor, Masons. Address: Fountains of Palm Beach, 4702 Fountain Drive South #203, Lake Worth, Florida 33463.■

SEYMOUR JEFFREY RUBIN

Executive Director, Professor. Personal: Born in Chicago, Illinois, in 1914; Married Janet B. Education: A.B., University of Michigan, 1936; LL.B. magna cum laude 1938, LL.M. 1939, Harvard Law School. Career: Law Clerk, Honorable A. N. Hand, 2nd Circuit, 1939-40; Various Government Positions, 1940-48; Assistant Legal Advisor, Department of State; Head of the United States Delegation on N.A.T.O. Tax Treaties, 1951-52; Deputy Administrator, Mutual Defense Assistance Administration, 1952-53; General Counsel Agency on International Development and United States Minister to Development Assistance Committee, 1962-64; Private Law Practice, 1964-73; Member, Inter-American Juridicial Committee, 1974 to present; United States Representative to the United Nations Commission on Transnational Corporations, 1975 to present; Executive Director, American Society of International Law; Professor of Law, American University Law School. Organizational Memberships: American Society of International Law, Executive Vice President 1975 to present; Member United States Panel, International Center for Settlement Investment Disputes, 1981 to present. Community Activities: United Nations Commission on International Trade Law, United States Representative, 1968-70; Special Expert Committee, United Nations Security Council, United States Representative 1964-65; Mutual Assistance Control Act, Deputy Administrator, 1951-53; Special Ambassador to Bolivia, 1962. Published Works: Author of Numerous Work in the Field of International Investment Law and Policy, Expropriation, Compensation and Protection of Private Foreign Investment and International Procedures, including *Private Foreign Investment — Legal and Economic Realities*, 1956. Honors and Awards: Sesquicentennial Award, University of Michigan, 1966; Grand Cross of Austria, 1965. Address: 1675 35th Street N.W., Washington D.C. 20007.■

NUNILO G. RUBIO

Physician. Personal: Born October 22, 1943; Son of Leopoldo and Emilia Rubio; Married Elenita I., Daughter of Pedro and Francisca Ignacio; Father of Nunilo Jr., Noel, Nathaniel. Education: Associate in Arts (pre-med) 1962, Doctor of Medicine 1967, Far Eastern University; Internship, Grant Hospital of Chicago, 1967-68; Residency, Grant Hospital of Chicago (general practice) 1968-69, Hines Veterans Hospital (internal medicine) 1969-71; Fellowship in Endocrinology, Hines Veterans Hospital, 1971-72. Career: Senior Delegate FE to SPMA, 1967; Clinical Instructor, Loyola Stritch Medical School, 1972-77; Clinical Assistant Professor, Loyola Stritch Medical School, 1977 to present; President, RVR Medical Specialty Group, Ltd.; Assistant Chief, Metabolic Department, Hines Veterans Hospital, 1976 to present; Co-Director of Metabolic Section, Grant Hospital of Chicago, 1977; Vice-Chairman, Department of Medicine, St. Elizabeth's Hospital, 1977; Chairman, Department of Medicine, St. Elizabeth's Hospital, 1978-80; President-Elect, St. Elizabeth's Hospital Medical Staff, 1983; Private Practice; Consultant and Attending Physician, Westlake Community Hospital, Melrose Park, Illinois; Attending Physician, Hines Veterans Hospital, Hines, Illinois; Consultant and Attending Physician, Grant Hospital of Chicago, Chicago, Illinois; Consultant and Attending Physician, St. Elizabeth's Hospital, Chicago, Illinois; Consultant, Bethany Garfield Hospital, Chicago, Illinois. Organizational Memberships: Alternate Delegate to Chicago Medical Society, 1981-82; Executive Committee Member, St. Elizabeth's Hospital, 1978-80; Committee Chairman, Pharmacy Department, Grant Hospital, 1980-81; Committee Chairman, Utilization Review, St. Elizabeth's Hospital; Treasurer, Far Eastern University Medical Alumni Foundation, Midwest Chapter, 1976; Trustee, Far Eastern University Medical Alumni National Society; Board of Governors, Far Eastern University Midwest Chapter, 1977 to present; Board of Governors, Philippine Medical

Association of Chicago, 1977-79, 1981-82; Chicago Medical Society; American Society of Internal Medicine; American Diabetes Association; Illinois Society of Internal Medicine; Illinois Medical Society; Philippine Medical Association of Chicago; Chicago Society of Internal Medicine; Local 11 Chicago Foundation of Medical Care, 1976-77; Fellow, American College of Utilization Review Physicians; Fellow, American College of Physicians. Community Activities: President, Cavite Association of America, 1978-81; Overall Chairman, Philippine Week Celebration, Chicago and Midwest, 1980; Trustee, Jose Rizal McArthur Foundation, 1980 to present; Philippine Heritage Society; Coordinator, Health-O-Rama for 3 Years at Fil-Am Center, 1977-80; Delegate to Fil-American Council, 1978 to present; Governor, Fil-American Council, 1982-84. Published Works: Author *Starvation and Obesity; Alcoholism and Osteoporosis* (ready for publication). Honors and Awards: Distinguished Achievement Award, 1981-82; Scholar, Far Eastern University College of Medicine; Intern of the Year, St. Lukes' Hospital, Quezon City, Phillippines, 1967; Caviteno of the Year, 1976; Listed in *Who's Who in the Midwest*. Address: 6555 Cochise Drive, Indianhead Park, Illinois 60525.■

WILLIAM VAUGHN RUCH

Associate Professor. Personal: Born September 29, 1937; Son of Dorothy D. (Daubert) and Weston H. (both deceased). Education: J.D., Western State University College of Law, 1983; Ph.D., Rensselaer Polytechnic Institute, Troy, New York, 1980; M.B.A, Fairleigh Dickinson University, Madison, New Jersey, 1972; M.A., Syracuse University, Syracuse, New York, 1969; B.A., Moravian College, Bethlehem, Pennsylvania, 1959. Career: Associate Professor, School of Business, San Jose State University, 1983 to Assistant Professor, College of Business Administration, San Diego State University, San Diego, California, 1979 to present; Lecturer, School of Business and Public Administration, California State University, 1977-79; Assistant Professor, School of Business, Bloomsburg State College, Bloomsburg, Pennsylvania, 1975-76; Assistant Professor, School of Business Administration, Fairleigh Dickinson University, Madison, New Jersey, 1974-75; Field Representative, United States Army Recruiting Command Account, N. W. Ayer and Son Inc., New York, New York, 1972-73; Assistant Editor, *The Bell System Technical Journal*, Bell Telephone Laboratories, Murray Hill, New Jersey, 1969-71; Technical Writer/Editor assigned to Space Technology Center, General Electric Company, King of Prussia, Pennsylvania with Engineering Consultants and Publications, Upper Darby, Pennsylvania, 1969; Financial Editor 1967-69, Advertising Assistant 1966-67, Sales Promotion Writer 1965-66, Pennsylvania Power and Light Company, Allentown, Pennsylvania; Assistant Editor, *Dixie News*, Dixie Products Division, American Can Company, Easton Pennsylvania, 1964-65; English Conversation Teacher, Jonan Senior High School, Matsuyama, Japan, United Church of Christ, New York, New York, 1960-62; Reporter, Call-Chronical Newspapers, Allentown, Pennsylvania, 1959-60. Organizational Memberships: American Business Communication Association; International Association of Business Communicators; Academy of Management; International Platform Association. Community Activities: Toured the Soviet Union as a Representative of the Citizens' Exchange Corps, Summer of 1970. Religion: Member United Church of Christ, Taught School in Japan as a Representative of the Church, 1960-62. Address: 661 McClellan Avenue, Monterey, California 93940.■

HOWARD FREDERICK RUDD, JR.

Professor of Management. Personal: Born February 28, 1944; Son of Howard Frederick (deceased) and Louise Martineau Rudd; Married Vicki Ross Hill; Father of Kimberly Butterfly, Nathalie Ashley. Education: B.S. Mechanical Engineering 1965, M.B.A. 1967, Syracuse University; D.B.A., Texas Tech University, 1973. Military: Served in the United States Air Force, Captain and Assistant Hospital Administrator, 1967-71. Career: Professor of Management, California State College, Bakersfield, 1973 to present; Instructor and Research Assistant, Texas Tech University, 1971-73; Applications Engineer 1967 (summer) and Factory Planner 1965 (summer), Carrier Corporation. Organizational Memberships: Small Business Institute Director's Association, President Region IX 1978-79, Vice President 1977-78; A.I.D.S.; A.S.P.A.; Academy of Management. Community Activities: Girl Scouts, Joshua Tree Council, Member Personnel Committee; College Chapter of American Society of Personnel Administrators, Faculty Advisor; Kiwanis, Member Boys and Girls Committee. Religion: First United Methodist Church, Bakersfield, California, Member Administrative Board. Honors and Awards: Beta Gamma Sigma, 1976; Sigma Iota Epsilon, 1969; Editorial Advisory Board Appointment, *Journal of Small Business Management*, 1982-84; S.B.A. District Best Case Award, 1979; United States Air Force Commendation Medal 1973, Outstanding Unit Award 1967-68; Listed in *Who's Who in the West, Personalities of America, Personalities of the West and Midwest*. Address: 2807 Sunset Avenue, Bakersfield, California 93304.■

WILLIAM J. RUDLOFF

Attorney. Personal: Born February 19, 1941; Son of Mrs. Alta Rudloff; Married Rita, Daughter of Mrs. Pauline Howton; Father of Daniel, Andrea, Leslie, Susan. Education: A.B. with honors, Western Kentucky University, 1961; J.D., Vanderbilt University, 1965; National Defense Fellowship, University of Nebraska, 1961-62. Career: Attorney. Organizational Memberships: Association of Insurance Attorneys; American Counsel Association; Defense Research Institute; Kentucky Defense Counsel; American, Kentucky State and Bowling Green Bar Associations. Community Activities: International Platform Association; United States Magistrate, Western District of Kentucky, 1971-75. Honors and Awards: Listed in *Who's Who in American Law, Men of Achievement, International Register of Profiles, Outstanding Young Men of America*. Address: 517 Ashmoor Drive, Bowling Green, Kentucky 42101.■

SANDRA ROSENBLOOM RUDNITZKY

Social Worker. Personal: Daughter of Howard Rosenbloom (deceased) and Thelma Olitzky; Married Elliot M. Rudnitzky; Mother of Robyn Helene, Michelle Randi. Education: Bachelor of Music, Boston University; Master of Arts, Columbia University, 1970; M.S.W., Hunter College School of Social Work, 1974. Career: Social Worker. Community Activities: Chairperson, Middlesex County Child Placement Review Board; Board of Directors and Chapter Sponsor, Parents Anonymous of New Jersey. Religion: Vice President, Board of Directors, Jewish Family Service of Northern Middlesex County. Honors and Awards: Certified Social Worker in New York State, Academy of Certified Social Workers; Cum Laude Graduate; Phi Kappa Lambda; Listed in *Who's Who in the East*. Address: 98 James Street, Edison, New Jersey 08837.■

PHILIP REED RULON

Professor of History. Education: B.A. History, Washburn University, Topeka, Kansas, 1963; M.A. History, Kansas State Teachers College, Emporia, Kansas, 1965; E.D. History and Higher Education, Oklahoma State University, Stillwater, Oklahoma, 1968; Postdoctoral Visitor, University of Texas, Department of Cultural Foundations of Education and Community College Leadership Program, Fall 1974. Military: Served with the United States Army, 24 Months. Career: Emporia State University, Graduate Assistant in History 1963-64, Assistant Professor in History at N.D.E.A. Institute in American History Summer 1967, E.P.D.A. Institute in American History Summer 1969; Oklahoma State University, Graduate Assistant in History 1964-65, Graduate Assistant in History at N.D.E.A. Institute in European History Summer 1965, Instructor in History 1965-67; Northern Arizona University, Assistant Professor in History, Associate Professor of History 1980 to present, Professor of History 1980 to present; Director (with Edgar Bruce Wesley), First Annual Northern Arizona University History of Education Institute, Summer 1969; Director, Second, Third, Fourth and Fifth Annual Northern Arizona University History of Education Institute, 1970-73, Director 1970-73; Director, American History of Education Institute, 1970-73; Director, American Historical Association Service Center Regional Conference on the Teaching of History, Northern Arizona University, February 1970; Director, Indian Education Oral History Project, 1976-77; Director, College Board Workshop in American History, Northern Arizona University, Summer 1980. Published Works: Author Numerous Articles to Professional Journals including "Academy, Female," in *Encyclopedia U.S.A.* 1981, "Henry Bernard," in *Encyclopedia U.S.A.* 1981, "The Education of Lyndon Baines Johnson," *Presidential Studies Quarterly* (in press), "Freedom and Survival: The Twin Cornerstones of Education in the Coming Decade," in *The Social Science Journal* 1977; Author Several Books including *Oklahoma State University* 1975,

Letters from the Hill Country: The Correspondence of Rebekah and Lyndon Baines Johnson 1981. Honors and Awards: Recipient of Fifteen Competitive Research Grants awarded by Northern Arizona University, Lyndon Baines Johnson Foundation, American Historical Association, The College Board. Address: Northern Arizona University, Flagstaff, Arizona 86011.∎

CHARLES C. RUSH

Insurance Company Executive. Personal: Born November 16, 1932; Son of Mr. and Mrs. R. O. Rush; Married Charlotte St. Martin; Father of Deborah A., C. Coleman. Education: B.A., Louisiana State University. Career: Chairman and President, Southern National Life Insurance Company; Senior Vice President and Director, Post American Corporation, Louisiana; Chairman of the Board, Group Legal Consultants Inc., Dallas, Texas; Director, Cox Resources Corporation, Dallas, Texas. Organizational Memberships: Texas Legal Reserve Officials Association; Consumer Credit Insurance Association; National Association of Life Companies; American Management Association. Community Activities: Dallas Chamber of Commerce; Greater Dallas Planning Council; North Texas Commission; Dallas Central Business District Association; Dallas Democratic Forum. Religion: Episcopal. Address: 5129 Radbrook Place, Dallas, Texas 75220.∎

DAVID H. RUSH

Executive. Personal: Born April 18, 1921; Son of Joseph and Ida Rush (both deceased); Married Miriam Nelson; Father of Barbara Lanzar, Joel L. Education: Attended Rutgers University, 1939-40; B.S., New York University, 1942. Military: Served in the United States Army Air Force. Career: Chairman of the Board, Vexilar, Inc.; President, Chairman of the Board, ACR Electronics, Inc.; President, Chromalloy Electronics Division, 1948-60; Director, Group Vice President 1955-77, Vice President Electronics Group 1967-77, Chormalloy American Corporation; President, Rush Photo, 1945-48. Organizational Memberships: First Federal of Broward Savings and Loan Association, Director 1979 to present; Miami Branch, Federal Reserve Bank of Atlanta, Past Chairman 1980-82; Better Business Bureau, Director. Community Activities: United Way of Broward County, Past President; Greater Hollywood Chamber of Commerce, Past Chairman; Easter Seal of Broward County, Past President; National Multiple Sclerosis Society, New York City, Director; Holy Cross Hospital, Fort Lauderdale, Director. Honors and Awards: Silver Medallion, National Conference of Christians and Jews, 1979. Address: 4804 Banyan Lane, Tamarac, Florida 33139.∎

JAMES EUGENE RUSNAK

Computer Scientist. Personal: Born August 1, 1937; Son of Grace Rusnak; Married Catherine Ann McGovern, Daughter of Marie McGovern; Father of Lance, Jimmy, Nicole Marie. Education: B.A. Economics and Mathematics, University of Washington. Military: Served in the United States Air Force Reserve, 1957-59, attaining the rank of First Lieutenant Acft. Maintenance Officer. Career: Computer Scientist specializing in Health Care and Hospital Information Systems. Organizational Memberships: Hospital Management Systems Society; Hospital Information Systems Sharing Group; SCAMC, 1980 to present; NCHCDPA, 1978 to present; International Hospital Federation. Community Activities: Fremont Unified School District, SIP Representative and Served on Several Parent Committees, 1976-80; Junior Chamber of Commerce, International Director of Project Kerala Committee, Seattle, 1962-65; Young Men's Christian Association Indian Guides, Local Officer, 1973-75; Odd Fellows Lodge, 1977 to present, Noble Grand 1979. Religion: Roman Catholic. Honors and Awards: Certified Data Processor, 1966; Spoke Award, Junior Chamber of Commerce, 1963; Appointed to Editorial Advisory Board, Hospital Information Management Magazine. Address: 181 Celada Court, Mission San Jose, California 94539.∎

FINDLAY EWING RUSSELL

Research Professor of Pharmacology. Personal: Born September 1, 1919, in San Francisco, California; Son of William and Mary Jane Russell (both deceased); Married Marilyn R. Strickland; Father of Christa Ann, Sharon Jane, Robin Emile, Constance Susan, Mark Findlay. Education: B.A., Walla Walla College, 1941; Attended the University of Southern California, 1946; M.D., Loma Linda University, 1950. Military: Served in the United States Army, 1943-46. Career: Intern, White Memorial Hospital, Los Angeles, 1950-51; Research Fellow, California Institute of Technology, 1951-52; Giannini Honor Fellow, California Institute of Technology, 1952-53; Chief Physiologist, Institute of Medical Research, Huntington Memorial Hospital, 1953-55; Assistant Professor of Neurophysiology 1955-58, Associate Professor of Neurophysiology 1958-61, Professor of Neurophysiology 1961-66, Research Professor of Neurosurgery 1966 to present, Loma Linda University; Professor of Neurology, University of Southern California School of Medicine 1966-80; Professor of Biology, University of Southern California, 1968-80; Professor of Physiology, University of Southern California School of Medicine, 1969-80; Director of Laboratory of Neurological Research and Venom Poisoning Center, Los Angeles County/University of Southern California Medical Center, 1955-80; Adjunct Professor, Neurology, University of Southern California School of Medicine, 1980 to present; Lecturer, University of California at Los Angeles School of Medicine, 1958 to present; Lecturer Loma Linda University School of Medicine, 1955 to present. Organizational Memberships: American College of Physicians, Fellow; American College of Cardiology, Fellow; Royal Society of Tropical Medicine, Fellow; New York Academy of Science, Fellow; American Association for the Advancement of Science, Fellow; International Science, Fellow; International Society on Toxinology, Fellow; Herpetologist's League, Fellow; Royal Society of Medicine, Fellow; San Diego Zoological Society, Fellow; American Physiological Society; Sigma Xi; Society of Experimental Biology and Medicine; Society of Experimental Biology, England; American Association of University Professors; American Society of Ichthyologists and Herpetologists; Cambridge Philosophical Society; Western Pharmacology Society; International College of Surgeons. Published works: Author of Over 200 Papers Related to Toxinology, Physiology, Pharmacology, Medicine and Literature; Five Books; 20 Chapters in Textbooks. Honors and Awards: President, International Society of Toxinology, 1961-66; President, Western Pharmacology Society, 1972-73; Chairman, Humanities Division, L.A.C./U.S.C. Medical Center, 1967-74; Chairman, Section Committee on Biological Standardization, WHO, 1967; Chairman, Ad Hoc Committee on Marine Fish Poisoning, WHO, 1972; Consulant on Venoms and Venomous Animals, National Academy of Sciences, American Medical Association, American Association of Poison Control Centers, United States Armed Forces, International Red Cross, National Science Foundation, National Institutes of Health, Office of Naval Research, NASA, FDA; Walter Reed Society; Awards from Ein Shams University 1964, Academia Nacional Medicine Buenos Aires 1966; F. Redi Award, 1967; Student-Faculty Award, 1968; Skylab Achievement Award, 1974; Loma Linda University Alumni Award, 1976; Institute Jozef Stefan Gold Award, 1977; Listed in *American Men of Medicine, American Men of Science, Dictionary of International Biography, Leaders in American Science, Notable Americans, Who's Who in the West, World Who's Who in Science*. Address: P.O. Box 125, Portal, Arizona 85632.∎

GRACE JARRELL WILLIAMS RUSSELL

Artist, Writer, Teacher. Personal: Born in Memphis, Tennessee; Daughter of Aubrey Hamilton Williams, Lill Senter Jarrell Williams (deceased); Married Henry Ewell Russell, 1945; Mother of Margaret Lill Rudolph (Mrs. Bill), Rose Ellen Weiner (Mrs. Bob), Henry E. III, Stephen A., Betty Grace House (Mrs. Phillip). Education: Honor Student, Humboldt; B.A., Southern Methodist University, 1946. Career: Teacher of Private Art Classes; Architectural and Interior Decoration Plans for Work in Churches and Parsonages; Teacher of High School English, Dyersburg, Tennessee, 1964-65; Magazine Cover Design, One-Man Art Shows; Speaker at Church and Civic Gatherings; Executive Secretary to District Superintendent, Dyersburg District United Methodist Church. Community Activities: Delta Delta Delta; Church Women United Bible Study Teacher, 1968-72; Certified Lay Speaker United Methodist Church, 1983; Susanna Wesley Circle of Ministers Wives, Memphis Conference President, District President, Several Districts; District Superintendents Wives, President of Jurisdictional; Woman's Club; Tennessee American Mothers Committee, State Historian, State Art Chairman; National League of American Penwomen, State President 1980-82; Delegate to Christian Heritage in Government Conference, London, 1981; Delegate to World Methodist Conference, Honoluu, 1981. Honors and Awards: State and National Honors for Writing; Named Duchess of Paducah, 1972; Represented (with her husband) Memphis Conference of the United Methodist Church at Reopening of City Road Chapel in London, 1978; World Methodist Conference, Honolulu, 1981; Christian Heritage in Government Conference, London, 1981; Listed in *World Who's Who of Women, International Who's Who of Intellectuals, Dictionary of International Biography, Notable Americans, Book of Honor, Men and Women of Distinction, International Register of Profiles*. Published Works: Author of 3 Books, *How I See England, Rings and Things, Hope in My Heart*; Newspaper Column "Gracelines"; Articles, Poetry and Study Materials. ∎

HENRY EWELL RUSSELL

Clergyman. Personal: Born in Paducah, Kentucky; Son of H. Ewell Russell, Margaret Wurst Russell (deceased); Married Grace Jarrell Williams, 1945; Father of Margaret Lill Rudolph, Rose Ellen Weiner, Henry E. III, Stephen A., Betty Grace Houser. Education: Attended Paducah Junior College; B.A., Lambuth

College, Jackson, Tennessee, 1943; M.Th., Perkins School of Theology, Southern Methodist University, 1947; D.D., Lambuth College, 1972. Career: Pastor, United Methodist Church, Appointed to Wickliffe (Kentucky) 1946-49, Reidland (Kentucky) 1949-50; Pastor, Churches in Ellendale (Tennessee) 1950, Fulton (Kentucky) 1955 58, Organized St. Stephens (Memphis, Tennessee) 1950-55, Dyersburg First Church 1958-65; Preaching Mission in Cuba; World Methodist Council Ministerial Exchange, Serving The Albert Hall, Manchester, England; Brownsville District Superintendent 1965-67, Broadway Paducah (Kentucky) 1967-72, St. Luke's (Memphis) 1972-78; District Superintendent, Dyersburg District; Built Wesley Homes of Dyersburg Inc., 1981. Organizational Memberships: Memphis Annual Conference; World Methodist Conference, Honolulu, Delegate 1981; Christian Heritage in Government Conference (London), Chairman Delegate and Discussion Leader 1981. Community Activities: Lambuth College, Board of Trustees; Methodist Hospital, Cabinet Representative, Board of Directors; Dyersburg Housing Authority; Mayor's Advisory Board, Paducah; Lions Club; Kiwanis; Rotary Club; Junaluska Associates (Lake Junaluska, North Carolina), Board Member Several Years; Board of Trustees, Parkview Methodist Hospital, Dyersburg, 1983. Published Works: Wrote Newspaper Column "Vertical Horizons." Honors and Awards: Tennessee House of Representatives Passed Resolution Honoring Dr. Russell for Contribution to State, 1976; Named Duke of Paducah, 1972; Represented Memphis Conference at Reopening of City Road Chapel, London, 1978; Listed in *International Register of Profiles*, *Who's Who in Religion*, *Personalities of the South*, *Dictionary of International Biography*, *Notable Americans*, Various Other Reference Volumes.■

RALPH TIMOTHY RUSSELL

Insurance Company Executive. Personal: Born May 26, 1948; Son of Mr. and Mrs. Ralph Russell; Married Sanda Schultz, Daughter of Mr. and Mrs. Paul Schultz; Father of Karen M., Kevin T., Kenton L. Education: B.S. Accounting, University of Alabama, 1970; M.B.A., University of South Alabama, 1975; C.P.C.U., Society of Chartered Property Casualty Underwriters, 1979. Military: Served in the United States Army, 1970-72, attaining the rank of Captain; United States Army Reserve, 1972 to present. Career: Vice President, Insurance Company. Organizational Memberships: Society of C.P.C.U., 1979 to present; National Association of Mutual Insurance Companies, National Committee Chairman 1981; Alabama Insurance Planning Commission, 1982. Community Activities: President, South Baldwin Chamber of Commerce, 1982; President, Foley Rotary Club, 1978; President, South Baldwin United Way, 1980-81; National Vice President, University of Alabama Alumni Association, 1977-78; Chairman of the Board, Riviera Utilities, 1980; Regional Blood Services Committee, American Red Cross, 1981-82; Chairman of the Board, Foley Public Library, 1980. Religion: Chairman, Catholic Charities Appeal Drive, Foley, Alabama, 1983; Member Board of Trustees, St. Benedicts School, Elberta, Alabama; Member St. Margaret's Catholic Church, Foley, Alabama. Honors and Awards: Merit Society, National Association of Mutual Insurance Companies, 1980; Army Commendation Medal, United States Army, 1972; Listed in *Who's Who Among Students in American Universities and Colleges*, *Outstanding Young Men of America*, *Personalities of America*. Address: 117 West Rosette Avenue, Foley, Alabama 36535.■

IRMA HAYDEE ALVAREZ DE RUSSO

Pathologist and Research Scientist. Personal: Born February 28, 1942; Daughter of Jose Maria Alvarez (deceased) and Maria Carmen Martinez; Married Jose Russo, Son of Felipe and Teresa; Mother of Patricia Alexandra. Education: B.A., Escuela Norma M.T.S.M. de Balcarce, Mendoza, Argentina, 1955-59; M.D., School of Medicine, University of Cuyo, 1961-70; Residency in Pathology, Wayne State University School of Medicine, 1976-80. Career: Co-Director, Pathology Reference Laboratory, Department of Pathology, Michigan Cancer Foundation, Detroit, Michigan, 1982 to present; Assistant Member, Michigan Cancer Foundation, Detroit, Michigan, 1982 to present; Assistant Member, Michigan Cancer Foundation, Detroit, Michigan, 1982 to present; Member, Medical Staffs (Pathology), Harper-Grace Hospitals, Detroit, Michigan, 1980-82; Assistant Professor, Department of Pathology, Wayne State University School of Medicine, 1978-80; Resident Physician, Department of Pathology, Wayne State University School of Medicine, Detroit, Michigan, 1976-78; Visiting Research Scientist, Experimental Pathology Laboratory, Department of Biology, Michigan Cancer Foundation, Detroit, Michigan, 1976-82; Research Scientist, Experimental Pathology Laboratory, Department of Biology, Michigan Cancer Foundation, Detroit, Michigan, 1973-75; Research Associate, Experimental Pathology Laboratory, Division of Biological Sciences, 1972-73; Associate Professor of Histology, Faculty of Physical, Chemical and Mathematical Sciences, University of Cuyo, San Luis, Argentina, 1970-72; Research Assistant and Instructor, Institute of Histology and Embryology, School of Medicine, University of Cuyo, Argentina, 1963-71; Guest Lecturer, Department of Obstetrics, School of Medicine, University National of Cuyo, Mendoza, Argentina, 1965-71. Organizational Memberships: American Society of Clinical Pathologists; American Association for Cancer Research; Michigan Society of Pathologists; American Medical Association; Electron Microscopy Society of America; Michigan Electron Microscopy Forum; Sigma Xi. Published Works: Numerous Publications in Field; Research on Pathogenesis and Prevention of Breast Cancer. Religion: Roman Catholic. Honors and Awards: Grants and Contracts from Rockefeller Foundation 1972-73, University of Miami, Florida Institute Molecular Cellular Evolution Immunoreproduction, National Cancer Institute 1978-81, 1984-87, Department of Pathology Michigan Cancer Foundation, Detroit, Michigan. Address: 1226 Audubon, Groose Pointe Park, Michigan 48230.■

CLARENCE ALFRED RUSTVOLD

Executive Director. Personal: Born February 13, 1930; Son of Al and Lilly Rustvold; Married Donna J.; Father of Gordon, Jeralyn, Tamra, Linda, Alison, Karen. Education: A.A., Itasca Junior College, 1950; Attended University of Idaho, 1951; B.S.M.E., Texas A&M University, 1960; M.S., Rensselaer Polytechnic Institute, 1964; D.O.D., Computer Institute, 1970. Military: Served with the United States Air Force with rank of Lieutenant Colonel, 1951-71; Served as Command Pilot and Missileman during the Korean Conflict and Vietnam War. Career: Executive Director, E.E.O. Services, Fountain Valley, California, 1974 to present; Vice President and Officer, Boyden International Group, Inc., 1971-74; President, R & R Aeronautics, Inc., 1976-78; Director, Career Development Systems, Inc., 1978-80; Director, Execudex, Inc., 1975; Director, Boyden Australia Pty., 1972-74; Executive Officer to the Director of Operation and Administration of the Defense Nuclear Agency, 1970-71; Program Manager and Project Engineer for the Space and Missile Systems Organization of the United States, 1967-70. Organizational Memberships: Air Force Association; Combat Pilots Association; Aircraft Owners and Pilots Association; Forward Air Controllers Association; International Platform Association. Community Activities: Newcomen Society; Town Hall; Lions CLub International. Religion: Catholic. Honors and Awards: Received Numerous Medals and Awards from the United Sttes Air Force; Listed in *Who's Who in the West*, *Who's Who in California Business and Finance*. Address: 18195 Santa Adela Circle, Fountain Valley, California 92708.■

JAMES W. RUTHERFORD

Mayor. Personal: Born April 23, 1925; Father of Marcia Rutherford Allard, Michelle Marie, Michael James, James Andrew. Education: A.A., Flint Community Junior College, 1958; B.S. 1960, M.S. 1964, Michigan State University. Military: Served in the United States Navy, 1945-47. Career: Mayor, City of Flint, Michigan, Elected 1975, Re-elected 1979; Flint Police Department, 1948; Detective Lieutenant 1953-63, Deputy City Manager 1963, Inspector 1965, Chief of Police 1967. Community Activities: Riverfront Advisory Committee; F&M Lodge #174; Chairman, Tri-County Human Resources Committee; Chairman, Downtown Development Authority; Bruin (Mott Community College) Boosters Executive Committee; Chairman, Membership Committee, I.A.C.P.; United States Conference of Mayors; Chairman, Genesee County Police Chiefs; Governor's Crime Commission; Board of Directors Tourist and Convention Council; Trustee, Historic Flint AutoWorld Foundation; Board of Directors, Flint-Genesee Corporation; Board of Directors, Flint Renaissance Inc.; Forward Development Corporation. Honors and Awards: Named One of Ten Outstanding Officers in the United States, 1966; Recipient of Michigan Fraternal Order of Eagles

"Reverence for Law Award," 1968; Recipient of Flint Exchange Club "Golden Deeds Award," 1969; Gideon's Civic Award, 1971; J. Edgar Hoover Memorial Award, 1973; C. S. Mott Citizen of the Year Award, 1982. Address: 1713 Chelsea Circle, Flint, Michigan 48503.■

ROGER K. RUTLEDGE

Psychiatric Social Worker. Personal: Born February 27; Son of Mr. and Mrs. Talmadge D. Rutledge; Married Catherine Dowdey; Father of Mark Hampton Hood, Bryan Kent. Education: B.A. Sociology, University of Southern California, 1966; M.A. Social Work, University of Chicago, 1968. Career: Psychiatric Social Worker, Private Practice, Columbia Psychiatric Association, 1973 to present; Psychiatric Social Worker, Sumter (South Carolina) Mental Health Clinic, 1968-72; Instructor in Sociology, Clemson University, Sumter, 1969-70; Medical Social Worker, South Carolina Department of Social Services, 1972-73; Service Consultant to Twelve Nursing Homes, 1969 to present; Consultant, Columbia School Autistic Children; Recipient Stipend South Carolina Department of Mental Health, 1966-68; Registered Social Worker, South Carolina Certified Instructor Parent Effectiveness Training. Organizational Memberships: President, Columbia Stepfamily Association, 1980 to present; National Association of Social Workers; Carolina Society of Adolescent Psychiatry. Community Activities: North Lakes Sertoma; Masons. Religion. Lutheran. Address: 1401 Laurel Street, Columbia, South Carolina 29201.■

ROBERT J. RUTMAN

Professor. Personal: Born June 23, 1919; Married First Wife Julia Zabroff; Second Wife Geraldine Burwell; Father of Rose, Randy, Stephen, David, Ellen. Education: B.S., Pennsylvania State University, 1940; Ph.D., University of California, 1950; Honorary M.S., University of Pennsylvania, 1975. Career: Professor of Biochemistry, Molecular Biology, Department of Animal Biology, University of Pennsylvania; Visiting Professor, External Examiner, University of Ibadan, Nigeria, 1973-74. Organizational Memberships: American Society of Biological Chemists; American Association for the Advancement of Science; Veterinary Oncology Society; American Association of Veterinary Educators; American Association for Cancer Research, Program Committee, 1980. Community Activities: President, C. W. Henry Home School Association, 1961-62; President, Philadelphia Citizens Committee on Public Education, 1963; Philadelphia Board of Education Committee on Non-Discrimination, 1963; Chairman, Delaware Valley Peace Council, 1967-68; Chairman, Delaware Valley SANE, 1968; Steering Committee, A.F.N.A. Medical Career Program; Co-Chairperson, A.F.N.A. Science Program; Acting Director, Philadelphia M. L. King Junior Center; Treasurer, M. L. King Jr. Support Committee; Board of Directors, Southeast Pennsylvania Leukemia Society; Board of Directors, Parkside Human Services, 1983; Board of Directors, Ile-Ife Center for Humanities, 1983.■

DIANA MEREDITH HUBBARD RYAN

Consultant. Personal: Born September 24, 1952; Daughter of L. Ron and Marysue Hubbard; Married John, Son of Dora Ryan; Mother of Roanne Lee Marysue. Education: Honor, Royal Academy of Arts, 1966. Career: Consultant; Former Occupations include Positions as Executive on Cultural Exchange, Composer, Pianist, Public Speaker, Social Reform Consultant. Organizational Memberships: H.A.S.I., Associate Member. Community Activities: American Cultural Association, 1979-81; Applied Scholastics, Inc., 1970-81. Religion: Scientologist, 1965 to present. Honors and Awards: Burbank Policeman's Association Award, 1980; Italian Arts Award, 1980; Inter-American Cultural Association Award, 1981; Keys to Long Beach; Various Scientology Awards. Address: 4751 Fountain Avenue, Los Angeles, California 90029.■

STANLEY ARTHUR RYAN

Senior Training Representative and Consultant. Personal: Son of Silas Ryan and Gladys Ryals-Ryan. Education: B.A. English, South Carolina State College, Orangeburg, 1967-71; M.A. English, University of Virginia, Charlottesville, 1971-73; Ph.D. Candidate in English, Emory University, Atlanta, Georgia; Student, Ph.D. Program, Columbia University Teacher's College. Career: Senior Training Representative, Philip Morris, Inc., 1981 to present; Training Representative, Consolidated Edison of New York, Inc., 1979-81; Instructor of English, Morehouse College, Inc., 1977-78; Training Specialist, Consolidated Edison of New York, Inc., 1974-76; Lecturer in English, State University of New York at Albany, 1973-74. Organizational Memberships: American Society for Training and Development. Community Activities: South Carolina State College Alumni Association; Omega Psi Phi Fraternity, Inc.; National Urban League's Black Executive Exchange Program, Visiting Professor; One Hundred Black Men, Inc. Published Works: "I'm Somebody," in *Proud Black Images* 1971. Honors and Awards: English Instructor at Governor's School of North Carolina, Summer 1978; Honor Society, 1968-71; Martin Luther King Fellow, 1971-73; Outstanding Contributions as Black Executive Exchange Program Professor, Voorhees College, Denmark, South Carolina, 1980; Certificate of Appreciation as Black Executive Exchange Program Professor, National Urban League, New York City, 1981; Certificate of Merit as Black Executive Exchange Program Professor, Jarvis Christian College, Hawkins, Texas, 1981; Listed in *Who's Who in America, Outstanding Young Men of America, Personalities of America*. Address: 109-52 134 Street, South Ozone Park, New York 11420.■

UNA SCULLY RYAN

Professor of Medicine. Personal: Born December 18, 1941; Daughter of Mrs. H. Scully; Married James W.; Mother of Tamsin Spencer Smith, Amy Jean Susan. Education: B.S., Bristol University, Bristol, England, 1963; Ph.D., Cambridge University, Cambridge, England, 1968. Career: Research Student, Department of Zoology, University of Cambridge, England, 1963-67 (leave of absence 1964-66); Predoctoral Fellow, Department of Biology, University of Virginia, Charlottesville, Virginia, 1964-66; Predoctoral Fellow, Department of Biology, University of Miami, Miami, Florida, 1966-67; Visiting Investigator, Laboratories for Cardiovascular Research, Howard Hughes Medical Institute, Miami, Florida, 1967-71; Director, Laboratory for Ultrastructure Studies, Howard Hughes Medical Institute, Miami, Florida, 1970-71; Adjunct Assistant Professor of Biology, Department of Biology, University of Miami, 1968-71; Senior Scientist, Papanicolaou Cancer Research Institute, Miami, Florida, 1972-77; Instructor in Medicine 1967-72, Assistant Professor of Medicine 1972-77, Associate Professor of Medicine 1977-80, Research Professor of Medicine 1980 to present, Department of Medicine, University of Miami School of Medicine, Miami, Florida. Organizational Memberships: American Society for Cell Biology; Society for Neuroscience; Tissue Culture Association; Council on Basic Research, Council on Circulation, American Heart Association; European Society for Microcirculation; American Microcirculatory Society; American Thoracic Society; New York Academy of Science. Community Activities: Chairman, National Heart Lung and Blood Research Review Committee A, 1978-81; Pulmonary Diseases Advisory Committee, 1973-77; Editor, *Tissue and Cell*, Longman Publishers, Inc. Religion: St. Stephen's Church, Coconut Grove, Florida, Member of Vestry, Board of Trustees St. Stephen's School. Honors and Awards: Established Investigator, American Heart Association, 1972-77; B.S. with First Class Honors in Zoology, Chemistry and Microbiology; Bristol University Open Exhibition, 1960; United Kingdom State Scholarship, 1960; County Major Scholarship, 1960; D.S.I.R. Research Fellowship, 1963; Ethel Sargant Research Fellowship, 1964 and 1965; Science Research Council Research Fellowship, 1966; Member Pulmonary Disases Advisory Committee, National Heart, Lung and Blood Institute, National Institutes of Health, 1972-76; Visiting Faculty, Thoracic Disease Division, Department of Internal Medicine, Mayo Clinic, Rochester, Minnesota, 1974; Primary Review Committee for Contract, Identification of Lung Cells, Division of Lung Disease, National Heart, Lung and Blood Institute, National Institutes of Health, 1975; Faculty of W. Alton Jones Cell Science Center, Lake Placid, 1977 to present; Member Molecular Biology Special Study Section, National Institutes of Health, 1979; Ad Hoc Member, Hematology Study Section, National Heart, Lung and Blood Institute, 1979; Reviewer for Veterans Administration Merit Review Board in Respiration, 1979; Reviewer for Veterans Administration Career Development Program, 1979; Director, Course on Isolation and Culture of Blood Vessel Derived Cells, W. Alton Jones Cells Science Center, 1981; Chairperson, N.H.L.B.I., Review of Cell, Cell Interaction in the Developing Lung, 1981. Address: 3420 Poinciana Avenue, Miami, Florida 33133.■

S

HILDEGARDE L.A. SACARELLO

Industrial Hygienist. Personal: Born February 2, 1955; Daughter of Rudolf J. and Vina F. Staninger; Married Rafael M. Sacarello. Education: A.A. Liberal Arts 1976; B.S. Biological Sciences (Microbiology) 1977, M.S. Secondary Education Science 1980, University of Central Florida, Orlando, Florida; Ph.D. Industrial Toxicology, Kensington University, Glendale, California, 1982. Career: Industrial Hygienist, Martin Marietta Aerospace, Orlando Division, 1981 to present; Industrial Hygienist, State of Florida, Bureau of Industrial Safety and Health, 1980-81; Instructor, Geometry, Elementary Algebra and General Mathematics, Merritt Island High, 1979-80; Book Revisor, Brevard Community College, Math-Science Division, Cocoa, Florida, July 1980-August 1980; Field Evaluator, Mr. Clark Maxwell, Property Appraiser, Titusville, Florida, 1977-79; Instructor, Science and English, Clearlake Middle School, Cocoa, Florida, February 1979-June 1979; Instructor, General Math, Consumer Math, Algebra I and Astronomy, Merritt Island High Adult Education, 1979-80; Graduate Assistant, Personnel, University of Central Florida, June 1979-August 1979; Instructor, Titusville High Adult Education, 1978-80; Student Assistant, Employment Section of Personnel, University of Central Florida, 1974-77. Organizational Memberships: American Association for the Advancement of Science; American Society for Microbiology; American Industrial Hygiene Association; American Institute of Biological Science; Association for Women in Science; University of Central Florida's Alumni Association. Religion: Roman Catholic. Published Works: Author of Dissertation "Mutagenic, Carcinogenic and Teratogenic Effects on Pregnant Women in the Workplace," 1982; Author of Safety Operating Procedures Manual "Hand and Arm Protection" 1982, and other papers and manuals. Honors and Awards: Transworld Airlines Science Awareness Award, 1970; Table Tennis Award for Intermurals, 1970; Soccer Award for Intermurals, 1970; Social Studies and Latin Award, Astronaut High School, 1973; Chi Kappa Scholarship, 1973; Third Place Ribbon, Season of Sailboat Racing, Titusville Yacht Club; Three Harry P. Leu Free Enterprise Scholarships, 1980; Competing for Association of Women in Science Doctoral Grants, 1983; Listed in *Who's Who in the South and Southwest, Who's Who in the World of Women, Personalities of the South*. Address: 15828 Deep Creek Lane, Tampa, Florida 33624.■

ROBERT GEORGE SACKETT

Agronomist. Personal: Born June 29, 1920; Son of Walter O. and Louise M. (Burzlaff) Sackett (both deceased); Married Emily M. Swanson; Father of Carol M. Martensen; Richard R. Sackett, Connie E. Fifer. Education: B.S. with honors 1959, M.S. 1963, University of Wyoming; Postgraduate Studies, Colorado State University, 1965-66; Military: Served in the United States Coast Guard, 1942-45. Career: Associate Agronomist, University of Arizona; Executive Secretary, Arizona Crop Improvement Association; University of Wyoming, Supply Instructor 1959-67, Instructor 1967-69; Farmer Near Rochester, Minnesota, 1945-52. Organizational Memberships: National Certified Alfalfa Variety Review Board, Member 1972-73 and 1978-80, Chairman 1974-75 and 1980-82; Crop Science Society of America; American Society of Agronomy; American Seed Trade Association; Western Seed Certification Officials; Pacific Seedsmen Association; Pima County Farm Bureau; Association of Official Seed Certifying Agencies, Executive Board 11 years, President 2 years; Sigma Xi; Gamma Sigma Delta; Alpha Zeta; Chi Gamma Iota; Associate Member, Farm House; AZ Cotton Planting Seed Association. Community Activities: Lions Club, Tucson and Laramie, Wyoming; Twice Director, Chairman High School Book Scholarship Committee, 2 years; Boy Scouts, Laramie, Wyoming; Chairman, Committee to Develop Uniform Methods and Procedures for Field Inspections for Official Seed Certifying Agency Inspectors, 1973; Chairman, Committee to Develop Operational Procedures of the National Certified Variety Review Board, 1978. Religion: Member of Christ Church United Methodist; Lay Leader, 1977-78; Chairman, Administrative Board 1976, and many other committees; Head Usher. Honors and Awards: Trophy for Reserve Champion in Agronomy, University of Wyoming Little International, 1957; Burpee Scholarship, 1958; Outstanding Seedsman for State of Wyoming, 1969. Address: 6802 East Rosewood Circle, Tucson, Arizona 85710.■

ROBERT J. SAGER

Professor. Personal: Born December 26, 1942; Son of Russel C. and Arlene H. Sager; Married Ingrid Davies. Education: B.S., Wisconsin State University, 1964; M.S., University of Wisconsin, 1966; J.D., Western State University School of Law, 1977. Career: Assistant Professor of Geography, California State University, 1967-71; Visiting Professor of Geography, Chapman College-World Campus Afloat, 1971-72; Professor of Earth Science, West Los Angeles College, 1974 to present. Organizational Memberships: Association of American Geographers; National Council for Geographic Education; National Marine Education Association; American Society of International Law; National Association of Geology Teachers. Community Activities: Oceanic Society, Los Angeles Chapter, Board of Directors, Legislative Chair, 1978-80; Local Coastal Plan Task Force, City of Laguana Beach, 1979-81; Conservation and Open Space Committee, City of Laguana Beach, 1978-80. Published Works: Co-Author, *Introduction to Physical Geography* 1975, *Essentials of Physical Geography* 1977, 2nd 1982, *World Geography Today* 1984; Author, *Papua New Guinea* 1976, *Coastal Morphology* 1982, *Southeast Alaska* 1983, *The Hawaiian Islands* 1984. Honors and Awards: Thomas Olson Memorial Geology Award, 1964; Departmental Honors Graduate, 1964; National Science Foundation Scholarship, Summer 1969; Department of Energy Participantship, Summer 1978; Instructional Research Grant, 1980; Graduate Teaching Assistantships, 1964-67; Listed in *Directory of Distinguished Americans, Personalities of America*. Address: 840 Catalina, Laguna Beach, California 92651.■

HARDEO SAHAI

Statistician. Personal: Born January 10, 1942; Son of Sukhdeo Prasad and Roopwati Srivastava; Married Lillian Sahai; Father of Amogh Sahai. Education: B.Sc. Mathematics, Statistics and Physics, First Division, Fourth in Class, Lucknow University, India, 1962; M.Sc. Mathematics, First Division, First in Class, Barnaras Hindu University, Varanasi, India, 1964; M.S. Statistics, University of Chicago, Illinois, 1968; Ph.D. Statistics, University of Kentucky, Lexington, 1971. Career: Professor, Department of Mathematics of the University of Puerto Rico-Rio Piedras, 1981 to present; University of Puerto Rice-Mayaguez, Associate Professor 1976-80, Research Investigator at Water Resources Research Institute 1975-76, Assistant Professor Department of Mathematics 1972-76; Visiting Research Professor, Department of Statistics and Applied Mathematics, Federal University of Ceara, Fortaleza, Ceara, Brazil, 1978-79; Consultant, Puerto Rico University Consultant Corporation, Puerto Rico, 1977; Statistical Consultant, Puerto Rico Driving Safety Evaluation Project, San Juan, 1973; Management Scientist, Management Systems Development Department, Burroughs Corporation, Detroit Michigan, 1972; University of Kentucky-Lexington, Research Assistant in Department of Statistics 1969-71, Teaching Assistant in Department of Statistics 1968-69; Statistical Programmer for Chicago Health Research Foundation, Chicago Civic Center, Chicago, Illinois, 1968; Statistical Programmer for Cleft Palate Center, University of Illinois-Chicago, 1967; Statistician for Research and Planning Division, Blue Cross Association, Chicago, Illinois, 1966; Assistant Statistical Officer, Durgapur Steel Plant, Durgapur, West Bengal, India, 1965; Lecturer in Mathematics and Statistics, Banaras Hindu University, Varanasi, India, 1964-65. Organizational Memberships: Institute of Mathematical Statistics; Bernoulli Society for Mathematical Statistics and Probability; Biometrics Society, Eastern North American Region; Indian Statistical Association; American Statistical Association; Japan Statistical Society. Community Activities: Lecturer at Numerous National and Foreign Universities such as Universidade Estadual de Campinas, Brazil, Universidade de Brasilia, Brazil, Universidade de Sao Paulo, Brazil, Universidad National de Trujilos, Peru, Universidade Nacional de Columbia. Published Works: *A Dictionary of Statistical Terms: English-Spanish and Spanish-English* 1981, *Random Effects Analysis of Variance: Estimation of Various Components, Part I: Balanced Data and Part II: Unbalanced Data* 1982; *The Analysis of Variance: Fixed, Random and Mixed Models* 1983; Contributor of Articles to a Variety of Professional and Educatioal Journals in the United States, United Kingdom, West Germany, Japan, India, Spain, Australia; Referee for *Biometrics* Canadian Journal of Statistics; Reviewer, *Mathematical Reviews* and *International Statistical Review*; Editorial Board Member, *Lecturas en Matematicas*, Sociedad Colombiana de Matematicas. Honors and Awards: Fellow, Council of Scientific and Industrial Research, Government of India, 1964-65; Fellow, University of Chicago, 1965-68; U.P. Board Merit Scholarship, 1957-59; Government of India Merit Scholarship, 1959-64; Banaras Hindu University Medal, 1964; New York Academy of Sciences; Listed in *American Men and Women of Science, Personalities of America, Book of Honor, Directory of Distinguished Americans, Men of Achievement, International Who's Who of Intellectuals.* Address: Calle I, D-25, Diudad Universitaria, San Juan, Puerto Rico 00760.■

CHARLES VIRGIL ST. JOHN

Executive. Personal: Born December 18, 1922; Son of Clyde W. and Elsie V. (Kintner) St. John (deceased); Married Ruth Ilene Wilson; Father of Janet Sue St. John Amy, Debra Ann St. John Mishler. Education: A.B., Manchester College, North Manchester, Indiana, 1943; M.S., Purdue University, West Lafayette, Indiana, 1946. Career: Eli Lilly and Company, Vice President, Production Operations Division 1977 to present, Chemist 1946, Department Head of Antibiotic Production Control 1951, Department Head of Antibiotics Final Purification 1953, Manager of Chemical and Antibiotics Production 1956, Assistant Director of Antibiotics Production and Agricultural Products Finishing l965, Director 1966, Director of Engineering and Materials Operations 1967, Director of Chemical Manufacturing 1969, Assitant General Manager and Director of Operations 1971, General Manager 1974; Research Chemist, Manhattan District Atomic Energy Project, 1944-46. Organizational Memberships: American Chemical Society. Community Activities: Greater Lafayette Chamber of Commerce, Board of Directors; Manchester College Board of Trustees; Board of Directors, Purdue National Bank, Lafayette Life Insurance Company; Purdue Research Foundation; Lafayette Symphony Foundation, Board of Trustees; Purdue President's Council; Lay Advisory Council, St. Elizabeth Hospital, Lafayette, Chairman 1978-81, Member 1974-81. Religion: Member of First United Methodist Church, West Lafayette, Indiana; Treasurer; Administrative Board. Honors and Awards: Cited for Effective Service and Essential Work During World War II by Secretary of War Henry Stimson, 1945. Address: 320 Overlook Drive, West Lafayette, Indiana 47906.■

DAVID SAITY

Executive. Personal: Born December 29, 1930; Son of Itzhak and Nina Saity; Married Chaya Polonsky in 1965. Education: Attended New York University, 1966-68. Career: President, CDS Enterprises, Limited; President, Saity Originals, Inc. Organizational Memberships: Jewelers of America, Inc.; Chamber of Commerce of America. Honors and Awards: Listed in *Who's Who in Finance and Industry, Who's Who in the World.* Address: 240 West 73 Street, New York, New York 10023.■

JUDITH-ANN SAKS

Artist. Personal: Born December 20, 1943; Daughter of Julien D. and Lucy-Jane (Watson) Saks; Married Haskell Irvin Rosenthal; Mother of Brian Julien. Education: Attended Texas Academy of Art, Houston, Texas, 1957-58; Attended Houston Museum of Fine Arts, 1962; Attended Rice University, 1962; B.F.A., Sophie Newcomb College of Tulane University, New Orleans, 1966; Postgraduate Studies, University of Houston, 1967. Career: Artist; Former Positions include Curator of Student Art, University of Houston, 1968-72. Organizational Memberships: Houston Museum of Fine Arts; Houston Art League; Artist Equity. Community Activities: Lady Washington Chapter, National Society of the Daughters of the American Revolution, Curator 1983-84, Constitution Week Chairman 1982-83; Sisterhood Temple Beth Israel, Board of Directors 1974-76, Historian 1977-78; Donated Works, Oil Paintings, Cruiser Houston Memorial Exhibit, M.D. Anderson Library, University of Houston 1981, Three Oil Paintings, Texas Children's Hospital 1979, City of Deer Park, Texas 1979, Tapestry Design for Podium, Temple Beth Israel 1977, Three Oil Paintings, Temple Beth Israel 1975, Directory Cover Design, Sisterhood Temple Beth Israel 1974, Houston Central Library 1974, Etching, Johnson Space Center Museum 1973, Harris County Heritage Society Museum 1971, Houston Chamber of Commerce Christmas Card 1971, Paintings Given for Auction, Cancer Society 1981, Assistance League 1979, Museum of Medical Science 1978, Houston Symphony Orchestra 1976, Memorial Chapter B'nai B'rith 1975, and others. Honors and Awards: Archives of American Art, Smithsonian Institution, 1980; American Revolution Bicentennial Artist for Port of Houston Authority, 1975-76; Lithographs of Same Accepted by President Jimmy Carter, Queen Elizabeth of England for Royal Library at Windsor Castle and Many Museums and Libraries; Print Among Twenty-one Selected for Year's Travel Tour, Mississippi Art Association, 1970-7l; Houston Art League, First Prize Water Color 1969, First Prize Graphics 1969, First Prize Sculpture 1968; Honorable Mention, First National Drawing and Small Sculpture Show, Del Mar College, Corpus Christi, Texas, 1967; Arthur Q. Davis Award for Drawing, Newcomb College, 1966, and others; Personal Appearances on Television, Radio and Before Clubs. Address: c/o Mrs. S.B. Weiner, 434 Hunterwood, Houston, Texas 77024.■

FRANK A. SALAMONE

Anthropologist. Personal: Born March 26, 1939; Son of Frances and Angelo Salamone; Married Virginia; Father of Frank Charles, Catherine Ann-Frances, Mark John, Stephen, David, Patrick, Robert. Education: B.A. History, St. John Fisher College, l96l; M.A. History, University of Rochester, 1966; Ph.D. Anthropology, State University of New York-Buffalo, 1973. Career: Chairperson, Department of Social Sciences, Elizabeth Seton College, Yonkers, New York; Anthropologist; Former Positions include High School Teacher; Psychiatric Administrator. Organizational Memberships: Fellow, American Anthropological Association, 1973 to present; Fellow, African Studies Association, 1979; Anthropology and Diplomacy, Founding Fellow, Member of the Board 1981 to present; Fellow, American Ethnological Association; Fellow, International Conference of Anthropologists and Ethnologists. Community Activities: Consultant, Upward Bound, Marist College, 1981; Consultant, Public Administration Program, Dominican College, 1980-81; New York State African Studies Council, 1970-74. Honors and Awards: Fellowship, American Philosophical Society, 1976; Fellowship, National Endowment for the Arts, 1976; Wenner-Gren Fellowship, 1979-80; Alternative, N.E.H. Summer 1983, A.C.L.S. 1983, many others. Address: 23 West Street, White Plains, New York 10605.■

DALE ALAN SALISBURY

Agronomist/Soil Scientist. Personal: Born June 23, 1944; Son of William Royce Salisbury (deceased) and Beverly R. Lizee; Married Barbara Nelson; Father of Jennifer Alyn. Education: B.S. 1978, M.S. 1980, Agronomy/Soil Science, California State University. Military: Served in the United States Army, 1966-

TWO THOUSAND NOTABLE AMERICANS

68, attaining rank of Sargeant. Career: Agronomist and Soil Scientist; Former Position as Produce and Truck Broker. Organizational Memberships: Western Kern Resource Conservation District, Director, Secretary/Treasurer, 1981 to present; American Society of Agronomy; Soil Science Society of America; Crop Science Society of America; Soil Conservation Society of America; International Soil Science Society; Weed Science Society of America. Community Activities: Director, Buttonwillow Health Center Inc., 1981-82; Troop Leader, Greater Cleveland Council Boy Scouts of America, 1971-73; Lions Club, Neenah, Wisconsin, 1982; Lions Club, Lost Hills, California, 1980-82; Vice President, Parent Teacher Association, Lost Hills, California, 1980-82. Religion: Member of Protestant Church; Sunday School and Youth Work, 1970-82. Honors and Awards: Agriculturalist of the Year, California State University-Fresno, 1978; Scholarships, Western Growers Association, 1977-79; Scholarship, Association of California Water Agencies, 1977-78; Alpha Zeta Fraternity; Listed in *Who's Who in the West, Personalities of America, Community Leaders of America.* Address: 126 Klompen Court, Neenah, Wisconsin 54956.■

FRANK BOYER SALISBURY

Professor. Personal: Born August 3, 1926, in Provo Utah; Married L. Marilyn Olson, 1949; Father of Frank Clark, Steven S., Michael J., Phillip B. (deceased), Rebecca L., Blake C. Education: B.S. Botany 1951, M.A. Botany and Biochemistry 1952, University of Utah; Ph.D. Plant Physiology and Geochemistry, California Institute of Technology, 1955; Atomic Energy Commission Predoctoral Fellow, 1953-54. Military: Served in the United States Army Air Force, 1945. Career: Photographer, Boyart Studio, 1949-50; Part-time Portrait-Commercial Photography, 1950 to present; Assistant Professor of Botany, Pomona College, 1954-55; Assistant Professor of Plant Physiology, Colorado State University, 1955-61; Professor of Plant Physiology, Colorado State University, 1961-66; National Science Foundation Postdoctoral Fellow, Tubingen, Germany, and Innsbruck, Austria, 1962-63; Utah State University, Professor of Plant Physiology and Head of Plant Science 1966-70, Professor of Plant Physiology 1966 to present, Professor of Botany 1968 to present; Board of Trustees, Colorado State University Research Foundation, 1960-62; Technical Representative in Plant Physiology, United States Atomic Energy Commission, Germantown, Maryland (now Department of Energy), 1973-74. Organizational Memberships: American Society of Plant Physiologists; American Institute of Biological Sciences; Fellow, American Association for the Advancement of Science; Former Consultant, Aerial Phenomena Research Organization; Botanical Society of America; Ecological Society of America; Phi Kappa Phi; Sigma Xi; Utah Academy of Arts, Letters and Science; Western Society of Naturalists; Editorial Board Member, *Plant Physiology* 1967 to present, *Bioscience* 1972-78; Consultant to N.A.S.A.; Served on N.A.S.A./A.I.B.S. Space Biology Panel to Evaluate Research Proposals, 1974-79; A.I.B.S. Governing Board Member-at-Large, 1975-78. Religion: Church of Jesus Christ of Latter-Day-Saints, Missionary to German-Speaking Switzerland 1946-49. Published Works: Author of Five Books, *The Flowering Process, Truth by Reason and by Revelation, The Biology of Flowering, The Utah UFO Display: A Biologists Report, The Creation;* Co—Author, *Vascular Plants: Form and Function, Plant Physiology* 2nd edition, *Botany* 2nd Edition; Over 130 Technical Papers and Articles Concerning Flowering and Time Measurement in Plants, Physiological Ecology, Space Biology (plant responses to gravity, etc.), Unidentified Flying Objects, and Science and Religion. Honors and Awards: Award of Merit from the Botanical Society of America, 1982. Address: 2020 North 1250 East, North Logan, Utah 84321.■

BERNARD SALTZBERG

Administrator, Professor. Personal: Born April 21, 1919; Son of David and Pearl Saltzberg (both deceased); Married Evalyn Freidin; Father of Steven, Larry, Dale, Eugene, Gwen. Education: B.S. 1952, M.S. 1953, Illinois Institute of Technology; Ph.D., Marquette University, 1972. Military: Served in the United States Air Force, 1943-46, attaining the rank of Sergeant. Career: Head, Information Analysis, Texas Research Institute of Mental Sciences; Professor, University of Texas Medical School; Adjunct Professor, Rice University, Baylor College of Medicine and University of Houston; Tulane University, Professor Electrical and Biomedical Engineering, Director of Biomathematics Research; Professor, Department of Psychiatry and Neurology, Tulane University Medical School; Senior Scientist, TRW Corporation and Bissett-Berman Corporation. Organizational Memberships: Vice President, Neuroelectric Society, 1978 to present; Consultant, National Institute of Health, 1970 to present; Member of Board of Directors, Advanced Instrument Development Corporation, 1976 to present; Member, Advisory Committee, National Institute of Health, 1970-74; Board of Directors, General Scientific Corporation, 1984 to present. Community Activities: Council Member, Alliance for Engineering in Medicine and Biology, 1975 to present; Board Member, Institute for Comprehensive Medicine, 1970 to present; Institute for International Education, Volunteer Member, Supporter. Honors and Awards: Schlieder Scholar Award of Tulane University, 1964; First Prize, American Institute of Electrical Engineering Graduate Paper Award, 1954; Honor Societies, Sigma Xi, Tau Beta Pi, Eta Kappa Nu, 1952. Address: 7449 Brompton, Houston, Texas 77025.■

MARY ANN SAMS

Administrator. Personal: Born September 14, 1933; Daughter of Carmen H. and Helen F. (Struak) Pacella; Married Wendell Morris Sams; Mother of Derek John Thomas. Education: A.B. cum laude, Home Economics/Child Development, Mundelein College, Chicago, 1958; M.Ed., Elementary Counseling, University of Puget Sound, 1970; Certificate, Elementary Education, Chicago Teachers College, 1960; Certificate, Special Education, University of Kansas, 1964; Certificate, Montessori Certification for Early Childhood Education and Teacher Training, American Montessori Teacher Training Institute, 1966; Certificate, Gessell and ILG Developmental Placement Examiner, Central Washington State College, 1969; Certificate, Parent Effectiveness Trainer, Teacher Effectiveness Trainer, Effectiveness Training Associates, 1972; Certificate, School Administration, San Francisco State University, 1973; Ed.D Candidate, University of San Francisco, 1977 to present. Career: Administrator, Piedmont Avenue Child Development Center, Oakland, California; Graduate Instructor, Early Childhood Educational Administration, University of San Francisco, 1983; Director, Children's Centers Department, Oakland Unified School District, 1979-80; Program Manager, Children's Centers Department, San Francisco Unified School District, 1978-79; Supervisor, Personnel, San Francisco Unified School District, 1975-78; Program Director, Western Region, Mini-Skools, Limited, Irvine, California, 1974-75; Coordinator, Reading and English as a Second Language, Department of Defense, Military Dependent Schools, Pacific Area (Japan), 1973-74; Executive Director, Curriculum and Personnel, Sullivan Preschool Centers and Sullivan Schools, Irving California, 1971-73; Director, Sullivan Preschool and Sullivan School, Redwood City, California, 1971; Project Manager, Project Learn, Behavioral Research Laboratories, Menlo Park, California, 1970-71; Early Childhood Specialist, Franklin Pierce Public School District, Tacoma, Washington, 1969-70; Instructor, University of Puget Sound, 1969-70; Teacher, Annie Wright Seminary, Tacoma, Washington, 1968-69; Master Teacher and Teacher Trainer, Park Ridge Montessori School, Park Ridge, Illinois, 1966-67; Master Teacher and Teacher Trainer, Spring Valley Montessori School, Federal Way, Washington, 1967-68; Teacher, Kindergarten-Primary Grades, Chicago, Illinois, 1964-66; Social and Personal Adjustment Teacher, Vocational Rehabilitation Division, Topeka, Kansas, 1962-64; Special Services Teacher, Kindergarten and Primary Grades, Chicago Public Schools, 1958-61; Consultant to Hoffman Educational Systems, Duarte, California, Behavioral Research Laboratories, Palo Alto, California, Sullivan Associates, Palo Alto, Photo and Sound, San Francisco, McGraw Hill and Company Webster Division, Chicago, Psyhcotechnics, Glenview, Illinois, Many Public School Systems and Others. Organizational Memberships: California Child Developmental Administrator's Association, State Executive Board 1979-81; Member-at-large 1979-81; Phi Delta Kappa; Association of California School Administrators; United Administrators of Oakland Schools; National Association for Education of Young Children; Council for Exceptional Children; National Black Child Development Institute; American Association of School Personnel Administrators; American Society for Personnel Administrators; Bay Area School Personnel Association; American Montessori Society; Association Montessori Internationale; Fellow, International Biographical Association. Community Activities: Children's Lobby of California, 1978 to present; Retreat Volunteer, Cenacle Convent of Chicago, 1951-60. Religion: Retreat-Promotion Speaker, Cenale Convent of Chicago. Published Works: "A Very Good Year", 16mm Sound Film, 1974; "Sullivan Individualized Reading Program", 35mm Slide-Cassette Tape, 1972; "Safety the Montessori Way" 1967. Honors and Awards: Certificate of Appreciation, San Francisco Unified School District, 1978; Special Tribute, Board of Education, Oakland Unified School District, 1980; Resolution, Childrens' Center's Leadership Advisory Committee, 1980; Certificate of Excellence, California Child Development Administrator's Association, 1980, 1981; Keeper of the Dream Award, California Child Development Administrator's Association, 1981; Listed in *Who's Who in the West, World Who's Who of Women, Who's Who in the World of Women, Personalities of the West and Midwest, Directory of Distinguished Americans, International Who's Who of Intellectuals, Book of Honor.* Address: 76 Los Cerros Avenue, Walnut Creek, California 94598.■

WALTER MacDONALD SANDERS

Associate Director. Personal: Born December 5, 1930; Son of Mrs. Mary E. Sanders; Married Emily Joyce; Father of Emily Graham, Walter McDonald, IV, Albert Brian, Steven Craig. Education: B.S.C.E., Virginia Military Institute, 1953; M.S.S.E. 1956, Ph.D.S.E. 1964, John Hopkins University. Military: Served in the United States Air Force Medical Service Corps, 1953-55, attaining the rank of First Lieutenant. Career: United States Environmental Protection Agency, Associate Director for Water Quality Research, Athens Environmental Research Laboratory 1975 to present; Sanitary Engineer Consultant, Division of

TWO THOUSAND NOTABLE AMERICANS

International Health 1956-58, Assistant Chief, Water Supply Section 1958-60, Research Sanitary Engineer, Chief Ecological Energetics Section, Clemson University 1962-65; Senior Sanitation Engineer, Athens, Georgia 1965-66; Research Sanitary Engineer, Chief National Pollutants Fate Research Program, United States Department of the Interior, 1966-70; Senior Sanitary Engineer, Chief National Pollutants Fate Research Program, Environmental Protection Agency, 1970-75. Organizational Memberships: American Society of Civil Engineers; American Association for the Advancement of Science; Sigma Xi; Technical Advisory Committee, Cheasapeake Bay Program; Project Officer, United States-Egyptian Project; Research Associate; Graduate Faculty of Ecology, University of Georgia, Athens, Georgia; Sigma Xi. Community Activities: American Orchid Society; Athens West Rotary Club, Board of Directors 1975-79, President 1977-78; President, Alps Road Parent-Teacher Association, 1970-71; Vice President, Timothy Estates Association. Religion: Elder, Friendship Presbyterian Church, 1966 to present; Member, Synods Committee on Campus Christian Life, Presbyterian Church, 1969-74; Chairman, Campus Christian Life Committee, 1972-74; Presbytery Committee of Minister and Works, 1978 to present; Presbytery Commission, 1981 to present. Honors and Awards: Eagle Scout with Four Palms; Listed in *Outstanding Young Men of American, Who's Who in the Southeast, Dictionary of International Biography, American Men and Women of Science, Who's Who in Technology Today.* Address: 195 Xavier Drive, Athens, Georgia 30606.■

PAUL EVERETT SANFORD

Professor, Nutritionist. Personal: Born January 14, 1917; Married Helen L. Crenshaw; Father of Paula Louise Schubert, Patricia Kathleen Banning, Carolyn Ruth Elmore. Education: B.S. Agriculture, Kansas State University, 1941; M.S. 1942, Ph.D. 1949, Poultry Nutrition, Iowa State University. Served in the United States Army, 1943-46, attaining the rank of Sergeant. Career: Kansas State University, Professor and Nutritionist, Department of Animal Sciences and Industry 1960 to present, Associate Professor 1949-60; United States Army, 1943-46; Iowa State University, Senior Teaching Fellow 1946-47, Graduate Research Assistant 1947-78, Graduate Assistant 1948-49. Organizational Memberships: Chairman General Program Committee, Poultry Science Association, 1980-81; World's Poultry Science Association; Secretary, American Poultry Historical Society, 1967-70. Community Activities: Project Leader, Lee Hilltoppers 4-H Club; Treasurer, Elementary Parent Teacher Association; President, Senior High Parent Teacher Association; Manhattan Chamber of Commerce, Chairman of Agriculture Committee, Chairman of City Beautification Committee, Member University Affairs Committee; City of Manhattan Environmental Board; Chairman, City of Manhattan Citizens Involvement Committee; Precinct Committeeman, Republican Party. Religion: Member of Presbyterian Church, Ordained Elder 1960-66, Ordained Deacon 1960-66; Member of Westminster Foundation Local Committee, 1951-70; Chairman Building Committee for New Center. Honors and Awards: Fellow, American Association for the Advancement of Science, 1961; Honorary Member, Broiler Society of Japan, 1963; Senior Faculty Award of Merit, Kansas State University, 1973; E. Walter Morrison University Foundation Award, 1976; Outstanding Faculty Advisor, College of Agriculture, 1981; Distinguished Scholar Award, National Association of Colleges and Teachers of Agriculture, 1982; Quaker Oats Fellowship, Iowa State University, 1941-42. Address: 343 North 14th, Manhattan, Kansas 66502.■

MARGARET WALKER ALICEA SANTIAGO

Museum Registrar. Personal: Born October 22, 1931; Daughter of Lee Walker (deceased) and Mozell Murray; Married Ismael Alicea Santiago, Sr.; Mother of Carmelita A.S. Williams, Ismael Alicea Santiago, Jr., Fredric Alicea Santiago, Cheryl Ann Alicea Santiago. Education: Graduate of Carver High School, Spartanburg, South Carolina; Attended A & T College, Greensboro, North Carolina, in English, Mathematics, Psychology, Art Appreciation and Negro History, 1949; Attended Cardoza Evening School, Washington, D.C. in Office Practice, Typing, 1956; Smithsonian Office of Personnel Administration, Certificate in Personnel Management for Supervisors 1967, Certificate in Supervisors Role in Equal Opportunity 1973; Credit from American University, Washington, D.C. in Management of Institutional Records Systems, 1971-72; Certificate in Introduction of Automated Data Processing, Civil Service Commission, Washington, D.C., 1974; United States Department of Agriculture Graduate School, Credit in Administrative Procedures 1965; Credit in Electronic Data Processing 1975, Certificate in Creative Career Development 1976, Certificate in Practical Approach to the Role of the Federal Women's Program Coordinator 1978, Credit in Information Storage and Retrieval by Computer; Completed Forty Hours of Training in Computer Operations, Office of Computer Services, Smithsonian Institution, 1975; Certificate in Packing and Shipping, Smithsonian Workshop 1980; Certificate in Human Resource Management, McClure-Lundberg Associates, Inc., 1980. Career: Smithsonian Institution, Museum Registrar, National Museum of Natural History 1977 to present, Supervisory Museum Technician 1970-77, Clerk-Typist, Office of the Registrar 1960-70. Organizational Memberships: Smithsonian Registrars Council; American Association of Museums, Registrars Committee, Registrars Nominating Committee 1980; Northeast Museums Conference, Registrars Committee, Membership Secretary 1981; Afro-American Museum Association; Smithsonian Women's Council, Chairperson 1982, Special Assistant on Minority Women's Affairs 1981, Vice Chairperson 1980. Community Activities: Victorians Civic Club, 1960's; Lamond-Riggs Civic Association, 1960's to present; North Carolina A&T College Alumni Association, 1960's to present; The National Council of Negro Women, Metropolitan Area Section, Member 1978 to present, Section President 1984, Section First Vice President 1983, Member Mid-Atlantic Bethune Recognition Committee 1983, Co-Chair Mid-Atlantic Bethune Recognition Committee 1984, Member Bethune Celebration Committee 1983, Member International Committee 1982, Member Life Members Guild; Gospel Solo Artist, Annual Concert to Benefit Charitable Organizations, 1963 to present. Religion: Member of Gethsemane Baptist Church, 1961 to present; Senior Choir, Mass Choir, Unit #3; Formerly Member of Gospel Chorus, Progressive Club, Twice Chairperson of Women's Day Activities, Chairperson Church Anniversary, Produced Many Musical Concerts. Honors and Awards: Certificate, National Association for the Advancement of Colored People, 1966; Certificate for Outstanding Achievement, National Council of Negro Women, 1982 and 1983; Outstanding Service Through Song, Gethsemane Baptist Church, 1981; Honorary Citizen of Tucson, Arizona, 1983; Key to the City of San Jose, California, 1980; ABIRA Life Fellow and National Advisor; Listed in *World Who's Who of Women, International Registry of Profiles, International Who's Who of Intellectuals, Personalities of America, Biographical Roll of Honor.* Address: 29 Tuckerman Street, Northwest, Washington, D.C. 20011.■

ARMEN SARAFIAN

University President. Personal: Born March 5, 1901, in Van Nuys, California; Father of Joy, Winston, Norman. Education: A.B. magna cum laude, La Verne College; M.A., Claremont Graduate School; Ph.D., University of Southern California; LL.D., La Verne College. Career: President, La Verne College (now University of La Verne), 1976 to present; President Pasadena City College, Superintendent Pasadena Area Community College District, 1965-76; Administrative Dean for Instruction, Pasadena City College, 1959-65; Adjunct Professor of Community College Administration, University of Southern California, 1968-78; Coordinator, Secondary and Junior College Education, Pasadena City Schools, 1951-59; Summer and Part-time Teaching in 12 Colleges and Universities including University of California-Los Angeles, Occidental, Claremont and California State Colleges, 30 Years; Junior College Teacher of English, United States History and Political Science, Pasadena Junior College District, 1947-51; In the Field of Elementary and Secondary Education, Chairman Banning High School English Department, 5 Years; Stockroom Manager, S. H. Kress Company, Pomona; Foreman, Dudley-Parker River Ranch, Norco; Consultant to Business, Industry and Government; Numerous Other Professional Activities. Community Activities: President, La Verne Chamber of Commerce, 1978-79; President, New Century Club of Pasadena, 1975-76; Founder and Member Executive Committee, Pasadena Hall of Science Project, 1965-76; Native Sons of the Golden West; Pasadena Arts Council; South Pasadena Oneonta Club; Vice President, Pasadena Chamber of Commerce, 1972; Vice President, Pasadena Kiwanis Club, 1971; President, California Conservation Council, 1966-68; Founder and Adult Advisor, Pasadena Area Youth Council, 1953-66; Past Member, Honorary Advisory Board, Pasadena Area Chapter, American Red Cross; Past Member, Board of Directors, Pasadena Urban Coalition; Past Member, St. Luke Hospital Advisory Board; Past Member, Mayor's Committee on Children and Youth; Past Member, Mayor's Committee for Pasadena Centennial Celebration; Past Chairman, Committee to Select South Pasadena City Manager; Chairman, Annual Committee to Select Distinguished Young Man of the Year for Pasadena Jaycees, 1967-76; Judge, Los Angeles Times Scholarship Award Contest; Arcadia Coordinating Council; Pasadena Historical Society; Patron, Pasadena Area Mexican-American Scholarship Committee; Former Management Advisor to City of Pasadena Municipal Government; Founding Board of Trustees Chairman for American Armenian International College. Honors and Awards: Life Membership Gold Seal Bearer, California Scholarship Federation; Full Tuition Scholarship to Claremont Graduate School; Honorary Life Member, Pasadena Council of Parents and Teachers; Honorary Life Member, Associated Student Body of Pasadena City College; Distinguished Community Service Award of Pasadena Education Association; Conservation Merit Award of California Conservation Council; Omicron Mu Delta Distinguished Service Award; Meritorious Service Award of Pasadena City College Faculty Senate; "Citizen of the Day" Award of Sierra Madre City Council; Phi Delta Kappa Special Recognition Award; Ralph Story Award for Outstanding Service to Education; University of Southern California Service Award; United States Public Health Service Recognition Award; Honorary Life Membership Award of Pasadena Chamber of Commerce; Western Association of Student Financial Aid Administrators Award; Salvation Army "Others" Award, 1975; Arthur Noble Award, Pasadena City Board of Directors, as Most Distinguished Citizen of Pasadena, 1976; Recognition Award, Pasadena Arts Council, 1976; Delta Epsilon Distinguished Lecturer for 1973, University of Southern California; Numerous Biographical Listings. Address: P.O. Box 1624, Glendora, CA 91840.■

TWO THOUSAND NOTABLE AMERICANS

VINOD KUMAR SARIN

Senior Staff Scientist. Personal: Born January 29, 1944; Married Rani Gupta; Father of Annika, Amit. Education: B.Sc., University of Wisconsin-Madison, 1965; M.Sc., University of Michigan-Ann Arbor, 1966; Sc.D., Massachusetts Institute of Technology, 1971. Career: Senior Staff Scientist, G.T.E. Laboratories; Former Positions include Senior Research Scientist, Adamas Carbide; Research Metallurgist, Sandvik AB, Sweden; Pool Officer, National Physical Laboratory, India; Lecturer, I.I.T., New Delhi, India. Organizational Memberships: Sigma Xi; American Powder Metallurgy Institute; Machinability Committee, American Society of Metals; American Society of Carbide and Tool Engineering. Religion: Hindu. Honors and Awards: Non-Resident Tuition Scholarship, University of Wisconsin, 1961-65; General Electric Fellow, University of Michigan, 1965-66; INCRA Fellow, Massachusetts Institute of Technology, 1968-71; First Prize, International Metallographic Exhibition, 1975; Other Metallographic Prizes, 1974-78; Several Technical Papers and Patents; Listed in *Who's Who in the East*. Address: 7 Diamond Road, Lexington, Massachusetts 02173. ■

LILI-CHARLOTTE (LOLO) SARNOFF

Artist (Sculptor). Personal: Born January 9, 1916; Daughter of Baroness Robert von Hirsch and Willy Dreyfus; Married Stanley J. Sarnoff; Mother of Daniela M. Sarnoff Bargezi, Robert L. Sarnoff. Education: Graduate of Reinmann Art School, Berlin, 1936; Studied at the University of Berlin and the University of Florence, 1934-37. Career: Research Assistant, Harvard School of Public Health, 1948-54; Research Associate, National Heart Institute, 1954-59; President, Rodana Research Corporation, 1959-61; Vice President, Cartrix Corporation, 1959-61; Sculptor. Organizational Memberships: The Cultural Alliance of Washington, D.C. Slide Registry; Artists Equity Association; International Sculpture Center; Washington Project for the Arts; Washington Women's Art Center; American Federation of Arts. Community Activities: Trustee, Corcoran Gallery of Art; Women's Committee of the Washington Opera; Women's Committee of the Washington Performing Arts Society; Director, The Art Barn, Washington, D.C.; Founder, the National Museum of Women's Art. Honors and Awards: Accademia Italia delle Arti e del Lavoro "Madaglia d'Oro" 1980. Address: 7507 Hampden Lane, Bethesda, Maryland 20814. ■

LAURENCE J. SASSO, JR.

Administrator. Personal. Born December 28, 1942; Son of Mr. and Mrs. Laurence J. Sasso, Sr.; Married Kathryn M. Gray; Father of Lauryn Ethne. Education: B.A. 1965, M.A. 1967, University of Rhode Island. Career: Director, Office of News and Information, Rhode Island College, Former Editorial Assistant, Observer Publications, Smithfield, Rhode Island; Free-Lance Writer, Poet; Poetry Editor, *Journal-Bulletin*, Providence, Rhode Island, 1970-77; Founder Co-Publisher, Editor, *The Greyledge Review*, 1979; Author, *Harvesting the Inner Garden*. Organizational Memberships: Council for Advancement and Support of Education; Rhode Island Press Club. Community Activities: Vice President, Historical Society of Smithfield, 1981; District Moderator, Voting District 5, Smithfield, Rhode Island, 1976-78, 1978-80, 1980 to present. Honors and Awards: *Sou'Wester* Magazine's Poetry Award, 1976; UNICO Foundation Literary Contest, 4th Place in Nation, 1978; Winner, Major Poetry Award, Worcester County Poetry Association, 1981; Listed in *Who's Who in the East*. Address: 142 Mann School Road, R.F.D. 3, Smithfield, Rhode Island 20917. ■

ROBERT THAYER SATALOFF

Associate Professor of Otolaryngology, Chairman of Department of Voice Science. Personal: Born February 22, 1949; Married Dahlia Mishell. Education: Graduate of Lower Merion High School, Ardmore, Pennsylvania, 1967; B.A., Haverford College, 1971; M.D., Jefferson Medical College, Thomas Jefferon University, 1975; D.M.A. Voice, Coombs College, Philadelphia, Pennsylvania, 1982; University of Michigan, House Office I, Department of Surgery 1975-76, Resident, Department of Otorhinolaryngology 1976-80, Fellow in Otology, Neuro-Otology and Skull Base Surgery 1980-81; Certified Instructor in Occupational Hearing Loss, Colby College, Waterville, Maine, 1973; Certified in Head and Neck Surgery, American Board of Otolaryngology, 1980. Career: Academy of Vocal Arts, Philadelphia, Pennsylvania, Professor and Chairman, Department of Voice Science 1982 to present, Annual Course, Lecture Series in Vocal Pedagogy 1980 to present; Department of Otolaryngology, Jefferson Medical College, Thomas Jefferson University, Philadelphia, Pennsylvania, Associate Professor 1984 to present, Assistant Professor 1981-84, Instructor 1980-81; International Symposium on Care of the Professional Voice, Julliard School of Music, Faculty 1982 to present, Co-Director 1983 to present; Chief Resident, Department of Otorhinolarngology, University of Michigan-Ann Arbor, 1979-80; Attending Physician, Thomas Jefferson University Hospital, Graduate Hospital of the University of Pennsylvania, Saint Joseph's Hospital; Consultant, Wills Eye Hospital; Annual Course on Occupational Hearing Loss, University of Maine, 1979 to present; Course Instructor, American Academy of Otolaryngology, Head and Neck Surgery, 1981 to present; Associate Director, Institute in Occupational Hearing Loss, University of Maine-Orono, 1982 to present; Faculty, Interdisciplinary Colloquium on the Use and Care of the Human Voice, University of Minnesota, 1982; Faculty, Microsurgery of the Larynx and Voice Conservation, Boston, Massachusetts, 1983 to present. Organizational Memberships: Physiological Society of Philadelphia, 1971; American Medical Association, 1971; Centurion Club, 1976; American Council of Otolaryngology, 1977; Junior Member, American Academy of Facial, Plastic and Reconstructive Surgeons, 1978; Walter Work Society, 1978; Member of Standing Committee on Membership, Philadelphia County Medical Society, 1981; Pennsylvania State Medical Society, 1980; Fellow, Philadelphia College of Physicians and Surgeons, 1981; Fellow, American Academy of Otolaryngology, Head and Neck Surgery, 1981; Associate Fellow, Philadelphia Society of Facial and Plastic Surgeons, 1981; Solomon Solis-Cohen Medical Literary Society, 1982; Pan American Otolaryngology Society, 1982; Associate Fellow, American Academy of Facial, Plastic and Reconstructive Surgeons, 1982; Fellow, American Neurology Society, 1982; Association for Research in Otolaryngology, 1983; Medical Club of Philadelphia, 1983; Pennsylvania Academy of Ophthalmology and Otolaryngology, 1983. Community Activities: The Voice Foundation, Scientific Advisory Board 1983; Trustee and Medical Director, Foundation for Voice and Ear Research 1983; Bylaws Committee of the Executive Committee, Alumni Association, Jefferson Medical College, 1982 to present; Alumni Council, Haverford, 1982; Board of Governors, Volunteer Faculty Association of Jefferson Medical College, 1982; Eagle Scout, 1962; Professional Baritone, 1967; Conductor, Thomas Jefferson University Choir, 1970-75, 1980 to present; Hearing Conservation Noise Control, Board of Directors 1975, Vice-President 1981; Chairman, Board of Directors, Pennsylvania Alliance for American Music, 1981; President, Haverford College Club of Philadelphia, 1982. Published Works: Author of Book *Hearing Loss* 1980; Author of Articles "Professional Singers: The Science and Art of Clinical Care," *American Journal of Otology* 1981, "The 4,000 Cycle Dip: Not Always Noise," *Ear, Nose and Throat Journal* 1980, and over 40 others. Honors and Awards: Phi Beta Kappa, 1970; Richard W. Foster Prize for Outstanding Contribution to Academic Programs, Thomas Jefferson University, 1975; Clinical Surgery Prize Honorable Mention, Thomas Jefferson University, 1975; Outstanding Young Men of America, 1982. Address: 1721 Pine Street, Philadelphia, Pennsylvania 19103. ■

ABRAHAM SATOVSKY

Attorney at Law. Personal: Born October 15, 1907; Son of Samuel and Stella Satovsky (both deceased); Married Toby Nayer; Father of Sheldon B., James B. Education: Graduate of Detroit Central High School, 1924; B.A. 1928, LL.B. and Juris Doctor 1930, University of Michigan. Career: Attorney at Law. Organizational Memberships: Michigan Bar Association; Oakland County Bar Association; American Bar Association; American Judicature Society; Detroit Bar Committees; Past Chairman, Friends of Court and Family; Public Advisory Committee for Judical Candidates, 1974-82; Constitution Committee. Community Activities: Public Panel Member, War Labor Board; Public Panel Member, American Arbitration Association, 1972-82; United Foundation and Torch Drives, 1945-52; University of Michigan Law School Campaigner, 1973-82; Past President, B'nai B'rith Detroit Lodge, 1947-48; Past Vice President, B'nai B'rith Metropolitan Detroit Council, 1949-50; Chairman of Interfaith Committee of Catholics, Jews and Protestants, 1946; Past Board Member, Jewish Welfare Federation, 1960-63; Allied Jewish Campaign, Co-Chairman Professional Division and Advisor, Active Member 1935-82; Detroit Service Group, Board Member 1960-82, Headed Mission to Israel 1964; Detroit Jewish Community Council Representative, 1960-77; Past President, Phi Beta Delta, Ann Arbor, 1928; Pi Lambda Phi, Ann Arbor; O.R.T.; Zionist Organization of America; Life Member of Mens Group, Hadassah; Vice President, Moies Chetim Organization of Detroit, 1966-82; Board Member, Michigan Jewish Historical Society, 1969-82; Coronado Building Co-Chairman, Great Miami Federation Campaign, 1975-82; American Jewish Congress; Detroit Round Table of Catholics, Jews and Protestants; Emeritus Club of Michigan. Religion: National Federation of Jewish Men's Clubs, Past President 1956-58, Life Member; Great Lakes Region of N.F.J.M.C., Founding President 1953, Life Board Member; Congregation Shaarey Zedek, President 1961-62, Life Board Member; Men's Club of Congregation Shaarey Zedek, Honorary President and Life Board Member 1951-82; Trustee, Clover Hill Park Cemetary, 1979-82; Advisory Council, United Synagogue of America, 1958-60; United Hebrew Schools; Aventura Jewish Center of North Miami Beach, Florida, 1976-82. Honors and Awards: Fiftieth Year Certificate, State of Michigan Bar Association, 1980; First Annual Service Award, Congregation

Shaarey Zedek Men's Club, 1978; Certificate of Merit, Metropolitan Detroit B'nai B'rith Council and Detroit Lodge #1374, 1978; Great Lakes Region of National Federation of Jewish Men's Club, 1977; Merit Award, National Federation of Jewish Men's Club, 1973; Jerusalem Award, State of Israel Bond Organization, 1969; Allied Jewish Campaign Award to Co-Chairman of Professional Division, 1958 and 1959; Detroit Service Group Victory Award, 1957-58; Campaign Award, United Federation of Metropolitan Detroit, 1952 and subsequent years; Seminary Award, Jewish Theological Seminary, 1952; Various Awards for Service, Detroit Torch Drive, 1945-48; Various Merit Awards for Services, Jewish Welfare Federation; Appreciation Award, Congregation Shaarey Shomiem, 1937. Address: 22500 Saratoga, Southfield, Michigan 48075.■

MARY L. SAUER

Civic Leader. Personal: Born June 26, 1923; Daughter of Maurice Edward and Sarah Katherine Kieffer (Steinhilber); Married; Mother of Elisabeth Ruth, Gordon C., Jr., Margaret Louise, Amy Kietter Sauer Doyle. Education: Graduate of Cleveland Heights High School; B.M.E., Northwestern University; Post Graduate Studies at the University of Missouri-Kansas City. Career: Substitute Teacher for Kansas City Schools. Organizational Memberships: Mu Phi Epsilon; American Guild of Organists; Kansas City Musical Club, Associate Member, Co-Chairman. Community Activities: American Association of University Women; President, Philharmonic League, 1959-60; Women's Committee Conservatory of Music, University of Missouri-Kansas City, President 1963-64, Trustee 1980-82; Board of Directors, Women's Council of University of Missouri-Kansas City, 1977-80; Co-Chairman, Kansas City Chamber Choir, 1971-74; Board of Directors, Regional Auditions, Metropolitan Opera Guild, 1965-69; Board of Directors, Nettleton Retirement Home, 1975-80; Research Hospital Junior Auxiliary, 1957-60; Shepherd Center Music Director, 1980; Daughters of the American Revolution, Westport Chapter; Lyric Opera Women's Guild, 1960. Religion: Presbyterian; Board of Women's Fellowship, 1960-76; Circle Leader, 1960-62, 1964-66; Pianist; Choir Member; Lay Pastor, 1981-82. Honors and Awards: Volunteer in Education, 1971-72, 1974-75; Listed in *Personalities of the West and Midwest, Book of Honor, Men and Women of Distinction, International Register of Profiles, Notable Americans, Community Leaders and Noteworthy Americans, Notable Americans of the Bicentennial Era.* Address: 830 West Fifty-eighth Terrace, Kansas City, Missouri 64113.■

GRETCHEN SUSAN SAVAGE

Executive. Personal: Born January 15, 1934; Daughter of Mr. and Mrs. F.D. Wardell; Married Terry R. Savage; Mother of Terry C., Christopher W., Richard T. Education: B.A., University of California-Los Angeles, 1955; Graduate Work in Library and Information Science, Education and Data Processing, 1957-73; Life Credential in Librarianship, State of California, 1970. Career: President, Savage Information Services, 1977 to present; Librarian, Goleta Schools, 1970-73; Consultant in Library and Information Science, Washington D.C., Santa Barbara, and Los Angeles, 1965-77; Manager, NASA Scientific and Technical Information Facility, Documentation Incorporated, Bethesda, Maryland, 1964-65; Head Librarian, Missiles and Space Systems, Douglas Aircraft Company, 1957-64; Teacher, Santa Monica Schools, California, 1955-57. Organizational Memberships: Special Libraries Association, Chairman of Consultation Section, Information Management Division, Secretary of Information Technology Division; American Society for Information Science; Association of Records Managers and Administrators; Alpha Phi Sorority. Honors and Awards: Phi Beta Kappa; Delta Phi Upsilon; Pi Lambda Theta. Address: 30000 Cachan Place, Rancho Palos Verdes, California 90274.■

ALICE TREMBLAY SAVARD

Artist Writer. Personal: Born May 5, 1919, in Jonquière, Canada; Married Henri Savard; Mother of Charlotte, Gaston, Gilles, Lina. Education: B.S.Ed., University of Quebec at Chicoutimi, 1978. Career: Professor of Plastic Art, Tome III Artists du Quebec, 1977-78; Paintings, Sculptures, Etchings, Seriographs and Photographs in Approximately 30 Group Exhibitions and 11 One-Woman Shows at Cegepien au Centre National d'exposition de Jonquie²re, at the Arts Center of Mont-Royal (Montreal), at the Gallery of Arts La Minerve du Quebec, at the Museum of Sept-Iles, at the Maison du Quebec de Terre des Hommes a Montreal, at the Fleuralies de Montreal, and at the 4th International Festival of Arts '84 at the Palace of Congress in Montreal. Organizational Memberships: Fellow of the Board, International Biographical Association, Cambridge, England; Secrétaire Trésorière Commerciale; Parchemin de la Foire Commercialle Industrielle-Culturelle de la Chambre de Commerce de Jonquière; Society of Canadian Writers in the French Language; Conceil Regional de la Culture Saguenay lac St-Jean; The Institute of Arts of Saguenay Lac St-Jean; The Council of Media Usage of Sagamie; International Biographical Association; Society of Studies and Lectures (Saguenay Lac-St-Jean Section); Federation of Women of Quebec; Quebec Federation of Leisure Photography; Museums of Quebec; Association of Quebec-Perche; Chorale de Notre Dame de Fatima. Published Works: *La Famille* (1982). Honors and Awards: Certificat du Merite Jonquierois en Reconnaissance de la Contribution Personnelle au Développement de la Communauté Jonquièroise; Medal of Arts and 2 Merit Awards, Gallery of Minerve of Quebec Festival of Painting; Tropy of La Minerve, 1983; Several Cultural Merit Awards of the Ville of Jonquiere; Parchment of la Maison du Quebec a Terre des Hommes a Montreal; Recipient Commemorative Awards from the International Biographical Centre of Cambridge; Listed in *World Who's Who of Women.* Address: 3760 rue Saint-Jules, Case postale 202, Jonquière, Quebec, Canada G7X 2K5.■

LORENA BERUBE SAVARD

Financial Coordinator. Personal: Born August 30, 1942; Daughter of J. Alfred and Florence H. Berube; Married Roger D. Savard; Mother of Dean R. Education: Postgraduate Certificate of Achievement in General Business, Hartford Adult School, 1962; Bookkeeping Certificate, Dudley Hall Business College, 1968; A.S. Management 1978, A.S. Accounting 1976, Quinebaug Valley Community College; Computer Courses, Thames Valley Technical College, Quinebaug Valley Community College, 1979; Computer Awareness Certificate, Northeast Connecticut Regional Adult Education Program, 1981; Attending Nichols College, Dudley, Massachusetts. Career: Financial Coordinator, Spectrum Information Systems, Inc., Woodstock, Connecticut; Calculator Clerk, Phoenix Mutual Life Insurance Company, Hartford, Connecticut, 1961-63; Teller, Citizen's National Bank, Putnam, Connecticut, 1966-67; Invoice Records Clerk, Catalog Clerk, Montgomery Ward and Company, Putnam, 1968-70; Manager, DKH Credit Union, Putnam, 1974-80; Sales Representative, Southwest Telephone Company, Putnam, 1981-82; Office Manager, Waters Brothers Oil Company, Putnam, 1982 to present. Organizational Memberships: National Association of Female Executives; International Platform Association; Life Patron, American Biographical Institute Research Association. Community Activities: Volunteer, Day Kimball Hospital Annual Giving Appeal, 1981; Class Representative, Hartford Adult School, 1961-62; Teacher Aide, Putnam Elementary School, 1972-76; Central New England; Volunteer, Quinebaug Valley Community College Business Office, 1974; Yearbook Staff Member, Quinebaug Valley Community College, 1975-76; Treasurer, Northeast Connecticut Association for Children with Learning Disabilities, 1978-82; Steering Committee, Career Planning Support System for Local Students, 1980-81; Board Member, Quinebaug Valley Youth Services Bureau, 1981-82. Honors and Awards: Dean's List, Quinebaug Valley Community College, 1974-78; Merit Certificate, Hartford Adult School, 1962; Listed in *World Who's Who of Women, Who's Who of American Women, Who's Who Among Students in American Junior Colleges, Personalities of America, Directory of Distinguished Americans, Community Leaders of America, Book of Honor, International Book of Honor, International Who's Who of Intellectuals, Personalities of the East, Others.* Address: F.R.D. 1, Putnam, Connecticut 06260.■

FRIEDA JOYCE SAVITZ

Artist, Teacher. Personal: Born December 3, 1931. Education: Attended Cooper Union, New York City, 1953-54; Scholarship to Attend Hans Hoffman School, 1954-55; B.S., M.A., Art Education, New York University, 1956-57; Master of Painting honoris causa Diploma, Universitai delle Arti, Accademia Italia, Parma, Italia, 1983. Career: Solo Exhibits, State Capital of New York (Albany) l983, Arizona State University-Tempe 1978, Hansen Galleries (New York City) 1977-78, Southern Vermont Art Association (Manchester) 1978, Rockland Community College (New York) 1976, Hudson River Museum (New York) 1973, Saint Thomas Aquinas College (New York) 1973; Group Exhibitions, Barcelona 84 (Traveling Exhibition) 1984, Salon of the Nations (Paris) 1984, Louisiana World Expo Women's Art 100 Years 1984, Air & Space Museum of the Smithsonian Institution 1984, 10th Independent International Print Expo (Yokahoma, Japan) 1984, Salon of the Nations (Paris, France) 1983, Biennel Internationale de Gravure (Yugoslavia) Summer 1983, Fourth Permanent Exhibition at Palazzo delle Manites, Tazioni Accademia (Parma, Italy) 1983-84, West/Art and the Law Exhibition 1982, Views by Women Artists 1982, Rutgers National Exhibition 1982-82, People '81 Hudson River Museum (New York) 1981, Hampton International Expo (New York) 1981, International Platform Association (Washington D.C.) 1981, Group Art Exposition 1981, World Tour, San Francisco Brigade Exhibit 1981, Sixth International Independents Exhibition of Prints (Yokohama,

Japan) 1980, International Festival at Carlsberg Glystoteck Museum, World Women's United Nations Conference (Copenhagen, Denmark) 1980, World Print Exhibition (New Orleans, Louisiana) 1980's, Everson Museum (Syracuse, New York) 1976-80, World Print Exhibition, San Francisco Museum of Modern Art 1977, International Ford Foundation Traveling Exhibition 1975-76, International XX Women's Pictures on Charletteborg (Copenhagen, Denmark) 1975, Hudson River Museum (New York) 1976, Brooklyn Museum (New York City) 1975-76, Newark Museum (New Jersey), Smithsonian National Museum (Washington, D.C.) 1957, Chrysler Museum (Massachusetts and Washington, D.C.), Vermont Art Association (Manchester) 1977-78, Guild Hall (East Hampton, New York) 1979-82; Art in Private, Public and Corporate Collections such as Accademia Italia, Parma, Italia, Chrysler Museum, Washington, D.C., Smithsonian Institution Archives of American Art 1981, Sophia Smith Collection at Smith College in Women's History Archives, Northampton, Massachusetts 1980, Syracuse Print Collection, Syracuse, New York, Women's Archives of Carlsberg-Glystotech Museum, Copenhagen, Denmark 1980, Southern Vermont Art Association of Manchester 1978 to present, San Francisco Museum of Modern Art Print Collection 1977, Bibliotheque Nationale, Paris, France, Hudson River Museum, New York 1978, World Print Council, San Francisco, California 1978, A.T.&T. Collection, Minolta Collection, Philip Morris Collection, Guild Hall, East Hampton, New York 1979; Teacher of Painting, Drawing, Composition and Various Related Visual Areas, New York City and New Jersey, 1954-60, 1973-81. Organizational Memberships: Accademia of Italia Parma, Italy; International Platform Association, Washington, D.C.; C.A.A., V.A.G.A.; A.E.A.; W.C.A.; N.Y.W.C.A.; W.W.A.C.; National Organization of Women; New York Ethical Society; World Print Council; International Artists Association; American Biographical Institute Research Association. Religion: American Ethical Society. Published Works: Poems, Fables and Articles, 1951-82. Honors and Awards: World Culture Prize, Statue of Victory, Centro Studi delle Nazioni, 1984; Accademico D'Europa, 1983; International Parliament for Safety and Peace (U.S.A.), 1983; Gold Metal for Artistic Merit; Master of Painting honoris causa, Accademia Italia, 1983; Golden Centaur Award, Accademia Italia, Parma, Italia, 1982; West/Art and the Law Exhibition Award, St. Paul, Minnesota, 1982; Honorary Diploma of Merit, Universitai delle Arti, Parma, Italia, 1981; Commemorative Award, American Biographical Institute Research Association, 1981; Gold Medal and Elected to Accademia Italia delle Arti del Lavoro, Parma, Italy 1980; Commemorative Award, International Biographical Centre, Cambridge, England, 1979; Grant, New York Foundation for the Arts Artist in the School, National Endowments for the Arts Pilot Program, 1979; World Print Exhibition, San Francisco Museum of Modern Art, 1977; International Women's Award, Ford Foundation, 1975-76; Listed in *International Biographies, International Book of Honor, Arthur and Elizabeth Schlesinger Library, History of Women in History, Who's Who in American Art, Who's Who in International Art, World Who's Who of Women, Who's Who of American Women Artists, Dictionary of International Biography, Directory of Distinguished Americans, Personalities of America, Encyclopeadia of Contemporary Personalities, Book of Honor, Art Bibliographies, Dictionary of Contemporary Artists, Two Thousand Notable Americans, Art Diary, The World's Art Guide, Tendenze and Testimonianze dell Arte Contemporanea, History of International Art, Community Leaders of America, International Who's Who of Intellectuals, Catalog of the Golden Centaur Award, History of Contemporary Art, Who's Who in the East, Foremost Women of the 20th Century, American Artists, International Register of Profiles,* Others. Address: 109 West Clarkstown Road, New City, New York 10956.■

THOMAS EDGAR SAWYER

Executive. Personal: Born July 7, 1932; Son of Sidney Edgar and Ruth (Bickham) Sawyer; Married Joyce Mezzanatto; Father of Jeffrey Thomas, Scott Alan, Robert James, Julie Anne. Education: B.S., University of California-Los Angeles, 1959; M.A., Occidental College, 1969; Ph.D., Florida State, 1971. Military: Served in the United States Marine Corps, 1950-53, attaining the rank of Sargeant. Career: President, Sage Institute International, 1983 to present; President and Chairman, MESA Corporation, 1978-83; Associate Professor of Business Management, Brigham Young University, 1974-78; Deputy Director, Office of Economic Opportunity, 1972-74; Principal and General Manager, Planning Research Corporation, 1969-72; Special Assistant to Governor Reagan, State of California, 1967-69; Manager of Development Operations, TRW Systems, 1960-67; Project Engineer, Garrett Corporation, 1954-60. Organizational Memberships: American Management Association; American Society for Public Administration; Director of Insul Chemical Corporation, Nooraid Chemical Corporation, World Diary and Food Research Corporation, Enviro Etch Chemical Corporation; Utah Council of Small Business. Community Activities: Chairman, Indian Education Advisory Committee, Utah State School Board, 1976 to present; Chairman, Southern Paiute Tribal Restoration Committee, 1982 to present; Chairman, Utah State Board of Indian Affairs, 1981 to present; Chairman, National Advisory Council on Indian Education, 1982 to present; Utah Endowment for the Humanities, Board of Trustees and Executive Committee, 1974-80; Chairman, Board of Trustees, Virginia Young Men's Christian Association, 1969-73; Virginia Governor's Businessman's Efficiency Task Force, 1970; Federal Government Procurement Commission, 1970. Religion: Member of the Church of Jesus Christ of Latter Day Saints (Mormons). Address: 548 West 630 South, Orem, Utah 84058.■

VINOD KUMAR SAXENA

Professor. Personal: Born May 23, 1944; Son of Mr. Kishori L. and Mrs. Uma Saxena; Married Indra Saxena; Father of Rita Nigam Saxena. Education: B.S. 1961, M.S. 1963, Agra University, India, Ph.D. University of Jaipur, India, 1967; Post-Doctoral, University of Missouri-Rolla, 1968-71. Career: Associate Professor of Atmospheric Sciences, Marine, Earth and Atmospheric Sciences Department, North Carolina State University; Research Associate Professor, University of Utah-Salt Lake City, 1977-79; Cloud Physicist and Lecturer, University of Denver, Colorado, 1971-77; Assistant Professor, University of Sagar, India, 1967-68; Research Fellow, University of Rajasthan, Jaipur, India, 1964-67; Lecturer, Agra College, India, 1963-64. Organizational Memberships: American Association for the Advancement of Science; American Meteorological Society; American Geophysical Union; American Water Research Association; Sigma Xi; Fellow Member, American Biographical Institute. Community Activities: International Platform Association, 1982 to present; Center for Reflection on the Second Law, 1982 to present. Religion: Member of the Himalayan International Institute of Yoga Science and Philosophy, 1978 to present. Honors and Awards: Meteorological Award, University of Utah, 1979; Merit Scholarship, Agra College, 1961-62; Listed in *American Men and Women of Science, Who's Who in the West, Notable Americans of the Bicentennial Era, Notable Americans of 1976-77, Community Leaders and Noteworthy Americans, Dictionary of International Biography, Men of Achievement, International Who's Who in Community Service, The International Who's Who of Intellectuals, Notable Americans of 1978-79, Personalities of America, Book of Honor, Dictionary of Distinguished Americans, Who's Who in Technology Today, Men and Women of Distinction, International Book of Honor, International Register of Profiles, Registry of American Achievement.* Address: 3616 Greywood Dr., Raleigh, North Carolina 27604.■

VINCENT ANTHONY SCARCELLA

Student. Personal: Born November 30, 1962; Son of Santi and Maria Scarcella. Education: Graduate of Saint Peter's Boys High School, 1980; Currently Attending Wagner College, Studying Business Administration/Accounting. Community Activities: Wagner College Volunteer Income Tax Assistance (VITA) Program; Pianist/Keyboard/Singer, Songwriter and Composer; Pianist for School Plays; Pianist at and Director of School Plays; Appeared as Extra in Upcoming Motion Picture; Member of Stage Crew; Band Member; Piano and Vocal Recitals at Wagner College; Community Concerts; Volunteer at Wagner College Functions and Activities and in the Community; Tutor at Saint Peter's High School in Mathematics, English, Accounting; Newspaper Staff, Saint Peter's High School, Member, Reporter, Writer, Sports Editor; Library Aide; Office Aide; Entertainment Editor and Writer, Wagner College Newspaper; Member, Accounting Society; Disc Jockey for WCBG 64 AM Wagner College Radio Station; Wagner College Yearbook Staff; Intramural Sports, Football, Baseball, Softball, Basketball; Player in Staten Island Softball League. Religion: Member Saint Joseph's Catholic Church, Altar Boy 1969-76, Church Organist, Church Commentator, Church Helper. Published Works: Author of Articles in *The Eagle* (Saint Peter's High School Newspaper), *The Wagnerian* (Wagner College Newspaper), *The Staten Island Advance.* Honors and Awards: Who's Who Among American High School Students Second Year Award; Social Studies Award, 1976; Farewell Address Reader, Grammar School Graduation, 1976; Saint Peter's High School Academic Honor Roll, 1976-80; Saint Peter's High School Honor Awards, Honor Certificates, Letters of Achievement and Commendation, 1976-80; Saint Peter's High School National Honor Society, 1977-80; Saint Peter's High School Italian Honor Roll, 1978-79; Merit Achievement Award, 1978-79; First Prize, Christian Youth Organization Talent Show, 1979; Saint Peter's High School Italian Award, 1980; Full Scholarship to Wagner College; Wagner College Dean's List; Two-Time Winner in the Staten Island Advance Sports Letter Contest; Listed in *Who's Who Among High School Students,*

TWO THOUSAND NOTABLE AMERICANS

International Youth in Achievement, Young Community Leaders of America, Young Personalities of America, Directory of Distinguished Americans, National Dean's List, Who's Who Among Students in American Universities and Colleges, Men of Achievement. Address: 14 Shaughnessy Lane, Staten Island, New York 10305.■

SUSAN SCHARY

Artist. Personal: Daughter of S. Stanley and Fay M. Schary (both deceased); Mother of Jennifer Lyn Gestri, Karima Ann Zedan. Education: B.F.A. with honors, Tyler School of Fine Arts, Temple University, 1960; Graduate of Philadelphia High School for Girls, 1954. Career: Artist; Art Instructor, Harcum Junior College, Bryn Mawr, Pennsylvania, 1960-62; Art Instructor, Fleisher Art Memorial, Philadelphia, 1967-68; Exhibitions - Louis Newman Galleries, Los Angeles 1982-84, Ten California Artists Salute the Los Angeles Bicentennial, California Museum of Science and Industry 1981, Civic Center Museum 1968, 1971, 1974, Samuel S. Fleisher Art Memorial Faculty Exhibition 1968, Grabar Art Gallery 1967, Philadelphia Artists Self Portraits Art Alliance 1967, One Hundred Distinguished Philadelphian Artists from 1840 to the Present 1967, Philadelphia Women in Fine Arts Annual Exhibitions at Moore Institute 1962-66, Arno and Florence Art Galleries, Florence, Italy 1965; Commissions - City Hall, Philadelphia 1964, Villanova University 1960, Temple University 1966-67, Thomas Paine Center 1967, Several Princes and Sheiks in Saudi Arabia 1981-82, Innumerable Private Collections. Organizational Memberships: Artist's Equity Association; International Platform Association. Honors and Awards: B.W. Gottlieb Memorial Prize, Samuel S. Fleisher Art Memorial Faculty Exhibition, 1968; Dean's Prize in Student Exhibition, 1958; Two Gimble Awards in Elementary School and High School. Address: 228 Saint Albans Avenue, South Pasadena, California 91030.■

HOWARD JAMES SCHAUBEL

Physician, Surgeon. Personal: Born May 29, 1916; Married Marjorie Moody; Father of Candice, Janis, Wendy, Gayla Sue. Education: Graduate of Union High School, Grand Rapids, Michigan, 1934; A.S., Grand Rapids Junior College, 1936; A.B., Hope College, 1938; M.D., University of Michigan Medical School, 1942; Intern and Assistant Ortho-resident, Duke University Medical Center, 1942-43; Resident, North Carolina Orthopedic Hospital, 1943-44; Chief Orthopaedic Resident, Duke University Medical Center, 1944-46; State Certificate of Proficiency in the Basic Sciences in Michigan, New Mexico, Florida; State Medical Licenses in Michigan, New Mexico, Texas, Florida. Military: Served in the United States Army, 1952-54, attaining the rank of Reserve Commission Major. Career: Private Practice in Orthopaedic Surgery, Grand Rapids, Michigan, 1946 to present; Hospital Appointments at Butterworth Hospital, Ferguson Hospital, and as Deputy Examiner, Texas Division of Disability Determiniation, 1946 to present. Organizational Memberships: Diplomat, American Board of Orthopaedic Surgery; Fellow Emeritus, American Academy of Orthopaedic Surgeons; Michigan Orthopaedic Society; Chairman, Piedmont Orthopaedic Society, 1963; Emeritus Member, Eastern Orthopaedic Association; Fellow, International College of Surgeons; Life Member, Southern Medical Association; Fellow, American Fracture Association; Galen's Honorary Medical Society of the University of Michigan; Michigan State Medical Society; American Medical Association; Ottawa County (Michigan) Medical Society; Kent County (Michigan) County Medical Society; Officer, Phi Pho Sigma Medical Fraternity, Zeta Chapter, 1941-42. Community Activities: Retired, Rotary International; 32nd Degree Mason; Shriner, Saladin Temple; Director, Royal Order of Jester, Court #11, 1966; The Century Club; International Good Neighbor Council; Board of Directors, Camp Blodgett; United Community Fund, President 1973, Member 1971-73; Life Fellow, International Oceanographic Foundation; Spring Lake Country Club, Michigan; Rancho-Viejo Country Club, Brownsville, Texas. Religion: Member of Mayflower Congregational Church, Grand Rapids, Michigan. Published Works: Author of Fifteen Articles to date, including "Modified Anterior Ilio-Femoral Approach to the Hip Joint", *International Surgery* 1980, "Cervical Spine Problems", *Piedmont Correspondence* 1953, "Injectable Robaxin: A Proven Muscle Relaxant", *The American Journal of Orthopaedic Surgery* 1959. Honors and Awards: Distinguished Service Award, Saladin Temple Crippled Children's Clinic, 1947-73; Appreciation Award, Chicago Shriner's Hospital, 1950-73; Service Award, Ferguson Hospital, 1962-73; Service Award, Fisherman's Hospital of the Florida Keys, 1974-76; Distinguished Service Award, Monroe County Medical Society, 1977; Service Award, Key's Memorial Hospital, 1977; Physician's Recognition Award, American Medical Association, 1973-82; Distinguished Alumni Award, Grand Rapids Junior College, 1967; Blue Key National Honorary Society, Hope College, 1937-38; Distinguished Service Award, Camp Blodgett, United Community Fund, 1973; Listed in *Who's Who in American Colleges and Universities, American Men of Medicine, Who's Who in the Midwest, Cyclopaedia of American Biography, Who's Who in America.* Address: 456 Cherry Street, Southeast, Grand Rapids, Michigan 49503.■

ALEXANDER GEORGE SCHAUSS

Director of American Institute for Biosocial Research. Personal: Born July 20, 1948; Son of Frank and Anna Schauss; Married Sharon L. Education: B.A. 1970, M.A. 1972, University of New Mexico; Additional Post Graduate Studies at Several Universities. Career: Director, American Institute for Biosocial Research; Research Director, Graduate School, City University of Washington State; Training Officer, Washington State Criminal Justice Training Commission, Olympia; Director for Adult Probation Services, Pierce County, Washington; State Assistant Administrator for Corrections, South Dakota; Federal Criminal Justice Planner, New Mexico. Organizational Memberships: American Public Health Association; American Association for the Advancement of Science; New York Academy of Sciences; Fellow, American Orthopsychiatric Association; Academy of Criminal Justice Sciences; American Society of Criminology; International College of Applied Nutrition; Fellow, German Academy of Color Sciences; American Correctional Association; American Association of Correctional Psychologists. Community Activities: Board Member, New England Salem's Children's Trust, 1980 to present; Board Member, National Foundation for Nutrition Research, 1982 to present; Board Member, Price Pottinger Nutrition Foundation, 1980 to present; Pierce County, Washington Law and Justice Committee, Chairman Corrections Sub-Committee, Executive Committee 1977-78; Conference Moderator, Washington State's First Conference on Domestic Violence, 1977; Washington State Criminal Justice Training Commission, 1977-78; Washington State House of Representatives Institutions Committee Advisory Task Force, 1979-81; Instructor, AFL-CIO Community Service Program, 1977-82; Instructor, South Dakota Committee on the Humanities, 1975-77; Advisory Council Member, South Dakota Department of Social Services, 1975-77; Governor's Committee on Criminal Justice Standards and Goals of New Mexico, 1974-75; Chairman City County Goals Committee, Middle Rio Grande Council of Governments, 1973-75; Chairman, Addictions Services Council of Albuquerque/Bernalillo County, 1972-74; Junior League Advisory Council of Albuquerque, 1971-74; Track Coach, Police Athletic League Women's Track and Cross Country Team, 1973-75; Albuquerque Public School's Education Advisory Committee, 1970-73. Honors and Awards: Mayor of New York Citation, 1966; National American Legion Award, 1966; Sid Morris Young Men's Christian Association Scholarship Award, 1966-70; Albuquerque Gerneral Addiction Treatment Effort Award for Community Service, 1975; Southwest Valley Youth Program Award for Community Service, 1975; American Personnel and Guidance Association's Public Offender Counseling Association Award, 1978; Award of Appreciation, San Diego County Sheriff's Department, 1980; Speaker's Award, International College of Applied Nutrition, 1981; Visiting Scholar, Kansas Association of Colleges and Universities, 1982; Invited Lecturer, First National Conference on Nutrition and Behavior, University of Texas-Austin, 1982; Invited Lecturer, Oxford University, McGarrison Society, 1983; Invited Lecturer, First International Nutritional Medicine Symposium, Australia, 1983; Invited Lecturer, First South Pacific Conference on Nutrition and Health, New Zealand, 1984; Listed in *American Men and Women of Science, Personalities of America, Personalities of the West and Midwest, Who's Who in the West, International Who's Who in Community Service, Men of Achievement, International Who's Who of Intellectuals, Notable Americans, Men and Women of Distinction.* Address: P.O. Box 1174, Tacoma, Washington, 98401.■

WINFRIED GEORGE SCHENDEL

Insurance Company Executive. Personal: Born June 19, 1931; Son of Mrs. Margarete Gassner; Married Joanne Wiiest; Father of Victor Winfried, Bruce Lawrence, Rachelle Laureen. Education: B.S., Electrical and Industrial Engineering, Hannover-Stadthagen University, Hannover, West Germany, 1952. Career: Electrical Draftsman, Corrosion Technology, Transcontinental Gas Pipeline Company, Houston, l957-59; Electrical Engineer, Ken R. White Consulting Engineers, Denver, Colorado, 1959-61; Sales Engineer, Weco Division Food Machinery and Chemical Corporation, 1961-64; New York Life Insurance Company, Denver, Colorado, Insurance Field Underwriter 1964-66, Assistant Manager 1966-70, Management Assistant 1970-71, General Manager 1971-77, Sales Manager 1979 to present; Ind. General Agent, Denver, 1978-79; Sales Manager for Denver General Office of New York Life, Denver Colorado. Organizational Memberships: Mile High Association of Life Underwriters, Vice President in Charge of Membership 1984; National Association of Life Underwriters; Colorado Association

TWO THOUSAND NOTABLE AMERICANS

of Life Underwriters; General Agents and Managers Association; International Salesmen with a Purpose Club. Community Activities: Boy Scouts of America, Institutional Representative, Advancement Chairman, Denver Area Council, 1968-72; Precinct Chairman, Jefferson County, Colorado, Republican Party, 1976-78; Lakewood Chamber of Commerce, President, People-to-People, Membership Chairman 1982-83; Lions Club; Edelweiss; International Order of Rocky Mountain Goats; Masons; Shriners. Religion: Presbyterian, Elder. Honors and Awards: Recipient of Cof. National Management Award, General Agents and Managers Association, 1975; Centurion Award, 1966; Northwestern Region Leader Manpower Development Award, New York Life Insurance Company, 1968; Jefferson County Salesman of the Year, 1981, 1983; Readers Digest Award for People-to-People Program; International Positive Mental Attitude Award, 1975. Address: 13802 West 20th Place, Golden, Colorado 80401.■

CLARENCE HENRY SCHERER

Executive Director. Personal: Born April 21, 1926; Son of Clem and Anna Scherer (deceased); Married Elaine J.; Father of Andrew, Bonnie, Mary, Susan, Theresa, David. Education: Graduate of Timber Lake High School, 1943; Completed United States Army Airborne School, 1945; Completed United States Army Medical Technician School, 1946; B.S. Chemistry and Biology, St. John's University, 1950; M.S. Environmental Sciences, Trinity University, 1953; Graduate Work Toward Ph.D. in Chemistry and Environmental Sciences; Short Courses in Water Utilities Operation and Management, Texas A&M University; Completed Course in Nuclear Chemistry and Physics, United States Public Health Service, 1954; Completed Course in Emergency Preparedness for National Nuclear Disaster, 1956; Attending Courses in Speed Reading, Management, Communications, Small Business Management and others, Amarillo College, 1958 to present. Military: Served in the United States Army Airborne Infantry, 1945-47, attaining the rank of Medical Laboratory Corpsman. Career: Partner and Executive Director of Water and Environmental Technology, 1978 to present; Owner-Director of Chemlab Service of Amarillo, 1960 to present; Water Superintendent for City of Amarillo, Texas, 1954 to present; Research Scientist, University of Texas-Austin, 1953-54; Director of Citrus Canning Waste Research Project, Texas State Department of Health, Donna, Texas, 1951-53; Chemist, Wastewater Treatment Plant, City of San Antonio, Texas, 1950-51. Organizational Memberships: Past President, Texas Water Utilities Association; Water Pollution Control Federation; American Water Works Association; American Public Works Association; Texas Water Pollution Control Association. Community Activities: Vice Chairman, Lake Meredith Water Quality Control Committee; Past President, Association Board of Certification for Water and Wastewater Utilities Operators; Chairman, Training Advisory and Coordinating Committee for Water Utilities, State of Texas; Vice Chairman, Water Utilities Advisory Certification Committee, Texas State Department of Health; Chairman, Panhandle Regional Water Utilities Regional Association and Short School; Chairman, Training and Education Committee, Texas Water Utilities Association. Religion: St. Laurence Parish Board of Directors; Choir Director, St. Laurence Cathedral, 1956-72. Published Works: Author of "Manual for Wastewater Treatment Plant Operators" 1978, "Reclamation and Industrial Re-use of Amarillo's Wastewater", *Journal of American Water Works Association* 1971, "A Complete Personnel Development Program", *Southwest Water Works Journal* 1968, and others. Honors and Awards: Water Pollution Control Federation, George Bradley Gascoigne Award, 1953 and 1971, William D. Hatfield Award 1970; Listed in *Who's Who in the Southwest, Personalities of the South, Men of Achievement, Dictionary of International Biography, Who's Who in Municipal Government, International Who's Who of Intellectuals*. Address: 1012 Melody Lane, Amarillo, Texas 79108.■

FREDERICK AUGUSTUS SCHILLING, JR.

Geologist. Personal: Born April 12, 1931; Son of Frederick and Hope Schilling; Married Ardis I. Dovre; Father of Frederick Christopher, Jennifer Dovre. Education: B.S., Washington State College, 1953; Ph.D., Stanford University, 1962. Military: Served in the United States Army, 1953-55. Career: Geologist, Various Organizations in California, Oregon, Idaho, Alaska, 1956-61; United States Geological Survey, California 1961, Kentucky 1962-64, Colorado 1964, Keradamex Inc., Anaconda Company, M.P. Grace, Reserve Oil and Minerals, and Ranchers Exploration and Development Corporation, Grants and Albuquerque, New Mexico, 1968 to present; Engineer, Climax Molybdenum Corporation, Colorado, 1966-68. Organizational Memberships: Geological Society of America; American Association of Petroleum Geologists; Society of Mining Engineers of A.I.M.E.; Rocky Mountain Association of Geologists; Albuquerque Geological Society. Community Activities: Fellow, The Explorers Club, International Platform Association; Masons, Albuquerque, 1977 to present. Religion: Presbyterian. Honors and Awards: Sigma Gamma Epsilon, 1952-53; Sigma Xi, 1959 to present; Representative of Stanford University at Concordia College, Presidential Inauguration, 1975; Address: 11413 Biscayne, Northeast, Albuquerque, New Mexico 87111.■

HOWARD AUGUST SCHIRMER, JR.

Consulting Geotechnical Engineer/Engineering Manager. Personal: Born April 21, 1942 in Oakland, California; Son of Mr. and Mrs. H. A. Schirmer; Married Leslie Mecum; Father of Christine Nani, Amy Kiana, Patricia Leolani. Education: B.S.C.E. 1964, M.S.C.E. 1965, University of California-Berkeley; M.B.A. Program, University of Hawaii-Manoa, 1968-70; Continuing Education in Soil Dynamics, Hawaiian Geology, University of Hawaii, 1967; Engineering Management, University of Michigan Graduate School, 1982. Career: Dames and Moore International, Managing Director 1983 to present, Chief Operating Officer 1981-83, Regional Manager/Partner (Pacific, Far East and Austrialia) 1978-81, Partner and Managing Principal-in-Charge 1975-78, Associate 1972-75, Chief Engineer 1969-72, Acting Chief Engineer 1968-69, Staff Engineer 1967-68, Assistant Engineer 1965-67; Professional Engineer, Hawaii 1968, Guam 1972; Dames and Moore San Francisco, Assistant Engineer 1965, Engineering Analyst 1964-65; Engineer-in-Training, State of California, Division of Highways, Materials and Research Laboratory, Sacramento, 1960-64. Organizational Memberships: American Consulting Engineers Council, Chairman Geotechnical Engineering Committee 1976, 1977, Member Organization Committee 1975, A/E Procurement Committee 1980-81, Planning Cabinet 1981-83, Professional Liability Committee 1984 to present, Secretary Committee on Engineering Management at the Individual Level 1983 to present; Member Committee on Engineering Management at the Individual Level, American Society of Civil Engineers, 1978 to present; American Society of Civil Engineers, Hawaii Section, President 1974, First Vice President, Second Vice President, Treasurer, Chairman, Auditing Committee, Employment Practice Committee, Chairman, Private Practice Subcommittee for Employment Practices; Chairman Nominations Committee, Co-Chairman Seminar on Professionalism in the Practice of Engineering in the Pacific Basin 1979; Chairman 1975 Meeting, Pacific-Southwest Council, American Society of Civil Engineering; Consulting Engineers Council of Hawaii, National Director 1973, President 1972, Vice President 1971, Treasurer 1970, Chairman Past National Directors Committee, Chairman Awards Committee, Chairman Education Committee, Chairman Engineering Practices Committee, Chairman Constitution and By-Laws Revision Committee, Chairman Program Committee, Co-Chairman Professional Practices Committee, Chairman Nominating Committee; Consulting Engineers Council of California; Engineering Association of Hawaii, 2nd Vice President 1977-78, Director 1976-77, Chairman Awards and Special Projects Committee, Member Program Committee; International Society of Soil Mechanics and Foundation Engineering; American Public Works Association, Director 1979 and 1980, Secretary 1977 and 1978; l5th Chairman, Committee on Industrial Participation, International Coastal Engineering Conference, 1976; Consulting Engineers Association of California; Chi Epsilon Board of Trustees, University of Hawaii Chapter, 1980; University of California Engineering Alumni, Past Honolulu Regional Chairman; Honolulu Community College, Chairman Advisory Committee for Engineering Technology 1975-79; Past Member, University of Hawaii Engineering Liasion Committee; Past Member, Engineers Committee, Construction Industry Legislative Organization; Structural Engineers Association of Hawaii; Committee Member for Ladies Activities, Western States Council of Structural Engineers Assoiations, 1979; Society of American Military Engineers. Community Activities: Aloha United Way, Engineer Section Chairman 1974, Budget Committee 1975-77; Founder and Patrol Leader, Mauna Kea Ski Patrol, 1969-72; National Ski Patrol System, National Status 1975 appointment, Certified Ski Proficiency Instructor 1971-79; American Red Cross First Aid Instructor, 1971-79; Outrigger Canoe Club, Past Member, Sailing Committee, Instructor; La Canada/Flintridge Chamber of Commerce, Sigma Phi Epsilon. Religion: Episcopal. Honors and Awards: Chi Epsilon Chapter Honor Member, University of Hawaii, 1979; National A.S.C.E. Edmund Friedman Young Engineers Award for Professional Achievement, 1974; Listed in *Who's Who in America, Who's Who in the West, Who's Who in Engineering, Who's Who in Technology, Men of Achievement, Who's Who in the World, Leading Consultants in Technology*. Address: 827 Inverness Drive, Flintridge, California 91011.■

REINHOLD E. SCHLAGENHAUFF

Administrator. Personal: Born August 14, 1923; Married Erika Krimm; Father of Annette, Stephen. Education: M.D., 1951. Career: Director, Department of Neurology, Erie County Medical Center; Associate Professor of Neurology, State University of New York-Buffalo. Organizational Memberships: Academy of Neurology; American Medical Electroencephalographic Association; American Institute of Ultrasound in Medicine. Published Works: Author of 42 Papers on Neurology, Electroencephalography, Electromyography, Ultrasound. Address: 41 Chaumont Drive, Buffalo, New York 14221.■

TWO THOUSAND NOTABLE AMERICANS

RICHARD H. SCHLOSBERG

Research Management. Personal: Born May 23, 1942; Son of Ruth Schlosberg; Married Pamela Graham, Daughter of Alice Graham; Father of Laura E., Jacqueline A., Joseph M. Education: B.S., Queens College, 1963; Ph.D., Michigan State University, 1967; Postdoctoral Studies, Organic Chemistry, Case Western Reserve University, 1967-69. Career: Research Management, Exxon Research and Engineering Company; Former Professor of Organic Chemistry, University of Wisconsin at Whitewater. Organizational Memberships: American Chemical Society, Fuel Division Program Chairman 1985, Organic Chemistry Division; American Institute of Chemical Engineers. Religion: Treasurer and Vice President, Summit J.C.C., 1979-82. Honors and Awards: 10 Patents in Area of Coal Conversion, 1975 to present; Petroleum Research Fund Grant, 1969-73. Address: 800 Amsterdam Road, Bridgewater, New Jersey 08807.■

VICKI LOUISE SCHMALL

Gerontology Specialist. Personal: Born March 14, 1947; Daughter of Grant and Iona Flagan; Married Rodney A. Schmall. Education: B.S., Montana State University, 1969; Ph.D., Oregon State University, 1977. Career: Gerontology Specialist, Oregon State University Extension Service; Director, Program on Gerontology, Oregon State University, 1975-78; Research Associate, Applied Systems Research and Development, 1977-78; Teaching Assistant, Family Life Department, Oregon State University, 1971-75; Field Instructor/Supervisor, Program on Gerontology, Oregon State University, 1973-74; Research Assistant/ Trainer, National Nutrition Program for the Elderly, Oregon State University, 1972-73; Instructor, Wilsall Consolidated Schools, 1969-70. Organizational Memberships: Gerontological Society of America; Editorial Board, Western Gerontological Society, 1980 to present; Editorial Board, National Council on Family Relations, 1981 to present; Publications Advisory Board, American Home Economics Association, 1980-82; National Council on Aging; Board of Directors, Oregon Gerontological Association, 1981 to present; Oregon Council on Family Relations; Oregon Home Economic Association; Oregon Extension Association. Community Activities: Conducted Over 200 Workshops on a Volunteer Basis for Public Service Agencies and Volunteers Working in Programs Serving Older Adults; Consultant, Community Nutrition Institute, Washington, D.C., 1980-82; Delegate, Oregon White House Conference on Aging, 1981; Governor's Task Force, White House Conference on Families, 1980; Hospice Development Committee, Benton County, 1978-80; Task Force on Housing for the Elderly, 1978-80; Reviewer for KWIC/ASTRA Training Resources on Aging, Duke University, 1978-80; Chairman Budget and Nutrition Committees, Area Agency on Aging Advisory Committee, 1977-80; Governor's Technical Advisory Committee on Aging, 1976-77. Religion: Workshops on Various Subjects Regarding Aging to Community Religious Leaders and Members of Congregations. Published Works: Over 25 Professional Articles, Two Educational Games and Three Media Productions. Honors and Awards: Superior Award, Agricultural Communicators in Education, for Educational Game "Sex and Aging: A Game of Awareness and Interaction", 1981; Phi Kappa Phi; Omicron Nu; Coach of the Year, 1970; Listed in *Outstanding Young Women of America, Outstanding Young Women of Oregon, Who's Who of International Women, Who's Who of American Women.* Address: 835 Marylhurst Circle South, West Linn, Oregon 97068.■

PHYLLIS KANE SCHMERTZ

Executive. Personal: Born March 2, 1949; Daughter of Martin and Rhoda Kane; Married Robert J. Schmertz (deceased). Education: B.S., New York University. Career: Vice Chairman, Universal Video Enterprises Ltd. Organizational Memberships: International Platform Association. Community Activities: Robert J. Schmertz Memorial Games; Democratic House and Senate Council. Address: 1020 Fifth Avenue, New York City, New York 10028.■

BENJAMIN EARL SCHMIDT

Lapidary and Jewelry Craft Instructor. Personal: Born November 11, 1903, Madison, South Dakota; Son of Rudolph August and Martha Maelar Schmidt Rebbert; Married Ruth Jerman Fry, June 29, 1940; Father of Martha Schmidt Rebbert. Education: B.S., Dakota State College, Madison, South Dakota, 1927; M.A., Columbia University, New York, New York, 1935; Postgraduate Studies, University of Minnesota 1928-39, University of Maryland 1940-50. Career: Instructor of Lapidary and Jewelry Making, Evening School of Adult Education, Baltimore City School System; Instructor, Industrial Art, R. J. Reynolds High School (Winston Salem, North Carolina) 1927-30, Baltimore City College 1930-70, Baltimore Junior College (Engineering Drawing) 1948-58. Organizational Memberships: Iota Lambda Sigma Fraternity, Nu Chapter, University of Maryland; Eastern Federation of Mineralogical and Lapidary Societies, Inc.; American Federation of Mineralogical Societies, Inc.; Gem Cutter's Guild of Baltimore, Inc., Charter Member 1950, President Gem Cutters Guild #1970072, Board of Directors 1972-73; Eastern Federation of Mineralogical and Lapidary Societies, Rules Committee; American Federation of Mineralogical Societies, Sub-Rules Committee; Retired Public School Teachers Association; American Association of Retired Persons. Community Activities: Senior Judge of Jewelry and Lapidary Displays for Local, Regional, National, and International Exhibits; Displays by Invitation his Own Handcrafted and Originally Designed Jewelry in Local, Regional, National, and International Shows (Non-Competitively). Religion: University Baptist Church, Baltimore, Maryland, Bible Teacher, Chairman Committee on Committees, Chairman Lord's Supper Committee, President Men's Club 1955-56, Member Board of Deacons, Member Various Other Committees. Published Works: Numerous Articles for *Lapidary Journal*; Articles in Local and Regional Newsletters. Honors and Awards: Listed in *Speakers' Directory, Society of Manufacturing Engineers, Notable Americans, The National Register of Prominent Americans and International Notables, Community Leaders and Noteworthy Americans, International Men of Achievement, Who's Who in the East, International Who's Who in Community Service, Dictionary of International Biography.* Address: 1315 Windemere Avenue, Baltimore, Maryland 21218.■

WILLIAM MAX SCHMIDT

Conglomorate Executive. Personal: Born November 23, 1947; Married Marylea O'Reilly. Education: B.S., Wharton College, 1969; M.B.A., Northwestern University, 1971. Career: Director, Marketing Research, Moody's Investors Service, Inc., 1971-73; Associate Consultant, William E. Hill & Company, Inc., 1973-75; Manager, Marketing Analysis, White Papers Group, International Paper Company, 1975-77; Production Supervisor, Carbonizing Tissue, 1977-79; Director, Market Analysis, U.S. Industries, 1979 to present. Organizational Memberships: Board of Directors, University of Pennsylvania Association of New York City; North American Society of Corporate Planning; American Marketing Association. Community Activities: Newcomen Society of North America; Sons of the American Revolution, Life Member; Sandbar Beach Club; The University Glee Club of New York City; Westport Astronomical Society; Wharton Business School Club of New York; Sigma Chi; Interviewing Committee, St. Bartholomew Community Club; Advisor, Junior Achievement; Knickerbocker Republican Club. Religion: St. John's United Church of Christ. Honors and Awards: Listed in *Dictionary of International Biography.* Address: 89 Partrick Road, Westport, Connecticut 06880.■

CAROLYN SUE SCHMITT

Vocational Counselor. Personal: Born December 19, 1940; Daughter of Charles Lee and Louise Mary de Hainaut Jarrett; Married Carveth J. R. Schmitt, Son of Clarence Charles and Thelma June White (deceased) Schmitt. Education: Diploma, South Charleston High School (Charleston, West Virginia), 1958; B.S. Business Administration, University of Charleston, Morris Harvey College, 1962; Certificate in Human Services, University of California at Riverside, 1971; M.A. Education/Manpower Administration, University of Redlands, 1974; B.S. Liberal Studies, University of the State of New York, 1978; B.A. Social Science, Thomas A. Edison State College, 1979; Postgraduate Studies undertaken at the University of California Extension at Riverside (1967-82), at Los Angeles (1966-67), at Davis (1972); Various Teaching Credentials in State of California. Career: Administrative Assistant, TRW Inc., Defense & Space Systems, 1962-63; Administrative Assistant, Insurance Department, Southern California Mortgage and Loan Corporation, San Bernardino, 1963-66; Employment Counselor, Employment Development Department, State of California, 1966-78; Instructor, Pacific American Institute/Whitehead College, 1979; Senior Vocational/Supervising Rehabilitation Counselor, Westside Counseling Center, 1979-80; Vocational Counselor, Carolyn Sue Schmitt, Private Vocational Counselor, 1980 to present. Organizational Memberships: California Personnel and Guidance Association; California Career Guidance Association; California Rehabilitation Counselor Association; International Association of Personnel Employees, Vice President Local Chapter 1970. Community Activities: American Philatelic Society; Arrowhead Stamp Club; American Topical Association, Life Member; Rex Alumni Association; Thomas A. Edison State College Alumni Association; University of Charleston Alumni Association; Friends of the Library Association of the University of Redlands; Republican Party; National Travel Club; University of Redlands Alumni

TWO THOUSAND NOTABLE AMERICANS

Association; The Rosicrucian Order, AMORC; University of Redlands Fellow; Valley Prospectors; Anthenaeum University of Redlands. Honors and Awards: Homecoming Queen's Court, University of Charleston/Morris Harvey College, 1959, 1960; Christmas Queens Court, 1961; Phi Kappa Kappa, Greek Government Representative, 1960, 1961; Certificate of Recognition for "Outstanding Service," Westside Counseling Center, 1980; Listed in *Personalities of America*, *Community Leaders of America*, *Personalities of the West and Midwest*, *Who's Who in California*, *The World Who's Who of Women*, *California Who's Who of Executive Women*, *Dictionary of International Biography*, *Five Thousand Personalities of the World*, *Who's Who of California Executive Women*, *The Directory of Distinguished Americans*, *International Book of Honor*. Address: 538 North Pampas Avenue, Rialto, California 92376.■

CARVETH JOSEPH RODNEY SCHMITT

Internal Auditor. Personal: Born September 10, 1934; Son of Clarence Charles and Thelma June White Schmitt (mother deceased); Married Carolyn Sue, Daughter of Charles Lee and Louise Mary Jarrett, on May 14, 1965. Education: Diploma, Beaumont High School (Beaumont, California), 1953; Diploma in Business Administration and Accounting, Skadron College of Business, 1959; A.A. Business Management, San Bernardino Valley College, 1962; B.S. Business Administration, University of Riverside, 1970; M.A. Education/Manpower Administration, University of Redlands, 1975; B.S. Liberal Studies, University of the State of New York, 1977; Certificate in Human Services, University of California at Riverside, 1977; B.A. Social Science, Thomas A. Edison State College, 1978; Postgraduate Work undertaken at the University of California Extension at Riverside, 1976-80; Various California Teaching Credentials. Military: Served in the United States Air Force, 1954-58. Career: Registered Representative, Ernest F. Boruski, Jr., New York, 1956-61; Accountant, Barnum & Flagg, San Bernardino, 1959-70; Credit Manager, Stationers Corporation, 1970-77; Registered Representative, Inland American Securities Inc., 1966-70; Life and Disability Agent, Inland American Life Agency Inc., 1966-70; Registered Representative, Parker-Jackson & Company, 1970-73 (part-time); Registered Representative, LeBarron Securities Inc., 1974 (part-time); Office Manager/Credit Manager, Stationers Corporation, 1977-83; Internal Auditor, Stockwell & Binney Office Products Centers, San Bernardino, 1983 to present. Community Activities: American Philatelic Society; Arrowhead Stamp Club; Colorado Mining Association; Northwest Mining Association; Nevada Mining Association; Gold Prospectors Association of America, Charter Member; National Travel Club; National Geographic Society; Myrtle Beach Lodge 353, A.F.M.; National Rifle Association, Life Member; Rex Alumni Association; Thomas A. Edison State College Alumni Association; University of Redlands Alumni Association; Republican Party; Friends of the Library Association, University of Redlands; The Rosicrucian Order - AMORC; University of Redlands Fellows; Anthenaeum University of Redlands; Fontana Tour Club; M&M Tour Club. Honors and Awards: National Defense Service Medal; Good Conduct Medal; Listed in *Who's Who in the West*, *Personalities of America*, *Community Leaders of America*, *Men of Achievement*, *International Book of Honor*, *Personalities of the West and Midwest*, *Who's Who in California*, *Dictionary of International Biography*, *Community Leaders of the World*, *The Directory of Distinguished Americans*, *The International Who's Who of Contemporary Achievement*. Address: 538 North Pampas Avenue, Rialto, California 92376.■

HARRISON HAGAN SCHMITT

Consultant, Former United States Senator. Personal: Born July 3, 1935, in Santa Rita, New Mexico; Son of Harrison A. and Ethel Hagan Schmitt. Education: B.S., California Institute of Technology, 1957; Undertook Postgraduate Studies (Fulbright Fellow), University of Oslo, 1957-58; Ph.D. (N.S.F. Post-doctoral Fellow), Harvard University, 1964; D.Eng. (honors), Colorado School of Mines, 1973; D.Sc. (honorary), Franklin and Marshall, 1977; D.Eng. (honorary), Rensselaer Polytechnic Institute, 1981; D.Astro.Sci., Salem College, 1982. Career: Geologist, United States Geological Survey, 1964-65; Astronaut, National Aeronautical and Space Administration, 1965-74; Lunar Module Pilot, Apollo 17, December 1972; Special Assistant to Administrator, 1974; Assistant Administrator, Office of Energy Programs, 1974-75; Member, U.S. Senate, New Mexico, 1977-83. Organizational Memberships: Geological Society America, Honorary Fellow; New Mexico Geological Society, Honorary Life Member; Norwegian Geological Society, Honorary Member; American Geophysical Union; American Association for the Advancement of Science; American Association of Petroleum Geologists; Fellow, A.I.A.A.; American Institute of Mining, Metallurgical and Petroleum Engineers, Honorary Fellow; Sigma Xi. Honors and Awards: J.S.C. Superior Achievement Award, 1970; Distinguished Service Medal, National Aeronautics and Space Administration, 1973; Arthur S. Fleming Award, 1973; National Order of the Lion (Senegal), 1973; Others. Address: Box 8261, Albuquerque, New Mexico 87198.■

HANS JUERGEN SCHNEIDER

Author, International Orator, Publisher, Pilot. Personal: Born April 25, 1935, in Breslau, Germany; Son of Alfred and Marga (Henkel) Schneider; Moved to United States, 1958; Married Inger Korneliussen, 1967; Father of Roy, Thomas, Helen, Josef, Rose Sharon. Education: Academic Secondary Schooling, Extensive Professional and International education; Evelyn Wood Reading Dynamics Course; Certificate of Merit, F.A.A. Physiological Training Program; Certificate, American National Red Cross Standard and Advanced Courses; Certificates, International Platform Association's Professionalizing Programs, Meetings and Seminars. Career: Founder and President, HJSWWE 1961 to present, World Wide Publishing Corporation 1977 to present. Published Works: "Masters of Legalized Confusion & Their Puppets" 1968, "Timely & Profitable Help for Troubled Americans" 1976, "Flying to Be Free" 1978. Honors and Awards: Ministerial Ordination Certificate; Listed in *Contemporary Authors*, *Above It All: Profiles of American Aviators*, *Books in Print*. Address: P.O. Box 105, Ashland, Oregon 97520.

LAWRENCE S. SCHOENFELD

Professor. Personal: Born December 22, 1941; Son of Irving and Muriel Schoenfeld; Married Heidi B., Daughter of Julian Buchbinder; Father of Jennifer Dawn, Jessica Leah. Education: B.A., Ohio Wesleyan University, 1963; M.A. 1965, Ph.D. 1967, University of Florida. Military: Served with the United States Public Health Service as a Senior Assistant Scientist, 1967-69. Career: Professor, Departments of Psychiatry and Anesthesiology, University of Texas Health Sciences Center, San Antonio; Former Positions include Director of Residency Training in Clinical Psychology, Coordinator of Adult Psychology Service at Robert B. Green Hospital, Supervisor of Southeast Treatment Unit of Alcohol Treatment Program, Adjunct Professor at Trinity University. Organizational Memberships: American Psychological Association; Texas Psychological Association; Bexar County Psychological Association. Community Activities: Board of Trustees, Planned Parenthood of San Antonio; Board of Trustees, Julie Jordan Free Clinic; Professional Advisory Committee, Parents without Partners; Chairman, Review Committee, Metropolitan Youth Agency Advisory Committee; Professional Advisory Board, Mental Health Association of Bexar County. Honors and Awards: Fellow, American Psychological Association, 1982; Diplomate, American Board of Professional Psychology, 1977; Citation, The National Volunteer Awards, 1974. Address: 16002 Wolf Creek, San Antonio, Texas 78232.■

SHARON LYNN SCHOLL

Professor. Personal: Mother of Laura Ann, Lynn Carol. Education: B.Mus., Trinity University; M.M.E., Indiana University; Ph.D., Florida State University. Organizational Memberships: Board Member, National Association for Humanities Education; Florida Endowment for the Humanities; Society for Integrative Studies; American Association of University Professors. Community Activities: Jacksonville Historical and Cultural Commission; Co-Founder, Preservation Association of Tree Hill, 1970; Planning Council, Leadership Jacksonville; Delegate, Governor's Conference on Public Leadership; Hospice of Northeast Florida; Revision Committee, Educational Testing Service Teacher Certification Examination, 1979; Central Committee Member, Jacksonville Campus Ministry; Board of Directors, Florida Community College Museum. Religion: Assistant Choir Director/Organist, Arlington Presbyterian Church. Published Works: *Music and the Culture of Man* 1970, *Death and the Humanities* 1983. Honors and Awards: Professor of the Year, Jacksonville University, 1974; Humanist of the Year, 1977; Four Year Service Award, Florida Endowment for the Humanities; Listed in *Outstanding Educators of America*. Address: 6854 Howalt Drive, Jacksonville, Florida 32211.■

TWO THOUSAND NOTABLE AMERICANS

RICHARD WEAVER SCHRAM

Naval Officer. Personal: Born August 4, 1940; Son of Capt. Richard A. and Marjorie W. Schram; Married Sharon F., Daughter of Ray Frost. Education: B.S., Purdue University, 1963; Armed Forces Staff College, 1975. Career: Commander, U.S. Navy, Serving as Aviation Support Liaison Officer in Office of Secretary of Defense, Washington, D.C.; Director, Community Relations Division, Chief of Information, Washington D.C.; Naval Officer, Has Flown over 250 Combat Missions in Grumann A-6 *Intruder*; Former Corporate Pilot. Organizational Memberships: Order of Daedalians; National Press Club; Aviation/Space Writers Association; American Institute of Aeronautics and Astronautics; Experimental Aircraft Association; Aerobatic Club of America; Tailhook Association; Association of Naval Aviation; American Aviation Historical Society; National Air Racing Group; Air Force Association; U.S. Naval Institute; Naval Order of the United States; National Aviation Club; Quiet Birdman. Honors and Awards: Three Distinguished Flying Crosses; Meritorious Service Medal; 26 Air Medals; Vietnamese Air Gallantry Cross; Several Personal Decorations; Listed in *Who's Who in Aviation, Who's Who in the South and Southwest, Who's Who in Government*. Address: 3732 Redwood Farm Drive, Virginia Beach, Virginia 23452.■

ROBERT NICHOLAS SCHREINER, JR.

Deputy Assistant Project Manager. Personal: Born January 12, 1935; Son of Robert Nicholas and Martha Louise (Picard) Schreiner, Sr.; Married Anne Louise Wendt, 1956; Father of Sue Anne, Wendy Louise, Robert Edward, Kurt Nicholas, Martha Elizabeth, David Paul. Education: B.S., Capital University, Columbus, Ohio, 1956; Graduate Studies, University of Southern California, Los Angeles, 1956-58. Career: Engineer, Northrop Corporation, Hawthorne, California, 1956-1959; TRW Inc., Staff Engineer, Engineering and Applied Mechanics 1959-65, Manager of Interactive Computer Graphics Advanced Technology 1965-68, Manager of Industrial/Educational Cooperative Research and Development 1968-72, Manager of Real Time Computer Application Design and Development 1972 to present; Lecturer in Mechanical Engineering and Advanced Computer Technology to Universities and Industrial Firms, 1965-72; Contributor of Articles to Professional Journals and Presentations to Professional Societies in Mechanical Engineering and Computer Technology, 1960-72. Community Activities: West Coast Regional Chairman during Centennial Anniversary of Capital University's Alumni Association, 1967. Religion: Regional Chairman, Lutheran Ingathering for Education, 1968. Religion: Lutheran Lay Assistant Pastor, Saint Paul's Lutheran Church of Palos Verdes, California, 1972 to present; Lutheran Church Council, 1958-75. Honors and Awards: Listed in *Who's Who in Computers and Data Processing, Who's Who in the West, Dictionary of International Biography, Men of Achievement, Community Leaders and Noteworthy Americans, Who's Who Distinguished Citizens of North America, Personalities of the West and Midwest, International Who's Who in Community Service, Men and Women of Distinction, The American Scientific Registry, Community Leaders of America, The Anglo-American Who's Who, Who's Who in Technology Today, The Directory of Distinguished Americans, Who's Who in California, Personalities of America, Contemporary Personalities, International Book of Honor, Biographical Roll of Honor, International Who's Who in Engineering, Five Thousand Personalities of the World, International Who's Who of Contemporary Achievement*. Address: 30520 Via Rivera, Rancho Palos Verdes, California 90274.■

WOLFRAM GERHARD SCHUETZENDUEBEL

Scientist/Engineer. Personal: Born February 17, 1932, in Alt-Landsberg, Germany; Son of G. E. and K. (deceased) Schuetzenduebel; Married Ingeborn Jutta Lesch, in 1960. Education: B.S.M.E. 1956, M.S.M.E. 1958, M.S. Power Engineering 1958, Technical University Berlin, Berlin, Germany; D.Sc. Engineering, University of Beverly Hills, 1979. Career: Development Engineer, Manager of Boiler Engineering Department, Riley Stoker Corporation, Worchester, Massachusetts, 1958-61; Senior Research and Development Engineer, Boiler Design/Development, Supervisor of System Development, Combustion Engineering, Inc., Windsor, Connecticut, 1961-68; System Coordinator of Fort St. Vrain Steam Generators, Section Leader for Program Group of Heat Exchange Equipment Department, Manager of Technical Services in Steam Generator Program, Manager of Steam and Water Systems of Fort St. Vrain Project, Senior Staff Specialist of Fort St. Vrain Project, General Atomic Company, San Diego, California, 1969-79; Director of Utilities, Solvent Refined Coal Project, The Pittsburg and Midway Coal Mining Comapny, SRC-II Project, Denver, Colorado, 1979-80; Director of Utilities, Solvent Refined Coal International, Inc., Denver, 1980-81; Director of Utilities, Gulf Science and Technology Company, Engineering Division, Houston, Texas, 1981-83; President, Endyne International Inc., Houston, Texas, 1983-84; Director of Engineering, Blount Energy Resource Corporation, Montgomery, Alabama, 1984 to present; Registered Professional Engineer, Mechanical Engineering-Germany, Nuclear Engineering-California, Corrosion Engineering-California; Accredited Corrosion Specialist, National Association of Corrosion Engineers; United States Correspondent to Technical German Publications, *Energie* (Energy), *Waerme* (Heat), *Energy Developments*; 39 Patents in the United States, Australia, Belgium, Canada, France, Great Britain, Japan, Sweden, Switzerland. Organizational Memberships: VDI (Association of German Professional Engineers); National Association of Corrosion Engineers; DAFe.V. (German Atomic Forum); American Nuclear Society, San Diego Section, 1976-79; American Society of Mechanical Engineers; Sea Horse Institute, F.L. LaQue Corrosion Laboratory, 1965; American Society of Mechanical Engineers, Nuclear Engineering Division, Nuclear Heat Exchanger Committee Vice Chairman 1975-76, Chairman 1976-78, Nuclear Codes and Standards Review Committee 1974-78, Program Committee 1976-78; Executive Committee 1976-78, Liaison Officer to Heat Transfer Division 1977-78. Published Works: 92 plus Scientific and Engineering Papers in the United States, Germany, Great Britain, Canada, Switzerland; Co-Author of Book on Nuclear Steam Generators. Honors and Awards: Listed in *Who's Who in the West, Who's Who in America, Dictionary of International Biography, Men of Achievement, Community Leaders and Noteworthy Americans, Notable Americans in the Bicentennial Era, International Who's Who of Intellectuals, Personalities of the West and Midwest, Men and Women of Distinction, International Who's Who in Community Service, Personalities of America, Who's Who in California, Who's Who in Community Service, Book of Honor, American Scientific Registry, Who's Who in Technology Today*. Address: 4748 Regal Drive, Montgomery, Alabama 36116.■

FRANK CARL SCHULZ, JR.

Educator. Personal: Born September 6, 1945; Son of Frank and Ethel Schulz. Education: B.S., Texas A&I University, 1967; M.S. Chemistry, New York University, 1975; D.D., University of Missouri, 1980; Ph.D., Columbia University, 1982; Management Diploma, Iowa College, 1978; Conservation Law Diploma, Cornell University, 1969. Military: Served in the United States Air Force Reserve, 1967-69; Instructor of Physics, New York Military Academy, 1969-72. Career: Teacher, Physics and Chemistry, J.C.S. Chemistry Department; Former Professional Consultant to Reader's Digest Books and Borden Company. Organizational Memberships: Society of American Military Engineers; New York Academy of Sciences; American Association for the Advancement of Science; American Chemical Society. Community Activities: Appointed Farm Manger, Muscout Farm, County of Westchester, 1976-78. Honors and Awards: County Outstanding Achievement Award, Washington D.C., 1978; Woodrow Wilson Fellow in Chemistry, Princeton University, 1982; Listed in *Who's Who, Men and Women of Distinction, International Book of Honor*. Address: Cooper Hill, North Creek, New York 12853.■

VICTOR ARTHUR SCHULZ

Administrator. Personal: Born February 5, 1982; Son of Lucas J. and Maria M. Schulz; Married Elsa R. Esparicia; Father of Ronald Arthur, Leroy Edgard. Education: B.A. Theology, River Plate College, 1964; Graduate Studies, Ohio University, 1975-76; M.Div. 1978, Ph.Div. 1979, Andrews University. Career: Director of Foreign Work, Indiana Conference, 1977-82; Directory of Foreign Work, Ohio, 1973-76; College Bible Teacher, Evangelist, Urguay, 1970-73; Pastor-Evangelist, Argentina, 1964-69. Organizational Memberships: Biblical Numismatic Society, 1978-82; Archaeological Institute of America, 1979-82; Biblical Archaeology Society, 1979-82. Community Activities: President, O.C.C.H.A. (Spanish-American Association), Ohio, 1975; Member of Various Boards and Associations; Led Several Family Seminars, Stop-Smoking Clinics and Other Programs to Benefit the Community in Ohio, Indiana, Texas and Louisiana. Religion: Conducted Six Different Tours to the Holy Land and Europe for Different Organizations. Honors and Awards: Honorary Citizenship and Gold Key, City of New Orleans, 1977; Honorary Citizenship, City of Houston, 1980; Distinguished Service to the Community Award, 1979; Listed in *Men of Achievement, Personalities of America*. Address: 3296 West 74th Place, Merrillville, Indiana 46410.■

ALEXANDER SCHURE

University Chancellor. Personal: Born August 4, 1920; Son of Harry and Bessie (Ginsberg) Joshua (both deceased); Married Dorothy Rubin; Father of Barbara, Matthew, Louis, Jonathan. Education: A.S.T., Pratt Institute, 1943; B.S., City College of New York, 1947; M.A. 1948, B.S. 1947, Ed.D. 1953, New York University. Military: Served United States Army, Signal Corps, 1941-45. Career: Chancellor, New York Institute of Technology, 1982 to present; Chancellor, Nova University, Florida, 1970 to present; President, New York Institute of Technology, 1955-82; President, Crescent Electronics Corporation, 1951-55; President, Crescent School of Radio and Television, 1948-55; Assistant Director, Melville Radio Institute, 1945-48; Film Producer; Designer, Automated Teaching Machine; Buile One of the World's First Computer-Controlled Anthropomorphic Speech Devices, 1959. Organizational Memberships: A.L.L.T.E.L. Committee, Council on Professional Accrediting Agencies, 1981 to present; New York State Education Department, Advisory Committee on Learning Resources, 1982 to present; Nassau County Consortia on Higher Education, 1971 to present; Institute of Electrical and Electronics Engineers, Inc.; Long Island Association of Commerce and Industry, 1971 to present; American Society for Training and Development; American Society for Engineering Education; Long Island Television Educational Council, Inc., President Board of Directors and Trustee 1977-79; New York Academy of Science; Electronic Industries Association, Chairman Task Force on Curriculum Development; Regents Regional Coordinating Council for Post-Secondary Education in New York City, 1973 to present; Alfred P. Sloan Foundation, Advisory Committee for Expanding Minority Opportunities in Engineering, 1974; National Association State Advisory Council, Representative 1975 to present; New York Title IV Advisory Council, Chairman 1975-77; Long Island Regional Advisory Council, Steering Committee 1974 to present; Committee on Independent Colleges and Universities, Member and Trustee Executive Committee; Advisory Council on Learning Technologies, 1982 to present; National Education Association; Consultant to Various State Departments of Education; Consultant to U.N.E.S.C.O.; Consultant to United States Office of Education; Phi Delta Kappa; Delta Mu Delta; Director of Numerous Research Projects. Published works: Author, Editor of Textbooks. Honors and Awards: Patentee in Field (7); Honorary Degrees include LL.D. from College of Boca Raton (Florida) 1976, D.Sc. from New York Institute of Technology 1976, Eng.Sc.D. from Nova University (Florida) 1975, Doctor of Humane Letters from Columbia College (California) 1983, LL.D. from Long Island University 1983; Aerospace Education Foundation Medal of Achievement, 1968; Long Island Distinguished Leadership Award, Long Island Business Review, 1978; Statewide Learning Technology Fair (Albany, New York), Certificate of Appreciation, 1982.■

LAWRENCE JAMES SCHUT

Physician, Clinical Professor. Personal: Born September 13, 1936; Son of Henry (deceased) and Hazel Schut; Married Loretta Fay Klemz; Father of Sherry, Maribeth, Ronald, David, James. Education: A.B., Hope College, 1968; B.S., M.D., University of Minnesota, 1962; Fellowship in Neurochemistry, 1966-67. Military: Served in the United States Army Reserve, 1963-69. Career: Resident in Neurology, University of Minnesota Medical School, 1963-66; Clinical Professor of Neurology, University of Minnesota Medical School; Neurological Coordinator, North Memorial Medical Center, 1972-83; Medical Director, Geriatric Research, Educational and Clinical Center, Minneapolis Veterans Administration Medical Center, 1983 to present; Physician Specializing in Neurology. Organizational Memberships: Secretary/Treasurer, Minnesota Society of Neurological Sciences, 1979 to present; Association of Neurologists of Minnesota, Secretary/Treasurer 1979 to 1982, President 1983 to present; Vice Chairman of Interspecialty Council, Minnesota Medical Association, 1982-83; American Medical Association. Community Activities: National Ataxia Foundation, Medical Director 1971 to present, Board Member 1980 to present; President, Accessible Space Inc., 1979 to present; Medical Adivsor of North Central Chapter, Committee to Combat Huntington's Disease, 1973 to present. Religion: Northern Pines of Minnesota Christian Conference Center, Board of Directors 1973-79, Trustee 1979 to present; Bryn Mawr Presbyterian Church, Minneapolis, Minnesota, Elder 12 years, Trustee 1979-81. Honors and Awards: Graduated cum laude, 1958; Faculty Honors 1958; Listed in *Who's Who in the Midwest*. Address: 434 Yosemite Avenue North, Minneapolis, Minnesota 55422.■

LORETTA J. SCHWARTZ-NOBEL

Journalist, Analyst. Personal: Born September 28, 1943; Daughter of Mr. and Mrs. A. Rosenberg; Married Joel J. Nobel, Son of Golda Nobel; Mother of Ruth, Rebekah. Education: B.A. English, Seattle University, 1969; M.A. English, University of New Mexico, 1971; Ph.D. Coursework, Indiana University, 1972. Career: Journalist, Contributing Editor, *Philadelphia Magazine*; Senior Policy Analyst, Plymouth Institute; Former Lecturer in English, St. Josephs College. Organizational Memberships: Sigma Delta Chi. Published Works: *Starving in the Shadow of Plenty*, 1981; Numerous Professional Articles. Honors and Awards: Sigma Delta Chi National Award for Public Service for "Nothing to Eat," 1975; Robert F. Kennedy Award for Outstanding Coverage of Problems of the Disadvantaged, 1975; Society of Professional Journalists Regional Award for "The Kids Nobody Wants," 1976; Sigma Delta Chi National Public Service Award, 1976; Society of Professional Journalists Regional Award, 1976; Pennsylvania Prison Society Award, 1976; American Bar Association Award, 1976; National Penny Missouri Award, 1976; Outstanding Young Leader of the Year, Philadelphia Jaycees, 1976; Sigma Delta Chi Award for "The Forgotten Children," 1977; Sarah Award, Women in Communications, 1977; National Women in Communications Clarion Award, 1977; National Magazine Award, 1977; Robert F. Kennedy Award for "Hungry Women in America," 1978; National Mental Health Media Award for "The Punishment Cure," 1979; National Women in Communications Award for "The Last Suppers," 1981; Chapel of the Four Chaplains Legion of Honor Award, 1981; Women in Communications Sarah Award, 1982; Society of Professional Journalists Award, 1982. Address: 1434 Monk Road, Gladwyne, Pennsylvania 19035.■

MONA MORRIS SCHWEHM

Artist, Photographer, Free-lance Writer. Personal: Born August 29, 1904, Chicago, Illinois; Married Ray F. on September 29, 1928. Education: Attended Business College; Additional Special Courses; Studies in Art at Evanston Art Center; Instruction from Harry Mintz of the Chicago Art Institute, William Stipe of Northwestern University, Erwin Kummer of *Who's Who of American Landscape Painters*, Charles Emerson of La Jolla Museum of Art. Career: Photography Instructor to Navy Veterans, Navy Hospital, Downey, Illinois; Chairman Chicagoland in Pictures, Chicago Historical Society, 25 Prints Accepted for Permanent Files 1953; Two Salon Prints in Gulf Oil Touring Show, 1955; Annual One-Woman Shows in La Jolla Gallery, Commissions and Invitational Exhibits; Lecturer and Judge for Print and Colour Slide Competitions. Organizational Memberships: North Shore Art Guild, Chicago, Program Chairman 1963-65; Rogers Park Women's Club, Art Chairman 1962, Treasurer 1963-65; Palette and Chisel Academy of Fine Art, Chicago, Exhibiting Artist; La Jolla Art Association, Social Chairman 1967-69; San Diego Art Institute, Exhibiting Artist; National League of American Pen Women, La Jolla, California Branch, Art Chairman 1977-78, Vice President 1978-79. Community Activities: Trained Red Cross Volunteer in Clinics and Hospitals; Gray Lady, Chairman to Red Cross Blood Donor Center; Civilian Recruiter for Women's Army Corps, Chairman First Ward; Donated Large Seascape Painting to Scripps Memorial Hospital, La Jolla, California, 1973. Honors and Awards: Army-Navy Silver E Pin for Work during World War II at Milwaukee Center; Print of the Year Trophy, Chicago Historical Society, 1953-55; Star Rating Photographic Society of America; Merit Award and Bronze Medal Pictorial Division of Photographic Society of America; Twentieth Year Anniversary Service Award, Chicago Area Camera Clubs, 1956; Illinois Federation of Women's Clubs purchased Painting to be hung in a Public School; Hung in San Diego 200th Anniversary Exhibit and La Jolla Museum of Art (both juried shows); Recipient Sixty Awards in Three Categories, Art, Photography and Volunteer Service; Listed in *World Who's Who of Women, International Who's Who of Intellectuals, International Register of Profiles*, and in the Archives of the San Diego Museum of Art. Address: 439 J. Church Avenue, Chula Vista, California 92010.■

GERTRUDE SCHWEITZER

Artist, Painter, Sculptor. Career: Solo Exhibitions at Montclair Art Museum (New Jersey), Washington Water Color Club, Cavuga Museum of History and Art (Auburn, New York), Potsdam Gallery of Art at State Normal School Currier Gallery of Art, Manchester, New Hampshire, Bevier Gallery at Rochester Institute of Technology, Erie Public Museum (Pennsylvania), Cortland Library (New York), Norton Art Gallery and School of Art (West Palm Beach, Florida), Galerie Charpentier (Paris, France), Galleria Al Cavallineo (Venice, Italy), Gallerie 11 Naviglio (Milan, Italy), High Museum (now Atlanta Art Association Galleries, Atlanta, Georgia), Florida Southern College (Lakeland, Florida), Witte Memorial Museum (San Antonio, Texas), Hanover Gallery (London, England), Galleria L'Lobelisco (Rome, Italy), Worth Avenue Gallery (Palm Beach, Florida), The Philadelphia Art Alliance (Pennsylvania), Hokin Gallery (Palm Beach, Florida), Pratt Manhattan Center (New York City), The New Britain Museum of American Art (Connecticut), Lakeland College (Florida); Exhibited at Corcoran Gallery (Washington, D.C.), Art Institute of Chicago (Illinois), Rhode Island School of Design, Denver Society, New York City, Los Angeles County Fair, University of Minnesota, University of Fine Arts (Santa Fe, New Mexico), Museum of the Legion of Honor (San Francisco, California), Menina, Sicily at Exhibition "Viaggio Intorno al Mondo," Albi Museum Contemporary Collection, France (first American represented), Metropolitan Museum of Art's 200 Years of American Water Colors; Works Held in Private Collections in United States, England, France, Denmark, Italy, Milan, Venice, Italy; Works in Permanent Collections in the Brooklyn Museum (New York), Toledo Museum of Art (Ohio), Hackley Art Gallery (Muskegon, Michigan), Davenport Municipal Art Gallery (Iowa), Canajoharie Library and Art Gallery (New York), Norton Art Gallery and School of Art (West Palm Beach, Florida), Atlanta Art Association Galleries (formerly High Museum, Atlanta, Georgia), Witte Memorial Museum (San Antonio, Texas), The Montclair Art Museum (New Jersey), Museum of Modern Art (Paris,

France), Albi Musieu (France), Walker Art Museum of Bowdin College (Brunswick, Maine), Rochester Memorial Art Gallery (Rochester, New York), Metropolitan Museum of Art (New York, New York), Whitney Museum of American Art (New York, New York), Chicago Art Institute (Illinois), The New Britain Museum of American Art (Connecticut), The National Academy of Design, The Society of the Four Arts (Palm Beach, Florida), Museum of Fine Arts (Santa Fe, New Mexico). Community Activities: Arts and Skills Corps of American Red Cross, Fort Jay Regional Hospital, Governor's Island, New York (Head during World War II). Published Works: Peintures et Dessins, 1965; Outstanding Women Artists of America, 1975. Honors and Awards: Bronzes, Stainless Steel Sculptures in Private College 10-foot S/S at Columbia University, New York City; 8-foot Sculpture, Permanence College Museum of Fine Arts, New Mexico; Honorary Doctor of Fine Arts, Pratt Institute; Elected to National Academy of Design, 1951; The Youth Friends Awards, Highest Honor of the School of Art League and Board of Education, New York; American Water Color Society Medal; Philadelphia Water Color Prize, Pennsylvania Academy of Fine Arts; American Artists Professional League Medal, State of New Jersey; First Prize, Norton Gallery and School of Art League and Board of Education, New York; American Water Color Society Medal; Philadelphia Water Color Prize, Pennsylvania Academy of Fine Arts; American Artists Professional League Medal, State of New Jersey; First Prize, Norton Gallery and School of Art, West Palm Beach, Florida; Grand National Exhibition, Miami, Florida; First Prize, Best Woman Painter, New Jersey State Exhibition, Miami, Florida, Montclair Art Museum; American Artists Professional League, New York State Award for the National Arts Club and Honor Roll Award; First Prize, Medal Award, Seton Hall University, Newark, New Jersey; Eleanor S. Higgines Award, 197th Annual New Jersey State Exhibition, Montclair Art Museum; First Grumbacher Purchase Award, Audubon 17th Annual Exhibition, New York City; Pauline Wick Award, American Artists Professional League, National Arts Club, New York, New York; Society of the Four Arts, Palm Beach, Florida; Listed in *Who's Who in America, Who's Who of American Women, Who's Who in the World, Who's Who in the South and Southwest, Who's Who in the East, World Who's Who in Art and Antiques, Dictionary of International Biography, Personalities of the South, Outstanding Women Artists of America, Men and Women of Distinction, National Register of Prominent Americans, Contemporary Personalities, International Directory of the Arts, Personalities of America, American Artists of Renown, World Who's Who of Women.* Address: Stone Hill Farm, Colts Neck, New Jersey 07722.■

HEINRICH SCHWEIZER

Composer, Conductor. Personal: Born September 5, 1943; Son of A. Schweizer. Education: Studied under Paul Muller in Zurich, Switzerland; International Masters Course of Composition, Bonn, Germany; Diploma as Orchestra Musician, 1967; Diploma as Teacher in Music Theoretical Themes, 1974. Career: Composer, Conductor, 1967 to present; Member of Cape Town Symphony Orchestra, 1970-71; Member of Zurich Tonhalle Orchestra under such Conductors as Otto Klemperer, Rudolf Kempe, Karl Boehm and Jean Martinon. Organizational Memberships: Composers, Authors and Artists of America, New York Chapter. Community Activities: Lecturer on "Music in West Africa" at Many Schools and on the Radio. Religion: Protestant. Published Works: "Concerto for Piano and Orchestra" 1981, "Serenade for Harp and Woodwind Quintet" 1980, "Carter String Serenade" for String Orchestra 1978, "Serenade" for String Sextet 1976, "Historical Symphony" 1975, "Concertino" for Xylophone and Orchestra 1974, "Five Songs" for Soprano and Piano 1972, "Overture for Orchestra" 1971, "King Drosselbart" Children's Musical 1970, "September Song" for Soprano and Piano 1967, "String Trio" 1967. Address: 35 West 67th Street, New York, New York 10023.■

CHARLES CARLO SCLAFANI

Professor of Italian. Personal: Born April 13, 1941; Son of Leonardo and Leonarda Sclafani; Married Emilia; Father of Dina, Sandra. Education: B.A., City College of New York, 1964; M.A., Rutgers University, 1971; Ph.D. Candidate, Rutgers University. Career: Associate Professor of Italian and Spanish 1976 to present, Language Laboratory Director 1974 to present, Assistant Professor of Italian and Spanish 1971-76, Westchester Community College; Instructor of Italian and Spanish, State University of New York at Stony Brook, 1970-71; Adjunct Faculty, Suffolk County Community College, 1967-70; Substitute Teacher, New York City School System, 1966. Organizational Memberships: American Association for Teachers of Italian; American Association of Teachers of Spanish and Portuguese; Italian Historical Society of America; New York State Association of Foreign Language Teachers; American Council of the Teaching of Foreign Languages; American Italian Historical Association; New York Association of Junior Colleges. Religion: Catholic. Honors and Awards: Award from Student Council of Westchester Community College for Outstanding Contributions to Student Activity Program, 1980-81, 1974-75; Nominated and Recommended Twice for New York State Chancellor's Award for Excellence in Teaching; Award from Columbian Police Association of Westchester for "tireless efforts in promoting and preserving the rich Italian heritage and culture of his people in Westchester County," 1979; Award from the Italian Club of Westchester Community College for Contributions and Guidance, 1980; Award from the Arabic Society "in recognition of outstanding leadership and service to the college and community," 1979; Westchester Community College Yearbook Dedicated to Him, 1980; Phi Sigma Iota; La Sociedad Nacional Hispanica Sigma Delta Pi; Others Awards; Listed in *Who's Who in the East.* Address: 56 Atlantic Avenue, Hawthorne, New York 10532.■

ALVIN DOUGLASS SCOTT

Chaplain. Personal: Born August 3, 1952; Son of Mr. and Mrs. Odell Young Scott (father deceased). Education: B.A., Texas Southern University, 1975; M.Div., Candler School of Theology, Emory University, 1980; Graduate, Basic Chaplain School, Fort Monmouth, New Jersey, 1983. Career: Battalion Chaplain attached to Battery A, 7th Training Battalion, United States Army Field Artillery Training Center, Fort Sill (Oklahoma); Former Director of Campus Ministry, Atlanta Baptist Student Union, Department of Student Ministries, Georgia Baptist State Missions Program; Former Pastor, Arbor Grove Baptist Church (LaGrange, Georgia); Educator, Atlanta Board of Education. Organizational Memberships: Alpha Kappa Mu; Lambda Iota Tau. Religion: Associate Minister, Grace Covenant Baptist Church, Atlanta, Georgia. Published Works: Poetry Published in *Brown Earthern Verse* and *America Sings.* Honors and Awards: Award Presented by St. Paul's Episcopal Church for Annual Prayer Breakfast, 1982; Award from St. Anthony's Catholic Church for Black History Week Revival, 1983; Outstanding Teenager of America, 1970; Listed in *Who's Who Among Students in American Universities and Colleges.* Address: Box 140, DeQuincy, Louisiana 70633.■

IRENA McCAMMON SCOTT

Researcher. Personal: Born July 31, 1942; Daughter of James and Gay McCammon; Married John Watson, Son of Sarah Scott. Education: Attended Cartography School (St. Louis, Missouri) 1965, Strategic Institute (Washington D.C.) 1968, Photography School (Colorado) 1968; B.S., Ohio State University, 1965; M.S., University of Nevada, 1972; Ph.D., University of Missouri, 1976. Career: Researcher, Ohio State University Medical School and Battelle Memorial Institute; Assistant Professor, St. Bonaventure University, 1978-79; Research Associate, Cornell University, 1977-78; Graduate Research Assistant, University of Missouri, 1972-76; Graduate Research Assistant 1970-72, Graduate Teaching Assistant 1972, University of Nevada; Intelligence Research Specialist, D.I.A., 1967-69; Cartographer, St. Louis, 1965-67. Organizational Memberships: Association for the Advancement of Science; Sigma Xi; Gamma Sigma Delta; American Physiological Society; American Dairy Science Association; Missouri Academy of Science. Community Activities: Coordinator, Mensa Writer's Group, Columbus, Ohio; Volunteer, Ohio State/Ohio Wesleyan University Radio Telescope; Ohio State University Astronomy Club; Verse Writer's Guild of Ohio; Olentangy Poets; Archaeological Society of Ohio. Religion: Volunteer, Lewis Center Methodist Church. Honors and Awards: Bausch and Lomb Honorary Science Award, 1960; Grantee, St. Bonaventure University, 1978; Graduate Fellowship, University of Missouri, 1972-76; Listed in *Who's Who in the Midwest, Personalities of America, World Who's Who of Women, Personalities of the West and Midwest.* Address: 6520 Bale Kenyon, Galena, Ohio 43021.■

MAE RANKIN SCOTT

Mortgage Company Executive. Personal: Born January 1, 1940, in Birmingham, Alabama; Daughter of William Roscoe Rankin, Annie Mae Dobbs Rankin Johnson; Mother of Leslie Ann Scott Garris, William Eugene Jr. Education: Attended University of Alabama Extension, 1959-61. Career: with Heritage Corporation of New York, 1962-67; Assistant Vice President 1967-73, Senior Vice President 1973-78, Executive Vice President 1978 to present, King's Way Mortgage Company (Miami, Florida); Corporate Secretary, Veritas Insurance Company, Alpha Inc.; Vice President, Pan American Mortgage Corporation; Approved Underwriter, Federal Home Loan Bank, Federal National Mortgage Association. Organizational Memberships: Mortgage Bankers Association of South Florida; Mortgage Bankers Association of America; South Florida Home Builders Association; National Association of Revenue Appraisers, Certified Revenue Appraiser; Various South Florida Real Estate Boards; International Institute of Valuers, SCV. Community Activities: Association for the Prevention of Blindness. Published Works: Contributor of Articles to Professional Publications. Honors and Awards: Listed in *Who's Who in the South and Southwest, Who's Who of American Women, Personalities of the South, Personalities of America.* Address: 9315 Southwest 71st Avenue, Miami, Florida 33156.■

TWO THOUSAND NOTABLE AMERICANS

ROBERT GORDON SCRUGGS

Housing Specialist. Personal: Born August 7, 1947; Son of R. W. Scruggs. Education: Attended Air Force N.C.O. Leadership School, 1969; Air Force Management Analysis School, 1968; A.A.S., Asheville-Buncombe Technical College, 1972; B.S.B.A., Mars Hill College, 1974; Additional Courses at Western Carolina University, Wake Technical College; M.R.E. (in progress), Southeastern Baptist Theological Seminary. Military: Served in the United States Air Force, E-4 Sergeant, 1966-70. Career: Housing Specialist, North Carolina Housing Finance Agency; Former Positions as Loan Specialist with Farmers Home Administration, Rehabilitation Placement Specialist with the North Carolina Employment Security Commission. Community Activities: American Legion, Post Commander; Department Veterans Affairs and Rehabilitation Commission, District Commander; Disabled American Veterans, District Commander 4 Years, Department Assistant Adjutant, Department Treasurer; Veterans of Foreign Wars, Post Commander and District Commander; A.M.V.E.T.S.; Wake County Veterans Council, President, Secretary-Treasurer, Trustee; Sons of Confederate Veterans, First Lieutenant Commander; Sons of Union Veterans of the Civil War; Trout Unlimited, President; National Wildlife Federation; National Historical Society; Henderson County Genealogical Society; Federation of Fly Fisherman; N.R.A. Religion: Southern Baptist, Sunday School Teacher, Discipleship Training Teacher, Choir Member, Media Center Director. Honors and Awards: American Legion, Veterans of Foreign Wars and Disabled American Veterans Membership Recruitment Awards, 1972-84; American Legion National Achievement Award, 1977; Disabled American Veterans Outstanding District Commander of the Year Award, 1980; Distinguished Service Pin, Veterans of Foreign Wars, 1978; 5-Gallon Donor Pin, Red Cross, 1984; 100- and 300-Hour Volunteer Pin and Certificates, Veterans Administration, Veterans of Foreign Wars and American Legion; American Legion Department Achievement Award, 1977. Address: P.O. Box 18626, Raleigh, North Carolina 27619.■

WILLIAM DONALD SEAGROVE

University Administrator. Personal: Born July 21, 1946; Son of Mr. and Mrs. Carl Seagrove; Married Patrice Graves, Daughter of Mr. and Mrs. E. M. Graves; Father of Christopher Patrick, Stephen Bradford. Education: B.A. Political Science and History 1968, B.A. Economics 1969, Mississippi State University; M.P.A., University of Tennessee, 1971; M.B.A., J.D., Mississippi College, 1972-79. Career: Director of Personnel, University of Mississippi Medical Center; Wage and Salary Administrator, U.M.C., 1974-77; Personnel Officer, Board of Trustees, Institutions of Higher Learning, 1977-78. Organizational Memberships: American Management Association; Society for Advancement of Management; Alpha Kappa Psi; Pi Sigma Alpha; Pi Sigma Epsilon. Community Activities: American Farm Bureau Federation; Mississippi Farm Bureau; Hinds County Farm Bureau; Ross Barnett Reservoir Association; Mississippi Wildlife Federation; Tau Kappa Epsilon. Religion: Church of Christ. Honors and Awards: Listed in *Who's Who in the South and Southwest, Personalities of the South, Personalities of America, Men of Achievement, Directory of Distinguished Americans*. Address: P.O. Box 4693, Jackson, Mississippi 39216.■

VERNOL ST. CLAIR SEALY

Clinial Laboratory Hematologist. Personal: Born August 18, 1928; Married Josephine S. D. Nanton, Daughter of Mrs. Margaret Nanton; Father of Vernetta, Vernol Jr. Education: General Certificate of Education, University of London, 1962; LL.B., LaSalle Extension University, 1967; B.S. Zoology 1968, Studies in Medical Technology 1969, M.S. Microbiology 1971, Howard University; M.P.H. Epidemiology and Public Health Laboratory Practice, University of Michigan, 1974; Licensed Practical Nurse, Maryland Board of Nurses, 1968; Certified Medical Technologist, American Society of Clinical Pathologists, 1969; Registered Microbiologist, American Academy of Microbiology, 1972; Hematologist, American Society of Clinical Pathologists, 1973. Career: Clinical Laboratory Hematologist, St. Joseph Mercy Hospital, Ann Arbor, Michigan, 1973 to present; Medical Technologist, D.C. General Hospital, 1970-73; Nurse, Freedmen's Hospital, Washington D.C., 1967-70; Nurse, Eugene Leland Hospital, Riverdale, Maryland, 1965-67; Former Positions as High School Teacher and Physiotherapist. Organizational Memberships: American Society of Clinical Pathologists; Fellow, Royal Society of Health (England); National Registry of Microbiologists; American Public Health Association; Royal Institute of Public Health and Hygiene; American Association for the Advancement of Science; New York Academy of Sciences; Academy of Political Sciences. Community Activities: The British Red Cross Society, Trinidad and Tobago Branch, Northern Division, Section Leader, Head Section Leader, Quarter Master of Detachment 3, Commmandant of Detachment 19M, Assistant Area Officer (Area 3 of East St. George); Boy Scouts Association, Tenth Port-of-Spain Boy Scout Troop, Patrol Leader, Troop Leader, Assistant Scout Master; Fellow, International Biographical Association. Honors and Awards: King Scout, Bushman's Thong, Gold Allround Cord, Several Proficiency Badges, Boy Scouts Association; Merit Badge, The British Red Cross Society; Listed in *Men of Achievement, International Who's Who of Intellectuals, Dictionary of International Biography, Five Thousand Personalities of the World, International Who's Who of Contemporary Achievement*. Address: 2104 Glencoe Hills Drive, Ann Arbor, Michigan 48104.■

CARL THOMAS SEBASTIANELLI

Media Psychologist. Personal: Born December 12, 1943; Son of Carlo and Antonio Sebastianelli. Education: B.S magna cum laude Psychology, University of Scranton, 1965; M.A. General Psychology, Temple University, 1967; Ph.D. Candidate, Clinical Psychology, Long Island University, 1970; Ph.D. Clinical Psychology, Clayton University, 1983. Career: Private Practice in Clinical Psychology, Media Psychologist; Former Positions include Clinical Psychologist and Adjunct Faculty (Psychology Department, University of Scranton and Pennsylvania State University); Clinical Psychologist, Harrisburg State Hospital (Psychiatric Treatment Center 1977-79, Family Therapy Center and Psychology Lab 1971-77, Director 1976-77) and Farview State Hospital (1967-68). Organizational Memberships: American Psychological Association; Pennsylvania Psychological Association, General Assembly Member and Chairman Public Information Committee 1981-83; Northeastern Pennsylvania Psychological Association, Secretary 1980-82, Executive Council 1983; Society of Behavioral Medicine; American Academy of Behavioral Medicine; Academy of Psychologists in Marital Sex and Family Therapy. Community Activities: Pennsylvania Social Services Union, Board Member and Chapter President 1974-75; Guest Speaker at Community Organization Meetings/Dinners on Various Psychological Topics, 1979 to present; Radio and Television Presentations of Psychological Topics, 1979 to present; Workshops on Psychological Topics for the General Community and Professional Psychologists, 1979 to present. Published Works: Poems and Non-Refereed Articles Published, 1979 to present. Honors and Awards: Award for Enhancing the Diabetics Education, 1980; Listed in *Who's Who in the East, Personalities of America, International Biographical Roll of Honor, Biographical Roll of Honor*. Address: Comprehensive Health Services Center, Suite 100, 1416 Monroe Avenue, Dunmore, Pennsylvania 18509.■

THOMAS A. SEBEOK

Distinguished Professor of Linguistics and Semiotics. Personal: Born 1920 in Budapest; Immigrated to United States 1937, Naturalized Citizen 1944. Education: B.A., University of Chicago, 1941; M.A. 1943, Ph.D. 1945, Princeton University. Career: Distinguished Professor of Linguistics 1967-78, Distinguished Professor of Linguistics and Semiotics 1978 to present, Professor of Anthropology, Professor of Uralic and Altaic Studies, Fellow of the Folklore Institute, Member of Russian and East European Institute, Chairman of Research Center for Language and Semiotic Studies, Chairman Graduate Program in Semiotic Studies, Director of Human Relations Area Files 1965-69, Director of Air Force Language Training Program, Founder and First Chairman of Department of Uralic and Altaic Studies, First Director of the Uralic and Altaic Language and Area Center, Indiana University; Visiting Appointments at University of Michigan (1946, 1958), University of Puerto Rico (1949), University of New Mexico (1963, Chairman of Visiting Committee for the Program in Linguistics and Language Pedagogy, 1971), University of Arizona (1958-59), University of Vienna (1963), University of Bescancon (1965), University of Hamburg (1966), University of Urbino (1966, 1981), University of Bucharest (1967, 1969), University of Illinois (1968), University of Colorado (1969), Consultant to Provost's Committee for the Humanities 1974, Member University of Colorado Advisory Committee on Semiotics 1976-78), Stanford University (1971), University of South Florida (1972, Linguistics Society of America Professorship 1974), Dalhousie University (Dorothy J. Killam Memorial Lecturer 1979), University of Toronto (Distinguished Visiting Professor in First International Summer Institute for Semiotic and Structural Studies 1980), Vanderbilt University (Distinguished Visiting Scholar in Second International Summer Institute for Semiotic and Structural Studies 1981); Member Visiting Committee at Harvard University (1973), Simon Fraser University (1975), Georgetown University (1977), Vanderbilt University (1977-78), Universidad Nacional Autonoma (1982). Organizational Memberships: Linguistic Society of America, Numerous Offices and Committee Memberships including Chairman of Search Committee for the Secretary/Treasurer 1977, Executive Committee 1968-76, President 1975, Vice President and Acting Secretary/Treasurer 1974; Semiotic Society of America, Secretary/Treasurer 1975, Executive Director 1976-80, Chairman of Editorial Board 1976-80, Vice President 1983, President 1984; Societe Linguistique de Paris; Fellow, American Anthropological Association; Fellow American Folklore Society; Fellow, American Association for the Advancement of Science; Deutsche Gesellschaft fur Semiotik; Osterreichische Gesellschaft fur Semiotik; Federation of American Scientists; International Society for the History of Rhetoric; New York Academy of Sciences, Fellow 1978 to present, Member 1975 to present; Permanent U.S. Member, International Organizing Committee, International Congress of Finno-Ugrists, 1965 to present; Executive Committee, International Association for Semiotic Studies, 1969 to present. Community Activities: Education Advisory Committee, Indianapolis Zoological Society, Inc., 1976 to present; International Brotherhood of Magicians; Science Advisory Board, The Explorer's Club, 1981 to present; Committee of 100, Newberry Library, 1981 to present; Honorary Member, Centro Comasco di Semiotica, 1981 to present; Honorary Sponsor, Institute for Cultural Progress, 1982 to present; Sigma Xi; Cosmos Club; Explorer Club, Fellow; Princeton Club; International House of Japan. Honors and Awards: Listed in *Who's Who in America, Who's Who in the Midwest, Dictionary of International Biography, Biographical Dictionary of the Phonetic Sciences, Men of Achievement, The Writer's Directory, Directory of American Scholars.* Address: 1104 Covenanter Drive, Bloomington, Indiana 47401.■

MARJORIE MARIE ALLISON SEBRING

Home Furnishing Executive. Personal: Born October 8, 1924, in Burnsville, North Carolina; Daughter of James William and Mary Will (Ramsey) Allison; Mother of Patricia Louise Banner Krohn. Education: Student, Mars Hill College 1943, Home Decorators School of Design (New York City) 1948, Wayne State University 1953; C.H.R., University of Virginia, 1982. Career: Position in the Decorating Division, Robinson Furniture, Detroit, 1953-57; Head Buyer, Tyner Hi-Way House, Ypsilanti, Michigan, 1957-63; Head Buyer, Town and Country, Dearborn, Michigan, 1963-66; Instructor, National Carpet Institute, 1963-65; Owner, Adams House, Inc., Plymouth, Michigan, 1966-70; Executive Vice President Marketing and Sales, Regional Sales and Marketing Manager, Triangle Industries, Los Angeles, 1972 to present; Co-Owner, Markham-Sebring Design and Development Corporation, St. Petersburg, Florida. Organizational Memberships: I.H.F.R.A.; International Delegate, 1978-83; International Home Furnishings Association; Florida Home Furnishings Representative Association, Officer; Florida Furniture Dealers Association. Community Activities; United States Coast Guard Auxiliary; National Audubon Society; Republican Party; International Platform Association. Published Works: Contributor Creative Display to *Better Homes and Gardens*, 1957-64. Honors and Awards: Recipient National Sales Awards; Recognition for Work with Youth and Aged; Listed in *Who's Who in Finance and Industry, Who's Who in American Women, Who's Who in the South and Southwest.* Address: 2601-3 Grist Mill Circle, New Port Richey, Florida 33552.■

MARILYN M. SEGAL

Professor. Personal: Born August 9, 1927; Daughter of Alice Mailman; Mother of Debbie, Richard, Betty Bardige, Patricia Lieberman, Wendy Masi. Education: B.A., Wellesley College, 1948; B.S., McGill School of Social Work, 1949; Ph.D., Nova University, 1970. Career: Professor of Child Development, Director of Family Center, Nova University; Positions Include Director of University School, Fort Lauderdale, Florida; Director of Preschool Head Start Demonstration Program, Hollywood, Florida; Social Case Worker, Boston Floating Hospital. Organizational Memberships: National Association for the Education of Young Children; Council for Exceptional Children; American Psychological Association; Florida Association of School Psychologists; Southern Association for Children Under Six; Broward Association for Children Under Six; Delta Kappa Gamma Society International. Chairperson, National Visiting Committee School of Nursing, University of Miami, 1982 to present; Committee on Allocations, Jewish Federation of South Broward, 1981 to present; State Steering Committee for Preschool Handicapped, 1981; Academic Affairs Committee, University of Miami Board of Trustees, 1980 to present; Community Resources Task Force, Superintendent's Commission on Public Education, Broward County, Florida, 1980; Health Planning Council of Broward County, Health Rehabilitation Services, Fort Lauderdale, Florida, 1976 to present; Trustee, University of Miami, Miami, Florida, 1970 to present; Advisory Board, Early Childhood Development Association, Fort Lauderdale, Florida, 1981 to present. Honors and Awards: Woman of the Year, B.P.W. Fort Lauderdale, 1981; First Annual Woman of the Year Award, Brandeis University National Women's Committee, Greater Hwd. Chapter, 1982; Citizen of the Year, Civitan Club, Hollywood, Florida, 1970; Outstanding Educators of America, 1971, 1973-75; Broward County Woman of the Year, Women in Communication, Inc., Atlantic Florida Chapter, 1975; Chief Award, President of Independent Colleges and Universities, 1982. Address: 919 Southlake Drive, Hollywood, Florida 33019.■

M. ANGELICE SEIBERT

President of Religious Order. Personal: Born January 16, 1922. Education: B.S. summa cum laude Chemistry, Ursuline College, Louisville, Kentucky, 1947; M.S. 1950, Ph.D. 1952 Biochemistry, Institutum Divi Thomae, Cincinnati, Ohio; Registered Specialist in Chemistry, American Society of Clinical Pathologists, 1954; Summer Fellow, National Endowment for the Humanities, 1974; Fulbright-Hays Visiting Professor of Biochemistry, University College, Galway, Ireland, 1968. Career: President, Ursuline Sisters of Louisville, Kentucky, 1980 to present; Fellow, Department of Health, Education and Welfare, New York, 1979; Professor and Chairperson, Division of Allied Health, Jefferson Community College, Louisville, Kentucky, 1970-78; Adjunct Professor of Biochemistry, Indiana University Southeast, 1976; Visiting Professor of Biochemistry, Smith College, Northampton, Massachusetts, 1969; President of Ursuline College, 1963-68. Organizational Memberships: Board of Directors, Bellarmine College, 1982; State Coordinating Committee, A.C.E. Project for Identification of Women in Higher Education Administration, 1978-82; Faculty Representative Advisory Board, Jefferson Community College, 1978-80; Board of Directors, American Society of Allied Health Professions, 1976. Community Activities: Fellow, United States Department Health Education and Welfare, 1979-80; Editorial Board, Journal of Allied Health Professions, 1976-79; Advisory Committee, West Louisville Health Professions, 1972-75; Member of National Identification Program for the Advancement of Women in Higher Education Administration, Kentucky State Planning Committee; Visiting Committee, Southern Association of College and Schools; Grant Evaluation Panel Committee, National Science Foundation. Religion: Member of the Ursuline Sisters of the Immaculate Conception of Louisville, Kentucky 1939 to present, President 1980-84. Honors and Awards: Bellarmine College Alumna of the Year, 1980; Certificate for Meritorius Service to Jefferson Community College, 1978; Certificate of Recognition for Outstanding Service to Higher Education, Louisville Chapter of Phi Delta Kappa, 1977; Woman of the Year, Young Women's Christian Association, 1976. Address: 3115 Lexington Road, Louisville, Kentucky 40206.■

CLIFFORD P. SEITZ

Consultant. Personal: Born July 19, 1912; Son of Henry G. and Frieda Seitz; Married Irene Metcalf; Father of Karl D., Ronald H. Education: B.A., Columbia College, 1934; M.A. 1936, Ph.D. 1939, Columbia University; Attended Duke University, 1936-37. Military: Served in the United States Naval Reserve, 1942-46, attaining the rank of Lieutenant Commander. Career: Consultant, Human Engineering, Safety, Training; Research Associate, Columbia University, 1934-36; Graduate Assistant, Duke University, 1936-37; Research Assistant, College of Physicians and Surgeons, Columbia University, 1934-36 and 1937-39; Instructor, City College, New York, 1937-39 and 1941-43; Instructor, University of Alabama, 1939-41; Adjunct Associate Professor, New York University, 1952-56; United States Naval Reserve, 1944-46; Chief Psychologist and Head Human Engineering Department, United States Naval Training Device Center, 1946-58; Grumman Aero Space Corporation, Chief Life Science 1958-70, Manager Future Business and Training 1970, Staff Special Project Military Space 1972; National Transportation Safety Board, Chief Bureau of Plans and Programs 1980-retired, Recommendations Manager 1973-76. Organizational Memberships: Diplomate, American Board Examiners in Professional Psychology; Fellow, American Psychological Association; Fellow, American Association for the Advancement of Science; American Institute Aeronautics and Astronautics; Aerospace Medical Association; Aerospace Life Sciences Association; Founding Member, Human Factors Society; Sigma Xi; Flight Safety Foundation; Systems Safety Society. Community Activities: Treasurer, School Board, Lloyd Harbor, New York; Centralization Committee, Lloyd Harbor and Cold Spring Harbor; Board of Education, Central District #2, Huntington, New York, Member Five Years, President One Year; Chairman, United Fund, Lloyd Harbor, 1963-64. Published Works: Author of Article "The Effect of Oxygen Deprivation on Complex Mental Functions," *Journal of Aviation Medicine* 1937, "A Psychosomatic Investory," *Journal of Applied Psychology*, "An Inexpensive Device for Measuring Rotational Speed," *American Journal of Psychology* 1939, and others. Honors and Awards: Distinguished Service in Achieving Safer Utilization of Aircraft Award, Flight Safety Foundation, 1967; Award for 22 Years Distinguished Service Devoted to Transportation Safety, National Transportation Safety Board, 1980, Citation for Community Service, United Fund of Huntington, New York, 1964; Listed in *Who's Who Who Knows and What, American Men of Science.* Address: 8861 Southeast Eaglewood Way, Hobe Sound, Florida 33455.■

TWO THOUSAND NOTABLE AMERICANS

ALAN DANIEL SELDITCH

Manager. Personal: Born September 8, 1926 in Philadelphia, Pennsylvania; Son of Jacob and Sarah Molly Selditch (both deceased); Divorced; Father of Gretchen, Edward, Michael, Ronald, Kimberly. Education: Engineering, Physics, Math, St. Lawrence University, Canton, New York, 1944-46; B.S. Engineering, Business, Public Administration, University of Southern California, 1948; Undertook Post Graduate Studies at Los Angeles City College, LaSalle University, California State Universities; M.S. 1982, Ph.D. 1983 Environmental Sciences, Heed University. Military: Served in the United States Naval Reserve, 1944-46, 1946-50. Career: Registered Professional Engineer, California; Certified in Material Management and Material Handling, International Material Management Society; Certified Instructor in M.T.M., University of Michigan and M.T.M. Society; Certified in Methods Engineering, Maynard Research Institute; Certified in Flow Measurement, Open and Confined Channels, Los Angeles County Sanitation District; Chief of Projects and Engineering, President, Sigma Associates, Los Angeles, 1950-57; Chief Industrial and Project Engineering and Plant Maintenance, Rexall Drug and Chemical Company, 1962-65; Regional Consulting Manager, H.B. Maynard and Company, Sherman Oaks, California, 1965-69; Assistant to the President, P.O.P. Systems/I.S.I., Santa Anna, California, 1970-72; Manager, Facilities and Corporate Planning, Systems Resource Recovery/System Associates, Long Beach, California, 1972-75; General Manager, Flowtrace, Los Angeles, 1975-77; Manager, Corporate/Environmental Affairs Group, Signetics, Sunnyvale, California, 1977 to present; President, A.D. Selditch and Associates, Newark, California, 1977 to present. Organizational Memberships: American Association for the Advancement of Science; American Institute of Industrial Engineers; American Society of Management; American Society of Standards; Association of Energy Engineers; California Society of Professional Engineers; International Material Management Society; Methods, Time-Measurement Association for Standards and Research; National Association for Solid Waste; National Association of Professional Engineers; American Society of Mechanical Engineers; American Society of Standards; American Academy of Environmental Engineers; American Institute of Plant Engineers; American Public Works Association; American Society of Metals; Governmental Refuse, Collection and Disposal Association; International Platform Association; Institute of Electrical and Electronic Engineers; Institute of Solid Wastes; Signet Society. Community Activities: Republican. Religion: Jewish. Published Works: Number of Articles Contributed to Professional Journals, including "Recovered Resources for Mixed Municipal Waste: A Sensitivity Analysis" 1975, "Proposal for the Design, Construction and Operation of Dade County, Florida, Solid Waste Resource Recovery System, 1973, and "Evaluation of Solid Waste as a Component of Cattle Feed" 1975. Honors and Awards: Listed in *Men of Achievement, Who's Who in California, Who's Who in the West, AEE Directory of Energy Engineering Pioneers, International Men of Achievement, Directory of Distinguished Americans, Personalities of America, International Book of Honor, Biographical Roll of Honor, Directory of International Biography, International Who's Who of Intellectuals, International Register of Profiles, Personalities of the West and Midwest, International Men of Science, National Council of Engineering Examiners, AEE Directory of Certified Energy Managers, Compendium of Environmental Engineers and Consultants, Directory of Environmental Consultants, Directory of Professional Engineers.* Address: 6267 #E Jaoquin Murieta Avenue, Newark, California 94560.■

DONALD J. SENESE

Assistant Secretary for Educational Research and Improvement. Personal: Born April 6, 1942; Son of Leo and Joan Senese (both deceased); Married Linda W.; Father of Denise Nicole. Education: B.S. History, Loyola University of Chicago, 1964; Master's (1966) and Doctoral (1970) Degrees in History, University of South Carolina, Columbia, South Carolina; Certificate of Accomplishment in Administrative Procedures, United States Department of Agriculture Graduate School, Washington, D.C., 1976; Specialized Study, Sophia University in Tokyo, Japan, Summer 1970, and National Chengchi University in Taipei, Taiwan, Summer 1971; Certificate of Achievement, Virginia Polytechnic Institute and State University Seminar in Economics, 1976; American Hospital Supply Corporation Government Fellow, 1978. Career: Associate Professor of History, Radford University, Radford, Virginia, 1969-72; Legislative Assistant and Newsletter Editor, Senator William L. Scott of Virginia, 1973; Chief Legislative Assistant, Representative Bill Archer of Texas, 1973-76; Senior Research Associate, House Republican Study Committee, United States House of Representatives, 1976-81; Assistant Secretary for Educational Research and Improvement, United States Department of Education, 1981 to present. Organizational Memberships: Vice Chairman, Subcommittee on Technology, F.I.C.E., 1981 to present; Federal Representative, Education Commission of the States, 1981 to present. Community Activities: Vice Chairman, Alexandria Republican City Committee, 1976-78; Board Member, University Professors for Academic Order, 1979-81; Alexandria Historical Records Commission, 1979-84; United States Delegate to the Centre for Education and Research Innovation, O.E.C.D., 1981 to present; Member General Administration Board, United States Department of Agriculture Graduate School, 1975-80, 1981 to present; Venerable, George Washington Lodge, Order Sons of Italy in America, 1979-80. Religion: Roman Catholic; Member Blessed Sacrament Parish, Alexandria, Virginia. Published Works: Author Articles and Book Reviews in Publications such as *American Education, Asia Mail, The Classical Outlook, Commonsense, Family Protection Report, Free Asia Report, The Freeman, Government Computer News, History Today, Human Events, ISI Campus Report, The Journal of Social and Political Studies, Korean Observer, Modern Age, New Guard, National Review, Policy Review, Private Practice, South Carolina Law Review, The State Factor, Universitas, The University Bookman*; Several Book Chapters; Author Books including *Asianomics: Challenge and Change in Northeast Asia* 1981. Honors and Awards: William P. Lyons Master's Essay Award, 1967; Outstanding Young Men of America Award, Jaycees, 1976 and 1978; Freedoms Foundation (Valley Forge) Award for Book *Modernizing the Chinese Dragon*, 1981; Certificate of Appreciation from the Minister of Education of the Republic of Korea for Promotion of Cultural Exchanges, 1984; Clara Barton Award for Excellence in Educational Leadership, 1981; Pi Gamma Mu; Phi Alpha Theta; Delta Sigma Rho; Tau Kappa Alpha; Listed in *Dictionary of American Scholars, Notable Americans of the Bicentennial Era, Outstanding Young Men in America, Who's Who in Virginia, Who's Who in North America, Congressional Staff Directory, International Who's Who in Education, Who's Who in American Politics, International Book of Honor, Who's Who in Washington.* Address: 7938 Bayberry Drive, Alexandria, Virginia 22306.■

DAVID JAMES SENN

Professor. Personal: Born November 12, 1940; Son of Mrs. Edward R. Senn; Married Ronda Keller; Father of Jonathan David, Amy Elisabeth; Timothy Andrew. Education: B.A., North Central College, 1962; M.A., Northern Illinois University, 1964; Ph.D., University of Massachusetts, 1967. Career: Professor in Psychology, Clemson University; Lecturer in Psychology, Smith College, 1967; Assistant Professor of Psychology, Franklin and Marshall College, 1967-70; Assistant Professor and Chairman, Monmouth College, 1970-73. Organizational Memberships: American Psychological Association; Southeastern Psychological Association; Chairman, Society of Southeastern Social Psychologists, 1980-81; South Carolina Psychological Association; Society for the Advancement of Social Psychology; Society for the Psychological Study of Social Issues. Community Activities: Anderson-Oconee-Pickens Mental Health Center, Needs Assessment Task Force, Utilization and Review Committee, Clinical Pastoral Education Program, Research and Evaluation Committee, 1973 to present; Family Vacation Camping Program, National Presbyterian Mariners, Director 1976, 1982, Resource Leader 1973; Advisory Committee, Community Mental Health Center; Basketball Coach, Young Men's Christian Association. Religion: Clemson United Methodist Church, Council on Ministries 1974 to present, Chairman 1978-80; Family Life Council, 1980-83; Delegate, South Carolina Annual Conference. Honors and Awards: Fellow, Labor Relations Research Center, 1965-66; Clemson University Faculty Senate, Member 1981 to present, Vice President/President Elect 1983-84, President 1984-85; Listed in *Who's Who Among Students in American Universities and Colleges, Outstanding Young Men of America, Outstanding Educators of America.* Address: 112 Lakeview Circle, Clemson, South Carolina 29631.■

DAVID MARTIN SENSENIG

Surgeon. Personal: Born May 4, 1921, in Gladwyne, Pennsylvania; Married Bernice; Father of Philip, David Jr., Andrew, Thomas, (Stepfather of) Judith, Diane, Deborah, Joanne. Education: Graduate of the Haverford School, 1938; B.S., Haverford College, Haverford, Pennsylvania, 1942; Attended the University of Pennsylvania School of Medicine, 1942-43; M.D., Harvard Medical School, Boston, Massachusetts, 1945; Rotating Internship, Allentown Hospital, Allentown, Pennsylvania, 1945-46; Surgical House Officer and Junior Assistant Resident, Peter Bent Brigham Hospital, Boston, 1948-50; Senior Assistant Resident and Resident Surgeon, New England Center Hospital, Boston, 1950-52; Surgical Resident, Westfield State Sanatorium, Westfield, Massachusetts, Cancer Section, 1952-53; Resident in Thoracic Surgery and Cardiac Surgery, University Hospital, State University of Iowa, 1957-59. Military: Served in the United States Army, 1943-48, attaining the rank of Captain, Medical Corps. Career: Assistant Chief, Surgical Service, and Director, Surgical Research Laboratory, Veterans Administration Medical Teaching Group Hospital, Memphis, Tennessee, 1953-55; Assistant Chief, Surgical Service, Veterans Administration Hospital, Albany, New York, and Instructor in Surgery, Albany Medical College, 1955-57; Instructor in Surgery 1957-58, Associate in Surgery 1958-59, University Hospitals, State University of Iowa, Iowa City; Chief, Thoracic Surgery Section, Veterans Administration Hospital, Philadelphia, 1959-60; Assistant Professor and Associate Professor of Surgery, University Hospitals, State University of Iowa, 1960-62; Cardiothoracic Surgeon, Pennsylvania Hospital, and Assistant Professor of Surgery, University of Pennsylvania, 1962-63; Assistant Chief, Surgical Service, and Supervisor, Animal Research Laboratory, Veterans Administration Hospital, Philadelphia; Assistant Professor of Surgery, University of Pennsylvania, 1963-66; Private Surgical Practice, Bangor, Maine, 1966 to present; Staff Surgeon,

Eastern Maine Medical Center, 1966 to present; Chief of Surgery, St. Joseph Hospital, 1973-78; Surgical Consultant, Penobscot Valley Hospital, Lincoln, Maine. Organizational Memberships: Phi Beta Kappa; Society of Sigma Xi; American Medical Association; American College of Surgeons; Pennsylvania Association for Thoracic Surgery; President, Penobscot County Medical Society; Maine Thoracic Society; American Association for the Advancement of Science; International Cardiovascular Society; American Geriatrics Society; Iowa Academy of Surgery; American College of Chest Physicians; Philadelphia Academy of Surgery; President, Bangor Medical Club; American Thoracic Society; President, Maine Vascular Society; Executive Committee, New England Surgical Society; New York Academy of Sciences; New England Society for Vascular Surgery. Community Activities: Cub Scout Master, Gladwyn, Pennsylvania, Troop #1964; President, Sebec Lake Association, Conservation Group, 1973. Religion: Protestant Episcopal Church. Honors and Awards: Phi Beta Kappa, Sigma Xi. Address: 436 State Street, Bangor, Maine 04401.■

John George Sevcik

General Manager. Personal: Born May 15, 1909; Married Rose Vanek; Father of Joanne Shea, John. Education: J.D. 1939, LL.D. 1958, DePaul University; B.Sc., Central College, 1945; M.B.A., University of Chicago, 1947; M.P.L. 1950, LL.M. 1954, John Marshall Law School; LL.D., St. Mary's College, 1956; LL.D., St. Procopius College (now Illinois Benedictine College), 1960. Career: DePaul University, Board of Trustees 1954 to present, Chairman of the Board of Trustees 1960-63, President of Alumni Association 1953-55, Chairman of 1952 Financial Campaign; Rosary College, Member Board of Trustees, Chairman 1966-69; Board of Trustees, St. Procopius College 1961-70, St. Mary's College 1957 to present; John Marshall Law School, Member Board of Trustees, President of Alumni Association 1968-71; University of Chicago, Citizens Board 1965-71, Advisory Council of School of Business, President of the Executive Program Club, M.B.A. Graduates 1949-50; Member and Vice Chairman, Board of Trustees, Illinois College of Podiatric Medicine; Lecturer, Numerous Colleges and Institutions; General Manager, McCormick Place, Chicago, 1971-81; President and Director, Burton-Dixie Corporation, 1949-71, Vice President Board of Directors 1971; Director, Brunswick Corporation; Director, Bus Capital Inc.; Director, Central National Bank; Director, Central Chicago Corporation; Director, Financial Marketing Services Company; Director, National Cotton Batting Institute; Chief Executive Officer, Chicago Investment Corporation, 1982; American Furniture Mart, Member Board of Governors, Chairman 1968-69; Editorial Advisory Board, *Bedding*; Chairman of the Board, Financial Marketing Service Inc. Organizational Memberships: Wisdom Society; National Association of Bedding Manufacturers, President 1959-60; Illinois Bar Association; American Bar Association; American Judicature Society; National Sales Executive Club; Chicago Association of Commerce and Industry, Director and Member Subscription Investigating Committee; National Association of Exposition Manufacturers; Illinois Manufacturers Association, Committee Member; Catholic Business Education Association, 1956-68; Institute of American Strategy, Vice President; Illinois Manufacturers Association. Community Activities: American Security Council, Vice President; United Cerebral Palsy Association, Past Chairman of the Board of Greater Chicago, Past President; Research and Educational Foundation, Inc., Board of Directors; Boy Scouts of America; Chicago Crime Commission, Board of Directors; Public Building Commission of Chicago, Commissioner 1956 to present; Dialogue Association for the Blind, Board of Directors; Youth Welcome Commission of Chicago; National Conference of Christians and Jews, Executive Board 1950-63, Illinois Brotherhood Chairman 1956, Steering Committee Chairman 1958; American Association of University Professors; Director of Catholic Charities; Citizens of Greater Chicago, Board of Governors Chairman 1960-65, Member Board of Governors and Board of Directors; Ivy Cancer Research Foundation, Board of Directors; Mayor's All Citizen's Committee of Chicago; Fund Raiser for the American Cancer Society, Catholic Charities, National Foundation of Medical Education, Easter Seals; Kiwanis Club; Illinois Chamber of Commerce, Membership Committee. Religion: Sponsor, B'nai B'rith Youth Organization Scholarship Program. Honors and Awards: Inducted as Knight of Malta, January 1984; Selected as 1 of 100 of Chicago's Outstanding Citizens, Loyola University, 1957; Knighted by His Imperial Highness Franz Josef, Archduke of Austria, Order of Knight Templar, for Outstanding Work in Charity 1956; Received Israel Prime Minister's Medal Study Israel Bonds 1968; Mother of World War II Certificate of Outstanding Achievement 1959, Veterans Administration Certificate for Volunteer Service 1959; Man of the Year, Furniture Industry, 1959; Phi Alpha Delta; Beta Gamma Sigma; Award from the University of Chicago, 1947; International Platform Association; Listed in *Who's Who in America*, *Who's Who in Commerce and Industry*, *Two Thousand Men of Achievement*, *National Social Directory*. Address: 2221 Ridgeland Avenue, Berwyn, Illinois 60402.■

Raymond B. Seymour

Professor. Personal: Born in 1912, in Boston, Massachusetts; Son of Walter A. and Marie E. Doherty Seymour (both deceased), Married Frances B. Horan; Father of David Ray, Peter Jerome, Philip Alan, Susan Jayne Seymour Smith. Education: B.S. 1933, M.S. 1935, University of New Hampshire; Ph.D., University of Iowa, 1937; Post-Doctoral Studies at Rensselaer Polytechnic Institute, Institute of Paper Chemistry, University of Utah. Military: Served as Officer in National Defense Executives Reserves, 1957 to present. Career: Distinguished Professor of Polymer Science, University of Southern Mississippi, 1976 to present; Professor of Chemistry, University of Houston, 1960-64; President, Loven Chemical of California, 1955-60; President, Atlas Chemical Corporation, 1949-55; Director of Research, Johnson and Johnson, 1948-49; Director of Research, University of Tennessee-Chattanooga, 1945-48. Organizational Memberships: Alpha Chi Sigma, 1932 to present; American Chemical Society, 1935 to present; American Association for Advancement of Science, 1945 to present; Society of the Plastics Industry, 1945 to present; American Institute of Chemical Engineers, 1945 to present; American Institute of Chemists, 1943 to present. Community Activities: Chairman, March of Dimes, 1952-53; Director, Rotary Club of Chattanooga, 1945-48; Director, Allentown Kiwanis Club, 1950-55; Alpine Rotary Club, 1960-64. Honors and Awards: International S.P.E. Education Award, 1983; Southern Chemists Award, 1981; Western Plastics Hall of Fame, 1981; American Institute of Chemists Honor Scroll, 1981; Chemical Manufacturers Association Catalyst Award, 1976; Plastics Pioneer Award, 1973; Southeastern Texas American Chemical Society Award, 1974; Western Plastics Award, 1968. Address: 111 Lakeside Drive, Route 10, Hattiesburg, Mississippi 39401.■

Tom Shachtman

Writer, Television Producer. Personal: Born in 1942; Married Harriet Shelare; Father of Noah, Daniel. Education: B.S., Tufts University, 1963; M.F.A., Carnegie-Mellon, 1966. Career: Writer, Television Producer; Author of Several Books, Producer of Television Documentaries and Fictional Programs for National Networks, Syndication, Local Stations, Government and Industry. Organizational Memberships: Writers Guild of America; Authors Guild. Community Activities: Broad of Trustees, The Caedmon School, New York City; Adjunct Lecturer, New York University. Published Works: Author of *Decade of Shocks* 1983, *The Phony War* 1982, *Edith and Woodrow* 1981, *The Day America Crashed* 1979, plus Several Books for Children; Producer of Television Documentaries and Fictional Programs for ABC, CBS, NBC, PBS, Syndication, Local Stations, Government, and Industry. Honors and Awards: Shubert Fellow, 1966; Golden Gate Award, San Francisco Film Festival, 1972; Three Gold Awards, Atlanta and Virgin Island Festivals, 1972-75; One Silver and Two Gold Awards, New York International Film and Television Festival, 1972-75; Six New York Area "Emmy" Awards, 1972-77; New York State Broadcasters Award; Catholic Broadcasters Award; and others. Address: 12 West Tenth Street, New York, New York 10011.■

Pauline Marie Shafer

Executive. Personal: Born March 21, 1925; Daughter of E. Paul and Ethel M. Dilling (deceased); Married Oscar F. Shafer; Mother of Bonita Marie, Byron Douglas. Education: B.S. Accounting, Indiana University of Pennsylvania, 1945. Career: President, P. & S. Developments, Inc.; Former Positions Include Secretary/Comptroller Oscar F. Shafer, Inc.; Treasurer/Comptroller, Cumberland Construction Company and R.S.E, Inc; Owner/Operator Mercury Accounting Service; Officer Manager, Eastern Overall Cleaning Company; Payroll Supervisor, Armstrong Cork Company. Organizational Memberships: Home Builders Association Auxiliary, Local President 1956-64 and 1977, State President 1962-63, National President 1964, Executive Committee 1959, Board of Directors 1959. Community Activities: Public Relations Chairperson, Service to Others Club, 1975; Developmental Disabilities Advocacy Network, Board of Directors, Executive Committee 1980 to present; Association for Children and Adults with Learning Disabilities, Local Secretary 1979-81, State Parliamentarian 1980-81, Treasurer 1982 to present; Cumberland Valley Citizens Curriculum Committee, Member 1976-78 and 1980, Treasurer 1982; President, Marysville Civic Club, 1970-72; President,

Silver Spring Women's Club, 1976-78; President, Birthright of Central Pennsylvania, 1979-81; Land Use Committee, League of Women Voters, 1976-78; Republican Club. Religion: Ordained Elder, United Presbyterian Church, 1977 to present; Member Session Silver Spring Presbyterian Church, 1977-81; Clerk of Session, 1980-81; Presbiterial of Presbyterian Church, Lesson Coordinator, 1980 to present; Commissioner to Presbytery of Carlisle, 1978; Various Presbytery Committees. Honors and Awards: Listed in *Who's Who of America* and Various other "Who's Who" Publications. Address: 43 Green Ridge Road, Mechanicsburg, Pennsylvania 17055.■

HOWARD JEFFREY SHAFFER

Psychologist. Personal: Born September 1, 1948. Education: B.A. Psychology, University of New Hampshire, 1970; M.S. 1972, Ph.D. 1974 Psychology, University of Miami; Licensed as Qualified Psychologist in Commonwealth of Massachusetts, State of New Hampshire, by National Register of Health Care Providers in Psychology. Career: Adjunct Faculty, University of Miami, 1974; Clinical Faculty, Barry College, Miami Shores, Florida, 1974-75; Field Faculty, Lone Mountain College, San Francisco, 1974-75; Teaching Consultant, University of Lowell, Massachusetts, 1975-76; Clinical Associate Professor, Boston University, Department of Counseling Psychology, 1976-78; Instructor in Psychology, Department of Psychiatry, Harvard Medical School, Cambridge Hospital, 1978-81; Faculty, Massachusetts Psychological Center, 1980 to present; Assistant Professor of Psychology in the Department of Psychiatry, Harvard Medical School, Cambridge Hospital, 1982 to present; Advisory Board and Faculty, Northeastern Comprehensive Service Institute, Danvers, Massachusetts, 1983; Research Director, Fellowship House, Psycho-Social Rehabilitation Center of Dade County, Inc., 1974-75; Clinical Director, Project Turnabout, Inc., Bingham, Massachusetts, 1975-78; Clinical Director, East Boston Drug Rehabilitation Clinic, East Boston, Massachusetts, 1976-77; Director, Special Consultation and Treatment Program for Women, Judge Gould Institute of Human Resources, Inc., Worcester, Massachusetts, 1977-78; Director, Drug Problems Resource Center, Department of Psychiatry, Harvard Medical School, Cambridge Hospital, North Charles Foundation for Training and Research, 1978-82; Council on Marijuana and Health, National Organization for the Reform of Marijuana Laws, 1981 to present; Coordinator of Psychiatric Education, Department of Psychiatry, Harvard Medical School, Cambridge Hospital, 1982 to present; Chief Psychologist, North Charles Institute for the Addictions, 1982 to present; Editorial Review Boards, *Journal of Psychoactive Drugs, Advances in Alcohol and Substance Abuse, Journal of Substance Abuse Treatment*; Associate Editor, *Bulletin of the Society of Psychologists in Addictive Behaviors*. Organizational Memberships: American Academy of Political and Social Sciences, 1975-77; American Psychological Association; American Association for the Advancement of Science; Society of Psychologists in Addictive Behaviors; Boston Computer Society. Published Works: Author of Articles "The Primary Prevention of Smoking Onset: An Inoculation Approach", *Journal of Psychoactive Drugs* 1983, "Drug History and Diagnosis: Some Unexpected Sex Differences", *Bulletin of Psychologists in Addictive Behaviors* 1983, "The Use of Contingency Contracts to Alter Self-Cutting in a Chronic Psychiatric Patient", *Journal of Psychiatric Treatment and Evaluation* 1983, and others; Author of Books *Myths and Realities: A Book About Drug Issues* 1977, *Classic Contributions in the Addictions* 1981. Honors and Awards: Psi Chi, 1968; First Place, University of New Hampshire Undergraduate Conference for Psychological Research, 1969; H.A. Carroll Award, University of New Hampshire, Department of Psychology, 1970; Phi Kappa Phi, University of Miami, 1974; Listed in *Who's Who in Frontier Science and Technology, Who's Who in the East, Personalities in America, Men of Achievement, Community Leaders of the World, Biographical Roll of Honor, Directory of Distinguished Americans*. Address: 171 Summer Street, Andover, Massachusetts 01810.■

NANDKUMAR S. SHAH

Chief of Research Services. Personal: Born May 6, 1928; Son of Shankarlal H. and Parvatiben Shah (deceased); Married Neeta N.; Father of Anita. Education: B.Sc. with honors 1953 and 1954, M.Sc. 1955, Poona University, India; Ph.D., University of Florida, Gainesville, Florida, 1965. Career: Chief Research Services, William S. Hall Psychiatric Institute, 1982 to present; Adjunct Professor, Department of Pharmacology, University of South Carolina School of Medicine, 1978 to present; Research Professor, Department of Neuropsychiatry and Behavioral Science, University of South Carolina School of Medicine, 1978 to present; Clinical Associate Professor, Department of Neuropsychiatry, University of South Carolina School of Medicine, 1975-78; Chief, Ensor Research Laboratory, William S. Hall Psychiatric Institute, Columbia, South Carolina, 1970 to present; Supernumerary Research Cadre Officer, Department of Pharmacology, Medical College, Baroda, India, 1968-70; Medical Research Associate III (Pharmacologist), Chief, Psychopharmacological Radioisotope Laboratory, Thudichum Psychiatric Research Laboratory, Galesburg, Illinois, 1965-67. Organizational Memberships: American Society for Pharmacology and Experimental Therapeutics; International Society for Neurochemistry; American Society for Neurochemistry; Society of Biological Psychiatry; The Division of Drug Metablism of the American Society for Pharmacology and Experimental Therapeutics; Association of Physiologists and Pharmacologists of India; The Society of Neuroscience; The South Carolina Academy of Sciences. Honors and Awards: Travel Award from the American Society for Pharmacolgy and Experimental Therapeutics to present a Paper at the 6th International Congress of Pharmacology, Helsinki, Finland, 1975; Travel Award from the American Society for Pharmacology and Experimental Therapeutics to present a Paper at the 7th International Congress of Pharmacology, Paris, France, 1978; Full Award to attend Workshop at the University of Colorado, Boulder, Colorado, from the National Institute of General Medical Sciences, 1980. Address: 2600 Quail Hollow Lane, West Columbia, South Carolina 29169.■

SHIRISH K. SHAH

College Professor and Department Chairperson. Personal: Born May 24, 1942; Son of Sushilaben and Kalyanbhai T. Shah; Married Kathleen Long; Father of Lawrence. Education: B.S. Chemistry and Physics, Gujarat University; St. Xavier's College; Ph.D. Physical Chemistry, University of Delaware, Newark, 1968; Additional Studies at Johns Hopkins University, Cornell University, University of Minnesota and Virginia Polytechnic Institute and State University. Career: Chairperson Computer Systems and Engineering Technologies and Professor of Science 1982 to present, Chairperson Technical Studies 1979-82, Associate Professor of Mathematics and Science and Coordinator of Academic Program Development 1976-79, Community College of Baltimore, Baltimore, Maryland; Associate Professor of Science and Coordinator of Vocational Program 1972-76, Assistant Professor of Science 1968-72, Chesapeake College; Director of Quality Control, Vita Foods, Inc., 1968-72. Organizational Memberships: Maryland Association of Community and Junior Colleges 1978-83, Vice President 1978, President 1979 to present; A.T.E.A., Life Member 1981 to present; American Vocational Association; Sigma Xi; Life Fellow, American Biographical Institute, 1984. Community Activities: Baltimore City's Adult Education Advisory Committee, Member 1982 to present, Chairperson Program and Development Committee; Back River Advisory Committee, Member 1981 (joint appointment by Mayor Schaffer and County Executive Mr. Hutchinson); Lung Association of Maryland, 1970-80; Chairperson Environmental Affairs Committee, 1979-80; President's Republican Task Force, 1982 to present. Religion: Catholic; Cathedral Mary Our Queen, Member Budget Committee 1983; St. Ignitius Church, Baltimore, Member Alpha Forum 1976-78. Honors and Awards: Nominated by Community College of Baltimore for Award as Outstanding Chemistry Professor, 1981; Nominated by Community College of Baltimore for Fellowship with the American Education Council as Faculty Member Most Likely to be a Successful Administrator, 1979; Nominated by Community College of Baltimore Harbor Campus as Outstanding Faculty Member, 1977; Nominated by Chesapeake College as an Outstanding Educator, 1972; Received Funds for Urban Transportation Program, 1980-81; Recieved C.E.T.A. Grant for Electronics, 1979-80; Received Grant for Food Technology Program, 1977-78. Address: 5605 Purlington Way, Baltimore, Maryland 21212.■

JAMES CURTIS SHAKE

Retired Associate Professor of Piano and Administrative Assistant. Personal: Born March 27, 1918; Son of Dr. Clarence A. and Clara J. Shake (both deceased); Married Cornelia Hughes; Father of James Curtis Jr., Thomas Hughes. Education: B.M., DePauw University, 1940; M.M., Eastman School of Music, 1941; Ph.D., Syracuse University, 1957. Career: Associate Professor of Piano and Administrative Assistant, School of Music, Syracuse University; Piano Teacher, Arthur Jordan Conservatory, Indianapolis, Indiana; Assistant Professor, West Virginia Wesleyan College, Buckhannon, West Virginia. Organizational Memberships: Phi Mu Alpha, Provincial Governor, 1962-70; Pi Kappa Lambda, Founder Local Chapter and First President, 1968-71; American Guild of Organists, Dean Local, 1974-76. Community Activities: Acting Assistant Dean for Music, 1971-72; Victorian Society in America, Local Founder and President 1978-80; Fischer Scholarship Fund, Director 1979-82; United Way at Syracuse University, 1950-83. Religion: Organist, St. Mark's Episcopal Church, 1953-59; St. Alban's Episcopal Church, Organist 1959-79, Vestryman 1979-82. Address: 1029 Westcott Street, Syracuse, New York 13210.■

ERWIN EMMANUEL SHALOWITZ

Government Official. Education: B.C.E., M.A. Public Administration. Military: Served in the United States Naval Reserve to Engineering Officer and Commanding Officer of Destroyer. Career: Government Official, Chief of Contract Support, General Services Administration; Former Chief Structural Research Engineer, Head Defense Research Section, Project Officer and Technical Advisor for Atomic Tests, U.S. Navy Department; Former Supervisor General Engineer, Special

TWO THOUSAND NOTABLE AMERICANS

Assistant for Protective Construction Programs, Project Manager for Building Systems, Chief Research Branch, Chief of Management Formation, Chief of Contracting Procedures, Chief of Contact Support, General Services Administration. Honors and Awards: Listed in *Who's Who in the South and Southwest, Who's Who in America, Who's Who in the World, Personalities of the South, Personalities of America, Notable Americans, Dictionary of International Biography, Who's Who in Government, Who's Who in American Jewry, Who's Who in World Jewry, Who's Who in Technology Today.* Address: 5603 Huntington Parkway, Bethesda, Maryland 20814.■

JAFAR SHARIF EMAMI

Personal: Born September 8, 1910; Son of Mohamed Hossein and Banu Kobra; Married Eshrat Moazami; Father of Shirin Gill, Simin Moazimi, Ali Sharif Emami. Education: Attended Deutsch Gewerbeschule and Sharaf, Teheram; Eisenbahn Zentralschurl, Technikum, Germany, 1929; Statens Tekniska Skolan, Sweden, 1939. Career: President, Third Constitutional Assembly, 1969; Chairman of the Board, Industrial and Mining Development Bank, 1964-78; Deputy Custodian, Pahlavi Foundation, 1962-78; Vice President, Red Lion and Sun Society, 1963-78; Member Board of Trustees, Pahlari University, National University, Aria Mehr Technological University. Community Activities: Iranian State Railways, Joined 1931, Technical Deputy General Director 1942; Managing Director, Independent Irrigation Corporation, 1946-50; General Director, State Railways, 1950; Minister of Roads and Communications, 1950-51; Member High Council and Managing Director Plan Organization, 1952-55; Senator from Teheran, 1955-57; Minister of Industries and Mines, 1957-60; Prime Minister, 1960-61, 1978; President of Senate, 1963-68. Honors and Awards: Dr.h.c., Seul University; Recipient 10 Iranian and 24 Foreign Decorations; President of 22nd International Conference of the Red Cross, 1963; President, Iranian Association of Engineers, 1966-78; President, International Banker's Association, 1975; Life Member, American Society of Civil Engineers, 1979. Address: 425 East 58th Street, New York, New York 10022.■

PAUL WILLIAM SHARKEY

Professor of Philosophy and Religion. Personal: Born March 22, 1945; Son of Paul R. Sharkey; Married Karen Kristine (Efker); Father of Erin Kathleen. Education: B.A. with high honors, California State University at Los Angeles, 1969; Ph.D., University of Notre Dame, 1973; Postdoctoral Research, Fuller Theological Seminary and University of California at Berkeley. Military: Served in the United States Navy, 1968-69. Career: Professor of Philosophy and Religion, Chairman Department of Philosophy and Religion, University of Southern Mississippi, Hattiesburg. Organizational Memberships: American Philosophical Association; Mississippi Philosophical Association, 1980-81; Institute for Advanced Philosophical Research, National Board of Advisors; Institute for Comparative Political and Economic Systems, Academic Advisory Board. Community Activities: Mississippi Committee for the Humanities, Scholar, Consultant, Evaluator; Philosopher in Residence, Forrest General Hospital and Hospice Planning Board. Religion: St. Thomas Aquinas Catholic Church, Lay Minister, Director of Adult Education, Newman Advisor. Honors and Awards: Excellence in Teaching Award, University of Southern Mississippi, 1979-80; Listed in *International Who's Who in Education.* Address: 128 Lakeside Drive, Hattiesburg, Mississippi 39401.■

GWENDOLYN IDELL SHAROFF

Educator. Personal: Born July 16, 1940, in Houston, Texas; Daughter of Leroy Lawrence and Harriett Idell (Galbreath) Anderson; Married Michael, June 20, 1970. Education: B.A., Baylor University, 1962; M.A., Baylor University at Dallas Theater Center, 1963; Ph.D., University of Southern California, 1981. Career: Teacher, Victoria (Texas) High School, 1963-64; Director, Galveston (Texas) Teen-Children's Theatre, 1964-66; Assistant Professor Speech and Drama, Director Theatre, Culver-Stockton College, Canton, Missouri, 1966-69; Instructor in Speech and Drama, Costumer, Bradley University, Peoria, Illinois, 1969-70; Production Supervisor, Studio Company, Academy Dramatic Art, Oakland University, Rochester, Michigan, 1970-71; Instructor Theatre, Fullerton (California) Junior College 1971-72; Cypress College 1971-73; California State College, San Bernardino, Instructor Theatre 1972-73, Lecturer Speech and Drama 1976-78; Assistant Professor Communications, Chapman College, Orange California, 1973-76; Lecturer Theatre, Saddleback College, Mission Viejo, 1978-79; Lecturer Theatre, Fullerton College, Fullerton, 1980 to present; Director, Fullerton College Children's Theatre, 1981 to present. Organizational Memberships: Speech Communication Association; A.N.T.A.; American Theatre Association; Chairman Region VIII Network for Women; Southern California Educational Theatre Association, Editor *Theatre of Focus*, Executive Secretary, Advisory Council; Alpha Lambda Delta; Alpha Chi; Tau Beta Sigma; Alpha Psi Omega; Pi Alpha Lambda, Parliamentarian, Historian; Theta Alpha Phi; Fullerton Alumni Chapter, Mu Phi Epsilon. Published Works: Contributor Book Reviews to Professional Journals. Honors and Awards: Winner of First University-College Theatre Association (of A.T.A.) Dissertation Award, 1982. Address: 2032 Victoria Drive, Fullerton, California 92631.■

SHARON BARTS SHARP

Deputy Director for Marketing. Personal: Born October 7, 1939; Daughter of Edwin and Gertrude Barts; Married Donald L. Sharp, Son of Claude (deceased) and Rita Sharp; Mother of Laura Sue, Christopher (Kip). Career: Deputy Director for Marketing, Illinois State Department of Commerce and Community Affairs, 1984 to present; Special Assistant to the Governor of the State of Illinois on Women, 1979-84; Government and Political Writer, 1974-78; Elected Elk Grove Township Clerk, 1977-79; Editor, *Elk Grove Township News*, 1975-77; Editor, Illinois Federation of Republican Women News, Views and Issues, 1977-78. Community Activities: Honorary Co-Chairperson, ERA Illinois, 1979 to present; Illinois Displaced Homemaker Advisory Board, 1980 to present; Director, LifeSpan, 1979 to present; League of Women Voters; Arlington Heights Friends of the Library; Altrusa, 1952-82; Chicago Area Public Affairs Group; The City Club, Chicago; Advisory Committee, Harper College Women's Program, 1980 to present; Friends of Harper College; Executive Club of Chicago; Women in Management; Support Chicago; Northwestern University Women's Community Advisory Committee, 1982 to present; Former Member, Illinois Community College Board; Former Advisor, Elk Grove Township Mental Health Committee; 1978 Republican Nominee to Illinois Secretary of State's Office (first woman to ever win a major statewide nomination); Co-Chairman, Republican Central Committee of Cook County, 1975 to present; Chairman, Women's Division, Republican Central Committee of Cook County, 1975; Chairman, Republican Cook County Search Committee; Director, Illinois Federation of Republican Women, 1975 to present; President, Women's National Republican Club, 1980-83; Illinois Women's Political Caucus; Republican Women's Task Force; 12th Congressional District Women's Republican Club; Former Elk Grove Township Committeewoman; Former President, Republican Women of Elk Grove Township; Chairman, Cook County Republican Candidate Committee; Chairman, Cook County Republican Reorganization Committee; Cook County Republican Executive Committee; Co-Founder, Republican Women for ERA, 1979. Honors and Awards: Subject of Harper College Political Science Film "Female Political Candidate" 1978; Subject of Public Television Film "The Political Woman" 1977; Charlotte Danstrom Women of Achievement Award, Northwest Suburban Chapter, Women in Management, 1982; Phi Theta Kappa Community College National Honors Society; Listed in *Who's Who of American Community Colleges, Who's Who of American Politics, Who's Who of American Women.* Address: 1306 West Cedar Lane, Arlington Heights, Illinois 60005.■

JAMES P. SHAVER

Professor, Associate Dean. Personal: Born October 19, 1933; Son of G. C. Shaver; Married Bonnie R. Pehrson; Father of Kim, Jay, Guy. Education: B.A., University of Washington, 1955; A.M.T. 1957, Ed.D. 1961, Harvard University. Career: Professor and Associate Dean of Research, Utah State University; Research Associate and Instructor, Harvard Graduate School of Education; Visiting Professor, University of Washington, Harvard University; Director, Social Studies Curriculum Center, The Ohio State University; Teacher, Peter Bulkeley Junior High School, Concord, Massachusetts, Roy High School, Sky View High School, Utah. Organizational Memberships: American Educational Research Association; National Council for the Social Studies, President 1976; American Association for the Advancement of Science; American Association of University Professors. Community Activities: National Commission on Educational Policy, Advisor 1965-67; Far West Laboratory for Educational Research and Development, Executive Panel 1970-74; American Bar Association Advisory Committee on Youth Education for Citizenship, 1975-81; Utah Commission for Law and Citizenship, 1978-83; Project '87 Education Committee, 1981 to present. Honors and Awards: Phi Beta Kappa; Faculty Honor Lecturer in the Humanities and Social Studies, Utah State University, 1972; Utah Council for Social Studies Outstanding University Service and Teaching Award, 1975, 1978; National Council for the Social Studies Citation for Exemplary Research in Social Studies Education, 1977. Address: P.O. Box 176, Hyrum, Utah 84319.■

ANDREW SHAW, JR.

Dean of Administration, Administrator. Personal: Born September 14, 1931; Son of Andrew (deceased) and Mary Shaw; Married Viola Mihalski; Father of Linda, Nancy, Robert. Education: Graduate of Plains (Pennsylvania) High School, 1949; B.S. Social Science, Wilkes College, 1958; M.S. Government Administration, Wharton Graduate School, University of Pennsylvania, 1960; M.P.A. 1976, D.P.A. 1978, Nova University. Military: Served in the United States Army, 1951-53. Career: Administrative Aide, City of Philadelphia, 1960; Transportation Researcher, Pennsylvania Economy League, Inc., 1972-74; Executive Director, Economy League, Lehigh Valley Branch, 1964-67; Branch Coordinator, Central D Division, Pennsylvania Economy League, 1967-68; Director of Research 1968-72, Director of Institute of Regional Affairs 1972 to present, Wilkes College; Dean of Management, Wilkes College, 1972 to present; Director of Small Business Center, Professor of Political Science, Wilkes College. Organizational Memberships: Governmental Research Association, United States and Canada; American Society of Public Administration, President N.E.P.A. Chapter; American Academy of Political and Social Science; Council on Basic Education; American Management Association; American Political Science Association; National Council of University Research Administrators. Community Activities: Susquehanna River Basin Association, President 1976-77, Treasurer 1978 to present; Wilkes-Barre Chamber of Commerce, Executive Committee; Downtown Development Company, Board Member Wilkes-Barre Industrial Development Authority, Advisory Board; Icaraus Energy Research Institute, Board Member; United Health and Hospital Association, Finance Committee; Economic Development Council/N.E.P.A., Finance Committee; Wyoming Valley United Way, Health Services Committee; Rotary Club of Wilkes-Barre, Chairman Vocational Committee, Education Committee; Susquehanna S.E.S. Project Committee, Advisory Group to Nuclear Steam Electric Plant; Wilkes-Barre Young Men's Christian Association, Board Member, Finance Committee; Pennsylvania Mountains Council/Boy Scouts of America, Financial Vice President; Pennsylvania Institute of Municipal Management, Chairman; Luzerne County Chairman of Labor/Management Committee; Pennsylvania County Commissioners Advisory Committee. Honors and Awards: Distinguished Pennsylvanian, 1978, Ben Franklin Club, Philadelphia; Citation for Service, Civil Defense Preparedness Agency, 1973; Distinguished Service Award, University of Pennsylvania, Fels Institute of State and Local Governments; Honorary Member, Association of Pennsylvania Municipal Managers; Listed in *Community Leaders of America, Who's Who in the East*. Address: 30 Peartree Lane, Dallas, Pennsylvania 18612.■

IMARA SHAW

Health Executive, Television Producer and Writer. Personal: Born January 4, 1946; Daughter of Mr. and Mrs. C. G. Leland; Married Stephen (deceased). Education: Attended Pasadena City College, 1965; American Saint Hill Organization, 1977-78. Career: Research Director, Hertz Lion, Beverly Hills, California, 1963-64; Fashion Model, Nina Blanchard, Los Angeles, California, 1964-65; Fashion Model, Model Service Agency, New York City, 1965-67; Director, Shelton Health Club, New York City, 1967-68; Communications Specialist, Hubbard Research Foundation Mediterranean, 1968-69; Technical Consultant, Beverly Hills Health Club, Beverly Hills, California, 1970-71; Manager, Shaw Health Centers, Reseda and Los Angeles, California, 1971-76; Chairman of the Board, Shaw Management Corporation, Los Angeles, California, 1976-82; Health and Management and Communications Consultant, 1977-82; Writer and Producer, "Feeling Good" Television Show, Los Angeles, California, 1981-82. Organizational Memberships: Board of Directors, Right Track; Board of Directors, Thomas Paine Institute for Human Action; Associate of Foundation for Advancement in Science and Education; Delphian Foundation; National Association of Women Business Owners; National Association for Female Executives; National Health Federation; Women's Health Network; Womens' Referral Service; Public Relations Society of America; Book Publicists of Southern California; Publicity Club of Los Angeles; Producers and Associates of Public Access; Direct Marketing Creative Guild; Los Angeles Area Chamber of Commerce; Hollywood Chamber of Commerce. Community Activities: Big Sisters of Los Angeles; Alliance for Survival; National Forrestry Association; Sierra Club; Audubon Society; Cousteau Society; Green Peace; National Wildlife Federation; Defenders of Wildlife; National Vivisection Society; Vegetarian Society International; Vegetarian Society of America; National Hygiene Society. Honors and Awards: Listed in *Who's Who in California, Who's Who in the West, Who's Who in America, Directory of Distinguished Americans, Personalities of America, Community Leaders of America, Dictionary of International Biography*. Address: 909 Via Coronel, Palos Verdes Estates, California 90274.■

LARRY DON SHAW

State Representative. Personal: Born January 29, 1953; Son of Larry and Bertie Shaw. Education: B.S. Agriculture Education, Texas Tech University, Lubbock, Texas, 1975. Career: Farmer, 1975 to present; Texas State Representative, 1980 to present. Organizational Memberships: Texas Farm Bureau and Texas Farmers Union, 1975 to present; Environmental Affairs Committee and Election Committee, 1981-82; Steering Committee House Democratic Caucus, Texas House of Representatives, 1983-84; Vice Chairman, Liquor Regulations Committee, County Affairs Committee and Consent and Calendar Committee, Texas House of Representatives. Community Activities: American Business Club; Kiwanis Club; Board of Directors, Big Spring Symphony Association; Cultural Affairs Council; Chamber of Commerce; Advisory Council, West Texas Children's Home; Board of Directors, Permian Basin Regional Planning Commission; Advisory Committee, Southwest Collegiate Institute for the Deaf, 1980 to present; Texas Delegate to the National Conference of State Legislators on Low-Level Nuclear Waste Disposal. Religion: Member First Baptist Church, Big Spring, Texas. Honors and Awards: Outstanding Young Man of America, 1981-83; Distinguished Service Award, Vocational Agriculture Teachers Association, 1983; Man of the Year in Agriculture Award, Texas County Agriculture Agents Association, 1983; Outstanding Young Man Award, Jaycees, 1984; Listed in *Who's Who in American Politics, Personalities of the South*. Address: 1307 Barnes, Big Spring, Texas 79720.■

WILLIAM JAMES SHAW

Psychologist and Assistant Professor of Psychiatry. Personal: Born March 11, 1947; Son of Mrs. William Shaw, Belleville, New Jersey; Married Catherine Jarvis. Education: Intern Certificate, University of Oklahoma Health Sciences Center, 1976; Doctor of Psychology, Baylor University, 1972-76; M.A.; Fairfield University, 1975; B.A., Iona College, 1968. Career: Psychologist, Assistant Professor of Psychiatry; Chief Psychologist and Director of Psychological Services, Oklahoma Department of Corrections, 1978-81; Private Practice, 1977-81; Graduate School, 1972-76; Teacher, Football Coach Bergen Catholic High School, Oradell, New Jersey, 1971-72; Teacher, Coach, Iona School, New Rochelle, New York, 1968-71. Organizational Memberships: American Psychological Association, Division 12, 18, 31, 1977 to present; Oklahoma Psychological Association 1976 to present, Board Member 1977-79, Treasurer 1979-81, Membership Chairperson 1977-79; Southwestern Psychological Association, 1976 to present, Chairman Publications Committee 1977-79; Association for the Advancement of Psychology 1977 to present, Nominee for Board of Trustees 1983; Society for Adolescent Medicine, 1982 to present; American Academy of Behavioral Medicine, 1981 to present; Society for Behavioral Medicine, 1981 to present; American Correctional Association, 1979-81; American Association of Correctional Psychologists, 1979-81. Community Activities: Oklahoma State Board of Examiners of Psychologists, Member 1979-82, Chairperson 1981-82 (appointed by Governor); Oklahoma Mental Health Association, 1977 to present; Parents Anonymous Child Abuse Program Volunteer, 1976-78; Oklahoma Breast Cancer Rehabilitation Network Volunteer, 1977-78; Financial Supporter of Oklahoma Medical Research Foundation, Baylor University, University of the South, St. Jude's Childrens Research Center, Heart Association. Religion: Member, Congregation of Christian Brothers, 1964-72. Honors and Awards: Distinguished Public Service Award, American Psychological Association, Division 18, 1979; Certificate of Appreciation, American Trial Lawyers Association, 1981; Diplomate, American Academy of Behavioral Medicine, 1981; National Merit Letter, 1964; New Jersey Scholarship, 1964; Listed in *Marquis Who's Who in the South and Southwest, National Register of Health Service Providers*. Address: 1506 Northwest 88th Street, Oklahoma City, Oklahoma 73114.■

CHARLES E. SHEARER, JR.

Lawyer, Financial Planner. Personal: Born September 2, 1922; Son of Charles E. and Helen L. Shearer; Married Ruth Mae Nicholson; Father of Kay Ellen Shearer Gardiner, Beth Ann Shearer Gould. Education: A.S., Kokomo Junior College, 1943; A.B., Indiana University, 1947; J.D., Indiana University School of Law, 1953. Military: Served in the United States Army, 1943-46, attaining the rank of Sergeant; Served in the United States Army Reserve, 1946-55, attaining the rank of Lieutenant. Career: Lawyer, Financial Planner; Former Positions include Industrial Relations Consultant, International Harvester; Personnel Director, Indianapolis Railways; Manager, Chamber of Commerce, Shelbyville, Indiana; Law Partnership, Supervisor, L. W. McDougal, Cleveland; Division Manager, Sales, College Life, Indianapolis; Senior Vice President, Export-Import, Bank of the United States. Organizational Memberships: District of Columbia Bar Association; Indiana Bar Association; Supreme Court of the United States; National Association of Life Underwriters; Chartered Life Underwriter. Community Activities: United States Jaycees, Past State President, National Vice President, President; United States Jaycee Foundation, Chairman of the Board 1980-82; Metropolitan Washington Young Men's Christian Association, Board Member, Vice Chairman 1982-83, Chairman 1984-85. Religion: Episcopalian. Honors and Awards: Y-Red Triangle Award, 1981; Named One of Three Outstanding Young Men in Indiana. Address: 6101 Walhonding, Bethesda, Maryland 20816.■

RUTH EASTER SHEARER

College Professor. Personal: Born April 3, 1920; Daughter of Dr. and Mrs. A. R. Mansberger (both deceased); Married Dr. Richard E. Shearer; Mother of Patricia Wilson, Suzanne Jones, Richard Judson. Education: B.A., Western Maryland College, 1941; M.Ed., University of Pittsburgh, 1943; Ed.D., Columbia University, 1963. Career: Professor of Education and Psychology, Alderson Broaddus College; Former High School Teacher of Latin, English, French. Organizational Memberships: Delta Kappa Gamma; Pi Lambda Theta; Kappa Delta Pi; Association of Teacher Educators. Religion: Executive Board, West Virginia Baptist Convention. Honors and Awards: West Virginia Mother of the Year, 1974; Mary Ward Lewis Prize, Awarded at the Undergraduate Level to the Outstanding Graduating Woman, 1941; Listed in *Who's Who of American Women, Who's Who in the East, Who's Who in the South and Southwest, Who's Who in American Education, World Who's Who of Women, Personalities of the South, Notable Americans, Outstanding Educators of America, Dictionary of International Biography, Leaders in Education.* Address: Alderson Broaddus College, Philippi, West Virginia 26416.■

CARRIE McDONALD SHEDD

Educator, Religious Worker, Community Developer. Personal: Born November 15, 1932; Daughter of Oscar L. (deceased) and Carrie B. Howell McDonald; Married Charles Clifton Shedd; Mother of Gwendolyn D. Todd-Dean, Vivian F. Ferguson-Sanders. Education: B.S. Elementary Education 1954, M.S. Educational Administration-Supervision 1961, Ph.D. Studies in Educational Administration-Curriculum Foundations 1970-71, Additional Studies 1959, 1962-63, Summers of 1964, 1965, 1969, all in Colleges in States of Alabama, Florida, New Jersey, Tennessee, and Ohio. Career: Teacher-Educator; Free Lance Writer; Served in Positions of College Registrar, Coordinator of Cooperative Education, College Instructor in Education Courses; Field Work with Clients Residing in Rural Regions of Southern Part of the United States. Organizational Memberships: National Education Association, 1954-70; United Teaching Profession, 1972; Parent-Teacher Association, 1954-70; Association for School Curriculum and Development, 1952-72; National Council of Collegiate Deans and Registrars, 1961-63; United Nations Association of the United States of America, 1972-74; Cooperative Education Association, 1979-80; John Dewey Society, 1972-74; National Council of Administrative Women in Education, 1962-64; Student Member, American Association of Higher Education, 1970-73; National Association of Women Deans and Counselors, 1962-64; President, Tuskegee Institute Chapter of American Association of University Professors, 1966; American Association of University Women, 1962-70; Society of Professors of Education, 1972-74; American Personnel and Guidance Association, 6 Branches, 1962-72. Community Activities: Blood Donor; Cotton Picker and Assistant Coordinator of Teacher-Educators in T.I.C.E.P. Program of the Office of Economic Opportunity; Brownie and Intermediate Girl Scout Leader, Coordinator, Poinsettia Neighborhood Girl Scouts; Participated with and Made Contributions to the United Fund, National Association for the Advancement of Colored People, and U.N.I.C.E.F. Fund Drives; Served with the Montgomery Improvement Association, 1956-58; Y-Teens and Young Women's Christian Association, 1948-50, 1950-54, 1972-75; Order of Eastern Star; Daughter of Isis; Co-Organizer (with husband) of Recreational Park's Little League and Adult Softball Club, 1967-70; League of Women Voters, 1963, 1967, Human Relations Council 1963, 1967; Recorder, International Women's Conference Economic Session, 1980; Women's Auxiliary of Catholic Hospital, 1974-76; Veterans Administration Hospital Volunteer, 1948-50, 1981 to present; Co-Organizer of Mobile Home Garden Club, 1983; Helped Promote Reading Interests among Religious Groups through Ministerial Guidance on Release of J. Allan Petersen's Book, *The Myth of the Greener Grass.* Religion: Vacation Bible School Teacher 1952, 1970, Adult Sunday School Teacher 1972-75, Church Steward, Secretary and Committee Member on Outreach and Evangelism; Completed Several Bible Courses and Conducted Two Seminar Sessions on "Women in Biblical Literature," 1981 and 1983. Honors and Awards: Achievements Recognized in Local Publications including "Help Your Child Learn How to Learn," *Essence Magazine* 1973, "Let's Resolve: For All the World's Children, A Childhood," *Tuskegee News* 1984, "Writer Cites Need for Master Teacher (Fulfilling an Obligation of 'Our Noblesse Oblige')" *Tuskegee News* 1982; "Republican Era to Make A Difference," *Tuskegee News* 1981, "Women in Business: A Look to the Future," *Business Gazette* Spring 1981, "Ebonite Queen of America," *Campus Digest* 1983; Author, *An AKA's Poetic Leisure* (book of specialty poems), 1981; Alpha Kappa Mu; Kappa Delta Pi; Pi Lambda Theta; Listed in *Who's Who of American Women, World Who's Who of Women, International Register of Profiles, International Who's Who of Intellectuals.* Address: P.O. Box 516, Tuskegee Institute, Alabama 36088.■

WILLIAM B. SHEEDER

University Administrator. Personal: Born January 21, 1938; Son of Fred T. and Amy F. Sheeder; Married D. Gayle Holden; Father of Lynn Suzanne, Traci JoAnn. Education: Graduate of Elmira Free Academy, Elmira, New York, 1956; A.B. Philosophy, Ottawa University, 1960; M.A. Human Relations, Ohio University, 1966. Career: Ottawa University, Ottawa, Kansas, Student Manager 1958-59, Student Council President 1959-60, President of Kansas Conference Student Association 1959-60; Ohio University, Athens, Head Resident of Men's Residence Hall 1960-62, Part-time Instructor in Human Relations and Social Science 1961-65, Associate Director of Baker University Center 1962-64, Assistant to the Dean of the College of Arts and Sciences 1964-66; University of Miami, Coral Gables, Director of Whitten Memorial Student Union 1966-73, Director of Student Activities and Whitten Student Union 1968-73, Vice President and Secretary of University Rathskeller Inc. 1972 to present, Assistant Vice President for Student Affairs 1973 to present, Dean of Students 1976 to present. Organizational Memberships: Association of College Unions International, Member 1967 to present, Enrichment Chairman 1975 Conference Planning Committee and Co-Host Director; International Association of Auditorium Managers 1971-74; Wesley Foundation, Dade County, Florida, Board of Directors, Treasurer 1971-73, Chairman 1973-77, Member 1971 to present; Centre for Experimental Learning and Living, Inc., Consultant 1976; National Association of Student Personnel Administrators; National Orientation Directors Association; American Association for Higher Education; American Personnel and Guidance Association/American College Personnel Association. Religion: Work Area on Higher Education and Campus Ministry, Florida Conference Council on Ministries of the United Methodist Church, 1976-80, 1981-84. Published Works: "Role Playing as a Method of Selecting Dormitory Counselors," 1963; "A Framework for Student Development in Higher Education," 1974; Introduction to *Guide to the Best, Most Popular and Most Exciting Colleges* 1982. Honors and Awards: Sigma Alpha Honor Society; Omicron Delta Kappa; Phi Delta Kappa; Orange Key, Leadership Recognition Society; Order of the Golden Leaf; Phi Kappa Epsilon, Outstanding Administrator Award and Honorary Member; Phi Mu Alpha; Faculty Honor Roll, Ohio University, 1965-66; Faculty Fellows Citation, Ohio University, 1965-66; Honorary Member, Federation of Cuban Students, University of Miami; Adjunct Brother, Zeta Beta Tau, 1971 to present; Listed in *Community Leaders of America, Community Leaders and Noteworthy Americans, Directory of Distinguished Americans, Dictionary of International Biography, International Who's Who in Community Service, International Who's Who of Intellectuals, Men of Achievement, Men of Distinction, Notable Americans, Outstanding Young Men of America, Personalities of America, Personalities of the South, Two Thousand Men of Achievement, Who's Who Among Students in American Colleges and Universities, Who's Who in the South and Southwest.* Address: 8315 Southwest 72 Avenue #301B, Miami, Florida 33143.■

RALPH ALBERT SHEETZ

Attorney. Personal: Born June 13, 1908, Halifax Township, Pennsylvania; Son of Harry Wesley and Manora Enders Sheetz; Married Ruth Lorraine Bender, May 19, 1938; Father of Ralph Bert. Education: Graduate with honors, East Pennsboro Township High School, 1926; Attended the University of California-Berkeley, Summer 1928; Ph.B., Dickinson College, Carlisle, Pennsylvania, 1930; Attended the University of Michigan School of Law, Summer 1932; LL.B., University of Alabama School of Law, 1933; J.D., University School of Law, 1969. Career: Admitted to Practice Law before the Supreme Court of Alabama 1933, Supreme Court of Pennsylvania 1934, Superior Court of Pennsylvania 1938, United States District Court for the Middle District of Pennsylvania 1944, Others; Solicitor, Peoples Bank of Enola (Pennsylvania), 40 Years; Selective Service Official for Appeal, Area #4, Pennsylvania, 1941; Attorney from Employees Loan Society, 1966-76. Organizational Memberships: American Bar Association; Pennsylvania Bar Association; Dauphin County Bar Association; Cumberland County Bar Association; Farrah Law Society, University School of Law. Community Activities: Perry Lodge #458, Free and Accepted Masons of Pennsylvania, Master Mason 1930, Worshipful Master 1971, Elected to represent Perry Lodge in Grand Lodge of Pennsylvania 1972; Harrisburg Masonic School of Instructions, Board of Directors; General Alumni Association, Dickinson College, Life Member; Harrisburg Forest #43, Tall Cedars of Lebanon, Drill Team Member 1934-44, Selected to Play Part of Prince Azariah in Pro-Logue and Royal Court at Ceremonials 1943, Life Membership for Muscular Dystrophy, Historian 1976 to present; Harrisburg Consistory, 32nd Degree, Ancient Accepted Scottish Rite; Zembo Temple, Ancient Arabic Order of Nobles of Mystic Shrine; Zembo Shrine Luncheon Club; York and Cumberland County Shrine Clubs; Harrisburg Council #499, Royal Arcanum, Regent 1952, Presided over Meeting of Executive Committee of Supreme Council of Royal Arcanum for United States and Canada 1952, Elected to Represent Harrisburg Council at Session of Grand Council of Royal Arcanum of Pennsylvania 1952, Committee on Laws, Chairman of Grand Council on Laws, Distinguished Service Member, Elected to Membership in Keystone Circle #3; East Pennsboro Township Republican Club; West Shore Twilight Baseball League, Umpire; East Pennsboro Township, Solicitor 1937-53, Assistant Solicitor 10 Years, Member of Planning Commission 3 Years, Vice Chairman, Chairman, Zoning Commission, Board of Adjustments Chairman; Royal Arch Mason in Perseverance Royal Arch Chapter #21, Most Excellent High Priest, Elected to Serve in Grand Holy Royal Arch Chapter of Pennsylvania; Harrisburg Council #7 Royal and Select Masters, Thrice Illustrious Master; Order of the Temple, Pilgrim Commandery #11, Knights Templar of Pennsylvania, Commander; Enola Boys Club, Incorporator 1950, Attorney, Treasurer; Harrisburg Chamber of Commerce; East Pennsboro Township Parent-Teacher Association, President 1951-53; Citizens Fire Company #1, Enola, Incorporator 1951, Honorary Member, Attorney; Order of Penn Priary #6, Knights of York Cross of Honour; East Pennsboro Township Senior Citizens Century Club, Charter Member 1979. Religion: United Methodist Church. Honors and Awards: Inducted into The Golden 50's Club, University of Alabama, 1983; Represented the University of Alabama at the Inauguration of Walter Consuelo Langsam as 8th President of Gettysburg College, 1952; Fifty Year Masonic Service Emblem, Grand Lodge of Pennsylvania and Certificate of Congratulations, Perry Lodge #458, Free and Accepted Masons; Past High Priest's Certificate, Perseverance Chapter #21; Red Ribbon Certificate of Eminent Commander, Order of the Temple, Pilgrim Commandery; Speaker, Dedication of New Highway between Overview and Marysville, Pennsylvania, 1938; Resolution by Senator Edwin S. Bower, 1945; Pin, Medal and Badge, Headquarters for Selective Service, Commonwealth of Pennsylvania, 1946; Order of the Silver Trowel, Council of Anointed Kings of the Commonwealth of Pennsylvania, 1948; Numerous Certificates of Recognition and Appreciation; Listed in *Dictionary of International Biography, National Society Directory, Who's Who in American Law, International Who's Who of Intellectuals, Book of Honor.* Address: 798 Valley Street, Enola, Pennsylvania 17025.■

VIOLET MAE SHEH

Journalist. Personal: Born June 3, 1919, in Prince Rupert, British Columbia, Canada; Daughter of Mr. and Mrs. Mah Bon Quen; Married Kenneth Sheh, February 19, 1948; Mother of Cheryl Irene de Haan, Douglas Wayne, Kenneth Warren. Education: Attended the Mun Yew School of Chinese Studies, Toishan, Kwangtung, South China, 1935-39. Career: Journalist; Social and Consumer Columnist and General Reporter, *Richmond Review,* 1967-72; Retired 1972. Organizational Memberships: Former Member, Media Club of Canada; Life Fellow, International Biographical Association. Published Works: Author Series of Articles for *Chinatown News* in Vancouver; Author Articles on Trips to Fiji, Peru and Argentina. Honors and Awards: Listed in *International Register of Profiles, World Who's Who of Women, Dictionary of International Biography, International Who's Who of Intellectuals, International Who's Who in Community Service, Men and Women of Distinction, Who's Who of American Women, Who's Who in the Commonwealth.* Address: 10251 Aintree Crescent, Richmond, British Columbia, Canada V7A 3T9.■

MARC LESLIE SHEINBEIN

Clinical Psychologist. Personal: Born December 11, 1945; Son of Isadore and Gloria Sheinbein; Married Andrea Merle Riff; Father of Amy Michelle, David Benjamin. Education: B.A., Vanderbilt University, 1967; M.A., University of Tennessee, 1969; Ph.D., University of Tennessee, 1972; Doctoral Internship, University of Oklahoma Medical School, 1971-72. Career: Clinical Psychologist in Private Practice, 1975 to present; Assistant Professor, University of Texas Health Sciences Center at Dallas, 1972-75. Organizational Memberships: American Psychological Association; Dallas Psychological Association; American Association of Marriage and Family Therapists; Dallas Association of Marriage and Family Therapists, Secretary 1980-82, Vice President 1984-85. Published Works: Author Numerous Professional Articles, Papers and Psychological Tests. Honors and Awards: Publisher's Prize in Psychology, Southwestern Psychological Association, 1972. Address: 8734 Clover Meadow, Dallas, Texas 75243.■

VICKI SHELL

Personnel and Training Manager. Personal: Born July 4, 1947; Mother of One Son. Education: B.S. cum laude 1968, M.A. 1969, M.A. (plus 30 hours) 1972, Murray State University; Ph.D., The Ohio State University, 1979. Career: Personnel and Training Manager, Ohio River Steel Corporation, Calvert City, Kentucky, 1983 to present; Training Director, Airco Carbide, Louisville, Kentucky, 1982-83; Safety and Training Manager, Airco Carbide, Calvert City, Kentucky, 1981-82; Coordinator of Special Activities, Department of Industrial Education, Murray State University, 1978-81; Research Associate, Interstate Curriculum Consortium, The Ohio State University, 1976-78; Distributive Education Coordinator and D.E.C.A. Advisor, Murray Area Vocational Education Center, 1972-76; Distributive Education Coordinator and D.E.C.A Advisor, North Marshall High School, 1969-71; Teaching Assistant, Murray State University, 1968-69. Organizational Memberships: American Industrial Arts Association, Convention Exhibitor; American Council in Industrial Arts Teacher Education; Kentucky Industrial Education Association; Epsilon Pi Tau; National Association of Distributive Education Teachers, Past National Secretary-Treasurer, Past Member National Public Relations Committee, Past Chairman National Nominating Committee, Past State Membership Chairman, Life Member; American Vocational Association, Member House of Delegates, Presenter for Distributive Education Sessions, Past Member Advisory Committee for Member Benefits, Member and Recorder for Distributive Education Sessions, Past Member Advisory Committee for Member Benefits, Member and Recorder for Distributive Education Policy and Planning Committee 1976-78; Kentucky Vocational Association, Past Vice President, Past Member State Nominating Committee, Past Distributive Education Membership Chairman, Presenter at Distributive Education Sessions; Distributive Education Clubs of America, Central Region Conference Consultant, Kentucky D.E.C.A. Board of Directors, Kentucky Constitution Committee, Kentucky Summer Camp Instructor, Chief Advisor for National Conference Area of Distribution Event, Ohio Fall Delegates Conference Judge, Ohio State Conference Judge; Council for Distributive Teacher Educators; Kentucky Association of Distributive Education Teachers, Past State President, Regional Secretary, Vice President; Phi Delta Kappa; American Vocational Education Research Association; American Educational Research Association; Parent-Teacher Association, Field Day Committee Chairman, President Murray, Kentucky. Community Activities: Murray Woman's Club, Kappa Department Past Treasurer and Parliamentarian; Murray Swim Team, Swim Meet Timer and Line Judge; Charity Ball, Murray, Kentucky, Past Decorations, Publicity and Food Committees; Murray Country Club, Past Social Chairman; Children's Hospital Fund Drive, Volunteer for Muirfield Golf Tournament; Murray-Calloway County Swim Team Board, 1981-84; Chairperson, First District Parent-Teacher Association Committee, 1981-82. Religion: First United Methodist Church, Hannah Circle, Past Treasurer, Bible School Teacher. Published Works; *Machine Shop State-of-the-Art Report* 1981; Number of Reports and Articles. Honors and Awards: Outstanding Young Woman of Kentucky, 1980; Kentucky Board of Occupational Education Appointed Member of Advisory Committee to Area Vocational Education; Selected as Member of Advisory Committee on Eligibility and Accreditation for United States Department of Health, Education and Welfare, 1975-78; Outstanding Distributive Education Teacher of Kentucky, 1975; Favorite Teacher of North Marshall High School, 1971; Listed in *Outstanding Young Women of America, Personalities of the South, Who's Who Among Students in American Colleges and Universities, Community Leaders of America.* Address: 1528 Oxford Drive, Murray, Kentucky 42071.■

BESSIE ELIZABETH SHELTON

Educator. Personal: Daughter of Robert (deceased) and Bessie P. Shelton. Education: B.A., West Virginia State College, 1958; M.S., State University of New York, 1960; Diploma, Universal Schools, 1971; Diploma, North American School of Travel, 1972; Diploma, Nashville School of Songwriting, 1975; Additional Study at Northwestern University, University of Virginia, Virginia Western College. Military: Served with the United States Navy, Personnelman 1951-55, Member of Great Lakes and WAVE Choirs. Career: Young Adult Librarian, Brooklyn Public Library; Assistant Head, Central Reference Division, Circulation Librarian, Art and Music Librarian, Queensborough Public Library, Jamaica, New York; Educator/Education Media Specialist, Lynchburg (Virginia) Public School System; Educator/Educational Media Associate, Board of Education of Allegany County. Organizational Memberships: National Education Association; Maryland State Teachers Association; Allegany County Teachers Association; American Association of Creative Artists; Intercontinental Biographical Association; American Biographical Institute Research Association; International Entertainers Guild; Vocal Artists of America, Lifetime Member; Clover International Poetry Association, Lifetime Danae Member; American Association of University Women; National Association for Female Executives; American Biographical Institute National Board of Advisors; International Platform Association; National Women's Hall of Fame; American Association for Women Deans, Counselors and Administrators. Community Activities: Guest Vocal Artist in Community and School Musical Programs; Brooklyn Philharmonia Choral Society; Fine Arts Center Chorus, Lynchburg; Community Chorus, Tri-State Community Concert Association; Young Women's Christian Association, Ethnic Studies Committee; Research Specialist for Educational Projects; Judge for Talent Competitions. Religion: Church Soloist, Choir Member, Youth Counselor. Honors and Awards: Certificate of Merit for Service as Soloist, U.S.N.T.C., Great Lakes, Illinois, 1951; Scholarship Award, 1957; Pi Delta Phi, President Beta Pi Chapter; Sigma Delta Pi; Certificate of Merit for Service to College Band as Majorette, West Virginia State College, 1958; B.A. with honors; First Prize Talent Award, 1969; Sweetheart of the Day, Radio Station WLVA, September 13, 1973; Listed in *Achievers International Record, Community Leaders and Noteworthy Americans, Community Leaders of America, Dictionary of International Biography, Five Thousand Personalities of the World, International Book of Honor, International Scholars Directory, International Who's Who in Community*

TWO THOUSAND NOTABLE AMERICANS

Service, International Who's Who of Intellectuals, Men and Women of Distinction, Notable Americans of the Bicentennial Era, Outstanding Americans (Bicentennial Edition), Outstanding Educators of America, Personalities of America, Personalities of the South, Who's Who Among Students in American Universities and Colleges, Who's Who in Library Service, Who's Who in the East, Who's Who in the South and Southwest, Who's Who of American Women, World Who's Who of Women. Address: P.O. Box 187, Cumberland, Maryland 21502.■

SANDRA MARY SHELTON

Medical Supplies Company Executive. Personal: Born September 6, 1943, in Knoxville, Tennessee; Daughter of Claude Earl and Mary Jane Eblen Hudson; Married John E. Shelton, February 17, 1973; Mother of Ingrid, David. Education: B.S. in Health Education, University of Tennessee at Knoxville, 1967. Career: Community Health Representative, Health and Welfare Division, Metropolitan Life Insurance Company, New York City, 1968; District Manager, Statistical Research Division, Research Triangle Institute, Research Triangle Park, North Carolina, 1973-75; Sales Representative, Lederle Pharmaceuticals Division, American Cyanamid Company, Pearl River, New York, 1975; with Mallinckrodt Inc., St. Louis (1975 to present), Southeast Regional Manager of Diagnostic Division 1981, Product Manager 1981 to present. Organizational Memberships: Society of Nuclear Medicine. Honors and Awards: Listed in *Who's Who in the South and Southwest.* Address: P.O. Box 12596, Creve Coeur, Missouri 63141.■

C. A. (NEIL) SHEPHERD, JR.

University Administrator. Personal: Born March 30, 1923, in Birmingham, Alabama; Son of Cornelious Alston Sr. and Reba Webb Shepherd; Married Betty Sue Garner, July 11, 1950; Father of Susanne Elizabeth, Jacquline Yvonne. Education: Graduate, Woodlawn High School (Birmingham, Alabama); Attended Auburn University; B.S., Howard College, 1948; J.D., Cumberland School of Law, Samford University, 1966. Military: Served in the United States Air Force, attaining the rank of First Lieutenant. Career: Director of Alumni Affairs, Samford University. Organizational Memberships: Alabama College Public Relations Association; American Association of University Administrators; Council for Advancement and Support of Education; Alpha Kappa Psi; Alpha Phi Omega; Kappa Delta Pi; Kappa Phi Kappa; Omicron Delta Kappa, Faculty Secretary 1976-81; Pi Gamma Mu; Phi Delta Kappa; Phi Delta Chi; Sigma Delta Kappa; Tau Kappa Alpha; 14th Air Force Association; Military Order of Foreign Wars of the U.S.; The Military Order of World Wars, Commander 1977-78; The Order of Lafayette. Community Activities: Shades Valley Rotary Club, Member 1968-80, Chairman Rotaract Committee 1972, 1973, 1974, 1975, 1976 and 1977, Club Director 1973, Club Treasurer 1977, District 686 Rotaract Chairman 1974 and 1979; Vestavia Hills Rotary Club, Member 1980 to present; Chairman, Samford University United Way Drive, 1975, 1976, 1977, 1978, 1979, 1980, 1981, 1982; Chairman, College and University Division, United Way, 1982; Chairman, Class of 1941 Woodlawn High School 40th Reunion; Homewood Chamber of Commerce, Vice President 1981, President 1982; American-Korean Cultural Foundation Advisory Board; American Cancer Society, Homewood Unit, President 1982; East Lake Lodge #480, Free & Accepted Masons; East Lake Chapter #154, R.A.M.; East Lake Council #80 R. & S.M.; East Lake Commandery #43 Knights Templar; Zamora Temple; National Sojourners Inc.; Sons of Confederate Veterans; Sons of the American Revolution, Vice President Birmingham Chapter 1978, President Birmingham Chapter 1979 and 1980, Vice President State Society 1980 and 1981, Senior Vice President State Society 1982; The Society of Colonial Wars of the State of Alabama, Secretary 1979, 1980 and 1981, Lieutenant Governor 1981, Deputy Governor 1982; National Society of Magna Charta Barons; Alabama Genealogical Society, Director 1980-82; Birmingham Genealogical Society, Vice President 1979-80, President 1980-81; National Society Sons and Daughters of the Pilgrims; St. Andrews Society of the Mid South; The Filson Club, Jamestown Society; Pi Kappa Alpha; Birmingham Monday Morning Quarterback Club; Birmingham Tip Off Club; Aircraft Owners and Pilots Association; Civil Air Patrol, Alabama Wing, Major; Birmingham Aero Club; Silver Wings Fraternity; International B-24 Liberator Club; The Confederate Air Force; Alabama Heart Association; Alabama Baptist Historical Association; Newcomen Society of North America; Religious Heritage of America; Sloss Furnace Association; The Birmingham Historical Society; The Birmingham-Jefferson Historical Society; The Executives Club of Birmingham, Vice President 1978-79, President 1979-80; American Aviation Historical Society. Religion: Member Ruhama Baptist Church, 1935-68 (Chairman Finance Committee, Deacon, Training Union Director); Member Vestavia Hills Baptist Church, 1968 to present (Chairman of Trustees, Executive Board Member to the Birmingham Baptist Association, 1977-82, Finance Committee 1978 & 1979, Sunday School Director, Deacon 1978-80 & 1982. Honors and Awards: Distinguished Flying Cross; American Campaign Medal; Asiatic-Pacific Medal; World War II Victory Medal; Good Conduct Medal; The China Medal; Cross of Military Service, United Daughters of the Confederacy, 1977; Woodlawn High School Hall of Fame, 1979; Civil Air Patrol, Alabama Wing, Meritorious Service Award, Grover Loeing Aerospace Award, Paul E. Garber Award; Listed in *Who's Who Among Students in American Universities and Colleges, Men of Achievement, Outstanding Educators of America, Personalities of the South, The Hereditary Register of the United States of America, Who's Who in Flying, Who's Who in the South and Southwest.* Address: 909 Southridge Drive, Birmingham, Alabama 35216.■

RONALD J. SHEPPARD

Market Development Executive. Personal: Born April 13, 1939; Son of Mr. and Mrs. Lester Sheppard; Married Shirley C.; Father of Jeffrey Brandon, Mark Justin. Education: B.S. Physics, Rensselaer Polytechnic Institute, 1961; M.S. 1962, Ph.D. 1965, Howard University; M.B.A., Rochester Institute of Technology, 1974; Course Work Toward Juris Doctor. Career: Manager Market Development, Imperial Clevite, Inc.; Director Strategy Analysis, Strategic Planning Department, General Motors Corporation; Former Positions include Product Planning Manager, Ford Motor Company; Group Program Manager, Xerox Corporation; Director, Space Sciences Laboratory, Teledyne Brown Engineering; Principal Consultant, Booz Allen Hamilton, Inc. Organizational Memberships: Engineering Society of Detroit; Detroit Economics Club; New Detroit, Inc. Community Activities: Rotary Club; Torch Club International; Rochester (New York) Montessori School, President Board of Directors; Jaycees; Shriner; Accounting Aid Society, Board of Directors. Honors and Awards: K. B. Weisman Human Relations Award, 1955, 1957; Harry Diamond Laboratories Graduate Student Award, 1963; Lawrence Institute of Technology, Community Service Award, 1980; Listed in *Personalities of the South, Men of Achievement.* Address: 19521 Burlington Drive, Detroit, Michigan 48203.■

THOMAS ALEXANDER SHERARD, JR.

Civil Engineer, Administrator. Personal: Born June 23, 1954; Son of Thomas A. and Olivia H. Sherard. Education: B.S.C.E., Clemson University, 1976. Career: Distribution Engineer, Supervisor of Properties Development, Duke Power Company, 1981 to present; Former Positions with Duke Power include Junior Engineer (Anderson, South Carolina) 1976-78, Assistant Distribution Engineer (Charlotte, North Carolina) 1978-81. Organizational Memberships: American Water Works Association, 1976-81; South Carolina Pollution Control Association, 1976-81; American Society of Civil Engineers, 1976 to present; National Society of Professional Engineers, 1976 to present. Community Activities: Young Life Leader, 1972-75; Boy Scouts of America, Unit Commissioner 1980-81, Assistant District Commissioner 1982 to present; Junior Achievement, Free Enterprise (Volunteer), 1982 to present. Religion: Presbyterian. Honors and Awards: Commissioner of the Year, Boy Scouts of America, 1982; Listed in *Biographical Roll of Honor, Who's Who in the South and Southwest, Personalities of the South, Personalities of America, Directory of Distinguished Americans.* Address: 937 Sardis Cove Drive, Matthews, North Carolina 28105.■

JOSEPH ANTHONY SHERMA

Professor. Personal: Born March 2, 1934, in Newark, New Jersey; Married Anita, Daughter of Mrs. A. Sture; Father of Karen Ann, James Joseph. Education: B.S, Upsala College, 1955; Ph.D., Rutgers University, 1958. Career: Joined Staff of Lafayette College 1958, Present Position Charles A. Dana Professor of Chemistry; Summer Positions in field with Harold Strain at Argonne National Laboratory, with James Fritz at Iowa State University, with Gunter Zweig at Syracuse University Research Corporation, with Joseph Touchstone at the Hospital of the University of Pennsylvania, with Brian Bidlingmeyer at Waters Associates and with Thomas Beesley at Whatman Inc. Organizational Memberships: American Chemical Society; Sigma Xi; Phi Lambda Upsilon; Society of Applied Spectroscopy; American Institute of Chemists, Life Fellow; American Association of University Professors. Published Works: Co-Author Volumes I and II of *CRC Handbook of Chromatography*, a Book on Paper Chromatography and 6 Volumes of Series *Analytical Methods for Pesticides and Plant Growth Regulators*;

Numerous Other Professional Publications. Honors and Awards: 2 Awards for Superior Teaching, Lafayette College; Distinguished Alumnus Award, Upsala College, 1979; Listed in *Who's Who in American Education, Who's Who in the East, American Men and Women of Science, Men of Achievement, Outstanding Educators of America, Personalities of America, Directory of Distinguished Americans.* Address: 1736 Millard Street, Bethlehem, Pennsylvania 18017.■

A. ROBERT SHERMAN

Professor of Psychology and Clinical Psychologist. Personal: Born November 18, 1942; Son of Mr. and Mrs. David R. Sherman; Married Llana Helene; Father of Jonathan Colbert, Relissa Anne. Education: B.A., Columbia University, 1964; M.S. 1966, Ph.D. 1969, Yale University. Career: Professor of Psychology, University of California at Santa Barbara; Psychologist in Private Practice; Psychological Consultant; Author. Organizational Memberships: American Psychological Association; American Association of University Professors, Chapter President for University of California at Santa Barbara 1978-79; Association for the Advancement of Behavior Therapy; Phi Beta Kappa, Chapter Treasurer 1971-74, Chapter Vice President 1975-77, Chapter President 1977-78 for University of California at Santa Barbara; Behavior Therapy and Research Society; Santa Barbara Area Psychological Association, President-Elect 1984; Psi Chi National Honor Society in Psychology, Chapter Faculty Advisor at University of California at Santa Barbara 1979 to present. Community Activities: Santa Barbara Mental Health Association, Board of Directors 1972-78 and 1981 to present, Chairman of Education Committee 1973-77, Executive Committee 1974-78 and 1984, First Vice President 1975-77, President 1978 and 1984; Mountain View School Site Council of Goleta Union School District, Council Member 1978 to present; Santa Barbara Continuing Education Advisory Council, Member 1979-83, Curriculum Committee 1979-83. Honors and Awards: Elected to Phi Beta Kappa, Columbia University, 1963; National Institutes of Mental Health Predoctoral Research Fellow, Yale University, 1964-69; Elected to Sigma Xi, Yale University, 1967; Received Research Grants, University of California at Santa Barbara, 1969-77; Received Faculty Fellowship, University of California at Santa Barbara, 1971; Received Research Grants from Exxon Education Foundation, 1973-76; Elected to Psi Chi, University of California at Santa Barbara, 1979; Listed in *Who's Who in the West, American Men and Women of Science, Contemporary Authors,* and Many Other Reference Works. Address: 961 Crown Avenue, Santa Barbara, California 93111.■

JEROME KALMAN SHERMAN

Professor of Anatomy. Personal: Born August 14, 1925; Son of Beatrice Sherman; Married Hildegard; Father of Karen, Marc, Keith. Education: A.B. Biology, Brown University, 1947; M.S. Biology, Case Western Reserve University, 1949; Ph.D. Zoology, University of Iowa, 1945. Military: Served in the United States Navy, 1943-46, Retired. Career: Research Associate in Urology, University of Iowa, 1952-54; Research Associate, American Foundation Biological Research, Madison, Wisconsin, 1954-58; Assistant Professor 1958-62, Associate Professor 1962-67, Professor of Anatomy, University of Arkansas College of Medicine, 1967 to present. Organizational Memberships: Society for Cryobiology, Charter Member, Editorial Board 1964-66; American Association of Tissue Banks, Charter Member, Board of Governors, Chairman Reproductive Council, 1976 to present; American Society of Zoology; American Association of Anatomists; American Physiological Society; Society Cryosurgery (honorary); Sigma Xi, Chapter President 1976. Community Activities: Arkansas Science Fair, Regional Director; Lion's Club, President; Great Decisions Discussion Leader; Young Men's Christian Association; Amelia Ives Day Care Center, Chairman Advisory Board; Men's Club, Vice President; E.O.A. Advisory Board Chairman; Boy Scouts of America, District Commissioner, Explorer Division District Chairman, Advisor, National Committeeman; Arkansas Eye and Kidney Bank, Board Member; N.C.C.J. Discussion Leader; Brown University National Alumni Schools Program, Area Chairman. Religion: Agudah Achim Synagogue, Board of Trustees; Temple B'nai Israel, Board of Governors, Board of Trustees, Program Chairman; National Jewish Committee, Boy Scouts of America. Honors and Awards: Lederle Medical Faculty Award, 1961-64; Fulbright Senior Research Award, University of Munich, 1965-66; Special Chair Professorship, Taiwan (Republic of China); National Chung Hsing University, National Science Council Award; National Shofar Award, Boy Scouts of America, 1978. Address: 3012 North Grant, Little Rock, Arkansas 72207.■

WILLIAM FARRAR SHERMAN

Lawyer, State Representative. Personal: Born September 12, 1937; Son of L. F. and Nancy Sherman; Married Carole Lynn Williams, Daughter of Millard Richardson; Father of John Farrar, Anna Katherine, Lucy Alden. Education: B.A. History, University of Arkansas, 1960; LL.B., University of Virginia, 1964. Military: Served in the United States Army, 1960-61; State Judge Advocate, Arkansas National Guard, 1981 to present. Career: Partner in Law Firm, Jacoway & Sherman; Arkansas Securities Commissioner, 1969-71; Assistant U.S. Attorney, Eastern District of Arkansas, 1966-69. Organizational Memberships: Pulaski County Bar Association; Arkansas Bar Association; American Bar Association; Arkansas Bar Foundation. Community Activities: Elected to Arkansas House of Representatives 1974, Re-elected to 5th term 1982; Elected to Arkansas Constitutional Convention; 1979; Law and Justice Committee, National Conference of State Legislatures; Sustaining Board of Advisors, Young Democrats of Arkansas; Liberal Arts Planning Council, University of Arkansas at Little Rock. Religion: First United Methodist Church. Address: 450 Midland, Little Rock, Arkansas 72205.■

SOL SHERRY

Distinguished Professor and Department Chairman. Personal: Born December 8, 1916; Son of Hyman and Ada Sherry (both deceased); Married Dorothy Sitzman; Father of Judith Ann McNelis, Richard Leslie. Education: B.A., New York University, 1935; M.D., New York University School of Medicine, 1939. Military: Served in the United States Air Force Medical Corp, Captain and Flight Surgeon, 1942-46. Career: Distinguished Professor and Chairman Department of Medicine, Temple University; Assistant Professor of Medicine, New York University; Director Medicine, Jewish Hospital of St. Louis; Professor and Co-Chairman, Department of Medicine, Washington University, St. Louis; Director, Thrombosis Research Center, Temple University. Organizational Memberships: Phi Beta Kappa; Alpha Omega Alpha; Sigma Xi, President Washington University Chapter 1962-63; American Physiological Society; American Society for Clinical Investigation; Association of American Physicians; Central Society for Clinical Research, Council 1962-64; Society for Experimental Biology and Medicine; Harvey Society; American Association for the Advancement of Science, Fellow; American College of Physicians, Master; American College of Cardiology, Fellow; American Therapeutic Society; American College of Clinical Pharmacology and Chemotherapy, Board of Regents 1965-67; Philadelphia College of Physicians; International Society on Thrombosis and Haemostasis, Council Chairman 1970-76, President 1975-77; International Society of Cardiology, Chairman Scientific Council on Thrombosis 1972-76; Association of Professors of Medicine, Councillor 1973-75, President-elect 1975-76, President 1976-77; Federated Council of Internal Medicine, Council 1975-78; Southeast Pennsylvania Chapter American Heart Association, President-elect 1977-78, President 1978-79; Association of Program Directors of Internal Medicine, Council 1978-81; American College of Angiology, Fellow; American Medical Association. Community Activities: Active in National Institute of Health, National Academy of Sciences National Research Concil, Veterans Administration, American National Red Cross, American Heart Association, International Committee on Haemostasis and Thrombosis; Office of the Surgeon General, Consultant to United States Army and Development Command 1964-69, Emeritus Consultant 1969 to present; Appointments to the New York University Alumni Awards Committee 1968 to present, Medical Advisory Board of Life Insurance Medical Research Fund 1970, Committee on Awards of American College of Physicians 1970-73, Board of Directors of Component Therapy Institute 1969-73; Judge of Cochems Competition of the University of Colorado 1962-73, Panel on Blood Diseases, National Heart, Blood Vessel, Lung and Blood Program of the National Heart Lung Institute 1972-73, Chairman Policy Board Anturane Reinfarction Trail, Honorary Degree Committee of Temple University 1975-79, Board of Trustees of Tott's Gap Research Institute 1978 to present, Pennsylvania Liaison Council of Internal Medicine 1978 to present. Honors and Awards: United States Army Typhus Commission Medal, 1945; Career Research Award, National

Institutes of Health, 1962-67; Modern Medicine Achievement Award, 1963; Distinguished Alumni Citation, New York University School of Medicine, 1966; Scientific Achievement Award, New York University School of Medicine, 1967; John Phillips Memorial Award, American College of Physicians, 1968; Franz M. Groedel Founder's Medal, American College of Cardiology, 1971; Outstanding Educator of America Award, 1972; Robert P. Grant Medal, International Society on Thrombosis and Haemostasis, 1977; Festschrift, Thrombosis and Haemostasis, Volume 38 December, 1977; Master, American College of Physicians, 1978; Julius B. Frankel Honorary Award, Department of Medicine, University of Chicago, 1978; Fellow, Royal College of Physicians, London, 1980; Honorary Doctor of Science, Temple University, 1980; Faculty Research Award, Temple University, 1980; Distinguished Professor, Temple University, 1983; Scientific Councils Distinguished Achievement Award, American Heart Association, 1983; Gold Medal Award, Pharmacia and Kabi Pharmaceutical Firms, 1983. Address: 408 Sprague Road, Narberth, Pennsylvania 19072.■

BRUCE ELDON SHERTZER

University Education Professor. Personal: Born January 11, 1928; Son of Edwin F. Shertzer (deceased); Married Carol M.; Father of Sarah, Mark. Education: B.S. 1948-52, M.S. 1952-53, Ed.D. 1953-58, Indiana University. Military: Served in the United States Army as Sergeant, 1946-48. Career: Professor of Education, Purdue University; Indiana State Director of Guidance, 1956-58; School District Director of Guidance, 1954-56; School Counselor, Secondary School Teacher, 1953-54. Organizational Memberships: Indiana Personnel and Guidance Association, President 1962-63; Association of Counselor Educators and Supervisors, President 1971-72; American Association for Counseling and Development, President 1973-74. Community Activities: National Advisory Council for Career Education, Chairman 1975-76, Member; State Advisory Committee for Indiana Division of Guidance, 1981 to present. Honors and Awards: Fulbright Senior Lecturer, Reading University, England, 1967-68; Listed in *Who's Who in America, Who's Who in the Midwest, Contemporary Authors, Men of Distinction*. Address: 1620 Western Drive, West Lafayette, Indiana 47906.■

JAMES EDWARD SHIFFLETT, JR.

Project Systems Analyst. Personal: Born July 23, 1950; Son of James Edward and Joyce Lee Shifflett. Education: B.S.A.E, University of Virginia, 1972; M.S.M.E., Princeton University, 1975; M.B.A. Finance, Washington University-St. Louis, 1980; M.S.C.S. (in progress), the Johns Hopkins University. Career: Project Systems Analyst, Bendix Corporation, 1982 to present; Program Manager, Harris Corporation, 1981-82; Systems Analyst, Gould, Inc., 1980-81; Engineer, McDonnell-Douglas Corporation, 1975-80. Organizational Memberships: Operations Research Society of America; The Institute of Management Sciences; International Platform Association. Community Activities: Toastmasters Club, President, Treasurer; Common Cause, Coordinator. Religion: Baptist. Honors and Awards: Scholarship and Grant, University of Virginia; Dean's List, High Honors, University of Virginia; National Honor Society; Listed in *Who's Who in the Midwest, Dictionary of International Biography, Who's Who of Intellectuals, Personalities of the West and Midwest, Men of Achievement, Who's Who in Finance and Industry, Biographical Roll of Honor, Who's Who on the Frontier of Science and Technology, International Who's Who of Contemporary Achievement, Community Leaders of the World* (First Commemorative Issue). Address: 605 U.S. Route 250 By-Pass, Charlottesville, Virginia 22901.■

MAX SHIFFMAN

Professor Emeritus, Mathematician. Personal: Born October 30, 1914; Father of Bernard, David. Education: B.S., College of City of New York, 1935; M.S., New York University, 1936; Ph.D., New York University, 1938. Career: Instructor, College of City of New York and St. John's University; Consultant, United States Government; Mathematician and Associate Professor, New York University; Mathematician, George Washington University and Rand Corporation; Professor of Mathematics, California State University at Hayward and Stanford University; Professor Emeritus, California State University at Hayward; Mathematician and Owner, Mathematico. Organizational Memberships: American Mathematical Society; Society for Industrial and Applied Mathematics; Mathematical Association of America. Community Activities: Aided in the United States Cuban Crisis of 1962, 1963; Helped Aid Israel and Obtain Truce in Egyptian-Israeli Conflict, 1969-73; Helped United States Withdraw and Make Truce in Vietnam, 1972; Helped Found the Peace and Freedom Party, 1966-68; California Republican League; Republican Party; Suggested Increasing Higher Educational and Economic Opportunities for Underprivileged Groups, 1966; Research in Mathematics, 1938 to present. Honors and Awards: Bulmenthal Fellow, New York University, 1935-38; Award of Merit, Highest Civilian Award to the United States Navy, End of World War II; Speaker at Problems of Mathematics Conference on 2000th Anniversary of Founding of Princeton University, 1946, and at 100th Anniversary of Riemann's Doctoral Dissertation, 1951; Various Plaques and Certificates for Distinguished Achievement, 1976 to present. Number of Biographical Listings. Address: 16913 Meekland Avenue #7, Hayward, California 94541.■

ROBERT THOMAS SHIRCLIFF

Management Consultant. Personal: Born May 20, 1928; Son of Mr. and Mrs. T. M. Shircliff; Married Carol Reed; Father of Laura S. Howell, Elizabeth S. Education: Graduate of Culver Military Academy, 1946; B.S. Marketing, Indiana University, 1950. Military: Served in the United States Army Reserves, retiring with the rank of Captain in Military Intelligence. Career: President, Robert T. Shircliff and Associates, Inc.; President, Pepsi-Cola Allied Bottlers, Inc., 1963-73. Organizational Memberships: National Pepsi-Cola Bottlers Association, President 1970-71. Community Activities: Jacksonville Chamber of Commerce, President 1977; United Way of Jacksonville, President 1975; Jacksonville University Council, President 1972; Speech and Hearing Center, President 1970; Rotary Club of West Jacksonville, President 1969; Rotary International, District Governor 1976; Northeast Florida Red Cross, Chairman 1968; St. Vincents Medical Center Board, Vice Chairman 1982 to present; Order of Malta; Jacksonville University Trustee, Chairman 1980-83; Cummer Museum Foundation, Trustee. Honors and Awards: Chairman of the Board of Trustees, Jacksonville Community Foundation; Top Management Award, S.M.E.J., 1973; Brotherhood Award, National Conference of Christians and Jews, 1975. Address: 4918 Prince Edward Road, Jacksonville, Florida 32210.■

ROBERT M. SHIRILLA

Vice President of Strategic Planning. Personal: Born March 21, 1949; Son of Michael and Jayne Shirilla. Education: B.A. magna cum laude, University of California-Los Angeles, 1971; M.B.A. with honors, Harvard Business School, 1975; Graduate of the United States Army Infantry, Airborne and Intelligence Schools. Military: Served as Chairman of the Junior Officers Council, 82nd Airborne Division, United States Army; Rank of Major, Military Intelligence, Brigade Staff, United States Army Reserves, 1979 to present; Captain and Company Commander, United States Army Reserves, 1977-79; Captain, Senior Aide-de-Camp to Division Commander, United States Army Reserves, 1975-77; Graduate of U.S. Army Command and General Staff College. Career: Vice President, Crocker Bank, 1983 to present; Citicorp, Diners Club, Carte Blanche, Vice President of Strategic Planning 1982 to present, Director of Strategic Planning 1981; Norton Simon Inc., Hunt-Wesson, Senior Marketing Manager of Wesson Oil Products 1980-81; Senior Marketing Manager of Hunt Tomato Products 1979-80, Marketing Manager of Hunt Convenience Products 1978-79, Product Manager of New Product Development 1977-78; Assistant Product Manager, General Foods Corporation, 1975-77; Consultant, Boston Consulting Group Inc., Summer 1974. Organizational Memberships: International Platform Association; International Biographical Association; American Biographical Institute; World Affairs Council of Los Angeles; Academy of Political Science, New York City; Harvard Club of New York City and Southern California. Community Activities: Hugh O'Brien Youth Foundation, Chairman; Los Angeles Business School, Chairman; March of Dimes, Chairman Advisory Committee, Board of Directors, Executive Committee; Los Angeles Junior Chamber of Commerce, Board of Directors; Charity Foundation, Board of Directors; Golf Foundation, Board of Directors; Board of Directors, American Management Association. Honors and Awards: First on Commandant's List, United States Army Infantry School; Army Commendation Medal; Alpha Kappa Psi Scholarship Award; Army R.O.T.C. Scholarship Award; Member Nine National Honor Societies; Corning Fellowship; Outstanding Service Award, Workshop in Business Opportunities; Outstanding Junior Officer, United States Army Reserves; Outstanding Achievement Award, Reserve Officers Association, United States Army; Meritorious Service Medal; Listed in *Directory of Distinguished Americans, Personalities of America, Community Leaders of America, Who's Who in the West, International*

TWO THOUSAND NOTABLE AMERICANS

Book of Honor, International Who's Who, Personalities of the West and Midwest, International Men of Achievement, International Register of Profiles, Who's Who in Finance and Industry. Address: 2000 Broadwalk #1002, San Francisco, California 94115.∎

JOE E. SHIVELY

Educational Researcher and Developer. Personal: Born March 3, 1945; Son of Mr. and Mrs. Russell Shively; Married Linda Kay Davis; Father of Mark Allen, Brenda Elaine. Education: B.S. 1967, M.S. 1968, Ph.D. 1970, Purdue University. Organizational Memberships: American Education Research Association; American Psychological Association; National Council on Measurement in Education; Association for Educational Data Systems; National E.B.C.E. Association; Phi Delta Kappa. Community Activities: Cub Scouts, Advisory Committee Chairman, 1971-73; Midget League Football Advisory Committee, Vice President and Acting President, 1974-76; Band Boosters Club, 1979-82; Kanawha Valley Civitan Club, Charter Member 1981, Board of Directors 1982 to present. Honors and Awards: Vocational Rehabilitation Scholarship, 1963-67; Disney Scholarship, 1963-67; U.S.O.E. Undergraduate Research Fellow, 1966-67; Dean's List, 1967; Kappa Delta Pi, 1968; U.S.O.E. Graduate Educational Research Fellow, 1968-70; Kentucky Colonel, 1979; Listed in *Personalities of the South, Dictionary of International Biography, International Who's Who in Community Services, Men of Achievement, Notable Americans, Men and Women of Distinction, Community Leaders and Noteworthy Americans,* Others. Address: 513 Dabney Drive, Charleston, West Virginia 25314.∎

MOHAMED H. K. SHOKEIR

Professor and Department Head. Personal: Born July 2, 1938; Son of H. K. (deceased) and Lolia M. Kira Shokeir; Married Donna Jean Nugent; Father of Marc Omar, Vanessa May. Education: M.B.B.Ch., Faculty of Medicine, Cairo University; D.Ch. 1963, D.Ch. (Orth.) 1964, School of Postgraduate Studies, Cairo University; M.S. 1965, Ph.D. 1969, Horace H. Rackham School of Graduate Studies, University of Michigan. Career: Fulbright Research Scholar, University of Michigan; Queen Elizabeth II Scientist, University of Manitoba and Saskatchewan; Associate Professor of Pediatrics, Head, Section of Clinical Genetics, University of Manitoba; Professor of Pediatrics and Director, Division of Medical Genetics, University of Saskatchewan. Organizational Memberships: American Pediatric Society; Society of Pediatric Research; Canadian Society of Clinical Investigations, Councillor 1974-76; Canadian Pediatric Society, Nominating Committee 1980 to present; American Society of Human Genetics; Western Pediatric Society; Midwestern Society for Pediatric Research; Canadian Society of Immunology; Genetics Society of America and of Canada; New York Academy of Science. Community Activities: Canadian Association of University Teachers, Academic Freedom and Tenure Committee 1979 to present; Scouts Movement of Canada, Vice-Chairman Saskatoon 1975-78; Nuclear Energy Advisory Committee; University Review Committee, 1976-78. Honors and Awards: Fulbright Scholar, 1964-69; Queen ELizabeth II Scientist,1969-75; Medical Research Council Grantee, 1970-76; Hamdy Award for Distinguished Contribution to Medicine (Gold Medal); John Phillips Award for Internal Medicine (Gold Medal), 1960; Solomon Award for Internal Medicine (Gold Medal), 1960; H. B. Day Award for Medicine (Gold Medal), 1960; Basic Sciences Award (Gold Medal), 1957. Address: 108 Riel Crescent, Saskatoon, Saskatchewan, Canada S7J 2W6.∎

L. ZANE SHUCK

Corporate Executive. Education: B.S.M.E., West Virginia Institute of Technology, Montgomery, West Virginia, 1958; M.S.M.E. 1965, Ph.D. 1970, West Virginia University, Morgantown, West Virginia; Additional Studies at Iowa State University, Wayne State University, Massachusetts Institute of Technology. Career: President, Technology Development, Inc., 1980 to present; Adjunct Professor, West Virginia University College of Engineering, 1980 to present; Science Advisor to West Virginia Governor J. D. Rockefeller IV, 1978-80; Associate Director, Engineering Experiment Station and Professor Mechanical Engineering and Mechanics, West Virginia University, 1976-80; Science and Technology Coordinator, West Virginia Legislature, 1979-80; Supervisory Mechanical Engineer, Morgantown Energy Research Center, Morgantown, West Virginia, 1970-76; National Science Foundation Science Faculty Fellow and Research Engineer, West Virginia University, Morgantown, 1968-70; Associate Professor and Chairman of Mechanical Engineering Department, Acting Director of Engineering (part-time), West Virginia Institute of Technology, 1959-68; Sales Engineer, West Virginia Armature Company, Bluefield, West Virginia, 1958-59; Engineering Consultant (part-time) 1959-70, FMC Corporation (South Charleston, West Virginia), United Fuel Gas Company (Charleston, West Virginia), Southern Public Service Company (Montgomery, West Virginia), West Virginia Air Pollution Control Commission (Charleston, West Virginia), Stonestreet Oil and Gas Company (Spencer West Virginia), Gravely Tractor Division, Studebaker Corporation (Dunbar, West Virginia), presently Consultant to M.E.T.C., D.O.E., Mound Laboratories and Various Oil and Gas Companies. Organizational Memberships: Tau Bet Pi; Sigma Xi; State of West Virginia Coal and Energy Advisory Committee; Associate Editor, *A.S.M.E. Transactions Journal of Energy Resources Technology;* Editorial Board, *In Situ Journal;* Editor Second Underground Coal Gasification Symposium Proceedings; Editoral and Program Reviewer for S.P.E., A.S.M.E., N.S.F. and D.O.E.; Chairman, A.S.M.E. Emerging Technology Committee. Published Works: Author 58 Publications; Numerous Invited Lectures and Television Appearances; Holder of 15 Patents with Others Pending; Producer of Four Technical Films for United States Department of Energy. Honors and Awards: Recipient of Four Ford Foundation Fellowships, Massachusetts Institute of Technology; Two National Science Foundation Fellowships, Iowa State University and Wayne State University; Sabbatical, West Virginia Institute of Technology; National Science Foundation Science Faculty Fellowship, West Virginia University; A.S.T.M. Materials Testing Award, 1970; West Virginia Registerd Professional Engineer; Certified by National Council of Engineering Examiners; Ralph James National Award for Outstanding Technical Contributions, 1980; Ohio Registered Engineer, 1984 to present; Listed in *American Men and Women in Science, Who's Who in the East, Who's Who in the South and Southwest, Men of Achievement, Who's Who in Engineering, Who's Who in Technology Today, Leading Consultants in Technology, International Who's Who in Engineering.* Address: 401 Highview Place, Morgantown, West Virginia 26505.∎

CARLTON ROGER SHULKIN

Executive. Personal: Born January 29, 1935; Son of Samuel H. and Faye Shulkin (deceased); Married Marlene, Daughter of Russell H. (deceased) and Helen Raskin; Father of Marsha Jan, David Ross. Education: B.A., University of Oklahoma, 1956. Military: Served to Major in the United States Army Artillery, 1957-69. Career: President, SIVAD of Texas, Inc., 1982 to present; Nutritional Consultation Service, Houston, 1975 to present; Distributor for SIVAD BioResearch Company, Madison Heights, Michigan, 1975 to present; Owner, SIVAD of Texas, 1975-82; Sales Manager, Imported Car Dealership, Houston, 1971-75; Supervisor, MOS Test Area, Texas Instruments Inc., Stafford, Texas, 1969-71. Organizational Memberships: Fellow, American Council of Applied Clinical Nutrition; Associate Member, International College of Applied Nutrition. Community Activities: Delegate, People to People Delegation to the Orient and People's Republic of China, 1981. Religion: Jewish. Honors and Awards: Bronze Star Medal with Three Oak Leaf Clusters. Address: 20214 Brondesbury Drive, Katy, Texas 77450.∎

MALCOLM DAVID SHUSTER

Engineer, Physicist. Personal: Born July 31, 1943, in Boston, Massachusetts; Son of Samuel Joseph and Sarah B. Shuster (mother deceased). Education: S.B. Physics, Massachusetts Institute of Technology; Ph.D. Physics, University of Maryland; M.S. Electrical Engineering, Johns Hopkins University. Career: Research Assistant, Department of Physics and Astronomy, University of Maryland, 1967-70; Engineer/Physicist, French Atomic Energy Commission (Paris, France), 1970-72; Instructor, University of Karlsruhe (Karlsruhe, West Germany), 1972-73; Lecturer, Tel-Aviv University (Tel-Aviv, Israel), 1973-76; Visiting Assistant Professor, Carnegie-Mellon University, 1976-77; Senior Member of Technical Staff, Computer Sciences Corporation (Silver Spring, Maryland), 1977-81; Staff Scientist, Business and Technological Systems, Inc. (Seabrook, Maryland), 1981 to present; Adjunct Graduate Professor, Department of Mechanical Engineering,

Howard University, 1983 to present. Organizational Memberships: American Astronautical Society, Senior Member; American Institute of Aeronautics and Astronautics, Associate Fellow; American Physical Society; British Interplanetary Society, Fellow; Institute of Electrical and Electronics Engineers, Senior Member. Published Works: Author of 24 Journal and Conference Reports in Theoretical Physics, Aerospace Engineering and Electrical Engineering. Honors and Awards: Bat-Sheva de Rothschild Foundation Award, 1974; N.A.S.A. Magsat Group Achievement Award, 1981; Sigma Xi, Eminent Scientist 1981; A.I.A.A. Survey Paper Citation, 1982; Tau Beta Pi, Eminent Engineer 1983; Listed in *Who's Who in Aviation and Aerospace, Who's Who in the East, Personalities of America, Community Leaders of the World, The Directory of Distingiushed Americans, Men of Achievement*. Address: P.O. Box 431, Glenn Dale, Maryland 20769.■

RAYMOND EDWARD SICARD

Assistant Professor of Biology. Personal: Born April 18, 1948; Son of Maurice and Jeannette Sicard; Married Mary Frances Lombard; Father of Kathleen Martha. Education: A.B., Merrimack College, North Andover, Massachusetts, 1969; M.S. 1972, Ph.D. 1975, University of Rhode Island, Kingston; Internship in Hematology, New England Deaconess Hospital, Boston, Massachusetts, 1970-73. Career: Lecturer, Department of Biology, Regis College (Weston, Massachusetts) and Research Associate, Department of Biology, Amherst College (Amherst, Massachusetts), 1983 to present; Editor, *Regulation of Amphibian Forelimb Regeneration*, 1985; Assistant Professor, Department of Biology, Boston College, 1976-83; Lecturer in Hematology, Division of Pharmacy and Allied Health, Northeastern University, Boston, 1975-76; Research Fellow, Department of Pediatrics, Shriners Burns Institute, Children's Service, Massachusetts General Hospital and Department of Pediatrics, Harvard Medical School, Boston, 1975-76; Research Associate, Department of Biology, Amherst College, 1974; Hematology Technologist, Department of Pathology, New England Deaconess Hospital, 1970-73; Junior Bacteriologist, Massachusetts Department of Public Health, Lawrence Experiment Station, Lawrence, Massachusetts, 1969. Organizational Memberships: American Association for the Advancement of Science; American Institute of Biological Sciences; American Society for Cell Biology; American Society of Clinical Pathologists; American Society of Zoologists; International Federation for Cell Biology; International Society for Comparative and Developmental Immunology; International Society of Developmental Biologists; New York Academy of Sciences; Phi Sigma Society; Sigma Xi; Society for Developmental Biology. Community Activities: Massachusetts State Science Fair, Judge 1975 to present; American Institute of Biological Sciences, Representative from Massachusetts for the Department of Government.Relations, 1980 to present. Religion: Studies at Marist Preparatory Seminary, Bedford, Massachusetts, 1961-64. Honors and Awards: Phi Sigma Society, University of Rhode Island Chapter, 1972; Elected to Membership in Sigma Xi, University of Rhode Island Chapter, 1973; Listed in *Outstanding Young Men of America, Who's Who in the East*. Address: 290 Edgell Road, Framingham, Massachusetts 01701.■

DANIEL ROBERT SIDOTI

Administrator. Personal: Born January 17, 1921; Son of John Sidoti; Married Gloria Virginia; Father of Lisa Stephanie. Education: Attended New York University, 1939-42; B.A. Chemistry/Science, Union College, 1947; M.S. Industrial Engineering, Stevens Institute of Technology, 1959. Military: Served in the United States Naval Reserves, 1942-46, attaining the rank of Lieutenant (jg). Career: Brand Development Manager, Research and Development, Anheuser-Busch Company, Inc.; Former Positions include Group Leader for New Ventures for Monsanto Company, Operations Manager for Carter-Wallace Company, Group Leader for Research and Development for General Foods Corporation, Quality Control Manager for Robert A. Johnston Company. Organizational Memberships: Institute of Food Technologists, National Councilor 1976 to present, St. Louis Chairman 1973; American Association of Cereal Chemists; American Society of Brewing Chemists. Community Activities: Advisory Committee, Food Science and Nutrition, University of Missouri; Business Partnership Program, St. Louis Schools. Honors and Awards: Several Patents in Yeast Technology and Egg Products. Address: 500 Wellshire Court, Ballwin, Missouri 63011.■

FRANCIS SILVER, V

Consulting Environmental Engineer and Boundary Surveyor. Personal: Born January 4, 1916; Son of Gray Silver and Kate Bishop; Married J. Nevelyne Wyndham. Education: Attended Virginia Military Institute, 1933-34; B.E. Gas Engineering, Johns Hopkins University, 1934-37; Graduate Studies, University of Maryland 1950, Massachusetts Institute of Technology 1980. Military: Served in the United States Army Ordinance, advancing through the ranks from Private to First Lieutenant, 1942-46. Career: Consulting Environmental Engineer and Boundary Surveyor, Berkeley County Court House, Martinsburg, West Virginia; Aircraft Weight Engineer, Fairchild Aircraft, Boeing Aircraft, 1951-57; Engineering and Management, John W. Bishop Company 1947-50, Standard Lime and Stone Company 1937-42. Organizational Memberships: Fellow, Royal Society for Health, 1971 to present; American Public Health Association; A.A.A.S.; American Chemical Society; American Society of Mechanical Engineers; Air Pollution Control Association, Diplomate; American Academy of Environmental Engineers; Society of Clinical Ecology, Associate Fellow, Director; Sigma Xi; New York Academy of Sciences; National Society of Professional Engineers; George Washington Chapter, West Virginia Society of Professional Engineers, President 1973; West Virginia Association of Land Surveyors, Vice President 1973, President 1975; Surveyor of Lands of Berkeley County, West Virginia, 1964 to present. Community Activities: Planning Commission, City of Martinsburg, 1951-57; General Adam Stephen Memorial Association, President 1968 to present; Berkeley County Historical Society, Director 1967 to present. Religion: Presbyterian. Honors and Awards: Surveyor of the Year 1976, Past Presidents Award 1976, West Virginia Association of Land Surveyors; Jonathan Forman Award for Contributions to the Field of Clinical Ecology, 1982; Called as Expert in Gas Toxicology to Testify on First Bill before United States Congress to Curb Automobile Exhaust 1958, and on Clean Air Act 1963. Address: 203 East Burke Street, Martinsburg, West Virginia 25401.■

HOWARD FINDLAY SILVER

Professor of Chemical Engineering, Consultant. Personal: Born September 16, 1930; Son of Marion M. Silver; Married Alice Graham; Father of Ronald Graham, James Howard, Carol Ann. Education: B.S., Petroleum Engineering, Colorado School of Mines, 1952; M.S.Ch.E. 1957, Ph.D. 1961, University of Michigan-Ann Arbor. Military: Served in the United States Army Chemical Corp, 1953-55, attaining the rank of Corporal. Career: Professor of Chemical Engineering, University of Wyoming, Laramie; Former Positions include Research Engineer, Chevron Research Corporation; Chemical Engineer, DuPont Company; Program Manager, Electric Power Research Institute. Organizational Memberships: American Institute of Chemical Engineers; American Chemical Society; Sigma Xi. Honors and Awards: Outstanding Engineering Faculty Award, 1976; International Scholars Directory, France, 1972; Tau Beta Pi; Sigma Gamma Epsilon; Phi Lambda Upsilon; Listed in *Who's Who in America, Who's Who in the West, Dictionary of International Biography, International Who's Who in Engineering, Men of Achievement, Directory of Distinguished Americans, Personalities of the West and Midwest, American Men and Women of Science, Who's Who in American Education, Who's Who in American Colleges and Universities*. Address: 607 24th, Laramie, Wyoming 82070.■

JOHN SAUNDERS SILVERTON

Plastic and Reconstructive Surgeon. Personal: Born May 8, 1943; Son of Dr. and Mrs. M. I. Silverton; Married AnneMarie; Father of Clare Frances, Julia Michelle. Education: Attended Eton College, Windsor, England, 1956-61; St. Bartholomew's Hospital Medical College, London, 1962-67; M.B. B.S., University of London, 1967; Full-time Course in Basic Medicinal Sciences, The Royal College of Surgeons of England, 1969-70; F.R.C.S., Edinburgh, 1973; F.R.C.S., England, 1974; E.C.F.M.G., 1974; F.L.Ex., 1975; Diplomate, The American Board of Plastic Surgery, 1978. Military: Served in the Royal Naval Reserve, 1965-71, attaining the rank of Surgeon Lieutenant. Career: Assistant Clinical Professor of Plastic Surgery, University of California at Davis, 1979 to present; Consultant Plastic Surgeon, Veterans Administration Hospital, Martinez, 1979-80; Plastic Surgeon in Private Practice, 1979 to present; Hospital Privileges at St. Joseph's Hospital (Stockton), Dameron Hospital (Stockton), Oak Park-St. Joseph's Hospital (Stockton), Lodi Community Hospital (Lodi, California), Lodi Memorial Hospital, Surgery Center (Sacramento); Chief Resident in Plastic Surgery, Emory University Affiliated Hospitals (Atlanta, Georgia), 1976; Resident in Plastic Surgery, West of Scotland Regional Plastic Surgery Service, Canniesburg Hospital (Glasgow), 1976; Resident in Plastic Surgery, Emory University Affiliated Hospitals, 1975; Registrar in Plastic Surgery, West of Scotland Regional Plastic Surgery Service, 1974-75; Senior House Surgeon, The Plastic Surgery Unit, Stoke Mandeville Hospital, 1973-74; The State Specialist Surgeon, The State of Brunei, Borneo, 1973; Registrar in General Surgery, Edgeware General Hospital, Middlesex, 1972-73; Senior House Surgeon, Southend General Hospital, Essex, 1971; Senior House Surgeon, The Royal Marsden Hospital, London, 1970-71; General Practice Assistant, Dr. Ezra, London, 1970; Senior House Officer, Accident and Emergency Department, Guy's Hospital, London, 1970; Resident House Officer, The Harley Street Clinic, London, 1969; House Physician, Harold Wood Hospital, Essex, 1968; House Surgeon, Southend General Hospital, 1968. Organizational

Memberships: The American Society of Plastic and Reconstructive Surgeons; The California Society of Plastic Surgeons; The California Society of Plastic and Reconstructive Surgeons; The Royal College of Surgeons of England, Fellow; The Royal College of Surgeons of Edinburgh, Fellow; San Joaquin County Medical Society. Community Activities: Institutional Review Committee, St. Joseph's Hospital; Admissions Committee, Budget Committee, Medical Assistants Committee, Medical Legal/Medical Practices/Public Relations Committees for San Joaquin Medical Society; Dameron Hospital Surgery Committee. Published Works: Co-Author Books *Essentials of Plastic Surgery* and *Scalp Tumors*; Various Presentations, Papers and Research Publications. Address: 6280 Amande Court, Stockton, California 95212.■

JAN SIMKO

Instructor in Shakespeare. Personal: Born October 30, 1920; Son of Terezia Simko; Father of Jan, Vladimir. Education: Teacher's Diplomas in English 1942, German 1943, and Ph.D. 1944, University of Bratislava (Czechoslovakia); M.Ph., University of London, 1967. Career: Professor of English, University of Bratislava, 1945-67; Fellow, Folger Shakespeare Library, Washington D.C., 1967-68; Professor of English, Rio Grande College, Ohio, 1968-75; Instructor, Foreign Service Institute, Washington, D.C., 1974; Examiner, Critical Languages Program, Kent State University, 1974 to present; Instructor in Shakespeare, Georgetown University, Washington, D.C., 1982 to present. Organizational Memberships: Modern Language Association of America, 1966 to present; Former Member, College English Association; The Medieval Academy of America, The Renaissance Society of America, Circle of Modern Philologists in Slovakia, President 1963-66. Community Activities: National Travel Club; Former Member International Platform Association; Organizer of College Students' Scholastic Creativity, 1955-65; Advisor to Publishing Houses on Shakespearean and Language Instruction Publications, 1950-67; Member of College Committee on Academic Policy; Donations to the Heart Fund, Columbia Lighthouse for the Blind, Others. Honors and Awards: Listed in *Personalities of the South, Notable Americans, Book of Honor, The International Who's Who of Intellectuals.* Address: 1356 East Capitol Street, Northeast, Washington, D.C. 20003.■

G. BALLARD SIMMONS

Dean Emeritus. Personal: Born April 9, 1897, in Ponce de Leon, Florida; Son of J. A. Simmons (deceased); Married First Wife Evalyn McNiel (deceased); Married Second Wife Edna Parker; Father of G. Ballard Jr., Evalyn S. Constans. Education: A.B. 1922, M.A. 1929, University of Florida; Ph.D., Johns Hopkins University, 1933. Military: Served in the United States Navy during World War II, Storekeeper Third Class, Lieutenant Colonel in Civil Air Patrol 1960. Career: Dean College of Education, Dean Emeritus 1967, Florida Atlantic University, Boca Raton, Florida; Acting Dean and Professor of Education 1941, Head of Department and Off-Campus Instruction 1948, College of Education, University of Florida; Teacher in Public Schools including City Schools of Panama City, Florida (Supervising Principal 1922-25), and City School System in Brooksville and Tallahassee, Florida (Supervising Principal, 1 year), 1922-28; Consultant to Civil Air Patrol, 1955-63; Organizational Memberships: Phi Kappa Phi; Kappa Delta Pi; Kappa Phi Delta; Phi Kappa Delta; Pi Gamma Mu; Life Member, National Education Association; Life Member, President 1941-42, Florida Education Association; President, Florida Retired Teachers Association, 1968-70; Associate Vice President, Area IV, National Retired Teacher's Association, 1970-74. Community Activities: Rotary International, President Gainesville, Florida Club 1936; Boca Raton Chamber of Commerce, Board of Directors, Vice President 1965-66. Published Works: Author, *Consolidations of Higher Education in Florida* 1980; Bulletins on Teacher Recruitment, "What Are You Looking For?" "School Improvement through Selective Recruitment of Teachers," "Teaching As A Career." Honors and Awards: Recipient of Distinguished Alumnus Award, University of Florida, 1975; Distinguished Service Award, Florida Atlantic University, 1975; World War I Veteran, United States Navy; Honored Upon Retirement from Florida Atlantic University. Address: 400 Northwest 14th Street, Boca Raton, Florida 33436.■

RUSSELL GENE SIMON

Finance Manager. Personal: Born November 9, 1948; Son of J. Rodney Simon. Education: B.S. Mathematics, University of Southwestern Louisiana, Lafayette, Louisiana, 1970; B.S.B.A. Accounting, University of North Dakota, Grand Forks, North Dakota, 1974; M.B.A. Finance, University of Santa Clara, Santa Clara, California, 1980. Military: Served in the United States Air Force as Captain and Missile Launch Officer, 1970-75. Career: Finance Manager in Information Processing Industry; Cost Accountant, Hewlett-Packard, 1975-79; Senior Cost Accountant and Cost Account Supervisor, Amdahl Corporation, 1979-81; Manager, Manufacturing Cost Analysis, Memorex (Bourroughs Company), 1981 to present. Organizational Memberships: National Association of Accountants; A.M.B.A. Honors and Awards: *Who's Who in the West.* Address: 2212 Calle de Primavera, Santa Clara, California 95050.■

DAN C. SIMONS

Realtor. Personal: Born January 30, 1936, in Murray, Utah; Son of Harold Earl and Fredda Simons; Married Sally Jane Anderson, 1954; Father of Eight Children. Education: Attended the University of Utah; Specialized Courses for Real Estate Knowledge. Career: Licensed Salesman with Bettilyon Realty, 1959; Sales Manager, Capson Investment Company, Eight Years; Licensed Broker, 1968; Former Broker and President, Bettilyon and Simons Realtors; Broker and President, Simons & Company; President, Real Estate Consultants; Certified Real Estate Instructor for State of Utah, Taught at University of Utah, Brigham Young University, Utah State University, Weber State University, Westminster College, Henagars Business College, Dixie College; Member Board of Directors, Valley Mortgage Corporation, Utah Academy of Gymnastics, Pioneer Dodge, Peck and Shaw Fine Cars, Frontier Automotive, Eagles Talents, Simons and Company, Real Estate Consultants, Bettilyon and Simons, American International Real Estate. Organizational Memberships: National Association of Realtors, Regional Vice President of Rocky Mountain Region 1981-82, National Director 1972-82, Steering Committee, Legislation Committee, Federation Taxation Subcommittee, Education Committee, State and Urban Affairs Committee, Local Board, Property Management Committee, Land Use Subcommittee, State and Local Taxation Committee, Chairman 1982 Environment, Energy and Development Committee; Utah Association of Realtors, President 1979-80, Vice President 1977-78 and 1978-79, State Director 1970-79, Legislation and Taxation Committee, Advisory Committee, Nominating Committee, Membership Committee, New Industry Committee, Budget Committee; Salt Lake Board of Realtors, President 1974-75, Vice President 1971-72, Board Director 1972-76, Advisory Council, Awards Committee, Budget Committee, Legislation and Taxation Committee, First Chairman of Make America Better Committee, Membership Committee, Zoning and Planning Committee, Vice Chairman of Salesmen Division; Utah Apartment Association, President 1970-71 and 1971-72; National Apartment Association, National Director 1970-76; Organized and Chaired Utah Council on Housing and Land Use; Realtors National Marketing Institute; Farm and Land Institute; Women's Council of Realtors; National Association of Review Appraisers; National Association of Real Estate Appraisers; American Institute of Real Estate Appraisers; International Council of Shopping Centers; Retail Merchants Association. Community Activities: Republican Party, Past Voting District Chairman, Senatorial District Chairman, Platform Chairman for Salt Lake County, Candidate Recruitment Chairman for Salt Lake County, Executive Committee, State Convention Delegate, County Convention Delegate; Life Member, U.R.P.A.C. and R.P.A.C.; Work with Heart Fund, Polio, United Fund, Scout Drives. Religion: Church of Jesus Christ of Latter-day Saints, High Priest, Has Taught and Served in Presidencies of the Priesthood, Sunday School and Mutual Improvement Association at Ward and Stake Levels. Honors and Awards: Salesman of the Year, Salt Lake Board of Realtors, 1968; Realtor of the Year, State and National Honor for Utah Association of Realtors, 1976; Omega Tau Rho; Appointed by Governor of Utah to Original Blue Ribbon Planning Committee, Utah State Housing Finance Agency; Appointed by Governor to State Blue Ribbon Committee on Statewide Land Use Planning; Appointed to State 208 Water Study Committee (Served as Chairman).■

LOIS LUCILLE SIMONSEN

Community Leader. Personal: Born in Henry, South Dakota; Daughter of Robert John and Sarah Elizabeth McKay; Married Elmer; Mother of Robert. Education: Graduate, Henry High School; Nurses Training, Huron, South Dakota. Military: United States Naval Reserve; Career: 35 Years of Service with John Merrell

TWO THOUSAND NOTABLE AMERICANS

and Company; Currently with the Volunteers Chaplain Service Veterans Administration. Community Activities: Navy Mother's Club, Commander 1974-76, State Commander 1974-76; Most Excellent Chief of the Pythian Sisters, 1976; Helped Organize a Canning Breakfast Group; Active in Faith Temple Choir. Honors and Awards: Recognition of Outstanding and Other Services to the United States Navy; Listed in *International Register of Profiles, Book of Honor, The American Registry Series*. Address: 4312 East 26th Street, Apartment 29, Sioux Falls, South Dakota 57104.■

CHARLES GREGG SINGER

Professor of Church History and Systematic Theology. Personal: Born June 3, 1910; Son of Arthur Gregg Singer (deceased); Married Marjorie Pouder; Father of Richard Gregg, Jean Singer Satterwhite, Terri Singer Speicher, Robert Adams. Education: A.B., Haverford College, 1933; M.A. 1935, Ph.D. 1940, University of Pennsylvania; D.Div., Atlanta School of Biblical Studies, 1984. Career: Professor of Church History, Systematic Theology, Atlanta School of Biblical Studies; Professor of History and Chairperson of Department at Wheaton College (Wheaton, Illinois), Salem College (Winston-Salem, North Carolina), Catawba College (Salisbury, North Carolina); Professor of History, Chairperson of Department, Vice President, Belhaven College, Jackson, Mississippi. Community Activities: War Manpower Commission, 1942-44; Special Advisor to Smith-McCarran Committee of Judiciary, 1951-53. Religion: President of Concerned Presbyterians, Ruling Presbyterian Elder 1951 to present, Lay Preacher 1949 to present. Published Works: Author *South Carolina in the Confederation, 1781-1789* (1940), *A Theological Interpretation of American History* (1964, 2nd edition 1981), *John Calvin: His Roots and Fruits* (1967), *Arnold Toynbee, A Critical Study* (1968), *The Unholy Alliance* (1975), *Christian Approaches to Philosophy and History* (1978), *From Rationalism to Irrationality* (1979), *The Church and the Sword* (1981, 2nd edition 1982); 200 Articles for the *Encyclopedia of Christianity* and 150 Articles to Similar Works. Honors and Awards: Phi Beta Kappa; Daughters of the American Revolution Mississippi Man of the Year. Address: 319 Wake Drive, Salisbury, North Carolina 28144.■

JEANNE WALSH SINGER

Composer, Pianist, Lecturer. Personal: Born August 4, 1924; Daughter of Professor and Mrs. Harold V. Walsh; Married Richard G. Singer; Mother of Richard V. Education: B.A. magna cum laude, Barnard College, 1944; Artist Diploma, National Guild of Piano Teachers, 1954. Career: Composer, Pianist, Lecturer, Private Teacher; Performed on Radio, Television, Lincoln Center; Performances in New York City, Canada, Europe, South America. Organizational Memberships: American Society of Composers, Authors and Publishers; National League of American Pen Women, National Music Chairman, Vice President New York City Branch 1979-81; Composers, Authors and Artists of America, Vice President 1971-78, Music Editor of Magazine; American Women Composers, Board of Directors 1976-78; International Platform Association; International Biographical Association, Life Fellow. Community Activities: Great Neck Community Concerts Association, Board of Directors, Executive Vice President 1978-81; North Shore Community Arts Center, Music Advisory Board 1978-81. Honors and Awards: Phi Beta Kappa; Special Award of Merit, National Federation of Music Clubs, 1976; Best Art Song Award, New York Poetry Forum, 1977; First Prize, Composers Guild, 1979; Hackleman Award, National League of American Pen Women, 1980; First Prize, Composers, Authors and Artists of America, 1981; First Prize, National League of American Pen Women, 1982; American Society of Composers, Authors and Publishers Special Awards, 1978-82; 1982 Grand Prize, Composers Guild; Life Fellow, American Biographical Institute. Listed in *Who's Who in the East*. Address: 64 Stuart Place, Manhasset, New York 11030.■

MALCOLM SCOTT SINGER

Research Chemist. Personal: Born July 31, 1940; Son of Beatrice L. Singer; Married Katherine Joyce; Father of Chris Hammer, Mark Hammer, Cathy Singer, Scott Singer. Education: B.S., University of Florida; M.S., Stanford University; Ph.D., University of Colorado. Career: Staff Research Chemist, Bio-Physical Correlations; Research Chemist, Organic Synthesis. Organizational Memberships: American Chemical Society, Pesticide Division, Organic Division; California Section, American Chemical Society, Alternate Councilor and Chairperson Urban Crisis Committee, Chairman-Elect 1984; Sigma Xi; Alpha Chi Sigma; American Association for the Advancement of Science. Community Activities: Coordinator, Tutor Richmond Youth, 1970 to present; Chevron Employees Association, President, Advisor, Treasurer, Social Chairman; Laurel Park Community Group, Treasurer 1970-72, Sergeant at Arms 1973; Coordinator Chevron's Toys for Tots. Honors and Awards: The Senate, California Resolution of the Senate Rules Committee for Public Service, 1972; National Honor Society, 1958. Address: 331 Midway Boulevard, Novato, California 94947.■

VIJAY P. SINGH

Professor and Coordinator of Water Resources Program. Personal: Born July 15, 1946; Son of Mr. and Mrs. Gurdayal Singh; Married Anita; Father of Vinay, Arti. Education: Bachelor of Science and Technology, U. P. Agril. University, 1967; M.S., University of Guelph, 1970; Ph.D., Colorado State University, 1974. Career: Professor of Civil Engineering 1983 to present, Associate Professor of Civil Engineering 1981-83, Louisiana State University; Associate Professor of Civil Engineering 1978-81, Mississippi State University; Associate Research Professor of Civil Engineering, George Washington University, 1977-78; Assistant Professor of Hydrology, New Mexico Tech, 1974-77; Assistant Engineer, Rockefeller Foundation, 1967-68. Organizational Memberships: American Society of Civil Engineers; American Water Resources Association; American Geophysical Union; International Association for Hydraulic Research; Indian Association of Hydrologists; Institution of Engineers; Indian Society of Agricultural Engineers; University of Guelph Alumni Association; Colorado State University Alumni Association; Indian Water Resources Society; Sigma Xi; National Board of Advisors, American Biographical Institute. Community Activities: Director, International Symposium on Rainfall-Runoff Modeling, 1981; Senior Judge, Science and Engineering Fairs, New Mexico, Maryland; Member of University Committee. Published Works: Editor, *Journal of Indian Association of Hydrologists*; Editor of Four Books. Honors and Awards: College Merit, 1965-66, 1966-67; Scholarship Award for Scholastic Achievement, 1966-67; CBIP Certificate of Merit for Outstanding Paper; N.S.F. and O.W.R.T. Research Grants; United States-Indian Exchange Scientist; Listed in *Who's Who in the South and Southwest, Who's Who in Technology Today, Directory of Distinguished Americans, Personalities of the South*. Address: 1043 Beckenham Drive, Baton Rouge, Louisiana 70808.■

DINESH PRASAD SINHA

Family Physician, General Practitioner, Surgeon. Personal: Born January 15, 1944; Son of Dr. G. S. Sinha and Mrs. Sharda Devi; Married Madhuri, Daughter of Mr. and Mrs. Muneshwar Prasad; Father of Simmi Rani, Sunil P., Sanjay P. Education: B.Sc., C.M. College (Bihar, India), 1962; M.B. B.S., R.M.C.H. Ranchi (Bihar), 1967; G.M.C., London, 1971; P.M.B. of N.S., 1972; M.C.F.P. (Canada), 1978. Career: Family Physician, General Practitioner and Surgeon; Resident in General Surgery, Saint John General Hospital, New Brunswick, Canada, 1970-73; Intern, St. John General Hospital, 1969-70; Senior Pediatric Resident and Family Planning Medical Officer Ranchi, Bihar, India, 1968-69. Organizational Memberships: President and Chief, Medical Staff of Eastern Shore Memorial Hospital; Chairman, Doctors and Nurses Liaison Committee, Sheet Harbour E.S.M. Hospital; Planning and Directing Group of Reproductive Care Program of Nova Scotia; Eastern Shore Medical Society, Member 1973 to present; Vice President/Secretary 1979; Medical Society of Nova Scotia;

TWO THOUSAND NOTABLE AMERICANS

Canadian Medical Association; College of Family Physicians of Canada; Indian Medical Association; Associate Member, Dalhousie Medical Alumni. Community Activities: Life Member, Vedant Ashram Society of Nova Scotia and Hindu Sanstha of Nova Scotia; Council Member, Board of Trade, Sheet Harbour; Lions Club; Donation, World Vision Canada. Religion: Hindu. Honors and Awards: Listed in *Community Leaders of America, Biographical Roll of Honor, Who's Who in the East.* Address: Sheet Harbour, Halifax County, Nova Scotia B0J 3B0, Canada.■

HARRY HALL SISLER

Distinguished Service Professor of Chemistry. Personal: Born March 13, 1917; Son of Harry C. and Minta A. (Hall) Sisler (both deceased); Married First Wife Helen Elizabeth Shaver; Married Second Wife Hannelore Lina Wass; Father of Elizabeth Ann, David F., Raymond K., Susan C. Education: B.S. with distinction, Ohio State University, 1936; M.S. Chemistry, University of Illinois, 1937; Ph.D. Chemistry, University of Illinois, 1939. Career: Instructor in Physical Science, Chicago City Colleges, 1939-41; Instructor in Chemistry 1941-42, Assistant Professor of Chemistry 1942-45, Associate Professor of Chemistry 1945-46, University of Kansas; Assistant Professor of Chemistry 1946-48, Associate Professor of Chemistry 1948-55, Professor of Chemistry 1955-56, Ohio State University; Head Professor of Chemistry 1956-64, Chairman Department of Chemistry 1964-68, Director Division of Physical Sciences and Mathematics 1964-68, Dean College of Arts and Sciences 1968-70, Executive Vice President 1970-73, Dean of Graduate School 1973-79, Director of Sponsored Research 1976-79, Distinguished Service Professor of Chemistry 1979 to present, University of Florida; Arthur and Ruth Sloan Visiting Professor, Harvard University, Fall Semester 1962-63. Organizational Memberships: Florida Academy of Science; Alpha Chi Sigma; American Chemical Society, Chairman-elect of Kansas City Section 1946, National Chairman of Division of Chemical Education 1957-58, Chairman of Florida Section 1962, Editorial Board of *Journal Chemical Education* 1955-58, Board of Publication *Journal Chemical Education* 1955-58; Former Member, American Association for the Advancement of Science. Religion: Methodist. Honors and Awards: Kappa Phi Kappa Award, Ohio State University, 1935; Phi Eta Sigma; Phi Delta Kappa; Phi Lambda Upsilon; Phi Kappa Phi; Kappa Delta Pi; Sigma Xi; Gamma Sigma Epsilon; University Fellow in Chemistry, University of Illinois, 1937-39; Outstanding S. E. Chemist Award, American Chemical Society, 1960; Southern Chemist Award, American Chemical Society, 1969; Florida Blue Key, 1970; Centennial Achievement Award, Ohio State University, 1970; Royal Order of the North Star, awarded by the King of Sweden, 1973; Doctorate Honoris Causa, University of Poznan, Poland, 1977; The James Flack Norris Award for Outstanding Contributions to the Teaching of Chemistry, 1979; Honorary Membership, Phi Beta Kappa; Listed in *Who's Who in America, Leaders in American Education, Who's Who in American Education, American Men of Science, Leaders in American Science, Who's Who in the World, Contemporary Authors, Florida Lives, International Biographical Dictionary, Leaders in Education, National Register of Prominent Americans and International Notables; Blue Book Writer's Directory, Who's Who in the South and Southwest.* Address: 6014 Northwest 54th Way, Gainesville, Florida 32606.■

LEIGHTON ESTEN SISSOM

University Administrator. Personal: Born August 26, 1934; Son of Mr. and Mrs. W. E. Sissom; Married Evelyn J. Lee, Daughter of Mr. and Mrs. T. T. Lee; Father of Terry Lee, Denny Leighton. Education: B.S., Middle Tennessee State University, 1956; B.S.M.E., Tennessee Technological University, 1962; M.S.M.E. 1964, Ph.D. 1965, Georgia Institute of Technology. Career: Dean of Engineering 1979 to present, Professor and Chairman of Mechanical Engineering 1965-79, Instructor in Mechanical Engineering and Engineering Science 1958-62, Tennessee Technological University; N.A.S.A. Faculty Fellow, Houston Manned Spacecraft Center, 1965; Mechanical Designer, ARO, Inc., Tullahoma, Tennessee, 1957-58; Principal, Leighton E. Sissom and Associates, Inc., 1978 to present. Organizational Memberships: Director, Accreditation Board for Engineering and Technology, 1980 to present; American Society of Mechanical Engineers, Council on Education 1976 to present, Professional Practices Committee 1968-73; American Society for Engineering Education; Commissioner, Engineering Acccreditation Commission, 1979 to present. Community Activities: Evaluator, Accreditation Board for Engineering and Technology, 1970 to present; Evaluator, Southern Association for Colleges and Schools, 1970 to present; Technical Reviewer for Four Journals, a Publishing Company and a Federal Agency, 1965 to present; Chairman, Tennessee Council of Engineering Deans, 1981-82; Board of Directors, National Engineering Deans Council, 1982 to present. Published Works: Editor-in-Chief, *Mechanical Engineering News,* 1977-80; Co-Author (with Donald R. Pitts), *Elements of Transport Phenomena* 1972, *Heat Transfer* 1977; Over 50 Papers to Various Publications. Religion: Church of Christ, Deacon 1965-81, Elder 1981 to present. Honors and Awards: N.A.S.A. Traineeship, 1962-65; Golden Medallion of A.S.M.E., Centennial Award for Contributions to Mechanical Engineering Education, 1980. Address: Route 14, Box A1, Cookeville, Tennessee 38501.■

LEIF T. SJOBERG

Professor of Scandinavian Studies and Comparative Literature. Personal: Born December 15, 1925; Married Inger Wallervik. Education: F.K. 1952, F.M. 1954, Fil. Lic. 1968, Fil.Dr.h.c. 1980, Uppsala University, Sweden. Career: Professor of Scandinavian Studies and Comparative Literature, Associate Professor 1968-72, State University of New York at Stony Brook; Lecturer and Assistant Professor, Columbia University, 1958-68; Lector in Swedish, Kings College, Newcastle-upon-Tyne, 1956-58; Realskolan, Vindeln, Sweden, 1954-56. S.A.S.S., Vice President 1965-67; A.S.F., 1958 to present; Ibsen Society; Ibsen Society of America; Isländska Sällskapet, Uppsala; American Association of University Professors; Comparative Literature Association; Others. Community Activities: American Scandinavian Foundation, Publication Committee 1965-77; A.S.F., Fellowships Committee 1958 to present; Scandinavian Seminar, New York City, 1965-77; Board of Trustees, American Swedish History Museum, Philadelphia, 1971-73; Colloquia in Comparative Literature, New York University, 1977 to present; Scandinavia Today, Academic Committee 1981-82; Donations of Art Works to the Museum of Modern Art (Olson, Baertling), The Guggenheim Museum (Baertling). Honors and Awards: Translation Award (with Muriel Rukeyser), Swedish Academy, 1966; Ida Bäckmann Prize, Swedish Academy, 1977; Fil.Dr.h.c., Uppsala University, 1980. Address: 50 Morningside Drive, New York, New York 10025.■

WILLIAM DALY SKEES

Computer Consultant Executive. Personal: Born March 27, 1939; Son of Raymond J. and Barbara A. Skees; Married Carol Ann; Father of Shannon Marie, William Edward, John Daniel. Education: Student, Fordham University, 1957-58; A.B. cum laude, St. Benedict's College, 1961; Postgraduate Work, American University 1961-62, Catholic University of America 1962-63; M.S., University of Illinois, 1964; University of Wisconsin, 1964-65; University of Kentucky, 1965-66; American University, 1968. Career: Computer Consultant Executive; Mathematician-Programmer, United States Naval Weapons Laboratory, Dahlgren, Virginia, 1961-62; Project Leader, AC Electronics, Milwaukee, 1964-65; Manager, Operating Systems, University of Kentucky Computer Center, Lexington, Kentucky, 1965-67; Manager Time Sharing System Development, C.E.I.R./Control Data Corporation, Washington, D.C., 1967-69; Assistant Director, Computer Science Division Operations, Research, Inc., Maryland, 1969-74; President, Skees Associates, Inc., 1974 to present. Organizational Memberships: Association for Computing Machines, Reviewer 1966-76; Pi Mu Epsilon, Mathematician 1965-66. Community Activities: Montgomery County Chamber of Commerce, Vice President 1983; Georgetown Hill Elementary School Parent Teacher Association, President 1973-74. Published Works: Author *Computer Software for Data Communications* (1981), *Writing Handbook for Computer Professionals* (1982), *Before You Invest in a Small Business Computer* (1982), *The Doctor's Computer Handbook* (1984). Honors and Awards: American Legion Citizenship Award, 1957. Address: 531 South Fairfax Street, Alexandria, Virginia 22314.■

JAMES ALBERT SKIDMORE

Executive. Personal: Born June 30, 1932; Married Peggy Ann Young; Father of Jacqueline Sue, James Albert III. Education: B.A. Economics, Muhlenberg College, 1954. Military: Served in the United States Marine Corps, 1954-57, attaining the rank of Captain. Career: Customer Sales Representative to District and Area Sales Manager to Division Marketing Manager, New Jersey Bell Telephone Company, 1957-66; President, United States Jaycees, 1965-66; Assistant to the President for Public Affairs, PepsiCo Inc., 1966-69; National Field Director of Citizens for Nixon-Agnew, 1967-68; Assistant to the President, White House Transition Staff, 1968-69; Vice President, Handy Associates, 1969; Board of Directors, Danline (Newark Brush Company), 1971; President and Chief Executive Officer, Science Management Corporation and Handy Associates, 1972; Chairman of the Board, Science Management Corporation, 1975; Board of Directors, The Coca-Cola Bottling Company of New York, Inc., 1977; Board of Directors, Franklin State Bank, Somerset, New Jersey, 1977; Board of Directors, National Business Consortium for Educating Gifted and Talented Children, 1981; Board of Directors, Mariner Communications, Inc., Cincinnati, Ohio, 1981; Board of Directors, Muhlenberg College, 1981; Board of Directors, New Jersey State Chamber of Commerce, 1982; Chairman, President and Chief Executive Officer, Science Management Corporation. Community Activities: National Council on Crime and Delinquency, 1965-66; Commission for Youth Employment, 1965-66; National Advisory Committee of Keep America Beautiful, 1965-67; State Chairman, New Jersey National Foundation, March of Dimes, 1966; Board of Directors, Project Concern, 1966; Advisory Commission on Youth Employment, 1966-67; Vice President and Director, Barry Sadler Foundation; Chairman of the Board, United States Jaycees, 1966-67; UNESCO Appointment, 1967; Treasurer, Junior Chamber International, 1967-68; Economic Social Commission of the United Nations, 1967-68; Citizen's Advisory Board on Youth Opportunity, 1969; President Project Concern Inc. and Director of Amdoc Corporation, San Diego, 1968; Advisory Commission on Small Business Administration, 1970; National Advisory Board of Directors of the American Security Council, 1970; Executive Board Member, Washington Area Council, Boy Scouts of America, 1972; Director, New York Urban League, 1972; Director, Granite State Machine Company (Manchester, New Hampshire), 1972; Board of Governors, Alpha Tau Omega, 1973; Young President's Organization, New Jersey Chapter, 1974; Appointment to Citizens Committee on Priorities, Berkeley Heights, New Jersey, 1975; Ambassador for Burlington County, the Economic Development Committee of Burlington County, 1975; Advisory Trustee, Board of Trustees, Brick Township Hospital, Inc., 1976; Vice Chairman of the Board of Governors, Alpha Tau Omega, 1977; Vice Chairman, Economic Development Task Force, 1977; Chairman of 1977-78 Annual Alumni Fund Campaign for Muhlenberg College; Area Managers Group, 1981; Re-elected to three year term, Alpha Tau Omega Board of Governors, 1981; Others. Honors and Awards: Selected as One of New Jersey's Five Outstanding Young Men, 1965; Received as U.S. Jaycee President, Freedom Foundation's George Washington Medal of Honor, U.S. Chamber of Commerce Award for "Outstanding Contribution in the Political Action Course in Practical Politics and Freedom versus Communism" and the National Clean-up Bureau's First Award in 50 Year History for "Outstanding Contribution to the Communities of our Nation," 1965-66; Cited by Director of U.S. Aid Mission to Vietnam for Instituting the Program "Adopt a Village," 1966; Distinguished Service Award, 1966; Muhlenberg College Alumni Award for "Outstanding Achievement in Life," 1966 (youngest individual to receive award); Award for Outstanding Leadership in Fight Against Birth Defects, The National Foundation, March of Dimes, 1967; International Communications Institute "Speech of the Month" (*The True Test of Leadership*) Recorded and Distributed to Over 35000, 1967; One of Nation's Ten Outstanding Young Men, 1968; Trinidad and Tobago Award, 1970; Invested as Associated Officer by Her Majesty the Queen of England into the Order of St. John, 1971; Received First Ambassador Award Presented to New Jersey Jaycee, 1977; International Understanding Award, Brussels, Belgium, 1977; Society for Advancement of Management Human Relations Award, 1982; Listed in *Great Britain's Blue Book, Who's Who in America, Who's Who in the East, Who's Who in Finance and Industry, National Social Directory, National Register of Prominent Americans and International Notables*. Address: 641 Ocean Avenue, Sea Girt, New Jersey 08750.■

RUSSELL ALTON SKIFF

Executive. Personal: Born February 26, 1927; Son of Albert Alton (deceased) and Leah Gladys Allen Skiff; Married Dolores Theresa Molnar; Father of Russell James, Sandra Lee, Eric Alan, Rebecca Lynn. Education: B.S. Chemistry and Mathematics, University of Pittsburgh, 1950. Military: Served in the United States Army Air Force, 1944-46, attaining the rank of Staff Sergeant. Career: Metallurgical Chemist, Jones and Laughlin Steel Company, Aliquippa, Pennsylvania, 1950-51; Research and Development Chemist, General Electric Company, Erie, Pennsylvania, 1951-57; Manager, Tech. Sales and Plant Operation, Hysol Corporation of California, El Monte, California, 1957-60; Senior Research Engineer, Autonetics Division, North American Aviation, Downey, California, 1960-62; President, Delta Plastics Company, Visalia, California, 1962 to present. Organizational Memberships: National Federation of Independent Business; California Federation of Independent Business; Society of Plastics Engineers; American Chemical Society; American Society for Testing and Materials; United States Senatorial Business Advisory Board. Community Activities: Exchange Club of Visalia, President 1981-82; Vasalia Breakfast Lions Club, Vice President 1981-82; Visalia Chamber of Commerce. Religion: Presbyterian. Honors and Awards: Member of First United Manufacturer's People-to-People Goodwill Delegation to China, 1980; Holder of Nine United States Patents. Address: 5525 West Pershing, Visalia, California 93291.■

CHARLES GORDON SKINNER

Coordinator of Research and Department Chairman. Personal: Born April 23, 1923; Married Lilly Ruth Brown; Father of Robert Gordon, Gary Wayne. Education: B.S. 1943, M.S. 1947, North Texas State University, Denton, Texas; Ph.D., University of Texas at Austin, Austin, Texas, 1952. Military: Served in the United States Army, Infantry, 1944-46; Career: Coordinator of Research, Assistant Dean Basic Science 1976-79, Texas College of Osteopathic Medicine; Chairman Basic Health Sciences, Chairman Department of Chemistry 1970-76, North Texas State University; Research Scientist, Clayton Foundation Biochemistry Institute, Austin, Texas, 1953-64. Organizational Memberships: Consultant, A.I.D. Consulting Engineers, 1981 to present; Associate Member, Joint Board, Council on Environmental Improvement, 1979; Associate Member, Council Committee on Chemical Safety, 1979; American Society of Biological Chemistry, 1958 to present; American Chemical Society, 1944 to present; Sigma Xi; Phi Lambda Upsilon; Alpha Chi Sigma; Fellow, American Institute of Chemists; Fellow, Texas Academy of Science; Board of Research, Denton Diabetic Association. Published Works: Author of Over 100 Scientific Articles; Holder of 8 Patents. Honors and Awards: W. T. Doherty Recognition Award, American Chemical Society, Dallas/Fort Worth Section, 1978. Address: P.O Box 5006, North Texas Station, Denton, Texas 76203.■

MARY McGOWAN SLAPPEY

Writer, Artist, Retired Navy Officer. Personal: Born November 22, 1914, in Kittrell, North Carolina; Daughter of Walter Gordon and Mary McGowan Slappey. Education: Honors Certificate, Corcoran Art, 1950's; A.B., George Washington University, 1947; J.D., International School of Law, 1977; Cultural Doctorate in Literature (honorary), World University, 1981. Military: Served as a Naval Officer during World War II; United States Naval Reserves, 1943 to present, Retired Lieutenant Commander. Career: Free-lance Writer, Contributor to *Liguorian, Rosicrucian Digest, Business Education World*, Others; Former Editor United States Catholic Conference (Washington) and Teacher for the National Business School (Washington). Organizational Memberships: Federal Poets, Affiliate of the National Association of State Poetry Societies, President 1976-78; Columbian Women of George Washington University, Historian 1981-83. Community Activities: Chairman, D.C. Art Week for National American Artists Professional Association of New York City, 1950's; Volunteer Assistance to Foreign Students with English Language and Americanization Problems. Published Works: Playwright, *Amethyst Remembrance* (1981-83); Author Novels, Novelettes, Non-Fiction including *Miracle of Believing* (1981), *Causes of War and Peace* (1983). Honors and Awards: United States Naval Commendation Ribbon for Sending Seabees Around the World, 1945; United Poets Laureate International Laurel Wreath, 1978; Accademia Italia delle Arti Gold Medal, 1979; Leonardo da Vinci Society Honors Diploma, 1981; Alumni Award, Central High, 1981. Address: 4500 Chesapeake Street N.W., Washington, D.C. 20016.■

DAVID BRUCE SLAVSKY

Astronomer and Professor. Personal: Born September 18, 1951; Son of Max (deceased) and Lillian Slavsky. Education: B.S., Brown University, 1973; M.S., Harvard University, 1975; Ph.D. Astronomy, University of Texas, 1983. Career: Astronomer; Professor; Columnist on Astronomy; Talk Show Host, "Science and Society," KLBJ-AM, Austin Texas; Director, Painter Hall Observatory, Austin, Texas; Research in Planetary Rotation Periods, 1977-81; Research in Astrochemistry, 1980 to present; Lecturer at Texas Superintendent of Schools Symposium, 1982; Inservice Speaker to Teachers in Central Texas, 1980-82. Organizational Memberships: Sigma Xi; American Astronomical Society; American Association for the Advancement of Science; American Meteorological

Society. Religion: Jewish. Honors and Awards: Welch Foundation Predoctoral Fellow, 1981; United States-Israel Bi-National Science Foundation Grant, 1981; Visiting Astronomer, Cerro Tololo Inter-American Observatory, Chile, 1980. Address: 6972 North Sheridan #312, Chicago, Illinois 60626.∎

STEVEN L. SLES

Artist, Multilingual Poet, Author, Inventor. Personal: Born June 16, 1940, in Jersey City, New Jersey. Education: Attended Bard College, 1958-60; B.A. English Literature, Swarthmore College, 1960-62; Private Lessons with Hans Hofmann, Provincetown, Massachusetts, 1957; Instituto de San Miguel de Allende, Mexico, 1958; Summer Study, University of Madrid, 1959; Mexico City University, 1961; Arts Students League, New York City, 1962. Career: Collections with H.R.H. Princess Anne (Buckingham Palace), Bertrand Russell Peace Foundation, Swarthmore College, Numerous Private Collections; Individual Shows at Swarthmore College 1961, Metiers d'Art (Carribbean Art Center, Fort-de-France, Martinique) 1963, Centro de Estudios Norteamericanos (Valencia, Spain) 1967, Circulo de la Amistad (Cordoba, Spain) 1970, Petchburi Gallery (Bangkok, Thailand) 1971, IBM Exhibition Hall (Princeton, New Jersey) 1971, Wrigley Mansion (now Mansion Club, Phoenix, Arizona) 1981, Ross Gallery (Scottsdale, Arizona) 1981, Real Life Photography (Tucson, Arizona) 1982, Others; Selected Group Shows include Provincetown Art Association 1963, Jersey City Museum and Provincetown Art Association 1964, Provincetown Art Association 1965, Galeria Toison (Madrid, Spain) 1969, Galeria Alerta (Santander, Spain) 1970, Jersey City Museum 1971 and 1973, New Jersey State Museum (Trenton, New Jersey) 1974, Saint Phillip's in the Hills Art Gallery (Tucson, Arizona) 1978, Ross Gallery (Scottsdale, Arizona) 1982. Organizational Memberships: Former Member of Art Exhibition Council of London, England; Free Painters and Sculptors Society (England), Poetry Society of London, England; Jersey City Museum (New Jersey), Art Exhibition Council of New Jersey, Auckland Society of Art (Australia), "Arte Actual" — Contemporary Arts Society of Valencia, Spain, Amigos de la Poesía (Valencia, Spain), Arts Community Association of Arizona (Tucson, Arizona); Lifetime Member of "Vereinigung der Mund-und Fussmalendan Künstler in aller Welt, Vaduz, Leichtenstein (Worldwide Association of Mouth- and Foot-Painting Artists), Fellow Royal Society of Arts (London, England), International Arts Guild (Monte Carlo), National Society of Literature and the Arts (Washington D.C.); Current Member, Artists Equity Association Inc. (New York City), Tucson Museum of Art (Tucson, Arizona), International Society of Artists (Marion, Ohio), Others. Published Works: Author Numerous Publications including (most recent) *Autobiography* 1982, *Prose* 1982, *Multilingual Poetry* 1982, *Poems of 1981*, *Prose of 1980*; "Sles Art Corporation Worldwide" (Tucson, Arizona), "Struggle Towards Immortality" 1976, "That He Might See Again" 1976, "That I Might Say For You Through Movements" 1976, "And As You Look On These Small and Gentle Children" 1976, "The Poetry of Life Is But A Simple Act" 1976, Proposals, Observations and Suggested General Pathways Concerning Handicapped Individuals in American Society" (essay for White House Conference on Handicapped Individuals) 1976, "Eliminating Society's Barriers, Creatively" (essay for National White House Conference on Handicapped Individuals) 1977, "The Artistic Career of Steven L. Sles" 1977, Numerous Others. Honors and Awards: Pearson Gallery Purchase Prize, Swarthmore College, Swarthmore, Pennsylvania, 1962; Ruth Sherman Gallery Award, New York City, New York, 1963; Kenny Rehabilitation Institute, Minnesota, Third Prize 1966, First and Second Prizes 1972; Tracy Long Memorial Award, New Jersey, 1968; Charles Bainbridge Award, New Jersey, 1970; Fabian Zaccone Prize, New Jersey, 1972; Galerie de Bourdeaux, France, Second Prize, 1973; Prix Jéricho, Diplome d'Honneur, Paris, France, 1974; Gold Medal, Accademia Italia delle Arti e del Lavoro, Parma, Italy, 1979; Lessing J. Rosenwald Award, Philadelphia, Pennsylvania, 1981; Elected Fellow, Royal Society of Arts, London, England; Elected Fellow, International Biographical Association, London, England; Invited Member by Mr. James Michener, National Society of Literature and the Arts; Elected Academic of Italy, Accademia Italia delle Arti e del Lavoro, Parma, Italy; Titular Member, International Arts Guild, Monte Carlo; Delegate, Arizona White House Conference on Handicapped Individuals, Arizona; Advisor, National White House Conference on Handicapped Individuals, Washington D.C.; Listed in *International Directory of Arts, Who's Who in American Art, Heráldica, Anuario de la Aristocracia y Alta Sociedad: Quién es Quien, International Who's Who of Art and Antiques, Dictionary of International Biography, International Who's Who in Poetry, International Who's Who of Intellectuals, Men of Achievement, Who's Who in the West, Personalities of the West and Midwest, Dictionary of Contemporary European Artists*. Address: P.O. Box 13334, Tucson, Arizona 85732.∎

PARKER ADAMS SMALL, JR.

Physician, Educator. Personal: Born July 5, 1932, in Cincinnati, Ohio; Son of Adams and Grace (McMichael) Small; Married Natalie Settimelli Parker on August 26, 1956; Father of Parker Adams, Peter McMichael, Carla Edmea. Education: Student, Tufts University, 1950-53; M.D., University of Cincinnati, 1957; Medical Intern, Pennsylvania Hospital, Philadelphia, 1957-58; Research Associate, National Heart Institute, National Institutes of Health, Washington, 1958-60; Research Fellow, St. Mary's Hospital, London, 1960-61. Military: Served with the United States Public Health Service, 1958-60. Career: Senior Surgeon, N.I.M.H., Washington, 1961-66; Professor of Immunology and Medical Microbiology 1966 to present, Chairman Department 1966-75, Professor of Pediatrics 1979 to present, University of Florida, Gainesville; Visiting Professor, University of Lausanne (Switzerland) 1972, University of Lagos (Nigeria) 1982; Visiting Scholar, Association of American Medical Colleges, Washington, 1973; Consultant in Field; Developer of the Patient-Oriented Problem Solving System for Medical Education. Organizational Memberships: American Association of Immunologists; Phi Beta Kappa; Sigma Xi; Theta Delta Chi. Community Activities: Oakmont, Maryland, Secretary-Treasurer 1964-65, Mayor 1965-66; Chairman, Citizens for Public Schools, Gainesville, 1969-70. Published Works: Editor, *The Secretory Immunologic Systems* 1971; Editorial Board, *Infection and Immunity* 1974-76, *Journal of Medical Education* 1978-80. Honors and Awards: Named Teacher of the Year, University of Florida, College of Medicine, 1978-79; Co-Chairman Life Sciences Panel Associateship Program, National Science Foundation, 1981; National Institute of Health, Special Fellow 1960-61, Research Grantee 1966 to present. Address: 3454 Northwest 12th Avenue, Gainesville, Florida 32605.∎

RICHARD DAVID SMALL

Senior Engineer. Personal: Born January 6, 1945; Son of Sydney and Gertrude Goldberg Small; Married Tsipora, Daughter of Mrs. Pnina Mierson; Father of Eileen Lara, Carrie Ayala. Education: B.S. 1967, M.S. 1968, M.Phil. 1969, Ph.D. 1971, Rutgers University. Military: Served in the Israeli Army, 1977. Career: Senior Engineer, Pacific-Sierra Research Corporation; Former Positions include Instructor at Rugters University, Senior Lecturer in the Department of Aeronautical Engineering at Technion (Israel Institute of Technology), Senior Lecturer at Tel Aviv University, Visiting Assistant Professor at the University of California at Los Angeles. Community Activities: Neighborhood Architectural Committee, 1981-82. Religion: Bar Mitzvah, 1958. Honors and Awards: Scholarships, 1963-67; N.D.E.A. Title IV Fellowship, 1967-70; Rothschild Prize, 1973; Listed in *Who's Who in the West, Personalities of America, Who's Who in Aviation and Aerospace, Directory of Distinguished Americans, Men of Achievement, Who's Who in Frontier Science and Technology, Who's Who in California*. Address: 1416 Valecroft Avenue, Westlake Village, California 91361.∎

ERNEST THOMAS SMERDON

Educator, Administrator. Personal: Born January 19, 1930; Son of John Erle and Ada Davidson Smerdon (both deceased); Married Joanne D.; Father of Ernest T. Jr., Katherine S. Myers, Gary J. Education: B.S. Agricultural Engineering 1951, M.S. Agricultural Engineering 1956, Ph.D. Agricultural Engineering and Civil Engineering 1959, University of Missouri. Military: Served with the United States Air Force Weather Service as a Meteorologist from 1951-55, attaining the rank of First Lieutenant. Career: Professor of Civil Engineering and Director of the Center for Research in Water Resources, University of Texas at Austin; Vice Chancellor for Academic Affairs, The University of Texas System, 1976-82; Assistant Dean for Research 1974-76, Professor and Chairman in the Department of Agricultural Engineering 1968-74, University of Florida; Professor of Civil Engineering and Director of Water Resources Institute 1964-68, Professor of Agricultural Engineering 1962-68, Associate Professor 1959-62, Texas A&M University. Organizational Memberships: American Society of Civil Engineers, Management Group D 1982 to present, Executive Committee, I&D Division 1975-79 and 1982 to present; A.S.A.E., Fellow Research Committee 1969-79, International Relations Committee 1979-84; U.C.O.W.R., Delegate 1982 to present, Executive Board 1968-74, Vice Chairman 1968-69 and 1970-71, Chairman 1972-74; N.A.S.U.L.G.C., Water Resource Committee 1972 to present, Vice Chairman 1976-77, Chairman 1977 to present, Energy and Environment Committee 1980 to present; National Research Council, N.A.S.-N.A.E.; American Association for the Advancement of Science, Fellow. Community Activities: Symphony Square (Austin), Advisory Board 1978-80; Celebrity Auction, KLRN-KLRU, Planning Committee 1978-80; Rotary Club, Gainesville, Florida, 1970-76. Religion: Ruling Elder, Session 1966-68, Chairman Pulpit Nominating Committee 1967, Board of Deacons 1963-66 (Chairman 1966), First Presbyterian Church, Bryan. Honors and Awards: Missouri Honor Award for Distinguished Service in Engineering, University of Missouri-Columbia, 1982; Winner, Special Award for Outstanding Service, Florida Section A.S.A.E., 1972; Winner, 1961 A.S.A.E. Technical Paper Contest (for paper "Critical Triactive Forces in Cohesive Soils"); Honorable Mention, 1960 Technical Paper Contest (for paper "Canopy Inlet for Closed Conduits"). Address: 2902 Scenic Drive, Austin, Texas 78703.∎

TWO THOUSAND NOTABLE AMERICANS

MARTIN SMETTER

Manufacturing Company Executive. Personal: Born March 2, 1941; Son of Cele Altman; Father of Michael. Education: M.B.A., Pepperdine University, 1972. Military: Served in the United States Navy, 1959-64. Career: President, Western Case Manufacturing Company; Former Positions include Customer Engineer for IBM, Account Executive for E. F. Hutton & Company, Sales Representative for Mohawk Data Sciences, Product Manager for Vector General, Director of Corporate Development for Tax Corporation of America. Organizational Memberships: American Management Association; Irvine Industrial League. Community Activities: Balboa Yacht Club. Address: 428½ Begonia, Corona Del Mar, California 92625.■

ARNOLD C. SMITH

Retired Diplomat and International Statesman; Educator and Writer. Personal: Born January 1915, in Toronto, Ontario, Canada; Son of Victor Arnold and Sarah Cory (Cantwell) Smith (deceased); Married Evelyn Hardwick Stewart; Father of Alexandra (Mrs. Harvey Gaylord Jr.), Stewart Cantwell, Matthew Cantwell. Education: Attended Upper Canada College, Toronto; Lycé Champolén, Grenoble, France; B.A. Political Science and Economics, University of Toronto, 1935; Rhodes Scholar for Ontario, Christ Church, Oxford, 1935; B.A. 1937, M.A. and B.C.L. 1938. Career: Editor, *The Baltic Times*, Tillinn, Estonia, 1939-40; Associate Professor of Political Economics, University of Tartu, Estonia, 1939-40; Representative British Council for Estonia, and Press Attaché, British Embassy, Cairo, Egypt, 1940-41; Special Lecturer, Political and Economics, Egyptian State University, Cairo, 194-42; Head of Propaganda Division, U.K. Minister of State for Middle East, 1941-43; Editor-in-Chief, "Akhbar el Harp," "Aera" and "Cephe" (Cairo), 1941-43; Transferred to Canadian Diplomatic Service and Proceeded to Kuibyshev, U.S.S.R., as Secretary Canadian Legation, 1943; Canadian Embassy, Moscow, 1943-45; Member Economic Division, Department of External Affairs, Ottawa, 1946-47; Associate Director, National Defense College of Canada, Kingston, Ontario, 1947-49; Served as Advisor on Various Committees and Councils, Representative for Canada at United Nations Meetings, becoming Principal Advisor, Permanent Delegate of Canada to United Nations and Canadian Delegate to United Nations General Assembly, 1949; Alternate Representative of Canada on United Nations Security Council and Atomic Energy Commission, Lake Success, 1949-50; Counsellor, Canadian Embassy, Brussels, and Head of Canadian Delegation to Inter-Allied Reparations Agency, 1950-53; Special Assistant to Secretary of State for External Affairs, 1953-55; Canadian Commissioner on International Truce Supervisory Commission for Cambodia, 1955-56; Canadian Minister to the United Kingdom, 1956-58; Ambassador to the United Arab Republic 1958-61, to the U.S.S.R. 1961-63; Assistant Under Secretary of State for External Affairs, Canada, 1963-65; Elected First Secretary-General of the Commonwealth, London, England, 1965-75; Lester Pearson Professor of International Affairs, Carleton University, 1976-81; Adjunct Professor, 1981 to present; Invested Companion of Honour by H.M. Queen Elizabeth II, 1975; Visiting Centennial Professor, University of Toronto, 1967; Visiting Cecil and Ada Green Professor, University of British Columbia, 1978; Visitor and Lecturer in Moscow, Guest of Soviet Academy of Science, 1977. Organizational Memberships: Chairman of the Board 1976-83, Honorary Chairman 1983 to present, International Peace Academy, United Nations Plaza, New York; Chairman of the Board, North-South Institute of Canada, 1976 to present; President, Canadian Bureau of International Education, 1976-79; Trustee, Hudson Institute, New York, 1976-81; Vice President (Life), Royal Commonwealth Society, London; Honorary President, Royal Commonwealth Society of Canada; Honorary President, Canadian-Mediterranean Institute, 1981 to present; Member Executive Committee and Council, Duke of Edinburgh's 5th Commonwealth Study Conference, Canada, 1980. Community Activities: Le Cercle Universitaire, Ottawa; Athenaeum, London. Published Works: Author, "Stitches in Time - The Commonwealth in World Politics" 1981, "The We-They Frontier - from International Relations to World Politics" 1983. Religion: Anglican. Honors and Awards: Awarded R. B. Bennett Commonwealth Prize, Royal Society of Arts, 1975; Honorary D.C.L., Michigan 1966, Oxford 1975, Bishop University 1977; LL.D., Ricker 1964, Queen's 1966, British Columbia, Toronto 1968, New Brunswick 1969, Leeds 1975, Trent 1979; Zimbabwe Independence Medal, 1980; Honorary Fellow, Lady Eaton College, Trent University; Beta Theta Pi. Address: 260 Metcalfe Street, Apt. 4B, Ottawa, Ontario, Canada K2P 1R6.

BOYCE MILES SMITH

Stockbroker. Personal: Born April 3, 1924; Son of William Pinkston and Alice Vivian Smith (both deceased); Married Helen Marguerite; Father of Sherry De Los Santos, Stanley Miles, Sally Anne, Scott Anthony. Education: B.S.Ch.E., University of Arkansas, 1952; Graduate Work in Meteorology, University of Texas, 1961; Master's Degree in Atmospheric Science, Colorado State University, 1965. Military: Served in the United States Air Force, 1943-80, attaining the rank of Colonel. Career: Stockbroker; Former Positions with the United States Air Force including Chemist, Navigator, Supply Liaison Officer, Radar Bombadier, Weather Forecaster, Squadron Commander; Special Staff Officer, United States Navy; Member of Army Special Staff Forces Command. Organizational Memberships: American Meteorological Society, 1959 to present; Alpha Chi Sigma, 1951 to present; American Geophysical Union, 1966 to present. Religion: Methodist. Honors and Awards: Legion of Merit; Meritorious Service Medal with Device; Air Medal with Device; Air Force Commendation Medal; Republic of Vietnam Campaign Medal; Republic of Vietnam Gallantry Cross with Device; United Nations Service Medal; Air Force Outstanding Unit Award with V Device; Air Force Outstanding Unit Award with L Device; World War II Victory Medal; Vietnam Service Medal; National Defense Service Medal with One Device; Air Force Longevity Service Ribbon with Six Devices; Korean Service Medal with Two Devices; European-African-Middle Eastern Campaign Medal with Three Devices; Good Conduct Medal, United States Army; Armed Forces Reserve Medal; American Campaign Medal; Small Arms Expert Marksmanship Ribbon. Address: 4120 Morning Trail, College Park, Georgia 30349.■

CAMERON O. SMITH

Corporate Executive. Personal: Born July 29, 1950; Son of William F. II and Jane B. Smith; Married Liza Vann. Education: Attended The Hotchkiss School, 1968; Princeton University, 1972; Pennsylvania State University, 1975. Career: President, Taconic Petroleum Corporation; President, The Catawba Corporation; Director, Borealis Exploration Limited; Trustee, The Hembdt Trust; Master of English, the Hotchkiss School. Organizational Memberships: American Association of Petroleum Geologists; Society of Petroleum Engineers of American Institute of Metallurgical Engineers; Petroleum Exploration Society of New York; Tulsa Geological Society. Community Activities: Trustee, Treasurer, Indian Mountain School, 1976-80; Class Agent, The Hotchkiss School, 1975-77, 1981 to present; Governor, The Union League Club of New York, 1976-81. Honors and Awards: Captain, Princeton University Soccer Team (honorably mentioned all-ivy), 1972; Summa Cum Laude Graduate, 1972; Phi Beta Kappa, 1968, 1972. Address: South Main Street, Sharon, Connecticut 06069.■

CHARLES WILLIAM SMITH

Associate Professor of Education. Personal: Born July 6, 1933; Son of Albert Glenn Smith; Married Miriam Louise Hogue. Education: B.S. Elementary Education, Indiana University of Pennsylvania, 1955; M.Ed. Educational Administration 1963, Ed.D. Elementary Education 1970, The Pennsylvania State University. Military: Served in the United States Army, 1956-58. Career: Associate Professor of Education, Northern Illinois University, DeKalb, Illinois, 1968 to present; Public School Teacher, Western Beaver County (Pennsylvania) Schools, 1955-67. Organizational Memberships: Life Member, National Education Association; Life Member, Phi Delta Kappa. Religion: Former Secretary, Board of Trustees and Elder, Presbyterian Church. Honors and Awards: Speaker, The International Symposium on Educational Testing, The Hague, The Netherlands, 1973. Address: 345 Miller Avenue, DeKalb, Illinois 60115.■

CORNELIA MARSCHALL SMITH

Professor Emeritus. Personal: Born October 15, 1895; Daughter of Ernst and Lucy Meusebach Marschall (both deceased); Married Dr. Charles G. Smith. Education: B.A., Baylor University, 1918; M.A., University of Chicago, 1923; Ph.D., Johns Hopkins University, 1928. Career: Professor Emeritus, Professor of Biology 1940-67, Chairman of Biology Department 1943-67, Director of Strecker Museum 1943-67, Assistant Professor 1930-35, Instructor in Botany 1928-30, Baylor University; Professor of Biology and Chairman of Biology Department, J. B. Stetson University, 1935-40. Organizational Memberships: Texas State Board of Examiners of Basic Sciences, Member 1949-67, Secretary-Treasurer 1959-67; American Society of Zoologists; Botanical Society of America; National Audubon Society; Texas Ornothological Society. Community Activities: American Association of University Women; American Association of University Professors; Modern Language Association; Sigma Xi; Beta Beta Beta; Alpha Epsilon Delta; Kappa Kappa Gamma. Religion: First Baptist Church of Waco, Texas, 1918 to present. Honors and Awards: Mortar Board, 1973 to present; Women's Day Outstanding Faculty Member, 1963; Minnie Piper Professor of the Year, 1961; Teacher of the Year, 1965-66; Outstanding Alumnae Award, 1972; Baylor University Cornelia M. Smith Professorship in Biology, Initiated in 1980; Fellow, American Association for the Advancement of Science; Texas Academy of Science. Address: 801 James, Waco, Texas 76706.■

DAVID E. SMITH

Educator, Physician. Personal: Born February 7, 1939, in Bakersfield, California; Son of Elvin and Dorthy Smith; Married Millicent Buxton; Father of Christopher Buxton-Smith, Julia, Suzanne. Education: Graduate of East Bakersfield High School, 1956; A.A., Bakersfield College, 1958; B.A., University of California-Berkeley, 1960; M.S. 1964, M.D. 1964, University of California-San Francisco; Intern, San Francisco General Hospital, 1965; Postdoctoral Fellowship, Pharmacology and Toxicology, University of California-San Franiscco, 1965-67; Ph.D. Program, Institute for Advanced Study of Human Sexuality, 1979 to present. Career: Founder and Medical Director, Haight Ashbury Free Medical Clinic, 1967 to present; Consultant, Drug Abuse, Gladman Memorial Psychiatric Hospital, Oakland, California, 1978 to present; Consultant on Drug Abuse, Department of Psychiatry, San Francisco General Hospital, 1967-72; Director, Alcohol and Drug Abuse Screening Unit, San Francisco General Hospital, 1965-72; Physician, Contra Costa Alcoholic Clinic, 1965-67; Physician, Presbyterian Alcoholic Clinic, 1965-66; Assistant Clinical Professor of Toxicology, Department of Pharmacology, University of California Medical Center, 1967-75; Lecturer in Criminology, University of California-Berkeley, 1958-69; Co-Director, National Training Center for Drug Education, San Francisco, 1970; Preceptor, Community Medicine Preceptorship Program, University of California-San Diego, 1971-73; Faculty, National College of Juvenile Justice, University of Nevada-Reno, 1971 to present; Honorary Lecturer, Department of Medicine, Addiction Research Foundation Clinical Institute, Toronto, Canada, 1975 to present; Associate Clinical Professor of Behavioral Pharmacology, University of Nevada Medical School, 1975 to present; Associate Clinical Professor of Behavioral Pharmacology, University of Nevada Medical School, 1975 to present; Associate Clinical Professor of Toxicology, Department of Pharmacology, University of California Medical Center, San Francisco, 1975 to present; Consultant, Drug Abuse, Veterans' Administration Hospital, 1968 to present; Consultant, National Association of State Drug Abuse, 1972 to present; Advisory Board fo PHARMCHEM Research Foundation, 1975 to present; Advisory Council on Narcotics and Drug Abuse, Sacramento; Advisory Committee on Controlled Substances, Food and Drug Administration, 1978-82; Associate Principal Investigator, San Francisco Polydrug Project, 1974-77; Consultant, Department of Psychiatry, San Francisco General Hospital, 1966 to present; Consultant, Peralta Chemical Dependence Hospital, Marin A.C.T. Chemical Dependence Program 1979 to present. Organizational Memberships: San Francisco Medical Society; California Medical Association, Consultant on Drug Abuse; Phi Beta Kappa; Sigma Xi; F.A.S.E.B.; Youth Projects Inc., President 1967 to present; American Public Health Association, Mental Health Section, 1968 to present; American Academy of Clinical Toxicology, Charter Member; California Society for the Treatment of Alcoholism and Other Drug Dependencies, Charter Member, Chairman Editor Committee 1973 to present, President 1980-83; San Francisco Society Board of Medical Quality Assurance Committee, 1979; Western Pharmacology Society; California Medical Association. Community Activities: Health Advisor to Jimmy Carter, 1976; Democratic National Platform, Alcoholism and Drug Abuse Sub-Committee 1976; Governor's Advisory Panel on Narcotics and Drug Abuse, 1977; Consultant, F.D.A Controlled Substances Advisory Committee, 1978 to present; Consultant, National Institute of Drug Abuse, 1976 to present. Published Works: Founder and Editor, *Journal of Psychoactive Drugs* (formerly *Journal of Psychedelic Drugs*), 1966 to present; Editorial Board, *The Journal*, Toronto Addiction Research Institute, 1974 to present; Editorial Board, *Clinical Toxicology*, 1975 to present; Author of Many Professional Articles, Books and Drug Abuse Films. Honors and Awards: Survey of Anesthesiology Research, 1964; Bordon Research Award, 1964; S.A.M.A. Research Award, 1966; California Junior College Alumnus of the Year, 1969; Chancellor's Award for Community Service, University of California-San Francisco, 1974; 16th Annual *San Francisco Examiner* "Ten Most Distinguished Award," 1974; American Medical Association Physician's Recognition Award in Continuing Education; Martin Luther King Humanitarian Award, Glide Church, San Francisco, 1980. Address: 409 Clayton Street, San Francisco, California 94117.■

ELIZABETH MARY SMITH

Assistant Professor. Personal: Born December 15, 1940. Education: B.A. 1960, M.S.W. 1962, University of Nebraska, Lincoln; Ph.D., Washington University, St. Louis, 1978. Career: Assistant Professor, Department of Psychiatry, Washington University School of Medicine; Chief Social Worker, Outpatient Psychiatric Clinic, Barnes Hospital, St. Louis, Missouri. Organizational Memberships: National Association of Social Workers, Secretary 1980-82; Missouri Chapter, National Association of Social Workers, President 1979-81; Midwest Coalition, National Association of Social Workers, Co-Chairman 1979-81; Council on Social Work Education; American Public Health Association; American Association of University Professors. Community Activities: Missouri Abortion Rights Alliance, Board of Directors 1972-79, President 1977-78; Reproductive Health Services, Inc., Board of Directors and Secretary 1973 to present; Missouri Association for Social Welfare; American Civil Liberties Union. Honors and Awards: N.I.A.A.A. Grant for Research on Alcohol and Women, 1978-81; Academy of Certified Social Workers, 1981; Theta Sigma Phi, National Journalism Honorary; Various Publications in Professional Journals. Address: 8408 Winzenburg Drive, St. Louis, Missouri 63117.■

GEORGE DEE SMITH

Company Executive. Personal: Born November 23, 1929; Son of George F. and Vera H. Smith (both deceased); Married Jeannine Meacham; Father of Dee Ann. Education: A.B., University of North Carolina, 1951; Advanced Management Program, Harvard University, 1982; Correspondence Course in Higher Education, La Salle University. Military: Served in the United States Naval Reserve, Lieutenant, 1951-55. Career: R. J. Reynolds Tobacco Company, Several Accounting Positions 1955-70, Comptroller and Member Board of Directors 1970, Vice President and Comptroller 1972, Senior Vice President 1973, Chairman and Chief Executive Officer of Macdonald Tobacco (R. J. Reynolds Canadian Subsidy) 1974, President and Chief Executive Officer R. J. Reynolds Tobacco International 1976, Senior Vice President and Assistant to Chairman 1980, Executive Vice President 1981 to present. Community Activities: United Way Board of Directors, 1984 to present; Winston-Salem Chamber of Commerce, Board of Directors, First Vice President, Executive Committee; The Arts Council, Board of Trustees and Chairman 1983; Old Salem, Inc., Board of Trustees; University of North Carolina at Greensboro and its Excellence Foundation, Board of Trustees, Chairman Major Gifts Campaign 1982-84; Business Advisory Council, Western Carolina University; Winston-Salem Rotary Club; Board of Trustees, Carolina Medicorp, Inc.; City/County Utilities Commission, 1982-84. Religion: Home Moravian Church, Member, Chairman of the Board Moravian Home Inc. 1982-84. Address: 317 Sherwood Forest Road, Winston-Salem, North Carolina 27104.■

GLORIA JEAN SMITH

Actuary. Personal: Born February 27, 1929, in Hollis, Oklahoma; Daughter of Benjamin J. and Lena B. Edwards Roy; Married Wilbert Sims Sr., December 3, 1946; Married Second Husband, Mayfield Wesley Smith Sr., December 12, 1956; Mother of Wilbert B. Sims Jr., William David Sims, Evelyn Jo Cheatham, Mayfield Wesley Smith Jr. Education: Attended the City College of San Francisco 1952, University of California at San Francisco 1964, London School of Journalism 1967-70. Career: Insurance Agent, Watchtower Life Insurance, Dallas, 1949-50; Manager, Business Office, San Francisco Medical Associates, 1960-61; Assistant Bookkeeper, I. Magnin & Company, San Francisco, 1961-65; Assistant Actuary, Coates, Herfurth & England, San Francisco, 1967-70; Assistant Consulting Actuary, San Francisco, 1970 to present. Organizational Memberships: American Management Association; National Writers Club; Research Institute of America. Community Activities: American Red Cross; Smithsonian Institution; San Francisco Women's Democratic Forum; St. Mary's College Guild. Honors and Awards: Listed in *Who's Who in the West*. Address: 2674 Sacramento Street, San Francisco, California 94115.■

IAN CORMACK PALMER SMITH

Principal Research Officer, National Research Council. Personal: Born September 23, 1939; Son of Cormack and Grace M. Smith; Married Eva Gunilla Landvik; Father of Brittmarie, Duncan, Cormack, Roderick. Education: B.S. with honors 1961, M.S. 1962, University of Manitoba, Winnipeg; Ph.D., Cambridge University, England, 1965. Career: Principal Research Officer, Former Head Molecular Biophysics, National Research Council, Ottawa; Research Scientist, Bell Laboratories, Murray Hill, New Jersey, 1966-67; Postdoctoral Fellow, Stanford University, 1965-66. Organizational Memberships: Biophysical Society, Council Member

1978-81; Canadian Biochemistry Society, Council Member 1980-83; Chemical Institute of Canada, Council Member 1978-80, Chairman Biological Chemistry Division 1976-77; Royal Society of Canada, Rapporteur 1983-85. Community Activities: Ottawa Memorial Society, Board of Directors 1969-70, 1980-82; Coach of Youth Baseball and Ringette. Published Works: Author 250 Articles in Journals and Chapters in Books. Honors and Awards: Fellow, Chemical Institute of Canada, 1973; Fellow, Royal Society of Canada, 1977; Merck, Sharp and Dohme Award, Chemical Institute of Canada, 1978; Ayerst Award, Canadian Biochemistry Society, 1978; Barringer Award, Canadian Spectroscopy Society, 1979; Labatt Award, Chemical Institute of Canada, 1984. Address: 550 Rivershore Crescent, Ottawa, Canada K1J 7Y7.

JAMES GILBERT SMITH

Professor and Laboratory Director. Personal: Born May 1, 1930; Married Barbara Ann; Father of Julie. Education: B.S.E.E. 1957, M.S.E.E. 1959, Ph.D. 1967, University of Missouri at Rolla. Military: Served in the United States Army, Sergeant, 1951-53. Career: Professor and Director, Lightening Research Laboratory, Department Chairperson Electrical Sciences and Systems Engineering 1971-80, Southern Illinois University-Carbondale; Engineer, Boeing Company, Emerson Electric and General Telephone and Electronics. Organizational Memberships: American Society for Engineering Education, Chairman Illinois/Indiana Section 1970-71; Institute of Electrical and Electronic Engineers; American Association for the Advancement of Science. Community Activities: Rotary International, 1973 to present. Honors and Awards: National Science Foundation Faculty Fellowship, 1962-63; Phi Kappa Phi; Tau Beta Pi; Eta Kappa Nu; Sigma Pi Sigma. Address: 2604 Sunset Drive, Carbondale, Illinois 62901.■

JOHN JULIUS SMITH

Pure Abstract Mathematical and Physical Research. Personal: Born May 28, 1941; Son of Julius Freeman and Lottie Winfred Smith; Married; Father of Derrick Daniel, John Julius II. Education: B.S. Mathematics, B.S. Physics, University of Arizona, 1969; M.A. Mathematics, Temple University, 1973; Ph.D. Mathematics, Ph.D. Physics, Southeastern University, 1981; C.C. Electronics, Newark College of Engineering, 1959; C.C. Mathematical Physics, College of William and Mary, 1971; M.S. Mathematics, Lehigh University, 1971; Further Studies undertaken at Penn State University, Bloomsburg State, University of Wisconsin. Military: Served in the United States Army, 1964-66, attaining the rank of First Lieutenant. Career: Pure Abstract Mathematical and Physics Research; Former Positions include Instructor, Tutor, Senior Engineer, Scientist, Sanitarian, Environmental Protection Specialist, N.A.S.A. Aerospace Technologist, Statistician, Head Programmer, Assistant Programmer, Project Assistant, Post Office Distribution Clerk. Organizational Memberships: Chairman of Ad Hoc Committee of tie between National Science Teachers Association and the American Association of Physics Teachers, 1982-84; Elected to Advisory Board of the American Biographical Institute; Fellow, A.P.T., M.A.A., A.M.S., American Association for the Advancement of Science. Community Activities: Boy Scouts of America, Assistant Scout Master 1970-76; American Legion; Wings Field Pilot Association; Apprenticeship Resources Center, Teacher/Tutor for G.E.D. for High School Dropouts, 1981-82; Appointed to 1982 National Board of Advisors, American Biographical Institute. Honors and Awards: National Science Foundation Candidate, 1966; Merit Awards, United States Army, 1971; Listed in *Who's Who in Finance and Industry, Who's Who in the World, Who's Who in the East, Who's Who in America, Who's Who in Science, Men of Achievement, Men of Intellect, American Registry Series*, Others. Address: 679 Cedar Hill Drive, Allentown, Pennsylvania 18103.■

JOSEPH NEWTON SMITH, III

Vice President of Interior Design. Personal: Born July 4; Son of Oneal K. Smith; Married Gloria; Father of Gordon. Education: B.S. 1948, B.Arch. 1949, Georgia Institute of Technology; Attended University of Tampa 1943-44, Emory University 1943, Georgia Institute of Technology 1943-44, 1946-49. Military: Served in the United States Navy, Lieutenant (j.g.). Career: Vice President of Interior Design; Assistant Dean, Georgia Institute of Technology. Organizational Memberships: A.I.A., Fellow, President Atlanta Chapter 1979, President Georgia Association 1983. Honors and Awards: Birch Burdette Long Memorial Award, Architectural League of New York, 1954; Special Award for Delineation, Florida Association of Architects, 1955; Award of Merit for Key Biscayne Presbyterian Church, South Atlantic Region, A.I.A., 1964; Honored as Artist of the Year, Young Women of the Arts, 1974. Address: 2466 Ridgewood Road, Northwest, Atlanta, Georgia 30335.■

JUDITH JOHNS SMITH

Administrator. Personal: Born October 27, 1937; Daughter of Ruth Agar Johns. Education: B.A. cum laude in English, College of William and Mary, 1960; M.S.Ed., Special Education, Old Dominion University, 1970; Ph.D. Special Education, University of New Mexico, 1981. Career: Director of Dissemin/Action, National Significance Project Funded by United States Department of Education; Founder, Director of Atlantic Academy, Proprietary School for Disturbed Adolescents, Norfolk and Virginia Beach, Virginia; Chief Editor and Technical Writing Instructor, The Stanwick Corporation, Norfolk and Arlington, Virginia; Instructor, University of Virginia, Hampton Roads Center; Psychometrician and Adolescent Therapist, Psychiatric Associates of Tidewater, Inc., Norfolk; Teacher of English and Social Studies, Northside Junior High School, Norfolk. Organizational Memberships: International Council for Exceptional Children, Member-at-Large to the Executive Committee, Teacher Education Division 1980 to present; National Council for the Accreditation of Teacher Education, Site Visitation Team 1979 to present; Editorial Board Member, *Teacher Education and Special Education, Journal of Special Education, The Pointer, Education and Training the Mentally Retarded, Jash.* Community Activities: Muscular Dystrophy Association, Area Leader, Telethon Liaison 1968-71; Committee for the Rights of the Handicapped, Albuquerque, New Mexico, Public Information Chairman 1975-76; United States Department of Education and Office of Developmental Disabilities of the Former Rehabilitation Services Administration, Field Reader, Panelist; Dissemination Forum of the National Institute of Education and United States Office of Education, Steering Committee 1978. Honors and Awards: Award for Significant Contribution to the Division of Mental Retardation of the International Council for Exceptional Children, 1977; Award, Edna St. Vincent Millay Memorial Poetry Contest, 1957; Listed in *World Who's Who of Women, Directory of Distinguished Americans, Who's Who in the South and Southwest.* Address: 750 McDonald Drive, Reno, Nevada 89503.■

KATHLEEN MARY SMITH

College Dean of Students and Member of Religious Order. Personal: Born September 26, 1945; Daughter of Michael W. and Mary E. (Cronin) Smith. Education: B.A. Mathematics, College Misericordia, Pennsylvania, 1969; M.A. Student Personnel Services, Indiana University of Pennsylvania, 1974; Ph.D. Higher Education Administration, The University of Michigan, 1982. Career: Dean of Students, Saint Xavier College; Dean of Student Services, Director of Financial Aid, Instructor, Admissions Counselor, Resident Director, Mount Aloysius Junior College, Cresson, Pennsylvania; Research Assistant, Consultant, The University of Michigan; Title III Consultant, Washtenaw Community College, Ann Arbor, Michigan; High School Mathematics Teacher, Sacred Heart High School and Bishop McCort High School, Pennsylvania. Organizational Memberships: Pennsylvania Association of Student Financial Aid Administrators, Executive Council 1977-79; National Association of Student Personnel Administrators; American Association of Higher Education; Association for the Study of Higher Education; American Association of Community and Junior Colleges, Conference Presenter 1983; Michigan Admission Counselors and Registrar Officers, Conference Presenter 1980; Mercy Higher Education Colloquium, Chair of Membership Subcommittee 1983-85; Illinois College Personnel Association; Chicagoland Deans of Students Association. Community Activities: Johnstown Flood Relief Program Volunteer, 1977; Cambria County Special Olympics, 1979 and 1983; Office of Education Financial Aid National Review Board, 1978; K.E.Y. Specialized Foster Care Services, Inc., Board Member 1983; Cambria City Teens Club, 1972-73; Retreat State Hospital Volunteer, 1966-67. Religion: Roman Catholic; Religious Sisters of Mercy, Province of Scranton, Fiscal Management Commission 1977-79 and 1982 to present, Formation Council 1983, Due Process Procedure Arbitration 1981-85, Higher Education Advisory Council 1978-79, Corporation of the Sisters of Mercy of Cresson Board 1974-79, 1982-83 (Treasurer 1974-79). Honors and Awards: White House Fellowship, Regional Finalist, 1982; General University of Michigan Scholarship,

TWO THOUSAND NOTABLE AMERICANS

1979-80; University Fellowship, 1980; P. I. Murrill Scholarship, 1980; School of Education Merit Award, 1981; Listed in *Who's Who in America, Personalities of America*. Address: 10024 South Central Park Avenue, Chicago, Illinois 60642.■

ROBERT JUNIUS SMITH

Financial Executive. Personal: Born December 25, 1920; Son of Samuel Francis and Lulu Jane Hatch Smith (both deceased); Married Lola Nielson, Daughter of Ernest E. (deceased) and Lavina D. Nielson; Father of Junola Smith Bush, Lynn Robert, Lynette Smith Lyman, Shirley Smith Ricks, LaRae Smith Blake, Jeanine Smith Denton, Larry Kay, Sheldon Ray. Education: B.S. Accounting and Business Administration, Brigham Young University, 1948; M.B.A. Accounting, Northwestern University, 1949; D.B.A. Accounting, Indiana University, 1957. Military: Served in the United States Naval Reserve, 1944-46, attaining the rank of Electronic Technician's Mate, Second Class. Career: Brigham Young University, Assistant Professor of Accounting 1949-50, Associate Professor 1950-57, Professor 1957 to present, Chairman Accounting Department 1952-55 and 1959-62, Acting Dean of the College of Business 1963-64, Assistant Academic Vice President 1968-71, Associate Academic Vice President 1971-78, Financial Vice President 1979-84, Administrative Vice President 1984 to present; Partner, Tenney, Western & Smith, 1961-65; Faculty Resident, Arthur Andersen & Company, 1964-65; Consulting Partner, Main Lafentz & Company, 1966-67. Organizational Memberships: President, Southern Chapter, Utah Association of CPA's, 1962-63; American Accounting Association; American Institute of CPA's; Alpha Kappa Psi; Beta Alpha Psi; Beta Gamma Sigma; Phi Kappa Phi; Utah Association of CPA's. Community Activities: United Way of Utah County, 13 Years Service including Office of President 1972; Utah National Parks Council Boy Scouts of America, Controller 1982-84, Treasurer 1984 to present. Religion: Member Church of Jesus Christ of Latter-day Saints; Latter-day Saint Mission, Southern States, 1942-44; Bishop 1959-61 and 1966-67; Stake Presidency, 1961-64 and 1967-78 (President 1973-78); Welfare Services Region Agent, 1979 to present. Honors and Awards: Elijah Watt Sells Gold Medal Award, American Institute of Certified Professional Accountants for Highest Grades in May, 1949 CPA Examination; Karl G. Maeser Outstanding Teaching Award, Brigham Young University, 1967; National Association of Accountants, Winner of Outstanding Manuscript Award in Salt Lake City Chapter, 1957-58, 1959-60, 1963-64; Brigham Young University Alumni Distinguished Service Award, 1982. Address: 2465 North 820 East, Provo, Utah 84604.■

ROGER PERRY SMITH

Clinical Assistant Professor. Personal: Born January 31, 1949; Son of Dr. and Mrs. Stanley E. Smith, Jr.; Married Barbara A.; Father of Scott A., Jeffrey T. Education: B.S., Purdue University, West Lafayette, Indiana, 1965-68; B.S.M., M.D., The Medical School, Northwestern University, Chicago, Illinois, 1968-72; Licensed in the State of Illinois, 1973; Certified by the American Board of Obstetrics and Gynecology, 1978. Career: Straight Surgical Internship, Chicago Wesley Memorial Hospital, Chicago, Illinois, 1972-73; Resident in Obstetrics and Gynecology, Northwestern Memorial Hospital-McGaw Medical Center, The Prentice Women's Hospital and Maternity Center, Chicago, Illinois, 1973-76; Attending Staff, Carle Foundation Hospital, Urbana, Illinois; Courtesy Staff, Burnham City Hospital, Champaign, Illinois; Courtesy Staff, Mercy Hospital, Urbana, Illinois; Courtesy Staff, McKinley Hospital, Urbana, Illinois; Courtesy Staff, Paris Community Hospital, Paris, Illinois; University of Illinois, School of Basic Medical Sciences, Urbana, Illinois, Clinical Associate 1977-79, Clinical Instructor 1979-81; University of Illinois, School of Clinical Medicine, Urbana, Illinois, Clinical Advisor 1980 to present, Clinical Assistant Professor 1981 to present. Organizational Memberships: American College of Obstetricians and Gynecologists, Fellow, Junior Fellow Section Chairman (Illinois) 1978-79; The Central Association of Obstetrics and Gynecology; American Institute of Ultrasound in Medicine; Association for the Advancement of Medical Instrumentation; Illinois Obstetrical and Gynecological Society, 'Secretary 1976-79, 1979 to present, Program Director 1978, 1979; Illinois Association of Maternal and Child Health, Board of Directors 1979-81; East Central Illinois Health Systems Agency; American Medical Association; Illinois State Medical Association; Chicago Medical Society, 1971-76; Champaign County Medical Society, Program Committee 1980-81; American Federation for Clinical Research. Community Activities: Charter Member, WILL Associates; Carle Foundation Circle of Friends; Champaign-Urbana Apple Users Group, Board of Directors 1982-83, Newsletter Editor 1982-83; Musical Box Society International. Published Works: Contributor Numerous Articles to Professional Journals, Chapters to Books; Several Exhibits, Films, Slide and Tape Programs. Honors and Awards: Phi Eta Sigma, Purdue University, 1965-66; Alpha Epsilon Delta, Indiana Beta Chapter, Purdue University, 1966, President 1967-68; Tomahawk, Purdue University, 1966-67; Gables Scholarship Key, Purdue University, 1965-66; President's Academic Honors Award, Purdue University, 1968 and 1969; Mensa; 1979 Community Hospital Award, the Central Association of Obstetrics and Gynecologists for Paper "The Objective Evaluation of Dysmenorrhea Therapy"; Sociedad Peruana de Obstetricia y Ginecologia, Honorario, 1980; 1983 Community Hospital Award, the Central Association of Osbetricians and Gynecologists for Paper "Distribution Analysis of Intrauterine Pressure in Nonpregnant Dysmenorrheic Women"; Listed in *Who's Who in the Midwest, Personalities of America, Personalities of the West and Midwest, Men of Achievement*. Address: 2204 Galen Drive, Champaign, Illinois 61821.■

SAM SMITH

City Councilman. Personal: Born July 21, 1922; Son of Rev. and Mrs. Steve Smith (both deceased); Married Marion King, Daughter of Mr. and Mrs. Glover King (both deceased); Father of A. Carl, Amelia I., Anthony E., Donald C., Ronald C., Stephen K. II. Education: Bachelor of Social Science, Seattle University, 1951; B.A. Economics, University of Washington, 1952; Graduate Work undertaken in Economics and Political Science, University of Washington, 1953. Military: Served in the United States Army, 1942-46, attaining the rank of Warrant Officer. Career: Full-time City Councilman for the City of Seattle, Washington; Former Positions include State Legislator for the State of Washington, Full-time Lead Expeditor for The Boeing Company (17 Years). Organizational Memberships: National League of Cities; National Black Caucus of Local Elected Officials; Northwest Conference of Black Elected Officials, Regional Director. Community Activities: Chairman Public Safety and Justice Committee, Member Finance Committee, Chairman Housing, Recreation and Health Committee of City Council; Former Member of Board of Managers, American Baptist Churches, U.S.A.; Life Member, National Association for the Advancement of Colored People; Seattle Urban League; Human Resources Committee, National Congress of Cities. Religion: Member of Mt. Zion Baptist Church (Seattle), Church School Teacher 28 Years, President of Men's Fellowship Group 23 Years. Honors and Awards: Commended for Effective Leadership as President of Seattle City Council by Seattle King County Municipal League, 1978; Prince Hall Scottish Rite Gold Medal Achievement Award, 1978; Medal of Honor, Daughters of the American Revolution, 1980; Distinguished Alumnus Award, Seattle University, 1976; Distinguished Service Award, Central Area Jaycees, 1974; Exemplary Leadership Award, Mount Zion Baptist Church, 1973; Community Service Award, 1971; Seattle Urban League Annual Award, 1968; Legislator of Year Award, State House of Representatives, 1967; 33rd Degree Mason; Pioneer Award, Goodwill Baptist Church, Seattle, Washington, 1984; Recognition from Kiwanis Club, Young Men's Christian Association, Other Civic Organizations. Address: 1814 31st Avenue, Seattle, Washington 98122.■

TIMOTHY ANDRE SMITH

University Professor. Personal: Born January 9, 1937; Son of Raphael and Florence Smith; Married Namida; Father of Linda, Mark, Maura, Alicia. Education: B.S., Marquette University, Milwaukee, Wisconsin, 1954-58; M.A. 1958-61, Ph.D. 1961-63, University of North Carolina at Chapel Hill. Career: Assistant Instructor, University of North Carolina at Chapel Hill, 1961-62; Instructor 1962-63, Assistant Professor 1963-69, Florida State University, Tallahassee, Florida; Associate Professor 1969-73, Professor 1973 to present, Professor of Community Dentistry and Education and Counseling Psychology 1973 to present, University of Kentucky, Lexington. Organizational Memberships: American Psychological Association; American Educational Research Association; Kentucky Psychological Association; American Association of Dental Schools; International Association for Dental Research; American Association of Public Health Dentists. Honors and Awards: B.S. Degree cum laude, Marquette University, 1958; Ford Behavior Science Fellowship, University of North Carolina, 1958-59; National Science Foundation Intermediate Fellowship, University of North Carolina, 1960-61; Fellow in Preventive and Social Medicine, Harvard School of Medicine, 1976. Address: 1178 Indian Mound Road, Lexington, Kentucky 40502.■

TOM E. SMITH

Corporate Executive. Personal: Born May 2, 1941; Son of Ralph Eugene and Cora Belle (Ervin) Smith; Married Catherine Conway Wallace; Father of Leigh Ann, Nancy Thompson. Education: A.B. Business Administration, Catawba College, 1964. Military: Served in the United States Army Reserve, 1968-72; Career: Position with Del Monte Sales Company, 1964-70; Food Town Stores, Inc., Buyer 1970-74, Vice President of Distribution 1974-77, Executive Vice President 1977-81, Board of Directors 1977 to present, President of Save-Rite 1973 to present, President Food Town 1981. Organizational Memberships: Director of North Carolina National Bank, 1974 to present; National Association of Retail Grocers of the United States, 1979 to present; Board of Directors, North Carolina Food Dealers, 1981-83; Board of Directors, Salisbury Sales Marketing, 1981. Community Activities: Board of Directors, United Way, 1975-

77; Director, Rotary, 1975-76; Board of Directors, Chamber of Commerce, 1975-77. Honors and Awards: Honorary Citizen of Prince George County, Virginia; Catawba College Distinguished Alumnus Award, 1982; Listed in *Who's Who in the Southeast, Who's Who in America, Who's Who in the World, Who's Who in Finance and Industry.* Address: 620 Catawba Road, Salisbury, North Carolina 28144. ■

TROY ALVIN SMITH

Aerospace Engineer. Personal: Born July 4, 1922; Son of Wade Hampton and Augusta Mabel Lindsey Smith (both deceased). Education: B.C.E., The University of Virginia, 1948; M.S.E. 1952, Ph.D. Engineering Mechanics 1970, The University of Michigan. Military: Served in the United States Navy, 1942-46. Career: Structural Engineer, Corps of Engineers, United States Army, 1948-59; Chief Structural Engineer, Brown Engineering Company, Inc., Huntsville, Alabama, 1959-60; Structural Research Engineer, United States Army Missile Command, Redstone Arsenal, Alabama, 1960-63; Aerospace Engineer, United States Army Missile Command, Redstone Arsenal, 1963 to present. Organizational Memberships: The Society of Sigma Xi; The New York Academy of Sciences; The Association of the United States Army. Community Activities: Professional Engineering, Virginia 1948 to present, Alabama 1959 to present; Benevolent and Protective Order of Elks, Lodge #1648, Huntsville. Honors and Awards: Secretary of the Army Research and Study Fellowship, The University of Michigan, 1969. Address: 2406 Bonita Drive, S.W., Huntsville, Alabama 35801. ■

WARREN THOMAS SMITH

Professor of Church History, Clergyman-Educator. Personal: Born October 20, 1923; Son of Warren T. and Lola May Jones Smith (deceased); Married Barbara Sullards; Father of James Warren. Education: Attended Maryville College, 1942-43; B.A., Ohio Wesleyan University, 1945; B.D., Emory University, 1948; Ph.D., Boston University, 1953; D.D., Lincoln Memorial University, 1958; Postdoctoral Work, Graduate School of Emory University, 1974; Research, Yale University, Summers 1978, 1980. Career: Professor of Church History, The Interdenominational Theological Center; Ordained Minister in the United Methodist Church, Peachtree Road Methodist Church (Atlanta); Director of Religious Life, Young Harris College; Pastor, Trinity Methodist Church (Atlanta); Director of Ministerial Recruitment with the General Board of Education of the Methodist Church; Pastor, Young Harris Methodist Church (Athens, Georgia), North Decatur Methodist Church, College Park First United Methodist Church (College Park, Georgia). Organizational Memberships: American Society of Church History; American Historical Association; Wesley Historical Society, England. Religion: United Methodist Minister, Member North Georgia Conference, Chairman North Georgia Commission on Archives and History, Georgia Commission on Higher Education, Interpreter for American Methodism's Bicentennial. Published Works: Author, *Thomas Coke, Foreign Minister of Methodism, Heralds of Christ, Writings of Thomas Coke, At Christmas, Preludes: Georgia, Methodism, The American Revolution, Augustine: His Life and Thought, And the Play Goes On: Characters in the Biblical Drama, Harry Hosier: Circuit Rider.* Honors and Awards: Grant from National Endowment for the Humanities for a Biographical Study of Thomas Coke; Brotherhood Award, Anti-Defamation League of B'nai B'rith. Address: 3460 Hemphill Street, College Park, Georgia 30337. ■

WILLIAM (BILL) SMITH, II

Department Supervisor. Personal: Born November 30, 1941; Son of William and Willie Mae Smith; Father of William III, Maurice. Education: B.S., Tuskegee Institute, 1964; Postgraduate Studies undertaken at Washington University, 1968-70. Military: Served in the United States Naval Reserves, honorably discharged in 1981. Career: Engineering Department Supervisor; Former Positions include Equipment Engineer with The Boeing Company, Plant Design Engineer with McDonnel Douglas Corporation, Project Manager for the Saint Louis County Government, Area Engineer for E. I. duPont de Nemours & Company, Engineering Manager for Westinghouse Corporation, Safety Engineer and Safety Conservationist for the Denver Public School System. Organizational Memberships: American Society of Safety Engineers; Colorado Association of School Energy Coordinators; Mayor's Citizens Advisory Commission on Energy Conservation; American Association of Blacks in Energy. Community Activities: Tuskegee Institute National Alumni Association; Colorado Council of Local Energy Officials; Black Administrators and Supervisors Association; United Way Volunteer, Wiring Homes for the Elderly; Boy Scouts of America, Committee Member. Honors and Awards: President's National Award for Energy Conservation, 1980; Listed in *Who's Who in America, Who's Who in the West, Community Leaders of America, Five Thousand Personalities of the World, Men of Achievement, Biographical Roll of Honor, Who's Who in Colorado, The Directory of Distinguished Americans, Personalities of the West and Midwest.* Address: 102 South Balsam Street, Lakewood, Colorado 80226. ■

MICHAEL LOUIS SMOLANOFF

Executive. Personal: Born May 11, 1942; Son of Beatrice Smolanoff; Married Patricia; Father of Jason, Lauren, Nicole. Education: B.Mus., M.S., Juilliard School of Music; D.Mus., Combs College of Music. Military: Served in the United States Air Force, 1967-71. Career: President, Real to Reel Productions; Former Positions include Editor with E. B. Marks Music Corporation, Teacher at the Philadelphia Musical Academy and Rutgers University (7 Years), Composer for Children's Books and Records, Writer of Movie Screen Play and Four Animated Cartoons. Organizational Memberships: American Society of Composers, Authors and Publishers; National Academy of Television Arts and Sciences; Juilliard Alumni Association; Phi Mu Alpha Sinfonia of America; Philadelphia Art Alliance. Honors and Awards: First Prize, "Canticle for Band," 1964; American Song Festival Award, 1982; American Society for Composers, Authors and Publishers Award, 1966 to present. Address: 14A La Bonne Vie Drive, East Patchogue, New York 11772. ■

WILLIAM JOHN SMOLLEN

Treasurer. Personal: Son of Hugh Joseph and Alice Scribner Smollen (deceased); Married Helen. Education: B.S. Business, Columbia University; Additional Studies at Harvard University, Fordham University and University of California at Los Angeles; Certified Public Accountant in New York and California. Military: Served in the United States Air Force as Warrant Officer. Career: Treasurer, Dart International; Former President and Chairman, Space Ventures, Inc.; C.F.O., Ford Overseas. Organizational Memberships: Director, Financial Executive Institute, 1978 to present; President, Los Angeles Treasurers Club, 1974 and 1975; President, Planning Executives Institute, 1969; Western Pension Conference, National Association of Accountants; California and New York State Certified Public Accountants Societies; American Bar Association. Community Activities: Trustee, Centinela Hospital Medical Center, 1976 to present; United Way, Regional Director 1972-82, Administration and Finance Committee 1965 to present; Newcomen Society. Religion: Roman Catholic. Honors and Awards: Fellow, Planning Executives Institute, 1972. Address: 3044 Arrowhead Drive, Los Angeles, California 90068. ■

CAROLYN E. SMOOT

Staff Associate. Personal: Born September 24, 1945; Daughter of Mary Hickman; Married Douglas Bruce Smoot; Mother of Caroline Trucia. Education: B.S. Education, West Virginia State College, 1967; M.P.A., West Virginia College of Graduate Studies, 1975. Career: Staff Associate, Office of Development, West Virginia State College; Former Commissioner of Employment Security for the State of West Virginia. Organizational Memberships: President, Business and Professional Club, 1983 to present; Shawnee Community Center Board of Directors, 1980 to present. Community Activities: Appointed to Kanawha County Private Industry Council 1983, Member of Executive Committee; First Vice President, Charleston National Association for the Advancement of Colored People, 1983 to present; National Women's Political Caucus, 1982; Co-Chairman of Charleston Area Political Caucus, 1981 to present; Job Corps Community Relation Council, Charleston, 1983 to present; West Virginia Commission on Aging, 1977-78. Honors and Awards: Participant in First White House Conference on National Growth and Development, 1978; Listed in *Who's Who in Black America, Who's Who of American Women, Community Leaders of America, Directory of Distinguished Americans, Personalities of America, Who's Who in West Virginia.* Address: Box 222, Institute, West Virginia 25112. ■

ALFRED HAYWOOD SNIPES (DECEASED)

Architect. Personal: Born January 17, 1909, in Cameron, North Carolina; Son of Alfred Marshall and Bessie Inez McLaurin Snipes; Married Annie Laurie

TWO THOUSAND NOTABLE AMERICANS

Trevvett; Father of Laure Anne McKinnon (Mrs. Charles N. Jr.), Alfred Haywood Jr. Education: Attended Duke University 1928-29, North Carolina State College 1929-30, Richmond Business College; B.Arch., Catholic University of America, 1942; Miscellaneous Postgraduate Courses and Workshops. Career: Various Construction Jobs, 1925-30; with the United States Government R.M.S., 1930-45; with Various Architectural Firms in Virginia, New Mexico and Missouri, 1945-50; Individual Architectural Practice, 1951-81. Organizational Memberships: American Institute of Architects, 1958-81; Missouri Association of Architects, 1962-81. Community Activities: Board of Governors 1972-81, Board of Directors 1972-75, The Eye Research Foundation of Missouri; Missouri Lions State Sight Conservation Committee, Member 1959-77, Chairman 1965-75; Easter Seal Society for Crippled Children and Adults of Missouri, Board of Directors 1973-81, Vice President 1977-80; Statewide Health Coordinating Council of Missouri, Member 1976-81, Vice Chairman 1978, Acting Chairman 1979, Chairman 1980 and 1981; Missouri Area V Health System Agency Council Inc., Member of Governing Body 1976-81; Region VII Center for Health Planning Advisory Board, 1977-79; Drafting Design and Advisory Council, Three Rivers Community College, 1969-81; Business Opportunities for the Missouri Blind, Board of Directors 1960-68, President 1962-64; The Poplar Bluff Lions Club, Member 1951-81, President 1956-57; Council of Governors, Multiple District 26, Lions International 1958-59, (Chairman of Council 1958-59); Past District Governors Club 1959-81, Secretary 1973-74, Lions International. Religion: Member of the First Baptist Church of Poplar Bluff (Missouri). Honors and Awards: Distinguished Service Award for 18 Years Service to Lions State Sight Conservation Service 1977, 18 Years Service to the Lions Eye Tissue Bank 1978, Lions of Missouri; Life Membership Award for Outstanding Service in Poplar Bluff Lions Club 1979, Senior Master Key Award 1972, Lions International; Lion of the Year Award, Poplar Bluff Lions Club, 1970; Certificate of Appreciation, Conservation Federation of Missouri, 1970; Appreciation Award, State of Missouri and Missouri Health Coordinating Council, 1976-81; Appreciation Awards, Southeast Missouri Council of Boy Scouts of America, 1978, 1979, 1980; Business Opportunities for Missouri Blind Appreciation Award, 1968; Supreme Extension Award, Lions International, 1967; Bridge Cotton Belt Sectional Tournament A.C.B.L. Section First, Memphis, Tennessee, 1963; International Counselor's Award 1959, District Governor's 100% Award 1959, Lions International; New Mexico West Texas Open Championship Golf, Third Flight Winner, 1949; Sportmanship Awards, Richmond (Virginia) Young Men's Christian Association, 1934-35, 1935-36; Numerous Other Service and Appreciation Awards from Lions International, Poplar Bluff Lions Club, Other Organizations. Listed in *Who's Who in the Midwest*, *Community Leaders and Noteworthy Americans*, *Dictionary of International Biography*, *Men of Achievement*. Address: Westwood Hills Country Club Road, Route 7, Box 426, Poplar Bluff, Missouri 63901.■

HELEN FOSTER SNOW

Author and Researcher. Personal: Born 1907; Daughter of John Moody Foster. Education: Attended the University of Utah, Yenching University (Peking, China). Career: Retired Certified Genealogist. Organizational Memberships: Society of Woman Geographers. Community Activities: Madison (Connecticut) Bicentennial Commission, 1976; Co-Founder, Gung Ho Chinese Industrial Cooperatives (for refugee relief), 1938; Vice-Chairman, American Committee in Aid of Chinese Industrial Cooperatives, 1947-52; American Committee for Industrial Cooperatives, Founder 1981. Published Works: Author of Eight Books, including *My China Years* (an autobiography) 1984; Published Three Dramatized Histories for Madison Bicentennial, *The Madison Story*, *The Guilford Story* and *The Saybrook Story*. Religion: Unitarian-Universalist. Honors and Awards: Honorary Doctorate in Literature, St. Mary of the Woods, 1981; Nominated for Nobel Prize for Peace, 1981. Address: 148 Mungertown Road, Madison, Connecticut 06443.

DEE ANN SODER

Financial Executive. Personal: Daughter of Keats E. (deceased) and Dorothy Ann Soder. Education: B.A. with special distinction 1969, M.S. 1972, Ph.D. 1976, University of Oklahoma. Career: Vice President, Human Resources Development, Prudential Insurance Company, Newark, New Jersey, 1981-84; Staff Psychologist, Equal Employment Opportunity Commission, 1981; Corporate Psychologist, Rohrer, Hibler and Replogle, 1980-81; Advisor to the District of Columbia Government, 1979-80; Chief, Policy, Research and Development Branch, Washington Metropolitan Police Department, 1978-79; Team Leader, President's Reorganization Project, Law Enforcement, Executive Office of the President of the United States, 1977-78; Personnel Research Psychologist, United States Civil Service Commission, 1974-78; Assistant Director, National Association of State Directors of Law Enforcement Training, 1973-74; University of Oklahoma, Director of Juvenile Personnel Training Program, Director of Evaluation, Psychometrist for Security Force Training and Post Office Programs, Personnel Research Assistant to the Medical Center, 1969-74. Organizational Memberships: Human Resources Planning Society Roundtable; American Management Association; Community Health Law Association, Board of Directors; American Psychological Association; Personnel Testing Council, Founder and Former Treasurer; International Personnel Management Association, Former Executive Board Member for Washington, D.C. Area; Epilepsy Foundation of America, Board of Directors New Jersey Chapter. Community Activities: Considerable pro bono Service to the Handicapped, Women's Organizations and Law Enforcement. Honors and Awards: Advisor, President's Committee on Mental Retardation, 1974; Outstanding Pledge, Alpha Chi Omega, 1965; Outstanding Performance Rating Award, District of Columbia, 1979; Certificate of Appreciation, President of the United States, 1978; Listed in *Directory of Distinguished Americans*, *Who's Who of American Women*, *American Men and Women of Science*, *Personalities of the South*, *Community Leaders of America*. Address: 1200 Springfield Avenue, New Providence, New Jersey 07974.■

GENE SANDRA SOGLIERO

Senior Research Scientist and Statistician. Personal: Daughter of Frank and Sarah Taggart Cianfarani (both deceased). Education: A.M. Mathematics, Brown University, 1954; Ed.B. Mathematics/Science, Rhode Island College, 1947; Ph.D. Mathematical Statistics, 1970. Career: Senior Research Scientist/Statistician; Senior Research Engineer, Senior Mathematician, United Technologies Research Laboratory; Professor of Mathematics, University of Zaire, Zaire, Africa; Assistant Professor of Mathematics, Trinity College, Hartford, Connecticut. Organizational Memberships: American Statistical Society; American Institute of Aeronautics and Astronautics; Institute of Mathematics Statistics. Community Activities: Undergraduate College Activities include President of International Relations Club 1946-47, Secretary of Student Council, Vice President of Women's Athletic Corps, President of Kappa Delta Pi. Published Works: Author of Several Technical and Scientific Papers. Honors and Awards: Special Achievement Award, U.S.C.G. Research and Development Center, 1981; NASA Summer Faculty Fellowship, 1979; Listed in *Who's Who of Intellectuals*, *World Who's Who of Women*, *Who's Who in the East*. Address: 324 Thames Street #5, Groton, Connecticut 06340.

RUELL FLOYD SOLBERG, JR.

Research and Development Engineer. Personal: Born July 27, 1939; Son of Ruel and Ruby Rogstad Solberg; Married Laquetta Jane Massey; Father of Chandra Dawn (Mrs. J. Mark Hamilton), Marla Gaye. Education: B.S.M.E. 1962, M.S.M.E. 1967, University of Texas at Austin; M.B.A., Trinity University, 1977. Military: Served with the United States Army. Career: Research Engineer, Applied Research Laboratories, Austin, Texas, 1962-67; Assistant Supervisor, Mechanical Engineering Section, Austin, 1966-67; Southwest Research Institute, San Antonio, Texas, Research Engineer in Department of Applied Electromagnetics 1967-70, Senior Research Engineer 1970-74, Electromagnetics Division 1974-75, Department of Electromagnetic Engineering 1975 to present; Literature Reviewer, *Shock and Vibration Digest*, 1979 to present; Technical Assistant, *Applied Mechanics Reviews*, 1980 to present. Organizational Memberships: American Society of Mechanical Engineers; American Society for Metals; Robotics International; Society for Manufacturing Engineers; New York Academy of Sciences; National Society of Professional Engineers; Texas Society of Professional Engineers. Community Activities: Bosque Memorial Museum; Norwegian-American Historical Association; Vesterheim Genealogical Center; Norwegian Society of Texas, Charter Member; Nordland Heritage Foundation, Charter Member; Norwegian-American Museum; Friends of the Northwest Library; Leon Valley Crime Prevention Association; Foundation of Christian Living; Oak Hills Terrace Elementary School, Helping Hand; Bronstad-Rogstad Family Reunion, President; Lutheran Marriage Encounter, San Antonio Community, Census Couple. Religion: Lutheran. Honors and Awards: Theta Pi Epsilon, 1959; Pi Tau Sigma, 1962; Tau Beta Pi, 1962; Sigma Xi, 1970; Sigma Iota Epsilon, 1977; American Society of Mechanical Engineers, Past Chairman Certificate 1974, Charles E. Balleisen Award, San Antonio Section, 1976, 1978, Council Certificate

1977, 1979, 1980, 1981, Centennial Medallion 1980, Centennial Award Region X 1980, Board of Governors Certificate 1981, 1982, 1983; Howell Instruments Scholarship, 1961; Listed in Numerous Biographical Publications including *Who's Who in Engineering, International Who's Who in Engineering, Who's Who in Technology Today, American Men and Women of Science, Men of Achievement, Who's Who in the South and Southwest, Dictionary of International Biography, International Who's Who in Engineering.* Address: 5906 Forest Cove, San Antonio, Texas 78240.■

INGEBORG HILDEGARD SOLBRIG

Professor of German, Author. Personal: Born July 31, 1923; Daughter of Reinhold J. and Hildegard M. Adelheid Ferchland-Solbrig (both deceased). Education: Abitur and Diploma in Chemistry, Germany; B.A. summa cum laude, California State University-San Francisco, 1964; Undertook Graduate Studies at the University of California-Berkeley, 1964-65; M.A., Stanford University, 1966; Ph.D. Humanities, German Literature and Philology, Stanford University, 1969. Career: Chemical Engineer, Schoeller Company, Osnabruck, West Germany; Assistant, Stazione Zoologica, Naples, Italy; Assistant Professor of Modern Languages, University of Rhode Island-Kingston 1969-70, and University of Tennessee-Chattannoga 1970-72; Assistant Professor of German, University of Kentucky-Lexington, 1972-75; Associate Professor of German 1975-81, Professor of German 1981 to present, University of Iowa, Iowa City. Organizational Memberships: I.V.G. (International Association of Germanic Studies); Modern Language Association of America; American Association of Teachers of German; Goethe Society of North America, Founding Member; Goethe Society Weimar; Deutsche Schiller-Ges; American Council for Study of Austrian Literature; American Society of 18th Century Studies; Association of German Studies. Community Activities: Numerous Collegiate and Departmental Committees; Faculty Senate, University of Iowa, 1978-81; Judicial Commission of the University of Iowa, 1979-82; Governor's Committee on German-Iowa Heritage; Organized Symposia and Exhibitions; Lectured at Congresses and Scholarly Conferences and at Civic Organizations. Published Works: Author of 3 Books; Numerous Articles and Reviews. Honors and Awards: Stanford University Fellow, 1965-66; Tuition Grants, Stanford University, 1965-68; Dissertation Fellow, Stanford, 1968-69; Fellow, Austrian Ministry of Education, 1968-69; Faculty Research Grant, University of Tennessee, 1971; Teaching Improvement Grant, University of Kentucky, 1972; Research Grant, Kentucky, 1973; Gold Medal, Austria, 1974; Old Gold Fellow, Iowa, 1977; Grant-in-Aid, American Council for Learned Societies, 1979; Developmental Leave, University of Iowa, Spring 1980; Financial Aid for Foreign Travel, Iowa, 1980; Grant from German Academic Exchange Service, 1980; Current Research for a Book on Islam in Western Literature; University of Iowa Senior Fellowship, 1983. Address: 1126 Pine Street, Iowa City, Iowa 52240.■

KARAM FARAG ATTIA SOLIMAN

Professor and Director of Basic Sciences. Personal: Born in Cairo, Egypt; Son of Mr. and Mrs. Farah A. Soliman; Married Samia S.; Father of John K., Gina K., Mark K. Education: B.S., Cairo University, 1964; M.S. Physiology 1971, Ph.D. Endocrinology 1972, University of Georgia. Career: Professor and Director of Basic Sciences, Associate Profesor 1975-79, College of Pharmacy, Florida A&M University; Assistant Professor, School of Veterinary Medicine, Tuskegee Institute, 1972-75; Research and Teaching Assistant, University of Georgia, 1968-72. Organizational Memberships: President, Florida A&M University Sigma Xi Club; Endocrine Society; American Physiological Society; Neuroscience Society. Religion: Christian Orthodox. Honors and Awards: N.A.S.A. Grantee, 1977 to present; National Institutes of Health Grantee, 1976-78, 1979-81, 1982-84; Outstanding Teacher of the Year, Florida A&M University, 1979; Invited to West Germany N.A.T.O., Australia, Endocrine Society, 1980; Listed in *Who's Who in the South and Southwest, Who's Who in Frontier Science and Technology.* Address: 2414 Blarney Drive, Tallahassee, Florida 32308.■

GERALD SOLK

Law Professor. Personal: Born July 20, 1942; Son of Louis and Serene Solk. Education: B.A., Pepperdine University, 1964; J.D., University of California Law School, Berkeley, 1967; LL.M., New York University Law School, 1972; Ph.D., Sussex College (U.K.), 1981; M.L.A. Candidate, Harvard University. Career: Law Professor, Suffolk University Law School, Boston, Massachusetts; Former Positions include Law School Associate Dean, Attorney. Organizational Memberships: California State Bar; Hawaii State Bar; Ohio State Bar; New York State Bar; Massachusetts State Bar; District of Columbia Bar. Community Activities: Los Angeles Municipal Court, Judge pro tem, 1978-80; American Arbitration Association, Arbitrator; Business Law Arbitration Panel, Los Angeles County Superior Court, Arbitrator 1979-81; Bar Association of the United States Supreme Court, Secretary-Treasurer. Honors and Awards: Outstanding Service Award, San Fernando Valley Bar Association, 1979; Law Teacher of the Year, 1978; Distinguished Service Award, American Civil Liberties Union, 1970. Address: 41 Temple Street, Boston, Massachusetts 02114.■

IVAN SOLL

Professor. Personal: Born March 29, 1938, in Philadelphia, Pennsylvania. Education: A.B. Philosophy, Princeton University, 1960; Graduate Studies in Philosophy undertaken at Harvard University 1960-61, University of Munich 1961-62; Ph.D., Princeton University, 1966. Career: Instructor in Philosophy 1964-66, Assistant Professor in Philosophy 1966-69, Associate Professor in Philosophy 1969-73, Professor in Philosophy and Titular Professor of Education Policy Studies 1973 to present, University of Wisconsin; Professor of Philosophy, University of Michigan/University of Wisconsin Program in Florence, Italy, 1983. Organizational Memberships: American Philosophical Association; International Hegel Society; Board of Consultants in the Humanities for *World Book Encyclopedia*, 1977 to present; Organizing Committee, Program Committee, Nietzche Society of North America. Published Works: Book *An Introduction to Hegel's Metaphysics*, 1969; Various Essays and Reviews. Honors and Awards: Full Scholarship to Princeton University, 1956-60; A.B. summa cum laude, 1960; Warbecke Prize in Aesthetics; Phi Beta Kappa; Woodrow Wilson Fellowship, 1960-61; Fulbright Fellowship, 1961-62; Fellowship for Graduate Study at Princeton University, 1962-64; Spencer Foundation Grant, 1973; National Endowment for the Humanities Younger Humanist Grant, 1974; A.C.L.S. Travel Grants, 1972, 1976; Council for European Studies Travel Grant, 1972; Research Grants from the University of Wisconsin Graduate School, 1966, 1967, 1970, 1972, 1974, 1976, 1978, 1979; Fellow, Institute for Research in the Humanities in Madison, 1976; Resident Scholar at the Rockefeller Study and Conference Center, the Villa Serbelloni, Bellagio, Italy, 1979; Listed in *Who's Who in the Midwest, Who's Who in America, Men of Achievement, Men and Women of Distinction, Dictionary of International Biography, Dictionary of American Scholars, Wisconsin Men of Achievement, International Authors and Writers Who's Who, The Writer's Dictionary, Contemporary Authors, International Who's Who of Intellectuals, Personaggi Contemporanei.* Address: Department of Philosophy, University of Wisconsin, Madison, Wisconsin 53706.■

PONISSERIL SOMASUNDARAN

Professor. Personal: Born June 28, 1939; Son of Mr. and Mrs. M. G. K. Pillai; Married Usha, Daughter of Dr. and Mrs. K. V. Nair. Education: B.Sc., Kerala University, 1958; B.E., Indian Institute of Science, 1961; M.S. 1962, Ph.D. 1964, University of California at Berkeley. Career: La Von Duddleson Krumb Professor, Columbia University; Former Positions include Research Chemist for Reynolds Industries, Research Engineer for International Minerals and Chemicals, Research Engineer and Teaching Assistant at the University of California at Berkeley. Organizational Memberships: Society of Mineral Engineers, Board of Directors 1982 to present, Chairman of Mineral Processing Division 1982-83, Vice Chairman 1981-82; American Institute of Chemical Engineering, Interfacial Committee; American Chemical Society; International Association of Coll. Interfacial Science; Fine Particle Society; Chairman, International Symposium on Resources Engineering and Technology, 1979; Chairman, International Symposium on Fine Particles Processing, 1980; Chairman, National Science Foundation Workshops, 1975, 1978. Community Activities: President, Keralasamajam of Greater New York, 1974-75; Board of Directors, Federation of Indian Associations, 1977 to present; Board of Directors, Volunteers in Service to Education in India, 1974 to present; Plenary Lecturer, International Mineral Processing Congress, Warsaw, 1979; Keynote Lecturer, International Conference on Complex Sulfides, Rome, 1980; Opening Lecturer, Symposium on Colloid and Surface Chemistry, Melbourne, 1977; Special Foreign Lecturer, Rehbinder Symposium, Moscow, 1981; National Academy of Science's Committee on Accessory Elements-Phosphates, 1976-78. Published Works: Editor in Chief, *Colloids and Surfaces*, 1979 to present; Associate Editor, *International Journal of Mineral Processing*, 1977 to present. Honors and Awards: Distinguished Member, Society of Mining Engineers of A.I.M.E., 1983; Chaired Professor, Columbia University, 1983; Mill Man of Distinction, Society of Mining Engineers of the American Institute of Mining Engineers, 1983; Antoine M. Gaudin Award, Society of Mining Engineers, 1982; Most Distinguished Achievement in Engineering, A.I.N.A., 1980; Publications Board Award, Society of Mining Engineers, 1980; University of Melbourne Fellowship for Research, Melbourne, 1977; Grants from National Science Foundation, National Institutes of Health, Department of Energy, American Iron and Steel Institute, Corporations; Prime Minister Nehru Scholarship Award, 1961. Address: 748 Route 9W, Nyack, New York 10960.■

TWO THOUSAND NOTABLE AMERICANS

PAUL ALLEN SOMMERS

Assistant Administrator. Personal: Born April 9, 1945; Son of Mrs. Rosalie Sommers. Married Carol Ann Newsom; Father of Eric Paul, Marc Allen. Education: B.S. Behavioral Science and Physical Education, University of Wisconsin, 1967; M.S. Behavioral and Learning Disabilities, Southern Illinois University, 1969; Ph.D. Administration and Research, Southern Illinois University, 1971. Career: Assistant Administrator, Gundersen Clinic; Executive Director, Comprehensive Child Care Center, Director of Learning Disabilities Section, Instructor for Pediatric House Staff, Gundersen Clinic, 1980-84; Administrator, Comprehensive Child Care Center, Marshfield Clinic, Marshfield, Wisconsin, 1975-80; Administrator, Division of Services for Children with Exceptional Health and Learning Needs, Wausau (Wisconsin) District Board of Education, 1973-75; Administrator, Division of Services for Children with Exceptional Health and Learning Needs, Cooperative Educational Service Agency #4 (Cumberland, Wisconsin), 1972-73; Evaluation Consultant, Minnesota State Department of Education, St. Paul, 1971-72. Organizational Memberships: American Public Health Association, 1976-82; National and State Councils of Administrators of Special Education, Past Regional Executive Officer; Council for Exceptional Children and Division on Learning Disabilities; National and State Epilepsy Associations, Past Center Executive Officer; East Seal Society of Wisconsin, Past Executive Officer; Wisconsin Association of Perinatal Centers, Board of Directors 1977-80; Wisconsin Association for Children with Learning Disabilities, Professional Advisory Board 1982-85. Community Activities: La Crosse (Wisconsin) Area Chamber of Commerce, Chairman Committee on Marketing; Wisconsin Association for Children with Learning Disabilities, Professional Advisory Board 1982-85; Midstate Epilepsy Center, Past President for Central Wisconsin 1975-80; Neurodevelopmental Institute for Cerebral Palsy, Wausau Medical Center, 1973-75; Sunburst Youth Homes for the Emotionally Disturbed, Education Policy Committee 1975-80. Honors and Awards: State of Wisconsin Scholarship, 1967; Elected to Phi Kappa Phi, 1969; State of Illinois Master's Honors Fellow, 1970; National Doctoral Honors Fellow in Administration, 1970-71; Distinguished Service Award, Midstate Epilepsy Center, 1980; Outstanding Service Citation, American Academy of Pediatrics Program of Preparing Physicians to Care for Children with Handicaps 1982; Listed in *Who's Who in the Midwest, Men of Achievement, Personalities of the West and Midwest. Personalities of America.* Address: 221 13th Avenue South, Onalaska, Wisconsin 54650.■

PAUL C. SOUDER

Bank Executive. Personal: Born December 2, 1920, in Greencastle, Indiana; Son of Dewey Clayton and Julia Dowell Souder; Married Dorrie Elliott; Father of Douglas Paul, Julie Jan. Education: B.A. Economics (Rector Scholar), DePauw University, 1941; Graduate, Harvard Graduate School of Business Administration (United States Naval Supply Corps), 1943; Graduate, Rutgers University Graduate School of Banking, 1951. Military: Served in the United States Naval Reserve, Commissioned Ensign 1952, Honorable Discharge as Lieutenant Commander 1946. Career: Position with Commercial Credit Corporation, 1941-42; Michigan National Bank 1946 to present, Credit Manager 1946-47, Assistant Vice President 1947-52, Vice President 1952-61, Senior Vice President 1961-71, Executive Vice President 1971-72, President 1972-80, Vice Chairman Michigan National Bank/Chairman Michigan National Corporation Outstate Banks 1980 to present; Director, Auto-Owners Insurance Company, Auto-Owners Life Insurance Company, Detroit and Mackinac Railway Company, Home Owners Mutual Insurance Company, Jameson Corporation, Lake Huron Broadcasting Corporation, Michigan Bank of Huron (Chairman), Michigan National Bank, Michigan National Bank of Detroit, Michigan National Bank-Michiana (Chairman), Michigan National Bank-Mid Michigan (Vice Chairman), Michigan National Bank-Valley (Chairman), Michigan National Bank-West (Chairman), Michigan National Corporation, Michigan National Bank-Midland, Owners Insurance Company, Property-Owners Insurance Company, W. F. McNally Company. Organizational Memberships: Detroit Bankers Club; Economic Club of Detroit; Independent Petroleum Association of America; Michigan Oil and Gas Association. Community Activities: Country Club of Lansing; Otsego Ski Club; Robert Morris Associates; Saginaw Club; Michigan State University Development Fund, Trustee; Michigan Wildlife Foundation, Trustee; Frank N. Andersen Foundation, Vice President and Director; Numerous Former Civic Activities. Published Works: Author, *Financing Oil Production in Michigan* 1951. Address: 2800 Maurer Road, Charlotte, Michigan 48813.■

WENDELL LORAINE SOWELL

College Administrator. Personal: Born August 17, 1917; Son of Larkin A. (deceased) and Sallie Brewer Sowell; Married Alva Webb (deceased); Father of Bashaba S. Gibbons, Wendell L. Jr., Darrell B. Education: B.S. Chemistry 1947, M.S. Biological Sciences 1955, Auburn University; LL.B., Jones Law School, 1960; Ph.D. Preventive Medicine and Public Health/Toxicology, University of Oklahoma, 1967. Military: Served in the United States Army Military Police, 1941-42, with Medical Discharge in 1944. Career: Director, Patrick Henry State Junior College Division of Law Enforcement, 1977 to present; Associate Professor, Jacksonville State University School of Law Enforcement, 1971-77; Associate Professor of Biology, Livingston University, Alabama, 1968-71; State Toxicologist, State of Ohio, 1968; Assistant Superintendent, B.C.I.&I., London, Ohio, 1968; Director and Developer, Crime Laboratory, City of Fort Worth, Texas, 1960-65; Associate Toxicologist in Charge of Auburn Division, State of Alabama Department of Toxicology, 1947-60; Director, Sowell School of Realty, Anniston, Birmingham, Gadsden, Mobile and Jacksonville, Alabama; Owner, Sowell Realty, 1971-78; Policeman, City of Mobile, Alabama, 1941-44. Organizational Memberships: American Academy of Forensic Sciences; Forensic Science Society; International Association of Forensic Toxicologists, Charter Member; Gamma Sigma Delta Honor Society of Agriculture, Auburn University; Southern Association of Criminal Justice; Academy of Criminal Justice Sciences; Sigma Delta Kappa Intercollegiate Law Fraternity. Religion: First Baptist Church, Monroeville, Alabama. Honors and Awards: Listed in *American Men and Women of Science, Who's Who in the South and Southwest, Notable Americans of the Bicentennial Era, Personalities of the South, Men of Challenge, Who's Who in Technology.* Address: 4414 Brush Hill Road, Nashville, Tennessee 37216.■

SHARON E. SOZA (SHARI)

Writer, Micro-Computer Consultant, Independent Software Vendor, Networker, Legal Researcher. Personal: Born June 21, 1945, in Port Arthur, Texas; Daughter of Francis Theodore and Mary Elizabeth (Grubbs) Newton; Married Albert Rudolph Soza; Mother of (by previous marriage) Ravi Narayan Seth. Education: M.S./Ph.D. (in progress), Columbia Pacific University; Attended the College of Siskiyous 1978, Rice University 1975, University of Houston 1969; B.S. Chemistry, Lamar State College of Technology, 1968. Career: Proofreader, Beaumont Enterprise, 1967-68; Technical Writer, Federal Electric (ITT), NASA, Houston, 1968-69; Systems Programmer, Texas Instruments 1969-70, Electronic Component Testing Systems; Systems Programmer, Consultant, Urban Systems and Services, Houston, 1970-72; Message-Switching Systems, 1970-72; Systems Programmer, Pipeline Control Systems, SCI Incorporated, Houston, 1972-73; Contract Consultant/Programmer, Traffic Control Systems, TRW Systems, Clear Lake, 1974; Developer of Software Products in Electronic Cottage and Direct Mail Modes, 1977 to present; Volunteer Systems Consultant, 1977 to present. Published Works: Author, *Toxin Release* 1978, *The State of Jefferson Program* 1975, *List-Master* 1975, Project: *Control-Z-UpArrow* (includes Justicia, a court-assistance system, and The Swan, a peace-process-facilitating message-switching system in process), *Herbal Cross-Index, Truth, Trust and Trading Starship!* 1977 to present, *Calendar Judge, Proposer, Determinor, Reviewer, Parallel Elements;* Manuscript on Brainwave Coordination, Levels-of-Awareness, the Cosmic Memory/Mass Unconscious and Time Matrix Translation. Honors and Awards: Listed in *Who's Who in California, Who's Who of American Women, World Who's Who of Women, Who's Who in the West, Personalities of America, Personalities of the West and Midwest, The Directory of Distinguished Americans, Who's Who of California Executive Women, The International Who's Who of Intellectuals.* Address: P.O. Box 81, Yreka, California 96097.

HAROLD CHARLES SPEAR

Thoracic and Cardiovascular Surgeon. Personal: Born September 29, 1923; Son of Harold Spear; Married Suzanne Bowmall; Father of Laurinda Spear Fort, Harold Charles III, Alison Lelyn. Education: Diploma, Lawrenceville School, 1941; B.S., Yale University, 1944; M.D., Harvard Medical School, 1947. Military: Served in the United States Air Force, MC Captain (retired), 1951-53. Career: Group Practice of Thoracic and Cardiovascular Surgery. Organizational Memberships: American Association for Thoracic Surgery; Society of Thoracic Surgeons, Founder Member; American College of Surgeons; American Medical Association; President Florida Chapter, American College of Chest Physicians. Community Activities: North Shore Medical Center, Board of Trustees 1977 to present, Chairman 1981 to present; Harvard Club of Miami, Board of Directors 1975-80; Heart Association of Greater Miami, Vice President 1961; President Medical Staff, North Shore Hospital 1964, Palmetto General Hospital 1971; Committee of One Hundred of Miami; Chief of Thoracic Surgery, Parkway General

TWO THOUSAND NOTABLE AMERICANS

Hospital, North Miami General Hospital and North Shore Hospital. Religion: Miami Shores Presbyterian Church, 1956 to present. Honors and Awards: Various Scholarship Awards, Lawrenceville, Yale University and Harvard Medical School. Address: 9325 North Bayshore Drive, Miami Shores, Florida 33138.■

FRANKLIN SCOTT SPEARS

Supreme Court Justice. Personal: Born August 20, 1931; Married Rebecca; Father of Franklin Scott Jr., Carleton Blaise, John Adrian. Education: B.B.A., J.D., University of Texas at Austin. Military: Served in the United States Army Military Police Corps, 1955-56, attaining the rank of Lieutenant. Career: Justice, Supreme Court of Texas, 1979 to present; Former Attorney at Law, San Antonio (Texas). Organizational Memberships: State Bar of Texas. Community Activities: State Representative in Texas Legislature, 1958-61; State Senator in Texas Legislature, 1961-66; Judge, 57th District Court, San Antonio, 1968-78. Religion: Presbyterian, Elder and Deacon. Honors and Awards: Friars Society, University of Texas; Outstanding Young Man of San Antonio, 1962; Tenor in International Championship Barbershop Quartet, Mark IV, 1969. Address: 2705½ Stratford, Austin, Texas 78746.■

HENRY LOSTON SPENCE

Electronics Engineer. Personal: Born October 26, 1943; Son of Neahmiah E. and Laura A. Grimstead Spence; Married Justine Spencer; Father of Adrienne Reil, Laurietta Sharaga, Henry Loston Jr. Education: A.S., Norfolk State University, 1971; B.S.E.E. 1977, M.S.E.E. and M.S.E.D. 1979, Metropolitan Collegiate Institute; M.S. Candidate in Management, Columbia Pacific University, 1984; Honorary D.Div., Church of Gospel Ministry, 1976. Military: Served in the United States Air Force, 1965-69, attaining the rank of Sergeant. Career: Electronics Engineer; Former Position as Senior Systems Engineer, Communication ITT World Commission. Organizational Memberships: Institute of Electrical and Electronics Engineers; A.F.C.E.A.; American Notary Society of Washington, D.C.; State-wide Notary of Virginia; American Entrepreneurs Association; American Federation of Government Employees. Community Activities: National Technical Association; Freedom Jaycees, Past President; Kawaida Jaycees, Past Chairman of the Board. Religion: Baptist. Honors and Awards: Honorary Doctor of Divinity, 1977; National Honor Society; Corporate Leadership Utilizing Business Award, 1979; Plank Honor Award, United States Navy USS Virginia 1976; American Notary Society; Statewide Notary of Virginia, 1979-87; Listed in Marquis Who's Who of American East, Directory of Distinguished Americans, Community Leaders of America, Personalities of America, International Who's Who of Intellectuals. Address: 1421 Palmetto Avenue, Virginia Beach, Virginia 23452.■

THOMAS MORRIS SPENCER

College President. Personal: Born November 30, 1916, in Nolan County, Texas; Son of Thomas Monroe and Della Whitley Spencer; Married Rachel Bradham, November 26, 1936; Father of Betty Dell, Thomas Morris Jr., Anna Lou, Vera Sue (deceased), Willie Jo. Education: Graduate, Denton Senior High School, 1932; B.S. 1935, M.A. 1939, Sam Houston State University; Ed.D., The University of Houston, 1947. Career: High School Principal, Holland, Texas, 1935-37; Superintendent, Thrall Public Schools (Thrall, Texas) 1937-41, Llano Public Schools 1941-42; Deputy State Superintendent of Public Instruction, 1942-43; Superintendent, Cypress-Fairbanks Public Schools (Cypress, Texas), 1943-47; President, Blinn College (Brenham, Texas) 1947-57, South Plains College (Levelland, Texas) 1957-61, San Jacinto College (Pasadena, Texas) 1961 to present. Organizational Memberships: Past President, Association of Texas Colleges and Universities; Past President, Texas Public Junior College Association; Past Member, Governor's Advisory Committee on Post Secondary Educational Planning; Past Member, Advisory Committee, Statewide Study of Continuing Education; Past Member, American Association of Junior Colleges Commission on Governmental Affairs; Past Member, Texas Council on Aerospace Education; Past Member, Board of Directors, Texas Surplus Property Agency; Past Member, House Committee on Vocational-Technical Education. Community Activities: Board of Directors, District Salvation Army; Legislative Affairs Committee, Past Member Board of Directors, Pasadena Chamber of Commerce; Master Mason; Scottish Rite; Knights Templar; Shrine; Woodmen of the World; Knight Commander of the Court of Honor, Ancient and Accepted Scottish Rite of Free Masonry; Past President, Pasadena Rotary Club; Past President, Lions Club; Past County Chairman, American Red Cross; Past Director, United Fund Drives. Religion: First Christian Church, Past Chairman Board of Elders, Past Chairman Official Board. Honors and Awards: Distinguished Alumni Award, University of Houston, 1981; Citizen of the Year, Pasadena Chamber of Commerce, 1979; Daughters of the American Revolution Honor Medal, 1982; Listed in Who's Who in America. Address: 4624 Fairmont Parkway, Suite 201, Pasadena, Texas 77504.■

DANIEL SPERBER

Professor of Physics. Personal: Born May 8, 1930, in Vienna, Austria; Son of Aniela E. Sperber; Married Ora; Father of Ron E. Education: M.S., The Hebrew University, Jerusalem, Israel, 1954; Ph.D., Princeton University, Princeton, New Jersey, 1960. Military: Served in the Israeli Army as Captain. Career: Teaching Assistant, The Hebrew University, Jerusalem, Israel, 1954; Teaching Assistant, Israel Institute of Technology, Haifa, Israel, 1955; Research Assistant 1956-57, Teaching Assistant 1958-60, Princeton University, Princeton, New Jersey; Associate Physicist 1960-62, Research Physicist 1962-64, Senior Physicist 1964-66, Scientific Advisor 1966-67, I.I.T. Research Institute, Chicago, Illinois; Instructor 1960-62, Lecturer 1962-64, Associate Professor 1964-67, I.I.T., Chicago, Illinois; Associate Professor 1967-72, Professor 1972 to present, Rensselaer Polytechnic Institute, Troy, New York; Nordita Professor, Niels Bohr Institute, Copenhagen, 1973-74. Organizational Memberships: American Physical Society; Israel Physical Society, Founding Member; Society of Sigma Xi; New York Academy of Sciences. Honors and Awards: Fellow, American Physical Society; Nordita Professor, Copenhagen. Address: 1 Taylor Lane, Troy, New York 12180.■

KIP SPERRY

Librarian, Genealogist, Author, Editor, Educator. Personal: Born May 25, 1940; Son of Sherman Alfred Sperry (deceased) and Anna Effie Morse; Married Elisabeth Anne, Daughter of Henry R. and Mary A. Pearson; Father of Daniel Kip. Education: B.S. American Genealogical Research 1971, M.L.S. 1974, Brigham Young University. Military: Served in the United States Army, 1961-64. Career: Former Collection Department Supervisor, American Reference Unit, Genealogical Library, Salt Lake City; Instructor in Family History, Brigham Young University Salt Lake Center; Former Senior Reference Consultant and Senior Research Specialist at the Genealogical Library. Organizational Memberships: Utah Genealogical Association, Board of Directors 1976-81; National Genealogical Society; New England Historic Genealogical Society; Ohio Genealogical Society; Connecticut Society of Genealogists; Rhode Island Genealogical Society; Others. Community Activities: Elected Member, Timpanogos Club of Utah, 1982 to present. Published Works: Editor, Genealogical Journal, Quarterly of the Utah Genealogical Association; Author Four Books, Various Periodical Articles, Many Book Reviews. Religion: Church of Jesus Christ of Latter-day Saints. Honors and Awards: Accredited Genealogist; Certified Genealogists; Fellow, Utah Genealogical Association; Award of Merit, National Genealogical Society, Washington, D.C., 1981. Address: P.O. Box 11381, Salt Lake City, Utah 84147.■

DOROTHY MARIE SPETHMANN

Assistant Professor of Education. Personal: Born April 7, 1935; Daughter of John and Jo Haggerty; Married Robert; Mother of Mary Jo. Education: B.S. Elementary Education, College Misericordia, Dallas, Pennsylvania, 1960; M.A. Education, University of South Dakota, Vermillion, South Dakota, 1977; Attended Villanova University (Pennsylvania), University of Detroit (Michigan), University of Dallas (Dallas, Texas). Career: Assistant Professor of Education, Dakota State College; Educator, Dakota State College (Madison, South Dakota) 1974-81, Washington Elementary School (Madison, South Dakota) 1970-71, Elkton Public School (Elkton, South Dakota) 1969-70, Elementary and Junior High School (Watertown, South Dakota) 1966-69, Senior High and Elementary School (Webster, South Dakota) 1964-69, Elementary and Preschool (Dallas, Texas) 1960-64, Senior High and Elementary School (Detroit, Michigan) 1956-60, Elementary School and Orphans, Reading (Scranton and Hudson, Pennsylvania) 1954-56. Organizational Memberships: American Association of University Women; South Dakota Council of Teachers of Math; National Council of Teachers of Math; Delta Kappa Gamma; Orton Gillingham Society. Community Activities: Every Citizen Counts Organization; Hospital Auxilliary Member; Dakota State Women; Advisor for Young Republicans. Religion: Catholic, Served as Nun in the

Franciscan Order, 1953-69. Honors and Awards: Listed in *Who's Who in the Midwest, World Who's Who of Women, Personalities of America, Outstanding Young Women.* Address: 904 Northwest 5th Street, Madison, South Dakota 57042. ■

THEODORE JOHN SPETNAGEL

Civil Engineer. Personal: Born May 26, 1948, in Chillicothe, Ohio; Son of Theodore Scott and Lucille Stuckey Spetnagel; Married Nancy Cunningham; Father of Theodore Allen. Education: B.S., Clemson University, 1970; M.S., Georgia Institute of Technology, 1972. Career: Registered Professional Engineer, Georgia, Kentucky, North Carolina, South Carolina, Tennessee, Virginia and West Virginia; Deputy Engineer, HQ Second U.S. Army, Fort Gillem, Georgia, 1984 to present; Chief, Minor Construction Section, HQ U.S. Army Forces Command, Atlanta, Georgia, 1979-84; Civil Engineer, HQ Fort McPherson, Atlanta, Georgia, 1978-79; Chief Design Engineer, Atlantic Building Systems, Inc., Atlanta, 1971-78; Graduate Research Assistant, Georgia Institute of Technology, 1970-71; Civil/Structural Engineer, Appalachian Consultings Engineers, Summers and Vacations 1967-70. Organizational Memberships: American Society of Civil Engineers, Georgia Section, 1974; National Society of Professional Engineers 1974, Professional Engineers in Government Board of Governors 1981; Georgia Society of Professional Engineers, Professional Engineers in Industry 1973-78, Nomination Committee 1977-78, Professional Engineers in Government 1978-81, Chairman Young Engineers 1978-79, Vice Chairman Professional Engineers in Government 1979-80, Chairman Professional Engineers in Government 1980-82, Awards Committee 1982; Atlanta Chapter of Georgia Society of Professional Engineers, Chairman Refugee Engineer Committee 1975-76, Chapter Director/P.E.I. 1976-77, Chairman Interprofessional Relations Committee 1976-77, Chairman Public Relations Committee 1976-77, Treasurer 1977-78, Chapter Director/P.E.G. 1979-80, Chairman Intergovernmental Affairs Committee 1980-81; Society of American Military Engineers, Assistant Secretary of Atlanta Post 1981, Director of Atlanta Post 1982-83; Chi Epsilon; Tau Beta Pi. Community Activities: Atlanta Neighborhood Planning Unit "C" 1976 to present; Board of Directors, Wildwood Civic Association, 1980-83; High Museum of Art, 1977-82; Atlanta Civic Opera, 1978-80; Timpanist, Atlanta Community Orchestra, 1977-80; Goergia Conservancy, 1974 to present; WABE/WETV, Charter Member 1976 to present; Atlanta Music Club, 1978-80. Religion: North Decatur Presbyterian Church, Deacon 1973-76, Chairman Property Committee 1975-76; Trinity Presbyterian Church, Elder 1978-81, Adult and Family Activities 1978-79, Choir 1978-80, Music and Worship 1978-80, Chairman Volunteer Personnel Services 1980-81, Assimilation Committee 1982-83. Honors and Awards: Atlanta Chapter of Georgia Society of Professional Engineers, Engineer of the Year in Industry 1977, President's Award 1978, Young Engineer of the Year 1980; Engineer of the Year in Government, 1982; Young Engineer of the Year, 30 Greater Atlanta Engineering Organizations, 1984; Listed in *Who's Who in the South and Southwest, Personalities of the South, Men of Achievement, Personalities of America, Directory of Distinguished Americans.* Address: 855 Kipling Drive, Northwest, Atlanta, Georgia 30318. ■

VINCENT EDWARD SPEZZANO

Publishing Company Executive. Personal: Born April 3, 1926; Son of Mr. and Mrs. Frank Spezzano; Married Marjorie Elliott; Father of Steve, Mark, Judy, Christine. Education: Graduate, York Central School (Retsof, New York), 1944; Attended Sampson College, School of Engineering, 1946-47; B.A., Syracuse University, School of Journalism, 1950. Military: Served in the United States Navy Air Corps, 1944-46. Career: Reporter, *The Livingston Republican* (Geneseo, New York) 1950-51, *The News* (Lynchburg, Virginia) 1951-54, *The Globe-Democrat* (St. Louis, Missouri) 1954-55; Political Writer, *The Times-Union* (Rochester, New York), 1955-64; Director of Public Service and Research, *The Times Union*, 1964-68; Public Service Director 1968-71, Dierctor of Promotion/Public Service 1971-75, Gannett Company, Inc., Rochester, New York; President and Publisher, Cape Publications, Inc., Cocoa, Florida, 1975 to present; Assistant Vice President 1977-78, Vice President 1978-79, Gannett/South, Gannett Company, Inc.; President, Gannett/Southeast Newspaper Group, Gannett Company, Inc., 1979-82; Executive Vice President 1982, President 1983, *USA Today*; President and Publisher, Cape Publications, Inc.; Senior Vice President/Communications, Gannett, 1983 to present. Organizational Memberships: Director, Gannett Company, Inc.; Board of Directors, Barnett Bank of Cocoa; Journalism Endowment Advisory Committee, University of Florida; Board of Directors, Wuesthoff Memorial Hospital; Board of Directors, Cape Canaveral Hospital; Trustee, Brevard Art Center and Museum; Board of Directors, United Way of Brevard County; Board of Directors, Florida Press Association; American Newspaper Publishers Association; Past President, International Newspaper Promotion Association (1970-71). Community Activities: Civilian-Military Community Relations Council; Cocoa Beach Chamber of Commerce. Honors and Awards: I.N.P.A. Silver Shovel, 1975; Award for Public Service Reporting, American Political Science Association, 1963; Distinguished Service Award (for non-members), Kiwanis Club, 1963; Citizen of the Year, Citizens Club of Rochester, 1960; News Writing Award, Virginia Press Association, 1953; Pulitzer Nominations, 1954, 1963; Boss of the Year, Florida Chapter, National Secretaries Association, 1977. Address: 855 South Atlantic Avenue, Cocoa Beach, Florida 32931. ■

ELLEN BRUBAKER SPILLER

Instructor in English. Personal: Born July 17, 1932; Daughter of George Nunley (deceased) and Lou Brubaker; Married Samuel Christopher; Mother of Katherine Quesney Spiller Gordon, Georgianne. Education: Bachelor of Journalism, University of Texas at Austin, 1954; M.A. English, University of Houston, Central Campus, 1965; M.A. College Teaching, University of Houston at Clear Lake City, 1980. Career: Instructor in English, Lee College; Editor, *Texas Future Farmer*, 1955-57; Editor, House Organs and Magazines, St. Luke's/Texas Children's Hospitals, 1957; Teacher of English, Aldine Junior High School, Houston, Texas, 1959-61; Teacher of English, Weltrip Senior High School, Houston, 1961-65. Organizational Memberships: Texas Junior College Teachers Association; American Association of University Professors; National Council Teachers of English; Conference on College Composition and Communication; Conference of College Teachers of English; Lee College Faculty Assembly, First Vice President 1981-82, Secretary 1984-86. Community Activities: Lee College Faculty Women's Club 1965 to present, Vice President 1980-81, President 1981-82. Religion: Altar Guild, All Saints Episcopal Church, 1975-82. Honors and Awards: T. I. Larsen Scholarship, University of Texas, 1953; Theta Sigma Phi; Women in Communications, 1953-54; First Prize, *Truckliner* Magazine Writing Contest; Excellence in Education Award, Exxon, 1982. Address: 211 Rue Orleans, Baytown, Texas 77520. ■

JOHN L. SPINKS

Company Executive. Personal: Born June 19, 1924; Son of Lucy Spinks Stockwell; Married Marion; Father of Susan, Douglas. Education: B.S.M.E., University of Kentucky, 1951; Postgraduate Studies, University of Southern California and University of California at Los Angeles, 1951-58; Attended the Police Academy, 1977. Military: Served in the United States Air Force Space Division as Lieutenant Colonel, Deputy Director of Engineer Division, 1961-73; Transport Commander on Troop Ships, 1943-46; Active Engineering Reserve, 1946-73; Retired 1973. Career: President, Environmental Emissions Engineering Company, 1983 to present; Supervising Engineer, Southern Coast Air Quality Management District, 1956-83. Organizational Memberships: American Academy of Environmental Engineers; Institute for the Advancement of Engineering; American Society of Mechanical Engineers; Air Pollution Control Association; National Society of Professional Engineers; California Society of Professional Engineers; Institute of Environmental Science; Society of Environmental Engineers, London; American Society of Engineering Education, Society of Engineering Science; Society of American Military Engineers; Delaware Association of Professional Engineers; Louisiana Association of Energy Engineers; International Platform Association; Member College Fellows, Institute for the Advancement of Engineering. Community Activities: American Alpine Club; Austrian Alpine Club; Alpine Club of Canada; United States Olympic Society; National Athletic Health Institute; Himalayan Rescue Association; American Medical Jogging Association; International Seniors Olympic Association; American College of Sports Medicine; Aerobics International Research Society; Mountain Safety Research Society; International Backpackers Association; Appalachian Trail Conference; Sierra Club; Seniors Track Club; Triangle Engineering Fraternity; California P.O.S.T. Certified Class I Reserve Police Officer, Hermosa Beach Police Department; Instructor Rock and Ice Mountaineering; Lecturer Marathon Running; Manager, Little League Baseball; Director, A.Q.M.D. Golf League; The Honorable Order of Kentucky Colonels. Religion: Usher, St. Francis Episcopal Church. Published Works: Pioneered Development of Engineering Principles and Technology for Air Pollution Control Techniques; Developed Air and Water Pollution Control Programs for United States Air Force; Co-Author, "Air Pollution Engineering Manual," First Edition 1967, Second Edition 1973. Honors and Awards: Diplomate, American Academy of Environmental Engineers; Honorary Member, National Advisory Board, American Biographical Institute; Fellow, Institute for the Advancement of Engineering; Fellow, International Biographical Association; Fellow, American Biographical Institute; United States Air Force Commendation Medal for Engineering; Consultant; Certified Energy Manager, A.E.E.: United States Presidential Sports Award; Commissioned a Kentucky Colonel by Governor John Y. Brown, Jr.; Registered Professional Engineer in California, Kentucky, Texas, Delaware,

TWO THOUSAND NOTABLE AMERICANS

New Hampshire, Louisiana, Wisconsin, Oklahoma and Mississippi; Listed in *Who's Who in the World, Men and Women of Distinction, Who's Who in America, Who's Who in Engineering, Men of Achievement in the World, International Who's Who of Intellectuals, Directory of Distinguished Americans, Who's Who in Technology Today, Book of Honor, American Men and Women of Science, Dictionary of International Biography*, Others. Address: 26856 Eastvale Road, Rolling Hills, California 90274.

PEGGY WEEKS SPOHN

Banking Regulatory Agency Official. Personal: Born August 23, 1944, in Kingston, Pennsylvania; Daughter of Edwin Rice and Maudie Hewitt Weeks. Education: B.A., Le Moyne College, 1966; M.A. Sociology, Fordham University, 1967; Special Student in Sociology, Syracuse University, 1965-66; Special Student in Cross Cultural Community Development, Cornell University College of Agriculture, 1964. Career: Program Analyst, Concentrated Employment Program, Bronx, New York, 1967-68; Group Work Supervisor, Self Help Enterprises, Inc., Modesto, California, 1968-69; Research Analyst, Organization for Social and Technical Innovation, Cambridge, Massachusetts, 1969-70; Senior Analyst, ABT Associates, Cambridge, Massachusetts; Research Associate, The Urban Institute, Washington, D.C., 1970-74; Corporate Secretary and Deputy Director, The Housing Allowance Office, South Bend, Indiana, 1974-76; Manager, D.C. Office Contract Research Corporation 1976-78; Co-Founder, Corporate Officer Network for Housing Research, Inc., Washington, D.C., 1968 to present; Deputy Director Office of Community Investment, Federal Home Loan Bank Board, Washington, D.C., 1978 to present; National Housing Conference, 1976 to present; Volunteer Team Leader, Community Development Effort, International House, Le Moyne College, Mexico, 1962-66; Volunteer Developer of Hope Village, A Cooperative Community, Inc., 1968. Address: Federal Home Loan Bank Board, 1700 G Street, Northwest, Washington, D.C. 20552.■

WILLIAM CLARK SPRAGENS

Professor of Political Science. Personal: Born October 1, 1925; Son of T. Eugene and Edna Grace Clark Spragens; Married Elaine Jean Dunham. Education: Graduate of Lebanon High School, Kentucky, 1943; A.B. Journalism 1947, M.A. 1953, University of Kentucky; Ph.D., Michigan State University, 1966. Military: Served in the United States Army, 1943-45, with the rank of Private. Career: Professor of Political Science, Bowling Green State University; Former Newspaper Reporter and Editor. Organizational Memberships: American Political Science Association; Midwest Political Science Association; Center for the Study of the Presidency; Academy of Political Science. Community Activities: Bowling Green Kiwanis Club, Former Member, Program Chairman. Religion: First Presbyterian Church, Bowling Green, Adult Education Committee. Published Works: Author of Four Books; Numerous Articles in Professional Journals. Honors and Awards: Grant from Lyndon B. Johnson Foundation, 1978, 1979; National Endowment for the Humanities Ethical Issues Seminar, A.P.S.A., 1980; Grants from National Science Foundation, 1972, and Bowling Green University Faculty Research Committee, 1969-81; Computer Science Trainee, National Science Foundation Sponsored, 1974; Falk Fellow, Michigan State University, 1960-61; Ford Legislative Intern, 1961. Address: 607 Lafayette Boulevard, Bowling Green, Ohio 43402.■

WILLIAM L. SPRINGER

Congressman. Personal: Born April 12, 1909, in Sullivan, Indiana; Son of Otha L. and Daisy E. Springer; Married Elsie Mattis in May 1942; Father of Katherine, Anne, Georgia. Education: B.A., DePauw University, 1931; LL.B., University of Illinois Law School, 1935. Military: Served in the United States Navy. Career: State's Attorney of Champaign County, 1940-42; County Judge of Champaign County, 1946-50; Elected to 82nd Congress 1950, Re-elected to each succeeding Congress through and including the 92nd Congress, from 22nd Congressional District of Illinois; Ranking Minority Member, House Committee on Interstate and Foreign Commerce; Ranking Minority Member, Subcommittees Transportation and Aeronautics, Communications and Power, Public Health and Environment, Commerce and Finance, Special Subcommittee on Investigations; Vice Chairman, National Republican Congressional Campaign Committee; Delegate, First United States-Mexico Interparliamentary Conference, Guadalajara, Mexico 1961, Chairman Delegation of Subcommittee on Foreign Trade; Delegate to Second Conference, Washington, D.C., 1962; Delegate to Third Interparliamentary Conference, Alliance for Progress Committee, 1963; Delegate to European Civil Air Conference in Strasbourg, 1955; Delegate, International Telecommunications Union Conference in Geneva 1963 and the Conference in 1965; Delegate to United States-British Bilateral Parliamentary Conference in Oxford, England, 1967; United States Congressional Delegate to World Health Organization Conferences in Geneva, 1963 and 1967; Delegate to Tripartite Conference, United States-France-Britain, 1968; United States Delegate, Conference on International Energy, Geneva 1959; Delegate, General Agreements on Trade and Tariffs, 1958, 1959, 1961; United States Representative (with Herbert Hoover, Jr.) to Conference on Near East Oil Compacts, 1953; Retired, 1972; Appointed by President Nixon as Member of Federal Power Commission 1973-75, Vice Chairman 1974, Delegate to International Conference on Liquified Natural Gas in Algeria, 1974; Appointed by President Ford to Federal Election Commission, 1976-77. Published Works: Author, Public Law 480, the Surplus Agriculture Trade and Development Act of 1954; Author with Senator Hubert Humphrey of Renewal of Legislation in 1961 as "Food for Peace Program" 1961, and "Food for Freedom Program" 1963. Honors and Awards: Honorary LL.D. from Lincoln College 1966, DePauw University 1972, Eastern Illinois University 1981, Millikin University 1984. Address: 900 West Park Avenue, Champaign, Illinois 60650.■

JACK MARION SPURLOCK

Academic Administration, Consultant. Personal: Born August 16, 1930; Son of Joseph M. Spurlock (deceased); Married Phyllis Ridgway, Daughter of Mildred S. Ridgway; Father of Barbara S. Chumley, Scott Edward, Paul Andrew, Teresa Anne. Education: B.Ch.E., University of Florida, 1952; M.S.Ch.E., Georgia Institute of Technology, 1958; Ph.D., Georgia Institute of Technology, 1961. Military: Served in the United States Air Force, 1952-72, attaining the rank of Captain. Career: Academic Administration and Consulting, Georgia Institute of Technology; Former Positions include President of Health and Safety Research Institute, Professor and Research Engineer, Consultant to Government and Industry, Quality Control Engineer in Industry. Organizational Memberships: Fellow, Royal Society of Health; Fellow, American Institute of Chemists; Associate Fellow, Aerospace Medical Association; Associate Fellow, American Institute of Aeronautics and Astronautics; Chairman, Committee SC-9 "Spacecraft Environmental Control Systems," Society of Automotive Engineers. Community Activities: Life Sciences Advisory Council, National Aeronautics and Space Administration, 1972-78; Biomass Panel of the Energy Research Advisory Board, United States Department of Energy, 1979-81; High Technology Task Force, Georgia Chamber of Commerce, 1980-83. Religion: Presbyterian Church in the United States, Ruling Elder 1966-69 and 1976-79, Elder 1966 to present, Adult Church School Teacher 1971 to present. Honors and Awards: M. A. Ferst Sigma Xi Award, Georgia Tech Chapter, for Ph.D. Dissertation, 1961; Outstanding Service Recognition Awards, Fourteenth Air Force 1962, Society of Automotive Engineers 1981, "Intersociety Conference on Environmental Systems" Steering Committee 1977. Address: 293 Indian Hills Trail, Marietta, Georgia 30067.■

NANJAPPA SREENIVAS

Physician, Psychiatrist. Personal: Born February 18, 1945; Son of Nanjegowda and Nanjamma; Married Sumitramma; Father of Rashmi. Education: M.B.B.S., Banalore Medical College, 1967; M.D., Educational Council for Foreign Medical College, 1974. Career: Medical Officer, Bangalore, India, 1968-72; Senior House Officer, Wrexham Group Hospital, United Kingdom, 1972-74; Resident in Psychiatry, Hyden Donhue Mental Health Institute, Oklahoma, 1976-79; Staff Psychiatrist, Central Oklahoma Mental Health Center, Norman, Oklahoma, 1979-81. Organizational Memberships: American Medical Association; American Psychiatric Association; American Psychiatric Association of Psychiatrists from India; Alumni Association of College of Medicine, University of Oklahoma. Community Activities: Joint Secretary, East and West Art Form, Oklahoma, 1979-81; Special Advisor, United States Congressional Advisory Board, 1982. Religion: Hindu. Honors and Awards: American Physician Recognition Award, 1980. Address: 2610 Emerald Lake Drive, Harlingen, Texas 78550.■

HENRY MICHAEL STAHR

University Professor. Personal: Born December 10, 1931; Married Irene F. Sondey; Father of Michael G., John C., Mary T., Patrick J., Matthew G. Education: B.S. Chemistry, South Dakota State University, 1916; M.S. Chemistry, Union College, Schnectady, New York, 1961; Ph.D. Food Technology, Iowa State

University, Ames, Iowa, 1976. Military: Served in the United States Marine Corps, 1949-52. Career: Professor, Veterinary Diagnosis Laboratory, Iowa State University; Former Positions as Senior Scientist, Development and Research and Analytical Chemist. Organizational Memberships: American Chemical Society 1956 to present, Committee Editor East New York Section; Society of Applied Spectroscopy, 1960 to present; American College of Veterinary Toxicology, Association of American Chemists, 1969 to present; American Association of Veterinary Laboratory Diagnosticians, 1978 to present. Community Activities: School Board Directors, Ogden Community Schools, 1976 to present; Ogden Lions Club, President 1977-78; Lions International: American Legion, Post 55, Commander 1978-80, Current Treasurer; Knights of Columbus, Ogden, President, 1976, 1977; Boy Scout Commissioner, 1969 to present; Isaac Walton Director, Ames Chapter, 1969-71; Environmental Council, Iowa State University, 1969-74. Religion: Roman Catholic. Honors and Awards: Outstanding Senior, South Dakota State University, 1956; Outstanding Patent, General Electric Company, 1961; Sigma Xi; Delta Sigma Gamma, 1975; Governor's Science Council, 1975 to present. Address: Box 180, Route 1, Ogden, Iowa 50212.∎

WILSON ALFRED STAIR, JR.

Environmental Designer. Personal: Born February 9, 1946; Son of Wilson Stair; Married Jan H. Education: Bachelor of Science Environmental Design 1973, Bachelor of Architecture 1974, Master of Architecture 1974, University of Oklahoma, Norman, Oklahoma. Military: Served in the United States Air Force, Staff Sargeant, 1966-70. Career: Environmental Designer; Former Positions as Architectural Designer, Urban Designer and Urban Planner. Organizational Memberships: American Planning Association; American Society of Landscape Architects; National Trust for Historic Preservation; The Nature Conservancy. Honors and Awards: Tau Sigma Delta. Address: 782 Village Lake Terrace #206, St. Petersburg, Florida 33702.∎

SANDRA ORNECIA STANLEY

Medical Student. Personal: Born July 6, 1950; Daughter of McKinley and Thelma Stanley. Education: Graduate, Lincoln High School (Jersey City, New Jersey), 1968; B.A., Ottawa University (Ottawa, Kansas), 1972; Attended Jersey City State College, 1973; M.S.Ed., University of Kansas at Lawrence, 1975; Ph.D., University of Kansas Medical Center, 1980; Currently a Medical Student at St. George's University School of Medicine, Grenada, West Indies. Career: Educational Diagnostician, Specialist, Consultant; Director/Coordinator, Training and Observation, University of Kansas Bureau of Child Research, Juniper Gardens Children's Project, 1979-82; Research Assistant, Department of Special Education, University of Kansas, 1977-79; Instructional Media/Materials Trainee, University of Kansas, 1976-77; Special Education Instructor, Joan Davis School for Special Education, Kansas City, Missouri, 1975-76; Director/Head Teacher, Salem Baptist Accredited Nursery School, Jersey City, New Jersey, 1972-73. Organizational Memberships: The Council of Exceptional Children; Council of Learning Disabilities; Black Caucus-Minority Exceptional Children; Association for Supervision and Curriculum Development; Women's Educational Network, Kansas City; National Association for Female Executives; International Platform Association. Community Activities: Urban League; National Association for the Advancement of Colored People; Easter Seal Society for Crippled Children and Adults of Missouri; College Women Inc., 1972-73 (now inactive); Women's Education Society of Ottawa University; Human Relations and Civil Rights Commission, Ottawa University, Recording Secretary 1968-69, Member 1968-72; University Union Hostesses, 1970-72; Search Committee for Chairperson, Department of Special Education, University of Kansas, 1978-79; Lecturer on Black English, Kansas Youth Trust School for Juvenile Delinquents; Project-Parent's Awareness of Student Attendance, Southeast High School (Kansas City) 1982; Oral Roberts Ministry; Salesian Mission; Father Flanagan's Boys Home; Emmanuel Baptist Educational Project, 1981; Muscular Dystrophy; World Vision Sponsor, 1982; Unity; Heart Fund. Religion: Member Salem Baptist Church. Published Works: Author of Several Articles and Educational Research Manuals. Honors and Awards: Plaque, Salem Baptist Accredited Nursery School, 1973; Master's Traineeship, Department of Special Education, 1974-75; Grantee, Alpha Gamma Delta's Founders Memorial Foundation, National Easter Seal Society Scholarship Program, 1975; Program Assistantship, Department of Special Education, 1976-77; Scholarship, College Women, Inc., 1977; Doctoral Fellowship, Department of Special Education, 1977-79; Honors, Comprehensive Exam, 1978; Listed in *Who's Who Among Students in American Universities and Colleges, Outstanding Young Women of America, Who's Who in the Midwest, Who's Who of American Women, Personalities of America, Personalities of the West and Midwest, Biographical Roll of Honor, World Who's Who of Women*. Address: 70 Madison Avenue, Jersey City, New Jersey 07304.∎

JANOS STARKER

Concert Cellist and Distinguished Professor. Personal: Born July 5, 1924, in Budapest, Hungary; Married Rae Busch; Father of Gabrielle, Gwen. Education: Graduate of Franz Liszt Academy. Career: Concert Cellist and Distinguished Professor of Music, Indiana University-Bloomington, 1958 to present; Solo Cellist, Chicago Symphony 1953-58, Metropolitan Opera 1949-53, Dallas Symphony 1948-49, Budapest Opera 1945-46. Organizational Memberships: American Federation of Musicians. Published Works: Over 85 L.P.'s on Angel, Phillips, Mercury, Decca, Deutsche Grammophon, Victor Japan, Japan Columbia; Originator of Starker Bridge. Published Works: Author *An Organized Method of String Playing, Bach Suite, Concerto Cadenzas, Schubert-Starker Sonatina, Bottermund-Starker Variation, Dvorak Concerto, Beethoven Sonatas and Variations* and Other Editions; Contributor of Many Articles and Essays to Various Magazines. Honors and Awards: Honorary Doctor of Music, East West University 1982, Williams College 1983, Cornell College 1978, Chicago Conservatory 1961; Ed Press Award, 1983; Kodaly Commemorative Medallion, 1983; Grand Prix du Dusque, 1948; George Washington Award, 1972; Sanford Fellowship, Yale University, 1974; Herzl Award, 1978; Honorary Member, Royal Academy, London, England, 1981. Address: Indiana University, Department of Music, Bloomington, Indiana 47401.∎

RUDOLF STARKERMANN

University Professor. Personal: Born April 12, 1924; Son of Anna Starkermann; Father of Renate, Brigitte. Education: Diploma Masch.Ing. 1949, Dr.Sci.Techn. 1964. Career: University Professor, 1970 to present; Theoretical Studies in Automatic Control of Thermal Machines and Consulting Engineer, Brown Boveri and Cie, Baden, Switzerland, 1950-56; Systems Engineer in Frequency-Load Control, Minneapolis-Honeywell, Philadelphia, 1956-58; Group Leader and Consulting Engineer in Multiple Automatic Control of Thermal Machines, Brown Boveri and Cie, Baden, Switzerland, 1958-70. Organizational Memberships: Schweizerische Gesellschaft fuer Automatik; The American Society of Mechanical Engineers; Society for General Systems Research; International Association of Science and Technology for Development; Association pour la Promotion des Techniques de Modélisation et de la Simulation dan l'Entreprise; Canadian Industrial Computer Society; The International Association for Mathematical Modelling. Community Activities: Canadian Figure Skating Association, Gold Judge in Dancing, Compulsory Figures and Free Skating. Honors and Awards: Listed in *International Who's Who in Education, International Who's Who of Intellectuals, Men of Achievement, Who's Who in the Commonwealth, International Register of Profiles, Dictionary of International Biography, Personalities of America, International Who's Who of Contemporary Achievement, International Register of Personalities, Biographical Roll of Honor*. Address: 172 Riverview Drive, Fredericton E3B 6Y1, Canada.

MARION H. STARRETT

Genealogist. Personal: Born November 14, 1930; Daughter of John and Theodora Horischak Hosko; Married Robert H. Starrett, Son of Henry F. and Irma Behrens Starrett. Education: A.S., Bay Path Junior College, 1950; Studies at the National Institute of Genealogical Research, National Archives, 1975, 1976; Certified Genealogical Researcher, 1977. Career: Administrative Assistant, WNHC-TV, 1950-57; Executive Secretary, WTIC-TV, 1957-58; Administrative

TWO THOUSAND NOTABLE AMERICANS

Assistant, Graceman Advertising Inc., 1958-60; Executive Secretary, Barnes Group, 1960-65; Corporate Secretary, Starrett Associates, Inc., 1966-75; President, Surveys, Inc., 1971-73; Staff Genealogist, National Society Daughters of the American Revolution Library, 1974-75; Professional Genealogist, 1975 to present; Lecturer, National Institute on Genealogical Research, National Archives, Washington, D.C., 1977-79; Lecturer, National Society Daughters of the American Revolution Volunteer Genealogical Training Program, 1977. Organizational Memberships: National Genealogical Society; Connecticut Society of Genealogists; New England Historical Genealogical Society; Old Maine Cemetery Association. Address: (Winter) 8712 Winthrop Drive, Alexandria, Virginia 22308; (Summer) Sprucewood, Boothbay Harbor, Maine 04538.■

MARCEA BLAND STATEN

Legal Counsel. Personal: Born October 12, 1948; Daughter of Mr. and Mrs. Ralph Bland; Married Randolph W. Staten; Mother of Randy Jr., Shomari Bland. Education: B.A. Sociology/B.S. Psychology, Knox College, 1968; J.D., Northwestern University, 1971. Career: International Counsel, Medtronic Inc.; Senior Attorney, Montgomery Ward and Company, Chicago, Illinois; Attorney, The Pillsbury Company, Minneapolis, Minnesota; Staff Counsel, The Ghetto Project, American Civil Liberties Union. Organizational Memberships: National Bar Association; American Bar Association; Minnesota Bar Association; Minnesota Association of Black Lawyers. Community Activities: Minneapolis Young Women's Christian Association, Board of Trustees; Minneapolis Urban Coalition, Vice President Board of Directors; The Links Incorporated; Iota Phi Lambda Professional Black Women's Group; Central Minnesota Legal Services Corporation, Director; Minnesota Women's Political Caucus. Religion: Zion Baptist Church, Parliamentarian. Address: 2515 12th Avenue North, Minneapolis, Minnesota 55411.■

CHARLES WILLIAM STEELE

Consultant. Personal: Born December 1, 1905; Son of William Deward and Katheryn S. Steele (both deceased); Married Mabelle C.; Father of Charles William Jr., Mary Louise (Steele) Apgar (deceased), Richard Earl, Linda Maybelle (Steele) Lux. Education: B.A. 1927, M.A. 1929, University of Missouri; M.S., Harvard Medical School, Boston, Massachusetts, 1931. Military: Served with the United States Army Medical Corps, Active Duty 1942-45, attaining the rank of Lieutenant Colonel; Served in Active Medical Corps Reserve, 1946-66, promoted to Full Colonel 1953. Career: Medical Consultant to Maine Social Security Administration; Medical Consultant to Vocational Rehabilitation Bureau, State of Maine; Private Practice in Internal Medicine; Cardiologist, Senior Visiting Physician, Chief of First Intensive Cardiology Service in Maine, Central Maine Medical Center, Lewiston, Maine; Consultant in Internal Medicine to the General Surgical and Medical Hospital, Veterans Hospital, Togus, Maine, 1974-78. Organizational Memberships: Androscoggin County Medical Society, 1935 to present; Maine Medical Association, 1935 to present; American Medical Association, 1935 to present; American Heart Association, 1936 to present; American Diabetic Association, 1969 to present; New England Heart Association, 1940-70; Pan-American Medical Association, Certified 1964, 1964-70; International Society of Internal Medicine; American Chemical Society; American Society of Internal Medicine, 1960 to present; Society of Internal Medicine of Maine, President 1955, Member 1952 to present; Maine Heart Association, President 1955, Member, 1950 to present; Maine Arthritis Association, 1948 to present; National Rehabilitation Association, 1960 to present. Community Activities: Maine State Deputy Civil Defense Director No. 3, responsible for Medical and Special Weapons, 1949-56; Advisor to Maine State Civil Defense Director on Medical and Special Defense, 1957-70; United States Civil Defense Council 1956-78, Member Advisory Committee on Health Services 1957-78, Chairman 1958; Committee on Civil Defense, American Medical Association, 1954-62; Committee on Civil Defense, American Diabetic Association; Advisor to United States Public Health Service, Division of Emergency Health Services, Family Division of Health Mobilization, 1960-70; Committee on Civil Defense, American Chemical Society, 1958-60; Advisor to Region I Council on Civil Defense of United States Civil, 1952-73; Rotary International, 1936-72. Religion: Baptist 1934 to present, Deacon 6 Years. Honors and Awards: George Washington Freedom Foundation Award, Freedom Foundation, Valley Forge, Pennsylvania, 1952; Scroll Award for Service as Commander, 333rd General Hospital, 1962; Gold Seal of Merit, Maine Civil Defense and Public Safety, 1957; Pfizer Company Award of Merit, United States Civil Defense Council, 1960; Outstanding Community Service by a Physician Award, Robins Company, 1964; Recognition Award for Outstanding Service Performed on behalf of the Society, American Society of Internal Medicine, 1972; Maine Heart Association Citation for Outstanding Public Service, 1972; Plaque for Outstanding Public Service, United States Civil Defense Council, Region I, 1973; Listed in *Community Leaders and Noteworthy Americans*. Address: 1 Wakefield Street, Lewiston, Maine 04240.■

ROBERT MILLER STEELE

Retired. Personal: Born April 8, 1921, in Argyle, Lee County, Iowa; Son of Kenneth Earl (deceased) and Ruth Irene (Miller) Steele; Married Lou Scott Pendleton; Father of Kenneth Martin, Luanne Scott. Education: B.S. Education, Northwest Missouri State University (formerly State Teachers College), 1943. Career: Position with Centre College, Danville, Kentucky, 1943-44; Tennessee Eastman Corporation (Y-12), Electromagnetic Process, Oak Ridge, Tennessee, 1944; Miles Consolidated Schools, Miles, Iowa, Spring Term 1945; Development of Proximity Fuses, University of Iowa, Testing Station, Clinton, Iowa, Summer 1945; Kemper Military School, Boonville, Missouri, 1945-46; Union Carbide Corporation, Oak Ridge, Tennessee, K-25 Gaseous Diffusion Facility 1946-50, X-10 Oak Ridge National Laboratory, Research and Development of Reactors until 1973; Teacher, State Technical Institute of Knoxville; Retired. Organizational Memberships: New York Academy of Science, 1982 to present; American Association for the Advancement of Science, 1949 to present; Past Member, American Crystallographic Association, Chemistry Society, Society for Metals. Community Activities: Scoutmaster for Local Boy Scout Troop 141. Published Works: Author Several Professional Publications including "The Preparation and Crystal Structure of Molybdenum (III) Fluoride" in *Journal of American Chemistry Society* (with D.E. LaValle and H. L. Yakel) 1960, "Identification of a Beta-Tungsten Phase in Tungsten-Rhenium Alloys" (with J. I. Federer) 1965, "Rhenium Nitrogen Fluoride and Rhenium Tetrafluoride" (with D. E. LaValle and William T. Smith Jr.) in the *Journal of Inorganic Nuclear Chemistry* 1966. Honor and Awards: Listed in *Dictionary of International Biography, I.B.A. Yearbook and Biographical Directory, International Who's Who of Intellectuals*, Others. Address: 1517 Ebenezer Road, Knoxville, Tennessee 37922.

RONALD ALBERT STEFFENHAGEN

Professor. Personal: Born November 6, 1923; Married Marie Shirley; Father of Eric Ronald, Mark Lee, Lori Ann. Education: B.A., University of Buffalo, 1950; M.S.A., Wayne State University, 1953; Ph.D., State University of New York at Buffalo, 1966. Military: Served in the United States Army Air Force as Corporal, 1943-46. Career: Professor, University of Vermont; Public Health Educator, Louisville, T.B. Association, 1954-55; Associate Professor, Rochester Institute of Technology, 1955-56. Organizational Memberships: American Society of Clinical Hypnosis; International Hypnosis Society; International Society for Professional Hypnosis; American Psychological Society; American Sociological Society. Community Activities: Volunteer Work in Corrections, Public Lectures on Drug Education. Religion: Catholic. Honors and Awards: Haupt Award for Excellence in Sociology; National T.B. Association Grant; Graduate Assistantship, University of Rochester; Health, Education and Welfare Research Grant; Alpha Kappa Delta; Listed in *American Men of Science*. Address: 167 Curtis Avenue, Burlington, Vermont 05401.■

JOHN COLBURN STEINMANN

Architect. Personal: Born October 24, 1941, in Monroe, Wisconsin; Son of John Wilbur and Irene Marie (Steil) Steinmann; Married Susan D. Koslosky on August 12, 1978. Education: B.Arch, University of Illinois, 1964; Postgraduate Work, Illinois Institute of Technology, 1970-71. Military: Served in the United States Army Reserve, 1964-66, attaining the rank of First Lieutenant C.E. Career: Project Designer, C. F. Murphy Associates, Chicago, Illinois, 1968-71; Steinmann Architects, Monticello, Wisconsin, 1971-73; Design Chief, Chief Project Architect, State of Alaska, Juneau, 1973-78; Project Designer, Mithun Associates, Architects, Bellevue, Washington, 1978-80; Owner, Principal, John C. Steinmann Associates; Architect, Kirkland, Washington, 1980 to present; Lecturer, Illinois Institute of Technology, 1971-72; Principal Works include Grant Park Music Bowl (Chicago) 1971, Menomonee Falls (Wisconsin) Medical Clinic 1972, Hidden Valley Office Building (Bellevue) 1978, Kezner Office Building (Bellevue) 1979, Sunriver Condominiums (Sun River, Oregon) 1980, Second and Lenora Highrise (Seattle) 1981, Bob Hope Cardiovascular Research Institute Laboratory Animal Facility (Seattle) 1982, Washington Court (Bellevue) 1982, Anchorage Business Park (Anchorage, Alaska) 1982, Private Residences; Registered Architect in Washington, Oregon, California, Arizona, New Mexico, Utah, Alaska, Wisconsin, Illinois. Organizational Memberships: American Management Association; National Council Architectural Registration Boards; American Institute of Architects; Alpha Rho Chi. Community Activities: Republican Party; University of Washington Yacht Club. Religion: Roman Catholic. Honors and Awards: Decorated Bronze Star. Address: 4316 106th Place, Northeast, Kirkland, Washington 98033.■

TWO THOUSAND NOTABLE AMERICANS

DEBORAH HASSELO STELLER ─────────────────────

Elementary School Principal. Personal: Born November 21, 1947; Daughter of Mrs. Sarah Hasselo; Married Arthur Wayne Steller, Son of Mrs. Bonnie Steller. Education: B.S., Florida State University, 1970; M.Ed. 1973, Ed.D. 1979, Mississippi State University. Career: Elementary School Principal; First, Fifth and Sixth Grade Teacher, Tinker School; Graduate Assistant in Institutional Research, Mississippi State University; Curriculum Intervention Specialist, Lanier School; Head Teacher, Lanier School; Elementary Curriculum Supervisor, 1977-79; Third Grade Teacher, Progress Village School. Organizational Memberships: Kappa Delta Pi, Life Member; Phi Delta Kappa, Life Member; American Association of School Administrators; Association for Supervision and Curriculum Development; National Association for Elementary School Principals; West Virginia Association for Elementary School Principals; West Virginia Association for Supervision and Curriculum Development; Ohio Alliance for Arts in Education. Community Activities: Florida State Alumni Association, Life Member; League of Women Voters; Mississippi State Alumni Association; Chi Omega Alumni Association; Cleveland Chi Omega Alumnae Association; Friends of the Public Library, Shaker Heights; Lomond Community Association; Nordonia Hills Boosters Club; Shaker Heights Historical Society; Longwood Young Men's Christian Association Advisory Committee; Counselor/Group Leader, Judeo-Christian Coalition Clinic, 1979-81; Tampa (Florida) Chi Omega Alumnae Association, Treasurer 1978-80. Religion: Administrative Board, Palma Ceia United Methodist Church, Tampa, Florida, 1980; Member Plymoth Church, Shaker Heights, 1982 to present. Honors and Awards: Selected for 1981-83 Curriculum Commission of 75 of the Association for Supervision and Curriculum Development; Selected by Freedoms Foundation to Attend a Week-Long Summer Seminar at Valley Forge, Pennsylvania, 1982; Proctor and Gamble Leadership Institute for Consumer Education; Listed in *Who's Who in the South and Southwest, World Who's Who of Women, Personalities of the South.* Address: 4223 San Luis, Tampa, Florida 33609.∎

MARILYN L. STEMBER ─────────────────────

University Professor. Personal: Born November 11, 1945; Daughter of Carl and Lillian Hanson; Married Ronald E. Education: B.S., Augustana College, 1967; M.S., University of Washington, 1970; M.A. 1974, Ph.D. 1975, University of Colorado. Career: University Professor; Former Positions as Program Evaluator, Public Health Nurse, School Nurse and Staff Nurse. Organizational Memberships: American Nurses Association; American Public Health Association; American Sociological Association; Association of Operating Room Nurses, Chairman Approval Board 1979-82; Colorado Nurses Association, Scholarship Program and Research Committees; Colorado Public Health Association, Board of Directors 1979-81, Chairman Public Relations Committee 1978-80; Sigma Theta Tau, Research Committee; Tithaynos, President 1966-67; Western Society for Research in Nursing; Western Social Science Association, Nominations Committee 1981-82. Community Activities: Denver Visiting Nurse Service, Research Consultant 1975-80, United Way, Community Needs Assessment Task Force 1980, Allocation Criteria Task Force 1979-80; Loveland Ski Patrol, First Aid and Rescue Work 1972 to present, Secretary 1974-75, Board of Directors 1974-75, Bylaws Committee Chairman 1975-76, Public Relations Committee 1975-77; Task Force on Teen Pregnancy, 1977-78; Statistical Consultation to Colorado State Health Department, 1979 to present; Program Evaluation Consultant to Seattle Pacific University, 1981; Curriculum Consultant, Mesa College, 1981; Research Consultant, Veteran's Hospital, 1980-81; Statistical Consultant, Colorado Health Insititute, 1979-80; University of Colorado, Graduate Coordinating Committee Chairman 1977-78, Graduate Memberships Committee 1978-79, 1982 to present, Subcommittee on Doctoral Admissions 1978-82, Discipline Appeals Committee 1979-82, Research Committee Chairman 1981-82, Faculty Council 1981-82, Distinguished Professor Committee 1981 to present, Faculty Status Committee 1981 to present, Committee on Tenure Standards and Procedures 1981-82. Published Works: Numerous Publications in *Communicating Nursing Research, Nursing Administration Quarterly, Introduction to Nursing Practice, Keeping the Public Healthy, Community Health Nursing, Planning Methodologies for Predicting Nurse Manpower Requirements, Environmetrics '81.* Honors and Awards: Student Nurse of the Year, 1967; Certificate of Appreciation, National Ski Patrol System, 1975; Outstanding Ski Patrol Pin and Citation, 1976; Citation, Denver Department of Health and Hospitals; Sigma Theta Tau Research Award, 1978; Colorado Nurses' Association Nurse of the Year, District 20, 1980; Nurse Scientist Grant, 1971-75; National Research Service Award for Postdoctoral Training, 1982-83; Sigma Theta Tau Honorary Nursing Society, 1970; Listed in *Who's Who in Health Care, Who's Who of American Women, Who's Who Among Contemporary Nurses, Who's Who in the West.* Address: 31753 Ponderosa Way, Evergreen, Colorado 80439.∎

DAVID BENTHEIM STENZEL ─────────────────────

Professor of History. Personal: Born January 5, 1927; Son of Mr. and Mrs. Roland Stenzel (deceased); Married Muriel Rosalie; Father of Christina, Eric, Carl. Education: B.S., School of Foreign Service, Georgetown University, 1951; M.A. 1954, Ph.D. 1957, University of California at Berkeley. Military: Served in the United States Army, 1945-47, as Technical Sergeant; Served in the United States Air Force, 1951-53, attaining the rank of Captain. Career: Professor of History, California State College, Stanislaus; Owner, Tempo Travel, Torlock; Former Occupations include Teaching at the University of California at Berkeley (summer) 1958, Stanford University 1957-59, United States Air Force Academy (summer) 1958. Community Activities: Member and Chairman, Stanslaus County Planning Commission, 1972-81; President, California County Planning Commissioners Association, 1977; Member and Past President, Turlock Rotary Club; Past District Chairman, Yosemite Area Council, Boy Scouts of America. Religion: Shepherd Lutheran Church, Past Chairman Church Council. Honors and Awards: Phi Beta Kappa, University of California at Berkeley; Paul Harris Fellow, Rotary. Address: 761 East Toolumme Road, Turlock, California 95380.∎

JOHN ERLE STEPHEN ─────────────────────

Attorney and Consultant. Personal: Born September 24, 1918; Son of John Earnest and Vida Klein Stephen; Married Gloria Yzaguirre; Father of Vida Leslie, John Lauro Kurt. Education: LL.B., J.D., University of Texas; Postgraduate Studies at the University of Mexico, Northwestern University, United States Naval Academy Postgraduate School, Naval War College. Military: Served to Commander in the United States Navy. Career: General Manager, Station KOPY, Houston, Texas, 1946; General Attorney, Executive Assistant to the President, Texas Star Corporation, Houston, 1947-50; Partner, Hofheinz and Stephen, Houston, 1950-57; Vice President and General Counsel, Television Broadcasting Company, Texas Radio Corporation, Gulf Coast Network, Houston, 1953-57; Special Counsel, Executive Assistant to Mayor, City of Houston, 1953-56; Vice President and General Counsel, Amway Corporation, Ada, Michigan, 1971-83. Organizational Memberships: American Bar Association, Council, Former Chairman Section of Public Utility Law; Federal Bar Association Council; World Peace Through Law Center, Geneva, Former Chairman International Aviation Law Committee; The District of Columbia State Bar; State Bar of Texas; State Bar of Michigan; Federal Communications Bar Association; Association of Interstate Commerce Commission Practitioners; American Judicature Society. Religion: Baptist. Published Works: United States Editor, *Yearbook of Air Law and Commerce;* Articles Published in Numerous Professional Journals. Honors and Awards: Member and Advisor to the United States Delegations to Diplomatic Conferenes, Warsaw Treaty and Hague Protocol, Bermuda Agreement, Tokyo Crimes Treaty, Montreal Liability Agreement; Visiting Lecturer, Harvard Graduate Business School, Washington Foreign Law Society, Pacific Agribusiness Conference; Chief of Protocol, City of Houston, 1953-56; Advisor, Consulates-General of Mexico in the United States, 1956-66; Advisor, United States Air Route Delegations to the United Kingdom, France, Belgium, Netherlands, in the United States 1956-66; Advisor, United States Air Route Delegations to the United Kingdom, France, Belgium, Netherlands, South Korea, Japan, Spain, Australia, Brazil, Argentina; Honorary Member, Japanese Air Law Society, Venezuelan Society of Air and Space Law; Honorary Faculty Member, University of Miami School of Law; Accredited Correspondent, United Nations; Republican and Democratic Conventions; Navy Unit Commendation with Bronze Star, 9 Battle Stars; Expert Marksman Medal; Expert Pistol Shot Medal; Listed in *Who's Who in the World, Who's Who in America, World Who's Who in Commerce and Industry, Who's Who in American Law, Who's Who in Finance and Industry, Who's Who in the South and Southwest, Who's Who in the Midwest, Who's Who in Aviation, Who's Who in World Aviation and Astronautics, Who's Who in American Universities and Colleges.* Address: 6904 Ligustrum Cove, Austin, Texas 78750.∎

JAMES O. STEPHENSON, JR.

Acquisitions and Mergers Executive. Personal: Born July 7, 1933; Son of James O. Stephenson, Sr.; Father of Suzanne, James O. III. Education: B.S., University of Missouri, 1955; M.B.A., New York University, 1962. Military: Served with the United States Army Artillery, 1955-57, attaining the rank of Lieutenant. Career: Head of Corporate Acquisition Program, The PQ Corporation; Former General Manager of Acquisitions, Mallinckrodt, Inc., St. Louis; Former Director of Planning and Acquisitions, Peabody International, Stamford, Connecticut. Organizational Memberships: Association for Corporate Growth, New York and Philadelphia Chapters, 1971-81; American Chemical Society, 1983; North American Society for Corporate Planning, 1983-84. Community Activities: River Bend Association, 1976-80; Sigma Alpha Epsilon Fraternity Alumnus, 1955-81. Honors and Awards: Listed in *Who's Who in the Midwest, Men of Distinction*. Address: 1307 Barkway Lane, West Chester, Pennsylvania 14380.■

ROBERT L. STEPHENSON

Archeologist. Personal: Born February 18, 1919, in Portland, Oregon; Son of George A. and Myrtle L. Stephenson (both deceased); Married Georgie Ellen Boydstun (deceased), Daughter of George and Mary Boydstun (both deceased). Education: B.A. Anthropology 1940, M.A. Anthropology 1942, University of Oregon; Ph.D. Anthropology, University of Michigan, 1956; Graduation Certificate, United States Department of Agriculture Management Development School, 1962. Military: Served in the United States Marine Corps Reserves, 1942-63, retiring with the rank of Major. Career: Archeologist; Student Crewman Excavating Catlow Cave, Southeastern Oregon, Summer 1937; Student Crewman Excavating Catlow and Roaring Springs Caves and Other Southeastern Oregon Sites, Summer 1938; Archeological Survey of Warner Valley, Southeastern Oregon, August 1938; Field Assistant Excavating Fort Rock Cave (9800-year old sandals) and other sites in Southeastern Oregon for University of Oregon, Summer 1939; Organized and Initiated Archeological Salvage in area to be Flooded by Grand Coulee Dam, Eastern Washington, Fall 1939; Field Assistant Excavating Sites in Northern California and South-Central Oregon, Summer 1940; Laboratory Supervisor for University of Texas in University of Texas/W.P.A. Project, 1940-41; Assistant Professor, Washington and Jefferson College, Summer 1941; Assistant Curator, Museum of Natural History, University of Oregon, 1941-42; Owned and Pperated First Street Food Store, 1946-47; Sold Rock-Wool Insulation, Austin, Texas, 1947; Field Director, Texas River Basin Surveys, 1947-51; Analyzed Large Collection of Excavated Specimens at Accokeek Creek Site, Southern Maryland, Summer 1952; Chief, Missouri Basin Project, River Basin Surveys, Smithsonian Institution, Lincoln, Nebraska, 1952-63; Assistant Professor, University of Nebraska, 1960-61; Acting Director, River Basin Surveys, Smithsonian Institution, Washington, D.C., 1963-66; Granted First Sabbatical Leave Ever granted by Smithsonian Institution, 1966-67; Coordinator, Nevada Archeological Survey, University of Nevada-Reno and Research Professor of Anthroplogy, 1966-68; Director, Institute of Archeology and Anthroplogy, University of South Carolina, 1968 to present; South Carolina State Archeologist, 1968 to present; Research Professor of Anthropology, University of South Carolina, 1968 to present. Organizational Memberships: American Anthropological Association, Fellow; American Association for the Advancement of Science, Fellow, Chairman of Finance Committee for "International Conference on Arid Lands in a Changing World" 1967-69; American Association for State and Local History; American Society for Conservation Archeology, Legislative Action Committee; American Society for Ethnohistory; Anthropological Society of Washington, D.C.; Archeological Societies of Texas, Oregon, California, Missouri, Oklahoma, Nevada, Virginia, West Virginia, Maryland, North Carolina, South Carolina, Georgia, Florida, Tennessee, Arkansas, Michigan; Condon Club, Pacific Northwest Geology Honorary; Conference on Historic Sites Archaeology, Director; Council on Abandoned Military Posts, National Director 1979-83, Regional Vice President 1976-78, National Vice President 1981-85; Explorer's Club of New York; Great Basin Archeological Conference; Historical Societies of Oregon, Nebraska, South Carolina; National Association of State Archeologists, Charter Member, President 1980-82; National Trust for Historic Preservation; Plains Anthropological Conference, Past Chairman; Society for American Archeology, American Committee for Archeological Conservation, Public Education Committee, Committee on Public Archeology, Past Assistant Editor of Journal 1960-63; Society for Historical Archeology, Charter Member, Past Conference Chairman; Society of Professional Archeologists, Charter Member, National Director 1977-79; Sigma Xi; Society of Vertebrate Paleontology; South Carolina Council of Professional Archeologists, Organizing Chairman 1975-79; South Carolina Federation of Museums, President 1971-73; Southeastern Archeological Conference, Past Chairman 1970. Community Activities: South Carolina Review Board for National Historic Preservation Act, 1969 to present; Ex-Officio Member, Camden Historical Commission, 1971 to present; South Carolina Heritage Trust Advisory Board, 1976 to present; Archeological Advisory Committee, Tennessee Valley Authority, 1972 to present; Baruch Associates, Belle W. Baruch Institute for Marine Biology and Coastal Research, University of South Carolina, 1976 to present; Toastmasters International, District Lieutenant Governor 1965-69; Lincoln (Nebraska) Community Council on Alcoholism, 1960-63. Religion: Episcopal, Lay Reader 1955-60. Published Works: Editor, Institute of Archeology and Anthropology *Notebook*, 1969 to present; Author Numerous Professional Publications. Honors and Awards: Lakeview Logging Company Graduate Fellowship, 1941-42; Alice L. L. Fergeson Memorial Fellowship, 1951-52 and 1954-56. Address: 5831 Satchel Ford Road, Columbia, South Carolina 29206.■

T(HOMAS) H(ULBERT) STEVENSON

Historian, Political Scientist, Author, Editor, Translator, Lecturer, Researcher. Personal: Born September 7, 1919; Married Dorothy A. Ruggles; Father of Mary Anne Stevenson Marchio, James Randolph. Education: A.B., Oberlin College, 1941; A.M. 1945, Ph.D. 1964, University of Chicago. Military: Served in the United States Army Air Force, 1942-43. Career: Historian, Political Scientist, Author, Editor, Translator, Lecturer, Researcher; Former Positions as College and University Faculty Member, Assistant to the President of Foundation for Voluntary Welfare. Organizational Memberships: A.H.A., 1965-71; Mensa, 1974-75. Community Activities: Delegate, Wayne County (Nebraska) Republican Party Convention, 1978, 1980, 1982; Alternate Delegate, Nebraska State Republican Convention, 1980; Election Night Commentator, Radio Station KEXL, Norfolk, Nebraska, 1980 and 1982, and on Various Elections Nights on Television Stations in San Jose, Marquette, Wayne and Other Cities. Published Works: Author *Politics and Government* (1973); Co-Author *Political Science* (1951, 1955, 1959, 1965; Japanese Edition 1976), *World Politics* (1962, 1966); Contributing Author *Soviet Power and Policy* (1966), *Soviet Total War* (1956); Editor, *Building Better Volunteer Programs* (1958, 1971); Author, Translator and Translator/Abstractor of Arts in Journals and Encyclopedias. Honors and Awards: Encyclopaedia Britannica Fellow in Medieval History, University of Chicago, 1946-47; Grant for Postdoctoral Research in Medieval History, Wayne State Foundation, 1968. Address: 711 Logan Street, Wayne, Nebraska 68787.■

DAVID WAYNE STEWART

Associate Professor of Management. Personal: Born October 23, 1951; Son of Wesley A. Stewart Jr. and Edith R. Moore; Married Lenora Francois, Daughter of Curtis Francois; Father of Sarah Elizabeth, Rachel Dawn. Education: B.A., Northeast Louisiana University, 1972; M.A. 1973, Ph.D. 1974, Baylor University. Career: Associate Professor of Management, Owen Graduate School of Management, Vanderbilt University; Associate Professor of Business and Psychology, Jacksonville State University, 1978-80; Research Manager, Needham Harper & Steers Advertising, Chicago, 1976-80; Research Psychologist, State of Louisiana Department of Mental Health, 1974-76. Organizational Memberships: Newsletter Editor, Division of Consumer Psychology, The American Psychological Association, 1981-83; Executive Committee, Division of Consumer Psychology, 1981 to present; American Marketing Association; Association for Consumer Research; Psychometric Society; Institute of Management Science. Community Activities: Marketing Task Force, Middle Tennessee Council of Boy Scouts of America, 1981; Beta Gamma Sigma, National Business Honor Society. Religion: Member Judson Baptist Church, Nashville, Tennessee. Published Works: Associate Editor, *Psychology and Marketing*; Member Editorial Board, *Journal of Marketing Research*. Honors and Awards: Phi Kappa Phi National Honor Society, 1972; Research Grant, Owen Graduate School of Management Dean's Fund, 1981, 1982, 1983; Research Grant, Marketing Science Institute, 1983. Address: 812 Fireside Circle, Brentwood, Tennessee 37027.■

ELIZABETH VICTORIA STEWART

Educator. Personal: Born February 20, 1910; Daughter of William and Ellen Stewart (both deceased). Education: Diploma, Freedmen's Hospital School of Nursing, Washington, D.C., 1933; B.S.N.E., The Catholic University of America, 1945; M.S., University of Maryland School of Nursing, 1971. Career: Public School Teacher, Grades 1-3, Madison County, Virginia, 1929-30; Professional Nurse, Staff 1939-41, Head Nurse 1941-45, Teaching Supervisor 1945, Department

Supervisor 1945-50, Administrative Nurse Supervisor 1950-54, Assistant Director of Nursing 1954-58, P.M. Charge Supervisor 1958-61, Student Health Director and Maternal-Child Instructor 1969-71, Archivist School of Nursing 1970-71, Nurse Specialist (Secondary Nurses Examination Board, D.C., 1971-73), Retired, Freedmen's Hospital; Assistant School Nurse, Howard University, Washington, D.C., 1935-36; Assistant School Nurse, Howard University, Washington, D.C., 1935-36; Assistant School Nurse, Virginia State College, Ettrick, Virginia, 1936-39. Organizational Memberships: Prince George's Mental Health Association; District of Columbia Nurses' Association, Longterm Care Counsel of D.C. League for Nursing, Member and Past Chairperson of Freedmen's Hospital Historical Source Committee; District of Columbia Nurses' Association, Board Member and Board Representative to the Graduate Nurses Association of the District of Columbia, Official Registry, Private Duty Section, 1 Term. Community Activities: American Red Cross; Smithsonian Associate; Alumni Associations of Freedmen's Hospital School of Nursing, Maryland University and University of Maryland Alumni Association International; The Catholic University of America School of Nursing Alumni Association. Religion: St. Luke's Episcopal Church, Active Member Cluster of Churches concerned with the Mission of Christians in the World, St. Luke's Greeters for Meeting New Members, Coffee and Conversation Hostess, Past Vestry Member; St. Mary's Guild, Church of the Atonement, Chairperson. Honors and Awards: Award for Devoted Service to All Men, Freedmen's Hospital Alumni Association, 1973; Appreciation Plaque, District of Columbia League for Nursing, 1974; Edith M. Beattie Award, Highest Award of Professionalism given by the District of Columbia Graduate Nurses Association, 1977; The Glowing Lamp for 33 Years of Service to Nursing, Faculty of Freedmen's Hospital School of Nursing, 1968. Address: 77 Watkins Park Drive, Upper Marlboro, Maryland 20772.

PAUL ALVA STEWART

Consultant. Personal: Born June 24, 1909; Son of William O. and Achsah B. Stewart (both deceased); Married; Father of David Enos, Seth Michael. Education: B.S. 1952, M.S. 1953, Ph.D. 1957, Ohio State University. Career: Consultant, Blackbird-Starling Problems; Research Entomologist, United States Department of Agriculture, 1965-73; Research Biologist, United States Fish and Wildlife Service, 1959-65; Assistant to Director, Indiana Division of Fish and Game, 1958; Research Fellow, Ohio Cooperative Wildlife Research Unit, 1952-57. Organizational Memberships: American, British, South African, Royal Australasian Ornithological Unions; Wilson and Cooper Ornithological Societies; American Society of Mammalogists; Donor, Paul A. Stewart Awards for Ornithological Research, Wilson Ornithological Society. Honors and Awards: Elective Member, American Ornithologists Union. Address: 203 Mooreland Drive, Oxford, North Carolina 27565.■

JOHN LAWRENCE STILL

Director of Staff Development. Personal: Born June 9, 1933; Son of Garland E. and Winnie V. Still; Married Patricia Susan Matheson; Father of John Lawrence Jr., Christopher Mark, Todd Alexander, Susan Rebecca. Education: B.S., Davidson College, 1956; M.A. (Andrew Carnegie Fellow), George Peabody College, 1957; Ph.D. (Administrative Leadership Intern), Florida State University, 1972. Military: Served in the R.O.T.C. at Davidson College, 1952-56. Career: Instructor in High School, Junior College, Adult Education, 1956-65; Director of Interns and Assistant Professor, University of South Florida, 1965-66; Visiting Instructor, Jacksonville University; County Curriculum Consultant, 1966-68; Supervisor of Social Science, 1968-80; Director of Staff Development and Assessment Center, 1980 to present. Organizational Memberships: Florida Council for Social Studies, President 1968-70; American Association of School Administrators; Association of Supervision and Curriculum Development; National Council for Social Studies, Chairman Steering Committee 1971; American Society for Training and Development; National Staff Development Association, Convention Speaker; Florida Staff Development Association, Planning Committee, 1983 to present; Phi Delta Kappa. Community Activities: Vice Chairman Fund Raising, Mease Hospital, Dunedin, Florida, 1980; Chairman, Pinellas County Committee on Consumer/Economic Education, 1978-80; Member Dunedin Fine Arts and Cultural Society; Pinellas Historical Society; President, Dunedin North Rotary Club; State Task Force Committee for General Adult Education; Chairman, State Competency Committee; Representative for Pinellas County to University of South Florida Regional Planning Council; Suncoast Chamber of Commerce; Chairman, American Education Week. Religion: Grace Lutheran Church, Member 1978-83, Superintendent of Sunday School and Member Church Council 1972-75, Confirmation Class Instructor 1982 to present. Honors and Awards: Star Teacher Award, Florida Chamber of Commerce, 1965; Administrative Leadership Award for Ph.D., 1968-72; J. R. Skretting Florida State Leadership Award, 1972 and 1980; Grantee Universities of Accra (Ghana) and Ibaddan (Nigeria), 1974-75; Speaker at American Association of School Administrators National Conventions, 1978-80; Program Chairman Awards for Directing State Conventions, 1971, 1980, 1983; Listed in *Who's Who in the South and Southwest*. Address: 2312 Jones Drive, Dunedin, Florida 33528.■

JOE LEE STOCKARD

Medical Officer. Personal: Born May 5, 1924. Education: B.S., Yale University, 1945; M.S., University of. Kansas, 1948; M.P.H., Johns Hopkins University, 1961. Military: Served in the United States Medical Corps, 1952-55. Career: Medical Officer (Tropical Medicine), Agency for International Development; Chief of Medicine, 8228 Mobile Army Surgical Hospital, Korea, 1953; Research Physician, Walter Reed Army Institute of Research, Korea and Malaya, 1954-55; Assistant Professor of Preventive Medicine and Rehabilitation, University of Maryland, School of Medicine, 1955-58; Deputy Director and Chief of Epidemiology, Pakistan, SEATO Cholera Research Laboratory, 1960-63. Organizational Memberships: American Society of Tropical Medicine and Hygiene; Royal Society of Tropical Medicine and Hygiene; American Association for the Advancement of Science; American Public Health Association; New York Academy of Sciences. Community Activities: Assistant Chief Epidemiology, Division of Foreign Quarantine, United States Public Health Service, 1963-64; Chief Preventive Medicine, A.I.D. Saigon, Republic of Vietnam, 1964-67; Deputy Associate Director, Multilateral Programs, Office of International Health, D.H.E.W., 1967-69. Religion: Baptist. Honors and Awards: Listed in *Men of Achievement*. Address: 12807 Falmouth Drive, Colesville, Maryland 20904.■

JONE C. STOKES

Management Communications Consultant (Retired). Personal: Born April 18, 1915, in Charlotte, North Carolina; Married Dorothy Jewell; Father of Kenneth. Education: Graduate, Air War College; Attended the American Foreign Service Institute, the University of Southern California, George Washington University. Military: Served in the United States Air Force, retiring in 1973 with the rank of Lieutenant Colonel. Career: Consultant, Department of Commerce/National Telecommunications and Information Administration 1978-80, White House Office of Telecommunications Policy 1976-78, U.S.I.A. Foreign Service Officer Selection Board 1976, National Institute of Health 1975, National Advisory Council on Indian Education 1974, U.S.I.A. Motion Picture & Television Service 1973-74, White House Technology Assessment Task Force 1972, President's Advisory Council on Management Improvement 1970-73, Atomic Energy Commission/Computer Science Corporation 1967; President, Televisual Systems Corporation 1976-82; Former Vice President, Teletrac Systems Corporation; Past President, Federal Design Council; Presidential Task Force Member, First Federal Design Assembly/National Arts Endowment; Federal Bureau of the Budget, 1947-51. Organizational Memberships: Vice President, Board Member, Public Members Association of the Foreign Service; American Association for the Advancement of Science; Past Member, Center for the Study of the Presidency, American Institute of Aeronautics and Astronautics, American Foreign Service Association, National Space Club, Air Force Association, The Retired Officers Association; Former Member, National Board of Governors, Information Film Producers of America. Honors and Awards: Legion of Merit, Meritorious Service Medal, Commendation Medal with Three Oak Leaf Clusters, United States Air Force; Cindy Award, Information Film Producers of America; Silver Anvil Award, Sigma Chi; Listed in *Who's Who in the World, Five Thousand Personalities of America, International Book of Honor*, Who's

TWO THOUSAND NOTABLE AMERICANS

Who in Aviation, Who's Who in Finance and Industry, Men of Achievement, International Who's Who of Intellectuals, World Biographical Hall of Fame. Address: 7119 Westchester Drive, Temple Hills, Maryland 20748.■

ELAINE MURRAY STONE

Author, Realtor, Composer, Television Host and Producer. Personal: Born January 22, 1922; Daughter of Mrs. Catherine Murray-Jacoby; Married F. Courtney Stone; Mother of Catherine Rayburn (Mrs. Robert), Pamela Webb (Mrs. Don), Victoria Francis. Education: Graduate of Ashley Hall, Charleston, South Carolina, 1939; Attended Juilliard School of Music, New York City, 1939-41; Graduate in Piano, New York College of Music, 1943; Graduate in Organ with Licentiate Degree, Trinity College of Music, London, England, 1947; Further Studies at Florida Institute of Technology and University of Miami. Career: Host of "Focus on History," a Television Show on WMDG-TV, Melbourne, Florida, 1982-83; Television Writer and Producer, 1978-80, KXTX-TV, Dallas, Texas; Radio Executive, WTAI, Melbourne, 1971-74; Editor, Cass Inc., Melbourne, 1970-71; Organist, New York, New Jersey, Florida, Fort Lauderdale, 1953-54; Cape Canaveral Branch, National League of American Pen Women, President 1979-80; Regent of Rufus Fairbanks Chapter, Daughters of the American Revolution, 1981-82, 1983; Episcopal Diocese of Southern Florida, Diocesan Board of Promotion, 1961-62. Community Activities: Melbourne Bicentennial Commission, 1975-76; Editor of the *Trumpet*, Publication of Brevard Symphony, 1965-75; Daughters of the American Revolution, Librarian Abigail Wright Chamberlin Chapter 1964-66; Florida Daughters of the American Revolution, Chairman of Music 1964-66; Abe Lincoln Radio-Television National Awards, Southern Baptist Radio-Television Commission, Judge 1980; Brevard Poetry Club, Judge 1981. Religion: Vice President, Episcopal Churchwomen, Holy Trinity Episcopal Church, Melbourne, 1970; Third Order of St. Francis, 1955-65; Author of Articles in *The Living Church, Christian Life, Logos,* Others. Published Works: Author of 100 Articles; *The Taming of the Tongue* 1954, *Love One Another* 1957, *Pedro Menendez de Aviles* 1969, *Melbourne Bicentennial Book* 1976, *Uganda: Fire and Blood* 1977, *Tekla and The Lion* 1981. Honors and Awards: First Place, Piano, South Carolina State Music Contest, 1939; First Place in Journalism, Florida State Contest, National League of American Pen Women, 1964; First Place in Sales, Engle Realty, 1975-, 1976, 1977, 1978; First Place in Books in Texas State Contest 1979, National League of American Pen Women, for *Uganda: Fire and Blood*; First Place in Short Story Contest, Texas State Contest, National League of American Pen Women, 1979. Address: 1945 Pineapple Avenue, Melbourne, Florida 32935.■

LEROY ALLEN STONE

Forensic Clinical Psychologist. Personal: Born September 13, 1931; Son of Hilda Stone; Married Patricia Joan Stone; Father of Erika D. Stone. Education: A.B. Psychology 1953, M.A. Psychology 1954, San Jose State University; Ph.D. Psychology, University of North Dakota, 1962. Military: Served in the United States Army, E-4, 1954-55. Career: Present Position in Forensic Clinical Psychology; Former Positions as College Professor, President of Psychological Services Consulting Corporation, Head of Research Laboratory, Head of Department in Research Institute, Consultant to Regional Mental Health Centers, Research Consultant. Organizational Memberships: American Psychological Association; Psi Chi; Sigma Xi; Psychonomic Society; Psychometric Society. Community Activities: Harpers Ferry Civil War Roundtable. Honors and Awards: Perceptual-Cognitive Development Director, 1969; N.I.M.H. Special Research Fellow, 1966-68; Listed in *American Men and Women of Science, Who's Who in the West, Who's Who in the Midwest, Dictionary of International Biography, Community Leaders of America, Who's Who Among Authors and Journalists, Outstanding Professionals in Human Service, Who's Who in the South and Southwest.* Address: P.O. Box 395, Harpers Ferry, West Virginia 25425.■

THADDEUS C. STOPCZYNSKI

State Representative. Personal: Born February 16, 1940; Son of Stephen and Cassie Stopczynski; Married Judith E., Daughter of Mr. and Mrs. Steve Drost; Father of Suzanne, Peggy, Lawrence, Gregory, Judith Joy, Matthew, Timothy, Elizabeth, Rebecca Lynne, Thaddeus G., Johnathon G. Education: Graduate, St. Augustine High School, 1958; Chrysler Millwright Apprentice Program, 1962; Detroit Police Academy, 1962. Career: State Representative; Former Police Officer, Detroit Police Department. Organizational Memberships: Detroit Board of Education, Chairman Region 6 School Board 1971-72. Community Activities: Pulaski Homeowners Association, Board Member; Northeast Council of Homeowners; Fraternal Order of Eagles #2495; 14th Congressional District Democratic Party; Honorary Member, PLAV Post #169; Polish Century Club; St. Raymond's Dad's Club; Immaculate Conception Parent's Club; Polish Falcons Nest #31; Michigan Polish-American Retirees-Senior Citizens. Religion: Member Immaculate Conception Ukrainian Church (Catholic). Honors and Awards: Selected as Legislator of the Year by Veterans of Foreign Wars; Legislator of the Year Award, Police Officers Association of Michigan. Address: 19214 Goulburn, Detroit, Michigan 48205.■

RALPH SHIRLEY STOWE

Chiropractor. Personal: Born March 1, 1945, in Kankakee, Illinois; Married Sandra Lee Groner; Father of Todd Jeffrey, Brian Scot, Nathanael Shirley, Erin Elizabeth, Abigail Eileen. Education: Graduate, Lockport Township High School (Lockport, Illinois), 1962; Attended Joilet Junior College (Joliet, Illinois) 1962-68, University of Washington at Seattle Summer 1969, Elmhurst College (Elmhurst, Illinois) Summer 1971, Illinois Institute of Technology (Chicago) 1967-70, National College of Chiropractic (Lombard, Illinois) 1972-75, College of Dupage (Glen Elyn, Illinois) Fall 1976, National-Lincoln School of Postgraduate Education (Lombard, Illinois) 1975-81, Clayton University (St. Louis) 1980. Military: Served in the United States Marine Corps, 1963. Career: Chiropractor, Crest Hill Chiropractic Clinic, Ltd.; Adjunct Professor of Biomechanics, National College of Chiropractic; Former Positions include Author, Business Manager, Carpenter, Cement Finisher, Commercial Pilot, Computer Programmer, Draftsman, Electrician, Experimenter and Junior Engineer, Hard Hat Diver, Inventor, Laboratory Assistant (Physiology, X-Ray), Lecturer, Physician, Professor, Salesman, Scientist, Scuba Diver and Instructor, Security Guard, Welder, Writer. Organizational Memberships: American Chiropractic Association; American Nuclear Society; American Society of Oceanography; Fellow, American Council of Applied Clinical Nutrition; Delta Tau Alpha; Knock Research Foundation, Board of Directors; Foundation for Chiropractic Education and Research; Professional Association of Diving Instructors; Radiation Research Society; Scientific Research Society of North America; Society for Computer Medicine; The International Oceanographic Foundation. Published Works: (include) "Reply to Dr. Sherlock" 1981, "Computer Modeling of cervical Spine Motions Based on Orthogonal X-ray Measurements *in vivo*" (with J. W. Butler) 1980, "Acupuncture Treatment of Bell's Palsy" (with Paul A. Jaskoviak, Andries M. Kleynhans and Norman A. Frigerio), Many Others. Honors and Awards: Included in *Chiropractic Doctors: An Amazing Profile of America's Most Effective Drugless Healers*; Kentucky Colonel, 1982; Listed in *Who's Who Among Students in American Universities and Colleges, Who's Who in Chiropractic, Men of Achievement.* Address: 19W168 Millbrook Drive, Downers Grove, Illinois 60516.■

JOHN GEORGE STRACHAN

Retired Administrator, Lecturer, Program Consultant, Author. Personal: Born May 23, 1910, in Montreal, Quebec, Canada; Son of Thomas Henry and Blanche Elizabeth Strachan (both deceased); Married Jane Ragland; Father of Roger Thomas, John A. (deceased). Education: Attended the University of Dayton (Ohio), St. John's College (New York), Pace and Pace Institute (New York); Graduate, Yale School of Alcohol Studies, 1950. Military: Served in the United States Air Force, 1941-45. Career: Helped Organize the Wisconsin Council and State Bureau, the Milwaukee Information Referral Center, and Some of Earliest Treatment, Community and Industrial Programs on Alcoholism; Helped Establish Alcohol Study Sessions, University of Wisconsin (now Mid-West Institute), Marquette Labor College, Three Schools at University of Alberta (first in Canada); Founded and Directed Alberta's First Impaired Drivers Program; Organized and Directed Alcoholism Foundation of Alberta, 1953-65; Milwaukee Information and Referral Center, 1947-53; Spearheaded Formation of Canadian Council on Alcoholism (now Canadian Addictions Foundation), 1954; Former Officer and Board Member, North American Association of Alcoholism Programs (now Alcohol and Drug Problems Association); Alcoholism Consultant, Department of the Attorney-General, Alberta, 1969-73; President, Gillain Foundation, 1972-80; President and Executive Director, Gillain Manor Ltd., Sidney, British Columbia, 1972-80. Organizational Memberships: North American Association of Alcoholism Program, Chairman 1960 Annual Conference; British Medical Association and International Council on Alcoholism Addictions Co-Sponsored to World Assembly, London, England, 1964; Royal Glenora Club; Canadian Authors Association; Association Litteraire et Artistique Internationale. Community Activities: E. M. Jellinek Memorial Fund, Board Member. Published Works; Author of Three Books, *Alcoholism: Treatable Illness, Practical Alcoholism Programming, Recovery from Alcoholism.* Honors and Awards: Life Membership, Alcohol and Drug Problems Association of North America; Fellow, Royal Society of Arts,

TWO THOUSAND NOTABLE AMERICANS

London; Honorary Doctor of Laws, University of Alberta, 1973; Distinguished Service Award and Life Membership, Canadian Addictions Foundation, 1976; Queen Elizabeth Silver Jubilee Medal, 1977; Alberta Alcoholism and Drug Abuse Commission's First Ever Distinguished Service Award, 1983; Library of the Alberta Alcoholism and Drug Abuse Commission renamed the J. George Strachan Library; Listed in *International Writers Biography, Dictionary of International Biography, Who's Who in the West, Men of Achievement, Community Leaders and Noteworthy Americans, International Who's Who in Community Service.* Address: 2035 Summergate Boulevard, Sidney, British Columbia, Canada V8L 4K6.■

NELLIE CORA STRAUB

Personal: Born December 20, 1898; Daughter of Mattie Mareny Gregory; Mother of Evelyn Elizabeth Straub Savage. Education: University of Illinois-Urbana, College of Commerce, 1921 (3 yrs). Religion: Methodist, Champaign, Illinois; Baptist, Honolulu, Hawaii. Address: 1777 Ala Moona, Honolulu, Hawaii 96815.■

JOSEPH PETER STRELKA

Professor of German and Comparative Literature. Personal: Born May 3, 1927; Son of Joseph (deceased) and Maria Strelka; Married Brigitte; Father of Alexandra Sascha. Education: Ph.D., University of Vienna, 1951. Career: Professor of German and Comparative Literature, State University of New York at Albany; Former Positions include Professor in Pennsylvania and California, Free-lance Critic in Vienna, Administrator in Austria, Visiting Professor at Several Universities in West Germany, Italy, South Africa. Organizational Memberships: International Comparative Literature Association; International Association of German Studies; International PEN Club (U.S. Center, Austrian Center, Center for German Authors Abroad); Board of Governors, Humboldt Society in West Germany; Founding Member, International Robert Musil Society; Others. Published Works: Author of a Dozen Books on Literature; Editor, Four Book Series in the U.S. and Switzerland; Member Several Editorial Boards of Journals and Book Series. Honors and Awards: Award from the Theodor Koerner Foundation in Vienna, 1954, 1955, 1956; Award of the City of Vienna, 1959; Austrian Cross of Honor for the Arts and Sciences, First Class, 1978. Address: 1188 Avon Road, Schenectady, New York 12308.■

JUDITH MITCHELL STRINGHAM

Equipment Sales Executive. Personal: Born May 9, 1939, in Hartford, Connecticut; Daughter of William Joseph and Irene Elizabeth Campton Mitchell; Married Varick Van Wyck Stringham, Jr., June 15, 1963; Mother of Amanda, Pamela, Varick Van Wyck III, Rebecca. Education: A.A.S., Fashion Institute of Technology, 1959; B.S., Cornell University, 1961; M.S., State University of New York at New Paltz, 1964. Career: Teacher, Fishkill (New York) Elementary School, Lamar Elementary School and Presbyterian High School (Kingsville, Texas) 1961-65; Secretary-Treasurer, North Atlantic Equipment Sales, Inc., Wappingers Falls, New York, 1972 to present. Community Activities: Former Member of the Board of Directors, Junior League of Poughkeepsie, League of Women Voters; Past Treasurer, Past President, Former Member Board of Directors, Community Children's Theatre; President, Past Secretary, Community Experimental Repertory Theatre; Secretary Advisory Committee, Former Member Board of Directors, Dutchess County Arts Council; Charter Member Board of Directors, Secretary, Cunneen-Hackett Cultural Complex; Former Crew, Hudson River Sloop Clearwater; Former Member Board of Directors, First Vice President Program Parent-Teacher Association; Cornell Secondary Schools Committee; National Association of Female Executives; National Organization of Women; American Association of University Women; Preservation League of New York State; Cornell University Alumni Association; Cornell College Human Ecology Alumni Association; Cornell Chorus Society; Dutchess County Historical Society; Fishkill Historic Society; County Players; Dutchess County Landmarks; Mt. Gulian Society; Mental Health Association in Dutchess County; Century Club of Vassar Brothers Hospital Association; American National Red Cross; Dutchess County S.P.C.A.; Paul Harris Sustaining Member, Rotary Foundation of Rotary International. Religion: Reformed Church in America. Honors and Awards: Listed in *Who's Who of American Women, World Who's Who of Women, Personalities of America.* Address: Dogwood Hill Road, Wappingers Falls, New York 12590.■

SAMUEL DAVID STROMAN

Professor. Personal: Father of Brenda D. Gumbs, Jamileh S. D., Sherolyn D., Synthia D., Samuel David II. Education: A.B., South Carolina State College, 1950; M.A., Howard University, 1964; M.S., University of Wisconsin-Milwaukee, 1972; Ph.D., The American University, 1976; Studies at the United States Army Command and General Staff College and Other Military Schools. Military: Served in the United States Army, 1941-45, rising through the ranks to First Sergeant; Regular Army Officer, 1950-76, Second Lieutenant to Full Colonel. Career: Assistant Professor, Department of Military Science, Howard University, 1959-63; Chairman, Department of Military Science, University of Wisconsin-Milwaukee, 1969-72; Chairman, Department of Military Science, Howard University, 1972-76; Army Officer, Platoon Leader, Company Commander, Battalion Commander, Inspector General, N.C.O. Academy Commandant, Senior Advisor, Vietnamese Infantry School; Department of the Army Branch Chief; Professor, South Carolina State College. Organizational Memberships: American Personnel and Guidance Association; South Carolina Personnel and Guidance Association; American Association for Counselor Education and Supervision; American Association for Non-White Concerns in Education; South Carolina Association for Non-White Concerns in Education; American Association of University Professors. Community Activities: Phi Delta Kappa, Vice President for Programs, Orangeburg Chapter 1980-81; National Association for the Advancement of Colored People, Chairman Legal Redress Committee, Orangeburg Chapter, 1977-79; Appointed to National Board of Advisors of American Biographical Institute, 1982; Chairman to Symposium on "Scientific Process of Decision Making," 81st Annual Convention of the American Psychological Association, Montreal, Canada, 1973; Board of Directors, Vasquez Association, Educational Research and Consulting Firm; Phi Kappa Phi; Kappa Delta Pi; Phi Delta Kappa. Published Works: Editorial Board, *Education* Magazine; Editorial Board, *Journal of Instructional Psychology.* Honors and Awards: Special Award from Students for Distinguished Teaching and Unselfish Devotion, 1977; Veterans of Foreign Wars Distinguished Service in Education Award, 1978; Veterans of Foreign Wars Award for Dedicated Service and Inspirational Leadership, 1981; Outstanding College Teacher of the Year, Orangeburg Chapter, Phi Delta Kappa, 1978-79; Inducted into South Carolina State College Army R.O.T.C. Hall of Fame, 1978; Award for Outstanding Service, Orangeburg Alumni Chapter, Kappa Alpha Psi, 1978; Southeastern Province Kappa Alpha Psi Achievement Award, 1978; Gold Medal Educator for the 1980's, 1980; Army Legion of Merit with Oak Leaf Cluster; Army Meritorious Service Medal with Oak Leaf Cluster; Army Commendation Medal with Oak Leaf Cluster; Army General Staff Badge; Bronze Star Medal; Listed in *Personalities of the South, Dictionary of International Biography, Who's Who in the South and Southwest, Book of Honor, American Biographical Directory, International Who's Who of Intellectuals, International Register of Profiles, Personalities of America, Men of Achievement, Men and Women of Distinction, Community Leaders of America, Biographical Roll of Honor, Five Thousand Personalities of the World.* Address: P.O. Box 1601, South Carolina State College, Orangeburg, South Carolina 29117.■

THOMAS TRACY STURROCK

University Professor of Botany and Assistant Dean. Personal: Born December 9, 1921; Son of Mr. and Mrs. David Sturrock (deceased); Married Jeanne Norquist; Father of Nancy Elizabeth, John David, Barbara Jeanne (Sturrock) Morris, Catherine Ann (Sturrock) Hilliard, Robert Charles Sturrock. Education: Diploma, Palm Beach Junior College, 1941; B.S.A. with honors 1943, M.S.A. 1943, Ph.D. 1961, University of Florida. Military: Served in the United States Air Force, 1943-46, attaining the rank of Captain, Pacific Area WWII; United States Air Force Reserves, Lieutenant Colonel, Retired. Career: Professor of Botany and Assistant Dean, Florida Atlantic University, Boca Raton, Florida; Partner, Sturrock Tropical Fruit Nursery, West Palm Beach, Florida, 1946-56; Inspector, State Plant Board of Florida, 1956-57; Teacher, Palm Beach High School, 1957-58; Research Assistant, University of Florida, 1958-60; Instructor, Palm Beach Junior College, 1960-64; Assistant Professor, Associate Professor, Professor and Assistant Dean, Florida Atlantic University, 1964 to present. Organizational Memberships: Florida State Horticultural Society; Florida Academy of Sciences, Florida Mango Forum; American Society for Horticultural Science. Community Activities: West Palm Beach Junior Chamber of Commerce, President 1951-52; Boy Scouts of America, Served in Various Leadership Positions including (currently) Vice President for Program of Gulf Stream Council, West Palm Beach, Florida. Religion: Presbyterian, Deacon and Elder. Honors and Awards: Silver Beaver Award, Boy Scouts of America, 1951. Address: 1010 Camellia Road, West Palm Beach, Florida 33405.■

THOMAS CHASE STUTZMAN

Attorney at Law. Personal: Born August 1, 1950; Son of Leon H. and Mary Louise Stutzman; Married Wendy Jeanne, Daughter of Fred and Margie Craig; Father of Sarah Anne. Education: B.A. high honors, University of California at Santa Barbara, 1972; J.D. cum laude, University of Santa Clara School of Law, 1975. Career: Attorney at Law. Organizational Memberships: Santa Clara City Bar Association, Chairman Environmental Law Section 1976-78; California Trial Lawyer's Association. Community Activities: San Jose Host Lions, Director 1976-78, Third Vice President 1981-82, Second Vice President 1982-83; Scottish Rite; Golden Rule Free & Accepted Masons; San Jose Elks; San Jose Jaycees, Director 1976-79; Santa Clara/Santa Cruz County Campfire, Board of Directors. Religion: Member Pilgrim Congregational Church. Honors and Awards: Phi Beta Kappa; Director of the Year, Jaycees, 1976-77; Instructor, San Jose State University, 1977-78. Address: 3164 Linkfield Way, San Jose, California 95135.■

TSUNG-CHOW JOE SU

Associate Professor of Ocean Engineering. Personal: Born July 9, 1947; Son of Chin-Shui Su and Chen-lin Shih Su; Married Hui-Fang Angie Huang; Father of Julius Tsu-Li, Jonathan Tsu-Wei, Judith Tus-Te. Education: B.S. Civil Engineering, National Taiwan University, 1968; M.S. Aeronautics 1970, Ae.E. Aeronautics 1973, California Institute of Technology, 1973; Eng.Sc.D. Ocean Engineering, Columbia University, 1974. Military: Served in the Chinese Army, 1968-69, attaining the rank of Second Lieutenant. Career: Associate Professor of Ocean Engineering, Florida Atlantic University, 1982 to present; Graduate Teaching/Research Assistant, California Institute of Technology, 1970-72; Research Assistant, Columbia University, 1972-73; Naval Architect/Structural Engineer, John J. McMullen Associates, Inc., 1974-75; Assistant Professor of Civil and Ocean Engineering, Texas A&M University, 1976-82. Organizational Memberships: American Institute of Aeronautics and Astronautics; American Society of Engineering Education; American Society of Mechanical Engineers; American Society of Civil Engineers; American Academy of Mechanics; Registered Professional Engineer, Texas; Appointed Judge, 1983 State Science and Engineering Fair, Florida. Honors and Awards: Elected Member, American Academy of Mechanics, 1982. Address: 8298 Brant Drive, Boca Raton, Florida 33431.■

ROBERTA LUCILLE SUDDITH

Cardiovascular Specialist, Registered Nurse. Personal: Born June 30, 1945; Daughter of Beaman and Effie L. Suddith (both deceased). Education: Diploma: Lutheran Hospital School of Nursing, Fort Wayne, Indiana; Student in Psychology, St. Francis College, Fort Wayne. Career: Staff Nurse, Lutheran Hospital, 1966-68; Assistant Head Nurse, Coronary Care Unit, Lutheran Hospital School of Nursing Alumni, Secretary 1969-70, Various Committees. Community Activities: American Heart Association, Northeast Indiana Chapter, Board of Directors; Cardiopulmonary Resuscitation Certified Instructor/Trainer, Chairperson Professional Education Committee. Honors and Awards: Good Heart Award 1973, Bronze Service Medllion 1974, Silver Service Medallion 1975, Gold Service Medallion 1977, American Heart Association; Listed in *Who's Who of American Women*, *World Who's Who of Women*, *Personalities of the West and Midwest*. Address: 9720 Hosler Road, Leo, Indiana 46765.■

JAMES MASANOBU SUGIHARA

University Administrator. Personal: Born August 6, 1918; Son of William B. and Takeyo Sugihara (both deceased); Married May Murakami, Daughter of Harry K. and Kogiku Murakami; Father of John Thomas, Michael James. Education: A.A., Long Beach Junior College, 1937; B.S. Chemistry, University of California at Berkeley, 1939; Ph.D. Chemistry, University of Utah, 1947. Career: Dean of Graduate School and Director of Research Administration, North Dakota State University at Fargo, 1974 to present; Dean of College of Chemistry and Physics and Dean of College of Science and Mathematics, North Dakota State University, 1964-74; Instructor, Assistant Professor, Associate Professor, Professor, University of Utah, 1947-48, 1949-64; Research Associate, Ohio State University, 1948-49. Organizational Memberships: American Chemical Society, Chairman Red River Valley Section 1970-71; Geochemical Society; Sigma Xi; Phi Kappa Phi; Midwestern Association of Graduate Schools, Membership Committee 1979-81, Audit Committee 1982 to present; Council of Graduate Schools. Community Activities: United Way of Cass Clay, Board of Trustees 1980 to present, Chairman Admissions Committee 1981 and 1982, Second Vice President 1982; Resources Research Committee of the North Dakota Legislative Council, 1974-78; Member U.S. Delegation (Department of Energy) which met with U.S.S.R. Oil Experts in Moscow, Volvograd and Leningrad, 1978; Steering Committee, Southeast Area Health Education Center, University of North Dakota, 1975 to present. Honors and Awards: Doctor of Service Award, North Dakota State University, 1972. Address: 1001 Southwood Drive, Fargo, North Dakota 58103.■

EARL ISEMAN SULLIVAN

Administrator. Personal: Born June 28, 1923; Son of Jesse Iseman and Birdie Melton Sullivan (both deceased). Education: B.A. English, Western Kentucky University, 1964; Graduate Study at Western Kentucky University, 1965. Military: Served in the United States Army, 1947-48. Career: Director, Army Education; Former Positions as Education Counselor and College Instructor. Organizational Memberships: Adult Education Association. Community Activities: Development of Military Career-Change Seminar for Pentagon, 1976-77; Metropolitan Organ Society of Washington, D.C., Vice President 1976; Smithsonian Institution, Volunteer Information Specialist 1977-79; Little Colonel Theater, Louisville, Kentucky, Assistant Director 1958-59; Junior Chamber of Commerce, Louisville, Speaker's Panel 1957. Religion: Fourth Avenue Methodist Church, Louisville, Kentucky, 1957 to present. Honors and Awards: Meritorious Civilian Service Award for Outstanding Professional Contributions to the United States Army Education at the Pentagon, 1978; Outstanding Performace Awards, 1978-80; Awards for Poetry and Non-Fiction, 1970-75; Listed in *Notable Americans*, *Men of Achievement*, *Personalities of the South*, *Dictionary of International Biography*, *Men and Women of Distinction*, *International Book of Honor*, *Personalities of America*, *Who's Who in the South and Southwest*. Address: 4 West Howell Avenue, Alexandria, Virginia 22301.■

JOSEPH PIERCE SULLIVAN

Professor of Psychology. Personal: Born November 1, 1929; Married Harriet Craig Holland; Father of George David, John Craig, Joseph Pierce Jr., Price Holland. Education: Bachelor of Civil Engineering, Georgia Institute of Technology, 1951; B.A. History 1955, M.A. Religion 1961, Baylor University; M.A. Psychology, University of Texas, 1966; B.Div., Southwestern Baptist Theological Seminary, 1960. Military: Served in the United States Air Force during the Korean War, Second Lieutenant; Retired Lieutenant Colonel United States Air Force 1981, United States Air Force Reserve. Career: Professor of Psychology, San Antonio College; Civil Engineer, United States Air Force, 1952-53; Teaching Assistant and Research Assistant, University of Texas, 1962-66; Pastor, First Baptist Church, Hackberry, Louisiana, 1960-62; Professor of Psychology, San Antonio College, 1966 to present. Organizational Memberships: Nominated for Piper Professor, 1975; Chi Epsilon Honorary Civil Engineering Fraternity. Community Activities: Democratic Candidate for United States Congress, 21st District of Texas, 1974, 1976, 1978; Democratic Nominee for United States Congress, 21st District of Texas, 1980; Democratic Candidate for United States Senate, Texas, 1982. Religion: Pastor, Minister of Music, Pianist and Organist, Soloist. Honors and Awards: Omicron Delta Kappa; Eagle Scout; Listed in *Who's Who in the South and Southwest*. Address: 117 Shalimar Drive, San Antonio, Texas 78213.■

WILLIAM LESCALETTE SULLIVAN, JR.

Public and Investor Relations Executive. Personal: Born May 15, 1935; Son of Mr. and Mrs. William L. Sullivan. Education: B.A. English and Philosophy, Johns Hopkins University, Baltimore, Maryland, 1959. Military: Served in the United States Navy, Lieutenant, (j.g.), 1959-63. Career: Manager, News Service, Association of American Railroads, Washington, D.C.; 1971-73; Director of Public Relations, American Bankers Association, Washington, D.C., 1973-76; Director of Communications, National Micrographics Association, Silver Spring, Maryland, 1976-79; Director of Public Relations and Communications, Chesapeake Corporation, 1980 to present. Organizational Memberships: National Press Club, Washington, D.C.; Public Relations Society of America; National Investor

Relations Institute; Richmond Public Relations Association. Community Activities: Past President and Director, West Point Kiwanis Club, 1982-83. Address: 826 Lee Street, Box 1165, West Point, Virginia 23181.■

DAVID ARVID SUTHERLUND

Attorney at Law. Personal: Born July 1929, Stevens Point, Wisconsin; Son of Arvid E. and Georgia M. Stickney Sutherlund. Education: B.A., University of Portland, 1952; J.D., University of New Mexico, 1957; Additional Studies, University of Wisconsin, 1957. Career: Special Agent in United States, Japan, and Korea, Counter-Intelligence Corps, 1952-54; Admitted to D.C. Bar 1957, Supreme Court Bar 1961; Attorney, I.C.C., Washington, 1957-58; Counsel, American Trucking Association, 1958-62; Associate and Partner, Law Firm of Morgan, Lewis & Bockius, 1962-72; Counsel, Firm of Turney & Turney, 1972-75; Partner, Firm of Fulbright & Jaworski, Offices in Washington D.C., and Houston, TX, 1975-83; Special Counsel, Firm of LaRoe, Winn & Moerman, Washington; Executive Director, Film, Air and Package Carriers Conference, Washington, 1962-72; Director of General Counsel, National Film Service, 1962-75. Organizational Memberships: Member Family Division Panel, Public Defense Service for District of Columbia, 1972-76; Founder and Member Board of Governors, *Transportation Law Journal*, 1967-74; National Panel of Arbitrators, American Arbitration Association, 1970 to present; American, Federal, and D.C. Bar Associations; Transportation Lawyers Association; Transportation Practitioners Association; American Judicature Society; National Lawyers Club. Community Activities: Vice Chairman, National Capitol Area Council, Boy Scouts of America, 1975-78; Served on Numerous Civic Committees; Smithsonian Society of Smithsonian Institution; National Alumni Advisory Council, University of Portland. Address: 2130 Bancroft Place, North West, Washington, D.C. 20008.■

TIMOTHY LACHLAN SUTTOR

Visiting Fellow in Renaissance Studies. Personal: Born May 11, 1926; Married Patricia Francis; Father of Carmel, Gregory, Felicity, Edward. Education: B.A., New England, Australia, 1947; M.A., Sydney, Australia, 1949; Ph.D., Canberra, Australia, 1960. Career: Visiting Fellow, Renaissance Studies, Yale University; English Literature, University of Sydney, 1947-54; Computer, 1955-57; Australian History, Australian National University, 1957-58; Modern European History, Canberra College University of Melbourne, 1959-61; Ancient History, Australian National University, 1962-64; Theology, Toronto, 1964-68; Religious Studies, Windsor, Ontario, 1968 to present. Organizational Memberships: Canadian Theological Society, 1965 to present; Catholic Historical Society, United States, 1965 to present; Canadian Society Church History, 1965 to present, President 1973-76; Canadian Catholic History Society, President 1970-72. Community Activities: National Educational Television Scripts and Interviews, Australia, 1962-64, 1967, Canada 1966-67; Consultant, Ped. Executive, Democratic Labor Party, Australia, 1963-66; Expert Witness in Court, Canadian Civil Liberties Association, 1970-76; Editor, *Study Sessions*, 1970, 1971, 1972; Canadian Catholic Historical Association; Originating Committee, Birthright Canada, Keynote Speaker at First Pan American Birthright Conference in Toronto 1973. Published Works: Author, *Canadian Nudist Primer*, Eastern Canadian Sunbathing Association. Religion: Preacher (3 times per month), Catholic St. Clair's Parish, Windsor, 1969-71. Address: 137 Fountain Street #B6, New Haven, Connecticut 06515.■

SRIKANTA MAYASANDRA NANJUNDIAH SWAMY

Professor of Electrical Engineering. Personal: Born April 7, 1935, in Bangalore, India; Son of M. K. Nanjudiah and M. N. Mahalakshamma; Married Leela Sitaramiah; Father of Saritha, Nikhilesh, Jagadish. Education: B.Sc. (Honors), University of Mysore, India, 1954; D.I.I.Sc., Indian Institute of Science, Bangalore, 1957; M.Sc. 1960, Ph.D. 1963, University of Saskatchewan, Canada. Career: Government of India Scientist, Indian Institute of Technology, Madras, 1963-65; Assistant Professor of Mathematics, University of Saskatchewan, 1964-65; Assistant, Associate and Professor of Electrical Engineering, Nova Scotia Technical College, Halifax, 1965-68; Professor of Electrical Engineering, Sir George Williams University, Montreal, 1968-69; Professor of Electrical Engineering, University of Calgary, 1969-70; Professor and Chairman of Electrical Engineering, Concordia University, Montreal, 1970-77; Dean of Engineering, Concordia University, 1977 to present. Organizational Memberships: Institute of Electrical and Electronics Engineers, Fellow, Vice President Circuits and Systems Society 1976, Program Chairman International Symposium on Circuit Theory in Toronto 1973; American Association of Engineerng Education, Director Mathematics Sub-Commitee 1973-75; Canadian Society for Electrical Engineering, Chairman Publications Council 1981 to present; Engineeirng Institute of Canada, Fellow; Institute of Electronics and Telecommunication Engineers, India, Fellow; Institution of Electrical Engineers (U.K.), Fellow; Institution of Engineers, India, Fellow; American Biographical Institute Research Association, Life Fellow; International Biographical Association, Life Fellow; Eta Kappa Nu. Community Activities: International Student's Club, University of Saskatchewan, Secretary 1960, President 1963; India-Canada Association, Saskatoon, General Secretary 1960, President 1960; Bharatiya Sangeeta Sangam, Montreal, President 1978-80. Published Works: Co-Author *Graphs, Networks and Algorithms* 1981; Author/Co-Author Over 100 Research Papaers Published in Leading Technical Journals, including *I.E.E.E. Transactions on Circuit Theory, Proceedings of I.E.E.E, Journal of the Franklin Institute, Radio and Electronic Engineer, Alta Frequenza*; Editorial Board, *Fibonacci Quarterly*; Associate Editor, *Journal on Circuits, Systems and Signal Processing*. Honors and Awards: Listed in *Dictionary of International Biography, Who's Who in the West, I.B.A. Yearbook, International Register of Profiles, American Men and Women of Science, International Who's Who of Intellectuals, Book of Honor, Registre Social du Canada*. Address: 275 Des Landes, St. Lambert, Quebec, Canada J4S 1V9.■

WILLIAM EDWARD SWARTZ, JR.

Professor and Chairman. Personal: Born August 16, 1944; Son of W. E. Sr. and Catherine Swartz; Married Sandra Y.; Father of Jennifer Elizabeth, Edward Robert. Education: B.S. Chemistry, Juniata College, 1962-66; Ph.D. Chemistry, Massachusetts Institute of Technology, 1966-71. Career: Professor and Chairman, Department of Chemistry, University of South Florida; Postdoctoral Research Associate, University of Georgia, 1971; Postdoctoral Research Associate, University of Maryland, 1972; Assistant Professor 1972-77, Associate Professor 1977-82, University of South Florida; Research supported by the Air Force, Research Corporation and Petroleum Research Fund of the American Chemical Society; Consultant with Numerous Industrial Laboratories throughout the United States. Organizational Memberships: American Chemical Society; American Vacuum Society, Chairman Florida Chapter 1980; Society for Applied Spectroscopy, Chairman Florida Section 1980-81; American Society for Testing and Materials; American Association for the Advancement of Science. Honors and Awards: Pennsylvania Bureau of Rehabilitation Scholarship, 1962-66; National Institutes of Health Pre-Doctoral Fellowship, 1967-71. Address: Department of Chemistry, University of South Florida, Tampa, Florida 33620.■

JAMES EDWARD SWEENEY

Communications/Electronics Officer. Personal: Born July 6, 1940; Son of Mr. and Mrs. Howard Sweeney; Married Hyang H., Daughter of Mr. and Mrs. Pan Dong Cho. Military: Service in the United States Air Force, attaining the rank of Captain. Education: Graduate, Cass Technical High School (Detroit, Michigan), 1969; B.S., Eastern Michigan University, 1975; Attended Officer Training School, 1977; M.A., University of Northern Colorado, 1979. Career: Communications/Electronics Officer, United States Air Force; Former Secondary School Teacher. Organizational Memberships: Junior Officers Council, Recorder 1980; Armed Forces Communications-Electronics Association; Air Force Association. Community Activities: Life Member, Air Force Aid Society. Honors and Awards: American Legion School Award, 1965; Charles Palmer Davis Current Events Award, 1964; Highest Honors Graduate, Cass Technical High School, 1969; Honor Graduate, Chanute Technical Training Center, 1969; Honor Student, Eastern Michigan University, 1973-75; Air Force Commendation Medal, 1979. Address: 313 Campus Drive, Belleville, Illinois 62221.■

KEVIN J. SWICK

Professor of Education. Personal: Born June 23, 1943; Son of Mrs. Howard Swick; Married Susan L.; Father of Melissa, Timothy, James. Education: B.A. Education 1965, M.Ed. 1966, Bowling Green University; Ph.D., University of Connecticut, 1970. Career: Assistant Professor 1970-73, Associate Professor

TWO THOUSAND NOTABLE AMERICANS

1974-76, Southern Illinois University; Associate Professor 1976-79, Professor of Education, University of South Carolina. Organizational Memberships: S.A.C.U.S., Vice President 1982-83; A.C.E.I., Research Committee 1982-84; N.A.E.Y.C. Community Activities: President, South Carolina Association on Children Under Six, 1980-81. Honors and Awards: Recipient A.C.E.I. Service Award, 1979; S.A.C.U.S. Service Award, 1982; Listed in *Who's Who in the South, Who's Who in the Southeast.* Address: 75 Juarez Court, Columbia, South Carolina 29206.■

MIKE SYNAR

Congressman. Personal: Born October 17, 1950, in Vinita, Oklahoma; Son of Ed and Virginia Synar. Education: Graduate, Muskogee Central High School (Muskogee, Oklahoma), 1968; B.A. Business Administration, University of Oklahoma, 1972; M.S. Management, Northwestern University, 1973; Postgraduate Studies in Economics undertaken at the University of Edinburgh (Edinburgh, Scotland), 1974; J.D., University of Oklahoma Law Center, 1977. Career: Elected to the United States House of Representatives, 96th Congress, 1978; Re-elected to 97th and 98th Congresses; Member of House Committee on Government Operations (Chairman Subcommittee on Environment, Energy and Natural Resources), House Committee on Energy and Commerce (Subcommittee on Energy Conservation and Power, Subcommittee on Fossil and Synthetic Fuels), House Committee on the Judiciary (Subcommittee on Monopolies and Commercial Law, Subcommittee on Courts, Civil Liberties and the Administration of Justice), House Select Committee on Aging (Subcommittee on Retirement Income and Employment, Subcommittee on Housing and Consumer Interests), Regional Whip for States of Oklahoma, Arkansas and Kansas in 97th and 98th Congresses; Attorney, Eastern Oklahoma Land and Cattle Company, Muskogee, Oklahoma, 1977-78; Assistant to the Oklahoma Attorney General, Civil Division, 1977; Advisor, Cooperative Black Farmers Organization, State of Illinois Department of Employment, 1972; Management Trainee, U.S. Forest Service, Department of Agriculture, Black Hills National Forest, South Dakota, 1972; Real Estate Broker, Eastern Oklahoma Land and Cattle Company, 1968-78; Rancher, Muskogee, Oklahoma, 1967 to present. Honors and Awards: One of Ten Outstanding Young Men of America, U.S. Jaycees, 1980; Rotary International Scholar, 1973; Man of Distinction, University of Oklahoma, 1972; Oklahoma Youth Delegate to the White House Conference on Aging, Appointed by Governor of Oklahoma and Approved by the President, 1971; Chairman of the Student Congress, University of Oklahoma, 1971; Inducted in the Oklahoma 4-H Hall of Fame as Outstanding 4-H Member in Oklahoma, 1970; One of Top Ten Freshmen, University of Oklahoma, 1969; Outstanding 4-H Member in the United States, 1969; Outstanding 4-H Public Speaker in the United States, 1968; One of Top 200 Young Men Leaders in America, William Danforth Foundation, 1968; Oklahoma State 4-H Vice President, 1967, 1968; Winner of Numerous Other 4-H and Public Speaking Awards. Address: c/o Congress of the United States, House of Representatives, Washington, D.C. 20515.■

ZOFIA SYWAK

Administrator. Education: B.A., Albertus Magnus College, 1964; M.A. 1966, Ph.D. 1975, St. John's University; Further Studies at Warsaw University (Warsaw, Poland) and American University (Washington D.C.). Career: Registrar, Kean College of New Jersey; Director, Rhode Island Historical Records Survey; Archivist, Kelly Institute, St. Francis College; Archivist, New Haven, Colony Historical Society; Lecturer, Poznan University, Poznan, Poland; Lecturer, Warsaw University, Warsaw, Poland; Manager, New York Telephone Company; American Editor, *Paderewski*, 1980; Co-Author, *Poles in America: Bicentennial Essays*, 1978. Organizational Memberships: Society of American Archivists, Status of Women Committee 1980 to present; American Association for the Advancement of Slavic Studies; Association of Records Managers and Administrators, Vice President State Chapter 1981-82; New England Archivists; Polish Institute of Arts and Sciences in America. Community Activities: Rhode Island Ad Hoc Committee on Records, Gubernatorial Appointment, 1980-82; New York Metropolitan Reference and Research Library Agency, Archives Task Force 1978-79; The Ukrainian Museum, Board of Trustees 1979 to present; Rhode Island Historical Society, Library Committee 1980-82. Honors and Awards: International Research and Exchange Fellowship, Research Fellowship, Poland, 1977-78; Alfred Jurzykowski Grant, Hoover Institution, Stanford University, 1977; Kosciuszko Foundation Grant, Foreign Office, London, England, 1972; Polish Ministry of Higher Education Fellowship, Poland, 1968-70, 1972; Kosciuszko Foundation Travel Grant, 1968. Address: 888 Westfield Avenue, Elizabeth, New Jersey 07208.■

VICTOR G. SZEBEHELY

Professor of Aerospace Engineering. Personal: Born August 10, 1921; Married Jo Betsy, Daughter of R. J. Lewallen; Father of Julie. Education: Doctor of Engineering, Technical University of Budapest, 1945. Career: Professor of Aerospace Engineering, University of Texas, 1968 to present; Associate Professor of Astronomy, Yale University, 1963-68; Manager of Space Dynamics Research, General Electric Company, Philadelphia, 1957-63; Lecturer, University of Maryland and George Washington University, 1951-57; Manager of Ship Dynamics Research, U.S. Navy Bureau of Ships, 1951-57; Associate Professor of Applied Mechanics, Virginia Polytechnic Institute, 1948-51. Organizational Memberships: United States National Academy of Engineering, 1982 to present; American Institute for Aeronautics and Astronautics, Fellow, Chairman Astrodynamics Committee 1962-63; American Astronomical Society, Chairman Division on Dynamical Astronomy 1973-74; International Astronomical Union, President Commission on Celestial Mechanics 1977-80; Director, NATO Advanced Study Institute, 1972, 1975, 1978, 1981, 1984. Published Works: Author Over 200 Technical Journal Articles and Fifteen Books. Honors and Awards: Knighted by Queen Julianna of Holland, 1957; Celestial Mechanics Research Awards (Brouwer), American Astronomical Society (1978) and the American Astronautical Society (1982); Outstanding Service Award, United States Air Force R.O.T.C., 1979; Endowed Chair of Engineering (Cockrell), University of Texas, 1982 to present; Chairman, Department of Aerospace Engineering, University of Texas, 1977-81. Address: 2501 Jarratt Avenue, Austin, Texas 78703.■

EMERIC SZEGHO

Retired Professor. Education: Attained a Licence at Law, University of Cernauti, Rumania, 1938; Doctor Juris Universi, University of Cluj, Rumania, 1947; Diploma as Attorney-at-Law, Rumanian Bar Association, Bucharest, 1941. Career: Founder, Center for International Security Studies of the American Security Council Education Foundation; Practicing Attorney-at-Law, 1941-60; Retired Professor, Alliance College, Cambridge Springs, Pennsylvania. Organizational Memberships: Emeritus Member, American Association of University Professors. Community Activities: Life Member, Republican National Committee; National Defense Task Force; National Advisory Board, American Security Council; Member, American Security Council Education Foundation (formerly the Institute for American Strategy); United States Senatorial Club, Founding Member; International Platform Association; International Biographical Association, Fellow; American Biographical Institute, Fellow; United States Congressional Advisory Board, State Advisor; Member, Republican Presidential Task Force; United States Defense Committee. Religion: Member United Presbyterian Church, Cambridge Springs, Pennsylvania. Published Works: Author of Two Books, *Crime and Punishment, The Problem of Crime* and *The Way of Life and the Crime*. Honors and Awards: Award of Merit, United States Congressional Advisory Board; Honorary Appointment to the National Board of Advisors, American Biographical Institute; Special Recognition for the Cause of a Stronger America, American Security Council; Certificate of Leadership, Republican Party of Pennsylvania; Special Recognition Award, Center for International Security Studies; National Republican Victory Certificate; Certificate of Recognition, National Republican Congressional Committee; Special Recognition, National Security Educational Leadership; Award of Tenure, Alliance College; The Statue of Victory "Personality of the Year" 1984; Distinguished Leadership Award, American Security Council Foundation; Listed in *International Who's Who of Community Service, International Who's Who of Intellectuals, International Register of Profiles, Men of Achievement, Dictionary of International Biography, Who's Who in North America, Notable Americans of the Bicentennial Era, Community Leaders of America, Notable Americans, Directory of Distinguished Americans, American Registry Series, Book of Honor, Hungarians in America, Personalities of America, Community Leaders and Noteworthy Americans, Men and Women of Distinction, Contemporary Personalities.* Address: 215 Ross Avenue, Cambridge Springs, Pennsylvania 19403.■

DEBORAH SZEKELY

Executive. Personal: Born May 3, 1922; Mother of Livia, Alex. Education: High School; Further Studies in New York, Tahiti, California. Career: Co-Founder, Rancho La Puerto, 1940; Founder/President, 'Golden Door' Inc. Organizational Memberships: President's Council on Physical Fitness and Sports, 1975-77; United States Delegate to U.N.E.S.C.O. and Fifth International Conference on Physical Fitness, Paris, France, 1977 (one of two delegates). Community Activities: The Menninger Foundation, Board of Trustees, Executive Committee and Vice Chairman for Clinical Services; Combined Arts and Education Council of San Diego, Founder, Board of Directors; Old Globe Theatre, San Diego, Board of Directors; University of California at San Diego, Board of Overseers, Chairman 1977 and 1978; San Diego Zoo Horticultural Committee; Travelers Aid Society, Board of Directors; Japanese Friendship Garden Association; California

School of Professional Psychology, Board of Trustees; National Center for Citizen Involvement, Board of Directors. Honors and Awards: Woman of the Year, The President's Council of Women's Service, Business and Professional Organizations of San Diego, 1982; Volunteer of the Year, National Society of Fund-Raiser Executives, 1979; Honorary Doctor of Letters, California School of Professional Psychology, 1978; Charter 100/City Club Woman of the Year, 1979; Small Businessperson of the Year, Small Business Administration, 1976. Candidate for Congress, 1982 California Primary. Address: 3232 Dove Street, San Diego, California 92103.■

T

BETTY JO TAFFE

State Legislator. Personal: Born November 19, 1942; Daughter of Elizabeth O. Miller; Married William J. Taffe; Mother of Daniel David, Michael Andrew. Education: B.A., Juniata College, 1964; M.A.T., University of Chicago, 1968. Career: State Legislator; High School Teacher; Dormitory Head Resident. Organizational Memberships: Education Commission of the States (New Hampshire Commissioner 1981 to present); National Council of State Legislatures, Education Committee, Executive Committee, 1981-82. Community Activities: Lakes Region Mental Health Center, Board Member 1979-81; Sceva Speare Hospital, Board Member 1980 to present; New Hampshire School Boards Association, Executive Council 1980-83; Governor's Task Force on Handicapped Educational Services, Appointed 1981; New Hampshire House of Representatives, Member 1976 to present, Vice Chairman House Education Committee 1978 to present; Rumney School Board, Member 1976-83, Chairman 1976-81, 1982-83; Grafton County Executive Committee, Member 1976 to present, Clerk 1978 to present. Address: Quincy Road, Rumney, New Hampshire 03266.■

RONDA CAROL TALLEY

Coordinator of Assessment/Placement Services. Personal: Born November 21, 1951; Daughter of Jack Howard and Ronda Mae McCoy Talley. Education: B.S. Early Childhood Education, Western Kentucky University, 1973; M.Ed. Special Education 1974, Ed.S. Administration and Supervision of Special Education Programs 1976, University of Louisville; Ph.D. School Psychology, Indiana University, 1979. Career: Adjunct Professor and Director School Psychology Program, Spalding University, Louisville, Kentucky, 1984 to present; President and Founder, Tri-T Associates, Inc., Louisville, Kentucky, 1982 to present; Coordinator Assessment/Placement Services, Exceptional Child Education, Jefferson County Public Schools, Louisville, Kentucky, 1981 to present; Adjunct Professor, University of Louisville, 1981-83; Learning Disabilities Resource Specialist, Whitney Young Elementary, Jefferson County Public Schools, Louisville, Kentucky, 1980-81; Administrative Intern at Bureau of Education for the Handicapped, Principal Investigator in Technical Assistance on Administrative Strategies to Integrate Handicapped Students, 1978-80; Research Coordinator, Children's Television Workshop, New York, New York, Summer 1978; Research Assistant, Center for Innovation in Teaching the Handicapped, Indiana University, Bloomington, Indiana, 1977-79; Supervisor, School Psychology Externs, Monroe County Community School Corporation, Bloomington, Indiana, 1977-78; Associate Instructor, Educational Psychology Department, School of Education, Indiana University, Bloomington, Indiana, Fall 1977; Research Assistant, Program Research in Integrated Multi-ethnic Education, University of California-Riverside, Summer 1977; Learning Disabilities Consultant, Bartholomew County Special Education Cooperative, Seymour Community Schools, Seymour, Indiana, 1976-77; Teacher of Children with Learning Disabilities, Jeffersontown Elementary School (Jefferson County Public Schools, Louisville, Kentucky) 1975-76, Blue Lick Elementary School (Jefferson County Public Schools, Louisville, Kentucky) 1974-75, Blake Elementary School (Jefferson County Public Schools, Louisville, Kentucky) 1973-74; Research Consultant, Department of Educational Research, Western Kentucky University, Bowling Green, Kentucky, 1974-79. Organizational Memberships: Comprehensive SOMPA Certificate and SOMPA Instructor's Certificate, Institute for Pluralistic Assessment Research and Training; Educational Mediator, Neighborhood Justice Center of Atlanta; Indiana School Psychologist; Kentucky Supervisor of Special Education Programs; Kentucky Standard School Psychologist. Kentucky Standard Elementary Teaching Certificate #407-68-1403 (grades 1-8), Kindergarten Classroom Teaching, Neurologically Impaired (grades 1-12); Learning Potential Assessment Device, Level I Certificate (Vanderbilt University), Advanced Certificate (Hadassah-Wizo-Canada Research Institute, Israel); Licenses, Indiana State Board of Examiners in Psychology, Kentucky Board of Psychology; Appointed Member, Kentucky School Psychological Services Handbook Development Committee 1983-84; Liaison and Public Relations Chairperson, Kentucky Association for Psychology in the Schools, 1983 to present; Executive Council Member and Kentucky Association for Psychology in the Schools Delegate to Kentucky Psychological Association, 1983 to present; Co-Chairperson, Committee on Urban School Psychology, National Association of School Psychologist, 1983 to present; Chairperson, Committee for Administrators of School Psychological Services, Division of School Psychology, American Psychological Association, 1982 to present; Invited Participant, Olympia Conference on the Future of School Psychology, Oconomowoc, Wisconsin, 1981; Chairperson, Student Affiliates in School Psychology, Division of School Psychology, American Psychological Association, 1977-82; Consulting Editor, *Behavioral Disorders*, the Council for Exceptional Children, 1978-81; *The School Psychologist*, Regional Editor 1978-81, Student Editor 1978-79; Student Research Grant, Bureau of Education for the Handicapped, United States Office of Education, Department of Health, Education, and Welfare, Washington, D.C., 1978-79; WHAS Crusade for Children Scholarship, University of Louisville, 1973. Community Activities: Honorable Order of Kentucky Colonels; Kappa Delta Alumnae Association, 1981 to present. Honors and Awards: Phi Delta Kappa, Alpha Chapter, 1979; Listed in *World Who's Who of Women, Biographical Roll of Honor, Five Thousand Personalities of the World, International Who's Who of Intellectuals, Personalities of the South, Who's Who in Frontier Science and Technology, Who's Who in the South and Southwest, Who's Who of Contemporary Achievement, Who's Who of American Women, Directory of Distinguished Americans, Personalities of America*, Others. Address: 9104 Hurstwood Court, Louisville, Kentucky 40222.■

NEVA BENNETT TALLEY-MORRIS

Lawyer, Educator, Author. Personal: Born August 13, 1909; Daughter of John and Erma Bennett (both deceased); Widow. Education: Graduated Valedictorian of Judsonia High School, 1926; B.A. magna cum laude, Ouachita University, 1930; M.Ed., University of Texas, 1938; Postgraduate Education and Pre-Law, University of Texas, 1939-42. Military: Served in the United States Army Service Ordnance as Head Line Inspector, a Civil Service Wartime Appointment, 1942-46. Career: Lawyer, 1947 to present; Educator; Writer; Judge of Legal Essay Contests and Publications. Organizational Memberships: World Association of Lawyers, Founding Member 1973-85; American Bar Association, Family Law Section Chairman 1969-70, House of Delegates 1970-74, Associate Judge Schwab Memorial Legal Writings 1982-85; National Association of Women Lawyers, President 1956-57, Life Member, Member Executive Council; Arkansas Bar Association, House of Delegates 1974-78, Desk Book Committee Chairman 1981-82; American Academy of Matrimonial Lawyers, Board of Governors 1974-80; Licensed Lawyer, All Arkansas Counties 1947 to present, United States Supreme Court 1950 to present, United States District Court of Eastern Arkansas 1947 to present. Community Activities: Arkansas Bar Foundation, Hall of Fellows 1968 to present, Founding Fellow, Board of Directors 1980-85, Chairman Legal Writers Award Committee 1981-85; Special Committee for Arkansas Supreme Court, Chairman Client Security Fund 1980-82; North Little Rock Business and Professional Women, President 1950-52, Life Member Little Rock Branch; American Association of University Women; Delegate, World Peace through Law Biennial Conferences, 1975-85. Religion: Park Hill Baptist Church, Charter Member 1946-50; Little Rock Second Baptist Church, 1950 to present. Honors and Awards: Delta Kappa Gamma, University of Texas Scholarship, 1938; Special Memberships Service Certificate 1979, Merit Award for Associate Judge of Writers Contest 1980-83, American Bar Association; Special Legal Service Award, Arkansas Bar Foundation, 1970; Annual Lawyer-Citizen Award, Arkansas Bar Association and Arkansas Bar Foundation, 1980; Special Service Award, National Association of Women Lawyers, 1961. Address: P.O. Box 67, Judsonia, Arkansas 72081.■

ENG M. TAN

Physician, Biomedical Scientist. Personal: Born August 26, 1926; Married Liselotte, Daughter of Mr. and Mrs. K. Filippi; Father of Philip Kee, Peter Carl. Education: A.B., Johns Hopkins University, 1952; M.D., Johns Hopkins University School of Medicine, 1956. Organizational Memberships: Western Association of Physicians; Western Association of Physicians, Vice President 1979-80; American Society for Clinical Investigation; American Association of Immunologists;

American Association of Pathologists; President, American Rheumatism Association, 1984-85. Community Activities: National Arthritis Advisory Board, Department of Health and Human Services; Arthritis Foundation Advisory Committee on Standardization of Antinuclear Antibodies, Chairman 1981 to present. Honors and Awards: Keynote Lecturer, Canadian Rheumatism Association 1980, Australia Rheumatism Association 1980; Macy Foundation Faculty Scholar Award, 1981; United Scleroderma Foundation Research Award, 1981; Keynote Lecturer, Japan Rheumatism Association, 1982. Address: 8303 Sugarman Drive, La Jolla, California 92037.■

OWEN T. TAN

Professor of Electrical Engineering. Personal: Born August 30, 1931; Son of Mrs. Lan H. Tan; Married Martha G. Liem; Father of Joyce Yolanthe, Edward H., Cindy Liliane. Education: B.Sc. 1953, M.Sc. 1955, Electrical Engineering, Technological Faculty, Bandung (Indonesia); Ph.D., Electrical Engineering, Eindhoven University of Technology (The Netherlands). Career: Full Professor, Associate Professor and Assistant Professor of Electrical Engineering, Louisiana State University (Baton Rouge), 1966 to present; Senior Lecturer, Lecturer in Electrical Engineering, Bandung Institute of Technology (Indonesia), 1962-66; Research and Development Engineer, Smit-Slikkerveer (Rotterdam, The Netherlands), 1956-62. Organizational Memberships: Institute of Electrical and Electronic Engineers; Royal Institute of Engineers, Holland; Eta Kappa Nu. Honors and Awards: Institute of Electrical and Electronic Engineers/I.A.S. Prize Paper Award, 1981; Research Fellowship, Eindhoven University of Technology, 1977; Research Fellowship, Siemens Schuckert, West Germany, 1962. Address: 649 Rodney Drive, Baton Rouge, Louisiana 70808.■

BERNICE SALPETER TANNENBAUM

Chairman of American Section of World Zionist Organization; National Chairman of Hadassah Medical Organization. Personal: Daughter of May and Isidore Franklin; Married Nathan Tannenbaum; Mother of Richard Salpeter. Education: B.A., Brooklyn College. Career: National Chairman, Hadassah Medical Organization, 1980 to present; Hadassah, National President 1976-80, National Vice President 1968-72, National Secretary 1964-68, Chairman of Press/Radio/Television Department 1961-64, National Chairman of Junior Hadassah 1957-60, President of Long Island Region of Hadassah 1954-57, National Youth Aliyah Chairman 1968-71, National Memberships Chairman 1964-68, Co-Chairman of Hadassah National Conventions 1961, 1962. Organizational Memberships: National Conference on Soviet Jewry, Executive Board 1978 to present; American-Israel Public Affairs Committee, Vice President, Member 1978 to present; World Zionist Organization, Chairman of American Section 1982 to present; World Jewish Congress, American Section, Executive Board 1971 to present; Governing Board 1976; General Assembly of Jewish Agency, Executive Board 1971 to present; World Confederation of United Zionists, Co-President; First Mid-Winter Conference in Israel, Chairman 1986; Hadassah Medical Organization, Chairman Fund Raising 1975-76; Hebrew University, Governing Board 1976 to present; Long Island Women's Division of State of Israel Bonds, Chairman 1957-58; Queens Women's Division of United Jewish Appeal, Chairman 1959-60; United Israel Appeal Board, 1972 to present; Member, Mayor Koch's Holocaust Commission for the City of New York; Delegate to United Nations Mid-Decade Conference on Women held in Copenhagen, 1980. Published Works: Co-Editor, *The Hadassah Idea*; Contributor of Monthly Articles to "President's Column," *Hadassah* Magazine; Editorial Board, *Hadassah* Magazine, 1972 to present. Honors and Awards: Henrietta Szold Award, Queens Region, 1981; Myrtle Wreath Award, New York Chapter 1980, Orange County and Long Beach Chapters 1980, Westchester Region 1979, Lower New York State Region 1979, Brooklyn Region 1979, Suffolk Region 1979, Southern New Jersey Region 1978, Nassau Region 1977, Eastern Pennsylvania Region 1976, Upper New York State Region 1975, Queens Region 1974; Negev Award, State of Israel Bonds, 1980; Citizen's Award, New England Region, 1979; Woman of the Year Award, Kew Gardens Chapter; Fellow of the Year, Hadassah Speakers Bureau. Address: Hadassah, 50 West 58th Street, New York, New York 10021.■

VIRGINIA TANZMANN

Architectural Firm Chief Executive Officer. Education: B.A. School of Architecture 1968, B.Arch. Graduate School of Architecture 1969, Syracuse University. Career: Principal, The Tanzmann Associates, 1978 to present; Staff Architect, Southern California Rapid Transit District, 1975-78; Project Architect, SUA Inc., 1974-75; Project Architect, Daniel L. Dworsky, F.A.I.A., 1972-74; Intern Architect, Burke Kober Nicolais Archuleta, 1969-72; Exhibits at Monterey Design Conference 1981, Los Angeles 1979, Seattle 1979, Paris (France) 1978, Los Angeles 1978, Ramsar (Iran) 1976. Organizational Memberships: American Institute of Architects, Chairwoman of National Task Force on Women in Architecture 1978-80, Board of Directors of Los Angeles Chapter 1980-82; Association for Women in Architecture, Board of Directors, Past President; Architectural Guild, Board of Directors; L'Union Internationale des Femmes Architectes. Community Activities: Volunteer Center of Los Angeles, Board of Directors, Vice President; Young Women's Christian Association of Los Angeles, Board of Directors, Chairwoman Facilities Committee, President; Mayor's Advisory Council on Voluntarism; United Way, Building Plans and Sites Committee; Frequent Speaker at Schools, Community Groups and Professional Groups. Honors and Awards: California Women in Government Certificate of Achievement Award; Achievement Award of the Soroptimist Club of Los Angeles; Architectural Award for Victory Park Recreation Center; Outstanding Young Women of America; Listed in Numerous Biographical Reference Publications. Address: The Tanzmann Associates, The Bradbury Building, 304 South Broadway, Los Angeles, California 90013.■

JAMES HENDERSON TATSCH

Geologist, Geophysicist. Personal: Born December 7, 1916, in Eldorado, Texas; Son of Henry Charles and Ella Mae (Specht) Tatsch; Married Helen Gailis in July 23, 1946; Father of James Alexis Wolfgang, Karyn Jo. Education: B.S., United States Naval Academy, 1940; Ph.D. Program, University of Arizona, 1960-63. Military: Served in the United States Marine Corps, Commissioned Second Lieutenant, advanced through grades to Lieutenant Colonel 1960, Assignments include Quantico 1941, Guadalcanal 1942, Bougainville 1943, Guam 1944, Okinawa 1945, Washington 1948-52, Japan 1955-56, Venezuela 1959-60, Retired 1960. Career: Senior Staff Research Scientist, Collins Radio Company, Cedar Rapids, Iowa, 1963-64; Director, Advance Economic Planning, Ingersoll Milling Machine Company, Rockfort, Illinois, 1965-67; Principal Engineer, Raytheon Company, Sudbury, Massachusetts, 1967-70; President, Tatsch Associates, Sudbury, 1970 to present. Organizational Memberships: A.A.A.S.; British Association for the Advancement of Science; American Geophysics Union; Seismological Society of America; Geochemical Society; Society Exploration Geophysicists; European Association Exploration Geophysicists; Southeast Asia Petroleum Exploration Society; Northwest Mining Association; Nuclear Research Council; Geothermal Research Council. Published Works: Author, *The Earth's Tectonosphere* 1972, *Mineral Deposits* 1973, *The Moon* 1974, *Petroleum Deposits* 1974, *Copper Deposits* 1975, *Gold Deposits* 1975, *Uranium Deposits* 1976, *Geothermal Deposits* 1976, *Earthquakes* 1977, *Coal Deposits* 1980; Contributor Articles to Professional Journals. Honors and Awards: Decorated Bronze Star. Address: Lland Rt., Box 103-Q, Fredericksburg, Texas 78624.■

GUNTHER TAUTENHAHN

Composer. Personal: Born December 22, 1938. Education: Studied Composition in New York. Career: Composer; Author; Conductor; Inventor of Clockface whereby a Child Can Learn to Tell Note Values and Time. Organizational Memberships: American Society of Composers, Authors and Publishers; A.S.U.C.; National Association of Composers of the U.S.A.; I.C.A.; A.M.C. Community Activities: Manhattan Beach Cultural Arts Committee. Published Works: Author of *The Importance of One* 1972, *Controlled Expressionism* 1976, *Fiber Movements* 1978, *The Silent Form* 1983; Composer of *Numeric Seranade*, *Brass Quintet*, *Concerto for D/Bass and Orchestra*, *Double Concerto for French Horn and Timpani with Orchestra*, Others. Honors and Awards: Young American Composers Award, 1963; Charter Member, National Association of Composers of the U.S.A., 1975; A.S.C.A.P. Standard Awards, 1982-83; Listed in *Who's Who in Music*, *Who's Who in California*, *Who's Who in the West*, *Who's Who in America*, *Who's Who of Intellectuals*, *A.S.C.A.P. Directory and Symphony Catalog*, *A.M.C. Catalog*, *Chamber Music Catalog*, *Directory of New Music*, *Contemporary American Composers*, *Men of Achievement*, *International Register of Profiles*, *Dictionary of International Biography*, *International Who's Who in Music*, *Personalities of the West and Midwest*. Address: 1534 3rd Street, Manhattan Beach, California 90266.■

ERNEST AUSTIN TAYLOR, JR.

Retired Electrical Engineer. Personal: Born January 18, 1918; Son of Ernest A. Taylor Sr. (deceased) and Alma Robinson; Married Charleen Morgan; Father

of Rachel Alma T. Clay, Charles Ernest. Education: B.S.E.E., Georgia Institute of Technology, Atlanta. Military: Served in the United States Navy, 1943-45, as Electrician's Mate, serving on repair ships in four invasions in the Pacific Theater. Career: Retired 1982; Senior Specialist in Electrical Engineering, Monsanto Company (Decatur, Alabama), 1956-82; Electrical Engineer, Electrical Equipment Company (Augusta, Georgia), 1951-52; Electrical Engineer, Patchen and Zimmerman (Augusta, Georgia), 1952-56; Electrical Engineer, Phillips Petroleum Company (Bartlesville, Oklahoma), 1948-51. Organizational Memberships: National Society of Professional Engineers; Alabama Society of Professional Engineers; Fluid Power Society. Community Activities: Member and Secretary, Board of Directors, International Bible College (Florence, Alabama), 1972 to present; Secretary Bicycle Committee, City of Decatur, 1974. Religion: Hatton Church of Christ (Town Creek, Alabama), Education Director 1974 to present; Austinville Church of Christ (Decatur, Alabama), Education Director 1958-64; Beltline Church of Christ, Decatur, Education Director, Elder, 1964-72; Beech Street Church of Christ, Decatur, Educational Director, 1972-74. Published Works: Numerous Proprietary Reports, Monsanto Company; "Thrusts of Free and Submerged Jets," Fluidic State-of-the-Art Symposium, Harry Diamond Laboratories, Washington D.C., 1974. Honors and Awards: Norbett P. No-No Fellowship Award, 1972; Holder of 18 United States Patents and Numerous Foreign Patents. Address: 5212 Jules Verne Court, Tampa, Florida 33611.■

FLORENCE (FROSTY) IRENE TAYLOR

Editor. Personal: Born April 9, 1937; Daughter of Emmet and Rena Waul; Married Duane M. Taylor, Son of Mervin and Gladys Taylor; Mother of Kent Duane, Dana Sue. Education: Graduate, Atlantic (Iowa) High School, 1955; Communication Courses, Scottsdale (Arizona) Community College. Career: Editor, Paradise Valley Press/Northwest News; Former Reporter, Columnist, Photographer. Organizational Memberships: National Photographers Association; National Press Women; Arizona Press Women; Sigma Delta Xi; Copperstate Photographers Association; Arizona Press Club; Paradise Valley Press Club; Paradise Valley Business and Professional Women's Club; Paradise Valley Chapter, American Business Women's Club; Paradise Valley Chamber of Commerce. Community Activities: Community Education Advisory Council, Member 1976-80, Secretary 1977; Vocational Education Advisory Council, 1974-82; Charter Member, Paradise Valley Lioness Club; Charter Member, Paradise Valley Business and Professional Women's Club; Charter Member, Paradise Valley Chapter, American Business Women; Paradise Valley Federation of Women's Clubs; Little League East, Secretary 1971; Paradise Valley Athletic Association, Secretary 1970. Honors and Awards: Mrs. Nebraska, 1964; Outstanding Little League Service Award, 1973; Girl Scout Community Service Award, 1974, 1980; Jaycees Community Service Award, 1977; Little Angel Senior Citizens Award, 1979; Jewel of Bellevue (Nebraska), 1965; Admiralcy of Nebraska Navy, 1964; Arizona Press Women Writing Award, 1977-78; Arizona Press Club Awards, 1975; Listed in *Outstanding Young Women of America, Who's Who of American Women, Who's Who in the West, Personalities of America*. Address: 3521 East Gold Dust, Phoenix, Arizona 85028.■

GRIER CORBIN TAYLOR

Musician and Performer. Education: Graduate, Bryn Mawr School in Baltimore, Maryland; B.A. Music and Voice, Towson University; Studied at the Chautauqua Institute under Francis Yeend. Career: Soloist on a Concert Tour of Europe singing Lieder in England, Holland, Austria, Germany, and at the Notre Dame Cathedral in Paris, France with a Baltimore College Choir; Presented Radio Broadcast Concert on WBJC-FM for the Cathedral of Mary Our Queen Concert Series; Appeared (2 times) on WBAL Television 11 as Soloist for Ecumedia's Program, "Man on the Move"; Performed Recitals for St. Paul's Church Center Forum Concert Series, Towson Senior and Junior Women's Clubs, Maryland Poetry Society, Pickwick Senior Citizens, Ladies' and Men's Auxiliary of Yedz Grotto, Azoans Donor Luncheon, the Friendship Club, and the Auxillary of the Baltimore County General Hospital; Performed at the Blue Crest, Regency Terrace, the Forum, Belvedere Hotel, the Surburban Club, Mercantile Club and Eudowood Gardens; Soloist at the Baltimore City Fair; Performed for Mayor Schaefer's Special Project at the War Memorial Plaza, Baltimore; Performed the Roles of Winnifred in "Once Upon a Mattress," and Madame Ernestine in "Little Mary Sunshine"; Sang as Soloist for the Student Assistantship Recital under the auspices of the Saratoga Potsdam Choral Institute, also Performed in the Chorus with the Philadelphia Orchestra under Eugene Ormandy; Presented a Full Recital at Barker Hall, Washington D.C.; Soloist at the Church of Christ Scientist in Essex, Maryland, and at the Howard Park Methodist Church in Baltimore (currently). Published Works: Poems Published by the National Poetry Press of California in *Pegasus* and the *National Collegiate Poetry Review*. Honors and Awards: Dean's List Student, Bryn Mawr School, Baltimore, Maryland; Graduated in High Academic Standing with Bachelor of Arts Degree, Towson University; Honorable Mention in Voice, Towson University Lindasey Contest; Talent Award, Miss Towson University Competition; Honorable Mention, American Opera Society's Voice Contest in Washington D.C.; Recipient of the Mu Phi Epsilon Memorial Foundation Scholarship to Study at the Chautauqua Institute; Winner in Voice, Concerto Competition, Chautauqua Institute; Full Assistantship, Saratoga Potsdam Choral Institute; Transylvania College Poetry Prize; Second Prize in Maryland State Poetry Society's Youth Contest; Award of Merit in Spanish at Berlitz in Baltimore; Listed in *The World Who's Who of Women, Book of Honor*.■

HUBERT LEE TAYLOR

Judge. Personal: Born March 30, 1943; Son of James Jason and Lois Wells Taylor; Married Aurelia Glosser; Father of Hubert Glosser, James Ellis. Education: Attended the United States Naval Academy, 1962; B.A. 1964, B.S. 1966, LL.B. 1967, University of Alabama. Military: Served in the United States Navy. Career: Judge, Alabama Court of Criminal Appeals; Former Attorney with Taylor and Cunningham, Gadsden, Alabama. Community Activities: Alabama House of Representatives, 1974-78; Judge, Alabama Court of Criminal Appeals, 1983 to present. Religion: Ordained Deacon, United Methodist Church. Honors and Awards: Named Outstanding Young Citizen of Gadsden, 1975, 1976; Named Outstanding Orator, Alabama Press Association, 1976; Selected as One of the Outstanding Men of Alabama and America. Address: 2714 Hazel Drive, Gadsden, Alabama 35901.■

JAMES DANIEL TAYLOR

Corporate Executive. Personal: Born November 21, 1930; Son of Mr. and Mrs. James D. Taylor; Married Teresa Francis; Father of Anita Teresa, Andrea Ella, Alex James. Education: Attended Bates College, Georgetown University School of Foreign Services, University of Mexico, Mexico City College, Aterico de Manila, Harvard Business School. Military: Served in the United States Army, 1946-48, attaining the rank of Staff Sergeant. Career: Owner and President of Three Corporations; Former Position as Marketing Executive with Exxon Corporation; Management Consultant, Price Waterhouse. Organizational Memberships: American Marketing Association; Sales Executive Club. Community Activities: Jaycees; Board of Education, Mountainside, New Jersey, 1971-72; Union County Board of Education, New Jersey, 1972; Jaycee Senate 1964 to present, Vice President Jaycees International; Tar Boosters Club and Tangerine Bowl Committee, 1976 to present; Georgetown University Alumni Interviewers Board of Governors, 1979 to present; Educational Consultant to Florida Senate, 1973; President, Winter Park Racquet Club, 1983; Board of Directors, Economics Club of Orlando. Honors and Awards: Schlitz Brewing Company, Inner Circle, Wholesaler Advisory Council, 1978-80; Businessman of the Year Nominee, Orlando Chamber of Commerce, 1982. Address: 30 Cypress Lane, Winter Park, Florida 32789.■

JOHN CALVIN TAYLOR

Dentist, Evangelist, Author. Personal: Born July 22, 1914; Son of John Calvin V. and Elizabeth Siehl Taylor; Father of Sarah Elizabeth, Margaret Louise, Virginia Alden, John Calvin VII, Frederick Christian, Adah Alison, Carla Susan. Education: B.S., Muskingum College, 1937; B.D., Reformed Presbyterian Theological Seminary, 1939; Certificate, Landour Language School (Mussoori, India), 1941; Certificate, Henry Martin School of Islamics (Mussoori), 1941; Diploma, Northwestern School of Taxidermy, 1952; Diploma, Academy of General Dentistry, 1975; Attended the Medical College of Virginia School of Dentistry, 1945-46; D.D.S., University of Pittsburgh School of Dentistry, 1949. Career: Dentist, Evangelist, Author and Member of Three Foreign Mission Boards; Missionary, First Appointed under Denominational Salary then Pauline Type, Professionally Self-Supported; Ordained Minister of the Gospel; Pastored Several Congregations; Farmer; Carpenter; House Painter; Fence Builder; Big-Game Hunting Guide and Outfitter; Taxidermist; Photographer; Protector and Tamer of Wildlife for Parks; Missionary Dentist, Inc., Asian Representative since 1953. Organizational Memberships: Missionary Evangelist and Superintendent, Reformed Presbyterian Mission, India, 1940-45; Superintendent, Presbyterian Denomination Home Mission Board, 1947-52; Director, Dental Clinic Methodist Mission Hospital, Bariely, India, 1954-55; Founder and Director, Dental Clinic of Landour Community Hospital, 1955-59; American Dental Association; Academy

TWO THOUSAND NOTABLE AMERICANS

of General Dentistry; Became Ministerial Member of the Presbyterian Church of America Denomination, 1982. Community Activities: Rotary Club, Mount Union, Pennsylvania, 1960-64; Speaker to Civic and Religious Groups, including Rotarians, Lions Club, Sportsmen and Dental Societies; Missionary Helper of Medical Missionary Parents and Registered Nurse Wife's Dispensary, 1940-45; Stated Supply Pastor, Fairview Church (Industry, Pennsylvania), 1946-47; Wildlife Preservation Society of India, Organizing and Life Member 1954 to present; Teacher of Emergency Dentistry at Vallore Medical College, 1958; Establisher, E.L.W.A. Hospital Dental Clinic (Monrovia, Liberia, Africa), 1977; Worldwide Brotherhood Exchange Representative to Shanta Bhawan Hospital, Nepal; General Synod of the R.P.E.S. Denomination, Active Advisory Member; Key Commissioner to Negotiate Indian Presbyteries to Form a Synod in India; Builder and Founder, Oral Clinic Center (Dera Dun, India), 1978-80; Overseas Training Seminars, Teacher for Missionary Dentists, Mexico, 1981; United States Congress and White House Advisor on Crucial Issues. Religion: Hindu, Moslem and Christian Debate Participant, 1927-30, 1940-41; Student Volunteer, Movement Activity, Muskingum College, 1933-37; Deputation Speaking to Many Churches, East to West Coasts, 1937-40; Preacher, Evangelist and Interpreter; Ordained in the Western Presbytery of Reformed Presbyterians, 1939; Elected Moderator of Reformed Presbyterian Denomination, 1946; Member, Monongahela Presbytery of United Presbyterian Denomination, Reordained 1953. Published Works: Author *Wildlife in India's Tiger Kingdom* 1981 and Others. Honors and Awards: Athlete of the Year, Woodstock High School, 1931; 4-Letter Man, Muskingum College Sports, 1933-37; Several Medals, M Sweater and M Blanket; Winner, International Deck Tennis, Tennis Singles Match with Prize, 1953; Past President Diamond-Studded Medallion, Mt. Union Rotary Club, 1965; Lecturer's Award for Serving 7th District Rotary Club International; Fellow, International Biographical Association; Listed in *Who's Who in the East, Who's Who in North America, Dictionary of International Biography, Men of Achievement, Reformed Presbyterian Archives, International Who's Who of Intellectuals, Personalities of America, The American Registry Series, International Register of Profiles.* Address: 110 Highland Avenue, Herminie, Pennsylvania 15637.■

JOHN MICHAEL TAYLOR

Director of Public Utilities and City Engineering. Personal: Born August 25, 1950; Son of Mr. and Mrs. J. M. Taylor; Married Judy Ann H., Daughter of Mr. and Mrs. Robert Atwood. Education: A.A.S. Civil Engineering, Guilford Community College, Jamestown, North Carolina, 1971; Postgraduate Work, University of North Carolina at Wilmington; B.S. Public Administration, North Carolina State University, Raleigh, 1979 to present. Career: Director of Public Utilities and City Engineering, present; Assistant County Engineer, New Hanover County, Wilmington, North Carolina, 1978-80; Construction Superintendent, P. J. Coble Construction Company, Burlington, North Carolina, 1977; Construction Superintendent, Beamans Projects, Greensboro, North Carolina, 1976; Project Engineer, Davis, Martin, Powell and Associates, High Point, North Carolina, 1972-76; Engineering Technician, North Carolina D.O.T., Winston-Salem, 1970-72. Organizational Memberships: American Water Works Association; American Public Works Association; North Carolina Rural Water Association; North Carolina Water Works Operators Association; North Carolina Water Pollution Control Association; Federal Water Pollution Control Federation; American Management Association; Institute for Water Resources, Solid Waste Management Association. Community Activities: A.W.W.A. Committee Member, Seminars and Workshops; Boy Scout Leader, High Point, 1963-65. Religion: Protestant. Honors and Awards: Received County (New Hanover) Recognition for Outstanding Work Performed on Solid Waste Disposal, 1980; Listed in *Personalities of the South, Book of Honor, Community Leaders of America, Who's Who in the South and Southwest, Directory of Distinguished Americans, International Book of Honor, Men of Achievement, Two Thousand Distinguished Southerners.* Address: Route 1 Box 367, Henderson, North Carolina 27536.■

LISA TAYLOR

Museum Director. Personal: Born January 8, 1933; Daughter of Theo von Berger-Maier and Martina Weincerl (both deceased); Married Bertrand L. Taylor III; Mother of Lauren, Lindsay. Education: Attended Johns Hopkins University, 1956-58; Georgetown University, 1958-62; Cocoran School of Art, Washington, D.C., 1958-65; Private Studies in Painting, Pottery, Weaving, Photography, Film-Making; D.F.A. (hon.), Parsons School of Design 1977, Cooper Union 1984. Career: Director, Cooper-Hewitt Museum, the Smithsonian Institution's National Museum of Design, New York, 1969 to present; Program Director, Smithsonian Institution, Washington, 1966-69; Membership Director, Corcoran Gallery, Washington D.C., 1962-66; Administrative Assistant, President's Fine Arts Committee, Washington, D.C., 1958-62; Part-Time Program Advisor, Johns Hopkins University Young Men's Christian Association, Baltimore, Maryland, 1956-58. Organizational Memberships: National Council for Interior Design, Member Qualifications Board; American Society of Interior Designers, Honorary Member; American Institute of Architects, Honorary Member; Smithsonian Institution, Honorary Life Member. Community Activities: National Endowment for the Arts, Museum Panel 1972-75; Member Mayor's Advisory Committee on Design; Association of Art Museum Directors; Bank Street College, New York, Visiting Committee; Fashion Institute of Technology, New York, Visiting Committee; University of Cincinnati, Advisor; Art Deco Society, Board Member; Municipal Arts Society; Architectural League; I.C.P.; American Institute of Architects, Honorary Member. Published Works: Editor, *Urban Open Spaces, Cities,* and *The Phenomenon of Change.* Honors and Awards: Trailblazer of the Year Award, Nominee 1977, Winner 1981; Nominee, Woman of the Year, 1977; Smithsonian Women's Council Award, 1979; Bronze Apple Award, 1977; Thomas Jefferson Award, 1976; Bronze Plaque, Johns Hopkins University Young Men's Christian Association, 1958; American Legion Medal of Honor, 1948; Smithsonian Institution Exceptional Service Award, 1969; Listed in *Who's Who in the World, International Who's Who of Intellectuals, Who's Who in America, Who's Who in Art, Who's Who in Government.* Address: 1115 Fifth Avenue, New York, New York 10028.■

ROBERT WALTER TAYLOR

College Professor, Soil Scientist. Personal: Born March 1, 1947; Son of Harry and Iva Taylor; Married Beverly Ann Redfield, Daughter of Willie and Alma Redfield; Father of Derrick Cornelius, Thyneice Rochelle. Education: B.S. Agronomy, Tuskegee Institute, Alabama, 1970; M.S. Soil Microbiology 1972, Ph.D. Soil Chemistry 1977, Michigan State University, East Lansing, Michigan. Career: College Professor (Soil Scientist), Alabama A&M University, present; Co-Investigator, Tennessee State University, Nashville, Tennessee, 1979-81; Research Agronomist/Soil Scientist, Bahamas Agricultural Research Center, Andros, Bahamas, 1977-79. Organizational Memberships: American Society of Agronomy; Soil Science Society of America; New York Academy of Sciences; American Association for the Advancement of Science. Community Activities: Head Soccer Coach, Tennessee State University, 1981; Coach of Eagles Soccer Club, Nashville, Tennessee, 1981; Coach of Youth Soccer Team, Huntsville, Alabama, 1982-83. Honors and Awards: Beta Kappa Chi, Scientific Honor Society, 1969; Alpha Kappa Mu, Honor Society, 1969; Alpha Zeta, Agricultural Honor Society, 1976. Address: 2608 Skyline Drive Northwest, Huntsville, Alabama 35810.■

THELMA JEAN TAYLOR

Corporate Executive. Personal: Born August 21, 1932; Married Robert L. Hiltenbrand; Mother of Myra Gail Taylor, Jerry Cam Taylor, Tim Taylor. Education: Student, Memphis State University, 1975-78; Student, Mary Baldwin College, 1978-79; "Women and Small Business Ownership," Shelby State Community College, 1979; Certified Records Manager. Career: President, Owner, Founder 1979, Archives, Inc., present; Records Manager Consultant and Security Records Consultant. Organizational Memberships: Association of Commercial Record Centers, Director; Association of Record Managers and Associates; Toastmasters International; Data Processing Management Association; Planning Executives, Secretary 1981; Sales and Marketing Executives, Career Women's Committee. Religion: Presbyterian 1978 to present; Methodist 1957-77, Sunday School Teacher. Honors and Awards: Lifetime Membership Award, United Methodist Women, 1956; Most Professional Display, S.M.E., 1981; Winner of "Incredible Dutch Experience," 1982; Memphis Advertising Federation, Annual Pyramid Awards Competition; William Olsten Award for Excellence in Records Management, 1982. Address: 496 Sutton Place, Memphis, Tennessee 38119.■

TIMOTHY DAVIES TAYLOR

Psychotherapist. Personal: Born January 25, 1943; Son of Tom Taylor Sr. Education: B.A. Education, Central University, 1968; M.Ed., University of Puget

Sound, 1975; Ph.D. Psychology, United States International University, 1980. Military: Served in the United States Army to E-5, 1968-74. Career: Private Practice Psychotherapy. Community Activities: Associate General Chairman, Pierce County United Way, 1981 and 1982; Pierce County March of Dimes, Chairman 1980-81; West Tacoma Optimist Club, President 1976-77; Young Men's Christian Association, Fund Raising Captain; United Way of Pierce County, Associate Chairman, 1981 and 1982. Honors and Awards: Optimist of the Year, 1977; Listed in *Outstanding Young Men of America, Who's Who in the West, Men of Achievement, Book of Honor*. Address: 4416 West 27th, Tacoma, Washington 98407.■

BETTY TAYMOR

Director of College Program. Personal: Born March 22, 1921; Married; Mother of Michael, Laure, Julie. Education: B.A., Goucher College, 1942; M.A., Boston University, 1957. Career: Director, "Program for Women in Political and Governmental Careers," Boston College, 1973 to present; Instructor, Metropolitan College, "Master in Urban Affairs," Boston University, 1973-74; Consultant, Office of the President, University of Massachusetts, 1973-74; Instructor in Government, Northeastern University, 1969-71; Lecturer and Field Work Supervisor, "Program for Women in Political and Administrative Service," Simmons College, 1968-69. Organizational Memberships: Democratic National Committee, 1976-84; Democratic State Committee, 1956-84. Community Activities: John F. Kennedy Library Consortium, 1976; Democratic National Convention, Delegate-at-Large 1976, Leader of Minority Peace Plank Report in Delegation 1968, Secretary Democratic Rules Committee 1964, Massachusetts Delegate-at-Large 1960, 1964; Governor's Commission on the Status of Women, 1975; Democratic National Charter Commission, 1973-74; Massachusetts Women's Political Caucus, Steering Committee 1972; Americans for Democratic Action, Vice-Chairman 1971, Executive Vice Chairman 1954-46; Newton Coalition for New Politics, Steering Committee 1970 to present; Massachusetts Democratic State Reform Committee on Party Organization, Co-Chairman 1970-72; Newton Campaign Coordinator for Robert Drinan for Congress 1970, Senator Edward M. Kennedy 1962-64, Senator John F. Kennedy 1958, Stevenson for President Committee 1956; National Platform Committee, 1960-68; Massachusetts Dollars for Democrats Campaign, Chairman 1960; United States National Commission for United Nations Educational, Science and Cultural Organization, 1960-66; Massachusetts Democratic State Committee, Vice-Chairperson 1956-68; Massachusetts State Democratic Convention, Delegate 1954-72. Honors and Awards: Elizabeth King Elliocott Fellow, Goucher College, 1959. Address: 14 Eliot Memorial Road, Newton, Massachusetts 02158.■

JOHN D. TELFER

Director of Campus Facilities and Services. Personal: Born December 21, 1926; Son of Mrs. James G. Telfer; Married Virginia K., Daughter of Mrs. Harry W. Kilgore; Father of Carleton K., Carlyle H. Military: Served in the United States Army Infantry, 1945-47, as Private First Class; Army Specialized Training Program, A.S.T.P., 1944-45. Career: Director of Campus Facilities and Services, Queens College, Flushing, New York; Secretary of the University, Vice President University of Tampa, Florida, 1979-82; Vice President for Facilities Planning and Professor of Architecture, State University at Buffalo, 1972-79; Assistant Vice President for Physical Planning, Columbia University, New York, 1968-72; University Planner, The University of Michigan, 1961-68; Professor of Engineering and Division Head, Abadan Institute of Technology, Iran, 1957-59. Organizational Memberships: Founder, Society for College and University Planning 1966, Executive Director 1966-72, International President 1974-78; American Institute of Certified Planners, Member 1965 to present. Community Activities: Commissioner and Chairperson, Yipsilanti, Michigan, City Planning Commission, 1962-67; Commissioner, Washtenaw County Planning Commission (Michigan), 1967-68; Executive Committee of Morningside Heights, Inc., New York City, 1968-71; Consultant Member of Directors Audubon New Community, Amherst, New York, 1974-78; Chamber of Commerce, Greater Tampa, Florida Area, Member/Chairman Waterfront Development Task Force 1980-82; Member Board of Research Advisors, Institute for Advanced Studies, Walden University, 1980 to present. Religion: Presbyterian Church, Ruling Elder, Michigan 1960-66, W.N.Y. 1972-78, Florida 1982; United Methodist Church, Trustee of United Theology Seminary, Dayton, Ohio, 1972-80; Secretary of Institutional Relations Committee 1973-75, Member Special Charter Revision Committee 1976-80. Honors and Awards: Tau Sigma Delta, Honor Society in Architecture and the Applied Arts, 1960; Society for College and University Planning, Distinguished Citation, Atlanta, Georgia, 1972; Honorary Doctor of Laws Degree for Outstanding Contributions in Education Facilities Planning, Eastern Michigan University, Board of Regents, 1974. Address: 15-28 215th Street, Bayside, New York 11360.■

EDWARD TELLER

Physicist. Personal: Born January 15, 1908; Son of Max and Ilona (Deutch) Teller; Father of Paul, Susan Wendy. Education: Ph.D., University of Leipzig, Leipzig, Germany, 1929-30; University of Munich, Munich, Germany, 1928; Karlsruhe Technical Institute, Germany, 1926-28. Career: Senior Research Fellow, Hoover Institution, Stanford University, 1975 to present; Consultant, Lawrence Livermore National Laboratory, 1975 to present; Research Associate, Leipzig, 1929-31; Research Associate, Gottingen, 1931-33; Rockefeller Fellow (with Niels Bohr), Copenhagen, 1934; Lecturer, University of London, 1934-35; Professor of Physics, The George Washington University, Washington D.C., 1935-41; Professor of Physics, Columbia University, New York City, 1941-42; Physicist, University of Chicago, 1942-43; Physicist, Manhattan Engineer District, 1942-46; Physicist, Los Alamos Scientific Laboratory, 1943-46; Professor of Physics, University of Chicago, 1946-52; Assistant Director, Los Alamos Scientific Laboratory (on leave, University of Chicago), 1949-52; Consultant, Livermore Branch, Radiation Laboratory, University of California, 1952-53; Professor of Physics, University of California, 1953-60; Associate Director, Lawrence Livermore Laboratory, University of California, 1954-58; Director, Lawrence Livermore Laboratory, University of California, 1958-60; Associate Director, Lawrence Livermore Laboratory, University of California, 1960-75; Professor of Physics-at-Large, University of California, 1960-70; Chairman, Department of Applied Science, University of California Davis/Livermore, California, 1963-66; University Professor, University of California, 1970-75; Visiting Professor, Arthur Spitzer Chair of Energy Management, Pepperdine University, 1976-77. Organizational Memberships: American Academy of Achievement, Board of Governors; American Academy of Arts and Sciences; American Association for the Advancement of Science; American Conservation Union Task Force on Energy; American Defense Preparedness Association; American Friends of Tel Aviv University Board of Governors; American Geophysical Union; American Nuclear Society Fellow; American Physical Society Fellow; Americans for More Power Sources, Advisory Board; Atlantic Union, Sponsor; Coalition for Asian Peace and Security; Committee of Protectors of Andrei Sakharov; Committee on the Present Danger; Committee to Unite America, Inc.; Defense Intelligence School, Board Member Emeritus; Association to Unite the Democracies, Board of Directors; International Platform Assocation; International Academy of Quantum Molecular Science; National Academy of Sciences; Scientific Advisory Board, United States Air Force; Scientists and Engineers for Secure Energy; Society of Engineering Scientists; ThermoElectron, Board Member; White House Science Council. Published Works: Author Many Books including *Nuclear Energy in the Developing World* 1977, *Energy from Heaven and Earth* 1979, *Pursuit of Simplicity* 1980. Honors and Awards: Honorary Doctor of Science Degrees from Yale University 1954, University of Alaska 1959, Fordham University 1960, The George Washington University 1960, St. Louis University 1960, Rochester Institute of Technology 1962, Clemson University 1966, Clarkson College 1969; Honorary Doctor of Law Degrees from Boston College 1961, Seattle University 1961, University of Cincinnati 1962, University of Pittsburgh 1963, Pepperdine University 1974, University of Maryland, Heidelberg 1977; Honorary Doctor of Humane Letters Degree from Mount Mary College 1964; Honorary Ph.D: from Tel Aviv University, 1972; Honorary Doctor of Natural Science from De La Salle University, 1981; Doctor of Medical Science honoris causa, Medical University of South Carolina, 1983; Harrison Medal, American Ordnance Association, 1955; Joseph Priestly Memorial, Dickinson College, 1957; Albert Einstein, 1958; General Donovan Memorial, 1959; Midwest Research Institute, 1960; Research Institute of American Living History, 1960; American Academy of Achievement Golden Plate, 1961; Thomas E. White, 1962; Enrico Fermi, 1962; Robins Award of America, 1963; Leslie R. Groves Gold Medal, 1974; Harvey Prize, Technion Institute, Israel, 1975; Semmelweiss Medal, 1977; Albert Einstein Award, Technion Institute of Israel, 1977; Henry T. Heald, Illinois Institute of Technology, 1978; American College of Nuclear Medicine Gold Medal, 1980; ARCS Man of the Year, 1980; Paul Harris Award, Rotary, 1980; A. C. Eringen Award, Society of Engineering Science, Inc., 1980; Distinguished Scientist, National Science Development Board, 1981; Distinguished Scientist, Phil-American Academy of Science and Engineering, 1981; American Academy of Achievement Gold Medal, 1982; The Lloyd Freeman Hunt Citizenship Award, 1982; National Medal of Science for 1982; Joseph Handleman Prize, Jewish Academy of Arts and Sciences, 1983. Address: Hoover Institution, Stanford, California 94305.■

HOWARD M. TEMIN

Professor of Oncology. Personal: Born December 10, 1934; Son of Mr. and Mrs. Henry Temin; Married Rayla, Daughter of Mr. and Mrs. Morris Greenberg; Father of Sarah Beth, Miriam Judith. Education: B.A., Swarthmore College, 1955; Ph.D., California Institute of Technology, 1959; D.Sc. (honorary), Swarthmore College, 1972; D.Sc. (honorary), New York Medical College, 1972; D.Sc. (honorary), University of Pennsylvania, 1976; D.Sc. (honorary), Hahnemann Medical College, 1976; D.Sc. (honorary), Lawrence University, 1976; D.Sc. (honorary), Temple University, 1979; D.Sc. (honorary), Medical College of Wisconsin, 1981. Career: Professor of Oncology, University of Wisconsin, 1969 to present; Harold P. Rusch Professor of Cancer Research, 1980 to present; American Society Professor of Viral Oncology and Cell Biology, 1974 to present; Steenbock Professor of Biological Science, 1982 to present; Wisconsin Alumni Research

Foundation Professor of Cancer Research, 1971-80; Public Health Service Research Career Development Award, NCI, 1964-75; Associate Professor of Oncology, University of Wisconsin, 1964-69; Postdoctorate Fellow, California Institute of Technology, 1959-60. Organizational Memberships: Associate Editor, *Journal of Cellular Physiology* 1966-77, *Cancer Research* 1971-74; Editorial Board, *Journal of Virology* 1971 to present, *Intervirology* 1972-75, *Archives of Virology* 1975-77, *Proceedings of the National Academy of Science* 1975-80; American Society of Microbiology; American Association for Cancer Research; National Academy of Science; American Academy of Arts and Science; American Philosophical Society; Fellow, Wisconsin Academy of Science, Arts and Letters. Community Activities: Waksman Award Committee, U.S. Steel Award Committee, National Academy of Science U.S.A.; Sponsor, Federation of American Scientists, 1976 to present; Advisory Committee to Direct National Institute of Health. Religion: Beth Israel Synagogue. Honors and Awards: Warren Triennial Prize of Massachusetts General Hospital, 1971 (Shared); Pap Award of the Papanicolaou Institute, Miami, 1972; Bertner Award, M.D. Anderson, Houston, 1972; U.S. Steel Foundation Award in Molecular Biology, National Academy of Science, 1972; Waksman Award, Theobald Smith Society, 1972; American Chemical Society Award in Enzyme Chemistry, 1973; Modern Medicine Award for Distinguished Achievement, 1973; 1972 Griffuel Prize, Villejuif, France, 1973; Gairdner Foundation International Award, Toronto, 1974 (Shared); Albert Lasker Award in Basic Medical Research, 1974; Nobel Prize for Physiology or Medicine, 1975 (Shared); Lucy Wortham James Award in Basic Research, 1976; Alumni Distinguished Service Award, California Institute of Technology, 1976; Lila Gurber Research Awardee, American Academy of Dermatology, 1981. Address: 3401 Lake Mendota Drive, Madison, Wisconsin 53705.■

CAROLYN JENNY TENNANT

Dean of Student Life. Personal: Born June 19, 1947, in Janesville, Wisconsin; Daughter of Mr. and Mrs. Ralph Jenny; Married Raymond Frank Tennant. Education: B.A. English Education 1969, M.A. English Education 1973, Ph.D. Education Administration and Supervision 1979, University of Colorado. Career: Dean of Student Life, North Central Bible College, Minneapolis, Minnesota; Director, Institute for Cognitive Development, Aurora, Colorado, 1979-83; Principal, Montbello Christian School (Denver), 1980; Director, Gifted/Talented and Instructional Staff Development, Denver/Adams County School District #12, 1978-79; Special Programs Consultant, Denver/Adams County School District #12, 1974-78; Teacher of English and Reading, Adams County School District #12, 1969-73. Organizational Memberships: Association of Supervision and Curriculum Development; National Association for Gifted Children; Colorado Association for Gifted and Talented; Colorado Language Arts Society; International Reading 1973-74; National Society for the Study of Education; International Reading Association. Community Activities: Adjunct Professor, University of Colorado at Boulder, University of Northern Colorado; Consultant in Fields of Gifted/Talented and Thinking Skills, Administrative Techniques; Planning Committee for State Title I Convention, 1978. Religion: Assemblies of God Church. Honors and Awards: Director of E.S.E.A. Title I Program Named One of Top 12 in U.S. by U.S. Office of Education, 1974; Colorado Teacher's Scholarship, 1972, 1973; Nominated for Fulbright Award to Taiwan, 1981; Listed in *Who's Who in the West*. Address: 9753 Utica Road, Bloomington, Minnesota 55437.■

FOREST SEARLS TENNANT, JR.

Executive Director of Community Health Projects. Personal: Born January 23, 1941; Married Miriam Tennant. Education: A.A., Hutchinson Junior College (Kansas), 1960; B.A., University of Missouri, 1962; M.D., University of Kansas Medical School, 1967; Internship in Internal Medicine, University of Kentucky, 1967; Residency, University of Texas, 1968; M.P.H. 1973, Residency in Preventive Medicine 1974, D.P.H. 1974, University of California at Los Angeles. Military: Served in the United States Army to the Rank of Major, 1968-72. Career: Executive Director of Community Health Projects, Inc.; Professor in Division of Epidemiology 1972 to present, United States Public Health Service Postdoctoral Fellowship for School of Public Health, University of California at Los Angeles; Chief Physician for Special Action Office for Alcohol and Drug Abuse 1971-72, Major in Medical Corps 1970-71, Captain in Medical Corps 1968-70, United States Army. Organizational Memberships: Southern California Association of Physicians in Drug Dependence, Past President; American Association for the Advancement of Science; American Geriatrics Society; California Public Health Association; Association of Teachers of Preventive Medicine; American Medical Association; California Medical Association; Los Angeles County Medical Association; American College of Preventive Medicine, Fellow. Community Activities: City of West Covina City Councilman, 1980-84; Consultant to California State Department of Justice, California State Rehabilitation Center; Past President, West Covina Chamber of Commerce; Rotary Club; Delhaven Community Center, Fund Raising Chairman; We T.I.P. Advisory Board; American Red Cross; American Cancer Society. Honors and Awards: United States Army Commendation Medal, 1971; Meritorious Service Medal, 1972; Student American Medical Association Research Award, 1973; Student American Medical Association Research Forum 1st Place in Neuropsychiatry, 1973; Small Business Award for Innovative System to Lower Health Care Costs, California State Chapter of Commerce, 1977; Citizen of the Year, West Covina, California, 1979; Director of the Year, West Covina Chamber of Commerce, 1979. Address: 1744 Aspen Village Way, West Covina, California 91791.■

JERALD L. TENNANT

Ophthalmologist. Personal: Born June 28, 1949; Son of Harold and Nellie Tennant; Married Marilyn Dickenson, Daughter of Clayton and Ruth Dickenson; Father of Scott, John, Tom, Jared, Tasha. Education: Attended Texas Tech University, 1957-60; M.D., University of Texas Southwestern Medical School, 1960-64; Internship, Methodist Hospital of Dallas, 1964-65; Resident in Ophthalmology, Parkland Memorial Hospital of Dallas, 1965-68; Certified by the American Academy of Ophthalmic Plastic and Reconstructive Surgery, 1972. Career: Eye Surgeon (Opthalmologist); Author Teacher; Realtor; Inventor. Organizational Memberships: Dallas County Medical Society; Dallas Academy of Ophthalmology; Texas Medical Association; Texas Opthalmological Society, Texas Society of Opthalmology and Otolaryngology; American Medical Association; American Intra-Ocular Implant Society, Scientific Advisory Board 1976-79; International Implant Club; The Royal Society of Medicine; Outpatient Ophthalmic Surgical Society, Co-Founder and Vice President, 1980 to present. Community Activities: The Greater Dallas Board of Realtors; Boy Scout Leader; Active in Civic Organizations, Committees, and Councils, Serving through Offices, Public Appointments, Volunteer Activities and Public Donations. Religion: Church of Jesus Christ of Latter-Day Saints, High Councilman, Executive Secretary. Honors and Awards: Valedictorian, 1957; Phi Eta Sigma Freshman Honor Society, 1958; Alpha Epsilon Delta Pre-Med Honor Society, 1958; Named A.S.A.L.O.E. Pre-Med Student of the Year, 1958; Phi Kappa Phi International Honor Society, 1959; Methodist Hospital, S.N., Intern of the Year Award, 1965.■

ROBERT ARTHUR TERRY, JR.

Professor of English and Philosophy, Pastor. Personal: Born February 10, 1938; Son of Dr. Arthur Terry; Married Diana Nunneley, June 10, 1964; Father of Natasha Elizabeth, David Matthews. Education: A.B. cum laude, Hendrix College, 1960; Attended Union Theological Seminary, 1960-61; M.A., University of Arkansas, 1963; Ph.D. University of Arizona, 1969; Attended Brown University, 1976. Career: Professor of English and Philosophy, Southern Arkansas University; Pastor, Village/Ebenezer Methodist Charge; Amway Distributor; Assistant Professor of English and Head Department of English, University of Alaska, 1969-73; Instructor in English and Assistant Director of Freshman English, University of Arizona, 1963-69; Graduate Teaching Assistant in English, University of Arkansas, 1961-63; Pastor, Emerson Methodist Church, 1977. Organizational Memberships: S.C.M.L.A.; A.P.A.; A.C.T.E., Vice President 1973; A.T.C.E., Vice President 1981-82, President 1982 to present; A.E.H., Executive Board 1977 to present, Vice President 1979-80, Co-President 1980 to present; S.H.C.; C.C.T.E., University Coordinator 1976-77. Community Activities: Columbia County Red Cross Board, Chairman 1978-79; Columbia County United Way Board, 1978-79. Religion: Little Rock Methodist Conference Commission on Archives and History, 1980 to present; Camden Methodist District, Director of Methodist Men 1976-78, Council on Ministries 1981 to present; First Methodist Church of Magnolia, Administrative Board, PPR Committee, Committee on Personnel, Sunday School Teacher 1973-78. Honors and Awards: National Endowment of the Humanities Summer Fellow, Brown University, 1976; National Teaching Fellow, 1973-74, 1974-75; Rockefeller Brothers Theological Fellow, 1960-61; National Merit Scholar, 1956-60; Alpha Chi, 1959-60; Alpha Tau, 1957-58; Pine Bluff (Arkansas) Rotary Club Scholar, 1956-57. Address: 1902 North Jackson, Magnolia, Arkansas 71753.■

SHOHIG SHERRY TERZIAN

Director of Mental Health Information Service. Personal: Daughter of Ardashes Garabed and Ebraxe Momjian Terzian (both deceased). Education: A.B. cum laude English Literature, Radcliffe College of Harvard University; M.S., Columbia University Graduate School of Library Services; Postgraduate Courses, New School for Social Research, Columbia University, University of Wisconsin, University of California at Los Angeles. Career: Director of Mental Health Information Service of the Neuropsychiatric Institute 1975 to present, Faculty Member of the Department of Psychiatry and Biobehavioral Science in the School of Medicine 1969 to present, Librarian of the Neuropsychiatric Institute of the Center for Health Science 1961-74, University of California at Los Angeles; Librarian, Prudential Insurance Company of American Western Home Office, Los Angeles, California, 1948-61; Research Librarian, Time Inc., New

York, New York, 1947-48; Picture Editor and Research Assistant, United States Department of State Office of International Information and Cultural Affairs, New York, New York, 1943-46; Assistant Vassar College Library, Poughkeepsie, New York, 1942-43; First Librarian, Neurological Institute of Columbia-Presbyterian Medical Center, New York, New York, 1940-41. Organizational Memberships: Literature Consultant on Genocide, Institute for the Study of Social Trauma of Shalvata Psychiatric Center, Israel; Literature Consultant on Genocide, Simon Wiesenthal Center for Holocaust Studies, Los Angeles; Association of Western Hospitals, Founder and First Chairman, Hospital Librarians Section; Special Librarians Association, President Southern California Chapter, Chairman Employment and Public Relations Committees, Chairman First Behavioral Science Committee and Other Local and National Committees; California Library Association, President Hospital and Institutions Roundtable. Community Activities: Association for Mental Health Affiliation with Israel, Chairman Southern California Library Committee; Columbia University Alumni of Southern California, Vice President, Newsletter Editor; Valley College Library/Media Technology Program Advisory Committee; University of California Graduate School of Library Service, Specialist Advisor/Consultant; Los Angeles Trade Technical College, Member Advisory Committee which Initiated Library Technicians Program; California State Personnel Board, Member Panels for Oral Interviews for the Statewide Positions of Librarian; State Department of Mental Hygiene, Chairman Workshop Planning Committee for First Training Workshop on Modern Psychiatric Librarianship for Librarians of California; Psychiatric Librarians Roundtable, Pilot Meeting at the Mental Hospitals Institute, American Psychiatric Association; Psychiatric Librarians of Los Angeles, Founder, First Chairman; Guest Lecturer at University of California at Los Angeles Graduate School of Library Service, University of Southern California Graduate School of Library Science and Immaculate Heart College School of Library Science; Radcliffe Club of Southern California, Vice President, Public Relations Director, Harvard Affiliate; Harvard Club of Southern California, Newsletter Columnist; Los Angeles County Commission on the Status of Women, Committees on Health, Employment and Senior Women. Honors and Awards: Lifetime/Honorary Member, Association for Mental Health Affiliation with Israel; "George Santayana and the Genteel Tradition" Radcliffe Honors Thesis Citation for Distinction, Department of English of Harvard University and Personal Review by George Santayana; Certificate, *International Who's Who of Intellectuals*; Listed in *American Registry, Anglo-American Who's Who, Book of Honor, Armenian Academic Personnel in the United States, Biographical Dictionary of Librarians in the United States and Canada, Biographical Dictionary of Librarians in the Field of Slavic and Central European Studies, Community Leaders and Noteworthy Americans, Dictionary of International Biography, Directory of Armenian Scholars, International Who's Who in Community Service, International Who's Who of Intellectuals, Men and Women of Distinction, Notable Americans, Personalities of America, Personalities of the West and Midwest, Who Knows and What, Who's Who in California, Who's Who in Community Service, Who's Who in Library Science, Who's Who in the West, Who's Who of American Women, World Who's Who of Women, Who's Who in Library and Information Services.* Address: 11740 Wilshire Blvd. #2502, Los Angeles, California 90025.■

BETTY WERTHEIMER TEVIS

Educational Consultant. Personal: Born April 7, 1929; Mother of Kathleen, Cynthia, Thomas, Mary Lynn. Education: B.A. 1950, B.S. 1950, M.A. 1951, Ph.D. 1972, Texas Woman's University. Career: Education Consultant; Former University Professor, Voluntary Health Agency Staff, Physical Educator. Organizational Memberships: Association for the Advancement of Health Education, Board of Directors 1981-84; American School Health Association, Governing Council 1976-79; Texas Association for Health, Physical Education and Recreation, Vice President for Health 1975-76; Texas School Health Association, President 1980-81, Executive Treasurer 1982 to present; Texas Public Health Association, Governing Council 1973-76; Various Other Professional Memberships. Community Activities: Board of Directors, American Cancer Society (Lubbock Division), American Heart Association (Lubbock Chapter), American Lung Association (West Texas Area), Lubbock Council on Alcoholism, Tel-Med of Lubbock; South Plains Association of Governments, Alcoholism Advisory Council; Chairman Schools and Colleges Committee, American Heart Association, Texas Affiliate; Schools and Colleges Committee, American Cancer Society, Texas Division; Consultant to Texas Department of Health, Louisiana Department of Education, Various Heart Associations throughout the United States; Host of TV Show "What in Health is Going On" on KTXT, Lubbock, 1973-76. Religion: Active in Single Young Adults Class, Lovers Lane Methodist Church. Honors and Awards: Bryant Memorial Award, Texas Public Health Association, 1976; Honor Award, Texas Association for Health, Physical Education and Recreation, 1976; Electronic Media Award, Texas Hospital Association, 1977; Eisenhower Award, American Heart Association, Texas Affiliate, 1978; Distinguished Service Award, 1981; Delta Psi Kappa; Eta Sigma Gamma; Phi Delta Kappa. Address: 9620 Bryson Drive, Dallas, Texas 75238.■

MARGIE LOUISE THAMS

Travel Executive, Counselor. Personal: Born October 6, 1937; Daughter of Charles (deceased) and Margaret Gates; Mother of Susan Lawson, Donald Lawson. Education: Attended Citrus Junior College, 1964; Attending Coastline Community College, 1981 to present. Career: Commercial Account Executive, Executive Travel Service, 1982; Commerical Travel Counselor, Thomas Cook Travel Inc., 1981-82; Administrative Assistant to the President, Occidental Research Corporation, 1974-80; Executive Secretary to Six Officers and Directors, Dahle Importers Inc., 1973-74; Executive Secretary to Corporate Treasurer, VSI Corporation, 1972-73; Personnel Administrator, Executive Secretary to Controller and Executive Vice President, Executive Secretary to New Products Development Manager, ORMCO Corporation, 1966-70; Executive Secretry to Corporate Controller, Kern Foods Inc., 1965-66; Administrative Secretary to Director of Material, Hycon Manufacturing Company (now Actron), 1963-65. Honors and Awards: Listed in *Who's Who in the West, Personalities of the West, World Who's Who of Women.* Address: 2220 Park Newport #215, Newport Beach, California 92660.■

CARLTON JAMES THAXTON

Retired Library Director. Personal: Born May 23, 1935; Married Donna Bradley; Father of James Bradley, Carl Stanton. Education: B.A. Journalism, University of Georgia, 1957; M.S. Library Science, Florida State University, 1958. Military: Served in the United States Army Reserve, Private First Class, 1955-57; U.S. Coast Guard Reserve, Yeoman Second Class, 1957-63; Serving in the U.S. Naval Reserve, Intelligence Specialist Second Class, 1979 to present. Career: Director, Lake Blackshear Regional Library Americus, Georgia, 1980-82; Director, Division of Public Library Services, State Department of Education, Atlanta, Georgia, 1968-79; Director, Coastal Plain Regional Library, Tifton, Georgia, 1958-68. Organizational Memberships: American Library Association; Southeastern Library Association; Georgia Library Association; President, Georgia Library Association, 1979-81 Biennium. Community Activities: Appointed by President Jimmy Carter to Serve on the Advisory Committee of the White House Conference on Libraries and Information Services, 1979-80. Religion: Member First United Methodist Church, Americus, Georgia; Senior High Sunday School Class Teacher, Ousley Methodist Church, Lithonia, Georgia, 1975-79. Address: 412 Judy Lane, Americus, Georgia 31709.■

EDWARD LOUIS THELLMANN

Administrator. Personal: Born May 16, 1927; Married; Father of Mark, Leah, Kenn, Kim. Education: B.S. Math/Chemistry, Cleveland State University, 1959; Certificate in Metallurgy, Fenn College, 1963. Military: Served in the United States Navy, 1945-46. Career: Manager of Applied Materials Technology; Former Manager of Powder Metallurgy. Organizational Memberships: American Society for Metals; American Powder Metallurgy Institute, Chairman Local Chapter 1974-75; American Defense Preparedness Association; S.A.M.P.E. Community Activities: Chairman, Walton Hills Lake Club, 1967-68; Chairman, Walton Hills Men's Club, 1975-76; Village of Walton Hills (Ohio) Planning Commission, 1975 to present; Village of Walton Hills City Council, 1982 to present. Honors and Awards: John C. Vaaler Award, 1966; American Society for Metals Materials Award Competition, 1967; IR 100 Award 1979, Fellow 1982, American Society for Metals; Holder of 10 Patents; Author Over 20 Technical Papers. Address: 18307 Orchard Hills Drive, Walton Hills, Ohio 44146.■

RADU AMZA SERBAN THEODORESCU

Professor. Personal: Born April 12, 1933; Son of Dan (deceased) and Ortensia Theodorescu; Father of Dan. Education: B.Sc., M.Sc., University of Bucharest, 1954; Ph.D., Academy of Romania, 1958; D.Sc., University of Bucharest, 1967. Career: Professor, Laval University; Former Assistant Professor (Research Fellow) 1954-57, Senior Assistant Professor (Senior Research Fellow) 1957-60; Associate Professor and Science Section Instructor, Mathematics Academy,

Romania, 1960-64; Professor, Department Head, Center for Mathematical Statistics, Romania, 1964-68; Professor, University of Bucharest, 1968-69; Guest Professor and Lecturer, Universities in Europe and North America. Organizational Memberships: Canadian Mathematical Society; American Mathematical Society; International Statistics Institute; Canadian Statistics Society; Institute of Mathematical Statistics; German Mathematics Society. Honors and Awards: G. Lazar Prize, Academy of Romania, 1960; Listed in *Who's Who in America, Men of Achievement, Who's Who in Community Service, National Register of Prominent Americans and International Notables.* Address: 1603-9 Jardins Merici, Quebec, Quebec G1S 4S8, Canada.■

PAUL JOSEPH THIEL

Administrator. Personal: Born December 16, 1926; Son of Joseph J. Thiel (deceased); Married Rita M., Daughter of Clarence J. Madden (deceased); Father of Paula, Christine, Julie, Janet, Bruce, Kevin, Susan, Kurt. Education: B.M.E., Marquette University, 1949. Military: Served in the United States Navy as a Radarman, 1944-46. Career: Manager, Columbia Operations, Wrenn Handling Inc.; Former Positions include Vice President and General Manager of Ann Realty Group Inc., President of State Machinery Company, Manager of Field Operations for WABCO Construction and Mining Equipment Group of American Standard Company, President of Denver Fire Clay Company. Organizational Memberships: South Carolina Equipment Distributors Association, President 1977-78; Associated Equipment Distributors, National Lieutenant Director 1975-77; Lexington Toastmasters, President 1980, 1984. Community Activities: WABCO Distributor Advisory Council, Chairman 1975; President, Deercreek Horizontal Property Regime, 1981-82 & 1983; Chairman, South Carolina Product Liability Task Force, 1978. Address: Route 6, Box 338K-2, Columbia, South Carolina 29210.■

MORRIS L. THIGPEN, SR.

Department of Corrections Commissioner. Personal: Born December 25, 1939; Son of Delwin Thigpen; Married Sue Hart, Daughter of Harold and Bessie Hart; Father of Morris Lee Jr., Scot Allen. Education: A.A., Meridian Junior College, Meridian, Mississippi; B.S., Millsaps College, Jackson, Mississippi, 1963; M.Ed., Mississippi State University, 1969. Career: Commissioner, Mississippi Department of Corrections, present; Deputy Commissioner, Mississippi Department of Corrections; Personnel Director and Director of Community Services, Mississippi Department of Youth Services; Special Counselor, Vocational Rehabilitation, Mississippi Department of Education; Sales, Smith, Kine and French Laboratories; Teacher, Jackson, Mississippi Public Schools. Organizational Memberships: Southern States Correctional Association, Treasurer 1982, Secretary 1983; Board Member, National Rehabilitation Counseling Association. Community Activities: Board Member, Millsaps College Alumni Association; Advisory Committee, Social and Rehabilitation Services, U.S.M.; State Vocational Advisory Council; Council on Crime and Delinquency, Mississippi Criminal Justice Planning Division; Governor's Task Force on Corrections; Board Member, Mississippi State Mental Health Association. Religion: Member Galloway United Methodist Church, Jackson, Mississippi, Sunday School Teacher and Youth Counselor. Honors and Awards: Honorary Member, Pi Alpha Alpha, Mississippi State University; Counselor of the Year for Mississippi, National Rehabilitation Counseling Association. Address: 5175 Reddoch Drive, Jackson, Mississippi 39211.■

K. G. THIMOTHEOSE

Corporate Executive Director, Chief Executive Officer and Board of Directors Chairman. Personal: Born February 11, 1938; Son of K. G. and Mariamma Varghese; Married Mariamma; Father of Geebee, Sonia. Education: M.A.; M.Ed.: M.A.; Ph.D.; C.S.W.; C.A.C.; Certified Psychologist; Diplomate-American Board of Psychotherapy; Certified Alcoholism Therapist. Career: Executive Director, Chief Executive Officer, Chairman Board of Directors, Central Therapeutic Services, Inc., Southfield, Michigan, 1981 to present; Former Positions include Clinical Director, Alexandrine House, Inc., Detroit, Michigan; Professor and Head of the Department of Educational Psychology, Teachers College, Kerala, India; Director, Ananndanilyam Orphanage and Widow Center, Kerala, India. Organizational Memberships: American Psychological Association, Clinical Member; Academy of Psychologists in Marital, Sex and Family Therapy; American Institute of Counseling and Psychotherapy, Clinical Member; Kerala University Forum of Educational Research and Studies, Vice President. Community Activities: University of Calicut, India, Member, Faculty of Education 1968-75; Advisory Board Member, Kerala Government Trivandrum Medical College Hospitals. Published Works: Former Editor, *Kerala Journal of Education*; Publisher of Textbook in Educational Psychology for B.Ed. Students. Honors and Awards: First Class and First Rank, University of Kerala for Master's Degree in Educational Psychology; Listed in Marquis *Who's Who,* and in International Biographical Centre and American Biographical Institute Publications. Address: 21701 Parklawn, Oak Park, Michigan 48237.■

BARBARA N. THOMAS

Secretarial School Executive Director, Institute Director. Personal: Born September 8, 1936. Education: B.S. Business, West Virginia University, 1959; Graduate Work in Guidance and Supervision Completed at West Virginia University, 1966-71. Career: Executive Director, Northamerican Secretarial School; President/ Director, Allentown Business; Director, Thompson Institute of Philadelphia; Director, Washington School for Secretaries, 1984 to present; Director, Katharine Gibbs, Inc., 1982-84; Board of Directors, Private Business Schools, Pennsylvania Department of Education; Former Occupations include Executive Director, Business Education Teacher, Coordinator and Director of Vocational Office Training, Legal Secretary and Supervisor of Student Teachers. Organizational Memberships: Education Director, Sales and Marketing Executives; Board of Directors, S.M.E., 1982; Board of Governors, Manpower Area Planning Council; Board of Governors, Chamber of Commerce (Allentown-Lehigh County); Chairman, Volunteers Involved Together in Lehigh; Chairman, Executive Women's Task Force, Chamber of Commerce; Board of Directors, Lehigh County Vocational Education Association; American Management Association; Management Education Committee; Associaton of Independent Colleges and Schools, National and Pennsylvania Business Education Associations; Region II Planning Commission; Pennsylvania Association of Private School Administrators; Soroptimist International; Zonta International. Religion: Sunday School Teacher. Honors and Awards: Named News-Maker of the Week, *Dominion-Post* for Outstanding Contributions to the Business and Education Community, 1979; Nominee for Woman of the Year, Business and Professional Women, 1975; Sales and Marketing Executives Award (international), D.S.A., 1982; Citizenship Award, 1960. Address: 1850 47th Place, N.E., Washington, D.C. 20007.■

GRACE FERN THOMAS

Psychiatrist, Expert Court Witness. Personal: Born September 23, 1897; Daughter of Mr. and Mrs. George W. Thomas (both deceased). Education: B.S., University of Nebraska, 1924; M.A. Biochemistry, Creighton University, Omaha, Nebraska, 1926; M.D., University of Southern California, Los Angeles, 1935; M.A. Religion, University of Southern California, Los Angeles, 1968. Military: Served in the United States Army Medical Corps, 1944-46, Commissioned Captain, World War II. Career: Private Practice in Psychiatry, Expert Court Witness; Director of Mental Health Clinics, New Mexico (V.A.), Ohio State (Canton and Norwalk), California (San Bernardino, Ukiah, Sonora); Director of Psychiatric Education, Mississippi State Hospital; Instructor in Chemistry and Biology, Duchesne College, Omaha, Nebraska. Organizational Memberships: Fellow, American Psychiatric Association, 1983; American Medical Association; International Soroptimist Club; Fellow, International Biographical Association, 1980. Community Activities: Lecturer in Mental Health Subjects in Ohio, California and New Mexico; Former Member, American Platform Association. Religion: Ordained in United Methodist Church, 1968; Adult Church School Instructor, Methodist Church, Canton, Ohio, 1955-58. Honors and Awards: Phi Beta Kappa, 1924; Sigma Xi, 1924; Phi Kappa Phi, 1934; Elected Fellow of International Biographical Association, 1981; Elected Life Fellow of American Psychiatric Association, 1982; Listed in *Who's Who in California, Who's Who in the West, Dictionary of International Biography, Who's Who of American Women, World Who's Who of Women, Two Thousand Women of Achievement, International Who's Who of Intellectuals, Directory of Medical Specialists.* Address: 2001 La Jolla Court, Modesto, California 95350.■

HELEN THOMAS

White House Correspondent. Personal: Married Douglas B. Cornell. Education: B.A., Wayne State University. Career: United Press International, Chief White House Correspondent, Employee since 1943. Organizational Memberships: White House Correspondents Association, President; Women's National Press Club,

TWO THOUSAND NOTABLE AMERICANS

President; Sigma Delta Chi Hall of Fame. Honors and Awards: Newspaper Woman of the Year, 1968; Headline Award, Women in Communication. Address: 2501 Calvert Northwest, Washington, D.C. 20008.■

MILDRED THOMAS

Professional Musician, Composer, Writer, Poet, Photographer, Teacher, Civic Leader. Personal: Born September 28, 1901, in New Sharon, Maine; Married John S. Sanders. Education: B.S. Education 1936, M.S.Ed. 1938, Boston University; Mus.B. 1950, Ph.D. Musicology 1970, Chicago Music Conservatory; Doctor of Science in Education (honorary), Nasson College, Springvale, Maine, 1980. Career: Teacher (1st grade), Supervisor of Reading, Demonstrator in a Teacher's College, Substitute Teacher and Tutor in Maine, Massachusetts, New Hampshire, Florida and Kentucky, 1923-73; Research in Musical Instruments of the Middle Ages. Organizational Memberships: Past President, American Pen Women; Past Branch President, League of American Pen Women in Winter Park, Florida; Founder and President, Writers' Work Shop, Orlando, Florida; Held Many Offices at the State of Maine Writers' Conference; Member, National League of American Pen Women; President, Clay County Retired Teachers Association, Florida; Founder and Director, Writers' Workshop in Green Cove Springs, Florida. Community Activities: Active in Civic Activities; Collector of Dolls from All Over the World, lending them to Interested Groups; Past President, World Wide Philathea, University of Maine Alumni Association in Massachusetts, Acquaintance Club, Florida Club of Ocean Park, Maine; American Association of University Women; Council on Aging, Lexington, Kentucky; Retirement Community, Penney Farms, Florida. Religion: The Christian Science Church, Boston, Massachusetts. Published Works: Author Several Books on Education, Teaching and Art; Contributor Articles on Education, Teaching, Art, and Travel to Educational Magazines; Poetry Published in Popular Magazines; Composer of Songs, Musical Plays for Children, Hymns, Duets, Vocal Solos, Violin and Cello Solos with Piano Accompaniment, Organ and Piano Duets and Piano Solos. Honors and Awards: Third Prize for Words and Music of "Owl Song" in Florida Pen Womens' Song Contest; Recchia Silver Medal for Service to the State of Maine Writers' Conference; Two Plaques for Honorable Mention in the *Portland Press Herald* "Clearing House" Poetry Contest; Appears in *Maine Composers and Their Music*, Published by the Maine Historical Society; Gained Recognition for Writing the Words and Music of Dedicatory Hymn for the New Organ in Henderson Memorial Church; Listed in *Who's Who of Women, Dictionary of International Biography, Who's Who in Community Service, Community Leaders and Noteworthy Americans, International Register of Profiles, International Who's Who of Intellectuals, Maine Composers and Their Music.* Address: P.O. Box 251, Penney Farms, Florida 32709.■

PEGGY R. THOMAS

Executive. Personal: Born December 19, 1933; Daughter of Sidney D. and Ruth M. Coffman; Married Donald Edward Thomas; Mother of Gene Lowell Gustafson, Richard Lynn Gustafson. Education: Graduate of Mangum (Oklahoma) High School, 1951; Attended the University of Oklahoma 1951-52, Southwestern State College 1952-53. Career: Chief, Supply Management Division, Alaska Railroad (Anchorage); Owner and Chief Executive Officer, XPRT Consultants (Government Contracts and Personnel Matters); Chief, Purchasing Division, Municipality of Anchorage, 1979; Chief Contracting and General Services Division, United States Fish and Wildlife Service, Anchorage, 1978-79; Chief, Services and Construction Contracts Division, Elmendorf Air Force Base, Alaska; Deputy Chief of Procurement, Mountain Home Air Force Base, Idaho, 1972-76; Chief, Supply Procurement Branch, United States Air Force (Civilian), Altus Air Force Base (Oklahoma) and Mountain Home Air Force Base (Idaho), 1966-71; Contract Specialist, United States Air Force (Civilian), Altus Air Force Base, 1962-66; Procurement Specialist, United States Air Force (Civilian), Altus Air Force Basse, Dyess Air Force Base (Texas), Clinton-Sherman Air Force Base (Oklahoma). Organizational Memberships: National Association of Female Executives; American Society of Professional and Executive Women; American Association of Individual Investors; American MENSA Ltd.; The Heritage Foundation; National Writers Club. Community Activities: Director, Civic Recycling Program, National Federation of Business and Professional Women, Mountain Home, 1973-75. Honors and Awards: Outstanding Performance Award, 1965, 1976; Air Force Service Award, 1966, 1975; Air Force Incentive Award, 1967, 1972; Air Force Certificate of Achievement for Resources Conservation, 1968, 1975, 1976; Military Airlift Command Personal Achievement Award, 1971; Tactical Air Command Personal Achievement Award, 1973; National Program Public Service Award for Keeping America Beautiful, 1973; Governor's Distinguished Public Service Award, State of Idaho, 1974. Address: SRA 85-T, 6001 Barry, Anchorage, Alaska 99516.■

PHILIP ROBINSON THOMAS

Operational Management Consultant Executive. Personal: Born December 9, 1934; Son of Leslie R. and Margaret L. Thomas; Married Wayne Heirtzler, Daughter of Claude A. and Aline Heirtzler; Father of Martin N. R., Stephen D. R. Education: B.Sc. Physics and Math, M.Sc. Physics, Ph.D. Engineering, University of London. Military: Served with the British Royal Air Force, 1953-54. Career: Operational Management Consultant Executive, Texas Instruments Corporation, 1961-72; Operations Manager, Dallas 1963-72, Bedford, England 1961-63; Vice President, General Manager, MOS/LSI Division General Instruments Company, New York City, 1972-73; General Manager, MOS Product Division, Fairchild Camera and Instruments Corporation, Mountainview, California, 1973-75; Vice President, Solid State Division RCA, Somerville, New Jersey, 1975-78; President, Chief Executive Officer, Thomas Group Inc., Ethel, Louisiana, 1978. Organizational Memberships: Institute of Electrical and Electronic Engineers, British Instruments Radio and Electronics Engineers. Address: Route 1, Box 181, Ethel, Louisiana 70730.■

ANDREW BOYD THOMPSON, JR.

Corporate Executive. Personal: Born March 30, 1930; Son of Mr. and Mrs. A. B. Thompson, Sr.; Married June Guy, Daughter of Mr. and Mrs. Leon D. Guy. Father of Guy Bradly, Eric Kiepp. Education: Graduate, Sidney Lanier High School, Montgomery, Alabama, 1948; Attended Auburn University, Auburn, Alabama, 1948-49; Completed G.E.D. Tests for First and Second Year College Level, 1952; Completed 8th Infantry Division's Leaders Course 1951, Third Army's Chemical Defense School Part I 1951, Third Army's Army Discussion Leaders Course 1951, United States Army Officer Candidate School 1952, Chemical Associate Company Officer Course 1953, Chemical Corps' Smoke Service Course 1953, Infantry Officer Career Course 1965, United States Army Command and General Staff Officer Course 1969, National Security Management Course (correspondence) 1974. Military: Joined Alabama National Guard 1949, Active Duty with United States Army 1951-53, Commissioned Second Lieutenant in Chemical Corps 1952, Assistant Training Officer in Chemical Replacement Training Center at Fort McClellan, Alabama 1952, Platoon Leader with 388th Chemical Smoke Generator Company in Korea 1953, Served with United States Army Reserve 1954-80, Assistant Plans and Training Officer with 466th Engineer (Combat) Battalion 1954, Command and General Staff Officer Course Instructor 1970-80, Detachment Commander of Montgomery Branch of 3385th United States Army Reserve School 1975-80, Retired with the rank of Lieutenant Colonel 1980. Career: Materials Engineer Assistant, Alabama Highway Department, 1949-51; Laboratory Manager, Technician, Montgomery Branch of Southern Testing Laboratories, 1955; Salesman and Store Manager, Mel's Photo/Shop 21, Montgomery, Alabama; Insurance Agent, The Prudential Insurance Company of America, 1957-58; Furniture Salesman, Sears, Roebuck and Company, 1966; Vice President, General Manager, Editor, National Photo Pricing Service Inc., 1966-81; President, National Pricing Service, Inc., 1981 to present. Organizational Memberships: Photo Marketing Association International; Photographic Manufacturers and Distributors Association; National Audio-Visual Association; Professional Photographers of America; Life Member, Reserve Officers Association of the United States; National Association of Atomic Veterans. Community Activities: The Military Order of the World Wars; Montgomery Area Chamber of Commerce; Alabama Chamber of Commerce; International Platform Association; Epilepsy Chapter of the Montgomery Area, Co-Founder, President, Chairman of Board of Directors, Past President, Past Vice President, Past Secretary; 31st Infantry "Dixie" Division Club, Past President, Past Vice President, Past Secretary; Mensa; Life Patron, American Biographical Institute; Fellow, American Biographical Institute Research Association; Life Fellow, International Biographical Association; Pi Kappa Alpha Social Fraternity; The American Legion; Past Member, Veterans of Foreign Wars; Alabama Governor James' Task Force on Epilepsy; Assistant Scoutmaster, Cub Roundtable Commissioner with Boy Scouts of America; Instructor of Photography Merit Badge Course, Girl Scouts of America. Honors and Awards: American Legion Medal for Outstanding Platoon Leader in High School Reserve Officers Training Corps, 1948; Competed for General Gorgas Science Scholarship, Awarded Money and Title of General Gorgas Scholar, 1948; Decorated Army Commendation Medal, Good Conduct Medal, National Defense Service Medal, Korean Service Medal with 2 Campaign Stars, Army Reserve Components Achievement Medal with 2 Oak Leaf Clusters, Armed Forces Reserve Medal with 10-Year Device, United Nations Service Medal, Meritorious Unit Commendation with Oak Leaf Cluster, 2 Republic of Korea Presidential Unit Citations, Expert Marksmanship Badge for Pistol, Sharpshooter Marksmanship Badges for Rifle and Carbine; American Red Cross 4-Gallon Blood Donor Award; Honorary Member, Editorial Advisory Board, American Biographical Institute, 1980-81, 1981-82; Certificates of Appreciation from Civic Groups for Talks on Photography; Listed in *Dictionary of International Biography, Men of Achievement, International Who's Who in Community Service, Men and Women of Distinction, International Register of Profiles, Who's Who in the South and Southwest, Personalities of the South, Notable Americans, Personalities of America, Community Leaders of America, The American Registry Series, Book of Honor, The Directory of Distinguished Americans, Contemporary Personalities.* Address: 4353 Amherst Road, Montgomery, Alabama 36116.■

TWO THOUSAND NOTABLE AMERICANS

BARBARA STORCK THOMPSON

Education Consultant. Personal: Born October 15, 1924; Daughter of John Storck; Married Glenn T. Thompson; Mother of David C., James T. Education: B.S., University of Wisconsin at Platteville, 1956; M.S. 1959, Ph.D. 1969, University of Wisconsin at Madison; Honorary Doctorate of Human Letters, Carroll College, 1974; Further Studies at the University of Iowa, Mt. Mary College, Edgewood College, University of Wisconsin at Milwaukee. Career: Education Consultant, Wisconsin Department of Public Instruction, 1973 to present; Wisconsin State Superintendent of Public Instruction, 1973-81; Consultant, Wisconsin Department of Public Instruction, 1964-73; Administrator, Principal, School Supervisor, Reading Specialist, College Instructor, Curriculum Coordinator, Classroom Teacher, 1944-64. Organizational Memberships: National Council of Administrative Women in Education; National Council of State Consultants in Elementary Education, President 1974-75; American Association of School Administrators; Wisconsin Association of School District Administrators; National, Wisconsin, Southwestern Wisconsin, Southeastern Wisconsin Associations for Supervision and Curriculum Development; National and Wisconsin Elementary School Principals Associations; Pi Lambda Theta; Alpha Beta; Parent Teacher Association; National Education Association; Wisconsin Education Association, Life Member; Southern Wisconsin Education Association; Wisconsin Education Research Association; National Department of Elementary-Kindergarten-Nursery Education; National Association of Childhood Education International; Madison Branch, Association of Childhood Education; National Association for the Advancement of Colored People; Delta Kappa Gamma; Education Commission of the States. Honors and Awards: Outstanding Service to National Advisory Committee on Child Abuse, Education Commission of the States; Concerned Educator of the Arts Award, Wisconsin Arts Education Association; Degree of Honorary American Farmer, National Future Farmers of America; Honorary D.E.C.A. Member, Distributive Education Clubs of America, Wisconsin Vocational Student Organization, 1978; County 4-H Club Recognition Award, Dane County 4-H Club Organization, 1977; State 4-H Alumni Recognition Award, Cooperative Extension Service, 1977; Distinguished National Alumnus Recognition Award, National 4-H Clubs of America, 1977; Honorary Association Membership, Wisconsin Association of Agricultural Instructors, 1977; Distinguished Alumnus Award, University of Wisconsin at Platteville, 1977; Honorary State Farmer, Future Farmers of America, 1976; Certificate of Appreciation, Wisconsin Library Association, 1976; Certificate Awarded for Creation of Committee for Non-Sexist Textbooks, Wisconsin Women's Political Committee, 1976; Certificate of Membership, International Association of Lion's Clubs Lioness Club, 1976; Certificate of Appreciation, Wisconsin School Food Services A.S.F.S.A. and W.S.F.S.A, 1976; Certificate of Membership, Educare, University of Wisconsin-Oshkosh, 1976; Certificate of Distinguished Service, American Legion, Badger Boys State, 1975; Certificate of Appreciation, Wisconsin Secondary School Administrators; Outstanding Service Award, Wisconsin Association of Vocational Agricultural Instructors, 1974; Distinguished Service Award, Bloomer Chapter, Future Farmers of America, 1974; State Conservation Award, Madison Lions Club, 1974; Woman of the Year, National Council of Administrative Women in Education, 1974; Featured as "Your Madisonian," November 1, 1970; Waukesha Freeman Recipient to Attend Two-Week Workshop on Use of Newspaper in the Classroom, University of Iowa; Nominated to *Who's Who in America, Who's Who in Government, Leaders in Education;* Listed in *Dictionary of International Biography, Personalities of the West and Midwest.* Address: 3591 Sabaka Trail, Verona, Wisconsin 53593.■

DAMON LEON THOMPSON

Professor of English. Personal: Born May 14, 1930; Son of Mr. and Mrs. B. F. Thompson (deceased); Married Jean Sheets. Education: Attended Sinclair College, 1953-54; B.F.A., Ohio State University, 1957; M.F.A., University of Iowa, 1961; Postgraduate Studies at Ohio State University, Bucknell University. Military: Served in the United States Army Signal Corps, 1951-53, attaining the rank of Corporal. Career: Instructor in English, Marshall University, 1961-63; Instructor in English, Dakota State College, 1963-64; Instructor in English, Slippery Rock University, 1964-67; Assistant Professor in English 1967-78, Professor of English 1978 to present, Williamsport Area Community College. Organizational Memberships: National Education Association; Pennsylvania State Education Association; W.A.C.C.E.A. Community Activities: Lycoming County (Pennsylvania) Historical Society; Friends of the J. V. Brown Library (Williamsport, Pennsylvania). Honors and Awards: First Prize, Winning Story, N.S.A.L.,1959; Literary Scholarship, University of Iowa, 1960; Literary Fellow, University of Iowa, 1960-61; Medalist Certificate, Columbia University, 1972; Plaque in Recognition of Contributions to Arts and Education, Historical Preservations of America, 1982. Address: 638 Fourth Avenue, Williamsport, Pennsylvania 17701.■

JACK W. THOMPSON

Executive. Personal: Born August 12, 1925; Son of Mrs. Willis E. Thompson; Married Pollie Ann, Daughter of Mrs. Irving Newcomb; Father of Sharon Layne, Jon Randall, Susan Gay, Jay Rodger. Education: Attended Texas A&M University, 1943-44; B.S.M.E., Southern Methodist University, 1949. Military: Served in the United States Army during World War II, attaining the rank of First Lieutenant. Career: Executive Vice President, Senior Vice President and Regional Manager 1980-83, Sam P. Wallace Company; Executive Vice President, Wallace International, 1976-80; Manager and Vice President, Sam P. Wallace Company, Dallas Division, 1971-76; Executive Vice President, George Linskie Company, Inc., 1964-71; Vice President and Division Manager, Natkin and Company, Lincoln, Nebraska, 1959-64; General Manager, Fagan A/C Company, Little Rock, Arkansas, 1951-59. Organizational Memberships: M.C.A.A., Board of Directors 6 Years; A.S.H.R.A.E., Director and Regional Chairman 6 Years, Director at Large 1 Year; N.E.B.B., Director 3 Years; M.C.A. of Texas and Dallas; Dallas Chapter, A.S.H.R.A.E.; Founding Member, North Texas Contractors Association; National Society of Professional Engineers; Texas Society of Professional Engineers; American Society of Mechanical Engineers. Community Activities: United Fund; Young Life Campaign; Chairman, Mechanical Code Committee, N.C.T.C.O.G.; City of Dallas Mechanical Appeals Board; Chairman Mechanical Code Committee, City of Dallas. Honors and Awards: Distinguished Service Award 1971, Fellow 1974, Engineer of Year in Dallas Chapter 1975, A.S.H.R.A.E.; Distinguished Service Award, Mechanical Contractors Association of America, 1981. Address: 215 Steeplechase Drive, Irving, Texas 75062.■

MARGARET DRODY THOMPSON

Association Founder, Editor and Publisher, Business Owner, Genealogist, Writer. Personal: Born April 21, 1931; Daughter of Harold Orson and Bernice Alice Floyd Drody (deceased); Married K. Reed, Son of Howard (deceased) and LaRue Head Thompson; Mother of Larry Stephen, Fred Lamar. Education: Private Voice Instruction with Ruby Leite, Dean Pryor, Eula Transou Ligon, Nicolo Lomascolo; Atlanta Academy of Modeling, 1950; B.S. Music, Radford College, 1970. Career: Founder, The Genealogical Association for Uncommon Surnames; Editor and Publisher, Journals Reporting Research; Owner, Personally Yours Tours; Genealogist; Former Occupations as Private Secretary, Concert Performer, Writer, Public Relations Person, Public School Music Instructor; Feature Story Interviews as Newspaper Reporter have included Stars of the Operatic Stage, Movie Personalities, Television Stars and Political Statesmen. Organizational Memberships: Thursday Morning Music Club, Director, Vice President, Recording Secretary, Concert Series Sales Coordinator, 1959-63; Mu Phi Epsilon; Kappa Delta Pi; Representative, Roanoke County Education Association, 1978-80. Community Activities: League of Women Voters, Moderator 1959-61, Voter's Service Chairman 1957-59; Den Mother, Cub Scouts, 1957-63; Boy Scouts Merit Badge Counselor, 1971-74; Instructor, Viginia Music Camp, 1972-74; Public Relations for Schools; Founder and President, Clan Macivor Society in America, 1982 to present. Religion: Church Soloist, 1945-77; Director of Youth and Adult Choirs. Honors and Awards: Member 1973 Visiting Committee for Southern Association of School Accreditation; Awards of Merit, Southeastcon '79 Conference of Electrical and Electronic Engineers, for Contribution as Social Chairman of Conference; Roanoke County Education Association Recognition for Outstanding Service for Salary Negotiations for 1980-81; Named Citizen Mother, League of Women Voters, 1962 to present; Guest Editor, *Roanoke World News* in conjunction with Municipal Days Celebration; Member Rebecca Motte Chapter, Charleston, South Carolina, Daughters of the American Revolution; Roanoke Chapter, United Daughters of the Confederacy, Current Third Vice President; Seventeenth Century Colonial Dames; Hugenot Society of South Carolina. Address: 4528 Wyndale Avenue, S.W., Roanoke, Virginia 24018.■

ROBERT NORMAN THOMPSON

Professor of Political Science, Publishing Company Executive. Personal: Born May 17, 1914; Married Hazel Maxine Kurth, May 4, 1939; Father of Grace Arlone Brunner, Alice Maxine Miller, George Raymond, David Dale, Lois Marie, Paul Andrew, Robert Makonner, Stephen Jones. Education: B.Sc. and Teacher's Certificate, 1934; D.C., Palmer College, 1939; F.R.G.S. (London), 1950; LL.D., Wheaton College, 1972. Military: Served in the Royal Canadian Air Force, Squadron Leader; Imperial Ethiopian Air Force, Colonel; 78th Frazer Highlander, Lieutenant Colonel Retired. Career: Professor of Political Science, 1965 to present; President, Omega Publications, 1981 to present; Executive Director, Kildonan Foundation; Chairman, Board of Trustees, Aavangen Foundation; Chairman, Board of Directors, Fraser Academy; Board of Directors, Roman Corporation, World Concern of Canada, Samaritan Purse Inc.; Parole Board, Province of British Columbia; Member of Parliament, Canada, 1962-72; Superintendent of Education, 1952-60; Director General, Education, Ethiopia, 1946-52; Headmaster, Secondary School, 1945-46; Teacher and Lecturer, 1934-37; President 1960-62, Party Leader 1962-67, Social Credit Party of Canada; Fellow, Royal Geographic Society, 1950 to present. Community Activities: Registrar, War Mobilization, Canada; Commissioner, Boy Scouts, 1947-48; Gideon International,

TWO THOUSAND NOTABLE AMERICANS

1960 to present; Rotary International, 1962 to present; Centennial Committee of Canada, 1964-65. Religion: Free Church of Canada, Priorities Commission 1978-79; Evangelic Free Church, Canada. Honors and Awards: Grand Officer, Star of Ethiopia, 1967; Silver Star, Royal Life Saving, 1981; Knight Commander, Order of St. Lazarus, 1964; Jubilee Medal, 1975; Centennial Medal, 1967. Address: 180 Madrona Drive, Anacortes, Washington 98221.■

VIVIAN O. THOMPSON

Charge Nurse. Personal: Born November 30, 1925; Daughter of Luther and Cora (Baugh) Thompson (deceased). Education: Diploma, Richlands High School, Richlands, Virginia, 1944; Diploma, Knoxville General Hospital School of Nursing, Knoxville, Tennessee, 1947; Classes and Seminars in Nursing, Southwest Community College, Richlands, Virginia, 1973-82. Career: Charge Nurse 11-7, Obstetrical Department, C.V.C. Hospital, Richlands, Virginia, 1979-82; Supervisor, Obstetrical Department, General Hospital, Knoxville, Tennessee, 1947-48; General Duty, C.V.C. Hospital, Richlands, Virginia, 1948-52; Industrial Nursing, Morocco, Africa, 1952-56; Supervisor, C.V.C., Richland, Virginia, 1957-61; Charge Nurse, Bluefield Sanitarium, Bluefield, West Virginia, 1961-65; Charge Nurse, Rochingham Memorial Hospital, Harrisonburg, Virginia, 1965-68; Supervisor, C.V.C. Hospital, Richland, Virginia, 1968-69. Organizational Memberships: National League of Nursing; Virginia League of Nursing; Registered Nurse in Tennessee, West Virginia, Virginia; Former Member, American Association of Industrial Nurses and the United States Corps of Nurses. Religion: Member Richlands Presbyterian Church. Honors and Awards: Certificate of Achievement, C.V.C. Hospital, Richlands, Virginia, 1979. Address: 205 Pennsylvania Avenue, Richlands, Virginia 24641.■

PAUL E. THOMS

Educator, Musician. Personal: Born April 16, 1936; Son of Augusta and S. C. Thoms (deceased); Married Marion Cox, Daughter of Virginia and M.A. Cox (deceased); Father of Melinda Thoms-Unklesbay, Monica Thoms-Frederking. Education: Attended Kentucky Wesleyan College; B.Mus., University of Kentucky; Private Study in New York with Katherine Oaks, Norman Myrvik; M.Mus., Miami University; Postgraduate Studies and Workshops at Indiana University, Millikin University, California State College, Baldwin-Wallace Conservatory, Ohio State University, Others; Professional Supervisors Certificate; Permanent Special Certificate in Music. Career: Curriculum Coordinator, Fairfield City Schools; Appearances in Opera and Musical Plays including "Dido and Aneas," "The Mikado," "Down in the Valley," "The Barber of Seville," "Hansel and Gretel," "South Pacific," "Carousel," "Guys and Dolls," "Showboat," "Kiss Me Kate," "Amahl and the Night Visitors"; Solo Appearances in Handel's "Messiah," Bach's "Christmas Oratoria" and "Coffee Cantata," Mendelssohn's "Elijah," Haydn's "The Creation," Mozart's "Requiem" and Shubert's "Mass in G"; Numerous Solo Appearances with the Hamilton Symphony Orchestra and the Hamilton Choral Society; Former Baritone Soloist for Temple Beth Israel and First Church of Christ Scientist, Both in Hamilton (Ohio); Roles in "Our Town," "Hayfever," "Romeo and Juliet," Others; Founder and Director, Nationally Acclaimed Fairfield Choraliers; Seminars and Workshops Taught at University of Cincinnati, University of Southern California, Murray State University, University of Iowa, Others; Staff Announcer, Radio WHOH-FM, Hamilton; with WOMI, Owensboro, Kentucky, 2 Years. Organizational Memberships: Association for Supervision and Curriculum Development; Alliance for Arts in Education; National Association of Jazz Educators; American Choral Directors Association, Life Member; International Platform Association; Federation Internationale des Choeurs d'Enfants; Kappa Delta Phi; Alpha Psi Omega; Phi Mu Alpha; National Thespian Society, Honorary Life Member; Tempo Club, Honorary Life Member; Kiwanis International, Honorary Life Member; National School Public Relations Association; Actors Equity Association; Life Member, Ohio Music Education Association; Life Member, Music Educators National Conference; Modern Music Masters; Ohio Valley Curriculum Council; President-Elect, Ohio Music Education Association; President-Elect, Tri-M International Music Honor Society; Ohio Representative to National Committee of Jazz and Show Choirs, American Choral Directors Association. Community Activities: Active Clinician in Areas of Music Administration and Public Relations, Frequent Appearances as Speaker on State, National and International Conference Programs; Executive Board, Torch International, Butler County; Executive Board, Drugs on Alert; National Adjudication Panel, Johnny Mann's Great American Choral Festival; Advisory Board, Queen City Suburban Press; Adjudicator for State and Regional Choral Festivals. Published Works: Columnist for *School Musician* Magazine; Books in Progress, *Public Relations — The Image of Your Total Music Program* and *Administering the Successful School Music Program*. Honors and Awards: Honored by Ohio Senate Resolution; "Paul Thoms Day" Established by Mayoral Proclamation and by Resolution of Board of Education; One of Ten Most Outstanding School Music Directors in the United States and Canada, *School Musician* Magazine; Listed in *International Who's Who in Music, Personalities of America, Men and Women of Distinction, Community Leaders of America, Dictionary of International Biography, Men of Achievement, Who's Who in American Music, Notable Americans of the Bicentennial Era, Personalities of the West and Midwest, Community Leaders and Noteworthy Americans, The Directory of Distinguished Americans, International Who's Who in Community Service.* Address: 128 South D Street, Hamilton, Ohio 45013.■

MINNIE ESTHER THORNE

Educator, Supervisor of Public Health Nurses, Registered Nurse. Personal: Born November 3, 1901; Daughter of Ichabod Redmond and Mary Etta Greene Thorne. Education: Studies for Teaching Certificate at East Carolina University, University of North Carolina at Chapel Hill, Appalachian State University; Graduate of the Medical College of Virginia; Postgraduate Study, University of North Carolina at Chapel Hill; Attended College of William and Mary. Career: Teacher, Wilson County School System, 8 Years; Public Health Nurse, Onslow, Duplin, Hertford and Johnston Counties, North Carolina, 23 Years; Supervisor of Public Health Nurses, Johnston County, North Carolina Health Department, 1945-60; Rural Pioneer Health Nurse, Onslow County, North Carolina, 1937, Established Maternity and Infancy Clinics, School Inspections, and Instructed Midwives in Health Care for Mothers and Babies. Organizational Memberships: Former Member, North Carolina State Nurses Association, North Carolina Legislative Committee (appointed twice); Former Member, United States Public Health Association. Community Activities: Instrumental in Initiating Action among Various Civic and Religious Groups for Contributions Sufficient to Establish a Crippled Children's Clinic as Part of Johnston County, North Carolina Health Department, 1955; Provide Local Radio Programs, Johnston County, North Carolina on Home and Office Safety and Fire Prevention and Safety for the Aging, 15 Years; Solicited Funds, Materials, Labor to Construct a Complete Home for Destitute Tuberculin Family in Johnston County, North Carolina, 1950; Executive Board, Girl Scouts of America, Duplin, Hertford and Johnston Counties, North Carolina, 20 Years; Memberships in Senior Citizens, Church, Grange, United Daughters of the Confederacy, Religious Organizations in Wilson County, North Carolina; Appointed to Five County Council of Governments (2 terms), Region L, Advisory Council for the Aging, Rocky Mount, North Carolina; Participates in Various Clubs, Membership Drives and Projects to Generate Funds for Local Scholarship and Loan Funds for Worthy Students; Business and Professional Women's Club, Smithfield, North Carolina, 15 Years; First Historian, Harper House Bentonville Chapter, United Daughters of the Confederacy, Four Oaks, North Carolina. Religion: Member Pleasant Hope Baptist Church, Elm City, North Carolina. Honors and Awards: Recipient One-Year Scholarship for Postgraduate Study at College of William and Mary, Richmond, Virginia; First Student Nurse of Medical College of Virginia to Have an Article Published in the *American Journal of Nursing* (article described a procedure developed by her for pediatric care that was both economical and time-saving); Awarded Key from Medical College of Virginia for Participation in Dramatic and Glee Clubs; First Supervisor of Public Health Nurses in Johnston County, North Carolina Health Department, 1945-60; First Registerd Nurse in North Carolina to Pass Social Service Merit Examination for Position with Welfare Department as Case Worker; Recognized by the National Foundation for Infantile Paralysis for Ten Years of Outstanding Service and Inspiring Leadership in Fight Against Infantile Paralysis; Article on Home Safety Chosen for Publication by National Safety Council of Chicago, Illinois, in *Home Safety Inventory*, 1955; Received Personal Letter from Governor James B. Hunt of North Carolina for Outstanding Contributions to Public Health Work in North Carolina. Address: Route 3, Box 46, Elm City, North Carolina 27822.■

ALMA LANE KIRKLAND THORPE

Religious Broadcaster. Personal: Born December 20, 1941; Daughter of Pierce and Dolly Odessa Kirkland; Mother of Margie Ann. Education: Graduate, Anniston High School, Anniston, Alabama, 1960; Student, Trevecca Nazarene College, Nashville, Tennessee, 1960-61; Attended Columbia School of Broadcasting, Atlanta, Georgia. Career: Religious Broadcaster; Former Position with Southern Bell Telephone and Telegraph; Former City of Atlanta Recreation Leader. Community Activities: Miss Queen of the Southern Horse Show Participant, Anniston, Alabama, 1953-54 (sponsor: Malard Cleaners); Miss Good Posture

TWO THOUSAND NOTABLE AMERICANS

Queen Participant, Anniston, Alabama, 1959 (sponsor: Dr. Jimmy Carter, Chiropractor); Miss Maid of Cotton Participant, Anniston, Alabama, 1961 (sponsor: Anniston Country Club). Honors and Awards: Listed in *Personalities of America, Marquis Who's Who, World Who's Who of Women.* Address: 963 Beecher Street Southwest, Atlanta, Georgia 30310.■

RICHARD LEE THURMAN

Associate Professor. Personal: Born April 4, 1940, in Detroit, Michigan; Son of Mr. and Mrs. S. L. Thurman; Father of Tamara Lynn. Education: B.S.Ed., University of Houston, 1962; M.S.Ed., Southern Illinois University, 1968; Ph.D., St. Louis University, 1974. Career: Certified by American Association of Sex Educators, Counselors and Therapists as Sex Educator; Licensed by Missouri Board of Nursing Home Administrators as Nursing Home Administrator; Associate Professor 1981 to present, Assistant Professor in Special Education 1974-81, Instructor in Special Education 1972-74, University of Missouri at St. Louis; Director of Vocational Rehabilitation, St. Louis State School and Hospital, 1971-72; Vocational Rehabilitation Counselor, St. Louis State Hospital, 1967-71; Counselor/Teacher, 1962-67; Special Education Area Leader, University of Missouri-St. Louis, 1981 to present; Designed and Directed International Travel Study Courses in Denmark 1975, at University of Copenhagen and England 1975 to present, at University of London and Dillington House; Consultant to Missouri State Department of Education, Missouri Department of Mental Health, Numerous School Districts, Head Start Projects, Mental Health Association, 1968 to present. Organizational Memberships: Council for Exceptional Children, Division on Mental Retardation; American Association for Mental Deficiency; Council for Children with Behavioral Disorders. Community Activities: Assistant Director of Project Upswing, Federal Grant Program at University of Missouri at St. Louis, 1972-73; Director of Vocational Rehabilitation, St. Louis State School Hospital, 1971-72; Vocational Rehabilitation Counselor, St. Louis State Hospital, 1968-71; Industrial Therapist, St. Louis State Hospital, 1967-68; Neighborhood Youth Corps Counselor, Jefferson City, Missouri, 1966-67; Physical Education Instructor and Recreational Therapist, St. Louis State Hospital, 1963-66. Honors and Awards: Most Spirited Player, University of Houston, 1962; Listed in *Who's Who in the Midwest, Men of Achievement, Personalities of America, Personalities of the West and Midwest, Dictionary of International Biography.* Address: 1227 Weleba, St. Louis, Missouri 63121.■

DONALD HAROLD TICE

Pastor, Educational Administrator. Personal: Born April 15, 1930; Son of Mr. and Mrs. Harold S. Tice (both deceased); Married Margaret Beall, Daughter of Mr. and Mrs. Joshua James Henry Beall (both deceased); Father of Thomas Marshall, Jonathan William. Education: B.S. Business Administration (Accounting), Bob Jones University. Career: Pastor; Chairman of the Board of Directors, Goldsboro Christian School, 1975 to present; Manager of Financial Affairs, Bob Jones University, 1971-74. Religion: President, Bridgeton Christian School, 1965-68; Founder/President, Ambassador Christian Academy, 1966-68; President, Gloucester County Christian School Board of Directors, 1966-70. Honors and Awards: President of Sophomore Class, Bob Jones University, 1950; Listed in *Who's Who Among Students in American Universities and Colleges.* Address: 6100 Morningside Avenue, Sioux City, Iowa 51106.■

REIN TIDEIKSAAR

Assistant Professor. Education: Studies in Psychology/Sociology, University of Maryland, 1972-74; B.A. Sociology, Hofstra University, 1974; Certificate of Professional Achievement, State University of New York at Stonybrook, 1976; B.S. Physician Assistant, Stonybrook University, 1976; Certified 1976, Recertification 1979, Physician Assistants National Board; Post-Baccalaureate Multidisciplinary Gerontological Studies Certificate, Adelphi University, 1979; M.S. Gerontology, Columbia Pacific University; Ph.D. Geriatrics and Gerontology, Columbia Pacific University, 1980. Career: Assistant Professor, Allied Health and Family Medicine, Health Science Center, State University of New York at Stonybrook, 1980 to present; Clinical Faculty Appointment, State University of New York at Stonybrook, 1979; Clinical Assistant Professor, College of Allied Health Professions, Hahnemann Medical College, 1982; Adjunct Lecturer, Harlem Physician Assistant Program, City University of New York. Organizational Memberships: American Academy of Physician Assistants, Chairman Geriatric Care Section; American Association of Public Health; American Medical Writers Association; New York State Society of Physician Assistants; New York City Public Health Association; Gerontological Society of America; Executive Board, Newsletter Editor, Chairman Publications Committee, Northeast Gerontological Society; Contributing Editor, *Health Practitioner* Magazine; Consulting Editor, *Hospital Physician*; Editor for Geriatric Health Letter, 1978-79. Honors and Awards: Henry L. Schwartz Brookdale Foundation Scholarship for the Pursuit of Gerontological Studies, 1978-79; Placed First in 14th Annual Scientific Journal Contest, Long Island Jewish-Hillside Medical Center/Queens Hospital, 1979; Achievement Award in Medical Writing, 16th Annual Scientific Journal Contest, 1981; Placed 2nd in 17th Annual Scientific Journal Contest, 1982; Best Medical Lecturer for Academic Year 1980-81, Long Island University Physician Assistants Program, New York; Listed in *International Authors and Writers Who's Who, Men of Achievement.*■

HOPE ELIZABETH JOHNSON TIEMEYER

Advertising Company Executive. Personal: Born May 20, 1908, in Fort Wayne, Indiana; Daughter of Edward Tibbens and Burton Meyers Johnson; Married Edwin H. Tiemeyer (deceased), October 30, 1929; Mother of Ann Elizabeth T. Lewin, Edwin Houghton (deceased). Education: B.A., University of Cincinnati, 1932. Career: Owner, Mail-Way Advertising Company (Cincinnati), 1955 to present. Community Activities: Daughters of the American Revolution, Cincinnati Chapter, Regent 1956-58, Chairman of National School Survey Committee 1961-62, National Vice Chairman of Americanism Manual for Citizenship 1962-65, Continental Congress Program Committee 1962-65, Congress Marshall Committee 1966-68, Congress Hostess Committee 1969-75; President, Officers Club, 1974-77; National Chairmen's Association, Recording Secretary 1969-71; Children of the American Revolution, Senior National Membership Chairman 1958-60, Senior National Recording Secretary 1960-62; Mountain School, National Chairman 1962-64, Honorary Senior National Vice President 1963-64, Senior National First Vice President 1964-66, Senior National President 1966-68, Honorary National Life President 1970 to present; National Officers Club, First Vice President 1965-69, President 1970-73, Honorary Senior Life President of Ohio Society; Ohio Congress of Parent-Teacher Associations, Honorary Life Member, Treasurer 1957-62, Vice President and Director of Department of Health 1962-63; National Congress of Parent-Teacher Associations, Honorary Life Member; Kappa Alpha Theta Mothers Club, Life Member, President 1958-59; Cincinnati Symphony Orchestra, Vice President Women's Committee 1964-65; University of Cincinnati Parents Club, President 1959-61, Vice President 1963-64; State House Conference on Education, Area Chairman 1953; American Association of University Women, Director 1963-64; Cincinnati Social Health Board, Member 1950-78, Executive Committee 1965-70, Vice President 1973-78, Treasurer 1975-78, Life Trustee 1978; Singleton's of Cincinnati Club, President 1969-71, Travelers Board President 1973-74, Art Committee 1971 to present, Memberships Committee 1973-78; Newtown Garden Club, President 1947-49; City Panhellenic Association, President 1930-32, National Admissions Committee 1933-35; Craftshow for Handicapped, Life Member; Zonta Club of Cincinnati, Chairman Amelia Earhart Fellowship Committee 1963-64, Program

Chairman 1964-65, Orientation Chairman 1965-67, International Relations Chairman 1967-68, Director 1969-74, Executive Committee 1969-73, National Nominating Committee 1970-73, Vice President 1971-73; Cincinnati Women's Club, Music Committee, Tearoom Committee 1969 to present; Queen City Chapter, National Association of Parliamentarians, Treasurer 1965-69; Cincinnati Chapter, Freedoms Foundation of Valley Forge, Vice President 1974-76, President 1978-80, Secretary 1980-83. Honors and Awards: Jonathon Moore Citation and Award, Sons of the American Revolution, 1967; Good Citizenship Medal, National Society, 1967; National Platform Association; English Speaking Union; Order of Kentucky Colonels; National Gavel Association. Address: 2786 Little Dry Run Road, Cincinnati, Ohio 45244.■

BILL W. TILLERY

Professor. Personal: Born September 15, 1938; Married Patricia Weeks Northrop; Father of Tonya Lynn, Lisa Gail. Education: B.S., Northeastern University, 1960; M.A. 1965, Ed.D. 1967, University of Northern Colorado. Career: Professor, Department of Physics, Arizona State University; Associate Professor, Arizona State University, 1973-75; Associate Professor and Director of Science and Mathematics Teaching Center, University of Wyoming, 1969-73; Assistant Professor, Florida State University, 1967-69; Teacher, Jefferson County (Colorado), 1962-64; Physics and Chemistry Teacher, Guthrie (Oklahoma), 1960-62. Organizational Memberships: National Science Teachers Association; Association for the Education of Teachers in Science; National Association for Research in Science Teaching; Arizona Science Teaching Association. Community Activities: Arizona Advisory Council on Energy Education, 1979 to present; State Resource Committee on Energy Education, 1980 to present; Arizona Science Teachers Association Editorial Board, 1980 to present; Flinn Foundation Advisory Council on Health Education, 1982 to present. Published Works: Editor, *Arizona Energy Education*, 1977 to present; Editor, Journal of the Arizona Science Teachers Association, 1978 to present; Author of Co-Author of 20 Books, 18 Sets of Audiovisual Materials, 29 Energy Monographs. Honors and Awards: Fellow, American Association for the Advancement of Science, 1971; Elected Outstanding University Educator, University of Wyoming, 1973. Address: 9103 South Kachima Drive, Tempe, Arizona 85284.■

CELESTINE TILLMAN

Associate Professor of Chemistry. Personal: Born December 12, 1933, in Trout, Louisiana; Daughter of Elbert Lee Sr. and Lillie Tillman (both deceased). Education: B.S. Chemistry and Mathematics, Southern University, 1955; M.S. Inorganic/Analytical Chemistry, Howard University, 1957; Doctoral Fellow, Inorganic/Analytical Chemistry, Pennsylvania State University, 1958-61; Further Studies at Louisiana State University (1968-72), Southern University (Summers 1979, 1980, 1981). Career: Associate Professor of Chemistry 1979 to present, Assistant Professor of Chemistry 1963-79, Instructor in Chemistry 1957-63, Southern University; Graduate Research Assistant, Pennsylvania State University, 1959-61; Graduate Teaching Assistant, Howard University, 1955-57; Research Associateship, Navy Ocean Systems Center, San Diego, Summers 1982 and 1983. Organizational Memberships: American Association for the Advancement of Science; American Chemical Society; National Organization for the Professional Advancement of Black Chemists and Chemical Engineers; Louisiana Academy of Sciences; Association for Women in Science; Baton Rouge Analytical Instrument Discussion Group. Honors and Awards: Research Grant, "Stability of Amberlite LA-2 to Acid Nitrite Solutions," Supported by Atlantic Richfield Hanford Company, 1976-77; NORCUS Research Summer Fellow, Atlantic Richfield Hanford Company, Summer 1973, Summer 1977; National Science Foundation Faculty Fellow, Louisiana State University, Summers 1968, 1969, 1971; Graduate Research Fellow, Pennsylvania State University, 1958-61. Community Activities: Delta Sigma Theta, Golden Life Member; National Council of Negro Women, State Organizer; The Eye Foundation of America; Community Association for the Welfare of School Children; Young Women's Christian Association; National Association for the Advancement of Colored People; Audubon Council Girl Scouts; League of Women Voters; Louisiana Council on Human Relations. Honors and Awards: Service Award, Southern University Chapter, Phi Delta Kappa International, 1982; Chemistry Teacher of the Year, Southern University, 1978-79; Phi Delta Kappa; Iota Sigma Pi; Sigma Delta Epsilon; Beta Kappa Chi; Alpha Kappa Mu; Kappa Delta Pi; Phi Sigma; Listed in *International Who's Who of Intellectuals, World Who's Who of Women, Who's Who in America, Who's Who in the South and Southwest, Book of Honor, The Directory of Distinguished Americans, Community Leaders of America, Personalities of America, Personalities of the South*. Address: 10761 South Gibbens Drive, Baton, Rouge, Louisiana 70807.■

MAYRE LUTHA TILLMAN

Field Representative. Personal: Born August 24, 1928; Mother of Daniel Parl, Shayla Denise. Education: Attended Florida State University, Tallahassee, Florida; Alladin Business College, Eau Gallie, Florida. Career: Field Representative, Department of Insurance and State Treasurer Tampa Service Officer, Tampa, Florida, 1982 to present; Consultant and Lobbyist, Self-Employed, 1980-82; Administrative Assistant, E. F. Hutton and Company, Tampa, Florida, 1979-80; Executive Assistant, Florida Democratic Party, Tallahassee, Florida, 1976-78; Counselor, Hillsborough County Housing Assistance Department, Tampa, Florida, 1976; Administrator of Property Management, Tampa-Hillsborough County Expressway Authority, Right of Way Division, Tampa, Florida, 1973-74; Tax Clerk, Clerk of the Circuit Court, Hillsborough County Courthouse, Tampa, Florida, 1970-73; Office Manager, Bumby and Stimpson, Inc., Plant City, Florida, 1968-70; Administrative Assistant, Dave Gordon Enterprises, Tampa, Florida, 1965-68; Administrative Assistant and Loan Officer, Lakeland Federal Savings and Loan Association, Lakeland, Florida, 1965; Administrative Assistant, Space Technology Laboratories, Cape Canaveral, Florida, 1960-64. Organizational Memberships: American Right of Way Association, Florida Chapter #26, 1973-64; Community Activities: Business and Professional Women's Club, Chairman of Convention 1982, President of Plant City Club 1967-69, Chairman of Membership and Expansion for District VII, Chairman of Legislative for District VII, Chairman of Talent Bank for Florida Federation 1970, Organized First Talent Bank in State to Promote More Women to Become Active in seeking Appointments for Policy Making Positions in Government 1970, Chairman of Legislation for Florida Federation; Plant City Women's Club, Chairman of Public Affairs 1978-80, Parliamentarian 1980-82; East Hillsborough County Historical Society; Democratic Executive Committee of Florida, Vice Chairman for 7th Congressional District on Central Committee 1974-76 and 1980 to present, Chairman for 7th Congressional District on Central Committee 1976-77, Campaign Committee 1976, 1978 and 1980, Convention Committee 1975, 1977, 1979, 1981, 1983, Member of Central Committee-at-Large 1974, Rules Committee, Credentials Committee, ERA Coordinator for Florida, National Committeewoman for Florida 1980-84; Democratic Women's Clubs of Florida, Inc.; Hillsborough County Democratic Executive Committee; Executive Assistant for Florida Democratic Party, President and Charter Member of East Hillsborough Democratic Club; 1980 Candidate for Florida House of Representative; Elected Director of Southern Region for the National Federation of Democratic Women, 1981-82; Member Duke University Forum on Presidential Nominations; Worked on Many Committees for Local and State Party Functions and Candidates; Appointed by Governor Askew to the Florida Host Committee for the 1972 Democratic National Convention at Miami Beach; Served on Sub-Committee for Woman's Activities: Carter-Mondale Steering Committee, 1976-80; Florida Delegate-at-Large for Jimmy Carter, 1976 Democratic National Convention in New York City; Elected Delegate for 8th Congressional District to the Democratic National Mid-Term Conference in Memphis, Tennessee, 1978; Elected Delegate for Jimmy Carter for 8th Congressional District to the Democratic National Convention in New York City, 1980; Appointed to Credential Committee for the National Federation of Democratic Women 1980, Chairperson 1981; Consultant and Campaign Chairman for Representative James T. Hargrett, Jr.; Chairman of Southern Region, Women's Caucus of the Democratic National Committee. Honors and Awards: Honorary Colonel, State of Mississippi; Honorary Colonel, State of Kentucky. Listed in *Who's Who in American Politics, Community Leaders and Noteworthy Americans, Personalities of the South, Prominent People in Florida Government, The Directory of Distinguished Americans, The American Registry Series, The World Who's Who of Women, Personalities of America, Who's Who of American Women*. Address: P.O. Box 97, Dover, Florida 33527.■

RALPH H. TINDALL

Retired Professor of Psychology. Personal: Born March 29, 1914; Son of Louis F. and Ednah B. Tindall (deceased); Married Thelma Barth, Daughter of Fred and Susie Barth (deceased). Education: B.A., Cedarville College, 1935; M.A., Ohio State University, 1946; Ph.D., Ohio State University, 1952. Military: Served in the Army Ground Forces, Mediterranean Theatre, 1943-45. Career: Director of Psychological Services, Milwaukee Public Schools, 1953-63; Professor of Psychology, University of South Carolina. Organizational Memberships: President Division 16, American Psychological Association, 1963-64; President, South Carolina Psychological Association, 1965. Community Activities: Sponsored the Establishment of the South Carolina School Psychological Association; One of the Fonders of Wisconsin School Psychological Association; Former Board Member, Lad Lake Inc., Dousman, Wisconsin; One of Founders of *Journal of School Psychology*. Religion: Humanist. Honors and Awards: Outstanding Contribution as a Psychologist, South Carolina Association of School Psychologists, 1979. Address: 2859 Gervais Street, Columbia, South Carolina 29204.■

TWO THOUSAND NOTABLE AMERICANS

THOMAS P. TINNIN

Insurance and Real Estate Development. Personal: Born May 15, 1948, in Albuquerque, New Mexico; Son of Robert and Francis Tinnin. Education: Diploma, New Mexico Military Institute; Attended the University of New Mexico 1967-69, University of Maryland 1970-71; Bachelor of Arts, University of New Mexico, 1973. Career: General Agent, Transamerica Occidental Life Insurance Company; President, Tinnin Investments Inc.; President, Tinnin Enterprises; Occidental Life Insurance Company, Albuquerque, 1972-77; Aide to U.S. Senator Clinton Anderson, 1969-72. Organizational Memberships: Million Dollar Round Table, 1982 to present; National Association of Life Underwriters, 1976 to present; New Mexico Life Leaders Association, 1981; Better Business Bureau, Board of Directors 1983. Community Activities: Greater Albuquerque Chamber of Comemrce, Member 1973 to present, Member Board of Directors 1977-78 and 1980 to present, Chairman Ambassador's Committee 1983; Albuquerque Country Club, 1973 to present; Boy Scouts of America, Manzano District, Chairman 1981-82, Finance Chairman 1983; Albuquerque Rotary Club, 1982 to present; Albuquerque Convention and Visitor's Bureau, Board Member 1982 to present; Albuquerque Armed Forces Advisory Association, Treasurer 1983; Board of Directors, St. Joseph Hospital and Health Care Foundation, 1983. Honors and Awards: Group Study Exchange Team to South and Southwest Africa, International Rotary Foundation, 1978; Honorary Commander, 1551st Flying Training Squadron, United States Air Force; Featured on Cover Story of *Money* Magazine, March 1984; Listed in *Men of Achievement, Outstanding Young Men of America, International Register of Profiles, International Book of Honor, Personalities of the West and Midwest, Personalities of America.* Address: 2700 Vista Grande, Northwest Unit #2, Albuquerque, New Mexico 87120.■

JAMES MCCALL TIPTON

Educator, Corporation Executive. Personal: Born July 20, 1948; Son of Mr. and Mrs. James Reed Tipton; Married Barbara Ann Miller, Daughter of Marie Miller; Father of James Christopher. Education: B.S. Economics, University of Tennessee-Knoxville, 1971; M.B.A. Finance 1976, M.A. Economics 1978, Ph.D. Economics 1981, University of Florida. Military: Served in the United States Army, 1971-74, attaining the rank of First Lieutenant. Career: Professor of Finance, Baylor University; President, J. M. Tipton & Associates, Inc.; Director, Financial Services, International Consulting Group, Richardson, Texas; Former Positions include Financial Consultant to Several Large Texas Banks and Savings & Loan Associations, Research Assistant to the Florida Public Utility Research Center, Treasury Analyst to Chicago Northwestern Transportation Company. Organizational Memberships: Financial Management Association; American Finance Association; American Economic Association; Southwestern Finance Association; Western Finance Association; Western Economic Association; American Institute for Religious Science. Community Activities: Sigma Chi, Eta Omega Chapter Advisor, Financial Advisor, House Corporation President, Member of Various Committees; Kiwanis International, Various Volunteer Activities and Committee Memberships; Omicron Delta Kappa, Faculty Secretary at Baylor University; Omicron Delta Epsilon, Faculty Sponsor; Financial Management Association Honor Society, Faculty Sponsor, Member Various Public Service Projects. Religion: Southern Baptist. Honors and Awards: Omicron Delta Kappa Leadership Society; Scabbard & Blade Honor Society; Omicron Delta Epsilon; Florida Public Utility Research Fellow, 1976; Outstanding Paper, Florida Public Research Center, 1977; Various Academic Honors. Address: 1016 Hummingbird Drive, Waco, Texas 76710.■

EDWARD A. TIRYAKIAN

Professor of Sociology. Personal: Born August 6, 1929; Son of Keghinee A. Tiryakian; Married Josefina Cintron, Daughter of Mr. and Mrs. Carlos Cintron; Father of Edmund Carlos A., Edwyn Ashod. Education: Associate Professor 1965-67, Professor of Sociology 1967 to present, Duke University; Lecturer, Harvard University, 1962-65; Assistant Professor, Princeton University, 1957-62; Instructor, Princeton, 1956-57; Visiting Professor, Laval University, 1978; Visiting Assistant Professor, Bryn Mawr College, 1957-59; Visiting Lecturer, University of the Philippines, 1954-55. Organizational Memberships: President, American Society for the Study of Religion, 1981-84; Executive Council, International Association of French-Speaking Sociologists, 1971 to present; American Sociological Association, Chairman Theory Section 1974-75. Religion: Armenian Gregorian Church. Honors and Awards: Summa Cum Laude Graduate, Princeton University; Phi Beta Kappa; Fulbright Research Fellowship, 1954-55; Princeton Bicentennial Preceptorship, 1959-62; Ford Foundation Faculty Fellow, 1971-72; Director, National Endowment for the Humanities Summer Seminar, 1978, 1980, 1983; Invited Fellow, Center for the Behavioral Sciences. Address: 1523 Hermitage Court, Durham, North Caroina 27707.■

TOBIE R. TITSWORTH, III

Educational Administrator. Personal: Born May 13, 1945; Son of Mr. and Mrs. T. R. Titsworth; Married Laura Jeanne Barnes, Daughter of Mr. and Mrs. Ralph Dewhirst; Father of Scottie Richard, Stephanie Ann. Education: B.S. 1967, M.S. 1973, Ed.D. 1976, Agricultural Education, Oklahoma State University; Coursework for Superintendent's Certification, Oklahoma State University, 1980; Additional Study at Texas Christian University, Washington State University, Texas A&M University, Rogers State College. Military: Served in the United States Air Force as an Aircraft Maintenance Officer, 1967-71, attaining the rank of Captain; Service in the United States Air Force Reserve since 1972, attaining the rank of Major and presently serving as Commander of the 403 Combat Logistics Support Squadron. Career: Vice President for Continuing and Technical Education, Rogers State College; Former Positions include Assistant Professor in Agricultural Engineering Department at Texas A&M University, Graduate Research Assistant in Agricultural Education Department at Oklahoma State University, Vocational Agriculture Instructor, Miami (Oklahoma) Public Schools. Organizational Memberships: American Technical Education Association, Life Member; Oklahoma Technical Society, Life Member; American Society of Agricultural Engineering, Chairman 218 Committee; American Association of Community and Junior Colleges; Council on Occupational Education; Higher Education Alumni Council. Community Activities: Oklahoma Health Systems Agency, Sub Area I, Fund Review and Nominations Committee, 1981-83; Claremore Area Chamber of Commerce, Board of Directors 1980 and 1982 to present; Northeastern Counties of Oklahoma, Board of Directors 1980 and 1981; Parent Teacher Organization, 1974 to present; Future Farmers of America Alumni Association. Religion: First Baptist Church, Deacon 1982, Sunday School Teacher 1982, 1983, 1976-78. Honors and Awards: Outstanding Teacher, Collegiate Future Farmers of America, Texas A&M University, 1978; Air Force Commendation Medal, 1980; Outstanding Student Teacher in Agricultural Education, Oklahoma State University, 1966; Listed in *International Who's Who of Intellectuals, Who's Who in the South and Southwest, Outstanding Young Men of America, Personalities of the South, Personalities of America, Who's Who Among Students in American Universities and Colleges.* Address: 1461 Paradise Park, Claremore, Oklahoma 74017.■

BARBARA TOBER

Editor-in-Chief. Personal: Born August 19, 1934; Married Donald G. Tober. Education: Studies undertaken at the Fashion Institute of Technology (New York, New York), Traphagen School of Fashion (New York, New York), New York School of Interior Design (New York, New York), Dwight-Morrow (Englewood, New Jersey), Kent Place (Summit, New Jersey). Career: Editor-in-Chief, *Bride's Magazine*, 1966 to present; Copy Editor, *Vogue Pattern Book*; Associate Beauty Editor, *Vogue*; Associate Food Editor, *Look*; Advertising and Promotion Department, Jack Braunstein Resident Buyers; Media Department, Hilton Ruggio Advertising, Geyer, Newell and Ganger Advertising. Organizational Memberships: The Fashion Group, Lifestyle Committee Chairman 1980, Member 1976-78; American Society of Magazine Editors; American Society of Interior Designers, Press Associate; National Academy of Television Arts and Sciences; Women in Communications, Inc.; Intercorporate Group. Community Activities: Wine and Food Society, Chief of Protocol 1981, Events Committee; Dames d'Escoffier; Golden's Bridge Hounds; International Side-Saddle Organization; North Salem Bridle Trail Association; National Association of Underwater Instructors; American Ballet Theater, National Council; Vivian Woodard Council of Fine Arts, 1964-65; Pan-Pacific Southeast Asia Women's Association, Inc., Communications Director 1982, National President 1982, Delegate International Conference 1981; Asia Society; China Institute; Japan Society; Arlington House Publishers, Equestrian Book Club, Connecticut, Advisory Board; Traphagen School of Fashion, New York, Advisory Board; Tobe-Coburn School for Fashion Careers, Advisory Board; Sugar Foods Corporation (Sweet'n'Low Marketing), New York, Secretary Board of Directors; Confrerie de la Chaines des Rotisseurs, Member Board of Directors and Charge de Presse, New York Baillage; Contributing Editor, *Gastronome*. Published Works: *The Bride; China: A Cognizant Guide* 1980; "Chaine Manners a Table," *Gastronome* Magazine, 1980; *The ABC's of Beauty*, 1963. Honors and Awards: *Bon Appetit* Great Cook Award, 1981; ALMA Award, 1968; Penney-Missouri Award, 1972; Traphagen Alumni Award, 1975; Tournament of Roses Rose Parade Judge, 1979; Traphagen School of Fashion Diamond Jubilee Award, 1983; Listed in *Who's Who of America, Who's Who of American Women.* Address: 620 Park Avenue, New York, New York 10021.■

EUGENIA TODD

Journalist, Assistant Activity Director, Registered Nurse, Executive. Personal: Born January 14, 1925; Daughter of Joseph and Mary Korchevsky; Married

TWO THOUSAND NOTABLE AMERICANS

Robert L.; Mother of Robert Joseph, John Burton. Education: B.S., State Teacher's College (Jersey City, New Jersey), 1947; R.N., Medical Center, Jersey City (New Jersey), 1947. Career: Journalist, "Mediapolis News"; Assistant Activity Director, Registered Nurse, Vice President and Secretary of North Hill Medical Building; Supervisor, Medical Center, Jersey City, New Jersey, 1947; General Duty, Mountainside Hospital, Glen Ridge, New Jersey, 1947-48; General Duty, Veteran's Hospital, Dearborn, Michigan, 1948-50; President, Hawkeye Nursing Registry, 1955. Organizational Memberships: Alumni Association Medical Center, Jersey City, New Jersey, 1947 to present; Officer, North Hill Medical Building, 1947 to present. Community Activities: North Hill School Parent Teacher Association, Treasurer (in the late 1950's); Citizens Committee to Save St. Francis Hospital, (late 1950's); Den Mother, Boy Scouts of America, 1950-60; Model for Norman Rockwell, 1942. Honors and Awards: Boy Scouts of America 10-Year Citation, 1960; Life Membership Art Guild of Burlington, Iowa; Listed in *Who's Who in the Midwest, Social Directory, The National Register of Prominent Americans and International Notables, Who's Who of Women of the World.* Address: 823 North Sixth Street, Burlington, Iowa 52601.■

ROBERT J. TOLLEFSON

Professor of Philosophy and Religion. Personal: Born April 6, 1927; Married; Father of Becky, Beth T. Goudschaal, Priscilla, Jeff. Education: B.S.E.E. with honors, Michigan Technological University, 1950; B.D. 1954, Th.M. 1956, Princeton Theological Seminary; Ph.D., The University of Iowa, 1963. Military: Served in the United States Naval Reserve, 1945-46 and 1950-51. Career: Professor of Philosophy and Religion, Buena Vista College, 1967 to present; Part-time Community Resource Person, Midwest Center of the National Endowment for the Humanities, 1973; Pastor, 1955-58; Graduate Assistant in Electrical Engineering, Princeton University, 1951-55; Part-time Instructor of Mathematics, Whitworth College, 1950-51. Organizational Memberships: American Society of Church History; American Academy of Religion; Society for the History of Technology; Institute of Society, Ethics and Life Sciences. Community Activities: Storm Lake Area Arts Council, First President; Storm Lake Area Advisory Council on Environmental Concerns, Chairperson; Citizens Advisory Council, Curriculum Committee; Kiwanis, Local President 1968, Lieutenant Governor of Old Division IX 1970-71; Spiritual Aims, District Chairman 1981-82; Kiwanis International Foundation, District Chairman 1982-83. Religion: Pastor, 1955-58; Congregational Presbytery, Synod and National Committees; Moderator, Synod of Lakes and Prairies, 1976-77. Honors and Awards: Faculty Study Grants, Buena Vista College, 1968, 1971; Outstanding Educator, 4 Times; National Endowment for the Humanities Summer Seminar, University of California at Los Angeles; Visiting Scholar, University of Cambridge, England, 1978-79; Listed in *Dictionary of International Biography, Dictionary of American Scholars, International Scholars Dictionary, International Who's Who of Intellectuals, Who's Who in American Education, Who's Who in Religion.* Address: 1305 Shoreway, Storm Lake, Iowa 50588.■

JOHN JARVIS TOLSON, III

United States Army Officer (Retired). Personal: Born October 22, 1915; Son of Mr. and Mrs. John J. Tolson, Jr.; Married Margaret Young; Father of David C., John J. IV, Harriet B. Education: Attended the University of North Carolina, 1932-33; B.S., United States Military Academy, 1933-37; United States Army Parachute School, 1941; Armed Forces Staff College (equivalent); Air Command and Staff College (equivalent), 1947; British Staff College, 1951; United States Army War College, 1953; United States Army Aviation School, 1957; Management, University of Pittsburgh, 1960; United States Military Assistance Institute, 1961. Military: Served in the United States Army from 2nd Lieutenant to Lieutenant General, 1937-73. Career: Officer, Regular United States Army, 1937-73; Secretary, North Carolina Department of Military and Veterans Affairs, 1973-77. Organizational Memberships: Association of the United States Army, Vice President 1974-76 & 1977-78, President 1976-77; The Airborne Association, President 1975-77; Army Aviation Association of America; American Helicopter Society; Order of Daedalians; Legion of Valor; Military Order of the Purple Heart; American Legion; Veterans of Foreign Wars; Disabled American Veterans; Retired Officers Association. Community Activities: The Army Aviation Museum Foundation, Inc., President 1977-82, Board Chairman; The Tammy Lynn Memorial Foundation, Inc., Board of Directors 1980-82, Vice President 1981-82; Budleigh Community Watch, Chairman 1979-82; Occoneechee Council of Boy Scouts of America, Executive Board 1980-84; Triangle Area Chapter, American Red Cross, Board of Directors 1982 to present; Lees McRae College Board of Advisors, 1978-82; North Carolina Governor's Blue Ribbon Study Commission on Transportation Needs and Financing, Chairman Aviation Committee 1978-80. Religion: Kanuga Episcopal Center, Board of Visitors 1979 to present; Christ Church (Raleigh, North Carolina), Vestry 1977-79; Episcopal Faith Alive Weekends, Visitor Team Member and Witness, 1977 to present; Lay Reader, Diocese of Southern Alabama, 1957-59; Episcopal Diocese of Atlanta 1955-56. Honors and Awards: Army Aviation Hall of Fame, 1975; Distinguished Service Cross; Distinguished Service Medal with 2 Oak Leaf Clusters; Silver Star; Legion of Merit with 2 Oak Leaf Clusters; Distinguished Flying Cross; Bronze Star Medal; Air Medal with 44 Oak Leaf Clusters; Army Commendation Medal; Purple Heart; Presidential Unit Citation; Combat Infantryman Badge; Master Parachutist Badge; Master Army Aviation Badge; National Guard Bureau Meritorious Service Award; Boy Scouts of America Silver Beaver Award; Distinguished Service Medal, State of North Carolina; Static Line Award, General of the Year, 1980. Address: 1610 Canterbury Road, Raleigh, North Carolina 27608.■

HENRY DALTON TOMLINSON

Corporate Executive. Personal: Born June 14, 1926; Married Anne Frost; Father of Kenneth, Hank, Diane. Education: B.S. Civil Engineering, University of Tennessee, Knoxville, 1948; M.S. Sanitary Engineering, Massachusetts Institute of Technology, Cambridge, 1955; Ph.D. Environmental Engineering, Vanderbilt University, Nashville, 1970. Military: Served with the United States Public Health Service as Senior Assistant Sanitary Engineer, 1952-53. Career: Senior Sanitary Engineer, Tennessee Stream Pollution Control Commission, Nashville, Tennessee, 1948-52; Senior Assistant Sanitary Engineer, United States Public Health Service, Boston, Massachusetts, 1952-53; Graduate Student, Research Assistant and Institute Sanitary Engineer, Massachusetts Institute of Technology, Cambridge, Massachusetts, 1953-55; Principal Sanitary Engineer, Kentucky Water Pollution Control Commission, Louisville, Kentucky, 1955-60; Sanitary Engineer, Metcalf and Eddy, Boston, Massachusetts, 1960; Associate Professor, Environmental and Sanitary Engineering Graduate Program, Washington University, St. Louis, Missouri, 1960-70; Senior Vice President, Envirodyne Engineers, Inc. (Ryckman, Edgerley, Tomlinson and Associates), St. Louis, Missiouri, 1970-79; Vice President, Environmental Engineering, Reynolds, Smith and Hills, Architects-Engineers-Planners, Inc., Jacksonville, Florida, 1979 to present. Organizational Memberships: Air Pollution Control Association; American Society of Civil Engineers; American Water Works Association; New York Academy of Sciences; Water Pollution Control Federation, National Program Committee 1976-81; Florida Engineering Society, Executive Committee 1982-83; National Society for Professional Engineers; Society of Military Engineers, Corporate Liaison Officer from Reynolds, Smith and Hills 1981-83. Religion: Member Lakewood United Methodist Church, Jacksonville, Florida, 1980 to present, General Member of Board 1983; Member Webster Hills United Methodist Church, Webster Hills, Missouri, 1960-80, General Board Member, Sunday School Teacher, Vice President and President of Gordon Ellis Sunday School Class, Stewardship Committee Member. Honors and Awards: Registerd Professional Engineer in California, Florida, Georgia, Illinois, Indiana, Kansas, Kentucky, Maryland, Massachusetts, Missouri, Nevada, North Dakota, Tennessee, Wisconsin; Society of Sigma Xi, 1961; Recipient of National Science Foundation Fellowship in Science and Engineering Education, Vanderbilt University, 1964; Vanderbilt University Teaching Fellowship, 1965; Water Pollution Administration Research Fellowship, Vanderbilt University, 1966 and 1967; Diplomate, American Academy of Environmental Engineerng, 1970; Chi Epsilon, 1979; Listed in *Who's Who in the Midwest, American Men of Science, Dictionary of International Biography, Who's Who in Florida, Who's Who in the South and Southwest, Who's Who in Engineering, Men of Achievement.* Address: 7958 Los Robles Court, Jacksonville, Florida 32216.■

KATHLEEN M. TOMS

Director of Nursing Service. Personal: Born December 31, 1943; Daughter of Phyllis J. Stewart; Mother of Kathleen Marie, Kelly Terese. Education: R.N., A.A., City College of San Francisco, 1963; B.P.S., Elizabethtown College (Pennsylvania), 1973; M.S.Ed., Temple University, 1977. Military: Service with the United States Army Reserve Nurses Corps with the rank of Major, 1973 to present; Appointed Chief Nurse, 361st Hospital, December 1983. Career: Director

TWO THOUSAND NOTABLE AMERICANS

of Nursing, Riverside Osteopathic Hospital (Wilmington, Delaware), 1980 to present; Medical Surgical Nurse, St. Joseph Hospital (Fairbanks, Alaska), 1963-65; Emergency Room Nurse, St. Joseph Hospital (Lancaster, Pennsylvania), 1965-69; Blood, Plasma and Compenents Nurse, 1969-71; President, F. E. Barry Company (Lancaster), 1971 to present; Director of In-service Education, Lancaster Osteopathic Hospital, 1971-75; Coordinator of Practical Nursing Program, Vocational Technical School (Coatesville, Pennsylvania), 1976-77; Director of Nursing, Pocopson Home (West Chester, Pennsylvania), 1978-80; Inventor of Auto-infusor for Blood Components, 1971. Organizational Memberships: Delaware Nurses Association; Pennsylvania Nurses Association, Director 1974-78; Temple University and Elizabethtown College Alumni Associations. Community Activities: Delaware Health Council; Medical-Surgical Task Force, 1980 to present; Member of Pennsylvania Governors Council on Drug Abuse and Alcoholism, 1974-76; Nurses Advisory Committee of the American Cancer Society, 1971-75; Director and Founder, Lancaster Community Health Center, 1973-76; Nurses Advisory Committee of the American Cancer Society, 1971-75; Director and Founder, Lancaster Community Health Center, 1973-76; Lecturer for N.I.D.A.—H.E.W. through N.F.C.C., 1973-76; Sustaining Member, Republican National Committee; International Associate of Coatesville Veterans Administration Medical Center (Coatesville, Pennsylvania), 1983 to present. Honors and Awards: Army Achievement Medal, 1983; Army Commendation Medal, 1978; Community Service Award, Citizens United for Better Public Relations (Pennsylvania), 1974; Outstanding Citizen Award, WGAL-TV, 1975; Sertoma Award, Sertoma Club of Lancaster. Address: 400 Summitt House, 1450 West Chester Parkway, West Chester, Pennsylvania 19380.■

LOUIS JOHN TOPEL, S. J.

Associate Professor of Theology, Ordained Roman Catholic Priest. Personal: Born August 9, 1934, in Seattle, Washington; Son of Mrs. Helen Topel. Education: Valedictorian of Seattle Preparatory School, 1952; B.A. Classical Languages magna cum laude 1958, M.A. Philosophy magna cum laude 1959, Gonzaga University; S.T.M. Dogmatic Theology summa cum laude, Santa Clara University, 1959; S.S.L. Biblical Exegesis magna cum laude, Pontifical Biblical Institute, Rome, 1969; Ph.D. Religious Studies magna cum laude, Marquette University, 1973. Career: Instructor of Greek and Latin, Bellarmine High School (Tacoma, Washington), 1959-62; Teaching Assistant in Theology, Marquette University, 1969-70; Director of Master's Degree Program in Religious Education 1971-76, Assistant Professor of Theology 1973-76, Associate Professor of Theology 1976 to present, Seattle University; Visiting Professor, Sophia University International College (Tokyo) 1979, Pontifical Biblical Institute (Rome) 1981. Organizational Memberships: Catholic Biblical Association of America; Society of Biblical Literature; Alpha Sigma Nu. Religion: Member of the Society of Jesus (Jesuits), August 14, 1952 to present; Ordained Roman Catholic Priest, June 12, 1965, in Spokane, Wasington; Rector for the Jesuit Community of Seattle University, 1975-78. Published Works: Numerous Scholarly Book Reviews in *America, Biblica, The Catholic Biblical Quarterly, The Homiletic and Pastoral Review, Theological Studies, Worship*; Articles "Rahner and McKenzie on the Social Theory of Inspiration" 1964, "Ways the Church Selected its Bishops" 1972, "On the 'Injustice' of the Unjust Steward" 1975, "On Being Parabled" 1976; Book *The Way to Peace. Liberation through the Bible*, 1979. Honors and Awards: Grant from the Jesuit Council on Theological Reflection for Book on the Biblical Bases of Liberation Theology, 1974; Grant from the Jesuit Council on Theological Reflection for Research on Prison Reform in Alameda County, 1975; Catholic Biblical Association Visiting Professorship at the Pontifical Biblical Institute in Rome, 1978. Address: Loyola Hall, Seattle University, Seattle, Washington 98122.■

JULIA TORRES

Retired Pastor. Personal: Born April 9, 1904; Daughter of Jose H. and Oliva Torres (deceased). Education: Graduate, Ponce High School, 1922; Normal Diploma 1925, B.A. Education 1942, University of Puerto Rico; Master's Degree in School Supervision, New York University, 1955; Advanced Studies, Union Seminary of Rio Piedras and Scarrit College. Career: United Methodist Pastor (Elder), Retired; Former Occupations include Public School Elementary Teacher and High School Teacher, Junior High School Principal (until 1957), Ordained Deacon 1957, Pastor in Santurce 1957, Elder 1960, Pastor in Ponce Playa (until 1972), Board Member of the Women's Division and Board of Global Ministries of the United Methodist Church, National Division. Organizational Memberships: Puerto Rico Teachers Association; National Education Association; Evangelical Ministers Association. Community Activities: American Red Cross, Secretary 1925-30, Active Member; Civil Defense Organization, Instructor and Group Leader, 1940-57; Organizer and One of the First Members of the Center of Guidance and Service at Ponce Playa, Co-Worker with Sister Isolina Ferré; Administrator Voluntary Chaplain at Ponce Girls Lyceum 1962-72. Religion: President, Epworth League, 1920-24; President, Methodist Women Association, 1932-41, 1954-56; President, United Women, 1944-46; President, Ministers' Association, 1962-64. Honors and Awards: Distinguished Citizen of Ponce City, 1969; One of the *Ten Century Women of Ponce*, 1975; Phi Beta Kappa 75th Anniversary Distinguished Educator, 1981; United Women Association Distinguished Member of the International Year of Women. Address: Apartment 605 Mayor Eld. Tower, 12 Mayor Street, Ponce, Puerto Rico 00731.■

ANA MARIA TORRES AYBAR

Educator and School Administrator. Personal: Born October 25, 1935; Daughter of Francisco J. Torres and Maria P. Aybar. Education: Bachelor of Philosophy, Siena Heights College, 1960; Master's Degree in Administration and Supervision, Master of Science 1970, Guidance and Counseling 1975, Barry College; Guidance and Counseling, Catholic University of Puerto Rico, 1975; Doctoral Degree in Higher Education (in progress), Nova University. Career: Assistant Superintendent of Catholic School; Supervisor of Schools; Principal of Schools; Assistant Principal of Schools; College Professor; Elementary and Secondary School Professor. Organizational Memberships: American Association of University Professors; Association for Supervision and Curriculum Development; Association for Supervision and Curriculum Development Puerto Rico; P.G.A.; P.G.A. Puerto Rico; A.E.E.E., Vice President 1977-79; Phi Delta Kappa, Sub-Treasurer 1981-83; C.A.T.P., President 1976-83; C.O.R., President 1971-73; A.P.O.R.E.; E.L.C.A. Community Activities: J.A.C. Coordinator, 1960-66; Co-Founder, Co-op System in the Dominican Republic, 1965-66; Founder of Old Peoples' Home in the Dominican Republic, 1965-66; Representative of Puerto Rico in Panama, 1972; Representative of Puerto in the United States, Educational Committee, 1973; Representative of Puerto Rico and the Virgin Islands in Region II, New York, 1975-79; Representative of Puerto Rico and the Virgin Islands in Washington, Office of Education, 1980-83; Member of Two School Boards in Ponce, Puerto Rico, 1979-83; Educational Consultant to Two Schools in Ponce, Puerto Rico; Consultant to Federal Programs in Puerto Rico and the Virgin Islands, 1975-83. Religion: Roman Catholic Instructor and Speaker at Various Activities. Honors and Awards: Kappan of the Year, 1982; Educator of the Year, 1980; Special Citations from A.E.E.E. 1979, 1980, 1966; Listed in *Who's Who in the South, Personalities of America, Personalities of the South, Who's Who in the World, One Thousand Outstanding Personalities, The Biographical Roll of Honor*. Address: Jardines Fagot-Calle 3 #E15, Ponce, Puerto Rico 00731.■

BASIL P. TOUTORSKY

Pianist, Composer, Professor, Doctor of Music. Personal: Born January 10, 1896, in Novotcherkask, Russia; Married Maria T. Howard on August 18, 1936. Education: Educated by Private Tutors, beginning a Musical Education at the Age of Four; Studied Violin with Professor Stadji, Age Ten; Graduate of the Novotcherkask Gymnasya and the Novotcherkask Musicak College; Graduate Studies under Professors of the Moscow Conservatory of Music; Obtained Law Degrees from the Moscow Imperial Lycee-University of Tsarevitch Nicholas and the University of Moscow. Military: Served as Midshipman and Appointed to the Staff of the Commander-in-Chief of the Black Sea Fleet (Navy) during World War I; Received Commission as a Naval Officer Continuing Service with the Naval Forces in the Black Sea. Career: Taught in Istanbul, Turkey, 2½ Years; Toured United States, Mexico, Canada and Europe as Concert Pianist; Founded and Directed Toutorsky Studio-Salon and Academy of Music, Los Angeles, 1923-36; Taught in Washington D.C.; Head of the Piano Department, Chevy Chase College, 1943-50; Organized Benefit Performances and Lecture Series and Judged Numerous Musical Competitions; Authoritative Interpreter of Chopin and the Russian Composers. Organizational Memberships: Washington Performing Arts Society, Patron; International Platform Association; D.C. Chapter, National Association for American Composers, Vice President 1967-74; Military Order of World Wars, Perpetual Member; National Trust for Historic Preservation, Smithsonian Institution; Life Patron, American Biographical Institute; Life Fellow, International Biographical Association. Published Works: Numerous Articles on Russian Music (including "Musical Development of Russia," "Nationalism in Music," and "Chords and Discords"); Compositions include *Valse in A Major*, Written in Celebration of the Bicentennial Year and Jubilee of Queen Elizabeth II, *Mazurka*, Written in Celebration of the Election of Pope John Paul II, *Elgie in B Minor*, in Memory of Sergie V. Rachmaninoff, *Valse in C Major*, in Memory of Anna Pavlova, *Poeme* and Other Compositions Reflecting the Style and Moods of His Generation. Honors and Awards: Doctor of Music Degree, American International Academy, 1937; Grand Prix Humanitarie de Belgique, Chevialier de Grand Croix, 1939; Diploma de Medaille d'Or Compagnie Theatrale Philanthropique, France, 1947; Listed in *Who's Who in Music, Two Thousand Men of Achievement, Dictionary of International Biography, International Register of Profiles, Notable Americans of the Bicentennial Era, Community Leaders and Noteworthy Americans, The Directory of Distinguished Americans, International Book of Honor*, Others. Address: 1720 16th Street, Northwest, Washington D.C. 20009.■

TWO THOUSAND NOTABLE AMERICANS

STATHIS TRAHANATZIS

Artist Painter, Painting Specialist. Personal: Born August 8, 1939, Caesariani, Athens, Greece; Became U.S. Citizen June 15, 1978; Son of Sophia and Athanasius. Education: Art Studies, Ecole des Beaux Arts, Paris, France, 1956-59; Byzantine Illuminated Manuscripts, Bibliotheque Nationale Paris; Byzantine Traditional Painting of Icons and Mural with Iconographer Photis Condoglou and Studies at the Old Monasteries in Greece and Yugoslavie, 1962-68. Career: Artist Painter; Specialist in Palaeography of Greek Papyri and Manuscripts and in Byzantine Traditional Painting; Iconographer Muralist; Miniaturist; Teacher of Byzantine Art, Rosary College, River Forest, Illinois, 1968; Byzantine Manuscripts and Illumination and Paintings, University of Chicago, 1977; Painted Greek Orthodox Cathedral of Annunciation, San Francisco, California, 1975; Currently Painting Greek Orthodox Cathedral of Annunciation, Chicago, Illinois; Various Exhibitions in Greece and the U.S.A.; Interviews on Art. Organizational Memberships: Folkloric Association of Greece. Published Works: Author Numerous Articles on Art. Honors and Awards: Medal, Royal Hellinic Air Force, 1961, Devoted to Painting the Interior of Military Base Chapel, Eleusina, Athens, Greece, 1960-61; Medal, Pope Paul VI, 1967; Medal, City Hall of the Island Cos, Greece, 1971; Appreciation from American Folklife Center, Library of Congress, Washington, D.C., 1977; Appreciation from Ecumenical Patriarch of Constantinople Demetrios I; Cited in *Religious and Ethical Encyclopedia*, Greece, 1966; Cited in *Encyclopedia Britannica* since 1974; Listed in *Who's Who of Intellectuals, Men of Achievement*. Address: San Francisco, California.■

FRITZ A. TRAUGOTT

Consulting Mechanical Engineer. Personal: Born March 18, 1928; Son of Johann and Maria Traugott (both deceased); Married Frances Fortier. Education: B.S.M.E., Government Engineering School, Austria, 1947; Graduate Study, Syracuse University, 1953. Career: Robson & Woese, Inc., Executive Vice President/Senior Partner and Treasurer 1977 to present, Vice President in Charge of HVAC Design 1970-77, HVAC Department Head 1968-70, Supervising Project Engineer 1958-68, Design and Specification Writer of Consulting Engineering Firm 1955-57; District Engineer, Stefan Ammann & Sohn-Austria, 1953-55; Engineer-in-Training, Carrier Corporation 1952-53. Organizational Memberships: A.S.H.R.A.E., Nominating Committee 1982-83, Honors and Awards Committee 1982-83, Finance Committee 1979-81, Director and Regional Chairman of Region I 1976-79; TC9.1 "Large Building A/C Systems," Member 1975 to present, Chairman 1980 to present; Nominating, Standards, Regional Subcommittees, Technical Programs, Workbook 1966-79; Central New York Chapter, President 1968-69, Secretary 1966-67; American Consulting Engineers Council; Technology Club of Syracuse. Community Activities: Rotary Club of Syracuse, Membership Committee Chairman 1978-79, 1981-82, Hospitality Committee Chairman 1977-78, Secretary 1982-83, Treasurer 1983-84; Century Club, 1977 to present; Cazenovia Ski Club, 1963 to present. Honors and Awards: United States Achievement Award, 1952; Engineer of the Year, City of Syracuse, 1969; Distinguished Service Award, 1979; A.S.H.R.A.E. Fellow 1980, Region I Regional Award of Merit 1981, Paul Harris Fellow Award 1982, Guest Lecturer, Syracuse University, 1972 to present. Address: 3996 Pompey Hollow Road, Cazenovia, New York 13035.■

JAMES PATRICK TRAYNOR

Government Official. Personal: Born December 10, 1954; Son of James Francis and Agnes Ruth Traynor. Education: B.A. with honors in Government Administration, Shippensburg College, 1976; M.P.A. (Public Administration), Maxwell School of Citizenship and Public Affairs, Syracuse University, 1978; J.D., Syracuse University College of Law, 1980. Career: Presidential Intern, United States Department of Labor, Washington D.C., 1978 to present; Cabinet Intern, Pennsylvania Insurance Commissioner's Staff, 1975; Staff Member, Syracuse Journal of International Law and Commerce, 1977-78. Organizational Memberships: Presidential Management Alumni Group; American Society for Public Administrators; American Management Association; Academy of Political Science. Community Activities: National Democratic Club; Corcoran Gallery of Art; Menninger Foundation; Smithsonian Associates; Folger Theater; College Planning Commission, 1974; Faculty Curriculum Committee, 1974; College Student Senate, 1974; College Freshman Senate, 1973. Religion: Roman Catholic. Honors and Awards: Selected Presidential Intern, 1978; Gold Medal for Distinction in the Social Sciences, Honorable Mention in Theology and Spanish, 1972. Address: 217 Prospect Drive, Wilmington, Delaware 19803.■

ARNULFO D. TREJO

Professor. Personal: Born August 15, 1922; Son of Petra and Nicolas Trejo (deceased); Married Annette, Daughter of Karl and Marie Foster; Father of Rachel, Rebecca, Ruth, (Stepfather of) Linda. Education: B.A. Education, University of Arizona, 1949; M.A. Spanish Language and Literature, Universidad de las Americas (Mexico City), 1951; M.A. Library Science, Kent State University, 1953; Litt.D. with honors, National University of Mexico (Mexico City), 1959. Military: Served in the United States Army, 143rd Infantry Division, 1942-45, attaining the rank of Sergeant. Career: Reference Librarian, University of California at Los Angeles, 1954-59; Library Administrator, Long Beach State University, 1959-66; Associate Professor of Library Science and Latin American Bibliographer 1966-68, Associate Professor of Library Science and English 1970-75, Professor of Library Science 1975 to present, University of Arizona; Consultant and Administrator, Caracas, Venezuela, 1968-70. Organizational Memberships: American Library Association, Council Member 1974-78, Nominating Committee Chairman 1979-80; American Association of University Professors; Arizona State Library Association; National Association of Spanish-Speaking Librarians in the United Sttes, President 1972-74; Beta Phi Mu; Phi Delta Kappa; Sigma Delta Pi. Community Activities: President and Founder, El Tiradito Foundation, Local Historic Preservation Organization, 1972-75; Board Member; Delegate-at-Large, White House Conference on Library and Information Services, 1979. Honors and Awards: Distinguished Alumnus Award, Kent State University School of Library Science, 1969; Simon Bolivar Award, Colegio de Biblioteconomos y Archivistas de Venezuela for "meritorious and distinguished contribution to the development of libraries in Venezuela," 1970; "El Tiradito Award," El Tiradito Foundation, Inc. (in recognition of outstanding service to the people of the Barrio), 1973; Annual Award, League of Mexican American Women (for dedicated service to the community), 1973. Address: 240 East Yvon Drive, Tucson, Arizona 85704.■

OLYMPIA DAVIS TRESMONTAN

Psychotherapist, Counselor and Consultant. Personal: Born November 27, 1925; Daughter of Peter Konstantin and Mary Hazimanolis Davis (both deceased); Married Robert Baker Stitt, March 21, 1974. Education: B.S., Simmons College, Boston, Massachusetts, 1946; M.A., Wayne State University, Detroit, Michigan, 1960; Ph.D., University of California-Berkeley, 1971. Career: Private Practice Psychotherapist, Counselor and Consultant, 1970 to present; Director, Studio Ten Services, San Francisco, California, 1973 to present; Director, Promise for Children, San Francisco, 1981 to present; Clinical Consultant, Childworth Learning Center, San Francisco, 1976-80; Teacher, Chapman College Graduate Division 1971-74, University of California-San Francisco Extension Division 1971-73; Sensitivity Trainer, National Science Foundation Science Curriculum Improvement Project of University of California-Berkeley, 1967-68; Social Worker, San Francisco Child Welfare, 1964-66. Organizational Memberships: American Psychological Association, 1970 to present; American Orthopsychiatric Association, 1974 to present; American Association of Marriage Therapists, 1973 to present; California Association of Marriage and Family Therapists, 1973 to present. Community Activities: Childworth Learning Center, San Francisco, Board of Directors 1976-80; Friends of the San Francisco Public Library, 1972 to present; International Hospitality Committee of the Bay Area, 1974 to present; National Association of Social Workers, 1947-49; Commonwealth Club of California, 1978 to present; American Association of University Women, 1980 to present. Honors and Awards: Wayne State University, Honors Convocation 1949-50, 1960; Shaefer Foundation Grantee, 1969-70; Pi Lambda Theta Honor Society for Women, University of California-Berkeley Chapter, 1967 to present; Honoring of Women, Thomas Starr King School of Religious Leadership, Berkeley, California, 1981. Address: 2611 Lake Street, San Francisco, California 94121.■

EDNA GANNON TREUTING

Director of Nursing Section. Personal: Born December 16, 1925; Daughter of Alphonse and Clara Gannon (both deceased); Married August Raymond Treuting; Mother of Keith, Karen, Madeline, Jaime, Jay. Education: Diploma, Charity Hospital School of Nursing, 1946; B.S.N.Ed., Louisiana State University School of Nursing, 1953; M.P.H. 1972, F.N.P. 1973, D.P.H. 1978, Tulane University School of Public Health and Tropical Medicine; Director, F.N.P. and P.N.P. Programs, 1972-81; Instructor of Public Health, 1972-74; Associate Professor of Public Health, 1977 to present; Director O.H.N., 1977-80; Nursing Educator, Louisiana State University School of Nursing/Maternal Child Health and Pediatrics; Nursing Educator, Charity Hospital School of Nursing/Pediatrics; Industrial Nurse, Shell Oil and American Sugar Refinery; Head Nurse, Pediatrics and Pre-Mature Nursery, Charity Hospital; Private Duty Nurse. Organizational Memberships: American Nurses Association; National League of Nursing; Southern Region Education Board; Council on Primary Health Care Nurse Practitioners.

Community Activities: Consultant, Louisiana State Health Department, Home Health Inc., Teagle Foundation, Regional Medical Program and Tri-Way Hospital, City of Lafayette, Ross Laboratories, Louisiana Industrial Nurses Association, Medical Personnel Pool; Research Consultant to American Association of Critical Care; Editorial Consultant to *Nurse Practitioners Journal*; Speaker for National, Regional and Local Groups; Developed and Conducted Workshops for University of Hawii, University of Southern Mississippi, National League of Nursing. Religion: Catholic; Holy Cross High School Board, 1966-72; Archidocese Seminarian Physical Examinations, 1962-69; School Nurse, St. Francis Cobrini, 1960-69; Senior Trip Nurse, Dominican High School, 1974. Published Works: Contributor to Various Journals, O.H.N. Book; American Nursing Administration Book in Progress. Honors and Awards: Delta Omega, Eta Chapter, Member 1976 to present, President 1981-82; Delta Omega Nominee Merit Award, 1978; School of Nursing Honor Society 1979, Mortar Board Outstanding Women's Day Speaker 1981, Louisiana State University; Sigma Theta Tau, 1982; International Citizen Ambassador to South America, 1979; University of Hawaii School of Public Health and School of Nursing Invitational Workshop, 1977. Address: 8040 Morrison Road, New Orleans, Louisiana 70126.∎

JAMES EDGAR TREVER

Computer System Engineer. Personal: Born September 1, 1945; Son of Dr. and Mrs. John Trever; Father of Elizabeth Agnes, Stephen Cecil. Education: B.S. Biology, Baldwin-Wallace College, 1968; Attended the University of Southern California, 1964-67; Graduate Work in Human Morphology, Brown University, 1971-72; Research Assistant, Vertebrate Paleontology, National History Museum of Los Angeles County, 1968-74. Military: Served in the United States Navy as a Flight Officer 1969-71 and as a Maintenance/Material Control Officer 1971-73, attaining the rank of Lieutenant. Career: Flight Instructor 1967-71, Chief Ground Instructor 1968-69, Gunnell Aviation, Santa Monica Airport; Founder and Director of Cordo Enterprises, 1977 to present. Organizational Memberships: Data Processing Management Association, Vice President Pensacola Chapter 1982; President, Flying Club of the University of Southern California, 1966-67. Community Activities: Sustaining Member, Republican National Committee, 1981 to present; Board Member, Occidental International Masters Championships, 1976-77; Camp Counselor for Underprivileged Children, Cleveland, Ohio, 1963; Visiting Lecturer on National History of Fossils for Public School Systems, Raleigh (North Carolina) and Pensacola (Florida), 1975 to present. Religion: Visiting Lecturer on the Dead Sea Scrolls, 1976 to present. Honors and Awards: National Honor Society, 1961-63; Various Science Awards, 1961-63; Distinguished Naval Graduate, 1969; Navy Achievement Medal, 1972; Special Achievement Award, United States Navy, 1982 (with quality step increases); Listed in *Outstanding Young Men of America, Who's Who in the South and Southwest*. Address: 4618A Bellview Avenue, Pensacola, Florida 32506.∎

DOROTHY L. TRICE

Physician and Medical Director. Personal: Married James E. Willie (deceased). Education: R.N., Lincoln School for Nurses, New York, 1945; B.S.Ed., Hunter College, 1947; M.D., Woman's Medical College of Pennsylvania, 1956; M.P.H., Columbia University School of Public Health and Administrative Medicine, 1959. Career: Physician and Medical Director, Neposnit Home for the Aged, 1979-82; Director of Ambulatory Care and Community Medicine, Queens General Hospital Affiliate of Long Island Jewish Medical Center, 1977-79; Physician, Health Officer, Bourough Director, Deputy Commissioner and Regional Director, New York City Department of Health, 1957-77. Organizational Memberships: Medical Society of the County of Kings, Past Trustee, Secretary; Provident Clinical Society of Brooklyn Inc., Past President; Brooklyn Tuberculosis and Lung Association, Community Education Committee; New York Diabetes Association, Clinical Society; Brooklyn Home for the Aged and Brooklyn Visiting Nurse Association, Professional Advisory Committee; American Cancer Society, New York City and Queens Chapters. Community Activities: Community Health Planning Boards of Districts 1, 3, 4, and 8 of Brooklyn, 1972-77; Willing Workers for Human Rights, 1963-70; Brooklyn Chapter of Soroptimist International of the Americas, 1976-84; Soroptimist International of Montclair, California, 1984 to present; Kings County Hospital Community Board, 1970-77. Religion: St. George's Episcopal Church, Vestry 1972 to present; Diocesan Convention Delegate, 1972-83; Diocesan Council Member, 1981 to present; Church Charity Foundation Member, 1973-78. Honors and Awards: St. George's Episcopal Church Scholarship Fund Award for Service, 1976; Susan Smith McKinney Stewart Medical Society Award, 1978. Address: 4199 Steamboat Drive, Montclair, California 91763.∎

VIJAY SHANKAR TRIPATHI

Geochemist. Personal: Born August 16, 1952; Son of Mr. Rajkeshwar Tripathi and Mrs. Kesari Tripathi; Married Utpala, Daughter of Mr. T. D. Shukla and Mrs. P. Shukla; Father of Vandana. Education: B.Sc. Geology and Chemistry 1971, M.Sc. 1973, Banaras Hindu University, India; M.S. Geochemistry 1976, M.S. Statistics 1981, Ph.D. Geochemistry 1982, Stanford University. Career: Geochemist. Organizational Memberships: International Association of Geochemistry and Cosmochemistry; American Association for the Advancement of Science; Geochemical Society; New York Academy of Sciences; Sigma Xi. Honors and Awards: La Touche Medal from the Mining, Geological and Metallurgical Institute of India; Banaras Hindu University Gold Medal; Master N. L. Sharma Gold Medal. Address: 120 C Escondido Village, Stanford, California 94305.∎

RICHARD STUART TROWBRIDGE

Research Scientist. Personal: Born April 3, 1942; Son of Walter H. and Lamia A. Trowbridge; Married Sue Hitchcock; Father of John Richard. Education: B.S. 1964, M.S. 1966, Ph.D. 1971, University of Massachusetts-Amherst. Career: Research Scientist in Virology and Mammalian Cell Biology; Clinical Microbiologist; Public Health Bacteriologist; Public Health Inspector; Sanitarian. Organizational Memberships: American Society for Microbiology, 1964 to present; Tissue Culture Association, 1976 to present; The New York Academy of Sciences, 1981 to present. Community Activities: Staten Island Rotary Club, 1979 to present; Staten Island's Meals on Wheels, Board of Directors 1979 to present, Vice President 1981 and 1982, President 1982 to present; Boy Scouts of America, District Committee Member-at-Large 1978 to present, Council Executive Committee 1981 to present, Scoutmaster 1977 to present, Troop Committee Chairman Pro-Tem 1977-78, Webelos Den Leader 1976-77, Cub Pack Committee 1977-78. Honors and Awards: N.D.E.A. Fellowship, 1968-70; Listed in *Who's Who in the East*. Address: 180 Woodward Avenue, Staten Island, New York 10314.∎

CHARLES WESLEY TRUE, JR.

Instructor. Personal: Born July 26, 1916; Son of Charles W. True (deceased); Married Ruth Hulen Smith, Daughter of Walter Lewis Hulen; Father of Marthe Ann Lebne Strunk, Charles W. III. Education: B.S. Agriculture, Texas A&I University, 1941. Military: Served in the United States Army during World War II. Career: Instructor of Horticulture, El Paso (Texas) Junior College; Former Positions include Chief of Land Management for the United States Air Defense Center (Fort Bliss, Texas), Research Agronomist at the Southwest Research Center (San Antonio, Texas), Range Conservationist for the United States S.C.S., Fertilizer Sales Representative for Umbaugh Chemical Company, Loan Supevisor for the United States Department of Agriculture Farm Security Administration and Soils Research Technician at Texas A&M University. Organizational Memberships: American Society of Agronomy; Crop Science Society of America; Weed Science Society of America; American Society of Range Management; Society of American Military Engineers. Community Activities: President, Beautify El Paso Association, 1977; Co-Founder and Secretary, Rio Bravo Turf and Golf Course Superintendents Association, 1968 to present; Secretary, El Paso Post, American Society of Military Engineers, 1973-76; Secretary, Benevides (Texas) Lions Club, 1952; 4-H Club Leader, 1954-59; Boy Scout Leader, 1955-61. Religion: United Methodist Church, Member for Over 50 Years, Member of Administrative Board Over 25 Years. Honors and Awards: Department of Defense Citation for Meritorious Achievement, 1974; Professional Crop Scientist Citation, 1978; Professional Agronomist, 1983; Silver Spur Award, Texas A&I University Alumni Association, 1982. Address: 9324 McFall Drive, El Paso, Texas 79925.■

DUANE PHILLIP TRUEX III

Museum Director. Personal: Born August 30, 1947; Married Brenda; Father of Adriane Michelle. Education: B.A. Music, Ithaca College. Career: Museum Director, Roberson Center for the Arts and Sciences, Binghamton, New York, 1978 to present; Executive Director, Arts and Humanities Council of Greater Baton Rouge, Inc.; Executive Director, Baton Rouge Symphony Association; Director of Public Relations, Kansas City Philharmonic; Assistant Director of Student Activities, Oklahoma State University. Organizational Memberships: Phi Mu Alpha National Professional Music Fraternity; Beta Gamma Sigma, Oklahoma State University Chapter, 1971. Community Activities: The Unknown Theater Company, Inc., Vice-Chairman, Board of Directors 1970-72; National Entertainment Conference, National Board of Directors 1972; National Bureau of Discovery, Board of Directors 1976-78; Binghamton Rotary Club, Board of Directors 1981; New York State Association of Museums, Secretary 1981-83; Vice-Chairman Commission on Architecture and Urban Design, 1978 to present. Honors and Awards: Listed in *Outstanding Young Men of America, Who's Who in the East, Who's Who in America.* Address: 5½ Haydn Street, Binghamton, New York 13905.■

NICHOLAS TSOULFANIDIS

Educator, Administrator. Personal: Born May 6, 1938; Son of Stephen Tsoulfanidis; Married Zizeta; Father of Stephen, Lena. Education: B.S. Physics, University of Athens (Greece), 1960; M.S. Nuclear Engineering 1965, Ph.D. Nuclear Engineering 1968, University of Illinois. Military: Served in the Greek Army. Career: Professor and Head, Department of Nuclear Engineering, University of Missouri-Rolla; Engineer/Consultant, Arkansas Power and Light Company, Summers 1976-79; Senior Engineer, General Atomic Company, 1974-75. Organizational Memberships: American Nuclear Society; Missouri Society of Professional Engineers; National Society of Professional Engineers. Honors and Awards: Fellowship Awarded by Greek Government, 1955-59; Fellowship Awarded by University of Illinois, 1965-67; Outstanding Teacher Award, University of Missouri at Rolla, 1968-69 and 1970-71. Address: Route 6 Box 523, Rolla, Missouri 65401.■

WIE-MING TU

Historian and Philosopher. Personal: Born February 26, 1940, in Kunming, China; Son of Shou-tsin and Shu-li Tu; Father of Eugene Lung-sun Tu. Education: B.A. Chinese Studies, Tunghai University, Taichung, Taiwan, 1961; M.A. East Asian Regional Studies 1963, Ph.D. Joint Degree in History and Far Eastern Languages 1968, Harvard University. Military: Served in the Reserve Officer Training Corps, Tunghai University, Taiwan, 1958-61; Served as Second Lieutenant, Platoon Leader, 1961-62. Career: Visiting Lecturer in the Humanities, Tunghai University, Princeton University, 1966-67; Visiting Lecturer in Oriental Studies 1967-68, Assistant Professor in East Asian Studies 1968-71; University of California-Berkeley, Assistant Professor of History 1971-73, Associate Professor of History 1973-77, Professor of History 1977-81; Professor of Chinese History and Philosophy, Harvard University; Research, Confucian Thought, Chinese Intellectual History, Religious Philosophy of East Asia. Organizational Memberships: Association for Asian Studies, Board of Directors 1972-75; American Historical Society; Society for Asian and Comparative Philosophy, Founding Member, American Academy of Religion; China Society of Japan; American Association for the Advancement of Science; Phi Tau Phi. Community Activities: Consultant, National Endowment for the Humanities; Chinese Cultural Foundation of San Francisco, Board of Directors; Ministry of Education, Singapore, Consultant. Religion: Residential Fellow, Center for the Study of World Religions, Harvard University, 1970-71; Member, Committee on the Study of Religion, Harvard University; Chairperson Group Major in Religious Studies, University of California-Berkeley, 1979-80. Honors and Awards: Harvard-Yenching Fellow 1962-64, Graduate Fellowship 1964-67, Harvard University; Princeton Humanities Fellowship, 1968-69; American Council of Learned Societies Fellowship, 1970-71; Mellon Fellow, Aspen Institute for Humanistic Studies, 1974; Humanities Fellowship, University of California-Berkeley, 1974-75; Senior Scholar Award, Committee on Scholarly Communication with the Peoples' Republic of China of the National Academy of Sciences, 1979-80. Published Works: Co-Author with James T. C. Liu, *Traditional China; Neo-Confucian Thought in Action — Wang-Ming's Youth; Centrality and Commonality: An Essay on Chung-yung; Humanity and Self-Cultivation: Essays in Confucial Thought;* Numerous Articles and Reviews in Various Professional Journals. Address: Department of East Asian Languages and Civilizations, Harvard University, Cambridge, Massachusetts 02138.■

DAVID L. TUBBS

Physicist, Consultant. Personal: Born May 22, 1951; Son of Donna Tubbs. Education: B.A., University of Wisconsin at Madison, 1973; Graduate Study at the University of Texas-Austin, 1973-74; Ph.D. Physics, University of Chicago, 1977. Career: Physicist, Los Alamos National Laboratory; Consultant, Lawrence Livermore National Laboratory; Former Positions include Research Fellow at the Kellogg Radiation Lab of Cal Tech, Research Associate at the University of Chicago, Instructor in the Collegiate Division of the University of Chicago, Consulting Physicist for the Special Studies Group of Lawrence Livermore National Laboratory. Organizational Memberships: American Physical Society; American Astronomical Society; Royal Astronomical Society; Phi Beta Kappa. Honors and Awards: Phi Beta Kappa; Marc Perry Galler Award, University of Chicago (for outstanding student research), 1978. Address: X-2, MSB 220, Los Alamos National Laboratory, Los Alamos, New Mexico 87545.■

EDWARD LANE TUBBS

Banker. Personal: Born April 17, 1920; Son of Clifton and Mary Lane Tubbs (deceased); Married Grace, Daughter of Roy and Clara Dyer (deceased); Father of Steven, Alan, William. Education: B.S., Iowa State University, 1941; Graduate School of Banking, University of Wisconsin. Military: Served in the United States Army, 1942-43. Career: Chairman, Maquoketa State Bank; Chairman, First Central State Bank, DeWitt, Iowa; Former Agricultural Extension Director, Veterans Agricultural Instructor, Farmer and Farm Manager. Organizational Memberships: Iowa Bankers Association, President 1980-81, Treasurer 1978-79; President, Mid-America Bankers Agricultural Service Company, Inc., 1982 to present; Director, Interstate Bankers Insurance Services, 1981-83; President, Ohnward Bancshare Inc; Director, American Bankers Association, 1983 to present; International Platform Association; President's Circle, Iowa State University. Community Activities: Director, Mabsco Bankers Service, Inc., 1981 to present; Treasurer, City of Maquoketa 1976-80, Maquoketa Community Services 1976-80; Director, Timber City Development Corp 1972-78 (Vice President 1972-78), Iowa Business Growth Corporation 1981 to present; President, Elwood (Iowa) School Board, 1956-62; People-to-People Delegate to the Soviet Union, 1959. Religion: Moderator, Maquoketa United Church of Christ. Honors and Awards: Gamma Sigma Delta; 4-H Alumni Award; Jaycees Boss of the Year; Order of the Knoll; Iowa Extension Award, 1982. Address: 820 Niles, Maquoketa, Iowa 52060.■

CARSON LINWOOD TUCKER

Manager. Personal: Born September 26, 1947; Son of Mr. and Mrs. R. E. Tucker; Married Sandra F., Daughter of Mr. and Mrs. P. C. Flansburg. Education: B.A. English, Virginia Military Institute, 1970; M.A. English, College of William and Mary, 1971; Certificate Management Development, J. Sargeant Reynolds Community College, 1979. Career: Manager of Management Development and Organization, Philip Morris U.S.A.; Former Positions as Manager of Technical Training, Editor, Instructor-Writer, Factory Supervisor. Organizational Memberships: A.S.T.D.; I.A.Q.C.; A.M.S., Board of Directors 1982-83; I.M.C., President 1977; I.M.C., National Vice President and Member Executive Committee 1982-83; Institute of Certified Professional Managers, Chairman of the Board of Regents 1981-83; N.M.A.; A.S.P.A. Community Activities: Concerned Citizens of Powhatan County, Inc., President 1978-81; Junior Achievement, 1978; Madison University State Department of Education Committee on Vocational Programs, 1982; Adjunct Professor at J. Sargeant Reynolds College, John Tyler College, Virginia Commonwealth University; Consulting for Richmond Metro Chamber of Commerce, Richmond Public Schools, Richmond Toastmasters, National Research Council. Honors and Awards: Certified Professional Manager, 1979 to present; Certified American Tree Farmer, 1977 to present; Society of Cincinnati, 1970, Woodrow Wilson Fellow, 1971; Valedictorian, 1970; Cum Laude Graduate, 1970; Summa Cum Laude Graduate, 1979; Distinguished Military Graduate, 1970; Listed in *Who's Who in the South and Southwest.* Address: Route 1 Box 124X, Powhatan, Virginia 23139.■

TWO THOUSAND NOTABLE AMERICANS

DOROTHY M. TUCKER

Professor of Psychology. Personal: Born August 22, 1942; Daughter of James Anderson and Cleo Christine Fant Tucker. Education: B.S. Bowling Green University, 1960; M.Ed., University of Toledo, 1968; Ph.D., The Ohio State University, 1972; Ph.D., California School of Professional Psychology, 1976. Career: Professor of Psychology; Associate Professor, Florida International University; Associate Professor, Charles R. Drew Postgraduate Medical School; Director of Clinical Training in Psychology, The Wright Institute Graduate School, Los Angeles; Special Assistant to the Speaker of the California State Assembly, Willie C. Brown, Jr. Organizational Memberships: California Psychology Examining Committee, Exceptional Children's Foundation, Board of Directors, 1982 to present; Black Women in Psychology, Founder/Convenor 1981 to present; United Negro College Fund of Southern California, Chairperson 1980-81; American Psychologists Association; Association of Black Psychologists; California State Psychological Association. Community Activities: California State Democractic Party Committee, 1979 to present; Alan Cranston for Senate Committee, Field Director, 1980; Judicial Nominees Evaluation Committee, 1980-81; Inglewood Housing Commission, 1980-81; Charter Review Commission of Inglewood, 1981 to present; National Women's Continuation Committee, 1977 to present. Honors and Awards: Ford Foundation Fellow; N.D.E.A. Fellow; Pi Lambda Theta; Citation, Outstanding Service, Florida Board of Regents; Listed in *Who's Who of Women in America*, *Who's Who of International Women*. Address: 107 South Broadway #8009, Los Angeles, California 90012. ■

EVERETT TUCKER, JR.

Executive. Personal: Born July 7, 1912; Son of Dewitt Everett and Will Lynn Alexander Tucker (deceased); Married Francis Williams, Daughter of Robert W. (deceased) and Marion Clarke Williams; Father of Robert W., Everett III, Marion Tucker Glatter. Education: Attended the Sewanee Military Academy, 1927-30; B.S. Commerce, Washington and Lee University, 1934; Attended Harvard Business School 1942-43, University of New Mexico Law School 1947-48. Military: Served in the United States Army Air Corps, 1942-47, Retired for Disability as Major. Career: President, Industrial Development Company; Director, Industrial Department, Little Rock Chamber of Commerce, 1949-53. Organizational Memberships: Managing Partner, Tucker Plantation (Tucker, Arkansas), 1958 to present; Director, Superior Federal Savings and Loan, 1953 to present; Director, Commercial National Bank, 1965 to present; Member and Past President, American Industrial Development Council; Member and Past President, Southern Industrial Development Council; Director, Arkansas National Stockyards, 1957-82. Community Activities: Director, Pulaski County Tuberculosis Association, 1950-72; Trustee, Little Rock University, 1959-60; Member and Past President, Little Rock Air Force Base Community Council; Member and Past President, Little Rock School Board (during school integration controversy); Appeared on CBS "Face the Nation" and NBC "Today" Show; Little Rock City Planning Commission, 1959; Chairman, Advisory Board, Salvation Army, 1978-79; President, Board of Trustees, Baptist Hospital Health Foundation, 1982; Founding Member and Past President, Fifty for the Future, 1973-83; Alumni Board, Sewanee Military Academy, 1971-78; Advisory Board, Catholic High School, 1964-66. Religion: Episcopalian, Member of Vestry 1973-76. Honors and Awards: Omicron Delta Kappa; President, Alumni Board 1974-75, Designated a Distinguished Alumnus 1975, Honorary LL.D. 1982, Washington and Lee University. Address: 4601 Kavanaugh Blvd., Little Rock, Arkansas 72207. ■

FLORENCE D. TUCKER

Human Resource Manager. Personal: Born November 12, 1925; Daughter of Victor Amos Denslow and Martha Buchanan Binkley (both deceased); Married Joseph N. Jr. (deceased), Son of J. Nathaniel Tucker (deceased) and Rose McLeod Tucker; Married Noel F. Parrish, Son of Garland J. and Lucille Lambert Parrish (both deceased), June 25, 1983; Mother of Joseph N. III, F. Steven, James D. Education: Diploma in Piano, Ward Belmont, 1945; Private Student of Michael Field, Concert Pianist, New York, New York, 1945-46; B.M.E., Delta State University, 1960; M.S. Counseling, University of Southern Mississippi, 1971; Ed.D. Human Resource Development, George Washington University, 1982. Career: Teacher of Music, Gulfport City Schools, Gulfport, Mississippi, 1959-63; Recreation Therapist, Veterans Hospital, PM&R Division, Gulfport, Mississippi, 1964-70; Education Counselor, United States Air Force, Keesler Air Force Base, Mississippi 1971-72, Kadena Air Force Base, Okinawa, Japan 1972-74; Education Services Officer, United States Air Force, Kunsan Air Base, Korea, 1974-75; Assistant Director, Senior Training, United States Air Force, Civil Air Patrol National Headquarters, Maxwell Air Force Base, Alabama, 1975-77; Equal Employment Opportunity Officer, D.C. Department of Labor, Washington D.C., 1977-80; Visiting Professor, Kunsan, Korea Teachers College and Kunsan Junior College, 1974-75; Bureau Chief, Complaints Processing and Adjudication, Office of Equal Employment Opportunity, National Headquarters, United States Geological Survey, Reston, Virginia, 1980-82; Human Resources Manager, Minerals Management Service, Reston, Virginia, 1982 to present; Independent Consultant, Management Development, Career Counseling, International Human Resource Development, 1971 to present. Organizational Memberships: Member Board of Directors 1983, Chairman National Affairs Committee 1983, Metropolitan Washington D.C. Chapter, American Society for Training and Development; Member Board of Directors, Wake Associates, Ltd., International Management Consulting Firm, Washington D.C., 1980 to present; American Association for the Advancement of Science, 1982; American Society for Public Administrators; Phi Delta Kappa; Women in Communications, Inc.; National Association for Female Executives; Adult Education Association; American Society of Professional and Executive Women; Society for International Development; Gulfport and Mississippi Teacher's Associations; American Personnel and Guidance Association; Washington D.C. Women's Network. Community Activities: Member United States Geological Survey Fine Arts Committee, representing the Director's Office; Conducted or Made Presentations in Approximately 300 Seminars and Workshops on Topics including Mental Health, Career and Life Planning, Education Practices, Discrimination and Affirmative Action, Counseling Techniques, Program Administration, Seminar Design and Development, Management and Executive Development, National and Internationally, 1967 to present; Gulfport Yacht Club, 1962-66; Broadwater Country Club, Gulfport, Mississippi, 1966-70; Les Danseuses, Gulfport, Mississippi, 1968-72; Gulfport Teacher's Association, 1959-63; Mississippi Teacher's Association, 1959-63; Westminster Presbyterian Church, Gulfport, Mississippi, Charter Member 1961-76; Parents Without Partners 1962-64, Organized and Served as President for Two Terms, the First Chapter in Mississippi; Civic Music Association, Gulf Coast Symphony, Belles Buouys Square Dance Club, Little Theater, Gulfport, 1960-72; Metropolitan Dinner Club, 1971-72; Smithsonian Resident Associates, 1977 to present; Organist, Pianist or Conductor for Numerous Civic Music Programs in Greenville, Mississippi, and Gulfport, Mississippi, 1956-70; Member Chapel Advisory Council, Kunsan Air Base, Korea, 1974-75. Published Works: Author Professional Articles in Federal Agency Newsletters; Co-Author, Position Papers on Education, Training Topics and Issues which effected Policy Changes. Honors and Awards: Scholarship, Ward-Belmont College, 1943; President's List Scholar and Dean's Scholar, Delta State College, 1958-60; Appointed Adjunct Professor for Two Korean Colleges, by the Korean Ministry of Education, Lecturing to Faculty and Students, 1974-75; Recipient of Outstanding Visiting Professor Award from Kunsan (Korea) Teachers College, 1974; Recipient of Award for Promoting Teacher Exchange Program from Kunsan (Korea) Junior College, 1975; Recipient of Certificate of Appreciation for Outstanding Assistance to the Civil Air Patrol, United States Air Force, 1977; Letter of Commendation from Plan B, Inc., 1979; Listed in *1982 International Consultants Directory*, *Marquis Who's Who in the South and Southwest*, *Who's Who of American Women*, *Personalities of the South*, *The World Who's Who of Women*, *Who's Who in International Human Resource Development*. Address: 4701 Kenmore Avenue, Apartment 1310, Alexandria, Virginia 22304. ■

ROSALIE L. TUNG

University Professor. Personal: Born December 2, 1948; Daughter of Andrew and Pauline Lam; Married Byron Tung; Mother of Michele Christine. Education: B.A., York University, 1972; M.B.A. 1974, Ph.D. Business Administration 1977, University of British Columbia. Career: University Professor, The Wharton School, University of Pennsylvania. Organizational Memberships: Academy of International Business; Academy of Management; American Management Association; American Economic Association; American Institute of Decision Sciences; American Psychological Association; International Association of Applied Psychology. Published Works: Author of Five Books, *Management Practives in China* (1980), *U.S.-China Trade Negotiations* (1982), *Chinese Industrial Society after Mao* (1982), *Business Negotiations with the Japanese* (1984) and *Key to Japan's Economic Strength: Human Power* (1984). Honors and Awards: Listed in *World Who's Who of Women*, *Who's Who of American Women*, *Book of Honor*, *Directory of Distinguished Americans*, *Personalities of America*, *Who's Who in Frontier Science*, *Who's Who in the East*. Address: P.O. Box 8253, Philadelphia, Pennsylvania 19101. ■

ROSALYN TURECK

Concert Artist, Author, Educator. Personal: Born December 14, 1914, in Chicago, Illinois; Daughter of Samuel and Monya Lipson Tureck. Education: Studied with Sophia Brilliant-Liven and Jan Chiapusso; Graduated cum laude, Juilliard School of Music, 1935. Career: Touring Concert Artist, United States 1937 to present, Europe 1947 to present, South Africa 1959, South America 1963, Israel 1963, Far East (Hong Kong, India, Australia) 1971; Conductor/Soloist with the London Philharmonic 1958, New York Philharmonic 1958, Collegium Musicum (Copenhagen), Tureck Bach Players (London) 1958 to present, San Antonio Symphony and Oklahoma Symphony 1962, Scottish National Symphony 1963, Israel Philharmonic 1963, Kol Israel Orchestra 1970, Nashville Symphony Orchestra 1977, Tureck Bach Players (London) 1980, Tureck Bach Players (United Staes) 1981, St. Louis Symphony Orchestra 1981; Television Appearancs; Professor of Music, University of Maryland 1982 to present, University of California at San Diego 1967-72; Visiting Professor of Music, Washington University

(St. Louis), 1963-64; Instructor, Columbia University 1953-55, Juilliard School of Music 1943-44, Mannes College of Music 1940-44, Philadelphia Conservatory of Music 1935-42; Visiting Fellow, St. Hilda's College, Oxford University, 1974; Honorary Life Fellow, St. Hilda's College, 1974 to present; Visiting Fellow, Wolfson College, Oxford University, 1975 to present; Founder/Director, Composers for Today 1951-55, Tureck Bach Players (London) 1957 to present, International Bach Society Inc. 1966, Institute for Bach Studies 1968, Tureck Bach Institute Inc. 1981. Organizational Memberships: American Music Scholarship Association, Honorary President; Music Library, Hebrew University, Jerusalem; Societe Johann Sebastian Bach de Belgique; Honorary Life Member, The Bohemians, New York; American Musicological Society; New Bach Society; Royal Musical Association; Royal Philharmonic Society; Oxford Society. Published Works: *An Introduction to the Performance of Bach* (3 Volumes) 1969-70 (Japanese Translation 1966, Spanish Translation 1975), *Tureck Bach Urtext Series: Italian Concerto* (1983), *Lute Suite in E minor set for classical guitar* (1983); Transcriber of Music, 1960; Numerous Periodical Articles, Recordings, Film Performances. Honors and Awards: First Prize Award for Debut, Age 9, 1923; First Prize, Greater Chicago Piano Playing Tournament, 1928; Winner, Schubert Memorial Contest, 1935; National Federation of Music Clubs Competition, 1935; Phi Beta Award for Excellence; First Town Hall Endowment Award, 1938; Honorary Fellow, Guildhall School of Music and Drama, London, 1959; Honorary Mus.D. Degree, Colby College 1964, Roosevelt University 1968, Wilson College 1968, Oxford University 1977; Fellow, Macdowell Colony, 1978; Officers Cross of the Order of Merit of the Federal Republic of Germany, 1979; Nominee, Grammy Award, 1980. Address: Columbia Artists Management, 165 West 57th Street, New York, New York 10019.■

THOMAS NORMAN TURK

Manufacturing Executive. Personal: Born December 9, 1938; Son of Charles J. and May C. Turk; Married Coleen, Daughter of John and Mayme Budd; Father of Tommy, Casey, Tiffany. Education: A.A., Golden West College, Huntington Beach, California, 1973; B.A., California State University, Long Beach, California, 1976; M.B.A., National University, San Diego, California, 1982; Certificate in Inventory Management, San Diego State University, 1980. Military: Served in the United States Marine Corps, 1956-58. Career: Production Control Manager, 1978 to present. Organizational Memberships: Society of Manufacturing Engineers; American Production and Inventory Control Society, Vice President Membership 1980-81, Vice President Education 1981-82; Computer Automated Systems Association. Honors and Awards: C.M.F.G.E., Certified as Manufacturing Engineer by the Society of Manufacturing Engineers; C.P.I.M., Certified as a Professional in Production and Inventory Management by the American Production and Inventory Control Society. Address: P.O. Box 2202, Costa Mesa, California 92626.■

ALLEN A. TURNBULL, JR.

Consulting Psychologist. Personal: Born June 21, 1947; Son of Allen A. and Mary D. Turnbull. Education: B.A., University of Virginia, 1969; M.A., College of William and Mary, 1971; Ph.D., Carleton University, 1977. Career: Consulting Psychologist; President, Bike Virginia, Inc.; Former University Professor, Management Analyst. Organizational Memberships: American Psychological Association; American Society for Training and Development; World Future Society; International Association of Quality Circles; Evaluation Research Society. Community Activities: President, Williamburg Bicycle Association, 1977-82. Honors and Awards: Psi Chi; Canada Council Doctoral Fellowship; Lilly Postdoctoral Fellowship; Listed in *Who's Who in the South and Southwest*. Address: 109 Laurel Lane, Williamsburg, Virginia 23185.■

CARL JEANE TURNER

International Business Development Specialist, Electronics Engineer. Personal: Born July 27, 1933, in Sevierville, Tennessee; Son of Kenneth Albert and Lenna Faye Christopher Turner (both deceased); Married Flossie Pearl Ingram, December 11, 1954; Father of Marcia, Kenneth, Theresa, Christopher, Robin. Education: B.S.Ed. and B.S.E.E. 1980, M.B.A. 1982, Columbia Pacific University. Military: Served in the Florida Air National Guard, 1948-50, until called to Active Duty for Korean Conflict; Served in the United States Air Force, 1950 until retirement in 1972. Career: G.T.E. Corporation, Manager Export Marketing, 1981 to present; Itek Corporation 1972-77, 1978-81, Applied Technology Division; Manager, International Program Planning and Control, Resident Manager-German Programs Office (Ulm, West Germany), Optical Systems Division, Program Development Manager (Athens, Greece); E-Systems Inc., Senior Engineer/Analyst and Chief Instructor, Greenville, Texas, 1977-78. Organizational Memberships: International Platform Association; American Society of Professional Consultants; Institute of Electrical and Electronic Engineers; Air Force Association; Association of Old Crows; Armed Forces Communications and Electronics Association; Order of Seasoned Weasels. Community Activities: Republican Presidential Task Force. Religion: Baptist. Published Works: Author/Editor, Electronic Warfare Management Courses and International Business Guides. Honors and Awards: Presidential Achievement Award, 1982; President's Medal of Merit, Ronald Reagan, President of the United States, 1982; George Washington Honor Medal, Freedom Foundation, 1965; Listed in *Who's Who in Finance and Industry, Who's Who in the West, Jane's Who's Who in Aviation and Aerospace, The Directory of Distinguished Americans, Personalities of America, Community Leaders of America, International Book of Honor, Personalities of the West amd Midwest, Who's Who in California, Men of Achievement, Dictionary of International Biography*. Address: GSD/GIC, 600 West John Street, Hicksville, New York 11802.■

GLADYS T. TURNER

Social Work Administrator. Personal: Born September 16, 1935; Daughter of Willis and Mary Bluford Turner; Married Frederick Marshall Finney. Education: B.A., A.M.&.N. College (now University of Alabama at Pine Bluff), 1957; M.S.W., Atlanta University, 1959. Career: Social Work Administrator; Clinical Social Worker. Organizational Memberships: National Association of Social Workers, Miami Valley Chapter, Secretary 1961, 2nd Vice President 1974, President 1975-76, Delegate to Delegate Assembly 1979, National Nominating Committee Member 1971-72 and Chairperson 1973. Community Activities: Montgomery County Children's Services, Advisory Board 1969-75; Dayton Board of Education, Advisory Committee for Special Education 1974; Montgomery County Combined General Health District Professional Advisory Committee 1974-77; Wright State University Medical School, Medicine in Society Steering Committee 1975-76; Miami Valley Hospital Social Work Directors Organization, Co-Founder; Parents Association on Non-Ambulatory Retarded Children, Co-Founder. Religion: College Hill United Presbyterian Church, Elder 1976 to present, Nominating Committee Chairperson 1981; Miami Presbytery Committee for the Self-Development of People, Chairperson 1981 to present. Honors and Awards: Social Worker of the Year, Miami Valley Chapter, National Association of Social Workers. Address: 1107 Lexington Avenue, Dayton, Ohio 45407.■

HERMAN NATHANIEL TURNER, JR.

Educator. Personal: Born November 6, 1925, in St. Louis, Missouri; Son of Herman Nathaniel Sr., and Rosie Mae Williams Turner; Married Terrance Diane Parker on October 5, 1980, in St. Louis; Father of Anthony Cabot, Mark Courtney, Herman Nathaniel III, Erik Alexander (by previous marriage) and Marian Terese Simmons, Mariesta Marcella Simmons, Melita Diane Simmons (stepdaughters). Education: Graduate, Vashon High School, St. Louis, 1944; B.S., Bradley University, 1951; Undertook Postgraduate Work at Bradley University, 1951-52. Military: Served with the United States Marine Corps during World War II in the South Pacific as Radar Operator, 1944-46. Career: Instructor of Mathematics at Vaux Junior High School and Stoddart-Fleisher Junior High School (Philadelphia, Pennsylvania) 1956-59, Washington Senior High School (Caruthersville, Missouri) 1961-62, United Township High School (East Moline, Illinois) 1965-66, and Northwest High School (St. Louis) 1968 to present; Mathematician, White Sands Proving Ground, Flight Determination Laboratory, Data Reduction Branch, Optical Reduction Section, Las Cruces, New Mexico, 1954-55; Cartographic Photogrammetric Aide, Aeronautical Chart and Information Center, Photogrammetry Division, Topography Branch, St. Louis, 1953-54. Organizational Memberships: Mathematical Association of America, 1962 to present; American Federation of Teachers, 1969 to present; American Mathematical Society, 1977 to present; Northwest High School Public Relations Committee, 1978 to present. Community Activities: Kiwanis Club of East Moline, Illinois, Chairman of Public Relations Committee 1965-66. Religion: Presbyterian. Honors and Awards: Fellow, International Biographical Association, 1978 to present; Fellow, American Biographical Institute, 1979 to present; Honorary Fellow, Anglo-American Academy, 1980 to present; Certified Teacher in Missouri, Illinois, Pennsylvania, New Jersey and New York; Certificate of Appreciation, Kiwanis Club of East Moline, 1965; Scroll of the Anglo-American Academy, 1980; Received Numerous Awards of Appreciation from Students at Northwest High

School, including Teacher of the Month (October-November, 1979) and Teacher of the Year, 1980; Listed in *Who's Who in the Midwest, International Who's Who of Intellectuals, Personalities of the West and Midwest, Community Leaders and Noteworthy Americans, Book of Honor, Personalities of America, Men of Achievement, International Who's Who in Community Service, Dictionary of International Biography, International Biographical Association Yearbook, International Book of Honor, Anglo-American Who's Who, Contemporary Personalities, Community Leaders of America*. Address: P.O. Box 1028, St. Louis, Missouri 63188.■

PATRICIA RAE TURNER

Regional Manager. Personal: Born May 15, 1935; Daughter of James Ray and Linnie Watson; Married Donald H., Son of John and Becky Turner. Education: B.B.A. 1971, M.B.A. 1974, Ph.D. Candidate, East Texas State University. Career: Regional Manager, South Central Texas Regional Training Center, Texas Engineering Extension Service, The Texas A&M University System, 1978 to present; Division Head, Special Programs Training Division, Texas Engineering Extension Service, The Texas A&M University System, 1978; Associate Director, Community Service, El Centro College, Dallas Community College District, Dallas, Texas, 1976-77; Director, Student Development, East Texas State University, 1974-76; Director, Division of Adult and Continuing Education, Angelo State University, San Angelo, Texas, 1974; Assistant Director, Community Service, Mountain View, Dallas County Community College District, Dallas, Texas, 1972-73; Program Coordinator, Division of Continuing Education, East Texas State University, 1970-72. Organizational Memberships: American Vocational Association; Texas Press Women; National Federation Press Women; American Society of Training and Development; National University Continuing Education Association; Iota Lambda Sigma; Kappa Delta Phi; Phi Delta Kappa; Alpha Chi. Community Activities: Alamo Area Council of Governments; Private Industry Council; City of San Antonio Industrial Development Authority, Board of Directors; Alamo Area Council of Governments Regional Development and Review Committee; Greater San Antonio Chamber of Commerce Business Expansion Task Force Committee Member, Consular Liaison Committee Member, Legislative Committee Member; United Way, Budget Allocations Panel; United San Antonio, Vocational and Technical Advisory Committee; Comprehensive Employment Training Act Reauthorization Roundtable Discussion Committee. Published Works: Editor; Contributing Author to *Handbook for Employing Handicap* and Handicap Articles to the Texas Rehabilitation Community TPEA Monthly Newsletter. Religion: Baptist. Honors and Awards: Certificate of Appreciation, United States Department of Navy; Appreciation Resolution, Board of Regents, East Texas State University; "Today's Woman," *The San Antonio Light Newspaper*, 1982; Distinguished Citizen Award for Participation in Vocational Education, City of Guatemala; Listed in the American Society of Training and Development's *Who's Who Training Directory*, Directory of National Women Administrators in Vocational Education *WAVE, Who's Who in the South and Southwest, Who's Who of American Women*. Address: 1506 Caper Lane, San Antonio, Texas 78232.■

R. CHIP TURNER (RALPH W. JR.)

Religious Administrator. Personal: Born January 18, 1948; Son of Ralph W. Turner, Sr.; Married Sandra Aymond, Daughter of Mrs. J. D. Aymond, Sr.; Father of Christopher Layne, Cory Wilson. Education: B.A., Louisiana College; M.R.E., New Orleans Baptist Theological Seminary. Career: Director of Media Services, Louisiana Baptist Convention; State Director of the American Christian Television Systems (ACTS); Former Positions include Associate Director of Missions of the New Orleans Baptist Association, Associate Pastor and Minister of Education at the First Baptist Church of Farmerville (Louisiana), Summit (Mississippi), Port Arthur (Texas), Beaumont (Texas), Slidell (Louisiana). Organizational Memberships: Louisiana Vice President, Ministers in Broadcasting; Baptist Public Relations Association; Southern Baptist and Louisiana Baptist Religious Education Associations; National Federation of Local Cable Programmers; National Association of Local Church Communicators, Board of Governors 1983 to present; International Television Association; A.E.C.T.; L.A.E.C.T.; National Audio-Visual Association. Community Activities: Boy Scouts of America, National Protestant Committee, National Board of Association of Baptists for Scouting, Executive Boards of Scout Councils in New Orleans (Louisiana), Beaumont (Texas), Alexandria (Louisiana); Church Commission for Civic Youth Serving Agencies, National Board; Rotary Club; Lions Club. Religion: Contract Teacher for New Orleans Baptist Theological Seminary. Published Works: Author of Articles and Series in 10 Denominational Magazines as well as Boy Scouting Articles. Honors and Awards: Silver Beaver 1982; Good Shepherd Award, 180; Outstanding Student Teacher; Alexandria Civitan Citizenship Award; Vice President, Louisiana College Student Body; American Christian Television System Advisory Board; State Consultant, Baptist Telecommunication Network. Address: 207 Arrowhead Drive, Pineville, Louisiana 71360.■

TERRANCE DIANE (PARKER) TURNER

Organization Executive. Personal: Born June 7, 1947, in St. Louis, Missouri; Daughter of Marion Willard Sr. and Esther Agusta (Hackett) Parker; Married Herman Nathaniel Turner Jr., Son of Herman Nathaniel Sr. and Rosie Mae (Williams) Turner; Mother of Marian Terese Simmons, Mariesta Marcella Simmons, Melita Diane Simmons (all by previous marriage); Stepchildren Anthony Cabot Turner, Mark Courtney Turner, Herman Nathaniel Turner III, Erik Alexander Turner. Education: Diploma, Sumner High School, St. Louis, Missouri, 1964; Certificate of Course Completion in Keypunch, O'Fallon Technical Center, Adult Education, St. Louis, Missouri, 1967. Career: Bindery Assistant, Con P. Curran Printing Company (St. Louis, Missouri) 1970-72, John S. Starks Printing Company (Manchester, Missouri) 1972-75; Pressperson, Lianco Container Corporation, Bridgeton, Missouri, 1975-79; Area Commander (with husband), from the Honorable Mayor Vincent C. Schoemehl Jr., Area F, Region #9, Operation Brightside (St. Louis Cleans Up), St. Louis, Missouri, June 5, 1982; Secretary, Block Unit #962, Urban League, St. Louis, Missouri, 1972 to present. Organizational Memberships: International Brotherhood of Bookbinders Association, Local #55, Creve Coeur, Missouri, 1970-75; Graphic Arts Local #505, Master Printers of America, Creve Coeur, Missouri, 1975-79. Community Activities: Mother's Club, Walnut Park School 1971-77, Cupples School 1977-79, Northwest High School 1979-82, St. Louis, Missouri. Religion: Non-Denominational. Honors and Awards: Letter of Introduction, Lianco Container Corporation, Bridgeton, Missouri, 1979; Listed in *Personalities of America, Community Leaders of America, Personalities of the West and Midwest*. Address: P.O. Box 1028, St. Louis, Missouri 63188.■

WELD WINSTON TURNER

Industrial Psychologist. Personal: Born July 25, 1931; Son of Frank and Hazel Weld Prevratil (deceased); Married Helen Theo Syrios (divorced 1969); Father of Jean Ann, Alan Weld. Education: Attended Wichita University, 1952-53; B.S. Oklahoma A&M College (now Oklahoma State University), 1954; M.S. 1955, Ph.D. 1959, Purdue University. Military: Served in the United States Army, 1950-51, attaining the rank of Corporal. Career: Industrial Psychologist; Former Positions as Sheetmetal Worker and Bookkeeper. Organizational Memberships: Midwestern Psychological Association 1955-59; American Psychological Association, 1955 to present; Society for Industrial and Organizational Psychology, 1955 to present; Metropolitan Psychological Association, 1968-71. Community Activities: Veterans of Foreign Wars, 1952-81; Veterans of Foreign Wars National Home, 1981; Part-Time Lecturer for the Adult Education Division of the University of Akron 1960-61, Executive Study Conference of the Educational Testing Service 1960-70; Talks on Industrial Psychology; Conducted Many Symposiums on Industrial/Organizational Psychology. Published Works: Article in the *Journal of Applied Psychology*, 1960. Honors and Awards: Phi Kappa Phi, 1954; Pi Gamma Mu, 1954; Sigma Xi, 1955; Certified as a Psychologist in New York, 1971. Address: 601 East Rosery Road, Apartment 3905, Largo, Florida 33540.■

YVONNE WILLIAMS TURNER

Community Resources Specialist. Personal: Born April 5, 1927; Daughter of John Harvey Williams and Leitha Williams Stevens; Married James Leroy Sr.; Mother of Philandus Christopher, Roderick Gerard, Keith Harvey, Leitha Bernadette, Stanley Mayo Oko. Education: Attended Booker T. Washington Junior College of Business, 1952; Graduate, Dale Carnegie Courses 1960, Rosetta Reifer of New York Modeling and Charm School 1954, Anna Watson School of Millinery 1958-68; Divers-Hayden Music Studio, 1950-52. Career: Community Resources Specialist, U.S. Department of Housing and Urban Development, Birmingham, Alabama; Program Aide, Community Planning and Development Division, Manager's Office, Birmingham Area Office, Department of Housing and Urban Development; Former Representative, Emps Association; Former Secretary, A. G. Gaston Interest 18 Years, Clyde Kirby Insurance Agency 1 Year; Booker T. Washington Business Junior College Alumni Club; American Federal Government Employees Union; Board Birmingham Creative Dance School; Board Birmingham Festival of Arts; Board Youth Development Headquarters; Advisory Board, Parent Education Program for City Schools; Former President, Wilkerson Elementary and A. H. Parker High School Band Boosters. Community Activities: Attended 100 Approved Workshops in Various Areas; Volunteer, Alabama Election Law Commissioner; Supportor of Area Churches; Jazz Hall of Fame; Southern Regional Opera; Town and Gown Theatre; Former President, Alabama State University Band Boosters; Member Alabama Christian Movement; 1978 Chairwoman for S.C.L.C.'s National Convention in Birmingham; Supporter, A. G. Gaston Boy's Club and Help One Another Inc.; Sang with Birmingham Civic Chorale, 4 Years; Appointed by City Council to Birmingham Design Review Committee for Revitalization of Historic Business Districts. Religion: Catholic. Published Works: Contributing Writer to *Birmingham World Newspaper*; "Cooking of Dr. Arrington" December 17, 1977, "Parker Band Boosters Club Treasurer Praised" March 15, 1980, "Black Business: To Be or Not

To Be" July 19, 1980, "The Price of Glory is High" *Birmingham Times Newspaper* December 11, 1980. Honors and Awards: Woman of Distinction, Iota Phi Lambda Sorority Inc., 1981; Mother of Distinction, Roderick, Turner and Family; Award of Appreciation, Alabama State University Bands; 1980 Service Award, Parker High Bands; 1979 Nominee Birmingham Board of Education; Wilkerson Elementary Outstanding Service Plaque, 1977, 1978, 1980, 1981; U.N.C.F. Awards; Certificate of Merit and Outstanding Service, 1978, B.T.W. Business College and Alumni; 1976 Nomination for Birmingham Woman of the Year, Downtown Business Women's Clubs; Listed in *Personalities of the South.* Address: 504 10th Court West, Birmingham, Alabama 35204.■

TERESA JORDAN TUZIL

Clinical Social Worker, Psychotherapist. Personal: Born May 13, 1948; Daughter of Kathleen G. Jordan; Married Joseph Tuzil III, Son of Joseph and Eleanore Tuzil; Mother of Joseph IV, Brian Joseph. Education: B.A., St. Johns University, 1970; M.S.W., Hunter College School of Social Work, 1973; Certificate in Gerontology, 1977. Career: Program Consultant, Community Council of Greater New York, 1978-79; Senior Social Worker, Jewish Association for Service to the Aged, 1973-78; Social Worker, Salvation Army Foster Care and Adoption Service, 1971-72; Private Practice, Consultation, Treatment and Supervision, Seaford, New York, 1976 to present. Career: National Association of Social Workers; Academy of Certified Social Workers; Certified, Registered, Clinical Social Worker. Community Activities: Field Instructor, Hunter College Graduate School of Social Work, Rutgers University School of Social Work, Columbia University School of Social Work. Religion: Catechist and Grade Chairperson, St. William the Abbot Roman Catholic Church Office of Religious Education. Published Works: Editor, *Journal of Gerontological Social Work*; Contributed Several Articles to Professional Publications in Social Work, Family Therapy, Gerontology. Honors and Awards: Listed in *Who's Who of American Women, International Directory of Who's Who of Women, Directory of Distinguished Americans.* Address: 3859 Tiana Street, Seaford, New York 11783.■

PAUL BASSET TWEED

Business Manager. Personal: Born September 22, 1913; Son of Jacob and Ida Tweed (deceased); Married Mildred Emma Haycock; Father of Bradford, Joel. Education: B.S. 1934, M.S. 1935, Rensselaer Polytechnic Institute; M.A., New York State College for Teachers, 1937. Military: Served as a Civilian Employee of the United States Army, 1940-62. Career: Business Manager, We Care Inc. (Suicide Prevention); Engineer, Martin Marietta Corporation, Orlando, Florida, 1966-76; Engineer, Avco Corporation, Wilmington, Massachusetts, 1962-66; Chemical Engineer, Picatinny Arsenal, Dover, New Jersey, 1940-62; Chemist, American Hard Rubber Company, Butler, New Jersey, 1936-40. Organizational Memberships: Mutual Weapons Development Team, 1958, 1960; American Defense Preparedness Association, Member 1954-78, Government Consultant to Loading Section 1957-62; Chairman Explosives Subcommittee for Ordnance Engineering Handbooks 1955-62; American Institute of Chemists, Fellow 1968-76, Accreditation Committee 1974-76. Community Activities: Instructor, Henry George School of Social Science, 1940-60; Lake Holden (Florida) Water Advisory Board, 1974-83. Religion: Morristown (New Jersey) Unitarian Fellowship, Member 1955-66, Treasurer 1957-59; Orlando Unitarian Church, Member 1977 to present. Honors and Awards: National Honor Society; New York State Scholarship, 1930-34; R.P.I. Scholarship, 1930-34; R.P.I. Graduate Scholarship, 1934-35; Sigma Xi; Guest Lecturer on Explosives, Franklin Institute, Philadelphia, 1970. Address: 4624 Tinsley Drive, Orlando, Florida 32809.■

DENNIS G. TWIGGS

Psychologist. Personal: Born February 5, 1946; Son of James and Velra Twiggs; Married; Father of Jason. Education: B.A. 1969, M.A. 1973, Appalachian State University; Ph.D., Tulane University, 1977. Military: Served with the United States Army Special Forces, 1969-71, attaining the rank of Lieutenant. Career: Psychologist, Private Practice, present; Psychologist, Mexia State School, Texas, 1977-78; Director of Rehabilitation Therapy, San Antonio State School Hospital, 1978-80. Organizational Memberships: Association for Retarded Citizens, Forsyth County, President 1980; Sigma Xi, 1977; Association for Advancement of Science, 1978. Community Activities: American Red Cross Board of Directors, 1980-83; Lions Club, 1982; Ambucs, 1982; Piedmont Coalition for Handicapped, Board of Directors 1981. Honors and Awards: Listed in *Who's Who in the South and Southwest, Personalities of America, Directory of Distinguished Americans.* Address: 3232 Luther Street, Winston-Salem, North Carolina 27107.■

BARBARA S. UEHLING

University Chancellor. Personal: Born June 12, 1932; Daughter of Mr. and Mrs. Roy W. Staner; Married Stanley Johnson; Mother of David, Jeff. Education: B.A. Psychology, Wichita State University, 1954; M.A. 1956, Ph.D. 1958, Northwestern University. Career: Chancellor, University of Missouri-Columbia, 1978 to present; Provost, University of Oklahoma at Norman, 1976-78; Dean of Arts and Science, Illinois State University, 1974-76; Academic Dean, Roger Williams College, 1972-74; Psychology Professor, University of Rhode Island 1970-72, Emory University 1966-69; Faculty Member, Oglethorpe University, 1959-64. Organizational Memberships: American Association for Higher Education, Board of Directors; American Council on Education, Board of Directors; Meredith Corporation, Board Member; Mercantile Bancorporation, Board Member; Carnegie Foundation for the Advancement of Teaching; Advisory Council of Presidents, Association of Governing Boards; Editorial Board, *National Forum Magazine*, Phi Kappa Phi. Community Activities: North Central Association of Schools and Colleges, Accreditation Team; National Association of State Universities and Land Grant Colleges, Policies and Issues Committee; N.C.A.A. Select Committee on Athletics; United Way, Board of Directors. Honors and Awards: Distinguished Alumni Award, Wichita State University; Honorary Degree, Drury College; Honorary Doctor of Laws, Ohio State University; 100 Young Leaders of the Academy, *Change* Magazine; Missouri Institute of Public Administration Award for Outstanding Contributions to Public Administration; Listed in *Who's Who in America, Who's Who in the Midwest, Dictionary of International Biography, American Men and Women of Science, Men of Achievement.* Address: Chancellor's Residence, Columbia, Missouri 65201.■

WALTER E. ULRICH

Deputy Commissioner. Personal: Born January 30, 1921, in New York City, New York; Son of Edward and Elisabeth Ulrich (both deceased); Married Bernice Marjorie Janssen, Daughter of William and Mary Janssen (both deceased); Father of Walter E. Jr., Marilyn Elisabeth Lynn. Education: Attended Catawba College (Salisbury, North Carolina), Columbia University (New York City); L.L.B., John Marshall School, 1948. Military: Served in the United States Army as Commanding Officer of the Medical Detachment/Evacuation Hospital, European Theatre Operations, World War II, with the rank of Captain. Career: Deputy Commissioner, New Jersey Department of Human Services, 1982 to present; Surrogate-Judge of Union County, New Jersey, 1979-82; Senior Supervisor, Claims and Legal Department, Hartford Accident and Indemnity, Newark, New Jersey (Retired); Manager, Stevens & Mathias (Law Firm); Elected Charter Commissioner, Rahway, 1953; Councilman, Rahway, New Jersey, 1955-65; Board of Chosen Freeholders, Union County, 1963-78; Deputy Director, Board of Chosen Freeholders; Advisory Board of Managers, John E. Runnells Hospital, Union County. Organizational Memberships: International Narcotics Enforcement Officers Association; National District Attorneys Association. Honors and Awards: Annual Award, Mental Health Association; Bronze Key Award, National Council on Alcoholism; Outstanding Recognition Award for Invaluable Service, Retired Seniors Volunteers Program, Union County; Association for Retarded Citizens/Union County Service Award; Citation for Ten Years Dedicated Public and Community Service, Rahway, New Jersey; Others. Address: 8 Pasadena Drive, Hamilton Township, New Jersey 08619.■

ROBERT C. UNDERWOOD

Illinois State Supreme Court Justice. Personal: Born October 27, 1915, in Gardner, Illinois; Son of Marion L. and Edith L. Frazee Underwood (both deceased); Married Dorothy L. Roy, February 2, 1939; Father of Susan Louise Barcalow (Mrs. John C. III). Education: Graduate, Gardner-South Wilmington Township High School, 1933; A.B., Illinois Wesleyan University, 1937; LL.B. (J.D.), University of Illinois College of Law, 1939. Career: Admitted to Illinois Bar, 1939; Private Practice, Bloomington, Illinois, 1939-46; City Attorney, Normal, Illinois; Assistant States Attorney, McLean County, Illinois, 1942-46; Judge of County Court of McLean County, 1946-62; Justice of the Supreme Court of Illinois, 1962 to present; Chief Justice, Supreme Court of Illinois 1969-75. Organizational Memberships: Conference of Chief Justices, Member 1969-75, Executive Council 1971-75, Vice Chairman 1974-75; Chairman Board of Elections, American Bar Association, 1974-77; McLean County Bar Association, Past President; Illinois State Bar Association; Chicago Bar Association, Honorary Member; Appellate Lawyers Association, Honorary Member; Director, American Judicature Society, 1975-79; Illinois Representative on the Council of State Court Representatives of the National Center for State Courts, 1979-81. Community Activities: Illinois Commission on Children, Vice Chairman; Illinois Wesleyan University, Former Member Board of Trustees; McLean County Mental Health Center, Former Member Board of Directors; Fellow, Pennsylvania Mason Juvenile Court Institute; Chairman, Board of Higher Education Committee to Survey Legal Education Needs in Illinois; Bloomington Consistory; Sigma Chi Social Fraternity; Pi Kappa Delta National Honorary Forensic Fraternity; Honorary Member, Rotary International; Honorary Member, Kiwanis International; Bloomington Country Club; Bloomington Club. Religion: Member First Methodist Church of Normal. Published Works: Author Various Professional Articles. Honors and Awards: Distinguished Service Award, United States Junior Chamber of Commerce, 1948; Good Government Award, United States Junior Chamber of Commerce, 1953; Illinois Welfare Association Annual Citation for Public Service, 1960; Outstanding Citizens Award, Normal Chamber of Commerce; 33rd Degree Mason, 1964; Certificate of Outstanding Achievement, University of Illinois College of Law, 1969; Honorary Doctoral Degree, Loyola University 1969, Illinois Wesleyan University 1970, Eureka College 1970; Honorary LL.D., Illinois State University, 1984; Elected Member, American Law Institute, 1970-77; Annual Distinguished Service Award, Illinois Scottish Rite, 1970; Significant Sig Award, 1971; Award of Merit, Illinois State Bar Association, 1976; Listed in *American Bench, American Patriot's of the 1980's, The Blue Book: Leaders of the English Speaking World, Community Leaders and Noteworthy Americans, Dictionary of International Biography, Directory of Distinguished Americans, International Who's Who in Community Service, Men of Achievement, National Register of Prominent Americans, Notable Americans of 1978-79, Personalities of America, Personalities of the West and Midwest, Prominent Americans of the Eighties, Who's Who in America, Who's Who in American Law, Who's Who of American Lawyers, Who's Who in American Politics, Who's Who in Government, Who's Who in Illinois, Who's Who in the Midwest, Who's Who in the United States, Who's Who in the World, Contemporary Personalities.* Address: #11 Kent Drive, Normal, Illinois 61761.■

HOWARD ALBERT UNGER

College Professor, Artist, Photographer. Personal: Born October 13, 1944; Son of Howard and Florence Unger; Married Anrita Abelow; Father of Christopher Howard. Education: B.F.A. 1966, M.A. 1968, Kent State University; M.Ed. 1972, Ed.D. 1975, Postdoctoral Studies in Educational Administration 1978, Teachers College, Columbia University; Studies with the Art Students League (New York) 1960-61, School of Visual Arts (New York) 1975-76, New York Institute of Holography 1976. Career: Professor, Ocean County College, Toms River, New Jersey; Photography Columnist, *The Soho Weekly News*, 1977-78; Photography Critic, *The Village Voice*, 1976-77; Artist/Photographer, Coordinator of Photography and Art, R.C.A. Records, New York, 1969-70. Organizational Memberships:

TWO THOUSAND NOTABLE AMERICANS

National Education Association; New Jersey Education Association; Society of Photography Educators. Community Activities: Chinese Cultural Development Council (New York), Producer of Documentary Videotape on Chinese Classical Music 1970; Dr. Martin Luther King Health Center (Bronx, New York), Producer and Director of Television Program on Oral Health Education 1972; Nutritional Education Program for Head Start in Conjunction with the Urban League of Westchester County (New York), Producer of Photographic Exhibition 1973; Young Men's Christian Association Photography Club (Manhattan, New York), Judge of Photography Show 1974; Westchester County Urban League (Port Chester, New York), Graphic Designer of Brochures on Health Education with Photogrpahic Illustration 1975; United States Navy (Lakehurst, New Jersey), Photography Exhibition Judge 1976; New Jersey Equine Society of the State Department of Agriculture, Art Show Judge 1977. Religion: Lutheran; Director of Video Production "Black Poets" for Inter-church Center, Union Theological Seminary (New York City), 1971. Published Works: Co-Author (with William Maxwell), *Printmaking: A Beginner's Handbook*, 1977. Honors and Awards: First Place, The American Greeting Card Competition, 1966; "Photographic Societas Photographis" Photography Show, Columbia University, New York, 1971; Photography Exhibition, Ziegfield Gallery (New York), 1972; Honorarium, Department of Curriculum and Teaching, Teachers College, Columbia University, 1973; Annual Faculty Art Show, Ocean County College, 1972-81; Featured in *Science and Technology in the Arts, A Tour through the Realm of Science plus Art*, 1974; Listed in *Who's Who in the East*. Address: 437 East 67th Street, New York, New York 10021. ■

HAL J. UPBIN

Executive. Personal: Born January 15, 1939; Son of David Upbin and Evelyn Stiefel (both deceased); Married Shari Kiesler; Father of Edward, Elyse, Danielle. Eduation: B.B.A. Accounting, Pace College, 1961; C.P.A., Certified Public Accounting Examination, 1965. Career: President, Triton Group Ltd. (formerly Chase Manhattan Mortgage and Realty Trust, New York, New York), 1978-84; Executive Vice President and Chief Financial Officer, Chase Manhattan Mortgage and Realty Trust, 1975-78; President, Wheelabrator Financial Corporation (New York, New York), 1974-75; Treasurer, Wheelabrator Frye, Inc. (New York, New York), 1972-75; Tax Manager, Price Waterhouse and Company (New York, New York), 1965-71; Tax Senior on Audit Staff, Peat, Marwick, Mitchell and Company (New York, New York), 1961-65. Organizational Memberships: New York State Society of Certified Public Accountants, Guest Speaker, Municpal and Local Taxation Committee; American Institute of Certified Public Accountants, Guest Speaker, Various Seminars. Community Activities: Isomedics Inc., Chairman of the Board and Director; Pace University, Guest Speaker at Seminars, Member Finance and Facilities Planning Committee of the Board of Trustees and Alumni Advisory Members; Interval Timeshare Association of New York, Inc., Vice President; Temple Beth-El (Somerset, New York), Past President; Jaycees of Somerset County (New Jersey), Past Vice President; Metropolitan Opera Guild; Metropolitan Museum of Art; Museum of Modern Art. Religion: Temple Beth-El. Published Works: Articles on Taxation, *The Journal of Accountancy*. Honors and Awards: Listed in *Who's Who in America, Who's Who in Finance and Industry, Notable Americans of 1978-79, The American Registry, Men of Achievement, Dictionary of International Biography, Directory of the United States Banking Executives, Community Leaders of America, Men and Women of Distinction, The International Who's Who of Intellectuals, International Who's Who in Community Service*. Address: 45 East 89th Street, New York, New York 10028. ■

WALTER J. URBAN

Research Psychoanalyst. Personal: Born April 20, 1932. Education: B.A. cum laude Psychology 1953, M.A. Clinical School Psychology 1954, City College of New York; Ph.D. Clinical Psychology, International College (Los Angeles), 1977; Certification in Psychoanalysis, National Psychological Association for Psychoanalysis (New York), 1958-65; Certificate in Mental Health Consultation, Postgraduate Center for Mental Health (New York), Department of Community Education and Services, 1967-70; Family Therapy Training with Dr. Nathan Ackerman, Family Institute, New York, 1966; Certificate in Hypnosis, Ethical Hypnosis Training Center (South Orange, New Jersey), 1976; Certificate of Attendance in Polarity Therapy, Orange, California, 1973; Gestalt Workshops with Elana Rubinfeld, Dr. Julian Silverman and Others, Esalen Massage, Esalen Institute (Big Sur, California), 1973; Basic Course in Jin Shin Jyutsu, Acupressure Workshop (Los Angeles, California), 1976. Career: Private Practice Research Psychoanalyst in Individual Group, Marital, Family and Integrative Therapy, 1962 to present; Tutor, International College, Los Angeles; Director, Health and Longevity Center, El Reposo Spa (Desert Hot Springs, California); Consultant, Postgraduate Center, Wright Institute of Angeles; Director, Theodor Reik Consultation Center, New York, 1976; Faculty, Humanistic Psychology Center of New York, 1976; Board of Directors, Education Committee and Faculty Member, National Psychological Association for Psychoanalysis, New York, 1976; Supervisor, Association for Psychotherapy, New York, 1976; Producer and Host, One-Hour Weekly Television Program "Psychoanalysis" for Manhattan Cable Television Channel D, 1976; Consultant, Matteawan State Hospital for the Criminally Insane (Beacon, New York), Sponsored by National Institute of Mental Health, 1968-71; Supervisor and Faculty Member, Postgradute Center for Mental Health, Department of Community Education and Services, 1968-71; Family Therapist, Jewish Family Service (Brooklyn, New York), 1967-69; Senior Therapist, Community Guidance Service, 1966-69; Administrative Director, Mental Health Consultation Center (New York, New York), 1962-64; Attending Psychologist, Rockland County Clinic for Mental Health (Monsey, New York), 1961-67; School Psychologist, Putnam County Board of Cooperative Educational Services (Carmel, New York), 1961-62; Instructor, Department of Teacher Education, Brooklyn College, 1960; Remedial Reading Therapist, Hoffman School (Riverdale, New York), 1959-60; Jewish Child Care Association (New York), 1959-60; Director of Remedial Education, Wiltwych School for Boys (New York), 1959-61; Teacher, Children's Village (Dobbs Ferry, New York), 1959; Special Education Teacher, Rockland County Center for Physically Handicapped (New York, New York), 1957-59; Teacher, Orangeburg Grammar School (New York), 1956; Speech Therapist, Monmouth Memorial Hospital (Longbranch, New Jersey), 1955-56; Fellow, Department of Speech, City College of New York, 1953-54; Teacher, Bernby Play Group (New York City), 1953-54. Organizational Memberships: California State Psychological Association; American Psychological Association; National Psychological Association for Psychoanalysis, Training Analyst, Control Analyst, Clinical Supervisor; New York Society of Clinical Psychologists, Full Member, Former Chairman Awards Committee; American Society of Group Psychotherapy and Psychodrama; International Council of Psychologists; Council of Psychoanalytic Psychotherapists, Full Member, Former Chairman Elections Committee, Membership Committee; The Association for the Integration of the Whole Person; New York Society of Freudian Psychologists, Former Member-at-Large of Board of Directors, Training and Control Analyst, Co-Chairman Psychoanalytic Consultation Center; Psychologists Interested in the Advancement of Psychotherapy; Association of Applied Psychoanalysis, Executive Council and Education Chairman, Delegate to Board of Affiliates of Council of Psychoanalytic Psychotherapists; Rockland County Psychological Society; Association for Humanistic Psychology; National Accreditation Association of the American Examining Board of Psychoanalysts, Certificate in Psychoanalysis #122; Association for Holistic Health. Published Works: *Integrative Therapy: The Foundation for Holistic and Self-Healing*, 1978; "Integrative Therapy," in *Innovative Psychotherapies*, 1981. Honors and Awards: Listed in *Who's Who in the West, Community Leaders of America*. Address: 6320 Drexel Avenue, Los Angeles, California 90048. ■

ANTHONY VACCO

Mayor/Village President. Personal: Born September 24, 1924; Married Patricia; Father of Sandra, Anthony Jr., Darlene. Military: Served in the United States Army Medical Corps, 32 Months. Career: Mayor/Village President, Appointed in 1968, Elected in 1969, Re-elected in 1973, 1977 and 1981; Deputy Sheriff of Cook County, 1966-68; District Manager, Home Deliveries for Field Enterprises, Inc. Newspaper Division, *Chicago Sun-Times*, 16 Years. Community Activities: Chairman, Zoning Board of Appeals, 1961-65; Village Trustee, 1965-68; Executive Board of the Council of Governments of Cook County, 1973 to present; Vice Chairman, Council of Governments, Elected 1976; Cook County Development Advisory Council, 1975 to present; Illinois Municipal League; Vice President of Board of Directors, Illinois Municipal League, Elected 1975, Re-elected 1976-84; President, C.A.T.S. Southwest Council of Mayors, 1976-84; Public Safety Committee, National League of Cities, 1974-78; Community and Economic Development Committee, National League of Cities, 1979-84; Past President, Evergreen Park Regular Republican Organization; Past President, Worth Township Regular Republican Organization; Executive Board, United Homeowners of Evergreen Park; Worth Township Regular Democratic Organization; Evergreen Park Regular Democratic Organization; Christmas Basket Program, United Homeowners of Evergreen Park; Leukemia Research Foundation; Park Law School; Garden School for the Handicapped; St. Xavier College President's Council; United Cerebral Palsy Telethon; March of Dimes; 1977 Christmas Seal Chairman, Evergreen Park; Board of Directors, Evergreen Park Cancer Society; Member of Suburban Mayor's Committee for Little City, Palatine, Illinois; State Chairman, Sons of Italy Birth Defects Drive, 1979-83; Honorary Mayor, Little City Foundation, 1980-84; Trustee, Worth Township Schools, Elected for 6-year Term 1967, Re-elected 1973; President, Worth Township School Trustees, Elected 1975, Re-elected 1977; American Legion, Evergreen Park Post #854; Past Senior Vice-Commander, Veterans of Foreign Wars; Southeast Improvement Association; Mustang Boosters Parent Association of Evergreen Park High School; Evergreen Park Chamber of Commerce; Honorary Member, Rotary Club of Evergreen Park, Kiwanis Club; Honorary President, Evergreen Park Lodge #2200 Order Sons of Italy; Grand State President, State of Illinois Order Sons of Italy in America, Elected 1983-85; Former Coach, Evergreen Park Athletic Association/Little League Baseball; General Chairman, Evergreen Park 75th Diamond Jubilee Anniversary Committee 1967-68; Honorary Charter Member, Evergreen Park Jaycees, 1980. Honors and Awards: Citizen of the Year, Evergreen Park Chamber of Commerce, 1983; Man of Year, Italics Club of Chicago, 1976; Golden Gallon Award (for donating one gallon of blood to Evergreen Park Blood Plan), 1975; State of Illinois 78th General Assembly House of Representatives Resolution #1185 (for years of continued service to the community), 1974; Appreciation Award, Evergreen Park Chamber of Commerce, 1973, 1980; Citation of Appreciation, American Business Women's Association; Certificate, National Foundation, March of Dimes (for distinguished leadership in birth defects prevention), 1974; Southwest Sertoma Club Appreciation Award, 1969; Honorary Member, Junior Girl Scout Troop #270, 1971; Boy Scout Pack 3656 Award; Appreciation Award, Evergreen Park Kiwanis Club, 1973, 1976, 1978, 1981; Library of Human Resources of the American Heritage Research Association, 1975; Christ Hospital Celebrity Brunch Committee Member Certificate; Saint Xavier College Service Award; 95th Street Beverly Hills Business Men's Association Appreciation Award; Distinguished Service Award, Illinois Bicentennial Commission; Honorary Cub Scout, Troop #4488; Good Turn Award, Friend of Scouting Woodland District, 1977; American Legion Citation for Meritorious Service; American Cancer Society Merit Citation; Mayor of the Sixth Annual King Richards Fair, July 1978; Award of Merit, Mount Greenwood Civic Association, 1979; Service and Leadership Award, March of Dimes Birth Defects Drive, 1980; Evergreen Park High School Executive Internship Program, Certificate of Appreciation, 1980; Listed in *Personalities of the West and Midwest, Who's Who in the Midwest, Who's Who in American Politics, Who's Who in Government, Community Leaders and Noteworthy Americans, Dictionary of International Biography*. Address: 9440 South Ridgeway Avenue, Evergreen Park, Illinois 60642.■

CAROLE DOUGHTON VACHER

Clinical Psychologist. Personal: Born December 31, 1937; Daughter of Harold and Mamie Doughton; Married A. Ray Mayberry; Mother of Eizabeth M. Vacher. Education: B.A., West Virginia Wesleyan, 1960; M.A., Ohio University, 1962; Ph.D., North Carolina State University, 1973; Clinical Internship in Psychology, Vanderbilt University School of Medicine, 1972-73. Career: Birth Defects Coordinator, West Virginia Medical School, 1962-63; Research Associate, University of North Carolina Medical School, 1965-70; Research Psychologist, North Carolina Department of Mental Health, 1973-75; Assistant Professor of Psychology, Family Practice Residency Program, East Tennessee University School of Medicine, 1975-77; Community Services Consultant, Overlook Mental Health Center, Knoxville, Tennessee, 1977 to present; Private Practice in Clinical Psychology, Maryville Psychiatric Services, Maryville, Tennessee, 1974 to present. Organizational Memberships: American Psychological Association 1975 to present, Division 29 (Psychotherapy) 1979 to present, and Division 27 (Community Psychology) 1979 to present; Tennessee Psychological Association, 1975 to present; Knoxville Area Psychological Association, 1977 to present; Consultant, Knox County Child Abuse Review Team, 1977 to present; Organizer, "Worry Clinic" on Pre-Teen and Teenage Alcohol and Problems for Knox County and Surrounding Counties, 1981. Community Activities: Tennessee Medical Association Auxiliary, Board Member, State Mental Health Chairman, 1981-82; Knoxville Medical Association Auxiliary, Board Member, Mental Health Chairman, 1980 to present; Member of Speakers Bureau, Mental Health Association of Knox County, 1979 to present; Board Member, Orange County Mental Health Association, North Carolina, 1967-68. Religion: Volunteer Mission Work to Rural Areas Near Les Cayes, Haiti, 1979; Helped to Organize Contact Teleministries, Blount County, Tennessee; Organized and Helped Conduct Training Program for Contact Teleministries, 1981-82; Mental Health Training to Life Line Ministries, Australia, 1982. Published Works: Co-Author of Book *Consultation Education: Development and Evaluation* 1976; Author of *Self Help Directory: Knox County and Surrounding Area*; Author and Co-Author of Several Journal Articles, including "Development of a Prevention Program at Overlook Mental Health Center", "Mental Health Report - A Few Minutes of Prevention Can Forestall a Lifetime of Illness", *Tennessee Medical Journal*, "The Self-Concept of Underachieving Freshmen and Upperclass Women College Students", *Journal of College Student Personnel*; Author of "Stress Management", Chapter in *Wellness Manual*; Wrote and Produced Four Mental Health Television Programs "Preventing Problems by Finding Alternatives". Honors and Awards: Outstanding Volunteer Service to Tennessee Department of Human Services, 1978; Certified Licensed Ph.D. Clinical Psychologist, Tennessee, 1975 to present; Mental Health Scholarship Recipient, North Carolina Department of Mental Health, 1970-71; Phi Kappa Phi; Psi Chi, 1961; Haught Literary Society, 1959; President, Alpha Psi Omega, 1959-60; Wesleyan Key Award, 1960. Address: Route 23, Charlton Drive, Knoxville, Tennessee 37920.■

AGATHA MIN-CHUN FANG VAETH

Nurse, Businesswoman. Personal: Born February 19, 1935; Daughter of Yung-Cheng Fang; Married Randy H.; Mother of David Sun, Elizabeth Cheng, Philip Cheng. Education: Diploma, Maryview Hospital, School of Nursing, 1959; Studies in Fine Art, Oklahoma State University, 1969-74; Bachelor of Science in Professional Art, St. Joseph's College. Career: Nurse; Businesswomen. Organizational Memberships: American Nurses Association; Louisiana Nurses Association; Baton Rouge District Nurses Association, 1975-81; Art and Artists Guild; Diamite Corporation; International Platform Association. Community Activities: American Red Cross Association; American Red Cross Volunteer Nurse, 1975-79; Arts and Humanities Council of Greater Baton Rouge. Honors and Awards: High Quality Performance, U.S.P.H.S. H.E.W., 1978; Dedication and Recognition to Clinical Branch, N.H.D.C., U.S.P.H.S. D.H.H.S., 1981; Recognition and Appreciation, Clinical Branch, N.H.D.C., U.S.P.H.S. D.H.H.S., 1983; Outstanding Young Leader in Allied Health in Southwest National Center for Allied Health Leadership, 1983. Address: 855 Flannery Road, Apartment 721, Baton Rouge, Louisiana 70815.■

LINDA ANN VALDEZ

Executive. Personal: Born October 9, 1946; Daughter of Charles and Joy Valdez. Education: B.S. Business Administration, University of Colorado, 1968; Life Certification, Special Graduate Internship Program, University of California, 1973; Work Towards Masters of Public Administration, 1973-75; Management Certificate, University of Southern California, 1978; Management Certificate, Guest Lecturer, Northeastern University, 1980; Executive Vice President, Metro Consultants, Inc., 1980-82; Assistant Executive Director, San Antonio (Texas) Convention and Visitors Bureau, 1980 to present; Manager Marketing Department, Via Metropolitan Transit, San Antonio, Texas, 1978-80; Supervisor Market Information, Regional Transportation District, Denver, 1975-78; Assistant Alumni Director, University of Colorado, Boulder, 1972-75; Business Teacher, Dublin High School, Dublin, California, 1970-72; Tour Executive/Travel Consultant, Wholesale and Retail Divisions, Howard Tours, Inc., Oakland, California, 1968-70. Organizational Memberships: American Public Transit Association: National Vice President Marketing, National Board of Directors and Executive Committee, National Task Force of Women in Transit, National Task Force on Training in Transit, National Marketing Steering Committee, Speaker at State, Regional and National Conference; Urban Mass Transportation Administration, Seminar Committee for National and Regional Conferences on Marketing, National Transit Awareness Task Force, Marketing Management Seminar; Director San Antonio Board, American Marketing Association; Women in Communication, American Alumni Council. Community Activities: Vice President, San Antonio Ballet Association; Children's Hospital Foundation, Board of Directors, Chairperson, Marketing Committee; Awards, Promotion and Development Committees, Downtown Denver, Inc.; Gamma Phi Beta/Beta Rho, Board of Directors, President; National Assembly Committee, Council for Advancement and Support of Education; President's Chancellors Search Committee, University of Colorado; President's Occupations Advisory Board, Community College of Denver. Honors and Awards: American Marketing Association, Marketing Firm of the Year 1980, Marketing Person of the Year 1980; American Advertising Association in Texas, Six Local Awards, Two District Awards, Outstanding Young Women of America, 1974. Address: 6517 Honey Hill, San Antonio, Texas 78229.■

ROBERT G. VANDUYN

Retired United States Foreign Service Officer, Consultant on Educational Development, Businessman. Personal: Born February 12, 1913; Son of Robert Grover and Anna Gladys VanDuyn (deceased); Married Florence Elizabeth Noyer; Father of Elizabeth Ann Woods, Robert Mitchell. Education: B.A. 1934, M.A. 1939, Ball State University; Graduate Studies at Harvard University, Columbia University; Studies at the Danish Folk School, Copenhagen, 1953; Ph.D., University of Chicago, 1953. Career: Teacher, Public School System, 1934-42; Dean and Teacher, Morgan Park Military Academy, 1943-44; Faculty Member, University of Chicago, 1945-48; Associate Direcctor, W. K. Kellogg Foundation, 1949-56; Special Consultant to Minister of Education and to the President of the University of the Philippines, Philippine Islands, 1955-57; Deputy Chief Education Officer 1957, Chief Education Officer 1958-60, United States Operations Mission to Thailand for State Department and Agency for International Mission to Thailand for State Department and Agency for International Development, Bangkok; Assisted in Creation and Establishment of Peace Corps, 1961; Deputy Director, Office of Institutional Development for the Africa/European Bureau (Washington, D.C.), 1962-67; Evaluation Specialist, Program Office, State Department's United States Operations Mission to Thailand, 1968; Staff Member, Office of Regional Economic Development, United States Embassy, Bangkok, 1968-71; Administrator and Consultant, United Nations Educational, Scientific and Cultural Organization, 1972-75; Consultant for U.N.D.P. and U.N.E.S.C.O. to United Nation's Children's Emergency Fund in Indonesia; Analyst for State Department/A.I.D. and Technical Assistance/Education, Health and Rural Development, 1976; Special Assistant to the United States Senate, 1977; Consultant on Education Development and Management; Partner in Private Business. Organizational Memberships: National Committee to Study Rural Youth Organization in the United States; International Committee, National Association of Educational Broadcasters; United States Committee for a National Project in Agriculture Communications; Rangoon (Burma) Conference on Southeastern Asian Problems in Higher Education; Organized, First Director, Consultant to Executive Board (6 Years), Asian Institute of Technology; United States Delegate to Preparatory Commission on Southeastern Asian University Problems and to Conference of Heads of Southeastern Asian Universities (Karachi, Pakistan); Attended U.N.E.S.C.O. Conference on Development of Higher Education in Africa; Task Force on Technical Assistance of Agency for International Development of United States Institutions of Higher Learning, Member Committee to Review Indonesian Education System and Propose a Comprehensive Program for Further Development. Honors and Awards: Walgreen Fellow, University of Chicago, 2 Years; Distinguished Service Award, Government of Thailand, 1959, 1961; Distinguished Service Award, Government of Indonesia 1975, Government of South Korea 1972; Lifetime Status of Full Professor, Government of Indonesia; Distinguished Service Award, Bethune-Cookman College, 1952; Distinguished Service Award, Ball State University Alumni Association, 1962; Honorary Citizen of the Philippines; U.S. Government Service Award for Many Years of Service and Great Contributions, 1976; Listed in *International Who's Who of Intellectuals, International Who's Who in Community Service, Who's Who in America, Who's Who in the East, Who's Who in Government.* Address: 21 West 88th Street, New York, New York 10024.■

MAN MOHAN VARMA

Scientist, Professor. Personal: Son of Ishar Dass and Bhagirithi Oevi; Married Kiran; Father of Mohit, Umang. Education: B.S.C.E., Alabama Polytechnic Institute, Auburn, Alabama, 1957; M.S. Sanitary Engineering, Iowa State College, Ames, Iowa, 1958; M.S. Highway and Soils, Oklahoma State University-Stillwater, 1960; Ph.D. Engineering Sciences, University of Oklahoma-Norman, 1963. Career: Scientist and Professor. Organizational Memberships: American Water Works Association; Water Pollution Control Federation, Chairman A.T.P. Measurement, 1975 to present; American Society for Testing and Materials, Water Committee 1977 to present, Chairman In-Vitro Mutagenicity Testing Procedures; Water Pollution Control Federation; American Chemical Society; New York Academy of Sciences; American Society of Testing and Materials; American Public Health Association, Glossary Committee 1975 to present, Chairman A.T.P. Measurement 1975 to present; Organization International de Normalization, United States Technical Advisory Group on Water Quality Measurement, 1975 to present; National Environmental Health, Chairman, Energy Committee, 1975-79. Honors and Awards: Consultant, World Health Organization, l972 to present; Consultant, Ministry of Public Health, Kuwait, 1976 to present; Visiting Professor, Harvard University, 1975-76; Diplomate, American Academy of Environmental Engineers; Reviewer of Technical Papers, *Journal of Water Pollution Control Federation, Environmental Health Journal, Radiation Health Journal. Water Research, B10/Technology, Environmental Health Journal* . Address: 704 Chichester Lane, Silver Spring, Maryland 20904.■

RAJENDRA VARMA

Administrator. Personal: Born December 26, 1942; Married Ranbir S.; Mother of Two Sons, Rajeev and Sunil. Education: B.S. 1958, M.S. 1960, University of Delhi, India; Ph.D. Biochemistry, University of New South Wales, Sydney, Australia, 1966; Career: Director, Biochemistry Department, Warren State Hospital, Warren, Pennsylvania, 1971 to present; Associate Professor, Edinboro State College, Pennsylvania, 1969-71; Assistant Professor, Alliance College, Cambridge Springs, Pennsylvania, 1968-69; Postdoctoral Fellow, Purdue University, Lafayette, Indiana 1968, Iowa State University-Ames 1967; Lecturer, Sydney Technical College, Sydney Australia, 1963-66; Lecturer and Research Worker, University of Delhi, India, 1960-62. Organizational Memberships: Fellow, American Institute of Chemists, 1976; American Chemical Society, 1967; Sigma Xi Society, 1968; New York Academy of Sciences, 1979; Published Works: About 50 Research Papers in International Journals; Two Medical Books. Honors and Awards: Medical Research Scientist Achievement Awards, Commonwealth of Pennsylvania, 1974-77, 1980; Presiding Officer, National Meetings of American Chemical Society, San Francisco, California 1976, Montreal, Canada 1977, Washington, D.C. 1979, Las Vegas, Nevada 1980, New York, New York 1981, Kansas City, Missouri 1982. Address: 305 Monroe Street, Warren, Pennsylvania 16365.■

ANTHONY C. VASIS

Professor. Personal: Born October 2, 1926, in Chicago, Illinois. Education: B.S. Industrial Arts and Social Sciences, University of Wisconsin-Platteville, 1950; M.S. Industrial Education, University of Wisconsin-Stout, 1951; Diploma, Automotive Testing Technician, Sun Electric Corporation, 1953; M.Ed., Educational Administration, Loyola University, 1962; Graduate Studies, Northern Illinois University, 1963. Military: Served in the United States Navy, 1945-46, Inactive Reserve 1946-51. Career: Teacher of Industrial Education, Wisconsin School for Boys, 1951; Teacher of Auto Shop, Senn High School, 1951-57; Teacher, Chicago Teachers College-South, 1956-57; Chicago State University-South, Associate Professor of Occupational Education 1976 to present, Student Teacher Supervisor, Teacher of Industrial Education Courses, Thesis Advisor, Industrial Technology Coordinator 1957 to present; Chicago State University-Sabin, Audio-Visual Coordinator, Teacher of Industrial Education Courses, Teacher of Education Courses 1958-61; Chicago State University-Crane, Administrative

Assistant, Audio-Visual Coordinator, Teacher of Industrial Education Courses, Acting Chairperson, Fine and Applied Arts Department 1962-66; Wood Shop Teacher, Jewish Community Centers of Chicago, 1966-76; Union Auto Mechanic, Summers 1952-56; Juried Sculpture Art Exhibits, 57th Street Art Fair 1959-70, Design Derby 1961, Old Town Holiday 1961-72, New Horizons in Sculpture McCormick Place Art Gallery 1962, Chicago Arts Festival McCormick Place 1962, Illinois Vocational Association Pick-Congress Hotel 1963, Art of Wood Sculpture Skokie Art Guild 1968, Art Lounge University of Illinois Medical Center 1968, Sculpture Gallery in St. Louis 1968, Sybil Gallery Chicago 1969-70, Kaplan Center Art Exhibit 1972, Cultural League of St. Demetries Art Exhibit 1972, Sculpture Show Chicago State University l972, Collectors Choice Art Show 1975, Oak Park Village Mall Exhibit 1976. Organizational Memberships: Life Membership, American Council on Industrial Arts Teacher Education; Life Membership, American Vocational Association; Industrial Education Teacher's Meetings, Chicago Board of Education, 195l to present; American Industrial Arts Association, 1954 to present; Illinois Vocational Association, 1954 to present; Illinois Industrial Education Association, 1954 to present; Illinois-Indiana Industrial Arts Teacher Education Conference, 1958 to present; Illinois Automotive and Aircraft Teacher Association, 1968 to present; Charter Member, National Association of Industrial Technology, 1968 to present; Illinois Power Mechanics Teacher Association, 1968 to present; Charter Member, Council of Vocational Educators, 1980 to present. Community Activities: Chicago Council on Foreign Relations; Field Museum of Natural History; Smithsonian Institution; Art Institute of Chicago; Lincoln Park Zoological Society, Inc.; Sponsor, Safety Club; Set up Wood Laboratory, Rogers Park Jewish Community Center-Chicago 1969, Mayer Kaplan Jewish Community Center-Skokie 1970; St. Scholastica High School Board of Education, 1972; Citizens School Committee; American Legion Post #47l, Board of Education 1963 to present, Adjutant 1968, Finance Officer 1969, Junior Vice Commander 1970, Senior Vice Commander 1971, Commander 1972, Executive Committee 1968 to present, First District Children and Youth Officer 1979, Poppy Chairman 1979 to present. Published Works: Author of Articles "From Snow Shovels to Walking Sticks", *Industrial Education* 1980, "The Professional Teacher", *I.I.E.A. Newsletter* 1979, "A Micro-Teaching System Employing an Evaluation Form", *Illinois Career Education Journal* 1978, and numerous others; Also Author of Teaching Handbooks, Book Reviews and Forwards. Honors and Awards: Epsilon Pi Tau, 1956 to present; Red Ribbon, West Central Art Exhibit, 1960; One Man Show, Rogers Park Library, 1963; Superior Rating as High School Auto Shop Teacher; American Vocational Association Life Membership Award, Illinois Technology Association, 1976; Certificate of Recognition and Response, Nikon Corporation, 1977; Listed in *Who's Who in Industrial Arts Teacher Education, Who's Who of Greek Origin in Institutions of Higher Learning, American Hellenic Who's Who in Business and the Professions, Who's Who in the Midwest.* Address: 6083 North Albany, Chicago, Illinois 60659.■

JOHN THOMAS VAUGHAN

Educational Administrator. Personal: Born February 6, 1932; Son of Henry Asa and Mary Howard Vaughan (deceased); Married Ethel Evelyn Sell; Father of John Thomas, Faythe, Michael Sell. Education: D.V.M. 1955, M.S. 1963, Auburn University. Career: Dean, School of Veterinary Medicine, Auburn University, 1977 to present; Professor and Head, Department of Large Animal Surgery and Medicine, School of Veterinary Medicine, Auburn University, 1974-77; Professor and Director, Large Animal Hospital, New York State College of Veterinary Medicine, Cornell University, 1970-74; Instructor 1955-59, Assistant Professor 1959-64, Associate Professor 1964-70, Department of Large Animal Surgery and Medicine, School of Veterinary Medicine, Auburn University. Organizational Memberships: American College of Veterinary Surgeons, President 1980, Chairman Board of Regents 1981; American Association of Equine Practitioners, President 1981; American Association of Veterinary Medical Colleges, Council of Deans, Chairman 1985; American Veterinary Medical Association; Alabama Veterinary Medical Association. Community Activities: Rotary Club. Religion: Methodist. Honors and Awards: Phi Eta Sigma; Phi Kappa Phi; Phi Zeta; Upjohn Award; Sigma Xi; Gamma Sigma Delta; New York Academy of Sciences; Listed in *Who's Who in the South and Southwest, American Men and Women of Science, Who's Who in Frontier Science and Technology*; Nominated to *The Blue Book, Personalities of America, Men of Achievement*. Address: P.O. Box 373, Auburn, Alabama 36830.■

JOHANNES DOUGLES VELDHUIS

Physician, Professor, Researcher in Medical Sciences. Personal: Born July 23, 1949; Son of Mr. and Mrs. Johannes M. Veldhuis; Married Marcia Gellert, Father of Nathan J.D., Ingrid R., Olivia L., Stefan M. Education: B.A. Chemistry, Rockford College, 1970; M.D., Milton S. Hershey Medical Center of Pennsylvania State University, 1974; Resident in Internal Medicine, Mayo Graduate School of Medicine, 1974-77; Special Studies in Molecular Endocrinology and Techniques of Hormone Action, Training Course by Bert W. O'Malley and William Schrader, 1979; Licensed by States of Minnesota, Pennsylvania, Virginia; Certified by National Board of Medical Examiners, American Board of Internal Medicine; Diplomate in Endocrinology and Metabolism. Career: Associate Consultant, Section of Preventive Medicine, Division of Internal Medicine, Mayo Clinic, 1977; Milton S. Hershey Medical Center, Pennsylvania State University, Clinical Endocrinology Fellowship 1977-78, Research Endocrinology Fellowship 1977-79, Assistant Professor of Medicine, Division of Endocrinology 1979-81, Associate Professor of Medicine 1981 to present. Organizational Memberships: Associate, American College of Physicians; Pennsylvania State Medical Society; Dauphin County Medical Society; American Federation for Clinical Research; The Endocrine Society; Society for the Study of Reproduction; Southern Society for Clinical Investigation; American Andrology Society; New York Academy of Sciences. Community Activities: Vice President, International Society for Philosophical Enquiry, 1982 to present; Recruitment Officer of the Mega Society, 1983; Medical College Representative, Faculty Research Forum of the University of Virginia; Pennsylvania State University School of Medicine, Human Radiation Safety Committee 1979-81, Student Research Project Review Committee l980-81. Religion: Elder and Board Member, Christian Missionary Alliance. Published Works: Author of Numerous Articles in Professional Journals and Books, including Most Recently "The Use of Calcium Antagonists in the Treatment of Esophageal Dysfunction", *Internal Medicine for the Specialist* 1983, "Influence of a Calcium-Influx Blocker, Diltiazem, on Anterior-Pituitary Hormone Release in the Human", *Journal Clinical Endocrenology Metabolism* 1983, "A Critical Role for Cell Density in the Expression of Estrogen Action on the Ovary", *Endocrinology* 1983. Honors and Awards: Phi Beta Kappa; Phi Kappa Phi; International Mensa Society; Alpha Omega Alpha; National Science Foundation Scholar in Mathematics, 1967; Presidential Merit Scholar, Aratus Kent Scholar and Valedictorian, 1970; Roche Outstanding Achievement Award in Medicine, Pennsylvania State University College of Medicine, 1974; Mayo Graduate Travel Award in Medicine, Mayo Clinic, 1977; National Research Service Award, National Institute of Child Health and Human Development, 1978-80; Faculty Initiation Research Award, Pennsylvania State University, 1979-80; Institutional Research Award, American Cancer Society, 1979-80; National Institutes of Health, Biomedical Research Support Awards to University of Virginia School of Medicine, 1981-82; University of Virginia, National Institutes of Health, Diabetes Center Grant, 1982-83; N.I.D.A.-National Institutes of Health Grant, 1983; National Institute of Child Health and Human Development-National Institutes of Health Grant, 1983; American Diabetes Association Grant, 1983.■

WILLIAM GARY VENDEVER

Banker, Investor. Personal: Born June 17, 1925; Son of Gary York and Allene (Vawter) Vendever; Married Margaret Glenn, December 1967; Father of Gary York, William Gary (from previous marriage). Education: M.S., St. Johns Military Academy, 1943; Student, Tulsa University 1945-47, New York University 1948. Military: Served with the United States Air Force, 1943-45. Career: Chairman of the Board, President, The Vandever Company, Inc., Tulsa, 1974 to present; Director, MidAmerican Federal Savings and Loan Association, 1959 to present; Vice President, Chairman Executive Committee, Director, First National Bank Stigler, Oklahoma, 1966 to present; President, Director, WGVI Financial Advisors, Inc., Tulsa, 1971 to present; President, Director, W. G. Vandever and Company, Inc., Tulsa, 1974 to present; President, Director, Tulsa Petroleum Corporation, 1978 to present; President, Director, Oklahoma Drilling Corporation, 1978 to present; President, Director, Mohawk Oil and Gas Corporation, 1979 to present; President, Director, Oklahoma Conveyance Corporation, 1979 to present; President, Director, Kansas Energy Corporation, 1980 to present. Community Activities: Trustee, American, Youth Performs Foundation, New York City, 1966 to present; Board of Directors 1952 to present, Vice President 1960-70, Tulsa Philharmonic Society; Member President's National Office of Emergency Planning, 1963 to present; Board of Directors, Arkansas Basin Development Association, Tulsa, 1960-65; Advisory Board, Tulsa Civic Ballet Association, 1965 to present; Advisory Board, Tulsa Opera, Inc., 1960-75; Member President Kennedy's Bi-racial Committee, 1963-64; Council Metropolitan Opera New York, 1960-63; Board of Directors, Tulsa Psychiatric Foundation, 1964-68; Board of Directors, Tulsa Broadway Theatre League, 1958-65; Board of Directors, Tulsa Community Chest, 1962-69; YMCA of Tulsa, 1960-68; Advisory Board, Downtown Tulsa Unltd., 1962-69; Tulsa

Chamber of Commerce, Director, 1956-69; Alpha Tau Omega Alumni Association; Tulsa Club; South Hills Country Club; Summit Club. Address: 1306 East 25th Street, Tulsa, Oklahoma 74114. ■

ESWARAHALLI S. VENKATESH

Assistant Professor. Personal: Born January 30, 1949; Son of Mrs. E.S. Lokamata; Married Vijaya E.; Father of Vinay Sundararajan, Vinita E. Education: B.Sc. Physics and Mathematics, Bangalore University, India, 1969; B.E. Metallurgy, Indian Institute of Science, India, 1971, M.S. Materials Engineering, Brown University, 1973; Ph.D. Metallurgy, New Mexico Institute Mining Technology, 1977; M.S. Petroleum Engineering, University of Oklahoma, 1980. Career: Assistant Professor, Petroleum and Mechanical Engineering, University of Alaska; Former Positions include Research Metallurgist in the Product Research Division of Conoco Inc., Instructor at the University of Oklahoma and Cornell University, Research Assistant at Brown University and New Mexico Institute Mining Technology, Research Associate at University of Rochester (New York), Research Engineer with I.N.T.E.V.E.P., Venezuela. Organizational Memberships: S.P.E.-A.I.M.E.; A.S.M.; Alpha Sigma Mu; Sigma Xi; Tau Beta Pi; Pi Epsilon Tau; T.M.S.-A.I.M.E.; E.M.S.A. Community Activities: Secretary, Cornell India Association; Secretary, New England Kannada Koota Association; President, International Students Association, New Mexico Institute Mining Technology. Honors and Awards: Elected Member to Several Honorary Societies, Alpha Sigma Mu, Sigma Xi, Tau Beta Pi, Pi Epsilon Tau; Best Speaker Award of Albuquerque Chapter of A.S.M., 1977; Listed in *Who's Who in the South and Southwest, International Men of Achievement*. Address: 722-A North Chandalar Avenue (UAF), Fairbanks, Alaska 99701. ■

W. EDWIN VERBECKE

Poet, Painter, Playwright, Recitalist. Personal: Born July 21, 1913; Son of Walter Earle and Dora Abhigail VerBecke (deceased); Married Countess Eugenia Chavessey (deceased); Father of Ghizella Anne (deceased), Joseph. Education: Attended the Minneapolis School of Fine Arts 1932, University of Minnesota 1937, Duluth State Teachers College; Private Study with David Erikson, Knute Heldner. Career: Poet, Painter, Playwright, Recitalist; Former Teacher of Art, University of Minnesota; Co-Director of Arts International of Chicago; Display Director, Sachs Interiors, New York City; Teacher, Abbey Institute, New York City. Organizational Memberships: Dramatist Guild, New York City, 1950; American Poetry Society, 1970; Minnesota Art Associatio, 1935. Community Activities: New York Delegate, Council on Aging, 1981; Founder/Director, Sausalito Little Theatre (California), 1950; Founder/Director, Galleries by the Sea (Sausalito, California), 1940-52; Founder, San Francisco Community Theatre, 1955; Founder, Drama Readers Laguna Beach (California), 1957; Co-Director, San Francisco Goethe Festival, 1945; One-Man Show, Royal Court Theatre ("Tragedy of Oscar Wilde"), 1980; Theatrical Producer, Hollywood. Religion: Ordained Universal Church of Master, 1953; Founder, U. R. God Center, Fort Lauderdale, Florida, 1971-80; Recital, Riverside Church, New York, 1983. Published Works: Author *Line in Painting, Poems of the Spirit, Life of Virgin Mary, Story of Mary* (Cassette). Honors and Awards: Joint Recital with Freida Hemple, San Francisco Opera House, 1952; "Isadora Duncan Recital," Rutgers University, 1981; Recital, Congressional Breakfast, 1981; Lecturer, New York Engineers Club, 1982-83; Art Exhibitions, One-Man Shows, McCormick Place (Chicago) 1965, University of Washington 1945, Robinson Gallery (New Orleans) 1937, Bucharest (Romania) 1970, Long Beach (California), Los Angeles Art Museum, Shreveport (Louisiana), Court Gallery (New York City), Duncan Gallery (Paris); Listed in *Men of Achievement*. Address: 840 8th Avenue, Capitol Apartments, Suite 6M, New York City, New York 10019. ■

EVELYN I. VERNON

Professor (retired). Personal: Born June 1, 1911; Daughter of G.A. and Mary V. Elsen (both deceased); Married Clinton D. Vernon; Mother of Evelyn Marlene, Frances Yvonne (Bonnie) V. Lloyd. Education: B.A. English and Psychology, George Washington University, 1933; M.A. Speech Education, Columbia University Teachers College, 1936; Summer School, Sorbonne, Paris 1955, University of Hawaii 1958. Career: University of Utah, Assistant Professor of Educational Psychology 1975-77, Supervisor of Reading Classes for General Education 1971-75, Instructor in Educational Psychology Department 1963-71, Instructor in Speech Department 1960-63; Teacher, John Robert Powers Finishing School, Salt Lake City, Utah, 1955-60; Instructor in Speech and Drama Departments, 1936-40; Insurance Supervisor, United States Government Home Owners Loan Association, 1933-35. Organizational Memberships: International Reading Asociation, 1965-75; College Reading Association, Member 1967-77, Director 1975; Utah Branch Secretary, National Association of Higher Education, 1972; American Association of University Professors, 1970-77; President, University Faculty Women, 1969-70; International Platform Association, 1981-82. Community Activities: Maryland State Rural Women's Lecturers, 1937-40; Utah State Society, Washington, D.C., Vice President, President, 1933-34; President, Women's State Legislative Council of Utah, 1951-53; League of American Pen Women, Local President 1950-52, State President 1952-54, State Parliamentarian 1977-82; Salt Lake Council of Women, Chairman 1979-82, First Vice President 1982-83; Friendship Force, Volunteer Ambassador to 3 Countries, Venezuela, Korea and West Berlin, Germany 1978-82; Public Lectures and Book Reviews, 1940-82; Over 100 Hours Yearly Volunteer Service, Assistance League of Salt Lake City. Religion: Latter-Day Saints Church; President, Young Women's Mutual Association, Washington, D.C., 1933-35; President, Primary Children's Organization, Wastach Ward, 1958; Relief Society Teacher of Literature and Cultural Arts, 1950-60, 1968-78; Teacher Development Leader, Stake Sunday School, 1977-82; Teacher in Most Organizations. Honors and Awards: Inducted into Hall of Fame, Salt Lake City Council of Women, 1983; Twenty Dollar Gold Piece for Being Most Outstanding Girl in Activities for 4 Years of College, George Washington University, 1933; Honor Roll, *Salt Lake Evening Telegram*, 1951; Graduate School of Education Plaque, 1977; Merit of Honor Award, Emeritus Club, University of Utah, 1982. Address: 1044 Oakhills Way, Salt Lake City, Utah 84108. ■

JACK BYRON VIAR

Mental Health Counselor and Consultant. Personal: Born September 28, 1935; Son of Mrs. Fred W. Viar; Married Virginia Walk, Daughter of Mr. and Mrs. Hall Walk; Father of Julie Ann, Andrew Jay, Amy Lynn. Education: Attended Baker University, 1953-55; B.S. Psychology, Central Missouri State University, 1959; M.S.W. Social Work, Missouri University, 1964; Certificate in Mental Health Consultation, Tulane University, 1972. Military: Served in the United States Air Force Reserves, 1958-62. Career: Mental Health Counseling and Consultation; Former Positions include Director of Tri-County Mental Health Center and Director of East Central Missouri Mental Health Center. Organizational Memberships: National Association of Social Workers, Member 1964 to present, Vice Chairman for Central Missouri 1971-73; National Council of Community Mental Health Centers, Missouri Chairman 1972-81, Legislative Chairman 1972-78; A.D.A.M.H., Region VII Technical Assistance Task Force, Chairman 1978, Missouri Chairman 1978-81; Missouri Coalition of Community Mental Health Centers, Chairman 1971, 1972, 1976. Community Activities: Mexico Community Chest, Chairman 1970-72; Curriculum Advisory Board, Mexico Area Vocational-Technical School; Chancellor's Advisory Committee, Metroplitan Junior Colleges, 1978-81. Honors and Awards: Listed in *Who's Who in the Midwest, Who's Who in America, Who's Who in Health Care, International Register of Profiles, Dictionary of International Biography*. Address: 202 Northwest 43 Terrace, Kansas City, Missouri 64116. ■

AUSTIN LAFAYETTE VICK

Civil Engineer. Personal: Born January 28, 1929, Cedervale, New Mexico; Married Norine E. Melton, July 18, 1948; Father of Larry A., Margaret J., David A. Education: B.S.C.E. 1950, M.S.C.E. 1961, New Mexico State University. Career: Chief Projects Section, Data Reduction Branch, 1955-58; Chief Projects Office, 1958-64; Chief Performance Evaluation Division, 1964-73; Chief Data Collection Division, 1973-82; Technical Assistant to Director, National Range Operations, 1982 to present; White Sands Missile Range, New Mexico. Organizational Memberships: American Defense Preparedness Association; Association United States Army, Rio Grande Chapter Vice President 1970; Senior Member, American Astronautical Society. Published Works: "Future Space Program and Impact on Range and Network Development" 1967; "Space Technology and Earth Problems" 1971; Numerous Technical Papers. Honors and Awards:

TWO THOUSAND NOTABLE AMERICANS

Secretary Army Award for Outstanding Achievement in Equal Opportunity, 1982; Outstanding Performance Award, White Sands Missile Range, 1972; Special Act Awards, 1967, 1971, 1975. Address: 4568 Spanish Dagger, Las Cruces, New Mexico 88001.■

JAMES FRANK VICKREY

University President. Personal: Born February 6, 1942, in Montgomery, Alabama; Son of Mrs. F. G. Murray; Father of John. Education: A.B. English and Speech, Auburn University, 1964; M.A. Rhetoric and Public Address, Auburn University, 1965; Ph.D. Speech Communication, Florida State University, 1972. Career: President, University of Montevallo; Former Positions include Executive Assistant to the Chancellor and Director of Public Affairs of Florida's Nine-University Board of Regents-Run State University System, Assistant to the President and Director of University Relations at the University of Florida and Administrative Assistant to the Executive Vice President at Florida State University. Organizational Memberships: Council for the Advancement and Support of Education; American Association of State Colleges and Universities; American Council on Education; American Association of University Administrators; Speech Communication Association; Alabama Association of College Administrators; Alabama Association of Colleges and Universities; National Presidents Advisory Council of the National Association of Intercollegiate Athletics, Chairman. Community Activities: Montevallo Rotary Club, Honorary Member; Montevallo Chamber of Commerce; Birmingham Chamber of Commerce; United Way, Board of Directors; Alabama Symphony Orchestra, Director of Board; Kiwanis Club; Alabama Film Commission. Religion: Member Montevallo United Methodist Church. Honors and Awards: Phi Eta Sigma; Phi Kappa Phi; Omicron Delta Kappa; Alpha Kappa Psi; Spades (honor society at Auburn University); Algernon Sydney Sullivan Award, Auburn University, 1964; Phi Eta Sigma National Scholarship, 1964; S. Allen Edgar Fellowship, Auburn University, 1965; Phi Delta Phi Award as Outstanding First Year Law Student at University of Alabama, 1969; Participation in 1970 Doctoral Honors Seminar of the Speech Communication Association at the University of Texas; University Fellow, Florida State University, 1970; Exceptional Achievement Award 1976, Grand Award 1977, Council for the Advancement and Support of Education; One of 100 Outstanding Young Leaders in American Higher Education, *Change* Magazine; Educator of the Year, Kappa Phi Kappa, 1982; Listed in *Who's Who in America*. Address: University of Montevallo-Flowerhill, Montevallo, Alabama 35115.■

JUDI VICTOR

Company President, Owner. Personal: Born April 12, 1949; Daughter of Mr. and Mrs. H. R. James; Married David Victor; Mother of David, Laurie, Andrew. Education: B.F.A. cum laude, University of Arizona, 1970. Career: President and Owner, The Producers, Inc.; President, Way Out West Productions, 1974 to present; Broadcast Production Manager, Mullen Advertising, 1973-74; Copy Director, Diamonds, 1971-73; Copywriter, Broadway-Hale, 1970-71; Columnist, Tucson Newspapers, Inc., 1970. Organizational Memberships: President, Women in Communications, 1978-79; I.A.B.C.; Charter 100, Publicity Committee 1981-82, Secretary 1982-83; Sigma Delta Chi; National Association of Television Arts and Sciences. Community Activities: Board Member, Phoenix Park Foundation, 1980 to present; Phoenix Environmetal Quality Commission, 1979-80. Honors and Awards: Western Region Woman of Achievement Award, Women in Communications, 1979; National TELLY Award, First Place for Fritz Scholder Television Commercial, 1980; Listed in *World Who's Who of Women*, *Western Hemisphere Who's Who of Women*, *Who's Who of American Women*. Address: 3835 East Sahuaro Boulevard, Phoenix, Arizona 85028.■

JULIO VIDAL

Educator. Personal: Born August 1, 1952; Son of Miguel Vidal and Lydia Vazquez. Education: A.B.D., Working on Doctoral Dissertation, State University of New York-Albany; M.A. International Affairs of Latin America, Florida State University, 1975; B.A. Political Science, Catholic University of Puerto Rico, 1973. Career: Instructor, Political Science, Catholic University of Puerto Rico, Ponce, Puerto Rico. Organizational Memberships: Latin American Studies Association; American Society for Public Administration; American Political Science Association; Center for Cuban Studies; The Political Science Academy; Phi Delta Kappa; Pi Gamma Mu. Community Activities: Reviewer for Grant Proposals, Division of Public Programs, National Endowment for Humanities; Conferences on the Community. Honors and Awards: Graduate Fellowships, State University of New York-Albany, 1979-81; Pi Gamma Mu; Phi Delta Kappa; Listed in *National Directory of Latin Americanists*, *Who's Who in the South and Southwest*, *Directory of Scholars and Specialists in the Third World Studies*, *Men of Achievement*, *Personalities of America*, *Personalities of the South*. Address: B #113, Santa Maria B, Ponce, Puerto Rico 00732.■

CAROLE A. VIER

Program Manager. Personal: Born October 5, 1948; Daughter of Frank and Mildred Wilson; Married Wayne William, Son of Gale and Irene Veir. Education: Attended Colorado State University, 1966-68; University of Guadalajara, Mexico, 1969; University of Utah, 1970-80; B.A. Spanish Education; M.Ed. Special Education; Ed.D. Educational Administration; J.D. Candidate, Southland University. Career: Program Manager, Office of Exceptional Children, State Department of Education, Alaska; Assistant Professor, Department of Special Education, A.S.U.; Administrator, Maricopa County Community College, Mesa, Arizona; Instructor, University of Utah, Salt Lake City, Utah; Administrator and Teacher, Granite Schools, Salt Lake City, Utah; Private Educational Consultant, Intermountain Consulting and Educational Services. Organizational Memberships: Phi Delta Kappa; Treasurer, Pi Lambda Theta; Sigma Delta Pi; A.E.R.A.; N.O.L.P.E.; C.E.C.; N.A.B.E.; A.U.A.; T.E.S.O.L. Community Activities: Vice President and Member Board of Directors, Tempe Community Council, Tempe, Arizona, 1980-82; Governors Committee for the Handicapped, 1982; Planning Committee, Tempe Leadership Conference, 1982; Council for Exceptional Children, National Convention Co-Chairperson, 1982; League of Women Voters, Public Relations 1980-82, International Committee, Grant Blocks Program, Education Committee; Advisory Board Bilingual Education, Mesa Community College, 1980-82; Faculty Sponsor, Phi Theta Kappa, 1980-81; Girl Scout Leader, 1978-79; President, Student Advisory Council, University of Utah, 1979-80; Treasurer, Pi Lambda Theta, 1981-82; ABA Youth Committee. Honors and Awards: Academic Honors, University of Utah, 1970-71; Official Delegate to U.S. University Educators Goodwill Tour to China, Japan, Hong Kong; Phi Theta Kappa, Meritorious Service and Leadership, 1981; Sigma Delta Pi, National Spanish Honor Society, 1971; Phi Delta Kappa, International Honor Fraternity, 1979; Pi Lambda Theta, National Fraternity, Outstanding Educational Readers, 1981; Listed in *World Who's Who of Women*, *Who's Who in the West*, the *Biographical Roll of Honor*, the *Dictionary of International Biography*. Address: 3-6000 Suite 163, Juneau, Alaska 99801.■

CRISTOBAL EUGENIO VIERA

Surgeon. Personal: Born September 6, 1941; Son of Mr. and Mrs. Cristobal J. A. Viera; Father of Estelle Marie, Chris. Education: Attended Candler College, Cuba, 1960; B.S. 1966, M.D. 1970, University of Miami; American Board of Surgery, 1977; Fellow, American College of Surgeon; Fellow, American College of Gastroenterology, 1980; Fellow, American Society of Abdominal Surgeons, 1981; Clinical Instructor, Department of Surgery, University of Miami School of Medicine, 1976-80; Clinical Assistant, Professor, University of Miami, School of Medicine. Military: United States Army Reserve, Captain MC. Career: Surgeon, Vascular and General Surgery; Straight Surgical Internship, Department of Surgery, University of Miami School of Medicine, 1970-71; Assistant Resident, Department of Surgery, University of Miami School of Medicine, 1971-72; Resident, Department of Surgery, University of Miami, 1972-73; Senior Resident, Department of Surgery, University of Miami, 1973-74; Chief Resident, Department of Surgery, University of Miami, School of Medicine, 1974-75; Part-time Clinical Instructor, Department of Surgery, University of Miami, School of Medicine. Organizational Memberships: Phi Chi Medical Fraternity, Treasurer 1968, President 1969-70; Student Research Day, Honorable Mention. Community Activities: Dade County Medical Society; Florida Medical Association; American Medical Association; American College of Surgeons; Phi Chi Medical Society; Southern Medical Association; Active Member, American Cancer

Society; American Gastroenterology Association. Religion: Roman Catholic. Honors and Awards: Selected as Most Effective and Popular Housestaff Teacher. Address: Mercy Professional Building, 3661 South Miami Avenue, Florida 33133.■

JAMES RICHARD VILKITIS

Educator, Consultant. Personal: Born October 31. Education: B.S. Fisheries and Wildlife, Michigan State University, 1965; M.S. Wildlife Management, University of Idaho, 1968; Ph.D. Wildlife Biology 1970, Postdoctorate Studies 1973, University of Massachusetts-Amherst. Career: Associate Professor, Natural Resources Management Department, Environmental Services Concentration, California Polytechnic State University; Associate Consultant, Ertec Western Inc. (The Earth Technology Corporation) and Robert L. Stollar and Associates; Principal and Managing Partner, Carlozzi, Sinton and Vilkitis Inc., Regional Natural Resource Consultants and Planners, 1971-80; Partner, The Total Environment Group Ltd., 1971-78; Lecturer, Division of Continuing Education, Department of Forestry and Wildlife, University of Massachusetts-Amherst, 1971-78; Assistant Professor, Department of Biological Sciences, Mount Holyoke College, 1979; Owner, TLC Leather Works, 1976-82; Partner, Rams Head Leather Works Ltd., 1976-79. Organizational Memberships: Association of Environmental Professionals, Director 1980, Executive Vice President 1983; The American Forestry Association; Wildlife Society; Xi Sigma Pi; Project Management Institute; Northeast Deer Study Group; Cal Poly University Club; National Rifle Association; National Audubon Society; Trout Unlimited. Community Activities: Big Brother Program; Gratus Consulting to Minority Groups; City and State Involvement with Student Internships; California Agricultural Teachers Association. Religion: Taoist. Published Works: Author/Co-author Various Professional Publications, including "Coastal Management as an Academic Program" 1981, "Characteristics of big hame law violators and sportsmen in Maine" 1978, "Wildlife habitat as an integral component of a planned unit development" 1978, "A development in harmony with wildlife" 1976. Honors and Awards: Listed in *The Directory of Distinguished Americans, The Anglo-American Who's Who, Dictionary of International Biography, Who's Who in the East, Contemporary Authors, American Men and Women of Science, Men of Achievement, The International Authors and Writers Who's Who, Who's Who in America, The Biographical Roll of Honor, International Who's Who of Intellectuals, Contemporary Personalities.* Address: 4942 Martin, Detroit, Michigan 48210.■

WILLIAM MACON VINING, JR.

Industrial Hygienist. Personal: Born December 19, 1947; Son of William M. and Eddie B. Vining. Education: B.A., Texas Christian University, 1970; M.S., University of Texas-Dallas, 1978. Career: Corporate Senior Industrial Hygienist, Dresser Industries, Inc., 1981 to present; Corporate Senior Industrial Hygienist, Texas Industires, Inc., 1977-81; Safety and Health Technician, Globe-Union Battery Division of Johnson Controls, 1973-77; Vice President Health Services (Consultant), O.E.C., Inc., 1981 to present; Certified in Comprehensive Practice of Industrial Hygiene, American Board of Industrial Industrial Hygiene; Diplomate of American Academy of Industrial Hygiene. Organizational Memberships: American Industrial Hygiene Association, National Engineering Committee 198l to present, President North Texas Section 1983, President-Elect 1982, Chairman Technical Committee 1981; American Society of Safety Engineers, Professional Member, Vice President Communications 1976-77, Vice President Professional Development 1977-78. Community Activities: Science Fair Judge, Dallas Independent School District, 1979. Honors and Awards: Listed in *Who's Who in the South and Southwest, Personalities of the South.* Address: 7001 Fair Oaks, #233, Dallas, Texas 75231.■

CLARENCE D. VINSON, JR.

Educator. Personal: Born June 23, 1933; Son of Clarence D. and Pearl P. Vinson (both deceased); Married Frances H. Poole; Father of Two Stepchildren. Education: Graduate, Oxford High School, Oxford, Alabama, 1950; B.S. 1954, M.S. 1957, Jacksonville State University; Ph.D., University of Alabama, 1977; Additional Graduate Work at University of Northern Colorado-Greeley and University of Wyoming-Laramie. Military: Served with United States Army as First Lieutenant, Chemical Corps, 1955-57. Career: Associate Professor of Science, Jacksonville State University, 1969 to present; Science Teacher and Coach, Saks High School, Anniston, Alabama, 1957-65; Science Teacher and Coach, Munford High School, Munford, Alabama, 1965-69; Organizational Memberships: National Education Association; Alabama Education Association; Local Education Association; Assistant Director, Northeast Alabama Regional Science Fair; Associate Counselor, Northeast Region of the Alabama Junior Academy of Science. Community Activities: Numismatic Association; Calhoun County Coin Club; American Bowling Congress; Member Board of Directors, Anniston Bowling Association, 1978 to present. Religion: Attends Baptist Church, Teacher of Bible Study Class, Deacon, 1977. Honors and Awards: Balfour Medal for Academic Achievement in High School, 1950; Elected to Kappa Phi Kappa, 1954; Scabbard and Blade, 1954; Phi Kappa Phi, 1969; Listed in *Who's Who in the South and Southwest, Personalities of the South.* Address: 435 Arnold Drive, Anniston, Alabama 36201.■

SUSAN JOSEPHINE VISCO

Educator, Psychologist. Personal: Daughter of Hugh (deceased) and Rose M. Visco. Education: A.A. Liberal Arts, Massachusetts Bay Community College, 1965; B.S. Elementary Education/Psychology, Suffolk University, 1967; M.Ed. 1973, Special Education, Boston College; Internship, Psychoeducational Evaluation, Boston Children's Hospital Medical Center, Developmental Evaluation Clinic, 1970-72; Certified as Licensed Psychologist, School Psychologist, Teacher of Elementary and Special Education, Special Education Administrator, State of Massachusetts. Career: Professor, Director College Learning Program, Bradford College, 1980-82; Psychologist and Coordinator of Evaluation Program and Advanced Crisis Center, 1970 to present; Consultant and Advisor in Special Needs Programming, Public School Systems, 1968-78; Stonehill College, Assistant Professor, Director of Child Development Department, Director of Special Needs and Learning Center 1971-76, Director of Stonehill Psychoeducational Evaluation and Learning Center 1972-76; Visiting Professor, Lowell University, Summers 1974 and 1975; Administrator Screening Program, Taunton Public Schools, September 1974; Screened Children and Implemented Programs to Identify Special Needs Children, State of Massachusetts, 1974-75; Visiting Professor, Learning Disabilities Courses, Salem State College, 1971-72; Supervisor of Special Education Student Teachers, Boston College, 1970-71; Visiting Professor, Language Arts in Learning Disabilities, Southeastern Massachusetts University, 1969; Teacher, Brookline Public Schools, 1969-71; Teacher Learning Disabilities, Wakefield Public Schools, 1968-70; Teacher, Saugus Public Schools, 1967-68; Instructor of Music Applied Harmony and Music Appreciation, Teacher of the Emotionally Disturbed and Mentally Retarded, Faelten Pianoforte School (Boston), 1960-65; Consultant, Nahant Public Schools, 1971-74; Consultant, Winthrop Public Schools, 1971-74; Consultant, North Shore School Systems, Massachusetts, 1971-74. Organizational Memberships: National Association of Children with Learning Disabilities; Council on Exceptional Children, National and Massachusetts Chapters, Division of Children with Learning Disabilities, Division of Children with Communication Disorders, Teacher Education Division. Community Activities: Director, Volunteer Preschool Child Development Screening Programs, North Shore Community School Systems, Massachusetts, 1966-73; Treasurer, Council on Exceptional Children, Massachusetts Division of Children with Learning Disabilities, 1973-74; Speaker, Numerous Lectures, Addresses, Workshops in Massachusetts, Connecticut, Florida, New Hampshire, New York and Rhode Island. Published Works: Author of Articles "The Performance of Normal and Learning Disabled Children on Tasks of Non-Verbal Auditory Perception" *Orton Society Bulletin* 1974, "Visco Child Development Program" *Educational Activities* 1982, and Others; Author of Book Reviews on "The Myth of Hyperactivity" *Linacre Quarterly* 1976, "And Say What He Is: The Life of a Special Child" *Linacre Quarterly* 1976, and Others. Honors and Awards: Listed in *Who's Who of American Women, Who's Who in America, World Who's Who of Women.* Address: 438 Essex Street, Saugus, Massachusetts 01906.■

SARALEE AMY NEUMANN VISSCHER

Professor. Personal: Born January 9, 1929; Daughter of Otto and Sarah Mershon Neumann; Married Paul Hummison Visscher; Mother of Kirby Alan Van Horn, Constance Van Horn, Amy Roena Visscher, Ernst Warren Visscher. Education: B.S. Biology, University of Montana-Missoula, 1949; M.S. Applied Science in Entomology 1958, Ph.D. Entomology 1963, Montana State University. Career: Montana State University, Professor of Entomology 1972 to present, Associate Professor of Entomology 1967-72, Assistant Professor of Entomology 1962-67; Postdoctoral Fellow, University of Virginia, 1965-66; Instructor in Biology, University of Kansas, 1958-59; Elementary Teacher, Denton, Montana, 1947-48. Organizational Memberships: American Society for Zoologists, 1965 to present; Entomological Society of America, Member 1963 to present, Memberships Chairman for Montana 1980 to present; Society for Developmental Biology, 1965 to present; American Society for the Advancement of Science, Fellow 1967, Member 1966 to present; Pan American Acridological Society, 1979 to present; Society for the Sigma Xi, Montana State University Chapter, President 1978-79, Member 1963 to present; Montana Academy of Sciences, Board of Directors 1976-79, President 1979-80, Member 1962 to present. Community Activities: Founder, Mershon Past President Award for Outstanding Contribution to Science in Montana of the Montana Academy of Sciences, 1981; Organizer, Rocky Mountain Regional Conference for Developmental Biology,

Yellowstone National Park, 1970; Organizer and Moderator, First International Symposium on Insect Embryology, XV International Congress of Entomology, Washington, D.C., 1976; Organizer and Moderator, Symposium on Grylloblattoidea, XVI International Congress of Entomology, Kyoto, 1980; Lewistown Member and Officer, American Association of University Women; High School Commencement Speaker, Geyser, Montana 1976, Belt, Montana 1977, Fort Benton, Montana 1981. Religion: Episcopal Church, National Youth Commission, 1945-46; Organist, St. James, Lewistown and Churches in Bozeman, 1959-62. Honors and Awards: Honorable Guest Member, Japanese Society of Arthropodan Embryology, 1982; One of Eight Outstanding Women of Montana, *Montana* Magazine, 1979; Dynamic American, *Dynamic Years* Magazine; Rockefeller Foundation Research Grant, 1980-81; National Science Foundation MONTS Grant, 1980-82; Dow Chemical U.S.A. Research Grant, 1980-81; AgRISTARS Grant, 1980-81; United States-Japan Cooperative Research Grant, 1977-80; National Institute of Health Research Grants, Co-Investigator, 1962-69; National Science Foundation Travel Grant to XIIth International Congress of Entomology, London, 1964; National Institute of Health Postdoctoral Fellowship, University of Virginia, 1965-66; National Science Foundation Predoctoral Fellowship, Montana State University, 1960-61; Honor Scholarship, University of Montana, 1945-46. Address: 516 South Sixth Avenue, Bozeman, Montana 59715.■

WILLIAM FRANCIS VITULLI

Professor. Personal: Born July 17, 1936; Son of Mr. and Mrs. William Vitulli; Married Betty Jean Sheubrooks; Father of Paige Ann, Quinn Anthony, Sheri K. Denise. Education: B.A. Psychology/Philosophy 1961, M.S. Research Psychology 1963, Ph.D. Research Psychology 1966, University of Miami, Florida. Military: Reserve Officer Training Corps, University of Miami, 1954-55. Career: Professor of Psychology, (Teaching and Researching), University of South Alabama; Former Positions include Graduate Research Assistant; Life Guard; Swimming Instructor. Organizational Memberships: American Psychological Association, 1966 to present; Alabama Board of Examiners, Member 1980-85, Vice Chairman 1982; Sigma Xi, 1981 to present; Alabama Academy of Science, 1968 to present; American Society of Primatologists, 1982 to present; Southeastern Psychological Association, 1965 to present; Alabama Psychological Association, Member 1967 to present, President 1975. Community Activities: Board of Directors, Cornerstone, Inc., 1976 to present; Chairman Historical/Cultural Committee, Italian-American Cultural Society of South Alabama, 1983. Religion: Member of Roman Catholic Church. Honors and Awards: Professor of the Quarter, Alpha Lambda Delta, 1977-78; Outstanding Educators of America, 1975-77; Faculty Advisor to Psi Chi, National Honorary Society in Psychology, 1972-80. Address: 2025 Maryknoll Court, Mobile, Alabama 36609.■

VICTORIA MAE VOGE-BLACK

Aerospace Medicine Specialist. Personal: Born June 27, 1943; Daughter of Veryl Voge; Married Gerald Ralph Black. Education: B.A., University of Minnesota, 1965; M.D., National Autonomous University of Mexico, 1971; M.P.H., Johns Hopkins University School of Hygiene and Public Health, 1977. Military: Service in the United States Navy, 1972 to present, holding the rank of Commander. Career: Aerospace Medicine Specialist, Flight Medicine Branch, United States Air Force School of Aerospace Medicine (San Antonio, Texas); Previously Stationed at the Naval Safety Center in Norfolk, Virginia. Organizational Memberships: American Medical Association; Aerospace Medical Association; S.A.F.E. Association; American Public Health Association; International Academy of Aviation and Space Medicine. Religion: Church of Jesus Christ of Latter-day Saints, 1973 to present. Honors and Awards: Wiley Post Award for Operational Physiology, 1980. Address: P.O. Box 35430, Brooks Air Force Base, Texas 78235.■

MOLLY T. VOGT

Director of Institutional Review Board Management and Professor. Personal: Born April 15, 1939; Daughter of Gordon (deceased) and Evelyn Thomas; Mother of William Brian, Keith Thomas. Education: B.S. with honors, Biological Chemistry, Bristol University, England; Ph.D., University of Pittsburgh, 1967. Career: University of Pittsburgh School of Health-Related Professions, Pennsylvania, Associate Dean and Professor 1977 to present, Associate Professor and Chairman 1972-76, Assistant Professor of Biochemistry 1971-72. Organizational Memberships: Associate Editor and Member Editorial Board, *Journal of Allied Health*, 1972-79; American Society of Allied Health Professions, Education Committee Chairman 1979 to present, Chairman, Task Force on Status of Women 1980 to present, Planner/Organizer, National Conference on Continuing Education 1978-81; American Association for the Advancement of Science; American Women in Science; American Association of Higher Education; National Association of Women Deans and Counselors. Community Activities: Presidential Task Force on Research, 1979-80; Elected Member-at-Large, Council of Individual Members, 1977-79; President, University of Pittsburgh Chapter of Sigma Xi, 1979-81; Consultant, Pennsylvania State Department of Education, 1976; Executive Women's Council of Greater Pittsburgh Coordinating Committee, 1975-81; Phi Delta Gamma. Honors and Awards: Certificate of Merit for Excellence in Writing and Outstanding Contribution to the Literature of Allied Health Professions, American Society of Allied Health Professions, 1978; Fellow, American Council of Education Academic Administration Internship Program, 1974-75; Fellow, American Society of Allied Health Professions, 1983; J. Warren Perry Distinguished Author Award, 1983. Address: 242 Race Street, Pittsburgh, Pennsylvania 15218.■

ROBERT VOLPE

Professor. Personal: Born March 6, 1926; Married Ruth Pullan; Father of Catherine Lillian, Elizabeth Anne, Peter George, Edward James, Rose Ellen. Education: M.D., University of Toronto, 1950; F.R.C.P.(C.) 1956; F.A.C.P., 1965. Military: Royal Canadian Naval Volunteer Reserve, 1943-45. Career: Professor, Department of Medicine, University of Toronto; Physician-in-Chief, The Wellesley Hospital, Toronto; Director, Endocrinology Research Laboratory, Wellesley Hospital. Organizational Memberships: American Thyroid Association, President 1981-82; Canadian Society of Endocrinology and Metabolism, Past President; Endocrine Society; Toronto Society for Clinical Research, Past President; Royal Society of Medicine, London; Canadian Society for Clinical Investigation; Alpha Omega Alpha; American Federation of Clinical Research; American College of Physicians, Governor for Ontario 1977-82. Community Activities: Medical Research Council of Canada, Endocrine Committee 1975-78; National Institutes of Health of the United States, Task Force for Funding of Endocrinology Research 1978-79; Numerous University of Toronto Committees; Wellesley Hospital Medical Advisory Committee, Chairman 1981-83; Hospital Council for Metropolitan Toronto. Published Works: Author 140 Articles or Books dealing with Immunology of the Endocrine System. Honors and Awards: Goldie Prize for Medical Research, University of Toronto, 1972; State of the Art Lecturer, Endocrine Society, 1975; Jamieson Prize of the Canadian Society of Nuclear Medicine, 1980; Honorary Membership, Endocrine Society of Chile; State of the Art Lecturer, Department of Medicine, University of Toronto, 1981; Numerous Visiting Professorshps. Address: 3 Daleberry Place, Don Mills, Ontario M2B 2A5, Canada.■

JAMES FRANCIS VONDRUSKA

Research Veterinarian. Personal: Born February 8, 1940; Son of James J. (deceased) and Helen B. Vondruska; Married Joan E. Broxham; Father of James F. Jr., Juliet E, Jonathan L. Education: Attended Loyola University, Chicago, Illinois, 1958-59; D.V.M., Ohio State University, Columbus, Ohio, 1964; Graduate Studies in Pathology, Northwestern University, Chicago, Illinois, 1969-72. Military: Served in United States Army Veterinary Corps, 1965-66, attaining the rank of Captain. Career: Research Veterinarian, Quaker Oats Company; Former Positions include Senior Research Scientist and Director of Laboratory Animal Resources, Searle Laboratories, Skokie, Illinois; Staff Veterinarian, Industrial Bio-Test Laboratories, Northbrook, Illinois; Staff Veterinarian, Chicago Zoological Society, Brookfield, Illinois; Several Positions in Practice of Small Animal Medicine. Organizational Memberships: American Veterinary Medical Association; American College of Laboratory Animal Medicine; American Society of Laboratory Animal Practitioners; Illinois State Veterinary Medical Association; American Association of Industrial Veterinarians; American Association of Veterinary Nutritionists; American Society of Veterinary Clinical Pathologists. Community Activities: Phi Zeta Veterinary Honor Society, 1964; School Board, St. Louise de Marillac School, La Grange Park, Illinois, 1971-72; Consulting Veterinarian, The Hinsdale Humane Society, Hinsdale, Illinois, 1978 to present; Columnist, *The Hinsdale Doings*, 1981-82; Board of Directors, Illinois Society for Medical Research, 1981. Address: 241 Meadowbrook Lane, Hinsdale, Illinois 60558.■

TWO THOUSAND NOTABLE AMERICANS

WILLIAM JOHN VOOS

College President. Personal: Born July 2, 1930; Son of William F. (deceased) and Dollie M. Voos; Married Louise Madeleine Huddle; Father of Nancy Elizabeth, Susan Lynn, Patricia Ann. Education: B.F.A., Washington University, St. Louis, Missouri, 1952; M.F.A., University of Kansas, 1953. Served in the United States Army, 1953-55, attaining the rank of Corporal. Career: Atlanta College of Art, President 1975 to present, Dean 1973-75; Associate Professor and Associate Dean, Washington University, 1968-73; Humanities Division Chairman and Associate Professor, St. Louis Community College-Florissant Valley, 1964-66; Chairman, Art Department, McCluer High School, 1956-64. Organizational Memberships: Chairman, Alliance of Independent Colleges of Art, 1981-83; Chairman, University Center in Georgia, 1982-83; Executive Board, National Association of Schools of Art and Design, 1967-73; President, Area Coordinating Council for the Arts in St. Louis, 1973; College Art Association. Community Activities: Metropolitan Atlanta Rapid Transit Authority Council for the Arts; Executive Board, Atlanta Arts Festival, 1947-77; Advisory Board, United Nations International Children's Emergency Fund. Religion: Member of Covenant Presbyterian Church, Marietta, Georgia, 1980 to present; Deacon Hazelwood Presbyterian Church, St. Louis, Missouri, 1964-66. Honors and Awards: Eleven Solo Art Shows; Numerous Art Awards; Omicron Delta Kappa, 1952. Address: 3229 Wendwood Drive, Marietta, Georgia 30062.■

CARMEN DELGADO VOTAW

Executive. Personal: Married Gregory B. Votaw; Mother of Stephen Gregory, Michael Albert and Lisa Juliette. Education: B.A. International Studies, The American University, School of International Service; D.D.S., School of Business Administration, University of Puerto Rico; Doctorate in the Humanities (honorary), Hood College, Maryland. Career: Vice President, Information and Services for Latin America; President, Inter American Commission of Women, 1978-80; Co-Chair, National Advisory Committee on Women; Member, U.S. Foreign Service Promotion Board Review Panel, 1976; President, National Conference of Puerto Rican Women; Federal Programs Specialist, Office of the Commonwealth of Puerto Rico, Washington, D.C.; President, Inter American Commission of Women of the Organization of American States; Consultant to U.S. Department of State, United States Representative to the Commission related to the U.S. OAS Mission and International Organization Affairs Bureau of the Department; Participant in World Conference on the United Nations Decade for Women, Mexico and Copenhagen (Denmark) and Numerous International Fora; Vice President, Overseas Education Fund, League of Women Voters of the United States, Board Member 1968-81, Executive Board, Executive Committee, Program Development, Latin American and Publications Committees; Director, Caribbean Seminar on Women in Development; Co-Chair, National Advisory Committee for Women, Appointed by the President of the United States; Commissioner, United States Commission on the Observance of International Women's Year 1977, Executive Committee, Chair of Selection Committee; Federal Programs Specialist, Federal Plans and Programs Section, Office of the Commonwealth of Puerto Rico, Washington, D.C.; Executive Assistant to the Administrator of the Office of the Commonwealth of Puerto Rico, Washington, D.C.; Short-term American Grantee, U.S. Department of State; Government Development Bank for Puerto Rico, San Juan, Puerto Rico, Secretary to the President and to the General Counsel, Editor of *Ecos* Personnel Information Publication of the Bank, Editor of *Caribbean Highlights*; Teacher, Benedict Business School, San Juan, Puerto Rico. Organizational Memberships: Board Member, Equity Policy Center; Pan American Development Foundation; Americans for Democratic Action; Board of Directors and Employment Task Force, National Urban Coalition; Wonder Woman Foundation; Advisory Committees/Boards, Puerto Rican Family Institute, New York; Women's Educational Equity Action League, Washington, D.C., Aspira of America Fellowships Program, Ad Hoc Coalition for Women's Appointments, National Women's Political Caucus; Board of Directors, National Puerto Rican Coalition, Coalition for Internatinal Development; Foreign Service Selection Board, U.S. Department of State; Board, Public Members Association of the Foreign Service; National Conference of Puerto Rican Women, National President, President of D.C. Chapter 1975, National Board until 1980; Advisor and Participant in Series of Conferences on Cross Disciplinary Perspectives on Bilingual Education, Center for Applied Linguistics, 1976; Advisory Committee on Women of the Secretary of Labor of the United States; Advisory Committee, Committee on International Interdependece, U.S. National Commission on the Observance of International Women's Year; Board of Directors, Hispanic Women's Center, Washington, D.C.; Trainee, Institute for Creative Leadership, Greensboro, North Carolina; Participant, White House Conference on Bilingual Education; Political Participation of Women's Task Force, Women's Action Alliance; Overseas Education Fund, Director, Vice President 1968-72; Steering Committee of Aspen Institute Project on Governance in the Western Hemisphere; World Bank Wives in Voluntary Service, Founding Member, Executive Committee Member 1969-72. Community Activities: Promoted and Implemented Plans for the Creation of a Hispanic First Credit Union to serve the Hispanic Community in the District of Columbia Metropolitan Area; Collaborated in the Program Development and Design of Leadership Seminars and Activities to Promote Civic Participation and Action in Community Involvement to Improve Communities in Latin America and Domestically; Directed and Guided the Growth of a National Organization Functioning in Ten States and Improved Its Organizational Development Patterns to Achieve Effective, Relevant National Recognition to Advance Opportunities for Hispanics and Women; Establishment, Direction and Management of the National Advisory Committee for Women until 1979. Published Works: Writer and Editor of Numerous Studies and Publications as Well as Articles and News Features Such as *Foundation Support to Puerto Ricans*, *The Process of Self Determination During the Last Two Decades*, *A Study of Federal Public Assistance Payments to Puerto Rico*, *Puerto Rican Women: Some Biographical Profiles* (book), *Women in Development*. Honors and Awards: Listed in *Who's Who of American Women;*, *Women's International Register*. Address: 6717 Loring Court, Bethesda, Maryland 20817.■

AUSTIN LAFAYETTE VRICK

Civil Engineer. Personal: Born January 28, 1929, in Cedervale, New Mexico; Married Norine E. Melton; Father of Larry A., Margaret J., David A. Education: B.S. 1950, M.S. 1961 Civil Engineering, New Mexico State University. Military: Served in the United States Air Force, 1951-71, attaining the rank of Captain. Career: White Sands Missle Range, Chief Projects Section, Data Reduction Branch 1955-58, Chief Projects Office 1958-64, Chief Performance Evaluation Division 1964-73, Chief Data Collection Division 1973-82, Technical Assistant to Director, National Range Operations 1983 to present. Organizational Memberships: American Defense Preparedness Association; Rio Grande Chapter Vice President, Association United States Army, 1970; Senior Member, American Astronautical Society. Published Works: "Future Space Program and Impact on Range and Network Development" 1967, "Space Technology and Earth Problems" 1971; Numerous Technical Papers. Honors and Awards: Secretary of the Army Award for Outstanding Achievement in Equal Opportunity, 1982; Outstanding Performance Award, White Sands Missile Range, 1972; Special Acts Awards, 1976, 1971, 1975. Address: 4568 Spanish Dagger, Las Cruces, New Mexico 88001.■

PAVLA GABRIEL FRANK VRSIC

Student, Psychiatric Technician. Personal: Born May 30, 1964, in Brownwood, Texas; Daughter of Prof. Dr. and Mrs. G. Frank Vrsic. Education: Graduate, Hawkins High School, 1981; Attending Brigham Young University. Career: Psychiatric Technician, Utah State Prison, Bluffdale. Honors and Awards: High School Salutatorian; NMSQT/PSAT National Merit Letter; MENSA (Member at Age 16); National Honor Society; Published Poetess; Region III Talented Youth; Rotary Student of Month; Numerous Awards in UIL Speech, Drama, Voice, Spelling, Poetry and Prose Contests; Honorable Mention, National Poetry Contest; Third Place, Miss Senior F.T.A.; 4th Place, District UIL Spelling and Poetry Contests; Second Place, Rotary Speaking Contest; Library Trophies; Listed in *Who's Who Among American High School Students*, *International Youth in Achievement*, *Community Leaders of America*, *Personalities of America*, *The Directory of Distinguished Americans*, *Personalities of the West and Midwest*. Address: Broadmore Apts., 1065 East 450 North, Unit #2, Provo, Utah 84601.■

DORIS HOMAN WADDELL

Chemist and Laboratory Supervisor. Personal: Born April 28, 1933; Daughter of Agnes Homan; Mother of Robert Kenneth. Education: B.S. Chemistry 1957, Teacher Certificate 1959, University of Miami; Certificate, Florida Computer College, 1969. Career: Chemist, Laboratory Supervisor, Preston Laboratory, Hialeah, Florida; Former Positions include Chemist in Quality Control Laboratory, Assistant Senior High School Science Teacher and Laboratory Technician. Organizational Memberships: American Chemical Society; American Water Works Association; Association of Women in Science. Community Activities: Guest Lecturer at Florida Water and Pollution Control Operators Association Short School 1979, 1980 and 1981, Toxic Task Force 1980. Honors and Awards: Education Crisis Honor Roll, Classroom Teachers' Association, 1968; Dean's List, University of Miami, 1956; Listed in *Who's Who of the South and Southwest*. Address: 549 Miller Drive, Miami Springs, Florida 33166.■

BETTE HOPE WADDINGTON
(STAGE NAME: ELIZABETH CROWDER)

Violinist. Personal: Born July 27, 1921, in San Francisco, California; Daughter of John and Marguerite Crowder Waddington (both deceased). Education: A.B. Music and Art, University of California at Berkeley, 1945; M.A. Music and Art, San Francisco State University, 1953; Postgradute Study undertaken at the University of California, San Jose State University, Juilliard School of Music; General California Teaching Credentials, Kindergarten through 12th Grades, Junior High Librarianship; California Junior College Life Credentials, Music and Art; Studies in Violin under Daniel Bonsack, Felix Khuner, Naoum Blinder, Louis Ford, Frank Gittelson, Melvin Ritter, Dr. D.C. Dounis. Career: Violinist with the St. Louis Symphony, 1958 to present; Former Positions include Librarian for the National Aeronautics and Space Administration, Librarian for the Children's Public Library in San Jose, Public School Teacher in Alameda and San Francisco Counties (California) and Erie (Pennsylvania), Violinist with the Dallas Symphony, Concert Mistress with the Peninsula Symphony (Redwood City and San Mateo, California), Carmel Bach Festival (California); Violinist in Erie Symphony (Pennsylvania), Conducted by Fritz Mahler, 1950-51; Violinist with the Dallas Symphony, Conducted by Walter Hendl, 1957-58. Organizational Memberships: Alpha Beta Alpha; American String Teachers Association. Community Activities: Sierra Club; University of California Alumni Association; San Jose State University Alumni Association; San Jose State University Alumni Association; United Services Organization and Red Corss Violin Soloist, 1940-48; Soloist at Camp in Yosemite, California. Religion: Presbyterian; Violin Soloist for Various Churches in Bay Area and High Sierra (California), Erie (Pennsylvania), New York City (New York). Honors and Awards: Scholarship as Student of Joseph Fuchs, Juilliard School of Music, 1950; *Time* Magazine Gave St. Louis Symphony National Ratings as Second Highest in United States, 1983; Extensive Travel throughout the United States, Europe, Canada, Mexico and Egypt Studying Art and Music. Address: Heritage House Apartments, 3800 Olive Street, St. Louis, Missouri 63103.■

MARY CARROLL WADE

Educator, Government Official, Psychologist. Personal: Born September 1, 1909; Daughter of Seaborn Rosa and Dollie Hill Carroll (both deceased); Married Richard Rudolph Wade (deceased). Education: B.A., Maryville College, 1931; Postgraduate Study undertaken at the French School, University of the South, Summer of 1937; M.A., George Washington University, 1948; Ed.D., American University, 1970. Career: High School Teacher and Drama Coach; Clerk Typist, War Department; Library Assistant, Library of Congress; Planner, Planner-in-Charge, Chief of Data Forms Section, United States Government Printing Office; Consultant Psychologist, Virginia Department of Rehabilitation; Chairman, Federal Women's Program, United States Government Printing Office; Lecturer, Montgomery College; Consultant. Organizational Memberships: American Psychological Association; Virginia Psychological Association; District of Columbia Psychological Association; Psi Chi, Secretary 1965; Kappa Delta Epsilon; Business Forms Management Association, Secretary 1980-81; Washington Craftsmen's Club; Washington Litho Club; Franklin Technical Society. Community Activities: Washington Cerebral Palsy Association, Board Member 1970-82; Northern Virginia Altrusa Club, Member 1977 to present, Vice President 1970-82, Secretary 1982-84; Scholarship Committee Board, Secretary 1982-84; Community Services, Chairman 1978; Business and Professional Women's Club of Fairfax, Vice President 1974-75, President 1975-76, Scholarship Chairman 1978; Phi Delta Gamma, Chapter President 1957-58, Secretary 1948-49, National Council Representative 1968-72; Columbian Women, Secretary 1983-84; Corporation of Alexandria Hospital, 1980 to present; Alexandria Inter-Service Club Council, Secretary 1981; Northern Virginia Toastmistress Club, President 1973, Vice President 1973, Secretary 1972, Treasurer 1972, Delegate to National Convention 1974 and 1982, Club Delegate to Council 1981; National Trust for Historic Preservation; Poetry Society of Virginia. Religion: Former Sunday School Teacher, Union Congregation Church, 1925-26; Member, Maryville Providence Presbyterian Church. Honors and Awards: Honorary Member of Staff of Tennessee Senator Anna Belle Clement O'Brien; Distinguished Service Award, United Service Organization, 1946; Six Certificates of Merit 1962-65, Superior Service Awards 1963 and 1966-68, Special Achievement Awards 1971-72, United States Government Printing Office; Nominee for Federal Woman of the Year Award, 1975; Chairman, Government Printing Office Federal Women's Program, 1972-73; Equal Employment Opportunity Service Award, 1974-75; National Committee for Standardization of Optical Character Recognition Forms, 1973-74; Graduate of Maryville College Art Department, 1931. Address: 614 Bashford Lane, Apartment 103, Alexandria, Virginia 22314.■

ROYCE ALLEN WADE

Corporate Executive. Personal: Born April 30, 1932; Son of Mrs. Charles Wade; Married Corinne Mae Weber; Father of Suzanne Mae, Debra Ann. Education: B.S., University of Wisconsin-Stevens Point, 1954; M.Div. Garrett Theological Seminary, Evanston, Illinois, 1960; M.S. Adult Education, University of Wisconsin-Milwaukee, 1960; Graduate Work in Adult Education, University of Wisconsin-Madison, 1970-75. Military: Served in the United States Army, Counter Intelligence Corps, 1954-56, as Intelligence Analyst. Career: Vice President and Director of Growth and Development, Professional Products and Services, Inc.; Curriculum Consultant in the University of Wisconsin School of Nursing, Instructor Small Group Seminar at the University of Wisconsin, and Director Adult Study Center (Portage, Wisconsin), 1974-76; Pastor, Poynette (Wisconsin) United Methodist Church, 1969-74; Associate Pastor, St. Luke United Methodist Church (Sheboygan, Wisconsin), 1968-69; Pastor, Simpson and Gardner United Methodist Churches, Milwaukee, Wisconsin, 1966-68; Associate Pastor, Community Methodist Church, Whitefish Bay, Wisconsin, 1962-66; Guidance Counselor at Edgerton (Wisconsin) Senior High School and Sales Training Manager with Hunt Water Softener Company (Fort Atkinson, Wisconsin), 1961-62; Pastor, Asbury United Methodist Church, Janesville, Wisconsin, 1958-61; Pastor, Richmond (Wisconsin) United Methodist Church, 1956-58. Organizational Memberships: Adult Education Association of United States of America; Phi Delta Kappa;

American Society for Training and Development; American Association for the Advancement of Science; Association of Official Analytical Chemists, Regular Executive Board Member. Community Activities: Adult Education Instructor, Wisconsin Conference, United Methodist Church, 1964-69; Village Trustee, Poynette, Wisconsin, 1977-81; Police Auxiliary, Whitefish Bay, Wisconsin, 1962-66; Consultant, Adult Education, Organizational Management, Human Relations, 1974 to present; Board of Directors, North Shore (Milwaukee) Council on Human Relations, 1964-66; Milwaukee Inter-Faith Council; Charter Member, Pynette (Wisconsin) Optimists International, 1979 to present. Religion: Ordained Elder in the United Methodist Church, 1960. Honors and Awards: Academic Scholarship, University of Wisconsin-Stevens Point, 1950; Listed in *Who's Who in the Midwest, Who's Who in Finance and Industry.* Address: 122 East Washington Street, Poynette, Wisconsin 53955.■

COE WILLIAM WADELIN

Chemist. Personal: Born August 18, 1927; Married Carolyn Gould Walker; Father of Jeffrey William. Education: B.S., Mt. Union College, 1950; M.S. 1951, Ph.D. 1953, Purdue University; Attended Massachusetts Institute of Technology, Center for Advanced Engineering Study, 1968-69. Military: Served in the United States Army, 1946-47, attaining the rank of Sergeant. Career: Chemist, Goodyear. Organizational Memberships: American Chemical Society, Analytical Division, Rubber Division. Religion: Member, United Methodist Church. Address: 3117 Orchard Road, Cuyahoga Falls, Ohio 44224.■

ASPI RUSTOM WADIA

Senior Project Engineer. Personal: Born April 17, 1953; Son of R. C. Wadia; Married Aban; Father of Farah, Shernaz, Holly. Education: Indian School Certificate Examination, Loyola School, India, 1970; Bachelor of Technology with honors, Indian Institute of Technology, Kharagpur, 1975; Master of Science in Aerospace, Cornell University; Ph.D., University of Texas-Arlington, 1979. Career: Senior Project Engineer, Turbine Aerodynamics Heat Transfer, DDA/GM, Indianapolis; Former Positions as Design Engineer with Garrett Turbine Engine Company (Phoenix, Arizona), Teaching Associate at the University of Texas-Arlington, and Research Assistant, Cornell University (Ithaca, New York). Organizational Memberships: Tau Beta Pi; Sigma Xi; Sigma Gamma Tau; A.S.M.E.; New York Academy of Sciences; Accomodations Coordinator, A.I.A.A. Regional Conference, 1977. Community Activities: Executive Student Member, Committee on International Student Affairs, Cornell University, Ithaca, New York, 1976-77; Consultant, C.D.C. Minnesota, 1980; Reviewer for A.S.M.E. and A.I.A.A. Journals, 1980-82. Religion: Zorastrian. Honors and Awards: John DeYoung Research Award, Department of Aerospace Engineering, University of Texas/Arlington, 1979; Sigma Xi Research Award for Outstanding Ph.D. Student Research, University of Texas-Arlington Chapter, 1978; Minta Martin Student Paper Competition Certificate of Merit, First Prize, Graduate Division, A.I.A.A., 1977; A.I.A.A. Student Branch Lecture Award, Cornell University, Ithaca, 1976; Listed in *Who's Who in the West, Who's Who in Finance and Industry, Men of Achievement, Personalities of America, Personalities of the West and Midwest.* Address: 11347 Oldfield Drive, Carmel, Indiana 46032.■

ANDREW JAMES WAGNER

Meteorologist. Personal: Born April 12, 1934; Son of Andrew and Ruth M. Wagner; Married Betty C. Ritenour. Education: B.A. with honors in Physics, Wesleyan University, 1956; M.S. Meteorology, Massachusetts Institute of Technology, 1958. Career: Meteorologist, National Weather Service. Organizational Memberships: Sigma Xi; American Meteorological Society; American Geophysical Union; Royal Meteorological Society; National Weather Association; American Scientific Affilation; Washington Academy of Sciences, Manager-at-Large 1982-85. Community Activities: Fairfax Resolves Chapter, Sons of the American Revolution, Third Vice President 1982-83, Chaplain 1980-85; Lake Beverly Forest Civic Association, President 1977-79, Vice President 1979-81. Religion: Church of Northern Virginia, Treasurer 1969-76, Building Chairman 1978-80, Elder 1968 to present, Trustee 1970 to present. Address: 7007 Beverly Lane, Springfield, Virginia 22150.■

IWANA B. WAGNER

Finance Officer, Coordinator in Home Rehabilitation Program, Historic Preservation Officer, Energy Advisor and Chairman Sister Cities Activities. Personal: Born July 5, 1932; Daughter of Okley T. Lee; Mother of Kenneth C. Jr., Alana Lee. Education: Graduate of East High School, Akron, Ohio, 1950; Graduate of Comptometer Business School, Akron, 1950; Accounting Courses, North Central Technical College, Mansfield, Ohio. Career: Payroll Supervisor, National Seating Company; Owner, Iwana's Seamstress Business; Finance Officer, Home Rehabilitation Coordinator, Historic Coordinator, Energy Advisor, Sister City Coordinator, City of Mansfield, Ohio. Organizational Memberships: M.O.A.B.W.A. Charter Chapter, American Business Women's Association, President 1973. Community Activities: Zonta of Mansfield, President 1981; Area Secretary, Senator Robert Taft's Campaign Committee, 1969; Precinct Committeewoman, Republican Party, 1974-77; Jaycees Wives President, 1960; Women's Coalition for Political Action, Treasurer, 1983-84. Religion: President, Women's Association, First United Presbyterian Church, Mansfield, Ohio, 1973. Honors and Awards: Woman of the Year, American Businesswomen's Association, M.O.A.B.W.A. Charter Chapter, 1973; Personality of the Week, *Mansfield News Journal,* 1976. Address: 576 Sherwood Drive, Mansfield, Ohio 44904.■

PATRICK A. WAGNER

Director of Psychological Services. Personal: Born February 7, 1946; Son of Mr. and Mrs. H. E. Wagner. Education: A.B. Psychology 1969, M.S. Educational Psychology 1971, Ph.D. School Psychology 1976, Indiana University. Career: Director of Psychological Services, New Hope of Indiana; Staff Psychologist, Marion County Association for Retarded Citizens; School Psychologist, Metropolitan School District of Martinsville, Indiana; Part-Time Professor, Indiana Central University. Organizational Memberships: American Psychological Association; Indiana Psychological Association; American Association on Mental Deficiency; American Association for the Advancement of Science; Biofeedback Society of Indiana. Community Activities: Guest Speaker on Stress Management to Shelbyville (Indiana) Lion's Club 1981, Shelbyville Rotary Club 1981, Northwest Sertoma Indianapolis 1981, Shelbyville Zonta Club 1982; Guest Speaker on Mental Retardation to Indiana Central University 1979, Indiana Girls' School 1980, Crispus Attucks High School 1982. Honors and Awards: Undergraduate Assistantship, Indiana University, 1968-69; School of Education Fellowship, Indiana University, 1972-73; Private Practice Certificate, Indiana Board of Examiners in Psychology, 1980. Address: 1710 Centurion Parkway, Indianapolis, Indiana 46260.■

PAUL A. WAGNER

Associate Professor. Personal: Born August 28, 1947; Son of Paul A. Wagner, Sr.; Married Karen S.; Father of Nicole Scroka, Eric Paul, Jason George. Education: B.S. Political Science/Economics, Northeast Missouri State University, 1969; M.A. Philosophy 1976, M.Ed. 1972, Ph.D. Philosophy of Education 1978, University of Missouri-Columbia. Military: Served in the Missouri National Guard, 1970-76. Career: Associate Professor, University of Houston; Instructor Philosophy of Education, University of Missouri-Columbia, 1976-78; Instructor Philosophy and Political Science, Moberly Area Junior College, 1974-75. Organizational Memberships: Fellow, Philosophy of Education Society; Philosophy of Science Association; American Philosophical Association; American Educational Studies Association; Br. Philosophy of Science Association; Southwest Educational Research Association. Community Activities: Vice Chairperson, Human Rights Commission, Columbia, Missouri, 1976-79. Religion: Catholic. Published Works: Author of Over 50 Articles in Professional Journals. Honors and Awards: Chancellor's Distinguished Service Professor, 1984; Atrium Circle Distinguished Research Professor, 1981-82; Graduate Teaching Award, University of Missouri,

Columbia, 1977; Omar E. Robinson Scholarship, 1969-70; Groessle Scholarship, 1967-68; Member Editorial Board, *Journal of Thought*, 1981 to present; Editorial Board, Focus on Learning, 1983 to present. Address: 2622 Plymouth Rock Drive, Webster, Texas 77598.■

FRANK BERNARD WAHL, JR.

Editor-in-Chief. Personal: Born September 13, 1948; Son of Frank and Lorraine Wahl; Married Barbara Ellen Kostlan, Daughter of Robert and Helen Kostlan; Father of Michael Anthony, Christina Michelle, Timothy Matthew. Education: B.S. Systems Engineering, U.S. Naval Academy, 1970; M.B.A. Business, National University, 1977; M.S. Systems Management, University of Southern California, 1981. Military: Served in the United States Navy 1970-75, United States Naval Reserve-R 1975, LCDR. Career: Editor-in-Chief, D.A.T.A. Books; Former Professional Occupations include Corporate Strategic Planner-General Dynamics, Logistic Analyst-General Dynamics, Project Engineer ARINC Research, Site Manager SAI Comsytems, Naval Officer. Organizational Memberships: I.E.E.E., Committee SCC11.9, J.E.D.E.C. Committee JC-10, I.E.E.E.-A.N.S.I. Standards 432.14; Senior Member, C.A.S.A. Community Activities: San Diego Navy Federal Credit Union, Treasurer Board of Directors, 1982. Honors and Awards: COLTS Award for Most Original Project in Systems Engineering, 1970; Listed in *Who's Who in the West*, *The Directory of Distinguished Americans*, *Personalities of America*. Address: 11767 Papagallo Court, San Diego, California 92124.■

LOUIS EDWARD WAITE

Vice President, Operations. Personal: Born February 11, 1926; Son of Clarence and Bessie Hoover Waite; Married Frances Clara Jackson; Father of Yvonne B. McClain, Louis Jr., Duane D., John T. Education: Graduate of Camden School, Kipton, Ohio, 1944; Oberlin College, Ohio, 1950. Military: Served in the United States Army from 1944-45 in the 304th Infantry Regiment, 76th Infantry Division, European Theatre of Operations, France, Belgium, Luxembourg and Germany, attaining the rank of Private First Class. Career: Vice President Operations, TLI, Inc., 1976 to present; Manager, Truck Transportation, Inland Container Corporation, Indianapolis, Indiana, 1970-76; REA Express, Minneapolis/St. Paul Division Manager 1968-70, Various Supervisory Positions 1953-68; Diesel Engineer, City of Oberlin, Ohio, 1950-53. Organizational Memberships: Delta Nu Alpha Transportation Fraternity, 1969; Indiana Motor Truck Association, Director Executive Board 1972-76, Chairman Private Carrier Division 1973-76; American Trucking Association, Director Private Carrier Conference 1975 to present; National Council of Physical Distribution; Missouri Truck and Bus Association. Community Activities: Volunteer Fireman, 1947-52; Boy Scouts of America, Committeeman, Kipton, Ohio, 1947-52; Kiwanis International, Greenwood, Indiana, 1970-76; Parent-Teacher Association, Greenwood, Indiana, President 1964-65; Toastmasters Club, Indianapolis, Indiana, 1973; Masonic Lodge, Greenwood, Indiana, 1962; Scottish Rite, 32nd Degree, Indianapolis, Indiana, 1971; Murat Shrine, Indianapolis, Indiana, 1971; S.P.E.B.S.Q.S.A., Florissant, Missouri, 1980. Religion: Sunday School Teacher, Various Times and Locations; Minister of Music, New Providence Baptist Church, Missouri, 1965-68; Choir President, First Baptist, Afton, Missouri, 1968-69. Honors and Awards: International Platform Association, 1982; Honorary Kentucky Colonel, State of Kentucky, 1973; Named Honorary Louisiana Colonel, State of Louisiana, 1983; Listed in *Who's Who in Business and Finance*, *Who's Who in the Midwest*, *Who's Who in America*, *Who's Who in the World*, *Personalities of America*, *Directory of Distinguished Americans*. Address: 2265 Brook Drive, Florissant, Missouri 63033.■

RUDOLPH ORSON WAITON

Physician and Surgeon. Personal: Born June 11, 1922; Married Marilyn, Daughter of Mr. and Mrs. George Pentland; Father of Richard, Corryann, Melanie, Thomas. Education: B.S., University of Pittsburgh, 1949; M.A. 1954, Ph.D. 1956, Stanford University; D.O., Kirksville College of Osteopathic Medicine, 1965; M.D., University of Oregon, 1974. Military: Served in the United States Air Force "Flying Tigers," 1942-56, attaining the rank of Lieutenant Colonel. Career: Physician and Surgeon; Former Positions include Associate Professor C.O.M.P., Teacher in Salinas (California), Director of Bacteriology at Curtis and Thompkins (San Francisco), Federal Inspector Subsistance for the Armed Forces. Organizational Memberships: International Academy of Preventive Medicine; Association of Medical Rehabilitation Directors and Coordinators; American Academy of Family Physicians; Osteopathic Physicians and Surgeons of California; American Academy of Osteopathy; Orthomolecular Medical Society; American College of Sports Medicine; International Academy of Holistic Health and Medicine; American Congress of Physical Medicine and Rehabilitation; American Academy of Physical Medicine and Rehabilitation; F.A.A. Medical Examiner; American Osteopathic Association; American Medical Association; California Medical Society; Santa Clara County Medical Society; Union of American Physicians and Dentists; American Arbitration Association. Religion: Member Los Gatos Christian Church, 1976 to present. Honors and Awards: Distinguished Flying Cross; Air Medal; Purple Heart; Charter Fellow, International College of General Practice; President and Chairman of Board, California Institute of Rehabilitation and Preventive Medicine; Director, West Coast Coma Center; Fellow, International College of Applied Nutrition. Address: 120 Carlton Street, #54, Los Gatos, California 95030.■

WESLEY H. WAKEFIELD

Evangelist. Personal: Born August 22, 1929; Son of William James Elijah and Jane Mitchell Halpenny Wakefield (both deceased); Married Mildred June Shouldice, October 24, 1959. Education: Graduate of Vancouver Public Schools, Wesleyan Theological Studies (until 1951); Special Studies in Constitutional Law and Addictions. Career: Evangelist and International Leader, Bishop-General, The Bible Holiness Movement, 1949 to present; Editor, Truth on Fire! 1949 to present, Christian Social Vanguard 1961-62; Manager, Liberty Press, 1966 to present; Manager, Evangelistic Book Services, 1951 to present; Director, Cumo Resources Limited, 1979 to present; Director, Seastar Resources Limited, 1981 to 1984; Administrator, Imperial Security Guard Service Limited, 1979 to present. Organizational Memberships: Christian Holiness Association; Evangelical Fellowship of Canada; National Black Evangelical Association; Anti-Slavery Society for the Protection of Human Rights; British Columbia Family Council; Christians Concerned for Racial Equality; Canadian Bible Society; Religious Information Centre, Chairman 1978 to present; Canadians for the Protection of Religious Liberty; Religious Freedom Conference of Christian Minorities, Chairman 1978. Community Activities: British Columbia Family Conference, Delegate 1974-75; Citizens Committee, Penticton, British Columbia, Chairman 1956; Canadians United for Separation of Church and State, 1977 to present; United Citizens for Integrity, Research Director 1976 to present; Japan Evangelistic Band, Board Member 1977 to present; National Association for the Advancement of Colored People; Canadian Bible Society. Religion: Conservative Wesleyan Evangelical. Published Works: *Bible Doctrine* 1951, *Bible Basis of Christian Security* 1957, *Jesus is Lord* 1974; Editor, *Wesleyan Annotated Edition of the Bible* 1981, *Hallelujah Songbook* 1981, Others. Honors and Awards: Twice Awarded International Honor for Community Service; Opened First Legislature of New Democratic Party Government, British Columbia, 1972; Listed in *Who's Who in Religion*, *Who's Who in Canada*, *Dictionary of International Biography*. Address: P.O. Box 223, Postal Sta., Vancouver, British Columbia, Canada V6C 2M3.■

KATHRYN MORRIS WAKELAND

Real Estate Owner and Manager of Properties. Personal: Born June 9, 1934; Daughter of Mr. and Mrs. Clarence Gilbert Morris (deceased); Married J. Baldwin Wakeland, Sr.; Mother of Jack Baldwin Jr., Misty Kathryn. Education: B.A., Belhaven College, 1982; M.S. in Communication, Mississippi College graduting with honors. Career: Real Estate Owner and Manager of Properties; Former Secretarial Position with Southern Bell Telephone Company; Editor, *Taste of the South*, 1984. Community Activities: President, Capitol Opti-Mrs Club, 1968-69; President, Meh Lady Club, 1973-74; President, Jackson Ballet Guild, 1978-79; Chairman, Mississippi Wheelchair Reception, 1976; Chairman, Symphony League Brown Bag Concert, 1976; Chairman, Symphony League Pops Concert, 1978; Chairman, Positions for Three Major Goodwill Benefits; Chairman, Two "Tastevins" Major Fund-raising Project for Jackson Ballet Guild; Chairman, First Civic/Arts Calender, Jackson Ballet Guild, 1978; Co-Chairman, Jackson Symphony Ball, 1982; Co-Chairman, Mississippi Art Association's "Japanese Pavallion" for Mississippi Art Festival, 1973; Hospitality Committee for International Ballet Competition, 1979, 1982; Board of Directors, Jackson Ballet Guild, 1979-80; Advisory Committee to the Academics and Performing Arts Complex, Jackson Municipal Separate Schools, 1982 to present. Religion: President Christian Women's Fellowship, First Christian Church, 1971-72, 1977-78; Executive Committee for Mississippi Billy Graham Crusade, 1975. Honors and Awards: Summa Cum Laude Graduate, Belhaven College, 1982; McRae's Great Lady Award, 1978; One of Twenty of Mississippi's Leading Hostesses, Mississippi Art Association, 1971; Cited for Outstanding Work in Sunday School by Church, 1975; Cited for Outstanding Women's Civic Work by Capitol Optimist Club, 1970; Listed in *Personalities of the South*, 1979, and 1983. Address: 4018 Eastwood Place, Jackson, Mississippi 39211.■

TWO THOUSAND NOTABLE AMERICANS

RAYMOND ERNEST WALDNER

Professor. Personal: Born May 2, 1950; Son of Ernest H. (deceased) and Betty E. Waldner. Education: A.A. Biology, Palm Beach Junior College, 1970; B.S. Zoology 1973, M.S. Aquatic Biology 1975, Florida Atlantic University; Ph.D. Biological Oceanography, University of Puerto Rico, 1981. Career: Assistant Professor of Biology, Palm Beach Atlantic College, West Palm Beach, Florida. Organizational Memberships: Association of Island Marine Laboratories of the Caribbean; American Society of Ichthyologists and Herpetologists; Florida Academy of Sciences; Western Society of Naturalists. Community Activities: Volunteer Hyperbaric Chamber Operator, University of Puerto Rico, 1976-80; Volunteer Hyperbaric Chamber Supervisor, Inter-City Recompression Chamber, Inc., 1980-82. Honors and Awards: National Science Foundation International Travel Grant, 1977; National Science Foundation Dissertation Grant, 1978; Phi Kappa Phi Honor Society, 1975; Graduate Assistantship, Florida Atlantic University, 1974-75; Graduate Assistantship, University of Puerto Rico, 1975-76 and 1977-79; Research Assistantship, University of Puerto Rico, 1976 and 1979-80. Address: 1812 Barbados Road, West Palm Beach, Florida, 33406.■

CAROLYN PEYTON WALKER

Educational Administrator, Lecturer. Personal: Born September 15, 1942; Daughter of Clay M. and Ruth Newman Peyton. Education: B.A. American History and Literature, Sweet Briar College, 1965; Certificate in French, Alliance Francaise, Paris, France, 1966; Ed.M. Education and Reading, Tufts University. 1970; Ph.D English Education, College Reading and Composition, Stanford University, 1977. Career: Stanford University, Director Learning Assistance Center, Lecturer School of Education, 1977 to present, Assistant Director and Reading/Writing Specialist, Learning Assistance Center, Lecturer English Department 1972-77, Lecturer School of Education 1974-84; Lecturer, Undergraduate Studies, Stanford, 1975-82; Reviewer, *Research in the Teaching of English*, Random House Publishers, 1983 to present; Consultant, Right to Read, California State Department of Education, 1977 to present; Consultant, Basic Skills Task Force, United States Office of Education, 1977-79; Consultant, ETS/College Board, 1983; Consultant, Program for Gifted and Talented, Fremont Unified School District, 1981-82; Consultant, San Francisco Association of Gifted and Talented, 1981, 1983; Evaluation Consultant, Institute for Professional Development, San Jose, California, 1975-76; Instructor, School of Business, University of San Francisco, 1973-74; Instructor, Humanities Division, Canada College, Redwood City, California, 1973 and 1976-78; Instructor, The Reading Institute, Boston, Massachusetts, 1969-70; Teacher, Blue Ridge School, Summer 1970; Teacher, Rock Hill Academy, Summer 1967; Teacher, Newark (California Unified School System), 1970-72; Substitute Teacher, Boston City Schools, 1969-70; Teacher, Gai-Matin, Institut D'Enfants, Chesieres, Switzerland, 1967-69; Teacher, J.F. Kennedy School, Jamaica Plain, Massachusetts, 1966-67; Has Presented Many Professional Papers and Organized Numerous Workshops in the Field of Reading Education. Organizational Memberships: American Association of University Professors, 1976 to present; Modern Language Association, 1975 to present; California Professors of Reading, 1975 to present; National Reading Conference, 1974 to present; Northern California College Reading Association, Member 1973 to present, Secretary/Treasurer 1976-78; Western College Reading and Learning Association 1973 to present, Treasurer, Member Board of Directors 1982-84; National Council of Teachers of English, 1972 to present; California Teacher's Association, 1970-72; Newark Teacher's Association, 1970-72; The Resource Center for Women, 1975-76; Board of Directors, High Technology Science Center, 1980-82; Board of Directors, Junior League of Palo Alto, 1974 to present. Published Works: "ESL Courses for Faculty and Staff: An Additional Opportunity to Serve the Campus Community" (with Bruce Henderson), *Proceedings of the Sixteenth Annual Conference of the Western College Reading Association*, Fall 1983; "Helping Math/Science Students When You Are Not a Math/Science Person Yourself" (Carolyn Walker et al), *Proceedings of the Fifteenth Annual Conference of the Western College Reading Association*, 1982; "Learning Center Courses for Faculty and Staff: Reading, Writing and Time Management," *Proceedings of the Fourteenth Annual Conference of the Western College Reading Association*, 1981; *Academic Tutoring at the Learning Assistance Center* (Carolyn Walker et al) 1980, Abstract in *Resources in Education* 1980; Others. Address: 2350 Waverley Street, Palo Alto, California 94301■

ERNEST LEE WALKER

Engineer. Personal: Born February 12, 1941; Son of Mrs. Mae R. Walker; Married Vivian L. Education: Graduate of Jasper County High School, 1958; B.S. Electrical Engineering, Indiana Institute of Technology, Fort Wayne, Indiana, 1967; M.S. Electrical Engineering, Syracuse University, 1972; Ph.D., North Carolina State University, 1982. Military: Served in the United States Army Signal Corps, l960-64. Career: Advisory Engineer, International Business Machines Corporation. Organizational Memberships: Institute of Electronic and Electrical Engineers; Communications Group; Information Theory Group; Optical Society of America. Community Activities: Southern Poverty Law Center; National Association for the Advancement of Colored People; Life Member, Kappa Alpha Psi Fraternity; Founder, Poughkeepsie Alumni Chapter Kappa Alpha Psi and Polemarch, 1973-74; United Negro College Fund; Rust College. Religion: Member of Saint Joseph's A.M.E. Church; Member of Steward Board. Honors and Awards: Two Invention Awards: Five United States Patents Issued, Two Soviet and French Patents Filed; Outstanding Young Man of America, 1973; Listed in *Who's Who in Black America, Men of Achievement*. Address: 117 Warren Way, Chapel Hill, North Carolina 275l4.■

FRANCIS C. WALKER

Consulting Industrial Psychologist. Personal: Born February 1, 1926; Son of Ivan Banks (deceased) and Hazel Walker; Married Donna J., Daughter of Clara Whitmer; Father of Gregory C., Taffy. Education: B.A. Humanities with honors 1949, M.A. Psychology 1950, Bradley University. Military: Served in the United States Air Force, 1944-46, attaining the rank of Corporal. Career: President, Frank Walker Associates, Inc., 1970 to present; Vice President 1969-70, Consultant 1970-71, Rutenberg Homes, Inc.; Secretary and Director of Administrative Services, Byron Harless, Schaffer, Reid and Associates, Inc., 1960-69; Industrial Relations Consultant, Sangamo Electric Company, Inc., 1955-60; Industrial Psychologist, Byron Harless and Associates, Inc., 1955; Personnel Counselor, Caterpillar Tractor, 1950-55. Organizational Memberships: International Association of Applied Psychologists; American Psychological Association, Divisions 13, 14, 23, 31, 42; Southeastern Psychological Association; Bay Region Chapter, Florida Psychological Assocation, President 1972-73; Tampa Bay Psychological Association, President 1966; National Rehabilitation Association; Professional Member, National Rehabilitation Counseling Association. Community Activities: Greater Tampa Chamber of Commerce, Past Chairman Law Enforcement Council; Boys Clubs of Tampa, Chairman Nominating Committee; University Club of Tampa; Exchange Club of Tampa; Instructor, Bradley University 1951-53, Springfield Junior College 1956, University of South Florida 1974, University of Tampa 1975-77, Hillsborough Community College 1975; President, Sheridan Village Homeowners Association, 1951-53; Richwoods Township Board of Education, Peoria, Illinois, 1951-55; Republican Precinct Committeeman, 1953-55 and 1966-68; Board of Directors, Illinois Association for Mental Health, 1956-60; Board of Directors 1960-76, Treasurer 1965-67, Florida Association for Mental Health; President, Hillsborough County Republican Club, 1964-66; Pine Island Property Owners Association, 1981 to present. Religion: Member Bayshore United Presbyterian Church, Past Clerk of Session. Published Works: Co-Author, "The Effectiveness of a Therapeutic Campaign Program for Delinquent Adolescents" 1976; Author "Motivating the Fund Raising Volunteer and Donor" 1978 and "Recruitment and Training" 1968 (unpublished works). Honors and Awards: National Honor Society, 1941-43; Bradley Federation of Scholars, 1948-49; Psi Chi National Honorary Society in Psychology; Listed in *National Register of Health Service Providers in Psychology, Who's Who in the South and Southwest, Who's Who in Consulting, Men of Achievement, Directory of Certified Psychologists, Personalities of the South, Personalities of America, Notable Americans 1976-77, Dictionary of International Biography, National Social Directory, Community Leaders and Noteworthy Americans*. Address: 215 South Hesperides, Tampa, Florida 33609.■

GLYNDA MARIE WALKER

Director of Communications Department. Personal: Born May 31, 1940; Daughter of Mr. and Mrs. Robert Glenn Walker. Education: B.S., Southern Illinois University, 1962; M.A., Ohio State University, 1968; Ohio License in Speech Pathology, 1975. Career: Director of Communications Department and Speech/Language Pathologist, Wheeling Society for Crippled Children, West Virginia, Over l8 Years. Organizational Memberships: American Speech/Language and Hearing Association, 1962 to present; Council of Exceptional Children, 1968 to present; Zeta Alpha Eta; Zeta Phi Eta; Association for Retarded Citizens, Board Member 1975 to present, Treasurer 1977-78, Vice President 1979-80; Russell Nesbitt-Ohio County Council for Retarded Children, Board Member 1981 to present, Corresponding Secretary 1981-82; Advisory Board Member, Headstart Agency, 1975 to present; Board of Directors, Northern Panhandle Headstart Agency, 1983 to present; Developmental Disabilities and Mental Retardation Steering Committee, Northern Panhandle Mental Health, 1977 to

present; Handicapped United Organization, 1980 to present. Community Activities: Sunshine Friday Social Club for Retarded Teenagers and Young Adults, Founder, Volunteer Coordinator, 1975 to present; Sponsor, Emoclew Handicapped Young Adult Club, 1962 to present; Volunteer Coordinator, Ohio Valley Stroke Club, 1978 to present. Religion: Vance Memorial Presbyterian Church; Sunday School Teacher, Christ Methodist Church, 1962. Honors and Awards: Certificate of Clinical Competence in Speech Pathology, American Speech/Language and Hearing Association, 1961 to present; Jaycette State and Local Awards, Spokette First Place Local and Second Place State 1973-74, Spunkette First Place Local and First Place State 1975-76, Spunkette First Place Local and Second Place State 1976-77, Local Speak-Up Award and Hillhopper Visitation Awards 1973-77; Outstanding Young Women of America Award in Recognition of Personal and Professional Accomplishments, 1977; Outstanding Alumna Award for State of West Virginia, West Virginia Delta Zeta Sorority, 1977; February Citizen of the Month, Wheeling, West Virginia, Community Award Presented by the Jaycees, 1978; Distinguished Service Award, Wheeling Jaycees, 1982; Member, American Biographical Institute Research Association, 1981; Listed in *Who's Who in the South and Southwest, World Who's Who of Women, Personalities of America.* Address: 200 B Betty Street, Wheeling, West Virginia 26003. ∎

JULIUS WALKER, JR.

Junior High School Principal. Personal: Born February 9, 1945; Son of Odessa Walker Grimes; Married Katie Johnson, Daughter of William and Louise Johnson; Father of Shawn Edward, Kendra Lynette. Education: B.S., Elizabeth City State University, Elizabeth City, North Carolina, 1967; M.S., North Carolina Central University, Durham, North Carolina, 1974; Educational Specialist Degree, East Carolina University, Greenville, North Carolina, 1980. Career: Elementary School Teacher, Washington County Union School, Roper, North Carolina, 1967-74; Principal, Creswell Elementary School, Creswell, North Carolina, 1974-77; Principal, Washington County Union School, Roper, North Carolina, 1977 to present. Organizational Memberships: Chairman, Social Studies Accreditation Committee, 1982-83; Member Principals Information Research Center; American School Board Journal; Association Elementary School Principal (Associations of Supervision and Curriculum Development); North Carolina Association of Educators; Delegate, N.C.A.E. Convention; Washington County Calendar Committee and Washington County Guidance Committee; Washington County Teacher of the Year Committee. Community Activities: Board of Directors, Washington County United Way, 1982; Democratic Judge, Lees Mill Precinct, 1971-74; Delegate, Washington County Precinct Convention, 1981; Board of Directors, Washington County Special Olympics, 1979-82; Board of Directors 1972-79, Vice Chairman 1981, Chairman 1981-82, Washington County Recreation Commission; Board of Directors, Washington County Heart Fund, 1978-79; Board of Directors, Roanoke Developmental Center, 1982-83; Commissioner, Men's Softball League, Washington County, 1976; N.A.A.C.P.; North Carolina Athletic Officials Association; Boy Scout Master, Troop 255; Kappa Alpha Psi Fraternity; Rising Moon Masonic Lodge; Selective Service Board, Elizabeth City Alumni Chapter Member and Past President. Religion: Delegate District Conference A.M.E. Zion Church, 1980-81; Assistant Steward to Pastor; Steward to Pastor; Primary Sunday School Teacher; Class Leader in Church. Honors and Awards: R.C.A.A. Coach of the Year, 1969; Teacher of the Year Award, Washington County, 1972-73; Principals Research and Information Center, 1977; Washington County Heart Fund Leadership, 1979; Outstanding Achievement Service to Easter Seals, 1979-80; Service Award, Student Athletes, 1979-80; Listed in *Who's Who in the South and Southwest, Personalities of America, Personalities of the South, Directory of Distinguished Americans, Biographical Roll of Honor, Men of Achievement.* Address: P.O. Box 358, Roper, North Carolina 27970. ∎

LORNA ANN WALKER

Nutritional/Allergy Consultant. Personal: Born June 19, 1950; Daughter of Orville and Clara Hussey; Married Philip M. Walker; Mother of Brent Alan. Education: B.S. Medical Technology, University of Rhode Island, Newport School of Medical Technology, Newport, Rhode Island, 1971; Current Post Graduate Work on Masters of Nutrition and Metabolic Studies, Antioch University, Yellow Springs, Ohio. Career: Medical Technologist, Chula Vista (California) Community Hospital, 1972-74; Tri-Counties Blood Bank, Santa Barbara, California, 1974; Instructor, Laboratory Sciences, Charron Williams College, Fort Lauderdale, Florida, 1981-82; Nutritional/Allergy Consultant, Sunrise, Florida, 1979 to present; Nutritional/Allergy Consultant, Chiropractic Care Center, Lauderhill, Florida, 1982 to present. Organizational Memberships: Board of Directors and Lecturer/Consultant, Hypoglycemia Research Foundation, Inc.; American Society of Clinical Pathologists, 1972 to present; American Society of Medical Technology, 1976-78; International Academy of Nutritional Consultants; Human Ecology Action League. Published Works: Author of Four Articles for the Hypoglycemia Research Foundation. Honors and Awards: Newport Engineering Society Award for Promotion of the Arts and Sciences; Lambda Tau Honorary Medical Technologists Society Award, 1968; Listed in *Who's Who of American Women.* Address: 11091 Northwest Twenty-first Court, Sunrise, Florida 33322. ∎

NATHAN BELT WALKER

State Representative. Personal: Born April 18, 1952; Son of Wendell and Azalea Walker. Education: B.S. Agricultural Journalism 1974, M.S. Community Development 1975, University of Missouri-Columbia. Career: State Representative, 12th District of Missouri, at present; Minority Whip, Missouri General Assembly, 1982 to present; Former Positions include Owner/Publisher/Editor, *Macon County Press* Newspaper; Missouri House of Representatives, Research Analyst, Legislative Assistant; Assistant, Missouri Lieutenant Governor's Office. Organizational Memberships: National Republican Convention, Alternate Delegate 1976, Delegate 1980; Member, Community Development Society. Community Activities: Executive Board Member, Missourians Against Hazardous Waste; Board Member, Longbranch Industries Sheltered Workshop; Macon Jaycees; La Plata Lions Club; Macon Chamber of Commerce; Macon Lodge B.P.O. Elks #999; Clarence Lodge #662 AF and AM; Ararat Temple A.A.O.N.M.S. Shrine of Kansas City; Vice Chairman, Advisory Board of Community and Public Services, University of Missouri; Life Member, National Rifle Association; Little League Coach; Speaker, Numerous Community and Public Meetings. Religion: Member, Clarence (Missouri) Christian Church; Outreach Sunday School Class; Part-Time Sunday School Teacher. Honors and Awards: Elks Outstanding Leadership Award, 1970; Outstanding Young Men of America Award, 1979; Missouri 4-H Outstanding Recognition Award, 1982. Address: Rural Route 1, Anabel, Missouri 63431. ∎

DEBORAH SUE WALLACE

Associate Professor. Personal: Born April 16, 1947; Daughter of Richard S. and Mary E. Wallace. Education: B.S.Ed., Ohio University, Athens, Ohio, 1969; M.A. 1974, Ph.D. 1976, The Ohio State University, Columbus, Ohio. Career: Associate Professor, Department of Special Education, Georgia State University, Coordinator Special Education Administration Program, Atlanta, Georgia, 1976 to present; Instructor, Individualized Instruction and Applied Supervision, Kent State University, Summer 1976; Team Leader of Parent Training Program in Exceptional Children Department 1976, Graduate Research Associate, Student Teacher Supervisor and Seminar Instructor (all 3 positions in 1976), Team Leader of Individualized Instruction Workshop 1975, Graduate Research Associate and Coordinator of Thurber School Project 1974, Graduate Research Assistant of Learning Disabilities Project 1973-74, The Ohio State University, Columbus, Ohio; Team Leader, Individualized Instruction Workshop, Baltimore, Maryland, 1975; Consultant, Learning Disabilities and EMR Workshop, Division of Special Education, Ohio Department of Education, Columbus, Ohio, 1974; Evaluation Team, Individualized Instruction Workshop, 1974; Teacher, Math and Reading, Summer School Program, Lancaster, Ohio, 1972; Teacher, Math and Biology, Summer School Program, Lancaster, Ohio, 1971; Tutor, Neurologically Handicapped, Lancaster, Ohio, 1970-73; Teacher, Title I Program, Summer Program, Lancaster, Ohio, 1970; Teacher, Individualized Intensive Instruction Unit, Lancaster, Ohio, 1969-73; Teacher, Head Start Program, Lancaster, Ohio, 1969. Organizational Memberships: Council for Exceptional Children; Council for Children with Behavior Disorders; Division for Children with Learning Disabilities; Teacher Education Division; Georgia Council for Administrators in Special Education; Pi Lambda Theta; Kappa Delta Epsilon, Georgia State University Faculty Advisor, Southeast Regional Director; Georgia Association for Behavior Analysis. Community Activities: Chairman, Needs Assessment, Fulton County Public Schools, 1983; Vice President, Board of Directors, Tommy Nobis Center for the Mentally Retarded, 1983 to present; Advisory, Board Member, Atlanta Public Schools, Program for Exceptional Children, 1983 to present; Southeast Regional Director, Kappa Delta Epsilon, 1983 to present; Evaluation Consultant, Center on Aging, Atlanta University, Atlanta, Georgia, 1982 to present; Numerous Other Memberships and Consultantships. Published Works: Author Articles, Book Reviews, Manuals, and Other Media Products. Honors and Awards: American Council on Education Fellows in Academic Administration, University Nominee; Tommy Nobis Center Service Award; Alumni Foundation Teaching Award, Georgia State University; International Women's Year Recognition Recipient; Martha Holden Jennings Scholar; Listed in *Who's Who of Women*, *Who's Who of American Women*, *Five Thousand Personalities of the World*, *Personalities of America*, *Personalities of the South*. Address: 2727 Godby Road, Apartment 0-8, College Park, Georgia 30349.■

JERRY JIM WALLER

Agronomist. Personal: Born June 23, 1932; Son of Hazel M. Waller; Married Sue, Daughter of Mr. and Mrs. D. S. Long; Father of Don, Bob, Jim, Carol. Education: A.A., Paris Junior College, 1951; B.S., East Texas State University, 1953; M.S., Texas A&M University, 1961; M.R.A., University of Montana, 1976. Military: Served in the United States Army, 1954-56, attaining the rank of Corporal. Career: United States Department of Agriculture-S.C.S., Soil Conservation Trainee (Stephenville, Texas) 1953, Soil Conservationist (DeLeon, Texas) 1953-54, Soil Conservationist (Groesbeck, Texas) 1956-59, Range Conservationist (Goldthwaite, Texas) 1960-61, Soil Conservationist (Waco, Texas) 1961-65, District Conservationist (Big Spring, Texas) 1965-66, Agronomist Serving Gulf Coast and Southern Texas 1966-67, Agronomist Serving North Central and Northeast Texas 1967-72, State Agronomist (Bozeman, Montana) 1972-76, State Agronomist (Temple, Texas) 1976 to present; Research Assistant, Texas A&M, 1959-60; Assistant Extension Agent, Texas Agricultural Extension Service, 1961. Organizational Memberships: Certified Professional Agronomist; American Society of Agronomy; Texas Chapter, American Society of Agronomy; Soil Conservation Society of America. Community Activities: Youth Baseball Coach, 1967-73; Boy Scouts of America, Service as Scoutmaster, Assistant Scoutmaster, Community Chairman, 1968-75. Religion: First United Methodist Church (Temple, Texas), Usher, Youth Council Advisor 1982. Honors and Awards: State Farmer Degree, Future Farmers of America, 1948; McWherter Agriculture Scholarship, 1950-51; Texas Transportation Institution Research Assistant, 1959-60; U.S.D.A.-S.C.S. Graduate School, 1975-76; Certificate of Merit 1978, Outstanding Performance Award 1980, U.S.D.A.-S.C.S. Address: 2103 Pamela, Temple, Texas 76502.■

BRUCE LEE WALLERSTEIN

Psychologist. Personal: Born May 23, 1943; Son of Mildred Wallerstein. Education: A.B., Boston University, 1965; M.S., University of Pennsylvania, 1967; Ph.D., California Western University, 1975. Career: Group Psychotherapy Association of Southern California, Member 1968-82, President 1975-77; Otto Rank Association, l974-82; American Ortho Psychiatric Association, l975-82; California Association of Marriage and Family Therapists, l968-80. Organizational Memberships: United Cerebral Palsy Association of Los Angeles, Member 1972-82, Vice President, 1975-81; President, Harbor View House Association, 1975-79; Board of Directors, American Civil Liberties Union, Southern California, 1972-75; Long Beach Chamber of Commerce; Naples Island Business Association. Religion: Jewish. Honors and Awards: Outstanding Member, Group Psychotherapy Association of Southern California, 1979; American Civil Liberties Union Award, 1975; National Institute of Mental Health Award, 1965-67. Address: Long Beach Marina, Long Beach, California 90803.■

BEN A. WALLIS, JR.

Attorney. Personal: Born April 27, 1936; Son of Ben and Jessie Wallis; Father of Ben A. III, Jessica. Education: B.B.A., University of Texas, 1961; J.D., University of Texas School of Law, 1966; Postgraduate Studies undertaken at the Southern Methodist University School of Law. Career: Licensed to Practice before the United States Supreme Court, United States Court of Appeals for Fifth, Eighth, Eleventh and District of Columbia Circuits, United States District Courts for District of Columbia and Northern, Southern and Western Districts of Texas, Northern District of California and Eastern District of Wisconsin; Investigator/Prosecutor, Texas State Securities Board, 1967-72; Attorney in Private Practice, Dallas, Texas, 1972; Vice President of Development, Club Corporation of America, 1973; Associate Counsel, United States House of Representatives Committee on the Judiciary Impeachment Inquiry, 1974; Attorney in Private Practice, San Antonio, Texas, 1975 to present; Hunting Preserve Operator, 1962 to present. Organizational Memberships: American Bar Association; National Cattlemen's Association; Federal Bar Association; District of Columbia Bar Association; Delta Theta Phi Legal Fraternity; State Bar of Texas; Dallas Bar Association; San Antonio Bar Association; Delta Sigma Pi Business Fraternity; Life Member, American Biographical Institute. Community Activities: Chairman, National Land Use Conference, 1979-81; President, Institute for Human Rights Research, 1978-82. Religion: Baptist. Honors and Awards: Honorary Member, Boundary Waters Conservation Alliance (Minnesota), 1980; Honorary Member, San Antonio Society of Association Executives, 1982; Adopted Member, Lac La Croix Indian Tribe (Ontario), 1979; Listed in *Who's Who in American Law*, *Who's Who in the Southwest*, *Who's Who in the South and Southwest*, *Who's Who in Real Estate*, *Directory of Distinguished Americans*, *Two Thousand Notable Americans*, *Biographical Roll of Honor*, *Dictionary of International Biography*, *Personalities of America*, *International Book of Honor*, *International Register of Profiles*, *International Who's Who of Contemporary Achievement*. Address: 13623 Inwood Park, San Antonio, Texas 78216.■

JAMES DAVID WALSH

Broadcasting Executive. Personal: Born December 17, 1947; Son of James A. Walsh and Dorothy S. Walsh (deceased); Married Mary Ellen Budge. Education: Northwestern College. Military: Served in the United States National Guard, 1967-73. Career: Announcer, WFLY-FM, Troy, New York, 1971-72; Account Executive and Announcer, WABY—AM, Albany, 1972-74; Account Executive, WPTR-AM, Albany, New York, 1974; Founder, General Manager, President, WWWD—AM Radio, Schenectady, 1975 to present; President, Walvon Communications, Inc. Organizational Memberships: Platform Speakers of America, 1981. Community Activities: Deputy Sheriff, Schenectady County, 1980 to present; Basketball Coach, Young Men's Christian Association-Church League, 1966-68; Basketball Coach, Boy's Club, 1968-70; Rotterdam Men's Recreation League, Basketball Coach, Official, 1971-76; Tri-City Comets Local Semi-Professional Basketball Team, Founder 1974, Manager and Coach 1974-76. Religion: Church Sunday School Teacher, 1967-68. Published Works: Co-Author, *Greenburg's Guide to American Flyer Trains* 1980. Honors and Awards: Three Platinum Albums, Fifteen Gold Records for Contributions to Success of Hit Phonograph Recordings; Nominated Music Director of the Year, Medium Market, 1976. Address: 142 Putnam Road, Schenectady, New York 12306.■

JOHN P. WALTER

Professor. Personal: Born July 22, 1941. Education: B.A. Mathematics, California State University at Northridge, 1967; M.S. Systems Engineering (Analysis Option), West Coast University, 1969; D.E.A., University of Paris, 1970; Doctorate, Applied Computer Science, University of Paris Faculty of Sciences, 1971; Industrial Engineer Professional Registration, California, 1974; Certificate in Data Processing, I.C.C.P., 1975; General Mathematics Qualification, Society of Actuaries, 1976; Lifetime Teaching Credentials in Mathematics, Engineering, Computer and Related Technologies, California Community Colleges, 1977; EDP Auditor Certification, 1979. Career: Professor of Information Systems; Former Chairperson of the Department of Accounting/Information Systems/Law, California State University at Dominguez Hills; Former Positions and Consultancies with American Telephone and Telegraph, Bechtel International Corporation, California State Polytechnic University, California State University at Los Angeles, CEGOS-Tymshare (France), Centre d'Analyse Socio-Economique (Paris), Computer Communications Inc., East Los Angeles College, Litton Guidance and Control Systems Division, New Vistas Systems Inc., Rockwell Liquid Metal Engineering Center, Santa Clara Valley Water District, System Development Corporation, University of California at Los Angeles Extension, United States Atomic Energy Commission, United States Small Business Administration.■

GEORGE WILLIAM WALTERS, JR.

Insurance Agent and Broker. Personal: Born September 3, 1950; Son of Luther and Majorie Esdaile. Education: Attended South Central Community College, New Haven, Conneticut, 1969; The Life Underwriters Training Council, 1976; The Huebner School of C.L.U. Studies, American University, 1979; Licensed in New York. Career: Insurance Agent and Broker; Former Positions Include Drug Counselor; Machine Operator Trainee; Drug Education Assistant; Drug Program Coordinator. Organizational Memberships: National Life Underwriters Association, 1974 to present; Connecticut Life Underwriters Association, 1978 to present; New Haven Life Underwriterss Association, 1978 to present; California Life Underwiters Association, 1974 to present; San Francisco Life Underwriters Association, 1974-75; American Society of Notaries, 1978-79. Community Activities: National Association for the Advancement of Colored People, 1982; Connecticut Afro-American Historical Society, 1982; Association of African Americans, 1982; New Haven (Conneticut) Honorary Sheriff's Club; New Haven Young Men's Christian Association, 1961-73; Boy Scouts of America, 1958-65; Co-Spokesman, Hillhouse High Black Student Union, New Haven, Conneticut, 1968-69. Religion: Men's Club of St. Luke's Episcopalian Church, 1977 to present; Minister of Universal Life Church, 1975 to present. Honors and Awards: Certified Life Insurance Company, Grand Award 1974-76, Wall of Fame Award 1976, President's Club 1974-77. Address: 70 Fountain Terrace, New Haven, Conneticut 06515; 1101 Stewart Avenue #307, Garden City, New York 11530. ■

ORTIZ MONTAIGNE WALTON

Author, Director of Institute. Personal: Son of Peter L. Walton; Married Kara; Father of Omar. Education: B.S. Psychology, Roosevelt University, 1966; M.A. 1970, Ph.D. 1973 Sociology, University of California-Berkeley. Career: Author and Director of Multi-Ethnic Institute for Research and Education; Former Positions Include Professor of Sociology, University of California-Berkeley; Member of Boston Symphony Orchestra; Principal Investigator of Study on Use of Alcohol and Drugs Among Adolescents and Young Adults, National Institute on Alcohol Abuse and Alcoholism. Organizational Memberships: American Sociological Association. Address: 1442-A Walnut Street, Berkeley, California 94709. ■

REBECCA HERRICK WANBAUGH

Professor. Personal: Born April 12, 1923; Daughter of Mrs. Chandler Bowden; Married Robert Clarence Wanbaugh Jr.; Step-Mother of Susan Jean. Education: B.A. Sociology 1945, M.A. History 1964, Ph.D. History 1980, University of Maine-Orono; Attended Andover-Newton Theological School, 1956-57. Career: Vocational Rehabilitation Counselor, New York State Department of Education, Division of Vocational Rehabilitation, Rochester, New York, 1958-59; Instructor of Sociology, University of Maine-Orono, 1959-62; University of Maine-Presque Isle, Dean of Women 1963-74, Assistant/Associate Professor of History 1963-82, Professor of History 1982 to present. Organizational Memberships: American Association of University Professors, 1961-76; American Historical Association, 1971 to present; American Sociological Association, 1961 to present; Charter Member, Maine Sociological Society; National Educational Association, 1963 to present; Maine Teachers Association, 1963 to present; National Association of Women Deans, Administrators and Counselors, 1963-74. Community Activities: Chairman, University of Maine-Presque Isle Chapter, Presque Isle United Fund Drive, 1964-67; General Assembly of the Maine State Young Men's Christian Association, Northern District, Model United Nations, Third Committee-Social, Humanitarian, Cultural-1965; Consultant and Lecturer in Sociology "Poverty in Affluence", Sponsored by Title I of Higher Education Act, 1968; Presque Isle-University of Maine Presque Isle Drug Education Team, State of Maine Drug Education Workshop, 1971-73; Advisory Council, Alcohol Information and Referrel Services, 1976-83; Maine Association for Retarded Citizens, 1965 to present; University of Maine-Presque Isle Faculty Representative to the University of Maine Board of Trustees, 1979-82; Academic Planning Committee on Student Life, University of Maine Board of Trustees, 1979-80. Religion: College Forum of the Congregational Church, Presque Isle, Organized and Sponsored, 1963-67; Presque Isle Ministerial Conferences, Consultant in Sociology, 1968-70. Honors and Awards: Sigma Mu Sigma; Alpha Kappa Delta; Phi Alpha Theta; Listed in *Who's Who in American College and University Administration, Maine's Most Prominent People, World Who's Who of Women in Education, Who's Who in the East, Directory of Distinguished Americans, Dictionary of International Biography.* Address: P.O. Box 1311, Presque Isle, Maine 04769. ■

RICHARD G. WANDERMAN

Physician. Personal: Born April 17, 1943; Son of Herman and Helen Wanderman (Schneider); Married Judy Rosenberg; Father of Richard Jr., Gregory Lloyd, Shana Abraham, Adam Joseph. Education: B.A., Western Reserve University, 1965; M.D., Downstate Medical Center, State University of New York, 1969; Intern, Kings County Hospital Center, 1969-70; Resident, Kings County Hospital Center 1970-71, Long Island Jewish-Hillside Medical Center 1971-72; Diplomate, American Board of Pediatrics, 1974; Diplomate, National Board of Medical Examiners, 1970. Career: Doctor of Pediatric and Adolescent Medicine in Private Practice, Associate 1972-74, Solo Practice 1974-78 and 1981 to present, With Associate 1978-80; Attending in Adolescent Clinic, Long Island Hospital, 1972-74; Physician-in-Charge of Adolescent Clinic, Charleston Area Medical Center, 1974-78; Supervisor in General Appointments Clinic, LeBonheur Children's Hospital, 1978-83; Assistant Instructor in Pediatrics, Downstate Medical Center, State University of New York, 1970-71; West Virginia University Medical School, Clinical Assistant Professor in Pediatrics 1974-78, Clinical Associate Professor 1978; Clinical Associate Health Sciences, 1979-. Organizational Memberships: New York State Medical Society, 1972-74; Nassau County Medical Society, 1972-74; Nassau County Pediatric Society, 1972-74; West Virginia State Medical Society, 1974-78; Kanawha County Medical Society, 1974-78; American Physician Fellowship Inc., 1974 to present; Southeast Pediatric Cardiology Society, 1976-78; Tennessee Medical Association, 1978 to present; Memphis-Shelby County Medical Society, 1978 to present; Memphis-Shelby County Pediatric Society, 1978-82; Society for Adolescent Medicine, 1973 to present; American Academy of Pediatrics, 1975 to present; A.A.P. Section on Adolescent Medicine, 1978 to present; Tennessee Pediatric Society, 1982 to present; Society for Clinical Ecology, 1983; Chairperson, West Virginia State School Health Task Force, 1975-76; Community Mental Health Center of Region 3 Inc. Task Force on Consultation and Education, 1976; Chairman, District III Parenting Education Coalition of Parent-Teacher Association, 1976-78; Chairman Parent Advisory Committee Headstart Program for Counties of Kanawha, Boone and Committee on School and College Health, 1978; LeBonheur Children's Medical Center Long Range Planning Task Force Committee on Education and Research, 1981; Grievance Committee of the Memphis-Shelby County Medical Society, 1982. Community Activities: M.E.N.S.A.; Zeta Beta Tau Fraternity, Lambda Chapter; Area Council of Jewish National Fund, 1981 to present; Memphis Jewish Community Center, Coach Swim Team 1979-80, Chairman Task Force on Adolescent Problems 1980; Les Amis du Vin, 1979-81; Life Fellow, American Biographical Institute; Board Member, Midsouth Area Jewish National Fund, 1983. Religion: Sunday School Teacher at the Temple Israel of Memphis, 1978-80. Honors and Awards: Honorary Appointment to the National Board of Advisors, American Biographical Institute, 1982; Listed in *Who's Who in the South and Southwest, Notable Americans, Personalities of the South, Personalities of America, Dictionary of International Biography, International Who's Who of Intellectuals, Men and Women of Distinction, Men of Achievement, Directory of Medical Specialists, How to Live With the New 20th Century Illness.* Address: 2536 Ashburton Place North, Cordova, Tennessee 38018. ■

CHIA PING WANG

Research Physicist, Professor. Personal: Born September 1; Son of Guan Can and Tah Wang (both deceased). Education: B.Sc., University of London, 1950; M.Sc., University of Malaya, 1951; Ph.D., Universities of Malaya and Cambridge, 1953; D.Sc. Physics, University of Singapore, 1972. Career: Assistant Lecturer, University of Malaya, 1951-53; Associate Professor of Physics 1954-56, Professor of Physics 1956-58, Head of Electron Physics Division 1955-58, Steering Committee of Nuclear Physics Division 1956-58, Nankai Tientsin University; Head, Electron Physics Division, Lanchow Atomic Project, 1958; Senior Lecturer, Professor, Acting Head, Departments of Physics and Mathematics, Hong Kong Univerisity and Chinese University of Hong Kong, 1958-63; Research Associate, Laboratory of Nuclear Studies, Cornell University, Ithaca, New York, 1963-64; Associate Professor of Space Science and Applied Physics, Catholic University of America, Washington, D.C., 1964-68; Associate Professor of Physics, Case Institute of Technology, Case Western Reserve University, Cleveland, Ohio, 1966-70; Visiting Scientist, Visiting Professor, Universities of Cambridge (England), Leuven (Belgium), United States Naval Research Laboratory and University of Maryland (concurrently), Massachusetts Institute of Technology, 1970-75; Research Physicist, United States Army Natick Research and Development Laboratories, 1975 to present. Organizational Memberships: American Physical Society; Institute of Physics, London; Society of Sigma Xi; Life Member, American Association for the Advancement of Science; New York Academy of Sciences; Italian Physical Society; American Geophysical Union; American Association of University Professors. Community Activities: Guest of the British Council, London, 1962; Hong Kong Delegate, 1962 International Conference on High Energy Physics, C.E.R.N., Geneva, Switzerland; Delegate, United States, United Kingdom, 1967 International Conference on Cosmic Rays, Calgary,

TWO THOUSAND NOTABLE AMERICANS

Canada; 1972 International Conference on High Energy Physics, Batavia, Illinois; 1978 International Symposium on Standardization of Radiation Dosimetry, Atlanta, Georgia; International Atomic Energy Agency, Vienna, Austria; 1969, 1971 International Conference on Elementary Particles at Lund, Sweden and Amsterdam, the Netherlands. Published Works: Author and Co-Author of Numerous Articles in Scientific Journals, Author of a Book. Honors and Awards: Converted for the First Time Picosecond Time Intervals into Pulse Heights, 1963; Deduced from Over 50 Experiments on Particle Multiplicity Distributions the Many-Subunits (now referred to as partons) Structures of the Nucleons and Other Hadrons, 1968; Deduced the 3-quark-boson (meson) Cloud Nucleon Model from the Structure, Functions and Momentum Distribution Spectra in High Energy Collisions, including Electron-Nucleon and Neutrino-Nucleon Collision, 1971-72; First Observed with O.R. Frisch (at the Cavendish Laboratory, University of Cambridge) the Sinusoidal Light Waves with a Laser Interferometer, 1970; Performed One of the First Experiments with the then 200 GeV Proton Accelerator at the Fermi National Laboratory, Batavia, Illinois, 1972; Formulated the General Integral Survival Fractions for Bacteria during Thermal Sterilization, 1978; Outstanding Performance Award 1980, Quality Increase Award 1980, Department of the Army; Citation, Consistently High Quality Performance in the Fields of Classical Quantum, Mechanical and Experimental Physics, and Keen Ability to Use the Skills to Solve Practical Problems in Research and Development of the Food Irradiation Process. Address: 28 Hallett Hill Road, Weston, Massachusetts 02193. ■

ESTHER M. WARBER

Counseling Psychologist. Personal: Born March 21, 1923; Daughter of Alex and Helena Schippers (both deceased). Education: B.S., University of Michigan, 1951; Master of Psychology, Wayne State University, 1958; Graduate Work, Harvard University, Tufts University, Boston University, 1967-77; Doctoral Candidate Public Administration, Nova University. Military: Served in the United States WAVES, 1943-46, attaining the rank of Machinists Mate First Class. Career: Medical Technologist; Vocational Rehabilitation Counselor; Counseling Psychologist, Veterans Administration. Organizational Memberships: American Psychology Association, 1958; American Personnel and Guidance Association, 1958; American Society of Personnel Administrators, 1977; President's Committee on the Handicapped, 1967 to present; Licensed Psychologist, 1973 to present; National Vocational Rehabilitation Association, 1956 to present. Community Activities: Michigan State Constitutional Convention Planning, 1957-58; Civil Defense, Volunteer 1951-62, Technology Instructor 1953-61; Red Cross, Instructor, First Aid, Home Nursing 1951-67; Michigan Governor George Romney Human Resource Council, 1964-66; Vice President Hubert Humphrey Human Resource Council, 1964; Peace Corps in Ecuador, National Public Health Instructor, Community Action Worker, 1962-64; Head Start Community Action Volunteer, 1964-67; Six Television Segments, United Nations Student Advisory, 1967; Detroit Mayor's Committee on Skid Row Problems, 1958-62; Massachusetts Health Council; New Hampshire Occupational Education Planning Council. Honors and Awards: Pi Lambda Theta National Honor Society, 1958; Graduate Scholarship in Rehabilitation, Department of Health, Education and Welfare; Dean's Scholarship, President's Scholarship, Wayne State University; Papers Accepted, University of Michigan Graduate Library; Listed in *Who's Who of American Women, Creative Personalities, International Who's Who of Women*. Address: 410 Faxon Commons, 1047 South Artery, Quincy, Massachusetts 02169. ■

DONALD EARL WARD

Associate Professor. Personal: Born November 30, 1946; Son of Earl R. and Dorothy H. Ward; Married Susan Jane Gordon; Father of Christopher Andrew, Jennifer Anne. Education: B.A. Psychology, DePauw University, Greencastle, Indiana, 1969; M.S. 1970, Ph.D. 1973 Counseling, Purdue University. Career: Pittsburg State University, Pittsburg, Kansas, Associate Professor of Psychology and Counseling, Counseling Psychologist in University Counseling Center. Organizational Memberships: American Association for Counseling and Development; Associate for Specialists in Group Work, Editorial Board Member; Association for Counselor Education and Supervision; Kansas Association for Counseling and Development, Executive Council, Past Chairperson Professional Development, Standards and Ethics Committee, President-elect; Past President, Kansas Association for Specialists in Group Work; K.V.G.A.; K.M.H.C.A.; K.A.C.E.S.; K.C.P.A.; Past President, Southeast Kansas Association for Counseling and Development. Community Activities: Kansas Department of Educational Guidance Advisory Council, 1978 to present. Honors and Awards: Edward Recter Scholar, DePauw University, 1965-69; Psi Chi National Psychology Honorary Society, 1968 to present; N.D.E.A. Title IV Fellow, Purdue University, 1969-72; Besser-Lindsey Award for Scholarship, Leadership and Athletics, Sigma Alpha Epsilon National Fraternity, 1969 to present; All-Conference Football Player, Indiana Collegiate Conference, 1967; Phi Kappa Phi National Academic Honorary Society, 1972 to present. Address: 2002 Countryside Drive, Pittsburg, Kansas 66762. ■

WILLIAM THEOPHILUS THOMAS WARD, SR.

Educator, Historian, Anthropologist. Personal: Born March 9, 1919; Son of John Wilmer, Sr. and Nancy Carter Ward (both deceased); Married Isabel Salvador; Father of Nancy Lee, John Wilmer II, Catherine Lavinia, William Theophilus Thomas, Jr. Education: A.B.; B.S.; M.A.; Ph.D. Career: Educator, Redstone Arsanel Huntsville, Alabama, 1983-; Historian, 13th Air Force, 1951-1983; Director, Community Relations, Clark Air Base, Philippines, 1964; Chief, Information Officer, 1962-63; Assistant Information Officer, 1959-62; Lecturer, University of the Philippines, 1954-55; Anthropologist, Trust Territory of Micronesia, 1950-51; Teacher, Pago Pago, American Samoa, 1949-50; Teacher, Marietta, Georgia, 1948-49. Organizational Memberships: Numerous Professional Associations. Religion: St. John's Episcopal Church, Florence, South Carolina. Published Works: Author, Numerous Historica and Anthropological Publications, including *The Death of President Roxas* 1960, *The Taiwan Straits Difficulty* 1958, 214 Volumes of 13th Air Force, 6th Air Division, 6200th Air Base Wing and 405th Fighter Wing Histories, 1951-79. Honors and Awards: Phi Kappa Phi, (University of the Philippines); Blue Key (University of South Carolina); Merritissimur-graduate work (University of Santo Tomas); Certificate of Appreciation, University of Philippines, 1959; Delegate, 7th Pacific Science Congress, (Pre-History Division), Manila, Philippines, 1956; Delegate, 8th Pacific Science Congress (Pre-History Division) Bangkok, Thailand, 1957; Member, Numerous Scholastic Honorary Societies. Address: 500 South Warley Street, Florence, South Carolina 29501. ■

ELEANORE BURTIS WARNER

Educator. Born January 14, 1923, in Allentown, New Jersey; Married Dr. L. Richard Warner; Mother of Five. Education: B.S.Ed., Trenton State College, 1947; M.Ed. 1958, Ed.D. 1965, Rutgers Graduate School of Education, Rutgers University. Career: Classroom Teacher, Grades 2, 4, 5, 8, New Jersey Schools, 1946-58; Curriculum Supervisor, Grades K-8, Two Schools, Little Silver, New Jersey, 1958-64; Director, Escola Americana De Santos, Santos, Brazil, 1965-67; Demonstration Teacher, Grade 6, Antheil School, Laboratory School for Trenton State College, 1967-69; Associate Professor, Department of Elementary/Early Childhood Education and Reading, Trenton State College, 1969 to present; Trenton State College Exchange Professor to Worcester College of Higher Education, Worcester, England, 1980-81. Organizational Memberships: National Education Association, 1947 to present; New Jersey Education Association, Member 1947 to present, Delegate Assembly 1958-64; Co-Editor, New Jersey Association of Teacher Educators, 1976-78; Association for Supervision and Curriculum Development, Active Member 1958-65, Member 1980-81; Tri-County Reading Association, 1976-78; Graduate School of Education Alumni Association, Rutgers State University, Vice President 1977-78, President 1978-79; New Jersey State College Faculty Association; Mercer County Education Association, 1967 to present; Monmouth County Education Association, 1950-65; Bergen County Education Association, 1946-50. Community Activities: People-to-People International, Homestay Coordinator 1978-80, Host Family 1973, 1975, 1978, 1979, Trenton Chapter Representative to Harrogate, England 1980, Grangemouth, Scotland 1980; Capital Squares Square Dance Club, Trenton, New Jersey; Princeton Masqueraders Square Dance Club, Princeton, New Jersey; Co-Ordin-8's Square Dance Club, Blakedown, England; Stourbridge Square Dance Club, Step-A-Round Dance Club, Stourbridge, England; Trenton State College, Faculty Dames, Gourmet Club, Travel Club; Teachers Corps Program, Wilson School; Competency Based Teacher Educational Program; Department of Elementary Early Childhood Education and Reading Language Arts Conference, 1977-80; Committee on Promotions, Reappointments and Tenure, Social Committee, Curriculum Revision Committee; Traffic Appeals Board; Teacher Education Advisory Board; Academic Calendar Committee; Academic Policies Committee; Academic Progress Committee, Secretary, Chairperson; College and Community Relations Committee, Secretary, Chairperson; Committee on Travel and Exchange; Faculty Senate, Elected 1981; Graduate School of Education, Rutgers University, Dean's Search Committee 1978-79, Dean's Invitational Conference 1973 to present, Phonothon 1977-83, School of Education Professional Enrichment Conference, 1971, 1972, Faculty Colloquium, "British Education", 1982; Featured Speaker, Bi-National Schools of South American Conference, Buenos Aires, Argentina, 1967; Language Arts Workshops, Escola Americana de Campinas, Brazil, Coordinator, Speaker 1967; American Schools Association, Language Arts Coordinator, Eastern Brazil Conference, 1966; Sao Paulo

University, Doctoral Committee for Doctoral Candidate, 1966; Kappa Delta Pi, Delta Xi Chapter, Scholarship Committee, Editor/Historian 1970-75, Vice President 1975-76; President 1976-78, Lecture-slide Presentations; National Foreign Policy Conference for Leaders in Teacher Education, Invitational Conference Department of State, 1972; Multi-Media Presentations; Radio Interviews, Soviet Culture and Education; Trenton Chapter Representative, Lord Mayor of Stoke-on-Trent, England, 1981; Mercer County Association for Gifted and Talented Children, Saturday Morning Program, Science Activities Teacher, 1981-82. Religion: West Trenton United Presbyterian Church, 1970 to present; Allentown, New Jersey, Presbyterian Church, 1923-50; Asbury Park, New Jersey, Presbyterian Church, 1950-70. Honors and Awards: Citation, Bi-National Schools of South American Conference, Buenos Aires, Argentina, 1967; Certificate of Merit, Escola Americana De Santos, Santos, Brazil, 1967; Compatriot in Education, National Kappa Delta Pi Award, 1976; Delta Xi Chapter, Kappa Delta Pi, 1956 to present; Phi Delta Kappa, Greater Trenton Area Chpater, 1971 to present; Certificate of Appreciation, Graduate School of Education Alumni Association, 1979; Distinguished Service Award, Rutgers University Graduate School of Education, 1982; Listed in *World Who's Who of Women in Education, Dictionary of International Biography, International Who's Who of Intellectuals, Notable Americans.* Address: 2060 Pennington Road, Trenton, New Jersey 08618.■

ALAN EVERETT WARRICK

Municipal Court Judge. Personal: Born June 18, 1953; Son of John Warrick and Geri Crisman; Father of Alan II, Whitney Blair. Education: B.A. magna cum laude, Howard University, Washington, D.C.; Doctor of Jurisprudence, Indiana University School of Law. Career: Attorney, Branton and Mendelsohn, Inc., 1978-82; Intern, Marion County Prosecutor's Office, Indianapolis, Indiana, 1977-78; Campaign Aide, U.S. Senator R. Vance Hartke, Indianapolis, Indiana, 1976-77; Civil Rights Specialist, Indiana Civil Rights Commission, Indianapolis, Indiana, 1975-76; Research Assistant, Joint Center for Political Studies, Washington, D.C., 1972-74. Organizational Memberships: American Bar Association; National Bar Association, Judicial Council; American Judicature Society; Association of Trial Lawyers of America; State Bar of Texas, Municipal Judges Section, Secretary-Treasurer, 1982-83; Texas Young Lawyers Association; Texas Trial Lawyers Association; San Antonio Bar Association; San Antonio Young Lawyers Association; San Antonio Trial Lawyers Association, Board of Directors; San Antonio Black Lawyers Association, Vice President. Community Activities: Dignowitty Hill Area Neighborhood Association, President, 1982 to present; San Antonio Festival, Inc., Board of Directors, 1982 to present; N.A.A.C.P., San Antonio Branch, 3rd Vice President, 1980-81; United Negro College Fund, Executive Committee, 1980-81; San Antonio Symphony, Board of Directors, 1980-81; Small Business Association, Area Advisory Council, 1980-81; Leadership San Antonio, Participant in Chamber of Commerce Sponsored Program Designed to Develop Young Leaders in the Community, 1979-80; Ella Austin Community Center, Board of Directors, Parliamentarian, 1979-80. Honors and Awards: Phi Beta Kappa, Howard University, 1975; Pi Sigma Alpha, Political Science Honor Society, 1974; Associate Editor, *Indiana Law Review*, 1977-78; First Place Award Winner, American Bar Association, Regional Moot Court Competition, 1978; Listed in *Who's Who Among Students in American Universities and Colleges*, 1976-77, 1974-75. Address: 509 Burleson, San Antonio, Texas 78202.■

GENE EDWARD WASHINGTON

Executive. Personal: Born August 12, 1931; Son of Horace Webster Washington; Married Jacqualin Ann Kaiser; Father of Robert Todd, James Allen, Steven Lee, Darren Scott. Education: B.S., Oklahoma State University, 1951; M.B.A., University of Chicago, 1970. Military: Served in the United States Air Force, 1952-56, attaining the rank of Captain, Instructor Pilot, Base Adjutant. Career: Systems Assurance and Financial Corporation, Chairman, President, Director; Environmental Chemic Systems, Inc., Past Director, Former Chairman, Former President; Senior Vice President and Group Executive, Boothe Computer Corporation, San Francisco, California, 1971-73; Greyhound Computer Corporation, Director, Vice President, 1968-70; International Business Machines, Senior Marketing Representative 1956-63, Marketing Manager 1963-67; Director, Greyhound Time-Sharing Corporation, Greyhound Computer of Canada Limited, Computer Personnel Consultants Inc., Boothe Computer of Canada Limited, Boothe Management Systems Inc., Boothe Computer Marketing Inc., Boothe A.G. (Zurich), CLS of South Africa. Organizational Memberships: Alpha Kappa Psi; Treasurer, Arnold Air Society, 1951-52; Blue Key; Computer Lessors Association; Data Processing Management Association; Gamma Theta Psi; Mu Kappa Tau; Scabbard and Blade; Treasurer, Sigma Chi, 1951-52. Community Activities: H.O.P.E., Founder, Director, 1961-62; Precinct Treasurer, Republican Party, 1965-66; Director, Junior Achievement, 1958-59; Common Wealth Club, 1970-71. Religion: Deacon, First Presbyterian Church, Bloomfield Hills, Michigan, 1964-65. Honors and Awards: International Business Machines, Manager of the Year 1966, Industry Leader 1962, Sales Training Number One Graduate 1957, Golden Circle 1958, Regional Managers Award 1960, 1962, 1963, Quota Club 1957-66; Listed in *Who's Who in America, Who's Who in Finance and Industry, Who's Who in the West, Men of Achievement, Community Leaders of America, Who's Who in California, Directory of Distinguished Americans, Personalities of America, International Book of Honor, Biographical Roll of Honor, Two Thousand Notable Americans, Five Thousand Personalities of the World, Dictionary of International Biography, Community Leaders of the World, Personalities of the West and Midwest, International Register of Profiles.* Address: 1427 Buchanan Street, Novato, California 94947.■

ROBERT O. WASHINGTON

Dean. Personal: Born February 8, 1935; Son of R. L. Washington; Married Mary; Father of Robert, Glynnis, Nathan, Cheryl, Allyson, Terrence, Candace. Education: B.S. General Studies, Hampton Institute, 1956; M.A. Social Psychology, Marquette University, 1966; Advanced Certificate in Guidance and Counseling, University of Missouri, 1968; Ph.D. Social Planning, Brandeis University, 1973. Military: Served in the United States Army Artillery, June 1956 to November 1956. Career: Dean and Professor, School of Social Work, University of Illinois-Urbana-Champaign, 1982 to present; Dean and Professor, College of Social Work, Ohio State University, Columbus, Ohio, 1976-82; School of Social Welfare, University of Wiscosin-Milwaukee, Associate Dean, Associate Professor of Social Planning, Senior Research Associate, Center for Advanced Studies in Human Services, 1974-76; School of Applied Social Sciences, Case Western Reserve University, Cleveland, Ohio, Assistant Professor of Evaluative Research, Senior Research Associate, Manpower Planning and Delivery Systems, Human Services Design Laboratory, 1972-74; Research, Manpower Planning and Educational Consultation, Greenleigh Associates Inc. 1968-72; Senior Research Associate, Research and Management Consultants, 1971-72; Lecturer, Social Research, School of Social Work, Simmons College, Boston, Massachusetts, 1970-72; Milwaukee Vocational, Technical and Adult Schools, Instructor 1957-61, School Social Worker 1961-65, Chairman of Student Personnel Services 1965-67. Organizational Memberships: Phi Beta Sigma Fraternity; American Public Welfare Association; Council on Social Work Education; Consulting Editor, *Humboldt Journal of Social Relations*; International Association of Schools of Social Work; National Association of Black School Workers; National Association of Social Workers; National Conference on Social Welfare; Ohio Citizen's Council; Ohio Welfare Conference; Consulting Editor, *Urban Education*; Commissioner, C.S.W.E. Commission on Accreditation, 1978-81. Community Activities: Visiting Committee, Board of Overseers, Case Western Reserve University School of Applied Social Sciences, 1977-79; Board of Trustees, Columbus Area Community Mental Health Center, 1980 to present; Board of Trustees, Columbus Area International Program, 1976 to present; Committee of Deans, Commission on Interprofessional Education and Practice, 1977 to present; Education Advisory Committee, Columbus Urban League, 1976 to present; Board of Directors, Family Financial Foundation, 1979 to present; Godman Guild, Board of Trustees, 1976-80; Board of Trustees, Guardian Services, Limited, 1979 to present; Community Advisory Board, Interdisciplinary Health Care for the Aged; Steering Committee, Mayor's Awards for Voluntary Service, 1979 and 1980; Mid-Ohio Health Planning Federation; University Director, National Council of Black Mayors/University Year for Action, 1979 to present; Board of Trustees, St. Vincent Children's Center, 1980 to present; Committee Member, Suicide Prevention Planning Committee for Senior Citizens, 1979 to present; Advisory Board, Young Women's Christian Association, Columbus, 1980 to present; Urban League of Champaign County, Illinois, 1983; Governors Commission on Guardianship and Advocacy, 1984. Honors and Awards: N.D.E.A. Fellow, 1967-68; Graduate Fellowship, S.R.S., 1972-73; Listed in *Who's Who in Health Care, Who's Who in the Midwest, Men of Achievement, Personalities of the West and Midwest, Dictionary of International Biography, Who's Who in the Midwest, Personalities of America, Who's Who in America.* Address: 1207 West Oregon Street, Urbana, Illinois 61801.■

HANNELORE LINA WASS

Professor of Educational Psychology. Personal: Born September 26, 1926; Daughter of Herman and Mina Kraft (deceased); Married Harry H. Sisler, Son of Harry and Minta Sisler (deceased); Mother of Brian. Education: Ph.D., University of Michigan. Career: Elementary Teacher, Mannheim, Germany, 1947-51; Teacher Trainee, Cultural Exchange Program, United States Office of Education, Washington, D.C., 1951-52; Middle School Teacher (Experimental Program), Foreign Language Instructor and Supervisor, School Camp Coordinator, 1952-57; Coordinator of Mannheim City Schools English Language Instruction, German-American School Relations Advisor for Mannheim City Schools, 1954-57; Teacher in Elementary Schools, Pittsfield, Massachusetts, 1957-58; Supervising Teaching, University School, University of Michigan and University of Chicago, 1958-64; Faculty, National Science Foundation Workshop, University of Michigan, Summer 1959; Faculty, Human Relations Workshop, University of Michigan, Summer 1960; Faculty, Headstart Training, Eastern Michigan University, Summer 1967; Research Associate for Professor Ned Flanders, University of Michigan, 1967-68; Associate Professor, Eastern Michigan University, 1965-69; Associate Professor in Psychological Foundations of Education 1969-71, Associate Professor 1971-74, Professor of Educational Psychology and Associate of the Center for Gerontological Studies 1975 to present, University of Florida. Organizational Memberships: American Psychological Association; International Work Group in Death, Dying and Bereavement; The Gerontological Society; International Board of Advisors, Forum for Death Education and Counseling; Board of Trustees, The Center for Thanatology Research and Education, Inc.; The Foundation of Thanatology; The National Council on Aging; The Southern Gerontological Society; The Florida Council on Aging; The Society for the Psychological Study of Social Issues; The Menninger Foundation; American Education Research Association; Association for Humanistic Education. Community Activities: North Central Florida Hospice Inc., Trainer, Volunteer; Gainesville Chapter, The Compassionate Friends, Board of Directors; Memorial Society of Alachua County, Board of Directors; Alachua General Hospital Corporation. Published Works: Co-Author, The Professional Education of Teachers, 1974; Senior Author, Humanistic Teacher Education - An Experiment in Systematic Curriculum Innovation, 1974; Editor and Co-Author, Dying - Facing the Facts, 1979; Senior Author, Death Education - An Annotated Resource Guide, 1980; Senior Editor, Helping Children Cope With Death: Guidelines and Resources 1982, Second Edition 1984; Childhood and Death 1984; Senior Author, Death Education: An Annotated Resource Guide Volume II, 1984; Author Numerous Professional Articles and Chapters in Books; Editor and Founder, *Death Education* (Pedagogy-Counseling-Care) International Bimonthly; Consulting Editor, *Educational Gerontology* International Bimonthly Journal; Consulting Editor, Series in *Death Education, Aging and Health Care,* 1979 to present. Honors and Awards: United States Office of Education Traineeship, Cultural Exchange Program, 1951-52; Principal Investigator, EDPA Fellowship Grant in Early Childhood Education, Eastern Michigan University, 1968; University of Florida Summer Faculty Research Award, 1971; Principal Investigator, USOE-NEI Small Contract Research Grant, 1972; Faculty Released Time for Research, Institute for the Development of Human Resources and College of Education, 1973; Minisabbatical, Winter Quarter, Office of Instructional Resources, 1974; Research Support from University of Florida Graduate School, 1974; Principal Investigator, HRS Training Grant, State of Florida, 1978; Co-Principal Investigator, NIA Grant for Research on "Supportive Networks and Coping in Bereaved Elderly" with Stein Gerontological Institute, Miami, 1981-83; Listed in *Personalities of the South, Who's Who in the Southeast, Leaders in Education, Who's Who of American Women, The World Who's Who of Women, Dictionary of International Biography, Who's Who in Frontier Science and Technology.* Address: 6014 Northwest 54th Way, Gainesville, Florida 32606.■

THOMAS LYLE WATERS

Educator, Consulting Engineer. Personal: Born March 11, 1929; Son of Theodore E. (deceased) and Lucile Taylor Waters; Married E. Yvonne Miller; Father of Wendy, Timothy Alan. Education: B.E.E.E., Youngstown State University, 1953; M.S. Systems Management, Florida Institute of Technology, 1973; M.S. Education, University of Southern California, 1975; Ph.D. Higher Education, American University, 1981. Military: Served in the United States Army, 1953-76, attaining the rank of Lieutenant Colonel, Retired. Career: College Teacher, Consulting Engineer; Former Positions include Military Officer; Military Research and Development; College Administrator, Two Colleges. Organizational Memberships: Society of Logistics Engineers; Society of American Military Engineers; Association of the United States Army; American Association of Higher Education; National Academic Advising Association; American Society of Engineering Education. Community Activities: Boy Scouts of America, Commissioner, Sustaining Membership Enrollment, Chairman, Scouting Program Chairman, Scoutmaster, Camp Director. Religion: Lutheran Church Lutheran Church of America, Usher 1978 to 1983; Lutheran Church, Korea, Usher, 1973-75; Lutheran Church Missouri Synod, Killeen, Texas, Member 1970-73, Elder, Usher. Honors and Awards: Legion of Merit, 1970; Two Bronze Star Medals, 1966-67; Meritorious Service Medal, 1972-73; Three Army Commedation Medals, 1959-60, 1960-64, 1966; Boys Scouts of Korea Medal of Appreciation, 1975; Boy Scouts of America Award of Merit, 1975. Address: P.O. Box 459, West Sand Lake, New York 12196.■

GEORGE WILLARD WATSON

Retired. Personal: Born July 28, 1909; Married Mary Ellen Bates; Father of Jo Anne Lyle, James Knox, John Kevin. Education: B.S. Biology, Muskingum College, 1931; M.S.P.H., University of Michigan, 1936. Military: Served in the United States Naval Reserve, 1943-57, attaining the rank of Lieutenant Commander. Career: Librarian, Ohio Department of Health (Columbus), 1939-42; Lieutenant Commander and Malariologist, United States Naval Reserves, 1943-45; Director of Health Education, Dayton Division of Health, Ohio, 1948-51; Non-Medical Administrator, Baltimore City Health Department, Maryland, 1951-56; Director of Health Education, Calhoun County Health Department, Battle Creek, Michigan, 1956-60; Chief Public Health Educator, Georgia Department of Health (Atlanta), 1961-64. Organizational Memberships: American Public Health Association, Fellow. Community Activities: Civil Defense Director, Muskingum County, Ohio, 1965-67. Published Works: Prepared Two Booklets for the Ohio Department of Public Health Alphabet (on nutrition); Initiated the "Doc Snork" Letters for School Children of Dayton. Honors and Awards: Meritorious Service Citation, President's Committee to Employ the Physically Handicapped, 1960. Address: 1725 Friendship Drive, Route 2, New Concord, Ohio 43762.■

JACK BORDEN WATSON, JR.

Assistant Professor of Sociology. Personal: Born January 15, 1954; Son of Mr. and Mrs. Jack B. Watson, Sr.; Married Rita Nelson; Father of Trey, Mary. Education: B.A. Sociology, Northeast Louisiana University, Monroe, Louisiana, 1976; M.A. Sociology, Texas Christian University, 1978; Completed Course Work for Ph.D. in Sociology, North Texas State University. Career: Assistant Professor of Sociology, Mississippi College, Clinton, Mississippi; Former Positions include Teaching Fellow, Department of Sociology, and Senior Research Assistant, Center for Studies in Aging, North Texas State University. Organizational Memberships: American Sociological Association; Gerontological Society of America; Mid-South Sociological Association; Association for the Scientific Study of Religion: Southwest; Mississippi Council on Family Relations. Community Activities: Social Security Advisory Committee, Third Congressional District of Mississippi; Childbirth Education Association of Metropolitan Jackson. Religion: Member of First Baptist Church, Clinton, Mississippi. Honors and Awards: Alpha Kappa Delta, International Sociology Honor Society, 1977; Pi Gamma Mu, International Social Science Honor Society, 1982; Listed in *Who's Who Among College and University Students.* Address: 503 Dahaja Circle, Clinton, Mississippi 39056.■

LITA LEA WATSON

Executive. Personal: Born May 23, 1931; Daughter of Veta E. Smallwood; Married Robert J. Watson; Mother of Jeannine Roberta, Robert Neal, James Kevin, Mary Elizabeth, Frederic Michael. Education: Graduate of Lovettsville, Virginia Grade and High Schools. Career: Secretary, Household Finance Corporation, Silver Spring, Maryland, 1948-52; Secretary, El Paso Natural Gas Company, El Paso, Texas, 1956-59; Sales Manager, Sara Coventry Jewelry, Newark, New York, 1959-67; Regional Manager, Snelling and Snelling Employment Agencies, Paoli, Pennsylvania, 1967-71; Secretary/Treasurer, Robert J. Watson Enterprises, Santa Anna, California, 1971 to present; President, B & W Enterprises, Irvine, California, 1972 to present; Owner, Manager, Dennis and Dennis Inc., Orange, California, 1978 to present. Organizational Memberships: International Platform Association; American Employment Association; California Association of Personnel Consultants, President (State Level), 1967 to present; National Association of Personnel Consultants, Hostess for International Convention. Community Activities: Orange County Chamber of Commerce, 1971 to present; Better Business Bureaus of Orange and Los Angeles Counties, 1971 to present. Religion: Catholic. Honors and Awards: J. R. Pierce Award, California Association of Personnel Consultants, 1982 and 1984; Jean Widdecomb Award, 1983. Address: 594 Turnabout Road, Orange, California 92669.■

DOYLE WARREN WATTS

College Department Chairperson. Personal: Born July 29, 1936; Son of Mr. and Mrs. T. A. Watts; Married Betty Howlett; Father of Gregg, Karla, Grady. Education: B.S., Abilene Christian College, 1962; M.A. 1972, Ed.D. 1975, Texas Tech University. Career: Northwestern Oklahoma State University, Chairperson, Department of Education/Psychology, Director of Teacher Education, Former Assistant Professor of Education/Psychology 1975-79; Part-time Instructor, Texas Tech University, 1975; Ropes Public Schools, Middle School Principal 1972-75, Classroom Teacher 1964-72. Organizational Memberships: American Psychological Association; Oklahoma Psychological Association; Institutional Representative, American Association of College and Teacher Education; Institutional Representative, Oklahoma Association of Colleges of Teacher Education; Institutional Representative, Teacher Education Council of State Colleges and Universities, Association for Supervision and Curriculum Development, Higher Education Alumnia Council of Oklahoma. Community Activities: Oklahoma's Professional Standards Board, 1979-83; Oklahoma Regents's Task Force on Teacher Education, 1981 to present; Steering Committee on Oklahoma's Teacher Certification Testing Program, 1981; Chairman, Committee for Revising Oklahoma's Teacher Accreditation System, 1983; Alva Public School's Staff Development Committee, 1982; President, Alva Parent-Teacher Association, 1982; Referee, *Journal of Teacher Education,* 1982 to present; State Department of Education Accreditation Teams. Published Works: Author of Articles in Fourteen Journals of International Circulation on the Teaching Profession of International Circulation; Article reprinted in *High School Debate Reader.* Honors and Awards: Phi Delta Phi, 1973; Honorary Member, Kappa Delta Pi, 1981; Phi Delta Kappan,

1984; Consultant, Oklahoma Association of Secondary Principals, 1982; Cited for Outstanding Teaching, Academic Dean, 1980, 1981, 1982; Consultant to Numerous State Legislative Committees. Address: 1901 Maple Street, Alva, Oklahoma 73717.■

LLOYD THOMAS WATTS, JR.

Air Force Officer. Personal: Born February 12, 1944; Education: B.S. Business Administration, University of Florida, 1967; M.B.A., Golden Gate University, 1970; Squadron Officers School, 1975; Air Command and Staff College, 1980; Air War College, 1982. Military: Served in United States Air Force, 1970 to present. Career: Lieutenant Colonel, United States Air Force. Organizational Memberships: Air Force Association; American Defense Preparedness Association; American Society of Quality Control; Society of Logistics Engineers; Programs Chairman, National Contract Management Association. Honors and Awards: Bronze Star, 1973; Meritorious Service Medal, 1979; Air Force Commendation Medal, 1977; Company Grade Officer of the Quarter, Wright-Patterson Air Force Base, Ohio, 1978. Address: 10322 Mockingbird Pond Court, Burke, Virginia 22015.■

DAVID MICHAEL WAYNE

Psychiatrist. Personal: Born December 7, 1906; Widower; Father of Robert Andrew. Education: B.A., Syracuse University, 1929; M.D., University of Vienna Medical School, 1934; Postgraduate Studies undertaken at the University of Pennsylvania, 1936. Military: Served in the United States Marine Corps, 1942-46, attaining the rank of Captain. Career: Psychiatrist; Director, Bluefield Mental Health Center (Bluefield, West Virginia). Organizational Memberships: American Medical Association; American College of Psychiatrists, Fellow; American Psychiatric Association; Southern Medical Association; West Virginia Medical Association; Mercer County Medical Association. Honors and Awards: Grant from the Southern Regional Education Board. Address: 421 Monterey Hill, Bluefield, West Virginia 24701.■

DANIEL J. WEATHERS

Corporate Safety Manager. Personal: Born October 14, 1945; Son of Mr. and Mrs. James A. Weathers; Married Phyllis L.; Father of Kari Beth, Tad Daniel. Education: B.A. Psychology 1971, M.S. Industrial Safety 1972, Central Missouri State University. Military: Served in the United States Air Force, 1966-70, attaining the rank of E-4, Nuclear Weapons Specialist. Career: Manager, Corporate Safety, Utah International, Inc.; Former Positions include Senior Corporate Safety Engineer, Kerr-McGee Corporation; Plant and Division Safety Engineer, Ford Motor Company; Instructor, Industrial Safety and Hygiene, Graduate Assistant, Central Missouri State University; Certified for Comprehensive Practice, Board of Certified Safety Professionals; Certified at Master Level by Board of Certified Hazard Control Managers. Organizational Memberships: Board of Directors, Mine Inspectors Institute of America, 1980 to present; Professional Member, American Society of Safety Engineers, 1974 to present; Professional Member, Board of Certified Safety Professionals, 1978 to present; Professional Member, Certified Hazard Control Managers, 1978 to present; Secretary, National Safety Council Mining Section, 1980 to present; American Mining Congresss, Resolution Committee 1979 to present, Executive Member Coal Mine Safety and Health Committee 1979 to present; National Society of Professors, 1972 to present; Chairman, Charter Student Section, American Society of Safety Engineers, 1972. Community Activities: Central Missouri State University Alumni Association, 1971; Masons, Wyandotte Lodge Number 3, Kansas City, Kansas, 1966; Northern California Golf Association, 1979; Girl Scouts of America; National Safety Council. Published Works: Author of "Automated Records Maintenance and Scheduling: A Cobol Computer Program", Utah International Inc. 1982, "A.S.S.E. Goes to College", *Journal of Professional Safety* 1972, and numerous others. Honors and Awards: Wm. H. Cameron Award Winner for Outstanding Contribution to Mine Safety and Health, National Safety Council, 1979 and 1981; Phi Kappa Phi National Honor Society, 1971; Elected to World Safety Organization, 1978; Advisor to the Eighth Institute on Mine Safety and Health, 1981 and 1982; Toastmaster's International, Public Service Award 1976, Designated Competent Toastmaster 1978; Research Fellowship, Central Missouri State University, 1972; Listed in *Who's Who in the West, Who's Who in America*. Address: 6072 Della Court, Rohnert Park, California 94928.■

GEORGE FREDERIC WEATON

Retired Educator, Mining Executive. Personal: Born August 19, 1911; Son of George F. and Gertrude L. Weaton (both deceased); Married Lois Irene Nordin Landis; Father of Brenda Whittaker, Janet Johnson. Education: B.S. Mining Engineering 1936, E.M. Mining Engineering 1940, Carnegie Institute of Technology; Graduate Study in Management Training, University of Wisconsin, 1953. Military: Served in the United States Navy, 1943-53, attaining the rank of Lieutenant. Career: Retired Professor of Mining Engineering, University of Minnesota (1976-82); Vice President, Mining, Colorado Consolidated Metals Corporation, 1978 to present; Mining Consultant, Commissioner of Revenue, Minnesota, 1958-75; Mining Consultant, Department of Revenue, Arizona, 1964-75; Mine Superintendent 1955-58, Shift Foreman to Mine Captain 1947-55, St. Joe Minerals Corporation; General Administrator and General Mine Foreman, Cerro de Pasco Copper Corporation, Yauricocha and Casapalca, Peru, 1937-47. Organizational Memberships: Society of Mining Engineers of the American Institute of Mining Engineers, Has Held Numerous Offices on Both Local and National Levels 1936 to present, Director of Twin City Subsection 1981 to present, Gem Chairman and Membership Chairman of Minnesota Section 1981. Religion: Lay Reader, Chalice Bearer, St. George's Episcopal Church (St. Louis Park, Minnesota), 1977 to present. Honors and Awards: Public Service Award, Citizens for the Taconite Amendment Committee, 1962; Service and Achievement Award, Minnesota Section American Institute of Mining Engineers, 1971; 46-Year Member Award 1979, National Membership Awards 1975, 1979, 1980, American Institute of Mining Engineers. Address: 2925 Toledo Avenue South, Minneapolis, Minnesota 55416.■

ALLEN DALE WEAVER

Professor. Personal: Born November 15, 1911; Son of Harry D. and Grace Allen Weaver (deceased); Married Irene Fraser; Father of James A., Peggy Weaver Nix. Education: B.S. Physics, Knox College, Galesburg, Illinois, 1933; M.S. Physics, University of Michigan, 1947; Ph.D. Science Education, New York University, 1954. Military: Served in the United States Army, 1941-46 (active duty), 1933-41 (reserve). Career: Professor of Physics Emeritus; Science Teacher, Illinois Public Schools, 1935-40; Teacher of Physical Science and Physics, State Teachers College, Salisbury, Maryland, 1947-55; Northern Illinois University, Associate Professor of Physics 1955-60, Professor 1960-81. Organizational Memberships: American Association of University Professors, President, Northern Illinois University Chapter 1961-64, President, Illinois Conference 1965-68; President, N.I.U. Local #1673, American Federation of Teachers, 1968-71; National Association for Research in Science Teaching, 1956 to present; National Science Teachers Association, 1955 to present; American Association of Physics Teachers, 1947 to present. Community Activities: Vice President, Citizens for Better Government, DeKalb, Ilinois, 1968-69; President, DeKalb Householders Association, 1959-63; Member Advisory Council to DeKalb Board of Education, 1960-70; DeKalb-Ogle County Central Labor Council, Delegate 1965-82, President 1972-74, Secretary 1974-82. Religion: Member of University Methodist Church; Board Member, Wesley Foundation, 1962-70. Honors and Awards: Phi Delta Kappa Key, 1969. Address: 591 Garden Road, DeKalb, Illinois 60115.■

KATHERINE GREY DUNLAP WEAVER (KITTY)

Writer. Personal: Born September 24, 1910, in Frankfort, Kentucky; Daughter of Arch Robertson Dunlap (deceased) and Rebecca Johnson (deceased); Married Henry B. Weaver. Education: Summer School, Sorbonne University, Paris, France, 1929; A.B., College of William and Mary, Williamsburg, Virginia, 1932; Study with Dr. Alfred Adler, Vienna, Austria, Summer 1932; M.A., George Washington University, Washington, D.C., 1933; B.S. Agriculture, University of Maryland, College Park, 1947; Graduate Work, Russian Area Studies, Georgetown University, Washington, D.C., 1964-67; Attended Graduate School of Education, University of Pennsylvania, Philadelphia, 1967-68. Career: Teacher, Reading and English, St. Petersburg Junior High Schools; Poultry Farmer, Aldie, Virginia, 1947-55; Author. Organizational Memberships: International Platform Association; American Committee for Early Childhod Education. Community Activities: Fauquier-Loudoun Graden Club, Past Horticulture Chairman; Aldie Horticulture Society, Past President; Garden Club of Virginia, Accredited Flower Show Judge; Certificate, Ikebana, Japanese Flower Arranging; Loudoun Hospital, Ladies Board; Delegate, White House Conference on Children; Volunteer Work, Cancer, Community Chest; Irish Wolfhound Club of America, Hostess Two Annual Specialty Shows; Virginia Museum of Fine Arts, Hostess Benefit Art Show; Sulgrave Club, Washington, D.C.; Acorn Club, Philadelphia, Past Member; River Club, New York; Middleburg Tennis Club, Virginia. Published Works: Author, *Lenin's Grandchildren*, Simon and Schuster, 1971; *Russia's Future*, Praeger, 1981. Address: "Glengyle," Aldie, Virginia 22001.■

TWO THOUSAND NOTABLE AMERICANS

BERNICE LARSON WEBB

University Professor. Personal: Daughter of Mrs. Ida Larson; Mother of William Carl Schear, Rebecca Rae Gentry (Mrs. Cowan E. Gentry, Jr.). Education: A.B. 1956, M.A. 1957, Ph.D. 1961, University of Kansas; Doctoral Research and Study, University of Aberdeen, Scotland, 1959-60. Career: University Professor. Organizational Memberships: Louisiana State Poetry Society, President 1981-82, 1978-79, First Vice President 1979-81, Second Vice President 1976-78, Corresponding Secretary 1970-74, Editor 1970 to present; Southwestern Louisiana Association of Phi Beta Kappa, President 1983-84, Vice President 1982-83, President 1976-77, Vice President 1975-76, Secretary-Treasurer 1965-71; Southwest Louisiana Poetry Society, Treasurer 1975 to present, Publicity Chairman 1970-75; American Association of University Women, State Division Editor 1967-71, Lafayette Branch Board of Directors 1966-67; Deep South Writers Conference, Inc., Board Member 1979 to present; Popular Culture Association, Book Reviewer 1980 to present; American Culture Association, Book Reviewer 1980 to present; Modern Language Association; College English Association; American Folklore Society; National Federation of State Poetry Societies, Inc.; South Central Modern Language Association; South Central College English Association; Louisiana Folklore Society; Louisiana Association for Post-Secondary Language Arts. Community Activities: Acadiana Open Channel, Inc. (community television), 1982 to present; Louisiana Talent Bank of Women, 1978 to present; Talent Bank, Mayor's Commission on the Needs of Women, 1978 to present; Playwrights' Theater of Louisiana, Local and Off-Off Broadway, 1978 to present; Acadiana Arts Council, Director of Poetry Workshops, 1977 to present; Lafayette Parish School System, Consultant in Poetry, 1976 to present; Lafayette Little Theater, Acting and Backstage Work, 1963-76; Coordinator, Poetry-in-the-Schools, 1974; Webb's Writers, Sponsor 1974 to present; Bayou Girl Scout Council, Editor Newsletter, Troop Outdoor Leader, 1962-66; Parent Teachers Association, 1953-68; U.S.L. Speakers Brochure, Volunteer Speaker; Co-Donor, Carl and Ida Larson Endowed Scholarship, 1976 to present. Religion: Roman Catholic. Published Works: Author of Four Books including *The Basketball Man* 1973 (translated into Japanese and published in Japan 1981 to present); Publication of Poems, Essays and Articles, Short Stories, Reviews, and Plays; Honors and Awards: Phi Beta Kappa, 1955; Recipient of Nine American University Scholarships and Fellowships, 1954-61; Foreign Exchange Scholarship, 1959-60; Pi Delta Phi,1958; American Association of University Women Educational Foundation Research Grant, 1978-80; Faculty Research Support Program Grant, 1980-81; Seaton Award, 1980; 125 Awards in Poetry, Fiction, Nonfiction and Drama, 1946-81. Address: 159 Whittington Drive, Lafayette, Louisiana 70503.■

CHARLES H. WEBB

University School of Music Dean. Personal: Born February 14, 1933; Son of Charles and Marion Webb; Father of Mark Charles, Kent Paul, Malcolm McGibbon, Charles H. III. Education: B.A. 1955, M.M. 1955, Southern Methodist University; D.M., Indiana University, 1964. Military: Served in the United States Army, 1955-57. Career: Indiana University School of Music, Bloomington, Indiana, Faculty Member 1960 to present, Manager of Musical Attractions 1960-64, Assistant Dean 1964-69, Associate Dean 1969, Associate Dean for Academic Affairs 1969-71, Dean 1973 to present. Organizational Memberships: Pi Kappa Lambda; Phi Mu Alpha; Phi Delta Theta. Community Activities: Commissioner, Indiana Arts Commission; Chairman Advisory Board, International Music Festivals; Member Advisory Panel, The Music Foundation; Member Recommendation Board, Avery Fisher Prize Program; Busoni Foundation. Religion: Organist, First Methodist Church, 1961 to present. Honors and Awards: Honorary Degree, Anderson College, 1979; Distinguished Alumni, Southern Methodist University, 1980. Address: 648 Woodscrest Drive, Bloomington, Indiana 47401.■

LANCE WEBB

Bishop of the United Methodist Church. Personal: Born December 10; Son of John N. S. and Delia Lance Webb (deceased); Married Mary Elizabeth Hunt; Father of Gloria Jeanne (Mrs. David B. Davis), Mary Margaret (Mrs. Lee G. Edlund), Ruth Elizabeth (Mrs. Allen Lindstrom). Education: B.A., McMurray College, 1931; B.S. and M.A., Southern Methodist University, 1934; Postgraduate Work, Union School of Theology, 1937, 1939 to present. Career: Clergy as Bishop of the United Methodist Church; Resident Bishop of Illinois Area 1964-76, Iowa Area 1976-80, Retired 1980 to present; Author; Pastor, North Broadway Methodist Church, Columbus, Ohio, 1953-64; Pastor, University Park Methodist Church, 1941-52; Pastor, Eastland Methodist Church 1939-41, Shamrock 1938-40; Chaplain and Professor of Religion, McMurry College, 1937-38; McCullough-Harrah Methodist Church, 1934-37. Organizational Memberships: President, North Central Jurisdiction College of Bishops, 1979-80; Consultant to the Upper Room on Spiritual Formation, 1980 to present; Chairman, General Commission on Worship, 1966-72; World Methodist Commission on Worship and Liturgy, Co-Chairman 1965-70, Executive Vice Chairman 1970-75, Chairman 1975-80; Member of General and Jurisdictional Conferences of the Methodist Church, 1956, 1960, 1964. Community Activities: One of the Founders of the Dallas Federation of Churches, 1950; Chairman-elect, Ohio Pastors Conference, 1964; Chaplain, Civitan International, 1952; 33rd Degree Scottish Rite Mason and Member of Supreme Council, 1976; Chaplain, Ohio State Senate, 1963; Torch Club, Columbus, Ohio, 1955-64; Member and Officer, Mayor's Committee on Human Relations, Columbus, Ohio, 1956-64. Honors and Awards: Honorary Degrees include D.D. from McMurry College 1948, D.D. from Ohio Wesleyan University 1960, McMurry College (Jacksonville, Illinois) 1967, LL.D. from Southern Methodist University 1966, H.H.D. from Illinois Wesleyan University, 1966, Litt.D. from Simpson College 1969, Litt.D. from Morningside College 1977. Address: 10321 Van Dyke Road, Dallas, Texas 75218.■

WILLIAM YATES WEBB

Retired. Personal: Born October 12, 1910, in Shelby, North Carolina; Married Laura Mae Brown, October 12, 1941; Father of Shirley Webb McCall. Education: Graduate of Shelby High School; Attended Wake Forest University; B.A. 1932, M.A. 1933, Columbia University; Graduate Fellowships, Duke University 1933-34, New York University 1934-35 and 1936-37, Brookings Institution 1935-36. Military: Served in the Materials Division, Executive Office of the Navy Secretary, 1941-46, with promotions from Lieutenant (j.g.) to Commander; Retired 1970. Career: Industrial Economist (retired); Office of the Secretary of Defense, 1965, 1969; Vulnerability Analyst, Office of Civil Defense, 1961-65; Industrial Specialist, Office of the Secretary of Defense, 1954-61; Industrial Specialist, Munitions Board, 1951-53; Industrial Engineer, Office of Naval Material, 1946-51; Naval Officer, Executive Office of the Secretary of the Navy, Munitions Board, 1942-46; Economist, W.P.B., 1942; Chief Oil and Gas Section, Mines and Quarries Division, Census Bureau, 1940-42; Economist, Bituminius Coal Consumers Council, 1937-40; Economist, Tin Investigating Committee, 1934. Organizational Memberships: A.E.A.; American Defense Preparedness Association; A.A.R.P.; American Security Council. Community Activities: American Legion; Metro Police Boys and Girls Club; National Symphony Orchestra Fund; National Economists Club; National Conference of St. Soc.; North Carolina Democratic Club of Washington, D.C.; North Carolina Society of Washington; Navy League; Reserve Officers Association; Roanoke Island Historical Association; Cleveland County Historical Association; Kappa Alpha Order; Pi Gamma Mu; Alto Clarinetist, Palisades Community Orchestra and Alexandria Citizens Band; Kenwood Golf and Country Club; Women's National Democratic Club; Duke, Columbia, and Wake Forest University Alumni Associations. Religion: Methodist, Men's Club of Metropolitan Memorial United Methodist Church; Played Clarinet in Church's Former "Metrotones." Published Works: Co-Author, "Price Fixing in the Bituminous Coal Industry," TNEC Monograph 32, Government Printing Office, 1941; Author, "Material Availability and Conservation," Society of Plastics Industry, 1952. Honors and Awards: Graduate Fellowships, Duke University, New York University, Brooking Institution; Commendations, Secretaries of the Army, Navy, Defense, Joint Chiefs of Staff, Industrial College of the Armed Forces, and Office of Emergency Planning; Kenwood Golf and Country Club Champion Bowling Teams, 1976-77, 1979-80. Address: 3614 Warren Street, Northwest, Washington, D.C. 20008.■

DARRELL JACK WEBER

Educator. Personal: Born November 16, 1933; Son of John and Norma Weber; Married Carolyn Foremaster; Father of Brad, Becky, Todd, Kelly, Jason, Brian, Trent. Education: B.S. 1958, M.S. 1959, Biochemistry, University of Idaho; Ph.D. Plant Pathology, University of California-Davis, 1963; Postdoctoral Work in Biochemistry undertaken at the University of Wisconsin 1965, and Michigan State University 1976. Military: Served in the United States Air Force Reserve Officer Training Corps for two years. Career: Professor of Botany, Brigham Young University; Associate Professor, University of Houston, 1965-69; Research Associate of Biochemistry, University of Wisconsin, 1963-65; Research Assistant, University of California-Davis, 1959-63; Research Assistant, University of Idaho-Moscow, 1958-59. Organizational Memberships: Alpha Zeta; American Society of Microbiologists; Sigma Xi; American Institute of Biological Scientists; American Mycological Society, Editor; American Botanical Society, Editor; American Phytopathological Society; Phytochemical Society. Religion: Bishopric 1957-59 and 1983, High Councilman 1967-82, Church of Jesus Christ of Latter-day Saints (Mormon). Published Works: Author, Over 70 Scientific Articles and Three Books; Research on Physiology of Fungi, Plant Diseases, Allergy Caused by Plants, Salt Tolerance of Plants, Medical Value of Plant Products.

Honors and Awards: Recipient of 17 Research Grants Worth $500,000; Elected Fellow, Utah Academy of Sciences, 1972; Karl G. Maeser Research Award of $3000, 1974. Address: 560 East Robin, Orem, Utah 84057.■

ALVIN STANLEY WEBSTER

Clinical Psychologist. Personal: Born June 5, 1926; Son of Norma Webster; Married Esther Rosalie Slovis on April 2, 1959; Father of Ashley Alexandria. Education: B.A. 1948, M.A. 1949, West Virginia University; Ph.D. 1952, Postdoctoral Fellow 1952-53, University of Tennessee. Career: Adjunct Professor of Psychology, Florida Institute of Technology, 1979 to present; Professor of Psychology, International Graduate University, 1979 to present; Associate Professor of Psychology, University of Tennessee, 1951-76; Practice Psychology, Knoxville, Tennessee, 1952-73; Chief Psychologist, Lakeshore Mental Health Institute, Knoxville, Tennessee, 1952-73; Assistant Superintendent for Clinical Support 1973-83, Director Overlook Mental Health Center (Lakeshore Mental Health Institute), Knoxville, Tennessee, 1973-75; President Hensco, Knoxville, Tennessee, 1969 to present; Knox County Council for Retarded Children, Knoxville, Tennessee, 1955-56. Organizational Memberships: American Psychological Association; Southeastern Psychological Association; Tennessee Psychological Association; Inter-American Society of Psychology; Council for Retarded Children. Honors and Awards: Award of Merit, City of Knoxville and Knox County Council for Retarded Children, 1955; Certificate of Appreciation, Multiple Sclerosis Society, 1978; Listed in *American Men of Science, Men of Science, Who's Who in the South and Southwest, Community Leaders and Noteworthy Americans, Who's Who in Tennessee, Personalities of the South, Outstanding Professions in Human Services*. Address: 7041 Stockton Drive, Knoxville, Tennessee 37919.■

BURNICE HOYLE WEBSTER

Physician, College Administrator. Personal: Born March 3, 1910, in Leeville, Tennessee; Son of Thomas Jefferson and Martha Ann Melton Webster; Married Georgia Kathryn Fogleman, 1939; Father of Brenda Kathryn (Mrs. James A. Hamilton III), Adrienne Elise, Philip Hoyle. Education: B.A. 1936, M.D. 1940, Vanderbilt University; Th.B. 1968, S.T.D. 1969, D.Sc. 1971, Holy Trinity College; D.D., Ph.D., Florida Research Institute, 1972. Career: Intern, Assistant Resident, Resident, St. Thomas Hospital and Vanderbilt Hospital, 1940-45; Assistant in Medicine, Vanderbilt University, 1949 to present; Private Practice in Internal Medicine, 1945 to present; President, Holy Trinity College, 1965 to present; Chairman, Tennessee Selective Medical Service, 1971 to present. Organizational Memberships: Nashville Academy of Medicine; President, Arthritis Foundation; Fellow, American Medical Association; President, Muscular Dystrophy Society; Fellow, American College of Chest Physicians; Fellow, Royal Society of Health. Community Activities: President Andrew Jackson and Tennessee Chapters, National Trustee, Sons of the American Revolution; Vice President General, Sons of the War of 1812; Deputy President and General, Sons of Colonial Wars; President, Baptist and Protestant Hospitals; Commander-in-Chief, Sons of Confederate Veterans; Commander, Order of Stars and Bars. Published Works: Author Over 50 Scientific Articles. Honors and Awards: Patriot Award; Southern Heritage Award; Silver Stethoscope Award; Kentucky Colonel; Georgia Colonel; Arkansas Traveller. Address: 2315 Valley Brook Road, Nashville, Tennessee 37215.■

HENRY WECHSBERG

Dentist, Implantalogist. Personal: Born June 29, 1919; Father Orin, Wendee Wechsberg Cartee. Education: Carolinum (Germany), 1934; University of California at Los Angeles, 1937-39; Clark University, 1943; University of Denver, 1946-47; D.D.S., Washington University School of Dental Medicine, 1947-51. Military: United States Army Counterintelligence, 1941-46. Career: Dentist, Implantalogist; Work on Film of Blade Implantology with Ten Years Follow Up. Community Activities: Past President, B'nai B'rith Southern California. Honors and Awards: Past President Alpha Omega, Member O.K.U. Dental Honorary, Academy Award Dental Medicine; Fellow, Royal Society of Health; Many Guest Lectures. Address: 3542 Coral Way, Miami, Florida 33145.■

MARY T. WEED

Assistant Professor, Clinical Psychologist. Personal: Born November 11, 1928; Daughter of Mr. and Mrs. John George Theophilos (both deceased); Mother of Heather. Education: B.A., University of Miami, 1953; M.A., University of Chicago, 1960. Career: School Psychologist, Chicago Board of Education, 1960-62; Assistant Professor of Psychology, Chicago City College, 1962 to present; Part-time Private Practice in Clinical Psychology. Organizational Memberships: American Psychological Association; Illinois Psychological Association. Community Activities: Laboratory Schools, University of Chicago, Middle School Chairperson 1980-81. Honors and Awards: Registered Psychologist in Illinois; Listed in *National Register of Health Service Providers in Psychology*. Address: 5534 South Harper, Chicago, Illinois 60637.■

PAUL LINCOLN WEIDEN

Physician. Personal: Born August 21, 1941, in Portland, Oregon; Married; Father of Two Children. Education: Graduate of Menlo-Atherton High School, California; B.A. summa cum laude, Harvard College, Cambridge, Massachusetts, 1963; M.D. cum laude, Harvard Medical School, 1967; Licensure, Washington, California, Ohio; Diplomate, National Medical Board of Examiners 1968, American Board of Internal Medicine 1972, Subspecialty of Medical Oncology, American Board of Internal Medicine 1973. Career: Clinical Associate, Immunophysiology Section, Metabolism Branch, National Cancer Institute, National Institute of Health, Bethesda, Maryland, 1969-71; University of Washington School of Medicine, Seattle, Oncology and Hematology Fellow 1971-73, Instructor in Division of Oncology 1973-74; Assistant Professor 1974-78, Associate Professor 1978-80, Clinical Associate Professor of Medicine 1981 to present; Fred Hutchinson Cancer Research Center, Seattle, Washington, Assistant Member 1973-78, Associate Member 1978-80, Affiliate Investigator in Medical Oncology 1981 to present; Physician, Section of Hematology-Oncology, The Mason Clinic, Seattle, Washington, 1981 to present; Medical Consultant, V.I.S.T.A., Seattle, 1972 to present. Organizational Memberships: American Medical Association; Abstracts Editorial Board, *Transplantation Proceedings*, 1981-84; American College of Physicians, Fellow; American Society of Hematology; International Society of Experimental Hematology; American Society of Clinical Oncology; *Experimental Hematology*, Editorial Board 1981-83. Community Activities: King County Animal Control Advisory Board, 1975 to present. Honors and Awards: Detur Prize, Harvard College, 1960; Phi Beta Kappa, 1963; Alpha Omega Alpha, 1966; Dean's Prize for Performance in Pre-Clinical Years, Harvard Medical School, 1967; Junior Faculty Clinical Fellowship, American Cancer Society, 1974-77; Listed in *Who's Who in the West, Personalities of the West and Midwest, Men of Achievement*. Address: The Mason Clinic, 1100 Ninth Avenue, P.O. Box 900, Seattle, Washington 98111.■

ELEANOR PERLSTEIN WEINBAUM

Poet, Businesswoman. Personal: Born in Beaumont, Texas; Daughter of Hyman Asher and Mamie Gordon Perlstein; Mother of Charles Jr. Education: Graduate of Beaumont High School; Ward-Belmont College; Benjamin School of New York, NY; Studied Poetry under Clement Wood and Attended Various Poetry Conference at Boulder University. Career: Real Estate Management Executive; Partner, 23rd Street Shopping Center; Freelance Writer and Poet. Organizational Memberships: Fellow, Intercontinental Biographical Association; International Poetry Institute; Poetry Society of Texas; United Poets Laureate International; World Poetry Society; International Academy of Poets; Life Member, League of Women Voters; Charter Member, Heritage Society; State and National Press Women; Beaumont Chamber of Commerce; Woodall Poetry Int; The Beaumont Club. Community Activities: Donated Eleanor Poetry Room at Lamar University, Beaumont, Texas; Sponsors Lecture by a Distinguished Poet Each Year; Helped to Establish New Poetry Room at Southern Methodist University, Dallas, Texas; Established *PULSE*, the Literary Magazine of Lamar University; Advisory Board Member, Texas Council for the Promotion of Poetry. Published Works: *From Croup To Nuts*, 1941; *The World Laughs With You*, 1950; *Jest For You*, 1954; *Shalom America*, 1970; *Conrad's Scrabble Babble*, 1977; *God's Eternal Word*, 1978; Numerous Short Stories and Poems in Various Jours and Anthologies. Honors and Awards: Resolution of Appreciation, Lamar University; Doctor of Modern Humanities Degree, International Academy; Distinguished Service Citation, World Poetry Society; Doctor of Humane Letters Diploma, University of Libre (Asia); Honorary Member, Gamma Nu Chapter, Sigma Tau Delta; Chosen as One of International Women of 1975 with Laureate Honors, UPLI Philippines; Subject of Feature

TWO THOUSAND NOTABLE AMERICANS

Article in 1977 *Cardinal*, the Yearbook of Lamar University; Recipient, 2nd Place Award for Public Relations Material, Texas Press Women, 1981; Listed in *Dictionary of International Biography, Two Thousand Women of Achievement, American Mosaic Anthology, Directory of British and American Writers, Community Leaders of America, International Who's Who in Poetry, National Register of Prominent Americans.* Address: 1215 Beaumont Savings Building, Beaumont, Texas 77701.■

STEVEN WEINBERG

Theoretical Physicist. Personal: Born May 3, 1933. Education: A.B., Cornell University, 1954; Attended the Copenhagen Institute of Theoretical Physics, 1954-55; Ph.D., Princeton University, 1957. Career; Theoretical Physicist. Organizational Memberships: National Academy of Sciences; Royal Society of London; American Philosophical Society; American Academy of Arts and Sciences, Councilor 1982-85; American Physical Society; Council for Foreign Relations; International Astronomical Union. Community Activities: Consultant to the United States Arms Control and Disarmament Agency, Institute for Defense Analysis, Stanford Research Institute; President's Committee on the National Medal of Science; Council of Scholars of the Library of Congress; Board of Overseers of SCC Accelerator; Director, Jerusalem Winter School of Theoretical Physics. Honors and Awards: Honorary D.Sc. Degrees, Knox College 1978, University of Chicago 1978, University of Rochester 1979, Yale University 1979, City University of New York 1980, Clark University 1982; Oppenheimer Prize, 1973; Heinemann Prize, 1977; Nobel Prize in Physics, 1979; Cresson Medal, 1979. Address: c/o Physics Department, University of Texas, Austin, Texas 78712.■

ARTHUR MARTIN WEIS

Corporate Executive. Personal: Born April 3, 1925; Son of Jerome and Lillie Feier Weis (both deceased); Married Bernice Shapiro; Father of Eric M. Education: Attended the New York School of Engineering; B.S. Aerospace Engineering, Rensselaer Polytechnic Institute, 1949; United States Naval Academy; New York University School of Law; J.D., Rutgers University of Law, 1968. Career: President and Founder, Capintec, Inc.; President and Director, Brevatome, U.S.A., 1966-70; Manager of Marketing, Nuclear Materials and Equipment Corporation, 1959-64, concurrently President of Muminco; Project Engineer, Systems Engineer, Research Engineer, Test Engineer, Assistant Patent Attorney, Marketing Manager, Curtiss Wright, 1947-59. Organizational Memberships: Society of Nuclear Medicine; American Management Association; New Jersey Bar Association. Address: 195 Fernwood Avenue, Upper Montclair, New Jersey 07043.■

JAMES ATHANASIUS WEISHEIPL

Dominican Priest, Educator. Personal: Born July 3, 1923; Son of John Joseph and Mary Ann (Gralla) Weisheipl. Education: S.T.Lr., Dominican House of Studies, River Forest, Illinois, 1950; Ph.D., Pontifical University of St. Thomas Aquinas, Rome, Italy, 1953; D.Phil., University of Oxford, U.K., 1957. Career: Lecturer in Medieval Thought 1957-58, Professor 1958-65, Pontifical Faculty of Philosophy, River Forest, Illinois; Visiting Lecturer 1963-64, Associate Professor 1964-68, Professor 1968 to present, Pontifical Institute of Mediaeval Studies, Toronto, Canada. Organizational Memberships: Member and Officer of Academic Organizations. Published Works: Author Books and Journal Articles on Medieval Science and Philosophy. Honors and Awards: Recipient of Numerous Awards. Address: Pontifical Institute of Mediaeval Studies, 59 Queen's Park Crescent E., Toronto, Ontario M5S 2C4.■

SHERRY JACOBS WEISLER

School Psychologist. Personal: Born May 18, 1951; Daughter of Barnet Jacobs (deceased) and Eve Jacobs; Married Jeffrey Mark Weisler; Mother of Stacey Melissa, Robert Allen. Education: B.S. cum laude Psychology, Brooklyn College, 1972; M.S. and Certificate in School Psychology, Brooklyn College, 1974. Career: Brooklyn College, Adjunct Lecturer in Psychology 1972, Adjunct Lecturer in Counseling in the School of Education 1972-74, College Assistant in Testing and Research 1973-75; School Psychologist in Training, Bureau of Child Guidance, New York City Board of Education, 1974-75; School Psychologist, Kennedy Learning Center, Brooklyn, New York, 1974-76; Assistant Research Scientist, Child Psychiatric Education and Research Unit, New York Department of Mental Hygiene, Brooklyn, New York, 1976; Psychologist, Comprehensive Mental Health Services, Inc., Clearwater, Florida, 1978-80; Social Sciences Instructor, St. Petersburg Junior College, St. Petersburg, Florida, 1977-80; Psychologist and Consultant, Pinellas County Head Start, 1980 to present; Licensed School Psychologist. Organizational Memberships: Association of School Psychologists of Brooklyn College; Florida Association of School Psychologists; Southeast Association of School Psychologists. Community Activities: Women's American ORT, 1976 to present; Health Advisory Board of Pinellas County Head Start, 1980 to present. Honors and Awards: Listed in *Who's Who of American Women, Personalities of America.* Address: 2868 Meadow Oak Drive East, Clearwater, Florida 33519.■

VLADIMIR STANLEY WEISS

Engineering Executive. Personal: Born August 23, 1931; Son of Bogdan Michael and Gjurgjica Duda Weiss (deceased); Married Branka-Marie Papa, Daughter of Peter and Vjekoslava Papa; Father of Theodore Daniel, Tamara Duda. Education: B.Sc. 1954, M.Sc. 1956, University of Zagreb (Yugoslavia); M.Sc., University of Vienna (Austria), 1957. Career: Department Head (Engineering), Brueder Warchalowski, Vienna, Austria, 1956-57; Research Engineer, Montreal Locomotive Works Ltd., Montreal, Quebec, Canada, 1957-65; President, Weiss & Associates, Montreal, Quebec, Canada, 1965 to present; President, Con-Des Inc., Montreal, 1966 to present; President, Weiss Engineering Ltd., Mississauga, Ontario, Canada, 1976 to present; President, Weiss Consultants Inc., Calgary, Alberta, Canada, 1979 to present. Organizational Memberships: American Association of Engineering Societies; American Institute of Chemical Engineers; Association of Professional Engineers, Geophysicists and Geologists of Alberta; Association of Professional Engineers of Ontario; Canadian Federation of Independent Business; Canadian Pulp and Paper Association; Canadian Society for Professional Engineers; Canadian Society of Mechanical Engineers; Engineering Institute of Canada; Instrument Society of America, Vice President 1970-72; Massachusetts Society of Professional Engineers; New York State Society of Professional Engineers; Order of Engineers of Quebec. Honors and Awards: Distinguished Society Service Award, Instrument Society of America, 1973; Distinguished Service to Community, Instrument Society of America (Montreal Section), 1976 and 1983; Listed in *Who's Who in the East, Personalities of America, Community Leaders of America, Who's Who in Engineering, Canadian Who's Who.* Address: 69 Maplewood Road, Mississauga, Ontario L5G 2M7.■

DONALD T. WELLS

Financial Executive. Personal: Born December 26, 1931, in Henderson, Kentucky; Son of Mr. and Mrs. Melvin J. Wells; Married Josephine G., 1954; Father of Renetta G., Kathy L. Education: Graduate of Barret High School, Henderson, Kentucky; B.S. Marketing/Finance, University of Kentucky, 1957; Graduate Studies, University of Indiana, 1957-59. Military: Served in the United States Armed Forces, 1951-53, as Instructor for the Counter Intelligence Section. Career: Lecturer; Financial and Tax Consultant; Assistant Secretary-Treasurer, Von Hoffman Press, Inc., St. Louis, Missouri, 1963-68; President, Treasurer, American Mortgage Equipment Leasing Corporation, St. Louis, Missouri, 1968-71; Group Controller, Interlake Steel Corporation, Dallas, Texas, 1971-73; Corporate Controller, Fiscal Officer, Multi-Amp Corporation, Subsidiary Thyssen-Bornemisza, Inc., Dallas, Texas, 1973 to present; Director, Prairie Creek Bootery, Inc. Organizational Memberships: National Association of Accountants; American Management Association; Institute of Corporate Controllers, Financial Executive Institute. Community Activities: Masons; Kiwanis; Chamber of Commerce. Religion: Baptist; Deacon, Vice Chairman Deacon Council, Chairman of Budget and Finance Committees, Sunday School Superintendent, Lay Speaker, Pioneer Mission Development Activities. Honors and Awards: Honorable Kentucky Colonel; Listed in *Who's Who in the South and Southwest, Who's Who in Finance and Industry, Personalities of the South, Personalities of America, Men of Achievement.* Address: Multi-Amp Corporation, Subsidiary of Indian Head, Inc., 4271 Bronze Way, Dallas, Texas 75237.■

ERNEST HATTON WELLS

Engineer and Scientist. Personal: Born August 1, 1921, in Crossville, Tennessee; Son of Noah and Chloe Burgess Wells (both deceased); Married Signa Faye

Stinett, 1954; Father of David Allen (deceased), William Ernest, Ronald Eston, Lawrence Robert. Education: Graduate with Distinction of Cumberland County High School, 1940; Attended Georgia Tech (Atlanta), North Carolina State University (Raleigh), Bendix, Philco Schools for Electronics, No. 5 Radio School, Clinton, Ontario, Boca Raton, Florida, Radar Training, Air Force Radar and Electronics School; B.S.E.E. Tennessee Technological University, 1951; D.Sc 1973, Ph.D. 1974, Sussex College of Technology, England; Over 33 Postgraduate Courses, Ten Colleges and Universities; First Class and Amateur Federal Communications Commission Radio Licenses. Military: Served in the United States Signal Corps, 1942-43, and in the United States Air Force, 1943-46, in the Position of Radar Chief in Guam and Iwo Jima; Honorable Discharge, 1946. Career: Operator, Wells Radio Service, until 1941; Washington National Airport; Research and Development Project Engineer, Leader, Expeditions to Greenland Ice Cap for Research on Guidance Systems, ERDL Fort Belvoir, Virginia; Radar Engineer, Navy Department; Telemetry Engineer for Cape Canaveral Redstone Firings, Project Engineer for White Sands, New Mexico Firings, ABMA Wernher Von Braun Rocket Team, Redstone Arsenal, Huntsville, Alabama, from 1957; Supervisor Four Laboratories, Electronics and Optics; National Aeronautics and Space Administration, MSFC, AST Space Scientist on Geophysical Satellites 1962, Assigned to Lunar Surface Studies, Optics and Planetology, Discovered Water on Mars, Designed SSL Solar Observatory, Pursued Research in Solar Phenomena, Raman Spectroscopy, Remote Sensing of Natural Resources, Water and Air Contamination, Space Instruments, Design of Solar Stimulators and Space Telescopes, Comets and Meteors, Manager Study for Rocket-Borne Manned Telescope for Lunar Use, Staff of the Optics and RF Systems Division EC31, Marshall Space Flight Center, Alabama; Electronics Instructor, Tennessee Technological University, 1947-48; Instructor, Courses in Religion and UFOs and World Mysteries, Mountain Gap School and University of Alabama, 1978; Research, Phenomena, Genealogy, Galactic Dynamics, Solar System Origin, Properties and Origin of the Moon, Solar H-Alpha, Solar Wind, Arctic Ice Radar and Electromagnetic Properties, Optical Radar Telescopic Optics, Atmospheric Pollution, Antennas, UFOs, Artificial Gravity; Founder, Director, The Order of Magnitude, Correspondence School for Inspiration and High Attainment. Organizational Memberships: American Rocket Society, Past Member; American Astronomical Association, Past Member; Rocket City Astronomical Association, Past Member; Institute of Radio Engineers, Past Senior Member and Memberships Chairman; Society of Professional Engineers, Tennessee Chapter; Broadcast Music Institute; International Biographical Center, Fellow; Optical Society of America, Huntsville Chapter; Mutual UFO Network; Huntsville Radio Club. Community Activities: Candidate Explorer's Club; Boy Scouts of America, Committee Chairman Troop 17, Assistant Scoutmaster Troop 382; Designed Telescope and Donated Dome, Madison Academy Wells Observatory. Religion: Past Teacher, Genesis, Central Church of Christ; Teacher Science/Religion and Biblical Archaeology, Fanning Heights Church of Christ. Published Works: Author, 54 Papers and Reports (many published in Professional Journals); Author, Books, *Astronomy Finds the Days of Creation, Search for Life in Space*; Many Other Manuscripts; Writer of Two Songs, "Impeachment Blues," "America Stand Up and Sing." Honors and Awards: 30-Year Service Award, Many Participation Awards, including Apollo-Soyuz Award and Medal 1969, Award of Achievement 1969, Space Shuttle Certificate of Recognition, National Aeronautics and Space Administration, Consultant to Teledyne Brown Engineering, Radar. Address: 712 Kilkenny Street, Northwest, Huntsville, Alabama 35805.■

JOHN CORSON WELLS

Professor of German. Personal: Born February 3, 1918; Son of Frederic Lyman Wells (deceased); Married Paula Kessler, Daughter of Hermann A. Kessler (deceased); Father of Peter S. Wells. Education: B.A. cum laude, Harvard College, 1940; Attended the Middlebury College Summer School of German, 1940, 1941; M.A. 1942, Teaching Fellow in German 1943-47, Ph.D. 1952, Harvard University; Attended the University of Freiburg (Germany), 1952-53. Military: Served in the United States Army Air Forces Technical Training Command, 1942-43, attaining the rank of Corporal. Career: Instructor, Assistant Professor, Associate Professor, Professor of German, 1947-83, Professor Emeritus 1983, Tufts University; Temporary Instructor in Modern Languages, Massachusetts Institute of Technology, 1945-46. Organizational Memberships: American Association of Teachers of German (Boston Chapter), Director of German Radio Hour and Chairman of Program Committee 1959-61, In Charge of National German Contest for High School Students in Eastern Massachusetts Area 1959-61; Modern Language Association; Mediaeval Academy of America; Dictionary Society of North America. Community Activities: Boy Scouts of America, Troop 382, Troop Treasurer 1960-62. Published Works: Compiler and Editor, *Althochdeutsches Glossenwörterbuch* (*Dictionary of Old High German Glosses*), 1972-84. Honors and Awards: Deutscher Akademischer Austauschdienst Fellowship, 1952-53; National Endowment for the Humanities, Eight Grants, 1967-81; Full-time Research Scholar under a Mellon Foundation Grant to Tufts University, 1982-83; Cross of the Order of Merit, First Class, Federal Republic of Germany, 1961. Address: 239 Mystic Valley Parkway, Winchester, Massachusetts 01890.■

PATRICIA A. BENNETT WELLS

Educator in Management/Organizational Behavior. Personal: Born March 25, 1935; Daughter of Benjamin Beekman Bennett (deceased) and Alice Catherine Bennett Breckinridge; Mother of Bruce Bennett, Barbara Lea. Education: A.A. Business, Allen Hancock College, Santa Maria, California, 1964; B.S. magna cum laude Business, College of Great Falls, Montana, 1966; M.S. Business Education, University of North Dakota, 1967; Ph.D. Business and Vocational Education, University of North Dakota, 1971; Certified Administrative Manager, 1979; New York State Permanent Certification in Business Subjects and Social Studies, Grades 7-12; California Community College Instructor Credential, Valid for Life. Career: Professor of Business Administration, Oregon State University, 1974 to present; Associate Professor, Chairman Department of Business Education, Virginia State University, 1973-74; Visiting Professor, University of Southern California, 1972; Visiting Professor, Chapman College, 1971-72; Summer Visiting Professor, University of Montana, 1972; Instructor, Western New England College, 1967-69; President, Chairman of the Board, Administrative Organizational Services, Inc., 1967 to present; Civilian Medical Services Accounts Officer, United States Air Force, 1962-64. Organizational Memberships: American Management Association; Administrative Management Society, Member 1974 to present, Chairman of Education Committee of Eugene Chapter 1976, Certified Administrative Manager Committee 1977, Chapter Achievement Program Committee 1978, Committee of 500 1978, Education Committee 1979, Cam of 1979; American Association of University Professors, Member 1968 to present, Chapter Secretary 1968, Chapter Board Member 1982-83, State Conference President 1983-85; American Business Women's Association, Member 1973 to present, Secretary 1974-75, Division Director 1975-76, Special Events Chairman 1977-78, Vice President 1977-78, President 1978-79, Education Chairman 1979-80; American Vocational Association, Member 1967 to present, Nominating Committee 1976; American Business Communication Association, Member 1975 to present, Regional Chairman of Business Liaison Committee 1976, Methodology Committee 1976, 1979 International Program Chairman, Proceeding Committee Chairman 1979-80, International Board of Directors 1980-83, Northwest Vice President 1981-82, Second Vice President 1982-83, First Vice President 1983-84; Corvallis Word Processing Management Group, Founder, Charter Member 1975 to present; Data Processing Management Association; Delta Pi Epsilon Graduate Honorary Society, Alpha Nu Chapter, 1967 to present, Program Director, Registration Chairman 1978-81; International Word Processing Association, Member 1974 to present, Chairman Task Force on Professional Certification 1978-79, Steering Committee, Educators Advisory Council 1978-81; Willamette Valley Chapter, International Word Processing Association (now Association Information Systems Professionals), Member 1974 to present, Charter Member, Chairman Nomination Committee 1974, Board of Directors 1974-80, New Chapter Committee; President 1977-78 and 1978-79, Nominated to International Board of Directors 1979, Joint Data Processing Management/International Word Processing Association Show and Symposium Co-Chairman 1980; Associated Oregon Faculties, 1978 to present; Oregon State Employee Association, Member 1974-80, President O.S.U. Chapter 47, Professional Certification 1978-79, Steering Committee, Educators Advisory Council 1978-81; National Business Education Association; National Association of Teacher Educators for Business Office Education, Member 1970 to present, Program Chairman 1973 Convention, Vice President 1975-76, President 1976-77, Chairman Public Relations Committee 1978-81, Life Member 1976 to present; Sigma Kappa Sorority; Western Business Education Association, 1974-80. Community Activities: Numerous Positions in University Service, Oregon State University, 1975-82; Numerous Continuing Education Short Courses and Conferences, 1970-81; Human Relations Committee, 1968; Higher Education Representative, Oregon Business Education Association Council, 1977-79; Newman Foundation, Board Member 1977-80, President 1978-79; Rosewood Estates Road District, Budget Committee 1978; Linn Benton Tax Relief Steering Committee, 1978; Lane Community College, Business Advisory Board 1978-79; Judge, Philomath Frolic Queen Contest, 1979; American Council on Education, State Panel Member, Oregon Identification Program for Women in Administration 1979; Consultant, Numerous State, Local, Professional, Academic, Research, Civic Organizations; Benton County Association for Retarded Citizens, Board of Directors 1981. Published Works: Office Systems; Information/Word Processing: A Management View; Numerous Papers and Journal Articles, including "Word Processing in the Typewriting Classroom," "Alcoholism Drug Abuse in the Work Force," "Evaluating Seminars." Honors and Awards: Phi Kappa Phi; Delta Epsilon Sigma National Undergraduate Honorary Society; Delta Kappa Gamma Women's Educational Honorary Society; Inscribed Plaque for Outstanding Contributions to the National Association of Teacher Educators in Business and Office Education, 1976; Listed in *Who's Who in the West, Who's Who Among American Women*. Address: 2145 Primrose Loop, Philomath, Oregon 97376.■

CAROL JUNE WELSH

Educator. Personal: Born October 31, 1931; Daughter of Clyde William and Redith K. Summerlot; Married Robert Walter Welsh; Mother of Phillip Paul,

Robin Walter. Education: Graduate of Honey Creek High School, Terre Haute, Indiana; B.S., Indiana State University, Terre Haute, Indiana. Career: Personnel Manager, Secretary-Treasurer, X-Tra Quality Laundry and Dry Cleaners; Former Positions include Physical Education Teacher, Science Teacher, Drivers Education Teacher, Kindergarten Teacher. Community Activities: Marshall Illinois Home Extension Council; Parent-Teacher Association, Marshall, Illinois, Council Member, Second Vice President; Wabash Extension Unit; Numerous Committees; Alpha Sigma Alpha Sorority, Terre Haute, Indiana; Athenaeum Club, Indiana State University. Religion: Armstrong Methodist Church, Marshall, Illinois, Women's Society of Christian Service; Philosophy Instructor, Concept Therapy Institute, San Antonio, Texas. Honors and Awards: Sportsman Award 1949, Attendant to Queen 1949, Honey Creek High School Girls Athletic Association; Class and Sorority Volleyball and Basketball Teams, Indiana State University. Address: P.O. Box 377, Cedar Crest, New Mexico 87008.■

ROBERT LEROY WENDEL

University Department Chairman. Personal: Born April 14, 1937; Son of Roy and Etna Wendel; Married Mary Jo; Father of David, Catherine. Education: B.A., University of North Carolina, 1959; M.A. 1960, Ed.D. 1967, University of Northern Colorado. Career: Chairman Department of Teacher Education, Miami University; Former Positions include High School English and Social Studies Teacher, Teacher/Advisor at Songea Secondary School (Songea, Tanganika, East Africa), Professor of Secondary and Adult Education at Northern Illinois University (DeKalb, Illinois). Organizational Memberships: Phi Delta Kappa; Adult Education Association; A.A.C.T.E.; Association of Teacher Educators. Community Activities: Community Sports Program for Children. Honors and Awards: Outstanding Man-Field of Education Award, University of Northern Colorado. Address: 505 Glenview Drive, Oxford, Ohio 45056.■

NORMA RUTH WENDELBURG

Composer, Pianist and Educator. Personal: Born March 26, 1918; Daughter of Mr. and Mrs. Henry Wendelburg (deceased). Education: B.M., Bethany College, Lindsburg, Kansas, 1943; M.M., University of Michigan, Ann Arbor, 1947; M.M. 1951, Ph.D. 1969, Eastman School of Music, Rochester, New York; Postgraduate Studies (Fulbright Award), Mozarteum (Salzburg, Austria) and Academy of Music (Vienna, Austria), 1953-55. Career: Composer, Pianist and Private Instructor; Professional Occupations College and University Teaching including Graduate Teaching and Chair Positions at Wayne State College (Wayne, Nebraska), Bethany College (Lindsborg, Kansas), University of Northern Iowa (Cedar Falls), Hardin-Simmons University (Abilene, Texas), Southwest Texas State University (San Marcos), Dallas Baptist College (Dallas, Texas). Organizational Memberships: Sigma Alpha Iota; MacDowell Colonists; American Women Composers; American Music Center; American Society of Composers, Authors and Publishers. Community Activities: New Music Performance; Festivals and Programs at Schools Served including the Organization and Implementation of Annual Festival at Hardin-Simmons University 1958-66, Copland (in person) and His Music for Area Colleges in Dallas 1975; Performer and Lecturer for Women's Clubs, Music Clubs, Teachers' Organizations and Other Groups, also at the State Fair of Texas 1959; Program Annotator for Civic Music, Abilene Symphony Orchestra (during tenure) 1958-60; Business and Professional Women; Young Women's Christian Association; Other Community Activities. Religion: Church Choir Director, Various Locations; Adult Church School Teacher, 1977-80; Served as Pianist, Committee Member (various committees). Published Works: Between 80 and 90 Compositions, including a Symphony, 2 String Quartets, Man Chamber and Choral Works, also Compositions for Solo Voice, Piano, Organ and Percussion, Some Unpublished. Honors and Awards: Recipient 2 Fulbright Awards to Austria; Scholarship from Berkshire Music Center, Lenox, Massachusetts; Scholarship from Composers' Conference, Bennington, Vermont; Resident Fellow for 3 Periods at Huntington Hartford Foundation, Los Angeles; Resident Fellow for 3 Periods at McDowell Colony; Graduate Assistantship in Research, Eastman School; "Meet the Composer" Award, Station WNYC, New York City; Sigma Alpha Iota; Listed in *Who's Who of American Women, International Who's Who of Community Service, Who's Who in the Midwest, Dictionary of International Biography, Community Leaders and Noteworthy Americans, World Who's Who of Women, Personalities of America, American Heritage Research.* Address: 2206 North Van Buren, Hutchinson, Kansas 67502.■

CHARLES WILLIAM WENDT

Professor. Personal: Born July 21, 1931; Son of Charles G. and Winnie Mae Wendt (deceased); Father of Charles Diller, John William, Elaine Anne, Cynthia Lynn. Education: B.S. Agronomy 1951, Ph.D. Soil Physics 1966, Texas A&M University; M.S. Agronomy, Texas Technological College, 1957. Military: Served in the United States Army, 1951-53, attaining the rank of First Lieutenant. Career: Professor, Associate Professor 1969-74, Texas Agriculture Experimental Station, Lubbock, Texas; Research Assistant 1953-55, Instructor of Agronomy 1957-61, Assistant Professor of Agronomy 1963-65, Texas Technological College; Research Assistant 1965-66, Research Associate 1966-69, Texas A&M University. Organizational Memberships: Soil Science of America; American Society of Plant Physiologists; Sigma Xi; Phi Kappa Phi; American Association for the Advancement of Science; 1981 British Plant Growth Regulator Group; Texas Representative and Secretary, Chairman-Elect, GPC-1 Committee on Evapotranspiration of Great Plains Agricultural Council on Plant Modification for More Efficient Water Use; Chairman Advisory Committee on Secondary Recovery Study, Ogallala Aquifer. Community Activities: Delegate to Lubbock County and State Republican Conventions, 1978; Optimist, Director 1978-79, First Vice President and Director 1981-82; Hale Center Lions Club, Secretary-Treasurer 1962; Texas Representative and Chairman to Committee on Evapotranspiration of Great Plains Agricultural Council; Chairman Advisory Board, Secondary Recovery Study, Ogallala Aquifer; Hale County Farm Bureau, Secretary-Treasurer 1954. Religion: Representative to Synod of Sun; Presbyterian Church 1976, Elder and Clerk of Session of Westminister Presbyterian Church. Published Works: Author, *Office of Technology and Assessment Report on Dryland Agriculture.* Honors and Awards: Agricultural Research Scientist of the Year Award, High Plains Research Foundation, 1982; Listed in *American Men and Women of Science, Who's Who in the South and Southwest, Who's Who in America, Who's Who in Technology Today, Personalities of America, Directory of Distinguished Americans.* Address: 4518 22nd Street, Lubbock, Texas 79407.■

CAROLYN CHARLES WENGER

Association Director, Editor. Personal: Born December 27, 1943; Daughter of Mr. and Mrs. Hiram M. Charles; Married Robert C. Education: A.B. English, Eastern Mennonite College, Harrisonburg, Virginia, 1965; M.A., University of Pennsylvania, Philadelphia; Attended A.A.S.L.H. Seminar on Administration of Historical Agencies and Museums and its Historical Publications Seminar, German Script Seminar. Career: Director, Lancaster Mennonite Historical Society; Editor, *Pennsylvania Mennonite Heritage*; Teacher, Lancaster Mennonite High School, Lancaster, Pennsylvania, 1965-67, 1968-69; Instructor in English, Eastern Mennonite College, Harrisonburg, Virginia, 1970-71. Organizational Memberships: American Association of Museums; American Association for State and Local History; Middle Atlantic Regional Archives Conference; Mennonite Historians of Eastern Pennsylvania; Friends of Germantown; Mennonite Historical Associaton of the Cumberland Valley; Juniata Mennonite Historical Society; Lancaster County Historical Society; Heritage Center of Lancaster County; Herr House Foundation; Others. Community Activities: East Petersburg Historical Society, Secretary 1975-76. Religion: East Petersburg Mennonite Church, Member; Historical Committee of Mennonite Church, Secretary 1973-81; Mennonite Historical Asssociates of the Lancaster Mennonite Historical Society, Founder 1972, Served as First Secretary. Honors and Awards: Ashton Fellowship, University of Pennsylvania, 1968. Address: 402 South State Street, Ephrata, Pennsylvania 17522.■

DONALD RAYMOND WESELY

State Senator. Personal: Born March 30, 1954; Son of Mr. and Mrs. Raymond Wesely; Married Geryl Williams, Daughter of Mr. and Mrs. David L. Williams. Education: B.A., University of Nebraska-Lincoln. Career: State Senator; Former Financial Advisor, Researcher. Community Activities: Lions Club; Mason; Rotary Club; University of Nebraska Alumni Association; United Nations Association, U.S.A.; Community Development Society of America; Nebraska Czechs of Lincoln, Board of Directors; Consumer Credit Counseling Service; Past Member, Innocents Society, Izaak Walton League, Lincoln-Lancaster County Goals and Policies Committee. Religion: Member, St. John's Catholic Church. Honors and Awards: Nebraska Water Conservation Award, 1982; Nebraska State Education Association "Friend of Education" Award, 1982; Lincoln Education Association "Friend of Education" Award, 1981-82; Outstanding Young Man of America, U.S. Jaycees, 1980; United Nations Association of Distinguished Service Award; Listed in *Men of Achievement.* Address: 903 North 66th, Lincoln, Nebraska 68505.■

DOROTHY ANNE WEST

Speech and Hearing Therapist. Personal: Born March 21, 1936; Daughter of Dr. Phillip W. West; Mother of Jeffrey West Freeman. Education: B.S. Education 1958, M.Ed. 1973, 48 Hours above Master's Degree, Louisiana State University. Career: Speech and Hearing Therapist; Assistant to Dean of Women, Louisiana State University; Compliance Consultant. Organizational Memberships: American Speech-Language-Hearing Association; Louisiana Speech and Hearing Association; Association of Teacher Educators; Phi Delta Kappa. Community Activities: Diamondhead Community Association, Board of Directors 1981; Lakeside Villa Condominium Association, Board of Directors 1978 to present, Secretary-Treasurer 1978, 1979, President 1980, 1981, 1982; Baton Rouge Mortar Board Alumnae Chapter, President 1960-62; Delta Gamma Fraternity, International Positions, Membership Study Committee 1962-64, Fraternity Scholarship Chairman 1965-59, Nominating Committee 1968-70, Province Collegiate Chairman 1970-75, Fraternity Awards Chairman 1975-79, Louisiana State University Advisory Board Chairman 1960-61, 1979-82, Pledge Advisor 1959-60, Scholarship Advisor 1978-79, Rush Consultant at Louisiana State University, University of Alabama, Tulsa University, Morehead University, Memphis State University, University of Arkansas, William Woods College, Baylor University, University of Southern Mississippi, Southern Methodist University. Religion: Sunday School Teacher, Choir Member, Building Committee, 1959-61. Honors and Awards: Silver Anchor 1968, Gold Anchor 1978, Cable Award 1980, $1000.00 Name Grant Scholarship Honoree, Delta Gamma. Address: 976 Baird Drive, Baton Rouge, Louisiana 70808.■

FRANK ELMER WEYER

Educator, Retired. Personal: Born January 14, 1890; Son of John and Elizabeth Weyer (both deceased); Married Mabelle Carey (deceased); Father of Mary Elizabeth Nutting, Dorothy Creigh (deceased), Phyllis Lucille Garriss. Education: A.B., Hastings College, 1911; M.A. 1916, Ph.D. 1940, University of Nebraska at Lincoln; Attended Columbia University 1916-17 and Summers of 1917 and 1932; Attended Stanford University, Summer 1924. Career: Principal, Newport (Nebraska) Public Schools, 1911-13; Superintendent, Atkinson (Nebraska) Public Schools, 1913-16; Professor of Education and Psychology, Kendall College, Tulsa, Oklahoma, 1917-18; Professor of Education and Dean 1918-60, Retired Dean Emeritus and Historian, Hastings College; Member of Faculty, United States Army University, Biarritz, France; Fulbright Lecturer, Ministry of Education, Pakistan, 1960-61; Visiting Professor of Education, Head of Education Department 1961-71, Professor Emeritus, Campbell College, Buies Creek, North Carolina. Organizational Memberships: Nebraska Education Association, President District 4, 1943; National Education Association, Vice President 1944; Nebraska Schoolmasters Club, President 1959; Phi Delta Kappa; North Central Association of Academic Deans, President; American Association of University Professors; North Central Association of Academic Deans, President; American Association of University Professors; Nebraska Council of Teacher Education, Past President. Community Activities: Adams County Selective Service Draft Board, 1943-60; Hastings Kiwanis Club, Vice President. Religion: Presbyterian Elder, Atkinson (Nebraska) 1915, Tulsa (Oklahoma) 1917, Hastings (Nebraska) 1919-59. Honors and Awards: LL.D. 1950, New Men's Dormitory Named Weyer Hall 1950, Alumni Citation 1975, Citation of Appreciation 1960, Hastings College; Paul Harris Award, Rotary Club, 1982. Address: 503 East 6th Street, Hastings, Nebraska 68901.■

WILLIAM POLK WHARTON, JR.

Counseling Psychologist. Personal: Born April 6, 1913; Married Lillian Andersen; Father of Christine E. (Mrs. James S. Leonard). Education: B.A., Yale University, 1934; M.A., Teacher's College, 1949; Ph.D., Columbia University, 1952. Military: Served in the United States Army, Enlisted 1940, Company Commander of The Adjutant General's School 1944-46; United States Army Reserves, Lieutenant Colonel, Retired 1973. Career: Counseling Psychologist, Independent Practice; Director of Counseling and Professor of Education, Director of The Educational Guidance Clinic, Allegheny College, Meadville, Pennsylvania, 1952-74; Advertising Research Manager and Assistant Sales Promotion Manager, Esquire Magazine, 1934-40; National Education Salesman; Associate Editor, *The Insider*. Organizational Memberships: N.V.G.A., Professional Member, 1956 to present; Fellow, Pennsylvania Psychological Association, 1961 to present; Licensed in Pennsylvania, 1973 to present; Diplomate, American Board of Professional Psychology, 1965 to present; A.P.A.; A.A.C.D.; P.P.A.; P.P.G.A.; American Association of University Professors; National Education Association; R.O.A. Community Activities: Past President, Crawford County Mental Health Center, Board of Directors 1959-60; State Memberships Chairman, American College Personnel Association, 1956-57; Editorial Board, *Psychotherapy*, 1966-68; Research Advisory Council, The Educational Development Center, Berea, Ohio, 1970-73; MH/MR Board of Crawford County, Chairman 1970-73, Member 1967-70; Committee Chairman, Drug and Alcohol Council, Crawford County, 1973-76; Delegate to Pennsylvania Mental Health Association, Crawford County Mental Health Association, 1973-76; Ethics Committee Co-Chairman, Northwest Pennsylvania Psychological Association, 1977-79. Published Works: Author of Numerous Articles in Professional Journals including "Ideas and Imagery," *A.A.S.M.I. Newsletter*, 1982; "Higher Imagery and the Readability of College History Texts," *Journal of Mental Imagery*, 1980; "The Clerk's Tale," *National Review*, 1975. Honors and Awards: Phi Beta Kappa, Yale University, 1934; Phi Delta Kappa and Kappa Beta Pi, 1949 to present; Romiett Stevens Scholar, Columbia University, 1950-51; Visiting Research Fellow, Psychotherapy Research Group, University of Wisconsin Psychiatric Institute, 1960-61; Diplomate (Counseling Psychology), American Board of Professional Psychologists, 1965 to present. Address: 415 North Main Street, Meadville, Pennsylvania 16335.■

SHARON MARIE WHEELOCK

Publisher, Columnist, Editor. Personal: Born June 23, 1938; Divorced; Mother of Robyn Renee, James Sidney, Londa Sue, Chris Marie and Lance Michael. Education: Attended Hyannis and Denver Public Schools. Career: Newspaper Publisher, Columnist and Editor; Columnist, Reporter, Manager, Owner/Manager 1976 to present, *The Grant County News*. Organizational Memberships: Nebraska Writers Guild; National Federation of Press Women; Nebraska Press Association; International Clover Poetry Association; Society of American Poets; Society of Professional Journalists. Religion: Christian. Honors and Awards: Citation from Nebraska Unicameral Legislature; Listed in *Who's Who of American Women, World Who's Who of Women, Personalities of America, Who's Who of the Midwest, International Who's Who of Intellectuals, International Book of Honor, Biographical Roll of Honor*, Others. Address: PO Box 134, Hyannis, Nebraska 69350.■

MARGARET MAIE WHELTLE

Educator, Lecturer. Personal: Born October 19, 1934; Daughter of Albert F. Sr. and Ruth Morse Wheltle (both deceased). Education: Attended Cathedral School, Baltimore, Maryland; Graduate of Notre Dame of Maryland Preparatory School, Baltimore; B.A. Commerce, Mount Saint Agnes College, Baltimore, 1956; J.D., University of Maryland School of Law, Baltimore, 1959; Study toward a C.P.A. Degree, Loyola Evening College, Baltimore, 1960-61; Attended Catholic University of America School of Theology, Washington, D.C., 1967-69; S.T.M., St. Mary's Seminary and University, Baltimore, 1972. Career: Swimming Instructor, American Red Cross, Summer 1955; Typist, Freeman and Requardt Insurance Company, Baltimore, Summers 1957, 1958; Student Assistant Director, Graduate Students Resident Hall Development Office, Catholic University, 1968, 1969; Department Director and Instructor of Theology, Instructor of Business Law, Harmony Hill High School, Watertown, South Dakota, 1969-70; Associate, Harley, Wheltle, Victor and Rosser, Law Firm, 1959-64; Assistant to the President, Director of Development, Television Production Coordinator, Mount Saint Agnes College, 1964-67; Coordinator of Religious Education for Adults and Public School Students, St. Agnes Roman Catholic Congregation, Inc., 1971-74; Theology Instructor 1978 to present, Religion Department Chairperson 1979 to present, Mount de Sales Academy; Lecturer, Theology and Law with Related Fields. Community Activities: Mount Saint Agnes College, National Alumnae President 1961-65, President's Council 7 Years; International Federation of Catholic Alumnae, Maryland Chapter Vice Governor 1964-66; Papal Volunteers for Latin America, Board of Directors of Fund Raising Project, 1 Year; Catholic University of America, Student Records Committee Observer, 1 Year; Saint William of York, Baltimore, Sodality Prefect 2 Years, Confraternity of Christian Doctrine 6 Years, Teaching Certificate 1968, Parish Planning

Team for Total Christian Education 1971, Total Parish Education Committee 1975-76, Adult Education Instructor 1976, National Catechetical Directory, Steering Committee 1975, Member 1977; St. Agnes Church, Parish Planning Team for Total Christian Education, 1971; Speaker's Bureau, Howard County Right to Life 1974-83, Archdiocese of Baltimore, Adult Education 1976 to present; Birthright of Maryland Inc., Speakers Bureau 1975-78, Vice Chairman 1975-76; St. Martin's Home for the Aged, Lecturer 1975, Ladies Auxiliary, Co-Founder and First Board Chairperson 1973-76, Board Member 1976 to present, Advisor 1977-82; Little Sisters of the Poor, Advisor 1977-82; Archdiocese Pastoral Council, Archdiocese of Baltimore Public Relations Committee 1975-76; Mount de Sales Academy, Board of Trustees 1979-82. Honors and Awards: 20 Year Appreciation Certificate for Service to Catholic Education, Archdiocese of Baltimore, 1981; Mount de Sales Academy Certificate of Appreciation, 1982; Listed in *Outstanding Young Women of America, Who's Who of American Women, Who's Who in the East, Directory of International Biography, Two Thousand Women of Achievement, Personalities of the South, International Who's Who in Community Service, Bicentennial Edition of Personalities of the South, Notable Americans of the Bicentennial Era, Community Leaders and Noteworthy Americans, Notable Americans of 1976-77, Personalities of America, World Who's Who of Women, Who's Who in American Law, Virginia, Maryland, Delaware and D.C. Legal Directory, People Who Matter, International Who's Who of Intellectuals, Men and Women of Distinction, Anglo-American Who's Who, Directory of Distinguished Americans, Five Thousand Personalities of the World, International Book of Honor.* Address: 515 Stamford Road, Baltimore, Maryland 21229.■

WALTER WHIPPLE

Computer Scientist, Professional Electrical Engineer. Personal: Born June 23, 1940; Son of Rear Admiral and Mrs. Walter Jones Whipple; Married Jean Anne Ewer; Father of Sara Marie, Kathryn Ann. Education: B.S. Engineering Science, Harvey Mudd College, 1962; M.S.E. Computer Information and Control Engineering 1974, Ph.D. Candidate 1976, University of Michigan. Career: Principal Engineer, Electrical Engineering Department, Electromagnetic Systems Division, Raytheon Company, Goleta, California, 1983 to present; Supervisor System Engineering Laboratory, Project Leader Simulation Productivity, Project Leader Weapon Computer Systems Research, Principal Investigator High Order Languages, Chairman Technical Advisory Committee for Software, General Dynamics, Pomona, California, 1978-83; Senior Electrical Engineer, Professional Services Division, Control Data Corporation, Waltham, Massachusetts, 1969-78; Engineer, Space and Information Systems Division, Raytheon Company, Sudbury, Massachusetts, 1967-69; Field Service Representative, Ordnance Department, General Electric Company, Pittsfield, Massachusetts, 1962-65; Engineering Aide, Vidya Division, Itek Corporation, Palo Alto, California, 1961; Visiting Professor of Computer Science, Harvey Mudd College. Organizational Memberships: Association for Computing Machinery, Chairman Arrowhead AdaTec, 1982-84; Institute of Electrical and Electronic Engineers, Senior Member; American Institute for Aeronautics and Astronautics, Associate Fellow; Society for Computer Simulation; National Society of Professional Engineers; Armed Forces Communication and Electronics Association; American Association of University Professors; Pascal Users Group; National Management Association; Association of Old Crows. Community Activities: University of Michigan Alumni Association; Harvey Mudd College Alumni Association, Board of Governors 1981-83; ACM Annual Conference, Boston, Simulation Session Chairman 1970; Winter Computer Simulations Conference, Sacramento, Financial and Econometric Session Chairman 1972; Harvey Mudd College Galileo Society, 1980-82. Honors and Awards: Quartermaster Award, Boy Scouts of America, 1957; Registered Professional Electrical Engineer, California; Registered Business Programmer, D.P.M.A.; Eta Kappa Nu, Honorary Fraternity for Electrical Engineering; Listed in *Who's Who in Engineering, Who's Who in the Midwest, Who's Who in California, International Who's Who in Engineering, Notable Americans.* Address: 1678 Spruce View Drive, Pomona, California 91766.■

WALTER EMMETT WHITACRE

Aerospace Engineer. Personal: Born September 28, 1931, in Detroit, Michigan; Son of Arthur James (deceased) and Reba Adeline England Whitacre; Married Donna Lee Longstreet, on November 26, 1950; Father of Donn Arthur, Kirk Alexander, Chris Martin. Education: Graduate of Central High School, Muncie, Indiana, 1949; B.S. Aeronautical Engineering 1959, M.S. Industrial Administration 1968, Purdue University; Graduate Study in Research and Technology Management, Southeastern Institute, 1980 to present. Career: Aerodynamics Engineer, Lockheed Missiles and Space Company, Sunnyvale, California, 1959-63, and Huntsville, Alabama, 1963-64; Aerospace Engineer, National Aeronautics and Space Administration, Marshall Space Flight Center, Huntsville, Alabama, 1964 to present. Organizational Memberships: American Society for Public Administration. Community Activities: Benevolent and Protective Order of the Elks, 1979 to present; Huntsville Power Squadron, Assisted in Teaching Safe Boating, Taught Seamanship Course, 1970-80; Young Men's Christian Association, Board of Management, Southeast Branch, 1965-67; Boy Scouts of America, San Jose, California, Cub Pack 360 Committee Chairman 1961-62, Cubmaster 1962-63, Committeeman 1963-64; Huntsville, Alabama, Cubmaster Pack 314 1963-64, Helped Form Cub Pack 364 1966, Formation of Boy Scout Troop 314 1964, Scoutmaster 1964-66, Formation of Troop 364 1966, Scoutmaster 1966-67, 1968 to present; Sea Explorers, Ship 364, Formation 1968, Skipper 1968-70; Ship 666, Formation 1970, Skipper 1970 to present; Order of the Arrow, Chapter Advisor Caddo Chapter 1976-80, Associate Advisor Kaskanampo Lodge 310 1979 to present, District Committee 1968 to present, District Training Staff 1969-73, Chairman Several District Camporees, Chief Event Judge Baden-Powell Jamboree 1972, Chairman Heart-of-Dixie Sea Explorer Rendezvous 1973, Scoutmaster Council Contingent to Philmont 1974; von Braun Chapter, National Eagle Scout Association, Organized 1975, Advisor 1975-76, Staff Area Wood Badge Course 1978, Director Area Wood Badge Course 1979, 1981, 1983, Scoutmaster Council Troop to National Jamboree 1981, Chairman King Neptune Sea Explorer Rendezvous 1975, 1977-83, Chairman Area IV Sailing Championship 1976, 1978-81, Chairman Area IV Sea Exploring 1978-81, Committee Member Southeast Region 1978 to present, Director Regional Sea Badge Conference 1981, 1982, Classroom Events Coordinator of T. J. Keane Rendezvous 1979-82, Chairman Sea Exploring for Southeast Region 1981 to present. Religion: Sunday School Teacher, Trinity Presbyterian Church, San Jose, California, 1962-63; Latham United Methodist Church, Huntsville, Alabama, Member 1963 to present, President of the Men's Club 1966-67, Scouting Coordinator, Chairman Scouting/Exploring Committee 1968 to present, Board of Trustees 1972-78, Grounds and Maintenance Committee 1972 to present, Administrative Board 1982 to present. Honors and Awards: Scouter's Key, Cub Scouts, 1964; Scouter's Training Award 1965, Scouter's Key 1967, Wood Badge 1970, Valley Scouter Awards (District Award of Merit) 1971, Scouter's Key 1975, William H. Spurgeon III Award 1977, Sea Badge 1978, Sea Exploring; Thanks to You Award, Huntsville Metropolitan Kiwanis Club, 1973; Liberty Bell Award, Madison County Bar Association, 1979; Youth Group Conservation Award, Alabama Environmental Quality Association, 1981; Service to Mankind Award, Huntsville Sertoma Club, 1981; National Eagle Scout Association's Scoutmaster Award for Alabama, 1982. Address: 301 Belvidere Drive, S.E., Huntsville, Alabama 35803.■

RONALD MARTIN WHITAKER

Licensed Professional Engineer. Personal: Born January 30, 1933, in Fullerton, Nebraska; Son of Leonard Bert and Margaret Mary (Seely) Whitaker; Married Janet Louise Spitz on April 12, 1955; Father of Mark David, Jeffrey Keith, Wendy Elaine. Education: Attended Central Technical College, Hastings, Nebraska; Franklin University, Columbus, Ohio; Ohio University, Lancaster, Ohio. Military: Served with the United States Army in Korea as Combat Engineer. Career: Manager, Spitz Foundry, Inc., Hastings, Nebraska, 1965-78; Plant Engineer, the Lattimer-Stevens Company, Columbus, Ohio, 1978-80; Vice President Engineering, The Lattimer-Stevens Company, Columbus, 1980 to present; Teacher, The Engineer Center, Fort Belvior, Virginia, 1953. Organizational Memberships: Registered Professional Engineer, California; Certified Manufacturing Engineer; Chairman and Senior Member, Society of Manufacturing Engineers; Senior Member, American Foundrymen's Society. Community Activities: Scoutmaster 1970-78, District Camping Director 1975-78, Order of the Arrow Advisor 1976-78, Overland Trails Council, Grand Island, Nebraska; Eagle Scout Extraordinary Minister, Roman Catholic Church; Endowment Member, National Rifle Association, Certified Marksmanship Instructor; Life Member, Nebraska Rifle and Pistol Association, Omaha, Nebraska; Life Member, National Reloaders Association; Eagle Scout and Member Eagle Scout Association; National Photographic Society; Central Ohio Council for International Visitors; Former Director, Jaycees, Hastings, Nebraska. Honors and Awards: Honorable Discharge from the United States Army, Good Conduct Medal, Combat Infantry Badge, Meritorious Unit Commendation, Sygman Rhee Citation, Korean Campaign Medal, United Nations Forces Medal. Address: 7411 Woodale Drive, Carroll, Ohio 43112.■

ELLA ELIZABETH WHITE

Administrator. Personal: Born October 20, 1948; Daughter of Mr. and Mrs. Herschel S. White, Sr. Education: B.S., Southern University, 1970; M.M., Miami University, 1971; Ph.D., Kansas State University, 1976. Career: Associate Director of Department of Federal Affairs, Research Associate in Department of Governmental Relations, Director of the Department of Governmental Relations, Howard University; Coordinator of Resource Development, ACCTION Consortium, 1976-77; Instructor and Choral Director, Alcorn State University, 1971-74. Organizational Memberships: Council for the Advancement and Support of Education, National Governmental Relations Committee; National Council for Research Administrators; American Association of University Women; American Educational Research Association; Society for Research Administrators; Association for Supervision and Curriculum Development; Delta Sigma Theta Public Service Sorority; Phi Delta Kappa; Kappa Delta Pi; Phi Delta Gamma; Mu Phi Epsilon International Music Fraternity; Prince Georges County Chapter, Links, Inc., Parliamentarian. Community Activities: Vice President, Young Women's Christian Association (Washington, D.C.), National Capital Area Board of Directors; International Student House, Board of Directors; Hannah Harrison Career School, Board of Directors. Religion: Methodist. Honors and Awards: Mu Phi Epsilon Achievement Award, 1970; Southern University Music Scholarship, 1966-70; Miami University Research Grant, 1971; Miami University Fellowship, 1970-71; Kansas State University Fellowship, 1974, 1975, 1976; Delta Sigma Theta Grant, 1970, 1971; Listed in *Outstanding Young Women of America, International Who's Who of Intellectuals, International Register of Profiles, The Biographical Roll of Honor*. Address: 3003 Van Ness Street, Northwest, Washington, D.C. 20008.■

JUDITH ANN WHITE

Educator, Theatre Director. Personal: Born November 11, 1955; Daughter of Harry C. and Jennie E. White. Education: M.S. Education, Illinois State University, 1976; M.S. Education (in progress), Western Illinois University. Career: Teacher of English; Assistant Director of Theatre; Part-time Radio Announcer, WVIK-FM, Rock Island; Part-time Radio Announcer, WQUA-AM, Moline; WEMO-FM, East Moline; Part-time Map Research Analyst, Rock Island County Voter Registration; Office of the Rock Island County Clerk, Rock Island, Illinois; Coding/File Clerk, John Deere Insurance, Moline, Illinois. Organizational Memberships: National Education Association, 1978 to present; Illinois Education Association 1978 to present, Region 18 Vice Chairperson 1972 to present, Region 18 Public Relations Chairperson 1982 to present; Classroom Teachers Association 1978 to present, Sabbatical Leave Committee 1981-83, Inservice Committee Chairperson 1980, Secretary 1981-82; Chairperson, Illinois Political Action Committee for Education, 1982-83; National Council for Teachers of English 1978 to present; Illinois Association of Teachers of English, 1978 to present; Illinois Association of Teachers of English, 1978 to present; American Association of University Women 1978 to present, Membership Committee 1980-81; Illinois Theatre Association, 1981 to present; Illinois Speech and Theatre Association, 1981 to present; Association for Supervision and Curriculum Development 1980-81, 1982 to present; American Field Service Faculty Liaison, 1979 to present; Council for Basic Education, 1978-81. Community Activities: International Platform Association, 1982 to present; The Hastings Center, 1982 to present; Associate Member, The Smithsonian Institute, 1981 to present; American Association for the Advancement of the Humanities, 1979-82; American Civil Liberties Union, 1982 to present; Illinois State University Friends of the Arts, 1976 to present; Kappa Delta Pi Honorary Education Society, 1975 to present; GESTERS, Ltd. (community theatre organization), 1981 to present; National Organization for Women, 1980 to present; Miss Blackhawk Valley Scholarship Pageant Corporation 1980 to present, Charter Member 1980, Entries Chair 1980, Corporate Vice-President 1982 to present; Tri-City Symphony Orchestra Auxiliary, 1981 to present; Metropolitan Opera Guild, 1980 to present; Illinois State University Alumni Association, 1976 to present; Community Theatre Work, 1972 to present (Genesius Guild, Quad-City Music Guild); Class of 1982 Sponsor, United Township High School, 1978, 1983; Senator Don Wooten Re-election Committee, 1980; Adlai Stevenson for Illinois Campaign Worker, 1982; Democratic Party Volunteer Worker, Rock Island County, 1982; Zeta Tau Alpha International Fraternity for Women 1974 to present, Charter Member Eta Phi Chapter 1974, House Manager, Scholarship Chairperson, Music Chairperson 1974-76; Rho-Mates of Alpha Gamma Rho Fraternity, Beta Delta Chapter 1975-76, Alumni Secretary 1975. Religion: St. Mary's, East Moline, Illinois, School Board of Education, 1980-83; St. Mary's Church Choir, 1968-80; Frequent Church Soloist at All Area Churches. Honors and Awards: Danforth Graduate Fellowship Nominee, 1976; Miss Moline, 1976; Semi-Finalist, Miss Illinois, 1976; High Academic Grade Point Averages; Quad City Music Guild Trainig Grants and Scholarship, 1974-75; Illinois General Assembly Scholarship, 1973; Sweetheart Beta Delta Chapter, Alpha Gamma Rho Fraternity, 1975; Listed in *World Who's Who of Women, Personalities of the Midwest, Personalities of America, Who's Who in the Midwest, Outstanding Young Women of America, Who's Who Among American High School Students*. Address: 3913-18 Avenue, East Moline, Illinois 61244.■

MORRIS EDWARD WHITE

Attorney. Personal: Born August 13, 1892; Married Louise Ruffin; Father of Mrs. Louise Cooke, Mrs. Frances Klay, Mrs. Martha Blalock. Education: B.S. 1913, M.A. 1915, LL.B. 1915, University of Mississippi. Military: Served in the United States Army, World War I First Officers Training Camp, Fort Logan H. Roots, Arkansas, 1917; Senior First Lieutenant, Company A, 348th Infantry, 87th Division, Camp Pike, Arkansas; Brigadier General, William F. Martin Staff, 1917; Captain, Command Headquarters Company, 348th Infantry, France, 1918, returned 1919. Career: Attorney. Organizational Memberships: American Bar Association; Florida Bar; International Bar Association; Federation of Insurance Council; International Association of Insurance Council; American College of Trial Lawyers. Community Activities: Public Recreation Board, City of Tampa; Tampa Port Authority; Board of Directors, University of Tampa; Commander USS Post #5, American Legion, 1929-30; President, Community Chest; County Defense Counsel, World War I; Board of Directors, U.S.O. Religion: Member, St. Andrews Episcopal Church. Honors and Awards: Honorary Degree, Doctor of Laws, University of Tampa. Address: 916 Golfview Avenue, Tampa, Florida 33629.■

NELSON H. WHITE

Bishop, Corporate Director, Author. Personal: Born October 29, 1938; Son of Dr. T. Robert and Edith Eyra White (mother deceased); Married Anne; Education: A.A. Electronics, San Bernardino Valley College, 1961; B.A. 1968, Graduate Studies 1968, University of the Redlands; Teaching Credentials received from the University of California at Los Angeles, 1969-70; D.Div., Light of Truth Church, 1973. Military: Served in the United States Navy as Hospital Corpsman, 1956-58. Career: Reserve Deputy Sheriff, San Bernardino County Sheriff's Motorcycle Possie, 1960-61; Electronics Inspector, 1969-70; Customs Officer, 1970; Co-Founder, Vice President, Church of Hermetic Science, 1970-73; Inspector General, Ordo Templi Astarte, 1970-73; Bishop, Corporate Director, Light of Truth Church. Organizational Memberships: Southern California Representative, Aquarian Anti-Defamation League, 1972-78; Grand Master, Temple of Truth, 1972 to present. Published Works: Author *The Best of The White Light—The Middle Years, Introduction to Magick, What and Why of Magick, Magic and the Law* (Volumes 1-5), *Index to the Spirits Given in Honourius, The Complete Exorcist, Student Reports, Ten Year Index to The White Light*; Co-Author (with Anna White) *Success in Candle Burning, Secret Magick Revealed, Lemegeton: Clavicula Salomonis, Index and Reference Volume to the Lemegeton of Solomon, Working High Magick, Selected Conjurations from the Lemegeton*; Editor, *The White Light*, 1973 to present. Honors and Awards: Listed in *Personalities of America, Personalities of the West and Midwest, International Book of Honor, Community Leaders of America, Directory of Distinguished Americans, Men of Achievement, Dictionary of International Biography, Who's Who in the West, Who's Who in California*. Address: P.O. Box 93124, Pasadena, California 91109.■

ROBERT JOSEPH WHITE

Professor. Personal: Born January 21, 1926, in Duluth, Minnesota; Married Patricia R. Murray; Father of Robert T., Christopher E., Patricia E., Michael J., Daniel J., Pamela M., James W., Richard P., Marguerite L., Ruth A. Education: B.S., University of Minnesota, 1951; M.D. with honors, Harvard University, 1953; Ph.D. Neurosurgery and Physiology, University of Minnesota, 1962. Military: Served in the United States Army in the South Pacific, 1944-45. Career: Professor, Case Western Reserve University School of Medicine; Director of the Department of Neurosurgery and the Brain Research Laboratory, Cleveland Metropolitan General Hospital; Mayo Clinic, Rochester, Minnesota, Assistant Professor to Associate Professor 1961-66, Research Associate to Neurophysiologist 1959-61, Assistant to Staff Member 1958-59; Resident, Boston Children's Hospital and Peter Bent Brigham Hospital, Boston, Massachusetts, 1954-55; Surgical Intern, Peter Bent Brigham Hospital, Boston, Massachusetts, 1953-54; First to Isolate the Brain in the Experimental Animal and Keep it Alive Outside the Body; First to Successfully Transplant and Hypothermically Store the Brain of an Experimental Animal; Introduced New Technique Employing Low Temperature Phenomena to treat Acute Spinal Cord Trauma and protect the Brain during Operation and Following Injury. Organizational Memberships: Cleveland Academy of Medicine, Board of Directors, President 1978-79; Society of University Neurosurgeons, Past President; American College of Surgeons, Officer, Committee on Trauma; Member of the Foremost Research and Surgical Societies, United States and Europe; Officer in Numerous National Organizations. Community Activities: University Hospitals, Associate Neurosurgeon; Veterans Administration Hospital, Visiting Staff; Lakewood Hospital of Greater Cleveland, Visiting

TWO THOUSAND NOTABLE AMERICANS

Staff; *Surgical Neurology*, Editor; *Resuscitation*, Editor; *The Journal of Trauma*, Editor; *Neurological Research*, Editor; Extensive Lectures in the United States, China, Europe and the Soviet Union. Religion: Recipient of Private Papal Audiences with Pope Paul VI 1972-77 and John Paul II to Discuss His Clinical and Experimental Work, 1980 and 1981. Published Works: Author of Over 400 Publications on Clinical Neurosurgery, Brain Research, Medical Ethics, and Health Care Delivery; Writings Translated into Many Languages including Russian and Chinese. Honors and Awards: Knight of Malta; Papal Knighthood; Svien Lectureship of the Mayo Clinic, 1978; L. W. Freeman Award, National Paraplegia Foundation, 1977; Alumni Research Award, Mayo Clinic; Medical Mutual Honor Award of Northeast Ohio; Honorary Doctor of Science Degrees, John Carroll University 1979, Cleveland State University; Listed in *Who's Who in the World*, *Who's Who in America*, *Who's Who in the Midwest*, *American Men of Science*, *National Registry of Prominent Americans*, *Royal Blue Book*, *Dictionary of International Biography*. Address: 2895 Lee Road, Shaker Heights, Ohio 44120.■

EMMA WHITE-REMBERT

Assistant Dean of Education. Personal: Born February 6; Daughter of Mrs. Jessie White Davis. Education: A.B., M.Ed., Florida A&M University; Ed.D., Syracuse University. Career: Assistant Dean of Education, Florida International University; Former Positions include Secondary School Supervisor, Educational Consultant, Charles E. Merrill Publishing Company, Reading Clinician, English Teacher. Organizational Memberships: International Reading Association; College Reading Association; National Council of Teachers of English. Community Activities: South Dade Young Women's Christian Association, Advisory Board; Hemispheric Women's Congress, Advisory Board; International Women's Year, State Coordinating Committee and National Delegate; Black Child Development Institute, Advisor; Delta Sigma Theta, Past Local President and Vice President. Honors and Awards: Florida Outstanding Teacher Educator, 1981; Florida Teacher Competence Award, 1964 and 1965; E.P.D.A. Fellow, Syracuse University. Address: 1318 North 13th Street, Fort Pierce, Florida 33450.■

MARVIN DELBERT WHITEHEAD

Plant Pathologist, Company Owner. Personal: Born December 18, 1917, in Paoli, Oklahoma. Son of Chester Arthur and Lola Elizabeth Whitehead (deceased); Married Verna Mae; Father of James Mark. Education: B.S. Agronomy and Botany 1939, M.S. Agronomy and Plant Pathology 1946, Oklahoma State University, Stillwater, Oklahoma; Ph.D. Plant Pathology and Mycology, University of Wisconsin, Madison, Wisconsin, 1949; Attended Institute for College Teachers, Microbiology, New York University, Niagra, 1963; Institute for College Teachers, Plant Pathology, Washington State University, 1972. Military: Served in the United States Army Air Force, 1941-46, Pacific Theatre Operations. Career: Plant Pathologist; Owner, Marvern Plant Health, Inc., "Every Living Thing Needs Health," Soil Conservation Service; Assistant Agricultural Aide, United States Department of Agriculture, Oklahoma, 1936-38; Assistant in Agronomy, Oklahoma State University, 1939-40; Senior Seed Analyst, Federal State Seed Laboratory, Alabama, 1940-42; Assistant Plant Pathology, University of Wisconsin, 1946-48; Research Fellow, University of Wisconsin, 1948-49; Assistant Professor Plant Pathology, Texas A&M University, 1949-55; Associate Professor Plant Pathology, University of Missouri, 1955-60; Professor of Plant Pathology, Edinboro State College, Pennsylvania, 1960-63; Professor Plant Pathology, Georgia Southern College, 1963-68; Professor Plant Pathology and Botany, Georgia State University, Atlanta, 1968-75. Organizational Memberships: American Association for the Advancement of Science; American Phytopathological Society, Chairman Seedborne Diseases 1950-55; Mycological Society of America; American Institute of Biological Sciences; Botanical Society of America; Crop Science Society of America; American Society of Agronomy; Official Seed Analyst for North America; Wisconsin Academy of Science; Georgia Academy of Science; Druid Hills Golf Club, Atlanta, Georgia. Religion: Baptist. Honors and Awards: Contributed 54 Journal Publications in Agronomy, Plant Pathology and Mycology; Scholarship, University of Wisconsin, Department of Plant Pathology, 1948. Address: 817 Clifton Road, Northeast, Atlanta, Georgia 30307.■

BETTY BLUE WHITEMAN

Association Executive. Personal: Born June 2, 1914; Daughter of William and Blanche Blue (deceased); Married George Dewey, Son of Elizabeth Whiteman Hagen (deceased); Mother of Dewey Dean, Peggy Louise Ganzeveld, Sharon Elizabeth Canfield, Janice Kay Louser. Education: Teaching Certificate, State Normal College, Dillon, Montana, 1937; Life Certificate, State Normal College, 1942; B.A., Western Montana College, 1976. Career: Secretary, Richey Historical Society, present; Teacher, Rural Schools Dawson and Richland Counties, Montana, 9 Years; Teacher in Richey Elementary School, Richey, Montana, 26 Years; Retired 1978. Community Activities: Secretary-Treasurer, Richey Health Center, 1975-79; Communication Chairman, American Legion Auxiliary, 1978-81; Vice President, American Legion Auxiliary, 1981-84; Vice President, Senior Citizens, 1981-84; Donates Time to Richey Historical Museum. Religion: Secretary, United Methodist Church, 1981-84; Chaplain, American Legion Auxiliary, 1978-81. Honors and Awards: Richey's Outstanding Citizen, 1974-75; Runner-up Certificate, Diana Award, 1979, Distinguished International Academy of Noble Achievement. Address: Box 218, Richey, Montana 59259.■

ORIS RAYMOND WHITLEY

Retired. Personal: Born October 24, 1912; Son of John Columbus and Ella (Blacklock) Whitley (both deceased); Married Billie V.; Father of Patricia Ball, Kay Keener, Deborah Ross. Education: B.S. (Associate), Little Rock University (now University of Arkansas at Little Rock), 1932; Attended United States Postal Service Academy, 1947; LaSalle Extension University, 1933-35; Military: Served in the United States Navy, MAM 2/C, 1944-46; United States Naval Reserve, 1946-48. Career: Manager, Kroger Company, 1933-37; Supervisor, United States Post Office, Little Rock, Arkansas, 1937-47; Postal Inspector, Pittsburgh, Pennsylvania, 1947-48; Postal Inspector, St. Louis, Missouri, 1948-56; Postal Inspector, Des Moines, Iowa, 1956-62; P.O.D. Training Officer, Firearms Coordinator, St. Louis Division, 1962-71. Organizational Memberships: President, Saline County N.A.R.F.E. 1975-78; President, Southern Region, National Association of Retired Postal Inspectors, 1982-84; Post Office Department of Civil Defense, Coordinator for the State of Iowa, 1956-62; Headed Interdivisional Postal Auditing Team, 1965-71; Special Investigator, Medical Fraud Team, Washington D.C., 1961-64. Community Activities: Special Examiner, United States Civil Service Commission, 1963-70; Commander Post #19, American Legion, 1981-83; Member Board of Directors, Kiwanis Club of Benton; Chairman, Site Advisory Council, Central Arkansas Area Agency on Aging; Member Board of Directors, Saline County Senior Adult Center, Benton, Arkansas; A.A.R.P., Saline County; Coached Girls' Softball Teams in Summer, Benton, 1974-78. Honors and Awards: Featured in Book, *Fraud* by E. J. Kahn, Jr., Harper and Row, 1973; Numerous Citations and Letters of Commendation by Post Office Department and United States Attorneys while Employed; "Bass Master," Bass Anglers Sportsman Society, 1974; Arkansas Deputy Sheriff (honorary), 1972-76; Listed in *Personalities of the South*. Address: 400 Denton Drive, Benton, Arkansas 72015.■

OSGOOD JAMES WHITTEMORE

Professor and Institute Director. Personal: Born January 24, 1919; Son of Mrs. O. J. Whittemore; Married Barbara E. Greenwood; Father of Donald O., Bonnie Turner, Julie A. Education: B.S. Ceramic Engineering 1940, Professional Ceramic Engineer 1950, Iowa State University; M.S. Ceramic Engineering, University of Washington, 1941. Career: Professor Ceramic Engineering, University of Washington; Director, Washington Mining and Mineral Resources Research Institute, present; Research Associate, Norton Company, 1946-64; Group Leader, Manhattan Project, Massachusetts Institute of Technology, 1944-46; Fellow, Mellon Institute, 1941-44. Organizational Memberships: American Ceramic Society, Vice President 1975-76, Held Numerous Other Offices 1950-82; National Institute Ceramic Engineers, President-elect, 1974-75; Society of Mining Engineers of A.I.M.E.; British Ceramic Society; Associacao Brasileira Ceramica, Brazil. Community Activities: Director, Washington Mining and Mineral Resources Research Institute, 1982 to present; Wachusett Regional High School Committee, Holden, Massachusetts, 1962-64; Advisory Committee, Town of Princeton, Massachusetts, 1959-62; Boy Scouts, Scoutmaster, Cubmaster, Others, 1942-60. Honors and Awards: Associacao Award, Associacao Brasileira Ceramica, Brasil 1982, Azevedo Award 1979; Trinks Industrial Heating Award, 1955; Admiral Earle Award, Worcester Engineering Society, 1949; Honorary Member, Tau Beta Pi 1957, Keramos, 1952. Address: 10015 Lakeshore Boulevard Northeast, Seattle, Washington 98125.■

TWO THOUSAND NOTABLE AMERICANS

EUNICE BAIRD WHITTLESEY

Legislative Liaison. Personal: Daughter of Stuart J. Baird (deceased), Mrs. Stuart J. Baird; Married Joseph Insull Whittlesey; Mother of Anne B. Donlan. Education: B.A. cum laude, State University of New York-Albany. Career: Executive Director, New York Statue of Liberty Celebration Foundation, 1982 to present; Former Legislative Liaison, 1979-1983; New York State Committee on Commerce and Economic Development, 1979-82; Organizaer and Executive Director, New York State Environmental Council Program, "Keep New York State Clean"; Consultant and Program Associate, New York State Environmental Health Services Unit, Pure Waters Division, 2 Years; Supervisor, Classified Document Library, Knolls Atomic Power Laboratory, 5 Years; Statistical Assistant, Animal Genetics Department, Cornell University; Teacher of English, Speech and Drama, New Hartford High School and Springfield Central School. Community Activities: State University of New York-Albany, National Chairman Fund Drive, Member of the Foundation; New York State Legislative Forum; State University of New York-Albany Foundation, Board Member; Schenectady County Republican Women's Club; Schenectady County Historical Society; State University of New York Agricultural and Technical College, Past Council Member 16 years; Schenectady County Volunteer Bureau, Past Board Member, Advisory Committee; Family and Child Service of Schenectady County, Past Board Member; Schenectady County Department of Social Services, Past Member and Secretary, Advisory Committee; Tuberculosis and Respiratory Disease Association, Past Board Member, Clean Air Committee; Volunteers Tie-Line, Past Organizer and Chair at Request of Governor Rockefeller; President Ford Campaign, New York Vice-Chairman; "People for Ford" State Co-Chairman; Nixon Lodge Volunteers, Schenectady County Chairman; "Housewives for Rockefeller" State Co-Chairman. Religion: Union Presbyterian Church. Honors and Awards: Distinguished Alumni Award 1979, Excellence in Service Awards 1978, State University of New York-Albany; Grant Honoree, Gift in Her Name Contributed to National Research Fund, American Association of University Women; Creator of Environmental Circle, Symbol of First Earth Day, New York State; Listed in *Who's Who in the East, Directory of Distinguished Americans.* Address: 118 Acorn Drive, Scotia, New York 12302.■

MARION RUSSELL WIEMANN, JR.

Biologist, Microscopist. Personal: Born September 7, 1929; Son of Marion R. Sr. and Verda (Peek) Wiemann; Father of Tamara Lee Wiemann. Education: B.S., Indiana University, 1959; Certificates for Professional Training in Microscopy, McCrone Research Institute, 1967, 1968, 1970, 1971. Military: Served in United States Navy in Fighter Squadron Forty-Two aboard *U.S.S. Midway*, 1951-53. Career: Principle Biologist/Microscopist, Marion Wiemann and Associates (consulting, research, and development), at present; University of Chicago, Histo-research Technician 1959, Research Assistant 1959-62, Research Technician 1962-64 and 1965-67, Senior Research Technician 1967-70, Research Technologist 1970-79; Science Teacher, Westchester Township School Corporation, 1964-66. Organizational Memberships: State Microscopical Society of Illinois, President 1970-71, Vice Preident 1969-70; Fellow, Royal Microscopial Society, 1971; Member of Numerous Other Scientific Societies During Career. Community Activities: Former Commissioner, Boy Scouts of America. Honors and Awards: Dean's Honor List, Indiana Univeristy, 1952, 1956; Scholarships, McCrone Research Institute, 1968; Boy Scouts of America, Scouter's Key 1968, Arrowhead Honor Award 1968; Society for Technical Communication, Award of Merit 1973, Distinguished Technical Communicator Awad 1974; Listed in *Personalities of America, Biographical Roll of Honor, Men of Achievement.* Address: P.O. Box E, Chesterton, Indiana 46304.■

JIMMY DON WIETHORN

Contractor, Engineer. Personal: Born March 6, 1950; Son of Mr. and Mrs. Herb Wiethorn; Married Jan Marstaller, Daughter of Mrs. W. E. Marstaller. Education: B.A. Mathematics and Physics, Baylor University, 1971; B.S. cum laude Architectural Engineering 1973, M.S. Architectural Engineering 1975, Ph.D. Architectural Engineering (in progress), University of Texas. Career: Contractor/Engineer, Former Structural Engineer. Organizational Memberships: National Society of Professional Engineers; Texas Society of Professional Engineers; Contract Specifier Institute; Associated General Contractors. Community Activities: Baylor Alumni Board of Directors, Appointed Director, 1981-82; Wiethorn Information Center, Baylor University, 1980; Baylor University Football Scoreboard, 1982; United States Congressional Advisory Board, 1983. Honors and Awards: Tau Beta Pi, National Honorary Engineering Fraternity, Chi Epsilon, National Honorary Civil Engineering Fraternity; Listed in *Biographical Roll of Honor, Men of Achievement, International Book of Honor, Who's Who in the South and Southwest, Personalities of the South.* Address: 3424 MacArthur Drive, Waco, Texas 76708.■

GUNNAR WIKSTROM, JR.

College Administrator. Personal: Born April 23, 1936; Son of Gunnar and Anna Wikstrom; Married Marilyn M.; Father of Jeffrey Alan, Daryl Lyn, Milton Curtis, Byron Kent. Education: A.B., Tufts University, 1958; B.D., Hartford Seminary, 1961; M.A., Syracuse University, 1967; Ph.D., University of Arizona, 1973. Career: Vice President Academic Affairs, College of Idaho, Caldwell, Idaho; Professor of Political Science, Buena Vista College, Storm Lake, Iowa; Former Minister in Local Churches, United Church of Christ (Congregational), in Minnesota and Washington. Organizational Memberships: American Political Science Association; Midwest Political Science Association; Tour Conference on Political Scientists; American Society for Public Administration, Siouxland Chapter. Community Activities: Storm Lake City Councilperson, Storm Lake, Iowa, 1977 to present; Parliamentarian, Buena Vista County Democratic Central Committee; Director, "Meeting Panel Needs and Problems" (program designed to help local government with long-range planning); Advisory Board, Northwest Iowa Planning and Development Commission, 1977-81. Religion: Member, Newell Congregational Church, Newell, Iowa; Standing with Northwest Association of Iowa Conference of United Church of Christ. Honors and Awards: Editor (with Nelson Webster), *Municipal Grant* 1982; Lilly Foundation Fellow, 1978-81 (faculty development grant). Address: 915 Russell Street, Storm Lake, Iowa 50588.■

J. ROSS WILCOX

Company Chief Ecologist. Personal: Born January 13, 1942; Son of Grant S. and Mary M. Wilcox (both deceased); Married Janice B.; Father of Scott, Laurie. Education: B.A. Biology, Kalamazoo College, 1963; M.S. Oceanography 1968, Ph.D. Oceanography 1972, University of Rhode Island. Career: Chief Ecologist, Florida Power and Light Company; Former Positions include Biologist with the Harbor Branch Foundation (Fort Pierce, Florida), and Graduate Assistant at the University of Rhode Island. Organizational Memberships: American Association for the Advancement of Science; American Society Limnology and Oceanography; Society of Sigma Xi; Ecological Society of America. Honors and Awards: Coordinator, Workshop on Cycling and Effects of Toxic Substances, Carmel, California, sponsored by Electric Power Research Institute, 1980; Loaned Employee, Electric Power Research Institute, 1980-81; Expert Testimony, Florida Power and Light Company, St. Lucie Nuclear Power Plant, State Certification Proceedings, 1980; Member Biological Subcommittee, Edison Electric Institute, 1979-80; Consultant, Sea Turtle Recovery Team, National Marine Fisheries Service, 1978 to present; Member Task Force on Environment, Electric Power Research Institute, 1977-79; Participant, Nuclear Power Generation and the Environment, University of Florida, 1976; Delegate U.S.A., F.A.O. Technical Conference on Aquaculture, Kyoto, Japan, 1976; Referee, Chesapeake Science, 1975, 1978, 1979; Book Reviewer, Science Books, American Association for the Advancement of Science, 1971-79; Treasurer, Graduate Student Association, University of Rhode Island, 1968; National Defense Education Act (N.D.E.A.) Title IV Scholarship, University of Rhode Island, 1964-67. Address: 9008 Gardens Glen Circle, Palm Beach Gardens, Florida 33410.■

JOHN HAZARD WILDMAN

Professor Emeritus. Personal: Born January 22, 1911; Son of Alexander James and Rachel Greene Whitaker Wildman (both deceased). Education: Ph.B. 1933, M.A. 1934, Ph.D. 1937, Brown University. Military: Served in the United States Army Air Force as T/Sergeant in Intelligence, 1942-45. Career: Professor Emeritus of English, Instructor in English 1940-46, Assistant Professor of English 1946-51, Associate Professor of English 1951-58, Professor of English 1958-80, Louisiana State University; Instructor in English, Brown University, 1940-46. Organizational Memberships: Modern Language Association of America; American Association of University Professors, Former Secretary-Treasurer and President Louisiana State University Chapter; South Central Modern Language Association. Community Activities: Cardinal Newman College Associate, 1982 to present; Speaker to Clubs and Other Organizations. Religion: Active in Newman Club, Catholic Student Center, Louisiana State University, Baton Rouge, 1946-62. Honors and Awards: Phi Beta Kappa, Brown University, 1933.■

WILLIAM EDWARD WILKINSON

Director of Health Nursing, Occupational Health Management Consultant. Personal: Born September 9, 1953; Son of William E. Wilkinson; Married Connie Sue. Education: B.S.N., Northwestern University, 1977; M.P.H., Tulane University, 1978; Dr.P.H., University of Texas, 1982. Career: Director Occupational

Health Nursing, University of Washington-Seattle; Former Positions include Occupational Health Management Consultant, University Faculty Member, Emergency Room Nurse, Operating Room Nurse. Organizational Memberships: American Public Health Association; American Industrial Hygiene Association; American Nurses Association; American Association of Occupational Health Nurses; Society for Occupational and Environmental Health. Community Activities: American Cancer Society; American Red Cross; Social Activities Chairman, Tulane University; Blood Drive Chairman, Tulane University; Boy Scouts of America; Karate Instruction (Black Belt). Religion: Presbyterian. Honors and Awards: National Institute for Occupational Safety and Health Educational Resource Center Traineeship Recipient; University of Texas at Houston, School of Public Health, 1979-82; Professional Nurse Traineeship Grant, Tulane University, New Orleans, Louisiana, 1977-78; Professional Nurse Traineeship Grant, Northwestern State University, Shreveport, Louisiana, 1976-77; Sigma Alpha Chi, Life Member; Listed in *Outstanding Young Men in America*, 1980. Address: 15029 66th Court, Northeast, Bothell, Washington 98011.■

ANNE O. WILLARD

Physical Therapist. Personal: Born August 4, 1916, in Cleveland, Ohio; Daughter of Rt. Reverend John Lorraine and Olga Carolina Wellington Oldham. Education: B.A., Rollins College, 1940; Attended the University of Wisconsin, School of Physical Therapy, 1942-45; Undertook Postgraduate Studies, University of Pennsylvania, 1959; Ph.D., Hamilton State University, 1974; Continuing Education Programs to date. Military: Served as First Lieutenant, United States Army, 1940-46; Retired Captain of the Reserves. Career: Chief Physical Therapist, Rex Hospital, Raleigh, North Carolina, 1949-51; Chief Physical Therapist, Lawton Memorial, Lawton, Oklahoma, 1951-53; Chief Physical Therapist, National Polio Foundation, Buffalo, New York, 1953-54; Head Physical Therapist, 17 Counties, State Crippled Childrens Service, State of Alabama, 1954-57; Therapist for Special Services, Cerebral Palsy Society, Fort Worth, Texas, 1957-60; Organized and Directed Physical Therapy Department, Crippled Childrens Society, Mineral Wells, Texas, 1960-61; Organized and Directed Physical Therapy Department, Crippled Childrens Society, Mineral Wells, Texas, 1960-61; Organized and Directed Physical Therapy Department, Flow Memorial Hospital, 1961-71; Organized and Directed Physical Therapy Department, Collin Memorial Hospital, McKinney, Texas, 1971 to present; Private Practice, 1957 to present; Relief Chief Therapist, St. Joseph's Hospital, Paris, Texas. Organizational Memberships: American Physical Therapy Association; Lancaster-Pittard Professional Association, Advisor-Consultant; Business and Professional Women's Club, Finance Chairman 1977, President-elect 1978-79, President 1979-80; International Platform Association. Community Activities: Alpha Phi; National Wildlife Federation; Order of Eastern Star, Officer 7 Years; Soroptimist, Denton Chapter, Vice President, President, Chief Delegate, Chairman of Ways and Means Committee; St. Monica's Episcopal Church Guild, Past President; Rainbow Girls, Board of Directors; Tarrant and Collin Counties Humane Societies, Past President Collin County Humane Society. Religion: Episcopalian. Honors and Awards: Listed in *World Who's Who of Women*, *Who's Who of American Women*, *Who's Who of Women*, *Who's Who of the South and Southwest*, *International Who's Who of Intellectuals*, *Who's Who in the United States*, *Personalities of the South*, *Royal Blue Book*, *Notable Americans*, *International Register of Profiles*, *Directory of International Biography*, *National Social Directory*, *Two Thousand Women of Achievement*, *I.B.A. Yearbook and Biographical Directory* (1979-80). Address: P.O. Box 703, McKinney, Texas 75069.■

ARNOLD LEE WILLEMS

Professor of Curriculum and Instruction, Department Head. Personal: Born September 16, 1942; Son of Abe and Ruth Willems; Married Wanda Lucille; Father of Emily Marie, David Arnold. Education: B.A., Goshen College, 1964; M.A., Western Michigan University, 1968; Ed.D., Indiana University, 1971. Career: Head Department of Curriculum and Instruction and Professor of Curriculum and Instruction, University of Wyoming, Laramie, Wyoming; Elementary School Teacher, 1964-69; Associate Instructor, Indiana University, 1970-71. Organizational Memberships: Phi Delta Kappa; Kappa Delta Pi; Association for Supervision and Curriculum Development; Association of Teacher Educators; National Council of Teachers of English; National Science Teachers Association; International Reading Association; National Education Association. Community Activities: High Plains Harriers; Little League Umpire. Religion: Member, United Presbyterian Church. Honors and Awards: Indiana University School of Education Fellowship, 1970-71; Meritorious Classroom Teaching Award, University of Wyoming, 1981; Listed in *Outstanding Educators of America*, *Who's Who in the West*, *Personalities of America*, *Community Leaders of America*. Address: 1810 Barratt, Laramie, Wyoming 82070.■

MARK HINCKLEY WILLES

Executive Vice President and Chief Financial Officer. Personal: Born July 16, 1941; Son of Joseph and Ruth Willes; Married Laura Fayone; Father of Wendy Anne, Susan Kay, Keith Mark, Stephen Joseph and Matthew Bryant. Education: A.B., Columbia College, 1963; Ph.D, Columbia Graduate School of Business, 1967. Career: Executive Vice President and Chief Financial Officer; President, Federal Reserve Bank of Minneapolis, 1977-80; Federal Reserve Bank of Philadelphia: First Vice President, 1980; Vice President and Director of Research, 1971; Director of Research, 1970; Senior Economist, 1969; Economist, Consulting Economist, 1967-69; Economic Advisor to Special Assistant to the President of the United States for Consumer Affairs, Member, Cost of Living Council, 1971; Assistant Professor of Finance and Visiting Lecturer, Wharton School of Finance and Commerce, University of Pennsylvania, 1967-71; Faculty, Graduate School of Banking, University of Wisconsin, 1970 to present; Research Economist, Committee on Banking and Currency, 1966; Instructor in Finance, Columbia University Graduate School of Business, 1965. Organizational Memberships: Member Board of Directors: Northwestern National Bank of Minneapolis, The Toro Company, Gelco Corporation, InterStudy; Member: National Advisory Council, Brigham Young University, 1978 to present; Economic Advisory Board, Columbia University, 1979 to present. Religion: Mormon, Church of Jesus Christ of Latter Day Saints; President, Minneapolis Minnesota Stake, 1979 to present. Honors and Awards: Spokesperson for a New Economic Theory Known as "Rational Expectations." Address: 555 North Pineview Lane, Plymouth, Minnesota 55441.■

AVON NYANZA WILLIAMS, JR.

Attorney, Senator. Personal: Born December 22, 1921, in Knoxville, Tennessee; Son of Avon Nyanza Sr. and Carrie Belle Williams (both deceased); Married Joan Marie Bontemps; Father of Avon Nyanza Williams III, Wendy Janette Williams. Education: B.A., Johnson C. Smith University, 1940; LL.B. 1947, LL.M. 1948, Boston University School of Law. Military: Served in United States Army Reserve, attaining rank of Lieutenant Colonel, JAGC (Retired). Career: Attorney; Admitted to Massachusetts Bar 1948, Tennessee Bar 1948; Admitted to Practice United States Court of Appeals Sixth Circuit 1953, United States Military Appeals 1956, Supreme Court of the United States 1963; General Practice of Law, Knoxville, Tennessee, 1949-53; General Practice in Association with Honorable Z. Alexander Looby, Nashville, Tennessee, 1953-69; Private Practice, Nashville, 1969 to present. Organizational Memberships: American Bar Association; American Judicature Society; Nashville Bar Association; Tennessee Bar Association; Former Member, Davidson County Trial Lawyers Association. Community Activities: Senator, 19th District of Tennessee, 1968 to present; Delegate, National Democratic Convention, 1972; Tennessee Voters Council, Board of Directors 1962 to present, Founding Member 1962, General Chairman 1966 to date; Davidson County Independent Political Council, Board of Directors 1962 to present, Founding Member 1962, Former President 1962-66; Member, State Democratic Steering Committee, 1964; Omega Psi Phi; Sigma Pi Phi; Davidson County Citizens for TVA, 1953; Board of Directors, Family and Children's Service, 1956-1960; Davidson County Anti-Tuberculosis Association, 1962-66; Executive Committee, Nashville Branch National Association for the Advancement of Colored People, 1953 to date; Appeals and Review Committee, Meharry Medical College, 1970 to present; Board of Directors, Southern Regional Council, 1968 to present. Published Works: Author of "Nashville's Greatest Challenge," *Nashville Magazine*, 1975; "Does a Child Have a Right Not to be Brainwashed by Adults?" *Peabody Journal of Education*, 1973; "Negro Subculture, The White Man's Problem," *New South* 1961, republished under title "Race Relations — A Community Problem," *Negro Digest* 1962. Honors and Awards: Citation for Achievement in Civil Rights Cases, East Nashville Community Club, 1957; Outstanding Citizen of the Year, Omega Psi Phi Fraternity, 1963; Citation for Outstanding Service in Civil Rights, Nashville Branch, National Association for the Advancement of Colored People, 1965; Award for Meritorious Service, General Alumni Association, Johnson C. Smith University, 1967; Certificate of Merit, Agora Assembly, 1968; Citizen of the Year Award, Nashville Frontiers Club, 1972; Citizen of the Year Award for Achievements in Civil Rights, Grand Lodge, FA and M of Tennessee, Prince Hall Masons, 1972; Award for Dedicated Religious Service, St. Andrews Presbyterian Church, 1976; Recognition Award for Services to Community and to Tennessee State University

(TSU), TSU Women's Association, 1976; Distinguished Achievement Award for Legal Leadership, Humanistic Concerns in Education and Civil Rights, TSU, 1977; Legislator of the Year Award, Black Caucus of Tennessee General Assembly, 1978; M. G. Ferguson Distinguished Community Service Award, Black Expo, 1979; Public Service Award, Tau Lambda Chapter, Alpha Phi Alpha Fraternity, 1981; Martin Luther King Jr. 53rd Birthday Award, Interdenominational Ministers Fellowship of Nashville and Vicinity, 1982. Address: 1818 Morena Street, Nashville, Tennessee 37208.■

BARBARA ELIZABETH WOMACK WILLIAMS

Guidance and Family Counselor. Personal: Born February 4, 1938; Daughter of W.A. Womack; Married Leon Franklin Williams; Mother of Mark Franklin, Alice Kathleen, Stephanie Todd. Education: B.A. 1966, M.Ed. 1968 American University; Postgraduate Studies, University of Virginia and Virginia Polytechnical Institute and State University. Guidance Counselor, Hidden Valley Junior High School, Roanoke, Virginia; Licensed Family and Guidance Counselor, Military and Security Redstone Arsenal, Huntsville, Alabama, 1956-57; Foreign Agriculture Section, United States Department of Agriculture, Washington, D.C., 1968-72; Teacher of English, Humanities and Psychology, Glenvar High School, Roanoke, Virginia, 1968-72. Organizational Memberships: Life Member, National Educational Association; Corresponding Secretary, National Council Teachers of English; Virginia Educational Association; Faculty Representative/Chairman Professional Services Committee, Roanoke County Educational Association; Roanoke Valley Mental Health Association; Roanoke Area Professional and Guidance Association. Community Activities: Party Founder, Farmingdale Civic League. Religion: Member, Windsor Hills United Methodist Church; Member of Official Board, Farley Methodist Church, Huntsville, Alabama. Honors and Awards: Madison County Leadership Award, Elks Club, 1966; Americanism Award, National Sojourners, 1966; Daughters of the American Revolution Award, 1966. Address: 5556 McVitty Road, Southwest, Roanoke, Virginia 24018.■

CHARLES VERNON WILLIAMS III

Corporate Manager. Personal: Born May 26, 1940; Son of Mr. and Mrs. Charles V. Williams, Jr.; Married Marie C., Daughter of Mr. and Mrs. Tenes Lespinasse; Father of Joann, Monique, Michelle C. Education: Modern School of Photography, 1975; A.A.S., Community College of the Air Force, 1977; B.G.S., University of Nebraska, 1974; M.S., Central Michigan University, 1977. Military: Served in the United States Air Force, Master Sergeant, 1958-80. Career: Manager, Mead Reinsurance Corporation, present; Former Professional Occupation as Superintendent, Budget and Logistics, Headquarters (AFLC) Air Force Logistics Command. Organizational Memberships: American Management Association; Society for the Advancement of Management; Miami Valley Management Association; Association of Information Systems Professionals, Board Member; Southwestern Ohio Word Processing and Administrative Support; International Pilots Association; NCO Academy Graduates Association, Vice President, 1978. Community Activities: Associate Editor, Ohio Prince Hall Grand Lodge Publication, *The Lamp*. Religion: Church Administrator, 1958-80. Honors and Awards: Bronze Star Medal, 1969; Meritorious Service Ribbon, 1980; Air Force Commendation Medal, 1978; Word Processing Achievement Award, 1981; 33rd Degree Mason, 1974; Listed in *Who's Who in America, Men of Achievement, Who's Who in Industry and Finance, International Register of Profiles*. Address: 2174 Malvern Avenue, Dayton, Ohio 45406.■

DAVID RUSSELL WILLIAMS

Professor, Administrator. Personal: Born October 21, 1932; Son of Mr. and Mrs. Russell Williams; Married Elsa Buhlmann. Education: A.B. 1954, M.A. 1956, Columbia University; Ph.D., University of Rochester, Eastman School of Music, 1965. Military: Served in the United States Army, attaining the rank of Sergeant First Class, Chief Instructor, Band Training School, Fort Chaffee, Arkansas, 1957-59. Career: Professor and Chairman, Music Department, Memphis State University; Eastman School of Music, Rochester, New York, Associate Professor of Theory 1965-80, Opera Coach 1962-65; Director of Music, Windham College, Putney, Vermont, 1959-62. Organizational Memberships: Secretary, College Music Society, 1973-83; President, Memphis Alumni Chapter, Phi Beta Kappa, 1983; Secretary, Region 8, National Association of Schools of Music, 1983; Secretary, Tennessee Association of Music Executives in Colleges and Universities, 1981-83; New York State Chairman of Theory and Composition, Music Teachers National Association, 1971-74. Community Activities: Rochester Philharmonic Orchestra, Secretary, Board of Directors, 1975-78; Rochester Chamber Orchestra, Board of Directors 1974-80, Vice President; Opera Theatre of Rochester, President Board of Directors 1973-74, Vice President 1974-76, Chairman Patron Committee; Board of Directors, Rochester Community Players, 1969-74; Chairman, Board of Directors, American Ritual Theatre, Rochester, New York, 1978-81; Member Executive Board, Opera Memphis, 1980; Member Board of Sponsors, Mid-South Regional Board of Directors, Memphis Youth Symphony, Board of Directors 1983 to present; Memphis Symphony League; Ballet Guild; Tennesseans for the Arts; Southeastern Composers League. Published Works: Two Books, One Article, One Record Album, Five Musical Compositions, Editing of Newsletters and Columns, Numerous Book Reviews. Honors and Awards: Eastman School of Music Publication Award, 1970; Edward Benjamin Contest for Tranquil Music, 1963; American Society of Composers, Authors and Publishers; Bibliotheque Internationale de Musique Contemporaine, Paris, France; Honorary Member, Phi Mu Alpha; Honorary Member, Phi Kappa Lambda, Liberal Arts Honor Society; Black Student Association, Memphis State University. Address: 295 Central Park West, #2, Memphis, Tennessee 38111.■

RICHARD LEE WILLIAMS, SR.

Business Executive and Psychologist. Personal: Born September 13, 1943; Son of C. L. and Julie Williams; Father of Richard Lee Jr., Tracey Lee, Michael Marshall. Education: B.A. Psychology, University of West Florida, 1969; M.S. Psychology 1972, Ph.D. Psychology 1979, University of Southern Mississippi. Military: Served in the United States Army, 1961-64, as Sgt-E5, Honorable Discharge 1961-64. Career: Systems and Test Engineer (Nuclear), Nuclear Test Engineer, Westinghouse, Pensacola, Florida; Nuclear Test Technician, Litton Industries, Pascagoula, Mississippi. Organizational Memberships: America Psychological Association; Oklahoma Psychological Association; Tulsa Psychological Association; Southwest Psychological Association; American Academy of Behavioral Medicine, Diplomate. Community Activities: Chairman of the Board, Rainbow Foundation, Inc. Religion: Methodist. Honors and Awards: *Directory of Distinguished Americans, Who's Who in Finance and Industry, Biographical Roll of Honor, Personalities of America, Men of Achievement, Who's Who in Frontier Science and Technology, Who's Who in the South and Southwest*. Address: 425½ East 4th, Claremore, Oklahoma 74017.■

W. R. WILLIAMS

Accounting Executive. Personal: Born March 15, 1930; Son of Eddie S. and Edna Rashall Williams (both deceased); Father of Julie Marie, Janet Lynn. Education: B.S. with high honors, University of Arkansas, 1956. Military: Served in the United States Air Force, 1948-52. Career: Peat, Marwick, Mitchell & Co., Personnel Committee, Petroleum Committee; Managing Partner, Tulsa Office, Peat, Marwick, Mitchell & Co, 1970-74; Partner, 1968 to present; Continental Europe Firm's Operating Committee; Senior Partner, German Practice, 1974-78; Board of Directors, Operating Committee, Vice Chairman, Peat, Marwick, Mitchell & Co. Organizational Memberships: Oklahoma State Board of Public Accountancy (past chairman; past secretary); American Institute of Certified Public Accountants, 1959 to present; Oklahoma Society of Certified Public Accountants (past member, board of directors; past president, member 1958-74, Tulsa Chapter); National Association of Accountants, 1973 to present; American Accounting Association, 1973 to present; National Association of State Boards of Accountancy, 1969-74; Downtown Optimist Club of Tulsa (past first vice president; member, 1970-74); Tulsa University Accounting Conference (past general chairman; member, 1970-74) Petroleum Society of Accountants, 1969-74. Community Activities: University of Arkansas Alumni Association (life member); Frankfurt International School, Germany (chairman); United States Chamber of Commerce (past member); American Chamber of Commerce in West Germany, 1974-78; Tulsa Chamber of Commerce, 1970-74; Houston Grand Opera Association (past governing board; member, 1979 to present); Forum Club of Houston, 1981 to present; Tulsa Press Club, 1970-74; Southern Hills Country Club, 1970-74; Tulsa Club, 1970-74; Summit Club, 1969-74; Frankfurt Golf Club, 1973-

74; Houston Club, 1978 to present; Houston Athletic Club, 1978 to present; Houston Racquet Club, 1979 to present; The Houstonian, 1980 to present; Brae Burn Country Club, 1980 to present; Lakeside Country Club, 1982 to present; Toastmasters International; Magic Empire Toastmasters Club, Tulsa, Oklahoma; Oklahoma State University Development Council of Tulsa County, Oklahoma (charter member, 1973-74). Honors and Awards: Accountant of the Year, Alpha Iota Chapter, Beta Alpha Psi, University of Arkansas, 1978, 1980; Frankfurt International School became First Institution in the World to be Jointly Accredited by Both European Council of International Schools and Middle State Association in the United States while under Chairmanship of Mr. Williams; Beta Gamma Sigma; Beta Alpha Psi; Alpha Kappa Psi. Address: 5555 Del Monte Drive #305, Houston, Texas 77056.∎

BEVERLY R. WILLISCROFT

Attorney-at-Law, Real Estate Broker, Business Co-Owner. Personal: Born February 24, 1945; Daughter of Paul and Gladys Williscroft. Education: B.A. Music, Southern California College, Costa Mesa, California, 1967; Additional Studies at San Jose State University; J.D., John F. Kennedy University, School of Law, Orinda, California, 1977. Career: Attorney-at-Law; Real Estate Broker; Co-Owner, Secretarial Service; Elementary School Teacher, 1968-72; Instructor for Real Estate Examination Preparation, 1979-80; Frequent Lecturer to Real Estate and Lending Professionals, Students, and Professional Organizations; Public Speaking and Personal Growth Teacher (especially to businesswomen); Bar Examination Grader, 1979 to present. Organizational Memberships: California Women Lawyers; Contra Costa County Bar Association; Contra County Bar Association; Contra Costa Barristers; American Bar Association; California State Bar. Community Activities: Redevelopment Advisory Committee, City of Concord, 1984-86; Community Development Advisory Committee, City of Concord, 1981-83; Status of Women Committee, City of Concord, 1979-81; Co-Chairperson, Longshore Morning Forum, Fundraising Breakfast Club for City Councilwoman Diane Longshore 1980 to present; Soroptomists International of Concord, Member 1979-82, Financial Secretary 1980-81; Contra Costa Musical Theatre, Inc., Performer 1977 to present, Vice President-Production Manager 1981-82; Mount Diablo Council, Boy Scouts of America, Executive Board, 1981 to present; Mount Diablo Health Care Foundation, Board of Trustees 1981-83; 337 Club, Mt. Diablo; Health Care Foundation, Director 1982 to present; National Organization for Women, 1977 to present; National Women's Political Caucus, 1979 to present; Member (Sponsor) American Red Cross, Mount Diablo Chapter, 1981 to present; Concord Chamber of Commerce, Board of Directors 1981 to present, Chairperson Legislative Affairs Committee, 1982-83; Todos Santos Business and Professional Women, Co-Founder and Charter First Vice President 1979-81, Third Vice President 1981-82, Public Relations Chairperson 1982-83, President 1983-84. Honors and Awards: Woman of Achievement, Todos Santos Business and Professional Women, 1980; Several Outstanding Achievement Awards from Bay Valley District of Business and Professional Women; Community Leadership Award, Chamber of Commerce, 1982. Address: 2108 Grant Street, Concord, California 94520.∎

ERNEST DWIGHT WILLOUGHBY

Government Official. Personal: Born March 6, 1932, in Flint, Michigan; Son of Ernest Clyde and Marion Amelia (Fletcher) Willoughby; Married Ann Harper on June 11, 1960; Father of Ernest Frank. Education: B.S., Wayne State University, Detroit, 1955; Postgraduate Studies in Humanities, 1960-65. Military: Served in the United States Army, Germany, 1955-57. Career: Various Positions Occupational Research, Michigan Employment Security Commission, Detroit, 1959 to present; Manager Occupational Research, 1975-82; Member, Federal Occupational Analysis Coordinating Committee, 1980-82; Michigan Occupational Information Coordinating Committee Advisory Committee on Career Information for the Disabled; United Nations Technical Expert Occupational Research, Tanzania and Ethiopia, 1972-73; International Manpower Development Advisor, United States Agency for International Development, Jamaica, 1982; Lecturer in Field; Career-job Placement Service Advisory Board, Detroit Public Schools, 1977-80; Career Information Consultant to Prisons, Community Agencies and Other School Systems; Expert in Occupations in American Economy, Primarily Metalworking; Research in Computer-Assisted Analysis and Classification of Work Organization. Organizational Memberships: American Management Association; International Personnel Management Association; Mensa; The Econometric Society, 1975. Religion: Episcopalian; Chairperson, Michigan Combined Episcopal Services Appeal, 1972. Published Works: Author, Occupational Analysis and Classification, Tanzania, 1975; Many Occupational Definitions in the Metal, Chemical, Woodworking Industries, Dictionary of Occupational Titles, 1965, 1977. Honors and Awards: Recognized for Career Education Work, Michigan Legislative Resolution, 1977; Listed in *Who's Who in Finance and Industry, Who's Who in the Midwest, The Directory of Distinguished Americans, Personalities of America, Men of Achievement, Dictionary of International Biography, Who's Who in the World.* Address: 15945 Curtis Avenue, Detroit, Michigan 48235.∎

DON B. WILMETH

University Professor and Department Chairman. Personal: Born December 15, 1939; Son of P. D. and Pauline Wilmeth; Married Judy Eslie; Father of Michael Tyler. Education: B.A., Abilene Christian University, 1961; M.A., University of Arkansas, 1962; Ph.D., University of Illinois, 1964; M.A. ad eundem, Brown University, 1970; Additional Studies at Cornell University and University of Colorado. Career: Chairman Department of Theatre Arts, Professor Theatre Arts and English, Brown University; Former Position as Chairman Department of Drama, Eastern New Mexico University. Organizational Memberships: American Society for Theatre Research, Executive Board 1977-79, 1980-83; Theatre Library Association, Vice President 1981 to present; Institute for American Theatre Studies, Board of Directors 1981 to present; Society for the Advancement of Education, Board of Trustees 1977 to present; American Theatre Association, Chairperson Publications 1975-77; New England Theatre Conference; International Federation for Theatre Research; University/College Theatre Association, Publications Committee 1981 to present. Community Activities: Board of Directors, Providence Players, 1972-74; Consultant, Core Collection for College Libraries, 1970-75; Chairperson, George Freedley and TLA Book Award Committee 1973 to present; Theatre Editor, *Intellect Magazine* and *USA Today*, 1974-80; Book Review Editor, *The Theatre Journal*, 1978-80; Advisory Editor, *Nineteenth-Century Theatre Research*, 1977 to present; Advisory Editor, *Modern Language Studies*, 1980 to present; Consultant, *Theatre Dictionary*, 1975 to present; Advisory Board, East Lynn Theatre Company, Jersey City, New Jersey, 1981 to present; Special Issues Committee, American Society for Theatre Research, 1980 to present; Chairperson Membership Committee, A.S.T.R., 1978 to present. Published Works: Author *The American Stage to World War I 1978, George Frederick Cooke: Michiavel of the Stage 1980, American and English Popular Entertainment 1980, The Language of American Popular Entertainment 1981, Variety Entertainment and Outdoor Amusements 1982, Plays by William Gillette 1983;* Contributor to Six Other Books and *World Book Encyclopedia* (9 entries); Essays Published in *Theatre Survey, Intellect, Theatre Notebook, Theatre Documentation, Journal of the Illinois Historical Journal, Theatre Journal, Educational Theatre Journal, USA Today, Quarterly Journal of Speech;* Book Reviewer for *Providence Journal, Nineteenth-Century Theatre Research,* Others. Honors and Awards: Alpha Psi Omega, 1959; Alpha Chi Scholastic Society, 1960; Phi Kappa Phi, 1974; Phi Beta Kappa, 1977; Wriston Grant, Brown University, 1981; Barnard Hewitt Theatre History Award, American Theatre Association, for *George Frederick Cooke* 1980; Guggenheim Fellowship, 1982. Address: 525 Hope Street, Providence, Rhode Island 02906.∎

ARTHUR JESS WILSON

Clinical Psychologist. Personal: Born October 25, 1920; Married Lillian Wilson; Father of Warren David, Anton Francis. Education: B.S. 1935, M.A. 1949, Ph.D. 1961, New York University; LL.B., Saint Lawrence University, 1940; J.D., Brooklyn Law School, 1967. Served in the United States Navy, 1943-45 as a Classification Specialist. Career: Clinical Psychologist in Private Practice; Former Positions Include High School Teacher; College Instructor in Psychology; Special University Lecturer in Rehabilitation Medicine; High School Principal; Municipal Director of Adult Education; State Supervisor of Rehabilitation; Psychiatric Hospital Staff Clinical Psychologist; Director of New York State Drug Abuse Rehabilitation Center; Medical Center Director of Rehabilitation; Personnel Executive in Private Industry; Author of Books and Articles. Organizational Memberships: New York Academy of Sciences; American Psychological Association; New York State Psychological Association; New York Society of Clinical Psychologists; Westchester County (New York) Psychological Association; American Association of School Administrators. Community Activities: Public Lecturer in Psychology, Education, Rehabilitation; Consulting Psychologist, New York State Education Department; Consultant, United States Department of Health and Human Services; Consulted by Eleanor Roosevelt on Rehabilitation; Presented Free Illustrated Slide-Lectures to Senior Citizens on World Travels to the Middle East, People's Republic of China; Professional Services as Psychological Consultant Contributed to North Broward County Community Mental Health Board, Florida; Advisory Boards of Rehabilitation Agencies; Participant in Numerous Professional Workshops in Psychology and Rehabilitation. Published Works: Contributor to Professional Journals in Psychology, Education, Law and Rehabilitation;

Author of Article "Law and Precedent", *Montana Law Review*. Honors and Awards: Complimented by Justice Felix Frankfurter of the United States Supreme Court on Article "Law and Precedent" (see above under published works); Honorary Membership, International Mark Twain Society; Honored as Westchester, New York, Author, Westchester County Historical Society; Kappa Delta Pi; Phi Delta Kappa; Epsilon Pi Tau; Called a Pioneer by New York State Narcotic Addiction Control Commission for Launching Governor Rockefeller's Drug Abuse Rehabilitation Program; Listed in *Who's Who in the East, Who's Who in American Education, Dictionary of International Biography*. Address: 4121 Northwest 88th Avenue, Coral Springs, Florida 33065.■

CHARLES WILLIAM WILSON

Medical Doctor. Personal: Born August 12, 1916; Son of Jacob Resor and Estella Cherrie Wilson (both deceased); Married Francis Preshia Stephenson; Father of Charles William II, Walter Stephen, Cherrie, James Robin. Education: B.A., University of Wichita, 1938; M.D., University of Kansas School of Medicine, 1942; Intern, Harper Hospital, Detroit, Michigan, 1942-43; Resident Physician in Neurology, University Hospitals, Iowa City, Iowa, 1946-47; Resident Physician in Psychiatry, Central State Hospital, Norman, Oklahoma, 1964-67. Military: Served in the United States Naval Reserves on Active Duty, 1943-46, as Lieutenant, Medical Corps. Career: Medical Doctor specializing in Psychiatry, Medical Hypnosis, 25 Years Clinical Research in the Function and Treatment of the Unconscious Mind, Cause and Treatment of Neuroses and Psychosomatic Disorders; Development and Use of Rapid Psychotherapies, Reality Insight Therapy, Body Image Therapy, Sleep-Teach Therapy, and Indirect Remote Psychotherapy (each averaging 10 to 20 hours in psychotherapy), Santa Maria, California, 1971 to present; Staff Psychiatrist in Community Mental Health Centers, Atascadero State Hospital, California 1975-79, San Luis Obispo, California 1973-75, Ponca City, Oklahoma 1967-71; Director, Mental Health Clinic for Students, Oklahoma State University-Stillwater, Oklahoma 1968-71; Private Practice, Psychiatry and Medical Hypnosis, Ponca City, Oklahoma, 1967-81; General Practice, St. Francis, Kansas, 1947-62, and Lacrosse, Kansas, 1962-64. Organizational Memberships: American Medical Association; American Psychiatric Association; Southern California Psychiatric Society; Academy of Parapsychology and Medicine; Society for Clinical and Experimental Hypnosis; International Society of Hypnosis; American Society of Hypnosis, Charter Member; American Academy of General Practice; American Association for the Advancement of Science; Northwest Kansas Medical Society, President 1951. Community Activities: Parent-Teacher Association; American Legion; Mason; Eastern Star; Phi Lambda Phi; Men of Webster; Phi Beta Pi; Delta Upsilon; Rotary International, Member St. Francis, Kansas and Ponca City, Oklahoma for 19 Years, President St. Francis, Kansas, 1955; Boy Scouts of America, Scout, Scoutmaster, Explorer Leader, Neighborhhod Commissioner, Council Trainer of Scouters, 23 years; International Platform Association; Elementary School Board, St. Francis, Kansas. Religion: Methodist Church, Lacrosse, Kansas; Sunday School Teacher; Church Committee Member; Lay Leader, 1963. Honors and Awards: Letter of Citation, National Parent-Teacher Association; Eagle Scout, Silver Award, Scoutmasters Key, Wood Badge, Boy Scouts of America; Listed in *Who's Who in the West, Who's Who in America, Who's Who in the World, Book of Honor, Notable Americans, Personalities of America, Personalities of the West and Midwest, Men of Achievement, Dictionary of International Biography, International Who's Who of Intellectuals, International Who's Who of Community Service, Men and Women of Distinction, National Social Registry*, and Others. Address: 4655 Basque Drive, Santa Maria, California 93455.■

FRANCES PRESHIA WILSON

Registered Nurse, Psychiatric Nurse, Co-Counselor and Receptionist. Personal: Born March 13, 1919; Daughter of Walter P. Stephenson (deceased); Married Charles William, Son of Jacob Resor Wilson and Estella Cherrie Wilson (both deceased); Mother of Charles William II, Walter Stephen, Cherrie, James Robin. Education: B.S. Nursing, Graduate Nurse Certificate, University of Kansas, 1940. Career: Registered Nurse, Psychiatric Nurse, Co-Counselor and Receptionist for Husband's Psychiatric Practice, present; Instructor and Assistant Director, School of Nursing, Axtell-Christian Hospital, Newton, Kansas, 1940-41; Administrator and Chairman, Student Health Program, Grace Hospital, Detroit, Michigan, 1941-43; Office Nurse and Receptionist, Norton, Kansas, 1944-46; Instructor of Psychiatric Nursing, In-Service Department, Central State Hospital, Norman, Oklahoma, 1964-67. Organizational Memberships: American Nurses Association; National League of Nursing Education; American Red Cross Nursing Service; Kansas State Nurses Association, 1940-64; Michigan State Nurses Association, 1941-43; Oklahoma State Nurses Association, Organizer and First Chairman of Geriatric Nursing Division 1964-67, Member 1964-67; Northwest Kansas Medical Auxillary, President 1951-53, 1947-62. Community Activities: American Red Cross Water Safety Instructor, Chairman of Water Safety Program, Board of Directors, Cheyenne County, Kansas, 1948-62; Girl Scouts of America, Key Trainer, Troop Organizer, Brownie Scout Leader, Assistant Girl Scout Leader, Camp Nurse, Member Program Committee of Sunflower Council, Kansas; Boy Scout Den Mother, 1959-62; Alpha Chi Omega; Eastern Star; Federated Women's Club; American Legion Auxilliary; Parent Teacher Association; Rotary Anns, Ponca City, Oklahoma, President 1968-69, Member 1967-71; California Central Coast Alpha Chi Omega Alumnae, President 1974-76; Member 1971 to present; Santa Maria Panhellenic Club, 1971-79; American Association of University Women, President Cheyenne County, Kansas Branch 1948-49, Member 1947-62; Fellow, International Platform Association; Medical Wives Club, Santa Maria, 1971 to present. Religion: Christian; Life Member, Women's Society of Christian Service, President St. Francis, Kansas, Methodist Church 1961-62, Member 1948 to present, Board Member 1960-62; Methodist Youth Fellowship Sponsor, La Crosse, Kansas, 1962-64; Sunday School Teacher of Children, College Students, Adults in Methodist Churches in St. Francis, La Crosse, Kansas, Ponca City, Oklahoma; Ordained Minister; Honorary Doctor of Divinity. Honors and Awards: Co-Researcher and Developer of Four Very Rapid Psychotherpies, Sleepteach Therapy, Reality Insight Therapy, Body Image Therapy, Programmed Personality Integration and Indirect Remote Psychotherapy (each therapy averages ten hours in length); Co-Developer of Motivation Program; National Honor Society, 1935; Sigma Tau Theta National Honorary Nursing Fraternity, 1940 to present; Girl Scouts of America Most Outstanding Scouter, Cheyenne County, Kansas, 1968-72; Listed in *Personalities of America, Directory of Distinguished Americans, International Book of Honor, The World Who's Who of Women*. Address: 4655 Basque Drive, Santa Maria, California 93455.■

JACQUES MARCEL PATRICK WILSON

School Principal. Personal: Born August 4, 1920; Son of James F. D. Wilson (deceased) and Mrs. Simone M. E. Wilson; Married Clotilde Tavares de Lima, Daughter of Joao Batista Tavares da Silva (deceased) and Luisa Tavares de Lima; Father of Jacqueline M. W. Martin, James F. T. Wilson, Alfred R. T. Wilson, John P. T. Wilson, Gregory B. T. Wilson, Guy M. T. Wilson. Education: B.A. 1941, M.Ed. 1960, University of Miami; Ph.D., University of Texas, 1966; Additional Studies, University of Havana, Sophia University, Purdue University. Military: Served in United States Army Air Corps and Air Force, 1941-57, attaining rank of Captain. Career: Principal, Miccosukee Indian School, at present; Past Positions include Executive Director, Miami International Institute of Technology Transfer; Director, Jacaranda Enterprises; Consultant, Foreign Languages and Bilingual Education, State of Florida; Assistant Provost, International Programs, University of West Florida; Chairman, Faculty of Foreign Languages, University of West Florida; Associate Director, Institute of Inter-American Studies, University of Miami; Chairman, Foreign Languages Department, Our Lady of the Lake College; Director, Three NDEA Institutes in Teaching of English to Speakers of Other Languages at OII, Texas. Organizational Memberships: Modern Language Association; Southern Conference on Language Teaching; American Association of Teachers of Spanish and Portuguese; American Council on Teaching of Foreign Languages; National Education Association; FEA; Phi Delta Kappa; Latin American Studies Association; Asocia¹cion de Prof. de Ingles del Ecuador; Caribbean Studies Association; American Association for the Advancement of the Humanities. Community Activities: Member, Steering Committee, Annual Conference on Western Hemisphere Relations and the Commonwealth of the Caribbean; Consultant, Bilingual Education, Harlandale (Texas) Independent School District; Consultant, Bilingual Education Matters, Rhodes Project; Consultant, Bilingual Education, Ad Hoc Committee, American Association of Teachers of Spanish and Portuguese; Expert Witness, Special Subcommittee on Bilingual Education, U.S. Senate Committee on Labor and Public Welfare; Expert Witness, Special Subcommittee on Education, U.S. House of Representatives Committee on Education and Labor; Expert Witness, Language and Educational Needs of Children of Limited English-speaking Ability in Florida's Public Schools, Florida Constitutional Revision Commission; Others. Religion: Member of Roman Catholic Church. Honors and Awards: Iron Arrow, University of Miami, 1941; NDEA Foreign Language Fellowship, University of Texas, 1962-64; Visiting Professor, Fulbright Commission in Ecuador,

1964, 1965, 1970; Guest Lecturer, Fourth Centennial of Camoes' Writing of the Epic *Os Lusiadas*, Convocation in Maringa, Parana, Brazil, 1972. Address: 5533 Alhambra Circle, Coral Gables, Florida 33146.■

JOHN WILLIAM WILSON, JR.

Retired Chemist/Researcher. Personal: Born April 1, 1916 in Albany, New York; Son of John William and Lena May (Gardner); Married Margaret Shaw Marshall Cunningham; Father of John William III, Elizabeth Anne. Education: Graduate cum laude, Albany Academy; A.B. cum laude Honors Chemistry, Amherst College, 1934-38; Graduate Work in Organic Chemistry, Massachusetts Institute of Technology, 1938-39; Advanced Work in Electron Microscopy, Cornell University, 1952; Continuing Education Course on Water Quality Engineering for Industry, The American Institute of Chemical Engineers, 1972; Advanced Seminar, Characterization of Surfaces and Elastohydrodynamic Lubrication, American Society of Lubrication Engineers, 1976. Career: Mobil Research and Development Corporation (formerly Research Department, Mobil Oil Corporation), 1940 to retirement in 1981; Mobil Oil Corporation, Supervising Chemist, Advanced Lubrication Technology 1972-81, Supervising Chemist, Water Base Lubricants 1970-72, Manager Industrial Lubricants Division, Research and Technical Service Department Mobile Oil Company Ltd. 1968-70, Supervising Chemist, Metal Processing Fluids June 1968-October 1968, Senior Research Chemist Structure of Greases 1948-68, Research Chemist Grease Group 1942-48, Analytical Chemist 1936-42, Service Station Lubrication Specialist 1934-35. Organizational Memberships: Electron Microscopy Society of America; Philadelphia Electron Microscope Society, Former Member, Chairman 1962-63; Local Chairman, Fifth International Congress for Electron Microscopy, 1962; Sigma Xi; New York Academy of Sciences; Institute of Petroleum; Lifetime Accredited Professional Chemist, American Institute of Chemists. Community Activities: Principal First Aid Instructor, Redding, Connecticut Volunteer Fire Company Number 1, 1941-60; Chairman, Transportation Committee, Redding Board of Education, 1947-51, 1956-60; Executive Board, Barclay Farm Civic Association, 1961-64; Cherry Hill, New Jersey, Advisory Committee on Education, 1960-64; Account Executive and Division Chairman, United Way of Camden County, 1966-68, 1971-81; Volunteer Teacher, Cherry Hill Public School System, 1981 to present; Volunteer Teacher, Moorestown Friends' School, 1980-81; Delaware Valley Ornithological Club, 1962-64; Wildfowl Trust, 1968-71; Royal Society for the Protection of Birds, 1968-71; National Audubon Society, 1971 to present; Philadelphia Museum of Art, 1975 to present; Smithsonian Institution, National Associate 1975 to present, Contributing Member 1982; Friends of Independence National Historical Park, 1976 to present; Pennsylvania Horticultural Society, 1977 to present; American Museum of Natural History, 1981 to present; East African Wildlife Society, 1981 to present; Nature Conservancy, 1982 to present; Legion of Honor of the Chapel of the Four Chaplains, Philadelphia, Pennsylvania, 1977; Honorary Fellow, Anglo-American Academy, 1978; Eleven Gallon Blood Donor, American Red Cross, 1941-78; National Wildlife Federation, 1982; Laboratory of Ornithology, Cornell University, 1982; Active in Boy Scouts of America, Mauwehu Council, Camden County Council, Area, Region, National and International, including Wood Badge Course Director 1970 to present and Staff Advisor 1976 to present, Northeast Region Advisory Board 1982 to present, National Council 1962 to present, National Volunteer Training Committee 1977 to present and Vice Chairman 1977 to present, Vice Chairman National Committee on Insignia and Uniform 1983 to present, Corporate Member United States Foundation for International Scouting 1977 to present, Member World Training Committee 1979 to present. Religion: Charter Member, St. Bartholomew's Church, Vestryman 1972-73, Stewardship Chairman 1966-68, Sunday School Superintendent 1963-68, Licensed Lay Reader 1975 to present; Member Christ Church, Vestryman 1953-56 and 1957-60, Sunday School Superintendent 1951-54, Diocesan Convention Delegate 1950-53. Published Works: Author of Numerous Articles, and Holder of Patent. Honors and Awards: Boy Scouts of America, Arrowhead Honor 1952, Scouter's Key Scoutmaster 1955, Explorer Advisor 1957, Commissioner 1965, District Award of Merit 1963, Silver Beaver Award 1966, Silver Antelope Award 1973, Eagle, Silver Explorer Award, St. George (Episcopal) Award 1981; Listed in *International Who's Who in Community Service, Community Leaders of America, American Men of Science, Who's Who in the East, Chemical Who's Who, Dictionary of International Biography, Royal Blue Book, Two Thousand Men of Achievement, Notable Americans of the Bicentennial Era, Community Leaders and Noteworthy Americans, Men and Women of Distinction, International Who's Who of Intellectuals, Five Thousand Personalities of the World, The Biographical Roll of Honor*. Address: 117 Saw Mill Court, Barclay Farm, Cherry Hill, New Jersey 08034.■

WILLIAM FEATHERGAIL WILSON

Geologist. Personal: Born December 25, 1934; Married Elizabeth Gail Wilson; Father of Clayton, Douglas, Wendy. Education: B.A. English 1957, B.S. Geology 1960, M.S. Geology 1962, University of Texas-Austin. Career: Placid Oil Company, Vice President, Chief Geologist 1981 to present, Texas Exploration Manager 1977-81; Senior Exploration Geologist to Exploration Manager of the Eastern Hemisphere, Tesoro Petroleum Corporation, 1974-77; Account Executive, Merrill Lynch, 1970-74; Environmental Geologist, Alamo Area Council of Government, 1970; Independent Petroleum Geologist, 1966-70; Senior Exploration Geologist, El Paso Natural Gas Company, 1965-66; Developmental Geology, Texaco, Inc., 1961-65. Address: 7918 Briaridge, Dallas, Texas 75248.■

GLEN ELBERT WIMMER

Engineer. Personal: Born February 16, 1903, in Creston, Iowa; Married Mildred G. McCullough; Father of Frank Thomas. Education: B.S.M.E. 1925, M.S.M.E. 1933, Iowa State University; M.B.A., Northwestern University, 1936. Military: Served in the United States Army Reserve Corps, 1925-38 (active duty, 1925-28). Career: Engineer, Engineering Department, General Electric Company, Fort Wayne, Indiana, 1925-29; Assistant Engineer, Western Electric Company, Chicago, Illinois, 1929-36; Engineering Staff, Michigan Technological University in Houghton, 1936-37; Firestone Tire and Rubber Company, 1937-38; Engineer in Charge of Design, Ditto Inc., 1938-39; Assistant to the Chief Engineer, Victograph Corporation, 1939-41; Designer of Industrial Machinery, Pioneer Engineering and Manufacturing Company; Designer and Checker, Engineering Service Corporation, 1941-42; Checker and Assistant Superintendent of Design, Norman E. Miller and Associates, 1942; Engineering Checker, Lee Engineering Company, 1942-43; Head, Design and Development Department, Cummins Perforator Company, 1943-45; Staff Engineer in Charge of Design and Development Projects, Tammen and Denison Inc., 1945-58; Instructor of Cost Accounting, Evening Division Classes, Illinois Institute of Technology, 1946-47; Staff Engineer, Barnes and Reinecke Inc., 1958-69; Engineer, Alpha Services, Inc., 1969-70; Retired, 1971; Part-time Consulting Professional Engineer and Management Consultant. Organizational Memberships: Illinois Engineering Council, 1958-66; Illinois Society of Professional Engineers; National Society of Professional Engineers; American Defense Preparedness Association; Society of Automotive Engineers; Society of Manufacturing Engineers; Delta Chi; International Platform Association; Intercontinental Biographical Association; Fellow, International Biographical Association. Honors and Awards: Holder of U.S. and Canadian Patents; Listed in *Who's Who in Engineering, Leaders in American Science, International Blue Book of World Notables, Dictionary of International Biography, Community Leaders and Noteworthy Americans, Personalities of the West and Midwest, International Register of Profiles, Two Thousand Men of Achievement, Notable Americans of the Bicentennial Era, National Social Directory, The Blue Book, Men of Achievement, International Who's Who of Intellectuals, Who's Who in the West, International Who's Who in Community Service, Illinois Lives, Social Directory of the United States, Who's Who in the Midwest, Profiles of Freedom - The Impressions of the American Historical Society, Men and Women of Distinction, Personalities of America, Book of Honor, Who's Who in California, American Patriots of the 1980's, The American Registry Series, California Who's Who in Business and Finance, Who's Who in Technology Today*. Address: 3839-48 Vista Campana South, Oceanside, California 92056.■

S. COLLEEN WINSTON

Office Director. Personal: Born August 29, 1937; Daughter of Wright and Marian Bacon Winston. Education: A.B. English/Secondary Education, Thomas More College, Edgewood, Kentucky, 1955; M.S. Biology, St. Mary College, Winona, Minnesota, 1972; M.A. Communications/Theology, University of Dayton, Ohio, 1977; Studies at Marquette University, Milwaukee, Wisconsin, Edgewood College, Cincinnati, Ohio, and University of Cincinnati, Ohio. Career: Director, Office of Communication, Catholic Diocese of Covington, Kentucky, 1981 to present; Former Positions include Consultant and Writer for Various Groups and Audiences; Archdiocese of Cincinnati, Media Consultant to Religious Education Office, Newsletter Editor of Office of Purchasing; Freelance Producer, Writer, Photographer, Slide/Filmstrip Programs for Religious Education; Lecturer, Teacher, Writer, Consultant in Media, Local, Regional and National Levels; High School Teacher of English, Sciences, Media, Religion and History. Organizational Memberships: Unda-U.S.A., Member National Board, Regional Representative, 1982 to present; Catholic Committee of Appalachia; American Benedictine Academy; Benedictine Musicians of America; Salesian Guild; Religious Futurists Network. Community Activities: Villa Madonna Academy, Board of Directors 1976-80 and 1983 to present, Secretary 1977-78; Campbell County Cable Citizens Advisory Board, 1982 to present; Kentucky Council of Churches, Delegate and Member of Media Commission 1982 to present, Chairperson of Media Commission 1983 to present. Religion: Roman Catholic, Member of Community of Benedictine Sisters of Covington, 1959 to present; Co-Founder and Coordinator, Mannafold Time and Space House, 1974 to present; Planner, Coordinator, Writer and Musician, Innumerable Prayer and Reflection Experiences.

TWO THOUSAND NOTABLE AMERICANS

Honors and Awards: Fellowship, *Wall Street Journal*, 1962; Fellow, National Science Foundation, 1964-68; Scholarships, Catholic Communications Foundation, 1981 and 1984; Listed in *Who's Who of American Women, Men and Women of Distinction, Personalities of the West and Midwest, Community Leaders, Dictionary of International Biography, World Who's Who of Women, Directory of Distinguished Americans*. Address: 2500 Amsterdam Road, Covington, Kentucky 41016.■

JOHN A. WISE, JR.

Attorney at Law. Personal: Born March 30, 1938; Son of John A. Wise and Blanche Parent Wise (deceased); Married Helga Margrit Bessin, Daughter of Ingeborg Bessin de Blohm; Father of Monique Elizabeth, John Eric. Education: A.B. cum laude, Holy Cross College, Massachusetts, 1959; University of Vienna, Austria, 1957-58; J.D., University of Michigan Law School, 1962; Ford Foundation Grant to Study German Law, University of Munich Law Faculty, 1962-63. Career: Partner, Dykhouse and Wise, present; Associate, Dykema, Wheat, Spencer, Goodnow & Trigg, Detroit, 1962-64; Assistant to the President, International Economic Policy Association, Washington D.C., 1964-66; Associate, Parsons, Tennent, Hammond, Hardig & Ziegelman, Detroit, 1967-70. Organizational Memberships: Detroit and Michigan Bar Associations; American Bar Association. Community Activities: Director, Colombian-American Friends, Inc., 1974 to present; Member Board of Trustees, Chairperson Finance Committee, Friends of School in Detroit, 1977-81. Address: 1221 Yorkshire, Grosse Pointe Park, Michigan 48230.■

LOUISE SCHAUB WITT

Author, Publisher, Consultant. Personal: Born February 6, 1914; Daughter of Russell and Stella Turner Schaub (deceased); Married Keith L.; Mother of Marjorie W. Stevens, Thomas K., Philip K., Mary Catherine W. Russell, Susan. Education: Associate Degree. Career: Internationally Recognized Author on Collectors Plates and Collectibles; Conductor, "Wonderful World of Plates" Tours to Factories in Europe; Special Consultant for First Book Hummel; Consultant to Factories on Limited Editions; Editorial Board, Plate World Magazine, Collectors Edition Magazine; Lecturer on Collectors Items from London to California; Registered Bridal Consultant. Organizational Memberships: National League of American Pen Women; I.P.A. Community Activities: United States Congressional Advisory Board; Daughters of the American Revolution. Religion: Presbyterian. Published Works: Author Wonderful World of Plates, First Book on Collectors Plates; Contributor Numerous Articles to Periodicals. Honors and Awards: Guest of Honor, Third International Plate Collectors Convention; Owner and Operator of The Gallery, Prairie Village, Kansas; Listed in *Who's Who of American Women, World Who's Who of Women, Personalities of America, The Directory of Distinguished Americans*. Address: 4324 West 70 Terrace, Prairie Village, Kansas 66208.■

JOHN STANLEY WODARSKI

Research Center Director. Personal: Born February 27, 1943; Son of Mrs. Estelle Wodarski; Married Lois Ann Moon, Daughter of Mr. and Mrs. Moon; Father of Ann Christine. Education: B.S. Social Work, Florida State University, 1965; M.S.S.W. Social Work, University of Tennessee, 1967; Ph.D. Social Work, Washington University, 1970. Career: Director, Research Center, School of Social Work, University of Georgia, present; Instructor, Sam Houston State University, 1967-68; Assistant Professor/Research Associate, Washington University, 1970-74; Grant Development Consultant, Johns Hopkins University, 1975-77; Associate Professor, University of Maryland, 1975-78. Organizational Memberships: National Association of Social Workers; American Psychological Association; Council on Social Work Education; American Sociological Association; Association for the Advancement of Behavior Therapy, National Council on Crime and Delinquency, American Correctional Association. Community Activities: M.S.W. Curriculum Committee, Chairperson; Doctoral Development for the School of Social Work, Chairperson; Curriculum Committee; Extended Degree Program Committee; Faculty Executive Committee, Chairperson; Administrative Advisory Committee to the Dean; Graduate Faculty Committee; Human Subjects Committee; Research Advisory Committee to the Vice President for Research; Alcohol Awareness Committee. Honors and Awards: Fellowship, Children's Bureau, Washington University, 1968-70; First Place, Professional Paper Award, Georgia Conference on Social Welfare, 1979; Listed in *Personalities of the South*. Address: 150 Green Hills Road, Athens, Georgia 30605.■

SOPHIE MAE WOLANIN

Tutor, Lecturer, Civic Worker, Scholar. Personal: Born June 11, 1915; Daughter of Stephen Wolanin and Mary Fijalka (both deceased). Education: B.S. (cum laude) Business Administration, University of South Carolina, 1948; Certificate, Secretarial Science, University of South Carolina, 1946; Certificate, Specialized Study, Engineering, Science and Management War Training Program, 1944. Career: Tutor, Lecturer, Civic Worker, Scholar, at present; Westinghouse Credit Corporation, Associate Editor, WCC News 1971-76, Assistant Editor 1968-71, Reporter 1967-68, Senior Secretary 1972-80, Executive Secretary 1954-1972, Charter Employee 1954-80; Westinghouse Electric Corporation, Confidential Secretary 1949-54, Order Service Department Secretary 1939-44, Manufacturing Department Coil Winder and Assembler 1937-39; University of South Carolina, School of Business Administration Instructor 1946-48, School of Commerce and of Liberal Arts Student Office Secretary 1944-46; Secretary and Receptionist, Medical Research Scientist's Office, 1934-37; Clerk and Secretary, Mercer County Tax Collectors Office, 1932-34. Organizational Memberships: Business and Professional Women's Club of Pittsburgh, Chairman Public Relations and Publicity 1971-80, Chairman World Affairs Committee 1970-71, Historian 1969-70, Chairman Roster and By-Laws Committee 1966-68, Numerous Other Offices; Life Member, Academy of Political Science; Life Member, American Association of University Women; Life Member, American Counselors Society; National Association of Executive Secretaries; National Federation of Business and Professional Women's Clubs; International Federation of University Women; International Platform Association; American Academy of Political and Social Science. Community Activities: University of South Carolina Alumni Association, Fellow Educational Foundation 1976, Chairman Pennsylvania State Fund Drive 1967-68, General Chairman Tri-State Area Alumni 1959; Allegheny County League of Women Voters; Life Member, Allegheny County Scholarship Association; American Bible Society; Friends of the Churchill Memorial and Library; Life Member, Mercer County Historical Society; National Advisory Board of the American Security Council; National Archives Associates; Active and Supporting Member, National Trust for Historic Preservation; Colonial Member, New England Historic Genealogical Society; National Charter Member, Smithsonian Institution Associates; Associate Member, American Museum of Natural History; Founding Charter Member, Anglo-American Historical Society; Early American Society; Founding Member, National Historical Society; Supporting Member, Women's Hall of Fame; Associate Member, Metropolitan Opera Guild; Polish American Numismatic Association; Polonus Philatelic Society; Charter Member, Republican Presidential Task Force; United National Association of the U.S.A.; Charter Member, Jonathan Maxcy Club, University of South Carolina; University Catholic Club of Pittsburgh; Honorary Member, College of Sharon Club; Numerous Other Activities. Religion: Catholic; Life Member, Liturgical Conference of North America; Music Patron, St. Paul's Cathedral Altar Society. Published Works: Contributed Articles to Newspapers including *The Oakland News* 1961-72, *Commercial Leader* 1969, *The South Bergen Review* 1969, *The North Arlington Leader* 1968, *The Bergen Sunday Leader* 1968, *Leader-Free Press* 1968, *WCC News* 1967-76, *Pittsburczanin* 1968-72. Honors and Awards: Medal of Merit, President Ronald Reagan; Special Recognition Award, Graduate School of Georgetown/Center for International Security Studies/American Security Council Education Foundation/Pentagon Education Center; Life Fellow, American Biographical Institute, 1979; Life Member, American Biographical Institute Research Association, 1977; Founder Fellow, International Institute of Community Service, 1974; Woman of the Year, Business and Professional Women's Club of Pittsburgh, 1972; Valedictorian, Pennsylvania State College Engineering Science and Management War Training Program, 1944; Honorary Ph.D. in Business Administration, Colorado State Christian College, 1972; Honorary Election to Key Club, Pennsylvania Federation of Business and Professional Women's Clubs, 1973; Societe Commemorative de Femmes Celebres; Numerous Other Awards; Listed in *Who's Who of American Women, Who's Who in the East, Who's Who in the World, Community Leaders of America, World Who's Who of Women, International Who's Who of Intellectuals, Directory of Distinguished Americans*, Over 32 Other Biographical References. Address: 5223 Smith-Steward Road, S.E., Girard, Ohio 44420.■

EVELYNE ROBERTS WOLF

Psychotherapist. Personal: Born April 2, 1921; Daughter of Mr. Morris H. Eddelman (deceased) and Mrs. Belle Eddelman; Married Ted George Wolf; Mother of Jane Roberts, Kevin S. Roberts, Richard E. Roberts, (stepmother of) Amy Wolf Lautin, Steven A. Wolf. Education: A.B. Education, Hunter College, 1941; M.S.W., Horace Rackham School of Graduate Studies, University of Michigan School of Social Work, 1948; Ph.D., Florida Institute of Technology, School of Professional Psychology, 1982. Military: American Red Cross, Psychiatric Hospital Case Work. Career: Psychotherapist, present; Part-time Instructor of Case Work, St. Michael Hospital School of Nursing, 1959-62; Part-time Instructor, "Women in Transition," "Coping Techniques," Women's Center at Broward Community College, 1983. Organizational Memberships: National Association of Social Workers; Association for Children and Adults with Learning Disabilities;

International Rodin Society, Patron; National Orton Dyslexia Society; American Association for Mentally Retarded; Academy of Certified Social Workers; National Clinical Registry of Social Workers. Community Activities: Governor of Michigan's Committee to Investigate Race Riot, 1942; Member Civil Defense and Blood Donor Activities, Michigan, 1942; Volunteer Leader for Adolescents in Community Center of Detroit, 1941-43; Secretary, Community Chest, Cresskill, New Jersey, 1953; Manager, Girl Scout Summer Day Camp, Cresskill, New Jersey, 1954; Co-Chairman, American Red Cross Fund Drive, South Orange, New Jersey, 1956; Den Mother, Boy Scouts of America; Program Chairman, Parent Teacher Association, South Orange Mountain School, 1959; Board Member, Children's Institute, West Orange, New Jersey, 1969; Director of Volunteers, Northwestern Guidance Clinic, Garden City, Michigan, 1971-73; Volunteer Activities with American Cancer Society, American Heart Association, Head Start Programs, Fair Housing Council. Honors and Awards: Patriotism Award; Basil O'Connor Award, 1946; Bamberger's "Woman in the News," 1966. Address: Developmental Resource Center, 2740 Hollywood Boulevard, Hollywood, Florida 33020.■

HENRY DaVEGA WOLFE

Executive. Personal: Born September 2, 1953, in Florence, South Carolina. Son of Mr. and Mrs. Joe L. Wolfe, Jr. Education: B.S. Honors Zoology, Clemson University, 1976; Continuing Education includes Seminars Time and Money Management, John F. Adams III, Freeport, Bahamas, 1979; Strategic Planning for Business, American Management Association, New York, New York, 1981; Transactional Analysis for Management, Abe Wagner, 1981; How to Sell or Buy a Business, University of North Carolina-Charlotte, 1982; Neurolinguistic Programming, Charlotte Bretto, Abaco, Bahamas, 1982; Psychology for Well People, Image Unlimited, Inc., Florence, South Carolina, 1982-83. Career: Chairman and Chief Executive Officer, DaVega and Wolfe Industries, Inc; Former Positions include City Ice and Fuel Company, Inc., Executive Vice President, Plant Manager. Organizational Memberships: American Entrepreneurs Association. Community Activities: Florence Rotary Club, Chairman of Program Committee 1981-82, Board of Directors 1981-82 and 1982-83; Toastmasters International, President Florence South Carolina Club 1981, Governor Area 2 of District 58 South Carolina 1981; Cypress Point Owners Association, President 1979, Treasurer 1980, Chairman of the Board 1981 and 1982; Chairman of Advisory Council District III of South Carolina, Future Business Leaders of America, 1981-82; United Way of Florence County, Team Captain 1981, Division Chairman 1982, Vice Chairman and Cabinet Member 1983, Cabinet Member and Chairman Pacesetter Division; Florence Family Young Men's Christian Association, Chairman of Physical Committee 1981 and 1982, Vice President 1982-83, President 1983-84, Board of Directors 1979-83; Crusade Volunteer, American Cancer Society, 1980; Greater Florence Chamber of Commerce, Chairman Executive Dialogue Group II 1982 and 1983, Chairman of Small Business Council 1982-83 and 1983-84; Boy Scouts of America, Chairman Florence County District 1982, Board of Directors, Pee Dee Area Council 1982 and 1983; Florence Ballet Company, Board of Directors, 1982; Crime Stoppers of Florence, Board of Directors, 1983; American Red Cross of Florence County, Board of Directors, 1983-84. Religion: Member of St. John's Episcopal Church, Florence, South Carolina, 1977 to present. Honors and Awards: Community Service Award, Phillips Petroleum Company, 1980; Outstanding Young Man of the Year, City of Florence, South Carolina, 1980; Outstanding Young Man of the Year, State of South Carolina, 1980; Outstanding Young Men of America, 1982; Listed in *Who's Who in America in Finance and Industry, Personalities of the South, Who's Who in the South and Southwest, International Who's Who of Contemporary Achievement*. Address: 700 South Cashua, #8B, Florence, South Carolina 29501.■

LEO WOLLMAN

Physician, Psychiatrist. Personal: Born March 14, 1914; Son of Joseph and Sarah Wollman; Married Eleanor Rakow Wollman; Father of Arthur Lee, Bryant Lee. Education: B.S., Columbia University, 1934; M.S., New York University, 1938; M.D., Edinburgh Medical School, 1942. Career: Physician: Psychiatrist. Organizational Memberships: American Society of Psychosomatic Dentistry and Medicine, President 1968-72, Journal Editor 1968-84, Executive Director 1974 to present; Society for Scientific Study of Sex, Past President 1979-81; Royal Medical Society, President, 1940; American Society of Clinical Hypnosis, Life Fellow; Society of Clinical and Experimental Hypnosis, Life Fellow; American Medical Writers Association, Life Fellow; American Society of Psychical Research, Life Fellow; National Association on Standard Medical Vocabulary, Secretary 1964 to present; Academy of Psychosomatic Medicine, Secretary 1965-66. Published Works: *Write Yourself Slim*, 1966; *Eating Your Way to a Better Sex Life*, 1982; Films, including *I Am Not This Body* 1970, *Strange Her* 1971, *Let Me Die A Woman* 1978; International Editor, *Revista Ibero Americana de Sofrologia* (Argentina), *Revista Latino Americana de Orientacion Biopsicosocial* (Argentina), *Revista Latino Americana de Hipnosis Clinica* (Argentina), *Instituto Peruano de Anestesiologia* (Peru), *Psychotherapy International* (International Society for Non-Verbal Psychotherapy, Switzerland); Consulting Editor, *Ressegna de Ipaosi e Psicosomoatica Medicina* (Italy); Numerous Others Editorial Assignments; Author, "Sexual Disorders Managed by Hypnotherapy" in Appendix to *How to Solve Your Sex Problems with Self-Hypnosis* (by Frank S. Caprio), 1964; "A Chronic Anxiety Patient Improves" in *Clinical Papers Related to Psychiatric Educational Seminars* (by Matthew Brody and Morton M. Golden), 1964; Other Contributions. Honors and Awards: Elected to Royal Medico-Psychological Association of England, 1970; Certificates of Award, American Society of Psychosomatic Dentistry and Medicine, 1966, 1964; Pioneer in Hypnosis Award, Jules Weinstein Annual Award, 1964; Certificate of Award for Significant Contribution to the Advancement of Hypnosis in the Therapeutic Arts, American Society of Clinical Hypnosis, 1968; Certificate of Award, Academy of Psychosomatic Medicine, 1962. Address: 4505 Beach 45 Street, Brooklyn, New York 11224.■

ROBERT E. WOLVERTON

Administrator. Personal: Born August 4, 1925; Son of Mrs. Vivian Overton; Father of Robert Jr., Laurie, Edwin, Gary. Education: A.B. Honors, Hanover College, 1948; M.A., University of Michigan, 1949; Ph.D., University of North Carolina, 1954. Career: Vice President for Academic Affairs, Mississippi State University; Former Positions include President, College of Mount St. Joseph on the Ohio; Dean of Graduate School and Research, Miami University; Associate Dean of Graduate College and Associate Professor of Classics, University of Illinois; Associate Professor of Classics and Director of Honors Programs, Florida State University; Assistant to Associate Professor of Classics and History and Assistant to Dean of Graduate School, Tufts University; Assistant Professor of Classics, University of Georgia. Organizational Memberships: President, American Classical League, 1972-76; American Philological Association; Executive Committee, National Council of Chief Academic Officers, 1981-83; American Association of Higher Education. Community Activities: President, Starkville Community Theatre, 1981-83; Mississippi Committee for the Humanities, 1982 to present; Chamber of Commerce; Former Member, Ohio Committee for the Humanities; Ohio Council on Economic Education; Trustee of St. Francis Hospital, Cincinnati; Trustee and Vice President of Consortium of Greater Cincinnati Colleges and Universities; The Literary Club; Rotary; Kiwanis; Torch Club. Religion: President, Diocese of Jackson, Mississippi, Pastoral Council 1980-82, President Parish Council 1979-80. Honors and Awards: Doctor of Letters Degree, College of Mount St. Joseph on the Ohio, 1977; Alumni Achievement Award, Hanover College, 1971; Fellow in Academic Administration, American Council on Education, 1965-66; Phi Kappa Phi; Omicron Delta Kappa; Phi Delta Kappa; Listed in *Who's Who in America, Who's Who in the United States*. Address: l08 Edinburgh Drive, Starkville, Mississippi 39759.■

SHARON GENELLE WOMACK

Director of Department of Library, Archives and Public Records. Personal: Born June 13, 1940; Daughter of Ted and Mary Martin; Widow. Education: B.S.B.A. 1972, Master of Library Science 1976, University of Arizona; Attended Phoenix College, 1961-67. Career: Department of Library, Archives and Public Records, State Capitol, Phoenix, Arizona, Director, Deputy Director; Director, Maricopa County Library; Director, Miami Memorial-Gila County Library; Reference Librarian, University of Arizona Social Sciences Department; Library Assistant, University of Arizona Government Documents Section. Organizational Memberships: Arizona State Library Association (president, 1977-78); Southwest Library Association (executive board, 1977-78); American Library Association (advisory committee, 1976 to present). Address: 6810 N. 29th Lane, Phoenix, Arizona 85017.■

GUY YOU WONG

Professor. Personal: Born April 8, 1935; Son of Mr. and Mrs. Fong G. Wong; Married Barbara Jean; Father of Andrew Wyatt-Mingyin, Brian Alan-Mingway. Education: M.D., University of Washington School of Medicine, 1962; Internship, Medical College of Virginia, 1962-63; Residency in Ophthalmology, Medical College of Virginia Hospital Division, 1963-66; Fellowship in Disorders of Ocular Motility 1968-69, Fellowship in Vitreous Retina Disorders 1975-76, Pacific Medical Center, San Francisco, California. Military: Served in the United States Air Force, 1966-68, attaining the rank of Captain. Career: Water Chemist, United States Fish and Wildlife Service, 1957-58; Chief of Ophthalmology Service, 810 Medical Group, Fairchild Air Force Base, Washington, 1966-68; Chief of Ophthalmology Department, Santa Clara Kaiser Permanente Medical Center, 1970 to present; Co-Director, Strabismus Service, Stanford University Medical Center, 1973-75; Clinical Associate Professor, Division of Ophthalmology, Stanford University Medical Center, 1974 to present; Faculty, Stanford Basic Course in Ophthalmology, 1974 to present; Consultant, Palo Alto Veterans Administration Hospital. Organizational Memberships: American Academy of Ophthalmology, Senior Instructor 1975-79, Fellow 1968 to present; Fellow, International Strabismological Association; Fellow, Military Society of Ophthalmologists; Charter Member, American Association of Pediatric Ophthalmology and Strabismus. Community Activities: Secretary/Treasurer, Caduceus Club, 1957; Attending Ophthalmologist, Lions Club Eye Clinic, San Francisco, California, 1968-69; International Order of Odd Fellows, 1979 to present; Executive Committee, Santa Clara Kaiser Permanente Medical Center; Chairman, Jampolsky Fellows Meeting, San Francisco, California, 1981. Honors and Awards: Scholarship, Lions Club, 1954; Training Grant, National Institute of Health, 1963-66; Phi Sigma, Biological Honorary Society, 1957; Research Grants, Kaiser Foundation Institute, 1970-78 and 1980-82. Address: 900 Kiely Boulevard, Santa Clara, California 95051.■

ARLETTA RENEE WOOD

Booking Agency, President and Founder. Personal: Born April 19, 1945; Daughter of Clem and Sarah Hairston (both deceased). Education: Graduate, East High School, Columbus, Ohio, 1963; Business Administration/English, Howard University, 1964-66. Career: Founder and President, Affiliated Enterprises, Inc., Booking Agency, 1967 to present; Beauty Instructor, 1971-79; President of Better Informed to Counsel His/Her Eclat Success, a Subsidiary Corporation of A.E.I.; Executive and Administrative Positions with Howard University's Botany Department, American Federation of Teachers, Americans United for Separation of Church and State, Air Transport Association of America, Ohio State Department of Education. Organizational Memberships: International Platform Association; International Toastmistress Association; International Toastmasters Association; American Society of Professional and Executive Women; American Management Association; American Film Institute; American Federation of Musicians; Employees Association of Air Transport Association, President. Community Activities: Notary Public, State of Maryland, Montgomery County, 1978-80. Honors and Awards: Arletta Renee Day Proclamation by Mayor Marion Barry Jr., Washington D.C., January 8, 1982; Listed in *Who's Who in Finance and Industry*, *Who's Who in the South*, *Directory of Distinguished Americans*, *World Who's Who of Women*, *Marquis Who's Who in the World*, *International Book of Honor*, *Who's Who Among Black Americans*, *Who's Who in the East*, *Distinguished Blacks in Washington*. Address: 2418 Homestead Drive, Silver Spring, Maryland 20902.■

FRANK BRADSHAW WOOD

Professor. Personal: Born December 21, 1915; Son of Thomas Frank and Mary Bradshaw Wood (deceased); Married Elizabeth Pepper; Father of Ellen, Eunice, Mary Elizabeth, Stephen. Education: B.S., University of Florida, 1936; M.A. 1940, Ph.D. 1941, Princeton University; Attended University of Arizona, 1938-39. Military: Served in the United States Navy Reserve, 1941-46, attaining the rank of Lieutenant Commander. Career: Professor of Astronomy, University of Florida; Former Positions include Assistant Professor, Associate Professor of Astronomy, University of Arizona and University of Pennsylvania. Organizational Memberships: International Astronomical Union, President Commission 42, 1967-70, President Commission 38, 1982; Member Council, American Astronomical Society, 1957-60; Secretary Section D, American Association for the Advancement of Science, 1958-70; President, Florida Academy of Sciences, 1983-84. Community Activities: Kiwanis Club; Visiting Lecturer, American Astronomical Society, 1958 to present. Religion: Member of Episcopalian Church. Honors and Awards: Air Medal, 1946; Fulbright Fellow, Australian National University, 1957-58; Fulbright Fellow, Instituto de Astronomia y Fisica del Espacio, 1977; National Academy Sciences Research Fellow, University of Arizona and University of California, 1946-47; NATO Senior Fellow, University of Canterbury, Christchurch, New Zealand, 1973. Address: 714 Northwest 89th Street, Gainesville, Florida 32607.■

LINCOLN JACKSON WOOD

Technical Supervisor. Personal: Born September 30, 1947; Son of William H. and Sarah S. Wood. Education: B.S. with Distinction, Cornell University, 1968; M.S. 1969, Ph.D. 1972, Stanford University. Career: California Institute of Technology, Technical Group Supervisor, Future Mission Studies Group, Navigation Systems Section, Jet Propulsion Laboratory 1981 to present, Visiting Associate Professor of Systems Engineering 1978 to present, Member Technical Staff, Navigation Systems Section, Jet Propulsion Laboratory 1977-81, Visiting Assistant Professor of Systems Engineering 1976-78, Lecturer in Systems Engineering 1975-76, Bechtel Instructor in Engineering 1972-74; Staff Engineer, Systems Analysis Laboratory, Space and Communications Group, Hughes Aircraft Company, El Segundo, California, 1974-77. Organizational Memberships: Senior Member, American Astronautical Society; American Institute of Aeronautics and Astronautics; Institute of Electrical and Electronics Engineers; American Association for the Advancement of Science. Community Activities: Associate Editor, *Journal of the Astronautical Sciences*, 1980 to present; Space Flight Mechanics Committee, American Astronautical Society, 1980 to present; Delegate, California Democratic Council Convention, 1978; Stanford Alumni Association; Cornell Alumni Association of Southern California; Planetary Society; Los Angeles County Museum of Art. Honors and Awards: Sigma Xi; Tau Beta Pi; Phi Kappa Phi; Phi Eta Sigma; National Science Foundation Trainee, 1968-72; Dean's List, 1964-68; Scholarship, Annie F. and Oscar W. Rhodes, 1964-68. Address: La Canada, Flintridge, California 91011.■

LARRY (MARYLAIRD) WOOD

Journalist. Personal: Born in Sandpoint, Idaho; Daughter of Edward Hayes and Alice McNeel Small; Married W. Byron Wood on January 30, 1942 (divorced May 1975); Mother of Mary, Marcia, Barry. Education: B.A. magna cum laude, University of Washington, 1938; M.A., 1940; Undertook Postgraduate Studies at Stanford University 1941-42, University of California-Berkeley, 1943-44; Certificate in Photography, 1971; Postgraduate Studies in Journalism, University of Wisconsin 1971-72, University of Minnesota 1971-72, University of Georgia 1972-73. Career: Feature Writer/Correspondent, *Linguapress* International Newsmagazine, Paris, France; Feature Writer, *Westways* and *Motorland*, AAA Magazines in West; By-line Columnist, *Oakland Tribune* (California), *San Francisco Chronicle*, 1946 to present; Feature Writer, *Western Region Christian Science Monitor*, SCM Radio Syndicate and International News 1973 to present, Time-Mirror Syndicate 1981 to present, Chevron U.S.A., Register and Tribune Syndicate, Des Moines 1975 to present, *California Today Magazine*; Stringer, *Travelday Magazine*, 1976 to present; Northern California Contributing Editor *Fashion Showcase*, Dallas; Regional Correspondent, *Spokane Magazine*; Feature Writer, Travel Section, *San Jose Mercury-News*; Photographer/Feature Writer, Scholastic Publications, 1974 to present; California Correspondent, *Seattle Times Sunday Magazine*; Contributing Editor, *Fashion Showcase*, Dallas; Freelance Writer Magazines including *Parents'*, *Sports Illustrated*, *Family Circle*, *Mechanix Illustrated*, *Oceans*, *Sea Frontiers*, *House Beautiful*, *Family Handyman*, *American Home*, *Parade*, *Off-Duty*, *Chevron U.S.A.*, Other National Magazines, 1946 to present; Feature Writer, Donnelley Publications, Oak Brook, Illinois, Meridian Business Publications, Xerox Education Publications, Scholatic Publications; Contributing Editor, *Fodor Travel Guides*, 1981 to present; Consultant, Feature Writer, Metropolitan Transportation Commission, Northern California, 1970 to present; Assistant Professor of Journalism, San Diego State University, 1975 to present; Professor of Journalism, San Jose State University, Spring 1976; Assistant Professor of Journalism, California State University, Hayward; Professor Environmental/Scientific Journalism, University of California Journalism Extension, 1979; Professor of Journalism, University of Pacific, Spring 1979; Director of Public Relations, Northern California Association Phi Beta Kappa, 1969 to present; Keynote Speaker, California State University Women in Communications Conference 1979, 1982, National Association Educational Journalism, Society Professional Journalism Conference 1979, Society American Travel Writers Convention 1979; Chairman, National Travel Writing Contest for United States University Journalism Students Assocaition for Education in Journalism, Society of American Travel Writers, 1979 to present; Director of Public Relations and Consultant in Field of Scientific and Environmental Affairs and Recreation to Numerous Firms, Institutions, and Associations. Organizational Memberships: Public Relations Society of America; National School Public Relations Association; Environmental Consultants of North America; International Environmental Consultant; Oceanic Society; International Oceanographic Society; American Association of Education in Journalism, Executive Board National Magazine Division 1978 to present, Newspaper Division 1974-77; University of Washington Ocean Sciences Alumni Association, Charter Member; American Management Association; Investigative Reporters and Editors; Society Travel Writers America; Society Professional Journalists; Women in Communications; California Academy Environmental News Writers; National Press Photographers Association;

San Francisco Press Club; Eastbay Women's Press Club; California Writers Club, Officer 1967, 1972. Community Activities: Public Relations Consultant to Alta Bates Hospital (Berkeley), Merrit Hospital (Oakland), Alameda Hospital, and Others; Delegate to National Press Photographers Flying Short Course, 1979; Public Relations Director, Young Women's Christian Association, Young Men-Young Women USO, Seattle 1942-46, Young Women's Christian Association, Oakland, California 1946-56, Children's Home Society of California 1946-56, Children's Medical Center Northern California 1946-70, Eastbay Regional Park District 1946-58, California Spring Garden Shows 1946-58, Girl Scouts U.S.A., Oakland 1948-56; Speaker for Educational Institutions and Professional Groups, 1946 to present; Secretary, Junior Center of Arts, Oakland, 1952 to present; Volunteer Public Relations, American Cancer Society, Young Men's Christian Association, Oakland, 1944-52; Public Relations Writer, American Red Cross, 1946-56; Consultant, Oakland Park Department, Young Men's Christian Association, Seattle, Oakland; Board of Directors, Camp Fire Girls, Oakland, Public Relations Chairman, Annual Film Festival, Joaquin Miller Parent Teacher Association, Oakland; Trustee, California State Parks Foundation, 1976 to present; World Wildlife Fund; Sigma Delta Chi; Theta Sigma Phi. Honors and Awards; Honoree, Checvon USA, 1983; Press Dignitary, Selected to Cover Visit of Queen Elizabeth II and Prince Philip to USA/West; Appeared on TV Documentary, "Larry Wood Covers Visit of Queen"; Selected "vip" press for Covering National Park Service's National Conference on Science, Citation by National Park Service for Work on First National Historic Reserve, Eby's Landing; Selected for National Press Tour of Preview of New Orleans World's Fair, May 1983, Guest of Texas, Washington State, Florida, Tennessee, on Special Economic and Development Press Previews, 1983-84, Guest of Government of Mexico; Coverage of First Women in Space (Sally Ride) and First USN Hydrofoil Missileships; Recipient USN Award for Reporting on Classified/Confidential Missileships; Works Selected for Archives of California Room, Oakland/San Francisco Public Libraries for University of Washington, Seattle Library; Recipient Citations from United States Forest Service 1975, National Park Service 1976, 1978, 1979, Oakland Museum Association 1977-79; Named California Woman of Achievement, 1979, 1980; Winner of Special Award, Discover America Travel Organization; Award for Architectural Coverage and Art Coverage, Oakland Museum; Citation for Features on Nation's First National Historical Reserve, Ebey's Landing on Whidbey Island and for Work on Bald Eagles in Klamath National Wildlife Refuge with United States Fish and Wildlife Service; Chosen to Join Selected Press in Covering the United States Navy's New Patrol Hydrofoil Missileship Squadron; Representing Press at First International Hydrofoil Conference, Nova Scotia, 1981; Numerous Other Honors and Awards; Listed in Professional, Journalistic and Photographic Rosters and in *Who's Who in America, Who's Who of American Women, Who's Who in the West, Who's Who in Finance and Industry, Who's Who in the World*, Others. Address: 6161 Castle Drive, Oakland, California 94611.■

SANDRA ELAINE WOOD

Systems Analyst/Programmer. Personal: Born June 27, 1944; Daughter of Mr. and Mrs. W. L. Wood, Sr. Education: Diploma, Big Island High School, 1962; 2-Year Executive Secretary Certificate, Phillips Business College, 1970; Certified Professional Secretary Rating, Institute for Certifying Secretaries, 1972; B.A. cum laude in Business Administration/Management 1982, M.B.A. (in progress), Lynchburg College. Career: Systems Analyst/Programmer, Owens-Illinois, Inc., 1977 to present; Sales Clerk, G. C. Murphy, 1962; Sales Clerk, Baldwin's, 1962-63; Secretary, C. W. Hancock and Sons, Inc., 1964-66; Secretary in Various Positions with Owens-Illinois, Inc., 1967-73; Data Processing Supervisor, 1974-76. Organizational Memberships: Data Processing Management Association, Member 1977 to present, Secretary 1978, Executive Vice President 1979, President, 1980; C.P.S. Associates, Member 1972 to present; Professional Secretaries International, Coordinator 1982 Southeast District Conference, Chapter Treasurer 1971-73, Chapter First Vice President 1973-74, Chapter President 1974-75, Chapter Director 1977-78, Seminar Chairman 1972-73, Chapter First Vice President 1973-74, Chapter President 1974-75, Chapter Director 1977-78, Seminar Chairman 1972-73, Chairmanships on both Chapter and Division Levels 1969 to present, Member 1966 to present. Community Activities: Bedford County Transportation Safety Commission, Secretary 1974 to present; Participation in Women's Focus, 1983; Answered Telephones for the Jerry Lewis Telethon, 1979, 1980, 1981; Interviewed for September 1981 Issue of Data Management Magazine, "Game Plan for Women in Management." Religion: Member Court Street United Mehodist Church 1967 to present, Secretary Official Board 1975-76; Big Island United Methodist Church, Choir Member 1956-64, Sunday School Superintendent 1962-64. Honors and Awards: High School Valedictorian, 1962; Beta Club, 1961-62; Chapter Secretary of the Year, 1970; Outstanding Alumni, Phillips Business College, 1972; B.A. cum laude, 1982; Gold Key Honor Society, Lynchburg College, 1982; Outstanding Young Women of America, 1978; Listed in *Who's Who of American Women, Personalities of America, Personalities of the South, The World Who's Who of Women, The Biographical Roll of Honor*. Address: P.O. Box 303, Big Island, Virginia 24526.■

SUMNER WOOD, SR.

Lawyer. Personal: Born in 1902; Married Mary Rawlings (deceased), Second Wife Peggy Angel; Father of Sumner Jr., David Eliab, Judson Rawlings, Brooks C. B., Octavia Wood Cooper, Wriley C. A. Education: B.S., Harvard University, 1925; LL.B., George Washington University, 1968, with honors, George Washington University School of Law, 1968. Career: Lawyer in District of Columbia, 1933 to present; Co-Trustee with Two Banks. Organizational Memberships: Harvard Club of District of Columbia. Community Activities: Mason, 1922 to present; Rotary Club of Rockville, Maryland; District of Columbia Society of Mayflower Descendants. Religion: Vestry Christ Episcopal Church. Published Works: *Malta*, 1935; *The Virginia Bishop*, 1961; *Laws Everyone Should Know*, 1941; *The Wood Family Index*, 1966; *Cupid's Path in Ancient Plymouth*, 1957; *The Horseshoe of the Potomac*, 1973. Honors and Awards: J.D. with honors, 1968. Address: 19430 Beallsville Road, Beallsville, Maryland 20839.■

DOROTHY MARIE WOODARD

Industrial Developer. Personal: Born February 7, 1932; Daughter of Gerald E. and Bessie Katherine Floeck (both deceased); Married Jack W. Woodard (deceased). Education: Studies at New Mexico State University, 1950, 1980, 1981; Thomas Hill Insurance Course Degree, United Nations Insurance Company, 1968. Career: United Nations Insurance Company, Broker, Agent, District Manager, 1968-74; Western National Life Insurance Company, Broker, Agent, 1976-81; Industrial Development, Executive Director for City of Tucumcari, New Mexico, 1979 to present; Owner, Manager, Western Oil Company, 1950 to present. Organizational Memberships: Regional Eastern Plains Council of Governments, Board of Directors; Bravo Dome CO_2, Board of Directors; Resource Conservation and Development Area Council, Board of Directors; Railroad Planning Conference Panel, State of New Mexico. Community Activities: New Mexico Industrial Development Executive Association; Chamber of Commerce; National Association for Female Executives, Inc., International Travelers Association; Mesa Country Club. Honors and Awards: Top Agent, United Nations Insurance Company, 1968, 1969. Address: P.O. Box 823, Tucumcari, New Mexico 88401-0823.■

NATALIE NESBITT WOODLAND

Professor. Personal: Born April 12, 1914; Daughter of Mary and Edgar Nesbitt; Married Robert H., Son of Florence and Louis Woodland; Mother of Nancy Couch. Education: B.S., Memphis State University, 1941; M.A., George Peabody College, 1950; Doctor of Arts, Middle Tennessee State University, 1977. Career: Retired; Part-time Professor of English, Tennessee Technological University; Former Professional Occupations include Teaching in Public Schools of Tennessee, Texas, and North Carolina, at Oklahoma Baptist University in Shawnee, Oklahoma, at City Schools of Clarksville, Tennessee and at Tennessee Technological University. Organizational Memberships: National Education Association; Tennessee Educational Association; American Association of University Women; Tennessee Philogical Association; South Atlantic MLA; Browning International Society, Charter Member; Guardian Angels, Fano Club; International Host Association for International Students. Community Activities: Board Member, Children's Drama, Cookeville, Tennessee; Clarksville City Teachers, Past President; Member International Hospitality Committee for International Students (past 15 years). Religion: Board Member, Agape Center for Pre-school Children; Active in Women's Circles; Past Sunday School Teacher. Honors and Awards: Certificate of Merit in Teaching; United Daughters of the Confederacy Scholarship at Peabody; Publication of *The Satirical Edge of Truth in the "Ring and the Book," Studia humanitatis*, directed by Bruno M. Damiani, The Catholic University of America. Address: 2185 Massa Avenue, Cookeville, Tennessee 38501.■

TWO THOUSAND NOTABLE AMERICANS

JEAN LEIGH WOODRUFF

Assistant Professor and Department Chairman. Personal: Born September 19, 1950; Daughter of Mrs. Jean Tulli. Education: B.S. History, University of North Carolina-Greensboro, 1972; M.B.A. Marketing, Emory University, 1974; Studied at Clemson University, 1975-80; Certificate in Norwegian, University of Oslo, Norway, Summer 1979; Work Toward Ph.D. Marketing and Management Science, University of Georgia, 1977-80; Certificates in Norwegain and Economics Policy, University of Oslo, Summer 1982. Career: Clemson University, Chairperson of Marketing and Management Seminars of the Office of Professional Development 1975-81, Instructor 1974-81; Editor, *Textile Marketing Newsletter*, 1981; Assistant Editor, *Textile Marketing Letter*, 1975-80; Assistant Professor, Department Chairperson 1982-83, Western New England College. Organizational Memberships: American Marketing Association; Southern Marketing Association; Proceedings Editor, Mid-Atlantic Marketing Association, 1980; Western Massachusetts International Trade Association; Phi Gammu Nu; The Institute of Management Science. Community Activities: Western New England College Women; Faculty Associate, Western New England College Student Chapter of Advertising and Marketing Club, 1981; Faculty Advisor, Clemson Collegiate Civitan, 1975-81; Faculty Advisor, Phi Gamma Nu, 1975-81; Troop Leader, Girl Scouts of America, 1974-81; University Women's Club, 1974-81; American Association of University Women, 1974-81; League of Women Voters, 1974-76; Helping Hands, 1979-81; Volunteer, Quadrangle Association, 1981. Religion: New Life Baptist Church; Women's Bible Conference, 1981; Bill Gothard Conferences, 1978. Honors and Awards: Young Careerist of the Month, Anderson, South Carolina, September 1977, Business and Professional Women's Club; Certificate of Outstanding Service, South Carolina Civitan, 1981; Certificate of Recognition, South Carolina Department of Social Services, 1981; Listed in *Outstanding Young Women of America, Who's Who in the South and Southwest, Personalities of the South, World Who's Who of Women, International Who's Who of Intellectuals, Personalities of America, International Youth in Achievement*. Address: 108 Breckwood Circle, Springfield, Massachusetts 01119.■

JOSEPH FRANKLIN WOODRUFF

Research Manager (retired). Personal: Born August 8, 1913; Son of Frank and Carolina Parks Woodruff (both deceased); Married Marie M. Miller on June 17, 1938; Father of Joanne Marie W. Wedder, Carolyn Jeanette W. Vail. Education: B.S., Capital University, Columbus, Ohio, 1935; Attended Ohio State University, Columbus, Ohio, 1935-36. Career: Armco, Inc., Manager 1968-77, Supervising Spectrochemist 1958-68, Senior Spectrochemist 1951-58, Spectrochemist 1946-51, Junior Research Engineer 1945-46, Spectroanalyst 1943-45, Chem-Analyst 1941-43; Instructor of Chemistry and Head of Science Department, McClain High School, Greenfield, Ohio, 1939-41; Instructor of Mathematics, Greenhills High School, Cincinnati, Ohio, 1938-39; Instructor of Mathematics, Physics and Chemistry, Kings Mills High School, Ohio, 1936-38. Organizational Memberships: Life Member, National Educational Association; Ohio School Board Association; Society of Applied Spectroscopy; Canadian Society of Applied Spectroscopy; Miami Valley Spectrographic American Institute of Physics; Optical Society of America; American Management Association; Cleveland Society of Spectroscopy; Committees E-2, E-4, S-17, American Society of Testing and Materials; C.O.R.V.A. Northern Sub-Area Council; Ohio Valley Spectrographic Society. Community Activities: Hospice of Middletown, Board of Trustees 1983 to present; Free and Accepted Masons 760; R.A.M. #87; Middletown Council #136; Middletown Commandery #71; Middletown Safety Council; Middletown Area United Way; Middletown Chamber of Commerce; Forest Hills Country Club; Lions Club of Middletown; Butler County Mental Hygiene Association; Butler County Heart Association; Middletown High School Boosters Club; F.A.M.A. of Fenwick High School; Life Member, Lemon-Monroe and Middletown Band Association; Moose Lodge; Middletown Area Young Republicans; Ohio Historical Society; Butler County Council on Aging; Middletown Board of Education, President Seven Years, Member 1952-63, 1971, 1973; Chairman, Five-County Science Awards Competition, l955-56; Co-Chairman, Red Cross Drive, Middletown, 1943; Ohio School Board Association, Chairman, Hospitality Committee, Convention 1956, Finance Committee Chairman 1959-63; Executive Board 1957-63; Executive Board, Southwestern Ohio School Boards Association, 1951-63; Chairman, Middletown Heart Association Drive, 1955; Captial University Alumni Association Board, 1953-56; Citizens Advisory Committee of the Special Service Bureau, Miami University, 1956-63; Franklin, Ohio, Air Raid Warden, 1942; District War Bond Salesman, Franklin, Ohio, 1942; Boy Scouts of America, Pokey District, Organizational and Extension Committee, 1949-52; Initiated Establishment of Miami University Extension Campus, Middletown, Ohio, 1962; Advisory Committee, Research Bureau of Miami University, 1961-65; Chairman, Community-Wide Appreciation Night for Howard Cromwell, Retiring Superintendent of Schools, 1966; Administrative Council, Middletown School District, 1967-69; Initiated Parent-Teacher Organizations and Parent-Teacher Associations, Middletown City School District; Chairman, Armco Research Employee Representatives, 1945; Chairman, Research Benefit Association, 1946. Religion: First Baptist Church, Middletown, Ohio, Board of Christian Education, Building Committee, Remote Control Engineer for Radio Broadcasts 1955-59; Sunday School Teacher for Elementary, Junior High, Senior High, and Young Married Classes, First Baptist Churches in Greenfield and Kings Mills, Ohio. Published Works: Author of Articles "Application of Vacuum Optical Emmission Spectroscopy in the Steel Industry", *Industrial Heating* 1967, "The Use of Briquetted Samples in the Spectrochemical Analysis of Carbon and Alloy Steels and Other Metals", *Journal of the Optical Society of America* 1950, "Quality Control of Steel Using Clock-and-Chart Recording Photoelectric Spectrometers", *Developments in Applied Spectroscopy, I,* 1962, "Introduction", *Sampling, Standards, and Homogeneity*, "Rapid Spectrochemical Analysis for Control of Basic Oxygen and Open Hearth Shops", *Open Heat Proceedings* 1964, Numerous Other Articles and Contributions to Books. Honors and Awards: Outstanding Layman Award, Ohio Association of Elementary School Principals, 1976; All-Southwest Honorary School Board, 1973; Middletown Jaycees Good Government Award, 1958; Annual Lay Award, Middletown Classroom Teachers Association and Ohio Education Association, 1966; Distinguished Service Award, Jaycees, 1964; American Society for Testing and Materials, H.V. Churchill Award 1974, Joseph F. Woodruff Steel Ingot Award 1973, Award of Merit 1978, Honorary Life Member 1975, Fellow 1970; Honorary Doctor of Science, Capital University, 1981; Listed in *The International Yearbook and Statesman's Who's Who, World Who's Who, Who's Who in Commerce and Industry, International Who's Who in Commerce and Industry, Who's Who in the Midwest, Who Knows-And What, American Men of Science, Notable Americans of the Bicentennial Era, Men of Achievement, Men and Women of Distinction, Dictionary of International Biography, Directory of Distinguished Americans, Who's Who in Aviation and Aerospace*. Address: 3457 Central Avenue, Middletown, Ohio 45043.■

ARLENE SITLER WOODS

Research Fellow. Personal: Born May 14, 1919; Daughter of Jerry and Hannah (Buschert) Sitler (both deceased); Married John O. Woods. Education: B.A., Goshen College, 1944; M.A., Teachers College, Columbia University, 1960; M.S.W., University of Kentucky, 1972; Ed.D., Indiana University, 1968. Career: Research in "The Role of Education in the Development of Self Reliance in Rural Youth of the Third World," 1981 to present; Higher Education and Research, 1960-81; Visiting Research Fellow, University of the West Indies, Institute of Social and Economic Research; Consultant in Grantsmanship, Thiel College, Greenville, Pennsylvania; Associate Professor, School of Social Work, Memorial University of Newfoundland, St. Johns, Newfoundland; Administration in Social Work, Mennonite Central Committee, 1944-56; Overseas Appointments include Post-War II Europe, London, England, Basel, Switzerland, and Post-Korean War, Loaned as Director Christian Children's Fund. Organizational Memberships: American Association of University Women; Council on Social Work Education; Thiel Women's Club; Canadian/International Federation of University Women. Community Activities: Social Action Committee, Trinity Lutheran Church, Greenville, Pennsylvania; Canadian Association for Mental Retardation; International Grenfell Association; United Nations Association, Town Chairperson, Stratford, Connecticut, 1970; Canadian Association Schools Social Work; National Association of Social Work; Association for Higher Education; Social Action Committee, Greater Bridgeport Council of Churches, 1969-71; Marion Community, St. John's, Newfoundland, 1975-79. Honors and Awards: P.R.A. Fellowship, Organization of American States, Jamica, 1981; Citation for Child Welfare Services, Ministry of Social Welfare, Republic of Korea, 1955. Address: 113 Plum Street, Greenville, Pennsylvania 16125.■

LARRY DAVID WOODS

Lawyer and Educator. Personal: Born September 10, 1944; Son of Mrs. Loyce Woods; Married Jinx Schwenke; Father of Rachel, Allen, Sarah. Education: B.A., Emory University, 1966; J.D., Northwestern University, 1969. Career: Lawyer/Teacher. Organizational Memberships: Tennessee Advisory Committee on Legal Services, Chairman; Tennessee Bar Association, House of Delegates; Nashville Bar Association; Continuing Legal Education, Education Committee. Community Activities: Committee to Re-elect Congressman Allen, Chairman 1976, 1978; Tennesseans for McGovern, 1972; Middle Tennessee Civil Liberties Union, Board of Directors 1972-79; Barkley Forum Foundation, Chairman 1972-73, 1977; Tennessee Democratic Telethon, Director 1972; National Alliance of Handgun Control Organizations, Inc., Director and General Counsel. Honors and Awards: United States Law Week Award; Ford Foundation Grant for Legal Research, Northwestern National Moot Court Team; First Place, Midwestern United States Moot Court Competition; Award for Best Brief, Midwestern United States Moot Court Competition; American Jurisprudence Award in Federal Courts. Address: 121 - 17th Avenue South, Nashville, Tennessee 37203.■

WILLIE G. WOODS

College Educator. Personal: Daughter of Reverend John and Mrs. Jessie Woods. Education: B.A., Shaw University, 1965; M.Ed., Duke University, 1968; Additional

Studies Pennsylvania State University, Temple University, University of New Hampshire, New York University. Career: Harrisburg Area Community College, Professor English/Education 1982 to present, Division Coordinator Tutorial Services 1972-78, Supervisor Writing Center 1975-78, PT Teacher Community Resources Institute 1975-78, Director Act 101/Basic Studies Program 1978 to present, Member/Chairperson of Numerous Committees Within College; Adult Basic Education Teacher, Preston School, 1968-69; Fifth Grade Teacher, Preston School, 1967-69; Language Arts and Social Studies Teacher, Berry O'Kelly School, 1965-67. Organizational Memberships: Pennsylvania Association of Developmental Educators, Board of Directors 1979 to present, Charter Member, State Conference Chairperson 1980 and 1981, Secretary 1981-82, Treasurer 1982-83; Western Region Act 101 Directors Council, Executive Committee 1978 to present, Sub-Regional Representative 1980-81, Council Chairperson 1981-82; Pennsylvania Black Conference on Higher Education, Representative Council 1972 to present, Secretary 1977-79, State Conference Committee 1978-80 and 1981-82, Advisory Committee of *BCOHE Journal* 1982 to present, Assistant Editor of *Journal* 1981 to present; National Council of Teachers of English; National Education Association; American Association of University Professors. Community Activities: Executive Board, People for Progress, 1970-73; Harrisburg Area Young Men's Christian Association, Board of Advisors Youth Urban Services 1981 to present, Camp Curtin Branch — Board of Managers 1971-79, Chairperson Planning Committee, Member Program Committee; Board of Directors, Alternative Rehabilitation Communities, 1978 to present; Adult Leader, 4-H Club, 1967-69; National Association for the Advancement of Colored People; Alpha Kappa Alpha; Volunteer Worker, Morrison for Judge Campaign, 1971; Consultant/Workshop Leader, Several Community and Professional Groups; Board of Directors, Dauphin Residences. Religion: Member of Harmony Missionary Baptist Church; Former Member Church Choir, 12 years; Speaker, Several Special Events and Activities. Honors and Awards: Alpha Kappa Mu National Honor Society; Certificate of Merit for Community Services, Harrisburg, 1971; Meritorious Faculty Contributor, Harrisburg, 1977; Outstanding Service Award, Pennsylvania, 1980; Listed in *Who's Who Among Students in American Colleges and Universities, Who's Who in the East, Personalities of America, Two Thousand Notable Americans, Directory of Distinguished Americans, Community Leaders of America, The Book of Honor, Personalities of the East, International Who's Who of Intellectuals, The International Register of Profiles.* Address: 610 Humphrey Court, Apt. 302, Harrisburg, Pennsylvania 17109.■

AMOS JARMAN WORD, III

Associate and Project Architect. Personal: Born March 10, 1949; Son of A. J. Word, Jr (deceased) and Mary F. Davis Word. Education: Liberal Arts, University of Mississippi, 1967-69; Bachelor of Architecture, Auburn University, 1969-73. Career: Associate and Project Architect, The Ritchie Organization; Architect, Brewer, Godbold and Associates, 1973-78; Architect, Blondheim, Williams and Golson, Inc., 1978-79. Organizational Memberships: American Institute of Architects, Chairman Food and Drink Committee for State Convention. Religion: Member, All Saints Episcopal Church. Honors and Awards: Award for Excellence in Masonry given to Miami Valley Hospital (project architect), 1983; Listed in *Who's Who in the South and Southwest, Personalities of the South, Personalities of America, International Book of Honor.* Address: 101 Gillon Drive, Birmingham, Alabama 35209.■

GEORGE F. WORKER, JR.

Agronomist, Superintendent of Field Station. Personal: Born June 1, 1923; Son of George F. Worker, Sr.; Married Donna Rae; Father of Debbie (deceased), Kent, Stephanie Shoup, Cathy, Melinda Jones. Education: Graduate of Del Nort High School, Colorado, 1941; Attended Adams State College, Colorado, 1941-43, 1946; B.S., Colorado State University, 1949; M.S., Nebraska University, 1953. Military: Served in the United States Army Air Corps, 1943-47. Career: Assistant in Agronomy (Lincoln), Assistant County Agent (Holdrige), University of Nebraska; Agronomist and Superintendent of Imperial Valley Field Station, University of California, El Centro; Consultant, Agronomist, Dr. Tamayo, Venezuela; Manager, Field Trials, Kufra Agricultural Project, Libya; Agronomist, Hawaiian Agronomics, Iran; Agronomist, IRI, North Yemen. Organizational Memberships: Agronomy Society of America, Member Western Section Crop Science, Member California Chapter; Gamma Sigma Delta. Community Activities: Rotary Club, 1955 to present; Meadows Union School Board, El Centro, California; Holtville Unified School Board. Published Works: Author, Chapter 8, *Agriculture in Semi-Arid Environment*; Numerous Research Papers in *Journal of Agricultural Sciences, Agronomy Journal, Crop Science Journal, California Agriculture.* Honors and Awards: Developed and Released Meloland Grain Sorghum and UC Signal Barley; Paul Harris, Sustaining Member. Address: 1004 East Holton Road, El Centro, California 92243.■

NANCY L. WORLEY

Educator. Personal: Born November 7, 1951; Daughter of Lillian S. Worley. Education: B.A., University of Montevallo, 1973; M.A., Jacksonville State University, 1974; Postgraduate Study, Birkbeck College, University of London, University of Edinburgh, University of Alabama. Career: Teacher of Latin, Speech, English. Organizational Memberships: National Junior Classical League, Southeast Membership Chairman, Dramatic Reading Chairman; Alabama Junior Classical League, Promotion Committee; Classical Association of the Middle West and South, Membership Committee, Vice President 1981 to present; Decatur Education Association, President 1979-80, Vice President 1978-79, Board of Directors 1980-83, Secretary 1977-78, Legislative Chairman, A-vote Chairman, Faculty Representative to State Assembly 9 Years; U.T.P. Uniserv Council 5, President 1979-80; Alabama Education Association, President 1983-84, President-elect 1982-83, Board of Directors 1979-82, Legislative Commission, Public Relations Commission, Negotiations Team, IPD Commission; National Education Association, Resolutions Committee Alternate, Delegate to Representative Assembly, 8 Years; Alabama Classroom Teachers Association, President 1982-83, Vice President 1980-82, President-elect 1981-82; Decatur Classroom Teachers Association, President 1980-81, Board of Directors 1977-80, Secretary 1978; Virgilian Society of England and the United States; Alabama Foreign Language Teachers Association, President 1982-83, Vice President 1981-82; National/Alabama Council for Teachers of English; Alabama Speech and Theatre Association; Huntsville Literary Association; International Association for Human Relations Literary Training. Community Activities: Opportunity Toastmistress Club, Vice President, Secretary, Parliamentarian, Speech Contest Chairman, Southeast Regional Audit Committee; Delta Kappa Gamma, Gamma Beta Chapter, Vice President; Kappa Delta Pi; American Association of University Women, President 1981-83, Division Community Area Representative, Division Parliamentarian, Decatur First Vice President, Decatur Secretary/Treasurer, Scholarship Committee, Creative Writing Committee, Art Fair Committee; Morgan County League of Women Voters; American Field Service, Student Sponsor; Alabama/Madison County Young Democrats; Alabama Women's Campaign Organization; Phi Mu Alumnae of Northeast Alabama, Secretary; Huntsville Broadway Theatre League, Faculty Sponsor; Huntsville Little Theatre Alabama Shakespeare Festival, Patron; University of Montevallo Alumni Association, Scholarship Committee; Town and Gown Theatre of Birmingham; Alabama Cystic Fibrosis Foundation, Morgan County Chairman 2 Years; Wheeler Basin Library Reading for the Blind; Morgan County Mental Health Association, Education Committee; Decatur Concert Association, Membership Worker; International Bus Stop, Publicity Chairman; Donations to St. Jude's Research Hospital, Chamber of Commerce Education Committee; Project HOPE Girl Scouts of America, Junior Achievement, Alabama Sheriff's Boy's and Girl's Ranches. Religion: Youth Choir Pianist. Honors and Awards: Alabama's Outstanding Young Educator, 1980; Morgan County Outstanding Young Educator, 1979; Latin Scholarship Award, 1970, 1971; Phi Mu Scholarship Award, 1970, 1971, 1972; Sigma Tau Delta English Honorary Society; Kappa Delta Pi Education Honorary Society; Eta Sigma Phi Scholarship Honorary Society; Dean's List, 1969; President's List, 1970, 1971, 1972; Cum Laude Graduate, 1973; Two Young Leaders of Decatur, 1980; Listed in *Who's Who Among Students in American Universities and Colleges, Personalities of the South, Book of Honor, Personalities of America, Directory of Distinguished Americans, Community Leaders of America, Outstanding Young Women of America.* Address: P.O. Box 162, New Hope, Alabama 35760.■

ROBERT CHARLES WORREST

Associate Professor. Education: B.A., Williams College, Williamstown, Massachusetts, 1957; M.A., Wesleyan University, Middletown, Connecticut, 1964; Ph.D., Oregon State University, Corvallis, Oregon, 1975; Other Graduate Work at Boston College 1967, Northeastern University 1968-69, Boston University 1970-71. Career: Associate Professor, Senior Research, Department of General Science, Oregon State University, Corvallis, Oregon, 1981 to present; Project Leader, Photobiology Program, United States Environmental Protection Agency, Corvallis, Oregon, 1980-82 (temporary intergovernmental assignment from Oregon State University); Assistant Professor of Senior Research 1977-81, Research Associate 1975-77, Instructor of General Biology 1971-72, Teaching Assistant General Biology 1971-72, Oregon State University, Corvallis, Oregon; Biology and Mathematics Teacher, Belmont Hill School, Belmont, Massachusetts, 1959-71; Biology, Chemistry and Mathematics Teacher, Canterbury School, New Milford, Connecticut, 1957-59. Organizational Memberships: American Association for the Advancement of Science; American Society for Photobiology; American Society of Limnology and Oceanography; The Ecological Society of America; Estuarine Research Federation; Pacific Estuarine Research Society; Radiation Research Society; Sigma Xi; Society for Risk Analysis. Honors and Awards: VIII International Congress on Photobiology Travel Grant, American Society for Photobiology, 1980; VII International Congress on Photobiology Travel Grant, National Research Council, 1976; Environmental Health Sciences Center Traineeship, 1972-75; Society of Sigma Xi Grant-in-Aid of Research, 1974;

TWO THOUSAND NOTABLE AMERICANS

Fifth International Congress of Radiation Research Travel Grant, Radiation Research Society, 1974; National Science Foundation In-Service Institution Tuition Grant, Boston University, 1970-71; A.E.C.-N.S.F Research Participation Grant, Oregon State University, 1968; A.E.C.-N.S.F. Summer Institute Grant, Boston College, 1967; A.E.C.-N.S.F. Summer Institute Grants, Wesleyan University, 1960-63. Address: Department of General Science, Oregon State University, Corvallis, Oregon 97331.■

JOHN LAWRENCE WRAY

Corporation Executive. Personal: Born June 17, 1935; Son of Lawrence P. Wray; Married Sally Gerdes; Father of Mary, Nancy, Carolyn. Education: B.S.M.E., M.S., Stanford University, 1958; M.B.A., University of Santa Clara, California, 1966. Military: Served in the United States Air Force, 1958-62. Career: President, Systrol, Inc., 1984 to present; Quadrex Corporation, Vice President of Computer Systems and Operations 1982-84, Vice President of Engineering 1980-82, Director of Engineering Services at N.S.C. 1978-80, Manager of Mechanical Engineering at N.S.C. 1978; General Electric Company, San Jose, California, Manager of Market Research and Planning 1976-78, Manager of Product Planning 1972-76, Area Sales Manager 1970-72, Manager of Licensing and Safety Engineering 1968-70, Manager of Mechanical, Electrical and Chemical System Engineering 1967-68, Manager of Core Proposal Engineering 1965-67, Proposal Engineer 1963-65, Program Engineer 1962-63; University of Virginia Instructor, George Mason College, Arlington, Virginia, 1961-62. Organizational Memberships: American Society of Mechanical Engineers; American Nuclear Society, Professional Divisions Committee 1980-83; Registered Professional Engineer, States of California, Illinois, New York, North Carolina, Ohio, Oregon, Michigan, Minnesota, Texas, Missouri, Oklahoma, Pennsylvania. Community Activities: Elementary School District, Saratoga, California, Financial Committee 1974-75. Honors and Awards: United States Air Force Commendation Medal. Address: 14961 Haun Court, Saratoga, California 95070.■

ANITA KAY WRENTMORE

Mathematics Instructor. Personal: Born December 3, 1955; Daughter of Mr. and Mrs. Lloyd Wrentmore. Education: M.S. Mathematics, Ohio University, 1979; B.S. Mathematics and Teaching Certificate, Ohio University-Lancaster, 1978. Career: Instructor of Mathematics, Central Ohio Technical College, 1983 to present; Lecturer in Mathematics Department, Ohio State University-Newark, 1980-83; Guest Lecturer and Part-time Instructor in Business Department, Central Ohio Technical College, Newark, Ohio, Spring 1983, Fall 1982, Summer 1982, Spring-Summer 1981; Visiting Lecturer Mathematical Sciences, Denison University, Granville, Ohio, 1980; Teacher, Circleville City Schools, Circleville, Ohio, 1979-80; Graduate Teaching Associate in Mathematics, Ohio University, Athens, Ohio, 1978-79; Developmental Mathematics Program Assistant, Ohio University, Lancaster, Ohio, 1975-77. Organizational Memberships: Life Member, National Council of Teachers of Mathematics, Ohio Council of Teachers of Mathematics, Phi Kappa Phi and Kappa Delta Pi Honor Societies, Association of Teacher Educators; Mathematics Association of America; American Mathematical Society; School Science and Mathematics Association; Ohio Mathematics Association of Two-Year Colleges; Newark Council of Teachers of Mathematics; Central Ohio Chapter of the Association for Computing Machinery; Association for Computing Machinery; Association for Individually Guided Education; Council for Basic Education; Association for Supervision and Curriculum Development; National Retired Teachers Association; Ohio Association of Two-Year Colleges; Licking County Business and Professional Women's Club; American Association of University Women. Religion: Member, Pleasant Hill United Methodist Church. Honors and Awards: Nominated for 1981 Teacher of Excellence Award for Ohio State University-Newark; Nominated for 1981 Young Career Woman of the Year, Licking County Business and Professional Women's Club; Listed in *Who's Who in the Midwest, Personalities of America, Personalities of the Midwest, World Who's Who of Women, International Book of Honor*. Address: 103 Ramona Avenue, Newark, Ohio 43055.■

BESSIE M. WRIGHT

Landscape Architect. Personal: Born May 23, 1905, in Centralia, Kansas; Daughter of Onbey Roscoe and Sarah Elizabeth (Shrontz) Roberts; Married Loyd Kenneth Wright (deceased) on February 6, 1924; Mother of John Robert. Education: Attended the American School of Landscape Architecture and Gardening, Newark, New York, 1927; College Southern Idaho, 1965 and 1981 (foreign language). Career: Secretary and Treasurer, Kimberly Nurseries, 1928-78, Treasurer 1978 to present. Organizational Memberships: National Federation Independent Business; American Nurseryman; Idaho Nursery Association. Community Activities: Twin Falls Chamber of Commerce; Twin Falls Fish and Wildlife Conservation Corp; Republican Party; Daughter of the Nile, Past President Zenobia Club #2, Twin Falls; Life Member, Charter Member, Hagerman Valley Historical Society, Hagerman, Idaho; Twin Falls Historical Society, Member of the Board; The Magic Valley Gem Club, Twin Falls, Idaho; The Snake River Archaeology Society of Idaho, Twin Falls, Idaho; The Twin Falls Fish and Wildlife Conservation Corp, Twin Falls, Idaho; Biblical Archaeology Review, B.A.R.; Archaeology Institute of America; National Association of Watch and Clock Collectors; National Member, Smithsonian Associates. Honors and Awards: Life Fellow, American Biographical Institute, National Board of Advisors; Life Fellow, International Biographical Association, Cambridge, England. Listed in *Who's Who in the West, Two Thousand Notable Americans, International Who's Who of Intellectuals, Foremost Women of the 20th Century, Five Thousand Personalities of the World*. Address: Box L, Kimberley, Idaho 83341.■

H. DALE WRIGHT

Hospital Department Director. Personal: Born January 16, 1935; Son of Mr. and Mrs. C. E. Wright (deceased); Married Barbara Jean. Education: Graduate, Acadia Baptist Academy, Eunice, Louisiana, 1952; B.A., Louisiana College, 1955; B.S. 1959, Th.D. 1964, New Orleans Baptist Theological Seminary; Internship Chaplain, Southern Baptist Hospital, New Orleans, 1965; Residency, Chaplain, Southern Baptist Hospital, New Orleans, 1966. Career: Director, Department of Pastoral Care, Baptist Memorial Hospital; Associate Director, Department of Pastoral Care, Southern Baptist Hospital, New Orleans; Pastor, Lakeshore Baptist Church, Lakeshore, Mississippi; Pastor, Harmony Baptist Church, Deville, Louisiana. Organizational Memberships: Louisiana Chaplains' Association, 1972-74; College of Chaplains, American Protestant Hospital Association, President 1981-82; Association for Clinical Pastoral Education, House of Delegates 1980-83; Kansas City Society for Theological Studies, 1977 to present. Community Activities: Family Study Center, University of Missouri in Kansas City, 1979 to present; Greater New Orleans Federation of Churches, Chairman Chaplains' Division, 1968-72. Honors and Awards: Plaque presented in Recognition of Services as President, College of Chaplains, American Protestant Hospital Association, 1982; Plaque for Outstanding Service, Louisiana Chaplains' Association, 1975; Certificate of Merit for Outstanding Service, 1970; Greater New Orleans Federation of Churches. Address: 201 West 70th Street, Kansas City, 64113.■

JEANETTE T. WRIGHT

Junior College President. Personal: Born September 8, 1927; Daughter of Julius and Ida Tornow (both deceased); Married Wilfred D. Wright. Education: B.A. 1956, M.A. 1959, George Washington University; Ed.D., Boston University, 1967. Career: Private Practice in Psychotherapy, Licensed by Commonwealth of Massachusetts; Teacher of Emotionally Disturbed Children, Arlington County Public Schools, Arlington, Virginia; Bay Path Junior College, President, Former Vice President, Dean of College, Dean of Students, Chairman of Department of Behavioral Sciences, Instructor in Psychology. Organizational Memberships: American Psychological Association; Massachusetts Psychological Association, Fellow; National Council of Independent Junior Colleges, Executive Committee, Board of Directors; New England Junior College Council, Board Member. Community Activities: Governor's Commission on the Status of Women, Commissioner 1973-74; Baystate Medical Center, Corporator 1980 to present; Community Savings Bank, Trustee 1982 to present; Springfield Adult Education Council, Board Member; Auto Club of Springfield, American Automobile Association, Director; Carew Girls' Club, Chairman of the Board 1967-70; Girls' Club of America, New England Regional Chairman, National Board Member, 1970-71; Women's Symphony League; Joint Civil Agencies, Women's Division; Springfield Boys Club, Board Member 1969-80; Springfield Mental Health Association, Vice President 1968-69; Longmeadow Professional Council; Springfield Women's Club; Springfield Young Women's Christian Association, Past Trustee. Honors and Awards: Golden Boy Award, Boys Club of America, 1974; Meritorious Achievement Award for Significant Accomplishment in Educational Administration, *Outstanding Educators of America*, 1971. Address: 130 Arlington Road, Longmeadow, Massachusetts 01106.■

MARTIN JUDD WYAND

Educator. Personal: Born May 28, 1931 in Greenwich, Connecticut; Married Margaret A. Knox. Education: B.A. Social Science 1953, M.A. Economics 1954, Pennsylvania State University; Ph.D. Economics, University of Illinois, Urbana, 1964; J.D., University of Denver, 1969; Graduate, Professional Military Education, Air War College, Command and Staff College, Industrial College of the Armed Forces. Military: Served in the United States Air Force, Active Duty at Andrews Air Force Base, Washington, D.C. 1954-56, attaining the rank of Lieutenant; Serves in the United States Air Force Reserves at Lowry Air Force Base, Denver, Colorado, 1956 to present, attaining the rank of Colonel. Career: Lowry Air Force Base, Denver, Colorado, Chairman of Air War College Seminar Division 1974, Academic Instructor in Armed Forces Intelligence Training Center 1978; Instructor of Economics, Pennsylvania State University, 1956-57; Administrative Assistant, Bell Telephone Company of Pennsylvania, 1957-60; Graduate Teaching Assistant in Economics, University of Illinois; Assistant, Associate and Full Professor of Economics, University of Denver, 1964 to present; Accreditation Examiner, North Central Association of Colleges and Universities. Organizational Memberships: American Economics Association; Association for Evolutionary Economics; Rocky Mountain Social Sciences Association; Air Force Association; Reserve Officers Association, Commander, Geddes Chapter; North Central Association of Colleges and Universities; American Collegiate Schools of Business. Community Activities: Colorado Right-to-Work Association, Board of Directors; University of Denver, Faculty Marshall, Commencement Exercises). Religion: Park Methodist Church, Denver, Colorado, Administrative Board of Directors, Bass Singer in Chancel Choir. Published Works: Author, Various Articles Published in Professional Journals; Author, Book Review on Roger Sherman's *Economics of Industry*; Author, Textbook, *The Economics and Law of Antitrust Policy*, in Progress. Honors and Awards: Shell Oil Company Research Grant, 1966; University of Denver Faculty Research Grant, 1976; Listed in *Who's Who in the Men of Achievement, Outstanding Educators of America, Community Leaders and Noteworthy Americans, American Men and Women of Social Science, Personalities of America, Personalities of the West and Midwest, People Who Matter, Noteworthy Americans of 1978.* Address: 15740 East Greenwood Drive, Aurora, Colorado 80013.■

FOREST KENT WYATT

University President. Personal: Born May 27, 1934; Son of Mr. and Mrs. Forest Wyatt; Father of Tara Wyatt Mounger, Elizabeth. Education: B.S. Education, Delta State University, 1956; M.Ed., University of Southern Mississippi, 1960; Ed.D., University of Mississippi, 1975; Advanced Study, Harvard University. Military: Served in the United States Army, 1957-58. Career: President, Delta State University, present; Former Professional Occupations include Mathematics Teacher and Coach in High Schools in Alabama and Mississippi, Principal at Merigold School in Merigold, Mississippi, Alumni Secretary, Administrative Assistant to the President, Director of Administrative Services, and Associate Professor of Education at Delta State University. Organizational Memberships: Mississippi Association of Educators; American Council on Education; American Association of School Administrators; American Association of State Colleges and Universities, Athletic Committee Chairman; Southern Association of Colleges and Schools; Vice President, Mississippi Committee for the Humanities; Past President, Gulf South Conference, Red Red Rose, Kappa Delta Pi; Past President, Phi Delta Kappa; Past President, Parent Teacher Association; Past President, Mississippi Association of Colleges Omicron Delta Kappa. Community Activities: Past President, Board of Governors, Metropolitan Dinner Club; Past President, Cleveland Lions Club; President, Chamber of Commerce; Member of Board, Grenada Banking System; Past President, Industrial Development Foundation; Board of Directors, United Givers Fund; Chairman, Boy Scouts of America Awards Banquet; Board of Directors, Cleveland County Club; Kappa Alpha Order; Past President, Crosstie Arts Council; Member of Board, Mississippi Economic Council; Past Chairman, Mississippi Economic Council "Leadership Mississipi Advisory Committee." Religion: Member First Baptist Church, Member Board of Trustees, Executive Committee, Southern Baptist Theological Seminary. Honors and Awards: Listed in *Who's Who in America, Who's Who in American Colleges and Universities, Outstanding Young Men of America, Personalities of the South.* Address: Box A-1, Delta State University, Cleveland, Mississippi 38733.■

KIONNE ANNETTE WYNDEWICKE

Educator. Personal: Daughter of Clifton Thomas and Missouria Johnson. Education: B.S. Social Science, Illinois State Normal University, 1960; Graduate Study, National College of Education, 1972-81; Attended Williams College, Innovative Teacher Training Institute. Career: Teacher, Chicago Board of Education; Former Positions include Case Worker, Cook County Department of Public Aid, Chicago, Illinois. Organizational Memberships: Illinois Speech and Theatre Association, Past Member; Speech Communications Association; C.A.R.A. Community Activities: Professional Women's Auxiliary of Provident Hospital, Charter Member, Corresponding Secretary 1965, Installation Committee 1963, Yearbook Committee 1964, 1965, 1967, Constitution Committee 1969, Dinner Dance Committee 1969, Publicity Committee Member 1969, 1976, Co-Chairman 1975, Chairman 1974, Volunteer Service Committee 1967, Hospitality Committee 1967, Benefit Committee 1973, Numerous Other Committees 1960 to present. Religion: Christ the Mediator Lutheran Church; Church Council 1978-81, Altar Guild 1960, 1961, 1962. Honors and Awards: One of 25 Black Women Selected in Chicago to Receive Kizzy Award, 1978; Community Service Award from South Central Community Committee, Honored 1981, The Beatrice Caffrey Youth Service, Inc.; M.Ed., National College of Education. Address: 533 East 33rd Place, Apartment 1100, Chicago, Illinois 60616.■

EARL M. WYSONG, JR.

Professor/Consultant. Personal: Born June 3, 1925; Son of Mary E. Wysong; Married Lois A. Wysong; Father of Joyce W. Gordy, Cheryl W. Dankulich. Education: B.A., Eastern Washington University, Cheney, Washington; M.B.A., D.B.A., George Washington University, Washington, D.C.; Military: Served in the United States Air Force to the rank of Major, 1943-46, 1949-62. Career: Professor/Consultant; Accountant/Auditor; Electronic Data Processing Systems Evaluator and Consultant; Aircraft Pilot. Organizational Memberships: Association for Systems Management, International Director 1981-84; Association of Government Accountants, Chairman of Automated Data Processing Committee 1975-78; American Institute of Certified Public Accountants; Institute of Internal Auditors. Community Activities: Calverton Citizens Association, Assistant Treasurer 1970-73, Auditor 1974-81. Honors and Awards: Certified Public Accountant; Certified Information Systems Auditor; Certified Manager; Career Development Award 1968, Literary Award 1967, 1973, United States General Accounting Office; Distinguished Service Award, Association for Systems Management, 1978; Achievement of the Year Award, Association of Government Accountants, 1975. Address: 213 Farmgate Lane, Silver Spring, Maryland 20904.■

ROBERT E. YAGER

Professor of Science Education. Education: B.A., University of Northern Iowa, 1950; M.S. 1953, Ph.D. 1977, University of Iowa. Career: Teacher of High School Science, Chapin, Iowa, 1950-52; Teacher of Basic Education, United States Army, 1953-55; High School Science Teacher/Department Chairman, The University of Iowa Laboratory School, 1956-74; Assistant Professor to Professor of Science Education, The University of Iowa, 1956 to present; Directed 100 National Science Foundation Institutes and Special Projects; Supervied 75 Ph.D. Dissertations; Authored 200 Research Papers; Headed Several Evaluation Teams; Served on Numerous Committees, Task Forces, Boards. Organizational Memberships: Phi Delta Kappa; Sigma Xi; Association for Supervision and Curriculum Development; A.E.R.A.; N.S.S.A.; C.E.S.I.; H.P.A.; S.C.S.T.; President, School Science and Mathematics Association, 1969-70; President, National Association of Biology Teachers, 1970-71; President, Iowa Academy of Science, 1973-74; President, Association of Education of Teachers in Science, 1973-74; President, National Association for Research in Science Teaching, 1974-75; President, National Science Teachers Association, 1982-83. Honors and Awards: National Association of Biology Teacher's Special Citation for Leadership, 1970; National Science Teacher's Association Robert H. Carleton Award, 1977; Iowa Science Teacher's Outstanding Service Award, 1977.■

PRESTON MARTIN YANCY

College Assistant Professor, Newspaper Columnist. Personal: Born October 18, 1938; Son of Margaret R. Yancy; Married Marilyn Leonard, Daughter of Hazel Leonard; Father of Robert James. Education: B.A., Morehouse College, 1959; M.H., University of Richmond, 1968; M.S.S. 1974, Ph.D. 1979, Syracuse University. Career: College Assistant Professor; Newspaper Columnist; Former Civilian Supply Officer for the United States Department of Defense. Organizational Memberships: American Association of University Professors. Community Activities: General Advisory Committee, Richmond (Virginia) Technical Education Center, 1975-78; Trustee, Union Theological Seminary, Richmond, 1969-70; Commonwealth of Virginia Governor's Committee to Hire the Handicapped, 1970-71; City of Richmond Human Relations Commission, 1969-71. Religion: Deacon, All Souls Presbyterian Church, 1966-68. Honors and Awards: National Newspaper Publishers Association Column Awards, 2nd Best 1975, 2nd Best 1976, 3rd Best 1977, 3rd Best 1978, 2nd Best 1980; Danforth Associates Program, 1980-86; United Negro College Fund Strengthening the Humanities Faculty Program Grant, 1981-82. Address: 3360 Mountain Drive #S-203, Decatur, Georgia 30032.■

MARY MARGARET YANKER

Executive, Management Training and Consulting Specialist. Personal: Born March 3, 1936; Daughter of Mary Frances Crawley; Married Robert Henry; Mother of Mary Anne, Robert Jr., Rodney, Randall, Holly. Education: Attended Vanderbilt University (Nashville, Tennessee), 1953-55; A.B. Anthropology 1960, Doctoral Program in Sociology 1962, 1963, and 1966, University of Pittsburgh (Pennsylvania); M.S. Ed. 1969, Ed.D 1973, Northern Illinois University (Dekalb). Career: Instructor in Management Sociology, Anthropology, Education and Behavioral Science, Northern Illinois University, Illinois Waubonsee Community College, Illinois West High School, University of Pittsburgh, 1962-72; Chairperson of Social and Behavioral Science Division 1973-79, Associate Professor of Behavioral Science 1973-81, Dean of Graduate Studies 1979-81, Aurora College (Illinois); Director/Officer, Chicago Consulting Group, 1975-77; President, Owner, Yanker Associates, Management Training and Consulting Specialists, 1978 to present. Organizational Memberships: Chicago Association of Women Business Owners, Board of Directors. Community Activities: Young Women's Christian Association, Board of Directors; Drug Abuse Council, Board of Directors; Family Support Center, Board of Directors; United Way, Board of Directors, Executive Committee; Mercy Center, Institutional Review Committee; Illinois Commission on the Status of Women, Education, Employment and Pensions Committees; City Alderwoman; National Humanistic Education Center, Value Trainer Network; In-service Workshops, over 10,000 Teachers and Administrators in Illinois, Indiana, Michigan, Florida; Workshops, Consulting, School-Related Groups, Businesses and Business Organizations, Police Departments and other Governmental Agencies, Private Social and Community Agencies and Organizations, Health-Related Groups; Core Staff Member, Four-Person Team, Three-Year Grant for Values Education Development, Aurora Schools; Numerous Speaking and Consulting, Management, Values, Decision-Making, Leadership, Motivation, Communication, Stress and Time Management, Team- Building, Women and Consumer Issues. Published Works: Numerous Publications, including "Management Skills for Women in Engineering and Science," "Consumer Complaints for Product and Service Industries," "Humanizing Through Value Clarification." Honors and Awards: Kellogg Fellow (for faculty development), 1977; Danforth Associate for Innovative Teaching and Interest in Values, 1976; Woman of the Year, Aurora, Illinois, 1979; Listed in *Who's Who of Women in Illinois Education*, *Who's Who of American Women*. Address: 7143 Springdale Drive, Northeast, Brookfield, Ohio 44403.■

KEMP PLUMMER YARBOROUGH

Educator. Personal: Born April 29, 1912; Son of William Henry and Eloise Hill Yarborough (both deceased); Married Brigitte Margarete (nee Freiin Roeder von Diersburg), Daughter of Kurt Freiherr and Sophie Freifrau Roeder von Diersburg (both deceased); Father of Victoria Hill Poyser, William Andrew, Charles Christopher. Education: B.A. University of North Carolina at Chapel Hill, 1933; Attended Wake Forest College Law School, 1935-36; M.A. University of South Carolina, 1950; Ph.D. Columbia University, 1963. Military: Served in United States Army, Field Artillery, Active Duty 1942-48 and 1951-53, attained the rank of Captain; Served in United States Army Reserve, attained the rank of Major. Career: Professor (retired), Part-time Teacher; Formerly Codification Assistant (Lawyer), North Carolina Department of Justice, 1941-42; Teaching Assistant and Part-time Instructor, University of South Carolina, 1948-51; Social Studies Chairman and Dean of Faculty, 1954-65, St Mary's College of Maryland; Associate and Full Professor of History and Government 1965-82, Department Chairman 1969-78, Emeritus 1982 to present, Texas Woman's University. Organizational Memberships: American Historical Association; Southers Historical Association; Texas Association of College Teachers; American Association of University Professors. Community Activities: Vice-President, St Mary's County (Maryland) Parent-Teachers Association, 1963-64; Denton Kiwanis Club, Member of Numerous Committees and Chairman of Program Committee, 1974 to present; Contributor to Denton Children's Clinic, United Way, Food Service, and CARE. Religion: Lifelong Member of Episcopal Church; Chapel of Ascension, Lexington Park, Maryland, Chapel Committee 1954-65; St. Barnabas, Denton, Texas, served on Vestry 1967 to present, Senior Warden 1979. Honors and Awards: Phi Beta Kappa, University of North Carolina, 1932; Phi Alpha Theta 1965, Outstanding Faculty Member Award 1968, Texas Woman's University; Campaign Stars for Ardennes, Rheinland, Central Europe (75th Division), 1945; Bronze Star in Korea (623rd F.A. Bn.), 1952. Address: 2522 Emerson Lane, Denton, Texas 76201.■

CLAUDE LEE YARBRO, JR.

Life Scientist. Personal: Born September 26, 1922; Son of Claude Lee Sr. and Laura Belle Yarbro (both deceased); Married Mary Clare Frazier; Father of Laura Anne, Elizabeth Mary, David Lee. Education: B.A. magna cum laude, Lambuth College, 1943; Graduate Studies in Biochemistry undertaken at Vanderbilt University, 1949-51; Ph.D. Biochemistry, University of North Carolina at Chapel Hill, 1954. Military: Served in the United States Naval Reserves, Active Duty 1943-46, Inactive Duty 1947-70, retiring with the rank of Commander. Career: Acting Professor, Mathematics and Physics, Lambuth College, 1946-

47; Instructor, Physics, Union University, 1948; Instructor, Biochemsitry, Vanderbilt University, 1949-51; Instructor, Research Associate, University of North Carolina at Chapel Hill, 1954-60; Biologist, United States Atomic Energy Commission, Oak Ridge, Tennessee; Biological Scientist, United States Energy Research and Development Administration, 1975-78; Life Scientist, United States Department of Energy, Oak Ridge. Organizational Memberships: Society of Sigma Xi, 1954 to present; New York Academy of Sciences, 1954 to present; Elisha Mitchell Scientific Society, 1954-60; American Association for the Advancement of Science, 1953 to present; American Institute of Chemists, Fellow 1968 to present; Ecological Society of America, 1975 to present; American Forestry Association, 1975 to present. Community Activities: Oak Ridge Parent-Teacher Association, 1960-78; Oak Ridge Band Parents, 1968-78; St. Andrews Society. Honors and Awards: Coker Award, Elisha Mitchell Scientific Society, 1954; Sustained Superior Performance Award, United States Atomic Energy Commission, 1966; Superior Job Performance Award, United States Department of Energy, 1952; Military Decorations, American Theatre, Asiatic Pacific Theatre, World War II Victory Medal, Naval Reserve Medal, Armed Forces Medal, Philippines Liberation Medal. Address: 147 Alger Road, Oak Ridge, Tennessee 37830.■

JOYCE L. YARBROUGH

Executive. Personal: Born October 7, 1948; Daughter of Dr. William S. Yarbrough (deceased) and Mrs. Hortense Jackson. Education: B.A. Political Science, Fisk University, 1970; M.B.A. Management, Golden Gate University, 1977. Career: Adminstrative Operations Supervisor, Department of Commerce, Bureau of the Census, 1980 Census; Sales/Statistician, Macy's of California, 1971 to present; Special Projects Coordinator, Economic Opportunity Council of San Francisco, 1971-79; President, Le Nore Company, 1978 to present. Community Activities: Scott-Wada Youth Fund, Treasurer 1977 to present; Westside Community Health, Board of Directors 1971-79, Treasurer 1976-78; Bay Area Urban League, Board of Directors 1973-79; United Way of the Bay Area, Panelist 1971-76; San Francisco Mental Health Association, Board of Directors 1972-78; Catholic Youth Organization, Secretary 1977 to present. Honors and Awards: National Mortar Board Scholastic Society, 1970 to present; Listed in *Who's Who of American Women*. Address: P.O. Box 15117, San Francisco, California 94115.■

FREDA E. KNOBLETT YEAGER

Educator. Personal: Born February 23, 1928; Daughter of Fred and Julia Knoblett (both deceased); Mother of Debra Alayne. Education: B.A., Franklin College (Indiana), 1965; M.A., Sam Houston State University, 1970; Ph.D., Texas A&M University, 1977. Career: Teacher, Columbus (Indiana) Senior High School, Three Years; Part-time Instructor, Texas A&M University, One Year; Fellowship 1968, Instructor while pursuing Ph.D. 1971, Associate Professor, Sam Houston State University. Organizational Memberships: Kappa Delta Pi; Phi Alpha Theta, President Beta Sigma Chapter 1965; C.C.T.E., 1981; S.C. Modern Language Association. Community Activities: Huntsville Planned Parenthood, Board Advocacy Council, Chairman Finance Committee 1981 & 1982; Huntsville National Organization for Women, Treasurer 1981 & 1982; Sam Houston State University, Business Manager *Texas Review* 1980, 1981 & 1982, Nonfiction Editor *The Texas Review*. Religion: St. Stephens Episcopal Church, Huntsville, Texas. Honors and Awards: Knobe Prize Awards for Creative Writing, 1964, 1965; Alpha Honor Society, 1965; Magna Cum Laude Graduate, Franklin College, 1965; Listed in *World Who's Who of Women in Education, World Who's Who of Women, International Who's Who of Intellectuals, Personalities of America, Dictionary of International Biography*. Address: 508 Hickory Drive, Huntsville, Texas 77340.■

JETHRO SUTHERLAND YIP

Retired Entomologist. Personal: Born July 28, 1895, in Victoria, B.C., Canada; Son of Wan Shang Yip and Grace Mark; Married Mabel Leo, on July 6, 1936. Education: B.S. 1921, M.S. 1923, University of California at Berkeley. Career: Control Chemist, F A. Frazier Company, Richmond California, 1924-25; Research Entomologist, California Spray Chemical Company, Watsonville, California, 1925-29; Standard Oil Company of California, San Francisco, 1930-31; Growers Chemical Company, San Francisco, 1932; Pyrethrum Advisor to the Division of Drug and Related Plants, Entomologist Bureau of Plant Industry of United States Department of Agriculture, Washington, C.C., 1934-36 (discovered Pyrethrum cultivated hydroponically can yield two and a half times the total Pyrethrin content found in ordinary soil grown plants); Undertook Personal Inspection of Pyrethrum Transplantation and Observation of Its Adaptive Ability in Lafayette (Indiana), Fort Collins (Colorado), Huntley Experimental Farms (Huntley, Montana), University of Nebraska Agricultural Experimental Station (Lincoln, Nebraska), Umitilla Field Station (Hermiston, Oregon), U.S. Cotton Field Station (Shafter, California), Oregon State Experimental Station (Corvallis, Oregon), Arizona University Agricultural Station (Tucson, Arizona), U.S. Cotton Breeding Station (Greenville, Texas), University of Tennessee Agricultural Station (Knoxville, Tennessee), California Spray Company, Semi-Com. Test Plot (Five Acres in Natividad, California); Developed (in cooperation with Food and Drug Related Plants Engineering Division) a Stripping Machine to Strip Pyrethrum Flowers with Minimum Amount of Stems, Resulting in Less Color Choropfl Extract and a Reduction of Extracting Fluid Required; Research Associate, Division of Plant Nutrition, University of California at Berkeley, 1936-41; Research at the Bureau of Plant Industry, United States Department of Agriculture, Washington D.C. on the Destruction of Seeds of Weed *Cracca virginiana* by Several Insects; Chemist and Entomologist, Twining Laboratory, Fresno, California; Baseball Player. Published Works: Contributor Articles to Professional Journals including *Journal of Economic Entomology, Pyrethrum Culture, Pennsylvania Farmer, Industrial Engineering Soap and Chemicals*. Honors and Awards: Distinguished Service Entomologist Award, London, England, 1939 and 1973; Recipient Numerous Commemorative Awards form London, England; American Bicentennial Recognition Award, 1976; Notable Chinese-American Plaque Award, Chinese Consolidated Benevolent Association, Fresno, 1976; Others; Listed in *World Who's Who in Commerce and Industry, Two Thousand Men of Achievement, Dictionary of International Biography, International Who's Who of Intellectuals, International Register of Profiles, Men of Achievement, Men and Women of Distinction, American Men of Science, Leaders in American Science, Community Leaders and Noteworthy Americans, Notable Americans of the Bicentennial Era, Book of Honor, Personalities of the West and Midwest, Notable Americans*. Address: 3901 East Dakota, Fresno, California 93726.■

DANIEL CHARLES YOEST

Vocational Agriculture Instructor. Personal: Born December 4, 1951; Son of Andrew and Mary Yoest; Married Susan Catherine Hawkins, Daughter of James and Catherine Hawkins; Father of Elizabeth Catherine, Cynthia Susan. Education: Attended State Fair Community College, Sedalia, Missouri, 1969-70; B.S. 1973, M.Ed. 1975, University of Missouri at Columbia. Career: Vocational Agriculture Instructor, Secondary Level, South Callaway School District, Hermann, Missouri, 1982 to present; Instructor Vocational Agriculture, Salem, Missouri, 1973-74; Agriculture Engineering Research Assistant, University of Missouri at Columbia, 1974-75; Instructor Vocational Agriculture, Department Head, Hermann, Missouri, 1975-81; Professional Renovation and Construction, 1979-81; Line Foreman, Gulf Central Pipeline, Santa Fe Industries, 1981-82. Organizational Memberships: American Vocational Association, 1975 to present; Missouri Vocational Association, 1975 to present; National Vocational Agriculture Teachers Association, 1975 to present; Missouri Vocational Agriculture Teachers Association, Past Secretary and Treasurer, Member of Executive Committee and President South Central District 1978-79. Community Activities: Gasconade County Fair, Board of Directors and Director of FFA Farm Mechanics Show, 1975-81; Historic Hermann Inc, Board of Directors, 1977 to present; Hermann Jaycees, 1975-78; Renovation and Restoration of Historic Building in Hermann, 1977 to present; Mayor of Hermann, 1982 to present; Missouri State Department of Education, State FFA Update Committee and State In-service Education Committee 1976-81. Religion: Member of St. George Catholic Church, Hermann, Missouri; Member, Knights of Columbus, 1981 to present. Honors and Awards: Honorary Chapter Farmer, Hermann Chapter of Future Farmers of America (FFA), 1978; Alpha Tau Alpha, 1972; Gamma Sigma Delta, 1975; Listed in *Who's Who in the Midwest, Men of Achievement*. Address: P. O. Box 57, Hermann, Missouri 65041.■

JANG H. YOO

Professor of Economics. Personal: Born February 11, 1941; Son of Jung-Ja Yoo; Married Chong-Cha, Daughter of Chang-Sup Song; Father of Alex, Kenneth. Education: B.A. Economics, Seoul National University, 1963; M.A. Economics, University of California at Los Angeles, 1969; Ph.D. Economics, Texas A&M University, 1972. Career: Professor of Economics, Virginia Commonwealth University; Former Positions include Assistant Professor of Economics at Clark University, Visiting Professor of Economics at Seoul National University, Associate Professor of Economics at Virginia Commonwealth University. Organizational Memberships: American Economics Association; Econometric Society; Board Member, Committee of Asian Economic Studies; Editor, *Journal of Economic Development*. Community Activities: National Program Committee, National Tax Association, 1980-81; Board Member, Committee of Asian Studies, 1983 to present. Published Works: Author *Macroeconomic Theory* 1975, *New York City's Financial Crisis* 1975; Articles Published in *Public Finance Quarterly, KYKLOS, Journal of Economic Development,*

Journal of Development Studies, Social Sciencies Journal, Others. Religion: Executive Council, Hanover Presbytery, 1983-86. Honors and Awards: Research Grant, National Science Foundation, 1981-82; Research Award, Social Science Research Council, 1976. Address: 3219 Nuttree Woods Drive, Midlothian, Virginia 23113.■

NATALIE ANN CATHERINE YOPCONKA

Senior Systems Analyst, Computer Specialist. Personal: Born July 21, 1942; Daughter of Mr. and Mrs. Michael J. Yopconka. Education: B.S. Business Administration, University of Maryland, 1965; M.B.A. Information Technology, George Washington University, 1976; Additional Studies undertaken at American University, United States Department of Agriculture Graduate School; Further Studies undertaken at Virginia Polytechnic Institute and State University, Prince Georges Community College, University of the District of Columbia, Towson State University, University of Maryland, George Washington University. Career: Senior Systems Analyst and Computer Specialist; Former Computer Specialist Auditor, Computer Programmer, Senior Administrative Applications Analyst Programmer, Senior Programmer Analyst, Consultant. Organizational Memberships: Electronic Data Processing Auditors Association; Data Processing Management Association; Association for Computing Machinery (education committee, instructor, 1978-79, education committee, 1980-81, professional development committee, 1982-83, Nat Sig on Security, Audit, and Control); F.A.D.P.U.G. including Special Interest Groups on Security and Auditing, Standards and Quality Assurance, Information Resources, Career Development and Training. Community Activities: Various Positions in Federal Government, Primarily in Computer Field, 1960-78; Various Positions Teaching Computer Science at Professional Association, Junior College, Data Entry School, Universities, 1978-84; Federal Automatic Data Processing Users Group, including the Special Interest Groups on Security and Auditing, Career Development and Training, Standards and Quality Assurance, Information Resources, 1979 to present; Takoma Park Disability Committee, 1980-81; Phi Delta Gamma, Scholarship Committee, Social Committee, Hospitality Committee, Committee Membership in Various Years; Federal Poets Club. Religion: Our Lady of Sorrows Catholic Church, Choir Member 1977-82, Catholic Alumni Club 1976 to present; Sodality, St. Jeromes Catholic Church, 1972-74; Catholic Alumni Club Christmas Choirs, 1976, 1981, 1982. Honors and Awards: Certificate of Appreciation, Association for Computing Machinery, Washington, D.C. Chapter, 1979, 1981; Recommended for Inclusion in Various Who's Who Publications; Certificates of Distinguished Scholarship, Dean's List, Alpha Lambda Delta, Pi Kappa Phi, Beta Gamma Sigma, Graduate with high Honors, University of Maryland; Phi Delta Gamma, George Washington University, Address: 7401 New Hampshire Avenue #1115, Hyattsville, Maryland 20783.■

JOAN E. S. YORK

Counselor. Personal: Born January 18, 1940; Daughter of Julius and Lottie Smith. Education: B.A., West Virginia State College, 1962; M.Ed., Trenton State College, 1980; Non-Degree Student in Doctorate Program, Teacher's College, Columbia University. Career: Counselor, Employee Advisory Service, State of New Jersey; Former Positions include Assistant Director of Work Release Program in Richmond City Jail, Outreach Counselor for Portsmouth Child/Family Service, WIN Social Worker for Hampton Department of Social Services, Social Worker for New York Department of Social Service and Claims Examiner for New Jersey Division of Employment Security. Organizational Memberships: Secretary 1980-82, Advisory Board, Trenton Detox-Alnaa TAP; First Vice President, New Jersey Task Force on Women and Alcohol, 1980-82; Association of Black Psychologists; American Association of Counseling and Development; National Black Alcoholism Counselors; New Jersey Alcoholism Association. Community Activities: Part-time Evening School Program Counselor, Trenton State Prison, 1981-82; Part-time Counselor, Delaware Valley Psychological Clinic, 1982 to present. Religion: Baptist. Honors and Awards: Certified as Alcoholism Counselor, State of New Jersey. Address: 138 Sanhican Drive, Trenton, New Jersey 08618.■

CHESTER RAYMOND YOUNG, SR.

Professor of History. Personal: Born July 2, 1920; Son of Joseph Alexander and Gertrude May Cole Young (deceased); Married Florence Alice Baird, Daughter of Lorenzo Dorland and Charlotte Galloway Baird (deceased); Father of Charlotte May Young Humphreys, Chester Raymond Jr., Virginia Ruth. Education: B.A., Berea College, 1943; M.Div 1949, Th.M. 1959, Southern Baptist Theological Seminary; M.A., University of Hawaii at Honolulu, 1964; Ph.D., Vanderbilt University, 1969. Military: Served in the United States Army Signal Corps, 972nd Signal Service Batallion, Honolulu, 1943-45. Career: Professor of History, Cumberland College; Missionary in Hawaii Stationed in Honolulu, Southern Baptist Foreign Mission Board, 1949-65; Mission Pastor, Columbia Baptist Church, Columbia, Kentucky, 1946-49; Archivist, National Archives, 1942. Organizational Memberships: Society of American Archivists; Associates of the Institute of Early American History and Culture; Virginia Historical Society. Community Activities: Assistant Scoutmaster (Columbia, Kentucky) 1937-38, Scoutmaster (Honolulu, Hawaii) 1945-46 and 1950-53, Boy Scouts of America; Second Vice President, Kalihi-Palama Community Council, Honolulu, 1958-64; Assistant to the Chaplain, Oahu Prison, Honolulu, 1959-64. Religion: President, Hawaii Baptist Convention, 1952-54; Moderator, Honolulu Baptist Association, 1963-64; Deacon, First Baptist Church, Jellico, Tennessee, 1969-70; Deacon, First Baptist Church, Williamsburg, Kentucky, 1972-74, 1976-78, 1983 to present. Published Works: Editor, *Westward into Kentucky: The Narrative of Daniel Trabue*, 1981; Author, *"The Win the Prize": The Story of the First Baptist Church at Williamsburg, Kentucky, 1883-1983*, 1983; Author of Six Articles in Learned Journals, 11 Entries in Dictionaries, 1 Article in Memorial Volume; 5 Historical Essays in Popular Periodicals. Address: Puu Kahea, Becks Creek Road, Williamsburg, Kentucky 40769.■

CLYDE WILLIAM YOUNG

Professor of Music. Personal: Born August 14, 1919; Son of Clyde A. and Rose M. Young (deceased); Married; Father of Martha Rose, Anne Marie, William Geoffrey. Education: B.S.Ed., Diploma in Organ, Southwest Missouri State University, 1941; M.Mus., University of Michigan, 1949; Ph.D. Musicology 1957, M.S. Library Science 1958, University of Illinois. Career: Teaching Assistant, Fellow, University of Michigan, 1949-53; Librarian, University of Illinois, 1957-58; Assistant Professor of Music, State University of New York at Cortland, 1958-60; Assistant Professor, Librarian, University of Nebraska, 1960-61; Assistant Professor, Associate Professor, Nebraska Wesleyan University, 1961-65; Associate Professor of Music 1965-73, Professor 1973 to present, Wayne State University. Organizational Memberships: American Musicological Society. Community Activities: Organist/Chorister, Springfield (Missouri), St Louis (Missouri), New York City, Ann Arbor (Michigan), Lincoln (Nebraska), Chicago, Detroit, Grosse Pointe (Michigan). Religion: Episcopalian. Honors and Awards: Pi Kappa Lambda; First Degree with High Distinction; Listed in *Who's Who in the Midwest, Who's Who in America, Who's Who in the World, Men of Achievement*. Address: 498 Barrington Road, Grosse Pointe Park, Michigan 48230.■

JAMES VAN YOUNG

Professor of Political Science. Personal: Born June 12, 1936; Son of Robert A. and Edith M. Young; Married Virginia Ann, Daughter of F.B. and Eleanor Hudson; Father of Ann Elizabeth, James Hudson. Education: B.A. 1958, J.D. 1960, Ph.D. 1964, The University of Iowa. Career: Professor of Political Science, Central Missouri State University; Assistant Professor of Political Science, St. Olaf College (Northfield, Minnesota), 1964-68; Instructor in Political Science, The University of Iowa, 1964. Organizational Memberships: Missouri Political Science Association; Pi Sigma Alpha, Advisor to Zeta Omicron Chapter at Central Missouri State University. Community Activities: Former Member, Warrensburg Jaycees, 1972-74; Warrensburg Tiger Booster Club, President 1978-79; Central Missouri State University Mules Booster Club and Century Club, 1975-81; University of Iowa National Lettermen's Club, 1974-82; I Club (University of Iowa), 1979-82; Mule Relays Officials Association, 1982 to present; Warrensburg Chamber of Commerce, 1982 to present; Sustaining Member, Warrensburg Jaycees, 1982 to present. Honors and Awards: T.F.A./U.S.A. All-America Award (Masters Track & Field, Shot Put), 1981; Missouri Valley AAU Indoor Shot Put Champion, 40-49 Age Group, 1980 & 1981; 1974 Physical Fitness Leadership Award, City of Warrensburg Jaycees; Phi Beta Kappa; Order of the Coif; Big Ten Medal Athletics and Scholarship, 1959; B.A. summa cum laude; J.D. magna cum laude; Author Two Books. Address: 320 Goodrich Drive, Warrensburg, Missouri 64093.■

MARY LAWRENCE YOUNG

Director of Corporate Communications. Personal: Born August 2, 1938; Daughter of Lawrence (deceased) and Mary Irwin; Mother of John Richard Jr., Lawrence Irwin, Mary Taylor. Education: A.A. Business 1958, B.A. History 1960, University of Louisville. Career: Director of Corporate Communications, The Bingham Companies; Associate Editor, Book Division, *The Courier-Journal* and *The Louisville Times*; Editorial Writer, WHAS-TV and Radio; Newspaper in Education Coordinator, *The Courier-Journal* and *The Louisville Times*. Organizational Memberships: International Association of Business Communicators, President

TWO THOUSAND NOTABLE AMERICANS

(1983-84), Vice President Programs, Vice President Membership, Vice President Placement. Community Activities: Kentucky Governor's Task Force on Education, 1977. Honors and Awards: Various Writing Awards and Awards for Developed Programs. Address: 9838 Longwood Circle, Louisville, Kentucky 40223.■

PATTI K. YOUNG

Stockholder, Executive. Personal: Born December 9, 1944; Daughter of Edmund and Mary B. King Nuss. Education: Attended the University of Oklahoma 1963-65, West Texas State University 1965, Amarillo College 1965-67; Selected Real Estate and Financing Courses, Selected Computer Science Courses. Career: Stockholder, Director, President, The Service Corporation, Mortgage Banking Firm (Dallas, Texas), 1983 to present; 50% Stockholder, Director, Treasurer, Dallas-Apple Tree, Inc., Developer of Long Term Hold & Resale of Housing, 1982 to present; 100% Stockholder, Director, President, International Condominium Enterprises, Inc., 1981 to present; 100% Stockholder, Director, President, Sun & Fun Management Inc., Investment Management (Dallas), 1981 to present; 50% Stockholder, Director, Treasurer, Hulsey Enterprises, Inc., Aircraft, 1978 to present; 50% Stockholder, Director, Southwest Hot Tubs and Spas, Inc. (Dallas), 1978 to present; 100% Stockholder, Director, President, Real Realty Corporation, Commercial and Residential Real Estate (Dallas, El Paso, Amarillo), 1974 to present; 50% Stockholder,l Director, Secretary/Treasurer, Real Condominiums, Inc. (Dallas), 1979-81; INCO, Inc. (Dallas) 1979-81; REAL Designs, Inc. (Dallas) 1975-81; REAL Investments, Inc. 1974-81; Vice President, Hibbard, O'Connor & Weeks, Inc., Stock Brokerage/Mortgage Banking (Houston, Fort Lauderdale, New York), 1974; Executive Vice President, Kirk-Mac Mortgage Company (Dallas, Fort Worth, Houston), 1971-74; Assistant to the President, National BioMedical Laboratories, Inc. (San Antonio), 1971; Production Scheduler, Bell Helicopter (Amarillo), 1968-70; Continuity Writer, WFAI Radio (Fayetteville, North Carolina), 1968; Traffice Director/Continuity Director, KIXZ Radio (Amarillo), 1964-67; Secretary, First National Bank (Amarillo), 1964; Secretary, Advertising Department, Citizens National Bank (Oklahoma City, Oklahoma), 1963. Organizational Memberships: National Association of Realtors; Texas Association of Realtors; Greater Dallas Board of Realtors; El Paso Board of Realtors; Texas Real Estate Political Action Committee, Life Member; Condominium Committee (active in development of new Texas Uniform Condominium Act). Community Activities: Board Member, Park Meadow Homeowners Association, Bell Meadow Homeowners Association, Catillian Homeowners Association, Averille House Homeowners Association, North Park Homeowners Association, TownHouse Row Homeowners Association, Baltimore House Homeowners Association, Hollows North Homeowners Association; University Place Homeowners Association, La Fontaine Homeowners Association, Birchbrook Manor Homeowners Association, Birchbrook II Homeowners Association, Danbury Homeowners Association, Apple Tree Homeowners Association, Douglas Place Homeowners Association (all in Dallas, Texas); Board of Directors, Thunderbird Homeowners Association (El Paso, Texas); Villa Pree Homeowners Association (Amarillo, Texas); Alpha Phi Social Fraternity, Phi Chapter. Published Works: Contributor to *Condominium Conversions*; Various H.U.D. Reports to Congress; Various Reports to the Urban Land Institute. Honors and Awards: Listed in *Who's Who of American Women, International Register of Profiles, Five Thousand Personalities of the World, International Book of Honor*. Address: 3420 Douglas, Dallas, Texas 75219.■

CHESTER EDWARD YOUNGBLOOD

Professor. Personal: Born January 19, 1928; Son of Edward T. and Eunice A. (Russell) Youngblood (deceased); Married Blanca Delia Miramontos, Daughter of Jose and Hilaria Miramontos; Father of Edward Joseph, Claudia Lizette, Alberto Tomas. Education: A.A., Shreiner College, 1948; B.A. 1949, M.Ed. 1951, D.Ed. 1961, North Texas State University; Post-Doctoral Study, North Texas State University 1971, Columbia University 1972, University of Texas-Austin 1973, 1974. Military: Served in United States Army Reserve, 1946-47 and 1951, attaining rank of Second Lieutenant. Career: Associate Professor of Education, College of the Virgin Islands, 1974 to present; Elementary Teacher, Texas Public Schools, 1949-54; Primary Teacher, United States Army Dependents Schools, France, 1954-55; Primary School Principal, Texas Public Schools, 1955-59; Teaching Fellow in Education and Psychology, North Texas State University, 1959-61. Organizational Memberships: Association for Childhood Education International, Committee on Research 1963-66, Committee on Infancy 1975-77, Committee on Intercultural/International Relations 1977-82; Association for Supervision and Curriculum Development; Member, Early Childhood Special Interest Group, National Association for Bilingual Education; National Association for the Education of Young Children; National Association of Early Childhood Teacher Educators; National Council for the Social Studies, Early Childhood Elementary Special Interest Group, Advisory Committee on Early Childhood Education 1977-79; Southern Association on the Education of Children Under Six; National Black Child Development Institute; American Educational Research Association Special Interest Groups on Early Education and Child Development, and on Research in Social Studies Education. Community Activities: Member, Virgin Islands Panel on Education of Handicapped Children, 1978 to present; Member, State Inter-Agency Council for Young Handicapped Children, 1980-82; State Head Start Educational Advisory Committee, Member 1980 to present, Curriculum Consultant for Revision of Virgin Islands Head Start Curriculum 1981; St. Croix Council on Child Abuse, Member 1982 to present, Committee on Educational Programs for School Age Children on Sexual Abuse 1982-83; St. Croix Schol Committee on the International Year of the Child, 1979; Member, Sub-Committee on *St. Croix Directory of Children's Services*. Religion: Member of Community United Methodist Church in St. Croix; Member, Committee on Church Operations, 1979; Consultant, Kindergarten and Day Care Programs, 1978-80; Member, Board of Directors Kindergarten-Day Care Center, 1981-83. Honors and Awards: Honor Graduate, Schreiner College, 1948; Elected Membership, Collegiate National Honor Societies Phi Theta Kappa, Alpha Chi, and Kappa Delta Pi; Recipient First Annual North Texas State University Outstanding Graduate Student Award for Leadership, Scholarship, Service, 1961; Teaching Fellowship, North Texas State University, 1959-61; College Teacher Training Program Fellowship, Columbia University, 1972; Huston-Tillotson College Faculty Fellowship, University of Texas-Austin, 1973; United Methodist Church Board of Education Fellowship, University of Texas-Austin, 1974; Listed in *Who's Who Among Students in American Universities and Colleges*. Address: P.O. Box 1962, Kingshill, United States Virgin Islands 00850.■

DAVID EUGENE YOUNT

Educator, Department Chairman. Personal: Born Jun 5, 1935; Son of Robert Ephram (deceased) and Jeanette Judson Yount; Married Christel Marlene; Father of Laura Christine, Gregory Gordon, Steffen Jurgen Robert, Sonja Kate Jeannette. Education: B.S. Physics, California Institute of Technology, 1957; M.S. Physics 1959, Ph.D. Physics 1963, Stanford University. Career: Professor of Physics and Chairman of the Department of Physics and Astronomy, University of Hawaii; Former Research Associate, Stanford Linear Accelerator Center; Former Assistant Professor, Princeton University. Organizational Memberships: Sigma Xi; American Physical Society; Undersea Medical Society; American Chemical Society; American Association of University Professors. Honors and Awards: Graduated with Honor from Caltech, 1957; Sigma Xi, The Scientific Research Society, 1961; Minnesota Mining and Manufacturing Postdoctoral Fellow, Princeton University, 1963; National Science Foundation Postdoctoral Fellowship, Orsay, France, 1964-65. Address: 5468 Opihi Street, Honolulu, Hawaii 96821.■

JONES GEORGE YOVICICH

Civil Engineer. Personal: Born June 2, 1927; Married Sofia, 1960; Father of One Son. Education: B.S.C.E. 1951, M.S.C.E. 1966, Ph.D. Business Administration 1958, Northwestern University. Career: Civil Engineer, Hollabird and Root, Chicago, 1956-57; Professional Engineer and General Manager 1956-70, Chairman of the Board 1970 to present, Arcadia Engineering International, Inc.; Overseas and Domestic Projects, United States Corps of Engineers, 1951-54; Professor of Structural Engineering, Northwestern University; Chairman of Economics, University of Illinois at Chicago; Legislative Assistant, General Assembly, Illinois; Board Chairman, Oakton College; President, Hamilton State University; President, Tetrakear & Associates, Inc.; Director, Board Member, First National Bank of Chicago and Skokie Community Hospital. Organizational Memberships: American Society of Civil Engineers; Professional Engineers Society of United States. Community Activities: Four Committees, State Legislative General Assembly, Illinois. Published Works: *The Pneumatic Tube Goes Modern* 1958, *Opportunities in Construction* 1960, *Management and Labor* 1962; Contributor to *Engineering News Record*. Honors and Awards: Honors Doctorate in Economics, University of Florida. Address: P.O. Box 712, Skokie, Illionis 60076.■

DANIEL DUWHAN YUN

Physician, Administrator. Personal: Born January 20, 1932; Son of Kap Ryong Yun; Married Rebecca Sungja Choi; Father of Samuel, Lois, Caroline, Judith. Education: Pre-Medical Graduate College of Science and Engineering, 1954; Graduate, College of Medicine, Yon Sei University, Seoul, Korea, 1958; Graduate Study, Trudeau School of Tuberculosis and Other Pulmonary Diseases, Saranac Lake, New York 1962; University of Pennsylvania Graduate School of Medicine 1963; Internship, Quincy City Hospital, Massachusetts, 1960; Residency, Internal Medicine, Presbyterian-University of Pennsylvania, Philadelphia, 1961-63; Fellowship, Cardiology, Presbyterian-University of Pennsylvania, Philadelphia, 1964-65. Career: Philip Jaisohn Memorial Foundation, Inc., Founder, President; Medical Director, Philip Jaisohn Memorial Medical Center, 1975 to present; Rolling Hill Hospital, Elkins Park, Pennsylvania, Director of Special Care Unit 1966-79, Medical Staff 1966 to present; Medical Director, Paddon Memorial Hospital, Happy Valley, Labrador, Canada; Medical Missionary among Deep-

Sea Fishers, Northern Labrador, International Grenfell Association, 1965-66; Clinical Professor of Medicine, University of Xochichalo, Guernavaca, Mexico, 1979. Organizational Memberships: American Association of Internal Medicine; American College of Cardiology; Council on Clinical Cardiology, American Heart Association; Philadelphia County Medical Society; Pennsylvania Medical Society; American Association for the Advancement of Science; American Medical Association; Fellow, Royal Society of Health; Fellow, American College of International Physicians; American College of Contemporary Medicine and Surgery; Montgomery/Bucks Professional Standards Review Organization; World Medical Association; Federation of State Medical Boards of the United States; United States Sentorial Business Advisory Board; United States Congressional Advisory Board; Co-founder, Republican Presidential Task Force; Honorary Member, Advisory Council on Peaceful Unification Policy of Korea. Community Activities: Honorary Member, International Cultural Society of Korea; Advisor, Korean and American Friendship Society; American Law Enforcement Officers Association; Director of Bank of World. Published Works: Author, Several Professional Articles, Nurses' Manual for Intensive Care Nursing. Honors and Awards: Human Rights Awards, City of Philadelphia, 1981; Distinguished Community Service Award, Korean American Association, 1971, 1979. Address: 3903 Somers Drive, Huntingdon Valley, Pennsylvania 19006.■

HELEN YURA

Professor of Nursing, Graduate Program Director. Personal: Born August 1, 1929; Daughter of Michael and Anna Yura. Education: B.S.N.E., University of Dayton, 1953; M.S.N. 1962, Ph.D. 1970, Catholic University of America. Career: Professor of Nursing and Graduate Program Director, Old Dominion University; Assistant Director, Division of Baccalaureate and Higher Degree Programs, National League for Nursing, New York, 1972-79; Chairman, Department of Nursing, St. Joseph College, 1970-72; Instructor, Assistant Professor 1964-70, Mental Health Integrator, The Catholic University of America School of Nursing; Instructor in Nursing, Sacred Heart Hospital School of Nursing, Allentown, Pennsylvania, 1953-60, 1962-64; Staff Nurse, Assistant Head Nurse, Head Nurse, Sacred Heart Hospital, 1950-53. Organizational Memberships: American Nurses Association; American History of Nursing Society, Charter Member 1981 to present; North American Diagnoses Association, Charter Member 1982 to present; National League for Nursing; National Association of Women Deans, Administrators and Councilors. Community Activities: Curriculum Module Coordinator for Research Project "Professional Practice of Nurse Administrators in Long Term Care Facilities" Conducted Jointly by American Nurses Association and American College of Nursing Home Administrators, 1982-84; Board of Directors, Seton Family Center, Emmittsburg, Maryland, 1970-72; Faculty Senate, Old Dominion University, 1980-83. Published Works: Co-Author, *The Nursing Process* (with M. B. Walsh), *Human Needs and the Nursing Process* (with M.B. Walsh), *Nursing Leadership: Theory and Process* (with D. Ozimek and M. B. Walsh); Numerous Publications on Nursing Accreditation, Curriculum Development, Teacher Preparation in Nursing; Member Editorial Board, *Health Care Supervisor*, 1982 to present. Honors and Awards: Honorary Doctorate, Villanova University, 1984; Sigma Theta Tau; Phi Kappa Phi; Special Achievement Alumni Award, University of Dayton, 1979; Outstanding Achievement Award, Field of Nursing, The Catholic University of America, 1978; Fellow, American Academy of Nursing, 1977; Outstanding Educator of America, 1972; Listed in *Who's Who of American Women, Who's Who in the South and Southwest, World Who's Who of Women.* Address: 1210 Spotswood Avenue, Norfolk, Virginia 23507.■

LADESSA JOHNSON YUTHAS

Educator, Specialist in Remedial and Developmental Reading. Personal: Married; Mother of Four Children. Education: B.S. Sociology, Colorado State University, 1949; M.S.Ed., Purdue University, 1954; Ph.D. Reading, University of Colorado at Boulder, 1969. Career: Professor of Reading, Department Chairman, Metropolitan State College (Denver, Colorado), 1966 to present; Consultant, Right-to-Read College Technical Assistant, Colorado Department of Education, 1973-79; Second Grade Teacher, Fort Collins, Colorado, 1955-56; Remedial Reading Supervisor, West Lafayette (Indiana) Public Schools, 1952-55; First Grade Teacher, Aurora, Colorado, 1951-52; Graduate Assistant, Office of Dean of Students, Washington State University at Pullman, 1949-51; Summer Workshop Consultant, Purdue University, 1953, 1954; Graduate Assistant in Reading Center 1968-69, Director of E.P.D.A. Institute 1970 & 1971, Graduate Extension Course 1970, University of Colorado; Visiting Professor, Fort Lewis College (Durango, Colorado), 1969; Consultant, E.S.E.A. Migrant Education, Colorado State Department of Education 1968-71, Bureau of Indian Affairs for the State of New Mexico 1969-70, Division of Youth Services of the State of Colorado 1969-71, Adams County SJ/29 J. Bennett Right-to-Read Program 1975-76. Organizational Memberships: International Reading Association, Nominating Committee 1975-76, Colorado Council Board of Directors 1969-74, President 1972-73; Colorado Optometric Association, Advisory Board Annual Forum on Vision and Learning; Children's Hospital Conference on Learning Disabilities, Advisory Board. Published Works: Author Articles Contributed to Various Professional Journals, including *Journal of Rocky Mountain Reading Specialists, Journal of Reading, Colorado Read.* Honors and Awards: Listed in *World Who's Who of Women, World Who's Who of Women in Education, Who's Who in Colorado, Who's Who Biographical Record of Child Development Professionals, Outstanding Educators of America.* Address: Reading Department, Metropolitan State College, 1006 Eleventh Street, Box 17, Denver, Colorado 80204.■

Z

ROBERT RONALD JOHN MARIA ZABOROWSKI

Provincial Archbishop, Prime Bishop. Personal: Born May 14, 1946, in Detroit, Michigan. Education: Attended LaSalle Extension University; D.D. 1971, J.C.D. 1974, S.T.D./Ph.D. 1976, St. Ignatius Bishop and Martyr Old Catholic Seminary. Career: Church Organist and Choirmaster, St. Elizabeth's Roman Catholic Church (Wyandotte, Michigan) and St. Henry's Roman Catholic Church (Lincoln Park); Priest, Old St. Mary's Roman Catholic Church (Detroit), St. Peters Lithuanian Roman Catholic Church (Detroit), St. Anthony's Lithuanian Roman Catholic Church (Detroit), St. Hedwig Polish Roman Catholic Church (Detroit); Ordained to Sacred Priesthood, Old Catholic Church, 1968; Parochial Assistant, Holy Cross Old Catholic Church (Chicago), 1968; Established Small Parochial Mission (Wyandotte), 1969; Bishop-Elect, 1971; Consecrated to Sacred Episcopate, 1972; Archbishop, 1972; Re-established and Re-organized Former Province of North America of Mariavite Old Catholic Church of Poland, 1974; Prime Bishop with Ecclesiastical and Episcopal Jurisdiction extending throughout North America and into Western Germany, France and Puerto Rico; Lecturer; Historian of Old Catholicism; Para-Professional Counselor. Organizational Memberships: St. Irenaeus Institute, France; Knight of the Grand Cross of the Sovereign Order of St. John of Jerusalem Knights of Malta, Rome; Knight of Justice of the Sovereign Order of St. John of Jerusalem Knights Hospitaller, Malta; Prelate of the Sovereign Military Teutonic Order of the Levant, England; Count of the City of Santo Stefano Alberto 1 Policastro, Prince of Manche-Normandia, Sovereign Titular of Crete, Italy; International Congress of Literature and Arts, France; Honorary Consul of the Republic of Free Poland (in exile). Published Works: Author of Numerous Works in regard to the Mariavite Old Catholic Church; Articles in Secular and Religious Newspapers and Periodicals. Honors and Awards: Honorary Degrees, Institute of Sainte Pierre, France. Address: Mariavite Old Catholic Church, Province of North America, Administrative Center, 2803 Tenth Street, Wyandotte, Michigan 48192-4994.■

VIRGINIA ZACHERT

Research Professor. Personal: Born March 1, 1920, in Jacksonville, Alabama; Daughter of Reinhold E (deceased) and Cora M. Zachert. Education: A.B. Mathematics, Georgia Women's College, 1940; M.A. Experimental Psychology, Emory University, 1947; Ph.D. Industrial Psychology, Purdue University, 1949; Postdoctoral Studies in Statistics undertaken at Virginia Polytech Institute, 1957. Military: Served in the WAVES, 1944-46; Captain, WAF, 1951-52. Career: Statistician, Davison's, Atlanta (Georgia), 1940-44; Aviation Psychologist, Human Resources Research Center, Lackland Air Force Base, San Antonio (Texas), 1949-52; Research Psychologist, Human Resources Research Institute, Air Force Personnel and Training Research Center, Maxwell Air Force Base, Montgomery (Alabama), 1953-55; Research Associate, Auburn Research Foundation, Auburn University, 1955-58; Director of Mathematics Division and Vice President, Sturm-O'Brien Consulting Engineers, Auburn (Alabama), 1958-59; Project Field Director, Automated-Prototype Project (Programmed Instruction), Educational Science Division, U.S. Industries, Kessler Air Force Base, Biloxi (Mississippi), 1959-62; Private Consultant, Programmed Instruction, Norman Park (Georgia), 1960-71; Private Consultant, Programmed Instruction, Good Hope (Georgia), 1971 to present; Visiting Professor, Department of Psychology, University of Georgia at Athens, 1963 to present; Associate Professor, Department of Obstetrics and Gynecology, Medical College, Medical College of Georgia, 1963-70; Professor, Department of Obstetrics and Gynecology, Medical College of Georgia, 1970 to present; Consultant, Silver-Haired Legislature of Georgia, Senate Committee on Health, 1980 to present. Organizational Memberships: American Psychological Association, Fellow Divisions 5, 14 and 19, Fellowship Committee of Division 14 1976-79 and 1981-84 (Chairman 1977-78), Subcommittee on CE Sponsor Approval 1982-84, Committee on Professional Practice 1982; Sigma Xi, Medical College of Georgia Program Committee 1977-78, President-Elect and President of Medical College of Georgia Chapter 1979-81; Georgia Psychological Association, Fellow 1956 to present, Policy and Planning Board Member 1961, Chairman Division IV 1964, Publicity Secretary and Editor 1968-69, Editor Georgia Psychologist 1976-77, Committees Secretary 1969-70, Chairman Membership Committee 1972-75; Alabama Psychological Association, President Division IV 1970-71, Program Committee 1973-74, Chairman Southeastern Regional Conference Meeting 1977; American Association of State Psychology Boards; National Society for Programmed Instruction, National Secretary 1967-68, Medical Program Chairman 1973, Consultant to Board of Directors 1968-70; Georgia State Board of Examiners of Psychologists, Member 1974-79, President 1978-79; Department of Obstetrics and Gynecology, School of Medicine, Medical College of Georgia, Senate Member 1974-82, Executive Board Member 1975-80 and 1982-83, Representative to Academic Council 1979-80, Senate Secretary 1977-78, Committee on Committees 1979-80; Faculty Member, Medical College of Georgia Space Utilization Committee, 1979-83; Academic Council, Medical College of Georgia, Member 1976-84, Educational Policies Committe 1977-79, Executive Committee 1979-83, Rules Committee 1980-84; Association of Professors of Gynecology and Obstetrics, Department Correspondent Affiliate Member 1979 to present. Community Activities: Board Member, Serendipity House Inc., Denver, Colorado, 1976-78; American Association of University Professors, President Medical College of Georgia Chapter 1977-78; American Association of Retired Persons, President Chapter 266 1981; Adjunct Professor, McCormick Theological Seminary, 1977-80; Board Member, Health Center Credit Union, 1980-81; National Council on Aging, 1981 to present; Augusta Senior Enrichment Association, 1981 to present; Board of Directors, Senior Citizens Council of Augusta, 1981 to present; Chairman, Mayor of Augusta Senior Citizen Advisory Board, 1982; President, New Bordeaux Association, 1981 to present. Religion: Modoc Baptist Church (Modoc, South Carolina), Member 1973 to present, Building Committee and Chairman of Fund Raising Subcommittee 1978 to present, Constitution Committee 1980 to present. Published Works: Author/Co-Author Numerous Professsional Publications (including) "Evaluation of Pharmacy Education: The Viewpoint of a Generalist" (1975), "Summary and Recommendations of the Workshop on Teaching Cancer Epidemiology and Early Detection in Oncology Training Programs" (1974), "Future Recommendations" (1973), "The Kessler Study: Electronic Technicians-Four Year Evaluation of Three Types of Training" (1973), "Programmed Pathology in a Coordinated Medical School Curriculum" (with Margaret Jones, 1971). Honors and Awards: Senior Superlative, Georgia State Women's College, 1940; Honorary Citizen, Natchitoches, Louisiana, 1960; Georgia State Women's College Alulmni Day Honors Speaker, Valdosta, Georgia, 1960; Presidential Citation, National Society for Programmed Instruction, 1968, 1973; Outstanding Member, National Society for Programmed Instruction, 1969; American Medical Association Service Recognition, Viet Nam Medical School Project, 1972; Alumni of Year, Valdosta State College, 1980; Delegate to Georgia White House Conference on Aging, 1981; Delegate from Georgia to White House Conference on Aging, Washington, D.C., 1981; Listed in Who's Who in America, Who's Who in the World. Address: 1126 Highland Avenue, Augusta, Georgia 30904.■

GEORGE ZACK

Music Director/Conductor. Personal: Born July 8, 1936; Son of Mr. and Mrs. George Zack (father deceased); Married Kerry Sheehan; Father of Katherine Eugenia, Melissa Sheehan. Education: B.Mus. cum laude, Wichita State University, 1958; M.Mus., University of Michigan, 1960; Ph.D., Florida State University, 1972. Career: Music Director/Conductor, Lexington Philharmonic and Warren (Ohio) Chamber Orchestra; Associate Professor of Music, Hiram College (Hiram, Ohio), 1964-72; Instructor of Music, University of Michigan, 1962-64; Music Director, Wooster (Ohio) Symphony; Music Director, Lexington Musical Theatre Society, 1972-75. Organizational Memberships: American Symphony Orchestra League; Conductor's Guild; American Federation of Musicians, Local 118; Honorary Member, American Federation of Musicians, Local 554-635; Board Member, Central Kentucky Youth Music Society, 1972 to present. Community Activities: Lexington Council of the Arts, 1972-76; Lexington Talent Education Association, 1973-77; Guest Conductor, Central Kentucky Youth Orchestra, 1978; Life Member, Fayette County Parent-Teacher Association; Picnic with the Pops Commission, Appointment by Mayor of Lexington. Religion: Greek Orthodox. Honors and Awards: Guest Conductor, National State Orchestra of Salonika, Greece, 1982; Guest Conductor, Louisville Orchestra, 1976; Guest

Conductor, Romantic Festival in Indianapolis, Indiana, with Louisville Orchestra, 1976; Guest Conductor, Charleston (South Carolina) Symphony Orchestra, 1983; Listed in *Men and Women of Distinction, Who's Who in the South and Southwest, Dictionary of International Biography, Men of Achievement, Notable Americans*. Address: 237 Woodspoint Road, Lexington, Kentucky 40502.■

MARK ALAN ZASTOUPIL

Corporate Engineering Manager. Personal: Born August 29, 1953; Son of Mr. and Mrs. Arthur Zastoupil; Father of Jeanna Kay. Education: B.S.I.E., University of Wisconsin, 1973; Business Management Diploma, LaSalle Extension University, 1976. Career: Corporate Engineering Manager, Sundor Brands, Inc., Previous Engineering Management Positions with Green Giant Company 1973-78. Organizational Memberships: Institute of Industrial Engineers, Senior Member of Central Florida Chapter; American Association of Cost Engineers; American Society of Heating, Refrigeration and Air Conditioning Engineers. Community Activities: Rotary Club of Mt. Dora, Director 1980-82; Chairman of Club Service Committee 1981; Mt. Dora Chamber of Commerce; University of Wisconsin Alumni Association; Advisory Board Committee for Mt. Dora High School Business Department, 1980-82; International Platform Association. Religion: First United Methodist Church of Mt. Dora, Administrative Board 1983 and 1984. Honors and Awards: Fellow Member, Member National Board of Advisors, American Biographical Institute; Served on Governor's Industrial Task Force on Energy for State of Florida, 1981; Listed in *Who's Who in the South and Southwest, Personalities of the South, Book of Honor, Community Leaders of America, Directory of Distinguished Americans, Personalities of America, Men of Achievement, Dictionary of International Biography*. Address: P.O. Box 1184, Mt. Dora, Florida 32757.■

WENDELL EVANS ZEHEL

General Surgeon. Personal: Born March 6, 1934; Son of Emma Zehel; Married Joan; Father of Lori Ann, Wendell Jr. Education: B.A., Washington and Jefferson College, 1956; M.D., University of Pittsburgh, 1960. Military: Served in the United States Air Force, 1961-63, attaining the rank of Captain. Career: General Surgeon. Organizational Memberships: American College of Surgeons; American Medical Association; National Advisory Board, American Biographical Institute; New York Academy of Sciences; Association for Advancement of Medical Instrumentation; American Association for the Advancement of Science. Honors and Awards: Listed in *Who's Who in the East, Personalities of America, Directory of Distinguished Americans, The International Register of Profiles, International Who's Who of Intellectuals, International Who's Who in Community Service, Men of Achievement*. Address: 53 Harrogate Drive, Pittsburgh, Pennsylvania 15241.■

JOHN WILLIAM ZEHRING

College Administrator. Personal: Born September 9, 1947; Married Donna Taber; Father of Micaela Ruth, Jeremiah Donald. Education: B.A., Eastern College, 1969; M.A., Rider College, 1971; M.R.E., Princeton Theological Seminary, 1971; M.Div., Earlham School of Religion, 1981; Advanced Graduate Study, Rhode Island College. Career: Vice President for Development, Bangor Theological Seminary, 1983; Special Assistant to the President, Earlham College; Former Positions include Assistant Dean at Barrington College, Director of Career Planning and Placement at Earlham College; Consultant to Business, Government, Education and Non-Profit Organizations. Organizational Memberships: Council for the Advancement and Support of Education; Yokefellow Institute, Vice Chairman Board of Directors. Religion: Ordained Minister, United Church of Christ. Published Works: Author of Five Books, *Preparing for W*O*R*K, Making Your Life Count, Implications, Careers in State and Local Government, Get Your Career in Gear*; Author of More than 150 Articles in Magazines, including *Yankee, The Black Collegian, Seventeen, The Journal of College Placement, The Chronicle of Higher Education, Christian Herald, Clergy Journal*; Member Editorial Team for *Career Information for College Graduates* and *The College Placement Annual*. Honors and Awards: Exceptional Achievement Award for Public Relations, Special Merit Award for News and Information, Council for the Advancement and Support of Education, 1982; Book of the Year Award, *Group Magazine*, 1982; Listed in *Who's Who in the Midwest, Outstanding Young Men of America, Notable Americans, Dictionary of International Biography, Personalities of America*. Address: 90 Saratoga Avenue, Bangor, Maine 04401.■

S. MICHAEL ZIBRUN

Executive. Personal: Born 1945; Son of Steve and Elizabeth Zibrun; Married Carol Ann, Daughter of Dominic and Mary Salerno; Father of Michael, Jennifer. Military: Served in the United States Naval Reserve, 1968-71. Education: B.A. Business Administration, Elmhurst College, 1968; M.B.A., Illinois Benedictine College, 1982. Career: President, S. Michael Associates; Director, Corporate Communications, Mark Controls Corporation, 1979-81; Director of Advertising, Patten Industries, 1968-79. Organizational Memberships: Chairman Phone Committee 1983, Chairman Internship Committee, Business/Professional Advertising Association. Community Activities: Bellwood Commission on Pornogrpahy, 1980 to present; Bellwood Zoning Board of Appeals, 1976 to present; Secretary, Zoning Board and Plan Commission, 1977 to present. Religion: Lector and Commentator, St. John Chrisostom Church, Bellwood, Illinois, 1974-82. Honors and Awards: Certified Business Communicator; Annual Associate, American Biographical Institute Research Association; Listed in *Who's Who in the Midwest, Who's Who in Finance and Industry, International Who's Who of Intellectuals, Personalities of America*. Address: 346 South 48 Avenue, Bellwood, Illinois 60104.■

JEFFREY L. ZIMMERMAN

Assistant Professor, Clinical Instructor. Personal: Born July 29, 1951; Son of Leonard and Rhoda Zimmerman. Education: B.A., Johns Hopkins University, 1973; M.A. 1977, Ph.D. 1980, University of Virginia. Career: Assistant Professor in the Department of Psychiatry and Behavioral Sciences, Instructor in the Department of Psychiatry and Behavioral Sciences 1980 to present, Clinical Instructor in the Department of Pediatrics 1981 to present, Clinical Instructor in Department of Orthopedic Surgery 1981 to present, Oklahoma University Health Sciences Center. Organizational Memberships: Associate Member, Sigma Xi Scientific Research Society; American Psychological Association, Division 38 and 12; Society for Behavioral Medicine; Society of Pediatric Psychology; Oklahoma Psychological Association. Honors and Awards: Research Grant, "Parameters of Therapeutic Effectiveness in Camp Programming for Chronically Ill Children" (Principal Investigator), National Science Foundation. Address: 217 West Eubanks, Oklahoma City, Oklahoma 73118.■

SHIRLEY L. ZIMMERMAN

Educator and Researcher. Personal: Born November 23, 1925; Daughter of Harry and Rose Schwartz (deceased); Married; Mother of Michael, Danny, Cassey, Julie. Education: B.A. 1947, M.S.W. 1967, Ph.D. 1977, Postdoctoral Studies 1977-78, University of Minnesota. Career: Educator and Researcher, Family Policy, 1982 to present; Social Science Researcher, 1970-73; Chief Welfare Consultant, 1967-69; Case Worker, 1947-49. Organizational Memberships: Board Member, Minnesota Council on Family Relations, 1982; Board Member, Minnesota Human Genetics League, 1981; Chairman, Institutes, Minnesota Social Service, 1979-80; Advisory Committee, National Association of Social Services, Minnesota Chapter, 1980 to present. Community Activities: Group Facilitator, Reach, Minnesota Mental Health Association, 1982 to present; University Senate Committee on Social Concerns, 1981 and 1982; Governor's Task Force on Family and Work, 1981; Advisory Committee, Interreligious Bio-Medical Ethics Committee, 1981 to present; President, National Council of Jewish Women, 1961-63. Honors and Awards: Phi Kappa Phi Honorary Society; Post-doctoral Fellowship, Family Impact Analysis, 1977-78. Address: 3843 Glenhurst, Minneapolis, Minnesota 55416.■

ELIAS PAUL ZINN

Entrepreneur. Personal: Born November 7, 1954; Son of Mr. and Mrs. Julius Zinn; Married Janis Ann. Education: University of Texas, 1972-74. Organizational

Memberships: APRO. Community Activities: Houston Chamber of Commerce; Houston Better Business Bureau; Dallas Better Business Bureau. Religion: Member, United Jewish Appeal, Member, Elutronu Representatives Association. Honors and Awards: Listed in *Who's Who in the Southwest, Personalities of America*. Address: 1480 Sugar Creek Boulevard, Sugarland, Texas 77478.■

ELEMER K. ZSIGMOND

Educator. Personal: Born May 16, 1930; Son of Elemer Zsigmond, J.D., Ph.D. (deceased); Married Kathryn; Father of William Zoltan. Education: M.D., University of Budapest Medical School, 1955; Resident in Anesthesiology, Allegheny General Hospital, Pittsburgh, Pennsylvania, 1961-63. Career: Clinical Anesthesiologist, Director Anesthesiology Research Laboratory, Allegheny General Hospital, 1963-68; Professor, Department of Anesthesiology, University of Michigan, 1968-79; Professor, Department of Anesthesiology, University of Illinois, 1979 to present. Organizational Memberships: American Society of Anesthesiology; Illinois Society of Anesthesiology; Cook County Medical Society; Illinois State Medical Society; American Medical Association; American Society of Regional Anesthesia; International Anesthesia Research Society; American Society of Anesthesiologists. Community Activities: Integrated Curriculum Committee, 1969-71; Pharmacy and Therapeutics Committee, 1971-72 and 1979-81; Civil Liberties Board, 1978-79. Honors and Awards: Numerous Professional Awards. Address: 6609 North LeRoy Avenue, Lincolnwood, Illinois 60646.■

JEROLD JAY ZUCKERMAN

Educator. Personal: Born February 29, 1936, in Philadelphia, Pennsylvania; Son of Harry Earle (deceased) and Evlyn Weisman Zuckerman; Married Rose Elizabeth Stinson, on June 4, 1959; Father of Lesley Jeanne, Thomas Abraham, Amanda Joy, Kathryn Jane, Amy Jo Allyn. Education: B.S., University of Pennsylvania, 1957; A.M. 1959, Ph.D. 1960, Harvard University; Ph.D. 1962, Sc.D. 1976, University of Cambridge, England. Career: Chemist, Smith Kline and French Laboratories, Philadelphia, Summer 1956; Chemist, Houdry Process Corporation, Marcus Hook, Pennsylvania, Summer 1957; Teaching Fellow, Harvard University, 1957-60; Chemist, Massachusetts Institute of Technology, Lincoln Laboratories, Lexington, Massachusetts, Summer 1958; Supervisor of Students in Chemistry, Sidney Sussex College, University of Cambridge, 1961-62; Assistant Professor, Cornell University, 1962-68; Assistant Professor, Harvard University Summer School, 1967; State University of New York at Albany, Associate Professor 1968-72, Professor of Chemistry 1972-76, Director for Research 1972-73; Associate Professor, Harvard University Summer School, 1970; Visiting Professor, Technical University of Berlin, Germany, 1973; Chairman of the Department of Chemistry 1976-80, Professor 1976 to present, University of Oklahoma-Norman; Professeur Associé, Universitié d'Aix, Marseille III, France, 1979, 1982. Organizational Memberships: Alpha Chi Sigma Professional Chemical Fraternity; Fellow, American Association for the Advancement of Science; American Association of University Professors; American Institute of Chemists, Fellow; American Society for Testing Materials; Association of Harvard Chemists; Association of University of Pennsylvania Chemists; The Cambridge Society; Phi Lambda Upsilon Honorary Chemical Fraternity; The Royal Society of Chemistry of London; The Society of the Sigma Xi; *Inorganic Reactions and Methods*, Verlag Chemie, Managing Editor; *Review of Si, Ge, Sn, Pb Compounds*, Editorial Advisory Board; American Chemical Society, Inorganic Chemistry Subcommittee, Examinations Committee, Division of Chemical Education, Past Chairman Committee on Nominations and Symposia Planning, Past Program Chairman, Division of Inorganic Chemistry; NRC-NAS, Past Chairman Ad Hoc Panel on Mössbauer Data Evaluation, Numerical Data Advisory Board; Pergamon Press, Past Regional Editor, Inorganic and Nuclear Chemistry Letters; Academic Press, Past Editor Determination of Organic Structures by Physical Methods; Wiley-Interscience National Science Foundation, Panelist; Consultant, Thiokol/Carstab Corporation, National Institute of Occupational Safety and Health, Bethesda, Maryland, Walter de Gruyter Company (Berlin), Midwest Research Institute, Kansas City, Life Systems Inc., ICAIR Systems Division (Cleveland). Community Activities: Brunswick Common School District, President Board of Trustees 1972-76. Published Works: Author, Over 140 Scientific Papers, Over 90 Communications at Scientific Meetings; Editor of Nine Books; Article on "Molecular Structure," 15th Edition, *Encyclopedia Britannica*; Editor, *Determination of Inorganic and Organometallic Structure by Physical Methods*. Honors and Awards: Philadelphia Board of Education Scholarship, 1953-57; Edgar Fahs Smith Scholarship, 1956-57, University of Pennsylvania; Summer Fellowship 1959, Research Grant 1964 to present, National Science Foundation; National Institute of Health Fellowship, 1958-60, 1960-62; National Institute of Health/ National Cancer Research Grant, 1963-68; Research Corporation Grant, 1968-70; American Chemical Society, Petroleum Research Fund Research Grant, 1968-71; North Atlantic Treaty Organization Grant, 1977-79; Office of Naval Research Grantee, 1977 to present; Alexander von Humboldt Senior Fellowship Award, 1973; Docteur honoris causa, Universitie d'Aix-Marseille III, Marseille, France, 1982; Listed in *Who's Who in the South and Southwest, Men of Achievement, Community Leaders of America, Outstanding Educators of America, Registry of American Achievement, Who's Who in America*. Address: 1608 Chestnut Lane, Norman, Oklahoma 73069.■

LOUIS ANTHONY ZURCHER

Educator, Social Psychologist. Personal: Born May 13, 1936; Son of Louis Anthony and Kathleen Walsh Zurcher (deceased); Married Susan Lee Shrum, Daughter of Amy Shrum; Father of Anthony Walsh, Nora Breen. Education: B.A. Psychology, University of San Francisco, 1961; M.A. Psychology 1963, Ph.D. Psychology 1965, University of Arizona at Tucson. Military: Served in the United States Navy, 1955-59, attaining the rank of Petty Officer; Service in the United States Naval Reserve Medical Service Corps, 1982 to present, with the rank of Commander. Career: Research Social Psychologist, Division of Social Science Research, The Menninger Foundation, Topeka, Kansas, 1965-68; Assistant Professor 1968-69, Associate Professor 1969-73, Professor 1973-78, Acting Department Chairperson 1974-75, Department of Sociology, The University of Texas at Austin; Associate Graduate Dean, Office of Graduate Studies, The University of Texas at Austin, 1975-78; Professor, Department of Sociology, Virginia Polytechnic Institute and State University, 1978-79; Associate Provost and Dean of the Graduate School, Virginia Polytechnic Institute and State University, 1978; Ashbel Smith Distinguished Professor, School of Social Work and Department of Sociology, The University of Texas at Austin, 1979 to present; Acting Dean, School of Social Work, The University of Texas at Austin, 1980-81. Organizational Memberships: American Sociological Association; Fellow, American Psychological Association; Society for the Study of Social Problems; Southwestern Sociological Association; Fellow, Inter-University Seminar on Armed Forces and Society, Executive Board; Society for the Study of Symbolic Interaction; International Sociological Association; Association of Voluntary Action Scholars, Board of Directors 1976 to present, Vice President for Research 1978-79, President 1979-80; Council on Social Work Education; Distinguished Contribution to Scholarship Awards Committee, American Sociological Association, 1983-85; Editor, *The Journal of Applied Behavioral Science*, 1979 to present. Honors and Awards: Alpha Kappa Delta; Psi Chi; Sigma Xi; Phi Beta Kappa; Abraham Maslow Visiting Fellow, Western Behavioral Sciences Institute, 1970; Fellow, American Psychological Association; Fellow, Division of Personality and Social Psychology, American Psychological Association; Fellow of the Society for the Psychological Study of Social Issues; Address: 7623 Rockpoint Drive, Austin, Texas 78731.■

Addendum

TWO THOUSAND NOTABLE AMERICANS

WILMA WILLIAMSON BAITSELL

Retired Art Teacher Supervisor. Personal: Daughter of Glen H. and Luetta Newell Williamson (deceased); Married Victor H. Baitsell (deceased); Mother of Corin Victor, Coby Allan, Corrine B. Robideau. Education: B.S., M.S. Career: Retired Art Teacher Supervisor. Organizational Memberships: New York State Art Association; National Art Association. Community Activities: Order of the Eastern Star; G.O.P.; County and Local Historical Society; Art Guild; Alumni Association. Religion: Member of the Methodist Church, Administrative Board. Honors and Awards: World Anglo-American Academy; Listed in *Dictionary of International Biography, Who's Who in America, Who's Who in Art, Directory of Distinguished Americans, Personalities of America.* Address: 3027 Whittemore Road, R.F.D. 4 Box 330, Oswego, New York 13126.■

KARAN ANN BERRYMAN

Library Director. Personal: Born June 26, 1956; Daughter of John R. and Wilda F. Berryman. Education: A.A. Humanities cum laude, Andrew College, 1974; B.S. Social Science with high honor, Auburn University, 1977; M.S. Library Science, University of North Carolina at Chapel Hill, 1979. Career: Director, Pitts Library, Andrew College, 1980 to present; Professor of English, Andrew College, 1979-80. Organizational Memberships: Georgia Library Association; Southeastern Library Association; American Library Association; Thronesstesska Heritage Foundation; Original Muscogee County Genealogical Society; Phi Kappa Phi; Phi Theta Kappa Alumni Association. Community Activities: Pilot Club; Volunteer Tour of Homes Worker; Volunteer College and Town Archivist. Religion: Member First Baptist Church, Former Church Library Director. Honors and Awards: Miss Andrew College, 1975; Phi Theta Kappa National Alumni Hall of Fame, 1978; Andrew College Sponsor of the Year, 1981, 1982; Listed in *Outstanding Young Women of America, Who's Who in the South and Southwest, Personalities of the South.* Address: P.O. Box 234, Cuthbert, Georgia 31740.■

JEAN DE SALES BERTRAM

Educational Administrator, Professor. Personal: Born in Burlington, Iowa. Education: B.A., University of North Carolina at Greensboro; M.A., University of Minnesota, 1951; Ph.D., Stanford University, 1963. Career: Reporter, *Greensboro News-Record,* 1942-43; Founder and Organizer, Public Relations Department, Burlington Industries, 1943-49; Assistant to the Dean of Education, University of North Carolina at Greensboro, 1949-50; Director of Radio Broadcasting Studio, Minneapolis Vocational High School, 1951-52; Instructor to Associate Professor 1952-71, Professor of Theatre Arts 1972 to present, Director of Committee for Lectures, Arts & Special Programs 1981 to present, San Francisco State University; Special Research in Ear Training and Listening, 1964; Founder and Director, Readers Repertory, San Francisco State University, 1968 to present; Founder and Director, Jean De Sales Bertram Players, 1972 to present; Author and Producer, California Cameos, American Revolution Bicentennial Commission, 1973-74; Author and Producer, American Cameos, 1976; Workshops in Freeing the Voice for Speech and Singing (with Dr. Sven Vedin). Organizational Memberships: Speech Communication Association; California Academy of Sciences. Published Works: Author of *The Oral Experience of Literature* 1967, *Cosmorama* 1972, *The Actor Speaks: A Handbook for Actors and Students of the Voice* 1979, 1980, 1981. Honors and Awards: Phi Beta Kappa; Delta Phi Lambda; Towzer Foundation Scholarship, 1951; Woodrow Wilson Fellowship, 1962; Listed in *Directory of American Scholars.* Address: Department of Theatre Arts, 1600 Holloway Avenue, San Francisco State University, San Francisco, California 94132.■

PAMELA PATRICIA BESCHE-WADISH

Homemaker, Civic Worker. Personal: Born August 15, 1939; Daughter of Mary H. M. Besche; Married Peter Paul Wadish, June 10, 1972; Mother of Andrew Leslie Wadish, Malcolm Stuart Wadish. Education: B.S. Speech Pathology, Newcastle-upon-Tyne University (England),, 1969; M.A. Speech Pathology/Communication Disorders and Sciences, Wayne State University, 1976. Career: Director/Teacher E.S.E.A. Title I in Chinook (Montana) Public Schools, Director of Blaine County (Montana) Adult Education Program, Psychological Evaluator for Chinook School District 10, 1978-80; Lecturer, Clinical Placement Supervisor, Tutor, The College of Speech Sciences, London (England), 1976-77; Post-Diploma Branch Visiting Lecturer, The National Hospitals for Nervous Diseases, Hampstead, London (England), 1976-77; Speech Pathologists/Psychological Evaluation and Consultation, Chinook Public Schools (District 10), 1971-73; Senior Speech Clinician/Supervisor for Graduate Students, Montana State University, Bozeman, 1971; Center Director, Easter Seal Speech and Hearing Center (Billings, Montana), 1970; Speech Pathology Consultant at Camp for Mentally Retarded Children, E.S.E.A. Title IV Superintendent of Public Instruction (Helena, Montana), Summer 1970; Speech Pathologist, University of Montana, Missoula, Summer 1970; Speech Pathologist, Easter Seal Speech and Hearing Center (Butte, Montana) and Headstart Program (Butte), 1969-70; Speech Pathologist, Glenrose School Hospital (Edmonton, Canada), 1969; Inspector/Executive Officer, Ministry of Health and Social Security (Bedford, England), 1962-65; Assistant Science Mistress, Convent of the Holy Ghost School (Bedford, England), 1960; Technical Assistant Biochemistry Laboratory, Unilevers Research Department, 1959-60. Organizational Memberships: Fellow, International Biographical Association; International Neuropsychological Society; Montana Association of School Psychologists; Delta Kappa Gamma, Secretary of Iota Chapter 1980-82; College of Speech Therapists (England), M.C.S.T.; Montana Speech and Hearing Association; British Chiropody Association; Association for Supervision and Curriculum Development; The Council for Exceptional Children. Community Activities: Order of the Eastern Star, Line Officer 1972-80, Matron of Chinook Chapter 1980-81 and 1981-82, Grand Committee Member of the Grand Chapter of Montana 1981-82, Grand Officer (Grand Sentinel) in the Grand Chapter of Montana 1982-83; Order of the Rainbow for Girls, Mother Advisor 1980-81, Rainbow Advisory Board 1977-83; Institute of Advanced Motorists; Welcome Wagon. Honors and Awards: Graduate Assistant Scholarship, Speech Pathology Department, Wayne State University, 1975 (declined due to necessity for orthopedic surgery); University Bursary, Newcastle-upon-Tyne University, 1968; County Major Scholarship, England, 1965; Licentiateship of Surgical School of Chiropody, England, 1964; Other Academic Awards; British Institute of Advanced Motorists Award; Medals and Certificates at Competitive Highland Festivals; Grading and Teaching Certificates in Ballet; Various Sports Awards; Listed in *International Register of Profiles, The World Who's Who of Women.* Address: P.O. Box 1261, Chinook, Montana 59523.■

M. ELOISE BETHELL

Painter and Art Educator. Personal: Born May 7, 1934, in Savannah, Georgia; Daughter of William Craig Pinckney Bethell (deceased) and Mary Guerrant Mitchener Bethell; Mother of Mikhael Bethell Wilkinson. Education: B.A., Converse College; Studies at Various Institutes of Fine Art including Académie de la Grande Chaumière (Paris, France), Instituto Allende (San Miguel Allende, Mexico), Institute Nacional de Bellas Artes (Mexico City and San Miguel Allende), Portland State College (Oregon), New York University; Studies on the Master's Degree Level in Dynamic Symmetry, Mural, Fresco, Oil, Watercolor, Drawing, Gouache, Chinese Ink. Career: Instructor in Fine Art, New York City, Paris, San Miguel Allende, 1953-60; Instructor, Summer Academy of Fine Arts, Aley, Lebanon, 1960; Lecture on Creative Process, Unitarian Church, New York City, 1961; Director of Arts and Crafts, Fort Clark Springs (Texas), 1974-75; Instructor of Watercolor and Drawing, Fine Arts Center (Roanoke, Virginia), 1976; Instructor of Oil, Watercolor and Drawing, Cultural Arts Council of Vinton (Virginia), 1976-78; Instructor of Watercolor, Pastel and Charcoal, Roanoke County (Virginia), 1977; Inservice Training for Public School Teachers, Vinton (Virginia), 1977; Instructor and Owner of Bethell Studio of Fine Art, Roanoke (Virginia), 1976-78; Instructor/Owner, Bethell Studio, 1978 to present; Artist in Residence, Instructor, Deacon Gallery, 1979-80; Instructor, Southeastern Community College, Brunswick County (North Carolina), 1979-80; Instructor, Y.W.C.A., 1981; Instructor, Wrightsville Beach (North Carolina) Recreation Department, 1979; Weekend Workshop in Oil and Watercolor, Lumberton Art Association and Robeson Technical Institute (Lumberton, North Carolina), 1979; Workshop in Watercolor, Rose Hill Art Association (North Carolina), 1980; Workshops in Watercolor, Flying Fish Gallery (Long Beach, North Carolina), 1981; Workshop in Composition, Design and Techniques, Long Beach Art Guild, 1981;

Workshops, Bethell-Golden Painting, 1981 to present; Instructor, Drawing and Watercolor, Community Arts Center (Wilmington, North Carolina), 1982; In-service Training for Public School Teachers, 1982; Demonstrations for Elementary School Children, 1982; One-Man Shows include Greenwich Village Gallery (New York City) 1950, Converse College Gallery (Spartanburg, South Carolina) 1953, Collectors Gallery (New York City) 1957 & 1958, St. John's Gallery (Wilmington, North Carolina) 1958, San Miguel Allende (Mexico) 1958 & 1959, Toronto (Canada) 1959, Portland (Oregon) 1959, Ligoa Duncan Gallery (New York City) 1962, A Creative Experiment in the Arts (New York City) 1965, A Creative Effort by Bethell and Inman (Dialogue between Painter and Poet) 1965, Fort Clark Springs (Texas) 1974 & 1975, Figure Eight Yacht Club (Figure Eight Island, North Carolina) 1978, Deacon Gallery (Wilmington, North Carolina) 1979, Riverbend Gallery (Wilmington, North Carolina) 1982; Two-Man Shows include Collectors Gallery (New York City) 1956, Aley (Lebanon) 1960, Raymond Duncan Gallery (Paris, France) 1962; Juried and Award Exhibits include Museo Nacional de Bellas Artes (Mexico City) 1960, New Jersey International 1962 & 1963, Prix de Paris (France) 1962, Raymond Duncan Gallery (Paris, France) 1962, Museo Nacional de Bellas Artes (San Miguel Allende) 1968, 1969, 1970, 1971, Polyforum de Siqueiros Museum (Mexico City) 1972 & 1973; Riverbend Gallery (Wilmington Art Association Exhibit) 1982, Watercolor Society of North Carolina 1982; Permanent Collections in North and Latin America, Europe and the Middle East. Organizational Memberships: Artists Equity; Associate, American Watercolor Society; Watercolor Society of North Carolina; Associated Artists of Southport (North Carolina); Wilmington Art Association, Vice President 1983. Honors and Awards: Listed in *Two Centuries of Art in New Hanover County, Salome, Artists/USA, Who's Who in the South and Southwest, Personalities of the South, Personalities of America, The Directory of Distinguished Americans, The Biographical Roll of Honor.* Address: 1218 Windsor Drive, Wilmington, North Carolina 28406.■

TOM BEVILL

Congressman. Personal: Born March 27, 1921; Married Lou Betts; Father of Susan, Donald, Patricia. Education: B.S., University of Alabama, 1943; L.L.B., University of Alabama School of Law, 1948. Military: Served in the United States Army, 1943-46, achieving the rank of Captain; Served in the United States Army Reserves, 1943-66, attaining the rank of Lietenant Colonel. Career: Congressman, 90th Congress , Re-Elected to 91st, 92nd, 93rd, 94th, 96th, 97th and 98th Congresses; Former Lawyer. Organizational Memberships: Walker County Bar Association; Alabama Bar Association; American Bar Association. Religion: Baptist. Honors and Awards: L.L.D. (honorary), University of Alabama, 1981. Address: 3827 North Military Road, Arlington, Virginia 22207.■

KARL ALTEN BEVINS

Musician, Teacher. Personal: Born May 30, 1915; Son of Daniel James Bevins (deceased); Married Blanche Albert; Father of Jean. Education: B.S.E.E., Georgia Institute of Technology, 1939; Fellowship and Certificate in Traffic Engineering, Bureau of Highway Traffic, Yale University, 1941; Studied Clarinet and Other Woodwinds under Carl T. Rundquist, Hymie Voxman, Clarence Warmelin, H. Charles Stumph, Michiel Fusco, Frank Chase; Studied Piano under Mrs. Henry Shields, Charles Beaton; Studied Harmony, Arranging and Conducting at the University of Iowa Summer School, 1930, 1931, 1932. Career: Assistant Engineer, Office of the Transportation Engineer, Georgia Power Company, 1940; Traffic Engineer, Georgia Power Company, 1941-49; City Traffic Engineer, Atlanta, Georgia, 1949-78; Solo Clarinet, Band of Atlanta, 1958-74; First Clarinet, Municipal Theatre of the Stars, 1954 to present; Principal Clarinet, Atlanta Symphony Orchestra, 1945-66; Principal Clarinet, Atlanta Pops Orchestra, 1945 to present; Principal Clarinet, Atlanta Philharmonic Orchestra, 1935, 1936; First Clarinet, University of Iowa Summer Symphony Orchestra, 1931, 1932; Instructor in Clarinet, Music Department, Georgia State University, 1964 to present; Private Lessons, 1933 to present; Assistant in Instrumental Music Department, Public Schools, Washington, Iowa, 1933-34; Assistant Director, Hq. Band, Georgia State Guard, 1941-46; Student Conductor, Georgia Tech Band, 1936-39; Assistant Director, Washington, Iowa, Municipal Band, 1934. Organizational Memberships: Registered Professional Engineer, State of Georgia; Institute of Traffic Engineers, President Southern Section 1955, Director District 5 1955-56; Georgia Society of Professional Engineers; Georgia Engineering Society; American Institute of Electrical Engineers; Kappa Kappa Psi, Iota Chapter, President 1938; Atlanta Music Club, Vice President Young Artists Division 1946-47; Atlanta Federation of Musicians, Executive Board 1954 to present, President 1967 to present. Community Activities: Kiwanis Club of Northside Atlanta; City of Atlanta Traffic Commission, Chairman 1949-54; Southern Safety Conference, Chairman Traffic Engineering Section 1952-53; Joint Atlanta-Fulton County Bond Committee on Streets and Highways, 1957-62; Georgia Motor Club, President 1971-72; A.A.A., National Director 1973-75. Honors and Awards: One of Atlanta's 100 Leaders of Tomorrow, Atlanta Chamber of Commerce and *Time* Magazine, 1953; Good Government Award, Junior Chamber of Commerce, 1962; Award for Outstanding Service, Georgia Society of Professional Engineers, 1966; Herman J. Hoose Distinguished Service Award, 1978; First Place, Clarinet Solo, Iowa High School Music Festival, 1933; 2nd Place, Clarinet Solo, National High School Music Festival, Evanston, Illinois, 1933. Address: 110 Laurel Forest Circle N.E., Atlanta, Georgia 30342.■

GERHARD KLAUS BIENEK

Consultant and University Instructor. Personal: Born October 20, 1943; Son of Fritz (deceased) and Hildegard Bienek; Married Rosemarie Edeltraud; Father of Klaus Gerhard, Peter Ralph, Diane Rose. Education: B.A. magna cum laude 1971, Ph.D. 1974, University of Utah. Career: Consultant and Instructor, Utah State University; Former Positions include Endangered Species Coordinator, Scientific Advisor to U.S. Interior Officials (Washington, D.C.), Wildlife Biologist, Environmental Coordinator, Research Biologist, Director of Environmental Sciences. Organizational Memberships: New York Academy of Science; Sigma Xi; American Society of Parasitologists; Rocky Mountain Society of Parasitologists; Ecological Society of America. Community Activities: Cub Scout Master; District Committee Member, Boy Scouts of America; Expert Witness for Endangered Species for Community of Barrow, Alaska; Endangered Species Advisor for Delta (Utah) Residents. Religion: Church of Jesus Christ of Latter-day Saints. Honors and Awards: Affiliate Associate Professor of Ecology, University of Alaska; Full Member, Sigma Xi; Listed in *Who's Who in America, Who's Who in the West, Personalities of America.* Address: 485 K-Street, Salt Lake City, Utah 84103.■

ERMA WOOD CARLSON

Retired Educator and Librarian. Education: B.S., Minnesota University, 1924; B.S., Black Hills Teacher's College, Spearfish, South Dakota, 1930; Further Studies at Drexel Institute, Philadelphia, Pennsylvania, 1932. Career: High School English Teacher, Monticello, Minnesota; Organizer of College Library in Baytown, Texas; Retired. Published Works: Author of Two Books, *The Everlasting Light* and *The Manifestation of God's Law of Abundance*. Honors and Awards: Carnegie Grant for Excellence in Organization of College Library. Address: 4747 Sunset, La Crescenta, California 91214.■

RICHARD CHARLES KARWOSKI

Professor. Personal: Born October 3, 1938. Education: B.F.A., Pratt Institute, 1961; M.A., Columbia University, Teachers College, 1963; Doctoral Equivalency, City University of New York, 1974. Career: Professor of Art, 1969 to present; Book Designer; Illustrator; Art Director, *Family Circle* Magazine; Administrative Assistant and Designer, Simon and Schuster Book Company. Organizational Memberships: Advisory Board, New York Artists Equity Association, 1982 to present; National Arts Club, 1982 to present. Community Activities: Art and Design High School, Advisory Board 1978 to present, Chairperson Alumni Association 1978 to present; Grace Gallery, New York City Technical College, Director 1970-80, Associate Director 1981 to present. Honors and Awards: Commencement Speaker, Art and Design High School, 1979; Materials Award, Pennsylvania Watercolor Society, 1981; First Prize, Juried Art Show, Adelphi University, 1982; Purchase Awrd, Prints, Exxon and Pratt, 1982; Second Prize Watercolor Category (Purchase Award), Art Marketing Letter, 1984; Listed in *Who's Who in American Art*. Address: 28 East 4th Street, New York, New York 10003.■

EMMA NAVAJAS-SOUFFRONT

Administrator. Personal: Born March 26, 1947; Daughter of Emma Souffront de Navajas; Married Arthur James Rytting (deceased). Education: B.A. magna cum laude, Catholic University of Puerto Rico, 1967; J.D. magna cum laude, Catholic University of Puerto Rico Law School, 1971. Career: Director (currently), Attorney-Advisor 1977-78, Director Legal Counsel Division 1978-79, Deputy Director 1979-81, Acting Director 1981-82, Puerto Rico Federal Affairs Administration (formerly Office of the Commonwealth of Puerto Rico in Washington D.C.); Law Enforcement Program Lecturer I, Harford Community College, Athens, Greece, 1973-74; Trial Attorney, Criminal Division, Department of Justice, 1971-73; Associate Professor, History Department, Catholic University of Puerto Rico, 1967-68. Organizational Memberships: Bar of the Commonwealth of Puerto Rico; Bar of the District of Columbia; United States Supreme Court Bar; American Bar Association; Federal Bar Association; Phi Alpha Theta; Alpha Mu Gamma; Phi Alpha Delta. Community Activities: Puerto

TWO THOUSAND NOTABLE AMERICANS

Rico Statehood Commission, Membership Committee 1982 to present; American Junior Red Cross, 1960-64; President Ponce Schools Chapters, 1963-64; Represented United States in the 1963 Goodwill Trip to Latin America. Religion: Member Athenai Air Force Base Catholic Church Parish Council, 1974-76. Honors and Awards: Undergraduate and Graduate Scholarship Recipient; Magna Cum laude Graduate, B.A. and J.D., Valedictorian College of Arts and Humanities, Catholic University of Puerto Rico, 1967. Address: 8101 Connecticut Avenue, Chevy Chase, Maryland 20815.■

LUGO DOMINGO VALENTIN

Company Executive. Personal: Born September 18, 1935; Son of Domingo Lugo Ruiz (deceased); Married Angela Soto, Daughter of Patrio Soto (deceased); Father of Elvin, Alvin D., Alberto, Raul D. Education: Graduate, Dr. Perea School, 1955; Associate Degree in Electronics Engineering, University of Puerto Rico, 1977. Career: Vice President, Former Field Service Engineer, Ortiz Music and Vending; Owner, Doluba Electronics; Vice President, Ramos and Lugo Music Corporation. Organizaitonal Memberships: Institute of Electricl and Electronic Engineers, 1976; President, Radio and Television Technical Association, 1978-79; Counselor, Western Amateur Radio Club, 1980. Community Activities: Guanajibo Sertoma Club, Charter Member 1981, President 1978-79, Lieutenant Governor 1979, Treasurer 1974-77, Sertoma Heart Campaign 1978, National Campaign Crippled Boys and Adults 1973. Religion: Catholic Church, Active Member. Honors and Awards: Gem Award 1972, Tribune Award 1976, Senator Award 1977-78, Award of Merit 1978-79, Life Member 1980, Sertoma International. Address: P.O. Box 656, Moca, Puerto Rico 00716.■

CAROLE A. VEIR

Program Manager. Personal: Born October 5, 1948; Daughter of Frank and Mildred Wilson; Married Wayne William, Son of Gale and Irene Veir. Education: Attended Colorado State University 1966-68, University of Guadalajara (Mexico) 1969; University of Utah 1970-80; Received B.A. Spanish Education, M.Ed. Special Education, Ed.D. Educational Administration; J.D. Candidate, Southland University. Career: Program Manager, Office of Exceptional Children, State Department of Education, Alaska; Assistant Professor, Department of Special Education, A.S.U.; Administrator, Maricopa County Community College, Mesa, Arizona; Instructor, University of Utah, Salt Lake City, Utah; Administrator and Teacher, Granite Schools, Salt Lake City, Utah; Private Educational Consultant, Intermountain Consulting and Educational Services. Organizational Memberships: Phi Delta Kappa; Treasurer, Pi Lambda Theta; Sigma Delta Pi; A.E.R.A.; N.O.L.P.E.; C.E.C.; N.A.B.E.; A.V.A.; T.E.S.O.L. Community Activities: Tempe Community Council, Tempe, Arizona, Vice President, Member Board of Directors, 1980-82; Governor's Committee for the Handicapped, 1982; Planning Committee, Tempe Leadership Conference, 1982; Council for Exceptional Children, National Convention Co-Chaiperson, 1982; League of Women Voters, Public Relations, International Committee, Grant Blocks Program, Education Committee; Advisory Board, Bilingual Education, Mesa Community College, 1980-82; Facultor Sponsor, Phi Theta Kappa, 1980-81; Girl Scout Leader, 1978-79; President, Student Advisory Council, University of Utah, 1979-80; Treasurer, Pi Lambda Theta, 1981-82; A.B.A. Youth Committee. Honors and Awards: Academic Honors, University of Utah, 1970-71; Official Delegate to United States University Educators Goodwill Tour to China, Japan, Hong Kong; Phi Theta Kappa, Meritorious Service and Leadership, 1981; Sigma Delta Pi, 1971; Phi Delta Kappa, 1979; Pi Lambda Theta; Listed in *World Who's Who of Women, Who's Who in the West, Biographical Roll of Honor, Dictionary of International Biography*. Address: 3-6000 Suite 163, Juneau, Alaska 99801.■

Appendix I

TWO THOUSAND NOTABLE AMERICANS

JOSEPH B. GAVIN, Ph.D., S.J.
Campion College, University of Regina, 3769 Winnipeg Street,
Regina S4S 0A2 Canada
President, Campion College, University of Regina, Regina, Canada

CARRIE LEIGH GEORGE, Ph.D., M.Div., Ed.S., M.A., D.Rel.
1652 Detroit Avenue, NW, Atlanta, Georgia 30314 USA
*Research Associate and Assistant Professor of Curriculum and Instruction,
Georgia State University; Ordained Clergywomen, Consultant, Researcher,
Educator*

ANTONIO GIRAUDIER, F.A.B.I., L.P.A.B.I.
215 East 68th Street, New York City, New York 10021 USA
Writer, Author, Poet, Artist, Musician

LEWIS DANIEL HOUCK, JR., Ph.D., L.F.I.B.A., F.A.B.I.
11111 Woodson Avenue, Kensington, Maryland 20795 USA
*Project Leader for Economic Research Service, United States Department of
Agriculture; Management Consultant, Author, Educator, Businessman*

MOZELLE BIGELOW KRAUS, Ed.D., L.A.A.B.I.
The Willoughby, No. 925N, 5500 Friendship Blvd., Chevy Chase,
Maryland 20815 USA
Private Psychology Practice, Psychotherapist

JOHN F. KURTZKE, M.D., F.A.C.P.
7509 Salem Road, Falls Church, Virginia 22043 USA
*Vice Chairman and Professor of Neurology, Georgetown Medical School,
Washington D.C.; Neurologist, Epidemiologist, Consultant, Author*

ENRIQUE ROBERTO LARDE, M.G.A., F.A.B.I.
Post Office Box 2922, Old San Juan, Puerto Rico 00903 USA
*Director, South Continental Insurance Agency, Inc.; Director and President,
Corporacion Insular de Seguros; Researcher, Business Executive*

RUBY STUTTS LYELLS, L.H.D.
1116 Isiah Montgomery Street, Jackson, Mississippi 39203 USA
*Federal Jury Commissioner, United States District Court, Southern District
of Mississippi; Trustee, Prentiss Institute; Writer, Researcher, Librarian*

KRISHNA SHANKAR MANUDHANE, Ph.D., F.A.B.I.
5211 Meadowview Avenue, North Bergen, New Jersey 07047 USA
*Director of Technical Services, Zenith Laboratories, Inc., Northvale, New Jersey;
Researcher*

ROBERT C. McGEE, JR., F.A.B.I.
Box 29540, Richmond, Virginia 23229 USA
*President, Swan Industries, Inc.; Business Executive, Aeronautical Engineer,
Consultant, Administrator*

ROD McKUEN
Post Office Box G, Beverly Hills, California 90213 USA
*Poet, Composer-Lyricist, Author, Performer; President, Stanyan Records, Discus
New Gramophone Society, Mr. Kelly Productions, Montcalm Productions,
Stanyan Books, Cheval Books, Biplane Books, Rod McKuen Enterprises*

HERBERT B. MOBLEY, Ph.D., D.D., S.T.D., L.P.A.B.I.
Post Office Box 165, Summit Station, Pennsylvania 17979 USA
*Pastor Emeritus, St. Mark's (Brown's) United Church of Christ, Summit
Station; Acting Pastor, St. Peter's United Church of Christ, Frackville,
Pennsylvania*

MAKIO MURAYAMA, Ph.D.
5010 Benton Avenue, Bethesda, Maryland 20814 USA
Research Biochemist, National Institute of Health

VIRGINIA SIMMONS NYABONGO, Ph.D.
935 34th Avenue North, Nashville, Tennessee 37209 USA
*Professor Emeritus of French, Research, Tennessee State University; Researcher,
Author, Educator*

MIHAIL PROTOPAPADAKIS
Square Ambidrix 32, 1040 Brussels, Belgium
Deputy, European Parliament

ROLAND B. SCOTT, M.D.
1723 Shepherd Street, NW, Washington, DC 20011 USA
*Distinguished Professor of Pediatrics and Child Health and Director, Sickle
Cell Disease Center, Howard University; Educator, Administrator*

SIR JAMES SIDNEY RAWDON SCOTT-HOPKINS, M.E.P.
2, Queen Anne's Gate, London, SW1H 9AA England
Member of the European Parliament

DR. CHOOMPOL SWASDIYAKORN
196 Phaholyothin Road, Bangkhen, Bangkok 10900 Thailand
Secretary-General, National Research Council of Thailand

HERBERT H. TARSON, Ph.D., F.A.B.I.
4611 Denwood Rod, La Mesa, California 92041 USA
*Senior Vice President, National University, San Diego, California; Researcher,
Educator*

ANDREW B. THOMPSON, JR., F.A.B.I., L.P.A.B.I., L.F.I.B.A.
Post Office Box 3008, Montgomery, Alabama 36109 USA
President, National Pricing Service, Inc.

BASIL P. TOUTORSKY, D.Mus., L.P.A.B.I., F.A.B.I., L.F.I.B.A.
1720 16th Street, NW, Washington DC 20009 USA
Director, Toutorsky Academy of Music; Professor, Composer, Pianist

WALTER E. ULRICH
8 Pasadena Drive, Hamilton Township, New Jersey 08619 USA
Deputy Commissioner, New Jersey State Department of Human Services

AYIYAH W.M. VON NUSSBAUMER, Ph.D., D.Th.
11110 Hazen Road, Houston, Texas 77072 USA
Research Librarian, Published Author, Educator

ROGER LODGE WOLCOTT
4796 Waterloo Road, Atwater, Ohio 44201 USA
*Former Specialist in Aeromechanical Research and Development; Engineering
Department, Goodyear Aerospace Corporation, Akron; Secretary, The Lighter
Than Air Society; Aviation Pioneer, Inventor, Association Executive*

Appendix II

The American Biographical Institute, Inc.
HONORARY EDUCATIONAL
ADVISORY BOARD

THE HONORARY EDUCATIONAL ADVISORY BOARD is a sizeable group of professionals which also advises the *Institute* in the area of editorial nominations and publication recommendations. This Board, however, is specialized in the area of education. There is a National Section and an International Section. There are seven Divisions within this board structure. A member may belong to one or more of the following seven Divisions:

DIVISION OF YOUTH RESEARCH
Nominations should encompass outstanding youths (ages 16-30) in academic, early career, organizational or community leaderships.

DIVISION OF ADMINISTRATIVE RESEARCH
Nominations should encompass administrative/academic leadership (college presidents, academic deans, etc.).

DIVISION OF FACULTY RESEARCH
Nominations should encompass outstanding educational instructors, departmental chairmen, committee chairmen, coaches, etc.).

DIVISION OF LIBRARY RESEARCH
Nominations should encompass leadership in educational research and library organization. Advisory relation of individual library interest in reference acquisition as well.

DIVISION OF FRATERNAL RESEARCH
Nominations should encompass leadership within fraternal organizations (professionals or student members).

NATIONAL AND INTERNATIONAL DIVISIONS

TWO THOUSAND NOTABLE AMERICANS

Freeman, Nelson
Gathy, Vera
Goggans, Kenny
Grondona, Mary
Gucer, Dogan
Gunther, Bruno
Gupta, Gian
Haber, J.
Harris, Lamar
Hayes, Dale
Heinrich, Adel
Hohenfellner, Rudolf
Howell, Roger
Ingles, Jose
Jackson, Linda
Jain, Sohan
Jarvis, Drake
Kashiwazaki, Hiroshi
Keller, Don
Kerr, Alexander
Khatri, Chinubhai
Kriel, Jacques
Krishnamurthy, G. R.
Krudop, James
Kuran, Witold
Lamkin, Billy
Laughlin, Charles
Lenk, Hans
Lentczner, Bennett
Letiche, John
Lidman, Mark
Liebowitz, Harold
Lineberger, Marilyn
Loke-Ming, Chou
Luedeman, John
Malone, Jean
Marchant, Mary
Martin, Gary
McCartney, James
McCaslin, Rosemary
McGee, George
McGuigan, F.

Meredith, Geoffrey
Miehsler, Herbert
Miller, Janet
Miller, Richard
Miller-Thompson, Brenda
Mims, Troy
Morton, Florence
Moura, Jose
Munoz, Jesus
Nelson, Ray
Norman, Cassandra
Nzegwu, Ifeanyi
Odamtten, Helen
Oktaba, Wiktor
Olesiak, Zbigniew
Olivera, Julio
Olson, David
Onat, Altan
Ordona, Irene
Palickova-Patkova, Jarmila
Paolucci, Anne
Papa, Sergio
Papacosta, Pangratios
Parker, Harriet
Parker, Willie
Parthasarathy, K.
Patrick, Danny
Pearn, John
Penland, Arnold
Perry, Emma
Phillips, Ivory
Picken, Stuart
Pietschmann, Herbert
Pirkle, Leon
Pitchlyn, Marlena
Pollack, Robert
Polvino, Geri
Pourciau, Lester
Prasad, Umapati
Rahman, A. H. M.
Rainosek, Alvin
Raunikar, Robert

Ray, Mohit
Rayburn, L.
Rayson, Jack
Reeves, James
Reeves, Joy
Rembert, Emma
Renfroe, Clarence
Rennert, Owen
Reynolds, Richard
Rhyne, David
Ridgel, Gus
Rizvi, Iftikhar
Roark, Jacquelyn
Roberson, Edward
Robertson, Harold
Rodahl, Kaare
Roy, Jean
Rudowski, Witold
Salam, Abdus
Salgueiro, Lidia
Schiflett, Mary
Schneider, Mary
Sebor de Wsseborzicz, Milos
Setty, M. G.
Sharma, Arun
Sharp, Paul
Sharpe, Thomas
Shelton, Bessie
Shively, Joe
Siddiqui, Salimuzzaman
Siegel, Betty
Sisler, Harry
Slimmer, Virginia
Smith, Harry
Snyder, Darl
Sodher, Myra
Sorber, Charles
Sprague, Ginger
Starr, Douglas
Stealy, Dave
Steinfield, Jesse
Straw, Richard

Sturgeon, Mary
Su, Tsung-Chow
Swamy, Ramnath
Szebehely, Victor
Tanja, Jon
Teague, William
Tipton, James
Tucker, Albert
Turner, Dean
Twum-Barima, K.
Tyra, Thomas
Uhlig, George
Uhlir, G.
Vasilescu, Dan
Velez, Joseph
Verbeke, Roger
Vermeer, Donald
Verrastro, Ralph
Vitulli, William
Voss, David
Wagner, Paul
Waldner, Raymond
Walia, Jasjit
Washington, Robert
Weaver, Marie
Webb, Bernice
Webster, Muray
Weeks, Beverly
Welch, Olga
Weldon, John
White, Katie
Williams, David
Wilson, Elizabeth
Wodarski, John
Wood, Frank
Yeh, Chai
Young, Trent
Zacur, Susan
Zatlin, Linda
Zehring, John
Zentner, Mary
Zwemer, Thomas

Appendix III

The American Biographical Institute, Inc.
RESEARCH BOARD OF ADVISORS

THE RESEARCH BOARD OF ADVISORS encompasses an extensive body of individuals which advises the *Institute* in the area of editorial nominations. Quarterly Nomination Campaigns are conducted annually. Appointment to this Board enables each member to influence the content of *ABI* publications, promote permanent biographical documentation and bring selective biographical credentials to light. There is a National Division as well as an International Division.

NATIONAL AND INTERNATIONAL DIVISIONS

TWO THOUSAND NOTABLE AMERICANS

Cleveland, Hattye
Clift, Annie
Closser, Patrick
Coatie, Charles
Cockrell, Claude
Cohen, Norman
Coke, C.
Colbert, Annie
Cole, Eugene
Coleman, Shalom
Collier, Louis
Collins, Clarence
Collins, Patrick
Collins, Wilma
Combier, Elizabeth
Combs, Janet
Combs, Willie
Comfort, Christine
Condon, Donald
Conner, Eunice
Consigli, Joseph
Conte, Gerard
Cook, David
Cooley, Carolyn
Cooley, J.
Conney, John
Cooper, Imelda
Copple, Ray
Core, Carolyn
Corsello, Lily
Cote-Beaupre, Camille
Couch, M.
Coval, Naomi
Covin, Theron
Cowan, Henry
Cowlishaw, Alan
Cox, Clark
Cranshaw, R.
Crews, Harold
Crofford, Helen
Cross, Rose
Crownover, Kenneth
Croxton, Jr., Thoms
Cucin, Robert
Culbertson, John
Cullen, Richard
Cullingford, Ada
Culpepper, Charles
Cushing, Eva
Custer, Dorothy
Daniel, Eunice
Darity, Evangeline
Davey, Thomas
Davidson, Hanna
Davidson, Mabel
Davis, Alexander
Davis, Dorothy
Davis, Evelyn
Davis, Gordon
Davis, Kenneth
Davis, Lottie
Davis, Rosie
Davison, Kenneth
Day, Stacey
Dean, Bennett
Dean, Lloyd
Deboutteville, Edouard
deJaeger, Herman-Karel
De los Cobos Villasenor, I.
De Luca, Carlo
Demos, Aryola
Dencker, Klaus
Denton, Thomas
Derera, Nicholas
de Rodriguez, Adelaida
Deroubaix, Jeanne
Derrick, Homer
Desika, S. A. S.
DeSomogyi, Aileen
Deters, David
Dettman, G.
de Vallbona, Rima Gretel
DeVane, Jessie
De Vito, Albert
De Vos, W.
DiBona, Darrell
Dijak, Denise
Dilsaver, Donna
Doelle, Horst
Doherty, Elizabeth
Dolar, Salvador
Dolcet-Buxeres, Luis
Domes, Jurgen
Dorminey, Clay
Dorough, Virginia
Douglas, Pauline

Dow, Marguerite
Drake, Josephine
Draper, Line
Driscoll, Nancy
Drisko, Barbara
Drown, Eugene
Drucker, Meyer
Dubey, Ph.D., Satya
DuBroff, Diana
Dudley, Joyce
Dula, Joanne
Duncan, Dyna
Dunetz, Anneliese
Dunkel, Lawrence
Dunlap, M.S., Estelle
Dunn, Helen
Duplechain, Lucy
Dupree, Kathryn
Dupuis, DeLores
Durbney, Clydrow
Durrant, Laurice
Earley, Joie
Edwards, Angela
Edwards, Del
Edwards, H.
Edwards-Taylor, Otrie
Eie, Leif
Eisenstein, Alfred
Eiss, Albert
Eizenga, Wietze
Ekeh, Peter
Eldh, Brita
Elam, Oscar
Elder, Gloria
Elguin-Body, Gita
Ellerbee, Estelle
Elliot, Sondra
Elziere, Roger
Emneus, Hans
Emrick, Raymond
Eng, Joe
Engelbrecht, Arthur
Engineer, Jai
Enwonwu, Cyril
Erwin, Jean
Escaler, Ernesto
Escandon, Ralph
Esparza, Thomas
Essenwanger, Oskar
Ester, Mary
Evans, Jo Fred
Evans, Peter
Everett, E.
Falt, Olavi
Farguhar, Betty
Farkas, Zoltan
Farley, Dorothy
Farr, Charles
Farrar, Ph.D., Margaret
Fawcett, Roscoe
Featherstone, Mary
Fedelle, Estelle
Feher, Leslie
Fenske, Virginia
Feodoroff, Nicholas
Ferguson, Harry
Fernandes, Agostinho
Fetterman, David
Feytmans, Ernest
Finch, Thomas
Fink, Aaron
Fiorentino, Carmine
Fish, Robert
Fitts, Stanton
Fleck, Florian
Fleming, A.
Fly, Claude
Forman, Ruth
Foster, Caroline
Foster, Cheryl
Foster, Dudley
Foster, Harold
Fox, Abraham
Fox, Laurette
Fox, Vivian
Framji, Kavasji
Frazier, Marzetta
Fread, Danny
Frederick, Harland
Freeman, Lanny
Freeze, Elizabeth
Freund, E.
Freyler, William
Fuller, Althia
Fuller, James
Fulop, Tamas

Fumi, Fausto
Gailey, APD, Marguerite
Gainer, Ruby
Gallaway, Lowell
Galvan, Sabino
Game, David
Gan, Woon
Gardine, Juanita
Garfinkle, Martin
Garnham, Frank
Garrett, Carol
Gary, Gayle
Gasser, Mariellen
Gaudron, Alfred
Gauthier, Thomas
Gebo, Robert
Geck, Francis
Geizer, Robert
Geneux, Edmond
Gentry, Marlene
George, Carrie
German, Finley
Gewant, Haji
Gibson, Weldon
Gilchrist, Dee
Gillissen, Gunther
Gillum, Perry
Glass, Wendy
Glenn, Lonnie
Gloe, Donna
Glogower, Debi
Gober, Grace
Golden, Constance
Golightly, A.
Gomez, Nelida
Gommel, William
Gonzales, Lucille
Gonzalez, Barbara
Gonzalez Torres, Rafael
Goode, Wade
Goodkin, Sanford
Goodman, David
Goodman, Jess
Goodrich, James
Gospodaric, Mimi
Gould, Carlene
Graham, Edmund
Grant, Geraldine
Gravina, Robert
Gray, Dora
Gray, Nolan
Green, Albert
Green, Virginia
Greenaway, Millicent
Greenberg, Lewis
Greene, Sharon
Greenspan, Adam
Greenway, V. W. H.
Gregory, Sheila Esther
Grier, William
Griffin, Dorothy
Griffin, Patricia
Griggs, Ione
Grigory, H.A.S., Mildred
Gugl, Wolfgang
Gulli, Kathleen
Gundara, Narindar
Guterman, Howard
Haas, Arthur
Haas, D.M.D., Charles
Hackett, William
Hackney, Howard
Hagrup, Knut
Hai, Tran
Hale, J.
Halferty, Diane
Hall, Charles
Hall, Sarah
Halpern, Patricia
Hamajima, Bin
Hamilton, Linda
Hamilton, Madrid
Hammer, Lillian
Hammons, Thomas
Hampton-Kauffman, Margaret
Hanford, William
Hanns, Christian
Hansor, Joseph
Hantgan, George
Harada, Keiichi
Harahap, Marwall
Harbani, Suharnoko
Harbert, Sheila
Hantgan, George
Harbet, Sheila
Hardman, Patricia

Haring, Patricia
Harrell, James
Harrell, Sherrie
Harris, David
Harris, Louise
Harris, Marian
Harris, Patricia
Harris, Paul
Harris, Rae
Harris, Troy
Harris, Vander
Harrison, Winnie
Harshman, Laurian
Hartwell, Linda
Hash, J.
Haulsee, Anne
Havard-Williams, Peter
Havenga-Coetzer, A.
Hawkins, Dourniese
Hayes, June
Hayes, Marcie
Head, William
Heald, Tee
Heckart, Robert
Heggers, John
Hegstrom, Robert
Heilman, Marilyn
Heimdal, Halvard
Heinrich, Busshoff
Hemingway, Eric
Hemleben, Sylvester
Hempler, Orval
Henschel, Jean
Herbert, Edward
Herren, Peter
Herrick, Kathleen
Hertzer, William
Hew, Ah
Hickman, Graham
Hicks, Anna
Hicks, Billy
Hill, Amelia
Hill, James
Hiller, E.
Hillion, Dr.
Hipscher, Jerome
Hitchens, Charles
Hodge, David
Hoens, D.
Holbrook, P.E., F.I.B.A., Edward
Holder, Doyle
Hollin, J.D., Shelby
Hollinger, Sylvia
Hollingsworth, Paul
Holloway, Ernest
Holloway, Warren
Holman, M.D., B.
Holm-Nielsen, Lauritz
Holmstrom, Gustaf
Holsti, Keijo
Hong, Zuu-Chang
Hopkins, Megan
Hori, Jun-ichi
Horiguti, Sinsak
Horn, Marion
Hornsby, J.
Horswell-Chambers, Margaret
Horwitz, Louis
Hostie, Raymond
Houseal, Reuben
Houseal, Ruth
Houser, Edna
Hsia, Han-Min
Hsieh, An-Tien
Hsu, Joseph
Hu, Chua
Huber, Joan
Hubner, Ferdinand
Huggins, Cannie
Hulvey, Larry
Hunley, Ann
Hunter, John
Huraj, Helen
Hutchinson, Ira
Hyett, Evangeline
Hymer, Jack
Iko, Moses
Iley, Martha
Imasogle, Osadolor
Imbach, Jean-Louis
Imbody, Norma
Ingram, Arbutus
Ingram, Benny
Inoguchi, Takashi
Ipes, Jr., Thomas
Issari, M.

Iverson, Virginia
Iyer, R.
Jackson, Ernest
Jackson, Maria
Jacobs, Peter
Jacobsen, William
Jarvinen, Pentti
Jarvis, Elizabeth
Jassal, Kirpal
Javellas, A.C.S.W., Ina
Javier, Concepcion
Jayakody-Vengadaselam, Mr.
Jaye, Robert
Jenkins, Will
Jinadasa, Nial
Johnson, Dorothy
Johnson, Dwight
Johnson, Fred
Johnson, Julian
Johnson, Kenneth
Johnson, Leanne
Johnson, Mohamed
Johnson, Rufus
Jones, Geraldine
Jones, Ruthanne
Jones, Virgil
Joyner, Delores
Kachel, Chanina
Kahar, Adrin
Kakrabah-Quarshie, Ray
Kalb, Roland
Kales, Robert
Kamdar, Hasmukh
Kane, Flora
Kane, Robert
Kang, Byung-Kyu
Kappa, Margaret
Karr-Bertoli, Julius
Kasachkoff, Alisa
Kasperbauer, James
Kato, Hidetoshi
Kauffman, Margaret
Kauppinen, Tero
Kay, Stanley
Keating, Keith
Kedia, P.
Keeler, Sally
Keiser, Edmund
Keishow, Beulah
Kelleher, Bryan
Kelley, Russell
Kelly, Margaret
Keogh, Frances
Kernaleguen, Anne
Keroher, Grace
Kershaw, Beulah
Kersler, Darrel
Kiddell, Sidney
Kilpatrick, Allie
Kim, Dong
Kirby, Ellen
Kirkpatrick, Phillip
Kirkwood, El Wanda
Kitada, Shinichi
Kjartansson, Kristjan
Kline, Tex
Knight, Gloria
Knoedler, Reinhard
Ko, Yih-Song
Kobayashi, Chris
Koch, Frances
Koehler, Isabel
Koehler, Wanda
Koinanoe, Joseph
Kolo, Sule
Korczak-Krzeczowski, George
Kristjonsdottir, Johanna
Kronfol, Zouhair
Kruger, Jeffrey
Kuei-shien, Lee
Kuosma, Kauko
Kurata, Tatsu
Kurjakovic, Mira
Kuttner, Bernard
Kymissis, Pavlos
Lacy, Wilson
Ladson, Barbara Maria
Lair, Helen
Lamb, Charles
Lamoutte, Sylvia
Landers, Ed.D., Vernette
Landy, Eugene
Lane, Mary Frances
Laney, Audrey
Lang, Gloria
Langlois, Aimee

Lant, Jeffrey
Larkin, Gertie
LaRue, DeRette
Laska, Vera
Laudenslager, Wanda
Lauer, Frances
Lawson, Kenneth
Lazenberry, Lillian
Leader, Harry
Leake, John
Leasure, Betty
Leavitt, Charles
Leba, Samuel
LeCocq, Rhoda
Ledbetter, P.
Lee, Min
Lee, Virginia
Lee, William
Lee, Yoo
Leecing, Walden
Leeson, Janet
Lefevre, Margaret
LeGrand, A.
Leibbrandt, Gottfried
Leonard, Nels
Leonard, Jr., Lawrence
Lepage, Robert
Lessenberry, Robert
Lettenmaier, Bernice
Leuterio, Gumersindo
Levin, Michael
Levine, Barbara
Levy, Olivier
Lewis, Erv
Lewis, John
Li, Choh-Luh
Liebe, Ruth
Lin, Ping-Wha
Lin, Yueh-Hwa
Lindberg, Elayne
Linder, Robert
Lingenfelser, Angelus
Lin-Quek, Muriel
Lipscomb, Ph.D., Peggy
Littlejohn, Joan
Littrell, Terril
Lizut, Nona
Lobo, Victor
Loggie, Jennifer
London, Mary Ellen
Long, Shirley
Lorenz, Marian
Love, Joann
Lovejoy, L.L.S., Dallas
Loving, Mary
Loviza, Joseph
Lowman, Pat
Lu, Nien-Tsing
Lugaras, George
Luk, King
Lunn, Joseph
Lyons, Phillip
Macebuh, Sandy
Machen, Roy
Madeira, D.
Magargal, M.D., F.A.C.S., Larry
Mahabir, Ramkhelawan
Mahrer, David
Malami, Alhaji
Malola, Mary
Mamaril, Cezar
Manahan, Manny
Mansir, M.
Maples, Carolyn
Marais, Jan
Marcucci, Silvestro
Marcus, Hellmut
Markham, Reed
Marsh-Edwards, Michael
Martin, Ann
Martin, Carolann
Martin, Wayne
Maruyama, Koshi
Masera, Francesco
Mason, M.D., Dean
Master, Bachoo
Masuda, Gohta
Mathov, Estrella
Matsumoto, Junji
Mauch, Diane
Mauldin, Jean
Mayo, Cynthia
Mazique, Edward
McAnally-Miller, Virginia
McBride, David
McBride-Petonic, Vickie

McCabe, Donald
McCasland, Jean
McCleave, Mildred
McCloskey, R.S.M., Mary
McCoin, John
McCollough, Constance
McConnell, James
McCormack, Grace
McCoy, Frank
McCoy, Patricia
McCurdy, Betty
McDonald, Ian
McDonald, Marjorie
McDuffie, Richard
McFarland, Martha
McGowan, Edward
McIlroy, H.
McLean, Stephen
McNabb, Sue
McNabney, JoAnn
McNurlan, Glen
McQuiddy, M.
McRee, Janice
Mejias, Cristina
Meldrum, Alexander
Mellert, Lucie
Mellinger, Michael
Melton, Sr., Ira
Mendell, Jay
Messerlian, Zaven
Michaels, Mary
Michna, Marienka
Middleton, Anthony
Miller, Arlene
Miller, Virginia
Mills, Margie
Minervini, Francesco
Mishima, Yoshitsugu
Mishra, R.
Mitchell, Peggy
Mitra, Gopal
Moir, Gertrude
Mollenhauer, Bernhard
Money, Donald
Montgomery, Alice
Moore, Elaine
Moore, Jan
Moore, Lynn
Moore, Ola
Morales-Dominguez, Arturo
Mori, Marianne
Morris, Neva Bennett
Morris, R.D.H., Richard
Morrison, Errol
Morrison, Francine
Morrison, Patricia
Morton, Jean
Mosley, Maxine
Mosley, II, James
Motter, Roberta
Movchan, Julian
Moxley, Thomas
Mozingo, Margaret
Mreiden, Alain
Muir, Robert
Mukoyama, Helen
Muller, Gerhard
Muller, Phillippe
Muller, Werner
Murayama, Makio
Murray, Avery
Murray, Karen
Naglee, Elfriede
Nagy, Eva
Nakamae, Tadashi
Natividade, Irene
Naylor, Jr., Pleas
Neef, Hazel
Neeper, Ralph
Neethling, Jacobus
Neetzel, Raymond
Nembhard, M.
NeSmith, Vera
Neumann, Bernhard
Newbern, Captola
Ng, Yew-Kwang
Nicoletti, Francois
Nisbet, Robert
Nohe, B.
Nolen, M.
Northup, William
Nozaki, Masako
Nucci, Annamaria
Nugroho, Mr.
Nwangwu, Peter
Oaera-Oruka, H.

O'Banion, Marguerite
Oberman, Samuel
O'Briant, Lois
Odawara, Ken'ichi
O'Dogherty, Pascual
Ogata, Katsuhiko
Ogletree, David
Oh, May
Okoro, Eugene
O'Meara, Sara
Opas, Philip
Orsi, Gloria
Osborn, III, Prime
O'Toole, Stanley
Owens, Graham
Page, Jane
Pan Davidson, Hanna
Pantle, Wanda
Papadopoulos, Constantine
Parke, Margaret
Parker, Maryland
Parker-Jackson, Maria
Parks, Olivia
Parr, Maria
Pathak, Dev
Patterson, Lloyd
Patterson, Zella
Patton, R.D.H., Celestel
Pavelic, Zlatko
Pavelka, Elaine
Payne, Margaret
Paynter, Dorothy
Pearson, Alice
Pearson, Norman
Peavoy, Sharon
Peck, Baey
Pederson, Trudy
Pekic, Borislav
Pellerin, Mary
Penttila, Rayno
Perry, R.
Peters, Marguerite
Peters-Barnes, Symiria
Peterson, Hans
Peterson, Patricia
Petonic, Vickie
Petracek, Herbert
Petterson, Sylvia
Pfister, Maria
Piemontese, Fanny
Pimenta, Alvaro
Pindera, Jerzy
Pirkle, Estus
Plum, Mary
Plummer, Edna
Plyler, Bob
Poehner, Raymond
Polley, Elizabeth
Polome, Edgar
Ponds, Otis
Ponomarew, Zygmunt-Serge
Popov, Stephan
Popovici, Aleva
Popovici, Petru
Porcar, Alfredo
Porter, Michael
Powell, Russell
Prachaksha, Saisang
Prescott, Lawrence
Price, Ruby
Prichard, Thora
Pringle, Edna
Prodan, James
Propst, L.F.I.B.A., E.
Pross, Harry
Provda, Lois
Pugel, Robert
Pulitano, Concetta
Pupo-Netto, Trajano
Purcell, George
Purdy, N.
Purvis, Dorothy
Purvis, Mary
Radion, Stepan
Ragan, S.
Rahmin, Phillip
Rainford, Henry
Randall, Eugene
Randell, John
Rani, S.
Ratnam, Chaluvadi
Ray, Alice
Reber, Ed.D., Donald
Recktenwald, Lester
Redd, Vivian
Reed, John

TWO THOUSAND NOTABLE AMERICANS

Reemelin, Angela
Reevy, Ph.D., William
Regnier, Claire
Reichle, Frederick
Reihel, Dorothy
Reilly, Jeanette
Reinhardt, Michael
Rejda, Theofil
Replogle, Eleanor
Reuben, Lucy
Rhodes, Ph.D., Veula
Rice, Alice
Richardson, Joyce
Richmond, Quinton
Rickgarn, Ralph
Ridgely, Josephine
Riebe, Norman
Rigg, Margaret
Riggs, Karl
Ringsfdorf, Jr., W.
Robbins, Ruby
Robbins, Viola
Robbins, Wayne
Roberts, C.
Roberts, Josephine
Roberts, Kathleen
Roberts, Roy
Roberts Sammye
Robichaud, Phyllis
Robinson, B.
Robinson, Dorris
Robinson, Mildred
Rodden, Donna
Rodenburg, D.D.S., Carl
Rodine-Pederson, Trudy
Rodkiewicz, Czeslaw
Rodrigues, Louis
Roemer, William
Rogell, Irma
Rogers, Gifford
Rolle, Alvan
Rollins, David
Rolston, Margaret
Romain, Margaret
Roney, Alice
Ronningen, Knut
Roode, Johanna
Rorschach, Martha
Rose, Delbert
Rose, Marian
Rosenthal, Leonard
Ross, Monte
Roth, Frederic
Rothman, Barry
Roudybush, Franklin
Roush, Mildred
Ruane, Richard
Rubin, Luce
Rubly, Grant
Rubly, Lucille
Ruby, Ralph
Ruiz, Jaime
Rulan, Phili
Ruse, Woody
Russo, Jose
Rustvold, Clarence
Rutsch, Alexander
Ryan, James
Rytting, Emma
Rzeminski, Peter
S., Rafael
Sabet, Mohsen
Saenz-Larrasquitu, Ray
Sail, Alcides
Salamon, Adalbert
Saleh, Mohamad
Sams, Mary
Sanchez, Juan
Sandred, Karl
Sanford, Paul
Sano, Keiji
Santos, Gonzalo
Sarraga, Dante
Sarver-Schultz, Sharon
Saunders, Ramsey
Savard, Lorena

Sawyer, Valerie
Saxton, Beryl
Schary, Susan
Schauss, Alexander
Schiffer, Joseph
Schindelin, Juergen
Schlee, Walter
Schmidt, Werner
Schmueckle, Jean
Schoedel, Vicki
Schroth, Evelyn
Schultz, Roy
Schulze, P.
Schuster, Helmut
Schwartz-Moscovici, Jeanna
Schwarzott, Wilhelm
Scott, Ainsworth
Scott, Elizabeth
Scott, Patricia
Sena, Patrick
Seneris, P.
Sengelaub, Mary
Seshacharlu, S.
Sexauer, Arwin
Shadle, George
Shalowitz, Erwin
Shaw, Ernest
Shecter, Pearl
Shehata, Ramzy
Shelton, Bessie
Shepard, Charles
Sherman, A.
Sherman, Eric
Shoenight, Pauline
Shrider, James
Siddelley, Barbara
Sigler, W.
Simeck, Clyde
Simpson, Barbara
Simpson, Jack
Simpson, M.S.W., Carole
Sincock, John
Singh, Vijay
Sjostedt, Ulf
Skiff, Russell
Skold, Hans
Skyllstad, Kjell
Sletager, Janice
Sliger, Halfdan
Small, Fay
Small, Rosemary
Smeeton, Patricia
Smith, Candace
Smith, Diane
Smith, Donna
Smith, Joseph
Smith, Ruth
Smith, Sam
Smith, Valentine
Smyth, Dacre
Smythe-Wood, Ian Alastair
Snell, June
Snydelaar, Margaret
Soboyejo, Olujimi
Sokoya, J. A.
Sommer, Patricia
Southward, B.
Spelts, Richard
Sperry, S.
Spethman, Dorothy
Spinks, John
Spira, Phyllis
Spitler, Lee
Spriggs, Garry
Spruce, Frances
Staaf, Anders
Stalder, Henry
Stallings, Viola
Standertskjld-Nordenstam, Carl-Gustaf
Stanford, Billy
Stenback, Guy
Stertmeyer, Randall
Stockman, Herbert
Strandell, Marjatta
Street, Julia

Stripling, Johnnie
Stroman, Ph.D., Samuel
Stromille, Mario
Strong, Leah
Strother, Hazel
Stuhl, Oskar
Su, Der-Ruenn
Suddith, Roberta
Sukaiman, T.
Suliin, Sheila
Suma, Kozo
Sun, Teresa
Sundardi, Florentinus
Swamy, M.N.S.
Swantz, Maria
Swarthout, Walter
Sweet, Jay
Sweezy, John
Sweitzer, Harry
Switaj, Lawrence
Syrkin, Lev
Szegho, Emeric
T. Ragan, S.
Tabuena, Romeo
Tadlip, Marilou
Taguchi, Kazumi
Taguchi, Yoshihiro
Takino, Masuichi
Talley-Morris, Neva
Tan, John
Tasman-Jones, Clifford
Tautenhahn, Gunther
Tay, John
Taylor, Catherine
Taylor, Cora
Taylor, Otrie
Taylor, Timothy
Taylor, Walter
Teck-Huat, Ang
Terpening, Virginia
Thagard, Sara
The Duke de Grantmeasnil
Theodore, Joseph
The Prince Palalologos, Petros
Thom, James
Thomas, Leslie
Thomas, William
Thompson, William
Thongcharoen, Prasert
Thrash, Sara
Tiemeyer, Hope
Tierney, Robert
Tillman, Celestine
Tipton, Gary
Tipton, Rains
Tisch, Johannes
Tonogbanua, Francisco
Torre, Elizabeth
Torers, Rafael
Torres-Aybar, M.D., Francisco
Touw, J.
Trevor, Joy
Trosper, Milt
Trotta, Geneva
Tseglakoff, Mark
Tulong, Joseph
Tune, Raymond
Tunick, Phyllis
Turner, Jr., Herman
Twum, Michael
Ulrich, Walter
Usategui, Jose
Vaeth, Agatha
Vallbona, Rima
Vandagriff, Jon
Van der Merwe, Johannes
Vanhanen, Tatu
Van Vrooman, Richard
Van Wyk, Carl
Vapaatalo, Heikki
Varma, M.
Varner, Barbara
Vassar, Barbara
Vaughn, Howard
Vaughn, Pearl
Veach, Betty

Vedin, Bengt-Arne
Venditto, James
Veneracion, Andrea
Vernon, Evelyn
Vetlesen, Robert
Vijayasenan, M.
Vilaplana, J.
Villar-Palasi, Jose
Vlachos, Estella
Volkmar, Lloyd
Volpe, Robert
Volpert, Don
Vyas, Gopal
Waddington, Bette
Wade, Thomas
Wainwright, Mary
Walchars, John
Walden, Kathryn
Walker, Glynda
Walker, J.
Wallace, Joel
Wanderman, Richard
Wang, Sing-wu
Ward, Shirley
Waren, Allan
Washburn, Sharon
Watanabe, Ryokichi
Watson, Alan
Weber, Gertrude
Webster, M.D., Ph.D., B.
Weeks, Maudie
Weiling, Franz
Weiser, Norman
Wellman, Gail
Wenck, Josephine
Westpheling, Paul
Whitacre, Walter
Whitaker, Margaret
White, Loraine
White, Norman
Whitfield, Vallie
Whittaker, Willie
Wienstroer, Ann
Wilcox, Colleen
Wilds, Jr., Jetie
Williams, Anita
Williams, Annie
Williams, Clyde
Williams, Felton
Williams, Leola
Williams, Patrick
Williams, Willie
Wilson, Ginny
Wilson, Wanda
Windheim, Paul
Winn, LaNelle
Winston, William
Wipf, Karl
Wirtschafter, Irene
Wolfe, Janet
Woodard, Dorothy
Woods, Margaret
Woods, Willie
Workman, Virginia
Worthington, E.
Wrancher, Elizabeth
Wright, Bessie, M. S.
Wright, Dana
Wyndewicke, Kionne
Yamada, Ryoji
Yamamoto, Yoshinori
Yamasaki, Yoshito
Yanosko, Elizabeth
Yarbrough, Sara
Yates-Edwards, Ella
Yazzie, Rena Mercedes
Yokely, Ronald
Yopconka, Natalie
Yost, Faye
Young, Francis
Young, James
Young, Sonia
Zastoupil, Mark
Zehel, Wendell
Zimmerman, Richard
Zuckerman, J.
Zundel, Georg

Appendix IV

Appendix IV

Roster of Life and Annual Members
The American Biographical Institute
Research Association

THE AMERICAN BIOGRAPHICAL INSTITUTE RESEARCH ASSOCIATION (ABIRA) was established in 1979. Functional aims of this organization are channeled to further extend the biographical research begun by The American Biographical Institute in 1967 when it published its first biographical reference volume and thus expand the objectives of the Institute, to provide a framework for individuals of diverse backgrounds and environments to join together to share knowledge and interests, and ultimately to offer incentive for dedication and stimulation. All members of the ABIRA are chosen by a special Executive Council based on individual merit and these individuals comprise an alliance of almost one thousand members. They are drawn from all regions of the world and are involved in a search for social, intellectual, and cultural enrichment in general. Backgrounds are varied with wide-ranging educations, outstanding professional careers, and extensive involvement in public affairs on community, state, regional, national and/or international levels. Benefits of the organization include group assemblies, media coverage, biographical research, consultation, advertising, member magazine (the Digest), memberships booklet (ABIRA Annual Membership Roster), newsletters, book discounts and incentive awards.

PROFESSIONAL/ADMINISTRATIVE STAFF

CHAIRMAN . . . . JANET MILLS EVANS
Vice Chairman . . . . J. S. Thomson
Director of Administrative Services . . . . Edith R. Curtis
Director of Promotional Services . . . . Andrew R. Holland
Communications Assistant . . . . Sandra J. Brown

Reference: Gale Encyclopedia of Associations
I.S.S.N.: 0196-0652

Forward all communications or membership inquiries to:

Chairman, ABIRA
5126 Bur Oak Circle
P.O. Box 31226
Raleigh, North Carolina 27622 U.S.A.

LIFE PATRONS

Allison, Frank
Aly, Said
Anderson, Vivian
Aragona, Guylaine
Aragona, Ronald
Au, Chang-Hung
Ayers, Anne
Barbour, Judy
Barcynski, Leon
Barnes, Melver
Barr, Nona
Baruwa, Abraham
Batal, A.
Baxter, Ruth
Bebawi, Girgis
Belisle, Lenore
Bell, Deanne
Benner, Richard
Benskina, Margarita
Berkey, Maurice
Blakely, Martha
Bohmfalk, Johnita
Bomkamp, Loraine
Boulton, Shauna
Break, Virginia
Carnevale, Dario

Carver, George
Cecconi-Bates, Augusta
Chambers, Lois
Chilton, Howard
Chin, Sue
Christensen, R.
Clark, James
Cole, Eddie-Lou
Collier, Richard
Cook, David
Cook, J.
Coriaty, George
Crause, Herman
Crihan, Herman
Croxton, Thomas
Dansby, Huddie
Davis, Alexander
Davis, Gordon
Davis, Robert
Dennison, Jerry
Denton, Thomas
Di Ponio, Concetta
DuBroff, Diana
Dumouchel, Anne
Duncan, Dyna
Duncan, Gertrude

Ellerbee, Estelle
Erwin, Jean
Everett, Thelma
Farmakis, George
Fergus, Patricia
Ferguson, Harry
Fisher, Mary
Follingstad, Henry
Ford, Gordon
Fox, Pauline
Fox, Vivian Estelle
Freeze, Elizabeth
Freund, E.
Gebo, Robert
Gershowitz, Sonya
Ghattas, Sonia
Giraudier, Antonio
Goh, Han
Gomez, Nelida
Goodman, Jess
Goulding, C.
Griffith, Reginald
Haas, Arthur
Hackett, William
Hanns, Christian
Hanson, Freddie

Harbani, Suharnoko
Harpster, V.
Harris, Louise
Harris, Thomas
Harrison, Winnie
Harz, Frances
Hatajack, Frank
Headlee, William
Heckart, Robert
Hendricks, Robert
Herren, Peter
Holland, Ray
Hornsby, J.
Houseal, Reuben
Houseal, Ruth
Howard, Adeline
Hubbard, L.
Huff, Cherry
Huff, Norman
Huraj, Helen
Ilo, Moses
Johnson, Rufus
Jordan, Lan
Kagey, F.
Kales, Robert
Karpen, Marian

TWO THOUSAND NOTABLE AMERICANS

Kaufman, Irene
Kerr, Catherine
King, Joseph
Kjartansson, Kristjan
Ko, Yih-Song
Kokenzie, Henry
Larde, Enrique
Laudenslager, Wanda
Leavitt, Charles
Lewis, Loraine
Long, Shirley
Lowry, Dolores
Malone, June
Manogura, Ben
Marchetti, Jean
Martin, Deborah Louise
Mashhour, Abdel-Hay
Mason, Madeline
Mathewson, Hugh
McCoy, Patricia
McCullough, Constance
McLaughlin, Sybil
Michna, Marienka
Miller, Virginia
Mills, George
Mills, William
Mitra, Gopal
Mobley, Herbert
Mollenhauer, Bernhard
Mooney, John

Moore, Dalton
Morahan, Daniel
Morgan, Branch
Mori, Marianne
Morrison, Francine
Music, Edward
Nazareno, Jose
Nicholls, James
Nikolai, Lorraine
Ogden, R.
O'Malley, William
O'Neal, Robert
Overby, George
Overby-Dean, Talulah
Pace, Jon
Parks, Anna
Payton, Ralph
Peachey, Christine
Pearson, Norman
Phillips, Karen
Phillips, Virginia
Pirkle, Estus
Plewinski, Gustaw
Plewinski, Teresa
Pollack, Stephen
Powell, Russell
Prichard, Thora
Puh, Chiung
Purvis, Mary
Puskarich, Michael

Raatz, Sherry
Rahimtoola, S.
Rasmussen, Helen
Rex, Lonnie
Reyman, Maria
Rhemann, Eugene
Richmond, John
Riemann, Wilhelmina
Roberts-Wright, Bessie
Robeson, Lillyan
Robinson, Ralph
Rodkiewicz, Czeslaw
Rodriguez, Beatriz
Rosenberg, Claire
Rowe, Iris
Rubly, Lucille
Sabella, Emmanuel
Savard, Lorena
Sawyer, Joseph
Seale, Ruth
Shah, Shirish
Sharif, Mohammed
Sheh, Violet
Simeck, Clyde
Smith, Norvel
Stein, David
Stevens, Myrtle
Stimach, Janet
Straub, Nellie
Stueber, Gustav

Sutton, Doris
Sweeney, James
Switaj, Lawrence
Szegho, Emeric
Tashiro, Noboru
Tekle, Afewerk
Thomas, William
Thompson, Andrew
Torres-Aybar, Francisco
Toutorsky, Basil
Urry, Vern
Van der Kuyp, Edwin
Vaughn, Pearl
Volpert, Don
Wainwright, Mary
Walden, Kathryn
Walker, Glynda
Waters, Raymond
Waters, Rowena
Webb, Rozana
Weinbaum, Eleanor
Whisenant, Mary
Wiemann, Marion
Williams, Annie
Williams, Melva
Williams, Yvonne
Wolanin, Sophie
Wolf, Joseph
Woods, Willie
Young, James

LIFE FELLOWS

Abba, Hilda
Abba, Raymond
Abrell, Ronald
Adetoro, J.
Al Bahar, Adnan
Al Seif, Khaled
Allen, Edgard
Allison, William
Ames, John
Amir-Moez, Ali
Anderson, Gordon
Anderson, Thelma
Anderson, Ursula
Aston, Katherine
Atkinson-Killian, Hulda
Attiah, Hassan
Averhart, Lula
Ayim, Emmanuel
Babajide, Solomon
Bair, Mary
Baker, Elsworth
Barbachano, Don
Bare, Jean
Baum, Carl
Beardmore, Glenn
Benebig, Roger
Bennett, Stefanie
Benson, Opral
Besche-Wadish, Pamela
Bethell, M.
Binford, Linwood
Bitters, Robert
Black, Larry
Blakeney, Roger
Bolton, Douglas
Bossert, Michael
Bourne, Geoffrey
Boyer, Theodore
Brame, Arden
Brown, Earle
Brown, F.
Bullard, Ethel
Bunnag, Srichitra
Burgess, Caroline
Burley-Allen, Madelyn
Burns, Maretta
Bush, Wendell
Bushbaum, Marianne
Campbell, Caroline
Carpenter, Charles
Carroll, Beatrice
Carson, William
Castro, Manfredo
Cauthen, Deloris
Chan, Kum Peng
Chang, Hong-Lou
Chang, Woo Joo
Char, Wai
Chisholm, William
Chretien, LaVerne

Chun, Sae-il M.D.
Ciancone, Lucy
Cintron, Emma
Clark, Fred
Clemente, Patrocinio
Cleveland, Hattye
Clift, Annie
Cohen, Irwin
Corniffe, Doris
Corsello, Lily
Couch, M.
Cullingford, Ada
D'Agostino, Ralph
Davis, Evelyn
Delphin, Jacques
Dillon, Robert
Doelle, Horst
Doherty, Elizabeth
Dolezal, Henry
Dorion, Robert
Dow, Marguerite
Drummond, Malcolm
D'Silva, Roby
Dunn, Helen
Dyer, Eileen
Eastland, Mary
Edwards, Angela
El-Sayeh, Ramzy
Emrick, Raymond
Enyi, Brown
Errazuriz, Rafael
Essenwanger, Oskar
Evans, Roymond
Fadahunsi, Samuel
Fairweather, Gladstone
Farley, Dorothy
Farrar, Margaret
Fawcett, James
Feist, Marian
Field, Elizabeth
Fink, Aaron
Francis, Mabel
Fries, Herluf
Frym, Janet
Fuchs, Helmuth
Gambrell, Mildred
Gan, Woon
Garcia, Henry
Gardine, Juanita
Garrison, Patricia
Gausman, Harold
Gauthier, Thomas
German, Fin
Gibson, Curtis
Gibson, Weldon
Glaze, Diana
Goerigk, Wolfgang
Goodman, Julius
Gospodaric, Mimi
Gossge-Blue, Edna

Gray, Dora
Greene, Sharon
Groeber, Richard
Guest, Bernette
Guyton, Suzanne
Haastrup, Adedokun
Hackney, Howard
Hale, Arnold
Hall, Wilfred
Hamilton, Madrid
Hammer, Jane
Hammons, Thomas
Hanf, James
Hanif, Akhtar
Hansen, Kathryn
Haritun, Rosalie
Hearn, Charles
Hedtke, Delphine
Hobdy, Frances
Holland, Ruby
Holmstrom, Gustaf
Hooper, Marjorie
Huck, Larry
Hui, Stephen
Hunter, Cannie
Huq, Syed
Hussaini, Hisham Rushdi
Huzurbazar, Vasant
Jacobsen, Parley
Jacobsen, William
Javed, Muhammad
Jensen, Helen
Johnston, Ruth
Jones, Bernard
Jordan, W.
Kaltenbach, Anneliese
Kanagawa, Robert
Kar, Anil
Karl, Dorothy
Kellogg, Bruce
Kelly, John
Kemp, Dorothy
Khan, Muzaffar
Kiehm, Tae M.D.
Kim, Un
King, Edwin
King, Helen
Kitada, Shinichi
Knaebel, Jeff
Knelson, Nelda
Koch, Frances
Kolb, Florence
Kolman, Laurence
Kong, Lim
Kraus, Pansy
Kritjanson, Harold
La Claustra, Vera
Landers, Newlin
Landers, Vernette
Le Cocq, Rhoda

Leeds, Sylvia
Lennox, William
Lim, Phillip
Lindberg, Elayne
Little, Florence
Littlejohn, Joan
Loening, Sarah
Long, Leonard
Lonneker, Arleen
Loper, Marilyn
Luahiwa, Judith
Lundell, Frederick
Lutzker, Edythe
Maass, Vera
Mabe, Ruth
MacLennan, Beryce
Magargal, Larry
Maigida, Umaru-Sanda
Malami, Alhaji
Malin, Howard
Manahan, Manny
Marais, Jan
Martin, James
Mason, Aretha
Massier, Paul
Masuda, Gohta
Matsumoto, Junji
McAdoo, Phyllis
McAvoy, Joseph
McCoin, John
McCormack, Grace
McNabb, Sue
Meldrum, Alex
Mellichamp, Josephine
Mello, Henry
Meskell, Una
Mestnik, Irmtraut
Meyer, G.
Miller, C.
Miller, Laverne
Miller, Robert
Mills, Rosemary
Min, Frank
Morler, Edward
Morris, Rich
Moseley, Laurice
Moses, Elbert
Mosonyi, Emil
Murayama, Makio
Naidu, Shrinivas
Naylor, Pleas
NeSmith, Vera
Nevel, Eva
Newbern, Captola
Newman, Michele
Nichols, Thomas
Njoku, Rose
Norby, Alice
Northup, William
Novak, Lela

xxvi

TWO THOUSAND NOTABLE AMERICANS

Nwankwo, Ochia
O'Dougherty, Pascual
Oh, May
Oien, Arthur
Okafor, Andrew
Okigbo, Pius
Oloruntoba, Barnabas
Opalka, Joyce
Osborn, Prime
Owelle, Frank
Oyeleye, Victor
Pai, Chung-Ruei
Pak, Chan
Palombo, Thomas
Parker, Lucy
Pasricha, Manohar
Pastor, Lucille
Perks, Barbara
Perry, Emma
Persch, Ruth
Peterson, Daniel
Philpott, Emalee
Pine, Charles
Pirs, Joze
Pollard, Joseph
Polley, Elizabeth
Porter, Michael
Prentice, Sartell
Price, Thomas
Putnam, Michael
Raddatz, Otto
Ragan, Bryant
Ramovs, Primoz

Regan, Helene
Reinhardt, Siegfried
Reynolds, Clayton
Richards, John
Richards, Novelle
Rifaat, Alsayed
Roberts, C.
Roberts, Josephine
Rodenburg, Carl
Rodkiewicz, Czeslaw
Rogers, Gayle
Rogers, Gifford
Roode, Johanna
Roth, Frederic
Rozenbaum, Najman
Ruas, Vitoriano
Rubly, Grant
Rutledge, Varian
Saheed, Mohammed
Sanders, Frances
Santiago, Margaret
Saxton, Beryl
Schabbel, Helen
Schirripa, Dennis
Schliephake, Erwin
Schwarzott, Wilhelm
Scott, Wilton
Sealy, Vernol
Sebastianelli, Mario
Seegar, Charlon
Segan, B.
Sewer, Pauline
Silvers, Morgan

Simpson, Jack
Singer, Jeanne
Slack, Florence
Slowik, Richard
Smith, Cecile
Snookal, Donald
Snyder, John
Soekanto, R.
Southward, B.
Speir, Kenneth
Sreenivas, Nanjappa
Steiner, A.
Stevens, Ben
Stewart, Elizabeth
Stewart, Roberta
Stilgenbauer, Robert
Stockton, Barbara
Stonebridge, Jerry
Stromillo, Mario
Stuhl, Oskar
Suleiman, Suleiman
Swamy, M.
Tabuena, Romeo
Talley-Morris, Neva
Tanzil, H. O. K.
Terao, Toshio
Tew, E.
Thomas, K.
Thomas, V.
Thomasson, Raymond
Todd, Vivian
Todres, Bernice
Torres, Rafael

Towne, Dorothea
Toyomura, Dennis
Tran, Quang
Tsau, Wen
Tulong, Joseph
Tung, Rosalie
Turk, Oscar
Turkay, Osman
Turyahikayo-Rugyema, Benon
Tyson, Helen
Umber, Anna
Vlachos, Estella
Voss, Arthur
Vukovic, Drago
Wallis, Ben
Walters, Helen
Walters-Godfree, Dorothy
Wanderman, Richard
Ward, William
Weber, Gertrude
Webster, Burnice
Welsh, Carol June
Whitfield, Vallie Jo
Wilhelm, Willa
Williams, Harvey
Willoughby, Clarice
Wilson, Jeanne
Woo, Po-Shing
Wrentmore, Anita
Wright, Jean
Wyslotsky, Ihor
Yee, Phillip
Yopconka, Natalie

LIFE ASSOCIATES

Breazeale, Morris
Dunlap, Estelle
Gaither, Dorothy

James, Shaylor
Lauer, Frances
McDowell, Margaret

Meeks, Elsie
Overton, Dean
Pasternak, Eugenia

Purcell, George
Sliwinski, M.
Small, Fay
Weaton, George

ANNUAL ASSOCIATES

Adewole, Olufunmilayo
Aldrich, Stephanie
Alexander, Samuel
Allen, Johnny
Amer, Nabil
Angus, J.
Baily, Doris
Banik, Sambhu
Basu, Debatosh
Beaman, Margarine
Bera, Sudhir
Bernard, Jonathan
Berresford, Brady
Bjornsson, Petur
Bjornsson, Sigurjon
Boim, Leon
Bomberger, Audrey
Bothwell, Shirley
Boykin, Frances
Bradley, Ramona
Brady, Bryan
Britton, Michael
Brod, Joseph
Brost, Eileen
Brott, Alexander
Brown, Edward
Brunale, Vito
Bryant, Sylvia
Burns, Marjorie
Campazzi, Betty
Capitol, Viola
Carter, Marion
Cassidy, Virginia
Cellini, William
Chappell, Mae
Chesney, Rose
Chor Fook Sin, Bill
Choun, Robert
Christensen, Don
Christias, Christos
Clark, Richard
Colston, Freddie
Corey, Margaret
Crafton-Masterson, Adrienne
Cucin, Robert
Dabbousi, M.
Davidson, Mabel

de Bettencourt Barbosa, Maria
de Brault, E.
Dean, Lloyd
DeJoia, Ruth
Dell, Margaret
Denktas, Raul
Deyton, Camilla
Dixon, Lawrence
Dossett, Betty
Downing, Everett
Drake, Josephine
Durbney, Clydrow
Dwyer, Marie
Engle, Patricia
Ester, Mary
Fales, DeCoursey
Fehrman, Cherie
Fenske, Virginia
Filos, Alberto
Forman, Ruth
Fuertes, Abelardo
Fuller, James
Fulling, Kay
Galamaga, Donald
Gallipeau, Joan
Garcia Olivero, Carmen
Gardner, Nord
Garnham, Frank
Gary, Gayle
Gibson, Jacquelyn
Gil del Real, Maria
Golton, Margaret
Goodstone, Geraldine
Gregory, Calvin
Groesbeck, E.
Gruber, Rosalind
Gugl, Wolfgang
Guy, Edward
Hagan, Paul
Hain, Violet
Hardy, Carole
Harris, Vander
Hartmann-Johnsen, Olaf
Hasumi, Toshimitsu
Havilland, Ben
Helgi, Johannes
Hemenway, Dorothy

Herring, Michael
Horswell-Chambers, Margaret
Howell, James
Hsu, Wen-ying
Hu, John
Hulsey, Ruth
Hunt, Edward
Ijiri, Yutaka
Jackson, Linda
Jamison, Maggie
Jeffrey, Margie
JemmottWilliams, Maxwell
Joannou, Michael
Jones, Myrtle
Joseph, Cuthbert
Kachel, Henry
Kane, Flora
Kang, Byung-Kyu
Kaplan, Richard
Kawano, Ietoshi
Keenan, Retha
Keroher, Grace
Kiddell, Sidney
Kihlstenius, Alf-Roger
Kjoss-Hansen, Bente
Kline, Tex
Klit, Erik
Knauf, Janine
Knepper, Eugene
Koehler, Isabel
Kopfler, Judith
Kraus, Mozelle
Ksiazek, Marilyn
Lair, Helen
Lane, Cynthia
Lang, Helmer
Larkin, Gertie
Lauterbach, Kathryn
Lawrie, Eileen
Leader, Harry
Learnard, James
Leba, Samuel
Lemire, David
Lester, William
Levandowski, Dr. Barbara
Lewis, Cecelia
Lim, Ho-Peng

Lim-Quek, Muriel
Littell, Bertha
Loret de Mola, Maria
MacLellan, Helen
Mader, Eileen
Mahaffey, Joan
Makinen, Kauko
Mallon, Thomas
Marcucci, Silvestro
Marshall, Patricia
Martin, Chippa
Martins, Micael
Masse, Louis
Mavros, Constantin
Mayer, Jacob
McCabe, Donald
McCune, Weston
McDowell, A.
Meghji, Mohamed
Melton, Ira
Mendieta, Marcelo
Messerlian, Zaven
Moore, Martha
Morgan, Clyde
Morris, William
Morse, Genevieve
Moutote, Daniel
Moya, Aury
Mozingo, Margaret
Muhlanger, Erich
Munson, Norma
Muss, Peter
Naouri, Issa
Neeper, Ralph
Nelson, Lorraine
Nelson, Robert
Nelson, Thomas
Newell, Virginia
Ney, Judy
Nicholson, Rosemary
Nicklin, Helen
Nicole, Christopher
Nohe, B.
Norby, Alice
Norton, Alan
Nozaki, Masako
Nzegwu, Ifeanyi

TWO THOUSAND NOTABLE AMERICANS

Olsen, Virginia
Orata, Pedro
Oswald, Roy
Ovenstone, Irene
Papamichael, Anna
Parson, Erwin
Paschall, Amy
Patten, Clara
Patterson, E.
Perate, Hannah
Peterson, Constance
Peterson, Mary
Pilioko, Aloi
Pizer, Elizabeth
Poehner, Raymond
Posta, Elaine
Prydz, Svein
Pulliainen, Erkki
Pulliam, Paul
Rahming, Philip
Rao, A.
Reicher, Arthur
Reichle, Frederick
Reid, Douglas
Reifler, Henrietta
Reinl, Harry
Ringsdorf, W.
Ritter, Olive

Rogell, Irma
Rogers, Carol
Roney, Alice
Rughani, M.
Saleh, Mohamad
Salsbury, Barbara
Salter, Margaret
Sanchez, Juan
Sanford, Paul
Snataella, Irma
Schioldborg, Ragnhild
Scott, J.
Seltzer, Ronni
Seppala, Arvo
Shaw, Imara
Sheetz, Ralph
Shelton, Bessie
Shiffman, Max
Shragai, E.
Simmons, Troy
Slappey, Mary
Smith, Mary
Smythe-Wood, Ian
Sperry, S.
Sproll, Heinz
Staffeld-Madsen, Alfred
Stanat, Ruth
Stankovic, Milorad

Stanley, Sandra
Stephens, Rupert
Stevens, Grace
Stewart, Joan
Stiefel, Betty
Stoeger, Keith
Stottsberry, Teresa
Studley, Helen
Stuhl, Johannes
Sulaiman, Suliantono
Takino, Masiuchi
Tamari, Moshe
Tan, It-Koon
Taylor, John
Tekelioglu, Meral
Terpening, Virginia
Thomas, Peggy
Tipton, Dorothy
Tipton, Rains
Tisch, J.
Tompkins, James
Touw, J.
Tunick, Phyllis
Turner, Terrance
Tzafestas, S.
Ulrich, Walter
Varner, Barbara
Vilgrain, Jacques

Vinokooroff, Leonide
Waddington, Bette
Walker, Lorna
Wallace, Betty
Wallace, Deborah
Walton, Fernie
Warner, J.
Way, Tsung-To
Wayne, David
Webb, William
Welch, Fern
Wells, Marrion
White, Margaret
Wierbicki, Eugen
Wilford, Rowland
Wilkinson, George
Wilson, Reba
Winston, William
Wolfe, Janet
Womack, William
Wong, Robert
Wood, Sandra
Wright, Dana
Yanosko, Elizabeth
Yap, Meow
Zelner, Estelle
Zibrun, S.
Zimmerman, Richard

ABIRA FOUNDING MEMBERS

Acker, Louise
Bardis, Panos
Benton, Suzanne
Brownell, Daphne
Kalvinskas, John
Westerfield, Hilda
Williams, Patrick

Appendix V

The American Biographical Institute
ROSTER OF FELLOW MEMBERS

THE ROSTER OF FELLOW MEMBERS constitutes a learned society of internationally acclaimed advisors and distinguished associates devoted to the principles of educational and professional advancement, public service and cultural enrichment of humanity. These individuals' careers, signal honors and accomplishments have been recognized and published in the Collector Editions of THE BOOK OF HONOR and through this review and selection have been elected unanimously to the Fellowship of The American Biographical Institute. This is an honorary and permanent seating.

John Gregory Abernethy
Christian Campbell Abrahamsen
Bergljot Abrahamson
Diane M. Abrahamson
Anthony (Tony) Salvatore Accurso
Louise Ida Acker
Cecile Neomi Walker Adams
Rev. Leroy Adams
Harold V. Addison
Steven V. Agid
Hugh Stephen Ahern
John Madison Airy
Ralph Hardie Akin, Jr.
Esther Ann Teel Albright
Signe Henreitte Johnson Aldeborgh
Larry J. Alexander, Ed.D.
Byron Paul Allen
Edgard Yan Allen
John Eldridge Allen
Rev. Thomas G. Allen
Frank E. Allison, Sr.
Mujahid Al-Sawwaf, Ph.D.
Peter C. Altner, M.D.
Thelma L. Alvarez
Ali Reza Amir-Moez, Ph.D.
Doris Ehlinger Anderson, J.D.
Gloria Long Anderson, Ph.D.
Harriet Idell Anderson
Herbert Frederick Anderson, M.D.
Rozena Hammond Anderson
Ursula M.Anderson, M.D., D.P.H.,
M.R.C.S.,
    L.R.C.P., D.C.H., F.A.A.P.
George Fredrick Andreasen, D.D.S.
Hyrum Leslie Andrus, Ph.D.
Walter Thomas Applegate, Ph.D., D.D.
Mahmoud Zaky Arafat, Ph.D.
Pedro Alfonzo Araya
Wendell Sherwood Arbuckle, Ph.D.
Violet Balestreri Archer, D.Mus.
Sylvia Argow
Floro Fernando Arive, M.D.
Edward James Arlinghaus
Claris Marie Armstrong
Naomi Young Armstrong, D.H.L.
William Harrison Armstrong, Jr.
Kenneth D. Arn, M.D.
James Edward Arnett, Ph.D.
Dwight Lester Arnold, Ph.D.
Florence M. Arnold
Edward Lee Arrington, Jr.
Albert J. Arsenault, Jr.
Franzi Ascher-Nash
Dell Shepherd Ashworth
Chuck Aston
Katharine Oline Aston
Grace Marie Smith Auer
Aurelia Marie Richard Augustus
Beryl David Averbook, M.D.
William Marvin Avery, Jr.
Florence M. Gotthelf Axton, Ph.D.
Roderick Honeyman Aya
Anne Louise Ayers
James Wilbur Ayers
Catherine Beatrice Aymar
Edith Annette Aynes

Peter J. Babris, Ph.D.
Rosalie Wride Bacher
Manson Harvey Bailey, Jr.
Daljit S. Bais
Judge Anna Dorthea Baker
Elsworth Fredrick Baker
John A. Baker
Justine Clara Baker
Roberta Rymer Balfe
Howard Balin, M.D.
Iris Georgia Ball
Louis Alvin Ball
Joseph G. Ballard, Sr.
Susan Lee Ballew
Betsy Ross Anne Ballinger
Lloyd Kenneth Balthrop, Th.D.
Barbara A. Bancroft
Helen Virginia Bangs
Candace Dean Bankhead
Jean Bare
Vivian Miller Barfield
Alexander John Barket
Herman Zulch Barlow, Jr., Ed.D.
George Hugh Barnard, J.D.
Frances Ramona Barnes
Marylou Riddleberger Barnes, Ed.D.
Melver Raymond Barnes
Charlotte A. Barr
Nona Lee Barr
Kathleen Corlelia Parker Barriss
Margaret Bentley Hamilton Barrows
Mihaly Bartalos, M.D.
Arline Ruth Barthlein
Larry H. Barton
Florence S. Bartova
G. Robert Bartron, M.D.
Nina M. Barwick
Henrietta Elizabeth (Beth) Bassett
Harold Ronald Eric Battersby
R. Ray Battin, Ph.D.
Ethel Hines Battle
Carl Edward Baum, Ph.D.
Donald Otto Baumbach, Ph.D.
Magdalena Charlotte Bay ('Magdalena')
Everett Minot Beale
Gary Floyd Beard
Donald Ray Beason
Roberta Ann Beaton
Mary Dawn Thomas Beavers
Adeline C. Becht
Harriet Perry Beckstrom, D.O.
Rexine Ellen Beecher
Phyllis Tenney Belcher
Lenore Breetwor Belisle, Ed.D.
George Wilbur Bell
James Milton Bell, M.D., F.A.P.A.
    F.A.C.P.
Harold James Bender
John A. Benedict
Christopher Aaron Bennett
Margarita Orelia Benskina
Betty Jones Benson
Dailey J. Berard
Julia Irene Berg
Muriel Mallin Berman

Harmon Gordon Berns
Leonard Bernstein
Frank Weldon Berry, Sr.
Irving Aaron Berstein
Norman M. Better, Ed.D.
Clifford Allen Betts
Laura Elizabeth Beverly
Brian William Louis Bex
Awinash P. Bhatkar, Ph.D.
Henrietta DeWitte Bigelow
Annette C. Billie
Novella Stafford Billions
Carol H. Bird
Donald Raymond Black
Harold Stephen Black
Willa Brown Black
Joe Ronald Blackston
Frank Blair
Ilene Mills Blake
Terri Blake (AKA-Theresa Blalock)
William H. Blakely, Jr.
Roger Neal Blakeney, Ph.D.
B. Everard Blanchard, D.Div.
Ronald Gail Blankenbaker, M.D.
Maija Sibilla Blaubergs
Gustav Henry Bliesner
Edna J. Gossage Blue
Wendell Norman Bodden
Carmen Page Bogan
Johnita Schuessler Bohmfalk
Gerald L. Boland
Oran Edward Bollinger, Ph.D.
Robert Howard Boltz
Suzanne Poljacik Bolwell
Loraine Mary Bomkamp
Dr. Floyd A. Bond
Drew Adrian Bondy
Tal D. Bonham, Th.D.
Ophelia Calloway Bonner
Earl James Eugene Books
Emily Clark Kidwell Linder Boone
Myron Vernon Boor
Mary Elizabeth Borst
Metodij Boretsky, Ph.D.
Raymond Paul Botch
Shirley Marie Oakes Bothwell
Harvey John Bott
Wilhelmina Wotkyns Botticher
Badi Mansour Boulous, M.D., Ph.D.
Mary Bancroft Boulton
Jean A. H. Bourget
Geoffrey Howard Bourne, D.Sc., D.Phil.
Gloria Diane Parrish Bousely, Ph.D.
Mildred Hazel Bowen
Theodore Stanley Boyer
Frances L. Boykin
Mervell Winzer Bracewell, R.N. DR.P.H.
Margaret Anowell Brame, Jr. II
Sister M. Teresa Bramisiepe
Wayne Keith Brattain
Helen Raymond Braunschweiger
Pius Brazauskas
Ruby Blanche Franklin Breads
Virginia Huffman Break
Arnold Brekke, Ph.D.
George Matthew Brembos

Lynn D. Brenneman
Charlotte Mae Brett
Anne A. Brevetti
Virginia Rose Alexander Brewer
Ethel Craig Brewster
A. Morgan Brian, Jr.
Joan Briggs
Juanita Sumner Brightwell
Angie R. Brinkley
Willis R. Brinkmeyer
Bobby Leroy Brisbon, Ed.D.
Jan Leeman Brooks
June Brooks Brooks
Margaret Alyce Page Brooks
Edith Petrie Brown, M.D.
Edward Kinard Brown, Ed.D.
Gwendolyn Ruth Brown
Hazel Claire MacCalla Brown
Jerry Joseph Brown
Joseph Leandrew Brown
Louis Daniel Brown, J.D.
Luther Daniel Brown, Ph.D.
Thomas Cartwright Brown
Thomas Lewis Brown
May L. Brumfield
Nancy Louise Bruner
Lillian Sholtis Brunner
Jacob Franklin Bryan, III
Elizabeth Ann Bryant
Kathryn Henriette Bryant
Richard John Brzustowicz
Wesley F. Buchele
Henry L. Buckardt
Bronius Budriunas
Richard S. Budzik
Vera Mildred Buening
Elizabeth Whitney Buffim
Ethel Munday Bullard
Claire R. Cohen Burch
Jewel Calvin Burchfield
Patricia Ann Burdette
Suanna Jeanette Burnau
Alta Hazel Burnett
William Earl Burney, D.R.E.
Grover Preston Burns, D.Sc.
Billie Burrow
Barbara J. Burton
Elizabeth Allene Burtt
Anna Gardner Butler
Broadus Nathaniel Butler, Ph.D.
Elaine Ruth Marjorie Mallory Butler, Ph.D
Joseph Buttinger
Mercy Lynne Buttorff
Frederick D. Byington
Joseph Keys Byrd
Edward Joseph Cabbell
John F. Cahlan
Joseph Alexander Cain
Ardith Faulkner Caldwell
Gladys Lillian Caldwell
Stratton Franklin Caldwell
John Calhoun, LL.D., Ph.D.
Carey S. Callaway
Alfonso De Guzman Calub, Ph.D.
Victor Joseph Camardo
Victor Joseph Camardo

TWO THOUSAND NOTABLE AMERICANS

George B. Camboni
Agnes Knight Campbell
Bruce Alexander Campbell
Clay Reese Campbell
Jean Chidester Campbell
Robert Craig Campbell, III, J.D.
Winnie B. Campbell
Louis J. Camuti, D.V.M.
Julia Elizabeth Cane
Joseph Peter Cangemi
Nixon Louis Cannady
Antonio Capone, M.D.
Wayne Caraway, Ph.D.
Patricia Jean Carey
Darol Wayne Carlson
Erma Wood Carlson
Martha Lu Carlson
William Howard Carlson
Arthur Commons Carmichael, Jr.
Rebecca L. Carner, Ed.D.
Dario Carnevale
Charles Whitney Carpenter, II, Ph.D.
Beatrice Johnson Carroll
Elizabeth Boyd Carroll
Mitchell Benedict Carroll, J.D., LL.D.
William Edwards Carson
Anna Curry Carter
Charlotte Radsliff Carter, Ph.D.
Joyce Elaine Arndt Carter
Marion Elizabeth Carter, Ph.D.
Nettie Mae Carter
Grace W. Cartwright
Emily Roxana Carus
Dorothy Lee Eskew Carver
George William Casarett, Ph.D.
Paul Conway Case
Francis W. Cash
Francois Cassagnol, Ph.D.
Dianne Marie Cassidy
Patricia Anne Cassner
Robert Woods Castle
Alan Cathcart
Deloris Vaughan Cauthen
Marguerite E. Cavanagh
Mary Magdalene Cavasina
Vernal G. Cave, M.D.
Joseph Douglas Cawley, Ph.D.
Billie Jean Cawood
Augusta Cecconi-Bates
Jose David Lujan Cepeda
Mary Ellen Cerney, Ph.D.
Robert A. Chahine, M.D.
Bobby Lee Chain
Hwa Ying Chang
Carlton J. Chapman
Wai Sinn Char, D.D.S.
Susan Charnley
E. Charles Chatfield
Tapan Kuman Chaudhuri, M.D.
John L. Childs
Howard Goodner Chilton
John Camillo Chinelly, Sr.
Andrew J. Chishom
Stanley Matthew Chittenden
Jerry Melvin Christensen, P.E.
Louis Washington Christensen
Ruth Ellen Christensen, M.D.
Odis Dwain Christian
Kenneth E. Christoff
A. John Christoforidis, M.D., M.M.Sc.
   Ph.D.
Sister Mildred Christoph, A.S.C.
Kyung-Cho Chung, LL.D., Litt.D.
Young Sup Chung, Ph.D.
Avery Grenfell Church
Lloyd Eugene Church, D.D.S., Ph.D.
Lillian Cicio
Robert Henry Cilke
John Henry Cissik, Ph.D.
Eugen Ciuca
John (Jack) P. Clancy, Ph.D.
Vance Curtis Clapp, Ed.D.
Stewart Clare, Ph.D.
Tema Shults Clare
Ann Nolan Clark
Bill P. Clark, Ph.D.
Lillie Robecca Clark
Marie Tramontana Clark
Marion Jo Clark
Elsie Catoe Clarke
John G. P. Cleland
Emma Walker Cleveland
Hattye Mae Johnson Cleveland
Patrick Denton Closser
LaVerne Carole Clouden
John Daniel Clouse, J.D.
Robert Clunie
Patricia Ann Clunn
Charles E. Coatie
Annetta P. Cobb
McKendree Thomas Cochran, Jr.
Richard Earle Cochran

Claude O'Flynn Cockrell, Jr.
Gail Debbie Cohen, F.I.B.A.
Irwin Cohen
Chauncey Eugene Coke, Ph.D.
Mary Catherine Coleman
Zelia S. Coleman
Dr. Johnnie Colemon
Barbara W. Colle
Louis Malcolm Collier
Evelyn Padgett Collins
Zelma Mitchell Collins
Bundy Colwell, J.D.
Allen J. Comeaux
Archimedes Abad Concon, M.D.
Jo W. Conibear
James Frederick Louis Connell, Ph.D.
James H. Conrod, D.Min.
Patricia Cochran Cook
J. F. Cooley, D.C.L., D.D.
Robert Tytus Coolidge
Mariel Coombes
George Augustin Cooney, J.D.
Eldo J. Coons, Jr., Ph.D.
Herbert Press Cooper, Ph.D.
Jimmy Lee Cooper
Patricia Evelyn Pennington Cooper
Gretchen J. Corbitt
George Bronnie Corder
Erlinda Balancio Corpuz-Ambrosio
Leota Rae Cornett
Ernest S. Corso
Lyn Cortlandt
Evelyn M. Costello
Robert W. Costley, Sr.
Constantinos Haralampos Coulianos
Naomi Miller Coval, D.D.S.
Mary E. Cox
Yvonne Peery Cox
Ella Hobbs Craig
Vernon Eugene Craig
Marlene Rae Cram
Ira Carlton Carndall, Ph.D. D.S.Sc.
   D.Litt., Ed.D.
Josephine Lackey Crawford
Ioan Crihan
Adrian Loreto Cristobal
Charles Harrison Criswell
Tillie Victoria Swanson Croft
Charles Marion Cromer
Rev. Irvie Keil Cross
Joe George Crowell, D.D.S.
Carolyn Ann Crutchfield, Ed.D.
Randall Edward Culberson
Alfred Samule Cummin, Ph.D.
Sylvia E. Cummin
Anne Bernice Smith Cunningham
David S. Cunningham, Jr.
Frank Earl Curran
Alton Kenneth Curtis, Ph.D.
Dorothy Massie Custer
Patsy Smith Czvik
Rev. Lawrence C. Dade
Bradford Ivan Daggett
Leola Lenora Dahlberg
Abdulhusein S. Dalal, Ph.D.
Charlotte Owens Dalo
Ruth C. Dameron
Frances Mueller Danforth
Huddie Dansby
Wayne Martel Daubenspeck
Ethel Hinton Daughtridge
Mabel Elizabeth Davidson
Alexander Schenck Davis
Beatrice Grace Davis, J.D.
Chaplain Rev. Dr. Clarence Davis, Jr.
Claudine Davis
Ernest Davis, Jr.
Evelyn Marguerite Bailey Davis
Father Francis R. Davis
Col. Gordon William Davis
Irma Blanche Davis
Lowell Livingston Davis
Mable Wilson Davis
Robert Wilson Davis
William Ackelson Davis
William Claude Davis
Kenneth Arthur Davison
Mary McCoy Deal
Michael Thomas Dealy
Robert Gayle Dean, Jr.
Walter John Deane
Patricia Ann de Champlain
David Michael DeDonato
Thelma B. DeGraff, Ph.D.
Dolores Tejeda de Hamilton
Michael Dei-Anang, Litt.D.
Jose C. Roman de Jesus
Elias Demetrios Dekazos, Ph.D.
Curtis Martin Delahoussaye
Violette de Mazia
Eugene F P C de Mesne
Aryola Marieanne Demos

Judianne Densen-Gerber
Sarah Lee Creech Denton
Mary Jane Denton-Learn, Ed.D.
Adelaide Batista De Rodriguez
Lawrence Aloysius DeRosa
Veena Balvantrai DeSai
Kenneth Noel Derucher
Ruth S. de Treville
Robert Marshall DeuPree
Adele K. Devera
Julia Anne Bonjour DeVere
Albert Kenneth De Vito, Ph.D., Mus.D.
Inez Stephens Dewberry
Franklin Roosevelt DeWitt, J.D.
Muriel Herrick DeYoung
Teipal Singh Dhillon, M.D.
G. Di Antonio
Darrell Thomas Dibona
June M. Dickinson
Joan T. Diedolf
Russell E. Diethrick, Jr.
H. Brent Dietsche, Ph.D.
Rudolph Gerard Di Girolamo
Anne Holden Dill
William G. Dilley
Otis B. Dillon
Priya Chitta Dimantha
Evelyn Lois Dittmann
Loy Henderson Dobbins, Ph.D.
Sofia Hilario Doctor
Jeannette Betts Dodd
Elizabeth C. Doherty, Ph.D.
Henry Dolezal
Sylvia Maida Dominquez, Ph.D.
Norbert Frank Dompke
Richard Francis Domurat
Mary H. O'Neill Dooley
Susan Sherley Dorsey
Robert F. Doster
Richard Bary Douglass
Helen Jeannette Dow, Ph.D.
Marguerite Ruth Dow
Charyl Wayne Kennedy Dragoo
Josephine Eleanor Drake
Zelphia Pollard Drake
Claude Evans Driskell, D.D.S.
Eugene Ardent Drown
Satya Deva Dubey, Ph.D.
Diana D. DuBroff
George William Dudley
Anne Marie Marcelle Dumouchel
Diedra Renee Duncan
Dyna Duncan
William Archibald Duncan
Helen Faye Kindle Dungee
Lawrence Dunkel, Ph.D.
Estelle Cecilia Diggs Dunlap
Elsie Hyder Dunn
Mildred Elaine Dunn
Clydrow John Durbney
Lewis M. Durden, D.D., Ph.D.
Nancy E. Dworkin, Ph.D.
Robert Francis Dyer, Jr., M.D.
Edith Wuergler Dylan
Thomas Capper Eakin
John Benjamin Ebinger (d. 1979)
Bertha Elizabeth Eckman
Elly Helen Economou, Ph.D.
Alan Michael Eddington
Harold W. Edomonson
Adrian Rose Edwards
Louis Mavis Way Eggleston, D.Litt (d. 1979)
Gordon Frederick Ehret, P.E.
Lois Eleanor Eisenmann
Alfred Eisenstein
Monday U. Ekpo
Oscar Reed Elam, Jr.
Norman Orville Eldred
Mohamed Tawfik El Ghamry, Ph.D.
Sami El Hage, Ph.D.
Johnnie Carl Eli, Jr., D.D.S.
Rosemary Taylor Elias
Afton Yeates Eliason
Donald J. Ely
Bessie Miriam Embree
Raymond Terry Emrick, Ph.D.
Elizabeth Lois English, Ph.D.
Charles Thomas Epps, Ph.D., Ped.D.
Rev. William Saxe Epps
Eugenia Eres
Ellsworth Burch Erickson
Anita Bonilla Ernouf, Ph.D.
Dorothy W. Erskine
Jean Hocking Erwin, Ph.D.
Billie Lee Eskut
Oskar M. Essenwanger, Ph.D.
Gene Gordon Essert, M.D.
Ann H. M. Estill
Eddie Estrada
L. Ken Evans, D.D.S.
Louis Evans, Ph.D.
Tuula Jokinen Fabrizio, D.M.S.

Mary Waring Falconer
Sally Basiga Famarin
Sadie Patton Fant
Francisco Cabreros Farinas
Dr. Dorothy Anne Farley
George Leonard Farmakis, Ph.D.
Helen Horne Farr, Ed.D.
Margaret Marion Farrar, Ph.D.
George E. Farrell, M.D.
Darlene Faucher
George D. Fawcett
Marie Ann Formanek Fawcett
Blair Fearon, M.D.
Eugene W. Fedorenko, Ph.D.
Shirley Feinstein
Gary Spencer Felton, Ph.D.
Tse-Yun Feng, Ph.D.
Nicholas Vasilievich Feodoroff
Patricia Marguerita Fergus
Anthony Ralph Fernicola, M.D.
Elizabeth Ashlock Field
Donald George Finch
Donnie Wayne Finch
Alice Elizabeth Fine
Richard I. Fine, Ph.D.
Aaron Fink, Ph.D.
Joan Lockwood Finn
William Francis Finn, M.D.
Carmine Fiorentino
O. Y. Firestone, J.D.
Charles Frederick Fisher, D.Ed.
Mary Hannah Fisher
H. William Fister, M.D.
Leonard Donald Fitts, Ph.D.
Stanton T. Fitts
Admiral Gerald Joseph FitzGerald
Harold Alvin Fitzgerald
Paul Leo Flicker, M.D.
Edward Francis Flint, Jr.
William Mathew Floto
Donald Ray Flowers, Sr.
Henry Bascom Floyd, III
Lyman John Floyd
Luella Lancaster Floyd, D.Min.
Claude Lee Fly, Ph.D.
Frank Foglio
Elinor R. Ford, L.H.D., LL.D.
Prof. Dr. Gordon Buell Ford, Jr.
Judith Anne Ford
Lee Ellen Ford, J.D.
Ruth VanSickle Ford
Gary Walton Fordham
Willmon Albert Fordham
Luella Helen Formanek
Virginia Ransom Forrest
Jane L. Forsyth, Ph.D.
Caroline Robinson Foster
Marietta Allen Foster
Inez Garey Fourcard
Clara M. Fouse
Abraham Harvey Fox
Lauretta Ewing Fox, Ph.D.
Arthur Norman Foxe, M.D.
Charles Leonard Foxworth, Ph.D.
Florence Gerald Foxworth
Dr. Irving A. Fradkin
Dorothy Killian Franchino
Donald Ely Frank
Elaine Koenigsdorf Frank
Richard Symons Frazer, Ph.D.
Danny Lee Fread, Ph.D.
Annie Belle Hamilton Freas
Eldine A. Frederick
Leonard Harland Frederick
Elizabeth Hicks Freeman
Elizabeth Bouldin Freeze
Ruth Evelyn French
Joyce Chlarson Frisby
Mary Elizabeth Louise Foustet
Louise Scott Fry
Wilhelmine E. Fuhrer
Fred Franklin Fulton
Gary Sudberry Funderburk
Mrs. Courtney H. Funn
Quint E. Furr
Diana Ruth Gabhart
Ruby Jackson Gainer, Ph.D.
Dorothy L. W. Gaither
John J. Gajec
Lilyan King Galbraith, Ed.D.
Lorraine S. Gall, Ph.D.
Joan Mildred Gallipeau
Mario R. Garcia-Palmieri, M.D.
Arwin F. B. Garelick
Lawrence Garrison
Ricardo F. Garzia
Sharon Lee Gates
Alexander V. J. Gaudieri
Charles Gottliev Geltz
Meta Wade George
Sonya Ziporkin Gershowitz
Mary Frances Gibson

TWO THOUSAND NOTABLE AMERICANS

Milton Eugene Gibson, M.D.
Weldon B. Gibson, Ph.D.
Katherine Jefferson Strait Giffin
Margaret Gill
Edna Avery Gillette
Rev. Perry Eugene Gillum
Antonio Giraudier
Perry Aaron Glick
Alberic O. Girod
Emilio R. Giuliani, M.D.
Arthur G. Glass
Joseph William Givens Godbey, Ph.D.
Joseph Gold
Patricia Anne Goler, Ph.D.
Nelida Gomez
William Raymond Gommel
E. Larry Gomoll
Carlos La Costa Gonzalez
Rafael A. Gonzalez-Torres, Ph.D.
Pamela J. Gonzlik
Hope K. Goodale, Ph.D.
Robert Thomas Gordon, M.D.
Mimi Gospodaric
Edna Jenkins Gossage
William B. Graham
Queenette Faye Grandison
Peter Hendricks Grant, Ph.D.
Edwin Milton Grayson
Frank Joseph Greenberg, Ed.D., Ph.D.,
L.F.I.B.A.
Janelle Garlow Greene
Edna Jensen Gregerson
Walter Greig, Sci.D., D.C.S.
Charles Allen Griffith, M.D.
Ione Quinby Griggs
Wilbur Wallace Griggs, Jr.
James Dehnert Gross, M.D.
Clarence Edward Grothaus, Ph.D.
Ivan H. Grove
Raymond Louis Guarnieri
Halldor Viktor Gudnason, M.D., Ph.D.
Laura Guggenbuhl, Ph.D.
Sr. St. Michael Guinan, Ph.D.
Rev. Jon Crawford Gulnac
Howard L. Gunn
Evelyn Coleman Gunter
Nina Nadin Gutierrez
Mildred Dorothy Guy
Merrill W. Haas
Maj. William David Hackett
Howard Smith Hackney
Lorena Grace Hahn
Major Arnold Wayne Hale
Dr. Tenny Hale
Gladys Murphy Haley
Karen Louise Haley
David Gunther Hall
Mildred Verzola Hall
Wilbur A. Hall
Jean-Pierre Hallet
Gerald Halpin, Ed.D.
Glennelle Halpin, Ph.D.
Earle Hartwell Hamilton
Madrid Turner Hamilton
Lillian Hammer
Eugene Kirby Hammett, Jr.
Frances LaCoste Hampson
Charles Robert Hamrick
Dr. Joyce McCleskey Hamrick
Laura Alice Green Hamrick
Franklin Jesse Hannah
Alberta Pierson Hannum
Kathryn G. Hansen
Freddie Phelps Hanson, Ph.D.
Vera Doris Hanson
Maria Harasevych
Jakob Harich, Ph.D.
Bobbye Roberts Harkins
Ethel Harper
V. Aileene Harpster, D.D., Th.D.
Hardy Matthew Harrell
Florence H. Harrill
Paul R. Harrington, M.D.
Louise Harris
Mary Imogene Harris, Ed.D.
Thomas Lee Harris
Virgil William Harris, III, Ph.D.
Daniel D. Harrison, Ph.D.
Shirley M. Harrison
Winnie M. Harrison
Newman Wendell Harter, D.D.S.
William O. Hartsaw, Ph.D.
Eleanor T. M. Harvey
Frances Marie Kirkland Harz
Nora Mae Rucker Hashbarger
James S. Haskins
Beatrice Giroux Jones Hasty
Col. Benjamin Frank Hatfield
Robert S. Hatrak
Jacob Hauser
Orressa Harris Hauser
Joseph Key Hawkins

Robert A. Hawkins, Ed.D.
Willard Hayden Hawley
Mildred Fleming Haworth
George Austin Hay
Arthur C. Hayes
Charles Patrick Hayes
D. Virginia Pate Hayes
Mary Katherine Jackson Hays
Mattie Sue Martin Hays
H. Lynn Hazlett, D.B.A.
William Hugh Headlee, Ph.D.
Gladys Levonia Moyers Heath
Robert Hezron Heckart, D.D.
Henrietta Irene Henderson
Morris Henderson
Graham Fisher Hendley
Donald Wayne Hendon, Ph.D.
Phyllis Jean Hendrickson
Robert Lee Henney, Ph.D.
Martha Alice Grebe Henning
Beverly Jean Smith Henschel, Ed.D.
Kirby James Hensley
Peter Hans Herren
Howard Duane Herrick, M.D.
Lettie Marie Herrman
Irene Rose Hess
Ah Kewn Hew
Carl Andreas Hiaasen, J.D.
Elizabeth Blake Hiebert
Doris Ross Higginbotham
Claudette D. Hill
George B. Hill
William Harwood Hinton, Ph.D.
Aurora Tahala Hipolito, M.D.
Charles Norwood Hitchens
Lore Hirsch, M.D.
Jane Richter Hoade, J.D.
Sidney LaRue Hodgin
Loren H. Hoeltke
Elise Hoffman, Ph.D.
Judy Hogan
Edward Lionel Holbrook
Dorothy Turner Holcomb
Gene 'Scotty' Grigsby Holland
Ray G. L. Holland, M.D.
Ruby Love Holland
Shelby W. Hollin, J.D.
Lawrence Milton Holloway, M.D.
Helen Marie Holzum
Daisy Bishop Honor
Burrell S. Hood III, Ed.D.
Thomas Richard Hood
Marjorie Seaton Hooper
Alice Elizabeth Hoopes
Albert Bartow Hope
Annie Pearl Cooke Horne
J. Marie Hornsby
J. Russell Hornsby
Louis A. Horwitz
Franziska Porges Hosken
Lewis Daniel Houck, Jr., Ph.D.
Reuben Arthur Houseal, Th.D. Ph.D., LL.D.
Ruth Arnold Houseal, D.R.E, L.H.D.
Edmund L. Housel, M.D.
Edna Gertrude Houser
Thelma L. Howard, M.D.
Lyman H. Howe, III, Ph.D.
John S. Hoyt, Jr., Ph.D.
Jean Ayr Wallace Hrinko
Joseph Jen-Yuan Hsu, Ph.D.
Wen-ying Hsu
Yao Tsai Huang
Elizabeth Desmond Hudson
Norman Nelson Huff
Phyllis Huffman
Edwin McCulloc Hughes, Ed.D.
Janice Baxter Hull
S. Loraine Boos Hull, Ph.D.
Hazel Lucia Humphrey
Lugene G. Hungerford
Geraldine Grosvenor Hunnewell
John DuBois Hunt, J.D.
Lula Mai Hung
Cannie Mae Hunter
Miriam Eileen Hunter
Priscilla Payne Hurd, D.D.
Abdo Ahmed Husseiny, Ph.D.
Edward Lee Husting, Ph.D.
Janet Lois Hutchinson
Colonel John K. Hyun, J.D.
Francis Joseph Ibranyi, Ph.D., D.S.T.
Celina Sua Lin Ing
Thomas Peter Ipes, D.Min.
Linda Jean Garver Iungerich
Anna Mitchell Jackson, Ph.D.
Carolyn Jane Jackson
Harvey L. Jackson, Jr.
Ruby L. Jackson
Thomas William Jackson
Gordon Waldemar Jacobs, M.D.
Benjamin William Henry Jacobs
Michael Harold Jacobson

Edward Louis John, Sr.
Paula Hermine Sophie Jahn
Advergus Dell James, Jr.
Robert Bleakley James, Jr.
Isabel Jansen
Nana Belle Clay Jarrell
Diane M. Jasek
Ina J. Javellas
Maria Bustos Jefferson
Woodie Rauschers Jenkins, Jr.
Ronald Paul Jensh, Ph.D.
Sue Allen Jent
Lester Earl Jeremiah, Ph.D.
Ann Elizabeth Jewett, Ed.D.
Hugh Judge Jewett, M.D.
Mary Alice Jezyk
Herta Helena Jogland, Ph.D.
Rev. Charlie James Johnson
Dorothy P. Johnson
Esta D. Johnson
James Andrew Johnson, Sr.
Patricia Lee Johnson
Colonel Rufus Winfield Johnson
Scott Edwin Johnson
Rev. William R. Johnson
Agueda Iglesias Johnston, D.H.L.
Lillian B. Spinner Johnston
George Jones
Faye C. Jones
Mallory Millettte Jones
Myrtis Idelle Jones
Patricia Jones, Ed.D.
Professor Vernon A. Jones
Gary Blake Jordan, Ph.D.
Lan Jordan, Ph.D.
Carmen A. Jordan-Cox
Kathleen Doris Jorgenson
Leslie James Judd
John Louis Juliano
Felix Joseph Jumonville, Jr. Ed.D.
Willa Dee June
Msgr. Francis M. Juras
Ioliene Justus
Woodland Kahler
Faith Hope Kahn, R.N., O.R.N., R.M.S.
Julian Kahn
Krishan K. Kaistha, Ph.D.
Nora Evelyn Kalbhin
Robert Gray Kales
Shirley M. Kales
Ted Reimann Kalua
Robert Kiyoshi Kanagawa
Joseph Kapacinskas
Anne Kaplan
Dorothy Theresa Karl
Marian Joan Karpen
Nikolai Kasak
Michael Kasberg
Nicolai Nicolaevich Kashin
Robert Stephen Kaszynski
Hilda Katz
Alvina Nye Kaulili
Rita Davidson Kaunitz
Lawrence Kayton, M.D.
Anita M. Kearin
Helen Revenda Kearney, Ph.D.
Jean Clarke Keating
Rosalie Ausmus Keever
Shirley Yvonne Kellam, M.D.
Paul Dudley Kelley, M.D., F.A.C.S.
Louise Salter Kelley
Doris Lilliam Kelly
Margaret McLaurin Ricaud Kelly
Greta Kempton
Charles William Kenn
D. James Kennedy, D.D., Ph.D.
Bettie Ilene Cruts 'Bik' Kenny
Donald Keith Kenny
Ethel Marie Kerchner
Minuetta Shumiatcher Kessler
Maj. Frank Howard Kiesewetter
Joseph Eungchan Kim
Keith Kim
Mary Lee Evans Kimball
Dr. Clifton W. King
Ethel Marguerite King, Ph.D.
Helen Blanche King
J. B. King, Jr.
Jospeh Jerone King
Louise Willis King
Sarah Nell King
Mattie Armstong Kinsey
Ellen Irene Groves Kirby
Henry Vance Kirby, M.D.
Mayme Clark Kirby
Nellie Woll Kirkpatrick
Sister Joan Kister, F.M.M.
Dorothea M. Klajbor
Dr. Edgar Albert Klein
I. Maxine Klein
Martin John Herman Klein
Jean Ross Kline

Tex R. Kline
Kurt L. Klippstatter
Paul E. Klopsteg, Ph.D., Sc.D.
Arthur Alexander Knapp, D.Opth.
Gloria Ann Mackey Knight
William Albert Koch
Dr. Boris Kochanowsky
Dr. Constantin Neophytos Kockinos
Dorothy June Koelbl
Lawrence Compton Kolawole
Adam Anthony Komosa, Ph.D.
Jin Au Kong, Ph.D.
Elaine Ferris Decker (Sunny) Korn
D. G. Kousoulas
Father William Armstrong Kraft
Father Ljubo Krasic
Mozelle De Witte Bigelow Kraus
Pansy Daegling Kraus
Dr. Rev. Violet Joan Krech-Cisowski
Adrian Henry Krieg
Yu Hsiu Ku, Sc.D., LL.D.
Ruth Peyton Kube
Isaac Newton Kugelmass, M.D.
Ida Carolyn Kugler, Ph.D.
William John Kugler
Stanley A. Kulpinski, Th.D.
Ina West Kurzhals
Leigh Elena Kurchinsky, Ph.D., M.D.
Lubomyr Ihor Kuzmak, M.D., D.Sc.
Christine Irene Kwik-Kostek, M.D.
V. Duane Lacey
Lloyd Hamilton Lacy
Shue-Lock Lam, Ph.D.
Lawrence Webster Lamb
Eleanor Lambert
E. Henry Lamkin, Jr., M.D.
Selma H. Lamkin
Labelle David Lance
Edward Clark Lander
Newlin J. Landers
Vernette Trosper Landers, Ed.D.
Georgina Barbara Landman
Mary Frances Kernell Lane
Audrey Pearl Knight Laney
Enrique Roberto Larde
Lena Schultz Larsen
Agnes D. Lattimer, M.D.
Elaine Marie Laucks
Frances Louise Peacock Lauer
Ralph Aregood Law, Jr.
Betty N. Lawson
Verna Rebecca Lawson
Obert M. Lay, M.D.
Harry Christopher Layton, D.D., Ph.D.
D.F.A., H.H.D.
Lillian Frances Warren Lazanberry
Albert Lazarus Leaf, Ph.D.
Miriam Leahy
Walden Albert Leecing
Sylvia Leeds
Dwight Adrian Leedy
Helen Ames Leete-Spaulding
Frank Edward LeGrand, Ph.D.
Silvia Weiner Leiferman
Elen A. Leinonen, Ph.D.
Yoko Ono Lennon
Professor Willkiam Robert Lennox
John Anthony Lent, Ph.D.
Mae Grace Leone, Ph.D.
Barbara C. LeRoy
William M. Lester
Lois May Letch
Elmer A. Letchworth, Ed.D.
Harold A. Levenson
Phillip Levine, M.D.
Keith Kerton Lewin
Edlwyn Ernest Lewis, Ph.D.
Leon Starks Lewis
Loraine Ruth Lewis
Shirley Jeane Lewis
William Howard Lewis, D.D.
Carol Ann Liaros
Eugene Aaron Lichtman
Ruth Dorothy Liebe
Morris B. Lieberman, Ph.D.
Luan Eng Lie-Injo, M.D.
Janis Lielmezs
Carol Asnin Liff
Rosalind Caribelle Lifquist
David Arthur Liggett
Dr. Delmore Liggett
Harriett Anna Grimm Lightfoot
Ping-Wha Lin, Ph.D., P.E.
Dorothy Insley Linker
Ivan L. Lindahl
Helge W. Lindholm
Mary Frances Lindsley, D.H., D.L.A.
Timothy Young Ling, Ph.D.
Elizabeth Charlotte Lippitt
Peggy Elaine Lipscomb
Darin V. Liska, P.E.
Robert Baarry Litman, M.D.

TWO THOUSAND NOTABLE AMERICANS

Bertha Felder Littell
Florence Elizabeth Herbert Little
Terril D. Littrell, Ph.D., D.D.
Si-kwang Liu, Ph.D.
Richard W. Livesay, M.D.
Von Edward Livingston, J.D.
Addie Mae Curbo Lloyd
Dame Jean Loach, D.C.M.S.A., D.C.T., C.C.A., F.M.L., F.I.B.A.
Floyd Otto Lochner, Ed.D.
L. W. Locke
David M. Lockwood, Ph.D.
Louisa Loeb
Sarah Elizabeth Larkin Loening
Hazel Anderson Loewenstein
Leslie Celeste Logan
Dr. Jennifer Mary Hildreth Loggie
Pauline Teresa Di Bitose Longo
ArLeen Patterson Lonneker
Rita A. Lopes
Anna M. Gonzalez Lopez
Maria Trinidad Lopez
Evelyn June Lorenzen, Ph.D., M.D.
Ann Louise Lotko
Joann Love
Dallas Landon Lovejoy, L.L.S.
Thelma Spessard Loyd
Judith Bagwell Luahiwa
Lilibel Pazoureck Lucy
Ruby Ballard Ludwig
Archie William Luper
Edythe Lutzker
Adelheid Wilhelmine Luhr
Ruby Elizabeth Stutts Lyells
Angela Yaw-Guo Lyie
Jerry Lee Lyons, P.E.
Vera Sonja Maass, Ph.D.
Roy Walter Machen, Th.D., D.D., D.R.E., D.Min.
Ruth Jean Maddigan
Eugenie Cassatt Madeina
Visweswara Laxminarayana Madhyastha, Ph.D.
William August Maesen, D.S.W.
Larry Elliot Magargal, M.D.
Albert A. Magee, Jr.
Thomas Harold Mahan
Francis Elizabeth Dougherty Maierhauser
James I. Maish, Ph.D.
Americo Bartholomew Makk
Raymond Howard Malik, Ph.D.
Wilfred Michael Mallon, S.J.
Mary E. Tranbarger Malola
June Culler Malone
Dr. Lucinda Johnson Malone
Joyce Morgan Maloof
Rt. Rev. Lucien Malouf, B.S.O.
James Darwin Mann
Santa Singh Mann
Colonel Filomena Roberta Manor
Krishna Shankar Manudhane, Ph.D.
Mamie Jane Jimerson Marbley
Paula Dee Thompson Markham
John D. Marks
V. Steven Markstrom
Don Welch Marsh
Milton Marsh
Otis 'Dock' Marston
James Larence Martin, D.D.S.
Melvin D. Martin
Paul J. Martin, M.D.
Peggy Smith Martin
Ernesto Pedregon Martinez
John S. Martinez, Ph.D.
Ellen Marxer
Aretha H. Mason
Dean T. Mason
Frank Henry Mason
Madeline Mason
Joseph F. Masopust
Elinor Tripato Massoglia, Ed.D.
John Ross Matheson, C.D., U.E.
Helen K. Mathews
Hugh Spalding Mathewson, M.D.
Bill G. Matson
Jean Foster Matthew, Ph.D.
Alvin Leon Matthews
Elsie Catherine Spears Matthews
Norma Jean Humphries Mauldin
Rev. Charles Alexander Maxell
Katherine Gant Maxwell, Ph.D.
Wythel Louween Killen Mayborn
Cynthia Francis May-Cole
Frederick J. Mayer
Edythe Beam Mayes
James Thomas Mayne
Lawrence Clayton McAlister
Bernice Jacklyn Lyons McAllister
Van A. McAuley
Honorable Rita Cloutier McAvoy
William V. McBride

Judge Daniel Thompson McCall, Jr.
Robert John McCandiss, M.D.
William Harroll McCarroll, M.D.
Mildred M. McCleave
Dr. Sherwin D. C. McCombs
Grace McCormack
Irene McCrystal, Ph.D.
Constance M. McCullough, Ph.D.
John Phillip McCullough, Ph.D.
(Betty) Martha Elizabeth McCurdy, Ph.D.
Henry Arwood McDaniel, Jr.
Khlar Elwood McDonald, M.D.
Theresa Beatrice Pierce McDonald
Barbara Ann McFarlin
Ambassador Gale W. McGee
Robert C. McGee, Jr.
William A. McGee, III
Helen McGinty
Marjorie Frances McGowan
Sterling Fisher McIlhany
Donald D. McKee
Marion Elizabeth McKell
Malcolm F. McKesson
Harry J. McKinnon, Jr., M.D.
Mary Cannon McLean, Ed.D.
Robert George McLendon
Gwen Edith McMillan
Ambrose M. McNamara
Thomas Parnell McNamara, Sr.
Esther M. Mealing
Dr. M. S. Megahed
Ira B. Melton, Sr.
Sol Mendelson, Ph.D.
Carlos Mendez-Santos
Samuel D. Menin
Vasant V. Merchant, Ph.D.
Addie Hylton Merrimee
Ruth Evelyn Parks Mertz
Juozas Meskauskas, Ph.D., M.D.
Dorothy Taylor Mesney
Maqbul A. Mian, M.D.
Cyril Michael
Barbara Falgout Michaelis
Hubert Sheldon Mickel, M.D.
Capt. Alfred Alexander Mickalow, Jr.
Mildred M. Milazzo
Charles E. Miles
Robert William Miles
Vivian Turner Millard
C. Edward Miller
Carol Miller Miller
Dolphus O. Miller
Dorothea Welsh Miller
Earl Beauford Miller
Maj. Gen. Frank Dickson Miller
J. Malcolm Miller
Jeanne-Marie A. Miller, Ph.D.
L. T. Miller, Jr., Ph.D.
Mary Frances Miller
Robert J. Miller
William A. Mills
Jewel Brooks Milner
John Herbert Milnes
Frank Kuipong Min
Giulio Romano Antonio Minchella, M.D., D.S.
Horst Minkofski-Garrigues
Barry Leonard Steffan Mirenburg
George Miskovsky, J.D.
Kegham Aram Mississyan, Ph.D.
Barbara Jean Mitchell
George E. Mixon, Ph.D.
Marjorie Frances Griner Mixon
Dr. Herbert Brooks Mobley
Edward Francis Mohler, Jr.
Gertrude M. F. Moir
John Troup Moir, Jr.
Eleanor Moore Montgomery
Dan Tyler Moore
Frank E. Moore
Hershell Edward Moore
Paul Richard Moore
Phyllis Clark Moore, Ph.D.
Dr. George Alexander Moorehead
Daniel M. Morahan
Kenneth Carol Morgan
Felix Cleveland Moring
Alvin E. Morris, Ed.D.
Eugene Morris
Florence Eden Morris
Irving Morris
Ruth Morris
Sue Hannah Morris
Francine Reese Morrison, D.S.M., D.D.
Leger R. Morrison, Ed.D.
Samuel Alton Morse, D.B.A.
Hans Birger Mortensen
Helen Luella Morton, M.D.
Walter Graydon Morton
Wilbur Young Morton
Dr. Herbert Frederick Moseley
Dr. James Anthony Moses, Jr.

James P. Mosley
Tommye Atkinson Moss
Beatrice Carroll Mullen
J. B. Mumford
Walter John Mumm, Ph.D.
Makio Murayama, Ph.D.
Walter John Mumm, Ph.D.
Wanda M. Penrod Munson, M.A.
Noveree Murdaugh
Percy Murdock
Mary Kathleen Connors Murphy, Ph.D.
William Joseph Murphy, Jr.
Joan Murray
Edward Cecil Music
Tofigh Varcaneh Mussivand, Ph.D.
Fred L. Myrick, Jr., Ph.D.
Toyozo W. Nakarai, Ph.D.
Hiromu Nakamura, Ph.D.
John B. Nanny
Sunil Baran Nath, Ph.D.
Pleas C. Naylor, Jr.
William Arthur Nebel, M.D.
Lucien Needham
Clarence E. Neff
America Elizabeth Nelson, M.D.
Lorraine Lavington Nelson
Robert Lee Nelson, Ph.D., D.D.
Thomas Harry Nelson
Elsie Paschal Nespor
Lois H. Neuman
Sister Laurine Neville, O.P.
Joyce Nevitt
Capitola Dent Newbern, Ed.D.
Martha R. Newby, Ed.D.
Virginia Shaw Newell
Emma Read Newton
Annette Evelyn Nezelek
Rev. James Harold Nicholls
Thomas S. Nichols
William Roger Niehaus
Mary Martin Niepold
Masami 'Sparky' Niimi
Lorraine C. Nikolai
George Washington Noble
Mark Gerard Noel
Patricia Joyce Brownson Norman
William Carlton Northup
Joachim Robert Nortmann
Marie A. Norton
Allen Stanislaus Motoyuki Numano
Walenty Nowacki
Crosby Llewelle Grant Nurse
Gene S. Obert
Paul M. Obert, M.D.
Robert Paul O'Block
D. Susan J. O'Brien
James P. O'Flarity
Wilson Reid Ogg
Clifton Oliver, Jr.
Hester Grey Ollis
Jaime Alberto Olmo, M.D.
Carl Edwin Olsen
M. Eugene Olsen
Benedict Bernard O'Malley, Ph.D.
William Joseph O'Malley
Col. Robert Palmer O'Neal
Paul de Verez Onffroy, Ph.D.
Helen Marie Opsahl
William Dabney O'Riordan, M.D.
Henry Orland, Ph.D.
Margaret Roberta Carlson Orlich
Robert Lois Ory, Ph.D.
Roman Sviatoslav Oryshkevich, D.D.S., M.D.
Prime F. Osborn, III
Cyrus Warren Ostrom
Marshall Voigt Otis
Edward Thomas O'Toole, Ph.D.
Marie Louise Molera O'Toole
George Robert Overby, Ph.D.
J. Homer Harold Overholser
Ronald Overholser
Edwin Dean Overton
Esen Sever Ozgener, Ed.D.
Margaret Ann Pace
Edward Thurston Pagat, M.D.
Marcelo Pagat, Jr.
Matthew John Page, M.D.
Thomas J. Pallasch, D.D.S.
Kayton R. Palmer
Rt. Rev. Dr. Louis Alexander Palumbo, Jr.
Robert Boisseau Pamplin, Jr.
Marciano Vega Pangilinan
John Pao
Spyros Demitrios Papalexiou
Leah Ann Pape
Margaret Pardee
Ruby Inex Myers McCollum Parham
Margaret Bittner Parke, Ed.D.
Boots Farthing Parker
Charles W. Parker, Jr.
Earl Melvin Parker, Sr.

Jacquelyn Susan Parker
Loislee M. Parker
Marilyn Morris Parker
William Dale Parker, Ph.D., Sc.D.
Belvidera Ashleigh Dry Parkinson, Ph.D.
D. C. Parks
Olivia Maxine Parks
Sanda Lou Parks
George N. Parris, J.D.
Andrew Mentlow Parsley, Ph.D.
Eugenia Pasternak
Lucille E. Pastor
John R. Pate
Bebe Rebeca Patten, Ph.D.
Priscilla Carla Patten, Ph.D.
Tom Patten
Celestel Patton
James Edward Payne
Virginia Alice Thompson Paysinger
Ralph Reed Payton
Reginald A. Pearman, Sr.
Betsy DeCelle Pearson
Norman Pearson
Judge John Wesley Peavy, Jr.
William Henry Peckham, III
Mary Ann Pellerin
Eugene Falero Pereda
Francisco Arriola Perez
Lynn Perkins Perez, J.D.
Anna Rebecca Perkins
Iris Francis Perkins
Robert Ronald Perkinson, Ph.D.
Alex G. Peros, D.C.
Robert J. Perry
Ruth Lucille Persch
Martin Ross Petersen
Norvell Louis Peterson, M.D.
Nan Dee Phelps
Helen Cecelia Phillips, LL.D.
Jacqueline Anne Mary Phillips
Karen Phillips
Michael Joseph Phillips, Ph.D.
Alyre Joseph Picard, M.D.
Patricia Jobe Pierce
Mary Isabelle Plum, M.A.
Alan L. Plummer, M.D.
Bob Lee Plyler
Marianna Cicilia Pisano
William M. (Bill) Pitchford
James Harvey Platt, Ph.D.
Father Joseph Kieran Pollard
Elizabeth Marie Polley
Gertrudee Pollitt
Lauren Lester Pond, Jr.
Nelda Lee Pool
Finis Winston Poole
Bishop Mary Maude Pope
Darwin Fred Porter
Milton C. Porter, H.H.D.
Roy E. Posner
Roy Wilson Potter
Nancy D. Potts
Russell Francis Powell
Ruth Hollowell Powell
Sartell Prentice, Jr.
James Travis Price
John Michael Price
Richard Lee Price
Ruby J. Timms Price
E. Allen Propst
Lois M. Provda
Ava Fay Pugh
George R. Purcell
William F. Purkiss
Walter Lee Pursell
Mary Belle Purvis
Seaborn Bryant Timmons Ragan
Karen Louise Ragle
Shahbudin Hooseinally Rahimtoola, M.D.
Robert Anton Rajander
Rawleigh H. Ralls, D.B.A.
Edward Ramov
Gerald Robert Randall
Helen Marietta Rasmussen
Maye Mitchell Ratliff
Ajit Kumar Ray, D.Sc.
Ollie Mae Ray, Ph.D.
Robert Benjamin Read, P.E.
Donald David Reber, Ed.D.
Judge Thomas J. Reddick, Jr.
Paschal E. Redding, Jr.
Pannala Jagan Mohan Reddy, M.D., D.P.M. F.R.C.P., A.B.P.N.
Maxwell Scott Redfearn, Ph.D., D.V.M.
Princess Red Wing
Minerva Tabitha Smith Reeve
William R. Reevy, Ph.D.
Frederick A. Reichle, M.D.
Lota Spence Reid
Siegfried Gerhard Reinhardt
Harry Charles Reinl
Regina F. Relford

TWO THOUSAND NOTABLE AMERICANS

Friedrich Otto Rest. A.B., B.D., D.D.
Benjamin Joseph Reynolds
Michael Eugene Reynolds, D.Min.
Randall Oscar Reynolds, D.D.S.
Movelda Earlean Rhine
O. W. Richard
Christine-Louise Richards
Frederick Douglass Richardson, A.A., C.S.R.
James M. Richcreek, Ed.D.
John Richmond, Ph.D.
Mossie J. Richmond, Jr., Ed.D.
Quinton Blaine Richmond
Jarnagin Bernad Ricks
Norman J. Riebe, D.Sc.
Jose M. Rigau-Marques, M.D.
Professor Margaret R. Rigg
Karl A. Riggs, Ph.D.
Elias R. Rigsby
Edna E. Riley
Warren Marshall Ringsdorf, Jr., D.M.D.
Florence L. Rippel
Mabel Amelia Rippel
Nicolas Nogueras Rivera
Arliss Lloyd Roaden, Ed.D.
Maj. Beverly Kay Roberts
Lt. Col. Edward Hartwell Roberts, Jr.
Evelyn Hoard Roberts, Ed.D.
Gertrud Hermine Kuenzel Roberts
Gertrude Brill Roberts
Josephine Frances Rees Roberts
Mark George Roberts
Lillyan Rose Robeson
Phyllis Isabel Robichaud
Erwin Robin, M.D.
Miriam B. Robins, Ph.D.
James D. C. Robinson, Ed.D.
Colonel James Hill Robinson
Ralph Rollin Robinson, M.D.
John D. (Jay) Rockefeller, IV
Donna Strickland Rodden
Carl E. Rodenburg, D.D.S.
William Harry Rodgers, Sr.
Czeslaw Mateusz Rodkiewicz, Ph.D.
Juan Francisco Rodriguez-Rivera, D.D.
Gifford Eugene Rogers
Rolf Ernst Rogers, Ph.D.
Thomas H. Rogers
David T. Rollins, Ph.D.
Fred G. Rollins, Sr., D.D.S.
Margaret Ann Romain
Clare Rose, Ed.D.
Wesley H. Rose
DeAnne Rosenberg
Julius L. Rothman, Ph.D.
Frederick Hull Roth
Agnes Brown Rowbotham
Iris Gordon Rowe
Grant Russell Rubly
Lucille Alyce Pickering Rubly
Aldelmo Ruiz
Philip Reed Rulon, Ed.D.
Bob R. Rundell
Mary Russell
Phebe Gale Russell
Robert Rowland Russell, Jr.
Mary Anne Petrich Rust, Ph.D.
Katharine Phillips Rutgers
James William Rutherford
Varian Palmer Rutledge
Mike Sablatash, Ph.D.
E. 'Steve' M. Sadang, M.D.V., Ph.D.
Stanley Cecil Winston Salvary, Ph.D.
Dorothy Vermelle Sampson, J.D.
Archbishop Mar Athanasius Yeshue Samuel
Carol Lee Sanchez
James Julian Sanchez, M.D.
Betty M. Sandella
Sylvia Ann Santos
Mary Louise Steinhilber Sauer
Robert Leonard Sawyer, Sr., Th.D.
Frank John Scallon
Helen Carol Schabbel
Lucrezia C. Schiavone
William Michael Schimmel, D.M.A.
Dolores F. Schjaastad
Minnie Anne Schmidt
Carl E. Schmollinger
George Ferdinand Schnack, M.D.
Mary E. Schwappach. M.D.
Wilhlem Schwarzotto
James L. Scott
Marie M. Scott
Col. Wilton C. Scott

Clara Kalhoefer Searles
Lorraine E. King Seay
Margielea Stonestreet See
JoAnn Semones
Doris Shay Serstock
John George Sevci, J.D.
Dr. John Charles Sevier
Flossie Tate Sewell
George Miller Shadle, M.D.
Erwin E. Shalowitz
Lucille M. Hogue Shealy
Ernest Shell
Vincent George Sheridan
Roy Allen Shive, Ph.D.
Mary F. Barnie Shuhi
Carrie Spivey Shumate
James McBride Shumway
C. Leroy Shuping, Jr., J.D.
Myrtis Irene Siddon
Howard M. Siegler, M.D.
Jan Simko, Ph.D.
Alyne Johnson Simpkins
Marion Carlyn Simpson
Eric John Sing, Ph.D.
Bhagwant Singh, Ph.D.
Kathern Ivous Sisk
James Dudley Sistrunk
Lydia Arlene Sitler, Ed.D.
Florence K. Slack
James Merritt Small, D.D.
Mary Ann U. Small
Ada Mae Blanton Smith, Ph.D.
Bettye L. Sebree Smith
Dock G. Smith, Jr.
Jessie Adie Smith
Norvel Emory Smith
Robert J. Smith
Wayne Delarmie Smith, D.V.M.
John Joseph Snyder, O.D.
Birger Kristoffer Soby
Walter W. Sohl
Ruell Floyd Solberg, Jr.
Donald Wayne Solomon, M.D., Ph.D.
Donald Henry Soucek, D.D.S.
Hattie T. Spain
Ellen Wilkerson Spears
James Parker Spillers
William Herschel Spinks
Ruth Evans Stadel
Edwin Henry Stamberger
Jacqueline J. Stanley
Linnie Marie Stearman
Lt. David Eric Stein
Andre Louis Steiner, D.Sc.
William Mark Stenzler
Dorothy Elizabeth Shay Stickman
Barbara Marshall Stockton
Willard Stone, D.H.A.
Jeremy Averill Stowell, M.D.
Dr. John George Strachan
Peer MacDonald Strang
Nellie Cora Straub
C. Clarke Straughan
Gustav Stueber
Glory Sturiale
Lakshminarayana Subramaniam
Eugene Y. C. Sung
M. N. Srikanta Swamy, Ph.D.
Arleen Wiley Swanson
Bonnie Ethel Wolfe Swickard
Maria Swiecicka-Ziemianek, Ph.D.
Ruby B. Sykes, D.D.S.
Emeric Szegho. J.D.
Neva Bennett Talley-Morris, M.Ed.
Peter J. Talso, M.D.
Noboru Tashiro, L.L.B.
Gunther Tautenhahn
Bertrand Leroy Taylor, III
Grier Corbin Taylor
Rev. Horace Melvin Taylor, Th.M.
Lisa Taylor
Wesley Daniel Taylor, M.D.
Neal Gary Tepper
Esther Irene Test
Harry Pemberton Thatcher
Joseph Theodore, Jr.
Kadakampallil G. Thimotheose, Ph.D.
Alan Thomas, Ph.D.
J. C. Thomas, Jr.
Lowell Thomas
Minna Lee Thomas
Mary Diel Thomason
Henry George Thompson

William LaMont Thompson
Jean Kaye Tinsley
Betty Ann Tinsley-Brown
George John Tiss, M.D.
Vivian Edmiston Todd, Ph.D.
Hugh Pat Tomlinson
Francisco G. Torres-Aybar, M.D.
Basil P. Toutorsky, L.L.M.
Dennis Takeshi Toyomura
June Traska
Evelyn Ladene Trennt
Harvey W. Trimmer, Jr.
Laura McCleese G. Trusedell
Wanda Hall Tucker
Dr. Arthur E. Turner
Herman Nathaniel Turner, Jr.
Helen Flynn Tyson
Robert Takeo Uda
Friedrich Karl Urschler, M.D.
M. Lois Valakis
Henry Valent
Verne Leroy van Breemen, M.D., Ph.D.
Barbara Jane Dixon VanGilder
Richard C. Van Vrooman
Henry Varner, Jr.
Larry Ivan Vass, D.D.S.
Mary Vaughn
Prudence Melvina Veatch
June J. Veckerelli
Marion G. Vedder
James Joseph Venditto
Josefina Vera
Sister Mary Vernice (Makovic), S.N.D.
Santos Luis Villar, Ph.D.
Anthony Joseph Viuscido, D.D.S.
Estella Maria Vlachos
John J. Vollmann, Ph.D.
Robert Volpe, M.D., F.R.C.P.
Arthur Voobus, Th.D.
Greta Evona Wade
Gerald Richard Wagner, Ph.D.
Betty Joanne Wahl
Mary Lee Sellers Wainwright
Edwin Prescott Wald
Kathryn Law Carroll Walden
Roy Willard Walholm, Jr.
Claudius R. Walker, Jr.
Iris Walker
Westbrook Arthur Walker, Ph.D.
William David Waller
James Arthur Waln
Doris E. Walsh
Bert Mathew Walter
Robert Ancil Walters
Rosie Reella Graham Ward
Marie Haley Warren
Lillian Frances Warren-Lazenberry
John Edward Warthen
Sharon Margaret Washburn
Lidia Cherie Wasowicz
Sydney Earle Watt
George Frederic Weaton, Jr.
Henry Weaver
Dr. Bernice Larson Webb
Ernest Packard Webb
Rozana Webb
Earl C. Weber
Gertrude Christian Weber
Sheila K. Weber, Ph.D.
Burnice Hoyle Webster, S.T.D., D.Sc., D.D., Ph.D.
Ernest Wesley Webster
Ruth S. Wedgworth
George C. Wee, M.D.
Milo Pershing Weeren
Diana Yun-Dee Wei, Ph.D.
Charles Kenneth Weidner
Norman Sidney Weiser
James Athanasius Weisheipl, Ph.D., D.Phil.
John W. Welch
Fay Gillis Wells
Josephine Mildred Wenck
L. Birdell Eliason Wendt
William W. Wendtland, Mus.D.
Wasyl Weresh, Ph.D.
Julian Ralph West
Lee Roy West, L.L.M.
Robert Warren Whalin, Ph.D.
William Polk Wharton, Jr., Ph.D.
Arline Z. Wheeler
James Edwin Wheeler
Charles Safford White
Ethyle Herman White

Frances R. Marjorie White
John Dudley White, Jr.
Mary Geraldine White
Saundra Sue White
Thurman James White, Ph.D.
Anna Whitefield
Alice McLemore Jones Whitehead
Edward Augustus Whitescarver
Vallie Jo Fox Whitfield
Cuthbert Randolph Whiting
Edward G. Whittaker
Grace Evelyn McKee Whittenburg
Carol Ann Wick
Jetie Boston Wilds, Jr.
William Garfield Wilkerson, M.D.
Harold Lloyd Wilkes, D.D.
Anne Oldham Willard
Carol Jane Petzold Willard, M.Ed.
Jack A. Willard
Albert J. Williams, Jr.
Anita T. J. L. Williams
Annie John Williams
Ather Williams, Jr.
Charlotte Evelyn Forrester Williams
Clarence Leon Williams, Ph.D.
Donald Jacob Williams
Dorothy Parmley Williams
Harvey Williams, Ph.D., D.Div.
Jean Taylor Williams
Leola K. Williams
William Harvey Williamson, Ph.D.
Francena Willingham
Mary Jane Willingham
James H. Willis
William Clarence Willmot
David Roger Willour, N.G.T.S.
Parker O. Willson
Charles William Wilson, M.D.
Cora Morgan Wilson
E. C. Wilson, Jr.
Hugh Edward Wilson
James Walter Wilson, Ph.D.
Leigh R. Wilson
Nevada Pearl Brown Wilson
Dorr Norman Wiltse, Sr.
Glen Elbert Wimmer
Lt. Gregory Lynn Winters
Nora Edna Wittman
Sophie Mae Wolanin, Ph.D.
Seymour "Sy" Wolf
Bradley Allen Wolfe
Deborah Cannon Partridge Wolfe, Ed.D.
Rev. Francis Wolle
Muriel Sibell Wolle
Colin Chockson Wong, D.D.S., F.R.S.H. F.A.G.D., F.A.D.I., F.I.C.D., F.A.C.D.
Marylaird (Larry) Wood
Stella Woodall, D.Lit., D.H.L.
Geraldine Pittman Woods, Ph.D., D.Sc.
Margaret Herbert Ratrie Woods
Margaret S. Woods
Clifton Ward Woolley, M.D., F.A.A.P.
Darrell Wayne Woolwine
Bertrand Ray Worsham, M.D.
Elizabeth Wrancher
John Lawrence Wray
Eugene Box Wright, J.D.
Inez Meta Maria Wright
Kenneth Kun-Yu Wu, M.D.
William Lung-Shen Wu, M.D.
Doris Stork Wukasch
Angela Jane Wyant
Rev. Claude S. Wyatt, Jr.
Kionne Annette Wyndewicke
Darlene Fry Wyatt
Alex Peralta Yadao, M.D.
Elizabeth Juanita Yanosko
Claude Lee Yarbro, Jr., Ph.D.
James Edgar Yarbrough
Fowler Redford Yett, Ph.D.
Jethro Sutherland Yip
Luella May Nafzinger Yoder
Ronald Eugene Yokely
James N. Young
Patrick J. H. Young
Adele Linda Younis, Ph.D.
Lawrence Thomas Zagar, Ph.D.
Edward Francis Zampella
Estelle M. Zelner
Dr. Melvin Eddie Zichek
Gladys Avery Zinn
Howard John Zitko, D.D.
Herman David Zweiban